July 12–16, 2014
Vancouver, BC, Canada

Association for
Computing Machinery

Advancing Computing as a Science & Profession

GECCO'14

Proceedings of the 2014 Genetic and Evolutionary Computation Conference

Sponsored by:

ACM SIGEVO

Association for
Computing Machinery

Advancing Computing as a Science & Profession

The Association for Computing Machinery
2 Penn Plaza, Suite 701
New York, New York 10121-0701

Notice to Past Authors of ACM-Published Articles
ACM intends to create a complete electronic archive of all articles and/or other material previously published by ACM. If you have written a work that has been previously published by ACM in any journal or conference proceedings prior to 1978, or any SIG Newsletter at any time, and you do NOT want this work to appear in the ACM Digital Library, please inform permissions@acm.org, stating the title of the work, the author(s), and where and when published.

ISBN: 978-1-4503-3275-0 (Digital)

ISBN: 978-1-4503-3266-8 (Print)

Additional copies may be ordered prepaid from:

ACM Order Department
PO Box 30777
New York, NY 10087-0777, USA

Phone: 1-800-342-6626 (USA and Canada)
+1-212-626-0500 (Global)
Fax: +1-212-944-1318
E-mail: acmhelp@acm.org
Hours of Operation: 8:30 am – 4:30 pm ET

Printed in the USA

Welcome

On behalf of the Organizing Committee, I would like to welcome you to Vancouver for the 2014 Genetic and Evolutionary Computation Conference (GECCO 2014). This year's GECCO is comprised of 20 tracks, including the new Artificial Immune Systems and Hot Off the Press (HOP) tracks. The latter offers authors of outstanding research recently published in journals and other conferences the opportunity to present their work to the GECCO community. Under the guidance of Editor-in-Chief Christian Igel, the Track Chairs and Program Committee have selected 180 out of the 544 submissions received in all tracks (excluding HOP) for oral presentation as full papers, resulting in an acceptance rate of 33%. Close to 100 short papers will be presented in the poster session.

Highlights of the conference include keynote talks by Yoshua Bengio on "Deep Learning and Cultural Evolution", and by Dario Floreano on "Bridging Natural and Artificial Evolution", as well as an invited talk by Sumit Gulwani in the Genetic Programming track. Altogether 32 tutorials cover topics ranging from broad and introductory to specialized and at the frontier of current research. GECCO also hosts fifteen workshops, including several new ones as well as at least one that predates GECCO itself. Further high points include the 11th Annual "Humies" Awards for Human-Competitive Results, which are again generously supported by John Koza, and five competitions, ranging from Art, Design, and Creativity to the Industrial Challenge. Finally, Evolutionary Computation in Practice continues to be an important and integral part of GECCO.

I would like to thank the entire Organizing Committee for their work and dedication over the past year. Thanks also go to the Track Chairs and the Program Committee for their careful reviewing of the large number of submissions received. Finally, thanks are due to Roxane Rose and Cara Candler from *Executive Events*, who have been in charge of logistical aspects and registration, Lisa Tolles and her team at *Sheridan Communications* for the production of the proceedings, Mark Montague and his team at *Linklings* for their conference management tool and support of the reviewing process, and Gerardo Valencia for artwork and website management.

I wish you all a productive and enjoyable conference.

Dirk Arnold
General Chair

A Word from the Chair of SIGEVO

Welcome to the Proceedings of GECCO 2014, the sixteenth GECCO, the "recombination" of the 23rd International Conference on Genetic Algorithms (ICGA) and the 19th Genetic Programming Conference (GP). This year, Dirk Arnold was General Chair of GECCO 2014 acting with great diligence and care. Christian Igel, the Editor-in-Chief of GECCO-2014 has done an excellent job at coordinating the reviewing process and leading the effort to select papers for publication. The results of the effort of them and their team are presented here.

GECCO is the premiere venue for presenting papers in the area of Genetic and Evolutionary Computation worldwide. The quality of papers submitted to GECCO is very high, and GECCO has a rigorous paper selection process. This means that the best and most important work in Evolutionary Computation and on related topics is presented at GECCO. Our conference is consistently ranked at the top of Evolutionary Computation conferences, exceeding in citation counts well known journals and other venues.

If you were not able to attend GECCO 2014 in person, the Proceedings are in the ACM Digital Library; they are globally accessible and readily found, which benefits both readers and authors.

ACM SIGEVO

Members of ACM SIGEVO, sponsor of GECCO, continue to draw major benefits from joining ACM. First is a discount at SIGEVO sponsored conferences, at GECCO as much as $100 per registrant. Members have, for a fee, access to the ACM Digital Library, a large and continuously growing resource for research in computing. Another key benefit is the outstanding newsletter *SIGEVOlution* produced by Pier Luca Lanzi and his excellent editorial board. If you are accessing these proceedings and are not a member of SIGEVO, please consider joining (for the low price of $25/year for non-students, and $10/year for student members). This will help us a lot in promoting our community.

Involvement in ACM SIGEVO

SIGEVO became a Special Interest Group (SIG) of the ACM in 2005. ACM considers its SIGs as the lifeblood of the organization. We are governed by bylaws available on the SIGEVO web pages. There, you also find a list of members of the 18-member Executive Committee.

Since 2011, I serve as chair of SIGEVO, together with a team of officers: Una-May O'Reilly (Vice-Chair), Marc Schoenauer (Secretary), and Franz Rothlauf (Treasurer). The Executive, its Officers and I are dedicated to continuously improve our organization. If you have any suggestions how to make GECCO or SIGEVO better, please let us know.

Wolfgang Banzhaf
SIGEVO Chair

Table of Contents

Track: Artificial Immune Systems

Track: Artificial Life, Robotics, and Evolvable Hardware

Track: Biological and Biomedical Applications

Track: Digital Entertainment Technologies and Arts

Track: Estimation of Distribution Algorithms

Track: Evolution Strategies and Evolutionary Programming

Track: Evolutionary Combinatorial Optimization and Metaheuristics

Track: Evolutionary Machine Learning

Track: Evolutionary Multiobjective Optimization

Track: Genetic Algorithms

Track: Genetic Programming

Track: Integrative Genetic and Evolutionary Computation

Track: Parallel Evolutionary Systems

Track: Real World Applications

Track: Search Based Software Engineering

Track: Self-* Search

Track: Theory

Organizers

General Chair:	Dirk V. Arnold, *Dalhousie University*
Editor-in-Chief:	Christian Igel, *University of Copenhagen*
Publicity Chair:	Christian Gagné, *Université Laval*
Local Chair:	Elena Popovici, *Icosystem Corporation*
Students Chair:	Petr Pošík, *Czech Technical University*
Tutorials Chair:	Mengjie Zhang, *Victoria University of Wellington*
Workshops Chair:	Per Kristian Lehre, *University of Nottingham*
Competitions Chair:	Amy K. Hoover, *University of Central Florida*
Late Breaking Abstracts Chair:	Dirk Sudholt, *University of Sheffield*
Evolutionary Computation in Practice Chairs:	Thomas Bartz-Beielstein, *Cologne University of Applied Sciences* Anna I. Esparcia-Alcázar, *S2 Grupo* Jörn Mehnen, *Cranfield University*
Business Committee:	Jürgen Branke, *University of Warwick* Darrell Whitley, *Colorado State University*

Track Chairs

Anne Auger, *INRIA Saclay*
Jaume Bacardit, *Newcastle University*
Dimo Brockhoff, *INRIA Lille*
Stefano Cagnoni, *Università degli Studi di Parma*
Kalyanmoy Deb, *Michigan State University*
Benjamin Doerr, *École Polytechnique de Paris*
James Foster, *University of Idaho*
Tobias Glasmachers, *Ruhr-Universität Bochum*
Emma Hart, *Edinburgh Napier University*
Malcolm I. Heywood, *Dalhousie University*
Hitoshi Iba, *University of Tokyo*
Christian Jacob, *University of Calgary*
Thomas Jansen, *Aberystwyth University*
Yaochu Jin, *University of Surrey*
Marouane Kessentini, *University of Michigan*
Joshua D. Knowles, *University of Manchester*
William B. Langdon, *University College London*
Pedro Larrañaga, *Technical University of Madrid*
Sean Luke, *George Mason University*
Gabriel Luque, *Universidad de Málaga*
John A. W. McCall, *Robert Gordon University Aberdeen*
Marco A. Montes de Oca, *University of Delaware*
Alison Motsinger-Reif, *North Carolina State University*
Yew Soon Ong, *Nanyang Technological University*
Michael Palmer, *Stanford University*
Konstantinos E. Parsopoulos, *University of Ioanninia*
Günther Raidl, *Vienna University of Technology*
Sebastian Risi, *IT University of Copenhagen*
Guenther Ruhe, *University of Calgary*
Tom Schaul, *New York University*
Thomas Schmickl, *Karl-Franzens-Universität Graz*
Bernhard Sendhoff, *Honda Research Institute Europe*
Kenneth O. Stanley, *University of Central Florida*
Thomas Stützle, *Université Libre de Bruxelles*
Dirk Thierens, *Universiteit Utrecht*
Julian Togelius, *IT University of Copenhagen*
Carsten Witt, *Technical University of Denmark*
Christine Zarges, *University of Birmingham*

Program Committee

Abbass, Hussein, *University of New South Wales*
Abdelbar, Ashraf, *Brandon University*
Abraham, Ajith, *Machine Intelligence Research Labs*
Acampora, Giovanni, *Nottingham Trent University*
Adamatzky, Andrew, *University of the West of England*
Adami, Chris, *Michigan State University*
Affenzeller, Michael, *University of Applied Sciences Upper Austria*
Aguirre, Hernan, *Shinshu University*
Ahn, Chang Wook, *Sungkyunkwan University*
Ahrens, Barry, *Nova Southeastern University*
Aickelin, Uwe, *University of Nottingham*
Akimoto, Youhei, *Shinshu University*
Alba, Enrique, *Universidad de Málaga*
Alden, Kieran, *University of York*
Aler, Ricardo, *Universidad Carlos III de Madrid*
Alfaro-Cid, Eva, *Universidad Politécnica de Valencia*
Allmendinger, Richard, *University College London*
Alshahwan, Nadia, *University College London*
Amoretti, Michele, *Università degli Studi di Parma*
Amos, Ng, *University of Skövde*
Andrews, Paul, *University of York*
Antoniol, Giuliano, *École Polytechnique de Montréal*
Arcuri, Andrea, *Simula Research Laboratory*
Arias Montaño, Alfredo, *CINVESTAV-IPN*
Arita, Takaya, *Nagoya University*
Arredondo, Antonio D. Masegosa, *Universidad de Granada*
Arvin, Farshad, *University of Lincoln*
Avigad, Gideon, *Braude College of Engineering*
Aydin, Nizamettin, *Yildiz Technical University*
Azad, Raja Muhammad Atif, *University of Limerick*
Babovic, Vladan, *National University Singapore*
Bader-El-Den, Mohamed, *University of Essex*
Bai, Ruibin, *University of Nottingham Ningbo*
Ballester, Pedro J., *European Bioinformatics Institute*
Bandyopadhyay, Sanghamitra, *Indian Statistical Institute*
Bankovic, Zorana, *IMDEA Software Institute*
Banzhaf, Wolfgang, *Memorial University of Newfoundland*
Barbosa, Helio J. C., *National Laboratory for Scientific Computation, Brazil*
Bardenet, Remi, *University of Oxford*
Barros, Marcio, *Universidade Federal do Estado do Rio de Janeiro*
Bartz-Beielstein, Thomas, *Cologne University of Applied Sciences*
Basgalupp, Marcio, *Universidade Federal de São Paulo*
Bassett, Jeffrey K., *George Mason University*
Basseur, Matthieu, *Université d'Angers*
Bastos Filho, Carmelo J. A., *University of Pernambuco*
Batista, Lucas, *Universidade Federal de Minas Gerais*
Beal, Jacob, *BBN Technologies*
Bechikh, Slim, *University of Michigan–Dearborn*
Bennell, Julia, *University of Southampton*
Bentley, Peter J., *University College London*
Bergstra, James, *University of Waterloo*
Bernardino, Heder, *Universidade Federal de Juiz de Fora*
Bernt, Matthias, *University of Leipzig*
Berry, Rod, *University of Technology, Sydney*
Bersano, Tom, *Google Inc.*
Besada-Portas, Eva, *Universidad Complutense de Madrid*
Beyer, Hans-Georg, *Vorarlberg University of Applied Sciences*
Bezerra, Leonardo, *Université Libre de Bruxelles*
Bhanu, Bir, *University of California at Riverside*
Biazzini, Marco, *INRIA Rennes*
Bielza, Concha, *Universidad Politécnica de Madrid*
Biesinger, Benjamin, *Technische Universität Wien*
Birattari, Mauro, *Université Libre de Bruxelles*
Blackwell, Tim, *Goldsmiths, University of London*
Blekas, Konstantinos, *University of Ioannina*
Blesa, Maria J., *Universitat Politècnica de Catalunya*
Blum, Christian, *University of the Basque Country*
Bollegala, Danushka, *University of Tokyo*
Bongard, Josh, *University of Vermont*
Booker, Lashon, *The MITRE Corporation*
Bosman, Peter A.N., *Centrum Wiskunde & Informatica*
Boudjeloud, Lydia, *Université de Lorraine*
Boumaza, Amine, *Université de Lorraine*
Bouvry, Pascal, *University of Luxembourg*
Bown, Ollie, *University of Sydney*
Brabazon, Anthony, *University College Dublin*
Branke, Jürgen, *University of Warwick*
Bredeche, Nicolas, *Université Pierre et Marie Curie*
Breen, David E., *Drexel University*
Bringmann, Karl, *Max Planck Institut für Informatik*
Browne, Will N., *Victoria University of Wellington*
Brownlee, Alexander E. I., *University of Stirling*
Buarque, Fernando, *University of Pernambuco*
Bui, Lam Thu, *Le Quy Don Technical University*
Bui, Thang, *Penn State*
Bull, Larry, *University of the West of England*
Bullinaria, John A., *University of Birmingham*
Burelli, Paolo, *Aalborg University*
Burjorjee, Keki Mehernosh, *Brandeis University*
Burke, Edmund, *University of Stirling*
Butz, Martin V., *University of Tübingen*
Buzdalov, Maxim, *Saint-Petersburg National Research University of Information Technologies, Mechanics & Optics*
Buzdalova, Arina, *Saint-Petersburg National Research University of Information Technologies, Mechamics & Optics*
Cagnina, Leticia, *Universidad Nacional de San Luis*
Cairns, David, *University of Stirling*
Campelo, Felipe, *Universidade Federal de Minas Gerais*
Campo, Alexandre, *Université Libre de Bruxelles*
Cangelosi, Angelo, *University of Plymouth*
Capodieci, Nicola, *University of Modena and Reggio Emilia*
Carvalho, Andre, *Universidade de São Paulo*

Castelli, Mauro, *Universidade Nova de Lisboa*
Castellini, Alberto, *University of Verona*
Ceschia, Sara, *University of Udine*
Chakraborty, Uday, *University of Missouri*
Chang, Pei-Chann, *Yuan Ze University*
Chelly, Zeineb, *University of Tunis*
Chen, Ying-ping, *National Chiao Tung University*
Chen, Tianshi, *Chinese Academy of Sciences*
Cheong, Yun-Gyung, *IT University of Copenhagen*
Chiarandini, Marco, *University of Southern Denmark*
Chicano, Francisco, *Universidad de Málaga*
Chiong, Raymond, *University of Newcastle*
Chipperfield, Andrew J., *University of Southampton*
Chong, Siang Yew, *University of Nottingham*
Christensen, Anders, *University Institute of Lisbon*
Christensen, David Johan, *Technical University of Denmark*
Chu, Dominique, *University of Kent*
Chuang, Chung-Yao, *Carnegie Mellon University*
Clark, John, *University of York*
Clerc, Maurice
Clune, Jeff, *University of Wyoming*
Coelho, Leandro, *Pontifícia Universidade Católica do Paranà*
Coello Coello, Carlos A., *CINVESTAV-IPN*
Cohen, Myra, *University of Nebraska–Lincoln*
Colby, Mitch K., *Oregon State University*
Colmenar, J. Manuel, *Universidad Complutense de Madrid*
Colton, Simon, *Imperial College London*
Congdon, Clare Bates, *University of Southern Maine*
Connelly, Brian, *University of Washington*
Cook, Michael, *University of London*
Cordon, Oscar, *European Centre for Soft Computing*
Corns, Steven M., *Missouri University of Science and Technology*
Correia, Luís, *Universidade de Lisboa*
Costa, Lino António, *Universidade do Minho*
Costa, Ernesto, *University of Coimbra*
Cotta, Carlos, *Universidad de Málaga*
Cowling, Peter, *University of York*
Craenen, Bart G.W., *Brunel University*
Cui, Wei, *University College Dublin*
Cummins, Ronan, *University of Greenwich*
Cussat-Blanc, Sylvain, *University of Toulouse*
D'Ambrosio, David B., *University of Central Florida*
Dahal, Keshav, *University of the West of Scotland*
Dahlskog, Steve, *Malmö University*
Dahlstedt, Palle, *University of Gothenburg*
Dang, Duc-Cuong, *University of Nottingham*
Darabos, Christian, *Dartmouth College*
Das, Swagatam, *Indian Statistical Institute*
Datta, Dilip, *Tezpur University*
Datta, Rituparna, *Indian Institute of Technology Kanpur*
David, Cornforth, *University of Newcastle*
De Causmaecker, Patrick, *KU Leuven*
De Jong, Kenneth, *George Mason University*
de la Fraga, Luis Gerardo, *CINVESTAV-IPN*
de la Ossa, Luis, *University of Castilla–La Mancha*
Deakin, Anthony, *University of Liverpool*
Della Cioppa, Antonio, *University of Salerno*
Delong, Andrew, *University of Toronto*
Derbel, Bilel, *INRIA Lille*
Dhaenens, Clarisse, *INRIA Lille, CNRS*
Di Caro, Gianni, *IDSIA*
Di Gaspero, Luca, *University of Udine*
Di Penta, Massimiliano, *University of Sannio*
Diaconescu, Ada, *Télécom ParisTech*
Ding, Yongsheng, *Donghua University*
Dinh, Huy, *University of Tokyo*
Dinneen, Michael J., *University of Auckland*
Dittrich, Peter, *Friedrich-Schiller-Universität Jena*
Divina, Federico, *Pablo de Olavide University*
Doerr, Carola, *Université Pierre et Marie Curie, CNRS*
Doncieux, Stéphane, *Université Pierre et Marie Curie*
Dorin, Alan, *Monash University*
Dorronsoro, Bernabe, *Université Lille Nord de France*
Dozal, León, *Centro de Investigación Científica y de Educación Superior de Ensenada*
Drugan, Madalina, *Vrije Universiteit Brussel*
Drugowitsch, Jan, *Université de Genève*
Dubois-Lacoste, Jérémie, *Université Libre de Bruxelles*
Ebner, Marc, *Ernst-Moritz-Universität Greifswald*
El-Abd, Mohammed, *American University of Kuwait*
Emmerich, Michael T. M., *Universiteit Leiden*
Engelbrecht, Andries P., *University of Pretoria*
Epitropakis, Michael, *University of Stirling*
Eremeev, Anton V., *Sobolev Institute of Mathematics, Omsk*
Esponda, Fernando, *Instituto Tecnológico Autónomo de México*
Evelyne, Lutton, *INRIA Saclay*
Everson, Richard, *University of Exeter*
Fan, Patrick, *Virginia Tech*
Farooq, Muddassar, *Institute of Space Technology, Pakistan*
Feldt, Robert, *Chalmers University of Technology*
Fenet, Serge, *Université Lyon 1*
Ferariu, Lavinia, *"Gheorghe Asachi" Technical University of Iaşi*
Fernandez, Jose David, *Universidad de Málaga*
Fernández de Vega, Francisco, *Universidad de Extremadura*
Festa, Paola, *Universitá degli Studi di Napoli*
Fialho, Álvaro, *GE Global Research*
Fieldsend, Jonathan Edward, *University of Exeter*
Figueredo, Grazziela, *University of Nottingham*
Filipic, Bogdan, *Jožef Stefan Institute*
Finck, Steffen, *Vorarlberg University of Applied Sciences*
Fink, Andreas, *Helmut Schmidt University Hamburg*
Fischer, Asja, *Ruhr-Universität Bochum*
Fleming, Peter, *University of Sheffield*
Folino, Gianluigi, *Institute of High Performance Computing and Networking, Italy*
Fraser, Gordon, *University of Sheffield*
Freisleben, Bernd, *Universität Marburg*

Freitas, Alex A., *University of Kent*
Friedrich, Tobias, *Friedrich-Schiller-Universität Jena*
Frowd, Charlie, *University of Winchester*
Gagliolo, Matteo, *Vrije Universiteit Brussel*
Gagné, Christian, *Université Laval*
Gallagher, Marcus R., *University of Queensland*
Galvan, Edgar, *Trinity College Dublin*
Galway, Leo, *University of Ulster*
Gambardella, Luca Maria, *IDSIA*
Gamez, Jose A., *Universidad de Castilla–La Mancha*
Gandibleux, Xavier, *Université de Nantes*
Gandomi, Amir Hossein, *University of Akron*
Gao, Yang, *Nanjing University*
Garcia-Nieto, Jose, *Universidad de Málaga*
Garcia-Piquer, Alvaro, *Institute of Space Sciences, Mexico*
García-Martínez, Carlos, *Universidad de Córdoba*
García-Sánchez, Pablo, *Universidad de Granada*
Garnier, Simon, *New Jersey Institute of Technology*
Garousi, Vahid, *University of Calgary*
Garrett, Deon, *Icelandic Institute for Intelligent Machines*
Gaspar-Cunha, Antonio, *Universidade do Minho*
Geem, Zong Woo, *Gachon University*
Gelareh, Shahin, *Université d'Artois*
Gershenson, Carlos, *Universidad Nacional Autonoma de México*
Gervasi, Osvaldo, *University of Perugia*
Giacobini, Mario, *University of Torino*
Giagkiozis, Ioannis, *University of Sheffield*
Giavitto, Jean-Louis, *Institut de Recherche et Coordination Acoustique/Musique, France, CNRS*
Gießen, Christian, *Christian-Albrechts-Universität zu Kiel*
Giraldez Rojo, Raul, *Pablo de Olavide University*
Giustolisi, Orazio, *Technical University of Bari*
Goeffon, Adrien, *Université d'Angers*
Goh, Chi-Keong, *Rolls-Royce*
Goldbarg, Marco César, *Universidade Federal do Rio Grande do Norte*
Goldman, Brian W., *Michigan State University*
Gomez-Pulido, Juan A., *Universidad de Extremadura*
Gong, Wenyin, *China University of Geosciences*
Goodman, Erik D., *Michigan State University*
Grasemann, Uli, *University of Texas, Austin*
Greenfield, Gary, *University of Richmond*
Greensmith, Julie, *University of Nottingham*
Greiner, David, *Universidad de Las Palmas de Gran Canaria*
Grewal, Gary William, *University of Guelph*
Gross, Roderich, *University of Sheffield*
Grouchy, Paul, *University of Toronto*
Gu, Feng, *Kingston University London*
Guerreiro, Andreia P., *University of Coimbra*
Guinand, Frederic, *Université du Havre*
Gutjahr, Walter J., *University of Vienna*
Hagelbäck, Johan, *Blekinge Tekniska Högskola*
Hamann, Heiko, *University of Paderborn*
Hamel, Lutz, *University of Rhode Island*
Hamzeh, Ali, *Shiraz University*
Hanafi, Said, *University of Valenciennes*
Handa, Hisashi, *Kindai University*
Handl, Julia, *University of Manchester*
Hansen, Nikolaus, *IRIA Saclay*
Hao, Jin-Kao, *Université d'Angers*
Harman, Mark, *University College London*
Harvey, Inman, *University of Sussex*
Hasegawa, Yoshihiko, *University of Tokyo*
Hasle, Geir, *SINTEF ICT*
Hastings, Erin, *University of Central Florida*
Hauert, Sabine, *Massachusetts Institute of Technology*
Hauschild, Mark W., *University of Missouri–St. Louis*
He, Jun, *Aberystwyth University*
Heckendorn, Robert, *University of Idaho*
Heidrich-Meisner, Verena, *Christian-Albrechts-Universität zu Kiel*
Helbig, Marde, *Council for Scientific and Industrial Research, South Africa*
Hendtlass, Tim, *Swinburne University of Technology*
Hereford, James, *Murray State University*
Hernandez, Daniel Eduardo, *Centro de Investigación Científica y de Educación Superior de Ensenada*
Hernández-Aguirre, Arturo, *Centre for Research in Mathematics, Mexico*
Hernández-Díaz, Alfredo G., *Pablo de Olavide University*
Hidalgo, J. Ignacio, *Universidad Complutense de Madrid*
Hingston, Philip, *Edith Cowan University*
Holdener, Ekaterina, *Exegy, Inc.*
Holladay, Kenneth, *Southwest Research Institute*
Holmes, John H., *University of Pennsylvania*
Hoover, Amy K., *University of Central Florida*
Hornby, Gregory S., *University of California at Santa Cruz*
Howard, Gerard, *Commonwealth Scientific and Industrial Research Organisation*
Hsiao, Michael S., *Virginia Tech*
Hu, Bin, *Technische Universität Wien*
Hu, Jianjun, *University of South Carolina*
Husbands, Phil, *Sussex University*
Hutter, Frank, *University of Freiburg*
Iclănzan, David Andrei, *Sapientia Hungaryan University of Transylvania*
Iida, Fumiya, *ETH Zürich*
Ikegami, Takashi, *University of Tokyo*
Inführ, Johannes, *Technische Universität Wien*
Iori, Manuel, *University of Modena and Reggio Emilia*
Ishibuchi, Hisao, *Osaka Prefecture University*
Istvan, Juhos, *University of Szeged*
Jackson, David, *University of Liverpool*
Jakob, Wilfried, *Karlsruhe Institute of Technology*
Janikow, Cezary Z., *University of Missouri–St. Louis*
Jayadeva, *Indian Institute of Technology Delhi*
Jiang, Siwei, *Nanyang Technological University*
Johannsen, Daniel, *SAP Innovation Center*
Johansson, Ulf, *University of Boråas*

Johnson, Colin Graeme, *University of Kent*
Jones, Ben, *University of Birmingham*
Joshi, Ayush, *University of Birmingham*
Jourdan, Laetitia, *INRIA Lille*
Joó, András, *Sapientia University*
Juarez, Reyes, *Universidad Autónoma de Baja California*
Julstrom, Bryant Arthur, *St. Cloud State University*
Kaban, Ata, *University of Birmingham*
Kaboudan, Mak, *University of Redlands*
Kampouridis, Michael, *University of Kent*
Karsai, Istvan, *East Tennessee State University*
Karthik, Sindhya, *University of Jyväskylä*
Kattan, Ahmed, *Umm Al-Qura University*
Kendall, Graham, *University of Nottingham*
Khaled Ahsan Talukder, A. K. M., *George Mason University*
Khan, Gul Muhammad, *University of Engineering & Technology Peshawar*
Khare, Vineet, *Amazon Development Centre, India*
Kirshenbaum, Evan, *HP Labs*
Kisi, Ozgur, *Canik Basari University*
Klamroth, Kathrin, *University of Wuppertal*
Klazar, Ronald, *University of Pretoria*
Knust, Sigrid, *University of Osnabrück*
Köppen, Mario, *Kyushu Institute of Technology*
Komosinski, Maciej, *Poznan University of Technology*
Kontis, Lysimachos, *University of Ioannina*
Korb, Oliver, *Cambridge Crystallographic Data Centre*
Kordon, Arthur K., *Dow Chemical*
Kotsireas, Ilias, *Wilfrid Laurier University*
Kötzing, Timo, *Max Planck Institut für Informatik*
Kovacic, Miha, *University Of Nova Gorica*
Kramer, Oliver, *University of Oldenburg*
Kratica, Jozef, *Serbian Academy of Sciences and Arts*
Krause, Oswin, *University of Copenhagen*
Krawiec, Krzysztof, *Poznan University of Technology*
Kritzinger, Stefanie, *Johannes Kepler Universität Linz*
Kronberger, Gabriel, *University of Applied Sciences Upper Austria*
Kubalik, Jiri, *Czech Technical University in Prague*
Künnemann, Marvin, *Max Planck Institut für Informatik*
Lamont, Gary Byron, *U.S. Air Force Institute of Technology*
Lampinen, Jouni, *University of Vaasa*
Landa-Silva, Dario, *University of Nottingham*
Langer, Philip, *Technische Universität Wien*
Lanzi, Pier Luca, *Politecnico di Milano*
Lara, Adriana, *CINVESTAV-IPN*
LaTorre, Antonio, *Universidad Politécnica de Madrid*
Lau, Henry, *University of Hong Kong*
Lau, Hoong-Chuin, *Singapore Management University*
Legrand, Pierrick, *Université Bordeaux*
Leguizamon, Guillermo, *Universidad Nacional de San Luis*
Lehre, Per Kristian, *University of Nottingham*
Leibnitz, Kenji, *National Institute of Information and Communications Technology, Japan*
Lengler, Johannes, *ETH Zürich*
Leo, Cazenille, *Université Paris Diderot*
Leon, Coromoto, *Universidad de La Laguna*
Leung, Kwong Sak, *Chinese University of Hong Kong*
Lewis, Peter R., *Aston University*
Lewis, Matthew, *Ohio State University*
Li, Ke, *City University of Hong Kong*
Li, Xianneng, *Waseda University*
Li, Bin, *University of Science and Technology of China*
Liang, Feng, *Nanyang Technological University*
Liang, Yiwen, *Wuhan University*
Liao, Tianjun, *Université Libre de Bruxelles*
Liapis, Antonios, *IT University of Copenhagen*
Lichodzijewski, Peter, *Dalhousie University*
Liefooghe, Arnaud, *Université Lille Nord de France*
Limmer, Steffen, *University of Erlangen-Nuremberg*
Ling, Ping, *Jiangsu Normal University*
Lioret, Alain, *Université de Vicennes à Saint-Denis*
Lipinski, Piotr, *University of Wroclaw*
Lissovoi, Andrei, *Technical University of Denmark*
Liu, Bo, *Chinese Academy of Sciences*
Lobo, Daniel, *Tufts University*
Lobo, Fernando G., *University of Algarve*
Loiacono, Daniele, *Politecnico di Milano*
Lones, Michael, *Heriot-Watt University*
López-Ibáñez, Manuel, *Université Libre de Bruxelles*
López-Jaimes, Antonio, *CINVESTAV-IPN*
Loshchilov, Ilya, *École Polytechnique Fédérale de Lausanne*
Louis, Sushil, *University of Nevada*
Lozano, Manuel, *Universidad de Granada*
Lozano, Jose A., *University of the Basque Country*
Lucas, Simon, *University of Essex*
Lukasiewycz, Martin, *TUM CREATE, Singapore*
Luna, Francisco, *Universidad de Extremadura*
Luna, J. M., *Universidad de Córdoba*
Luo, Wenjian, *University of Science and Technology of China*
Lust, Thibaut, *Université Pierre et Marie Curie*
Mabu, Shingo, *Yamaguchi University*
Machado, Penousal, *University of Coimbra*
Macia, Nuria, *Universitat Ramon Llull*
Madureira, Ana Maria, *Polytechnic Institute of Porto*
Majercik, Stephen, *Bowdoin College*
Malago, Luigi, *Università degli Studi di Milano–Bicocca*
Malo, Pekka, *Aalto University*
Mambrini, Andrea, *University of Birmingham*
Mancoridis, Spiros, *Drexel University*
Manderick, Bernard, *Vrije Universiteit Brussel*
Mandziuk, Jacek, *Warsaw University of Technology*
Manzoni, Luca, *Université Nice Sophia Antipolis*
Marchiori, Elena, *Radboud University Nijmegen*
Marinakis, Yannis, *Technical University of Crete*
Maringer, Dietmar, *University of Basel*
Marks II, Robert, *Baylor University*
Marmion, Marie-Eleonore, *Université Lille Nord de France*
Martin, Andrew, *University College London*
Martinez, Hector P., *IT University of Copenhagen*

Martinez, Ivette C., *Universidad Simon Bolivar*
Mascia, Franco, *Université Libre de Bruxelles*
Maslov, Igor V., *EvoCo Inc.*
Matsui, Shouichi, *Central Research Institute of Electric Power Industry, Japan*
Mauri, Giancarlo, *Università degli Studi di Milano–Bicocca*
Mayer, Helmut A., *University of Salzburg*
McDermott, James, *University College Dublin*
McEwan, Chris, *Microsoft Research*
McIntyre, Andrew Ryan, *Dalhousie University*
McKay, Bob, *Seoul National University*
McMinn, Phil, *University of Sheffield*
McPhee, Nicholas Freitag, *University of Minnesota, Morris*
Meignan, David, *University of Osnabrück*
Melab, Nouredine, *Université Lille Nord de France*
Melkozerov, Alexander, *Tomsk State University of Control Systems and Radioelectronics*
Mendes, Rui, *Universidade do Minho*
Mendiburu, Alexander, *University of the Basque Country*
Menzel, Stefan, *Honda Research Institute Europe*
Merelo-Guervós, Juan-Julián, *Universidad de Granada*
Mesejo Santiago, Pablo, *Université d'Auvergne*
Meyer, Bernd, *Monash University*
Meyer-Nieberg, Silja, *Universität der Bundeswehr, München*
Mezura-Montes, Efrén, *Universidad Veracruzana*
Miconi, Thomas, *The Neurosciences Institute*
Middendorf, Martin, *University of Leipzig*
Miettinen, Kaisa, *University of Jyväskylä*
Miikkulainen, Risto, *University of Texas, Austin*
Miklic, Damjan, *University of Zagreb*
Miller, Julian, *University of York*
Minai, Ali, *University of Cincinnati*
Minku, Leandro, *University of Birmingham*
Miramontes Hercog, Luis, *Self-Organizing Solutions*
Misir, Mustafa, *Singapore Management University*
Mitchell, George, *CCKF Ltd.*
Mjolsness, Eric, *University of California at Irvine*
Moen, Hans Jonas Fossum, *Norwegian Defence Research Establishment*
Mohan, Chilukuri K., *Syracuse University*
Montanier, Jean-Marc, *Norwegian University of Science and Technology*
Montemanni, Roberto, *IDSIA*
Moore, Jason, *Dartmouth College*
Mora, Antonio, *Universidad de Granada*
Moraglio, Alberto, *University of Birmingham*
Moses, Melanie, *University of New Mexico*
Möslinger, Christoph, *Karl-Franzens-Universität Graz*
Mostaghim, Sanaz, *Karlsruhe Institute of Technology*
Mouret, Jean-Baptiste, *Université Pierre et Marie Curie, CNRS*
Muelas, Santiago, *Universidad Politécnica de Madrid*
Müller, Christian Lorenz, *New York University*
Mumford, Christine Lesley, *Cardiff University*
Musliu, Nysret, *Technische Universität Wien*
Nagata, Yuichi, *Tokyo Institute of Technology*
Nakib, Amir, *Laboratoire LISSI*
Narukawa, Kaname, *Honda Research Institute Europe*
Nashed, Youssef, *Università degli Studi di Parma*
Naujoks, Boris, *Cologne University of Applied Sciences*
Nebro, Antonio, *Universidad de Málaga*
Neirotti, Juan, *Aston University*
Nejati, Shiva, *University of Luxembourg*
Neri, Ferrante, *University of Jyväskylä*
Neumann, Frank, *University of Adelaide*
Nguyen, Huy, *Misfit Wearables*
Nguyen Xuan, Hoai, *Hanoi University*
Nicolau, Miguel, *University College Dublin*
Nievola, Julio Cesar, *Pontifícia Universidade Católica do Paraná*
Nobile, Marco, *Universitàdegli Studi di Milano–Bicocca*
Nojima, Yusuke, *Osaka Prefecture University*
Noman, Nasimul, *University of Newcastle*
Ó Cinnéide, Mel, *National University of Ireland, Dublin*
O'Neill, Michael, *University College Dublin*
O'Riordan, Colm, *National University of Ireland, Galway*
Ochoa, Gabriela, *University of Stirling*
Ofria, Charles, *Michigan State University*
Oh, Choong Kun, *U.S. Naval Research Laboratory*
Okabe, Tatsuya, *Honda R&D Co., Ltd.*
Olhofer, Markus, *Honda Research Institute Europe*
Oliveira, Pedro N. F. P., *Universidade do Minho*
Oliveto, Pietro S., *University of Sheffield*
Oliwa, Tomasz, *University of Georgia*
Olmo, Juan Luis, *Universidad de Córdoba*
Ombuki-Berman, Beatrice, *Brock University*
Omran, Mohammed, *Gulf University for Science & Technology*
Ono, Isao, *Tokyo Institute of Technology*
Ortega, Julio, *Universidad de Granada*
Ouni, Ali, *Université de Montréal*
Özcan, Ender, *University of Nottingham*
Palafox, Leon, *University of Tokyo*
Pang, Wei, *University of Aberdeen*
Parque, Victor, *Toyota Technological Institute*
Pasquier, Philippe, *Simon Fraser University*
Pedro, Castillo, *Universidad de Granada*
Pellegrini, Paola, *Université Libre de Bruxelles*
Pereira, Francisco Baptista, *Instituto Superior de Engenharia de Coimbra*
Perez Caceres, Leslie, *Université Libre de Bruxelles*
Peña, Jose-Maria, *Universidad Polytécnica de Madrid*
Phelps, Steve, *University of Essex*
Philippides, Andrew, *University of Sussex*
Pibernat, Hugo, *King Games Inc.*
Polani, Daniel, *University of Hertfordshire*
Poles, Silvia, *EnginSoft*
Poloczek, Jendrik, *University of Oldenburg*
Pop, Petrica, *North University of Baia Mare*
Popovici, Elena, *Icosystem Corp.*
Porumbel, Daniel, *Université Lille Nord de France*

Pošík, Petr, *Czech Technical University in Prague*
Potter, Walter, *University of Georgia*
Poulding, Simon, *University of York*
Prandtstetter, Matthias, *Austrian Institute of Technology*
Prestwich, Steve, *University College Cork*
Preuss, Mike, *Technische Universität Dortmund*
Price, Kenneth
Puchinger, Jakob, *Austrian Institute of Technology*
Puente, Cesar, *Universidad Autónoma de San Luis Potosi*
Puerta, Jose Miguel, *Universidad de Castilla–La Mancha*
Punch, William F., *Michigan State University*
Purshouse, Robin, *University of Sheffield*
Qin, Kai, *RMIT University*
Randall, Marcus Christian, *Bond University*
Ranjithan, Ranji S., *North Carolina State University*
Rasheed, Khaled, *University of Georgia*
Ray, Tom, *University of Oklahoma*
Ray, Tapabrata, *University of New South Wales*
Read, Mark, *University of Sydney*
Reed, Patrick M., *Cornell University*
Reif, David, *U.S. Environmental Protection Agency*
Rhee, Phill Kyu, *Inha University*
Rhyd, Lewis, *Cardiff University*
Riff, Maria Cristina, *Universidad Técnica Federico Santa Maria*
Robert, Wille, *University of Bremen*
Robilliard, Denis, *Université Lille Nord de France*
Rohlfshagen, Philipp, *SolveIT Software*
Roper, Marc, *University of Strathclyde*
Ross, Brian J., *Brock University*
Ross, Peter, *Edinburgh Napier University*
Rothlauf, Franz, *Universität Mainz*
Rowe, Jonathan, *University of Birmingham*
Rudolph, Günter, *Technische Universität Dortmund*
Ruhul, Sarker, *University of New South Wales*
Ruiz, Ruben, *Universidad Polytécnica de Valencia*
Runkler, Thomas, *Siemens AG*
Ryan, Conor, *University of Limerick*
Sagarna, Ramon, *University of the Basque Country*
Sahin, Erol, *Middle East Technical University*
Sahraoui, Houari, *Université de Montréal*
Salem, Ziad, *Karl-Franzens-Universität Graz*
Sanchez, Luciano, *Universidad de Oviedo*
Santana, Roberto, *University of the Basque Country*
Santibáñez Koref, Iván, *Technische Universität Berlin*
Sarro, Federica, *University College London*
Sato, Hiroyuki, *University of Electro-Communications*
Sato, Yuji, *Hosei University*
Sawada, Hideyuki, *Kagawa University*
Schillaci, Massimiliano, *Dora S.p.A.*
Schoenauer, Marc, *INRIA Saclay*
Schütze, Oliver, *CINVESTAV-IPN*
Scully, Peter, *Aberystwyth University*
Segura, Carlos, *Universidad de La Laguna*
Sekanina, Lukas, *Brno University of Technology*
Semet, Yann, *Thales*
Sen, Sandip, *University of Tulsa*
Seppi, Kevin, *Brigham Young University*
Serpell, Martin, *University of the West of England*
Sevaux, Marc, *Université de Bretagne-Sud*
Shaheen, Fatima, *Loughborough University*
Shaker, Noor, *IT University of Copenhagen*
Shakya, Siddhartha, *British Telecom*
Shapiro, Jonathan Lee, *University of Manchester*
Shengxiang, Yang, *De Montfort University*
Shihab, Emad, *Rochester Institute of Technology*
Shukla, Pradyumn Kumar, *Karlsruhe Institute of Technology*
Siarry, Patrick, *Université Paris–Est Créteil*
Silva, Fernando, *Universidade de Lisboa*
Sim, Kevin, *Edinburgh Napier University*
Simões, Anabela, *Polytechnic Institute of Coimbra*
Sinha, Ankur, *Aalto University*
Sipper, Moshe, *Ben-Gurion University*
Skurikhin, Alexei N., *Los Alamos National Laboratory*
Smith, Jim, *University of the West of England*
Smith, Stephen L., *University of York*
Smith, Alice, *Auburn University*
Smyth, Tamara, *University of California at San Diego*
Snoek, Jasper, *Harvard University*
Solnon, Christine, *Institut National des Sciences Appliquées de Lyon*
Song, Andy, *RMIT University*
Sossa, Humberto, *Instituto Politécnico Nacional, México*
Souza, Jerffeson, *State University of Ceara*
Spector, Lee, *Hampshire College*
Spicher, Antoine, *Université Paris–Est Créteil*
Squillero, Giovanni, *Politecnico di Torino*
Standish, Russell, *High Performance Coders*
Stepney, Susan, *University of York*
Stibor, Thomas, *GSI Helmholtz Centre for Heavy Ion Research*
Stich, Sebastian, *ETH Zürich*
Stonedahl, Forrest, *Northwestern University*
Stouch, Daniel W., *Charles River Analytics*
Straccia, Umberto, *Istituto di Scienza e Tecnologie dell'Informazione*
Stracquadanio, Giovanni, *Johns Hopkins University*
Stradner, Jürgen, *Karl-Franzens-Universität Graz*
Sudholt, Dirk, *University of Sheffield*
Sun, Xiao-yan, *China University of Mining and Technology*
Sun, Yi, *Google Inc.*
Sun, Chaoli, *Taiyuan University of Science and Technology*
Sutton, Andrew Michael, *Friedrich-Schiller-Universität Jena*
Suzuki, Reiji, *Nagoya University*
Swan, Jerry, *University of Stirling*
Takadama, Keiki, *University of Electro-Communications*
Talbi, El-Ghazali, *INRIA Lille*
Tan, Ying, *Peking University*
Tanaka, Kiyoshi, *Shinshu University*
Tanev, Ivan, *Doshisha University*
Tang, Ke, *University of Science and Technology of China*
Tarantino, Ernesto, *Institute of High Performance Computing*

and Networking, Italy
Tauritz, Daniel R., *Missouri University of Science and Technology*
Tavares, Jorge, *Microsoft*
Tavares, Roberto, *Universidade Federal de São Carlos*
Taylor, Tim, *Goldsmiths, University of London*
Terashima Marín, Hugo, *Tecnológico de Monterrey*
Tettamanzi, Andrea G. B., *Université Nice Sophia Antipolis*
Teuscher, Christof, *Portland State University*
Textor, Johannes, *Universiteit Utrecht*
Teytaud, Fabien, *Université Lille Nord de France*
Teytaud, Olivier, *INRIA Saclay*
Thawonmas, Ruck, *Ritsumeikan University*
Thiele, Lothar, *ETH Zürich*
Thompson, Tommy, *University of Derby*
Timmis, Jonathan, *University of York*
Ting, Chuan-Kang, *National Chung Cheng University*
Tino, Peter, *University of Birmingham*
Tiwari, Santosh, *General Motors Company*
Tiwari, Ashutosh, *Cranfield University*
Tomassini, Marco, *Université de Lausanne*
Tonda, Alberto Paolo, *Institut National de la Recherche Agronomique, France*
Topchy, Alexander, *Nielsen Media Research*
Torres-Jimenez, Jose, *CINVESTAV-IPN*
Torresen, Jim, *University of Oslo*
Trefzer, Martin, *University of York*
Trianni, Vito, *Institute of Cognitive Sciences and Technologies, Italy*
Trujillo, Leonardo, *Instituto Tecnológico de Tijuana*
Tsang, Edward, *University of Essex*
Tuci, Elio, *Aberystwyth University*
Tufte, Gunnar, *Norwegian University of Science and Technology*
Tušar, Tea, *Jožef Stefan Institute*
Tutum, Cem Celal, *Michigan State University*
Twycross, Jamie, *University of Nottingham*
U, Man Chon, *University of Georgia*
Ugolotti, Roberto, *Università degli Studi di Parma*
Urbanowicz, Ryan, *Dartmouth College*
Urquhart, Neil, *Edinburgh Napier University*
Vašíček, Zdeněk, *Brno University Of Technology*
Van den Herik, H. Jaap, *Tilburg University*
Vanneschi, Leonardo, *Universidade Nova de Lisboa*
Vatolkin, Igor, *Technische Universität Dortmund*
Ventura, Sebastian, *Universidad de Córdoba*
Verel, Sebastien, *Université du Littoral Côte d'Opale*
Vergilio, Silvia, *Federal University of Paraná*
Viana, Ana, *Polytechnic Institute of Porto*
Vladislavleva, Ekaterina, *Evolved Analytics Europe*
Von Zuben, Fernando J., *Universidade Estadual de Campinas*
Vrahatis, Michael N., *University of Patras*
Wagner, Tobias, *Technische Universität Dortmund*
Waldock, Antony, *BAE Systems*
Walsh, Paul, *Cork Institute of Technology*
Wang, Yong, *Central South University*
Wang, Ziyu, *University of British Columbia*
Wanka, Rolf, *University of Erlangen-Nuremberg*
Weimer, Westley, *University of Virginia*
Weise, Thomas, *University of Science and Technology of China*
Werfel, Justin, *Harvard University*
Wessing, Simon, *Technische Universität Dortmund*
Whigham, Peter Alexander, *University of Otago*
White, David, *University of Glasgow*
Wilkerson, Josh, *Missouri University of Science and Technology*
Wilson, Garnett, *Afinin Labs Inc.*
Wilson, Stewart W., *Prediction Dynamics*
Wimmer, Manuel, *Technische Universität Wien*
Wineberg, Mark, *University of Guelph*
Winkler, Stephan, *University Of Applied Sciences Upper Austria*
Wong, M. L. Dennis, *Swinburne University of Technology*
Woodward, John R., *University of Stirling*
Wright, Alden H., *University of Montana*
Wrobel, Borys, *Adam Mickiewicz University*
Wu, Zheng Yi, *Bentley Systems*
Wu, Annie S., *University of Central Florida*
Xie, Huayang, *Oracle New Zealand*
Yamada, Takeshi, *NTT Communication Science Labs*
Yamamoto, Lidia, *Université de Strasbourg*
Yannakakis, Georgios, *IT University of Copenhagen*
Yeh, Wei-Chang, *National Tsing Hua University*
Yoo, Shin, *University College London*
Yu, Tina, *Memorial University of Newfoundland*
Yu, Tian-Li, *National Taiwan University*
Yu, Yang, *Nanjing University*
Zafra, Amelia, *Universidad de Córdoba*
Zahadat, Payam, *Karl-Franzens-Universität Graz*
Zaharie, Daniela, *West University of Timisoara*
Zambetta, Fabio, *RMIT University*
Zapf, Michael, *Georg Simon Ohm University of Applied Sciences Nuremberg*
Zapotecas Martínez, Saúl, *CINVESTAV-IPN*
Zell, Andreas, *Universität Tübingen*
Zexuan, Zhu, *Shenzhen University*
Zhang, Mengjie, *Victoria University of Wellington*
Zhang, Fu, *Mathworks*
Zhang, Yuanyuan, *University College London*
Zhang, Byoung-Tak, *Seoul National University*
Zhong, Yanfei, *Wuhan University*
Zhou, Aimin, *East China Normal University*

Best Paper Nominations

Track: Generative and Developmental Systems

Track: Genetic Algorithms

Track: Genetic Programming

Track: Parallel Evolutionary Systems

Track: Real World Applications

Track: Search Based Software Engineering

Track: Theory

An Improved Multi-Start Particle Swarm-based Algorithm for Protein Structure Comparison

Hazem Radwan Ahmed
School of Computing, Queen's University
25 Union Street, Kingston, Ontario,
Canada K7L 3N6.
hazem@cs.queensu.ca

Janice I. Glasgow
School of Computing, Queen's University
25 Union Street, Kingston, Ontario,
Canada K7L 3N6.
janice@cs.queensu.ca

ABSTRACT

This paper proposes a novel particle-swarm based approach for protein structure alignment and comparison. Applying heuristic search to discover similar protein substructure patterns can be easily trapped in certain regions of the sparse and challenging problem search space. Diversification, or restarting the heuristic search, is one of the common strategies used to escape local optima. Agile Particle Swarm Optimization (APSO) is a recent multi-start PSO that addresses the question of when to best restart swarm particles. This paper focuses on where and how to restart the swarm. Another challenge of applying a heuristic search to protein structures is that the fitness landscape does not necessarily guide to the optimal region. To address this issue, we propose the Targeted Agile PSO (TA-PSO) that uses a dynamic window-based search for automatic, variable-size pattern discovery in protein structures. The TA-PSO automatically builds a guiding list of potential patterns and uses it during the search process, which helps to find better solutions faster. The proposed TA-PSO showed up to 4 times improved performance that is ~3.5 times faster and 6 times more robust/consistent compared with the traditional 'non-targeted' search.

Categories and Subject Descriptors

I.2.8 [**Artificial Intelligence**]: Problem Solving, Control Methods, and Search—*Heuristic methods*

Keywords

particle swarm optimization; proteomic pattern discovery; contact map overlap; multi-start search; stagnation; speedup technique.

1. INTRODUCTION

Protein structure comparison remains one of the fundamental tasks in computational biology [3], with important applications to protein structure prediction, function annotation and drug design.

GECCO '14, July 12–16, 2014, Vancouver, BC, Canada.

ACM 978-1-4503-2662-9/14/07…$15.00.
http://dx.doi.org/10.1145/2576768.2598212

Analyzing the three-dimensional structure of proteins is not a straightforward task. That is why two-dimensional representations of protein structures, such as protein distance maps and contact maps, have been widely used as promising alternatives that offer efficient ways to analyze the 3D structure using 2D feature maps [10]. This is because they are readily amenable to machine learning and optimization algorithms, while also capturing useful spatial and topological information about protein conformation (represented in residue-residue interactions). Thus, both distance and contact maps provide a simple, yet robust representation of protein 3D structures.

The Maximum Contact Map Overlap (Max-CMO) has received continued scientific attention during the past decade for pairwise protein structure comparison [1]. In Max-CMO, the similarity between protein structures is represented as the maximum global overlap of their contact maps. Max-CMO tries to find the best global pairwise structure alignment that maximizes the number of common contacts between protein pairs [16]. Several studies have been proposed in the literature to tackle the Max-CMO problem using different techniques that vary from Integer Programming approaches [4] using the Branch-and-Cut method [7], to a Memetic Evolutionary Algorithm [6], and a more-efficient problem approximation using heuristic approaches such as Lagrangian Relaxation [5] and Variable Neighborhood Search [17]. The MaxCMO problem has also been tackled as a Maximum Clique problem [19], and more recently as a Branch-and-Bound (B&B) splitting problem [24].

Unlike Max-CMO that tries to find pairwise *global* alignments between protein structures, this study focuses on finding *local* alignments instead. The ability of PSO algorithm to scale well in high dimensional search spaces makes this study extendable to not only pairwise structure comparison but also to multiple structure comparison. To the best of our knowledge, no attempt has been made in the literature to apply PSO neither to the CMO problem nor to proteomic pattern analysis/structure alignment problems.

Particle Swarm Optimization (PSO) was proposed by James Kennedy and Russell Eberhart in 1995, drawing inspiration from the sociological behavior associated with bird flocking [13]. Since then, a nearly-exponential growing number of PSO applications have been explored in several domains due to the simplicity, efficiency and fast-convergence nature of PSO algorithms. Several comprehensive technical reports made extensive reviews of PSO and their applications. Among over a thousand PSO publications, the survey in [18] considered around 350 papers as proposals for improvements and extensions to the original PSO algorithm. Such a large number of PSO variants has allowed PSO to be capable of solving several kinds of optimization problems, ranging from unconstrained, single-objective or static problems to constrained, multi-objective or dynamic problems.

Stagnation is a well-known issue of PSO. A swarm stagnates when the particles' private memory of their best positions become very similar to the swarm's global best position, which makes the rate of position changes (or velocities) that attract particles to the global best position, is almost zero. This situation, if left unhandled, may lead the swarm to being trapped in a local optimum, from which it cannot escape nor generate new better solutions. This issue is particularly prominent for protein contact maps, in which PSO can be easily trapped in the region around the dense diagonal area of the short-range local contacts, especially when the optimal solution is hidden in the sparse off-diagonal area of the long-range remote contacts (as shown in (Figure 1(b)). A common strategy to help recover a swarm from a stagnation situation is to restart the particles when they prematurely converge. Agile PSO (APSO) is a recent approach for a Multi-Start PSO (MPSO) proposed to address this issue, using a fitness-based criterion to detect an imminent stagnation situation and restart the swarm.

A key question concerning MPSOs is *what* actually to restart. Different studies have used numerous strategies that vary from restarting the particle positions and/or changing their velocities to also resetting particle memories. These strategies have been applied either to 1) only the global best particle since it has the most influence on the rest of the swarm [11], 2) to a random percentage of the swarm (e.g., 10% [12]), or 3) to all swarm particles except the global best to help them discover better positions [23]. Unlike the aforementioned strategies, in this study, the positions of *all* swarm particles are re-initialized, as well as their velocities and memories are reset to *instantly* change the overall search trend and *remove* previous search bias, while keeping a *dictionary* of all previously found best search results. Recording the performance before each restart is important because it is not necessarily the case that the performance is going to improve after each full restart – the swarm may get trapped in another even worse local optimum especially in complex multimodal problems. Thus, in the proposed approach, while all particle memories, velocities and their positions are reset, or lost, after each restart, their best global performances over all number of restarts are kept in a performance dictionary. This approach guarantees to eventually pick the historically best performance (achieved over all number of restarts), which does not necessarily have to happen at the end of the last iteration.

In this study, the proposed Targeted Agile PSO (TA-PSO) method uses a dynamic window-based search for variable-size pattern discovery in protein contact maps. The TA-PSO automatically builds a guiding list of potential contact patterns from the larger contact map that are descendingly ordered by their size. Then, it performs a targeted search approach while focusing the search process on the most promising search subspaces, with the top largest contact patterns. Experimental results over two benchmark protein datasets [15; 19] showed the use of the proposed guiding list has remarkably improved the overall performance, and demonstrated a more robust, effective and efficient behavior compared with the 'non-targeted' APSO, in which particles are mainly guided by their fitness values only (as in many other PSOs).

The paper is organized as follows: Section 2 provides a brief background on distance and contact maps and the Max-CMO problem. Section 3 describes the proposed TA-PSO algorithm for the automatic discovery of common variable-size proteomic patterns in contact maps. Section 4 discusses the experimental settings, results and observations. Lastly, the Conclusions section summarizes the key findings and contributions of the study, and suggests a further potential direction for future research.

2. BACKGROUND

2.1 Distance and Contact Maps

One challenge of protein structure comparison stems from the fact that the 3D coordinate information of each protein structure has a fixed coordinate space. However, in order to reliably compare different protein structures, they need to be represented in a coordinate-independent space that is translation and rotation invariant, such as distance and contact maps [10].

Not only is a protein distance map an effective alternative representation of the protein structure, but also it is simpler and more compact two-dimensional representation of the three-dimensional coordinate information of the protein. This relatively reduces the complexity of proteomic pattern discovery problem from the comparison of protein 3D structures to the comparison of 2D matrices or feature maps. A distance map, D, for a protein of n amino acids is a symmetric n x n matrix that represents all pairwise distances between α-carbon atoms of protein amino acids in 3D space. Each axis in distance maps represents the protein sequence. As shown in Figure 1(a), the darker the distance map color, the closer the distance between its corresponding amino acid pair. A distance map can be used to construct another thresholded, binary matrix of same size called a contact map.

A contact map, C, is a two-dimensional binary symmetric matrix that represents all pairwise interactions of protein residues. Residue-residue interactions fold a protein into a unique three-dimensional structure, which essentially determines its specific function. A pair of amino acids is defined to be interacting if the distance between their α-carbon atoms is less than or equal a given distance threshold (usually measured in Ångstroms), as shown in Figure 1(b). A contact map can be used to infer some important structural features of the original 3D structures. It has been found that different secondary structures (e.g., α-helices and β-sheets) have distinctive structural patterns in contact maps. For example, an α-helix appears as an unbroken row of contacts between i, i ± 4 pairs along the main diagonal (short-range contacts), while β-sheets appear as an unbroken row of contacts in the off-diagonal areas (long-range contacts). A row of contacts that is parallel to the main diagonal represents a pair of parallel β-sheets, while a row of contacts that is perpendicular to the main diagonal represents a pair of anti-parallel β-sheets [26]. The reconstruction of the original 3D structure from distance or contact maps is fortunately possible. Although the 3D structure reconstruction from a distance map is simpler (due to the more information it encodes compared with the thresholded contact map), a number of studies have shown some potential in

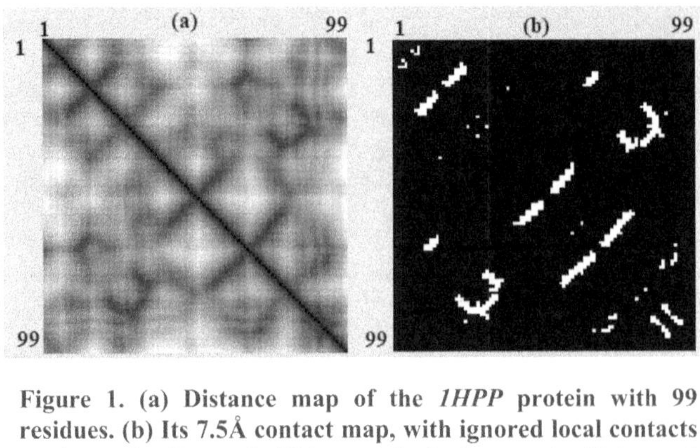

Figure 1. (a) Distance map of the *1HPP* protein with 99 residues. (b) Its 7.5Å contact map, with ignored local contacts at the main diagonal. This protein is the most widely used strain in the study of potential drugs against HIV.

reconstructing the 3D structure from contact maps [21]. Similar to this study [16], a distance threshold of 7.5Å was adopted in our experiments without taking into account local contacts or contacts between neighboring amino acids of at most two residues apart (unless otherwise specified).

An element of the ith and j^{th} residues of a contact map, $C(i,j)$, can be defined as follows [10]:

$$C(i,j) = \begin{cases} 1; & \text{if } D(i,j) \leq \text{threshold} \\ 0; & \text{otherwise} \end{cases}$$

Where, $D(i,j)$ is the distance between amino acids i and j, ***one*** denotes a pairwise inter-residue *contact* (or white in color space), and **zero** denotes *no contact* between corresponding residue pairs (or black in color space).

In protein structure comparison using contact maps, the local contacts between each residue and itself on the main diagonal are typically ignored. This is because even too distant contact maps will share a similar main diagonal anyway, so comparing the main diagonal of contact maps will neither add meaningful information for their similarity nor their dissimilarity. Moreover, local or neighboring contacts of at most two residues apart at protein backbone are ignored in this study, since they almost always occur in any contact maps.

3. METHODOLOGY

Agile PSO (APSO) is a recent type of an MPSO that triggers the restart mechanism using a Performance-based Stagnation Indicator (PSI) to detect an imminent stagnation situation and restart the swarm to escape potential local optima, which showed to be more efficient and effective compared with the commonly used distance-based criteria [9; 20]. The PSI criterion effectively triggers the restart mechanism when the average fitness of all swarm particles becomes almost the same as the global best particle, as shown in (4). The efficiency of the PSI criterion stems from the fact that it makes use of the already calculated fitness values stored in each particle's memory, without the overhead of calculating particle distances to the global best particle (unlike distance-based criteria).

$$\frac{Average\,(f(P_i))}{f(P_g)} \geq \psi, \; f(P_g) > 0 \tag{4}$$

Where: f is the objective (maximization) function, $f(P_i)$ is the corresponding fitness vector of particles' historically best positions, $f(P_g)$ is the fitness value of the global best particle position, and ψ is the *PSI threshold*, which is a positive percentage value defined by the user. The smaller the value of ψ, the more frequent the restart mechanism will be triggered. Thus, PSI value clearly affects the algorithm's sensitivity to triggering the restart mechanism. It was empirically found that this approach works well when the PSI threshold is set between 90% for low-dimensional problems and 70% for high-dimensional problems. Higher-dimensional problems would generally require lower PSI threshold, because the chance of stagnation situation usually increases as the problem dimensionality increases. Thus, a more sensitive restart mechanism for higher-dimensional problems would be needed. In this 5- dimensional problem, PSI threshold is set at 80%.

Thus far we have discussed *why* and *when* to restart particles. The other key questions to be addressed with respect to MPSOs in this paper are *how* and *where* to restart. Another important question concerning MPSOs is *how* to initialize and re-initialize swarm particles. Initializing particle positions using a uniform random distribution is an easy and simple answer to this question. However, it has been found that the resulting set of particle positions using this approach does not evenly cover the whole search space [8]. This issue becomes prominent in high-dimensional or complex search spaces when the optimum region is hidden or is not easy to reach, which is often the case in the generally sparse contact maps. One approach to address this issue is to use a robust initialization scheme for particles that evenly covers the entire search space as "regular" as possible to avoid missing the optimum region when it is fully surrounded by bad or non-attractive areas. Clerc tested several PSO initialization methods [8] and concluded that the use of Hammersley distribution [22] is the best to initialize particle positions, especially on complex, multimodal and/or multidimensional search problems [8]. That is the reason why it is adopted in the proposed TA-PSO to better initialize/re-initialize particle positions for the generally sparse contact maps.

Another key question concerning MPSOs is w*here* to initialize and re-initialize swarm particles. Traditional search strategies initialize particles evenly all over the entire search space. Applying this approach to contact maps with an MPSO using Hammersley distribution can generally help not to miss the optimum regions. However, the search process may take longer to discover hidden optimum region(s), if they are surrounded by a low-fitness, non-attractive area for the flying particles. This commonly happens when the optimum region is isolated in an off-diagonal area with just a few sparse contacts around (as shown earlier in Figure 1(b)). In this case, the fitness landscape or the gradient of the search space will not generally guide to such an isolated optimum region. Thus, in order to speed the discovery of the optimum regions, when they are out of particles' sight, this paper suggests the use of a targeted search strategy, as will be discussed in the following section.

3.1 Targeted Agile PSO (TA-PSO)

TA-PSO uses an expanding window-based search approach for the automatic discovery of common variable-size patterns in protein contact maps. Each particle in TA-PSO has a five-dimensional position vector: X_1, Y_1, X_2, Y_2, and L which represents a pair of 2D points in the contact map pair and the size of a flying square window pair L. In particular, X_1 and Y_1 represent the upper-left corner of a flying $L \times L$ window on the first contact map, and X_2 and Y_2 represent the upper-left corner of another flying window on the other contact map. Each pair of flying windows has the same size, $L \times L$, which is initially set to some small value and then *iteratively* gets expanded as needed. The first question regarding this approach is: what are the lower and upper bounds to be used during the expansion process for flying window pairs.

In this study, we started with an initial minimum window size of 5X5. It is known that proteomic patterns of less than five-residue length can abundantly re-occur even in non-evolutionary related proteins (especially at the dense diagonal area of local contacts) [2], because they simply may occur as a result of the general folding constraints of proteins. Thus, similarities of less than 5X5 window are ignored in this study.

Unfortunately, however, it is not as easy to decide on the maximum window size. Without an informed search strategy in a pair of contact maps of two proteins with sizes L_1 and L_2, there is no definite upper-bound of the expanding window size. All what is known is that the ultimate maximum window size should never go beyond the size of the smaller contact map, $min(L_1,L_2)$, which may be used as an ultimate upper-bound. The proposed TA-PSO, however, determines the upper bound using a more efficient strategy compared with using the ultimate maximum window size.

As discussed earlier, TA-PSO automatically builds a guiding list of potential contact patterns (with largest connected white regions in the larger contact map) in a descending order according to their size.

Then, a targeted search is performed on the smaller contact map while focusing the search on the larger contact map within the boundaries of the most potential patterns. The first advantage of this approach is that the upper-bound of the window size can now be determined more efficiently according to the size of the largest pattern in the guiding list, which is almost always going to be much less than the aforementioned ultimate maximum window size. Justifiably, there is no need to expand the search window beyond the size of the largest pattern in the larger contact map. This more efficient strategy is found to save considerable time during the expansion process and improved the overall computation speed.

The next question regarding the use of dynamically changing window size is when to stop the expansion process. In this study, the expansion stops the sooner of reaching the upper-bound of the expanding window, or reaching an iteration that does not improve the number of common contacts after just increasing the window size. At the dense diagonal area, however, the bigger the window size, the more the common contacts is normally expected to be found, often regardless of the actual pair-wise pattern similarity. Thus, in this study, we used a similarity threshold of 80%, below which the expansion process terminates (as will be later discussed in the Results section). Then, the fitness value and the square window size L before terminating the expansion process is given to the 5-dimesnional particle residing at that location, which represents a pair of 2D points in the two contact maps and the square window size.

3.2 Objective Function

Jaccard's Coefficient (J) is a well-known binary similarity measure and is a particularly suitable measure for contact map similarity, where binary values do not carry equal information. In this study, we are more interested in contacts (ones) than 'no contacts' (zeros). Moreover, J does not consider counting common zero elements (i.e., no-contacts in contact map pairs), which removes the effect of the "double absence" that has neither meaningful contribution to the similarity, nor the dissimilarity, of contact maps, as shown in (5).

$$J = \frac{C_{11}}{S - C_{00}} \tag{5}$$

Where C_{11} is the count of nonzero, white elements (common contacts) between each discovered pair of contact patterns of both contact maps, C_{00} is the count of zero, black elements (no-contacts) between the pair of square contact patterns, and S is the size of the square window (i.e., *L x L*). It is worth emphasizing here that the objective function, or particle's fitness value to be maximized is not set to J, but to C_{11}. In this study, J was only used as a part of the stopping criteria for the window expansion process. In summary, the square, expanding window pair at each particle position starts with a 5X5 size in this study, and iteratively expands as long as 1) C_{11} is increasing, 2) J is greater than 80%, and 3) the upper-bound of the window size is not reached.

3.3 TA-PSO vs. Max-CMO

As discussed earlier, the Maximum Contact Overlap (Max-CMO) problem aims to find a *global* structure alignment between pairs of proteins. In Max-CMO, protein structure is represented as an undirected contact graph, as shown in Figure 3. The nodes in the graph correspond to protein amino acids, while edges correspond to residue-residue interactions. That is, there is an edge between any two nodes of the contact graph if their corresponding amino acids are in contact, i.e., their positions in the three-dimensional structure of the protein are within a predefined distance threshold (6.0 Å in the example shown in Figure 3). Thus, the Max-CMO problem has been modeled as a type of the maximum clique problem in an alignment graph (or maximum edge-induced sub-graph problem). Different approaches based on Integer Programming [4] and Lagrangian Relaxation [5], among others, have been successfully used in the past decade to align protein structures by maximizing their common sub-graph. The amount of similarity between two proteins is, therefore, determined according to the size of the maximum common contacts (edges) in their contact graphs. More specifically, the amount of similarity represents the number of edges that connect two equivalent nodes in both alignment graphs. Both MaxCMO and the proposed TA-PSO can be used to compare protein structures, but there are a number of major differences between the two approaches. Firstly, TA-PSO uses a dynamic window-based search directly on the binary adjacency matrix of residue-residue interactions without the need of converting protein contact maps to contact graphs. Secondly, because the discovered similar *local* structural patterns of contact maps can be eventually used as building blocks in a bottom-up approach for protein structure prediction [10], TA-PSO is concerned with discovering similar *local* patterns (local alignment), as opposed to finding the *global* pairwise alignment that may maximize the contact map overlap but not necessarily finds the common structural building blocks between the query and template proteins.

The following example, adapted from [24], is used to illustrate the different problem representation in Max-CMO versus TA-PSO. The example uses a pair of small mainly-alpha proteins, cow insulin (*1cph)* and chicken villin *(1vii)*, as shown in Figure 2, which are two of other collected proteins in the Sokol benchmark dataset [19]. Figure 3 shows an instance of CMO with 18 aligned residues (or dashed lines of common contacts), resulting from the global alignment between the two proteins. Figures 4 shows a sample run of TA-PSO, which discovered a 7-residue match with 13 common contacts (C_{11} = 13 and J = 86.7%) between **H2** of 1cph and **H3** of 1vii, which is a good local alignment between the two proteins that the method repeatedly managed to locate (Figure 4-b). It is worth emphasizing that the used objective function to be maximized in this problem is the number of common contact C_{11}, and not the actual Jaccard similarity (J). In fact, we tried using Jaccard similarity as the objective function at first, but the search was observed to be so conservative with no preference to expand the window size beyond the given minimum size of 5X5. This is because the bigger the window size, the larger the number of common contacts (C_{11}), and the smaller or same Jaccard similarity (J). Thus, the objective of maximizing J would conflict with the objective of maximizing the window size. On the other hand, when C_{11} was used alone as the objective function to be maximized, the search showed the opposite

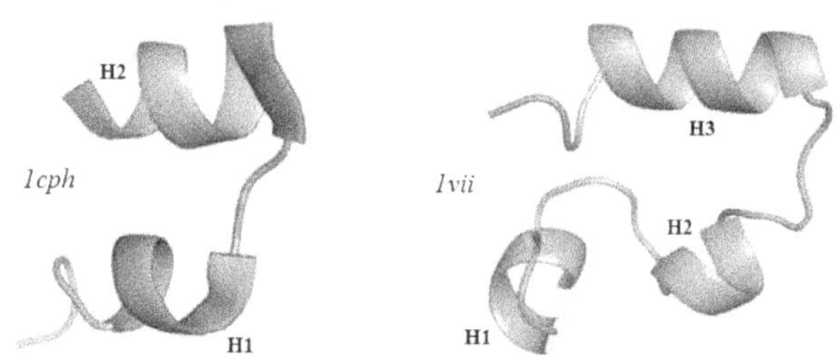

Figure 2. A pair of small mainly-alpha proteins: *1cph* and *1vii*. The left protein (*1cph*, 21 resuides) has two α-helices (*H1 and H2*). The other protien (*1vii*, 36 resuides) has three α-helices (*H1, H2 and H3*).

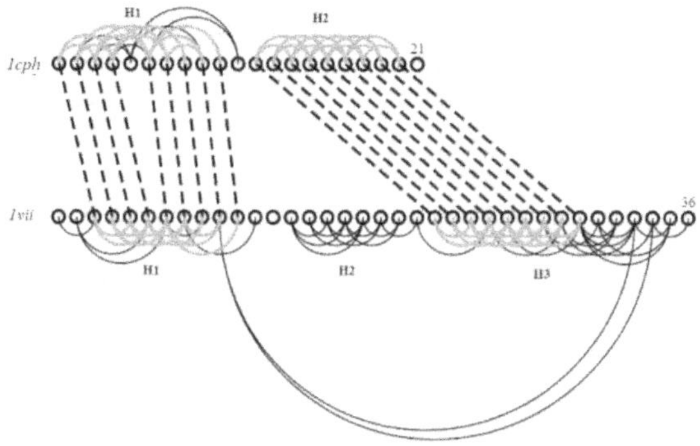

Figure 3. An instance of CMO between *1cph* (21 residue) & *1vii* (36 residues), using a 6Å distance threshold to define interacting residues. Solid arcs represent the edges of the contact graph for each protein, dashed lines indicate a global alignment of residues, and bold solid arcs correspond to the 24 overlaps that result from this alignment instance. Adapted from [24].

behavior. It was biased to find larger patterns with lower similarity (mostly up to the maximum window size). To address this issue, we used C_{11} as the objective function while also setting a minimum similarity threshold of 80%, after which the window expansion process stops even if C_{11} is still increasing. In the previous example, for instance, if the minimum 80% similarity threshold is slightly relaxed, a bigger local alignment of 8 residues with 14 common contacts (C_{11} = 14) can be located, but with lower similarly (J = 70%), between **H1** of *1cph* and **H3** of *1vii*, as shown in Figure 4(f).

While the upper bound of the aforementioned CMO instance was presented in [24], it is worth noting that this upper bound is less relevant to our study since it represents the maximum *global* overlap (like most state-of-the-art algorithms), not the maximum *local* alignment that this study is attempting to discover instead, which as mentioned earlier can be eventually used as building blocks in our future research on protein structure modeling from contact map [14]. In this study, however, similar to the original example in [24], local and consecutive contacts at the main diagonal are not taken into consideration since they always occur in any contact maps. Also, the lower triangle was ignored due to the symmetrical nature of contact maps. As discussed earlier, TA-PSO approach builds a guiding list of the top N largest patterns in the larger contact map, where in this example N was set to 3 (**H1**, **H2**, and **H3**) of *1vii* protein. The largest pattern in this guiding list is **H3** with 11-resuide length. Thus, the expanding window size starts with *5X5* up to *11X11*, instead of going up to the ultimate maximum window size *21X21*, which is the size of the smaller contact map (*1cph*). The use of the guiding list did not only help to use a more targeted search that only focused on potential patterns of interest, but also it considerably cut the expansion time to almost half in this example. While the initialization/re-initialization on the larger contact maps was targeted to mainly focus on the largest contact patterns, particles fly over the *entire* search space of the other smaller contact map. The use of Hammersley distribution to restart particle positions allowed particles to almost always cover the entire search space evenly, as shown in Figure 4(c), for instance.

Last but not least, the same boundary conditions of APSO were used in TA-PSO. In particular, the restricted damping condition was used for vertical and horizontal boundaries and the invisible damping condition was used for the diagonal boundary of contact maps. Restricted damping boundary condition acts as a *'hard wall'* that resets the position of all particles trying to cross a boundary at any

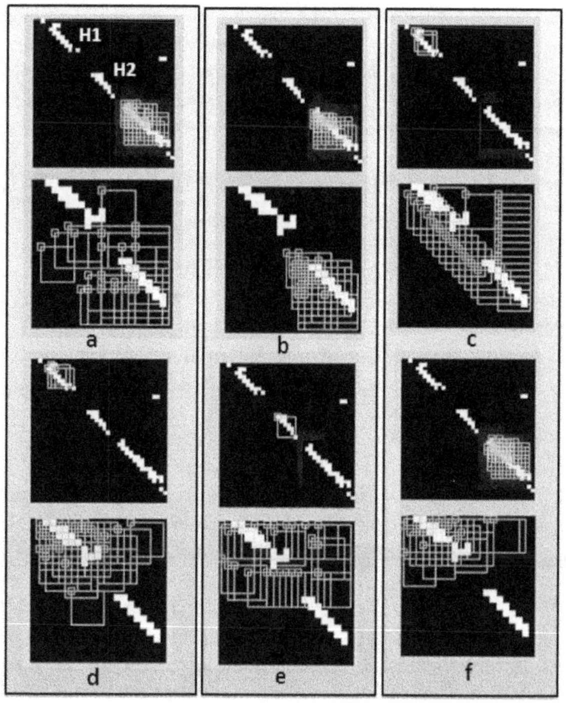

Figure 4. Sample run of TA-PSO (using Top3, 50 particles and 80% for J & Ψ) on a pair of 6Å contact maps: *1vii* protein on the upper contact map and *1cph* protein on the lower one. (a) Particles are targeted to the largest pattern H3 in the top contact map for the larger protein *1vii*, while a Hammsersly distribution is used over the other smaller contact map. (b) Particles are almost converged and rapidly discovered a good local alignment between H3 of *1vii* and H2 of *1cph*. (c) & (e) Restart mechanism is triggered: Particles on the top contact maps have switched focus to the next largest pattern H1 then H2 of *1vii*, and particle positions are re-initialized using Hammersley distribution to evenly cover the upper triangle of the smaller contact map. (d) Particles are about to converge, and the restart mechanism is about to get triggered again. (f) When the minimum J similarity threshold is relaxed, particles were able to locate a larger alignment between H3 of *1vii* and H1 of *1cph* with C_{11} = 14 but with lower similarity (J = 70%).

dimension to that boundary location and changes their velocity to the opposite direction. Whereas, invisible damping boundary condition acts as a *'soft wall'* that does not reset the position of errant particles, but rather resets their fitness value to zero and inverses their motion direction to eventually have them attracted back to the allowed search space [25].

4. RESULTS AND DISCUSSION

An all-against-all analysis was performed on two benchmark protein datasets (Sokol with 45 instances of protein pairs from three different fold families [19]) and Skolnick with 820 instances of protein pairs from five different fold families [15]), using Clerc's constriction model with χ = 0.729 and c_1=c_2=2.05 over 10 independent runs, with a swarm of 50 particles and 200 iterations per each pairwise comparison (unless otherwise specified). All experiments used 7.5Å contact maps without local contacts up to two residues apart. As discussed earlier, TA-PSO builds a guiding list of the top N largest patterns from the larger contact map. The first question about this approach is how many N largest patterns to consider. Different N values are tested ranging for Top1 to Top7. As shown in Figure 5, Top2 seems to work best (i.e., achieved the largest number of common contacts) among other tested values. The reason of this could be due to the fact that Top1 makes a kind of greedy approach that considers the top largest pattern only, whereas Top3+ distracts the search with over 3 targets (or, actually makes it 'less targeted'). The J threshold is another search parameter used to tune the minimum allowed Jaccard similarity, which is utilized to terminate the window expansion process. Different values for J thresholds were tested ranging from a stringent approach of 100% similarity to a very relaxed threshold of only 40% similarity. As shown in Figure 6, using J threshold of 100% similarity achieved the lowest number of common contacts, which is expected because the search in this case becomes very restrictive and refuses any patterns unless they have a perfect 100% match. Moreover, there is an almost increasing trend of the number of common contacts as the J threshold decreases, but the performance difference appears quite negligible with less than 80% J thresholds (e.g., 0.05% difference when J=70% and 1.9% at the very relaxed J threshold of 40%). Thus, a J threshold of 80% is considered a good value that makes a balance between search flexibility and search effectiveness.

As for the number of particles, Figure 7 shows the effect of varying swarm sizes (from 20 to 80 particles) on the performance. As expected, there is a general increasing trend on the search performance as the swarm size increases. We observed an 8% performance improvement, on average, by increasing the swarm size from 20 to 80 particles; however, the algorithm apparently becomes less sensitive to swarm size after using over 40-50 particles. For example, the difference between using 50 and 80 particles is only 1.8%. A swarm size of 50 is therefore considered a good value that makes a balance between search effectiveness and search efficiency.

As for the PSI threshold, its range is generally found to best start from 90% for low-dimensional problems to 70% for high-dimensional problems. The use of 80% PSI threshold is empirically found, in a previous study, suitable for 4-D pairwise pattern discovery with fixed window size. In this 5-D pairwise pattern discovery problem with dynamically expanding window size, the same PSI value of 80% seems to still work well. As shown in Figure 8, among different tested PSI thresholds from 95% to 65%, a PSI value of 80% achieved the best median performance over 10 runs.

The number of iterations in any heuristic search plays an influential role in the search performance. In this study, we set a maximum number of iterations per each pairwise comparison. In general, more iteration is preferred for better solution quality, but this comes at the cost of search efficiency. Thus, a sufficiently good number of iterations are necessary to make a trade-off between search time and solution quality. Figure 9 shows the number of common contacts discovered in the Sokol dataset at various iteration choices, ranging from 25 to 1000 iterations, per each pairwise comparison. The normally increasing trend of discovered common contacts with more iteration is expected. An interesting observation, however, is that the average results over 10 independent runs when using 1000 iterations is almost the same as using 600 iterations (0.1% difference), and even when using 400 iterations (0.6% difference). Moreover, the average results when using 200 iterations can hardly be distinguished from using more iteration. For example, there is only 2.6% difference when increasing the number of iteration from 200 to 1000 iterations. Thus, the maximum number of iterations per pairwise comparison is set to 200 in this study.

Another interesting observation from Figure 9 is that the difference between the upper and lower quartiles of the performance over 10 independent runs is becoming negligible when using 200 iterations or more. For example, there is less than 1% performance difference between the 25th percentile (i.e., the performance of the worst 25% runs) and the 75th percentile (i.e., the performance of the best 25% runs) when using 200 iteration. This difference approaches zero when using more iteration, and it generally increases with less iteration (e.g., 2% difference when using 100 iterations and 6% difference when using 25 iterations). The lesser the performance difference between the worst and best runs, the more robust and consistent the heuristic search is, and the less dependent it is on different initial random seeds. This essentially highlights the main contribution of the proposed targeted search approach, as opposed to the traditional 'non-targeted' search approach, as will be discussed in the following paragraph.

Figure 10 shows the number of common contacts discovered in the Sokol dataset using the 'non-targeted' search approach at different number of iterations, ranging from 25 to 1000. Not only is the median performance of TA-PSO *four* times better, on average, than non-targeted APSO median performance, but also it is *six* times more robust, on average, compared with the non-targeted approach. The robustness here is measured in terms of the performance difference between the 25% worst runs (lower quartile) and 25% best runs (upper quartile) for both approaches. TA-PSO has an average performance difference of 37 common contacts, as opposed to APSO with 239 common contacts (i.e., over 6 times bigger difference on average). Besides the robustness and effectiveness of the proposed targeted approach, it is also more efficient than non-targeted approach. In this experiment, TA-PSO is found to be over *3.5* times faster than APSO. The computation speed is expected due to the better ability of the targeted approach to decide on the maximum expanding window size, as opposed to the non-targeted approach that tries up to the ultimate maximum window size (i.e., the size of the smaller contact map, as discussed in Section 3.1).

Lastly, Figure 11 shows the performance of TA-PSO on the larger Skolnick dataset of 820 instances of protein pairs, using best parameter values as previously discussed in Sokol dataset, namely Top2, 50 particles, 80% for J and PSI thresholds at various numbers of iterations per each pairwise comparison. The first quick observation from this figure is that the number of discovered common contacts in Skolnick dataset is justifiably in order of magnitude bigger than the previously tested smaller Sokol dataset. Another observation is that there is an expected increasing trend of discovered common contacts as the number of iteration increases. Moreover, similar to the aforementioned Sokol results, the search robustness/consistency increases with more iteration. For instance, there is only 0.6% performance difference between the upper and lower quartiles when using 200 iterations, as opposed to 1.1% when using 100 iterations. Also similar to Sokol results, this difference approaches zero with more iteration (e.g., 0.28% difference when using 1000 iterations and 0.15% difference when using 2000 iterations).

Unlike Sokol results, however, the performance improvement when increasing the number of iterations from 200 to 1000 is relatively bigger (12%), as opposed to 2.6% in Sokol. This suggests that the use of extra iterations is more preferable in the more challenging Skolnick dataset, although the performance with 200 iterations still achieved fairly decent results. We therefore tested more choices of iteration values in this experiment. The performance improvement with more iteration is observed to keep decreasing after 200-300 iterations (although not as strongly decreasing as in Sokol). But eventually there was less than 1% performance improvement when the number of iterations is doubled from 1000 to 2000.

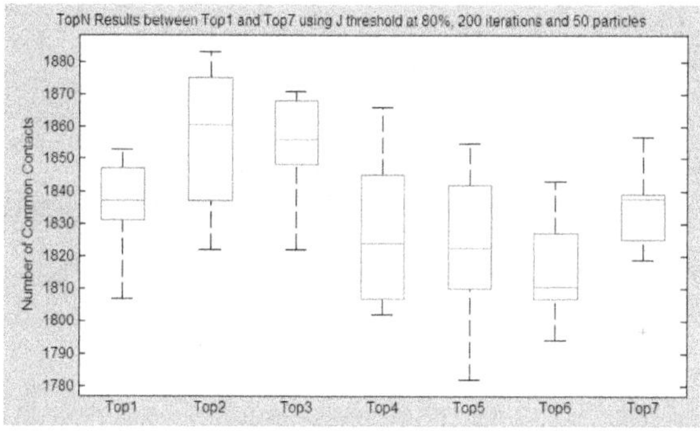

Figure 5. No. of common contacts with various Top N values (Sokol).

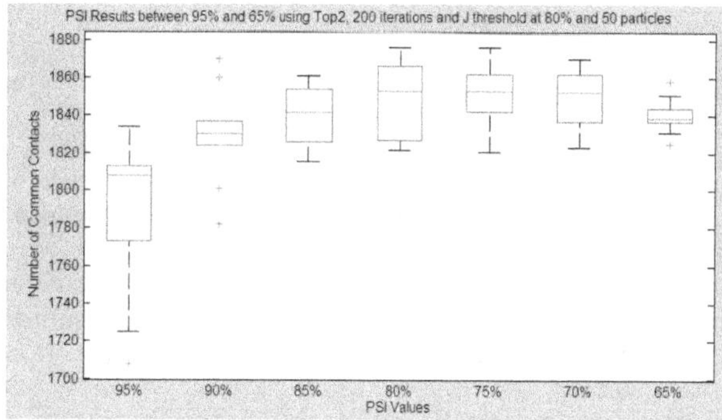

Figure 8. No. of common contacts with various PSI thresholds (Sokol).

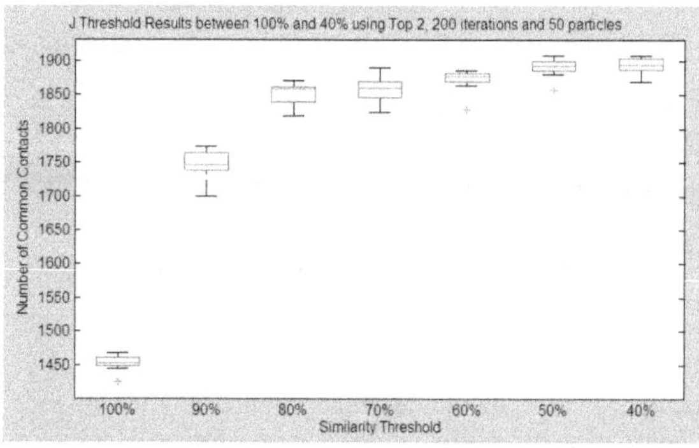

Figure 6. No. of common contacts with various J similarity thresholds (Sokol).

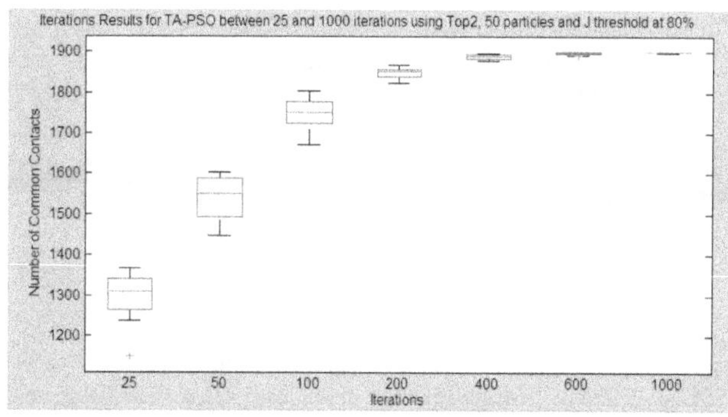

Figure 9. TA-PSO applied to Sokol dataset at different number of iterations.

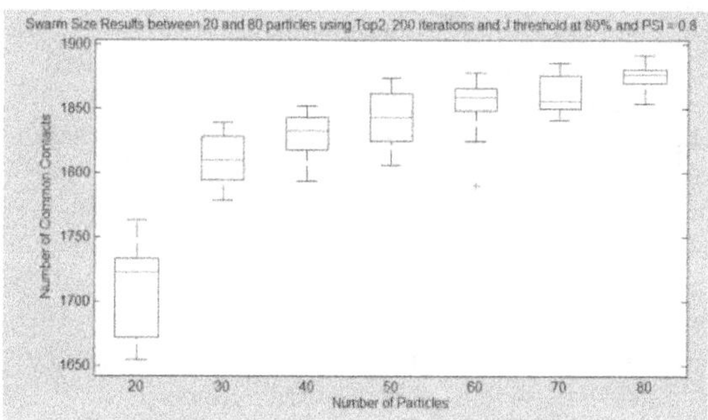

Figure 7. No. of common contacts with various swarm sizes (Sokol).

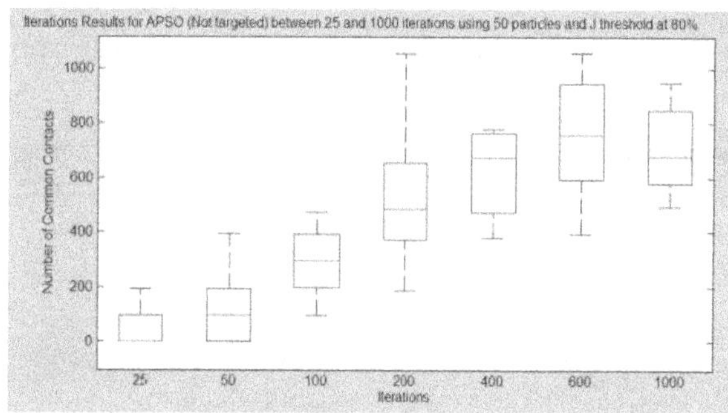

Figure 10. APSO applied to Sokol dataset at different number of iterations.

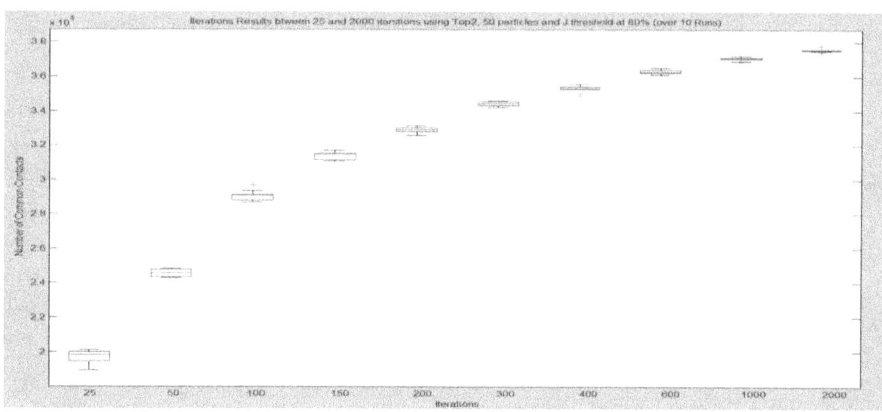

Figure 11. TA-PSO applied to Skolnick dataset at different number of iterations, using best parameter values (Top2, 50 particles, 80% for J & PSI thresholds).

5. CONCLUSIONS

Making use of the simplicity and efficiency of Particle Swarm Optimization (PSO), this paper proposed a targeted, dynamic window-based search approach, called Targeted Agile PSO (TA-PSO), for protein local structure alignment and pairwise structure comparison. To the best of our knowledge, this is the first study in the literature to investigate the applicability of PSO to proteomic pattern analysis and structure alignment problems. TA-PSO addresses the well-known stagnation issue of PSO by restarting particle positions and resetting their velocities and memories when an imminent stagnation situation is detected, using an efficient fitness-based criterion for stagnation detection.

This paper focuses on how and where to restart particles in order to escape local optima, and speed convergence to better solutions. Instead of using the simple, yet less effective, uniform random distribution to initialize/reinitialize particle positions, the more robust Hammersley distribution that better covers the entire search space evenly is used to increase the chances of finding hidden optimum regions, which is often the case in the generally sparse protein contact maps. Moreover, the proposed TA-PSO uses a targeted search approach by focusing the search on the most promising regions, using an automatically built guiding list of largest contact patterns. Experimental results on two protein benchmark datasets (45 and 820 instances of protein pairs, respectively) have showed the proposed targeted search method to be more effective (4 times better) and more efficient (~3.5 times faster) compared with the traditional 'non-targeted' search method, as well as 6 times more robust/consistent over 10 independent runs.

The main objective of this study was to investigate the applicability of PSO to pairwise protein structure comparison, but possible future work includes comparing the effectiveness of the proposed approach with other evolutionary algorithms, such as Differential Evolution, as well as extending the TA-PSO to simultaneous multiple protein structure comparison/alignment.

6. REFERENCES

[1] Andonov, R., Malod-Dognin, N., and Yanev, N., 2011. Maximum contact map overlap revisited. *Journal of Computational Biology 18*, 1, 27-41.

[2] Betancourt, M.R. and Skolnick, J., 2004. Local propensities and statistical potentials of backbone dihedral angles in proteins. *Journal of molecular biology 342*, 2, 635-649.

[3] Bourne, P.E. and Shindyalov, I.N., 2003. Structure comparison and alignment. *Structural Bioinformatics, Volume 44*, 321-337.

[4] Caprara, A., Carr, R., Istrail, S., Lancia, G., and Walenz, B., 2004. 1001 optimal PDB structure alignments: integer programming methods for finding the maximum contact map overlap. *Journal of Computational Biology 11*, 1, 27-52.

[5] Caprara, A. and Lancia, G., 2002. Structural alignment of large—size proteins via lagrangian relaxation. In *Proceedings of the sixth annual international conference on Computational biology* ACM, 100-108.

[6] Carr, R., Hart, W., Krasnogor, N., Hirst, J., Burke, E., and Smith, J., 2002. Alignment Of Protein Structures With A Memetic Evolutionary Algorithm. In *GECCO*, 1027-1034.

[7] Carr, R., Lancia, G., and Istrail, S., 2000. *Branch-and-cut algorithms for independent set problems: Integrality gap and an application to protein structure alignment.* Sandia National Laboratories.

[8] Clerc, M., 2008. Initialisations for particle swarm optimisation, Available Online at http://clerc.maurice.free.fr/pso.

[9] Evers, G.I. and Ben Ghalia, M., 2009. Regrouping particle swarm optimization: a new global optimization algorithm with improved performance consistency across benchmarks. In *Systems, Man and Cybernetics, 2009. SMC 2009. IEEE International Conference on* IEEE, 3901-3908.

[10] Glasgow, J., Kuo, T., and Davies, J., 2006. Protein structure from contact maps: A case-based reasoning approach. *Information systems frontiers 8*, 1, 29-36.

[11] Higashitani, M., Ishigame, A., and Yasuda, K., 2007. Particle swarm optimization with controlled mutation. *IEEE Trans on Electrical & Electronic Engineering 2*, 2, 192-194.

[12] Hu, X. and Eberhart, R.C., 2002. Adaptive particle swarm optimization: detection and response to dynamic systems. In *Evolutionary Computation, 2002. CEC'02. Proceedings of the 2002 Congress on* IEEE, 1666-1670.

[13] Kennedy, J. and Eberhart, R., 1995. Particle swarm optimization. In *Neural Networks, 1995. Proceedings., IEEE International Conference on* IEEE, 1942-1948.

[14] Kuo, T.C. and Glasgow, J., 2014. Predicting helix pair structure from fuzzy contact maps. *Applied Soft Computing 14*, 357-362.

[15] Lancia, G., Carr, R., Walenz, B., and Istrail, S., 2001. 101 optimal PDB structure alignments: a branch-and-cut algorithm for the maximum contact map overlap problem. In *Proceedings of the fifth annual international conference on Computational biology* ACM, 193-202.

[16] Malod-Dognin, N., 2010. Protein Structure Comparison: From Contact Map Overlap Maximisation to Distance-based Alignment Search Tool. PhD thesis, University of Rennes.

[17] Pelta, D., González, J., and Vega, M.M., 2008. A simple and fast heuristic for protein structure comparison. *BMC Bioinformatics 9*, 1, 161.

[18] Poli, R., 2007. An analysis of publications on particle swarm optimization applications. *Technical Report, Department of Computer Science, University of Essex, UK.*

[19] Strickland, D.M., Barnes, E., and Sokol, J.S., 2005. Optimal protein structure alignment using maximum cliques. *Operations research 53*, 3, 389-402.

[20] Van Den Bergh, F., 2002. An analysis of particle swarm optimizers. PhD Thesis, Department of Computer Science, University of Pretoria, South Africa.

[21] Walsh, I., Vullo, A., and Pollastri, G., 2006. XXSTOUT: Improving the Prediction of Long Range Residue Contacts. In *Proceedings of the the 14th Int'l Conf. on Intelli. Systems for Molecular Biology (ISMB'06)* (2006).

[22] Wong, T.-T., Luk, W.-S., and Heng, P.-A., 1997. Sampling with Hammersley and Halton points. *Journal of graphics tools 2*, 2, 9-24.

[23] Worasucheep, C., 2008. A particle swarm optimization with stagnation detection and dispersion. In *IEEE Congress on Evolutionary Computation, 2008 (CEC'08)* 424-429.

[24] Xie, W. and Sahinidis, N.V., 2007. A reduction-based exact algorithm for the contact map overlap problem. *Journal of Computational Biology 14*, 5, 637-654.

[25] Xu, S. and Rahmat-Samii, Y., 2007. Boundary conditions in particle swarm optimization revisited. *Antennas and Propagation, IEEE Transactions on 55*, 3, 760-765.

[26] Yuan, X. and Bystroff, C., 2007. Protein contact map prediction. In *Computational Methods for Protein Structure Prediction and Modeling* Springer, 255-277.

SPSO2011 – Analysis of Stability, Local Convergence, and Rotation Sensitivity

Mohammad Reza Bonyadi
School of Computer Science
The University of Adelaide
mrbonyadi@cs.adelaide.edu.au

Zbigniew Michalewicz
School of Computer Science
The University of Adelaide
zbyszek@cs.adelaide.edu.au

ABSTRACT

In a particle swarm optimization algorithm (PSO) it is essential to guarantee convergence of particles to a point in the search space (this property is called stability of particles). It is also important that the PSO algorithm converges to a local optimum (this is called the local convergence property). Further, it is usually expected that the performance of the PSO algorithm is not affected by rotating the search space (this property is called the rotation sensitivity). In this paper, these three properties, i.e. stability of particles, local convergence, and rotation sensitivity are investigated for a variant of PSO called Standard PSO2011 (SPSO2011). We experimentally define boundaries for the parameters of this algorithm in such a way that if the parameters are selected in these boundaries, the particles are stable, i.e. particles converge to a point in the search space. Also, we show that, unlike earlier versions of PSO, these boundaries are dependent on the number of dimensions of the problem. Moreover, we show that the algorithm is not locally convergent in general case. Finally, we provide a proof and experimental evidence that the algorithm is rotation invariant.

Categories and Subject Descriptors

I.2.8 **[Problem Solving, Control Methods, and Search]**: Heuristic methods; G.1.6 **[Optimization]:** Unconstrained optimization;

General Terms

Algorithms

Keywords

Particle swarm optimization, stability analysis, local convergence, rotation invariance

1 INTRODUCTION

Particle swarm optimization (PSO) is one of the stochastic population-based optimization methods that was developed by Kennedy and Eberhart [1] in 1995. The algorithm has been successfully applied to many problems such as artificial neural network training, function optimization, and pattern classification [2, 3], to name a few. Due to the fast convergence to acceptable solutions and the ease of implementation, PSO has received more attention in recent years [3]. Also, since 1995, different aspects of the original version of PSO [1] have been modified and many *variants* have been proposed. Because of the emergence of many variants during the past years, some researchers have attempted to define standard versions for the PSO algorithm [4-6]. The standard version is updated every several years incorporating new advances. The most recent standard version for PSO was defined in 2011 [5]; it is called Standard PSO2011 (SPSO2011). SPSO2011 was applied to standard continuous space optimization problems and its results were reported to set a baseline for further research [6]. However, there have not been any attempts to investigate some aspects of SPSO2011 including stability of particles (like the ones in [7, 8] that was done for other PSO variants), local convergence (like the ones in [9, 10] that was done for other PSO variants), and rotation sensitivity (like the one in [11] that was done for another PSO variant).

In this paper, stability of particles, local convergence, and rotation sensitivity of SPSO2011 are analyzed. For the stability analysis, we propose an algorithm (called Estimate Coefficients Boundaries, ECB) which can estimate the boundaries of coefficients for a PSO variant so that particles are stable. ECB is applied to estimate the boundaries of coefficients for a PSO variant for which these boundaries are known. Our comparisons show that the proposed algorithm can estimate the boundaries for that PSO variant. ECB is used to estimate the coefficients of the velocity updating rule of SPSO2011. Also, we investigate the local convergence property of the algorithm and we prove that the algorithm is not local convergent in the general case. A simple approach is proposed which addresses this issue, however, detailed analyses is left for future works. Finally, it is proven that the algorithm is rotation invariant. This property of the algorithm is also tested experimentally and it is compared with earlier PSO variants. Note that the experimental evidence is only to show the difference between rotation invariant and rotation variant PSO variants.

The rest of the paper is organized as follows. In section 2 some background information about PSO and some of its variants are provided. We describe existing approaches for stability analysis of PSO variants and we discuss stability analysis for SPSO2011 in section 3. In section 4, some analyses conducted by earlier studies for local convergence property of PSO variants are reviewed and this property for SPSO2011 is investigated. In section 5, we start with an overview of existing rotation sensitivity analyses for some PSO variants and then we provide a proof and experimental evidence that SPSO2011 is rotation invariant. Section 6 concludes the paper.

2 PARTICLE SWARM OPTIMIZATION

Each particle in the Original PSO (OPSO) [12] contains three vectors:

- *Position* ($\vec{x}_t^i$) — is the position of the ith particle in the tth iteration. This is used to evaluate the particle's quality.
- *Velocity* ($\vec{V}_t^i$) — is the direction and length of movement of the ith particle in the tth iteration.

GECCO '14, July 12–16 2014, Vancouver, BC, Canada

http://dx.doi.org/10.1145/2576768.2598263

- *Personal best* ($\vec{p}_t^i$) — is the best position[1] that the ith particle has visited in its lifetime (up to the tth iteration). This vector serves as a memory for keeping knowledge of best found solutions [12].

At every iteration, the velocity of each particle is updated by

$$\vec{V}_{t+1}^i = \vec{V}_t^i + \varphi_1 R_{1t} \underbrace{(\vec{p}_t^i - \vec{x}_t^i)}_{\substack{Personal \\ Influence\,(PI)}} + \varphi_2 R_{2t} \underbrace{(\vec{g}_t - \vec{x}_t^i)}_{\substack{Social \\ Influence\,(SI)}} \quad 1$$

where φ_1 and φ_2 are two real numbers called *acceleration coefficients*[2] and $\vec{p}_t^i$ and $\vec{g}_t$ are the personal best (of the particle i) and the global best vectors, respectively, at iteration t. Also, the role of vectors $PI = \vec{p}_t^i - \vec{x}_t^i$ (Personal Influence) and $SI = \vec{g}_t - \vec{x}_t^i$ (Social Influence) is to *attract* the particles to move toward known quality solutions, i.e. personal and global best vectors. Moreover, R_{1t} and R_{2t} are two $d \times d$ diagonal matrices[3] [13, 14], where their elements are random numbers distributed uniformly ($\sim U(0,1)$) in the interval [0, 1]. Note that matrices R_{1t} and R_{2t} are generated at each iteration for each particle separately. The position of the particles is updated by

$$\vec{x}_{t+1}^i = \vec{x}_t^i + \vec{V}_{t+1}^i \quad 2$$

OPSO was studied by many researchers since 1995 and many new variants were proposed. As an example, the velocity updating rule was modified [15] where previous velocity ($\vec{V}_t^i$) was multiplied by an inertia weight (ω) to control the impact of $\vec{V}_t^i$ on the movement of particles (we call this PSO variant as Inertia PSO, IPSO, in this paper). In fact, the velocity updating for IPSO was written as

$$\vec{V}_{t+1}^i = \omega\vec{V}_t^i + \varphi_1 R_{1t}(\vec{p}_t^i - \vec{x}_t^i) + \varphi_2 R_{2t}(\vec{g}_t - \vec{x}_t^i) \quad 3$$

where ω is inertia weight. As many new PSO variants emerged (see [16] for a review paper on some variants), it became almost impossible to point to one of those as a standard version. This was causing difficulties for researchers to compare their new PSO variants with a baseline algorithm to find out if their method performs acceptably well. Thus, some researchers designed standard version of PSO that was updated frequently (every couple of years)[4]. The standard PSOs were updated according to new findings related to the algorithm, including new values for coefficients, population size, topology, velocity updating rule, and adaptations (see for example [4]).

The most recent standard PSO algorithm (SPSO2011) was proposed in [5] and applied to some standard benchmarks [6]. In SPSO2011, the velocity updating rule was written as:

$$\vec{V}_{t+1}^i = \omega\vec{V}_t^i + \mathcal{H}_i(\vec{G}_t^i, \|\vec{G}_t^i - \vec{x}_t^i\|) - \vec{x}_t^i \quad 4$$

where $\mathcal{H}_i(\vec{G}_t^i, \|\vec{G}_t^i - \vec{x}_t^i\|)$ is a spherical distribution with the center $\vec{G}_t^i$ and radius $\|\vec{G}_t^i - \vec{x}_t^i\|$, $\vec{G}_t^i = \frac{\vec{L}_t^i + \vec{P}_t^i + \vec{x}_t^i}{3}$, where $\vec{P}_t^i = \vec{x}_t^i + c_1(\vec{p}_t^i - \vec{x}_t^i)$ and $\vec{L}_t^i = \vec{x}_t^i + c_2(\vec{l}_t^i - \vec{x}_t^i)$. In [6], the values of c_1 and c_2 were set to $\varphi_1 R_{1t}$ and $\varphi_2 R_{2t}$, respectively. We will use the SPSO2011 variant which was described in [6] unless specified.

[1] In general, personal best can be a *set* of best positions, but all PSO types listed in this paper use single personal best.

[2] These two coefficients control the effect of personal and global best vectors on the movement of particles and they play an important role in the convergence of the algorithm. They are usually determined by a practitioner or by the dynamic of the particles' movement.

[3] Alternatively, these two random matrices are often considered as two random vectors. In this case, the multiplication of these random vectors by PI and SI is element-wise.

[4] Some source codes and documentation for these standard PSOs can be found in http://www.particleswarm.info/Programs.html

Note that, in [5], it was suggested that if $\vec{l}_t^i = \vec{p}_t^i$ then calculate $\vec{G}_t^i = \frac{\vec{P}_t^i + \vec{x}_t^i}{2}$, which was not mentioned in [6]. It was claimed that SPSO2011 is rotation invariant; however, no proper proof for this claim was provided.

3 STABILITY ANALYSIS

In this section we discuss some earlier studies related to stability analysis of IPSO. Afterwards, we analyze the stability of particles in SPSO2011.

3.1 Stability analyses for IPSO

One of the earliest convergence analysis of stochastic optimization algorithms took place on 1965 [17], which was followed by [18, 19]. An iterative stochastic optimization algorithm (optimization algorithm in short) is said to converge in probability (to converge in short) if

$$\forall \varepsilon > 0 \ \lim_{t\to\infty} P(|x_t - X| < \varepsilon) = 1 \quad 5$$

where P is the probability measure, x_t is a generated solution by the optimization algorithm (a point in the search space) at iteration t, ε is a small positive value, and X is a point in the search space. Analysis of convergence to a point (also known as stability analysis) is usually conducted for an iterative stochastic optimization algorithm to understand whether the sequence of the generated solutions by the algorithm is convergent. Stability analysis was done for IPSO in [7, 20-22]. One of the aims of the stability analysis for IPSO was to find boundaries for the coefficients (i.e. inertia weight and acceleration) of velocity vector so that position of particles converges to a point in the space (this boundary of coefficients for a PSO variant is called *convergence boundary* in this paper).

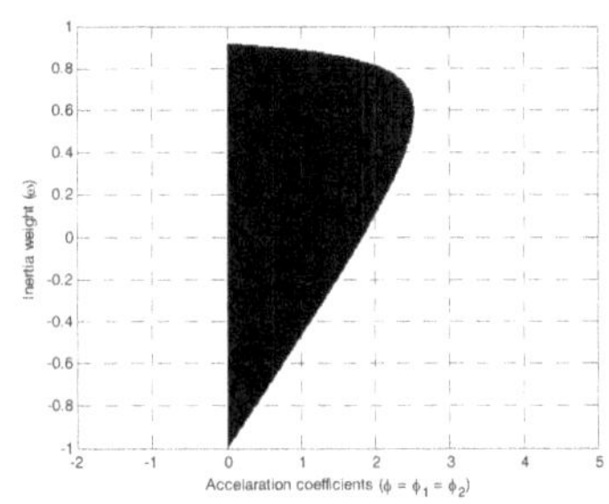

Fig. 1 The dark area represents the convergence boundary for IPSO that was reported in [21] through some theoritical analysis.

The position for a particle in IPSO is called a *stable position* (also known as *equilibrium point* [8]) if $\vec{x}_{t+1}^i = \vec{x}_t^i$ (particle does not move anymore) for all $t>t'$. In this case, it is obvious that $\vec{V}_{t+1}^i$ should be zero because $\vec{x}_{t+1}^i = \vec{x}_t^i + \vec{V}_{t+1}^i$ [8, 20]. Note that, in the equilibrium point, because $\vec{V}_{t+1}^i$ should be zero, it is essential that $\vec{p}_t^i = \vec{x}_t^i$ and $\vec{p}_t^i = \vec{g}_t$ for all i (see also [20] for detailed analysis). There have been several articles on stability analyses of IPSO [7, 8, 21-23] to identify convergence boundary for the algorithm. As an example, Fig. 1 shows the convergence boundary for IPSO that was identified in [21].

Because the aim of stability analysis is to find convergence boundary for a PSO variant, it is considered that $\vec{p}_t^i$ and $\vec{g}_t$ are not updated during the run. Also, usually velocity and position updating rules are analyzed for an arbitrary particle i in a one dimensional space. The reason for considering a one dimensional space is that in IPSO all calculations (including generation of the random values on the diagonal of R_{1t}^i) are done in each dimension independently, hence, all analyses in one dimensional case is generalizable to the multi-dimensional case as well [20].

3.2 Stability analysis for SPSO2011

All stability analyses for IPSO were done for a one dimensional particle and, as each dimension was updated separately in IPSO, the results were generalizable to any number of dimensions. However, this assumption is not applicable for stability analysis of SPSO2011 because the velocity vector in SPSO2011 is not updated for each dimension separately. The reason is that the operator $\vec{c} = \mathcal{H}_i(\vec{a}, b)$ (for an arbitrary vector $\vec{a}$ and value b) generates a random point in the space with center $\vec{a}$ according to the radius b. Hence, the process of generating $\vec{c}$ is not decomposable to a dimension-wise process. Thus, any approach that is going to analyze stability of particles for SPSO2011 needs to consider a general case of the n-dimensional space, i.e. $||\vec{V}_t^i|| = 0$ at the equilibrium point, rather than considering dimension-wise analysis, i.e. $\vec{V}_t^i = 0$ in a one dimensional space at the equilibrium point. Whereas repeating previous analyses that were done for IPSO is not applicable in a general n-dimensional case, we conduct an experimental study to estimate the convergence boundary for SPSO2011.

Algorithm ECB (Estimate Convergence Boundaries)
Inputs: $\varphi_a, \varphi_s, \varphi_e, \omega_a, \omega_s, \omega_e, d, r, maxIter$
Output: *Y*

1. *Set the desired value of d (number of dimensions)*
2. *For* $\varphi = \varphi_a : \varphi_s : \varphi_e$
   a. $\varphi_1 = \varphi_2 = \varphi$
   b. *For* $\omega = \omega_a : \omega_s : \omega_e$
      i. *Run the PSO algorithm for a predefined number of iterations (maxIter*d) and number of runs (r) for the given* $\varphi_1 = \varphi_2 = \varphi$ *and* ω
      ii. $\vec{K}_{avr}$*=average of the final velocity vectors over r runs (separately for each dimension)*
      iii. $\vec{U}_{avr}$*=average of the initial velocity vectors over r runs (separately for each dimension)*
      iv. $K_\omega = log_{10}(norm(\vec{K}_{avr})/norm(\vec{U}_{avr}))$
   c. *End for*
   d. $Y_{\varphi,\omega}^d = K_\omega$ *for all* ω *in* $\omega_a : \omega_s : \omega_e$
3. *EndFor*

To conduct stability analysis, we assume that the personal best and global best vectors are equal for all time from the current time ($\vec{p}_t^i = \vec{g}_t$ for all $t \geq t'$) and personal best is not updated ($\vec{p}_{t+1}^i = \vec{p}_t^i$ for all $t \geq t'$, i.e. personal best is not updated after t'), as it was assumed in earlier stability analysis for IPSO. We also assume that $\vec{x}_{t'}^i = \vec{p}_{t'}^i$ because the point $\vec{p}_{t'}^i$ is sampled by $\vec{x}_{t'}^i$. Also, we assumed arbitrary number of particles in the swarm. However, because $\vec{g}_t$ is not updated for any $t > t'$, we can safely analyze one particle (particle *i*) in the swarm. Note that the presence of other particles in the swarm *does not* influence the behavior of particle *i* because the only information that is propagated through particles is the position of $\vec{g}_t$, which is not changed anymore. This assumption is also correct in the case of other topologies ($\vec{l}_t^i$ for each particle rather than $\vec{g}_t$) as the personal best for other particles can be assumed to be steady as well. For the sake of simplicity, we assumed that $\varphi = \varphi_1 = \varphi_2$ (this was also assumed in [20] for analyses). Also, without losing generality, we assume *t'=0* and *i=1*. With these settings, we propose an experiment (called Estimate Convergence Boundary, ECB) that is able to estimate the convergence boundary for a PSO algorithm. In ECB, we change the value of coefficients (φ and ω) and, for each value, we run the PSO algorithm for $maxIter$ iterations *r* times. The final velocities for these *r* runs are averaged for each dimension and the norm of the resulted vector (this vector is called $\vec{K}_{avr}$) is divided by the norm of the average of $\vec{V}_0^i$s (initialized velocities) for all runs (this vector is called $\vec{U}_{avr}$). The value of $log_{10}(norm(\vec{K}_{avr})/norm(\vec{U}_{avr}))$ is stored in $Y_{\varphi,\omega}^d$ for each ω and φ (see Algorithm ECB, Estimate Convergence Boundaries). Thus, $Y_{\varphi,\omega}^d$ shows the logarithm of the overall rate of changes in the norm of the velocity vector ($||\vec{V}_t^i||$). Also, we initialize $\vec{x}_0^i = \vec{p}_0^i$ as well as $\vec{V}_0^i$ to random values in the *d* dimensional space in each run separately. It is expected that if the setting of coefficients (ω and φ) for a run are in the convergence boundary, the value of $||\vec{V}_t^i||$ shrinks with regard to $||\vec{V}_0^i||$. Thus, we expect that the value of $Y_{\varphi,\omega}^d$ is small if ω and φ are in the convergence boundary.

The matrix $Y_{\varphi,\omega}^d$ represents the average rate of changes in the *norm* of velocity vectors over *r* runs for different values of $\varphi = \varphi_1 = \varphi_2$ and ω. If the PSO algorithm is convergent for a value of ω and φ then $Y_{\varphi,\omega}^d$ is small ($||\vec{V}_t^i||$ has shrink during the run), otherwise, it is relatively big (relative to other values in $Y_{\varphi,\omega}^d$).

To test the validity of this experimental approach (ECB algorithm) for identifying convergence boundary, we applied this approach to find the convergence boundary for IPSO with $\varphi_a = -2, \varphi_s = 0.1, \varphi_e = 8.5, \omega_a = -1.3, \omega_s = 0.01, \omega_e = 1.3, r = 10,$ $maxIter = 2000 * d$ for *d=1* and *d=50* (see Fig. 2).

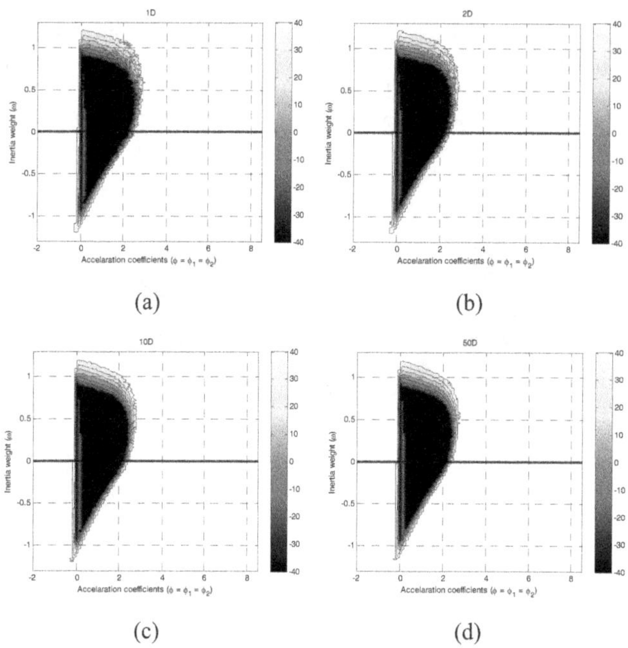

Fig. 2 The boundaries for ω and φ so that IPSO is convergent. The darker the areas, the smaller the value of velocity. Thus, the darker the areas, the more probable that the algorithm is convergent with those coefficients. The color spectrum shows the value of the matrix $Y_{\varphi,\omega}^d$. Experiments were conducted for (a) *d=1*, (b) *d=2*, (c) *d=10*, and (b) *d=50*.

The color spectrums in Fig. 2(a-d) show the value of $Y_{\varphi,\omega}^d$ for IPSO for different values of inertia weight and acceleration coefficients. In the boundaries where $Y_{\varphi,\omega}^d$ is relatively small (dark areas), it is highly probable that the particles become stable. Also, as it is clear in Fig. 2(a-d), when $\omega = 0$ the stability of the particles is very probable for all values of φ and *d*. This was in fact expected as if $\omega = 0$, and because $\vec{x}_0^i = \vec{p}_0^i$ and $\vec{p}_t^i = \vec{g}_t$ for all *t*, the value of $\vec{V}_t^i$ becomes zero for all t, which imposes stability. Fig. 2 (a-d) shows that the convergence boundary for IPSO is similar for different number of dimensions (the value of $Y_{\varphi,\omega}^d$ for *d=1, 2, 10,* and *50* is very close for the tested ω and φ). To test this similarity, we draw the value of $|Y_{\varphi,\omega}^{50} - Y_{\varphi,\omega}^1|$ (see Fig. 3)

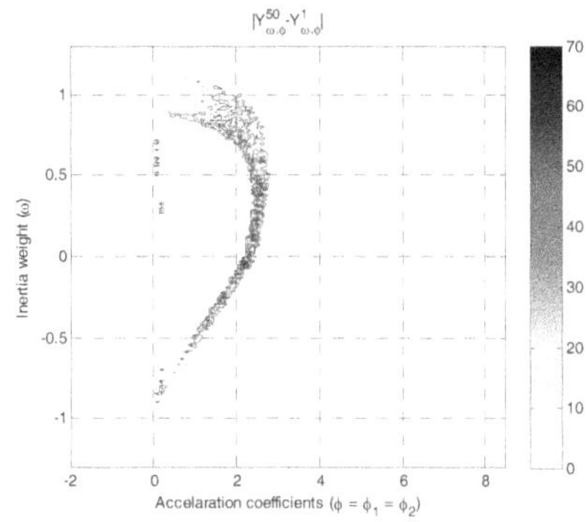

Fig. 3 The graph of $|\mathbf{Y}_{\varphi,\omega}^{50} - \mathbf{Y}_{\varphi,\omega}^1|$ for different values of φ and ω. The farther the values of $\mathbf{Y}_{\varphi,\omega}^{50}$ and $\mathbf{Y}_{\varphi,\omega}^1$, the darker the areas.

From Fig. 3, it is clear that the value of $|Y_{\varphi,\omega}^{50} - Y_{\varphi,\omega}^1|$ is close to zero in most of the cases for different values of φ and ω. This indeed confirms the assumption by earlier analyses (e.g. [8]) for IPSO that the analysis for 1 dimensional space is generalizable to analysis for n-dimensional space. Also, these results are very similar to what was reported in [20, 21] for the stability of particles (see also Fig. 1 and compare it with Fig. 2 (a)). This in fact confirms that the experimental study proposed in this paper (algorithm ECB) can estimate the convergence boundary of IPSO.

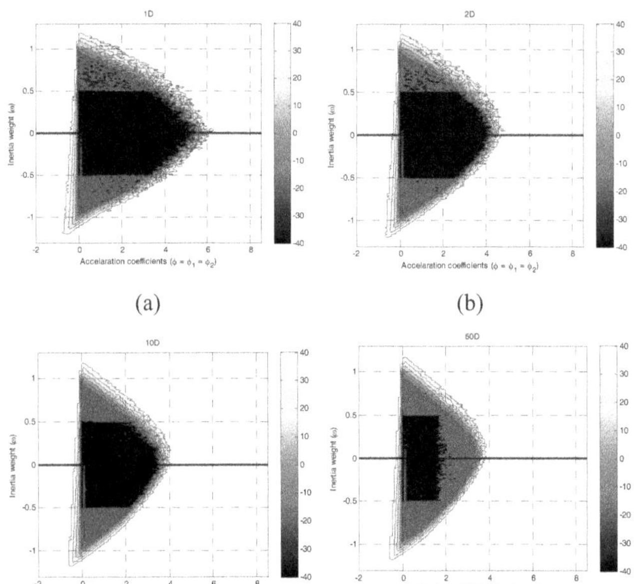

Fig. 4 The matrix $Y_{\varphi,\omega}^d$ for different number of dimensions (a) 1-D, (b) 2-D, (c) 10-D, and (d) 50-D.

We now apply ECB to find the convergence boundary for SPSO2011. We used the following parameters for ECB: $\varphi_a = -2, \varphi_s = 0.1, \varphi_e = 8.5, \omega_a = -1.3, \omega_s = 0.01, \omega_e = 1.3, r = 10,$ $maxIter = 2000 * d$ for *d=1, d=2, d=10, and d=50* (see Fig. 4).

Fig. 4 shows that the convergence boundary for SPSO2011 is changed by changing the number of dimensions. Also, the boundaries look very different from the one for IPSO.

To test that the estimated convergence boundary are correct (the particles become stable if the coefficients are chosen from the darker area), we applied SPSO2011 to a sphere function ($f(x) = \sum_{i=1}^{d} x_i^2$) for $d = 2$ and $d = 50$ with two different settings for (ω, φ)—the first setting $(0.73, 1.5)$ that is frequently used in PSO literature for IPSO (see [7, 13] for example) and the second setting $(0.72, 1.1)$ selected because SPSO2011 is convergent for both $d = 2$ and $d = 50$ with this setting according to the results from ECB algorithm. The value for $Y_{\varphi,\omega}^d$ for the first setting ($(\omega, \varphi) = (0.73, 1.5)$) was $Y_{0.73,1.5}^2 = -14.39$ and $Y_{0.73,1.5}^{50} = 12.64$ and for the second setting ($(\omega, \varphi) = (0.72, 1.1)$) was $Y_{0.72,1.1}^2 = -15.95$ and $Y_{0.72,1.1}^{50} = -13.92$. These values suggest that the particles should become stable in all cases except when SPSO2011 is applied to the sphere function with *d=50* with the first setting ($(\omega, \varphi) = (0.73, 1.5)$). We applied SPSO2011 to the sphere function with the two aforementioned settings and for *d=2* and *d=50*, 100 times each, and recorded the *norm* value of the velocity vector of a randomly selected particle at each run. The average of this norm value over 100 runs for each case is shown in Fig. 5.

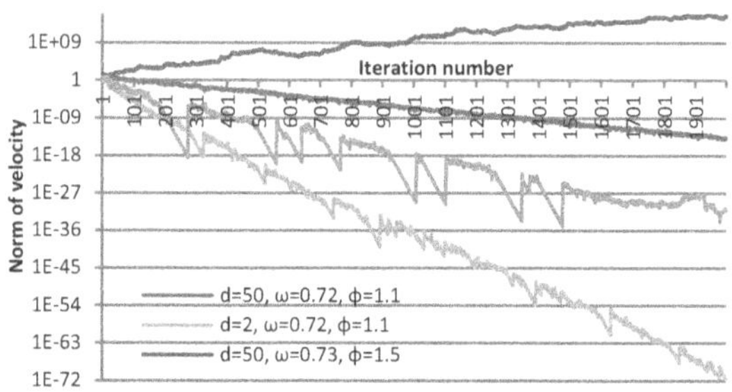

Fig. 5 Average value of the norm of the velocity for a randomly selected particle over 100 runs for different settings.

It is clear in Fig. 5 that for the first setting of coefficients ($\omega = 0.73$ and $\varphi = 1.5$), the velocity of the randomly selected particles decreased over iterations for sphere function with *d=2*, while it increased to 1E+12 for the sphere function with *d=50*. However, this value was decreased for the sphere function with *d=2* or *50* when the second setting of coefficients ($\omega = 0.72$ and $\varphi = 1.1$) was considered. This experiment confirms that the estimated convergence boundary was correct.

4 LOCAL CONVERGENCE

In this section, some earlier studies which have analyzed the local convergence of IPSO are briefly reviewed and then the local convergence for SPSO2011 is investigated.

4.1 Local convergence for IPSO

Local convergence for IPSO has been investigated in [10, 24]. A PSO algorithm is said to be locally convergent if it guarantees finding a local optima in the search space. As it was mentioned in [10], if $\vec{p}_t^i = \vec{g}_t = \vec{x}_t^i$, then $\vec{x}_t^i$ is moved in the next step if $\omega\vec{V}_t^i$ is non-zero. However, it might be the case that $\vec{V}_t^i$ becomes zero, which results in $\vec{V}_{t+1}^i = 0$ and, consequently, no movement takes place in the next step. Also, as $\vec{V}_{t+1}^i = 0$ and $\vec{p}_t^i = \vec{g}_t = \vec{x}_t^i = \vec{x}_{t+1}^i$, thus there is no movement in even further steps (the particle is in its equilibrium). As no claim has been made about the equilibrium point, it is not clear whether $\vec{x}_t^i$ is a local optimum while it is not updated in the next steps. Thus, IPSO algorithm is not local convergent in general case. A mutation operator was proposed in [10] that generated a random point (according to some distribution) around current $\vec{g}_t$ and moved the global best particle (the particle which its personal best is $\vec{g}_t$) to that random point rather than moving the particle according to its velocity. In this case, even if all particles stop moving, the global best particle still continue movement randomly around $\vec{g}_t$, which prevents complete stop of that particle (the algorithm was called Guaranteed Convergent PSO, GCPSO). It was proven that the algorithm is local convergent.

The local convergence property of IPSO was also investigated in [24]. It was proven that, in a one dimensional space, IPSO is local convergent if $n > 1$ and coefficients are set in the convergence boundary. However, the algorithm might not converge to a local optimum if $d > 1$. To address this issue, a strategy was proposed to detect if $\|\vec{V}_t^i\| + \|\vec{g}_t - \vec{x}_t^i\|$ is smaller than a constant δ. In this case, the velocity vector of particle i was regenerated randomly within a hyper-rectangle with the side length δ. It was proven that by using this approach for the velocity vector the algorithm is locally convergent.

4.2 Local convergence for SPSO2011

We show that there are at least two cases that SPSO2011 is not local convergent:

Case 1: assume that $\vec{p}_t^i = \vec{l}_t^i = \vec{x}_t^i$ in SPSO2011. The value of $\vec{G}_t^i$ in Eq. 4 is then calculated by

$$\vec{G}_t^i = \frac{\vec{x}_t^i + \varphi_2 R_{2t}(\vec{l}_t^i - \vec{x}_t^i) + \vec{x}_t^i + \varphi_1 R_{1t}(\vec{p}_t^i - \vec{x}_t^i) + \vec{x}_t^i}{3} = \vec{x}_t^i$$

Thus, in this case, $\|\vec{G}_t^i - \vec{x}_t^i\|$ is zero, which implies that $\mathcal{H}_i(\vec{G}_t^i, \|\vec{G}_t^i - \vec{x}_t^i\|) = \vec{G}_t^i = \vec{x}_t^i$. Hence, the value of velocity for $t+1$ is $\vec{V}_{t+1}^i = \omega \vec{V}_t^i$. This is exactly the same as the case we discussed in section 4.1 (i.e. if $\vec{V}_t^i = 0$, there is no chance for the particle to move in further iterations). By using the same analysis in section 4.1, SPSO2011 is not local convergent in general case. This issue also exist in the formulation explained in [5] because if $\vec{p}_t^i = \vec{x}_t^i$:

$$\vec{G}_t^i = \frac{\vec{x}_t^i + \varphi_1 R_{1t}(\vec{p}_t^i - \vec{x}_t^i) + \vec{x}_t^i}{2} = \vec{x}_t^i$$

Case 2: we also prove that SPSO2011 is not local convergent for any one dimensional problem when $n = 1$, under specific initialization for x_0 and V_0 that happen with non-zero probability.

Theorem 1: *SPSO2011 is not local convergent for any one dimensional problem if* $n = 1$, *the particle is initialized at a point* x_0 *which is not a local optimum, the objective function is monotonically decreasing at* x_0, $0 < \omega < 1$, $x_0 < a$, $0 < V_0 < \frac{(a-x_0-\varepsilon)(1-\omega)}{\omega}$, *where* a *is the closest local optimum to* x_0 *in the direction of* V_0 *and* $0 < \varepsilon < a - x_0$.

Proof: clearly, $x_0 = g_0 = p_0$, which results in $V_1 = \omega V_0$ with any initialization. Also, $x_1 = x_0 + V_1 = x_0 + \omega V_0$. It is clear that $\omega < \frac{\omega}{1-\omega}$ which implies that $x_0 + \omega V_0 < x_0 + \frac{(a-x_0-\varepsilon)(1-\omega)\frac{\omega}{1-\omega}}{\omega} = a - \varepsilon$. Also, as $V_0 > 0$, thus $x_0 < x_1 < a - \varepsilon$. Because a is the closest optimum to x_0 and the objective function is monotonically decreasing, x_1 is a better point than x_0 for any value of $0 < \omega < 1$, which results in updating $g_1 = p_1 = x_1$. In this case, it is clear that $V_2 = \omega V_1$ which results in $x_2 = x_1 + V_2 = x_0 + V_0(\omega + \omega^2)$.

As it is obvious that $\omega + \omega^2 < \frac{\omega}{1-\omega}$, thus $x_2 = x_0 + V_0(\omega + \omega^2) < x_0 + \frac{(a-x_0-\varepsilon)(1-\omega)\frac{\omega}{1-\omega}}{\omega} = a - \varepsilon$. Also, as $V_0 > 0$, it is clear that $x_1 < x_2 < a - \varepsilon$. Because $x_2 < a - \varepsilon$, x_2 is better than $g_1 = p_1$. Thus, $g_2 = p_2 = x_2$. By continuing the same strategy (note that $\omega + \omega^2 + \cdots + \omega^t \le \frac{\omega}{1-\omega}$ for any t), x_t is calculated by:

$$x_t = x_0 + V_0 \sum_{i=1}^{t} \omega^i < x_0 + \frac{V_0 \omega}{1-\omega} = x_0 + \frac{(a - x_0 - \varepsilon)(1-\omega)\frac{\omega}{1-\omega}}{\omega} = a - \varepsilon$$

Also, as the objective function is monotonically decreasing, thus $x_0 < \cdots x_{t-1} < x_t < a - \varepsilon$. Hence, x_t moves towards a in each iteration but never meets a, which completes the proof for the theorem. ■

In fact, the particle always moves towards the local optimum a, however, the velocity decreases in every iteration to a portion (ω), and, consequently, it does not arrive to the local optimum if the velocity is initialized inappropriately. Also, note that the probability of this initialization is non-zero.

A simple fix for these two cases is to bound the value of $\|\vec{G}_t^i - \vec{x}_t^i\|$ to a small number $\delta > 0$. This in fact fixes the issue in both cases. In the case 1, by setting $\|\vec{G}_t^i - \vec{x}_t^i\| > \delta$, we make sure that the value of velocity is always non-zero, which guarantees movement. Also, in the case 2, because $\|\vec{G}_t^i - \vec{x}_t^i\| > \delta$, $\mathcal{H}_i(\vec{G}_t^i, \|\vec{G}_t^i - \vec{x}_t^i\|)$ is not equal to $\vec{x}_t^i$, which causes theorem 1 invalid. The proof for local convergence of SPSO2011 with this fix is left for future research.

5 ROTATION SENSITIVITY

In this section some earlier studies on rotation sensitivity of IPSO are reviewed. We also investigate the rotation, scale, and translation sensitivity of SPSO2011.

5.1 Rotation sensitivity of IPSO

It has been proven that IPSO is scale invariant while it is *rotation variant* [11, 25]. An algorithm is said to be rotation variant if its performance is change by rotating the search space. Note that, intuitively, the performance of algorithm should remain the same by rotating the search space as the search space remains unchanged. It has been proven that linear PSO (a PSO which uses the same random value for all dimensions, all values on the diagonal of R_{1t} and R_{2t} are equal) is scale and rotation invariant (this variant is called LPSO). However, in LPSO, if $(\vec{p}_t^i - \vec{x}_t^i) \| (\vec{g}_t - \vec{x}_t^i)$ and $\vec{V}_t^i \| (\vec{p}_t^i - \vec{x}_t^i)$, the particle i starts oscillating between its personal best and the global best (see also [26]), which is considered as a defect in the algorithm. A new PSO variant was proposed in [11] that was rotation invariant. The algorithm (called Rotation invariant PSO, RPSO) used random rotation matrices rather than random diagonal matrices to rotate the velocity vector. An approximation idea (an exponential map) was used for generating the rotation matrices to reduce the computational expenses arising from matrix multiplication. In the exponential map, a rotation matrix M is generated by:

$$M = I + \sum_{i=1}^{max_i} \frac{1}{i!}\left(\frac{\alpha\pi}{180}(A - A^T)\right)^i \qquad 6$$

where A is a $d \times d$ matrix with elements generated randomly in the interval [-0.5, 0.5], α is a real value representing the angle, and I is the identity matrix. The generated matrix M is a random rotation matrix with the angle α. It is clear in Eq. 6 that the matrix M becomes a more accurate estimation of a rotation matrix with the angle α when max_i is larger. In that article the value of max_i was set to 1, limiting the approximation to one term of the summation only. Thus, the approximation error of the random rotation matrix method grows with the rotation angle (α). Note that for larger values of max_i, the time complexity of generating rotation matrices grows rapidly. The time complexity for generating and multiplying the approximated rotation matrix (with max_i=1) into a vector is in $O(d^2)$, i.e. including generating the approximated matrix ($O(d^2)$) plus vector-matrix multiplication ($O(d^2)$).

In [27], it was shown that IPSO performs poor comparing to covariance matrix adaptation ES (CMA-ES) [28] and Differential Evolution (DE) [29] when it is facing non-separable optimization problems. Because of the fact that rotating a landscape makes an optimization problem non-separable [30], IPSO performs also poor when the landscape is rotated (it is rotation variant). The same comparison was also conducted in [31]. This study confirmed that, although IPSO performs well in separable optimization problems, its performance in non-separable optimization problems is poor. The authors argued that the main reason behind this poor performance is that all calculations in IPSO are done for each dimension separately [31], which makes the algorithm rotation variant.

5.2 Rotation sensitivity of SPSO2011

It is well-known that a PSO algorithm is rotation, scalar, and translation invariant (RST invariant) if for all $t>0$ $\hat{x}^i_{t+1} = sQ\vec{x}^i_{t+1} + \vec{b}$ (i.e. updating the position of particle i and then rotating, scaling, and translating the search space is the same as rotating, scaling, and translating the search space and then updating the position) for any scalar s, orthogonal matrix Q, and vector $\vec{b}$, and $\hat{x}^i_{t+1}$is the position vector in the rotated, scaled, and translated space [11, 32] at iteration $t+1$. Let's calculate $sQ\vec{x}^i_{t+1} + \vec{b}$ for SPSO2011:

$$sQ\vec{x}^i_{t+1} + \vec{b} = sQ\left(\vec{x}^i_t + \omega\vec{V}^i_t + \mathcal{H}_i\left(\vec{G}^i_t, \|\vec{G}^i_t - \vec{x}^i_t\|\right) - \vec{x}^i_t\right) + \vec{b} \quad (7)$$

It is clear that $\vec{V}^i_t = \vec{x}^i_t - \vec{x}^i_{t-1}$, thus Eq. 7 is written as

$$sQ\vec{x}^i_{t+1} + \vec{b} = sQ\vec{x}^i_t + sQ\omega\left(\vec{x}^i_t - \vec{x}^i_{t-1}\right) + sQ\mathcal{H}_i\left(\vec{G}^i_t, \|\vec{G}^i_t - \vec{x}^i_t\|\right) - sQ\vec{x}^i_t + \vec{b} \quad (8)$$

Also, to calculate $\hat{x}^i_{t+1}$:

$$\hat{x}^i_{t+1} = \hat{x}^i_t + \hat{V}^i_{t+1} = sQ\vec{x}^i_t + \vec{b} + \omega\left(sQ\vec{x}^i_t + \vec{b} - sQ\vec{x}^i_{t-1} - \vec{b}\right) + \hat{\mathcal{H}}_i\left(\vec{G}^i_t, \|\vec{G}^i_t - \vec{x}^i_t\|\right) - sQ\vec{x}^i_t - \vec{b} \quad (9)$$

By comparing Eq. 8 and 9, it is clear that, in order to guarantee $\hat{x}^i_{t+1} = sQ\vec{x}^i_{t+1} + \vec{b}$ (and consequently guarantee that the algorithm RST invariant), the following equality must be satisfied:

$$\hat{\mathcal{H}}_i\left(\vec{G}^i_t, \|\vec{G}^i_t - \vec{x}^i_t\|\right) = sQ\mathcal{H}_i\left(\vec{G}^i_t, \|\vec{G}^i_t - \vec{x}^i_t\|\right) + \vec{b} \quad (10)$$

Note that, according to the definition of RST invariance, if $\mathcal{H}_i\left(\vec{G}^i_t, \|\vec{G}^i_t - \vec{x}^i_t\|\right)$ is RST invariant then the equality in Eq. 10 is true. Also, it is clear that generating a random point in a hyper-sphere with a given radius and center ($\mathcal{H}_i(.,.)$) and then rotating, scaling, and translating the search space is the same as rotating, scaling, and translating the search space and then generating a random point in a hyper-sphere with the same radius and the transformed center. Thus, the operator $\mathcal{H}_i(.,.)$ is RST invariant, which implies that SPSO2011 is RST invariant.

Although the above proof is sufficient to guarantee rotation invariance of SPSO2011, in order to see the impact of this characteristic in different algorithms, we applied the algorithms (SPSO2011, IPSO, RPSO, LPSO, and GCPSO) to a benchmark problem designed in [33] for analyzing the rotation invariance of PSO variants. The benchmark is a two dimensional Ellipse that is rotated in the space (from 0 to 180 degree) and the algorithms are applied 20 times to find an optimum point in the search space (see Fig. 6).

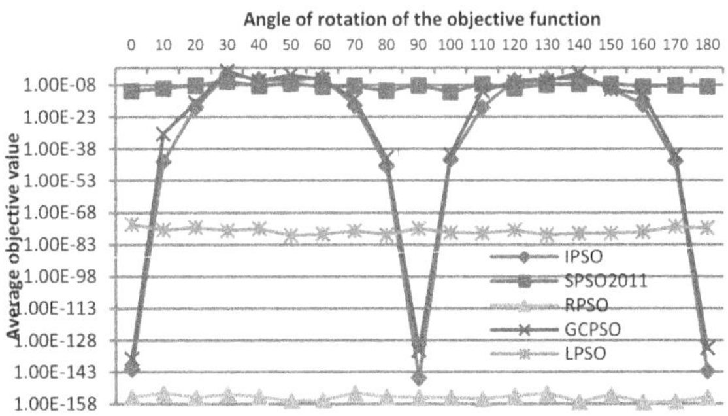

Fig. 6 Application of five PSO varients to a two dimensional Ellipse function.

According to Fig. 6, it is clear that the performance of SPSO2011, LPSO, and RPSO is not significantly changed by rotating of the search space with different angles. The slight changes in the performance of these methods are because of random components in the methods. However, performance of IPSO and GCPSO is substantially changed by rotating the search space, which shows that IPSO and GCPSO are not rotation invariant in general case (this test case serves a counter example for the statement "IPSO or GCPSO is rotation invariant").

6 CONCLUSIONS AND FUTURE WORKS

In this paper, the stability of particles, local convergence, and rotation sensitivity of SPSO2011 were investigated. In the stability analysis, we proposed an experimental approach (called Estimate Convergence Boundary, ECB) which could estimate the convergence boundary (the boundary of coefficients for a PSO variant where the particles converge to a point in the search space) for PSO variants. ECB was applied to estimate the convergence boundary for a PSO variant (called IPSO) that its convergence boundary is known. Results indicated that the proposed ECB algorithm can estimate the convergence boundary for IPSO. ECB was applied to estimate the convergence boundary for SPSO2011. Results showed that the convergence boundary for SPSO2011 looks different from that of IPSO. Also, it was shown that, unlike IPSO, the convergence boundary for SPSO2011 is changed when the number of dimensions changed. Further experiments showed that picking previous frequently-used coefficients for PSO variants are not necessarily good choices for SPSO2011. In terms of local convergence, it was proven that SPSO2011 is not able to guarantee locating a local optimum in the search space. A simple approach was proposed to overcome this issue; however, detailed analyses for that approach were left for future works. Finally, it was proven that SPSO2011 is rotation, scale, and translation invariant. Theoretical analysis of stability of particles in SPSO2011 is a potential future work in this area of research.

7 ACKNOWLEDGEMENT

This work was partially funded by the ARC Discovery Grant DP130104395 and by grant N N519 5788038 from the Polish Ministry of Science and Higher Education (MNiSW).

8 REFERENCES

[1] J. Kennedy and R. Eberhart, "Particle swarm optimization," in *International Conference on Neural Networks*, IEEE, 1995, pp. 1942-1948.

[2] A. P. Engelbrecht, *Fundamentals of computational swarm intelligence*. Hoboken, NJ: Wiley, 2005.

[3] R. Poli, "Analysis of the publications on the applications of particle swarm optimisation," *Journal of Artificial Evolution and Application,* pp. 1-10, 2008

[4] D. Bratton and J. Kennedy, "Defining a standard for particle swarm optimization," in *Swarm Intelligence Symposium*, IEEE, 2007, pp. 120-127.

[5] M. Clerc. (2011). *Standard Particle Swarm Optimisation* Available: http://hal.archives-ouvertes.fr/hal-00764996

[6] M. Zambrano-Bigiarini, M. Clerc, and R. Rojas, "Standard Particle Swarm Optimisation 2011 at CEC-2013: A baseline for future PSO improvements," in *Congress on Evolutionary Computation*, IEEE, 2013, pp. 2337-2344.

[7] M. Clerc and J. Kennedy, "The particle swarm - Explosion, stability, and convergence in a multidimensional complex space," *IEEE Transactions on Evolutionary Computation,* vol. 6, pp. 58-73, Feb 2002

[8] I. C. Trelea, "The particle swarm optimization algorithm: convergence analysis and parameter selection," *Information Processing Letters,* vol. 85, pp. 317-325, Mar 31 2003

[9] P. K. Lehre and C. Witt, "Finite First Hitting Time versus Stochastic Convergence in Particle Swarm Optimisation," *CoRR,* vol. abs/1105.5540, 2011

[10] F. Van den Bergh and A. P. Engelbrecht, "A Convergence Proof for the Particle Swarm Optimiser," *Fundamenta Informaticae,* vol. 105, pp. 341-374, 2010

[11] D. N. Wilke, S. Kok, and A. A. Groenwold, "Comparison of linear and classical velocity update rules in particle swarm optimization: Notes on scale and frame invariance," *International journal for numerical methods in engineering,* vol. 70, pp. 985-1008, 2007

[12] R. Eberhart and J. Kennedy, "A new optimizer using particle swarm theory," in *International Symposium on Micro Machine and Human Science*, IEEE, 1995, pp. 39-43.

[13] M. A. M. de Oca, T. Stützle, M. Birattari, and M. Dorigo, "Frankenstein's PSO: A Composite Particle Swarm Optimization Algorithm," *IEEE Transactions on Evolutionary Computation,* vol. 13, pp. 1120-1132, Oct 2009

[14] M. Clerc, *Particle swarm optimization*: Wiley-ISTE, 2006.

[15] Y. Shi and R. Eberhart, "A modified particle swarm optimizer," in *World Congress on Computational Intelligence*, IEEE, 1998, pp. 69-73.

[16] R. Poli, J. Kennedy, and T. Blackwell, "Particle swarm optimization an overview," *Swarm Intelligence,* vol. 1, pp. 33-57, 2007

[17] J. Matyas, "Random optimization," *Automation and Remote Control,* vol. 26, pp. 246-253, 1965

[18] F. J. Solis and R. J.-B. Wets, "Minimization by random search techniques," *Mathematics of Operations Research,* vol. 6, pp. 19-30, 1981

[19] N. Baba, "Convergence of a random optimization method for constrained optimization problems," *Journal of Optimization Theory and Applications,* vol. 33, pp. 451-461, 1981

[20] R. Poli, "Mean and Variance of the Sampling Distribution of Particle Swarm Optimizers During Stagnation," *IEEE Transactions on Evolutionary Computation,* vol. 13, pp. 712-721, Aug 2009

[21] M. Jiang, Y. P. Luo, and S. Y. Yang, "Stochastic convergence analysis and parameter selection of the standard particle swarm optimization algorithm," *Information Processing Letters,* vol. 102, pp. 8-16, Apr 15 2007

[22] F. Van den Bergh and A. P. Engelbrecht, "A study of particle swarm optimization particle trajectories," *Information Sciences,* vol. 176, pp. 937-971, 2006

[23] M. Jiang, Y. Luo, and S. Yang, "Particle swarm optimization–stochastic trajectory analysis and parameter selection," *Swarm intelligence focus on ant and particle swarm optimization. I-TECH Education and Publishing, Wien,* 2007

[24] M. Schmitt and R. Wanka, "Particle Swarm Optimization Almost Surely Finds Local Optima," in *Genetic and Evolutionary Computation Conference*, ACM, Amsterdam, The Netherlands, 2013, pp. 1629-1636.

[25] D. Wilke, "Analysis of the particle swarm optimization algorithm," Master Thesis, University of Pretoria, 2005.

[26] M. R. Bonyadi, X. Li, and Z. Michalewicz, "A hybrid particle swarm with velocity mutation for constraint optimization problems," in *Genetic and Evolutionary Computation Conference*, ACM, Amsterdam, The Netherlands, 2013, pp. 1-8.

[27] N. Hansen, R. Ros, N. Mauny, M. Schoenausr, and A. Auger, "PSO facing non-separable and ill-conditioned problems," *INRIA,* 2008

[28] N. Hansen and A. Ostermeier, "Adapting arbitrary normal mutation distributions in evolution strategies: The covariance matrix adaptation," in *Congress on Evolutionary Computation*, IEEE, 1996, pp. 312-317.

[29] R. Storn and K. Price, "Differential evolution–a simple and efficient heuristic for global optimization over continuous spaces," *Journal of Global Optimization,* vol. 11, pp. 341-359, 1997

[30] R. Salomon, "Reevaluating Genetic Algorithm Performance under Coordinate Rotation of Benchmark Functions - A survey of some theoretical and practical aspects of genetic algorithms," *BioSystems,* vol. 39, pp. 263-278, 1995

[31] A. Auger, N. Hansen, J. P. Zerpa, R. Ros, and M. Schoenauer, "Empirical comparisons of several derivative free optimization algorithms," in *Acte du 9ieme colloque national en calcul des structures (Proceedings of the 9th National Symposium in calculation of structures)*, 2009.

[32] M. R. Spiegel, *Theory and problems of vector analysis*: Schaum's Outline Series, 1959.

[33] W. M. Spears, D. T. Green, and D. F. Spears, "Biases in particle swarm optimization," *International Journal of Swarm Intelligence Research,* vol. 1, pp. 34-57, 2010

Identifying and Exploiting the Scale of a Search Space in Particle Swarm Optimization

Yasser Gonzalez-Fernandez
School of Information Technology
York University
Toronto, Canada
ygf@yorku.ca

Stephen Chen
School of Information Technology
York University
Toronto, Canada
sychen@yorku.ca

ABSTRACT

Multi-modal optimization involves two distinct tasks: identifying promising attraction basins and finding the local optima in these basins. Unfortunately, the second task can interfere with the first task if they are performed simultaneously. Specifically, the promise of an attraction basin is often estimated by the fitness of a single sample solution, so an attraction basin represented by a random sample solution can appear to be less promising than an attraction basin represented by its local optimum. The goal of thresheld convergence is to prevent these biased comparisons by disallowing local search while global search is still in progress. Ideally, thresheld convergence achieves this goal by using a distance threshold that is correlated to the size of the attraction basins in the search space. In this paper, a clustering-based method is developed to identify the scale of the search space which thresheld convergence can then exploit. The proposed method employed in the context of a multi-start particle swarm optimization algorithm has led to large improvements across a broad range of multi-modal problems.

Categories and Subject Descriptors

I.2.8 [**Artificial Intelligence**]: Problem Solving, Control Methods, and Search—*Heuristic methods*

Keywords

Metaheuristics; particle swarm optimization; fitness landscape; thresheld convergence; multi-start methods

1. INTRODUCTION

An effective optimization algorithm must consider two essentially conflicting tasks, namely exploration and exploitation [21]. The first task entails the global exploration of the search space to locate regions with high-quality solutions, and the second task requires a local exploitation around the best solutions in order to improve them to an optimal level. The ratio at which these two task should be balanced is closely related to the characteristics of the optimization problem. In multi-modal search spaces, it is expected that a considerable search effort – i.e. function evaluations (FEs) – should be expended in finding the most promising areas of the search space before concentrating the search in these regions. Nonetheless, many search heuristics do not explicitly separate these processes [6, 17].

Particle swarm optimization (PSO) [14] is an example of such a heuristic with no explicit distinction between global and local search. Each particle is attracted towards its personal best position and the best position of a neighbouring member of the swarm. Even with the use of a local communication topology, these attractors quickly concentrate the search around a few regions of the search space. This level of convergence can work well in unimodal search spaces, but it can lead to poor performance on multi-modal problems.

"Thresheld convergence" [6, 17] is a technique specially designed to separate the processes of exploration and exploitation in search heuristics. It is based on the hypothesis that concurrent exploration and exploitation can interfere with the correct assessment of the quality of an "attraction basin" (regions in which greedy descent will lead to the same local optimum). If the promise of an attraction basin is estimated by the fitness of a single solution, an attraction basin represented by a random solution will often appear to be less promising than an attraction basin represented by its local optimum – even if the optimum in the first attraction basin is fitter than the optimum of the second. In order to prevent these biased comparisons, local search is "held back" during the initial phases of the search heuristic by means of a distance threshold.

Ideally, thresheld convergence should use a threshold value that is correlated to the size of the attraction basins in the search space. However, earlier uses of thresheld convergence in PSO [6, 7] have not tried to estimate this value, but they have instead set the initial threshold to a fraction of the main diagonal of the search space and then used simple mechanisms to reduce the threshold over time. In this paper, we develop a clustering-based method to explicitly identify the scale of the search space which thresheld convergence can then exploit. The proposed method is employed in the context of a multi-start particle swarm optimization algorithm where it achieves positive results on a broad range of multi-modal problems.

The development of this result begins with the necessary background on PSO and thresheld convergence in Section 2 before illustrating our research motivation in Section 3. Sec-

GECCO'14, July 12–16, Vancouver, BC, Canada.

ACM 978-1-4503-2662-9/14/07 ...$15.00.
http://dx.doi.org/10.1145/2576768.2598280.

tion 4 then presents the clustering approach for the identification of the scale of the search space and the newly-proposed multi-start PSO with thresheld convergence. The performance of the new technique is then empirically studied in Section 5 before Section 6 gives a summary of the main results and the conclusions of the paper.

2. BACKGROUND

The first part of this section briefly describes the variant of PSO considered as the baseline of our study. Thresheld convergence and its integration with PSO is then presented.

2.1 Particle Swarm Optimization

The initial development of PSO includes inspirations from "bird flocking, fish schooling, and swarming theory" [14]. PSO keeps a group of candidate solutions to the optimization problem – deemed as particles in a swarm – and performs updates to their positions until a termination criterion is satisfied. In addition to its position, each particle maintains a velocity vector that represents a displacement with respect to its current position which is used to move the particle in the search space. The velocity is updated at each iteration by attracting each particle to the best position it has found so far and towards the best position achieved by any neighbouring particle. For each individual particle, a neighbourhood is defined as a group of particles in the swarm that it is able to communicate with.

A particle identified with the index i among a swarm of size S is represented in PSO by three n-dimensional real vectors: 1) its position in the search space x_i; 2) the best position it has individually found $pbest_i$; and 3) its velocity v_i. Additionally, the neighbourhood notion allows us to identify by $lbest_i \in \mathbb{R}^n$ the best position achieved by any neighbouring particle, and consequently the best position globally in the swarm by $gbest \in \mathbb{R}^n$.

The initial positions are sampled from a continuous uniform distribution within the bounds of the search space, while the velocities are initialized to zero [9]. At each iteration, PSO updates the swarm by updating the velocity and the position of each particle $i = 1, \ldots, S$ in every dimension $j = 1, \ldots, n$ according to

$$v_{i,j} = \chi \left(v_{i,j} + c_1 \epsilon_{1j} (pbest_{i,j} - x_{i,j}) + c_2 \epsilon_{2j} (lbest_{i,j} - x_{i,j}) \right)$$
$$x_{i,j} = x_{i,j} + v_{i,j};$$

where $\epsilon_1, \epsilon_2 \in (0,1)^n$ are uniform random vectors simulated independently for each particle that perturb the differences $(pbest_{i,j} - x_{i,j})$ and $(lbest_{i,j} - x_{i,j})$, respectively; c_1 and c_2 are constants that scale the influence of the cognitive component $(pbest_{i,j} - x_{i,j})$ and the social component $(lbest_{i,j} - x_{i,j})$; and χ is a parameter known as constriction factor that balances the global and local search capabilities of the update rule. If after updating a particle it goes out of the search space boundaries, its position and velocity will be reset following the Reflect-Z technique [10].

The use of a swarm of 50 particles ($S = 50$) in a ring topology (every particle connected to two other particles in a circular network) with $c_1 = c_2 = 2.05$ and $\chi = 0.72984$ corresponds to our implementation of the standard PSO 2007 [4]. This configuration is used as the baseline of the study presented in the paper.

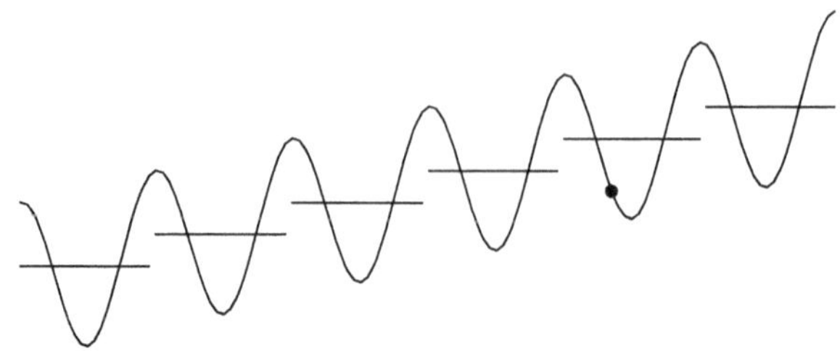

Figure 1: A search space with attraction basins of the same size and shape. The horizontal lines represent the average fitness of a random solution taken from each attraction basin. A better-than-random solution – represented by the dot – may be fitter than random solutions drawn from better basins.

2.2 Thresheld Convergence

Thresheld convergence [6, 17] is based on the hypothesis that concurrent exploitation and exploration can interfere with the effectiveness of a search technique's processes for exploration. For heuristic search techniques to exhibit a good behaviour on multi-modal fitness landscapes, they require a combination of both exploratory and exploitative moves. The exploratory part of the search process entails finding the regions of the search space where the best local optima are located, while the exploitative part must find the best possible solution – i.e. a particular local optimum – within a given region.

In general, heuristic optimization techniques estimate the promise of a region of the search space based on the evaluation of random solutions. PSO maintains a population of *pbests* and, in order to redirect the focus of the search to another (more promising) region of the search space, a sample solution from the new region that is better than the existing *pbest* representative(s) of the current region must be found. However, simultaneously combining exploration and exploitation can interfere with the process of correctly assessing the quality of a newly sampled region.

Figure 1 presents a search space with attraction basins that are all of the same size and shape – e.g. a sinusoid super-imposed over a linear slope. The average fitness of random solutions from an attraction basin is correlated to the fitness of the local optimum within that basin. Thus, given two random solutions from different attraction basins, there is a reasonable expectation that the fitter solution will be from the basin with the fitter local optimum. However, the same cannot be said for the comparison of a random solution from one attraction basin with a better-than-random solution from a second basin.

Starting from an initial solution, let us define any change that leads to a solution in a new attraction basin as an exploratory/global search step and any change that leads to a solution in the same basin as an exploitative/local search step. Without any other information, the first solution from an attraction basin can be considered to be a random solution. Subsequently, a second solution in the same basin that is better than the first solution can be considered to be a better-than-random solution. Concurrent exploitation, which can cause existing attraction basins to become represented by better-than-random solutions, can interfere with a search technique's exploratory processes by biasing its assessment of attraction basins to favour currently discovered (and partially exploited) basins.

The goal of thresheld convergence is to delay exploitation/local search and thus prevent inaccurate comparisons of attraction basins. Convergence is delayed by disallowing local search steps that are less than a distance threshold. As the threshold value decays to zero, greedier local search steps become possible. Conversely, until the threshold is sufficiently small, the search technique is forced to focus on the global search aspect of finding the best attraction basin in the search space.

The positive effects of thresheld convergence have been demonstrated on multiple metaheuristics (see e.g. [2, 3, 7]). The use of thresheld convergence in these techniques is based on the addition of a minimum step-size to the mechanisms that control the exploration/exploitation balance. In PSO, the threshold function is used during the update rule for the *pbests*. The following pseudo-code shows the original *pbest* update condition:

> **if** $f(x_i) < f(pbest_i)$ **then**
> $pbest_i \leftarrow x_i$
> **end if**

while the code fragment below shows the update condition for PSO with thresheld convergence proposed in [7]:

> **if** $f(x_i) < f(pbest_i)$ **and**
> distance(x_i, $pbest_i$) $\geq$ *threshold* **and**
> distance(x_i, $lbest_i$) $\geq$ *threshold* **then**
> $pbest_i \leftarrow x_i$
> **end if**

With thresheld convergence, a *pbest* is updated only if the new position is located a minimum distance away from both the old *pbest* and *lbest* positions. Ideally, each of these three solutions will be in different attraction basins, and the elimination of local search can remove a source of bias from the comparison of the potential fitness of these attraction basins.

3. MOTIVATION

In order to illustrate the research motivation, we have chosen the well-known Rastrigin's function as defined in [19] (hereafter simply Rastrigin). This function is a non-convex minimization problem frequently used as a performance test for numerical algorithms. It constitutes a typical example of a non-linear and multi-modal function, defined as

$$f(\mathbf{x}) = An + \sum_{i=1}^{n} \left[x_i^2 - A\cos(2\pi x_i)\right],$$

where $A = 10$ and $x_i \in [-5.12, 5.12]$. The function has a single global minimum at $\mathbf{x} = \mathbf{0}$ with $f(\mathbf{x}) = 0$, but it is a fairly difficult optimization problem due the large number of local minima. The local optima are located at the integer values of a regular grid of size 1 – thus, there are n^{11} local optima in the n-dimensional search space defined above.

By analyzing the function definition, we know that the minimum distance between adjacent local optima is 1 and the maximum distance is $\sqrt{n}$. These values represent moving from one local optimum to another only through one dimension or through the diagonal, respectively. Also, given a search point, the nearest local optima in the same basin can be obtained by rounding each component to its nearest integer value. As will be shown, this information is very

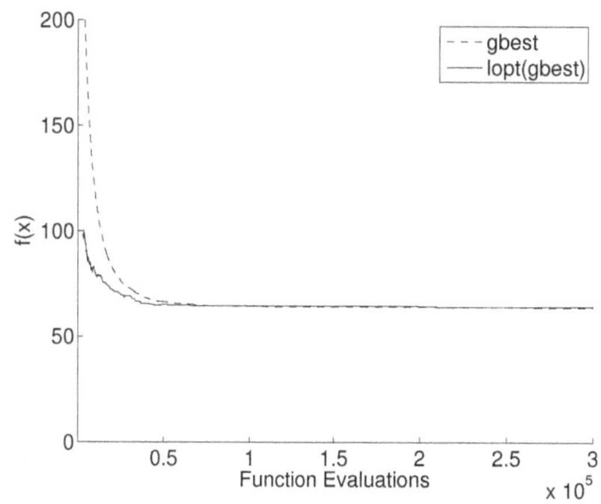

Figure 2: Results of PSO on Rastrigin for $n = 30$. The plot shows the average performance over 51 trials: mean $f(x)$ of *gbest* is 63.8.

useful for understanding the results of PSO on this problem and to design a strategy to improve its performance.

To provide a baseline, standard PSO was run 51 times on Rastrigin for $n = 30$ dimensions. Figure 2 illustrates the progress of the algorithm in terms of the FEs up to a maximum allocation of 300,000. The dashed line represents the fitness of the best solution found so far, and the solid line the fitness of the local optimum corresponding to that solution (i.e. the local optimum in the same attraction basin). Therefore, changes in the solid line represent global search, and the convergence of the dashed line onto the solid line is evidence of local search.

From the plot, it can be seen that the solid line quickly plateaus after the first 10–20% of the FEs. This suggests that PSO uses 10–20% of its running time looking for a promising area in the search space and 80–90% performing local search in this area to find the corresponding local optimum. Since only the best generated solutions are stored as *pbests*, PSO eventually becomes highly exploitative around the regions of the search space containing these *pbest* positions as the velocities slow down to zero [8], even with the (local) ring topology.

This strong convergence is a property that makes PSO a very effective method for unimodal search spaces, but it is not an appropriate strategy for multi-modal functions. In order to obtain better results on highly multi-modal problems, PSO needs better global search capabilities – e.g. the ratio of global and local search should be inverted. Several PSO extensions tackling this drawback have been proposed in the literature, including niching techniques (see e.g. [1, 5]), multi-swarm systems (see e.g. [11, 22]), thresheld convergence (covered in Section 2.2), and many others.

One of the most simple alternatives (studied in detail in [20]) is running PSO multiple times from different initial solutions in order to increase the chance of convergence to the global optimum. Figure 3 shows the results of a simple multi-start strategy consisting of five completely independent restarts with a static allocation of 60,000 FEs each. The use of multiple restarts improves the performance on Rastrigin by 21.6% due to the additional exploration of the search space introduced by the resampled initial solutions. Nonetheless, going back to solutions sampled uniformly within the bounds of the search space wastes most of

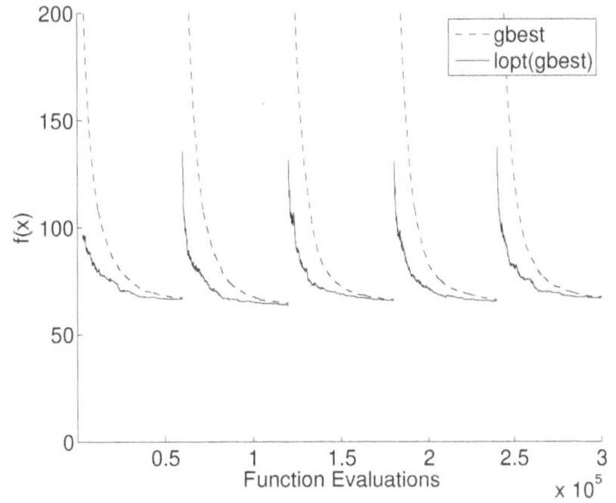

Figure 3: Results of five restarts of PSO – with 1/5 of the allotted FEs each – on Rastrigin for $n = 30$. The plot shows the average performance over 51 trials: mean $f(x)$ of *gbest* is 50.0. The discordance between this value and the chart is caused by the line plot averaging the individual restarts and not the best global result of each trial.

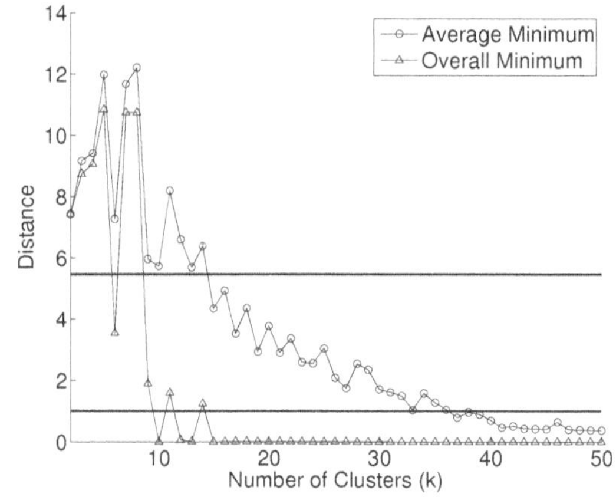

Figure 4: Average and overall minimum distance between the centroids of every pair of the $k \in [2, 50]$ clusters obtained from the population of *pbests*. The horizontal lines show the minimum and maximum distance between adjacent local optima in Rastrigin for $n = 30$.

the FEs and the algorithm produces, on average, five replicas of the behaviour of the single-run version.

Resetting the particles' positions – and in particular the *pbests* that lead the swarm – can increase the probability of convergence to the global optimum. However, relying solely on restarts does not provide an explicit mechanism to influence the exploration/exploitation balance. Thresheld convergence – by means of the threshold parameter – can control the amount of local search performed: large threshold values (in particular greater than the distance between local optima in adjacent basins) prevent the algorithm from doing any local search, while setting the threshold to zero allows PSO to converge freely. In the next section, we propose a strategy to identify and exploit the scale of the search space as the foundations for designing a PSO extension that combines thresheld convergence and multiple restarts.

4. IDENTIFYING AND EXPLOITING THE SCALE OF THE SEARCH SPACE

As illustrated in Section 3, in order to obtain better results with PSO on multi-modal problems, the ratio of global vs. local search needs to be increased. To fulfil this aim, we combine thresheld convergence and multiple restarts. Thresheld convergence allows us to have explicit control over the exploration/exploitation balance in PSO, while restarts introduce new solutions into the swarm. This section focuses on thresheld convergence, the main component around which the multi-start strategy is built.

Earlier algorithms using thresheld convergence have set the initial value of the threshold to a fraction of the main diagonal of the search space and have used a formula in terms of the total FEs (see e.g. [2, 6, 17]) or an adaptive approach (see e.g. [3, 7]) to reduce the threshold as the algorithm proceeds. A different method is proposed in the context of multi-starts: appropriate threshold values are selected automatically from an analysis of the search space and used to run different restarts of PSO with thresheld convergence, followed by a final local search step to exploit the discovered attraction basins. The goal is to make PSO search at different scales of the search space in order to focus only on a subset of the attraction basins at a given time.

The social component of the swarm update rule presented in Section 2.1 attracts connected particles towards the best positions in their neighbourhood. Due to the limited global communication of the (local) ring topology, it takes several communication cycles for this information to spread throughout the entire swarm. This situation favours the formation of groups of nearby solutions in the population of *pbests*, which constitute a promising set of solutions for the identification of threshold values. Accordingly, a method to get information about the scale of the search space expressed as the distance among neighbouring (groups of) *pbests* is required. We recur to cluster analysis and k-means in particular (see [12] for an introduction), which has been used successfully for similar purposes in the context of multi-swarm systems [13]. k-means splits the points into k groups that minimize the within-cluster sum of squared differences with respect to the centroid of the cluster, which is in concordance with the purpose of identifying groups of nearby solutions that are hopefully in different attraction basins.

Motivated by the behaviour of PSO observed in Rastrigin, the population of *pbests* after the first 10% of the total FEs is considered as the input set of solutions for k-means. Figure 4 illustrates the feasibility of this approach with a representative trial. The plot shows the average and overall minimum distance between the cluster centroids obtained with k-means for k between 2 and 50 (the swarm size). The horizontal lines correspond to the values 1 and $\sqrt{n}$ – i.e. the minimum and maximum distance between adjacent local optima, respectively.

A minimum cluster distance near zero indicates that k is so large that points which belong in the same cluster are forced to be in separate clusters. Thus, as k decreases, there should be a value at which the minimum cluster distance "spikes up" from zero. Across all fifty-one trials, there were visible spikes and these spikes often matched the known minimum distance between local optima of 1. Further, at the value of k with the spike, the average minimum distance for clusters was often close to the known maximum distance between adjacent local optima of $\sqrt{n}$.

The following procedure automates the identification of a value of k corresponding to these reference threshold values by targeting the observed spike. From $k = 50$ and decreasing iteratively towards $k = 2$, we start collecting the sample of the overall minimum distances. We select the first value of $k \leq 35$ in which the deviation of the overall minimum distance with respect to the mean of the collected sample differs by more than 10 standard deviations. For example, in Figure 4, the overall minimum distance for $k = 14$ is around 200 standard deviations away from the mean of the values for $k \in [15, 50]$. The condition is only applied for $k \leq 35$ in order to collect a reasonable sample of the overall minimum distance. If $k = 2$ is reached and the condition is never satisfied, the function is considered unimodal and the reference threshold values are both set to zero. This relatively simple heuristic performed consistently well on extensive experiments with different input sets of solutions.

Based on this heuristic, we propose the following multi-start PSO strategy with thresheld convergence. It is divided into three phases:

1. First, PSO is run for 10% of the allotted FEs. The final population of *pbests* is processed using the heuristic described above in order to obtain an estimation of appropriate threshold values for the search space. For further reference, let a and b denote the values of the average and overall minimum distance selected with the heuristic, respectively. This phase is responsible for the identification of the scale of the search space.
2. Next, the information collected during the first phase is exploited using thresheld convergence. Four restarts of PSO with thresheld convergence and different constant threshold values are run, each one for 20% of the total FEs. The thresholds for each restart are: a, $(a + b)/2$, $2b$ and b (a and b were defined in the description of the first phase). In the first restart of PSO with thresheld convergence, the information of the particle corresponding to the *gbest* of the initial phase is kept and the others are reset uniformly within the search space boundaries. In the other restarts only the threshold value changes.
3. Finally, standard PSO is run for the remaining 10% of the total FEs, starting from the *pbests* at the end of the fourth restart of PSO with thresheld convergence. The purpose of this phase is to perform local search which will find the (local) optima in the attraction basins discovered during the second phase.

Notice that at this point we have minimized the use of resets – i.e. particles are only reset after the first phase. Consequently, the use of thresheld convergence in phase two corresponds to a step threshold function. We have prioritized presenting a solid foundation to solve highly multi-modal problems based on an appropriate balance between global/local search. In the next section, a computational study of the proposed strategy on a wider range of benchmark problems is presented, and we then build an improved heuristic by incrementally adjusting phases two and three for better performance.

5. COMPUTATIONAL STUDY

This section presents an extensive computational study of the multi-start PSO with thresheld convergence introduced in the previous section. The test suite from the CEC 2013 Special Session on Real-Parameter Optimization [16] (CEC'13 benchmark for short) is considered for the evaluation of the performance of the heuristic in $n = 30$ dimensions. It includes 28 minimization problems with known global optimum, divided into three groups: unimodal functions (1–5), basic multi-modal functions (6–20), and composition functions (21–28). The second group is of particular interest to this study, given that the proposed technique was specially designed for such problems.

The experimental setup closely follows the guidelines of the CEC'13 benchmark. Fifty-one randomized trials with a maximum of 300,000 FEs were performed on each function, reporting the mean and standard deviation of the fitness errors achieved by the algorithms. In addition, the relative difference on the mean errors (%-diff) is given when two algorithms are compared. The %-diff of the mean error m_1 of a first algorithm with respect to the mean m_2 of a second algorithm is given by $100(m_1 - m_2)/\max(m_1, m_2)$. Hence, positive %-diff values indicate that the first algorithm performs better than the second one, and *vice versa*. A t-test between the two samples is also performed to focus the comparison on statistically significant differences at the 5% level.

5.1 Initial Results

Table 1 shows the results on the CEC'13 benchmark of standard PSO and the initial version of the multi-start PSO with thresheld convergence (as presented in Section 4). The proposed heuristic obtains average improvements over 5% on both the multi-modal test problems and the composite functions. On the multi-modal functions, nine results are significantly better, three are worse, and the remaining three are indistinguishable – which evidences that the clustering approach designed in terms of the observed behaviour on Rastrigin is also applicable to other multi-modal functions. In order to build a better-performing technique, the next section presents a first extension to the basic algorithm that resets the particles' positions and *pbests* during the second phase of the heuristic.

5.2 Resetting Positions and pbests

The multi-start technique described in Section 4 only resets particles during the transition between phases one and two – i.e. as part of the initialization of the first restart of PSO with thresheld convergence. In this section, resets are also introduced during the initialization of the second, third, and fourth restarts of PSO with thresheld convergence. However, to reuse earlier-obtained information about the search space implicitly encoded in the swarm, only partial resets are considered.

In the first restart of PSO with thresheld convergence, the *gbest* of the first phase is kept and the other particles are discarded, since it would not be profitable applying thresheld convergence to a swarm that has converged beyond the radius of the threshold size. Conversely, the other restarts offer more flexibility to reuse a greater number of particles because of the decreasing threshold values. Specifically, we propose keeping the positions and *pbests* of the $s > 1$ best particles from the previous restart, and completing the S particles in the initial swarm with reinitialized solutions.

Table 1: Results of PSO and the initial version of multi-start PSO with thresheld convergence (PSO+TC) – including only the step threshold function – on the CEC'13 benchmark. Bold %-diff values indicate statistical significance.

func.	PSO mean	PSO std dev	Multi-Start PSO+TC (step threshold func.) mean	Multi-Start PSO+TC (step threshold func.) std dev	%-diff	t-test
1	0.00e+0	0.00e+0	2.81e−9	2.01e−8	-100.0%	0.32
2	2.07e+6	7.82e+5	8.00e+6	3.67e+6	**-78.3%**	0.00
3	6.75e+7	7.06e+7	9.15e+7	1.31e+8	-46.1%	0.29
4	1.80e+4	4.55e+3	2.70e+4	1.75e+4	**-47.0%**	0.00
5	0.00e+0	0.00e+0	7.44e−7	2.35e−6	**-100.0%**	0.02
1–5					-74.3%	
6	1.67e+1	4.34e+0	3.03e+1	1.44e+1	**-53.0%**	0.00
7	6.37e+1	1.74e+1	3.39e+1	9.54e+0	**50.0%**	0.00
8	2.09e+1	5.51e−2	2.09e+1	5.76e−2	0.0%	
9	2.86e+1	1.95e+0	2.39e+1	2.35e+0	**16.5%**	0.00
10	1.32e−1	5.53e−2	4.80e+0	2.72e+0	**-97.9%**	0.00
11	6.47e+1	1.51e+1	3.81e+1	9.90e+0	**43.7%**	0.00
12	7.85e+1	1.72e+1	6.52e+1	1.95e+1	**16.1%**	0.00
13	1.44e+2	2.21e+1	1.23e+2	2.63e+1	**14.%**	0.00
14	2.63e+3	3.80e+2	1.91e+3	4.66e+2	**28.3%**	0.00
15	3.95e+3	6.25e+2	4.59e+3	6.64e+2	**-14.6%**	0.00
16	1.66e+0	3.51e−1	1.58e+0	3.53e−1	3.8%	0.27
17	1.01e+2	1.55e+1	7.69e+1	1.16e+1	**25.2%**	0.00
18	1.70e+2	2.68e+1	1.57e+2	3.12e+1	**7.2%**	0.00
19	5.76e+0	1.30e+0	3.67e+0	7.82e−1	**39.0%**	0.00
20	1.17e+1	5.12e−1	1.17e+1	4.84e−1	0.0%	
6–20					5.27%	
21	2.20e+2	5.30e+1	2.30e+2	4.57e+1	-4.1%	0.31
22	2.96e+3	5.15e+2	1.97e+3	5.34e+2	**34.2%**	0.00
23	4.66e+3	7.06e+2	4.76e+3	7.97e+2	-2.2%	0.51
24	2.76e+2	5.64e+0	2.61e+2	7.88e+0	**5.3%**	0.00
25	2.92e+2	7.12e+0	2.77e+2	6.53e+0	**5.2%**	0.00
26	2.13e+2	4.61e+1	2.13e+2	4.30e+1	0.7%	0.92
27	1.03e+3	7.43e+1	8.99e+2	6.09e+1	**13.3%**	0.00
28	3.00e+2	0.00e+0	2.96e+2	2.80e+1	1.2%	0.32
21–28					6.7%	

Table 2: Results of multi-start PSO with thresheld convergence (PSO+TC) – including uniform resets – on the CEC'13 benchmark. The %-diff and t-test values are with respect to the PSO results in Table 1. Bold %-diff values indicate statistical significance.

func.	Multi-Start PSO+TC (uniform restarts) mean	Multi-Start PSO+TC (uniform restarts) std dev	%-diff	t-test
1	0.00e+0	0.00e+0	0.0%	
2	6.81e+6	3.59e+6	**-75.5%**	0.00
3	1.51e+8	2.06e+8	**-73.0%**	0.01
4	2.40e+4	1.55e+4	**-39.4%**	0.01
5	1.52e−6	8.23e−6	-100.0%	0.19
1–5			-57.6%	
6	3.10e+1	1.50e+1	**-55.4%**	0.00
7	2.46e+1	7.21e+0	**64.2%**	0.00
8	2.09e+1	5.84e−2	0.0%	
9	2.04e+1	2.56e+0	**29.0%**	0.00
10	4.82e+0	3.69e+0	**-98.2%**	0.00
11	3.73e+1	1.19e+1	**44.0%**	0.00
12	5.05e+1	2.17e+1	**33.7%**	0.00
13	1.03e+2	2.79e+1	**28.6%**	0.00
14	1.56e+3	5.24e+2	**41.0%**	0.00
15	3.87e+3	8.57e+2	0.6%	0.57
16	1.34e+0	3.46e−1	**19.1%**	0.00
17	6.71e+1	9.62e+0	**34.9%**	0.00
18	1.22e+2	2.70e+1	**28.4%**	0.00
19	3.01e+0	7.13e−1	**49.7%**	0.00
20	1.12e+1	6.40e−1	**4.4%**	0.00
6–20			14.9%	
21	2.30e+2	5.71e+1	-4.8%	0.37
22	1.39e+3	4.37e+2	**54.4%**	0.00
23	3.92e+3	7.54e+2	**15.9%**	0.00
24	2.53e+2	7.93e+0	**8.3%**	0.00
25	2.68e+2	7.63e+0	**8.4%**	0.00
26	2.00e+2	2.12e−1	**10.2%**	0.04
27	7.85e+2	7.30e+1	**24.4%**	0.00
28	3.00e+2	1.23e−1	0.0%	
21–28			14.6%	

In order to be able to choose a small (yet effective) s value, the particles that are kept are then re-spaced equally among the S particles in the ring topology. This structure ensures that the information about the best solutions found so far is more accessible to all of the particles. Two reinitialization approaches for the $S - s$ particles are studied.

In the first approach, the particles are resampled uniformly within the bounds of the search space. The number of particles that are kept was set to 10, which showed the best performance among the tested values of $s \in \{2, 5, 10, 25\}$. Table 2 summarizes results of the proposed heuristic with uniform resets during the second phase, compared to the PSO baseline. The beneficial effects of the uniform resets on the overall behaviour of the algorithm are clear: the average performance of the heuristic on the three groups of problems was improved. In particular, the improvement on the targeted group of multi-modal functions is now close to 15%. The newly sampled solutions introduce diversity into the swarm, which translates into better exploration and less risk of stagnation.

The second reinitialization variant is motivated by the fact that the uniformly sampled solutions do not exploit information about promising search space regions already acquired by the algorithm. As it was illustrated in Section 3 using PSO with simple restarts, this can result in a considerable waste of FEs. To make use of this information implicitly encoded in the population of *pbests*, a sampling strategy inspired by the univariate marginal distribution algorithm (UMDA) for continuous domains [15] is used. Each component $j = 1, \ldots, n$ of a reinitialized solution is sampled from a univariate normal distribution $\mathcal{N}(\mu_j, c_\sigma \sigma_j^2)$, where μ_j and σ_j are respectively the mean and standard deviation of the sample of the variable j in the final population of *pbests* of the previous restart. The additional parameter c_σ is a factor that scales the variance of the sampling distribution, which was set empirically to 0.5 after experiments with the values of 0.5, 1.0, and 1.5.

Table 3 shows the results of the proposed technique including normal resets. It produces consistent improvements on the multi-modal problems reaching a mean performance improvement of around 21% in this group. Compared to the results using uniform resets, the effect on the other two groups is negligible. Therefore, the normal resets are selected over the uniform resets to be incorporated into the algorithm. The next section focuses on improving the local search step in the third phase of the heuristic.

5.3 Improving the Local Search Phase

A closer look at the results of the proposed strategy with normal resets presented in Table 3 shows that the two functions with negative results among the multi-modal functions share common characteristics in terms of the fitness landscape. Functions 6 (rotated Rosenbrock's) and 10 (rotated Griewank's) present a flat region that the algorithm must

Table 3: Results of multi-start PSO with thresheld convergence (PSO+TC) – including normal resets – on the CEC'13 benchmark. The %-diff and t-test values are with respect to the PSO results in Table 1. Bold %-diff values indicate statistical significance. Compare to the results in Table 2.

func.	Multi-Start PSO+TC (normal restarts)		%-diff	t-test
	mean	std dev		
1	0.00e+0	0.00e+0	0.0%	
2	7.77e+6	3.89e+6	**-78.4%**	0.00
3	1.06e+8	2.28e+8	-70.9%	0.25
4	2.03e+4	1.49e+4	-30.0%	0.32
5	2.75e−7	9.96e−7	-100.0%	0.05
1–5			-55.9%	
6	2.90e+1	1.10e+1	**-47.9%**	0.00
7	2.19e+1	7.61e+0	**66.7%**	0.00
8	2.09e+1	6.24e−2	0.0%	
9	1.96e+1	3.07e+0	**31.9%**	0.00
10	3.35e+0	1.87e+0	**-96.9%**	0.00
11	2.63e+1	8.46e+0	**61.1%**	0.00
12	3.13e+1	2.42e+1	**58.2%**	0.00
13	6.87e+1	2.92e+1	**53.1%**	0.00
14	1.47e+3	3.66e+2	**45.0%**	0.00
15	3.55e+3	8.71e+2	**8.2%**	0.01
16	1.39e+0	4.64e−1	**14.6%**	0.00
17	6.02e+1	9.12e+0	**41.7%**	0.00
18	1.10e+2	3.24e+1	**35.7%**	0.00
19	2.85e+0	7.56e−1	**52.8%**	0.00
20	1.13e+1	6.75e−1	**3.7%**	0.00
6–20			21.8%	
21	2.30e+2	5.38e+1	-4.7%	0.27
22	1.61e+3	5.95e+2	**46.2%**	0.00
23	3.91e+3	9.38e+2	**15.4%**	0.00
24	2.52e+2	7.74e+0	**8.8%**	0.00
25	2.68e+2	6.62e+0	**8.3%**	0.00
26	2.06e+2	2.89e+1	5.6%	0.35
27	8.10e+2	6.79e+1	**22.0%**	0.00
28	2.96e+2	2.79e+1	1.2%	0.33
21–28			12.9%	

Table 4: Results of the final version of multi-start PSO with thresheld convergence (PSO+TC) – including normal resets and improved local search – on the CEC'13 benchmark. The %-diff and t-test values are with respect to the PSO results in Table 1. Bold %-diff values indicate statistical significance.

func.	Multi-Start PSO+TC (imp. local search)		%-diff	t-test
	mean	std dev		
1	0.00e+0	0.00e+0	0.0%	
2	4.32e+6	3.53e+6	**-67.8%**	0.00
3	1.00e+8	2.66e+8	-81.2%	0.41
4	1.42e+4	1.04e+4	**6.2%**	0.02
5	0.00e+0	0.00e+0	0.0%	
1–5			-28.5%	
6	2.02e+1	6.03e+0	**-19.9%**	0.00
7	2.13e+1	6.27e+0	**68.3%**	0.00
8	2.09e+1	6.20e−2	0.0%	
9	1.95e+1	2.74e+0	**32.0%**	0.00
10	2.64e−1	2.17e−1	**-68.1%**	0.00
11	2.89e+1	1.39e+1	**56.7%**	0.00
12	3.80e+1	3.42e+1	**41.7%**	0.00
13	7.63e+1	3.90e+1	**46.8%**	0.00
14	1.54e+3	6.22e+2	**40.7%**	0.00
15	3.87e+3	1.23e+3	-1.3%	0.67
16	1.31e+0	4.50e−1	**18.5%**	0.00
17	6.14e+1	8.38e+0	**40.4%**	0.00
18	8.65e+1	4.64e+1	**47.3%**	0.00
19	2.82e+0	9.00e−1	**52.9%**	0.00
20	1.10e+1	6.78e−1	**5.6%**	0.00
6–20			24.1%	
21	2.25e+2	5.60e+1	-2.%	0.60
22	1.54e+3	7.18e+2	**48.7%**	0.00
23	4.29e+3	1.19e+3	5.6%	0.05
24	2.51e+2	9.18e+0	**9.1%**	0.00
25	2.69e+2	6.63e+0	**8.0%**	0.00
26	2.06e+2	2.79e+1	5.9%	0.32
27	8.00e+2	8.10e+1	**23.0%**	0.00
28	3.00e+2	0.00e+0	0.0%	
21–28			12.3%	

transverse during the optimization. Our hypothesis is that the algorithm becomes stalled on these regions because of insufficient local search to reach a local optimum.

In order to improve the local search capabilities of the third phase of the multi-start strategy, the swarm is reduced to the 10 best particles (i.e. the same number kept on restarts 2, 3, and 4 of PSO with thresheld convergence). This change both accelerates the communication among the particles and allows PSO to perform a greater number of generations within the same 10% of the allotted FEs. Additionally, the initial positions are set equal to the *pbests* and the initial velocities are set to the difference vectors between the corresponding *pbest* and the *gbest*. The goal is to ensure a quick convergence to the best local optimum in the attraction basins discovered during the previous phase.

Table 4 summarizes the results of the proposed multi-start PSO including the normal resets and the changes for better local search described above. The mean performance on the principal group of multi-modal functions has been raised to just over 24% and the results on both functions 6 and 10 are better. After having adjusted phases two and three of the proposed technique for better performance on the wide range of multi-modal problems included in the CEC'13 benchmark, 11 out of the 15 problems exhibit statistically significant performance improvements, and most of them constitute sizable differences of over 40%.

6. SUMMARY AND CONCLUSIONS

Thresheld convergence is a generally applicable mechanism for improving the performance of search heuristics on multi-modal problems. It is based on the hypothesis that simultaneous exploration and exploitation processes can interfere with a correct assessment of the potential fitness of a newly sampled region. Ideally, thresheld convergence will use a minimum distance threshold that is correlated to the size of the attraction basins in the search space. This paper examined the use of a clustering-based method in the context of a multi-start PSO to identify the scale of the search space which thresheld convergence can then exploit.

As a conclusive note on the effect of the proposed multi-start PSO algorithm with thresheld convergence, we show the performance of the final version of the algorithm (discussed in Section 5.3) on Rastrigin. Figure 5 clearly illustrates the effect of each component of the strategy and the important differences with respect to the behaviour of standard PSO shown in Figure 2. Note the effect of thresheld convergence in delaying convergence (i.e. the gap between the two lines) and to effectively increase global search in a controlled manner (i.e. the continuous decrease of the solid line and the dips that occur when the threshold values change, e.g. at 150,000 FEs). The effect of the local search step is also illustrated after 270,000 FEs when the two lines

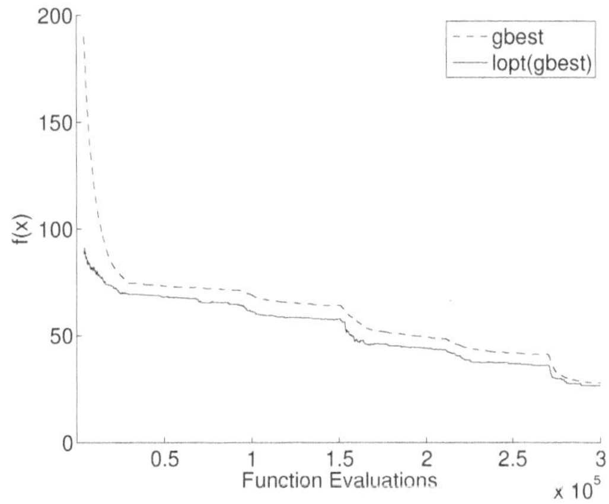

Figure 5: Results of the final version of multi-start PSO with thresheld convergence – including normal resets and improved local search – on Rastrigin for $n = 30$. The plot shows the average performance over 51 trials: mean $f(x)$ of *gbest* is 27.9.

converge quickly. Overall, the proposed strategy obtains a 56.2% performance improvement on this function.

The proposed technique not only outperformed standard PSO on Rastrigin, but it also led to large improvements across a broad range of multi-modal optimization problems. The reported experimental study validated the robustness of the proposed clustering approach to identify appropriate threshold values. Interestingly, the use of a similar approach on differential evolution (DE) with thresheld convergence led to divergent results [18]. The attraction vectors in PSO promote the formation of distinct clusters, whereas DE exhibits a more homogeneous convergence which does not produce the clusters which the proposed cluster-based method is designed to identify. These results constitute key insights for future research on thresheld convergence and its integration with different heuristics.

7. REFERENCES

[1] S. Bird and X. Li. Adaptively choosing niching parameters in a PSO. In *8th Annual Conference on Genetic and Evolutionary Computation*, 3–10, 2006.

[2] A. Bolufé-Röhler and S. Chen. Minimum population search – lessons from building a heuristic technique with two population members. In *IEEE Congress on Evolutionary Computation*, 2061–2068, 2013.

[3] A. Bolufé-Röhler, S. Estévez-Velarde, A. Piad-Morffis, S. Chen, and J. Montgomery. Differential evolution with thresheld convergence. In *IEEE Congress on Evolutionary Computation*, 40–47, 2013.

[4] D. Bratton and J. Kennedy. Defining a standard for particle swarm optimization. In *IEEE Swarm Intelligence Symposium*, 120–127, 2007.

[5] R. Brits, A. P. Engelbrecht, and F. van den Bergh. A niching particle swarm optimizer. In *4th Asia-Pacific Conference on Simulated Evolution and Learning*, 692–696, 2002.

[6] S. Chen and J. Montgomery. A simple strategy to maintain diversity and reduce crowding in particle swarm optimization. In *24th Australian Joint Conference on Artificial Intelligence*, 281–290, 2011.

[7] S. Chen and J. Montgomery. Particle swarm optimization with thresheld convergence. In *IEEE Congress on Evolutionary Computation*, 510–516, 2013.

[8] M. Clerc and J. Kennedy. The particle swarm – explosion, stability, and convergence in a multidimensional complex space. *IEEE Transactions on Evolutionary Computation*, 6(1):58–73, 2002.

[9] A. Engelbrecht. Particle swarm optimization: Velocity initialization. In *IEEE Congress on Evolutionary Computation*, 70–77, 2012.

[10] S. Helwig, J. Branke, and S. M. Mostaghim. Experimental analysis of bound handling techniques in particle swarm optimization. *IEEE Transactions on Evolutionary Computation*, 17(2):259–271, 2013.

[11] T. Hendtlass. WoSP: A multi-optima particle swarm algorithm. In *IEEE Congress on Evolutionary Computation*, 727–734, 2005.

[12] L. Kaufman and P. J. Rousseeuw. *Finding Groups in Data: An Introduction to Cluster Analysis*. Wiley, 1990.

[13] J. Kennedy. Stereotyping: Improving particle swarm performance with cluster analysis. In *IEEE Congress on Evolutionary Computation*, 1507–1512, 2000.

[14] J. Kennedy and R. Eberhart. Particle swarm optimization. In *IEEE International Conference on Neural Networks*, 1942–1948, 1995.

[15] P. Larrañaga, R. Etxeberria, J. A. Lozano, and J. M. Peña. Optimization by learning and simulation of Bayesian and Gaussian networks. Technical Report EHU-KZAA-IK-4/99, University of the Basque Country, Spain, 1999.

[16] J. J. Liang, B. Y. Qu, P. N. Suganthan, and A. G. Hernández-Díaz. Problem definitions and evaluation criteria for the CEC 2013 special session on real-parameter optimization. Technical Report 201212, Zhengzhou University, China and Nanyang Technological University, Singapore, 2013.

[17] J. Montgomery and S. Chen. A simple strategy for maintaining diversity and reducing crowding in differential evolution. In *IEEE Congress on Evolutionary Computation*, 2692–2699, 2012.

[18] J. Montgomery, S. Chen, and Y. Gonzalez-Fernandez. Identifying and exploiting the scale of a search space in differential evolution. In *IEEE Congress on Evolutionary Computation*, 2014. In press.

[19] H. Mühlenbein, M. Schomisch, and J. Born. The parallel genetic algorithm as function optimizer. *Parallel Computing*, 17(6–7):619–632, 1991.

[20] F. van den Bergh. *An Analysis of Particle Swarm Optimizers*. PhD thesis, University of Pretoria, South Africa, 2002.

[21] M. Črepinšek, S.-H. Liu, and M. Mernik. Exploration and exploitation in evolutionary algorithms: A survey. *ACM Computing Surveys*, 45(3):35:1–35:33, 2013.

[22] S. Z. Zhao, J. J. Liang, P. N. Suganthan, and M. F. Tasgetiren. Dynamic multi-swarm particle swarm optimizer with local search for large scale global optimization. In *IEEE Congress on Evolutionary Computation*, 3845–3852, 2008.

Stepsize Control on the Modified Bacterial Foraging Algorithm for Constrained Numerical Optimization

Betania Hernández-Ocaña
Universidad Juárez Autónoma de Tabasco
Tabasco, México
betania.h.o@gmail.com

Ma. Del Pilar Pozos-Parra
Universidad Juárez Autónoma de Tabasco
Tabasco, México
pilar.pozos@ujat.mx

Efrén Mezura-Montes
Facultad de Física e Inteligencia Artificial
Universidad Veracruzana
Xalapa, Ver., México
emezura@uv.mx

ABSTRACT

The stepsize value is one of the most sensitive parameters in the bacterial foraging optimization algorithm when solving constrained numerical optimization problems. In this paper, four stepsize control mechanisms are proposed and analyzed in the modified bacterial foraging optimization algorithm. The first one is based on a random value which remains fixed during the search, the second one generates a random value per cycle, the third one is based on a non-linear decreasing function and the last one is an adaptive approach. Seven experiments are proposed to evaluate the abilities of each mechanism to: (1) obtain competitive final results, (2) find feasible solutions, (3) find the feasible global optimum, (4) promote successful swims, and (5) decrease the constraint violation. A comparison against two state-of-the-art algorithms is considered to evaluate the performance of the most competitive control mechanism. A well-known set of constrained numerical optimization problems is used in the experiments as well as six performance measures. The results obtained show that the control mechanism based on the nonlinear decreasing function is the most competitive and provides the ability to generate better solutions late in the search.

Categories and Subject Descriptors

G.1.6 [**Optimization**]: [Constrained optimization]

General Terms

Algorithms, Experimentation, Performance

Keywords

Swarm intelligence, Bacterial Foraging, Parameter control

GECCO'14, July 12–16, 2014, Vancouver, BC, Canada.
Copyright © 2014 ACM 978-1-4503-2662-9/14/07...$15.00.
http://dx.doi.org/10.1145/2576768.2598379.

1. INTRODUCTION

Swarm Intelligence Algorithms (SIAs) [6], which are based on the cooperative behavior of some species, particularly foraging tasks, have been gaining popularity along with Evolutionary Algorithms (EAs) [3] to solve complex optimization problems [28]. Originally designed to deal with unconstrained search spaces, SIAs and EAs can be added with constraint-handling techniques so as to solve constrained numerical optimization problems (CNOPs) [13]. Among the most popular SIAs found in the specialized literature to solve CNOPs there are the Particle Swarm Optimization (PSO) [9, 17] and the Artificial Bee Colony (ABC) [8, 14]. More recently, the Bacterial Foraging Optimization Algorithm (BFOA), originally proposed by Passino [23] to solve unconstrained optimization problems, has been adapted to solve CNOPs as well [18, 19].

Without loss of generality, a CNOP can be defined as to minimize $f(\vec{x})$ subject to $g_i(\vec{x}) \leq 0$, $i = 1, ..., m$, and $h_j(\vec{x}) = 0$, $j = 1, ..., p$, where $\vec{x} = [x_1, x_2, \ldots, x_n] \in R^n$, is the solution vector and each decision variable x_i, $i = 1, ..., n$ is bounded by lower and upper limits $L_i \leq x_i \leq U_i$, which define the search space S; m is the number of inequality constraints and p is the number of equality constraints (in both cases, the constraints can be linear or nonlinear). If F denotes the feasible region, then it must be clear that $F \subseteq S$. As it is commonly found in the specialized literature of nature-inspired algorithms to solve CNOPs [1, 13, 16] an equality constraint is transformed into an inequality constraint by using a small tolerance. In this paper, this tolerance is dynamic [14] and controlled as indicated in Equation 1:

$$\xi(G+1) = \frac{\xi(G)}{dec} \tag{1}$$

where ξ is an user-defined tolerance for equality constraints, G is the current cycle of the algorithm and dec is a user-defined decreasing rate ($dec > 1$). The ξ value decreases until it reaches the value of 1E-4.

A recent review of the state-of-the-art in BFOA to solve CNOPs showed that the penalty function is the most popular constraint-handling technique. Moreover, such review concluded that BFOA is particularly sensitive to the stepsize used in its main variation operator, known as the tumble-swim movement. There are different ways to control the stepsize: (1) keep it static during the search process (as in the original BFOA) [18, 7, 30], (2) using random values [24, 29], using a dynamic variation [22, 21], or adopting an adaptive mechanism [26, 19]. However, such proposals were stated mainly for specific optimization problems and, to the best of the authors' knowledge, there are no studies devoted to the stepsize control in BFOA for constrained search spaces. This is the main motivation of this work, where four stepsize control mechanisms are added to a BFOA-based algorithm to improve its performance in different constrained optimization problems. The four proposals are analyzed in seven experiments by using performance measures and final results as well. The bacterial foraging optimization algorithm adopted in this work is the Modified BFOA (MBFOA for short) [18], which is a simplified version of the original BFOA but designed to solve CNOPs, MBFOA is detailed later in the document.

The structure of the paper is organized as follows: Section 2 briefly introduces BFOA's biological inspiration. After that, MBFOA and its four main processes are explained. Section 3 presents the proposed control mechanisms for the stepsize. Afterwards, Section 4 describes the experimental design and shows the results obtained by the different stepsize control mechanisms in MBFOA and the observed behaviors are discussed. Moreover, a comparison against two state-of-the-art algorithms is presented. Finally, Section 5 summarizes the general conclusions and establishes the future work.

2. MODIFIED BACTERIAL FORAGING OPTIMIZATION ALGORITHM (MBFOA)

BFOA emulates the behavior of the E.coli bacterium in its foraging process. Each bacterium tries to maximize its obtained energy per each unit of time spent on the foraging process, while avoiding noxious substances. Moreover, bacteria can establish communication with others in the neighborhood. A swarm of bacteria presents the following process [23]:

1. Bacteria are distributed at random in the map of nutrients.
2. Bacteria locate high-nutrient regions in the map by chemotaxis movements (tumble and swim).
3. Bacteria in regions with noxious substances or low-nutrient regions will die and disperse, respectively.
4. Bacteria in high-nutrient regions will reproduce by splitting. They will also attempt to attract other bacteria by generating chemical attractors.
5. Bacteria then disperse to seek new nutrient regions in the map.

BFOA was designed to solve unconstrained optimization problems and the details of such version can be found in [23]. A BFOA's general algorithm is presented in Figure 1.

MBFOA, originally proposed in [13] and extended in [19, 20], is based on the original BFOA [23] but it is focused on solving CNOPs. A set of feasibility rules proposed by Deb [2] is adopted in MBFOA as the constraint-handling mechanism, employed as selection criteria when bacteria are compared: (1) between two feasible bacteria, the one with the best objective function value is chosen, (2) between one feasible bacterium and another infeasible one, the feasible is chosen, and (3) between two infeasible bacteria, the one with the lowest sum of constraint violation is chosen. MBFOA

```
Begin
   Create a random initial swarm of bacteria
   Evaluate each bacterium in the population
   For l=1 to N_ed Do
      For k=1 to N_re Do
         For j=1 to N_c Do
            For i=1 to S_b Do
               Update the fitness value of each bacterium
               by emulating the swarming process
               Perform the chemotaxis process
               (tumble-swim) for all bacteria
               controlled by the N_s parameter
            End For
         End For
         Perform the reproduction process by sorting
         all bacteria in the swarm based on fitness
         deleting the S_r worst bacteria and duplicating
         the remaining S_b - S_r
      End For
      Perform the elimination-dispersal process by
      eliminating each bacteria with probability 0 <= P_ed <= 1
   End For
End
```

Figure 1: BFOA pseudocode. Input parameters are number of bacteria S_b, chemotactic loop limit N_c, swim loop limit N_s, reproduction loop limit N_{re}, number of bacteria for reproduction S_r (usually $S_r = S_b/2$), elimination-dispersal loop limit N_{ed}, stepsizes C_i for the tumble-swim (they depend of the dimensionality of the problem) and probability of elimination dispersal p_{ed}.

inherits the four main processes used in BFOA: (1) chemotaxis, (2) swarming , (3) reproduction and (4) elimination-dispersal [13]. However, they were adapted with the aim to eliminate one loop and some parameters. In MBFOA a bacterium i represents a potential solution to the CNOP (i.e., a n-dimensional real-value vector identified as $\vec{x}$ in Section 1), and it is defined as $\theta^i(j,G)$, where j is its chemotaxis loop value and G is the current cycle of the algorithm. The processes are detailed as follows.

2.1 Chemotaxis

In this process, each bacterium in the current swarm performs a tumble-swim movement. The tumble, as proposed by Passino [23], consists of a search direction $\phi(i)$ generated at random as presented in Equation 2:

$$\phi(i) = \frac{\Delta(i)}{\sqrt{\Delta(i)^T \Delta(i)}} \tag{2}$$

where $\Delta_{(i)}$ is a randomly generated vector of size n with elements within $[-1, 1]$ and T is the transpose of $\Delta_{(i)}$.

The swim allows the bacterium $\theta^i(j,G)$ to follow the search direction and move to a new position $\theta^i(j+1,G)$. Two swims in the same direction are carried out per iteration of each bacterium in its chemotaxis loop. The first swim is computed as indicated in Equation 3:

$$\theta^i(j+1,G) = \theta^i(j,G) + C(i)\phi(i) \tag{3}$$

where $C(i)$ is the stepsize vector defined by the expression in Equation 4:

$$C(i)_k = R * (\frac{\Delta\vec{x}_k}{\sqrt{n}}), k = 1, ..., n \tag{4}$$

where $\Delta\vec{x}_k$ is a vector composed by the difference between upper and lower limit of each variable x_k: $U_k - L_k$, n is the number of variables and R is a user-defined parameter to scale the stepsize value. This vector remains fixed during the all search process.

A second swim starting with the same original position $\theta^i(j,G)$ in the same direction ϕ is computed as detailed in Equation 5:

$$\theta^i(j'+1,G) = \theta^i(j,G) + R\phi(i) \quad (5)$$

where the same R value used in the first swim to scale the stepsize is now adopted to directly scale the values of the search direction vector ϕ. Therefore, the first swim will get larger values (i.e. it will favor exploration) while the second swim will provide shorter values favoring exploitation.

If one of the two new positions, $\theta^i(j+1,G)$ and $\theta^i(j'+1,G)$ has a better fitness (based on the feasibility rules), with respect to the original position $\theta^i(j,G)$, another two swims in the same direction will be carried out by taking this best solution as the new starting position. Otherwise, a new tumble is computed. The process stops after N_c attempts (also defined by the user).

2.2 Swarming

MBFOA includes an attractor movement which let each bacterium in the swarm to follow the bacterium located in the most promising region of the search space. The movement is detailed in Equation 6:

$$\theta^i(j+1,G) = \theta^i(j,G) + \beta(\theta^B(G) - \theta^i(j,G)) \quad (6)$$

where $\theta^i(j+1,G)$ is the new position of bacterium i, $\theta^i(j,G)$ is the current position of bacterium i, $\theta^B(G)$ is the current position of the best bacterium in the swarm so far at cycle G, and β (user-defined parameter) defines the closeness of the new position of bacterium i with respect to the position of the best bacterium $\theta^B(G)$. The attractor movement is applied one time within the chemotaxis loop. In the remaining steps, the tumble-swim movement is used. Both, the tumble-swim and swarming movements can generate variable values outside their limits. Therefore, a simple repair mechanism is used [10], where the violated value is multiplied by 2 and the violated limit is subtracted (i.e. $x_{valid} = 2 * x_{invalid} - violated\_limit$).

2.3 Reproduction

The swarm is sorted based on the feasibility rules and the best S_r bacteria are cloned, and the worst bacteria are eliminated. This process must keep a fixed size of the swarm at each cycle. To reduce premature convergence due to bacteria cloning, the reproduction takes place at certain cycles of the search process (defined by the RepCycle parameter).

2.4 Elimination-dispersal

This process only eliminates the worst bacterium $\theta^w(j,G)$ based on the feasibility rules, and a new randomly generated bacterium is inserted as a replacement.

The corresponding pseudocode is presented in Figure 2 and in its caption the user-defined parameters are summarized.

```
Begin
  Create randomly an initial swarm of bacteria θ^i(j,0)
  ∀i, i = 1,...,S_b
  Evaluate θ^i(j,0) ∀i, i = 1,...,S_b
  Calculate R using any of the strategies
  For G=1 to GMAX Do
    For i=1 to S_b Do
      For j=1 to N_c Do
        Perform the chemotaxis process with Eq. 2, 4, 3, 5 and
        the attractor operator with Eq. 6 for bacteria θ^i(j,G) by
        considering the feasibility rules as selection criteria
      End For
    End For
  If (G mod RepCycle == 0)
  Perform the reproduction process by sorting all bacteria in
  the swarm based on the feasibility rules and deleting
  the S_r worst bacteria and duplicating the remaining S_b − S_r
  End If
  Perform the elimination-dispersal process by eliminating
  the worst bacterium θ^w(j,G) in the current swarm by
  considering the feasibility rules
  End For
End
```

Figure 2: MBFOA pseudocode. Input parameters are number of bacteria S_b, chemotaxis loop limit N_c, number of bacteria for reproduction S_r, scaling factor β, the reproduction cycle RepCycle, the number of cycles $GMAX$, the tolerance of constraint violation ξ and its decreasing rate dec

3. STEPSIZE CONTROL MECHANISMS

Four control mechanisms for the R parameter, directly related with the stepsize used in the chemotaxis loop, are tested in this section. They are the following:

1. **Static stepsize** : A random value $\in (0, 0.01]$ fixed during the search.

2. **Random stepsize** : A random value $\in (0, 1)$ generated at each cycle of the algorithm.

3. **Dynamic stepsize** : A nonlinear decreasing function [25] is used to also decrease the R value at each cycle as in Equation 7:

$$R(G+1) = (G/GMAX)^4 \quad (7)$$

where $GMAX$ is the maximum number of cycles of the algorithm.

4. **Adaptive stepsize** : Inspired by the adaptive mechanism used in Evolution Strategies (ES) [15], an adaptive mechanism proposed in [19] is revisited. According to the number of successful swims of each bacterium in the chemotaxis process, the R value is updated. A successful swim is counted when a bacterium improves its solution after a tumble-two-swim movement. The value is updated with Equation 8:

$$R(G+1) = \begin{cases} R(G) * SSA & if \quad SR < 0.015 \\ R(G)\frac{1}{SSA} & otherwise \end{cases} \quad (8)$$

where $SSA = 0.7$ is an user-defined parameter to control the change of the stepsize value and SR is the average number of successful swims of all swims made by all the bacteria in the current cycle. The initial value of R is generated at random $\in (0, 1]$. Unlike the adaptive rule in ES, where the 20% success rate is sought, in this case a smaller rate was more suitable (1.5%). This issue requires more research and it is considered in the future work.

In the third step of the algorithm in Figure 2 the R value is updated based on one, out of four, stepsize control mechanisms.

4. RESULTS AND DISCUSSION

Four MBFOA variants were generated, each one with one stepsize control mechanism. They are identified as follows: the MBFOA variant with the static stepsize is called Alternative MBFOA with Static stepsize (sMBFOA), the MBFOA variant with random stepsize values per generation is called Alternative MBFOA with Random stepsize (rMBFOA). In the same way, the variant with Dynamic stepsize is called dMBFOA and the Adaptive variant is called aMBFOA.

Each variant was used to solve 24 well-known CNOPs found in [11]. Due to space restrictions the complete details of the test problems are not included. However, their main characteristic are presented in Table 1.

Table 1: summary of the 24 test problems. n is the number of variables, ρ is the estimated ratio between the feasible region and the search space, *li* is the number of linear inequality constraints, *ni* is the number of nonlinear inequality constraints, *le* is the number of linear equality constraints, *ne* is the number of nonlinear equality constraints, a is the number of active constraints and $f(\vec{x}^*)$ is the best known feasible solution

function	n	type of function	ρ	li	ni	le	ne	a	$f(\vec{x}^*)$
g01	13	quadratic	0.0111%	9	0	0	0	6	-15
g02	20	nonlinear	99.9971%	0	2	0	0	1	-0.803619104
g03	10	polynomial	0.0000%	0	0	0	1	1	-1.0005001
g04	5	quadratic	52.1230%	0	6	0	0	2	-30665.53867
g05	4	cubic	0.0000%	2	0	0	3	3	5126.496714
g06	2	cubic	0.0066%	0	2	0	0	2	-6961.813876
g07	10	quadratic	0.0003%	3	5	0	0	6	24.30620907
g08	2	nonlinear	0.8560%	0	2	0	0	0	-0.095825041
g09	7	polynomial	0.5121%	0	4	0	0	2	680.6300574
g10	8	linear	0.0010%	3	3	0	0	6	7049.248021
g11	2	quadratic	0.0000%	0	0	0	1	1	0.7499
g12	3	quadratic	4.7713%	0	1	0	0	0	-1
g13	5	nonlinear	0.0000%	0	0	0	3	3	0.053941514
g14	10	nonlinear	0.0000%	0	0	3	0	3	-47.76488846
g15	3	quadratic	0.0000%	0	0	1	1	2	961.7150223
g16	5	nonlinear	0.0204%	4	34	0	0	4	-1.905155259
g17	6	nonlinear	0.0000%	0	0	0	4	4	8853.539675
g18	9	quadratic	0.0000%	0	13	0	0	6	-0.866025404
g19	15	nonlinear	33.4761%	0	5	0	0	0	32.65559295
g20	24	linear	0.0000%	0	6	2	12	16	0.2049794
g21	7	linear	0.0000%	0	1	0	5	6	193.7245101
g22	22	linear	0.0000%	0	1	8	11	19	236.4309755
g23	9	linear	0.0000%	0	2	3	1	6	-400.0551
g24	2	linear	79.6556%	0	2	0	0	2	-5.508013272

The maximum number of evaluations (max_fes) allowed for each test problem was 240,000. The final tolerance for equality constraints was $\xi = 1E-4$.

The following measures [11] were computed in the comparison. The first four were taken from [11], while the last two are proposed for this comparison:

- **Feasible run**: a run where at least one feasible solution is found within max_fes.
- **Successful run**: a run where a feasible solution $\vec{x}$ satisfying $f(\vec{x}) - f(\vec{x}^*) \leq 0.0001$ is found within max_fes.
- **Feasible rate** = (number of feasible runs) / total runs.
- **Success rate** = (number of successful runs) / total runs.
- **Successful swim**: A swim/attractor movement where the new position is better (based on the feasibility rules) with respect to the original position.
- **Successful swim rate** = (number of successful swims) / total swims, where total swims $=s_b \times 2 \times n_c \times GMAX$.

The values of the input parameters used by MBFOA are shown in Table 2. Such values are common to the four MBFOA variants and they were fine-tuned by the iRace tool [12]. The only fixed parameter was $GMAX$ related with the termination condition of 240,000 evaluations.

Table 2: MBFOA variants common parameter values obtained by the iRace tool [12]

Parameter	Value
s_b	20
n_c	20
s_r	1
β	1.5
$RepCycle$	100
$gmax$	value to reach 240,000 evaluations
ξ	1.2
dec	1.08

Seven experiments were carried out to analyze the behavior of the four stepsize control mechanisms in MBFOA. The first experiment focus on the final results obtained by each variant in the complete benchmark. The second experiment is designed to observe the ability of each variant to reach the feasible region of the search space. The third experiment measures the capacity of the variants to find the neighborhood of the feasible global optimum. The fourth experiment aims to evaluate the ability of each stepsize control mechanism to favor successful swims. The fifth experiment evaluates the capacity of each variant to decrease the constraint violation over time. The sixth experiment considers the adaptive behavior of aMBFOA. Finally, the seventh experiment compares the final results of the most competitive MBFOA variant against those of two state-of-the-art algorithms to solve CNOPs.

4.1 Experiment 1

Table 3 presents, for each test problem, the best, average, and standard deviation values obtained from 25 independent runs by each MBFOA variant. No MBFOA variant was able to find feasible solutions in three test problems g20, g21 and g22. Furthermore, aMBFOA was unable to find feasible solutions also in problems g13, g14, g15 and g17. The four variants consistently found the feasible global optimum in test problem g11.

From the results in Table 3 dMBFOA provided better results in ten test problems g01, g02, g04, g06, g07, g08, g09, g12, g18, and g19. On the other hand, rMBFOA was clearly better in test problems g15 and g23 and sMBFOA outperformed the other variants in test problem g05. aMBFOA was competitive, but not clearly better, in test problems g10 and g16. In test problem g03 both, rMBFOA and sMBFOA found the best results. In problem g13, rMBFOA found the best result but dMBFOA was more robust (better mean and standard deviation values). In problem g14 the most robust variant was rMBFOA but the best result was found by sMBFOA. In problem g17 the most robust variant was sMBFOA but the best result was found by dMBFOA. Finally, in test problem g24 aMBFOA was slightly better with respect to dMBFOA.

The 95%-confidence Wilcoxon signed-rank test was applied to the results in Table 3. The summary of the statistical tests is presented in the lower part of Table 3. It is then

Table 3: Results obtained by the four MBFOA variants and a comparison of results against those obtained by Memetic-SAMSDE and IPSO. The 95%-confidence Wilcoxon signed-rank test results are presented below. In boldface the best results are remarked. '-' indicates that no feasible solutions were found. '+' means that the results of the first algorithm are significantly better than those of the second one. '/' means that the results of the first algorithm are significantly worse than those of the second one, and '=' means that there is no significant difference between the results of the two algorithms.

$f(x^*)$	Stat	rMBFOA	sMBFOA	dMBFOA	aMBFOA	Memetic-SAMSDE	IPSO
	Runs	25	25	25	25	25	30
	FEs	239,267	239,200	239,200	239,200	240,000	160,000
g01	Best	-12.71	-11.42	**-14.99**	-14.95	**-15**	**-15**
-15	Average	-9.0557	-7.6267	**-14.9133**	-14.8271	**-15**	**-15**
	Std.	2.12E+00	2.20E+00	9.01E-02	**8.30E-02**	0	0.00E+00
g02	Best	-0.7052681	-0.3795004	**-0.8035107**	-0.7346371	**-0.8036191**	-0.802629
-0.8036191	Average	-0.5508	-0.3102	**-0.7093**	-0.68311	**-0.8036191**	-0.713879
	Std.	5.87E-02	3.70E-02	5.19E-02	**2.51E-02**	0	4.62E-02
g03	Best	-1.00047	**-1.00048**	-0.99143	-0.9992	**-1.005**	-0.641
-1.0005	Average	**-1.0004**	-1.0003	-0.82	-0.7927	**-1.005**	-0.154
	Std.	**0**	2.00E-04	1.28E-01	1.68E-01	0	1.70E-01
g04	Best	-30662.345	-30593.6367	**-30665.5387**	-30655.99671	**-30665.539**	**-30665.539**
-30665.5387	Average	-30378.8117	-30196.618	**-30665.5384**	-30628.05037	**-30665.539**	**-30665.539**
	Std.	2.91E+02	2.53E+02	**4.00E-04**	1.39E+01	0	7.40E-12
g05	Best	5137.3697	**5128.6938**	5134.8775	-	**5126.497**	5126.502
5126.4967	Average	5137.3697	**5128.6938**	5557.7082	-	**5126.497**	5135.521
	Std.	**0**	**0**	3.48E+02	-	0	1.23E+01
g06	Best	-6961.8124	-6961.79248	**-6961.81387**	-6961.03051	**-6961.813875**	**-6961.814**
-6961.81388	Average	-6961.7912	-6961.7142	**-6961.8139**	-6955.090598	**-6961.813875**	**-6961.814**
	Std.	1.09E-02	6.84E-02	**1.45E-05**	3.71E+00	0	2.81E-05
g07	Best	32.2645	144.2565	**24.3960**	25.0482	**24.3062**	24.366
24.3062	Average	561.6848	1277.4473	**24.7146**	42.2303	**24.3062**	24.691
	Std.	6.75E+02	1.03E+03	**2.47E-01**	1.28E+01	0	2.20E-01
g08	Best	**-0.095825**	**-0.095825**	**-0.095825**	**-0.09581**	**-0.095825**	**-0.095825**
-0.095825	Average	-0.0958	-0.0888	**-0.0958**	-0.0957	**-0.095825**	**-0.095825**
	Std.	3.22E-10	1.01E-02	**9.40E-18**	1.00E-04	0	4.23E-17
g09	Best	682.97	746.56	**680.68**	**680.68**	**680.63**	680.638
680.63	Average	1851.3353	6994.1909	**680.6821**	692.2547	**680.63**	680.674
	Std.	5.13E+03	2.78E+04	**3.39E-02**	5.88E+00	0	3.00E-02
g10	Best	9164.86299	10465.11966	**8002.0291**	7322.630605	**7049.24802**	7053.963
7049.24802	Average	13304.969	14664.8471	10557.9725	**9169.400**	**7049.24802**	7306.466
	Std.	3.21E+03	3.24E+03	1.44E+03	**1.13E+03**	0	2.22E+02
g11	Best	**0.7499**	**0.7499**	**0.7499**	**0.7499**	**0.7499**	**0.7499**
0.7499	Average	**0.7499**	**0.7499**	**0.7499**	**0.7499**	**0.7499**	0.753
	Std.	1.47E-07	9.38E-05	**7.65E-07**	1.00E-04	0	6.53E-03
g12	Best	**-1**	-0.9998	**-1**	**-0.9999**	**-1**	**-1**
-1	Average	-0.9966	-0.993	**-1**	-0.9999	**-1**	**-1**
	Std.	3.10E-03	6.70E-03	**0**	1.48E-06	0	0.00E+00
g13	Best	**0.055784**	0.086864	0.081754	-	**0.053942**	0.066845
0.053941	Average	0.4269	1.7568	**0.408**	-	**0.053942**	0.430408
	Std.	2.81E-01	2.77E+00	**1.61E-01**	-	0	2.30E+00
g14	Best	-47.21327	**-47.5851**	-46.327887	-	**-47.764888**	-47.449
-47.764888	Average	**-45.584**	-45.1138	-44.0341	-	**-47.764888**	-44.572
	Std.	**9.57E-01**	1.63E+00	1.43E+00	-	0	1.58E+00
g15	Best	**961.71504**	961.71509	961.71506	-	**961.71502**	961.715
961.71502	Average	**961.9617**	964.0536	961.8524	-	**961.71502**	962.242
	Std.	6.19E-01	2.68E+00	**4.09E-01**	-	0	6.20E-01
g16	Best	-1.901861	-1.882024	**-1.904699**	-1.895311	**-1.905155**	**-1.905**
-1.905155	Average	-1.7469	-1.6121	-1.8064	**-1.8647**	**-1.905155**	**-1.905**
	Std.	1.16E-01	1.82E-01	7.14E-02	**1.79E-02**	0	2.42E-12
g17	Best	8871.66724	8971.787	**8864.4728**	-	**8853.5397**	8863.293
8853.53967	Average	9032.6511	**8973.1112**	9036.7973	-	**8823.5397**	8911.738
	Std.	1.41E-02	**1.87E+00**	1.21E+02	-	0	2.73E+01
g18	Best	-0.865638	-0.759252	**-0.866025**	-0.856673	**-0.866025**	-0.865994
-0.866025	Average	-0.6921	-0.4403	**-0.8656**	-0.5239	**-0.866025**	-0.862842
	Std.	1.58E-01	1.45E-01	**7.00E-04**	1.88E-01	0	4.41E-03
g19	Best	50.87558	73.783047	**36.585541**	44.672686	32.655593	33.967
32.655592	Average	79.2473	223.2578	**46.631**	56.8306	32.655593	37.927
	Std.	2.90E+01	1.07E+02	**6.30E+00**	9.44E+00	0	3.20E+00
g20	Best	-	-	-	-	-	-
0.204979	Average	-	-	-	-	-	-
	Std.	-	-	-	-	-	-
g21	Best	-	-	-	-	**193.72451**	193.758
193.72451	Average	-	-	-	-	**193.72451**	217.356
	Std.	-	-	-	-	0	2.65E+01
g22	Best	-	-	-	-	**236.370313**	-
236.430975	Average	-	-	-	-	**245.738829**	-
	Std.	-	-	-	-	**9.05939**	-
g23	Best	**-214.508**	-44.9945	-69.3804	-0.0471	**-400.0551**	-250.707
-400.0551	Average	**-9.4519**	1.3133	4.6749	-0.0282	**-400.0551**	-99.598
	Std.	9.80E+01	2.28E+01	6.06E+01	**1.18E-02**	0	1.20E+02
g24	Best	-5.508011	-5.507963	**-5.508013**	**-5.508013**	**-5.508013**	**-5.508**
-5.508013	Average	-5.4609	-4.9452	**-5.508**	**-5.508**	**-5.508013**	**-5.508**
	Std.	1.60E-01	4.16E-01	3.10E-11	**9.06E-16**	0	9.03E-16

Algorithms	Criterion	p-value	Decision
rMBFOA-sMBFOA	Best fitness	3.74E-03	+
rMBFOA-dMBFOA	Best fitness	5.23E-02	/
rMBFOA-aMBFOA	Best fitness	2.34E-01	=
sMBFOA-dMBFOA	Best fitness	6.14E-03	/
sMBFOA-aMBFOA	Best fitness	1.39E-02	/
dMBFOA-aMBFOA	Best fitness	7.11E-01	=
dMBFOA-Memetic-SAMSDE	Best fitness	1.77E-02	/
dMBFOA-IPSO	Best fitness	2.71E-02	+

confirmed that dMBFOA was the most competitive MBFOA variant based in the final results (dMBFOA was better than sMBFOA and rMBFOA, and despite being considered as equal based on the statistical test, dMBFOA solved more test problems than aMBFOA).

4.2 Experiment 2

In Table 4 the feasible rates obtained by each MBFOA variant are presented. Aside from problem g23, dMBFOA obtained the best feasible rates among the four variants, followed by rMBFOA, sMBFOA and aMBFOA as the worst of them.

Table 4: Feasible rate obtained by each MBFOA variant

function	rMBFOA	sMBFOA	dMBFOA	aMBFOA
g01	100	100	100	100
g02	100	100	100	100
g03	100	100	100	100
g04	100	100	100	100
g05	4	4	80	-
g06	100	100	100	100
g07	100	100	100	100
g08	100	100	100	100
g09	100	100	100	100
g10	100	96	100	100
g11	100	100	100	100
g12	100	100	100	100
g13	100	76	100	-
g14	100	100	100	-
g15	100	100	100	-
g16	100	100	100	100
g17	20	8	68	-
g18	96	88	100	100
g19	100	100	100	100
g20	-	-	-	-
g21	-	-	-	-
g22	-	-	-	-
g23	80	64	32	36
g24	100	100	100	100

4.3 Experiment 3

Table 5 includes the success rate obtained by each variant. Even they are capable of reaching a good approximation of the feasible optimum solution (based on the results in Table 3), it is clear that such solutions do not satisfy the tolerance used in this experiment. The most competitive variant regarding success rate was dMBFOA.

Table 5: Success rate obtained by each MBFOA variant

function	rMBFOA	sMBFOA	dMBFOA	aMBFOA
g01	-	-	-	-
g02	-	-	-	-
g03	92	40	-	-
g04	-	-	60	-
g05	-	-	-	-
g06	-	-	100	-
g07	-	-	-	-
g08	100	56	100	48
g09	-	-	-	-
g10	-	-	-	-
g11	100	92	100	36
g12	28	-	100	100
g13	-	-	-	-
g14	-	-	-	-
g15	12	4	8	-
g16	-	-	-	-
g17	-	-	-	-
g18	-	-	44	-
g19	-	-	-	-
g20	-	-	-	-
g21	-	-	-	-
g22	-	-	-	-
g23	-	-	-	-
g24	88	8	100	100

4.4 Experiment 4

To further analyze the effect of the four stepsize control mechanisms, the number of successful swims and the successful swim rates were computed in two representative test problems: $g03$ and $g20$. Both problems have a tiny feasible region. However, the four variants obtained a 100% feasible rate in the first one and 0% in the last one.

The successful swims by cycle of the run located in the median value of the 25 independent runs reported in Table 3 are plotted in Figure 3 for test problem g03 and in Figure 4 for test problem g20.

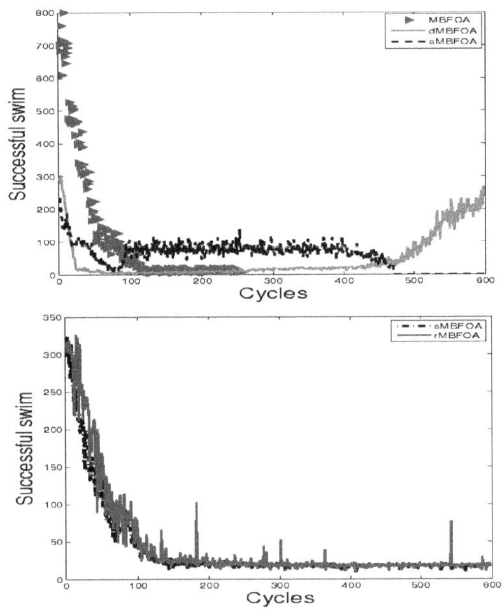

Figure 3: Successful swims per cycle of the four MBFOA variants in problem g03. The results of the original MBFOA are included as a reference [18]

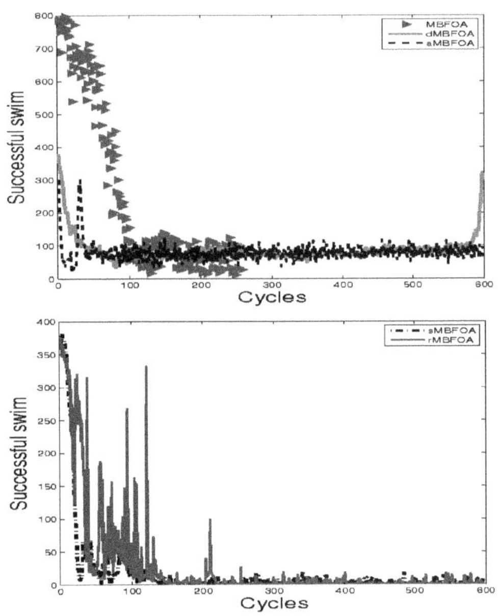

Figure 4: Successful swims per cycle of the four MBFOA variants in problem g20. The results of the original MBFOA are included as a reference [18]

The successful swim rates in problem g03 for rMBFOA, sMBFOA, dMBFOA and aMBFOA were 11.24%, 9.68%, 11.40% and 14.59%, respectively. Regarding g20, the values were 6.91%, 4.42%, 21.67% and 19.70% for rMBFOA, sMBFOA, dMBFOA and aMBFOA, respectively.

It is important to remark, from Figures 3 and 4, the ability of dMBFOA of generating successful swims late in the search process for both test problems. This behavior let this MBFOA variant to find better solutions with respect to the other variants (as reported in Table 3) which had a behavior of several successful swims at the beginning and very few at the end.

4.5 Experiment 5

To analyze the effect of the stepsize control mechanisms in the way the feasible region is reached, the average constraint violation per cycle was measured in the run located in the median value of the 25 independent runs in the four MBFOA variants for test problem g20 (where all variants were incapable of generating feasible solutions). The original MBFOA is included as a reference [18]. Figure 5 shows this information. The plot suggests that all four stepsize control mechanisms are able to improve, in a similar way, the approaching to the feasible region of the search space with respect to the original MBFOA. This behavior may lead to consider special operators [27] or local search [4] to favor the generation of feasible solutions.

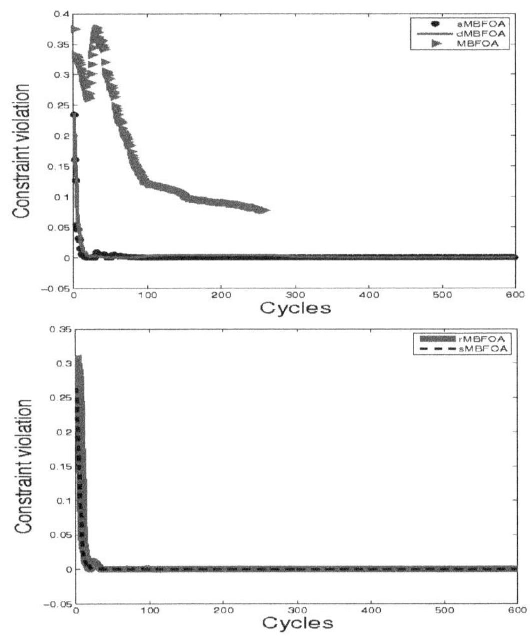

Figure 5: Constraint violation per cycle by each MBFOA variant in test problem g20

4.6 Experiment 6

For test problems g03 and g20 the behavior of the only adaptive control mechanism (aMBFOA) is depicted in Figure 6, where the stepsize values per cycle in the run located in the median value of 25 independent runs are plotted. For test problem g03, where the performance of this variant was good, just one stepsize value increase before cycle 100 was detected. After that, very small stepsize values are reported.

On the other hand, for test problem g20, where the feasible region was almost reached, larger stepsize values are reported at the beginning and a small increment is seen before cycle 50. After that, small stepsize values are reported. The aforementioned behavior, coupled with the poor behavior shown in the results in Table 3, suggest the inability of such adaptive stepsize control mechanism to avoid premature convergence.

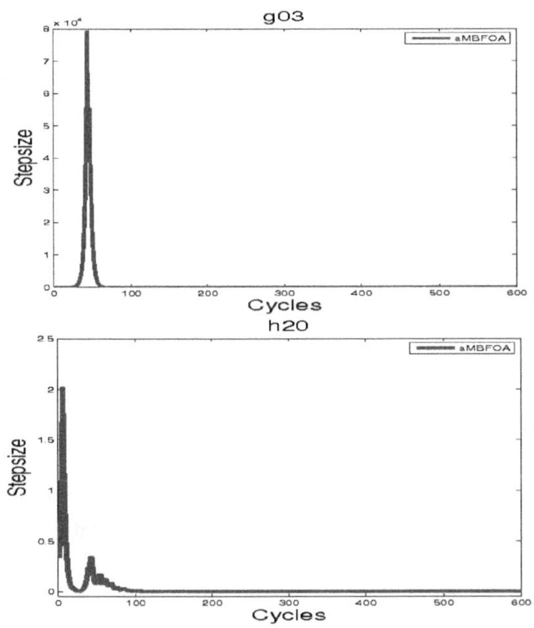

Figure 6: aMBFOA behavior in test problems g03 and g20

4.7 Experiment 7

Finally, in Table 3 a comparison of the final results of dMBFOA and two state-of-the-art algorithms for solving CNOPs: Memetic-SAMSDE [5] and Improved Particle Swarm Optimization (IPSO) [17], are presented. The first one is an approach where several Differential Evolution variants are combined with a local search algorithm in a framework to solve CNOPs, while the second one is an improved PSO version based on local-best leader selection and constriction factor velocity update. Regarding the first algorithm, dMBFOA was competitive in eight test problems: g04, 06, g08, g11, g12, g15, g18 and g24. However, SAMSDE had better overall results. Regarding IPSO, dMBFOA was competitive in twelve test problems: g02, g03, g04, g06, g07, g08, g09, g11, g12, g15, g18, and g24. The results of the 95%-confidence Wilcoxon signed-rank test applied to such comparisons showed that dMBFOA provided a better performance with respect to IPSO, but was outperformed by Memetic-SAMSDE.

5. CONCLUSIONS

This paper presented a study of four stepsize control mechanisms added to the modified bacterial foraging algorithm to solve constrained numerical optimization problems. The first mechanism was based on a random value generated at the beginning of the search, which is kept unchanged until the end of the process. The second mechanism generated a random stepsize value at each cycle of the algorithm. The third mechanism was based on a nonlinear decreasing function and the last mechanism was based on the number of successful swims performed by bacteria in the current swarm. Seven experiments were designed and six performance measures were adopted to solve a well-known benchmark found in the specialized literature to analyze the final results of each variant and their ability to reach the feasible region and the feasible global optimum as well. The number of successful swims and the capacity to decrease the constraint violation promoted by each variant were also analyzed. Finally, the behavior of the adaptive control mechanism was observed and also the most competitive variant (the dynamic approach based on the nonlinear decreasing function) was compared against two state-of-the-art algorithms for CNOPs.

The results obtained in the experiments showed that, besides providing the best final results in the benchmark adopted, the dynamic stepsize control mechanism (dMBFOA) was the most competitive to find the feasible region of the search space and also to locate the vicinity of the feasible global optimum. An encouraging finding was the fact that dMBFOA was able to promote successful swims late in the search process. Another promising conclusion was the fact that all four stepsize control mechanisms were able to decrease the constraint violation in a better way with respect to the original MBFOA. Regarding the adaptive control mechanism (aMBFOA), even it provided an expected behavior, the results were not as good as expected and it was outperformed by dMBFOA. Finally, dMBFOA was able to outperform IPSO (but requiring more evaluations), and provided good results, but not good enough, with respect to Memetic-SAMSDE. However, this last algorithm requires a significant effort to implement it with respect to dMBFOA.

The findings of this work set a good base towards the design of a highly competitive MBFOA to solve CNOPs. The future research includes the improvement of the ability to find the feasible region in those problems where the algorithm almost generated feasible solutions. Moreover, aMBFOA will be revised to improve its capability by changing the criteria to modify the stepsize values. Finally, dMBFOA will be used as the base algorithm to test special operators [27] and local search operators [4].

6. ACKNOWLEDGMENTS

The first author acknowledges support from UJAT and the Mexican Consejo Nacional de Ciencia y Tecnología (CONACyT) through a scholarship to pursue PHD studies at Universidad Juárez Autónoma de Tabasco, MEXICO.

7. REFERENCES

[1] C. A. Coello Coello. Theoretical and Numerical Constraint Handling Techniques used with Evolutionary Algorithms: A Survey of the State of the Art. *Computer Methods in Applied Mechanics and Engineering*, 191(11-12):1245–1287, January 2002.

[2] K. Deb. An Efficient Constraint Handling Method for Genetic Algorithms. *Computer Methods in Applied Mechanics and Engineering*, 186(2/4):311–338, 2000.

[3] A. Eiben and J. E. Smith, editors. *Introduction to Evolutionary Computing*. Natural Computing Series. Springer-Verlag, 2003.

[4] S. Elsayed, R. Sarker, and D. Essam. Integrated strategies differential evolution algorithm with a local search for constrained optimization. In *2011 IEEE Congress on Evolutionary Computation (CEC'2011)*, pages 2618–2625, New Orleans, USA, July 2011. IEEE Press.

[5] S. M. Elsayed, R. A. Sarker, and D. L. Essam. On an evolutionary approach for constrained optimization problem solving. *Applied Soft Computing*, 12(10):3208 – 3227, 2012.

[6] A. P. Engelbrecht. *Fundamentals of Computational Swarm Intelligence*. John Wiley & Sons, 2005.

[7] H.-C. Huang, Y.-H. Chen, and A. Abraham. Optimized watermarking using swarm-based bacterial foraging. *Information Hiding and Multimedia Signal Processing*, 1(1):51–58, 2010.

[8] D. Karaboga and B. Basturk. Powerful and efficient algorithm for numerical function optimization: Artificial bee colony (abc) algorithm. *Journal of Global Optimization*, 39(3):459–471, 2007.

[9] J. Kennedy and R. C. Eberhart. *Swarm Intelligence*. Morgan Kaufmann, UK, 2001.

[10] S. Kukkonen and J. Lampinen. Constrained Real-Parameter Optimization with Generalized Differential Evolution. In *2006 IEEE Congress on Evolutionary Computation (CEC'2006)*, pages 911–918, Vancouver, BC, Canada, July 2006. IEEE.

[11] J. Liang, T. P. Runarsson, E. Mezura-Montes, M. Clerc, P. Suganthan, C. A. Coello Coello, and K. Deb. Problem definitions and evaluation criteria for the cec 2006 special session on constrained real-parameter optimization. Technical report, School of EEE Nanyang Technological University, Singapore, September 2006.

[12] M. López-Ibáñez, J. Dubois-Lacoste, T. Stützle, and M. Birattari. The irace package, iterated race for automatic algorithm configuration. Technical Report TR/IRIDIA/2011-004, IRIDIA, Université Libre de Bruxelles, Belgium, 2011.

[13] E. Mezura-Montes, editor. *Constraint-Handling in Evolutionary Optimization*, volume 198 of *Studies in Computational Intelligence*. Springer-Verlag, 2009.

[14] E. Mezura-Montes and O. Cetina-Domínguez. Empirical analysis of a modified artificial bee colony for constrained numerical optimization. *Applied Mathematics and Computation*, 218(18):10943 – 10973, 2012.

[15] E. Mezura-Montes and C. A. Coello Coello. A Simple Multimembered Evolution Strategy to Solve Constrained Optimization Problems. *IEEE Transactions on Evolutionary Computation*, 9(1):1–17, February 2005.

[16] E. Mezura-Montes and C. A. Coello Coello. Constraint-handling in nature-inspired numerical optimization: Past, present and future. *Swarm and Evolutionary Computation*, 1(4):173–194, 2011.

[17] E. Mezura-Montes and J. I. Flores-Mendoza. Improved particle swarm optimization in constrained numerical search spaces. In R. Chiong, editor, *Nature-Inspired Algorithms for Optimization*, volume 193, pages 299–332. Springer-Verlag, Studies in Computational Intelligence Series, 2009, ISBN: 978-3-540-72963-1., 2009.

[18] E. Mezura-Montes and B. Hernández-Ocaña. Modified bacterial foraging optimization for engineering design. In C. H. Dagli and et al., editors, *Proceedings of the Artificial Neural Networks in Enginnering Conference (ANNIE'2009)*, volume 19 of *Intelligent Engineering Systems Through Artificial Neural Networks*, pages 357–364, St. Louis, MO, USA, November 2009. ASME Press.

[19] E. Mezura-Montes and E. A. López-Dávila. Adaptation and local search in the modified bacterial foraging algorithm for constrained optimization. In *Proccedings of the IEEE Congress on Evolutionary Computation 2012*, pages 497–504. ISBN:978-1-4673-1508-1, 2012.

[20] E. Mezura-Montes, E. A. Portilla-Flores, and B. Hernández-Ocaña. Optimum synthesis of a four-bar mechanism using the modified bacterial foraging algorithm. *International Journal of Systems Science*, 45(5):1080–1100, 2014.

[21] B. Niu, Y. Fan, H. Xiao, and B. Xue. Bacterial foraging based approaches to portfolio optimization with liquidity risk. *Neurocomputing*, 98(0):90 – 100, 2012.

[22] N. Pandit, A. Tripathi, S. Tapaswi, and M. Pandit. An improved bacterial foraging algorithm for combined static/dynamic enviromental economic dispatch. *Applied Soft Computing*, 0(12):3500–3513, 2012.

[23] K. M. Passino. Biomimicry of bacterial foraging for distributed optimization and control. *IEEE Control Systems Magazine*, 22(3):52–67, 2002.

[24] P. Praveena, K. Vaisakh, and S. R. M. Rao. A bacterial foraging and pso-de algorithm for solving dynamic economic dispatch problem with valve-point effects. In *First International Conference on Integrated Intelligent Computing*, pages 227–232. IEEE, 2010.

[25] M. M. Reyes Sierra. *Use of Coevolution and Fitness Inheritance for Multi-Objective Particle Swarm Optimization*. PhD thesis, Centro de Investigación y de Estudios Avanzados del Instituto Politécnico Nacional, Ciudad de México, México, Agosto 2006.

[26] A. Y. Saber. Economic dispatch using particle swarm optimization with bacterial foraging effect. *Electrical Power and Energy Systems*, 0(34):38–46, 2012.

[27] S. Salcedo-Sanz. A survey of repair methods used as constraint handling techniques in evolutionary algorithms. *Computer Science Review*, 3(4):175–192, 2009.

[28] P. Siarry and Z. Michalewicz, editors. *Advances in Metaheuristic Methods for Hard Optimization*. Springer, Berlin, 2008. ISBN 978-3-540-72959-4.

[29] K. Vaisakh, P. Praveena, S. R. M. Rao, and K. Meah. Solving dynamic economic dispatch problem with security constraints using bacterial foraging pso-de algorithm. *Electrical Power and Energy Systems*, 0(39):56–67, 2012.

[30] Y. Zhang, L. Wu, and S. Wang. Bacterial foraging optimization based neural network for short-term load forecasting. *Computational Information Systems*, 6(7):2099–2105, 2010.

A Tribal Ecosystem Inspired Algorithm (TEA) For Global Optimization

Ying Lin [a], Jing-Jing Li [b] (Corresponding Author), Jun Zhang [c] and Meng Wan [d]

[a] Department of Psychology, Sun Yat-sen University

[b] School of Computer Science, South China Normal University

[c] School of Advanced Computing, Sun Yat-sen University

[d] Center for Science and Technology Development, Ministry of Education

jingjing.li1124@gmail.com

ABSTRACT

Evolution mechanisms of different biological and social systems have inspired a variety of evolutionary computation (EC) algorithms. However, most existing EC algorithms simulate the evolution procedure at the individual-level. This paper proposes a new EC mechanism inspired by the evolution procedure at the tribe-level, namely tribal ecosystem inspired algorithm (TEA). In TEA, the basic evolution unit is not an individual that represents a solution point, but a tribe that covers a subarea in the search space. More specifically, a tribe represents the solution set locating in a particular subarea with a coding structure composed of three elements: *tribal chief*, *attribute diversity*, and *advancing history*. The tribal chief represents the locally best-so-far solution, the attribute diversity measures the range of the subarea, and the advancing history records the local search experience. This way, the new evolution unit provides extra knowledge about neighborhood profiles and search history. Using this knowledge, TEA introduces four evolution operators, *reforms*, *self-advance*, *synergistic combination*, and *augmentation*, to simulate the evolution mechanisms in a tribal ecosystem, which evolves the tribes from potentially promising subareas to the global optimum. The proposed TEA is validated on benchmark functions. Comparisons with three representative EC algorithms confirm its promising performance.

Categories and Subject Descriptors

I.2.8 [**Artificial Intelligence**]: Problem Solving, Control Methods, and Search – *heuristic methods*.

General Terms

Algorithms, Experimentation

Keywords

Evolutionary computation (EC), global optimization, tribe

1. INTRODUCTION

Evolutionary computation (EC) is a kind of probabilistic optimization algorithms inspired by the evolution mechanisms of complex systems in nature. Given an optimization problem, an EC algorithm is initialized with a population in which each individual represents a candidate solution. The fitness of individuals is evaluated in a way that the quality of represented solutions can be reflected proportionally. Evolution operators are designed to implement the principles of inheritance, variation, and selection in natural evolution. The EC algorithm performs the evolution operators for evolving the population towards the global optimum in an iterative manner.

The above evolution steps allow EC algorithms to solve an optimization problem without requiring any problem-specific knowledge other than a quantitative criterion for evaluating the quality of solutions. Such flexibility and simplicity encourage the applications of EC algorithms in a wide range of fields. However, despite the success of EC algorithms on solving many problems, they still suffer from the weakness of lengthy computational time and potentially premature convergence. Therefore, how to design algorithms that can find the global optimum in short time remains to be one of the most promising yet challenging research topics in the field of EC.

In the literature, the most notable and promising methods for addressing the above topic include adapting parameters to strike a dynamic balance between global exploration and local exploitation [1]-[3], designing novel evolution operators to achieve better search efficiency [4][5], applying niching methods to preserve the diversity of the population [6][7], hybridizing with local search techniques [8][9], and using multi-population strategies [10][11], etc. The underlying strategies of the above methods for improving the optimization accuracy and efficiency are based on introducing sophisticated operations or refinement in the entire optimization process. However, their algorithms remain *solution-based*. That is, the basic evolution unit in these EC algorithms is solutions - discrete points in the search space. Nevertheless, a solution can only provide the position and quality information of itself, but cannot provide information about the surrounding area (neighborhood). The lack of neighborhood information is the essential cause of bind and repetitive search, slowing down the search speed or even causing prematurity.

A tribe is a social group of people that unite under one chief and share similarities in physical and cultural attributes. In a tribal ecosystem comprising heterogeneous tribes, a tribe seeks development from both inner- and inter-tribe cooperation [12]. Inspired by the evolution mechanisms in tribal ecosystems, this paper proposes a new EC mechanism, namely tribal ecosystem inspired algorithm (TEA). In TEA, each tribe is mapped to the solution set in a particular subarea in the search space. Specifically, the best solution found in the subarea is analogous to the tribal chief and the range of the subarea is interpreted as the diversity of the tribe in attributes. The search experience of

GECCO'14, July 12–16, 2014, Vancouver, BC, Canada.

http://dx.doi.org/10.1145/2576768.2598253

exploiting the subarea is also attached to the tribe as a record of its self-advancing history. By doing so, TEA is differentiated from traditional solution-based EC algorithms as the basic evolution unit has been changed from discrete solution points to solution sets in different subareas in the search space.

Given an optimization problem, TEA initially partitions the search space into a set of zones with uniform size and initializes the tribal society by founding tribes on a subset of evenly distributed zones. After initialization, TEA performs four novel operators iteratively to simulate the evolution procedure of real tribes. In each generation, a *reforms* operator is first performed to reorganize the structure of the tribal society based on the similarities of existing tribes. An existing tribe may split into new tribes, merge into another tribe, or remain unchanged. Then a *self-advance* operator is carried out to simulate the process that a tribe seeks development through inner cooperation. As in tribal ecosystems, TEA gives tribes with fitter chiefs and more successful self-advancing history large opportunities to undergo self-advance. The inner-tribe cooperation in the self-advancing process brings in homogeneity, which is reflected by a decreasing diversity in the attributes of tribes. Thirdly, a *synergistic combination* operator is executed to emulate the inter-communication among tribes. New tribes are formed by combining attributes of existing tribes. Finally, TEA uses an *augmentation* operator to imitate the process that the tribal society extends to less populated areas in seek of more living resources. Such augmentation process results in the formation of new tribes in less explored subareas of the search space.

Using tribes as the basic evolution unit brings TEA a number of benefits. Firstly, the *reforms* operator compels the resulting tribes to represent solution sets in subareas different from each other. As a result, TEA avoids converging in a particular subarea and reduces the possibility of prematurity. Secondly, with the tribal structure, not only solutions, but also information of their surrounding neighborhoods, are inherited from generation to generation. The impact of the neighborhood information is twofold. First, it facilitates subsequent exploitation in their neighborhoods. Second, it guides TEA to efficiently identify promising subareas in the search space. The effectiveness and efficiency of TEA is validated on a diverse set of benchmark functions. Comparisons of TEA with a number of representative EC algorithms confirm the advantage of the tribal structure.

The remaining sections of this paper are organized as follows. Section 2 introduces details of the proposed TEA. Experimental results and comparisons are displayed in Section 3. Section 4 draws a conclusion to the whole paper.

2. THE PROPOSED TEA

Without loss of generality, we introduce the proposed TEA in the context of the following n-dimensional minimization problem:

$$\min_{l \le x \le u} f(\boldsymbol{x}), \tag{1}$$

where $\boldsymbol{x}$ is a candidate solution in the search space $[\boldsymbol{l}, \boldsymbol{u}]$ and $f(\cdot)$ is the fitness function. In TEA, each variable in the optimization problem is considered as a personal attribute and a society $\boldsymbol{S}$ of N tribes is evolved. Each tribe T_i is characterized by a tribal chief $\boldsymbol{c}_i$, an attribute diversity $\boldsymbol{d}_i$, and a historical record h_i, i.e.,

$$T_i = <\boldsymbol{c}_i, \boldsymbol{d}_i, h_i>. \tag{2}$$

The chief $\boldsymbol{c}_i = (c_{i,1}, c_{i,2}, \ldots, c_{i,n})$ is the one that achieves the best fitness in T_i. $c_{i,j}$ denotes the j-th attribute of $\boldsymbol{c}_i$. The diversity $\boldsymbol{d}_i = (d_{i,1}, d_{i,2}, \ldots, d_{i,n})$ measures the diversity of T_i on all the n attributes. The smaller $d_{i,j}$ is, the more homogeneity T_i has on the j-th attribute. With $\boldsymbol{c}_i$ as the centroid and $\boldsymbol{d}_i$ as the radius, the coverage of T_i can be described as $[\boldsymbol{c}_i - \boldsymbol{d}_i, \boldsymbol{c}_i + \boldsymbol{d}_i]$. The historical record h_i records the self-advancing history of T_i. A larger h_i value implies a greater success of T_i in the previous self-advancing process. Treating tribes coded by the above structure as the basic evolution unit, the evolution procedure of TEA comprises the following five steps.

2.1 Initialization

In the initialization phase, TEA chooses a parameter m and divides each dimension of the search space into m even segments. The search space is thus partitioned into (m^n) zones with uniform size. M zones are selected from the search space according to a pre-generated *orthogonal array* [13], where M is the total of level combinations in the array. The tribal society $\boldsymbol{S}$ is initialized with the chief of each tribe randomly generated in a selected zone. Suppose that '$\otimes$' denotes a inner multiplication operator between two vectors with equal dimensionality. Then the initialization of $\boldsymbol{c}_i$ can be formulated as

$$\boldsymbol{c}_i = \boldsymbol{l} + (\boldsymbol{com}_i + \boldsymbol{r}_i - 1) \otimes (\boldsymbol{u} - \boldsymbol{l}) / m, \tag{3}$$

where $\boldsymbol{r}_i \in (0,1)^n$ is an n-dimensional normalized random vector and $\boldsymbol{com}_i \in [1,m]^n$ is the i-th level combination in the orthogonal array. The attribute diversity $\boldsymbol{d}_i$ and the historical record h_i are initialized as their initial values $\boldsymbol{d}_0$ and h_0, respectively. For the sake of simplicity in the implementation, $\boldsymbol{d}_0$ and h_0 are calculated here by

$$\boldsymbol{d}_0 = (\boldsymbol{u} - \boldsymbol{l})/m, \tag{4}$$

$$h_0 = \exp(\varepsilon_{\min}), \tag{5}$$

where $\varepsilon_{\min} \in (0, 1)$ is a predefined constant.

The orthogonal property of orthogonal arrays guarantees that the M selected zones are uniformly distributed in the search space [13]. The tribal society initialized by the above method is thus able to scan the search space evenly, which helps TEA to gain a general image of the overall fitness distribution.

2.2 Reforms

The tribes are reformed by clustering existing tribes on both scales of fitness and attributes. A clustering technique termed *polythetic division* is applied for doing so. This technique is used because it can achieve satisfying clustering performance without the need of setting extra parameters or using iterative optimization procedure. Due to length limit, please refer to [14] for details of polythetic division. Detailed steps of the reform process are introduced afterwards.

Successful application of polythetic division requires a distance metric and a criterion for judging whether a group can be further divided. In the proposed TEA, the distance $\delta_{i,k}$ between two tribes T_i and T_k ($i, k = 1, 2, \ldots, N, i \ne k$) is defined as follows:

$$\delta_{i,k} = \begin{cases} |f(\boldsymbol{c}_i) - f(\boldsymbol{c}_k)|, & \text{on the scale of fitness} \\ \sqrt{(\boldsymbol{c}_i - \boldsymbol{c}_k)^{\mathrm{T}}(\boldsymbol{c}_i - \boldsymbol{c}_k)}, & \text{on the scale of attributes} \end{cases}. \tag{6}$$

With respect to the dividable criterion, it is defined as the maximum depth of the corresponding classification tree. With the above definition, the reforming process of TEA is given below:

Step 1) Apply the polythetic division technique to cluster the N tribes in $\boldsymbol{S}$ until the depth of the classification tree reaches the predefined upper bound D_f. Denote the resulting set of groups as $\boldsymbol{G}' = \{G_1', G_2', \ldots, G_{N'}'\}$, where N' is the number of groups in $\boldsymbol{G}'$ and $N \leq 2^{D_f}$.

Step 2) Apply the polythetic division technique to further cluster the tribes in each group $G_i' \in \boldsymbol{G}'$ on the scale of attributes. This clustering process continues until the depth of the corresponding classification tree reaches the predefined upper bound D_a. Denote the set of obtained groups as $\boldsymbol{G} = \{G_1, G_2, \ldots, G_N\}$, where N is the number of groups in $\boldsymbol{G}$ and $N \leq 2^{D_f + D_a}$.

Step 3) A new tribe $T_i' = < \boldsymbol{c}_i', \boldsymbol{d}_i', h_i >$ is defined based on each group $G_i \in \boldsymbol{G}$. Suppose that $T_{\text{best}}^{(i)} = < \boldsymbol{c}_{\text{best}}^{(i)}, \boldsymbol{d}_{\text{best}}^{(i)}, h_{\text{best}}^{(i)} > \in G_i$ is the tribe whose chief has the best fitness among all the tribes in G_i. Then T_i' is defined as

$$\boldsymbol{c}_i' = \boldsymbol{c}_{\text{best}}^{(i)}, \tag{7}$$

$$d_{i,j}' = \frac{1}{2}\left[\max_{T_k \in G_i}(c_{k,j} + d_{k,j}) - \min_{T_k \in G_i}(c_{k,j} - d_{k,j})\right], j = 1, 2, \ldots, n \tag{8}$$

$$h_i' = h_{\text{best}}^{(i)}. \tag{9}$$

The N tribes derived from the groups in $\boldsymbol{G}$ compose a new generation of $\boldsymbol{S}$.

Figure 1 exemplifies the above reforming process on a one-dimensional search space with $\boldsymbol{S} = \{T_1, T_2, \ldots, T_{10}\}$, $D_f = 2$, and $D_a = 1$. It can be observed that with $D_f = 2$, the ten tribes in $\boldsymbol{S}$ are divided into four groups on the scale of fitness, i.e., $G_1' = \{T_1, T_3, T_7, T_{10}\}$, $G_2' = \{T_4, T_6, T_8, T_9\}$, $G_3' = \{T_2\}$, and $G_4' = \{T_5\}$. Then the reforming process proceeds into the scale of attributes, as indicated by the arc arrows in Figure 1. Tribes in the above four groups are further clustered based on the attributes of their chiefs. With D_a=1, G_1' and G_2' are further divided into four groups as $G_1 = \{T_8, T_9\}$, $G_2 = \{T_4, T_6\}$, $G_3 = \{T_1, T_3\}$, and $G_4 = \{T_7, T_{10}\}$. G_3' and G_4' are not further divided as they have only one tribe. Consequently, with each of the six groups G_1, G_2, G_3, G_4, G_3', and G_4' defining a tribe, the reforming process reorganizes a ten-tribe society into a society of six tribes.

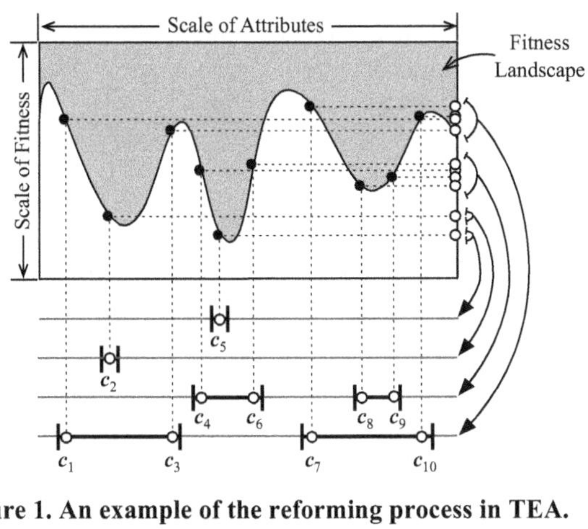

Figure 1. An example of the reforming process in TEA.

2.3 Self-advance

The probability for a tribe to self-advance depends on two factors: the leading power of its chief and its self-advancing history. A chief with better fitness is supposed to have the highest leading power, while a larger value of the historical record suggests a more successful self-advancing history. Suppose that in comparison with T_i, the society $\boldsymbol{S}$ contains F_i tribes that have less powerful chiefs and H_i tribes that have less successful self-advancing history. The self-advancing probability of T_i is calculated as follows:

$$p_{\text{adv}}(i) = \eta - (\eta - 1)\left[N - \sum_{1 \leq k \leq N}^{k \neq i} I_{F,H}(i,k)\right], \tag{10}$$

where $\eta \leq 1$ is a coefficient and $I_{F,H}(i,k)$ is a function indicating whether or not T_i surpasses T_k by satisfying one of the following two criteria: (i) $F_i + H_i > F_k + H_k$ or (ii) $F_i + H_i = F_k + H_k$ and $F_i > F_k$, i.e.,

$$I_{F,H}(i,k) = \begin{cases} 1, & \text{if (i) or (ii) satified} \\ 0, & \text{otherwise} \end{cases}, \tag{11}$$

From (10) and (11), it can be known that tribes with more powerful chiefs and more successful self-advancing history are given higher self-advancing probabilities, which is consistent with the situations in tribal ecosystems.

To avoid the trouble of tuning η, the value of η is set as:

$$\eta = \exp\left(\frac{E}{E_{\max}}\right) \tag{12}$$

where $E > 0$ is the number of fitness evaluations (FEs) and $E_{\max}$ is the predefined upper limit of E. By doing so, η increases from one to e as the algorithm proceeds. The growing η, on the one hand, facilitates TEA to explore the search space in the early phase because a small η allows more tribes to do self-advancement. On the other hand, as the η value increases, TEA focuses more on exploiting several most promising tribes and thus accelerates the convergence speed.

Based on the self-advancing probabilities calculated as above, a subset of tribes is randomly selected from the society. The self-advancing process of each selected tribe T_i iterates a direction prediction phase and a directional advance phase. As shown in Figure 2, detailed implementation of the above two phases are described as follows:

1) Phase of Direction Prediction: In this phase, an advancing direction $\boldsymbol{adv}_i = (adv_{i,1}, adv_{i,2}, \ldots, adv_{i,n})$ is predicted through the cooperation of the tribal population in T_i. In detail, a set of M trial points is sampled from the population according to a pre-generated orthogonal array with n factors and three levels per factor. The three levels correspond to three actions on a value, which are increment, decrement, and unchanged, respectively. Suppose that the k-th level combination in the orthogonal array is denoted as $\boldsymbol{com}_k = (com_{k,1}, com_{k,2}, \ldots, com_{k,n})$, where $com_{k,j} \in [1,3]$ is the level of the j-th factor in $\boldsymbol{com}_k$, $k = 1, 2, \ldots, M$, and $M = 3^{\lceil \log_3(3n-2) \rceil}$. The k-th trial point $\boldsymbol{v}_k$ is generated by $\boldsymbol{c}_i + \boldsymbol{d}_i \otimes (\boldsymbol{com}_k - 2)$. Based on the fitness of the M trial points, the advancing direction $\boldsymbol{adv}_i$ is predicted as

$$adv_{i,j} = -2 + \arg\min_{1 \leq lev \leq 3} \sum\nolimits_{\boldsymbol{v}_k \in V_{j,lev}} f(\boldsymbol{v}_k), j = 1,2,\ldots,n, \tag{13}$$

where $V_{j,lev} = \{\boldsymbol{v}_k \mid com_{k,j} = lev, k = 1, 2, \ldots, M, lev \in [1, 3]\}$ is a subset of the M trial points. To validate whether the above prediction successfully predicts a beneficial direction, a trial point z_0 is generated as

$$z_0 = \boldsymbol{c}_i + \boldsymbol{d}_i \otimes \boldsymbol{adv}_i\ . \tag{14}$$

If $f(z_0)$ is better than $f(\boldsymbol{c}_i)$, the prediction is successful. The self-advancing process enters into the phase of directional advance for seeking further improvement. Conversely, the prediction fails when $f(z_0)$ is no better than $f(\boldsymbol{c}_i)$. In this case, $\boldsymbol{d}_i$ is shrunk by multiplying a parameter ρ_p. Suppose that α failures have occurred consecutively for predicting a beneficial direction, $\alpha \geq 1$. ρ_p is calculated as $\max(0.1, 0.9^{\alpha})$. The self-advancing process keeps trying to predict a beneficial direction until the total φ_p of unsuccessful prediction exceeds a predefined number Φ_p.

2) Phase of Directional Advance: The phase of directional advance is performed only when a beneficial direction is successfully predicted. In this phase, T_i continues to advance along $\boldsymbol{adv}_i$ step by step. For each advancing step k ($k \geq 1$), a trail point z_k is generated as

$$z_k = z_{k-1} + \boldsymbol{d}_i \otimes \boldsymbol{adv}_i\ . \tag{15}$$

The step succeeds if $f(z_k)$ is better than $f(z_{k-1})$. Otherwise, the step fails and z_k is replaced by z_{k-1}. After each advancing step, $\boldsymbol{d}_i$ is adjusted as

$$\boldsymbol{d}_i = \begin{cases} \rho_s \boldsymbol{d}_i, & \text{if } f(z_{k-1}) \leq f(z_k) \\ \boldsymbol{d}_i / \rho_s, & \text{otherwise} \end{cases}, \tag{16}$$

where ρ_s is calculated as $\max(0.1, 0.9^{\beta})$ and β is the number of consecutive successful (or unsuccessful) steps. The directional advance continues until the total φ_s of unsuccessful steps exceeds a predefined number Φ_s. Suppose that a total of λ steps have been performed by then. $\boldsymbol{c}_i$ is replaced by z_λ and h_i is updated as

$$h_i = \exp\left[\left(f_0 - f(\boldsymbol{c}_i)\right) / |f_0|\right] \tag{17}$$

where f_0 denotes the fitness of $\boldsymbol{c}_i$ at the very beginning of the self-advancing process.

The remaining problem of the above self-advancing process is how to set Φ_p and Φ_s. Since the optimal settings of Φ_p and Φ_s may vary in different problems or even different phases of the algorithm, it is more desired that the parameters can be tuned automatically after reasonable initial values are given. In this paper, we design an adaption strategy that adjusts Φ_p and Φ_s based on the improvement obtained. More specifically, the adjustment of Φ_p is made according the relative improvement achieved in one iteration of the self-advancing process, whereas the adjustment of Φ_s is made based on the relative improvement obtained from one step in the phase of directional advance. Detailed adaption rules are listed as follows:

Rule 1) Φ_p (or Φ_s) is increased by one if the relative improvement obtained in the current iteration (or step) exceeds the upper bound ξ_{max}, which is defined as

$$\xi_{\max} = 10^{1+\lfloor \log_{10}(\Delta f) \rfloor}, \tag{18}$$

where Δf denotes the relative improvement obtained from the previous iteration (or step).

Rule 2) Φ_p (or Φ_s) is reduced by one if the relative improvement obtained in the current iteration (or step) drops below the lower bound ξ_{min} but remains non-zero. ξ_{min} is defined as

$$\xi_{\min} = \min(\varepsilon_{\min}, 10^{\lfloor \log_{10}(\Delta f) \rfloor})\ . \tag{19}$$

Rule 3) Φ_p (or Φ_s) is reduced by one if no improvement has been achieved for two consecutive iterations (or steps).

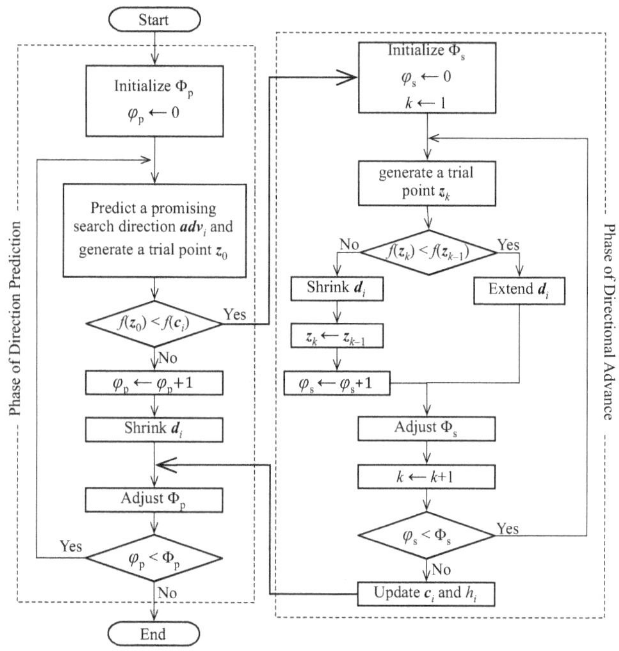

Figure 2. Flowchart of the self-advancing process of a tribe T_i.

2.4 Synergistic Combination

Among the N tribes in the society $\boldsymbol{S}$, the tribe whose chief has the best fitness is termed the *major tribe*. Without loss of generality, suppose that T_1 is the major tribe. Then synergy between T_1 and each of the other (N–1) tribes occurs and generates (N–1) new tribes. All the new tribes coexist with the original N tribes until the reforms operator reorganizes $\boldsymbol{S}$ in the next generation. Denote the new tribe generated by the synergy between T_1 and T_k as T_k^{syn}. The chief $\boldsymbol{c}_k^{syn}$ of T_k^{syn} combines the attributes of $\boldsymbol{c}_1$ and $\boldsymbol{c}_k$ as

$$c_k^{syn} = \begin{cases} c_{k,j}, & \text{if } r_{k,j} \leq (N - R_k)/2N \\ c_{1,j}, & \text{otherwise} \end{cases}, \tag{20}$$

where $r_{k,j} \in (0, 1)$ is a normalized random number and $R_k \in [1, N]$ is the rank of T_k in order of ascending fitness values. The attribute diversity and the historical record of T_k^{syn} are set as $\boldsymbol{d}_0$ and h_0, respectively.

From (20), it can be deduced that c_k^{syn} is more likely to be $c_{1,j}$ when R_i increases. Thus, the chief of a new tribe inclines to learn from the chief of the major tribe if the other tribe in synergy has a poor chief. The synergism process thus increases the chance for the new chiefs to achieve good fitness.

2.5 Argumentation

TEA keeps a census $\boldsymbol{U} = [u_{j,k}]_{n \times m}$ of the tribal society since the beginning of the algorithm. Each element $u_{j,k}$ in the census $\boldsymbol{U}$ records the number of tribal chiefs whose attribute on the j-th dimension falls into the range of

$$seg(j,k)=\left[l_j+\frac{(k-1)(u_j-l_j)}{m},l_j+\frac{k(u_j-l_j)}{m}\right]. \quad (21)$$

The probability to augment into $seg(j, k)$ is calculated based on the reverse of $u_{j,k}$ as

$$p_{\text{aug}}(j,k)=\frac{1}{1+u_{j,k}}. \quad (22)$$

By doing so, augmentation is biased towards areas with smaller population.

Based on the probabilities in (22), the augmentation process generates $2^{D_f+D_a}$ new tribes, all of which will enter the society. In detail, the chief $\boldsymbol{c}_k^{\text{aug}}$ of the i-th new tribe T_k^{aug} is generated as

$$c_{k,j}^{\text{aug}}=l_j+(K-1+r_{i,j})(u_j-l_j)/m,\ j=1,2,\ldots,n, \quad (23)$$

where $r_{i,j}\in(0,1)$ is a normalized random number and $K\in[1,m]$ denotes the segment picked out by the *roulette wheel selection* based on the probability distribution in (22). The attribute diversity and the historical record of T_k^{aug} are set as $\boldsymbol{d}_0$ and h_0, respectively.

TEA completes an evolution cycle after performing the augmentation operator. Since both the synergistic combination and augmentation operators generate new tribes, the number of tribes in the society rises, causing the N value to update after each evolution cycle.

3. EXPERIMENTS AND DISCUSSIONS

In this section, TEA is applied to minimize a set of seventeen benchmark functions with thirty dimensions (n = 30) [15][16]. Although the global minima of these functions are all zero, their properties are significantly different. The first four functions f_1 to f_4 are unimodal problems. Conducting experiments on these unimodal functions helps us to analyze the local search ability of TEA. The next eight functions f_5 to f_{12} are multimodal functions, each of which has a unique global optimum and multiple local optima. Experiments on these multimodal functions provide a systematic view into the ability of TEA in performing global search and avoiding prematurity. The last five functions f_{13} to f_{17} are shifted & rotated multimodal functions proposed by Suganthan *et al.* [16]. We test TEA on these functions for evaluating its performance on complex problems. Detailed definitions of the above test functions are given in Table 1. As can be seen, each function is attached with an accuracy level, which is the maximum error allowed for an acceptable solution.

Table 1 Benchmark Functions

Function	Search Domain	Accuracy Level
$f_1(\boldsymbol{x})=\sum_{i=1}^{n}x_i^2$	[−100, 100]n	10-10
$f_2(\boldsymbol{x})=\sum_{i=1}^{n}\lvert x_i\rvert+\prod_{i=1}^{n}\lvert x_i\rvert$	[−10, 10]n	10-10
$f_3(\boldsymbol{x})=\sum_{i=1}^{n}\left(\sum_{j=1}^{i}x_j\right)^2,\ \boldsymbol{y}=\boldsymbol{x}-\boldsymbol{o}$	[−100, 100]n	10-10
$f_4(\boldsymbol{x})=\sum_{i=1}^{n}\lfloor x_i+0.5\rfloor^2$	[−100, 100]n	10-10
$f_5(\boldsymbol{x})=\sum_{i=1}^{n-1}[100(x_{i+1}-x_i)^2+(x_i-1)^2]$	[−30, 30]n	100
$f_6(\boldsymbol{x})=-\sum_{i=1}^{n}x_i\sin(\sqrt{\lvert x_i\rvert})+418.9829n$	[−500, 500]n	10-10
$f_7(\boldsymbol{x})=\sum_{i=1}^{D}[x_i^2-10\cos(2\pi x_i)+10]$	[−5.12, 5.12]n	10-10
$f_8(\boldsymbol{x})=-20\exp\left[-0.2\sqrt{\sum_{i=1}^{n}x_i^2/n}\right]-\exp\left[\sum_{i=1}^{n}\cos(2\pi x_i)/n\right]+1$	[−32, 32]n	10-10
$f_9(\boldsymbol{x})=\sum_{i=1}^{n}x_i^2/4000-\prod_{i=1}^{n}\cos(x_i/\sqrt{i})+1$	[−600, 600]n	10-10
$f_{10}(\boldsymbol{x})=\frac{\pi}{30}\{10\sin^2(\pi y_1)+\sum_{i=1}^{n-1}(y_i-1)^2[1+10\sin^2(\pi y_{i+1})]+(y_n-1)^2\}+\sum_{i=1}^{n}u(x_i,10,100,4)$, where $\boldsymbol{y}=1+(\boldsymbol{x}+1)/4$	[−50, 50]n	10-10
$f_{11}(\boldsymbol{x})=1/10\{10\sin^2(3\pi x_1)+\sum_{i=1}^{n}(x_i-1)[1+\sin^2(3\pi x_{i+1})]+(x_n-1)^2[1+\sin^2(2\pi x_n)]\}+\sum_{i=1}^{n}u(x_i,5,100,4)$	[−50, 50]n	10-10
$f_{12}(\boldsymbol{x})=\sum_{i=1}^{n}\left[\sum_{j=1}^{n}(a_{i,j}\sin\alpha_j+b_{i,j}\cos\alpha_j)-\sum_{j=1}^{n}(a_{i,j}\sin x_j+b_{i,j}\cos x_j)\right]^2$	[−π, π]n	100
$f_{13}(\boldsymbol{x})=f_8(\boldsymbol{z}),\ \boldsymbol{z}=(\boldsymbol{x}-\boldsymbol{o})\cdot\boldsymbol{M}$	[−32, 32]n	21
$f_{14}(\boldsymbol{x})=f_7(\boldsymbol{z}),\ \mathrm{z}=(\boldsymbol{x}-\boldsymbol{o})\cdot\boldsymbol{M}$	[−5, 5]n	100
$f_{15}(\boldsymbol{x})=\sum_{k=0}^{20}\left\{\sum_{i=1}^{n}2^{-k}\cos\left[2\pi 3^k(z_i+0.5)\right]\right\}-n\sum_{k=0}^{20}2^{-k}\cos(3^k\pi)$, where $\boldsymbol{z}=(\boldsymbol{x}-\boldsymbol{o})\cdot\boldsymbol{M}$	[−0.5, 0.5]n	20
$f_{16}=\sum_{i=1}^{n-1}f_9\left(f_5(z_i,z_{i+1})\right)+f_9\left(f_5(z_n,z_1)\right)$, where $\boldsymbol{z}=\boldsymbol{x}-\boldsymbol{o}+1$	[−5, 5]n	10
$f_{17}(\boldsymbol{x})=\sum_{i=1}^{n-1}F(z_i,z_{i+1})+F(z_n,z_1)$, where $\mathrm{z}=(\mathrm{x}-\mathrm{o})\cdot\mathrm{M}$	[−100, 100]n	13

* In f10 and f11, the function u is defined as $u(x,a,k,m)=\begin{cases}k(x-a)^m, & \text{if } x>a\\ k(-x-a)^m, & \text{if } x<-a\\ 0, & \text{otherwise}\end{cases}$.

* In f12, $a_{i,j}$ and $b_{i,j}$ are random integers in the range of [−100, 100] and α_j is a random number in the range of [−π, π], i=1,2,…,n, j=1,2,…,n.
* In f13 to f17 $\boldsymbol{o}$ denotes a random vector in the search domain and $\boldsymbol{M}$ denotes an n by n orthogonal matrix.

* In f_{17}, the function F is defined as $F(x,y)=0.5+\frac{\sin^2(\sqrt{x^2+y^2})-0.5}{\left[1+0.001(x^2+y^2)\right]^2}$

To further validate the effectiveness and efficiency of TEA, its results are compared with three representative EC algorithms: evolutionary parallel local search (EPLS) [6], comprehensive learning particle swarm optimization (CLPSO) [4], and an adaptive differential evolution algorithm with an optional external archive (JADE) [3]. For the sake of fairness in the comparisons, all the four algorithms are programmed and complied with Visual C++ 6.0 in Windows XP (Service Pack 2). EPLS, CLPSO, and JADE use exactly the same parameter settings as their original papers, while the parameters of TEA are set as $m = 9$, $D_f = 2$, $D_a = 3$, $\varepsilon_{min} = 10^{-3}$, and $\Phi_p = \Phi_s = 2$. Using 300,000 FEs as the termination criterion ($E_{max} = 300{,}000$), the four algorithms report their average results obtained from fifty independent trials for comparison.

3.1 Unimodal Functions

Table 2 tabulates the results on the unimodal functions f_1 to f_4. As can be observed, TEA achieves the best solution accuracy on f_1 and f_2, followed by JADE, CLPSO, and EPLS. JADE obtains the best result on f_3, but the Mann-Whitney test indicates that TEA is still significantly better than EPLS and CLPSO. Each algorithm except for EPLS is able to find the global minimum zero on the non-continuous step function f_4 with a 100% successful rate. In general, TEA obtains the best solution accuracy on the four unimodal functions.

Table 3 tabulates the average FEs number for the algorithms to find the first acceptable solution. The successful rates, that is, the percentage of successful trials in which acceptable solutions are found, are also reported. From the table, it can be observed that on f_1, f_2, and f_4, TEA, JADE, and CLPSO all obtain 100% successful rates on the accuracy level at 10^{-10}. However, the average FEs number needed by TEA is significantly less than those of the other two algorithms. Take f_1 as an example: the average FEs number needed by TEA is 5596, which is less than 1/6 of the smallest average FEs number among the other three algorithms (JADE: 35313). The large gap in the average FEs number reveals the advantage of TEA in search speed. On f_3, TEA and JADE are the only two algorithms that find acceptable solutions on the accuracy level at 10^{-10}. JADE leads TEA in the successful rate by 4% and the average FEs number needed by JADE is smaller than that of TEA.

Table 2. Comparison of Solution Accuracy on Unimodal Functions[1]

Func	Alg	Best	Mean	Std.	Significance[2]
f_1	EPLS	5.13×10^{-28}	1.64×10^{-8}	7.37×10^{-8}	+1
	CLPSO	5.15×10^{-24}	2.36×10^{-23}	1.32×10^{-23}	+1
	JADE	2.26×10^{-149}	3.03×10^{-83}	2.14×10^{-82}	+1
	TEA	**0**	**0**	**0**	-
f_2	EPLS	8.01×10^{-14}	6.59×10^{-4}	3.58×10^{-3}	+1
	CLPSO	7.27×10^{-15}	1.41×10^{-14}	4.77×10^{-15}	+1
	JADE	2.15×10^{-76}	1.16×10^{-30}	8.19×10^{-30}	+1
	TEA	**0**	$\mathbf{9.08\times10^{-141}}$	$\mathbf{6.42\times10^{-140}}$	-
f_3	EPLS	2.94×10^{-8}	0.16596	0.51147	+1
	CLPSO	68.817	170.75	48.718	+1
	JADE	$\mathbf{7.91\times10^{-42}}$	$\mathbf{1.44\times10^{-37}}$	$\mathbf{5.05\times10^{-37}}$	−1
	TEA	5.03×10^{-41}	6.43×10^{-10}	3.18×10^{-9}	-
f_4	EPLS	0	0.92	1.9984	+1
	CLPSO	**0**	**0**	**0**	0
	JADE	**0**	**0**	**0**	0
	TEA	**0**	**0**	**0**	-

[1] The results marked in **boldface** are the best among the four algorithms.
[2] '+1', '−1', and '0' in the significance column indicate that compared to the result of TEA, the annotated result is significantly worse, significantly better, or insignificantly different, respectively.

Table 3. Comparison of Search Speed & Convergence Reliability on Unimodal Functions[1]

Func	Average FEs Number				Successful Rate (%)			
	EPLS	CLPSO	JADE	TEA	EPLS	CLPSO	JADE	TEA
f_1	183274	173335	35313	**5596**	76	**100**	**100**	**100**
f_2	196110	235871	63435	**54710**	12	**100**	**100**	**100**
f_3	-	-	**108117**	208264	0	0	**100**	96
f_4	138838	49624	9379	**2211**	64	**100**	**100**	**100**

[1] The results marked in **boldface** are the best among the four algorithms.

Figure 3 depicts the convergence curves of the four algorithms by plotting their median results obtained in the fifty trials along the FEs number. As can be observed, on f_1, f_2, and f_4, the convergence curves of TEA are much steeper than those of the other three algorithms. The advantage of TEA in search speed is thus confirmed on these three functions. With respect to f_3, the convergence curve of JADE exhibits the fastest descending rate. The convergence curve of TEA on f_3 is close to that of JADE and is much steeper than those of EPLS and CLPSO.

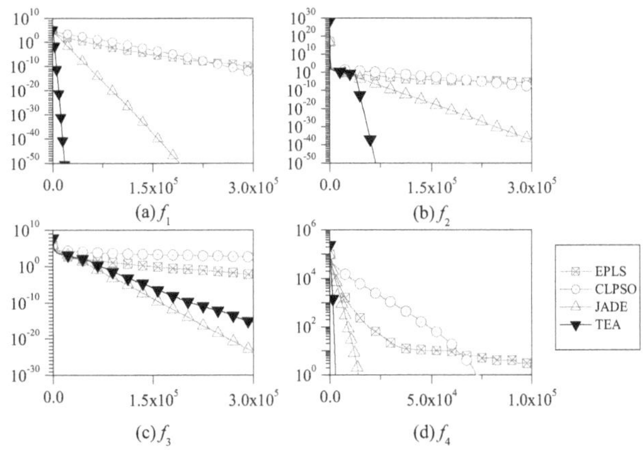

Figure 3. Convergence curves of EPLS, CLPSO, JADE, and TEA on unimodal functions f_1 to f_4.

The above results prove that TEA is capable of finding high-quality solutions to unimodal problems at fast speed. Compared to the other three algorithms, TEA possesses general advantage in both terms of solution accuracy and search speed. This is because the adaptive self-advancing processes of tribes endow TEA with powerful local search ability. Besides, since tribes with fitter chiefs and better self-advancing history are given higher self-advancing probabilities, TEA can bias exploitation towards promising areas where better solutions are more likely to be found. By doing so, TEA accelerates the convergence towards the global optimum.

3.2 Multimodal Functions

According to the results reported in Table 4, among the eight multimodal functions f_5 to f_{12}, the proposed TEA obtains the best average results on f_6, f_7, f_8, f_9, f_{10}, f_{11}, and f_{12}. Specifically, TEA completely avoids premature convergence on f_6 to f_{11}. The other algorithm that can do so is CLPSO. However, as shown by the average results on f_8 to f_{11}, the solution accuracy of CLPSO is significantly worse because CLPSO has to sacrifice the convergence speed for performing global exploration [4].

Table 5 reports the average FEs numbers and the successful rates for the four algorithms to find acceptable solutions on f_5 to f_{12}. As can be observed from the table, TEA always achieves the highest successful rate with the minimum or second minimum number of FEs. Specifically, compared to the other algorithms that achieve

100% successful rates on f_7 to f_{11}, the FEs number needed by TEA is much smaller.

Table 4. Comparison of Solution Accuracy on Multimodal Functions[1]

Func	Alg	Best	Mean	Std.	Significance[2]
f_5	EPLS	0.3605	71.27	45.60	+1
	CLPSO	0.09826	18.07	21.00	−1
	JADE	**0**	**0.07973**	**0.5638**	−1
	TEA	10.46	25.33	14.47	-
f_6	EPLS	355.3	934.1	341.12	+1
	CLPSO	**3.82×10^{-4}**	**3.82×10^{-4}**	3.60×10^{-13}	0
	JADE	**3.82×10^{-4}**	11.84	35.892	+1
	TEA	**3.82×10^{-4}**	**3.82×10^{-4}**	**3.06×10^{-13}**	-
f_7	EPLS	8.955	16.62	5.018	+1
	CLPSO	**0**	**0**	**0**	0
	JADE	**0**	**0**	**0**	0
	TEA	**0**	**0**	**0**	-
f_8	EPLS	5.46×10^{-11}	1.975	0.7895	+1
	CLPSO	7.55×10^{-15}	8.12×10^{-15}	2.42×10^{-15}	+1
	JADE	**4.00×10^{-15}**	**4.00×10^{-15}**	**0**	0
	TEA	**4.00×10^{-15}**	**4.00×10^{-15}**	**0**	-
f_9	EPLS	**0**	0.01632	0.02856	+1
	CLPSO	**0**	8.05×10^{-15}	2.99×10^{-14}	+1
	JADE	**0**	1.45×10^{-5}	1.05×10^{-3}	+1
	TEA	**0**	**0**	**0**	-
f_{10}	EPLS	2.25×10^{-27}	0.02695	0.08587	+1
	CLPSO	3.30×10^{-25}	1.94×10^{-24}	1.16×10^{-24}	+1
	JADE	**1.57×10^{-32}**	**1.57×10^{-32}**	**8.29×10^{-48}**	0
	TEA	**1.57×10^{-32}**	**1.57×10^{-32}**	**8.29×10^{-48}**	-
f_{11}	EPLS	1.26×10^{-20}	0.3626	0.7067	+1
	CLPSO	1.27×10^{-23}	8.47×10^{-23}	5.41×10^{-23}	+1
	JADE	**1.35×10^{-31}**	**1.35×10^{-31}**	**1.77×10^{-46}**	0
	TEA	**1.35×10^{-31}**	**1.35×10^{-31}**	**1.77×10^{-46}**	-
f_{12}	EPLS	565.6	10682	7665.6	+1
	CLPSO	2867.3	7860.1	2666.4	+1
	JADE	**1.84×10^{-12}**	9655.5	5822.3	+1
	TEA	0.1016	**4749.1**	**4105.8**	-

[1] The results marked in **boldface** are the best among the four algorithms.

[2] '+1', '−1', and '0' in the significance column indicate that compared to the result of TEA, the annotated result is significantly worse, significantly better, or insignificantly different, respectively.

Table 5. Comparison of Search Speed & Convergence Reliability on Multimodal Functions[1]

Func	Average FEs Number				Successful Rate (%)			
	EPLS	CLPSO	JADE	TEA	EPLS	CLPSO	JADE	TEA
f_5	79265	89115	11088	42471	88	**100**	**100**	**100**
f_6	-	149170	**114205**	163962	0	**100**	90	**100**
f_7	-	210691	158198	**112507**	0	**100**	**100**	**100**
f_8	239755	107912	56732	**10293**	2	**100**	**100**	**100**
f_9	188330	225950	38760	**12005**	38	**100**	98	**100**
f_{10}	174678	160845	33025	**9343**	68	**100**	**100**	**100**
f_{11}	206296	177754	42602	**23496**	46	**100**	**100**	**100**
f_{12}	-	-	**109457**	116074	0	0	4	**6**

[1] The results marked in **boldface** are the best among the four algorithms.

The above results demonstrate the effectiveness and efficiency of TEA in solving multimodal problems. Figure 4 depicts the convergence curves of the four algorithms on f_5 to f_{12} to further illustrate the search behavior of TEA on multimodal problems. From the figure, it is noticed that the search speed of TEA can be relatively slow in the early stage of the optimization procedure (as shown in Figure 4 (b), (c), and (g)). This is because TEA is trying to identify the basin of the global minimum from the set of areas defined by the tribes. Once the basin is found, the self-advancing process of the corresponding tribe will quickly bring the search procedure to the precise location of the global optimum.

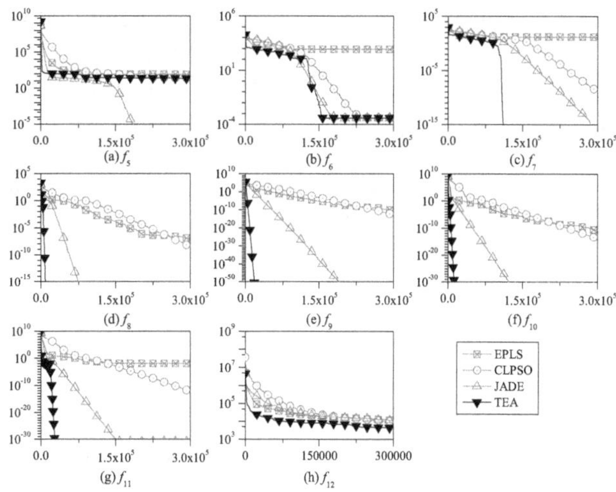

Figure 4. Convergence curves of EPLS, CLPSO, JADE, and TEA on multimodal functions f5 to f12.

3.3 Shifted & Rotated Multimodal Functions

The shifted & rotated multimodal functions f_{13} to f_{17} are particularly difficult to optimize because they comprise a huge number of local optima and their dimensions are non-separable. Table 6 shows that none of the four algorithms succeeds in finding the global optima of these functions. Nevertheless, TEA still obtains the best or the second best average results on four of the five functions. Meanwhile, as reported by Table 7, TEA is the only algorithm that finds acceptable solutions with over 80% successful rates on all the five functions. All the above results show that even in complex problems, TEA can maintain certain advantages in terms of solution accuracy, search speed, and reliability. These advantages can also be observed from the convergence curves depicted in Figure 5.

Table 6. Comparison of Solution Accuracy on Shifted & Rotated Functions[1]

Func	Alg	Best	Mean	Std.	Significance[2]
f_{13}	EPLS	**20.04**	**20.25**	**0.09444**	−1
	CLPSO	20.85	20.95	0.04492	+1
	JADE	20.77	20.93	0.04796	+1
	TEA	20.14	20.29	0.06480	-
f_{14}	EPLS	51.74	111.65	26.80	+1
	CLPSO	73.78	122.02	18.53	+1
	JADE	**22.52**	**33.58**	**4.483**	−1
	TEA	26.86	59.76	13.70	-
f_{15}	EPLS	22.51	29.85	3.689	+1
	CLPSO	22.30	26.12	1.705	+1
	JADE	26.85	32.91	3.622	+1
	TEA	**10.29**	**15.86**	**2.062**	-
f_{16}	EPLS	1.437	3.708	1.674	−1
	CLPSO	**0.5345**	**1.327**	**0.413**	−1
	JADE	1.312	1.572	0.124	−1
	TEA	2.309	5.587	1.967	-
f_{17}	EPLS	12.45	13.31	0.3259	+1
	CLPSO	12.03	12.88	0.1998	+1
	JADE	12.98	13.26	0.1385	+1
	TEA	**11.64**	**12.54**	**0.3404**	-

[1] The results marked in **boldface** are the best among the four algorithms.

[2] '+1', '−1', and '0' in the significance column indicate that compared to the result of TEA, the annotated result is significantly worse, significantly better, or insignificantly different, respectively.

Table 7. Comparison of Search Speed & Convergence Reliability[1]

Func	Average FEs Number				Successful Rate (%)			
	EPLS	CLPSO	JADE	TEA	EPLS	CLPSO	JADE	TEA
f_{13}	**14651**	95355	183811	48703	**100**	86	82	**100**
f_{14}	**25355**	242946	134641	32973	32	13	**100**	**100**
f_{15}	-	-	-	**27708**	0	0	0	**100**
f_{16}	**13781**	86337	34305	95808	98	**100**	**100**	98
f_{17}	**23489**	168756	203415	49684	16	76	8	86

[1] The results marked in **boldface** are the best among the four algorithms.

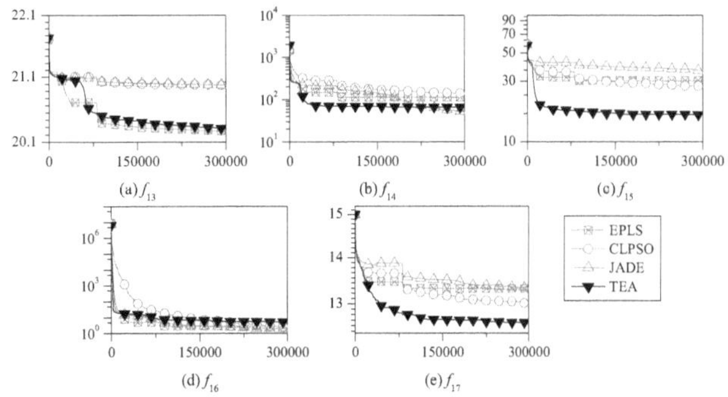

Figure 5. Evolution curves of EPLS, CLPSO, JADE, and TEA on shifted & rotated multimodal functions f12 to f17.

4. CONCLUSION

A new EC mechanism called TEA has been developed from the evolution mechanism of tribal ecosystems. An essential feature that differentiates TEA from other EC algorithms is that it uses the concept of tribes to extend the basic evolution unit from discrete solution points to solution sets in different subareas of the search space. Specifically, a tribe in TEA describes the solution set in a particular subarea with the locally best-so-far solution analogous to the tribal chief and the radius of the subarea analogous to the tribal diversity. The search experience in the subarea is also recorded as the self-advancing history of the tribe. Simulating tribal ecosystems, four evolution operators are designed for evolving tribes from roughly estimated promising subareas to the precise location of the global optimum.

The promising results of TEA on a diverse set of benchmark functions reveal the significance of our research in twofold. First, in terms of algorithmic design, we show that extending the basic evolution unit from solution points to solution sets in different subareas in the search space is beneficial for improving the performance of EC algorithms. This is because the extension allows more useful information to be involved in the evolution and thus facilitates the use of such information for helping the search procedure. Encouraged by the promising performance of TEA, it is worthwhile to investigate how the basic evolution unit can be further extended for incorporating more useful information efficiently. Second, in terms of performance, TEA provides an effective way for finding high-quality solutions at fast speed. Experimental results show that TEA has a general advantage against a number of representative EC algorithms, especially in terms of the search speed. It will be interesting to study the performance of TEA in practical problems.

5. ACKNOWLEDGEMENTS

This work was supported in part by the National High-Technology Research and Development Program (863 Program) of China No.2013AA01A212, in part by the NSFC for Distinguished Young Scholars 61125205, in part by the NSFC No. 61332002, No. 61300044 and No. 61170220.

6. REFERENCES

[1] J. Zhang, H. S. –H. Chung, and W. –L. Lo, "Clustering-based adaptive crossover and mutation probabilities for genetic algorithms," *IEEE Trans. Evol. Comput*, vol. 11, no. 3, pp. 326 – 335, June 2007.

[2] Z. –H. Zhan, J. Zhang, Y. Li, and H. S. –H. Chung, "Adaptive particle swarm optimization," *IEEE Trans. Syst. Man. Cyber. – B*, vol. 39, no. 6, pp. 1362 – 1381, Dec. 2009.

[3] J. Zhang and A. C. Sanderson, "JADE: adaptive differential evolution with optional external archive," *IEEE Trans. Evol. Comput.*, vol. 13, no. 5, pp. 945 – 959, Oct. 2009.

[4] J. J. Liang, A. K. Qin, P. N. Suganthan, and S. Baskar, "Comprehensive learning particle swarm optimizer for global optimization of multimodal functions," *IEEE Trans. Evolutionary Computation*, vol.10, no.3, pp.281-295, Jun. 2006.

[5] Y. Wang, Z. Cai, and Q. Zhang, "Differential evolution with composite trial vector generation strategies and control parameters," *IEEE Trans. Evol. Comput.*, vol. 15, no. 1, pp. 55 – 66, Feb. 2011.

[6] G. Guo and S. Yu, "Evolutionary Parallel Local Search for Function Optimization," *IEEE Trans. Syst. Man. Cyber. – B*, vol. 33, no. 6, pp. 864 – 876, Dec. 2003.

[7] X. Li, "Niching without niching parameters: particle swarm optimization using a ring topology," *IEEE Trans. Evolutionary Computation*, vol. 14, no. 1, pp. 150-169, Feb. 2010.

[8] X. Chen, Y. –W. Ong, M. –H. Lim, and K. C. Tan, "A multi-facet survey on memetic algorithms," *IEEE Trans. Evol. Comput.*, vol. 15, no. 5, pp. 591 – 607, Oct. 2011.

[9] Y.-S. Ong, M.-H. Lim, N. Zhu, and K.-W. Wong, "Classification of adaptive memetic algorithms: a comparative study," *IEEE Trans. Syst. Man. Cyber. – B*, vol. 36, no. 1, pp. 141 – 152, Feb. 2006.

[10] T. Park and K. R. Ryu, "A dual-population genetic algorithm for diversity control," *IEEE Trans. Evol. Comput.*, vol. 14, no. 6, pp. 865 – 884, Dec. 2010.

[11] H. Kwasnicka and M. Przewozniczek, "Multi-population pattern searching algorithm: A new evolutionary method based on the idea of messy genetic algorithms," *IEEE Trans. Evol. Comput.*, vol. 15, no. 5, pp. 715 – 732, Oct. 2011.

[12] M. H. Fried, *The Notion of Tribe*, California: Cummings Publishing Company, 1975.

[13] fA. Hedayat, N. Sloane, and J. Stufken, *Orthogonal Arrays, Theory and Applications*. New York: Springer-Verlag, 1999.

[14] B.S. Everitt, S. Landau,and M. Leese, *Cluster Analysis* (4th Edition), Oxford University Press, 2001.

[15] X. Yao, Y. Liu, and G. Lin, "Evolutionary programming made faster," *IEEE Trans. Evolutionary Computation*, vol.3, no.2, pp.82-102, Jul. 1999.

[16] P. N. Suganthan, N. Hansen, J. J. Liang, K. Deb, Y.-P. Chen, A. Auger, S. Tiwarki, "Problem definitions and evaluation criteria for the CEC 2005 special session on real-parameter optimization," *Technical Report, Nanyang Technological University, Singapore, and KanGAL Report Number 2005005*, May 2005.

Energy Aware Virtual Machine Placement Scheduling in Cloud Computing Based on Ant Colony Optimization Approach

Xiao-Fang Liu[a], Zhi-Hui Zhan[a]* (Corresponding Author), Ke-Jing Du[b], Wei-Neng Chen[c]

[a]Department of Computer Science, Sun Yat-sen University, Guangzhou, P. R. China, 510275

[a]Key Laboratory of Machine Intelligence and Advanced Computing, Ministry of Education, P.R. China

[a]Engineering Research Center of Supercomputing Engineering Software, Ministry of Education, P.R. China

[b]Department of Management Science, City University of Hong Kong, Kowloon, Hong Kong

[c]School of Advanced Computing, Sun Yat-sen University, P. R. China

*zhanzhh@mail.sysu.edu.cn

ABSTRACT

Cloud computing provides resources as services in pay-as-you-go mode to customers by using virtualization technology. As virtual machine (VM) is hosted on physical server, great energy is consumed by maintaining the servers in data center. More physical servers means more energy consumption and more money cost. Therefore, the VM placement (VMP) problem is significant in cloud computing. This paper proposes an approach based on ant colony optimization (ACO) to solve the VMP problem, named as ACO-VMP, so as to effectively use the physical resources and to reduce the number of running physical servers. The number of physical servers is the same as the number of the VMs at the beginning. Then the ACO approach tries to reduce the physical server one by one. We evaluate the performance of the proposed ACO-VMP approach in solving VMP with the number of VMs being up to 600. Experimental results compared with the ones obtained by the first-fit decreasing (FFD) algorithm show that ACO-VMP can solve VMP more efficiently to reduce the number of physical servers significantly, especially when the number of VMs is large.

Categories and Subject Descriptors

I.2.8 [**Artificial Intelligence**]: Problem Solving, Control Methods, and Search – *Heuristic methods.*

General Terms

Algorithms, Performance, Design, Experimentation

Keywords

Cloud computing, resource scheduling, virtual machine placement, ant colony optimization

GECCO '14, July 12–16, 2014, Vancouver, BC, Canada.

http://dx.doi.org/10.1145/2576768.2598265

1. INTRODUCTION

Cloud computing is a hot topic recently and is developing quickly. It refers to both the applications delivered as services over the Internet and the hardware and software in the data centers that provide those services [1]. Cloud computing provides computation and storage as services, which are made available as subscription-based services in pay-as-you-go mode to customers [2]. The services are divided to three major types: infrastructure as a service (IaaS), platform as a service (PaaS), and software as a service (SaaS).

The virtualization technology further makes cloud computing different from the traditional grid computing or cluster computing paradigms, and also makes cloud computing more suitable in the commercialization. Virtualization provides promising approach to re-divide the hardware and software resources of one or more physical servers into multiple parts and each part runs in independent environment. Through creating isolated virtual machines (VMs) for different applications, multiple applications are able to run on the same physical server even with different resources. That is, the size of CPU, memory, and, other resources in VMs can be configured according to the time-varying demand of customers. This way, the cloud resources are more efficiently used.

As virtualization is an important technology in cloud computing, the VM placement (VMP) problem has become a significant research topic in cloud computing. VMP is to find an optimal map to place the VMs to physical servers so as to make the cloud resources used efficiently [3]. As VMs are running on physical servers, great energy is consumed by maintaining the servers in data center and much cost is paid for cooling down the facilities [4]. In this sense, more physical servers means more energy consumption and more money cost. Therefore, a promising scheduling purpose in the VMP problem is to effectively use the physical resources to host the virtual resources, so as to reduce the number of running physical servers.

Obviously, a very simple scheduling strategy to solve the VMP problem is a random placement strategy. However, such a strategy may not obtain promising solutions. In the literatures, many works have been conducted to solve the VMP problem. Assigning VMs to the least number of servers has been simulated to study in [5]. A linear programming algorithm to minimize the number of physical servers for the VMP problem has been proposed in [6]. It optimizes the problem across multiple cloud providers. A simple greedy algorithm named first-fit decreasing (FFD) is also been presented [7]. Evolutionary computation approaches have developed fast in recent years [8][9] and have been applied to many practical applications [10]-[12]. In the literature, there are some works on using EC approaches to solve the VMP problem. A genetic algorithm (GA) based approach is proposed to optimize the physical locations of VMs [13]. The authors in [14] proposed a scheduling strategy on load balancing of VM resources based on GA. Ant colony algorithm (ACO) is also successfully applied on this problem. A load adaptive cloud resource scheduling model based on ACO is proposed in [15]. An algorithm based on MAX-MIN ant system (MNAS) heuristic for minimizing the number of physical servers used to support the current workload is proposed in [16].

In this paper, the VMP problem is formulated as a combinatorial optimization problem (COP) and is solved by using an ACO based approach. That is, given a set of VMs with various resource demands (e.g., the CPU and memory demands). How to optimally replace these VMs to a set of physical servers, so as to reduce the number of physical servers? The motivation of using ACO is that the VMP is formulated as a COP while ACO has been widely accepted as a promising approach to solve various COPs [17][18]. Specifically, an algorithm named ACO-VMP is proposed, which is based on ACO to solve the VMP problem for minimizing the number of physical servers. Different from other works that the pheromone is deposited between the physical server and the VM, we herein propose to deposit the pheromone between every two VMs to record the historical desirability of placing them in the same physical server. Moreover, the heuristic information is defined between the VM and physical server to measure how the resource utilization ratio can be improved if the VM is placed on this physical server. This way, the heuristic information can further help ACO-VMP to efficiently place VMs on the most suitable physical servers. In the beginning of the ACO-VMP approach, the number of physical servers is the same as the number of the VMs. In every generation during the optimization process, the number of physical servers is set as one less than the number of physical servers used in the global best solution. Therefore, the ACO-VMP approach tries to reduce the physical servers one by one.

The rest of this paper is organized as follows. In Section 2, the VMP problem in cloud computing is defined. Section 3 presents the ACO-VMP approach in detail. Experimental results are given in Section 4. Finally, Section 5 gives the conclusion and future work.

2. PROBLEM FORMULATION

In a cloud environment, a large number of physical servers are connected through a communication network. The physical servers are virtualized and all applications are running on the VMs. The VMP problem is to maps VMs to server nodes, which is similar to the bin packing problems. The physical servers represent the bins and VMs represent the items to be packed. Each server (bin) has capacity constraints of different resources it can supply, such as CPU and memory. A VM (item) is defined as a vector with CPU and memory resources demand.

Suppose that we are given a set of M physical servers denoted as I, and a set of N VMs denoted as J. Both physical server and VM are defined as multidimensional vector. Each dimension represents a kind of resource. For simplicity, we consider only CPU resource and memory resource in this paper. Each physical server i ($1 \le i \le M$) has CPU capacity PC_i and memory capacity PM_i. Each VM j ($1 \le j \le N$) has its CPU demand VC_j and memory demand VM_j. We assume that the resources demand of each VM is less than the resources that a physical server can supply. The formulation of the VMP problem is as:

$$Minimize \sum_{i=0}^{M} y_i \tag{1}$$

subject to:

$$y_i = \sum_{j=1}^{N} x_{ij}, \quad \forall\, i \in I \tag{2}$$

$$\sum_{i=0}^{M} x_{ij} = 1 \quad \forall\, j \in J \tag{3}$$

$$\sum_{j=1}^{N} VC_j \cdot x_{ij} \le PC_i \quad \forall\, i \in I \tag{4}$$

$$\sum_{j=1}^{N} VM_j \cdot x_{ij} \le PM_i \quad \forall\, i \in I \tag{5}$$

$$x_{ij} \in \{0,1\}, \ \forall i \in I \text{ and } j \in J \tag{6}$$

Eq. (2) shows that whether a physical sever is used (y_i=1) or not (y_i=0). Constraint (3) shows that a VM is assigned to only one of the physical server. The capacity constraint of the physical server is described in constraint (4) and (5) for the CPU and memory respectively. Constraint (6) defines the placement information of physical server i and VM j, x_{ij}=1 means VM j is placed on physical server i while x_{ij}=0 means not.

3. PROPOSED ALGORITHM

In this section, we introduce ACO-VMP approach for minimizing the number of servers used for VMs placement. First, we describe the construction of solution. Then the algorithm will be described and the pseudo code will be presented.

3.1 Objective Function

A solution to the problem can be defined as $S=\{S_1, S_2, ..., S_{Mt}\}$ where S_i is a server that is used to deploy some VMs. This S_i can be also regarded as a subset of the VMs. The VMs subsets deployed on different servers are disjoint with each other and each VM is placed and only placed on one physical server. The objective is to minimize the number of physical server. So we can calculate the objective value of the solution S as:

$$f(S) = w_1 \cdot \sum_{i=1}^{M_t^S} \left(\frac{1}{PC_i - UC_i + e} + \frac{1}{PM_i - UM_i + e} \right) + w_2 \cdot M_t^S \tag{7}$$

where w_1 and w_2 are weights, and e=1. PC_i and PM_i represent the CPU and memory capacities of server S_i, respectively. UC_i and UM_i represent the CPU and memory that have been used by all the VMs deposited on S_i. Moreover, M_t^S is the number of the physical servers used in the solution S.

The objective function of Eq. (7) is a minimization function. We can see from Eq. (7) that the w_1 term means the higher utilization of each server, the solution is better; the w_2 term means the less number of servers used, the solution is better.

Therefore, if two solutions use different number of physical servers, the solution uses less servers win. If two solutions use the same number of physical servers, the utilization of CPU and memory of the server is considered.

3.2 ACO Solution Construction

An ant's movement depends greatly on initialization state configurations, construction rule, and pheromone update. An example of the solution construction is shown in Fig. 1. In the example, 5 VMs are placed on physical servers where M_t=5 is the number of servers provided. The all possible deploy can be viewed as a matrix. Each element x_{ij} represents that whether the VM_j is deployed on the server S_i. If x_{ij} is selected, then x_{ij} is set to 1. Otherwise x_{ij} is set to 0. The total number of steps for an ant to construct a solution is the same as the number of VMs. For each step j, the ant selects a physical server to run the current VM_j. There is only one is selected in each column. The VMs selected on row i are deployed on server S_i (i=1, 2, 3, …, M_t). In Fig. 1, the ant's path (x_{11}, x_{32}, x_{23}, x_{44}, x_{25}) represents a solution S={S_1, S_2, S_3, S_4}, where VM_1 is deployed on server S_1, VM_3 and VM_5 are deployed on S_2, VM_2 is deployed on S_3, and VM_4 is deployed on S_4. S_5 is not used.

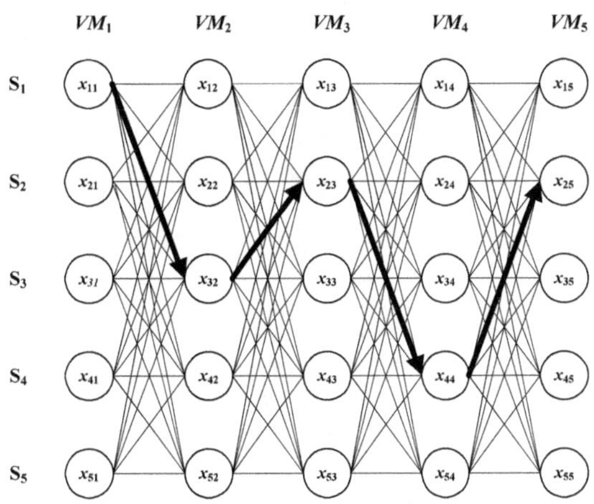

Fig. 1. Example of the construction of solution with N=11 and M_t=5

3.2.1 Initialization State Configurations

The solution construction is influenced by M_t. We want to find the minimizing number of servers used. In the beginning of the process, the number of physical servers is set as the number of VMs, i.e., N, representing that each VM is placed on a different physical server. Therefore in the initialization, we set M_t=N–1. That is, ACO-VMP tries to construct solutions with one less physical server than the current best feasible solution. During the process, if we find one solution, we can set M_t to M_t–1. Therefore, the M_t is adaptive to the search process as:

$$M_t = M^{\min}-1 \tag{8}$$

where $M^{\min}$ is the minimum number of physical servers used in the solution we have find until iteration t. So ants can adjust the grouping of VMs and find the best solution with $M^{\min}$–1 or fewer servers. In this way, the search direction is clear and the search is efficient.

The pheromone is deposited on VM pairs. We initial τ_0=1/N (N is the number of servers used in the beginning, i.e., the number of VMs).

3.2.1 State Transition Rule

In every iteration of the ACO-VMP approach, the purpose is to place the N VMs into M_t physical servers, so as to find a solution that can satisfy the constraints described in Section 2. Therefore, in each step j for an ant to construct the solution, as in Fig. 1, the ant selects a server i to place the VM_j. In ACO-VMP, pheromone is deposited on VM pairs. So we can calculate the average pheromone between the current VM_j and the VMs already on the server S_i. The average pheromone can be viewed as the desirability of placing the current VM VM_j on the server S_i, as follow:

$$T(i,j)=\begin{cases}\frac{1}{|S_i|}\sum_{k\in S_i}\tau(k,j), & \text{if } |S_i|\neq 0\\ \tau_0, & \text{otherwise}\end{cases} \tag{9}$$

where $T(i, j)$ represent the historic desirability of grouping VM_j and the VMs that are already on S_i. $|S_i|$ is the number of VMs that are already on S_i.

The heuristic information is also important in the solution construction. It represents the desirability to assign VM_j to on S_i. Good heuristic information guides the ants to move targeted. It's related to the improvement that VM_j can bring to the utilization of the server S_i. Mathematically, the heuristic information of placing VM_j on S_i can be calculated as:

$$\eta(i,j)=\begin{cases}\frac{1-|(PC_i-UC_i)-(PM_i-UM_i)|}{|PC_i-UC_i|+|PM_i-UM_i|+\delta}, & \text{if } i\in\Phi_j(S)\\ 0, & \text{otherwise}\end{cases} \tag{10}$$

where δ is a constant and it is set to 1.0. PC_i and PM_i represent the CPU and memory capacities of server S_i. UC_i and UM_i represent the CPU and memory that have been used of S_i after VM_j has been placed on it. $\Phi_j(S)$ is the set of servers that still have sufficient resources to host VM_j. That is:

$$\Phi_j(S)=\left\{\begin{array}{l} i\,|\,((\sum_{k=1}^{j-1}(x_{ik}\cdot VC_k)+VC_j)\leq PC_i)\wedge\\ ((\sum_{k=1}^{j-1}(x_{ik}\cdot VM_k)+VM_j)\leq PM_i),\\ i=1,2,\cdots,M_t \end{array}\right\} \tag{11}$$

With the pheromone and heuristic information, we calculate the probability for assigning VM_j to S_i as:

$$p(i,j)=\frac{T(i,j)[\eta(i,j)]^{\beta}}{\sum_{k\in\phi_j(S)}T(k,j)[\eta(k,j)]^{\beta}} \tag{12}$$

where β is a parameter. An ant selects a server according to the rule as follow:

$$i=\begin{cases}\arg\max_{k\in\phi_j(S)} p(k,j), & \text{if } q\leq q_0\\ I, & \text{otherwise}\end{cases} \tag{13}$$

where q_0 ($0\leq q_0\leq 1$) is a parameter, q ($0\leq q\leq 1$) is a random number. $\Phi(S)$ is the set of servers that still have sufficient resources to host VM_j. I is a random number selected according to probability distribution calculated by Eq. (12). This selection way can increase the randomness to avoid local optimum.

There is a special case that $\Phi_j(S)$ is empty. All servers fail to satisfy the constraints defined in Section II, the value of $\eta(i, j)$ is 0 for $i = 1, 2, 3, \ldots, M_t$. As a result, the probability defined by Eq. (10) is all zero and generating random number by probability distribution can't work. To solve this problem, a complementary rule is designed as follow:

$$i = \begin{cases} \arg\min_{1 \le k \le M_t} over(S_k), & \text{if } q < q_0 \\ rand(1, M_t), & \text{otherwise} \end{cases} \tag{14}$$

where

$$over(S_k) = |PC_k - VC_j - UC_k| + |PM_k - VM_j - UM_k| \tag{15}$$

where q is a random number. $over(S_k)$ calculates the sum of the absolute difference between utilization and capacity upper bound about CPU and memory after assigning VM_j to S_k. No matter it's overload or not, the value is better if it's closer to 0. If the value is smaller, VM_j can contribute more to the improvement of utilization of the server. The remaining CPU and memory resource of a server is more balanced. That is to say, it makes effective utilization of the resources in all dimensions and balance the resources left on each server along different dimensions [3].

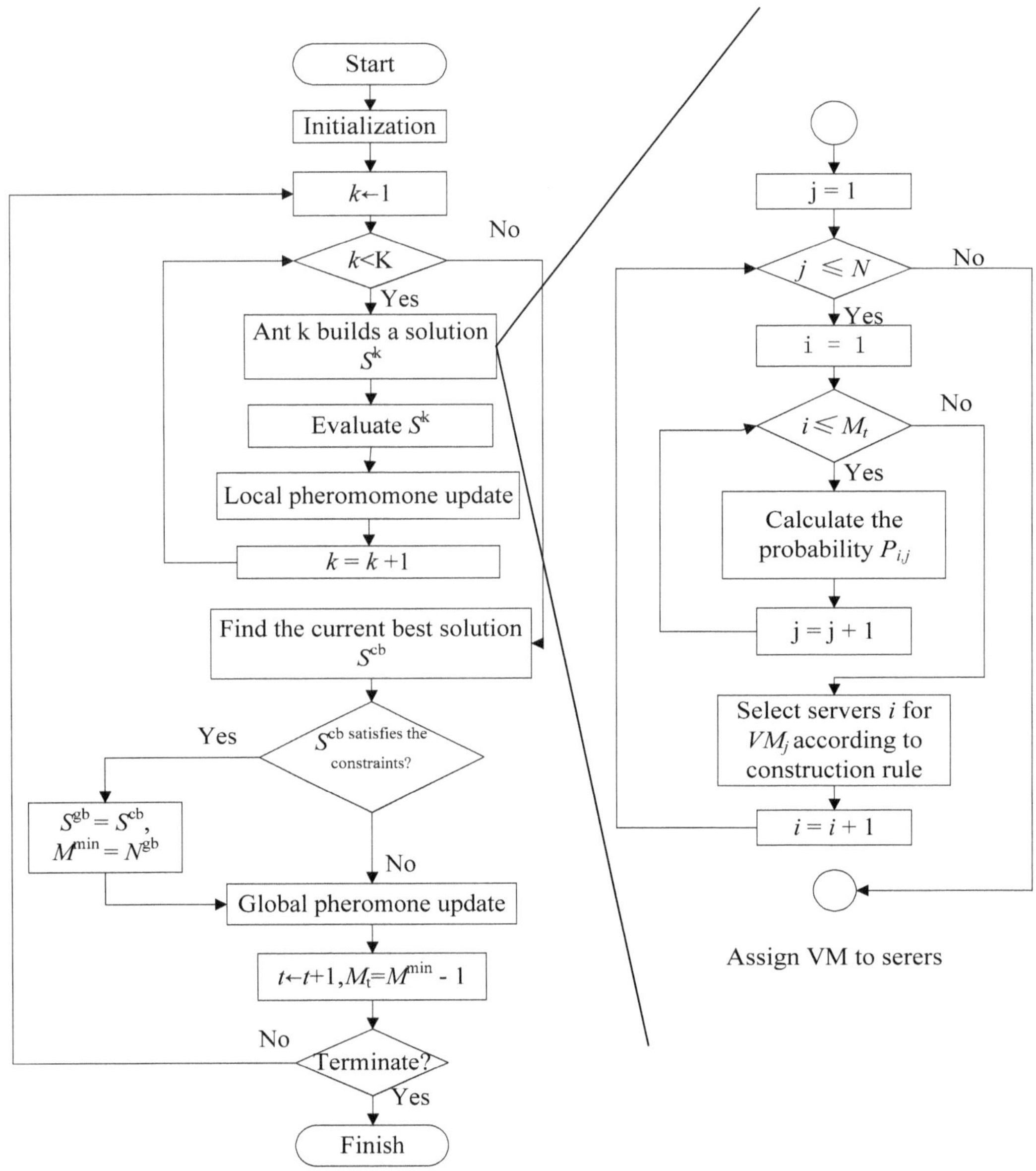

Fig. 2. The flowchart of the ACO-VMP algorithm.

```
Input: Set of VMs with resource demand and set of servers with capacity constraint
Output: The placement of VMs

/*Initialization*/
Set the value of the parameters
Initialize all the pheromone values between VMs to τ0
Initialize the Mt (the number of servers provided) to N-1 and M^min to N
Repeat
  For i=1 to K (number of ants) do
    For j = 1 to N(number of VMs)
     If there is servers set S not empty can load the VM Then
        For every server Si ∈ S
            Calculate the pheromone desirability of the movement according to Eq. (9)
          Calculate the heuristic probability of the movement according to Eq. (10)
      End for
      Generate a random number q
       If(q < q0) Then
           Select the server using the transition rule as Eq. (13)
       Else
           Select the server using the probability distribution as Eq. (12)
    Else //There is no server that can host the VM
        For every server
          Calculate the value according to Eq. (15)
        End for
        Generate random number q
        If(q < q0) Then
           Select the server according to Eq. (14)
        Else
           Rand select a server
    End for
    Adjust VM between the upload server and other server
    Local pheromone updating
  End for
  Calculate the value of objective for every ant
  Select the best ant
  Global pheromone update
  If the best solution satisfies the constraints defined in Section 2 Then
     Mt = Mt -1
Until the maximal generations met
```

Fig. 3. Pseudo code of the algorithm ACO-VMP.

3.3 Pheromone Updating Rules

The ants communicate indirectly through the pheromone information. The pheromone update comprises local update and global update. Local pheromone update is followed by an ant that has finished building its solution. To search more paths, pheromones evaporate on some VM pair. For each VM pair (j, k) in the solution, the local pheromone is update as:

$$\tau(j,k) = (1-\rho)\cdot\tau(j,k) + \rho\cdot\tau_0 \quad (16)$$

The global pheromone updating is applied after the best current solution is found. It increases the pheromone value on pairs in the best solution. In this way, the algorithm can converge faster. The pheromone of each VM pair (j, k) deployed on S_i in the current best solution is updated as:

$$\tau(j,k) = (1-\varepsilon)\cdot\tau(j,k) + \varepsilon\cdot\Delta\tau \quad (17)$$

$$\Delta\tau = \frac{1}{M_t+1} + \frac{1}{|PC_i - UC_i| + |PM_i - UM_i|} \quad (18)$$

where PC_i and PM_i represent the CPU and memory capacities, while UC_i and UM_i represent the CPU and memory that have been used of S_i in the current best solution.

These two pheromone updating rules are used to adjust the search behaviors of the ants. The effect of the local pheromone updating rule is to reduce the desirability of the visited edges by some ants. Evaporation of the pheromone on the visited edges makes them less attractive for the following ants. Hence it is useful for increasing the population diversity. The effect of the global pheromone updating rule is to increase the desirability of the edges on the best-so-far solution. This reinforcement can result in a higher convergence speed.

3.4 The Complete ACO-VMP Algorithm

The complete algorithm ACO-VMP is shown in Fig. 2 and its pseudo code is shown in Fig. 3. The step of ACO-VMP can be described as follow:

Step 1: Initialization. Set the parameters to the predefined value and initialize τ_0 and M_t.

Step 2: The K ants construct solutions according to the rule shown in Section 3.2. And local pheromone updating is applied after each ant finish building solution. Evaluate the solution by the objective function and calculate the number of servers needed to use really s_k for ant_k ($1 \le k \le K$). If the solution satisfies the constraints, $s_k = M_t$. Otherwise, $s_k = M_t - 1$.

Step 3: Select the current best solution S^{cb} in K solutions. The compare procedure includes two parts. Considering the number of servers need to use t_k firstly. And then compare the objective function.

Step 4: Update parameter and pheromone. If the current best solution satisfies the constraints defined in Section 2, the global best solution S^{gb} will be covered by S^{cb} and M_t will be set to M_t–1. Global update the pheromone on the VM pairs in the current best solution.

Step 5: Termination check. When the maximum number of iterations is reached, the algorithm terminates. Otherwise, set $k = k + 1$ and go to Step 2 for the next optimization.

4. Experiments and Comparisons

4.1 Test Cases

In this section, experiments are carried out to verify the performance of the ACO-VMP algorithm. The FFD [7] algorithm with multidimensional is used for comparison. FFD considers VMs in a decreasing order of utilization of a certain resource and places each VM into the first servers that has enough resource remaining [3].

For simplify, we suppose that all servers are homogeneous. The approach can also be used in nonhomogeneous environments. Moreover, we only consider CPU and memory resources. Without special instruction, all experiments for ACO-VMP use the same parameters. The parameters settings are as: the population size K=10, β=2, ρ=0.35, ε=0.35, q_0=0.7, and τ_0 =1/N. We conduct test cases with different number of VMs. The test instances are generated randomly. The instances are the demand of CPU and memory utilizations for VMs. In worst case, one VM must be assigned to one server individually. So the number of server is set to the number of VMs at the beginning.

We run 30 times for every test instance and take the average in the result for comparisons. FFD algorithm is run only one time because it's deterministic. All experiments are running on a PC with an Intel Pentium Dual CPU at 2.0 GHz and 2.0 GB RAM.

4.2 Experimental Results

The experiments are with different scales that have different numbers of VMs. The results are presented and compared in Table 1. The table compares the number of servers of each algorithm. From the table, we can see that ACO-VMP performs better than FFD algorithm. ACO-VMP uses less number of servers because of it is able to search in global space and make more effective use of the resources.

Table 1 Experimental Results for Different Test Cases with Different Number of VMs

Number of VMs	Number of Physical Severs			
	FFD	ACO-VMP		
		mean	best	worst
100	34	29.9	**29**	30
200	67	59.9	**59**	60
300	105	92	**92**	92
400	140	121.6	**121**	122
500	179	158.3	**158**	159
600	203	174.8	**174**	175

Moreover, the results are plotted in Fig. 4 to show how the number of physical servers varies with the increment of the number of VMs. The comparisons clearly show that the advantages of the ACO-VMP approach get more and more evident as the number of VMs become larger.

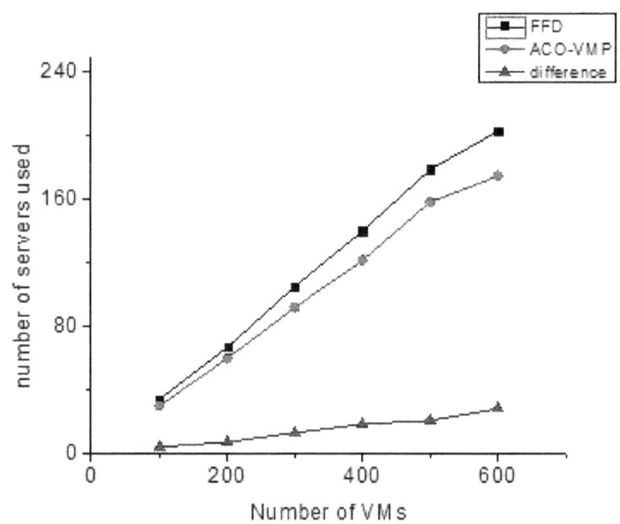

Fig. 4. Test results of FFD and ACO-VMP for VMP problem with different numbers N of VMs.

5. Conclusion

With the large energy cost for running the servers, it's essential to efficiently assign VM to physical servers and improve the resource utilization. In this paper, we propose an algorithm based on ant colony optimization for minimizing the number of servers used.

We evaluate the performance of the proposed ACO-VMP approach in solving VMP with the number of VMs being up to

600. Experimental results show that the algorithm is competitive and effective to make effective utilization of resources when compared with the ones obtained by FFD, especially when the number of VMs is large.

We test the above experiments in the simulative environment. So for future work, we will conduct our experiments under the real cloud environment such as the OpenStack cloud platform.

6. ACKNOWLEDGMENTS

This work was supported in part by the NSFC No.61379061, No.61309003, No.61202130, and No.61379060, in part by NSFC Joint Fund with Guangdong under Key Projects U1201258 and U1135005.

7. REFERENCES

[1] M. Armbrust, A. Fox, R. Griffith, A. D. Joseph, R. Katz, A. Konwinski, G. Lee, D. Patterson, A. Rabkin, I. Stoica, and M. Zaharia, "A View of Cloud Computing", in *Proc. Communications of the ACM*, vol. 53 no. 4, pp. 50-58 Apr. 2010.

[2] R. Buyya, S. Pandey, and C. Vecchiola, "Cloudbus toolkit for market-oriented cloud computing," in *Proc. 1st International Conference on Cloud Computing*, 2009, pp. 24–44.

[3] Y. Q. Gao, H. B. Guan, Z. W. Qi, Y. Hou, and L. Liu, "A multi-objective ant colony system algorithm for virtual machine placement in cloud computing," *Journal of Computer and System Sciences*, vol. 79, no. 8, pp. 1230-1242, Dec. 2013.

[4] G. International. "Make it green: Cloud computing and its contribution to climate change", 2010.

[5] M. Stillwell, D. Schanzenbach, F. Vivien, and H. Casanova. "Resource allocation algorithms for virtualized service hosting platforms", *Journal of Parallel and Distributed Computing*, vol. 70, no. 9, pp. 962-974, September 2010.

[6] S. Chaisiri, B. S. Lee, and D. Niyato, "Optimal virtual machine placement across multiple cloud providers", in *Proc. IEEE Asia-Pacific Services Computing Conference*, 2009, pp. 103–110.

[7] Y. Ajiro and A. Tanaka, "Improving packing algorithms for server consolidation", in *Proc. International Conference for the Computer Measurement Group (CMG)*, Computer Measurement Group, 2007.

[8] Z. H. Zhan, J. Zhang, Y. Li, and Y. H. Shi, "Orthogonal learning particle swarm optimization," *IEEE Transactions on Evolutionary Computation*, vol. 15, no. 6, pp. 832-847, Dec. 2011.

[9] Z. H. Zhan, J. Zhang, Y. Li, and H. Chung, "Adaptive particle swarm optimization," *IEEE Transactions on Systems, Man, and Cybernetics--Part B*, vol. 39, no. 6, pp. 1362-1381, Dec. 2009.

[10] Z. H. Zhan, J. Li, J. Cao, J. Zhang, H. Chung, and Y. H. Shi, "Multiple populations for multiple objectives: A coevolutionary technique for solving multiobjective optimization problems," *IEEE Transactions on Cybernetics*, vol. 43, no. 2, pp. 445-463, April. 2013.

[11] Z. H. Zhan, K. J. Du, J. Zhang, and J. Xiao, "Extended binary particle swarm optimization approach for disjoint set covers problem in wireless sensor networks," in *Proc. Conf. Technologies and Applications of Artificial Intelligence*, Tainan, Taiwan, 2012. pp. 327-331.

[12] M. Shen, Z. H. Zhan, W. N. Chen, Y. J. Gong, J. Zhang, and Y. Li, "Bi-velocity discrete particle swarm optimization and its application to multicast routing problem in communication networks," *IEEE Transactions on Industrial Electronics*, in press 2014

[13] H. Mi, H. Wang, G. Yin, Y. Zhou, D. Shi,n and L. Yuan, "Online self-reconfiguration with performance guarantee for energy-efficient large-scale cloud computing data centers," in *Proc. IEEE International Conference on Services Computing*, 2010, pp. 514-521.

[14] J. H. Hu, J. H. Gu, G. F. Sun, and T. H. Zhao, "A scheduling strategy on load balancing of virtual machine resources in cloud computing environment", in *Proc. 3rd International Symposium on Parallel Architectures, Algorithms and Programming*, 2010, pp. 89-96.

[15] X. Lu and Z. L. Gu, "A Load-adaptive cloud resource scheduling model based on ant colony algorithm", *in Proc. IEEE International Conference on Cloud Computing and Intelligence Systems* , 2011, pp. 296-300.

[16] E. Feller, L. Rilling, and C. Morin, "Energy-aware ant colony based workload placement in clouds", in *Proc. IEEE/ACM International Conference on Grid Computing (GRID)*, 2011, pp. 26-33.

[17] M. Dorigo and L. M. Gambardella, "Ant colony system: A cooperative learning approach to the traveling salesman problem", *IEEE Transactions on Evolutionary Computation*, vol. 1, no. 1, pp. 53-66, Apr. 1997.

[18] Z. H. Zhan, J. Zhang, Y. Li, O. Liu, S. K. Kwok, W. H. Ip, and O. Kaynak, "An efficient ant colony system based on receding horizon control for the aircraft arrival sequencing and scheduling problem," *IEEE Transactions on Intelligent Transportation Systems*, vol. 11, no. 2, pp. 399-412, Jun. 2010.

Consensus Costs and Conflict in a Collective Movement

Timothy Solum
Dept. of Computer Science and Network Engineering
Southern Nazarene University
Bethany, OK, USA
tsolum@mail.snu.edu

Brent E. Eskridge
Dept. of Computer Science and Network Engineering
Southern Nazarene University
Bethany, OK, USA
beskridge@snu.edu

Ingo Schlupp
Dept. of Biology
University of Oklahoma
Norman, OK, USA
schlupp@ou.edu

ABSTRACT

Aggregation, whether it be in natural or artificial systems, provides numerous benefits to both the individual and the group. However, aggregation has costs and frequently involves inter-individual conflict. Although conflicts in natural systems is understood to be at times beneficial, as well as detrimental, conflict in artificial systems, such as a team of robots, is frequently viewed as inhibiting consensus and, therefore, success. This is particularly the case in large-scale aggregations where ensuring consensus is especially challenging. In response, mechanisms are often integrated into the group's control systems to minimize, or even eliminate, conflicts of interest. As a result, the potential benefits of losing consensus, such as increased diversity and reduced consensus costs, are not available. Using a biologically-based collective movement model, we demonstrate that not enforcing consensus and allowing conflict to evolve as agents make decisions results in a system in which agents meet their own needs, thus minimizing consensus costs, while still maintaining group cohesion when possible. Simulations predict that conflict balances consensus costs with individual preferences such that both individual and group goals are met.

Categories and Subject Descriptors

I.2.11 [**Artificial Intelligence**]: Distributed Artificial Intelligence—*coherence and coordination, multiagent systems*

Keywords

conflict, collective movement, swarm robotics, coordination

1. INTRODUCTION

Group living provides significant benefits in nature, ranging from increased protection from predators to increased foraging success [45]. The same is true in artificial systems where multi-robot systems such as robot swarms provide robustness, flexibility, and scalability [40]. To maintain these benefits, cohesive aggregations and coordination are frequently necessary [35]. The flocking of birds [33], schooling of fish [25], and mass herds of migrating wildebeests [16] are just some of the examples of large-scale aggregation and coordination that have been observed and studied in natural systems.

GECCO'14, July 12–16, Vancouver, BC, Canada.
Copyright 2014 ACM 978-1-4503-2662-9/14/07 ...$15.00.
http://dx.doi.org/10.1145/2576768.2598357.

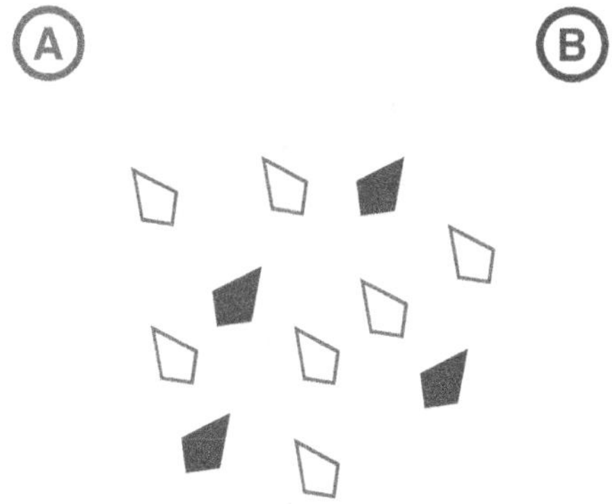

Figure 1: Group members preferring to go to destination B will incur consensus costs if the group collectively decides to go to destination A.

Although all members of a group usually participate in decision-making in large aggregations, not all members receive the same benefits. Participating in aggregations such as these frequently imposes *consensus costs* on individual group members [12, 14]. These costs can range from minor inconveniences to effectively preventing an individual from achieving its goal. Consider the situation depicted in Figure 1. If the group decides to go to destination A, which is favored by the majority of the group, the agents preferring to go to destination B will not reach their preferred destination. Although simple models for natural aggregations and their artificial analogues, robot swarms, often assume that all agents are the same, agents have differing needs, information, and cost to benefit ratios which introduces conflicts of interest into the decision-making process [5, 30].

Generally, conflict is viewed as something negative that imposes group-level costs in collective decision-making. As a result, efforts are frequently made to minimize it. However, conflict is a very general phenomenon observed universally in evolutionary biology, and can have positive effects. Unfortunately, research efforts on conflict's effects on aggregations, and specifically collective movement models, have primarily focused on navigation decisions [10] or on the benefits of different types of decision-making models [8], and not on the decisions involved in initiating and maintaining collective movements. What if consensus costs are actually more costly than conflict and should be the ones minimized?

In the work presented here, we use a biologically-based collective movement model to explore how conflicts of interest, especially as it pertains to consensus costs and collective decision-making, affects both individual and group success. We demonstrate that the introduction of conflict minimizes consensus costs for agents involved in collective decision-making based on quorum sensing rules. Furthermore, we demonstrate that although the introduction of conflict does impact the overall success of the group in completing a goal, it allows for significantly improved individual success.

2. RELATED WORK

In natural systems, a *consensus decision* is defined as "members of a group choos[ing] between two ore more mutually exclusive actions with the specific aim of reaching a consensus" [12]. Note that this definition precludes the option of compromise, which is not a viable possibility in many situations, such as decisions on *where* to go [44]. *Consensus costs*, therefore, are defined as members incurring reduced fitness by "forgoing their own optimal action to comply with the decision outcome" [12]. In many cases, the benefits of consensus decision-making, such as increased group cohesion and decision-making accuracy [46], outweigh the costs. However, the consensus costs can outweigh the benefits if the group is too large [31], unless a significant portion of the group has no strong preferences [30], are simply uninformed [15], or all share the same preferences [41]. In some cases, consensus costs are high because a minority of decision-makers have significant influence over the consensus decision [28]. However, even if decision-making is more democratic, consensus costs still exist [13].

If consensus costs incurred as a result of factors such as different goals or information become too high, group conflict can result which often incurs group level costs, such as increasing the amount of time required to reach consensus [30] or a loss of cohesion, and with it many of the benefits of group living [45]. Left unresolved, conflict can significantly impede group consensus, and ultimately success, in collective decision-making. Because of the emphasis on a consensus in robot swarms, considerable efforts have been made to mitigate, or even eliminate, conflict in swarms. A variety of techniques have been proposed, ranging from central control [7] to the use of aggression [39]. In spite of these efforts to resolve or avoid conflict, it does provide non-trivial group benefits. For example, conflict has been shown to increase the overall accuracy of group decision-making [9, 11]

In natural systems, conflict is resolved in a variety of ways. Compromise is a common means of resolving conflict, especially for "when" decisions, but, as noted above, it frequently is not a viable option, such as in "where" decisions. When consensus costs are low, compromise is frequently chosen as an acceptable outcome, even if the decision is favored by a minority [23]. However, when consensus costs are high, compromise is avoided.

Another common means of resolving conflict in natural systems is to allow the larger group to split, or *fission*, into separate subgroups [38]. Fissioning allows individuals to temporarily aggregate into smaller groups, with lower consensus costs. Examples of natural systems organized using the concept of group fission and fusion exist throughout nature and include species such as fish [18], dolphins [34], chimpanzees [29], hyaenas [42], spider monkeys [2], elephants [1], and bats [27]. In these examples, one of the most important points is that the fission–fusion process is the result of decision making at the individual level, not at the group level [3]. The fission process provides a solution to many problems arising from large groups and can be viewed as "an adaptive outcome where individual's interests conflict" [44].

The concept of splitting a larger group into subgroups is not uncommon in robot swarms, but the emphasis on a generalized approach in which decisions are based at the individual level is. One approach uses weighted voting and game theory to determine when to split a group into subgroups as a way to resolve conflicting interests [20]. However, the approach relied on a despotic leader robot that sent commands to other members of the group, a restriction that is impractical as the group is scaled. Another approach focuses on splitting a robot swarm into multiple groups using a biologically-inspired model, but the relative sizes of the subgroups are predefined and do not adapt to the current consensus costs of group members [4, 26].

3. METHODS

The simulations used for this work were performed using a modified version of a collective movement model developed through observations of collective movement attempts in a group of white-faced capuchin monkeys [24, 36], and was later confirmed in observations of sheep [37]. The model could be classified as a probabilistic finite state machine [6] and uses anonymous quorum-sensing to determine the rates of collective movement decisions. The anonymous quorum-sensing nature of the model means that leaders, whether successful or unsuccessful, cannot be recognized as such, and decision-making must rely on the number of participating individuals only. To integrate conflict and spatial movement into the model, significant modifications were required, including converting the model from the usage of continuous time to discrete time.

3.1 Collective Movement Model

The collective movement model uses three rules to govern the decision-making process involved in starting collective movements [36, 24]. The first rule assumes that all individuals within the group are identical and can initiate a collective movement attempt with a rate of $1/\tau_o$. While this assumption may not hold for groups with dominant leaders, studies have shown that it is a viable assumption for egalitarian animal groups, such as the capuchin monkeys used in the model's development. It is also a viable assumption for robot swarms, and is sometimes even a determining factor in a multi-robot systems classification as a robot swarm [40].

The second rule describes the rate at which followers join the collective movement attempt and is calculated by $1/\tau_r$. The time constant τ_r for the following rate is calculated using the following:

$$\tau_r = \alpha_f + \beta_f \frac{N - r}{r} \quad (1)$$

where α_f and β_f are constants determined through direct observation, N is the number of individuals in the group, and r is the number of individuals following the initiator. As the number of individuals following the initiator increases, the rate at which individuals join the movement also increases.

Not all initiation attempts are successful as initiators often cancel and return to the group. The third rule calculates this cancellation rate using the following:

$$C_r = \frac{\alpha_c}{1 + (r/\gamma_c)^{\varepsilon_c}} \quad (2)$$

where α_c, γ_c, and ε_c are constants determined through direct observation, and r is the number of individuals following the initiator. Simulations of the model included the implicit assumption that a successful collective movement required all of the members of the group to participate, since there was a non-zero probability of canceling even if all but one member participated. While this is not necessarily the case in nature, cohesive collective movements were the primary objective of this work and, as such, incomplete movements were considered failures.

3.2 Integrating Conflict

To investigate the effects of altering the rate at which individuals initiate, follow an initiator, and cancel a movement, Gautrais added an individual-specific constant, referred to as a "k factor," to the rate calculations of the collective movement model [24]. Initiation attempts were now calculated at the constant rate of k/τ_o, and the following and canceling rate calculations were modified as follows:

$$\tau_r = \frac{1}{k}\left(\alpha_f + \beta_f \frac{N-r}{r}\right) \quad (3)$$

$$C_r = k\left(\frac{\alpha_c}{1 + (r/\gamma_c)^{\varepsilon_c}}\right) \quad (4)$$

where the variables were the same as before. Since this k factor can either increase or decrease the three decision-making rates, it was an ideal means with which the effects of conflict could be incorporated into the model.

Like other work involving conflicts of interest [14], conflict was introduced by assigning individuals different preferred goal destinations. An equal number of individuals were given each preferred goal destination, thus ensuring that the initial amount of conflict would be the same, regardless of the initiator's destination. However, unlike other work, individuals were considered homogeneous, other than their different preferred destinations, and did not posses an individual "degree of assertiveness." This decision was made for two reasons. First, it minimized the number of confounding variables in the system, thus simplifying the analysis of results. Second, it was consistent with other work in the area of robot swarms in which swarm members are assumed to be identical [40].

The conflict value c_i for individual i in following a potential leader was calculated using the angle θ between the leader's observed vector of movement $\vec{v_l}$ and the vector $\vec{d}$ to the individual's preferred destination from the leader's current position as follows:

$$c_i = \frac{|\theta|}{\pi} \quad (5)$$

with θ having a range of $[-\pi, \pi]$ and calculated using the dot product of the vectors $\vec{v_l}$ and $\vec{d}$. If a potential leader was not moving, θ was defined to be π, the maximum value. Although neither the original model, nor the observations on which the model was based, discussed conflicts of interest for the individual animals involved, it was assumed that the individuals encountered moderate conflict. Therefore, the integration of conflict incorporated the concept of moderate conflict ($c_i = 0.5$), which produced the same results as the original model. Also, the magnitude with which low conflict affected the model would be the same as high conflict so as not to bias the model towards one conflict value over another. As a result, the conflict value c_i was then used to calculate k, as follows:

$$k = 2c_i \quad (6)$$

where the variables were the same as before. Since k had a non-inclusive lower limit of zero, the non-inclusive upper limit of two was chosen to ensure balance. In the simulations described below, conflict was limited to the range $[0.1 : 0.9]$ to ensure these limits were satisfied.

3.3 Conversion to Discrete Time

The collective movement model originally used continuous time events to simplify and speed up the algorithm. However, such an approach was not compatible with discrete time requirements in simulating spatial movement. As a result, significant modifications were made to the model's implementation algorithm. First, instead of using the individual decision rates to generate decision times from an exponential distribution, the decision rates were used to calculate the probability of the decision being made at any given time step. This was straightforward since the inverse of the decision rate is simply the instantaneous probability. Second, because it was possible that an individual would make a new decision at any given time step, a "do nothing" decision was added to the decision-making process. However, there were situations in which a decision to "do nothing" was not possible. For example, if a follower's leader canceled its movement or instead decided to follow another leader, the follower was required to make a decision to either follow a new leader or initiate its own movement.

To ensure that the order in which individuals made decisions did not affect the results (e.g., a leader's initiation affected the decision-making of a later individual), decisions for all individuals were made before any actions were taken. Once an individual reached its preferred goal destination, it stopped moving and did not perform any additional decision-making for the remainder of the simulation.

3.4 Numerical Implementation

Numerical simulations of the collective movement model were implemented in Java[1] using the original algorithm as a starting point [24]. However, as noted above, the algorithm was converted to use discrete time events, instead of the continuous time events in the original, and modified to allow for spatial movement.

The original model was only evaluated with a group size of 10, but previous results have shown that the success of collective movements increases as the group size is increased, with most success differences present in group sizes of 50 or less [21]. As such, evaluating different group sizes presented an opportunity to evaluate the effects of conflict with different group dynamics. For each evaluation environment, simulations were performed using group sizes from 10 to 50. Each treatment was simulated 2,000 times, each with a different random seed. Each simulation constituted an attempt

[1]Simulation source code and data analysis scripts are available for download from `https://github.com/snucsne/bio-inspired-leadership`.

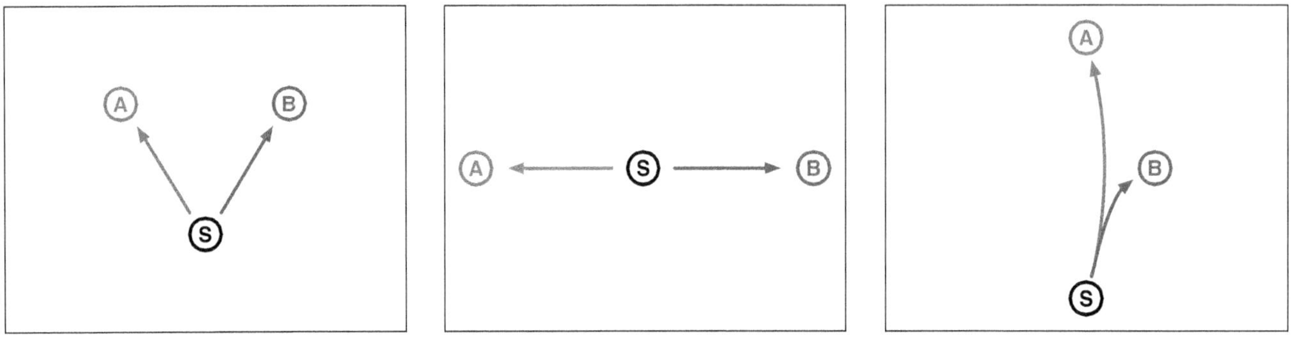

(a) Moderate initial conflict (b) Maximum initial conflict (c) Minimal initial conflict

Figure 2: The three different simulation environments used to evaluate the conflict's effect on consensus costs are shown. In each environment, individuals started the simulation at location S and were tasked with moving a goal location. Before the simulation began, half the individuals were randomly assigned with a preferred destination of A, while the other half were assigned destination B.

for each individual to move to their preferred destination and had a maximum of 20,000 time steps. Unlike the original model, multiple initiators were allowed and a cancellation was not classified as an immediate failure if other initiators were active. The model parameters used were the same as those used in the original model [24, 36].

Three different simulation environments were used to evaluate conflict's effect on consensus costs in a simulated robot swarm (see Figure 2). In the first environment, two goal destinations were located at the same distance from the starting area, but were separated by an angle of 74° (see Figure 2a). Individuals evaluated in this environment initially experienced moderate conflict in deciding to follow a leader moving towards the non-preferred destination. In the second environment, two goal destinations were located at the same distance from the starting are, but were separated by an angle of 180° (see Figure 2b). Because of the extreme angle, agents evaluated in this environment experienced the maximum level of conflict if they chose to follow a leader moving towards the opposite destination. In the last environment, one goal location was much further from the starting area than the other goal location, with an angle of 37° between them (see Figure 2c). Since the angle between the two goal locations was comparatively small as seen from the starting area, agents evaluated in this environment initially experienced minimal conflict when they chose to follow a leader to the non-preferred destination, especially if they preferred the closer destination. However, as the agents continued to follow the leader to the non-preferred destination, they experienced increasing levels of conflict.

4. RESULTS & ANALYSIS

To compare the effects of conflict on consensus decision-making, simulations were performed for three different treatments: *a*) all agents had the same preferred destination; *b*) agents had different preferred destinations, but conflict was not used; and *c*) agents had different preferred destinations and conflict was used. To quantify the effects of conflict in these two treatments, three different metrics were used: *a*) the median time for agents to reach their preferred destination, *b*) the mean percentage of agents that reached their preferred destination and *c*) the mean percentage of the swarm that is currently moving towards their preferred destination at each time step. The first metric allowed us to compare the costs for a swarm with agents having different goals, whereas the second and third metrics allowed us to compare the consensus costs incurred by agents in the swarm. Due the nature of the collective movement model and the consensus costs present, individuals frequently did not reach their preferred destination. To ensure the median time for reaching the preferred destination was a useful metric in these situations, the time to reach the preferred destination for these agents was truncated to the maximum number of timesteps.

Since there was no bias in the simulations towards one destination over another, the analysis of the simulations took into account that the identity of the destinations was not important. Rather, given the nature of consensus costs, the order in which destinations were reached was the important differentiator of the destinations. As such, simulation results were organized into first and second destination categories, as determined by the median times in which the destinations were reached in a given simulation.

Figure 3 shows the median number of timesteps required for agents to reach their preferred destination, with agents not reaching their preferred destination having their time truncated to the maximum number of timesteps. In simulations with conflict, almost all the agents were able to reach their preferred destination, while only approximately half of the agents were able to reach their preferred destination in simulations without conflict. As Figure 3 illustrates, this was primarily because agents were unlikely to succeed in splitting the group to move towards the other destination without the addition of conflict. The effects of conflict are also seen in the median number of timesteps to reach the second destination where group splitting was more successful as conflict increased. Simulations in the environment with maximum initial conflict yielded the fastest median times to the second destination, while the environment with minimal initial conflict yielded the slowest. Furthermore, larger groups resulted in faster times, regardless of the environment. This was due to the fact that, as previous work has shown, larger groups increased the likelihood of a successful initiation [21, 22].

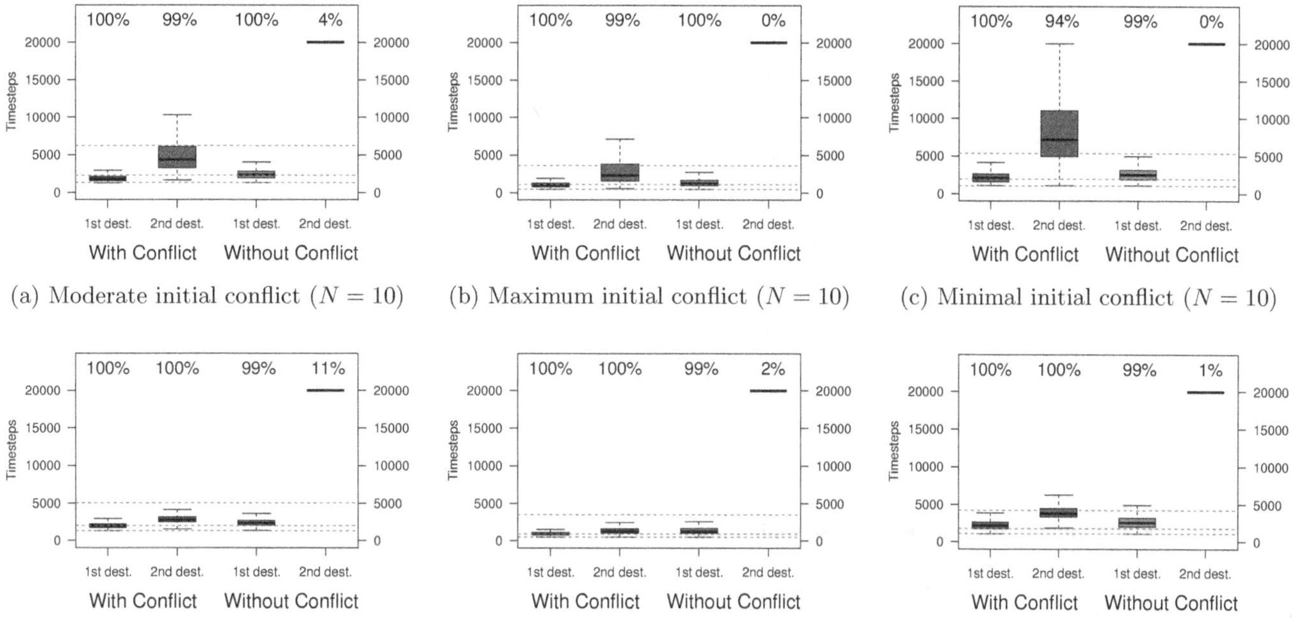

(a) Moderate initial conflict ($N = 10$) (b) Maximum initial conflict ($N = 10$) (c) Minimal initial conflict ($N = 10$)

(d) Moderate initial conflict ($N = 50$) (e) Maximum initial conflict ($N = 50$) (f) Minimal initial conflict ($N = 50$)

Figure 3: The median number of timesteps and the interquartile range needed for agents to reach their preferred destination are shown for each simulation environment and groups of size $N = 10$ and $N = 50$. Percentages indicate the fraction of agents that reached a particular, preferred destination. Horizontal dashed lines represent the minimum, mean, and maximum times for baseline simulations. Times for agents not reaching their preferred destination were truncated at the maximum number of timesteps.

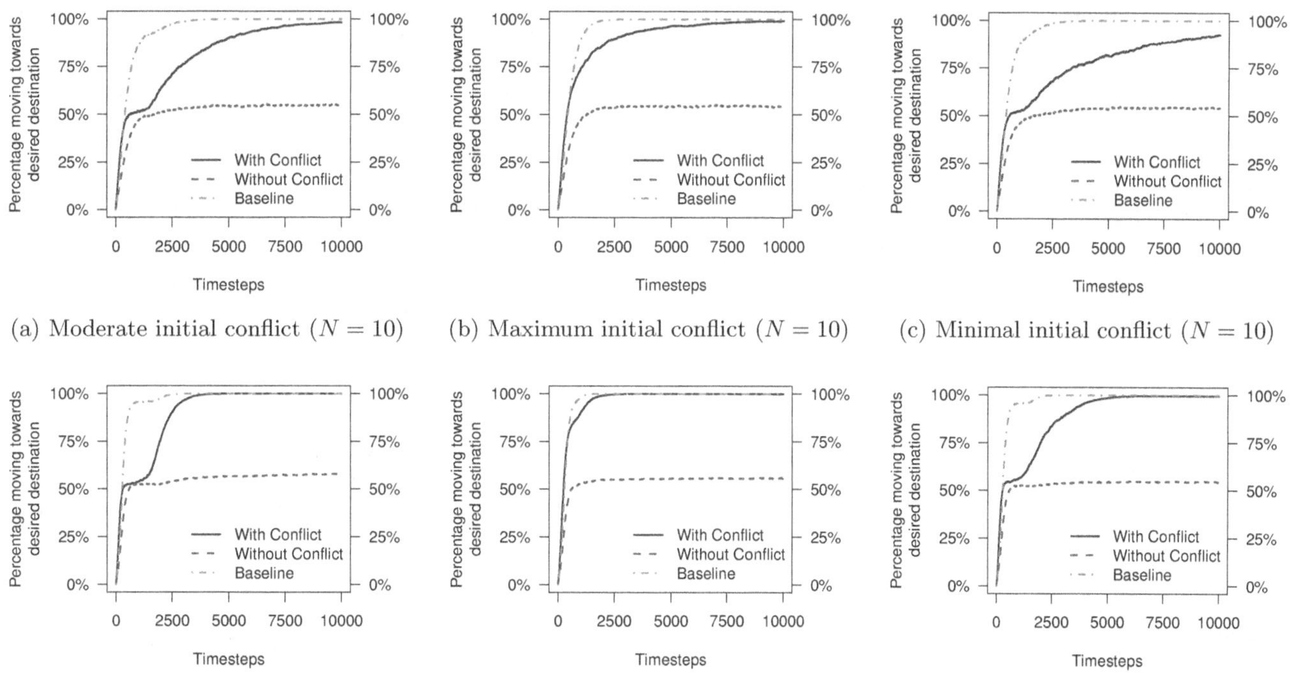

(a) Moderate initial conflict ($N = 10$) (b) Maximum initial conflict ($N = 10$) (c) Minimal initial conflict ($N = 10$)

(d) Moderate initial conflict ($N = 50$) (e) Maximum initial conflict ($N = 50$) (f) Minimal initial conflict ($N = 50$)

Figure 4: The percentage of the total number of agents moving towards their preferred destination are shown for each simulation environment and groups of size $N = 10$ and $N = 50$.

Environment	Group Size	Conflict With	Conflict Without
Moderate	10	9.9 ±0.3	5.6 ±1.1
	20	19.9 ±0.2	11.7 ±2.6
	30	29.9 ±0.2	17.8 ±4.1
	40	39.9 ±0.7	24.3 ±5.8
	50	49.9 ±0.3	30.5 ±7.1
Maximum	10	9.9 ±0.1	5.4 ±0.8
	20	19.9 ±0.1	11.1 ±1.7
	30	29.9 ±0.2	16.7 ±2.5
	40	39.9 ±0.2	22.4 ±3.2
	50	49.9 ±0.2	27.9 ±3.9
Minimal	10	9.8 ±0.7	5.4 ±0.8
	20	19.9 ±0.4	10.9 ±1.3
	30	29.9 ±0.4	16.4 ±1.8
	40	39.9 ±0.5	21.9 ±2.4
	50	49.8 ±1.0	27.2 ±2.6

Table 1: The mean number of agents that arrived at their preferred destination in each simulation are shown (mean ± std. deviation). All results for simulations with conflict are statistically significantly larger ($p << 0.0001$).

(a) Without conflict (b) With conflict

Figure 5: Representative movement histories in the environment depicted in Figure 2a are shown for simulations with and without conflict. Green and red lines depict the positions of agents having preferred destinations of A and B, respectively.

The fraction of agents that reached their preferred destination are also shown in Figure 3 for each destination. Table 1 lists the mean number of agents that arrived at their preferred destination by the end of the simulation for both destinations combined. In every environment and group size combination, simulations with conflict resulted in a statistically significantly higher number of individuals reaching their destination (Kolmogorov-Smirnov test, $p << 0.0001$). As Figure 3 shows, this difference was due to the inability of agents to successfully initiation a split from the group moving towards the other destination.

Figure 4 shows the percentage of agents that were moving towards their preferred destination over the course of a simulation. In each environment and group size combination, baseline simulations in which all agents had the same preferred destination outperformed simulations in which agents had differing preferred destinations, but no conflict. While the baseline simulations initially outperformed the conflict simulations, the addition of conflict allowed agents with a different preferred destination than the current group to eventually split and move towards their own preferred destination. This was most apparent for simulations with maximum initial conflict where most of the agents were moving towards their preferred destination soon after the start of the simulation (see Figures 4b and 4e). Simulations in the other two environments required more time for individuals preferring to go to the other destination to successfully split from the current group. As the simulations progressed, the percentage of the overall group moving towards their preferred destination increased, approaching 100% and the baseline results. As noted above, larger groups increased the likelihood of a successful initiation. This is illustrated in the "With Conflict" plots in Figures 4d, 4e and 4f where a larger percentage of the group was moving towards their preferred destination earlier in the simulation.

To illustrate the interpretation of these simulations, Figure 5 depicts the movement trajectories for agents in two representative simulations, one without conflict and one with conflict, in the environment with moderate initial conflict. More recent positions are darker and distant positions fade to gray. In the simulation without conflict, group members preferring to go to the second destination, in this case the red destination on the right, were unable to successfully split from the larger group and make it to their preferred destination. However, in the simulation with conflict, the entire group moved towards the red destination on the right, but group members preferring to go to the green destination on the left, successfully initiated a split from the group and were able to make it to their preferred destination[2].

5. DISCUSSION

Analysis of these simulation results provides a number of interesting insights. First, the addition of a simple concept of conflict was sufficient to reduce consensus costs for agents participating in collective movements. Without the addition of conflict, nearly all the agents in the group with preferences different from the consensus were unable to achieve their individual goal. In ignoring preferences of agents, a consensus decision-making can result in achieving a goal faster, but only in some cases. However, nature shows that individual preference plays a substantial factor in group movements. By integrating conflict, all of the agents were able to achieve their goals while maintaining group cohesion when possible with an acceptable increase to the time taken for the first objective to be completed.

Previous research using similar experimental methods, but with a different focus, found similar results [17]. In this other work, group cohesion was enforced, even when individuals had differing preferred directions of movement. Results showed that when the difference between preferred directions was large, the entire group moved in one of the pre-

[2]See the Supplemental Materials for videos of representative simulation runs for each environment.

ferred directions, instead of traveling in an average direction as it did when the difference was low. Since conflict was not used and cohesion was enforced, individuals were unable to avoid consensus costs.

Second, our results show that consensus costs increased as the size of the swarm was scaled up. As the group size was increased, the mean time required agents to arrive at a destination for simulations without conflict increased. Similar effects have been observed in natural systems in which the probability of a group fissioning due to consensus costs increases as the group is scaled up [32].

Lastly, these results must be tempered with the understanding that implicit in our simulations is the assumption that consensus costs were too high and individual goals must be met. There are situations in which group cohesion is paramount and individual goals are secondary. For example, if the resulting group size after a split in a natural system is too small, the agents could be at risk from predation. Furthermore, sometimes agents have incorrect information and the consensus resulting from collective decision-making minimizes these errors. Future work will expand on these findings by incorporating more authentic decision-making processes that incorporate these ideas.

6. CONCLUSIONS AND FUTURE WORK

There are two significant contributions of this work. First, these results show that the simple addition of conflict is able to balance consensus costs with individual preferences in a manner that still allows group level success, while significantly improving individual success. In simulations without conflict, only approximately half of all group members were able to achieve their individual goal. On the other hand, in simulations with conflict, almost every individual was able to achieve their individual goal. Second, the results also show that when agents in a swarm have different preferences, consensus costs can be significant to the point where agents having a different preference from the consensus will not achieve their goal. Furthermore, these consensus costs increase as the group size increases, something corroborated by observations of natural systems [32].

This work represents one aspect of a larger research effort. One of the next steps is to incorporate splitting costs into the model. The combination of consensus and splitting costs would allow us to evaluate the stability of consensus decisions and cohesion in a variety of environments. Another step is to expand our definition of conflict to a more general concept of "dissatisfaction with the current state." In simple collective movement task, this would expand the contributing factors to include variables such as time and energy. Also, agents in the swarm are currently modeled as self-propelled particles [19]. The next version of the simulator will use a more high-fidelity model for agents and include more detailed movement behaviors such as those found in flocking. Lastly, the current formulation of the movement model is not amenable to extensive parameter tuning. In the future, we wish to use a more general and tunable version of the model so we are better able to tailor the decision-making to tasks frequently assigned to robot swarms [43].

7. ACKNOWLEDGMENTS

This material is based upon work supported by the National Science Foundation under Grant No. BCS-1124837.

8. REFERENCES

[1] E. A. Archie, C. J. Moss, and S. C. Alberts. The ties that bind: Genetic relatedness predicts the fission and fusion of social groups in wild african elephants. *Proceedings of the Royal Society B: Biological Sciences*, 273(1586):513–522, 2006.

[2] N. Asensio, A. H. Korstjens, and F. Aureli. Fissioning minimizes ranging costs in spider monkeys: a multiple-level approach. *Behavioral Ecology and Sociobiology*, 63(5):649–659, 2009.

[3] F. Aureli, C. M. Schaffner, C. Boesch, S. K. Bearder, J. Call, C. A. Chapman, R. Connor, A. Di Fiore, R. I. Dunbar, S. P. Henzi, and C. P. v. Schaik. Fission–fusion dynamics: New research frameworks. *Current Anthropology*, 49(4):627–654, 2008.

[4] S. Berman, A. Halász, V. Kumar, and S. Pratt. Bio-inspired group behaviors for the deployment of a swarm of robots to multiple destinations. In *IEEE International Conference on Robotics and Automation*, pages 2318–2323. IEEE Press, 2007.

[5] N. Bode, D. Franks, and A. Wood. Leading from the front? Social networks in navigating groups. *Behavioral Ecology and Sociobiology*, 66(6):835–843, 2012.

[6] M. Brambilla, E. Ferrante, M. Birattari, and M. Dorigo. Swarm robotics: a review from the swarm engineering perspective. *Swarm Intelligence*, 7(1):1–41, 2013.

[7] L. Chaimowicz and V. Kumar. Aerial shepherds: Coordination among UAVs and swarms of robots. In R. Alami, R. Chatila, and H. Asama, editors, *Distributed Autonomous Robotic Systems 6*, pages 243–252. Springer, 2007.

[8] L. Conradt. Models in animal collective decision-making: information uncertainty and conflicting preferences. *Interface Focus*, 2(2):226–240, 2012.

[9] L. Conradt. Collective animal decisions: preference conflict and decision accuracy. *Interface Focus*, 3(6), 2013.

[10] L. Conradt, J. Krause, I. Couzin, and T. Roper. "Leading according to need" in self-organizing groups. *The American Naturalist*, 173(3):304–312, 2009.

[11] L. Conradt, C. List, and T. J. Roper. Swarm intelligence: When uncertainty meets conflict. *The American Naturalist*, 182(5):592–610, 2013.

[12] L. Conradt and T. Roper. Consensus decision making in animals. *Trends in Ecology & Evolution*, 20(8):449–456, 2005.

[13] L. Conradt and T. J. Roper. Group decision-making in animals. *Nature*, 421(6919):155–158, 2003.

[14] L. Conradt and T. J. Roper. Conflicts of interest and the evolution of decision sharing. *Philosophical Transactions of the Royal Society B: Biological Sciences*, 364(1518):807–819, 2009.

[15] I. D. Couzin, C. C. Ioannou, G. Demirel, T. Gross, C. J. Torney, A. Hartnett, L. Conradt, S. A. Levin, and N. E. Leonard. Uninformed individuals promote democratic consensus in animal groups. *Science*, 334(6062):1578–1580, 2011.

[16] I. D. Couzin and J. Krause. Self-organization and collective behavior in vertebrates. *Advances in the Study of Behavior*, 32:1–75, 2003.

[17] I. D. Couzin, J. Krause, N. R. Franks, and S. A. Levin. Effective leadership and decision-making in animal groups on the move. *Nature*, 433(7025):513–516, 2005.

[18] D. P. Croft, J. Krause, and R. James. Social networks in the guppy (*Poecilia reticulata*). *Proceedings of the Royal Society B: Biological Sciences*, 271(Suppl 6):S516–S519, 2004.

[19] A. Czirók and T. Vicsek. Collective behavior of interacting self-propelled particles. *Physica A: Statistical Mechanics and its Applications*, 281(1):17–29, 2000.

[20] P. Dasgupta and K. Cheng. Robust multi-robot team formations using weighted voting games. In *Distributed Autonomous Robotic Systems*, pages 373–387. Springer, 2013.

[21] B. E. Eskridge. Effects of local communication and topology on collective movement initiation. In *International Conference on the Simulation and Synthesis of Living Things*, volume 13, pages 155–162, 2012.

[22] B. E. Eskridge, E. Valle, and I. Schlupp. Using experience to promote the emergence of leaders and followers. In *European Conference on Complex Systems*. Complex Systems Society, 2013.

[23] D. Fleischmann, I. O. Baumgartner, M. Erasmy, N. Gries, M. Melber, V. Leinert, M. Parchem, M. Reuter, P. Schaer, S. Stauffer, et al. Female Bechstein's Bats adjust their group decisions about communal roosts to the level of conflict of interests. *Current Biology*, 23(17):1658–1662, 2013.

[24] J. Gautrais. The hidden variables of leadership. *Behavioural Processes*, 84(3):664–667, 2010.

[25] C. Hemelrijk and H. Hildenbrandt. Self-organized shape and frontal density of fish schools. *Ethology*, 114(3):245–254, 2008.

[26] M. A. Hsieh, Á. Halász, S. Berman, and V. Kumar. Biologically inspired redistribution of a swarm of robots among multiple sites. *Swarm Intelligence*, 2(2-4):121–141, 2008.

[27] G. Kerth and B. König. Fission, fusion and nonrandom associations in female bechstein's bats (*Myotis bechsteinii*). *Behaviour*, 136(9):1187–1202, 1999.

[28] A. J. King, C. Douglas, E. Huchard, N. J. Isaac, and G. Cowlishaw. Dominance and affiliation mediate despotism in a social primate. *Current Biology*, 18(23):1833–1838, 2008.

[29] J. Lehmann and C. Boesch. To fission or to fusion: effects of community size on wild chimpanzee (*Pan troglodytes verus*) social organisation. *Behavioral Ecology and Sociobiology*, 56(3):207–216, 2004.

[30] N. E. Leonard, T. Shen, B. Nabet, L. Scardovi, I. D. Couzin, and S. A. Levin. Decision versus compromise for animal groups in motion. *Proceedings of the National Academy of Sciences*, 109(1):227–232, 2012.

[31] B. Majolo, A. de Bortoli Vizioli, and G. Schino. Costs and benefits of group living in primates: group size effects on behaviour and demography. *Animal Behaviour*, 76(4):1235–1247, 2008.

[32] P. Michelena, A. M. Sibbald, H. W. Erhard, and J. E. McLeod. Effects of group size and personality on social foraging: The distribution of sheep across patches. *Behavioral Ecology*, 20(1):145–152, 2009.

[33] M. Nagy, Z. Ákos, D. Biro, and T. Vicsek. Hierarchical group dynamics in pigeon flocks. *Nature*, 464(7290):890–893, 2010.

[34] H. C. Pearson. Influences on dusky dolphin (*Lagenorhynchus obscurus*) fission–fusion dynamics in Admiralty Bay, New Zealand. *Behavioral Ecology and Sociobiology*, 63(10):1437–1446, 2009.

[35] O. Petit and R. Bon. Decision-making processes: The case of collective movements. *Behavioural Processes*, 64(3):635–647, 2010.

[36] O. Petit, J. Gautrais, J.-B. Leca, G. Theraulaz, and J.-L. Deneubourg. Collective decision-making in white-faced capuchin monkeys. *Proceedings of the Royal Society B: Biological Sciences*, 276(1672):3495–3503, 2009.

[37] M.-H. Pillot, J. Gautrais, P. Arrufat, I. D. Couzin, R. Bon, and J.-L. Deneubourg. Scalable rules for coherent group motion in a gregarious vertebrate. *PLoS ONE*, 6(1):e14487, 01 2011.

[38] L. W. Pyritz, C. Fichtel, E. Huchard, and P. M. Kappeler. Determinants and outcomes of decision-making, group coordination and social interactions during a foraging experiment in a wild primate. *PloS One*, 8(1):e53144, 2013.

[39] A. Rosenfeld, G. A. Kaminka, and S. Kraus. A study of scalability properties in robotic teams. In P. Scerri, R. Vincent, and R. Mailler, editors, *Coordination of Large-scale Multiagent Systems*, pages 27–51. Springer, 2006.

[40] E. Şahin. Swarm robotics: From sources of inspiration to domains of application. In *Swarm robotics*, volume 3342 of *Lecture Notes in Computer Science*, pages 10–20. Springer, 2005.

[41] T. D. Seeley. *Honeybee Democracy*. Princeton University Press, 2010.

[42] J. E. Smith, J. M. Kolowski, K. E. Graham, S. E. Dawes, and K. E. Holekamp. Social and ecological determinants of fission–fusion dynamics in the spotted hyaena. *Animal Behaviour*, 76(3):619–636, 2008.

[43] C. Sueur and J. Deneubourg. Self-organization in primates: Understanding the rules underlying collective movements. *International Journal of Primatology*, 32(6):1413–1432, 2011.

[44] C. Sueur, A. J. King, L. Conradt, G. Kerth, D. Lusseau, C. Mettke-Hofmann, C. M. Schaffner, L. Williams, D. Zinner, and F. Aureli. Collective decision-making and fission–fusion dynamics: a conceptual framework. *Oikos*, 120(11):1608–1617, 2011.

[45] C. Sueur and O. Petit. Shared or unshared consensus decision in macaques? *Behavioural Processes*, 78(1):84–92, 2008.

[46] D. J. Sumpter and S. C. Pratt. Quorum responses and consensus decision making. *Philosophical Transactions of the Royal Society B: Biological Sciences*, 364(1518):743–753, 2009.

Ant Colony Optimization with Group Learning

Gunnar Völkel
Theoretical Computer Science
Ulm University
gunnar.voelkel@uni-ulm.de

Markus Maucher
Medical Systems Biology
Ulm University
markus.maucher@uni-ulm.de

Uwe Schöning
Theoretical Computer Science
Ulm University
uwe.schoening@uni-ulm.de

Hans A. Kestler*
Medical Systems Biology
Ulm University
hans.kestler@uni-ulm.de

ABSTRACT

We introduce Group Learning for Ant Colony Optimization applied to combinatorial optimization problems with group-structured solution encodings. In contrast to the common assignment of one pheromone value per solution component in Group Learning each solution component has one pheromone value per group. Hence, the algorithm has the possibility to learn the optimal group membership of the components. We present different strategies for Group Learning and evaluate these in simulation experiments for the Vehicle Routing Problem with Time Windows using the problem instances of Solomon [10]. We describe a revised Ant Colony System (ACS) algorithm which does not use a local pheromone update while maintaining the general ideas of ACS. We evaluate the revised ACS experimentally comparing it to the original ACS. Our experimental results show that Group Learning is a valuable modification for Ant Colony Optimization. Additionally, the results indicate that the revised ACS performs at least as well as the original algorithms.

Categories and Subject Descriptors

I.2.8 [**Artificial Intelligence**]: Problem Solving, Control Methods, and Search – heuristic methods

General Terms

Algorithms

Keywords

ant algorithms, combinatorial optimization, transportation, empirical study

*corresponding author

GECCO'14, July 12–16, 2014, Vancouver, BC, Canada.

http://dx.doi.org/10.1145/2576768.2598214.

1. INTRODUCTION

The Ant Colony Optimization (ACO) metaheuristic is a class of algorithms, inspired by the foraging behavior of ants, which is used to solve combinatorial optimization problems. These optimization problems originate from different scientific disciplines (computer science, operations research or engineering). Many important combinatorial optimization problems are NP-hard. For these problems the best known algorithms have a worst-case runtime to find an optimal solution which grows exponentially in terms of the problem instance size.

A combinatorial optimization problem (COP, w.l.o.g. minimization) in terms of decision variables X_i ($i \in \{1, \ldots, N\}$) with finite domains $\mathcal{D}_i = \mathcal{D}(X_i)$ and an objective function $f : \mathcal{D}_1 \times \cdots \times \mathcal{D}_N \to \mathbb{R}$ is specified by the following properties

$$\begin{array}{rcl} f(X_1, \ldots, X_N) & \to & \min \\ \omega(X_1, \ldots, X_N) & = & \texttt{true}, \quad \forall \omega \in \Omega \\ X_i & \in & \mathcal{D}_i, \quad\quad i \in \{1, \ldots, N\} \end{array},$$

using additional constraints $\omega \in \Omega$ with $\omega : \mathcal{D}_1 \times \cdots \times \mathcal{D}_N \to \{\texttt{true}, \texttt{false}\}$ which restrict the set of feasible solutions. In other words the task is to find a feasible assignment $(X_1 = c_{1j_1}, \ldots, X_N = c_{Nj_N})$ for the variables $X_1, \ldots, X_N$ such that $f(X_1, \ldots, X_N)$ is minimized. It is assumed that the objective function f and the constraints ω can be computed efficiently (i.e. in polynomial time) for a given (partial) assignment. A feasible assignment is called a feasible solution s of the combinatorial optimization problem and the values c_{ij} are called solution components. A partial assignment $s' = (X_{i_1} = c_{i_1 j_{i_1}}, \ldots, X_{i_k} = c_{i_k j_{i_k}})$ is called a partial solution of the COP. A partial solution $s' = (X_{i_1} = c_{i_1 j_{i_1}}, \ldots, X_{i_k} = c_{i_k j_{i_k}})$ is called feasible if all constraints $\omega \in \Omega$ hold for the partial assignment. The set of solution components that can be added to a partial solution s' resulting in another partial solution is called the set of feasible components $C_\Omega(s')$. The brief notation $s = (c_{1j_1}, \ldots, c_{Nj_N})$ is used for solutions in the following.

The class of probabilistic construction algorithms named Ant Colony Optimization usually assigns a pheromone value $\tau_{ij} \in \mathbb{R}^+$ to each solution component c_{ij}. The pheromone value represents the desirability to choose this component during the solution construction. In the search process a predefined number of solutions is constructed per iteration. The solution construction adds solution components incrementally which are selected randomly with a probability proportional to the pheromone value of the particular component. After each iteration the pheromone values are updated. In many ACO variants the pheromone values of components in the best-so-far solution are increased while the pheromone values of the remaining components are decreased [5, 6]. Usually, the runtime of the algorithm is limited to a predefined number of iterations or a predefined period of time. A general description of Ant Colony Optimization can be found in [5, 6].

The linear solution encoding used by most ACO variants is not optimal for combinatorial optimization problems with solutions that are sub-structured into groups of solution components like the Vehicle Routing Problem with Time Windows [11]. We introduced Group-based Ant Colony Optimization (GB-ACO) [11] which uses a parallel construction principle based on a group-based solution encoding that is better suited for these kinds of problems. However, most ACO variants and GB-ACO share the mapping of solution components c_{ij} to pheromone values[1] τ_{ij}, which enables only local learning of the desirability of component c_{ij}. This paper introduces Ant Colony Optimization with Group Learning (ACO-GL) as an extension of Group-based Ant Colony Optimization. ACO-GL uses pheromone values[2] τ_{ijg} to represent the desirability that the corresponding component c_{ij} shall occur in group g. Hence, ACO-GL is also able to learn structural information additionally to the local information. In this paper a revised variant of Ant Colony System [4] is described and evaluated experimentally Finally, a combination of Ant Colony System and Group Learning (ACS-GL) is introduced and evaluated.

The paper is organized as follows. In Section 2 Ant Colony Optimization with Group Learning is described. The application of Group-based Ant Colony Optimization to the Vehicle Routing Problem with Time Windows (VRPTW) is explained first. Then the idea of group learning and the associated group learning strategies are described. Additionally, after a description of Ant Colony System two revised variants of Ant Colony System are introduced. Finally, Ant Colony System with Group Learning is defined. Section 3 contains the description of the experimental evaluation of the presented algorithms on the VRPTW followed by Section 4 with a discussion of the results.

2. ANT COLONY OPTIMIZATION WITH GROUP LEARNING

In this section the ACO metaheuristic is explained using the algorithm Group-Based Ant Colony Optimization (GB-ACO) [11] which is applied to the Vehicle Routing Problem with Time Windows (VRPTW). Then the algorithm Ant Colony Optimization with Group Learning (ACO-GL) is introduced as an extension of GB-ACO. Subsequently, the two variants of Ant Colony System are described and based on that two revised (global) pheromone update rules are presented. Finally, the combination of the ideas of ACS and ACO-GL is defined.

[1]Usual pheromone matrix for ACO when using construction graph $G_C = (V, E)$: $\tau \in (\mathbb{R}^+)^{|V|\times|V|}$

[2]Pheromone matrix for ACO with group learning with at most M groups: $\tau \in (\mathbb{R}^+)^{|V|\times|V|\times M}$

2.1 GB-ACO for the VRPTW

The Vehicle Routing Problem with Time Windows is a generalization of the Traveling Salesman Problem and defined as follows. Given a set of customers v_i each situated at location l_i $(i \in \{1, \ldots, N\})$ with a given demanded quantity q_i of a product and a depot v_{N+1} at location l_{N+1} the Vehicle Routing Problem with Time Windows is the problem to distribute the product quantities to all customers within their given time windows $[b_i, e_i]$ using a minimal number of vehicles with capacity C. Minimizing the total travel distance of all vehicles is a secondary goal.[3] For each customer v_i the delivery lasts for a service duration Δs_i and must start within the customer's time window. For each pair of locations (l_i, l_j) the distance d_{ij} and travel duration Δt_{ij} between them is specified. At most M vehicles are allowed to solve the VRPTW. A lexicographic order $\prec$ is used to compare two solutions. Let $N_V(s)$ be the number of vehicles used in solution s and $\Sigma d(s)$ the corresponding total travel distance. Then $s_1 \prec s_2$ if and only if

$$\begin{aligned} & N_V(s1) < N_V(s_2) \\ \vee \quad & \big(N_V(s_1) = N_V(s_2) \ \wedge \ \Sigma d(s_1) < \Sigma d(s_2)\big) \ . \end{aligned}$$

A survey on the Vehicle Routing Problem with Time Windows can be found in [2].

To apply Ant Colony Optimization to the VRPTW the construction graph $G_C = (V, E)$ is used with vertices $V = \{v_1, \ldots, v_N, v_{N+1}, \ldots, v_{N+M}\}$ where v_i $(i \in \{1, \ldots, N\})$ represents the i-th customer at location l_i and v_{N+j} $(j \in \{1, \ldots, M\})$ is a start node of the j-th vehicle at the depot location. A solution to the VRPTW is encoded as at most M paths through the graph each starting at one of the vehicle nodes $v_{N+1}, \ldots, v_{N+M}$ such that every customer node is visited in one of the paths. Thereby, the capacity constraint must be satisfied on every path as well as the time window constraints. The underlying construction graph was first described in [7].

Group-Based Ant Colony Optimization [11] employs a group-based solution encoding and a parallel construction principle. Solutions are encoded as a set of groups which contain the solution components formally written as

$$\begin{aligned} s &= (g_1, g_2, \ldots, g_M) \\ g_a &= (c_{a,1}, c_{a,2}, \ldots, c_{a,l_a}) , \quad 1 \le a \le M \ . \end{aligned}$$

In terms of the VRPTW a group g_i containing solution components corresponds to a tour t_i of a vehicle and each tour is defined by the visiting order of its customers:

$$\begin{aligned} s &= \overbrace{(g_1, g_2, \ldots, g_M)}^{=(t_1, t_2, \ldots, t_M)} \\ g_a &= (v_{N+i_a}, v_{j_{a,1}}, v_{j_{a,2}}, \ldots, v_{j_{a,l_a}}), \quad 1 \le a \le M \ . \end{aligned}$$

GB-ACO constructs the groups of a solution in parallel, i.e. a group is selected randomly with a probability proportional to the pheromone sum of its feasible components and then the component to add is selected randomly with a probability proportional to its pheromone value from the corresponding feasible components. For a given partial solution

$$\begin{aligned} s_k &= (g_{1,k}, \ldots, g_{M,k}) \\ g_{a,k} &= (c_{i_{a,1} j_{a,1}}, c_{i_{a,2} j_{a,2}}, \ldots, c_{i_{a,l_k} j_{a,l_k}}), \quad 1 \le a \le M \end{aligned}$$

[3]In early research the minimization of total travel distance was the primary goal.

the set of feasible components $C_\Omega(s_k, g_{a,k})$ for a group $g_{a,k}$ is defined as the set of components which can be added to this group resulting in a feasible partial solution. Using the pheromone values τ_{ij} and the problem-specific heuristic values η_{ij} for the solution components c_{ij} the probability to select the group $g_{a,k}$ is defined as

$$P(g_{a,k} \mid s_k) = \frac{\sum\limits_{c_{ij} \in C_\Omega(s_k, g_{a,k})} \tau_{ij}^\beta \cdot \eta_{ij}^\alpha}{\sum\limits_{q=1}^{M} \sum\limits_{c_{uv} \in C_\Omega(s_k, g_{q,k})} \tau_{uv}^\beta \cdot \eta_{uv}^\alpha} \qquad (1)$$

and the probability to select a feasible component $c_{i_{k+1}, j_{k+1}}$ of $C_\Omega(s_k, g_{a,k})$ for the selected group $g_{a,k}$ is

$$P(c_{i_{k+1}, j_{k+1}} \mid s_k, g_{a,k}) = \frac{\tau_{i_{k+1} j_{k+1}}^\beta \cdot \eta_{i_{k+1} j_{k+1}}^\alpha}{\sum_{c_{ij} \in C_\Omega(s_k, g_{a,k})} \tau_{ij}^\beta \cdot \eta_{ij}^\alpha} . \qquad (2)$$

For the application to the VRPTW in this paper we use $\eta_{ij} = d_{ij}^{-1}$. Similar to many other ACO algorithms GB-ACO uses weights $\alpha, \beta \in \mathbb{N}^+$ in the component ratings $\tau_{ij}^\beta \cdot \eta_{ij}^\alpha$ to adjust the influence of the heuristic values and pheromone values.[4] GB-ACO uses a fixed number of groups. For the VRPTW the exponential empty group punishment is used to guide the algorithm to solutions with a minimal number of used vehicles [11]. Using the modified value $p(\Sigma\tau, N_G, N_\emptyset)$ instead of $\Sigma\tau = \sum_{c_{ij} \in C_\Omega(s_n, g_{a,n})} \tau_{ij} \cdot \eta_{ij}$ in $P(g_{a,n} \mid s_n)$ is called *empty group punishment*. Exponential group punishment is defined by the function $p_{\exp}(\Sigma\tau, M, M_\emptyset) = \frac{\Sigma\tau}{10^{M - M_\emptyset}}$ where $M_\emptyset$ is the number of empty groups at the time when the probabilities are calculated. When solving VRPTW with GB-ACO a fitness proportional pheromone strategy is used with the pheromone initialization

$$\forall i, j : \tau_{ij} = g(s') = \frac{1}{(N + M) \cdot d(s')}, \quad d(s) = \sum_{c_{ij} \in s} d_{ij} ,$$

where s' is an initial solution constructed by a nearest neighbor heuristic. The initial pheromone value for all solution components is denoted as τ_0. The pheromone update is defined as

$$\tau_{ij}(n+1) = (1 - \rho) \cdot \tau_{ij}(n) + \begin{cases} \rho \cdot \mathsf{R}(\hat{s}(n)), & c_{ij} \in \hat{s}(n) \\ 0, & \text{otherwise} \end{cases} ,$$

where $\mathsf{R}(\hat{s}(n))$ is a reward for the components occurring in the best-so-far solution. For the VRPTW the fitness-proportional reward $\mathsf{R}(\hat{s}(n)) = \frac{1}{d(s(n))}$ is used.

With the choices mentioned before, Algorithm 1 describes GB-ACO. The algorithm performs N_I iterations constructing N_S solutions each. Local search can be applied to the constructed solutions if specified. The function PruneGraph removes the depot nodes that are not used in s' from the construction graph G_C. The probabilistic solution construction is described in Algorithm 2. The data structure containing the feasible components $C_\Omega(s_k, g)$ for every group g of the partial solution s_k is called the solution neighborhood $\mathcal{N}(s_k)$. Using the solution neighborhood $\mathcal{N}(s_k)$ the algorithm avoids to recalculate all sets of feasible components $C_\Omega(s_k, g)$ completely in each iteration by just updating the affected group and single components in the remaining groups. If the neighborhood $\mathcal{N}(s_k)$ of the current solution s_k is empty and unvisited nodes remain, the algorithm will try to repair s_k with a greedy completion heuristic [11].

[4]In contrast to previous work we named the weight for the heuristic value α due to our experiments with different pheromone structures.

Algorithm 1: Generic ACO

$\hat{s}(0) = s' =$ CreateInitialSolution(G_C) ;
$G'_C = (V', E') =$ PruneGraph(s', G_C) ;
$\tau_{ij}(0) = g(s') \quad \forall (i,j) \in E'$;
for $n = 1, \ldots, N_I$ **do**
  for $l = 1, \ldots, N_S$ **do**
    $s^l =$ SolutionConstruction($G'_C, \tau(n-1)$) ;
    if *local search enabled and* $\Omega(s^l) =$ **true then**
      $s^l =$ Improve(s^l) ;
  $S_\Omega = \{s \in \{s^1, \ldots, s^{N_S}\} \mid \Omega(s) = \mathbf{true}\}$;
  $\hat{s}(n) = \arg\min\{f(s) \mid s \in S_\Omega \cup \{\hat{s}(n-1)\}\}$;
  $\tau(n) =$ PheromoneUpdate($\hat{s}(n), \tau(n-1)$) ;
return $\hat{s}(N_I)$;

Algorithm 2: SolutionConstruction

$s_0 =$ CreateEmptySolution(G_C) ;
$\mathcal{N}(s_0) =$ InitializeNeighborhood(s_0) ;
$\mathcal{U}_0 =$ DetermineUnvisitedNodes(s_0) ;
$k = 0$;
while $\mathcal{U}_k \neq \emptyset$ **do**
  if $\mathcal{N}(s_k) = \emptyset$ **then return** TryCompletion($\mathcal{U}_k, s_k$);
  Choose $(g_a, c_{ij}) \in \mathcal{N}(s_k)$ with $P((g_a, c_{ij}) \mid s_k)$;
  $s_{k+1} =$ ModifySolution(s_k, g_a, c_{ij}) ;
  $\mathcal{U}_{k+1} = \mathcal{U}_k \setminus \{j\}$;
  $\mathcal{N}(s_{k+1}) =$ UpdateNeighborhood($\mathcal{U}_{k+1}, g_a, c_{ij}, \mathcal{N}(s_k)$);
  $k = k + 1$;
return s_k;

2.2 ACO with Group Learning

The probabilistic component selection of GB-ACO selects a group g and a corresponding component c_{ij} based on the current state of the pheromone matrix $\tau \in (\mathbb{R}^+)^{|V| \times |V|}$ which contains one pheromone value τ_{uv} for each component c_{uv}. In plain ACO the pheromone values τ_{ij} represent the desirability to use the solution components c_{ij}. The idea of *group learning* uses a pheromone matrix $\tau \in (\mathbb{R}^+)^{|V| \times |V| \times M}$ with pheromone values τ_{ijg} which represent the desirability to add the solution component c_{ij} to the group g. Therefore, the probability for selecting a group from Equation (1) is modified to

$$P(g_{a,k} \mid s_k) = \frac{\sum\limits_{c_{ij} \in C_\Omega(s_k, g_{a,k})} \tau_{ijg_{a,k}}^\beta \cdot \eta_{ij}^\alpha}{\sum\limits_{q=1}^{M} \sum\limits_{c_{uv} \in C_\Omega(s_k, g_{q,k})} \tau_{uvg_{q,k}}^\beta \cdot \eta_{uv}^\alpha} \qquad (3)$$

and the probability to select a component for the selected group from Equation (2) is changed to

$$P(c_{i_{k+1},j_{k+1}} \mid s_k, g_{a,k}) = \frac{\tau^{\beta}_{i_{k+1}j_{k+1}g_{a,k}} \cdot \eta^{\alpha}_{i_{k+1}j_{k+1}}}{\sum\limits_{c_{ij} \in C_\Omega(s_k, g_{a,k})} \tau^{\beta}_{ijg_{a,k}} \cdot \eta^{\alpha}_{ij}} \quad (4)$$

Let $\mathbb{U}_v$ denote the pheromone update rule with $\tau_{ijg}(n+1) = \mathbb{U}_v(\tau_{ijg}, \hat{s}(n), \rho)$. This pheromone update rule needs to be adjusted for group learning as well. The simple extension of the pheromone rule used in GB-ACO is

$$\mathbb{U}_{\text{simple}}(\tau_{ijg}, \hat{s}, \rho) = (1-\rho) \cdot \tau_{ijg} + \begin{cases} \rho \cdot \mathsf{R}(\hat{s}), & (c_{ij}, g) \in \hat{s} \\ 0, & \text{otherwise} \end{cases},$$

where $(c_{ij}, g) \in \hat{s}(n)$ means that the solution component c_{ij} is member of group g in the best-so-far solution $\hat{s}(n)$. This means that in the case $(c_{ij}, g') \in \hat{s}(n)$ the pheromone value τ_{ijg} with $g \neq g'$ receives no reward. With $\mathbb{U}_{\text{simple}}$ as update rule the pheromone matrix will only reflect that component c_{ij} in group g' is a good choice but not that c_{ij} separately might be a good choice as well even in one of the other groups $g \neq g'$. Therefore, adding a reward to τ_{ijg} might be beneficial. Hence, we suggest different pheromone update rules in the following, which adhere to the form

$$\mathbb{U}_v(\tau_{ijg}, \hat{s}, \rho) = \begin{cases} (1-\rho) \cdot \tau_{ijg} + \rho \cdot \mathsf{R}(\hat{s}), & (c_{ij}, g) \in \hat{s} \\ \mathcal{R}_v(\tau_{ijg}, \mathsf{R}(\hat{s})), & (c_{ij}, g') \in \hat{s},\ g \neq g' \\ (1-\rho) \cdot \tau_{ijg}, & \text{otherwise} \end{cases},$$

where $\mathcal{R}_v$ is the distinguishing pheromone reinforcement for the other groups $g \neq g'$ between the different rules. The first rule $\mathbb{U}_{\text{part}}$ is called *partial reinforcement* and is defined with

$$\mathcal{R}_{\text{part}}(\tau, \mathsf{R}) = (1-\rho) \cdot \tau + \sigma \cdot \mathsf{R}$$

using a smaller rate σ with $0 < \sigma < \rho$ which determines the ratio of the reward that is added. The *sublearn rule* $\mathbb{U}_{\text{sub}}$ uses a second evaporation rate $\varphi \in (0,1)$ and is defined via

$$\mathcal{R}_{\text{sub}}(\tau, \mathsf{R}) = (1-\varphi) \cdot \tau + \varphi \cdot \mathsf{R}\,.$$

For $\varphi < \rho$ the sublearn rule updates the pheromone values at a slower rate compared to the update rule for the case $(c_{ij}, g) \in \hat{s}(n)$. While in the early iterations of the algorithm a larger partial reinforcement for solution components in $\hat{s}(n)$ for the groups $g \neq g'$ might be beneficial, it might distract the algorithm during the last iteration since more exploitation than exploration is needed then. Therefore, we suggest the following two time-dependent partial reinforcement rules. The *linear time-dependent partial reinforcement* rule $\mathbb{U}_{\text{lin-td}}$ is defined by

$$\mathcal{R}_{\text{lin-td}}(\tau, \mathsf{R}) = (1-\rho) \cdot \tau + \sigma_{\text{lin}}(n) \cdot \mathsf{R},$$
$$\sigma_{\text{lin}}(n) = (1 - \frac{n-1}{N_I - 1}) \cdot \sigma_B + \frac{n-1}{N_I - 1} \cdot \sigma_E$$

where $0 < \sigma_B, \sigma_E < 1$. The *exponential time-dependent partial reinforcement* rule $\mathbb{U}_{\text{exp-td}}$ is defined with

$$\mathcal{R}_{\text{exp-td}}(\tau, \mathsf{R}) = (1-\rho) \cdot \tau + \sigma_{\text{exp}}(n) \cdot \mathsf{R},$$
$$\sigma_{\text{exp}}(n) = \sigma_0 \cdot 2^{-\frac{n-1}{t_{1/2}}}$$

where $0 < \sigma_0 < 1$ and the half-life $t_{1/2} \in \mathbb{N}^+$. Summarizing, *Ant Colony Optimization with Group Learning* (ACO-GL) is an extension of Group-based Ant Colony Optimization (GB-ACO) using the group learning idea described above. Since the pheromone update rules differentiate the variants of ACO-GL the variant using $\mathbb{U}_v$ is named ACO-GL$_v$ accordingly ($v \in \{\text{simple}, \text{part}, \text{sub}, \text{lin-td}, \text{exp-td}\}$).

2.3 Ant Colony System

Ant Colony System [4] differs from the ACO algorithms described previously in several aspects. ACS chooses components via the *pseudo-random proportional rule*, i. e. for a given partial solution $s_k = (c_{i_1,j_1}, c_{i_2,j_2}, \ldots, c_{i_k,j_k})$ using a linear solution encoding ACS chooses with probability $q_0 \in (0,1)$ the component $c_{i_{k+1},j_{k+1}}$ via

$$c_{i_{k+1},j_{k+1}} = \arg\max\{\tau_{ij} \cdot \eta_{ij} \mid c_{ij} \in C_\Omega(s_k)\}$$

and with probability $(1-q_0)$ a probabilistic selection is performed to choose $c_{i_{k+1},j_{k+1}}$ with probability

$$P(c_{i_{k+1},j_{k+1}} \mid s_k) = \frac{\tau^{\beta}_{i_{k+1}j_{k+1}} \cdot \eta^{\alpha}_{i_{k+1}j_{k+1}}}{\sum_{c_{ij} \in C_\Omega(s_k)} \tau^{\beta}_{ij} \cdot \eta^{\alpha}_{ij}}\,.$$

The random decision with q_0 selects between *exploitation* and *exploration*. The pheromone update of ACS is split into a local and a global pheromone update. The *local pheromone update* is performed immediately after a component c_{ij} is added to the solution to reduce its pheromone value by

$$\tau_{ij}(n+1) = (1-\rho) \cdot \tau_{ij}(n) + \rho \cdot \tau_0\,.$$

The *global pheromone update* is performed after all solutions of iteration n have been completed and the new best-so-far solution $\hat{s}(n)$ has been determined. Only the components c_{ij} of the best-so-far solution receive the following fitness-proportional reward

$$\tau_{ij}(n+1) = (1-\xi) \cdot \tau_{ij}(n) + \xi \cdot \mathsf{R}(\hat{s}(n))$$

with a different evaporation rate $\xi \in (0,1)$. ACS uses a *simultaneous solution construction*, i.e. one component is added to each solution iteratively before adding a second component to any of the solutions. This is in contrast to a *complete solution construction* (as in GB-ACO) where one solution is constructed completely before the construction of another solution is started. The effect of the simultaneous construction combined with the local pheromone update is that a component selected in a previous solution is chosen less likely for the next solutions. When the complete construction is used, there is no such influence on the construction of the first solution in the current iteration. The local update after the construction of a solution has a similar effect on the construction of the following solutions: components used in early solutions are less likely chosen for later solutions.

The MACS-VRPTW [7] algorithm uses a complete solution construction in contrast to the simultaneous solution construction of its predecessor ACS. Hence, the algorithm performs the local update for all components of the current solution before constructing the next solution. For the pheromone updates MACS-VRPTW uses the evaporation rate ρ for both updates: global and local.

This raises the question whether there is a significant difference between these two construction principles in terms of solution quality. This question leads to a subsequent question whether the local pheromone updates (after component addition or individual solution construction) are necessary for the solution quality of ACS. Therefore, we define two ACS variants $\mathtt{ACS}_{\mathrm{rev},1}$ and $\mathtt{ACS}_{\mathrm{rev},\Sigma}$ which do not use separate local pheromone update but modify the global pheromone update to include the pheromone evaporation of solution components used in the solution construction. The pheromone reinforcement function $\widehat{\mathcal{R}}(\tau, s)$ for components in the best-so-far solution and the pheromone evaporation function $\mathcal{E}(\tau)$ are defined as

$$\begin{aligned}\widehat{\mathcal{R}}(\tau, s) &= (1-\rho)\cdot\tau + \rho\cdot\mathsf{R}(s), \qquad \tau\in\mathbb{R}^+\\ \mathcal{E}(\tau) &= (1-\rho)\cdot\tau + \rho\cdot\tau_0\,.\end{aligned}$$

Let $\mathbb{1}_s(c_{ij})$ be the indicator function whether component c_{ij} occurs in solution s, $\Delta s(n)$ the set of solutions constructed in iteration n and $\mathbb{1}_{\Delta s(n)}(c_{ij}) = \sum_{s\in\Delta s(n)} \mathbb{1}_s(c_{ij})$ Then $\mathtt{ACS}_{\mathrm{rev},1}$ is the variant that applies the evaporation function only once to solution components that were used at least once in the current iteration. Its pheromone update is defined as follows

$$\tau_{ij}(n+1) = \begin{cases}\widehat{\mathcal{R}}\big(\tau_{ij}(n),\, \hat{s}(n)\big), & c_{ij}\in\hat{s}(n),\ \mathbb{1}_{\Delta s(n)}(c_{ij}) = 0\\ \widehat{\mathcal{R}}\big(\mathcal{E}(\tau_{ij}(n)),\, \hat{s}(n)\big), & c_{ij}\in\hat{s}(n),\ \mathbb{1}_{\Delta s(n)}(c_{ij}) \geq 1\\ \mathcal{E}\big(\tau_{ij}(n)\big), & c_{ij}\notin\hat{s}(n),\ \mathbb{1}_{\Delta s(n)}(c_{ij}) \geq 1\\ \tau_{ij}(n), & c_{ij}\notin\hat{s}(n),\ \mathbb{1}_{\Delta s(n)}(c_{ij}) = 0\end{cases}.$$

The last case corresponds to components that neither have been used in the solution construction of the current iteration nor occur in the current best-so-far solution. The second variant $\mathtt{ACS}_{\mathrm{rev},\Sigma}$ applies the evaporation function t times to components used in the current iteration where t is the number of solutions they are part of. This is defined by the following pheromone update

$$\tau_{ij}(n+1) = \begin{cases}\widehat{\mathcal{R}}\big(\tau_{ij}(n),\, \hat{s}(n)\big), & c_{ij}\in\hat{s}(n),\ \mathbb{1}_{\Delta s(n)}(c_{ij}) = 0\\ \widehat{\mathcal{R}}\big(\mathcal{E}^{(t)}(\tau_{ij}(n)),\, \hat{s}(n)\big), & c_{ij}\in\hat{s}(n),\ \mathbb{1}_{\Delta s(n)}(c_{ij}) = t\\ \mathcal{E}^{(t)}\big(\tau_{ij}(n)\big), & c_{ij}\notin\hat{s}(n),\ \mathbb{1}_{\Delta s(n)}(c_{ij}) = t\\ \tau_{ij}(n), & c_{ij}\notin\hat{s}(n),\ \mathbb{1}_{\Delta s(n)}(c_{ij}) = 0\end{cases},$$

where $\mathcal{E}^{(t)} = \mathcal{E}\circ\cdots\circ\mathcal{E}$ is the t-fold function composition of $\mathcal{E}$. ACS uses the pseudo-random proportional rule together with a pheromone update that only updates solution components that are either used in the current iteration or part of the best-so-far solution in contrast to the common rule [6] that updates the pheromone values of all components. To check whether the pseudo-random proportional rule in combination with a pheromone update of all components performs well in comparison to the ACS variants, we define $\mathtt{ACO}_{\mathrm{pseudo}}$ which uses this component selection rule, a linear solution encoding and a sequential construction, i.e. `ClassicACO` from [11] with the pseudo-random proportional rule.

2.4 Ant Colony System with Group Learning

Since Ant Colony System and the idea of group learning are not mutually exclusive, a combination of both suggests itself. Therefore, the probabilistic component selection and the pheromone update of `ACO-GL` need to be adjusted. The component selection of `ACO-GL` is adapted to perform the random exploitation versus exploration decision and use the component selection of `ACO-GL` (Equations (3), (4)) in the exploration step. The pheromone update rules of ACS must be adjusted to handle the case when updating c_{ijg} and $(c_{ij}, g') \in \hat{s}(n)$ with $g \neq g'$. This is an additional reinforcement that can be added to the pheromone update rule, e.g. for $\mathtt{ACS}_{\mathrm{rev},\Sigma}$ the pheromone update is extended as follows

$$\tau_{ijg}(n+1) = \begin{cases}\widehat{\mathcal{R}}\big(\mathcal{E}^{(t)}(\tau_{ijg}(n)),\, \hat{s}(n)\big), & (c_{ij}, g)\in\hat{s}(n),\\ & \mathbb{1}_{\Delta s(n)}(c_{ij}, g) = t\\ \mathcal{R}_{\mathrm{v}}\big(\mathcal{E}^{(t)}(\tau_{ijg}(n)),\, \hat{s}(n)\big), & (c_{ij}, g')\in\hat{s}(n),\ g\neq g'\\ & \mathbb{1}_{\Delta s(n)}(c_{ij}, g) = t\\ \mathcal{E}^{(t)}\big(\tau_{ijg}(n)\big), & c_{ij}\notin\hat{s}(n),\\ & \mathbb{1}_{\Delta s(n)}(c_{ij}, g) = t\end{cases},$$

where $\mathcal{R}_{\mathrm{v}}$ is one of the update rules of `ACO-GL` and $\mathcal{E}^{(0)}(\tau) = \tau$ is the identity function. The indicator functions are extended such that $\mathbb{1}_s(c_{ij}, g) = 1$ if $(c_{ij}, g) \in s$ and $\mathbb{1}_s(c_{ij}, g) = 0$ otherwise. The resulting Ant Colony System with Group Learning is denoted as `ACS-GL`.

3. COMPUTATIONAL EXPERIMENTS

This section contains the experimental evaluation of the discussed algorithms on the Vehicle Routing Problem with Time Windows. The problem instances used for the experiments are the Solomon instances[5] [10]. For a fair comparison of the algorithms we use the automatic configuration method provided by the `irace` package [9] to find a good parameter configuration for each algorithm. `irace` generates different candidates of parameter configurations for the selected algorithm and then performs a race of those candidates on distinct problem instance, i.e. all candidates are run on a predefined number of instances before the first statistic test is performed to remove the worst candidates. After that the test is performed each time after all remaining candidates have been run on the next instance until the iteration budget is exhausted or only few candidates remain. Usually, multiple races are performed containing the previous best candidates and newly generated ones until the total budget is exhausted. We use multiple runs of `irace` where the first tuning is used to narrow down the search space and the subsequent tuning to find a good configuration within the smaller search space. In the first tuning the following ranges are used: different rate parameters $\rho, q_0, \sigma, \varphi, \sigma_B, \sigma_E, \sigma_0, \xi \in (0.01, 1.0)$, the weighting constant $\alpha \in \{1, \ldots, 6\}$ and the half-life $t_{1/2} \in \{1, \ldots, 1000\}$. The parameter configurations of the second tuning experiment via `irace` for all algorithms can be found in the supplement. In the comparison experiment the algorithms are run on all Solomon instances repeatedly with several parameter configurations centered around the best ones found by `irace`. Each algorithm configuration is run 100 times per instance with different seeds for the pseudo-random number generator per repetition. Finally, we perform a Friedman test (level of significance 0.05) and a corresponding post-hoc test[6] [3] to determine the best algorithm and significant relations between the compared algorithms. We follow Gambardella et

[5]The Solomon instances are available at `http://www.sintef.no/vrptw`.

[6]also used in `F-Race` [1]

al. [7] and perform all experiments with $N_S = 10$ solution constructions per iteration. To limit the computational effort we use $N_I = 100$ iterations . In the experiments no local search is used, as we want to study the group learning idea and its combination with the ideas of ACS undisturbed of additional influences.

3.1 Group Learning Strategies

This section describes the experiments to evaluate the following group learning strategies: ACO-GL$_{\text{simple}}$, ACO-GL$_{\text{part}}$, ACO-GL$_{\text{sub}}$, ACO-GL$_{\text{lin-td}}$ and ACO-GL$_{\text{exp-td}}$. Those strategies are also compared with GB-ACO and a representative of ACO algorithms with a sequential construction principle using linear solution encoding named ClassicACO. For those two algorithms the optimal parameters found in [11] are used. Based on the results in [11] $\beta = 1$ and exponential group punishment were used.

After tuning, the experiment was performed using all combinations of the parameters listed in Table 1 including the best found parameter values. Table 1 shows the best ranked configurations per algorithm determined in the comparison experiment. ACO-GL$_{\text{exp-td}}$ with the configuration listed in Table 1 is the best ranked algorithm and according to the test result significantly better than 96% of all configurations over all algorithms (Friedman test, $p < 10^{-15}$) although there is no significant distinction to the best configuration of ACO-GL$_{\text{part}}$ (significantly better than $D = 87\%$ of the all algorithm configurations). The relation between the other algorithms with their respective best configuration is as follows. ACO-GL$_{\text{exp-td}}$ and ACO-GL$_{\text{part}}$ are significantly better than the remaining algorithms with their respective best configurations. There is no significant difference between ACO-GL$_{\text{sub}}$ ($D = 81\%$) and ACO-GL$_{\text{lin-td}}$ ($D = 73\%$) but ACO-GL$_{\text{sub}}$ has a better rank. Both are significantly better than GB-ACO, ACO-GL$_{\text{simple}}$ and ClassicACO. Finally, GB-ACO is significantly better than ACO-GL$_{\text{simple}}$ which is significantly better than ClassicACO.

3.2 Revised Ant Colony System

In this section the different algorithm variants using the ideas of Ant Colony System are compared. The original ACS with the simultaneous solution construction is denoted as ACS$_{\text{sim}}$. The ACS variant using the complete solution construction of MACS-VRPTW is named ACS$_{\text{compl}}$. In contrast to MACS-VRPTW ACS$_{\text{compl}}$ uses two different evaporation rates ρ and ξ similar to ACS$_{\text{sim}}$. The two revised ACS variants are ACS$_{\text{rev},1}$ and ACS$_{\text{rev},\Sigma}$. ACO$_{\text{pseudo}}$ is the ACO variant that uses only the pseudo-random proportional rule but not the ACS specific pheromone update. The best ranked configurations found in the comparison experiment of the ACS variants are listed in Table 1. The best ranked algorithm in the experiment is ACS$_{\text{rev},\Sigma}$ with the configuration listed in Table 1. This algorithm is significantly better than 89% of all configurations over all algorithms (Friedman test, $p < 10^{-15}$). However, although ACS$_{\text{rev},\Sigma}$ is better ranked there is no significant distinction between ACS$_{\text{rev},\Sigma}$, ACS$_{\text{compl}}$ ($D = 89\%$) and ACS$_{\text{sim}}$ ($D = 57\%$) with respect to their best configurations. There is no significant distinction between the best ACS$_{\text{rev},\Sigma}$ configuration and 26% of the ACS$_{\text{compl}}$ configurations. Only the best configuration of ACS$_{\text{sim}}$ is not significantly distinguishable from the best ACS$_{\text{rev},\Sigma}$ configuration. The previously mentioned three algorithms are significantly better than ACS$_{\text{rev},1}$ which is significantly better than ACO$_{\text{pseudo}}$.

3.3 Ant Colony System with Group Learning

The experiments to evaluate the different Ant Colony System with group learning variants are described in this section. Since ACS$_{\text{rev},\Sigma}$ has been the best ranked ACS variant it has been selected to evaluate the combination of ACS with group learning resulting in the following algorithms: ACS-GL$_{\text{part}}$, ACS-GL$_{\text{sub}}$, ACS-GL$_{\text{lin-td}}$ and ACS-GL$_{\text{exp-td}}$. The best ranked configurations found in the comparison experiment of the ACS variants are listed in Table 1. The best ranked algorithm in the experiment is ACS-GL$_{\text{exp-td}}$. This algorithm is significantly better than 97% of all configurations over all algorithms (Friedman test, $p < 10^{-15}$). With respect to the individual best configurations ACS-GL$_{\text{exp-td}}$ is significantly better than the other algorithms. ACS-GL$_{\text{sub}}$ is significant better than ACS-GL$_{\text{lin-td}}$. There is no significant distinction between the best configurations of ACS-GL$_{\text{part}}$ ($D = 81\%$), ACS-GL$_{\text{sub}}$ ($D = 86\%$) and ACS-GL$_{\text{lin-td}}$ ($D = 66\%$).

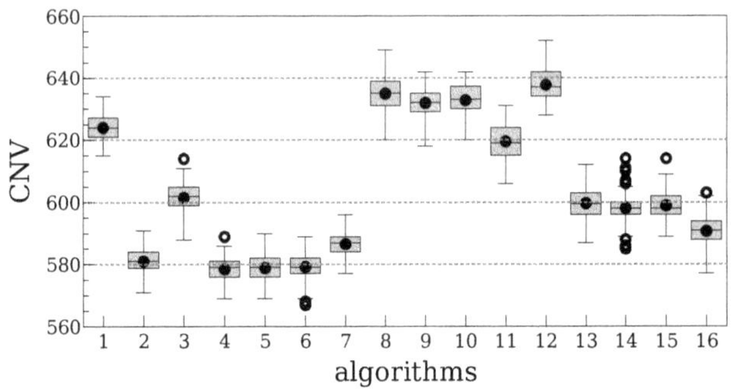

Figure 1: Cumulative number of vehicles per algorithm with the respective best found configuration. The algorithms are ordered as follows: (1) ClassicACO, (2) GB-ACO, (3) ACO-GL$_{\text{simple}}$, (4) ACO-GL$_{\text{part}}$, (5) ACO-GL$_{\text{sub}}$ (6) ACO-GL$_{\text{lin-td}}$, (7) ACO-GL$_{\text{exp-td}}$, (8) ACS$_{\text{sim}}$, (9) ACS$_{\text{compl}}$, (10) ACS$_{\text{rev},1}$, (11) ACS$_{\text{rev},\Sigma}$, (12) ACO$_{\text{pseudo}}$, (13) ACS-GL$_{\text{part}}$, (14) ACS-GL$_{\text{sub}}$, (15) ACS-GL$_{\text{lin-td}}$, (16) ACS-GL$_{\text{exp-td}}$.

4. DISCUSSION

The evaluation of the ACO algorithms with group learning confirms our assumption that it is not sufficient to only add a reward to the combination (c_{ij}, g) of the group and the component that occur in the best-so-far solution $\hat{s}(n)$. This is indicated by the results for ACO-GL$_{\text{simple}}$. In fact, the evaluation shows that a fitness-proportional, but smaller reward needs to be used for the pheromone value τ_{ijg} in the case $(c_{ij}, g') \in \hat{s}(n)$ and $g \neq g'$. We proposed four different strategies therefore. The strategy ACO-GL$_{\text{exp-td}}$ with the time-dependent exponentially decreasing rate ranked best in the evaluation but there is no statistically significant distinction to the constant rate strategy ACO-GL$_{\text{part}}$. Figure 1 shows a boxplot of the cumulative number of vehicles (CNV) for all algorithms with their particular best found parameter configuration. The CNV values of the four ACO-GL algorithms (except ACO-GL$_{\text{simple}}$) and GB-ACO are close which confirms that the group-based solution encoding is an im-

Algorithm	parameter ranges (tuning)						best found parameters						worse
	ρ	q_0	σ/φ	σ_B/σ_0	$\sigma_E/t_{1/2}$	ξ	$\rho*$	q_0^*	σ^*/φ^*	σ_B^*/σ_0^*	$\sigma_E^*/t_{1/2}^*$	ξ^*	
ClassicACO	0.01 – 0.05	–	–	–	–	–	0.03	–	–	–	–	–	75%
GB-ACO	0.04 – 0.08	–	–	–	–	–	0.06	–	–	–	–	–	50%
ACO-GL$_{simple}$	0.07 – 0.11	–	–	–	–	–	0.07	–	–	–	–	–	93%
ACO-GL$_{part}$	0.04 – 0.08	–	0.01, 0.015–0.03	–	–	–	0.07	–	0.02	–	–	–	85%
ACO-GL$_{sub}$	0.04 – 0.08	–	0.012 – 0.016	–	–	–	0.06	–	0.012	–	–	–	50%
ACO-GL$_{lin\text{-}td}$	0.05 – 0.1	–	–	0.04 – 0.1	0.04 – 0.1	–	0.07	–	–	0.04	0.04	–	99%
ACO-GL$_{exp\text{-}td}$	0.05 – 0.09	–	–	0.02, 0.03, 0.04	5, 10, 15, 20, 25	–	0.08	–	–	0.03	5	–	81%
ACS$_{sim}$	0.06 – 0.1	0.77, 0.79, 0.81, 0.83, 0.85	–	–	–	0.04 – 0.08	0.06	0.83	–	–	–	0.05	69%
ACS$_{compl}$	0.06 – 0.1	0.79, 0.81, 0.83, 0.85, 0.87	–	–	–	0.04 – 0.08	0.1	0.79	–	–	–	0.07	74%
ACS$_{rev,1}$	0.20, 0.22, 0.24, 0.26, 0.28	0.58, 0.60, 0.62, 0.64, 0.66	–	–	–	–	0.24	0.66	–	–	–	–	38%
ACS$_{rev,\Sigma}$	0.17 – 0.21	0.82, 0.84, 0.86, 0.88, 0.90	–	–	–	–	0.2	0.88	–	–	–	–	92%
ACO$_{pseudo}$	0.013 – 0.017	0.24, 0.29, 0.34, 0.39, 0.44	–	–	–	–	0.016	0.24	–	–	–	–	83%
ACS-GL$_{part}$	0.13, 0.16, 0.19, 0.22, 0.25	0.81, 0.83, 0.86	0.02 – 0.05	–	–	–	0.25	0.86	0.02	–	–	–	86%
ACS-GL$_{sub}$	0.20, 0.22, 0.24, 0.26, 0.28	0.81, 0.82, 0.84	0.01, 0.05, 0.08, 0.1	–	–	–	0.24	0.84	0.01	–	–	–	90%
ACS-GL$_{lin\text{-}td}$	0.13, 0.16, 0.19, 0.22, 0.25	0.87, 0.88, 0.90	–	0.03, 0.04, 0.05, 0.06	0.22, 0.24, 0.26, 0.28	–	0.25	0.87	–	0.03	0.28	–	87%
ACS-GL$_{exp\text{-}td}$	0.09, 0.12, 0.15, 0.18, 0.21	0.88, 0.89, 0.91	–	0.01, 0.04, 0.08, 0.09	30, 60, 70, 80	–	0.09	0.91	–	0.01	80	–	94%

Table 1: Used parameter values of the experiment. Best found parameters with percentage of other significantly worse configurations for the same algorithm (Friedman test, $p < 10^{-15}$). For α the best values determined in the tuning experiment are used: $\alpha = 5$ for ACO-GL$_{simple}$, $\alpha = 4$ for ACO-GL$_{exp\text{-}td}$, ACO$_{pseudo}$, $\alpha = 2$ for ACS$_{rev,\Sigma}$, ACS-GL$_{exp\text{-}td}$ and $\alpha = 3$ for the remaining algorithms.

provement. The fact that ACO-GL$_{exp\text{-}td}$ and ACO-GL$_{part}$ are significantly better than GB-ACO indicates that group learning leads to more robustness. The best configuration of the algorithm ACO-GL$_{lin\text{-}td}$ with the time-dependent linearly increasing or decreasing (depending on the parameters) rate is degenerated to ACO-GL$_{part}$ with $\sigma = 0.04$. Hence, it is not surprising that ACO-GL$_{lin\text{-}td}$ performs significantly worse than ACO-GL$_{part}$ with its best found rate $\sigma = 0.02$. In this case the best parameter values found by the tuning are inconsistent with the best values found in the experiment.

The revised Ant Colony System algorithm ACS$_{rev,\Sigma}$ ranked best in the evaluation but there is no significant difference between the best configurations of the algorithms ACS$_{rev,\Sigma}$, ACS$_{sim}$ and ACS$_{compl}$. Figure 1 shows that ACS$_{rev,\Sigma}$ achieves much better CNV values. The results of the evaluation also show that the idea of punishing solution components n-times provided that they were used multiple times during the construction is essential for the performance of ACS since the solutions of ACS$_{rev,1}$ are significantly worse than the solutions of ACS$_{rev,\Sigma}$, ACS$_{sim}$ and ACS$_{compl}$. The previous mentioned results indicate that no local pheromone update is needed for good solutions neither after adding a component in simultaneous construction[7] nor after constructing a solution in complete solution construction[8] provided that the global pheromone update punishes used components repeatedly, reinforces the components of the best-so-far solution and keeps the other pheromone values unchanged. Among the algorithm variants that combine group learning and Ant Colony System the algorithm ACS-GL$_{exp\text{-}td}$ ranked best. The algorithm ACS-GL$_{exp\text{-}td}$ combines the group learning strategy of ACO-GL$_{exp\text{-}td}$ with the ACS variant ACS$_{rev,\Sigma}$. The evaluation of different local search strategies to use with ACO-GL and ACS-GL is part of our future work since it is likely that

[7]Simultaneous construction as used in the original ACS [4]

[8]Complete solution construction as used in the construction of MACS-VRPTW [7]

the rewards of the improved solutions have an impact on the learn process of the group membership of solution components. Additionally, incorporation of local search will allow a fair comparison with other algorithms such as MACS-VRPTW [7]. Since there were considerable improvements in solution quality of `GB-ACO` compared to `ClassicACO` on the larger problem instances of Gehring & Homberger [8] we will evaluate the algorithms presented in this paper on those instances. None of the presented algorithms is limited to the Vehicle Routing Problem with Time Windows. Instead, they are applicable to any combinatorial optimization problem with solutions that are sub-structured into groups of solution components. Hence, the algorithms should be evaluated on other problems like Job Shop Scheduling or Cluster Analysis.

5. CONCLUSION

In this paper we introduced Ant Colony Optimization with Group Learning (`ACO-GL`) an extension of Group-based Ant Colony Optimization (`GB-ACO`). Additional to the group-based solution encoding of `GB-ACO` Ant Colony Optimization with Group Learning uses pheromone values for the combination of groups and solution components to enable the algorithm to learn the group membership of solution components. Apart from a straight forward extension of the pheromone update ($\texttt{ACO-GL}_{\text{simple}}$) we described and investigated four different strategies which do not only add rewards to the pheromone values of combinations of groups and components that are part of the best-so-far solution but also to the other groups that do not contain that component. In our experiments, $\texttt{ACO-GL}_{\text{exp-td}}$ and $\texttt{ACO-GL}_{\text{part}}$ have been significantly better than all the other `ACO-GL` variants and also significantly better than `GB-ACO`. Furthermore, we define two revised Ant Colony System algorithms and compare them experimentally with the original ACS and the construction procedure used in MACS-VRPTW. The experiment results show that the revised ACS algorithm $\texttt{ACS}_{\text{rev},\Sigma}$ does not need a local pheromone update while performing at least as well as the previous ACS algorithms. The algorithm $\texttt{ACS-GL}_{\text{exp-td}}$ is statistically significant better than the other combinations of ACS and group learning. We conclude that using group-based solution encoding can improve Ant Colony Optimization algorithms on combinatorial optimization problems with group-structures.

Acknowledgement

This work was funded partly by the German Federal Ministry of Education and Research (BMBF, Gerontosys II, Forschungskern SyStaR, project ID 0315894A) and the German Science Foundation (DFG, SFB 1074, project Z1).

6. REFERENCES

[1] M. Birattari. *The Problem of Tuning Metaheuristics as Seen from a Machine Learning Perspective*. PhD thesis, Université Libre de Bruxelles, Brussels, Belgium, 2004.

[2] O. Bräysy and M. Gendreau. Vehicle Routing Problem with Time Windows, Part I: Route Construction and Local Search Algorithms. *Transportation Science*, 39(1):104–118, 2005.

[3] W. Conover. *Practical Nonparametric Statistics*. Wiley, New York, NY, 3. edition, 1999.

[4] M. Dorigo and L. Gambardella. Ant Colony System: A cooperative learning approach to the traveling salesman problem. *IEEE Transactions on Evolutionary Computation*, 1(1):53–66, 1997.

[5] M. Dorigo and T. Stützle. *Ant Colony Optimization*. Bradford Books. MIT Press, 2004.

[6] M. Dorigo and T. Stützle. Ant Colony Optimization: Overview and Recent Advances. Technical Report TR/IRIDIA/2009-013, IRIDIA, Université Libre de Bruxelles, Brussels, Belgium, 2009.

[7] L. M. Gambardella, Éric Taillard, and G. Agazzi. MACS-VRPTW: A Multiple Colony System For Vehicle Routing Problems With Time Windows. In D. Corne, M. Dorigo, F. Glover, D. Dasgupta, P. Moscato, R. Poli, and K. V. Price, editors, *New Ideas in Optimization*, pages 63–76. McGraw-Hill, 1999.

[8] H. Gehring and J. Homberger. A parallel hybrid evolutionary metaheuristic for the vehicle routing problem with time windows. In *Proceedings of EUROGEN99 – Short Course on Evolutionary Algorithms in Engineering and Computer Science*, pages 57–64, 1999.

[9] M. López-Ibáñez, J. Dubois-Lacoste, T. Stützle, and M. Birattari. The irace package, Iterated Race for Automatic Algorithm Configuration. Technical Report TR/IRIDIA/2011-004, IRIDIA, Université Libre de Bruxelles, Belgium, 2011.

[10] M. M. Solomon. Algorithms for the vehicle routing and scheduling problems with time window constraints. *Operations Research*, 35:254–265, 1987.

[11] G. Völkel, M. Maucher, and H. A. Kestler. Group-Based Ant Colony Optimization. In *Proceedings of the Fifteenth Annual Conference on Genetic and Evolutionary Computation*, GECCO '13, pages 121–128, New York, NY, USA, 2013. ACM.

Anticipatory Stigmergic Collision Avoidance under Noise

Friedrich Burkhard von der Osten
Department of Computing & Information Systems
The University of Melbourne
Victoria 3010, Australia
fvon@student.unimelb.edu.au

Michael Kirley
Department of Computing & Information Systems
The University of Melbourne
Victoria 3010, Australia
mkirley@unimelb.edu.au

Tim Miller
Department of Computing & Information Systems
The University of Melbourne
Victoria 3010, Australia
tmiller@unimelb.edu.au

ABSTRACT

Reactive path planning to avoid collisions with moving obstacles enables more robust agent systems. However, many solutions assume that moving objects are *passive*; that is, they do not consider that the moving objects are themselves re-planning to avoid collisions, and thus may change their trajectory. In this paper we present a model, *Anticipatory Stigmergic Collision Avoidance* (ASCA) for reciprocal collision avoidance using *anticipatory stigmergy*. Unlike standard stigmergy, in which agents leave pheromones to indicate a trace of previous actions, anticipatory stigmergy deposits pheromones on intended future paths. By sharing their intended future paths with each other at regular intervals, agents can re-plan to attempt to avoid collisions. We experimentally evaluate ASCA over three scenarios, and compare with a state of art approach, Reciprocal Velocity Obstacles (RVO). Our evaluation showed that ASCA is consistently more robust in noisy environments in which transmitted information can be lost or degraded. Further, using ASCA without noise results in fewer collisions than RVO when agents are in formation, but more collisions when formed randomly.

Categories and Subject Descriptors

Computing methodologies [**Control methods**]: Motion path planning

Keywords

collision avoidance; stigmergy; simulation; cooperation

1. INTRODUCTION

Reactive path planning in dynamic environments is used to prevent agents (robots, vehicles, software agents) from colliding with moving objects [2]. Many reactive planning solutions assume that moving objects are *passive*, meaning that it is assumed that they will continue moving in a somewhat predictable manner. In multi-agent environments, such an assumption may not be valid, because other agents will also be reactively planning to avoid collisions.

Recent work on collision avoidance in multi-agent environments [6] has provided solutions to this problem [28]. However, existing solutions are mostly used for ground robots, and are not directly applicable to some problems due to the following assumptions:

1. *Stationary*: Agents can be stationary if moving resulted in a collision. In addition, they can stop suddenly or change directions arbitrarily.

2. *Perfect information*: Agents can accurately perceive the location of other agents in the environment, without any noise.

In some domains, such as unmanned aerial vehicles (UAVs) or unmanned underwater vehicles (UUVs), these two assumptions do not hold [17]: (1) UUVs require slow down time and have a large turning circle; and (2) noise in the environment (e.g. due to lack of visibility) will result in degraded perception or transmission of the location of other UUVs in a formation. Removing these assumptions results in cases in which it is impossible to completely avoid collisions, but with robust models, the number of collisions could be reduced.

In this paper, we present an approach to collision avoidance, *Anticipatory Stigmergic Collision Avoidance* (ASCA). This approach uses the notion of anticipatory stigmergy [10] for agents to coordinate with each other to avoid collisions. Unlike standard stigmergy-based models, in which agents deposit pheromones to inform other agents what actions they have taken, anticipatory stigmergy deposits pheromones to inform others of intended future actions. In the context of collision avoidance, we use anticipatory stigmergy for agents to inform others where they intend to travel, and then agents can re-plan their paths to attempt to avoid collisions.

We evaluate our model by comparing it to a state-of-the-art collision avoidance model for ground robots called Reciprocal Velocity Obstacles (RVO). The results show that in scenarios where agent locations are randomly initialised, RVO outperforms ASCA when there is no noise in the environment, but ASCA outperforms RVO in the presence of noise. In scenarios in which agents move in formations, ASCA also outperforms RVO under no noise, but this is due to an unusual characteristic of RVO. RVO is marginally more efficient with respect to the length of the re-planned path.

GECCO'14, July 12–16, 2014, Vancouver, BC, Canada.

http://dx.doi.org/10.1145/2576768.2598389.

This paper will be organised as follows: Section 2 describes the most closely related work in reactive path planning and stigmergy-based models. Section 3 introduces the ASCA approach for reactive path planning in multi-agent environments. Section 4 outlines an experimental evaluation in which ASCA is compared with RVO and a baseline of no collision avoidance, and Section 5 presents the results of this evaluation. Conclusions are presented in Section 6.

2. RELATED WORK

The most closely related literature to this paper is agent motion and path planning. Whereas most motion planning literature focuses on planning complete paths through an environment, path planning tries to find minimum cost plans. We view collision avoidance as the task of steering free of obstacles while following the global plan, and thus a sub-task of planning.

Approaches for path planning seek to find exact mathematical solutions to the given problem (optimal path planning) and the sub-problem of collision avoidance, such as optimal trajectories [2, 12], navigation functions [6, 19] or path search [23]. Dynamic window collision avoidance approaches, such as [7, 8, 25] or minimum cost models like [28] sample possible solutions and pick the best according to an objective function which usually minimises travelled distance or time. Many of those approaches do not take other agents' collision avoidance decisions into consideration, but still result in robust models.

One of the few exceptions is Reciprocal Velocity Obstacles (RVO) [25]. An agent in the RVO model takes into account other agents' positions and velocities and chooses a velocity that does not lead to a collision with other agents, or, if that is not possible, takes the velocity closest to its preferred velocity and resulting in a collision furthest away. This model assumes perfect sensing, and also that agents can stop suddenly and turn 360 degrees.

Although there are various extensions to the RVO model, dealing with large numbers of agents [26], movement constraints [27, 1, 22] and uncertainty [9], none of them incorporates those problems in one approach.

Behaviour based models are used to facilitate inter-agent communication. Examples are negotiation [3, 21] or non-equilibrium physics [20]. The downsides of behavioural models are high complexity, no guaranteed convergence to a solution, reliance on communication and poor performance under pressure, such as high agent densities.

As opposed to exact mathematical models, stigmergy [24] is a principle idea that approximates solutions probabilistically by means of indirect communication. It has been used in various areas for other purposes (such as routing [5], pedestrian dynamics [11], exploration [18] and optimisation [14, 15]), but is of interest in collision avoidance for its inherent properties: simplicity, decentralisation, scalability and robustness.

Some models using stigmergy have reversed it to indicate future rather than past actions and interpreting them for predictions, for example in vehicle routing [13] or traffic congestion management [4, 10]. None of these models explicitly consider collision avoidance, but lack of collisions is an implicit goal. However, their assumptions that agents can stop and turn at any angle lead to a different solution than ASCA.

Stigmergy also overlaps with swarm intelligence, where flocking [16] has been used as a collision avoidance behaviour as well, although again assuming perfect sensing of the environment. This paper introduces a model using anticipatory stigmergy to create a noise-robust multi-agent collision avoidance method that is less reliant on accurate sensor information about the environment, and is scalable, as it is decentralised.

3. ANTICIPATORY STIGMERGY COLLISION AVOIDANCE

In this section, we present our Anticipatory Stigmergy Collision Avoidance (ASCA) model. This model aims to help avoid collisions between multiple ASCA agents in an environment.

The model makes two assumptions not typically made in existing collision avoidance work:

1. *Agents cannot turn a full 360 degrees to avoid an imminent collision.* Instead, they can vary only up to a certain degree, assumed to be 40 degrees in our experimental evaluation.
2. *Perceptions can be noisy.* That is, an agents perception of the agents in its local neighbourhood can be incorrect. This assumption means that for any solution to be robust, it must allow for variation in trajectories.

Together, these assumptions imply that collisions are impossible to avoid in some cases, particularly in dense environments, as several agents converging onto a single location will not be able to avoid each other without significant and accurate lookahead.

3.1 Overview of model

ASCA agents use an anticipatory stigmergy-based solution [10] for collision avoidance. Unlike standard stigmergy-based models, in which agents deposit pheromones indicating where they have been, anticipatory stigmergy uses the principle of stigmergy in a different way. Instead of leaving interpretable information on the trail passed, agents deposit pheromones (i.e. information) on *future* trails to indicate their intended paths. This allows other agents to interpret this information in a temporal manner to decide on their own paths.

Anticipatory stigmergy solutions for traffic congestion solutions [10] use pheromones to "reserve" a space, thus preventing other agents from passing over this space at the time it is reserved by another agent. In highly-congested environments, this can lead to less efficient outcomes as an agent cannot find space to navigate towards its goal.

In essence, an ASCA agent deposits pheromones along the path it wants to take. Other ASCA agents will then avoid areas with high pheromone concentrations to reduce the likelihood of collisions. However, ASCA agents cannot reserve space.

When deciding its immediate path, an ASCA agent samples pheromones deposited by other agents on immediate paths towards its goal. An area with high pheromone count is likely to be congested, so the agent selects a path with a probability weighted by its likelihood of avoiding congestion, and therefore reducing the chance of collisions.

Figure 1 shows an example of how an ASCA agent samples paths in a 2-dimensional grid. A choice between three next

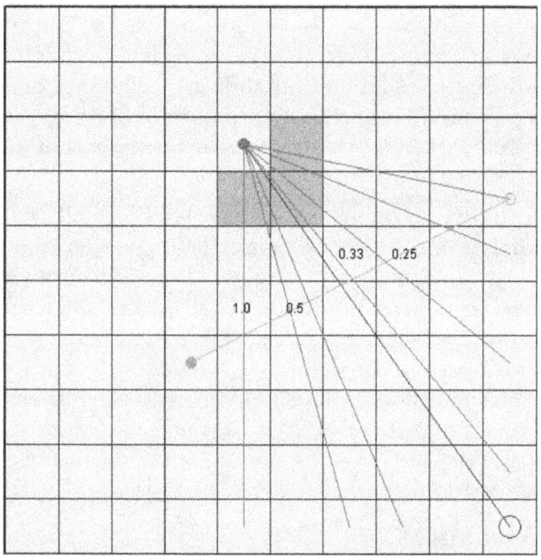

Figure 1: Example of an agent sampling different paths (red) up to $\theta = 40°$ around the optimal path to its goal (blue) with a step size of $\Delta_\theta = 10°$. The grey boxes are the resulting optional velocities. The green agent has already deposited some pheromones up to a lookahead distance $\phi = 4$.

steps must be made, but several paths that start at these points are sampled. Although two sampled paths might result in the same first step, they can have different pheromone densities, which increase/decrease the probability of taking that step next. Our model has been implemented on a 2-dimensional grid for the sake of simplicity, but we believe it can be extended into continuous and even 3-dimensional space. This is discussed further in Section 5.3.

3.2 Process

3.2.1 Path sampling

At regular, fixed intervals, each agent calculates its preferred path to its goal using some path planning algorithm. In our model, we use the Bresenham Line Algorithm to obtain the shortest straight path to the goal, however, any path planning algorithm could be used.

Agents plan their path up to a fixed distance of lookahead, called the *lookahead distance* ϕ. Planning the entire path is less efficient (computationally) while offering little benefit, as the probability of being on a cell on a path will decrease the further the cell is from the current location. If the originally-planned path is free up to ϕ steps ahead, the agent will choose it immediately, as this represents its preferred path and no other agent has signalled its intention to cross this path.

If the path is not free, the agent samples a specific number of *candidate paths*, and calculates the pheromone density of those paths and the original path. The set of candidate paths is the set of straight paths that vary from the optimal path by a fraction Δ_θ of some maximum degree θ. Figure 1 shows an example of path sampling.

3.2.2 Candidate path evaluation

Once a set of candidate paths has been identified, each candidate path is evaluated. The pheromone density of a path is evaluated by the weighing function:

$$w(ph_p) = \frac{1}{\sum_{i=1}^{\phi} ph(i)}, \tag{1}$$

in which $ph(i)$ is the pheromone density at the ith cell along path p. The pheromone density is simply the sum of all deposited pheromones on the cell:

$$ph(i) = \sum_{a \in \Lambda} d(a, i), \tag{2}$$

in which $d(a, i)$ is the pheromone density deposited at cell i by agent a (Λ is the set of all agents having deposited pheromones on that cell), defined in Equation 4.

Thus, the path is evaluated by summing the pheromones deposited at each cell on the path, and then weighting each cell inverse proportionally to the distance from the current cell. This is weighted because we are less certain about cells that are further away.

3.2.3 Path selection

After calculating optional and preferred paths, an agent then needs to choose which path to take. Using the weighting of paths, the least congested path is then chosen probabilistically. A path p has a probability defined as:

$$Pr(p) = \frac{w(ph_p)}{\sum_{j \in \theta} w(ph_j)} \tag{3}$$

where j are the set of paths sampled up to the maximum degree θ. The weighing function $w(ph)$ has the effect of assigning less congested paths higher probabilities.

If the selected path is not the original path, the pheromones are removed from the original path and placed on the new path. This mechanism replaces the typical pheromone decay used in stigmergy models. If the pheromones of an old path remained and slowly decayed, other agents would be limited in their path planning due to paths marked by other agents who have no intention of using them. Removing the path is also computationally more efficient than decaying pheromones over time.

3.2.4 Pheromone depositing

Each agent deposits pheromones along the intended path up to ϕ steps away according to the following pheromone deposit function:

$$d(a, i) = \frac{1}{i}, i \in [1, \phi] \tag{4}$$

This gives the amount of pheromones deposited by agent a on the ith cell of the chosen path. This models the fact that closer cells will be arrived at sooner, therefore increasing the need to avoid collisions, and that closer cells are more likely to be actually used by the pheromone-depositing agents than further away cells. The deposit function $d(a, i)$ thus makes the pheromone information temporally interpretable.

Pheromones are deposited as virtual pheromones, placed directly on the 2-dimensional grid that constitutes the environment for the agents.

As an example in a real-world application, agents could broadcast their virtual pheromones on GPS coordinates (or by means of alternative localisation methods) in a radius of ϕ. Such a broadcast would not require any message exchange and would be limited locally akin to ϕ. An agent would only need to broadcast its own intended path, which requires very little communication bandwidth. If an agent receives a broadcast, it integrates the received intended path into its worldview (local data structure). Thus there is no need for a global data structure (e.g. maps) to be stored or shared. This also allows the algorithm to be executed asynchronously. To account for communication or localisation failure, noise has been applied to the model; see Section 4.1.

Table 1 presents the model parameters and default values. The time/memory complexity of the algorithm is $O(\phi)$, as it only depends on the area the agent evaluates.

Table 1: Model parameters

Parameter	Explanation
$\phi = 10$	lookahead distance (in cells)
$d(a, i)$	pheromone deposit function on i^{th} cell of the path by agent a
$w(ph_p)$	pheromone weighting function on path p
$\theta = 40°$	sample degree (left and right of optimal path)
$\Delta_\theta = 10°$	sample degree step size
δ	noise level $\in [0, 1)$

4. EXPERIMENTAL EVALUATION

In this section we outline an experimental evaluation of ASCA. The goal of the experiments is to evaluate whether ASCA is effective at minimising collisions, while also efficiently arriving at its target. In addition, the optimal lookahead distance (ϕ) is estimated. As a baseline, all scenarios were run without any collision avoidance model, the agents simply take the default path to their destination.

Additionally, a comparison to the state-of-the-art method in collision avoidance, Reciprocal Velocity Obstacles (RVO) [25] is conducted to demonstrate ASCA's abilities in application. To enable a controlled comparison, the RVO model has been altered to limit its sampling of velocities to the same range as the ASCA model, i.e. a fixed speed of 1 cell per round, and a limited turning circle, i.e. only considered paths in a limited angle θ around the current direction.

For statistical aspects of the experiments see Section 5.2.3.

4.1 Independent variables

The independent variables tested are the two algorithms for collision avoidance and the baseline: (1) ASCA; (2) RVO; and (3) baseline (no collision avoidance).

In addition to this, we test three parameters of interest:

1. *Lookahead distance* ϕ, to estimate its optimal value for the remaining tests. Experiments are run for lookahead values $\phi \in \{2-20, 30, 40, 50, 100, 200\}$.

2. *Number of agents.* A high density of agents makes collisions impossible to avoid under the assumptions that agent movements are restricted. Experiments were conducted with increasing numbers of agents from 50 to 500 in increments of 50. This effectively increases the agent density on the grid, as the grid dimensions are fixed.

3. *Noise.* To evaluate the robustness of the approaches, they are tested over various *noise levels*, which aim to simulate unreliable communication channels or sensoring. Noise is implemented as a probability $\delta \in [0, 1)$ in increments of 0.1, indicating the likelihood of a failure of sensing/communication.

   In the RVO model, an agent checks for collisions with other agents in range using their position and velocity. For each agent in range, there is a probability δ that no information about that agents' velocity is received. However, all agents are perceived in their current location. In the ASCA model, an agent deposits pheromones on each cell along its path. For each cell, there is a probability of δ that no pheromones are deposited. Thus, missing pheromones affect all agents in range.

4.2 Measures

There are two main measures of interest:

1. *Number of collisions.* As collisions are not entirely avoidable under our assumptions, we measure the number of collisions occurring in a simulation. A collision occurs if two agents occupy the same grid cell at the same time. In such a case, the colliding agents continue to their goal.

2. *Efficiency.* This measures how efficiently agents reach their goal as a function of distance. Distance efficiency is calculated as the percentage of the optimal distance over the actual distance travelled.

$$\text{Eff}_d = 100 \times \frac{d_{optimal}}{d_{travelled}} \tag{5}$$

4.3 Scenarios

To assess the results under different conditions, experiments were performed under three scenarios, the first two of which are designed to create a high agent density. Each scenario is an unobstructed grid of 1000 × 1000 cells.

The scenarios are:

1. *Cross scenario, random initialisation.* For the first scenario, equal numbers of agents are placed in random positions in the four corners of the grid, with their destination being a random position diametrically opposite (see Figure 2). The agents will cross with each other, creating a high density area in which each agent must avoid other agents travelling in the same direction, in the opposite direction, and travelling across from both left and right. This scenario will be referred to as the *random corner* scenario.

2. *Cross scenario, formation initialisation.* The second scenario is set up similarly, but agents will be placed in a fixed square in each corner. This tests the case of agents attempting to travel in a fixed formation. This scenario will be referred to as the *formation corner* scenario.

3. *Random scenario.* In the third scenario, agents are placed at completely random coordinates with random destinations. It serves as verification of the results of the other two scenarios, as it does not involve any geometric positioning. The scenario will be referred to as the *random* scenario.

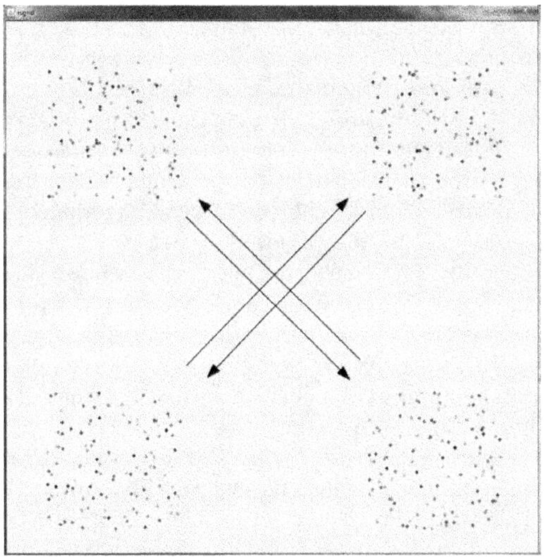

Figure 2: The *random corner* scenario

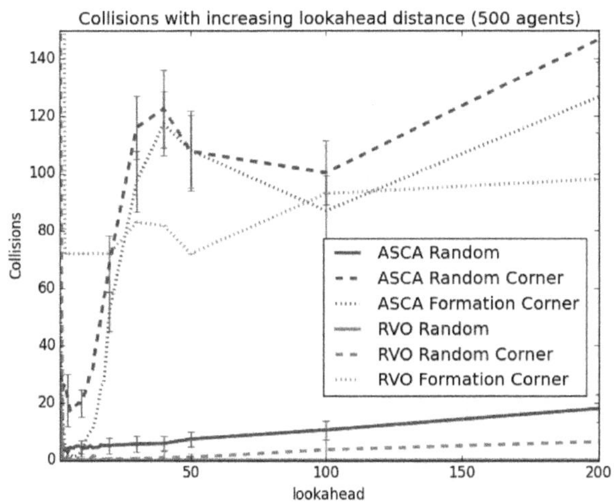

Figure 3: Collisions with increasing lookahead distance without noise

The collision avoidance algorithms are run on the same setup independently; e.g. for the *random corner* scenario, agents are placed at the same positions with the same destinations for the baseline, ASCA, and RVO.

5. RESULTS

In this section, we present the results of the evaluation outlined in Section 4.

5.1 Lookahead distance

The optimal *lookahead distances* ϕ for ASCA and RVO are empirically estimated as a trade-off between as little collisions as possible while maintaining a high distance efficiency. Figure 3 shows how the number of collisions evolved with increasing lookahead distance for the scenarios. Error bars represent the standard deviation.

The ASCA curves have a similar trend in all scenarios and suggest that small lookahead distances produce significantly less collisions, with the optimal value residing at approximately 10. Higher lookahead numbers allow a better evaluation of paths, but will also result in more pheromones being placed by all ASCA agents, which saturate the environment with pheromones, making it difficult to evaluate paths.

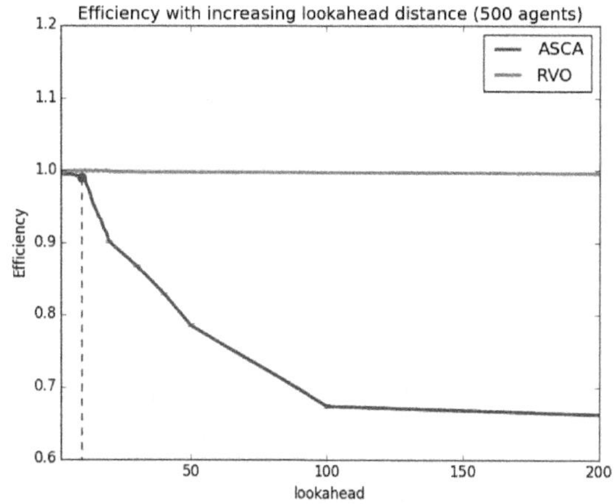

Figure 4: Efficiency with increasing lookahead distance on the formation corner scenario without noise

The reason lookahead distances under 10 result in high number of collisions for both models is that it limits the number of optional velocities.

As can be seen in Figure 3, RVO performs worse on the formation corner scenario, but better on the random corner scenario. This is due to model specifics that lead to an inability of avoiding collisions if a particular number of agents meet in a specific constellation. As an example, four agents will meet with diametrically opposite velocities at the same distance. If one of them tries to evaluate the penalties for the optional velocities, the penalties for the velocity obstacles with all three other agents will be exactly the same, thus a velocity leading to a collision is chosen.

Figure 4 shows that small lookaheads increase efficiency for ASCA in the formation corner, with the optimal value approximately 10. The curves for distance efficiency with increasing lookahead distance on the other scenarios are similar, so have been omitted. These results support our hypothesis that a higher lookahead will "crowd out" the environment, making it difficult to determine the less congested paths.

For the remainder of the experiments, a lookahead distance of 10 has been chosen for both models.

5.2 Agent density and noise

5.2.1 Collisions

Figure 5 shows 3D plots for the three scenarios, outlining the number of collisions under increasing agent density and noise.

From these figures, one can see that the number of collisions increases with both agent density and noise for both ASCA and RVO. However, RVO increases exponentially with an increase in noise, while ASCA seems to increase linearly, or close to. Similarly, as agent density increases, the collisions observed using RVO increase more rapidly than ASCA.

The results over a noise level of $\delta = 0$ are the only case where RVO partially outperforms ASCA. Figure 6 compares

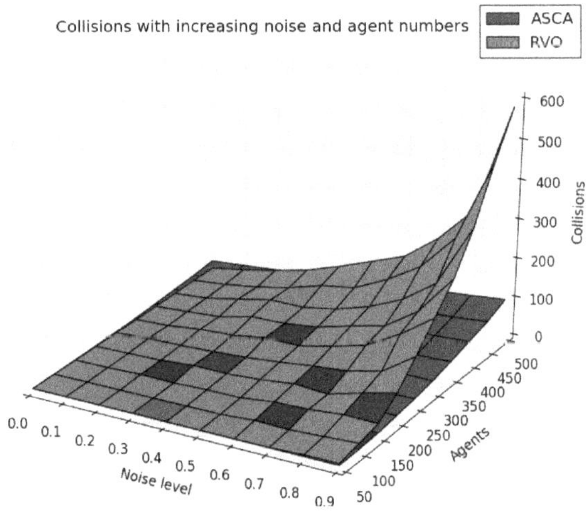

(a) Random corner scenario

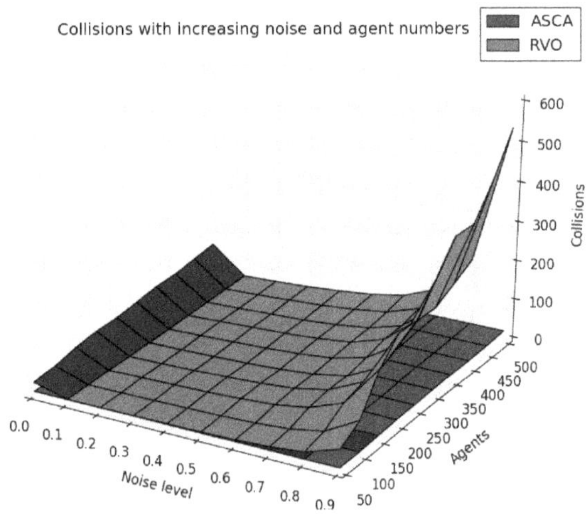

(b) Formation corner scenario

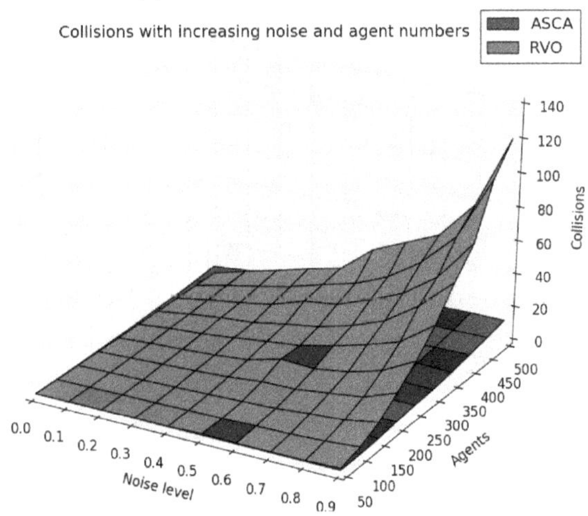

(c) Random scenario

Figure 5: Collisions with increasing agent numbers and noise

the two approaches for noise values 0.0 and 0.5, which are 2-dimensional slices of the same data from Figure 5.

On the random corner scenario, RVO has less collisions than ASCA without noise, whereas the inverse holds for the formation corner scenario. This differing result occurs for the same reason mentioned in the previous section (diametrically opposite velocities). Once noise is introduced, ASCA outperforms RVO in all evaluated cases.

Unexpectedly, RVO performs better under noise than without for the formation corner scenario, because the particular constellations that cause high collision rates do not appear as often (with noise other agents are not always perceived). Note that the number of collisions with RVO increases much faster than with ASCA under noise.

An interesting result is that in the formation corner scenario the number of collisions is generally lower. We attribute this to the geometric setup: the equal gaps between the agents allow for more room to manoeuvre when avoiding collisions, whereas in the random corner scenario, small gaps between agents that make collisions unavoidable occur more frequently. The increase in collisions is still steeper for the RVO model.

5.2.2 *Efficiency*

Figure 7 shows the distance efficiency for both models with increasing agent density and noise on the formation corner scenario. The curves on the other scenarios are similar so have been omitted. The trend shows decreasing efficiency with increasing agent density in all cases. The differences between RVO and ASCA are only marginal, but interestingly ASCA's efficiency improves under noise, while RVO's efficiency decreases. We attribute this to the perceived gaps in the pheromone grid, so more paths will be perceived as free and less diversions are taken to avoid collisions.

5.2.3 *Statistical analysis*

For each data point collected, 100 simulations with the same parameters but different random seeds are carried out. To verify the validity of the results, an ANOVA test ($F_{9,91}$) has been run over the entire dataset for each scenario. The results for the collision measure can be seen in Table 2 (the results for the efficiency measure are even lower, so have been omitted here). The p values are all significantly below 0.001, indicating no correlation between the two datasets for ASCA and RVO.

Table 2: ANOVA results

	Random Corner	Formation Corner	Random
F ratio	14.841	27.538	25.748
p value	0.00016	3.949e-7	8.933e-7

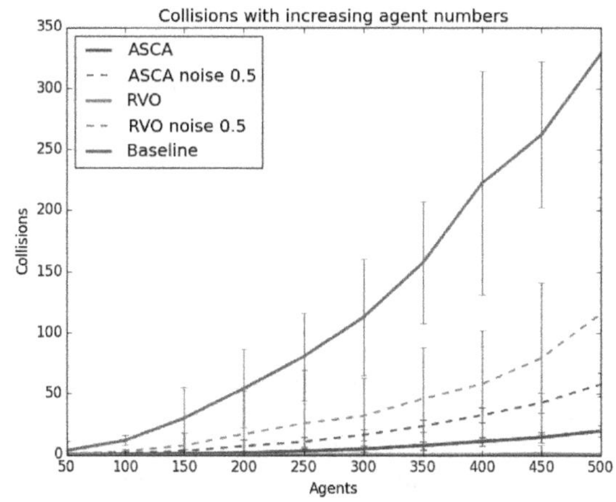

(a) Random corner scenario

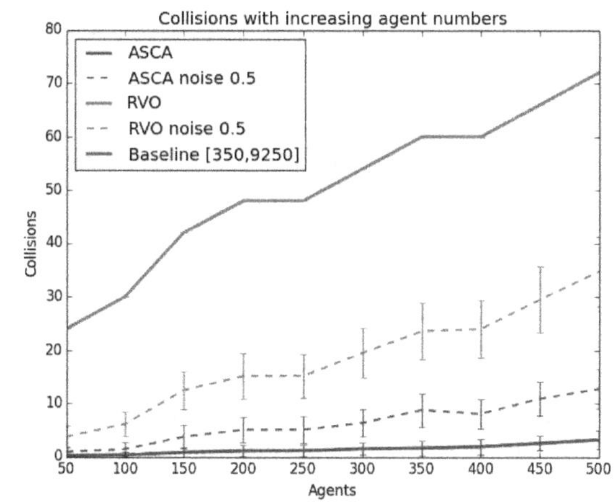

(b) Formation corner scenario

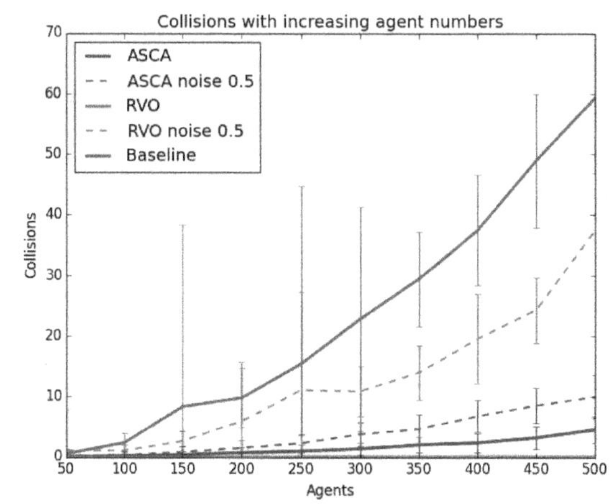

(c) Random scenario

Figure 6: Collisions with no noise and 0.5 noise

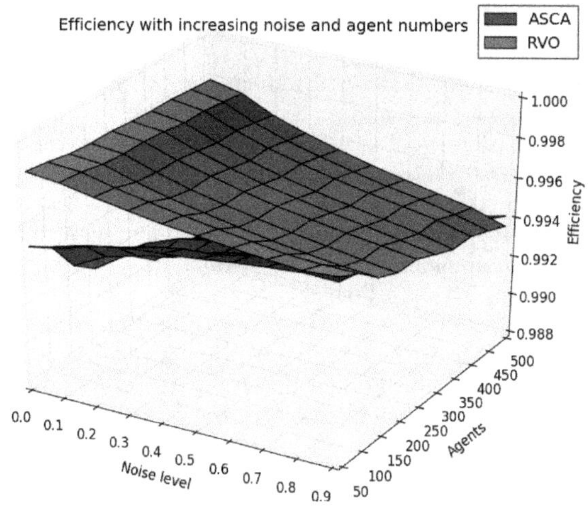

Figure 7: Efficiency with increasing agent numbers and noise on the formation corner scenario

5.3 Discussion

The results from the evaluation demonstrate that ASCA performs robustly in a noisy environment when compared to RVO. This is mainly due to the fact that RVO is designed for complete collision avoidance assuming robots with different characteristics; namely the ability to stop and turn quickly. Further, ASCA agents are able to get to their destination with comparable efficiency with RVO, although ASCA was less efficient for all parameters tested. The results support our hypothesis for applications such as multi-UUV environments, where perception is difficult and the vehicles have large turning circles and cannot stop quickly, existing collision avoidance models cannot be used directly.

While evaluating ASCA using a discrete, 2-dimensional grid, we believe that it would work well in a 3-dimensional grid too, although that would have to be proven with experiments. Further, we believe that the model could be applied in a continuous environment by discretising the environment to a suitable resolution. Additionally, it would be interesting to investigate different scenarios, such as following a moving target.

6. CONCLUSIONS AND FUTURE WORK

In this paper, we presented a simple and effective robust collision avoidance model called Anticipatory Stigmergic Collision Avoidance (ASCA). In ASCA, an agents' decision process is independent of other agents' decisions, while still taking other agents' behaviour into account. Unlike other models, we assume stricter constraints on how agents can move, making it suitable for applications such as aerial or aquatic vehicles. Compared with RVO, a state-of-the-art collision avoidance model designed without these constraints, ASCA results in less collisions in noisy environments, while offering similar efficiency.

In future work, we will extend the model to a continuous 3-dimensional space, and will include sampling of different velocities, which we believe can additionally improve the performance in terms of reducing collisions.

7. REFERENCES

[1] J. Alonso-Mora, A. Breitenmoser, M. Rufli, P. Beardsley, and R. Siegwart. Optimal reciprocal collision avoidance for multiple non-holonomic robots. In *Distributed Autonomous Robotic Systems*, pages 203–216. Springer, 2013.

[2] F. Belkhouche. Reactive path planning in a dynamic environment. *IEEE Transactions on Robotics*, 25(4):902–911, 2009.

[3] J.-P. Calliess, D.l Lyons, and U. D. Hanebeck. Lazy auctions for multi-robot collision avoidance and motion control under uncertainty. In *Advanced Agent Technology*, volume 7068 of *LNCS*, pages 295–312. Springer.

[4] R. Claes, T. Holvoet, and D. Weyns. A decentralized approach for anticipatory vehicle routing using delegate multiagent systems. *IEEE Transactions on Intelligent Transportation Systems*, 12(2):364–373, 2011.

[5] G. Di Caro, F. Ducatelle, and L. M. Gambardella. Swarm intelligence for routing in mobile ad hoc networks. In *Proceedings of the IEEE Swarm Intelligence Symposium*, pages 76–83, 2005.

[6] D. Dimarogonas, Loizou S., K. Kyriakopoulos, and M. Zavlanos. A feedback stabilization and collision avoidance scheme for multiple independent non-point agents. *Automatica*, 42(2):229–243, 2006.

[7] P. Fiorini and Z. Shiller. Motion planning in dynamic environments using velocity obstacles. *The International Journal of Robotics Research*, 17(7):760–772, 1998.

[8] D. Fox, W. Burgard, and S. Thrun. The dynamic window approach to collision avoidance. *IEEE Robotics & Automation Magazine*, 4(1):23–33, 1997.

[9] Daniel Hennes, Daniel Claes, Wim Meeussen, and Karl Tuyls. Multi-robot collision avoidance with localization uncertainty. In *Proceedings of the 11th International Conference on Autonomous Agents and Multiagent Systems-Volume 1*, pages 147–154. International Foundation for Autonomous Agents and Multiagent Systems, 2012.

[10] T. Ito, R. Kanamori, J. Takahashi, I. Maestre, and E. De La Hoz. The comparison of stigmergy strategies for decentralized traffic congestion control: Preliminary results. In *PRICAI 2012: Trends in Artificial Intelligence*, pages 146–156. Springer, 2012.

[11] J. Izquierdo, I. Montalvo, R. Pérez, and V.S. Fuertes. Forecasting pedestrian evacuation times by using swarm intelligence. *Physica A: Statistical Mechanics and its Applications*, 388(7):1213–1220, 2009.

[12] KG Jolly, R Sreerama Kumar, and R Vijayakumar. A Bezier curve based path planning in a multi-agent robot soccer system without violating the acceleration limits. *Robotics and Autonomous Systems*, 57(1):23–33, 2009.

[13] R. Kanamori, J. Takahashi, and T. Ito. Evaluation of anticipatory stigmergy strategies for traffic management. In *IEEE Vehicular Networking Conference*, pages 33–39. IEEE, 2012.

[14] N. Lemmens and K. Tuyls. Stigmergic landmark foraging. In *Proceedings of the 8th International Conference on Autonomous Agents and Multiagent Systems*, pages 497–504. IFAAMAS, 2009.

[15] N. Lemmens and K. Tuyls. Stigmergic landmark optimization. *Advances in Complex Systems (ACS)*, 15(8), 2012.

[16] R. Olfati-Saber. Flocking for multi-agent dynamic systems: Algorithms and theory. *IEEE Transactions on Automatic Control*, 51(3):401–420, 2006.

[17] C. Petres, Y. Pailhas, P. Patron, Y. Petillot, J. Evans, and D. Lane. Path planning for autonomous underwater vehicles. *IEEE Transactions on Robotics*, 23(2):331–341, 2007.

[18] B. Ranjbar-Sahraei, G. Weiss, and A. Nakisaee. A multi-robot coverage approach based on stigmergic communication. In *Multiagent System Technologies*, pages 126–138. Springer, 2012.

[19] G. Roussos, D. V. Dimarogonas, and K. J. Kyriakopoulos. 3D navigation and collision avoidance for nonholonomic aircraft-like vehicles. *International Journal of Adaptive Control and Signal Processing*, 24(10):900–920, 2010.

[20] A. Schadschneider, A. Kirchner, and K. Nishinari. Cellular automaton approach to collective phenomena in pedestrian dynamics. In *Cellular Automata*, pages 239–248. Springer, 2002.

[21] D. Sislak, P. Volf, and M. Pechoucek. Agent-based cooperative decentralized airplane-collision avoidance. *IEEE Transactions on Intelligent Transportation Systems*, 12(1):36–46, 2011.

[22] Jamie Snape and Dinesh Manocha. Navigating multiple simple-airplanes in 3d workspace. In *Robotics and Automation (ICRA), 2010 IEEE International Conference on*, pages 3974–3980. IEEE, 2010.

[23] A. Stentz. Optimal and efficient path planning for partially-known environments. In *IEEE International Conference on Robotics and Automation*, pages 3310–3317. IEEE, 1994.

[24] G. Theraulaz and E. Bonabeau. A brief history of stigmergy. *Artificial life*, 5(2):97–116, 1999.

[25] J. Van den Berg, M. Lin, and D. Manocha. Reciprocal velocity obstacles for real-time multi-agent navigation. In *IEEE International Conference on Robotics and Automation (ICRA)*, pages 1928–1935. IEEE, 2008.

[26] Jur Van Den Berg, Stephen J Guy, Ming Lin, and Dinesh Manocha. Reciprocal n-body collision avoidance. In *Robotics Research*, pages 3–19. Springer, 2011.

[27] Jur van den Berg, Jamie Snape, Stephen J Guy, and Dinesh Manocha. Reciprocal collision avoidance with acceleration-velocity obstacles. In *Robotics and Automation (ICRA), 2011 IEEE International Conference on*, pages 3475–3482. IEEE, 2011.

[28] K. Wang and A. Botea. Tractable multi-agent path planning on grid maps. In *International Joint Conference on Artificial Intelligence*, pages 1870–1875, 2009.

Differential Evolution Using Mutation Strategy With Adaptive Greediness Degree Control

Wei-Jie Yu [a], Jing-Jing Li [b] (Corresponding Author), Jun Zhang [c] and Meng Wan [d]
[a] Department of Psychology, Sun Yat-sen University
[a] Key Laboratory of Machine Intelligence and Advanced Computing, Ministry of Education
[a] Engineering Research Center of Supercomputing Engineering Software, Ministry of Education
[b] School of Computer Science, South China Normal University
[c] School of Advanced Computing, Sun Yat-sen University
[d] Center for Science and Technology Development, Ministry of Education
jingjing.li1124@gmail.com

ABSTRACT

Differential evolution (DE) has been demonstrated to be one of the most promising evolutionary algorithms (EAs) for global numerical optimization. DE mainly differs from other EAs in that it employs difference of the parameter vectors in mutation operator to search the objective function landscape. Therefore, the performance of a DE algorithm largely depends on the design of its mutation strategy. In this paper, we propose a new kind of DE mutation strategies whose greediness degree can be adaptively adjusted. The proposed mutation strategies utilize the information of top t solutions in the current population. Such a greedy strategy is beneficial to fast convergence performance. In order to adapt the degree of greediness to fit for different optimization scenarios, the parameter t is adjusted in each generation of the algorithm by an adaptive control scheme. This way, the convergence performance and the robustness of the algorithm can be enhanced at the same time. To evaluate the effectiveness of the proposed adaptive greedy mutation strategies, the approach is applied to original DE algorithms, as well as DE algorithms with parameter adaptation. Experimental results indicate that the proposed adaptive greedy mutation strategies yield significant performance improvement for most of cases studied.

Categories and Subject Descriptors

I.2.8 [**Artificial Intelligence**]: Problem Solving, Control Methods, and Search – *Heuristic methods*

General Terms

Algorithms

GECCO '14, July 12–16, 2014, Vancouver, BC, Canada

http://dx.doi.org/10.1145/2576768.2598236

Keywords

Adaptive control, differential evolution (DE), evolutionary algorithm (EA), global optimization, mutation strategy

1. INTRODUCTION

Differential evolution (DE), which was first proposed by Storn and Price in 1995 [1][2], is a simple and powerful evolutionary algorithm (EA) for global numerical optimization. During the last few years, DE has been successfully applied to a variety of real-world problems from diverse domains of science and engineering [3]–[6]. Similar to other EAs, DE employs three general evolutionary operators, i.e. mutation, crossover, and selection in each generation to evolve the population. In these three operators, the mutation operator which utilizes difference of parameter vectors to explore the search space mainly makes DE differs from other EAs. Therefore, how to design efficient mutation strategies for DE so as to improve the performance of the algorithm has become a significant and promising research topic in DE.

The five original and most frequently used DE mutation strategies in the literature were proposed by Storn and Price [3][4]. Among them, two mutation strategies, namely, DE/rand/1 and DE/rand/2 are performed in a random manner. For example, in the DE/rand/1 mutation, all the three parent vectors are selected randomly from the current population. Such mutation strategies with high degree of randomness are good at exploring and able to locate different promising regions of the search space. However, they may be poor at exploitation of the solutions and cause slow convergence of the algorithm [7]. On the contrary, the other three mutation strategies, namely, DE/best/1, DE/best/2, and DE/current-to-best/1 incorporate the best solution information. The best parameter vector with the best fitness value in the population is selected as one of the parent vectors involved in mutation. Such greedy mutation strategies can help improving the convergence performance. Nevertheless, due to the exploitative tendency, the population may lose its diversity too early and reduce its exploration ability to search new region of the search space. This way, individuals of the population are more likely to be trapped in some local optima, especially when solving complex multimodal problems.

As the above analysis shows, different DE strategies have different performance characteristics and are suitable for solving different optimization problems [8]–[10]. In addition, to optimize a specific problem, different phases of the optimization process also require different mutation strategies. Therefore, many researchers employed the concept of combing different mutation strategies in an ensemble and proposed enhanced DE algorithms such as SaDE [11], EPSDE [12], SaJADE [13], and CoDE [14], etc. The mutation strategies in the ensemble approach have distinct characteristics, so that they can be adaptively selected to exhibit distinct performance for different optimization phases when dealing with a particular problem.

In this paper, instead of utilizing the ensemble approach, we propose a new kind of mutation strategies whose greediness degree can be adaptively adjusted to fit for different optimization scenarios. Different from the original DE algorithm, in our approach, one of the parents involved in the mutation is randomly selected from the top t solutions in the current population. This greedy strategy benefits from fast convergence performance, and the new introduced parameter t controls the greediness degree. To adapt the greediness degree to the requirements of different problem scenarios, we design a simple yet efficient adaptive control scheme for adjusting the value of parameter t. Consequently, the proposed mutation strategies can provide fast convergence performance while maintaining the reliability of the algorithm at a high level. Moreover, the approach can be easily applied to other advanced DE variants with minimal changes.

To validate the effectiveness of our proposed adaptive greedy mutation strategies on DE, our approach is compared with the original DE algorithm with different mutation strategies. In addition, the proposed adaptive greedy mutation strategies are also applied to other DE variant with parameter adaptation. Experimental results show that our proposed adaptive greedy mutation strategies are able to enhance the performance of the original DE and the advanced DE with parameter adaptation for most of the cases studied.

The rest of this paper is organized as follows. Section 2 reviews the DE algorithm and the related works on variants of DE mutation strategies. Section 3 describes the proposed adaptive greedy mutation strategies in detail. In Section 4, experiments are carried out on benchmark functions to verify the influence of our proposed approach. Finally, Section 5 draws the conclusions.

2. DE ALGORITHM AND RELATED WORKS

2.1 Differential Evolution (DE) Algorithm

DE is a population-based stochastic algorithm designed for global numerical optimization. Similar to other EAs, DE searches for a global optimum in the feasible solution space with a population of parameter vectors $\{\mathbf{x}_{i,g} = [x_{i,1,g}, x_{i,2,g}, \ldots, x_{i,D,g}], i = 1,2,\ldots, NP\}$, where g denotes the current generation, D is the dimension of the search space, and NP is the population size. In generation g=0, the jth component of the ith vector can be initialized as

$$x_{i,j,0} = x_{\min,j} + \text{rand}(0,1)\cdot(x_{\max,j} - x_{\min,j}) \quad (1)$$

where rand(0,1) is a uniform random number on the interval [0,1], and $x_{\min,j}$, $x_{\max,j}$ are the prescribed minimum and maximum bounds of the jth dimension, respectively. After initialization, DE enters an evolutionary process which includes mutation, crossover, and selection operations.

Mutation: In each generation g, the mutation operation is applied to each individual $\mathbf{x}_{i,g}$ (also called target vector) to create its corresponding mutant vector $\mathbf{v}_{i,g}$. The six most frequently used mutation strategies are listed as follows.

- DE/rand/1:

$$\mathbf{v}_{i,g} = \mathbf{x}_{r1,g} + F\cdot(\mathbf{x}_{r2,g} - \mathbf{x}_{r3,g}) \quad (2)$$

- DE/best/1:

$$\mathbf{v}_{i,g} = \mathbf{x}_{\text{best},g} + F\cdot(\mathbf{x}_{r1,g} - \mathbf{x}_{r2,g}) \quad (3)$$

- DE/rand/2:

$$\mathbf{v}_{i,g} = \mathbf{x}_{r1,g} + F\cdot(\mathbf{x}_{r2,g} - \mathbf{x}_{r3,g}) + F\cdot(\mathbf{x}_{r4,g} - \mathbf{x}_{r5,g}) \quad (4)$$

- DE/best/2:

$$\mathbf{v}_{i,g} = \mathbf{x}_{\text{best},g} + F\cdot(\mathbf{x}_{r1,g} - \mathbf{x}_{r2,g}) + F\cdot(\mathbf{x}_{r3,g} - \mathbf{x}_{r4,g}) \quad (5)$$

- DE/current-to-rand/1:

$$\mathbf{v}_{i,g} = \mathbf{x}_{i,g} + F\cdot(\mathbf{x}_{r1,g} - \mathbf{x}_{i,g}) + F\cdot(\mathbf{x}_{r2,g} - \mathbf{x}_{r3,g}) \quad (6)$$

- DE/current-to-best/1:

$$\mathbf{v}_{i,g} = \mathbf{x}_{i,g} + F\cdot(\mathbf{x}_{\text{best},g} - \mathbf{x}_{i,g}) + F\cdot(\mathbf{x}_{r1,g} - \mathbf{x}_{r2,g}) \quad (7)$$

It can be seen that the mutant vector $\mathbf{v}_{i,g}$ is generated by combing a base vector with one or two scaled difference vectors. In the above equations, the indices r_1, r_2, r_3, r_4, and r_5 are distinct integers randomly selected from the range [1, NP], and all are different from the index i. $\mathbf{x}_{\text{best},g}$ is the vector with the best fitness value in the current generation. The factor F is a positive control parameter for amplifying the difference vectors.

Crossover: In order to enhance population diversity, a crossover operation exchanges some components of the mutant vector $\mathbf{v}_{i,g}$ with the target vector $\mathbf{x}_{i,g}$ to generate a trial vector $\mathbf{u}_{i,g}$. The process can be expressed as

$$u_{i,j,g} = \begin{cases} v_{i,j,g}, & \text{if } \text{rand}(0,1) \le CR \text{ or } j = j_{\text{rand}} \\ x_{i,j,g}, & \text{otherwise} \end{cases} \quad (7)$$

where rand(0,1) is a uniformly distributed random number as before. j_{rand} is an integer randomly generated from the range $[1, D]$, which is used to ensure the trial vector has at least one component different from the target vector. The crossover probability CR is another control parameter that determines the fraction of vector components inherited from the mutant vector.

Selection: To decide whether the target or the trial vector can survive to the next generation, the selection operation is finally performed. For a minimization problem, the vector with the lower fitness value enters the next generation, which can be expressed as follows:

$$\mathbf{x}_{i,g+1} = \begin{cases} \mathbf{u}_{i,g}, & \text{if } f(\mathbf{u}_{i,g}) \le f(\mathbf{x}_{i,g}) \\ \mathbf{x}_{i,g}, & \text{otherwise} \end{cases} \tag{8}$$

where $f(\mathbf{x})$ is the objective function for the minimization problem.

The above three operators are repeated until the algorithm meets a termination criteria, such as a maximum iteration number or a maximum number of fitness evaluations.

2.2 Variants of DE Mutation Strategies

In addition to the six most frequently used mutation strategies mentioned in Section 2.1, a lot of other variants have been proposed to further improve the performance of DE. Fan and Lampinen [15] proposed a trigonometric mutation to increase the convergence speed of DE. Kaelo and Ali [16] proposed a hybrid mutation operator which uses the attraction-repulsion technique of an electromagnetism-like algorithm. In order to balance the exploration and exploitation capabilities of DE, many researchers designed variants of some greedy mutation strategies [17]–[19]. These variants utilize the information of multiple good solutions instead of the single best solution in the entire population. However, the greediness degree of these variants remains unchanged during the evolution.

Besides developing new DE mutation strategies, some researchers investigated DE mutation frameworks that can be applied to different DE variants. For example, Epitropakis *et al.* [20] proposed a mutation framework in which the probability of selecting an individual to become a parent is inversely proportional to its distance from the individual undergoing mutation. Gong and Cai [21] proposed a kind of ranking-based mutation framework, where some of the parents in the mutation operator are proportionally selected according to their rankings in the current population. Cai and Wang [22] proposed a DE mutation framework that exploits the neighborhood and direction information of the population.

Unlike the above methods, some DE variants such as SaDE [11], EPSDE [12], SaJADE [13], and CoDE [14] employed an ensemble of different mutation strategies. In the ensemble approach, a pool of mutation strategies competes to produce successful offspring population. The mutation strategies present in a pool have diverse characteristics, so that they can exhibit distinct performance characteristics during different phases of the evolution, when optimizing a specific problem [5].

3. DE MUTATION STRATEGIES WITH ADAPTIVE GREEDINESS DEGREE CONTROL

In this section, we propose the adaptive greedy mutation strategies, where one of the parent vectors in the mutation is randomly selected from the top t solutions in the current population. Next, we discuss which parent vector in the mutation should be selected from the top t solutions and how to adaptively adjust the value of parameter t.

3.1 Vector Selection

Before performing mutation in each generation, we first find out the current top t solutions based on the fitness values. Then, the *base* vector in the mutation strategy is randomly selected from the current top t solutions, while the other vectors in the mutation are selected randomly as the original DE algorithm. Note that if the base vector in a mutation strategy is the target vector (e.g. DE/current-to-best/1), instead of the base vector, the *terminal* point of the difference vector is randomly chosen as one of the current top t solution.

By incorporating the vector selection scheme into the six original mutation strategies mentioned in Section 2.1, we develop three novel adaptive greedy variants as follows:

- DE/*at*best/1:

$$\mathbf{v}_{i,g} = \mathbf{x}^t_{\text{best},g} + F \cdot (\mathbf{x}_{r1,g} - \mathbf{x}_{r2,g}) \tag{9}$$

- DE/*at*best/2:

$$\mathbf{v}_{i,g} = \mathbf{x}^t_{\text{best},g} + F \cdot (\mathbf{x}_{r1,g} - \mathbf{x}_{r2,g}) + F \cdot (\mathbf{x}_{r3,g} - \mathbf{x}_{r4,g}) \tag{10}$$

- DE/current-to-*at*best/1:

$$\mathbf{v}_{i,g} = \mathbf{x}_{i,g} + F \cdot (\mathbf{x}^t_{\text{best},g} - \mathbf{x}_{i,g}) + F \cdot (\mathbf{x}_{r1,g} - \mathbf{x}_{r2,g}) \tag{11}$$

where $\mathbf{x}^t_{\text{best},g}$ is randomly chosen as one of the current top t solutions, t = 1, 2, …, *NP*. Among them, DE/*at*best/1 is derived from DE/rand/1 and DE/best/1, DE/*at*best/2 is derived from DE/rand/2 and DE/best/2, and DE/current-to-*at*best/1 is derived from DE/current-to-rand/1 and DE/current-to-best/1. Note that tuning the parameter t can control the greediness degree of the search process. In the following subsection, we describe how to adjust the value of parameter t.

3.2 Adaptive Control Scheme for Parameter t

To adapt the greediness degree to the requirements of different problem scenarios, we design a simple yet efficient scheme to adaptively adjust the value of parameter t. Each individual in the initial population is associated with an integer value of t which is randomly selected from the range [1, *NP*]. In the mutation process, each target vector produces mutant vector using its own value of parameter t. Then the crossover operator is applied to each pair of mutant vector and target vector to generate a trial vector. If the generated trial vector produced is better than the target vector, the value of parameter t is retained with trial vector which becomes the target vector in the next generation. Otherwise, if the trial vector is worse than the target vector, the target vector is randomly reinitialized with a new value of parameter t. This adaptive control scheme allows better values of parameter t to be more likely to survive and offspring would be produced by these better parameter values in the future generations.

3.3 DE With Adaptive Greedy Mutation Strategy

Combining the proposed adaptive greedy mutation strategy with DE, the DE algorithm using mutation strategy with adaptive greediness degree control (AGDE) is developed. Figure 1 illustrates the flowchart of the AGDE algorithm. It can be seen that AGDE maintains the simple structure of the original DE algorithm. In addition, since information of good solutions is utilized in the mutation, the algorithm benefits from fast convergence. The robustness of the AGDE can be further enhanced by the adaptive greediness control scheme. Moreover, the adaptive greedy mutation strategies are also able to integrate into other DE variants with minimal changes.

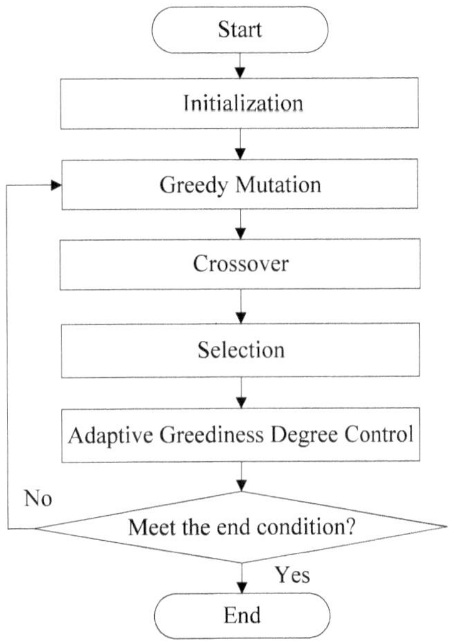

Figure 1. Flowchart of the AGDE algorithm.

4. EXPERIMENTAL RESULTS

4.1 Benchmark Functions

In this section, experiments are carried out to validate the performance of the proposed AGDE algorithms. We employ 25 benchmark functions from CEC 2005 special session on real-parameter optimization [23] as the test suite. Based on their characteristics, these functions can be divided into the four classes: 1) unimodal functions (F_1–F_5); 2) basic multimodal functions (F_6–F_{12}); 3) expanded multimodal functions (F_{13}–F_{14}); and 4) hybrid composition functions (F_{15}–F_{25}). More details of this benchmark suite can be found in [23].

4.2 Experimental Setup

In the experiments, we first test the influence of our approach on different mutation strategies in original DE. The performance of three AGDEs proposed in Section 3 (i.e. DE/*at*best/1, DE/*at*best/2 and DE/current-to-*at*best/1) is compared with their respective original algorithms. Then, we validate the effectiveness of the proposed mutation strategies on an advanced DE variant, namely, jDE [24]. jDE uses a self-adaptive approach to adapt the parameter values of F and CR, so that it can obtain promising results among various mutation strategies. To make a fair comparison, we employ the parameter settings for all of the compared DE algorithms as follows:

1) Function dimension: $D = 30$;

2) Population size: $NP = 100$ [7][10][24][25];

3) Function evaluations (FEs): FEs = 300 000;

4) Number of runs (NumR): NumR = 25.

To measure the performance of the algorithms, we calculate the average and standard deviation of the function error value $f(\mathbf{x}) - f(\mathbf{x}^*)$, where $\mathbf{x}$ is the best solution of each run and $\mathbf{x}^*$ is the global optimum of the benchmark function. For clarity, the results of the best algorithms are highlighted in **boldface** for each benchmark function. Moreover, we apply the paired Wilcoxon signed-rank test [26] to evaluate the statistical significant differences between two algorithms. Bases on the test, we mark the results with "+", "=", and "−", which indicate that the performance of our proposed algorithm is significantly better than, equal to, and worse than the corresponding algorithm, respectively.

4.3 Effects on Original DE With Different Mutation strategies

In this section, we evaluate the effectiveness of our proposed different mutation strategies in the original DE. Six mutation strategies [see (2)–(7)] are compared with their corresponding adaptive greedy variants [see (9)–(11)] in the experiment. As suggested in most of the literatures [2][24][27][28], the original DE algorithm set the values of F and CR to 0.5 and 0.9, respectively. The experimental results of DE/*at*best/1, DE/*at*best/2, and DE/current-to-*at*best/1 compared with their respective original algorithms are shown in Table 1, Table 2, and Table 3, respectively. From these results, we can find that, for the majority of the test functions, the AGDE algorithms achieve significantly better error values compared with their corresponding original DE algorithms.

1) For the unimodal functions F_1–F_5, it can be found that all the three AGDEs obtain significant better results than their corresponding original DEs on most of these functions. The only exception is that the performance of DE/*at*best/2 is deteriorated on 4 out of the 5 functions when compared with DE/best/2.

2) For the basic multimodal functions F_6–F_{12}, regardless of the mutation strategy used, the adaptive greedy DE variants consistently outperform the original DEs in most of the cases (23 out of 42). In the remaining 19 cases, AGDEs provide 13 similar results and 6 worse results compared with their corresponding original DEs, respectively.

3) For the expanded multimodal functions F_{13}–F_{14}, the adaptive greedy approach does not yield great performance improvement. The AGDEs exhibits improvement performance in 4 out of 12 cases, while in 4 cases the proposed scheme deteriorates the performance.

4) For the hybrid composition functions F_{15}–F_{25}, the AGDEs exhibit significant improvement on most of these functions, although they are very difficult to solve for most optimization algorithms. In all the 66 cases, AGDEs are significantly better than original DEs in 48 cases and worse than them in only one case. In particular, DE/*at*best/1 and DE/current-to-*at*best/1 are significantly better than DE/best/1 and DE/current-to-best/1 on all of the 11 functions, respectively.

Table 1. Effects on DE/rand/1 and DE/best/1 in Original DE

Fun.	DE/rand/1 Mean (Std.)	DE/best/1 Mean (Std.)	DE/*at*best/1 Mean (Std.)
F_1	**0.00E+00 (0.00E+00)** =	5.21E−13 (3.67E−12) +	**0.00E+00 (0.00E+00)**
F_2	2.81E−05 (1.87E−05) +	2.26E−12 (1.66E−12) +	**7.96E−14 (2.78E−14)**
F_3	3.84E+05 (2.58E+05) +	**1.72E+04 (1.02E+04)** −	8.35E+04 (4.98E+04)
F_4	1.74E−02 (2.07E−02) +	3.78E+02 (7.13E+02) +	**2.33E−09 (8.99E−09)**
F_5	5.78E+01 (4.58E+01) +	2.10E+03 (7.31E+02) +	**4.78E+01 (6.53E+01)**
F_6	**8.19E−02 (1.80E−01)** +	1.44E+00 (1.86E+00) +	4.78E−01 (1.29E+00)
F_7	**1.08E−03 (2.96E−03)** =	2.09E−02 (2.21E−02) +	1.15E−02 (1.17E−02)
F_8	2.10E+01 (4.90E−02) =	2.10E+01 (3.17E−02) =	**2.09E+01 (6.27E−02)**
F_9	1.31E+02 (2.37E+01) +	1.08E+02 (2.51E+01) +	**1.69E+01 (4.07E+00)**
F_{10}	1.81E+02 (1.05E+01) +	**1.48E+02 (3.52E+01)** =	**1.48E+02 (2.97E+01)**
F_{11}	3.94E+01 (1.01E+00) +	**2.21E+01 (1.93E+00)** −	3.83E+01 (5.99E+00)
F_{12}	**1.29E+03 (1.67E+03)** =	2.89E+03 (3.82E+03) =	2.17E+03 (2.54E+03)
F_{13}	1.53E+01 (1.01E+00) +	**6.92E+00 (2.34E+00)** =	8.62E+00 (4.31E+00)
F_{14}	1.33E+01 (1.40E−01) =	**1.20E+01 (6.53E−01)** −	1.32E+01 (2.00E−01)
F_{15}	4.08E+02 (4.45E+01) =	4.73E+02 (8.70E+01) +	**4.04E+02 (4.45E+01)**
F_{16}	2.12E+02 (9.97E+00) +	3.28E+02 (1.29E+02) +	**1.26E+02 (1.05E+02)**
F_{17}	2.25E+02 (1.36E+01) =	3.02E+02 (1.22E+02) +	**2.20E+02 (4.39E+01)**
F_{18}	9.00E+02 (3.83E+01) +	9.67E+02 (4.66E+01) +	**8.85E+02 (4.28E+01)**
F_{19}	9.04E+02 (1.33E+00) +	9.65E+02 (2.64E+01) +	**8.77E+02 (4.81E+01)**
F_{20}	9.04E+02 (1.07E+00) +	9.63E+02 (3.73E+01) +	**8.94E+02 (3.50E+01)**
F_{21}	**5.00E+02 (1.67E−13)** =	7.56E+02 (3.03E+02) +	**5.00E+02 (1.56E−13)**
F_{22}	9.08E+02 (1.05E+01) +	1.05E+03 (4.32E+01) +	**8.99E+02 (1.26E+01)**
F_{23}	**5.34E+02 (3.20E−04)** =	1.04E+03 (1.90E+02) +	**5.34E+02 (3.56E−04)**
F_{24}	**2.00E+02 (2.84E−14)** =	8.54E+02 (4.92E+02) +	**2.00E+02 (2.84E−14)**
F_{25}	**2.09E+02 (1.25E−01)** =	7.89E+02 (5.52E+02) +	**2.09E+02 (1.61E−02)**
+/=/−	14/11/0	18/4/3	−

"+", "=", and "−" indicate that the performance of our proposed algorithm is respectively better than, equal to, and worse than the corresponding algorithm according to the Wilcoxon signed-rank test at $\alpha = 0.05$.

Table 2. Effects on DE/rand/2 and DE/best/2 in Original DE

Fun.	DE/rand/2 Mean (Std.)	DE/best/2 Mean (Std.)	DE/*at*best/2 Mean (Std.)
F_1	7.88E−01 (3.04E−01) +	6.59E−14 (1.85E−14) +	**2.96E−14 (2.83E−14)**
F_2	7.59E+03 (2.05E+03) +	**2.64E−13 (8.34E−14)** −	2.72E+00 (9.40E−01)
F_3	5.32E+07 (1.35E+07) +	**1.46E+05 (7.24E+04)** −	9.23E+05 (2.25E+05)
F_4	1.58E+04 (2.45E+03) +	**1.31E−04 (3.89E−04)** −	4.97E+01 (1.16E+01)
F_5	8.13E+03 (6.36E+02) +	**1.07E+02 (2.03E+02)** −	8.54E+02 (1.18E+02)
F_6	4.89E+03 (1.74E+03) +	**4.78E−01 (1.30E+00)** −	6.01E+00 (1.37E+01)
F_7	6.97E+00 (2.74E+00) +	1.11E−02 (9.20E−03) +	**2.87E−06 (1.47E−06)**
F_8	**2.09E+01 (5.63E−02)** =	2.10E+01 (4.76E−02) +	**2.09E+01 (5.23E−02)**
F_9	2.16E+02 (1.08E+01) +	**1.82E+02 (1.51E+01)** =	1.92E+02 (8.87E+00)
F_{10}	2.41E+02 (1.06E+01) +	**1.97E+02 (1.28E+01)** =	2.04E+02 (9.12E+00)
F_{11}	3.96E+01 (1.08E+00) +	3.98E+01 (7.92E−01) +	**3.94E+01 (7.92E−01)**
F_{12}	5.25E+05 (6.62E+04) +	**1.28E+03 (2.36E+03)** −	2.26E+05 (1.46E+05)
F_{13}	2.06E+01 (8.38E−01) +	**1.55E+01 (1.41E−01)** −	1.71E+01 (1.17E−01)
F_{14}	1.35E+01 (1.33E−01) =	**1.33E+01 (2.16E−01)** =	**1.33E+01 (2.99E−01)**
F_{15}	4.06E+02 (6.84E+00) =	3.89E+02 (1.02E+02) =	**3.88E+02 (4.13E+01)**
F_{16}	2.69E+02 (1.27E+01) +	3.18E+02 (9.97E+01) +	**2.28E+02 (1.36E+01)**
F_{17}	3.02E+02 (1.65E+01) +	3.44E+02 (1.14E+02) +	**2.57E+02 (1.25E+01)**
F_{18}	9.40E+02 (4.00E+00) +	9.08E+02 (3.03E+00) =	**9.07E+02 (2.73E−01)**
F_{19}	9.40E+02 (3.03E+00) +	9.08E+02 (3.49E+01) −	**9.07E+02 (5.20E−01)**
F_{20}	9.39E+02 (3.92E+01) +	8.99E+02 (3.52E+01) =	**9.07E+02 (7.35E−01)**
F_{21}	**5.00E+02 (1.11E−01)** +	5.48E+02 (1.10E+02) +	**5.00E+02 (1.72E−13)**
F_{22}	1.02E+03 (1.36E+01) +	9.31E+02 (1.88E+01) =	**9.30E+02 (7.19E+00)**
F_{23}	5.35E+02 (4.68E−01) =	6.17E+02 (1.62E+02) +	**5.34E+02 (3.62E−04)**
F_{24}	**2.00E+02 (1.31E−01)** +	2.00E+02 (9.26E−13) =	**2.00E+02 (2.84E−14)**
F_{25}	2.29E+02 (3.60E+00) +	2.47E+02 (1.60E+02) +	**2.09E+02 (1.58E−01)**
+/=/−	21/4/0	9/8/8	−

"+", "=", and "−" indicate that the performance of our proposed algorithm is respectively better than, equal to, and worse than the corresponding algorithm according to the Wilcoxon signed-rank test at $\alpha = 0.05$.

Table 3. Effects on DE/current-to-rand/1 and DE/current-to-best/1 in Original DE

Fun.	DE/current-to-rand/1 Mean (Std.)	DE/current-to-best/1 Mean (Std.)	DE/current-to-*at*best/1 Mean (Std.)
F_1	6.57E+03 (1.31E+03) +	1.89E+03 (1.05E+03) +	**1.71E+03 (6.08E+02)**
F_2	6.91E+03 (1.57E+03) +	4.60E+03 (2.36E+03) +	**3.28E+03 (1.26E+03)**
F_3	3.81E+06 (2.06E+06) +	6.19E+06 (4.51E+06) +	**2.67E+06 (1.30E+06)**
F_4	3.09E+03 (1.49E+03) +	6.30E+02 (6.48E+02) +	**2.51E+02 (3.04E+02)**
F_5	5.84E+03 (1.16E+03) +	8.52E+03 (1.53E+03) +	**4.79E+03 (1.06E+03)**
F_6	1.10E+09 (4.76E+08) +	**1.43E+08 (1.31E+08)** −	2.39E+08 (2.14E+08)
F_7	3.35E+03 (3.67E+02) +	2.42E+03 (5.77E+02) +	**1.67E+03 (3.45E+02)**
F_8	**2.09E+01 (8.18E−02)** =	2.10E+01 (4.11E−02) =	**2.09E+01 (4.60E−02)**
F_9	1.54E+02 (1.11E+01) +	**8.43E+01 (2.25E+01)** =	8.54E+01 (5.56E+01)
F_{10}	1.78E+02 (1.35E+01) +	**1.19E+02 (2.72E+01)** −	1.57E+02 (2.82E+01)
F_{11}	3.91E+01 (9.69E−01) +	**1.47E+01 (1.79E+00)** −	3.32E+01 (9.62E+00)
F_{12}	2.64E+04 (1.37E+04) +	3.43E+04 (2.11E+04) +	**1.53E+04 (9.15E+03)**
F_{13}	1.38E+01 (8.82E−01) +	**4.90E+00 (3.19E+00)** −	1.22E+01 (1.07E+00)
F_{14}	1.27E+01 (3.09E−01) +	**1.20E+01 (3.72E−01)** −	1.24E+01 (2.84E−01)
F_{15}	4.78E+02 (8.69E+01) +	4.92E+02 (9.00E+01) +	**4.18E+02 (1.17E+02)**
F_{16}	1.86E+02 (1.13E+01) +	2.46E+02 (1.64E+02) +	**1.54E+02 (1.35E+02)**
F_{17}	**2.07E+02 (2.21E+01)** =	2.78E+02 (1.49E+02) +	2.10E+02 (7.17E+01)
F_{18}	**9.23E+02 (4.51E+01)** =	9.92E+02 (3.36E+01) +	**9.23E+02 (5.12E+01)**
F_{19}	9.13E+02 (4.44E+01) =	1.00E+03 (2.93E+01) +	**9.04E+02 (5.67E+01)**
F_{20}	**9.03E+02 (4.60E+01)** =	9.98E+02 (2.17E+01) +	9.25E+02 (4.75E+01)
F_{21}	1.03E+03 (1.32E+02) +	1.07E+03 (2.02E+02) +	**8.87E+02 (2.26E+02)**
F_{22}	9.38E+02 (1.48E+01) +	1.02E+03 (3.93E+01) +	**9.27E+02 (1.10E+01)**
F_{23}	1.00E+03 (1.49E+02) +	1.13E+03 (1.12E+02) +	**9.58E+02 (1.73E+02)**
F_{24}	6.96E+02 (9.76E+01) +	9.34E+02 (2.59E+02) +	**3.51E+02 (1.27E+02)**
F_{25}	1.09E+03 (2.82E+02) +	1.44E+03 (5.46E+01) +	**7.97E+02 (4.59E+02)**
+/=/−	20/5/0	18/2/5	−

"+", "=", and "−" indicate that the performance of our proposed algorithm is respectively better than, equal to, and worse than the corresponding algorithm according to the Wilcoxon signed-rank test at $\alpha = 0.05$.

Overall, based on the results and analysis, it can be seen that our proposed adaptive greedy approach is able to improve the performance of the original algorithm with different mutation strategies. In the next subsection, we will test the influence of the adaptive greedy mutation on advanced DE variant with parameter adaptation.

4.4 Effects on jDE With Different Mutation strategies

In order to study the effect of our approach more comprehensively, we further incorporate the adaptive greedy mutation strategies into an advanced DE variant, namely, jDE, which uses a self-adaptive approach to adapt the values of *F* and *CR* throughout the evolutionary process. The experimental results are shown in Tables 4–6. It can be found that, for the majority of the test functions, the adaptive greedy jDEs provide significantly better results compared with their corresponding jDEs. For example, jDE/*at*best/1 significantly improves the performance of jDE/best/1 on 19 out of 25 functions but only loses on 3 functions. jDE/current-to-*at*best/1 significantly outperforms jDE/current-to-rand/1 on 15 functions, whereas worse than it on only one function.

In general, from results shown in Tables 4–6, we can conclude that our proposed adaptive greedy mutation strategies are also capable of improving the performance of the advanced DE variant with parameter adaptation.

Table 4. Effects on DE/rand/1 and DE/best/1 in jDE

Fun.	jDE/rand/1 Mean (Std.)	jDE/best/1 Mean (Std.)	jDE/*at*best/1 Mean (Std.)
F_1	**0.00E+00 (0.00E+00)** =	1.05E−13 (6.87E−14) +	**0.00E+00 (0.00E+00)**
F_2	3.29E−06 (3.59E−06) +	1.28E−12 (1.24E−12) +	**2.59E−13 (1.49E−13)**
F_3	1.91E+05 (7.94E+04) +	**9.74E+03 (7.18E+03)** −	5.11E+04 (3.25E+04)
F_4	1.67E−01 (3.49E−01) +	4.37E+02 (5.60E+02) +	**1.51E−03 (3.82E−03)**
F_5	1.10E+03 (4.65E+02) −	3.05E+03 (5.58E+02) +	**1.64E+03 (4.09E+02)**
F_6	2.01E+01 (2.36E+01) +	**1.12E+00 (1.79E+00)** =	1.59E+00 (1.95E+00)
F_7	**1.22E−02 (9.57E−03)** =	2.32E−02 (2.22E−02) +	1.54E−02 (1.33E−02)
F_8	**2.09E+01 (4.91E−02)** =	2.10E+01 (2.82E−02) =	**2.09E+01 (3.36E−02)**
F_9	**0.00E+00 (0.00E+00)** =	6.90E+01 (1.70E+01) +	**0.00E+00 (0.00E+00)**
F_{10}	5.60E+01 (7.35E+00) +	9.28E+01 (1.67E+01) +	**3.49E+01 (1.11E+01)**
F_{11}	2.86E+01 (2.11E+00) +	**2.41E+01 (2.78E+00)** −	2.67E+01 (2.97E+00)
F_{12}	1.51E+04 (7.10E+03) +	1.59E+03 (2.15E+03) +	**1.06E+03 (1.58E+03)**
F_{13}	1.71E+00 (1.78E−01) +	3.44E+00 (1.26E+00) +	**1.65E+00 (1.07E−01)**
F_{14}	1.30E+01 (1.82E−01) =	**1.23E+01 (2.98E−01)** −	1.29E+01 (2.22E−01)
F_{15}	**3.47E+02 (8.92E+01)** =	3.97E+02 (6.40E+01) =	3.60E+02 (8.49E+01)
F_{16}	8.90E+01 (6.78E+01) +	1.85E+02 (8.94E+01) +	**7.97E+01 (7.19E+01)**
F_{17}	1.33E+02 (1.70E+01) +	2.53E+02 (1.28E+02) +	**8.67E+01 (6.85E+01)**
F_{18}	**9.06E+02 (1.82E+00)** =	9.52E+02 (2.16E+01) +	9.08E+02 (2.24E+01)
F_{19}	**9.07E+02 (1.76E+00)** =	9.47E+02 (2.22E+01) +	9.12E+02 (3.77E+00)
F_{20}	**9.02E+02 (2.01E+01)** =	9.56E+02 (2.21E+01) +	9.08E+02 (2.23E+01)
F_{21}	**5.00E+02 (1.33E−13)** =	6.83E+02 (2.69E+02) +	**5.00E+02 (1.64E−13)**
F_{22}	**9.05E+02 (8.35E+00)** =	9.70E+02 (3.76E+01) +	**9.05E+02 (1.11E+01)**
F_{23}	**5.34E+02 (3.01E−04)** =	7.47E+02 (2.44E+02) +	**5.34E+02 (5.04E−01)**
F_{24}	**2.00E+02 (2.84E−14)** =	3.27E+02 (3.42E+02) +	**2.00E+02 (2.84E−14)**
F_{25}	2.10E+02 (3.62E−01) +	2.95E+02 (2.81E+02) +	**2.09E+02 (3.47E−02)**
+/=/−	11/13/1	19/3/3	−

"+", "=", and "−" indicate that the performance of our proposed algorithm is respectively better than, equal to, and worse than the corresponding algorithm according to the Wilcoxon signed-rank test at $\alpha = 0.05$.

Table 5. Effects on DE/rand/2 and DE/best/2 in jDE

Fun.	jDE/rand/2 Mean (Std.)	jDE/best/2 Mean (Std.)	jDE/*at*best/2 Mean (Std.)
F_1	**0.00E+00 (0.00E+00)** =	6.14E−14 (1.54E−14) +	**0.00E+00 (0.00E+00)**
F_2	2.23E−03 (4.77E−03) +	5.07E−13 (1.65E−13) =	**3.55E−13 (3.05E−13)**
F_3	2.73E+05 (1.63E+05) +	**1.22E+04 (8.56E+03)** −	6.23E+04 (3.43E+04)
F_4	6.71E+00 (2.04E+01) +	3.34E+00 (7.48E+00) +	**1.77E−04 (3.11E−04)**
F_5	7.25E+02 (3.81E+02) =	2.13E+03 (6.71E+02) +	8.91E+02 (4.12E+02)
F_6	1.54E+01 (1.19E+01) +	1.92E+00 (2.00E+00) +	**4.99E−01 (1.08E+00)**
F_7	**4.14E−03 (4.76E−03)** −	1.27E−02 (1.34E−02) =	1.30E−02 (9.34E−03)
F_8	**2.09E+01 (4.46E−02)** =	**2.09E+01 (5.15E−02)** =	2.09E+01 (4.15E−02)
F_9	**0.00E+00 (0.00E+00)** =	1.12E+01 (9.61E+00) +	**0.00E+00 (0.00E+00)**
F_{10}	6.62E+01 (9.32E+00) +	7.16E+01 (1.58E+01) +	**4.61E+01 (9.12E+00)**
F_{11}	2.83E+01 (1.91E+00) =	**2.52E+01 (3.00E+00)** −	2.82E+01 (1.41E+00)
F_{12}	2.27E+04 (4.94E+03) +	**2.70E+03 (4.24E+03)** −	1.25E+04 (8.99E+03)
F_{13}	1.81E+00 (1.55E−01) +	1.87E+00 (2.17E−01) +	**1.74E+00 (1.60E−01)**
F_{14}	1.31E+01 (2.26E−01) =	**1.28E+01 (2.90E−01)** =	1.30E+01 (2.30E−01)
F_{15}	**2.70E+02 (1.76E+02)** −	3.81E+02 (8.03E+02) =	3.84E+02 (5.43E+01)
F_{16}	9.67E+01 (1.92E+01) +	1.44E+02 (8.78E+01) +	**7.65E+01 (2.21E+01)**
F_{17}	1.57E+02 (1.56E+01) +	1.58E+02 (1.11E+02) +	**1.23E+02 (2.25E+01)**
F_{18}	**9.08E+02 (1.51E+00)** =	9.16E+02 (4.05E+01) +	**9.08E+02 (1.91E+00)**
F_{19}	**9.07E+02 (1.40E+00) =**	9.11E+02 (1.73E+01) +	9.08E+02 (1.84E+00)
F_{20}	**9.07E+02 (1.24E+00) =**	9.21E+02 (2.93E+01) +	9.08E+02 (2.49E+00)
F_{21}	**5.00E+02 (1.07E−13)** =	6.30E+02 (2.47E+02) +	**5.00E+02 (1.65E−13)**
F_{22}	9.23E+02 (8.36E+00) +	9.46E+02 (2.28E+01) +	**9.03E+02 (9.93E+00)**
F_{23}	**5.34E+02 (2.59E−04)** =	7.23E+02 (2.66E+02) +	**5.34E+02 (2.78E−04)**
F_{24}	**2.00E+02 (6.25E−13)** =	**2.00E+02 (9.17E−13)** =	**2.00E+02 (2.84E−14)**
F_{25}	**2.09E+02 (2.73E−01)** +	**2.11E+02 (1.20E+00)** =	**2.09E+02 (2.31E−01)**
+/=/−	11/12/2	15/7/3	−

"+", "=", and "−" indicate that the performance of our proposed algorithm is respectively better than, equal to, and worse than the corresponding algorithm according to the Wilcoxon signed-rank test at $\alpha = 0.05$.

Table 6. Effects on DE/current-to-rand/1 and DE/current-to-best/1 in jDE

Fun.	jDE/current-to-rand/1 Mean (Std.)	jDE/current-to-best/1 Mean (Std.)	jDE/current-to-*at*best/1 Mean (Std.)
F_1	1.14E−14 (2.27E−14) +	5.23E−14 (1.85E−14) +	**0.00E+00 (0.00E+00)**
F_2	1.50E+01 (3.82E+01) +	**1.96E−12 (4.77E−12)** −	8.83E−02 (4.18E−01)
F_3	4.64E+05 (2.62E+05) +	**3.99E+04 (7.85E+04)** −	1.63E+05 (9.16E+04)
F_4	9.05E+01 (7.87E+01) +	**8.58E−01 (8.12E−01)** −	7.57E+00 (2.29E+01)
F_5	2.81E+03 (3.89E+02) +	2.30E+03 (7.24E+02) =	**2.29E+03 (5.41E+02)**
F_6	3.34E+01 (2.38E+01) +	1.31E+01 (2.89E+01) =	**1.30E+00 (1.50E+00)**
F_7	1.29E−02 (1.10E−02) +	2.21E−02 (2.78E−02) +	**8.36E−03 (1.16E−02)**
F_8	**2.09E+01 (5.19E−02)** =	**2.09E+01 (8.74E−02)** =	**2.09E+01 (4.12E−02)**
F_9	1.50E−12 (6.12E−12) +	5.00E−14 (1.85E−14) +	**0.00E+00 (0.00E+00)**
F_{10}	3.76E+01 (6.61E+00) +	4.80E+01 (1.08E+01) +	**3.51E+01 (6.57E+00)**
F_{11}	**2.50E+01 (1.37E+00)** =	2.53E+01 (1.14E+00) +	**2.50E+01 (1.71E+00)**
F_{12}	9.40E+03 (3.03E+03) +	**2.49E+03 (4.19E+03)** −	5.06E+03 (2.76E+03)
F_{13}	**1.66E+00 (1.82E−01)** =	1.69E+00 (1.79E−01) =	1.70E+00 (1.59E−01)
F_{14}	1.28E+01 (1.99E−01) +	1.27E+01 (2.37E−01) +	**1.26E+01 (2.83E−01)**
F_{15}	**2.15E+02 (9.32E+01)** −	3.52E+02 (1.42E+02) +	3.04E+02 (1.36E+01)
F_{16}	**6.57E+01 (1.14E+01)** +	1.74E+02 (1.51E+02) +	7.00E+01 (6.79E+01)
F_{17}	1.04E+02 (2.28E+01) +	2.02E+02 (1.52E+02) +	**9.31E+01 (2.95E+01)**
F_{18}	**8.75E+02 (5.65E+01)** =	8.87E+02 (5.51E+01) =	8.91E+02 (5.10E+01)
F_{19}	**8.71E+02 (5.83E+01)** =	9.19E+02 (2.53E+01) +	8.84E+02 (5.29E+00)
F_{20}	**8.86E+02 (534E+01)** =	8.89E+02 (5.58E+01) =	8.90E+02 (5.08E+01)
F_{21}	**5.00E+02 (1.51E−13)** =	6.29E+02 (2.43E+02) +	**5.00E+02 (1.61E−13)**
F_{22}	**9.26E+02 (1.01E+01)** =	**9.27E+02 (2.04E+01)** +	**9.21E+02 (1.15E+01)**
F_{23}	5.35E+02 (1.93E+00) +	6.30E+02 (2.13E+02) +	**5.34E+02 (6.50E−01)**
F_{24}	**2.00E+02 (1.03E−12)** =	**2.00E+02 (1.35E−12)** =	**2.00E+02 (2.84E−14)**
F_{25}	2.12E+02 (7.86E−01) +	2.61E+02 (1.93E+02) +	**2.11E+02 (6.81E−01)**
+/=/−	15/9/1	14/7/4	−

"+", "=", and "−" indicate that the performance of our proposed algorithm is respectively better than, equal to, and worse than the corresponding algorithm according to the Wilcoxon signed-rank test at $\alpha = 0.05$.

5. CONCLUSION

In this paper, adaptive greedy mutation strategies have been proposed for the DE algorithm. The proposed strategies utilize the information of top *t* solutions in the population. To adapt the greediness degree to fit for different optimization scenarios, an adaptive control scheme has been proposed for adjusting the value of parameter *t*. The adaptive greedy mutation strategies have been applied to the original DE and jDE. Experiments have been conducted on 25 benchmark functions from CEC 2005. The results demonstrate the effectiveness of the adaptive greedy mutation strategies to improve the overall performance.

The applications of the proposed strategies to other state-of-the-art DE variants will be studied in future work. The extension of the proposed strategies to multi-objective and dynamic optimization will be another future direction.

6. ACKNOWLEDGMENTS

This work was supported in part by the National High-Technology Research and Development Program (863 Program) of China No.2013AA01A212, in part by the NSFC for Distinguished Young Scholars 61125205, in part by the NSFC No. 61332002, No.61300044 and No. 61170220.

7. REFERENCES

[1] R. M. Storn and K. V. Price, "Differential evolution-a simple and efficient adaptive scheme for global optimization over

continuous spaces," TR-95-012, 1995 [Online]. Available: http://icsi.berkeley.edu/~storn/litera.html.

[2] R. M. Storn and K. V. Price, "Differential evolution-a simple and efficient heuristic for global optimization over continuous spaces," *J. Global Optim.*, vol. 11, pp. 341–359, 1997.

[3] K. V. Price, R. M. Storn, and J. A. Lampinen, *Differential Evolution: A Practical Approach to Global Optimization.* Berlin, Germany: Springer-Verlag, 2005.

[4] K. V. Price, "An introduction to differential evolution," in *New Ideas in Optimization*, D. Corne, M. Dorigo, and V. Glover, Eds. London, U.K.: McGraw-Hill, 1999, pp. 79–108.

[5] S. Das and P. N. Suganthan, "Differential evolution: a survey of the state-of-the-art," *IEEE Trans Evol. Comput.*, vol. 15, no. 1, pp. 4–31, Feb. 2011.

[6] F. Neri and V. Tirronen, "Recent advances in differential evolution: A survey and experimental analysis," *Artif. Intell. Rev.*, vol. 33, no. 1/2, pp. 61–106, Feb. 2010.

[7] N. Noman and H. Iba, "Accelerating differential evolution using an adaptive local search," *IEEE Trans. Evol. Comput.*, vol. 12, no. 1, pp. 107–125, Feb. 2008.

[8] D. K. Tasoulis, V. P. Plagianakos, and M. N. Vrahatis, "Clustering in evolutionary algorithms to efficiently compute simultaneously local and global minima," in *Proc. IEEE CEC*, vol. 2. 2005, pp. 1847–1854.

[9] M. G. Epitropakis, V. P. Plagianakos, and M. N. Vrahatis, "Balancing the exploration and exploitation capabilities of the differential evolution algorithm," in *Proc. IEEE CEC*, 2008, pp. 2686–2693.

[10] M. G. Epitropakis, D. K. Tasoulis, N. G. Pavlidis, V. P. Plagianakos, and M. N. Vrahatis, "Enhancing differential evolution utilizing proximitybased mutation operators," *IEEE Trans Evol. Comput.*, vol. 15, no. 1, pp. 99–119, Feb. 2011.

[11] A. K. Qin, V. L. Huang, and P. N. Suganthan, "Differential evolution algorithm with strategy adaptation for global numerical optimization," *IEEE Trans. Evol. Comput.*, vol. 13, no. 2, pp. 398–417, Apr. 2009.

[12] R. Mallipeddi, P. Suganthan, Q. Pan, and M. Tasgetiren, "Differential evolution algorithm with ensemble of parameters and mutation strategies," *Appl. Soft Comput.*, vol. 11, no. 2, pp. 1679–1696, Mar. 2011.

[13] W. Gong, Z. Cai, C. X. Ling, and H. Li, "Enhanced differential evolution with adaptive strategies for numerical optimization," *IEEE Trans. Syst., Man, Cybern. B, Cybern.*, vol. 41, no. 2, pp. 397–413, Apr. 2011.

[14] Y. Wang, Z. Cai, and Q. Zhang, "Differential evolution with composite trial vector generation strategies and control parameters," *IEEE Trans. Evol. Comput.*, vol. 15, no. 1, pp. 55–66, Feb. 2011.

[15] H. Y. Fan and J. Lampinen, "A trigonometric mutation operator to differential evolution," *J. Global Optim.*, vol. 27, no. 1, pp. 105–129, 2003.

[16] P. Kaelo and M. M. Ali, "Differential evolution algorithms using hybrid mutation," *Comput. Optimization Appl.*, vol. 37, pp. 231–246, Jun. 2007.

[17] S. Das, A. Abraham, U. K. Chakraborty, and A. Konar, "Differential evolution using a neighborhood-based mutation operator," *IEEE Trans. Evol. Comput.*, vol. 13, no. 3, pp. 526–553, Jun. 2009.

[18] J. Q. Zhang and A. C. Sanderson, "JADE: Adaptive differential evolution with optional external archive," *IEEE Trans. Evol. Comput.*, vol. 13, no. 5, pp. 945–958, Oct. 2009.

[19] S. M. Islam, S. Das, S. Ghosh, S. Roy, and P. N. Suganthan, "An adaptive differential evolution algorithm with novel mutation and crossover strategies for global numerical optimization," *IEEE Trans. Syst., Man, Cybern. B, Cybern.*, vol. 42, no. 2, pp. 397–413, Apr. 2012.

[20] M. G. Epitropakis, D. K. Tasoulis, N. G. Pavlidis, V. P. Plagianakos, and M. N. Vrahatis, "Enhancing differential evolution utilizing proximitybased mutation operators," *IEEE Trans Evol. Comput.*, vol. 15, no. 1, pp. 99–119, Feb. 2011.

[21] W. Gong and Z. Cai, "Differential evolution with ranking-based mutation operators," *IEEE Trans. Cybern.*,vol. 43, no. 6, pp. 2066–2081, Dec. 2013.

[22] Y. Cai and J. Wang, "Differential evolution with neighborhood and direction information for numerical optimization," *IEEE Trans. Cybern.*, vol. 43, no. 6, pp. 2202–2215, Dec. 2013.

[23] P. N. Suganthan, N. Hansen, J. J. Liang, K. Deb, Y.-P. Chen, A. Auger, and S. Tiwari, "Problem definitions and evaluation criteria for the CEC 2005 special session on real-parameter optimization," Nanyang Technol. Univ., Singapore, KanGAL Rep. No. 2005005, May 2005, IIT Kanpur, India.

[24] J. Brest, S. Greiner, B. Boskovic, M. Mernik, and V. Zumer, "Self-adapting control parameters in differential evolution: A comparative study on numerical benchmark problems," *IEEE Trans. Evol. Comput.*, vol. 10, no. 6, pp. 646–657, Dec. 2006.

[25] S. Rahnamayan, H. R. Tizhoosh, and M. M. A. Salama, "Opposition based differential evolution," *IEEE Trans. Evol. Comput.*, vol. 12, no. 1, pp. 64–79, Feb. 2008.

[26] J. Derrac, S. Garc´ıa, D. Molina, and F. Herrera, "A practical tutorial on the use of nonparametric statistical tests as a methodology for comparing evolutionary and swarm intelligence algorithms," *Swarm Evol. Comput.*, vol. 1, no. 1, pp. 3–18, Mar. 2011.

[27] J. Rönkkönen, S. Kukkonen, and K. V. Price, "Real-parameter optimization with differential evolution," in *Proc. IEEE Congr. Evol. Comput.*, 2005, pp. 506–513.

[28] U. K. Chakraborty, *Advances in Differential Evolution.* Berlin, Germany: Springer, 2008.

Constrained Multi-Objective Aerodynamic Shape Optimization via Swarm Intelligence

Saúl Zapotecas Martínez
Shinshu University
Faculty of Engineering
4-17-1 Wakasato, Nagano,
380-8553, Japan
saul.zapotecas@gmail.com

Alfredo Arias-Montaño
IPN-ESIME
Departamento de Ingeniería
Aeronáutica
México, D.F. 07340, MEXICO
aarias@ipn.mx

Carlos A. Coello Coello
CINVESTAV-IPN (EVOCINV)
Departamento de
Computación
México, D.F. 07360, MEXICO
ccoello@cs.cinvestav.mx

ABSTRACT

In this paper, we present a Multi-objective Particle Swarm Optimizer (MOPSO) based on a decomposition approach, which is proposed to solve Constrained Multi-Objective Aerodynamic Shape Optimization Problems (CMO-ASOPs). The constraint-handling technique adopted in this approach is based on the well-known ε-constraint method. Since the ε-constraint method was initially proposed to deal with constrained single-objective optimization problems, we adapted it so that it could be incorporated into a MOPSO. Our main focus is to solve CMO-ASOPs in an efficient and effective manner. The proposed constrained MOPSO guides the search by updating the position of each particle using a set of solutions considered as the global best according to both the decomposition approach and the ε-constraint method. Our preliminary results indicate that our proposed approach is able to outperform a state-of-the-art MOEA in several CMO-ASOPs.

Categories and Subject Descriptors

I.2.8 [**Computing Methodologies**]: Artificial Intelligence—*Problem Solving, Control Methods, and Search.*

Keywords

Constrained Multi-objective Optimization, Multi-objective Swarm Optimization, Aerodynamic Shape Optimization.

1. INTRODUCTION

Multi-objective Evolutionary Algorithms (MOEAs) have been successfully applied to the solution of a wide variety of problems in the fields of science and engineering [6, 7]. Although MOEAs were originally designed for solving unconstrained multi-objective optimization problems, most real-world applications require satisfying equality and/or inequality constraints. Generally, Constrained Multi-objective Optimization Problems (CMOPs) are difficult to solve, because finding feasible solutions may require substantial additional computational resources (i.e., an important number of extra objective function evaluations). In aeronautical systems design as well as in the design of propulsion system components, such as turbine engines, aerodynamics plays a key role. Thus, Aerodynamic Shape Optimization (ASO) is a crucial task, which has been extensively studied and developed. This discipline has recently benefited from the use of MOEAs, which have gained an increasing popularity in the last few years. For a detailed survey of applications of MOEAs in this field, the interested reader is referred to [3].

The simplicity and success of particle swarm optimization (PSO) algorithms, has motivated researchers to extend their use to solve Multi-objective Optimization Problems (MOPs) in the field of engineering and science, giving rise to the well-known Multi-Objective Particle Swarm Optimizers (MOPSOs). In recent years, the use of swarm intelligence applied to ASO problems has attracted the interest of several researchers. However, most of these approaches have been used to deal with single-objective ASO problems (see e.g. [20]) or with unconstrained MOPs (see e.g. [21]).

In this paper, we study the performance of a recent Multi-Objective Particle Swam Optimizer based on decomposition (called here DMOPSO[1]) [23], which was initially introduced for solving unconstrained MOPs. Here, we add to DMOPSO a constraint-handling mechanism based on the well-known ε-constraint method [19], which was proposed for single-objective optimization. The resulting approach is used to solve CMO-ASOs, which, are normally difficult to tackle in an efficient way, because of the high computational time that it is required to evaluate their objective functions. We argue that our proposed approach is a viable choice for solving CMO-ASOs in an effective and efficient way.

The remainder of this paper is organized as follows. In Section 2, we provide the basic concepts required for understanding the rest of the paper. Section 3 describes our proposed approach, including a detailed explanation of the adaptation of the ε-constraint method into DMOPSO in order to maintain a suitable balance between feasible solutions and convergence towards the Pareto optimal front. Section 4 presents the experimental study used for assessing the performance of our proposed algorithm. In Section 5, we provide a discussion of our results. Finally, in Section 6, we

GECCO'14, July 12–16, 2014, Vancouver, BC, Canada.
Copyright 2014 ACM 978-1-4503-2662-9/14/07 ...$15.00.
http://dx.doi.org/10.1145/2576768.2598372.

[1]The acronym DMOPSO (used in this paper) should not be confused with the Dynamic Multiobjective Particle Swarm Optimization (DMOPSO) presented in [11].

provide our conclusions and some possible paths for future research.

2. BASIC CONCEPTS

2.1 Constrained Multi-objective Optimization

A nonlinear Constrained Multi-objective Optimization Problem (CMOP) can be stated as (assuming minimization of all the objective functions):

$$\begin{array}{lll} \min & \mathbf{F}(\mathbf{x}) = (f_1(\mathbf{x}), \ldots, f_k(\mathbf{x}))^T & \\ \text{s.t.} & g_i(\mathbf{x}) \leq 0, & i = 1, \ldots, p \\ & h_j(\mathbf{x}) = 0, & j = 1, \ldots, q \\ & L_i \leq x_i \leq U_i, & i = 1, \ldots, n \end{array} \quad (1)$$

where $\mathbf{x} = (x_1, \ldots, x_n)^T \in \mathbb{R}^n$ is an n dimensional vector of decision variables, $g_i(\mathbf{x}) \leq 0$ and $h_j(\mathbf{x}) = 0$ represent the q inequality constraints and the p equality constraints, respectively. L_i and U_i are the lower and upper bounds of each of the decision variables x_i. The vector $\mathbf{F}$ consists of k objective functions f_i's $(i = 1, \ldots, k)$ to be minimized. The set of solutions that satisfy the constraints of problem (1) defines the feasible region $\Omega \subseteq \mathbb{R}^n$.

In order to describe the concept of optimality in which we are interested on, the following definitions are introduced [13]:

Definition 1. Let $\mathbf{x}, \mathbf{y} \in \Omega$, we say that $\mathbf{x}$ *dominates* $\mathbf{y}$ (denoted by $\mathbf{x} \prec \mathbf{y}$) if and only if, $f_i(\mathbf{x}) \leq f_i(\mathbf{y})$ and $f_i(\mathbf{x}) < f_i(\mathbf{y})$ in at least one f_i for all $i = 1, \ldots, k$.

Definition 2. Let $\mathbf{x}^\star \in \Omega$, we say that $\mathbf{x}^\star$ is a *Pareto optimal* solution, if there is no other solution $\mathbf{y} \in \Omega$ such that $\mathbf{y} \prec \mathbf{x}^\star$.

Definition 3. The *Pareto optimal set* PS is defined by: $PS = \{\mathbf{x} \in \Omega | \mathbf{x} \text{ is Pareto optimal solution}\}$, and the *Pareto optimal front* PF is defined as: $PF = \{\mathbf{F}(\mathbf{x}) | \mathbf{x} \in \mathcal{PS}\}$.

We thus wish to find the best possible *trade-offs* among the objectives, such that no objective can be improved without worsening another one. However, in this case, our solutions must also satisfy the constraints of problem (1). We are also interested in generating a set of solutions that are well-distributed along the Pareto front.

2.2 Decomposition of a Multi-objective Optimization Problem

It is well-known that a Pareto optimal solution to the problem (1), under certain conditions, could be an optimal solution of a scalar optimization problem in which the objective is an aggregation of all the objective functions f_i's. Many scalar approaches have been proposed to aggregate the objectives of an MOP. Among them, the Tchebycheff approach is one of most widely used methods reported in the specialized literature. In the following, we describe the Tchebycheff problem which is adopted in this study. Note however, that other scalarization approaches could also be easily coupled to this work–see for example those presented in [8, 13].

Tchebycheff approach

This approach transforms the vector of function values $\mathbf{F}$ into a scalar optimization problem which is of the form:

$$\begin{array}{ll} \min & g^{te}(\mathbf{x}|\mathbf{w}, \mathbf{z}) = \max_{1<j<k}\{w_j |f_j(\mathbf{x}) - z_j|\} \\ s.t. & \mathbf{x} \in \Omega \end{array} \quad (2)$$

where Ω is the feasible region, $\mathbf{z} = (z_1, \ldots, z_k)^T$, such that: $z_j = \min\{f_j(\mathbf{x}) | \mathbf{x} \in \Omega\}$ for each $i = 1, \ldots, k$ and $\mathbf{w} = (w_1, \ldots, w_k)^T$ is a weight vector, i.e., $w_j \geq 0$ for all $j = 1, \ldots, k$ and $\sum_{j=1}^{k} w_j = 1$.

For each Pareto optimal point $\mathbf{x}^\star$ there exists a weight vector $\mathbf{w}$ such that $\mathbf{x}^\star$ is the optimum solution of equation (2) and each optimal solution of equation (2) is a Pareto optimal solution of equation (1). An appropriate representation of the Pareto front could be reached by solving different scalarization problems. Such problems can be defined by a set of well-distributed weight vectors, which establish the search direction in the optimization process.

2.3 Constraint Violation Degree

The overall constraint violation $\phi(\mathbf{x})$ of a solution $\mathbf{x}$ can be given by the maximum of all constraints or the sum of all constraints.

$$\phi(\mathbf{x}) = \max\{\max_i\{0, g_i(\mathbf{x})\}, \max_j\{|h_j(\mathbf{x})|\}\} \quad (3)$$

$$\phi(\mathbf{x}) = \sum_i || \max\{0, g_i(\mathbf{x})\}||^\alpha + \sum_j ||h_j(\mathbf{x})||^\alpha \quad (4)$$

where α is a positive number, i.e. $\alpha \in (0, +\infty)$. Equality constraints can be transformed into inequality constraints by using [5]:

$$|h_j(\mathbf{x}) - \varepsilon| \leq 0, j = 1, \ldots, q \quad (5)$$

where ε is a small real-value threshold.

For methods that do not require gradient information, it does not matter if equation (5) is non-differentiable. Therefore, a CMOP with equality constraints can be stated as a CMOP having only inequality constraints. Assuming that all constraints of problem (1) are inequality constraints, the constraint violation in equations (3) and (4) can be computed as:

$$\phi(\mathbf{x}) = \max_{1 \leq i \leq p} \{0, g_i(\mathbf{x})\} \quad (6)$$

$$\phi(\mathbf{x}) = \sum_{i=1}^{p} || \max\{0, g_i(\mathbf{x})\}||^\alpha \quad (7)$$

Thus, we can say that without loss of generality, in this paper we consider only constraint functions of the form $g(\mathbf{x}) \leq 0$. Any equality constraint $h(\mathbf{x}) = 0$ needs to be transformed into an inequality constraint using equation (5).

2.4 The ε-Constraint Method

The ε-constraint method for single-objective optimization was proposed by Takahama and Sakai [19]. This constraint-handling technique adopts a lexicographic ordering with relaxation of the constraints. The basic idea is to define an ε level comparison in order to state an order relation on pairs consisting of the objective function value and the constraint violation value, $(f(\mathbf{x}), \phi(\mathbf{x}))$. If the violation of a constraint is greater than 0, then the solution is not feasible and its value will be low. Since the feasibility of a solution $\mathbf{x}$ is more important than the minimization of the objective function, the ε level comparisons are defined as a lexicographic order in which $\phi(\mathbf{x})$ precedes $f(\mathbf{x})$.

Let $f_1(f_2)$ and $\phi_1(\phi_2)$ be the function values and the constraint violation at a solution $\mathbf{x}^1(\mathbf{x}^2)$, respectively. Then, for any ε satisfying $\varepsilon \geq 0$, the ε level comparison $<_\varepsilon$ and $\leq_\varepsilon$ between (f_1, ϕ_1) and (f_2, ϕ_2) is defined as follows:

$$(f_1, \phi_1) <_\varepsilon (f_2, \phi_2) \Leftrightarrow \begin{cases} f_1 < f_2, & \text{if } \phi_1, \phi_2 \leq \varepsilon \\ f_1 < f_2, & \text{if } \phi_1 = \phi_2 \\ \phi_1 < \phi_2, & \text{otherwise} \end{cases} \tag{8}$$

$$(f_1, \phi_1) \leq_\varepsilon (f_2, \phi_2) \Leftrightarrow \begin{cases} f_1 \leq f_2, & \text{if } \phi_1, \phi_2 \leq \varepsilon \\ f_1 \leq f_2, & \text{if } \phi_1 = \phi_2 \\ \phi_1 < \phi_2, & \text{otherwise} \end{cases} \tag{9}$$

In case of $\varepsilon = \infty$, the ε level comparison $<_\infty$ and $\leq_\infty$ are equivalent to the ordinal comparison $<$ and $\leq$ between function values. Furthermore, the cases $\varepsilon = 0$, $<_0$ and $\leq_0$ are equivalent to the lexicographic order in which the constraint violation $\phi(\mathbf{x})$ precedes the function value $f(\mathbf{x})$.

2.5 The Framework of DMOPSO

The decomposition-based Multi-Objective Particle Swarm Optimizer (called here DMOPSO) [23], transforms a MOP into several scalarization problems. Therefore, an approximation of the Pareto front is obtained by solving the N scalarization subproblems in which a MOP is decomposed.

Considering $W = \{\mathbf{w}^1, \ldots, \mathbf{w}^N\}$ as a well-distributed set of weight vectors, DMOPSO finds the best solution to each subproblem defined by each weight vector using the Tchebycheff approach. The objective function of the jth subproblem is then defined by $g^{te}(\mathbf{x}|\mathbf{w}^j, \mathbf{z})$, where $\mathbf{w}^j \in W$ and $\mathbf{z} = (z_1, \ldots, z_k)^T$ is the artificial utopian vector whose component z_i is the minimum value found so far for the objective f_i.

At each generation, DMOPSO finds the best solution to each subproblem throughout the evolutionary process and maintains:

1. a population of N particles $P = \{\mathbf{x}^1, \ldots, \mathbf{x}^N\}$, where $\mathbf{x}^i$ is the current solution to the ith subproblem; the velocity $\mathbf{v}^i$, the age a^i and the personal best $\mathbf{x}^i_{pb}$ of each particle $\mathbf{x}^i$, for each $i = 1, \ldots, N$.

2. $F^1, \ldots, F^N$, where F^i is the F-value of each particle $\mathbf{x}^i$, i.e., $F^i = \mathbf{F}(\mathbf{x}^i)$ for each $i = 1, \ldots, N$;

3. the global best set $G_{best} = \{\mathbf{g}^1, \ldots, \mathbf{g}^N\}$ which constitutes the set of particles considered to be the best for the ith subproblem along the search process.

The general framework of DMOPSO is presented in Algorithm 1, where each particle in the swarm is evolved by updating both its velocity $\mathbf{v}^i$ and its position $\mathbf{x}^i$ according to the following equations:

$$\mathbf{v}^i = w\mathbf{v}^i + c_1 r_1(\mathbf{x}^i_{pb} - \mathbf{x}^i) + c_2 r_2(\mathbf{g}^i_{best} - \mathbf{x}^i) \tag{10}$$

and the new particle's position is updated according to the equation:

$$\mathbf{x}^i = \mathbf{x}^i + \mathbf{v}^i \tag{11}$$

Algorithm 1: General Framework of DMOPSO

Input:
a stopping criterion;
N: the number of the subproblems considered in εDMOPSO;
W: a set of weight vectors $\{\mathbf{w}^1, \ldots, \mathbf{w}^N\}$;
Output:
P: the final swarm of particles found by εDMOPSO.

Initialize a swarm of N particles $P = \{\mathbf{x}^1, \ldots, \mathbf{x}^N\}$;
$\mathbf{z} = (+\infty, \ldots, +\infty)^T$;
foreach $\{1, \ldots, N\}$ **do**
  $F^i = \mathbf{F}(\mathbf{x}^i)$;
  $\mathbf{v}^i = \mathbf{0}$;
  $\mathbf{x}^i_{pb} = \mathbf{x}^i$;
  $a^i = 0$;
  If $f_j(\mathbf{x}^i) < z_j$ then $z_j = f_j(\mathbf{x}^i)$, for each $j = 1, \ldots, k$;
end
$G_{best} = P$;
while *stopping criterion is not satisfied* **do**
  foreach $i \in \{1, \ldots, N\}$ **do**
    Select randomly a solution $\mathbf{g}^i_{best}$ from G_{best}, such that: $\mathbf{x}^i \neq \mathbf{g}^i_{best}$;
    if $a^i < T_a$ **then**
      // Using $\mathbf{g}^i_{best}$ and $\mathbf{x}^i_{pb}$ do:
      Update velocity $\mathbf{v}^i$ (equation (10));
      Update position $\mathbf{x}^i$ (equation (11));
      $a^i = a^i + 1$;
    else
      Reset the particle $\mathbf{x}^i$ (equation (12));
      $\mathbf{v}^i = \mathbf{0}$;
      $a^i = 0$;
    end
    Repair bounds of the particle $\mathbf{x}^i$ (equation (13));
    Calculate $\mathbf{F}(\mathbf{x}^i)$;
    If $f_j(\mathbf{x}^i) < z_j$ then $z_j = f_j(\mathbf{x}^i)$, for each $j = 1, \ldots, k$;
    // Updating $\mathbf{x}^i_{pb}$:
    if $g^{te}(\mathbf{x}^i|\mathbf{w}^i, \mathbf{z}) < g^{te}(\mathbf{x}^i_{pb}|\mathbf{w}^i, \mathbf{z})$ *or* $a^i = 0$ **then**
      $\mathbf{x}^i_{pb} = \mathbf{x}^i$;
      $a^i = 0$;
    end
    // Using Algorithm 2:
    $G_{best} = \mathit{update\_G_{best}}(P \cup G_{best}, W)$;
  end
end

where $w \geq 0$ represents the inertia factor, $c1, c2 \geq 0$ are the constraints on the velocity, r_1, r_2 are two random variables having a uniform distribution in the range $(0, 1]$, $\mathbf{v}^i$, $\mathbf{x}^i_{pb}$ and $\mathbf{g}^i_{best}$ represent the velocity, the personal best and the selected global best position for the ith particle, respectively.

If a particle does not improve its personal position in a flight cycle, then the particle increases (by one) its age. On the other hand, if a particle exceeds a certain (pre-defined) age threshold, the particle (including, its velocity, its age and its best personal) is reinitialized. DMOPSO employs a reinitialization mechanism based on a parametric probability density function, which involves the selected global best $\mathbf{g}^i_{best}$ and the personal best $\mathbf{x}^i_{pb}$ of the current particle $\mathbf{x}^i$. Therefore, the jth component of the new particle is reset according to the following equation:

$$x^i_j = N\left(\frac{g^i_{best,j} - x^i_{pb,j}}{2}, |g^i_{best,j} - x^i_{pb,j}|\right) \tag{12}$$

Algorithm 2: *update_G*$_{best}(Q, W)$

```
T = Q;
foreach i = {1, ..., N} do
    g^i = {x | min_{x∈T} g^te(x|w^i, z)}, where w^i ∈ W;
    T = T \ {x}
end
G = {g^1, ..., g^N};
return G;
```

where $N(m, \sigma)$ represents a random number using a Gaussian distribution with mean m and sigma σ.

When a particle goes beyond the boundaries of the decision variables, this particle needs to be repaired. DMOPSO adopts the *deterministic back* mechanism [4] to repair solutions that are generated outside the allowable bounds. Therefore, the jth bound of the particle's position $\mathbf{x}^i = (x_1^i, \ldots x_n^i)^T$ and of its velocity $\mathbf{v}^i = (v_1^i, \ldots, v_n^i)^T$, are re-established as follows:

$$\begin{aligned} x_j^i &= \begin{cases} x_j^L, & \text{if } x_j^i < x_j^L \\ x_j^U, & \text{if } x_j^i > x_j^U \end{cases}, \quad j = 1, \ldots, n \\ v_j^i &= -\gamma v_j^i, \quad j = 1, \ldots, n. \end{aligned} \tag{13}$$

where x_j^L and x_j^U are the lower and upper bounds in the component j^{th} (for each $j = 1, \ldots, n$) of the allowable decision variable values, respectively. In the same way than other MOPSOs [15, 14], DMOPSO adopts $\gamma = 1$.

In DMOPSO, a $(\mu + \lambda)$-selection mechanism is employed in order to obtain the global best set by using the current set of particles P and the current global best set G_{best}. In other words, DMOPSO updates the G_{set} set by finding the best solution for the ith subproblem from $\{P \cup G_{best}\}$ as it is shown in Algorithm 2. A more detailed description of DMOPSO can be found in [23].

3. OUR PROPOSED APPROACH FOR CONSTRAINED OPTIMIZATION

As indicated before, the proposed ε-constrained DMOPSO (εDMOPSO) is based on the ε-constraint method [19] and it adopts the decomposition-based Multi-Objective Optimizer (DMOPSO), which was initially introduced for dealing with unconstrained MOPs [23]. Our proposed εDMOPSO uses the information related to the whole swarm of particles in order to approximate solutions towards the Pareto optimal front while satisfying the constraints of the problem.

In the following description we assume that W is a set of well-distributed weight vectors $\{\mathbf{w}^1, \ldots, \mathbf{w}^N\}$. Along the search, εDMOPSO finds the best solution to each subproblem defined by the Tchebycheff approach (equation (2)) using each weight vector in W. In this way, the objective function of the jth subproblem is then defined by $g^{te}(\mathbf{x}|\mathbf{w}^j, \mathbf{z})$, where $\mathbf{w}^j \in W$ and $\mathbf{z} = (z_1, \ldots, z_k)^T$ is the artificial utopian vector whose component z_i is the minimum value found so far for the objective f_i.

At each generation, εDMOPSO finds the best solution to each subproblem according to the decomposition approach and the proposed ε level comparison. Throughout the search, εDMOPSO maintains:

1. a population of N particles $P = \{\mathbf{x}^1, \ldots, \mathbf{x}^N\}$, where $\mathbf{x}^i$ is the current solution to the ith subproblem;
2. $F^1, \ldots, F^N$, where F^i is the F-value of $\mathbf{x}^i$, i.e., $F^i = \mathbf{F}(\mathbf{x}^i)$ for each $i = 1, \ldots, N$;

In an analogous way, εDMOPSO adopts the same framework as DMOPSO (Algorithm 1). However, in order to satisfy the constraints of the problem, the updating algorithm (Algorithm 2) to select the global best set is modified. In the following section we present a detailed description of the proposed constraint-handling technique employed by εDMOPSO.

3.1 Normalized Constraint Violation Degree

In order to measure an appropriate constraint violation between two solutions, we use the normalized constraint violation degree. In the following description, we assume that the constraint violation degree of a solution $\mathbf{x}$ is computed using equation (7).

Let P be the set of particles found by εDMOPSO. Assuming p inequality constraints of the form $g_i \leq 0$ $(i = 1, \ldots, p)$, the normalized constraint violation of any solution $\mathbf{x}$ can be computed as:

$$\phi_N(\mathbf{x}) \quad = \quad \sum_{i=1}^{p} \left|\left| \max\left\{0, \frac{g_i(\mathbf{x})}{g_{\max}^i}\right\} \right|\right|^{\alpha} \tag{14}$$

where α is a positive number (in this work, $\alpha = 1$) and g_{max}^i is the maximum violation value for the ith constraint in the set of solutions P. To be more precise, g_{max}^i can be calculated by:

$$g_{\max}^i = \max_{\mathbf{x} \in P}\{0, g_i(\mathbf{x})\}, \quad i = 1, \ldots, p \tag{15}$$

Note however that if $g_{max}^i = 0$, all the solutions $\mathbf{x} \in P$ are feasible for the ith constraint and equation (14) cannot be computed. For this case, we set $g_{max}^i = 1$, thus penalizing the normalized constraint value $\phi_N(\mathbf{x})$ if solution $\mathbf{x}$ is not feasible for the ith constraint.

3.2 The ε level value

For the ε-constraint method, we use the formulation that prefers a solution with strictly less function value than other one, i.e., the order relation $<_\varepsilon$ (equation (9)). In our approach, the ε value is defined by:

$$\varepsilon = \phi_{N,min} + \tau \times (\phi_{N,max} - \phi_{N,min}) \tag{16}$$

where $\phi_{N,min}$ and $\phi_{N,max}$ are the minimum and the maximum value given by the normalized constraint violation of each solution $\mathbf{x}$ in P. To be more precise:

$$\begin{aligned} \phi_{N,max} &= \max_{\mathbf{x} \in P}\{\phi_N(\mathbf{x})\} \\ \phi_{N,min} &= \min_{\mathbf{x} \in P}\{\phi_N(\mathbf{x})\} \end{aligned} \tag{17}$$

τ represents a parameter given by the user, which tries to balance the generation of feasible solutions with the minimization of each subproblem defined by εDMOPSO.

The value of τ should be given in the range $[0, 1]$. If $\tau = 0$, the search is driven towards the generation of solutions with a normalized constraint value lower than $\phi_{N,min}$, i.e., preferring feasible solutions. If $\tau = 1$, the search is driven towards the generation of solutions with a lower cost for each subproblem, instead of preferring to satisfy the constraints of the CMOP.

3.3 Obtaining the global best set for constrained optimization

Along the cycles, each particle $\mathbf{x}^i$ in the swarm P gives the best solution to the ith subproblem. Considering N subproblems, the set W has the same number of elements, i.e., the cardinality of W is N. At the beginning, the set of particles P constitutes the global best set G_{best} (line 10 in Algorithm 1). Therefore, the number of solutions in G_{best} is also N. The following updates of the global set are carried out in two different stages.

1. Preferring convergence. Let $T = \{P \cup G_{best}\}$ be the set of solutions to be considered as the new global best set G_{best}. We select from T, the set of solutions $C^1 = \{\mathbf{a}^1, \dots, \mathbf{a}^N\}$ which minimize each subproblem defined by each $\mathbf{w}^i$ in W by using Algorithm 2, i.e., $C^1 = update\_G_{best}(T, W)$.

   With this, we prefer solutions with a lower function value for each separate subproblem even if they do not satisfy the constraints of the CMOP.

2. Satisfying constraints. Let $R = \{T \setminus C^1\}$ be the remaining solutions in T. In an analogous way, we define a new set $C^2 = \{\mathbf{b}^1, \dots, \mathbf{b}^N\}$ by using Algorithm 2, $C^2 = update\_G_{best}(R, W)$. It is worth noting that the selected solutions $\mathbf{a}^i$ and $\mathbf{b}^i$ correspond to the best solutions for the ith subproblem defined by $\mathbf{w}^i$.

   The tiebreaker for selecting a new solution as part of the new global best set G_{best} is carried out by using the ε-constraint method according to the next rule.

   Let $g_1^{te}(g_2^{te})$ and $\phi_N^1(\phi_N^2)$ be the function values given by the Tchebycheff aggregation function (equation (2)) and the normalized constraint violation at the solution $\mathbf{a}^i(\mathbf{b}^i)$, respectively. Then, for any ε satisfying $\varepsilon \geq 0$, the ε level comparison $<_\varepsilon$ between (g_1^{te}, ϕ_N^1) and (g_2^{te}, ϕ_N^2) is defined as follows:

$$(g_1^{te}, \phi_N^1) <_\varepsilon (g_2^{te}, \phi_N^2) \Leftrightarrow \begin{cases} g_1^{te} < g_2^{te}, & \text{if } \phi_N^1, \phi_N^2 \leq \varepsilon \\ g_1^{te} < g_2^{te}, & \text{if } \phi_N^1 = \phi_N^2 \\ \phi_N^1 < \phi_N^2, & \text{otherwise} \end{cases} \quad (18)$$

   Therefore, $\mathbf{g}_{best}^i = \mathbf{a}^i$, if and only if equation (18) is satisfied. Otherwise $\mathbf{g}_{best}^i = \mathbf{b}^i$, for each $i \in \{1, \dots, N\}$. The global best set for the next cycle of εDMOPSO is then constituted by:

$$G_{best} = \{\mathbf{g}_{best}^i, \dots, \mathbf{g}_{best}^N\}$$

With this, stage 1 finds convergence towards optimal values of each subproblem, while stage 2 promotes satisfying the constraints of the problem, i.e., by performing stage 2, the ε level will reduce its value along the cycles trying to satisfy the constraints of the CMOP.

4. EXPERIMENTAL STUDY

4.1 Constrained Multi-Objective Airfoil Shape Optimization Problems

In order to assess the performance of our proposed approach we employ CMO-ASOPs adapted from [18, 22, 12, 2]. Two different CMO-ASOPs were defined having two and three objectives and different numbers of constraints. Since the test CMO-ASOPs deal with airfoil shape geometries, next we describe the geometry parameterization used in them, which in turn defines the dimensionality of the search space.

Parameter	Lower bound	Upper bound
r_{leup}	0.0085	0.0126
r_{lelo}	0.0020	0.0040
α_{te}	7.0	10.0
β_{te}	10.0	14.0
Z_{te}	-0.0060	-0.0030
ΔZ_{te}	0.0025	0.0050
X_{up}	0.4100	0.4600
Z_{up}	0.1100	0.1300
Z_{xxup}	-0.90	-0.70
X_{lo}	0.20	0.26
Z_{lo}	-0.0230	-0.0150
Z_{xxlo}	0.05	0.20

Table 1: Parameter ranges for modified PARSEC airfoil representation

4.1.1 *Geometry parameterization*

Finding an optimum representation scheme for ASO problems is an important step for a successful aerodynamic optimization task.

In this case, the PARametric SECtion (PARSEC) airfoil representation [17] is used. Figure 1 illustrates the 11 basic parameters used for this representation. Where r_{le} is the leading edge radius, X_{up} is the location of maximum thickness for the upper surface (extrados), X_{lo} is the location of maximum thickness for lower surface (intrados), Z_{up} is the maximum thickness for upper surface, Z_{lo} is the maximum thickness for lower surface, Z_{xxup} is the curvature for upper surfaces, at maximum thickness location, Z_{xxlo} is the curvature for lower surfaces, at maximum thickness location, Z_{te} is the trailing edge coordinate, ΔZ_{te} is the trailing edge thickness, α_{te} is the trailing edge direction, and β_{te} represents the trailing edge wedge angle.

For the present case, the modified PARSEC geometry representation adopted allows us to define independently the leading edge radius, both for upper and lower surfaces. Thus, 12 variables in total are used. Their allowable ranges are defined in Table 1.

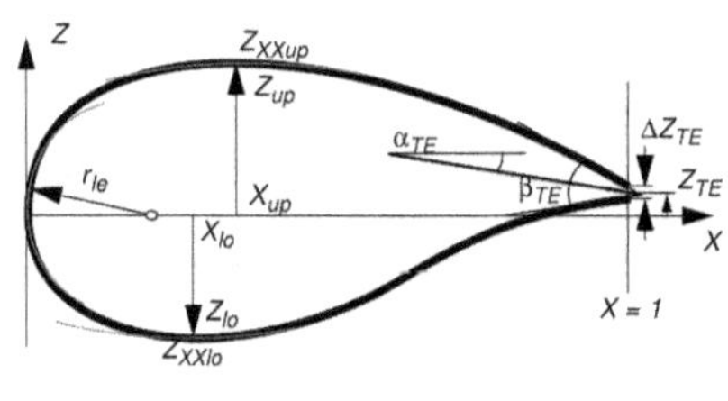

Figure 1: PARSEC airfoil parameterization

The PARSEC airfoil geometry representation uses a linear combination of shape functions for defining the upper and lower surfaces. These linear combinations are given by:

$$Z_{upper} = \sum_{n=1}^{6} a_n x^{\frac{n-1}{2}}, \quad Z_{lower} = \sum_{n=1}^{6} b_n x^{\frac{n-1}{2}}$$

In the above equations, the coefficients a_n, and b_n are determined as functions of the 12 described geometric parameters, by solving two systems of linear equations.

4.1.2 *Definition of the CMO-ASOPs*

The goal is to optimize the airfoil shape of a standard-class glider, aiming at obtaining optimum performance for this type of aircraft. In the following definition of CMO-ASOPs, common objectives are to maximize the aerodynamic efficiency, i.e., the lift to drag forces ratio C_l/C_d, to maximize the aerodynamic power efficiency, i.e., C_l^3/C_d^2, and to minimize the absolute value for the aerodynamic moment coefficient, C_m. These objectives reflect the global aerodynamic efficiency of a glider and are evaluated for different flight regimes, which are defined in terms of the airfoil's angle of attack (α), and the gliding velocity, given by the Reynolds (Re) and Mach (M) numbers. Note that in the CMO-ASOPs definition, all objectives are considered to be minimized, requiring, in consequence, the use of the inverse of C_l/C_d and C_l^3/C_d^2 ratios. For some airfoil designs, being evaluated, it can happen that its C_m value could be positive or negative. In this case, we consider the moment coefficient value squared as the objective to minimize. In some other situations, existing designs serve as reference values for the new designs. In this case, constraints are imposed in order to have better performing designs. The mathematical definition for the CMO-ASOPs is presented next:

Test Problem **CMO-ASOP1**

This problem considers two objective functions: *i)* to maximize the aerodynamic efficiency, i.e., the lift to drag forces ratio C_l/C_d, and *ii)* to minimize the absolute value for the aerodynamic moment coefficient. From the aerodynamic point of view, an airfoil's efficiency could be increased by reducing its thickness to chord ratio, t/c, leading to very thin airfoil shapes. In order to avoid this situation, one constraint is added to achieve a $t/c = 0.13$. This thickness ratio allows to reduce the wing weight while maintaining good structural strength. The mathematical definition for CMO-ASOP1 is:

i) $Minimize : C_d/C_l \text{ @ } \alpha = 4.0^o,\ Re = 2.0 \times 10^6,\ M = 0.1$

ii) $Minimize : C_m^2 \text{ @ } \alpha = 4.0^o,\ Re = 2.0 \times 10^6,\ M = 0.1$
s.t. $t/c = 0.13$

Test Problem **CMO-ASOP2**

This problem considers three objective functions: *i)* to maximize the aerodynamic efficiency, i.e., to maximize the C_l/C_d ratio at a first flight condition, *ii)* to maximize aerodynamic power efficiency, i.e., C_l^3/C_d^2 at a second flight, and *iii)* to maximize aerodynamic power efficiency, i.e., C_l^3/C_d^2 at a third flight condition. For this problem, four constraints are formulated. The first three aim to have a better aerodynamic objective function with respect to a reference airfoil shape commonly used in this application (the $a720$ airfoil) and reported in [18]. The fourth constraint aims to limit the t/c ratio in a similar way as was done in the previous problem. The mathematical definition for CMO-ASOP2 is:

i) $Minimize : C_d/C_l \text{ @ } \alpha = 1.0^o,\ Re = 4.0 \times 10^6,\ M = 0.3$

ii) $Minimize : C_d^2/C_l^3 \text{ @ } \alpha = 3.0^o,\ Re = 3.0 \times 10^6,\ M = 0.3$

iii) $Minimize : C_d^2/C_l^3 \text{ @ } \alpha = 5.0^o,\ Re = 2.0 \times 10^6,\ M = 0.3$

$$\begin{aligned} \text{s.t.} \quad & C_d/C_l && \leq 0.005201 \\ & C_d^2/C_l^3 && \leq 0.004462 \\ & C_d^2/C_l^3 && \leq 0.004458 \\ & t/c && = 0.13 \text{ for all flight operating conditions.} \end{aligned}$$

4.2 Performance Measures

Hypervolume

The Hypervolume (I_H) performance measure was proposed in [26]. This performance measure is Pareto compliant [27], and quantifies both convergence and spread of nondominated solutions along the Pareto optimal front. It is mathematically stated as:

$$I_H(P) = \Lambda\left(\bigcup_{\mathbf{p}\in P}\{\mathbf{x}|\mathbf{p} \prec \mathbf{x} \prec \mathbf{r}\}\right) \tag{19}$$

where Λ denotes the Lebesgue measure, P is the Pareto approximation to the true Pareto front and $\mathbf{r} \in \mathbb{R}^k$ denotes a reference vector being dominated by all valid candidate solutions in P. A high I_H value, indicates that the approximation P is close to PF and has a good spread towards the extreme portions of the Pareto front.

Feasibility Ratio

The feasibility ratio (I_F) indicator refers to the ratio of the number of feasible solutions found in the final approximation P to the Pareto front. It is mathematically stated as:

$$I_F(P) = \frac{P_f}{|P|} \tag{20}$$

where P_f denotes the number of feasible solutions in P and $|P|$ represents the cardinality of the population P.

4.3 Experimental Setup

To assess the performance over the CMO-ASOPs adopted, we compared the results obtained by our εDMOPSO with respect to those achieved by the proposal presented by Jan and Zhang in [9], which we call here cMOEA/D-DE. We selected cMOEA/D-DE for its ability to solve complex problems [9] and because it uses one of the most representative MOEAs based on decomposition, the well-known MOEA/D-DE. Additionally, its source code is in the public domain.

In order to allow a fair comparison, the set of weight vectors was the same for both algorithms, and they were generated in the same way using the procedure described in [25], i.e., the settings of N and $W = \{\mathbf{w}^1, \ldots, \mathbf{w}^N\}$ were controlled by a parameter H. More precisely, $\mathbf{w}^1, \ldots, \mathbf{w}^N$ are all the weight vectors in which each individual weight w_j^i ($i = 1, \ldots, N$ and $j = 1, \ldots, k$) takes a value from: $\{\frac{0}{H}, \frac{1}{H}, \ldots, \frac{H}{H}\}$. Therefore, the number of such vectors in W is given by $N = C_{H+k-1}^{k-1}$, where k is the number of objective functions.

Because of the high computational time required by the CMO-ASOPs adopted in our study, we used a low number of subproblems. Here, we use $H = 49$ (for the bi-objective problem) and $H = 13$ (for the three-objectives problem), i.e., we generated 50 and 105 weight vectors for each CMO-ASOP, respectively. It is worth noting that the use of large populations (greater than 200 individuals), could significantly increase the computational time (even requir-

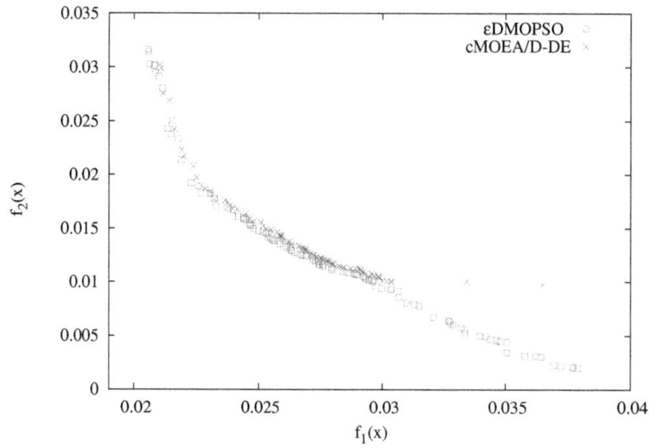

Figure 2: εDMOPSO and MOEA/D-DE for CMO-ASOP1.

ing days in some cases) that an optimizer requires (only for a single run) for solving these CMO-ASOPs.

For each CMO-ASOP, we performed 30 independent runs with each algorithm. The parameters for both algorithms where set as follows: $N = 50$ and $N = 105$ represent the number of weight vectors (and the population size) for CMO-ASOP1 and CMO-ASOP2, respectively. The maximum number of iterations was set as $N_{it} = 100$ for both test problems. Therefore, both algorithms performed 5,000 and 10,500 fitness function evaluations for each problem, respectively. For cMOEA/D-DE, the parameters were set as: $T_n = \lceil 0.1 \times N \rceil$ (neighborhood size) $\delta = 0.9$ (probability that parent solutions are selected from the neighborhood) $F = 0.5$ (the differential factor), $CR = 1$ (the crossover ratio), $\eta_m = 20.0$ (the mutation index), $P_m = 1/n$ (mutation rate) and $n_r\lceil 0.01 \times N \rceil$ (the number of solutions to be replaced). These values were set as it is suggested in [9]. For the constraint-handling technique, the parameters for cMOEA/D-DE we used were: $s_1 = 0.01$ and $s_2 = 20.0$, and they were set as in [9] (we used the best parameters settings found by Jan and Zhang in their comparative study).

For εDMOPSO, $\tau = 0.3$ and $T_a = 2$ represent the control parameter for equation (18) and the age threshold, respectively. The constraints on the velocity (c_1, c_2) and the inertia factor (w) were dynamically defined. As in DMOPSO [23], we adopted uniformly distributed values, such that: $c_1, c_2 \in (1.2, 2.0)$ and $w \in (0.1, 0.5)$.

5. DISCUSSION OF RESULTS

As indicated before, the results obtained by our proposed approach (i.e., εDMOPSO) were compared against those produced by cMOEA/D [9]. In Table 2, the hypervolume values were calculated using the reference vectors **r** given in this same table. According to the results presented in Table 2, εDMOPSO had a better performance than cMOEA/D-DE in the two CMO-ASPs adopted. This table provides a quantitative assessment of the performance of εDMOPSO in terms of the I_H and I_F indicators. That means that the solutions obtained by εDMOPSO achieved a better approximation of the Pareto optimal front than the solutions obtained by cMOEA/D-DE while maintaining an acceptable ratio of feasible solutions. Due to space limitations, we only show (in Figure 2) the performance of εDMOPSO when it is compared with respect to cMOEA/D-DE for CMO-ASOP1. As we can see, εDMOPSO produced solutions with better convergence to the extremes and most of them dominated those produced by cMOEA/D. This corroborates the results of the good performance of our proposed εDMOPSO regarding CMO-ASOP1. For CMO-ASOP2, numerical results showed that our proposed approach significantly outperformed cMOEA/D. In fact, a good value of I_H indicates that εDMOPSO achieved a better convergence towards the Pareto optimal front[2] than cMOEA/D.

In terms of the feasibility of the solutions, we can see from Table 2 that our proposed εDMOPSO obtained a better ratio of feasible solutions for both problems (CMO-ASOP1 and CMO-ASOP2). This means that our proposal of incorporating the ε-constraint method into DMOPSO, seems, at first sight, a good strategy to deal with expensive optimization problems. Although our proposed approach has been tested here only with CMO-ASOPs, it can clearly be applied to other real-world problems as well, and that is part of our ongoing research.

6. CONCLUSIONS AND FUTURE WORK

We have proposed a new approach based on DMOPSO for constrained multi-objective optimization. Our proposed εDMOPSO introduces a selection mechanism based on the ε-constraint method in order to define the set of global best solutions along the search process. Although the use of the new constraint-handling technique was adopted here for DMOPSO, this approach can be easily adopted by any other decomposition-based MOEA which uses a $(\mu + \lambda)$-selection mechanism to obtain optimal solutions (for example, the approach presented in [1]). Our preliminary results indicate that our proposed εDMOPSO is highly competitive with respect to a current state-of-the-art MOEA (i.e., cMOEA/D-DE) in the test problems adopted here. However, more test problems are required in order to draw more general conclusions about its performance.

As part of our future work, we would like to validate our proposed approach in many-objective optimization problems (i.e., multi-objective problems having more than 3 objectives). We also intend to focus on the design of a strategy that allows us to adjust, in a dynamic way, the value of ε employed by our proposed εDMOPSO. We are also considering the possibility of experimenting with a penalty function or another powerful constraint-handling technique such as stochastic ranking [16]. Furthermore, in order to deal in an efficient way with more complex CMOPs, the introduction of local search mechanisms to εDMOPSO seems as a promising path for future research. We believe that the use of an appropriate local search mechanism coupled with a MOEA (such as those presented in [10, 24]) could give rise to a powerful search engine capable of dealing with more complex CMOPs in a more effective and efficient way.

Acknowledgements

The second author acknowledges support from IPN-ESIME through the COTEBAL, EDI and SIBE programs.

[2]For CMO-ASOP1 and CMO-ASOP2, the true Pareto fronts are unknown.

Table 2: Results of I_H for εDMOPSO and cMOEA/D-DE

MOP	εDMOPSO		cMOEA/D-DE		reference vector **r**
	I_H	I_F	I_H	I_F	
	average (υ)	*average* (σ)	*average* (σ)	*average* (σ)	
CMO-ASOP1	**9.3477e-04** (1.0504e-05)	**81.37** (0.093454)	8.6921e-04 (1.5823e-05)	76.72 (0.021125)	$(0.065, 0.031)^T$
CMO-ASOP2	**1.5333e-12** (6.2821e-13)	**67.20** (0.012837)	9.0066e-16 (4.8502e-15)	44.72 (0.982360)	$(0.0053, 0.0045, 0.0045)^T$

7. REFERENCES

[1] A. Arias Montaño, C. A. Coello Coello, and E. Mezura-Montes. MODE-LD+SS: A Novel Differential Evolution Algorithm Incorporating Local Dominance and Scalar Selection Mechanisms for Multi-Objective Optimization. In *2010 IEEE Congress on Evolutionary Computation (CEC'2010)*, pages 3284–3291, Barcelona, Spain, July 18–23 2010. IEEE Press.

[2] A. Arias-Montaño, C. A. Coello Coello, and E. Mezura-Montes. Multi-Objective Airfoil Shape Optimization Using a Multiple-Surrogate Approach. In *CEC'2012*, pages 1188–1195, Brisbane, Australia, June 10-15 2012. IEEE Press.

[3] A. Arias-Montaño, C. A. Coello Coello, and E. Mezura-Montes. Multi-Objective Evolutionary Algorithms in Aeronautical and Aerospace Engineering. *IEEE Transactions on Evolutionary Computation*, 16(5):662–694, October 2012.

[4] M. Clerc. Confinements and Biases in Particle Swarm Optimisation, 2006.

[5] C. A. Coello Coello. Theoretical and numerical constraint-handling techniques used with evolutionary algorithms: A survey of the state of the art. *Computer methods in applied mechanics and engineering*, 191:1245–1287, 2002.

[6] C. A. Coello Coello and G. B. Lamont, editors. *Applications of Multi-Objective Evolutionary Algorithms*. World Scientific, Singapore, 2004. ISBN 981-256-106-4.

[7] C. A. Coello Coello, G. B. Lamont, and D. A. Van Veldhuizen. *Evolutionary Algorithms for Solving Multi-Objective Problems*. Springer, New York, second edition, September 2007. ISBN 978-0-387-33254-3.

[8] M. Ehrgott. *Multicriteria Optimization*. Springer, Berlin, 2nd edition, June 2005.

[9] M. A. Jan and Q. Zhang. Moea/d for constrained multiobjective optimization: Some preliminary experimental results. In *2010 UK Workshop on Computational Intelligence (UKCI)*, pages 1–6, 2010.

[10] P. Koch, O. Kramer, G. Rudolph, and N. Beume. On the hybridization of sms-emoa and local search for continuous multiobjective optimization. In *GECCO'2009*, pages 603–610, New York, NY, USA, 2009. ACM.

[11] W. F. Leong. *Multiobjective particle swarm optimization: Integration of dynamic population and multiple-swarm concepts and constraint handling*. PhD thesis, Oklahoma State University, 2008.

[12] A. López-Jaimes, A. Arias-Montaño, and C. A. Coello Coello. Preference Incorporation to Solve Many-Objective Airfoil Design Problems. In *CEC'2011*, pages 1605–1612, New Orleans, Louisiana, USA, 5-8 June 2011. IEEE Service Center.

[13] K. Miettinen. *Nonlinear Multiobjective Optimization*. Kluwer Academic Publishers, Boston, Massachuisetts, 1999.

[14] N. A. Moubayed, A. Petrovski, and J. A. W. McCall. A novel smart multi-objective particle swarm optimisation using decomposition. In *PPSN XI*, volume 6239, pages 1–10, 2010.

[15] M. Reyes-Sierra and C. A. Coello Coello. Multi-Objective Particle Swarm Optimizers: A Survey of the State-of-the-Art. *International Journal of Computational Intelligence Research*, 2(3):287–308, 2006.

[16] T. P. Runarsson and X. Yao. Stochastic Ranking for Constrained Evolutionary Optimization. *IEEE Transactions on Evolutionary Computation*, 4(3):284–294, September 2000.

[17] H. Sobieczky. Parametric airfoils and wings. In K. Fuji and G. S. Dulikravich, editors, *Notes on Numerical Fluid Mechanics, Vol.. 68*, pages 71–88, Wiesbaden, 1998. Vieweg Verlag.

[18] A. Szöllös, M. Smid, and J. Hajek. Aerodynamic optimization via multi-objective micro-genetic algorithm with range adaptation, knowledge-based reinitialization, crowding and epsilon-dominance. *Advances in engineering software*, 40(6):419–430, June 2009.

[19] T. Takahama, S. Sakai, and N. Iwane. Constrained Optimization by the ε Constrained Hybrid Algorithm of Particle Swarm Optimization and Genetic Algorithm. In S. Zhang and R. Jarvis, editors, *AI 2005: Advances in Artificial Intelligence*, volume 3809 of *Lecture Notes in Computer Science*, pages 389–400. Springer Berlin Heidelberg, 2005.

[20] Y.-y. Wang, B.-q. Zhang, and Y.-c. Chen. Robust airfoil optimization based on improved particle swarm optimization method. *Applied Mathematics and Mechanics*, 32(10):1245–1254, 2011.

[21] U. K. Wickramasinghe, R. Carrese, and X. Li. Designing airfoils using a reference point based evolutionary many-objective particle swarm optimization algorithm. In *CEC'2010*, pages 1857–1869, Barcelona, Spain, July 18–23 2010. IEEE Press.

[22] S. Zapotecas Martínez, A. Arias Montaño, and C. A. Coello Coello. A Nonlinear Simplex Search Approach for Multi-Objective Optimization. In *2011 IEEE Congress on Evolutionary Computation (CEC'2011)*, pages 2367–2374, New Orleans, Louisiana, USA, 5–8 June 2011. IEEE Service Center.

[23] S. Zapotecas Martínez and C. A. Coello Coello. A Multi-objective Particle Swarm Optimizer Based on Decomposition. In *GECCO'2011*, pages 69–76, Dublin, Ireland, July 2011. ACM Press.

[24] S. Zapotecas Martínez and C. A. Coello Coello. A Direct Local Search Mechanism for Decomposition-based Multi-Objective Evolutionary Algorithms. In *CEC'2012*, pages 3431–3438, Brisbane, Australia, June 2012. IEEE Press.

[25] Q. Zhang and H. Li. MOEA/D: A Multiobjective Evolutionary Algorithm Based on Decomposition. *IEEE Transactions on Evolutionary Computation*, 11(6):712–731,| December 2007.

[26] E. Zitzler and L. Thiele. Multiobjective Optimization Using Evolutionary Algorithms—A Comparative Study. In A. E. Eiben, editor, *PPSN V*, pages 292–301, Amsterdam, September 1998. Springer-Verlag.

[27] E. Zitzler, L. Thiele, M. Laumanns, C. M. Fonseca, and V. G. da Fonseca. Performance Assessment of Multiobjective Optimizers: An Analysis and Review. *IEEE Transactions on Evolutionary Computation*, 7(2):117–132, April 2003.

Automatic Path Planning for Autonomous Underwater Vehicles based on an Adaptive Differential Evolution

Chuan-Bin Zhang [a], Yue-Jiao Gong [a], Jing-Jing Li [b] (Corresponding Author) and Ying Lin [c]
[a] Department of Computer Science, Sun Yat-sen University
[a] Key Laboratory of Machine Intelligence and Advanced Computing, Ministry of Education
[a] Engineering Research Center of Supercomputing Engineering Software, Ministry of Education
[b] School of Computer Science, South China Normal University
[c] Department of Psychology, Sun Yat-sen University, P.R. China
jingjing.li1124@gmail.com

ABSTRACT

This paper proposes a path planner for autonomous underwater vehicles (AUVs) in 3-D underwater space. We simulate an underwater space with rugged seabed and suspending obstacles, which is close to real world. In the proposed representation scheme, the problem space is decomposed into parallel subspaces and each subspace is described by a grid method. The paths of AUVs are simplified as a set of successive points in the problem space. By jointing these waypoints, the entire path of the AUV is obtained. A cost function with penalty method takes into account the length, energy consumption, safety and curvature constraints of AUVs. It is applied to evaluate the quality of paths. Differential evolution (DE) algorithm is used as a black-box optimization tool to provide optimal solutions for the path planning. In addition, we adaptively adjust the parameters of DE according to population distribution and the blockage of parallel subspaces so as to improve its performance. Experiments are conducted on 6 different scenarios. The results validate that the proposed algorithm is effective for improving solution quality and avoiding premature convergence.

Categories and Subject Descriptors

I.2.8 [**Artificial Intelligence**]: Problem Solving, Control Methods, and Search – *heuristic* methods.

General Terms

Algorithms, Performance, Experimentation.

Keywords

AUVs, 3-D path planning, parallel subspace, differential evolution, adaptive parameters.

1. INTRODUCTION

Autonomous Underwater Vehicle (AUV) is a machine equipped with a series of on-board sensors, which is able to survive underwater independently and complete the setup tasks autonomously [1]. Nowadays, AUVs are sent to remote or dangerous ocean environments where they could not respond to human controllers immediately. Therefore, it requires AUVs to possess a level of intelligence so as to improve their ability to survive in those isolated environments. One of the most critical issues required to ensure the safety of AUVs in such environments is path planning. Path planning for AUVs is challenging, because it needs to consider the structure of AUV, the characteristics of the environment, energy consumption and security, etc.

In early years, many deterministic algorithms are used to solve the problem of path planning. Usually, these methods simply define the problem of path planning as optimization problems of shortest path or minimum power consumption. Latombe [2] presented many popular methods used in path planning, such as cell decomposition methods and potential field methods. In [3], the path planning problem was defined as an optimization framework on computational 2-D grid and a method based on mixed integer linear programming (MILP) is proposed. Cetin *et al.* [4] decomposed the problem space into cubes and propose a feasibility MILP method. An A* search procedure was also used to optimal paths on ocean environments with eddies and currents in [5].

However, path planning for AUVs is so complex that deterministic algorithms encounter deficiency when the problem scale increases. In recent years, many researchers adopt evolutionary algorithms to deal with the problem, such as genetic algorithm (GA) and particle swarm optimization (PSO). Guo and Gao [6] set up an environmental model of 3-D space which was separated into several parallel parts and developed a spiral particle pathway searching approach based on discrete particle swarm optimization (DPSO). In [7], path planning problem was formulated as a safe path with minimum energy cost and a GA-based path planner was developed. Zeng *et al.* [8] carried out a novel annular space decomposition scheme to describe problem space, then they proposed path planners based on GA and Quantum-behaved PSO. Moreover, some hybrid algorithms were developed and utilized for path planning [9]-[11]. Cheng *et al.* [9] combined GA with dynamic programming and proposed a path planner based on a Hybrid Genetic Algorithm (HGA). In [10], a path planning solution for unmanned aerial vehicles (UAVs) based on parallel GA and PSO was presented. This approach shortens the execution time and made it possible for real-time path planning.

In previous work, the influence of obstacles has not been carefully considered and search algorithms were not designed based on the characteristics of problem spaces. In this paper, our model considers the seabed and obstacles in 3-D underwater

GECCO'14, July 12–16, 2014, Vancouver, BC, Canada.

http://dx.doi.org/10.1145/2576768.2598267

environments, which is closer to real world. We simulate that obstacles are separate from the seabed and suspended in space, so navigation area for AUVs is narrower. Then, underwater environment is decomposed into parallel subspaces and each subspace is described by grids, which can distinguish the obstacles and hollowness area in subspaces. This decomposition method provides more detailed information to path planner. Each subspace contains only one waypoint of a path, hence, the path is generated by joining a set of waypoints in search space. DE algorithm [14] is applied to optimize the location of waypoints, thereby generating an optimal path. In addition, an adaptive parameter control strategy is employed to improve the performance of DE. The scaling parameter F is adapted according to population distribution and the crossover rate CR is associated to the blockage of subspaces so as to lead waypoints away from obstacles.

The rest of this paper is organized as follows. Section 2 presents the modeling of the environment and the encoding of paths. Section 3 defines a cost function to evaluate the quality of paths. Section 4 proposes a path planner based on improved DE through an adaptive parameter control strategy. We conduct experiments on different scenarios and compare the performance of the original DE, jDE, the original PSO and the proposed DE in section 5. Finally, section 6 draws conclusions.

2. MODELING

The first step of path planning is modeling environment and encoding path. In this paper, the 3-D underwater environment is modeled as a cuboid space. Obstacles are separate from the seabed and suspended in the problem space, so a parallel subspace model is develop to distinguish seabed and obstacles.

We have established the rectangular coordinate system of the problem space. The X-axis represents the width of the space; the Y-axis represents the depth of space and the Z-axis represents the length of space (see Fig. 1). Then the space is divided into p parallel subspaces numbered 1 to p along the Z-axis. A subspace perpendicular to the Z axis is expressed in grids and a block matrix is employed to represent the blockage of a subspace. A blocking position is the position where there is an obstacle at the same place in the subspace. In block matrix, the elements corresponding blocking positions are set to −1. On the contrary, the elements corresponding hollowness positions are set to 0 (see Fig. 2). Therefore, the 3-D underwater environment is separated into p subspaces and each subspace is described by a block matrix. Moreover, the model can describe the 3-D underwater environment more accurately by increasing the number of subspaces and grids.

Only one waypoint locates in each subspace, so a path consists of p+1 waypoints including the start-point and the target-point. In the process of path planning, the locations of waypoints change in subspaces. A path is generated by joining waypoints and encoded in a waypoint matrix that each row represents the 3-D coordinates of the corresponding waypoint, as shown in (1). A path is the optimal path if all waypoints of this path locate in the global optimal positions. The start-point $waypoint_0$ and the target-point $waypoint_p$ are fixed, which are not considered as variables during the optimization process once they are set.

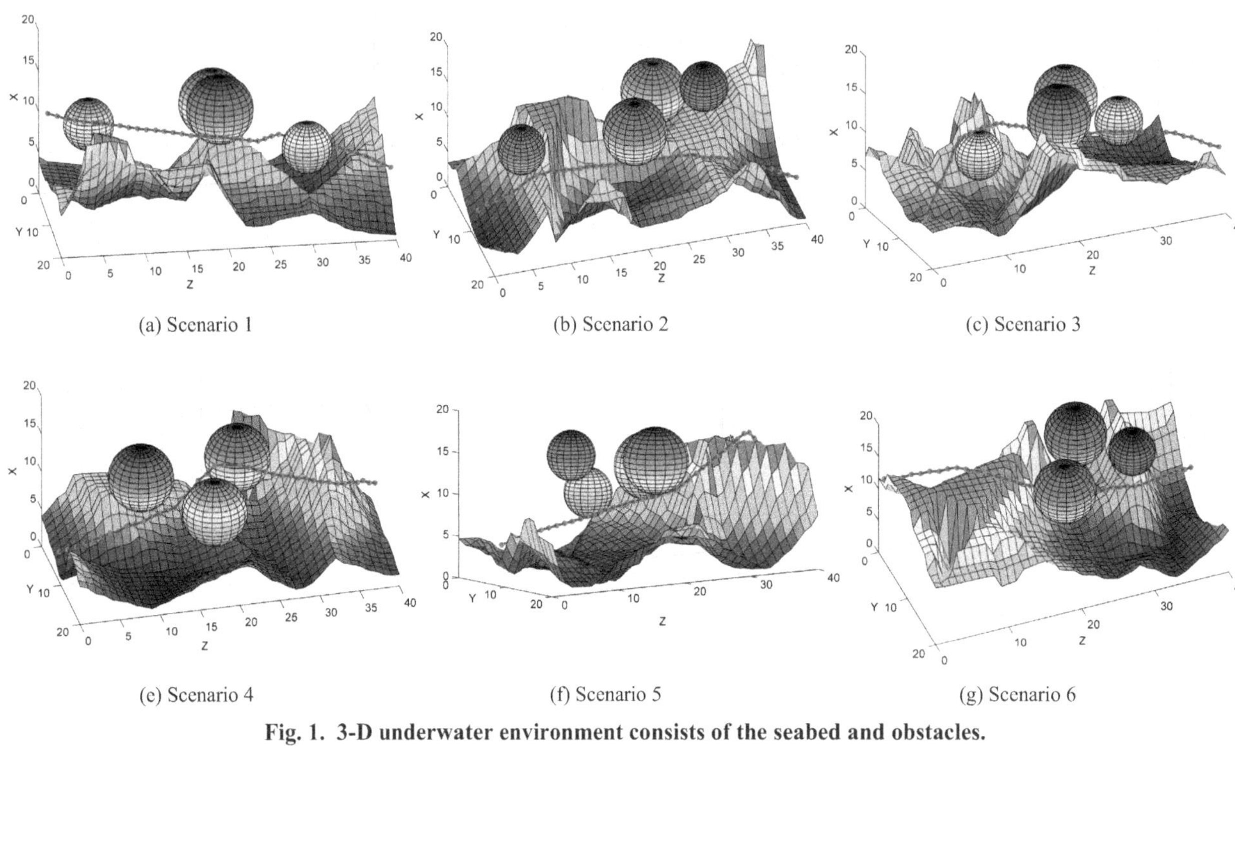

(a) Scenario 1 (b) Scenario 2 (c) Scenario 3

(e) Scenario 4 (f) Scenario 5 (g) Scenario 6

Fig. 1. 3-D underwater environment consists of the seabed and obstacles.

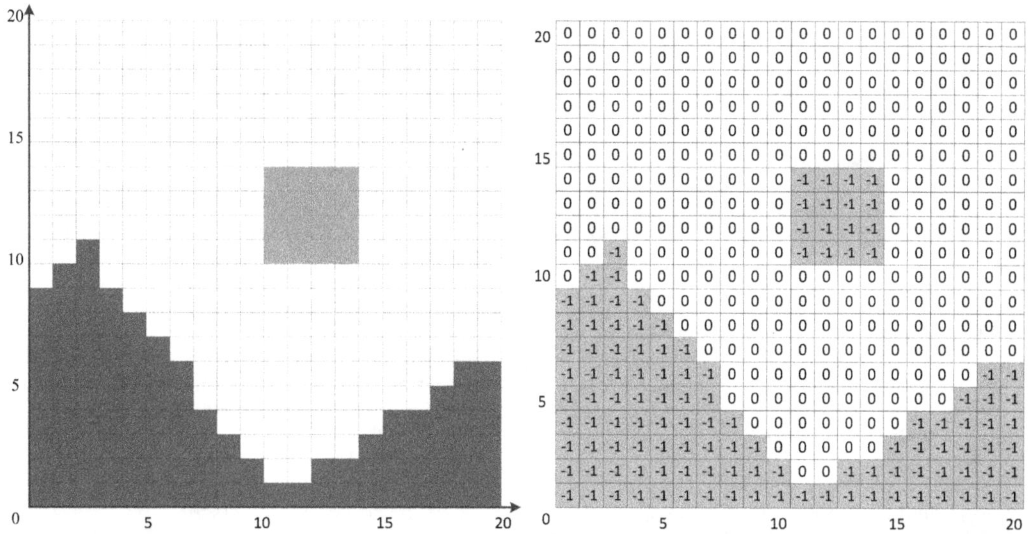

(a)A subspace is decomposed into grids. **(b)A block matrix representing the blockage of the subspace**

Fig. 2. A subspace and a block matrix.

$$path = \begin{pmatrix} waypoint_0 \\ waypoint_1 \\ \vdots \\ waypoint_p \end{pmatrix} = \begin{pmatrix} x_0 & y_2 & z_0 \\ x_1 & y_1 & z_1 \\ \cdots & \cdots & \cdots \\ x_p & y_p & z_p \end{pmatrix} \quad (1)$$

When path planner evaluates the quality of a path. The length of the path is the sum of Euclidean distance between waypoints. Furthermore, waypoints will be mapped to block matrixes. A waypoint is defined as a blocking waypoint, if it locates in blocking position. Oppositely, a waypoint is defined as a feasible waypoint, if it locates in hollowness position. We conclude that a path collides with obstacles if it contains blocking waypoints. In a word, we express continuous spaces and paths in a discretization method, which makes path planner simpler to store and manipulate data, and thus improve the performance.

3. COST FUNCTION

The quality of a path is influenced by the constraints of environment and AUVs capacity. In this paper, the complete set of constraints is length, energy consumption, safety and curvature of a path. Then, constraints are described in a cost function using penalty function method. In the cost function, C_{length} penalizes longer paths; C_{depth} penalizes paths with more snorkeling actions; C_{smooth} penalizes paths that cannot be smoothed; C_{block} penalizes paths colliding with obstacles.

In our definition, C_{length} is defined as

$$C_{length} = 1 - \frac{L_{PsPt}}{L_{path}}, C_{length} \in (0,1) \quad (2)$$

where L_{PsPt} is the direct Euclidean distance between the start-point P_s to the target-point P_t . L_{path} is the actual length of a path. A tortuous path will result in high cost.

C_{depth} is defined as

$$C_{depth} = \frac{D_{\max} - D_{\min}}{D}, C_{depth} \in (0,1) \quad (3)$$

where D_{max} and D_{min} are the maximum and minimum depth of a path. D is the maximum depth in our model. AUVs should avoid snorkeling actions as much as possible, because these actions consume a lot of energy.

C_{smooth} penalizes a path involving segments that are unable to be smoothed, which is defined as

$$C_{smooth} = \begin{cases} 2 + \frac{N_{unable}}{N_{segment}}, N_{unable} > 0 \\ 0, N_{unable} = 0 \end{cases}, C_{smooth} \in 0 \cup (2,3) \quad (4)$$

where N_{unable} is the number of impossible smoothing segment and $N_{segment}$ is the total number of segments. C_{smooth} is 0, if the path can be smoothed, otherwise it is larger than 2. We determine whether the segment can be smoothed by the following method.

In our implement, the direct Euclidean distance between P_s and P_t is l and the turning radius is θ, as show in Fig. 3. The distance between each subspace is fixed at l' and the maximum turning radius of AUVs is $\theta_{\max}$. Therefore, the maximum distance between 2 waypoints in a smooth path is

$$l_{max} = \frac{l'}{\cos\theta_{\max}} \quad (5)$$

Note that $\theta < \theta_{\max}$ if $l < l_{max}$ in this case. Because of this property, we can determine whether the segment can be smoothed by

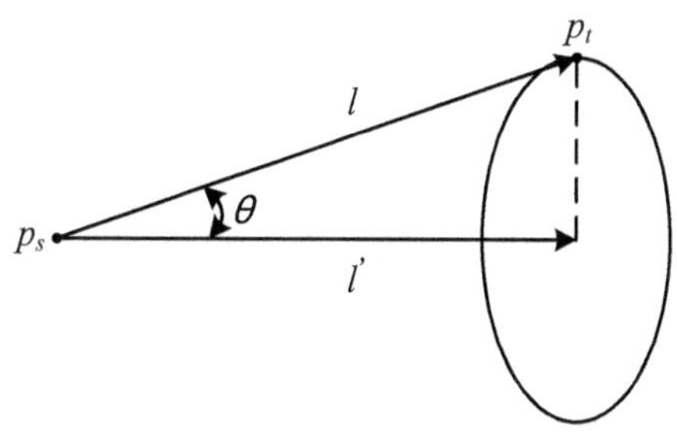

Fig. 3. How to determine whether the segment can be smoothed. The length from P_s to P_t is l and the offset angle is θ.

calculating the Euclidean distance between them.

C_{block} is defined as follows:

$$C_{block}=\begin{cases}2+\dfrac{N_{block}}{N_{space}}, N_{block}>0 \\ 0 \qquad\qquad , N_{block}=0\end{cases}, C_{block}\in 0\cup(2,3) \tag{6}$$

where N_{block} is the number of waypoints that collide with obstacles and N_{space} is the number of subspaces and also the total number of waypoints except start-point and target-point. C_{block} is 0, if the path does not collide with obstacles, otherwise it is larger than 2.

In general, penalty function method is very meaningful to the path planning algorithm which transforms the problem into a search for minimum value of the cost function. The cost function is defined as

$$F_{cost}=C_{length}+C_{depth}+C_{smooth}+C_{block} \tag{7}$$

C_{smooth} and C_{block} are feasibility criteria that guide the path planner to find out feasible solutions. Each feasibility criterion equals to 0 when the path is feasible, otherwise is in the range [2, 3]. C_{length} and C_{depth} are optimization criteria that each of them are defined to be in range [0, 1]. Optimization criteria are adopted to improve solution quality. It is to be noted that the value of the cost function will be smaller than 2 when the path is feasible, otherwise an F_{cost} larger than 2 indicates that the path is infeasible. In this way, the infeasible paths always possess higher cost than the feasible paths, which will be distinguished by algorithm quickly.

4. DE-BASED PATH PLANNER

Differential Evolution (DE) is a simple meta-heuristic for global optimization with fast convergence speed and good fitness value [14]. In this paper, the powerful algorithm is adopted to solve the path planning problem of AUVs. The specific steps of the proposed DE is described in this section.

4.1 Initialization

At the beginning of the differential evolution algorithm, *NP* arbitrary individuals are generated to initial the population. In our representation, an individual represents a path which is encoded in a waypoint matrix. The *j*th column in the waypoint matrix is the 3-D coordinate (x_j, y_j, z_j) of $waypoint_j$. A vector *X*, a vector *Y* and a vector *Z* are respectively defined as the first row (x_0, x_1,..., x_p), the second row (y_0, y_1, ..., y_p) and the third row (z_0, z_1, ..., z_p) in the waypoint matrix (see Fig. 4). The quality of a path is mainly decided by *X* and *Y*. *Z* does not be optimized because it is just fixed as serial number of subspaces. The proposed DE respectively conduct all operations on vector *X* and vector *Y* so as to find out the optimum path. For instance, the vector *X* of a path is initialized according to a random manner, for i=1, 2,..., *NP* and j=1, 2,..., *D*.

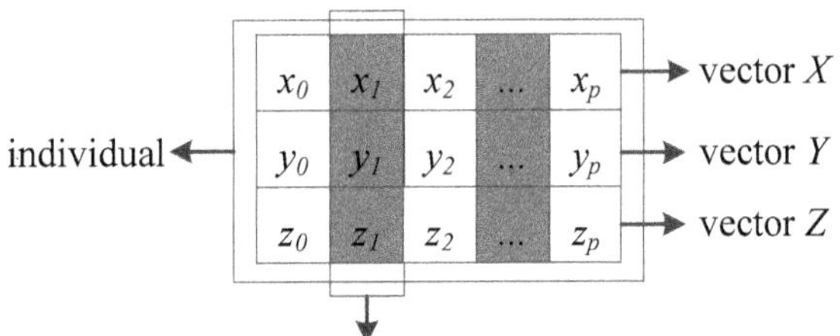

Fig. 4. Individual component.

$$x_{i,j}(0)=l+rand_1\times(u-l) \tag{8}$$

where u and l is the upper bound and lower bound of the width of problem space. The $rand_1$ is a uniformly distributed random within [0, 1]. *D* is the dimension of the individual and *NP* is the population size. The vector *Y* of a path is initialized in the same way. Each dimension of vector *Z* is set to corresponding serial number of subspaces. We take the operations of the vector *X* as an example when we describe the rest of operations, because both vectors conduct operations in the same way.

4.2 Mutation

After initialization, mutant vector is generated based on the current population. Various mutation strategies can be applied to mutation [15] [16]. In this paper, we use the DE/current-to-best/1.

For example, the mutant vector V_i^x for vector X_i is obtained by

$$\begin{aligned}v_i^x(G+1)&=x_i(G)+F\cdot(x_{best}(G)-x_i(G))\\&+F\cdot(x_{r1}(G)-x_{r2}(G)), r1\neq r2\neq best\neq i\end{aligned} \tag{9}$$

$r1, r2, r3\in[1, NP]$ are random indexes and different from the running indexes i and *best*. The $x_{best}(G)$ is the vector with the best fitness in the population at generation *G*. *F* is used to scale the difference vector and leads the population to convergence.

In [15], it is said that the fixed parameter *F* for the original DE is usually chosen in [0.5, 1]. However, this parameter setting does not perform well in our optimization problem. Therefore, an adaptive *F* is employed to adjust convergence rate so as to improve the performance of DE. A large *F* speeds up convergence when the population is dispersed. Whereas a small *F* keep the diversity of population in a crowd population. Suitable *F* can make population converge stably and increase the possibility of finding out potential solutions when DE is in the exploring stage. Increasing *F* is helpful for escaping from local optima when population is crowded. Parameters of adaptive PSO are adapted according to population distribution in order to avoid trapping into the likely local optimum [12]. Similarly, *F* adapts according to *d* in this paper. *d* is the mean Euclidean distance of the best individual to the other individuals, which is used to assess population distribution. The proposed DE calculates it every 100 generation. The factor *F* is obtained by (11).

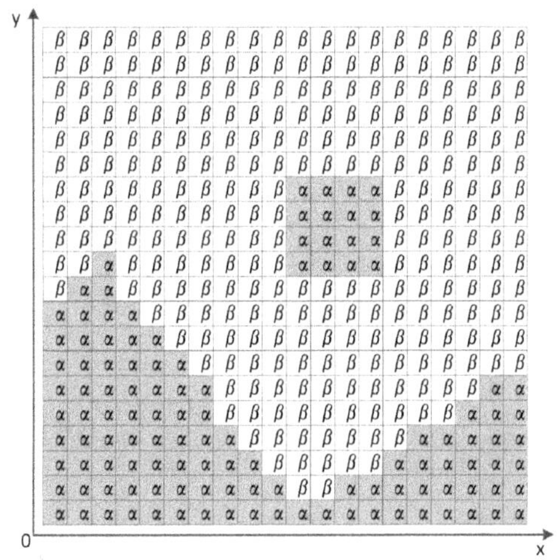

Fig. 5. The crossover matrix generated according to the subspace see in Fig. 2

$$d=\frac{\sum_{i=1,i\neq best}^{NP}\sum_{j=1}^{D}\sqrt{\left(x_{best,j}-x_{i,j}\right)^2+\left(y_{best,j}-y_{i,j}\right)^2}}{(NP-1)\cdot D} \tag{10}$$

$$F=\begin{cases}0.6+0.3\times\frac{d}{d_0} & ,\text{if } d>1\\ 1-0.4\times d & ,\text{if } d\leq 1\end{cases} \tag{11}$$

where d_0 is the mean distance of the best individual to other individuals after conducting initialization, *best* is the index of the best individual at current generation.

Note that some components of the mutant vector may violate boundary constraints because of the scaling method. The following formula is used to reset components of the trial vector when their values are out of boundary.

$$v_{i,j}(G)=l+rand_2\times(u-l),\ \text{if } v_{i,j}(G)<l \text{ or } v_{i,j}(G)>u \tag{12}$$

where $v_{i,j}$(G) is the *j*th dimension of *i*th vector, $rand_2$ is a uniformly distributed random within [0, 1]. It ensures that each dimension of a vector takes value in [*l, u*].

4.3 Crossover

Crossover is introduced to increase the diversity of the perturbed parameter vectors after mutation. The trial vector U_i^x for vector X_i is produced as follow

$$u_i^x(G+1)=\begin{cases}v_i^x(G+1),\text{if } (rand_3\leq CR) \text{ or } (j=randj)\\ x_i(G) \quad ,\text{otherwise}\end{cases} \tag{13}$$

where $rand_3$ is a uniformly distributed random value within [0,1]. $rand_j$ is a randomly chosen dimension index from 1 to *D* and ensures that each $u_i^x(G+1)$ gets at least one dimension from $v_i^x(G+1)$. *CR* controls how many components of the current individual are mutated. In the original DE, *CR* is a fixed parameter of crossover probability at all generations and takes value in range [0, 1].

In order to improve the quality of paths, blocking waypoints should be replaced by feasible waypoints as much as possible, on the other hand, blocking waypoints generated by mutation operation should be cautiously used to replace original waypoints. Thus, crossover matrixes are generated according to the blockage of subspaces. *CR* is β where the position in the subspace is hollowness, otherwise is α and set as low probability rate, α and β take values in range [0, 1]. For instance, a crossover matrix generated according to a subspace (see in Fig. 2) is shown in Fig. 5. For each dimension of a path, the proposed DE should obtain *CR* before proceeding crossover and *CR* is determined by the location of waypoints in each subspace (i.e., *CR* is β in the 5th dimension of an individual, because the 5th waypoint of a mutant path locates in (10.4, 1.5, 5) where is hollowness in Fig. 5). In this paper, α is set as 0 and β is set as 0.4. In other word, the proposed DE ignores mutant waypoints which are in the blocking position.

4.4 Selection

Finally, the trial vector is compared to the target vector using the greedy criterion. In this paper, the quality of an individual is evaluated by the cost function. The individual with the minimum cost is the optimal path in the problem space.

$$path_i(G+1)=\begin{cases}u_i^{path}(G+1),\text{if } f\left(u_i^{path}(G+1)\right)<f\left(path_i(G)\right)\\ path_i(G) \quad ,\text{otherwise}\end{cases} \tag{14}$$

```
1) Initialization
   Load 3-D underwater environment data;
   Model and decompose the 3-D underwater environment;
   Generate block matrixes for each subspace according to the blockage of the subspace;
   Enter the start-point and the target-point;
   Initialize paths, crossover matrixes and mutation parameter F;
2) Optimization
   Repeat
     Find out the individual with the minimum cost in current population;
     Generate mutation parameter F according to (16);
     For each individual
       Update mutation vector according to (11) and (12);
       Generate a random index j from rand(1,D);
       For each dimension
         Update each dimension of crossover vector according to (13);
       End for
       Evaluate the cost of the crossover vector;
       If the cost of the crossover vector is less
         Update the individual according to (14);
       End if
     End for
   Until termination criterion is satisfied
3) Display
   Save the results in files and visualize it through the graph in MATLAB™;
```

Fig. 6. Overall procedure of the path planning algorithm.

TABLE I MEAN VALUE AND VARIANCE OF PATHS GENERATED BY THE ORIGINAL DE, JDE, PSO AND THE PROPOSED DE

scenarios	start-point and target-point	F=0.6,CR=0.6 (the original DE)	F=0.7,CR=0.7 (the original DE)	F=0.8,CR=0.7 (the original DE)	F=0.9,CR=0.8 (the original DE)	jDE	PSO	the proposed DE
1	(13,8,0);(7,15,40)	**0.32161(0)**	**0.32161(0)**	0.361752(1.30E-2)	0.322263(1.02E-6)	0.32161(0)	5.885362(4.07E-3)	0.420127(4.02E-2)
	(6,8,0);(4 13,40)	0.181811(3.56E-3)	**0.160024(0)**	0.1710262(2.32E-3)	0.261668(3.31E-3)	0.194534(1.04E-2)	6.265734(1.23E-1)	0.388989(1.20E-5)
	(10,12,0);(6,16,40)	0.218510(4.38E-6)	**0.217680(1.78E 5)**	0.2214278(3.02E-7)	0.223989(3.42E-6)	0.218356(1.36E-4)	6.133394(1.21E-1)	0.259495(1.72E-5)
2	(5,13,0);(4,16,40)	0.430098(7.77E-3)	0.431772(7.68E-3)	**0.399786(1.13E-2)**	0.441091(2.64E-3)	0.409948(1.04E-2)	6.230536(1.46E-1)	0.428457(4.39E-2)
	(8,10,0);(6,17,40)	0.712991(3.32)	0.329094(1.74E-6)	**0.321613(1.79E-3)**	1.247008(1.32E+1)	0.728801(3.19)	6.038856(4.00E-2)	0.405546(5.12E-2)
	(7,15,0);(5,16,40)	0.3590629(9.07E-3)	**0.332051(1.01E-2)**	0.344161(1.13E-2)	0.385855(4.1E-5)	0.337701(1.36E-2)	6.0114(1.04E-1)	0.419288(9.92E-2)
3	(6,18,0);(8,18,40)	2.021282(1.46E+1)	1.699998(1.47E+1)	0.465378(7.17E-2)	1.330405(4.92)	1.236306(1.30E+1)	6.035746(7.60E-3)	**0.460605(1.23E-1)**
	(8,10,0);(6,17,40)	**0.220518(2.05E-1)**	0.758460(4.54)	0.454135(6.46E-2)	0.876345(3.94)	0.38422(9.38E-2)	6.244654(2.17E-1)	0.582667(3.01E-2)
	(7,15,0);(5,16,40)	1.155652(1.39E+1)	1.736358(1.52E+1)	0.978312(3.77)	0.937326(3,59)	1.404417(5.93)	6.139224(3.56E-2)	**0.580731(2.81E-2)**
4	(4,9,0);(7,7,40)	**0.349937(2.34E-3)**	0.438356(5.81E-2)	0.4614(1.04E-1)	1.316869(1.61E+1)	0.736643(2.97)	6.212246(9.47E-2)	0.626577(9.17E-2)
	(6,10,0);(8,7,40)	0.365456(2.85E-2)	**0.263352(1.61E-2)**	0.382284(6.44E-2)	0.365599(7.92E-2)	0.638990(3.41)	6.004548(4.29E-2)	0.536404(8.53E-5)
	(6,4,0);(4,13,40)	0.7396816(3.50)	0.305502(7.38E-3)	**0.260199(8.08E-3)**	0.812751(4.72)	0.306618(1.40E-2)	6.275336(2.09E-1)	1.461967(5.20)
5	(5,9,0);(12,11,40)	3.684434(4.41)	4.034565(3.34)	2.866557(1.04E+1)	2.147028(1.07E=1)	4.10767(3.54)	6.057614(1.35E-2)	**0.750541(9.66E-2)**
	(7,6,0);(13,12,40)	2.365852(1.03E-5)	2.82075(3.72)	2.36622(4.92E-2)	2.900671(1.10E+1)	2.033863(2.49)	6.05228(2.09E-1)	**1.005671(3.45)**
	(8,10,0);(14,11,40)	2.802434(3.34)	2.76165(3.47)	3.188622(5.35)	2.832843(1.13E+1)	2.350582(2.20E-3)	5.923244(1.19E-1)	**0.481749(1.07E-2)**
6	(13,2,0);(7,7,40)	4.590854(3.87E-3)	4.584307(1.24E-2)	4.1870112(3.65)	4.613735(3.96E-2)	4.656088(4.42-2)	6.072864(2.76E-2)	**1.007700(8.60E-1)**
	(14,2,0);(6,6,40)	4.734482(6.77E-2)	4.267592(2.88)	4.653034(2.17E-4)	4.232726(2.86)	4.666146(1.87E-2)	6.037644(3.19E-2)	**1.04268(3.59)**
	(15,3,0);(7,15,40)	4.199218(3.15)	3.804884(4.69)	4.594318(1.46E-3)	3.3687832(1.33E+1)	3.414078(4.81)	5.972792(9.78E-3)	**0.9187664(3.53)**

where $path_i(G)$ is the original $path_i$ *and* $u_i^{path}(G+1)$ is the treated path generated by mutation and crossover. The treated path replaces the original path, if the cost of former is less than the latter one.

4.5 General Procedure

So far, we have described all parts needed to implement the path planner for AUVs. Here, we describe the specific steps of the path planning algorithm. Firstly, path planner models an underwater environment and decomposes it into parallel subspaces and grids. Secondly, the start-point and target-point are required to enter, and then NP paths are initialized by initialization operation. Crossover matrixes are generated according to the blockage of parallel subspaces. d_0 is calculated and F is initialized to 0.9. Thirdly, the optimization operation based on the DE is repeated generation after generation until some specific termination criteria are satisfied. Finally, the results are stored in files and displayed in MATLAB™. The overall procedure of path planning algorithm is shown in Fig. 6.

5. EXPERIMENTAL RESULTS

All algorithms are coded in C and the results are visualized in MATLAB™ 2010. The configurations of the computer are Intel Core 2 Duo P7350 CPU 2.00 GHZ, 2 GB of memory. The proposed algorithm is compared with the original DE, jDE and the original PSO. We conduct experiments in 6 scenarios (Fig. 1) and each scenario test 3 pairs of start-point and target-point. The population sizes of all algorithms are 256. An individual consists of 41 dimensions corresponding to waypoints of a path. The maximum generations are set to 20,000.

1) The proposed DE: the original DE with self-adaptive strategy. The self-adaptive strategy is specifically designed for our model.
2) DE [14]: The original DE.
3) JDE [17]: jDE is a variant of DE with self-adapting parameters. F and CR values change in the process of optimization. F takes values from $[F_l, F_u]$ and CR takes values from $[CR_l, CR_u]$ in a random manner, τ_1, τ_2 represent

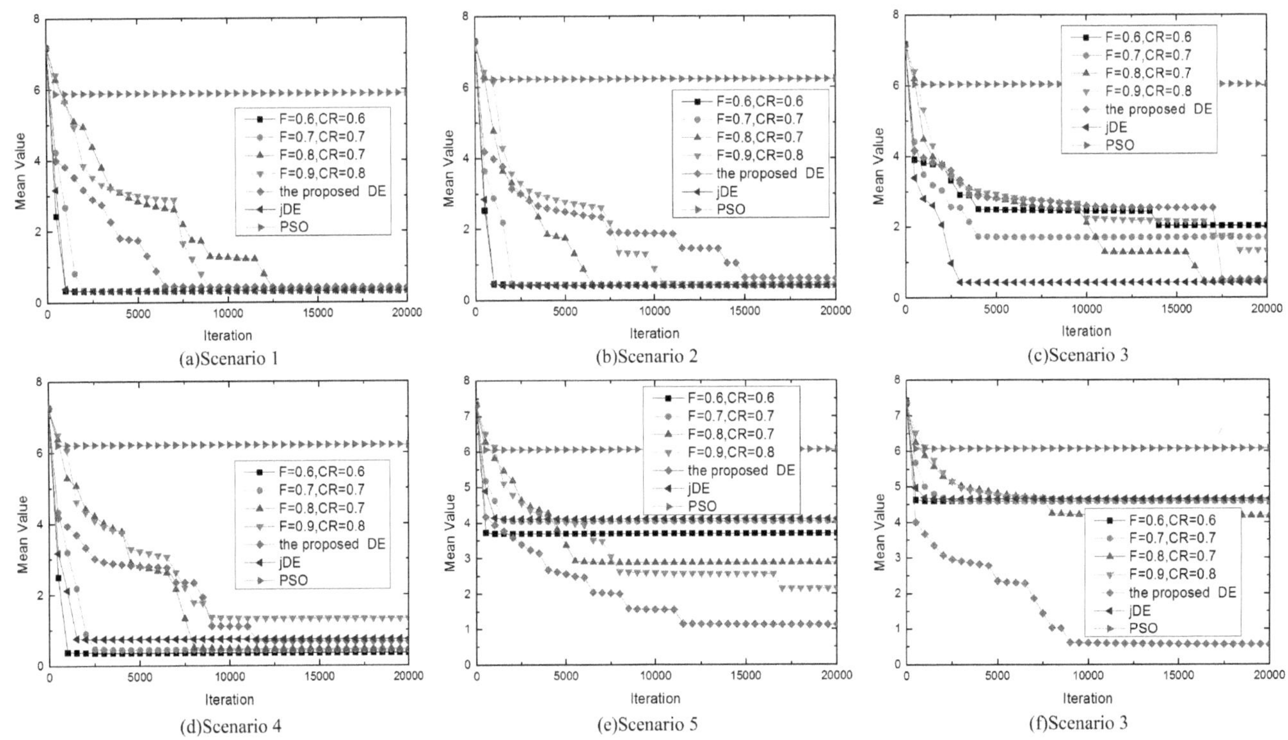

Fig. 7. Mean value of paths generated by four algorithms at each iteration for the scenarios

probabilities to adjust parameters respectively.

4) PSO [13]: the original particle swarm optimization.

The parameters setting for our proposed DE has been described in section 5. Four fixed parameter settings (*F*=0.6, *CR*=0.6; *F*=0.7, *CR*=0.7; *F*=0.8, *CR*=0.7 and *F*=0.9, *CR*=0.8) for the original DE are tested here. In our implementation for jDE, *F* takes values from [0.3, 0.7], *CR* takes values from [0.1, 0.7], initial *F* and *CR* are both set as 0.7, τ_1, τ_2 are 0.1. The inertia weight w of PSO is 0.6 and acceleration coefficients c_1 and c_2 are both 2.0.

The mean value and variance of paths generated by four algorithms over 30 independent runs are listed in Table 1. We plot the mean cost of paths (a set of start-point and target-point for each scenario) generated by four algorithms at each iteration for 6 scenarios in Fig. 7. Obviously, the proposed DE can find out optimal or sub-optimal paths on all scenarios. Though the proposed DE takes more iterations before finding a feasible path in simple environment models than the original DE, it has a higher success rate for planning optimal path than other algorithms in complex environment models. The original DE converge to global optima quickly in simple environment models, but it is usually trapped into local optimum in complex environment. The results show that our algorithm balances the convergence and diversity of population during the search. From the Table 1, we note that DE algorithms outperform the original PSO. The original PSO cannot find a feasible path in most cases; it is trapped into local optimum prematurely. However, important differences between DE algorithms with different parameter settings could be measured in the experiment, we cannot conclude that which fixed parameter setting of the original DE satisfies all environment models for planning optimal paths. The original DE with a special setting may outperform than other algorithms in some environment, yet, it cannot even find a feasible path in other complex environment. That is why we try to improve the performance of the original DE with adaptive parameters. The self-adaptive strategy for jDE just randomly changes the value of *F* and *CR*, not adjusts parameters according to features of environment models and characteristics of the population. Therefore, jDE cannot effectively improve the performance of DE in our path planning problem.

6. CONCLUSION

This paper proposes a path planner based on an adaptive DE for AUVs in 3-D underwater environment. The problem spaces are decomposed into parallel subspaces along the Z axis. A path is obtained by joining waypoints in each subspace. Moreover, a cost function involving the length, energy consumption, safety and curvature constraints is applied to evaluate the quality of a path. Then path planning is carry out in subspace. In order to improve the performance of DE, a self-adaptive parameter technique is incorporated into DE. At last, we conduct experiments in different scenarios and compare with results. The proposed DE outperforms other algorithms in most cases. It shows that our proposed algorithm provides an effective tool for path planning of AUVs in 3-D complex environments.

However, more constraints should be added to the cost function so as to evaluate paths better, for example, the influence of currents calls for future work. Future research may also focus on improving the performance of the path planner on much more complex problem space with more constraints.

7. ACKNOWLEDGMENTS

This work was supported in part by the High-Technology Research and Development Program (863 Program) of China No. 2013AA 01A212, in part by the NSFC for Distinguished Young Scholars 61125205, in part by the NSFC No. 61332002 and No.61300044.

8. REFERENCES

[1] Blidberg, D. R. 2001. The development of autonomous underwater vehicles (auvs); a brief summary. *IEEE Int. Conf. Robotics Automation*, 6500.

[2] Latombe, J. C. 2005. *Robot motion planning*. Norwell, USA: Kluwer.

[3] Yilmaz, N. K., Evangelinos, C., Lermusiaux, P. and Patrikalakis, N. M. 2008. Path planning of autonomous underwater vehicles for adaptive sampling using mixed integer linear programming. *IEEE J. Ocean. Eng.* 33, 4, 522-537.

[4] Cetin, B., Bikdash, M. and Hadaegh, F. Y. 2007. Hybrid mixed-logical linear programming algorithm for collision-free optimal path planning. *IET Control Theory and Applications*. 1, 2, 522–531.

[5] Garau, B., Alvarez, A. and Oliver, G. 2005. Path planning of autonomous underwater vehicles in current fields with complex spatial variability: an A* approach. in *Proc. IEEE Conf. Robotics and Automation*. 194-198.

[6] Guo, S.-X. and Gao, B.-F. 2009. Path planning optimization of underwater microrobots in 3-D space by PSO approach. in *Proc. IEEE Int. Conf. Robotics and Biomimetics*. 1655-1620.

[7] Alvarez, A., Caiti, A. and Onken, R. 2004. Evolutionary path planning for autonomous underwater vehicles in a variable ocean. *IEEE J. Ocean. Eng.* 29, 2, 418-429.

[8] Zeng, Z., Lammas, A. and Sammut, K. 2012. Optimal path planning based on annular space decomposition for AUVs operating in a variable environment. *IEEE/OES Autonomous Underwater Vehicles (AUV)*. 1-9.

[9] Cheng, C. T. Fallahi, Leung, K. H. and Tse, C. K. 2010. An AUVs path planner using genetic algorithms with a deterministic crossover operator. in *Proc. IEEE Int. Conf. Robotics and Automation*, Anchorage. 2995-3000.

[10] Roberge, V., Tarbouchi, M. and Labonte, G. 2013. Comparison of Parallel Genetic Algorithm and Particle Swarm Optimization for Real-Time UAV Path Planning. *IEEE Trans Industrial Informatics*. 9, 1, 132 – 141.

[11] Petres, C., Pailhas, Y., Patron, P., Petillot, Y., Evans, J. and Lane, D. 2007. Path planning for autonomous underwater vehicles. *IEEE Trans. Robotics*. 23, 2, 331-341.

[12] Zhan, Z. H., Zhang, J., Li, Y. and Chung, H. H. 2009. Adaptive particle swarm optimization. *IEEE Trans Systems, Man, and Cybernetics*. 39, 6, 1362-1381.

[13] Kennedy, J. and Eberhart, R. C. 1995. Particle swarm optimization. in *Proc. IEEE Int. Conf. Neural Netw.* 4, 1942–1948.

[14] Storn, R. and Price, K. 1997. Differential evolution–a simple and efficient heuristic for global optimization over continuous spaces. *Journal of global optimization*. 11, 4, 341-359.

[15] Mallipeddia, R., Suganthana, P. N., Panb, Q. K. and Tasgetirenc, M. F. 2011. Differential evolution algorithm with ensemble of parameters and mutation strategies. *Applied Soft Computing*. 11, 2, 1679-1696.

[16] Storn, R. 1996. On the usage of differential evolution for function optimization. Biennial Conference of the North American Fuzzy Information Processing Society. 519-523.

[17] Brest, J., Greiner, S., Boskovic, B., Mernik, M. and Zumer, V. 2006. Self-adapting control parameters in differential evolution: A comparative study on numerical benchmark problems. *IEEE Trans. Evol. Comput.* 10, 6, 646-657.

A Two-Leveled Hybrid Dendritic Cell Algorithm Under Imprecise Reasoning

Zeineb Chelly*
Department of Computer Science, High Institute of Management of Tunis
zeinebchelly@yahoo.fr

Zied Elouedi
Department of Computer Science, High Institute of Management of Tunis
zied.elouedi@gmx.fr

ABSTRACT

The Dendritic Cell Algorithm(DCA) is a bio-inspired algorithm based on the behavior of Dendritic Cells(DCs). The DCA performance relies on its data pre-processing phase where feature extraction and signal categorization are performed and which are based on the use of the Principal Component Analysis(PCA) technique. However, using PCA presents a limitation as it destroys the underlying semantics of the features after reduction. To overcome this limitation, Rough Set Theory(RST) was applied as a pre-processor; but, still the developed rough approach presents an information loss as data should be discretized beforehand. Indeed, DCA was known to be sensitive to the input class data order. This is due to the crisp separation between the two DCs contexts; semi-mature and mature. Thus, the aim of this paper is to develop a novel DCA version based on a two-leveled hybrid model handling the mentioned DCA shortcomings. In the top-level, our proposed algorithm applies a more adequate feature extraction technique based on Fuzzy Rough Set Theory(FRST) to build a solid data pre-processing phase. At the bottom level, our algorithm applies Fuzzy Set Theory to smooth the crisp separation between the DCs contexts. Results show that our proposed algorithm succeeds in obtaining significantly improved classification accuracy.

Categories and Subject Descriptors

I.2 [**Computing Methodologies**]: Artificial intelligence

General Terms

Algorithms, Experimentation, Performance.

Keywords

Artificial Immune Systems, Hybrid Algorithm, Classification, Fuzzy Set Theory, Rough Set Theory.

*Corresponding Author

GECCO'14, July 12–16, 2014, Vancouver, BC, Canada.

http://dx.doi.org/10.1145/2576768.2598217.

1. INTRODUCTION

As a bio-inspired algorithm, the Dendritic Cell Algorithm (DCA) [1] is one of the emerging algorithms within the field of Artificial Immune Systems. DCA is derived from behavioral models of natural immune cells called the Dendritic Cells (DCs). Lately, DCA has caught the attention of researchers due to the worthy characteristics expressed by the algorithm as it exhibits several interesting and potentially beneficial features for binary classification problems [2]. However, as the DCA is still a recent foundation, several studies have been conducted to address and resolve the DCA limitations by proposing new modified DCA models. These new algorithms can be categorized into three main heads based on their goals. The first class aims to improve the DCA algorithmic steps. Examples of works belonging to this category can be the deterministic version of the DCA (dDCA) [3]. dDCA aims at generating a lightweight algorithm in terms of running time by easing the calculation of the DCA crucial algorithmic information. dDCA was, also, modified in [4] where a Markov chain is used to generate synthetic data sets to investigate the antigen sample property of the dDCA. Other modified versions have tended to either add additional components to the algorithm or differ in their methods of implementation. For instance, in [5], a segmentation step was added to the DCA in order to perform periodic analysis on the processed information presented by the DCs. As a result it can effectively improve the anomaly detection speed. The second class of the modified DCAs aims to investigate the DCA pre-processing phase which is decomposed into feature reduction and signal categorization. More precisely, through the pre-processing phase, DCA selects a subset of features and classifies each feature into one of three categories; i.e., as "Danger Signal" (DS), "Safe Signal" (SS) and "Pathogen-Associated Molecular Pattern"(PAMP). The resulting correlation signal values are then classified to form an anomaly detection style of two-class classification. Initially, the DCA data pre-processing phase was based on the use of the Principal Component Analysis (PCA). The use of PCA aims to automatically reduce data dimension by generating new features to retain and to perform their categorization to their specific signal types (SS, DS, PAMP). Other dimensionality reduction techniques were defined including correlation coefficient and information gain. Nevertheless, applying data reduction techniques for data pre-processing destroys the underlying meaning behind the features present initially in the input database. This is seen as an undesirable property for many data pre-processing algorithms such as DCA [6, 7]. As for the DCA signal categorization, the second sub-step of the DCA data pre-processing phase, the PCA ranking in terms of variability was used. Attributes are mapped into the DCA input signal categories by correlating the PCA ranking with the ranking of signal categories which is in the order Safe, PAMP, and Danger [1]. However, this categorization reasoning could not be considered as a coherent categorization procedure. Consequently, other machine learning techniques for feature selection and signal categorization were introduced in the DCA data pre-processing phase. Recent addendums are the rough DCA versions [6, 7, 8]. The rough DCAs are based on the application of Rough Set Theory (RST) [9] as a pre-processor. To select features and based on the RST concepts, the algorithms remove the unnecessary attributes while keeping only the most informative ones, a subset termed reduct, that preserve nearly the same classification power of the original database. Moreover, the signal categorization step is based on the RST reduct and core concepts. It was shown that applying RST, instead of PCA, is more convenient for the DCA data pre-processing step yielding much better performance in terms of classification accuracy. More works have been focused on the functioning of the proposed rough DCAs and it was noticed that the application of RST as a pre-processor is reliant upon crisp data sets; the attribute values of the input database should be discretized beforehand. Consequently, important information may be lost as a result of quantization [10]. This information loss can influence the rough DCAs data pre-processing task and, thus, that will misguide the algorithms classification process by producing unreliable results. To overcome the RST applicability restriction, Fuzzy Rough Set Theory (FRST) [10] was introduced as it encapsulates the related but distinct concepts of vagueness (for fuzzy sets) and indiscernibility (for rough sets), both of which occur as a result of uncertainty in data. A method employing FRST can handle this uncertainty. Therefore, in [11, 12, 13], new fuzzy-rough DCAs were developed based on the FRST concepts. It was shown that the developed fuzzy-rough algorithms outperform the crisp rough DCAs in terms of classification results while avoiding the mentioned information loss.

The third and last class of the modified DCAs focuses on the behavior of the DCA as a binary classifier. In [3], it was noticed that the standard DCA version is sensitive to the input class data order and on this issue several investigations have been conducted to solve this limitation. Investigations have shown that the DCA makes more mistakes when the context changes multiple times in a quick succession unlike when the data are ordered between classes; i.e., class 1 and class 2. Thus, to obtain high and satisfactory classification results, the standard DCA was only applied to ordered data sets where all class 1 are followed by all class 2. Such a drawback is the result of an environment characterized by a crisp separation between the DC semi-mature context and the DC mature context. However, the reality is connected to imprecision by nature. Such imperfection may affect the DCA classification performance leading the algorithm being sensitive to the input class data order. Therefore, one idea was to combine Fuzzy Set Theory (FST) with the DCA to deal with imprecise contexts. In this sense, a first work named the Fuzzy Dendritic Cell Method (FDCM) [14] was developed to solve the DCA issue as being sensitive to the input class data order. FDCM is based on the fact of smoothing the mentioned crisp separation between the DCs contexts since we can neither identify a clear boundary between them nor quantify exactly what is meant by "semi-mature" or "mature". This was handled by the use of FST since it offers the possibility to the systems to deal with the ambiguity that can be found in the definition of a concept or the meaning of a word. Yet, FDCM despite of being a stable classifier was a user-dependent algorithm as its parameters have to be set by the user. Thus, in [15] a modified version of FDCM was developed named the Modified Fuzzy Dendritic Cell Method (MFDCM). MFDCM, as a stable classifier, is based on the fact of automatically generating the parameters of the system by using a fuzzy clustering technique to avoid false and uncertain values given by the user. Still, it is important to mention that these stable fuzzy DCAs, FDCM and MFDCM, apply the PCA for data pre-processing which is a non-adequate technique for feature reduction and signal categorization as shown in [6, 7]. Besides, the already discussed crisp rough and fuzzy-rough DCAs are only applied to ordered-classes data sets; i.e., these algorithms are sensitive to the input class data order. Accordingly and at this stage, it seems important to develop a general DCA characterized, first, by a robust data pre-processing phase based on the theory of fuzzy rough sets and, second, by being stable non-sensitive to the input class data order and a non-user-dependent algorithm. On these basics, we have developed a two-leveled hybrid bio-inspired classifier. In the top-level, our proposed algorithm uses FRST as a robust feature selection and signal categorization technique to ensure a more rigorous data pre-processing phase. In the second level, our algorithm uses FST to ensure a non-sensitivity to the input class data order and a fuzzy clustering technique to guarantee an automated generation of the algorithm's parameters.

2. FUZZY ROUGH SET THEORY

Basic Concepts: In the same way that crisp equivalence classes are central to RST [9], *fuzzy equivalence classes* are central to FRST [10]. The concept of crisp equivalence classes can be extended by the inclusion of a fuzzy similarity relation S on the universe, which determines the extent to which two elements are similar in S. The fuzzy lower approximation becomes $\mu_{\underline{R_P}X}(x) = inf_{y \in U} I(\mu_{R_P}(x,y), \mu_X(y))$ and the fuzzy upper approximation becomes $\mu_{\overline{R_P}X}(x) = sup_{y \in U} T(\mu_{R_P}(x,y), \mu_X(y))$. In the presented formulae, I is a fuzzy implicator and T is a t-norm. R_P is the fuzzy similarity relation induced by the subset of features P: $\mu_{R_P}(x,y) = \bigcup_{a \in P}\{\mu_{R_a}(x,y)\}$ where $\mu_{R_a}(x,y)$ is the degree to which objects x and y are similar for feature a. A fuzzy similarity relation can be constructed for this purpose: $\mu_{R_a}(x,y) = max(min(\frac{(a(y)-(a(x)-\sigma_a))}{(a(x)-(a(x)-\sigma_a))}, \frac{((a(x)+\sigma_a)-a(y))}{((a(x)+\sigma_a)-a(x))}), 0)$ where σ_a is the standard deviation of feature a. The tuple $< \underline{P}(X), \overline{P}(X) >$ is called a *fuzzy-rough set*. The difference between the fuzzy lower approximation, containing information regarding the extent of certainty of object membership to a given concept, and the fuzzy upper approximation, containing information regarding the degree of uncertainty of objects, generates the *fuzzy boundary region*; defined as: $\mu_{BND_{R_P}(X)}(x) = \mu_{\overline{R_P}X}(x) - \mu_{\underline{R_P}X}(x)$. This subset contains objects within the boundary region with less uncertainty.

Reduction Process: To search for the optimal subset of features, the fuzzy-rough reduct, the uncertainty for every concept has to be calculated. The uncertainty for a concept X using features in P can be calculated as follows: $U_P(X) =$

$\frac{\sum_{x\in U}\mu_{BND_{R_P}(X)}(x)}{|U|}$. This is the average extent to which objects belong to the fuzzy boundary region for the concept X. The total uncertainty degree for all concepts, given a feature subset P, is defined as: $\gamma'_P(Q) = \frac{\sum_{X\in U/Q} U_P(X)}{|U/Q|}$. A Fuzzy-Rough QuickReduct algorithm can be constructed for locating a fuzzy-rough reduct based on this measure. The task of the algorithm is to minimize the total uncertainty degree. When this reaches the minimum for the data set, a fuzzy-rough reduct has been found. An example on how to use the Fuzzy-Rough QuickReduct algorithm, based on the fuzzy boundary region, can be found in [10].

3. THE TWO-LEVELED HYBRID SOLUTION

In this Section, we present our newly proposed fuzzy rough DCA version within imprecise framework.

3.1 Top-Level : Data pre-processing Phase

As previously explained, it is more adequate to apply FRST instead of the crisp RST and data reduction techniques for the DCA data pre-processing phase. This important observation was highlighted in [11, 12, 13]. So back to these works proposed in [11, 12, 13], we notice that each of these algorithms relies on the use of a different FRST concept. The first fuzzy-rough DCA, named FRST-DCA [11], is based on the use of membership functions where the algorithm generates associated fuzzy sets for the used data set. Nevertheless, the complexity related to these calculations becomes prohibitively high for large feature subsets and, thus, a second fuzzy-rough DCA was proposed in [12]. The algorithm, named FLA-DCA, is based on the fuzzy lower approximation and fuzzy similarity relations instead of generating the associated fuzzy sets and, thus, avoiding the extra calculations performed by FRST-DCA. The proposed FLA-DCA was criticized in [13] since it uses, only, the fuzzy lower approximation for the evaluation of feature subsets. In fact, the fuzzy lower approximation contains information regarding the extent of certainty of object membership to a given concept. On the other hand, the fuzzy upper approximation contains information regarding the degree of uncertainty of objects, and hence, this information can be used to discriminate between subsets. For example, two subsets may result in the same fuzzy lower approximation, but one subset may produce a smaller fuzzy upper approximation. This subset will be more useful as there is less uncertainty concerning objects within the fuzzy boundary region. On these basics, the third fuzzy-rough algorithm, named FBR-DCA, was proposed in [13]. FBR-DCA is based on the fuzzy boundary region and fuzzy similarity relations. From these conclusions, we have based the data pre-processing phase of our newly proposed algorithm on the same FBR-DCA concepts. We have named our algorithm FBR-MFDCM.

3.1.1 *The Process of Feature Selection*

For antigen classification, our learning problem has to select high discriminating features from the original input database which corresponds to the antigen information data set. We may formalize this problem as an information table where universe $U = \{x_1, x_2, \dots, x_N\}$ is a set of antigen identifiers, the conditional attribute set $C = \{c_1, c_2, \dots, c_A\}$ contains each feature of the information table to select and the decision attribute D of our learning problem corresponds to the class label of each sample. The decision attribute D of the FBR-MFDCM input database has binary values d_k: either the antigen is collected under safe circumstances reflecting a normal behavior or the antigen is collected under dangerous circumstances reflecting an anomalous behavior. The decision attribute feature D is defined as follows: $D = \{normal, anomalous\}$. For feature selection, FBR-MFDCM has to determine, first of all, the fuzzy boundary region for both concepts; i.e., the two-class labels d_k. To do so, the fuzzy lower and the fuzzy upper approximations of each concept d_k, for each feature c_i and for all objects x_j have to be calculated. The fuzzy lower approximation, the fuzzy upper approximation and the fuzzy boundary region are denoted by: $\mu_{\underline{R_{c_i}}(\{d_k\})}(x_j)$, $\mu_{\overline{R_{c_i}}(\{d_k\})}(x_j)$ and $\mu_{BND_{R_{c_i}}(d_k)}(x_j)$, respectively. Once the fuzzy boundary regions are measured, FBR-MFDCM calculates the uncertainty degrees for each attribute c_i for each concept d_k, denoted by $U_{c_i}(d_k)$. To find the fuzzy-rough reduct, FBR-MFDCM starts off with an empty set and moves to calculate the total uncertainty degrees for each feature c_i; defined as $\gamma'_{c_i}(D)$. The attribute c_m having the smallest total uncertainty degree among all the calculated total uncertainty degrees of the remaining features is added to the empty fuzzy-rough reduct set. Once the first attribute c_m is selected, FBR-MFDCM adds, in turn, one attribute to the selected first attribute and computes the total uncertainty degrees of each obtained attributes couple $\gamma'_{\{c_m,c_i\}}(D)$. The algorithm chooses the couple having the smallest total uncertainty degree. The process of adding each time one attribute to the subset of the selected features continues until the total uncertainty degree of the obtained subset results in the minimal uncertainty for the data set. The obtained fuzzy-rough reduct includes the most informative features that preserve nearly the same classification power of the original data set. Those features will be the most relevant for the FBR-MFDCM next data pre-processing sub-step.

3.1.2 *The Process of Signal Categorization*

Throughout this phase, FBR-MFDCM has to assign for each selected attribute included in the generated fuzzy-rough reduct its specific signal category. In literature, two possible methods for signal categorization were proposed in [6, 7]. The first work, named RST-DCA [6], proposes to assign only one attribute to form both SS and PAMP. As for the DS categorization, RST-DCA combines the rest of the reduct features and assigns the resulting value to the DS. The second work, named RC-DCA [7], proposes to assign different features for different signal types; i.e., a specific feature is assigned to be either as SS or as a PAMP signal. Same as RST-DCA, RC-DCA combines the rest of the reduct features and assigns the resulting value to the DS. In [8], a comparative study was made to compare the two signal categorization processes presented in [6, 7]. In [8], it was shown that the fact of assigning for each selected feature a specific signal category leads to improve the classification performance of the algorithm than assigning the same attribute to both SS and PAMP. Based on these clarifications, FBR-MFDCM will assign a specific feature to each type of signal. Besides, the general guidelines for signal categorization are based on the semantic of each signal type [1]:

• SSs: Their presence certainly indicates that no anomalies are present. • PAMPs: The presence of PAMPs usually means that there is an anomalous situation. • DSs: Their presence may or may not show an anomalous situation, however the probability of an anomaly is higher than under normal circumstances.

Based on the semantics of the mentioned signals, a ranking can be performed. More precisely, both SSs and PAMPs are more informative than DSs which means that both of the former signals can be seen as indispensable attributes; i.e., reflecting the first and the second ranking positions. To represent this level of importance, our method uses the first obtained couple of features through the fuzzy-rough reduct generation. On the other hand, DSs are less informative than PAMPs and SSs; i.e., reflecting the last and third ranking position. Therefore, our method discards initially the two first selected attributes that are already chosen to represent the SS and PAMP signals, and then our algorithm uses the rest of the fuzzy-rough reduct attributes in order to represent the DSs. Technically, our method processes as follows: as FBR-MFDCM has already calculated the total uncertainty degree of each attribute c_i apart, $\gamma'_{c_i}(D)$, FBR-MFDCM selects the first attribute c_m having the smallest total uncertainty degree to form the SSs. This is because c_m is considered as the most informative first feature added to the fuzzy-rough reduct. With no additional computations and since FBR-MFDCM has already computed the total uncertainty degree of each attributes couple $\gamma'_{\{c_m,c_i\}}(D)$ when adding, in turn, one attribute c_i to the selected first attribute c_m, FBR-MFDCM chooses the couple having the smallest total uncertainty degree. More precisely, FBR-MFDCM selects that second attribute c_r having the smallest $\gamma'_{\{c_m,c_r\}}(D)$ among the calculated $\gamma'_{\{c_m,c_i\}}(D)$. That attribute c_r is chosen to form the PAMP signals. Finally, the rest of the fuzzy-rough reduct attributes are combined and used to represent the DSs.

Once the signal categorization sub-step is achieved, our method calculates the values of each signal category using the same process used by the standard DCA [1]. The output is, thus, a new information table which reflects the signal database. In fact, the universe U of the induced signal data set is $U = \{x'_1, x'_2, \ldots, x'_N\}$ a set of antigen identifiers and the conditional attribute set $C = \{SSs, PAMPs, DSs\}$ contains the signal types. Once data pre-processing is achieved, FBR-MFDCM moves to its second level where a fuzzy process is performed allowing the algorithm to accomplish its classification task within imprecise circumstances.

3.2 Bottom-Level : Fuzzy Process

The second level of FBR-MFDCM is composed of five sub-steps. Each sub-step is based on the basics of FST.

3.2.1 Defining the Inputs-Output Variables

Once the signal database is ready and based on the same process performed by the standard DCA, seen in Section 2, FBR-MFDCM processes the signal base values to get the cumulative values; i.e., the semi-mature signal value and the mature signal value. These signal values are seen as a mapping with the immune DC semi-mature context and the DC mature context. To describe each of these two contexts, we have used linguistic variables. The semi-mature context is denoted C_s while the mature context is denoted C_m. Both C_s and C_m are considered as the two input variables of the FBR-MFDCM fuzzy process phase. The final state "maturity" relative to the final maturity state of a DC is chosen as the output variable and is denoted S_{mat}. These linguistic variables are defined as follows: $C_s = \{\mu_{C_s}(c_{s_j})/c_{s_j} \in X_{C_s}\}$, $C_m = \{\mu_{C_m}(c_{m_j})/c_{m_j} \in X_{C_m}\}$ and $S_{mat} = \{S_{mat}(s_{mat_j})/s_{mat_j} \in X_{S_{mat}}\}$; where c_{s_j}, c_{m_j} and s_{mat_j} are, respectively, the elements of the discrete universe of discourse X_{C_s}, X_{C_m} and $X_{S_{mat}}$. μ_{C_s}, μ_{C_m} and $\mu_{S_{mat}}$ are, respectively, the corresponding membership functions.

3.2.2 Defining the Term Sets

S_{mat} is specified via the term set $T(S_{mat})$ which is defined as: $T(S_{mat}) = \{Semi-mature, Mature\}$. Each term in $T(S_{mat})$ is characterized by a fuzzy subset in a universe of discourse $X_{S_{mat}}$. The *Semi-mature* term set might be interpreted as a data instance having a normal behavior. The *Mature* term set might be interpreted as an object having an anomalous behavior. Similarly, the input variables C_s and C_m are described using the following term set: $T(Q) = \{Low, Medium, High\}$; where Q = C_s and C_m, respectively.

3.2.3 Membership Function Construction

In order to specify the range of S_{mat}, we have run the FBR-MFDCM and we have recorded a list of all the cumulative semi-mature signal values and the cumulative mature signal values generated for each antigen present in the signal data set. Once the latter values are recorded, we picked up their minimum and maximum values in order to fix the borders of the S_{mat} range which are defined as follows:

$$min(range(S_{mat})) = min(min(range[C_m]), min(range[C_s]))$$

$$max(range(S_{mat})) = max(max(range[C_m]), max(range[C_s]))$$

In the same way, the borders ranges of the C_s and C_m input variables are fixed. At this stage, the parameters of each linguistic variable have to be automatically fixed by our algorithm in order to have a non-user depend algorithm. The needed parameters reflect the extents and midpoints of each membership function of the inputs and output. To achieve this parametrization process, our algorithm applies the fuzzy Gustafson-Kessel clustering algorithm. Now, a mapping has to be performed between the clustering context and the FRST basics. Therefore, each cluster is considered as a membership function while the number of clusters is relative to the number of the membership functions of each variable; i.e, inputs and output.

3.2.4 The Rule Base Description

Positioned at the fourth sub-step of the FBR-MFDCM fuzzy process, a knowledge base comprising rules has to be built to support the algorithm fuzzy inference procedure. The different rules are extracted from the information reflecting the effect of each immune signal on the state of a DC. This was previously pointed in the itemized list figuring in the FBR-MFDCM signal categorization phase Section. The generated rule base is defined in the following itemized list where all the mentioned signals are taken into account implicitly in the FBR-MFDCM fuzzy inference process.

1. If (C_m is Low) and (C_s is Low) then (S_{mat} is Mature)
2. If (C_m is Low) and (C_s is Medium) then (S_{mat} is Semi-mature)
3. If (C_m is Low) and (C_s is High) then (S_{mat} is Semi-mature)
4. If (C_m is Medium) and (C_s is Low) then (S_{mat} is Mature)
5. If (C_m is Medium) and (C_s is Medium) then (S_{mat} is Semi-mature)
6. If (C_m is Medium) and (C_s is High) then (S_{mat} is Semi-mature)
7. If (C_m is High) and (C_s is Low) then (S_{mat} is Mature)
8. If (C_m is High) and (C_s is Medium) then (S_{mat} is Mature)
9. If (C_m is High) and (C_s is High) then (S_{mat} is Mature)

3.2.5 *The Fuzzy Context Assessment*

This final sub-step includes the classification task of FBR-MFDCM. FBR-MFDCM is based on the "Mamdani" composition method and the "centroid" defuzzification mechanism. The inputs go through a fuzzification process and the centroid value, reflecting the output, is generated. Once this is accomplished, the cell context has to be fixed by comparing the output value to the middle of the S_{mat} range. In fact, if the generated centroid value is greater than the middle of the output range then the final context of the data instance is "Mature"; i.e., indicating that the collected antigen may be anomalous. Otherwise, the collected antigen is likely to be normal. Once the context is fixed for all antigens and same as the standard DCA, the MCAVs are calculated to allow FBR-MFDCM to perform its classification task. This is done by comparing the $MCAV$s to an anomalous threshold which is generated automatically from the data. More precisely, those antigens whose $MCAVs$ are greater than the anomalous threshold are classified into the anomalous category while the others are classified into the normal one.

4. EXPERIMENTAL SETUP

4.1 Used Benchmarks

To test the FBR-MFDCM performance, our experiments are performed on two-class databases from [16]. The used databases, described in Table 1, are composed of real-valued attributes.

Table 1: Description of Databases

Database	Ref	♯ Instances	♯ Attributes
Sonor	SN	208	61
Molecular-Bio	Bio	106	59
Cylinder Bands	CylB	540	40
Chess	Ch	3196	37
Ionosphere	IONO	351	35
Sick	Sck	3772	30
Horse Colic	HC	368	23
German-Credit	GC	1000	21
Labor Relations	LR	57	16
Red-White-Win	RWW	6497	13

4.2 Algorithms under Comparison

It is likely that not all of the attributes presented in the mentioned databases, described in Table 1, are required to determine the class of each instance. Hence, feature selection is needed. In [15], this was achieved by applying PCA. However, in [6, 7], it was shown that applying PCA for such task is not convenient. It was, also, shown that applying RST, instead of PCA, leads to improve the classification performance of the algorithm. It is important to note that the works proposed in [6, 7] deal with the standard DCA version and not MFDCM. Thus, a first work was recently proposed in [17] based on the MFDCM version and coupling it with RST for data pre-processing. The work named RST-MFDCM [17] was compared to the MFDCM when applying PCA for data pre-processing and again it was shown that applying RST, instead of PCA, is more adequate for the MFDCM classifier while improving its classification performance. However, as the data sets presented in Table 1 are entirely composed of real-valued attributes, RST-MFDCM has to perform data discretization before performing its task of feature selection. This is clearly a potential source of information loss. By applying the present work, we try to show that our FBR-MFDCM can avoid the mentioned information loss while generating better classification results than when applying the crisp RST. Thus, we will compare FBR-MFDCM to RST-MFDCM. As previously stated, in [17], RST-MFDCM applied RST as a pre-processor. However, to select the right set of features, RST-MFDCM generates all possible reducts that can be produced from data. Obviously, this is an expensive solution to the problem and is only practical for very simple data sets. Most of the time only one reduct is required as, typically, only one subset of features is used to reduce a data set, so all the calculations involved in discovering the rest are pointless. On the other hand, RST-MFDCM may either generate one reduct or a family of reducts. So, to perform the signal categorization process, the algorithm proposes different solutions for each of these two cases. This is seen as a time consuming task. Furthermore, for the signal categorization process, RST-MFDCM proposes to assign only one attribute to form both SS and PAMP. Indeed, let us remind that our FBR-MFDCM model generates only one reduct based on the use of the Fuzzy QuickReduct algorithm. FBR-MFDCM proposes to assign a specific feature to be either as SS or as a PAMP signal. So, it is clear that a comparison between FBR-MFDCM and RST-MFDCM is not possible. Thus, to make the comparison possible, we propose a second version of RST-MFDCM that we dub QR-MFDCM. We have based QR-MFDCM on the same process of selecting features and same reasoning of signal categorization as FBR-MFDCM. Instead of using the fuzzy QuickReduct algorithm, QR-MFDCM is based on the crisp QuickReduct algorithm [10]. We aim to show that QR-MFDCM can be an alternative to RST-MFDCM capable of finding a trade-off between generating satisfactory classification results and having a lightweight in terms of running time in comparison to RST-MFDCM. This is because QR-MFDCM generates only one reduct. Consequently, it will be possible to compare FBR-MFDCM and QR-MFDCM. Secondly, we aim to show that applying FRST with our FBR-MFDCM new model, instead of RST applied to QR-MFDCM and RST-MFDCM, is more convenient to the MFDCM data pre-processing phase as information loss is avoided.

4.3 Parameters Description

Each data item is mapped as an antigen, with the value of the antigen equal to the data ID of the item. In all experiments a population of 100 cells is used and 10 DCs sample the antigen vector each cycle. The migration threshold of an individual DC is set to 10 to ensure this DC to survive over multiple iterations. To perform anomaly detection, a threshold is applied to the MCAVs. The threshold is calculated by dividing the number of anomalous data items presented in the used data set by the total number of data items. So, if the MCAV is greater than the anomaly threshold then the antigen is classified as anomalous, else it is classified as normal. For each experiment, the results presented are based on mean MCAVs generated across 10 runs. Weightings are derived from empirical immunological data. All the experiments are based on a 10 cross validation test.

Concerning both QR-MFDCM and RST-MFDCM, a discretization phase has to be performed before the feature selection step. To do so, the Equal-width binning technique is used. Using the Weka software, the parameters set to the discretization technique are as follows: The "findNumBins" parameter is set to "True" to optimize the number of equal-width bins, the "ignoreClass", the "makeBinary" and the "useEqualFrequency" parameters are set to "False". Finally, the "invertSelection" parameter is set to "False" to let only selected (numeric) attributes to be discretized. But, before this all the qualitative terms of all attributes are coded using natural numbers.

4.4 Used Metrics

We evaluate the performance of the MFDCM versions in terms of number of extracted features, running time, sensitivity, specificity and accuracy which are defined as: $Sensitivity = TP/(TP+FN)$; $Specificity = TN/(TN+FP)$; $Accuracy = (TP+TN)/(TP+TN+FN+FP)$; where TP, FP, TN, and FN refer respectively to: true positive, false positive, true negative and false negative. All experiments are run on a Sony Vaio G4 2.67 Ghz machine.

Adding to these criteria and to further validate the obtained results, we will compare the performance of our FBR-MFDCM to the standard DCA when applying PCA (PCA-DCA) and when applying the QuickReduct algorithm (QR-DCA) [8], PCA-MFDCM, QR-MFDCM, the Support Vector Machine (SVM), the Artificial Neural Network (ANN) and the Decision Tree (DT). Please, note that PCA-DCA, QR-DCA, QR-MFDCM and PCA-MFDCM are based on the concept of assigning different features to different signal categories. Using the Weka software, the used SVM is the LibSVM and more precisely the C-support vector classification (C-SVC), the used ANN is the multilayer perceptron (MLP) and the used DT is C4.5. The parameters of these algorithms are set to their defaults values given by Weka. The comparison made is based on statistical tests which are given in what is next.

4.5 Adopted Statistical Methodology

Our experimental study involves algorithms that are non-deterministic, i.e., that may provide different results over multiple repeated runs. To handle such stochastic aspect of results, the use of statistical testing is mandatory. Since we are comparing more than two algorithms, we choose to use the Kruskal-Wallis test [18]. The latter is non-parametric alternative to the ANOVA test and it does not require verifying whether the data sets are normally distributed or not. We perform 30 runs and analyze the statistical difference of results with a 95% confidence level ($\alpha = 0.05$). The Kruskal-Wallis test verifies the null hypothesis H0 that the obtained results of all algorithms are samples from continuous distributions with equal medians, as against the alternative that they are not, i.e., H1. The p-value of the Kruskal-Wallis test corresponds to the probability of rejecting the null hypothesis H0 while it is true (type I error). A p-value that is less than or equal to α (≤ 0.05) means that we accept H1 and we reject H0. However, a p-value that is strictly greater than α (> 0.05) means the opposite. To perform this test, we have used the MATLAB routine *kruskalwallis()*. Nevertheless, the shortcoming of this test consists in the fact that one algorithm could be different from the others; however the others are all statistically similar. For this reason and after the use of the *kruskalwallis()* function, we add another MATLAB function which is *multcompare()* to perform additional follow-up testing. This function allows to detect statistical differences in a pairwise way (one-versus-one).

5. RESULTS AND ANALYSIS

5.1 Comparison of the MFDCM Classifiers

Starting the comparison between RST-MFDCM and QR-MFDCM and from Table 2, we can notice that QR-MFDCM can find a trade-off between generating satisfactory classification results and processing in less time than RST-MFDCM. QR-MFDCM has either the same number of features as RST-MFDCM or more features. This is explained by the fact that QR-MFDCM, by applying the QuickReduct algorithm, follows the features path that generates the highest dependency degree. Consequently, the taken path may either lead to a final reduct including the smallest number of features or to a path including more selected features. For instance, applying QR-MFDCM to the IONO database, the number of selected attributes is set to 22. However, when applying RST-MFDCM, the number of selected features is set to 19. Applying the two rough MFDCM models to the Ch database, the number of the selected features is the same: 11. In terms of classification accuracy, we can notice that QR-MFDCM outperforms RST-MFDCM. For instance, the classification accuracy of RST-MFDCM when applied to the SN database is set to 87.98% which is less than 92.30% generated by QR-MFDCM. This is explained by the fact that RST-MFDCM differs from QR-MFDCM in the signal categorization phase. QR-MFDCM assigns different features to different signal categories. However, RST-MFDCM uses the same attribute to assign it for both SS and PAMP. From these results, we can conclude that it is crucial to assign for each signal category a different feature. These results endorse the results obtained in [8]. The main advantage of our QR-MFDCM is that it takes less time to process than RST-MFDCM. For example, when applying the algorithms to the CylB database, the amount of time taken by QR-MFDCM to process is 14.61(s) which is less than the time taken by RST-MFDCM which is 1426.73(s). The QR-MFDCM lightweight in terms of running time is explained by the advantage of using the QuickReduct algorithm as it attempts to calculate a reduct without exhaustively generating all possible subsets. In contrast, RST-MFDCM generates all possible subsets and retrieves those with a maximum rough set dependency degree. This is an expensive solution and all the calculations involved in discovering all the reduct sets are pointless. To summarize, QR-MFDCM can be seen as an interesting classification technique proposed as an alternative to RST-MFDCM. QR-MFDCM is capable of generating better classification results than RST-MFDCM while having a lightweight in terms of running time. Once we have shown the advantages of our QR-MFDCM crisp rough model, we can compare its obtained results to our second developed algorithm; i.e., the FBR-MFDCM fuzzy-rough approach.

Let us remind that both QR-MFDCM and FBR-MFDCM generate only one reduct. Both algorithms are based on the same process of feature selection and signal categorization; except that QR-MFDCM is based on the crisp RST and FBR-MFDCM is based on FRST. We aim to show that applying FRST, instead of RST, can avoid the information loss caused by the mandatory step of data quantization. We, also, aim to show that by leaving the attribute values unchanged, FBR-MFDCM is able to select fewer fea-

Table 2: Comparison Results of the MFDCM Versions

Database	Sensitivity(%)			Specificity(%)			Accuracy(%)			Time(s)			♯ Attributes		
	MFDCM			MFDCM			MFDCM			MFDCM			MFDCM		
	FBR	QR	RST	FBR	QR	RST	FBR	QR	RST	FBR	QR	RST	FBR	QR	RST
SN	98.19	90.99	90.09	98.96	93.81	85.56	98.55	92.30	87.98	28.41	10.03	1695.96	9	22	20
Bio	90.56	83.01	66.03	94.33	84.90	58.49	92.45	83.96	62.26	17.09	9.56	1617.02	9	19	19
CylB	98.50	98.00	97.00	98.71	98.39	97.43	98.63	98.24	97.26	32.69	14.61	1426.73	5	7	7
Ch	99.78	98.92	98.20	99.80	99.60	99.21	99.76	99.24	98.68	722.13	586.93	1700.10	4	11	11
IONO	99.20	97.61	96.03	99.55	97.77	98.22	99.43	97.72	97.43	47.15	19.81	599.42	9	22	19
Sck	96.96	97.83	97.40	99.40	97.96	96.89	99.25	97.95	96.92	725.99	529.17	1401.70	14	22	20
HC	98.61	98.14	96.75	98.02	96.05	92.10	98.36	97.28	94.83	45.06	23.75	94.29	5	14	14
GC	90.87	92.33	87.95	92.28	92.69	90.35	91.90	92.60	89.70	210.04	141.09	507.87	10	17	17
LR	95.00	95.00	90.00	97.29	97.29	94.59	96.49	96.49	92.98	0.72	0.64	0.81	5	5	5
RWW	99.61	99.40	99.26	99.18	99.62	99.31	99.50	99.46	99.27	1653.87	1032.01	2251.47	3	8	6

tures than QR-MFDCM which will better guide the FBR-MFDCM classification process. This is confirmed by the results obtained from Table 2. For instance, applying FBR-MFDCM to the Bio database, the number of selected attributes is 9. However, when applying QR-MFDCM to the same database, the number of selected features is set to 19. This is explained by the fact that FBR-MFDCM, by applying the Fuzzy-rough QuickReduct algorithm, incorporates the information usually lost in crisp discritization by utilizing the fuzzy boundary region to provide a more informed technique. Results show that FBR-MFDCM selects features without much loss in information content. Furthermore, we can notice that FBR-MFDCM outperforms QR-MFDCM in terms of classification accuracy. For instance, when applying the algorithms to the Sck data set, the classification accuracy of FBR-MFDCM is set to 99.25%. However, when applying QR-MFDCM to the same database, the accuracy of the algorithm is set to 97.95%. Same remark is observed for the specificity and the sensitivity criteria. When comparing results in terms of running time, we can notice that FBR-MFDCM needs more time to process than QR-MFDCM due to the attachment of the fuzzy component. We can, also, notice that the time taken by FBR-MFDCM to process is less than the time needed by RST-MFDCM as the latter algorithm generates all the set of possible reducts. For example, when applying the algorithms to the Bio database, the amount of time taken by FBR-MFDCM to process is 17.09(s) which is less than the time taken by RST-MFDCM which is 1617.02(s) and a bit longer than the time taken by QR-MFDCM which is set to 9.56(s). In the next Section, we will further validate these obtained results using statistical tests.

5.2 Comparison with State-of-the-art Classifiers

In this Section, we will compare the performance of our FBR-MFDCM to the standard PCA-DCA, to QR-DCA [8], to PCA-MFDCM, QR-MFDCM, C-SVC, MLP and to C4.5. For the sake of comparison, we have numbered the used algorithms as follows: (1) reflects the FBR-MFDCM algorithm, (2) reflects the QR-MFDCM algorithm, (3) reflects PCA-MFDCM, (4) reflects QR-DCA, (5) reflects PCA-DCA, (6) reflects C-SVC, (7) reflects MLP and (8) reflects C4.5.

Table 3 shows the comparison results in terms of medium accuracies for the used data sets and for all algorithms. In each row of Table 3, for each database, we find the medium accuracy of each algorithm. Under every medium accuracy value we find the algorithms numbers which are statistically different from the algorithm in that column. For example, for the database SN, the medium accuracy value of FBR-MFDCM is set to 97.95%. FBR-MFDCM is statistically different from algorithm (2)QR-MFDCM, (3)PCA-MFDCM, (5)PCA-DCA, (6)C-SVC, (7)MLP and (8)C4.5. The last column reflects the calculated p-value of each database.

From Table 3, we can notice that the obtained p-values are less than $\alpha = 0.05$. Thus, a statistical comparison can be made for the used algorithms. To begin with, Table 3 shows that in most databases the (5)PCA-DCA algorithm is statistically different from (6)C-SVC, (7)MLP and (8)C4.5. We can notice that PCA-DCA is outperforming these algorithms mainly (7)MLP and (8)C4.5 confirming the results obtained from literature. Indeed, Table 3 shows that (4)QR-DCA is statistically different from (4)PCA-DCA while outperforming the latter algorithm. This confirms that applying RST as a pre-processor is more convenient for the DCA data pre-processing phase; i.e., instead of PCA.

Furthermore, we can see that in terms of the Kruskal-Wallis test (3)PCA-MFDCM is statistically better than (5)PCA-DCA; as in most data sets (3)PCA-MFDCM is statistically different from (5)PCA-DCA. This confirms that applying a fuzzy process to the DCA is more convenient for the algorithm to handle the imprecision within the definition of the two DCs contexts. The fact of coping with this imprecision leads to an improvement of the algorithm performance. From these remarks, we can conclude that if we hybridize both RST and the fuzzy process, we will obtain a better performance of the classifier. Based on this, we can clearly notice that our hybrid (2)QR-MFDCM developed model outperforms both (3)PCA-MFDCM, which only applies FST, and (4)QR-DCA which only applies RST.

Most importantly, the most interesting results are noticed for our (1)FBR-MFDCM algorithm. In most data sets (1)FBR-MFDCM is statistically different from the rest of the classifiers including (2)QR-MFDCM, (3)PCA-MFDCM, (4)QR-DCA, (5)PCA-DCA, (6)C-SVC, (7)MLP and (8)C4.5. In some databases (1)FBR-MFDCM is statistically similar to (2)QR-MFDCM. Hence, endorsing the results obtained from Table 2. These promising (1)FBR-MFDCM results are explained by the appropriate application of FRST to the MFDCM data pre-processing phase. This makes the MFDCM a better classifier by generating more reliable and more pertinent results.

To summarize, we have firstly proposed QR-MFDCM as an alternative to RST-MFDCM. We have shown that QR-MFDCM is capable of generating better classification results than RST-MFDCM while having a lightweight in terms of running time. Secondly, we have proposed a fuzzy rough data pre-processing phase for MFDCM. We have shown that

Table 3: Comparison Results in terms of Medium Accuracies (%)

Database	FBR-MFDCM (1)	QR-MFDCM (2)	PCA-MFDCM (3)	QR-DCA (4)	PCA-DCA (5)	C-SVC (6)	MLP (7)	C4.5 (8)	p-value
SN	97.95 2,3,5,6,7,8	91.90 1,3,4,5,6,7,8	82.69 1,2,5,6,8	88.39 2,5,6,7,8	78.11 1,2,3,4,8	75.96 1,2,3,4,7	82.21 1,2,4,6,8	71.15 1,2,3,4,5,7	1.5298e-046
Bio	91.33 2,3,4,5,6,7,8	83.04 1,3,5,6,7,8	49.25 1,2,6,7,8	77.72 1,5,6,7,8	40.88 1,2,4,7,8	39.13 1,2,3,4,8	36.41 1,2,3,4,5	31.69 1,2,3,4,5,6	1.8443e-047
Clyb	98.51 3,4,5,6,7,8	97.91 3,4,5,6,7,8	93.77 1,2,5,6,7,8	96.88 1,2,5,6,7,8	91.31 1,2,3,4,7,8	81.66 1,2,3,4,8	79.55 1,2,3,4,5	77.77 1,2,3,4,5,6	1.9327e-047
Ch	99.59 2,3,4,5,6,7	99.19 1,3,4,5,6,8	94.76 1,2,4,5,7,8	98.54 1,2,3,5,7,8	93.74 1,2,3,4,6,7,8	95.43 1,2,5,7,8	99.34 1,3,4,5,6	99.43 2,3,4,5,6	3.0530e-047
IONO	98.97 2,3,4,5,6,7,8	97.32 1,5,6,7,8	96.55 1,6,7,8	96.00 1,6,7,8	94.24 1,2,6,7	88.60 1,2,3,4,5,8	91.16 1,2,3,4,5	91.45 1,2,3,4,6	7.8271e-047
Sck	99.00 2,3,4,5,6,7	97.85 1,3,4,5,6	94.98 1,2,5,8	97.45 1,2,5,6,8	93.85 1,2,3,4,7,8	93.87 1,2,4,7,8	97.18 1,5,6,8	98.86 3,4,5,6,7	8.0063e-046
HC	97.95 2,3,4,5,6,7,8	97.15 1,3,5,6,7,8	89.22 1,2,5,6,7	93.25 1,5,6,7,8	83.04 1,2,3,4	82.60 1,2,3,4	80.43 1,2,3,4,8	85.32 1,2,4,7	1.4628e-046
GC	91.83 2,3,4,67,8	92.22 1,3,4,5,6,7,8	88.78 1,2,6,7,8	89.88 2,6,7,8	86.99 1,2,7,8	75.10 1,2,3,4,8	71.60 1,2,3,4,5	70.50 1,2,3,4,5,6	1.4720e-046
LR	96.35 3,5,6,7,8	96.49 3,4,5,6,7,8	75.04 1,2,4,5,6,7	90.99 2,3,5,7,8	82.21 1,2,3,4,8	89.47 1,2,3,8	85.96 1,2,3,4,8	73.68 1,2,4,5,6,7	6.0315e-046
RWW	99.15 3,5,7,8	98.89 3,4,5,7	98.11 1,2,4,5,6,7,8	98.83 2,3,5,7	97.59 1,2,3,4,6,7,8	99.07 3,5,7	99.53 1,2,3,4,5,6,8	98.70 1,3,5,7	8.4801e-037

FBR-MFDCM has the advantages of selecting fewer features than QR-MFDCM and RST-MFDCM. FBR-MFDCM is, also, capable of avoiding the discussed information loss. This led to improve the classification performance of the algorithm. Adding to these interesting notes, FBR-MFDCM is coping with the crisp DCs contexts as it relies within an imprecise framework.

6. CONCLUSION AND FUTURE WORKS

In this paper, we have developed a new hybrid DCA bio-inspired model. Our proposed algorithm relies on a powerful information extraction technique that can guarantee the algorithm high and satisfactory classification results. Indeed, our proposed algorithm relies on an imprecise framework where it copes with the crisp separation between the two DC contexts. This hybridization based RST and FST leads to a smoothed fuzzy rough DCA binary classifier which is more reliable in terms of classification results. As future works, we aim to verify further the validity of our method obtained results using more challenging databases and more statistical measures for comparison. We also aim to boost the DCA data pre-processing phase by extending the application of FRST to databases with missing and noisy data.

7. REFERENCES

[1] J. Greensmith, U. Aickelin, and S. Cayzer. Introducing dendritic cells as a novel immune-inspired algorithm for anomaly detection. In *ICARIS*, pages 153–167, 2005.

[2] J. Greensmith and U. Aickelin. Articulation and clarification of the dendritic cell algorithm. In *ICARIS*, pages 404–417, 2006.

[3] J. Greensmith and U. Aickelin. The deterministic dendritic cell algorithm. In *ICARIS*, pages 291–302, 2008.

[4] J. Musselle. Insights into the antigen sampling component of the dendritic cell algorithm. In *ICARIS*, pages 88–101, 2010.

[5] G. Feng, J. Greensmith, and U. Aickelin. Integrating real-time analysis with the dendritic cell algorithm through segmentation. In *GECCO*, pages 1203–1210, 2009.

[6] Z. Chelly and Z. Elouedi. Rst-dca: A dendritic cell algorithm based on rough set theory. In *ICONIP*, pages 480–487. Springer, 2012.

[7] Z. Chelly and Z. Elouedi. Rc-dca: A new feature selection and signal categorization technique for the dendritic cell algorithm based on rough set theory. In *ICARIS*, pages 152–165. Springer, 2012.

[8] Z. Chelly and Z. Elouedi. Qr-dca: A new rough data pre-processing approach for the dendritic cell algorithm. In *ICANNGA*, pages 140–150. Springer, 2013.

[9] D. Massart B. Walczak. Rough sets theory. *Chemometrics and Intelligent Laboratory Systems*, 47:1–16, 1999.

[10] R. Jensen and Q. Shen. New approaches to fuzzy-rough feature selection. *IEEE Transactions on Fuzzy Systems*, 17:824–838, 2009.

[11] Z. Chelly and Z. Elouedi. A new data pre-processing approach for the dendritic cell algorithm based on fuzzy rough set theory. In *GECCO*, pages 163–164. ACM, 2013.

[12] Z. Chelly and Z. Elouedi. Supporting fuzzy-rough sets in the dendritic cell algorithm data pre-processing phase. In *ICONIP*, pages 164–171. Springer, 2013.

[13] Z. Chelly and Z. Elouedi. A fuzzy-rough data pre-processing approach for the dendritic cell classifier. In *ECSQARU*, pages 109–120. Springer, 2013.

[14] Z. Chelly and Z. Elouedi. Fdcm: A fuzzy dendritic cell method. In *ICARIS*, pages 102–115, 2010.

[15] Z. Chelly and Z. Elouedi. Further exploration of the fuzzy dendritic cell method. In *ICARIS*, pages 419–432, 2011.

[16] http://mlearn.ics.uci.edu/MLRepository.html , UCI Machine Learning Repository.

[17] Z. Chelly and Z. Elouedi. A new hybrid fuzzy-rough dendritic cell immune classifier. In *ICSI*, pages 514–521, 2013.

[18] M. Hollander and D. Wolfe. *Nonparametric Statistical Methods*, volume 17. Wiley, 1973.

Clonal Selection based Fuzzy C-Means Algorithm for Clustering

Simone A. Ludwig
Department of Computer Science
North Dakota State University
Fargo, USA
simone.ludwig@ndsu.edu

ABSTRACT

In recent years, fuzzy based clustering approaches have shown to outperform state-of-the-art hard clustering algorithms in terms of accuracy. The difference between hard clustering and fuzzy clustering is that in hard clustering each data point of the data set belongs to exactly one cluster, and in fuzzy clustering each data point belongs to several clusters that are associated with a certain membership degree. Fuzzy c-means clustering is a well-known and effective algorithm, however, the random initialization of the centroids directs the iterative process to converge to local optimal solutions easily. In order to address this issue a clonal selection based fuzzy c-means algorithm (CSFCM) is introduced. CSFCM is compared with the basic Fuzzy C-Means (FCM) algorithm, a genetic algorithm based FCM (GAFCM) algorithm, and a particle swarm optimization based FCM (PSOFCM) algorithm.

Categories and Subject Descriptors

I.2.8 [**Artificial Intelligence**]: Problem Solving, Control Methods, and Search

Keywords

Evolutionary computation, fuzzy c-means algorithm, data clustering

1. INTRODUCTION

Data mining is a relatively broad field that deals with the automatic knowledge discovery from databases, and is one of the most developed fields in the area of artificial intelligence. Given the rapid growth of data collected in various realms of human activity and their potential usefulness requires efficient tools to extract and make use of the potentially gathered knowledge [1]. One of the important data mining tasks is classification, which is an effective method that is used in many different fields. The main idea behind the classification task is to build a model (classifier) that assigns items in a collection to target classes with the goal to accurately predict the target class for each item in the data [2]. There are many techniques that can be used to do a classification process such as decision trees, Bayes networks, genetic algorithms, genetic programming and many others [3]. Another important data mining technique used when analyzing data is clustering [4]. The main goal of clustering algorithms is to divide a set of unlabeled data objects into different groups called clusters (each group has common specifications between the group members). The cluster membership measure is based on a similarity measure. To obtain high quality clusters, the similarity measure between the data objects in the same cluster is to be maximized, and the similarity measure between the data objects from different groups is to be minimized.

There are several definitions of how a cluster can be formulated depending on the objective of clustering. In general, a cluster is a group of objects that are more similar to one another than to members of other clusters [5, 6]. The term "similarity" is defined in terms of mathematical similarity with a distance norm. Distance can be measured among the data items or as a distance from a data item to some object (prototype) of the cluster. Since the objects are usually not known beforehand, they are determined by the algorithms during the clustering steps. The objects can be of the same dimension as the data objects, or can be defined as "higher-level" geometrical objects such as linear or nonlinear functions. The performance of most clustering algorithms is influenced by the geometrical shapes and densities of the individual clusters. However, it is also influenced by the spatial relations and distances of the clusters.

Many clustering algorithms have been introduced and clustering techniques can be categorized depending on whether the subsets of the resulting classification are *fuzzy* or *crisp* (hard). In *hard clustering* an object either belongs or does not belong to a cluster. In *fuzzy clustering* however, the objects belong to several clusters exhibiting different degrees of membership. Fuzzy clustering is seen as more natural than hard clustering since the objects on the class boundaries do not need to fully belong to one of the classes. The objects are assigned membership degrees between 0 and 1.

In recent years, fuzzy based clustering approaches have shown to outperform state-of-the-art hard clustering algorithms in terms of accuracy. Fuzzy c-means clustering [5] is a common and effective algorithm, however, the random initialization of the centroids directs the iterative process to converge to local optimal solutions easily. Therefore, evolutionary algorithms and swarm intelligence techniques

GECCO'14, July 12–16, 2014, Vancouver, BC, Canada.

http://dx.doi.org/10.1145/2576768.2598270.

have been successfully applied such as genetic algorithms, ant colony optimization, and particle swarm optimization in order to tackle this problem.

This paper proposes another evolutionary algorithm technique belonging to the category of artificial immune systems. A clonal selection mechanism is combined with the fuzzy c-means algorithm. The paper is structured as follows: Section 2 presents related work starting with general categories of fuzzy clustering and ending with a list of work related to using evolutionary methods for fuzzy clustering. In Section 3, first the fuzzy c-means algorithm and the clonal selection algorithm are introduced before the proposed method is described. Section 4 lists the experimental setup and the data sets used. In Section 5, the results of the experiments are given and discussed. Section 6 concludes this paper with a summary of the findings.

2. RELATED WORK

Due to the algorithmic approach, fuzzy clustering can be categorized into three categories: hierarchical fuzzy clustering methods, graph-theoretic fuzzy clustering methods and fuzzy clustering based on objective functions [7]. Hierarchical clustering methods correspond to the determination of "similarity" trees, which is based on fuzzy equivalence relations.

Hierarchical clustering methods generate a hierarchy of partitions by means of agglomerative and divisive methods [7]. The agglomerative algorithms produce a sequence of clusters of decreasing number at each step merging two clusters from the previous level. The divisive algorithms work the other way around. Lee [8] proposed a hierarchical clustering algorithm to cluster business processes identified during business systems planning. The best number of clusters is determined by a matching approach. Another technique called fuzzy equivalent relation-based hierarchical clustering method deals with the cluster problem without a predefined number of clusters [9].

Graph-theoretic fuzzy clustering methods are based on the idea of connectivity of nodes of a graph representing the data set. In graph-theoretic fuzzy clustering, the graph representing the data structure is a fuzzy graph and different notions of connectivity lead to different types of clusters. The idea of fuzzy graphs is first mentioned in [10] whereby the fuzzy analogues of several basic graph-theoretic concepts such as bridges, cycles, paths, trees are introduced. In [11], fuzzy graphs were first used for cluster analysis.

Fuzzy clustering based on objective functions results in the most precise formulation of the clustering. The fuzzy C-Means clustering model (FCM) was first introduced in 1974 [12], and later extended and generalized in [5]. Since then, some variations of the method and model improvements are suggested.

The Gustafson-Kessel (GK) algorithm [13] is a fuzzy clustering technique that can estimate local covariance and partition data into subsets, which can be well fitted with linear submodels. However, considering a general structure for the covariance matrix can have substantial effect on the modeling approach, and therefore, the Gath-Geva algorithm [14] was proposed. The Fuzzy C-Varieties (FCV) [15] clustering algorithm is a fuzzy clustering algorithm where the prototype of each cluster is a multi-dimensional linear variety.

By replacing the Euclidean distances with other distance measures and enriching the cluster prototypes with further parameters, other shapes than just the spherical clusters can be discovered. Clusters might be ellipsoidal, linear, manifolds, quadrics or even differ in volumes [7]. Fuzzy clustering has been proven to handle ambiguous data that share properties of different clusters using membership degrees to assign data objects.

The use of fuzzy clustering especially the FCM algorithm has been shown to be effective in image segmentation [16]. However, the FCM algorithm still lacks enough robustness to noise and outliers, especially in absence of prior knowledge of noise. The time of segmenting an image depends on the image size, and hence the larger the size of the image, the longer the segmentation time [17].

Evolutionary algorithms and swarm intelligence techniques have been successfully applied such as Genetic Algorithms (GA), Ant Colony Optimization (ACO), and Particle Swarm Optimization (PSO). The key features of these evolutionary and swarm intelligence based algorithms compared to other global optimization techniques are their swarm-based collective learning ability, flexibility and robustness.

Many evolutionary computation methods have been applied for clustering. A hybrid technique based on combining the k-means algorithm, Nelder-Mead simplex search, and PSO was applied for cluster analysis in [18]. Another algorithm based on the combination of GA, k-means and logarithmic regression expectation maximization [19] was introduced. An introduced k-means algorithm that performs correct clustering without preassigning the exact number of clusters was proposed in [20]. A genetic k-means algorithm for cluster analysis was introduced in [21], and a GA based method to solve the clustering problem and experiment on synthetic and real life data sets to evaluate the performance was proposed in [22] - a basic mutation operator specific to clustering called distance-based mutation is the novelty of this approach. A GA algorithm that exchanges neighboring centers for k-means clustering has been presented in [23]. A combination of evolutionary algorithm with a ACO algorithm for the clustering problem was introduced in [23, 24].

Artificial Immune Systems (AIS) based clustering methods have also been proposed. A so called fuzzy artificial immune system clustering approach was proposed in [25]. The approach is based on artificial immune networks and fuzzy system. The authors compared their approach with the k-means algorithm and reported better results achieved by their proposed algorithm. Another algorithm is proposed in [26]. The algorithm is based on the immune mechanism, whereby the data to be clusters is represented as the antigens, and the centroids are represented as the antibodies. The clustering is therefore driven by the generation of antibodies to recognize the antigens. The solution converges towards finding the optimal antibodies for the capture of the antigens. The results showed that the proposed algorithm increases the convergence speed by avoiding local optima. The next algorithms makes use of an immunodomaince operator that is introduced to the clonal selection algorithm in [27]. This operator allows to gain prior knowledge and the sharing of information among the different antibodies. Their method was compared with the standard FCM and a GA-based FCM algorithm. The results showed that their proposed algorithm performed better than the others, in particular in avoiding the local optimum trap. Another algorithm based on artificial immune system and ant colony optimization was proposed in [28]. The authors proposed an Immunity-based Ant Clustering Algorithm (IACA) in order to perform the clustering task automatically by finding the correct number of clusters.

Even though AIS based approaches have been explored for data clustering in the past, however, this paper proposes an approach based on the combination of standard FCM algorithm with the clonal selection principle of AIS. The FCM algorithm is a very powerful algorithm, however, it suffers from the initialization problem easily converging to suboptimal solutions. In order to overcome this clonal selection is used applying operators such as cloning, mutation, reselection and displacement.

3. PROPOSED APPROACH

This section gives an introduction of the fuzzy c-means algorithm first followed by a discussion of the clonal selection approach. Afterwards the proposed clonal selection based fuzzy c-means algorithm is described in detail.

3.1 Fuzzy c-Means Algorithm

In fuzzy clustering each data point belongs to several clusters that are associated with a certain membership degree.

The FCM algorithm is an iterative partitional clustering technique first introduced by Dunn [12], and was further extended by Bezdek [5]. FCM is a standard least squared error model that generalizes an earlier and very popular non-fuzzy c-means model that produces hard clusters of the data. An optimal c partition is produced iteratively by minimizing the *weighted within group sum of squared error* objective function:

$$J = \sum_{i=1}^{n} \sum_{j=1}^{c} (u_{ij})^m d^2(y_i, c_j) \tag{1}$$

where $Y = [y_1, y_2, ..., y_n]$ is the data set in a d-dimensional vector space; n is the number of data items; c is the number of clusters which is defined by the user where $2 \leq c \leq n$. u_{ij} is the degree of membership of y_i in the jth cluster; m is a weighted exponent on each fuzzy membership; c_j is the center of cluster j; $d^2(x_i, c_j)$ is a squared distance measure between object y_i and cluster c_j.

A solution with c partitions can be obtained via an iterative process which is as follows:

1. Input c, m, threshold value ϵ, Y.
2. Initialize the fuzzy partition matrix $U = [u_{ij}]$.
3. Iteration starts by setting $t = 1$.
4. Calculate the c cluster centers with U^t:
$$c_i = \frac{\sum_{i=1}^{n} (u_{ij})^m y_i}{\sum_{i=1}^{n} (u_{ij})^m} \tag{2}$$
5. Calculate the membership U^{t+1} using:
$$u_{ij} = \frac{1}{\sum_{k=1}^{c} (\frac{d_{ij}}{d_{kj}})^{\frac{2}{(m-1)}}} \tag{3}$$
6. If one of the stopping criteria is not met, then increment t and go to Step 4. The stopping criteria are the maximum number of iterations achieved and no significant improvement compared to the previous iteration is made based on ϵ.

3.2 Clonal Selection Algorithm

De Castro and Von Zuben developed the Clonal Selection Algorithm (CSA) [29] based on the biological clonal selection theory and the shape space model of the biological immune system. The main idea is that only cells that are capable of recognizing an antigen will proliferate. CSA is very similar to a genetic algorithm, however, CSA does not have a crossover operator. The algorithm works as follows:

- Step 1. *Initialization*: Randomly initialize a population of individuals P.
- Step 2. *Evaluation*: Present each input I to the population P, and determine its affinity with each element of P.
- Step 3. *Selection and cloning*: Select n of the highest affinity elements of P, and clone these individuals proportionally to their affinity with the antigen. The higher the affinity, the higher the number of copies.
- Step 4. *Hypermutation*: Mutate all these copies with a rate proportional to their affinity with the input pattern - the higher the affinity, the smaller the mutation rate.
- Step 5. *Receptor editing*: Add these mutated individuals to the population P, and reselect m of these maturated individuals to be kept as memory cells.
- Step 6. Repeat Steps 2-5 until a certain criterion is met.

3.3 Proposed Clonal Selection based FCM Algorithm - CS-FCM

Our proposed CSFCM algorithm uses the objective function of FCM and the principles of clonal selection in order to find the optimal centroids given the membership matrix. In particular, CSFCM is designed to find the optimal membership matrix and the centroids by minimizing Equation 1.

For the notation used in the algorithm description below, the term antibody represents the centroids, antigen represents the membership matrix, and the memory cell represents the best solution or best centroids.

The CSFCM algorithm works as follows:

- **Step 1**: The antibody population is randomly generated.
- **Step 2**: The first iteration of the algorithm begins by calculating the affinity of the antibody population using the following equation:
$$f = \frac{1}{1 + J} \tag{4}$$
where f is the fitness of an antibody.
- **Step 3**: The n highest affinity antibodies are selected to compose a new set of high-affinity antibodies, and the highest affinity memory cell is found. Next follows the cloning stage. The n selected antibodies are cloned based on their antigenic affinities to generate the clone set C. The number of clones for an antibody is fixed to

$n+1$. Therefore, the total number of clones generated n_c is defined as:

$$n_c = \sum_{i=1}^{n}(n+1) = n^2 + n \quad (5)$$

This function allows the optimization to get closer to the solution by increasing the average affinity.

- **Step 4**: The next step is mutation. Each antibody in the clone set C gets the opportunity to produce mutated offspring abiding by the law that the higher the affinity, the smaller the mutation rate. In order to achieve this, the affinity of the antibodies are normalized (f_{norm}) to be in the range of [0,1]. The mutation rate is adaptively determined by:

$$p_m = exp(-2 \times f_{norm}(antibody)) \quad (6)$$

where p_m is the mutation rate (in the range of [0,1]), and 2 is the decay coefficient. The mutation process is a very important step in the algorithm. It generates a random real value using a uniform distribution (u) in the range between the minimum and the maximum. The function is defined as:

$$\Delta(I, u) = u(1 - r^{(1-i/I)^{\lambda}}) \quad (7)$$

where r is a random value in the range of [0,1], i is the current iteration, I is the maximum number of iterations defined, and λ is the nonconforming degree factor. This step is crucial for the algorithm since the mutation step helps to avoid local optima. One antibody is kept in order to keep the search stable. Then, the affinity of the matured clones is calculated. Afterwards, the antibodies with the highest affinity are replacing the ones with the lowest affinity, and the one with the highest affinity is set to be the memory cell. During the iteration, this memory cell is only updated if there was an improvement compared to the previous iteration. Then, the antibodies with the lowest affinity are replaced by newly randomly generated antibodies.

- **Step 5**: The stopping criterion is the maximum number of iterations reached. If the stopping criterion is not fulfilled, then the algorithm proceeds with Step 2.

- **Step 6**: Calculate the validity indices (described in Section 4.2).

4. EXPERIMENTAL SETUP

This section describes the parameter setup and the data sets used as well as describes the validity measures proposed in literature that are being used for the experiments.

4.1 Parameter Setup and Data sets

The parameters of the CSFCM algorithm are set to:

- Population size (antibodies) = 20
- Maximum number of iterations = 100
- Number of selected antibodies = 8
- Number of displaced antibodies = 5
- Fuzzy weighting exponent = 2

The data sets used for the experiments are given in Table 1. The number of records, dimensions, and number of clusters are listed. 30 independent runs were performed for each data set.

Table 1: Data sets

Data set	Records	Dimensions	Clusters
Iris	150	4	3
Wine	178	13	3
Vowel	871	3	6
Glass	214	10	6
Ecoli	336	7	8
Liver disorder	345	7	2
Vowel2	528	10	11

4.2 Validity Indices

To measure the quality of the resulting clusters, several cluster validity measures have been proposed in literature. The cluster validity is a measure of the relative performance of a partitioned structure of the data set. All clustering algorithms generate a partition matrix and other useful information regarding the cluster structure by identifying centroids. Partition and centroids jointly determine the "goodness" of a cluster structure. The validity indices used in this study are explained below.

4.2.1 *Partition Coefficient (PC) Index*

The Partition Coefficient (PC) is defined as [5]:

$$PC = \frac{1}{n}\sum_{i=1}^{n}\sum_{j=1}^{c} u_{ij}^2 \quad (8)$$

PC obtains its maximum when the cluster structure is optimal.

4.2.2 *Partition Entropy (PE) Index*

The Partition Entropy (PE) is defined as [15]:

$$PE = -\frac{1}{n}\sum_{i=1}^{n}\sum_{j=1}^{c} u_{ij} log_b(u_{ij}) \quad (9)$$

where b is the logarithmic base. PE obtains its minimum when the cluster structure is optimal.

4.2.3 *Davies-Bouldin (DB)*

The Davies-Bouldin (DB) fuzzy validity index is defined as the ratio of the sum of within-cluster scatter to between-cluster separation [30]:

$$DB = \frac{1}{c}\sum_{i=1}^{c} R_i \quad (10)$$

where c is the number of clusters, $R_i = \max_{i \neq j}\{S_i + S_j)/l_{ij}\}$. The scatter with the jth center is $S_j = (1/|C_j|)\sum_{x \in C_i} ||y - z_j||^2$. The distance between the ith cluster center and the jth cluster center is $l_{ij} = ||z_i - z_j||^2$. DB achieves the minimum when the cluster structure is optimal.

4.2.4 *Partition Coefficient And Exponential Separation (PCAES) Index*

The Partition Coefficient And Exponential Separation (PCAES) index [31] is defined as:

$$PCAES = \sum_{i=1}^{n}\sum_{j=1}^{c}\frac{(u_{ij})^2}{u_M} - \sum_{k=1}^{c} exp(-\min_{k \neq i} ||z_i - z_k||^2/\beta_T) \quad (11)$$

where $u_M = \min_{1 \le j \le c}\{\sum_{i=1}^{n} u_{ij}^2\}$ and $\beta_T = (\sum_{j=1}^{c} ||z_j - \bar{z}||^2)/c$. $\bar{z} = \sum_{i=1}^{n}(y_i/n)$. PCAES reaches its maximum when the cluster structure is optimal.

4.2.5 Pakhira-Bandyopadhyay-Maulik Fuzzy (PBMF) index

The Pakhira-Bandyopadhyay-Maulik Fuzzy (PBMF) index for fuzzy clustering is defined as [32]:

$$PBMF = (\frac{1}{c} \times \frac{E_1}{J_m} \times D_c)^2 \tag{12}$$

where

$$E_1 = \sum_{i=1}^{n} ||y_i - z|| \tag{13}$$

E_1 is a constant determined by the data set, with z being the centroid of the data set.

$$D_c = \max_{i,j=1}^{c} ||z_i - z_j|| \tag{14}$$

PBMF obtains its maximum when the cluster structure is optimal.

4.2.6 Xie-Beni (XB) Index

Xie and Beni proposed a validity function in 1991 [33] and later it was modified by Bezdek in 1995 [34].

$$XB = \frac{J_m}{n \times \min_{i \ne j} ||z_i - z_j||^2} \tag{15}$$

XB reaches its minimum when the cluster structure is optimal.

5. RESULTS

The results of applying the different validity indices are shown in Tables 2-7. The comparison values for FCM, GAFCM and PSOFCM are taken from [35]. The comparison algorithms used the following parameters. FCM was run for 100 iterations. GAFCM used a population size of 50 chromosomes, a crossover rate of 0.85, and a mutation rate of 0.008, and was run for 100 iterations. PSOFCM used a swarm size of 50 particles, the maximum and minimum inertia weight were set to 0.9 and 0.4, respectively, the constants c_1 and c_2 were both set to 2, with the number of iterations set to 120.

Table 2 lists the comparison of FCM, GAFCM, PSOFCM and CSFCM in terms of the PC validity index applied to the given data sets. It can be seen that the CSFACM algorithm achieves 3 out of 7 times the best PC validity index tied with the FCM algorithm. GAFCM as well as PSOFCM achieve the highest PC index on one data set each.

Looking at Table 3, the PE validity index for all algorithms measured on the data sets is given. It shows that CSFCM achieves the lowest values and therefore best values for 4 data sets, again tied with the FCM algorithm.

From Table 4 it can be seen that the CSFACM algorithm achieves the best DB validity value 5 out of 7 times, whereas FCM obtains the best index in 4 cases, and GAFCM only in 1.

The PCAES validity index values are given in Table 5. Our CSFCM algorithm outperforms the other techniques scoring the highest PCAES validity values on 5 data sets. The PSOFCM algorithm scores best on 2 data sets.

CSFCM obtains the highest PBMF validity index on 6 data sets as seen in Table 6. FCM scores the best value on 3 data sets, and PSOFCM obtains the highest score on the Liver disorder data set.

Table 7 contains the XB validity values. Again, CSFCM scores best obtaining the lowest and therefore best score on 5 data sets, whereas FCM scores best 3 times. GAFCM and PSOFCM achieve the best value on 1 data set each.

Overall, our CSFCM algorithm obtains the better validity values for 4 of the 6 validity indices. For the other 2, CSFCM is tied with FCM.

Figure 1 summarizes the results graphically. It can be seen by the number of wins, draws, and losses that CSFCM outperforms the other algorithms followed by FCM. A win is defined as having the best validity index (highest or lowest) compared to the other algorithms, a loss is defined as not having the best validity index, and a draw is defined if two or more algorithms achieved exactly the same best validity index. The number of wins, draws and losses are summed over all data sets.

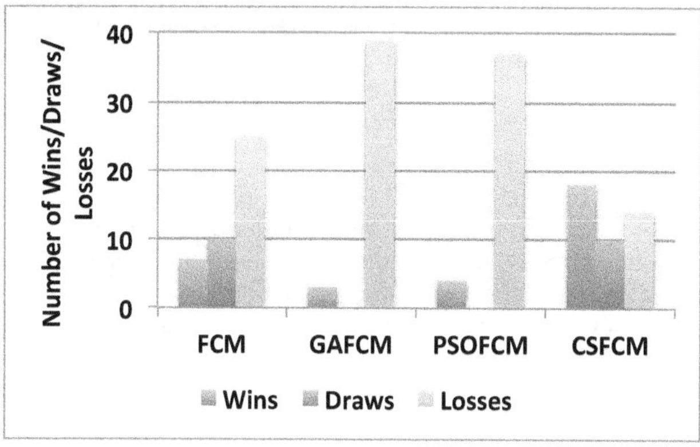

Figure 1: Number of wins, draws, and losses of all algorithms

However, it has to be mentioned that our CSFCM algorithm used the highest number of Function Evaluations (FE) with 9,700 FE (20 antibodies plus 72 clones plus 5 displacement antibodies times 100 iterations). The FCM achieving very good results only needed 100 FE, and GAFCM used 5,000 FE (50 chromosomes times 100 iterations), and PSOFCM ran with 6,000 FE (50 particles times 120 iterations).

6. CONCLUSION

Fuzzy based clustering approaches have shown to outperform state-of-the-art hard clustering algorithms. The difference between hard clustering and fuzzy clustering is that in hard clustering each data point of the data set belongs to exactly one cluster, and in fuzzy clustering each data point belongs to several clusters that are associated with a certain membership degree. Fuzzy c-means clustering is a well-known and effective algorithm, however, the random initialization of the centroids directs the iterative process to converge to local optimal solutions easily. This paper proposed a clonal selection based fuzzy clustering algorithm (CSFCM) in order to overcome this issue. The algorithm makes use of clonal selection theory by applying methods such as cloning, mutation, reselection and displacement as well as using the objective function of the FCM algorithm.

Seven data sets were chosen and the CSFCM algorithm was compared to the basic fuzzy c-means algorithm (FCM),

Table 2: **Comparison of FCM, GAFCM, PSOFCM, CSFCM in terms of PC validity index**

Data set	FCM	GAFCM	PSOFCM	CSFCM
Iris	**0.7832±3.7633e-16**	0.75823±0.01351	0.77417±0.0099931	0.7618±1.91761e-5
Wine	**0.79094±1.1.4057e-12**	0.79004±0.0011282	0.78845± 0.0024337	0.79004±1.6337-7
Vowel	0.54976±9.3088e-8	0.49496±0.018895	0.52674± 0.012648	**0.55004±4.2974e-8**
Glass	0.50173±0.006688	**0.51232±0.059044**	0.49461±0.095027	0.50827±7.1837e-9
Ecoli	0.30873±0.001027	0.27437±0.011477	**0.37804±0.031598**	**0.37804±6.1944e-6**
Liver disorder	0.82993±3.7026e-16	0.82488±0.01628	0.81221 ±0.080893	**0.83103±2.4917e-8**
Vowel2	**0.22873±0.0013672**	0.12554±0.0035406	0.18685± 0.0055172	0.2182±5.2344e-6

Table 3: **Comparison of FCM, GAFCM, PSOFCM, CSFCM in terms of PE validity index**

Data set	FCM	GAFCM	PSOFCM	CSFCM
Iris	**0.39593±3.341e-16**	0.43395±0.021827	0.4133±0.018546	0.40857±1.349e-9
Wine	**0.38041±1.5985e-12**	0.38204±0.0015792	0.3855±0.0049499	**0.38041±4.8934e-8**
Vowel	**0.92244±9.6191e-7**	1.0216±0.034679	0.97007±0.026595	0.92293±7.6243e-7
Glass	0.96943±0.02053	1.4308±0.12146	1.0842±0.17089	**0.9479±2.9477e-8**
Ecoli	1.5333±0.011206	1.9196±0.034903	1.6449±0.082692	**1.5296±1.2673e-4**
Liver disorder	**0.28813±2.7948e-16**	0.29613±0.023051	0.30998 ±0.11027	0.29017±1.3728e-7
Vowel2	1.8882±0.0032484	2.228±0.014348	1.5143±0.027739	**1.4378±3.8373e-5**

a genetic algorithm based FCM algorithm (GAFCM), as well as a particle swarm optimization based FCM algorithm (PSOFCM). Six validity indices were used in order to compare the algorithms with each other. The results showed that CSFCM outperformed the other algorithms for four of the validity indices, and scored equally well compared to FCM on the other two validity indices in terms of best validity value achieved.

Future work will address the second shortcoming of FCM with the number of clusters needing to be predefined. Furthermore, in order for the algorithm to be applicable on big data sets, a parallelization of the algorithm is paramount.

7. REFERENCES

[1] A. Ghosh and L. C. Jain, "Evolutionary Computation in Data Mining Series: Studies in Fuzziness and Soft Computing", vol. 163, Sprinter, 2005.

[2] P. Tan, M. Steinbach, and V. Kumar, "Introduction to Data Mining", Addison-Wesley, May 2005.

[3] H. Jabeen and A. R. Baig. "Review of Classification Using Genetic Programming", International Journal of Engineering Science and Technology, vol. 2, no. 2, pp. 94-103, 2010.

[4] J. Han, "Data Mining: Concepts and Techniques", Morgan Kaufmann Publishers Inc., San Francisco, CA, USA, 2005.

[5] J. C. Bezdek, "Pattern Recognition with Fuzzy Objective Function Algorithms", Kluwer Academic Publishers Norwell, MA, USA, 1981.

[6] A. K. Jain and R. C. Dubes, "Algorithms for Clustering Data, Prentice-Hall, Inc., Upper Saddle River, NJ, 1988.

[7] M. S. Yang, "A survey of fuzzy clustering", Math. Comput. Modelling, 18, pp. 1-16, 1993.

[8] H. S. Lee, "Automatic clustering of business process in business systems planning", European Journal of Operational Research, 114, pp. 354-362, 1999.

[9] G. J. Klir, B. Yuan, "Fuzzy Sets and Fuzzy Logic Theory and Application", Prentice Hall PTR, Upper Saddle River, NJ, 1995.

[10] A. Rosenfeld, Fuzzy graphs, in: L. A. Zadeh, K. S. Fu, M. Shimura (Eds.), "Fuzzy Sets and their Applications to Cognitive and Decision Processes", Academic Press, New York, 1975.

[11] D. W. Matula, "Cluster analysis via graph theoretic techniques", Proceedings of the Louisiana Conference on Combinatorics, Graph Theory and Computing, Winnipeg, 1970.

[12] J. C. Dunn, "A Fuzzy Relative of the ISODATA Process and Its Use in Detecting Compact Well-Separated Clusters", Journal of Cybernetics 3: 32-57, 1973.

[13] V. P. Guerrero-Bote, C. Lopez-Pujalte, F. de Moya-Anegon, V. Herrero-Solana, "Comparison of neural models for document clustering", Int. Journal of Approximate Reasoning, vol. 34, pp. 287-305, 2003.

[14] I. Gath and A. B. Geva, "Unsupervised optimal fuzzy clustering", IEEE Transactions on Pattern Analysis and Machine Intelligence, vol. 11(7), pp. 773-781, 1989.

[15] J. C. Bezdek, C. Coray, R. Gunderson and J. Watson, "Detection and Characterization of Cluster Substructure - Linear Structure, Fuzzy c-Varieties and Convex Combinations Thereof", SIAM J. Appl. Math., vol. 40, no. 2, pp. 358-372, 1981.

[16] Y. Yang and S. Huang, "Image Segmentation by Fuzzy C-Means Clustering Algorithm with a Novel Penalty Term", in Computing and Informatics, vol. 26, pp. 17-31, 2007.

[17] W. Cai, S. Chen and D. Zhang, "Fast and robust fuzzy c-means clustering algorithms incorporating local information for image segmentation", Pattern Recognition, vol. 40, no. 3, pp. 825-838, 2007.

[18] Y. T. Kao, E. Zahara, I. W. Kao, "A hybridized approach to data clustering", Expert Systems with Applications 34 (3), 1754-1762, 2008.

Table 4: Comparison of FCM, GAFCM, PSOFCM, CSFCM in terms of DB validity index

Data set	FCM	GAFCM	PSOFCM	CSFCM
Iris	**0.91204±1.0549e-15**	0.92938±0.0086253	0.92095±0.010754	0.91317±1.8342e-8
Wine	**116.44±1.4355e-14**	116.68±0.77969	116.66±0.86855	**116.44±6.5433e-12**
Vowel	**187.6±1.7698e-14**	193.78±0.0731	192.13±0.6523	**187.6±2.17236e-11**
Glass	2.179±0.029096	2.425±0.5164	2.673±0.645	**2.1714±2.7583e-13**
Ecoli	3.9223±0.46362	**3.851±0.623**	4.0258±0.704	3.8552±3.0548e-6
Liver disorder	**45.843±0**	45.967±0.57959	46.641±3.3651	**45.843±0**
Vowel2	2.3076±0.035978	2.632±0.1304	2.512±0.2164	**2.189±4.2840e-3**

Table 5: Comparison of FCM, GAFCM, PSOFCM, CSFCM in terms of PCAES validity index

Data set	FCM	GAFCM	PSOFCM	CSFCM
Iris	1.972±0.52633	1.8809±0.46614	**2.33±0.89747**	2.1348±4.2327e-4
Wine	2.2064±0.77077	2.0673±0.80591	2.1656±0.86423	**2.1361±4.5722e-5**
Vowel	2.0828±0.95751	2.7142±0.2415	2.202±0.724	**2.7902±3.4975e-3**
Glass	8.0692±0.1788	9.109±0.636	9.047±0.638	**9.1543±3.9547e-4**
Ecoli	2.822±0.7289	2.3986±0.7279	2.911±0.222	**2.9159±7.5678e-3**
Liver disorder	3.136±0.104	3.9429±0.4519	2.8944±0.2186	**4.2523±2.2852e-3**
Vowel2	3.0307±0.1848	3.8321±0.9351	**8.0544±0.2493**	4.5275±4.1387e-4

Table 6: Comparison of FCM, GAFCM, PSOFCM, CSFCM in terms of PBMF validity index

Data set	FCM	GAFCM	PSOFCM	CSFCM
Iris	**1.1343±4.7263e-16**	1.0228±0.065783	1.0807±0.06328	**1.1343±3.4721e-12**
Wine	**1.0407±1.0589e-12**	1.0353±0.004563	1.0248±0.01489	**1.0407±5.2125e-11**
Vowel	**0.15345±4.2779e-7**	0.14099±0.0066558	0.15033±0.005635	**0.15345±7.2195e-9**
Glass	0.56154±0.0037025	0.28959±0.04661	0.42935±0.054079	**0.5874±2.6235e-8**
Ecoli	0.24857±0.0029411	0.15323±0.017463	0.24285±0.048303	**0.2278±2.6487e-4**
Liver disorder	0.28445±2.5327e-16	0.27592±0.021256	**0.29362±0.066964**	0.27364±6.1446e-8
Vowel2	0.15191±0.0019245	0.12853±0.0056154	0.12436±0.026612	**0.16173±1.7485**

Table 7: Comparison of FCM, GAFCM, PSOFCM, CSFCM in terms of XB validity index

Data set	FCM	GAFCM	PSOFCM	CSFCM
Iris	**0.13711±5.9074e-16**	0.20954±0.04634	0.142±0.01772	**0.13711±5.3491e-9**
Wine	0.12566±3.6067e-12	**0.12522±0.001930**	0.12846±0.00484	0.12582±5.3189e-10
Vowel	**0.18933±4.492e-8**	0.48874±0.20922	0.25009±0.074111	**0.18933±3.7648e-10**
Glass	0.94653±0.047904	1.1628±0.57795	**0.31815±0.21906**	0.91448±2.6478e-8
Ecoli	0.91204±0.08645	1.6848±0.66646	0.90928±1.0236	**0.8013±4.1698e-5**
Liver disorder	**0.12617±1.2928e-16**	0.13726±0.034688	0.14235±0.09482	**0.12617±2.1773e-10**
Vowel2	0.60571±0.2154	1.6359±0.50056	1.2361±0.2064	**0.5073±6.1847e-4**

[19] D. N. Cao, J. C. Krzysztof, "GAKREM: a novel hybrid clustering algorithm", Information Sciences 178, 4205-4227, 2008.

[20] K. R. Zalik, "An efficient k-means clustering algorithm", Pattern Recognition Letters 29, 1385-1391, 2008.

[21] K. Krishna, Murty, "Genetic k-means algorithm", IEEE Transactions of System Man Cybernetics Part B-Cybernetics 29, 433-439, 1999.

[22] U. Mualik, S. Bandyopadhyay, "Genetic algorithm-based clustering technique", Pattern Recognition 33, 1455-1465, 2000.

[23] M. Laszlo, S. Mukherjee, "A genetic algorithm that exchanges neighboring centers for k-means clustering", Pattern Recognition Letters 28 (16), 2359-2366, 2007.

[24] P. S. Shelokar, V. K. Jayaraman, B. D. Kulkarni, "An ant colony approach for clustering", Analytica Chimica Acta 509 (2), 187-195, 2004.

[25] Z. Liu, X. Jin, R. Bie, X. Gao, "FAISC: A Fuzzy Artificial Immune System Clustering Algorithm", Proceedings of the Third International Conference on Natural Computation (ICNC), 2007.

[26] T. Liu, Y. Zhou, Z. Hu, Z. Wang, "A New Clustering Algorithm Based on Artificial Immune System", Proceedings of the Fifth International Conference on Fuzzy Systems and Knowledge Discovery, 2008.

[27] R. Liu, Z. Shen, L. Jiao, W. Zhang, "Immunodomaince based clonal selection clustering algorithm", Proceedings of the 2010 IEEE Congress on Evolutionary Computation (CEC), 2010.

[28] C. Chui-Yu, C.-H. Lin, "Cluster Analysis Based on Artificial Immune System and Ant Algorithm", Proceedings of the Third International Conference on Natural Computation, 2007.

[29] L. N. De Castro and F. J. Von Zuben, "Learning and optimization using the clonal selection principle", IEEE Transactions on Evolutionary Computation, vol. 6, no. 3, pp. 239-251, 2002.

[30] D. L. Davies and D. W. Bouldin, "A cluster separation measure", IEEE Transactions on Pattern Analysis and Machine Intelligence, (2), 224-227, 1979.

[31] K. L. Wu, and M. S. Yang, "A cluster validity index for fuzzy clustering", Pattern Recognition Letters, 26(9), 1275-1291, 2005.

[32] M. K. Pakhira, S. Bandyopadhyay, U. Maulik, "Validity index for crisp and fuzzy clusters", Pattern Recognition, 37, 487-501, 2004.

[33] X. L. Xie, and G. Beni, "A validity measure for fuzzy clustering", IEEE Transactions on Pattern Analysis and Machine Intelligence, 13(8), 841-847, 1991.

[34] N. R. Pal, and J. C. Bezdek, "On cluster validity for the fuzzy c-means model", IEEE Transactions on Fuzzy Systems, 3(3), 370-379, 1995.

[35] C. Li, J. Zhou, P. Kou, J. Xiao, "A novel chaotic particle swarm optimization based fuzzy clustering algorithm", Journal of Neurocomputing, Elsevier, vol. 83, no. 1, 2012.

On the Runtime Analysis of Stochastic Ageing Mechanisms

Pietro S. Oliveto
Department of Computer Science
University of Sheffield
Sheffield, S1 4DP, United Kingdom

Dirk Sudholt
Department of Computer Science
University of Sheffield
Sheffield, S1 4DP, United Kingdom

ABSTRACT

Ageing operators are applied in the field of artificial immune systems (AIS) to increase the diversity of the population during the optimization process. Previous theoretical analyses have shown how static ageing operators can successfully escape local optima by implicitly performing a restart of the algorithm. However, showing naturally that ageing in an AIS is more effective than a conceptually simpler restart strategy has proved to be a hard task. We present a rigorous analysis of stochastic ageing mechanisms and show that superior performance compared to just simple restarts can be achieved. Since standard stochastic pure ageing is only effective for small population sizes, we present a hybrid pure ageing operator that achieves the same performance independent of the population size. For a benchmark function used in dynamic optimisation we rigorously prove that hybrid pure ageing allows to escape local optima beyond restarts while static pure ageing is inefficient. The results also apply to the non-dynamic setting. An analytical general framework for the analysis of standard stochastic pure ageing is presented along the way.

Categories and Subject Descriptors

F.2.2 [**Analysis of Algorithms and Problem Complexity**]: Nonnumerical Algorithms and Problems

Keywords

Artificial immune systems, ageing, runtime analysis, theory

1. INTRODUCTION

Artificial Immune Systems (AIS) are a class of general purpose algorithms based on the immune system of vertebrates [6]. Most AIS algorithms for optimisation are inspired by Burnet's clonal selection theory [1]. Popular ones are the B-Cell algorithm (BCA) [15], Opt-IA [4] and Clonalg [7]. Apart from the absence of crossover operators, the main distinguishing features of AIS compared to Evolutionary Algorithms (EAs) are hypermutation operators such as contiguous somatic mutation or inversely fitness-proportional mutation rates and the presence of ageing operators to enhance diversity in the population. Although the concept of ageing has been introduced in EAs [19], it is rarely used.

In recent years the amount of theoretical work analysing the performance of AIS has rapidly increased. While previously only convergence analyses were available [5], nowadays runtime analyses exploring the effectiveness of several typical AIS operators have appeared together with time complexity analyses of standard algorithms, such as the BCA, for classical combinatorial optimisation problems. Concerning typical hypermutation operators, the inversely fitness proportional mutation rate was analysed in [21, 22], hypermutations with mutation potentials were analysed in [13] as well as the contiguous somatic hypermutations (CSM) [11]. All these works considered the hypermutation operators within a very simple algorithmic framework on simple example problems to understand the power and limitations of the operators. Concerning CSM, the work was a basis which enabled the analysis of the full BCA for standard combinatorial optimisation problems such as vertex cover [10] and the longest common subsequence problem [14].

On the other hand, there is still a limited understanding of the effectiveness of the ageing operators used in algorithms such as Opt-IA [4] and IMMALG [3] amongst others. Theoretical studies of static pure aging have shown how an AIS with ageing has far superior performance compared to an AIS without ageing on example function classes containing a local optimum on an easy-to-find path and a global optimum on a harder-to-find path [9, 11]. The superior performance comes from static pure ageing's capability of implicitly restarting the whole population once it is trapped on the local optimum if the aging parameter is not too low. Quoting from [9]: "Thus, a simple EA with restarts is efficient too. It is an open problem to strengthen the results such that aging becomes necessary". Recently an example problem has been presented where static pure ageing can achieve a speed up that cannot be achieved with a restart strategy [12]. However, for the algorithm to be effective k-point crossover is required, an operator that is not usually found in AIS algorithms.

In this paper we present a study of stochastic ageing operators, and show that they are effective in a natural setting where restarts do not work. To this end we choose a well studied instance class from dynamic optimisation called BALANCE [18, 16]. Since optimising the function is hardest

GECCO'14, July 12–16, 2014, Vancouver, BC, Canada.

ACM 978-1-4503-2662-9/14/07 ...$15.00.
http://dx.doi.org/10.1145/2576768.2598328.

at low frequencies of change, the results also apply to the static setting for escaping large local optima beyond restarts. Before the analysis for BALANCE we show that the stochastic operators can also implicitly perform restarts in the fashion of static pure ageing on functions where a simple restart strategy is an effective way to find the optimal solution. To show this we perform the analysis on the LOCALOPT_k function that was previously used in literature to prove the effectiveness of static pure ageing [11]. Since the standard "stochastic pure aging" [3, 2] operator is efficient only if the population size is not too large, we present a hybrid pure ageing mechanism that is effective also for large populations.

In the next Section we present a formal definition of static, stochastic and hybrid pure ageing together with the complete algorithmic framework. Just like in [11] we choose to embed ageing in the minimal (μ+1) EA framework allowing the study of the ageing operators in isolation. In the same section we will also present the LOCALOPT_k and the BALANCE functions.

In Section 3 we present the analysis of the LOCALOPT_k function and show that the (μ+1) EA equipped with stochastic pure ageing and small population size can efficiently optimise the function in the same fashion as the (μ+1) EA with static pure ageing, while hybrid pure ageing is efficient for any polynomial population size.

In Section 4 we show how the hybrid pure ageing operator can efficiently escape the local optimum of the BALANCE function while the (μ+1) EA with a restart strategy or equipped with static pure ageing are inefficient.

We conclude the paper with a discussion of the results.

2. PRELIMINARIES

2.1 Ageing and Algorithmic Framework

We use the same algorithmic framework as in previous theoretical work on ageing [9, 11]. Essentially we consider a standard (μ+1) EA equipped with a pure ageing mechanism, see Algorithm 1. A population of μ individuals of age 0 is initialised uniformly at random. In each generation each individual's age is increased by 1 and an individual x is selected uniformly at random for reproduction. The offspring y is obtained by applying standard bit mutation to a copy of x and is assigned the same age as x unless it has better fitness (i. e., if $f(y) > f(x)$ then $y.age := 0$). In the selection phase a random individual with minimal fitness is removed from the population if the current size is greater than μ (i. e., no individuals have been removed due to their age). If the population size is smaller than μ, then it is filled up to size μ by creating new individuals uniformly at random (i. e., birth phase).

The idea behind ageing is to increase the diversity of the population by removing old individuals that have been in the population for a long time. A birth phase concludes each generation inserting new individuals and ensuring that the population size remains the same throughout the run. In AIS two main ageing mechanisms are common, static pure ageing [4] and stochastic pure ageing [3, 2]. In *static pure ageing* a threshold τ is used to indicate the deterministic life time of individuals. When individuals reach age $\tau + 1$ they are automatically removed from the population. The static pure ageing mechanism is formalised in Operator 2.

In *stochastic pure ageing* individuals are given an expected life time. In each generation an individual has a probability

Algorithm 1 Algorithmic Framework [11].

1. **Initialisation**
   a) Create a random population $P = \{x_1, x_2, \dots, x_\mu\}$.
   b) For all $x \in P$ set $x.age := 0$.
2. **Ageing: Growing older**
   For all $x \in P$ set $x.age := x.age + 1$.
3. **Variation**
   a) Select $x \in P$ uniformly at random.
   b) Create y by copying x.
   c) Flip each bit in y with probability $1/n$.
   d) If $f(y) > f(x)$ then $y.age := 0$
   else $y.age := x.age$
4. **Removal due to age**
   (either static, stochastic or hybrid pure ageing)
5. **Selection**
   If $|P| > \mu$ then remove one $x^* \in P$ with minimal fitness.
6. **Birth phase**
   While $|P| < \mu$ insert randomly created individuals in P.
7. **Stopping**
   If stopping criterion not met continue at line 2.

Operator 2 Static Pure Ageing [11].

For all $x \in P$ if $x.age > \tau$ then set $P := P \setminus \{x\}$.

to survive of $p_{\text{live}} = e^{-\frac{c}{\tau'}}$ (i.e., hence a probability to die of $p_{\text{die}} = 1-e^{-\frac{c}{\tau'}}$) where c is usually a constant and τ' the main parameter of the operator. Hence, the expected life time of an individual is $E[\tau] = 1/p_{\text{die}}$. The stochastic pure ageing mechanism is formalised in Operator 3. From the analyses

Operator 3 Stochastic Pure Ageing [3].

For each $x \in P$ set $P := P \setminus \{x\}$ with probability p_{die}

presented in Section 3 for LOCALOPT_k we learn that the stochastic ageing operator is effective in achieving implicit restarts and in escaping local optima beyond restarts only if the population size is not too large. In order to allow for larger population sizes we introduce a hybrid mechanism which has features of both pure static and pure stochastic ageing in an attempt of taking advantages from both operators. Just like static ageing, *hybrid pure ageing* does not act on an individual until its lifetime reaches a deterministic value τ. This allows to "protect" an individual from dying for τ generations. All the individuals with age greater than τ survive with probability p_{live} and are removed from the population with probability $p_{\text{die}} = 1 - p_{\text{live}}$ like in stochastic ageing. This may allow, even in large populations, both complete restarts and the possibility for some individuals to survive after they have escaped a local optimum. The hybrid pure ageing mechanism is formalised in Operator 4.

Operator 4 Hybrid Pure Ageing.

For all $x \in P$, if $x.age > \tau$ then
set $P := P \setminus \{x\}$ with probability p_{die}

In literature an alternative ageing operator, namely *genotypic ageing* [11], has been introduced to allow for restarts and also perform random walks across plateaus of equal fitness. Genotypic ageing achieves this by resetting the age of

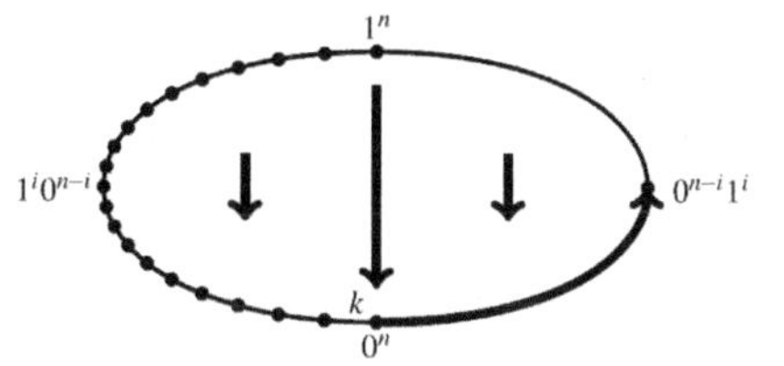

Figure 1: Sketch of the LocalOpt function.

individuals of equal fitness that are genotypically different from their parents. However, if a local optimum consists of several neighbouring points of equal fitness, then genotypic ageing would not allow for complete restarts at all. This is the case for the BALANCE function considered in this paper.

2.2 The LocalOpt Function

The LOCALOPT$_k$ function class is defined as follows.

DEFINITION 1. *For $n \in \mathbb{N}$ and $2 \leq k = O(1)$ the function* LOCALOPT$_k$*: $\{0,1\}^n \to \mathbb{R}$ is defined for $x \in \{0,1\}^n$ by* LOCALOPT$_k(x)$ =

$$\begin{cases} n \cdot (i \cdot k + 1) & \text{if } x \in \{1^{i \cdot k}0^{n-i \cdot k} | i \in \{1, 2, \ldots, \lfloor n/k \rfloor\}\}, \\ n \cdot (i+1) & \text{if } x \in \{0^{n-i}1^i | i \in \{1, 2, \ldots, \lfloor n/2 \rfloor\}\}, \\ n - \sum_{i=1}^{n} x[i] & \text{otherwise.} \end{cases}$$

A sketch of the function class is given in Figure 1. For most of the search space the function is ZEROMAX guiding randomised search heuristics towards the 0^n bitstring. From there two separate paths start. An "easy-to-find-path" is found if i rightmost 0-bits are flipped into 1-bits (i.e., $i \in \{1, 2, \ldots, \lfloor n/2 \rfloor\}$). This path leads to a local optimum represented by the $0^{n/2}1^{n/2}$ bitstring with fitness value $n \cdot (\lfloor n/2 \rfloor + 1)$. A "harder-to-find" path is found if exactly $i \cdot k$ leftmost bits are flipped into 1-bits (i.e., $i \in \{1, 2, \ldots, \lfloor n/k \rfloor\}$). This path leads to the global optimum 1^n of value $n \cdot (\lfloor n/k \rfloor \cdot k + 1)$. Jansen and Zarges [11] have shown how a (μ+1) EA cannot find the global optimum efficiently because there is a high probability that the algorithm finds the easy path and ends up being stuck on the local optimum. On the other hand static pure ageing can implicitly restart the population allowing it to escape from the local optimum and to eventually find the path leading to the global optimum. In Section 3 we will show how the (μ+1) EA equipped with stochastic and hybrid pure ageing can also optimise the function in a similar fashion.

2.3 The Dynamic Function Balance

The BALANCE function [18, 16] was introduced by Rohlfshagen et al. [18] to disprove the conjecture that the higher the frequency of change, the harder it is to optimise a dynamic function. It is defined as follows (see also Figure 2):

DEFINITION 2. *Let $a, b \in \{0,1\}^{n/2}$ and $x = ab \in \{0,1\}^n$. Then,* BALANCE(x) =

$$\begin{cases} n^3 & \text{if } \mathrm{LO}(a) = n/2, \text{ else} \\ |b|_1 + n \cdot \mathrm{LO}(a) & \text{if } n/16 < |b|_1 < 7n/16, \text{ else} \\ n^2 \cdot \mathrm{LO}(a) & \text{if } |a|_0 > \sqrt{n}, \text{ else} \\ 0 & \text{otherwise.} \end{cases}$$

where $|x|_1 = \sum_{i=1}^{n} x_i$ and $\mathrm{LO}(x) := \sum_{i=1}^{n} \prod_{j=1}^{i} x_j$ counts the number of leading ones.

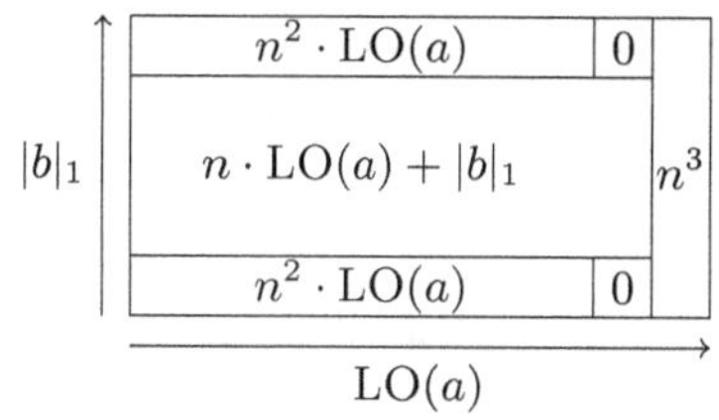

Figure 2: Visualisation of BALANCE [18].

Each search point of BALANCE consists of a prefix of length $n/2$ and a suffix of the same length. The fitness of a search point is determined by the number of leading ones in the prefix and by the number of 1-bits (i.e., ONEMAX) in the suffix. A globally optimal search point has the maximal value $n/2$ of leading ones (i.e., $\mathrm{LO}(a) = n/2$) in the prefix. However, before reaching the global optimum the algorithm may reach the two trap regions corresponding to search points with less than $n/16$ 0-bits or less than $n/16$ 1-bits in the suffix. The trap regions and the global optimum are separated by a region of 0-fitness of length $\sqrt{n}$ that makes it prohibitive for search heuristics to reach the optimum from the traps.

We use the XoR framework to impose dynamics to the stationary BALANCE function in exactly the same way as done in previous work [18, 16].

The framework can be used with any stationary pseudo-Boolean function by means of a bit-wise *exclusive-or* operation that is applied to each search point $x \in \{0,1\}^n$ prior to each function evaluation. The dynamic fitness function is simply $f(x(t) \oplus m(\pi))$ where $\oplus$ is the *xor* operator and $m(\pi) \in \{0,1\}^n$ is a binary mask. The period index $\pi = \lceil t/\varphi \rceil$ is determined by the duration $\varphi > 0$ between changes. Hence, the *frequency of change* is defined by $1/\varphi$.

Following [18, 16] we apply the XoR framework to achieve cyclical dynamics on the function by using the following mask m as a function of the period index π:

$$m(\pi) := \begin{cases} 0^{n/2}0^{n/2} & \text{if } \pi \bmod 2 = 0, \text{and} \\ 0^{n/2}1^{n/2} & \text{otherwise.} \end{cases}$$

As a result, only the suffix of the search points is affected and the magnitude of change is $n/2$. During odd periods π, the fitness increases with the increase of suffix 0-bits while for even π it increases with the increase of 1-bits. If the frequency of change is high, then the function is easy because a randomised search heuristic does not have enough time to optimise the ONEMAX suffix before the suffix-dependent part of the function changes into ZEROMAX and vice versa. Hence, the algorithm balances along the centre of the suffix (the centre of the y-axis in the figure) and efficiently optimises the leading ones in the prefix [18].

Oliveto and Zarges [16] have shown that for sufficiently low frequencies of change (i.e. $\varphi > 20\mu n$) the (μ+1) EA requires exponential expected optimisation time for sublinear population sizes (i.e. $\mu \leq n^{1/2-\epsilon}$). However, as the population size increases towards linear sizes (i.e., $\mu = \Omega(n)$), the algorithm becomes efficient for any value of φ. In Section 4 we will show that the (μ+1) EA equipped with hybrid ageing can optimise BALANCE for any value of φ while using static pure ageing leads to exponential runtimes for small frequencies of change and for the static setting.

3. LOCALOPT ANALYSIS

In this section we concentrate on the instance class where static pure ageing was previously shown to be efficient [11]. We first show that stochastic pure ageing can optimise LOCALOPT$_k$ if the population size is not too large. Afterwards we will show that the hybrid ageing operator is efficient independent of the population size.

3.1 Stochastic Pure Ageing Works for Small Populations

The roadmap for the analysis is as follows. We first consider the time for reaching some local optimum. If the wrong local optimum $0^{\lceil n/2\rceil}1^{\lfloor n/2\rfloor}$ is reached, the (μ+1) EA can escape by performing a restart where all individuals die in the same generation. Once a local optimum with leading ones is reached, there is a good chance for the (μ+1) EA to climb up these local optima to reach the global optimum.

The following lemma describes a random walk, which will serve as a pessimistic model for the evolution of individuals with current best fitness.

LEMMA 1. *Consider a random walk X_t on $\{0,1,\dots,\mu\}$ such that $\Pr(X_{t+1} = X_t - d \mid X_t) = \ell^d$ for all $1 \le d \le X_t$, and $\Pr(X_{t+1} = X_t + 1 \mid X_t) = 1 - \sum_{d=1}^{X_t} \ell^d$. If $\ell \le 1/40$, and the random walk starts in state μ, then the expected first hitting time of state 0 is at least $(6\ell)^{-\mu}$. Moreover, the probability that state 0 is reached within t generations starting in state μ is at most $t \cdot (6\ell)^\mu$.*

Using Lemma 1, we are able to tell how quickly, and with what probability, the (μ+1) EA with stochastic ageing manages to improve its current best fitness.

LEMMA 2. *Consider the (μ+1) EA with stochastic ageing using $p_{\text{die}} \le 1/(320\mu^2)$ and let f be the minimum fitness in the population. Assume that every mutation of an individual of fitness at least f has a probability at least s of creating an offspring with fitness $f^+ > f$. The expected time until the (μ+1) EA first reaches a population of minimum fitness f^+ or the best current fitness drops below f is at most $O(\mu/s + \mu \log \mu)$.*

The probability that in that case a minimum fitness of f^+ is reached is at least $1 - O((\mu/s + \mu\log\mu) \cdot (48\mu p_{\text{die}})^\mu)$.

Proof. Due to stochastic ageing, the population may continually lose individuals of high fitness. We therefore first analyse the Markov chain describing the number of individuals X_t with fitness at least f at generation t. This number may decrease in case individuals die and worse offspring are accepted, or the population is being filled with newborn random individuals. Let $p_{i,j}$ denote the transition probabilities in the Markov chain describing X_t.

A necessary event for X_t dropping by $d \ge 1$ is that d individuals among these die:

$$p_{i,i-d} \le \binom{i}{d} p_{\text{die}}^d (1 - p_{\text{die}})^{i-d} \le (i p_{\text{die}})^d := p'_{i,i-d}.$$

A sufficient condition for $X_t = i < \mu$ to increase by 1 is that no individual dies, including the new offspring, and the new offspring has fitness at least f. The latter can be achieved by simply selecting a parent of fitness at least f and not flipping any bits during mutation. Hence,

$$p_{i,i+1} \ge (1 - p_{\text{die}})^{\mu+1} \cdot \frac{i}{\mu} \cdot \left(1 - \frac{1}{n}\right)^n \ge \frac{i}{8\mu} := p'_{i,i+1}$$

using $(1-p_{\text{die}})^{\mu+1} \ge (1-\frac{1}{2(\mu+1)})^{\mu+1} \ge 1/2$ and $(1-1/n)^n \ge 1/4$ for $n \ge 2$. In the same way, we obtain $p_{\mu,\mu} \ge 1/(8\mu) := p'_{\mu,\mu}$. We proceed using the primed transition probabilities as pessimistic estimations of the real ones. Furthermore, we pessimistically speed up the Markov chain by eliminating self-loops for all states except for state μ. We define transition probabilities $p''_{i,j}$ for $1 \le i \le \mu - 1$ without self-loops by conditioning on the event that a transition to a higher or lower state happens. Thus, for $1 \le d \le i$

$$p''_{i,i-d} := \frac{p'_{i,i-d}}{\sum_{j=1}^{i} p'_{i,i-j} + p'_{i,i+1}} \le \frac{p'_{i,i-d}}{p'_{i,i+1}} = \frac{8\mu}{i} \cdot (i p_{\text{die}})^d.$$

For state μ, we get

$$p''_{\mu,\mu-d} := \frac{p'_{i,i-d}}{\sum_{j=1}^{i} p'_{\mu,\mu-j} + p'_{\mu,\mu+1}} \le \frac{p'_{\mu,\mu-d}}{p'_{\mu,\mu}} = \frac{8\mu}{i} \cdot (i p_{\text{die}})^d.$$

Define $\ell := 8\mu p_{\text{die}}$, then for all $1 \le i \le \mu$ and all $1 \le d \le i$ $p''_{i,i-d} \le \ell^d$. Since $\ell \le 1/40$, this describes the random walk analysed in Lemma 1. The probability for increasing the current state $1 \le i \le \mu - 1$ is at least

$$1 - \sum_{j=1}^{i} \ell^i = 1 - \ell \cdot \frac{1-\ell^i}{1-\ell} \ge 1 - 40\ell/39.$$

We use these transition probabilities to estimate the expected time for an individual to discover a solution of fitness at least f^+ and for individuals with fitness at least f^+ to take over the whole population.

As long as the population contains at least one individual of fitness at least f, the probability of creating an offspring with fitness f^+ is at least $1/\mu \cdot s$, and the expected time for such an event to happen is at most μ/s. A sufficient condition for raising the minimum fitness in the population to at least f^+ is that in the subsequent generations the number of individuals with fitness at least f^+ steadily increases. Let X_t^+ denote the corresponding Markov chain and note that it has the same properties as X_t, allowing us to use the same pessimistic transition probabilities.

A sufficient condition for reaching X_t^+ is that in steps where X_t^+ changes, we only see an increase. We speak of a successful trial if this happens, and a failure otherwise, that is, if there is a step decreasing X_t^+. The probability for a successful trial, starting with $X_t^+ = 1$, is at least

$$\prod_{i=1}^{\mu-1} \left(1 - \sum_{j=1}^{i} \ell^j\right) \ge \prod_{i=1}^{\mu-1} (1 - 40\ell/39)$$
$$\ge 1 - 40\mu\ell/39 = 1 - 320\mu^2 p_{\text{die}}/39 \ge 1/2.$$

The expected time for this to happen, or X_t^+ decreasing, can be bounded using $p'_{i,i+1} \ge i/(8\mu)$ as $\sum_{i=1}^{\mu-1} \frac{8\mu}{i} = 8\mu H(\mu)$, $H(\mu) \le (\ln \mu) + 1$ denoting the μ-th Harmonic number. In case of a failed trial, we repeat the argument. Altogether, the expected time for finding an improvement and a successful trial that raises the minimum fitness to f^+ – or decreasing the current best fitness below f – is $\mathrm{E}(T) = O(\mu/s + \mu \log \mu)$.

To show the second claim, we use the second statement of Lemma 1 with respect to X_t. We get that the probability of decreasing the best fitness below f before time T above is at most

$$\sum_t \Pr(T = t) \cdot t \cdot (6\ell)^\mu$$
$$= \mathrm{E}(T) \cdot (6\ell)^\mu = O\Big(\big(\tfrac{\mu}{s} + \mu \log \mu\big) \cdot (48\mu p_{\text{die}})^\mu\Big). \qquad \square$$

Knowing how long the (μ+1) EA with stochastic pure ageing takes to find a better fitness allows us to estimate the time until some local optimum is reached. The following lemma applies not just to LOCALOPT$_k$, but to any function with a bounded number of fitness values.

LEMMA 3. *Consider the (μ+1) EA with stochastic ageing on a function with at most d function values. If*

$$p_{\text{die}} \le \min\left\{\frac{1}{320\mu^2}, \frac{1}{48\mu} \cdot \left(\frac{1}{cd\mu n}\right)^{1/\mu}\right\}$$

for a sufficiently large constant $c > 0$, the expected time for the (μ+1) EA to reach some local optimum is $O(\mu dn)$.

Proof. As long as no local optimum has been reached, every individual can be improved by flipping only one specific bit. Applying Lemma 2 with $s := 1/n \cdot (1 - 1/n)^{n-1} \ge 1/(en)$ at most d times and taking the union bound over all failure probabilities yields that with probability $\Omega(1)$ the (μ+1) EA finds a local optimum before the best current fitness decreases as described in Lemma 2. If this happens, we repeat the argument. In expectation $O(1)$ trials are sufficient. $\square$

For LOCALOPT$_k$ we get the following main result.

THEOREM 4. *The expected optimisation time on LOCALOPT$_k$ of the (μ+1) EA with stochastic pure ageing, population size $\mu = O(1)$ and*

$$p_{\text{die}} = \min\left\{\frac{1}{320\mu^2}, \frac{1}{48\mu} \cdot \left(\frac{1}{c\mu n^{k+1}}\right)^{1/\mu}\right\}$$

for a sufficiently large constant $c > 0$, is at most

$$O\Big(\mu n^{k+1} + n^{k-1} \cdot p_{\text{die}}^{-\mu-1}\Big) = O\Big(n^{2k+(k+1)/\mu}\Big).$$

The condition on p_{die} reveals a sound parameter choice for p_{die}. The term $(1/(c\mu n^{k+1}))^{1/\mu}$ is chosen such that the expected time for μ individuals dying at the same time is $p_{\text{die}}^{-\mu} \ge c\mu n^{k+1}$, which is a good estimate for the time needed to climb up the path to the global optimum. The chosen value for p_{die} ensures that the path can be climbed with good probability, as confirmed in the following proof. On the other hand, p_{die} is large enough to allow the (μ+1) EA to quickly escape from the wrong local optimum.

Proof of Theorem 4. Consider the population after initialisation, or after a full restart where all $\mu+1$ individuals have died. By Lemma 3 the (μ+1) EA finds some local optimum within expected $O(\mu n^2)$ generations. The probability to enter the path to the global optimum given that either path is entered is $\Omega(1/n^{k-1})$ [11]. If this does not happen, we wait for a full restart, which happens with probability $p_{\text{die}}^{\mu+1}$, hence in expected time $p_{\text{die}}^{-\mu-1}$, and repeat the argument. The total expected time for finding a local optimum on the path to the global optimum is hence bounded by

$$T_1 = O\Big(n^{k-1} \cdot (\mu n^2 + p_{\text{die}}^{-\mu-1})\Big) = O\Big(n^{k-1} \cdot p_{\text{die}}^{-\mu-1}\Big)$$

as $p_{\text{die}}^{-\mu-1} \ge \mu n^2$.

Assume that a local optimum on the path to the global optimum has been reached. So long as no better or equally good individual with trailing ones is created, the probability of reaching the next local optimum on that path in one mutation is at least $1/(en^k)$. Applying Lemma 2 with $s := 1/(en^k)$ yields that the next local optimum is reached with probability at least $1 - 1/n$, if c is chosen large enough. Repeating this for all n/k local optima, the probability that the population will climb to the global optimum is at least $1 - n/k \cdot 1/n \ge 1/2$. The expected time for this to happen is at most $T = O(\mu n^{k+1})$.

There is a risk that, while the population contains individuals on a local optimum with leading ones, individuals might evolve that develop trailing ones and hence follow the path to $0^{n/2}1^{n/2}$. Once these individuals reach an equal or better fitness than the one on the path to the global optimum, the former might take over the population. However, in order for this to happen, evolution must cross a "fitness valley" of worse search points as only search points with at least k trailing ones have a better or equal fitness. The Hamming distance between any such points is at least $2k$. Such a lineage is unlikely to evolve, as it is more likely that the individuals on the local optimum will take over the population before the mentioned $2k$ bits can be flipped by mutation. It follows that the probability of reaching any point with equal or better fitness within $T = O(\mu n^{k+1})$ generations is $o(1)$.

Together, the expected optimisation time is bounded by

$$\frac{O(\mu n^{k+1}) + T_1}{1/2 - o(1)} = O\Big(\mu n^{k+1} + n^{k-1} \cdot p_{\text{die}}^{-\mu-1}\Big). \qquad \square$$

For large population sizes, stochastic pure ageing fails to work efficiently. If $p_{\text{die}} > 1/\mu$, in expectation more than one individual dies in each generation. If one individual (including the offspring) dies, the surviving μ individuals form the next population, regardless of the fitness of the offspring. In other words, in these generations the population evolves without guidance by fitness. If more than one individual dies, the same happens, and additionally the population is being filled with random individuals. Experiments show that then the population resembles a collection of random individuals, unable to optimise even the ONEMAX part of LOCALOPT$_k$.

On the other hand, if $p_{\text{die}} \le 1/\mu$, and the population size μ is large, the population will need a long time to escape from the local optimum $0^{n/2}1^{n/2}$. The probability of all $\mu + 1$ individuals dying in the same generation is $p_{\text{die}}^{\mu+1} < \mu^{-\mu-1}$, and the expected time for this is $\mu^{\mu+1}$ and hence exponential in μ. The population may also die out incrementally, as not all individuals have to die in exactly the same step. But our analysis gives strong indications that for all parameters $p_{\text{die}} \le 1/\mu$ the expected time to escape from $0^{n/2}1^{n/2}$ is exponential in μ. This poses no problem for small μ, but for large μ, say $\mu \ge n^\varepsilon$, the expected optimisation time on LOCALOPT$_k$ would then be exponential in n.

3.2 Hybrid Pure Ageing Always Works

We first prove some general results regarding the (μ+1) EA with hybrid pure ageing in the following two lemmas. Afterwards we will prove the main result of this subsection. We call *genuine restart* the event that the whole population dies in the same generation. If at least one individual (or an offspring) survives we call the event a *failed restart*. Lemma 5 gives a lower bound on the age parameter

τ to allow the operator to achieve a restart and escape from a local optimum.

LEMMA 5. *Let the whole population be on a local optimum. Then, as long as a better local optimum is not found first and no individual reaches age $\tau+1$, all the individuals will have the same age in expected time $O(\mu^3)$.*

Proof. Let X_t be the largest number of individuals in the population having the same age. After $X_t = \mu$ for the first time all individuals will have the same age, unless individuals die from ageing or a better search point is found. Recall that an individual passes on its age to its offspring, if the fitness of the offspring is not larger than that of its parent. While $X_t < \mu$, the number of individuals can be increased by selecting one of X_t individuals of that age group, creating a clone, and removing an individual from another age group. We have

$$\Pr(X_{t+1} = X_t + 1 \mid X_t) \geq \frac{X_t \cdot (\mu - X_t)}{\mu(\mu+1)} \cdot \left(1 - \frac{1}{n}\right)^n.$$

The value of X_t can decrease if another age group expands in the same fashion, unless the latter becomes the new largest age group. Hence

$$\Pr(X_{t+1} = X_t - 1 \mid X_t) \leq \Pr(X_{t+1} = X_t + 1 \mid X_t).$$

We consider *relevant steps*, defined as generations where $X_{t+1} \neq X_t$. As $X_0 \geq 1$, a sufficient condition for reaching $X_t = \mu$ is that during $t := \mu^2$ relevant generations the number of relevant steps I increasing X is at least $t + (\mu+1)/2$. The number I follows a binomial distribution with parameters t and $1/2$. The variance of the binomial distribution implies $\Pr(I \geq t + (\mu+1)/2) \geq \Omega(1)$.

If this does not happen, we repeat the argument with another period of $t = \mu^2$ relevant steps. In expectation, $O(\mu^2)$ relevant steps are required. A single relevant step occurs with probability at least

$$\frac{\mu - 1}{\mu(\mu+1)} \cdot \left(1 - \frac{1}{n}\right)^n \geq \frac{1}{3\mu} \cdot \frac{1}{4} = \frac{1}{12\mu}$$

for all $\mu \geq 2$ and all $n \geq 2$. Hence, the expected waiting time for a relevant step is at most 12μ. Multiplying this with $O(\mu^2)$ yields the claim. □

Lemma 6 gives bounds on the probabilities of genuine and failed restarts from local optima. Furthermore it also calculates the probability that a given individual survives and may allow to escape a local optimum.

LEMMA 6. *Let the whole population be on a local optimum and have the same age greater than τ. Let $p_{\text{live}} = 1/\mu$. Then the probability of a genuine restart in the next generation is at least $(4e)^{-1}$. The probability that a genuine restart fails is at least $(2e)^{-1}$ and the probability that one defined individual survives is at least $(2e\mu)^{-1}$.*

Proof. The probability one individual dies is $p_{\text{die}} = 1 - p_{\text{live}}$. Hence, the probability the whole population dies is $p_{\text{FullRestart}} = (1 - 1/\mu)^{\mu+1} \geq 1/(4e)$. For a genuine restart to fail it is sufficient that one individual survives. Since each individual survives with probability $p_{\text{live}} = 1/\mu$ and there are $\mu + 1$ individuals in total we get $p_{\text{FailRestart}} = \mu \cdot 1/\mu \cdot (1 - 1/\mu)^{\mu} \geq 1/(2e)$. Finally one defined individual survives with probability $p_{\text{live}} = 1/\mu$ and the remaining μ are removed with probability p_{die}. Hence, $p_{\text{survivor}} = 1/\mu \cdot (1 - 1/\mu)^{\mu} \geq 1/(2e\mu)$. □

THEOREM 7. *Let $k = O(1)$, $p_{\text{live}} = 1/\mu$ and $\tau = \omega(\log(n) \cdot (n^k + \mu n) + \mu^3)$. The ($\mu$+1) EA with hybrid pure ageing optimises* LOCALOPT$_k$ *in expected time $O(\tau n^{k-1} + n^{k+1})$.*

Proof. We mainly follow the proof for the (μ+1) EA with static pure ageing [11] and show that the algorithm with hybrid pure ageing follows a similar trajectory. We pessimistically assume the local optimum is found before the global optimum. This requires expected $O(n^2 + \mu n \log n)$ generations due to Witt's proof for the (μ+1) EA [20]. Once the local optimum is reached, in expected time $O(\mu \log \mu)$ all the individuals of the population are on the local optimum (by standard takeover arguments [20]). Now we calculate the time for the individuals to all have the same age. By Lemma 5 the expected number of generations for this event is $O(\mu^3)$. Hence, after a total number of $O(n^2 + \mu n \log n + \mu \log \mu + \mu^3) < \tau$ generations all the individuals are on the local optimum and have the same age $a < \tau$. Since only copies are accepted and these inherit their parent's age all the population will reach age $\tau+1$ at the same generation and each individual will die with probability p_{die}. By Lemma 6 both a genuine restart and a failed restart (i. e., at least one individual survives) happen with at least constant probabilities. Overall, the time to reach the local optimum and to achieve a restart is $O(\tau + n^2 + \mu n \log n + \mu^3)$.

If a failed restart happens we wait for all the surviving individuals to die. Unless the surviving individuals achieve an improvement (i. e., their age is reset), they will each die with probability $1 - 1/\mu$ in the next generation. The probability that all not improving survivors die in the next generation is at least $(1 - 1/\mu)^{\mu+1} \geq 1/(4e)$. So the new phase starts after expected $4e$ generations and all the individuals of the population with have an age between 0 and $4e$.

We now concentrate on the required number of genuine restarts. In this case we are in the setting analysed by Jansen and Zarges for static pure ageing [11] and we follow their proof again. Since the probability to enter the path to the global optimum given that either path is entered is $\Omega(1/n^{k-1})$ [11], $O(n^{k-1})$ expected genuine restarts are required before the right path is entered. This gives a runtime of $O(\tau n^{k-1} + n^{k+1} + \mu n^k \log n + \mu^3 n^{k-1})$ to enter the path to the optimum. This time is the same as that in the Theorem statement since $\tau n^{k-1} = \Omega(\mu n^k \log n)$ and $\tau n^{k-1} = \Omega(\mu^3 n^{k-1})$. From now on we will remain in the same setting as static pure ageing since as proven by Jansen and Zarges [11] there is a high probability of reaching the optimum without the best individual ever reaching age τ in a time that is dominated by the time to enter the path to the global optimum. □

4. BALANCE ANALYSIS

For the BALANCE function the (μ+1) EA has been shown to be inefficient for sublinear population sizes (i.e., $\mu \leq n^{1/2-\epsilon}$ for any constant $0 < \epsilon < 1/2$) if the frequency of change is small and when the function is static. For larger population sizes the algorithm solves the problem independent of the frequency of change [17]. In this section we show that static pure ageing does not help when the (μ+1) EA is inefficient, while stochastic ageing operators are efficient.

We believe that stochastic pure ageing is efficient on BALANCE for small (i. e., constant) population sizes as well, and that this can be proven with the analytical framework developed in Section 3.1. However, due to space restrictions, we leave this for future work and concentrate on showing that hybrid pure ageing works for any value of μ (i. e., $\mu \leq n^{1/2-\epsilon}$) for which the ($\mu$+1) EA with and without static pure ageing provably fail.

4.1 Static Pure Ageing Does Not Work

The following theorem shows that the (μ+1) EA with static pure ageing fails for any value of τ. If τ is not large enough to allow the individuals to improve their fitness before reaching age τ, then no local optimum will be found at all. For larger values of τ it is shown that with overwhelming (w. o. p.). the trap is reached before the global optimum. Consequently, when the individuals are eventually restarted they end up in the trap all over again w. o. p.

THEOREM 8. *Let $\varphi > 38\mu n^{3/2}$ and $\mu \leq n^{1/2-\epsilon}$. Then the ($\mu$+1) EA with static pure ageing requires at least $2^{\Omega(\sqrt{n})}$ generations to optimise* BALANCE *w. o. p. for every value τ.*

Proof. W. l. o. g. we assume the time phase is such that ONEMAX has to be optimised in the suffix. According to Theorem 1 by Oliveto and Zarges [17] the whole population of the (μ+1) EA converges to the trap in $38\mu n^{3/2}$ generations with probability at least $1 - 2^{-\sqrt{n}}$. Using similar reasoning to the proof of Witt [20] and that $\mu \leq n^{1/2-\epsilon}$, $m := n/4$ leading ones in the prefix are optimised in less than cm^2 generations with probability less than $2^{-\Omega(m)} = 2^{-\Omega(n)}$. So with probability $1 - 2^{-\Omega(n)} - 2^{-\sqrt{n}}$ the whole population reaches the trap before optimising $m := n/4 - \sqrt{n}$ leading ones. Given that the probability to find a better point is $n^{-\Omega(\sqrt{n})}$, the individuals will die when they reach age $\tau + 1$ and new random individuals will be generated. With the same calculations as above these new individuals will also end up in the trap with overwhelming probability (w. o. p.) unless the function changes to ZEROMAX due to the ending of an interval φ. In this case all the individuals outside the trap will optimise ZEROMAX w. o. p. in another $38\mu n^{3/2}$ generations before optimising the remaining $m' := n/4 - \sqrt{n}$ leading ones in the prefix. Since $\varphi > 38\mu n^{3/2}$ at most one function change may happen before each individual reaches the trap after it is re-initialised and since for large enough n, $2 \cdot 38 n^{2-\epsilon} < cm^2 = c(n/4)^2$, the proof is completed. □

4.2 Hybrid Pure Ageing Works

For the sake of simplicity we analyse a (μ+1) RLS (randomised local search) equipped with hybrid pure ageing rather than the standard (μ+1) EA. This allows us to prove that the ageing mechanism is useful in a more simple setting. To this end, we adapt Lemma 1 of Oliveto and Zarges [17] for the (μ+1) EA to the (μ+1) RLS. The proof follows the same calculations up to constant factors.

LEMMA 9. *Let $\mu \leq n^{1/2-\epsilon}$. If the global optimum is not found first, in expected time less than $6\mu n$ iterations all individuals of the (μ+1) RLS on* BALANCE *have a suffix b with $|b|_1 < n/16$ or $|b|_1 > 7n/16$ (i.e., all are in the trap).*

Now we can prove the main result of the subsection.

THEOREM 10. *Let $\mu \leq n^{1/2-\epsilon}$, $\tau > c\mu n \ln n$ and c a large enough constant. Then the expected time for the (μ+1) RLS with hybrid pure ageing to optimise the* BALANCE *function is $O(\mu^2 n^3)$ for any frequency of change $\varphi > 0$.*

Proof. We pessimistically assume the trap is found before the global optimum by all individuals. By Lemma 9 they all converge to the trap in expected time $O(\mu n)$. Once in the trap we calculate the time for the algorithm to reach the maximum number of trap leading ones (i.e., $m := n/2 - \sqrt{n}$). This requires $O(n^2)$ steps by adapting Witt's proof for the (μ+1) EA for Leading Ones [20] to the RLS version by considering that if $i < \mu$ individuals with j leading ones are in the population, then another individual with j leading ones is created with probability at least $i/(2\mu)$ by selecting one of the i individuals and flipping any of the $n/2$ suffix bits. Once an individual with m leading ones is created it will never be removed by selection because no other trap point has higher fitness and the RLS cannot escape the trap by making 1-bit flips. After expected time $O(\mu \log \mu)$ all individuals will have the same number of leading ones by similar arguments as above (i.e., the probability of creating a "copy" of a current best individual is $i/(2\mu)$ if there are i individuals with m leading ones). Now we apply Lemma 5 (adapting it to the RLS version by replacing constant factors in the proof) to show that in expected $c'\mu^3 < \tau$ generations all the individuals have the same age.

Now we need to show that with constant probability when the individuals reach age $\tau + 1$ there will be at least one individual with exactly $n/16+1$ zeroes (i.e., it will escape the trap if it flips a 1-bit of the suffix and survives the restart). Recall that in the trap all the points with the same number of leading ones have the same fitness. Hence there is a drift towards the border of the trap at $n/16$ suffix 1-bits. By standard drift analysis [8] we get an expected drift of

$$E(\Delta) > \frac{(7/16)n}{n} - \frac{n/16}{n} = \frac{6}{16}$$

and an expected time of $E[T] \leq \frac{n/16}{6/16} = n/6 = O(n)$ steps to reach the border of the trap. The expected return time to the border for one individual is:

$$E(\text{ReturnTime}) \leq \frac{15}{16} \cdot 1 + \frac{1}{16}\left(1 + \frac{16}{6}\right) = 7/6$$

because with probability 15/16 the border is not left and with probability $(n/16)/n = 1/16$ another suffix 1-bit is flipped. In the latter case the return time is the 1 step in which the border has been left plus 16/6 expected steps to return achieved by drift analysis again. Finally, the probability the individual is on the border at any time step (including generation $\tau + 1$) is greater than $1/E(\text{ReturnTime}) = 6/7$. This holds for a population of only one individual. Given the drift towards the border, the probabilities of at least one individual being at the border at any generation can only be higher with greater population sizes.

By Lemma 6 the probability that at generation $\tau + 1$ we get a complete restart apart from the offspring surviving is $1/(2e\mu)$ and the probability that the offspring is outside the trap is $(n/16)/n \cdot 6/7 = 3/56$. In the next generation the survivor is selected for reproduction and increases its number of leading ones with probability $1/(\mu n)$. Overall, the expected number of restarts before we get exactly one survivor outside the trap is $(56/3) \cdot (2e\mu) \cdot (\mu n) = O(\mu^2 n)$ and since we require $O(\mu n + n^2 + \mu \log \mu + \mu^3 + \tau)$ generations for a restart to happen by pessimistically assuming we always achieve genuine restarts the trap is escaped after expected $O(\mu^2 n \cdot n^2) = O(\mu^2 n^3)$ generations. The other $\mu - 1$ individuals that have been initialised again would require expected time $\Omega(\mu n)$ to reach the trap while in expected $O(\mu \log \mu)$ generations they will have been taken over by the survivor. Finally, the survivor will reach the global optimum in expected time $O(n\sqrt{n})$ by optimising the remaining $\sqrt{n} - 1$ leading ones by considering once again that it can create "copies" of the individual with most leading ones with constant probability by flipping a bit in the suffix and that points with more than $(7/16)n$ ones or $(7/16)n$ zeroes in the suffix will be rejected due to their 0 fitness.

Now, there is a chance that the best individual might die on its way to the global optimum, if it does not manage to continually find improvements before τ generations. The probability the current best is selected and increases its leading ones value is at least $1/(\mu n)$. Hence, the probability it doesn't improve is at most $1 - 1/(\mu n)$ and the probability it doesn't improve in τ generations is at most $(1 - 1/(\mu n))^{c\mu n \ln n} \leq e^{-c \ln n} = n^{-c}$. By the union bound, with high probability all required improvements are achieved before the current best individual reaches age τ. □

5. CONCLUSION

An analytical framework for the analysis of the standard stochastic pure ageing operator has been introduced. More specifically Lemmas 2 and 3 are independent of the fitness function and we predict they will be useful in other settings. We rigorously show that stochastic pure ageing is efficient for not too large populations and give theoretical guidance for the optimal settings for parameter p_{die}. However, if the population size is large (i.e., $\mu \geq n^{\epsilon}$), our analysis indicates that, independent of the value of the parameter, the operator is inefficient. To this end we present a hybrid pure ageing operator that allows for the same effective performance independent of the population size and we rigorously prove this for two example functions from the literature. Interestingly, the parameter setting for efficient hybrid pure ageing is at opposite sides of the spectrum compared to that of stochastic pure ageing. While the latter operator requires a "high" probability of surviving (i.e. p_{live} close to 1) the former requires a "low" survival probability (i.e. $p_{\text{live}} = \Theta(1/\mu)$).

Acknowledgment: The research leading to these results has received funding from the European Union Seventh Framework Programme (FP7/2007-2013) under grant agreement no 618091 (SAGE).

6. REFERENCES

[1] F. M. Burnet. *The Clonal Selection Theory of Acquired Immunity.* Cambridge University Press, 1959.

[2] V. Cutello, G. Nicosia, and M. Pavone. A hybrid immune algorithm with information gain for the graph coloring problem. In *Proc. of GECCO 2003*, pages 171–182, 2003.

[3] V. Cutello, G. Nicosia, and M. Pavone. An immune algorithm with stochastic aging and kullback entropy for the chromatic number problem. *Journal of Combinatorial Optimization*, 14:9–33, 2007.

[4] V. Cutello, G. Nicosia, M. Pavone, and J. Timmis. An immune algorithm for protein structure prediction on lattice models. *IEEE Transactions on Evolutionary Computation*, 11(1):101–117, 2007.

[5] V. Cutello, G. Nicosia, M. Romeo, and P. S. Oliveto. On the convergence of immune algorithms. In *Proc. of FOCI 2007*, pages 409–415, 2007.

[6] L. de Castro and J. Timmis. *Artificial Immune Systems: A New Computational Intelligence Approach.* Springer, 2002.

[7] L. de Castro and F. Zuben. Learning and optimization using the clonal selection principle. *IEEE Transactions on Evolutionary Computation*, 6(3):239–251, 2002.

[8] J. He and X. Yao. Drift analysis and average time complexity of evolutionary algorithms. *Artificial Intelligence*, 127(1):57–85, 2001.

[9] C. Horoba, T. Jansen, and C. Zarges. Maximal age in randomized search heuristics with aging. In *Proc. of GECCO 2009*, pages 803–810, 2009.

[10] T. Jansen, P. S. Oliveto, and C. Zarges. On the analysis of the immune-inspired B-Cell Algorithm for the vertex cover problem. In *Proc. of ICARIS 2011*, LNCS 6825, pages 117–131. Springer, 2011.

[11] T. Jansen and C. Zarges. Analyzing different variants of immune inspired somatic contiguous hypermutations. *Theoretical Computer Science*, 412(6):517–533, 2011.

[12] T. Jansen and C. Zarges. On the role of age diversity for effective aging operators. *Evolutionary Intelligence*, 4(2):99–125, 2011.

[13] T. Jansen and C. Zarges. Variation in artificial immune systems: Hypermutations with mutation potential. In *Proc. of ICARIS*, pages 132–145, 2011.

[14] T. Jansen and C. Zarges. Computing longest common subsequences with the B-Cell Algorithm. In *Proc. of ICARIS 2012*, LNCS 7597, pages 111–124, 2012.

[15] J. Kelsey and J. Timmis. Immune inspired somatic contiguous hypermutation for function optimisation. In *Proc. of GECCO 2003*, pages 207–218, 2003.

[16] P. S. Oliveto and C. Zarges. Analysis of diversity mechanisms for optimisation in dynamic environments with low frequencies of change. In *Proc. of GECCO 2013*, pages 837–844. ACM Press, 2013.

[17] P. S. Oliveto and C. Zarges. Analysis of diversity mechanisms for optimisation in dynamic environments with low frequencies of change. Technical report, 2013. URL: http://staffwww.dcs.shef.ac.uk/people/P.Oliveto/papers/DynamicTechRep.pdf.

[18] P. Rohlfshagen, P. K. Lehre, and X. Yao. Dynamic evolutionary optimisation: an analysis of frequency and magnitude of change. In *Proc. of GECCO '09*, pages 1713–1720. ACM Press, 2009.

[19] H. Schwefel and G. Rudolph. Contemporary evolution strategies. In *Proc. of ECAL*, pages 893–907, 1995.

[20] C. Witt. Runtime analysis of the (μ+1) EA on simple pseudo-Boolean functions. *Evolutionary Computation*, 14(1):65–86, 2006.

[21] C. Zarges. Rigorous runtime analysis of inversely fitness proportional mutation rates. In *Proc. of PPSN X*, LNCS 5199, pages 112–122. Springer, 2008.

[22] C. Zarges. On the utility of the population size for inversely fitness proportional mutation rates. In *Proc. of FOGA 2009*, pages 39–46. ACM Press, 2009.

An Improved Immune Inspired Hyper-Heuristic for Combinatorial Optimisation Problems

Kevin Sim
Institute for Informatics and Digital Innovation
Edinburgh Napier University
Edinburgh, Scotland, UK
k.sim@napier.ac.uk

Emma Hart
Institute for Informatics and Digital Innovation
Edinburgh Napier University
Edinburgh, Scotland, UK
e.hart@napier.ac.uk

ABSTRACT

The *meta-dynamics* of an immune-inspired optimisation system NELLI are considered. NELLI has previously shown to exhibit good performance when applied to a large set of optimisation problems by sustaining a network of novel heuristics. We address the mechanisms by which new heuristics are defined and subsequently generated. A new representation is defined, and a mutation-based operator inspired by clonal-selection introduced to control the balance between exploration and exploitation in the generation of new network elements. Experiments show significantly improved performance over the existing system in the bin-packing domain. New experiments in the job-scheduling domain further show the generality of the approach.

Categories and Subject Descriptors

Computing Methodologies [**Artificial Intelligence**]: Problem Solving, Control Methods and Search

Keywords

Hyper-heuristics; Artificial Immune Systems

1. INTRODUCTION

The previous two decades have seen significant advances in meta-heuristic optimisation techniques that are able to quickly find optimal or near-optimal solutions to problem instances in many combinatorial optimisation domains. Hyper-heuristic approaches to optimisation have attempted to raise the generality of approaches by focusing on techniques that work well across large sets of problems, often using simple deterministic heuristics in combination to provide rapid solutions to problems. Although this inevitably results in some loss of performance when compared to search algorithms that are specifically designed and tuned on particular problem sets, some trade-off between quality and speed is considered acceptable to practitioners in the real-world. In an article analysing the mismatch between the efforts of researchers who make substantial contribution to the field of evolutionary computation and the number of real-world applications ([15]), it is suggested that the typical tendency in academia to focus on finding global optima is in some sense misguided, noting first that in business, the concept of a global optima is different than in academia, secondly that decision makers have seconds to react rather than spending significant time in searching for optima, and thirdly, robust quality solutions are preferable as the environment is likely to change.

GECCO'14, July 12–16, Vancouver, BC, Canada.
Copyright 2014 ACM 978-1-4503-2662-9/14/07 ...$15.00.
http://dx.doi.org/10.1145/2576768.2598241.

In [17, 19], the authors attempted to address these points in developing a hyper-heuristic system that *generalised* over large sets of problem instances, exhibited *memory* so that it could rapidly find solutions to new instances that were similar to those solved in the past, and *adapted* over time. The core of this system, dubbed NELLI (Network for Life Long Learning), was inspired by processes apparent in the natural immune system, recognising the mapping between the required properties of *memory, generalisation adaptation* and the characteristic properties of the immune system.

One the key elements of NELLI is a *meta-dynamic* process that generates a continuous steam of novel heuristics using a tree-based representation, which then self-organise into a self-sustaining network of heuristics that efficiently cover the problem space. Although [19] demonstrated successful results on bin-packing problems, analysis of the generated heuristics showed they rarely exploited problem characteristics such as bin capacity and free space, effectively resulting in a sequence of nodes that caused items to be packed. In recognition of this, we propose a more efficient representation, and then introduce new meta-dynamic processes to provide a better balance between exploration and exploitation of the heuristic space that combine clonal selection with heuristic generation.

A brief coverage of the background to this paper is provided before NELLI is described in detail. We then provide details of the novel components introduced, providing results that show a significant improvement over the previous system on the bin-packing corpus. Additionally, we provide new results in the domain of Job Shop Scheduling where a diverse set problem instances are tackled, showing the generality of the approach.

2. RELATED WORK

Although many mechanisms have been proposed to explain immune function, of most relevance to this work is the idiotypic network model proposed by [13] as a possible mechanism for explaining long-term memory. Challenging existing thinking at the time, Jerne proposed that antibodies produced by the immune system interact with each other to form a self-sustaining network of collaborating cells, that collectively embodies a memory of previous responses. [3] proposed that the engineering community might benefit from developing algorithms inspired by double plasticity of the network view of the immune system: *parametric* plasticity provides an adaptive mechanism that adjusts parameters while executing a task to improve performance while *structural* plasticity enables new elements to be incorporated into network and elements to be removed, thereby enabling the network to adapt to a time-varying environment.

Idiotypic network theory has been translated into a number of computational algorithms within the Artificial Immune System (AIS) field in machine-learning, optimisation and engineering domains (see [21] for an overview). However, very few of these applications really address problems in the kind of complex, dynamic environments envisaged by [3]. [16] describe a system based on an idiotypic network for tracking evolving clusters in noisy data-streams, finding it to be both capable of learning and scalable. However, the majority of relevant work evolving learning and/or memory is found in the robotics domain [23]. Within optimisation, [9] considers problems whose fitness function changes over time, but not scenarios in which the fitness function remains static but the characteristics of the problems themselves change.

In the hyper-heuristic domain, there are many examples of systems that either *generate* novel heuristics or *select* from a set of pre-defined heuristics to solve a problem and are shown to be capable of good performance across large problem sets, see [4] for a recent and comprehensive overview. However there is little work that *combines* these approaches (see the authors work in [17, 19] for an exception). Furthermore, we are unaware of any work other than our previously published work on NELLI [17, 19] that combines hyper-heuristics with AIS in an optimisation system that learns and adapts over time.

3. APPLICATION DOMAINS

Two application domains are utilised, noting that scheduling and packing problems are amongst the most widely addressed in the hyper-heuristic literature, e.g. [20] and [5] describe recent generative hyper-heuristics for each of these domains respectively.

The objective of the Bin-Packing Problem (BPP) is to find a packing which minimises the number of containers, b, of fixed capacity c required to accommodate a set of n items with weights $\omega_j : j \in \{1 \ldots n\}$ falling in the range $1 \leq \omega_j \leq c, \omega_j \in \mathbb{Z}$, while enforcing the constraint that the sum of weights in any bin does not exceed the bin capacity c.

The Job Shop Scheduling Problem (JSSP) requires that J jobs have to be processed on each of M machines in a predefined order that can vary for each job. Each of the M operations making up job j has to be processed on a specified machine m and is denoted by (j_i, m_i). Each operation has a corresponding processing time of p_{jm}. The objective is to minimise the total makespan; the time between starting the first operation and completing the last operation across all machines.

The reader is referred to [4] for a detailed overview of hyper-heuristics within these application domains.

4. NELLI

Introduced in [17] and described in detail in [19], NELLI comprises of three main parts: a stream of problem in-

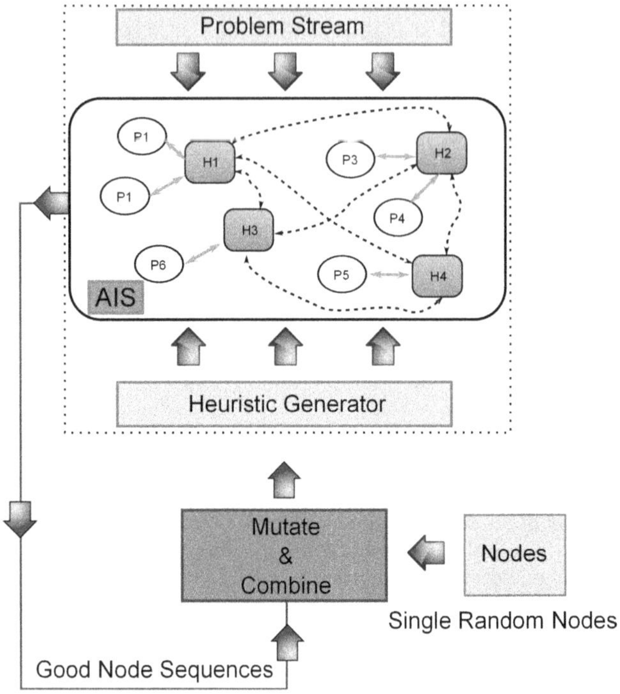

Figure 1: A conceptual view of the system: Problems and heuristics are continuously injected into the AIS. The dynamics and meta-dynamics of the system result in a self-sustaining network of heuristics and problems. Heuristics and problems that receive no stimulation are removed. Solid lines show *direct* interactions between components, dashed lines represent *indirect* interactions. The original system is shown surrounded by a dotted line. The heuristic generator now allows for new heuristics to be created randomly, as before, or by mutating or concatenating heuristic sequences already sustained by the system.

stances, a continuously generated stream of novel heuristics and a network that sustains co-stimulating components (heuristics and problem instances). Illustrated in Figure 1, NELLI is designed to run continuously; problem instances and heuristics can be added in any quantity at any point. The AIS is responsible for governing the dynamic processes that enable heuristics and problem instances to be incorporated (stimulated) or rejected (suppressed) by the network.

The three components of the original system are illustrated in Figure 1 surrounded by a dotted line. The components outside this boundary represent the improvements to the system which are detailed in subsequent sections.

The dynamics of the system are visualised in Figure 2 In this diagram, the Figure (a) shows a set of problems that have entered the system. In Figure (b) 4 heuristics are added; problems are allocated to the heuristic that solves them best. The problems denoted $P1$ and $P2$ are encompassed by two heuristics, signifying that the heuristics each produce an equal quality solution to those problem instances. H2 is clearly subsumed by H1 and H3.

As a result of applying the network dynamics, the situation in (c) results; H2 is removed as it does not add to the collective ability of the set of heuristics. Problems P1 and P2 are removed as the best found solutions to these prob-

$$h_{stim} = \sum_{p \in \mathcal{P}} \delta_{bins} \begin{cases} \delta_{bins} = \min(bins_{\mathcal{H}'_p}) - bins_{h_p} & : \text{ if } \min(bins_{\mathcal{H}'_p}) - bins_{h_p} > 0 \\ \delta_{bins} = 0 & : \text{ otherwise} \end{cases} \tag{1}$$

$$p_{stim} = \sum_{h \in \mathcal{H}} \delta_{bins} \begin{cases} \delta_{bins} = \min(bins_{\mathcal{H}'_p})) - bins_{h_p} & : \text{ if } \min(bins_{\mathcal{H}'_p}) - bins_{h_p} > 0 \\ \delta_{bins} = 0 & : \text{ otherwise} \end{cases} \tag{2}$$

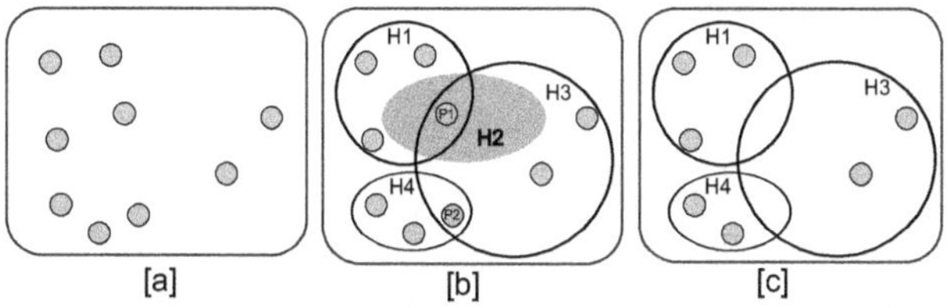

Figure 2: Diagram [a] shows the problems that the system is currently exposed to $\mathcal{E}$. The middle diagram [b] shows a set of generated heuristics that cover the problems in $\mathcal{E}$. The problems $P1$ and $P2$ shown are equally solved by one or more heuristics and therefore not required to map the problem space. The shaded heuristic is redundant as it does not have a niche. The right-hand diagram [c] shows the resulting *network* $\mathcal{N}$ that sustains the minimal set of problems and heuristics required to describe the space.

lem instances are implicitly retained by heuristics H3 and H4 that best solve them.

The central AIS network component of NELLI remains faithful to the original implementation and is described by Algorithm 1 where[1]:

- $\mathcal{U}$ - the complete set of 1370 problem instances.
- $\mathcal{E}$ - the current environment, i.e. the set of problems we are currently interested in solving, i.e. $\mathcal{E} \subset \mathcal{U}$
- $\mathcal{E}^*$ - the set of *all* problems to which the system has been exposed during its lifetime
- $\mathcal{N}$ - the immune network, comprised of a set of problems and a set of heuristics
- $\mathcal{P}$ - the set of *problems* currently sustained in the immune network $\mathcal{N}$, i.e. $\mathcal{P} \subset \mathcal{E}^*$
- $\mathcal{H}$ - the set of *heuristics* currently sustained in the immune network $\mathcal{N}$

NELLI captures the three essential concepts of an immune network as proposed by [22] – structure, dynamics, and meta-dynamics. The term *structure* refers to the interactions between components of the network, in this case, problems and heuristics as described by steps 5 and 6 of Algorithm 1 and Equations 1 and 2. *Dynamics* refers to the variations in time of the concentration and affinities between components of the network, and crucially, describes how the network adapts to itself and the environment (steps 7-9 in Algorithm 1). Finally, the network *metadynamics* refers to a unique property of the immune system, that is the ability to continuously produce and recruit novel components, in this case, heuristics and problems.

[1]The parameter values used in Algorithm 1 are described later in Section 7

Algorithm 1 NELLI Pseudo Code

Require: $\mathcal{H} = \emptyset$:The set of heuristics
Require: $\mathcal{P} = \emptyset$:The set of current problems
Require: $\mathcal{E} = \mathcal{E}_{t=0}$:The set of problems to be solved at time t

1: **repeat**
2: *optionally* replace $\mathcal{E}$: $\mathcal{E}^* \leftarrow \mathcal{E}^* \cup \mathcal{E}$
3: Add n_h randomly generated heuristics to $\mathcal{H}$ with concentration c_{init}
4: Add n_p randomly selected problem instances from $\mathcal{E}$ to $\mathcal{P}$ with concentration c_{init}
5: calculate $h_{stim} \forall h \in \mathcal{H}$ using Equation 1
6: calculate $p_{stim} \forall p \in \mathcal{P}$ using Equation 2
7: increment all concentrations (both $\mathcal{H}$ and $\mathcal{P}$) that have concentration $< c_{max}$ and stimulation > 0 by Δ_c
8: decrement all concentrations (both $\mathcal{H}$ and $\mathcal{P}$) with stimulation ≤ 0 by Δ_c
9: Remove heuristics and problems with *concentration* ≤ 0
10: **until** *stopping criteria met*

The network $\mathcal{N}$ sustains a set of interacting heuristics and problems. Problems are *directly* stimulated by heuristics, and vice versa. Heuristics are *indirectly* stimulated by other heuristics.

A heuristic h can be stimulated by one or more problems. The total stimulation of a heuristic is the sum of its affinity with each problem in the set $\mathcal{P}$ currently in the network $\mathcal{N}$. A heuristic h has a non-zero affinity with a problem $p \in \mathcal{P}$ *if and only if* it provides a solution that uses fewer bins than any other heuristic currently in $\mathcal{H}$. If this is the case, then the value of the affinity $p \leftrightarrow h$ is equal to the improvement in the number of bins used by h compared to the next-best heuristic. If a heuristic provides the best solution for a problem p but one or more other heuristics give an equal result, then the affinity between problem p and the heuristic h is zero. If a heuristic h uses more bins than another heuristic on the problem, then the affinity between problem p and the heuristic h is also zero.

Although the implemented dynamics are simplified with respect to much research in AIS that relies on equations defined by [7], the system is shown in [17, 19] to provide heuristics that efficiently cover the problem and collectively minimise the total number of bins used to solve all problems the network is exposed to. A heuristic only survives if it is able to solve at least one problem better than any other heuristic in the system. This provides competition between heuristics which forces a heuristic to find an individual niche to ensure survival. Thus, although no quantitative value is calculated for heuristic$\leftrightarrow$heuristic interactions there is an *indirect* interaction arising from the method of calculating the problem$\leftrightarrow$heuristic interactions.

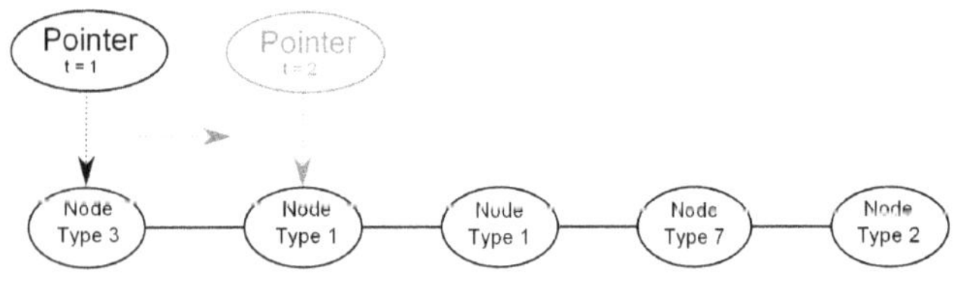

Figure 3: Heuristics are represented as linear sequences of nodes. A pointer keeps track of which node to apply next. The sequence restarts from the beginning after the last node is processed.

5. NOVEL IMPROVEMENTS TO NELLI

This section introduces the improvements made to both the representation used and the processes employed to generate a novel stream of heuristics for incorporation into NELLI.

5.1 Representation

A key feature of NELLI is the ability to generate a constant stream of novel heuristics. In [17, 19], heuristics were defined using a tree representation borrowed from Single Node Genetic Programming (SNGP) [12]. Trees were randomly constructed from a set of terminal nodes that encapsulated information about the problem (e.g. in the bin-packing domain, the free space in the bin and item size) and simple function nodes. In this paper we replace this tree representation with a linear sequence of heuristic-components, in which all nodes explicitly cause items to be placed into the solution. Each component, or node, constructs part of a solution, e.g. placing items in a bin in the bin-packing domain, or scheduling an operation in a scheduling domain.

Figure 3 shows a generic example showing a string of five heuristic components with a "pointer" used by an encompassing *wrapper* to indicate the current component position. For each problem instance the general concept for any problem domain is to apply each node in sequence until all objects are placed into the solution. When the pointer reaches the end of the string it is simply returned to the beginning. A wrapper — specific to the problem domain — controls the application of heuristics, testing whether the application of a heuristic was successful and specifying when to move to the next heuristic in the list.

The specific wrappers and set of heuristic components used in the BPP and JSSP domains are described in sections 6.1 and 6.2 respectively.

5.2 Heuristic Generation

Many AIS-based optimisation algorithm employ some form of clonal selection [6] in order to perform exploitation of the search space. Typically, new solutions are generated in numbers proportional to, and with a mutation rate in inverse proportion to the quality of the incumbent. The version of NELLI described in [17, 19] performed only exploration in continuously generating novel heuristics. To balance this, we introduce a simplified clonal selection approach that achieves exploitation but without incurring the overhead that would result from generating and applying a large numbers of cloned heuristics to large sets of problem instances.

A number of mutation operators are used in order to better guide the search for new heuristics towards promising areas of the landscape while maintaining an element of diversity and exploration by still injecting a smaller number of randomly generated heuristics. The dynamics of the system already favours good sequences of nodes, meaning that the number of "good node sequences" retained by the system should be significantly higher than bad combinations. Thus, new heuristics are created by either mutating or concatenating existing sequences currently sustained in the network. Randomly generated heuristics are also injected into the system to maintain an element of diversity and continual exploration of the changing search space. A number of mutation operators are used:

- Select a random heuristic from the network and swap the position of two random nodes.
- Select a random heuristic from the network and replace a random node with a new node selected randomly.
- Select a random heuristic from the network and remove a random node.
- Select a random heuristic from the network and add a random node at a randomly selected position.
- Select two random heuristics from the network and concatenate their nodes to generate a new heuristic.

6. HEURISTICS AND WRAPPERS

The wrappers and nodes specific to the BPP and JSSP are described in the following sections.

6.1 Bin-Packing

The nodes used are given in table 1 and include only nodes that cause items from the problem to be placed into a solution omitting the function nodes and terminal nodes that encapsulated information about the problem state used in the previous system. A key aspect of the improvements achieved in the bin-packing domain is the way that a sequence of nodes is applied and is described by Algorithm 2.

Algorithm 2 Bin-Packing Problem Wrapper

Require: $I \in \{i_1, i_2, ..., i_n\}$ {The set of items to be packed}
Require: $B = \emptyset$ {The set of bins which is initially empty}
Require: $N = (n_1 \dots n_j)$ {The sequence of nodes}
Require: $p = 1$ {At the start set the pointer to the first node}
repeat
  add a new bin b to B
  repeat
    $I' = I$
    $result = evaluate(n_p)$ {This may cause items from I to be packed into the current bin b}
    $p = p + 1$
    if $p > j$ **then**
      $p = 1$
    end if
  until $result < 0$ **or** $I = \emptyset$ **or** $I = I'$
  if $I = I'$ **and** $I \neq \emptyset$ **then**
    pack each remaining item in a new bin
  end if
until $I = \emptyset$

Unlike the previous application to the BPP the heuristic applied to pack each bin is not identical. If a node is successful in packing one or more items into a bin, then the pointer is advanced to the next node and the process continues with the current bin — when a node fails, a new bin is opened, the current one is closed and the pointer advances to the next node. The pointer is reset to the start after the evaluation of the last node in the sequence. This results in a different sequence of nodes being applied for each bin increasing the potential utility of the heuristic.

Table 1: BPP Nodes

B1	Packs the single largest item into the current bin returning 1 if successful or -1 otherwise
B2	Packs the largest combination of exactly 2 items into the current bin returning 1 if successful or -1 otherwise
B3	Works as for B2 but packs exactly 3 items
B4	Works as for B2 but packs exactly 4 items
B5	Works as for B2 but packs exactly 5 items
B2A	Packs the largest combination of up to 2 items into the current bin giving preference to sets of lower cardinality. Returns 1 if successful or -1 otherwise
B3A	As for B2A but considers sets of up to 3 items
B4A	As for B2A but considers sets of up to 4 items
B5A	As for B2A but considers sets of up to 5 items

6.2 JSSP

The component heuristics used in the linear sequence for JSSP are defined as follows:

Table 2: Scheduling Rules

Pseudonym	Packs an operation:
FCFS	Earliest in its job queue
LMT	Longest machine processing time so far
LORPT	Longest remaining job time including the operation
LOS	Longest remaining job time not including the operation
LOT	Longest operation time
LPT	Logest job duration
LRPT	Longest remaining job time not including the operation
RAND	At random
SMT	Shortest machine processing time so far
SORPT	shortest remaining job processing time including the operation
SOT	Shortest operation processing time
SPT	Shortest job processing time
SRPT	Shortest remaining job processing time not including the operation

Each of the thirteen rules described in Table 2 can be combined with one of three choices of conflict set described below which is used to determine which operation(s) should be scheduled next:

- **Conflict Set A** Based on Giffler and Thompson's pioneering work[10] gets the operation(s) that can be completed the earliest and selects the machine(s) that those operations are to be processed on. The set of operations returned includes all available operations waiting to be processed on those machines.
- **Constraint Set B** The set of all available waiting operations.
- **Constraint Set C** From [11] returns the subset of available operations that can be started the earliest.

As before, a wrapper advances a pointer through the sequence of nodes starting at the beginning an applying each in turn. Applying each heuristic schedules exactly one operation onto a machine at the earliest possible time. The dispatching rules themselves may return more than one possible operation — in this case one of these is selected randomly and returned to the wrapper to be scheduled.

7. EXPERIMENTS

NELLI as defined by Algorithm 1 requires a number of parameters to be set. The default parameters are detailed in Table 3 and justified in [17]. When applied to the BPP, NELLI was executed using the default parameters settings. On the JSSP the number of problems added each iteration, n_p, was reduced from 30 to 10 to take account of the reduced size of the problem set.

Parameter	Description	Value
n_p	number of problems added each iteration	30
n_h	number of heuristics added each iteration	1
c_{init}	initial concentration of heuristics/problems	200
Δ_c	variation in concentration based on stimulation	50
c_{max}	maximum concentration level	1000

Table 3: Default parameter settings for experiments

Two new parameters are introduced. The first, $prob_{mut}$, defines the probability that a new heuristic will be generated by mutating an existing heuristic with the remainder generated randomly. The second parameter, max_{len}, determines the maximum length that a randomly generated sequence of nodes can have (randomly selected between $[1 \ldots max_{len}]$). If mutation is applied to generate a new heuristic then the operator chosen is selected with equal probability. The maximum length of new heuristics generated by mutation is not fixed. The length of the sequence has no affect on the heuristics computational complexity. Nodes are simply evaluated cyclically until all items are placed into a solution.

The experiments conducted were designed to first test the utility of the representation and second the merit of using mutation to exploit good sequences and improve the speed of convergence. The results on the BPP are contrasted against those achieved using the original implementation with those obtained on the JSSP compared to the results obtained by applying the individual rules in isolation. Comparison to other hyper-heuristic approches is difficult as other authors have not used the same large data-set or have applied hyper-heuristics to generate individual heuristics for each problem to be solved. For example, [5] obtain excellent results on a subset of 90 of the problem instances we used, but evolve an individual heuristic per problem instance using 50000 evaluations each time. [18] learn a procedure to solve large sets of problems but test on a subset of 890 of the problems we use — previous results described in [19] showed that NELLI outpeformed this system. Comparison to state-of-the-art search methods designed to find global optima is not relevant for reasons outlined in section 1. Experiments were conducted on both problem domains using a range of different values of $prob_{mut}$ and max_{len}.

7.1 Bin-Packing Results

For the BPP, 1370 problems instances were used to test the system allowing a comparison to the original implementation where these instances are defined in detail [17, 19]. Results obtained here on the BPP are denoted NELLI* to distinguish them from those obtained previously, denoted for this section as NELLI.

Table 4 gives the results obtained by the best combination of the $prob_{mut}$ and max_{len} parameters. Figure 4 summarises the results obtained using each of the 20 different parameter settings. Each box in the plot shows the result of running NELLI* 30 times with each run terminated after 5000 iterations.

The table clearly highlights the benefit of the approach used by NELLI* in comparison to NELLI, both in terms of the number of problems solved optimally and in the total number of extra bins used across all problems; the number of extra bins is reduced from 308 to 171 and there is an increase in problems solved optimally from 82% to 88.2%. The graph shows the impact of the parameter settings, with a clear trend in improvement shown as the mutation rate is increased, resulting in more exploitation of existing heuristics. Note that even experiments in which the mutation rate was set to zero outperform the previous version of NELLI, indicating the superiority of the newly introduced representation over the previously used tree-structures.

The table shows a trade-off emerging between the number of heuristics sustained and the overall quality — the new exploitation process generates and sustains *additional* heuristics that fill *gaps* in the problem space. An additional experiment limited the maximum number of heuristics allowed in NELLI* to 6 to mimic NELLI — even with this constraint an increase in performance was obtained, of 281 bins over optimal.

Figure 5 expands 5 of the 20 plots (those denoted $010_{0.00} \rightarrow 010_{0.99}$) from Figure 4 plotting them against the results achieved previously using NELLI. It is apparent that NELLI* reacts just as rapidly as NELLI achieving comparable results within the first few iterations but that NELLI* continues to improve if given sufficient time to do so. It is also clear from Figure 5 that increasing the value of $prob_{mut}$ correlates to a more rapid response highlighting the benefit of a more directed search when compared to NELLI and results obtained using NELLI* with $prob_{mut} = 0$. This is reinforced by Figure 4 which highlights an increase in average solution quality with an increase in the probability of generating new heuristics using mutation.

Table 4: Extra bins (δ) required by NELLI* compared NELLI and the best known solutions from the literature on the complete set of 1370 benchmark problem instances

	Number of Problems Solved Requiring δ Extra Bins					
	$\delta = 0$	$\delta = 1$	$\delta = 2$	$\delta = 3$	$\delta = 4$	$\delta = 5$
NELLI	1126	202	26	12	2	2
NELLI*	1209	152	8	1	0	0

	Number Heuristics	Number Extra Bins
NELLI	6	308
NELLI*	39	171

Experiments were also conducted where the *concatenation* and *addition* mutation operators were removed from the system resulting in heuristics that never exceeded their initial length. These results are omitted due to space considerations but highlighted that utility of the concatenation operator in terms of both speed of convergence and final solution quality.

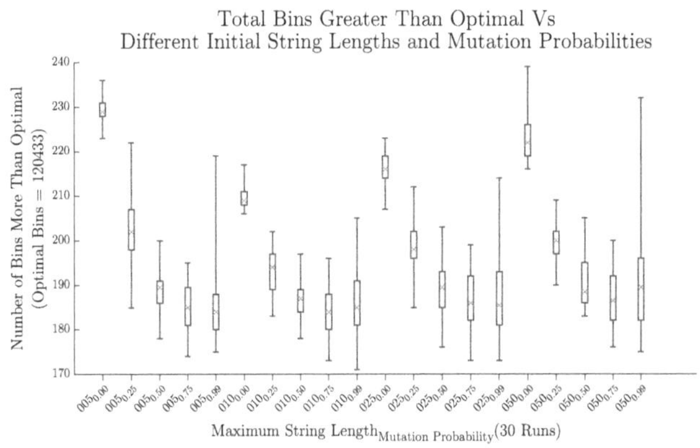

Figure 4: Comparison between different mutation probabilities, $prob_{mut}$, and different maximum string lengths, max_{len}, averaged over 30 runs. The original implementation of NELLI managed to solve these problems using between 308 and 309 extra bins. A t-test comparing the 2 systems (using the results shown here for $010_{0.75}$) show the results to by highly significant giving a P value of less than 0.0001

7.2 Job Shop Scheduling Results

A smaller study was carried out on the JSSP to investigate the ability of NELLI to generalise to other problem domains. A total of 62 problem instances were used as a test-bed which were taken from 5 publications, described below.

- 3 instances from Fisher and Thompson [8] referred to as $ft06, ft10$, and $ft20$.
- 40 instances from Lawrence [14]: referred to as $la01 - la40$.
- 5 instances from Adams et al. [1]: referred to as $abz05 - abz09$.
- 10 instances from Applegate and Cook [2]: referred as $orb01 - orb10$.

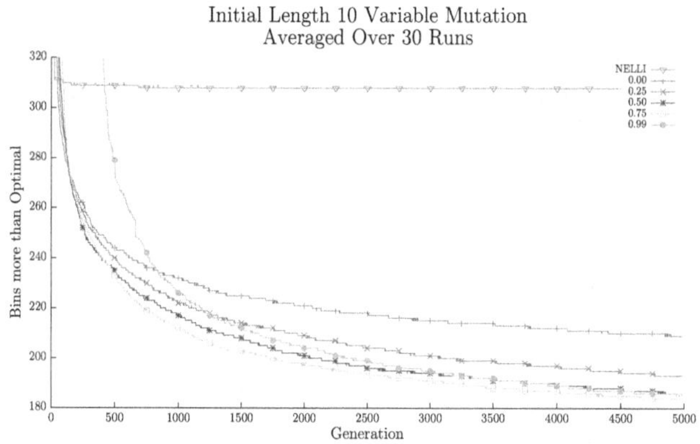

Figure 5: Comparison between NELLI and NELLI* using different mutation probabilities $prob_{mut}$ with an initial string length of $max_{len} = 10$. Results averaged over 30 runs.

- 4 instances from Yamada and Nakano [24]: referred as $yn01 - yn04$.

These problem instances are widely studied by practitioners and have best known solutions, obtained using more specialised metaheuristic techniques, that are superior in many cases to those presented here. Studies using NELLI have to date been limited to the BPP and even here, on the JSSP, the heuristic generator developed is limited to combining simple problem specific nodes with the objective of generating sets of constructive heuristics quickly that can collectively generalise over the problem space. No comparison is made here to other work due to the lack of publications addressing the JSSP in the hyper-heuristic literature. Instead the heuristics that emerge are contrasted against results obtained using each of the 39 nodes, described in Section 6.2 when applied in isolation. Results obtained using each of these 39 nodes are presented in Figure 6 which shows for each node the result of applying the rule 30 times to each problem instance.

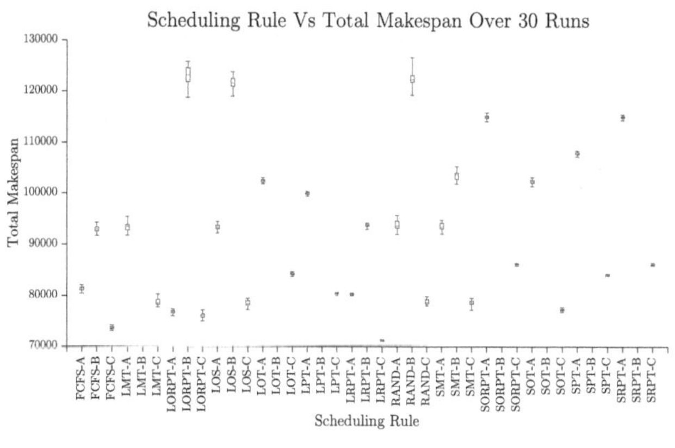

Figure 6: Comparison between scheduling rules applied in isolation taken over 30 runs.

Figure 7 shows the results of repeating the experiments described for bin-packing in which both the mutation rate and maximum string length are varied. The same pattern is observed — increasing the proportion of heuristics that are generated via mutation improves solution quality. In this study there is less of a difference in final solution quality with respect to the initial sequence length although if mutation is not used it is clear that the final solution quality is reduced. Results obtained, and omitted here, using longer initial sequences of dispatching rules showed a marked deterioration in solution quality which it is hypothesised is due to the fact that many more nodes are utilised here than on the BPP resulting in an increased size of the search space. As with the BPP, high mutation rates allow the search to be directed towards more useful sequences of rules although the stochastic nature of the scheduling rules causes new sequences to vary in performance (the same rule can return a different operation if there are still conflicts after they are applied).

The best known reported solutions to these problems have a total makespan summed across all 62 problem instances of 63318. In contrast the best result obtained by a *single* dispatching rule was achieved by LRPT-C which produced solutions with a total makespan of 71130 (12.3% more than the optimal). The best single result achieved using NELLI* gave a combined makespan of 65641 (3.6 % more than optimal).

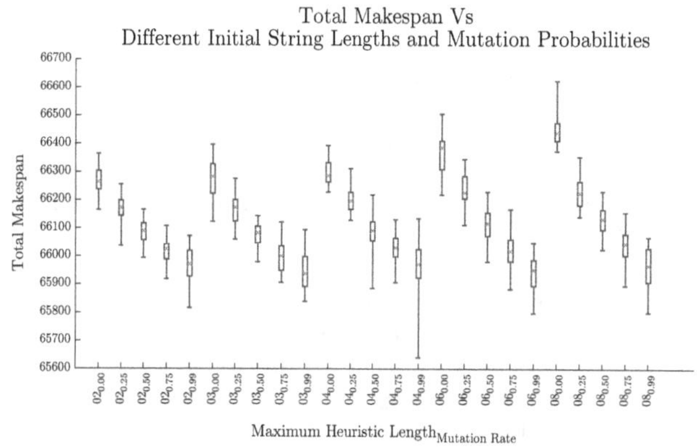

Figure 7: Comparison between different initial maximum string lengths and mutation probabilities taken over 30 runs.

8. CONCLUSION

An existing immune-inspired system NELLI that enables an optimisation system to solve large sets of problems has been improved by focusing on the *meta-dynamics* of the system, i.e. the mechanism by which the system generates novel heuristics. The original tree-based representation has been replaced with a linear sequence of nodes that is applied cyclically. A key result of this is that each bin is now potentially packed using a different heuristic in the case of bin-packing, and each operation potentially scheduled with a different heuristic for JSSP. A mutation mechanism is used to modify heuristics that are currently sustained in the system, acting as an exploitation mechanism. An experimental investigation proved the efficacy of this approach, and investigated the balance required between exploiting existing heuristics and generating completely novel ones. In contrast to previous work, the new representation results in each bin being packed with a (potentially) different heuristic which is hypothesised to contribute to the improvement in quality.

Results on a large set of bin-packing problems showed significant improvement compared both to the previous AIS and existing results in the literature. The system was also applied to a previously untested domain, that of JSSP. A new set of heuristic components and wrapper were defined, but the remainder of the system remains identical to that used for bin-packing. Results showed again that the system outperformed any individual heuristic, and that a balance could be found between exploitation and exploration.

9. REFERENCES

[1] J. Adams, E. Balas, and D. Zawack. The shifting bottleneck procedure for job shop scheduling. *Management Science*, 34(3):391–401, 1988.

[2] D. Applegate and W. Cook. A computational study of the job-shop scheduling problem. *ORSA Journal on Computing*, 3(2):149–156, 1991.

[3] H. Bersini. The endogenous double plasticity of the immune network and the inspiration to be drawn for engineering artifacts. In D. Dasgupta, editor, *Artificial Immune Systems and Their Applications*, pages 22–44. Springer Berlin Heidelberg, 1999.

[4] E. K. Burke, M. Gendreau, M. Hyde, G. Kendall, G. Ochoa, E. Ozcan, and R. Qu. Hyper-heuristics: A survey of the state of the art. *J Oper Res Soc*, pages –, July 2013.

[5] E. K. Burke, M. R. Hyde, G. Kendall, and J. Woodward. Automating the packing heuristic design process with genetic programming. *Evol. Comput.*, 20(1):63–89, Mar. 2012.

[6] F. M. Burnet. *The clonal selection theory of acquired immunity.* Cambridge University Press, Cambridge, UK, 1959.

[7] J. D. Farmer, N. H. Packard, and A. S. Perelson. The immune system, adaptation, and machine learning. *Phys. D*, 2(1-3):187–204, 1986.

[8] H. Fisher and G. L. Thompson. Probabilistic learning combinations of local job-shop scheduling rules. In J. Muth and G. L. Thompson, editors, *Industrial Scheduling*, pages 225–251. Prentice Hall, Englewood Cliffs, New Jersey, 1963.

[9] L. d. C. F.O. de Franca, F.J. Von Zuben. An artificial immune network for multimodal function optimization on dynamic environments. In *Proceedings of the Genetic and Evolutionary Computation Conference, GECCO 2005*, pages 289–296. ACM, 2005.

[10] B. Giffler and G. L. Thompson. Algorithms for solving production-scheduling problems. *Operations Research*, 8(4):487–503, 1960.

[11] E. Hart and P. Ross. A heuristic combination method for solving job-shop scheduling problems. In A. Eiben, T. Bäck, M. Schoenauer, and H.-P. Schwefel, editors, *Parallel Problem Solving from Nature PPSN V*, volume 1498 of *Lecture Notes in Computer Science*, pages 845–854. Springer Berlin / Heidelberg, 1998.

[12] D. Jackson. Single node genetic programming on problems with side effects. In C. Coello, V. Cutello, K. Deb, S. Forrest, G. Nicosia, and M. Pavone, editors, *Parallel Problem Solving from Nature - PPSN XII*, volume 7491 of *Lecture Notes in Computer Science*, pages 327–336. Springer Berlin Heidelberg, 2012.

[13] N. K. Jerne. Towards a network theory of the immune system. *Ann Immunol (Paris)*, 125C(1-2):373–89, 1974.

[14] S. Lawrence. Resource constrained project scheduling: An experimental investigation of heuristic scheduling techniques. Graduate School of Industrial Administration, Carnegie Mellon University, Pittsburgh., 1984.

[15] Z. Michalewicz. Ubiquity symposium: Evolutionary computation and the processes of life: The emperor is naked: Evolutionary algorithms for real-world applications. Ubiquity 2012(November), 3:1–3:13 (Nov 2012)

[16] O. Nasraoui, C. Uribe, C. Coronel, and F. Gonzalez. Tecno-streams: tracking evolving clusters in noisy data streams with a scalable immune system learning model. In *Data Mining, 2003. ICDM 2003. Third IEEE International Conference on*, pages 235–242, 2003.

[17] K. Sim, E. Hart, and B. Paechter. Learning to solve bin packing problems with an immune inspired hyper-heuristic. In G. N. S. N. Pietro Lió, Orazio Miglino and M. Pavone, editors, *Advances in Artificial Life, ECAL 2013: Proceedings of the Twelfth European Conference on the Synthesis and Simulation of Living Systems*, pages 856–863. MIT Press, 2013.

[18] P. Ross, J. Marín-Blázquez, S. Schulenburg and E. Hart (2003). Learning a procedure that can solve hard bin-packing problems: A new ga-based approach to hyper-heuristics. In Cantú-Paz *et al*, editors, *Genetic and Evolutionary Computation, GECCO 2003*, volume 2724 of *Lecture Notes in Computer Science*, pages 1295–1306. Springer Berlin Heidelberg.

[19] K. Sim, E. Hart, and B. Paechter. A lifelong learning hyper-heuristic method for bin packing. *Evolutionary Computation Journal*, In Press, January 2014.

[20] J. C. Tay and N. B. Ho. Evolving dispatching rules using genetic programming for solving multi-objective flexible job-shop problems. *Computers & Industrial Engineering*, 54(3):453–473, 2008.

[21] J. Timmis. Artificial immune systems—today and tomorrow. *Natural Computing*, 6(1):1–18, 2007.

[22] F. Varela, A. Coutinho, B. Dupire, and N. N. Vaz. Cognitive networks: immune, neural and otherwise. *Theoretical immunology*, 2:359–375, 1988.

[23] A. Whitbrook, U. Aickelin, and J. Garibaldi. Idiotypic immune networks in mobile-robot control. *Systems, Man, and Cybernetics, Part B: Cybernetics, IEEE Transactions on*, 37(6):1581 –1598, 2007.

[24] T. Yamada and R. Nakano. Genetic algorithms for job-shop scheduling problems. In *In Proceedings of Modern Heuristic for Decision Support*, pages 474–479. Morgan Kaufmann, 1997.

A Generic Finite Automata Based Approach to Implementing Lymphocyte Repertoire Models

Johannes Textor
Theoretical Biology & Bioinformatics
Universiteit Utrecht
Padualaan 8
3584 CH Utrecht, The Netherlands
johannes.textor@gmx.de

Katharina Dannenberg
Institute for Theoretical Computer Science
Universität zu Lübeck
Ratzeburger Allee 160
23538 Lübeck, Germany
k.dannenberg@hotmail.de

Maciej Liśkiewicz
Institute for Theoretical Computer Science
Universität zu Lübeck
Ratzeburger Allee 160
23538 Lübeck, Germany
liskiewi@tcs.uni-luebeck.de

ABSTRACT

Artificial immune systems (AIS) inspired by lymphocyte repertoires include negative and positive selection, clonal selection, and B cell algorithms. Such AISs are used in computer science for machine learning and optimization, and in biology for modeling of fundamental immunological processes. In both cases, the necessary size of repertoire models can be huge. Here, we show that when lymphocyte repertoire models based on string patterns can be compactly represented as finite automata (FA), this allows to efficiently perform negative selection, positive selection, insertion into, deletion from, uniform sampling from, and counting the repertoire. Specifically, for r-contiguous pattern matching, all these tasks can be performed in polynomial time. But even in NP-hard cases like Hamming distance matching, the FA representation can still lead to practically important efficiency gains. We demonstrate the feasibility and flexibility of this approach by implementing T cell positive selection simulations based on human genomic data using four different pattern rules. Hence, FA-based repertoire models generalize previous efficient negative selection algorithms to perform several related algorithmic tasks, are easy to implement and customize, and are applicable to real-world bioinformatic problems.

Categories and Subject Descriptors

D.2.8 [**Software Engineering**]: Metrics—*complexity measures, performance measures*; F.2.2 [**Analysis of Algorithms and Problem Complexity**]: Nonnumerical Algorithms and Problems—*Pattern matching*; I.2.6 [**Artificial Intelligence**]: Learning

General Terms

Artificial Immune Systems; Negative Selection; Immunology

GECCO'14, July 12–16, 2014, Vancouver, BC, Canada.

ACM 978-1-4503-2662-9/14/07 ...$15.00.
http://dx.doi.org/10.1145/2576768.2598331.

1. INTRODUCTION

Lymphocytes are the cognate elements of human immune systems. These cells carry individually different receptors that allow them to detect specific molecular patterns called *epitopes*, and trigger certain actions such as the initiation or suppression of an immune response. Molecular patterns examined by some B- and most T-lymphocytes are essentially short linear strings of amino acids – for instance, one famous epitope from HIV can be written as the string YNTVAT using the one-letter amino acid coding[1]. Lymphocyte-epitope interactions have inspired the development of a class of artificial immune systems (AIS) in which these interactions are modeled using string pattern matching [24]. In this paper, we call such AISs *repertoire models*. A particularly well-known repertoire model is the negative selection algorithm (NSA) [10], which is based on a process in the thymus where newborn T cells carrying random receptors are exposed to a population of peptides from the host organism. All cells recognizing such peptides are deleted, ensuring that cells leaving the thymus recognize many different foreign patterns but tolerate self. Other AISs based on string models of lymphocyte-epitope interactions include clonal selection (based on the principle of B cell affinity maturation) and the B cell algorithm (based on contiguous somatic hypermutation), which are used for optimization tasks.

Repertoire models have been applied in both computer science, particularly computer security [10], and in computational immunology [23]. The NSA in particular triggered a flurry of research after some initial enthusiasm [9], which however was soon replaced by skepticism about its computational cost [15, 28] and generalization capabilities, leading to its demise in the field of AIS. On the other hand, and largely unappreciated by the AIS community, repertoire models including NSA have been quite successfully applied in immunology, where their use as models of the real immune system continues to provide insight into fundamental principles of immunity and infection until recently [5, 6, 3], most notably in the field of HIV infection modeling [17, 18].

An issue pertaining to both application fields of repertoire models is the huge size of the repertoire sets that are typically required. For realistic immune system modeling, one

[1]Actually this epitope is usually written as SLYNTVATL, but only positions 3 through 8 from this string are in contact with the T cell receptor whereas the others are hidden in a carrier molecule called MHC [22].

aims to attain comparable size and diversity as in the modeled organism – for a mouse, this means on the order of 10^8 cells, and for a human, even 10^{10}. But also for uses in classification, empirical studies have often found the detector sets needed to achieve acceptable classification results to be prohibitively large (e.g. [15]). This problem can be solved by algorithms that generate polynomial sized compressed representations of repertoires [8] for the cases where the so-called r-contiguous [23] and r-chunk [1] matching rules are used to model T cell–peptide interactions. Here, we adopt this idea of repertoire compression and take it further by presenting a generic approach that uses deterministic finite automata (DFA) as a compressed representation of the lymphocyte repertoire. This representation allows us to perform six common tasks of repertoire modeling (defined below) in a rather flexible manner: The user only needs to supply code that generates a DFA that accepts strings encoding all detectors which match a given *single* sample string (Fig. 1). All other steps are then identical regardless the detector type.

Specifically, we show how the following tasks (used in e.g. [26, 5, 3]) can be performed using the DFA representation. Repertoire modeling often involves generating a set of patterns that do not match any string in an input dataset too strongly (*negative selection*) and/or weakly match at least one string from the same dataset (*positive selection*). Having obtained the initial repertoire, one usually examines a set of "antigens" (i.e., elements to classify), for which we search one or all matching detectors (*classification*). By *counting* the number of detectors from the repertoire which match an antigen string, we obtain a measure of dissimilarity between the antigen and the input set of self strings. But we may also wish to *sample* detectors explicitly from the whole repertoire or from the subset that also matches a given antigen in order to examine their properties or to perform further modifications on them (e.g., run a genetic algorithm). Lastly, we may wish to *manipulate* the repertoire, e.g. by deleting detectors that perform poorly or inserting mutated clones of those that perform exceptionally well.

This paper is divided into a theoretical and an empirical part. After some basic definitions, we first consider the DFA approach generally, i.e., independent of the detector type. We show how several tasks of lymphocyte repertoire modeling relate to each other and how they can be solved using DFAs. Then we give a general sufficient condition which implies efficient solutions for all of these tasks. Afterwards, we delineate the theoretical limitations of our approach by showing an example for which no efficient DFA based repertoire representation exists, even though the example is easily solved by other means. In the empirical part, we compare the space and time cost of the DFA based approach to the dominant existing approach of generating detectors one by one explicitly [13]. We perform this approach on "typical" data of immune system modeling, i.e., short strings from large proteomes [4]. We find that while space savings are indeed relatively modest for "difficult" detector types, time savings of 4-5 orders of magnitude are nevertheless achievable.

2. DEFINITIONS

Let Σ be an alphabet and let $S \subseteq \Sigma^L$ for a fixed positive integer L. A *detector* of type D is a string d of length L over an auxiliary alphabet Σ_D with an associated matching rule $m_D : (\Sigma_D)^L \times \Sigma^L \to \{+1, -1\}$. We define $D[S^-]$ as the set of all detectors that classify *all* elements of S *negatively*, i.e., for all $d \in D[S^-]$, $m_D(d, s) = -1$ for all $s \in S$, whereas $D[S^+]$ refers to the set of detectors that classify *one or more* element of S *positively*. Hence, $D[S^-]$ is the complement of $D[S^+]$ in $(\Sigma_D)^L$. By convention, $D[\emptyset^+] = \emptyset$ and hence $D[\emptyset^-] = (\Sigma_D)^L$.

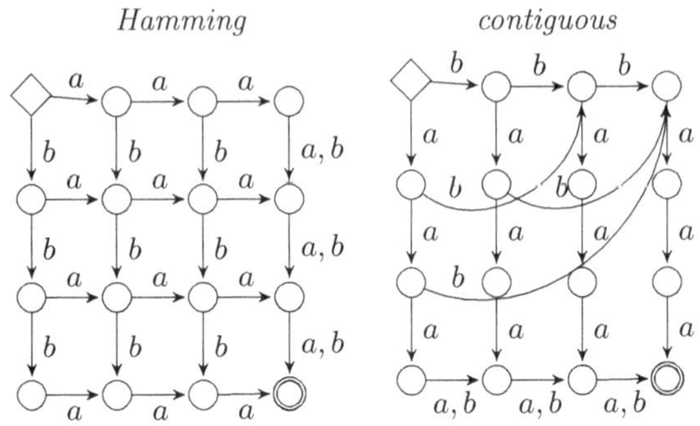

Figure 1: Finite automata encoding the detectors that match the string a^6 ($\Sigma = \{a, b\}$) for 3-Hamming and 3-contiguous matching (Definition 2). The left automaton accepts all strings $d \in \Sigma^6$ of Hamming distance ≤ 3 to the string a^6. The right automaton accepts all $d \in \Sigma^6$ such that d and a^6 are identical in ≥ 3 contiguous positions. The incomplete versions of the automata (i.e., without a sink state) are shown.

For formal definitions of DFAs and their accepted languages, see e.g. [12]. We say that a DFA is *complete* if for any state q and any symbol a there exists an edge starting in q and labeled with a. Any DFA can be made complete by adding one "sink" state and linking all missing transitions to this state. A DFA is called *minimal* (or *minimum-state* DFA) if no other DFA with fewer states accepts the same language.

The languages used in repertoire modeling are finite, and therefore are describable by DFAs that are acyclic, i.e. the transition graph of which is loop free. To minimize an acyclic automaton M we transform M to the complete automaton by adding the sink state and missing transitions, thus obtaining an automaton that is acyclic apart from a loop on the sink. An *m-level* DFA is a DFA in which all states (except the sink if the DFA is complete) can be partitioned into $m + 1$ levels with the following properties: (1) there is exactly one state at level 0 and it is the start state, (2) there is exactly one state at level m and it is the accept state, (3) every transition is from a state in level i to either a state in level $i + 1$ or to the sink state (if it exists), and (4) for any state, q, the accept state is reachable from q and q is reachable from the start state.

3. DFA-BASED REPERTOIRE MODELS

We now introduce the DFA-based approach to Repertoire modeling and prove some positive and negative results that characterize the promises and limitations of this approach.

3.1 Tasks of repertoire modeling

To handle the basic tasks of AIS and computational immunology efficiently, one needs an appropriate model for encoding detectors sets. Our approach here is to use DFAs for this aim. This modeling allows succinct representation of, typically huge, detector sets $D[S^+]$ and/or $D[S^-]$ and efficient manipulations of these sets. With this DFA representation, below we specify the tasks to be solved.

Definition 1. For given detector types D and D' we define the following tasks related to lymphocyte repertoire modeling. We are given two sample sets $S, S' \subseteq \Sigma^L$, two sequences of detector sets $T_1, T_2, T_3, \ldots \subseteq (\Sigma_D)^L$ and $T'_1, T'_2, T'_3, \ldots \subseteq (\Sigma_D)^L$, and a number n.

1. *Positive selection.* Output a DFA M s.t. $L(M) = D[S^+]$.
2. *Negative selection.* Output a DFA M s.t. $L(M) = D'[S'^-]$.
3. *Positive and negative selection.* Output a DFA M s.t. $L(M) = D[S^+] \cap D'[S'^-]$.
   Note that we allow the detector types to be different (e.g., we may use different matching radii for positive and negative selection).
4. *Repertoire manipulation.* First perform task (3) computing M_0 with $L(M_0) = D[S^+] \cap D[S'^-]$ and next for $i = 1, 2, \ldots$ compute iteratively DFAs M_i s.t.
   $$L(M_i) = (L(M_{i-1}) \setminus T_i) \cup T'_i.$$
5. *Counting the repertoire.* First perform any task of (1-4), then for the resulting DFA M output the cardinality of $L(M)$.
6. *Sampling from the repertoire.* Let M be the output of any task in (1-4). Output n strings from $L(M)$ uniformly at random (drawn with replacement).

First, we note that some further common tasks are special cases of the tasks above. Particularly, *classification*: given an S and a test string m determine if there is a detector in $D[S^-]$ which matches m, and *response simulation*: given an S and an antigen x choose randomly detectors in $D[S^-]$ which match x. The first task can be modeled as follows: compute a DFA M s.t. $L(M) = D[S^-] \cap D[\{m\}^+]$ and output m as "positive" if $L(M) \neq \emptyset$; otherwise output m as "negative". Similarly, in the second task we compute a DFA M s.t. $L(M) = D[S^-] \cap D[\{x\}^+]$ and next output strings from $L(M)$ uniformly at random.

3.2 Algorithms and complexity: good news

We start with the following obvious observation: The DFAs for tasks (1-3) listed in Definition 1 are acyclic. Moreover they can be transformed to complete L-level DFAs. Next we give a sufficient condition for implementing repertoire models efficiently.

LEMMA 1. *Let D, D' be detector types for which there is a polynomial time algorithm for positive selection. Then any task listed in Definition 1 can be solved by an algorithm whose runtime is polynomial in L, n, and the cardinalities of input sets.*

PROOF. With positive selection solved, we can solve negative selection by simply inverting the accepted states. Task 3 can then be solved by computing the intersection of the automata resulting from positive and negative selection. For task 4 any iteration can be done in polynomial time according to the output size of the previous iteration. This can be solved by removing or appending the strings in T_i and T'_i from the language accepted by M_{i-1} one-by-one, starting with M_0 given as output by task (3). Each string addition or removal can be done by adding at most L states and $L \cdot |\Sigma_D|$ transitions to M_{i-1}. A standard depth first search counting of accepting paths solves (5) because any M output by (1-4) must be deterministic and acyclic. Lastly, for random sampling from $L(M)$ (task 6), one can use e.g. the linear algorithm proposed by Bernardi and Giménez [2]. □

3.3 Algorithms and complexity: bad news

Below we analyze the computational complexity of tasks (1-4) in more details. For a given sample set $S \subseteq \Sigma^L$, let M_s, with $s \in S$, denote a minimum-state DFA s.t. $L(M_s) = D[\{s\}^+]$. Then, from the computational complexity point of view, task 1 can be equivalently formulated as: output a DFA M such that $L(M) = \bigcup_{s \in S} L(M_s)$. Similarly, if automata M'_s are minimum-state DFAs s.t. $L(M'_s) = D[\{s\}^-]$ then task 2 can be formulated as: output a DFA M' such that $L(M') = \bigcap_{s \in S} L(M'_s)$. We show that in general, these problems are computationally difficult – more strongly, even only deciding if $L(M) = \Sigma^*$, or equivalently if $L(M') = \emptyset$, is difficult.

We start with a very general setting and consider the problem called *the finite automaton intersection problem*, formulated as follows: Let $M_1, \ldots, M_k$ be k DFAs with a common alphabet Σ. The problem is to determine whether $\bigcap_{i=1}^k L(M_i)$ is nonempty. This problem is PSPACE-complete for DFAs with cycles [19]. For acyclic DFAs the complexity interestingly drops to NP but remains NP-complete, as we now show. First, it is easy to see that the problem for acyclic DFAs is in NP: simply "guess" a string $w \in \Sigma^*$ of length less or equal to the maximum number of states over all DFAs $M_1, \ldots, M_k$ and then check deterministically if $w \in L(M_i)$, for all $i = 1, \ldots, k$. To prove NP-hardness, one can modify the proof of Kozen [19]. However, in the context of our approach to repertoire representation we can prove an even stronger NP-completeness statement.

LEMMA 2. *There exist detector types D for which, if M'_s denotes a minimum-state DFA s.t. $L(M'_s) = D[\{s\}^-]$ then (1) for any $s \in \Sigma^L$ the number of states of M'_s is at most L^2, and (2) the problem to decide if for a given $S \subseteq \Sigma^L$ set $\bigcap_{s \in S} L(M'_s)$ is nonempty is* NP*-complete.*

PROOF. The lemma holds, e.g. for r-Hamming detectors D (see Definition 2), even for binary alphabets $\Sigma = \{a, b\}$. For this detector type it is easy to construct for any $s \in \Sigma^L$ a DFA M'_s for $D[\{s\}^-]$ having at most L^2 states (see Fig. 1 for an example automaton accepting $D[\{s\}^+]$, with $s = a^6$, which can be easily modified to obtain the required automaton M'_s). Property (2) follows directly from Theorem 2 in [21] that says that the problem to decide if for a given set $S \subseteq \Sigma^L$ the detector set $D[S^-]$ is nonempty, is NP-complete. Hardness for binary alphabets follows from the fact that the well-known farthest string problem is NP-complete even for binary strings [20]. □

In the next section we will provide a generic algorithm that allows to solve tasks (1-4) efficiently if the resulting automaton M, with $L(M) = \bigcup_{s \in S} L(M_s)$, has small size. However, we first give an example where the minimal automaton is huge: For an arbitrary alphabet $\Sigma = \Sigma_D$, consider the matching function $m(d,s) = +1$ iff (a) $d, s \in \{uu : \text{for } u \in \Sigma^{L/2}\}$ if L is even and (b) $d, s \in \{uau : \text{for } u \in \Sigma^{L/2}$ and $a \in \Sigma\}$ if L is odd.

LEMMA 3. *For the detector defined above, for any $s \in \Sigma^L$ the number of states of the minimum DFA M_s, with $L(M_s) = D[\{s\}^+]$, is at least $|\Sigma|^{L/2+1}$.*

PROOF. Assume $s = a^L$ for some $a \in \Sigma$, and let $S = \{s\}$. Then $D[\{s\}^+] = \{uu : \text{for } u \in \Sigma^{L/2}\}$ if L is even and otherwise $D[\{s\}^+] = \{uau : \text{for } u \in \Sigma^{\lfloor L/2 \rfloor}\}$. But in both cases, any state-minimal DFA for this language has at least $|\Sigma|^{L/2+1}$ states. □

However, note that tasks (1-4) are easily solvable in polynomial time for this detector type. Therefore, our example illustrates that not every repertoire model that is easy to implement has also an efficient DFA-based implementation.

3.4 A generic algorithm for positive selection

Lemma 1 shows that once positive selection is solved (or negative selection, for that matter), all other tasks can then be performed applying basic DFA-related algorithms on the resulting automaton. But also positive selection itself can be solved by combining a much simpler task with standard DFA manipulation, as we now show. Recall that our task is to compute for a given S a DFA M such that $L(M) = D[S^+]$. The following algorithm accomplishes this.

1. $M \leftarrow$ "DFA recognizing $\emptyset$".
2. For all strings $s \in S$ do
3. compute M_s such that $L(M_s) = D[\{s\}^+]$,
4. compute N such that $L(N) = L(M) \cup L(M_s)$,
5. minimize N,
6. set $M \leftarrow N$.
7. Return M.

Note that the only part of this algorithm that depends on the detector type is the construction of M_s in line 3. Therefore, we have now broken down all tasks of repertoire modeling to the construction of an automaton that accepts the language of all detectors matching a single input string (Fig. 1). Computing the DFA N in line 4 with $L(N) = L(M) \cup L(M_s)$ can be done in time $\mathcal{O}(L \cdot n \cdot n_s \cdot |\Sigma|)$, where n denotes the width of M (i.e. maximum, over all $i = 1, \ldots, L$, of number of states on level i) and n_s is the width of M_s. The minimization step in line 5 is optional, but can be important when the product automaton computed in line 4 is highly redundant. Using the linear time minimization algorithm for acyclic DFAs by Revuz [25] we can implement step 5 in time $\mathcal{O}(L \cdot n \cdot n_s \cdot |\Sigma|)$.

LEMMA 4. *If for any $S \subseteq \Sigma^L$ the number of states of minimum-state DFA M, s.t. $L(M) = D[S^-]$, is polynomial with respect to $|S|$, $|\Sigma|$, and L then the negative selection task can be solved in polynomial time.*

Since the union operation on languages is associative and commutative our generic algorithm can be implemented in other ways than presented here. Particularly, one can compute the resulting DFA M using the "divide and conquer" strategy, i.e. divide S into two disjoint S_1 and S_2 of almost the same size, compute M_1 for $D[S_1^+]$ and M_2 for $D[S_2^+]$ and M for $L(M_1) \cup L(M_2)$. This algorithm can be also implemented using a "dynamic programming" approach such that first automata $M_1, M_2, \ldots$ for $L(M_{s_1}) \cup L(M_{s_2})$, $L(M_{s_3}) \cup L(M_{s_4}), \ldots$ are computed, then for $L(M_1) \cup L(M_2)$, $L(M_3) \cup L(M_4), \ldots$ and so on.

4. DETECTOR-SPECIFIC RESULTS

The framework outlined in the last section is not only of practical interest, but it also provides a generic proof system for obtaining positive or negative (hardness) results on the computational complexity of specific detector types. More formal versions of the below definitions can be found in [29].

Definition 2. Throughout, d is a detector and s a string.

1. *r-contiguous detectors:* $d \in \Sigma^L$ matches $s \in \Sigma^L$ iff d and s are identical in $\geq r$ contiguous positions.
2. *r-pattern detectors:* $d \in (\Sigma \cup \{\#\})^L$ matches $s \in \Sigma^L$ at every non-# position and contains at most r "don't-care-symbols" #.
3. *r-Hamming detectors:* $d \in \Sigma^L$ matches $s \in \Sigma^L$ iff d and s differ in at most r positions.
4. *r-PMBEC detectors:* We use this additional detector type as a biologically motivated variation of the Hamming distance. Let $\Delta : \Sigma \times \Sigma \to \mathbb{Z}$ be a similarity function between the symbols in Σ. Then d matches s iff (1) d and s differ in at most r positions and (2) for all positions i where they do differ, $\Delta(d[i], s[i]) \geq \vartheta$. In our empirical evaluation, we use the PMBEC amino acid similarity matrix that has been designed for immunoinformatic purposes [16] and has recently been applied to T cell epitope modeling [4]. The recommended cutoff threshold for this matrix is $\vartheta = 5$ [16], allowing 17 letter pairs to substitute, e.g. `S` and `T`.

LEMMA 5. *Assume $S \subseteq \Sigma^L$ and let M be a minimum-state complete DFA, s.t. $L(M) = D[S^+]$, for r-contiguous detectors. Then DFA M has $\mathcal{O}(L \cdot r \cdot \min\{|S|, |\Sigma|^r\})$ states.*

PROOF. (Sketch). One can prove this by considering the equivalence relation over Σ^* defined as

$$u \sim v \quad \text{iff} \quad \forall z \in \Sigma^* (uz \in D[S^+] \Leftrightarrow vz \in D[S^+]).$$

This relation has $\mathcal{O}(L \cdot r \cdot \min\{|S|, |\Sigma|^r\})$ equivalence classes. By the Myhill-Nerode theorem, this matches the minimum number of states of a DFA recognizing $D[S^+]$. For details, see the full version of our paper. □

From Lemmas 5 and 4 together with Lemma 1, we now immediately obtain the following generalization from negative selection to repertoire models.

COROLLARY 1. *For r-contiguous detectors, all tasks listed in Definition 1 are solvable in polynomial time.*

These results illustrate how we can apply the DFA framework to obtain polynomial time algorithms for repertoire modeling. Unfortunately, for all other detector types defined above, we can only obtain hardness results. The corollary below follows immediately from the intractability results for r-Hamming detectors presented in [21].

COROLLARY 2. *For r-Hamming, r-pattern and r-PMBEC detectors, tasks (1-5) in Definition 1 are not solvable in polynomial time unless* P = NP.

For r-Hamming, even only deciding if $D[S^-] \neq \emptyset$ is already NP-hard [21]; therefore, also sampling (task 6) is not efficiently solvable in that case. For r-pattern, this decision problem is trivial to answer [21], but solving positive selection in polynomial time would allow an efficient solution of the more general counting problem (task 5), which is #P-hard. Therefore tasks (1-5), which all contain positive selection as a special case, cannot be solved efficiently unless P = NP. Note that the exclusion of task 6 in Corollary 2 is because there exist detector types [31] for which sampling can be efficiently solved although the other tasks cannot (assuming P $\neq$ NP).

5. EMPIRICAL EVALUATION

Computational immunology has been a fruitful application domain of repertoire models in general and the most fruitful one of negative selection algorithms in particular [5, 6, 17, 18, 3]. Therefore, we evaluate the practical performance of the DFA approach using typical data from that domain. The input dataset sizes were set similarly as in studies by Košmrlj and others [17, 18, 3]. In those studies, computational T cell repertoire models were used for predictive modeling of the real human immune system, which provided important insight into the dynamics of HIV infection [18]. Typically, those models use thousands to tens of thousands of input strings. As string length we use $L = 6$ (which is the number of amino acids that determine CD8 T cell recognition [22]), even though Košmrlj et al. [18] used $L = 5$ instead, perhaps for computational reasons.

As in the mentioned studies [17, 18, 3] we generated the input datasets S by applying so-called MHC-binding prediction algorithms to the human proteome (i.e., the set of protein sequences from all human proteins), which was downloaded from the UniProt database [7]. Potential T cell epitopes were predicted using the NetMHCPan algorithm [11][2]. This resulted in a candidate set of 180,000 potential epitopes (strings of length $L = 6$) that can potentially be used for negative and positive selection in the thymus. From these candidate epitope sets, we randomly generated subsets with cardinalities ranging from 4,000 to 32,000 strings (similar as in [18]) and used these sets as input S. We implemented custom algorithms for union and intersection of acyclic L-level DFAs that take advantage of some of the properties of these automata to achieve better runtime than more generic algorithms. For instance, our algorithms can assume that all DFAs have only a single accepting state, and can build the product automaton level by level. For other DFA manipulation tasks, such as minimization, we used the AT&T Finite State Machine library[3].

5.1 Space efficiency

Our DFA based approach can only be expected to perform better than simple exhaustive algorithms when the DFA representation is significantly more compact than the set of represented detectors. To empirically investigate the space efficiency of the DFA representation, we first need to introduce a quantitative measure of space efficiency. For this purpose, we use the compression ratio. We first define the *size* of an (incomplete) DFA M as $\text{size}(M) = (n+m)\lceil \log_2(n) \rceil$, where n is the number of states and m is the number of transitions –i.e., size(M) is the number of bits needed to store an adjacency list representation of M. Furthermore, we define the size of a string set $S \subseteq \Sigma^L$ as $\text{size}(S) = |\Sigma| \lceil \log(|\Sigma|) \rceil$ –i.e., size(S) is the number of bits needed to store S. Now we can define the compression ratio of an automaton M as $\text{comp}(M) = \text{size}(L(M))/\text{size}(M)$, e.g., $\text{comp}(M) = 10$ would mean that storing $L(M)$ explicitly would require 10 times more bits than storing M.

We addressed the compression ratios by applying positive selection to the predicted T cell epitopes as input data as described above. We do not present results for negative selection because these are expected to be very similar[4]. The results of our analysis are shown in Fig. 2. The resulting DFA sizes ranged from 10^1 to 10^6 states. In general, the matching parameter r turned out to be the most important determinant of the DFA size, and the largest DFAs were found around $r = 5$ for r-contiguous matching and $r = 3$ for r-Hamming and r-PMBEC matching. As expected from our theoretical understanding of the problem, we found the highest compression ratios with r-contiguous matching, where they ranged up to the order of $10,000 : 1$, and of course even higher in the trivial cases where $L(M)$ equals or almost equals Σ^L. Except for such cases, we obtained comparatively lower but still substantial compression ratios of around $10 : 1$ for the r-Hamming and r-PMBEC distances. In general, the DFA size was always well below the size of the string set, except for some of the degenerate instances $r = 6$ (for r-contiguous) and $r = 0$ (for the others), where $L(M) = S$.

As indicated above, the compression ratio can be a misleading measure for very large detector sets, because a "naive" implementation could also just store the much smaller complement instead. Therefore, we focused our further evaluation on those instances where $|D[S^+]| < 20^6/2$, and investigated the determinants of the compression ratio. From Fig. 2 it is apparent that the compression ratio correlates with r, but r itself is in turn correlated with $|D[S^+]|$. Hence, we used a linear regression analysis to investigate which of the two parameters more strongly determines comp(M).

5.2 Runtime efficiency

While we believe that the number of bits required to store M is a realistic measure for the space complexity of the DFA approach, there is no obvious machine-independent measure of practical (as opposed to asymptotic) runtime. Therefore, we compared the actual runtimes of a C++ implementation of naive positive selection and our C++ implementation of the DFA approach. To avoid skewing of our results due to potential paging between memory and hard-disk, we performed these experiments on an Intel(R) Xeon(R) X5680 server with 96GB of RAM. Although the machine had 12 processors with 6 cores each available, we did not parallelize our algorithms such that each experiment was run on a sin-

[2]More specifically, HLA-0201 MHC binders were predicted and the 6-mer from position 3 to 8, which are the T cell receptor contact residues for that MHC type, were extracted. For further details on binding prediction, see e.g. the textbook by Lund et al. [22].

[3]This library, written by Mehryar Mohri and Fernando C. N. Pereira and Michael D. Riley, can be accessed at www2.research.att.com/~fsmtools/fsm/ref.html

[4]We would only need to invert the DFA generated by positive selection. This is not completely trivial because the DFA is stored as an incomplete representation. However, it is easy to show that the size of an DFA M and its complement $\bar{M}$ can differ at most by factor $|\Sigma|$.

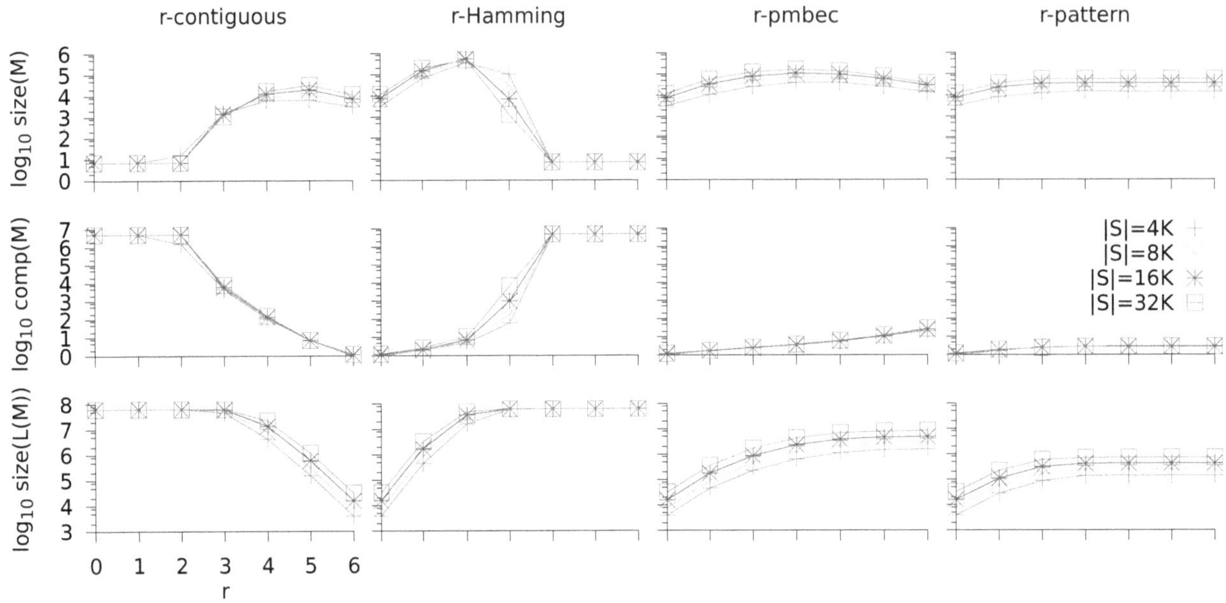

Figure 2: Empirical evaluation of the space efficiency of DFA-based representations of detector sets on proteomic data. The input sets S were generated using a human epitope prediction algorithm, i.e., $|\Sigma| = 20$ and $L = 6$, and positive selection was performed for each input dataset. Then the size $|D[S^+]| = |L(M)|$ of the generated repertoire was determined. Please note that the largest compression ratios achieved, i.e. for $\{0, 1, 2\}$-contiguous and $\{4, 5, 6\}$-Hamming are simply due to the fact that these parameters lead to the degenerate case $D[S^+] = (\Sigma_D)^L$ where all possible detectors match some input string.

gle core only. No other jobs were run on the machine at the same time such that cores were close to 100% occupied by the experiments.

The naive (i.e., exhaustive enumeration) positive selection algorithms were implemented according to the template pseudocode shown in Fig. 3. The only change for different detector types is the implementation of the matching function m_D. Although the outer loop that iterates over $(\Sigma_D)^L$ seems daunting, it is still quite feasible for our use case $|\Sigma| = 20, L = 6$ if S is not too large. For larger S, the runtime depends crucially on the matching probability between d and s (line 4). If this probability is for instance bounded from below by a constant p, then the inner loop terminates after $\mathcal{O}(1/p)$ iterations and the runtime becomes independent of $|S|$. In the worst case, if no detector can be found ($p = 0$), we have to iterate over all elements of S. This important role of the matching probability between d and s for naive implementations of repertoire models led to thorough theoretical investigations for the case of r-contiguous detectors [27].

Fig. 4 shows the results of our runtime analysis. For r-contiguous detectors, the runtime of the DFA approach is for most parameters superior to the naive approach, and even comes close to a Java implementation [31] of the fastest known dedicated algorithm for this case [8]. For r-Hamming, consistent with its theoretical difficulty, we find a less convincing speedup. Although it can still amount to some orders of magnitude for $r \leq 2$, it is not much better than exhaustive search for $r \geq 3$. However, the r-PMBEC version of the Hamming distance, which from a theoretical perspective is equally difficult, performed much better. Note that this difference between r-PMBEC and r-Hamming is *not* simply

1. $D \leftarrow \emptyset$
2. For all strings $d \in (\Sigma_D)^L$ do
3.   For all strings $s \in S$ do
4.   if $m_D(d, s) = +1$ then
5.   insert d into D
6.   continue with the next d
7. Output the cardinality of D.

Figure 3: Pseudocode for the "naive" exhaustive enumeration approach to positive selection used in our runtime analysis.

a consequence of the sizes of the resulting automata, which are in fact quite similar (Fig. 2). Instead, it is due to the sizes of the intermediate automata computed "on the way" to the final one. Lastly, the r-pattern detectors performed similar as in the r-PMBEC case, as already in the space complexity analysis.

Hence, while our empirical results partly reflect the theoretical hardness of the corresponding decision problems, especially for the Hamming case, it also emphasizes the obvious point that there can be enormous practical performance difference within these "hard" cases, rendering some practically tractable and putting others out of reach. Still, in general, the DFA implementation does seem preferable to the "classical" approach of generating detectors by exhaustive search or by random sampling [13]. For instance, we note that generating the "naive approach" data shown in Fig. 4 required about one week (171.7h) of CPU time on our Xeon server, whereas the DFA based data required only 1.5h.

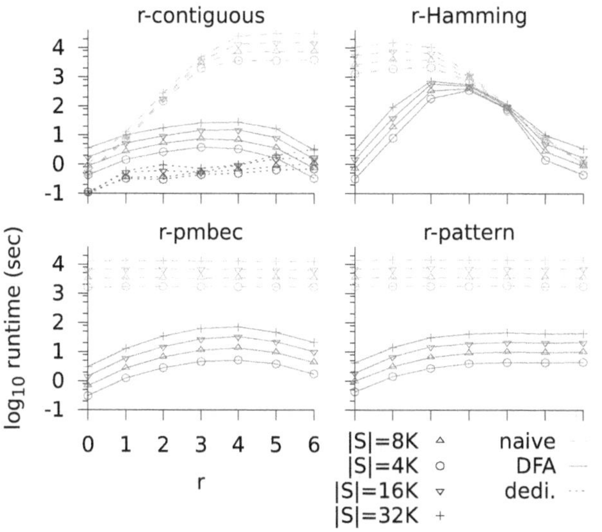

Figure 4: Empirical runtime analysis for repertoire counting after positive selection. We compare a naive implementation and the general DFA-based approach for $|S| \in \{4000, 8000, 16000, 32000\}$, $|\Sigma| = 20$ and $L = 6$. For r-contiguous detectors, we also run the dedicated *negative* selection implementation (dedi) by Textor [30] and convert the output to the positive selection count using the identity $|D[S^+]| = |\Sigma|^L - |D[S^-]|$.

6. DISCUSSION

Here we proposed a DFA based approach to implement lymphocyte repertoire models based on string patterns (detectors). This approach can be used to implement negative selection, positive selection, repertoire counting and sampling, classification, and allows on-line repertoire manipulation. To implement all these tasks for a certain detector type, the user only has to provide code that outputs a DFA describing the detectors that match a given string. We have explored the algorithmic and complexity theoretic issues of the DFA approach and implemented and tested it for four specific detector types using typical data from computational immunology.

DFAs are not the only conceivable formalism to support repertoire modeling – one could e.g. also use grammars or regular expressions. It is also not necessarily the best formalism – indeed, we have given an example where polynomial runtime is achievable but the DFA approach needs exponential time (Lemma 3). Nevertheless, DFAs subsume some other well-known string compression tools like tries or prefix DAGs and can therefore be expected to perform well when the string sets to be represented have at least some degree of regular structure (like for r-contiguous detectors). Because DFAs are a fundamental subject in computer science, there are also many highly efficient algorithms and software libraries for DFA processing available. This led us to choose this representation type over other options like regular expressions or grammars. An interesting perspective for future research would be to investigate whether nondeterministic FAs can be used to solve some repertoire modeling tasks approximatively that still require too many resources to be solved exactly. For instance, for all detector types considered here it is very easy to construct a polynomial size nondeterministic finite automaton (NFA) describing the language $D[S^+]$. Since a polynomial time algorithm exists to sample approximately at uniform from the language described by a given NFA [14], this could be an alternative approach for the repertoire sampling tasks.

The DFA based approach can of course not provide polynomial time repertoire modeling algorithms for Hamming distance and related detectors because these detector types lead to NP-hard decision problems [21]. Despite this, we still found substantial performance improvements compared to explicit detector generation at least for r-pattern and r-PMBEC detectors. It would now be very interesting to apply these detector types for anomaly detection tasks and compare their classification performance to r-contiguous and the related r-chunk detectors, which were so far the only detector types for which a thorough empirical comparison to other anomaly detection algorithms could be performed [30]. For space reasons, this could not be added to the present paper anymore. However, because the string lengths (6-10) [5], sample sizes (thousands) and alphabet sizes (<100) used in that study were similar to ours, we do expect this to be feasible for r-pattern detectors. The study also contained a protein anomaly detection problem for which the r-PMBEC detectors could be applied.

DFA-based string compression might be useful in other areas than AIS and computational immunology. For instance, many learning classifier systems use r-pattern-like matching rules, and may thus benefit from compressed rule representations when large rule sets are needed. Moreover, one could explore whether the DFA approach would allow evolutionary optimization algorithms to efficiently maintain and manipulate very large populations of candidate solutions, and whether that could improve optimization performance.

7. REFERENCES

[1] J. Balthrop, F. Esponda, S. Forrest, and M. R. Glickman. Coverage and generalization in an artificial immune system. In *Proc. of GECCO 2002*, pages 1045–1050, 2002.

[2] O. Bernardi and O. Giménez. A linear algorithm for the random sampling from regular languages. *Algorithmica*, 62(1-2):130–145, 2012.

[3] T. C. Butler, M. Kardar, and A. K. Chakraborty. Quorum sensing allows T cells to discriminate between self and nonself. *PNAS*, 110(29):11833–11838, 2013.

[4] J. J. A. Calis, R. J. D. Boer, and C. Kesmir. Degenerate T-cell recognition of peptides on MHC molecules creates large holes in the T-cell repertoire. *PLoS Comp Biol*, 8(3), 2012.

[5] D. L. Chao, M. P. Davenport, S. Forrest, and A. S. Perelson. A stochastic model of cytotoxic T cell responses. *J. Theor. Biol.*, 228:227–240, 2004.

[6] D. L. Chao, M. P. Davenport, S. Forrest, and A. S. Perelson. The effects of thymic selection on the range of T cell cross-reactivity. *Eur. J. Immunol.*, 35:3452–3459, 2005.

[5] More precisely, the actual sequence lengths were much larger and varied, but the anomaly detection was done using a sliding window of small size.

[7] T. U. Consortium. Ongoing and future developments at the universal protein resource. *Nucleic Acids Res.*, 39:D214–D219, 2011.

[8] M. Elberfeld and J. Textor. Negative selection algorithms on strings with efficient training and linear-time classification. *Theor. Comput. Sci.*, 412:534–542, 2011.

[9] S. Forrest, S. A. Hofmeyr, and A. Somayaji. Computer immunology. *Commun. ACM*, 40:88–96, 1997.

[10] S. Forrest, A. S. Perelson, L. Allen, and R. Cherukuri. Self-nonself discrimination in a computer. In *Proc. of the IEEE Symposium on Research in Security and Privacy*, pages 202–212. IEEE Computer Society Press, 1994.

[11] I. Hoof et al. NetMHCpan, a method for MHC class I binding prediction beyond humans. *Immunogenetics*, 61:1–13, 2009.

[12] J. E. Hopcroft, R. Motwani, and J. D. Ullman. *Introduction to automata theory, languages, and computation.* Pearson/Addison Wesley, 2007.

[13] Z. Ji and D. Dasgupta. Revisiting negative selection algorithms. *Evol. Comput.*, 15(2):223–251, 2007.

[14] S. Kannan, Z. Sweedyk, and S. Mahaney. Counting and random generation of strings in regular languages. In *Proc. of SODA 1995*, pages 551–557, 1995.

[15] J. Kim and P. J. Bentley. An evaluation of negative selection in an artificial immune system for network intrusion detection. In *Proc. of GECCO 2001*, pages 1330–1337. Morgan Kaufmann, 2001.

[16] Y. Kim, J. Sidney, C. Pinilla, A. Sette, and B. Peters. Derivation of an amino acid similarity matrix for peptide: MHC binding and its application as a Bayesian prior. *BMC Bioinformatics*, 10:394, 2009.

[17] A. Košmrlj, A. K. Jha, E. S. Huseby, M. Kardar, and A. K. Chakraborty. How the thymus designs antigen-specific and self-tolerant T cell receptor sequences. *PNAS*, 105(43):16671–16676, 2008.

[18] A. Košmrlj et al. Effects of thymic selection of the T-cell repertoire on HLA class I–associated control of HIV infection. *Nature*, 465:350–354, 2010.

[19] D. Kozen. Lower bounds for natural proof systems. In *Proc. of FOCS 1977*, pages 254–266, 1977.

[20] J. K. Lanctot, M. Li, B. Ma, S. Wang, and L. Zhang. Distinguishing string selection problems. *Information and Computation*, 185:41–55, 2003.

[21] M. Liśkiewicz and J. Textor. Negative selection algorithms without generating detectors. In *Proc. of GECCO 2010*, pages 1047–1054. ACM, 2010.

[22] O. Lund, C. Keşmir, M. Nielsen, C. Lundegaard, and S. Brunak. *Immunological Bioinformatics.* MIT Press, 2005.

[23] J. K. Percus, O. E. Percus, and A. S. Perelson. Predicting the size of the T-cell receptor and antibody combining region from consideration of efficient self-nonself discrimination. *PNAS*, 90(5):1691–1695, 1993.

[24] A. S. Perelson and G. F. Oster. Theoretical studies of clonal selection: minimal antibody repertoire size and reliability of self-non-self discrimination. *J. Theor. Biol.*, 81(4):645–670, 1979.

[25] D. Revuz. Minimisation of acyclic deterministic automata in linear time. *Theor. Comput. Sci.*, 92(1):181–189, 1992.

[26] D. J. Smith, S. Forrest, D. H. Ackley, and A. S. Perelson. Using lazy evaluation to simulate realistic-size repertoires in models of the immune system. *Bull. Math. Biol.*, 60:647–658, 1998.

[27] T. Stibor. Foundations of r-contiguous matching in negative selection for anomaly detection. *Nat. Comput.*, 8:613–641, 2009.

[28] T. Stibor, P. Mohr, J. Timmis, and C. Eckert. Is negative selection appropriate for anomaly detection? In *Proc. of GECCO 2005*, pages 321–328. ACM, 2005.

[29] J. Textor. *Search and Learning in the Immune System: Models of Immune Surveillance and Negative Selection.* PhD thesis, University of Lübeck, Germany, 2011.

[30] J. Textor. A comparative study of negative selection based anomaly detection in sequence data. In *Proc. of ICARIS 2012*, volume 7597 of *LNCS*, pages 28–41. Springer, 2012.

[31] J. Textor. Efficient negative selection algorithms by sampling and approximate counting. In *Proc. of PPSN 2012*, volume 7492 of *LNCS*, pages 32–41. Springer, 2012.

Adapting to a Changing Environment Using Winner and Loser Effects

Jeremy Acre
Dept. of Mathematics
Southern Nazarene University
Bethany, OK, USA
jeacre@mail.snu.edu

Brent E. Eskridge
Dept. of Computer Science and Network Engineering
Southern Nazarene University
Bethany, OK, USA
beskridge@snu.edu

Nicholas Zoller
Dept. of Mathematics
Southern Nazarene University
Bethany, OK, USA
nzoller@snu.edu

Ingo Schlupp
Dept. of Biology
University of Oklahoma
Norman, OK, USA
schlupp@ou.edu

ABSTRACT

Many animals form large aggregations that have no apparent consistent leader, yet are capable of highly coordinated movements. At any given time, it seems like an individual can emerge as a leader only to be replaced by another. Although individuals within a group are largely considered equal, even individuals in a homogeneous group are different. Clearly individuals will differ based on traits like sex, age, and experience. Of particular interest is the idea of individuals differing in their correlated traits, or personality. Different personalities can arise via complex interactions between genes and an environment and are often shaped by individual experience. For example, one would generally predict that individuals characterized as "bold" would more frequently be leaders. However, if the environment changes, how do once successful leaders respond to failure and how do newly successful leaders emerge? Using a biologically-based collective movement model, we demonstrate that a self-assessment mechanism using winner and loser effects is capable of producing transitory leaders who change roles in response to changes in the environment. Furthermore, simulations predict that this self-assessment mechanism allows the group to adapt to drastic changes in the environment and remain successful.

Categories and Subject Descriptors

I.2.11 [**Artificial Intelligence**]: Distributed Artificial Intelligence—*coherence and coordination, multiagent systems*

Keywords

collective movement, coordination, leadership, adaptation

GECCO'14, July 12–16, Vancouver, BC, Canada.

http://dx.doi.org/10.1145/2576768.2598355.

1. INTRODUCTION

Nature is abundant with examples of large animal aggregations that perform highly coordinated movements. While there is no consistent leader in these groups across all movements, leaders are evident in individual movements. However, these leadership positions are transitory with the leader of one movement being replaced by another in a later movement. How these leaders emerge is a widely studied question [13, 16, 21, 30]. Although individuals within such groups are largely considered equal, individuals still differ in a variety of ways. Of particular interest are differences in an individual's *personality*, or the set of correlated traits that play a role in the individual's decision-making process. Personalities are often shaped by an individual's experiences and can have long term effects on an individual [31]. Furthermore, research has shown that the addition of personality allows for differentiation and self-assignment of individuals into the roles of leader and follower in a collective movement [11].

Even though experience can shape personality, experience is not always reliable. Individuals can experience success or failure due to circumstances beyond their control. Furthermore, an individual can experience success in one environment, but failure in another. For example, one individual may have exceptional eyesight and be particularly effective during the day, while another may have superior hearing and be more effective at night. However, in other situations, which individual has the potential to be the most effective leader is not as apparent. Two individuals may have different information on the location of a food patch, only one of which is accurate, and the accurate location is only known after sampling the patch sites. To further complicate the situation, food patches can be depleted. A food patch can be abundant one day, and empty the next.

The ability for a once-effective leader, that is now ineffective, to adapt to a changing environment can be essential for the long-term success and fitness of the individual, and the group's as a whole. Unfortunately, uncertainty inhibits adaptation since time and energy limits constrain an individual's opportunities to fully sample and explore the current environment, and communication limitations make transferring full information to every member of a group impractical.

Although ecological uncertainty has been theorized to be a cause of personality [28], the mechanism that shapes personality using experience is not well understood [1, 6, 31].

In the work presented here, we use a biologically-based collective movement model to explore how personality, especially as it pertains to leaders and followers, can be shaped by experience in a changing environment. We demonstrate that a self-assessment mechanism using biologically-inspired winner and loser effects is capable of producing personalities that reflect stable, self-assigned leader and follower roles. Furthermore, we demonstrate that these roles are transitory through simulations involving drastic changes to the environment and the emergence of new leaders.

2. RELATED WORK

Animal personalities, also referred to as *behavioral syndromes*, are the focus of considerable recent research effort [35, 38]. Personalities refer to behavioral traits in animals that are frequently found together, such as an insensitivity to social information and an increased likelihood of leaving the safety of cover to forage for food. The most commonly described personalities lie along the bold-shy continuum [14, 17]. Animal personalities have three important properties that are of particular interest in this work.

First, individuals exhibiting a bold personality are frequently leaders in many group activities, with shy individuals frequently being followers [7, 16, 25, 27]. Although there are certainly situations where leaders have physiological traits that predispose them towards being leaders, the significance of personalities in the emergence of leadership is becoming increasingly apparent.

A second important property of animal personalities results is that groups having a combination of both bold and shy individuals can be more successful than either personality type alone [7]. The combination of bold leaders and shy followers results in a two level hierarchy that is found in many successful animal aggregations [5]. Furthermore, bold and shy personalities allow individuals to specialize in a niche role within the group, which can explain the maintenance of personality differences [29]. It has even been theorized that the fitness benefits of this niche specialization are so strong that personality differences can be maintained at the genetic level through "social heterosis" [29].

Lastly, animal personalities are thought to be in part affected by environmental change [36]. In fact, some contend that environmental uncertainty is the cause of personalities [28] as they provide default mechanisms for decision-making when information and experience are unreliable [4].

Individuals participating in group living must frequently adapt to perform in uncertain environments. One such situation is the establishment of dominance hierarchies. Dominance hierarchies are frequently established through fighting contests and the associated winner and loser effects [18]. Winner and loser effects are feedback mechanisms in which experience affects future success. In other words, a winner in a contest is more likely to win future contests and a loser is less likely. Winner and loser effects can exist both as a means of mutual assessment, learning about the capabilities of others in the group, or self-assessment [9, 19]. The latter type is of particular interest in the work presented here as it does not require communication with or identification of other individuals in the group. Furthermore, this self-assessment mechanism affects the individual's perception of its own abilities to the point where it can alter behavior without any actual change in ability [12]. Winner and loser effects have also been shown to affect animal personalities.

Although winner and loser effects are present in a variety of species, their effects differ both from one species to the next and from one situation to the next. For example, shy losers have been observed to become bold in some situations and more shy in others [14, 18]. In other cases, winner and loser effects differ based on the age and experience of the individual, with younger, naïve individuals having high loser effects and older, more experienced individuals exhibiting high winner effects [12]. Of particular interest to the work presented here is the result that winner and loser effects are rarely persistent and decay over time [18]. This can be the result of either the hormonal state produced by the contest itself or other behavioral and ecological factors [8, 22]. The primary benefit of winner and loser effect decay is that as the time since the assessment increases, the information gained is less reliable and certain [20, 22]. If no new information is gained through new experiences, the winner and loser effects can decay to the point where an individual behaves as if it had no experience in the first place [18].

3. METHODS

The simulations used for this work were built using a modified version of a collective movement model developed through observations of collective movement attempts in a group of white-faced capuchin monkeys [15, 32], and was later confirmed in observations of sheep [33]. The anonymous quorum-sensing nature of the model means that leaders, whether successful or unsuccessful, cannot be recognized as such, and decision-making must rely on the number of participating individuals only. Despite being a collective movement model, actual movement through an environment is not a part of the model. Rather, the focus of the model is on the decision-making process that precedes a movement. Examples of such situations are found in nature where individuals exhibit notifying behaviors indicating a preferred direction of movement during a predeparture period [34].

3.1 Collective Movement Model

The simulation model used in this study was developed through observations of collective movement attempts in a group of white-faced capuchin monkeys [32, 15], and was later confirmed in observations of sheep groups [33]. It uses anonymous mimetism [34] and consists of three probabilistic interaction rules to govern the decision-making process involved in starting collective movements. The first rule assumes that all individuals within the group can initiate a collective movement attempt (see the Supplementary Material for a full description of each rule). While this assumption may not hold for groups with dominant leaders, studies have shown that it is a viable assumption for egalitarian animal groups, such as the capuchin monkeys used in the model's development, and robot swarms [3].

The second rule describes the rate at which followers join the collective movement attempt. As the number of individuals following the initiator increases, the rate at which individuals join the movement also increases. Since the model assumes global communication, once an individual initiates a collective movement, all the other individuals in the group are assumed to have observed the initiation attempt and have the opportunity to follow the initiator.

The third rule describes the fact that not all initiation attempts are successful, as initiators often cancel and return to the group. As the number of individuals following the initiator increases, the rate at which the initiator cancels an initiation decreases. Also, simulations of the model include the implicit assumption that a successful collective movement requires all of the members of the group to participate, since there is a non-zero probability of canceling even if all but one member participates. While this is not necessarily the case in nature, cohesive, collective movements were the primary objective of this work and, as such, incomplete movements were considered failures.

3.2 Integrating Personality

To investigate the effects of altering the rate at which individuals initiate a movement, follow an initiator, and cancel a movement, Gautrais added an individual-specific constant, referred to as a "k factor," to the rate calculations of the collective movement model [15]. Since this k factor can either increase or decrease the three decision-making rates, it was an ideal means with which the effects of personality could be incorporated into the model.

Three important points were considered in integrating personality with the collective movement model. First, personality has been observed in natural systems to affect the events used in this model in different ways. For example, a bold personality should result in a higher initiation rate and lower following and canceling rates since bold individuals are generally less sensitive to the actions of others in the group [16, 26]. On the other hand, a shy personality should result in a lower initiation rate and higher following and canceling rates since they are more sensitive to others. Second, the magnitude with which a shy personality affects the model should be the same as a bold personality so as not to bias the model towards one personality over another. Since k had a non-inclusive lower limit of zero, the non-inclusive upper limit of one was chosen to ensure balance. In the simulations described below, personalities were limited to the range [0.1:0.9] to ensure these limits were satisfied. Lastly, although neither the original model, nor the observations on which the model was based, discussed the personality of the individual animals involved, it was assumed that the observed group members could be classified as having either bold or shy personalities. However, since the personalities of the observed individuals were unknown, all individuals were assumed to have had a default moderate personality ($p_i = 0.5$), which produced the same results as the original model (see the Supplementary Material for a full description of how personality was integrated into the model).

The initiator's personality was updated after every collective movement initiation attempt using the following standard update (or learning) rule [2, 23, 37]:

$$p_{t+1} = p_t(1 - \lambda) + \lambda r \tag{1}$$

where p_t was the initiator's personality for the current movement, p_{t+1} was the personality for the next movement, λ was the rate at which updates changed the personality, and r was the reinforcement value used to update the personality. When λ was low, the personality was primarily determined through long-term historical success and changes were minor. When λ was high, the personality was primarily determined through short-term success, namely the last initiation attempt, and changes from one attempt to the next

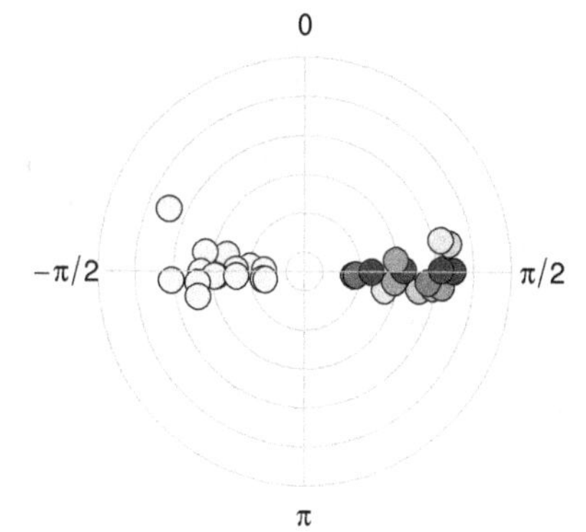

Figure 1: Representative preferred movement directions for a group size of 20 is shown. Each circle represents the preferred direction of movement of an individual and the color represents the effectiveness in the current environment with dark red denoting the most effective.

were significant. For the simulations described in this work, a low value of lambda was chosen ($\lambda = 0.02$) to emphasize long-term initiation success. For successful initiations, the reinforcement was $r = 1$, while it was $r = 0$ for unsuccessful initiations.

3.3 Environmental Change

In order to tie an individual's effectiveness to a particular environmental state, each individual was assigned a random preferred direction of movement, denoted d_i, that was drawn from a Gaussian distribution with either a mean of $\pi/2$ or $-\pi/2$, with the half of the group using one mean and half using the other (see Figure 1). A corresponding environmental direction, referred to as d_e, was also added and represented the optimal direction of movement, such as the true direction to a food patch. Note that individuals were unable to sense the preferred direction directly. The only way for an individual to evaluate their effectiveness in the environment was to successfully initiate a collective movement and gain direct experience. The personality update (see Equation 1) rule was modified to incorporate an initiator's effectiveness in the current environment as follows:

$$p_{t+1} = p_t(1 - \lambda) + \lambda r \frac{f(d_i - d_e, \mu, \sigma)}{f(0, \mu, \sigma)} \tag{2}$$

where $f(d_i - d_e, \mu, \sigma)$ computed the value in a normal distribution corresponding to the difference in the individual's preferred direction d_i and the optimal, environmental direction d_e using a given μ and σ, and $f(0, \mu, \sigma)$ computed the value corresponding to no difference. This modification has the effect of scaling winner effects by the effectiveness of an initiator in the current environment. Successful initiators with a preferred direction close to the optimal value received a reward close to the maximum, while initiators that lead followers in the wrong direction received no reward. For all simulations, $\mu = 0$ and $\sigma = 0.1$.

To evaluate the adaptability of leadership personalities, the environment's optimal direction was altered after a specified number of simulations. Two different types of change were evaluated in simulations. In the first, the optimal direction changed only once from $\pi/2$ to $-\pi/2$ and occurred halfway through the evaluation. This allowed enough simulations for personalities to emerge and stabilize before the environment changed. In the second, the optimal direction changed from $\pi/2$ to $-\pi/2$ and then back to $\pi/2$. This provided an opportunity to determine if the same individual that had once been a leader before the environmental change returned to a leadership role once the environment reverted to its original state.

Note that the success of a particular initiation attempt was not tied to an environmental state. Leadership success was only tied to an individual's ability to initiate a movement in which all members of the group participated. However, since environmental state did affect the individual's future personality, the success of the individual in initiating future movements, namely through the canceling rate, was affected by environmental state.

3.4 Personality Decay

After evaluating a number of possible decay functions, a decay function that minimally disrupted the overall success of the collective movement model, while still affording meaningful personality decay, was chosen (see the Supplementary Material for more information). This decay function, referred to as *momentum decay*, acted in a manner opposite to the more traditional exponential decay. Namely, small changes in personality were made when an initiation attempt was recent with the changes growing exponentially larger as the number of simulations since the initiation attempt increased. Since environmental changes were rare events, recent experiences were very likely to be accurate, hence the need for a decay function that did not make large changes to personality after only a few simulations. Decayed personalities were calculated as follows:

$$p_{t+1} = (p_l - p_i)\left(1 - e^{(\Delta t - d_t)/5}\right) + p_i \qquad (3)$$

where p_{t+1} was the decayed personality for the next simulation, p_l was the personality after the last initiation attempt, p_i was the initial personality, Δt was the number of simulations since the last initiation attempt, and d_t was the treatment's decay time. Since the number of individuals in the group affect the number of initiations an individual may make, the two different decay times evaluated were specified as a function of the group size N. The values evaluated were $100N$ and $500N$. Results from exploratory simulations showed that decay rates below the lower value were too disruptive and rates above the higher value did not produce significantly different results.

3.5 Numerical Implementation

Numerical simulations of the collective movement model were implemented in Java using a customized version[1] of the original algorithm [15]. The time of each event was calculated as a random number drawn from an exponential distribution calculated from the appropriate model rate equation. As such, the simulations used continuous time events, and not discrete time.

The original model was only evaluated with a group size of 10, but other work has shown that the success of collective movement initiations increases as the group size is increased, with most success differences present in group sizes of 50 or less and diminishing effects beyond a group size of 100 [10]. As such, evaluating different group sizes presents an opportunity to evaluate the effects of personality with different group dynamics. To evaluate the impact of the initial personality value, treatments were performed using the following personality values for all individuals within a group: shy ($p_v = 0.2$), moderate ($p_v = 0.5$), and bold ($p_v = 0.8$). Within each treatment, group sizes from 20 to 50 were used.[2] Fifty evaluations were performed for each group size, each with a different random seed. A single evaluation consisted of $2,000N$ simulations, where N was the group size. Each simulation constituted a single attempt at a collective movement and ended in either success (all individuals participating in the movement) or the initiator canceling. Individual personality values were reset at the beginning of each evaluation and persisted from one simulation to the next. The model parameters used were the same as those used in the original model [15, 32].

The R `changepoint` package was used to analyze trends in personality values of successive attempts in an evaluation [24]. This software package allowed for the identification of shifts in the mean personality value for a particular individual. These shifts, referred to as changepoints, represented a potential personality transition in our simulations. Since personalities were not constant and the analysis produced a linear approximation of a portion of a personality value time series, we defined a personality to be bold if a segment of the personality had a mean value greater than or equal to 0.85. The high threshold was needed to differentiate truly bold individuals from individuals with an initially bold personality (i.e., $p = 0.8$) that had not yet had an opportunity to gain experience.

4. RESULTS & ANALYSIS

Five broad types of simulation treatments were performed to evaluate the ability of individuals to adapt to a changing environment: *a*) no personality (baseline); *b*) personality, but no direction change or personality decay; *c*) personality with a direction change, but no personality decay; *d*) personality with a direction change and personality decay; and *e*) personality with two direction changes, but no personality decay. This broad range of treatments allowed comparisons between treatments with respect to environmental change and personality decay.

4.1 Leadership Success

The mean percentage of simulations in which individuals led a successful initiation were analyzed for each treatment and group size combination (see Figure 2). The addition of personality resulted in statistically significant improvements for all treatments except those using highly disruptive personality decay rates (see Figures 2b and 2c). As has been shown in previous work, a higher initial personality and a larger group generally led to increased overall success, regardless of the specific treatment. For simulations with a shy initial personality, there were minimal differences in success rate, regardless of environmental change or personality

[1]Simulation source code and data analysis scripts are available for download from `https://github.com/snucsne/bio-inspired-leadership`.

[2]A group size of 10 was not included in treatments since previous results indicate that the maximum number of leaders in such a group is one, thus limiting our ability to effectively evaluate the ability of personalities to adapt in a changing environment.

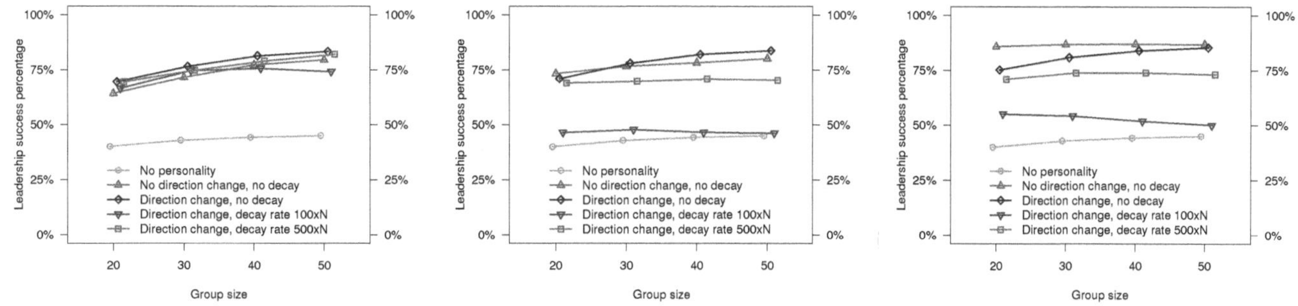

(a) Initial shy personality (b) Initial moderate personality (c) Initial bold personality

Figure 2: Comparisons of the mean percentage of all initiations by leaders that are successful between different simulation treatments are shown (mean/SE). Simulation treatments using the original collective movement model with the personality modification and treatments with the personality modification but no direction change in the environment are shown for comparison purposes.

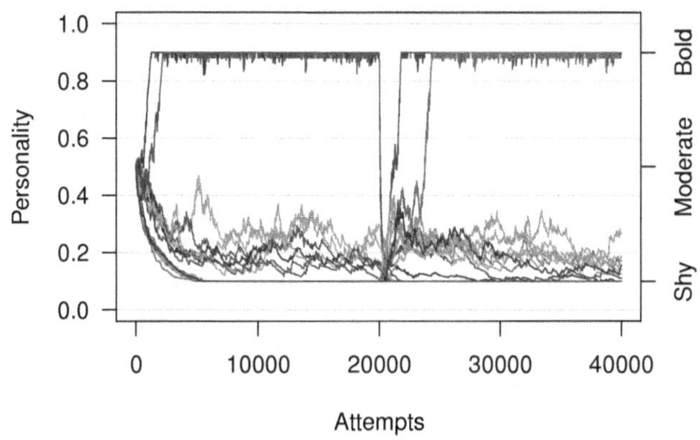

Figure 3: A representative plot of individual personalities from an evaluation of a group size of 20 and a change in environmental conditions halfway through the evaluation is shown.

decay. However, for treatments with bolder initial personalities, significant differences were apparent, with both environmental change and personality decay having negative effects on overall success. Also, treatments using a rapid personality decay rate of $100N$ and a bold initial personality had low leadership success, almost as low as treatments not using personality.

4.2 Adaptation to Environmental Change

Figure 4 shows representative personality histories in evaluations incorporating environmental change. Figures 4a and 4b depict two individuals in an evaluation with a group size of 20 and initially moderate personalities. In the initial environmental state, the first individual was an effective leader, while the second individual was effective after the change in the environment. Note that the initial leader's personality was immediately affected by the environmental change with a rapid decline after the halfway mark of 20,000 simulations. In contrast, the second leader required time to not only begin sampling the environment, but to also experience success and reach a bold personality.

Figures 4d and 4e depict two individuals in an evaluation with a group size of 20, initially moderate personalities, and personality decay. Note the differences between these histories and the histories of individuals without personality decay. With a lack of experience, personalities for shy individuals decayed to their initial moderate levels. Only with consistent failure did the personalities return to a shy value. Decay in bold personalities was not as visible since those individuals, by virtue of their bold personality, initiated movements frequently, thus gaining frequent experience.

4.3 Personality Decay

The number of overall simulations and initiations by a single individual required for an individual with a shy personality to gain enough successful experiences to become bold were compared for evaluations with a personality decay rate of $500N$ and without personality decay. Additionally, since the presence of a bold leader affects the rate at which subsequent leaders emerge, the number of simulations and initiations required for the first bold personality to emerge were also compared (see Table 1). For all treatments except one, the addition of personality decay resulted in statistically significant reductions in the number of initiations required for the first bold personality to emerge after the change in the environment (Kolmogorov-Smirnov test, $p < 0.05$).[3] For treatments using bolder initial personalities, statistically significant reductions in the total number of simulations and initiations required by a single individual to transition to a bold personality were observed, regardless of any bold personalities that may have previously emerged. In contrast, treatments not using personality decay outperformed those with personality decay during the initial adjustment period, especially with bolder initial personalities.

Personalities for individuals in treatments using a rapid personality decay rate of $100N$ rarely exhibited a clear bold or shy value. This was especially the case for large group sizes and treatments using an initial bold personality. In fact, for an initial bold personality, no individual reached the minimum threshold of 0.85 to be classified as a bold personality for treatments using a group size of 40 and 50. Figure 4f depicts a representative personality history for just such an individual. The individual was better suited to the

[3]See the Supplementary Material for the full results of statistical comparisons between treatments without personality decay and those with decay.

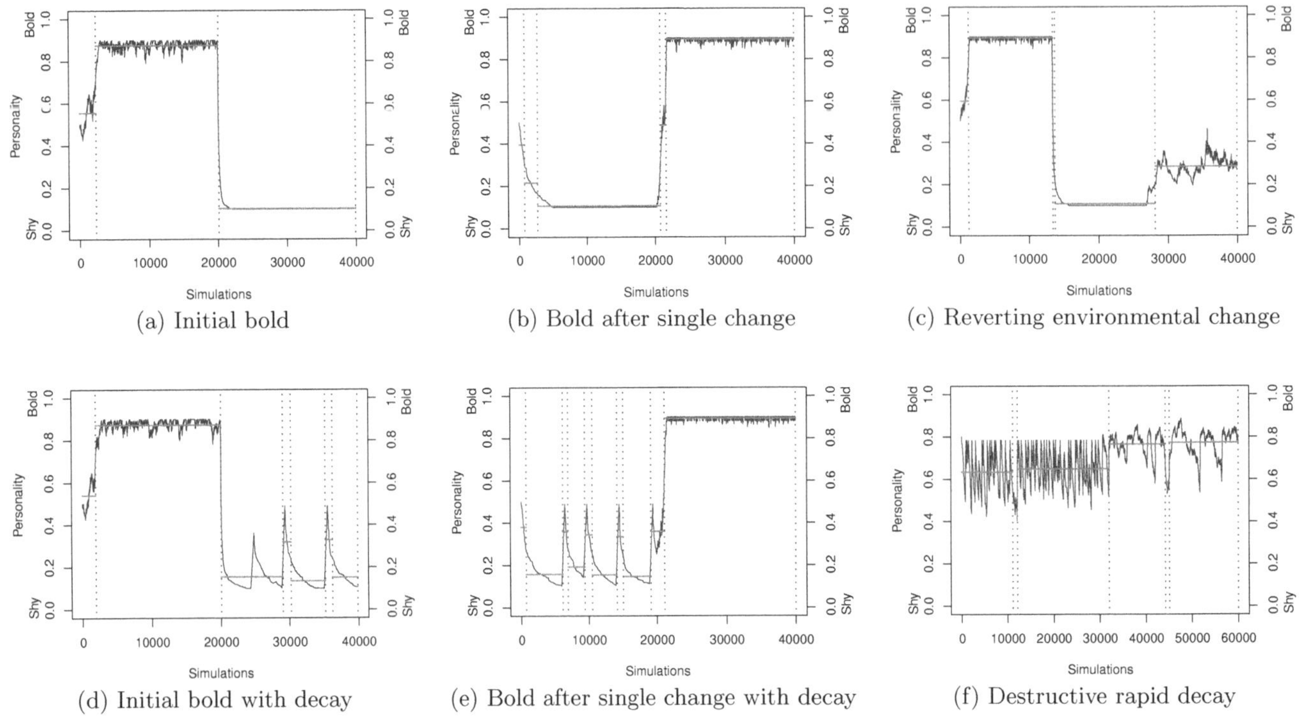

(a) Initial bold

(b) Bold after single change

(c) Reverting environmental change

(d) Initial bold with decay

(e) Bold after single change with decay

(f) Destructive rapid decay

Figure 4: Representative personality history plots for different treatments are shown. Horizontal red lines represent mean personality values and vertical dashed lines represent points at which the mean changed. Figures 4a and 4b depict bold leaders in an environment with a single change and no decay. Figure 4c depicts a leader in an environment that changed and then reverted back to its original state. Figures 4d and 4e depict bold leaders in a environment with a single change and decay. Figure 4f depicts an individual in a simulation with a rapid decay rate that inhibited the emergence of leaders.

Group Size	Adaptation	Bold statistic	Without decay		With decay	
20	Change	Simulations	2503.6 ±2663.2		2222.1 ±2861.2	*
		Simulations (first)	1470.1 ±431.3		1198.6 ±438.6	*
30	Change	Initiations	387.7 ±212.3		334.1 ±228.8	*
		Initiations (first)	210.9 ±37.3		158.6 ±40.1	*
		Simulations	5613.0 ±5213.0		5608.5 ±6523.2	*
		Simulations (first)	1791.9 ±416.3		1254.9 ±472.1	*
40	Initial	Initiations	238.5 ±152.4	*	262.5 ±163.4	
		Simulations	4946.9 ±5023.5	*	7002.5 ±8112.0	
	Change	Initiations	391.2 ±212.1		305.8 ±185.4	*
		Initiations (first)	194.2 ±29.1		130.4 ±31.9	*
		Simulations	8983.4 ±8321.4		8790.1 ±9145.3	*
		Simulations (first)	2364.6 ±432.7		1680.2 ±435.9	*
50	Initial	Simulations	6824.6 ±7155.9	*	8869.4 ±10034.7	
	Change	Initiations	357.1 ±169.9		307.5 ±188.4	*
		Initiations (first)	180.3 ±20.7		119.6 ±17.4	*
		Simulations	11320.3 ±9725.8	*	11479.1 ±11256.1	
		Simulations (first)	2812.4 ±450.6		2176.8 ±366.2	*

Table 1: The mean number of simulations and individual initiations required for an individual to become bold are shown for an initially moderate personality ($p = 0.5$) for evaluations both with and without personality decay (mean ± std. deviation). Differences calculated as statistically significant by the Kolmogorov-Smirnov test with $p \leq 0.05$ are denoted with an *. Statistics not calculated as statistically significant are omitted.

environment after the change in direction, as evident by a more consistent personality value, but note that it was unable to reach the minimum bold personality threshold.

4.4 Re-emergent Leaders

For evaluations in which the optimal environmental direction of movement returned to its original value, no individuals were observed to be leaders both during the initial and final stages when the optimal direction was the same. In each evaluation, individuals that were shy during the initial stage became bold during the final stage. However, despite not becoming bold, individuals with a preferred direction close to the environment's optimal direction did experience improved leadership success, as is shown by visible winner effects in Figure 4c.

5. DISCUSSION

Analysis of these simulation results provides a number of interesting insights. First, using winner and loser effects as a self-assessment mechanism alone is sufficient to produce rapid adaptations to either the initial, fixed environment or to an environment that has recently changed. Leaders that were once effective quickly adapted their personalities when they weren't successful, regardless of the personality distribution in the group, thus providing opportunities for shy individuals to initiate and gain up-to-date information on their effectiveness in the current environment. Beyond the ability to promote rapid adaptations, the simplicity of the mechanism itself is especially beneficial considering the complexity inherent in the system even before the number of individuals is scaled higher. A complex mechanism of individual recognition and memory required for mutual assessment is not required for success and would undoubtedly be problematic for larger groups.

Another insight is that the initial, or default, personality of an individual has significant implications for the overall performance of the group, especially with respect to personality decay. As is evident in the baseline treatments without personality in Figure 2, failed initiations are initially more common than successes. Since frequent failures make transitioning from a shy to a bold personality far easier than the reverse, personalities decaying to a high initial value inhibits the emergence of distinct personality types, thus reducing the overall success of the group. This is particularly the case for fast decay rates, such as the $100N$ rate used here. If personality decay is to be a useful mechanism for promoting the rapid emergence of bold personalities in a dynamic environment, this problem must be addressed, most likely through the use of a more sophisticated decay algorithm.

6. CONCLUSIONS AND FUTURE WORK

The contributions of this work are as follows. First, these results show that winner and loser effects, modified by environmental suitability, were able to produce rapid changes in personality, allowing individuals to adapt their decision-making to a changing environment. Bold leaders that gained frequent experience in the environment began experiencing failure immediately after the change in the environment and adapted their personality accordingly. Without an effective leader, shy followers had more opportunities to initiate, and therefore gain new experiences. As a result of more initiation attempts, individuals that were then effective in the environment were able to adapt their personality accordingly. Second, the results show that individual adaptations happened quickly and required relatively few initiation experiences. Also, the number of required initiations was further reduced in many situations through the use of personality decay. Lastly, in the absence of environmental change and the associated uncertainty, these results show that individuals used their personality to modify their decision-making process such that they were able to participate in successful movements, thus increasing the overall success of the group.

This work represents but one aspect of a larger research effort. The most significant opportunity for future work is to incorporate these results into simulations involving actual movement. Such simulations would provide a number of real-world constraints that would test the adaptability of individuals and their personalities, including such things as local communication, dynamic communication networks, and conflicts of interest. Furthermore, in the simulations presented here, adaptation occurred at long timescales between initiation attempts. For the adaptation mechanism to work in simulations involving actual movement, adaptation must occur within short timescales. One way to accomplish this may be through the use of multiplicative winner and loser effects, instead of the additive effects used here [18]. Lastly, these results indicate that personality decay provides benefits in many situations. Further investigation into how to better balance its benefits and detriments is warranted.

7. ACKNOWLEDGMENTS

This material is based upon work supported by the National Science Foundation under Grant No. BCS-1124837. Some of the computing for this project was performed at the OU Supercomputing Center for Education & Research (OSCER) at the University of Oklahoma.

8. REFERENCES

[1] R. Bergmüller and M. Taborsky. Animal personality due to social niche specialisation. *Trends in Ecology & Evolution*, 25(9):504–511, 2010.

[2] C. Bernstein, A. Kacelnik, and J. Krebs. Individual decisions and the distribution of predators in a patchy environment. *The Journal of Animal Ecology*, 57(3):1007–1026, 1988.

[3] M. Brambilla, E. Ferrante, M. Birattari, and M. Dorigo. Swarm robotics: a review from the swarm engineering perspective. *Swarm Intelligence*, 7(1):1–41, 2013.

[4] A. J. Carter, H. H. Marshall, R. Heinsohn, and G. Cowlishaw. Personality predicts decision making only when information is unreliable. *Animal Behaviour*, 86(3):633–639, 2013.

[5] I. D. Couzin, J. Krause, N. R. Franks, and S. A. Levin. Effective leadership and decision-making in animal groups on the move. *Nature*, 433(7025):513–516, 2005.

[6] N. J. Dingemanse and M. Wolf. Recent models for adaptive personality differences: a review. *Philosophical Transactions of the Royal Society B: Biological Sciences*, 365(1560):3947–3958, 2010.

[7] J. R. Dyer, D. P. Croft, L. J. Morrell, and J. Krause. Shoal composition determines foraging success in the guppy. *Behavioral Ecology*, 20(1):165–171, 2009.

[8] R. L. Earley, C.-K. Lu, I.-H. Lee, S. C. Wong, and Y. Hsu. Winner and loser effects are modulated by hormonal states. *Frontiers in Zoology*, 10(1):1–13, 2013.

[9] D. O. Elias, M. M. Kasumovic, D. Punzalan, M. C. Andrade, and A. C. Mason. Assessment during aggressive contests between male jumping spiders. *Animal Behaviour*, 76(3):901–910, 2008.

[10] B. E. Eskridge. Effects of local communication and topology on collective movement initiation. In *International Conference on the Simulation and Synthesis of Living Things*, volume 13, pages 155–162, 2012.

[11] B. E. Eskridge, E. Valle, and I. Schlupp. Using experience to promote the emergence of leaders and followers. In *European Conference on Complex Systems.* Complex Systems Society, 2013.

[12] T. W. Fawcett and R. A. Johnstone. Learning your own strength: winner and loser effects should change with age and experience. *Proceedings of the Royal Society B: Biological Sciences*, 277(1686):1427–1434, 2010.

[13] A. Flack, B. Pettit, R. Freeman, T. Guilford, and D. Biro. What are leaders made of? the role of individual experience in determining leader–follower relations in homing pigeons. *Animal Behaviour*, 83(3):703–709, 2012.

[14] A. Frost, A. Winrow-Giffen, P. Ashley, and L. Sneddon. Plasticity in animal personality traits: does prior experience alter the degree of boldness? *Proceedings of the Royal Society B: Biological Sciences*, 274(1608):333–339, 2007.

[15] J. Gautrais. The hidden variables of leadership. *Behavioural Processes*, 84(3):664–667, 2010.

[16] J. L. Harcourt, T. Z. Ang, G. Sweetman, R. A. Johnstone, and A. Manica. Social feedback and the emergence of leaders and followers. *Current Biology*, 19(3):248–252, 2009.

[17] J. L. Harcourt, G. Sweetman, R. A. Johnstone, and A. Manica. Personality counts: the effect of boldness on shoal choice in three-spined sticklebacks. *Animal Behaviour*, 77(6):1501–1505, 2009.

[18] Y. Hsu, R. L. Earley, and L. L. Wolf. Modulation of aggressive behaviour by fighting experience: mechanisms and contest outcomes. *Biological Reviews*, 81(1):33–74, 2006.

[19] Y. Hsu, I.-H. Lee, and C.-K. Lu. Prior contest information: mechanisms underlying winner and loser effects. *Behavioral Ecology and Sociobiology*, 63(9):1247–1257, 2009.

[20] S.-P. Huang, S.-Y. Yang, and Y. Hsu. Persistence of winner and loser effects depends on the behaviour measured. *Ethology*, 117(2):171–180, 2011.

[21] R. Johnstone and A. Manica. Evolution of personality differences in leadership. *Proceedings of the National Academy of Sciences*, 108(20):8373–8378, 2011.

[22] M. M. Kasumovic, D. O. Elias, S. Sivalinghem, A. C. Mason, and M. C. Andrade. Examination of prior contest experience and the retention of winner and loser effects. *Behavioral Ecology*, 21(2):404–409, 2010.

[23] E. Katsnelson, U. Motro, M. Feldman, and A. Lotem. Evolution of learned strategy choice in a frequency-dependent game. *Proceedings of the Royal Society B: Biological Sciences*, 279(1731):1176–1184, 2012.

[24] R. Killick and I. Eckley. *changepoint: An R package for changepoint analysis*, 2013. R package version 1.1.

[25] R. Kurvers, B. Eijkelenkamp, K. van Oers, B. van Lith, S. van Wieren, R. Ydenberg, and H. Prins. Personality differences explain leadership in barnacle geese. *Animal Behaviour*, 78(2):447–453, 2009.

[26] R. Kurvers, K. Van Oers, B. Nolet, R. Jonker, S. Van Wieren, H. Prins, and R. Ydenberg. Personality predicts the use of social information. *Ecology Letters*, 13(7):829–837, 2010.

[27] R. H. Kurvers, V. M. Adamczyk, S. E. van Wieren, and H. H. Prins. The effect of boldness on decision-making in barnacle geese is group-size-dependent. *Proceedings of the Royal Society B: Biological Sciences*, 278(1714):2018–2024, 2011.

[28] K. J. Mathot, J. Wright, B. Kempenaers, and N. Dingemanse. Adaptive strategies for managing uncertainty may explain personality-related differences in behavioural plasticity. *Oikos*, 121(7):1009–1020, 2012.

[29] P.-O. Montiglio, C. Ferrari, and D. Réale. Social niche specialization under constraints: personality, social interactions and environmental heterogeneity. *Philosophical Transactions of the Royal Society B: Biological Sciences*, 368(1618), 2013.

[30] S. Nakayama, J. L. Harcourt, R. A. Johnstone, and A. Manica. Initiative, personality and leadership in pairs of foraging fish. *PloS One*, 7(5):e36606, 2012.

[31] J. E. Oosten, C. Magnhagen, and C. K. Hemelrijk. Boldness by habituation and social interactions: a model. *Behavioral Ecology and Sociobiology*, 64(5):793–802, 2010.

[32] O. Petit, J. Gautrais, J.-B. Leca, G. Theraulaz, and J.-L. Deneubourg. Collective decision-making in white-faced capuchin monkeys. *Proceedings of the Royal Society B: Biological Sciences*, 276(1672):3495–3503, 2009.

[33] M.-H. Pillot, J. Gautrais, P. Arrufat, I. D. Couzin, R. Bon, and J.-L. Deneubourg. Scalable rules for coherent group motion in a gregarious vertebrate. *PLoS ONE*, 6(1):e14487, 01 2011.

[34] L. Pyritz, A. King, C. Sueur, and C. Fichtel. Reaching a consensus: Terminology and concepts used in coordination and decision-making research. *International Journal of Primatology*, 32(6):1268–1278, 2011.

[35] A. Sih, A. Bell, and J. C. Johnson. Behavioral syndromes: an ecological and evolutionary overview. *Trends in Ecology & Evolution*, 19(7):372–378, 2004.

[36] J. Stamps and T. G. G. Groothuis. The development of animal personality: relevance, concepts and perspectives. *Biological Reviews*, 85(2):301–325, 2010.

[37] R. S. Sutton and A. G. Barto. *Reinforcement Learning: An Introduction.* MIT Press, 1998.

[38] M. Wolf, G. S. van Doorn, O. Leimar, and F. J. Weissing. Life-history trade-offs favour the evolution of animal personalities. *Nature*, 447(7144):581–584, 2007.

Evolution of Biologically Plausible Neural Networks Performing a Visually Guided Reaching Task

Derrik E. Asher Jeffrey L. Krichmar Nicolas Oros
Department of Cognitive Sciences
2201 Social & Behavioral Sciences Gateway Building
University of California, Irvine, CA 92697-5100
{dasher, jkrichma, noros}@uci.edu

ABSTRACT

An evolutionary strategy (ES) algorithm was utilized to evolve a simulated neural network based on the known anatomy of the posterior parietal cortex (PPC), to perform a visually guided reaching task. In this task, a target remained visible for the duration of a trial, and an agent's goal was to move its hand to the target as rapidly as possible and remain for the duration of that trial. The ES was used to tune the strength of 15609 connections between neural areas and 4 parameters governing the neural dynamics. The model had sensory latencies replicating those found in recording studies with monkeys. The ES ran 100 times and generated very diverse networks that could all perform the task well. The evolved networks 1) showed velocity profiles consistent with biological movements, and 2) found solutions that reflect short-range excitation and long-range, contralateral inhibition similar to neurobiological networks. These results provide theoretical evidence for the important parameters and projections governing sensorimotor transformations in neural systems.

General Terms

Algorithms, Experimentation, Theory

Keywords

Neural Networks, Visually Guided Reaching, Evolutionary Strategy, Sensorimotor Transformation

1. INTRODUCTION

Primates have the impressive ability to perform fluid movements guided by visual and proprioceptive information. Complex neural architectures in the primate brain that are responsible for these sensory guided movements have emerged through the process of evolution and natural selection. In particular, experimental evidence has highlighted specific roles for the parietal, pre-motor and motor cortices. The parietal cortex has been viewed as an association area that combines different types of sensory information to form a single representation of space [1]. Evidence has implicated the posterior parietal cortex (PPC) as being necessary for transforming multiple sources of sensory information such as visual and proprioceptive information into actions [2, 3], and important for aspects of movement [4, 5]. Sensory integration for the control of reaching actions is primarily performed by a network of brain regions connecting the PPC, dorsal pre-motor (PMd) and, primary motor (M1) cortices [3, 6]. Interestingly, experiments have shown that the sensory inputs associated with the neural activity of reaching actions arrive in parietal brain regions with different latencies. It was found that proprioceptive inputs indicating the position of hand relative to the center of gaze arrives after a delay of approximately 30ms, and visual inputs from a stimulus arrive after a delay of approximately 90ms [7].

Computational models have contributed significantly towards our understanding of the neurophysiological activation associated with action execution and sensory-motor transformations [8-12]. Visually guided models of reaching actions have been used to show how sensory input combines to give rise to joint angle estimations [13], and the neural representations in distinct regions of the brain for competing reaching decisions [8]. However, the aforementioned models did not take into consideration the different sensory delays that must be accounted for in order to assemble a biologically realistic neural network model performing sensorimotor transformations. Furthermore, while they included feedforward projections from sensory to motor areas, they did not take into consideration the huge number and diversity of lateral connections within the PPC and feedback connections to the PPC.

Therefore, the main goal of the present work was to investigate if a neuroanatomical architecture with complex lateral and feedback connections could cope with sensory delays while performing a visually guided reaching task. The second goal of this work was to investigate the diversity of networks with the same general architecture but different parameter values that could perform the task well. Specifically, we used an evolutionary strategy (ES) algorithm to tune the large number of parameters (~15000) of our model. We ran the ES 100 times with different random seeds and analyzed the differences between the best solutions generated.

In the present work, we show that a biologically plausible neural architecture could be artificially evolved to perform accurate reaching movements to visual targets, and overcome sensory delays. The results suggest a neural architecture based on the parietal cortex for reaching, and provide theoretical evidence for the diversity of connection sets that can give rise to the behavior observed in humans and non-human primates. Such an architecture inspired by the primate brain highlights the great potential for neural based sensorimotor systems that can generate fluid sensory-guided movements.

2. METHODS

2.1 Visually Guided Reaching Task

Simulated agents were evolved through artificial selection to perform a visually guided task designed to test smooth and accurate movements in the presence of visual stimulus input (target). This task was designed to be similar to those carried out by humans and non-human primates [14]. An agent consisted of a

GECCO'14, July 12–16, 2014, Vancouver, BC, Canada.

ACM 978-1-4503-2662-9/14/07...$15.00.
http://dx.doi.org/10.1145/2576768.2598368

hand that could move on a 2D space, an eye that perceived the hand and the target in this space, and a neural network that processed sensory information into motor commands in order to move the hand towards the target. The 2D space was measured in degrees of visual angle from an agent's central fixation (0°, 0°) ranging from [-50°, 50°] in both the x and y directions. An agent's vision was fixed, implying that it could not move its eyes or head.

During a trial, the goal of an agent was to move its hand towards a target as fast as possible, and then hold it on the target for the remainder of the trial. An agent always started a trial with its hand located in the center of the 2D space (0°, 0°). The target was visible to the agent for the entire duration of a trial (50 timesteps simulating 500ms of real time).

Agents were evolved to reach eight targets situated at different locations on an invisible square. For this reason, each agent performed eight trials, one trial for each of the targets located 25° (two vertical and two horizontal targets) or 35° (four diagonal targets) from the center of the visual space.

2.2 Neural Network Architecture

A neural network based on the know anatomy of the primate brain was designed to perform a visually guided reaching task. The model consisted of 367 neurons distributed into four distinct regions (Figure 1): Vision, Proprioception, Posterior Parietal Cortex (PPC), and Premotor/Primary Motor Cortex (PMd/M1) with a fixed number of neurons per region. Excitatory topographic projections were made between the Vision area and the PPC, and inhibitory topographic projections between the Proprioception area and PPC (Figure 1 and Section 2.2.1). The PPC had lateral (recurrent) connections where neurons were fully connected to each other. The PPC was also fully connected to PMd/M1 neurons encoding movement of the hand (Up, Down, Left, and Right). Finally, these neurons projected back to the neurons in the PPC.

In our experiments, only the weights from the PPC to PMd/M1 (feedforward - 484 weights), from PMd/M1 to PPC (feedback - 484 weights), and of the lateral PPC connections were evolved (14641 weights). Therefore, the model had a total of 15609 evolvable connections, initialized randomly to values between [-1, 1] drawn from a uniform distribution.

For purposes of analyses, the parameters were separated into two distinct categories, neural firing and weights. The evolved parameters governing simulated neural firing rates (Section 2.2.2) were compared directly to determine significant relationships within and between neural layers. The evolved connections were first separated into three distinct weight sets (feedforward, feedback, and lateral) and compared accordingly. The feedforward and feedback weights were further separated into ipsilateral and contralateral. The ipsilateral weights consisted of connections between the PPC and PMd/M1 layers corresponding to the same side of the agent (e.g., left half of PPC neurons connected to the left PMd/M1 neuron), and the contralateral weights for the opposite side of the agent. Lateral connections were further separated into short, medium, and long-range weights determined by the distance between PPC neurons.

2.2.1 Sensory Inputs

An agent received visual information from both the hand and the target, along with proprioceptive input from the hand. Both Vision and Proprioception regions of the network consisted of 11x11 2D arrays of sensory neurons, spanning the space [-50°, 50°] with a resolution of 10°. The sensory information from the locations of the hand and the target was mapped into the activity of the corresponding neurons in the Proprioception and Vision areas (activity set to one). The activity of the other sensory neurons was set to zero. In the case of vision, if both the hand and target overlapped, the activity of the visual input neuron for that particular location was set to two.

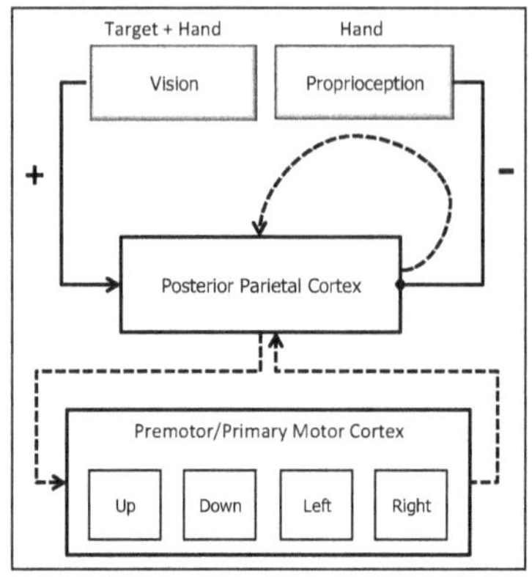

Figure 1. Neural architecture consisting of four areas: vision, proprioception, posterior parietal cortex (PPC) and premotor/primary motor cortex (PMd/M1). Dashed lines indicate evolvable connections.

The Vision to PPC connections were solely excitatory, whereas the Proprioception to PPC connections were solely inhibitory, allowing these sensory inputs to combine in a subtractive manner, similar to the empirically derived vector subtraction that seems be computed in the PPC [15]. The weight values of the projections from the Vision and Proprioception areas to the PPC neurons were assigned using 2D cosines as defined by Equation 1:

$$w_{ij} = f * cos^g\left(\frac{d}{20}\right) \tag{1}$$

where w_{ij} is the weight value connecting neuron j to neuron i, f is a scale factor set to 2 for vision and -4 for proprioception. The value of 2 was selected as the amplitude for the visual input signal. The value -4 was selected for the proprioceptive amplitude to approximately cancel the visual signal when the hand covered the target. The distance d was measured between a sensory and a PPC neuron. The peak of the 2D cosine resided at the location where a sensory neuron's coordinates were the same as a PPC neuron's coordinates ($d = 0$). The gain g was set to 200 to ensure that the projections from Proprioception and Vision to PPC displayed broad cosine tuning curves across multiple PPC neurons.

Based on empirical evidence [16], we implemented sensory latencies, which provided our model with delayed information on the location of the hand. It was observed that proprioceptive inputs have a latency of at least 30ms and visual inputs have a latency of about 90ms. To implement these latencies, the PPC neurons were provided with proprioceptive spatial information about the hand's location that lagged by three timesteps and visual information that lagged by nine timesteps. This implies that the model did not receive any visual input from the target or hand locations until the 9th timestep of every trial, rendering the model blind to the task for the first 1/5th of each trial. Proprioceptive information was received upon the 3rd timestep of each trial, though it provided no information about the target's location.

2.2.2 PPC and PMd/M1 Neural Firing

Neurons within the PPC and PMd/M1 regions of the model generated firing rates calculated with a sigmoid function that bounded activity between [0, 1]. The sigmoid function is described in Equation 2:

$$s_i(t) = \frac{1}{1 + exp^{(\Delta - I_i(t)) * k}} \tag{2}$$

where $s_i(t)$ is the firing rate for neuron i at timestep t, Δ is the bias for the sigmoid function that shifts the range of sensitivity, $I_i(t)$ is the synaptic input into neuron i from all connected neurons at timestep t, and k is the gain on the sigmoid function, which determines the sensitivity of the neurons. Neurons from the same area shared the same bias and gain values, but different areas could have different values. The synaptic input $I_i(t)$ was given by:

$$I_i(t) = \sum_j w_{ij} s_j(t-1) \tag{3}$$

where $I_i(t)$ is the input to a PPC or PMd/M1 neuron i at timestep t, w_{ij} is the weight connecting from neuron j to neuron i, and $s_j(t-1)$ is the firing rate for neuron j at the previous timestep $(t-1)$.

These bias and gain parameters were evolved for the PPC and PMd/M1 areas using the evolutionary strategy described below. Therefore, four neural firing parameters were evolved (two for each area) with the values of Δ and k being continuous and bounded within the ranges [-5, 5] and [0.1, 10] respectively.

2.3 Hand Movement

The reaching movements of the hand in the 2D space were calculated by a velocity vector defined by a rate of change in position (visual degrees/second) and a direction (angle). First we multiplied the activity of the PMd/M1 neurons with the sine and cosine of their respective angles in polar coordinates (Up: $\pi/2$, Left: π, Down: $3\pi/2$, and Right: 2π). The vector sum of these values was calculated and used to compute the horizontal and vertical components of the velocity vector. This method is commonly referred to as population coding [17]. The population coding method is described in Equation 4:

$$D_i = v * \sum_j \sin(\theta_j - \varphi_i) * s_j(t) \quad \begin{cases} i = 1,2 \\ j = 1, \dots, 4 \end{cases}$$

$$\theta_j = (j-1) * \frac{\pi}{2}$$

$$\varphi_i = (i-1) * \frac{\pi}{2} \tag{4}$$

where D is the velocity vector defined by vertical ($i=1$) and horizontal ($i=2$) components, j is the index representing the four PMd/M1 neurons, θ_j is the angle representing right, up, left, and down respectively, φ_i shifts the angle θ by pi/2 to take the cosine for the horizontal component of the velocity vector D, $s_j(t)$ is the firing rate for a PMd/M1 neuron j at timestep t, and v is a scalar set to 2. This value was chosen to set the maximum velocity of the hand to 2 degrees per timestep (200 degrees/second) if moving to a horizontal or vertical target (e.g., $D_1 = 2.0$ and $D_2 = 0$), and 2.83 degrees per timestep (283 degrees/second) if moving towards a diagonal target (e.g., $D_1 = 2.0$ and $D_2 = 2.0$). This rate of movement was chosen to match biological movement recorded in human and non-human primate reaching studies [18, 19].

2.4 Evolutionary Strategy

An evolutionary strategy algorithm, implemented in the Evolving Objects (http://eodev.sourceforge.net) library [20], was used to tune the neural networks over 25000 generations. At that point, the agent with the lowest fitness value was selected as the best agent. The free parameters and their ranges of values were: 1) 15609 connection weights [-1.0, 1.0] (Figure 1; dashed arrows), two biases [-5.0,5.0] (Δ in Equation 2) and two gains [0.1, 10] (k in Equation 2) for PMd/M1 and PPC areas (15613 total free parameters). All these parameters were continuous floats causing the search space to be extremely large. The ES used in our experiments was the evolution strategy algorithm named "mu comma lambda" (μ, λ) that includes elitism, crossover with roulette wheel selection, and mutation [21] with a population size of 20 agents. Each agent had a 40% chance of undergoing mutations. Mutations were applied randomly (probability of 0.5) to all free parameters by the addition of a small random number drawn from a Gaussian distribution G(0,0.3) for the weights, G(0, 3) for the biases, and G(0, 1.5) for the gains. The same ES was run 100 times with different random seeds to produce 100 independently evolved best agents. For the remainder of the manuscript the 100 independently evolved best agents will be referred to as the population.

2.4.1 Fitness Function

The fitness function was defined to reflect both an agent's speed and accuracy when reaching to the eight targets, as well as the ability to stay on the targets. Lower fitness values indicated better performance. Fitness was calculated by summing the Euclidian distance from the agent's hand to the target at each timestep, across all trials. The fitness function is given by Equation 5:

$$F = \sum_n \sum_t E_n(t) \quad \begin{cases} n = 1, \dots, 8 \\ t = 1, \dots, 50 \end{cases}$$

$$E_n(t) = \sqrt{(H_x(t) - T_{xn})^2 + \left(H_y(t) - T_{yn}\right)^2} \tag{5}$$

where F is an agent's fitness value, n represents the trial, t is the timestep in a trial, $E_n(t)$ is the Euclidian distance between an agent's hand and the target for timestep t during trial n, $(H_x(t), H_y(t))$ are the x and y components of hand position in 2D Cartesian space, and (T_{xn}, T_{yn}) is the 2D Cartesian coordinate of the target position for trial n.

The best (minimum) possible fitness value was 3563.4, which was the total amount of degrees of visual angle across all timesteps and trials that an agent would take to move to the eight targets at maximum velocity. Therefore, we subtracted off 3563.4 from all agents' fitness values to provide a normalized fitness per agent that was optimized at 0.

3. RESULTS

3.1 Fitness Evolution

Fitness values from the 100 agents generated by 100 ES runs show that fitness improved exponentially for the first 5000 generations and linearly from approximately generation 5000 to 25000 (Figure 2). It is clear from Figure 2 that the best agent evolved in coincidence with the population until generation 2000 (Figure 2; dashed line). From generations 2000 to 25000, the same ES consistently evolved a better fitness than the other 99 ES runs, resulting in a final fitness of 519.7 at generation 25000. The solid black line in Figure 2 is the mean fitness for the population of evolved agents with the width of the line showing the standard deviation around the mean for every generation, with a final average fitness of 1563.5 ± 363.9 at generation 25000.

3.2 Agent Behavior

To demonstrate that the agents evolved correct behaviors, we recorded the reach paths, velocity profiles, and target error (TE) for each of the 100 agents. The reach paths show the reaching trajectories across the trials, indicating precisely how an agent moved towards targets. The velocity profiles are complementary to the reach paths, in that they are derived from the reach path data, yet they provide a better understanding of why one agent's fitness was better than another. The TE shows how close an agent was to the target upon the last timestep of every trial, which was independent of an agent's reach path or velocity profile.

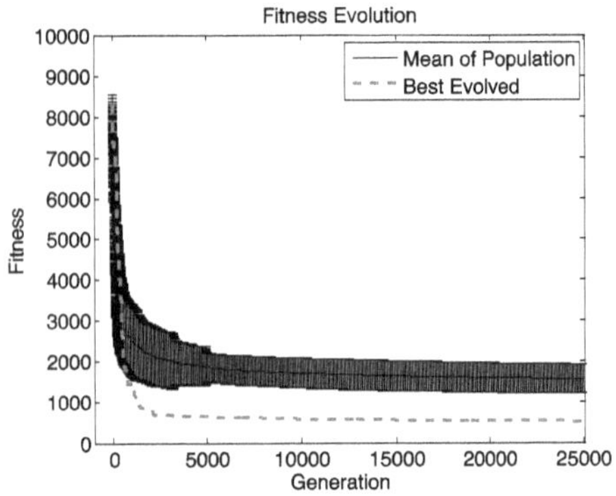

Figure 2. Fitness evolution over generations. The y-axis shows the fitness values. The x-axis shows generations. The thick solid line is the average fitness for the population. Dashed line shows the ES that produced the best agent.

3.2.1 Reach Paths

Reach paths for an agent's hand position at every timestep are shown in Figure 3 (a-c). Each data point represents either an agent's absolute hand position in space per timestep (Figure 3a-b), or the average hand position across the population per timestep (Figure 3c), with each line representing a trial. Distances between data points indicate the rate of movement.

Agents' trajectories in the visually guided reaching task reflect excellent performance corresponding to fitness values and distance from the target at the end of each trial (TE). We plotted the path of two individual agents: the best agent (agent #1) and the worst agent (agent #100). The mean reach path for the population of agents was calculated for every timestep across all agents and trials (Figure 3c). A comparison between the two individual agents illustrates one aspect of the diversity that emerged as a result of running 100 ES. The reach paths for agent #1 are clearly shorter (straighter) than that of agent #100. However, it can be seen that even agent #100 was able to correctly perform the reaching task. This point is emphasized with the average reach path from the population (Figure 3c).

The agents' reach paths provide a good understanding of the different reaching movements that emerged, but do not emphasize the rates at which the agents moved. We therefore investigated the velocity profiles of the agents.

3.2.2 Velocity Profiles

Figure 3 (d-f) shows the velocity profile for agent #1, agent #100, and the population. These were plotted using the average rate of movement per timestep (instantaneous rate) across the eight trials. It is important to note that the velocity profiles match up with the reach paths (Figure 3a-3c), implying that the velocity profiles (Figure 3; bottom row) reflect the average rate at which the hand moved through space in the reach path plots (Figure 3; top row).

The velocity profiles shown in Figure 3 (d-f) demonstrate that the agents' acceleration reached maximum velocity followed by deceleration until movement ceased. This data is similar to that observed from empirical studies with control subjects [18, 19].

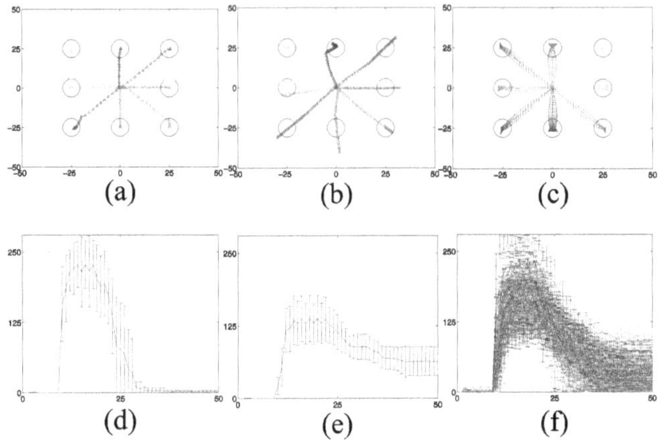

Figure 3. Reach paths and velocity profiles. (a-b) Reach paths for agent #1 and agent #100. (c) Average reach path for the 100 agents. (d-e) Average velocity profile for agent #1 and #100. (f) Overlapped average velocity profile for all agents. Error bars are standard error of the mean (SEM).

There are multiple differences between the two individual agents' data shown. Agent #1 (Figure 3d) moved its hand at a fast average rate then ceased movement at about 30 timesteps. Agent #100 moved about half as fast as agent #1 and had difficulty stopping. Figure 3f suggests that the population of agents were able to efficiently deal with sensory delays by the emergence of a single optimized movement towards the intended goal. A single-hump in the velocity profile suggests that the evolved architecture (Figure 1) allowed for sensory integration (proprioceptive and visual) of the hand positions through the trials, resulting in precise reaches to the visual targets (see Figure 3). Taken together, these results show that the population produced realistic behaviors.

3.2.3 Target Error (TE)

TE is a complementary measure of behavioral performance, which reveals the accuracy of the agents, independent of movement rate or path. TE corresponds to the distance between an agent and the target at the last timestep of each trial. Figure 4a shows that #100 was more accurate than #1 on half of the trials.

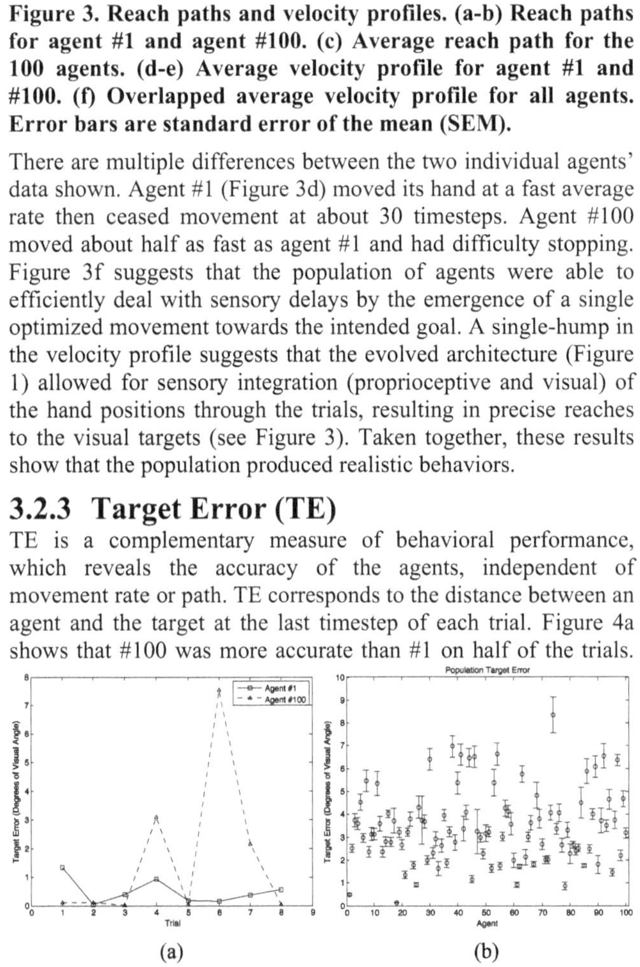

Figure 4. Target error (TE). Distance between target and hand at the last timestep per trial. Error bars show standard error of the mean (SEM). (a) TE across trials for agents #1 and #100. (b) Average TE per agent.

Interestingly, it is not clear from the TE metric that agent #1 has performed better than agent #100 across trials. This is due to the fact that TE does not take into account the rate of movement (velocity profile) or the distance (reach path) taken to reach the target. However, the TE metric does show how diverse behaviors were between the two agents across trials (Figure 4a). Moreover, average TE across the population reflects differences in behavior that independently evolved (Figure 4b).

Interestingly, we observed that the average TE for each agent was below the implemented 10° sensory (visual and proprioceptive) resolution. The TE metric emphasizes the fact that the evolved agents showed great accuracy despite the limited visual resolution. Further experiments will be conducted in order to investigate this emergent property.

3.3 Parameter Analysis

3.3.1 Population Diversity

We investigated the diversity of evolved parameters in the population of solutions to confirm that they were independent and non-degenerate. We used the moment of inertia (MoI) for quantifying population diversity of different parameters sets [22]. Values closer to 0 indicate less diversity, whereas greater values represent greater population diversity. Through the evolutionary process, diversity often decreases as the algorithm settles on a solution. Therefore, it is common practice to show the MoI in early vs. late stages of evolution to provide an understanding of how much diversity vanished as evolution progressed.

The amount of parameters along with standard deviation around an average parameter, the range of possible parameter values and the moment of inertia (MoI) calculation provide a decent approximation of population diversity (Table 1). The values in the rows of Table 1 are complementary, indicating that they are similar ways of assessing the diversity of a population. The amount of continuous parameters (Table 1; # Parameters) and their respective ranges (Table 1; Range) indicate the size of the search space that the solution(s) reside in. Given that the solution(s) are good, the average parameter values and their respective deviations indicate the relevant solution values and their ranges, provided that the population is diverse. Therefore, alternative metrics like MoI comparisons provide reinforcing evidence about population diversity.

Table 1. Population diversity measurements. Number of parameters, average parameter value (stdev), range of parameter values, and moment of inertia (MoI).

Parameter	# Parameters	Range	Mean (± s.d.)	MoI $_{[Gen\ 1]}$	MoI $_{[Gen\ 25000]}$
PPC Bias	1	[-5.0, 5.0]	1.831 ± 0.582	932.536	33.538
PPC Gain	1	[0.1, 10.0]	5.670 ± 2.483	912.125	610.539
PMd/M1 Bias	1	[-5.0, 5.0]	0.909 ± 0.852	965.219	72.917
PMd/M1 Gain	1	[0.1, 10.0]	1.906 ± 1.697	838.444	284.948
Weights: feedforward	484	[-1.0, 1.0]	0.006 ± 0.582	33.897	32.082
Weights: feedback	484	[-1.0, 1.0]	0.006 ± 0.577	33.673	32.972
Weights: lateral	14641	[-1.0, 1.0]	0.002 ± 0.577	33.978	32.997

In order to assess how much each evolved parameter contributed to the diversity of the population, the MoI was calculated for each parameter listed in Table 1 individually. It can be seen that the weights contributed the least to population diversity and showed minimal change after 25000 generations of evolution (Table 1; $MoI_{[Gen\ 1]}$ to $MoI_{[Gen\ 25000]}$, Weights: feedforward, feedback, and lateral). In contrast, the evolved gain and bias values contributed the most to diversity of the evolved population. Of these four parameters, PPC bias contributed the least to final population diversity, but had the greatest change in MoI (898.998), indicating a narrow range of solutions found by the ES, potentially indicating the importance of this parameter in good solutions. The PPC gain contributed the most to final population diversity, but had the smallest change in MoI (301.586), implying the flexibility of this parameter in the solutions. The PMd/M1 bias MoI was roughly double the PPC bias, but small relative to the MoI of the PPC gain, indicating that the narrow range of this evolved parameter could also be important for good solutions. The PMd/M1 gain, like the PPC gain contributed a large portion of the final population diversity, leaving the relative importance of this parameter in between the PMd/M1 bias and the PPC gain.

Together, the ES found a diverse set of good solutions indicated by the parameter metrics shown in Table 1 paired with the behavioral data shown in Figures 3-4. The population diversity metrics across the parameters provide insight into the potential importance of select parameters and their relative contributions to population diversity across the set of evolved solutions.

3.3.2 Neuron Parameters

To evaluate the relationship between parameters, pairwise linear sample correlation coefficients were calculated (Table 2). The significant comparisons (Table 2; bold red values) reflect the Pearson's correlation coefficient r, which indicates the strength and slope (positive or negative) of the relationship. The four evolved neuron parameters and fitness (Table 2) were considered in the pairwise linear comparisons to determine how the parameters influenced each other, and which parameters influenced fitness. The considered parameters were: PPC bias, PPC gain, PMd/M1 bias, PMd/M1 gain, and fitness. The majority of the pairwise comparisons did not show a linear relationship. Three linear comparisons showed a significant pairwise relationship: 1) PPC gain to PPC bias, 2) PMd/M1 bias to PPC bias, and 3) PMd/M1 gain to fitness. Alpha was 0.00036 Bonferroni corrected for multiple comparisons at the 99 percent confidence level. Indicating that these three parameter comparisons were highly significant ($p < 0.0001$), and reflected a strong negative linear relationship for the 100 evolved solutions.

Table 2. Pearson's sample correlation coefficients between pairs of evolved parameters and fitness. Sign indicates slope of the relationship and bold, red values indicate significance.

Parameter	PPC Bias	PPC Gain	PMd Bias	PMd Gain
PPC Bias	--	--	--	--
PPC Gain	-0.713	--	--	--
PMd Bias	-0.733	0.303	--	--
PMd Gain	0.129	-0.031	-0.1457	--
Fitness	0.260	-0.268	-0.068	-0.524

In order to further understand the relationship and differences between the parameters of the 100 solutions, a hierarchical cluster analysis was performed on the same parameters as shown in Table 2. The hierarchical clustering was calculated by taking the largest distance between data points, also called *furthest neighbor* or *complete-linkage clustering* (Figure 5a). Seven clusters were identified that represented a conservative hierarchical separation in agents' parameters (including fitness). The cluster threshold was selected to demonstrate conservative separation between parameter clusters. The cluster separation in the dendrogram (Figure 5a) was mapped directly to the pairwise parameter cluster comparisons shown in Figure 5(b-d). The colored polygons in the cluster plots simply connect the perimeter data points to outline each cluster for easier viewing. Parameter values for agents #1 and #100 (Figure 5) tie behavior to parameters.

The clusters reveal marked separations for the PPC gain vs. PPC bias (Figure 5b). Interestingly, the cluster of which the best solution (Figure 5b; #1) shares commonalities with six of the seven clusters, implicating that cluster as a range and domain for optimal PPC gain and PPC bias values. It is interesting to note that relative to the evolved population, solution #1 (best) evolved a high PPC gain and low PPC bias compared to solution #100 (worst), which evolved the opposite, a high PPC bias and low PPC gain. However, although there exists a significant linear relationship between these evolved parameters (Table 2), a conclusion cannot be inferred about behavioral performance.

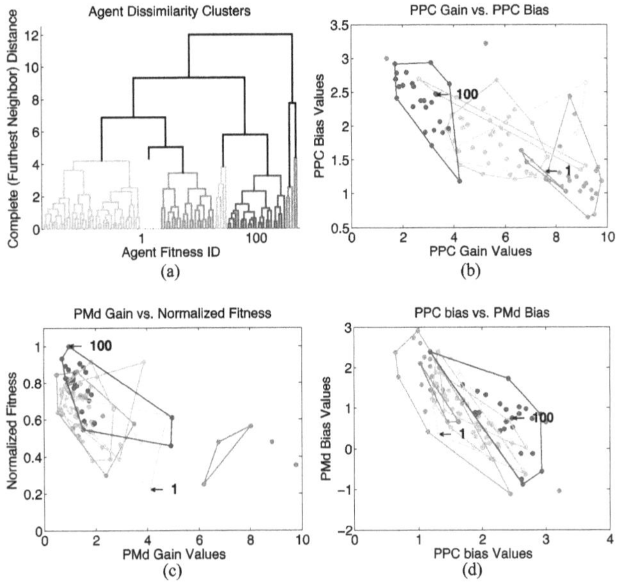

Figure 5. (a) Dendrogram of 7 hierarchical clusters based on evolved parameters and fitness for population. Cluster plots (b-d) show linear relationships between parameters. Enclosed points indicate clusters shown in dendrogram. (b) PPC gain vs. PPC bias. (c) Fitness vs. PMd/M1 gain. (d) PPC bias vs. PMd/M1 bias. Agents #1 and #100 are labeled in these plots.

In contrast to the diversity shown in the PPC parameters governing firing rates in the PPC layer, PMd/M1 gain vs. fitness (Figure 5c) revealed a large majority of solutions evolved PMd/M1 gain values between 0 and 2, which resulted in higher fitness values. Although similar to the yellow cluster overlap in Figure 5b, there is heavy overlap between five of the seven clusters in Figure 5c. However, the domain [0, 2] of PMd/M1 gain values did not lead to better fitness (Figure 5c). In fact, the data show that the top five agents (data points closest to 0 on the y-axis) evolved PMd/M1 gain values greater than 2, indicating that a PMd/M1 gain value greater than 2 was important for better fitness. Therefore, unlike the comparison between PPC gain and bias values, a PMd/M1 gain value greater than 2 led to better fitness, resulting in a better solution and behavior.

Interestingly, a significant linear relationship between the bias values in the two different layers (PPC and PMd/M1) evolved for the population (Figure 5d). The data show that the majority of solutions evolved PMd/M1 bias values between [0, 2] and PPC bias values between [1, 3]. This result suggests that these two parameters may have been critical for good solutions because of the narrow range and the significant linear relationship (Table 2). In addition, it is important to note that none of the evolved PPC bias values were below zero (all positive), whereas, several agents evolved negative PMd/M1 biases (Figure 5d). Furthermore, the overlapped clusters indicate that an optimal PMd/M1 and PPC bias value pair lies within a narrow range in 2-D Cartesian space.

Neuron parameters comparisons revealed three important aspects of the evolved parameters. 1) Population diversity remained after evolution (Table 1), indicating a diverse set of solutions found by the ES. 2) Significant linear relationships between evolved parameters emerged (Table 2). 3) Parameter clusters pertained to different agent behavior and fitness (Figure 5).

3.3.3 Weight Parameters

The average population weights were analyzed to determine their contributions towards the observed behavior. In particular, we investigated the connection length (distance between nodes), sign (excitatory or inhibitory), and strength. The weight parameters consist of the three sets of connections, 1) projections from the 121 (11x11) PPC neurons to the 4 PMd/M1neurons, 2) projections from the PMd/M1 neurons to the PPC neurons, and 3) recurrent projections between the PPC neurons. The first two sets of projections were analyzed with a comparison of the average connection strength of the 100 agents between half the PPC neurons and the corresponding PMd/M1 neuron (ipsilateral: e.g., upper (left) half of PPC neurons connecting to the *Up (Left)* PMd/M1 neuron), vs. the other half of the PPC neurons and the same PMd/M1 neuron (contralateral: e.g., lower (right) half of PPC neurons connecting to the *Up (Left)* PMd/M1 neuron).

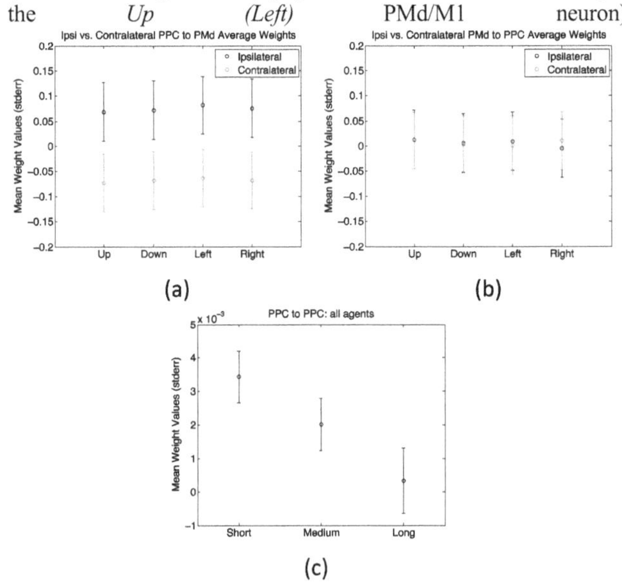

Figure 6. Analysis of evolved population weights. (a) Average ipsi vs. contra lateral feedforward weights (b) Average ipsi vs. contra lateral feedback weights. (c) Average short, medium and long lateral weights.

In contrast, recurrent PPC connections were analyzed by comparing connection length and average connection strength across the population of agents. Connection length was calculated with the Euclidian distance between each PPC neuron. The PPC connections were separated into short (distance < 5), medium ($5 <$ distance < 8), and long (distance > 8) range projections. The average relative strength per length provided a metric for how the different length connections contributed to the evolved behavior.

Due to the topographic organization of the sensory input layers and their projections to the PPC, the population of agents evolved ipsilateral excitatory and contralateral inhibitory feedforward PPC to PMd/M1 projections (Figure 6a). Two sample Kolmogorov-Smirnov tests of the population average PPC to PMd/M1 ipsilateral excitatory and contralateral inhibitory projections revealed strong significance ($p << 0.0001$). This result indicates that ipsilateral PPC projections corresponding to the intended direction of movement (the direction of the visual target) excited the PMd/M1 neuron to move in that direction. Furthermore, if the visual stimulus appeared in the contralateral region of PPC neurons, the projections inhibited that same PMd/M1 neuron, so movement towards the incorrect direction was inhibited.

In contrast to feedforward (PPC→PMd/M1) weights, feedback (PPC←PMd/M1) weights did not show significant differences when comparing ipsilateral to contralateral (Figure 6b). However, it is interesting to note that feedback ipsilateral and contralateral average projections were roughly the same (mean of zero), indicating that the feedback weights may not have contributed towards the observed behavior across the population of agents. Whereas, the ipsilateral vs. contralateral analysis revealed high significance in the feedforward projections and no significance in the feedback projections, the recurrent PPC length vs. average strength analysis resulted in a significant difference between short and long-range PPC projections (Figure 6c).

A two-sample Kolmogorov-Smirnov test was utilized to determine differences in weight values between the PPC short vs. medium, medium vs. long, and short vs. long-range weights. Neither the short vs. medium nor medium vs. long-range weight comparisons were significant, but short vs. long was significant ($p = 0.0134$; Bonferroni corrected for multiple comparisons) at the 0.05 confidence level. Furthermore, the significant difference between long and short-range weights across the recurrent PPC neurons indicates that on average, the population evolved short-range excitation and long-range inhibition. This result coincides with the significant difference found between feedforward ipsi and contra-lateral weights. These results help explain how the evolved weights contributed towards good task performance.

4. DISCUSSION

In this study, simulated agents were evolved through artificial selection to perform a visually guided task. We ran an evolutionary strategy algorithm 100 times to evolve a diverse set of biologically realistic neural networks. We found that 1) all 100 evolved agents successfully performed the task even though the parameter space was vast (15613 parameters), 2) the evolved parameters gave rise to velocity profiles consistent with visually guided reaching studies in control subjects [18, 19], 3) the population had high precision (<5°) despite the implemented sensory resolution (10°), 4) linear relationships between specific neuron parameters emerged, 5) the evolved agents coped with the sensory inputs corresponding to different delays, 6) ipsilateral projections from PPC to PMd/M1 tended to be excitatory and contralateral tended to be inhibitory, and 7) recurrent PPC projections had short-range excitation and long-range inhibition.

In the field of artificial intelligence, evolutionary computation (EC) is often used to design or tune neural networks that control agents [23, 24]. EC has been used in computational neuroscience to fit the activity of neuron models to electrophysiological recordings [25, 26]. Most relevant to our work, neural networks were evolved to perform a reaching task with intentions of investigating the interaction between evolution and individual learning [27]. In this simulation study however, the sensory inputs and neural architectures were abstract and not intended to investigate the mammalian brain or cortical interactions. More recently, neural networks were evolved in robotic platforms to investigate the relationship between selective attention and action selection by running experiments in a foraging task [28]. Similar to our work, they investigated the relationship between evolved architecture and the resulting behavior, but their neural architectures were not intended to model sensory integration or sensorimotor transformations, nor did their models provide any predictions pertaining to the underlying biology. Furthermore, these implementations did not constrain their neural network connectivity based on known neuroanatomy, consider empirically derived sensory delays, or attempt to use direct encoding for the evolution of a large parameter set (15613 parameters) that better reflects the intrinsic complexity of a brain network. Biologically plausible parieto-frontal neural networks performing sensorimotor transformations have been utilized to investigate the neural correlates between competing reaching decisions [8]. In these studies, the neural networks were hardwired, indicating that their connections were preset and unable to change. Additionally, the networks only received visual sensory input. In contrast, our model received both visual and proprioceptive sensory inputs with realistic latencies, and the connections giving rise to the reaching behavior were not determined *a priori*. These differences allowed our model architecture to demonstrate sensory integration and the sensorimotor transformations that led to smooth, accurate reaching movements. Biologically inspired network models with visual and proprioceptive inputs, capable of adaptive voluntary reaching actions, tend to emphasize motor learning based on motor error, which has previously been correlated with cerebellar neural activity [9, 10]. Our model was not designed or tested for corrective reaching actions, nor attempting to model cerebellar cortex, however, evidence suggests that the feedback connections from PMd/M1 to PPC carry a corollary discharge signal that could lead to corrective reaches [2, 15]. Therefore, we would anticipate that the model could be evolved to perform online corrective reaching movements, however, the model could be missing critical components without a cerebellar region predicting the sensory consequences of motor commands (error signal).

Many movements, including reaches, show a rapid acceleration after movement onset followed by deceleration as the hand approaches the target. These smooth, accurate movements (Figure 3), which match control subject behavior for visually guided reaching [18, 19], emerged as a result of the evolved parameters. As for velocity profiles, single-humped profiles evolved, which indicates an optimal trade-off between speed and accuracy. In a multi-humped velocity profile, each hump represents a sub-movement towards the motor goal that indicates a non-optimal trade-off between speed and accuracy, and the magnitude of each sub-movement is dependent on the distance to the target and the target size [29]. We predict that the absence or manipulation of any parameters within the model should result in non-optimal corrective movements or a multi-humped velocity profile.

An interesting result came with the high accuracy of evolved agents. Theoretical evidence has indicated that sensory integration (from multiple modalities) leads to a better signal-to-noise ratio (SNR) provided that each sensory input is sufficiently noisy [30]. Based on this evidence, we predict that the integration of two distinct sensory inputs with different latencies provided sufficient sensory noise, leading to a better SNR, and resulting in behavioral accuracy greater than the implemented sensory resolution (Figure 4). Analysis of population diversity was done through MoI and average evolved parameter values (Table 1), and behavioral data (Figures 3-4). This analysis provided conclusive evidence that the ES found 100 independent solutions. As for the relationship between evolved parameters, the results suggest that a biological population should have some linear relationships between parameters governing neural firing patterns, and that topography would be preserved in feedforward but not in feedback projections. Finally, the results provide theoretical evidence for short-range excitation and long-range inhibition in recurrent connections across the PPC. Together these results provide a theoretical basis for future empirical studies investigating the fine-grained relationships between neural firing patterns and the neural projections in a sensorimotor transformation task, such as reaching to a visual target.

The present study suggests how directly encoded evolved connectivity within an area such as the parietal cortex can lead to the construction of motor plans. These motor plans can overcome delays in sensory input, while still achieving accurate and rapid movements. Furthermore, predictions from the model suggest that there exists a diverse set of significant parameters governing these movements, and that manipulations of these parameters should lead to movement dysfunction. In future experiments, it would be of interest to implement indirect encoding of the weight parameters to investigate the importance of specific connectivity, and to see what types of excitation and inhibition emerge. In addition, it would be of interest to utilize the state of the art Covariance Matrix Adaptation (CMA) ES algorithm [31], and compare the evolutionary dynamics and evolved solutions with our current results.

5. REFERENCES

[1] Mountcastle, V. B., Lynch, J. C., Georgopoulos, A., Sakata, H. and Acuna, C. Posterior Parietal Association Cortex of Monkey - Command Functions for Operations within Extrapersonal Space. *Journal of Neurophysiology*, 38, 4 1975), 871-908.

[2] Andersen, R. A. and Cui, H. Intention, action planning, and decision making in parietal-frontal circuits. *Neuron*, 63, 5 (Sep 10 2009), 568-583.

[3] Sabes, P. N. Sensory integration for reaching, 1912011), 195-209.

[4] Andersen, R. A. and Buneo, C. A. Intentionalmaps Inposteriorparietalcortex. *Annual Review of Neuroscience*, 25, 1 2002), 189-220.

[5] Desmurget, M., Epstein, C. M., Turner, R. S., Prablanc, C., Alexander, G. E. and Grafton, S. T. Role of the posterior parietal cortex in updating reaching movements to a visual target. *Nat Neurosci*, 2, 6 (Jun 1999), 563-567.

[6] Caminiti, R., Chafee, M. V., Battaglia-Mayer, A., Averbeck, B. B., Crowe, D. A. and Georgopoulos, A. P. Understanding the parietal lobe syndrome from a neurophysiological and evolutionary perspective. *European Journal of Neuroscience*, 31, 12 (Jun 2010), 2320-2340.

[7] Mulliken, G. H., Musallam, S. and Andersen, R. A. Inaugural Article: Forward estimation of movement state in posterior parietal cortex. *Proceedings of the National Academy of Sciences*, 105, 24 2008), 8170-8177.

[8] Cisek, P. Integrated Neural Processes for Defining Potential Actions and Deciding between Them: A Computational Model. *Journal of Neuroscience*, 26, 38 2006), 9761-9770.

[9] Passot, J.-B., Luque, N. R. and Arleo, A. Coupling internal cerebellar models enhances online adaptation and supports offline consolidation in sensorimotor tasks. *Frontiers in Computational Neuroscience*, 72013).

[10] Shadmehr, R. and Krakauer, J. W. A computational neuroanatomy for motor control. *Exp Brain Res*, 185, 3 (Mar 2008), 359-381.

[11] Xing, J. and Andersen, R. A. Models of the posterior parietal cortex which perform multimodal integration and represent space in several coordinate frames. *J Cogn Neurosci*, 12, 4 (Jul 2000), 601-614.

[12] Zipser, D. and Andersen, R. A. A back-propagation programmed network that simulates response properties of a subset of posterior parietal neurons. *Nature*, 331, 6158 (Feb 25 1988), 679-684.

[13] Sober, S. J. and Sabes, P. N. Multisensory integration during motor planning. *J Neurosci*, 23, 18 (Aug 6 2003), 6982-6992.

[14] Batista, A. P. and Andersen, R. A. The parietal reach region codes the next planned movement in a sequential reach task. *J Neurophysiol*, 85, 2 (Feb 2001), 539-544.

[15] Buneo, C. A. and Andersen, R. A. The posterior parietal cortex: sensorimotor interface for the planning and online control of visually guided movements. *Neuropsychologia*, 44, 13 2006), 2594-2606.

[16] Mulliken, G. H., Musallam, S. and Andersen, R. A. Decoding trajectories from posterior parietal cortex ensembles. *J Neurosci*, 28, 48 (Nov 26 2008), 12913-12926.

[17] Trappenberg, T. P. *Fundamentals of computational neuroscience*. Oxford University Press, Oxford ; New York, 2010.

[18] d'Avella, A., Portone, A. and Lacquaniti, F. Superposition and modulation of muscle synergies for reaching in response to a change in target location. *J Neurophysiol*, 106, 6 (Dec 2011), 2796-2812.

[19] Perfetti, B., Moisello, C., Landsness, E. C., Kvint, S., Pruski, A., Onofrj, M., Tononi, G. and Ghilardi, M. F. Temporal Evolution of Oscillatory Activity Predicts Performance in a Choice-Reaction Time Reaching Task. *Journal of Neurophysiology*, 105, 1 2010), 18-27.

[20] Keijzer, M., Merelo, J. J., Romero, G. and Schoenauer, M. Evolving objects: A general purpose evolutionary computation library. *Lect Notes Comput Sc*, 23102002), 231-242.

[21] Kita, E. and Maruyama, T. *Genetic algorithm based on schemata theory*. City, 2011.

[22] Morrison, R. W. and De Jong, K. A. Measurement of population diversity. *Lect Notes Comput Sc*, 23102002), 31-41.

[23] Floreano, D., D\"u, r., Peter and Mattiussi, C. Neuroevolution: from architectures to learning. *Evolutionary Intelligence*, 12008), 47-62.

[24] Stanley, K. O., D'Ambrosio, D. B. and Gauci, J. A hypercube-based encoding for evolving large-scale neural networks. *Artif. Life*, 15, 2 2009), 185-212.

[25] Van Geit, W., Achard, P. and De Schutter, E. Neurofitter: a parameter tuning package for a wide range of electrophysiological neuron models. *Front Neuroinform*, 12007), 1.

[26] Rossant, C., Leijon, S., Magnusson, A. K. and Brette, R. Sensitivity of Noisy Neurons to Coincident Inputs. *Journal of Neuroscience*, 31, 47 (Nov 23 2011), 17193-17206.

[27] Cecconi, F. and Parisi, D. Evolving organisms that can reach for objects. In *Proceedings of the Proceedings of the first international conference on simulation of adaptive behavior on From animals to animats* (Paris, France, 1990). MIT Press, [insert City of Publication],[insert 1990 of Publication].

[28] Petrosino, G., Parisi, D. and Nolfi, S. Selective attention enables action selection: evidence from evolutionary robotics experiments. *Adaptive Behavior*2013).

[29] Meyer, D. E., Abrams, R. A., Kornblum, S., Wright, C. E. and Smith, J. E. Optimality in human motor performance: ideal control of rapid aimed movements. *Psychol Rev*, 95, 3 (Jul 1988), 340-370.

[30] Sabes, P. N. Sensory integration for reaching: models of optimality in the context of behavior and the underlying neural circuits. *Prog Brain Res*, 1912011), 195-209.

[31] Igel, C., Hansen, N. and Roth, S. Covariance matrix adaptation for multi-objective optimization. *Evol Comput*, 15, 1 (Spr 2007), 1-28.

Evolution of Honest Signaling by Social Punishment

David Catteeuw
Artificial Intelligence Lab
Vrije Universiteit Brussel
Pleinlaan 2, 1050 Brussels, Belgium
dcatteeu@vub.ac.be

The Anh Han
Artificial Intelligence Lab
Vrije Universiteit Brussel
Pleinlaan 2, 1050 Brussels, Belgium
h.anh@ai.vub.ac.be

Bernard Manderick
Artificial Intelligence Lab
Vrije Universiteit Brussel
Pleinlaan 2, 1050 Brussels, Belgium
bmanderi@vub.ac.be

ABSTRACT

When facing dishonest behavior of any form, individuals may choose to punish in order to enhance future honesty from others, even if it is costly for the punishers. Such behavior can be found ubiquitously in human and animal communications, suggesting that it may play an important role in the evolution of honest signaling or reliable communication. By applying Evolutionary Game Theory to the Philip Sidney game, we provide a computational model to investigate whether costly punishment can be a viable strategy for the evolution of honest signaling. We identify four different forms of dishonesty, and study how punishing them affects the level of honesty in the final outcome of evolutionary dynamics. Our results show that punishing those that lie can significantly boost honest signaling when conflicts are moderate and signals are cheap or cost-free. It hence provides an important alternative to the well-known Handicap Principle, which states that honest signaling can evolve only if signals are sufficiently costly for their senders. Furthermore, punishing greedy responses promotes honest signaling if conflicts of interest are high and signals are costly. Lastly, punishing timid or worried individuals does not lead to a clear improvement of honesty.

Categories and Subject Descriptors

I.2.11 [**Artificial Intelligence**]: Distributed Artificial Intelligence—*Multiagent Systems*

General Terms

Theory

Keywords

Philip Sidney game, punishment, honest signaling, evolutionary game theory

GECCO'14, July 12–16, 2014, Vancouver, BC, Canada.

ACM 978-1-4503-2662-9/14/07 ...$15.00.
http://dx.doi.org/10.1145/2576768.2598312.

1. INTRODUCTION

Communication is undoubtedly among the most important processes in human society as well as in the societies of many other species [39, 25]. It enables a smooth and efficient coordination among participants of a joint venture. Diverse examples of such behavior can be found in nature, such as the invention of human languages [28], the honey bees' waggle dance to indicate the location of a food source [41], and alarm calls in vervet monkeys [34]. In artificial multiagent systems, communication enables teamwork [2], such as in playing robotic soccer [4], in cooperative hunting [21], and wireless sensors that communicate to find an optimal route via which all data is sent to the sink node [45].

Despite the important benefits of communication, when there are conflicts of interests between communicating individuals, dishonesty may emerge leading to the breakdown of the communication systems [1, 8]. Conflicts of interest provide incentives to lie, and when most communication becomes unreliable, no one will respond to it and when that happens, it is best not to communicate since it is ineffective while being costly to the communicator. Hence, the (evolutionary) puzzle here is, why are communication systems so abundant in different societies even though conflicts of interests are largely unavoidable [24, 27, 39]?

This question of explaining the evolution of communication (also called evolution of honest signaling) has been actively investigated in several fields of research, most notably in biology, economics, and evolutionary linguistics [27, 32, 37]. The main and most influential explanation is the Handicap Principle [43, 44, 11], saying that when it is sufficiently costly to initiate the communication (or to send a signal), honest communication (signaling) can evolve and remains stable. However, it has been shown that there are communication systems where it is quite cheap to communicate, and several alternatives to the Handicap Principle have been proposed (see the surveys by Számadó [38] and Zollman [46]). For instance, other equilibria (called partial pooling and hybrid equilibria) exist where communication is slightly less informative—but still honest—and a lot less costly [23, 19]. Another alternative is based on the assumption (supported by examples) that it is more costly to the dishonest than honest signalers to send a signal [18, 24] (see Section 2 for further discussion). Differently, here we study how punishing dishonest signaling behavior can provide a pathway for the evolution of honest signaling. Note that a large body of evidence shows that in human and many other species' societies, individuals are willing to pay a personal cost in order to punish those that infringe their interests, such as the non-contributors of a public good or dishonest individuals in communication [7, 9, 12]. Punishment has been shown to promote cooperation in different scenarios, including the Prisoner's Dilemma and the Public Goods Game, e.g. in [15, 36, 16]. However, little effort has been provided to clarify the role of punishment in the emergence and stability of honest signaling or reliable communication systems.

In order to study this problem, we apply Evolutionary Game Theory methods in finite populations [30, 35] to an extension of the Philip Sidney game [26]. It is the standard game-theoretical framework to study honest communication in biology and economics, which best illustrates the Handicap Principle: when interests conflict, signals must be costly in order to maintain honesty [43, 44, 11]. We extend the Philip Sidney game to study four distinct types of punishment which target the four possible deviations from honest signaling, namely the liars, the timid, the greedy and the worried individuals (see definitions in Section 3.2). We show how each of them affects the level of honesty in the final outcome of the evolutionary dynamics.

The rest of the paper is structured as follows. Section 2 discusses relevant literature of honest signaling and punishment in different contexts. Section 3 describes our model of punishment within the context of the Philip Sidney game, and gives methods to analyze the model. Section 4 then shows our numerical results. Finally, in Section 5 we discuss the obtained results and describe some future directions.

2. RELATED WORK

The most influential explanation for the evolution of honest signaling is the Handicap Principle: costly signals can maintain honesty even if interests conflict [43]. Grafen [11] proved this mathematically but two issues remain: signal costs in nature are often smaller than predicted, and the signal cost makes other non-signaling equilibria (also called pooling equilibria) often more attractive to both senders and receivers [38]. Several alternatives to the Handicap Principle have been proposed that allow honesty with cheap or cost-free signals (see the surveys by Számadó [38] and Zollman [46]). A first alternative explanation is that *partially* honest communication can be an equilibrium at a much lower cost than completely honest communication. These are so-called partial pooling equilibria and hybrid equilibria. In a partial pooling equilibrium, communication is only partially honest, because the same signal is used in many different but closely related states [23]. In a hybrid equilibrium, senders may now and then signal dishonestly and receivers may sometimes ignore the sender [19]. Another alternative defines signals that are cheap when honest, but costly when dishonest. Hurd [18] and Lachmann et al. [24] give examples of such cost functions and prove that they maintain honesty. Several mechanisms that generate such cost functions have been suggested, including social punishment, but they remain implicit in these models [38, 46]. Instead, we explicitly analyze whether costly punishment can be a *viable* strategy for the evolution of honest communication systems.

There is a great body of literature, theoretical and experimental, showing the promoting role of costly punishment in the evolution of cooperation. Such theoretical models and experimental works are usually framed in the context of the Prisoner's Dilemma and the Public Good Games [15, 36, 7, 9, 12, 16]. To the best of our knowledge, this is the first effort to provide a computational model analyzing the role of costly punishment in the evolution of reliable communication systems, particularly within the context of the Philip Sidney game. As will be seen, punishment in the context of the Philip Sidney game (or signaling games in general [32]) is much richer and more complex to analyze. In the context of the study of the evolution of cooperation, punishment is usually carried out against those that defect or do not help others, which is similar to the punishment of greedy individuals in the current context. Signaling games exhibit the possibility to punish other types of dishonest behavior, including liars, timid and worried individuals. We discuss these differences into more detail in Section 5.

Last but not least, it is undoubtedly important to mention the large body of work on agent communication in multiagent systems research [2, 22, 42, 33]. One main concern of these works is to design and implement efficient and reliable communication systems in multiagent systems so as to allow coordination and teamwork [2], for example in wireless sensor networks [45] and playing robotic soccer [4], and also to collaboratively assess trust and reputation of others [22, 33]. In contrast, the current work studies how communication systems can remain reliable while it may be advantageous to act dishonestly, with the help of social punishment targeting different forms of dishonesty in signaling. As will be seen, the results from this work provide important insights into the design of more reliable communication systems in concrete domains, namely which forms of dishonesty should be targeted with punishment and under which circumstances—in order to achieve a high level of honesty.

3. MODEL AND METHODS

3.1 The Philip Sidney game

The Philip Sidney Game [26] is a signaling game: a two-player extensive-form game with asymmetric information (Figure 1). The first player, Sender, may be in one of two states: healthy or needy, with probability p and $1-p$, respectively. In each state, he may either signal at cost c ($0 \leq c \leq 1$) or stay quiet (at no cost). The second player, Receiver, does not know Sender's true state, but observes whether or not Sender signals and must then decide to donate his resource to Sender, or to keep it for himself.

We assume that Sender and Receiver are related such that Receiver may benefit from donating his resource to Sender. This is the principle of *inclusive fitness* [13]. Each player's payoff is the sum of his own survival probability plus a fraction r of the other player's survival probability (the benefit of survival is normalized), where r is the players' relatedness coefficient.

The survival probabilities depend on the outcome of the game (Table 1). Receiver is sure to survive if he keeps the resource, but if he donates the resource he is only sure to survive with probability $S < 1$. If Sender receives the resource he is sure to survive, otherwise his survival probability depends on his initial state: if he is needy, he will die; if he is healthy, he will survive with probability $V < 1$. As already mentioned, signaling is costly: Sender's survival probability is decreased by a factor $(1-c)$ if he signals.

The Philip Sidney game has sixteen pure strategies which are represented by a couple (S_i, D_j) (see Table 2). The first element (S_i) determines what to do when in the role of Sender, which can be either: always signal (S_A), never signal ($S_\emptyset$), signal only when healthy (S_H), or signal only when

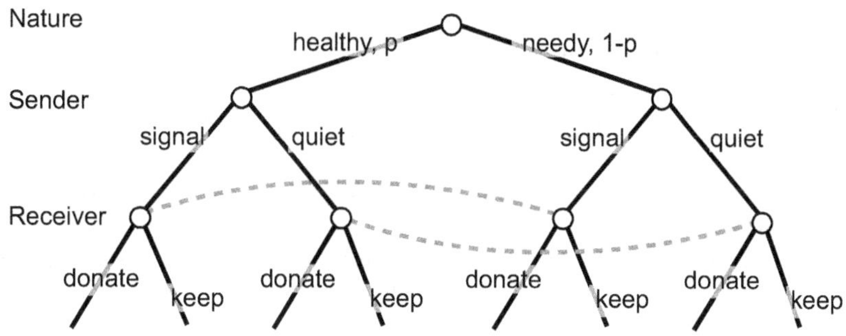

Figure 1: Philip Sidney game.

Table 1: Sender's and Receiver's survival probabilities for all possible outcomes of the Philip Sidney game.

	healthy		needy	
	donate	keep	donate	keep
quiet	$1, S$	$V, 1$	$1, S$	$0, 1$
signal	$1-c, S$	$V(1-c), 1$	$1-c, S$	$0, 1$

Table 2: Abbreviation and meaning of the four Sender and four Receiver strategies.

	strategy
S_A	always signal
$S_\emptyset$	never signal
S_N	signal only when needy
S_H	signal only when healthy
D_A	always donate
$D_\emptyset$	never donate
D_S	donate only when signal
D_Q	donate only when quiet

needy (S_N). The second element (D_j) determines what to do when in the role of Receiver, which can be either: always donate (D_A), never donate ($D_\emptyset$), donate only when signal (D_S), or donate only when quiet (D_Q). For example, the honest signaling strategy—signal only when needy, donate only when signal—is represented by (S_N, D_S). The payoffs of these pure strategies are calculated assuming that each strategy is equally likely to be in the role of Receiver or of Sender.

Note that players do not need to be related genetically. The relatedness factor r may simply represent the level of common interest [3]. If $r = 1$, interests are perfectly aligned. For smaller r the conflict of interest increases. Furthermore, depending on the other parameters of the game, there may be a conflict when Sender is needy, when Sender is healthy, in both cases, or never. We say there is a conflict if, knowing Sender's state, both players would prefer other outcomes, whether Sender signals or not. Concretely, there is a conflict when Sender is healthy if $r(1-V) < 1-S$ and $r(1-S) < (1-c)(1-V)$ [5]. Similarly, there is a conflict when Sender is needy if $r < 1-S$ and $r(1-S) < (1-c)$. Note that conflicts do not depend on the probability of Sender being healthy p [26]. If there is no conflict, we expect communication to emerge only if this is best for both players. When there is a full conflict, we expect no communication will emerge. The most interesting region is the one where there is a partial conflict [5].

3.2 Model

We consider new honest signaling strategies that punish dishonest behavior. We distinguish four different such strategies which target each of the possible deviations from honest signaling, namely punishment of lying (P_L), of greedy (P_G), of timid (P_T), and of worried opponents (P_W). An individual is lying (or simply a liar) if he signals when healthy; greedy if he keeps when Sender signals; timid if he remains quiet when needy; and worried if he donates when Sender is quiet.

Note that a strategist can be punished on several occasions. For example, the strategy 'signal only when healthy, donate only when quiet', (S_H, D_Q), is lying, greedy, timid, and worried simultaneously, albeit in different cases. When adopting this strategy, a healthy Sender is deemed a liar while a needy Sender a timid one.

In the new game, a player's survival probability is decreased by d if he punishes his opponent, and decreased by e if he is punished. As before, we apply inclusive fitness with relatedness factor r to the survival probabilities of the players. Punishing your opponent always lowers your own payoff even if the cost to punish $d = 0$, due to the relatedness to your opponent ($r > 0$) and decreasing his survival probability decreases your payoff. For example, if Sender punishes Receiver, Sender earns $u_S = (v_S - d) + r(v_R - e)$ and Receiver $u_R = (v_R - e) + r(v_S - d)$, where Senders and Receiver survival probability, v_S and v_R, depend on the game's outcome as shown in Table 1. If Receiver punishes Sender, the costs d and e are swapped. If no one punishes, the costs d and e are left out (as in the original Philip Sidney game).

While greedy and worried strategists are always revealed and hence are always punished by a strategy such as P_{GW}, liars and timid are only revealed with probability $q < 1$. Hence, they may sometimes (with probability $1-q$) escape punishment. Table 3 summarizes all parameters of the Philip Sidney game with punishment.

3.3 Evolution in Finite Populations

The numerical analysis in the following section is based on methods of Evolutionary Game Theory methods for finite populations [30, 20]. In such a setting, individuals' payoff represents their *fitness* or social *success*, and evolutionary dynamics is shaped by social learning [17, 35], whereby the

Table 3: Parameters of the Philip Sidney game with punishment.

	domain	meaning
p	$(0,1)$	probability of *Sender* being healthy
q	$[0,1]$	probability that the true state of *Sender* is revealed
r	$[0,1]$	relatedness factor
S	$(0,1)$	*Receiver*'s survival probability when donating resource
V	$(0,1)$	*Sender*'s survival probability when healthy but not getting resource
c	$[0,1]$	signal cost
d	$[0,1]$	cost payed to punish the opponent
e	$[0,1]$	cost incurred when punished

most successful individuals will tend to be imitated more often by others. In the current work, social learning is modeled adopting the so-called pairwise comparison rule [40]. It assumes that an individual A with fitness f_A adopts the strategy of another individual B with fitness f_B with probability given by the Fermi function, $(1+\exp(-\beta(f_B-f_A)))^{-1}$. The parameter β represents the 'imitation strength' or 'intensity of selection', i.e., how strongly the individuals decide to imitate based on fitness comparison. For $\beta=0$, we obtain the limit of neutral or random drift—the imitation decision is random. For large β, imitation becomes increasingly deterministic.

In the absence of mutations or exploration, the end states of evolution are inevitably monomorphic (i.e all individuals in the population adopt the same strategy): once such a state is reached, it cannot be escaped through imitation. We thus further assume that, with a certain mutation probability, an individual switches randomly to a different strategy without imitating another individual. In the limit of small mutation rates, the behavioral dynamics can be conveniently described by a Markov Chain, where each state represents a monomorphic population, whereas the transition probabilities are given by the fixation probability of a single mutant [20, 15, 36]. The resulting Markov Chain has a stationary distribution, which characterizes the average time the population spends in each of these monomorphic end states.

Let N be the size of the population. Suppose there are at most two strategies in the population, say, k individuals using strategy A $(0 \le k \le N)$ and $(N-k)$ individuals using strategy B. Thus, the (average) payoff of the individual that uses A and B can be written as follows, respectively,

$$\begin{aligned} \Pi_A(k) &= \frac{(k-1)\pi_{A,A} + (N-k)\pi_{A,B}}{N-1}, \\ \Pi_B(k) &= \frac{k\pi_{B,A} + (N-k-1)\pi_{B,B}}{N-1}, \end{aligned} \quad (1)$$

where $\pi_{X,Y}$ is the payoff an X-strategist obtains in an interaction with a Y-strategist.

The probability to change the number k of individuals using strategy A by ± 1 in each time step can be written as

$$T^{\pm}(k) = \frac{N-k}{N}\frac{k}{N}\left[1+\exp(\mp\beta[\Pi_A(k)-\Pi_B(k)])\right]^{-1}. \quad (2)$$

The fixation probability of a single mutant with a strategy A in a population of $(N-1)$ individuals using B is given by [40, 10]

$$\rho_{B,A} = \left(1 + \sum_{i=1}^{N-1}\prod_{j=1}^{i}\frac{T^-(j)}{T^+(j)}\right)^{-1}. \quad (3)$$

In the limit of neutral selection (i.e. $\beta=0$), $\rho_{B,A}$ equals the inverse of the population size, $1/N$.

Considering a set of strategies $\{1,...,Z\}$, these fixation probabilities determine a transition matrix $M=\{T_{ij}\}_{i,j=1}^{Z}$, with $T_{ij,j\neq i} = \rho_{ji}/(Z-1)$ and $T_{ii} = 1-\sum_{j=1,j\neq i}^{Z} T_{ij}$, of a Markov Chain. The normalized eigenvector associated with the eigenvalue 1 of the transposed of M provides the stationary distribution described above [10, 20], describing the relative time the population spends adopting each of the strategies.

Invasion and Replacement in Finite Populations.
We describe some key concepts of Evolutionary Game Theory in finite populations that we use to discuss the results presented in the next section. In finite populations, evolutionary stability is defined differently from the traditional concept of evolutionarily stable strategies [35]. It takes into account the population size N and is based on the dynamics described above. A strategy is evolutionarily stable in finite populations if selection (i) opposes any mutant strategy invading the population, and (ii) opposes any mutant replacing the entire population [30]. Strategy B is resistant to *invasion* if in a population where $N-1$ individuals adopt strategy B and one individual adopts the (mutant) strategy A, the fitness of the single mutant A is lower than that of the other individuals (the Bs): $\Pi_A(1) < \Pi_B(1)$ for all $A \neq B$. Together with Equation (1) this implies that for all $A \neq B$: $(N-1)\pi_{A,B} < \pi_{B,A} + (N-2)\pi_{B,B}$. Strategy B is resistant to *replacement* if the probability that any mutant A fixates in a population of individuals adopting B is smaller than the neutral fixation probability: $\rho_{B,A} < 1/N$ for all $A \neq B$. If selection pressure is weak $(\beta \ll 1)$, we simply have: $\pi_{A,A}(N-2) + \pi_{A,B}(2N-1) < \pi_{B,A}(N+1) + \pi_{B,B}(2N-4)$.

4. RESULTS

To study the effect of punishing dishonest behavior on the evolution of honest signaling, we consider a finite population of the sixteen (pure) strategies of the Philip Sidney game together with one of the punishment strategies described above. Then, we numerically compute stationary distributions of the strategies using the methods described in Section 3.3 for different configurations of the parameters.

4.1 Punishing Dishonest Signalers: Liars and Timid

Punishing liars. First, let us consider the honest signaling strategy that punishes those who signal when healthy: P_L. Figure 2a shows the frequency of honest signaling (i.e. the sum of the frequencies of P_L and of the pure honest signaling strategy) as a function of the signal cost c, and the relatedness level r. For a wide range of c and r, there is a high level of honest signaling. Interestingly, that occurs even for low values of c, which is not the case in the original Philip Sidney game [6, 43, 11]. So, punishment of liars can provide an alternative for the Handicap Principle, which states that,

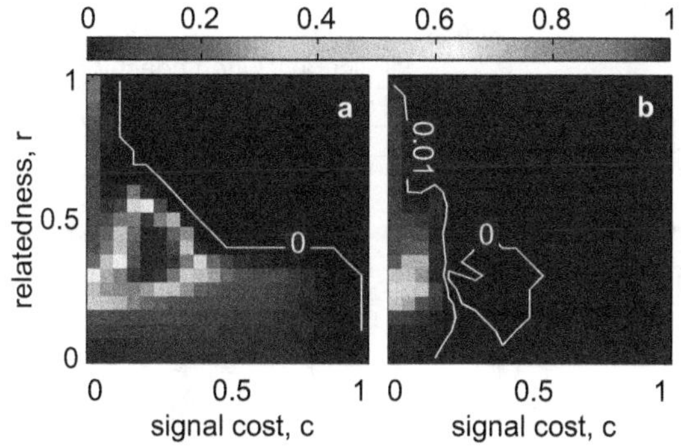

Figure 2: *a)* Total frequency of honest signaling in the Philip Sidney game with punishment of liars (P_L). *b)* Increase in frequency of honest signaling when P_L is present compared to when it is absent (being replaced with another pure honest signaling strategy). For small signal costs there is a clear increase in the frequency of honest signaling. There is also a region where punishment has a slightly negative effect ($\approx -10^{-3}$ inside the 0-contour line). Both figures were obtained for population size $N = 100$, selection pressure $\beta = 5$, $p = q = d = 1/2$, $S = V = 4/5$, $e = 1$, and varying signal cost c and relatedness level r.

under conflict of interest, honest signaling cannot evolve or has low frequency for low-cost signaling systems.

The effect of punishing liars on the level of honest signaling is clearer in Figure 2b, where we plot the increase in frequency of honest signaling when P_L is present in the population compared to the case where P_L is replaced by another pure honest signaling strategy. Irrespective of the relatedness level r, when signal cost c is small enough, the presence of P_L always has a positive effect on the level of honest signaling compared to when it is absent.

For higher signal costs c, the cost of punishment and honesty may not outweigh the benefits. Figure 2b shows a region where punishment has no effect and even slightly decreases the level of honest signaling (approximately -10^{-3}).

This interesting observation can be explained as follows. P_L is effective for small signal costs c since it is resistant to invasion by any mutant in that region whereas honest signaling without punishment can be invaded by mutants that 'always signal,' see Figure 3. In the original Philip Sidney game, honest signaling can be stable only if the signal cost $c > 0$. In the new model, honest signaling with punishment cannot be stable, since it can always be replaced by honest signaling without punishment through random drift. But except for the pure honest signaling strategy, punishment is stable even for cost-free signals, $c = 0$.

Moreover, punishment directly affects liars and indirectly affects other strategies that can replace liars. Figure 4 shows the Markov chain and the transition probabilities of the Philip Sidney game with P_L and without P_L (ignoring the P_L state with the arrows to and out of it). The strategies 'always signal, donate when signal,' (S_A, D_S), and 'always signal, never donate,' $(S_A, D_\emptyset)$, can replace honest signaling, but not honest signaling with punishment (P_L). P_L can only be replaced through random drift by honest signaling

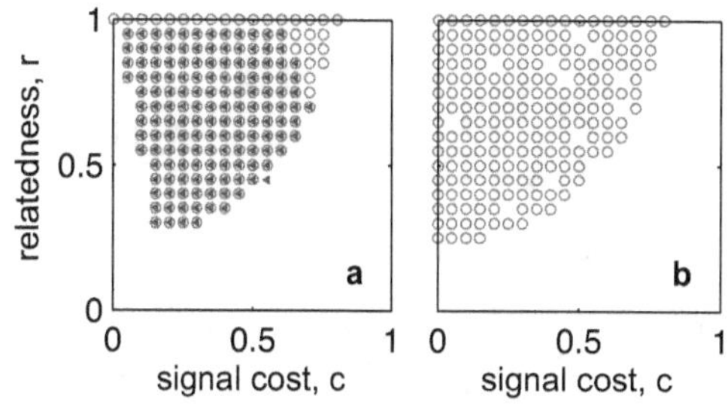

Figure 3: Red circles indicate resistance to invasion by any mutant strategy, blue triangles indicate resistance to replacement by any mutant. *a)* Honest signaling is evolutionarily stable in the colored area, but requires a minimum signal cost ($c > 0$). *b)* Honest signaling with punishment of liars is not evolutionarily stable, since it can always be replaced by honest signaling (without punishment) through random drift. But it is resistant to invasion for small signal costs. We used the same parameters as in Figure 2.

itself. As such, lying is less frequent when the punisher P_L is present. For example, the frequency of 'always signal, never donate,' $(S_A, D_\emptyset)$, and 'signal when healthy, donate when quiet,' (S_H, D_Q), dropped below the averaged frequency (i.e. $1/Z$ where Z is the number of strategies). Since liars are less frequent, other strategies that replace liars are also affected. The frequency of 'never signal, never donate,' $(S_\emptyset, D_\emptyset)$, for example, also dropped below the averaged frequency.

Although we call 'signal when healthy, donate when quiet' a liar, it is also honest in some sense. This strategy simply has the meaning of the signals 'signal' and 'quiet' reversed. When the signal cost c is very small (for example $c = 0.01$ as in Figure 4), this strategy is only slightly worse than honest signaling. When the signal cost $c = 0$, both strategies behave symmetrically and perform equally well. When signals have different costs, individuals have a common preference of when to signal what, and end up using the same signal under the same circumstances: the cost creates the meaning. When signals are cost-free there is no a priori common preference for one signal or the other. This does not only makes lying cheap, but also creates two equally valid honest signaling strategies: one where 'signal' means 'needy' and 'quiet' means 'healthy', and the other where 'signal' means 'healthy' and 'quiet' means 'needy'. Punishment deters lying, but can also teach others the preferred meanings.

These results show that costly, social punishment is indeed an alternative explanation for honest signaling. Signals do not need to be costly, as the Handicap Principle suggests; the cost may be paid by liars and punishers. This cost deters liars and so, is rarely paid.

Punishing timid signalers. A different form of deviation from honest signaling occurs when the signalers are 'so timid' that they do not signal even when they are needy. Our results show that punishing this behavior exhibits no clear improvement and its effect is significantly smaller than punishing the liars (Figure 6). The effect is mostly neutral, and even slightly negative for lower relatedness (dark blue region in Figure 5c). That is because in that case timid

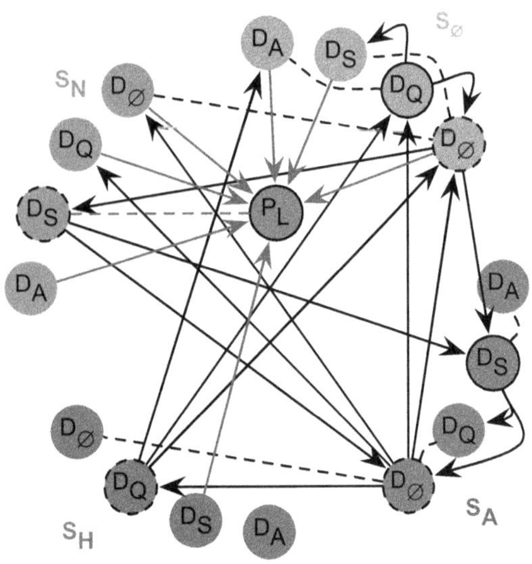

Figure 4: Transition probabilities and stationary distribution for all strategies of the Philip Sidney game (see methods described in Section 3.3 and strategy names in Table 2). Punishment of liars can only be replaced by honest signaling, (S_N, D_S), through random drift. Parameter values are $p = q = d = 1/2$, $S = V = 4/5$, $e = 1$, $c = 0.01$, and $r = 0.3$. Black borders indicate strategies which have above the average frequency $(1/Z)$; *dashed* black borders indicate strategies which have no longer above average frequency after the introduction of the punishment strategy (P_L). For clarity, we only draw transitions departing from strategies with above average frequency and transitions to the punishment strategy (P_L). Dashed lines indicate random drift.

strategies have very low frequencies, hence the effort to punish them is not worth the cost. Although for more efficient punishment (i.e. e/d and q are greater) a small improvement is observed for high signal cost c and low relatedness r, its overall average effect is negative (see Figure 6).

4.2 Punishing Dishonest Responders: Greedy and Worried

When being in the role of a signaler, the player can choose to punish those that deviate from the honest or helpful response, namely those that keep when the sender signals for help (greedy, P_G) and those that donate when the sender is quiet (worried, P_W).

Punishing greedy individuals improves honest signaling for low relatedness if signals are costly ($c > 0.2$ and $r < 0.3$). This region characterizes high conflicts of interest, where greed pays off in the original Philip Sidney game [5]. It may also decrease the frequency of honest signaling for small signal costs (blue region near $(c, r) = (0.1, 0.3)$ in Figure 5a).

Punishing worried individuals slightly improves honest signaling if there is a full conflict or no conflict at all. The improvement is too small to be visible in Figures 5b and 6. Its effect is mostly neutral and even negative when there is a conflict only when the sender is healthy ($0.2 < r < 1 - c$).

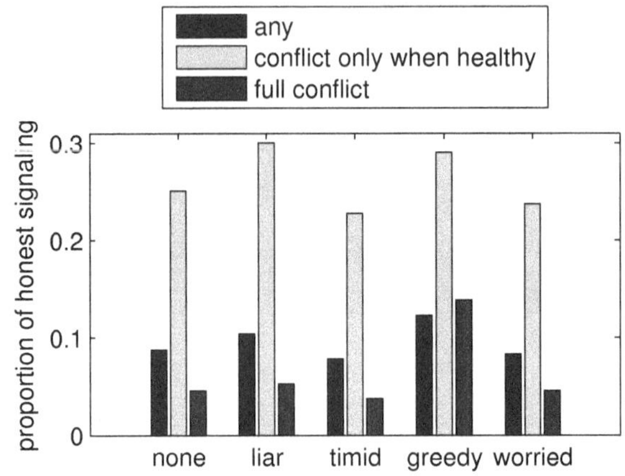

Figure 6: Frequency of honest signaling for different forms of punishment averaged over different regions of conflict as described in Section 3.1. The baseline model (labeled 'none') includes two honest signaling strategies without punishment. Punishing liars is most effective when there is a partial conflict when healthy. Punishing greedy is very effective when there is a full conflict. Punishing worried helps slightly when there is a full conflict. Punishing timid individuals is, on average, counterproductive for the evolution of honest signaling. We used the same parameter values as in Figure 2.

Note that greedy and worried strategists can always be detected, whereas lying and timid ones cannot (in all our experiments lying and timid behaviors are detected with $q = 50\%$ chance). We may expect that punishing greedy and worried is more effective than punishing liars, but this is not the case.

Finally, to have a better understanding on the overall effects of different forms of punishment, we measure the average (total) frequency of honest signaling in different regions of conflict, as described in Section 3.1. Figure 6 shows, varying r and c, the result for the entire region ('any'), the region where there is a conflict only when Sender is healthy, and the region of full conflict. The baseline mode replaces punishment strategies with another pure honest signaling strategy, and is labeled 'none'. Punishing liars is most effective when there is a partial conflict when healthy. Punishing greedy is very effective when there is a full conflict. Punishing worried is slightly effective when there is a full conflict and otherwise not. Punishing timid individuals shows no improvement on average. Additional analysis shows that these results are robust for varying probability q of detecting liars and timid, effectiveness of punishment e/d, and intensity of selection β.

5. DISCUSSION

Within the context of the Philip Sidney game, we studied the effects of punishing four different forms of dishonest behavior in communication—the lying, timid, greedy, and worried individuals—on the level of honest signaling. We have shown these distinct forms of punishment are not all beneficial for promoting the evolution of honest signaling or reliable communication, and when they are beneficial, it

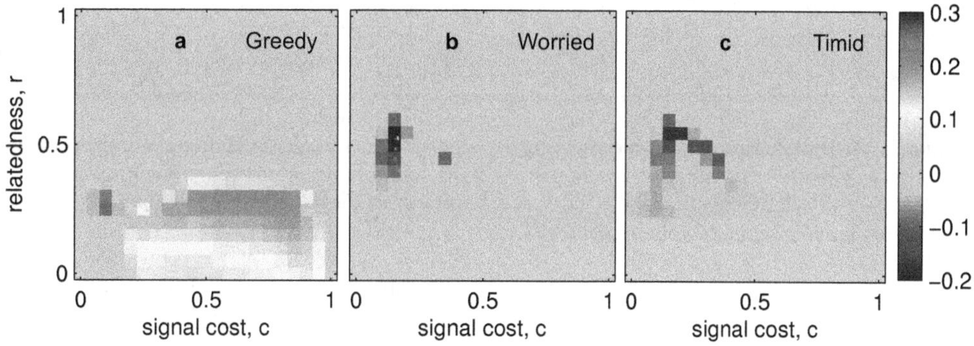

Figure 5: Increase in frequency of honest signaling when punishing *a)* greedy individuals (P_G), *b)* worried individuals (P_W), and *c)* timid individuals (P_T). We used the same parameter values as in Figure 2.

occurs in different regions of the signal costs and relatedness levels. Punishing liars increases the frequency of honest signaling when the signals are cheap and even cost-free. We deem this an important form of punishment because it clearly suggests an alternative for the Handicap Principle—the main and most influential explanation for the evolution of communication. Punishing greedy individuals increases the frequency of honest signaling when conflicts of interest are high (i.e. relatedness level is low) and signals are sufficiently costly. Finally and surprisingly, punishing timid or worried individuals is mostly counterproductive for the evolution of honest signaling. They do not lead to any clear improvement in general, and even result in an overall decrease of the frequency of honest signaling.

We have not yet taken into account anti-social (punishing honest signalers) and spiteful punishment (punishing everyone) [16]. As shown in the context of the study of the evolution of cooperation [31, 16], these types of punishment may destroy any benefit provided by the *social* punishment targeting dishonest signalers. However, as described in some recent works, antisocial and spiteful punishment may be avoided if reputation effects are taken into account [16] or prior agreements regarding posterior consequences of not honoring them are made [14]. In future work, we will analyze whether these mechanisms can still deal with anti-social and spiteful punishment in the context of the evolution of honest signaling. We expect they do, as there is evidence from nature and human societies showing that anti-social and spiteful punishment may be unlikely in this context [29].

In contrast to the analysis of honest signaling, there have been a great number of theoretical and experimental studies analyzing the role of costly punishment in the evolution of cooperative behavior, within the contexts of the Prisoner's Dilemma and the Public Goods Game (Section 2). It has been shown that, in general, social punishment (i.e. punishing those that defect or do not contribute to the Public Good) promotes the evolution of cooperation. However, in the context of the Philip Sidney (signaling) game, that is not generally the case. Herein punishment (even only social) is more complex, showing diverse possibilities which result in different outcomes. Defectors are similar to the greedy individuals herein, but the other types of dishonest behavior (liars, timid and worried) are not present in the Prisoner's Dilemma and the Public Goods Game.

In short, our work demonstrates that punishing dishonest behavior in communication promotes the evolution of honest signaling or reliable communication in several contexts, leading to higher levels of honesty. It provides a richer and more complex framework for the study of the evolutionary roles of punishment than in the context of cooperation. More effort and attention is required to further clarify the roles of punishment in the evolution of communication.

6. ACKNOWLEDGMENTS

The Anh Han acknowledges the support provided by the F.W.O. Belgium (postdoctoral fellowship 05_05 TR 7142).

7. REFERENCES

[1] G. A. Akerlof. The Market for "Lemons": Quality Uncertainty and the Market Mechanism. *Quarterly Journal of Economics*, 84(3):488–500, 1970.

[2] S. Barrett, N. Agmon, N. Hazon, S. Kraus, and P. Stone. Communicating with Unknown Teammates. In S. Devlin, D. Hennes, and E. Howly, editors, *Proceedings of the 13th Adaptive and Learning Agents workshop*, pages 46–52, Saint Paul, MN, USA, 2013.

[3] C. T. Bergstrom and M. Lachmann. Signalling among relatives. I. Is costly signalling too costly? *Philosophical Transactions of the Royal Society B: Biological Sciences*, 352(1353):609–617, May 1997.

[4] C. Castelpietra, L. Iocchi, D. Nardi, M. Piaggio, A. Scalzo, and A. Sgorbissa. Coordination among heterogeneous robotic soccer players. In *Proceedings of the IEEE/RSJ International Conference on Intelligent Robots and Systems*, pages 1385–1390. IEEE, 2000.

[5] D. Catteeuw and B. Manderick. Honesty and deception in populations of selfish, adaptive individuals. *The Knowledge Engineering Review*, 31(2):1–15, 2016.

[6] D. Catteeuw, B. Manderick, and T. A. Han. Evolutionary stability of honest signaling in finite populations. In *Proceedings of IEEE Congress on Evolutionary Computation*, pages 2864 – 2870. IEEE Computer Society, 2013.

[7] T. Clutton-Brock and G. Parker. Punishment in animal societies. *Nature*, 373:209–216, 1995.

[8] M. S. Dawkins and T. Guilford. The corruption of honest signalling. *Animal Behaviour*, 41(5):865–873, 1991.

[9] E. Fehr and S. Gächter. Altruistic punishment in humans. *Nature*, 415:137–140, 2002.

[10] D. Fudenberg and L. A. Imhof. Imitation processes with small mutations. *Journal of Economic Theory*, 131:251–262, 2005.

[11] A. Grafen. Biological signals as handicaps. *Journal of Theoretical Biology*, 144(4):517–46, June 1990.

[12] F. Guala. Reciprocity: Weak or strong? what punishment experiments do (and do not) demonstrate. *Behavioral and Brain Sciences*, 35(1):1, 2012.

[13] W. D. Hamilton. The genetical evolution of social behaviour. *Journal of Theoretical Biology*, 7(1):1–52, 1964.

[14] T. A. Han, L. M. Pereira, F. C. Santos, and T. Lenaerts. Good agreements make good friends. *Scientific reports*, 3(2695), 2013.

[15] C. Hauert, A. Traulsen, H. Brandt, M. A. Nowak, and K. Sigmund. Via freedom to coercion: the emergence of costly punishment. *Science*, 316(5833):1905–7, June 2007.

[16] C. Hilbe and A. Traulsen. Emergence of responsible sanctions without second order free riders, antisocial punishment or spite. *Scientific reports*, 2, 2012.

[17] J. Hofbauer and K. Sigmund. *Evolutionary Games and Population Dynamics*. Cambridge University Press, 1998.

[18] P. L. Hurd. Communication in discrete action-response games. *Journal of Theoretical Biology*, 174(2):217–222, May 1995.

[19] S. M. Huttegger and K. J. S. Zollman. Dynamic stability and basins of attraction in the Sir Philip Sidney game. *Proceedings of the Royal Society B: Biological Sciences*, 277(1689):1915–1922, June 2010.

[20] L. A. Imhof, D. Fudenberg, and M. A. Nowak. Evolutionary cycles of cooperation and defection. *Proceedings of the National Academy of Sciences of the United States of America*, 102:10797–10800, 2005.

[21] K. C. Jim and C. L. Giles. Talking helps: evolving communicating agents for the predator-prey pursuit problem. *Artificial life*, 6(3):237–54, Jan. 2000.

[22] A. Koster, J. Sabater-Mir, and M. Schorlemmer. Personalizing communication about trust. In *Proceedings of the 11th International Conference on Autonomous Agents and Multiagent Systems*, pages 517–524, 2012.

[23] M. Lachmann and C. T. Bergstrom. Signalling among Relatives II. Beyond the Tower of Babel. *Theoretical Population Biology*, 54:146–160, 1998.

[24] M. Lachmann, S. Szamado, and C. T. Bergstrom. Cost and conflict in animal signals and human language. *Proceedings of the National Academy of Sciences of the United States of America*, 98(23):13189–13194, Nov. 2001.

[25] D. K. Lewis. *Convention: A Philosophical Study*. Harvard University Press, Cambridge, 1969.

[26] J. Maynard Smith. Honest signalling: The Philip Sidney game. *Animal Behaviour*, 42:1034–1035, 1991.

[27] J. Maynard Smith and D. Harper. *Animal signals*. Oxford University Press, Oxford, UK, 2003.

[28] J. Maynard Smith and E. Szathmary. *The major transitions in evolution*. Oxford University Press, Oxford, UK, 1997.

[29] A. P. Moller. Social control of deception among signalling house sparrows Passer domesticus. *Behavioral Ecology and Sociobiology*, 20(5):307–11, 1987.

[30] M. A. Nowak, A. Sasaki, C. Taylor, and D. Fudenberg. Emergence of cooperation and evolutionary stability in finite populations. *Nature*, 428:646–650, 2004.

[31] D. G. Rand and M. A. Nowak. The evolution of antisocial punishment in optional public goods games. *Nature Communications*, 2:434, 2011.

[32] J. G. Riley. Silver signals: Twenty-five years of screening and signaling. *Journal of Economic Literature*, 39(2):432–478, 2001.

[33] E. Serrano, M. Rovatsos, and J. Botia. A qualitative reputation system for multiagent systems with protocol-based communication. In *Proceedings of the 11th International Conference on Autonomous Agents and Multiagent Systems*, pages 307–314, 2012.

[34] R. M. Seyfarth, D. L. Cheney, and P. Marler. Vervet monkey alarm calls: Semantic communication in a free-ranging primate. *Animal Behaviour*, 28(4):1070–1094, Nov. 1980.

[35] K. Sigmund. *The Calculus of Selfishness*. Princeton University Press, 2010.

[36] K. Sigmund, H. De Silva, A. Traulsen, and C. Hauert. Social learning promotes institutions for governing the commons. *Nature*, 466(7308):861–3, Aug. 2010.

[37] B. Skyrms. *Signaling: Evolution, Learning and Information*. Oxford University Press, New York, 2010.

[38] S. Számadó. The cost of honesty and the fallacy of the handicap principle. *Animal Behaviour*, 81(1):3–10, Jan. 2011.

[39] M. Tomasello. *Origins of Human Communications*. MIT Press, 2008.

[40] A. Traulsen, M. A. Nowak, and J. Pacheco. Stochastic dynamics of invasion and fixation. *Physical Review E*, 74(1):011909, July 2006.

[41] K. Von Frisch. *The dance language and orientation of bees*. Harvard University Press, Cambridge, MA, USA, 1967.

[42] S. A. Williamson, E. H. Gerding, and N. R. Jennings. Reward shaping for valuing communications during multi-agent coordination. In *Proceedings of the 8th International Conference on Autonomous Agents and Multiagent Systems*, pages 641–648, 2009.

[43] A. Zahavi. Mate selection - a selection for a handicap. *Journal of Theoretical Biology*, 53:205–214, Sept. 1975.

[44] A. Zahavi. The cost of honesty (further remarks on the handicap principle). *Journal of Theoretical Biology*, 67(3):603–5, Aug. 1977.

[45] W. Zhuang and M. Ismail. Cooperation in wireless communication networks. *Wireless Communications, IEEE*, (April):10–20, 2012.

[46] K. J. S. Zollman. Finding alternatives to handicap theory. *Biological Theory*.

Automated Generation of Environments to Test the General Learning Capabilities of AI Agents

Oliver J. Coleman
School of Computer Science and Engineering
University of New South Wales
Sydney, 2052, NSW, Australia
ocoleman@cse.unsw.edu.au

Alan D. Blair
School of Computer Science and Engineering
University of New South Wales
Sydney, 2052, NSW, Australia
blair@cse.unsw.edu.au

Jeff Clune
Evolving AI Lab
Computer Science Dept.
University of Wyoming
Laramie, WY, USA
jeffclune@uwyo.edu

ABSTRACT

Algorithms for evolving agents that learn during their lifetime have typically been evaluated on only a handful of environments. Designing such environments is labour intensive, potentially biased, and provides only a small sample size that may prevent accurate general conclusions from being drawn. In this paper we introduce a method for automatically generating MDP environments which allows the difficulty to be scaled in several ways. We present a case study in which environments are generated that vary along three key dimensions of difficulty: the number of environment configurations, the number of available actions, and the length of each trial. The study reveals interesting differences between three neural network models – Fixed-Weight, Plastic-Weight, and Modulated Plasticity – that would not have been obvious without sweeping across these different dimensions. Our paper thus introduces a new way of conducting reinforcement learning science: instead of manually designing a few environments, researchers will be able to automatically generate a range of environments across key dimensions of variation. This will allow scientists to more rigorously assess the general learning capabilities of an algorithm, and may ultimately improve the rate at which we discover how to create AI with general purpose learning.

Categories and Subject Descriptors

I.2.6 [**Artificial Intelligence**]: Learning-Concept Learning, Connectionism and Neural Nets

General Terms

Experimentation, Algorithms

Keywords

Evolutionary robotics, Generative encodings, Neural networks, Learning, Neuromodulation

GECCO'14, July 12–16, 2014, Vancouver, BC, Canada.

ACM 978-1-4503-2662-9/14/07 $15.00.
http://dx.doi.org/10.1145/2576768.2598257.

1. INTRODUCTION

A long-standing goal in artificial intelligence is producing agents that learn throughout their lifetime [24]. One technique for doing so is to combine evolutionary algorithms with algorithms for intra-life learning [1, 9, 19]. A challenge for scientists in this field is evaluating agents over more than a few environments [2, 6, 15, 17, 21–23, 26, 28, 33].

Designing environments is labour intensive, and any single given environment is potentially open to bias towards or against certain kinds of algorithms and models [9, 18]. Testing on only a few environments provides only a small sample size that may prevent accurate general conclusions from being drawn [9, 18].

To address these problems, we present a method for automatically generating environments for which the difficulty can be scaled in several key ways. This automated environment generation method allows a more rigorous assessment of the learning capabilities of new models and algorithms. In what follows, we first introduce the concepts behind automatically generating environments. We then present a brief case study that demonstrates how this technique can generate environments for which the difficulty can be varied over three dimensions. The study reveals differences between three neural network models that would not have been obvious without sweeping across these difficulty dimensions.

The overall goal of our paper is to encourage research into ways to automatically test algorithms across many different, important dimensions of variation. Doing so may ultimately improve the rate at which we discover how to create AI capable of general purpose learning.

2. PREVIOUS WORK

While the technique in this paper is potentially beneficial for any type of learning agent, in this paper we focus on its benefits in the field of evolving *plastic* neural networks, i.e. those that *learn within their lifetimes*. Evaluating the fitness of such agents requires testing the agent's ability to learn and exploit information about its environment to achieve goals. Such evaluations require producing environments that are different in some way each generation or that change during a fitness evaluation [6, 17, 26, 28].

Initial studies on evolving plastic neural networks that perform intra-life learning focused on supervised learning [2, 6, 12]. Nearly all subsequent research has focused on reinforcement learning [15, 17, 21–23, 26, 28, 33]. In most reinforcement learning experiments the fitness of an agent is the amount of reward it receives in its lifetime [17, 26, 28] or is strongly correlated with the reward received [15, 22].

To maximize rewards, agents typically must learn an association that changes during their lifetime, such as which colour flower provides the most nutrition in a simple bee foraging task [17, 20, 27], which object types are food or poison in a more complex foraging task [28], or which arm of a T-maze contains the highest-value reward [20, 21, 26].

There have been variations on these kinds of environments designed to increase their difficulty. For example variations on the T-maze include the double T-maze, which has four arms instead of two [20, 26], a version requiring the agent to learn a possibly non-linear association between the perception of objects and their reward value [21], and a continuous version where the only input to the controller, besides a reward signal, comes from 5 range-finder sensors [22].

Possibly one of the most difficult tasks studied to date, in terms of the size of the exploration space and the number of associations to memorise, is a purely associative task in which agents learn associations between each possible input and output pattern [33, 34]. Aside from an input reward signal, the input and output vectors were four binary values. To simplify the task only one bit of either was set to 1, the rest were 0. The number of possible combinations to learn is 16, or four times as many as the double T-maze.

Over all previous work on evolving plastic neural networks that perform intra-life learning, only a handful of environments or tasks have been considered. The tasks have typically required a simple exploration strategy to determine which of a small set of behaviours should be conducted.

In any given study a newly introduced algorithm or model, such as an encoding scheme or neural network model, is typically assessed on only one or two environments. Furthermore, the variations of environments typically alter the environment in a single way. While it is understandable that few environments are tested, because designing environments is labour-intensive, the unfortunate result is that we problematically attempt to draw general conclusions about new algorithms and models from a very small sample size.

A method for automatically generating a broad range of environments would be beneficial in order to more rigorously assess the learning abilities of new models and algorithms.

3. METHODS

In the field of reinforcement learning, environments are often represented by a Markov Decision Process (MDP) that consists of a finite set of discrete states [24]. To move from one state to another in the environment an agent must perform one of a finite number of actions (with some actions possibly having an effect only in some states). Some state transitions confer a reward value. The task for the agent is to maximise the reward it receives over its lifetime, usually by performing an exploration of the environment to determine the expected future reward for each action in each state and then exploiting this knowledge.

A key insight of this paper is that this traditional way of representing reinforcement learning environments permits us to algorithmically generate novel environment instances with tunable difficulty over multiple dimensions, hereafter referred to as *difficulty dimensions*. To generate an environment, each state is assigned a random mapping of actions to transitions to other states, and each state transition is assigned a randomly selected reward value.

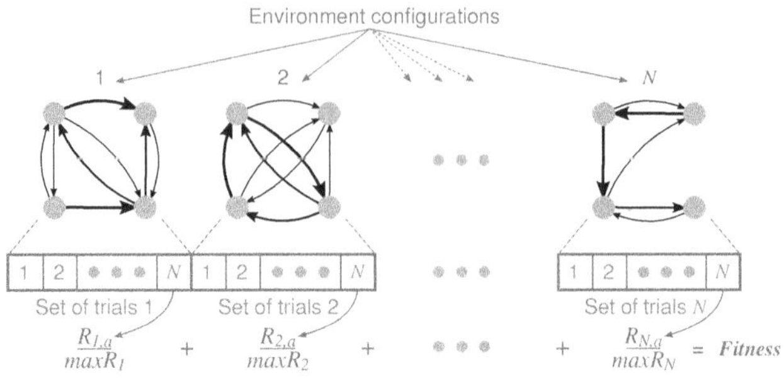

Figure 1: **Automatically Generated Environments.** For a single evolutionary run we generate N MDP environments that all have the same number of states and number of possible actions. We refer to these as *environment configurations*. A fitness evaluation consists of multiple *sets of trials*, with each environment configuration being presented for several consecutive trials – a set of trials – before the next environment configuration is presented for a set of trials. This process is repeated until all N environment configurations have been presented. Following [34], we reset the network at the beginning of each set of trials because we are testing the ability to learn, not the ability to forget and learn. Thus each set of trials simulates a lifetime for the agent, providing a more statistically informed evaluation of the general learning capabilities of the agent by avoiding the noise introduced by agents that just happen to work well for a particular ordering of the environment configurations. N equals the number of environment configurations, allowing an agent that can perform a good behaviour for each environment configuration to try each behaviour in turn within a set of trials until it discovers the best behaviour for the current configuration. The reward $R_{x,a}$ received by agent a in the last trial of each set of trials x, is the proportion of the maximum possible reward $maxR_x$ for the environment configuration presented in that set of trials. The fitness is calculated as the sum of these proportions over all sets of trials.

3.1 Assessing Learning Capabilities

As noted previously, assessing the learning capabilities of an agent in an evolutionary framework requires producing environments that are either different each generation or that change in some way during the agent's lifetime. Following from previous work, for the case study in this paper we adopt the latter approach.

Figure 1 describes how an agent's fitness is evaluated. The task of the agent is to determine, over a given set of trials, the current *environment configuration* it is in and adopt the optimal behaviour for that configuration. Switching between environment configurations during the agent's lifetime, with each configuration being presented for several consecutive trials before the switch, is similar in spirit to most environments from previous work on evolving plastic neural networks. For example, the T-maze environment has two configurations, one for each reward location. The agent must determine which configuration it is in and adopt the appropriate behaviour until the environment configuration changes.

One strategy an evolving agent can take, which frequently emerged in previous work [17, 21–23, 26, 28, 33], is for an agent to perform multiple fixed behaviours, one for each environment configuration, and iterate over those behaviours until the correct one is found in a given set of trials. The minimum number of trials per set of trials required for an agent to try each fixed behaviour in turn until it finds the correct one for the environment configuration being presented is thus the number of environment configurations. Thus in this case study the number of trials in a set of trials is the same as the number of environment configurations.

Only the reward received in the last trial of each set of trials contributes to the fitness. Including reward only from the last trial promotes agents that are able to determine which environment configuration they are operating in and to then adopt the best behaviour for that configuration, thereby collecting the highest reward in the last trial. Specifically, the fitness of an agent is calculated as the sum of the proportion of the maximum possible reward that can be earned in the last trial of each environment configuration the agent encounters in a lifetime. The agent – here, a neural network – is reset to its initial state between each set of trials.

Some of the dimensions over which the difficulty of this task can be varied are: the number of states; the number of available actions; the number of environment configurations; whether state transitions are probabilistic; whether the agent can directly observe the state of the environment; how regular the structure of the state transitions is (e.g. constraining transitions such that the states form a grid); and the length of a single trial.

In this case study we demonstrate how environments can be automatically generated along three different dimensions of variation. Where not specified, the number of actions and the length of trials are set to 4 and the number of environment configurations per run is 8. For any given state, the proportion of actions that have an effect – for which a state transition will occur – is 0.75, and the proportion of state transitions that provide a reward value is 0.5. When generating environments these proportions are evaluated probabilistically. All environments are deterministic, the environment state is directly observable by the agent and the structure of the environments is unconstrained.

For these environments, the complexity of the optimal behaviour for a configuration increases as the *available actions* and *trial length* difficulty parameters are increased.

3.2 Neural Network Models

Our case study examines three different neural network models, which control agents operating in MDP environments. We test these three treatments across three dimensions of environmental difficulty to demonstrate that automatically generated environments can reveal differences between neural models. The three neural network models are (1) non-plastic, fixed-weight, (2) Hebbian learning, and (3) neuromodulated Hebbian learning.

Fixed-Weight

The *Fixed-Weight* model is a typical fixed-weight, recurrent neural network in which the neurons have a sigmoidal, rate-based activation function [16].

Plastic-Weight

The *Plastic-Weight* model is identical to the *Fixed-Weight* model, but instead of fixed weights it has a more general form of Hebbian learning [13] introduced by Niv et al. [17]. Whereas Hebbian learning increases the strength of a connection if both the pre-synaptic and post-synaptic neuron fire together, the parametrised model allows connections to both increase or decrease, and do so in more situations. The model consists of four terms: *(A)* a correlation term that only adjusts the weight when the pre- and post-synaptic activation signals are correlated; *(B)* a pre-synaptic term that adjusts the weight based only on the pre-synaptic signal; *(C)* a post-synaptic term that adjusts the weight based only on the post-synaptic signal; and *(D)* a constant term that adjusts the weight only as a function of time, independently of pre- or post-synaptic activation signals.

The coefficients of these terms, as well as overall "learning rate" η, are the parameters of the model:

$$\Delta w = \eta(Axy + Bx + Cy + D) \quad (1)$$

where x and y are the pre- and post-synaptic activation signals respectively. A, B, C, D, and η are evolvable.

Modulated Plasticity

The *Modulated Plasticity* model is identical to the *Plastic-Weight* model, but adds a model of neuromodulation [22, 26], which allows learning to be turned on and off for a subset of connections based on environment stimuli and the state of other neurons. Thus the neural network can selectively turn learning on or off in a subset of connections depending on the situation that the agent is in. Our implementation of neuromodulation is identical to that of Risi and Stanley [22].

In this model some connections carry a modulatory signal rather than a normal activation signal. Every neuron has a modulatory activation level as well as the standard activation. The modulatory activation level is calculated similarly to that of the normal activation level:

$$m_i = \sum_{w_{ji} \in \text{Mod}} w_{ji} o_j \quad (2)$$

where m_i is the modulatory activation for neuron i, w_{ji} is the weight of the synapse connecting neuron j to i, o_j is the output of neuron j and Mod is the set of modulatory synapses. The modulatory activation level m_i modulates the plasticity of regular (i.e. non-modulatory) connections leading into neuron i. Based on the plasticity model from Niv et al. [17] this gives the updated plasticity rule:

$$\Delta w = \tanh(m_i/2)\eta(Axy + Bx + Cy + D) \quad (3)$$

3.3 HyperNEAT

This section is from [8] with minor modification. In 2007 an encoding was introduced called Compositional Pattern Producing Networks (CPPNs), which abstracts the process of natural development without requiring the simulation of diffusing chemicals [29]. When CPPNs encode ANNs, the algorithm is called HyperNEAT [30], which is described below. A key idea behind CPPNs is that complex patterns can be produced by determining attributes of their phenotypic components as a function of their geometric location. This idea is based on the belief that cells (or higher-level modules) in nature often differentiate into their possible types as a function of where they are situated in geometric space. For example, for some insects, a segment at the anterior pole should produce antennae and a segment at the posterior pole should produce a stinger.

Components of natural organisms cannot directly determine their location in space, so organisms have evolved developmental processes that create chemical gradients that organismal components use to figure out where they are and, thus, what to become [5]. For example, early in the development of embryos, different axes (e.g., anterior-posterior) are indicated by chemical gradients. Additional gradients signaled by different proteins can exist in the same area to represent a different pattern, such as a repeating motif. Downstream genes, such as Hox genes, can then combine repeated and asymmetric information to govern segmental differentiation [5]. Further coordinate frames can then be set up within segments to govern intra-module patterns.

3.3.1 CPPNs

One of the key insights behind CPPNs is that cells *in silico* can be directly given their geometric coordinates. The CPPN genome is a function that takes geometric coordinates as inputs and outputs the fate of an organismal component. When CPPNs encode two-dimensional pictures, the coordinates of each pixel on the canvas (e.g., $x = 2$, $y = 4$) are iteratively passed to the CPPN genome, and the output of the function is the color or shade of the pixel (Figure 2).

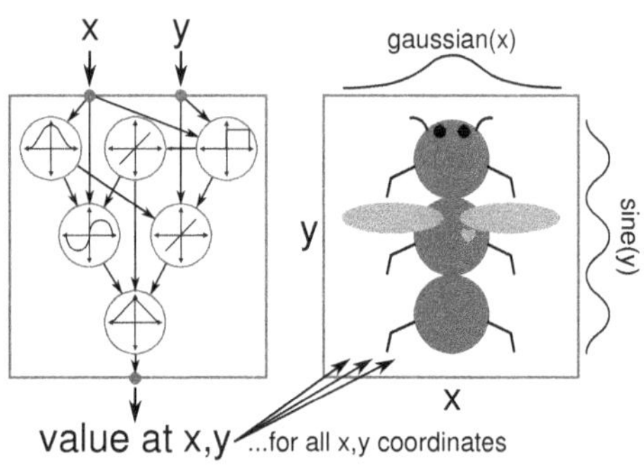

Figure 2: **Compositional Pattern Producing Networks.** CPPNs compose mathematical functions to generate regularities, such as symmetries and repeated modules, with and without variation. This figure is adapted from [29].

Each CPPN is a directed graph in which every node is itself a single function, such as sine or Gaussian. The nature of the functions can create a wide variety of properties, such as symmetry (e.g., a Gaussian function) and repetition (e.g., a sine function) that evolution can exploit. Because the genome allows functions to be comprised of other functions, coordinate frames can be combined and hierarchies can develop. For instance, a sine function early in the network can create a repeating theme that, when passed into the symmetrical Gaussian function, creates a repeating series of symmetrical motifs (Figure 2). This procedure is similar to the natural developmental processes described above [5].

The links that connect and allow information to flow between nodes in a CPPN have a weight that can magnify or diminish the values that pass along them. Mutations that change these weights may, for example, give a stronger influence to a symmetry-generating part of a network while diminishing the contribution from another part.

When CPPNs are evolved artificially with humans performing the selection, the evolved shapes look complex and natural (Figure 3) [25]. Moreover, these images display the features in natural organisms that indirect encodings were designed to produce, namely, symmetries and the repetition of themes, with and without variation.

3.3.2 Encoding ANNs with CPPNs

In the HyperNEAT algorithm, CPPNs encode ANNs instead of pictures, and evolution modifies the population of CPPNs [11, 30]. HyperNEAT evolves the weights for ANNs with a fixed topology. The ANNs in the experiments in this paper feature a two-dimensional, $m \times n$ Cartesian grid of inputs and a corresponding $m \times n$ grid of outputs. If an experiment uses an ANN with hidden nodes, the hidden nodes are placed in their own two-dimensional layer between the input and output grids. Recurrence is disabled, so each of the $m \times n$ nodes in a layer has a link of a given weight to each of the $m \times n$ nodes in the proximate layer, excepting output nodes, which have no outgoing connections. Link weights can be zero, functionally eliminating a link.

The inputs to the CPPNs are a constant bias value and the coordinates of both a source node (e.g., $x_1 = 0, y_1 = 0$) and a target node (e.g., $x_2 = 1, y_2 = 1$) (Figure 4). The CPPN takes these five values as inputs and produces one or two output values, depending on the ANN topology. If there is no hidden layer in the ANN, the single output is the weight of the link between a source node on the input layer and a target node on the output layer. If there is a hidden layer, the first output value determines the weight of the link between the associated input (source) node and hidden-layer (target) node, and the second output value determines the weight of the link between the associated hidden-layer (source) node and output-layer (target) node. All pairwise combinations of source and target node coordinates are iteratively passed as inputs to the CPPN to determine the weight of each ANN link. HyperNEAT can thus produce patterns in weight space similar to the patterns it produces in two-dimensional pictures (Figure 3).

An additional novel aspect of HyperNEAT is that it is one of the first neuroevolutionary algorithms capable of exploiting the geometry of a problem [7, 10, 11, 30]. Because the connection weights between nodes are a function of the geometric positions of those nodes, if those geometric positions represent aspects of the problem that are relevant to its solution, HyperNEAT can exploit such information. For example, when playing checkers, the concept of adjacency (on the diagonals) is important. Connection weights between

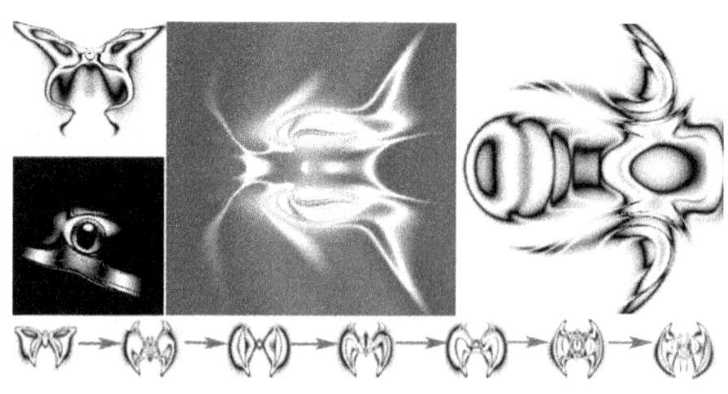

Figure 3: **Images Evolved with CPPNs.** Displayed are pictures from picbreeder.org [25], a website where visitors select images from a population evolved with the CPPN indirect encoding, which is also used in HyperNEAT. The bottom row shows images from a single lineage. Arrows represent intermediate forms that are not pictured.

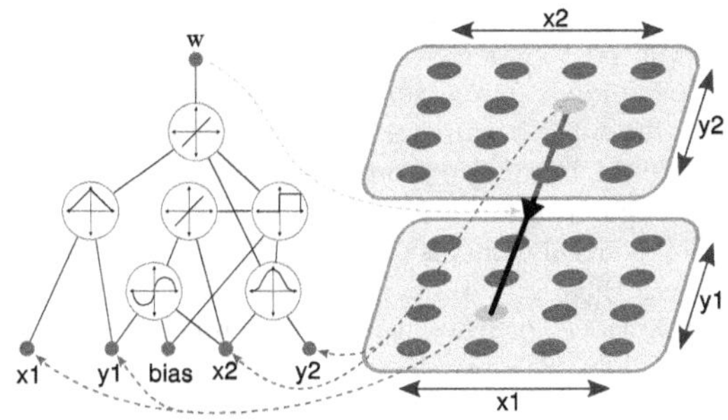

Figure 4: **HyperNEAT Produces ANNs from CPPNs.** Weights are specified as a function of the geometric coordinates of the source node and the target node for each connection. The coordinates of these nodes and a constant bias are iteratively passed to the CPPN to determine each connection weight. If there is no hidden layer, the CPPN has only one output, which specifies the weight between the source node in the input layer and the target node in the output layer. If there is a hidden layer in the ANN, the CPPN typically has two output values, which specify the weights for each connection layer. Alternatively inputs may be added to designate the z coordinates for the source and target nodes.

neighbouring squares may need to be different than weights between distant squares. HyperNEAT can create this kind of connectivity motif and repeat it across the board [10, 11]. Producing such a regularity would be more difficult with an encoding that does not include geometric information, because there would be no easy way for such an algorithm to identify which nodes are adjacent.

Variation in HyperNEAT occurs when mutations or crossover change the CPPNs. Mutations can add a node, which results in the addition of a function to the network, or change its link weights. Typical functions for CPPNs are sine, sigmoid, Gaussian, and linear. The evolution of the population of CPPN networks in HyperNEAT occurs according to the principles of the widely used NeuroEvolution of Augmenting Topologies (NEAT) algorithm [31]. NEAT, which was originally designed to evolve ANNs, can be fruitfully applied to CPPNs because a population of CPPNs is similar in structure to a population of ANNs.

The NEAT algorithm contains three main components [31, 32]. First, it starts with small genomes that encode simple networks and slowly complexifies them via mutations that add nodes and links to the network. This complexification enables the algorithm to evolve the network topology in addition to its weights. Second, NEAT implements a fitness-sharing mechanism via a speciation method that preserves diversity in the population and allows new innovations time to be tuned by evolution before forcing them to compete against rivals that have had more time to mature. Finally, historical information stored in genes helps to perform crossover in a way that is effective, yet avoids the need for expensive topological analysis. A full explanation of NEAT can be found in Stanley & Miikkulainen [31].

Our implementation of HyperNEAT differs in three ways from the original. First, speciation is implemented with a K-means clustering method. Second, in the original NEAT algorithm nodes are only added by splitting an existing connection, but in our implementation nodes could also be added anywhere along with two new connections to connect it to the existing network. Third, in the original formulation of HyperNEAT a connection is not expressed if the magnitude of the weight output of the CPPN is below a threshold, but in an extension called Link Expression Output (LEO) a separate output is used to determine whether a connection should be expressed. This method is employed in this case study. The key insight of LEO is that it makes it easier to evolve the pattern of which connections should exist independently from the pattern of weight values [35].

3.4 Synaptic Plasticity Parameter Classes

Rather than encoding each parameter of the synaptic plasticity model for each individual connection, we take the same approach as Stanley et al. [28], in which the genome defines the parameter values for several plasticity rules, or classes, and then encodes which rule each connection references. Two benefits of this approach are that it reduces the overall search space and the classes can be optimised separately from the genes that determine which class a connection belongs to. Additionally, this approach bears some resemblance to natural neural networks, which tend to have numerous, but specific, types of neurons, neurotransmitters, and synapses that perform different functions [3, 4, 14, 36].

Unlike the model in [28], which is based on a direct encoding, we adapt the approach to HyperNEAT by evolving CPPNs that have $n+1$ outputs that specify the class for a connection or a special no plasticity class, where the number of classes is n. This approach is employed for all plastic neural network models considered in this case study.

3.5 Experimental Details

For each treatment 50 runs of evolution are performed, with each run lasting 2000 generations. At the start of a run multiple environment configurations are generated – as determined by the environment configurations difficulty dimension setting – which are used throughout that run.

Each run starts with a different random seed, however the random seed used to generate environment configurations at the start of a run varies only as a function of the run number within a treatment. Thus for a given set of environment generation parameters, such as the number of states and actions, the same environment configurations are generated for the same run number for each of the different neural network model treatments. This allows a more direct and fair comparison between treatments.

The parameter settings for HyperNEAT are similar to those in [30] except for the following differences: the population size is 1000; the K-means speciation method uses 32 clusters; the available functions for CPPNs are Sigmoid, Gaussian, Sine, absolute, ramp, linear, and sign; the probabilities of adding a CPPN node by replacing an existing connection or adding a node with two new connections are both 0.02; and CPPN weights are mutated with 0.15 probability by perturbation from a normal distribution with σ=0.3.

Evolved neural networks consist of an input layer, a hidden layer and an output layer, with the input and output layer sizes based on the number of states and number of actions that the generated environments are composed of (Figure 5). The networks are potentially fully recurrent within and between all layers, except the input layer, with LEO determining whether a potential connection is expressed.

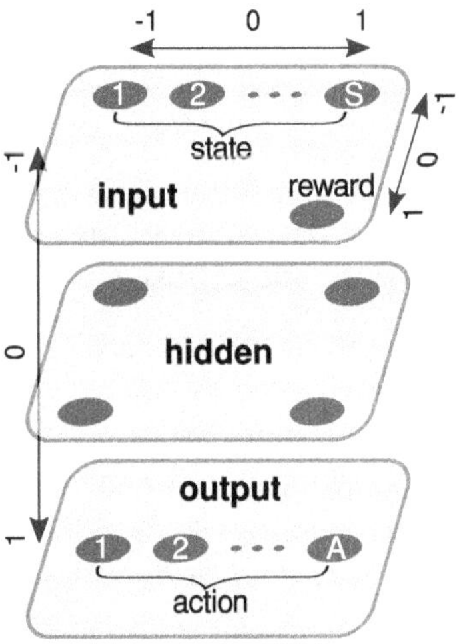

Figure 5: **Neural Network Topology for All Experiments.** S and A are the number of states and actions in the environment respectively.

All software, experiment settings, and data are available upon request or at *http://ojcoleman.com/publications*.

4. RESULTS AND DISCUSSION

We test the performance of three neural network models over automatically generated environments that sweep across three difficulty dimensions. Each dimension is scaled from easier to harder (Figure 6). We compare how the network models respond to changes in each difficulty dimension and across the difficulty dimensions. All statistical analyses in this case study are performed with R's Mann–Whitney–Wilcoxon rank sum test.

Across all difficulty dimensions, when the difficulty parameter is greater than or equal to 4, the Plastic-Weight and Modulated Plasticity models significantly outperform the Fixed-Weight model in nearly all cases ($p < 0.01$).

Interestingly, the Modulated Plasticity model does not typically perform significantly better than the Plastic-Weight model, and in fact the Plastic-Weight model significantly outperforms it when the number of actions is increased to 8 and beyond ($p < 0.001$; Figure 6b). The only case where the Modulated Plasticity model significantly outperforms the Plastic-Weight model ($p < 0.05$) is when the number of environment configurations is 16 (Figure 6a).

The results reveal differences between the neural network models that are not obvious without sweeping across these dimensions of difficulty. For example, as the number of actions is increased, the performance of the Modulated Plasticity model and the Plastic-Weight model diverge drastically, whereas these two models perform almost identically when sweeping across the other two dimensions of difficulty.

If we were to compare these neural network models over any one difficulty dimension, then very different conclusions could be drawn from the results. For example, if the number of actions is not considered then we may have drawn the general conclusion that the Modulated Plasticity and Plastic-Weight models are very similar in performance, and alternatively if only the number of actions are considered then we could draw the conclusion that, given a sufficient number of actions, the Plastic-Weight model outperforms the Modulated Plasticity model.

Similarly, if we compare these neural network models over any one difficulty parameter value then very different conclusions could be drawn from the results. For example, if only a difficulty parameter value of 4 is studied, we may draw the general conclusion that the Plastic-Weight and Modulated Plasticity models do not perform significantly differently. However if we study a difficulty parameter value of 8 only, then we may draw the conclusion that, at least in some cases, the Plastic-Weight model significantly outperforms the Modulated Plasticity model. More generally, without a wide sweep beyond 4 available actions the drastic difference between the Plastic-Weight and Modulated Plasticity models is not evident. Even a seemingly wide sweep of 2, 3, 4 and possibly even 5 available actions may not show the difference between the two models.

Another interesting performance difference that emerges between the different environment difficulty dimensions is that increasing the trial length beyond 4 does not affect the performance of any of the neural network models very much. On the other hand, increasing the number of environment configurations beyond 4 greatly reduces the performance of every neural network model. Thus if we do not sweep over all of these environment difficulty dimensions we may arrive at very different conclusions about how the performance of all neural network models are affected by increases in the difficulty of the environments.

These kinds of difficulty dimensions and difficulty parameter settings are reminiscent of those chosen in previous research on evolving plastic neural networks that learn during their lifetime [2, 6, 15, 17, 21–23, 26, 28, 33] in terms of the size of the memory requirements, kinds of environment exploration strategies, and complexities of behaviour required. For example, increasing the T-maze environment from a single T-maze, which can be solved with 2 fixed behaviours, to the double T-maze [26], which requires 4 fixed behaviours. Thus the results from the case study presented in this paper are relevant to the kinds of tasks and environments employed in our field to assess, and draw conclusions about, the learning capabilities of new models and algorithms. The results of this case study strongly suggest that a more rigorous assessment of learning capabilities, such as that provided by the automated environment generation method introduced in this paper, is not only useful but perhaps necessary to gain a more accurate picture of learning capabilities.

5. FUTURE WORK

While the scope of this paper is to introduce the automated environment generation method, in future work we will use this method to rigorously assess and analyze the performance characteristics of existing models and algorithms. For example, in the case study in this paper, the Modulated Plasticity model did not outperform the Plastic-Weight model. Testing many variants of these two models across different difficulty dimensions will allow us to better understand why.

The case study in this paper sweeps across only three of many possible difficulty dimensions, and studies only three neural network models. Future work will explore other difficulty dimensions and include more models and algorithms. We will also study not just environments that change *within*

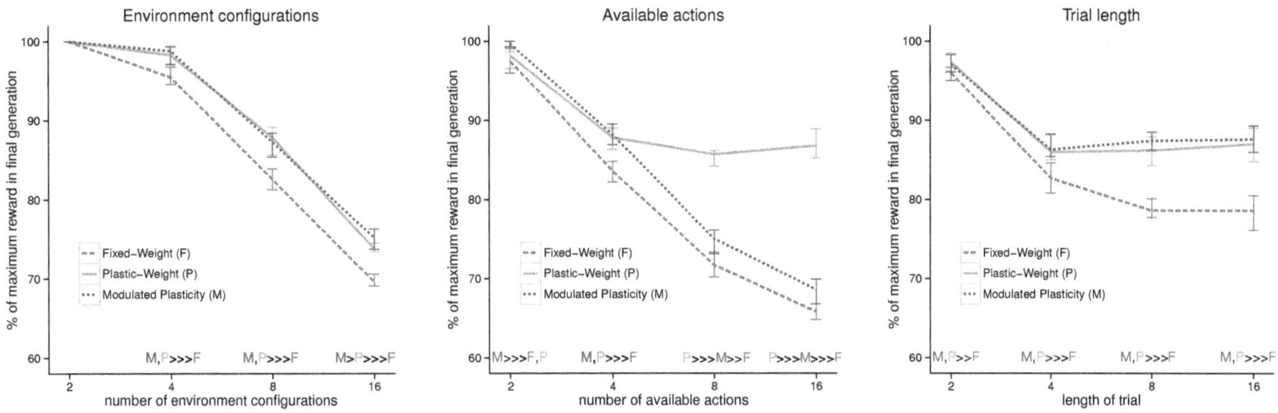

(a) (b) (c)

Figure 6: **Performance of the three neural network models over sweeps across three difficulty dimensions in automatically generated environments.** The median performance ($\pm 95\%$ bootstrapped confidence intervals) of the best performing neural network from the final generation over all runs are shown. Statistical significance is indicated by $>$ ($p < 0.05$), $>>$ ($p < 0.01$) and $>>>$ ($p < 0.001$).

a generation, but also environments that change *across* generations.

The discrete MDP environment in this paper cannot represent many real-world tasks. Two reasons are the inability to accurately represent continuous values and a lack of environment *dynamics*: environment states that change over time due to the laws of physics. Another direction for future work is adding the ability to automatically generate environments with continuous values and such physical dynamics. More generally, being able to automatically generate a broader class of environments will further increase our ability to assess the general properties of models and algorithms.

6. CONCLUSION

In this paper we have introduced a method for automatically generating environments for which the difficulty can be scaled in many dimensions. This method makes it easier to conduct a more rigorous assessment of the learning capabilities of agents that perform intra-life learning. The automated environment generation method addresses three key issues: (1) any single environment is potentially open to bias towards or against certain kinds of models and algorithms; (2) manually creating environments is labour intensive, at best taking time away from focusing on other aspects of research and, at worst, meaning that sweeps across key difficulty dimensions are not performed; and, most significantly (3) testing new models and algorithms on one or a few environments provides only a small sample size that may prevent accurate general conclusions from being drawn.

The utility of automated environment generation is not limited to assessing the learning capabilities of evolved agents or agents based on neural networks. Rather, the automated environment generation method could be applied to assessing the learning capabilities of any kind of agent that is able to operate in MDP environments, regardless of how the agent is developed or what kind of learning model the agent is based on. Thus the automated environment generation method presented in this paper has a potentially broad applicability to the field of artificial intelligence, and may ultimately accelerate the rate at which we discover how to create general purpose AI.

References

[1] D. Ackley and M. Littman. Interactions between learning and evolution. *Artificial life II*, 10, 1991.

[2] J. Baxter. The evolution of learning algorithms for artificial neural networks. *Complex Systems*, 1993.

[3] G. Bi and M. Poo. Synaptic modifications in cultured hippocampal neurons: Dependence on spike timing, synaptic strength, and postsynaptic cell type. *J. Neurosci.*, 18(24):10464–10472, Dec. 1998.

[4] R. Cantrup, R. Dixit, E. Palmesino, S. Bonfield, T. Shaker, N. Tachibana, D. Zinyk, S. Dalesman, K. Yamakawa, W. K. Stell, R. O. Wong, B. E. Reese, A. Kania, Y. Sauvé, and C. Schuurmans. Cell-type specific roles for PTEN in establishing a functional retinal architecture. *PLoS ONE*, 7(3), Mar. 2012.

[5] S. Carroll. *Endless forms most beautiful: The new science of evo devo and the making of the animal kingdom.* WW Norton & Company, 2005.

[6] D. Chalmers. The evolution of learning: An experiment in genetic connectionism. In *Proc. of the 1990 connectionist models summer school*, 1990.

[7] J. Clune, C. Ofria, and R. T. Pennock. The sensitivity of HyperNEAT to different geometric representations of a problem. In *Proc. of the 11th Annual Genetic and Evolutionary Computation Conference*, 2009.

[8] J. Clune, K. Stanley, R. Pennock, and C. Ofria. On the performance of indirect encoding across the continuum of regularity. *IEEE Transactions on Evolutionary Computation*, 15(3):346–367, 2011.

[9] D. Floreano and C. Mattiussi. *Bio-inspired artificial intelligence: theories, methods, and technologies.* The MIT Press, 2008.

[10] J. Gauci and K. Stanley. A case study on the critical role of geometric regularity in machine learning. In *Proc. of the 23rd AAAI Conference on Artificial Intelligence. AAAI Press*, 2008.

[11] J. Gauci and K. Stanley. Autonomous evolution of topographic regularities in artificial neural networks. *Neural Computation*, 2010.

[12] F. Gruau and D. Whitley. Adding learning to the cellular development of neural networks: Evolution and the baldwin effect. *Evolutionary Computation*, 1(3):213–233, 1993.

[13] D. O. Hebb. *The Organization of Behavior: A Neuropsychological Theory.* Wiley, New York, NY, USA, 1949.

[14] E. M. Izhikevich. Which model to use for cortical spiking neurons? *IEEE Transactions on Neural Networks*, 15(5):1063–1070, 2004.

[15] G. M. Khan, J. F. Miller, and D. M. Halliday. Evolution of cartesian genetic programs for development of learning neural architecture. *Evolutionary Computation*, 19(3):469–523, 2011.

[16] W. McCulloch and W. Pitts. A logical calculus of the ideas immanent in nervous activity. *Bulletin of mathematical biology*, 5(4):115–133, 1943.

[17] Y. Niv, D. Joel, I. Meilijson, and E. Ruppin. Evolution of reinforcement learning in uncertain environments: A simple explanation for complex foraging behaviors. *Adaptive Behavior*, 10(1):5–24, 2002.

[18] S. Nolfi and D. Floreano. *Evolutionary robotics: The biology, intelligence, and technology of self-organizing machines.* MIT press, Cambridge, MA, 2000.

[19] S. Nolfi, D. Parisi, and J. L. Elman. Learning and evolution in neural networks. *Adaptive Behavior*, 3(1):5–28, June 1994.

[20] S. Risi, C. E. Hughes, and K. O. Stanley. Evolving plastic neural networks with novelty search. *Adaptive Behavior*, 18(6):470–491, Dec. 2010.

[21] S. Risi and K. O. Stanley. Indirectly encoding neural plasticity as a pattern of local rules. In *11th International Conference on Simulation of Adaptive Behavior (SAB 2010)*, page 533–543, 2010.

[22] S. Risi and K. O. Stanley. A unified approach to evolving plasticity and neural geometry. In *Proc. of the International Joint Conference on Neural Networks (IJCNN).* IEEE, 2012.

[23] S. Risi, S. D. Vanderbleek, C. E. Hughes, and K. O. Stanley. How novelty search escapes the deceptive trap of learning to learn. In *Proc. of the 11th Annual Genetic and Evolutionary Computation Conference*, page 153–160, 2009.

[24] S. J. Russell, P. Norvig, J. F. Canny, J. M. Malik, and D. D. Edwards. *Artificial Intelligence: A Modern Approach*, volume 74. Prentice Hall, 1995.

[25] J. Secretan, N. Beato, D. D Ambrosio, A. Rodriguez, A. Campbell, and K. Stanley. Picbreeder: evolving pictures collaboratively online. In *Proc. of the Computer Human Interaction Conference*, page 1759–1768. ACM, 2008.

[26] A. Soltoggio, J. A. Bullinaria, C. Mattiussi, P. Dürr, and D. Floreano. Evolutionary advantages of neuromodulated plasticity in dynamic, reward-based scenarios. *Artificial Life*, 11:569, 2008.

[27] A. Soltoggio, P. Dürr, C. Mattiussi, and D. Floreano. Evolving neuromodulatory topologies for reinforcement learning-like problems. In *Proc. of the IEEE Congress on Evolutionary Computation*, page 2471–2478, 2007.

[28] K. O. Stanley. Evolving adaptive neural networks with and without adaptive synapses. In *Proc. of the IEEE Congress on Evolutionary Computation*, volume 4, 2003.

[29] K. O. Stanley. Compositional pattern producing networks: A novel abstraction of development. *Genetic Programming and Evolvable Machines*, 8(2):131–162, 2007.

[30] K. O. Stanley, D. B. D'Ambrosio, and J. Gauci. A hypercube-based encoding for evolving large-scale neural networks. *Artificial Life*, 15(2):185–212, 2009.

[31] K. O. Stanley and R. Miikkulainen. Evolving neural networks through augmenting topologies. *Evolutionary Computation*, 10:99–127, 2002.

[32] K. O. Stanley and R. Miikkulainen. Competitive coevolution through evolutionary complexification. *J. Artif. Intell. Res. (JAIR)*, 21:63–100, 2004.

[33] P. Tonelli and J. Mouret. Using a map-based encoding to evolve plastic neural networks. In *2011 IEEE Workshop on Evolving and Adaptive Intelligent Systems (EAIS)*, pages 9–16. IEEE, Apr. 2011.

[34] P. Tonelli and J.-B. Mouret. On the relationships between synaptic plasticity and generative systems. In *Proc. of the 13th annual Genetic and Evolutionary Computation Conference*, page 1531–1538, 2011.

[35] P. Verbancsics and K. O. Stanley. Constraining connectivity to encourage modularity in HyperNEAT. In *Proc. of the 13th annual Genetic and Evolutionary Computation Conference*, page 1483–1490, 2011.

[36] D. Weinreich and W. F. Wonderlin. Inhibition of calcium-dependent spike after-hyperpolarization increases excitability of rabbit visceral sensory neurones. *J. Physiol.*, 394(1):415–427, 1987.

Evolution of Communication and Cooperation

Jason Fairey
Electrical Engineering and Computer Science Department
Washington State University
Pullman, WA
jason.fairey@wsu.edu

Terence Soule
Computer Science Department
University of Idaho
Moscow, ID 83844-1010
tsoule@cs.uidaho.edu

ABSTRACT

In the wild, spotted hyenas have been observed to chase lions away from a recent kill. This is a high risk, high reward behavior that requires significant teamwork and decision making skills. Modeling this behavior and creating algorithms that can improve evolutionarily may lead to more adaptable artificial systems for robotics and other cooperative artificial agents. Previous research has shown that having a lead or "flag bearer" hyena can significantly improve evolution. Thus, the complex social dynamics and coordination abilities required for this problem make it interesting artificial intelligence task. This also suggests that the type and encoding of the sensory inputs has a significant effect on the evolutionary trajectory and overall success at the task. Additionally, in the wild genetic diversity is driven by the migration of young males between packs, which leads to interesting evolutionary questions. To address the role of input encodings we introduce two evolutionary neural network variants, one using absolute headings as inputs/outputs and one using relative headings as inputs/outputs (headings defined relative to environmental elements). Our results show that the networks with relative inputs and outputs evolve significantly faster and result in better performance, suggesting that a critical difference is the existence of easily accessible, problem relevant, references for defining movement vectors. Our results also show that the inclusion of a leader in the team structure can improve the rate at which cooperative behaviors are evolved, but does not lead to better overall behaviors. In addition, we examine the emerging behaviors as the teams go from random behavior to a circling pattern to an aggressive charge towards the goal.

Categories and Subject Descriptors

I.2.11 [**Artificial Intelligence**]: Distributed Artificial Intelligence—*Multiagent Systems*

General Terms

Multiagent

GECCO'14, July 12–16, 2014, Vancouver, BC, Canada.

http://dx.doi.org/10.1145/2576768.2598377

Keywords

Cooperation, communication, multi-agent

1. INTRODUCTION

Cooperation between agents, either artificial or natural, has been vital for the success of certain tasks. Schools of fish stick together to disorient predators. Shiny scales and fast, coordinated movements allow for a higher survival rate for the school as a whole when confronted with a small group of predators. Humpback whales are known to work with other whales by herding fish up towards the surface, then creating a ring of bubbles forcing the fish to stay in a small area. After the fish are properly herded, the whales will swim up through the school and eat [11]. Another type of dolphin will herd fish near a bank in the river and, as a synchronized whole, charge up onto the shore eating as many fish as they can. Without coordination, the entire process would be far less efficient, or perhaps even deadly, as a beached dolphin is in great risk [5].

Spotted hyenas also work together as a team. They will forage for food, and on occasion they will team up to chase off lions from a recent kill. This behavior is inherently risky, as lions are stronger than a solitary hyena, and will defend their kill. The hyenas must work together to ensure that there are enough of them to make the lions think twice about staying and fighting. A single hyena may lose against a lion, but five hyenas will have a much better chance. This cooperation can lead to a group of hyenas being able to eat a nutritious meal without expending the energy needing to kill it.

While this behavior alone is an interesting problem for artificial intelligence algorithms, the dynamics of their clan structure as well as their breeding habits lead to an even more interesting genetic algorithm problem. The social rankings of a given spotted hyena is based on the ranking of their mother. A female offspring of the leader of the clan will have a high social order and it is to her benefit to stay in that clan, leading to more available food. The males on the other hand, while able to survive easier by staying within the clan, have a lower chance of mating within said clan. This leads to most males emigrating away from their home clan and attempting to join a different clan. Immigrant males end up at the bottom of the social rankings in their new clan, but they also have a higher chance of mating, hence rewarding that behavior and increasing genetic diversity between clans.

Hyenas also have a great deal of sensory information to process. Information stemming from vision, hearing, smell, as well as taste and touch, are processed by the hyena brain. The amount of information is too much to handle at every level. As an extreme example, in making a decision a hyena (or any other animal) does not have to directly consider the amount of light reaching every rod and cone in its retina. Instead information is compressed into more manageable concepts. For example, the retina filters images for color and light contrast, then by edges, and eventually into shapes that can be categorized as an object and that information is used in making "higher level" decisions. In addition, compressed information from different sources, such as olfactory and auditory senses, are melded leading to recognition of important concepts. E.g., a rustle of leaves may be perceived through visual stimuli alone and considered to be simply a breeze, but with the addition of the sound of a growl or the smell of a lion's breath, the cause of the rustling leaves may be interpreted as a much bigger danger. By compressing raw data into information and melding it with information from other sources, much more complex concepts can be addressed. This process of compressing data into information is also very common in artificial agents where, for example, an image may be reduced to its component objects by an image processing routine, and then it is the identified objects that are passed to the decision making routines. In the process of compressing information for artificial systems it is necessary to choose a representation for the newly compressed information. This representation is likely to have a significantly impact on how easy it is to evolve successful behaviors.

In this paper we examine two very different approaches to representing the compressed information. One method uses absolute values, e.g. x and y coordinates, as both input and output. The other will use a relative system where each input and output is based on vector information. Each input is originally made up of a great deal of sensory inputs leading to a more complex concept such as the direction of the nearest lion. This compression allows us to simulate the evolved behavior without having to add the complexity involved in sight, sound, and smell. We will also explore the possibilities of using a neural network to simulate the portion of the hyena's brain responsible for this behavior as well as using a genetic algorithm to allow the network to learn. In a previous paper, this simulation was used with an expression tree instead of a neural network [7]. The results show that a neural network with the right inputs can lead to a more successful adaptation than the expression tree used before.

2. BACKGROUND

This section presents a brief background on genetic algorithms, neural networks, and the previous research conducted on the lions and hyena problem.

2.1 Genetic Algorithms

Genetic algorithms are designed to mimic the process of sexual genetic reproduction in animals. This process occurs when the genetic code of the parent organism is split into two sets, each containing a random selection of the genetic code. During fertilization, this genetic code will merge with the genetic code of the other parent organism creating a new genetic code for the offspring. The offspring will then develop according to their genetic code, and if that code has features that allow it to live longer and breed more, it is considered more "fit" and it is likely that genetic code will spread further. The opposite is true of any mistakes, as an organism with a weaker genetic code is more likely to have a lower fitness level and that genetic code will not spread as much [3].

This design is quite useful as often the correct behavior of a system is not completely known. A robot may be designed to handle a great many static situations, but as soon as it has to interface with a new environment, the hard coded behaviors may not be able to correctly control the robot's behavior. To combat this, artificial intelligence algorithms are used, and will "train" on real world data, trying to converge to a more correct behavior. While there are many different artificial intelligence algorithms, genetic algorithms are both successful as well as interesting when comparing artificial evolution to real world examples.

Genetic algorithms appear specifically apt when the entire control system can be represented by a set of values. These values can be treated as either individual genes or "alleles" which are groups of genes. A large set of these control systems can be generated and tested for success. The most successful ones are then run through the simulated reproduction process to create a new offspring. This process is repeated until a control system is considered to be the best, and is used for the final result.

2.2 Neural Network

As humans tried to develop artificial intelligence systems, it seemed appropriate to try to mimic the human brain. Initially the attempts were simple, such as state machines, but eventually attempts were made to model the neurons that are primarily responsible for intelligent behavior in most animals. Each neuron has a set of inputs from other neurons or sensory organs in the body. These inputs are modulated through amplitude and time and converge at the hillock of the neuron. Each signal that reaches this hillock is added together, some may be negative and some positive, and if the result is positive enough, the neuron will fire, sending out a pulse, or spike, that will become an input on another neuron, gland, or muscle [1].

An artificial neural network (ANN) simulates this behavior. While most designs ignore time modulation, each input into a neuron is multiplied by a weight, simulating the amplitude modulation of a real neuron. Each neuron then consists of a set of inputs, a set of weights for each input, and then an output. A real neuron's output is either a spike, or nothing. This is managed by the neuron sending a different number of spikes depending on how strong the input is. The artificial neuron simulates this by using any number between 0 and 1.

There is a long history of using evolved ANNs to control both simulated and physical agents (see for example [2, 6, 8]), which is why ANNs were chosen as the representation for comparison with the previous research on the lions and hyenas problem using tree based representation. Most of this research has focused on evolving network weights. However, several techniques have been developed for the evolution of neural network topology, most notably NEAT [9] and hyper-NEAT [12, 4]. Although these techniques would be promising avenues for future research in the current research only the weights in the neural network are evolved, not the network topology, which is fixed.

2.3 Lions and Hyenas

Previous research on the lion and hyenas used a fairly standard genetic programming technique [7]. Each hyena was controlled by a unique vector expression tree. The inputs were vectors to objects in the environment such as the nearest hyena, nearest lion and North. The output was another vector, which determined the direction of the hyena's movement. The expression tree was reevaluated at every timestep. (Note that we consider this vector an absolute movement command, Section 3.2 in that on a given timestep the expression tree returned a specific vector and the hyena moved in that direction. In contrast, a relative movement command would be a command such as "move towards the nearest lion".) This research showed that having a leader (or flag bearer) - a hyena that all other hyenas could observe - significantly improved the evolution of coordinated behaviors.

A significant weakness of the GP expression tree approach is that the output of the expression tree is typically limited to the same general type as the inputs. E.g. the inputs are a set of vectors and the output is a new vector determining the hyena's direction of movement. It is more complicated to have multiple outputs of different types. For example, generating movement commands that are not simple, absolute vectors. Clearly this is a coding issue that can be overcome, but that would involve a series of design decisions that are likely to have a significant impact on any experiments, thereby clouding the underlying science.

Thus, in this paper an artificial neural network (ANN) is used to control the hyenas. This is another commonly used control structure for mobile agents, but the use of an ANN makes it easier to change the outputs in a 'natural' way - in this case comparing generating absolute versus relative movement commands.

3. METHODS

The system used for evaluation is broken into three major components, the simulation environment, the evolution of the hyena population, and the individual hyena's control system.

3.1 Environment

The environment consists of an infinite, two-dimensional surface. All of the participants, hyenas, lions, and the zebra, begin in the same general area. The zebra is always placed at the origin; the two lions are placed randomly in a small radius around the zebra; and the hyenas are placed randomly in a large radius around the zebra (see Figure 3). The lions follow deterministic movement rules (described below), the hyenas move according to their evolved ANNs, and the zebra (actually the zebra corpse) remains stationary. In addition to moving hyenas can also "call". This is a deterministic behavior, when a hyena is within 8 units of a the zebra, the large circle in Figure 3, it begins calling. This effects how it is identified by other hyenas (see Section 3.2). Hyenas in the wild exhibit a similar behavior, loudly vocalizing when they approach the lions.

In each generation each team of (fourteen) hyenas is run through five tests, and their fitness is their average score across the five tests. Each test lasts for 100 simulated time steps. In each time step each hyena is given its set of inputs, computes its direction of travel, and then moves in that direction. After each time step, the fitness is calculated for each hyena based on the distance it is away from the zebra:

$$F_{zebra} = \frac{1}{1 + d_{zebra}}$$

in addition hyenas lose fitness for being too close (within 3 units) to a lion:

$$F_{lion} = 3 \times (d_{lion} - 3)$$

note that because this expression is only applied if d_{lion} is less than 3, it always gives a negative value, i.e. a fitness loss. This reflects a hyena being injured by a lion.

The fitness of a given hyena is F_{zebra} plus F_{lion} for each lion that would attack. Then each fitness value for each time step is added together to make up the total fitness for a specific hyena. A sum of each hyena's fitness is used as the team's overall fitness. Of course, F_{zebra} may not be strictly representative of the natural world - hyenas presumably do not receive a fitness reward for approaching a zebra (or any other food source), only for actually reaching it and obtaining some food. However, as a practical matter rewarding hyenas for approaching the zebra was necessary to create a sufficient fitness gradient for evolution to succeed.

Note that with this fitness function simply charging the lions alone is a poor strategy for a hyena. It would gain roughly 1 point of fitness every time step for being close to or on the zebra, but would lose close to 18 (= 2*3*-3) points per time step for being near the two lions. Thus, coordinated behavior to drive off the lion is necessary to get the zebra.

Lions only move if forced out of position by being outnumbered by hyenas by more than 3 to 1, a ratio consistent with field studies. If the number of hyenas within 5 units of a lion outnumber the lions within that range by more than 3 to 1 the lion moves directly away from the nearest hyena. E.g. with two lions it takes at least seven hyenas getting close to force the lions to move.

3.2 Input and Output

The inputs consists of values from the senses that each hyena has available to them, converted into a polar form. These inputs include the following scalar inputs:

- The number of calling hyenas
- The number of lions

and the following vector inputs:

- The previous move performed by this hyena

- The location of the zebra, but only if the hyena is close within 8 units of it (the large circle in figure 3)
- The location of the nearest lion
- The location of the nearest hyena
- The location of the nearest calling hyena (a hyena calls if its with 8 units of the zebra)

In some trials the following vector input was also included as it was one of the most vital input in the previous experiments [7]:

- The location of the leader hyena, if it is calling.

In the trials that include a leader hyena the leader is simply the first hyena in the team. Note that although it is referred to as a leader this hyena has no direct influence of the behavior of the other hyenas, they can simple "see" it if it is calling. In contrast, for non-leader trials other hyenas only see the *nearest* calling hyena (and know the number of calling hyenas).

Each vector input is relative to the location of the current hyena, E.g. if the hyena is closer to the zebra, the zebra location vector would have a shorter magnitude.

Input and output information was encoded in one of two methods, either *absolute* or *relative*.

3.2.1 Absolute Input/Output

In the absolute encoding agents move in absolute directions (defined using Cartesian coordinates). The output of the ANN is an absolute direction in that it is a direction that, once calculated by the ANN, be interpreted independently of any objects in the environment. Thus, in the absolute encoding each input vector is converted into Cartesian coordinates and the network's output is an absolute movement direction. This meant that the control system received an x and y offset for each input. I.e. the ANN had $2N + 2$ input nodes (plus a bias input), where N is the number of input vectors and the +2 is for the two scalar inputs (number of calling hyenas and number of lions). The output was a pair of values treated as the desired movement in the x and y direction respectively. This is considered an "absolute" representation because the output is an absolute movement from the hyena's current location.

3.2.2 Relative Input/Output

In the relative encoding agents moved relative to objects in the environment. E.g. whereas in the absolute encoding the output is an absolute direction ("go 15 degrees East of North"), in the relative encoding the output is defined relative to objects in the environment ("go between the nearest other hyena and the nearest lion"). The relative method used only the magnitude of each input vector as inputs. I.e. the ANN received $N + 2$ inputs (plus a bias input), where N is the number of input vectors and the +2 is for the two scalar inputs (number of calling hyenas and number of lions). This meant that the control system had no information about the direction of each input.

The output consisted of one value for each vector input. I.e. the ANN had N output nodes. Each output value was used as a scalar multiplier for a given input vector. I.e. each hyena's movement was determined by a weighted sum of the input vectors where the weights were generated each time step by the hyena's ANN. This is considered a "relative" representation because the output of the ANN is a command that is relative to the current state of the environment. E.g. if the output node associated with the vector to the nearest hyena returns a large value then the hyena will tend to move towards the nearest hyena - a relative, rather than an absolute, direction.

This can be analogous to the drive to move closer or further away from a given object, e.g. the hyena can try to move closer to the zebra (if the output node associated with the zebra direction generates a large value), but not get too close to the lion (if the output node associated with the lion direction generates a large negative value). So, after a certain point, the drive to stay away from the lion might counteract the drive to move closer to the zebra.

For both representations, the inputs are given to the control system (the evolving ANN) and the output is calculated as described above in each time step. Hyenas are limited to moving a distance of, at most, one unit per time step. They can move shorter distances.

3.3 The Neural Network

The control system evaluated for this experiment is a three layer neural network consisting of an input layer, a hidden layer, and an output layer. An additional node is created with a constant value of one to be used as a bias value for each hidden layer and output layer node. As noted above the number of inputs nodes is either $2N + 2$ or $N + 2$ depending on whether the absolute or relative encoding is used.

The nodes between each layer are fully connected, with each connection having its own weight value. The hidden layer nodes use a sigmoid activation function (in this case an arc tangent function) with the output bounded between 0 and 1, and the output nodes act as a weighted sum of the hidden layer nodes multiplied by their associated weights.

3.4 Generations

At the beginning of each trial, a new population of 100 teams is created. Each hyena is given a set of random values between -0.5 and 0.5. These values, or genes, are the weights used by the neural networks described in section 3.2 and can be equated with that hyena's genetic code. Each team in this population is tested in the manner described in section 3.1, and a fitness score is determined for each team.

Between each generation, a tournament process takes place, where five randomly selected teams are compared. Another set of five randomly selected teams is created, and the best team in each set is paired up as a "breeding" set. These two teams are run through a crossover algorithm to create two new teams. The algorithm pairs up each hyena in the team (the first hyena of the first team will pair up with the first hyena of the second team), and then a number of gene pairs equal to 50% of the size of the genetic code are swapped

Table 1: Parameters

Team Size	14
Population Size	100
Time Steps per evaluation	100
Retests per evaluation	5
Trials	40
Mutation Rate	10%
Generations	500
Selection	Tournament, size 5
Crossover	Uniform, 50%

between hyenas. The end result is two new teams consisting of a distribution of weights from both parent teams.

After this process is finished, each hyena in the new teams undergoes a mutation process. Each value has a 10% chance to mutate, adding a random value between -0.5 and 0.5 to the weight that value represents. This process allows for offspring to obtain values that neither parent possessed.

Fifty new teams are generated in this fashion with each new pair being selected from two new tournaments. The rest of the teams needed are generated through an all-star method. For each place in the team, five individual hyenas are compared to each other with the best being selected for the new team. After two teams are built in this manner, they undergo the same crossover and mutation processes that the normal tournament teams went through. The next generation population consists of 50 from team pairing and 50 from all-star pairing.

4. PARAMETERS

A population of 100 teams, each consisting of 14 hyenas, was used in each trial. Each hyena begins with a set of randomly generated ANN weights. Each team in each generation is run through a set of five simulated tests, with each test simulating one encounter with a pair of lions and their recent zebra kill. Each simulation lasts for 100 time steps, after each time step the fitness of each hyena is calculated. The fitness values are added together for the entire 100 time steps to calculate a hyena's fitness. The fitness of each member in the team is added together to generate the team's fitness. The fitnesses from all five tests are summed to get the overall fitness scores for each hyena and team. After each team in the population is evaluated, the average fitness value for the population is calculated and stored along with the fitness of the best team.

In each generation a new population is generated through the breeding process described above, and tested in the same manner that the previous generation was tested. This process continues 500 times, i.e. 500 generations, with each new population generated from the previous population. At the end of 500 generations, the average and best fitness values are stored and the next trial begins.

For each of the four experimental conditions, absolute versus relative encoding and leader versus no leader, 40 trials were run in the exact same manner, starting with a new, random population in each trial. The data for each trial is recorded and final results are averaged together to obtain the final fitness values. The improvement over time and final average fitness values are used to denote comparative success.

5. RESULTS

Table 2 shows the average and best fitness values for each experimental condition: the input/output method and if the leader was used is defined in the first and second columns. The absolute encoding method performed very similarly regardless of whether a leader was included, and the difference in average fitness (687.72 without a leader versus 746.90 with a leader) was not significant.

The relative encoding method performed much better overall. The average performance with the relative encoding, with or without a leader, was significantly better than the performance with the absolute encoding, with or without a leader. Interestingly, early in the evolutionary process the fitnesses were very similar for all conditions method, but they began to diverge around the 150th generation (Figure 1). This divergence led to a significant increase in fitness with the relative encoding leading to an average fitness of approximately 3900 in generation 500.

For the relative encoding method, the fitness difference between having a leader and not having one wasn't significant in the final generation. However, the second increase in fitness occurred, on average, in an much earlier generation with a leader (Figure 1).

6. DISCUSSION

Overall, the results show an interesting progression in behaviors from poor performance in early generations to higher fitnesses in later generations. Figure 3 shows typical behaviors in the early generations. A single hyena would be foolish to charge a lion, and early teams with this behavior obtain very low fitness values, leaving them with a low chance to breed to the next generation. More cautious teams obtain higher fitness values, and the next generation has a higher chance of inheriting some of that caution. Thus, although Figure 3 shows a few hyenas charging the lion, even in this early generation most of the team is avoiding the lion - more so than in the other teams, which is why this team was the best of the generation. Individualistic behavior like avoiding danger, can be observed in real hyenas, as different hyenas will react differently to a recording of lion sounds, with some hyenas running off and others appearing curious [10].

After roughly 30 generations, more sophisticated strategies begin to emerge. A clear example is hyenas which move quickly from their starting points into a holding pattern, either stationary or circling, which approaches the lions without getting too close (Figure 4). This allows the hyenas to stay close to the zebra, increasing their fitness value, while staying away from the lions and any attacks they may trigger if they get too close.

While the absolute system stops with this conservative behavior, the relative systems continue to evolve. After approximately 150 generations, the average fitness of these populations show another sharp increase as they transition from a circling pattern to a more aggressive strategy. This strategy includes aggressive movement towards the lions in order to drive them away from the zebra. The series of larger

Table 2: Fitness values after 500 generations with both the average fitness of every team tested, and the fitness of the best team in each trial. Two-tailed Student's t-tests were run comparing the average fitness of each test variant,* denotes significance at the P < 0.01 level while - denotes non-significance. Average fitness after 500 generations with the relative encoding was significantly higher than for the absolute systems. Additionally, a Kruskal-Wallis test was run on the average fitness of each test variant. Every case was shown to be from a separate distribution with a confidence of P < 0.01.

	Input/ Output	Leader	Average (std. dev.)	Best (std. dev.)	1	2	3
1	Absolute	False	687.72(44.16)	994.02(15.20)	-		
2	Absolute	True	746.90(34.92)	977.16(13.47)	*	-	
3	Relative	False	3427.94(264.40)	3953.51(276.50)	*	*	-
4	Relative	True	3306.64(127.97)	3868.80(102.46)	*	*	-

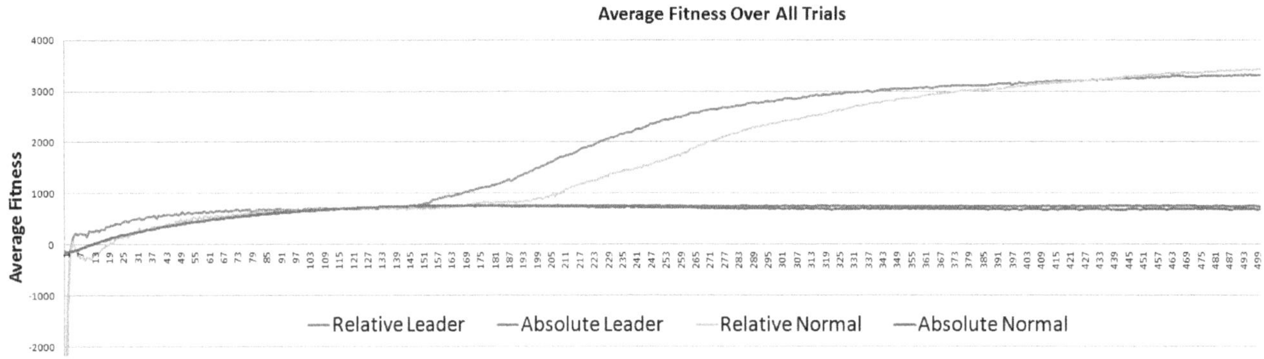

Figure 1: The global average fitness by generations over the four test conditions. The relative systems both perform significantly better in later generations than the absolute systems. The relative system with the leader input starts a second increase in fitness earlier than the relative system without the leader, but starts to fall behind in very late generations. The relative systems also start out with a much lower initial fitness value, although this is quickly corrected.

dots in Figure 5 shows the movement of the lions away from the zebra (toward the North in this case). This is the same strategy that was observed in previous research using GP expression trees as the hyenas control structure [7].

This behavior, once discovered by one of the clans in the population, quickly spreads through the rest of the population. This aggressive behavior is clear in Figure 5, the hyenas quickly converge on the center of the image, where the zebra and lions are, as a cohesive whole, which drives the lion away. This process may mimic how this behavior may have evolved in real hyenas, a few hyenas would not be able to drive off a lion, and would likely not be alive to breed for the next generation if they tried. But by hovering close to a kill hyenas may have been able to snatch bites of food or get first access to the remains after the lions leave. [1] If sufficient numbers of hyenas congregated, the chance of chasing off a lion could increase enough to warrant the continuation of that behavior to the next generation. Eventually this behavior could become common.

Of the two test conditions using the relative encoding, the one that included a leader hyena input made an earlier transition from the circling pattern to the more aggressive behavior. We hypothesize that this is due to some or all of the hyenas learning to coordinate movement towards the leader. With a group of hyenas coordinating to follow the leader, it would only require the leader to evolve to move towards the lions to cause the entire team, or a significant portion of the team, to move towards the lion. The ability to coordinate using either the lions, zebra, or leader as a reference point, instead of only the lions or zebra, may explain why this coordinated behavior appeared in earlier generations when a leader was present. However, the populations without a leader hyena also discovered this behavior, demonstrating that a lead is not a prerequisite for this type of behavior.

Interestingly, while the average fitness between populations with a leader and those without was not statistically significant, the best individual populations were all ones without a leader. This leads to the possibility of populations without a leader having more room for improvement, achieving higher fitness levels when the correct behavior is discovered. While the best populations were without a leader, the worst ones were as well, which lead to a decrease in the average fitness level over all leaderless populations. One possible explanation for this difference is that in some cases the leader delays the aggressive behavior. For example, the hyenas start at random locations if the leader happens to start relatively far from the zebra it may take more time for the hyenas to congregate on the leader and drive off the lions. In contrast,

[1] Hyenas have a pronounced ability to both eat enormous amounts of food very quickly, making them very efficient at snatching food, and have extremely powerful jaws, allowing them to benefit from picked over remains, e.g. by cracking large bones.

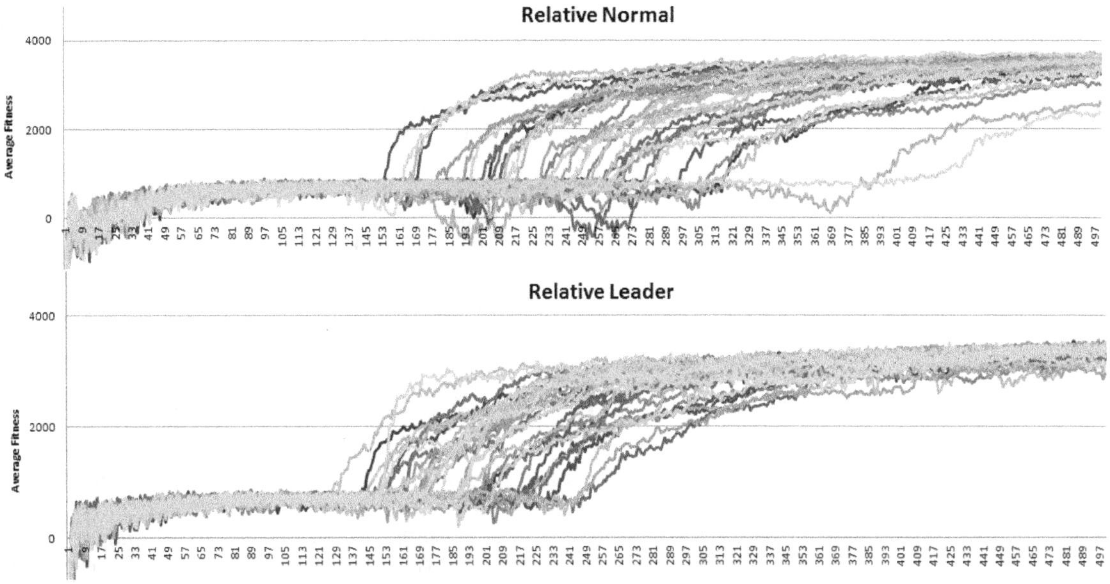

Figure 2: The average fitness of each trial population. While the global average shows a clear improvement of the relative systems over the absolute systems, the effect on the individual populations is much clearer when each of them is viewed separately. This shows that for most of the populations, the second increase is very rapid.

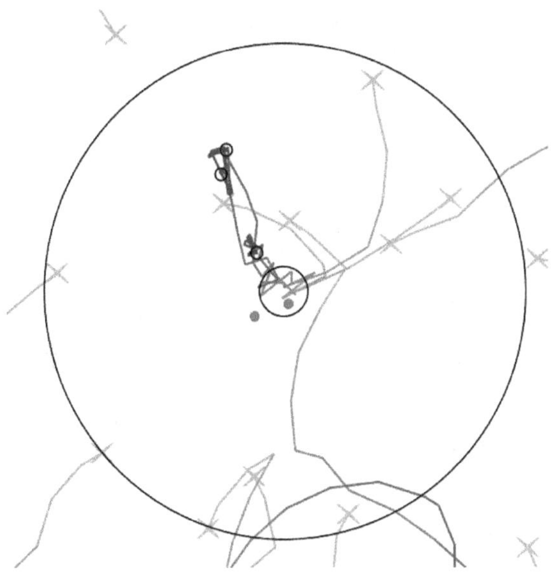

Figure 3: The best team from the 2nd generation, relative encoding with the leader input. The inner hollow circle is the location of the zebra, the outer hollow circle is the furthest away a hyena can be and still see the zebra. X's denote the hyenas' starting locations and small hollow circles denote the hyenas' end positions. The larger, filled (red) dots near the center of the image are the initial locations of the lions, which begin close to each other. At this generation the hyenas haven't obtained much of the knowledge required to make "intelligent" decisions, leading to them moving in seemingly random directions. Although even in this early generation much of the motion is away from the lions.

Figure 4: The best team from generation 47, relative encoding with the leader input. Some of the hyenas have learned that circling the lion without attacking it leads to a higher fitness level than just running away. This behavior mimics many animals' natural behavior when facing a dangerous, but potentially rewarding, threat.

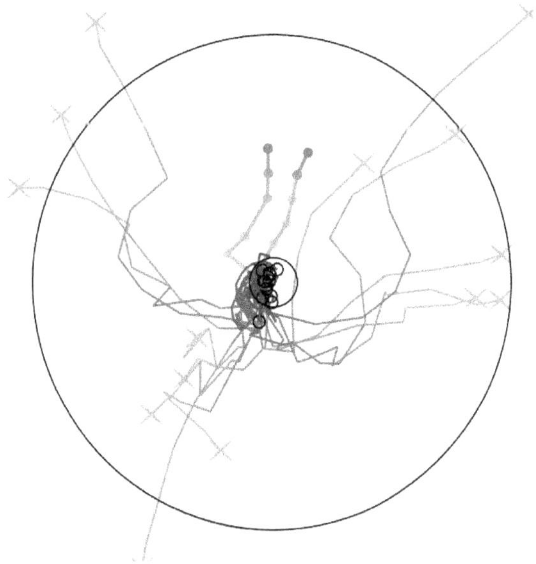

Figure 5: The best team from generation 269, relative encoding with the leader input. The hyenas have obtained the ability to team up and chase the lion away from the kill. This is close to what can be observed in real life in a successful capture of a recent kill.

without a leader it may be that the hyenas closest to the lions always converge immediately (recall that it only takes seven of the fourteen hyenas to drive off the lions) thereby reaching the zebra sooner on average. However, currently this is pure speculation and much more detailed observations of the evolved behaviors are necessary to determine the cause of the fitness difference, if any.

It's also worth noting that given many more generations of improvement, the leader hyena populations may evolve to become less reliant on the leader hyena, obtaining fitness values equal to the populations without the leader. Or indeed other, novel behaviors could evolve.

Due to the quicker improvement by the populations with the leader hyena, fitness averaged over all generations is higher for the populations with a leader (average fitness across all generations is 1992), than populations without the leader hyena (average fitness across all generations is 1756). These values are likely to converge given enough generations, as the system has a theoretical maximum fitness of 7000 assuming all hyenas are at the zebra and no lions are around.

7. CONCLUSIONS

We have presented a novel, ANN based, approach to the lions and hyenas problem. For some versions of the system we observe similar results to those previously observed using tree based GP - the hyenas evolve behaviors that allow them to coordinate sufficiently to drive off the lions. Interestingly, this behavior is only observed for the relative encoding - where the output of the ANN is a weighted sum of input vectors. Including a leader hyena, a hyena that all of the other hyenas could "see", improved the rate of evolution, but not the fitness reached in the final generations.

It is important to note that, given the complexity of this coordination problem, the control system is fairly simple with relatively few inputs and outputs. This, along with the difference in performance observed between the relative and absolute encoding systems, demonstrates that for this coordination problem, how inputs and outputs are represented may be a larger factor in evolving successful behaviors than actual structure of the control system. E.g. the neural network using an absolute encoding has the same basic components as the neural network using a relative encoding, and yet performs much poorer due to the extra effort it takes to map the inputs to an effective output.

8. REFERENCES

[1] A. Burkitt. A review of the integrate-and-fire neuron model: Ii. inhomogeneous synaptic input and network properties. *Biological Cybernetics*, 95(2):97 – 112, 2006.

[2] Dario Floreano, Francesco Mondada, et al. Automatic creation of an autonomous agent: Genetic evolution of a neural-network driven robot. *From animals to animats*, 3:421–430, 1994.

[3] James A. Foster. Evolutionary computation. *Nature Reviews Genetics*, 2(6):428–436, June 2001.

[4] Jason Gauci and Kenneth O Stanley. Autonomous evolution of topographic regularities in artificial neural networks. *Neural computation*, 22(7):1860–1898, 2010.

[5] Stephen Leatherwood. Some observations of feeding behavior of bottle-nosed dolphins (tursiops truncatus) in the northern gulf of mexico and (tursiops cf t. gilli) off southern california, baja california, and nayarit mexico. *Marine Fisheries Review*, 37(9), 1975.

[6] Orazio Miglino, Henrik Hautop Lund, and Stefano Nolfi. Evolving mobile robots in simulated and real environments. *Artificial life*, 2(4):417–434, 1995.

[7] Michael Solomon, Terence Soule, and Robert B. Heckendorn. A comparison of a communication strategies in cooperative learning. In *Proceedings of the Fourteenth International Conference on Genetic and Evolutionary Computation Conference*, GECCO '12, pages 153–160, New York, NY, USA, 2012. ACM.

[8] Kenneth O Stanley. Evolving neural networks. In *Proceedings of the fourteenth international conference on Genetic and evolutionary computation conference companion*, pages 805–826. ACM, 2012.

[9] Kenneth Owen Stanley et al. *Efficient evolution of neural networks through complexification.* The University of Texas at Austin, 2004.

[10] Heather E. Watts, Lisa M. Blankenship, Stephanie E. Dawes, and Kay E. Holekamp. Responses of spotted hyenas to lions reflect individual differences in behavior. *Ethology*, 116(12):1199–1209, 2010.

[11] David Wiley, Colin Ware, Alessandro Bocconcelli, Danielle Cholewiak, Ari Friedlaender, Michael Thompson, and Mason Weinrich. Underwater components of humpback whale bubble-net feeding behaviour. *Behaviour*, 148(5):575–602, 2011.

[12] Brian G Woolley and Kenneth O Stanley. Evolving a single scalable controller for an octopus arm with a variable number of segments. In *Parallel Problem Solving from Nature, PPSN XI*, pages 270–279. Springer, 2010.

The Evolution of Kin Inclusivity Levels

[Artificial Life Track]

Anya Elaine Johnson
BEACON Center for the Study of Evolution in Action
Michigan State University, U.S.A.
anyaejo@msu.edu

Heather J. Goldsby
BEACON Center for the Study of Evolution in Action
University of Washington, U.S.A.
goldsby@uw.edu

Sherri Goings
Carleton College, U.S.A.
sgoings@carleton.edu

Charles Ofria
BEACON Center for the Study of Evolution in Action
Michigan State University
U.S.A.
ofria@msu.edu

ABSTRACT

Altruism is a ubiquitous strategy among organisms ranging from microbes to mammals. Inclusive fitness theory indicates that altruistic strategies can be beneficial when an altruist acts to benefit organisms that share its genes. It is common for such altruistic strategies to be negatively affected by cheaters that do not act altruistically. A more subtle form of cheating involves altruists that are more selective. For example, a selective organism may benefit from a distant kin's altruistic actions without reciprocating. We consider an organism's kin inclusivity level to be the maximum number of mutational differences where the other organism will be considered kin. We use evolving computer programs (digital organisms) to explore competitions among organisms with different kin inclusivity levels. Using competition assays that vary environmental parameters, we find that high mutation rates favor more inclusive colonies. When we competed colonies with a wide range of kin inclusivity levels, we found that moderate mutation rates and populations sizes led to intermediate inclusivity levels winning the competitions, indicating that extreme inclusivity levels were not always optimal. However, when organisms could set their own kin inclusivity level, we found that high mutation rates selected for highly inclusive organisms.

Categories and Subject Descriptors

I.2.8 [**Artificial Intelligence**]: Problem Solving, Control Methods, and Search

GECCO'14, July 12–16, 2014, Vancouver, BC, Canada.

ACM 978-1-4503-2662-9/14/07 ...$15.00.
http://dx.doi.org/10.1145/2576768.2598283 .

Keywords

Digital evolution; Avida; kin altruism

1. INTRODUCTION

The term altruism is used to describe any act where an organism lowers its own fitness in order to raise another organism's fitness [24]. Altruistic behaviors are observed frequently within nature in organisms ranging from *E. coli* [1] to termites [20] to human beings [5]. For example, one variant of *E. coli* engages in suicidal behavior to release toxins (colicins) into the environment [1]. Specifically, when an *E. coli* colony encounters a rival group, some of the members will produce toxins and then explode. This explosion kills the colony member and releases toxins into the surrounding area. Close kin are resistant to the toxin, however members of the rival colonies are killed. Thus, the toxin reduces resource competition for the rest of the suicidal organism's colony. Altruism in general, and suicidal altruism in particular, is puzzling from the evolutionary perspective since an individual is harming or killing itself and therefore decreasing its ability to propagate its own genes. An explanation for this behavior is *kin-selection* (or *inclusive fitness*), where the sacrificial act makes it more likely that many of the organism's kin, which share some of its genes, will survive and flourish [12, 13, 3, 7, 15].

One challenge to the evolution of altruistic behaviors is cheating, where an organism performs the altruistic act less frequently or forgoes altruistic actions altogether [24, 4, 23, 6, 22, 14, 8]. A subtle form of cheating involves organisms that behave altruistically to close kin, but not to more distant kin that behave altruistically to them. We consider an organism's *kin inclusivity level* to be the maximum number of mutational differences where the other organism will be considered kin. If an organism has a high kin inclusivity level, then they will be altruistic to a wide range of related organisms (*clan altruists*). An organism with a low kin inclusivity level may only be altruistic toward their exact clones (*clone altruists*). In the case that a clan altruist is related to a clone altruist, the clan altruist will behave altruistically to the clone altruist, but the clone altruist will not reciprocate. In this case, the clone altruist would "cheat" their clan altruist relatives, demonstrating kin discrimination [18]. Without mechanisms in place for organisms to detect and prevent cheating behaviors based on kin inclusivity levels, clone altruists are likely to take over in highly-related populations. However, minimal kin inclusivity levels that allow only clonal offspring will prevent further adaptive evolution by killing mutants and thus limiting further adaptation. In this study, we explore the environmental conditions under which higher and lower kin inclusivity levels are adaptive.

To explore questions surrounding the evolution of kin inclusivity levels, we use the Avida digital evolution platform [17], which has been used previously to study the properties of evolving systems (e.g., [10] and [16]). Within Avida, digital organisms, which are computer programs that self-replicate and potentially incur mutations, compete with neighboring organisms for resources, including space. Using organic experimental systems to study the evolution of kin inclusivity levels is a time consuming and imperfect process. Even the fastest evolving natural organisms typically take months or years to undergo the thousands of generations necessary for evolution, whereas digital organisms take mere hours. Moreover, controlling factors such as kin inclusivity levels in natural organisms can be challenging, if not impossible. Because digital organisms evolve within a computer, we can rapidly perform experiments spanning thousands of generations with complete experimental control and data collection.

In previous work, we competed clone altruists (called 'kin-cheaters') against clan altruists [9]. We found that within genetically similar groups, the clone altruists frequently drove clan altruists out of the population. We also discovered that in larger populations clan altruists were occasionally able to outcompete initially genetically similar clone altruists. Here, we extend that work by exploring how a number of environmental factors influence whether higher or lower kin inclusivity levels are favored by evolution.

2. METHODS

For this study, we used the Avida digital evolution platform [17]. Figure 1 depicts a population of digital organisms that resides in a toroidal grid of cells within the Avida framework. Each digital organism has a genome, which is a circular list of instructions from a simple, assembly-like computer language. The Turing-complete instruction set from which this list is derived includes instructions for basic computation (e.g., addition and increment), control of genome instruction execution (e.g., jumps), and the instructions required for self-replication. An organism's hardware consists of a virtual CPU, several registers, and two stacks. An organism must execute instructions to replicate itself. When an organism replicates, its offspring is placed in a random cell adjacent to the parent organism. If the selected adjacent cell was occupied, the previous occupant is killed.

Our experiments use an instruction set that includes the default Avida instructions and several additional altruistic (*explode*) instructions. These instructions are modeled after the suicidal behavior of colicinogenic *E. coli*. When an explode instruction is executed by an organism, the organism explodes with a 5% probability. An explosion will kill the organism itself, as well as any non-kin within two grid cells. An organism considers a neighbor kin if the Hamming distance between its genome and the neighbor's genome is

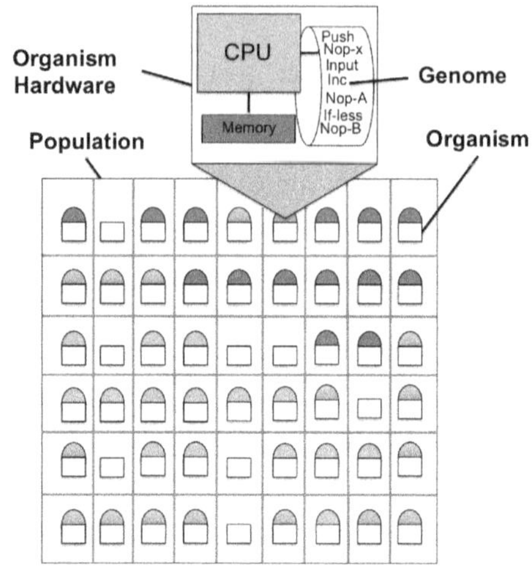

Figure 1: An Avida population, where half-circles represent organisms and boxes represent the cells that they live in. A single organism's hardware and genome are superimposed. Different colors represent different genomes.

less than its kin inclusivity level (χ). For example, if an organism has a kin inclusivity level of $\chi = 3$, it considers all neighboring organisms whose genomes differ by less than three instructions kin. All organisms' genomes were fixed at 100 instructions and insertion and deletion mutations are not permitted, therefore only substitution mutations could occur. The use of Hamming distance provides the organisms with a perfect measurement of genetic similarity instead of an approximation, such as kinship [2]. When an organism explodes, it kills all organisms with a Hamming distance greater than or equal to its kin inclusivity level. Thus, continuing with our example, an organism with a kin inclusivity level of 3 would kill all neighboring organisms whose genomes differed in three or more instructions. For some experiments, we fixed the kin inclusivity level of the organisms; for others we let the kin inclusivity level evolve. When the kin inclusivity level was fixed, it was statically set in a configuration file for a specific instruction. Organisms with a low kin inclusivity level recognize fewer organisms as kin. For example, clone altruists have a minimal kin inclusivity level ($\chi = 1$), and therefore kill any organism with one or more genomic differences upon exploding (Figure 2A). In contrast, organisms with higher kin inclusivity levels recognize more organisms as kin. For example, clan altruists have $\chi = 6$, so they kill organisms with six or more mutations in an explosion (Figure 2B).

Within our competition experiments, we required each organism to maintain one and only one copy of an explode instruction in its genome, whereas the rest of the genome still undergoes mutation based on the set mutation rate. This means an organism was not able to mutate its explode instruction to a different Hamming distance, as that would require that fixed instruction to mutate to a different instruction. Additionally, an organism was required to execute the explode instruction at least once (with a 5% chance of actually exploding) before the organism was allowed to reproduce. These constraints prevent the confounding ef-

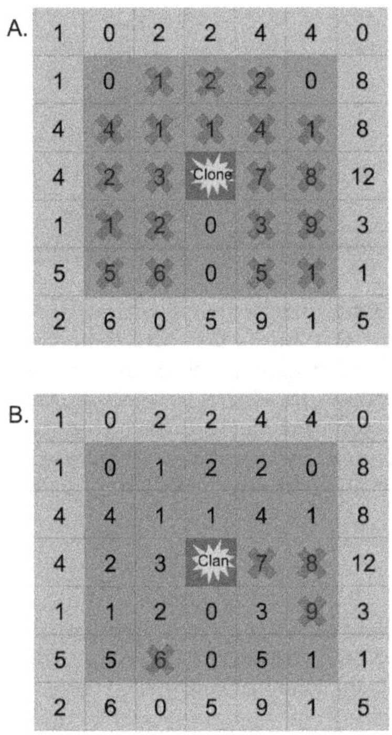

Figure 2: A depiction of the organisms killed when a clone altruist (A) or clan altruist (B) explodes. Each square represents an organism. The number in the square represents the Hamming distance between that organism and the organism depicted in the middle square. When that middle organism explodes as a clone altruist ($\chi = 1$), it kills all organisms within two cells of it (the red-shaded area) that have an edit distance of greater than or equal to one. When the middle organism is a clan altruist ($\chi = 6$) and explodes, it kills all organisms with an edit distance of greater than or equal to six within two squares of it. Organisms that were killed are overlaid with red X's.

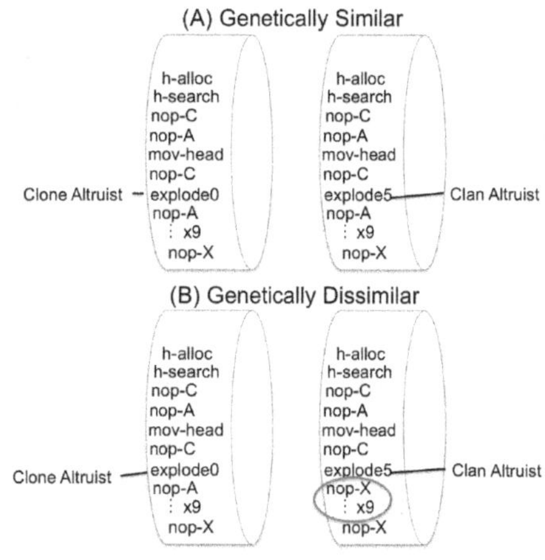

Figure 3: A pair of genetically similar (A) and a pair of genetically dissimilar (B) organisms. For the genetically similar case, there is a one-instruction difference between the two genomes. For the genetically dissimilar case, there is an eleven-instruction difference.

fects of organisms mutating to either avoid exploding or to explode multiple times with different kin inclusivity levels, therefore allowing us to determine which genotype is favored by evolution.

We performed competition assays in which we varied both the genetic relationship among the colonies and also the number of distinct colonies present within the population, where a colony is a group of organisms descended from the same ancestor organism and sharing the same explode instruction. Specifically, we started each competition assay with colonies that were either genetically similar or genetically dissimilar to each other. Figure 3 depicts sample clan and clone altruist genomes for both cases. In the genetically-similar treatments, the only instruction that varied between the colonies was the explosion instruction. Thus, in a two-colony experiment, the clan altruist considered the clone altruist kin, but the clone altruist did not consider the clan altruist kin. We created genetically dissimilar, but functionally equivalent, altruist genomes by inserting ten "no-operation" instructions into each colony's genome. Because the clan altruists (the most inclusive genotype tested) were set to have a kin inclusivity level below ten for our experiments ($\chi = 6$), this genomic change meant that no colony considered another colony to be kin. Thus, if a member of any colony exploded, it would kill members of the other colonies. In experiments with more than two competing colonies, the no-operation instructions were placed in different locations to make all colonies genetically dissimilar from all other colonies.

The goal of our competition experiments was to ascertain if a particular genotype was favored by evolution. As such, in the two-colony competition assays, we started both colonies at 50% of the population in two equal-sized patches filling the environment. In the multi-colony competition assays, all colonies also started at equal frequencies in six equal-sized patches made as close to perfectly square as possible.

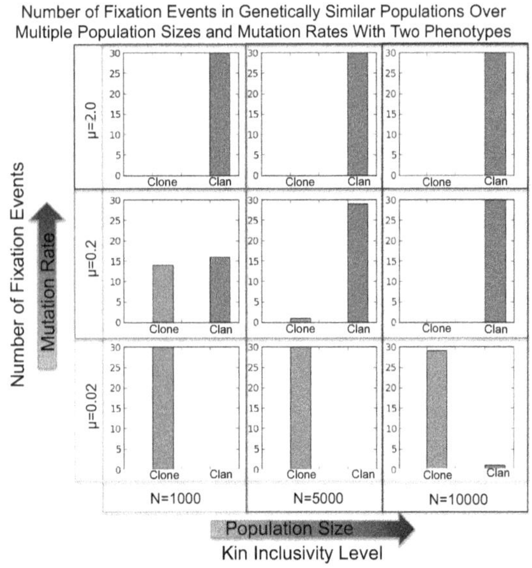

Figure 4: The number of fixation events by clone altruists (green) and clan altruists (purple) starting from equal proportions of genetically-similar clan altruists and clone altruists at three different mutation rates and three different population sizes. At the low mutation rate, the clone altruists fix in all but one replicate. At the medium mutation rate, however, the clan altruists win the majority of replicates. Finally, at the high mutation rate, the clan altruists fix in every replicate.

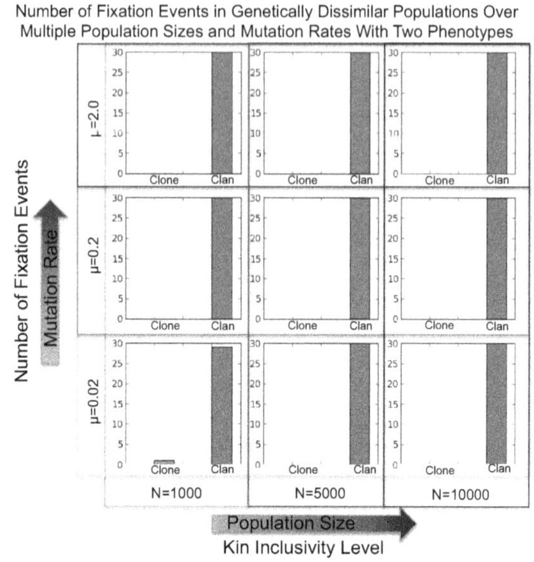

Figure 5: The number of fixation events by clone altruists (green) and clan altruists (purple) starting from equal proportions of genetically-dissimilar clone altruists and clan altruists at three different mutation rates and three different population sizes. The clan altruists were able to outcompete the clone altruists in all but one replicate across all treatments.

Replicates were run until one colony reached 100% of the population. We determined this by assigning a label to each colony at the beginning of the experiment and that label is inherited when an organism reproduces.

We used population sizes of 1000, 5000, and 10,000 for both the two-colony and six-colony competitions. We used genomic mutation rates of 2.0, 0.2, and 0.02. All treatments were replicated 30 times.

3. RESULTS

For this study, we first performed competition assays to examine the behavior of organisms that exhibit two extreme kin inclusivity levels (e.g., clone altruists with $\chi = 1$ and clan altruists with $\chi = 6$). We then expand our study to include organisms of intermediate kin inclusivity levels. Lastly, we allow organisms to set their own kin inclusivity level.

3.1 Clan and Clone Altruist Competition Assays

In our first experiment, we performed competition assays that started with one colony of clone altruists ($\chi = 1$) and one colony of clan altruists ($\chi = 6$). We varied whether or not the two groups started genetically similar to each other, the population size (N = 1000, 5000, or 10,000 organisms), and the genomic mutation rate (μ = 0.02, 0.2, or 2.0 expected mutations per organism reproduction).

Figures 4 and 5 present the results of our two-colony experiments with starting colonies that were genetically similar and dissimilar, respectively. When the colonies were genetically similar (Figure 4), at a high mutation rate (μ=2.0), the clan altruists outcompeted the clone altruists in all replicates at every population size. However, additional analysis revealed that the clone altruists were often unable to survive at the high mutation rate (μ=2.0), even in isolation, which likely confounded our results. Thus, we also tested a slightly lower mutation rate of μ=1.0. At this lower mutation rate, the clone altruists could consistently survive in isolation, but the clan altruists still fixed in all runs at every population size. When examined at a low mutation rate (μ=0.02), the clone altruists outcompeted the clan altruists in all replicates at the small and medium population size and 29/30 at the large population size. At the moderate mutation rate (μ=0.2), the clan altruists were able to win the majority of the replicates at each population size (16/30, 29/30, and 30/30 at the small, medium, and large population sizes, respectively). These results indicate that populations with more genetic diversity, due to a higher mutation rate or larger population size, permit individuals with a high kin inclusivity level (i.e., the clan altruists with $\chi = 6$) to drive colonies with a lower kin inclusivity level (i.e., the clone altruists with $\chi = 1$) out of the population.

Next, we performed the same series of competition assays, but used genetically dissimilar colonies as the initial populations. Our results are depicted in Figure 5. Under these conditions, the clan altruists won all but one of the competitions regardless of mutation rate and population size. To ensure these results were not driven by the clone altruists' problem with surviving at the high mutation rate (μ=2.0), we again tested a slightly lower mutation rate of μ=1.0. The clan altruists still won all 30 replicates even at this reduced mutation rate. These results, when compared to the previ-

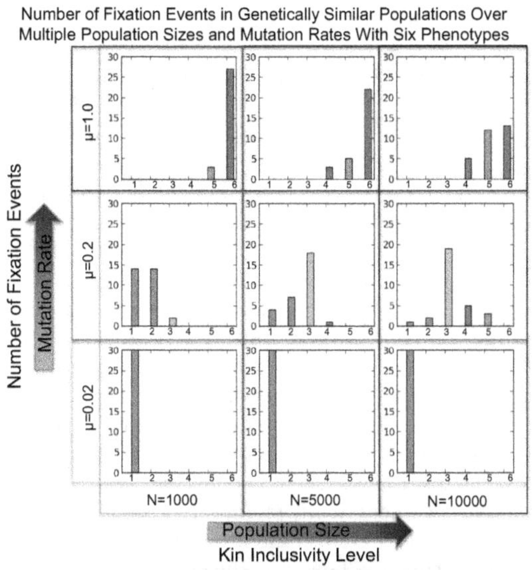

Figure 6: The number of fixation events by each of six genetically similar colonies with differing kin inclusivity levels ($\chi = 1$ through $\chi = 6$). We performed these competition assays across three different mutation rates and three different population sizes. Each panel represents the results of one competition assay. As mutation rate increases, colonies with larger kin inclusivity levels fix more frequently. At intermediate mutations rates, larger population sizes enable colonies with higher kin inclusivity levels to fix. At the highest mutation rate, larger population sizes enable a wider range of high-inclusivity-level colonies to reach fixation.

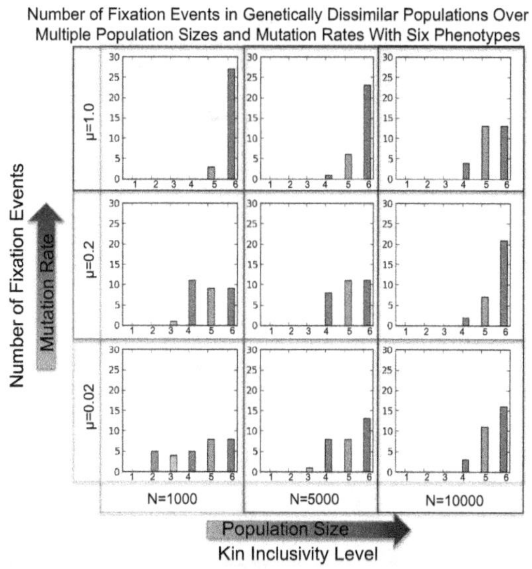

Figure 7: The number of fixation events by each of six genetically dissimilar colonies with differing kin inclusivity levels ($\chi = 1$ through $\chi = 6$). Panels represent three mutation rates and population sizes. As the population size and mutation rate increase, colonies with higher kin inclusivity levels fix more often, except at the highest mutation rate. At the highest mutation rate, larger population sizes enable a wider range of kin inclusivity levels to reach fixation.

ous genetically similar results, demonstrate that the genetic similarity (or dissimilarity) among colonies within the initial population strongly influenced which colony was able to reach fixation.

3.2 Intermediate Kin Inclusivity Levels Competition Assays

In nature, it is likely that organisms exhibit intermediate phenotypes (i.e., kin inclusivity levels that range between those selected for our clan and clone altruists), rather than constraining themselves to extreme phenotypes. Thus, in our second set of experiments, we performed competition assays among six different colonies of organisms, where each colony had a different kin inclusivity level (i.e., $\chi = 1$ through $\chi = 6$). In general, we examined the effects of these intermediate phenotypes under the same set of mutation rate and population size parameters we used for our two-colony experiments. However, because clone altruists ($\chi = 1$) are not able to survive in isolation at the highest mutation rate μ=2.0, we used a mutation rate of μ=1.0 as our highest mutation rate for these competition assays.

Figures 6 and 7 depict the results of our experiments when all six colonies started genetically similar or dissimilar to each other, respectively. When the colonies start genetically similar, mutation rate strongly influences the results of the competition (Figure 6). At a low mutation rate, (μ=0.02) colonies with $\chi = 1$ outcompeted all other colonies in all runs at all population sizes. At a high mutation rate (μ=1.0), colonies with $\chi = 6$ tended to fix. In a few cases, other high kin inclusivity level colonies (i.e., $\chi = 5$ or even $\chi = 4$) won the competitions. However, within the moderate mutation rate (μ=0.2) treatments, the intermediate phenotypes with $\chi = 2$ through $\chi = 5$ were able to win the majority of competitions.

Figure 7 depicts the results of our genetically dissimilar treatments with six colonies. Similar to the results presented for the two-colony experiments, the higher kin inclusivity level colonies generally outcompete the lower kin inclusivity level colonies at the moderate (μ=0.2) and high (μ=1.0) mutation rates. However, at the low mutation rate (μ=0.02), the organisms with intermediate inclusivity levels are favored by selection. At the smallest population size, a mix of intermediate and high kin inclusivity level colonies win the competitions. As the population size increases, the $\chi = 6$ colony (the clan altruist) wins more of the competitions.

The geographical starting positions of the six colonies in the initial population could potentially influence the competition results. To assess this dynamic, we performed five different sets of experiments that permuted the initial positions of the various colonies. The starting location of each colony is defined by which colonies directly neighbor the colony, so for the permutations we sought to test the majority of variations of direct neighbors for each colony. The results of these experiments were qualitatively identical, suggesting that the initial geography has little influence over the competition outcome.

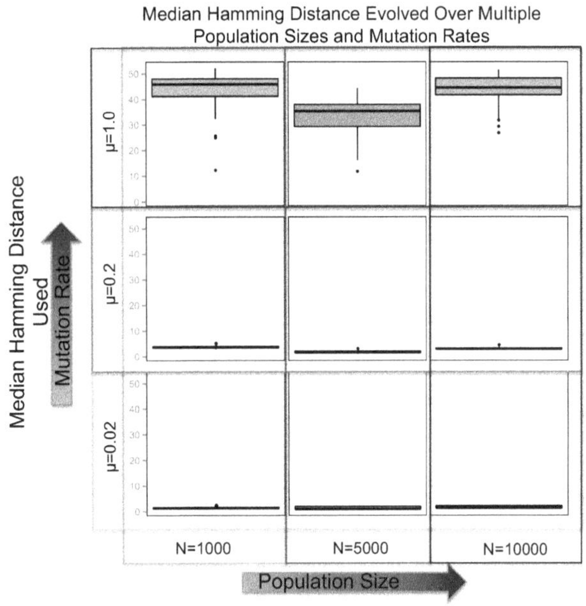

Figure 8: The median kin inclusivity levels evolved at three mutation rates and population sizes. As the mutation rate increase, organisms evolve higher kin inclusivity levels. At the low and medium mutation rate, organisms evolve a kin inclusivity level similar to clone altruists.

These results suggest that intermediate phenotypes affect the kin inclusivity level favored by evolution. For example, in the genetically-similar experiment with only two colonies at the intermediate population size (N=5000) and mutation rate (μ=0.2), the clan altruists ($\chi = 6$) reach fixation the majority of the time (29/30). However, when the intermediate inclusivity levels are included in the competition, the $\chi = 3$ colony (an intermediate phenotype) outcompetes the clan altruists (and all others) most of the time. These results indicate that extreme levels of altruistic inclusivity are sub-optimal under certain environmental conditions. Such intermediate cases are pertinent for extrapolating how altruistic organisms behave within nature where kin inclusivity levels can likely evolve more freely.

3.3 Evolving Kin Inclusivity Levels

To more fully understand the kin inclusivity levels favored by evolution within a given environment, we shift away from competition experiments where the kin inclusivity levels of the organisms are statically configured and allow the kin inclusivity level to be an evolvable trait. In our final experiments, when an organism explodes, we interpret the contents of one of its registers as its kin inclusivity level. Specifically, we take the value of the register modulo 100 (to constrain organisms to specifying kin inclusivity levels that are possible given their genome length of 100) as the organism's kin inclusivity level. We started each replicate of this experiment with only a single organism that replicated to fill the world with its descendants. We again performed treatments that varied the mutation rate and population size. Figure 8 shows the kin inclusivity levels evolved by the organisms within these treatments.

The mutation rate parameter appears to be a key factor in determining the kin inclusivity levels that were evolved. As the mutation rate increases, the organisms increase their kin inclusivity level. Organisms evolved with the low mutation rate (μ=0.02) exhibited a median kin inclusivity level of 1.433, 1.044, and 1.452 at the small (N=1,000), moderate (N=5,000), and large (N=10,000) population sizes, respectively. The median kin inclusivity level appreciably increases at the higher mutation rate (μ=2.0) to 45.934, 35.429, and 44.598 at the small, moderate, and large population sizes, respectively. The median kin inclusivity levels for the low (μ=0.02) and medium (μ=0.2) mutation rate treatments all are between 1 and 4. These treatments therefore, on average, consist of organisms with low kin inclusivity levels who are altruistic mostly to identical clones or individuals with a few mutations. These kin inclusivity levels are similar to the clone altruists from the first two-colony experiments, when the colonies started genetically similar and the mutation rate was low or moderate. At the medium mutation rate in the two-colony experiments, however, the clan altruists fixed the majority of the time. The result of this experiment with a median kin inclusivity level of 1.8-3.8 at the medium mutation rate suggests that a more intermediate kin inclusivity level in the two-colony competitions may have been more successful. At the high mutation rate, however, the average kin inclusivity level is much higher, between 35 and 46. These evolved kin inclusivity levels are much higher than any of the levels we previously tested. These organisms are a more extreme example of the clan altruist organisms in the first experiment. The emergence of this higher kin inclusivity level parallels the fixation of the clan altruists with their higher kin inclusivity level in the two-colony experiment when the colonies started genetically similar and the mutation rate was high.

4. DISCUSSION AND CONCLUSIONS

There is substantial research on the evolution of altruism and cheating within both theoretical and biological systems [4, 23, 6, 18, 22, 14, 8]. Here, we focus on studies that have explored evolutionary parameters similar to those explored in our study.

Goings *et al.* found that clan altruists would evolve from a non-altruistic ancestor, but lost in direct competition against genetically similar clone altruists [9]. However, one exception to this general rule occurred sometimes when, under larger population sizes, clan altruists outcompeted clone altruists. This original study served as inspiration for the current research.

Here we expand on the work of Goings *et al.* to determine how mutation rate, population size, and genetic similarity of ancestor organisms influences the outcome of competition between clone and clan altruists. The different factors varied in our experiments affect key portions of Hamilton's rule. Specifically, mutation rate affects the number of genetic differences between related organisms. The genetic similarity of ancestor organisms affects the potential benefits associated with suicidal altruism.

We found that as mutation rate increases, higher kin-inclusivity levels are selected for. This likely results from the same level of relatedness (i.e., parent-offspring or grandparent-grandoffspring) having a larger number of genetic differences as a result of an increased probability of mutation during replication. We also found that higher genetic similarity increases the competitive advantage of colonies with low kin-inclusivity levels. This effect most likely occurs as the result of organisms with low kin-inclusivity levels (i.e., clone altruists) receiving a benefit from related organisms with higher kin-inclusivity (i.e., clan altruists) without reciprocating. In contrast, genetic dissimilarity enables clan altruists to differentiate themselves from clone altruists. In addition, we found that larger population sizes confer an advantage to colonies with higher kin-inclusivity levels (i.e., clan altruists). This effect could result from larger population sizes enabling colonies to be isolated from competing colonies for more evolutionary time, thus allowing larger amounts of genetic dissimilarity to occur as a result of drift. This enables colonies with higher kin inclusivity levels to successfully behave altruistically to colony members, while killing competing colonies with lower inclusivity levels. Finally, we also found that organisms exhibiting intermediate kin inclusivity levels (i.e., levels 2-5) frequently were able to outcompete more extreme organisms.

Greig and Travisano explored the effects of population density in single-celled yeast that are known to cooperate in the wild [11]. They found that the cheating colony had higher fitness as the density of the population was increased across treatments. While this is not identical to our factor of population size, treatments with small world sizes fill more quickly than treatments with large world sizes. Therefore, small population sizes are likely to have higher population densities when averaged over the course of the treatment than larger population size treatments. When considering this, our study exhibits similar results across population size. Smaller population size treatments favor the clone altruists when the colonies are genetically similar and the clone altruists can be considered to be "cheating" on the clan altruists.

Two notable studies suggest that lower mutation rates favor altruism. First, Spector and Klein [21] explored how mutation rate and territorial structure affected competition between groups of kin altruists. The territorial structure determined how many neighbors along a ring an individual organism had the chance of being paired with. An organism's tag, which was inherited at birth, indicated the kin group of the organism. Organisms donated to other neighbors whose tags were within a tolerance amount of their own. Given these parameters, they found that tag-mediated altruism was more likely to evolve with lower mutation rates and smaller interaction radii. However, the salient difference from our work is that when the organisms' tags were mutated they were changed to a random value. Thus, the distance between tags (used to establish whether or not an organism would donate) did not measure genetic similarity unless the organisms had identical tags. In contrast, within our study, the edit distance between two genomes is a perfect measure of similarity.

Paolucci and Conte studied the effect of roost size and mutation rate on the evolution of altruism in simulated vampire bats [19]. Within this study, the mutation rate determined the probability that an offspring organism would be an altruist or a cheater. They found that high mutation rates increased the invasion of cheaters and that smaller roost sizes decreased the invasion rates. The apparent difference between these conclusions and those put forth by our study results from the implementation of the mutation operator. Our mutation operator can increase genetic differences between a parent and offspring without affecting whether or not the organism behaves altruistically.

There are many possible future directions for this study. First, to get a better understanding of the evolution of kin inclusivity levels in spatially-structured populations, we could explore how the distribution of kin inclusivity levels varies over space. Second, most organisms in nature have some form of communication. By allowing our digital organisms to communicate, it is likely that they will evolve to exhibit a more sophisticated strategy for determining when to behave altruistically. Within our current experiments, often organisms will explode when they are completely surrounded by their kin, due to the stochastic nature of the instruction. If we provide them with the ability to sense related (or unrelated) organisms around them, then new and interesting strategies that make use of the explosion instructions may develop, such as facultative cheating [6]. Finally, currently, the organisms are not able to move. If able to move in the environment, the organisms may strategically place themselves near unrelated organisms before executing the explode instructions, similar to various species of eusocial insects that strategically explode when a predator draws near [20].

5. ACKNOWLEDGEMENTS

We thank the DevoLab and BEACON Center for the Study of Evolution in Action for advice and support. This work was funded in part by the Clare Boothe Luce Foundation and the NSF. This material is based in part upon work supported by the National Science Foundation under Cooperative Agreement No. DBI-0939454 and No. OCI-1122620. Any opinions, findings, and conclusions or recommendations expressed in this material are those of the author(s) and do not necessarily reflect the views of the National Science Foundation.

6. REFERENCES

[1] L. Chao and B. R. Levin. Structured habitats and the evolution of anticompetitor toxins in bacteria. *Proceedings of the National Academy of Sciences*, 78(10):6324–6328, Oct. 1981.

[2] J. Clune, H. J. Goldsby, C. Ofria, and R. T. Pennock. Selective pressures for accurate altruism targeting: evidence from digital evolution for difficult-to-test aspects of inclusive fitness theory. *Proceedings of the Royal Society B: Biological Sciences*, 278(1706):666–674, Jan. 2011.

[3] R. Dawkins. The Selfish Gene. 2006.

[4] S. P. Diggle, A. S. Griffin, G. S. Campbell, and S. A. West. Cooperation and conflict in quorum-sensing bacterial populations. *Nature*, 450(7168):411–414, 2007.

[5] E. Fehr and U. Fischbacher. The nature of human altruism. *Nature*, 425(6960):785–791, Oct. 2003.

[6] F. Fiegna and G. J. Velicer. Competitive fates of bacterial social parasites: persistence and self-induced extinction of Myxococcus xanthus cheaters. *Proceedings of the Royal Society B: Biological Sciences*, 270(1523):1527–1534, July 2003.

[7] K. R. Foster, T. Wenseleers, and F. L. W. Ratnieks. Kin selection is the key to altruism. *Trends in Ecology & Evolution*, 2006.

[8] O. M. Gilbert, K. R. Foster, N. J. Mehdiabadi, J. E. Strassmann, and D. C. Queller. High relatedness maintains multicellular cooperation in a social amoeba by controlling cheater mutants. *Proceedings of the National Academy of Sciences*, 104(21):8913–8917, May 2007.

[9] S. Goings, J. Clune, C. Ofria, and R. T. Pennock. Kin selection: The rise and fall of kin-cheaters. In *Proceedings of the Ninth International Conference on Artificial Life*, pages 303–308, 2004.

[10] H. J. Goldsby, A. Dornhaus, B. Kerr, and C. Ofria. Task-switching costs promote the evolution of division of labor and shifts in individuality. *Proceedings of the National Academy of Sciences*, 109(34):13686–13691, Aug. 2012.

[11] D. Greig and M. Travisano. The Prisoner's Dilemma and polymorphism in yeast SUC genes. *Proceedings of the Royal Society B: Biological Sciences*, 271(Suppl 3):S25–S26, Feb. 2004.

[12] W. D. Hamilton. The evolution of altruistic behavior. *The American Naturalist*, 1963.

[13] W. D. Hamilton. The genetical evolution of social behaviour. II. *Journal of theoretical biology*, 1964.

[14] A. Khare, L. A. Santorelli, J. E. Strassmann, D. C. Queller, A. Kuspa, and G. Shaulsky. Cheater-resistance is not futile. *Nature*, 461(7266):980–982, Sept. 2009.

[15] L. Lehmann and L. Keller. The evolution of cooperation and altruism – a general framework and a classification of models. *Journal of Evolutionary Biology*, 19(5):1365–1376, Sept. 2006.

[16] R. E. Lenski, C. Ofria, R. T. Pennock, and C. Adami. The evolutionary origin of complex features. *Nature*, 423:139–144, May 2003.

[17] C. Ofria and C. O. Wilke. Avida: A software platform for research in computational evolutionary biology. *Artificial Life*, 10(2):191–229, Mar. 2004.

[18] E. A. Ostrowski, M. Katoh, G. Shaulsky, and D. C. Queller. Kin discrimination increases with genetic distance in a social amoeba. *PLOS Biology*, 2008.

[19] M. Paolucci and R. Conte. Roost size for multilevel selection of altruism among vampire bats. In *Multi-Agent-Based Simulation VII*, pages 69–79. Springer Berlin Heidelberg, Berlin, Heidelberg, 2007.

[20] J. R. Shorter and O. Rueppell. A review on self-destructive defense behaviors in social insects. *Insectes Sociaux*, 59(1):1–10, Dec. 2011.

[21] L. Spector and J. Klein. Genetic stability and territorial structure facilitate the evolution of tag-mediated altruism. *Artificial Life*, 12(4), Oct. 2006.

[22] J. E. Strassmann, O. M. Gilbert, and D. C. Queller. Kin discrimination and cooperation in microbes. *Annual Review of Microbiology*, 65(1):349–367, Oct. 2011.

[23] G. J. Velicer, L. Kroos, and R. E. Lenski. Developmental cheating in the social bacterium Myxococcus xanthus. *Nature*, 404(6778):598–601, 2000.

[24] S. A. West, A. S. Griffin, and A. Gardner. Social semantics: altruism, cooperation, mutualism, strong reciprocity and group selection. *Journal of Evolutionary Biology*, 20(2):415–432, Mar. 2007.

Overcoming Deception in Evolution of Cognitive Behaviors

Joel Lehman
University of Texas at Austin
1 Inner Campus Drive
Austin, TX 78712 USA
joel@cs.utexas.edu

Risto Miikkulainen
University of Texas at Austin
1 Inner Campus Drive
Austin, TX 78712 USA
risto@cs.utexas.edu

ABSTRACT

When scaling neuroevolution to complex behaviors, cognitive capabilities such as learning, communication, and memory become increasingly important. However, successfully evolving such cognitive abilities remains difficult. This paper argues that a main cause for such difficulty is deception, i.e. evolution converges to a behavior unrelated to the desired solution. More specifically, cognitive behaviors often require accumulating neural structure that provides no immediate fitness benefit, and evolution often thus converges to *non-cognitive* solutions. To investigate this hypothesis, a common evolutionary robotics T-Maze domain is adapted in three separate ways to require agents to communicate, remember, and learn. Indicative of deception, evolution driven by objective-based fitness often converges upon simple non-cognitive behaviors. In contrast, evolution driven to explore novel behaviors, i.e. novelty search, often evolves the desired cognitive behaviors. The conclusion is that open-ended methods of evolution may better recognize and reward the stepping stones that are necessary for cognitive behavior to emerge.

Categories and Subject Descriptors

I.2.6 [**Artificial Intelligence**]: Learning—*connectionism and neural nets, concept learning*

General Terms

Algorithms

Keywords

Diversity Maintenance; Evolutionary Robotics; Cognition; Deception

1. INTRODUCTION

A goal of neuroevolution research is to evolve artificial neural networks (ANNs) able to solve increasingly complex tasks. So far, most tasks have been largely *reactive*, i.e. behaviors that can result from reacting to current sensory input without persistent state or computation. It is still challenging to solve tasks that require cognitive behaviors such as communication, remembering previous states, or learning from experience. When such behaviors have been successfully evolved, artificial domain constraints [19, 26], specialized domain knowledge in the reward scheme driving evolution [13, 18], or specialized encodings [28] were often needed. Yet such special knowledge is difficult to come by and a more general solution would be desirable.

While it is easy to design fitness functions that *recognize* a successful instance of a cognitive behavior, it is more difficult to craft a fitness function that *paves* the path towards it [10]. In particular, to realize a cognitive behavior through an ANN often requires significant scaffolding structure, i.e. additional neurons and connections adapted to provide cognitive functionality. Yet building only one part of such scaffolding may provide no immediate fitness benefit, particularly if fitness is measured narrowly by how closely a behavior resembles evolution's target. As a result, evolution may often converge to locally optimal reactive policies, and there may be no performance gradient connecting such a reactive policy to the desired cognitive one. In such cases, evolution may remain deceived by non-cognitive local optima. This observation leads to the main hypothesis explored in this paper: deception is a significant factor making evolving cognitive behaviors difficult.

Previous studies have explored evolving cognitive behaviors such as communication [19, 26], memory [13, 28], and learning [17, 27]; yet overall, evolving sophisticated cognitive behaviors remains difficult. Importantly, some such studies support the idea that evolving cognitive behaviors may be deceptive [13, 17] and further suggest that methods that are based on novelty rather than fitness may be beneficial [17]. In particular, novelty search [8] rewards behaviors relative only to how different they are from those previously encountered during the search. Risi et al. [17] shows that novelty search succeeds significantly more often than objective-based search in evolving learning behavior.

This paper builds upon such previous results to evolve three separate cognitive behaviors. A T-Maze domain, similar to those used in previous evolutionary robotics (ER) studies [13, 17, 18, 28], is varied to form three separate tasks that require evolving communication, short-term memory, and learning from experience. Across such tasks, the performance of a variety of objective-based methods is compared to that of novelty search. To probe how such methods scale

GECCO'14, July 12–16, 2014, Vancouver, BC, Canada.

http://dx.doi.org/10.1145/2576768.2598300.

with increased complexity, a more difficult extended T-Maze domain is also tested. The goal is to verify that deception is problematic across a spectrum of cognitive behaviors, and determine how it is exacerbated by increased problem complexity.

The results support the hypothesis that deception is a significant factor in cognitive tasks. The conclusion is that the stepping stones towards cognitive behaviors may not be identified by traditional objective-based fitness functions. Instead, methods that open-endedly discover structure in a domain, thereby potentially accumulating such stepping stones, are needed.

2. BACKGROUND

This section first reviews previous approaches to evolving cognitive behaviors, then describes the NEAT and novelty search methods applied in this paper's experiments.

2.1 Evolving Cognitive Behaviors

The evolution of various cognitive behaviors has been studied in artificial life and ER [12, 13, 17, 19, 26–28]. It is helpful first to review mechanisms applied in these experiments to make evolution more tractable.

First, domains are often artificially restricted to isolate and encourage cognitive behavior's evolution [19, 26]. Without such restrictions, evolution may often converge to simpler non-cognitive policies that either fail to solve the task or solve the task in trivial or unintended ways [19]. For example, Werner and Dyer [26] introduced an experimental setup in which female animals are stationary but can produce signals, whereas male animals can sense signals from females but cannot produce them nor can they perceive the environment. The advantage of such an unrealistic setup is that communication offers the only way to solve the task, thereby reducing the potential for convergence to simpler non-communicative solutions.

Other experiments demonstrated that injecting additional knowledge can improve performance in cognitive domains. Such approaches include applying incremental evolution [21], refined fitness functions [18], more complicated neural models [28] or additional helper objectives [12, 13]. Ideally, however, it would not be necessary to uncover technical domain knowledge specific to new applications.

Similarly, the benefit of encouraging higher-level (e.g. behavioral) diversity has been demonstrated in several cognitive tasks [12, 13, 17, 25]. In particular, Risi et al. [17] demonstrated that driving search *only* towards behavioral novelty can sometimes more effectively evolve learning policies than evolution driven by an objective-based fitness function. By directly comparing diversity-driven and objective-driven search in this way, deception can be effectively isolated [8, 17]; the same approach is applied in this paper.

Overall, previous results demonstrate that it is possible to evolve cognitive behaviors, but it is difficult to do so without domain knowledge or specialized approaches. Furthermore, some such studies directly implicate deception as the main obstacle [13, 17].

2.2 NEAT

In experiments described in this paper, behaviors are evolved for robots that are controlled by artificial neural networks (ANNs). Thus a neuroevolution (NE) method is needed to underpin these experiments. The NEAT method is appropriate because it is widely applied [1, 8, 17, 22–24] and well understood.

The NEAT method was originally developed to evolve ANNs to solve difficult control and sequential decision tasks [22–24]. Evolved ANNs control agents that select actions based on their sensory inputs. Like the SAGA method [5] before it, NEAT begins evolution with a population of small, simple networks and *complexifies* the network topology into diverse species over generations, leading to increasingly sophisticated behavior. A similar process of gradually adding new genes has been documented in natural evolution [11]. This section briefly reviews the NEAT method; for comprehensive introductions see e.g. [23, 24].

To keep track of which gene is which while new genes are added, a historical marking is uniquely assigned to each new structural component. During crossover, genes with the same historical markings are aligned, producing meaningful offspring efficiently. Speciation in NEAT protects structural innovations by reducing competition among differing structures and network complexities, thereby giving newer, more complex structures room to adjust. Networks are assigned to species based on the extent to which they share historical markings. Complexification, which resembles how genes are added over the course of natural evolution [11], is thus supported by both historical markings and speciation, allowing NEAT to establish high-level features early in evolution and later elaborate on them. Further, NEAT's ability to evolve increasingly complex ANNs fits well with this paper's motivation of evolving cognitive behaviors, which require potentially complex evolved structure.

Note that as originally described, NEAT speciates the population to encourage genotypic diversity. Because some experiments in this paper explore the effects of diversity maintenance on search, NEAT is extended to run without speciation as a baseline, and speciation is also replaced in some setups by the age-layered population structure (ALPS; [6]), a diversity maintenance technique encouraging diversity among the age of genomes instead of among ANN topologies.

Additionally, in some experiments in this paper NEAT is also extended with a mechanism for lifetime adaptation. In particular, in the learning task described later, ANNs are augmented with neuromodulated plasticity, a biologically-plausible [3] method for behavioral plasticity applied in similar previous learning experiments [17, 21]. In this model, an unsupervised learning rule modifies connection weights based on postsynaptic activity. In addition, special neuromodulatory neurons can be added to the ANN by random mutations; their role is to modulate the magnitude of weight changes for the neurons to which they connect. In particular, for each non-modulatory neuron, the sum of incoming activation from modulatory neurons (which do not contribute to the non-modulatory neuron's traditional activation level) determines the magnitude of weight changes for the non-modulatory node's incoming connections. In this way, neuromodulatory neurons can allow an ANN itself to decide not only *how* to adapt connection weights but also *when*. Following Risi et al. [17], the particular plasticity rule is:

$$\Delta w_{ji} = \tanh(m_i/2) * 35.95 a_i, \tag{1}$$

where w_{ji} is the weight of the connection from neuron j to i, m_i is the sum of incoming modulatory activation, and a_i is the activation of neuron i.

2.3 Novelty Search

In contrast to most EAs, which tend to converge the population, novelty search is a *divergent* evolutionary technique. It is inspired by natural evolution's drive towards novelty. In novelty search, novel behavior is rewarded directly *instead* of progress towards a fixed objective [7, 8]. The idea is that novelty can act as a proxy for many creative forces in natural evolution. In this way, rewarding only novelty allows investigating the impact of such creative forces independent of adaptive pressure to better fit a particular niche. This paper applies novelty search both as a means of illustrating deception when compared with objective-driven search, and as a potential practical alternative to such objective-driven search when evolving cognitive behaviors.

Tracking novelty requires little change to an evolutionary algorithm aside from replacing a fitness function with a *novelty metric*. Such a metric measures how different an individual is from other individuals, thereby creating a constant pressure to do something new. The key idea is that instead of rewarding performance on an objective, divergence from prior behaviors is rewarded.

In order to implement novelty search, novelty needs to be measured. A novelty metric characterizes how far away the new individual is from the rest of the population and its predecessors in *behavior space*, i.e. the space of unique behaviors. A good metric should thus compute the *sparseness* at any point in the behavior space. Areas with denser clusters of visited points are less novel and therefore rewarded less.

A simple measure of sparseness at a point is the average distance to the k-nearest neighbors of that point. Intuitively, if the average distance to a given point's nearest neighbors is large then it is in a sparse area; it is in a dense region if the average distance is small. The sparseness ρ at point x is given by

$$\rho(x) = \frac{1}{k}\sum_{i=0}^{k} \text{dist}(x, \mu_i), \tag{2}$$

where μ_i is the ith-nearest neighbor of x with respect to the distance metric dist, which is a domain-dependent measure of behavioral difference between two individuals in the search space. Candidates from more sparse regions of the behavior space then receive higher novelty scores.

If novelty is sufficiently high at the location of a new individual, i.e. above some minimal threshold $\rho_{\min}$, then the individual is entered into the permanent archive that characterizes the distribution of prior solutions in behavior space. The current generation plus the archive give a comprehensive sample of where the search has been and where it currently is; that way, by attempting to maximize the novelty metric, the gradient of search is simply towards what is *new*, with no other explicit objective.

However, even without an explicit objective, novelty search is still driven by meaningful information. Behaving in a novel way often requires exploiting the structure of the domain. For example, if the novelty of a robot's behavior is measured across many independent trials, learning from experience in any way (i.e. not necessarily such that it improves objective performance) may help a robot to differentiate itself from previous behaviors that behave *uniformly* when exposed to repeated trials in the same environment. Importantly, such learning behavior, first evolved without objective benefit, may later facilitate evolving the task's solution.

Once objective-based fitness is replaced with novelty, the underlying evolutionary algorithm operates as normal, selecting the most novel individuals to reproduce. Over generations, the population spreads out across the space of possible behaviors.

3. THE T-MAZE DOMAIN

The approach in this paper is to compare the effectiveness of different reward schemes in variants of an ER domain designed to require evolving different cognitive abilities.

The common experimental setup consists of a simulated mobile robot embedded in a T-Maze domain typical of ER experiments [13, 17]. In the T-Maze, the robot begins in a corridor and travels to the corridor's end, where the path splits into two branches. At the end of one branch there is a high reward, while the other branch contains a low reward. The imposed time limit prevents a robot from traversing both branches, and the robot cannot differentiate rewards until one is collected. Thus a successful robot can only maximize collecting the high reward by intelligently deciding which branch to traverse.

An advantage of the T-Maze is that it offers a simple mechanism for isolating cognitive properties of robot behaviors through repeated trials of binary decision making. If the ANN controlling the robot is flushed between trials (i.e. each neuron's activation is reset), information from a robot's previous trials can affect successive trials only through explicit allowances in experimental design. For example, in experiments with communication, the goal is to evolve networks that extract information from a given trial and communicate it to the robot attempting the same task in the following trial. A task-specific output of the evolved ANN is recorded at a trial's end and is interpreted as a communication signal, which is given as an additional input to the robot at the beginning of the next trial. The task-specific output and input together constitute a single continuous-valued communication channel spanning trials; no other information can leak between trials. In this way, any systematic changes in behavior between such trials can be attributed to utilization of the communication channel. Thus if trials are sequenced such that success depends upon intelligently modulating behavior, a successful outcome ensures that the desired cognitive behavior has actually been evolved.

In contrast, when information is not isolated in such a way, evolution often discovers mechanisms simpler than intended. For example, it is often possible to exploit the environment as a form of external memory or to leverage neural activation between trials to differentiate behavior instead of through synaptic learning or explicit communication.

The robot and its ANN controller are shown in figure 1, and the two T-Maze maps such robots must explore in this paper's experiments are shown in figure 2. The Standard T-Maze map (figure 2a) is similar to the classic T-Maze imported from experiments in animal cognition [14], and has been previously explored in previous ER studies [13, 17, 21]. Note that in the Standard T-Maze map, to navigate from the starting point to one of the branches requires a relatively simple behavior: the robot must be able to go forward and decide which way to turn at the junction.

In contrast, in the Extended T-Maze map (figure 2b) the required behavior is more complex: The robot must success-

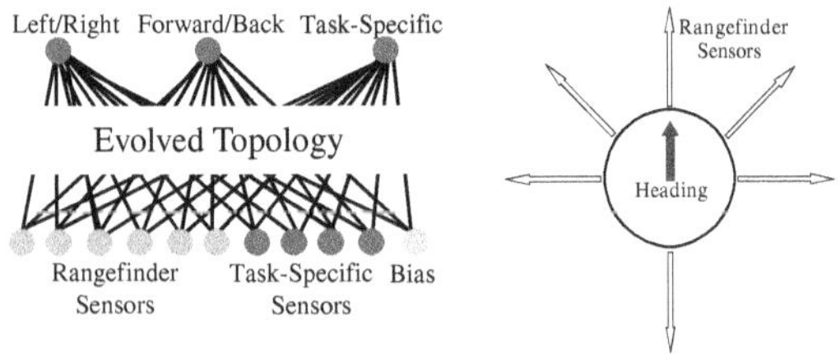

(a) Neural Network (b) Sensors

Figure 1: **The T-Maze Robot.** In the T-Maze domain studied in this paper, the ANN in (a) controls the robot. The environmental sensors of the ANN are augmented with task-specific inputs and outputs. In the Memory task, such inputs enable the robot to perceive external stimuli. In both the Communication and Learning tasks, such inputs allow the robot to perceive which reward it collects. Additionally, in the Communication task such neurons provide a channel through which to communicate and receive information between trials. The layout of the robot's sensors is shown in (b). Each arrow outside of the robot's body in (b) is a rangefinder sensor that indicates the distance to the closest obstacle in that direction. The solid arrow indicates the robot's heading.

(a) Standard T-Maze (b) Extended T-Maze

Figure 2: **T-Maze Maps.** In both maps, an unfilled circle represents the starting position of the robot and the R symbols represent the two reward locations. In each T-Maze instance, a high and a low reward will appear at the end of the maze's branches. The goal of a robot is to collect the high reward as often as possible over all of its trials. The Standard T-Maze is shown in (a), while (b) extends the T-Maze slightly to require an additional turn, interfering with the optimal turn decision later on in the maze. Note that while in both maps the high reward is depicted on the left, the rewards' locations will swap multiple times across the repeated trials of a robot's evaluation.

fully move forward, turn right, move forward to the junction, and only then decide whether to turn left or right. Thus while the extension to the maze may appear minor, the required behavior is much more complex. In this way, the idea is to explore the scalability of approaches and to determine whether deception is exacerbated as problem difficulty increases.

4. COGNITIVE TASKS

The three separate cognitive tasks tested in the underlying T-Maze domain are designed to require evolution of communication, memory, and learning (figure 3). In all three tasks, a robot is placed in either the Standard or Extended T-Maze for many independent trials (figure 4), with the goal of collecting the high reward as often as possible. However, the high reward switches branches systematically such that consistently collecting it requires evolving a particular cognitive behavior. Note that the robot's ANN is flushed between trials to control information flow between trials, and that to prevent overfitting, in each trial the robot's initial location and heading are slightly perturbed.

The Communication and Learning tasks are similar, but differ in the mechanism by which information from one trial can affect a robot's behavior in successive trials. In both tasks, robots are augmented with two sensors indicating which reward the robot reaches at the end of an evaluation. This reward information, combined with a mechanism for information transfer, makes it possible to modulate behavior intelligently in the future.

In the Communication task, such information transfer is provided by augmenting the robot's ANN with an additional output and input. Through such added neurons, the robot can communicate information to itself in the following trial (i.e. the added output is queried at the end of each trial, and is supplied to the robot as an additional input in the following trial). The communication input is set to 0 for the first trial because in that trial there is no previous communication to relay. Note that because the robot sends the signal to an identical ANN, the experiments do not investigate the evolution of language. Instead, the task tests the ability to distill information into a communication signal and to effectively modulate behavior through interpreting the signal. Thus a successful communicating agent will observe when it collects the low reward and communicate the need to visit the opposite branch to itself in the following trial.

In contrast, in the Learning task, networks are augmented with the ability to change network weights through neuromodulated plasticity as in several previous ER learning experiments [17, 21]. That is, NEAT in this particular task is extended with a model allowing the ANN to change its weights through modulated learning rules. While network activation is cleared between trials, connection weight modifications remain throughout an evaluation. Thus, a successful learning agent, after observing which reward it has collected at the end of a trial, can change its synaptic weights if necessary to guide it to the high reward in the following trial.

For the Communication and Learning tasks, how the reward location varies over the trials that constitute an individual's evaluation is shown in figure 4a. The idea is to keep the reward's location fixed long enough for adaptation to be beneficial; that is, if reward location is constant for at least three trials, an agent can consistently outperform a policy always taking the same branch by adapting to take the opposite branch whenever it collects the low reward.

The Memory task, unlike the Communication and Learning tasks, does not require learning *between* trials. As a result, no information from one trial of the robot is allowed to influence the next trial. The reason is that the tested behavior is to store information over the course of a single trial, as in [13]; in particular, the task is inspired by the AX-CPT working memory test [2] where two stimuli are presented in succession. Thus, to behave differentially over combinations of presented stimuli the ANN must remember the first one; such memory is possible in NEAT's ANNs through recurrent connections that maintain signals over time through feedback loops.

In the beginning of each trial in the Memory task, the ANN first receives as input either the A or the B stimulus. The ANN is then activated (without the robot being allowed to move) for 25 timesteps before the first stimulus is cleared. The ANN's inputs are cleared and it is then activated for 25

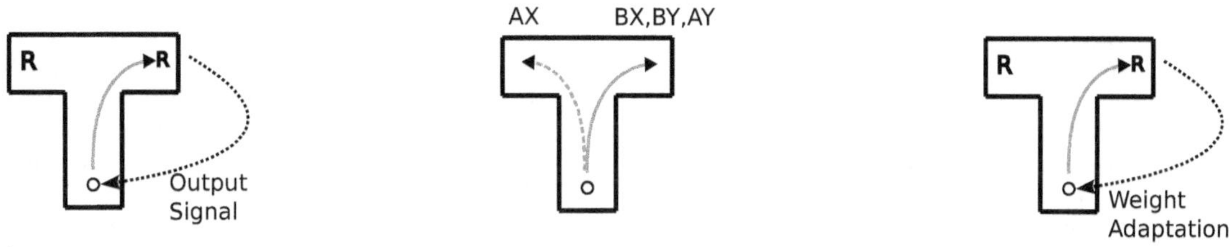

(a) Communication Task (b) Memory Task (c) Learning Task

Figure 3: **Separate Cognitive Tasks within the T-Maze Domain.** In all three tasks a robot's goal is to collect the high reward as often as possible. (a) In the Communication task, the robot must communicate between trials to consistently collect the high reward. An output added to the ANN is queried at the end of an evaluation, and communicated as an input in the following trial. (b) In the Memory task, a robot is first presented with time-delayed stimuli before it navigates the map. To consistently collect the high reward, the ANN must develop short-term memory through recurrent connections. (c) In the Learning task, the ANN model is extended such that a robot can modify its ANN's connection weights to maximize collecting the high reward before it switches locations again.

(a) Communication and Learning Tasks

(b) Memory Task

Figure 4: **Schedule of Reward Locations for Different Cognitive Tasks.** The locations of the high and low reward vary over the trials composing a robot's evaluation. Figure (a) shows the locations for the 50 successive trials of the Communication and Learning tasks and figure (b) the locations for the 24 successive trials of the Memory task. Filled rectangles indicate that the high reward is on the left branch of the T-Maze, while unfilled rectangles indicate that it is on the right branch. Note that the schedule is the same for the Communication and Learning tasks, and the number of trials before the reward switches is varied to prevent overfitting. In the Memory task, the presented stimuli cycle every four trials between AX, AY, BX and BY. Because the test is to distinguish AX from the other stimuli, in the first trial and every fourth succeeding trial the high reward is on the left branch, and for all others it is on the right branch.

additional timesteps without any stimulus. Then the ANN receives as input either the X or Y stimulus for 25 timesteps. Following the presentation of the stimuli, the robot is then allowed to navigate through the T-Maze. If the stimuli presented in a particular trial are A and X, then the high reward is placed on the left branch of the T-Maze; in the other three situations (i.e. AY, BX, and BY) the high reward is placed on the right branch. Thus when presented with either the X or Y stimulus, only by remembering whether the A or B stimulus had been presented previously can the robot consistently choose the correct branch. The schedule of reward locations for each trial in an individual's evaluation is shown in figure 4b.

5. METHODS COMPARED

For all experiments in this paper the underlying NEAT neuroevolution algorithm [23] is applied. However, the evolutionary incentive and type of diversity maintenance are varied to explore the degree of deception in cognitive domains. In particular, several objective-driven methods are compared to a non-objective search method.

For the objective-driven methods, the main evolutionary incentive is provided by an objective-based fitness function typical of such domains. In each trial a robot's fitness is 0 if it fails to collect any reward, 250 if it collects the low reward, and 500 if it collects the high reward. A robot's overall fitness is the sum of its fitness score over all of its trials. The intuitive motivation for this fitness function is that it reflects the desirability of outcomes and is similar to those applied in previous ER T-Maze domains [13, 17, 21].

The motivation for the objective-based methods is to apply a range of representative techniques. In total, four objective-based methods are evaluated:

- The **Baseline** method is a neuroevolution algorithm without any diversity maintenance. That is, for the baseline runs NEAT's standard diversity maintenance method, speciation, is disabled. The motivation is to determine whether a more sophisticated technique is necessary to solve the tasks, and to provide a baseline against which to compare more sophisticated methods.
- In the **High Mutation** method, mutation rates are increased to make adding neurons and connections to the ANN more likely; such increased structural mutation rates may encourage evolving more complex ANNs. This method follows a common practical principle of simply increasing mutation rates as remedy for premature convergence.
- The **Speciation** method is identical to the Baseline setup except genotypic speciation is enabled, i.e. this method is the standard NEAT algorithm as described in Stanley and Miikkulainen [23]. The purpose of genotypic speciation is to encourage exploring ANNs with diverse topologies. In this way, speciation may aid evolving cognitive behaviors because realizing them may require evolving more complex ANNs.
- Finally, the **ALPS** method augments NEAT with an implementation of ALPS [6], which is a popular ER diversity maintenance technique. The basic idea in ALPS is to protect younger genotypes from competing with older genotypes by segregating genomes based on their age. This method is complemented by regular infusion of randomly-generated genotypes. In this way, search never completely converges to a single local optimum. For a more complete description of ALPS, see Hornby [6]. Note that speciation is also disabled in this method so that there is only one diversity-maintenance mechanism being tested.

With the aim of illustrating deception, a non-objective-driven setup is also evaluated. In particular, the **Novelty** method rewards only behavioral novelty (through novelty search), instead of progress towards the desired objective. Note that NEAT's speciation is disabled in this method because preliminary experimentation showed that it decreased performance.

Applying novelty search requires defining a space of behaviors through which it can search. The approach taken in this paper is to define such a space from high-level summary properties of a robot's behavior across the trials of a cognitive task. The idea is to create a tractable space of behaviors that is similar in spirit to how a human might summarize a robot's performance. In this way the resulting measure of novelty might grossly reflect a human's measure of behavioral distance. For example, in the Memory task, one might summarize a robot's behavior according to which branches the robot most often visits and how often it collects the high and low rewards. Thus novelty search's behavioral characterization in this task includes four values: what fraction of trials the robot visits the left branch, visits the right branch, collects the high reward, and collects the low reward.

In the Communication and Learning tasks a human observer would likely pay special attention to a robot's behavior in the trials when the location of the high reward switches branches, and in the trial immediately following such a switch. Such trials are informative because they encompass when the robot is expected to make a mistake and then adapt its behavior. Thus in both these tasks, beyond the four fractions measured in the Memory task, four additional fractions are added to the behavioral characterization: the fraction of trials in which the robot reaches the high and low rewards, for both trials in which the rewards switch locations and the trials that immediately follow such a switch.

Note that when novelty search explores such a space, it is rewarded for finding combinations of such fractions different from those the search has encountered in the past, with no fixed objective. In other words, if neither behavior has yet been encountered, a behavior maximizing the robot's ability to crash without collecting any rewards is as viable as a behavior that consistently collects the high reward. A more granular behavioral characterization was explored in initial experimentation consisting of concatenating together the outcomes of each trial. However, it performed worse than the coarse behavioral characterization described in this section, which was then adopted for the experiments.

6. EXPERIMENTS

All experiments were run for 500,000 evaluations. For all methods except ALPS, the steady-state rtNEAT algorithm was applied with a population size of 500. For ALPS a generational algorithm based on Hornby [6] was implemented, with five age-layers of 100 individuals each (for a total population size of 500) with a polynomial aging scheme and an age gap of 20. For all methods except High Mutation, NEAT's add node mutation probability was 0.03 and its add link probability was 0.15. In High Mutation, these probabilities were raised to 0.1 and 0.3, respectively. For all methods, the weight mutation power was 2.5 and the survival threshold was set to 0.4.

Figure 5 compares the performance of the objective-based search methods with that of novelty search across the three cognitive tasks in the Standard T-Maze map. Indicative of deception, in these tasks novelty search evolves solutions in more than half of all runs, while the objective-based methods taken together evolve solutions in less than 20% of all runs. In particular, in every pair-wise comparison between novelty search and the objective-based variants in each domain, novelty search solves the task significantly more often (Fisher's exact test; $p < 0.01$). Additionally, of the 150 runs of novelty search in the Standard T-Maze map, only one failed to evolve a behavior that exceeded the performance of the simplest purely-reactive controller (i.e. one that always turns the same direction at the end of the T-Maze). In contrast, objective-based search more often failed to do so, particularly in the Memory task.

Figure 6 similarly compares performance in the more difficult Extended T-Maze. In every pair-wise comparison between novelty search and the objective-based variants, novelty search both solves the task more often and is more likely to evolve a policy outperforming purely reactive behavior (Fisher's exact test; $p < 0.01$). Overall, performance of all methods declines in this more difficult version of the T-Maze. However, novelty search still consistently evolves behaviors outperforming the basic reactive policy, and evolves solutions in a significant percentage of runs. In contrast, the only combination of objective-based method and cognitive task to be solved in more than two out of 50 runs was High Mutation evaluated on the Communication task. Performance degradation was particularly acute in the Memory task, where the objective-based methods never solved the task and novelty search solved it in only 16% of runs.

Based on a pair-wise comparison over all tasks and domains, Speciation was most effective out of the objective-based methods in exceeding the performance of a reactive agent (Fisher's exact test; $p < 0.01$). However, Speciation did not evolve *solutions* to tasks more consistently. Thus while directly encouraging accumulating ANN structure may sometimes help narrowly to increase performance it may not always be enough to overcome deception.

7. DISCUSSION AND FUTURE WORK

The results in this paper support the hypothesis that deception is a central factor underlying the difficulty to evolve cognitive behaviors. Such a result is important because it indicts objective-focused selection pressure rather than the encoding or evolutionary algorithm itself, which are more often the focus of refinement. The tendency of objective-based search to converge to reactive behaviors highlights that the necessary stepping stones leading to solving a cognitive task often may not lie conveniently on the gradient of increasing behavioral similarity to a task's solution. For example, Risi et al. [17] illustrated that the stepping stones towards evolving learning behavior often perform worse according to the task objective than the population so far. Similarly, figure 7 plots the objective fitness scores for the lineage of a solution for the Communication task in this paper: The innovations facilitating the desired cognitive behavior are not recognized by the objective-based fitness function. While deception has previously been shown to become increasingly problematic as problems become more complex [9, 10], this study is the first to show that deception may be systemic when evolving cognitive behaviors in particular. To overcome such deception likely requires refining selection. However, the results here show that diversity maintenance techniques alone are not always sufficient. The reason is that large digressions from the gradient of objective-based fitness are needed to establish the neural structure that enables cognitive behav-

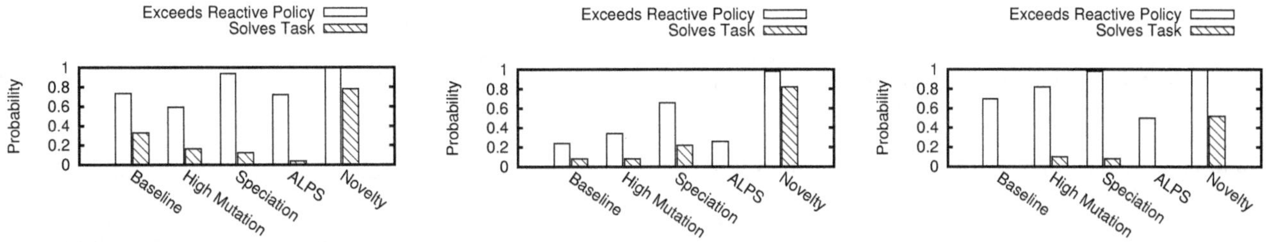

(a) Communication Task (b) Memory Task (c) Learning Task

Figure 5: **Performance in the Standard T-Maze across Cognitive Tasks.** The ability for different methods to exceed the performance of a reactive agent that traverses the same branch every trial, and to successfully solve the task, is shown for (a) the Communication task, (b) the Memory task, and (c) the Learning task. Indicative of deception, novelty search solves each of the tasks more consistently, and the objective-based methods fail to consistently evolve policies outperforming a purely-reactive one.

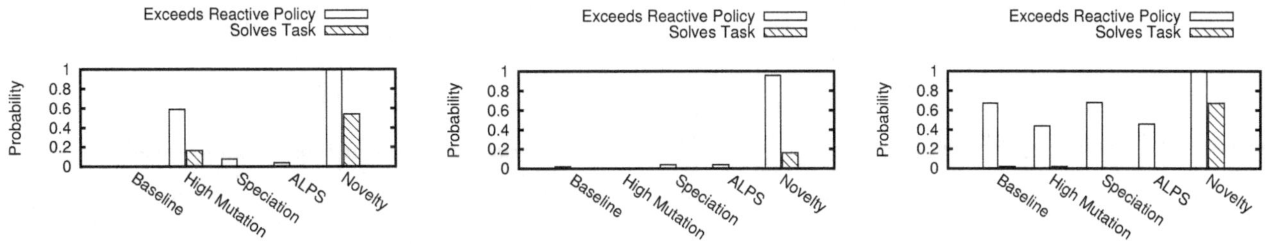

(a) Communication Domain (b) Memory Domain (c) Learning Domain

Figure 6: **Performance in the Extended T-Maze across Cognitive Tasks.** The ability for different methods to exceed the performance of a reactive agent that traverses the same branch every trial, and to successfully solve the task, is shown for (a) the Communication task, (b) the Memory task, and (c) the Learning task. Illustrating that deception is worse in this more complex T-Maze variation, all of the objective-based methods struggle to consistently evolve solutions outperforming reactive policies. Novelty search's performance also degrades, although it still solves each task in a significant percentage of runs.

ior. In particular, cognitive behavior often requires integrating multiple independent adaptations that taken alone do not increase performance in benchmark tasks like those studied in this paper. For example, for communication to improve performance in the T-Maze the information necessary for correctly adapting behavior in the following trial must be first distilled, such information must then be propagated to the communication output of the ANN, and the information from the communication input must be used to actually modify behavior in the following trial. In this way, developing any of these adaptations in isolation will not improve performance, which may undermine their evolution by objective-driven search.

In contrast, novelty search rewards fledgling instances of cognitive ability that enable novel behavior in the T-Maze even if it serves no objective purpose. The performance advantage of novelty search in this paper both highlights deception and points to the importance of open-ended search processes in general when tackling problems requiring higher-complexity behaviors. Beyond novelty search, other examples of more open-ended searches, such as multi-objectivization [12, 13, 25], artificial life virtual worlds [16], and methods driven by curiosity [15, 20] are thus also promising approaches for generating complex cognitive behaviors. In particular, combining pressure towards behavioral diversity with pressure towards an objective is often an effective approach in practice [10, 13, 25]; however, searching only for novelty (i.e. without any objective-based optimization [8]) is used in this paper to isolate the role of deception.

In addition to open-ended search processes, more open-ended *domains* may also be necessary to scale to increasingly complex cognitive tasks. The problem is that domains imported from animal cognitive tests, like the T-Maze, narrowly constrain possible agent behavior to a single highly-structured task. In doing so, such domains similarly constrain evolution's creativity, which may often proceed through exapting structures evolved for one purpose

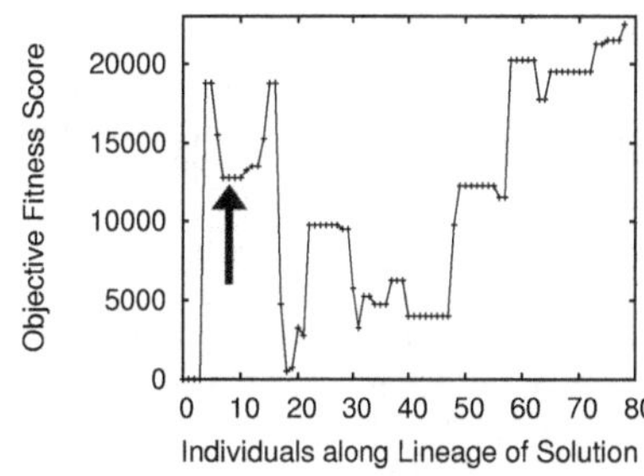

Figure 7: **Deceptive Stepping Stones in the Communication Task.** The objective fitness scores are shown for the ancestors of the eventual solution evolved in a representative run of novelty search in the Standard T-maze for the Communication task (crossover was disabled for this particular run to enable a single line of descent). Key innovations that facilitate the eventual solution receive lower fitness scores than their predecessors, and therefore would be unlikely to be preserved by objective-based search – yet novelty search can build on them because they are deemed more novel than their predecessors. For example, the ancestor highlighted by the arrow receives a fitness score of 12,750, which is a significantly worse than the one received by the simple reactive policy of always going to the same branch of the T-maze (18,750), discovered earlier in evolution (by the fifth individual in the lineage). Yet because the lower scoring policy reacts when the reward location changes, it proves to be a better stepping stone to an effective solution policy.

to suit another [4]; if every behavior must relate to navigating through a T-Maze, there is little to exapt. In other words, both objective-based search and constrained domains may serve to focus evolution, when what may sometimes be needed is *less* directed focus.

An interesting direction for future work is to apply novelty search to a single task that requires integrating multiple cognitive behaviors. For example, evolved agents able to communicate and learn could potentially enable effective teams for Robocup soccer or other complex group-based tasks.

8. CONCLUSION

This paper explored the hypothesis that deception complicates evolving ANNs capable of cognitive behavior. Evidence for such a hypothesis was provided through experiments contrasting objective-driven search with novelty search in tasks requiring communication, memory, and learning. Overall, novelty search more effectively evolved solutions across the tested tasks, although the performance of all tested methods declined in the harder domain variant. The conclusion is that evolving cognitive behaviors may require both increasingly open-ended search processes and domains.

9. ACKNOWLEDGEMENTS

This research was supported in part by NSF grants DBI-0939454 and IIS-0915038, by NIH grant R01-GM105042, and by the FRI program of the College of Natural Sciences at the University of Texas at Austin.

References

[1] T. Aaltonen et al. Measurement of the top quark mass with dilepton events selected using neuroevolution at CDF. *Physical Review Letters*, 2009.

[2] Todd S. Braver, Jonathan D. Cohen, and David Servan-Schreiber. A computational model of prefrontal cortex function. *Advances in Neural Information Processing Systems: 7*, 7:141, 1995.

[3] Thomas J. Carew, Edgar T. Walters, and Eric R. Kandel. Classical conditioning in a simple withdrawal reflex in aplysia californica. *The Journal of Neuroscience*, 1(12):1426–1437, 1981.

[4] Stephen Jay Gould and Elisabeth S. Vrba. Exaptation-a missing term in the science of form. *Paleobiology*, pages 4–15, 1982.

[5] Inman Harvey. *The Artificial Evolution of Adaptive Behavior.* PhD thesis, School of Cognitive and Computing Sciences, University of Sussex, Sussex, 1993.

[6] Gregory S. Hornby. ALPS: the age-layered population structure for reducing the problem of premature convergence. In *Proceedings of the Genetic and Evolutionary Computation Conference (GECCO-2006)*, pages 815–822, New York, NY, USA, 2006. ACM.

[7] Joel Lehman and Kenneth O. Stanley. Exploiting open-endedness to solve problems through the search for novelty. In *Proc. of the Eleventh Intl. Conf. on Artificial Life (ALIFE XI)*, Cambridge, MA, 2008. MIT Press.

[8] Joel Lehman and Kenneth O. Stanley. Abandoning objectives: Evolution through the search for novelty alone. *Evol. Comp.*, 19(2):189–223, 2011.

[9] Joel Lehman and Kenneth O. Stanley. Novelty seach and the problem with objectives. In *Genetic Programming in Theory and Practice IX (GPTP 2011)*, chapter 3, pages 37–56. Springer, 2011.

[10] Joel Lehman, Kenneth O. Stanley, and Risto Miikkulainen. Effective diversity maintenance in deceptive domains. In *Proceedings of the Genetic and Evolutionary Computation Conference (GECCO-2013)*. ACM, 2013.

[11] Andrew P. Martin. Increasing genomic complexity by gene duplication and the origin of vertebrates. *The American Naturalist*, 154(2):111–128, 1999.

[12] Charles Ollion, Tony Pinville, and Stéphane Doncieux. Emergence of memory in neuroevolution: impact of selection pressures. In *Proceedings of the fourteenth international conference on Genetic and evolutionary computation conference companion*, pages 369–372. ACM, 2012.

[13] Charles Ollion, Tony Pinville, and Doncieux Stéphane. With a little help from selection pressures: evolution of memory in robot controllers. In *Artificial Life*, volume 13, pages 407–414, 2012.

[14] David S. Olton. Mazes, maps, and memory. *American Psychologist*, 34(7):583, 1979.

[15] Pierre-Yves Oudeyer. Intelligent adaptive curiosity: a source of self-development. In *Proceedingsof the Fourth International Workshop on Epigenetic Robotics*. Lund University Cognitive Studies, 2004.

[16] Thomas S. Ray. Evolution, complexity, entropy and artificial reality. *Physica D: Nonlinear Phenomena*, 75 (1):239–263, 1994.

[17] Sebastian Risi, Charles E Hughes, and Kenneth O Stanley. Evolving plastic neural networks with novelty search. *Adaptive Behavior*, 18(6):470–491, 2010.

[18] Sebastian Risi and Kenneth O Stanley. A unified approach to evolving plasticity and neural geometry. In *Neural Networks (IJCNN), The 2012 International Joint Conference on*, pages 1–8. IEEE, 2012.

[19] Gregory M. Saunders and Jordan B. Pollack. The evolution of communication schemes over continuous channels. *From Animals to Animats*, 4:580–589, 1996.

[20] J. Schmidhuber. Developmental robotics, optimal artificial curiosity, creativity, music, and the fine arts. *Connection Science*, 18(2):173–187, 2006.

[21] Andrea Soltoggio and Ben Jones. Novelty of behaviour as a basis for the neuro-evolution of operant reward learning. In *Proceedings of the 11th Annual conference on Genetic and evolutionary computation*, pages 169–176. ACM, 2009.

[22] Kenneth O. Stanley, Bobby D. Bryant, and Risto Miikkulainen. Real-time neuroevolution in the NERO video game. *IEEE Transactions on Evolutionary Computation Special Issue on Evolutionary Computation and Games*, 9(6):653–668, 2005.

[23] Kenneth O. Stanley and Risto Miikkulainen. Evolving neural networks through augmenting topologies. *Evolutionary Computation*, 10:99–127, 2002.

[24] Kenneth O. Stanley and Risto Miikkulainen. Competitive coevolution through evolutionary complexification. *Journal of Artificial Intelligence Research*, 21:63–100, 2004.

[25] Paul Tonelli and Jean-Baptiste Mouret. On the relationships between synaptic plasticity and generative systems. In *Proceedings of the 13th annual conference on Genetic and evolutionary computation*, pages 1531–1538. ACM, 2011.

[26] Gregory M. Werner and Micheal G. Dyer. Evolution of communication in artificial organisms. In *Proceedings of the Second International Conference of Artificial Life*, pages 659–687, 1991.

[27] Brian M. Yamauchi and Randall D. Beer. Sequential behavior and learning in evolved dynamical neural networks. *Adaptive Behavior*, 2(3):219–246, 1994.

[28] Tom Ziemke and Mikael Thieme. Neuromodulation of reactive sensorimotor mappings as a short-term memory mechanism in delayed response tasks. *Adaptive Behavior*, 10(3-4):185–199, 2002.

Encouraging Creative Thinking in Robots Improves Their Ability to Solve Challenging Problems

Jingyu Li
Evolving AI Lab
Computer Science Dept.
University of Wyoming
Laramie High School
jingyuli@mit.edu

Jed Storie
Evolving AI Lab
Computer Science Dept.
University of Wyoming
jed.storie@gmail.com

Jeff Clune
Evolving AI Lab
Computer Science Dept.
University of Wyoming
jeffclune@uwyo.edu

ABSTRACT

Evolutionary algorithms frequently get stuck on local optima–and fail to find the global optimum–when local gradients do not point the search process toward the direction of the global optimum. A recent breakthrough called Novelty Search ameliorates this problem by enabling the search process to explore in every direction by encouraging the production of novel, or not-yet-seen, phenotypes (e.g. new robot behaviors). However, a problem with Novelty Search is that it can get lost on "novelty plateaus" wherein novel behaviors in offspring are not immediately produced by mutation and crossover (e.g. when a sequence of specific mutations is required to produce new behaviors, but the intermediate mutations are not rewarded because they do not produce novel behaviors). In such cases, Novelty Search and related approaches that reward behavioral diversity can get stuck. Here we introduce a new approach, borrowed from human psychology, that mitigates this problem: encouraging creative thinking. In addition to rewarding novel behavior, we encourage evolving neural networks to "think differently" by rewarding not-yet-seen firing patterns in hidden neurons, which we call the "Creative Thinking Approach." We hypothesize that encouraging novel thinking can reward stepping stones toward new behaviors. On a variety of challenging robotic control problems from previous publications we demonstrate that, as problem difficulty increases, adding the Creative Thinking Approach increasingly improves performance over simply encouraging novel behaviors. Our results suggest that the Creative Thinking Approach could help improve the scale and complexity of problems that can be solved by evolutionary algorithms.

Categories and Subject Descriptors

H.5 [**Information Interfaces and Presentation**]: Computing Methodologies:Artificial Intelligence

GECCO'14, July 12–16, 2014, Vancouver, BC, Canada.

ACM 978-1-4503-2662-9/14/07 ...$15.00.
http://dx.doi.org/10.1145/2576768.2598222.

Keywords

Novelty Search, Behavioral Diversity, Evolutionary Robotics, Creative Thinking Approach

1. MOTIVATION

Traditional Evolutionary Algorithms (EAs) have fitness functions that reward organisms more the closer they are to (or the higher they perform on) an objective. EAs often get stuck on local fitness optima, which are regions of high fitness surrounded by regions of low fitness. In such situations, the fitness gradient does not point in the direction that needs to be traversed to find the global optima, preventing further improvements in fitness [8]. In these deceptive problems, being unwilling to explore areas of low fitness prevents evolution from reaching its goal. Take the example of a Chinese finger trap. If we took fitness as maximizing distance between the two fingers, higher fitnesses are achieved by pulling, which is a counter-productive strategy that only more tightly traps the fingers. Instead, one has to first push together the fingers–temporarily lowering fitness–before escaping the trap [14]. The same is true for many problems: individuals must first move away from high fitness areas in order to reach the global goal [14]. It is thus helpful to reward stepping stones *on the path toward* desired solutions, which may not be *in the direction of* the final goal as judged by the fitness function; such stepping stones are often not rewarded by objective-based fitness functions [13, 14].

One approach is to reward stepping stones in deceptive problems by adding helper-objectives that are not directly related to performance, but that guide evolution to produce potentially useful behaviors. For example, it has been shown that adding objectives to promote behavioral consistency (i.e. encouraging similar behavior to be performed in the presence of noise) or reactivity (i.e. performing different behaviors in different scenarios) can increase performance [21, 15].

Most previous techniques for preventing premature convergence on local optima focus on increasing *genomic* diversity [26, 20, 24, 8]. In recent years, researchers have shifted toward rewarding diversity in the space of *behaviors*, such as by adding a behavioral diversity objective to a multi-objective algorithm [18, 6, 17]. A more extreme version of this idea is Novelty Search, which rewards only behavioral novelty and ignores the objective entirely [13, 14]. Both approaches substantially help EAs avoid getting trapped on local optima and often outperform EAs with genomic-based diversity metrics or no diversity pressure at all [18, 6, 17, 13, 14].

Algorithms that reward behavioral diversity or novelty require a *behavioral distance function* that quantifies how different the behaviors of two organisms are. Examples from previous work include the final location of a robot or its trajectory over time [13, 14, 17]. The specific behavioral distance function chosen makes a significant difference, placing a burden on the user to not only pick a behavioral distance function, but to pick a good one. Recent research has focused on creating behavioral distance functions that are generally applicable to many different problems, such as concatenating the entire sequence of inputs to and outputs from a neural network controller and then comparing this sequence to that of another robot [6, 17]. Modern computers and efficient algorithms enable comparisons even in such high-dimensional spaces, and the approach has been shown to work as well as human-designed custom behavioral distance functions [18, 6, 17].

All approaches that encourage behavioral diversity will have a problem if mutations to the current population do not produce novel behaviors. We call this phenomenon a *novelty plateau*. After a prolonged search for novel behaviors, it would not be surprising if the population reached a point wherein the creation of new behaviors required more than one mutation. One can imagine, for example, a situation in which five specific mutations would be required to produce a new behavior, but in which none of the intermediate mutations cause the behavior. In this situation, there is no selection gradient towards having all five mutations, since having four of the five is no better than having none of the five. Such novelty plateaus may significantly hurt the performance of EAs that encourage behavioral diversity, although the extent to which they do so is currently unknown. Of course, neutral genetic drift could lead the search out of a novelty plateau, just as drift could lead a population out of a fitness plateau [11, 23], but drift requires luck in exponentially increasing amounts as the number of specific mutations required to exit the plateau grows. For the same reason you may want to encourage behavioral diversity in objective-based search when there is no helpful gradient toward the objective, it could also be helpful to encourage thought diversity in behavior-based search when there is no behavioral diversity gradient. As seen in psychology, being stuck on a problem is a result of being locked into a certain way of thinking and thus new and creative thinking plays a large factor in getting unstuck on problems [22].

2. METHODS

2.1 The Creative Thinking Approach

To test the idea of encouraging thought diversity, we introduce the Creative Thinking Approach (CTA), which encourages robots to "think differently" than robots that have come before in the same run. Of course, suggesting that robots controlled by neural networks "think" at all is controversial: we only use the term "think" metaphorically. To the extent that neural networks do think in the most loose sense of the word, in that they perform computations to process inputs and generate outputs, our algorithm encourages them to think differently. In less metaphorical and more technical language, rewarding "creative thinking" simply means rewarding novel patterns of neural firing. In a nutshell, then, our algorithm rewards novel thoughts in addition to novel behaviors.

Technically, our work is an extension of the general behavioral diversity mechanism from Doncieux and Mouret [6, 17]. For the general behavioral diversity mechanism, over the course of a robot evaluation, all of the robot's inputs and outputs from each time step (or a sub-sample of time steps) are stored in a binary vector to represent the behavior of the individual (values > 0 are stored as 1, otherwise 0). This method is general because a user does not have to design a problem-specific behavioral characterization (such as the number of doors opened): the method will provide a behavioral metric and distance function for any problem in which a robot has inputs and outputs. The behavioral distance between two organisms is the Hamming distance between their binary vectors, which is computationally efficient to calculate with modern algorithms. The Hamming distance is the number of bits that differ between two binary sequences. This behavioral distance factors into a behavioral diversity objective in the NSGA-II multi-objective algorithm [4]: the other objective is performance on the task. Briefly, multi-objective algorithms seek to improve performance on all objectives in a way that maintains a diverse set of solutions that perform well to varying degrees on all objectives. For a review of multi-objective algorithms, the reader is directed to [5, 3].

In this paper, the general behavioral diversity mechanism just described [6, 17] is compared to the Creative Thinking Approach. Because that general behavioral diversity mechanism looks only at behavior (characterized by input and output values) [6, 17], we refer to this control as the *behavioral diversity only* (BDO) treatment.

To implement the Creative Thinking Approach, we extend the BDO method by adding the firing patterns of the hidden neurons to the binary vector describing the robot's behaviors (Figure 1). Note that the CTA is a superset of the BDO, in that it includes the behaviors (characterized by inputs and outputs) and adds to that a consideration of the firing patterns of hidden neurons. Thus, two robots that have identical inputs and outputs, but have different neural firing patterns, will be recognized as being different and thus rewarded. While technically a small change, there are consequences to consider. By adding hidden neurons, the computational cost of calculating the difference between two organisms increases. In our problems, this additional cost is minor compared to the cost of running the simulation to evaluate organisms, although it could become an issue for faster problem domains or larger neural networks. For the problems in this paper, we did not notice that the CTA ran slower than BDO. An additional complication is how to compare the hidden neurons in neural networks with different topologies, as can be the case if the topology evolves. To avoid that complexity in this first paper on the Creative Thinking Approach, the topology of the neural networks is fixed. In the discussion we propose ways of dealing with variable topologies.

Following [17], the neural network controllers for our experiments are Elman-Jordan networks [7], which are simple recurrent networks. The networks are represented with a direct encoding [27, 2].

Evolution was conducted in the Sferes2 evolutionary computation framework [16]. As previously mentioned, all runs feature the NSGA-II [4] multi-objective evolutionary algo-

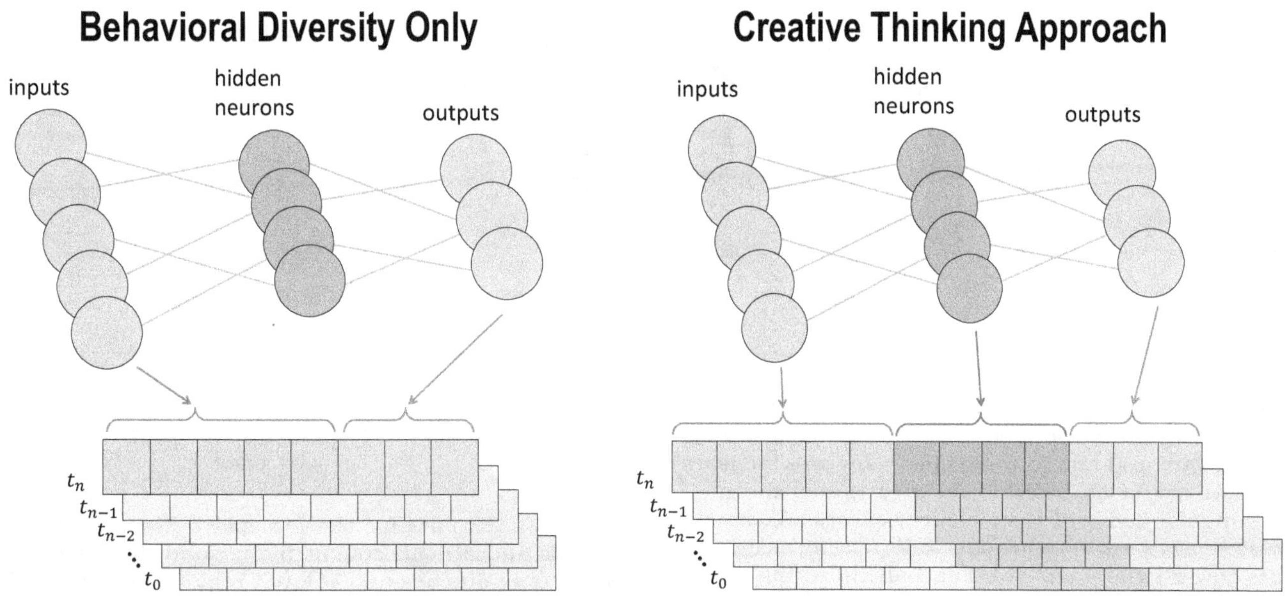

Figure 1: Comparing the behavioral diversity only (BDO) method from [6, 17] to the Creative Thinking Approach (CTA) proposed in this paper. At each time step t, a vector of the robot's input and output values for that time step are concatenated to a large vector that characterizes the robot's behavior.

rithm with two objectives: performance and diversity (either BDO or CTA). All statistics are performed with the non-parametric Mann-Whitney Wilcoxon test. Plots show medians (lines) and 95% bootstrapped confidence intervals of the median (shaded areas), which are calculated by resampling the data 5000 times. Confidence intervals are smoothed by a median filter with a window size of 101 to reduce noise. Asterisks below each plot indicate if the Creative Thinking Approach performs significantly better than the behavioral diversity only approach at that generation. The code and data for all experiments are available upon request.

3. EXPERIMENTS AND RESULTS

3.1 Easiest Problem: The Deceptive Maze

In this experiment, the objective is to evolve a neural network that is able to navigate its way through the maze from the start to the goal (Fig. 2). The problem is from Mouret and Doncieux 2012 [17] and is inspired by the deceptive "Hard Maze" from Novelty Search papers [14, 13]. It is deceptive because the performance objective rewards organisms for getting closer to the goal, but doing so results in getting trapped in the dead end above the start. While hard for traditional, objective-only EAs, solving this maze is relatively simple for EAs that do encourage behavioral diversity [17, 14, 13].

The neural network robot controllers for this problem have 7 input (sensor) neurons and two output neurons (Fig. 3). Sensors include three range sensors, which provide the normalized distance to the nearest obstacle in the direction that sensor points, and four pie-slice goal sensors that fire if the goal is within their purview, irrespective of intervening obstacles, and thus serve as a compass toward the goal. The two output neurons control the speed of each wheel. There are 7 hidden neurons. The experiment is run 50 times with a population size of 200 for 1500 generations.

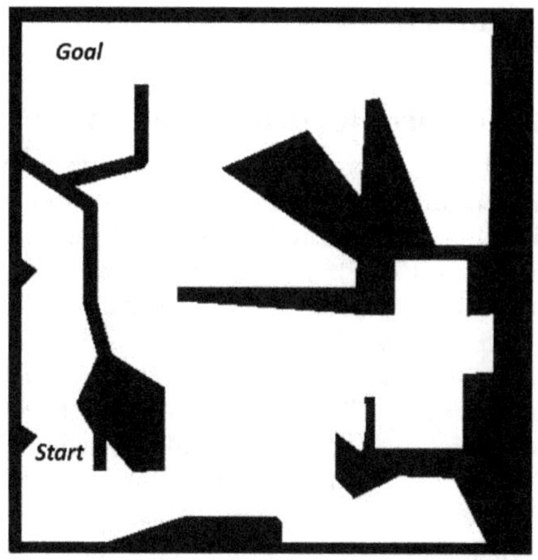

Figure 2: The Deceptive Maze Environment

The performance measure rewards getting closer to the goal [17]. Specifically, it is

$$performance = 1 - \frac{distance\ to\ goal}{size\ of\ maze} \quad (1)$$

On this problem there is no significant difference between the treatments ($p > 0.05$) and both treatments solve the problem in less than 1500 generations (Fig. 4). We hypothesize that the problem is not difficult enough for the Creative Thinking Approach to make a difference, and it may in fact slow the search process down by diluting the selection pressure on generating easily-produced behavioral diversity. We next investigate whether the Creative Thinking Approach is more advantageous on a harder problem.

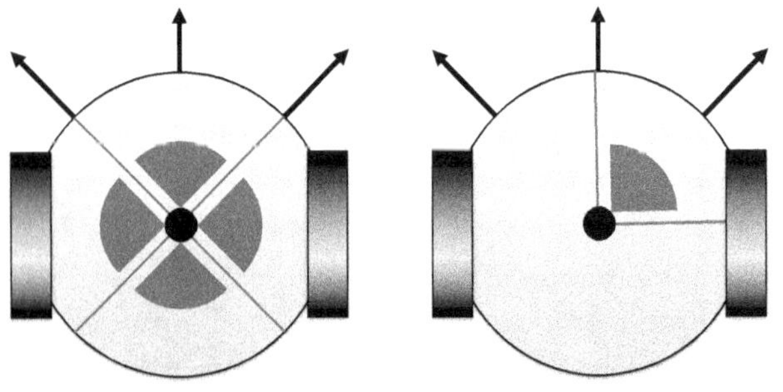

(a) (b)

Figure 3: The robots and their sensors. (a) The maze navigating robot has three distance-to-wall sensors (arrows) and four pie-slice "compass" sensors (blue wedges) that indicate the direction of the goal. The angular range of the pie-slice sensors are shown; these sensors can see through walls, acting as a compass toward the goal. (b) The ball collecting robot has three distance-to-wall sensors (arrows), two pie-slice sensors that detect the presence of balls, and two similar sensors with the same range that detect the basket. The range of the right pie-slice sensors is shown; the left pie-slice sensors are symmetric. See text for a full description of all sensors. Figure adapted from [17].

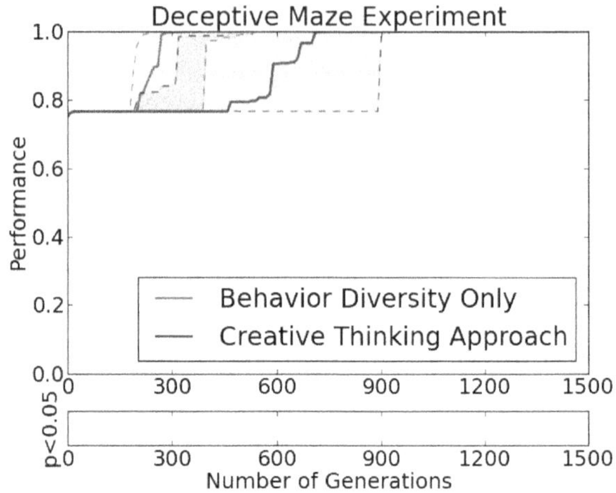

Figure 4: Results for the Deceptive Maze problem. In this and all subsequent plots, solid lines are medians over 50 runs and colored regions indicate 95% bootstrapped confidence intervals of the median. Asterisks appear in the lower panel if the treatments are statistically significantly different from each other with p < 0.05.

3.2 Harder Problem: Ball Collection

In this problem—from [6, 17]—a robot must navigate its way around an unknown environment, pick up a ball, place it in an illuminated area, and then repeat that process for eleven other balls (Fig. 5). A trial consists of three sub-trials. In each sub-trial, the robot starts at a different location and must collect four balls, the initial positions of which are the same for each sub-trial[1]. The three different starting locations for the robot are shown in Fig. 5. Those three different starting locations are the same for all subsequent versions of the ball collection problem, but are not pictured in subsequent figures to reduce clutter. For this version of the problem, trials stop at 9000 evaluations (3000 evaluations for each sub-trial). The setup, including the robot's neural network, is reset before each sub-trial.

Performance on this problem is measured as the fraction of balls placed in the lighted area. Note there is no pressure on speed or efficiency aside from the fact that being efficient may enable collecting more balls. In this version of the problem, the sequence in which balls are collected does not matter. If a ball is dropped outside the lighted region, the robot will be unable to pick it up again and fails to collect that ball.

There are 10 inputs to the neural network (Fig. 3) [17]: three laser range sensors that return normalized distances to the nearest obstacles, two bumpers that return a 1 when touching an obstacle and 0 otherwise, two basket-presence sensors that detect the basket when in the angular range of its sensors (Fig. 3) and not blocked by obstacles (contrary to the maze navigating robot, this robot cannot see through walls), two ball presence sensors with the same range and properties as the basket sensors, and one ball-carrying sensor that returns a 1 if the robot is carrying a ball and 0 otherwise. The robot has 3 outputs (Fig. 3): two that control the speed of each wheel and a third that controls an effector that can pick up a ball. To pick up a ball this output must be above 0.5 when the robot is over the center of the ball. Once a ball is collected, it is dropped any time this effector output drops below 0.05. There are 10 hidden neurons and 10 context neurons. Each input neuron is connected to all hidden neurons. Each hidden neuron is connected to exactly one context neuron and each context neuron is connected to itself and all hidden neurons. The recursive nature of these connections enables memory because the networks can maintain data from previous states. Each hidden neuron is connected to all output neurons [7, 17]. The population size is 200 individuals. In each experiment, both treatments are run 50 times. All other parameters are identical to those in [17].

This problem is hard because no reward is given unless a robot navigates to a ball, closes its gripper to pick the ball up, keeps that gripper in the closed position while navigating to the lighted area, and releases the ball in the lighted area. Because none of these intermediate stepping stone behaviors are rewarded via the performance objective, evolutionary algorithms that are guided by only performance never solve the task [17].

The BDO and CTA treatments in this paper, which both reward for behavioral diversity, achieve perfect performance on this problem on average (Fig. 5). The increased difficulty of the problem is reflected in the larger number of generations required to solve it compared to the Deceptive Maze Problem (compare the range of the y axes of Fig. 4 and Fig. 5) and the fact that some runs in both treatments do not solve the problem after 15000 generations. On this more difficult problem, the addition of the Creative Thinking Ap-

[1] A video showing some of the evolved robot behaviors can be viewed at `EvolvingAI.com`

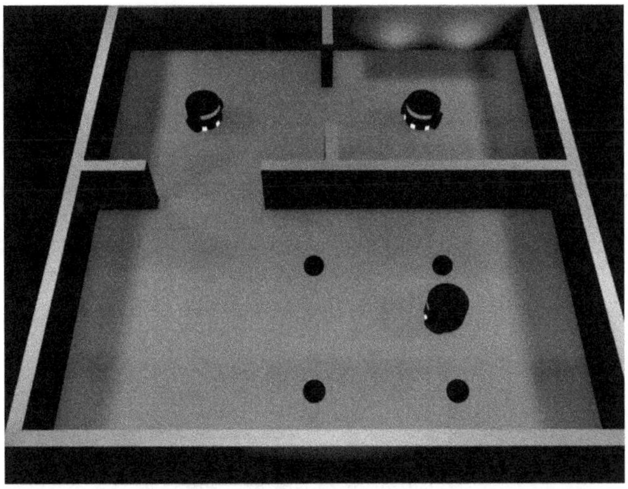

Figure 5: The Ball Collection Problem. The robot must collect balls one at a time and place them in the lighted area. There are twelve balls in total (four pictured). The robot's three starting locations (different location for each sub-trial) are shown. There are four balls per sub-trial whose initial locations are the same for all sub-trials.

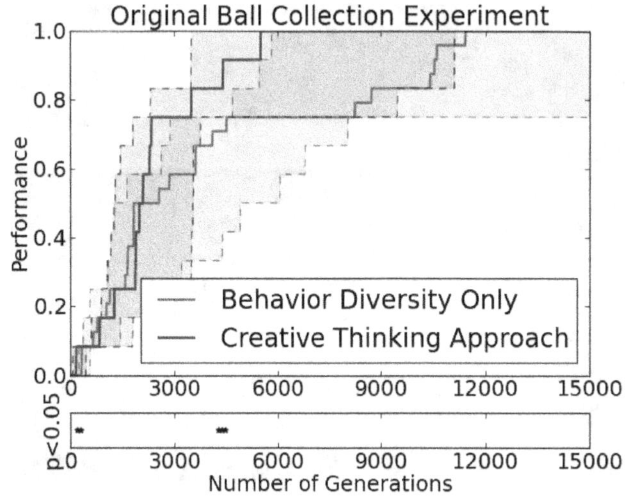

Figure 6: Results for the ball collection problem. Asterisks below the plot indicate generations in which the Creative Thinking Approach (CTA) performs significantly better than the behavioral diversity only (BDO) approach.

proach improves performance, although there is rarely any statistically significant advantage (Fig. 6).

3.3 An Even Harder Problem: Sequenced Ball Collection

To increase the difficulty further, in this problem a reward is only given if balls are placed in the lighted area in a predefined order (shown in Fig. 7). This order is the same for the three sets of four balls. On this more difficult problem, the addition of the Creative Thinking Approach improves performance, and does so significantly from around 38000 to 53000 generations (Fig. 8).

3.4 Another Hard Problem: The Balls in Corner Problem

To create another difficult version of the ball collection problem, we placed the balls in a compact area in a corner (Fig. 9). Doing so means that the robot is far less likely to encounter a ball by chance, for three reasons. First, the balls are in a smaller area, making it less likely for a robot to randomly encounter one of them. Secondly, in the default version of the problem, the balls surround the robot for one of its three starting positions (Fig. 5). While the robot's three starting positions remain the same for this version of the problem, because the balls are in the corner they no longer surround the robot, meaning that most directions from that starting location will not immediately lead to collecting a ball. Third, it is much less likely for a robot conducting a random or semi-random walk to make it deep into a corner due to collisions with walls. All three reasons make it less likely for the robot to initially, randomly encounter a ball, which greatly increases the difficulty of the problem. Recall that no fitness is gained until a ball is collected and placed in the lighted area, so there is no chance of a robot receiving any performance feedback if it does not at least first encounter a ball (let alone the other things it needs to do after picking a ball up).

On this difficult problem, the advantage of adding the Creative Thinking Approach is statistically significant at nearly every generation (Fig. 10). The median CTA run solves the problem in around 15000 generations, whereas the median run in the BDO treatment never solves the problem.

4. DISCUSSION

An objection to CTA may be its extra computational cost, especially as the size of the neural network and length of the evaluations increase. This same objection was mentioned as a potential problem with the behavioral diversity only (BDO) approach [6, 17], which includes all input and output values in the behavioral characterization [6, 17]. However, there are reasons why this objection is not a major concern. There are efficient algorithms for calculating Hamming distances between large vectors, and usually the computational cost of fitness evaluations dominates this cost [6, 17]. Moreover, while adding hidden neurons to the behavioral characterization increases the overall vector size, the number of hidden neurons is usually only a small factor larger than the number of input and output neurons, at least for most neural networks currently experimented with in the field of Evolutionary Robotics. As such, the algorithm is not slowed down exponentially. However, this concern could become a factor for neural networks with many times more hidden neurons than input and output neurons.

Techniques can also be applied to reduce computational costs while maintaining benefits of CTA. We can sample only a subset of neurons and/or time points. Additionally, techniques can be used to reduce the dimensionality of the data in the hidden-neuron vector, such as Principal Components Analysis [12], Independent Components Analysis [10], or more modern machine learning techniques [19, 1].

Even if the approach is computationally slower, it is better to have an approach that will eventually succeed if given

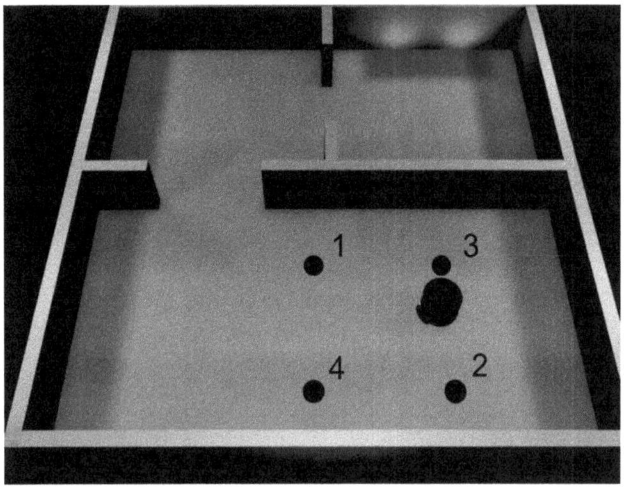

Figure 7: Sequenced Ball Collection Problem. Robots must collect the balls and place them in the lighted area in a predefined sequence. There are 12 balls in total (four pictured). The sequence for each set of four balls per sub-trial is the same.

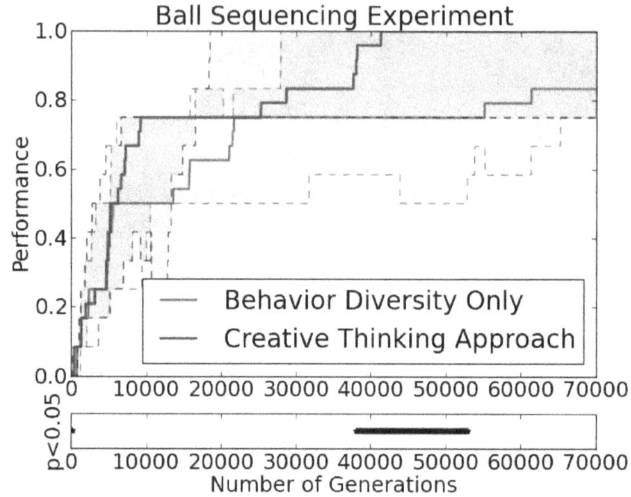

Figure 8: Results from the Sequenced Ball Collection problem.

enough computation, rather than an algorithm that will spin its wheels indefinitely. Similar arguments have been made for Novelty Search [14]. As such, if the CTA approach does increase the ability to solve some challenging tasks, as it appears to, it seems worthy of future investigation. Moreover, that the CTA can solve some problems in fewer generations than BDO suggests that it may actually save computation (Figs. 8 and 10). While these comparisons were made on generations, not actual running time, we did not notice that CTA ran slower: the fitness evaluations and the idiosyncrasies of evolutionary runs were the dominant factors that determined computational costs.

Another challenge for the Creative Thinking Approach is dealing with algorithms that evolve the number of hidden nodes, such as the NeuroEvolution of Augmenting Topologies algorithm [26]. Fortunately, that very algorithm offers a technical solution that makes it easy to conduct a principled comparison of vectors of hidden node activity even when those vectors are of different lengths. The answer is NEAT's historical marking scheme, which can keep track of which hidden neurons should be considered the same, from a historical (phylogenetic) perspective [26]. Explaining the details of that algorithm are beyond the scope of this paper, but NEAT's historical marking scheme, which can be applied to any topology-evolving neural network algorithm, should enable the CTA to align hidden node activation vectors in a principled fashion before calculating the Hamming distance between them. Neurons that are phylogenetically new in one network–and thus do not exist in the comparator network–can be compared to binary slots always set to zero in the comparator network's vector.

Another objection could be that the CTA is simply carrying out an exhaustive search. Importantly, however, while the CTA is exhaustively searching in neural firing space, that is far different from exhaustively searching in the much larger genomic search space. In fact, papers on the behavioral diversity only approach found that BDO worked as well as hand-designed behavioral characterizations that were much lower-dimensional [6]. That is because algorithms that reward behavioral diversity, like Novelty Search, search in the space of behaviors, which is not exhaustive search in the genome space [14, 13]. Like those algorithms, the CTA approach encourages evolution to learn how to produce new patterns of hidden neuron activity (in addition to behavior), which is a challenging space in which to search. It is not possible to simply search directly in the space of neural firing, because it is not known ahead of time which neural network topologies will lead to which patterns of behavior and hidden neuron firing. That problem is especially true when evolving neural networks with generative encodings, which feature an indirect mapping from the genome to a neural network, such as the popular HyperNEAT algorithm [25, 2, 9]. Thus CTA is not an exhaustive or random search in the extremely large genotype space (or even neural network space, for generative encodings). Rather, it searches for genomes that tend to produce novel thinking and novel behavior when mutated.

5. FUTURE WORK

As seen on the deceptive maze problem (Fig. 4), some problems do not require the Creative Thinking Approach and may be slowed down by it. It is thus useful to adjust the weight of rewards for diversity in hidden neurons accordingly. On harder problems, we see that the CTA and BDO are similar in performance (Figures 6, 8, 10) in early generations. We assume this is because generating novel behaviors is easier in early generations. We hypothesize that increasing the weight for diversity in hidden neurons as generation number increases will improve performance. Another, perhaps more informed and thus more effective approach, is to increase the reward for hidden neuron diversity as an inverse function of the behavioral diversity in the current generation. In other words, if the search is currently able to generate novel behaviors, do not add a reward for novel thinking; if the search for novel behaviors stagnates, increase the weight for creative thinking. Preliminary experiments suggest these approaches improve performance and in future work we will investigate them more thoroughly.

Another direction of future work is to investigate the Cre-

Figure 9: A harder version of the collection problem in which balls are hidden in the corner. Placing the balls in the corner makes the problem hard for three different reasons (see text), significantly increasing the problem difficulty.

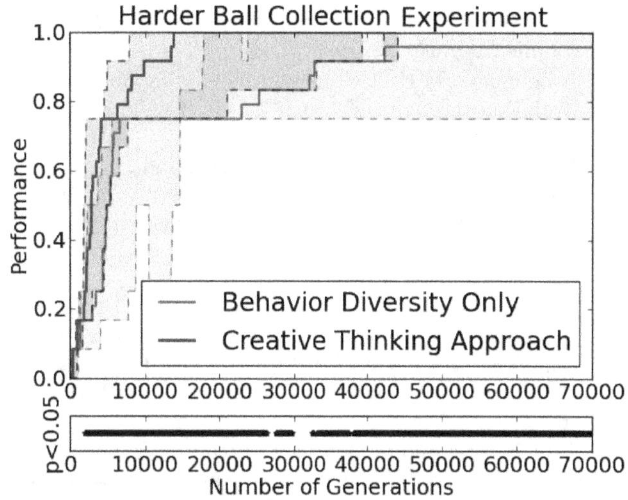

Figure 10: Results for the harder version of the ball collection experiment in which balls are hidden in the corner (Fig. 9). The addition of the Creative Thinking Approach significantly improves performance at nearly every generation.

ative Thinking Approach with recurrent neural networks on problems where remembering information would be helpful, but does not provide an immediate benefit. On such problems, the CTA could be a successful way of encouraging the search process to try creating robots that remember different things.

6. CONCLUSION

This paper introduced the Creative Thinking Approach, which encourages different patterns of firing in hidden neurons in addition to rewarding for novel behavior. In other words, thinking of neural networks as models of animal brains, it encourages robots to exhibit novel or creative thinking to help solve problems. We showed that, on challenging problems, the Creative Thinking Approach significantly outperforms a similar algorithm that rewards behavioral diversity only. We also introduced the concept of a novelty plateau, wherein the search process has no gradient to follow to produce new behaviors. Such novelty plateaus may help explain why rewarding creative thinking can help a search process: encouraging creative thinking rewards stepping stones on the path to generating new behaviors.

7. ACKNOWLEDGMENTS

We thank Jean-Baptiste Mouret, Stéphane Doncieux, Charles Ollion and the members of the Evolving AI Lab, especially Joost Huizinga, for their helpful roles in this research.

8. REFERENCES

[1] C.M. Bishop. *Pattern Recognition and Machine Learning (Information Science and Statistics)*. Springer-Verlag New York, Inc., Secaucus, NJ, USA, 2006.

[2] J. Clune, K.O. Stanley, R.T. Pennock, and C. Ofria. On the performance of indirect encoding across the continuum of regularity. *IEEE Transactions on Evolutionary Computation*, 15(4):346–367, 2011.

[3] C.A. Coello Coello. Evolutionary multi-objective optimization: a historical view of the field. *Computational Intelligence Magazine, IEEE*, 1(1):28–36, Feb 2006.

[4] K. Deb, A. Pratap, S. Agarwal, and T. Meyarivan. A fast and elitist multiobjective genetic algorithm: Nsga-ii. *Trans. Evol. Comp*, 6(2):182–197, April 2002.

[5] K. Deb. *Multi-Objective Optimization Using Evolutionary Algorithms*. John Wiley & Sons, Inc., New York, NY, USA, 2001.

[6] S. Doncieux and J.-B. Mouret. Behavioral diversity measures for evolutionary robotics. In *WCCI 2010 IEEE World Congress on Computational Intelligence, Congress on Evolutionary Computation (CEC)*, pages 1303–1310, 2010.

[7] J.L. Elman. Learning and development in neural networks: The importance of starting small. *Cognition*, 48(1):71–99, 1993.

[8] D. Floreano and C. Mattiussi. *Bio-inspired artificial intelligence: theories, methods, and technologies*. The MIT Press, 2008.

[9] J. Gauci and K.O. Stanley. Autonomous evolution of topographic regularities in artificial neural networks. *Neural Computation*, 22(7):1860–1898, 2010.

[10] A. Hyvärinen and E. Oja. Independent component analysis: Algorithms and applications. *Neural Netw.*, 13(4-5):411–430, May 2000.

[11] T. Jansen and I. Wegener. Evolutionary algorithms - how to cope with plateaus of constant fitness and when to reject strings of the same fitness. *Trans. Evol. Comp*, 5(6):589–599, December 2001.

[12] I.T. Jolliffe. *Principal Component Analysis*. Springer Verlag.

[13] J. Lehman and K.O. Stanley. Exploiting open-endedness to solve problems through the search

for novelty. In *Proceedings of Artificial Life XI*, volume 11, pages 329–336, 2008.

[14] J. Lehman and K.O. Stanley. Abandoning objectives: Evolution through the search for novelty alone. *Evolutionary Computation*, 19(2):189–223, 2011.

[15] J. Lehman, S. Risi, D.B. D'Ambrosio, and K.O. Stanley. Rewarding reactivity to evolve robust controllers without multiple trials or noise. In *Proceedings of the Artificial Life Conference*, volume 13, pages 379–386, 2012.

[16] J.-B. Mouret and S. Doncieux. SFERESv2: Evolvin' in the multi-core world. In *WCCI 2010 IEEE World Congress on Computational Intelligence, Congress on Evolutionary Computation (CEC)*, pages 4079–4086, 2010.

[17] J.-B. Mouret and S. Doncieux. Encouraging behavioral diversity in evolutionary robotics: an empirical study. *Evolutionary Computation*, 1(20), 2012.

[18] J.-B. Mouret and S. Doncieux. Overcoming the bootstrap problem in evolutionary robotics using behavioral diversity. In *Evolutionary Computation, 2009. CEC'09. IEEE Congress on*, pages 1161–1168. IEEE, 2009.

[19] K.P. Murphy. *Machine Learning: A Probabilistic Perspective (Adaptive Computation and Machine Learning series)*. The MIT Press, August 2012.

[20] E.S. Nicoară. Mechanisms to avoid the premature convergence of genetic algorithms. *Petroleum - Gas University of Ploiesti Bulletin, Mathematics - Informatics - Physics Series*, 61:87–96, 2009.

[21] C. Ollion, T. Pinville, and S. Doncieux. With a little help from selection pressures : evolution of memory in robot controllers. *Artificial Life*, 13:407–414, 2012.

[22] T. Rickards. *Creativity and Problem Solving at Work*. Gower Publishing, Ltd., 1997.

[23] A. Rogers and A. Prügel-Bennett. Genetic drift in genetic algorithm selection schemes. *IEEE Transactions on Evolutionary Computation*, 3(4):298–303, October 1999.

[24] C. Ryan. Reducing premature convergence in evolutionary algorithms, 1996.

[25] K.O. Stanley, D.B. D'Ambrosio, and J. Gauci. A hypercube-based encoding for evolving large-scale neural networks. *Artificial Life*, 15(2):185–212, 2009.

[26] K.O. Stanley and R. Miikkulainen. Evolving neural networks through augmenting topologies. *Evolutionary Computation*, 10(2):99–127, 2002.

[27] K.O. Stanley and R. Miikkulainen. A taxonomy for artificial embryogeny. *Artificial Life*, 9(2):93–130, 2003.

Coevolutionary Learning of Swarm Behaviors Without Metrics

Wei Li
Department of Automatic Control and Systems Engineering
The University of Sheffield, UK
wei.li11@sheffield.ac.uk

Melvin Gauci
Department of Automatic Control and Systems Engineering
The University of Sheffield, UK
m.gauci@sheffield.ac.uk

Roderich Groß
Department of Automatic Control and Systems Engineering
The University of Sheffield, UK
r.gross@sheffield.ac.uk

ABSTRACT

We propose a coevolutionary approach for learning the behavior of animals, or agents, in collective groups. The approach requires a replica that resembles the animal under investigation in terms of appearance and behavioral capabilities. It is able to identify the rules that govern the animals in an autonomous manner. A population of candidate models, to be executed on the replica, compete against a population of classifiers. The replica is mixed into the group of animals and all individuals are observed. The fitness of the classifiers depends solely on their ability to discriminate between the replica and the animals based on their motion over time. Conversely, the fitness of the models depends solely on their ability to 'trick' the classifiers into categorizing them as an animal. Our approach is metric-free in that it autonomously learns how to judge the resemblance of the models to the animals. It is shown in computer simulation that the system successfully learns the collective behaviors of aggregation and of object clustering. A quantitative analysis reveals that the evolved rules approximate those of the animals with a good precision.

Categories and Subject Descriptors

I.2.6 [**Artificial Intelligence**]: Learning—*Knowledge acquisition*; I.2.8 [**Artificial Intelligence**]: Problem Solving, Control Methods, and Search—*Heuristic methods*; I.2.9 [**Artificial Intelligence**]: Robotics—*Autonomous vehicles*

Keywords

animal behavior; coevolution; swarm robotics; evolutionary robotics; system identification; artificial life

1. INTRODUCTION

The scientific study of animal behavior, or ethology [2], is pursued not only because it is a subject of interest in itself, but also because the knowledge gained from it has several practical applications. For instance, models of animal decision-making processes can be used to predict their behavior in novel environments, which can help in making ecological conservation policy [26]. Knowledge about animal behaviors has also been applied for solving computational problems [8], and for constructing biologically-inspired robotic agents [22]. Swarm behaviors are emergent behaviors that arise from the interactions of a number of animals in a group, whose individual behaviors tend to be relatively simple [5]. A wide variety of swarm behaviors can be observed in nature, such as the aggregation of cockroaches [14] and foraging by ants [6]. Learning about the behaviors exhibited in such animal collectives is particularly challenging, as the individuals do not act independently of each other, and the motion of each individual is hard to predict.

Recent developments in science automation have shown that machines can autonomously conduct scientific investigations [15, 25]. In this paper, we propose a method that allows a machine to infer the rules of interaction between a group of homogeneous animals in an autonomous manner. The approach requires a replica that resembles the animal under investigation in terms of appearance and behavioral capabilities. It is based on a coevolutionary algorithm that comprises two competitive populations: one of *models*, to be executed on the replica, and the other of *classifiers*. The fitness of the classifiers depends solely on their ability to discriminate between the replica and the animals based on their motion. Conversely, the fitness of the models depends solely on their ability to 'trick' the classifiers into categorizing them as an animal. The approach does not rely on a pre-defined metric for judging the resemblance of models to the animal. Rather, such metrics are implicitly defined by the classifiers, and hence incorporated into the evolutionary process.

There are a number of works on system identification using coevolutionary algorithms [17, 16, 20]. Bongard and Lipson [4] proposed the *estimation-exploration algorithm*, a nonlinear system identification method to coevolve tests and models in a way that minimizes the amount of tests that have to be carried out on the system. They applied this method to evolve the parameters of models that approximate the morphology of a mobile robot after it undergoes physical damage. In [3], they reported that "in many cases the simulated robot would exhibit wildly different behaviors even when it very closely approximated the damaged 'physical' robot. This result is not surprising due to the

GECCO'14, July 12–16, 2014, Vancouver, BC, Canada.

http://dx.doi.org/10.1145/2576768.2598349.

fact that the robot is a highly coupled, non-linear system: thus similar initial conditions [...] are expected to rapidly diverge in behavior over time". Bongard and Lipson addressed this problem by using a more refined comparison metric reported in [3]. In [20], an alternative way of designing fitness functions based on Shannon information theory was used for model inference. All the works mentioned above rely on pre-defined metrics for gauging the difference between the target system and the model.

In experimental biology, researchers have used robots that interact with animals (e.g. ducks [27], cockroaches [12] and chicks [11]), in order to understand and model their behaviors. Robots can be created and systematically controlled in such a way that they are accepted as con- or heterospecifics by the animals in the group, which allows the researchers to learn the behavior of the animals [18, 24, 13]. We believe that this framework can be enhanced through the use of metric-free learning algorithms that infer the collective behaviors in an autonomous manner. In this paper, we present for the first time such an algorithm.

Li et al. [19] presented a coevolutionary approach for learning the behavior of a single animal that moved in a 1-D world. The system uses classifiers to distinguish between the models and the animal. Our system extends the framework in [19] to learn about the collective behavior of groups of animals. The classifiers decide whether an agent is an animal or the replica solely based on the motion data of this particular agent. We present two case studies in computer simulation showing that this information is sufficient to guide the learning of the collective behaviors of self-organized aggregation and object clustering.

This paper is organized as follows. Section 2 describes the animal simulation platform, the two swarm behaviors investigated in this paper as well as the implementation of the proposed coevolutionary algorithm. Section 3 discusses the results obtained. Section 4 concludes the paper.

2. METHODOLOGY

2.1 Animal Simulation Platform

We use the open-source library Enki [21]. Enki is able to model the kinematics and dynamics of the e-puck, which is a miniature, differential wheeled mobile robot [23]. The robot is a disk with a diameter of 7.4 cm and a height of 5.5 cm. The inter-wheel distance is 5.1 cm. The velocities of the left and right wheels along the ground can be set independently in $[-12.8, 12.8]$ cm/s. Enki generates noise for each wheel through multiplying its left and right speeds by random numbers in the range of $(0.95, 1.05)$ following uniform distribution.

The sensor of the robot is a line-of-sight sensor of unlimited range. At any given time, it returns one of a finite number of readings depending on what it is pointing towards. Note that it does not provide distance information. The sensor is implemented by projecting a line from the robot's front and checking whether it intersects with anything in the environment.

The length of the control cycle was set to 0.1 s, and the physics was updated at a rate of 10 times per control cycle. In the following, we refer to the simulated robots as 'animals' and 'replicas'.

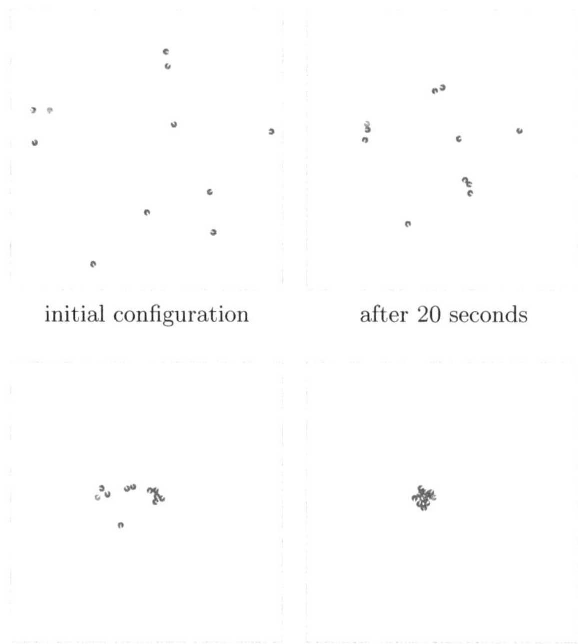

Figure 1: Snapshots of the aggregation behavior. A replica executing a model (red) is mixed into a group of ten animals (blue). All agents are observed by a population of classifiers, which co-evolve with the models. These classifiers attempt to tell apart the animals from the model.

2.2 Aggregation Behavior

2.2.1 *Rule of Aggregation Behavior*

We use the aggregation behavior reported in [10]. In this behavior, the line-of-sight sensor is binary: it gives a reading of $I = 1$ if there is an agent in the line of sight, and a reading of $I = 0$ otherwise. The environment is homogeneous, 2-D, and free of obstacles. The objective of the animals is to aggregate into a single, compact cluster as quick as possible. This behavior was validated with a swarm of 40 physical e-puck robots in [10].

Each animal decides how to move based on whether or not it can see another agent in its line of sight. Its rule is a mapping from each of the two possible sensor readings, $I = 0$ and $I = 1$, onto a pair of pre-defined velocities for the left and right wheels; it is an *if-then-else* rule. Let $\bar{v}_l, \bar{v}_r \in [-1, 1]$ represent the normalized left and right wheel velocities, respectively, where -1 (1) corresponds to the wheel rotating backwards (forwards) with maximum speed. The controller for the animal can be written as a quadruple,

$$\mathbf{p} = (\bar{v}_{l0}, \bar{v}_{r0}, \bar{v}_{l1}, \bar{v}_{r1}), \; \mathbf{p} \in [-1, 1]^4, \tag{1}$$

where $\bar{v}_{l0}$ refers to the normalized velocity of the left wheel when $I = 0$, and so on.

The optimal (memoryless) controller for aggregation was found by performing a grid search over the entire space of possible controllers within a finite resolution [10]. The resolution used was 21 settings per parameter, with each parameter taking values in the set:

$$\mathbf{s} = \{-1, -0.9, \ldots, -0.1, 0, 0.1, \ldots, 0.9, 1\}. \quad (2)$$

Therefore, $21^4 = 194481$ combinations were evaluated. The parameters of the optimal controller were given by

$$\mathbf{p}' = (-0.7, -1, 1, -1). \quad (3)$$

Now, we can describe the behavior of the animal as follows. When $I = 0$, it moves backwards along a clockwise circular trajectory. When $I = 1$, it rotates clockwise on the spot, with the maximum possible angular velocity. When employing this controller, a single robot provably aggregates with another robot, or cluster of robots [10].

2.2.2 *Experimental Setup*

In our setup, we use 11 agents (consisting of 10 animals and 1 replica that executes a model). They are initially placed in arbitrary positions, and facing in arbitrary directions in a (virtual) square of size 331.66 cm, such that the area per agent is, on average, 10000 cm^2. Fig. 1 shows snapshots of an example trial.

2.3 Object Clustering Behavior

2.3.1 *Rule of Object Clustering Behavior*

We use the object clustering behavior reported in [9]. The sensor of the animals used here is an extension of that in the aggregation behavior. Each animal has a line-of-sight sensor I, which indicates to the animal what it is pointing at: $I = 0$ if it is pointing at nothing (or the walls of the environment, if this is bounded), $I = 1$ if it is pointing at an object, and $I = 2$ if it is pointing at another agent. The aim of the animals is to push these objects into a single cluster as fast as possible. The behavior was validated using 5 physical e-puck robots and 20 cylindrical objects in [9].

The rule of the object clustering behavior is represented as a mapping from each of the three possible values onto a pair of velocities for the two wheels. The controller can thus be represented as a six-tuple:

$$\mathbf{q} = (\bar{v}_{l,0}, \bar{v}_{r,0}, \bar{v}_{l,1}, \bar{v}_{r,1}, \bar{v}_{l,2}, \bar{v}_{r,2}), \quad \mathbf{q} \in [-1, 1]^6, \quad (4)$$

where $\bar{v}_{l,0}$ denotes the normalized angular velocity of the left wheel when $I = 0$, etc. The controller was found using an evolutionary algorithm [9], and was given by:

$$\mathbf{q}' = (0.5, 1.0, 1.0, 0.5, 0.1, 0.5). \quad (5)$$

The behavior can be described as follows. When $I = 0$ and $I = 2$, the animal moves forward along an anti-clockwise circular trajectory, but with different linear and angular speeds. When $I = 1$, it moves forward along a clockwise circular trajectory.

2.3.2 *Experimental Setup*

In our setup, we use 10 cylindrical objects and 5 agents (consisting of 4 animals and 1 replica that executes a model). They are randomly placed in a (virtual) square of size 100 cm, so that the area per object is, on average, 1000 cm^2. Fig. 2 shows snapshots of an example trial.

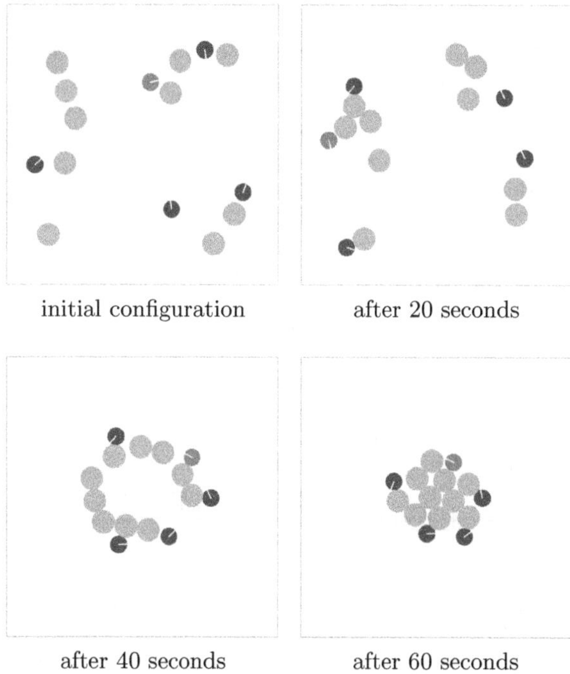

Figure 2: Snapshots of the object clustering behavior. There are 4 animals (blue), 1 replica executing a model (red), and 10 objects (green) to be pushed by them.

2.4 Coevolutionary Algorithm and Implementation

The coevolutionary algorithm is comprised of two populations: one of models, and one of classifiers, which coevolve with each other competitively.

The fitness of the classifiers depends solely on their ability to distinguish the behavior of the model from the behavior of the animals. The fitness of the models depends solely on their ability to mislead the classifiers into making the wrong judgment, that is, classifying them as an animal.

2.4.1 *Model Structure*

The model is executed on the replica, which resembles the animal under investigation in term of appearance and behavioral abilities. In particular, we assume that the replica has a disk body, two wheels and a line-of-sight sensor and that these are identical to the ones for the animal. The task is thus to estimate the parameters ($\mathbf{p}'$ and $\mathbf{q}'$), in the two behaviors. Note that different from Eqs. 1 and 4, the search space is unbounded. The fitness of the models depends solely on the performance of the classifiers, and that the latter do not have any knowledge about the model structure and parameters.

2.4.2 *Classifier Structure*

The structure of the classifiers is a recurrent Elman neural network [7] with two inputs, five hidden neurons, and one output neuron. Each neuron of the hidden and output layers has a bias. The network has a total of 46 parameters, which all assume values in $\mathbb{R}$. The activation function used in the hidden and the output neurons is the logistic sigmoid function, which has the range $(0, 1)$ and is defined as $\text{sig}(x) = 1/(1 + \exp(-(x)))\ \forall x \in \mathbb{R}$.

One of the inputs to the network is the linear speed (v) of the agent, and the other input is its angular speed (ω). In order to make the setup more feasible to implement on a physical system, it is assumed that the system cannot directly measure the linear and angular speeds of the agent, but rather its position and orientation at time t. The absolute value of the animal's linear speed is obtained by calculating the relative distance of the previous measured position and the current measured position, and then dividing the resulting number by the time interval between two measurements. When the angle between the animal's orientation and its direction of motion is smaller than 90 degrees (i.e. the animal is moving forward), we define the sign of the linear speed to be positive; otherwise, the linear speed is negative. The angular speed is calculated by subtracting the previous measured orientation from the current orientation, and dividing the resulting number by the time interval between two measurements.

In order to make a judgment between a model and an animal, the classifier observes the behavior (motion) of the agent over a period of time—here 10 s at 0.1 s intervals for a total of $T = 100$ time steps. After having iterated through all the time steps (a single trial), the final value of output neuron O is used to make a judgment: the classifier decides on a model if $O < 0.5$, and on an animal if $O \geq 0.5$. The memory of the classifier is reset after making a judgment. All the classifiers use the same data for each trial to make their own judgments. The initial positions of the animals and the replica are randomly generated in each trial.

2.4.3 *Optimization Algorithm*

The algorithm used here is based on a $(\mu + \lambda)$ evolution strategy with self-adaptive mutation strengths [1], and can be thought of as consisting of two sub-algorithms: one for the models, and another for the classifiers. The populations are treated identically, and they do not interact with each other except for the fitness calculation step (described in Sec. 2.4.4). The details of the implementation of the evolutionary algorithm can be found in [19].

2.4.4 *Fitness Calculation*

The populations in the coevolution comprise of 100 models and 100 classifiers. The fitness of each model is obtained by evaluating it with each of the classifiers in the competing population (100 in total). For every classifier that wrongly judges the model as being the animal, the model's fitness increases by 1. Therefore, the fitness takes a value in $\{0, 1, 2, \dots, 100\}$. The fitness value is then normalized to the interval $[0, 1]$.

The fitness calculation of the classifiers depends on the behavior investigated. For the aggregation behavior, in each trial, the fitness of each classifier is obtained by using it to evaluate 1 model and 10 animals. For the correct judgment of the model, the classifier's fitness increases by 0.5; for each correct judgment of the animal, the classifier's fitness increases by 0.05. Therefore, the fitness of each classifier in each trial is in the set $\{0, 0.05, 0.1, \dots, 1\}$. This evaluation is performed 100 times, and the fitness value of each classifier is then normalized to the interval $[0, 1]$. For the object clustering behavior, the method of calculation is analogous.

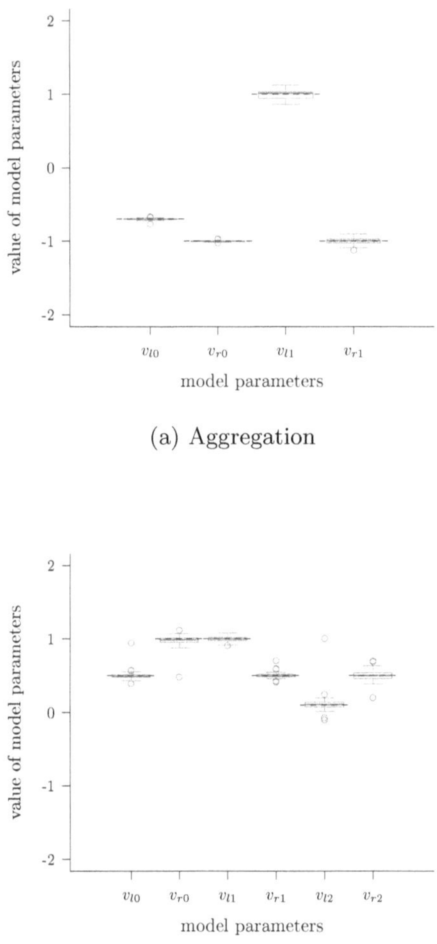

(a) Aggregation

(b) Object Clustering

Figure 3: This box-and-whisker plot shows the parameters of the evolved models with the highest subjective fitness in the 1000th generation in the coevolutions for (a) the aggregation behavior and (b) the object clustering behavior. Each box corresponds to 30 coevolutionary runs. The dotted lines correspond to the values of the parameters that the system is expected to learn (i.e. those of the animal).

3. RESULTS

3.1 Analysis of the Evolved Models

We performed 30 coevolutionary runs for each of the two setups described in Sec. 2. Each run lasted for 1000 generations. Fig. 3 shows a box plot[1] with the parameters of the evolved models with the highest subjective fitness in the final generation. As can be seen, the system identified the

[1]The box plots presented here are all as follows. The line inside the box represents the median of the data. The edges of the box represent the lower and the upper quartiles (25-th and 75-th percentiles) of the data, whereas the whiskers represent the lowest and the highest data points that are within 1.5 times the inter-quartile range from the lower and the upper quartiles, respectively. Circles represent outliers.

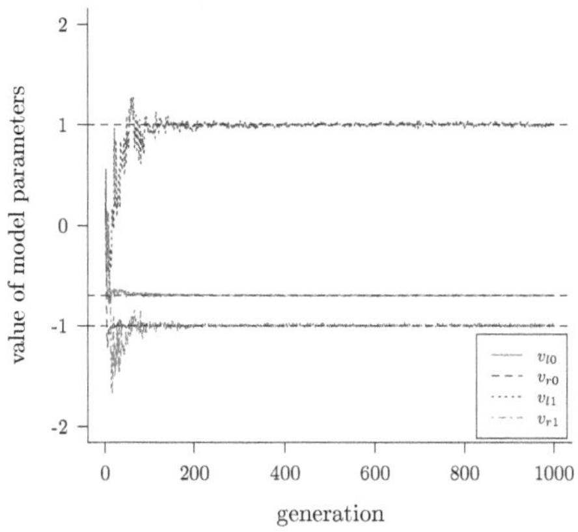

(a) Aggregation

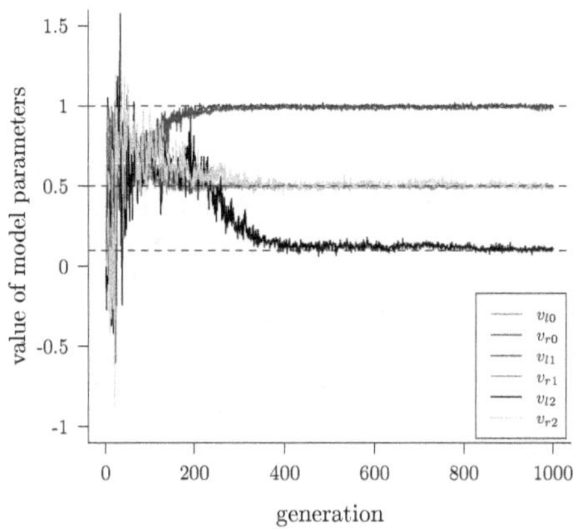

(b) Object Clustering

Figure 4: This plot shows how the model parameters evolve during the course of coevolution for (a) the aggregation behavior and (b) the object clustering behavior. The curves correspond to the median values from 30 coevolutionary runs.

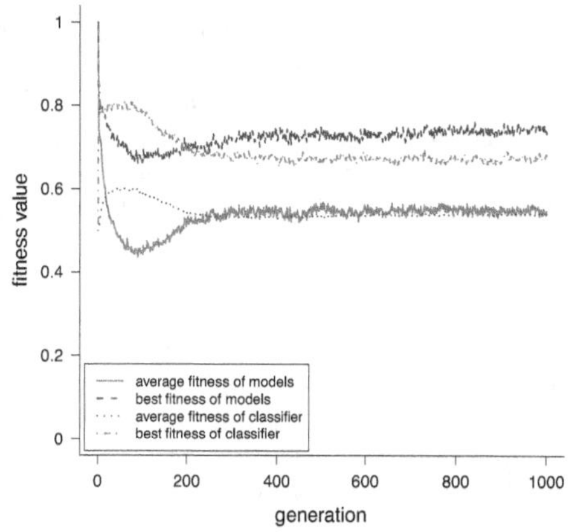

(a) Aggregation

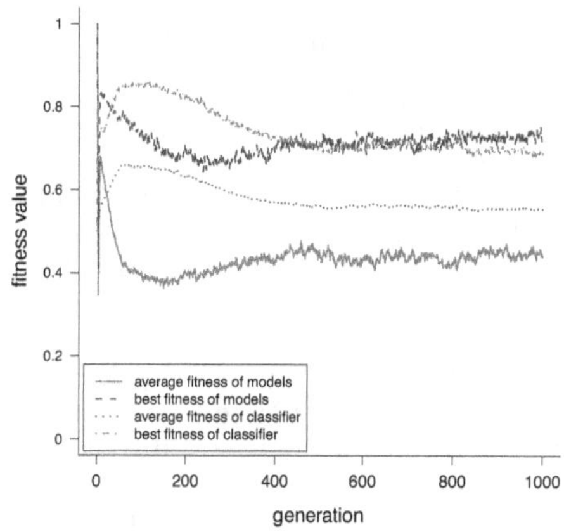

(b) Clustering Objects

Figure 5: This plot shows the subjective fitness of the classifiers and the models for (a) the aggregation behavior and (b) the clustering objects behavior. The curves show the average fitness across 30 coevolutionary runs.

parameters of these two behaviors with a good accuracy. For the case of aggregation, the relative error of the median of the four evolved parameters with respect to those of the animal is 0.23%, 0.13%, 1.03%, and 0.37%, respectively. For the case of object clustering, the relative error of each evolved parameters is 1.13%, 1.18%, 0.24%, 0.04%, 8.41%, and 0.36%, respectively.

We also investigate how the model parameters are learned during the course of coevolution for the two behaviors. Fig. 4 shows the convergence of the parameters over generations. In the aggregation behavior, the rule corresponding to $I = 0$ is first to be learned, as after about the 60th generation, both v_{l0} and v_{r0} closely approximated their true values (-0.7 and -1.0). For $I = 1$, it took about 140 generations for v_{l1} and v_{r1} to converge. This is due to the fact that the chance of the agents not seeing each other is higher than that of the agents seeing each other.

In the object clustering behavior, the parameters which correspond to the cases of $I = 0$ and $I = 1$ are learned faster than the other two parameters, as shown in the Fig. 4(b). After about 200 generations, v_{l0}, v_{r0}, v_{l1} and v_{r1} started to converge; however it took about 360 generations for v_{l2} and v_{r2} to approximate their true values. This phenomenon can be explained as follows. Since there are fewer robots than objects, the chance of the agents seeing each other is lower than that of the agents seeing objects or nothing.

A video showing both the learning process and a swarm of replicas (executing an evolved model of the final generation) is available in the supplementary material.

3.2 Coevolutionary Dynamics

In order to analyze how the classifiers and the models interact with each other during the course of the coevolution, we investigate the dynamics of the subjective fitness of the classifiers and the models as shown in Fig. 5.

In the aggregation behavior, at the beginning, the fitness of the classifiers is 0.5 as they output 1 for all the animals and models, which means the classifiers make uninformed decisions[2]. Therefore, the fitness of the models starts from 1.0, as all the classifiers judge them as the animal. Then, the fitness of the classifiers quickly increases, corresponding to the decline of model fitness. As the models learn to adapt, the fitness of the classifiers only increases slightly until about the 100th generation. After that, the fitness of the models starts to increase. The fitness of the models surpasses that of the classifiers after about the 200th generation; at this point, the fitness of the best models is around 0.7. This means that the models are able to mislead 70% of the classifiers into judging it as the animal. From the 200th generation onwards, the fitness of the classifiers and models remains "balanced" until the last generation.

The coevolutionary dynamics of the object clustering behavior is similar. However, the average fitness of classifiers remains higher than that of the models after the initial peak. This could be explained by the higher number of parameters and the higher complexity of the behavior to be evolved.

3.3 Post-Evaluation of the Evolved Classifiers

For the sake of simplicity, in the following sections, we only analyze the aggregation behavior. We analyze the best evolved classifiers from the last generation of each coevolutionary run; therefore, there are 30 classifiers to be evaluated in total. We evaluate the performance of each classifier when the parameters of the animals are disturbed. Here, we change one parameter at a time while keeping the other three parameters identical to those of the animal. We consider the parameter values shown in Eq. 2. Therefore, there are $21 \cdot 4 = 84$ combinations to be tested by each classifier. For each combination, we performed 100 trials and calculated the average fitness of the classifier.

In order to evaluate the performance of the classifiers, we defined the following metric:

$$W = \frac{1}{\Omega} \sum_{j=1}^{4} \sum_{\substack{i=1, \\ x_i \neq p_j}}^{20} \frac{\bar{f}_{ij}}{|x_i - p_j|}, \tag{6}$$

where, p_j is one of the parameters of the animal from Eq. 3, x_i is one of the parameter values from Eq. 2, and $\bar{f}_{ij}$ is the average fitness of the evaluated classifier over 100 trials where we assign a value x_i to the parameter p_j. $\Omega = 160.66$ is the maximum value that the double sum can achieve (i.e. if all the $\bar{f}_{ij}$'s are equal to 1). This metric penalizes small values of $\bar{f}_{ij}$ for each combination, and gives more emphasis to small distances of $|x_i - p_j|$. As all the classifiers have a low fitness value in the case of $x_i = p_j$, this is not considered in the metric.

The best classifier according to the metric (Eq. 6) had a value of $W = 0.81$. The average fitness of this classifier over 100 trials per combination is shown in Fig. 6. The classifier is most sensitive to changes in v_{r1}, followed by v_{r0}, v_{l0} and v_{l1}. There is a sudden jump when v_{r0} and v_{r1} deviate from the target value (of the animal), suggesting that the classifier can discriminate very well between the animal and models

[2]Note that in the implementation of the coevolutionary algorithm, the parameters of the models and classifiers are initialized to 0, which means all the classifiers are identical at the 1st generation.

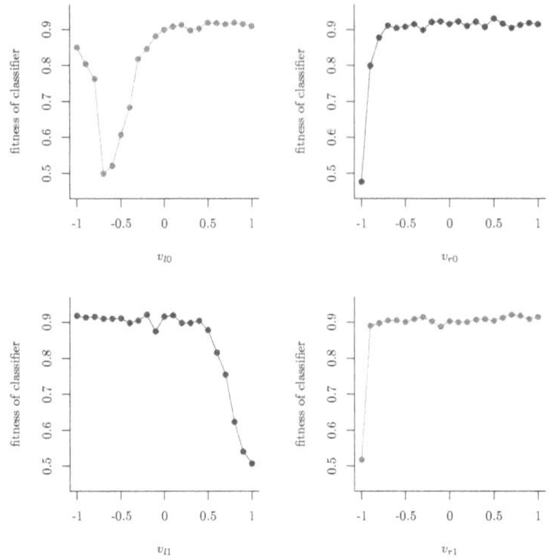

Figure 6: This plot shows the average fitness of the best classifier when the parameters of the animal are disturbed in the aggregation behavior. There is only one parameter changing at a time. See the text for details.

that do not approximate particular well these parameters. For the disturbance of the left wheel speed, v_{l0} and v_{l1}, the fitness curve of the classifier changes more smoothly. In all the four cases, when the parameter is close to its target value (i.e. the replica is behaving like the animals), the classifier has a fitness value of around 0.5. We have verified from the data that it judges almost every agent as an animal, which is correct when the model is *exactly* like the animal.

We also analyze the scalability of the best classifier with respect to the number of agents in the mixed group. Fig. 7 shows the average fitness of the best classifier over 100 trials when changing the number of animals. In each trial, the model parameters for a single replica are randomly generated in $[-1.0, 1.0]$. The average fitness of the classifier is not affected by the variation of the number of animals except for the cases that there are few animals in the group. For instance, in the case of 1 animal and 1 model, the fitness of the classifier declined to 0.82. Since there are only two agents in the environment, they do not interact with each other too often to reveal their full behavior. This influences the judgment of the classifier.

3.4 Noise Study

We conducted a study to investigate how the performance of the system is affected by noise on the measurements of the agents' position and orientation. As the e-puck robot has a maximum linear speed of 12.8 cm/s, the maximum distance that it can travel in one control cycle (0.1 s) is 1.28 cm. For this reason, we define a disturbance of 1.28 cm to an agent's position as a measurement error of 100%. Similarly, we define a 100% measurement error on the agent's orientation as the maximum change in orientation that an e-puck can undergo in one control cycle. This corresponds to 0.5 rad.

We conducted 5 sets of 30 coevolutions for the noise values $M = \{0, 25, 50, 75, 100\}\%$. In a coevolution with a noise value M, every measurement of an agent's position is perturbed in a random direction and by a random distance chosen uniformly in $[0, 1.28\frac{M}{100}]$ cm. Similarly, every orien-

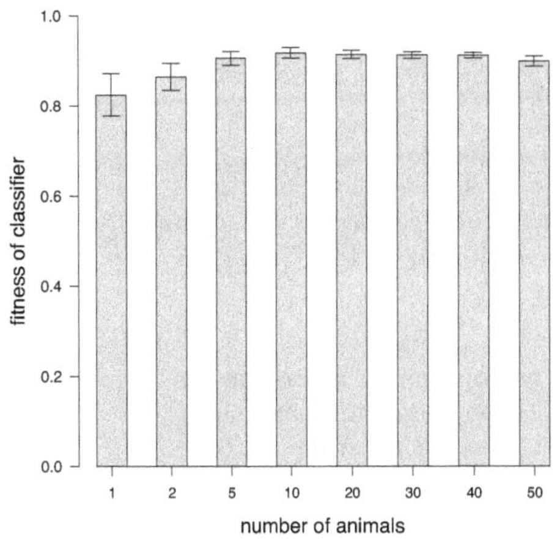

Figure 7: This plot shows the average fitness of the best classifier for different numbers of animals in the aggregation behavior. In each trial, a single replica was present and the model parameters were randomly generated in $[-1.0, 1.0]$.

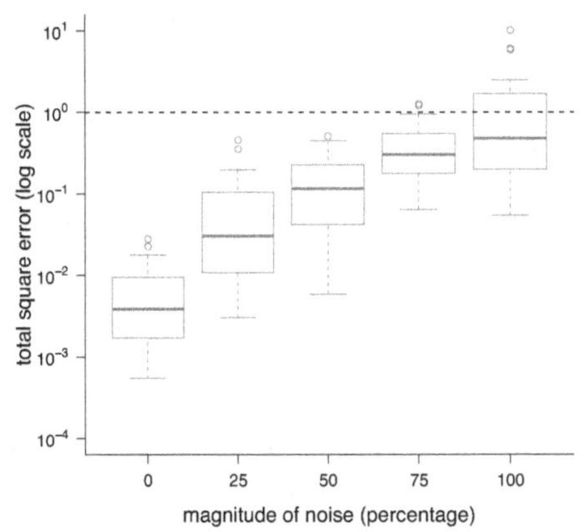

Figure 8: This plot shows the total square error of the evolved parameters when increasing the percentage of noise on the measurements of the agents' position and orientation in the aggregation behavior. Each box corresponds to 30 coevolutionary runs. See the text for details.

tation measurement is perturbed by a random angle chosen uniformly in $\left[-0.5\frac{M}{100}, 0.5\frac{M}{100}\right]$.

Fig. 8 shows the total square error of the evolved parameters in the final generations of the coevolutions. This plot reveals that the system still performs relatively well when a considerable amount of noise affects the agents' motion tracking system.

3.5 Scalability Study

We performed a further study on the aggregation behavior with 50 animals and 1 replica in the environment. However, instead of observing the trajectories of all the agents, the classifiers only observed the trajectory of the replica and of a single, randomly-chosen animal in each trial. Fig. 9 shows the parameters of the evolved models with the highest subjective fitness in the 1000th generation over 30 coevolutionary runs. All the four parameters are well approximated. The relative error of the median of the four evolved parameters with respect to those of the animal is 0.44%, 0.43%, 0.69%, and 0.38%, respectively.

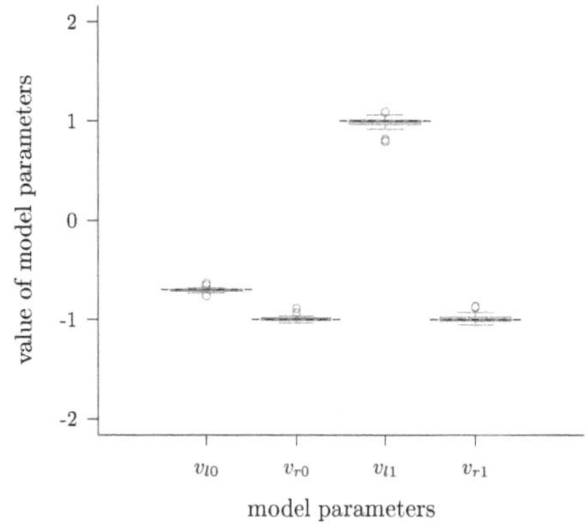

Figure 9: This plot shows the scalability of the coevolutionary approach. There are 1 replica and 50 animals in the group. The classifiers only observe two trajectories: one from the replica, the other from a randomly chosen animal.

4. CONCLUSIONS

This paper has presented a coevolutionary method that can autonomously learn the behavior of a group of animals, or other agents through observation. In principle, our approach does not require any prior information about the behavior. It does not rely on any pre-defined metric to gauge the difference between the animal and the model. Rather, such metrics are implicitly defined by the classifiers themselves, and hence incorporated into the evolutionary process. This eliminates the biasing effect that pre-defined metrics can have on the solutions obtained.

Using this approach, the system successfully learned two swarm behaviors (self-organized aggregation and object clustering) with a good accuracy in the model parameters obtained. We also analyzed the performance of the best classifier in the aggregation behavior, and found that it could discriminate between models and animals based on a relatively small difference in only a single parameter. When changing the number of animals in the environment, the judgment of the classifier was only affected if the number of agents was very low, which is not typical in a swarm behavior. The method proved robust with respect to noise in the motion tracking system.

The results suggest that what constitutes collective behaviors can be fully characterised by the effects that the interactions have on the individual in the group. In other words, rather than analyzing how a group of animals interact with each other, it is sufficient to observe the trajectory of a single individual. The major advantage of this approach is scalability. In principle, our learning technique would only have to processes a constant amount of information (e.g. data from 1 animal and 1 replica, as shown in this paper), regardless of the number of animals in the group.

In the future, we intend to perform experiments using physical robots and real animals, and apply our approach to other more complex social behaviors.

References

[1] H.-G. Beyer. *The Theory of Evolution Strategies*. Springer, Berlin, Heidelberg, Germany, 2001.

[2] J. J. Bolhuis and L.-A. Giraldeau. *The Behavior of Animals: Mechanisms, Function, and Evolution*. Wiley, Hoboken, NJ, 2004.

[3] J. Bongard and H. Lipson. Automated robot function recovery after unanticipated failure or environmental change using a minimum of hardware trials. In *Proceedings of 2004 NASA/DoD Conference on Evolvable Hardware*, pages 169–176, Seattle, WA, June 2004.

[4] J. Bongard and H. Lipson. Nonlinear system identification using coevolution of models and tests. *IEEE Transactions on Evolutionary Computation*, 9(4):361–384, 2005.

[5] S. Camazine et al. *Self-Organization in Biological Systems*. Princeton University Press, Princeton, NJ, 2001.

[6] C. R. Carroll and D. H. Janzen. Ecology of foraging by ants. *Annual Review of Ecology and Systematics*, 4:231–257, 1973.

[7] J. L. Elman. Finding structure in time. *Cognitive Sci.*, 14(2):179–211, 1990.

[8] D. Floreano and C. Mattiussi. *Bio-Inspired Artificial Intelligence: Theories, Methods, and Technologies*. MIT Press, Cambridge, MA, 2008.

[9] M. Gauci, J. Chen, W. Li, T. J. Dodd, and R. Groß. Clustering objects with robots that do not compute. In *Proceedings of the 13th International Conference on Autonomous Agents and Multiagent Systems*, IFAAMAS, Richland, SC. In press.

[10] M. Gauci, J. Chen, W. Li, T. J. Dodd, and R. Groß. Self-organized aggregation without computation. *International Journal of Robotics Research*. In press.

[11] A. Gribovskiy, J. Halloy, J.-L. Deneubourg, H. Bleuler, and F. Mondada. Towards mixed societies of chickens and robots. In *Proceedings of the 2010 IEEE/RSJ International Conference on Intelligent Robots and Systems*, pages 4722–4728, Boston, MA, October 2010.

[12] J. Halloy et al. Social integration of robots into groups of cockroaches to control self-organized choices. *Science*, 318(5853):1155–1158, 2007.

[13] J. Halloy, F. Mondada, S. Kernbach, and T. Schmickl. Towards bio-hybrid systems made of social animals and robots. In *Biomimetic and Biohybrid Systems*, volume 8064 of *Lecture Notes in Computer Science*, pages 384–386. Springer, Berlin, Heidelberg, Germany, 2013.

[14] R. Jeanson et al. Self-organized aggregation in cockroaches. *Animal Behaviour*, 69(1):169–180, 2005.

[15] R. D. King et al. The automation of science. *Science*, 324(5923):85–89, 2009.

[16] S. Koos, J. Mouret, and S. Doncieux. Automatic system identification based on coevolution of models and tests. In *Proceedings of 2009 IEEE Congress on Evolutionary Computation*, pages 560–567, Trondheim, Norway, May 2009.

[17] B. Kouchmeshky, W. Aquino, J. Bongard, and H. Lipson. Co-evolutionary algorithm for structural damage identification using minimal physical testing. *International Journal for Numerical Methods in Engeering*, 69(5):1085–1107, 2007.

[18] J. Krause, A. F. Winfield, and J.-L. Deneubourg. Interactive robots in experimental biology. *Trends in Ecology and Evolution*, 26(7):369–375, 2011.

[19] W. Li, M. Gauci, and R. Groß. A coevolutionary approach to learn animal behavior through controlled interaction. In *Proceedings of the 15th Annual Conference of Genetic and Evolutionary Computation*, pages 223–230, Amsterdam, Netherlands, July 2013.

[20] D. Ly and H. Lipson. Optimal experiment design for coevolutionary active learning. *IEEE Transactions on Evolutionary Computation*, PP(99):1–11, 2013.

[21] S. Magnenat, M. Waibel, and A. Beyeler. Enki: The fast 2D robot simulator, 2011.

[22] J.-A. Meyer and A. Guillot. Biologically inspired robots. In B. Siciliano and O. Khatib, editors, *Springer Handbook of Robotics*, Springer Handbooks, pages 1395–1422. Springer, Berlin, Heidelberg, Germany, 2008.

[23] F. Mondada, M. Bonani, X. Raemy, J. Pugh, C. Canci, A. Klaptocz, S. Magnenat, J.-C. Zufferey, D. Floreano, and A. Martinoli. The e-puck, a robot designed for education in engineering. In *Proceedings of the 9th Conference on Autonomous Robot Systems and Competitions*, volume 1, pages 59–65, 2009.

[24] T. Schmickl et al. Assisi: Mixing animals with robots in a hybrid society. In *Biomimetic and Biohybrid Systems*, volume 8064 of *Lecture Notes in Computer Science*, pages 441–443. Springer, Berlin, Heidelberg, Germany, 2013.

[25] M. Schmidt and H. Lipson. Distilling free-form natural laws from experimental data. *Science*, 324(5923):81–85, 2009.

[26] W. J. Sutherland. The importance of behavioural studies in conservation biology. *Animal Behaviour*, 56(4):801–809, 1998.

[27] R. Vaughan, N. Sumpter, J. Henderson, A. Frost, and S. Cameron. Experiments in automatic flock control. *Robotics and Autonomous Systems*, 31(1):109–117, 2000.

Evolving Joint-Level Control with Digital Muscles

Jared M. Moore
Dept of Computer Science and Engineering
Michigan State University
East Lansing, MI, USA
moore112@msu.edu

Philip K. McKinley
Dept of Computer Science and Engineering
Michigan State University
East Lansing, MI, USA
mckinley@cse.msu.edu

ABSTRACT

The neuromuscular systems of animals are governed by extremely complex networks of control signals, sensory feedback loops, and mechanical interactions. Morphology and control are inherently intertwined. In the case of animal joints, groups of muscles work together to provide power and stability to move limbs in a coordinated manner. In contrast, many robot controllers handle both high-level planning and low-level control of individual joints. In this paper, we propose a joint-level control method, called *digital muscles*, that operates in a manner analogous to biological muscles, yet is abstract enough to apply to conventional robotic joints. An individual joint is controlled by multiple muscle *nodes*, each of which responds to a control signal according to a node-specific activation function. Evolving the physical orientation of muscle nodes and their respective activation functions enables relatively complex and coordinated gaits to be realized with simple high-level control. Even using a sinusoid as the high-level control signal, we demonstrate the evolution of effective gaits for a simulated quadruped. The proposed model realizes a control strategy for governing the behavior of individual joints, and can be coupled with a high-level controller that focuses on decision making and planning.

Categories and Subject Descriptors

I.2.9 [**Computing Methodologies**]: Artificial Intelligence—*Robotics, Autonomous vehicles*

Keywords

Evolutionary robotics, digital muscles, joint-level control, simulation, bio-inspired design

1. INTRODUCTION

Biological organisms demonstrate a remarkable level of complexity in both their bodies and brains. Together, morphology and control coordinate movements among multiple joints [6,8], each of which is governed by groups of muscles. Multiple muscles work together to express different behaviors, from simple locomotion to fine motor skills [7, 12]. In contrast, robotic joints are often implemented using single degree of freedom (DOF) actuators, manipulated by robotic controllers that are relatively decoupled from the underlying robot morphology. Our work explores the integration and co-evolution of joint-level control and joint morphology, which together respond to high-level control signals in order to produce movements.

GECCO'14, July 12–16, 2014, Vancouver, BC, Canada.

http://dx.doi.org/10.1145/2576768.2598373 .

In this paper, we propose a digital muscle model that emulates the function of biological muscles, yet is abstract enough to apply to engineered systems and biological study. Receiving commands from a high-level controller, muscle groups define the movement repertoire of individual joints. The model integrates aspects of both morphology and control, which are evolved together. By delegating joint-level control to muscle groups, a high-level controller is free to address complex tasks and decision making.

The digital muscle model helps to bridge the gap between control and morphology. Instead of being explicitly encoded in the genome, aspects such as joint ranges *emerge* from the interaction between components of the model and the environment. Here, we apply the digital muscle model to the evolution of locomotion in quadruped animats. Evolved agents demonstrate effective gaits that exhibit symmetry and coordination among individual joints, even though they are driven by a single, shared sinusoidal control signal. We emphasize that this model is not intended to replicate the functionality of physical muscles, but rather to provide an abstraction of joint-level control that can be mapped into robotic systems or used to help understand the evolution of natural organisms.

The remainder of this paper is organized as follows. Background and related work are presented in Section 2. The proposed digital muscle model is described in Section 3. Experiments are detailed in Section 4 with results following in Section 5. Possible applications of the model are presented in Section 6, while Section 7 offers conclusions and discusses future work.

2. BACKGROUND AND RELATED WORK

Evolutionary robotics [3, 5, 10, 16, 24, 28] draws upon concepts from natural evolution and applies them to the design of (simulated or physical) robots [4,22]. Controllers such as artificial neural networks (ANNs) [31] and central pattern generators (CPGs) [18] are particularly amenable to evolutionary optimization, having proven successful in many forms of robotic locomotion, including salamander gaits [13], bipedal walking [27], and crawling [14]. Typically, these controllers produce high-level signals to govern the movement of each joint, such as specifying the desired angle of an actuator. In addition, a single control strategy often addresses multiple aspects of behavior, from high-level decision making down to the individual joint-level commands [21]. In contrast, the movement of natural organisms is a complex interaction between an individual's neuromuscular and musculoskeletal systems.

In nature, morphology and control evolve together to produce effective behaviors. In the case of a robot, the inclusion of morphology in the evolutionary process can greatly increase the robustness of an individual [2]. The embodiment of a controller within a morphology [26] allows for a high degree of integration between the two. Bongard and Paul [25] demonstrated the importance of co-evolving control and morphology in a biped robot platform; small changes to the robot's mass distribution had large effects on the resultant gait. Other studies have shown success in modular self-organizing systems [17] and the development of locomotion strategies for robots with different morphologies [1]. Doncieux and Meyer [9] have shown that it may be difficult, if not impossible, to develop complex control strategies without structural modularity in neural networks. In the proposed digital muscle model, we focus on evolving parameters that affect aspects of both joint control and joint morphology. Whether modularity associated with joint-level control adds further benefits remains an open question.

Lessin et al. [15] developed models of physical muscles that connect rigid bodies, with movement determined by a variable spring constant. Actuation occurs when the constant is changed, resulting in contraction or expansion of the simulated muscle. In these virtual creatures, the evolution of multiple behaviors was investigated, with natural looking movements provided by the muscle-based effectors. Geijtenbeek et al. [11] demonstrated virtual bipeds, controlled by simulated muscles, capable of walking on both flat and varying surfaces. Muscles are simulated with physical properties governing attachment points, contraction paths and actuation parameters that are determined through optimization. Gaits are effective in different morphologies, demonstrating realistic movements for the virtual creatures. While promising, these systems emulate physical muscles directly, which may complicate their mapping into some types of robotic actuators. The proposed digital muscle model does not consider muscles to be effectors in the traditional sense. Instead, the model is abstract, providing commands that govern the movement of actuators, while enabling evolved solutions to be mapped into joints driven by various types of actuators.

3. DIGITAL MUSCLE MODEL

Biological muscles provide the power necessary for organisms to move and interact with their environment [8]. Working in antagonistic pairs, muscles allow for flexion and extension of individual joints, coordinated by neural systems [6,7]. Although in some cases movement may appear to occur within a single DOF (for example, a knee extending), multiple muscles work together to both move and stabilize a joint. The proposed digital muscle model provides an abstract control layer that emulates the fundamental properties of biological muscles, while still being suitable for realization in terms of conventional robotic actuators. Aspects of both control and morphology are integrated in the model, allowing for both to be evolved simultaneously.

Figure 1 depicts a simple example of the digital muscle model. Movement of the lower segment is controlled by four muscle *nodes*, whose locations and activation functions are evolved. All nodes in a muscle group receive the same signal from a controller (in this paper a simple sinusoid), with the *activation function* of each individual node determining its behavior. The combined responses of the muscle nodes along with their evolved positions determine the behavior of the joint. In Figure 1 the muscle nodes are equally spaced around the joint, but in general these locations are evolved.

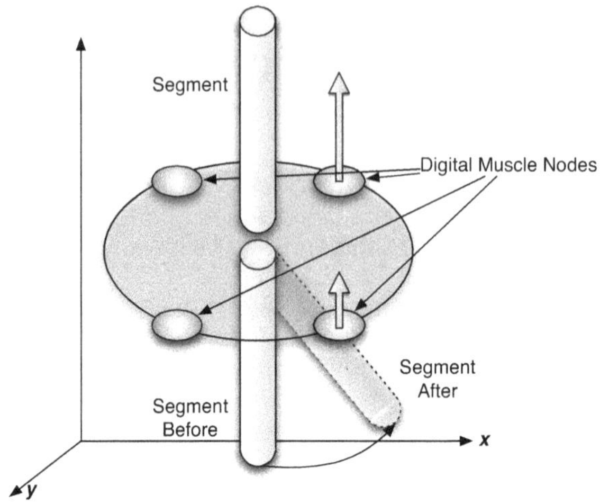

Figure 1: A digital muscle group controls one joint in an animat. The muscle group is composed of nodes, radially distributed around a joint on a 2D plane. Conceptually, nodes exert a pulling force, which draws the limb segment towards the node's position on the plane. Movement of a joint is calculated by aggregating the pulling forces. The outputs of a digital muscle group dictate the movement of a joint in a physics simulation engine. Antagonistic relationships can emerge between nodes leading to coordinated movement of a joint.

Control.

The activation function of a digital muscle node governs when and how strongly it *contracts*, that is, pulls on a limb segment. This pulling force determines how far and fast a limb segment moves toward the node's location relative to the joint. Activation functions can be any function that maps an input signal to a corresponding output value. For this study, activation functions are Gaussians with evolvable parameters: μ (center), σ^2 (spread) and α (magnitude). Nodes are limited to positive exertion values, similar to the function of natural muscles, which are only capable of active contraction. Consequently, at least two nodes, aligned as an antagonistic pair, are necessary to have both flexion and extension in a joint.

Morphology.

Figure 2 shows the spatial component of muscle nodes, namely, where they are located with respect to their associated joint. Each node has an evolvable parameter that defines its position on a unit circle around the joint. This position determines which direction the limb will be pulled when a node contracts. Relative positions of muscle nodes evolve over generations. The result may be a joint with a wide range of motion, as in a human shoulder, or one with limitations, as in a knee joint.

Motor Control Signal Generation.

The activation functions of the nodes in a muscle group collectively define the response of the joint to an input signal. Activation functions for a sample group with 4 nodes can be seen in Figure 3. In the figure, an input signal value of -0.5 results in nodes 0, 1, and 2 exerting themselves with activations of 0.77, 0.42, and 0.28, respectively. For example, if the nodes were aligned as shown in Figure 2, then movement of the limb would be away from node 3, which does not contract at inputs under -0.1.

Joint behavior is calculated by combining the activation outputs from all nodes in a group for a given input value. The outputs for

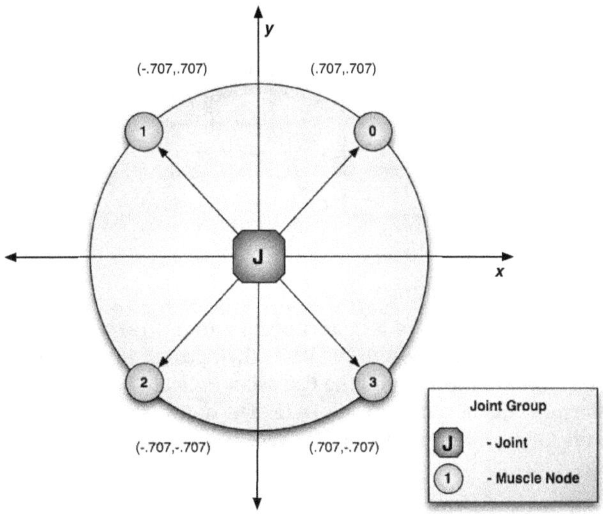

Figure 2: A top down view of an individual muscle group consisting of four nodes placed radially around a joint. Each node has both an activation function and a spatial component. Together, these determine the strength and direction of pull placed on a joint by the individual node.

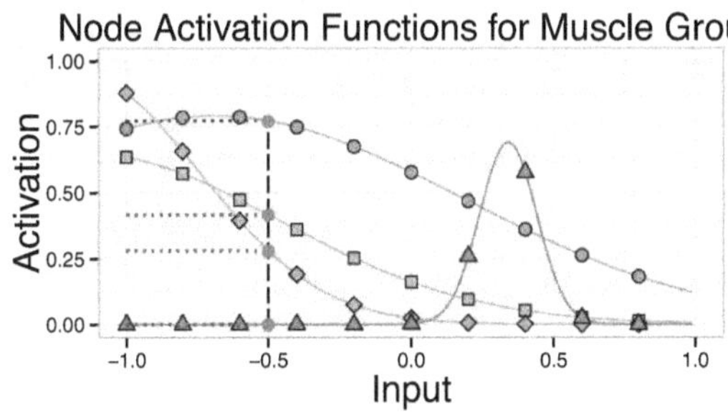

Figure 3: Activation functions for four nodes in a muscle group. An input signal determines the response of nodes according to the Gaussian activation functions for each. The values of the activation functions for an input signal of -0.5 are highlighted.

each node are projected into two values, one for each axis of the 2-DOF joint, according to the activation output and (x,y) coordinate of each node in a group. Figure 4 shows the results of aggregating the muscle node activations plotted in Figure 3. In this manner, both the activation function of each node and its spatial location contribute to the response of the joint. The response is an emergent property of the model, rather than directly dependent upon the specific activation function or single evolved parameter. Joint movement speeds are calculated as the difference between current and desired joint positions for the next time step. (The speed of movement may be included as an output in the model in future extensions.)

Figure 5 shows the mapping of a high-level control signal (in this case a simple sinusoidal wave) to the response of a hip joint in a quadruped. A muscle group, composed of multiple nodes, is mapped to a single joint in an animat. Each muscle group receives a single control signal which is distributed to the nodes. A high-level controller then needs only to provide one signal per joint, rather than unique signals for each muscle node.

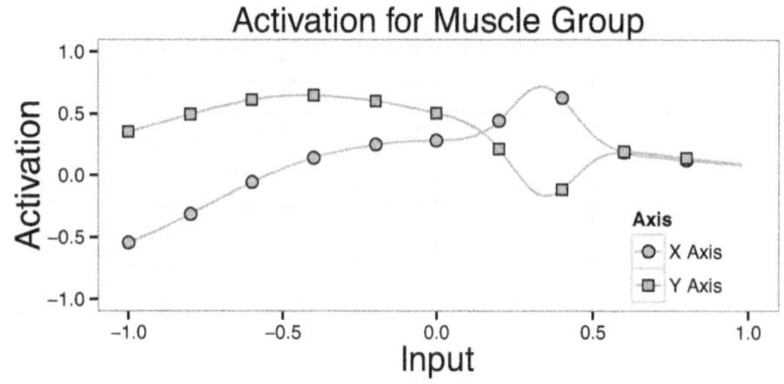

Figure 4: Aggregated activations for the 2 DOF controlled by a muscle group. The nodes depicted in Figure 3 map to the two commands seen in this figure. The humps in both around 0.4 are the result of Node 3, which is a Gaussian with $\mu = 0.4$. Aggregated activations take into account both the activation function for a node as well as its spatial location. Nodes for this muscle group are radially distributed at 45°, 135°, 225°, and 315° as in Figure 2.

4. EXPERIMENTS

We conducted experiments in evolving walking gaits for the quadruped animat shown in Figure 5f. This animat has two 2-DOF joints per leg. Evaluations were conducted using the Open Dynamics Engine (ODE), a 3D physics simulation environment [29]. ODE simulates forces such as gravity and friction while providing a collision engine for the robot. In the proposed model, 2-DOF joints allow the connected limb to move anywhere in 3D space, within the physical constraints of the animat. This approach also allows for fabricating evolved individuals in a physical robot using two servo motors, rotated 90 degrees to each other.

Treatment 1 - Digital Muscle Model.

Treatment 1 features individuals whose high-level control signal is a sinusoid. A population of 100 individuals evolves for 12,000 generations, using a conventional genetic algorithm, with both crossover and mutation applied at each generation. For each treatment, we execute 20 replicate runs, each initialized with a unique starting seed. Individuals contain 8 muscle groups, in which the positions of nodes are initially evenly distributed around the joint with randomized parameters for the nodes. During a simulation controllers are activated every 20 milliseconds. Fitness is the Euclidean distance from the starting location after 5 seconds of simulation time. The next generation is populated using 2-way tournament selection. Elitism is not used in this study. Crossover and mutation are applied with 10% and 2.5% probabilities, respectively. For purposes of crossover, individuals are treated as a composition of muscle groups. During the operation, a child individual is created from two parents, with muscle groups assigned to the corresponding joints. Genomes in this treatment consist of 128 parameters (8 muscle groups * 4 nodes * (3 gaussian + 1 position parameter)), resulting in an average of 3 mutations per genome. Individual parameters are mutated using a normal distribution around the current value with an approximate range of $\pm 10\%$ of the parameter value.

Treatment 2 - ANN Controller.

In the second treatment, individuals are controlled by ANNs evolved with the NEAT algorithm [30]. We emphasize that the proposed digital muscle model is not intended to compete with ANNs, but rather to complement ANNs and other high-level controllers.

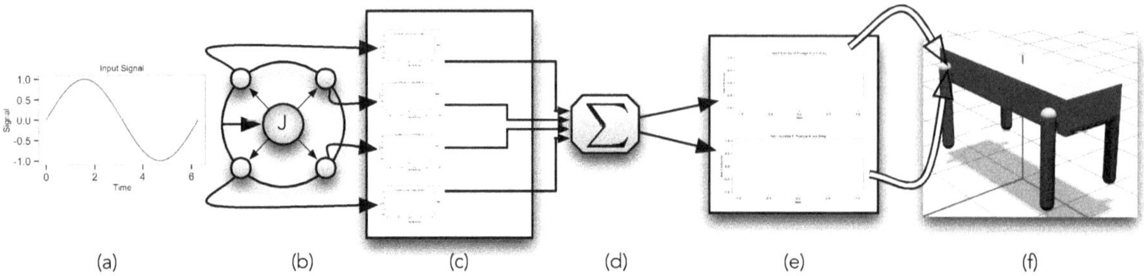

Figure 5: Example of an input signal being converted to joint commands in the rear hip of a quadrupedal animat. (a) A signal (in this case a simple sinusoid) from a higher level controller is distributed to each muscle group (b) which is then passed to all nodes in the group (c). Each node takes the input value and determines its output by finding the point on the Gaussian indicated by the input. This output is then combined with the spatial position of the node to determine the output for each DOF. The outputs of all nodes in the joint are aggregated (d) to derive the two motor movement commands for a joint in a robot (e). These commands are then sent to the motors (f) associated with the joint.

Here, we provide this benchmark comparison to ground results to a known method. ANNs are configured with a single input for the sinusoidal signal and 16 outputs, one for each DOF in the quadruped. ANN input is intentionally limited to the same information as in Treatment 1. Population size, the number of generations and number of replicate runs are the same as those of Treatment 1. Parameters specific to NEAT used in this study include: overall mutation rate of 33%, with specific weight mutation rate of 90%, add neuron probability of 10% and add link probability of 80%.

5. RESULTS

We first describe various gaits and behaviors that evolved in Treatment 1. Next, the evolution of symmetry between independent muscle groups, as well as functional specialization are discussed. Finally, comparisons to ANN based controllers are presented.

Sample of Evolved Muscle Model Gaits.

Several distinct gaits evolved using the digital muscle model; three examples are shown in Figure 6. A video of evolved gaits can be seen at: `http://youtu.be/42w3WW5916w`. The evolution of multiple different gaits across the replicates demonstrates the expressive capacity of the muscle model for a given morphology. The emergence of relatively complex gaits suggests that individual muscle groups evolve to coordinate with each other. As a whole, behaviors tend to balance speed (fore/aft movement of the limbs) with stability (splaying limbs outwards from the body).

Evolution of Symmetric Movements.

We observed the evolution of symmetric behavior among joints in the gait depicted in Figure 6a. In this gait, the rear legs provide forward propulsion, moving symmetrically, with the front acting to keep the body upright. A video showing snapshots during the evolution of this gait can be seen at the following address: `http://youtu.be/rKg3Cd4eicg`. Coordination among legs is evident, along with the evolution of left/right symmetry.

Figures 7 and 8 plot the two axes, at different points in the evolutionary process, of movement for the rear hips from the individual in Figure 6a. Early in evolution, individuals do not demonstrate symmetric or in-phase movement, exhibiting a less coordinated, shuffling gait. The symmetric, in-phase coordination between the rear hip joints is evident in later generations as the two joints evolve similar phase, amplitude and period. Perfectly symmetric movement is difficult to evolve, due to the high number of parameters and interaction between multiple muscle groups required to express effective gaits. Evolution of symmetric movement is apparent in Figure 8, wherein, movement away from the body is initially quite different between the hips. Over the course of evolution, these two muscle groups exhibit like behaviors, ultimately demonstrating similar phase, period, and amplitudes. Coordination in both axes of movement of the hips results in an effective forward bounding gait.

Figure 9 shows the movement paths for the rear hips at different points during evolution. Here, the early generation individual exhibits a shuffling gait where the right rear hip pulls the leg under the robot. Early generation individuals also exhibit random movement trajectories, with little observable coordination between the two axes of movement. This is illustrated by the erratic paths for both joints. Over the course of evolution, however, these movements smooth out, ultimately producing roughly ellipsoidal trajectories. In addition to the smooth movements within a joint group, the evolution of left/right symmetry can also be seen between the two hip joints.

Figure 10 shows the evolved configuration of the muscle nodes for both muscle groups in the rear hips. Here, three of the four nodes in each muscle group are relatively similar in spatial position. Even though the fourth nodes are not close to each other, the expressed behaviors, as indicated by the previously discussed figures, are quite similar. In the muscle model, similar behaviors can emerge, despite completely different muscle node configurations, as *both* activation and spatial positioning determine the contraction of each node.

Evolution of a Functional Knee.

Although joints in the animat have 2 DOF, the muscle model allows for functional specialization to 1 DOF joints. For example, in one of the replicates, the second joint of the rear left leg evolved to a functional knee joint. Figure 11 shows the evolution of this joint-level control, while a video can be seen at the following address: `http://youtu.be/Q7LvNMfuDlg`. In the first few generations, the joint flexes in response to the movement of other joints in the animat, as opposed to providing direct thrust for movement. This behavior serves to keep the animat stable while the other limbs provide thrust for movement. In later generations, however, the joint assumes an active role, as different muscle groups start exhibiting coordination across the animat. The expressed behavior in the muscle group evolves to an ellipsoid, elongating and narrowing. By generation 300, most of the reactive and jerky movements observed in earlier generations disappear. Planar movement and

(a)

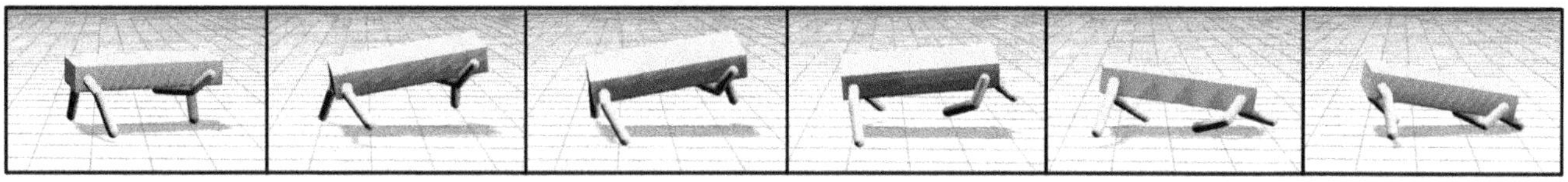

(b)

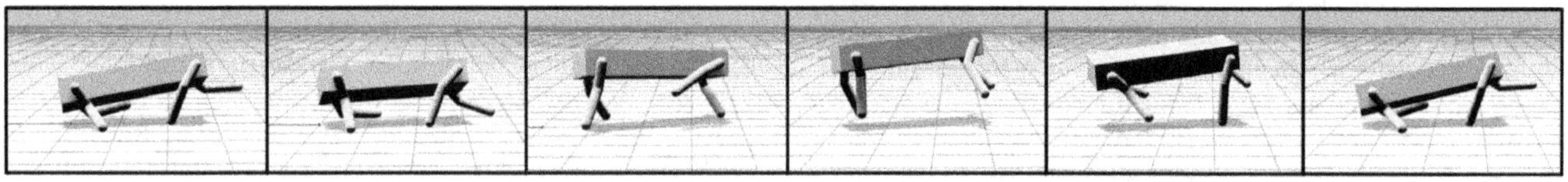

(c)

Figure 6: Examples of evolved in digital muscle based animats. (a) Rear leg driven bounding gait with left/right symmetric motion. (b) Three legged pace gait, where the left legs move in unison, out of phase with the right rear leg. (c) A three legged bounding gait with both left and the right rear leg moving in near unison.

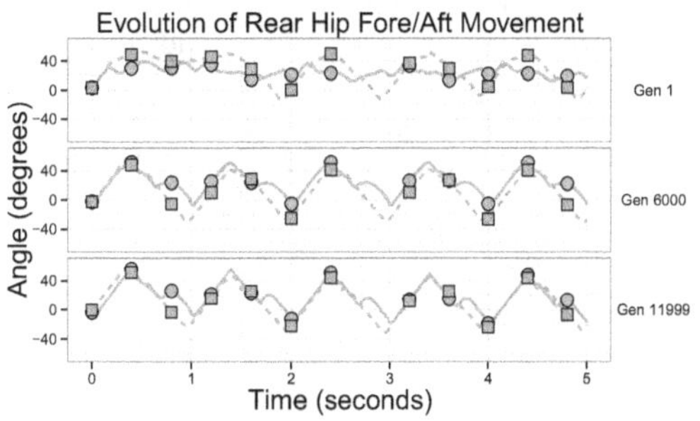

Figure 7: Evolution of forward and backward movement of the rear hips in a bounding individual. Positive angles indicate forward movement. Initially, the joint movements are not synchronized and differ in amplitude. As evolution progresses, the movement of the hips becomes synchronized, with the joint angles moving toward a common phase, amplitude and period.

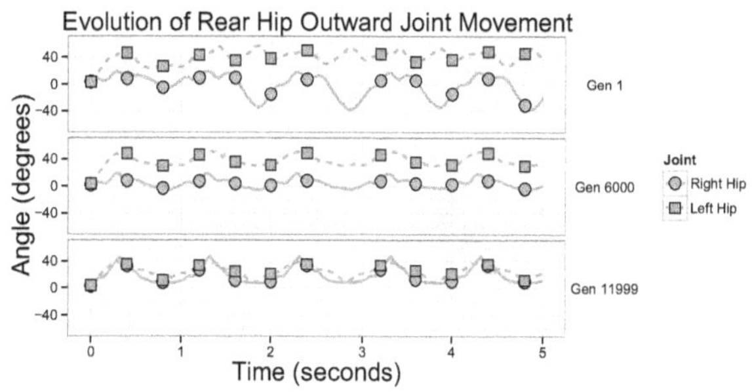

Figure 8: Evolution of movement away from the body in the rear hips of a bounding individual. Positive angles indicate movement away from the body. Movement of the rear hips is quite different, with the gap closing over the course of evolution to ultimately arrive at similar phase, period and amplitudes.

knee-like functionality are observable by generation 1,000, with this behavior becoming more refined in the final individual at generation 11,999.

ANN Evolved Controllers.

Evolved gaits with ANN controllers were also found to be effective, although the individuals tended to remain low to the ground, apparently to maintain stability. Figure 12 shows a representative gait evolved using NEAT. Many ANN-based controllers exhibited similar movement among all legs, rather than anti-phase movements, as in walking or pace gaits. This pattern emerged in the majority of the replicates. This behavior led to lower fitness than the gaits evolved in Treatment 1. The synchronous movement is likely due to the evolutionary method of complexification in NEAT, which results in the growth of networks from an initially fully connected state. In addition, the lack of environmental inputs forces the ANN to work with only a single stimulus. As a result, multiple legs receive the same or similar control signals from the ANN.

Performance Comparison.

Figure 13 plots the evolutionary trajectories and fitness performance for the two treatments. In this study, evolved muscle model controllers outperform ANN controllers, with the maximum and average fitnesses being significantly different ($p < 0.001$ t-test). Quantifying the behaviors across treatments is difficult due to the variety of gaits that evolve. However, one indicator of general behavior is the average height above the ground for the main body of the animat, plotted in Figure 14. Individuals with a muscle model controller tend to maintain higher main body positions than those with ANN controllers. Higher postures are indicative of walking, as opposed to a low crawl or shuffling gait. Observations of the sample gaits from each treatment support this interpretation, the individuals from Treatment 1 exhibit more vertical leg standing postures, whereas ANN based controllers limbs are splayed outward,

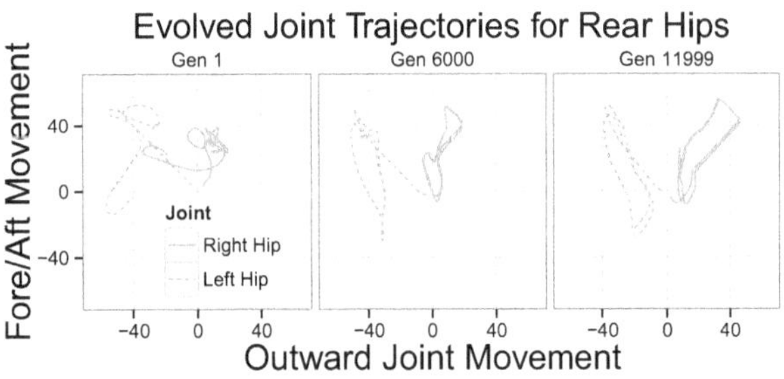

Figure 9: Evolution of the rear hip joint trajectories (Each plot represents the best individual for that generation). The x-axis represents movement toward and away from the body. Values near 0 represent movements near the robot, while larger values indicate movements away from the robot. For the right hip, negative values on the x-axis indicate movements under the robot, while positive values are associated with movements away from the body. In the left hip, the opposite is true. The right hip initially crosses over the 0 boundary, resulting in the leg being under the robot. Later generations exhibit symmetric movements mirrored about 0 on the x axis.

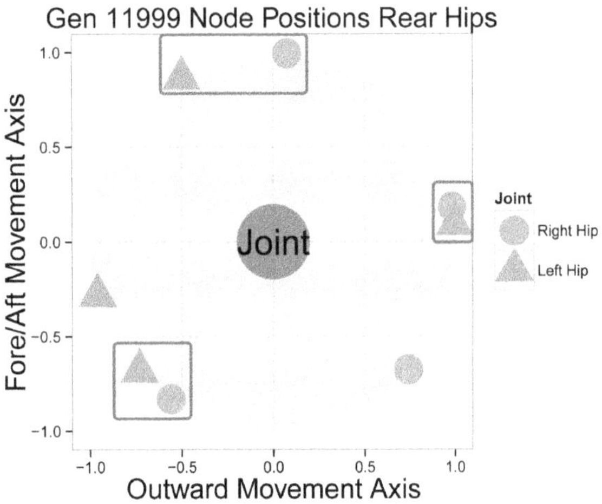

Figure 10: The evolved muscle node positions for the two rear hips do not directly mirror each other as only three of the four nodes, indicated by the red squares, have similar spatial positions. Instead, symmetry in the expressed joint movements is a combination of both node position and activation functions relating to each muscle node. Actual movements are symmetric and coordinated as seen in Figures 7, 8, and 9

with the main body often contacting the ground. Although it provides stability, such contact results in drag, reducing velocity. Individuals that avoid this behavior, as is often the case in Treatment 1, are able to move more effectively, resulting in higher fitness values.

6. POSSIBLE APPLICATIONS

As noted earlier, although the digital muscle model presented in this paper is compared to an ANN based control strategy, the two are not meant to be competitive. Instead, the muscle model is intended to provide a means to co-evolve joint-level control and joint morphology. High-level control strategies can be governed by an ANN or rule-based control strategy. The muscle model may then produce basic gaits without requiring much input from a higher level controller, freeing those resources to be applied to more complex maneuvers and decision making. Gaits evolved in Treatment 1 are driven using only a sinusoid control signal, in order to help us understand how the muscle model functions under controlled conditions. In future work, we plan to investigate multi-tiered control strategies.

In addition to serving as a robotic control strategy, information about evolved orientations of muscle nodes and activation functions can inform biology. Given the incomplete fossil record, evolutionary algorithms and simulation provide a means to test different hypotheses regarding joint-level control and its role in locomotion. Understanding the mechanics of specific motions and muscle configurations is of interest to the study of biological organisms [19, 22, 23]. Evolutionary experiments can yield insight into the biomechanics underlying basic movements [20]. However, finely detailed musculoskeletal simulations are impractical for use in computational evolution. In such musculoskeletal simulators, single experiments can require multiple days of computation time for a single analysis, with the process often requiring multiple iterations. Moreover, while these simulations provide insight into the neuromuscular control of living animals, they are limited in their ability to explore alternative morphologies or behaviors. The digital muscle model presented in this paper provides a way to simulate the basic mechanics underlying natural muscles without the high overhead cost of more detailed simulations. Individual runs (1.2 million evaluations) conducted for this study took approximately 24 hours using a server with 24 cores. Information obtained from this model can then be used as a basis for creating models in more detailed simulators, shortening the iterative cycle.

7. CONCLUSIONS

The digital muscle model presented in this paper is meant to provide a bridge between aspects of control and morphology at the joint level. Each muscle group provides a low-level control strategy that defines the behavior of an individual joint. In contrast to a comprehensive control strategy that supports high-level cognitive tasks (waypoint following, path planning), mid-level (walking, turning), and low-level (basic movements, extension, flexion), the muscle model is intended to function as a low-level controller only. Additionally, the proposed model serves as a computationally efficient tool to assist biological study when using computational evolution. These features, along with the abstract nature of the control strategy, allow the digital muscle model to map into robotic systems while also informing biological study. Results show that effective gaits can evolve using the digital muscle model with instances of functional specialization, coordination, and symmetry all appearing in evolved individuals. Future work will involve exploring more robust behaviors and integration with ANN-based high-level controllers.

Acknowledgments

The authors gratefully acknowledge the contributions and feedback provided by Anthony Clark, Xiaobo Tan, Anne Gutmann, Craig McGowan, and members of the BEACON Center at Michigan State University. This work was supported in part by National Science Foundation grants CNS-1059373, CNS-0915855, and DBI-0939454, and by a grant from Michigan State University.

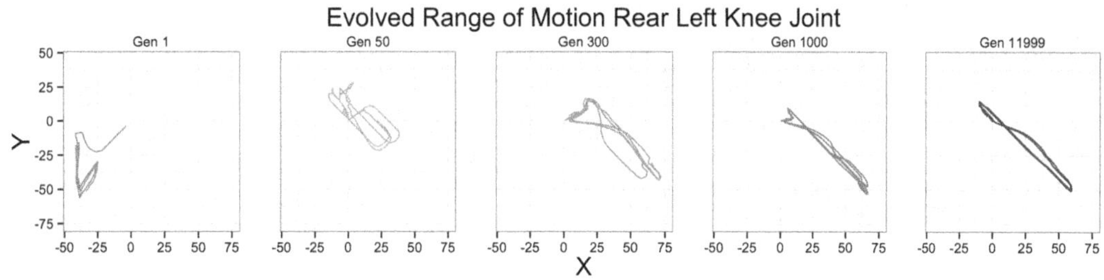

Figure 11: Joint movement for the left rear knee over evolutionary time. The joint initially moves somewhat erratically, in both degrees of freedom with a noticeable hitch. At generation 50, the joint has a balanced movement between both axes but still has jitter. This results in jerky movement of the lower limb. As evolution progresses, the movement becomes planar, using a combination of both degrees of freedom. A functional knee joint then arises with the lower limb moving steadily back and forth without much side-to-side movement.

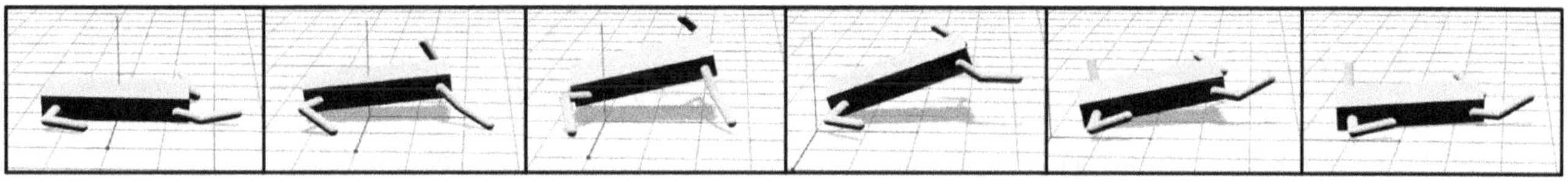

Figure 12: Evolved three legged bounding gait using an ANN-based controller. The main body remains low to the ground throughout the evaluation period, emphasizing stable locomotion. Limbs exhibit symmetric movements, likely due to the complexification of the ANN over evolutionary time.

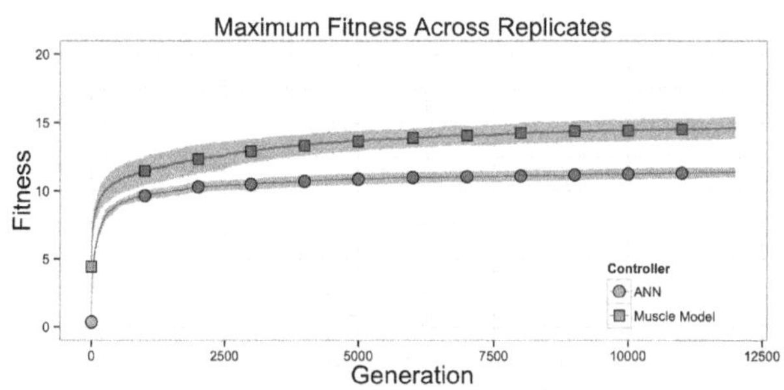

(a)

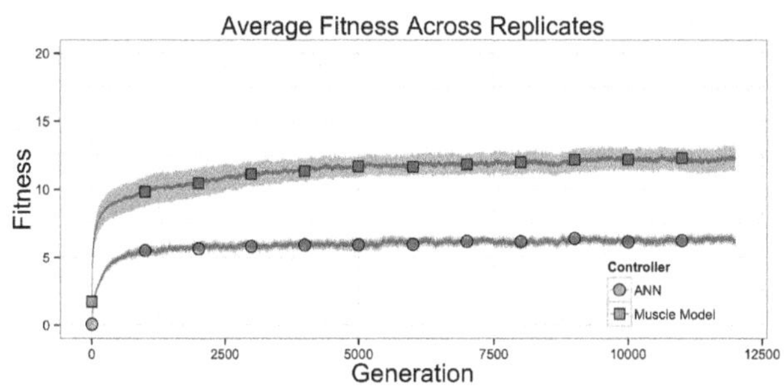

(b)

Figure 13: Evolutionary fitness progressions for both treatments. Shaded areas indicate the 95% confidence intervals across 20 replicate runs per treatment. Both the maximum fitness distribution and average fitness distribution are significantly different ($p < 0.001$ t-test).

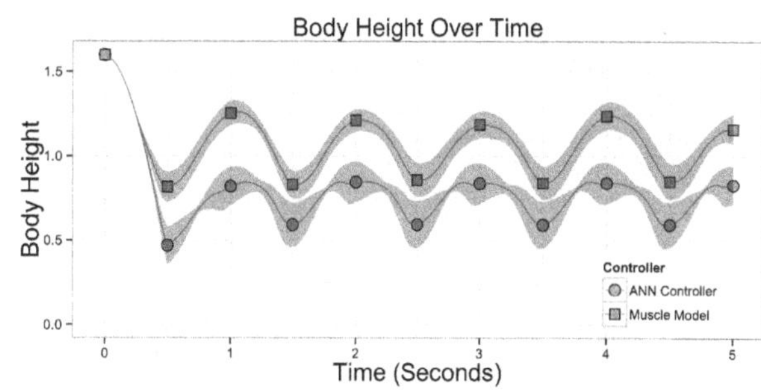

Figure 14: The average body height above the ground for all replicate runs between the two treatments. Shaded areas indicate 95% confidence intervals with the two distributions being significantly different ($p < 0.001$ t-test). As a whole, gaits from digital muscle model controllers evolve higher postures as legs are typically held closer to vertical. Whereas, ANN controllers evolve gaits that tend to remain closer to the ground, splaying the legs outward.

8. REFERENCES

[1] Joshua E. Auerbach and Josh C. Bongard. Dynamic resolution in the co-evolution of morphology and control. In *Proceedings of the Twelfth International Conference on Artificial Life*, pages 451–458, Odense, Denmark, 2010.

[2] Josh Bongard. Morphological change in machines accelerates the evolution of robust behavior. *Proceedings of the National Academy of Sciences*, 108(4):1234–1239, 2011.

[3] Rodney A. Brooks. A robot that walks; emergent behaviors from a carefully evolved network. *Neural Computation*, 1(2):253–262, 1989.

[4] Anthony J. Clark, Jared M. Moore, Jianxun Wang, Xiaobo Tan, and Philip K. McKinley. Evolutionary design and experimental validation of a flexible caudal fin for robotic fish. In *Proceedings of the 13th International Conference on the Simulation and Synthesis of Living Systems*, pages 325–332, East Lansing, Michigan, USA, 2012.

[5] Dave Cliff, Phil Husbands, and Inman Harvey. Explorations in Evolutionary Robotics. *Adaptive Behavior*, 2(1):73–110, 1993.

[6] MA Daley, G Felix, and AA Biewener. Running stability is enhanced by a proximo-distal gradient in joint neuromechanical control. *The Journal of Experimental Biology*, 210(3):383–394, 2007.

[7] Monica A Daley, Alexandra Voloshina, and Andrew A Biewener. The role of intrinsic muscle mechanics in the neuromuscular control of stable running in the guinea fowl. *Journal of Physiology*, 587(Pt 11):2693–2707, Jun 2009.

[8] Michael H. Dickinson, Claire T. Farley, Robert J. Full, M. A. R. Koehl, Rodger Kram, and Steven Lehman. How animals move: An integrative view. *Science*, 288(5463):100–106, 2000.

[9] S. Doncieux and J.-A. Meyer. Evolving modular neural networks to solve challenging control problems. In *Proceedings of the Fourth International ICSC Symposium on Engineering of Intelligent Systems (EIS 2004)*, pages 1–7, Madeira, Portugal, 2004.

[10] Dario Floreano, Phil Husbands, and Stefano Nolfi. Evolutionary Robotics. In *Handbook of Robotics*. Springer Verlag, Berlin, 2008.

[11] Thomas Geijtenbeek, Michiel van de Panne, and A. Frank van der Stappen. Flexible muscle-based locomotion for bipedal creatures. *ACM Transactions on Graphics*, 32(6):206:1–206:11, November 2013.

[12] K G Gerritsen, A J van den Bogert, M Hulliger, and R F Zernicke. Intrinsic muscle properties facilitate locomotor control - a computer simulation study. *Motor Control*, 2(3):206–220, Jul 1998.

[13] A.J. Ijspeert, A. Crespi, and J.M. Cabelguen. Simulation and robotics studies of salamander locomotion. *Neuroinformatics*, 3(3):171–195, 2005.

[14] K. Inoue, T. Sumi, and Shugen Ma. CPG-based control of a simulated snake-like robot adaptable to changing ground friction. In *Proceedings of the IEEE/RSJ International Conference on Intelligent Robots and Systems*, pages 1957 –1962, San Diego, California, USA, 2007.

[15] Dan Lessin, Don Fussell, and Risto Miikkulainen. Open-ended behavioral complexity for evolved virtual creatures. In *Proceedings of the 2013 ACM Genetic and Evolutionary Computing Conference*, pages 335–342, Amsterdam, Netherlands, 2013. ACM.

[16] Hod Lipson. Evolutionary robotics and open-ended design automation. In *Biomimetics*, pages 129–155. CRC Press, 2005.

[17] Daniel Marbach and Auke Jan Ijspeert. Co-evolution of configuration and control for homogenous modular robots. In *Proceedings of the Eighth Conference on Intelligent Autonomous Systems (IAS8)*, pages 712–719, Amsterdam, Netherlands, 2004.

[18] K. Matsuoka. Mechanisms of frequency and pattern control in the neural rhythm generators. *Biological Cybernetics*, 56:345–353, 1987.

[19] C.P. McGowan, R.R. Neptune, and W. Herzog. A phenomenological muscle model to assess history dependent effects in human movement. *Journal of Biomechanics*, 46(1):151 – 157, 2013.

[20] Craig P. McGowan, Richard R. Neptune, and Walter Herzog. A phenomenological model and validation of shortening-induced force depression during muscle contractions. *Journal of Biomechanics*, 43(3):449–454, 02 2010.

[21] Jared M. Moore, Anthony J. Clark, and Philip K. McKinley. Evolution of station keeping as a response to flows in an aquatic robot. In *Proceedings of the 2013 ACM Genetic and Evolutionary Computing Conference*, pages 239–246, Amsterdam, Netherlands, 2013. ACM.

[22] Jared M. Moore, Anne K. Gutmann, Craig P. McGowan, and Philip K. McKinley. Exploring the role of the tail in bipedal hopping through computational evolution. In *Proceedings of the 12th European Conference on Artificial Life*, pages 11–18, Taormina, Italy, 2013.

[23] Richard R. Neptune and Craig P. McGowan. Muscle contributions to whole-body sagittal plane angular momentum during walking. *Journal of Biomechanics*, 44(1):6–12, 2011.

[24] Stefano Nolfi and Dario Floreano. *Evolutionary Robotics: The Biology, Intelligence and Technology of Self-Organizing Machines*. The MIT Press, 2000.

[25] C. Paul and J. C. Bongard. The road less travelled: Morphology in the optimization of biped robot locomotion. In *Proceedings of the 2001 IEEE/RSJ International Conference on Intelligent Robots and Systems*, pages 226 – 232, Maui, Hawaii, USA, 2001.

[26] Rolf Pfeifer, Max Lungarella, and Fumiya Iida. Self-Organization, Embodiment, and Biologically Inspired Robotics. *Science*, 318(5853):1088–1093, 2007.

[27] T. Reil and P. Husbands. Evolution of central pattern generators for bipedal walking in a real-time physics environment. *IEEE Transactions on Evolutionary Computation*, 6(2):159–168, 2002.

[28] K Sims. Evolving virtual creatures. In *Proceedings of the 21st Annual Conference on Computer Graphics and Interactive Techniques*, pages 15–22, 1994.

[29] Russell Smith. Open Dynamics Engine, http://www.ode.org/, 2013.

[30] Kenneth O. Stanley and Risto Miikkulainen. Evolving neural networks through augmenting topologies. *Evolutionary Computation*, 10(2):99–127, June 2002.

[31] X. Yao. Evolving artificial neural networks. *Proceedings of the IEEE*, 87(9):1423–1447, 1999.

Directional Communication in Evolved Multiagent Teams

Justin K. Pugh
Department of EECS
University of Central Florida
Orlando, FL 32816 USA
jpugh@eecs.ucf.edu

Skyler Goodell
Department of EECS
University of Central Florida
Orlando, FL 32816 USA
goodsky@eecs.ucf.edu

Kenneth O. Stanley
Department of EECS
University of Central Florida
Orlando, FL 32816 USA
kstanley@eecs.ucf.edu

ABSTRACT

The question of how to best design a communication architecture is becoming increasingly important for evolving autonomous multiagent systems. Directional reception of signals, a design feature of communication that appears in most animals, is present in only some existing artificial communication systems. This paper hypothesizes that such directional reception benefits the evolution of communicating autonomous agents because it simplifies the language required to express positional information, which is critical to solving many group coordination tasks. This hypothesis is tested by comparing the evolutionary performance of several alternative communication architectures (both directional and non-directional) in a multiagent foraging domain designed to require a basic "come here" type of signal for the optimal solution. Results confirm that directional reception is a key ingredient in the evolutionary tractability of effective communication. Furthermore, the real world viability of directional reception is demonstrated through the successful transfer of the best evolved controllers to real robots. The conclusion is that directional reception is important to consider when designing communication architectures for more complicated tasks in the future.

Categories and Subject Descriptors

I.2.11 [**Artificial Intelligence**]: Distributed Artificial Intelligence—*intelligent agents, multiagent systems, coherence and coordination*; I.2.6 [**Artificial Intelligence**]: Learning—*connectionism and neural nets*

Keywords

Multirobot Teams; Coordination; Communication; Artificial Neural Networks; Evolutionary Algorithms; HyperNEAT

1. INTRODUCTION

Because there exists a substantial class of tasks that require more than one agent to solve [28], evolving multiagent robot teams has attracted significant interest. Due to the limitations inherent in centralized control systems [18], a popular alternative is to evolve controllers for multiple autonomous agents that confront the challenge of group coordination through distributed interactions. While some researchers have built controllers for non-communicating autonomous agents [4, 5], communication can potentially improve group coordination through sharing information about the sensed environment [17] or agent states [10]. The question then becomes how to design an effective communication scheme. While there are many important design features of communication systems to consider [14], this paper focuses on one of the most basic features: *directional reception* of signals. When this feature is present, agents can perceive the direction from which incoming signals originate.

Directional reception in the design of communication systems for autonomous robots is not a new idea [7, 8, 19, 33]. However, many systems without directional reception have also been proposed [3, 17, 22, 31] and despite the interest in both communication schemes with and without directional reception, few empirical studies have investigated the importance of directionality. The hypothesis in this paper, suggested by the prevalence of directional reception in natural communication systems, is that directional reception is beneficial to the evolution of communicating autonomous agents that must coordinate in a spatial environment. This hypothesis is important to confirm in particular to provide guidance to new researchers entering the field who may assume from prior such experiments that lacked directionality that such directionality is not necessary.

Consider the following thought experiment: Imagine that you are trying to help a friend who is on the other side of a crowded room to come to your location. If you can only communicate through text messages, the message you send may be similar to "come to the southwest corner of the room, near the grey statue," or, "turn 120 degrees to your left and walk towards me." However, by shouting across the room, you can simply say "come here." The reason the message complexity reduces is that the positional information that is explicit in the longer messages is implicit in the compact message because humans benefit from directional reception of auditory signals. Similarly, agents equipped with directional reception in a spatial environment should be able to communicate with less complex messages than those without directional reception, which benefits evolution because simpler signals are easier to evolve.

This hypothesis is validated by an experiment comparing the evolutionary performance of directional and non-

GECCO'14, July 12–16, 2014, Vancouver, BC, Canada.
Copyright 2014 ACM 978-1-4503-2662-9/14/07 ...$15.00.
http://dx.doi.org/10.1145/2576768.2598299.

directional communication schemes in a multiagent foraging domain designed to require a "come here" type of signal. Controllers in the experiment are evolved with the HyperNEAT algorithm for evolving large-scale artificial neural networks (ANNs) [11, 24], which has been successfully applied to multiagent domains in the past [3–5]. Unlike many neuroevolution methods, HyperNEAT can be informed by geometric information in the domain, making it an ideal platform for testing directional communication. Experimental results support the hypothesis that directional communication schemes are more evolutionarily tractable than their non-directional counterparts, highlighting that directional reception is important for enabling the evolution of group coordination tasks because it redirects evolutionary effort from learning a complex language to learning task-critical behaviors. Finally, the practical value of the evolved controllers is demonstrated by transferring the best teams to real-world Khepera III robots.

It is important to emphasize that while the main hypothesis may be intuitive, many robot coordination experiments in the past nevertheless have lacked such directional reception [3, 17, 22, 31]. The need for directional communication has in effect rarely if ever been addressed explicitly. Thus this paper makes a practical contribution by serving as a reminder that including directionality is often in practice more important than allowing complex communication when contemplating the setup of future experiments in evolved coordination.

2. BACKGROUND

This section reviews prior work in training communicating agents and summarizes the HyperNEAT neuroevolution algorithm featured in the experiments presented in this paper.

2.1 Communication in Multiagent Teams

Within the field of evolutionary computation, communication among agents has been studied from several perspectives. One of the most popular questions is how natural communication may have emerged under evolutionary pressure; Wagner et al. [30] provide a detailed review of past work in this area on the emergence of communication. One aspect of communication that is often present in simulated models but is rarely the subject of empirical testing is *directional reception*, which is the ability of an agent, upon hearing a message, to sense the direction of the message's source. Directional reception is one of the 13 design features of animal communication identified by Hockett [14] and is present in even the least advanced communicating mammals. Perhaps the reason its importance is not often tested is that when tracing the evolution of humans back to land mammals, directional reception co-occurs with communication as an immediate implication simply of having ears.

Communication is also often important for agents in a cooperative multiagent team. One situation in which agents benefit from communication is when each agent senses only a fraction of the observable state of the environment. In such tasks, communication facilitates sharing information among team members to increase the amount of environmental context available to each agent [17]. Communication may also be necessary in tasks in which agents have limited information about the state of other agents on the team, such as when an agent requires the assistance of other agents to solve a subgoal [10].

Realizing the importance of communication in solving cooperative tasks, researchers developing evolved or learned controllers for cooperative teams of robots have experimented with different forms of communication, many of which include a form of directional reception. For example, Yong and Mikkulainen [33] developed neural controllers that received as input the relative positions of all team members. Marocco and Nolfi [19] developed simulated robots with a single communication output that produces signals whose intensity and direction is perceived by team members through directional pie-slice sensors. Di Paolo [7] developed robots that could "speak" using simulated sound waves and who could thereby infer the relative position of a speaker through a set of ears positioned on opposite sides of the body. Floreano et al. [8] evolved physical robot controllers that communicate their positions through light.

Considerable effort has also been devoted to developing communicating agents that are not aware of the relative position of the speaker. In pioneering work on the evolution of communication, Werner and Dyer [31] evolved agents that communicate via three-bit binary signals to solve a task in which stationary "female" agents must guide blind "male" agents to their position on a discretized two-dimensional grid. Jim and Giles [17] evolved teams of agents to solve a discrete predator-prey task; each agent in the domain reads and writes bit strings to a shared message board. In a recent work, D'Ambrosio et al. [3] solved a multiagent synchronization task by evolving a neural controller that features direct neural connections between agents. In another recent work, Rawal et al. [22] evolved agents for a discrete predator-prey task in which blind predator agents receive real-valued communication signals from stationary predator agents. In each of Werner and Dyer [31], Jim and Giles [17], D'Ambrosio et al. [3], and Rawal et al. [22], positional information is critically important to solving the task even though it is not explicitly included in the communication scheme. The binary-string languages that subsequently emerged in Werner and Dyer [31] and Jim and Giles [17] and the real-valued languages from Rawal et al. [22] attach positional information to certain "words" in the language. D'Ambrosio et al. [3] in contrast achieved a solution by extracting positional information from assumptions about the starting positions and orientations of the agents.

This paper advances the hypothesis that knowing the relative location of a speaker is often critically important in solving group coordination tasks and that it is beneficial to include such information implicitly in the communication scheme so that evolutionary effort need not be expended incorporating it into the emergent language. A recent neuroevolution technique called HyperNEAT [11, 24] easily facilitates the evolution of agents with a position-aware communication scheme because HyperNEAT can take into account geometric information about the domain (such as the spatial relationship between an agent's vision or audition sensors), making it a good platform for testing this hypothesis. The following sections review the HyperNEAT approach, which is applied in the experiments in this paper.

2.2 Neuroevolution of Augmenting Topologies

The HyperNEAT approach is itself an extension of the original NEAT (Neuroevolution of Augmenting Topologies) algorithm that evolves increasingly large ANNs [25, 27]. NEAT starts with a population of simple networks that then *increase in complexity* over generations by adding new nodes and connections through mutations. By evolving ANNs in this way, the topology of the network does not need to be known a priori; NEAT searches through increasingly complex networks to find a suitable level of complexity. Because it starts simply and gradually adds complexity, it tends to find a solution network close to the minimal necessary size. However, as explained in the next section, the direct representation of nodes and connections in the NEAT genome cannot scale up to larger networks that can take advantage of domain geometry. For a complete overview of NEAT, see Stanley and Miikkulainen [25] or Stanley and Miikkulainen [27].

2.3 HyperNEAT

Like NEAT, many neuroevolution methods are *directly encoded*, which means each component of the phenotype is encoded by a single gene, making the discovery of repeating motifs expensive and improbable [32]. Therefore, indirect encodings [1, 2, 15, 20, 26] have become a growing area of interest in evolutionary computation.

One such indirect encoding designed explicitly for neural networks is in Hypercube-based NEAT (HyperNEAT) [11, 24], which is itself an indirect extension of the directly-encoded NEAT approach [25, 27] reviewed in the previous section. This section briefly reviews HyperNEAT; a complete introduction can be found in Stanley et al. [24] and Gauci and Stanley [11]. Rather than expressing connection weights as independent parameters in the genome, HyperNEAT allows them to vary across the phenotype in a regular pattern through an indirect encoding called a *compositional pattern producing network* (CPPN; [23]), which is like an ANN, but with specially-chosen activation functions.

CPPNs in HyperNEAT *encode* the connectivity patterns of ANNs as a *function of geometry*. That is, if an ANN's nodes are embedded in a geometry, i.e. assigned coordinates within a space, then it is possible to represent its connectivity as a single evolved function of such coordinates. In effect the CPPN paints a pattern of weights across the geometry of a neural network. Because the CPPN encoding is itself a network, it is evolved in HyperNEAT by the NEAT algorithm, which is designed to evolve networks of increasing complexity. To understand why this approach is promising, consider that a natural organism's brain is physically embedded within a three-dimensional geometric space, and that such embedding heavily constrains and influences the brain's connectivity. Topographic maps (i.e. ordered projections of sensory or effector systems such as the retina or musculature) in natural brains preserve geometric relationships between high-dimensional sensor and effector fields [16, 29]. In other words, there is important information *implicit* in geometry that can only be exploited by an encoding informed by such geometry.

In particular, geometric *regularities* such as symmetry or repetition are pervasive throughout the connectivity of natural brains. To similarly achieve such regularities, CPPNs exploit activation functions that induce regularities in HyperNEAT networks. The general idea is that a CPPN takes as input the geometric coordinates of two nodes embedded in the *substrate*, i.e. an ANN situated in a particular geometry, and outputs the weight of the connection between those two nodes (figure 1). In this way, a Gaussian activation function by virtue of its symmetry can induce symmetric connectivity and a sine function can induce networks with repeated elements. Note that because the size of the CPPN is decoupled from the size of the substrate, HyperNEAT can compactly

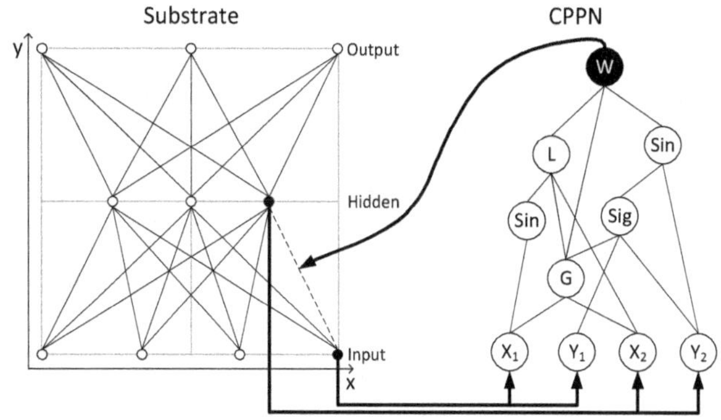

Figure 1: HyperNEAT example. An example substrate (left) for a simple ANN contains ten neurons that have been assigned (x, y) coordinates. The weight of every connection specified in the substrate is determined by the evolved CPPN (right): (1) The coordinates of the source (x_1, y_1) and target (x_2, y_2) neurons are input into the CPPN, (2) the CPPN is activated, and (3) the weight w of the connection being queried is set to the CPPN's output. CPPN activation functions in this paper can be *sigmoid (Sig), Gaussian (G), linear (L), or sine (Sin).*

encode the connectivity of an arbitrarily large substrate with a single CPPN.

Additionally, HyperNEAT can evolve controllers for *teams* of agents. This multiagent HyperNEAT algorithm was first introduced by D'Ambrosio and Stanley [5], D'Ambrosio et al. [4], and D'Ambrosio and Stanley [6]. It can be used to evolve both homogeneous and heterogeneous teams; however, the experiments in this paper only necessitate the homogeneous case. Controllers for homogeneous teams are created by evolving a single controller that is duplicated for each agent on the team.

3. EXPERIMENT

Each of the communication schemes reviewed in Section 2.1 that succeed without directional reception share a common feature: the domain in which they are applied is simplified. For example, the simulated worlds in Werner and Dyer [31], Jim and Giles [17], and Rawal et al. [22] consist of discrete two-dimensional grids, and while the world in D'Ambrosio et al. [3] is continuous, agents are restricted to only forward-backward movement, effectively narrowing actions to one dimension. To test the hypothesis that non-directional communication schemes require more evolutionary effort than their directional counterparts, a more challenging domain is proposed that takes place in a continuous two-dimensional world.

A team of five agents is placed in a large rectangular room bounded on all four sides by walls but otherwise free of obstructions. Agents must collect the greatest number of food items possible from the room within a time limit. Only one food item is present in the room at a given time; whenever one is collected, a new one spawns randomly somewhere in the room. The key mechanism encouraging communication is that food items are not collected until they are touched by three agents simultaneously. While it is possible for all three agents to arrive at a food item through random wandering (without communication), the second and third agents can find the food much faster if the first agent to find it signals its location. The type of communication that is required for the optimal behavior is thus relatively unsophisticated: agents must produce a *come here* signal upon discovering a food item. However, this type of signal is significantly more difficult to produce when directional reception is not embedded in the communication architecture because extra "words" must be discovered to describe the location of "here" (a concept that is implicit within directional reception). While this domain is relatively simple, the underlying dynamic of rallying a group of cooperating agents to salient locations in real time is fundamental to a range of important real world tasks such as rescue, patrol, and retrieval tasks. In this way, this experiment helps to highlight the potential importance of directional reception across a range of real-world problems.

In addition to a control scheme with no communication (**NoCom**), three different communication schemes are tested to determine the extent to which directional reception is important in solving this group foraging task. In the first scheme, **DirCom**, agents can emit signals on one channel (which can range from 0.0 to 1.0) and can hear signals coming from one of ten directions (equally spaced around the agent) via an array of ten pie-slice sensors. In the second communication scheme, **OneBit**, agents can also emit signals on only one channel, but cannot hear signals directionally. Instead, agents have five communication inputs for hearing signals from each of the five agents on the team. The input for sensing an agent's own signals is disabled for consistency with the DirCom scheme, in which agents cannot hear themselves either. The final communication scheme, **FiveBit**, is the same as OneBit except that agents can emit signals on five channels and have an array of 25 communication inputs (one for each channel on each agent). The extra "bits" can potentially make possible a more complex language capable of expressing the positional information necessary to compensate for a lack of directional reception. However, whether such a language is evolutionarily tractable will be determined experimentally.

Individual agents are equipped with several arrays of pie-slice sensors for the various senses that serve as inputs into a HyperNEAT-evolved ANN. The HyperNEAT substrate that serves as the basis for all the variant setups is shown in figure 2. This kind of *multi-spatial substrate* is shown effective for tasks with multiple modalities in Pugh and Stanley [21]. Agents sense the location of food items within a maximum radius of 100 units with a set of five equal-size pie-slice sensors that span the frontal 180 degrees of vision. Similarly, agents detect walls with a set of five 100-unit rangefinders arranged across the front of each agent in 36 degree intervals. Each agent also detects the location of other agents with a set of ten unlimited-range[1] pie-slice sensors that surround the agent. Figure 3 depicts the different sensor types. Each agent has the ability to move forward and to turn left or right (a set of three output neurons control the movement: left, forward, and right, where the direction and magnitude of each turn is decided by the difference between the left and right turn outputs).

DirCom, OneBit, and FiveBit agents are identical in every way except for their communication scheme, which differ as follows. DirCom (figure 4a) and OneBit (figure 4b) agents each have a single output neuron for sending simple communication signals, while FiveBit (figure 4c) has a set of five output neurons for sending more complex signals. DirCom agents have a set of ten input neurons for receiving communication signals (figure 5a), one for each pie-slice in their 360 degree non-overlapping array. OneBit agents have a set of five input neurons for receiving communication signals (figure 5b), one for each agent on the team (one of which is never activated because agents cannot hear themselves). FiveBit agents have a set of 25 input neurons for receiving communication signals (figure 5c), five for each of five agents on the team (five of which are never activated). Recall that because HyperNEAT is an indirect encoding, the dimensionality of the inputs is not an obstacle to effective learning [24].

The room is 1,000 by 900 units, and the five agents are initially arranged in a horizontal line in the center of the room spaced 100 units apart. Food items spawn randomly around the room, not closer than 40 units from a wall. During evolution, team performance is averaged over 20 trials to mitigate the evaluation noise caused by randomized food

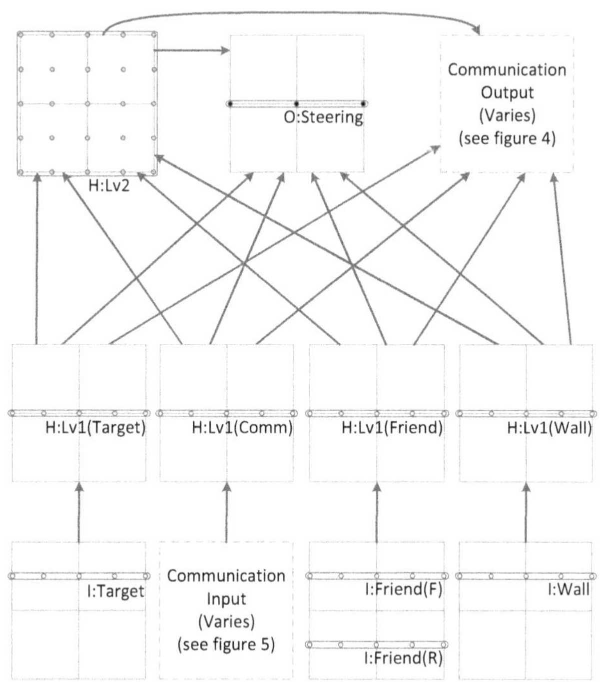

Figure 2: HyperNEAT substrate (all communication schemes). Each input and output modality and each hidden layer is placed on its own plane within the substrate, following the multi-spatial substrate configuration described in Pugh and Stanley [21]. The substrate is strictly feedforward: Each input modality feeds into a dedicated "level 1" hidden layer, all level 1 hidden layers feed into a common "level 2" hidden layer, and all hidden layers (level 1 as well as level 2) feed into all outputs. Individual neural connections are omitted for clarity. Instead, arrows indicate the existence of neural connections between two planes. Planes shown as connected are potentially fully connected (all neurons on the first plane are queried by HyperNEAT for connections to all neurons on the second plane). Communication input and output planes vary depending on communication scheme; see figure 4 for output planes and figure 5 for input planes.

[1]Activation of the friend sensors that detect other agents is floored at 20% if sensing an agent more than 500 units away.

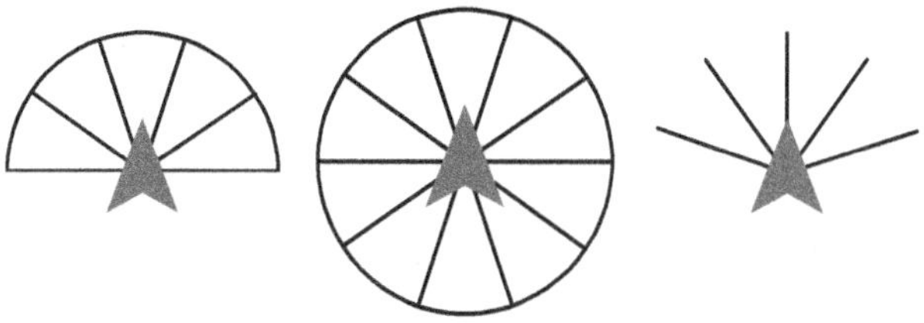

(a) Food (b) Friends, DirCom (c) Walls

Figure 3: Agent sensor types. Agents have pie slice sensors for detecting food (a) and friends (b), and a set of rangefinders for detecting walls (c). DirCom robots also have a set of pie slice sensors for sensing communication signals (b). The activation level of all sensor types is based on distance (i.e. it decreases linearly the farther the distance) except for DirCom communication sensor activation, which is based on the strongest signal received from each direction.

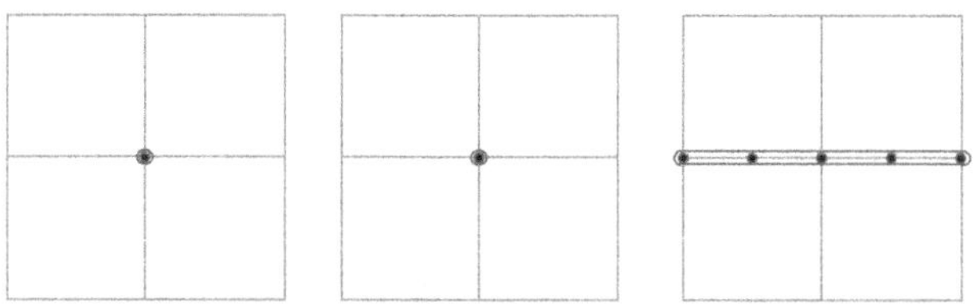

(a) DirCom (b) OneBit (c) FiveBit

Figure 4: Substrate: communication output planes. The number of neurons on the communication output plane corresponds to the size of the signal vector sent to all other agents on the team on each tick: one for DirCom (a) and OneBit (b), and five for FiveBit (c).

item spawn points. Each trial, teams are given 2,000 ticks of simulation time to collect as many food items as possible, up to a maximum of ten food items. Team fitness on a particular trial is determined by the number of food items seen, the number collected, and the time at which each was collected. More specifically, each food item is worth a maximum of 100 points, 10 of which are awarded when a single agent comes within range (the food is "seen"), 40 of which are awarded when three agents come within range (thus collecting the food), and 50 of which are time dependent (50 points are awarded if the food is collected on the first tick of simulation, diminishing to 0 points awarded if the food is collected on the last tick). The time component is included to provide a smoother fitness gradient for evolution to follow.

Evolution is run for 1,000 generations, by which time fitness inevitably stops improving. The training phase consists of 20 runs of evolution for each of the three communication schemes, after which the champions are tested according to a more stable metric: Testing performance is determined by the raw number of food items collected in 5,000 time ticks, averaged over 10,000 trials. During testing, there is no artificial limit of 10 food items, although there are practical limits due to the time it takes agents to travel across the room (agents move at a maximum rate of 5 units per tick and have a maximum turn rate of 36 degrees per tick).

Finally, to highlight the practical value of effective communication, the best performing teams are implemented on

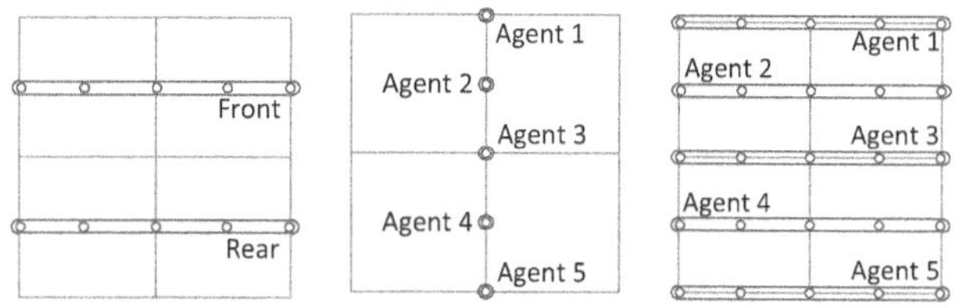

(a) DirCom (b) OneBit (c) FiveBit

Figure 5: Substrate: communication input planes. Communication input for DirCom (a) consists of two sets of five neurons corresponding to the front and rear pie-slice sensors. Each neuron in the communication input plane for OneBit (b) corresponds to an agent on the team and is activated when detecting signals from that agent. The communication input plane for FiveBit (c) consists of a 5×5 grid arranged as five horizontal groups. Each horizontal group corresponds to an agent on the team, and each neuron within a group corresponds to a different communication channel.

real-world Khepera III robots. In the real world implementation, several sensor types are implemented by a central station that reads each agent's position and orientation information on every tick via odometry on their wheel encoders. This information is synthesized to yield communication sensors, friend vision, and target vision. Hardware IR sensors serve as the wall sensors. While in practice positional information in the real world may not always be possible to compute through a central computing node, it is important to note that this setup approximates other real world setups that would convey similar information, such as true hardware-based emitters [8] or decentralized mutual localization techniques [9].

It is also important to note that in the real world the IR sensors also detect the presence of other robots as well as the target points (plastic cups), causing those entities to be treated like walls. This ambiguity is contrary to the case during evolution where wall sensors only activate when in range of a wall. To partially mitigate this potential discrepancy, walls in the real world are covered with retroreflective tape while robots and target points are not. Thus agents perceive a strong activation when seeing walls and a comparatively weak activation when seeing other solid objects in the room. The evolved policies are robust enough to work when transferred to the real world despite any remaining differences.

Because HyperNEAT differs from original NEAT only in its set of activation functions, it uses the same parameters [25]. The experiment was run with a modified version of the public domain SharpNEAT package [12]. The size of the population was 500 with 20% elitism. Sexual offspring (50%) did not undergo mutation. Asexual offspring (50%) had 0.96 probability of link weight mutation, 0.03 chance of link addition, and 0.01 chance of node addition. The coefficients for determining species similarity were 1.0 for nodes and connections and 0.1 for weights. The available CPPN activation functions were sigmoid, Gaussian, linear, and sine, all with equal probability of being added to the CPPN. Parameter settings are based on standard SharpNEAT defaults and prior reported settings for NEAT [25, 27]. They were

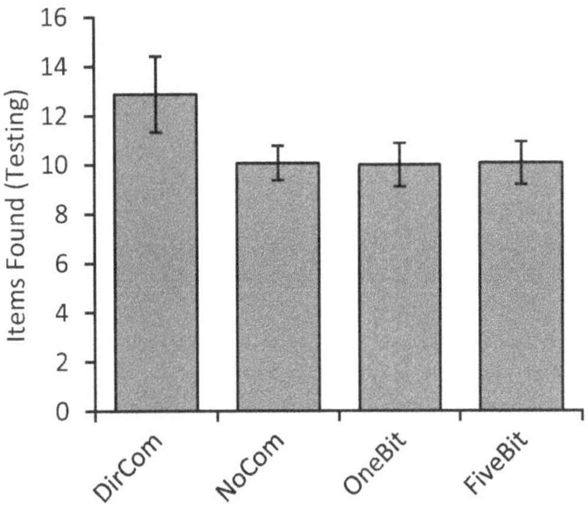

Figure 6: Test performance. The testing performance of a single run is determined by the average number of food items collected over 10,000 trials by the team with the highest training performance. Results for each communication scheme are averaged over 20 runs. Error bars depict a 95% confidence interval. The DirCom scheme performs significantly better than the other schemes ($p < 0.05$; Student's t-test).

found to be robust to moderate variation through preliminary experimentation.

4. RESULTS

For each communication scheme, each of the best performing genomes found after 1,000 generations of evolution (one for each of 20 runs) is evaluated according to the testing metric described in the previous section. The test performance for each communication architecture, averaged over the 20 champions, is presented in figure 6. The directional communication scheme significantly outperforms all others ($p < 0.05$; Student's t-test), while there is no significant difference between the OneBit, FiveBit, and NoCom architectures. The best performing NoCom champion collects 12.3 food on average during testing. Nine out of the 20 DirCom champions pass a success threshold of collecting more than 105% of the food collected by the best NoCom champion, while the number of such successes for OneBit and FiveBit are zero and one, respectively. It is important to note that the differences between DirCom and the other variants in figure 6 represent qualitatively very different behaviors.

For example, the best performing NoCom teams exhibit surprisingly effective exploratory behavior. The very best consists of a single agent closely following the walls and corners of the arena while the remaining four agents lag behind seeking the leading agent and at the same time checking the interior of the room. If food is discovered in the interior, the swarm of agents quickly collects it, and if food is discovered near a wall, the wall-exploring agent stops at it and the swarm of agents is able to catch up and thus collect the food in a reasonable time. However, this highly coordinated behavior is rare; most NoCom teams achieve scores closer to 10.0 through random wandering. The best OneBit teams exhibit a similar style of coordination as the best NoCom team, with scores of 12.7 and 12.6. All of the OneBit teams either send chaotic signals at all times, usually with no discernible purpose (signals changed little if at all when agents were in range of a target point or wall), or else do not send signals at all. In contrast, the best FiveBit team produces a rudimentary "come here" signal that allows it to achieve good results, with a score of 14.4. Agents on this team spread out and explore the map individually. When an agent finds the food, it sends a signal that causes all other agents to change behavior and begin to seek nearby agents. This inevitably causes the agents to capture the food, although it is clear that they do not know the location of the agent sending the signal because often all four of the remaining agents will join up before moving to the fifth (and thus the food). While this strategy is effective, that it was only achieved in one of the FiveBit runs suggests the difficulty of discovering it. From the behaviors of teams without directional communication, it is evident that they fail to express position even implicitly within their communication schemes because once the food is found by one agent, no teams approach it right away. Furthermore, while a more sophisticated communication strategy is conceivable whereby agents e.g. near the wall indicate that they are near a wall when they see food, no such strategy actually evolved with FiveBit, highlighting the difficulty of fully exploiting the increased bandwidth without a directional component.

In contrast to the non-directional schemes, half of the DirCom teams learned to produce a "come here" signal upon discovering the food. The testing performance of these teams varied (from 13.0 to 19.3) according to the effectiveness of non-communicative behaviors such as exploration and the reliability of turning towards a detected food item without moving past it (and thus out of range). The best DirCom team, with a test score of 19.3, combines "come here" signaling with efficient exploratory behaviors (agents tend to spread out as much as possible).

The five best performing DirCom teams were transferred to real Khepera III robots and placed in an open arena containing a single food item. Transferred teams demon-

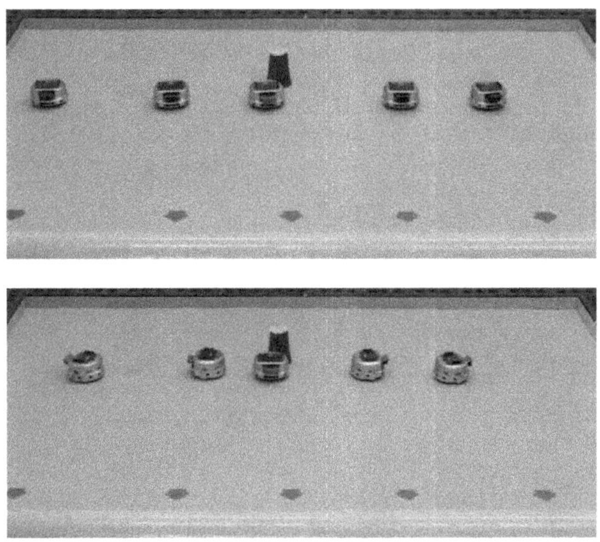

Figure 7: Real world implementation. In this example, the robots explore the arena by moving forward from their starting positions. The third robot finds the target point (top) and signals its location to the other robots who then begin moving towards it (bottom).

strated effective group coordination (figure 7), despite significant differences between the real world and the simulated world (e.g. robots can collide with each other in the real world, while they cannot do so in simulation). Real world teams are tested with varying team sizes of five, four, and three robots without losing the ability to solve the task. Videos of some of the transferred teams can be found at `http://tinyurl.com/DirComVideos`.

5. DISCUSSION

The results indicate that the communication scheme that includes directional reception is able to solve the task more efficiently than those schemes without directional reception. In fact, only one out of 40 teams across both non-directional communication schemes achieves a level of performance unreachable by non-communicating teams. By comparison, almost half of the teams with directional reception achieve such performance. This result demonstrates that even though it is possible to evolve effective communication without directional reception, doing so is less evolutionarily tractable than when directional reception is present in the system.

Messages in a system without directional reception must express directionality through a complex system of "words" that each contain different positional information. These words must be invented independently, and they may have little or no benefit until several have already been invented. This problem is difficult for evolutionary algorithms because there may exist no path of increasingly fit stepping stones to the discovery of the final working language. Directional reception alleviates this problem by incorporating positional information into the communication architecture itself so that agents automatically learn the entire vocabulary of positional information as soon as a single word is invented. In this way, effective signaling is more evolutionarily tractable because directionality can be discovered in a single step.

Directional reception can be implemented in the real world in a number of ways. For example, it is possible to perceive the direction of signals sent via sound or light [8]. However, naïve implementations of such approaches may not be robust to environmental factors such as bright rooms or poor acoustics. More promisingly, directional communication can also be simulated if robots have an accurate means of localization. The real world experiment in this paper demonstrates a centralized localization approach based on wheel encoder odometry that facilitates the real world implementation. However, stronger methods exist, such as the decentralized localization proposed by Franchi et al. [9], or the system for localized communication proposed by Gutiérrez et al. [13] that uses frequency modulation to overcome environmental IR-sensor noise.

The significant advantage demonstrated in the experiment by the communication scheme with directional reception over the non-directional approaches points to the importance of considering including directional reception when formulating multiagent communication architectures for future robot coordination problems. Furthermore, communication features other than directional reception likely have a significant impact on evolutionary performance, but have yet to be empirically tested. One such feature is directional projection - the ability of agents to project communication signals only in a specific direction. Overall, with realistic real world options for directional sensing and signal projection available, such schemes merit serious consideration for complex multiagent tasks.

6. CONCLUSIONS

This paper presented an empirical study of directional reception for the evolution of neural controllers applied to a group coordination task. A communication scheme with directional reception was compared to two non-directional schemes with different potentials for message complexity, as well as to a scheme in which communication is disabled. The results indicate that directional communication is more evolutionarily tractable than non-directional approaches because it eliminates the need to discover a complex language to express the positional information that is crucial to optimally solving the task. The real world viability of the directional communication scheme was demonstrated by successfully transferring the best evolved neural controllers to Khepera III robots. Thus this paper serves as a reminder of the importance of directional reception and suggests that it is an important language feature to consider when designing communication architectures for more complicated tasks in the future.

7. ACKNOWLEDGMENTS

This work was supported through a grant from the US Army Research Office (Award No. W911NF-11-1-0489). This paper does not necessarily reflect the position or policy of the government, and no official endorsement should be inferred.

References

[1] P. J. Bentley and S. Kumar. Three ways to grow designs: A comparison of embryogenies for an evolutionary design problem. In *Proceedings of the Genetic and Evolutionary Computation Conference (GECCO 1999)*, pages 35–43, 1999.

[2] J. C. Bongard and R. Pfeifer. Evolving complete agents using artificial ontogeny. *Morpho-functional Machines: The New Species (Designing Embodied Intelligence)*, pages 237–258, 2003.

[3] D. B. D'Ambrosio, S. Goodell, J. Lehman, S. Risi, and K. O. Stanley. Multirobot behavior synchronization through direct neural network communication. In *Proceedings of the 5th International Conference on Intelligent Robotics and Applications (ICIRA 2012)*, New York, NY, 2012. Springer-Verlag.

[4] D. B. D'Ambrosio, J. Lehman, S. Risi, and K. O. Stanley. Evolving policy geometry for scalable multiagent learning. In *Proceedings of the Ninth International Conference on Autonomous Agents and Multiagent Systems (AAMAS 2010)*, pages 731–738. International Foundation for Autonomous Agents and Multiagent Systems, 2010.

[5] D. B. D'Ambrosio and K. O. Stanley. Generative encoding for multiagent learning. In *Proceedings of the Genetic and Evolutionary Computation Conference (GECCO 2008)*, New York, NY, 2008. ACM Press.

[6] D. B. D'Ambrosio and K. O. Stanley. Scalable multiagent learning through indirect encoding of policy geometry. *Evolutionary Intelligence*, 2013. To appear.

[7] E. Di Paolo. Behavioral coordination, structural congruence and entrainment in a simulation of acoustically coupled agents. *Adaptive Behavior*, 8(1):27–48, 2000.

[8] D. Floreano, S. Mitri, S. Magnenat, and L. Keller. Evolutionary conditions for the emergence of communication in robots. *Current Biology*, 17(6):514–519, 2007.

[9] A. Franchi, G. Oriolo, and P. Stegagno. Mutual localization in a multi-robot system with anonymous relative position measures. In *Proceedings of the International Conference on Intelligent Robots and Systems (IROS 2009)*, pages 3974–3980. IEEE, 2009.

[10] A. Garland and R. Alterman. Multiagent learning through collective memory. In *Adaptation, Coevolution and Learning in Multiagent Systems: Papers from the 1996 AAAI Spring Symposium*, pages 33–38, 1996.

[11] J. Gauci and K. O. Stanley. Autonomous evolution of topographic regularities in artificial neural networks. *Neural Computation*, 22(7):1860–1898, 2010.

[12] C. Green. SharpNEAT homepage. `http://sharpneat.sourceforge.net/`, 2003–2006.

[13] A. Gutiérrez, A. Campo, M. Dorigo, D. Amor, L. Magdalena, and F. Monasterio-Huelin. An open localization and local communication embodied sensor. *Sensors*, 8(11):7545–7563, 2008.

[14] C. F. Hockett. The origin of speech. *Scientific American*, 203:88–111, 1960.

[15] G. S. Hornby and J. B. Pollack. Creating high-level components with a generative representation for body-brain evolution. *Artificial Life*, 8(3), 2002.

[16] D. Hubel and T. Wiesel. Receptive fields, binocular interaction and functional architecture in the cat's visual cortex. *The Journal of Physiology*, 160(1):106, 1962.

[17] K.-C. Jim and C. L. Giles. How communication can improve the performance of multi-agent systems. In *Proceedings of the Fifth International Conference on Autonomous Agents (ICAA 2001)*, pages 584–591, New York, NY, USA, 2001. ACM.

[18] J. L. King. Centralized versus decentralized computing: organizational considerations and management options. *ACM Computing Surveys*, 15(4):319–349, 1983.

[19] D. Marocco and S. Nolfi. Emergence of communication in embodied agents evolved for the ability to solve a collective navigation problem. *Connection Science*, 19(1):53–74, 2007.

[20] J. Miller. Evolving a self-repairing, self-regulating, french flag organism. In *Proceedings of the Genetic and Evolutionary Computation Conference (GECCO 2004)*, pages 129–139. Springer, 2004.

[21] J. K. Pugh and K. O. Stanley. Evolving multimodal controllers with HyperNEAT. In *Proceedings of the Genetic and Evolutionary Computation Conference (GECCO 2013)*, New York, NY, 2013. ACM Press. To appear.

[22] A. Rawal, P. Rajagopalan, R. Miikkulainen, and K. Holekamp. Evolution of a communication code in cooperative tasks. In *Artificial Life*, volume 13, pages 243–250, 2012.

[23] K. O. Stanley. Compositional pattern producing networks: A novel abstraction of development. *Genetic Programming and Evolvable Machines Special Issue on Developmental Systems*, 8(2):131–162, 2007.

[24] K. O. Stanley, D. B. D'Ambrosio, and J. Gauci. A hypercube-based indirect encoding for evolving large-scale neural networks. *Artificial Life*, 15(2):185–212, 2009.

[25] K. O. Stanley and R. Miikkulainen. Evolving neural networks through augmenting topologies. *Evolutionary Computation*, 10(2):99–127, 2002.

[26] K. O. Stanley and R. Miikkulainen. A taxonomy for artificial embryogeny. *Artificial Life*, 9(2):93–130, 2003.

[27] K. O. Stanley and R. Miikkulainen. Competitive coevolution through evolutionary complexification. *Journal of Artificial Intelligence Research*, 21:63–100, 2004.

[28] P. Stone and M. Veloso. Multiagent systems: A survey from a machine learning perspective. *Autonomous Robots*, 8(3):345–383, 2000.

[29] S. Udin and J. Fawcett. Formation of topographic maps. *Annual Review of Neuroscience*, 11(1):289–327, 1988.

[30] K. Wagner, J. A. Reggia, J. Uriagereka, and G. S. Wilkinson. Progress in the simulation of emergent communication and language. *Adaptive Behavior*, 11(1):37–69, 2003.

[31] G. Werner and M. Dyer. Evolution of communication in artificial organisms. In *Proceedings of the Second International Conference of Artificial Life (ALIFE 1991)*, pages 659–687, Redwood City, CA, 1992. Addison-Wesley.

[32] X. Yao. Evolving artificial neural networks. *Proceedings of the IEEE*, 87(9):1423–1447, 1999.

[33] C. Yong and R. Miikkulainen. Coevolution of role-based cooperation in multiagent systems. *IEEE Transactions on Autonomous Mental Development*, 1(3):170–186, 2009.

Generational Neuro-Evolution: Restart and Retry for Improvement

David Shorten
University of Cape Town
Private Bag X3
Rondebosch 7701
dshorten@cs.uct.ac.za

Geoff Nitschke
University of Cape Town
Private Bag X3
Rondebosch 7701
gnitschke@cs.uct.ac.za

ABSTRACT

This paper proposes a new *Neuro-Evolution* (NE) method for automated controller design in agent-based systems. The method is *Generational Neuro-Evolution* (GeNE), and is comparatively evaluated with established NE methods in a multi-agent predator-prey task. This study is part of an ongoing research goal to derive *efficient* (minimising convergence time to optimal solutions) and *scalable* (effective for increasing numbers of agents) controller design methods for adapting agents in neuro-evolutionary multi-agent systems. Dissimilar to comparative NE methods, GeNE employs tiered selection and evaluation as its generational fitness evaluation mechanism and, furthermore, re-initializes the population each generation. Results indicate that GeNE is an appropriate controller design method for achieving efficient and scalable behavior in a multi-agent predator-prey task, where the goal was for multiple predator agents to collectively capture a prey agent. GeNE outperforms comparative NE methods in terms of efficiency (minimising the number of genotype evaluations to attain optimal task performance).

Categories and Subject Descriptors

I.2.11 [**Distributed Artificial Intelligence**]: Intelligent agents

General Terms

Algorithms

Keywords

Neuro-Evolution, Conventional Neuro-Evolution, Multi-Agent Enforced Sub-Populations

GECCO'14, July 12-16, 2014, Vancouver, BC, Canada.

http://dx.doi.org/10.1145/2576768.2598295.

1. INTRODUCTION

Neuro-Evolution [29], [9] has been demonstrated as effective for evolving various problem-solving collective behaviors in agent based systems [11], [24]. Collective behaviors (those requiring agent cooperation) that emerge as the result of interactions of cooperative or specialised agent behaviors, have been demonstrated as adaptive, robust and efficient problem solvers in a broad range of tasks [18], [20], [21], [5]. For example, collective behaviors have been evolved to solve tasks such as multi-robot coordination and cooperation [18], [2], multi-agent game playing [27], and multi-agent pursuit-evasion [19], [5], [32].

However, an open research objective is to derive controller design methods that evolve *efficient* and *scalable* collective behaviors that are consistently effective across a broad range of tasks. In this study, *efficient* refers to the number of fitness (genotype) evaluations a method requires to reach an optimal solution, and *scalable* refers to the capability to retain efficient behavior as task complexity increases.

This paper introduces the *Generational Neuro-Evolution* (GeNE) method for automated controller design. GeNE contributes a tiered approach for selecting and evaluating progressively fitter genotypes during each generation. This allows low performance genotypes to quickly be removed and the population to be periodically re-initialized in the region of the fittest genotypes. This allows GeNE to rapidly focus its search in optimal parts of the fitness landscape.

For complex tasks, NE usually requires many fitness (genotype) evaluations before a near optimal or optimal solution is attained, and genotype evaluations are computationally expensive and time consuming [15]. This problem is exacerbated by multi-agent (collective behavior) tasks, where the interactions of multiple agents required to solve such tasks increases the dimensionality of the search space. Also, many collective behavior tasks, such as multi-robot cooperative transport and collective construction, are defined by noisy, discontinuous, multi-modal search spaces [26], [1].

Several methods have been proposed as a means of increasing *Evolutionary Algorithms* (EAs) efficiency. For example, the interpolation between genotypes to build a meta-model of the fitness function [16], the inheritance of fitness from ancestral genotypes [25], and clustering genotypes and assigning fitness to population sub-sets [17]. All of these approaches reduce the number of fitness evaluations required, increasing EA efficiency in their respective tasks.

However, there has been relatively little successful research into NE methods yielding increased efficiency and scalability in collective behavior tasks. To increase efficiency and scalability, GeNE combines techniques used in *Evolutionary Strategies* (ES) [4] and *Hill Climbers* [23]. That is, similar to ES, GeNE employs only *mutation* operators [7], and similar to *Hill Climbers* [23], the genotype population is periodically re-initialized in the neighbourhood of the current fittest solutions in the fitness landscape [3]. An initial experimental validation of GeNE's efficiency and scalability is conducted in controller adaptation in a multi-agent predator-prey (*pursuit-evasion*) task for a range of predator team sizes. *Conventional Neuro-Evolution* (CNE) [12], and *Multi-Agent Enforced Sub-Populations* (MESP) [32] are also tested in the pursuit-evasion task. CNE and MESP were selected as comparative methods since both have been successfully applied to the pursuit-evasion task [19], [32].

Pursuit-evasion is indicative of a broader range of multi-agent tasks that use emergent collective behavior such as cooperation to enable problem solving [6]. Such tasks include multi-robot surveillance [10], [20], collective construction [21], and coordinated movement and search [2]. The pursuit-evasion task in this paper used predator and prey agents moving at equal speeds in a wrap-around world. A consequence of this was that cooperation between predators was mandated for prey capture.

Results support the efficacy of GeNE using efficiency and scalability metrics in the pursuit-evasion task, and yield an initial insight into the type of collective behavior tasks to which GeNE is most suited as a controller design method.

1.1 Research Goal, Hypothesis, and Task

Research goal: Demonstrate that GeNE out-performs (with statistical significance) the CNE and MESP controller design methods in a multi-agent pursuit-evasion task. Efficiency and scalability metrics are used as the performance metrics.

Research hypothesis: GeNE's tiered genotype evaluation mechanism allows GeNE evolved predator teams to achieve a higher task performance (with statistical significance) in the pursuit-evasion task, compared to CNE and MESP evolved predator teams.

Pursuit-evasion task: Requires multiple predators to adapt their collective behavior such that they capture a prey agent [19]. The behavior of the prey is not adapted during simulation, but rather uses a static heuristic predator-evasion behavior from previous experiments [32].

2. METHODS

2.1 CNE: Conventional Neuro-Evolution

CNE [12] uses the NE process illustrated in *Figure 1(a)*. A *Genetic Algorithm* (GA) [7] is applied to evolve a population of *Artificial Neural Network* (ANN) controllers (section 3.1). Each team of predator controllers is represented in the genotype population as a vector of all ANN connection weights. CNE predator teams are heterogeneous in that the genotype encodes N distinct predator ANN controllers. Each generation of CNE, the team is evaluated in multiple task trials (predator team lifetimes), and an average fitness assigned to the genotype (predator team) being evaluated.

2.2 MESP: Multi-Agent Enforced Sub-Populations

MESP [32] uses cooperative co-evolution to adapt behaviors in a team of agent controllers (ANNs). Given N genotype populations, N controllers are evolved, and evaluated according to how well they solve a collective behavior task. MESP teams are heterogenous since each controller is evolved from a separate population. *Figure 1* illustrates an example of MESP applied to evolve three ANN predator controllers.

MESP evolves hidden layer neuron weights and within each population combines the fittest u neurons, selected from u sub-populations (in each population) into complete ANN controllers. Each sub-population evolves a neuron for a specific hidden layer position, where neurons are evaluated based on how well they function in a complete controller (determined by fitness evaluations). Yong and Miikkulainen [32] present a comprehensive description of MESP.

2.3 GeNE: Generational Neuro-Evolution

GeNE's genotype is the same as used by CNE. That is, a vector of all ANN connection weights for a team of N controllers. However, GeNE differs from CNE in the following respects:

1. GeNE uses mutation only. The motivation for this design choice was to investigate (within the context of a collective behavior task) the benefits of mutated solutions being applied, per generation, to progressively fitter regions of the genotype space.
2. GeNE is generational. At the end of each generation the population is re-initialized in a *Cauchy* distribution around the generation's fittest genotype.
3. GeNE's genotype evaluation uses a tiered structure. Initially, all genotypes are evaluated comparatively few times. Only genotypes which perform well on these evaluations are passed on to a subsequent tier of evaluations in which they are evaluated further. The process of passing fewer genotypes on to higher tiers continues until only one genotype remains. The population is re-initialized about this fittest genotype.

The GeNE process is enumerated in the following.

1. *Tiered Evaluation:* The genotypes are passed through T evaluation tiers. Tier t accepts n_t input genotypes, evaluates them in ρ_t task trials, and outputs the n_{t+1} fittest genotypes ($n_{t+1} < n_t$). These n_{t+1} fittest genotypes are then input to tier $t+1$. This process continues until one genotype is output by tier T. A task trial was z iterations of a simulation run, during which a genotype was evaluated.
2. *Re-initialisation:* At the end of each generation, the population is re-initialized around the generation's fittest genotype. Every weight of the fittest genotype has a random value drawn from a *Cauchy* distribution added to it. This process is similar to burst mutation [32].
3. *Stagnation Control:* The fittest genotype is recorded at each generation. Given that fitness values are normalized between 0 and 100, then if the fittest genotype of the current generation is not 20 units or fitter than the fittest genotype 3 generations ago, then stagnation has occurred. If so, GeNE is restarted.
4. *Stop condition:* Re-iterate steps [1, 3] until convergence is achieved (prey-capture in this study), or GeNE has run for Y generations. A generation is the pro-

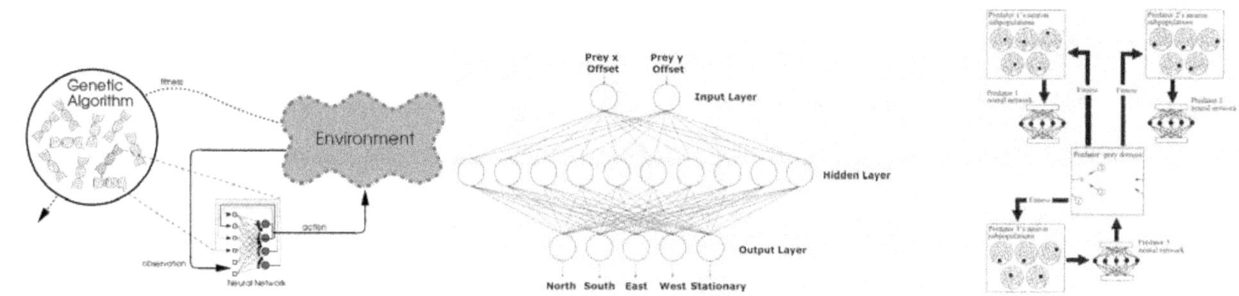

(a) (b) (c)

Figure 1: ***(a) Conventional Neuro-Evolution (CNE).*** **Complete ANN controllers are evolved from one population (Figure from Gomez et al. [12], used with the permission of the authors).** ***(b) Predator ANN Controller.*** **Connection weights were evolved by CNE, MESP or GeNE in pursuit-evasion experiments.** ***(c) Multi-Agent Enforced Sub-Populations (MESP).*** **Example of MESP applied to evolve three predator controllers in a pursuit-evasion task (Figure from Yong and Miikkulainen [32], used with the permission of the authors and the *IEEE*).**

cess whereby genotypes move up through the evaluation tiers followed by re-initialization around the fittest genotype.

Figure 2 illustrates the GeNE process.

3. PURSUIT-EVASION TASK

Pursuit-evasion requires a *predator* team to collectively capture a *prey* in a multi-agent simulation [32]. The environment was a 100 x 100 wrap-around grid. Predators always started in the top-left corner grid square, and the prey at a random position. Both predators and prey moved at equal speeds and had a global view of the environment (always sensing opponent positions). The task was for the predators to minimise the number of simulation (task trial) iterations to prey-capture. Prey-capture occurs when at least one predator moves onto the same grid-square as the prey. Given equal movement speeds, and a wrap-around environment, at least two predators are required to capture the prey [32]. Predator and prey movement was limited to *north*, *south*, *east* and *west*, and one grid square per iteration. Predators and prey *lived* for 150 iterations (one *task trial* in table 1).

3.1 Predator and Prey Controllers

Predator sensory inputs were mapped to motor outputs using a feed-forward *Artificial Neural Network* (ANN) controller (Figure 1, centre). Two input and five output neurons were fully connected to 10 *Hidden Layer* (HL) neurons. HL and output neuron activation values were computed by a *Sigmoid* function [14]. The output node with the highest activation value was selected as the output (action) of the given simulation iteration. This approach was selected since it was used in the NE controller evolution experiments of Yong and Miikkulainen [32]. Furthermore, the MESP method is re-implemented in this study with the goal of reproducing previous results [32], as well as comparing them with the CNE and GeNE methods.

The prey controller was a heuristic that directed the prey to move in the opposite direction of the closest predator.

3.2 Fitness Function: Predator Evaluation

Predator team prey capture behavior (evolved by CNE, MESP, and GeNE) was evaluated in terms of *efficiency* and *scalability*. That is, the number of fitness evaluations that elapsed before task completion, and the efficiency of evolved prey-capture behaviors as predator team size is increased.

The fitness function shown in equation 1 was used by CNE, MESP and GeNE, where d_e was the average distance between the predators and the prey at the end of a task trial, 100 was the environment length and width, and 200 was used to increase fitness awarded for prey capture.

$$f(d_e) = \begin{cases} 100 - d_e & \text{if the prey was not caught} \\ 200 - d_e & \text{if the prey was caught} \end{cases} \tag{1}$$

4. EXPERIMENTS

Experiments applied either CNE (section 2.1), MESP (section 2.2), or GeNE (section 2.3) to evolve the connection weights of ANN controllers (figure 1, centre), and thus adapt predator team behavior. One experiment was CNE, MESP or GeNE executed for Y generations, or until a threshold task performance was attained. Each experiment was executed for 200 runs. Table 1 presents the parameters used in these experiments.

The task performance threshold was defined as prey capture for at least 80% of agent starting positions. The prey had 100 possible starting positions in a 10x10 grid in the bottom left corner of the environment. An average fitness of CNE, MESP and GeNE evolved teams was calculated over all runs. CNE, MESP, and GeNE each tested predator team sizes: N = [3, 4, 5, 6]. Each generation of the GeNE, MESP, and CNE methods consists of multiple task trials. A task trial was one predator team executed for 150 simulation iterations (table 1). Each task trial tested different prey starting positions as a means of sampling the many possible starting positions.

To ensure a fair comparison, all methods used the same population size of 500 genotypes per predator, where team sizes of three to six predators were tested. As per previous work [12], the number of genotype evaluations varied, for different methods, as the predator team size increased.

Table 1 presents the simulation and NE method parameter settings. These parameter values were determined experimentally so as to maximize the performance of all the al-

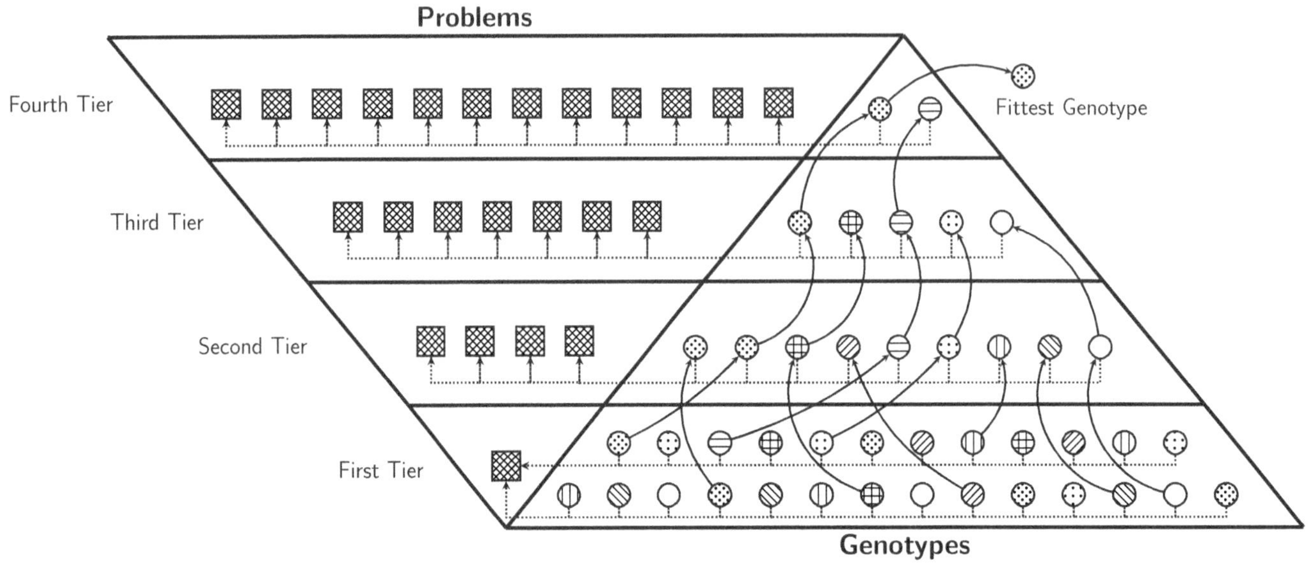

Figure 2: The tiered evaluation process of a generation of a hypothetical run of GeNE. The round nodes represent genotypes and the square nodes represent problems (or problem instances) on which they can be evaluated. A solid edge represents a genotype being promoted from a lower tier to a higher one. A dashed edge represents a genotype being evaluated on a problem. In the pursuit-evasion task multiple problem instances (agent starting positions) are evaluated.

gorithms involved. Minor changes to these values produced similar results for CNE, MESP and GeNE evolved teams. Unless otherwise specified, the parameters listed in table 1 apply to all NE methods.

Yong and Miikkulainen executed similar pursuit-evasion experiments on MESP [31]. They observed that the evolution of three predator teams capable of capturing the prey seven times, for nine different starting positions, required on average 108 000 evaluations (standard deviation of 42000). The experiments presented in this paper found that the evolution of three predator teams capable of capturing the prey eighty times, given one hundred different starting positions required, on average 94 000 evaluations (standard deviation of 112 000, table 3). This demonstrates that the higher task performance of GeNE evolved teams is not a result of parameter tuning issues in either method.

4.1 Cauchy Distribution

Cauchy distribution was used as a mutation operator in our experiments. The reasons for this are:

1. Testing on numerous instances with the Cauchy distribution indicated that it produced better task performance than the normal distribution.
2. In the related field of evolutionary programming, the Cauchy distribution has been found to yield higher performance than the normal [30].
3. There is precedent for using the Cauchy distribution in NE [32].

4.2 CNE: Setup

CNE (section 2.1) predator controllers were evolved from a population of N (predator team size) x 500 genotypes. Each genotype encoded N controllers as a vector of N x 70 real values. That is, two input neurons plus five output neurons fully connected to 10 hidden layer neurons. The CNE process was as follows.

Each gene (weight) in each genotype of the population was *initialized* to a random value from a *Cauchy* distribution ($x_0 = 0$ and $\gamma = 1$). Each genotype was decoded into N ANNs to derive a heterogeneous team of predator controllers. Each team (genotype) was then systematically selected and evaluated in the pursuit-evasion task for 20 task trials. Each team's fitness was calculated as an average over all task trials. At the end of each generation, genotypes in the fittest 25% of the population were randomly paired and *uniform crossover* [7] applied. Enough child genotypes were created to replace the least fit 50%. A child was mutated with a 0.4 degree of probability. If a child was selected for mutation, then N x 10 randomly chosen weights, were modified via adding a randomly drawn value from a *Cauchy* distribution ($x_0 = 0$ and $\gamma = 0.5$).

4.3 MESP: Setup

MESP (section 2.2) evolved N predator ANNs from N populations. Each population contained 10 sub-populations, where each sub-population contained 50 genotypes (hidden layer neurons). That is, the weights of 10 hidden layer neurons were evolved from 10 sub-populations to form complete ANN controllers. A MESP genotype was a vector of seven real values encoding the connection weights of two sensory inputs plus five outputs of a hidden layer neuron. The MESP process was as follows.

Each gene (weight) in each genotype of the population was *initialized* to a random value from a *Cauchy* distribution ($x_0 = 0$ and $\gamma = 1$). In line with the evaluation approach used in previous research [32], evaluation in MESP occurred over *10 task trial sets*. In each task trial set, 50 *groups* (where 50 was the sub-population size) of task trials were performed. A group to be evaluated was composed via

Table 1: Pursuit-Evasion Parameters. Simulation and Neuro-Evolution method settings.

Pursuit-Evasion Parameter Settings	
Simulation runs / Environment size / Predator team size (N)	200 / 100 x 100 / [3, 6]
Predator / Prey controller	Feed-Forward ANN / Heuristic
Predator ANN Input/ Output / Hidden layer neurons	2 / 5 / 10
Predator / Prey sensor range	Environment length
Genotype structure (CNE / MESP / GeNE)	N x ANN weights / Hidden neurons / N x ANN weights
Genotype length (CNE / MESP / GeNE)	N x 70 / 7 / N x 70
Genotype representation	Real valued vector
Generations / Trial iterations (team lifetime)	500 / 150
Mutation probability	0.4
Mutation *Cauchy* distribution γ (CNE / MESP / GeNE)	0.1 / 0.5 / see table 2
Crossover operator (CNE, MESP)	uniform
Population size (CNE, MESP, GeNE)	N x 500
Genotype populations (CNE/MESP/GeNE)	1 / [3, 6] / 1
Sub-populations / Sub-population size (MESP)	10 / 50
Parent selection (MESP, CNE) / (GeNE)	Elitist: top 25% / Tiered selection (section 2.3)
Population replacement	Lower 50% of population

randomly selecting a genotype g_{ij} from each sub-population p_{ij} ($1 \leq j \leq 10$). This was done for each population P_i ($1 \leq i \leq N$, $3 \leq N \leq 6$), where N is the number of predators in a team. Selected genotypes were marked so as they were not evaluated again in a given task trial set. This ensured that each genotype was evaluated the same number of times.

From these selected genotypes, N predator controllers were constructed, and this team was evaluated in six task trials. An average fitness (calculated over the task trials) was assigned to each genotype that participated in the task trial set. A genotype's fitness was calculated as its average fitness across 10 task trial sets.

At the end of each generation, genotypes in the fittest 25% of p_{ij} were randomly paired and *uniform crossover* applied. Enough child genotypes were created to replace the least fit 50%. A child was mutated with a 0.4 degree of probability. If a child was selected for mutation, then N x 10 randomly chosen weights, were modified via adding a randomly drawn value from a *Cauchy* distribution ($x_0 = 0$ and $\gamma = 0.5$).

4.4 GeNE: Setup

GeNE (section 2.3) evolves predator teams from a population of N x 500 genotypes, where each genotype encodes the connection weights of N predator controllers. So as to allow reuse of the MESP architecture, a variation on GeNE's initialisation and re-initialisation procedures (section 2.3) was used for these experiments.

For initialization, N MESP populations were initialized, where each population contained 10 sub-populations and each sub-population consisted of 100 genotypes (section 4.3). For the construction of each GeNE genotype, one MESP genotype was randomly chosen from each of the 10 sub-populations in each of the N populations. These N x 10 genotypes then represented one GeNE genotype.

Re-initialization occurred via mutating the weights of all MESP genotypes that composed the fittest GeNE genotype (for a given generation). This had the effect of re-initializing the corresponding sub-populations (from which the GeNE genotype was composed). Table 2 specifies the γ used for re-initialization and the parameter values used in GeNE's tiered evaluation. Table 2 also presents the number of genotypes (teams) selected for evaluation in each tier, and the number of task trials (ρ) per team evaluation per tier. These values were determined experimentally and found to work well for the pursuit-evasion task.

4.5 Lesion Studies

Lesion studies were done to ascertain the contribution of GeNE's tiered evaluation and re-initialization (section 2.3). For each lesion study, resultant data sets of GeNE evolved teams in non-lesioned studies (section 4.4) were compared with lesioned study results for statistically significant differences ($p < 0.01$) using independent two-sample t-tests [8].

Lesion study 1: This study tested only one tier of evaluation (four were used in the pursuit-evasion task) per GeNE generation. This tier had a size of 123 and ρ was set to 49. The goal was to elucidate the benefit of multiple tiers of evaluation. Supporting this, results indicated a higher (with statistical significance, $p < 0.01$) average task performance (for team sizes N = [3, 4, 5, 6]) of GeNE evolved teams in non-lesioned versus lesioned experiments (figure 3(b)).

Lesion study 2: This study tested four tiers of evaluation to elucidate the impact of GeNE's re-initialization procedure. To test this, this lesion study only mutated each

Table 2: Left: GeNE Tiered Evaluation. N genotypes (teams) are input to each tier. These teams are tested in ρ task trials. A fittest subset of teams is output (input for the next tier). ρ: Number of task trials a team is tested in. Right: γ values used for GeNE population re-initialization given the previous generation's fittest team's capture ratio.

Tier	Input Teams	Output Teams	ρ	Capture Ratio (r)	γ
1	2000	500	1	$0 \leq r < 0.1$	0.9
2	500	50	4	$0.1 \leq r < 0.2$	0.7
3	50	12	16	$0.2 \leq r < 0.3$	0.5
4	12	1	100	$0.3 \leq r < 0.5$	0.4
-	-	-	-	$0.5 \leq r < 0.6$	0.3
-	-	-	-	$0.6 \leq r < 0.8$	0.15

Table 3: Task performance of CNE, MESP, and GeNE evolved predator teams: Average number (in thousands) of fitness (genotype) evaluations until prey capture. Values in parentheses are standard deviations.

Method	3 Predators	4 Predators	5 Predators	6 Predators
CNE	3172.35 (863.60)	3981.20 (914.53)	4296.25 (741.06)	4633.80 (365.87)
MESP	93.51 (112.70)	48.70 (10.94)	44.84 (8.62)	44.04 (8.10)
GeNE	37.15 (22.64)	27.99 (16.87)	24.02 (10.57)	24.33 (9.15)
GeNE (Lesion study 1)	109.06 (84.11)	60.42 (43.35)	52.23 (32.19)	39.72 (22.31)
GeNE (Lesion study 2)	69.44 (59.50)	46.17 (35.34)	30.68 (17.46)	32.06 (17.35)

weight in a GeNE genotype with a 0.2 degree of probability. Lesion study 2 results indicated a higher (with statistical significance, $p < 0.01$) average task performance (for team sizes $N = [3, 4, 5, 6]$) of GeNE evolved teams in non-lesioned versus lesioned experiments (figure 3(b)).

5. RESULTS AND DISCUSSION

Figure 3(a) presents the average number of *fitness* evaluations (calculated over 200 runs for each method) required by CNE, MESP and GeNE evolved teams to achieve the task performance threshold for method *efficiency* (section 4). These results are also shown in table 3. The *scalability* (maintaining efficiency as team size increased) of CNE, MESP and GeNE evolved prey-capture behaviors was also tested for team sizes of three to six predators.

Statistical comparisons (two-sample independent t-tests, $p < 0.01$) indicated that GeNE evolved teams yielded a significantly higher average efficiency, where this higher efficiency was maintained for all team sizes tested. This partially addresses the research objective (section 1.1) in that results indicate that GeNE out-performs CNE and MESP according to the efficiency metric.

Figure 3(a) indicates that all methods were scalable across the different predator team sizes which were tested. There were no major differences in the number of evaluations required as the predator team size increased. This was theorized to be the result of the interactions of solution space dimensionality and the number predators in the simulation. That is, increasing the number of predators increased the dimensionality of the solution space, however, a larger team size also increased the likelihood that the prey would be captured during the team's lifetime. However, only predator team sizes in the range [3, 6] were tested. In order for scalability to be properly demonstrated, a wider range of predator team sizes would need to be tested. It is thus concluded that the second part of the research goal (demonstrating scalability) was not fully addressed.

Figure 3(b) presents the average number of genotype evaluations taken by GeNE evolved teams versus lesioned GeNE evolved teams (section 4.5), for team sizes of up to six predators. Statistical comparisons ($p < 0.01$) indicated that lesioned GeNE evolved teams yielded a significantly lower average efficiency, that was consistent across all team sizes tested. These lesion study comparisons support the hypothesis (section 1.1) that GeNE's tiered genotype evaluation mechanism allows it to achieve a higher task performance, compared to CNE and MESP evolved predator teams. That is, lesion study 1 results supported the benefits of GeNE's tiered evaluation process, and lesion study 2 results supported the benefits of GeNE's re-initialization process.

The comparatively high efficiency of GeNE is theorized to be a result of its tiered evaluation (section 2.3). Consider that this pursuit-evasion study required the evolution of a prey-capture behavior where prey-capture is exhibited above a given task performance threshold. The evaluation of prey-capture behavior required many task trials that sampled the space of initial states (prey start positions versus predator start positions). The more task trials used to evaluated a

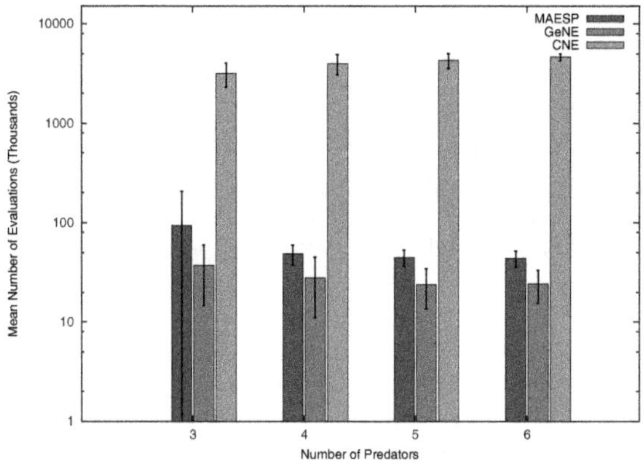

(a)

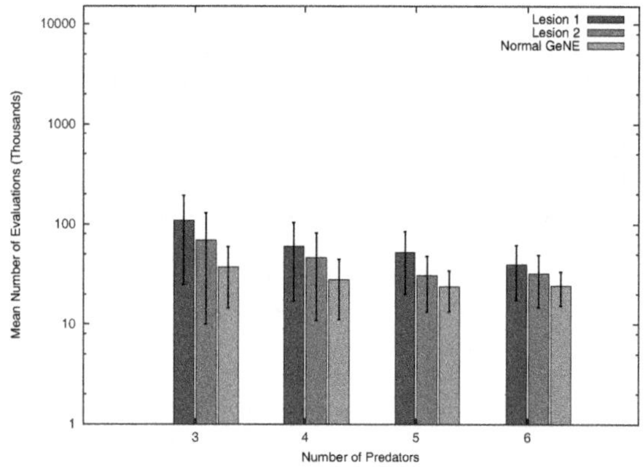

(b)

Figure 3: *(a)* CNE, MESP and GeNE evolved teams. Plots of average number of fitness (genotype) evaluations for predator team sizes: [3, 4, 5, 6]. Bars show the standard deviation. *(a)* Comparative plots for GeNE versus GeNE (lesioned) for predator team sizes: [3, 4, 5, 6]. Bars show the standard deviation. Note the logarithmic scale.

given genotype (prey-capture behavior), the more accurate that genotype's evaluation will be. Thus, via its tiered evaluation, GeNE was able to focus more evaluations on genotypes that were more likely to yield effective prey-capture behaviors, and thus attain a more accurate evaluation of these genotypes, and propagate these genotypes throughout the evolutionary process.

Furthermore, it is theorized that the re-initialization process enabled GeNE to achieve and maintain a high efficiency for all team sizes tested. That is, per generation of GeNE, the re-initialization process mandated a shift in search focus from exploration to exploitation in a given search space area. That is, GeNE's search was initially in a wide area of the fitness landscape (defined by the γ parameter in the burst mutation operator), around the current fittest genotype. As the fitness of the fittest genotype at each generation improved, γ decreased together with the size of the search space area. This tiered evaluation process is similar to the function of the self-adaptive σ parameter in *Evolutionary Strategies* (ES) [4]. Hence, one supposition is that GeNE will yield a comparative task performance on the same tasks in which ES yield optimal or near optimal performance. As such, future work will comparatively test GeNE and various ES on canonical optimization benchmark tasks [4].

Furthermore, it is theorized that particular features of the multi-agent pursuit-evasion search space, make it amendable to an efficient search by GeNE, where such efficiency is *scalable* (maintained for increasing team sizes). That is, compared to CNE and MESP, GeNE yielded faster convergence to search space optima (prey-capture above a task performance threshold) in ANN connection weight spaces of increasing dimensionality. However, the exact algorithmic and task environment mechanisms responsible for this result is the subject of ongoing research.

Also, most problems upon which NE methods yield a high task performance are presented in either a *general* or a *specific* form. In the pursuit-evasion task, predator agents can be adapted to catch prey starting from a given location (specific) or from a set of locations (general). Similarly, in the pole-balancing task [12], agents can be adapted to balance poles for a specific initial condition or for a range of initial conditions. Future work will also test if GeNE has an advantage where a range of starting conditions must be considered in order to evolve an optimal solution, since GeNE spend more of its evaluations sampling the task performance of genotypes with the potential to be highly fit.

6. CONCLUSIONS AND FUTURE WORK

This paper presented a new NE controller design method: *Generational Neuro-Evolution* (GeNE). In this study GeNE was applied to evolve predator agent controllers in a multi-agent pursuit-evasion task and was tested comparatively with *Conventional Neuro-Evolution* (CNE) and *Multi-Agent Enforced Sub-Populations* (MESP). Behaviors evolved by CNE, MESP and GeNE were measured in terms of *efficiency* and *scalability*. Efficiency was measured as the number of fitness (genotype) evaluations until a pursuit-evasion task performance threshold was attained. Scalability was measured as a method's capability to maintain efficiency as predator team size increased. Results supported part of this research objective, demonstrating that GeNE evolved collective prey-capture behaviors that were consistently more *efficient* (with statistical significance, $p < 0.01$) compared to those evolved by CNE and MESP. However, scalability was not fully demonstrated due to a lack of testing over a large range of team sizes. Results also supported the hypothesis that GeNE's tiered evaluation contributed to the higher efficiency and scalability of GeNE evolved prey-capture behaviors.

Several approaches to future work are currently underway. Future work will attempt to validate the efficacy of GeNE, using metrics of efficiency and scalability, but tested in single and multi-agent tasks. For example, controller adaptation in double-pole balancing [12], and multi-robot controller adaptation for collective behavior tasks such as cooperative transport [13], collective gathering [22], coordinated movement [2] or collective construction [28]. The efficacy of GeNE will also be tested for other controller types and genotype representations. ANNs and NE were selected since both are well established and as such considered appropriate for a preliminary study. Successful application of GeNE to canonical ES and NE benchmark tasks and more complex single and multi-agent tasks would contribute to establishing the efficacy of GeNE as an NE controller design method, and more generally as a broadly applicable evolutionary algorithm.

7. REFERENCES

[1] T. Arai, E. Pagello, and L. Parker. Advances in multi-robot systems. *IEEE Transactions on Robotics and Automation*, 18(5):655–661, 2002.

[2] G. Baldassarre, D. Parisi, and S. Nolfi. Distributed coordination of simulated robots based on self-organisation. *Artificial Life*, 12(3):289–311, 2006.

[3] D. Beasley, D. Bull, and R. Martin. A sequential niche technique for multimodal function optimization. *Evolutionary Computation*, 1(2):101–125, 1993.

[4] H. Beyer and H. Schwefel. Evolution strategies: A comprehensive introduction. *Natural Computing*, 1(1):3–52, 2002.

[5] D. D'Ambrosio and K. Stanley. Scalable multiagent learning through indirect encoding of policy geometry. *Evolutionary Intelligence*, 6(1):1–26, 2013.

[6] A. Eiben, G. Nitschke, and M. Schut. Evolving team behaviors with specialization. *Genetic Programming and Evolvable Machines*, 13(4):493–536, 2012.

[7] A. Eiben and J. Smith. *Introduction to Evolutionary Computing*. Springer-Verlag, Berlin, Germany, 2003.

[8] B. Flannery, S. Teukolsky, and W. Vetterling. *Numerical Recipes*. Cambridge University Press, Cambridge, 1986.

[9] D. Floreano, P. Dürr, and C. Mattiussi. Neuroevolution: from architectures to learning. *Evolutionary Intelligence*, 1(1):47–62, 2008.

[10] E. Folgado, M. Rincon, J. Alvarez, and J. Mira. A multi-robot surveillance system simulated in gazebo. In *Nature Inspired Problem-Solving Methods in Knowledge Engineering*, pages 202–211. Springer Berlin, Heidelberg, Germany, 2007.

[11] R. Goldstone and M. Janssen. Computational models of collective behavior. *TRENDS in Cognitive Sciences*, 9(9):424–429, 2005.

[12] F. Gomez, J. Schmidhuber, and R. Miikkulainen. Accelerated neural evolution through cooperatively coevolved synapses. *Journal of Machine Learning Research*, 9(1):937–965, 2008.

[13] R. Gross and M. Dorigo. Evolution of solitary and group transport behaviors for autonomous robots capable of self-assembling. *Adaptive Behavior*, 16(5):285–305, 2008.

[14] J. Hertz, A. Krogh, and R. Palmer. *Introduction to the Theory of Neural Computation*. Addison-Wesley, Redwood City, 1991.

[15] Y. Jin. A comprehensive survey of fitness approximation in evolutionary computation. *Soft Computing*, 9(1):3–12, 2005.

[16] Y. Jin, M. Olhofer, and B. Sendhoff. A framework for evolutionary optimization with approximate fitness functions. *IEEE Transactions on Evolutionary Computation*, 6(5):481–494, 2005.

[17] H. Kim and S. Cho. An efficient genetic algorithms with less fitness evaluation by clustering. In *Proceedings of the Congress on Evolutionary Computation*, pages 887–894, Seoul, Korea, 2001. IEEE.

[18] L. Li, A. Martinoli, and A. Yaser. Learning and measuring specialization in collaborative swarm systems. *Adaptive Behavior.*, 12(3):199–212, 2004.

[19] G. Nitschke. Designing emergent cooperation: a pursuit-evasion game case study. *Artificial Life and Robotics*, 9(4):222–233, 2005.

[20] G. Nitschke, M. Schut, and A. Eiben. Collective neuro-evolution for evolving specialized sensor resolutions in a multi-rover task. *Evolutionary Intelligence*, 3(1):13 29, 2010.

[21] G. Nitschke, M. Schut, and A. Eiben. Evolving behavioral specialization in robot teams to solve a collective construction task. *Swarm and Evolutionary Computation*, 2(1):25–38, 2012.

[22] S. Nouyan, R. Gross, M. Bonani, F. Mondada, and M. Dorigo. Teamwork in self-organized robot colonies. *IEEE Transactions on Evolutionary Computation*, 13(4):695–711, 2009.

[23] S. Russell and P. Norvig. *Artificial Intelligence, A Modern Approach. Second Edition.* University of Michigan Press, Ann Arbor, USA, 2003.

[24] R. Sarker and T. Ray. Agent based evolutionary approach: An introduction. In *Agent-Based Evolutionary Search, Adaptation, Learning, and Optimization*, pages 1–11. Springer, Berlin, Germany, 2010.

[25] K. Sastry, D. Goldberg, and M. Pelikan. Don't evaluate, inherit. In *Proceedings of the Genetic and Evolutionary Computation Conference*, pages 551–558, San Francisco, USA, 2001. Morgan Kaufmann.

[26] C. Schultz and L. Parker. In *Multi-robot Systems: From Swarms to Intelligent Automata*. Kluwer, Washington DC, USA, 2002.

[27] K. Stanley, B. Bryant, and R. Miikkulainen. Real-time neuro-evolution in the nero video game. *IEEE Transactions Evolutionary Computation*, 9(6):653–668, 2005.

[28] J. Werfel and R. Nagpal. Extended stigmergy in collective construction. *IEEE Intelligent Systems*, 21(2):20–28, 2006.

[29] X. Yao. Evolutionary artificial neural networks. *International Journal of Neural Systems*, 4(3):203–222, 1993.

[30] X. Yao, Y. Liu, and G. Lin. Evolutionary programming made faster. *Evolutionary Computation, IEEE Transactions on*, 3(2):82–102, 1999.

[31] C. Yong and R. Miikkulainen. Cooperative coevolution of multi-agent systems. *University of Texas at Austin, Austin, TX*, 2001.

[32] C. Yong and R. Miikkulainen. Coevolution of role-based cooperation in multi-agent systems. *IEEE Transactions on Autonomous Mental Development*, 1:170–186, 2010.

A Novel Human-Computer Collaboration: Combining Novelty Search with Interactive Evolution

Brian G. Woolley
Department of ECE
Air Force Institute of Technology
WPAFB, OH 45433, USA
brian.woolley@ieee.org

Kenneth O. Stanley
Department of EECS
University of Central Florida
Orlando, FL 32816, USA
kstanley@eecs.ucf.edu

ABSTRACT

Recent work on novelty and behavioral diversity in evolutionary computation has highlighted the potential disadvantage of driving search purely through objective means. This paper suggests that leveraging human insight during search can complement such novelty-driven approaches. In particular, a new approach called *novelty-assisted interactive evolutionary computation* (NA-IEC) combines human intuition with novelty search to facilitate the serendipitous discovery of agent behaviors in a deceptive maze. In this approach, the human user directs evolution by selecting what is interesting from the on-screen population of behaviors. However, unlike in typical IEC, the user can now request that the next generation be filled with *novel* descendants. The experimental results demonstrate that combining human insight with novelty search not only finds solutions significantly faster and at lower genomic complexities than fully-automated processes guided purely by fitness or novelty, but it also finds solutions faster than the traditional IEC approach. Such results add to the evidence that combining human users and automated processes creates a synergistic effect in the search for solutions.

Categories and Subject Descriptors:
I.2.6 [**Artificial Intelligence**]: Learning

General Terms: Algorithms

Keywords: Evolutionary computation, interactive evolutionary computation, human-led search, fitness, deception, non-objective search, novelty search, stepping stones, serendipitous discovery

1. INTRODUCTION

Several results in recent years have hinted at the limitations of traditional objective functions, wherein the more a candidate resembles the objective, the higher its fitness. An early hint that such an approach to fitness may be flawed was from experiments with the *novelty search* algorithm [13], which rewards novel behaviors instead of rewarding objective performance. Interestingly, novelty search significantly outperformed objective-based fitness in a deceptive maze-navigation domain [13, 16], showing counter-intuitively that in some deceptive cases it is possible that having no specific objective may work better than rewarding progress toward the objective. Other results with novelty search in recent years have echoed this outcome [10, 17, 20].

At the same time, interactive evolutionary computation (IEC) [32], wherein humans guide evolution through interactive breeding, has also shown promise at finding needles in the haystack of possibilities. For example, Woolley and Stanley [35] found that images evolved by human users on the Picbreeder online service [26] could not be re-evolved by the very same evolutionary algorithm when they are made the automated objective, suggesting that humans are uniquely adept at identifying promising stepping stones.

Yet both novelty search and IEC face their own challenges. Work with novelty search has shown that it may become lost in especially large spaces [12, 15], and Takagi [32] warns that IEC is limited by human fatigue. However, interestingly, the advantages of both approaches can potentially address each other's disadvantages. That is, the main insight in this paper is that the ability of humans to identify promising stepping stones is naturally complemented by the ability of novelty search to generate *candidate sets* of potential stepping stones. In other words, novelty search can mitigate the main weakness of IEC (i.e. that humans grow tired quickly [32]) by offloading most of the exploratory work, while IEC can mitigate the tendency of novelty search to get lost in vast behavior spaces.

In this paper, a hybrid approach, called *novelty-assisted interactive evolutionary computation* (NA-IEC), is compared via the evolution of neurocontrollers for robots in the deceptive mazes of Lehman and Stanley [16] to pure novelty search, objective-based search, and a human-led search without the novelty assistance. Interestingly, while novelty search was previously shown significantly more effective than objective-based search in this domain [16], NA-IEC outperforms novelty search by a multiple of three to four times, yielding by far the fastest solution on these deceptive problems. This work is complementary to recent results from Bongard and Hornby [1] and Hornby and Bongard [11] that showed that humans and more conventional objective-driven search can work together synergistically to solve practical control problems rather than just to explore creative domains. This paper builds on this idea by showing that novelty also has an important role to play in such a human-machine collaboration, in part to push the human out of his or her comfort zone to explore new ideas.

2. BACKGROUND

This section reviews deception in EC and the non-objective methods that are the basis for the approach introduced in this paper.

2.1 Deceptive Task Domains

The key question in research on deception is what causes evolutionary algorithms (EAs) to fail and how to mitigate such fail-

GECCO'14, July 12–16, 2014, Vancouver, BC, Canada.

ACM 978-1-4503-2662-9/14/07 ...$15.00.
http://dx.doi.org/10.1145/2576768.2598353.

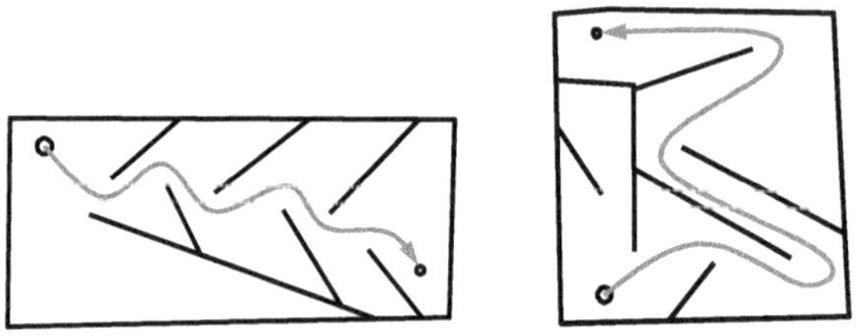

(a) Medium Map (b) Hard Map

Figure 1: Maze Navigation Maps (Lehman and Stanley [13, 16]). The deceptive maze domain is a metaphor for search and is *not* a path-planning problem. Rather, the aim is to evolve a neural network that drives a robot through the maze. The walls represent barriers to search and the cul-de-sacs represent local-optima that can deceive objective-based search.

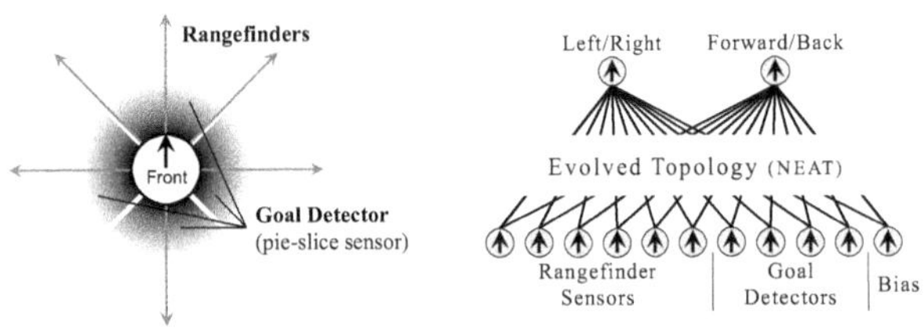

(a) Sensors (b) Neural Network

Figure 2: Maze Navigation Robot (Lehman and Stanley [13, 16]). The sensor package (a) includes six rangefinders that detect walls and four pie-slice sensors that signal the general direction to the objective. The navigation behavior, encoded as an ANN (b), maps sensor inputs to actions, i.e. turn rate (*left/right*) and velocity (*forward/backward*). Under this construction, navigators cannot see the whole maze and must evolve a control policy that traverses the maze based on sensory input.

ures [8, 34]. For the purpose of this work, we are interested in the case in which pursuing what appears to be a reasonable *objective* produces an unreasonable *objective function*. In this context, an intuitive definition of deception, as stated by Lehman and Stanley [16], is: "A deceptive objective function will *deceive* search by actively pointing the wrong way." That is, the fitness function can point the wrong way because not only must it reward the objective, but it must also reward the intermediate solutions (i.e. the *stepping stones*) that lead to the objective. Often these stepping stones do not improve performance on the objective function (and may even decrease it), causing search algorithms to forsake the most promising candidates.

A good example of a deceptive domain, which is also the experimental domain in this paper, is the deceptive maze domain introduced by Lehman and Stanley [13, 16], in which a simulated robot must navigate through a maze with deceptive cul-de-sacs (figure 1). The maze-navigation agents that act within the maze have a sensor package with six rangefinders that detect the walls and four pie-slice sensors that signal the direction to the goal (figure 2a). Each robot's navigation behavior, encoded as an artificial neural network (ANN), maps sensor inputs to actions, i.e. turn rate (*left/right*) and velocity (*forward/backward*), as shown in figure 2b. Under this construction, navigators must evolve a control policy that traverses the maze based on sensory input.

The medium (293 x 134 units) and hard (195 x 202 units) maps in figure 1 are deceptive by design because the maps contain cul-de-sacs that represent local optima in the search space. If fitness is assigned based on reducing the distance to the goal, then the objective function prunes out of the search the deceptive intermediate solutions (i.e. those that move away from the goal location) needed to reach the global objective. While an alternative objective function that rewards specific intermediate solutions is conceivable (and in fact will be explored later in this paper as well), the original point of this domain was to explore the effect of objective fitness when the precise stepping stones are *not known*, which is the typical predicament in most domains. In such cases, as in the standard objective function here, performance is generally rewarded for its proximity to the target behavior. Thus evolution driven by proximity to the goal often converges to a cul-de-sac from which the goal is inaccessible.

Despite extensive research, deception remains a significant problem in the field of EC [9, 18, 22]. The problem is that evolutionary algorithms (EAs) ultimately respond to the selection pressures created by the fitness function, which is often misleading. The challenge is to determine how to reward the intermediate steps that are required to reach the goal. In effect, what appears to be a reasonable heuristic may actually *prevent* the objective from being reached. Therefore, any similarity metric that guides the search toward an a priori objective is potentially a false compass to the optimal solution [28]. In this spirit, Lehman and Stanley [13, 16] introduced the idea of abandoning objectives as a search heuristic in deceptive domains, electing instead to reward individuals only for novel behaviors, as described next.

2.2 Novelty Search

Because pursuing objectives can be deceptive, Lehman and Stanley [13, 16] proposed that searching without regard to the objective, i.e. searching only for novel behavior, can be more effective at discovering solutions in some deceptive domains than rewarding objective performance.

Novelty search works with EAs by replacing the fitness function with a *novelty metric*. The novelty metric is a measure of the uniqueness of an individual's behavior at a given task. Instead of rewarding performance, novelty search rewards individuals in the population for finding new ways to complete the evaluation task, thus creating a constant pressure to do something new [16].

Because novelty search operates in *behavior space*, it is important first to characterize the space of unique behaviors in a way that is meaningful to the domain. The novelty search algorithm then computes the *sparseness* in the behavior space as the average distance to the k-nearest neighbors [2] around that behavior. The sparseness ρ of behavior x is given by

$$\rho(x) = \frac{1}{k}\sum_{i=0}^{k} \mathrm{dist}(x, \mu_i), \qquad (1)$$

where μ_i is the ith-nearest neighbor of x with respect to the distance function $\mathrm{dist}(x, \mu)$. In this way, if the average distance is large, then the candidate solution is considered to be in a sparse area of the behavior space, thus making it more likely to be selected by the EA. Optionally, as in coevolution [4], an archive of past behaviors may serve to avoid backtracking through the behavior space. If the novelty metric is sufficiently high for a new individual (i.e. above some minimal threshold $\rho_{\min}$), then the individual may be recorded in the permanent archive to provide a comprehensive sample of where the search has been, thereby increasing the pressure to discover new ways of behaving in the domain [13, 16].

Characterizing behaviors so that they can be compared is the most challenging aspect of novelty search. For the deceptive maze domain [13, 16] (figure 1), the behavior of a maze navigation robot is usually defined as its *final position*. In this way, the novelty metric rewards controllers that end at new locations in the maze. At first, the collection of behaviors may include robots that do nothing, get stuck in corners, run in circles, and so forth. However, at some point, the collection of simple behaviors becomes saturated and the pressure to do something new increases, i.e. evolution favors mutations that take the navigator to new places in the maze.

While the idea of selecting anything novel may sound potentially similar to exhaustive search, searching in the space of *behaviors* is often tractable because many points in the space of possible *genomes* collapse to a single behavior. Furthermore, when applied in conjunction with complexifying algorithms like NEAT [13, 15] and GP [14], simple behaviors become associated with minimal representations, and only mutations that increase the size of the genome and lead to novel behaviors are explored further. Therefore, this approach, operating without regard to an objective, moves into complex spaces in a meaningful way because new behaviors are those that could not be expressed at lower levels of complexity, i.e. complexity is rewarded when it is warranted.

However, experience has also shown that novelty search becomes lost in unrestricted domains [15]. In such domains there is an opportunity to leverage human knowledge rather than exhaustively exploring the space of all possible solutions. Thus the next section provides relevant background on the field of human-led evolution.

2.3 Interactive Evolutionary Computation

In *interactive evolutionary computation* (IEC) the traditional objective-function is replaced by a user who performs selection [32]. IEC is effective in creative domains [25] where the term *fitness* is subjective because what people experience as pleasing or interesting is based on individual preferences.

Like traditional EAs, IEC systems also typically begin from a random initial population that evolves over generations by selecting, mating and mutating members. However, IEC differs from traditional automated EAs in that a human user is now responsible for the evaluation and selection of promising candidate solutions. While this difference typically leads to smaller population sizes and higher mutation rates, the most profound implication is that evolution is no longer bound to a rigid expression of what is fit and unfit. While efforts have been applied to model human selection criteria [11], the human evaluator's breadth of experience makes it likely that his or her selection criteria will change over the course of evolution. Such an ability to make *serendipitous discoveries*, i.e. to identify and pursue important artifacts as they emerge, is an important motivation for the NA-IEC approach introduced in this paper.

To interface with the human evaluator, the majority of IEC systems are modeled after the original Blind Watchmaker *Biomorphs* application by Dawkins [3]. In this approach the user is presented with a panel of individuals (e.g. 3×4) from which the parents of the next generation are selected. The IEC system then mates, recombines, and mutates the genetic material of the parents to create the next generation, which is then presented to the user. This process is repeated at the user's direction until the user is satisfied.

Despite the benefits of having a human in the loop, such IEC systems are limited by user fatigue. According to Takagi [32], typical IEC only lasts 10–20 generations per session. The problem is that the vast majority of significant discoveries exist beyond the reach of a single-user session. One response, which has become known as *collaborative interactive evolution* (CIE) [31]), is to leverage the efforts of many users. That way, when one user fatigues, another can take over and continue the chain. One particular example is *Picbreeder* (`http://picbreeder.org` [26, 27]), where such CIE allows long chains of users to branch from each other's discoveries, which indeed demonstrates that when the generational limits of a single user are extended significantly, remarkable discoveries begin to accumulate (figure 3).

However, chaining users is not the only way to augment the power of a single user. An alternative approach is to combine a human with a form of automated search, thereby amplifying the human's capabilities. While recent work by Bongard and Hornby [1] and Hornby and Bongard [11] shows that evolution driven by an objective can help to push search farther than the human alone, the novel approach in this paper adds the option to run novelty search into the mix. That way, users can request that the computer quickly gather a set of unique stepping stones that the user can then assess to decide which path is most promising, as explained next.

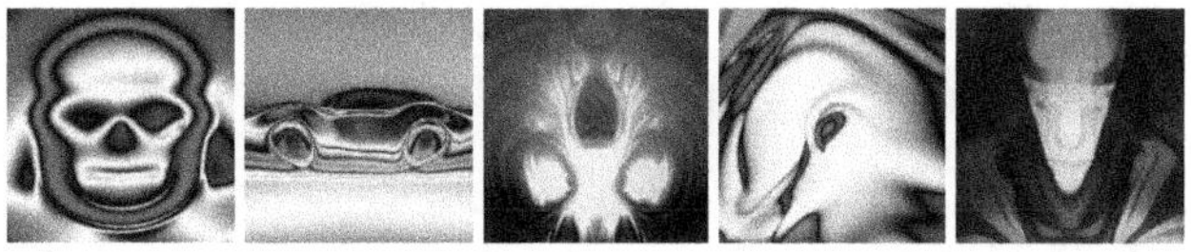

(a) Skull **(b)** Car **(c)** Mystic **(d)** Dolphin **(e)** Wizard

Figure 3: Images Evolved on Picbreeder (Secretan et al. [26]). These images were interactively evolved by a community of human users. They demonstrate the system's ability to discover interesting and meaningful images, including such seminal images as the *Skull* and the *Car*—which were evolved in 74 and 106 generations, respectively, by chains of users branching from each other.

3. NA-IEC FRAMEWORK

The main idea in this section is to combine for the first time the intuitive ability of human users to identify what is interesting and important in a domain, i.e. interactive evolutionary computation (IEC), with a stepping stone generator based on a short-term novelty search and an objective optimizer to create a synergistic effect that expedites the evolution of controller solutions. Under this new approach, called *Novelty-Assisted Interactive Evolutionary Computation* (NA-IEC), a human user is asked to select individuals from a population of candidate behaviors and then apply one of three evolutionary operations: a traditional IEC step, a short-term novelty search, or a fitness-based optimization.

In this way, the user can apply the evolutionary operations where appropriate, even changing the mode of evolution during the course of the search, to reach a satisfactory (or just interesting) solution. The ability of a human user to apply powerful automated approaches like objective-based search [5–8] and novelty search [13, 16] in short bursts and when appropriate is a key contribution of the NA-IEC approach. The primary hypothesis is that letting the user make a relatively small number of critical selections during evolution, and leaving the remainder of search to automated approaches seeded by those user selections, can significantly augment the pace of evolution and the quality of its discoveries.

Figure 4 shows the main interface for the system, where the user can choose among the *Step*, *Novelty*, and *Optimize* operations. Choosing the *Step* operation creates a new generation of offspring through the recombination and mutation of the selected candidate behaviors. This classic approach to IEC is simple and computationally inexpensive, i.e. it only creates a handful of new candidates.

Choosing the *Novelty* operation causes evolution to explore the space of agent behaviors without regard to an objective and then present the human evaluator with a broad view of where the evolutionary search can go from its current position. To accomplish this aim, the next IEC population is generated by seeding a larger population with variations of the user-selected candidate behaviors and then running novelty search in the background to find novel individuals (in comparison to what has been encountered previously in the search) based on the sparseness measure $\rho(x)$ from equation 1 and the threshold ρ_{min}. The underlying evolutionary algorithm is NEAT [29, 30], which is often the base algorithm under novelty search [13, 16]. Furthermore, to ensure that novelty is measured

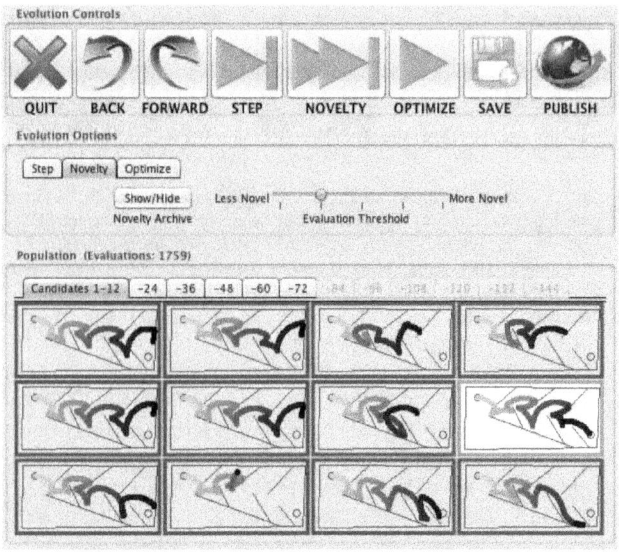

Figure 4: Screenshot of the NA-IEC user interface. The user interface for the NA-IEC framework consists of the *Evolution Controls*, the *Evolution Options*, and the *Evaluation Population*. Candidate solutions are represented by a gradient trail that shows the robot's behavior in a particular maze. Selected candidates are shown with a green border and solutions are highlighted with a white background. Unlike traditional IEC applications, the user can now select one of three evolution modes: *Step*, *Novelty*, and *Optimize*. The *Publish* button saves the results of a completed run for later analysis. Like Picbreeder, projects based on NA-IEC could additionally leverage crowdsourcing by implemented them an online format. [21].

with respect to the entire search completed so far, all individuals encountered during *both* traditional IEC steps and interleaved novelty searches throughout a session of NA-IEC are measured for their novelty and entered into the permeant archive if their novelty score is greater than the threshold $\rho_{\min}$.

The novelty search runs until *at least n* new individuals are added to the evaluation population (more than n such novel candidates may be found when the novelty search is first started by generating an initial pool of candidates based on the user-selected choices on the screen), where n is the size of an on-screen IEC population. At that point, the collected novel individuals become the next IEC generation and control is returned to the user. By convention, the n novel individuals are sorted by their novelty score before the NEAT-based speciation adjustment to place the most novel candidate behaviors on the first visible page of the on-screen IEC population (figure 4). While the *Novelty* operation is significantly more computationally expensive than the *Step* operation, it provides the human user with a breadth of stepping stones that would have been time-consuming or unlikely to discover on his or her own under the narrow view of a traditional single IEC step, which only presents the user with a handful of direct one-generation descendants. In a sense, the set of stepping stones returned to the user by novelty search is like the set of images evolved by *other* users from which a visitor to Picbreeder can branch: In both cases, someone or something else has put in effort to collect a set of interesting jumping-off points and present them to the user.

By augmenting the human-led interactive search with interleaved novelty searches, a small population can be constructed that contains a set of novel stepping stones around the currently-selected candidates. In the event that evolution cannot fill the next generation with a sufficient number of new archive members in a reasonable amount of time, or if the user cancels the operation, the search will return the most novel individuals yet discovered.

This approach does *not* imply that the set of novel agent behaviors presented to the evaluator will be good at a potential task. What is important is that they are *behaviorally* diverse; it is the human evaluator who will direct the search by recognizing what is promising for a given domain. The goal is to promote innovation through serendipitous discovery, and presenting the various directions that the search can take leverages the human evaluator's inherent ability to recognize what is important or interesting in a particular domain.

Finally, because objective-based optimization is likely the best option for *perfecting* well-formed behaviors already discovered, the user is also given the option to request seeding a traditional objective-based search with currently-selected individuals. The objective-based search will run until a specified solution criterion is met or until the user requests it to terminate, at which point the most fit individuals discovered so far will update the on-screen IEC population. Providing this traditional option will allow users to optimize candidates that are near an objective attractor that the user would prefer to approach automatically once it is within striking distance (i.e. once the search is no longer deceptive and the primary discovery is already made).

In this multifaceted approach, the user is free to change the mode of evolution between generations, thus allowing evolution to proceed in the capacity best suited for the current context. In this way, the human user may begin NA-IEC by exploring the space of behaviors agnostically, and once an interesting behavior is established, the mode of evolution may be changed to optimize it. For more information on NA-IEC, or to download the framework, please visit `http://eplex.cs.ucf.edu/naiec`.

4. EXPERIMENT

To demonstrate the synergistic effects of augmenting a human-directed search with novelty search, the experiment is conducted in the deceptive maze domain introduced by Lehman and Stanley [13, 16, Section 2.1]. That way, the NA-IEC approach can be compared against pure novelty search, fitness-based search, and a novelty-free IEC-based search directly. In the deceptive maze domain, the goal is to evolve a navigation behavior that drives a robot from the start to the finish of the medium maze or the hard maze shown in figure 1, which are constructed with several cul-de-sacs that create local optima in the fitness landscape. Because these local optima are so deceptive, Lehman and Stanley [13, 16] found that novelty search significantly outperforms objective-based search in both mazes. The question here is, can NA-IEC do even better?

To compare performance, each approach is evaluated over 30 runs on the medium and hard maps. While novelty search and fitness-based search are both automated algorithms, the NA-IEC approach requires a human evaluator. To accomplish the NA-IEC portion of this experiment, six users (who are not the authors) were recruited who were familiar with novelty search and EAs. These users were introduced to the NA-IEC framework and each asked to evolve five solutions to the medium map and five solutions to the hard map. The aim is to characterize the performance that can be reasonably expected from a practitioner in EC when evolving with NA-IEC. Users were permitted to restart if they felt that evolution had become stuck. However, all evaluations before such restarts were recorded as a part of the same run.

Inevitably, some will argue that such human guided runs have an unfair advantage because the user can see the path through the maze. To address this concern, an additional fitness-based experiment, inspired by Risi and Stanley [24] is conducted. In this additional experiment the primary deceptive element of the maze navigation domain, i.e. the attraction of agents to cul-de-sacs, is removed. In this alternative reward scheme, candidates are rewarded

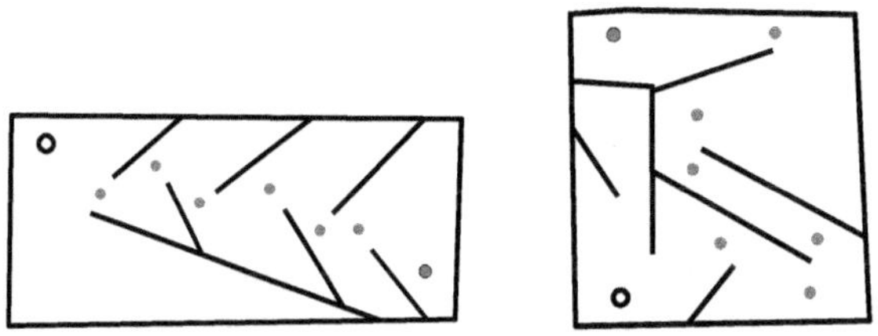

(a) Medium Map (b) Hard Map

Figure 5: Maze navigation waypoints. To compare how much advantage is gained from knowing the path to the goal, waypoints (which are *not* seen by the agent) are provided for the medium and hard maps. In this way, deception is removed by allowing a traditional fitness-based search to reward solutions that discover stepping stones that are on the path to the goal.

for progressing along a path that actually leads to the goal. Figure 5 shows the waypoints (which are invisible to the agent) in the medium and hard maps. In this waypoint-directed version of the experiment, the fitness function f is defined such that agents are rewarded for each waypoint crossed (including the goal); they also receive a partial reward for approaching the next waypoint:

$$f = n + (1 - d), \quad (2)$$

where n is the number of waypoints reached and d is the distance to the next waypoint (proportional to distance between waypoint w_n and w_{n+1}, in the range $[0, 1]$).

Some might still argue that the waypoint-directed search above is at a disadvantage. Thus an additional human-led experiment is also conducted to further characterize the specific advantage provided by the human evaluator. In fact, this experiment is identical to the NA-IEC experiment with two exceptions: (1) the short-term novelty operation is not available to the human user, and (2) the mutation rate of the step operation is matched to the rates of the other experiments. In this way, the human user can evaluate individual generations of candidate behaviors just as in IEC, but can then tune (without waypoints) their solutions with the optimize operation to achieve the final solution. In this setup, five human subjects performed six runs each on both mazes.

4.1 ANN Representation

In this experiment, as in Lehman and Stanley [13, 16], the ANN controllers in all variants of the deceptive maze experiment are evolved by the NeuroEvolution of Augmenting Topologies (NEAT) approach [29, 30]. More specifically, the NEAT algorithm starts with a population of simple ANNs and *complexifies* them over generations by adding new nodes and connections through structural mutations. By evolving networks in this way, the topology of the network does not need to be known a priori. As applied to maze navigation policies, this process begins with an initial population of simple behaviors that are represented by fully-connected networks with 22 connections, no hidden nodes, and the inputs/outputs in figure 2b. As the underlying networks add complexity (i.e. new nodes and connections), features and nuances emerge in the resulting behaviors that could not be expressed by the simpler ANNs.

4.2 Experimental Parameters

The evolutionary parameters in this experiment are based on the deceptive maze navigation experiment by Lehman and Stanley [13, 16] and on the established parameters for NEAT [29]. All experiments were run with a version of the public domain ANJI package augmented to support steady-state evolution, interactive evolution, and novelty search. The IEC population size was 12, while the novelty search and fitness-based search population sizes were 250, with each run limited to 250,000 total evaluations. Note that when the user initiates novelty search or optimization from within NA-IEC, a starting pool of 250 candidates are first generated from the user-selected candidates on the screen. The speciation threshold, δ_t, was 0.2 and the compatibility modifier was 0.3. Offspring in all automated runs, short-term novelty operations, and IEC step operations had a 5% chance of adding a node, a 10% chance of adding a link, a 1% chance of loosing a link, and the weight mutation power was 0.8. During optimization operations and Step operations in the NA-IEC experiment the connection weight mutation power was 0.1 to support behavioral fine-tuning. The ANN employed unsigned sigmoidal activation with recurrent connections, resulting in a shifted output range of $[-0.5, 0.5]$.

The parameters specific to novelty were also based on the original deceptive maze navigation experiment [13, 16]. They include the nearest neighbors value ($k = 15$) and the novelty threshold, $\rho_{\min}$, which begins at 3.0 and is adjusted after every 2,500 evaluations. Each navigation robot was given 400 time-steps to reach the goal, which only allows behaviors that proceed directly to the goal. It is important to note that the experiments of Lehman and Stanley [13, 16] were *re-run* with this setup to ensure a fair comparison and to validate our implementation.

5. RESULTS

As with the original experiment by Lehman and Stanley [13, 16], a navigation behavior that finishes within five units of the goal location is considered successful. The main result is that NEAT with NA-IEC discovers such solutions in significantly fewer evaluations than both NEAT with novelty search and fitness-based NEAT on the medium and hard maps. Furthermore, despite the expense of waiting on the human to evaluate a panel of candidate solutions, NA-IEC also consumes less wall-clock time in search, suggesting that the value of the user's direction easily offsets the delay of waiting for human input. Another result is that NA-IEC produces solutions with significantly fewer hidden nodes than both novelty search and fitness-based search, further suggesting the importance of allowing a human evaluator to make key decisions about the direction of evolution. While some may dismiss such improvements based on the human evaluator's ability to see the path through the maze, results from the waypoint-directed search, a non-deceptive fitness-based experiment, are on par with NEAT with novelty search, which is still well below the performance of NEAT with NA-IEC. Furthermore, NA-IEC not only succeeds in discovering solutions in significantly fewer evaluations than IEC without novelty, but also reduces fatigue by requiring many fewer user operations. The implication is that NEAT with NA-IEC not only exposes key stepping stones, but also provides evolution with subtle insights about the domain not easily incorporated into a traditional fitness function a priori.

On the medium map, users directing NEAT with NA-IEC found 30 solutions in an average of 6,729 (sd = $8,068$) evaluations. These results are significantly ($p < 10^{-6}$; Student's t-test) faster than NEAT with novelty search (22,116 evaluations, sd = $10,157$), fitness-based NEAT (55,066 evaluations sd = $47,339$), waypoint-directed NEAT (22,594 evaluations sd = $11,982$), and human-led NEAT without novelty (12,741 evaluations sd = $12,792$), each averaged over 30 runs (figure 6a). Furthermore, users solved the medium map in an average of 294 (sd = 359) seconds, which is 2.8 times faster than novelty search, 9.1 times faster than fitness-based search, and 2.0 times faster than the waypoint-directed search.[1] While solutions from the novelty-based, fitness-based, waypoint-

[1]Note that clock times are not reported for IEC without novelty because these runs took so long that users generally could not complete them in one sitting, which would confound the results.

directed, and human-led searches have on average 3.2 (sd = 1.9) hidden nodes, 2.9 (sd = 1.65) hidden nodes, 3.0 (sd = 1.8) hidden nodes, and 1.0 (sd = 3.1) hidden nodes respectively, solutions produced by NA-IEC are significantly simpler, averaging just 0.23 (sd = 0.5) hidden nodes per solution ($p < 10^{-10}$; Student's t-test).

On the hard map, the NA-IEC approach evolved 30 successful navigators in an average of 7,481 (sd = 6,610) evaluations, which is a significant ($p < 10^{-5}$; Student's t-test) improvement over not only NEAT with novelty search alone (33,320 evaluations, sd = 20,949), but also over the non-deceptive (i.e. waypoint-directed) version of fitness-based NEAT (26,954 evaluations, sd = 18,464) and the human-led NEAT without novelty (24,447 evaluations, sd = 26,691), each averaged over 30 runs. In the case of fitness-based NEAT, as in Lehman and Stanley [13, 16], no comparison could be made because only four of 30 runs evolved solutions for the hard map. Evaluations required to solve the hard map are shown in figure 6b. In addition to evolving successful navigators for the hard map in fewer evaluations, NA-IEC did so on average in just 402 (sd = 374) seconds, which is 3.5 times faster than NEAT with novelty search and 2.5 times faster than the waypoint-directed search. Regarding complexity, solutions from novelty search have on average 3.3 (sd = 1.8) hidden nodes, solutions from the non-deceptive waypoint-directed search have an average of 3.5 (sd = 2.0) hidden nodes, and solutions from the human-led search averaged 1.2 (sd = 1.4) hidden nodes, while those evolved by NA-IEC are significantly smaller with 0.5 (sd = 1.01) hidden nodes ($p < 10^{-8}$; Student's t-test).

Typical patterns of exploration for each approach in the medium and hard maps are shown in figure 7, which compares the distribution of all ending points visited during a typical run. As Lehman and Stanley [13, 16] discovered previously, the traditional fitness-based approach is attracted to the cul-de-sacs in the maze (figures 7a and 7b), while selecting for behavioral novelty allows NEAT to explore the space of possible behaviors more evenly (figures 7c and 7d). Such search distributions are the result of selection pressure; thus when the objective-function rewards agents for following the solution path (figures 7e and 7f) the cul-de-sacs no longer deceive evolution. Interestingly, when the points visited during IEC (figures 7g and 7h) and NA-IEC (figures 7i and 7j) are plotted in this way the signatures of the human selector becomes evident. As expected, the first of these is that there are far fewer points in the cul-de-sacs than in both novelty search and even the waypoint-directed search, demonstrating the intolerance of the human user for behaviors that explore these spaces. The second signature is that there are frequently tight groupings of points at key junctions in the map, indicating that the user is probing these areas of the search space for a behavior that can turn a corner and enter a new chamber of the maze. Such observations demonstrate how the human evaluator is contributing his or her insights to the search. Furthermore, it is interesting how these human effects are so readily visible in the points plotted. However, the key difference between the IEC runs (i.e. without the short-term novelty operator) and NA-IEC runs is the regularity with which solutions can be found in a small number of evaluations, highlighting the advantage of having the novelty search option.

Finally, it is also important to analyze the behavior of the human users, especially in light of the human susceptibility to fatigue in IEC systems [32]. In the IEC experiment without novelty, users found solutions to the medium map in an average of 148.8 (sd = 128.5) operations, 79.1% of which were *Step* functions and 20.9% were *Optimize* functions. Similarly, solutions found for the hard map required an average of 1,179.5 (sd = 1,837.9) user operations, of which 95.6% were *Step* functions and 4.4% were *Optimize*

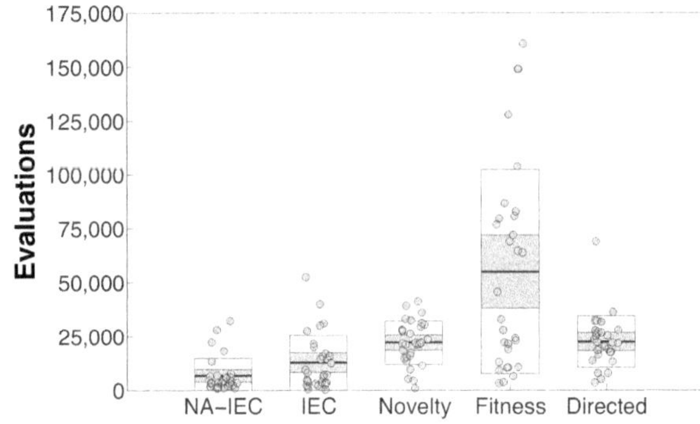

(a) Medium Map

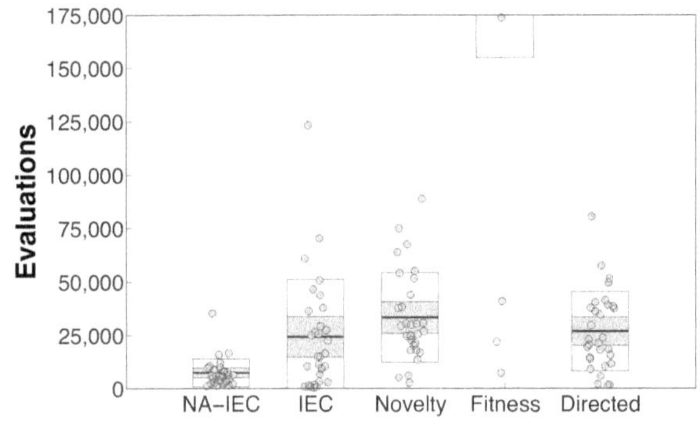

(b) Hard Map

Figure 6: Evaluations required to find solutions. The number of evaluations required by NEAT to find solutions are shown for the medium (a) and hard (b) maps with NA-IEC, IEC augmented with optimization only, novelty search, fitness-based search (pure), and waypoint-directed search. The average number of evaluations to reach a solution is marked by a line, boxed regions extend out to one and two standard-deviations, and the distribution of the individual data points is shown. As in work by Lehman and Stanley [13, 16], fitness-based search is generally deceived in the hard map and is unlikely to produce solutions. The main result is that the NA-IEC approach consistently finds solutions for the medium and hard maps in significantly fewer evaluations than any other approach.

functions. In contrast, users working with NA-IEC found solutions for the medium map in an average of just 30.1 (sd = 40.5) choices, applying the *Step* function 29.8% of the time, the *Novelty* function 47.8% of the time, and the *Optimize* function 22.4% of the time. On the hard map, solutions required an average of 32.0 (sd = 23.5) human choices, of which 29.2% were *Step* functions, 58.9% were *Novelty* functions, and 11.9% were *Optimize* functions. Furthermore, results show that users tended to employ novelty early in evolution and applied optimization at the end of evolution, i.e. once a solution has been established. Combined with the overall performance results, these statistics demonstrate the important role played by the *Novelty* operator in dramatically reducing both the overall cost of a run and the likelihood for user fatigue [32]. As these results also show, the human's ability to see through the maze in the IEC runs could not make up for the lack of novelty search, demonstrating again that search (even interactive search augmented with objective optimization) benefits significantly from novelty.

6. DISCUSSION

In the deceptive maze domain, humans in NA-IEC make a good team with novelty search and objective optimization, which helps to finish the job. In both mazes, users choose *Novelty* to generate the next set of choices significantly more frequently than the other options. The stepping-stone generator of novelty search provides

(a) Medium Map Fitness

(b) Hard Map Fitness

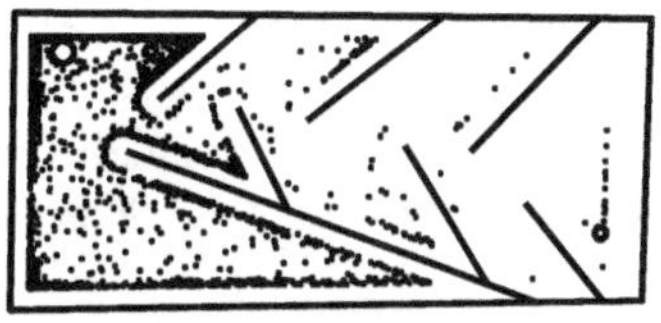

(c) Medium Map Novelty

(d) Hard Map Novelty

(e) Medium Map Directed

(f) Hard Map Directed

(g) Medium Map IEC

(h) Hard Map IEC

(i) Medium Map NA-IEC

(j) Hard Map NA-IEC

Figure 7: Distribution of final points visited. Each maze shows the final position for all candidates in a typical run. The density of points shows how fitness-based NEAT, NEAT with novelty search, waypoint-directed NEAT, IEC-based NEAT, and NEAT with NA-IEC behave in the deceptive maze domain. As in Lehman and Stanley [13, 16], fitness-based search is attracted to the cul-de-sacs, while the points visited by novelty search are more evenly distributed throughout the maze. When rewarded for progressing along the solution path, the waypoint-directed runs are less deceived. For the IEC and NA-IEC runs, the human user's influence is clearly visible, i.e. there are significantly fewer points in the major cul-de-sacs and tight groupings of points around key junctions. Such characteristics reveal how human selections are impacting evolution.

a desirable menu of possibilities to the human user, ultimately exceeding the performance of novelty search alone, as well as the reported performance of novelty–fitness multi-objective hybrids [19], by several times. Nevertheless, a natural question is whether such results are somehow specific to the maze domain. Perhaps humans harbor a particularly keen insight into the most promising robot behavior in mazes, but would lack such insight in other domains.

For example, one hypothesis might be that humans in effect know the right path through the maze because they can see the whole maze. Yet this interpretation is not entirely accurate. The correct path *through the maze* is not equivalent to the correct path *through the search space*. While some behaviors seem clearly dead ends (such as being caught in the most obvious cul-de-sac in the hard maze), others are less obvious. It is not necessarily the case that just because one behavior drives the robot farther down the correct path that it must be a more promising stepping stone. Some such behaviors are themselves dead ends that cannot push farther. Also, humans perceive more subtle and nuanced indicators that are also important, such as path smoothness or unnecessary loops in the robot trajectory. A behavior in which the robot doubles back on itself and then turns back onto the correct path may be just as ominous as being stuck in a dead end. Humans intuitively understand *these* kinds of dangers, yet to articulate them in an objective function would be quite challenging, and would almost certainly take more time than simply guiding the search away from them, whether they are easy to formalize or not.

Interestingly, the NA-IEC approach found solutions in significantly fewer evaluations and with fewer user operations compared to the IEC runs conducted without the novelty operator. In *both* of these human-led experiments, the evaluators had full insight into the correct route through maze and the robot path behaviors for each candidate, as well as the option to run optimization, yet those advantages alone without novelty were still less effective. The insight is that the ability to request a set of novel candidate behaviors (whether good or bad) plays an important role by affording the user a broad view of where evolution could go next. This additional information appears to facilitate better decisions that lead to increased efficiency.

While only future empirical results can settle this issue, there is reason to believe that humans would carry similarly critical insights into other domains. For example, in a biped-walking task [16, 23, 33], humans can see that certain kinds of leg oscillations are promising even if the robot falls down. Yet to describe exactly what makes them promising in a fitness function is likely prohibitive. The human's overhead view, and hence knowledge of the mazes, should be viewed metaphorically as like any intuitive understanding of the shape of a particular behavior space. Just as we can see in the maze that certain passageways must precede other passageways, so we can see in a biped robot that oscillations and balance must precede walking. While it is possible that the intuitive insight into some domains is less than in the maze domain, the highly significant advantage provided by such insight in the maze domain suggests that even if the advantage were less elsewhere, it could still be significant.

NA-IEC also may be important for more than just optimization. In some spaces, such as in morphological brain-body evolution or with sophisticated encodings, we may be more interested in *what is possible* than in achieving a particular end result. The apparent synergy that results from humans combined with novelty search could be leveraged in the future to show us more about such spaces than trying to solve specific problems. With all the limitations recently shown for objective-based search, NA-IEC provides an alternative without relinquishing our desire to have some say in the process.

7. CONCLUSION

This paper introduced the *novelty-assisted interactive evolutionary computation* (NA-IEC) approach, wherein the intuitive ability of human users to identify promising candidate behaviors is augmented by an agnostic stepping stone generator (i.e. novelty search) seeded with the behaviors selected by the user. In this way, the advantages from IEC and novelty search create a complementary effect that offsets each other's limitations. Humans in this study only spent up to ten minutes to make a few dozen selections among thousands of evaluations, much of which was automated by novelty search. This novel incorporation of single mutational steps, short-term novelty search, and fitness-based optimization into a single evolutionary tool resulted in an effective synergy that allowed human users to realize what was important for a given domain *during* evolution. Furthermore, such serendipitous exploration found solutions in fewer evaluations, at lower genomic complexities, and in significantly less time overall than the fully-automated processes (i.e. novelty search, fitness-based search, and the directed fitness search alone), while also reducing fatigue when compared to IEC without the novelty component. Thus the key contribution of the NA-IEC approach is that it can accelerate the rate and quality of evolution by leveraging human-level domain knowledge without burdening the user with the responsibility of evaluating every candidate created during evolution.

References

[1] J. C. Bongard and G. S. Hornby. Combining fitness-based search and user modeling in evolutionary robotics. In *Proceedings of the 15th annual conference on Genetic and evolutionary computation*, GECCO'13, pages 159–166, New York, NY, USA, 2013. ACM.

[2] T. M. Cover and J. Thomas. *Elements of Information Theory*. Wiley, Hoboken, NJ, 1991.

[3] R. Dawkins. *The Blind Watchmaker*. Longman, Essex, U.K., 1986.

[4] E. D. De Jong. The incremental pareto-coevolution archive. In *Proceedings of the 6th annual conference on Genetic and evolutionary computation*, GECCO'04, pages 525–536. Springer Berlin Heidelberg, 2004. ACM.

[5] K. A. De Jong. *Evolutionary Computation: A Unified Perspective*. MIT Press, Cambridge, MA, 2002.

[6] A. Eiben and J. Smith. *Introduction to evolutionary computing*. Springer-Verlag, 2003.

[7] D. B. Fogel. *Evolutionary computation: toward a new philosophy of machine intelligence, third edition*. Wiley-IEEE Press, 2006.

[8] D. E. Goldberg. *Genetic Algorithms in Search, Optimization and Machine Learning*. Addison-Wesley, Reading, MA, 1989.

[9] D. E. Goldberg and J. Richardson. Genetic algorithms with sharing for multimodal function optimization. In *Proceedings of the Second International Conference on Genetic Algorithms*, pages 148–154. San Francisco: Kaufmann, 1987.

[10] J. Gomes, P. Urbano, & A. Christensen. Evolution of swarm robotics systems with novelty search. *Swarm Intelligence*, pages 1–30, 2013.

[11] G. S. Hornby and J. C. Bongard. Accelerating human-computer collaborative search through learning comparative and predictive user models. In *Proceedings of the 14th annual conference on Genetic and evolutionary computation*, GECCO'12, pages 225–232, New York, NY, USA, 2012. ACM.

[12] S. Kistemaker and S. Whiteson. Critical factors in the performance of novelty search. In *Proceedings of the 13th annual conference on Genetic and evolutionary computation*, GECCO'11, pages 965–972, New York, NY, USA, 2011. ACM.

[13] J. Lehman and K. O. Stanley. Exploiting open-endedness to solve problems through the search for novelty. In *Proceedings of the Eleventh International Conference on Artificial Life (Alife XI)*, Cambridge, MA, 2008. MIT Press.

[14] J. Lehman and K. O. Stanley. Efficiently evolving programs through the search for novelty. In *Proceedings of the 12th annual conference on Genetic and evolutionary computation*, GECCO'10, pages 837–844, New York, NY, USA, 2010. ACM.

[15] J. Lehman and K. O. Stanley. Revising the evolutionary computation abstraction: minimal criteria novelty search. In *Proceedings of the 12th annual conference on Genetic and evolutionary computation*, GECCO'10, pages 103–110, New York, NY, USA, 2010. ACM.

[16] J. Lehman and K. O. Stanley. Abandoning objectives: Evolution through the search for novelty alone. *Evolutionary Computation*, 19 (2):189–223, 2011.

[17] J. Lehman and K. O. Stanley. Novelty search and the problem with objectives. In *Genetic Programming Theory and Practice IX (GPTP 2011)*, New York, NY, 2011. Springer.

[18] G. E. Liepins and M. D. Vose. Deceptiveness and genetic algorithm dynamics. Technical Report CONF-9007175-1, Oak Ridge National Lab., TN (USA); Tennessee Univ., Knoxville, TN (USA), 1990.

[19] J.-B. Mouret. Novelty-based multiobjectivization. In *New Horizons in Evolutionary Robotics*, volume 341 of *Studies in Computational Intelligence*, pages 139–154. Springer Berlin / Heidelberg, 2011.

[20] E. Naredo and L. Trujillo. Searching for novel clustering programs. In *Proceedings of the 15th annual conference on Genetic and evolutionary computation*, GECCO'13, pages 1093–1100, 2013.

[21] G. Newman, A. Wiggins, A. Crall, E. Graham, S. Newman, and K. Crowston. The future of citizen science: emerging technologies and shifting paradigms. *Frontiers in Ecology and the Environment*, 10(6):298–304, 2012.

[22] M. Pelikan and D. Goldberg. Escaping hierarchical traps with competent genetic algorithms. Technical Report 2001003, Illinois Genetic Algorithms Laboratory, University of Illinois at Urbana-Champaign, Urbana, IL, 2001.

[23] T. Reil and P. Husbands. Evolution of central pattern generators for bipedal walking in a real-time physics environment. *IEEE Transactions on Evolutionary Computation*, 6(2):159–168, 2002.

[24] S. Risi and K. O. Stanley. Enhancing es-hyperneat to evolve more complex regular neural networks. In *Proceedings of the 13th annual conference on Genetic and evolutionary computation*, GECCO'11, pages 1539–1546, New York, NY, USA, 2011. ACM.

[25] J. Romero and P. Machado. *The art of artificial evolution: A handbook on evolutionary art and music*. Springer-Verlag, New York, NY, 2008.

[26] J. Secretan, N. Beato, D. B. D.Ambrosio, A. Rodriguez, A. Campbell, J. T. Folsom-Kovarik, and K. O. Stanley. Picbreeder: A case study in collaborative evolutionary exploration of design space. *Evolutionary Computation*, 19(3):373–403, 2011.

[27] J. Secretan, N. Beato, D. B. D'Ambrosio, A. Rodriguez, A. Campbell, and K. O. Stanley. Picbreeder: Evolving pictures collaboratively online. In *CHI '08: Proceedings of the twenty-sixth annual SIGCHI conference on Human factors in computing systems*, pages 1759–1768, New York, NY, USA, 2008. ACM.

[28] K. O. Stanley. Searching without objectives. Speech presented at SPLASH 2010, Reno, Nevada. October 21, 2010. `http://www.infoq.com/presentations/Searching-Without-Objectives`.

[29] K. O. Stanley and R. Miikkulainen. Evolving neural networks through augmenting topologies. *Evolutionary Computation*, 10: 99–127, 2002.

[30] K. O. Stanley and R. Miikkulainen. Competitive coevolution through evolutionary complexification. *Journal of Artificial Intelligence Research*, 21:63–100, 2004.

[31] S. R. Szumlanski, A. S. Wu, and C. E. Hughes. Conflict resolution and a framework for collaborative interactive evolution. In *Proceedings of the 21st national conference on Artificial intelligence - Volume 1*, pages 512–517. AAAI Press, 2006.

[32] H. Takagi. Interactive evolutionary computation: Fusion of the capacities of EC optimization and human evaluation. *Proceedings of the IEEE*, 89(9):1275–1296, 2001.

[33] M. van de Panne and A. Lamouret. Guided optimization for balanced locomotion. In *Sixth Eurographics Workshop on Animation and Simulation*, volume 95, pages 165–177. Springer-Verlag, 1995.

[34] L. D. Whitley. Fundamental principles of deception in genetic search. *Foundations of genetic algorithms*, 1(3):221–241, 1991.

[35] B. G. Woolley and K. O. Stanley. On the deleterious effects of a priori objectives on evolution and representation. In *Proceedings of the 13th annual conference on Genetic and evolutionary computation*, GECCO'11, New York, NY, USA, 2011. ACM.

The views expressed in this paper are those of the authors and do not reflect the official policy or position of the United States Air Force, the Department of Defense, or the United States Government.

Wolfpack-Inspired Evolutionary Algorithm and a Reaction-Diffusion-based Controller are Used for Pattern Formation

Payam Zahadat
Artificial Life Lab of the
Department of Zoology
Karl-Franzens University Graz
8010 Graz, Austria
payam.zahadat@uni-graz.at

Thomas Schmickl
Artificial Life Lab of the
Department of Zoology
Karl-Franzens University Graz
8010 Graz, Austria
thomas.schmickl@uni-graz.at

ABSTRACT

The implicit social structure of population groups have been previously investigated in the literature representing enhancements in the performance of optimization algorithms. Here we introduce an evolutionary algorithm inspired by animal hunting groups (i.e. wolves). The algorithm implicitly maintains diversity in the population and performs higher than two state of the art evolutionary algorithms in the investigated case studies in this article. The case studies are to evolve a hormone-inspired system called AHHS (Artificial Homeostatic Hormone Systems) to develop spatial patterns. The complex spatial patterns are developed in the absence of any explicit spatial information. The results achieved by AHHS are presented and compared with a previous work with Artificial Neural Network (ANNs) indicating higher performance of AHHS.

Categories and Subject Descriptors

I.2.11 [**Computing Methodologies**]: Distributed Artificial Intelligence; F.1 [**Theory of Computation**]: Computation By Abstract Devices; I.m [**Computing Methodologies**]: Miscellaneous

Keywords

Evolutionary algorithms; reaction-diffusion-based system; pattern formation

1. INTRODUCTION

The use of sophisticated optimization techniques for automating the search for effective representations has been previously indicated [24] as a requirement in finding good function approximators. For example, evolutionary methods such as evolutionary strategies [17] and genetic algorithms [10] are of a wide use in the area of optimization and controller design. It has been shown [12] that considering an underlying social structure in the pool of possible solutions in an optimization algorithm can significantly enhance the quality of the search. This is evident by Particle Swarm Optimization (PSO) which was also inspired by a flock of birds that converges to search targets (goals) and where the influence of flock members is asymmetrically distributed, as was pointed out already from bird observations by Lorenz [13].

In the natural systems, the implicit evolutionary dynamics of population groups with social structure have been investigated by mathematical modelling several times. For example, Mangel and Clark 1988 [14] review several models of lions' collective foraging. The models predict, based on empirical data (by Schaller [18]), that the collective hunting of African lions (Panther leo L.) and the communal food sharing have a significant affect on evolutionary dynamics in comparison with individual (egoistic) hunting predatory felines like the cougar (Felis concolor L.) and the leopard (Panthera pardus L.). By using mathematical modelling based on empirical data from Ekman and Liliendahl [5], Mangel and Clark (2000) [15] predicted the starvation-related death of birds due to food shortages and positive impact of a social hierarchy on the predicted probability of survival of dominant birds over subordinate ones.

In this paper, we introduce a variation of evolutionary algorithms, called Wolfpack Evolutionary Algorithm (WEA), which is inspired by animal hunting groups, like packs of wolves that employ a strict hierarchy reflecting their fitness and compare it with some of the state of the art evolutionary methods in case studies of spatial pattern formation.

Pattern formation is chosen as a case study due to being a challenging subject both in biological and artificial organisms. Different forms with various levels of complexity are found everywhere in nature. One of the challenges in developmental biology is to understand the underlying processes that control pattern formation [11]. In addition, from the point of view of robotics, a proper behaviour emerges from a proper pattern of roles assigned to the robotic modules across the body of a robot.

A problem encountering pattern formation is symmetry-breaking. As it was suggested in a model by Wolpert [25] and found in biological systems, such as embryos of fruit fly Drosophila melanogaster ([4, 6]), the polarization of an or-

GECCO'14, July 12–16, 2014, Vancouver, BC, Canada.

http://dx.doi.org/10.1145/2576768.2598262.

ganism is induced by some maternal cue in the form of morphogen gradients in the early developmental phases. The process was proposed by Wolpert [25] as a French-flag model. The model is then used by many researchers of artificial evolutionary and developmental systems applying different approaches(e.g., [16, 1, 8]). For example, by using Boolean logic circuits [16], gene regulatory networks [2, 26], or neural networks [7, 3].

Artificial Homeostatic Hormone System (AHHS) [19, 20] have been previously used in applications such as single and multi-modular robotic applications (see [21], [9], [22], [27]). In this paper, AHHS is used to develop a number of patterns (including French flag) of different levels of difficulty without providing spatial information. AHHS is a reaction-diffusion-based system that uses virtual hormones as state variables of the system. Reaction-diffusion systems are inspired by signalling network of unicellular organisms. In a recent version of AHHS, *tunnelling* has been added to the system as a new mechanism of communication between adjacent cells in multi-cellular organisms. In contrast to diffusion, *tunnelling* can act against hormone gradients and generate directional influence in hormone transfer. The directional information that is potentially collected by *tunnelling* is especially beneficial when spatial information is not explicitly provided.

The contributions of this paper can be summarized as: (1) introducing a new evolutionary algorithm, WEA, that maintains implicit diversity in populations and comparing the proposed algorithm with examples of GA and ES. (2) Successful evolution of AHHS augmented by its new feature, *tunnelling*, for developing patterns in different levels of difficulty without spatial information and comparing its performance with an Artificial Neural Network (ANN) as a previously applied method.

2. WOLFPACK EVOLUTION ALGORITHM

2.1 Biological Motivation

The idea of Wolfpack Evolution Algorithm (WEA) is to perform Artificial Evolution (aka Evolutionary Computation) based on an underlying social network of the modelled population. A prominent example of such a social structure in nature is the social organization of animal hunting groups, like packs of wolves, troops of monkeys or prides of lions. In such social systems the members of the group have a rather strict hierarchy reflecting their fitness. This position in the hierarchy determines for example their access to food and their access to high-fitness mating partners thus, in turn affects the genomes of their offspring directly and their fitness (food access) indirectly. In such socially structured groups a high-ranking female will mate more likely with a high-ranking male and will have richer food supply than a low ranking female. More food means often more/better milk-supply in mammalians and thus higher survival chance and growth and resistance against diseases. In such social systems higher-ranking animals feed first on collectively predated food [13]. This in consequence means that low-ranking animals get only little or no food occasionally. This in turn lowers their fitness even more, making them less likely to be mating partners of high-ranking females and less likely to survive critical periods of food shortages. The algorithm we propose here tries to encapsulate these social mechanisms in a rather abstract way.

2.2 Algorithm Description

The algorithm maintains overlapping generations and considers a fixed maximum value for the population size reflecting a limited food resource in an animal group. Every evaluated offspring with high fitness is capable of removing the equal or lower fitness individuals from the population (neutrality is considered), which leads to free places for new offspring of high-fitness individuals. If the maximum size of the population is reached and all the individuals are evaluated, any random individual may get another chance to go over the whole population and remove the others with equal or lower fitness. This way, the population stays dynamic and hierarchical. Hierarchy is especially maintained by removing the individuals of equal (along with the lower) fitness which implicitly keeps the diversity of the population.

Figure 1 graphically describes the algorithm. A more formal description of WEA is as follows:

Initialize a population of randomly parametrized AHHS
for maximum number of evaluations **do**
  if there is an individual, e, in the population that is not evaluated yet **then**
    $current \leftarrow e$
    evaluate($current$)
  else
    $current \leftarrow r$ where r is a random member of the population
  end if
  for every evaluated individual, e in the population, where $fitness_e \leq fitness_{current}$ **do**
    eliminate e from the population with a probability of μ
  end for
  for all the empty places in the population **do**
    generate an offspring by mutating an individual that is selected by proportional selection (fitness-based) over the evaluated individuals
  end for
end for

3. SHORT SUMMARY OF AHHS

AHHS (Artificial Homeostatic Hormone System) [19] is a reaction-diffusion-based system. It is inspired by Turing process [23] that describes processes of natural pattern formation and growth. An AHHS consists of a number of underlying processes that drive the internal dynamics of the system. The underlying processes and their effects in producing patterns in different levels of diversity are previously investigated in an autonomous system in [27]. AHHS can be also seen as a Gene Regulatory Network (GRN) augmented by special communication processes. In the original versions of AHHS including its implementations in robotic scenarios, the system consists of a set of *hormones* which are state variables of the system, and a set of *rules* describing interactions between hormones in autonomous units (cells). The rules define influence of hormones on the concentration levels of other hormones within a unit. A diffusion process is defined in the system as the means of communication between neighbouring units. A new process, called *tunnelling*, has been later introduced to the system in [27]. The process uses a set of *tunnels* that determine how each hormone may affect another hormone by pumping it to the neighbouring units. This process defines an additional means of interac-

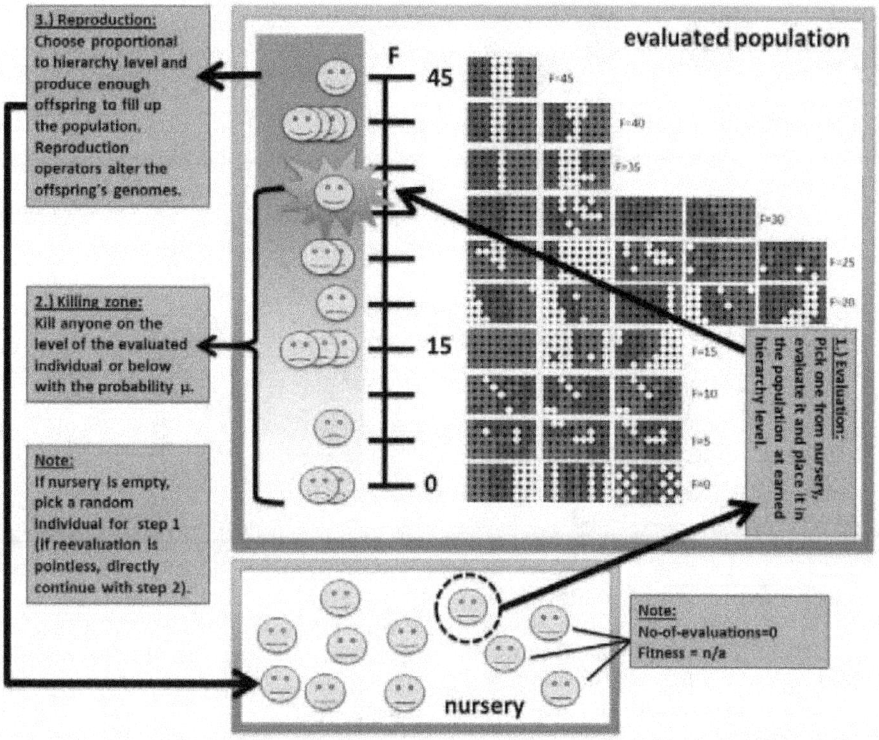

Figure 1: A demonstration of WEA. *Nursery* represents the set of individuals that have never been evaluated.

tion which can act against hormone gradients in the units. Note that, both *rules* and *tunnels* perform locally, meaning that rules apply to the hormone concentrations within a cell (same rules applied across all cells) and tunnels act between nearest neighbours.

In a formal representation, the dynamics of hormone concentration H at time t is defined for hormone h as follows:

$$\frac{\Delta H_h}{\Delta t} = \alpha_h + D_h \nabla^2 H_h(t) - \mu_h H_h(t) + \sum_i \mathcal{L}_i(t) - \sum_i (\mathcal{T}_i(t) + \sum_n \mathcal{T}_i^n(t)), \quad (1)$$

where α_h, D_h, and μ_h are base production rate, diffusion rate, and decay rate of hormone h, respectively. $\mathcal{L}_i(t)$ is the influence of a rule i, and $\mathcal{T}_i(t)$ is the influence of the tunnel i executed in the unit under consideration and $\mathcal{T}_i^n(t)$ is the influence of neighbouring unit n to the unit under consideration when tunnel i is executed in the neighbouring unit.

A rule is defined as:

$$\mathcal{L}_i(t) = \theta(H_k(t))(H_k(t)\lambda_i + \kappa_i), \quad (2)$$

The output is applied to hormone concentration $H_h(t)$ and the input is $H_k(t)$ ($h = k$ is allowed). λ_i and κ_i are two parameters of the rule called dependent dose and fixed dose. These values are allowed to be negative. Trigger function θ determines whether or not the rule is executed.

$$\theta(x) = \begin{cases} 1 & \text{if } min_i < x < max_i \\ 0 & \text{else} \end{cases}, \quad (3)$$

where min_i and max_i are parameters of the rule (between 0.0 and 1.0 in this implementation).

A tunnel is defined with an equation similar to a rule:

$$\mathcal{T}_i(t) = \theta(H_k(t))(H_k(t)\lambda_i + \kappa_i), \quad (4)$$

the difference is that the output of the tunnel's equation determines the amount of hormone concentration that is transferred from a unit to one of its neighbours. The target neighbour is determined by a parameter of the tunnel indicating the direction of the neighbour. This parameter, along with all the other parameters of AHHS are directly encoded in the genomes and are evolved in the context of given tasks.

4. EXPERIMENTS

In the following, WEA has been implemented to evolve AHHS for developing a number of spatial patterns as proposed in [3]. Four patterns, *two-bands*, *three-bands*, *circle* and *halfcircle*, with increasing levels of difficulty are introduced (see Figure 2, top). AHHS is used to determine the colour of every cell of the grid. That means, identical copies of an AHHS genome define the automonous controllers of the cells that determine their colours. The cells are linked to their nearest neighbours and communicate by diffusion and tunnelling. There is no spatial information provided for the AHHS and that is a task of evolution to figure out proper communication channels (tunnels) for the AHHS which are able to generate necessary spatial information.

Two sets of experiments are performed. In all the experiments, 5 hormones, 10 rules and 10 tunnels are randomly initialized in every AHHS and are subject to evolve.

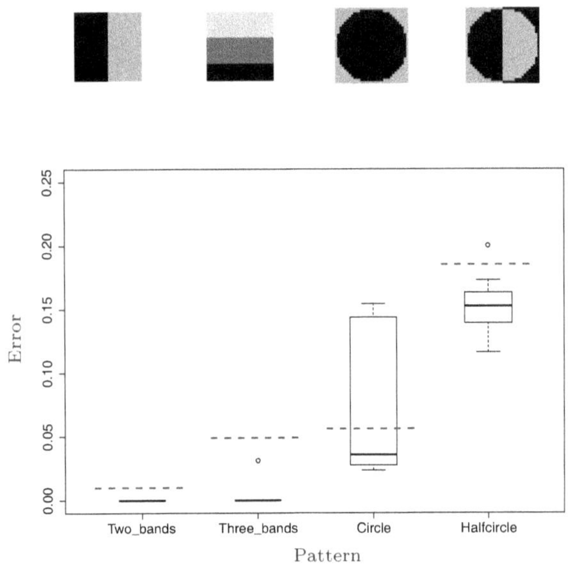

Figure 2: Comparison between fitness achieved by evolving AHHS and ANN (from [3]) for *two-bands*, *three-bands*, *circle* and *halfcircle* patterns. Dashed-lines represent the median values for ANN. The patterns are 32 and fitness are considered at time-step 128 after 250,000 evaluations.

In the first set of experiments, all the four patterns are developed with the same settings as [3] in order to investigate and compare the capability of AHHS with ANN (implemented in [3]). Fitness in this case is the number of correctly coloured cells of the generated pattern in a fixed number of steps (128 steps).

In the second set of experiments, AHHS is evolved for each of the four patterns with three different evolutionary methods: steady-state GA (SSGA) [10], ES [17], and WEA. ES and SSGA are chosen as two state of the art evolutionary methods. The implemented ES is $(\mu + \lambda)$ where in every non-overlapping generation, all the individuals produce an offspring by mutation. The offspring are then evaluated and the best individuals among all the parents and offspring form the new generation. Neutrality is considered in the replacement strategy (newer individual is considered of a higher rank than the older one with equal fitness). SSGA is chosen because of its similarity to the WEA in terms of overlapping generations and use of proportional selection to choose the parents. Hence, in every generation, a parent is chosen based on proportinal selection (proportional to fitness) to produce an offspring by mutation. The offspring is inserted to the population if it's fitness is higher or equal to the current lowest fitness in the population.

The fitness in the second set of experiments is the minimum number of correctly coloured cells of the generated pattern in the last 20 time-steps of development. That means, an AHHS with maximum fitness generates the correct pattern in at least all the last 20 time-steps. Hence, the evolved solutions develop more stable patterns comparing the first set of experiments. The resolution of the generated patterns in this case is lower (8×8 grid, see Figure 3) due to computational reasons. Table 1 summarizes evolutionary and developmental settings of the two sets of experiments.

Table 1: Evolutionary and developmental parameters in the two sets of experiments.

	AHHS vs. ANN[3]	WEA vs. ES, GA
number of runs	100	16
population size	10	10
no. of evaluations	250000	50000
μ (elimination)	1	1
no. of developments	64	128
pattern size	8	32×64

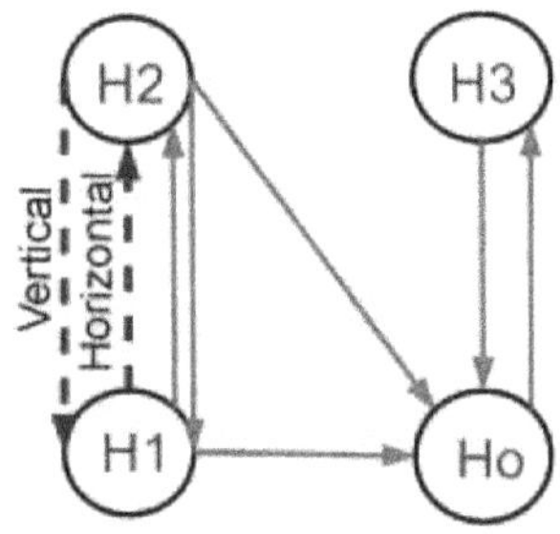

Figure 5: An example solution AHHS for generating a circle pattern. The evolved AHHS contains 4 effective hormones, 6 effective rules, and 2 effective tunnels. Every solid arrow represents the influence of one hormone to another indicated by a rule. The dashed arrows represent the influence of one hormone to another indicated by a tunnel. H1 pumps H2 from every cell to its right neighbouring cell. H2 pumps H1 upwards.

5. RESULTS AND DISCUSSION

Figure 2 demonstrates the results from the first set of experiments with 16 repetitions for each pattern. The dashed lines in the figure represents the medians of the results achieved by ANN in [3] indicating the higher performance of AHHS (represented by solid lines). It has to be mentioned that, since there is no external gradient or global spatial information in the system, AHHS without tunnelling is not able to generate the desired patterns. The capability of AHHS to break the symmetry of the cells and develop the patterns is due to tunnelling which generates directional information. The directional information in ANN is provided by the links between the neighboring cells.

An example evolved AHHS that develops a *circle* pattern is investigated in order to give an impression of the evolved solutions of AHHS and how the internal features of AHHS interact to perceive and exploit the spatial structure of the environment. Figure 5 represents the internal structure of the AHHS and Figure 6 represents the development of the desired pattern during 27 steps of development. As represented in Figure 5, the evolved AHHS consists of four hormones, 6 rules and 2 tunnels represented by the circles, solid arrows, and dashed arrows respectively. The two tunnels are responsible for generating the directional information for the system. One of the tunnels represents a directional influence of H1 to H2, and the other tunnel represents influence of H2 to H1 in another direction. In fact, H1 pumps a fraction of H2 from every cell to its right neighbouring cell and H2 pumps a fraction of H1 to the upper neighbouring cell. These two directional effects lead to the formation of verti-

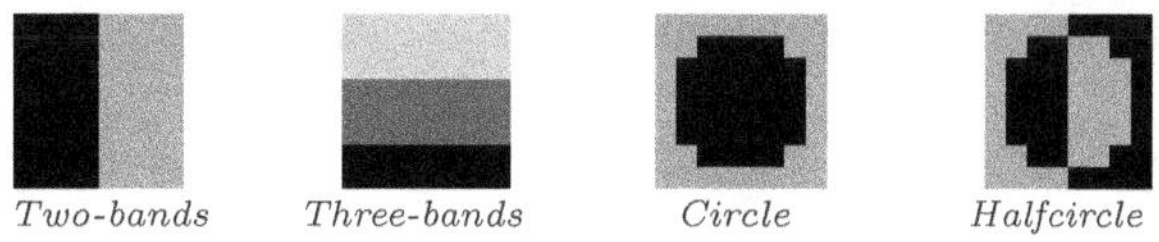

Figure 3: Desired patterns in the second set of experiments (to compare the evolutionary algorithms): *two-bands*, *three-bands*, *circle*, and *halfcircle*

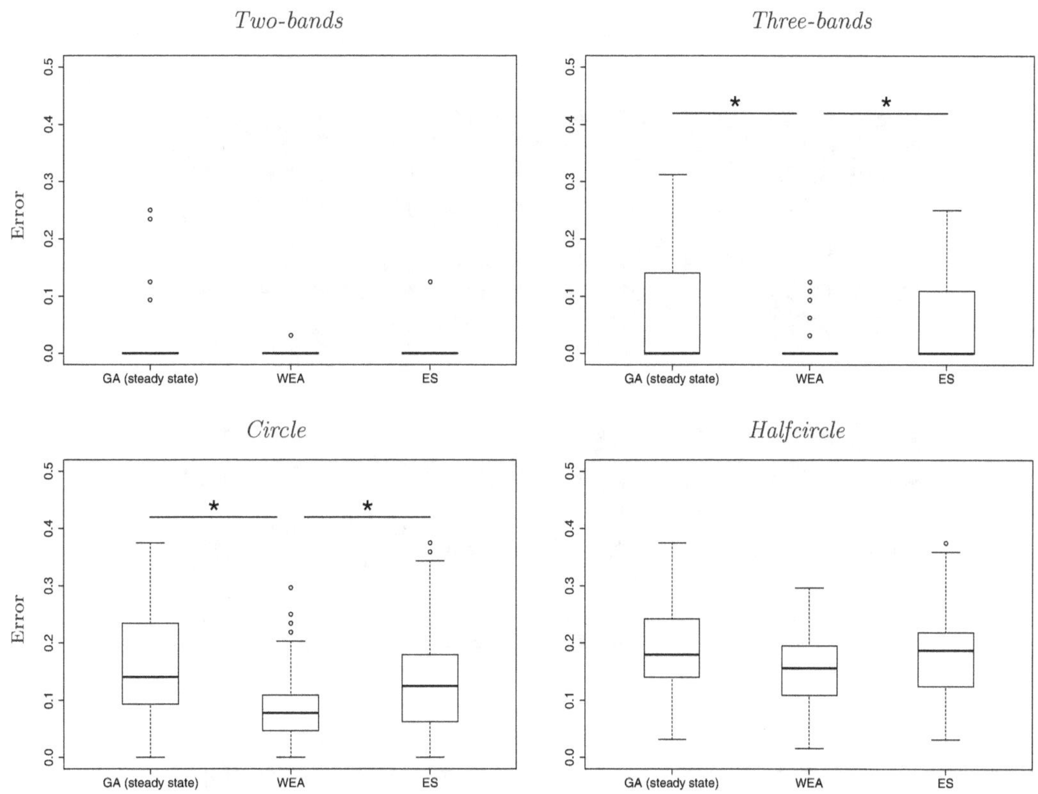

Figure 4: Comparison of fitness achieved by WEA, GA, and ES for the four different patterns in 100 independent runs. WEA performs significantly better than GA and ES in *three-bands* and *circle* patterns. Difference is not significant in very easy (*two-bands*) and very difficult (*halfcircle*) patterns (*:$p < 0.01$; Wilcoxon signed-rank test, unpaired date, "two.sided"-hypothesis). Box-plots indicate median and quartiles, whiskers indicate the most extreme data points which are no more than 1.5 times the length of the box away from the box, circles indicate outliers.

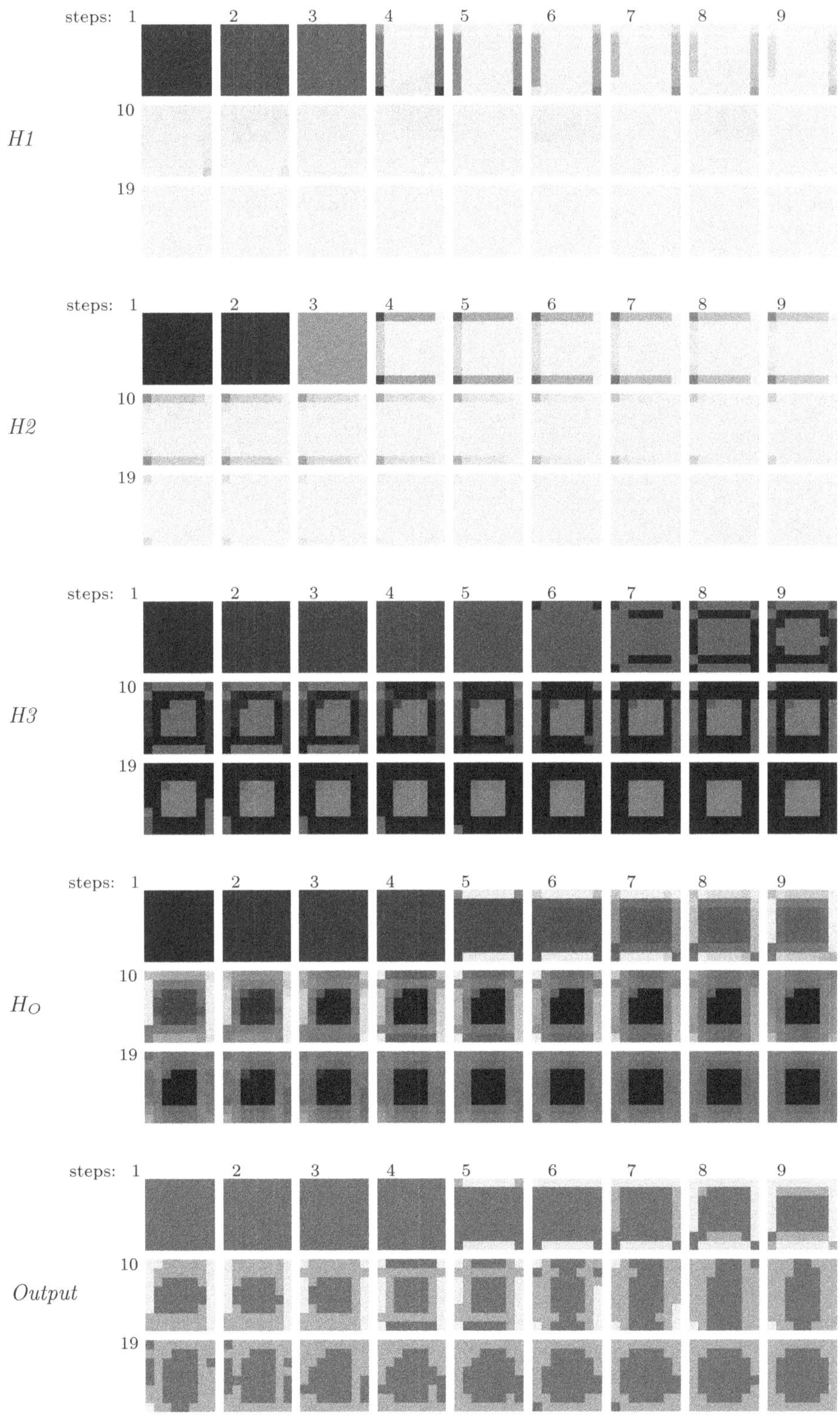

Figure 6: hormone concentration levels.

cal and horizontal edges by H1 and H2 (see Figure 6) and consequently an outer frame at the edges of the pattern by H3 and H_o that leads to the circular shape of the pattern in the later steps.

Figure 4 represents the results of the second set of experiments comparing different evolutionary methods in developing the patterns. The results are accumulated from 100 independent repetitions of the experiments. As the figure shows, WEA performs equally or significantly better in all the experiments. For the easiest pattern (two-bands) all the three evolutionary algorithms represent the highest achievable performance. For the patterns of the middle degree of difficulty (three-bands and circle), WEA performs significantly better. For the most difficult pattern (half-circle), the median error of WEA is lower than the other two algorithms although the difference between the results are not statistically significant.

We suspect that the higher performance of WEA in comparison with the other two methods is due to the dynamicity and diversity of the population during (overlapping) generations which are resulted from the elimination mechanism and strictly maintaining hierarchy in the population. The hierarchy is provided especially by removing individuals with a fitness of equal to (along with the lower than) the most recently evaluated individual. This mechanism implicitly prevents convergence of the population to a fixed point and keeps the diversity of the population. This can be seen in Figure 7 where the fitness values of the population for a successful run of every evolutionary algorithm is represented. The task is to generate a *circle* pattern. The population size is 10 and the populations are depicted for every 100 evaluations. The black dots represent the individuals that are present in the population and the grey dots for the ES and SSGA represent the offspring which are discarded in the immediate last generation. Since every individual in WEA gets a chance to stay in the population for at least one (overlapping) generation, no grey dot is shown for WEA. As represented in the figure, the population in WEA does not quickly converge to the best solutions which are discovered at any point of time, while the number of individuals around the high fitness is high. This way, diversity is kept implicitly which leads to the higher performance of the algorithm. Local optima are detectable in the figures as horizontal lines indicating a high number of individuals evaluated with similar fitness. More local optima are indicated in the WEA figure while the global optima has been also covered by the population.

WEA is also tested (data not shown) with different values for the probability of eliminating the individuals with lower or equal fitness (μ in Section 2.2), but no significant difference is detected except for the lowest possible value where the performance decreases. This indicates that the "presence" of the elimination mechanism is an important factor to generate the dynamics of the system and the method is not sensitive to the chosen value.

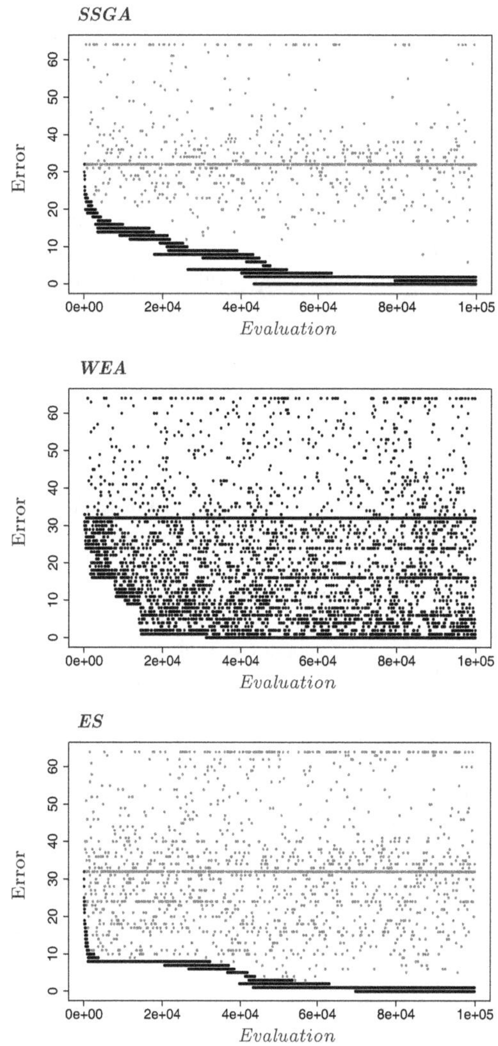

Figure 7: Examples of the poulation dynamics in successful runs by SSGA, WEA, and ES. The populations are depicted in every 100 evaluations. The black dots represent the individuals present in the population and the grey dots in ES and SSGA represent the offspring which are discarded in the last generation.

6. ACKNOWLEDGMENTS

This work is supported by: EU-ICT project 'CoCoRo', no. 270382; EU-ICT project 'ASSISI_bf', no. 601074; Austrian Federal Ministry of Science and Research (BM.W F).

7. REFERENCES

[1] C. P. Bowers. Simulating evolution with a computational model of embryogeny: Obtaining robustness from evolved individuals. In *In Advances in Artificial Life, Proceeding of the 8th European Conference on Artificial Life: ECAL 2005 (2005*, pages 149–158, 2005.

[2] A. Chavoya and Y. Duthen. Use of a genetic algorithm to evolve an extended artificial regulatory network for cell pattern generation. In *Proceedings of the 9th Annual Conference on Genetic and Evolutionary Computation*, GECCO '07, pages 1062–1062, New York, NY, USA, 2007. ACM.

[3] A. Devert, N. Bredeche, and M. Schoenauer. Robustness and the halting problem for multicellular artificial ontogeny. *IEEE Trans. Evolutionary Computation*, 15(3):387–404, 2011.

[4] W. Driever and C. Nusslein-Volhard. The bicoid protein determines position in the drosophila embryo in a concentration-dependent manner. *Cell*, 54(1):95–104, 1988.

[5] J. B. Ekman and K. Lilliendahl. Using priority to food access: fattening strategies in dominance-structured willow tit (parus montanus) flocks. *Behavioral Ecology*, 1993.

[6] A. Ephrussi and D. S. Johnston. Seeing is believing - the bicoid morphogen gradient matures. *Cell*, 116(2):143–152, 2004.

[7] D. Federici. Using embryonic stages to increase the evolvability of development. In *In Proceedings of the Genetic and Evolutionary Computation Conference (GECCO-2004)*. Springer Verlag, 2004.

[8] T. G. W. Gordon and P. J. Bentley. Bias and scalability in evolutionary development. In *Proceedings of the 2005 Conference on Genetic and Evolutionary Computation*, GECCO '05, pages 83–90, New York, NY, USA, 2005. ACM.

[9] H. Hamann, J. Stradner, T. Schmickl, and K. Crailsheim. Artificial hormone reaction networks: Towards higher evolvability in evolutionary multi-modular robotics. In H. Fellermann, M. Dörr, M. M. Hanczyc, L. L. Laursen, S. Maurer, D. Merkle, P.-A. Monnard, K. Støy, and S. Rasmussen, editors, *Proc. of the ALife XII Conference*, pages 773–780. MIT Press, 2010.

[10] J. H. Holland. *Adaptation in Natural and Artificial Systems*. Univ. Michigan Press, Ann Arbor, MI, 1975.

[11] J. Jaeger and A. Martinez-Arias. Getting the Measure of Positional Information. *PLoS Biology*, 7(3):e81+, Mar. 2009.

[12] J. Kennedy and R. C. Eberhart. *Swarm Intelligence*. Morgan Kaufmann, 2001.

[13] K. Z. Lorenz. *Das sogenannte Böse. Zur Naturgeschichte der Aggression*. Borotha-Schoeler, Wien, 1963 1963.

[14] M. Mangel and C. W. Clark. *Dynamic Modeling in Behavioral Ecology*. Princeton University Press, Princeton, 1988.

[15] M. Mangel and C. W. Clark. *Dynamic State Variable Models in Ecology*. Oxford University Press, New York, Oxford, 1988.

[16] J. F. Miller. Evolving developmental programs for adaptation, morphogenesis, and self-repair. In W. Banzhaf, T. Christaller, P. Dittrich, J. T. Kim, and J. Ziegler, editors, *Advances in Artificial Life. 7th European Conference on Artificial Life*, volume 2801 of *Lecture Notes in Artificial Intelligence*, pages 256–265, Dortmund, Germany, 2003. Springer.

[17] I. Rechenberg. *Evolutionsstrategie. Optimierung technischer Systeme nach Prinzipien der biologischen Evolution*. Frommann Holzboog, 1973.

[18] G. B. Schaller. *Dynamic State Variable Models in Ecology*. University of Chicago Press, Chicago, IL, 1972.

[19] T. Schmickl and K. Crailsheim. Modelling a hormone-based robot controller. In *MATHMOD 2009 - 6th Vienna International Conference on Mathematical Modelling*, 2009.

[20] T. Schmickl, H. Hamann, and K. Crailsheim. Modelling a hormone-inspired controller for individual- and multi-modular robotic systems. *Mathematical and Computer Modelling of Dynamical Systems*, 17(3):221–242, 2011.

[21] T. Schmickl, H. Hamann, J. Stradner, R. Mayet, and K. Crailsheim. Complex taxis-behaviour in a novel bio-inspired robot controller. In H. Fellermann, M. Dörr, M. M. Hanczyc, L. L. Laursen, S. Maurer, D. Merkle, P.-A. Monnard, K. Støy, and S. Rasmussen, editors, *Proc. of the ALife XII Conference*, pages 648–655. MIT Press, 2010.

[22] J. Stradner, H. Hamann, P. Zahadat, T. Schmickl, and K. Crailsheim. On-line, on-board evolution of reaction-diffusion control for self-adaptation. In C. Adami, D. M. Bryson, C. Ofria, and R. T. Pennock, editors, *Proceedings of the Thirteenth International Conference on the Simulation and Synthesis of Living Systems (Alife XIII)*, pages 597–598. MIT Press, 2012.

[23] A. M. Turing. The chemical basis of morphogenesis. *Philosophical Transactions of the Royal Society of London. Series B, Biological Sciences*, B237(641):37–72, 1952.

[24] S. Whiteson and P. Stone. Evolutionary function approximation for reinforcement learning. *Journal of Machine Learning Research*, 7:877–917, 2006.

[25] L. Wolpert. The French Flag problem: A contribution to the discussion on pattern development and regulation. In C. H. Waddington, editor, *The Origin of Life: Toward a Theoretical Biology*, pages 125–133. 1968.

[26] P. Zahadat, K. Crailsheim, and T. Schmickl. Evolution of spatial pattern formation by autonomous bio-inspired cellular controllers. In P. Lio, O. Miglino, G. Nicosia, S. Nolfi, and M. Pavone, editors, *12th European Conference on Artificial Life (ECAL 2013)*, pages 721–728. MIT Press, 2013.

[27] P. Zahadat and T. Schmickl. Generation of diversity in a reaction-diffusion-based controller. *Artificial Life*, 2014, In press.

Multiple Feature Construction for Effective Biomarker Identification and Classification using Genetic Programming

Soha Ahmed[1], Mengjie Zhang[1], Lifeng Peng[2] and Bing Xue[1]
[1]School of Engineering and Computer Science
[2] School of Biological Sciences
Victoria University of Wellington , PO Box 600, Wellington 6140, New Zealand
{soha.ahmed, mengjie.zhang, bing.xue}@ecs.vuw.ac.nz and lifeng.peng@vuw.ac.nz

ABSTRACT

Biomarker identification, i.e., detecting the features that indicate differences between two or more classes, is an important task in omics sciences. Mass spectrometry (MS) provide a high throughput analysis of proteomic and metabolomic data. The number of features of the MS data sets far exceeds the number of samples, making biomarker identification extremely difficult. Feature construction can provide a means for solving this problem by transforming the original features to a smaller number of high-level features. This paper investigates the construction of multiple features using genetic programming (GP) for biomarker identification and classification of mass spectrometry data. In this paper, multiple features are constructed using GP by adopting an embedded approach in which Fisher criterion and p-values are used to measure the discriminating information between the classes. This produces nonlinear high-level features from the low-level features for both binary and multi-class mass spectrometry data sets. Meanwhile, seven different classifiers are used to test the effectiveness of the constructed features. The proposed GP method is tested on eight different mass spectrometry data sets. The results show that the high-level features constructed by the GP method are effective in improving the classification performance in most cases over the original set of features and the low-level selected features. In addition, the new method shows superior performance in terms of biomarker detection rate.

1. INTRODUCTION

The discovery of fingerprints in transcproteomics, proteomics and metabolomics samples is attracting much research in the life sciences [5]. Identifying the variables (genes, proteins, metabolites) that distinguish different populations with certain groups is highly interesting. Such variables are commonly referred to as biomarkers [7].

GECCO'14, Jul 12–16, 2014, Vancouver, BC, Canada.

http://dx.doi.org/10.1145/2576768.2598292.

Mass spectrometry (MS) offers high throughput analysis of the biological samples by determining the elemental compositions of these samples [1,8]. The molecules in the mass spectrometer are usually ionized to facilitate the process of measuring the molecules, therefore, each of the molecules is associated with a mass to charge ratio (m/z). Mass spectrometer produces spectra which are composed of m/z values of the charged molecules in the sample and their corresponding abundances (intensities). The mass spectrometer is often accompanied by a liquid chromatography (LC) device. LC separates the molecules and elute them into the mass spectrometer at different retention times. This helps in reducing the complexity of the sample, and hence, increasing the identification numbers. The produced LC-MS spectra is composed of m/z values, retention times and intensities of the compounds in the sample. The number of features of the spectra is usually very large, exceeding thousands, and at the same time the number of samples is very small [27]. This makes biomarker identification extremely difficult [18,28].

Feature construction can provide a means for dimensionality reduction and producing new high-level features from the original low-level features. The new constructed features will also benefit in discovering the relationship between the original features, and therefore, improve the classification performance [22]. Existing feature construction methods can be classified into three main categories [4, 17], which are wrapper approaches, filter approaches, and embedded approaches. Wrapper approaches use a classification algorithm to evaluate the goodness of the constructed features while filter approaches are independent of any classification algorithm. Embedded approaches construct features during the learning process of a classification algorithm.

Genetic programming (GP) can dynamically build models for classification. Due to the nature of GP which automatically produces high-level features (construction) by combining the original features through the functions used in the evolved models, GP can be a good choice for feature construction. This capability of automatic feature construction can also help in discovering the hidden relationship between features [26], and therefore, increase the classification performance. GP is not limited to a specific transformation model like principle component analysis for example [12]. Moreover, GP can build different transformations without any predefined templates.

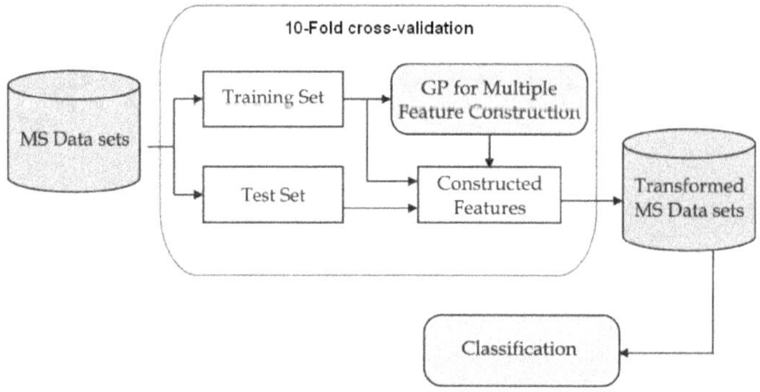

Figure 1: Overview of the GP-multiple feature construction system.

GP has been widely used for feature construction [12,17,21,22] with promising results in terms of improving classification accuracy. There have been different scenarios for the use of GP for feature construction, for example, in [9] GP was used as an embedded approach to construct features, while in [11,12], the authors used a wrapper approach to construct features. In addition, a filter approach was used in [22] to construct a single feature per class depending on the entropy measure.

Most of the GP based feature construction approaches were based on constructing a single feature and either using this single feature for classification or using this feature along with the original set of features. Using the single constructed feature alone might not achieve acceptable classification accuracy and using the combination of a single constructed feature along with the original set of features will increase the dimensionality [10,22]. Therefore, the second approach is completely inappropriate for high dimensional data like MS data, where the number of features exceeds thousands. However, none of these methods investigates the effect of constructing multiple features from a single tree during the evolutionary process of GP.

In this paper, we present a new GP approach to constructing multiple features, which uses GP to select a good subset of features and automatically construct new features. The new approach is expected to further decrease the dimensionality of the selected features and improve the classification performance. This method is also evaluated through its performance for biomarker detection on MS data.

Goals

The goal of the paper is to investigate the performance of the features constructed by GP in terms of the classification accuracy and biomarker identification. The new GP method works by taking an embedded approach, where the features are constructed by automatically generating high-level features from the combination of the original low-level features and the functions from the function set. The sub-trees and root nodes are used as the constructed features. Fisher criterion and p-values are used to measure the discriminating information between different classes. Specifically, we will investigate the following questions:

1. How can multiple features be automatically constructed from the evolved GP tree?

2. How can Fisher criterion and the p-values be used to construct a new fitness measure?

3. What is the effect of mixing several compounds of peptides or metabolites in terms of classification accuracy?

4. Whether the constructed features perform better than the low-level selected features?

5. How well can the new method detect the actual biomarkers?

Organisation

The rest of the paper is organised as follows. Section 2 describes the new GP approach. The experiment set-up, the data sets description and preprocessing are presented in section 3. Section 4 reports the experimental results along with the discussions. The conclusions of the paper are presented in section 5.

2. THE NEW GP ALGORITHM FOR MULTIPLE FEATURE CONSTRUCTION

2.1 Overall Structure

GP can automatically produce multiple outputs from its sub-trees and root nodes [32]. The use of subtree outputs (internal nodes) has shown to be effective for classification problems [32] which encourages us to use the internal nodes outputs for constructing new features. Unlike other approaches which use only the output of root node of the evolved tree as the constructed feature, the sub-tree nodes' output are also used as high-level features here. This will help in construction of more features from a single evolved tree and not from multiple trees (runs) and therefore, reduce the computational cost. The more high-level features can also improve the classification accuracy. The proposed GP method uses the original low-level features to construct multiple features. The constructed features are the outputs of the functions that are calculated using the original features. For example, if two original features from the terminal set are mixed with a multiply function, the constructed feature is the output of the multiplication of those two features. The constructed multiple features are used to transform the original data. Finally, the projected data is used for classification. The overview of the GP multiple feature construction system is shown in Figure 1.

The process is as follows: divide the data sets into training and test sets using ten-fold cross-validation. Use the training set with GP to construct new features, where the goodness of the features are measured using their discriminating power between the classes, which is calculated using Fisher

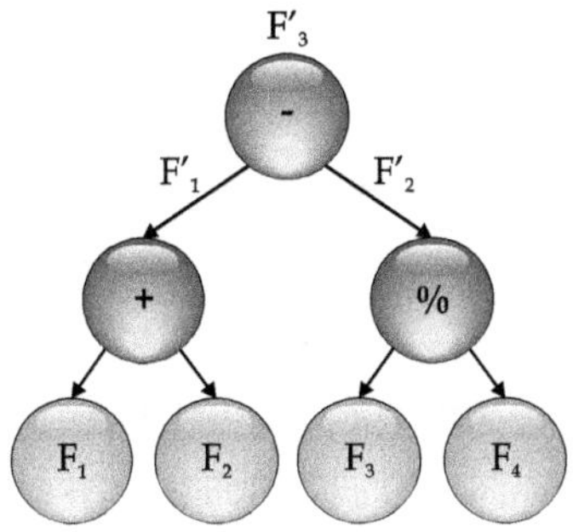

Figure 2: Example of how the features are constructed.

criterion and the p-values. The features are constructed by taking the output of the function on the original features in the evolved program. The new constructed features are used to project both the training and test sets, where different classification algorithms can be used to evaluate new features. Figure 2 shows an example of how the features are constructed from an evolved GP tree. As shown in Figure 2, the two features F_1 and F_2 construct a new feature F'_1, while the two features F_3 and F_4 construct the new feature F'_2. Finally, the new feature F'_3 which represents the final output of the tree is constructed from the new features F'_1 and F'_2. Therefore, this evolved tree will construct three new features from the four original selected features.

2.2 New Fitness Function

The fitness function determines how well a GP tree performs, which is one of the key components in a GP system. Usually, using a wrapper based fitness measure in GP for feature construction can achieve better classification performance than a filter based fitness measure [12], but the computational cost is higher as it requires training a classifier for each individual of the population. Meanwhile, the classification performance success depends more on the discrimination power of the classifier. Therefore, designing a fitness function as an embedded method can avoid those disadvantages.

The Fisher criterion [9] works by maximizing the *between-class* scatter and minimizing the *within-class* scatter. For a two-class problem, the Fisher criterion is defined as

$$\text{Fisher criterion} = \sum_{n=1}^{N} \left| \frac{\mu_i - \mu_j}{\sigma_i^2 - \sigma_j^2} \right| \tag{1}$$

where μ_i and μ_j are the means of the samples which belong to class i and class j, respectively. σ_i^2 and σ_j^2 are the variances of the samples which belong to class i and class j, respectively. N is the number of samples in the training set.

For c classes where $c > 2$, the Fisher criterion is firstly calculated for each adjacent pair of classes based on Equation (1) and the summation of those pairs is the final value of Fisher criterion.

In addition to the Fisher criterion, minimizing the p-value between the classes helps in the significant maximization of the distance between the classes. The p-values are calculated using the one way analysis of variance (one-way ANOVA) test which also measures the *between-class* and *within-class* separability. The new fitness function F_p is given by:

$$F_p = \frac{\text{Fisher criterion}}{P_{value}} \tag{2}$$

In Equation (2), the Fisher criterion is the measured distribution of between-class scatter over the within-class scatter of the GP program outputs. The P_{value} ensures that the degree of separation of the GP program outputs of different classes is significantly large. The objective is to maximize the fitness. Therefore, during the evolution, the p-value is minimized and the Fisher criterion is maximized (i.e. the between-class distance is maximized and the within-class distance is minimized).

3. EXPERIMENT SETUP

This section explains the design of the experiments including the data sets that were used in the experiments and the preprocessing of the data sets. The terminal set, the function set and the GP parameters are also explained in this section.

3.1 Data Sets and Preprocessing

In order to test the effectiveness of the new GP approach, eight MS data sets were used. In this section, the data sets characteristics and the preprocessing will be explained. Table 1 summarizes the characteristics of the data sets.

Preprocessing of the MS data involves several steps which is necessary for successful analysis of the data. The MS data sets include binary and multi-class classification problems which are described as follows.

- Pancreatic cancer data set [14]: This data set is acquired using a time-of-flight (TOF) mass spectrometer and the samples were analyzed using surface-enhanced laser desorption/ionization (SELDI). It is composed of 101 healthy samples and 80 cancerous samples. The preprocessing steps includes baseline subtraction where piecewise linear interpolation is used for regression of the baseline. Afterwards, filtering and normalization are performed using Gaussian filter and area under the curve respectively.

- Ovarian cancer low and high resolution data sets [23]: Both of these data sets were analyzed using SELDI-TOF technology. Although the high resolution mass spectra can generate more distinguishable sets of diagnostic features, the high resolution data is more complex than the low resolution data. Similar to the preprocessing of the Pancreatic Cancer data set, the preprocessing of these two data sets involves baseline adjustment, filtering and normalization. The final step performed is the alignment in order to remove the fluctuation in the m/z values. The ovarian cancer high resolution data set contains 121 cancer and 95 healthy samples, while the low resolution data set contains 162 cancerous samples and 91 healthy samples.

- Prostate cancer data set [24]: Samples of three different stages of Prostate Cancer and healthy samples were analyzed using low resolution SELDI-TOF mass spectrometer. It is composed of four classes which are: Healthy (63 samples), Benign (stage_1) (190 samples), Prostate Cancer stage_2 (26 samples) and Prostate Cancer stage_3 (43 samples).

- Toxpath data set [25]: Serum samples with toxicity-related biomarkers were analyzed using SELDI-TOF mass spectrometer. The data set consists of four classes

Table 1: Data sets characteristics

Data Set	# Features	# Samples	#Classes
Pancreatic cancer	6771	181	2
Ovarian cancer low resolution	15,154	253	2
Ovarian Cancer high resolution	15,000	216	2
Prostate cancer	15,000	322	4
Toxpath	7105	115	4
Arcene	10,000	200	2
Apple-plus	773	40	4
Apple-minus	365	40	4

which are: definite positive (34 samples), definite negative (28 samples), probable positive (10 samples) and probable negative (43 samples). The prostate and Toxpath data sets were already baseline adjusted. Therefore, both of the data sets were only filtered and normalized.

The above five data sets were downloaded from FDA-NCI Clinical Proteomics Program[1]. Those data sets are already binned therefore the number of features remains the same after preprocessing. Matlab [20] bioinformatics toolbox was used to perform the preprocessing of the data.

- Arcene data set [3]: Three different MS data sets were combined to produce the Arcene data set which contains 100 samples of cancer patients and 100 healthy samples. The data set is available after preprocessing and it is downloaded from the UCI machine learning repository [3].

- Apple extract data sets [8]: These two data sets are metabolomics data sets where twenty apples were analyzed using LC-MS technology. Four classes are created from the twenty apples where each class contains ten samples. Three classes contain a mixture of known compounds (biomarkers) while the fourth class is not spiked-in with those compounds. The negative and positive ion modes form the two different data sets. The total number of biomarkers is five and twelve in the negative and positive ion modes, respectively. The data sets are available in NetCDF format and it is preprocessed using XCMS [29] with the settings described in [8].

3.2 GP Settings

The standard tree-based GP is used in the experiments where each node outputs a single floating point [6,26]. The initial population is generated using the ramped half-and-half method [16].

The m/z and retention time variables represent the feature identities of the compounds and the corresponding intensity is the feature value [31]. Therefore, the terminal set is composed of the intensity variable which represents the abundance of the compound in the data. For each sample in a data set, a single floating-point value is produced by the program at the root of its evolved tree [16]. The function set is composed of the four mathematical operators $+, -, \times, \%$ in addition to the operators max, min and if then else ($max, min, IFTE$). The % is a protected division which returns zero for dividing by zero. All the function set members take two arguments except for $IFTE$, which takes three argument and it returns the second argument if the first argument is negative or it returns the third argument otherwise. The evolution terminates at a maximum number of generations of 50. This number is selected as there was no further improvement in increasing the number of generations. The size of population is set to 2000. The tree-depth has been set between 2 and 10. The crossover and mutation rates are set to 0.8 and 0.2, respectively. The tournament selection method is used here and the size is set to 7. An elitist method is taken to ensure the best individual in the next generation is not worse than the current generation and, therefore, keeps the performance monotonically increasing during the evolution [30]. The ECJ [19] package was used in our experiments for running GP. Table 2 shows the various settings of the new method.

[1]`http://home.ccr.cancer.gov/ncifdaproteomics/`

Table 2: GP settings

Function set	$+, -, \times, \%, max, min, IFTE$
Variable terminals	Intensity features
Initialization method	Ramped Half-and Half
Tree Depth	2-10
#Generations	50
Mutation rate	20%
Crossover rate	80%
Elitism	Yes%
Population Size	2000
Selection type	Tournament
Tournament Size	7

3.3 Benchmark Classification Algorithms

To evaluate the classification performance of the constructed features, various linear and non-linear classifier algorithms are used in the experiments. The WEKA package [13] is used to run the classification algorithms. The classification algorithms used are as follows.

1. Multi-layer perceptron (MLP) classifier: It is the implementation of artificial neural networks (ANN) which is a non-linear classifier where the input space is transformed into layers of networks.

2. Naive Bayes Tree (NB-tree): Uses Naive Bayes classifiers at the leave nodes of a decision tree.

3. Random Forest (RF): constructs a multitude of decision trees for training.

4. K- Nearest Neighbors (K-NN): it is the implementation of the nearest neighbors algorithm where the output class is the class of the nearest training example. K is set to 1.

5. Naive Bayes (NB): is a probabilistic method based on Bayes theorem.

6. J-48: The C4.5 decision tree classifier.

7. Decision table (DT): The possible subset of features are used to construct the decision tables. The test set samples are mapped to cells in the decision table. The samples in the test set are then classified according to the label of the majority of training samples of the cell they are mapped to in the table [15].

3.4 Comparison Methods

The performance of the proposed GP method is compared with several methods. Firstly, the original set of features of each data set are used with the seven classifiers for classification. Secondly, the proposed method firstly selects low-level features and through its operators form another set of high-level features. The objective here is to test whether the high-level features can perform better than the low-level features selected by the same method. Therefore, the features selected by the proposed method are compared against the features constructed by it. This method is annotated as $Method_1$. Finally, another method is used for comparison which is a GP-based feature selection method ($Method_2$) [2] for MS data. The reason for selecting $Method_2$ is its previous good performance on MS data. The settings and parameters of $Method_1$ and $Method_2$ are set to be the same as the proposed method on the eight data sets. $Method_1$ and $Method_2$ select the features which are used in the terminal nodes of the best individual. Both $Method_1$ and $Method_2$ are used with the same seven classifiers.

The classification performance of the new GP method for feature construction is compared to that of using all the original features, the low-level features selected by $Method_1$ and the low-level features selected by $Method_2$ [2]. For each set of the GP experiments, the GP process is repeated for 30 independent runs with 30 random seeds. A significance test (Z-test) is with 90% significance level is performed to compare the classification performances of the three methods.

4. RESULTS AND DISCUSSIONS

In Table 3, the new GP method is annotated as *GP-Constructed.* The mean ($\overline{x}$), best and the standard deviation (s) of the 30 runs for using the selected and the constructed features with the seven classifiers are reported in Table 3. "Avg#" shows the average number of selected or constructed features by each method. The evaluation of the seven classifiers is done through ten-fold cross validation. The accuracy of using all the original features is also reported in the same table and shown by "All".

In Table 3 the sign ^{T} means that the proposed method is significantly better than using all the features, while the sign † means that the proposed method is significantly better than $Method_1$. The sign * means the new method is significantly better than $Method_2$. The experiments were run on a machine with an Intel(R) Core(TM) i7-3770 CPU @ 3.40GHz, running Ubuntu 4.6 and Java 1.7.0_25 with a total memory of 8GByte.

4.1 Comparison of the Constructed Features with All the Original Features

As shown in Table 3, for all the data sets except for Apple-plus and Apple-minus, using the original set of features with MLP and NB-tree were both running out of memory and did not manage to produce the results due to the huge search space.

The best classification performance of the GP constructed features is better than using the original set of features on all the data sets except for Apple-plus and Apple-minus data sets, where their performance were both ideal. The average classification performance of the GP constructed features is significantly better than using all the original features on almost all the MS data sets excluding the LC-MS data sets (Apple-plus and Apple-minus). This suggests that GP can benefit in both selecting a good set of features and at the same time in discovering the hidden relationship between the features by constructing the new features that can perform better.

For all the seven classifiers, the features constructed by GP managed to improve the classification accuracy over using all the original features. On the Ovarian Low, Ovarian High, Apple-plus and Apple-minus data sets, the constructed features achieved 100.0% accuracy with most of the classifiers. For other data sets, the improvement of the accuracy of the seven different classifiers is 25.97-41.44% on Pancreatic Cancer, 14.5-27.5% on Arcene, and 2.55-27.79% on Prostate Cancer and Toxpath.

In addition to improving the classification performance, the proposed GP approach also helps in reduction of dimensionality. For example in Prostate Cancer data set, the mean number of the constructed features is 26.03, which means that GP reduced around 99.82% of the original dimensionality. The only exception is the Toxpath data set with J-48 classifier where the original features are slightly better than the average performance of the constructed features, but the best performance of the constructed features achieved the same performance. This is mainly due to the imbalance between the number of samples in each class and the embedded feature selection capability of J-48.

4.2 Comparison of the New Constructed Features with the Low-Level Selected Features

The features constructed by the new approach are also compared with the features selected by GP $Method_1$ (low-level features of the proposed method) and GP $Method_2$. The objective is to test whether the new smaller set of high-level features constructed by GP can perform better than the selected original low-level features.

Comparing the proposed method with $Method_1$: In most cases, the classification performance of the features constructed by the new approach (i.e. notated as GP-Constructed) is significantly better than that of the features selected by $Method_1$ (low-level features of *GP-Constructed*) for most classifiers. For example, On the Toxpath data set, GP-Constructed is significantly better than $Method_1$ with all the seven classifiers except for NB-tree, where their results are similar.

In terms of the dimension reduction, GP-Constructed further decreased the number of features over $Method_1$ on all the eight data sets. The average number is reduced by 7.9-29.26 in different data sets. Meanwhile, GP-Constructed either significantly improved or kept the same performance as the low-level selected features in almost all cases.

Comparing the proposed method with $Method_2$: In almost all data sets, the classification performance of the new approach is significantly better or similar to that of $Method_2$ for most classifiers. For example, GP-Constructed is significantly better than $Method_2$ on the Ovarian Low, Ovarian High, and Apple-plus data sets with almost all the seven classifiers, and on the Toxpath and Apple-minus data set with five of the seven classifiers.

The average number of the constructed features is smaller or much smaller than the average number of the features selected by $Method_2$. The new method reduces the number of features on average from 1 to 221 features over $Method_2$ on different data sets. With the smaller set of constructed

Table 3: Results of using the constructed, selected and original set of features with seven classifiers.

Data set	Classifier	All		GP-Constructed			$Method_1$			$Method_2$		
		Best	Avg#	Best	$\overline{x} \pm s$	Avg#	Best	$\overline{x} \pm s$	Avg#	Best	$\overline{x} \pm s$	Avg#
	MLP	-		95.55	**88.48±4.97**†*		94.44	86.17±4.40		82.60	74.56±6.12	
	NB-tree	-		96.66	89.57 ±3.77*		96.66	90.92 ±3.38		96.73	**92.94 ±2.87**	
	RF	58.56		100.0	**95.38 ±2.14**^{T*}		98.88	95.13 ±2.00		97.83	94.11 ±1.51	
Pan Cancer	K-NN	55.80	6770	98.88	95.56 ±1.80^{T}	36.20	98.88	95.70 ±2.16	65.46	100.0	**95.73 ±1.61**	257.66
	NB	51.38		77.77	**62.50 ±5.76**^{T†*}		64.44	57.26 ±3.44		56.52	54.57 ±0.91	
	J-48	50.82		92.77	87.82 ±2.77^{T}		94.44	**88.48 ±2.41**		92.93	88.42 ±2.16	
	DT	61.32		81.15	**72.36 ±5.33**^{T†*}		80.44	71.17 ±4.40		75.61	64.57 ±6.12	
	MLP	-		100.0	99.97±0.14*		100.0	**99.98±0.07**		100.0	99.23±0.66	
	NB-tree	-		100.0	**99.68 ±0.45**†*		100.0	99.55 ±0.43		100.0	99.06 ±0.68	
	RF	93.28		100.0	99.67±0.26^{T*}		100.0	**99.73±0.37**		100.0	99.21 ±0.46	
Ovarian Low	K-NN	92.09	15154	100.0	**99.95 ±0.20**^{T†*}	27.20	100.0	99.76 ±0.47	46.10	100.0	99.01 ±0.68	62.03
	NB	76.28		99.21	**96.91 ±1.42**^{T†*}		97.22	94.48 ±2.22		96.87	91.12 ±2.78	
	J-48	95.65		100.0	**98.76 ±1.06**^{T†*}		100.0	98.20 ±1.06		99.22	97.28 ±0.93	
	DT	92.49		100.0	97.97 ±1.39^{T*}		100.0	**97.98 ±0.49**		100.0	97.23 ±2.43	
	MLP	-		100.0	**99.93±0.28**†*		100.0	98.69±0.80		100.0	97.00±1.63	
	NB-tree	-		100.0	**99.55 ±0.90**†*		100.0	98.10 ±1.12		100.0	96.12 ±2.01	
	RF	87.04		100.0	**99.71 ±0.51**^{T†*}		100.0	98.33±0.92		100.0	97.17 ±1.08	
Ovarian High	K-NN	86.57	15000	100.0	**99.85 ±0.43**^{T†*}	27.26	100.0	98.97 ±0.83	48.23	99.10	96.10 ±1.38	63.00
	NB	83.79		100.0	**94.16 ±4.38**^{T*}		98.13	93.97 ±2.36		93.11	88.22 ±3.34	
	J-48	86.57		100.0	**96.76 ±2.72**^{T†*}		98.59	95.28 ±2.00		97.71	93.93 ±1.77	
	DT	82.87		97.93	**94.74 ±2.16**^{T†*}		97.00	93.69 ±3.20		96.21	92.00 ±3.45	
	MLP	-		99.00	95.48±2.98†		100.0	96.15±1.50		99.00	**95.78±1.70**	
	NB-tree	-		98.00	91.57 ±3.10†*		99.00	94.03 ±2.65		99.00	**94.73 ±3.01**	
	RF	72.50		100.0	97.28 ±0.51^{T*}		100.0	**97.50±1.27**		100.0	96.68 ±1.53	
Arcene	K-NN	84.50	10000	100.0	**96.73 ±1.48**^{T}	32.50	100.0	96.70 ±1.49	58.56	99.00	96.33 ±1.58	102.1
	NB	70.0		85.50	**72.75 ±7.53**		88.5	72.00 ±6.56		77.50	69.95 ±3.17	
	J-48	81.00		95.50	**90.43 ±2.76**^{T*}		93.50	90.15 ±2.59		94.50	88.65 ±2.45	
	DT	71.50		92.00	83.51 ±4.64^{T}		93.67	84.15 ±3.50		94.00	**85.78 ±2.35**	
	MLP	-		100.0	96.47±2.62†		99.68	**97.39±1.54**		99.39	96.69±1.59	
	NB-tree	-		98.58	95.09 ±2.04*		98.12	94.59 ±1.76		98.78	**96.29 ±1.43**	
	RF	98.75		100.0	**98.83 ±0.90**†*		98.75	97.82±0.76		100.0	98.80 ±0.80	
Pros. Cancer	K-NN	97.45	15154	100.0	**98.83 ±0.95**^{T†*}	26.03	99.37	97.72 ±0.98	41.76	100.0	97.74 ±1.04	40.83
	NB	58.13		84.91	**75.37 ±6.13**^{T†*}		82.18	70.34 ±5.25		80.79	69.85 ±6.91	
	J-48	95.00		94.33	**88.55 ±2.86**		90.62	87.71 ±2.13		92.07	87.75 ±2.46	
	DT	72.21		82.25	73.49 ±4.92†		81.25	72.39 ±5.54		83.39	**73.65 ±4.59**	
	MLP	-		99.12	**94.42±3.03**†*		98.25	93.07±2.95		96.72	91.45±4.56	
	NB-tree	-		99.12	89.56 ±4.82		97.36	**89.94 ±4.80**		96.72	89.84 ±5.75	
	RF	97.36		100.0	**97.92 ±1.39**†*		100.0	97.05±1.75		97.54	93.67 ±2.10	
Toxpath	K-NN	97.75	7105	100.0	**98.65 ±1.10**^{T†*}	37.1	100.0	97.75 ±1.14	59.40	96.72	92.57 ±1.54	177.80
	NB	58.12		82.45	**61.99 ±8.89**†*		60.52	51.23 ±4.93		54.91	49.72 ±2.72	
	J-48	89.47		89.47	**83.59 ±3.48**†*		89.47	81.46 ±4.78		88.53	80.19 ±3.68	
	DT	64.91		76.12	**67.42 ±3.03**^{T†*}		78.25	65.07 ±4.45		71.72	62.45 ±2.56	
	MLP	100.0		100.0	**100.0±0.0**†*		100.0	99.25±2.38		96.72	91.01 ±3.68	
	NB-tree	100.0		100.0	**100.0 ±0.0**†*		100.0	98.83 ±2.38		96.72	87.67 ±5.04	
	RF	100.0		100.0	**99.85 ±0.83**†*		100.0	92.65 ±2.33		97.54	91.01 ±3.68	
Apple plus	K-NN	100.0	773	100.0	**100.0±0.0***	32.30	100.0	**100.0 ±0.0**	46.73	98.36	95.24 ±1.94	33.26
	NB	100.0		100.0	95.83 ±1.75*		100.0	**95.93 ±1.87**		71.31	55.57 ±6.62	
	J-48	100.0		100.0	**93.29 ±2.28**†*		100.0	92.58 ±3.23		88.52	80.71 ±4.58	
	DT	100.0		100.0	**97.25 ±2.38**†*		100.0	96.35 ±3.23		96.72	91.01 ±3.68	
	MLP	100.0		100.0	**99.71±1.66***		100.0	99.58±1.87		100.0	98.26±3.63	
	NB-tree	100.0		100.0	99.03 ±2.27*		100.0	**99.75 ±1.01**		100.0	98.96 ±2.67	
	RF	100.0		100.0	**100.0 ±0.0**†*		100.0	99.63 ±0.63		100.0	99.86 ±0.53	
Apple minus	K-NN	100.0	365	100.0	**100.0±0.0**	28.43	100.0	**100.0 ±0.0**	36.33	100.0	**100.0 ±0.0**	41.33
	NB	100.0		100.0	**100.0 ±0.0**†*		100.0	99.58 ±1.33		100.0	92.08 ±9.94	
	J-48	100.0		100.0	**100.0 ±0.0***		100.0	**100.0 ±0.0**		100.0	90.76 ±9.15	
	DT	100.0		100.0	**99.19 ±1.66***		100.0	99.00 ±1.87		100.0	97.26 ±3.63	

features, the new approach still achieved similar or better classification performance than $Method_2$ in almost all cases.

4.3 Biomarker Identification

We tested the performance of biomarker identification of the proposed method on the Apple-plus and Apple-minus data sets because only in these two data sets, a set of compounds were spiked-in and predefined as the biomarkers.

Figure 3 shows an example of the approach used to count the number of identified biomarkers. As shown in Figure 3, the intersection between the selected features in the terminal nodes of the tree and the predifined set of biomarkers are used as an evaluation of the biomarker identification task.

Table 4 shows the biomarkers in Apple-plus and Apple-minus data sets (positive and negative modes of the ions).

Table 4: Identified spike-in biomarkers by the proposed GP method and Method_1 for the Apple data sets. The biomarkers are identified using their m/z values.

m/z values in Apple-plus data set (12 biomakers)	New Method		Method_2	
	Selection Status	% of GP runs	Selection Status	% of GP runs
331.21	✗	0	✓	100.0
471.09	✓	80.00	✓	50.00
107.05, 169.05, 238.05, 275.09, 456.11, 459.13	✓	100.0	✗	0.0
456.62, 475.10	✗	0.0	✗	0.0
449.11	✓	66.67	✓	88.0
229.09	✓	90.00	✗	0.0
m/z values in Apple-minus data set (5 biomakers)	New Method		Method_2	
	Selection Status	% of GP runs	Selection Status	% of GP runs
463.0	✓	86.67	✗	0.0
447.09	✓	100.0	✓	86.67
273.03	✓	100.0	✓	93.33
435.13	✓	100.0	✗	0.0
227.07	✓	93.33	✗	0.0

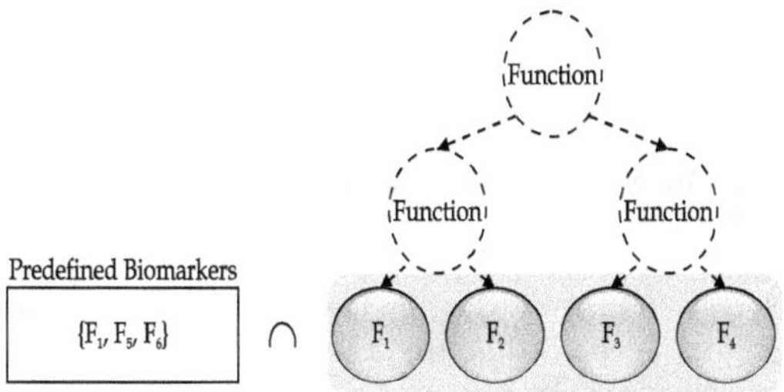

Figure 3: Biomarker Identification approach.

The table also shows the status of identification of the biomarkers by the proposed GP method and Method_2. The percentage of runs in which these biomarkers appear are shown in Table 4. As shown in Table 4, GP identified the complete set of biomarkers in Apple-minus data sets. Method_2 detected only two bimarkers in 93.33% and 86.67% of the runs, respectively. For Apple-minus data set, the new GP method detected three biomarkers in all its 30 runs and the remaining two in 86.67% and 93.33% of the runs. For the Apple-plus data set, nine out of the twelve biomarkers (75%) are detected by the proposed GP method, where seven biomarkers are identified in 100.0% of runs and the other three are selected in 66.67%, 80% and 90% of the GP runs. However, Method_2 identified only three of the twelve biomarkers. This suggests that the new proposed method can be successfully used for the task of biomarker identification as it constructs a new set of features that can achieve better classification accuracy and biomarker detection rate.

5. CONCLUSIONS AND FUTURE WORKS

The goal of this paper was to test the performance of GP in constructing multiple new high-level features and to examine the effect of these new features in terms of dimensionality reduction, classification performance and biomarker identification. The goal was successfully achieved by developing a new GP method, which takes an embedded approach by maximizing the significant discrimination between different classes. The performance of the high-level constructed features are compared to the whole original set of features and the selected set of low-level features from two methods with seven different classifiers. The results show that the new features performed better than the original set of features for all the data sets with most of the classifiers. The results also show that these smaller sets of new features achieved significantly better or similar performance to the selected low-level features on almost all the data sets. Moreover, the constructed features helped in reducing the dimensionality more than the selected features. The biomarker identification results of the proposed method showed that the new GP method can identify 100.0% of the biomarkers in the Apple-minus LC-MS data set and 75% of the predefined biomakers in the Apple-plus data set. Due to its better classification and biomarker identification performance, the new GP can be successfully applied to this task.

As for future directions, it can be tested if using numerical simplification of the evolved trees can reduce the number of constructed features. Furthermore, as there are no publicly available feature construction methods like feature selection, other feature construction methods will be implemented in the future to compare them to the proposed method.

6. REFERENCES

[1] S. Ahmed, M. Zhang, and L. Peng. Genetic Programming for Biomarker Detection in Mass Spectrometry Data. In *Proceeding of the 25 th Australasian Conference on Artificial Intelligence*, pages 266–278, 2012.

[2] S. Ahmed, M. Zhang, and L. Peng. Enhanced feature selection for biomarker discovery in lc-ms data using GP. In *Proceedings of 2013 IEEE Congress on Evolutionary Computation*, pages 584–591, 2013.

[3] K. Bache and M. Lichman. UCI machine learning repository, 2013.

[4] W. Banzhaf, F. D. Francone, R. E. Keller, and P. Nordin. *Genetic Programming: An Introduction: on the Automatic Evolution of Computer Programs and Its Applications.* Morgan Kaufmann Publishers Inc., San Francisco, CA, USA, 1998.

[5] C. Baumgartner, M. Osl, M. Netzer, and D. Baumgartner. Bioinformatic-driven search for metabolic biomarkers in disease. *Journal of Clinical Bioinformatics*, pages 1–3, 2011.

[6] C. M. Bishop. *Neural Networks for Pattern Recognition.* Oxford University Press, Inc., New York, NY, USA, 1995.

[7] G. Chen, T. G. Gharib, C.-C. Huang, D. G. Thomas, K. A. Shedden, J. M. G. Taylor, S. L. R. Kardia, D. E. Misek, T. J. Giordano, M. D. Iannettoni, M. B. Orringer, S. M. Hanash, and D. G. Beer. Proteomic analysis of lung adenocarcinoma: Identification of a highly expressed set of proteins in tumors. *Clinical Cancer Research*, 8(7):2298–2305, 2002.

[8] S. Datta. Feature Selection and Machine Learning with Mass Spectrometry Data. In R. Matthiesen, editor, *Mass Spectrometry Data Analysis in Proteomics*, volume 1007, pages 237–262. Humana Press, 2013.

[9] H. Firpi, E. Goodman, and J. Echauz. On Prediction of Epileptic Seizures by Computing Multiple Genetic Programming Artificial Features. In M. Keijzer, A. Tettamanzi, P. Collet, J. Hemert, and M. Tomassini, editors, *Genetic Programming*, volume 3447 of *Lecture Notes in Computer Science*, pages 321–330. Springer Berlin Heidelberg, 2005.

[10] H. Guo, L. Jack, and A. Nandi. Automated feature extraction using genetic programming for bearing condition monitoring. In *Proceedings of the 2004 14th IEEE Signal Processing Society Workshop*, pages 519–528, 2004.

[11] H. Guo and A. Nandi. Breast cancer diagnosis using genetic programming generated feature. In *2005 IEEE Workshop on Machine Learning for Signal Processing*, pages 215–220, 2005.

[12] H. Guo, Q. Zhang, and A. K. Nandi. Feature extraction and dimensionality reduction by genetic programming based on the Fisher criterion. *Expert Systems*, 25(5):444–459, 2008.

[13] M. Hall, E. Frank, G. Holmes, B. Pfahringer, P. Reutemann, and I. H. Witten. The weka data mining software: an update. *SIGKDD Explorer Newsletter*, pages 10–18, 2009.

[14] S. R. Hingorani, E. F. P. III, A. Maitra, V. Rajapakse, C. King, M. A. Jacobetz, S. Ross, T. P. Conrads, T. D. Veenstra, B. A. Hitt, Y. Kawaguchi, D. Johann, L. A. Liotta, H. C. Crawford, M. E. Putt, T. Jacks, C. V. Wright, R. H. Hruban, A. M. Lowy, and D. A. Tuveson. Preinvasive and invasive ductal pancreatic cancer and its early detection in the mouse. *Cancer Cell*, 4(6):437–450, 2003.

[15] R. Kohavi. The power of decision tables. In *Proceedings of the European Conference on Machine Learning*, pages 174–189. Springer Verlag, 1995.

[16] J. R. Koza. Introduction to genetic programming: tutorial. In *Genetic and Evolutionary Computation Conference,GECCO (Companion)*, pages 2299–2338, 2008.

[17] K. Krawiec. Genetic programming-based construction of features for machine learning and knowledge discovery tasks. *Genetic Programming and Evolvable Machines*, 3(4):329–343, 2002.

[18] Y. Li, Y. Liu, and L. Bai. Genetic algorithm based feature selection for mass spectrometry data. In *BioInformatics and BioEngineering, 2008. BIBE 2008. 8th IEEE International Conference on*, pages 1–6, 2008.

[19] S. Luke. *Essentials of Metaheuristics*. Lulu, second edition, 2013.

[20] MATLAB. *version 7.10.0 (R2010a)*. The MathWorks Inc., Natick, Massachusetts, 2010.

[21] K. Neshatian and M. Zhang. Unsupervised elimination of redundant features using genetic programming. In *Proceeding of the 22nd Australasian Conference on Artificial Intelligence*, pages 432–442, 2009.

[22] K. Neshatian, M. Zhang, and P. Andreae. A filter approach to multiple feature construction for symbolic learning classifiers using genetic programming. *IEEE Transactions of Evolutionary Computation*, 16(5):645–661, 2012.

[23] Petricoin, A. M. Ardekani, B. A. Hitt, P. J. Levine, V. A. Fusaro, S. M. Steinberg, G. B. Mills, C. Simone, D. A. Fishman, E. C. Kohn, and L. A. Liotta. Use of proteomic patterns in serum to identify ovarian cancer. *The Lancet*, 359(9306):572–577, 2002.

[24] E. F. Petricoin, D. K. Ornstein, C. P. Paweletz, A. Ardekani, P. S. Hackett, B. A. Hitt, A. Velassco, C. Trucco, L. Wiegand, K. Wood, C. B. Simone, P. J. Levine, W. M. Linehan, M. R. Emmert-Buck, S. M. Steinberg, E. C. Kohn, and L. A. Liotta. Serum Proteomic Patterns for Detection of Prostate Cancer. *Journal of National Cancer Institute*, 94(20):1576–1578, 2002.

[25] E. F. Petricoin, V. Rajapaske, E. H. Herman, A. M. Arekani, S. Ross, D. Johann, A. Knapton, J. Zhang, B. A. Hitt, T. P. Conrads, T. D. Veenstra, L. A. Liotta, and F. D. Sistare. Toxicoproteomics: Serum proteomic pattern diagnostics for early detection of drug induced cardiac toxicities and cardioprotection. *Toxicologic Pathology*, pages 122–130, 2004.

[26] R. Poli, W. B. Langdon, and N. F. McPhee. *A field guide to genetic programming*. Lulu Enterprises, UK Ltd, 2008.

[27] H. Ressom, R. S. Varghese, E. Orvisky, S. Drake, G. Hortin, M. Abdel-Hamid, C. A. Loffredo, and R. Goldman. Ant colony optimization for biomarker identification from maldi-tof mass spectra. In *Proceedings ofthe 28th IEEE Annual International Conference in Engineering in Medicine and Biology Society*, pages 4560–4563, 2006.

[28] H. W. Ressom, R. S. Varghese, L. Goldman, Y. An, C. A. Loffredo, M. Abdel-Hamid, Z. Kyselova, Y. Mechref, M. Novotny, S. K. Drake, and R. Goldman. Analysis of MALDI-TOF mass spectrometry data for discovery of peptide and glycan biomarkers of hepatocellular carcinoma. *Journal of Proteome Research*, 7(2):603–610, 2008.

[29] C. Smith, E. Want, G. O'Maille, R. Abagyan, and G. Siuzdak. XCMS: Processing mass spectrometry data for metabolite profiling using Nonlinear peak alignment, matching, and identification. *Analytical Chemistry*, pages 779–787, 2006.

[30] M. Smith and L. Bull. Feature Construction and Selection Using Genetic Programming and a Genetic Algorithm. In C. Ryan, T. Soule, M. Keijzer, E. Tsang, R. Poli, and E. Costa, editors, *Genetic Programming*, volume 2610 of *Lecture Notes in Computer Science*, pages 229–237. Springer Berlin Heidelberg, 2003.

[31] R. Wehrens, P. Franceschi, U. Vrhovsek, and F. Mattivi. Stability-based biomarker selection. *Analytica Chimica Acta*, 705:15–23, 2011.

[32] Y. Zhang and M. Zhang. A multiple-output program tree structure in genetic programming. In *Proceedings of The Second Asian-Pacific Workshop on Genetic Programming*, pages 1–12, Cairns, Australia, 2004.

Enhancing Genetic Algorithm-Based Genome-Scale Metabolic Network Curation Efficiency

Eddy J Bautista
Department of Chemical and Biomolecular Engineering,
University of Connecticut, Storrs, CT, USA
191 Auditorium Road
Storrs, CT 06226 USA
eddy.bautista@uconn.edu

Ranjan Srivastava
Department of Chemical and Biomolecular Engineering,
University of Connecticut, Storrs, CT, USA
191 Auditorium Road
Storrs, CT 06226 USA
srivasta@engr.uconn.edu

ABSTRACT
Genome-scale metabolic modeling using constraint-based analysis is a powerful modeling paradigm for simulating metabolic networks. Models are generated via inference from genome annotations. However, errors in the annotation or the identity of a gene's function could lead to "metabolic inconsistency" rendering simulations infeasible. Uncovering the source of metabolic inconsistency is non-trivial due to network size and complexity. Recently published work uses genetic algorithms for curation by generating pools of models with randomly relaxed mass balance constraints. Models are evolved that allow feasible simulation while minimizing the number of constraints relaxed. Relaxed constraints represent metabolites likely to be the root of metabolic inconsistency. Although effective, the approach can result in numerous false positives. Here we present a strategy, MassChecker, which evaluates all of the relaxed mass balance constraints in each generation prior to the next round of evolution to determine if they had become consistent due to recombination/mutation. If so, these constraints are enforced. This approach was applied to the development of genome-scale metabolic model of *B. anthracis*. The model consisted of 1,049 reactions and 1,003 metabolites. The result was a 60% reduction in the number of relaxed mass balance constraints, significantly speeding up the curation process.

Categories and Subject Descriptors
J.3 [**Life and Medical Science**]: Biology and genetics

General Terms
Algorithms.

Keywords
Metabolic modeling, computational biology, metabolic engineering, genetic algorithms, genome-scale modeling, flux balance analysis, systems biology

GECCO'14, July 12–16, 2014, Vancouver, BC, Canada.

1. INTRODUCTION
Genome-scale metabolic flux balance analysis (FBA) is a powerful tool for mathematically modeling metabolism [1]. The model is inferred by determining the presence or absence of metabolic pathways based on genome annotation. Due to the large number of variables, the model is generally underdetermined. Optimization theory is used to determine the optimal distribution of metabolic resources based upon an appropriate objective function and various biological constraints. Unfortunately, the genome annotation is often incomplete or may have errors, resulting in incorrect constraints, particularly with regard to the mass balances on metabolites. As a result, the model is mathematically inconsistent and thus not solvable. GAFBA is a genome-scale metabolic model curation methodology that combines a genetic algorithm (GA) with FBA to resolve inconsistency in constraints [1]. GAFBA finds the minimum number of metabolites with mass balance constraints that should be relaxed, in order to determine a feasible solution for the optimization problem. It is important to note that the feasible solution is not the correct solution; rather the information of interest is which constraints were relaxed. The constraints that require relaxing are the ones where the inconsistencies are likely to be present. Thus this approach identifies which metabolites to focus curation efforts on. Given that thousands of metabolites interacting with each other, identifying problematic metabolites is a non-trivial problem.

To resolve the inconsistency, five possible solutions may be applied to the network based on experimental studies or literature/database information. The options are: 1) change the directionality of a reaction, 2) add an exchange flux for the metabolite, 3) add a transport or intracellular reaction, 4) remove a reaction or metabolite from the model, or 5) no change. In a previous publication examples of each of the options were presented during the curation of *Mycoplasma gallisepticum*. [1].

GAFBA randomly generates an initial population of chromosomes for the GA. Each chromosome represents a potential genome-scale metabolic model for the microorganism. The chromosomes are binary encoded where each of the genes represents a mass balance constraint. If the gene has a value of zero, then the mass balance constraint is relaxed. If the value is one the mass balance is enforced. The population is evolved using the genetic operations of reproduction, crossover, and mutation to produce a better population and, ultimately, an accurate metabolic model.

The composition of the initial population in GAs has been reported to affect their convergence, their performance, and their ability to find the best possible solution [4; 8; 9; 11]. If the initial population is of high quality, the possibility of finding accurate solutions increases. However, the random generation of the initial population is useful because it increases the diversity among the population and can represent any region within the search space [11].

In GAFBA, during the generation of the initial population of solutions for use with the GA, whether a mass balance constraint is enforced or relaxed is determined randomly. As a result, some metabolites with a consistent mass balance are inaccurately labeled as "problematic" ones. These metabolites are referred to as "false positives." As new solutions evolve over the course of generations, the number of false positives decreases. However, these situations slow down the evolution of the model through the curation process. Moreover, the number of "false positives" at the end of a simulation increases with the size as the model. Therefore, a mass balance constraint consistency checker tool, MassChecker, was introduced. MassChecker was developed to find these false positives and adjust the chromosomes to keep them in the model as enforced mass balance constraints. MassChecker enhances the performance of GAFBA while reducing the number of simulations required during the curation process, as well as the total running time.

MassChecker was implemented in GAFBA and tested during the development of the genome-scale metabolic model for *Bacillus anthracis*. Here a comparison of the evolution of the model using GAFBA with and without MassChecker is presented. For convenience, the original version of GAFBA is referred to as GAFBA v1.0. The version with MassChecker is referred to as GAFBA v1.1.

2. MATERIALS AND METHODS

2.1 Model organism

The organism modeled and curated for this study was *Bacillus anthracis*. *B. anthracis* is the etiologic agent of anthrax. *B. anthracis* has a genome size of 5.2 MB. The metabolic model consisted of 1,049 reactions and 1,003 metabolites.

2.2 Genetic algorithm parameters

The GAFBA algorithm was modified to incorporate amass balance consistency checking, referred to as MassChecker. Additionally, a bottom re-seed operation was also incorporated. The bottom re-seed operation replaces the chromosomes of the bottom part of the population with new randomly generated chromosomes.

The following parameters were used for the GA: Population size was 30 chromosomes; crossover probability was 30%; and mutation probability was 1%. The Elite Selection was used with an elite fraction of 20%. Two-point crossover was performed, and bottom re-seed was not allowed. Both versions of GAFBA (v1.0 and v1.1) were run for 2,000 generations per simulation, and 10 simulations in total were carried out. All simulations were implemented on a 2.7 GHz Intel Core i5 computer. For the GAFBA v1.0 algorithm, each simulation (2,000 generations) took approximately 4 hours. Meanwhile, the running time for each simulation with GAFBA v1.1 took 3 hours. Thus the total time for the 10 simulations was 40 hours with GAFBA v1.0, and 30 hours with GAFBA v1.1.

2.3 Flux Balance analysis parameters

FBA is represented mathematically by the mass balance for each metabolite presented in the network under steady state conditions,

$$\bar{\bar{S}} \cdot \bar{v} = \bar{0} \quad (1)$$

where $\bar{\bar{S}}$ represents the stoichiometric matrix, while $\bar{v}$ represents the flux. The set of constraints are represented as

$$\alpha_j \leq v_j \leq \beta_j \quad (2)$$

where α_j and β_j are the respective lower and upper bounds of the j fluxes. The bounds for the reversible reactions were $-\infty \leq v_j \leq \infty$, whereas for the irreversible reactions, they were $0 \leq v_j \leq \infty$. The exchange fluxes bring metabolites into or out of the system. The exchange fluxes for nine metabolites were determined experimentally and are shown in Table 1. The remaining boundaries for the exchange fluxes were defined as $-\infty \leq v_j \leq \infty$ for metabolites in the media. For metabolites only secreted out of the system, the constraint used was $0 \leq v_j \leq \infty$. The media used was *iron reduced media* [2] consisting of glucose, arginine, leucine, methionine, cysteine, phenylalanine, histidine, isoleucine, valine, aspartate, proline, serine, thiamine, threonine, tryptophan, glutamate, Ca^{2+}, Cl^{-}, Fe^{3+}, K^{+}, Mg^{2+}, Mn^{2+}, Na^{+}, sulfate, and phosphate. The lower boundary of the non growth-associated maintenance value was set to 6.75 mmol/gram-dry-weight/hr based on the experimentally measured value for *Bacillus subtilis* [13].

$$Z = \sum_{j=1}^{N} c_j v_j, \quad (3)$$

Finally, the optimal metabolic flux distribution was determined using a linear objective function,
where Z represents the objective function to be maximized, which in this case was the biomass equation. The term c_j is a biologically determined coefficient that exhibited the contribution of v_j to the objective function Z. The objective function chosen for the optimization problem was the maximization of the biomass for *B. anthracis* based on compositions given in Tables 2 and 3.

Table 1. Experimentally measured fluxes used as constraints for the FBA model.

Rate	Flux (mmol/gram-dry-weight/hr)
Glucose uptake rate	-13.157
Carbon dioxide production rate	6.29
Oxygen uptake rate	-6.737
Lactate uptake rate	-0.973
Glutamic acid uptake rate	-0.266
Iron uptake rate	-0.00075
Bacillibactin production rate	0.0023
Petrobactin production rate	0.0163
Protocatechuate production rate	0.0241

Table 2. List of biomass reactants for *B. anthracis* model. The name, reaction, and stoichiometric coefficients are provided (Source of data - [3; 5-7; 10; 12; 14; 15])

	Species	mmol/gram-dry-cell-weight
Protein	Glycine	0.412078
	Alanine	0.433604
	Valine	0.329047
	Leucine	0.375175
	Isoleucine	0.293682
	Serine	0.182975
	Threonine	0.239866
	Phenylalanine	0.162986
	Tyrosine	0.132234
	Tryptophan	0.007688
	Cysteine	0.010763
	Methionine	0.083031
	Lysine	0.264468
	Arginine	0.184512
	Histidine	0.087643
	Aspartate	0.209114
	Asparagine	0.209114
	Glutamine	0.266005
	Glutamate	0.266005
	Proline	0.155298
RNA	AMP (ATP)	64.31000
	GMP (GTP)	0.131137
	CMP (CTP)	0.089431
	UMP (UTP)	0.096310
DNA	dAMP (dATP)	0.010802
	dGMP (dGTP)	0.006413
	dCMP (dCTP)	0.005738
	dTMP (dTTP)	0.010802
Ions	K	0.700573
	Mg	0.100903
	Fe(+3)	0.002030
	NH4	0.001285
	SO4	0.000031
	Ca2+	0.003179
Cofactors	coa	0.000128
	spermidine	0.000020
	ACP	0.000273
	Ornitine	0.000046
	NAD	0.018220
	NADP	0.001053
	NADPH	0.000237
	menaquinol 7	0.000150
	10-formyltetrahydrofolate	0.000207
Lipids	cardiolipin (tetrahexadecanoyl)	0.000740
	cardiolipin (stearoylcardiolipin)	0.000023
	1,2-dipalmitoyl-phosphatidylglycerol	0.005107
	phosphatidylglycerol (dioctadacanoyl)	0.000162
	1,2-dipalmitoyl-phosphatidylethanolamine	0.006196
	phosphatidylethanlamine (dioctadecanoyl)	0.000196
	1,2-dipalmitoyl-phosphatidylserine	0.000415
	phosphatidylserine (dioctadecanoyl, n-c18:0)	0.000013
	1,2-dipalmitoylglycerol	0.010908
	1,2-distearoyl-sn-glycerol	0.000339
	hexadecanoic/palmitic/palmitate	0.000572
	octadecanoic/stearic/stearate	0.000018
Cell wall	a peptidoglycan subunit	0.030270
	water	59.90000

Table 3. List of biomass products for *B. anthracis* model. The name, reaction, and stoichiometric coefficients are provided (Source of data - [3; 5-7; 10; 12; 14; 15]).

	Species	mmol/gram-dry-cell-weight
Growth associated maintenance	ADP	64.200000
	H+	64.200000
	Pi	64.190000
	PPI	0.458900
	Biomass	1.000000
tRNA recycling	Glycine	0.412078
	Alanine	0.433604
	Valine	0.329047
	Leucine	0.375175
	Isoleucine	0.293682
	Serine	0.182975
	Threonine	0.239866
	Phenylalanine	0.162986
	Tyrosine	0.132234
	Tryptophan	0.007688
	Cysteine	0.010763
	Methionine	0.083031
	Lysine	0.264468
	Arginine	0.184512
	Histidine	0.087643
	Aspartate	0.209114
	Asparagine	0.209114
	Glutamine	0.266005
	Glutamate	0.266005
	Proline	0.155298
	apo-ACP	0.000273109

2.4 Mass balance constraints consistency checker (MassChecker)

The algorithm is presented in Figure 1. After the initial population is randomly generated, an optimal flux distribution is determined by FBA for each of the chromosomes in the population. The fitness of each chromosome is scored based on the minimum number of mass balance constraints relaxed. However, if two chromosomes have the same number of mass balanced constraints relaxed, the chromosome with the higher growth rate is considered the better one. Next, the elite pool is selected based on the predetermined elite fraction, and MassChecker is applied to each of the chromosomes in the elite pool. MassChecker inspects each of the mass balances of the metabolites with relaxed constraints in the chromosome. It takes the flux distribution from FBA calculations and determines the summation of the fluxes through the reactions where the metabolite participates. If the summation is equal to zero, then by definition the mass balance constraint is fulfilled. In such a scenario, the gene of the corresponding chromosome is changed from zero to one, thus enforcing the mass balance constraint in future calculations.

After MassChecker analyzes all the chromosomes from the elite pool, they are then copied to the new population without further modification. Applying the genetic operations of crossover and mutation, the remainder of the population is bred. This process is kept running for 2,000 generations at which point the algorithm stops and the list of remaining problematic metabolites are generated. After the appropriate changes are made in the model based on the results, GAFBA can be initialized from the random generation of the initial population or by using the last population from the previous simulation. This process continues until the number of mass balance constraints relaxed equals zero and the growth rate is near the experimental one.

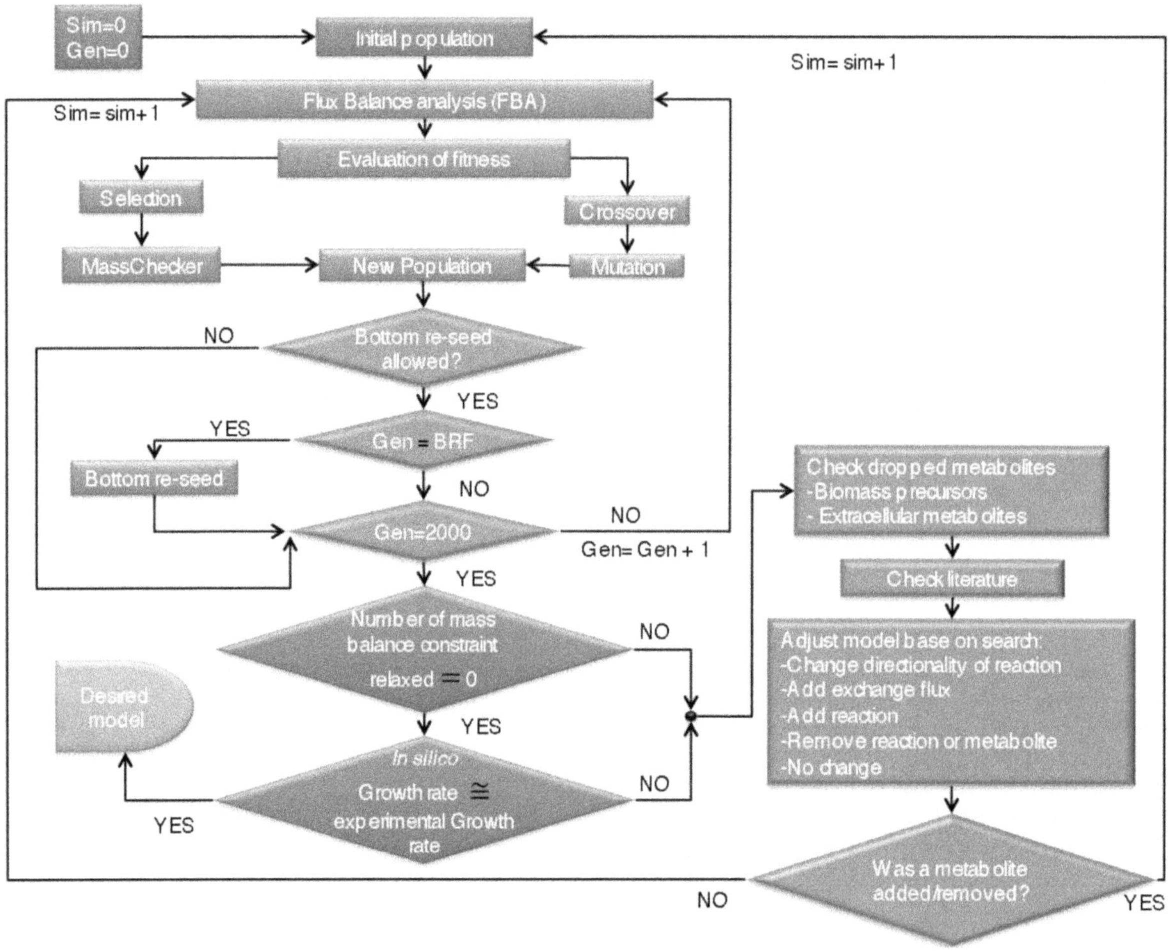

Figure 1. GAFBA v1.1. This version of the GAFBA algorithm includes the MassChecker. The steps in purple are operations performed by the user. Note that one simulation or "Sim" is equivalent to 2,000 generations or "Gen". BRF refers to bottom re-seed; BRF was not used in the current study.

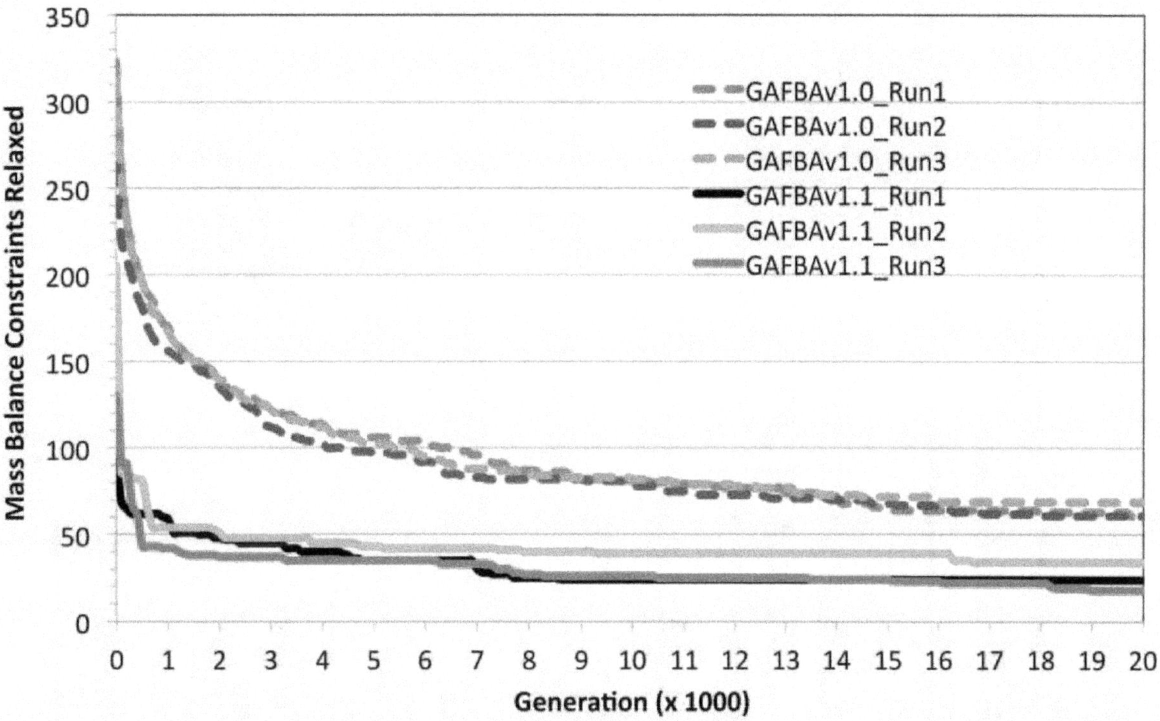

Figure 2. Comparison of the evolution of mass balance constraints on GAFBA v1.0 and GAFBA v1.1. For each algorithm three runs, consisting of 20,000 generations each, were made. Magenta (run 1), blue (run 2) and green (run 3) dotted lines are the results for GAFBA v1.0. Black (Run 1), cyan (Run 2), and red (Run 3) lines are the results for GAFBA v1.1.

3. RESULTS

The evolution of the number of mass balances constraints relaxed for *B. anthracis* is presented in Figure 2 for GAFBA v1.0 algorithm without MassChecker. Three trials were run with the same initial conditions and with random generation of the initial population. The number of mass balance constraints relaxed at generation zero was 323 for Run 1, 314 for Run 2, and 263 for Run 3.

The relaxed constraints slowly decreased to a final value of 60 for Run 1, 61 for Run 2, and 69 for Run 3. From generation 10,000 to 20,000, the change in the number of metabolites with relaxed constraints was 21 for Run 1, 19 for Run 2, and 13 for Run 3.

Figure 2 shows the evolution of the mass balance constraints relaxed for GAFBA v1.1, which includes the MassChecker tool. The same conditions were used as the trials in GAFBA v1.0. The number of mass balances constraints relaxed at simulation zero were 94 for Run 1, 205 for Run 2, and 130 for Run 3. It can be seen that MassChecker sped up the minimization of the number of problematic mass balances. After only 2,000 generations, it had fallen below 50 for all three trials. Moreover, from generation 10,000 to 20,000, the changes on the number of metabolites with mass balances constraints relaxed were 0 for Run 1, 5 for Run 2, and 8 for Run 3. Thus, only ten simulations were needed to start the analysis of the problematic metabolites since not much variation was seen beyond that point. More importantly only 24 (Run 1), 34 (Run 2), and 18 (Run3) metabolites needed to be analyzed with GAFBA v1.1, compared with the 60 metabolites (Run 1), 61 (Run 2), and 69 (Run 3) from GAFBA v1.0 without MassChecker.

The evolution of the number of false positives found on the chromosomes from the elite pool is shown in Figure 3. The values are only for Run 1 of GAFBA v1.1. Since the elite fraction was set to 20%, six chromosomes formed the elite pool. At generation zero, MassChecker found 212 false positives for chromosome one, 284 for chromosome two, 332 for chromosome three, 459 for chromosome four, 487 for chromosome five, and zero false positives for chromosome six. As the number of generations was increased, the number of false positives decreased substantially. This result was mainly because the effects of the random population generation had dissipated.

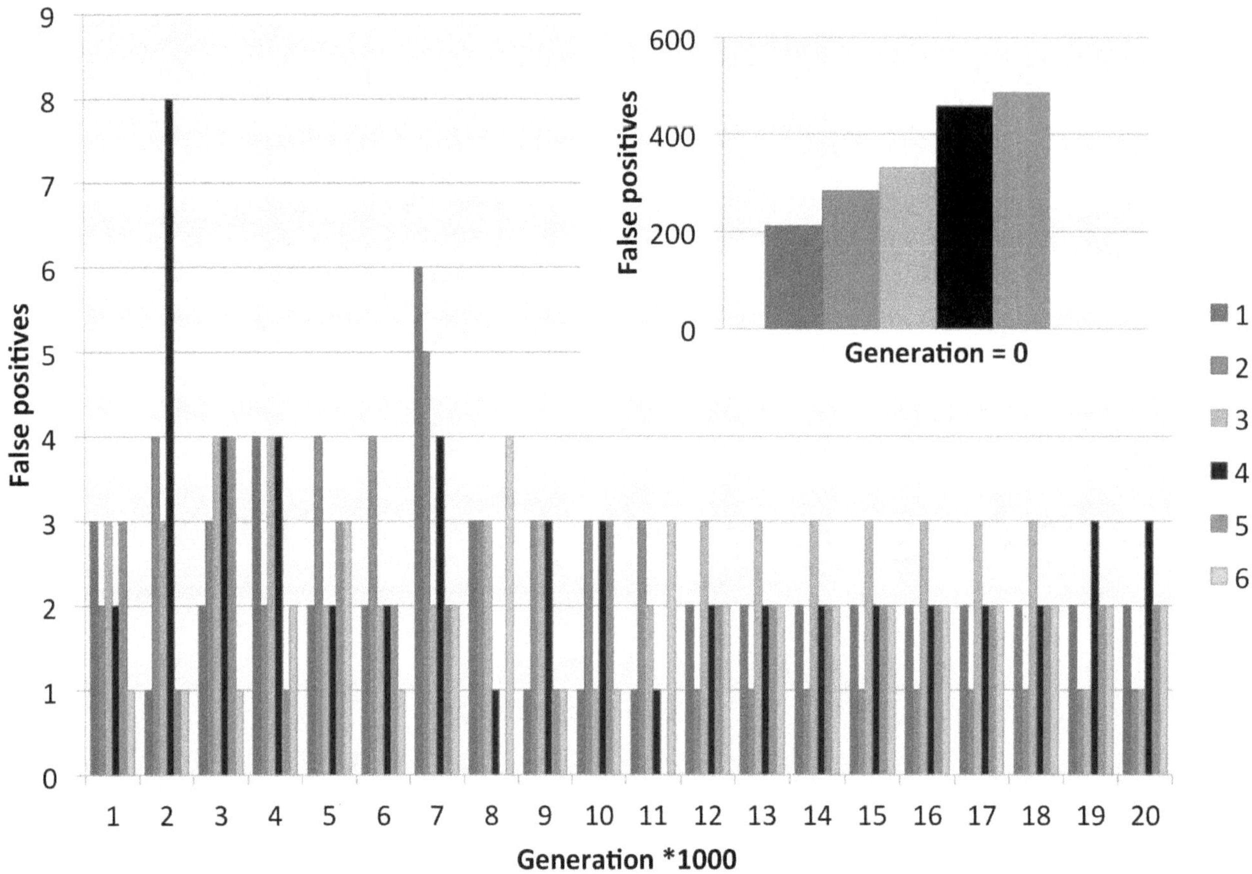

Figure 3. Evolution on the number of false positives in the elite pool for Run 1 using GAFBA v1.1. Given that the elite fraction was the top 20% of the total GA population of 30, the elite pool consisted of the best six chromosomes (1, 2, 3, 4, 5, 6 denoted by blue, red, green, black, pink, and cyan respectively). The inset chart shows the number of false positives found in the top elite chromosomes at generation number zero.

4. CONCLUSIONS

The random generation of the initial population for the GA portion of GAFBA v1.0 caused some metabolites with an already closed mass balance to be considered as problematic ones. MassChecker was developed to find these false positives and adjust the chromosomes to keep them in the model as enforced mass balance constraints.

MassChecker was developed as a consequence of the overwhelming number of false positives that could appear in the first runs of GAFBA v1.0. The main concern was the curation of large models, where the number of mass balance constraints dropped from the beginning of the reconstruction could confuse the curator. Furthermore, toward the end of the reconstruction process, the number of mass balances constraints relaxed in GAFBA v1.0 could hit a plateau before reaching the ideal scenario of all mass balance constraints being enforceable. As a result, the curator might think that something was wrong with the model when there really was no problem at all.

MassChecker was merged with GAFBA v1.0 in a new version of GAFBA v1.1. It allows for taking advantage of the random generation of the initial population while at the same time removing the debilitating effects of false positives. GAFBA v1.1 is faster and more efficient than the original version. The speed increase seen with the MassChecker tool is due to enhancement of the curation process by decreasing the number of simulations needed to run before achieving stabilization. Most important, the number of mass balances constraints relaxed was reduced by 60%,
from 63 ± 5 for GAFBA v1.0 to 25 ± 8 for GAFBA v1.1. As a result, this algorithm helps to allow an isolated focus on the metabolites that are truly biologically problematic rather than spurious artifacts.

5. ACKNOWLEDGMENTS

Support for this work was provided by NIH Grant 1R03LM009753-01. We want to thank to Diego F Martinez for his insightful comments and discussion during MassChecker development.

6. REFERENCE

[1] BAUTISTA, E.J., ZINSKI, J., SZCZEPANEK, S.M., JOHNSON, E.L., TULMAN, E.R., CHING, W.-M., GEARY, S.J., and SRIVASTAVA, R., 2013. Semi-automated Curation of Metabolic Models via Flux Balance Analysis: A Case Study with *Mycoplasma gallisepticum*. *PLoS Comput Biol 9*, 9, e1003208. DOI= http://dx.doi.org/10.1371/journal.pcbi.1003208.

[2] CENDROWSKI, S., MACARTHUR, W., and HANNA, P., 2004. *Bacillus anthracis* requires siderophore biosynthesis for growth in macrophages and mouse virulence. *Molecular Microbiology 51*, 2, 407-417. DOI= http://dx.doi.org/10.1046/j.1365-2958.2003.03861.x.

[3] DAUNER, M. and SAUER, U., 2001. Stoichiometric growth model for riboflavin-producing *Bacillus subtilis*. *Biotechnol Bioeng 76*, 2 (Sep), 132-143.

[4] DIAZ-GOMEZ, P.A. and HOUGEN, D.F., 2006. Pseudo Random Generation of the Initial Population in Genetic Algorithms: an Experiment. In *2nd Annual Computer Science Research Conference.* , University of Oklahoma.

[5] GARUFI, G., HENDRICKX, A.P., BEERI, K., KERN, J.W., SHARMA, A., RICHTER, S.G., SCHNEEWIND, O., and MISSIAKAS, D., 2012. Synthesis of lipoteichoic acids in *Bacillus anthracis*. *J Bacteriol 194*, 16 (Aug), 4312-4321. DOI= http://dx.doi.org/10.1128/JB.00626-12.

[6] KOGA, Y. and KUSAKA, I., 1970. Involvement of intracellular phospholipase C in autolytic fragmentation of cytoplasmic membranes of *Bacillus cereus*. *European Journal of Biochemistry 16*, 3, 407-413.

[7] LANG, D.R. and LUNDGREN, D.G., 1970. Lipid composition of *Bacillus cereus* during growth and sporulation. *J Bacteriol 101*, 2 (Feb), 483-489.

[8] MAARANEN, H., MIETTINEN, K., and MÄKELÄ, M.M., 2004. Quasi-random initial population for genetic algorithms. *Computers & Mathematics with Applications 47*, 12, 1885-1895. DOI= http://dx.doi.org/http://dx.doi.org/10.1016/j.camwa.2003.07.011.

[9] MAARANEN, H., MIETTINEN, K., and PENTTINEN, A., 2007. On initial populations of a genetic algorithm for continuous optimization problems. *Journal of Global Optimization 37*, 3 (2007/03/01), 405-436. DOI= http://dx.doi.org/10.1007/s10898-006-9056-6.

[10] OH, Y.-K., PALSSON, B.O., PARK, S.M., SCHILLING, C.H., and MAHADEVAN, R., 2007. Genome-scale Reconstruction of Metabolic Network in *Bacillus subtilis* Based on High-throughput Phenotyping and Gene Essentiality Data. *Journal of Biological Chemistry 282*, 39 (September 28, 2007), 28791-28799. DOI= http://dx.doi.org/10.1074/jbc.M703759200.

[11] POP, P.C., 2012. *Generalized Network Design Problems: Modeling and Optimization*. De Gruyter.

[12] RIVERA, J., CORDERO, R.J., NAKOUZI, A.S., FRASES, S., NICOLA, A., and CASADEVALL, A., 2010. *Bacillus anthracis* produces membrane-derived vesicles containing biologically active toxins. *Proc Natl Acad Sci U S A 107*, 44 (Nov 2), 19002-19007. DOI= http://dx.doi.org/10.1073/pnas.1008843107.

[13] SAUER, U., HATZIMANIKATIS, V., HOHMANN, H.-P., MANNEBERG, M., VAN LOON, A., and BAILEY, J.E., 1996. Physiology and metabolic fluxes of wild-type and riboflavin-producing *Bacillus subtilis*. *Applied and environmental microbiology 62*, 10, 3687-3696.

[14] SONENSHEIN, A.L., HOCH, J.A., and LOSICK, R., 2002. *Bacillus subtilis and its closest relatives*. ASM Press.

[15] STUY, J.H., 1958. The nucleic acids of *Bacillus cereus*. *J Bacteriol 76*, 2 (Aug), 179-184.

GA-Based Selection of Vaginal Microbiome Features Associated with Bacterial Vaginosis

Joi Carter
North Carolina A&T State University
Department of Computer Science
Greensboro, NC USA
jncarte1@ncat.edu

Daniel Beck
University of Idaho
Bioinformatics & Comp. Biology
Moscow, ID USA
beck5429@vandals.uidaho.edu

Henry Williams
North Carolina A&T State University
Department of Computer Science
Greensboro, NC USA
hwilliams18@gmail.com

Gerry Dozier
North Carolina A&T State University
Department of Computer Science
Greensboro, NC USA
gvdozier@ncat.edu

James A. Foster
University of Idaho
Biological Sciences
Moscow, ID USA
foster@uidaho.edu

ABSTRACT

In this paper, we successfully apply GEFeS (Genetic & Evolutionary Feature Selection) to identify the key features in the human vaginal microbiome and in patient meta-data that are associated with bacterial vaginosis (BV). The vaginal microbiome is the community of bacteria found in a patient, and meta-data include behavioral practices and demographic information. Bacterial vaginosis is a disease that afflicts nearly one third of all women, but the current diagnostics are crude at best. We describe two types of classifies for BV diagnosis, and show that each is associated with one of two treatments. Our results show that the classifiers associated with the 'Treat Any Symptom' version have better performances that the classifier associated with the 'Treat Based on N-Score Value'. Our long term objective is to develop a more accurate and objective diagnosis and treatment of BV.

Categories and Subject Descriptors

J.3 [**Life and Medical Sciences**]: Health

General Terms

Algorithms

Keywords

Bacterial Vaginosis, GEFeS, Genetic Algorithm, Human Microbiome

1. INTRODUCTION

Human beings have coevolved with bacteria. 90% of the cells in our bodies, and 99% of the genes, are bacterial rather than human. This "human microbiome" affects human health. Examples include the adult gut microbiome and obesity[1,2], the neonatal gut microbiome and sepsis[17], the lung microbiome and pulmonary infections[3] and cystic fibrosis[18], and the vaginal microbiome and bacterial vaginosis[4-6]. All known microbiome-associated diseases appear to be forms of dysbiosis, an ecological disturbance of the "normal" bacterial community in an individual, rather than the emergence of a pathogen. Therefore, the challenge to diagnosing such diseases is to uncover the features of a complex mélange of bacteria whose variation is associated with those diseases. This paper presents a new genetic algorithm, GEFeS (Genetic & Evolutionary Feature Selection), originally developed for image feature recognition, that successfully reveals the changes in the vaginal microbiome associated with bacterial vaginosis (BV), extending previous work on machine learning classifiers for BV [14].

BV affects nearly one third of all women at any given time[11], and is associated with increased risk for some sexually transmitted diseases and preterm birth. There are two clinical diagnostics for BV. The Amsel criteria (Any-Symptom approach) searches for the presence of at least three of the following criteria: the presence of discharge, a positive whiff test, the presence of clue cells, and a pH greater than 4.5[12]. The Nugent score (N-Score approach), a scale of 0-10 with anything over 7 indicating disease, is based counting gram-positive cells with morphologies similar to some Lactobacillus species (large rods) [13].

Both diagnostic criteria are problematic, resulting in up to 30% of BV diagnoses being for women who in fact have no observable symptoms [19]. Misdiagnosis can have serious adverse health consequences, since the prescribed treatment is systemic antibiotics, which would seem unnecessary, if not unethical, when there are no symptoms to treat. Both diagnostic tests assume that the predominance of Lactobacillus species indicates vaginal health, and their absence indicates disease, on the assumption that pH maintenance is the primary mechanism for maintaining health. However, different Lactobacillus species have very different mechanisms for acidification, and there are other species that provide the same function. More significantly, recent cultivation independent surveys of the vaginal microbiome have shown that healthy women, especially in minority communities, do not have Lactobacillus dominated vaginal communities[8,10] and that the "normal" vaginal micobiome varies significantly from day to day[15,20,21]. The two criteria frequently disagree, usually with the Nugent score indicating BV when Amsel does not. Amsel is

GECCO'14, July 12–16, 2014, Vancouver, BC, Canada.

the most commonly used diagnostic, since it is more amenable to a clinical setting. However, the "sniff test" is subjective, there are no "clue cells" that unambiguously identify BV, and the average pH of healthy black and Hispanic women are 4.7±1.04 and 5.0±0.74 respectively [15]. It would be helpful to have a diagnostic tool based on a small set of objective features, recognizing the dependence of BV on the complicated vaginal microbiome and characteristics of individual patients.

Our feature extraction algorithm shows that such an objective, symptomatic and microbiome-based diagnostic is possible. It takes as input a list of the relative abundances of all observed bacterial populations in the vaginal microbiome along with patient metadata such as demographics and sexual practices. Relative abundances are most accurately determined by a cultivation independent assay of a hypervariable regions of the 16S rRNA gene, obtained via next generation sequencing. The technique is to extract all DNA from a sample, amplify and sequence the target rRNA sequences, and then cluster the sequences into " operational taxonomical units" (OTUs). Standard practice treats OTUs clustered at 3% similarity as separate species, naming them by searching a database of all known sequences..

In this paper, we use GEFeS to evolve high-performance feature subsets in order to develop classifiers for determining whether a subject has BV based on: the Any-Symptom (Amsel criteria) approach or the N-Score (Nugent score) approach. The remainder of this paper is as follows. In Section II, we provide a brief overview of GEFeS. In Section III, describe our experiment and in Section IV we present our results. In Section V, we present our conclusions and future work

2. GEFES

GEFeS [25] has been successfully used for feature selection on a variety of recognition and classification problems. GEFeS evolves a population of candidate feature masks (FMs). A candidate FM, fmi, can be viewed as a triple, <Mi, ti, fi> , where Mi is set of N masks, Mi = {mi,0 , mi,1 , … , mi,n-1} where each mi,j □ [0..1] is associated with feature j in the original (baseline) feature set, where ti □ [0.1] is a masking threshold value, and fi is the fitness of the candidate FM, fmi . If mi,j < ti, then the jth feature of the original feature set is masked. GEFeS co-evolves the Mi and ti of candidate FMs, fmi .

GEFeS incorporates cross-validation in order to evolve FMs that generalize well. The evolutionary process is as follows. Initially, a random population of candidate FMs. Each candidate FM is then evaluated using the training set of feature templates and assigned a fitness that corresponds to the number of errors the candidate FM causes. Additionally, each candidate FM is evaluated using a validation set of feature templates. The best performing FM on the validation set is saved as FM*. After the initially population has been created and evaluated, two candidate FMs are selected and mated to form an offspring FM. The offspring FM is then evaluated and assigned a fitness value as above. The offspring FM is then evaluated using the validation set. If the offspring FM causes fewer errors than the current FM*, then it becomes the new FM*. This process is repeat for a user-specified number of candidate FM evaluations, after which FM* is returned to the user. Figure 1 provides an overview of the evolutionary process of GEFeS.

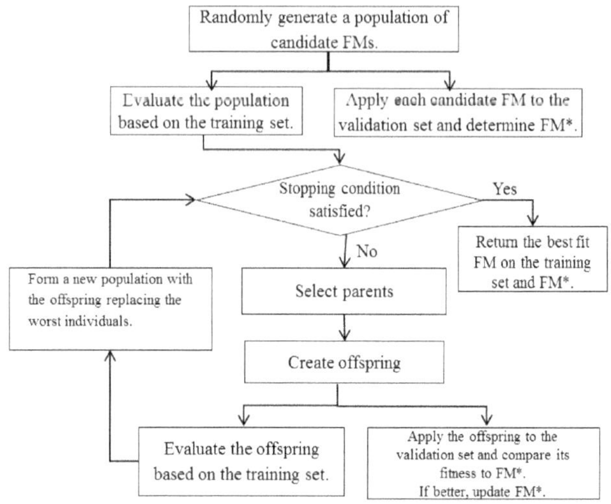

Figure 1. The Evolutionary Process of GEFe S

3. EXPERIMENT

The dataset used for our experiment consisted of 1601 instances with 410 features. The data include relative abundances of bacterial species determined by next-generation sequencing of 16S rRNA fingerprint sequences, demographic information, and behavioral and health data from daily journals from 25 women over a 10 week period[22]. The study received Institutional Review Board approval from the University of Maryland School of Medicine and sample collection followed the protocols from earlier studies[8,23,24]. This dataset was divided into a training set consisting of 60% of instances, a validation set consisting of 20% of the instances, and a test set that consisted of 20% of the instances. The objective of this experiment was to evolve FMs that generalized well to unseen instances.

In comparing two instances, the Manhattan distance between a probe and gallery feature (sub)vectors used calculated. After a probe instance has been compared to each gallery instance, the gallery instance that is closest to the probe is considered its mate. If the gallery instance came from a different sample than the probe instance, an error is recorded.

4. RESULTS

The results presented in this paper were created by applying GEFeS in an effort to evolve high-performance subsets of features associated with the N-Score and Any-Symptom BV problems. GEFeS is an instance of a steady-state GA found in the X-TOOLSS suite of Evolutionary Computations [25]. GEFeS evolved a population of 20 candidate FMs, used uniform crossover, a mutation usage rate of 1.0, and Gaussian mutation of the form 0.2N(0,1). GEFeS was run a total of 30 times for each of three stopping conditions, 2000, 4000, and 8000 function (candidate FM) evaluations, for a total of 90 runs on both the N-Score and Any-Symptom BV Problems.

In Table 1, the performances of GEFeS at 2000, 4000, and 8000 function evaluations are compared with the full feature sets (baseline) for the N-Score and Any-Symptom problems. The first column in Table 1 denotes the two methods used GEFeSnScore and GEFeSanySymptom , the second column the corresponding baseline accuracies of the full features set, and the 3rd, 4th, and 5th column are the average accuracies of the feature subsets.

Table 1: Comparison of the Performances of the Baseline Features Sets vs. the GEFeS Feature Sets for the N-Score and Any-Symptom BV Problems wrt Average Accuracy

Method	B	2000FE	4000FE	8000FE
$\mathbf{GEFeS_{nScore}}$	0.9252	0.9756	0.9764	0.9773
$\mathbf{GEFeS_{anySymptom}}$	0.9626	0.9945	0.9954	0.9953

The average performances of the evolved feature subsets at 2000, 4000, and 8000 function evaluations outperforms the performances of the baseline feature sets. On average, GEFeSanySymptom is a superior criterion to GEFeSnScore. The performance using GEFeSnScore increases with the number of evaluations in all cases, and using GEFeSanySymptom performance increases initially

Table 2 compares the average percentage of he full feature sest required for classification for both diagnostic criteria. On average, both criteria use reduced feature sets. The required number of features varies with the number of iterations.

Table 2: Comparison of the Performances of the Baseline Features Sets vs. the GEFeS Feature Sets for the N-Score and Any-Symptom BV Problems wrt the Average Percentage of Features Needed.

Method	B	2000FE	4000FE	8000FE
$\mathbf{GEFeS_{nScore}}$	100%	44.56%	42.82%	32.45%
$\mathbf{GEFeS_{anySymptom}}$	100%	46.87%	47.93%	47.00%

5. CONCLUSIONS & FUTURE WORK

In this paper we show that GA-based feature selection can increase classification accuracy of BV from microbiome data using fewer features, for either diagnostic criterion. But Any-Symptom induces a better baseline performance. Future research will expand this project using X-TOOLSS to compare GEFeS to other evolutionary techniques.

Future work includes a detailed analysis of the actual features that GEFeS discovered to be associated with BV. Since these features include both microbial and patient behaviors, they should be evaluated from both microbial ecology and clinical perspectives; proposing hypotheses about how specific collection of bacterial species or patient demographics and behavior contribute to health or disease, and how applicable these findings are to diagnostic evaluation in clinical settings (which rarely have access to next generation sequencing).

6. ACKNOWLEDGMENTS

Funded by NSF DBI0939454 and NIH P20GM016454. We thank Roxanne Hickey, Larry J. Forney, and Jacques Ravel for substantial help and for the data for this study.

7. REFERENCES

[1] Ley RE, Turnbaugh PJ, Klein S, Gordon JI. (2006) Microbial ecology: Human gut microbes associated with obesity. Nature 444: 1022-1023

[2] Turnbaugh PJ, Ley RE, Mahowald MA, Magrini V, Mardis ER, Gordon JI. (2006) An obesity-associated gut microbiome with increased capacity for energy harvest. Nature 444: 1027-1031

[3] Sibley CD, Parkins MD, Rabin HR, Duan K, Norgaard JC, Surette MG. (2008) A polymicrobial perspective of pulmonary infections exposes an enigmatic pathogen in cystic fibrosis patients. Proceedings of the National Academy of Science USA, 105: 15070-15075.

[4] Ling Z, Kong J, Liu F, Zhu H, Chen X, *et al.* (2010) Molecular analysis of the diversity of vaginal microbiota associated with bacterial vaginosis. BMC Genomics 11: 488

[5] Srinivasan S, Fredricks DN. (2008) The human vaginal bacterial biota and bacterial vaginosis. Interdisciplinary Perspectives on Infectious Diseases 2008

[6] Brotman RM. (2011) Vaginal microbiome and sexually transmitted infections: an epidemiologic perspective. Journal of Clinical Investigation 121: 4610-4617

[7] Amann RI, Ludwig W, Schleifer KH (1995) Phylogenetic identification and in situ detection of individual microbial cells without cultivation. Microbiological Reviews 59: 143-169

[8] Ravel J, Gajer P, Abdo Z, Schneider GM, Koenig SSK, *et al.* (2011) Vaginal microbiome of reproductive-age women. Proceedings of the National Academy of Science USA 108: 4680-4687

[9] Srinivasan S, Hoffman NG, Morgan MT, Matsen FA, Fiedler TL, *et al.* (2012) Bacterial communities in women with bacterial vaginosis: high resolution phylogenetic analysis reveal relationships of microbiota to clinical criteria. PLOS One 7: 6

[10] Zhou X, Bent SJ, Schneider MG, Davis CC, Islam MR, Forney LJ (2004) Characterization of vaginal microbial communities in adult healthy women using cultivation-independent methods. Microbiology, 150: 2565-2573.

[11] Koumans EH, Sternberg M, Carol B, McQuillan G, Kendrick J, *et al.* (2007) The prevalence of bacterial vaginosis in the United States, 2001–2004; Associations with symptoms, sexual behaviors, and reproductive health. Sexually Transmitted Diseases 34: 864-869.

[12] Amsel R, Totten PA, Spiegel CA, Chen KC, Eschenbach D, Holmes KK (1983) Nonspecific vaginitis. Diagnostic criteria and microbial and epidemiologic associations. American Journal of Medicine 74: 14-22

[13] Nugent RP, Krohn MA, Hillier SL. (1991) Reliability of diagnosing bacterial vaginosis is improved by a standardized method of gram stain interpretation. Journal of Clinical Microbiology 29: 297–301

[14] Beck D and JA Foster (2014, in press) Machine learning techniques accurately classify microbial communities by bacterial vaginosis characteristics. PLoS ONE.

[15] Hickey RJ, Zhou X, Pierson JD, Ravel J, Forney LJ. Understanding vaginal microbiome complexity from an ecological perspective. Transl Res. 2012 Mar 6

[16] Wang O, GM Garrity, JM Tiedje and JR Cole. (2007) Naïve Bayesian Classifier for Rapid Assignment of rRNA Sequences into the New Bacterial Taxonomy. Appl. Environ. Microbiol. 73(16):5261. DOI: 10.1128/AEM.00062-07.

[17] Madan JC, Salari RC, Saxena D, Davidson L, O'Toole GA, Moore JH, et al. Gut microbial colonisation in premature neonates predicts neonatal sepsis. Arch Dis Child Fetal Neonatal Ed. 2012 May 6.

[18] Madan JC, Koestler DC, Stanton BA, Davidson L, Moulton LA, Housman ML, et al. Serial analysis of the gut and respiratory microbiome in cystic fibrosis in infancy: interaction between intestinal and respiratory tracts and impact of nutritional exposures. mBio. 2012;3(4).

[19] Forney LJ, Foster JA, Ledger W. The vaginal flora of healthy women is not always dominated by Lactobacillus species. J Infect Dis. 2006 Nov 15;194(10):1468–9; authorreply1469–70.

[20] Ravel J, Brotman RM, Gajer P, Ma B, Nandy M, Fadrosh DW, et al. Daily temporal dynamics of vaginal microbiota before, during and after episodes of bacterial vaginosis. studies. 2013;19:20.

[21] Ravel J, Brotman RM, Gajer P, Ma B, Nandy M, Fadrosh DW, et al. Daily temporal dynamics of vaginal microbiota before, during and after episodes of bacterial vaginosis. studies. 2013;19:20.

[22] Ravel J, Personal communications. 2014.

[23] Forney LJ, Gajer P, Williams CJ, et al. (2010) Comparison of self-collected and physician-collected vaginal swabs for microbiome analysis. Journal of Clinical Microbiology 48:1741–1748. doi: 10.1128/JCM.01710-09

[24] Yuan S, Cohen DB, Ravel J, et al. (2012) Evaluation of methods for the extraction and purification of DNA from the human microbiome. PLoS ONE 7:e33865. doi: 10.1371/journal.pone.0033865.t004

[25] Williams, H., Carter, J., W. Campbell, Roy, K., Dozier, G. (to appear). "Genetic & Evolutionary Feature Selection for Author Identification of HTML Associated with Malware," *International Journal of Machine Learning and Computing.*

Predicting Patterns of Gene Expression During *Drosophila* Embryogenesis

Rotem Golan
Dept. of Computer Science
University of Calgary, Canada
grotem@ucalgary.ca

Christian Jacob
Dept. of Computer Science
University of Calgary, Canada
cjacob@ucalgary.ca

Savraj Grewal
Dept. of Biochemistry & Molecular Biology
University of Calgary, Canada
grewalss@ucalgary.ca

Jörg Denzinger
Dept. of Computer Science
University of Calgary, Canada
denzinge@cpsc.ucalgary.ca

ABSTRACT

Understanding how organisms develop from a single cell into a functioning multicellular organism is one of the key questions in developmental biology. Research in this area goes back decades ago, but only recently have improvements in technology allowed biologists to achieve experimental results that are more quantitative and precise. Here, we show how large biological datasets can be used to learn a model for predicting the patterns of gene expression in *Drosophila melanogaster* (fruit fly) throughout embryogenesis. We also explore the possibility of considering spatial information in order to achieve unique patterns of gene expression in different regions along the anterior-posterior (head-tail) axis of the egg. We then demonstrate how the resulting model can be used to (1) classify these regions into the various segments of the fly, and (2) to conduct a virtual gene knockout experiment. Our learning algorithm is based on a model that has biological meaning, which indicates that its structure and parameters have their correspondence in biology.

Categories and Subject Descriptors

J.3 [**Computer Applications**]: Life and Medical Sciences—*Biology and Genetics*; I.2.6 [**Artificial Intelligence**]: Learning—*Parameter Learning*

Keywords

Bioinformatics; Machine Learning; Prediction; Pattern Recognition and Classification; Local Search; Systems Biology; Gene Expression; Gene Regulatory Networks

GECCO'14, July 12–16, 2014, Vancouver, BC, Canada.

ACM 978-1-4503-2662-9/14/07 ...$15.00.
http://dx.doi.org/10.1145/2576768.2598250 .

1. INTRODUCTION

One of the favorite model organisms used by developmental biologists is *Drosophila melanogaster*, also known as the common fruit fly. Its development, from a fertilized egg to an adult fly, takes about 10 to 12 days at 25°C. Our work is focused on the first 24 hours of development where the fly's embryo is formed, a process that is known as embryogenesis. Figure 1 illustrates the key role that gradients of proteins play in *Drosophila*'s development.

At the beginning of embryogenesis, DNA is replicated rapidly and around 13 nuclear divisions occur, leading to the distribution of about 6000 cells throughout the internal surface of the egg. This layer of cells is called the cellular blastoderm, and is divided into 14 parasegments (Figure 1(b)). At the same time, gradients of proteins are produced along the anterior-posterior (head-tail) and the dorsal-ventral (top-bottom) axes of the egg (Figure 1(a)). The nuclei respond to the concentration of these proteins in their local environment in order to establish their patterns of gene expression, which consequently determine their cell functionality. Gene expression is defined as the process in which the information of a gene is used to synthesize (produce) gene products, such as proteins and functional RNAs. By the end of embryogenesis, the segments of the embryo (Figure 1(c)), which later give rise to the body segments of the adult fly (Figure 1(d)), can be distinguished; these include 3 head segments, 3 thoracic segments, and 8 abdominal segments (a total of 14 segments, which correspond to the parasegments in Figure 1(b)).

The fly's regulatory network, and gene regulatory networks in general, have a first impression of being highly complex with an overwhelming degree of connectivity. There are, however, ways to make these networks more understandable and identify modular subunits. Uri Alon [1] identifies network motifs which shed light on the dynamics of gene expression; they are defined as sub-structures of the biological network that appear in high frequency compared to random networks. These network motifs usually exhibit specific traits such as generating an oscillatory function, generating a FIFO (first-in-first-out) temporal order, and acting as persistent detectors. Motifs are also considered to have been conserved in the natural evolutionary process, and therefore, to play an important rule in the regulatory network [1].

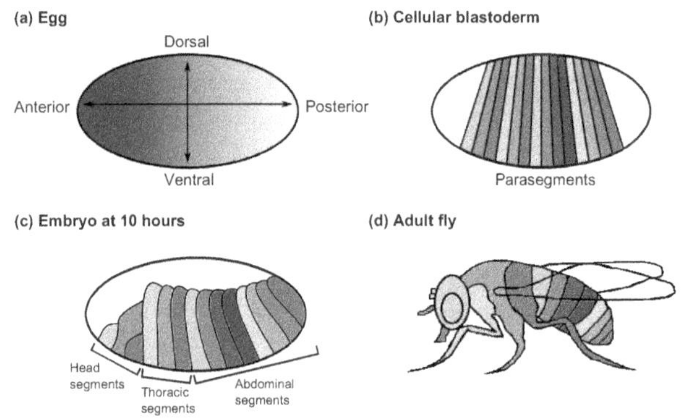

Figure 1: Gradients of proteins in the egg define parasegments in the cellular blastoderm, which later give rise to segments in the embryo and adult fly.

Regulatory networks can also be simplified by conducting biological experiments, such as gene knockout experiments, which can help determine the causality and dynamics between the various genes [4, 13, 18]. Such work reveals a hierarchical structure of the genes that regulate the embryogenesis process of the fly. At the top of the hierarchy we find the maternal effect genes, which establish the initial axes of the embryo via the formation of protein gradients [7, 8] (Figure 1(a)). These genes are interpreted by another group of genes that are called segmentation genes, which determine the segments of the embryo (Figure 1(c)); they can be arranged into 3 groups: gap genes, pair-rule genes, and segment polarity genes. Finally, both maternal and segmentation genes are used by the homeotic selector genes, composed of the bithorax and antennapedia genes, to specify the identity of each segment (Figure 1(d)).

In this paper, we will first discuss a way in which a model can be learned to predict the temporal patterns of gene expression throughout embryogenesis. We will then explore the possibility of adding spatial information in order to predict spatial patterns of gene expression as well. For this, we divided the egg into 28 vertical regions along its anterior-posterior axis; this means that each parasegment in Figure 1(b) is covered by exactly two vertical regions. Our learning algorithm is based on the following:

1. A binding regulatory network and a functional regulatory network, produced as part of the *Drosophila* modENCODE project [3, 17].
2. A dataset (Supplementary Table 17 in [6]), which specifies the expression levels of all modENCODE genes in *Drosophila* throughout its development.
3. A model, composed of hill functions and proposed by Uri Alon [1], which has biological meaning.
4. Data about the spatial distribution of gene products along the anterior-posterior axis of the egg [2, 7, 8, 10, 16, 18].

We will analyze the results of our learning algorithm, and demonstrate how one of its resulting models can be used to classify the regions along the anterior-posterior axis of the egg into the various segments of the fly. Finally, we will show how this model can also be used to conduct a virtual gene knockout experiment; more specifically, we will demonstrate how virtually knocking out the bithorax genes results in an embryo with an almost normal head, a long upper thorax, and no abdomen, which is a result similar to what is observed in biological experiments [4, 13].

2. LEARNING A PREDICTION MODEL

In this section, we will first describe the input data we used in our learning algorithm. We will define the model our learning algorithm is based on, and demonstrate its biological meaning by examining its potential to generate a FIFO (first-in-first-out) temporal order, and to act as a persistent detector. These two features have been observed in *Escherichia coli* [1, 12], but are assumed to appear in other organisms as well, including *Drosophila*. Finally, we will describe our learning algorithm, and demonstrate its ability to produce models with the above features.

2.1 Input data

The modENCODE project [3] is a research network with the goal of providing a comprehensive encyclopedia of genomic functional elements in the model organisms *C. elegans* and *D. melanogaster*. It has produced two regulatory networks for *D. melanogaster*: a physical (binding) regulatory network (bRN) and a functional regulatory network (fRN) [17].

The physical regulatory network (bRN) is comprised of 76 transcription factors (TF) and 52 microRNAs (miRNA), and is based on physical relationships between TFs, miRNAs, and their target genes. More specifically, there exists an edge between gene A and gene B if, and only if, the product of gene A (TF or miRNA) is experimentally observed to bind the genomic region of gene B.

The functional regulatory network (fRN) is comprised of 8,972 genes, and is based on predicted functional relationships between regulators and their target genes. These relationships derive from computationally integrating bRN with patterns of coordinated activity of regulators and targets. Note that the total number of known genes in *Drosophila* is about 17,000. So this network represents about half of *Drosophila*'s genome.

Supplementary Table 17 in [6] describes a dataset ($DS1$) which specifies the expression levels in FPKM (fragments per kilobase of exon per million fragments mapped) of 17,000 genes in *Drosophila* throughout development. The time period of embryogenesis is divided into 12 discrete time steps, each representing 2 hours out of the total 24 hours of the process.

There has been extensive research on embryogenesis in *Drosophila*. Consequently, much is already known about the spatial distribution of many gene products along the axes of the egg [2, 10, 16, 18]. Figure 2 describes the distribution of 19 gene products along the anterior-posterior axis of the egg, based on literature. Note that, in all 28 regions, the sum of frequencies for each gene is exactly 1. We used these distributions, together with the temporal values in $DS1$, to construct a new dataset ($DS2$) which specifies the expression levels of all genes throughout embryogenesis and in each one of the 28 regions of the egg. This was done by multiplying each frequency with the appropriate value in $DS1$, so that the expression level of a gene in $DS1$ at some developmental step is equal to the sum of its values in all regions in $DS2$ at that developmental step. Note that we use the same spatial distributions for all developmental steps when constructing

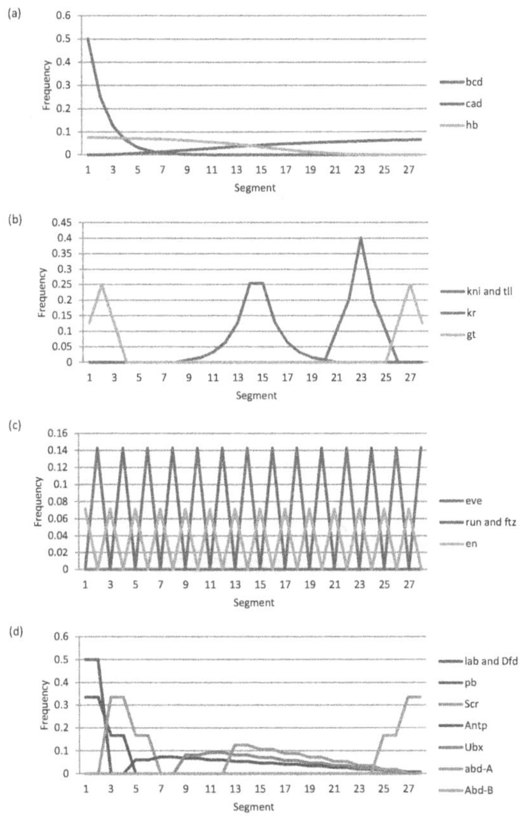

Figure 2: Distribution of 19 genes in each of the 28 regions along the anterior-posterior axis of the egg, based on literature. (a) Maternal and gap genes. (b) Gap genes. (c) Pair-rule and segment polarity genes. (d) Homeotic selector genes.

$DS2$. This means that we assume these distributions to be constant throughout embryogenesis.

Finally, we extracted a new regulatory network (sRN) out of bRN by considering only these 19 genes with their spatial distributions known. The main purpose of this network is to predict the expression patterns of the homeotic selector genes, which we later use in our classification algorithm. Therefore, we had to choose genes that (1) are relevant to the expression of the homeotic selector genes, and (2) whose temporal and spatial expression patterns are known. This means that sRN contains a path between any gene to at least one homeotic selector gene, and that the homeotic selector genes have no outgoing edges.

2.2 Model definition and properties

The problem of predicting patterns of gene expression is a function regression problem, so a number of candidate models, such as Artificial Neural Networks, come to mind as potential solutions. However, since the function we aim at predicting represents a biological phenomenon, we prefer a model that has biological meaning, which necessitates that its structure and parameters have their correspondence in biology. Achieving such a property will result in a model that biologists can better comprehend and appreciate. Moreover, it could be extended manually by adding insights from biological research.

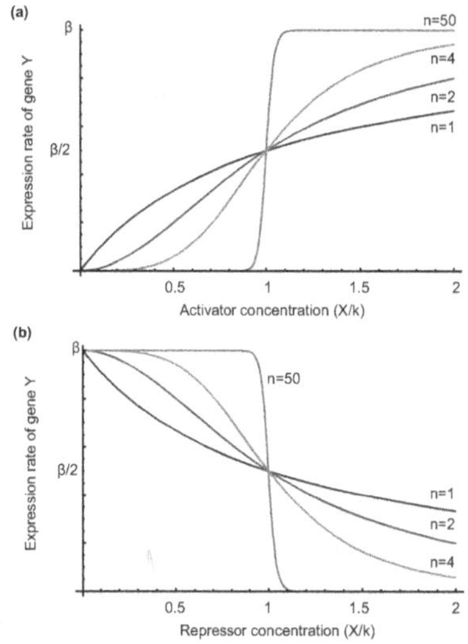

Figure 3: Hill functions with hill coefficient n=1, 2, 4, and 50, which describe the dynamics between the concentration of a single activator/repressor (X) and the expression rate of its target gene (Y). β is the maximal expression rate, and k is the value of X needed for 50% maximal activation/repression of gene Y.

Uri Alon [1] has suggested a model that could achieve such biological meaning. It is based on a gene regulatory network, where each gene (node) is associated with an input function that includes one or more hill functions of its regulators. The model's structure is defined according to the regulatory network it is applied for, and its input functions will be learned using our learning algorithm. Here, we will define this model and discuss its properties, including its biological meaning. Figure 3 describes ways in which the concentration of a single activator/repressor (X) can affect the expression rate of its target gene (Y) in this model.

The following input functions describe the expression rate of gene Y when X is an activator:

$$f(X,Y) = \frac{\beta X^n}{X^n + k^n} - \alpha Y, \tag{1}$$

and when X is a repressor:

$$f(X,Y) = \frac{\beta}{1 + (\frac{X}{k})^n} - \alpha Y. \tag{2}$$

Here, X and Y are the concentrations of their respective gene products. k is the activation coefficient, and is defined as the value of X needed for 50% maximal activation/repression of gene Y. It represents the threshold between activation and repression for large values of n (Figure 3). Among other factors, the value of k is related to the chemical affinity between the product of gene X and its binding site in the promoter of gene Y. β is defined as the maximal expression rate of gene Y. When X is an activator, maximal expression is reached when X is significantly greater than k ($X >> k$), i.e. there are enough products of gene X to constantly occupy their binding site in the promoter of gene Y; when X is a repressor, maximal expression is reached when $X = 0$, i.e., there are no repressors to prevent the expression of gene Y. α is the degradation rate which defines how much of gene Y's products are degraded in each developmental step. Finally, n is the hill coefficient governing the steepness of the hill function; the higher its value, the more step-like the hill function becomes (Figure 3).

It is interesting to note that while these parameters are learned using our learning algorithm, there is an equivalent to this process in nature: the process of evolution by means of natural selection. In other words, these values are under constant selection pressure and can change over the generations as environments change. For example, since the value of k is related to the chemical affinity between a protein and its binding site, it can be modified via a mutation in the DNA of either one; even a mutation in a single nucleotide can strengthen/weaken this chemical affinity.

In order to appreciate the biological meaning of Alon's model we move away from *Drosophila* and examine the process of flagella formation in *Escherichia coli*. A flagellum is a lash-like appendage that protrudes from certain cell bodies; its primary role is to enable cell movement (locomotion), usually in response to nutrition in its environment. We will examine a network motif called the multioutput FFL (feed-forward loop) which controls the formation of flagella in *E. coli* [1, 12], but is also assumed to play an important role in regulatory networks of other organisms, including *Drosophila*. There are two features of flagella formation that are of interest to us:

First, we know that *E. coli* produces its flagella only when nutrition in its local environment is scarce; this allows it to explore its environment for new sources of nutrition. Since it is likely that *E. coli* will find itself in a fluctuating environment, it has to find a way to keep producing the proteins necessary for flagella formation even when there are brief spikes in nutrition levels around it. Only when there is a significant and continuous level of nutrition around it, then it should stop the formation of the flagella, remain in its local environment, and focus on metabolizing nearby food molecules. As a result, our learning algorithm should be able to produce models that can act as persistent detectors.

Second, the flagellum is a complex structure that is composed of a number of parts, one of which is the flagellum motors. The flagella motors are composed of a number of proteins which have the intriguing property that the order in which they are expressed corresponds to the order in which they are used in the assembly process of the flagella motors; furthermore, the order in which these proteins are degraded is the same FIFO temporal order in which they are expressed [12]. This feature has evolved for thousands of years to conserve energy in *E. coli* by minimizing the expression of unneeded proteins that, without the need to form the flagella motors, have no usable function. Therefore, our learning algorithm should be able to produce models that can generate a FIFO temporal order.

Uri Alon [1] examined how these two features of flagella formation can be generated by a multioutput FFL (feed-forward loop). Figure 4 shows a diagram of a multioutput FFL where there are two regulators (X and Y) which, in addition to X activating Y, activate all output genes $Z_1, ..., Z_n$. Figure 5 demonstrates how, assuming certain activation thresholds, such a network motif can generate a FIFO temporal order for the expression and degradation of two output genes Z_1 and Z_2.

In addition to producing a FIFO temporal order, the multioutput FFL can act as a persistent detector for each one

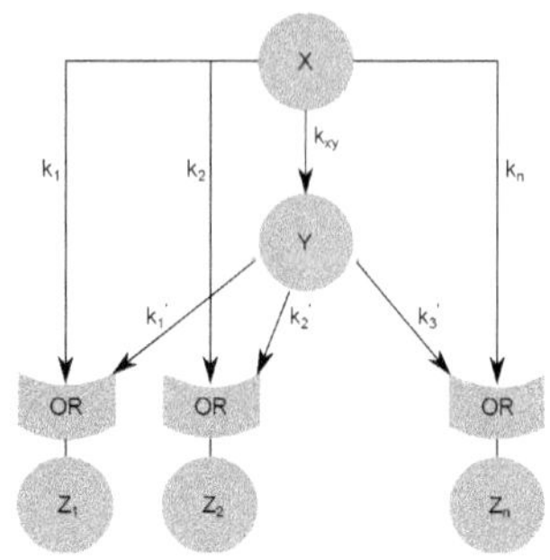

Figure 4: A diagram of a multioutput FFL (feed-forward loop). (©Uri Alon [1])

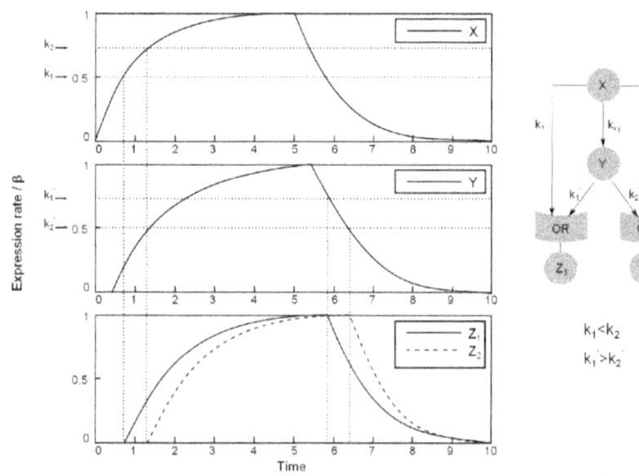

Figure 5: FIFO (first-in-first-out) order in a multioutput FFL (feed-forward loop) with OR logic input functions. The output genes Z_1 and Z_2 begin their expression when X crosses activation thresholds k_1 and k_2, respectfully; and stop their expression when Y goes below activation thresholds k_1' and k_2', respectfully. When the order of k_1 and k_2 is opposite to that of k_1' and k_2', FIFO order is obtained. (©Uri Alon [1])

of its output genes. Figure 6 demonstrates this property by looking at one output gene (Z) and its two regulators (X and Y). We assume that the products of gene X (proteins) are active only if there are no food molecules nearby. At $Time = 2$ there is a sudden and permanent spike in food molecules so the products of gene X are no longer active (shown as the sudden drop in the expression of X). The output gene Z is still expressed since it requires only one active regulator for it to be activated, and Y still has not reached k_{yz}. Once the expression level of Y goes below k_{yz}, Z's concentration is decreased. This means that a time delay was generated between the sudden drop in the expression of gene X to the decrease in the expression of gene Z. This time delay is used by the system to make sure that the spike in food molecules is not temporary. Once the time delay passes, the flagella proteins stop their expression, and instead of moving, *E. coli* remains in its local environment and focuses on metabolizing nearby food molecules.

2.3 Our learning algorithm

Our learning algorithm has two separate goals: the first goal ($goalA$) is to produce a model ($modelA$) which could predict the temporal patterns of gene expression in *Drosophila* throughout embryogenesis (as defined in $DS1$), for all genes in bRN or fRN; the second goal ($goalB$) is to pro-

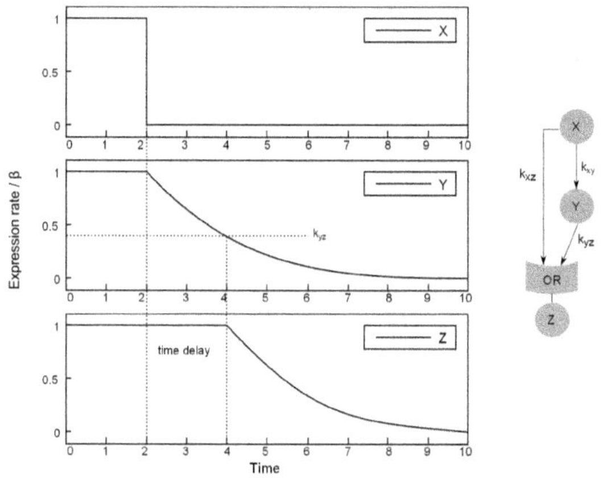

Figure 6: A simple FFL (feed-forward loop) which acts as a persistent detector for its output gene Z. A time delay is generated between the sudden drop in the expression of gene X to the decrease in the expression of gene Z.

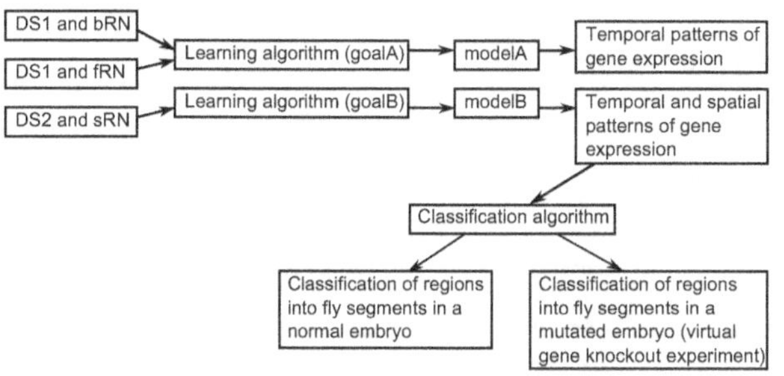

Figure 7: An information flow diagram of our experiments.

duce a model (*modelB*) which could predict the patterns of gene expression throughout embryogenesis and along the anterior-posterior axis of the egg (as defined in $DS2$), for all genes in sRN. Figure 7 shows the information flow diagram of our experiments.

In both cases, our learning algorithm is used to determine the input function of each gene (node) in a given network, so that the resulting model could be used to successfully predict the patterns of gene expression in a given dataset. Our learning algorithm allows each input function to combine a number of regulators through the summation of their respective hill functions (Equation 3). For example, assuming that genes X, Y, and W are parents of gene Z in a given regulatory network, our learning algorithm can enable gene X to be an activator and gene Y to be a repressor while ignoring the effect gene W might have on the expression of gene Z. As a result, the following input function will describe the expression rate of gene Z:

$$f(X,Y,W,Z) = \frac{\beta_a X^{n_a}}{X^{n_a} + k_a^{n_a}} + \frac{\beta_r}{1 + (\frac{Y}{k_r})^{n_r}} - \alpha Z \quad (3)$$

where the letters a and r are used to distinguish between the parameters of the activator X and of the repressor Y, respectfully. All other parameters are according to Equations 1 and 2 earlier.

Note that since an OR gate is essentially equivalent to the summation of two hill functions with large values of n, and since the regulatory networks we use as input contain multioutput FFLs, our learning algorithm has the potential to produce models, with the appropriate parameters, that can exhibit the biological meaning and features we described in the previous section.

Our learning algorithm is a hill climbing algorithm (local search), which we found to produce interesting results despite its simplicity and its known tendency to reach a local optimum. It can be described as follows: initially, a random set of candidate solutions is generated. Then, a candidate solution with the lowest average error is selected, and is used as a template to generate a new set of candidate solutions by means of mutation. This process is repeated until a fixed number of iterations is reached. At the end of the algorithm, a candidate solution with the lowest average error is returned.

Mutating a candidate solution is done as follows: given a regulatory network N and a candidate solution M (composed of a set of input functions, one for each gene in N), we randomly select a set of genes from N (according to a mutation rate). For each gene g in this set, we modify its input function by randomly executing one of the following operations:

- Randomly select a hill function that is included in g's input function, and
  - increase/decrease its k value by 5%
  - increase/decrease its n value by 5%
  - increase/decrease its β value by 5%
  - change its type from an activator to a repressor hill function, or vice versa
  - replace it with a randomly generated hill function of a new regulator (from g's parents as defined in N)
- Increase/decrease the α value of g's input function by 5%
- Add a randomly generated hill function of a new regulator (from g's parents as defined in N), or remove an existing one

Note that an input function of a gene might include two or more separate hill functions of the same regulator.

Algorithm 1 describes how the average error of a candidate solution is computed. The text in squared brackets describes the modifications needed for this computation to handle spatial patterns of gene expression in addition to temporal ones (*goalB*). Note that a candidate solution has no errors in the first developmental step (since it is initialized with these values), and when genes have no regulators (since it extracts their correct values from the dataset); this is reflected in rows 2, 7, and 13 of Algorithm 1.

3. RESULTS

In this section, we analyze the results of our experiments which proved to be accurate in the case of predicting temporal patterns, but had a significant reduction in accuracy when predicting spatial patterns as well. We will then discuss how, even with this reduction in accuracy, the resulting model can be used to (1) classify the regions along the anterior-posterior axis of the egg into the various segments of the fly, and (2) to conduct a virtual gene knockout experiment.

Algorithm 1 Computing the average error of a candidate solution

Input: a regulatory network N; a candidate solution M; a dataset DS
Initialize *predictedValues* to hold the values of all genes in N [at each of the 28 regions of the egg], according to their values in DS at the first developmental step
$errorSum \Leftarrow 0$
for each developmental step **do**
  for each gene g in N **do**
    [**for** each of the 28 regions of the egg **do**]
      Compute the new value (*newValue*) of g according to its input function (as defined in M) and its required values (as defined in *predictedValues*); if g has no parents in N (no regulators) then extract its new value from DS
      $errorSum \leftarrow errorSum + |newValue - correctValue|$ (*correctValue* is extracted from DS)
    [**end for**]
  end for
  Update *predictedValues* with the new values of all genes in N [at each of the 28 regions of the egg]
end for
$averageError \Leftarrow \frac{errorSum}{(numOfDevelopmentalSteps-1)\times(numOfGenes-numOfUnregulatedGenes)[\times 28]}$
Return $averageError$

In all prediction experiments, the coefficient of determination (R^2) is used to estimate the accuracy of the resulting models:

$$R^2 = 1 - \frac{SS_{res}}{SS_{tot}} = 1 - \frac{\sum_i (y_i - f_i)^2}{\sum_i (y_i - \overline{y})^2} \tag{4}$$

where $1 \leq i \leq numOfPredictedValues$, y_i is the i'th observed value, f_i is the i'th predicted value, and $\overline{y}$ is the average of all observed values.

Table 1 describes the properties of the different input data we used in our learning algorithm. Table 2 summarizes the results of our prediction experiments. We can see that running our learning algorithm with $DS1$ and bRN as input resulted in the most accurate model ($R^2 = 0.94$). We can also see that its accuracy, as measured by the coefficient of determination (R^2), was not significantly reduced ($R^2 = 0.9$ instead of $R^2 = 0.94$) when increasing the number of nodes from 72 to 8824 nodes. This provides us with some indication that our learning algorithm is scalable.

However, running our learning algorithm with the aim of capturing the spatial patterns of gene expression, in addition to temporal ones, has resulted in a model with a significant reduction in accuracy ($R^2 = 0.35$ without allowing the use of sin functions). We associate this reduction in accuracy with the small number of network nodes (19 nodes), together with the harder task of finding spatial patterns, and our assumption that these spatial distributions are constant throughout embryogenesis. To overcome this issue, we allowed our learning algorithm to use sin functions in this experiment. This means that the expression rate of gene Y could take the form of

$$f(X,Y) = \beta \sin(\frac{X^n}{X^n + k^n} \times \pi) - \alpha Y \tag{5}$$

when X is an activator, and

$$f(X,Y) = \beta \sin(\frac{1}{1 + (\frac{X}{k})^n} \times \pi) - \alpha Y \tag{6}$$

when X is a repressor.

It is important to note that the added sin functions have no direct biological meaning as there is no direct equivalent of sin functions in biology; however, we do find oscillatory processes in nature even if these are not a product of a single component but rather an emergent phenomenon of the system [14, 15].

Table 1: Properties of the input data

Input data	Nodes	Edges	Average value	SD	Unregulated nodes
$DS1$ and bRN	72	1297	38.42	48.61	0
$DS1$ and fRN	8824	203483	55.22	262.80	54
$DS2$ and sRN	19	145	0.57	4.90	1

Table 2: Results of our prediction experiments

Input data	Average error	SD of errors	R^2
$DS1$ and bRN	4.35	11.77	0.94
$DS1$ and fRN	20.51	82.77	0.90
$DS2$ and sRN	0.34	1.49	0.35
$DS2$ and sRN (with sin functions)	0.24	1.15	0.59

Allowing the use of sin functions improved the learning algorithm's ability to distinguish between the patterns of gene expression in the different regions of the egg, which is reflected in the improved (but still rather low) accuracy of the resulting model in this experiment ($R^2 = 0.59$ instead of $R^2 = 0.35$). It did not, however, result in any improvement in the case of bRN or fRN.

3.1 Classification of regions into fly segments

The goal of our classification algorithm is to classify each of the 28 vertical regions along the anterior-posterior axis of the egg into one of the 14 fly segments, which include head segments 0-2, thoracic segments 3-5, and abdominal segments 6-13. Having a model which can predict the patterns of gene expression throughout embryogenesis (12 developmental steps) and along the anterior-posterior axis of the egg (28 regions), even if its accuracy is rather low, allows us to design a simple and intuitive classification algorithm for achieving this goal. This algorithm can be viewed as a k-nearest neighbors algorithm with $k = 1$, which is one of the simplest classification algorithms in machine learning. Algorithm 2 gives a detailed description of our classification algorithm. Note that it only uses the 8 homeotic selector genes for classification since these are the genes that have been observed in biological experiments to specify the identity of each segment.

We use two methods for estimating the accuracy of our classification algorithm: standard accuracy (*standAcc*) and

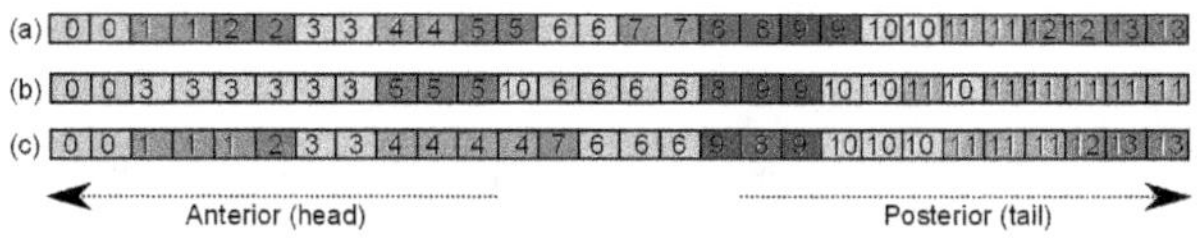

Figure 8: Classification of the 28 regions of the egg into the 14 segments of the fly in a normal embryo. (a) Correct segment numbers ($relaxAcc = 1$ and $standAcc = 1$). (b) Predicted segment numbers, without allowing the use of sin functions ($relaxAcc = 0.91$ and $standAcc = 0.39$). (c) Predicted segment numbers, allowing the use of sin functions ($relaxAcc = 0.96$ and $standAcc = 0.67$).

relaxed accuracy ($relaxAcc$). Here is a formal definition of these two methods:

$$standAcc = \frac{\text{number of correctly classified regions}}{\text{total number of regions}} \tag{7}$$

$$relaxAcc = 1 - \frac{\sum_{0 \le i \le 27} |predSN_i - corrSN_i|}{\sum_{0 \le i \le 27} max\{corrSN_i, 13 - corrSN_i\}} \tag{8}$$

where $predSN_i$ is the predicted segment number of the i'th region, and $corrSN_i$ is the correct segment number of the i'th region ($0 \le predSN_i, corrSN_i \le 13$).

Note that while the $standAcc$ method considers the classification of regions to be either correct or not, the $relaxAcc$ method takes into account the differences between the predicted and correct segment numbers of these regions; as a result, the $relaxAcc$ method will prefer models that minimize these differences. The motivation for this method comes from the understanding that the patterns of gene expression of two nearby fly segments are more similar than those of two distant ones; for example, head segments 1 and 2 have expression patterns that are much more similar than head segment 1 and abdominal segment 7.

Figure 8 indicates the correct segment numbers of all 28 regions in a normal embryo, compared to the predicted segment numbers of these regions (with or without allowing the use of sin functions). It suggests that accurate classification is achieved when using the $relaxAcc$ method to estimate the accuracy of our classification algorithm ($relaxAcc = 0.96$ when allowing the use of sin functions); and that allowing the use of sin functions improved the accuracy of our classification algorithm ($relaxAcc = 0.96$ instead of $relaxAcc = 0.91$, and $standAcc = 0.67$ instead of $standAcc = 0.39$).

3.2 Conducting a virtual gene knockout experiment

Edward Lewis was one of the first to appreciate the importance of the homeotic selector genes in development [4]. He managed to measure the effect knocking out the bithorax genes has on the differentiation of cells into segments in the living larva, before it develops into an adult fly; an important accomplishment since deleting these genes is a lethal mutation. Figure 9(a) indicates the correct segment numbers of all 28 regions in a mutated embryo where the bithorax genes were knocked out (deleted). It shows a normal head (segments 0-2), a long upper thorax (segment 3), and no abdomen.

In order to produce the same result as the mutated embryo in Figure 9(a), we executed a virtual experiment by running our classification algorithm (Algorithm 2) with the assumption that the bithorax genes had no expression at all. Figure 9 shows the results of the real gene knockout experiment, compared to the results of our virtual experiment (with or without allowing the use of sin functions). It suggests that accurate classification is achieved even when using the more strict $standAcc$ method to estimate the accuracy of our classification algorithm ($standAcc = 0.96$ when allowing the use of sin functions). In addition, allowing the use of sin functions improved the accuracy of our classification algorithm ($relaxAcc = 0.99$ instead of $relaxAcc = 0.97$, and $standAcc = 0.96$ instead of $standAcc = 0.85$). This result shows an embryo with an almost normal head (segments 0-2), a long upper thorax (segment 3), and no abdomen, which is a result similar to what is observed in biological experiments [4, 13].

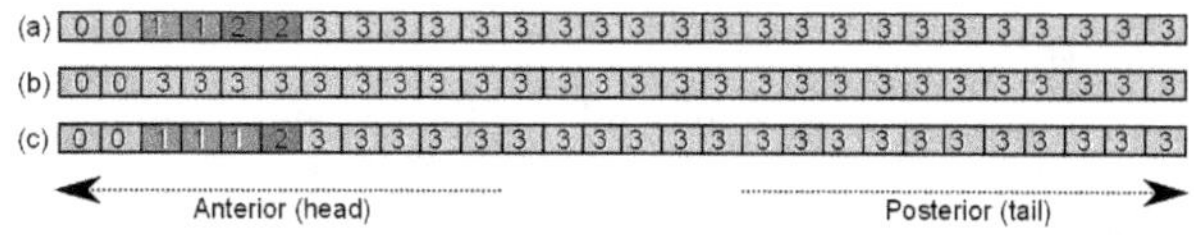

Figure 9: Classification of the 28 regions of the egg into the 14 segments of the fly in a mutated embryo where the bithorax genes were knocked out. (a) Correct segment numbers ($relaxAcc = 1$ and $standAcc = 1$). (b) Predicted segment numbers, without allowing the use of sin functions ($relaxAcc = 0.97$ and $standAcc = 0.85$). (c) Predicted segment numbers, allowing the use of sin functions ($relaxAcc = 0.99$ and $standAcc = 0.96$).

4. CONCLUSIONS

In this paper we showed how a model with biological meaning can be learned based on large biological datasets. It proved to be accurate in the case of predicting the temporal patterns of gene expression throughout embryogenesis, but had a significant reduction in accuracy when trying to predict spatial patterns as well. Nevertheless, we were able to demonstrate how it can be used to (1) classify the different regions of the egg into fly segments, and (2) to conduct a virtual gene knockout experiment. Achieving a more complete and accurate model will require a multidisciplinary effort from both the biology and computer science communities. Here, we examine the assumptions of our methodology, and give a few examples to how it can be improved and extended.

First, the data we use in our learning algorithm is key for the biological relevance of its resulting models. Therefore, it is essential to achieve a comprehensive regulatory network of all functional elements in *Drosophila*, a goal that is set by the modENCODE project [3]. In addition, we used the spatial data of only 19 genes due to the scarcity of datasets that take spatial information into consideration. Therefore, having datasets that are cell-line specific, or even tissue specific, should improve the accuracy and scope of future models; allowing them to classify cells into specific cell types, and not just into broad segments of the fly.

Second, extending our learning algorithm to consider additional biological processes will make it more comprehensive and realistic. For example, it is common for a group of regulators to become active (affect the expression of their target gene) only when they bind each other to form a multi-protein complex; therefore, instead of using summation and assuming independence between the regulators, our learning

Algorithm 2 Classification of regions into fly segments

1: Input: a regulatory network sRN; a model M; a dataset $DS2$
2: Generate a set of vectors $observedVectors = \{(o_{i1}, o_{i2}, \ldots, o_{i8}) \mid 0 \leq i \leq 13\}$ where o_{ij} is the correct value of the j'th homeotic selector gene at the i'th fly segment and at the last developmental step (as defined in $DS2$)
3: Generate a set of vectors $predictedVectors = \{(p_{k1}, p_{k2}, \ldots, p_{k8}) \mid 0 \leq k \leq 27\}$ where p_{kl} is the predicted value of the l'th homeotic selector gene at the k'th region of the egg and at the last developmental step (as predicted by M)
4: **for** each vector $u = (u_1, u_2, \ldots, u_8)$ in $predictedVectors$ **do**
5: Find the vector $v = (v_1, v_2, \ldots, v_8)$ in $observedVectors$ such that $\sum_{1 \leq i \leq 8} |u_i - v_i|$ is minimal
6: Classify the region that is associated with u into the segment that is associated with v
7: **end for**

algorithm should enable the combination of regulators in a way that corresponds to this biological process.

Third, we showed how some interesting results can be achieved despite the simplicity of both our learning and classification algorithms. There are a number of ways in which these can be improved. For example, our hill climbing algorithm can be extended to a more complex local search algorithm such as tabu search or simulated annealing which try to avoid reaching a local optimum; and our classification algorithm can be replaced with a more advanced classification algorithm such as the C4.5 algorithm for learning decision trees.

Finally, our work can be utilized in a broader context of a 3D simulation of embryogenesis. Such a simulation will respond to a challenge raised by Harel et al. [5, 9] to model the development of a complete multicellular organism as a reactive system. For this, we might consider using a 3D simulation environment (such as Lindsay Composer [11]), which can allow us to simulate a dynamic environment where gene products go through diffusion and degradation. This will enable us to break our assumption that the distributions of gene products in the egg are constant throughout embryogenesis.

5. ACKNOWLEDGMENTS

This research was funded by Alberta Innovates Technology Futures (AITF) as part of the Graduate Student Scholarships program.

6. REFERENCES

[1] U. Alon. *An introduction to systems biology: design principles of biological circuits.* CRC press, 2006.

[2] S. B. Carroll, A. Laughon, and B. S. Thalley. Expression, function, and regulation of the hairy segmentation protein in the *Drosophila* embryo. *Genes & development*, 2(7):883–890, 1988.

[3] S. E. Celniker, L. A. Dillon, M. B. Gerstein, K. C. Gunsalus, S. Henikoff, G. H. Karpen, M. Kellis, E. C. Lai, J. D. Lieb, D. M. MacAlpine, et al. Unlocking the secrets of the genome. *Nature*, 459(7249):927–930, 2009.

[4] E. Coen. *The Art of Genes: How Organisms Make Themselves.* Oxford University Press, 1999.

[5] J. Fisher, D. Harel, and T. A. Henzinger. Biology as reactivity. *Communications of the ACM*, 54(10):72–82, 2011.

[6] B. R. Graveley, A. N. Brooks, J. W. Carlson, M. O. Duff, J. M. Landolin, L. Yang, C. G. Artieri, M. J. van Baren, N. Boley, B. W. Booth, et al. The developmental transcriptome of *Drosophila melanogaster. Nature*, 471(7339):473–479, 2010.

[7] T. Gregor, W. Bialek, R. R. van Steveninck, D. W. Tank, and E. F. Wieschaus. Diffusion and scaling during early embryonic pattern formation. *Proceedings of the National Academy of Sciences of the United States of America*, 102(51):18403–18407, 2005.

[8] T. Gregor, E. F. Wieschaus, A. P. McGregor, W. Bialek, and D. W. Tank. Stability and nuclear dynamics of the bicoid morphogen gradient. *Cell*, 130(1):141–152, 2007.

[9] D. Harel. A grand challenge for computing: towards full reactive modeling of a multi-cellular animal. In *Verification, Model Checking, and Abstract Interpretation*, pages 323–324. Springer, 2004.

[10] P. Ingham and P. Gergen. Interactions between the pair-rule genes runt, hairy, even-skipped and fushi tarazu and the establishment of periodic pattern in the *Drosophila* embryo. *Development*, 104(Supplement):51–60, 1988.

[11] C. Jacob, S. von Mammen, T. Davison, A. Sarraf-Shirazi, V. Sarpe, A. Esmaeili, D. Phillips, I. Yazdanbod, S. Novakowski, S. Steil, et al. Lindsay virtual human: Multi-scale, agent-based, and interactive. *Advances in Intelligent Modelling and Simulation*, pages 327–349, 2012.

[12] S. Kalir, J. McClure, K. Pabbaraju, C. Southward, M. Ronen, S. Leibler, M. Surette, and U. Alon. Ordering genes in a flagella pathway by analysis of expression kinetics from living bacteria. *Science*, 292(5524):2080–2083, 2001.

[13] P. A. Lawrence et al. *The making of a fly: the genetics of animal design.* Blackwell Scientific Publications Ltd, 1992.

[14] D. Noble. Modeling the heart–from genes to cells to the whole organ. *Science*, 295(5560):1678–1682, 2002.

[15] D. Noble. *The music of life: biology beyond genes.* Oxford University Press, 2008.

[16] R. Rivera-Pomar and H. Jackle. From gradients to stripes in *Drosophila* embryogenesis: filling in the gaps. *Trends in Genetics*, 12(11):478–483, 1996.

[17] S. Roy, J. Ernst, P. V. Kharchenko, P. Kheradpour, N. Negre, M. L. Eaton, J. M. Landolin, C. A. Bristow, L. Ma, M. F. Lin, et al. Identification of functional elements and regulatory circuits by *Drosophila* modencode. *Science*, 330(6012):1787–1797, 2010.

[18] P. Russell. *iGenetics: A Molecular Approach, Third Edition.* Pearson Education, 2010.

Multiple Graph Edit Distance – Simultaneous Topological Alignment of Multiple Protein-Protein Interaction Networks with an Evolutionary Algorithm

Rashid Ibragimov
Max Planck Institute for Informatics, Saarland University, Germany
ribragim@mpi-inf.mpg.de

Maximilian Malek
Center for Bioinformatics, Saarland University, Germany
mmalek@mmci.uni-saarland.de

Jan Baumbach
Department of Mathematics and Computer Science, University of Southern Denmark, Denmark
jan.baumbach@imada.sdu.dk

Jiong Guo
Cluster of Excellence for Multimodal Computing and Interaction, Saarland University, Germany
jguo@mmci.uni-saarland.de

ABSTRACT

Motivation: We address the problem of multiple protein-protein interaction (PPI) network alignment. Given a set of such networks for different species we might ask how much the network topology is conserved throughout evolution. Solving this problem will help to derive a subset of interactions that is conserved over multiple species thus forming a 'core interactome'.

Methods: We model the problem as Topological Multiple one-to-one Network Alignment (TMNA), where we aim to minimize the total Graph Edit Distance (GED) between pairs of the input networks. Here, the GED between two graphs is the number of deleted and inserted edges that are required to make one graph isomorphic to another. By minimizing the GED we indirectly maximize the number of edges that are aligned in multiple networks simultaneously. However, computing an optimal GED value is computationally intractable. We thus propose an evolutionary algorithm and developed a software tool, GEDEVO-M, which is able to align multiple PPI networks using topological information only. We demonstrate the power of our approach by computing a maximal common subnetwork for a set of bacterial and eukaryotic PPI networks. GEDEVO-M thus provides great potential for computing the 'core interactome' of different species.

Availability:
http://gedevo.mpi-inf.mpg.de/multiple-network-alignment/.

GECCO'14, July 12–16, 2014, Vancouver, BC, Canada.

http://dx.doi.org/10.1145/2576768.2598390.

Categories and Subject Descriptors

J.3 [**Life and Medical Sciences**]: Biology and genetics

Keywords

Protein-Protein Interaction Networks, Multiple Network Alignment, Graph Edit Distance, Evolutionary Algorithm

1. INTRODUCTION

Recent advances in high-throughput technology have opened the way for large-scale reconstruction of biological networks. Huge amounts of protein-protein interaction (PPI) data have become available over the last years. Currently, more than 16 million protein-protein interactions can be accessed through the PSICQUIC web service [4] and may serve as an example for the ongoing "data explosion" here. While traditionally DNA sequence alignment was used to computationally infer biological function of genes and proteins, the availability of such huge data sets has paved the way to predict function from biological network alignment as well. Given a set of PPI networks, establishing a biologically meaningful correspondence between proteins and their interaction has become a central problem here.

Several formalizations of this problem have recently been proposed: protein clustering, network querying, pairwise or multiple network alignment. By combining DNA sequence data and network topology in different ways each formalization aims to reflect different sides of the initial idea: Find functionally and/or evolutionarily conserved parts of subnetworks amongst multiple species.

In this paper, we formulate a multiple network alignment problem by extending the formulation of pairwise global network alignment to multiple species. Here, we look for a set of one-to-one mappings between all proteins in every pair of the input networks. Similar to the pairwise case, the resulting alignment of the multiple input networks is likely to be biologically more meaningful if there are many aligned interactions between multiple networks simultaneously. Most of the existing methods and tools model pairwise global network alignment as finding a one-to-one mapping between a pair of PPI networks that maximize a function of the form $F = \alpha \cdot T + (1-\alpha) \cdot B$, where T and B correspond to topological score and biological quality of the resulting alignment, and $0 \leq \alpha \leq 1$ to a balance between their contribution to the final score. The ideas behind the proposed optimization methods vary from "seed-and-extend", greedy, and bipartite graph matching strategies (PISwap [5], SPINAL [1], MI-GRAAL [15], GHOST [21], and NETAL [19]) to relaxations of an integer linear program formulation (Natalie [7]) and bio-inspired heuristics (NABEECO [11], GEDEVO [10]).

Despite these *pairwise* graph alignment methods, several techniques have recently been proposed for multiple network comparison: C3Part-M [6], NetworkBlast-M [13], BEAMS [2], IsoRankN [16], MULE [14], Graemlin 2.0 [8], SMETANA [25], and NetCoffee [9].

Their objective is to cluster the proteins from multiple graphs into groups based on a combination of sequence similarity and topology similarity, which is used as a combined similarity function. A recent review over existing tools in the field of network alignment may be found in [18] and [17]. All approaches, in contrast to the one that we will introduce below, define multiple network alignment as a set of many-to-many mappings between the proteins in the different graphs, i.e. several proteins from one graph are allowed to be mapped to several proteins from other graphs. The intention behind this is to account for gene duplication events and to maximize biological significance scores, which are usually measured by Gene Ontology agreement (see for example [28]).

In contrast to existing approaches, we do not want to allow for many-to-many mappings but require each node from each graph to be mapped to exactly one node from each other graph. Our intention is to identify a solid 'core interactome', which we define as a set of proteins that we find topologically conserved in a set of multiple PPI networks. In contrast to existing approaches, we seek to ensure that a network, if aligned to multiple instances of itself, will give a result where all nodes from all instances are aligned to its corresponding copies, i.e. an accuracy of 100% in self-alignment. We will extend the Graph Edit Distance model to multiple graph instances and introduce GEDEVO-M, an evolutionary algorithm that minimizes the corresponding optimization function.

The rest of the paper is organized as follows. We first give necessary notations and formally define the topological multiple network alignment problem. We also introduce several indicators that are useful for evaluating the resulting alignment. We further describe an evolutionary algorithm and its operators to approach the problem. Next, we present experimental results from aligning multiple real PPI networks with GEDEVO-M. We conclude the paper with a short outline of future work.

2. PROBLEM DEFINITION

We consider PPI networks as undirected graphs. An *undirected graph* G is a pair $(V(G), E(G))$ with $E(G) \subseteq V \times V$; the elements of $V(G)$ are called nodes of the graph G, the elements of $E(G)$ are edges. The *size* of a graph G is the number of edges in $E(G)$, denoted by $|E(G)|$. The neighborhood of a node v in a graph G, denoted by $N_G(v)$, is the set of all nodes adjacent to v. The *degree* of v is $|N_G(v)|$.

Given two graphs G and H and a one-to-one mapping $f: V(G) \to V(H)$, *graph edit distance* (GED) is defined as $\mathrm{GED}_f(G,H) := |\{(u,v) \in E(G) : (f(u), f(v)) \notin E(H)\} \cup \{(u',v') \in E(H) : (f^{-1}(u'), f^{-1}(v')) \notin E(G)\}|$ (see Fig. 1 as an example). An edge $(u,v) \in E(G)$ is aligned if $(f(u), f(v)) \in E(H)$. *Edge correctness* (EC) is defined as

$$\mathrm{EC}_f(G,H) := \frac{|\{(v,u) \in E(G) : (f(v), f(u)) \in E(H)\}|}{\min(|E(G)|, |E(H)|)} \ .$$

For a node $v \in V(G)$, the *pair score* is defined as

$$\begin{aligned} p_f(v) := |\{u \in N_G(v) : f(u) \notin N_H(f(v))\} \cup \\ \{u' \in N_H(f(v)) : f^{-1}(u') \notin N_G(v)\}| / \\ (|N_G(v)| + |N_H(f(v))|) + d(v, f(v)) \ , \end{aligned}$$

where $d(u,u')$ measures the difference between $u \in G$ and $u' \in H$.

Let $\mathcal{G} = \{G_1, \ldots, G_N\}$ be a set of N graphs. A *multiple mapping* (*m-mapping*) from G_1 to $\mathcal{G}' \subseteq \mathcal{G} \setminus G_1$ is a set $\mathcal{F}' = \{f_{i,j} : G_i, G_j \in \mathcal{G}' \cup G_1\}$ of one-to-one mappings such that $f_{1,j} : V(G_1) \to V(G_j)$ and $f_{i,j}(v) = f_{1,j}(f_{1,i}^{-1}(v))$, for every $G_i, G_j \in \mathcal{G}'$ and $v \in G_i$. Given an m-mapping $\mathcal{F}'$, we define *multiple graph edit distance* ($mGED$) as

$$\mathrm{mGED}_{\mathcal{F}'} := \sum_{f_{i,j} \in \mathcal{F}'} \mathrm{GED}_{f_{i,j}}(G_i, G_j) \ .$$

Similarly, *multiple edge correctness* (mEC) is defined as

$$\mathrm{mEC}_{\mathcal{F}'} := \sum_{f_{i,j} \in \mathcal{F}'} \mathrm{EC}_{f_{i,j}}(G_i, G_j) / |\mathcal{F}'| \ .$$

We use the mGED to evaluate the quality of an m-mapping. However, mEC is more convenient to interpret for the user and reader of this paper, in particular on networks of different sizes, especially given that the optimal mGED value (minimum) is unknown *a priori* while the mEC scales between 0 and 1. Given an m-mapping $\mathcal{F}$ on $\mathcal{G}$, a pair $v, u \in V(G_1)$, is *k-aligned* if $|\{(f_{1,j}(v), f_{1,j}(u)) \in E(G_j) : G_j \in \mathcal{G}\}| = k$. If $k > 1$, we also refer to k-aligned pair as *k-aligned edge*. We denote the number of k-aligned pairs by k-AE. The *k-aligned edges ratio* is defined as

$$k\text{-AR} := \sum_{i=k}^{N} \frac{i\text{-AE}}{\max^i\{|E(G_1)|, \ldots, |E(G_N)|\}} \ ,$$

where $\max^i A$ is the i-th largest (or the $(N-i+1)$-th smallest) element in the set A. Given a *k-common graph* G that is built on the nodes that are incident to ℓ-aligned edges, for $\ell = k, \ldots, N$, the value of k-AR indicates the size of G opposed to the ideal case when $(k-1)$-many smallest graphs $\mathcal{G}'' \subset \mathcal{G}$ are all subgraphs of a graph $G \in \mathcal{G} \setminus \mathcal{G}''$. Given an m-mapping $\mathcal{F}'$ to $\mathcal{G}'$ and $v \in V(G_1)$, a *tuple* is a set $\{f(v)$, where $f : v \to V(G), G \in \mathcal{G}'\}$. A *tuple score* is defined as $P_{\mathcal{F}'}(v) := \sum_{f \in \mathcal{F}'} p_f(v)$. A *full score* S is defined as $\sum_{v \in V(G_1)} P_{\mathcal{F}}(v)$.

Given a set of graphs $\mathcal{G}$, we define the Topological Multiple Network Alignment problem (TMNA) as the problem of finding an m-mapping $\mathcal{F}$ on $\mathcal{G}$ such that $\mathrm{mGED}_{\mathcal{F}}$ is minimal over all possible m-mappings on $\mathcal{G}$. Clearly, TNMA is NP-hard even for two graphs. The intuition behind the formulation of TNMA is as follows. Ideally, a biologically meaningful alignment of multiple PPI networks should map functionally related proteins. At the same time, for closely

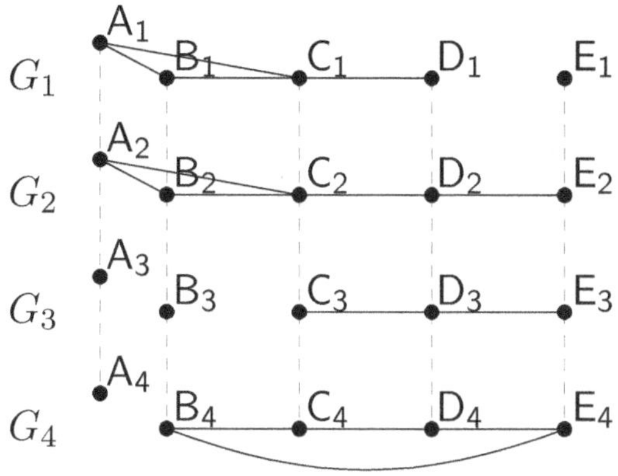

$\mathrm{GED}_{f_{1,2}}(G_1,G_2)=1$, $\mathrm{GED}_{f_{1,3}}(G_1,G_3)=4$,
$\mathrm{GED}_{f_{1,4}}(G_1,G_4)=4$, $\mathrm{GED}_{f_{2,3}}(G_2,G_3)=3$,
$\mathrm{GED}_{f_{2,4}}(G_2,G_4)=3$, $\mathrm{GED}_{f_{3,4}}(G_3,G_4)=2$

$\mathrm{mGED}_{\mathcal{F}}=\sum_{f_{i,j}\in\mathcal{F}}\mathrm{GED}_{f_{i,j}}(G_i,G_j)=17$

4-AE $=1$, 4-AR $=\frac{1}{2}$,

3-AE $=2$, 3-AR $=\frac{3}{4}$,

2-AE $=2$, 2-AR $=\frac{5}{4}$

Figure 1: An m-mapping $\mathcal{F}$ (dashed lines) on graphs G_1, G_2, G_3 and G_4. There is only one set of four edges that are mapped to each other in all graphs: the edges (C_1, D_1), (C_2, D_2), (C_3, D_3), (C_4, D_4), such that the frequency of edges aligning in all four graphs 4-AE equals to 1. The smallest number of edges in one of the input graphs is two, such that we have 4-AR=4-AE/2=1/2; similarly for the remaining values of k-AE and k-AR, for $k=\{2,3\}$.

related species, the overall difference in the corresponding PPI networks should be small due to evolutionary conservation of many interactions (edges in the graphs). This is thought to be achievable if many pairs of nodes induce smaller numbers of edge insertions and deletions. Similarly to the graph isomorphism problem, in TNMA, when aligning N copies of a network G, an optimal m-mapping should result in $|E(G)|$-many N-aligned edges and have mGED $=0$. However, with the current PPI data being noisy and incomplete, the requirement of strict correspondence of all edges is unrealistic. We therefore chose to model the multiple PPI network alignment as TNMA. Clearly, the definition of TMNA can be generalized to integrate external data such as edge weights and external node-to-node similarities (derived, for instance, from pairwise protein sequence alignments).

3. METHODS

To approximate Topological Multiple Network Alignments we propose a heuristic based on an evolutionary algorithm that extends a previous approach from [10] developed for the alignment of two graphs. An evolutionary algorithm (EA) describes a general procedure to optimize a certain "fitness" function over a set of individuals that represent sample solutions of the problem (see for example [12]). The set of individuals is called the population. A typical EA starts with an initial population and iteratively generates new individuals by applying problem specific evolutionary operators. Only individuals with the highest values as evaluated by the fitness function are passed to the next generation. The algorithm stops when a predefined criterion is fulfilled, such as the maximum number of iterations or when convergence of the best value of the fitness function is reached. Evolutionary algorithms have proven efficient in solving various hard optimization problems. Note that testing all possible mappings is already unfeasible for pairwise network alignment of two graphs. In TMNA, we also observe exponential growth of the search space with respect to the number of input networks N. The number of all possible m-mappings here corresponds to $O((n!)^N)$, where n is the number of nodes in the input networks.

Next we describe evolutionary operators that are specific for GEDEVO-M and essential for its performance. In GEDEVO-M, generating a new population we chose randomly a set $\mathcal{G}'\subseteq\mathcal{G}\setminus G_1$ and apply the following operators on $\mathcal{G}'$:

- In a *PMX-like mutation* a new individual is created by copying the m-mapping of a randomly selected individual from the previous generation. We randomly swap ("bad") tuples on $\mathcal{G}'$ that have tuple scores higher than a certain threshold. The threshold is defined as the average over all tuple scores on $\mathcal{G}'$.
- In a *random mutation* the tuples on $\mathcal{G}'$ with lower than the threshold values of their tuple scores are also given a certain chance to be swapped.
- A *crossover operator* constructs a new m-mapping from two or more "parent" individuals of the previous generation. We first compute tuple scores for every possible subset of $\mathcal{G}$ and sort them. Then, starting with larger subsets of $\mathcal{G}$, we repeatedly iterate over the corresponding tuple scores and assign some of these tuples to the new m-mapping until every subset is considered. Subsets having identical sizes are processed in random order. To maintain consistency (one-to-one requirement) in the new m-mapping, we set the tuple only if none of its element was already assigned in the previous steps. Finally, the unassigned images of the m-mapping are distributed randomly. We exploit three versions of the crossover operator. The first combines two individuals that have better values of fitness function achieved so far. The other two versions generate m-mapping from two and 3-8 parents: the parents here are selected randomly.
- A *directed mutation* selects a tuple t corresponding to $\mathcal{G}'$ and greedily looks for another tuple t' such that when t and t' are swapped the resulting m-mapping has the best improvement of the fitness function.
- A *greedy mutation* randomly chooses a set of tuples on $\mathcal{G}'$ of size at most 10 and changes the m-mapping

Table 1: Protein-protein interaction data sets used for evaluating GEDEVO-M.

Short name	Species	Proteins	Interactions	Citation
Dmela	*Drosophila melanogaster*	7569	23 017	[30]
Scere	*Saccharomyces cerevisiae*	5011	22 503	[30]
Celeg	*Caenorhabditis elegans*	2686	4079	[30]
Hsapi	*Homo sapiens*	2332	3305	[30]
cjejunihc	*Campylobacter jejuni*	1095	2988	[20]
Meso	*Mesorhizobium loti*	1803	3094	[29]
Syne	*Synechocystis sp.(PCC6803)*	1908	3102	[27]
ecolifi	*Escherichia coli*	1941	3989	[22]
hprd	*Homo sapiens*	9671	39 214	[23]

by testing every possible permutation of the chosen subset. The permutation that results in the best improvement of the fitness function is assigned to the m-mapping at the end.

- A *random m-mapping* results in random permutations of the tuples of $\mathcal{G}'$.

We use the score S as an indicator of the quality of an m-mapping. To increase population diversity, we also exploit the notion of the health of an individual, which is maximal when an individual is born and drops over time (number of iterations). If the health reaches or falls below zero, the individual is discarded. The health of the best 10% (according to S) of individuals remains unmodified; the health of the remaining 90% of individuals are subject to the following linear reduction: the best individual there remains unchanged and the worst one loses 90% of maximal health. Consequently, individuals with higher (worse) values of S and poor health have lower chances to survive and contribute to the future generations.

Similarly to [10] we utilize the notion of the so-called Graphlet-degree Signature Distance (GSD) [24]. In S we combine the accumulated GSD of the m-mapping and its actual mGED. The GSD serves as a topological indicator for the differences of the local neighborhoods of the potentially matched nodes. With the above defined set of operators and the score S describing the quality of an m-mapping, our evolutionary algorithm GEDEVO-M improves the resulting m-mappings by preferably keeping those elements of m-mappings unchanged that lead to the lower values of the fitness function and modify elements of the m-mappings that have higher ones.

The crossover operator is the most computationally expensive operation (more expensive than evaluation of an individual, random mapping and other operators). For an individual there are $T := n \cdot 2^{(N-1)}$ distinct tuples obtained from $2^{(N-1)}$ subsets of $\mathcal{G} \setminus G_1$ and the number n of nodes in input graphs. Computing a pair score requires $O(d)$ time, where d is the highest node degree. Thus, computing tuple scores for π parents in the crossover operator requires $O(\pi \cdot T \cdot d)$ time. Sorting all the tuples can be performed in $O(\pi \cdot T \cdot \log(\pi \cdot T))$ time. Assigning tuples to the new mapping requires at most $2^{(N-1)}$ passes on $\pi \cdot T$ values of tuples scores. In the final step, filling unassigned nodes is performed in $O(n \cdot 2^{(N-1)})$ time. Thus, the overall running time of the crossover operator on $\pi \leq 8$ parents is $O(\pi \cdot T \cdot (d + \log(\pi \cdot T)))$, which is not larger than $O(n \cdot 2^N \cdot (d + N + \log n))$. Given, that the evolutionary algorithm runs I iterations with population size P, its overall running time corresponds to $O(I \cdot P \cdot n \cdot 2^N \cdot (d + N + \log n))$. As for memory consumption, each individual requires $O(n)$ space to represent every mapping from G_1 to $G' \in \mathcal{G} \setminus G_1$. A significant amount of memory is needed to store the values of the distance matrices (used in the pair score) between every pair of input graphs. Thus, the overall amount of required space results in $O(P \cdot N \cdot n + \binom{N}{2} \cdot n^2)$.

4. NETWORK DATA

To evaluate GEDEVO-M we used the same source of network data previously used for pairwise graph alignments in [10] (see Table 1 for the summary). The PPI networks of four eukaryotic species were extracted from the DIP database (release July 7th, 2013), which contains experimentally detected and manually curated protein-protein interactions [30]. The two bacterial networks *cjejunihc* and *ecolifi* are well-studied high-confidence networks: the first network resulted from high-throughput yeast two-hybrid screens; the second network was constructed using experimental and computational data (see [22]). The *Syne* network was obtained through a modified high-throughput yeast two-hybrid assay and covers around half (52%) of the total protein coding genes; similarly for network *Meso* that involves 24% of the protein coding genes.

The *hprd* network is a PPI network obtained from the Human Protein Reference Database (HPRD), which is a repository storing high-quality, manually curated human interaction data.

5. RESULTS

In this section we provide experimental evaluation of the proposed algorithm. All executions of GEDEVO-M were performed on a 64-bit Linux 3.2.42 kernel running on AMD Opteron 6276 with 150GB RAM and 50 threads. From our testing experiments, despite the probabilistic nature, GEDEVO-M converged to similar mGEDs in all cases. We therefore present only the results for one GEDEVO-M run per input data set. The initial population size was set to 500 individuals. As the termination criterion we set GEDEVO-M to stop after 100k iterations or if no changes in the best value of GED has been observed in in last 3k iterations.

We aligned two sets of PPI networks: "eukaryotic" (*Dmela*, *Scere*, *Celeg*, *Hsapi*) and "bacterial" (*cjejunihc*, *Meso*, *Syno*, *ecolifi*). The properties of the resulting alignments are summarized in Table 2. Note, the values of mEC for randomly generated m-mappings (which are also used for the initial-

Table 2: The values of mGED, mEC and aligned pairs aligning two sets of bacterial and eukaryotic PPI networks. See text and Fig. 1 for an illustration of mGED, mEC, 4-AE, 3-AE, and 2-AE.

	achieved		random		k-aligned edges		
Set of networks	mGED	mEC	mGED	mEC	4-AE	3-AE	2-AE
Dmela, Scere, Celeg, Hsapi	139 024	24.16%	155 796	0.18%	310	638	4657
cjejunihc, Meso, Syno, ecolifi	30 287	25.27%	39 327	0.53%	328	503	1139

Table 3: Proportions of aligned edge aligning two sets of bacterial and eukaryotic PPI networks. See text and Fig. 1 for an illustration of 4-AR, 3-AR, and 2-AR.

Set of networks	aligned edges	proportion of aligned edges	4-AR	3-AR	2-AR
Dmela, Scere, Celeg, Hsapi	12 468	23.57%	9.38%	23.24%	24.91%
cjejunihc, Meso, Syno, ecolifi	5099	38.71%	10.98%	26.86%	63.51%

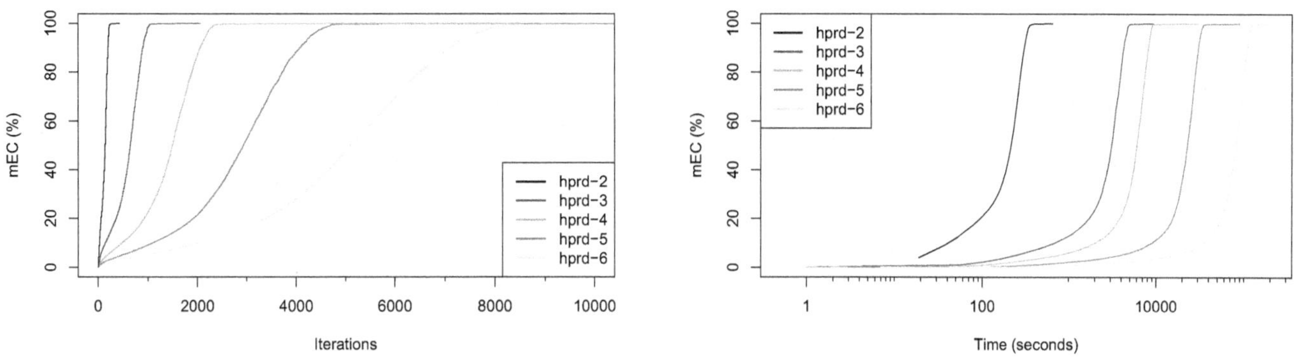

Figure 2: Development of the multiple Edge Correctness (mEC) over progressing iterations (and elapsing time) while aligning multiple copies of the *hprd* network. Note that a perfect alignment of a network to multiple copies of itself should reach an edge correctness of 100%, which is reached by GEDEVO-M.

ization step) are just 0.18% and 0.53% for eukaryotic and bacterial networks, respectively. Thus, GEDEVO-M substantially improved these values to 25.16% and 25.27%, respectively. In Table 3, we provide edge alignment ratios and the proportions of aligned edges. Note that almost every fourth edge of the eukaryotic networks has an aligned edge; for the bacterial networks more than one third of edges is matched (38.71%).

The common graphs that are built on 4-, 3-, 2-aligned edges of the m-mapping on eukaryotic networks consist of 490, 1290, 4923 nodes, respectively. For the bacterial networks these values correspond to 511, 1057, 1565, respectively. The edges and nodes of the common graphs may give hints to the "core interactome".

By the definition of TMNA, aligning multiple copies of a network to the resulting mGED should be 0 with an mEC of 100%. To demonstrate that GEDEVO-M is able to cope with this task, we aligned several copies of the comparably big *hprd* network. In Fig. 2, we show that GEDEVO-M successfully aligns multiple copies (i.e. 2-6x) of the *hprd* input network. In all tests GEDEVO-M achieved optimal values for mGED (0 edits) and mEC (100%). However, the time needed to reach this optimum grows exponentially with the number of input networks. This can be explained by the increasing number of the subsets of networks that can be generated when applying an evolutionary operator.

6. CONCLUSION AND OUTLOOK

We defined Topological Multiple Network Alignment, TMNA, as a an extension of the pairwise global network alignment problem to model the alignment of multiple graphs, particularly protein-protein interaction networks. As this problem is hard, even for only two graphs, we presented GEDEVO-M, a novel heuristic based on evolutionary computation for TMNA. By minimizing the total pairwise Graph Edit Distance between all input networks, GEDEVO-M finds edges that are conserved across the input PPI networks. On two sets of PPI networks we evaluated topological properties of the resulting m-mappings. On a big human PPI network, we demonstrate that GEDEVO-M is capable of finding an optimal alignment by comparing several copies of the network to itself.

In the future we will study the results of GEDEVO-M together with evolutionary biologists and functional genomics researchers. We expect our results to give new insights into the core interactome of life. We will further implement GEDEVO-M as Cytoscape plugin [26] to provide a one-click solution of GEDEVO-M. To reduce the search space and run times, we will also include sequence-based similarities [3] to pre-align nodes and to integrate this knowledge at generating initial population. GEDEVO-M and all used data sets are publicly available at http://gedevo.mpi-inf.mpg.de/multiple-network-alignment/.

Acknowledgements

The work was supported by the Cluster of Excellence Multimodal Computing and Interaction (MMCI) and the International Max Planck Research School for Computer Science (IMPRS).

7. REFERENCES

[1] A. E. Aladag and C. Erten. SPINAL: scalable protein interaction network alignment. *Bioinformatics*, 29(7):917–924, 2013.

[2] F. Alkan and C. Erten. BEAMS: backbone extraction and merge strategy for the global many-to-many alignment of multiple PPI networks. *Bioinformatics*, 30(4):531–539, 2014.

[3] S. F. Altschul, W. Gish, W. Miller, E. W. Myers, and D. J. Lipman. Basic local alignment search tool. *Journal of molecular biology*, 215(3):403–410, Oct. 1990.

[4] B. Aranda, H. Blankenburg, S. Kerrien, F. Brinkman, A. Ceol, E. Chautard, J. Dana, J. De Las Rivas, M. Dumousseau, E. Galeota, A. Gaulton, J. Goll, R. Hancock, R. Isserlin, R. Jimenez, J. Kerssemakers, J. Khadake, D. Lynn, M. Michaut, G. O'Kelly, K. Ono, S. Orchard, C. Prieto, S. Razick, O. Rigina, L. Salwinski, M. Simonovic, S. Velankar, A. Winter, G. Wu, G. Bader, G. Cesareni, I. Donaldson, D. Eisenberg, G. Kleywegt, J. Overington, S. Ricard-Blum, M. Tyers, M. Albrecht, and H. Hermjakob. PSICQUIC and PSISCORE: accessing and scoring molecular interactions. *Nature Methods*, 8(7):528–529–, 2011.

[5] L. Chindelevitch, C.-Y. Ma, C.-S. Liao, and B. Berger. Optimizing a global alignment of protein interaction networks. *Bioinformatics*, 29(21):2765–2773, 2013.

[6] Y.-P. Deniélou, F. Boyer, A. Viari, and M.-F. Sagot. Multiple alignment of biological networks: A flexible approach. In *CPM*, pages 263–273, 2009.

[7] M. El-Kebir, J. Heringa, and G. Klau. Lagrangian relaxation applied to sparse global network alignment. In M. Loog, L. Wessels, M. Reinders, and D. Ridder, editors, *Pattern Recognition in Bioinformatics*, volume 7036 of *Lecture Notes in Computer Science*, pages 225–236. Springer Berlin Heidelberg, 2011.

[8] J. Flannick, A. F. Novak, C. B. Do, B. S. Srinivasan, and S. Batzoglou. Automatic parameter learning for multiple local network alignment. *Journal of Computational Biology*, 16(8):1001–1022, 2009.

[9] J. Hu, B. Kehr, and K. Reinert. NetCoffee: a fast and accurate global alignment approach to identify functionally conserved proteins in multiple networks. *Bioinformatics*, 30(4):540–548, 2014.

[10] R. Ibragimov, M. Malek, J. Guo, and J. Baumbach. GEDEVO: an evolutionary graph edit distance algorithm for biological network alignment. In *GCB*, pages 68–79, 2013.

[11] R. Ibragimov, J. Martens, J. Guo, and J. Baumbach. NABEECO: biological network alignment with bee colony optimization algorithm. In *GECCO (Companion)*, pages 43–44, 2013.

[12] K. A. D. Jong. *Evolutionary computation - a unified approach*. MIT Press, 2006.

[13] M. Kalaev, V. Bafna, and R. Sharan. Fast and accurate alignment of multiple protein networks. *Journal of Computational Biology*, 16(8):989–999, 2009.

[14] M. Koyutürk, Y. Kim, S. Subramaniam, W. Szpankowski, and A. Grama. Detecting conserved interaction patterns in biological networks. *Journal of Computational Biology*, 13(7):1299–1322, 2006.

[15] O. Kuchaiev and N. Pržulj. Integrative Network Alignment Reveals Large Regions of Global Network Similarity in Yeast and Human. *Bioinformatics*, 27(10):1390–1396, Mar. 2011.

[16] C.-S. Liao, K. Lu, M. Baym, R. Singh, and B. Berger. Isorankn: spectral methods for global alignment of multiple protein networks. *Bioinformatics*, 25(12), 2009.

[17] S. Mohammadi and A. Grama. Biological network alignment. In M. KoyutâĄ£rk, S. Subramaniam, and A. Grama, editors, *Functional Coherence of Molecular Networks in Bioinformatics*, pages 97–136. Springer New York, 2012.

[18] L. A. Mueller, M. Dehmer, and F. Emmert-Streib. Comparing biological networks: A survey on graph classifying techniques. In A. Prokop and B. Csukás, editors, *Systems Biology*, pages 43–63. Springer Netherlands, 2013.

[19] B. Neyshabur, A. Khadem, S. Hashemifar, and S. S. Arab. NETAL: a new graph-based method for global alignment of protein-protein interaction networks. *Bioinformatics*, 29(13):1654–1662, 2013.

[20] J. Parrish, J. Yu, G. Liu, J. Hines, J. Chan, B. Mangiola, H. Zhang, S. Pacifico, F. Fotouhi, V. DiRita, T. Ideker, P. Andrews, and R. Finley. A proteome-wide protein interaction map for campylobacter jejuni. *Genome Biology*, 8(7):R130, 2007.

[21] R. Patro and C. Kingsford. Global network alignment using multiscale spectral signatures. *Bioinformatics*, 28(23):3105–3114, 2012.

[22] J. M. Peregrin-Alvarez, X. Xiong, C. Su, and J. Parkinson. The modular organization of protein interactions in *Escherichia coli*. *PLoS Comput Biol*, 5(10):e1000523, 10 2009.

[23] K. T. S. Prasad, R. Goel, K. Kandasamy, S. Keerthikumar, S. Kumar, S. Mathivanan, D. Telikicherla, R. Raju, B. Shafreen, A. Venugopal, L. Balakrishnan, A. Marimuthu, S. Banerjee, D. S. Somanathan, A. Sebastian, S. Rani, S. Ray, H. C. J.

Kishore, S. Kanth, M. Ahmed, M. K. Kashyap, R. Mohmood, Y. L. Ramachandra, V. Krishna, A. B. Rahiman, S. Mohan, P. Ranganathan, S. Ramabadran, R. Chaerkady, and A. Pandey. Human Protein Reference Database–2009 update. *Nucleic acids research*, 37(Database issue):D767–D772, Jan. 2009.

[24] N. Pržulj. Biological network comparison using graphlet degree distribution. *Bioinformatics*, 23(2):e177–e183, Jan. 2007.

[25] S. M. E. Sahraeian and B.-J. Yoon. SMETANA: Accurate and Scalable Algorithm for Probabilistic Alignment of Large-Scale Biological Networks. *PLoS ONE*, 8(7):e67995, 07 2013.

[26] R. Saito, M. E. Smoot, K. Ono, J. Ruscheinski, P.-L. Wang, S. Lotia, A. R. Pico, G. D. Bader, and T. Ideker. A travel guide to Cytoscape plugins. *Nat Meth*, 9(11):1069–1076, Nov. 2012.

[27] S. Sato, Y. Shimoda, A. Muraki, M. Kohara, Y. Nakamura, and S. Tabata. A large-scale protein-protein interaction analysis in synechocystis sp. pcc6803. *DNA Research*, 14(5):207–216, 2007.

[28] A. Schlicker, F. S. Domingues, J. Rahnenführer, and T. Lengauer. A new measure for functional similarity of gene products based on gene ontology. *BMC Bioinformatics*, 7:302, 2006.

[29] Y. Shimoda, S. Shinpo, M. Kohara, Y. Nakamura, S. Tabata, and S. Sato. A large scale analysis of protein-protein interactions in the nitrogen-fixing bacterium mesorhizobium loti. *DNA Research*, 15(1):13–23, 2008.

[30] I. Xenarios, L. Salwínski, X. Joyce, P. Higney, S.-M. M. Kim, and D. Eisenberg. DIP, the Database of Interacting Proteins: a research tool for studying cellular networks of protein interactions. *Nucleic acids research*, 30(1):303–305, Jan. 2002.

Virtual Photography Using Multi-Objective Particle Swarm Optimization

William Barry
Sheridan College
Trafalgar Campus
1430 Trafalgar Road
Oakville, Ontario
L6H 2L1, Canada
william.barry@sheridancollege.ca

Brian J. Ross
Brock University
Dept. of Computer Science
500 Glenridge Ave.
St. Catharines, Ontario
L2S 3A1, Canada
bross@brocku.ca

ABSTRACT

Particle swarm optimization (PSO) is a stochastic population-based search algorithm that is inspired by the flocking behaviour of birds. Here, a PSO is used to implement swarms of cameras flying through a virtual world in search of an image that satisfies a set of compositional objectives, for example, the rule of thirds and horizon line rules. To effectively process these multiple, and possible conflicting, criteria, a new multi-objective PSO algorithm called the sum of ranks PSO (SR-PSO) is introduced. The SR-PSO is useful for solving high-dimensional search problems, while discouraging degenerate solutions that can arise with other approaches. Less user intervention is required for the SR-PSO, as compared to a conventional PSO. A number of problems using different virtual worlds and user-supplied objectives were studied. In all cases, solution images were obtained that satisfied the majority of given objectives. The SR-PSO is shown to be superior to other algorithms in solving the high-dimensional virtual photography problems studied.

Categories and Subject Descriptors

I.2.11 [**Artificial Intelligence**]: Distributed Artificial Intelligence—*Intelligent agents*

General Terms

Experimentation

Keywords

particle swarm optimization, virtual photography, multiobjective optimization

1. INTRODUCTION

Recent research is investigating high-level software tools for assisting photographers create images adhering to artistic rules of composition. *Automated photography* refers to algorithmic techniques for the unsupervised automation of photographic composition, for images taken in both virtual and real-life environments. We adopt the term *virtual photography* to refer to automatic photography within a virtual 3D environment. The automated composition of such images is important, since images should comply to established norms of artistic composition. This technology is also applicable to automated editing of digital photographs. This may result in intelligent photographic assistants built into cameras that modify images to make them more compositionally pleasing and "professional". A related problem is *virtual world exploration* [14], where agents autonomously seek out desirable subject matter within a virtual environment.

Various algorithms, including optimization techniques, are used in virtual photography. Preuss *et al.* [22] apply a niching evolutionary algorithm to the virtual photography problem, in search for a diversity of results that satisfy compositional objectives. Bares and Kim [3] automate rules of composition by considering subject size, view angle, location, depth, exclusion, and occlusion. Swanson *et al.* use machine learning to learn compositional rules for virtual environments [24]. Related work in real-life photography includes [7, 25].

Particle Swarm Optimization (PSO) has been used in virtual photography. Ermetici *et al.* [8, 19] use a PSO to generate images in a virtual environment complying to a set of supplied constraints. These constraints specify the visibility of different game avatars, and their orientation with respect to the camera. Virtual photography has been applied to cinematography to assist in composition. Abdullah *et al.* [1] use a PSO to optimize cinematographic images via composition rules. Burelli and Preuss use multi-objective optimization for automatic cinematography [9].

This paper presents a new technique for virtual photography.[1] Like Ermetici *et al.* [8, 19], a PSO algorithm is used to harness a swarm of cameras to autonomously explore a virtual 3D world. Each camera will move through the world in search of an image that satisfies a supplied set of aesthetic rules. Since there are usually multiple compositional requirements to be satisfied, a multi-objective approach is taken here, in order to reconcile the multiple aesthetic objectives of images. When composing a picture with a camera, many things must be considered. The subject(s) of interest must be present, and the amount of image real estate

[1]See [4] for more details about this research.

GECCO'14, July 12–16, 2014, Vancouver, BC, Canada.
Copyright 2014 ACM 978-1-4503-2662-9/14/07 ...$15.00.
http://dx.doi.org/10.1145/2576768.2598210.

it covers must be considered. The subject should be positioned close to one of the four compositional loci of the rule of thirds. Other objects of interest will have similar considerations. The horizon rule states that it should reside at a 1/3 or 2/3 vertical position in the image. The colour palette of the image also may be of consideration. An advantage of multi-objective search is that the user is usually not required to specify how different objective scores are to be measured with respect to each other.

We introduce a new multi-objective PSO algorithm called the sum of ranks PSO. The SR-PSO borrows a multi-objective strategy used in high-dimensional genetic algorithms [5], which are used to optimize problems with a large number of conflicting objectives. Besides its ability to handle many problem objectives, images obtained with it are less likely to be *outlier* solutions (ones that satisfy a small minority of objectives). The sum of ranks strategy was found to be useful in evolutionary design problems (eg. [6]), since outlier solutions are often of neglible value compared to solutions satisfying multiple objectives. This is also the case with virtual photography.

Obvious applications for this research may be within video games, virtual reality portals (Google Streetview), and 3D building design software. For example, today's games strive to generate complex, realistic virtual worlds. These worlds also contain objects of interest to the game, which require time and effort for creating specific cameras to focus upon. Using the strategy proposed in this paper, game developers could have PSO agents automatically discover objects of interest, and return dramatically composed images of them. More advanced applications of this technology are conceivable. For example, one could imagine the PSO swarm to be autonomous robot helicopters [20].

The paper is organized as follows. Multi-objective problem solving is discussed in Section 2. Section 3 introduces the SR-PSO algorithm, as well as other PSO algorithms used in comparisons in later sections. The composition rules used in this research are discussed in Section 4. The system architecture is described in Section 5. Results and comparative analyses are given in Section 6. Comparisons to related research is given in Section 7. Section 8 gives conclusions and directions for future research.

2. MULTI-OBJECTIVE PROBLEMS

A multi-objective optimization problem has two or more objectives to be optimized [11]. These multiple objectives can interact in complex and conflicting ways. Often, the best one can hope for is that the majority of objectives can be balanced and satisfied to an acceptable degree.

2.1 Pareto Ranking

The most popular multi-objective scoring strategy is Pareto ranking [13]. Pareto ranking is based on the concept of Pareto dominance.

$$\begin{aligned} A\ dominates\ B \leftrightarrow\ & (\forall_{obj}\, f_{obj}(A) \leq f_{obj}(B)) \\ & \wedge (\exists_{obj}\, f_{obj}(A) < f_{obj}(B)) \end{aligned}$$

where $f_{obj}(P)$ is the score of objective obj in agent P, $1 \leq obj \leq n$ objectives, and f defines a minimization problem. A dominates B if it is superior to B in at least one objective, and equal to B in the remaining objectives.

Using the definition of Pareto dominance, a population of agents is examined (Table 1). The nondominated agents are assigned the Pareto rank of 1 and removed. The nondominated agents from the remaining population are assigned the rank of 2. This continues until all agents are ranked. Lower ranks are preferred. Pareto ranking is ineffective with more than 5 objectives, because most of the population becomes nondominated. In such cases, the sum of ranks scoring strategy should be considered.

	Objectives				Ranks			
	O_1	O_2	O_3	P	R_1	R_2	R_3	SR
1)	10	5	80	1	5	1	2	2.25
2)	6	50	80	3	4	3	2	2.55
3)	3	60	20	3	3	4	1	2.1
4)	2	40	20	2	2	2	1	1.4
5)	1	40	20	1	1	2	1	1.2
max:					5	4	2	

Table 1: Example of sum of ranks calculation. O_i are raw scores (lower preferred), P are the Pareto ranks, R_i is the rank of O_i, and *SR* is the (normalized) sum of ranks.

2.2 Sum of Ranks

The sum of ranks (or average rank) was originally proposed for solving high-dimensional multi-objective problems [5, 12]. Consider a problem with K objectives, each of which must be minimized. Each population member j is assigned a rank vector, in which each objective score for the objective is given a rank value $r (1 \leq r \leq N)$ for population size N: $R^j = < r_1, ..., r_K >$. Individuals with tied scores have the same rank value. These rank scores are always set relative to the current population. Hence, a rank $r_i = 1$ will be found in the vector of the individual that has the best score in objective i. The sum of ranks score S^j for each individual in the population is then:

$$SR^j = \sum_{i=1}^{K} \frac{w_i r_i}{max_i}$$

where w_i is an optional weight (default 1.0), and max_i is the maximum rank for each objective. Normalizing by max makes the rankings uniform between objective.

In Table 1, rows 1-5 represent the population, and objective scores are to be minimized. The ranks R_i replace the raw objective scores with rank orderings. SR is the sum of the normalized ranks in that row, which are found by dividing each R_i by the maximum rank for that objective (column). Note that the relative orderings of the SR scores and Pareto ranks (P) differ.

3. PARTICLE SWARM OPTIMIZATION

3.1 The Basic PSO Algorithm

Particle swarm optimization (PSO) is a population based search algorithm inspired by the social behaviour known as flocking [15]. Swarm individuals (particles, agents) have two important attributes: velocity and position. These two attributes are best thought of as a K size vector, for a problem with K values to optimize. Throughout a simulation, each individual updates its own position by its own velocity, and the velocity is modified by one value from within the population and one value from itself. The influence from the population is a global best *gbest*, which is the best individual from within the swarm. The influence from an individual agent is its personal best *pbest*, which is the best solution that the individual has seen. More formally, the attributes that contribute to the change of particle *i*'s state and velocity vectors are:

p_i:	particle position or state
v_i:	particle velocity
w:	an inertia value to control the velocity
pbest:	particle's personal best solution
r_1:	random number between (0,1)
c_1:	constant constraint for *pbest*
gbest:	swarm's best solution
r_2:	random number between (0,1)
c_2:	constant constraint for *gbest*

Using these attributes, individuals in a swarm update their velocity:

$$v_i = wv_i + c_1 r_1 (pbest - p_i) + c_2 r_2 (gbest - p_i) \quad (1)$$

A particle's position is then updated:

$$p_i = p_i + v_i \quad (2)$$

Algorithm 1: Particle swarm optimization

```
1  for i = 1 to N do
2      p_i ← randomize;
3      pbest_i ← p_i;
4      if f(p_i) < f(gbest) then
5          gbest ← p_i;
6      end
7      v_i ← randomize;
8  end
9  while Termination criteria not met do
10     for i = 1 to N do
11         Generate random numbers r_1, r_2;
12         Update v_i with Eqn. (1);
13         Update p_i with Eqn. (2);
14         if f(p_i) < f(pbest_i) then
15             pbest_i ← p_i;
16             if f(p_i) < f(gbest) then
17                 gbest ← p_i;
18             end
19         end
20     end
21 end
```

Algorithm 1 outlines the basic PSO. The algorithm assumes a swarm size of N, and D problem objectives or dimensions. Termination criteria will either be a maximum number of iterations of the algorithm, or the detection of a particle whose fitness is within a minimal requirement. The conventional PSO outlined is distinguished by the fitness evaluator f returning a single-value numeric result, where lower values are preferred. Should the problem in question have multiple objectives to satisfy, then a weighted sum formula is used:

$$f(\mathbf{p}) = \sum_{j=1}^{K} w_j f_j$$

where there are K constraints $\mathbf{p} = (f_1, ..., f_K)$, and w_j is a weight factor.

The next two sections present alternative ways of calculating the fitness of a particle optimizing a problem with multiple objectives.

3.2 The SR-PSO Algorithm

A new PSO algorithm, the sum of ranks PSO (SR-PSO), is introduced. It is largely the same as the PSO in Algorithm 1. The main difference is the method by which fitness scores are found in the multi-objective search space. Given a multi-objective problem to solve by the PSO, instead of using the conventional PSO's weighted sum formula (equation (1)), the sum of ranks scoring method discussed in Section 2 is used. This alternate scoring will be incorporated into line 12 of Algorithm 1.

In order to find $pbest_i$ and *gbest*, the SR-PSO uses *archives* of particle's multi-objective score vectors for determining sum of ranks scores. Each particle has its own *particle archive* of personal best vectors. Similarly, the swarm has a *global archive* recording best vectors seen overall. The sum of ranks calculation is applied to these archives during each iteration of the PSO. The lowest sum of ranks scores for the archives are used to identify the *pbest* for each particle, and the *gbest* for the swarm. An effect of this is that the current swarm's *gbest* may not coincide with the global archive's *gbest*. In such circumstances, the global archive's *gbest* will be a positive influence the swarm.

Archives are processed as follows. To update the global archive's *gbest*, the sum of ranks algorithm determines the current *gbest* from the population and adds this agent to the global archive. If there is a tied rank score for the current best, all tied vectors are added to the archive. The archive is then scored by sum of ranks, and the top scoring vector is selected as the simulation best. Particle archives are processed similarly. Since archives might grow large during long runs, a user-supplied size limit on archives is used.

3.3 The Pareto PSO

The multi-objective PSO algorithm of Mostaghim and Teich was selected as a comparison algorithm (see [21] for a more in-depth discussion). Each agent s assigned a fitness gradient (slope) value σ. For a 2-dimensional problem:

$$\sigma = \frac{f_1^2 - f_2^2}{f_1^2 + f_2^2} \quad (3)$$

N-dimensional problems have higher-dimensional gradients. A global archive of Pareto nondominated best solutions is maintained, along with their σ values. To determine the *gbest* to use for a particle, the Pareto nondominated particle in the archives with the closest gradient to that particle is determined, and is selected as the guide for the particle. If an agent is already considered to be Pareto optimal then it uses itself as the *gbest*. The rationale for this approach is that such a selected guide will direct the particle more directly towards the Pareto front. Each particle's *pbest* is computed in the conventional way as in Section 3.1.

3.4 Bootstrapping

An option called *bootstrapping* is available. Image evaluation rules in Section 4 such as object detection and rule of thirds are not measurable if an object of interest is not seen in an image. When this happens, only rules such as colour palette matching and horizon line return meaningful scores, and the swarm will optimize only these rules, and ignore the others. With bootstrapping, the PSO will repeatedly randomize particles until at least one particle has spotted an object of interest. Once such an object is found, object detection and rule of thirds will be measurable, and this will improve PSO performance across multiple objectives.

4. COMPOSITION RULES

Four composition rules are used. Experiments can use multiple instances of these constraints, possibly on different objects of interest. As elsewhere [1, 8, 19], composition rules are highly modular, and new rules can be readily added as desired.

4.1 Rule of Thirds

The rule of thirds is one of the most important composition rules [18]. An image is subdivided into thirds horizontally and vertically. The areas around the four intersections are positions where dominant objects of interest should reside. To implement the rule of thirds, the pixel mask for objects of interest is determined (Section 4.3). If an object of interest is found in the image, the centroid for its visibly rendered pixels (n total) is determined:

$$C_{x,y} = \frac{\sum [x,y]}{n}$$

Then the Euclidean distances between $C_{x,y}$ and each of the four rule of thirds locations is determined. The least distance found is assigned as the rule of thirds score.

4.2 Horizon Line

The horizon line rule also uses the concept of proportion of thirds. The horizon is the delineation line where the sky meets the land. The horizon line rule states that the horizon should reside at a proportion of either one-third or two-thirds vertically in an image[17]. The implementation of the horizon line rule first requires a mask image to be rendered, with the mask indicating the ground and sky in the scene. The horizon line, if visible, is easily determined from this mask. Note that cameras are not permitted to roll, and so the horizon will always be horizontal. Next, the shortest vertical distance between the horizon and one of the horizon rule lines (at the one-third and two-thirds positions) is calculated. The smaller of these distances is used as the horizon rule score.

4.3 Object of Interest

Subject matter is an important factor in photography. The automation of object recognition is an advanced computer vision topic beyond the scope of this research. Since we are working in a virtual 3D environment, however, we exploit the system's knowledge of the models rendered in an image. Each object is rendered with a colour-coded mask value. This mask image is examined to see whether a particular object of interest is rendered within it. Furthermore, the percentage of area of that object relative to the total image can be determined. Using this idea, we can specify a desired area (%) that an object of interest should have within an image.

4.4 Colour Palette

Colour is an important aspect of aesthetics, as it conveys mood in an image. It is also a means to help identify subject matter. The *Colour Histogram Quadratic Matching* algorithm [23] is used to determine the colour match between a rendered image from the PSO and the target colour image. A colour target image is supplied to the system. This image specifies a desired colour palette, as well as relative amount of each colour. A quantized colour histogram is generated for the colour target image at the beginning of a run. When evaluating a PSO image, the image is processed to generate another quantized colour histogram. Then the quadratic histogram distance is computed, which measures each colour of one histogram with every colour in the other, producing a relaxed measurement of colour correspondence.

5. SYSTEM ARCHITECTURE

Table 2: Rotation and field of view constraints

$Rotation_X$	$30° \leq R_x \leq 150°$
$Rotation_Y$	N/A (camera roll not allowed)
$Rotation_Z$	$0° \leq R_z \leq 360°$
FoV	$40° \leq fov \leq 72°$

Each agent in the swarm is a camera in a virtual environment capable of generating an image based on the direction it is facing. Three properties modify the camera: *Location* (x,y,z), *Rotation*, and *Field of View (FoV)*. To prevent gimbal lock (rotation issues from using Euler angles) in the camera from the *Rotation* and undesired rendering artifacts from the *FoV*, constraints were included (Table 2). These properties are stored in a vector, which every PSO agent uses to determine the camera location and viewpoint in the environment.

We implemented a virtual 3D environment with 3ds Studio Max [2]. A custom plug-in was written in *C#* and *MaxScript* to manipulate an agent's camera in the scene and render the current viewport of the camera. Three independent modules (Image Analysis, Particle Swarm Optimization and 3ds Max) are loaded and executed in parallel. The Image Analysis component analyzes an agent's image and return fitness values. The PSO algorithm uses these fitness values to update the swarm, by modifying every agent's state vector in the swarm. Then each agents vector is transferred to 3ds Max. 3ds Max updates the *Location*, *Rotation*, and *FoV* of the respective camera within the world, and renders a new image. Once all agents are updated, the process iterates until the simulation is complete.

6. RESULTS

Table 3: PSO parameters

Number of Runs	30
Swarm size	25
Max iterations	100
Inertia	0.8
Personal best constraint (c_1)	0.45
Global best constraint (c_2)	0.5

Table 4: Fitness ranges for objectives.

Fitness Objective	Fitness Range
Object Detection (OD)	$0 \leq f \leq 153600$
Rule of Thirds (ROT)	$0 \leq f \leq 800$
Horizon Line (HZ)	$0 \leq f \leq 240$
Colour Similarity (CS)	$0.0 \leq f \leq 1.0$

The virtual worlds used here are typical of those found in video games and computer animations. The problem specifications used have between 6 to 10 objectives. These are potentially challenging problems for the PSO, given that conflicting objectives will arise.

Table 3 are the PSO parameters used for all these examples. They were determined during exploratory runs, and are not claimed to be optimal. The c_1 and c_2 constraints are from Equation (1), which in turn is used in Algorithm 1. Table 4 give the expected ranges for different scores.

6.1 Sunrise

Table 5: Sunrise objectives

1.	Object detection: boat on land (10%)
2.	Object detection: boat in water (10%)
3.	Object detection: Sun (5%)
4.	Rule of thirds: boat on land
5.	Rule of thirds: boat in water
6.	Rule of thirds: Sun
7.	Horizon line
8.	Colour similarity

This example of an ocean sunrise scene uses 8 objectives in total (Table 5). There are two boats and a Sun as objects of interest, all of which should be composed with the rule of thirds. Each boat should use 10% of the image area. Figure 1(a) shows one view of the environment.

Two result images are shown in Figure 1 (b) and (c), and their objective scores are shown in Table 6. Image (b) is typical of the results obtained, and has tried to satisfy most of the requirements. However, it is difficult applying the rule of thirds to both ships and the Sun simultaneously, and so the boat in the water is off on this. On the other hand, image (c) is an example of an anomalous result image. It has missed both ship objects (see the poor OD and ROT scores for the ships in Table 6), but has obtained better Sun ROT and horizon scores. Although the sum of ranks scoring usually discourages such anomalies, they can sometimes arise. Therefore, PSO algorithms are almost always executed many times on a problem, in order to generate a set of solutions for consideration.

Table 6: Objective scores for images in Fig. 1.

Objective	(b)	(c)
OD boat land (%)	17.0	–
OD boat water (%)	19.3	–
OD Sun (%)	9.9	9.9
ROT boat land	0.33	800.0
ROT boat water	10.87	800.0
ROT Sun	75.89	22.32
HZ	18	2
CS	0.011	0.019

Table 7: Frequency that algorithm beat others on Sunrise scene objectives (95% confidence). Table values represent # objectives in which algorithm A beat algorithm B (maximum 8).

	B		
A	SRB	NB	PB
SRB	-	4	5
NB	1	-	4
PB	0	0	-

Images (d) through (f) in Figure 1 are screen captures from an animation of the swarm in action.[2] The initial state of the swarm is shown in (d), where the particles are scattered randomly throughout the environment. As the simulation proceeds in (e), the swarm begins to converge as the particles detect objects of interest. The swarm converges in (f), which almost always happened in all our runs.

A comparison is done of the bootstrapped sum of ranks (SRB), bootstrapped Pareto PSO (PB) from [21], and bootstrapped normal PSO (NB). Given the many objectives to consider, a statistical analysis was undertaken to clearly summarize the performance. Each algorithm was run 30 times, and 30 solutions were obtained. (For the Pareto PSO, an arbitrary rank 1 solution was taken from each run.) The non-parametric Mann-Whitney U test was used to test when one algorithm performed statistically better than another on a particular objective (95% confidence level). The number of times each algorithm outperformed another on each objective was tallied (Table 7). The table shows that both the sum of ranks PSO and conventional PSO outperformed the Pareto PSO on half or more of the objectives. The sum of ranks PSO also did better than the conventional PSO on half the objectives. This gives evidence that the sum of ranks PSO is indeed suitable for high-dimensional multi-objective search, as seen in the problem studied.

6.2 Space

Table 8: Space objectives

1.	Object detection: boat on land (10%)
2.	Object detection: boat in water (10%)
3.	Object detection: red moon (5%)
4.	Object detection: blue moon (5%)
5.	Rule of thirds: boat on land
6.	Rule of thirds: boat in water
7.	Rule of thirds: red moon
8.	Rule of thirds: blue moon
9.	Horizon line
10.	Colour similarity

This example enhances the previous scene, by replacing the Sun with two moons. The objectives are similarly defined (Table 8). Figure 2 shows 3 solution images, and Table 9 shows the scores. There is no perfect solution, given that the swarm struggles to position all four objects at one of

[2]`http://www.cosc.brocku.ca/~bross/psoPhotos/`

(a) Environment.

(b) Result 1.

(c) Result 2. Ships missing, but Sun and horizon composed well.

(d) Swarm in initial scattered state.

(e) Swarm starts to converge.

(f) Swarm close to convergence.

Figure 1: Sunrise experiment.

Table 9: Objective scores for images in Fig. 2.

Objective	(a)	(b)	(c)
OD boat land (%)	18.4	16.2	18.1
OD boat water (%)	19.0	19.2	19.4
OD red moon (%)	9.9	10.0	10.0
OD blue moon (%)	9.9	10.0	10.0
ROT boat land	1.33	43.52	13.62
ROT boat water	79.40	18.11	1.94
ROT red moon	31.48	37.67	31.69
ROT blue moon	45.88	24.40	37.42
HZ	11	27	1
CS	0.023	0.028	0.005

the rule of thirds loci, and satisfy object detection requirements. All three solutions show different compositional compromises in satisfying the competing criteria.

A comparison of the 3 PSO algorithms is shown in Table 10. The Pareto PSO was further outmatched by both the conventional PSO and sum of ranks PSO. Once again, the sum of ranks PSO statistically outperformed the other algorithms on more objectives simultaneously.

6.3 Table Conversation

This example highlights the effect of colour matching as a problem objective. Here, we are to find two specific people in a crowd of eight. The two people of interest will be identified via the colour similarity test, based on their clothing colour. Therefore, the PSO cannot rely on the OD algorithm to uniquely identify the pair of individuals, but instead must use the CS test to find them. The scene was set up so that

Table 10: Frequency that algorithm beat others on Space scene objectives (95% confidence). (See Table 7.)

	B		
A	SRB	NB	PB
SRB	-	4	8
NB	0	-	9
PB	0	0	-

Table 11: Table Conversation objectives

1.	Object detection: male face (10%)
2.	Object detection: female face (10%)
3.	Rule of thirds: male face
4.	Rule of thirds: female face
5.	Horizon line
6.	Colour similarity

the four male faces have the same model mask identifier, and similarly for the females. This means that all the people can satisfy the OD requirements, which forces the colour test to come into consideration. Table 11 lists the objectives for this simulation. The colour similarity image is also placed as a bitmap on the table (see Fig. 3(c)), which acts as a decoy to trick the swarm when evaluating colour similarity.

Three results are shown in Figure 3, and their objective scores are in Table 12. In 3(a), the simulation found multiple faces for both female and male but managed to find the two people of interest (both partially obscured by man in green

(a) Result 1. (b) Result 2. (c) Result 3.

Figure 2: Image results for the Space environment.

(a) Result 1: Top in CS, HZ. (b) Result 2: Top in OD male & female. Result 3: Top in OD female.

Figure 3: Image results for the Table Conversation scene.

Table 12: Objective scores for images in Fig. 3.

Objective	(a)	(b)	(c)
OD male (%)	19.7	**18.1**	19.5
OD female (%)	19.9	**19.7**	19.8
ROT male	10.79	**7.45**	8.54
ROT female	7.01	21.94	**0.10**
HZ	**0**	**0**	3
CS	0.061	0.086	**0.110**

shirt) by using the colour similarity. Image 3(b) manages to find multiple males and females in the scene, but focuses on the female subject in the yellow shirt. Image 3(c) finds the people of interest, and composes them well with the rule of thirds. The "decoy" bitmap on the table, although visible in the image, did not distract the swarm from obtaining good OD scores. This shows that the sum of ranks was not overly influenced by a single good-scoring objective. With Pareto, however, the decoy's excellent colour match score could mean all the other objectives would be ignored.

The above results show that solutions obtained in multi-objective problems are often compromises. As the scope and number of objectives increases, a balance must be found in satisfying objectives. For example, image (b) has the best object detection and rule of thirds scores for the male, but has poor OD and ROT scores for the female. These "democratic compromises" naturally arise with the sum of ranks strategy.

7. COMPARISON TO RELATED WORK

Di Gaspero *et al.* [8, 19] introduced the use of PSOs for virtual photography. They use upwards of 10 rules, which are divided into mandatory *hard objectives* and optional *soft objectives*. Their PSO requires the user to supply objective weights. Compared to our system, their rules require the user to specify a much lower level of detail, for example, positions within the frame, and object distances. We did not use weights (although they are optional). Our bootstrapping idea is similar to their hard constraints. Similarly, Abdullah *et al.* [1] use a conventional PSO for virtual photography. They also require user-supplied weights to balance objectives, which we did not require.

Recently, Burelli and Preuss used multi-objective optimization for automatic composition [9]. There, a nondominated hypervolume is used as a fitness measure. A comparison of their approach and our sum of ranks would be interesting.

8. CONCLUSIONS

We have proposed a new technique for automatic virtual photography. The SR-PSO is can handle the high number of conflicting objectives found in virtual photography problems. Empirical comparisons against a conventional PSO and a Pareto-based PSO showed its effectiveness. Furthermore, problem-specific weights were not required. This contrasts to other work with conventional PSO's, which require objective weights and user micromanagement of compositional specifications, for example, low-level measurement requirements of compositions.

Additional details of this research, such as additional algorithm comparisons and other experiments, are described in [4]. All runs were done on a dual quad core Intel running at 2.9 GHz with 4G RAM. Runs took between 11 and 21 hours to process, largly due to the raytraced rendering required. Although execution time of the PSO system was not of primary concern to us, future work should consider execution efficiency.

There are many other directions for future work. The introduction of more intelligent computer vision analyses is worth consideration, for example, automatic face recognition. More advanced virtual photography needs computer vision algorithms for object detection and recognition. These would be necessary if PSO photography were to be applied to non-virtual, real-world environments. More intelligent image analyses might also include knowledge-based approaches to virtual/real environment search. More intelligent search, perhaps looking for human subjects to photograph, would first look for instances of human habitation (towns, houses, roads, ...) within the virtual or real world, knowing that humans are likely to be found in such settings.

There has been much research in the field of multi-objective PSO [16]. The sum of ranks PSO should be empirically compared to other MOP PSO's on virtual photography problems, as well as other MOP problems in the literature. The issue of swarm diversity is also worth consideration. Adding diversity heuristics to a multi-objective PSO would result in a variety of alternative solution images from a single run.

There is also the opportunity to introduce more advanced rules of composition and aesthetics as found in [10, 17, 18]. However, implementing many of these sophisticated principles of composition requires advanced computer vision and artificial intelligence.

Acknowledgements: Thanks to Beatrice Ombuki-Berman, Vladimir Wojcik and Marcus Dos Santos for their helpful advice. This research is partially supported by NSERC DG 138467.

9. REFERENCES

[1] R. Abdullah, M. Christie, G. Schofield, C. Lino, and P. Olivier. Advanced composition in virtual camera control. *Proc. 11th Intl. Conf. on Smart Graphics (SG 11)*, pages 13–24, 2011.

[2] Autodesk. 3ds max 2009. *http://usa.autodesk.com/*, August 2012.

[3] W. Bares and B. Kim. Generating virtual camera compositions. In *Proc. 6th Intl. Conf. on Intelligent User Interfaces*, IUI '01, pages 9–12, New York, NY, USA, 2001. ACM.

[4] W. Barry. Generating aesthetically pleasing images in a virtual environment using particle swarm optimization. Master's thesis, Brock U., 2012.

[5] P. Bentley and J. Wakefield. Finding acceptable solutions in the pareto-optimal range using multiobjective genetic algorithms. In P. C. et al., editor, *Soft Computing in Engineering Design and Manufacturing*, pages 231–240. Springer-Verlag, 1998.

[6] S. Bergen and B. Ross. Evolutionary Art Using Summed Multi-objective Ranks. In *Genetic Programming - Theory and Practice VIII*, pages 227–244. Springer, May 2010.

[7] S. Bhattacharya, R. Sukthankar, and M. Shah. A Holistic Approach to Aesthetic Enhancement of Photographs. *ACM Trans. Multimedia Comp., Comm. and Apps.*, 7S(1):1–21, October 2012.

[8] P. Burelli, L. Gaspero, A. Ermetici, and R. Ranon. Virtual camera composition with particle swarm optimization. *Proc. 9th Intl. Symp. on Smart Graphics (SG 08)*, pages 130 – 141, 2008.

[9] P. Burelli and M. Preuss. Automatic camera control: a dynamic multi-objective perspective. In *Evostar 2014*. Springer, April 2014.

[10] P. Burian. *Mastering Digital Photography and Imaging*. Wiley, 2006.

[11] C. C. Coello, G. Lamont, and D. van Veldhuizen. *Evolutionary Algorithms for Solving Multi-Objective Problems*. Springer-Verlag, New York, 2006.

[12] D. Corne and J. Knowles. Techniques for highly multiobjective optimisation: Some nondominated points are better than others. In *Proc. GECCO*, pages 773–780, New York, NY, 2007. ACM.

[13] K. Deb. *Multi-Objective Optimization Using Evolutionary Algorithms*. Wiley, 2009.

[14] S. Desroche, V. Jolivet, and D. Plemenos. Towards plan-based automatic exploration of virtual worlds. *Proc. Int'l Conf. Central Europe on Computer Graphics, Visualization and Computer Vision (WSCG).*, 1:25–32, 2007.

[15] R. Eberhart and J. Kennedy. A new optimizer using particle swarm theory. *Proc. IEEE Intl. Conf. Neural Networks*, 4:1942 – 1948, 1995.

[16] J. Fieldsend. Multi-objective particle swarm optimisation methods. Technical report, TR419, Dept. Computer Science, U. Exeter, 2004.

[17] B. Fier. *Composition Photo Workshop*. Wiley, 2007.

[18] M. Freeman. *The Photographer's Eye: Composition & Design for Better Digital Photos*. Focal Press, 2007.

[19] L. D. Gaspero, A. Ermetici, and R. Ranon. Swarming in a virtual world: A pso approach to virtual camera composition. *ANTS 2008*, LNCS 5217:155–166, 2008.

[20] N. Michael, J. Fink, and V. Kumar. Cooperative manipulation and transportation with aerial robots. *Autonomous Robots*, 30(1):73–86, Jan 2011.

[21] S. Mostaghim and J. Teich. Strategies for finding good local guides in multi-objective particle swarm optimization (mopso). In *Proc. IEEE Swarm Intelligence Symp.*, 2003.

[22] M. Preuss, P. Burelli, and G. Yannnakakis. Diversified virtual camera composition. In *Proc. European Conf. on Applications of Evolutionary Computation*, pages 265–274, Malaga, Spain, 2012. Springer-Verlag.

[23] J. Smith and S. Chang. VisualSEEk: a fully automated content-based image query system. In *Proc. 4th ACM Intl. Conf. on Multimedia*, pages 87–98. ACM Press, 1996.

[24] R. Swanson, D. Escoffery, and A. Jhala. Learning visual composition preferences from an annotated corpus generated through gameplay. In *Computational Intelligence and Games*, pages 363–370. IEEE, Sept 2012.

[25] F.-L. Zhang, M. Wang, and S.-M. Hu. Aesthetic Image Enhancement by Dependence-Aware Object Re-Composition. *IEEE Trans. on Multimedia*, 15, June 2013.

Monte Mario: Platforming with MCTS

Emil Juul Jacobsen
IT University of Copenhagen
Rued Langgaards Vej 7
Copenhagen, Denmark
ejuu@itu.dk

Rasmus Greve
IT University of Copenhagen
Rued Langgaards Vej 7
Copenhagen, Denmark
ragr@itu.dk

Julian Togelius
IT University of Copenhagen
Rued Langgaards Vej 7
Copenhagen, Denmark
julian@togelius.com

ABSTRACT

Monte Carlo Tree Search (MCTS) is applied to control the player character in a clone of the popular platform game Super Mario Bros. Standard MCTS is applied through search in state space with the goal of moving the furthest to the right as quickly as possible. Despite parameter tuning, only moderate success is reached. Several modifications to the algorithm are then introduced specifically to deal with the behavioural pathologies that were observed. Two of the modifications are to our best knowledge novel. A combination of these modifications is found to lead to almost perfect play on linear levels. Furthermore, when adding noise to the benchmark, MCTS outperforms the best known algorithm for these levels. The analysis and algorithmic innovations in this paper are likely to be useful when applying MCTS to other video games.

1. INTRODUCTION

Monte Carlo Tree Search (MCTS) is a relatively recently devised statistical tree search method [2] that has proven to be remarkably good at playing classic board games such as *Go* [8]. MCTS has also shown promise when it comes to playing unseen games such as those in the *General Game Playing Competition* [6], partly due to not relying on a state evaluation function. In both of these domains, MCTS is arguably the best method available, as variations of this algorithm tops the leagues for computer players. Naturally, it has therefore been suggested that MCTS has much broader applicability than this, presenting a viable approach to all of game AI or perhaps even all of AI. However, in domains such as Go and general game playing[1] games are played in a relatively small number of discrete turns and the state of the game is discrete and can be described using a relatively small number of variables. In other words, not only are they discrete-time and discrete-state, both the time and state space are highly constrained.

Most games that we think of as "video games" are completely different from this. It is very common to emulate some of the physical aspects of the "real world", which at a human scale is continuous-time and continuous-space. While digital computers are by their nature discrete state machines, the state space of a computer is vast, and continuous state and time in a game world can be approximated using floating point numbers and multiple frames per second. Thus, first-person shooter games such as *Halo* or *Bioshock*, real-time strategy games such as *StarCraft* or *Age of Empires* and action adventure games such as *Tomb Raider* and *Skyrim* typically have game states that update 30 or 60 times per second, and where the position of each object or character is denoted by a 32 or 64 bit floating point value per dimension. These circumstances would seem to pose significant obstacles for any method based on evaluating all possible actions (moves) at each time step (turn). Therefore, we feel it is an open question whether MCTS can be made to perform well in pseudo-continuous game domains, and how.

There have been a few recent attempts to apply MCTS to such domains. In particular, there has been considerable work on applying MCTS to the Physical Travelling Salesman Problem (PTSP), which can be described as a mix between the classic TSP problem and a racing game. This game has pseudo-continuous space, but very few actions available per time step and a static game world. It was found that MCTS-based agents exhibit human-competitive performance, but only after several modifications, including macro-actions that constitute several smaller actions [10, 11]. MCTS has also been applied to small-scale combat scenarios in StarCraft with moderate success [4]. Multiple attempts has been made at applying MCTS to *Ms. Pac-Man* both for controlling the Pac-Man agent as well as for ghost enemy control with great success [12], [9].

In this paper, we consider the problem of playing *Super Mario Bros*, or more accurately the *Mario AI Benchmark*, which is based on a clone of that game, using MCTS. This is not only an important game representative of a very popular genre, but also provides a different kind of challenge than anything that has been attempted with MCTS so far. Though it shares some properties with Ms. Pac-Man as both games require realtime decision making and give the player the option of allowing the agent to "procrastinate" by not making any progress towards an end state. In the next

[1]With "general game playing", we are here referring to the type of games used in the existing GGP competition and expressible in that language, elsewhere referred to as "Stanford GDL"; other types are certainly possible and even proposed [5].

GECCO'14, July 12–16, 2014, Vancouver, BC, Canada.

ACM 978-1-4503-2662-9/14/07 ...$15.00.
http://dx.doi.org/10.1145/2576768.2598392.

two sections we give a brief background on both MCTS and the Mario AI Benchmark. We then describe the particular way in which we applied MCTS to the Mario AI Benchmark, and describe the unsatisfactory behaviour of "vanilla" MCTS. The next section describes a number of modifications to the algorithm that we developed specifically to counter the identified failures of MCTS on this problem. The results section details the quantitative performance of MCTS with and without the modifications, and compares it to A* search in state space, which has performed well on these levels. The results analysis section qualitatively discusses the behaviour of the algorithm for selected combinations of modifications. After noting that the deterministic nature of the benchmark does not exploit the strength of MCTS in handling unpredictable behaviour, we produce a noisy version of the benchmark, and again compare its performance to A*.

In the result tables in this paper, we compare each result with a specified other result and show how statistically significantly different they are. Statistical significance levels are denoted by stars (*) or daggers (†) and the levels are: * means $p \leq 0.05$, ** means $p \leq 0.01$ and *** means $p \leq 0.0005$,

2. MONTE CARLO TREE SEARCH

MCTS is a tree search algorithm in which evaluation of a node is done by performing random actions from the decision space until an outcome can be determined. MCTS is an *anytime* algorithm, meaning that it can be halted when a time limit expires and give the result that looks the most promising at the given time. Furthermore it often requires little, if any, domain knowledge because a basic implementation only requires knowledge of the action space and a means of simulating the outcome of an action.

Searching using MCTS is done by iteratively building a search tree where the nodes are different game states, and the edges are the actions leading to one state from another. A node is added to the tree during each iteration and recursively, based on the reward of the new node, the reward values of parent nodes are updated. A single iteration of the MCTS building process consists of these four steps:

1. Tree Policy (A node to be expanded is chosen)
2. Expansion (The node is expanded by simulating the associated action)
3. Default Policy (The game is simulated following a random path until a terminal node is reached)
4. Backpropagation (The result propagates up through the tree)

Upper Confidence Bound for Trees (UCT) is a bandit based approach to choosing the most urgent node to expand. The benefit from UCT is that it allows for prioritizing between exploitation of seemingly promising nodes (first term) and exploration of less tried nodes (second term).

$$UCB_j = \overline{X}_j + C_p \cdot \sqrt{\frac{2 \cdot \ln(n)}{n_j}} \quad (1)$$

Equation 1 is used for calculating the Upper Confidence Bound for node j. Here $\overline{X}_j$ is the average (i.e. expected) reward over the times (n_j) node j has been visited and C_p is a constant for adjusting the weight of the exploration term. n is the total number of expansions and n_j is the number of times node j was selected. Since the exploration term of the equation depends on how explored the node is compared to the parent, the confidence in a node will increase steadily until the node is eventually explored. The exploitation term will, however, make sure that good nodes will be explored more frequently than less promising ones.

3. THE MARIO AI BENCHMARK

Super Mario Bros (SMB), published by Nintendo in 1985, is one of the world's best-selling games and certainly one of the most influential. It introduced the canonical form of side-scrolling platform games, and its design has inspired countless games since. *Infinite Mario Bros* (IMB) is a Java-based clone of SMB by Notch. IMB is the basis for the Mario AI Benchmark, a benchmark for artificial intelligence that has been used in a series of international competitions [7].

In IMB, the player controls Mario, who can be made to walk or run left or right, jump, and can be upgraded to jump through bricks and spit fire. The main objective in each level is to reach the end (the rightmost point) of the level, which involves dodging or killing enemies and not falling into gaps. The original game is controlled with a joypad and two buttons; in the Mario AI Benchmark, an action is defined as 5 bits (buttons: left, right, down, a, b), yielding 32 possible actions. 25 times per second, the controller is presented with a representation of the area surrounding Mario (one screen) and asked to return what action to take.

The first Mario AI competition, which ran in 2009, was won by Robin Baumgarten who implemented an agent based on A* search in state space [14]. At every time step, the agent tried to find the shortest path towards the right edge of the current screen (that is, in the direction of the end of the level) using a simple heuristic based on horizontal position. This agent managed to consistenly clear the linear levels that was used in the 2009 competition, but lost its top position when levels that require backtracking were introduced in the 2010 competition [1].

4. MCTS IN MARIO

When searching the action space using MCTS we found the heaviest computation to be the simulation of actions on a given state. This makes it practically impossible to perform the rollout to termination and even in that case it would practically always be a death.

This led us to experiment with several different evaluation functions for calculating the reward value of a non-terminal state. The first logical solution would be to use the x-distance to the right edge of the screen (as far as Mario can see) and let the value be the fraction between the initial position (for this tick) and the edge of the screen. This, however, gave very bad results with Mario unable to clear even small obstacles and consistently running backwards when facing Bullet Bills flying towards him.

Another approach was to make the value relative to only the position of the parent node and let the maximum reward be the furthest you could potentially go by running directly to the right. This evaluation function shows much better performance and is what we have chosen to use.

$$reward_j = \frac{1}{2} + \frac{1}{2} \cdot \frac{x_j - x_p}{11 \cdot (1 + n_R)} \tag{2}$$

In Equation 2 x_j is the current node's final x-coordinate and x_p is the parent's. The denominator of the right term is the maximum x-distance Mario can run in one tick where n_R is the chosen rollout length cap. This value is always within the range of 0 to 1.

Since the levels generated in this version of Super Mario did not require the use of the "down" key, and including it among the possible actions degraded performance greatly, we removed that key from the action set.

For the simulation of future game states we use the LevelScene model by Robin Baumgarten [14] which was originally extracted from the game engine itself in order to obtain the correct behaviour of monsters and objects. This model is provided with the environment information given to the agent to start the simulation from the current game state. Each node in the search tree therefore contains the LevelScene as its state and the different childrens' states are the result of performing a specific action on the current node's state. Each node has capacity for a child corresponding to each possible action for the possibility to explore in all possible directions.

4.1 Parameters

Since we had to decide how long the roll out phase could continue for we had to determine the best rollout depth cap for our basic MCTS implementation. To do this we have performed a series of benchmarks. The results can be seen in Table 1 where we have highlighted the most promising value. The mean score in our benchmarking is the mean of x-distance traveled in each of the 100 levels. Due to how the levels are randomly generated their length can vary slightly but are generally around 4300 pixels.

The roll out depth cap we chose did not give the highest value, but has a low average completion time and has a score very close to the highest valued one.

We have done the same kind of parameter tuning for the C_p value (for UCB calculation). The results can be found in table 2. We chose the value of 0.25 for C_p since it has shown good results and behaviour on manual tests and the highest score is not significantly different. The rollout cap and C_p values chosen here have been used in all further tests and modifications.

Rollout Cap	Mean Score	Avg. Time Left
0	1220***	-
1	1430***	116
2	1790***	138
4	2684***	134
6	**3861**	**134**
8	3843	120
10	2930***	93
12	1724***	71
16	922***	11
$1 * 10^6$	248***	-

Table 1: Results of vanilla MCTS with various rollout depth cap. These calculations are performed with a C_p-value of 0.25 on 100 levels. The results are the mean score of all levels and the average time left from completed levels. The stars denote the statistical significance of difference from the results of all measurements and the result from using a rollout cap of 6.

C_p-value	Mean Score	Avg. Time Left
0	3319***	131
0.188 (1.5/8)	3993	134
0.25	**3950**	**131**
0.333	3868	132
0.5	3859	132
0.707 ($1/\sqrt{2}$)	3815	129
2	3886	132
5	3791	130
10	3868	130

Table 2: Results of vanilla MCTS with various C_p values with rollout depth cap of 6. These calculations are performed with a rollout depth cap of 6 on 100 levels. The results are the mean score of all levels and the average left over time from completed levels. The stars denote the statistical significance of difference from the results of all measurements and the result from using a C_p value of 0.25.

5. MODIFICATIONS TO MCTS

The performance of the MCTS-based agent was not dreadfully bad, but not satisfactory, and far from the elegance of Baumgarten's A* agent. There were several failures: Mario was sometimes unable to jump over tall cannons, was very reluctant to jump over gaps, sometimes fell into gaps and ran straight into enemies. Mario seemed shortsighted and cowardly. Based on this qualitative analysis, we suggested the following improvements.

5.1 Mixmax rewards

When calculating the confidence of a node by the average value of its children, the resulting behaviour of Super Mario will be quite defensive. This is because a single good path among many dangerous ones will only increase the average value slightly.

Mixmax Q-value	Mean Score	Avg. Time Left
0 (Avg.)	4029	131
0.125	**4103**	**146**
0.25	4093	149
0.375	3846**	151
0.5	4007	152
0.75	3753**	153
1 (Max)	2098***	153

Table 3: Results of using Mixmax backup with different Q values on 100 levels. The results are the mean score of all levels and the average time left from completed levels. The stars denote the statistical significance of the difference from each measurement to the result of using $Q = 0.125$

This can be alleviated by calculating the total reward as a mix between the average value and the maximum value between the children. Equation 3 show the use of the constant Q as a factor between the two values. This value will then be used for the UCB calculation (in Equation 1 replacing $\overline{X}_j$).

$$exploitation = Q \cdot max + (1 - Q) \cdot \overline{X}_j \quad (3)$$

Through experiments (See table 3) we have observed that a Q-value of 0.125 yields the best results and is better than both average ($Q = 0$) and maximum ($Q = 1$) while having a much better average completion time.

5.2 Macro-actions

In Super Mario, the pace at which new moves are to be decided is so fast that the search tree rarely gets deeper than 4-5 levels. This results in Mario making decisions based purely on the very nearest surroundings, and possibly taking a bad route on the macroscopic level. (E.g. choosing to jump into a pack of monsters instead of taking a peaceful route above them on another path). Because Macro Actions have been previously shown to be a good enhancement for MCTS allowing a tradeoff between precision and strategic quality in a realtime continous domain [11], it is interesting to see how it changes the performance of MCTS in Super Mario.

Macro Actions allows us to make better use of the limited search depth by simulating further into the level via a coarse path. This is achieved by modifying the expansion process such that instead of performing the action just once, it is repeated a predefined number of times before a child node is created. After an action has been decided upon, it is performed this same number of repetitions, thus leaving more time to expand on the same search tree.

In some cases the coarse route and the commitment to repeating an action a certain number of times is, however, not optimal. In particular, close to monsters or gaps there is a need for micro-planning where every action taken can be different. When close to monsters, the monsters must be avoided or hit correctly in order to stay alive, and when close to gaps, the best way to jump over them is to move close to the edge before jumping. Consequently our implementation switches to the normal action size of 1 when in danger, which is determined by being either close to a monster or a gap. The distance thresholds for being close have been determined by just a few loose experiments as this enhancement alone is not the focus of the study. This does include some domain-knowledge into the implementation of macro-actions.

5.3 Partial Expansion

Simulating a move in Super Mario has proven to be a relatively time consuming operation. Since about half the possible actions lead in the wrong direction with respect to where the finish line is, it seems superfluous to simulate them if it can be avoided.

The strategy "progressive unpruning" deals with the issue of having a large branching factor and little time, by first reducing the branching factor artificially, and then unprune actions when more time is available [3]. In Partial Expansion we follow this idea, but instead of reducing the branching factor, we simply add the option of traversing partially expanded nodes. In the tree policy step of MCTS the urgency of expanding a new child is calculated and compared to the confidences for each existing child. Only if the urgency for creating a new child exceeds any of the childrens' confidences a new child is created. With this change UCT can either choose to exploit a promising path, or expand another unexplored action.

$$UCB_c = k + C_p \cdot \sqrt{\frac{2 \cdot \ln(n)}{1 + c_n}} \quad (4)$$

Equation 4 calculates the urgency of creating a new child and is quite similar to Equation 1, but with some differences, since the non-existent nodes don't have a calculated reward and have never been visited. The k-value is the standard reward for non-existent children, we set this constant to 0.5. c_n is the number of expanded children on the current node. This way nodes will be gradually expanded with nodes higher in the tree being expanded more than lower ones.

This results in a deeper tree since the average branching factor of the nodes is significantly reduced, but when selecting the child to expand randomly you risk missing promising paths. The higher branches of the tree will, however, be expanded more than the lower, and since the deeper levels of the tree have less immediate effect on the state this risk isn't very high.

5.4 Roulette wheel selection

Our implementation of MCTS expand nodes through multiple iterations, and not all children at once. This requires that we decide an order in which children are to be generated. Normally this is chosen at random, but by introducing some domain knowledge, the generally most beneficial actions can be chosen for expansion first. Expanding some actions before others does not have a great impact on its own, but it does skew the search tree in a desirable direction, and is interesting in combination with other enhancements.

The method of Roulette Wheel Selection is implemented by associating a weight with each possible action. These weights are determined from prior observations of the algorithm playing Super Mario levels by recording which actions where used the most in successful playthroughs. When selecting which child to create while expanding a node, the weights are used in the random selection as tickets in a lottery, making actions with high weights more likely to be selected than actions with low weights - this without removing the possibility of any action, good or bad, being selected first.

Using Roulette Wheel Selection with MCTS has previously shown good results in determining what child to expand next [13].

5.5 Domain knowledge

Although MCTS can get a long way in Super Mario without introducing much domain knowledge, some challenges of the game are better tackled with some knowledge of the game. Since we had to ignore the down key, the action space consist of 16 actions. By removing actions that either don't add any new options (e.g. left + right + jump is equal to just jump) or that we deemed unnecessary we managed to reduce the set of actions to 10. This decreased the branching factor which lead to increasing the possible search depth in the same amount of time.

A relatively frequent challenge in Super Mario levels is gaps. Gaps can be of varying depth and if Mario touches the bottom he dies. The challenge with gaps is that their deadly property is only discovered if the algorithm is able to simulate steps all they way to the bottom. Deep gaps pose a problem as the shortsightedness of unmodified MCTS (Figure 1, yellow line) results in Mario going down the gap and ending up walljumping back and forth near the bottom of the gap if not dying straight away. By detecting when a position is inside a gap we can avoid them by drastically reducing the reward of positions inside gaps.

6. RESULTS

6.1 Individual modifications

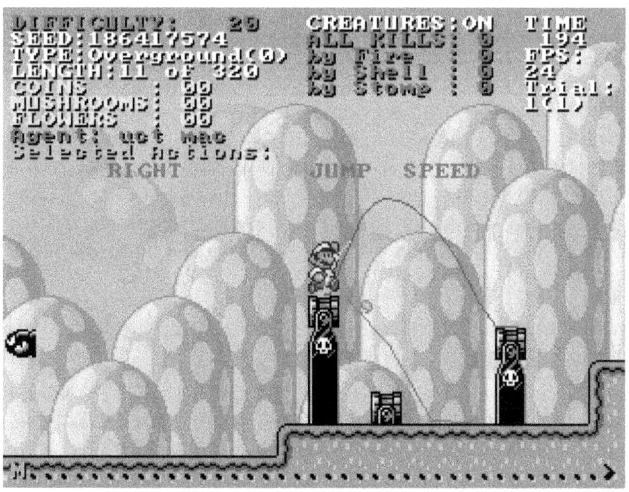

Figure 1: Illustrates the different search depths for three individual modifications. Red: Macro Actions, Yellow: Vanilla MCTS, Blue: Best Combination

Our experiment consist of 6 different enhancements, all of which are tested in combination with each other giving 64 different agents to test.

The agents are tested on the same 100 randomly generated levels on the hardest difficulty the Mario AI Framework allows. We use the "Wilcoxon signed-ranks test" to calculate p, and require $p < 0.05$ for the difference to be significant.

The calculated final x-position of mario in each level is the level score, and the mean of all levels is the score that

Modification	Mean Score	Avg. T Left
Vanilla MCTS (Avg.)	3918	131
Vanilla MCTS (Max)	2098***	153
Mixmax (0.125)	4093	147
Macro Actions	3869	142
Partial Expansion	3928	134
Roulette Wheel Selection	4032	139
Hole Detection	4196**	134
Limited Actions	4141*	137
(Robin Baumgarten's A*)	4289***	169

Table 4: Results of each individual modification on 100 levels. The stars denote the statistical significance in difference from each result to unmodified MCTS. We include results from running Baumgarten's A* implementation as reference.

the combination receives. Table 5 show the results of these tests.

In this section the behaviour of the individual and the most interesting combinations is described. Results from testing the individual enhancements can be found in table 4.

6.2 Vanilla MCTS

When adjusted with the optimal values for the constants C_p and rollout depth cap, the basic MCTS algorithm actually performs rather well. It completes 80 out of 100 levels. The main problems with this agent is the very limited search depth which is never more than 5 actions, constituting only 200ms ahead (See Figure 1, yellow line). This makes the agent vulnerable towards monsters falling from above and makes it hard to scale the tall cannon towers.

6.2.1 Mixmax

The higher weight of the largest reward beneath each node reduces the cowardness of Mario greatly. This change can, however, also in some cases result in reckless and dangerous behaviour, sometimes resulting in certain death. That is alleviated by only letting the maximum reward have a relatively low influence ($\frac{1}{8}$) compared to the average reward ($\frac{7}{8}$). This skews the simulation tree further towards the larger values exploring those nodes further while making it more certain that they are safe.

The Mixmax modification on its own doesn't show a significant difference from Vanilla MCTS as can be seen in table 4.

6.2.2 Macro Actions

The increased action size of Macro Actions enables the search to go further into the level without having more iterations (Figure 1, red line). This not only makes Mario take routes with less monsters, but also enables the agent to quickly scale tall cannons, which seems to be a challenge. This reduces the wasted time (and reduce timeout related losses), but since Mario is exposed to monsters when trying to find a way over the canon it also reduces the risk of dying from monsters.

6.2.3 Partial Expansion

Like the Macro Actions enhancement, using Partial Expansion enables the agent to search to a greater depth. This enables Mario to quickly and safely jump over gaps, and choose safer routes. The greater depth is obtained when some actions are clearly better than others (in terms of how much to the right Mario gets). This unfortunately means that Partial Expansion doesn't help in the case where Mario gets stuck in front of cannons, as none of the immediate moves give a high reward and thus exploration evens out the tree.

Method	Score	T	Method	Score	T
----	3918 †	131	---L	4141* †	137
X---	4093 †	147	X---L	4152* †	147
-M---	3869 †	142	-M--L	4025 †	143
XM---	3922 †	146	XM--L	4043 †	147
-P--	3928 †	146	-P-L	4214* †	146
X-P--	4109* †	140	X-P-L	4278*	150
-MP--	3997 †	134	-MP-L	4156* †	135
XMP--	4166* †	139	XMP-L	4220* †	143
--R-	4032 †	139	--R-L	4132* †	142
X-R-	3786 †	149	X-R-L	4134* †	150
-M-R-	3956 †	145	-M-R-L	4063 †	145
XM-R-	4088 †	146	XM-R-L	4031 †	150
-PR-	4271*	149	-PR-L	4275*	153
X-PR-	4281*	154	X-PR-L	4260*	156
-MPR-	4165* †	135	-MPR-L	3955 †	136
XMPR-	4182* †	141	XMPR-L	4145* †	140
---H-	4196* †	134	---HL	4161* †	139
X--H-	4221* †	145	X--HL	4281*	147
-M-H-	4182* †	142	-M-HL	4251*	141
XM-H-	4197* †	146	XM-HL	4260*	146
-P-H-	2679*†	96	-P-HL	4277* †	138
X-P-H-	3656* †	105	X-P-HL	4277*	147
-MP-H-	2692*†	112	-MP-HL	3970 †	125
XMP-H-	3583* †	105	XMP-HL	4237* †	138
--RH-	4212* †	139	--RHL	4211* †	142
X-RH-	4206* †	148	X-RHL	4195* †	150
-M-RH-	4189* †	143	-M-RHL	4204* †	141
XM-RH-	4240*†	145	XM-RHL	4248*†	147
-PRH-	4268*	148	-PRHL	4284*	152
X-PRH-	4274*	153	X-PRHL	4272*	155
-MPRH-	4071 †	126	-MPRHL	3692 †	126
XMPRH-	4189* †	132	XMPRHL	4061 †	131

Table 5: Results of all enhancement combinations. X: Mixmax, M: Macro Actions, P: Partial Expansion, R: Roulette Wheel Selection, H: Hole Detection, L: Limited Actions. The results are the mean score of all levels and the T value is the average time left on completed levels. Stars denote statistical significance in difference from unmodified MCTS. Daggers denote statistical significance in difference from a perfect score of 4289.

6.2.4 *Roulette Wheel Selection*

On its own Roulette Wheel selection doesn't make much of a difference to the behaviour. This is because all children of a node must be simulated before the next depth can be searched, thus the order in which children are created only makes a difference in the last level of expansion where not all children are created. Unless the values of the roulette are chosen badly this modification should give atleast the same results as without, since exploring more promising actions earlier should seem safer.

6.2.5 *Hole Detection*

This enhancement very clearly has a great effect on the ability to avoid going into gaps, which in turn reduces the number of gap-related deaths.

6.2.6 *Limited Actions*

Limiting the action space reduces the branching factor which increases the search depth. Since we had to remove the down key in our base algorithm the reduction isn't that big, and the effect of limited actions isn't very noticeable on its own.

6.3 No domain knowledge

A particularly interesting combination is Mixmax and Partial Expansion. This combination is the best agent consisting only of enhancements that do not add any domain knowledge to the agent. It performs better than Vanilla MCTS with a significant difference, but is still some way from a winning score. It seems that some domain knowledge is needed in order to really improve the performance of MCTS.

6.4 Partial Expansion + Roulette Wheel Selection

The combination of Partial Expansion with Roulette Wheel Selection has shown very good performance. The two enhancements separately only shows decent results, but in conjunction the algorithm is able to search a great distance into the level, which allows for planning on the macroscopic level, but with great detail in movement when need be. This combination in able to detect and avoid gaps by searching far enough to reach the opposite edge. They complement each other well since Roulette Wheel Selection is a solution the the problem that Partial Expansion wants to explore the most promising actions first and leave the rest for later.

6.5 Best combination

The combination that gave the best results was the one using all enhancements except Macro Actions. It is not the combination with the highest score in the benchmarking but was fast and more robust than other candidates. The feature that Macro Actions would give is the ability to search far into the level at the cost of presicion, but when using Partial

Expansion and Roulette Wheel Selection in conjunction this is achieved, even without losing the precision as is the case with Macro Actions (Figure 1, blue line). Hole Detection makes the search more focused on actions not leading into gaps, Limited Actions reduces the action space and Mixmax reduces the cowardly behaviour. This combination enables the agent to often search to the end of the screen. It is evident that this combination still can fail in certain difficult levels, but even here it rarely happens.

The variation observed is due to the fact that MCTS is not deterministic in that the chosen action can vary depending on what order the actions of a state are explored. Additionally the scheduling of the agentâĂŹs thread can vary, possibly yielding a different number of iterations of the algorithm, and thus possibly changing the choice of actions.

7. ANALYSIS OF RESULTS

The cowardly behaviour of Mario when using unaugmented MCTS is very interesting, as it points to a problem that is likely to recur in other video game domains. Essentially, the agent became very risk-averse: it refused to take actions that might lead to positive rewards (e.g. jumping over a gap) because most of the random rollouts would lead to substantial negative rewards (e.g. falling into the gap). To our best knowledge and mild surprise, this has not been identified as a problem with MCTS before. To understand why, it is instructive to look at the differences between the types of games to which MCTS is commonly applied and to games like SMB. In SMB, it is possible to "procrastinate" by standing still or moving back and forth. This is because no forward movement is enforced (the screen follows the player character) and there's no adversary to race or combat. The negative consequences of procrastinating – running out of time – only show up hundreds of seconds (tens of thousands of time steps) later, which is beyond the rollout depth of any MCTS agent. In contrast, board games such as Go necessarily approach the end of the game with every move, and a rollout of a manageable length will always reach an end state.

Given that many video games have more in common with Super Mario Bros than with Go, it stands to reason that the same modifications to MCTS that helped overcome the pathological behaviour of unaugmented MCTS on this problem would improve the efficiency of this algorithm on other problems. While it is always possible to incorporate domain knowledge in various forms, it is interesting to note that it was possible to achieve near-perfect play with only knowledge-free modifications. It is entirely plausible that Mixmax backups, partial expansion or roulette wheel selection would make MCTS work well in a first-person shooter or an open-world racing game.

The most surprising thing about the Mixmax backup modification is that we have not seen it described in the literature before. It is a very simple idea, which essentially gives us a "testosterone gauge" for Mario: the more of the max reward we mix in, the more risks Mario takes. It is possible that such a modification would never be useful in a game such s Go or Chess, which points to the influence and importance of the choice of benchmark problem when developing an algorithm.

Note that the modified MCTS agent still does not play better than the A* agent. The most likely reason for this is that it is not possible to play that set of levels better. As stated above, the main objective of the paper is not to develop a better-playing Mario agent, but rather to understand and improve the behaviour of the very promising MCTS algorithm on continuous-state continuous-time videogames without mandatory progress, a large category of games of which Mario is a good example. For clarity, it should be pointed out that a best-first search algorithm like A* would not perform well on playing any game which did not have a very fine-grained heuristic function or which was adversarial.

Still, it would be interesting to see if there was some version of the Mario AI benchmark where our improved MCTS algorithms would outperform A*. The stochastic nature of MCTS would seem to make it more adept at handling unpredictability, not only due to an opposing player but also due to the environment. A study of the paths the A* agent reveals that they depend on the environment being absolute predictable: Mario, as controlled by A*, jumps at the very last pixel before falling into a gap, and passes enemies with absolutely no margin. Such solutions would be very brittle in the face of any unreliability in the agent-environment coupling. We therefore undertook to investigate the effects of introducing such unreliability.

8. SECOND TEST: NOISY MARIO

In order to test our implementationâĂŹs rigidity against noise, we created a test scenario where 20% of an agentâĂŹs moves would be random regardless of what it actually wanted to do. This was implemented as a wrapper around the agent code, where in every interaction cycle there was a 0.2 chance that the command from the agent would be replaced with a random command. With these settings our best combination (all enhancements except macro actions) was benchmarked against the A* implementation on the same 100 levels as previously and the results are compared. During testing the A* implementation crashed occasionally in some levels, these two levels have been removed from both samples for fairness yielding a basis of 98 levels.

The results from the noisy action test reveals that our MCTS implementation performs significantly better than A* under these conditions. MCTS cleared three levels while A* died in all. Across the 98 levels MCTS achieved a mean of 1770 points while A* reached 1342 (see table 6). This difference suggests that the MCTS implementation is coping much better with the uncertainty under these conditions than A*. Both controllers performed much worse than either controller did in the noiseless case, which is because the noisy version of the problem is much more challenging.

AI	Mean Score
MCTS (X-PRHL)	1770
A* agent	1342**

Table 6: Results of evaluating the MCTS and A* agents with a 20% chance of a random action being performed instead of the selected one. The stars denote the statistical significance in difference from the selected variant of MCTS (X-PRHL)

It is interesting to note that the characteristics of the noisy version of the Mario AI Benchmark are almost diametrically opposed to those of the game which MCTS has had most pronounced success on, namely Go. Whereas Go has a high branching factor, relatively short average and maximum game length and is deterministic, the Mario AI Benchmark has very low branching factor, long average game length and very long maximum game length (if you do nothing, you have to wait tens of thousands of ticks to time out). Further, the noisy version of the benchmark is nondeterministic. The relative success of MCTS under these conditions points to that the core algorithm, with suitably chosen extensions, can provide good performance in conditions which are very different from those which it was originally designed for and tested on. It should be investigated further and more systematically which kinds of games MCTS can work well on.

9. CONCLUSION

In this paper, we investigated the performance and behaviour of MCTS on the Mario AI benchmark, and found that standard MCTS performed relatively badly. Based on the problems we identified with MCTS' behaviour on this benchmark, we then proposed a number of modifications, and tested all combinations of those. It was found that a judicious combination of these modifications yields an agent that plays near optimally. Two of the modifications are novel in the sense that we invented them and have not found them in the literature: mixmax backups and partial expansion. We then produced a noisy version of the Mario AI benchmark, and tested the algorithms on this benchmark. It was found that the improved MCTS controller clearly outperforms A* on this version of the benchmark. We hope to have helped clarify the role MCTS can play in video games, and suggested a few useful techniques for conquering continuous time and space.

10. REFERENCES

[1] S. Bojarski and C. Congdon. Realm: A rule-based evolutionary computation agent that learns to play mario. In *Computational Intelligence and Games (CIG), 2010 IEEE Symposium*, pages 83–90, 2010.

[2] C. Browne, E. Powley, D. Whitehouse, S. Lucas, P. Cowling, P. Rohlfshagen, S. Tavener, D. Perez, S. Samothrakis, and S. Colton. A survey of monte carlo tree search methods. *Computational Intelligence and AI in Games, IEEE Transactions on*, 4(1):1–43, 2012.

[3] G. M. J. Chaslot, M. H. Winands, H. J. V. D. HERIK, J. W. Uiterwijk, and B. Bouzy. Progressive strategies for monte-carlo tree search. *New Mathematics and Natural Computation*, 4(03):343–357, 2008.

[4] D. Churchill, A. Saffidine, and M. Buro. Fast heuristic search for rts game combat scenarios. *Proceedings of AIIDE*, 2012.

[5] M. Ebner, J. Levine, S. Lucas, T. Schaul, T. Thompson, and J. Togelius. Towards a video game description language. *Dagstuhl Follow-up. To appear., Preprint available at http://www. idsia. ch/˜ tom/publications/dagstuhl-vgdl. pdf*, 2013.

[6] M. Genesereth, N. Love, and B. Pell. General game playing: Overview of the aaai competition. *AI magazine*, 26(2):62, 2005.

[7] S. Karakovskiy and J. Togelius. The mario ai benchmark and competitions. *IEEE Transactions on Computational Intelligence and AI in Games*, 2012.

[8] C.-S. Lee, M.-H. Wang, G. Chaslot, J.-B. Hoock, A. Rimmel, O. Teytaud, S.-R. Tsai, S.-C. Hsu, and T.-P. Hong. The computational intelligence of mogo revealed in taiwan's computer go tournaments. *Computational Intelligence and AI in Games, IEEE Transactions on*, 1(1):73–89, 2009.

[9] T. Pepels and M. H. Winands. Enhancements for monte-carlo tree search in ms pac-man. In *Computational Intelligence and Games (CIG), 2012 IEEE Conference on*, pages 265–272. IEEE, 2012.

[10] D. Perez, P. Rohlfshagen, and S. M. Lucas. Monte-carlo tree search for the physical travelling salesman problem. In *Applications of Evolutionary Computation*, pages 255–264. Springer, 2012.

[11] E. Powley, D. Whitehouse, and P. Cowling. Monte carlo tree search with macro-actions and heuristic route planning for the physical travelling salesman problem. In *Computational Intelligence and Games (CIG), 2012 IEEE Conference on*, pages 234–241, 2012.

[12] S. Samothrakis, D. Robles, and S. Lucas. Fast approximate max-n monte carlo tree search for ms pac-man. *Computational Intelligence and AI in Games, IEEE Transactions on*, 3(2):142–154, 2011.

[13] F. W. Takes and W. A. Kosters. Solving samegame and its chessboard variant. In *Proceedings of the 21st Benelux Conference on Artificial Intelligence (BNAIC?09)(eds. T. Calders, K. Tuyls, and M. Pechenizkiy)*, pages 249–256, 2009.

[14] J. Togelius, S. Karakovskiy, and R. Baumgarten. The 2009 mario ai competition. In *Proceedings of the IEEE Congress on Evolutionary Computation*, 2010.

Semantic Aware Methods for Evolutionary Art

Penousal Machado
CISUC, Department of Informatics Engineering
University of Coimbra, 3030
Coimbra, Portugal
machado@dei.uc.pt

João Correia
CISUC, Department of Informatics Engineering
University of Coimbra, 3030
Coimbra, Portugal
jncor@dei.uc.pt

ABSTRACT

In the past few years the use of semantic aware crossover and mutation has become a hot topic of research within the Genetic Programming community. Unlike traditional genetic operators that perform syntactic manipulations of programs regardless of their behavior, semantic driven operators promote direct search on the underlying behavioral space. Based on previous work on semantic Genetic Programming and Genetic Morphing, we propose and implement semantic driven crossover and mutation operators for evolutionary art. The experimental results focus on assessing how these operators compare with traditional ones.

Categories and Subject Descriptors

I.3.3 [**Computer Graphics**]: Picture/Image Generation; I.2.m [**Artificial Intelligence**]: Miscellaneous

Keywords

Semantic Operators, Evolutionary Art, Genetic Programming, Computational Creativity

1. INTRODUCTION

The use of geometric semantic genetic operators [14] in the context of Genetic Programming (GP) is a recent field of research. While conventional GP perform syntactic changes to programs ignoring their behaviour, geometric semantic operators consider behaviour, thus allowing the direct search of the behavioral space. The theoretical advantages of such operators are huge: they induce a unimodal fitness landscape for all the problems consisting in matching input data with known outputs.

We revisit the early works of Sims [18] and Hart [7] concerning the generation of short animations through "genetic morphing" between individuals. We adapt their approaches, developing several semantic-inspired crossover and mutation operators. We use these operators in the context of evolutionary art and study their properties.

GECCO'14, July 12–16, 2014, Vancouver, BC, Canada.

ACM 978-1-4503-2662-9/14/07 ...$15.00.
http://dx.doi.org/10.1145/2576768.2598293 .

In Section 2 we make a short overview of geometric semantic operators proposed in GP literature, introducing several important concepts. Section 3 makes a short introduction to expression based evolutionary art and an overview of our evolutionary art system. The semantic-inspired genetic operators proposed in this paper are described in Section 4 and the results obtained through their use are summarized on Section 5. Finally we draw conclusions.

2. GEOMETRIC SEMANTIC OPERATORS

Traditional GP crossover and mutation operators perform syntactic manipulations of programs – e.g. sub-tree swapping – ignoring the semantics of the programs that they manipulate [14]. While semantic-blind operators have shown their merit, as it is demonstrated by the extensive list of valuable results and breakthroughs obtained by GP approaches, the definition of operators that are aware of the semantics of candidate solutions [2] is becoming an important area of research within the GP community.

The exact meaning of semantics in the context of GP is debatable, with several researchers adopting the definition proposed by Uy et al. [20] and Moraglio et al. [14] who consider semantics as the function computed by the program, more precisely, as the behavior of a program over a set of data, i.e., "input-output pairs making up the computed function". In simple terms, adopting this definition, where semantics equates behavior and applying it to expression-based evolutionary art, implies that the semantics/behavior of an individual is the image produced by the individual when executed over a set of x,y coordinate values.

Since traditional GP crossover and mutation ignore semantics, the consequences of the syntactic modifications performed by these operators on the behavior of the programs are difficult to predict. Moraglio et al. [14] recently introduced a new type of genetic operators, called geometric semantic genetic operators, that manipulate directly the behavior of the programs, ignoring their syntactic information. The ability to directly manipulate semantic information confers them several interesting properties, most notably: they induce a unimodal fitness landscape for all the problems consisting in matching input data with known target outputs. In other words, under these operators problems such as symbolic regression become trivial, in the sense that a program that reproduces the training data is found with little effort.

Unfortunately, they also possess a major disadvantage: these operators always produce offspring that are larger than their parents, which causes an exponential growth in program size. Thus, while it is trivial to solve problems such as symbolic regression, the size of the evolved programs is so large that, for most applications, it defeats the purpose. Although it is common to define symbolic regression as the problem of finding a mathematical expression that approximates or matches the training data, this definition is incomplete. Matching the training data is only a part of the problem and it can be solved trivially by a variety of methods, e.g. considering that your training data consists of n (x, y) pairs, with $x, y \in \mathbb{R}$ you can always use polynomial regression to derive polynomial of order $n-1$ that fits the data perfectly. Thus, the goal of symbolic regression is better defined as the problem of finding a **compact** expression that **approximates** the training data and that **generalizes** well. Analogously, in the context of evolutionary art, as demonstrated by Machado and Cardoso [12] finding the symbolic expression for the Mona Lisa, or any other given image, is both a trivial problem and a fruitless endeavor *per se*. However, finding a compact representation is a difficult and valuable problem, perhaps even central for evolutionary art [13], opening the door for a wide range of applications.

Considering the potential and the limitations of semantic operators their contribution to the field of evolutionary art is unclear, and should be scrutinized. Next we describe the semantic geometric crossover and mutation operators for real functions presented by Moraglio et al. [14].

Geometric Semantic Crossover: Given two parent functions $T_1, T_2 : \mathbb{R}^n \rightarrow \mathbb{R}$, the recombination returns the real function $T_X = T_1.T_R + T_2.(1 - T_R)$, where T_R is a random real function with codomain $[0, 1]$.

In simple terms, this geometric semantic crossover operator creates a program, T_3, that returns as output a weighted sum of the outputs of its parents T_1, T_2. This ensures that the operator is semantically driven and also that it is a geometric crossover on the semantic space, in the sense that when the parents and descendant are mapped onto the semantic space the descendant is bound to be between the parents and. Therefore, assuming that a target point in the semantic space exists the Euclidean distance between the descendant and that point is never larger than the distance of the farthest parent. Figure 1 illustrates this property. A formal demonstration and additional semantic geometric operators can be found in Moraglio et al. [14]

Geometric Semantic Mutation: Given a parent function $T : \mathbb{R}^n \rightarrow \mathbb{R}$, the mutation returns the real function $T_M = T + ms.(T_{R1} - T_{R2})$, where T_{R1} and T_{R2} are random real functions and ms is the mutation step.

The use of two random real functions, T_{R1}, T_{R2} ensures that the semantic perturbation is centered around zero while the mutation step, ms, allows one to control the degree of the perturbations. Moraglio et al. [14] formally prove that this operator induces a unimodal fitness landscape, corresponding to a box mutation on the semantic space.

3. EVOLUTIONARY ART

The seminal work of Sims [18] created what is now the most popular approach to evolutionary art, the *expression-based* approach. Each genotype is a tree that encodes a symbolic expression. The rendering of the expression results in a phenotype, i.e., an image. The genotype-phenotype mapping process varies, but, in general, the phenotype can be seen as a visualization of the output of the $s-expression$ over a set of variable values. Typically, evolution is user-guided although noteworthy exceptions exist [10, 17]. Some

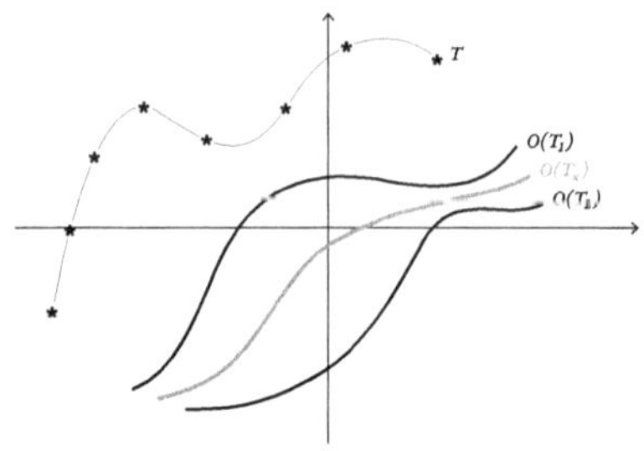

Figure 1: An illustration of geometric semantic crossover. The output of the descendant, $O(T_X)$, is bound to be between the outputs of the parents, $O(T_1), O(T_2)$, and, therefore, it is never farther from to the target, T, than the worst parent, T_2 in this case. Adapted from Vanneschi et al. [21].

examples of this *expression-based* approach can be found in [18, 19, 22, 12, 7]. A thorough survey of EA systems beyond the scope of this paper (see, e.g., [10] for a survey).

As Machado and Cardoso [12] point out, most *expression-based* EA systems are theoretically able to create any image. Nevertheless, in practice, the image space that is actually explored depends heavily on the particularities of the system (primitives, genetic operators, genotype-phenotype mapping, etc.). McCormack [13] identified the problem of finding a symbolic-expression that corresponds to a known "target" image as one of the open problems of evolutionary art. More exactly, the issue is not finding a symbolic-expression, since this can be done trivially [12], the issue is finding a compact expression that provides a good approximation of the "target" image taking advantage of its structure.

In spite of the importance of this specific open problem, it is important to mention that in most evolutionary art applications there is no "target" image to obtain. The goals can be as varied as satisfying the user, as is the case of interactive evolutionary art, satisfy a hard-wired or learned aesthetic criteria [1, 5, 12, 4, 11], create novel images [9, 3], respond to the "infections" of parasites in a co-evolutionary scheme [6], etc.

Nevertheless, the use of semantic operators, may result in increased evolvability, thus promoting the fruitful exploration of the search space and potentially lead to better results, independently of the criteria used to judge the quality of those results.

Those familiar with Sims [18] influential work may recall that in addition to the evolution of static images Sims also evolved short animations. These animations were produced by a process called *genetic cross dissolve*, given two symbolic expressions, corresponding to two images, this process creates an animation by generating intermediate frames through the "interpolation" between the symbolic expressions over time. As we will see in Section 4, in its simplest form, this process is analogous to the geometric semantic operator presented in the previous Section. Additionally, Sims also mentions using this approach to mate individuals. Thus, evolutionary art adopted semantic methods since its early beginning, in fact, as far as we know, Sims [18] was the first to use semantic methods in GP. However, due to the limitations of the method, this contribution is often overlooked.

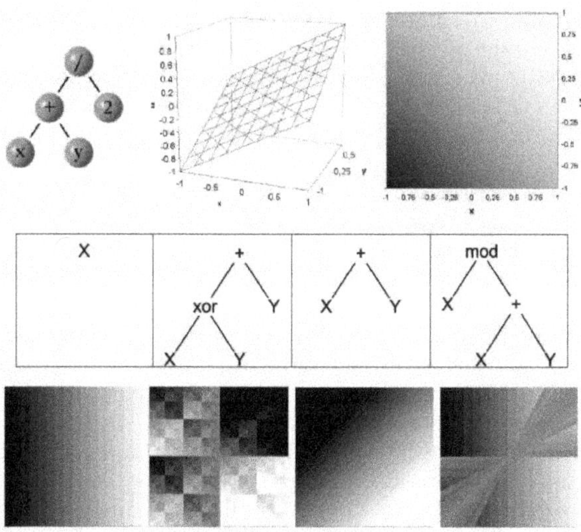

Figure 2: Representation scheme with examples of functions and the corresponding images.

3.1 Evolutionary Art Engine

The engine used in these experiments is inspired by the works of Sims [18]. It is a general purpose, expression-based, GP image generation engine that allows the evolution of populations of images. The genotypes are trees composed of a lexicon of functions and terminals. The function set is composed of simple functions such as arithmetic, trigonometric and logic operations. The terminal set is composed of two variables, x and y, and randomly initialized constants, these can be scalars or 3d vectors. The 3d vectors introduce color by specifying different values for the RGB color channels, e.g. #(0.1, 0.2, 0.1). Although a single tree is used for the 3 color channels, this tree can be decomposed into three different trees, one for each color channel, operating and returning real numbers. The phenotypes are images that are rendered by evaluating the expression-trees for different values of x and y, which serve both as terminal values and image coordinates. In other words, to determine the value of the pixel in the (0,0) coordinates, one assigns zero to x and y and evaluates the expression-tree (see figure 2). A thorough description of the GP engine can be found in [12]. Figure 3 displays typical imagery produced via interactive evolution using this system.

4. SEMANTIC METHODS FOR EVOLUTIONARY ART

In Section 2 we described geometric semantic crossover and mutation operators. Here, we describe our implementation of such operators and introduce novel semantic-inspired operators. These are based on the early work of Sims [18] and Hart [7] on the creation of short animations depicting smooth transitions between two evolved images.

The production of such animations relies on the use of the *lerp* function, which can be defined as follows:

$$lerp(A, B) = A.t + B.(t-1),$$

with $A, B : \mathbb{R}^n \to \mathbb{R}$ and $t \in [0, 1]$.

To generate a video one creates a new individual $lerp(A, B)$ and calculates its output for different values of

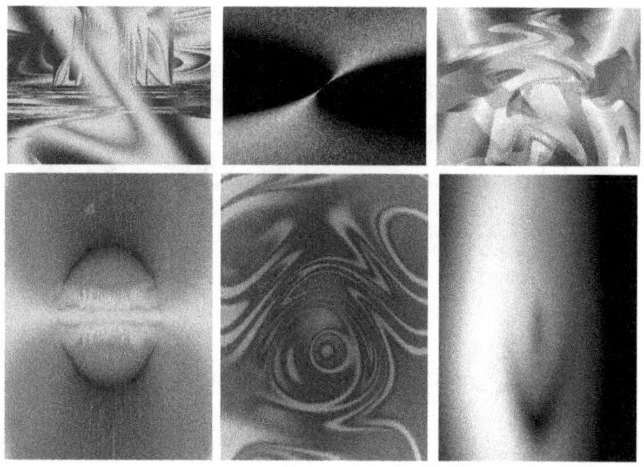

Figure 3: Examples of images generated by the evolutionary engine using interactive evolution.

t, starting with $t = 0$ and increasing t by a fixed step until $t = 1$, which produces a "fade" between A and B. In most cases, this results in rather uninteresting videos since it is simply a static morph between two images. Sims [18] proposes an approach based on *first-differences* alignment which allows him to obtain swift transitions between pairs of images while introducing the illusion of movement and change over time. Later Hart [7] refined this early approach introducing novel alignment schemes which extend the range of results producible through genetic cross dissolve.

The similarity between the *lerp* function and the geometric semantic crossover defined in Section 2 are striking. In fact, the only difference is the following: *lerp* uses the variable t to control the influence A and B on the outcome while the geometric semantic crossover uses a random function, T_R, with codomain $[0, 1]$ for the same effect.

To make them equivalent we redefine *lerp* as follows:

$$lerp(T_1, T_2, T_R) = T_1.sig(T_R) + T_2.(1 - sig(T_R)),$$

with $T_1, T_2, T_R : \mathbb{R}^n \to \mathbb{R}$, and $sig(x) = \frac{1}{1+e^{-x}}$.

Following the work of Vanneschi et al. [21], we use *sig* to map $\mathbb{R}$ into $[0, 1]$, thus removing the constraint of using as third argument a function with codomain $[0, 1]$.

In the next sections we describe several genotype alignment techniques and the corresponding genetic operators.

4.1 Crossover and Tree-Alignment

The first crossover operator described herein is similar to the semantic crossover operator presented in Section 2. The second results, directly, from the work of Sims [18], who used a similar technique for creating animations and performing crossover between parents with similar structures. The last two crossover operators are inspired on the work of Hart [7]. The difference between the four operators lies on the algorithm for aligning the genotypes, i.e. finding matches between pairs of genotypes [15, 16].

4.1.1 Root Alignment

This is the simplest alignment technique, the roots of both parents, A and B are aligned and no further alignments are made. Considering this technique the result of the crossover operator between any pair of individuals A and B is $lerp(A, B, T_R)$, where T_R is a randomly generated

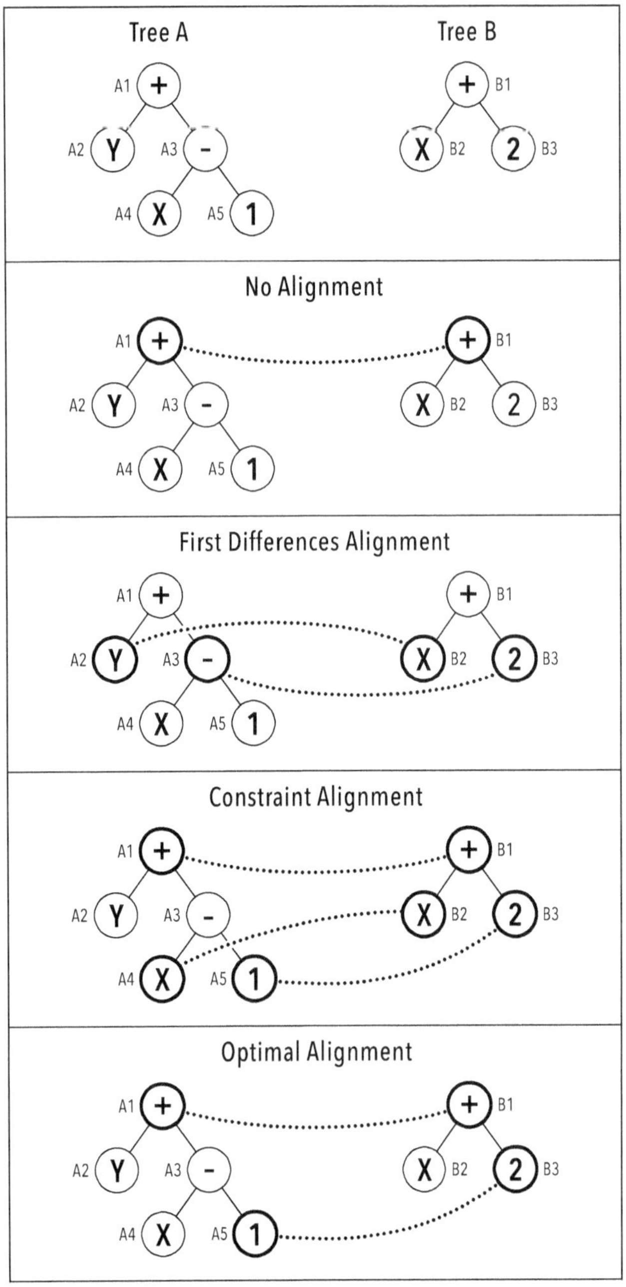

Figure 4: Alignments of A and B according to different algorithms.

tree. Thus, the crossover between the individuals depicted in figure 4 would result in: $lerp(+(y, -(x, 1)), +(x, 2), T_R)$. As previously mentioned, this operator is equivalent to the one presented in Section 2, sharing the exact same properties, and can, therefore, be classified as a geometric semantic operator.

4.1.2 First Differences Alignment

The first difference alignment algorithm can be described as follows: If the roots of the trees are equal call the alignment algorithm for each of their arguments (unless they are leafs); if the roots are different align both roots.

Running this algorithm for the example presented in figure 4 produces the following alignments: $(A2, B2)$ and $(A3, B3)$. Like previously, to produce the descendant one *lerp* node is introduced for each alignment, resulting in: $+(lerp(x, y, T_{R1}), lerp(-(x, 1), 2, T_{R2})$.

Although the operator is semantic-inspired, it can no longer be classified as a geometric semantic operator since the descendant is no longer necessarily "between" the two parents. In other words, considering a target image T and Euclidean distance, while *root alignment* crossover returns a descendant that is at least as close to T as the farthest of its parents, *first difference alignment* crossover may return a descendant that is farther from T than the farthest parent.

This approach was used by Sims [18] for creating his famous *genetic cross dissolves* between images. If the two expressions have different root nodes *first differences* and *root* alignment produce the same outcome. In Sims work, the resulting video would be a "traditional", and rather uninteresting, fade between the images. However, when the trees share a common structure (i.e., when they have at least the root node in common) interesting movements and unexpected, yet smooth, transitions tend to occur.

Since Sims [18] and Hart [7] where primarily focused on the production of videos, they control the influence of each parent on the outcome through the variable t. We use a random function for the same purpose, which introduces a subtle, but important, difference between the approaches. In the original version the relative influence of the parents is homogeneous across the image since it only depends on t, however, when a random function – which can use variables x and y, and as such return different outputs for different x, y coordinates – is used this is no longer true, e.g. the upper part of the image may be strongly influenced by the first parent while the bottom part is mainly influenced by the second.

4.1.3 Constraint Alignment

As noted by Hart [7], two genotypes are likely to have different root nodes, and the result of the previously described operators is likely to be a rather uninteresting blend of the two images. Thus, although *root* alignment may be a valuable operator for "conventional" GP applications such as symbolic regression, its interest in the context of evolutionary art appears rather limited. To some extent, the same applies to *first differences* alignment since, in most cases, it will give the same output as *root* alignment. Considering that it may be desirable to "continue matching nodes after encountering a difference between the trees, since the result of the blend will often move rather than fade" [7], Hart proposes two additional alignment techniques. Like *first differences* alignment, the resulting crossover operators are semantic-inspired, but cannot be classified as geometric semantic operators under Euclidean distance.

The first technique is *constraint alignment* which can be informally described as follows: Considering two trees, A and B, we begin by establishing a correspondence between the levels of the trees; since the trees may have different heights, we will randomly discard levels of the larger tree, so that the number of levels to be considered is the same (the root level is never discarded); the remaining levels are then matched in top to bottom fashion (and hence there is always a match between the two root levels); we then proceed in level by level fashion, randomly discarding nodes so that the number of nodes at each level coincides; the remaining nodes are aligned in left to right order.

In figure 4 we present a possible outcome of the *constraint alignment* crossover between two individuals. Parent A has a height of 3, B has a height of 2. Therefore, for alignment purposes, it is necessary to randomly discard a level of parent A (either level 2 or 3, since the root is never discarded). In this case level 2 was discarded, thus the first level A is matched with the first of B and the third level of A is matched with the second of B. Since the number of nodes per considered level is the same for both parents, it is unnecessary to discard further nodes. Finally the nodes are aligned per level from left to right resulting in the following alignments: $(A1, B1)$, $(A4, B2)$, $(A5, B3)$.

As previously, each alignment results in the introduction of *lerp* operators. Therefore the crossover of A and B results in: $lerp(+(y, -(lerp(x, x, T_{R1}), lerp(1, 2, T_{R2}))), +(lerp(x, x, T_{R3}), lerp(1, 2, T_{R4})), T_{R5})$.

4.1.4 Optimal Alignment

Based on the work of Jiang et al. [8] on the alignment of ordered phylogenetic trees, Hart [7] proposes an optimal alignment scheme. This algorithm calculates all possible alignments between pairs of nodes and forests of children, that is every node of the first parent is compared against every node of the second parent and every forest of children of a node of the first parent is compared against every forest of children of every node of the second. As is demonstrated by Jiang et al. [8], the algorithm they propose has a quadratic temporal complexity. The quality of each alignment between a pair of nodes, n_1, n_2 is determined by a function, μ, which penalizes alignments between nodes of different types. Hart [7] adapted μ to a GP context, proposing the following function: $\mu(a,b) = 0$ when $a = b$; $\mu(a,b) = 1$ when $a \neq b$ but a and b are of the same type (i.e., both are variables, constants, or functions); $\mu(a, \lambda) = mu(\lambda, a) = 1$ that is not aligning a node gives a penalty of 1; $\mu(a,b) = 2$ when $a \neq b$ and a and b are of different types. The quality of an alignment between two trees is given by the sum of the μ values of all alignments between nodes. The algorithm efficiently calculates an alignment that minimizes μ. There is always an alignment between the root nodes of the parents.

A thorough description of the optimal alignment algorithm is beyond the scope of this paper, so we redirect the reader to the original works of Jiang et al. [8] and Hart [7].

For the example presented in figure 4 the optimal alignment between parent A and B is $(A1, B1)$ and $(A5, B3)$. As such the result of the optimal alignment crossover operation is: $lerp(+(y, -(x, lerp(1, 2, T_{R1}))), +(x, (1, 2, T_{R2})), T_{R3})$.

4.2 Mutation

Our mutation operators take full advantage of the tree alignment methods that were previously described. Therefore we have *root*, *first differences*, *constraint* and *optimal* alignment mutations. All of these operators can be described as follows: $mutation(A) = crossover(A, B.ms)$, with $A, B : \mathbb{R}^n \to \mathbb{R}$, where B is a random function and ms is the mutation step. In other words to mutate an individual we perform a crossover between this individual and a random tree, using a specific alignment scheme.

For *root* alignment, this mutation operator is similar to the geometric mutation operator described in Section 2, since the use of the *sig* function ensures a codomain of $[0, 1]$ and since the outputs of our random trees are naturally centered around zero. Therefore, *root* alignment mutation is also a geometric semantic operator under Euclidean distance. However the same cannot be stated for the remaining mutation operators.

5. EXPERIMENTATION

The use of semantic genetic operators raises a practical problem, the growth of program size is so accentuated that, after a few generations, the individuals become so large that it becomes impossible to calculate their output by transversing the program tree. In some scenarios, it is possible to calculate the output of a program from the outputs of its parents [21], which circumvents this specific problem. However, this is only possible for the *root* alignment operators. When other types of alignment are used it would be necessary to use dynamic programing techniques to calculate and store intermediate results. Although these techniques postpone the problem for a while, they do not solve it. The same applies to the simplification of the symbolic expressions proposed by Moraglio et al. [14].

For these reasons performing long evolutionary runs is not feasible. As such we consider that, at least in the context of evolutionary art, the most promising applications of these semantic-inspired operators are the following:

1. Short evolutionary runs with large populations;
2. Long evolutionary runs using conventional operators by default and semantic operators on rare occasions;
3. Semantic recombination of highly fit individuals evolved using conventional operators;
4. Semantic mutation of highly fit individuals evolved using conventional operators;

5.1 Runs With Semantic-Inspired Operators

We conducted a series of interactive evolutionary runs using the proposed semantic-inspired mutation and crossover operators. In each run we selected one alignment scheme – *root*, *first differences*, *constraint*, *optimal* – and used the associated crossover and mutation operators. The experimental settings were the following: population size = 100; number of generations 10; crossover probability = 0.8; mutation probability = 0.2; tournament selection, with tournament size = 5; elitist strategy, with elite size = 1.

When we compare the results obtained using semantic-inspired operators with those obtained using conventional operators one can observe a striking difference: the use of semantic operators results in a dramatic reduction of population diversity. This is somewhat expected since geometric semantic crossover ensures that the descendants are "between" both parents (see Section 2). Therefore, in the absence of mutation, search is constrained to the regions between parents. After a few populations selection pressure guides evolution towards an even smaller sub-region of the space. Geometric semantic mutation may introduce novelty in the population. However, in the experimental conditions, the mutations are unable to introduce enough novelty to keep the runs sufficiently interesting, even when mutation steps, ms, as high as 1 are considered. The loss of diversity is particularly visible when using *root*, which is a geometric semantic operator, and *first differences* alignment,

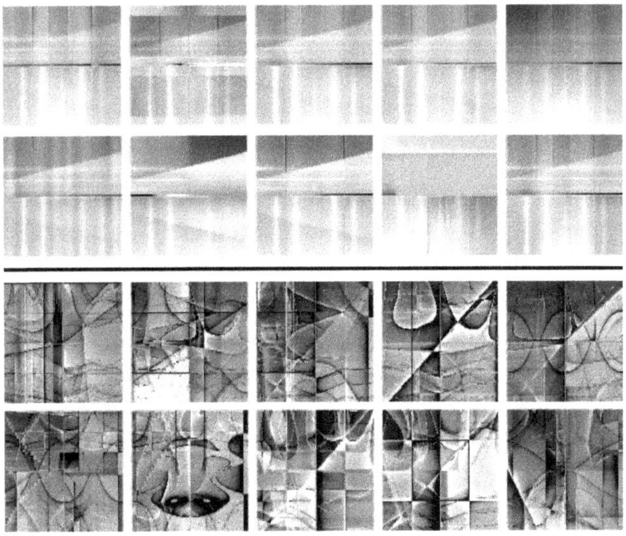

Figure 5: Partial screenshots of populations from runs using root (top two rows) and constraint (bottom two rows) alignment.

which behaves similarly to *root* alignment when the roots of the parents are different. Conversely, *constraint* and *optimal* alignment, which although semantic-inspired are not geometric operators, are able to sustain diversity for longer periods of time. In terms of user experience the runs using semantic-inspired operators can be considered largely disappointing, due to the lack of diversity, and also because the users feel, and to some extent are, committed to the choices made in the first few generations and unable to steer evolution in a different direction. In figure 5 we present partial snapshots of the 15th population of two runs using *root* and *constraint* alignment, highlighting the differences in diversity between the results.

We also conducted several runs using a hardwired fitness function similar to the one presented by Machado and Cardoso [12]. In terms of population diversity the results are comparable to those reported for interactive evolution runs. However, looking at these runs exclusively from an optimization point of view the differences between standard and semantic-inspired operators become less visible. That is, fitness increases along the evolutionary process and the differences of performance among operators are not statistically significant. Our explanation for this result is the following: although the theoretical properties of geometric semantic operators should give them an edge in optimization tasks, the runs are short and so these advantages are not visible.

5.2 Semantic Manipulation of Fit Individuals

The nature of semantic-inspired genetic operators and the quality of the *genetic cross dissolves* presented by Sims [18] and Hart [7] indicate that they can be particularly well-suited for recombining and mutating fit individuals. We conducted a series of tests using fit individuals evolved previously through interactive evolution using conventional genetic operators. These individuals were then recombined and mutated using semantic-inspired operators.

Figure 6 depicts typical examples of the recombination of individuals with similar structures, in particular with the same root node. As it can be observed, conventional

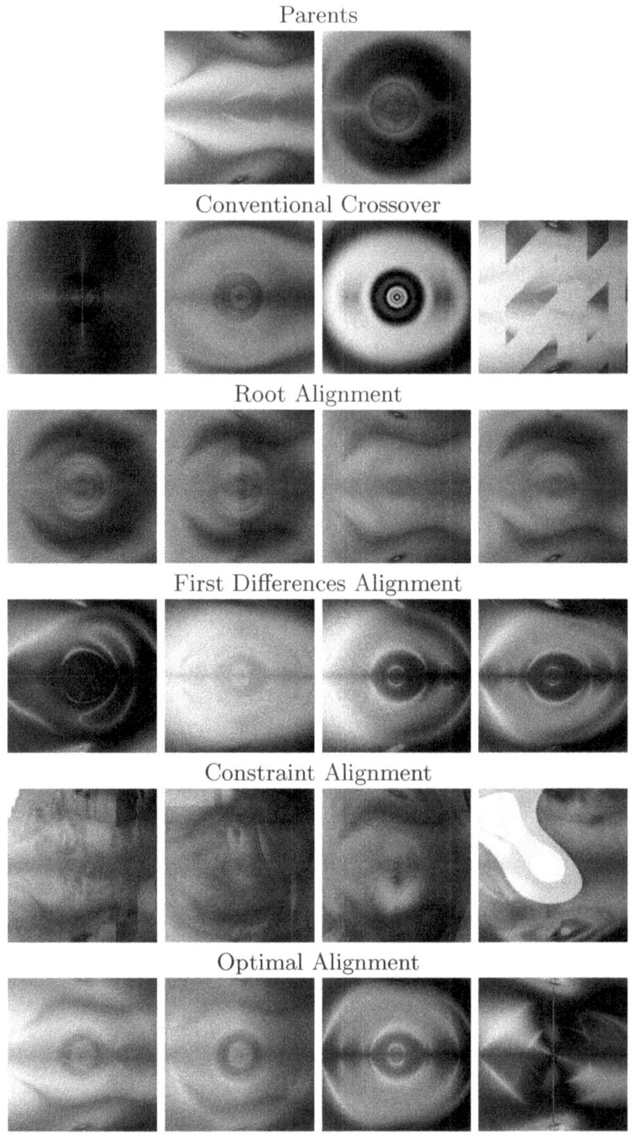

Figure 6: Examples of the recombination of individuals with similar structures.

crossover produces a wide variety of outputs that may show strong deviations from the parents, while *root* alignment produces fades between the two parents and, therefore, predictable results. *First differences* alignment produced a wide range of interesting results that, in our subjective opinion, appear to be a good compromise between diversity and inheritance of visual characteristics from the parents. The same can be stated regarding *optimal* alignment, although the results tend to be less varied. *Constraint* alignment produced unexpected results, it often produces descendants that close matches to one of the parents, fades between parents and totally unexpected images that bare little resemblance to any of the parents. Our explanation for this behaviour is the following: the alignments made using the *constraint* technique are largely arbitrary and so are the results. Considering the overall results, we find that semantic-inspired operators are valuable for the recombination of structurally similar individuals, and that *first differences* and *optimal* alignment tend to produce the best results.

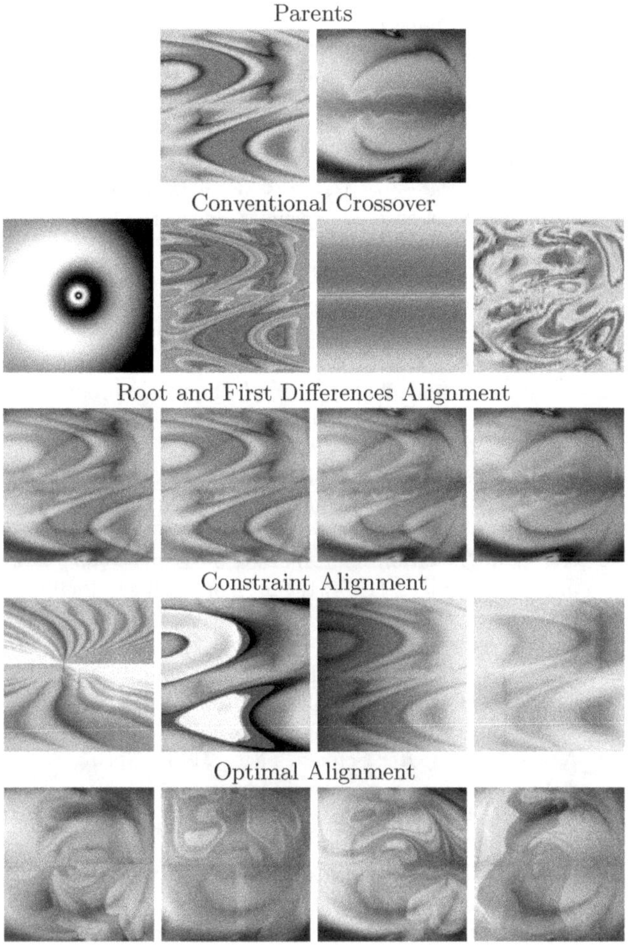

Figure 7: Examples of the recombination of individuals with dissimilar structures.

Figure 7 presents varied examples of the recombination of individuals with dissimilar structures. Since the root nodes are different *root* and *first differences* alignment are equivalent. As previously, conventional crossover produces a wide range of outputs and strong deviations from the parents are, apparently, more common than when the individuals have similar structures. *Root* alignment disregards the structure of the individuals and, as such, we obtain the same type of fades between parents that can be observed when recombining structurally similar individuals. The erratic behaviour of *constraint* alignment is accentuated and the individuals tend to fall on one of two extremes: a fade between the parents, an image that is apparently unrelated to any of them. *Optimal* alignment shows, by far, the highest percentage of recombinations that simultaneously inherit visual characteristics from both parents and depict some novelty. For this reason we considered it the most useful operator for the recombination of structurally dissimilar parents.

Figure 8 shows typical examples of the mutation operator. In general, the statements made regarding the crossover of individuals with different structures also apply to mutation. This is an expected result since, in essence, the semantic-inspired mutation operators perform the crossover of an individual with a randomly generated tree. The differences among semantic-inspired operators tend to less visible.

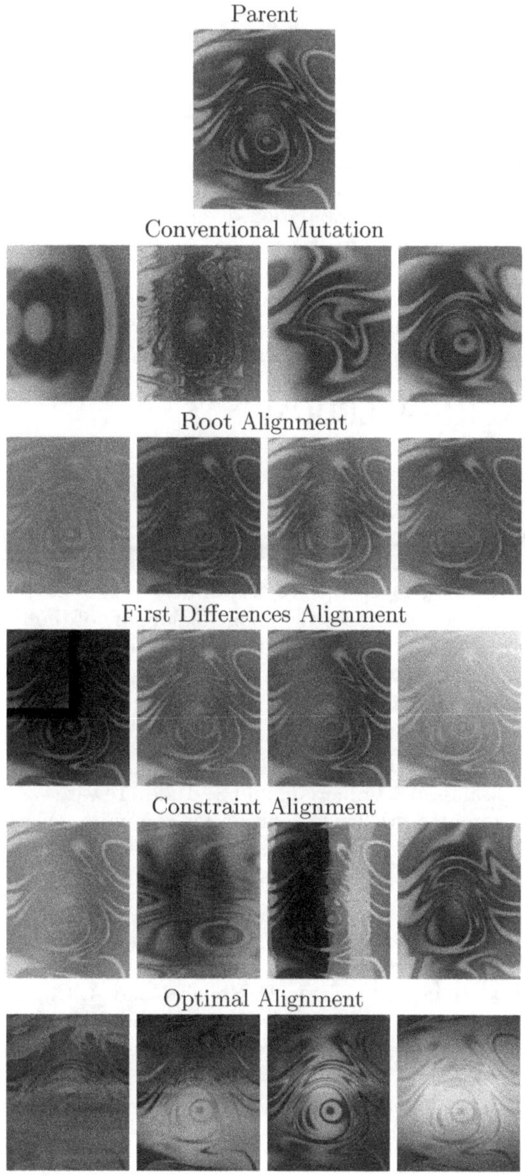

Figure 8: Examples of mutation operations.

Since the randomly generated trees are significantly smaller than the individuals used for crossover, the opportunities for alignment are scarcer, which dilutes the differences. Although semantic-inspired mutations may be useful for introducing subtle changes, in general, and in our subjective opinion, they offered little or no advantage over conventional mutation. In particular, they all tend to fail to systematically introduce novelty into the population and thus to keep the users interested in the evolutionary process.

6. CONCLUSIONS

We presented several semantic-inspired genetic operators using different genotype alignment techniques and applied them in the context of evolutionary art. The analysis of the experimental results indicates that, while these operators have practical limitations due to the exponential increase of program size, they are useful for specific tasks. In particular these semantic method are promising for the recombination of particularly fit individuals. On the other hand, performing long evolutionary runs, particularly interactive ones, appears to be unfeasible and tedious.

In the future we intend to conduct several interactive and automated runs using a combination of conventional and semantic operators. This combination may be useful for avoiding the lack of population diversity and the exponential growth of program size induced by the use of semantic operators, but still preserve their advantages. To achieve this, the semantic operators should be used seldom, which implies that identifying the occasions where their use is advantageous becomes an important research question.

7. ACKNOWLEDGMENTS

This research is partially funded by: iCIS project (CENTRO-07-ST24-FEDER-002003), which is co-financed by QREN, in the scope of the Mais Centro Program and European Union's FEDER; Fundação para a Ciência e Tecnologia (FCT), Portugal, under the grant SFRH/BD/90968/2012; project ConCreTe. The project ConCreTe acknowledges the financial support of the Future and Emerging Technologies (FET) programme within the Seventh Framework Programme for Research of the European Commission, under FET grant number 611733.

8. REFERENCES

[1] S. Baluja, D. Pomerlau, and J. Todd. Towards automated artificial evolution for computer-generated images. *Connection Science*, 6(2):325–354, 1994.

[2] L. Beadle and C. G. Johnson. Semantically driven mutation in genetic programming. In *IEEE Congress on Evolutionary Computation*, pages 1336–1342. IEEE, 2009.

[3] J. Correia, P. Machado, J. Romero, and A. Carballal. Feature selection and novelty in computational aesthetics. In P. Machado, J. McDermott, and A. Carballal, editors, *EvoMUSART*, volume 7834 of *Lecture Notes in Computer Science*, pages 133–144. Springer, 2013.

[4] A. Ekárt, A. Joó, D. Sharma, and S. Chalakov. Modelling the underlying principles of human aesthetic preference in evolutionary art. *Journal of Mathematics and the Arts*, 6(2-3):107–124, 2012.

[5] G. Greenfield. Evolving aesthetic images using multiobjective optimization. In *Evolutionary Computation, 2003. CEC '03. The 2003 Congress on*, volume 3, pages 1903–1909 Vol.3, 2003.

[6] G. R. Greenfield. On the co-evolution of evolving expressions. *International Journal of Computational Intelligence and Applications*, 2(1):17–31, 2002.

[7] D. A. Hart. Toward greater artistic control for interactive evolution of images and animation. In *Proceedings of the 2007 EvoWorkshops 2007 on EvoCoMnet, EvoFIN, EvoIASP,EvoINTERACTION, EvoMUSART, EvoSTOC and EvoTransLog*, pages 527–536, Berlin, Heidelberg, 2007. Springer-Verlag.

[8] T. Jiang, L. Wang, and K. Zhang. Alignment of trees – an alternative to tree edit. *Theoretical Computer Science*, 143(1):137–148, 1995.

[9] T. Kowaliw, A. Dorin, and J. McCormack. An Empirical Exploration of a Definition of Creative Novelty for Generative Art. In K. B. Korb, M. Randall, and T. Hendtlass, editors, *ACAL*, volume 5865 of *Lecture Notes in Computer Science*, pages 1–10. Springer, 2009.

[10] M. Lewis. Evolutionary visual art and design. In J. Romero and P. Machado, editors, *The Art of Artificial Evolution: A Handbook on Evolutionary Art and Music*, pages 3–37. Springer Berlin Heidelberg, 2007.

[11] Y. Li, C. Hu, L. L. Minku, and H. Zuo. Learning aesthetic judgements in evolutionary art systems. *Genetic Programming and Evolvable Machines*, 14(3):315–337, 2013.

[12] P. Machado and A. Cardoso. All the truth about NEvAr. *Applied Intelligence, Special Issue on Creative Systems*, 16(2):101–119, 2002.

[13] J. McCormack. Facing the future: Evolutionary possibilities for human-machine creativity. In J. Romero and P. Machado, editors, *The Art of Artificial Evolution: A Handbook on Evolutionary Art and Music*, pages 417–451. Springer Berlin Heidelberg, 2007.

[14] A. Moraglio, K. Krawiec, and C. G. Johnson. Geometric semantic genetic programming. In C. A. C. Coello, V. Cutello, K. Deb, S. Forrest, G. Nicosia, and M. Pavone, editors, *PPSN (1)*, volume 7491 of *Lecture Notes in Computer Science*, pages 21–31. Springer, 2012.

[15] S. B. Needleman and C. D. Wunsch. A general method applicable to the search for similarities in the amino acid sequence of two proteins. *Journal of molecular biology*, 48(3):443–453, 1970.

[16] C. Notredame. Recent progress in multiple sequence alignment: a survey. *Pharmacogenomics*, 3(1):131–144, 2002.

[17] J. Romero and P. Machado, editors. *The Art of Artificial Evolution: A Handbook on Evolutionary Art and Music*. Natural Computing Series. Springer Berlin Heidelberg, November 2007.

[18] K. Sims. Artificial evolution for computer graphics. *ACM Computer Graphics*, 25:319–328, 1991.

[19] T. Unemi. Sbart2.4: Breeding 2d cg images and movies, and creating a type of collage. In *The Third International Conference on Knowledge-based Intelligent Information Engineering Systems*, pages 288–291, Adelaide, Australia, 1999.

[20] N. Q. Uy, N. X. Hoai, M. O'Neill, R. I. McKay, and E. G. López. Semantically-based crossover in genetic programming: application to real-valued symbolic regression. *Genetic Programming and Evolvable Machines*, 12(2):91–119, 2011.

[21] L. Vanneschi, M. Castelli, L. Manzoni, and S. Silva. A new implementation of geometric semantic gp and its application to problems in pharmacokinetics. In K. Krawiec, A. Moraglio, T. Hu, A. S. Etaner-Uyar, and B. Hu, editors, *EuroGP*, volume 7831 of *Lecture Notes in Computer Science*, pages 205–216. Springer, 2013.

[22] L. World. Aesthetic selection: The evolutionary art of steven Rooke. *IEEE Computer Graphics and Applications*, 16(1), 1996.

Automatic Design of Sound Synthesizers as Pure Data Patches using Coevolutionary Mixed-typed Cartesian Genetic Programming

Matthieu Macret
School of Interactive Arts and Technology
Simon Fraser University
B.C., Canada V3T 0A3
mmacret@sfu.ca

Philippe Pasquier
School of Interactive Arts and Technology
Simon Fraser University
B.C., Canada V3T 0A3
pasquier@sfu.ca

ABSTRACT

A sound synthesizer can be defined as a program that takes a few input parameters and returns a sound. The general sound synthesis problem could then be formulated as: given a sound (or a set of sounds) what program and set of input parameters can generate that sound (set of sounds)? We propose a novel approach to tackle this problem in which we represent sound synthesizers using Pure Data (Pd), a graphic programming language for digital signal processing. We search the space of possible sound synthesizers using Coevolutionary Mixed-typed Cartesian Genetic Programming (MT-CGP), and the set of input parameters using a standard Genetic Algorithm (GA). The proposed algorithm coevolves a population of MT-CGP graphs, representing the functional forms of synthesizers, and a population of GA chromosomes, representing their inputs parameters. A fitness function based on the Mel-frequency Cepstral Coefficients (MFCC) evaluates the distance between the target and produced sounds. Our approach is capable of suggesting novel functional forms and input parameters, suitable to approximate a given target sound (and we hope in future iterations a set of sounds). Since the resulting synthesizers are presented as Pd patches, the user can experiment, interact with, and reuse them.

Categories and Subject Descriptors

H.5.5 [**Sound and Music Computing**]: Methodologies and techniques.

General Terms

Algorithms

Keywords

Cartesian Genetic Programming; Coevolution; Sound Synthesis

GECCO'14, July 12–16, 2014, Vancouver, BC, Canada.

ACM 978-1-4503-2662-9/14/07 ...$15.00.
http://dx.doi.org/10.1145/2576768.2598303.

1. INTRODUCTION

Replicating sounds using synthesis techniques is a problem frequently addressed in the field of computer music [12]. A well-researched problem is the following: Given a target sound and a synthesizer, what set of input parameters can replicate or approximate this sound. Manually estimating input parameters of a particular synthesizer is usually difficult and time consuming, especially when there is no intuitive relationship between the input parameter values and the sound produced. This search for input parameters is then a good candidate for an automatic optimization scheme. Thus, diverse optimization methods have been used for automatic calibration, such as Particle Swarm [11], HMM [34], Neural Nets [27], Cellular Automata [29] and Genetic Algorithms [12]. It has been suggested that evolutionary approaches such as Genetic Algorithms (GAs) are performing the best to matching musical instrument tones [27]. GAs have been used extensively for estimating the parameters of various synthesis techniques [1, 8, 13, 14, 17, 22, 28, 31] and real-world synthesizers [16, 33]. For instance, we developed a GA-based system [17] able to automatically calibrate a ModFM synthesizer to replicate harmonic instrument tones. We then worked on a more complex problem: calibrating the OP-1 synthesizer [16]. This commercial synthesizer contains several synthesis engines, effects and Low-Frequency-Oscillators, which make the parameter search space large, complex, but also discontinuous. In order to tackle this difficult problem we proposed using a Non-dominated Sorting Genetic Algorithm-II (NSGA-II) with multiple objectives.

In this work, instead of only searching the space of input parameters for a specific synthesizer, we attempt to solve the more general sound synthesis problem: given a sound, what program (sound synthesizer) and set of input parameters can generate that target sound? We propose a system in which we represent sound synthesizers as directed acyclic graphs using the graphical programming language: Pure Data (Pd). We search the space of possible sound synthesizers using Coevolutionary Mixed-typed Cartesian Genetic Programming (MT-CGP). The proposed algorithm co-evolves a population of MT-CGP graphs, representing *functional forms* of synthesizers, and a population of GA chromosomes, representing their *inputs parameters.* A fitness function based on the Mel-frequency Cepstral Coefficients (MFCC) evaluates the distance between the target and produced sounds. We run experiments using contrived and recorded target sounds. The resulting sounds and synthesizers presented as Pd patches are available online [5] and are discussed in Section 5.

2. RELATED WORK

Only a few attempts have been made at solving the general sound synthesis problem. The resulting systems differ from other GA sound matching systems [1, 8, 13, 14, 17, 22, 28, 31] in that they are not only searching the *inputs parameters* but also the *functional form* of the synthesizer.

Takala et al. [30] evolved what they called *Timbre Trees*. The nodes of these trees were arithmetic operations, analytic functions or noise generators. They defined a roulette-wheel selection operator as well as a crossover and mutation operator for trees. The user had to listen to the sounds generated using these trees and interactively evaluate them. Takala et al used the term Genetic Algorithm to describe their system but the term Genetic Programming (GP) seems more appropriate given the algorithmic process and genetic operators they defined. They implemented directly their system in C++ without using any generic sound synthesis library. While the authors reported that they successfully used their system to produce an entire class of bee-like sounds (ranging from mosquitos to chain saws), they did not present any proper evaluation.

More recently, Garcia [9] designed a Genetic Programming (GP) system for automatic generation of sound synthesis techniques. He encodes the instructions for building sound synthesis topology graphs in the GP expression trees. Production rules are defined to ensure that any valid expression tree will produce a valid topology. The nodes of the topologies are chosen from six different types of basis synthesizer components (oscillator, addition/multiplication operators, filters, etc). These topologies have two inputs parameters that are optimized by a canonical GA. He defined the fitness function as the least-squared error of the short-time spectra where the frequencies that are not heard by the average listener are ignored. The system was implemented directly in C++ and Matlab without using any generic sound synthesis library. Garcia tested his system with a FM woodwind instrument and verified that it could generate an expression tree with close similarity to the target FM equation used to design the instrument. However, there were higher energies at high frequencies. He also got modest results evolving a synthesizer for a sampled piano tone that sounded like a *string hit by a hammer*.

3. PURE DATA

Pure Data (Pd) [25] is a graphical programming environment for audio, video, and image processing popular among musicians, artists and sound designers. Pd programs (called *patches*) are made by arranging and connecting boxes within a visual *canvas*. There are four types of boxes: object, message, GUI (number boxes, toggles, sliders, etc.) and comment. Objects act as self-contained programs, each of which may receive inputs (through one or more visual *inlets*), generate outputs (through visual *outlets*), or both. Inputs and outputs can be of two types: *audio signal* or *control message* (trigger, integer or float). A connection can link the output of a given box and the input of another one (see Figure 1c). A connection can represent a control signal (represented in Pure Data by a thin link) or an audio signal (thick link). A control (audio) signal can only be produced by a control (audio) object. The presence of the sign $\sim$ in an object box indicates that it is an audio object (see Figure 1c). Audio (control) signals can only be transmitted between specifically defined audio (control) outlets and inlets.

We represent the synthesizers in Pd as directed acyclic graphs. Hundreds of object types are available in Pd. In order to limit the size of the search space, we select only objects that are the common building blocks of sound synthesizers in Pd. Table 1 shows a selection of Pd objects available to our search algorithm. This list includes arithmetic, trigonometric operations for controls and signals but also oscillators and filters. These objects are commonly used by Pd programmers [25] to implement major sound synthesis techniques such as additive, subtractive, FM, AM or PM synthesis. Each of these Pd objects has one to three inlets and only one outlet. Each inlet (outlet) is connected to one or more outlets (inlets). Figure 1c shows an example of Pd graphs evolved by our algorithm. In principle, any synthesizer can be represented as a Pd patch [25].

4. MIXED TYPED CARTESIAN GENETIC PROGRAMMING

Cartesian Genetic Programming (CGP) [21] is a form of Genetic Programming that encodes a directed acyclic graph representation of a computer program instead of a tree. The genotype, a string of integers, determines the functions of nodes in the graph, the connections between nodes, the connections to inputs and the locations in the graph where outputs are taken from. Using a graph representation is very flexible as many computational structures can be represented as a graph. Examples of this are artificial neural networks, electronic circuits or mathematical equations [21]. In this work, we represents Pd patches which are directed acyclic graphs in their general form.

This graph representation presents advantages over the classical tree-based GP representation. In a CGP graph, the output of a given node can be connected to one or more inputs of other nodes. It is not the case with a tree representation where a node output can only be connected to one other node. In addition, nodes of the graph are not necessary connected indirectly or directly to the output node of the program (e.g. second node see Figure 1b). As a result, nodes in the representation can have no effect on the output, a feature known in CGP as *neutrality*. This has been shown to be useful to the evolutionary process [21].

Mixed Typed Cartesian Genetic Programming (MT-CGP) is an extension of CGP [10] that handles multiple data types. Contrary to CGP, MT-CGP genotypes represent a linear string of nodes, without loss of generality. That is to say, only one row of nodes is used in contrast to CGP which can have a rectangular grid of nodes. The evolutionary algorithm usually used with MT-CGP is a $1 + 4$ Evolutionary Strategy [10].

To generate programs with multiple data types, MT-CGP uses an internal data type that can be cast to different data types. In MT-CGP, the functions inspect the types of the input values being passed to it, and determine the most suitable operation to perform. This in turn determines the output type of the function. In our implementation, we represent the functions as Pd objects and consider the two internal data types used in Pd: *signal* (for audio signal) and *control* (for float or integer messages). The functions inspect the types of the input values being passed to them, and, given a set of predefined rules (see Table 1), determine the most suitable Pd object type to implement. For example, consider a function with a type gene value equals to 0. This function takes two inputs and returns one output. There are 3 input cases that need to be considered: two controls, two signals and a signal and a control. The sum of two control is performed by the + object, the signal addition and sum of the signal and a control by the $+\sim$ object. In Figure 1a, the node 3 has a type gene value equals to 0. It is interpreted as a $+\sim$ Pd object (see Figure 1c) because its 2 inputs are respectively of type *signal* and *control*. This node has then an output of type *signal* (thick connection).

Figure 1a shows an example of a CGP chromosome (genotype) corresponding to the CGP graph (phenotype) in Figure 1b and the Pd patch in Figure 1c. In this first implementation, the first 3 genes are not interpreted as we enforce Pd patch inputs of type *control*. In future iterations of this system, we plan to use these genes to code for the type of the Pd patch inputs. A gene would then code for either a *control* input (type 0) or for a*signal* input (type 1). More inputs could be added by simply appending new genes at the beginning of the chromosome.

The following genes are grouped by 5 in genesets (between brackets). Each of these genesets represents a node of the MT-CGP graph and are numbered from left to right starting from 0. Each MT-CGP node represents a Pd object and is encoded with the five genes (four integers and one double) of the corresponding geneset. The first gene of a geneset specifies the Pd object type that the node represents. The next three genes are used to specify the nodes from which the Pd object obtains its inputs. These connection addresses are defined relative to the current node and specify how many nodes backwards in the genotype/graph to connect. If a relative address extends beyond the extent of the genome, a new connection address is computed by taking the relative address modulo 3 in order to get the address of one of the 3 input nodes. We consider only 3 genes coding for connections because in our system, the Pd objects available to the search algorithm have an arity of maximum 3 (see Table 1).

The final gene for each node is a floating point number that can be interpreted as either a function parameter, or used to generate values within the program. In our case, this extra parameter is used as constant for arithmetic operations (see gene value 9 in Table 1) and also to handle special cases to determine the most suitable Pd object type to use. For example, for the gene value 6 that represents the low pass filter (*lop* $\sim$), if there is no signal input, a new gene value is computed by taking the extra parameter modulo 4 in order to get a arithmetic object (gene value from 0 to 3) compatible with these inputs.

Table 2 gives the range of each gene types. The extra parameter can take integer values between 0 and 22500. 22500 is the Nyquist frequency for a sampling rate of 44.1 kHz and also the upper bound of the human hearing frequency range.

The decoded CGP graph (Figure 1b) is then embedded in the engine Pd patch (Figure 1c). Nodes that are not connected directly or indirectly to the output in the CGP graph are are not visible in the Pd patch as they have no effect on the sound produced.

Gene value	**Input 1**	**Input 2**	**Input 3**	**Extra param.**	**Pd Object**	**Description**	**Output type**
0	**c**	**c**	-	-	+	Addition	c
0	**s**	**c**	-	-	+~	Addition	s
0	**c**	**s**	-	-	+~	Addition	s
0	**s**	**s**	-	-	+~	Addition	s
...							
3	**c**	**c**	-	-	/	Division	c
3	**s**	**c**	-	-	/~	Division	s
3	**c**	**s**	-	-	/~	Division	s
3	**s**	**s**	-	-	/~	Division	s
4	**s**	**c**	-	-	osc~	Oscillator	s
4	**c**	**c**	-	-	osc~	Oscillator	c
...							
5	**s**	**c**	-	-	phasor~	Sawtooth oscillator	s
5	**c**	**c**	-	-	phasor~	Sawtooth oscillator	c
...							
6	**s**	**c**	-	-	lop~	Low pass filter	s
6	**c**	**s**	-	-	lop~	Low pass filter	s
6	**s**	s	s	**v**	lop~	Low pass filter	s
6	**c**	**c**	v	v	s.c.	Arithmetic function	c
...							
9	**s**	-	-	**v**	+~	Add a constant	s
9	**c**	-	-	**v**	+	Add a constant	c
...							

Table 1: Rules that determine the type of the Pd object that each node of the CGP graph represents given its respective gene value and its input types. s is for signal type, c for control type, v for the extra parameter and - for unused parameter. The inputs of the nodes that are considered for connection for the corresponding Pd object are set in bold. s.c. is a special case where the gene value is replaced by the value of the extra parameter modulo 4. The rule is then reapplied using the result as the new gene value.

4.1 Evolutionary algorithm and parameters

MT-CGP is used with a simple Evolutionary Strategy $1 + n$ with $n = 4$. In this setting, the best performing individual is selected as the parent. However, if the best performance is achieved by more than a single individual the ES chooses the one with the shortest program (i.e. the individual with the fewest connected nodes). When this choice is not unique, the newest individual is selected. Choosing the shortest program pushes evolution to find more compact programs. The preference to newer individuals has been shown to help MT-CGP find better solutions [10].

In keeping with the $1+n$ evolutionary strategy, MT-CGP does not use crossover. This *mutation-only* approach is typical in MT-CGP and it appears that a high mutation rate (10%) performs best [10]. The mutation rate is defined as the probability of each gene to be modified when generating an offspring. MT-CGP requires few parameters compared to other Evolutionary Algorithms [10], even in a distributed system.

$$[0, 0, 0, [5, 1, 4, 6, 295], [9, 2, 10, 5, 14773], [0, 2, 9, 7, 14300], [3, 5, 6, 1, 9520], [7, 9, 3, 3, 4108], [4, 3, 2, 4, 15775], [1]$$

(a) CGP chromosome (genotype)

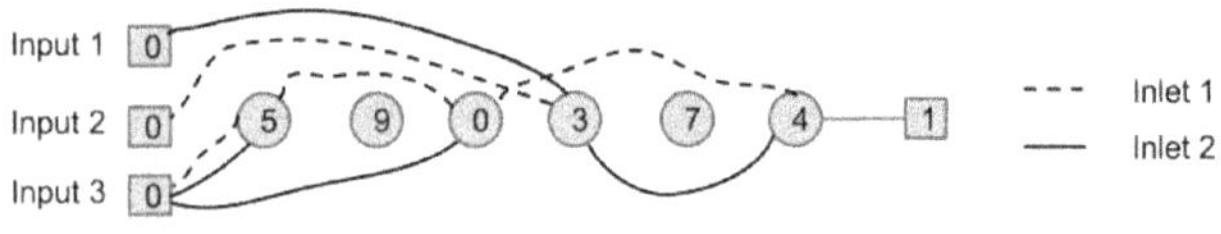

(b) CGP graph (phenotype)

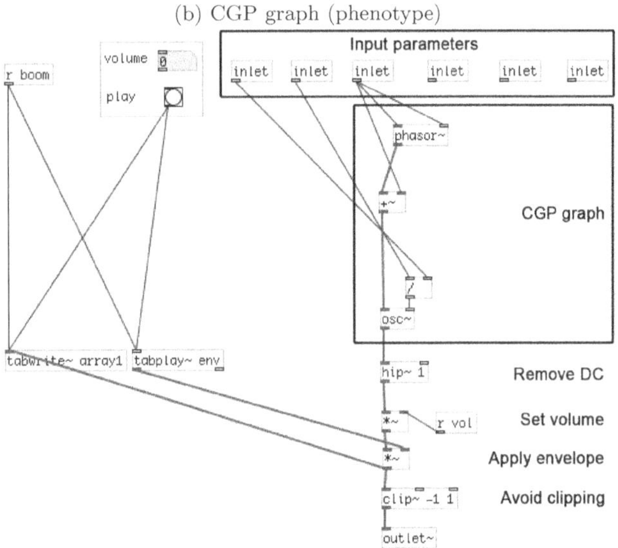

(c) Pd patch engine

Figure 1: Example of CGP chromosome decoding

Table 2 lists the parameters of our MT-CGP algorithm. These values have not been optimized, and therefore it may be possible to improve the performances of our system by conducting a parameter sensitivity analysis.

4.2 Similarity measure and fitness function

In this implementation, we consider the Mel-frequency Cepstral Coefficients (MFCC) to measure the similarity between the target sound and the sounds generated by the evolved patches. This sound feature has been initially developed for the task of speech recognition [20]. It also has been extensively used in Music Information Retrieval (MIR) systems [3, 4] and in automatic synthesizer calibration systems [27]. Yee-King and Roth [27] conducted a study to compare the performances of four parametric optimization techniques for automatic synthesizer calibration. The results of their study showed that the GA, with the MFCC fitness function, outperformed all the other optimization techniques in every experiments.

In the pre-processing steps of our algorithm, we extract the MFCC coefficients from the target sound on each time window. The same extraction is done on each candidate sound generated by the evolved Pd patches. Then, we calculate the Euclidean distances between the MFCC vector on each frame, sum them and finally divide this value by the number of frames.

Parameter (CGP)	Value
Max. number of generations	5000
Gene mutation rate	10%
Genotype length	50 genes
Number of inputs	3
Number of outputs	1
Type gene range	$[0, 14]$
Object input connections range	$[1, 50]$
Extra parameters range	$[0, 22050]$
Parameter (GA)	**Value**
Population size	150
Mutation probability	10%
Bitflip probability	10%
Crossover probability	80%
Tournament selection size	2
Elitism	3%
Bit-string size	$15 \times 3 = 45$

Table 2: CGP and GA parameters

Equation (1) shows how we compute this distance between the sound t and c.

$$d_{MFCC}(t, c) = \frac{\sum_{i=1}^{N_w} \sqrt{\sum_{j=1}^{N_c} (t_{i,j} - c_{i,j})^2}}{N_w} \tag{1}$$

The sampling rate is 44100 Hz and we set a window analysis size of 1024 samples (23 ms) and an overlapping of 512 samples (11.5 ms). N_w is the total number of windows. N_c is the number of MFCC coefficients that is set to 13. $t_{i,j}$ (resp. $c_{i,j}$) is the jth MFCC coefficient on the ith window for the sound t (resp. c).

The fitness function is then obtained by Equation (2) and gives a measure of similarity ranging from 0 (not similar) to 1 (perfect match).

$$fit = \frac{1}{1 + d_{MFCC}} \tag{2}$$

The goal of our optimization algorithm is then to find the synthesizer (Pd patch) and set of inputs parameters that maximize this fitness function.

4.3 Evaluation in Coevolutionary MT-CGP

In GP, CGP or MT-CGP, the fitness of a given generated program is, most of the time, evaluated given a dataset of inputs [10, 21]. For example, Harding and al. [10] used MT-CGP to generate programs that classify clinical data into two classes: cancer and non-cancer. They used the well known Wisconsin breast cancer dataset as dataset of inputs to evaluate theirs MT-CGP programs.

In our case, it is not possible to generate a generic dataset of inputs that would work for every synthesizers generated by MT-CGP. For a given synthesizer (MT-CGP program), it is not possible to know in advance what would be good input parameters to approximate the target sound. To deal with this issue, we coevolve a population of input parameters using a GA in parallel to the CGP population [15, 24]. In our system, the 3 input parameters of the Pd patches are integers ranging from 0 to 32767. These 3 integers are encoded as 15 bits bitstrings. Any floats or integers can then be obtained from a given input parameter using arithmetic or trigonometric Pd objects (see Table 1). Each CGP indi-

	Fitness (see Eq (2))				Nb. Pd Objects				
Contrived sound	max	min	std	mean	max	min	std	mean	target
additive	0.1572	0.1475	0.0055	0.1509	14	6	4.0415	10.333	20
FM	0.2467	0.1967	0.0273	0.2154	10	5	2.6458	8	7
phase	0.2171	0.1747	0.0225	0.1915	8	7	0.5774	7.3333	8
ring	0.2718	0.2407	0.0220	0.2563	14	10	2.8284	12	20
Recorded sound	max	min	std	mean	max	min	std	mean	target
op1	0.4265	0.4023	0.0580	0.4132	10	8	0.6534	9	X
transient	0.4126	0.4114	0.0001	0.4120	6	5	0.4171	5.3	X
clarinet	0.4212	0.4154	0.0041	0.4183	12	7	3.5355	9.5	X
cello	0.3977	0.3518	0.0325	0.3748	10	7	2.1213	8.5	X

Table 3: Experiment results

vidual is then evaluated using the inputs parameters taken from the GA population. The best fitness score obtained over the GA population is assigned to the CGP individual.

For each generation, once the 5 CGP individuals have been evaluated, each GA individual has been evaluated 5 times and consequently has 5 distinct fitness scores. The best score among these 5 fitness scores becomes the unique fitness score of the GA individual. This way, GA individuals, scoring high with CGP individuals that are not selected in the next generation, are more likely to be kept in the GA population. With this mechanism, we maintain diversity in the GA population (input parameters) and avoid to bias this population toward a specific CGP individual (synthesizer).

The GA population is then varied using a bitflip mutation and a 2-point crossover operator implementing an diversity preservation method (incest prevention strategy [26]). Table 2 lists the parameters used in the GA.

A neutral mutation is a mutation that does not change the CGP phenotype [21]. In order not to perform unnecessary evaluations, when neutral mutations is detected, the new CGP offspring is not evaluated but get the same fitness score than its parent. This offspring also replace its parents to encourage this kind of mutation that can lead to shorter graphs. Likewise, when the output of the last Pd object is of type control for a given CGP individual, the Pd patch does not produce any sound. The CGP individual is then not evaluated and it receives the minimal fitness score (0).

4.4 Pd patch design

Any sound synthesizer offers the functionality of changing the volume. In order to limit the complexity of the search, we normalize the sounds before evaluating them and provide a volume parameter on the Pd patch GUI for the user to adjust.

The difficulty in sound matching is mainly getting the right timbre and pitch [12]. The temporal envelope can easily be obtained using, for example, an envelope follower. Searching the temporal envelope in addition to the other parameters has shown to increase significantly the complexity of the problem [16]. Moreover, in most sound synthesizers, the temporal envelope is usually adjusted separately by the user. For example, the user may want a longer sustain and a shorter attack for the sound.

In our implementation, the temporal envelope is not optimized during the evolution. In the pre-processing steps of our algorithm, we extract the target envelope using an envelope follower. This envelope is then applied to the sound at the output of the CGP graph (see Figure 1c). One advantage of this approach is that the user can easily replace this envelope by an envelope of her choice: for instance, a *vline* ~ object generating an ADSR envelope.

4.5 Implementation

The evolved CGP graph is embedded in a Pd patch consisting of two canvas. The first canvas is the canvas that the user sees when opening the patch. This canvas is common to every patches evolved and acts as GUI. On this canvas, the user can change the input parameters and the volume. A bang object has to be triggered to set the input parameters to the values optimized by our search algorithm. Another bang object triggers the generation of the sound. This sound can be listened and its waveform visualized on a graph.

The second patch called *engine* embeds the CGP graph evolved by our algorithm (see Figure 1c). The outlet of the last object of this graph is connected to a high-pass filter (*hip* ~) to remove the DC component of the generated sound. It is then multiply by the envelope extracted from the target sound. This envelope is scaled by the *volume* parameter that can be adjusted on the GUI.

The implementation of the GA and MT-CGP uses the DEAP Python framework [6]. The MFCC coefficients are extracted using the Python wrapper for Yaafe [18]. The rules to determine the Pd object type given its inputs (see Table 1) are applied using the Python knowledge-based inference engine Pyke [7]. To speed up the execution of our search algorithm, we use the Bugaboo cluster that is part of Compute Canada/Westgrid [32]. We distribute the evaluation of the GA population for each CGP individual over 50 nodes. Pd is embedded in our algorithm using the Python wrappers offered by libpd [2]. CGP graphs from DEAP are converted into Pd file format that can be directly loaded with libpd from memory and processed to get the resulting sound. Using libpd makes possible to avoid parallel hard drive access. Instead of exporting the sound as a file, libpd directly provides Yaafe with the corresponding array of samples ready to be analyzed. This advantage can seem minor but it is actually significant in a distributed context where parallel hard drive access has to be avoided.

5. EXPERIMENTS

To demonstrate the validity of our approach, we have tested our algorithm with two types of target sounds: contrived sounds [23] and recorded sounds. The first category of sounds are sounds generated by Pd Patches. We generated four target sounds using additive synthesis, FM synthesis,

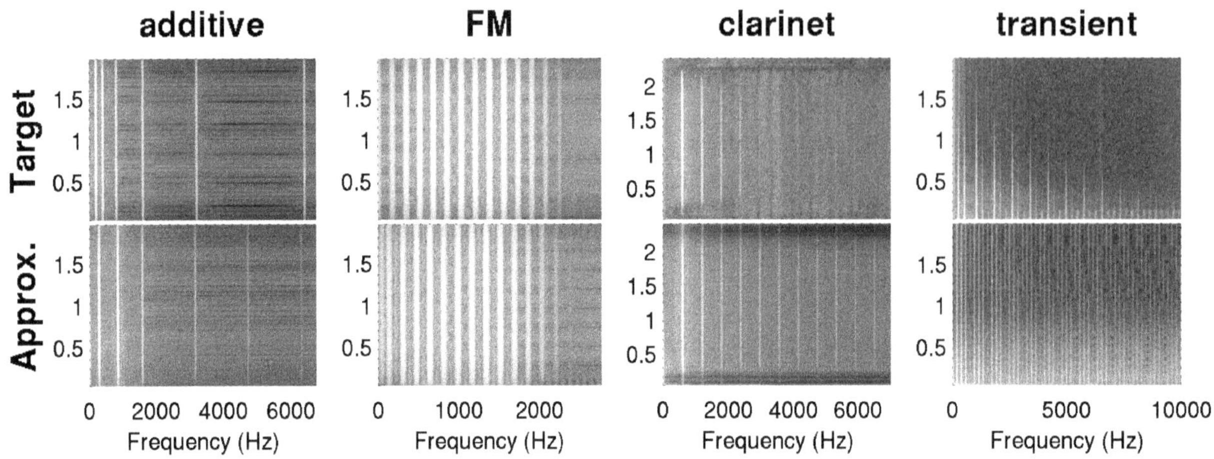

Figure 2: Spectra comparisons between approximated and target sounds

phase synthesis and ring modulation synthesis. In this experiment, we know that a solution exists in the Pd patches space that replicates perfectly this sound. We want to inquire whether our algorithm is able to reverse engineer the Pd patch or discover a novel way to approximate this sound.

The second category of sounds are recorded sounds that could be instrumental, natural or even synthesized by other means than Pd. We select four sounds: a clarinet sound, a cello sound, a transient sound and a sound synthesized by a commercial synthesizer (the OP-1). In this experiment, we want to see how well the synthesizers produced approximate these sounds, but also investigate what kind of program is found.

Table 3 gives the maximum, minimum, standard deviation and mean across 5 repetitions for each target sound. For the contrived sounds, one can notice that our system generates Pd patches that are more compact than the ones used to initially produce the target sounds. For a given target sound, the performance of our system is consistent across experimental repetitions ($std < 0.05$).

We report in the rest of this section the results of the most successful runs of our algorithm. Figure 2 compares the target spectra and their approximations by our algorithm for 2 contrived sounds (additive and FM) and 2 recorded sounds (clarinet and transient). The evolved Pd patches and sounds are available for download online [5].

Our system was unable to perfectly replicate the target sound in any of the experiments but it did approximate it using interesting synthesis methods. As the Pd patches are meant to be played with, it is relevant to look at the effect of changing an input parameter on the output sound. For example, in a Pd patch evolved for the flute sound, one input parameter was directly mapped to the pitch of the sound. It is then easy to generate another flute sound with a different pitch using this parameter.

For the additive target sound, the evolved synthesizer generates a spectrum that matches four of the five harmonics. When looking at the structure of the evolved patch, we can see that it is using additive synthesis. Oscillator objects ($osc \sim$) are added together using an addition object ($+ \sim$). Some patches even use Phasor objects ($phasor \sim$) (that generate sawtooth signals whose spectrum contains even and odd harmonics of the input frequency) instead of oscillator objects. Coupled with a low pass filter ($lop \sim$), it makes possible to generate spectra with a limited number of harmonics in a more compact way than adding together as many oscillators as there are harmonics.

For the FM target sound, the evolved synthesizer generates a spectrum very similar to a FM spectrum with a fundamental frequency and side bands frequencies of decreasing amplitudes. Looking at the structure of the evolved patch, it uses a combination of FM synthesis and ring modulation synthesis. Oscillator, Phasor and cosine waveshaper ($cos \sim$ objects output the cosine of two π times its signal input) objects are combined to approximate the target spectrum. The same observations can be made for the experiments using target sounds from ring and phase modulation.

We experimented with different recorded sounds. One of the most successful was the clarinet sound. Our system was able to find a very compact way of re-synthesizing this sound. It uses a Phasor centered on the fundamental frequency of the target clarinet sound and filters the high frequencies with a low pass filter. The result is a very suitable approximation of the target sound. As with the flute sound, the pitch of the sound was one of the input parameters evolved.

Our system was also to approximate sounds synthesized by other means than Pd. For example, for a sound generated by the OP-1, the evolved patch is able to match the frequencies of every harmonics but not their correct amplitudes. It is also able to match a transient sound even if there are some unwanted harmonics in the high frequency range. However, the results were less successful for sounds with time-varying spectrum such as piano sounds, voice sounds or synthesized sounds involving LFO.

6. DISCUSSION

Compared to Garcia's system [9], our system presents some advantages. First, the synthesizer structures are directly encoded in the CGP graphs while, in Garcia's system, the GP trees had to be mapped to the synthesizer structures using production rules. Second, acyclic directed CGP graphs are also more expressive representations than the GP trees. For example, in a CGP graph, an output of a given node can be connected to one or more inputs of other nodes. It is not the case with Garcia's representation where a node output can only be connected to one other node.

In Garcia's system, the input parameters of each synthesizer functions had to be optimized by a GA. Computational resources were wasted when trying to optimized input parameters for unpromising synthesizer functions. Co-evolving a GA population of input parameters in parallel of the CGP population does a better use of the computational resources. Synthesizer functions and input parameters are evolved in parallel. The potential of promising synthesizer functions are unveiled using fitter and fitter input parameters while maintaining diversity in the GA population to discover novel functions. This approach also makes possible to better distribute the input parameters search between the GA and CGP. Arithmetic operations and constants (using the extra parameter) are available to the CGP algorithm (see Table 1). The search for the best inputs parameters is then made in cooperation between the GA that adjusts the input parameters and the CGP that changes the way these parameters are used in the synthesizer function. For example, given an input parameter with value 4, a target value 8 can be obtained either by, directly modifying bits in the GA bitstring that encodes the value, or by applying a suitable arithmetic operation in the CGP graph (multiply by the constant 2, add 4, etc.) or both. This balance between GA and CGP in the input parameter search can be adjusted by modifying the number of input parameters. For example, if we reduce the number of input parameters from 3 to 2, more complexity would be required in the CGP graph to regenerate these 3 initial parameters internally using only 2 input parameters.

Another advantage of our system is the representation of the synthesizers as Pd patches [25]. Pd counts a large user base and has a popular commercial version (MAX/MSP) commonly used in professional audio production. The Pd patches evolved by our system can easily be modified and reused in other contexts or applications. Garcia took a different approach and developed his own library to represent the synthesizers. This library was designed especially to work with his GP system and was not thought to be easily modified or reused in other applications. Moreover, more synthesizer's components are available with Pd than in Garcia's system making possible to generate more complex synthesizers and match more complex sounds.

Finally, Garcia's system required 20 to 200 hours per experiments. As our algorithm is distributed on a cluster, we are able to limit the time to perform an experiment to 5 hours. For each experiment, we evolve 5000 generations that represents at most 3.75×10^6 evaluations ($5000 \times 5 \times 150$). This number could be highly reduced by fine-tuning the GA and CGP parameters (see Table 2). We also constrained the types of Pd objects accessible to our algorithm to the basic building blocks of synthesizers. Adding more complex objects, such as more sophisticated filters or envelopes, could lead to novel function discoveries and a better and faster convergence.

7. CONCLUSIONS AND FUTURE WORKS

We propose a new approach to automate the design process of sound synthesizers using Coevolutionary Mixed-typed Cartesian Programming. The approach is capable of evolving synthesizer structures for generating sounds similar to the target sound (according to the fitness function based on MFCC coefficients). We represent the synthesizer structures using acyclic directed graphs and optimize the synthesizer's input parameters in parallel using a GA. We run a small number of experiments but their results are promising and show the potential of using Coevolutionary Mixed-typed Cartesian Programming as an approach to automate the design of sound synthesizers.

Our proposed method involves quite many parameters (see Table 2). We plan to perform a parameter sensitivity analysis to investigate the robustness of our method and also determine how to set these parameters in a procedural fashion. We also plan on performing a more rigorous quantitative and qualitative comparison with previous similar systems [9, 30] using, for example, a same benchmark of target sounds and reporting on their respective performance.

In this work, we limited our search to only one target sound. We plan to extend our system to search the synthesizer space for synthesizers able to reproduce not only one sound but a set of sounds. For example, one could search for a synthesizer able to produce clarinet sounds but also oboe sounds just by changing the input parameters. Considering sound as a multi-dimensional object has shown to be helpful to better explore the sound space [16, 19]. For future work, we plan to take into account more sound features (psycho-acoustic, spectral or temporal) instead of only MFCC coefficients.

8. ACKNOWLEDGMENTS

This research was funded by a grant from the Canada Council for the Arts, and the Natural Sciences and Engineering Research Council of Canada.

References

[1] Bozkurt, B. and Yüksel, K. Parallel evolutionary optimization of digital sound synthesis parameters. In *Proceedings of the Conference on Applications of Evolutionary Computation* (2011), pp. 194–203.

[2] Brinkmann, P., Kirn, P., Lawler, R., McCormick, C., Roth, M., and Steiner, H. Embedding pure data with libpd. In *Proceedings of the Pure Data Convention* (2011).

[3] Brown, J. C., Houix, O., and McAdams, S. Feature dependence in the automatic identification of musical woodwind instruments. *The Journal of the Acoustical Society of America 109* (2001), 1064–1072.

[4] Casey, M., Veltkamp, R., Goto, M., Leman, M., Rhodes, C., and Slaney, M. Content-based music information retrieval: Current directions and future challenges. *Proceedings of the IEEE 96*, 4 (2008), 668–696.

[5] Experiment results for contrived and recorded sounds. `http://metacreation.net/mmacret/GECCO2014/` [Last accessed: April 2014].

[6] Fortin F., De Rainville F., Gardner M., Parizeau M. and Gagné C. DEAP: Evolutionary algorithms made easy. *Journal of Machine Learning Research 13* (2012), 2171–2175.

[7] Frederiksen, B. Applying expert system technology to code reuse with pyke. In *Proceedings of the conference on the Python Conference (PyCon)* (2008).

[8] FUJINAGA, I. AND VANTOMME, J. Genetic algorithms as a method for granular synthesis regulation. In *Proceedings of the International Computer Music Conference* (1994), pp. 138–146.

[9] GARCIA, R. Automating the design of sound synthesis techniques using evolutionary methods. In *Proceedings of the conference on Digital Audio Effects, Limerick, Ireland* (2001), Citeseer, pp. 1–8.

[10] HARDING, S., GRAZIANO, V., LEITNER, J., AND SCHMIDHUBER, J. MT-CGP: Mixed Typed Cartesian Genetic Programming. In *Proceedings of the international conference on Genetic and Evolutionary Computation Conference* (2012), ACM, pp. 751–758.

[11] HEISE, S., HLATKY, M. AND LOVISCACH, J. Automatic cloning of recorded sounds by software synthesizers. In *Proceedings of the Audio Engineering Society Convention 127* (2009).

[12] HORNER, A. Evolution in digital audio technology. In *Evolutionary Computer Music*. Springer, 2007, pp. 52–78.

[13] HORNER, A. AND BEAUCHAMP, J. Piecewise-linear approximation of additive synthesis envelopes: a comparison of various methods. *Computer Music Journal 20*, 2 (1996), 72–95.

[14] HORNER A. AND BEAUCHAMP J. AND HAKEN L. Machine tongues XVI: Genetic algorithms and their application to FM matching synthesis. *Computer Music Journal 17*, 4 (1993), 17–29.

[15] HRBACEK, R.AND SIKULOVA, M. Coevolutionary Cartesian Genetic Programming in FPGA. In *Advances in Artificial Life, ECAL* (2013), vol. 12, pp. 431–438.

[16] MACRET, M., AND PASQUIER, P. Automatic Tuning of the OP-1 Synthesizer Using a Multi-objective Genetic Algorithm. In *Proceedings of the Sound and Music Computing conference* (Stockholm, Sweeden, 2013), pp. 614–621.

[17] MACRET, M., PASQUIER, P. AND SMYTH, T. Automatic Calibration of Modified FM Synthesis to Harmonic Sounds using Genetic Algorithms. In *Proceedings of the Sound and Music Computing conference* (2012), pp. 387–394.

[18] MATHIEU, B., ESSID, S. AND FILLON, T., PRADO, J. AND RICHARD, G. YAAFE, an easy to use and efficient audio feature extraction software. In *Proceedings of the International Society for Music Information Retrieval* (2010).

[19] MCDERMOTT, J., O'NEILL, M., AND GRIFFITH, N. EC control of sound synthesis. *Evolutionary Computation Journal 18*, 2 (2010), 277–303.

[20] MERMELSTEIN, P. Distance measures for speech recognition, psychological and instrumental. *Pattern recognition and artificial intelligence 116* (1976), 374–388.

[21] MILLER, J., AND THOMSON, P. Cartesian genetic programming. In *Genetic Programming*. Springer, 2000, pp. 121–132.

[22] MITCHELL, T. Automated evolutionary synthesis matching. *Journal on Soft Computing* (2012), 1–14.

[23] MITCHELL, T. AND CREASEY, D. Evolutionary sound matching: A test methodology and comparative study. In *International Conference on Machine Learning and Applications* (2007), pp. 229–234.

[24] POPOVICI, E., BUCCI, A., WIEGAND, R. P., AND DE JONG, E. Coevolutionary principles. In *Handbook of Natural Computing*. Springer, 2012, pp. 987–1033.

[25] PUCKETTE, M. Pure data: another integrated computer music environment. In *Proceedings of the Second Intercollege Computer Music Concerts* (1996), pp. 37–41. `http://puredata.info/`.

[26] ROCHA, M. AND NEVES, J. Preventing premature convergence to local optima in genetic algorithms via random offspring generation. *Multiple Approaches to Intelligent Systems* (1999), 127–136.

[27] ROTH, M. AND YEE-KING, M. A comparison of parametric optimization techniques for musical instrument tone matching. In *Proceedings of the Audio Engineering Society Convention* (2011), pp. 972–980.

[28] SCHATTER, G. AND ZÜGER, E. AND NITSCHKE, C. A synaesthetic approach for a synthesizer interface based on genetic algorithms and fuzzy sets. In *Proceedings of the International Computer Music Conference* (2005), pp. 664–667.

[29] SERQUERA, J. AND MIRANDA, E. Evolutionary sound synthesis: rendering spectrograms from cellular automata histograms. *Applications of Evolutionary Computation* (2010), 381–390.

[30] TAKALA, T., HAHN, J., GRITZ, L., GEIGEL, J., AND LEE, J. . Using physicallybased models and genetic algorithms for functional composition of sound signals, synchronized to animated motion. In *Proceedings of the International Computer Music Conference* (1993), pp. 180–185.

[31] VUORI, J. AND VÄLIMÄKI, V. Parameter estimation of non-linear physical models by simulated evolution-application to the flute model. In *Proceedings of the International Computer Music Conference* (1993), pp. 402–402.

[32] Westgrid/ComputeCanada: Bugaboo cluster. `http://www.westgrid.ca/` [Last accessed: April 2014].

[33] YEE-KING, M. AND ROTH, M. Synthbot: An unsupervised software synthesizer programmer. In *Proceedings of the International Conference Music Conference* (2008), pp. 1–6.

[34] YOSHIMURA, T., TOKUDA, K., MASUKO, T., KOBAYASHI T. AND KITAMURA T. Simultaneous modeling of spectrum, pitch and duration in HMM-based speech synthesis. In *Proceedings of the conference on Speech Communication and Technology* (1999), pp. 1315–1318.

EVOR: An Online Evolutionary Algorithm for Car Racing Games

Samadhi Nallaperuma
School of Computer Science
The University of Adelaide
Adelaide, Australia

Frank Neumann
School of Computer Science
The University of Adelaide
Adelaide, Australia

Mohomad Reza Bonyadi
School of Computer Science
The University of Adelaide
Adelaide, Australia

Zbigniew Michalewicz
School of Computer Science
The University of Adelaide
Adelaide, Australia

ABSTRACT

In this paper, we present evolutionary racer (EVOR) that is a simulated car dynamically controlled by an online evolutionary algorithm (EA). The key distinction between EVOR and earlier car racing methods is that it considers car racing as a dynamic optimization problem which is addressed by an evolutionary algorithm. Our approach calculates a car trajectory based on a controller decision and adjusts this decision according to the suitability of its resultant trajectory with the current track status. Furthermore, it allows to integrate features such as opponent handling implicitly. Our experimental results show that EVOR outperforms current best AI controllers on a wide range of tracks.

Categories and Subject Descriptors

I.2 [**Computing Methodologies**]: Artificial Intelligence

Keywords

Dynamic Optimization; Online Algorithms; Simulated Car Racing

1. INTRODUCTION

Simulated car racing is a widely popular computer game. The open racing car simulator (TORCS) race engine [5] provides a good testbed to test car racing algorithms. The simulated car racing (SCR) championship series [10, 19] have enabled further expansion of these capabilities specially for artificial intelligence (AI) approaches. In recent years, there has been a boost of AI based car racing algorithms implemented on the TORCS framework. Rule based controllers [8, 11, 18], fuzzy inference systems [14, 16], and artificial neural networks [6, 7] are some examples of the existing methods for simulated car racing.

GECCO'14, July 12-16, 2014, Vancouver, BC, Canada.

http://dx.doi.org/10.1145/2576768.2598298

There are already some car racing methods in which the controller learn using an evolutionary algorithm though an off line process [1, 14, 18]. However, due to the optimization capabilities, evolutionary algorithms have great potential to be the core of the controller rather than an offline learning approach. Using an EA method as a car racer not only enables the controller designers to reduce the need for domain knowledge, but also reduces computational overhead in the pre-processing phase (e.g. neural network-based controllers) or parameter tuning phase. Note that preparing domain knowledge is not an easy task specially if there are not enough/accurate information available about the environment. It is well-known that fuzzy systems lead today's general controller design in computer games domain [14] as well as real-life control systems (such as cruise controllers [13]). EA can be a good alternative to this approach.

Controlling a car can be viewed as a dynamic optimization problem and EAs have been widely applied to dynamic optimization [12]. In fact a driver needs to apply optimal steer, acceleration, clutch, brake and gear controller values dynamically to drive fast and safe. In case of driving, the problem environment is represented by a diverse set of factors including car position, orientation, speed, current road condition as well as other environmental factors such as wind, rain and obstacles. All these factors are changing over the time deviating the current optimum from the previous optimum (controller values) to a new position in the search space. Accordingly, it would be beneficial to take these dynamic factors into account and try to find optimal solutions during the run. Simply this is the scenario almost any generic dynamic optimization process encounters. In this study, we investigate how dynamism in a car controlling environment can be addressed by an online evolutionary algorithm.

In an EA based car controller, the actuator values can be represented as the genes of the individual. Then the natural optimization problem would be to find the best combination of the controller values under dynamic circumstances. A feasible evaluation criteria is based on how much a car trajectory resultant from the current controller values in an individual would fit the current track. This strategy is simple to realize because it does not rely on heavy domain knowledge. Also, in such an approach, unlike other car racing approaches that need special mechanisms to handle opponents [2, 18], there is no need for such extra specialized modules. Instead, a fitness based strategy could implicitly optimize the trajectory considering opponents as another level in the fitness criteria. As a proof of concept, we present an implementation of a simulated driver EVOR consisting an evolutionary optimizer for its controller. We conduct a series of experiments to investigate the performance of this new driver on a diverse set of standard benchmark tracks. For the majority of the cases it outperforms existing best AI based drivers.

The organization of the paper is as follows. Section 2 describes strengths and limitations of existing AI approaches and also the widely used mechanisms in physical controllers. Section 3 explains the core of our evolutionary dynamic optimizer and section 4 describes additional features integrated to enhance overall performance. In Section 5 we conduct a series of experiments and analyses of the results. Finally, Section 6 concludes with the highlights and future directions.

2. BACKGROUND

The TORCS framework [5] is one of the most famous frameworks for simulated car racing. TORCS provides a free game engine with standard features such as sensory information, aerodynamics, friction and 3D graphics. The TORCS framework is used for many racing games and competitions. A customized version of TORCS was provided by the simulated car racing (SCR) championship [10] specially aiming for building AI controllers. This version uses a client server architecture where client bots are connected to the related server bots. The communication between clients and the server takes place through the user datagram protocol (UDP) socket connection. Researchers can develop their own drivers with the interface provided by the SCR client.

Current simulated car racing approaches include expert systems [8, 11, 18], artificial neural networks [6, 7] and fuzzy expert systems [14, 16]. Among these approaches Autopia [14] driver has won a great popularity due to its performance in simulated car racing (SCR) championship series [10] in recent years. The significance of Autopia is that it works equally well under different road conditions. The fuzzy controller in Autopia enables its smooth handling under different conditions. Mr.Racer [18], the winner of SCR championship at GECCO 2013 [10] is also a popular driver. This driver is based on an expert system as the core of the controller. Mr.Racer constructs a track model during its initial run on a new road. The runner up ICER IDDFS of the same competition is also an expert system. Some approaches incorporate evolutionary strategies to tune the parameters used in their formulas[18][14] or genetic programming to learn the controller program [1]. In both these cases the evolutionary process takes place in off-line mode that is prior to the actual driving/racing.

Although EAs are used for optimizing parameters and for learning the controller program in some current approaches, the core of these controllers are expert systems [18] or other AI approaches like fuzzy inferencing [14] or artificial neural networks [6]. None of these approaches have considered the possibility to use an evolutionary algorithm as the core of the online decision making process rather than to use it only for parameter tuning. By using an evolutionary algorithm as an online decision maker, there is no need for heavy domain knowledge (as for expert systems), pre-processing (as for neural networks), or tedious parameter tuning (as for off line tuning based controllers) any more. Similar kind of evolutionary dynamic optimizers have been used in decision making for other real time games and proves to successful [17].

There are simple and efficient control mechanisms used in physical automobiles on top of the raw actuator outputs, such as advanced brake system (ABS) [15] and traction control mechanisms [15] [4]. We can integrate these techniques to the evolutionary controller outputs to enhance the overall performance. Another popular feature is the auto gear system used in real vehicles at present. We can introduce this feature to the simulated environment also by introducing a direct mapping [4] of gear values to the engine rpm.

3. APPROACH

Our controller is based on an evolutionary algorithm having a population of one individual. The single individual of the EA represents the acceleration, brake and steer actuator values. Our driver is designed to have an auto gear system, therefore, we do not optimize gear dynamically. Instead, gear is applied through a direct mapping of the engine rpm (round per minute) to the gear. The clutch is also not included in this initial version of the driver considering its less relevance for the basic performance. Nevertheless, adding another control value is simplified with our algorithm. In fact, a new actuator introduces merely a new gene to the individual. The significance of the individual we use here is that it contains a set of heterogeneous genes having different ranges opposed to the standard binary or real valued vectors generally used in EA's. Hence, the standard crossover operators cannot be applied here. We use uniform mutation as the only variation operator.

As shown in Algorithm 1 the evolutionary optimization process runs forever. Once a new car state is received from the sensors the algorithm adapts the optimization process accordingly. At the end of a certain time interval the data in the current individual is converted to the actual controller values and applied to the car. In computer game environment this interval means the simulation server timeout. This asynchronous behavior is realized through a multi threaded model consisting separate threads for the EA and the input output (I/O) communication. In practice this algorithm provides robust dynamic car controlling that could either be used in autonomous vehicles or simulated car racing. Let us discuss the components of the evolutionary algorithm in detail.

Algorithm 1 (1+1)EA

$x \leftarrow$ an individual with a random set of controller values
repeat
  $y \leftarrow \text{Mutate}(x)$
  if $f(y) \geq f(x)$ **then**
    $x \leftarrow y$
  end if
until forever

The individual represents the set of actuators of the car including steer, acceleration and brake. Acceleration and brake are represented by a single floating point variable that has a continuous data range of -1 to +1 in which positive values represent acceleration and negative values represent brake. The floating point variable representing steer lies in a continuous range of -90 to +90 degrees. The actual steering controller values may stay in a more restricted range depending on the car. We consider this wide range for optimal steering. If the value of a variable, generated by the algorithm, exceeded its feasible range then it is mapped into the closest value in the feasible range. At the timeout of the server, a car controller output is created by converting the data in the individual to relevant actuators. The fitness of an individual is mainly based on how much it suits the current environment. First, We approximate the car trajectory resultant from the control values in the current individual applied to the current car status. Then this trajectory is evaluated based on the track. Here, the trajectory consists of two major factors: (1) the trajectory direction which is dependent on the optimal path and, (2) the velocity that is dependent on the current trajectory direction.

The strength of this fitness function is that the mutual dependency of the applied steer and the applied acceleration is implicitly addressed unlike most of other AI approaches where these actuator values are determined separately. In this model, a combination of these actuators are considered at once as they are contained within the individual. Hence, the acceleration is evaluated dependent on the steer value implicitly as the steer is considered in the trajectory direction for which acceleration is evaluated. These concepts will be discussed in detail within the trajectory evaluation criteria.

3.1 Car Trajectory Approximation

The car trajectory is estimated using basic physics [15] on motion. The trajectory is the expected path of the car defined by a particular set of controller values and a car state. We have considered two models for the trajectory estimation: the actual circular trajectory based on car dynamics and a linear approximation for the trajectory. For the circular trajectory, the radius of the circle is determined based on the centripetal force resultant from the lateral forces of the front and the rear wheels. The lateral force is formed in the opposite direction to the lateral velocity of the vehicle. The center of the circle is found using the current position of the car, the radius and the direction of the lateral forces. When the car is on a straight line this radius is infinite. Given the centripetal force F, velocity V and mass of the car M, using $F = MV^2/r$ the radius of the trajectory is calculated.

The centripetal force is formed by a combination of the lateral forces for front and rear wheels of the car and is denoted by $F_{centripital} = F_{lat,rear} + F_{lat,front} \cdot \cos(\delta)$ where δ representing the steering angle. These lateral forces are dependent on the slip angle α of the tires. For smaller angles the force has a linear correlation with the slip angle hence can be calculated by $F = c\alpha$ where c represents the cornering stiffness. Slip angles are calculated based on the lateral and longitudinal velocities of the car V_{lat}, V_{long}, the distances from the front (b) and the rear (c) axles to the center of gravity of the car, the angular motion ω and the steering angle δ. For the front wheels this angle is calculated using the formula $\alpha_{front} = \arctan[(V_{lateral} + \omega \cdot b)/V_{long}] - \delta \cdot sgn(V_{long})$ and for the rear wheels using $\alpha_{rear} = \arctan[(V_{lateral} - \omega \cdot c)/V_{long}]$. This actual trajectory is defined with the lateral and longitudinal velocities of the car, the angular motion, the size and the mass of the car and the steering angle. For the considered simulation platform, the mass and the dimensions of car are not available. Therefore, we use initial assumptions and utilize a low pass filtering technique to update the mapping function of the centripetal force, for a given slip angle. For a comprehensive description on this physics model we refer the interested reader to the textbook of Pacejka [15].

Our second model, the linear trajectory, is an approximation to the actual circular car trajectory. In this model, we find a straight line based on the car steering direction α and the current car position $P(x_p, y_p)$ using $Y - y_p = tan\alpha \cdot (X - x_p)$. This is based on the observation that for a small distance, a fraction of the circumference of a circle is close to a line. This approximation works well because, in practice, only the nearest fraction of the track is critical on the controlling decision. The initial implementation of EVOR performs well with both models although we maintain the second model due to the simplicity, adequacy for the game environment, and the minimal dependency on the domain knowledge.

3.2 Construction of the Track Model

When a driver is set on a track initially it can learn the track model and then use this model to support further driving on the same track. Usually, in both simulated and physical racing competitions, a brief warm up session is provided before the race [9]. When set on a new track, EVOR drives slowly for two laps to build the track model during the warm up phase. EVOR is capable of constructing the track model during the race even if there is no specific warm up phase provided.

The track model is comprised of line segments perpendicular to the axis or the heading direction of the original track, positioned on the track per each meter. This design enables our fitness calculation based on the trajectory intersection with these track segments. For each sensory reading, the segments related to the visible section of the track are calculated. These new segments are then translated and rotated to merge with the existing track segments. To calculate these segments, first the right and left boundaries of the visible track are estimated using the sensor information [1]. Then, relative to the current position of the car, the perpendicular segments connecting the right and left boundaries of the track are identified. This process is repeated for each meter of the visible section of the track, thus, constructing a segment per a meter. Using the information of the current distance from the track start position which is considered as the reference point of the coordinate system and the current rotation angle of the car relative to the axis of our coordinate system, these relative segments are merged to the existing track as absolute track segments. We use a single rotation and a translation to merge a new (or repeating) segment to the existing track model.

Additionally, the track is annotated with the bend information. Straight areas, small and sharp bends are classified based on the curvature of the track. The curvature is calculated by aggregating the heading changes of consecutive track segments. This bend information is useful in determining the optimal acceleration on a turn. A sample track model built using this mechanism is shown in Figure 1

3.3 Trajectory Evaluation

Fitness for the considered trajectory is incremented for each track segment that intersects with the trajectory as shown in Figure 2. For each of these intersecting track segments, the

[1]Note that the particular sensor distribution can be a property of the physical car or the simulation environment in case of gaming. For example, in the SCR default setting these sensors sample the space in front of the car every 10 degrees, spanning clockwise from -90 degrees up to +90 degrees with respect to the car axis

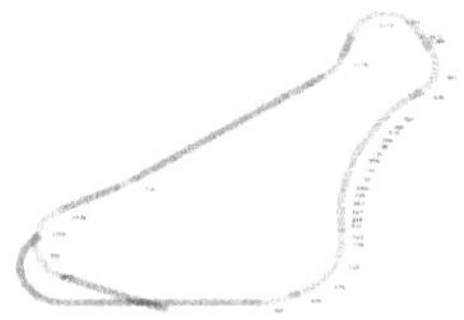

Figure 1: a sample track model

Algorithm 2 fitness function

for each visible track segment s **do**
  if trajectory intersects s at p inside the track **then**
    fitness += distance from p to the closest track boundary
    if maximum distance possible to stop < safe distance **then**
      fitness += speed at safe distance
    else
      fitness -= speed at safe distance
    end if
  end if
end for

fitness is incremented only if the intersect point lies within the left and right boundaries of the track. As shown in Algorithm 2, this fitness value is calculated based on the distance from the closest boundary to the intersection point.

As stated in the latter part of the Algorithm 2 we consider the trajectory based fitness for the acceleration also. First we calculate the distance to the intersection point where the current trajectory collides with one of the left or right boundaries of the track (possibly in a bend). Let us call this *safe distance*. This can be approximated using physics formulas on linear motion. Similarly, the *stop distance*, within which the car can be stopped if brake is applied to the current car status, is calculated. If the *safe distance* is larger than the possible *stop distance* this means the car can have a higher speed, still managing to stop before a collision, therefore we prefer to accelerate more. In this case fitness is incremented based on the calculated speed at the *safe distance*(i.e. the higher the speed is, the larger the fitness increment will be). In contrast to this scenario, if we are already too fast and close to the track boundary (possible collision), we prefer to brake and, hence, fitness is decremented based on the speed at the collision point (the higher the speed, the larger the fitness decrement).

3.4 Mutation

Our mutation operator is specialized for the heterogeneous genes in the individual. As explained in the beginning of the section 3, each individual consists of two different genes with varying data ranges. Therefore, we define two variations of the uniform mutation operator specialized for each gene. At a given mutation step the algorithm selects a mutation point uniformly at random. Then the specific mutation operator for the gene is applied. We have considered two standard mutation strategies relevant to our problem representation and the best is selected subsequently.

For steer we use uniform mutation that assigns a random value generated within the continuous range from -90 to +90. We have also studied another alternative a nonuniform mutation with a fixed distribution. This mutation changes the current value slightly by adding a small variable drawn from a Gaussian distribution. As observed experimentally, this operator had a tendency to make the algorithm converge quickly to a local optimum without exploring the search space. In contrast, uniform mutation could preserve the global exploration of the search space and enable the algorithm to converge within a reasonable time. For acceleration also we have considered the same uniform mutation operator with a different data range of -1 to +1.

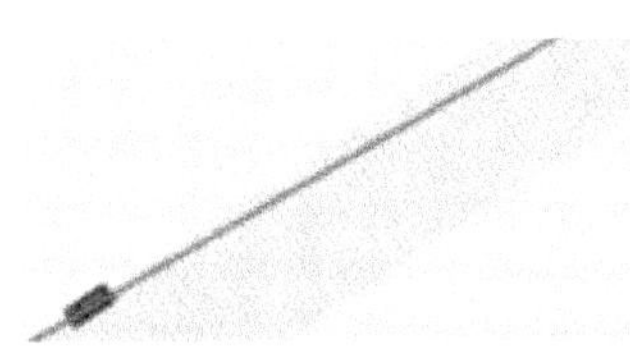

Figure 2: trajectory (long line in red) intersection with the track segments (short lines in grey)

4. ADDITIONAL FEATURES

In this section we describe the additional features introduced to enhance the overall performance of our evolutionary controller.

4.1 Opponents Handling

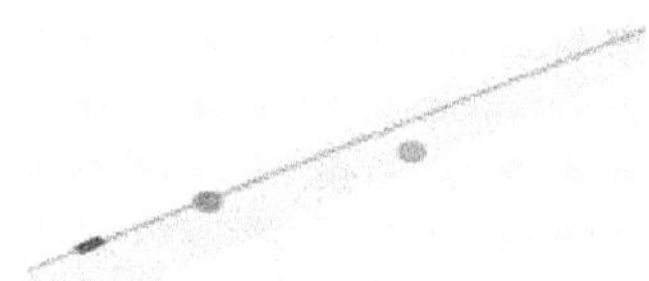

Figure 3: car (rectangle in blue) trajectory (long line in red) intersection with obstacles (circles in colors)

The opponents in front are considered as obstacles with which intersection would reduce the fitness of a trajectory. Based on this obstacle avoidance strategy the trajectories that do not intersect with the obstacles are preferred over the trajectories that intersect with the obstacles. For each intersecting obstacle the fitness is then reduced in terms of the distance from the car to the collision point as shown in Algorithm 3. For static obstacles when they are intersecting with the car trajectory closer to the current position of the car, fitness is reduced for that trajectory more. For example, as shown in Figure 3 the obstacle that intersects with the trajectory closer to the car position would reduce the fitness more than the other obstacle intersects with the trajectory at a greater distance in front. As per the moving obstacles the relative distance is dependent with the opponent's velocity. Hence, only if the opponent velocity is less than ours it is considered as a potential obstacle, otherwise it will not be colliding anyway.

Algorithm 3 fitness based on opponents

for opponent o detected **do**
  if o intersects and o's relative speed is less than 0 **then**
    dist := find the distance to collision point from current car position
    fitness -= (dist / max opponent car size)
  end if
end for

4.2 Fitness Adjustments for More Efficient Turning

The basic approach on fitness evaluation for acceleration discussed in section 3 is safe although it is not very efficient. Therefore, we introduce a slight adjustment to the fitness evaluation criteria for acceleration to increase the considered safe distance further where the actual distance is large or decrease it further where the actual distance is already small. This adjustment can mitigate any error due to track model building. We use two linear functions to adjust the safe distance based on the sharpness of the bend at the intersection point (in Algorithm 4) and the calculated safe distance value (in Algorithm 5). This adjustment changes the safe distance used in the original fitness function (in Algorithm 2). Then the last two lines of the basic fitness function is replaced by the Algorithm 6

Algorithm 4 angle based adjustment factor

$m := ((1.0 - 1.5)/(\pi/4))$
$c := 1.5$
turn angle α at wall := find turn angle from track
angle based adjustment factor := $m \cdot \alpha + c$

Algorithm 5 distance based adjustment factor

$m := (0.5/100)$
$c := 0.5$
distance based adjustment factor := $m \cdot$ distance to wall $+c$

Algorithm 6 fitness adjustment for efficient turning

```
safe distance d := find distance to wall
d *= angle based adjustment factor
d *= distance based adjustment factor
if distance to stop < d then
    fitness += speed at d
else
    fitness -= speed at d
end if
```

4.3 Stuck Management

Since EVOR always tries to find an effective trajectory, a stuck scenario is rather rare. Nevertheless, we have taken stuck management into account as it is still probable in the dynamic environment specially when racing against offensive opponents. Considering the small frequency of this scenario it is not covered in the basic EA used for driving. Alternatively, we incorporate stuck management into our evolutionary optimization model through another EA to optimize actuators on stuck situations. This EA is asleep usually, once stuck situation is observed it is awakened and the program control switches from the regular optimization process (driving EA) to this specialized EA. Once again, when the car is in safe position, this EA goes back to sleep mode saving its current stuck recovery controller values in its current parent individual. Then the regular EA runs and once again may call the stuck EA upon a stuck situation. Then the stuck EA resumes the optimization process from this saved individual.

If the car is at the same position without a velocity for a specified time we consider the car is stuck. For stuck management we use a simple fitness strategy. Here, the gear is fixed to be on reverse. The fitness is evaluated based on how much the car position is close to the track center and the car heads straight front. The design of this EA is similar to the basic EA used for regular driving except for this fitness criteria.

4.4 Auto Gear System, Traction Control and Advanced Brake System (ABS)

We incorporate some expert knowledge on standard vehicle controller design to our evolutionary driver where appropriate. The auto gear system is an example, that we can use the popular mapping on optimal gearing based on engine rpm [4]. For traction control also we use a few standard rules used in car physics [4, 15]. Similarly we apply ABS on top of the already chosen brake value from the optimizer. The details about these techniques are not discussed here, since its not of the major interest of this study. We refer the interested reader to the text books [4] and [15] for more information regarding these techniques.

4.5 Convergence and Runtime of the Algorithm

As described earlier, the EA runs forever. Based on our implementation the number of possible fitness evaluations between two consecutive status updates is around 2000. While a global convergence is not achieved within this time interval, a solution of close approximation from the global optima is always achieved. Note that a dynamic change does not cause re-optimization but only a reevaluation of the current individual immediately after the change. A typical run of the algorithm is observed to be effective. Furthermore, rigorous theoretical analysis is essential to obtain a deeper understanding on the underlying dynamic optimization process and its effectiveness.

5. EXPERIMENTAL ANALYSIS

As a proof of the concept that a simple EA works well as a car controller we have implemented a prototype version of EVOR to run on a simulated environment. We use a customized version of the TORCS [5] simulator with limited sensor information that is used in SCR competition [10]. We believe this setting is more realistic because in physical driving environment also, we have access to sensor information on the visible area of the track only. We developed EVOR as a client communicating with a SCR-server bot [9].

We have conducted a series of experiments to compare the performance of EVOR against other AI approaches. For that, we have chosen 3 other best competitors of SCR championship 2013 [10] Autopia [14] the all time winner, Mr Racer [18] the winner of SCR championship at GECCO 2013 and the runner up ICER IDDFS of the same competition. We have analyzed the behavior of these drivers for several groups of tracks oval, road and dirt provided by the TORCS simulator and also for a set of random tracks generated using the track generator by Cardamone et al. [3]. The size and the physical factors of the tracks in the first three classes have major differences.

We have evaluated our controller based on an established experimental set up inspired by the SCR competition [10].

This competition set up consists of 3 stages the warm-up, the individual race and the final race. Similar to the competition, for our experiments also 100000 game ticks are provided for the warm up session. During this stage drivers can build track models or tune any parameters. Then the cars race individually for 10000 game ticks. This time is approximately equal to 200 seconds as a game tick is around 20ms. In the final stage the drivers race together on each track for 10 laps. The starting positions of the competitors are determined according to the results of the individual race stage. Running on several laps means the experiment is repeated for several times, thus guarantees the fairness of the results like any other standard experimental setup.

Experiments were conducted in a Ubuntu Linux 12.04 PC with 64 bit Intel i5 $2.40GHz$ quad-core processor and $3.8GB$ memory. The experiments were run on SCR [9] patched version of TORCS 1.3.4 under the default mode. In the default mode the damage, the lap-time and the fuel limits are enabled.

5.1 Oval Tracks

Oval tracks represent speedways. The shapes and slopes slightly differ in the oval tracks provided with the TORCS simulator. Road friction, aerodynamic and other physical effects are quite similar in all oval tracks. The results of the four drivers raced individually on the oval tracks are shown in Figure 4. These results show that for 4 out of 5 oval tracks EVOR has bridged the largest distance within the given time budget of 10000 game ticks. It is evident that EVOR's trajectory optimization has provided the better path and the speed for these tracks than other drivers.

5.2 Road Tracks

The 15 road tracks shown in Figure 4 are diverse. They are significantly different to each other with regard to many aspects unlike oval or dirt tracks that share similar conditions within the group. The selected set of road tracks represent all different sub groups within the road group provided with the TORCS simulator. The road tracks can be of various shapes, widths, as well as of road friction. For example, the road friction may vary significantly from paved roads like *forza* to snowy slippery roads like *alpine-2*. And also the curvature of bends varies from mild bends in *forza* and *g-tracks* to large bends in *alpines* or sharp bends in *corkscrew*. EVOR has traveled the largest distance for the majority of the road tracks. For some tracks like *forza*, *wheel-2* and *g-track-2* having good road friction and moderate bends Mr.Racer was better. The major reason is that unlike Mr.Racer, EVOR was not specially tuned for specific friction parameters. Furthermore, for two tracks with a very sharp bend, *corkscrew* and *street-1* Autopia was the best. In this kind of sharp triangle shaped bends EVOR's race line optimization becomes weak. However, this kind of bends are rather unlikely in natural tracks. For all other road tracks including real tracks like *alpines*, *ruudskogen* etc., EVOR has reported the longest traveled distance.

5.3 Dirt Tracks

Dirt tracks are different from the other two groups with their sandy road conditions and bumps. The results of the four drivers raced individually on dirt tracks are shown in Figure 4. Results show that Autopia has bridged the longest raced distance for individual races for all dirt tracks while EVOR was catching up closely and the other competitors stayed reasonably behind. EVOR currently addresses the slipperiness of the tracks well with its traction control. We believe that by incorporating bump detection feature to EVOR, we can improve its performance on dirt tracks further.

5.4 Random Tracks

These tracks are generated from the TORCS compliant random track generator presented in Cardemone et al. [3]. These tracks consist of a combination of road and dirt conditions. Results show that EVOR has traveled the longest distance for the half of the random tracks (see Figure 4).

5.5 Race with Opponents

For all the tracks considered in the individual race round, we have then tested the racing performance with opponents also. For each track all the competitors were set to race together for 10 laps. The starting grid was based on the performance in the individual race. The results are shown in Table 1. The end results are quite similar to the previous experiment that generally the winners of the individual race are the winners of the race with opponents too. However, there are some interesting scenarios due to opponents observed during these experiments. Due to the strengths of opponent handing and stability EVOR could win three additional races in the final round than the previous individual race round. These were on tracks *forza* and *wheel-2* previously won by Mr.Racer and *torcello-mountain-snow* won by Autopia in the individual race round. These effects are depicted in the results shown in Figure 4 and Table 1. Although, EVOR has lost one track, namely *ole-road-1* that won in the previous individual race round. ICER with good bump detection capabilities won this race where as other drivers had problems with high damage rate in this high bumpy road thus could not complete the race. This was not observed in the individual race round as its only held for 10000 ticks within which most of the drivers could stay in the TORCS damage limit of 10000. Nevertheless, EVOR could win 19 out of 30 races in the opponents round that is even better than the 17 out of 30 in the individual race round. From the rest of 11 races EVOR could become the first runner up reporting a small time gap from the winner's time for most of the cases.

6. CONCLUSION AND FURTHER WORK

This study has remodeled the controlling of a vehicle as a dynamic optimization problem. The problem was then addressed by a simple evolutionary optimizer to optimize the actuator outputs in a dynamic environment. As a proof of the concept EVOR, a simulated driver implementation based on this approach is presented. Experiments were conducted to benchmark this driver on a diverse set of tracks and to compare the performance against existing best AI approaches. EVOR has outperformed current best AI controllers for the majority of the tested tracks. More broadly, this study reveals the potential of the evolutionary optimizer as a physical car controller specially in areas like cruise control where only fuzzy rule based controllers are currently being investigated. Future work will be concentrated on introducing bump detection and noise handing capabilities to EVOR to perform better on dirt tracks and in noisy environment.

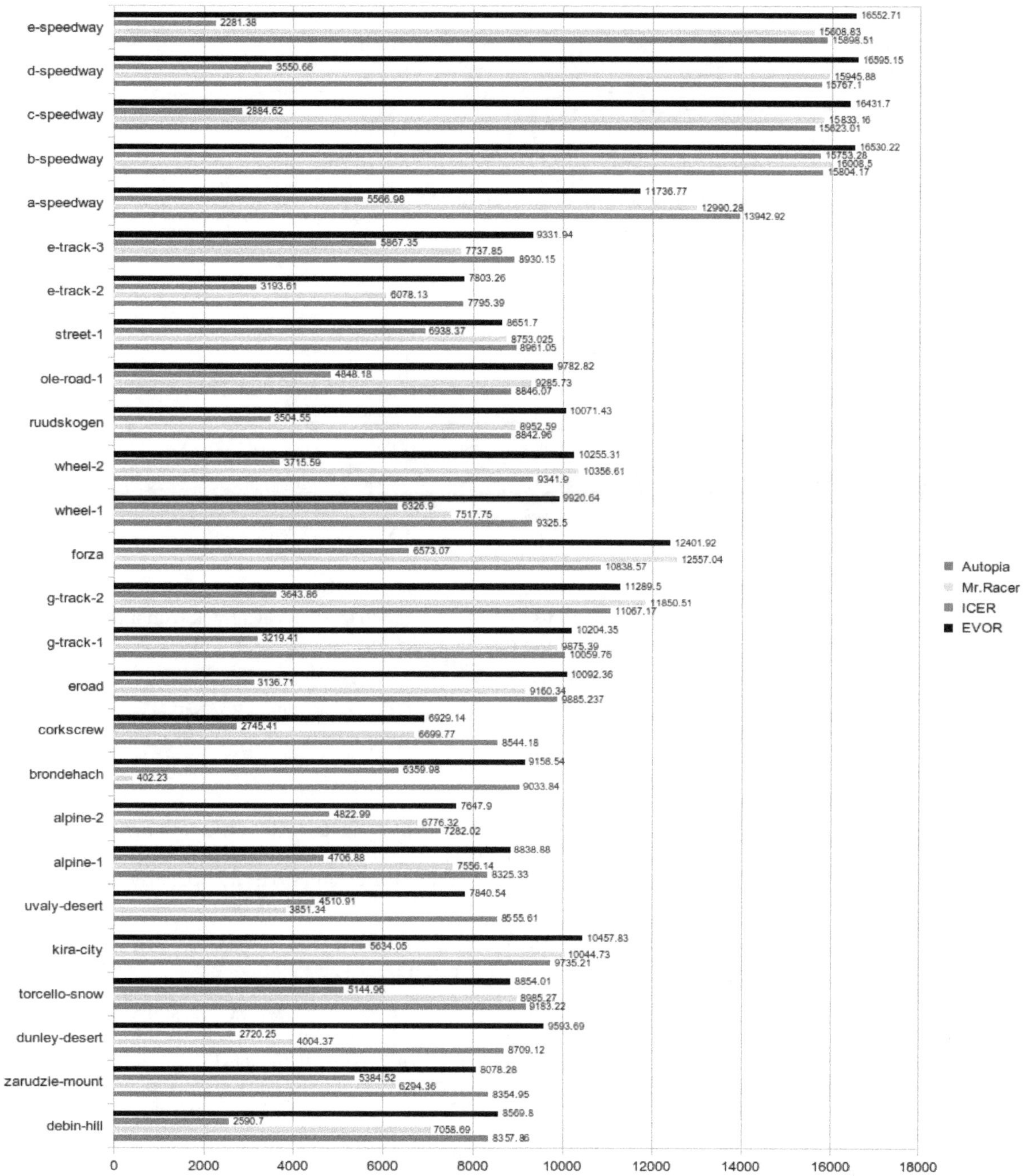

Figure 4: distance raced (in meters) for 10000 game ticks for oval, road, dirt and random tracks

7. ACKNOWLEDGEMENTS

We thank the organizers of SCR championship for the motivation and the feedback for the preliminary version of EVOR and also for sharing the sources of TORCS special version used for championship contest to conduct our experiments similar to SCR setting.

References

[1] A. Agapitos, J. Togelius, and S. M. Lucas. Evolving controllers for simulated car racing using object oriented genetic programming. In *Proceedings of the 9th Annual Conference on Genetic and Evolutionary Computation*, GECCO '07, pages 1543–1550, New York, NY, USA, 2007. ACM.

[2] L. Cardamone, P. L. Lanzi, D. Loiacono, and E. Onieva. Advanced overtaking behaviors for blocking opponents in racing games using a fuzzy architecture. *Expert Systems with Applications*, 40(16):6447 – 6458, 2013.

[3] L. Cardamone, D. Loiacono, and P. L. Lanzi. Interactive evolution for the procedural generation of tracks in a

road	winner		1st runner up		2nd runner up	
	name	time (m:s:ms)	name	winner+time	name	winner+time
a-speedway	Autopia	04:58:82	Mr.Racer	+09:24	**EVOR**	+26:79
b-speedway	**EVOR**	08:08:96	Mr.Racer	+21:85	Autopia	+22:65
c-speedway	**EVOR**	07:03:39	Autopia	+10:14	Mr.Racer	+19:16
d-speedway	**EVOR**	07:30:52	Autopia	+00:09	Mr.Racer	+00:17
e-speedway	**EVOR**	08:37:11	Mr.Racer	+17:80	Autopia	+1 lap
alpine-1	**EVOR**	23:35:53	Mr.Racer	+1 lap	ICER	+2 laps
alpine-2	**EVOR**	17:30:21	Autopia	+23:96	ICER	+ lap
brondehach	**EVOR**	14:12:96	Autopia	+08:19	Mr.Racer	+10:09
corkscrew	Autopia	14:39:02	**EVOR**	+1 lap	Mr.Racer	+2 laps
eroad	**EVOR**	11:10:32	Autopia	+07:69	Mr.Racer	+2 laps
g-track-1	**EVOR**	07:07:88	Autopia	+05:92	Mr.Racer	23:51
g-track-2	Mr.Racer	09:14:58	**EVOR**	+20:79	Autopia	+51:17
forza	**EVOR**	16:34:48	Mr.Racer	+01:12:59	Autopia	+10 laps
wheel-1	**EVOR**	15:12:70	Mr.Racer	+2 laps	ICER	+3 laps
wheel-2	**EVOR**	20:10:45	Mr.Racer	+04:16	ICER	+2 laps
ruudskogen	**EVOR**	11:25:40	Mr.Racer	+27:29	Autopia	+1 lap
ole-road-1	ICER	26:25:65	**EVOR**	+5 laps	Mr.Racer	+8 laps
street-1	Autopia	14:27:73	Mr.Racer	+53:78	**EVOR**	+01:08:67
e-track-2	**EVOR**	13:57:01	Autopia	+03:46	Mr.Racer	+2 laps
e-track-3	**EVOR**	15:48:82	Autopia	+16:57	Mr.Racer	+1 lap
dirt-1	Autopia	05:46:54	**EVOR**	+23:81	ICER	+4 laps
dirt-3	Autopia	10:53:26	**EVOR**	+08:74	ICER	+5 laps
dirt-4	Autopia	13:37:33	**EVOR**	+07:84	ICER	+1 lap
dirt-5	Autopia	05:35:30	**EVOR**	+46:95	ICER	+1 lap
debin-hill	**EVOR**	13:02:90	Autopia	+32:90	Mr.Racer	+1 lap
zarudzie-mountain	Autopia	14:32:58	**EVOR**	+17:06	ICER	+7 laps
dunley-desert	**EVOR**	11:53:22	Autopia	+16:63	ICER	+1 lap
torcello-mountain-snow	**EVOR**	16:10:45	Mr.Racer	+19:44	ICER	+1 lap
kira-yoshida-city	**EVOR**	13:12:28	Autopia	+01:00:92	Mr.Racer	+01:17:49
uvaly-desert	Autopia	13:36:75	**EVOR**	+55:71	Mr.Racer	+5 laps

Table 1: racing times of the winners of the final race with opponents on 30 tracks for 10 laps on each track (run under TORCS default settings, in visual mode and the starting grid is based on the results of the individual race round)

high-end racing game. In N. Krasnogor and P. L. Lanzi, editors, *GECCO*, pages 395–402. ACM, 2011.

[4] C. Edmondson. *Fast Car Physics*. The Johns Hopkins University Press, 1st edition, 2011.

[5] E. Espie and C. Guionneau. Torcs the open racing car simulator. `http://torcs.sourceforge.net/`.

[6] D. Galanopoulos, C. Athanasiadis, and A. Tefas. Evolutionary optimization of a neural network controller for car racing simulation. In I. Maglogiannis, V. P. Plagianakos, and I. P. Vlahavas, editors, *SETN*, volume 7297 of *Lecture Notes in Computer Science*, pages 149–156. Springer, 2012.

[7] K.-J. Kim, J.-H. Seo, J.-G. Park, and J. C. Na. Generalization of torcs car racing controllers with artificial neural networks and linear regression analysis. *Neurocomput.*, 88:87–99, July 2012.

[8] T. S. Kim, J. C. Na, and K. J. Kim. Optimization of an autonomous car controller using a self-adaptive evolutionary strategy. *Int J Adv Robot Syst*, 73(9), 2012.

[9] D. Loiacono, L. Cardamone, and P. L. Lanzi. Simulated Car Racing Championship: Competition Software Manual, Apr. 2013.

[10] D. Loiacono and P. L. Lanzi. Simulated car racing championship. `http://scr.geccocompetitions.com/`.

[11] J. Munoz, G. Gutierrez, and A. Sanchis. A human-like torcs controller for the simulated car racing championship. In *Computational Intelligence and Games (CIG), 2010 IEEE Symposium on*, pages 473–480, 2010.

[12] T. T. Nguyen, S. Yang, and J. Branke. Evolutionary dynamic optimization: A survey of the state of the art. *Swarm and Evolutionary Computation*, 6:1–24, 2012.

[13] E. Onieva, J. Godoy, J. Villagra, V. Milanés, and J. Pérez. On-line learning of a fuzzy controller for a precise vehicle cruise control system. *Expert Syst. Appl.*, 40(4):1046–1053, 2013.

[14] E. Onieva, D. A. Pelta, J. Godoy, V. Milanés, and J. Pérez. An evolutionary tuned driving system for virtual car racing games: The autopia driver. *Int. J. Intell. Syst.*, 27(3):217–241, 2012.

[15] H. Pacejka. *Tire and Vehicle Dynamics*. Elsevier, 3rd edition, 2012.

[16] D. Perez, G. Recio, Y. Saez, and P. Isasi. Evolving a fuzzy controller for a car racing competition. In *Proceedings of the 5th International Conference on Computational Intelligence and Games*, CIG'09, pages 263–270, Piscataway, NJ, USA, 2009. IEEE Press.

[17] D. Perez, S. Samothrakis, S. M. Lucas, and P. Rohlfshagen. Rolling horizon evolution versus tree search for navigation in single-player real-time games. In *GECCO*, pages 351–358, 2013.

[18] J. Quadflieg, M. Preuss, and G. Rudolph. Driving faster than a human player. In *Proceedings of the 2011 international conference on Applications of evolutionary computation - Volume Part I*, EvoApplications'11, pages 143–152, Berlin, Heidelberg, 2011. Springer-Verlag.

[19] J. Togelius, S. M. Lucas, H. D. Thang, J. M. Garibaldi, T. Nakashima, C. H. Tan, I. Elhanany, S. Berant, P. Hingston, R. M. MacCallum, T. Haferlach, A. Gowrisankar, and P. Burrow. The 2007 ieee cec simulated car racing competition. *Genetic Programming and Evolvable Machines*, 9(4):295–329, 2008.

Evolving Multimodal Behavior With Modular Neural Networks in Ms. Pac-Man

Jacob Schrum
Department of Computer Science
The University of Texas at Austin
Austin, TX 78712 USA
schrum2@cs.utexas.edu

Risto Miikkulainen
Department of Computer Science
The University of Texas at Austin
Austin, TX 78712 USA
risto@cs.utexas.edu

ABSTRACT

Ms. Pac-Man is a challenging video game in which multiple modes of behavior are required to succeed: Ms. Pac-Man must escape ghosts when they are threats, and catch them when they are edible, in addition to eating all pills in each level. Past approaches to learning behavior in Ms. Pac-Man have treated the game as a single task to be learned using monolithic policy representations. In contrast, this paper uses a framework called Modular Multiobjective NEAT to evolve modular neural networks. Each module defines a separate policy; evolution discovers these policies and when to use them. The number of modules can be fixed or learned using a new version of a genetic operator, called Module Mutation, which duplicates an existing module that can then evolve to take on a distinct behavioral identity. Both the fixed modular networks and Module Mutation networks outperform traditional monolithic networks. More interestingly, the best modular networks dedicate modules to critical behaviors that do not follow the customary division of the game into chasing edible and escaping threatening ghosts.

Categories and Subject Descriptors

I.2.1 [**Artificial Intelligence**]: Applications and Expert Systems—*Games*; I.2.6 [**Artificial Intelligence**]: Learning—*Connectionism and neural nets*

General Terms

Algorithms, Experimentation

Keywords

Games, Neural networks, Multi-objective optimization

1. INTRODUCTION

Ms. Pac-Man is among the most popular video games of all time. This popularity extends to AI research, as evidenced by numerous papers and two different competitions. Ms. Pac-Man is interesting because simple rules give rise to a game in which complex strategies are needed to succeed.

GECCO'14, July 12–16, 2014, Vancouver, BC, Canada.

http://dx.doi.org/10.1145/2576768.2598234.

Ms. Pac-Man is a predator-prey scenario, with a twist. Ms. Pac-Man is usually the prey of the ghosts, but if she eats a power pill, the situation is reversed: Ghosts temporarily become her prey. The switch in game dynamics requires a switch in play strategy. In other words, multimodal behavior is required to succeed. Despite the game's multimodal nature, most learning approaches to the game have focused on learning monolithic policies that control Ms. Pac-Man regardless of whether predator or prey ghosts are present.

In contrast, this paper evolves neural networks with multiple output modules using a new framework called Modular Multiobjective NEAT. Each module represents a different policy the agent can use, and special preference neurons are used to arbitrate between available modules. The number of modules can be fixed, or evolved using Module Mutation (also called Mode Mutation [21]). A new version of this structural mutation operator—called Module Mutation Duplicate because new modules copy the behavior of a previous module—is developed and evaluated in this paper.

The results show that modular networks are more likely to learn multimodal behaviors suited to this challenging game. Moreover, the best module division is unexpected: Modules are developed to handle critical behaviors, such as luring threat ghosts near a power pill in advance of eating them, and choosing how to escape when nearly surrounded.

The paper progresses as follows: Related work in multimodal behavior and Ms. Pac-Man is discussed in Section 2. The Ms. Pac-Man simulator is described in Section 3, and the need for multimodal behavior in Ms. Pac-Man is motivated in Section 4. Section 5 describes the evolutionary methods used to discover this behavior. Sections 6 and 7 describe experiments evaluating these methods, which are discussed in Section 8 before concluding in Section 9.

2. RELATED WORK

This section first discusses related research into multimodal behavior and modular neural network architectures, and then continues with previous work in Ms. Pac-Man.

2.1 Multimodal Behavior Research

Domains requiring multimodal behavior are common in both video game and robotics research, so various approaches have been implemented to deal with such domains. This section presents approaches that involve separately learned controllers, and single controllers with modular architectures.

2.1.1 Separately Learned Controllers

For complex tasks, it is common to combine controllers into a hierarchy. Such hierarchical controllers can be hand-designed [5], or learned: Togelius's evolved subsumption architecture [25] has been used in EvoTanks [24] and Unreal Tournament [26], and Stone's Layered Learning [23] was applied to simulated RoboCup Soccer. These approaches still require a programmer to divide the domain into constituent tasks and develop effective training scenarios for each task.

These hierarchical approaches are appealing because each component has a clear purpose. However, properly dividing a domain into subtasks requires significant human expertise. Therefore, instead of manually combining learned components, methods have been developed in which the learned controllers have built-in capacity to split up into separate modules, as will be discussed next.

2.1.2 Modular Architectures

Modular approaches automatically associate components of the architecture with specific functionality. For instance, Calabretta et al. [7] evolved neural networks to control robots using a duplication operator, which copies one output neuron with all of its connections and weights. The network then has two outputs for the same actuator, and needs to arbitrate between them. This is accomplished via selector units: The output neuron with the highest corresponding selector unit activation is chosen. Duplication can only be performed once per output.

A similar approach is Mode Mutation [21], which introduces complete modules rather than individual neurons; a single Mode Mutation adds enough output neurons to define a new policy, plus an additional neuron to arbitrate between modules. The behavior-defining neurons are called policy neurons, and the one arbitration neuron per module is called a preference neuron. Preference neurons are similar to the selector units used by Calabretta et al. Unlike the duplication operator, Mode Mutation can be performed multiple times, with no bound on the number of new modules produced. The name Mode Mutation suggests that each module encapsulates a single mode of behavior, which is not necessarily true: One module may exhibit multiple modes of behavior. So, it is more appropriate to rename this operation Module Mutation. Previous versions of Module Mutation initialized new modules either with random connections, or links to a previous module. This paper introduces Module Mutation Duplicate (MM(D)), which creates new modules via duplicating an old module (Section 5.3.2).

Other researchers have developed modular networks using generative and developmental methods [14, 27]. These approaches evolve modular neural networks assuming that distributing aspects of a problem across modules makes optimization of task-specific behavior easier. The concept of a module is less strictly defined in these contexts (they need not consist exclusively of output neurons). A module is simply a cluster of interconnected neurons with few connections to neurons in other clusters.

With so many approaches to learning multimodal behavior, it is surprising that none have been applied to Ms. Pac-Man, which is clearly composed of multiple sub-tasks. Regardless, there has been a great deal of research in the domain of Ms. Pac-Man, which is discussed next.

2.2 Ms. Pac-Man Research

Pac-Man (1980) and its sequel Ms. Pac-Man (1981) are among the most popular video games of all time. They feature similar gameplay that is simple, yet requires complex strategies for success. This combination has made the game appealing to computational intelligence researchers.

Until recently, individual researchers created their own simulators. This diversity was problematic because it made fair comparisons difficult, and because in some cases the custom simulators were less challenging than the original game. For example, Koza [12] used Genetic Programming (GP) to learn Pac-Man behavior in a custom simulator, but his variant of the game turned out to be much easier than the arcade version [13, 16].

Even the original Pac-Man is a poor choice for AI research, because ghost behavior is deterministic. Therefore, it is possible to maximize one's score by following memorized paths, without any strategic intelligence. For this reason, current research focuses on the non-deterministic Ms. Pac-Man. Its non-determinism makes evaluations noisy, which in turn makes learning hard. Another difference is that Ms. Pac-Man has four mazes in comparison to Pac-Man's one. These differences make success in Ms. Pac-Man depend more on generalization than memorization.

Microsoft's Revenge of Arcade port of this game was used in the annual Ms. Pac-Man screen-capture competition[1] at IEEE conferences from 2007 to 2011. Many approaches have been evaluated in this domain: influence maps [28], game-tree search [17], decision trees [9], and Monte-Carlo Tree Search (MCTS) [10]. A common conclusion is that the quality of any method is greatly affected by the quality of the screen-capture procedure used to assess the game state.

A simulator by Lucas and colleagues [13, 6, 17] avoids this complication. It has become a standard research platform since it was used in the Ms. Pac-Man vs. Ghosts competitions[2] in 2011 and 2012. This simulator includes a `Legacy` team that approximates the original ghosts. Several approaches have been evaluated against the `Legacy` team. GP was used with complex sensors and actions [1, 2], with simple sensors and primitive actions [4], and in conjunction with MCTS [3]. MCTS was also used on its own, though the best results occurred under unusual evaluation conditions (first maze only [18]). Ant Colony Optimization (ACO) [16] was also evaluated. Scores from these methods are compared with the results of this paper in Section 7.3.

Since this simulator is the most common, it will be used as a platform to learn multimodal behavior in this paper. Details of how it works are given next.

3. MS. PAC-MAN SIMULATOR

In Ms. Pac-Man, each maze contains several pills and four power pills. All pills and power pills must be eaten to clear a level. Each pill earns 10 points, and each power pill 50 points. To reduce learning time, evaluation ends when the fourth maze is cleared. There are 932 pills across all mazes.

In each evaluation, four hostile ghosts start in a lair near the center of the maze. They come out one by one and pursue Ms. Pac-Man according to different algorithms. If a ghost touches Ms. Pac-Man, she loses a life. However, if Ms. Pac-Man eats a power pill, then for a limited time the game dynamics are reversed, and Ms. Pac-Man can eat the ghosts. The 1st, 2nd, 3rd, and 4th ghosts eaten in sequence are worth 200, 400, 800, and 1600 points, respectively. The maximum score is achieved by eating all four ghosts after

[1] `http://tinyurl.com/mqcfzxf`

[2] `http://www.pacman-vs-ghosts.net/`

eating each power pill in each level. This goal becomes more challenging in each subsequent level, because the edible time decreases as the level increases.

The highest score that can be achieved across four levels is 58,120. Though Ms. Pac-Man normally has multiple lives, experiments in this paper only allow her to have one, both to reduce evaluation time and to make the behavior more consistent (since dying will have a large impact on fitness).

In the original game, the speed of all agents depends on various factors. The simulator simplifies movement by having agents usually move at the same speed. However, edible ghosts move at half speed, which is necessary for Ms. Pac-Man to have a chance at catching them.

Another change is the behavior of the `Legacy` ghost team. This team roughly approximates the behavior of ghosts in the original game using different path metrics for each ghost: The red, blue, and pink ghosts pursue Ms. Pac-Man along paths minimizing distance according to shortest path, Manhattan distance, and Euclidean distance, respectively. The orange ghost makes uniformly random movement choices, which is one source of non-determinism in the game. The other source applies to all ghosts: Normally, ghosts cannot reverse direction, but every time step there is a 0.15% chance that all ghosts will randomly reverse direction. Such random reversals are unpredictable events that can either help or harm Ms. Pac-Man. Reversals also occur deterministically whenever a power pill is eaten, so that edible ghosts flee Ms. Pac-Man.

This version of Ms. Pac-Man is challenging, has proven worthwhile as a benchmark (Section 2.2), and does not require screen capture. Therefore, it was used to carry out the experiments in this paper. The next section explains why multimodal behavior is required to succeed.

4. MULTIMODAL BEHAVIOR

Ms. Pac-Man requires multimodal behavior because she must respond differently to edible and threat ghosts. Although this distinction alone imposes a challenge, the game is actually more complicated than that. Usually, all ghosts are either threats or edible, but there are cases when ghosts of both types are in the maze at the same time. After a ghost is eaten it returns to the lair for a short time before reemerging as a threat, which can happen before the edible time has expired for the other ghosts. A learned policy must therefore not only have behaviors against threatening and edible ghosts, but also for the blended situations in between.

Although the threat/edible split seems obvious, other task divisions also have merit. Dealing with threat ghosts is actually a collection of tasks, since Ms. Pac-Man must avoid threats, collect pills, and decide when to eat power pills so that eating edible ghosts will be easy. This last behavior, a form of luring, will prove important in the experiments below: The best performing policies dedicate a network module almost completely to luring, which is a surprising and powerful result. The next section describes how these modular networks are evolved.

5. EVOLUTIONARY METHODS

Evolutionary multiobjective optimization is used to evolve controllers for Ms. Pac-Man. The evolved individuals are neural networks, and modular architectures are used to encourage multimodal behavior.

5.1 Evolutionary Multiobjective Optimization

The research community has always treated Ms. Pac-Man as a single-objective problem, where the goal is to maximize game score. Even though all that matters is the score, pill and ghost eating contribute to this score in different ways. In this paper, results in Ms. Pac-Man are evaluated according to the highest scoring individual in each population, but populations are evolved using multiobjective optimization to maximize pill and ghost eating scores separately. Optimizing with multiple objectives instead of one improves search by helping avoid local optima [11]. A principled way of dealing with multiple objectives is provided by the concepts of Pareto dominance and optimality:

Pareto Dominance: Vector $\vec{v} = (v_1, \dots, v_n)$ dominates $\vec{u} = (u_1, \dots, u_n)$, i.e. $\vec{v} \succ \vec{u}$, iff

1. $\forall i \in \{1, \dots, n\} : v_i \geq u_i$, and
2. $\exists i \in \{1, \dots, n\} : v_i > u_i$.

Pareto Optimality: A set of points $\mathcal{A} \subseteq \mathcal{F}$ is Pareto optimal iff it contains all points such that $\forall \vec{x} \in \mathcal{A}$: $\neg\exists \vec{y} \in \mathcal{F}$ such that $\vec{y} \succ \vec{x}$. The points in $\mathcal{A}$ are non-dominated, and make up the non-dominated Pareto front of $\mathcal{F}$.

The above definitions indicate that one solution is better than (i.e. dominates) another solution if it is strictly better in at least one objective and no worse in the others. The best solutions are not dominated by any other solutions, and make up the Pareto front of the search space. The next best individuals are those that would be in a recalculated Pareto front if the actual Pareto front were removed first. Layers of Pareto fronts can be defined by successively removing the front and recalculating it for the remaining individuals. Solving a multiobjective optimization problem involves approximating the *first* Pareto front as best as possible. In this paper this goal is accomplished using the Non-Dominated Sorting Genetic Algorithm II (NSGA-II [8]).

NSGA-II uses $(\mu + \lambda)$ elitist selection favoring individuals in higher Pareto fronts over those in lower fronts. Within a given front, individuals that are more distant from others in objective space are favored by selection so that the algorithm explores diverse trade-offs.

Applying NSGA-II to a problem produces a population containing an approximation to the Pareto front. This approximation set potentially contains multiple solutions. Usually, this set must be analyzed in order to determine which solutions fulfill the needs of the user, but for Ms. Pac-Man the notion of game score determines which solution is best.

NSGA-II is indifferent as to how these solutions are represented. In this paper, NSGA-II is used to evolve artificial neural networks.

5.2 Neuroevolution

Neuroevolution is the simulated evolution of neural networks. All behavior in this paper is learned via a version of NEAT (Neuro-Evolution of Augmenting Topologies [22]), a constructive neuroevolution method that starts with simple networks that become more complex from mutations across several generations. The initial population of networks has no hidden neurons, only input and output neurons.

Networks are modified by the usual three mutation operators in NEAT. Weight mutation perturbs the weights of existing network connections, link mutation adds new (potentially recurrent) connections between existing nodes, and node mutation splices new nodes along existing connections. Another key innovation of NEAT is topological crossover based on historical markers. Every new link and neuron introduced by mutation is given a unique innovation number to identify it. The genotype that encodes each neural network stores these innovations linearly in a consistent order across all members of the population. This representation makes it easy to align components with a shared origin within different genotypes, thus making crossover between networks computationally efficient.

The basic NEAT method described so far has been used to solve many challenging problems [20, 22], but the resulting networks only define a single control policy. The next section describes new methods for augmenting network architectures so that they possess multiple policies, making it easier to learn multimodal behavior.

5.3 Modular Networks

The modular networks of this paper can have multiple output modules. Each output module defines a different control policy. In fixed networks, evolution must discover how to use the existing modules, and when Module Mutation is used, evolution must also settle on an appropriate number of modules. Both approaches depend on preference neurons

5.3.1 *Preference Neurons*

Preference neurons make module arbitration possible. Each module's preference neuron outputs the network's relative preference for using that module. On each time step, the network module whose preference neuron output is highest is used to define the output of the network.

For example, assume a domain requires two outputs to designate the behavior of an agent, and a network has two modules (Fig. 1a). Then the network has six outputs: two policy neurons and one preference neuron for Module 1, and two policy neurons and one preference neuron for Module 2. Whenever the output of Preference Neuron 1 is higher than the output of Preference Neuron 2, the two policy neurons of Module 1 define the behavior of the agent. Otherwise, the policy neurons of Module 2 are used.

This architecture assumes that a designer specifies the number of modules. If a good guess at the number cannot be made, one option is to simply give a network lots of modules, and hope that it learns to ignore those it does not need. However, adding extra modules needlessly increases the size of the search space, defeating some of the benefits of constructive neuroevolution. However, new modules can also be introduced gradually, using Module Mutation.

5.3.2 *Module Mutation*

Module Mutation is any structural mutation operator that adds a new output module to a neural network. An unknown number of modules may be added in this way. Such networks depend on preference neurons for module arbitration. New populations start with a single module and a preference neuron that only becomes relevant after more modules are added. Each Module Mutation adds a new set of policy neurons and a new preference neuron.

Different versions of Module Mutation have been evaluated in prior research [21]. MM(P) initializes new modules with lateral inputs from a previous module. The new module is thus similar to the previous module, but not identical because of the tanh activation function. In contrast, MM(R) initializes new modules with random input link weights and sources. New MM(R) modules are often very different from existing modules, and explore the space of policies better,

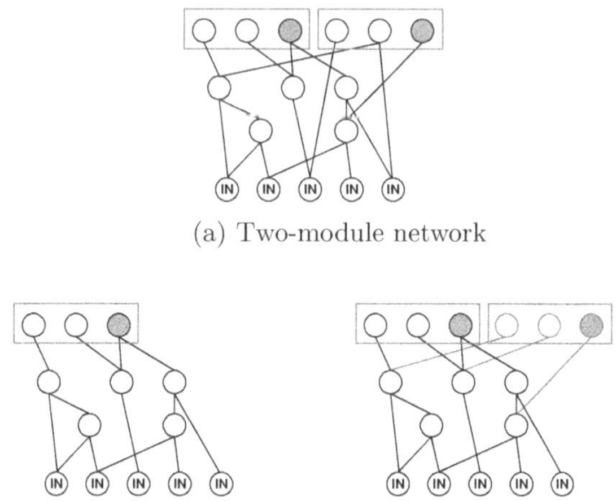

(a) Two-module network

(b) Network before MM(D) (c) Network after MM(D)

Figure 1: **Modular Networks:** These example networks are designed for a domain where two policy neurons define the behavior of an agent. Each output module is contained in its own red box. (a) A fixed network with two modules that uses preference neurons to determine which module to use. (b) A starting network in a population where Module Mutation is enabled. It has one module, and an irrelevant preference neuron. (c) After MM(D), the network gains a new module, and both the pre-existing and newly added preference neurons are relevant. The policy neurons in the new module are linked to the same neuron sources with the same link weights as policy neurons in the module that was duplicated. However, the new preference neuron is linked to a random source with a random weight so that the new module is used in different situations. Extra modules allow these networks to learn multimodal behavior more easily by associating a different module with each behavioral mode.

but they also have a higher chance of decreasing fitness. MM(R) was shown to be superior to MM(P) in two previous domains requiring multimodal behavior [21].

This paper presents a new approach combining Module Mutation with the idea of the duplication operator (Section 2.1.2). This new operator is called Module Mutation Duplicate (MM(D); Fig. 1c), because the new module duplicates the behavior of an existing module. For every link into a policy neuron in the original module, a duplicate link into the corresponding policy neuron of the new module is created that has the same source neuron and link weight as the link being copied. A network that undergoes MM(D) will have the exact same behavior as the original network. MM(D) provides a network with new structure for evolution to explore without altering the network's fitness. However, links to the new module's preference neuron are not copied from the parent module. Rather, the new preference neuron has a single link with a random source and weight, to encourage the module to be used in different circumstances.

It turns out that MM(D) is the most powerful Module Mutation approach in Ms. Pac-Man [19]. New MM(D) modules behave like previous modules (an improvement on MM(P)), but can diverge from previous modules because new links are created to define each new module (as with MM(R)). It is therefore the method of choice in this paper. Support for all varieties of modular networks, combined with the integration of NSGA-II, results in a new software framework called Modular Multiobjective NEAT (MM-NEAT)[3]. MM-NEAT's ability to discover multimodal behavior is demonstrated in the experiments described next.

[3]Download at `http://nn.cs.utexas.edu/?mm-neat`

6. EXPERIMENTAL SETUP

This section describes the policy representation, sensors, objectives, and specific network architectures used to evolve multimodal behavior in Ms. Pac-Man.

6.1 Direction-Evaluating Policy

A learned policy can control Ms. Pac-Man in several different ways (see Section 2.2), regardless of the method used to represent the function approximator defining the policy.

This paper uses an approach introduced by Brandstetter and Ahmadi (BA [4]). Direction-oriented sensors evaluate each available direction using a function approximator with a single output, and then the direction with the highest output value is picked. This approach is similar to the common Reinforcement Learning approach of evaluating afterstates to pick an action, but does not require a model, and has proven superior to previously attempted afterstate-based approaches to Ms. Pac-Man [13, 6].

The BA approach was chosen because it uses primitive actions and simple sensors. Other evolved Ms. Pac-Man agents [12, 1, 2] use high-level actions that bias learning and impose an additional programming burden. Primitive actions assure that intelligent behavior discovered is due to evolution, rather than sophisticated high-level actions. The sensors in this paper are similarly simple, as explained next.

6.2 Sensor Configuration

Previous approaches to learning Ms. Pac-Man nearly always made a distinction between edible and threat ghosts. Any sensor dealing with threat ghosts, such as the distance to the nearest one, was accompanied by a similar sensor that only gave information about edible ghosts. This design choice makes it clear how the sensor should be interpreted: Threat ghosts are always bad and edible ghosts are always good. In contrast, if there were simply a generic ghost sensor, there would be conflicting ways of interpreting it depending on the type of ghost. Thus splitting up the sensors into threat and edible sensors is another source of bias in learning. Such a bias makes learning easier [19], but requires knowledge that is not available in all domains.

This paper shows how modular networks can learn multimodal behavior even with unbiased sensors that do not suggest how to break up the domain into separate tasks. There are three sets of such sensors: direction-oriented ghost sensors, other direction-oriented sensors, and sensors that are not direction-oriented. Direction-oriented distances measure the shortest path starting in a particular direction and continuing without reversing. Distances have a maximum of 200, and all sensors are scaled to $[0, 1]$.

There are 16 direction-oriented ghost sensors: distances to the 1st, 2nd, 3rd, and 4th closest ghosts, whether each ghost is approaching, whether a directional path to each ghost contains junctions, and whether each ghost is edible. Because ghosts are sorted by directional distances, a different sorting could apply to each direction. The sorting ignores whether each ghost is edible, but this information is provided via the additional sensor for each ghost.

There are six remaining direction-oriented sensors: distances to the nearest pill, power pill, and junction, the maximum numbers of pills and junctions within 30 steps, and a special sensor called Options From Next Junction (OFNJ). OFNJ looks at the next junction in a given direction, and counts the number of subsequent junctions that can be safely reached from the first junction without reversing. The safety of a route can be determined by taking all agent distances into account and conservatively assuming ghosts will follow the shortest path to the target junction. No forward simulation is needed. OFNJ is the one sensor from this group that is not part of the BA approach. BA has a weaker version of this sensor that merely detects whether an upcoming junction is blocked by a threat. OFNJ makes it easier to avoid death, but high scores depend on eating edible ghosts, which are only detectable by the ghost sensors above.

The remaining eight sensors are not direction-oriented, i.e. they provide the same reading for each direction checked. They are a constant bias, the proportions of remaining pills, power pills, edible ghosts, and edible time, and Boolean sensors indicating whether any ghost is edible, all ghosts and threats are outside the lair, and Ms. Pac-Man is within 10 steps of a power pill. This last sensor is useful because it warns Ms. Pac-Man that a power pill is about to be eaten, which helps optimize the timing of this important event.

These sensors are sufficient to make intelligent decisions, but are challenging to use because they are so general. However, the results show that modular networks are able to make effective use of them.

Having explained how the evolved Ms. Pac-Man controllers sense their environment, it is now time to explain what the agents will try to achieve and how they will be evaluated.

6.3 Objectives and Performance

Populations are evolved with separate pill and ghost objectives. The `Pill Score` is simply the number of pills eaten. This fitness function treats power pills as regular pills, since both need to be eaten to clear levels. Because there are 932 pills across the four mazes and four power pills per maze, this objective has a maximum of 948.

The `Ghost Score` is more tricky to define. For each power pill eaten, the point value of each subsequently eaten ghost doubles, so this objective gives higher rewards for the ghosts that are worth more points. The 1st, 2nd, 3rd, and 4th ghosts are worth 1, 2, 4, and 8 points respectively. Therefore, it is possible to earn 15 `Ghost Score` points per power pill, which adds up to 60 points per maze, and 240 points across all four.

Because evaluation in Ms. Pac-Man is noisy, each neural network is evaluated 10 times. Fitness scores are the average scores across evaluations. Because 10 evaluations take a long time to carry out, a limit of 8,000 time steps is imposed for each maze, after which Ms. Pac-Man is killed. This restriction discourages behaviors that stay alive a long time without making progress, such as moving in circles while the ghosts chase from behind. This time limit is high enough to not affect the champions by the end of evolution.

The game score is almost a weighted combination of the `Pill Score` and `Ghost Score` (special handling of power pills causes a small discrepancy). Results in Section 7 are in terms of game scores. However, learning based only on game score would throw away valuable information about how these objectives interact; using both objectives along with NSGA-II allows evolution to explore different areas of the tradeoff surface to find skilled, multimodal behavior.

6.4 Evolving Networks

These experiments show the benefits of modular neural networks in a domain requiring multimodal behavior. Populations of networks with `One Module`, `Two Modules`, and `Three Modules` are evolved. Modular networks use preference neurons to decide which module to use on each time step. If either two or three modules happens to be the ideal number of modules for this domain, then learning to use these fixed modules should be easier than using Module Mutation (which must also discover how many modules to use). Populations of networks that start with one module, but can add more via `MM(D)`, are also evaluated.

Populations of each type are evolved 20 times for 200 generations each, with a population size of $\mu = \lambda = 100$. When offspring are produced, each network link has a 5% chance of Gaussian perturbation. Additionally, each network has a 40% chance of having a new random link added between existing neurons, and a 20% chance of a new neuron being spliced along a randomly chosen link. In MM(D) runs, Module Mutation is applied to 10% of offspring. Topological network crossover is applied 50% of the time offspring are produced, with parents chosen via tournament selection.

Networks are initialized with a randomly weighted link from each input neuron to each policy neuron. In modular networks, each preference neuron begins with only a single incoming link from a randomly chosen input, to more easily allow module arbitration to be swayed by mutations. Evolving populations of networks under these conditions leads to the results in the next section.

7. RESULTS

This section analyzes the results of learning, describes the behaviors exhibited by champion networks, and compares these champions to previous results in the literature.

7.1 Learning

The main result is that modular networks achieve better game scores than `One Module` networks throughout evolution (Fig. 2). `Two Modules` performs the best, then `Three Modules` followed by `MM(D)`. Learning curves show average scores across 20 champions for each method. Because these scores were achieved during evolution, each champion score is in turn an average across 10 game evaluations.

Such averaging mitigates some of the noise in evaluation, but to get a more reliable evaluation of the final results, they were also compared post-learning. The champion of each run was evaluated 100 times, and their average scores were compared for each method. The non-parametric Kruskal-Wallis test confirmed that there is a significant difference between at least two of the four methods ($H = 13.55, p \approx 0.0036$). Mann-Whitney U tests were then used to compare each modular approach to `One Module`: `Two Modules` ($U = 313, p \approx 0.0017$), `Three Modules` ($U = 316, p \approx 0.0013$), and `MM(D)` ($U = 283, p \approx 0.025$) are all significantly better than `One Module`. However, none of the modular approaches are significantly different from each other.

The average scores from post-learning evaluations are plotted in Fig. 3 against the percentage of the time that the most used module was chosen by that champion across all 100 evaluations. This figure is sufficient to understand the module usage behavior of all champions because, surprisingly, no modular champion uses more than two modules, including `Three Modules` and `MM(D)` champions. `MM(D)` champions all had two or three modules, but networks with as many as five modules also emerged in some runs. Extra modules are simply ignored (with usage less than 0.2%). For the modular methods, there are two large clusters, which can be analyzed by observing the behavior of networks in these clusters.

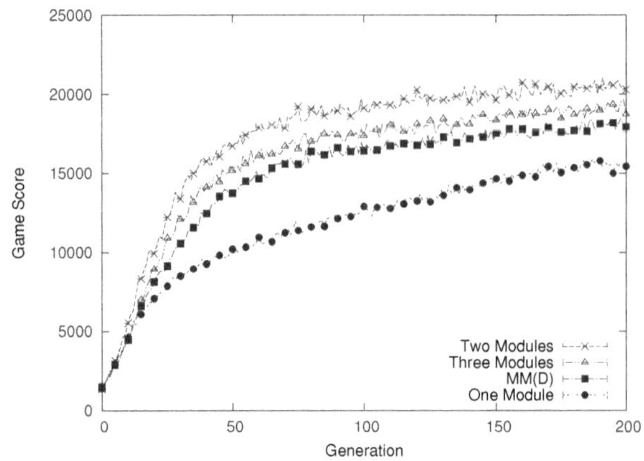

Figure 2: **Average Champion Scores Over Evolution:** Average scores across 20 runs of each method are plotted by generation. The modular approaches quickly split off from `One Module` and maintain superiority until the end. Therefore, modular networks attain better scores quicker, and overall.

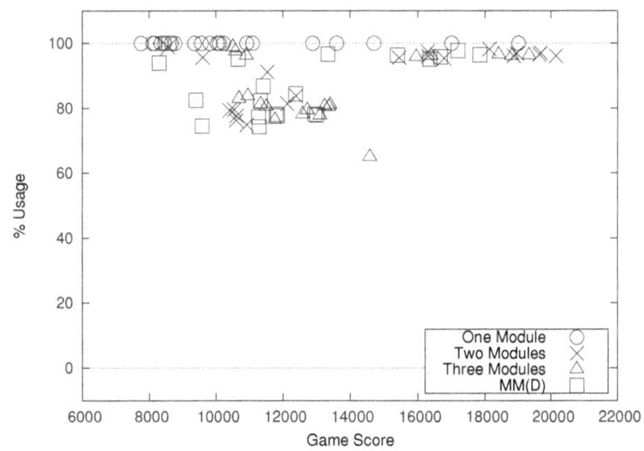

Figure 3: **Average Post-Learning Champion Scores vs. Primary Module Usage:** Each champion is evaluated 100 times, and the average scores are plotted against the percentage of the time each choses its most used module. Recall that networks process inputs for each direction in which Ms. Pac-Man can move; the "chosen" module is the one that the network used when fed inputs for the direction that Ms. Pac-Man ultimately chose to move in. All `One Module` networks use their single module 100% of the time, and most score below 11,000. Modular approaches that use one module around 80% of the time (scoring 9,000–14,000) generally use a threat/edible split. However, the best modular approaches (scoring 15,000–21,000) use one module over 95% of the time, because the other module, used for luring, is only needed a small percentage of the time when it really counts.

7.2 Behavior

Observing evolved behaviors reveals how multiple modules are used to implement successful behaviors. Videos of behaviors can be seen at `http://nn.cs.utexas.edu/?ol-pm`. There are two common module usage patterns: threat/edible split and luring.

The threat/edible split is the obvious way of splitting the domain: Ms. Pac-Man should behave differently around edible ghosts than around threat ghosts. However, ghosts of both types are sometimes present simultaneously. In these situations, Ms. Pac-Man generally uses the edible module until threat ghosts block the path to any remaining edible ghosts, which is a sensible strategy for staying alive.

This strategy achieves good scores (9,000–14,000), but occasionally has trouble eating ghosts. Sometimes it leads Ms. Pac-Man to eat power pills at inopportune times. The edible

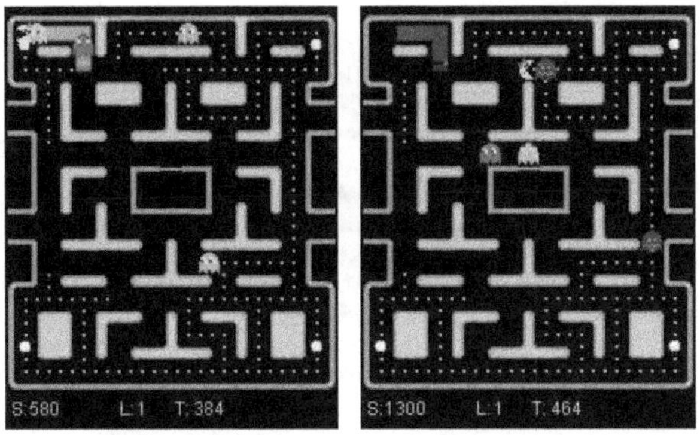

(a) Luring (b) After Luring

Figure 4: **Behavior With a Luring Module:** (a) Ms. Pac-Man waits at the junction for the ghosts to get close, then activates the luring module, which leads her and the ghosts to the power pill. The cells in the upper left shaded blue indicate locations in which the luring module was used. (b) After eating the power pill, Ms. Pac-Man quickly eats the ghosts that were chasing her, then chases the remaining ghosts. The luring module was not used after the power pill was eaten. Though it is rarely activated, half of the network's neural resources are dedicated to this module because it leads to such high scores. An animation of this behavior is at `http://nn.cs.utexas.edu/?ol-pm`.

time is so short that even though she immediately switches to a module that pursues the ghosts, she has a hard time catching them before time runs out. To eat more ghosts, Ms. Pac-Man needs to lure them close to power pills before eating them, so that the edible ghosts are easy to catch.

This is the strategy used by the best modular networks (those scoring 15,000–21,000; Fig. 4). Ms. Pac-Man uses one module for navigating the maze and eating pills while ghosts chase her, but sometimes she stops at a junction and waits for the ghosts to get closer. When she is almost captured, a luring module takes over and leads the pursuing ghosts toward a power pill, which she then eats. At this point, control returns to the first module, and Ms. Pac-Man quickly eats the now vulnerable ghosts. The luring module also helps Ms. Pac-Man escape dangerous situations even when no power pill is present. The basic behavior is the same: Lure the ghosts to a junction, then escape via the best route.

Networks that discover a luring module use it a small portion of the time (under 5%), but it is vital for increasing `Ghost Score`. However, it is surprising that the other module can support the different behavioral modes of running from threat ghosts and chasing edible ghosts. `Three Modules` and `MM(D)` runs that learn this behavior also use only two modules, even though other modules are available to take on these extra behavioral modes. In fact, the lower performance of these methods indicates that the extra modules are a harmful distraction in this domain.

The OFNJ sensor likely helps these behavioral modes coexist in the same module. If the urge to pursue ghosts is slightly overwhelmed by the pressure to go towards safety, then Ms. Pac-Man will head towards ghosts when they are edible, and run away from them when they are threats because the influence of OFNJ is stronger. However, luring is very different from these behaviors, which is why it tends to need a dedicated module in order to execute correctly.

The worst individuals are `One Module` networks that do not learn what to do when ghosts are edible: Ms. Pac-Man jitters helplessly, and tends to only eat them if they wander directly into her path. The worst modular networks also exhibit this behavior, but in these rare cases the network in question is mostly using only one of its available modules.

There are also five high performing `One Module` outliers. The best exhibits luring behavior, but its ability to chase ghosts suffers as a result, which is why modular luring networks achieve better scores. With only one module, improvements in one behavior often come at the expense of other behaviors, which is why even the best `One Module` champions have trouble exhibiting multimodal behavior.

Such multimodal behavior leads to high scores in the full game as well, as shall be shown in the next section.

7.3 Comparison

To compare performance with the literature, slight changes must be made in the game setup. In particular, scores discussed so far have been achieved using only one life, whereas results in the literature generally let Ms. Pac-Man start with three lives, and earn a fourth after achieving 10,000 points, as in the original game. This variant is called `FourMaze`, because evaluation is restricted to a single visit to each maze.

However, much of the literature describes entrants in the Ms. Pac-Man vs. Ghosts competitions (`MPMvsG` variant), and these scores were achieved under the following additional rules: (1) clearing the fourth maze leads back to the first maze, until each maze is visited four times (16 levels); (2) the per-level time limit is 3,000 time steps, but running out of time advances Ms. Pac-Man to the next level instead of killing her; and (3) Ms. Pac-Man is awarded half the score from remaining pills in the level when time runs out.

Furthermore, evaluations in both variants are timed, meaning Ms. Pac-Man only has 40ms to decide on each action. This time limit is seldom a problem for the evolved networks, but whenever an action is not returned in time, the action made on the previous time step is repeated.

To compare scores achieved by modular networks with those in the literature, champions from each run were evaluated an additional 100 times in both the `FourMaze` and `MPMvsG` variants (Table 1). The average scores of the modular networks are superior to average scores of all previous works in both `FourMaze` and `MPMvsG`. The maximum scores are also better in most cases. Even the best `One Module` champion beats previously published results, although typical `One Module` performance is lower.

The results demonstrate the success of multiobjective neuroevolution in general, and modular networks in particular, but there are many promising directions for future research.

8. DISCUSSION AND FUTURE WORK

Modular networks discover multimodal behavior more often than networks with one module. The worst modular networks are those that fail to use multiple modules, indicating that the potential of modular architectures is not always realized.

Therefore, one direction for future work is to investigate methods of encouraging use of modules that remain untapped. Multiobjective evolution should fill this role by encouraging exploration of trade-offs in objective space, but vanilla multiobjective evolution does not consistently capitalize on the potential of extra modules.

One extension of multiobjective evolution that could do so is Targeting Unachieved Goals [20]. This fitness-based shaping technique turns off objectives in which the population is performing well so that evolution can focus on the objec-

Method	FourMaze		MPMvsG	
	AVG	MAX	AVG	MAX
GP [1]	16,014	**44,560**	N/A	N/A
GP+Training Camps [2]	11,413	31,850	N/A	N/A
GP (BA) [4]	N/A	N/A	19,198	33,420
ACO [16]	N/A	N/A	36,031	43,467
GP+MCTS [3]	N/A	N/A	32,641	69,010
One Module	32,009	41,320	57,767	87,840
Two Modules	**32,959**	42,120	65,323	88,430
Three Modules	32,039	40,720	63,701	82,590
MM(D)	32,647	44,520	**65,447**	**100,070**

Table 1: **Post-Learning Scores in Full Ms. Pac-Man:** Champions from this paper are compared with results from the literature in two variants of the full game. Only results for champion networks with the highest average scores are reported. The best One Module scores are better than previous work as well, hinting that there is a benefit from using multiobjective neuroevolution with a challenging evaluation scheme (just one life), but keep in mind that the best One Module result is an outlier. Average modular network scores are higher than previously reported scores and One Module scores, especially in the MPMvsG variant.

tives that need it most. Such a change in focus encourages modular networks to use additional modules better [19].

Another shaping technique that is easily combined with multiobjective evolution is Behavioral Diversity [15]: An extra objective rewards individuals that exhibit behaviors substantially different from the norm of the population, and thus may encourage use of additional modules when the majority of the population is ignoring them.

Additional objectives could also be used to reward multiple modules directly, but care must be taken in how such objectives are defined. For example, simply encouraging equal usage of all available modules would be detrimental in Ms. Pac-Man, because the high-scoring networks that have a luring module use it only a small portion of the time. Even the threat/edible division does not result in an even split, because ghosts are more often threats than edible. Figuring out how to reward multiple module use without punishing corner cases like these is a challenging open question.

9. CONCLUSION

Ms. Pac-Man is a challenging game that requires multimodal behavior to succeed. Modular approaches are superior because they can dedicate separate modules to different modes of behavior. Some learn to handle threat and edible ghosts with separate modules, which is a sensible division, but others learn an even better, unexpected division that focuses one module on the behavior of luring ghosts near power pills, so that they can be easily eaten. Evolution of modular networks using MM-NEAT should be useful in other domains requiring multimodal behavior, especially if ways are found to evolve the best task divisions more reliably. Encouraging the evolution of these divisions via shaping is an interesting direction for future work.

10. ACKNOWLEDGMENTS

This research was supported in part by NSF grants DBI-0939454, IIS-0915038, and SBE-0914796, and by NIH grant R01-GM105042.

11. REFERENCES

[1] A. M. Alhejali and S. M. Lucas. Evolving diverse Ms. Pac-Man playing agents using Genetic Programming. In *UKCI*, 2010.

[2] A. M. Alhejali and S. M. Lucas. Using a Training Camp with Genetic Programming to evolve Ms Pac-Man agents. In *CIG*, pages 118–125, 2011.

[3] A. M. Alhejali and S. M. Lucas. Using Genetic Programming to evolve heuristics for a Monte Carlo Tree Search Ms Pac-Man agent. In *CIG*, 2013.

[4] M. F. Brandstetter and S. Ahmadi. Reactive control of Ms. Pac Man using information retrieval based on Genetic Programming. In *CIG*, pages 250–256, 2012.

[5] R. A. Brooks. A robust layered control system for a mobile robot. *Robotics and Automation*, 2(10), 1986.

[6] P. Burrow and S. M. Lucas. Evolution versus Temporal Difference Learning for learning to play Ms. Pac-Man. In *CIG*, pages 53–60, 2009.

[7] R. Calabretta, S. Nolfi, D. Parisi, and G. Wagner. Duplication of Modules Facilitates the Evolution of Functional Specialization. *ALife*, 6(1):69–84, 2000.

[8] K. Deb, A. Pratap, S. Agarwal, and T. Meyarivan. A Fast and Elitist Multiobjective Genetic Algorithm: NSGA-II. *Evolutionary Computation*, 6:182–197, 2002.

[9] G. Foderaro, A. Swingler, and S. Ferrari. A model-based cell decomposition approach to on-line pursuit-evasion path planning and the video game Ms. Pac-Man. In *CIG*, 2012.

[10] N. Ikehata and T. Ito. Monte-Carlo Tree Search in Ms. Pac-Man. In *CIG*, pages 39–46, 2011.

[11] J. D. Knowles, R. A. Watson, and D. Corne. Reducing Local Optima in Single-Objective Problems by Multi-objectivization. In *EMO*, 2001.

[12] J. R. Koza. *Genetic Programming: On the Programming of Computers by Means of Natural Selection.* MIT Press, Cambridge, MA, USA, 1992.

[13] S. M. Lucas. Evolving a neural network location evaluator to play Ms. Pac-Man. In *CIG*, 2005.

[14] J.-B. Mouret and S. Doncieux. MENNAG: a modular, regular and hierarchical encoding for neural-networks based on attribute grammars. *Evolutionary Intelligence*, 2008.

[15] J.-B. Mouret and S. Doncieux. Using behavioral exploration objectives to solve deceptive problems in neuro-evolution. In *GECCO*, pages 627–634, 2009.

[16] G. Recio, E. Martín, C. Estébanez, and Y. Sáez. AntBot: Ant colonies for video games. *TCIAIG*, 2012.

[17] D. Robles and S. M. Lucas. A simple tree search method for playing Ms. Pac-Man. In *CIG*, 2009.

[18] S. Samothrakis, D. Robles, and S. M. Lucas. Fast Approximate Max-n Monte Carlo Tree Search for Ms Pac-Man. *TCIAIG*, 3(2):142–154, 2011.

[19] J. Schrum. *Evolving Multimodal Behavior Through Modular Multiobjective Neuroevolution.* PhD thesis, University of Texas at Austin, 2014.

[20] J. Schrum and R. Miikkulainen. Evolving agent behavior in multiobjective domains using fitness-based shaping. In *GECCO*, 2010.

[21] J. Schrum and R. Miikkulainen. Evolving multimodal networks for multitask games. *TCIAIG*, 4(2), 2012.

[22] K. O. Stanley and R. Miikkulainen. Evolving Neural Networks Through Augmenting Topologies. *Evolutionary Computation*, 10:99–127, 2002.

[23] P. Stone and M. Veloso. Layered Learning. In *ECML*, 2000.

[24] T. Thompson, F. Milne, A. Andrew, and J. Levine. Improving Control Through Subsumption in the EvoTanks Domain. In *CIG*, pages 363–370, 2009.

[25] J. Togelius. Evolution of a subsumption architecture neurocontroller. *Intelligent and Fuzzy Systems*, 2004.

[26] N. van Hoorn, J. Togelius, and J. Schmidhuber. Hierarchical Controller Learning in a First-Person Shooter. In *CIG*, pages 294–301, 2009.

[27] P. Verbancsics and K. O. Stanley. Constraining connectivity to encourage modularity in HyperNEAT. In *GECCO*, pages 1483–1490, 2011.

[28] N. Wirth and M. Gallagher. An Influence Map Model for Playing Ms. Pac-Man. In *CIG*, 2008.

Minimal Walsh Structure and Ordinal Linkage of Monotonicity-Invariant Function Classes on Bit Strings

Lee A. Christie
IDEAS Research Institute
Robert Gordon University
Aberdeen, United Kingdom
l.a.christie4@rgu.ac.uk

John A. W. McCall
IDEAS Research Institute
Robert Gordon University
Aberdeen, United Kingdom
j.mccall@rgu.ac.uk

David P. Lonie
School of Computing Science
and Digital Media
Robert Gordon University
Aberdeen, United Kingdom
d.p.lonie@rgu.ac.uk

ABSTRACT

Problem structure, or linkage, refers to the interaction between variables in a black-box fitness function. Discovering structure is a feature of a range of algorithms, including estimation of distribution algorithms (EDAs) and perturbation methods (PMs). The complexity of structure has traditionally been used as a broad measure of problem difficulty, as the computational complexity relates directly to the complexity of structure. The EDA literature describes necessary and unnecessary interactions in terms of the relationship between problem structure and the structure of probabilistic graphical models discovered by the EDA. In this paper we introduce a classification of problems based on monotonicity invariance. We observe that the minimal problem structures for these classes often reveal that significant proportions of detected structures are unnecessary. We perform a complete classification of all functions on 3 bits. We consider non-monotonicity linkage discovery using perturbation methods and derive a concept of directed ordinal linkage associated to optimization schedules. The resulting refined classification factored out by relabeling, shows a hierarchy of nine directed ordinal linkage classes for all 3-bit functions. We show that this classification allows precise analysis of computational complexity and parallelizability and conclude with a number of suggestions for future work.

Categories and Subject Descriptors

I.2.8 [**Artificial Intelligence**]: Problem Solving, Control Methods, and Search

General Terms

Algorithms; Design; Performance; Theory

Keywords

Estimation of Distribution Algorithms; Linkage Learning; Monotonicity; Ordinal Selection; Perturbation Methods

GECCO'14, July 12–16, Vancouver, BC, Canada.

http://dx.doi.org/10.1145/2576768.2598240.

1. INTRODUCTION

There has been a long standing interest in understanding the role of *structure* in black-box function optimization such as estimation of distribution algorithms (EDAs). Structure, or *linkage*, refers to the interactions between variables in a function. Traditionally this was thought of as building blocks, which are potentially disrupted by mutation and recombination operators [7]. There are several approaches to overcoming the problem of disruption of structure [3]:

1. Evolving representations/operators
2. Probabilistic modeling (EDAs)
3. Perturbation methods (PMs)

In this paper, we consider the latter two approaches, due to their explicit models for variable linkage. Any analysis of problem structure runs across the issue that there are infinitely-many functions for even a fixed number of variables. Under many ordinal-selection–based algorithms, many functions are equivalent as they rank solutions equivalently. Negligible differences in value may be considered irrelevant to optimization.

EDAs build a probability distribution of high-quality solutions from a population and sample that distribution to find other high-quality solutions. Many EDAs use ordinal selection, such as tournament selection, which uses comparison between fitness values as opposed to selection based on absolute fitness values. Such approaches are invariant under monotone transformations of the fitness functions, even though the model-building stages of the EDA may not be. Perturbation methods (PMs) make small changes to candidate solutions in a controlled way and calculate the effect of changes to multiple variables to directly infer which variables interact. PMs partition the variables into typically non-overlapping subsets of mutually-interacting variables. Many PMs use *non-monotonicity detection*, that is detecting whether the setting of one variable affects the optimal setting of another, as opposed to whether the effect of both variables is a linear sum of the effect of each.

We define *equivalence classes* of monotonicity invariant functions as sets of all functions that rank solutions identically. To fully explore a subset of all possible functions, the functions used in this paper are restricted to length 3 bit strings, that is functions of the form $f : \{0,1\}^3 \to \mathbb{R}$. In this domain, we can explore the different classes of functions possible to gain theoretical insight into approaches which may be extended to higher-dimensional function spaces.

2. BACKGROUND

2.1 Estimation of Distribution Algorithms

Estimation of distribution algorithms (EDAs) are an offshoot of genetic algorithms. EDAs construct a population of candidate solutions and model the distribution to sample more high quality solutions. They are able to overcome the problem of building-block disruption faced by genetic algorithms, by explicitly modeling the interactions between variables. Early EDAs use a *univariate* model, examples include PBIL [1] and UMDA [10]. In *bivariate* and *multivariate* EDAs the model is often a probabilistic graphical model (PGM). The underlying PGM aims to estimate the linkage between variables.

EDAs can be classified as *univariate*, *bivariate*, or *multivariate*, according to the complexity of the probabilistic model built [14]. In addition, the same terms are also used to classify the complexity of the functions based on the complexity of interactions between the variables. Hence, it is desirable that the model built by an EDA mirrors the underlying structure of the function. Probabilistic graphical models have been used to create EDAs with directed structure (e.g. Bayesian networks [12]) or undirected structure (e.g. Markov random fields [16]).

2.2 Walsh-Hadamard Transform

EDAs such as the DEUM algorithm [16] use a Markov random field (MRF) model based on Walsh coefficients. This is an appropriate representation because any fitness function on bit strings may be rewritten using the Walsh-Hadamard transform, and the non-zero Walsh coefficients are indicative of the structure of the function [6]. Under this transform, the function is expressed as a sum of Walsh coefficients (α_k) multiplied by Walsh functions ($W_k(x)$) as given by Eqn. 1, 2. Here, k iterates over all possible subsets of L.

$$f(x) = \sum_{k \subseteq L} \alpha_k W_k(x) \tag{1}$$

where

$$\begin{aligned} L &= \{0, \cdots, \ell - 1\} \\ W_\emptyset(x) &= 1 \\ W_k(x) &= \prod_{i \in k} \begin{cases} 1 & \text{if } x_i = 1 \\ -1 & \text{if } x_i = 0 \end{cases} \end{aligned} \tag{2}$$

A column vector of Walsh coefficients ($\vec{\alpha}$) may be computed using the Hadamard matrix as given by Eqn. 3. A faster method for Walsh-Hadamard transform is given by Fino and Algazi [5], however, the simple method was sufficient for the experiments within this paper.

$$\vec{\alpha} = \frac{1}{2^\ell} H_\ell \vec{f} \tag{3}$$

where H_ℓ is the Hadamard matrix of order-ℓ:

$$\begin{aligned} H_0 &= \begin{bmatrix} 1 \end{bmatrix} \\ H_1 &= \begin{bmatrix} 1 & 1 \\ 1 & -1 \end{bmatrix} \\ H_\ell &= \begin{bmatrix} H_{\ell-1} & H_{\ell-1} \\ H_{\ell-1} & -H_{\ell-1} \end{bmatrix} = H_1 \otimes H_{\ell-1} \end{aligned} \tag{4}$$

and $\vec{f}$ is a reverse binary-ordered column vector of fitnesses:

$$\vec{f} = \begin{bmatrix} f(111\ldots 1) \\ \vdots \\ f(100\ldots 0) \\ f(000\ldots 0) \end{bmatrix} \tag{5}$$

The Walsh-Hadamard transform produces a column vector of Walsh coefficients $\vec{\alpha}$ i.e.

$$\vec{\alpha} = \begin{bmatrix} \alpha_\emptyset \\ \alpha_{\{0\}} \\ \alpha_{\{\ 1\}} \\ \alpha_{\{0,1\}} \\ \alpha_{\{\ \ 2\}} \\ \alpha_{\{0,\ 2\}} \\ \alpha_{\{\ 1,2\}} \\ \alpha_{\{0,1,2\}} \\ \vdots \\ \alpha_{\{0,1,\ldots,\ell-1\}} \end{bmatrix} \tag{6}$$

To maintain the ordering of function values, the constant term $\alpha_\emptyset$ is never necessary, as it is an offset added to every output. Setting this term to zero does not affect the ranking or the separation between function values. This can be achieved by calculating the mean fitness and subtracting the mean from each output. We refer to this process as normalization. There are $2^\ell - 1$ possible elements of structure for an ℓ-bit function, e.g. 7 coefficients for a 3-bit problem. These are represented by Figure 1. Each structure element has been labelled with a power of two (shown below Figure 1 in hexadecimal) allowing all possible combinations to be uniquely enumerated as shown in Figure 2.

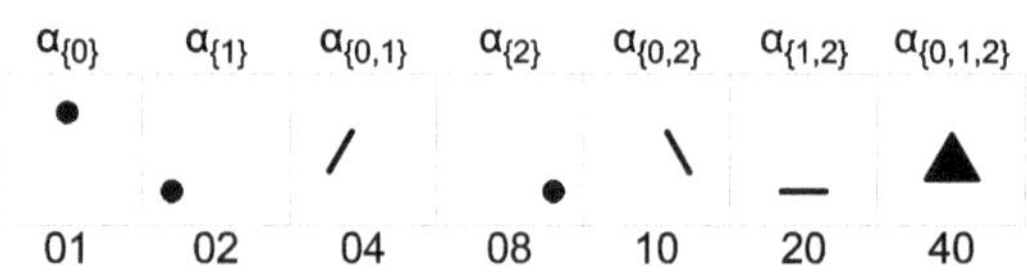

Figure 1: The parts of Walsh structure of a 3-bit function.

If we are interested in whether each coefficient is zero (not present in the structure) or non-zero (present in the structure), there are $2^{(2^\ell - 1)}$ possible structures (or 128 for a 3-bit function).

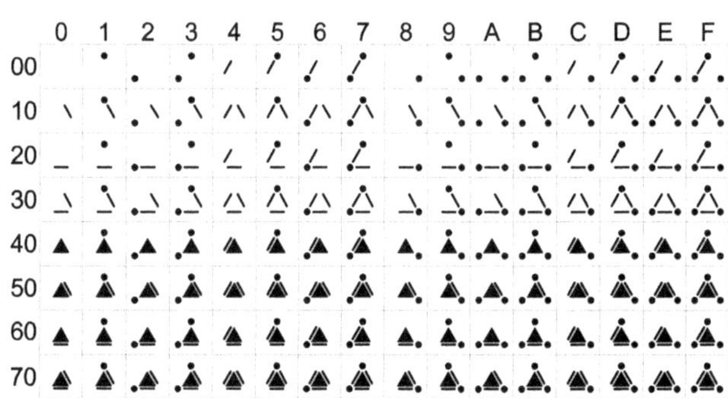

Figure 2: All 128 possible 3-bit Walsh structures after normalization.

2.3 Perturbation Methods

Like EDAs, perturbation methods (PMs) are a type of evolutionary algorithm which is able to overcome the problem of building-block disruption faced by genetic algorithms. In contrast to EDAs, PMs work by evaluating similar candidates with small changes (perturbations) and observe fitness difference $\Delta f_i(x)$:

$$\Delta f_i(x) = f(x[i \to 1]) - f(x[i \to 0]) \tag{7}$$
$$x[i \to b] = [x_0, \ldots, x_{i-1}, b, x_{i+1}, \ldots, x_{\ell-1}]$$

The fitness difference is the change in fitness caused by changing the value of a variable – to detect whether two variables are independent or interdependent.

The standard criterion for detecting interdependent variables is a non-linearity check [11]. This is a Boolean expression denoted by $\mathcal{L}(i,j)$ (Eqn. 8), and is a symmetric relation (Eqn. 9).

$$\mathcal{L}(i,j) \Leftrightarrow (\Delta f_j(x[i \to 1]) \neq \Delta f_j(x[i \to 0])) \tag{8}$$
$$\mathcal{L}(j,i) \Leftrightarrow \mathcal{L}(i,j) \tag{9}$$

A definition of variable linkage is non-linearity and non-monotonicity detection [11] given by Eqn. 10.

$$\begin{aligned} \mathcal{L}(i,j) &\Leftrightarrow \forall x (\neg P_{ij}(x) \vee M_{ij}(x)) \\ P_{ij}(x) &= \{\Delta f_i(x) > 0 \wedge \Delta f_j(x) > 0\} \\ M_{ij}(x) &= \{\Delta f_{ij}(x) > \Delta f_i(x) \\ &\quad \wedge \Delta f_{ij}(x) > \Delta f_j(x)\} \end{aligned} \tag{10}$$

The motivation behind non-monotonicity detection is that learning interactions, that only affect the magnitude of a variable's effect (and not the optimal setting), is not necessary when the objective is to locate a function optimum. This is therefore another way to define which structure is necessary.

Non-monotonicity detection checks that when a change in either variable increases fitness, the result of changing both also increases fitness. When using non-monotonicity detection there can be higher-order interactions, i.e. hierarchical interactions between groups [19].

2.4 Linkage Partition

Two variables, i and j, are considered to be in the same *linkage group* if they are interdependent, or transitively dependent through a chain of interdependent variables. In this sense, the linkage groups are connected components of an undirected graph formed by pairs of interdependent variables. A linkage group is a set of linked variables, with the kth linkage group is represented by $\gamma_k = \{X_i, X_j, \ldots\}$.

The *linkage partition* is the set of linkage groups in a problem, which are each non-overlapping: $\Gamma = \{\gamma_0, \gamma_1, \ldots \gamma_{n-1}\}$. The variables in γ_k are arranged into a *substring* (s_k). A function is considered to be an additively separable function (ASF) [13] if the linkage partition consists of more than one linkage group and therefore may be rewritten as a sum of *subfunctions* on substrings as in Eqn. 11.

$$f(x) = g_0(s_0) + g_1(s_1) + \ldots + g_{n-1}(s_{n-1}) \tag{11}$$

Because the effect on fitness of the change of one variable is only affected by the values of the variables in the same linkage group, each linkage group may be optimized without regard to the other linkage groups. The global optimum may be therefore be found by exhaustive evaluation of each linkage group in $O(2^k)$ time where k is the maximum size of any one linkage group. This is because all 2^k combinations of variables in the same linkage group must be tried to conclusively identify the optimum value for any. An ASF with small linkage group can be optimized relatively efficiently if the linkage can be discovered efficiently. It has been shown by Streeter [17] that learning the linkage of an ASF adds only an $\ell\, ln(\ell)$ term, meaning an ASF can be optimized efficiently in $O(\ell\, ln(\ell)\, 2^k)$ time.

3. BINARY BENCHMARK FUNCTIONS

In this section we consider well-known benchmark functions of bit strings, and discuss the structure of the 3-bit instances.

3.1 Ones and BinVal

The *Ones* (or MaxOnes/OneMax) function is a commonly-cited univariate benchmark function which is the sum of the bits in the bit string. (Eqn. 12)

$$\text{Ones}(x) = \sum_{i=0}^{\ell-1} x_i \tag{12}$$

The *BinVal* function [4] is an exponential univariate function which sums the bits in the bit string, weighted according to their position in the string. (Eqn. 13)

$$\text{BinVal}(x) = \sum_{i=0}^{\ell-1} 2^i x_i \tag{13}$$

The Walsh coefficients of the 3-bit Ones and BinVal functions are given by Table 1. The BinVal function has increasing Walsh coefficients because it is an *exponential function*, whereas the Ones function has constant Walsh coefficients, though, both are univariate functions.

	Ones	BinVal
$\alpha_\emptyset$	1.5	3.5
$\alpha_{\{0\}}$	0.5	0.5
$\alpha_{\{1\}}$	0.5	1.0
$\alpha_{\{2\}}$	0.5	2.0

Table 1: Walsh coefficients of the 3-bit Ones and BinVal functions.

Both the Ones function and BinVal function are univariate, hence have no interactions between the variables, thus the linkage partition is $\Gamma = \{\{0\}, \{1\}, \{2\}\}$.

3.2 Checkerboard (1-D)

The *Checkerboard* (1-D) function (Eqn. 14) is a 1-dimensional variation on a checkerboard function, which rewards for assigning opposite values to adjacent alleles [2] [9].

$$Checkerboard\,(x) = \sum_{i=0}^{\ell-2} g\,(x_i, x_{i+1}) \tag{14}$$

$$\text{where } g\,(y,z) = \begin{cases} 0 & \text{if } y = z \\ 1 & \text{if } y \neq z \end{cases}$$

The Walsh coefficients of the 3-bit Checkerboard (1-D) function are given by Table 2.

	Checkerboard
$\alpha_{\emptyset}$	1.0
$\alpha_{\{0,1\}}$	-0.5
$\alpha_{\{1,2\}}$	-0.5

Table 2: Walsh coefficients of the 3-bit Checkerboard (1-D) function.

Despite the relative simplicity of the Checkerboard (1-D) function, there is a linear chain of each variable connecting to the next. Thus, this is not additively separable. The linkage partition is $\Gamma = \{\{0,1,2\}\}$.

4. RANK-EQUIVALENCE CLASSES

There are an infinite number of ℓ-bit functions, however, if we consider functions which rank solutions in the same way to be equivalent, there are a finite number of such equivalence classes of functions for a given ℓ.

We define the *rank* of a solution x, in the domain of function f, denoted by $R_f\,(x)$ as the number of solutions with a strictly lower fitness value, given by Eqn. 15. Listing the ranks for a function f gives the class C_f as in Eqn. 16. Two functions, f and g, are said to be *rank-equivalent* if $C_f = C_g$.

$$R_f\,(x) = |\{y : y \in f_{\text{domain}} \wedge f\,(y) < f\,(x)\}| \tag{15}$$

$$C_f = [R_f\,(1\ldots1), \ldots, R_f\,(1\ldots0), R_f\,(0\ldots0)] \tag{16}$$

The transpose of C_f gives a *canonical* example fitness vector (Eqn. 5) in class C_f. For the 3-bit functions $f : \{0,1\}^3 \rightarrow \mathbb{R}$, there are 545 835 distinct rank-equivalence classes, considering permutations as distinct. The number of classes for each number of distinct ranks is given by Table 3. For a given number of distinct ranks n and a given bit string length ℓ, the number of classes, $c\,(n,\ell)$ is:

$$c\,(n,\ell) = n^{(2^\ell)} - \sum_{k=1}^{n-1} c\,(k,\ell) \cdot {}_nC_k \tag{17}$$

Here, ${}_nC_k$ denotes the binomial coefficient, n choose k.

Num. Ranks (n)	Num. Deltas	Num. Classes (c)
1	0	1
2	1	254
3	2	5 796
4	3	40 824
5	4	126 000
6	5	191 520
7	6	141 120
8	7	40 320
	Total	545 835

Table 3: The number of rank-equivalence classes for each number of distinct ranks for 3-bit functions.

5. NECESSARY WALSH STRUCTURE

There are existing notions of *unnecessary* structure. Some parts of model structure have been called unnecessary if they are undesirable with the aim of minimizing model complexity [8] and maximizing mixing [18] or if the structure discovered by the probabilistic graphical model is surplus to accurate modeling of the fitness function [15]. In our work, we argue that structure is unnecessary when the same ordering of solutions could be maintained without it.

Take as an example, the class of the Ones function, $C_{\text{Ones}} = [7,4,4,1,4,1,1,0]$. An instance of C_{Ones} is specified by the function minimum ($f_{\min}$) and 3 positive *delta* values i.e. $\delta_0, \delta_1, \delta_2 > 0$ as shown in Table 4 and illustrated in Figure 3. The specific case of the Ones function is defined by $f_{\min} = 0$, $\delta_0 = 1$, $\delta_1 = 1$, and $\delta_2 = 1$.

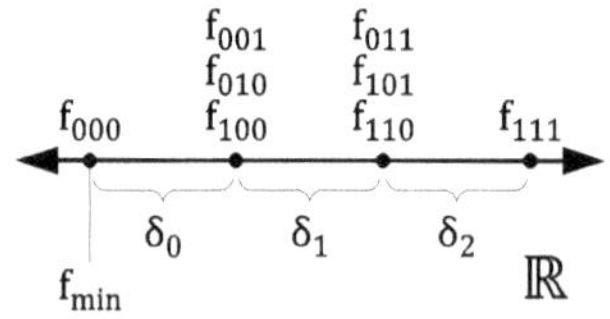

Figure 3: Illustration of the fitness values for the 3-bit class $C_{\text{Ones}} = [7,4,4,1,4,1,1,0]$ on the real number line, separated by delta values.

x	$f\,(x)$	Rank Expansion	$R_f\,(x)$
111	3	$f_{\min} + \delta_0 + \delta_1 + \delta_2$	7
011	2	$f_{\min} + \delta_0 + \delta_1$	4
101	2	$f_{\min} + \delta_0 + \delta_1$	4
001	1	$f_{\min} + \delta_0$	1
110	2	$f_{\min} + \delta_0 + \delta_1$	4
010	1	$f_{\min} + \delta_0$	1
100	1	$f_{\min} + \delta_0$	1
000	0	$f_{\min}$	0

Table 4: Fitness values, delta expansion, and ranks of the 3-bit ones function.

Performing the Walsh-Hadamard transform on the algebraic rank expansion (Table 4) with the arithmetic mean subtracted from each fitness gives a general, normalized set of Walsh coefficients in terms of delta expansion. In this class, they are given by Eqn. 18, 19, 20.

$$\alpha_{\{0\}} = \alpha_{\{1\}} = \alpha_{\{2\}} = \tfrac{1}{8}\,(\delta_0 + 2\delta_1 + \delta_2) \tag{18}$$

$$\alpha_{\{0,1\}} = \alpha_{\{0,2\}} = \alpha_{\{1,2\}} = \tfrac{1}{8}\,(\delta_2 - \delta_0) \tag{19}$$

$$\alpha_{\{0,1,2\}} = \tfrac{1}{8}\,(\delta_0 + \delta_2 - 2\delta_1) \tag{20}$$

As all δ are strictly positive, the univariate terms must be positive (hence, non-zero). The remaining possible structures are shown in Figure 4.

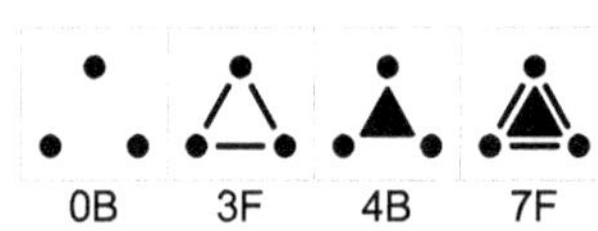

Figure 4: Minimal Walsh structure (0B) and all other possible Walsh structures of $C_{\text{Ones}} = [7,4,4,1,4,1,1,0]$.

In the general case, structure 7F will be produced. On the condition $2\delta_1 = \delta_0 + \delta_2$, the trivariate term becomes zero, producing structure 3F. On the condition $\delta_0 = \delta_2$, the bivariate terms become zero, producing structure 4B. If both of the above conditions hold, then $\delta_0 = \delta_1 = \delta_2$, then the univariate structure 0B is produced, as is the case with the canonical Ones function. We conclude that this univariate structure, 0B, is this minimum structure for this class.

The same analysis was repeated for the class $C_{\text{BinVal}} = [7, 4, 4, 1, 4, 1, 1, 0])$, which due to higher degrees of freedom, allows for a larger number of structures, 16, which we find to be the maximum possible for a 3-bit problem. The possible structures for C_{BinVal} are shown in Figure 5.

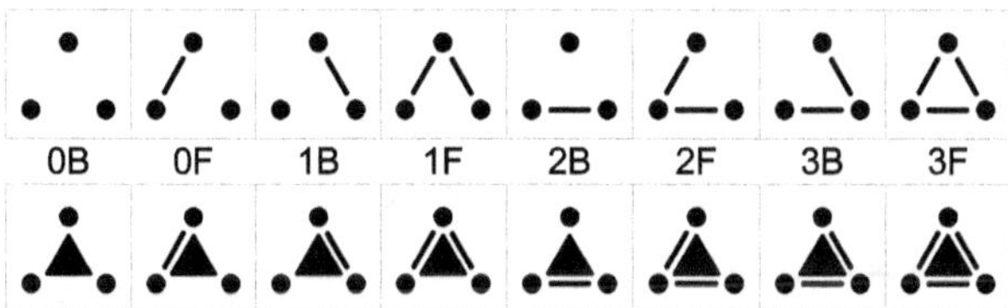

Figure 5: Minimal Walsh structure (0B) and all other possible Walsh structures of $C_{\text{BinVal}} = [7, 6, 5, 4, 3, 2, 1, 0]$.

For class $C_{Checkerboard} = [0, 2, 6, 2, 2, 6, 2, 0]$, we find that the bivariate terms between order-adjacent variables must be present, with an optional term between the start and end variables. No other parts of structure (univariate or trivariate terms) may be present in a function in this class. The possible structures for $C_{\text{Checkerboard}}$ are shown below in Figure 6.

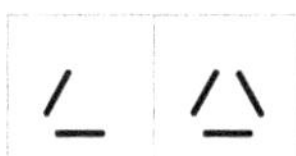

Figure 6: Minimal Walsh structure (24) and all other possible Walsh structures of $C_{\text{Checkerboard}} = [0, 2, 6, 2, 2, 6, 2, 0]$.

A complete analysis of all 545 835 classes of 3-bit functions was found by an automated process. By placing some restrictions on the types of functions considered, the Walsh-Hadamard transform could be computed of a well-defined large subset of functions for each class. These restrictions were to limit the image of the function to $y \in \mathbb{Z}, 0 \le y \le U$ and the deltas to $\delta \in \mathbb{Z}$.

The value chosen for U was 15. If a value for $U < 15$ was chosen, some structures for some classes were not detected. In the 3-bit case, a function may be constructed for any given Walsh structure where each $\alpha_I \in \{-1, 0, 1\}$. Using the expression $\vec{f} = H_3\vec{\alpha}$, the maximum value for any function value will be 7, and the minimum value will be -7 (a range of 15), therefore sampling from a set of $U = 15$ distinct integers is sufficient to generate any possible combination of negative, zero, and positive Walsh coefficients. It was confirmed experimentally, that for $U < 15$, some structures were not detected, and no additional structure were found for values $U > 15$ tried.

Table 5 shows the number of structures produced from each number of deltas. The result reveals that the Ones class has the maximum number of structures for any 3-delta class (4 structures) and that the maximum number of Walsh structures for any 3-bit class is 16. And we also see a positive correlation between number of deltas and the number of structures.

Num.	Num. Deltas							
Structs	0	1	2	3	4	5	6	7
1	1	254	2 744	6 720	4 032	-	-	-
2	-	-	3 052	16 072	23 856	10 080	-	-
3	-	-	-	11 760	30 240	21 504	8 064	-
4	-	-	-	6 272	41 664	53 760	14 784	2 688
5	-	-	-	-	12 096	41 664	34 944	5 376
6	-	-	-	-	8 064	24 864	24 192	9 408
7	-	-	-	-	5 376	18 816	16 128	2 688
8	-	-	-	-	672	15 456	25 536	8 064
9	-	-	-	-	-	-	-	-
10	-	-	-	-	-	2 688	6 720	5 376
11	-	-	-	-	-	-	-	-
12	-	-	-	-	-	2 688	9 408	4 032
13	-	-	-	-	-	-	-	-
14	-	-	-	-	-	-	-	-
15	-	-	-	-	-	-	-	-
16	-	-	-	-	-	-	1 344	2 688

Table 5: Number of structures produced from each number of deltas. Number of classes in each case is listed.

Analysis of the result shows that Walsh coefficients were not always simply necessary or unnecessary. For example, Figure 7 shows a case in which the trivariate structure $\alpha_{\{0,1,2\}}$, or one bivariate structure $\alpha_{\{0,2\}}$, or one univariate structure $\alpha_{\{0\}}$ may be considered unnecessary, but no more than one of those may be omitted. Another notable example is shown in Figure 8, where one bivariate structure $\alpha_{\{1,2\}}$ or the other two together (both $\alpha_{\{0,1\}}$ and $\alpha_{\{0,2\}}$) are required. This shows that from a rank-based perspective, some functions have a trade off between the presence of Walsh coefficients. Additionally, examples such as C_{ones} show that a symmetry is required to produce certain rank classes.

Figure 7: Three minimal Walsh structures (3F, 6F, and 7E) and the maximum structure (7F), the possible structures of the class $[5, 4, 2, 5, 5, 1, 0, 2]$.

6. DIRECTED ORDINAL LINKAGE

Linkage discovered by perturbation methods (PMs) is commonly regarded as bi-directional. i.e. $\mathcal{L}(j, i) \Leftrightarrow \mathcal{L}(i, j)$. We observe that using non-monotonicity detection perturbation, the dependence relationship between variables can in some cases be uni-directional, as illustrated in Figure 9. In this case, the optimum setting of X_0 can be inferred by sampling both values for X_0 at any point, whereas, identifying the optimal setting of X_1 depends on the value of X_0. By any previously-given definition of linkage (non-linearity or non-monotonicity), these variables are linked. We argue that this case of linkage places an ordering on the variables.

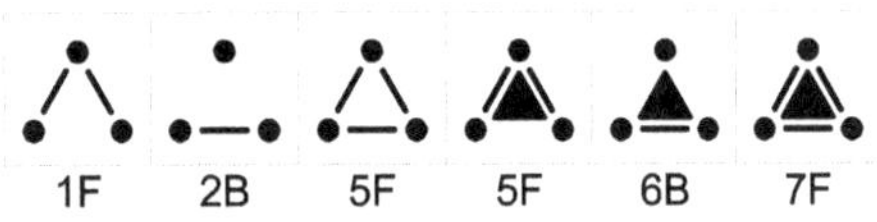

Figure 8: Two minimal Walsh structures (1F, and 2B) and four other possible structure of the class $[7, 4, 4, 2, 4, 2, 1, 0]$.

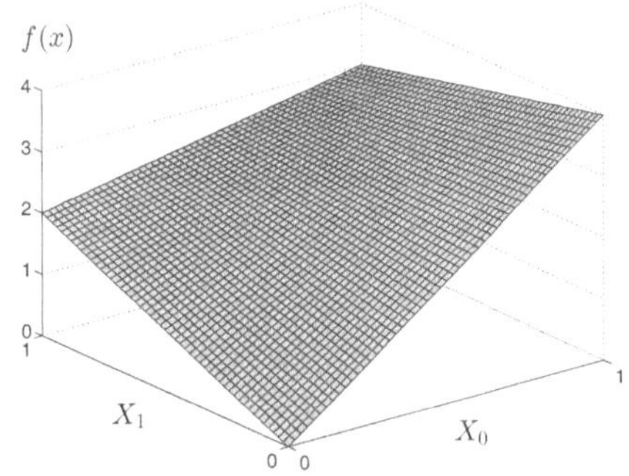

Figure 9: 2-bit fitness landscape illustrating unidirectional dependence $X_0 \rightarrow X_1$.

We provide a definition of *directed* linkage:

$$\mathcal{L}_O(i,j) \Leftrightarrow \exists\, x : sgn\left(\Delta f_j\left(x\left[i \rightarrow 1\right]\right)\right) \neq sgn\left(\Delta f_j\left(x\left[i \rightarrow 0\right]\right)\right) \tag{21}$$

The notation X_iX_j refers to interdependence:

$$X_iX_j \Leftrightarrow \mathcal{L}_O(i,j) \wedge \mathcal{L}_O(j,i) \tag{22}$$

The notation $X_i \rightarrow X_j$ refers to the unidirectional dependence j *depends on* i:

$$X_i \rightarrow X_j \Leftrightarrow \mathcal{L}_O(i,j) \wedge \neg\mathcal{L}_O(j,i) \tag{23}$$

The notation $X_i + X_j$ refers to independent variables:

$$X_i + X_j \Leftrightarrow \neg\mathcal{L}_O(i,j) \wedge \neg\mathcal{L}_O(j,i) \tag{24}$$

When referring to a general case without specifying the labelling of variables, the $\bullet$ operand may serve as a placeholder for variables, e.g. $\bullet\bullet \rightarrow \bullet$ may substitute for $X_0X_1 \rightarrow X_2$ but generalizes to any relabeling of the variables.

With this definition of directed linkage, a digraph with the same connected components as the undirected graph formed as a result of the conventional definition of linkage. Additionally, under our definition, each connected component may be regarded as one or more strongly-connected component (SCC).

Contracting each SCC to a single vertex produces a new directed acyclic graph (DAG) over the SCCs of the original graph. Assuming no higher-order dependencies, traversing this DAG with a topological ordering will give an order in which the SCCs of the original graph may be visited in which each SCC is optimized *after* its predecessors.

As with the interdependence relationships however, there can be higher-dimensional dependencies. We found experimentally that in the 3-bit case discussed in this paper, the higher-dimensional linkage can only exist where there is *no incoming edge* to a SCC of *two* vertices, thus, in these cases, it was checked whether the optimum setting of the two variables in the SCC depended on the third variable, and if so,

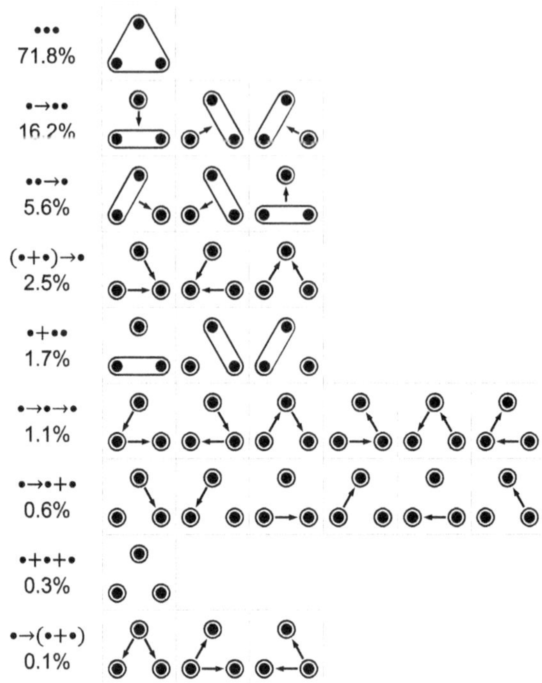

Figure 10: All 29 possible 3-bit directed linkage graphs with transitive linkages removed, grouped in to 9 cases according to relabeling invariance. The percentages show the proportion of rank-equivalence classes for different levels of structure complexity.

an incoming edge was added to correct the structure. Here, some classes in $\bullet\bullet \rightarrow \bullet$ are actually $\bullet\bullet\bullet$ and some classes in $\bullet + \bullet\bullet$ are actually $\bullet \rightarrow \bullet\bullet$.

Functions in the same rank-equivalence class as described in section 4 are indistinguishable by non-monotonicity detection PMs and hence, in contrast to the Walsh coefficients, each function in that class will have the same structure by this description.

With the removal of redundant transitive linkages (i.e. $X_0 \rightarrow X_2$ is redundant in the case that $X_0 \rightarrow X_1$ and $X_1 \rightarrow X_2$), there are 29 possible directed structures. These are shown in Figure 10, grouped into 9 cases according to invariance of relabeling of variables.

7. OPTIMIZATION SCHEDULES

Given the 9 cases of possible directed structures invariant under relabellings, these can be regarded as optimization schedules. There is a hierarchy of general to specific schedules. e.g. the most general schedule $\bullet\bullet\bullet$ regards all variables as interdependent and hence requires that the function be optimized by exhaustive evaluation, the most specific case $\bullet + \bullet + \bullet$ regard the variables as independent (univariate problem) to be optimized separately. If a problem is solvable by the more specific case, it is also solvable (though perhaps less efficiently) by the more general case. The tree in Figure 11 shows the relationship between the 9 cases, if a problem may be solved by an instance lower down the tree, it will also be solvable by all schedules reachable by following the edges of the tree. This ordering can be constructed by observing that to gain generality, an independence rela-

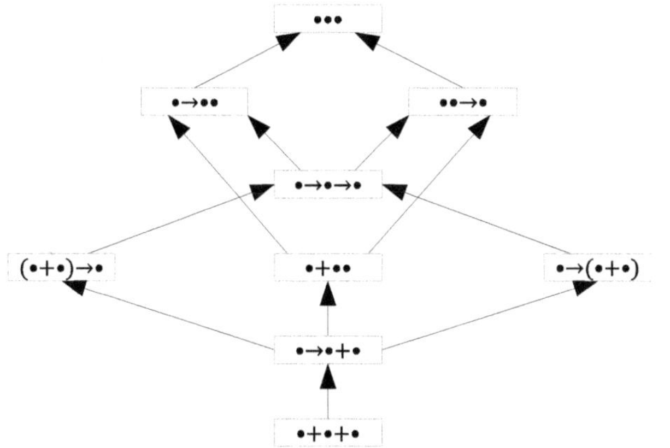

Figure 11: The relationship between the 9 ordinal linkage cases (see Figure 10). Any case may be solved processed as a case reachable by the edges in this graph.

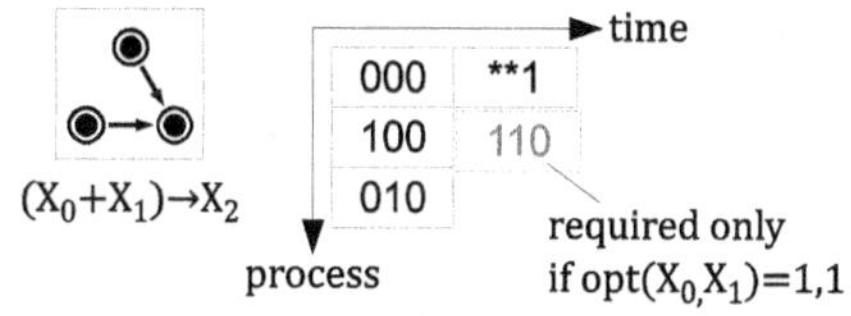

Figure 12: The 4 or 5 required function evaluations and 2 required time steps in the $(X_0 + X_1) \rightarrow X_2$ case. In the first time step, the optimum setting of X_0 and X_1 is determined, in the second time step, the optimum for the remaining variables is determined. This only requires evaluation of $f(1,1,0)$ if the optimum setting of the first two variables is both 1. The asterisks represent whatever optimum was determined in the previous time step.

tionship $\bullet + \bullet$ may be replaced by a dependence relationship $\bullet \rightarrow \bullet$, and a dependence relationship may be replaced with an interdependence relationship $\bullet\bullet$. The effect of these transformations is to *add* edges to the graph, allowing the schedule to be applicable to solve *more* cases.

The finesses which must be evaluated to determine a global optimum, given the structure of directed linkage is given by choosing one of the applicable schedules. The schedules differ in minimum number of function evaluations, ranging from 4 in the most specific case to 8 in the most general case.

Allowing for parallelization of evaluation, the schedules also differ in the minimum number of time steps required to achieve this minimum, ranging from 1 to 3, equaling the number of level sets in the contracted DAG. This is because the unidirectional linkage requires that the optimum for some variable(s) be determined before it is known which function evaluations will determine the optimum for some other variable(s).

As an example, Figure 12 shows the 4 or 5 required function evaluations and 2 required time steps in the $X_0 + X_1 \rightarrow X_2$ case. In the $**1$ function evaluation, the asterisks represent the optimum of the first two variables. The 5th functions evaluation, 110 is only required if the optimum setting of the first two variables is 11, otherwise the optimum of the third variable may be determined by comparing $**1$ to one of the first three evaluations. This is the only one of the 9 cases to have an evaluation which may or may not be required. Note that the function evaluations with asterisks are a result of uni-directional dependence enforcing an ordering of evaluation. After the first time step, an optimum of the first two variables may be substituted in the pattern to become 001, 101, 011, or 111, and only in the latter case, the optional 110 must be added on.

The necessary function evaluations are given in Figure 13 for one example labeling of each of the 9 cases. From this we see that the choice to move to another schedule may in some cases represent a trade-off between number of function evaluations and minimum number of time steps. This minimum depends on the number of evaluations which can be done in parallel.

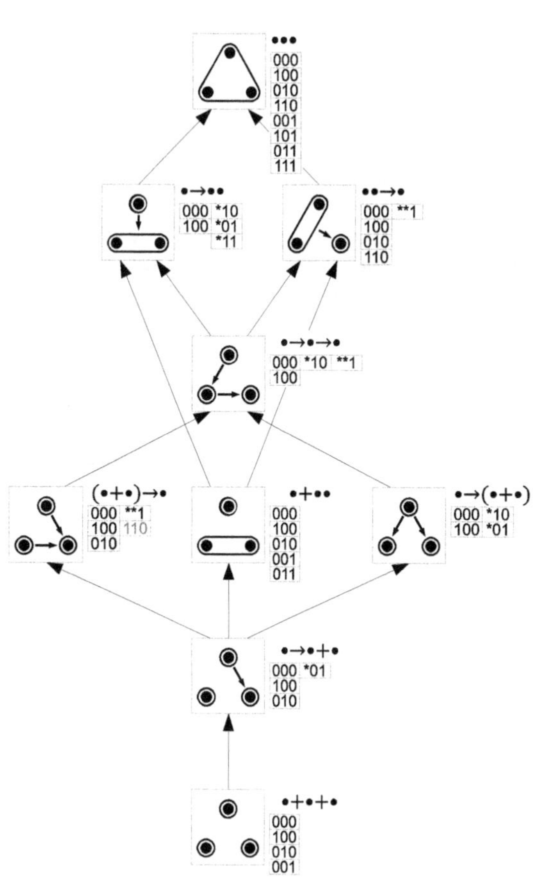

Figure 13: One example per ordinal linkage case (see Figure 10) with a linkage schedule (see Figure 12) which will locate a global optimum for the shown case. This figure is set out in the same arrangement as Figure 11

8. CONCLUSIONS

Many EDAs use linkage learning to determine which variables should be optimized together, but often construct models which use more information about linkage than is necessary. This leads to overly-complex models, which do not give an advantage over a simpler EDAs. This paper gives some theoretical insight in to the type of linkage which is strictly necessary from the point of view of a Markov network EDA or non-monotonicity-detection perturbation methods. Further, as the probability distribution modelled by *any* EDA could be represented as a Markov network, this view of unnecessary interactions may have implications for other EDAs.

In this paper we have given a method of classifying functions as being rank-equivalent, and given the number of instances in the 3-bit case for each of the possible number of different fitness levels. We have shown the minimal Walsh structure of the classes which the benchmark functions Ones, BinVal, and Checkerboard (1-D) belong to, and highlighted examples of equivalence classes which have a trade-off in necessary structure; and shown a positive correlation between number of deltas and the number of structures with the maximum at 16 for the 3-bit case. We have described how variables in non-monotonicity–detection perturbation methods can have uni-directional interactions, and enumerated all possible digraphs which may be formed in the 3-bit case. We have shown how these graphs dictate the minimum optimization schedules necessary to discover a global optimum for a given function and structure, and how the different possible optimization schedules are hierarchically related.

There are several directions for future work in this area. Modeling methods in EDAs may be adapted to look for minimal structures to avoid unnecessary computation. In bit string spaces, minimal Walsh structure may be estimated and the argument may be extended to other variable encoding. The adoption of perturbation methods for linkage detection allows consideration of choice of optimization schedule. The hierarchical classification on an unseen problem allows trade-offs to be made between computational effort / parallelizability and likelihood of optimality, which can be conditioned incrementally on evidence as the search progresses. Finally, the structure classification may be used to generate more representative benchmark problem sets.

9. REFERENCES

[1] S. Baluja and R. Caruana. Removing the genetics from the standard genetic algorithm. In *ICML*, pages 38–46, 1995.

[2] S. Baluja and S. Davies. Using optimal dependency-trees for combinatorial optimization: Learning the structure of the search space. Technical report, DTIC Document, 1997.

[3] C.-Y. Chuang and Y.-p. Chen. Likage identification by perturbation and decision tree induction. In *Evolutionary Computation, 2007. CEC 2007. IEEE Congress on*, pages 357–363. IEEE, 2007.

[4] S. Droste, T. Jansen, and I. Wegener. On the analysis of the (1+1) evolutionary algorithm. *Theoretical Computer Science*, 276(1):51–81, 2002.

[5] B. J. Fino and V. R. Algazi. Unified matrix treatment of the fast (walsh-hadamard) transform. *Computers, IEEE Transactions on*, C-25(11):1142–1146, 1976.

[6] D. E. Goldberg. Genetic algorithms and Walsh functions: Part i, a gentle introduction. *Complex Systems*, 3(2):129–152, 1989.

[7] D. E. Goldberg, B. Korb, and K. Deb. Messy genetic algorithms: Motivation, analysis, and first results. *Complex systems*, 3(5):493–530, 1989.

[8] M. Hauschild, M. Pelikan, C. F. Lima, and K. Sastry. Analyzing probabilistic models in hierarchical boa on traps and spin glasses. In *Proceedings of the 9th annual conference on Genetic and evolutionary computation*, pages 523–530. ACM, 2007.

[9] P. Larrañaga and J. A. Lozano. *Estimation of distribution algorithms: A new tool for evolutionary computation*, volume 2. Springer, 2002.

[10] H. Mühlenbein and G. Paaß. From recombination of genes to the estimation of distributions i. binary parameters. In *Proceedings of the 4th International Con-ference on Parallel Problem Solving from Nature, Lecture Notes In Computer Science*, volume 1141, pages 178–187, 1996.

[11] M. Munetomo and D. E. Goldberg. Identifying linkage groups by nonlinearity/non-monotonicity detection. In *Proceedings of the genetic and evolutionary computation conference*, volume 1, pages 433–440, 1999.

[12] M. Pelikan. Bayesian optimization algorithm. In *Hierarchical Bayesian Optimization Algorithm*, pages 31–48. Springer, 2005.

[13] M. Pelikan, D. E. Goldberg, and E. Cantu-Paz. Linkage problem, distribution estimation, and bayesian networks. *Evolutionary computation*, 8(3):311–340, 2000.

[14] M. Pelikan, D. E. Goldberg, and F. G. Lobo. A survey of optimization by building and using probabilistic models. *Computational optimization and applications*, 21(1):5–20, 2002.

[15] E. Radetic and M. Pelikan. Spurious dependencies and eda scalability. In *Proceedings of the 12th annual conference on Genetic and evolutionary computation*, pages 303–310. ACM, 2010.

[16] S. Shakya, A. Brownlee, J. McCall, F. Fournier, and G. Owusu. A fully multivariate deum algorithm. In *Evolutionary Computation, 2009. CEC'09. IEEE Congress on*, pages 479–486. IEEE, 2009.

[17] M. J. Streeter. Upper bounds on the time and space complexity of optimizing additively separable functions. In *Genetic and Evolutionary Computation–GECCO 2004*, pages 186–197. Springer, 2004.

[18] D. Thierens and P. A. Bosman. Optimal mixing evolutionary algorithms. In *Proceedings of the 13th annual conference on Genetic and evolutionary computation*, pages 617–624. ACM, 2011.

[19] M. Tsuji, M. Munetomo, and K. Akama. Metropolitan area network design using ga based on hierarchical linkage identification. In *Genetic and Evolutionary Computation–GECCO 2003*, pages 1616–1617. Springer, 2003.

Solving Building Block Problems Using Generative Grammar

Chris R. Cox
University of Southampton, UK
c.cox@soton.ac.uk

Richard A. Watson
University of Southampton, UK
r.a.watson@soton.ac.uk

ABSTRACT

In this work we demonstrate novel applications of generative grammar to evolutionary search. We introduce a class of grammar that can represent hierarchical schema structure in a problem space, and describe an algorithm that can infer an instance of the grammar from a population of sample phenotypes. Unlike conventional sequence-based grammars this grammar represents set-membership relationships, not strings, and is therefore insensitive to gene-ordering and physical linkage. We show that these methods are capable of accurately identifying problem structure from populations of above-average-fitness individuals on simple modular and hierarchically modular test problems. We then show how these grammatical models can be used to aid evolutionary problem solving by enabling facilitated variation; specifically, by producing novel combinations of schemata observed in the sample population whilst respecting the inherent constraint structure of the problem space. This provides a robust method of building-block recombination that is linkage-invariant and not restricted to low-order schemata.

Categories and Subject Descriptors

I.2.8 [**Artificial Intelligence**]: Problem Solving, Control Methods, and Search-Heuristic methods; J.3 [**Life and medical sciences**]: Biology and genetics

Keywords

genetic algorithms; evolutionary algorithms; generative grammar; compression; optimisation; metaheuristics

1. INTRODUCTION

A primary concern in understanding the full potential of evolutionary search as a problem solving mechanism is discovering how an evolutionary population can learn epistatic interactions of many different orders. From a computational perspective of evolution as combinatorial optimisation dealing with epistasis is fundamental, as problems without variable interdependencies can be solved with the simplest gradient-climbing methods and do not typically require our attention. And although the variable interactions which hard problems are sensitive to can be complex, there are often patterns in this complexity, which we refer to as problem structure, that if detected and exploited provide some hope of finding a good or even globally optimal solution to the problem. Understanding how problem structure can be modelled and exploited continues to be a topic of huge theoretical and practical importance in the field, and although many types of both implicit and explicit model-building mechanism have been proposed and tested, there is a great deal of potential to improve our understanding, techniques and results in this area. In this paper we contribute to this endeavour by showing for the first time how generative grammar can be used to model combinatorial structure, and demonstrate an application of this technique to evolutionary computation - specifically by using generative grammar to efficiently solve shuffled modular and hierarchically modular test problems.

The field of evolutionary computation has proposed a variety of both implicit and explicit mechanisms by which epistatic dependencies that offer a fitness advantage can be identified and then exploited in evolutionary search, starting with Holland's work on the Schema Theorem [8]. Holland was able to show that genetic recombination through crossover offers a scheme under which fit multivariate patterns known as schemata can grow in frequency in an evolutionary population. This was followed by the Building Block Hypothesis [4] which suggested that short, lower order, fit schemata ("building blocks") could recombine to form even larger schemata, effectively providing a means for evolutionary search to operate at multiple scales of organisation. These foundational theories were able to offer a theory of how genetic algorithms using simple genetic crossover might implicitly infer problem structure into the genetic makeup of a population and exploit it to find better solutions. However later results showed that in practice sexual GA's struggled to match the performance of even relatively simple hill-climbers on modular test problems [3].

More recently Estimation of Distribution Algorithms have been introduced (EDA's) that are able to explicitly model and then exploit useful variable interactions in a population (see [7] for a review). These methods typically attempt to build a probabilistic model of problem structure from a sample population, and then evolve the population by generating new offspring from the model. These explicit approaches to modelling tend to offer less in terms of plausibility of natu-

GECCO'14, July 12–16, 2014, Vancouver, BC, Canada.
Copyright 2014 ACM 978-1-4503-2662-9/14/07 ...$15.00.
http://dx.doi.org/10.1145/2576768.2598259.

ral occurrence, but more in terms of modelling sophistication and effectiveness on certain types of problem. Of particular note are the limitations of GA's with simple crossover on modular and hierarchically modular problems such as "Royal Roads" [3], "Hierarchical If and Only If" (HIFF) [26] and deceptive trap functions [2], and the comparative success of model-building algorithms such as the Bayesian Optimisation Algorithm (BOA) [18], the Building Block Hill Climber (BBHC) [9] and the Linkage Tree Genetic Algorithm (LTGA)[23] that are able to solve them using a sub-quadratic number of fitness evaluations.

In this paper we present an explicit method for modelling problem structure using generative grammar. Unlike previous model-building methods we define a method that builds a lossless rather than a probabilistic model from a sample population using grammatical inference. By a lossless model we mean a model from which the original samples can be recreated without any loss of information. Indeed, we will show that the grammar induction algorithm used here is a type of lossless compression that identifies common hyperplane partitions with which the sample population can be more compactly described. Furthermore, we show that the hierarchy of hyperplane partitions this process produces is encoded into the grammar as a hierarchy of symbols that are equivalent to genetic schemata, and thus we refer to the grammar as "schema grammar".

This paper is structured as follows. After a review of related work we introduce schema grammar, and an offline compression algorithm that is able to infer an instance of the grammar from a population of sample phenotypes. We then provide initial results from experiments that show problem structure being identified using schema grammar inference and then exploited using an evolutionary search algorithm. We use concatenated and hierarchical trap functions [2, 19] as our problem instances, and show that by inferring a grammar from local optima of these functions building blocks are successfully identified that allow search to proceed at a higher level of organisation and the global optima to these functions to be found.

2. RELATED WORK

The concept of generative grammar in an evolutionary context is not new. Of particular note are a class of grammar called Lindenmayer Systems (L-Systems), which provide an intriguing and often visually compelling model for growth in natural systems [12, 20], and Grammatical Evolution, in which genetic programs are generated using pre-defined grammars that provide a genotype to phenotype mapping [22], and can themselves be evolved [17]. Schema grammar differs from these approaches in two important respects. Firstly, we do not use either evolved or pre-defined grammars, and instead use grammatical inference to build a model of an evolutionary population. Secondly, schema grammar generates combinatorial as opposed to sequential languages, and the production rules it encodes expand to unordered sets of symbols rather than ordered sequences or strings. We combine this feature with the Messy GA encoding [5] that allows individuals to be modelled as unordered sets of symbols rather than sequential bit-strings. These features of the grammar offer two key advantages over the use of sequential grammar in genetic algorithms. Firstly, they remove the limitations of sequential order from the concept of co-occurrence: patterns of co-occurrence that are non-contiguous in nature can be represented symbolically in the grammar, allowing a complete range of epistatic interactions to be modelled. Secondly, they allow the recursive expansion of symbols to be contained within a fixed combinatorial problem space.

Our use of compression grammars for evolutionary problem solving builds on the concept of Compression Evolutionary Algorithms (Compression EA's) introduced by Toussaint [24]. Toussaint provided an interpretation of model-building algorithms as attempting to minimise the Kullback-Leibler divergence of a model to a population of fit phenotypes, and showed that compressing the population representation is one way to minimise this divergence. He then illustrated the concept using both EDA and GA style searches and a sequential L-System compression grammar model, which were applied to variable length hierarchical XOR problems. We directly follow the intuition and general approach of compression as model building that is suggested by Toussaint, and indeed our work can be considered an instance of a Compression EA. In this context, the key contributions of our work are to extend the capabilities of Compression EA's by enabling the modelling of non-contiguous structure using generative grammar, and to demonstrate the effectiveness of the Compression EA approach on classic building block test problems.

The evolutionary search framework in which we apply our modelling technique is a multi-scale (building block) hill-climbing search that uses schemata created from the grammar's symbol table as mutation operators. This is inspired by recent works that show for the class of problem we are studying here - decomposable modular and hierarchically modular test problems [26] - multi-scale search is highly effective as a problem solving method [9, 13]. This type of search algorithm contrasts with the canonical EDA approach of candidate generation through sampling of a probabilistic model, which could be implemented using schema grammar by probabilistically modelling and then sampling the compressed representation of the population (and indeed is the approach considered by Toussaint). We chose multi-scale hill climbing specifically for the class of problem we examine in this paper, however in future works we intend to explore using schema grammar models within different search frameworks.

The inference algorithm we will describe (see Section 4) uses a type of agglomerative clustering to encode each sample in the grammar. In this scheme a recursive substitution of symbol pairs simultaneously compacts each sample whilst creating a hierarchical schema structure in the grammar. We note some similarity between our algorithm and model-building algorithms including LTGA [23] and ECGA [6] which also employ agglomerative clustering. The key distinguishing feature of our approach is that the associations learned by the grammar are *point-wise* associations, which describe interactions between specific alleles and are not constrained by a model of physical linkage. In fact, the grammar has no concept of loci as variables and this allows the inferred schemata to freely overlap in locus space (see Section 3). As such the agglomeration in schema grammar inference is an agglomeration of allele expressions, rather than an agglomeration of loci. This contrasts with the aforementioned algorithms and linkage learning approaches more generally, which typically infer models of inter-locus linkage. For the class of problem studied here this is not pertinent as the problem structures do not contain complex overlap, however for many other types of problem this is not the case. Modelling such problems using schema grammar will be one avenue of future research.

3. SCHEMA GRAMMAR

Schema grammar is a type of context-free formal grammar (CFG) and is inspired by the "straight-line" context-free grammars that are typically used for sequential compression (see [10] for a review). In these grammars variables (known as a *non-terminal symbols*) are expanded into a strings of characters (known as *terminal symbols*) using recursive rewriting. Rewriting is specified using production rules that associate each non-terminal symbol with a string of symbols it should be substituted with, and by executing these rules recursively a single *start symbol* can produce a complete sequence of characters. Grammatical models can compress source data by encoding recurring, potentially hierarchical, patterns as non-terminal symbols and re-using these to create a compact, factorised representation of the original data. The straight-line properties of the grammar require that each non-terminal symbol in the grammar is only associated with one production rule and there are no loops in production. These properties ensure that each derivation from the grammar is deterministic.

Grammatical models have properties that make them useful for representing evolutionary populations. Non-terminal symbols and their associated production rules can be used to encapsulate complex and often hierarchical multivariate interdependencies in a factorised symbolic representation. By using this structure as a genotype-phenotype (G-P) map, individual genotypes can be represented in a reduced, symbolic space with a surjective mapping from genotype to phenotype. This allows evolutionary variation to be performed in an unconstrained way whilst respecting the inherent constraints of phenotype space (see [25] for a fuller exploration of these ideas). Our approach to modelling is therefore to infer a grammatical model of genotypes and a G-P map from a population of phenotypes, and use this to facilitate evolutionary search.

The key modification we make to traditional CFG's in schema grammar is to specify production rules using set membership rewriting as opposed to string rewriting, with no linear precedence constraints. We adopt the Messy GA encoding [5], which enables bit strings to be respecified using an unordered set of symbols, each defined as a $\langle position|value\rangle$ pair. So for example the bit string 0110 becomes $\{\langle 0|0\rangle, \langle 1|1\rangle, \langle 2|1\rangle, \langle 3|0\rangle\}$, which (being unordered) is equivalent to $\{\langle 3|0\rangle, \langle 0|0\rangle, \langle 2|1\rangle, \langle 1|1\rangle\}$. This also provides a natural way of modelling schemata: for example the schema 1**1**0 (using standard notation) can be modelled as the set $\{\langle 0|1\rangle, \langle 3|1\rangle, \langle 6|0\rangle\}$.

By combining the Messy GA encoding with set expansion in the grammar's production rules we can model individuals using the recursive expansion of a hierarchy of schemata of any defining length. For example, one way of representing the binary phenotype 110011 using the grammar is through the expression of a 2-level modular pattern as follows (with the recursive phenotype expansion of each symbol shown in the right column using standard schema notation):

Production rule	Phenotype expansion
$g \rightarrow \{\langle 2\|0\rangle, \langle 3\|0\rangle, s_0\}$	110011
$s_0 \rightarrow \{s_1, s_2\}$	11**11
$s_1 \rightarrow \{\langle 0\|1\rangle, \langle 5\|1\rangle\}$	1****1
$s_2 \rightarrow \{\langle 1\|1\rangle, \langle 4\|1\rangle\}$	*1**1*

where g is the genetic representation of the sample individual and s_0, s_1 and s_2 are non-terminal symbols that represent individual schemata. By using set membership rewriting and the Messy GA encoding, it is clear that the grammar has no intrinsic bias toward any specific ordering of genes. As we will see this also means that grammar inference is also insensitive to gene ordering, and inference of samples with inherent sequential structure (for example local optima of concatenated trap functions) produces the same grammatical characteristics as inference from the randomly shuffled versions of these functions.

We can now formally define schema grammar using the following 5-tuple:

$$\mathbb{G}_{Schema} = (V, G, S, \Sigma, R), \text{ where:} \quad (1)$$

- V is a set of non-terminal symbols (variables), each of which defines a sub-language of $\mathbb{G}_{Schema}$, where $V \ni \{G, S\}$ and $G \cap S \in \emptyset$
- G is a non-empty set of non-terminal symbols representing the genotypes in the sample population
- S is a set of non-terminal symbols representing genetic schemata, which may be empty
- Σ is the set of terminal symbols representing the complete set of alleles in an n-dimensional binary problem space encoded as $\langle position|value\rangle$ tuples, i.e. $\Sigma = \{\langle\lambda|\alpha\rangle | \lambda \in \{0, .., n\}, \alpha \in \{0, 1\}\}$.
- R is a finite set of production rules that relate each non-terminal symbol to the expansion of an unordered set of symbols, such that $R : V \rightarrow \{V \cup \Sigma\}^*$

Table 1 illustrates an example instance of schema grammar inferred from a population of three phenotypes in a 5-dimensional binary problem.

V	$\{G, S\}$		
G	$\{g_0, g_1, g_2\}$		
S	$\{s_0, s_1\}$		
Σ	$\{\langle 0\|0\rangle, \langle 0\|1\rangle, \langle 1\|0\rangle, \langle 1\|1\rangle, \langle 2\|0\rangle, \langle 2\|1\rangle, \langle 3\|0\rangle, \langle 3\|1\rangle, \langle 4\|0\rangle, \langle 4\|1\rangle\}$		
R	r_0	$g_0 \rightarrow \{s_0, \langle 2\|1\rangle\}$	01100
	r_1	$g_1 \rightarrow \{s_0, \langle 2\|0\rangle\}$	01000
	r_2	$g_2 \rightarrow \{s_1, \langle 0\|1\rangle, \langle 1\|1\rangle, \langle 2\|1\rangle\}$	11100
	r_3	$s_0 \rightarrow \{s_1, \langle 0\|0\rangle, \langle 1\|1\rangle\}$	01*00
	r_4	$s_1 \rightarrow \{\langle 3\|0\rangle, \langle 4\|0\rangle\}$	***00

Table 1: An example grammar for representing three bit-strings 01100, 01000 and 11100. The recursive phenotype expansion of each production rule is displayed to its right.

One important feature of the grammar is that the schemata it encodes can overlap in the space of both loci and alleles as illustrated by the following grammar:

Production rule	Phenotype expansion
$s_0 \rightarrow \{\langle 0\|1\rangle, \langle 1\|1\rangle, \langle 3\|1\rangle\}$	11*1
$s_1 \rightarrow \{\langle 0\|1\rangle, \langle 1\|1\rangle, \langle 3\|0\rangle\}$	11*0
$s_2 \rightarrow \{\langle 0\|0\rangle, \langle 2\|0\rangle, \langle 3\|1\rangle\}$	0*01
$s_3 \rightarrow \{\langle 1\|0\rangle, \langle 2\|1\rangle\}$	*01*

In this example s_0 and s_1 model two overlapping combinations of alleles from the eight possible at three specific loci, and s_2 and s_3 model two schemata that overlap with all others in the grammar both in terms of loci and alleles. This illustrates the flexibility of the grammar to capture epistatic interactions of different orders without being bound to specific models of physical linkage, and without being required to exhaustively model alternative combinations of alleles at specific loci.

3.1 Pre-terminal Symbols

We introduce a further definition that is required in the problem-solving section of this paper. We define every non-terminal symbol in S that includes a terminal symbol directly in its expansion as a pre-terminal symbol. The pre-terminal symbols P of the grammar $\mathbb{G}_{Schema}$ are therefore:

$$P = \{s \in S | p(s) \cap \Sigma \notin \emptyset\} \tag{2}$$

where $p(s)$ is the right hand side of the single production rule that has s as its left hand side. The pre-terminal symbols are the lowest level building blocks of the grammar schema hierarchy. All schema symbols are either pre-terminal symbols themselves or recursively expand to combinations of pre-terminals. We introduce the concept here as in the test problems we investigate below we use pre-terminal symbols as mutation operators during evolutionary search.

4. GRAMMAR INFERENCE

In this section we present an offline algorithm that is capable of inferring an instance of schema grammar from a collection of samples. The algorithm performs lossless combinatorial compression and is based on an adaptation of two existing sequential compression algorithms that use grammar codes: *RE-PAIR* (recursive pairing), an offline algorithm from Larrson et al. [11] and *SEQUITUR*, an online algorithm from Nevill-Manning et al. [16]. Both algorithms compress a sequence of characters by identifying frequently co-occurring symbols (digrams) and substituting these with non-terminal symbols. This process repeats recursively to build a hierarchy of symbols that expand into sequential motifs of various orders. In both cases the resulting grammar has an important property: no two symbols co-occur anywhere in the grammar more than once. Essentially, the compression process identifies recurring sequential structure present in the original string of symbols and refactors it into a hierarchical symbol table, resulting in a compressed version of the original with redundant structure removed.

In our algorithm we use the general offline dictionary-based approach of *RE-PAIR* and the rule utility constraints of *SEQUITUR* that collapse unnecessarily deep hierarchies of order-two productions into larger, flatter productions. The key conceptual adaptation we introduce is inference of production rules that expand to unordered sets rather than ordered sequences. This turns out to be a simple adaptation that results in grammars with similar properties to those inferred by sequential compression. To proceed we adopt an alternative definition of co-occurrence. In the following sequential production rule:

$$s \rightarrow ababc$$

we would consider the co-occurrences present to be all the pairs of ordered adjacent symbols in the right-hand-side of the rule, i.e.:

$$\{(a,b),(b,a),(a,b),(b,c)\}$$

In contrast we define the co-occurrences in a schema grammar production as all the un-ordered 2-combinations present in the right-hand-side of the rule. So for example the production rule:

$$s \rightarrow \{\langle 0|1\rangle, \langle 1|0\rangle, \langle 2|0\rangle\}$$

contains the three co-occurrences:

$$\{\{\langle 0|1\rangle, \langle 1|0\rangle\}, \{\langle 0|1\rangle, \langle 2|0\rangle\}, \{\langle 1|0\rangle, \langle 2|0\rangle\}\}$$

We initialise the grammar by encoding a set of genotype symbols G that directly map to the sample phenotypes. We proceed with compression by counting the frequency of each co-occurring pair of symbols across all production rules. A new non-terminal symbol is created that produces the most frequently co-occurring pair, and each instance of the pair in the rules is then substituted with the new symbol. If the frequencies of two or more co-occurrences are equal then one is selected randomly. This process repeats until no co-occurrence appears more than once anywhere in the production rules, as with sequential compression. Larger schema symbols are formed through the recursive substitution of co-occurring symbols, creating symbol hierarchies.

The rule utility constraint we adopt from *SEQUITUR* stipulates that non-terminal symbols that are referenced only once in the right-hand-side of the production rules should be removed as they are superfluous. This is best served by an example. Consider a frequently occurring schema 1111**** (for example if the population were local optima of concatenated trap-4 functions). Without the rule utility constraint this schema would be inferred into the grammar in a hierarchy like the following:

Production rule	Phenotype expansion
$g_0 \rightarrow \{s_2, \langle 4|1\rangle, \langle 5|1\rangle, \langle 6|1\rangle, \langle 7|1\rangle\}$	11111111
$g_1 \rightarrow \{s_2, \langle 4|0\rangle, \langle 5|0\rangle, \langle 6|0\rangle, \langle 7|0\rangle\}$	11110000
$s_0 \rightarrow \{\langle 0|1\rangle, \langle 1|1\rangle\}$	11******
$s_1 \rightarrow \{s_0, \langle 2|1\rangle\}$	111*****
$s_2 \rightarrow \{s_1, \langle 3|1\rangle\}$	1111****

In these production rules symbols s_0 and s_1 are only referenced once and are unnecessary in order to encode the schema 1111**** efficiently. By enforcing the rule utility constraint the production for s_0 would be back-substituted into s_1 and s_1 back into s_2, and the now-redundant symbols removed, leaving:

Production rule	Phenotype expansion
$g_0 \rightarrow \{s_2, \langle 4|1\rangle, \langle 5|1\rangle, \langle 6|1\rangle, \langle 7|1\rangle\}$	11111111
$g_1 \rightarrow \{s_2, \langle 4|0\rangle, \langle 5|0\rangle, \langle 6|0\rangle, \langle 7|0\rangle\}$	11110000
$s_2 \rightarrow \{\langle 0|1\rangle, \langle 1|1\rangle, \langle 2|1\rangle, \langle 3|1\rangle\}$	1111****

The offline compression algorithm for schema grammar is described in Algorithm 1, and a worked example of its execution is shown in Table 2. The algorithm is not fully deterministic as presented as there can be a random selection in step 2(b) when multiple symbol co-occurrences have the same frequency. The implication of this is that the same input samples can result in different grammars. The process can however be made fully deterministic by making an arbitrary but predictable choice in this situation, for example by

Algorithm 1: The offline compression algorithm for inferring an instance of schema grammar

1. Initialise production rules, directly encoding production of sample phenotypes
2. Identify the most frequent co-occurrence of symbols in the right-hand-side of all production rules:
   (a) If no two symbols co-occur more than once, then go to step 5
   (b) If two co-occurrences appear with the same frequency then select one randomly
3. Create a new non-terminal symbol and a production rule that re-writes the symbol to the two co-occurring symbols. Replace each co-occurrence with the new non-terminal symbol
4. Go to Step 2
5. For each non-terminal symbol that is referenced in only one production rule, substitute the non-terminal symbol for its production in the referenced rule, and delete the non-terminal symbol and its associated rule
6. End

hashing the co-occurrences and choosing the co-occurrence with the smallest hash value. It should also be noted that there is no guarantee that the inferred grammar will be the most compressed (or "best") grammar possible. In the realm of sequential grammars finding such a grammar is known as the "smallest grammar problem" (see [1] for a review) and is NP-complete [21].

In terms of computational complexity the initial scan of co-occurrences across each sample of the population is $\Theta(n^2)$, where n is the length of each phenotype. On each subsequent symbol substitution the frequency table requires an $O(n')$ update where n' is the current length of each sample, which incrementally reduces with each substitution. The overall complexity then is $\Omega(n^2)$, with exact scalability depending on the structure of the population and the implementation. We have empirically observed scalability in the range $O(n^2)$ to $O(n^3)$ in our own initial tests, although optimisation has not be performed and more work is required to analyse this rigorously.

5. EXPERIMENTS

5.1 Search Algorithm

In this section we report initial results from global optimisation experiments on test building-block problems. The search framework we employ is an iterative multi-scale hill-climbing search, and is similar in concept to both the Building Block Hill Climber (BBHC) [9] and MACRO [13], which both perform multi-scale search using mutation operators built from models of problem structure. Our approach is to identify an initial population of above-average fitness phenotypes using simple bit-flip hill climbing. The population is then modelled using schema grammar inference, capturing any structure present in the population in the hierarchical schema structure of the grammar. The resulting schemata

Step	Production Rules R	Action
0	$g_0 \rightarrow \{\langle 0\vert 0\rangle, \langle 1\vert 1\rangle, \langle 2\vert 1\rangle, \langle 3\vert 0\rangle, \langle 4\vert 0\rangle\}$	Initialise genotype
	$g_1 \rightarrow \{\langle 0\vert 0\rangle, \langle 1\vert 1\rangle, \langle 2\vert 0\rangle, \langle 3\vert 0\rangle, \langle 4\vert 0\rangle\}$	symbols from
	$g_2 \rightarrow \{\langle 0\vert 1\rangle, \langle 1\vert 0\rangle, \langle 2\vert 1\rangle, \langle 3\vert 0\rangle, \langle 4\vert 0\rangle\}$	sample phenotypes
1	$g_0 \rightarrow \{\langle 0\vert 0\rangle, \langle 1\vert 1\rangle, \langle 2\vert 1\rangle, s_0\}$	Substitute
	$g_1 \rightarrow \{\langle 0\vert 0\rangle, \langle 1\vert 1\rangle, \langle 2\vert 0\rangle, s_0\}$	$\{\langle 3\vert 0\rangle, \langle 4\vert 0\rangle\}$
	$g_2 \rightarrow \{\langle 0\vert 1\rangle, \langle 1\vert 0\rangle, \langle 2\vert 1\rangle, s_0\}$	(3 co-occurrences)
	$s_0 \rightarrow \{\langle 3\vert 0\rangle, \langle 4\vert 0\rangle\}$	
2	$g_0 \rightarrow \{s_1, \langle 2\vert 1\rangle, s_0\}$	Substitute
	$g_1 \rightarrow \{s_1, \langle 2\vert 0\rangle, s_0\}$	$\{\langle 0\vert 0\rangle, \langle 1\vert 1\rangle\}$
	$g_2 \rightarrow \{\langle 0\vert 1\rangle, \langle 1\vert 0\rangle, \langle 2\vert 1\rangle, s_0\}$	(2 co-occurrences)
	$s_0 \rightarrow \{\langle 3\vert 0\rangle, \langle 4\vert 0\rangle\}$	
	$s_1 \rightarrow \{\langle 0\vert 0\rangle, \langle 1\vert 1\rangle\}$	
3	$g_0 \rightarrow \{s_2, \langle 2\vert 1\rangle\}$	Substitute
	$g_1 \rightarrow \{s_2, \langle 2\vert 0\rangle\}$	$\{s_0, s_1\}$
	$g_2 \rightarrow \{\langle 0\vert 1\rangle, \langle 1\vert 0\rangle, \langle 2\vert 1\rangle, s_0\}$	(2 co-occurrences)
	$s_0 \rightarrow \{\langle 3\vert 0\rangle, \langle 4\vert 0\rangle\}$	
	$s_1 \rightarrow \{\langle 0\vert 0\rangle, \langle 1\vert 1\rangle\}$	
	$s_2 \rightarrow \{s_0, s_1\}$	
4	$g_0 \rightarrow \{s_2, \langle 2\vert 1\rangle\}$	Back-substitute
	$g_1 \rightarrow \{s_2, \langle 2\vert 0\rangle\}$	s_1 into s_2 as only
	$g_2 \rightarrow \{\langle 0\vert 1\rangle, \langle 1\vert 0\rangle, \langle 2\vert 1\rangle, s_0\}$	referenced once,
	$s_0 \rightarrow \{\langle 3\vert 0\rangle, \langle 4\vert 0\rangle\}$	and delete $s1$
	~~$s_1 \rightarrow \{\langle 0\vert 0\rangle, \langle 1\vert 1\rangle\}$~~	
	$s_2 \rightarrow \{s_0, \langle 0\vert 0\rangle, \langle 1\vert 1\rangle\}$	
5	$g_0 \rightarrow \{s_2, \langle 2\vert 1\rangle\}$	Stop (no co-
	$g_1 \rightarrow \{s_2, \langle 2\vert 0\rangle\}$	occurrences with
	$g_2 \rightarrow \{\langle 0\vert 1\rangle, \langle 1\vert 0\rangle, \langle 2\vert 1\rangle, s_0\}$	frequency > 1)
	$s_0 \rightarrow \{\langle 3\vert 0\rangle, \langle 4\vert 0\rangle\}$	
	$s_2 \rightarrow \{s_0, \langle 0\vert 0\rangle, \langle 1\vert 1\rangle\}$	

Table 2: A worked example of the offline compression algorithm incrementally compressing three sample individuals from a 5-dimensional binary population. Highlights in the grammar rules show changes made by each action.

are then used to continue the search using building-block hill climbing, allowing fit multivariate interactions to be exploited and modular interdependencies in the fitness landscape to be navigated.

The algorithm is passed a set of symbols that define the available mutations - each of which is either a terminal symbol (i.e. a single bit flip mutation) or a non-terminal symbol representing a schema. Mutants are created by recursively expanding the symbol into the phenotype, overwriting any existing alleles at the specified loci. On each iteration individuals are initialised by applying uniformly-drawn random mutations to an empty bit string until it is fully specified. Then, the hill-climbing algorithm randomises a sequence of the possible mutations and attempts each new mutation without replacement. If the fitness of each mutant is higher than current fitness then the mutation is kept and this continues until all mutations are attempted. When the mutation operators are created from the terminal symbols Σ (i.e. single bit flips) the search process is equivalent to a simple stochastic hill-climbing algorithm. The algorithm pseudo code is shown in Algorithm 2.

On the first iteration of hill-climbing bit-flip mutations are used to facilitate the search and generate a population of candidate phenotypes. On each subsequent iteration the current population is modelled using schema grammar, and the lowest-level building blocks in the grammar - the *pre-terminal symbols* (see Section 3.1) - are identified. The population is then regenerated with schema search using the pre-terminal symbols as mutation operators. This process is repeated until either the global optimum is found or no further improvements can be made to the population. The choice of pre-terminal symbols as mutation operators (rather than all non-terminal symbols, or those symbols present in

Algorithm 2: The schema search algorithm

```
input : mutation symbol set Λ
output: phenotype bitstring p_o
p_o ← empty bit string
while p_o not fully specified do
    ExpandInto(p_o, RandomChoice(Λ))
end
for λ ∈ RandomPermutation(Λ) do
    candidate_p ← p_o
    ExpandInto(candidate_p, λ)
    if F(candidate_p) > F(p_o) then
        p_o ← candidate_p
    end
end
```

the top-level compression of the population) avoids the problem of model over-fitting, which will occur when working with the test problems and search algorithm that we use here.

5.2 Deceptive Trap Functions

We use concatenated and hierarchical versions of deceptive traps [2, 19], which are also randomly shuffled, to investigate the efficacy of schema grammar in identifying and then exploiting modular and hierarchically modular structure. Each trap function is composed of k bits with two local optima, all-0's and all-1's, with the all-0's optimum typically having slightly less fitness (specified by f_{low}) than the all-1's optimum (specified by f_{high}). States between these two optima penalise the number of 1's present, creating a deceptive fitness gradient towards the lower optimum.

The concatenated trap problem specifies m conjoined trap functions of length k creating a problem size of $n = mk$. The fitness of each trap function $\tau \in T$ is independent from all others and is a function of the number of 1's present in the structure, u. For concatenated traps we use $f_{\text{low}} = 0.9$ and $f_{\text{high}} = 1.0$. The fitness of each function is given by:

$$f(\tau) = \begin{cases} f_{\text{high}} & : \text{if } u = k \\ f_{\text{low}}(1 - \frac{u}{k-1}) & : \text{otherwise} \end{cases} \quad (3)$$

and overall fitness is defined as:

$$f(T) = \sum_{\tau \in T} f(\tau) \quad (4)$$

The hierarchical trap problem introduces modular interdependency in the fitness landscape by defining trap functions in a logical hierarchy that operates at multiple scales (readers are referred to [19] for a more complete description than the one given here). Each problem contains L logical levels. At the lowest logical level the input string is divided into n/k trap functions just as with concatenated traps, with the input bits taken directly from the string and the overall fitness of the level calculated as the sum of the individual functions as before. The state of the k bits in each trap function are then mapped to a single logical bit value that is used to calculate fitness at the next logical level (all 0's to 0, all 1's to 1, otherwise null). Each successive level l therefore contains $1/k$ of the trap functions of the previous level but operates at larger scale, encompassing k^l bits. The fitness of each level is weighted by k^l and is equal to zero if there are any null bits, which is only possible at higher logical levels. At all levels except the top level we set $f_{\text{low}} = f_{\text{high}} = 1.0$, and at the top level we set $f_{\text{low}} = 0.9$, $f_{\text{high}} = 1.0$. The global optimum of this function is thus all 1's, however reaching this optimum requires modular co-ordination at successively larger scales.

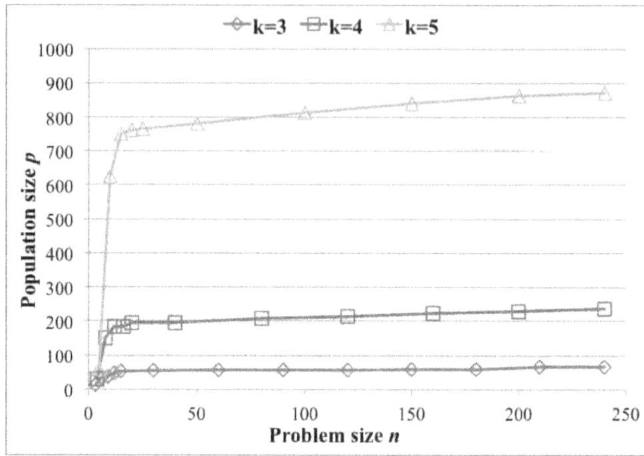

Figure 1: Population sizes (lowest population with 20 out of 20 successful trials) required to accurately detect the structure of concatenated trap problems.

5.3 Recognising Problem Structure

The key to solving the concatenated trap problem is to first identify the different trap functions present in the problem and their two local optima, and then search the 2^m combinations of these which lie on a unimodal and thus trivially solvable fitness landscape. In terms of the efficiency of schema grammar in performing the former, a sufficiently large population is required in order for the local optima of each block to be inferred into the grammar as distinct symbols so that they can be recombined in the second phase. In the first experiment we estimate the population size required to recognise every local optimum present in concatenated trap problems across a range of sizes. In each run we use schema search with terminal symbol (bit-flip) mutations to create the population and then run the offline grammar inference algorithm over it. The resulting schema structure is then compared against the structure of the problem, and is successful if each local optimum is recognised as a distinct symbol in the grammar's structure. We incrementally raise the population size until problem structure is correctly recognised in 20 out of 20 runs. The results from this experiment are shown in Figure 1.

These results suggest that the size of population required to correctly recognise the problem structure is asymptotically sublinear in n for any given k, which is consistent with recent analytical work [14]. Intuitively, the requirement is for the population to be large enough for each local optimum to occur at least twice, and in different contexts so that inference doesn't mistakenly infer that two separate local optima should always co-occur with each other. Figure 2 shows the derivation of an example individual from a grammar that has successfully inferred problem structure from a population of local optima. The figure shows the individual is a hierarchical composite of three local optima from the trap functions within the problem space. Each local optimum is represented by a distinct pre-terminal symbol.

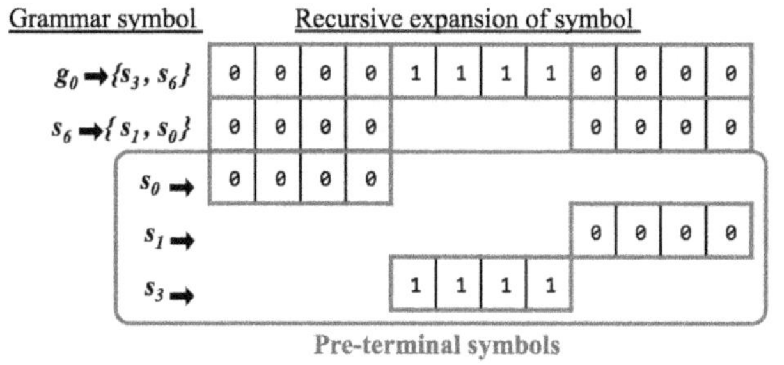

Figure 2: An example derivation of a single individual from a grammar that has successfully inferred the structure of a concatenated trap problem space ($k = 4$, $m = 3$, shown un-shuffled for presentation).

Hierarchical trap functions are more complex to solve as the fitness landscape is bi-modal at every level of the hierarchy. This requires the algorithm to solve the problem in L stages, with the grammar learning the modular structure of the problem at each stage. Additionally, at each stage the population needs to be perturbed enough to distribute individuals across the basins of attraction of every local optimum at that level. Despite this additional complexity the fundamental learning task for hierarchical traps is the same as for concatenated traps - to recognise trap structure from the current generation of the population. Therefore, for our experiments the sublinear scaling of required population in n enables us to fix the size of the population for a specific trap size k and successfully solve across a range of different problem sizes, for both variants of the problem.

5.4 Results

We ran the grammar search algorithm first on shuffled concatenated traps, and then on shuffled hierarchical traps of various sizes up to $n = 729$ where $k = 3$ and the population was set to 80 in all cases based on the approach outlined in the previous section. We report average fitness evaluations until the global optimum is reached for all successful trials (at least 9 out of 10 successes).

For the concatenated trap experiment we also ran a random restart hill-climber as a control and measure fitness evaluations until the global optimum is reached, or null if a maximum number of fitness evaluations is exceeded (set to 500,000 per trial). The results for the schema hill climbing and the control are shown in Figure 3. These results show that for the sizes of problem studied here, and with a fixed population size, an approximately linear scaling of fitness evaluations with respect to problem size n is achieved. They also show that the random restart hill climber scales exponentially, which is expected, with results where $n > 21$ not being returned within the maximum number of iterations. The results illustrate the difficulty of single-bit hill climbing to succeed across multiple deceptive functions, and the ability of the schema grammar to learn the structure of the problem and solve it in linear time using multi-scale variation.

For the third experiment we measured average fitness evaluations to reach the global optimum for the hierarchical version of the problem, and these results are shown in Figure 4. For comparison purposes we also plot the results for BBHC (reported in [9]) and hierarchical BOA (hBOA) (reported in

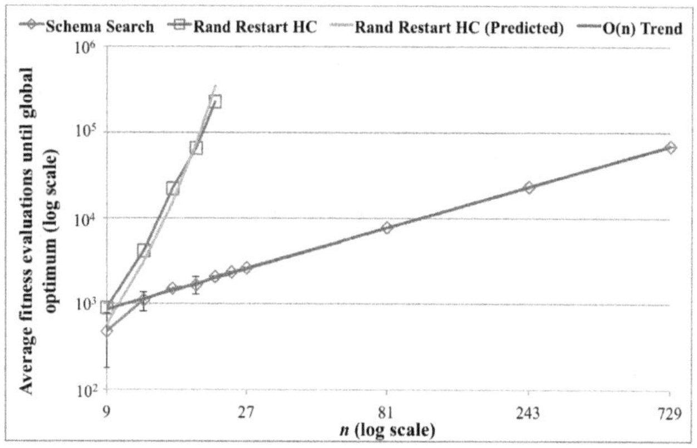

Figure 3: Average fitness evaluations versus problem size n on the concatenated trap problem where $k = 3$.

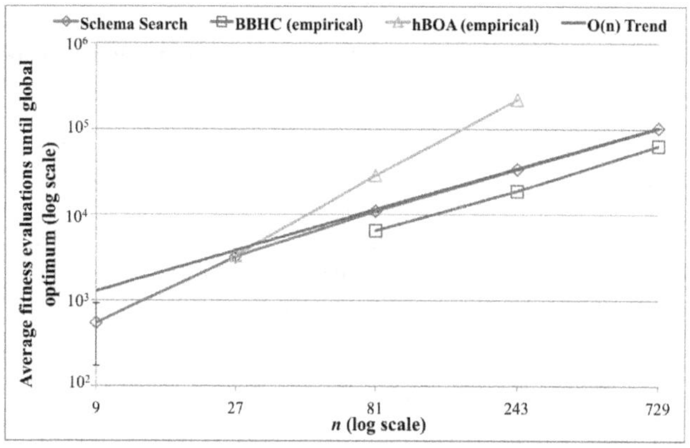

Figure 4: Average fitness evaluations versus problem size n on the hierarchical trap problem where $k = 3$.

[19]). The comparisons should be understood as providing an illustrative context in which to show the schema grammar results and not as direct performance comparisons, as the approaches to model-building, solving, parameterisation and methodology are different in each case.

The results for hierarchical traps also show that for the sizes of problem studied here approximately linear scaling of fitness evaluations with respect to problem size n is achieved. The explanation for linear scaling in our results has two different facets. Firstly, the local schema search algorithm uses sampling without replacement and is upper bounded by the number of mutation operators, so is $O(n)$ on the first iteration, rather than $O(n \log n)$ as would be the case in local search with replacement [15]. Secondly, if all blocks are recognised correctly on the first iteration then the concatenated traps problem will be solved on the first macro search using these blocks. For hierarchical traps the problem will be solved in L iterations, with each iteration requiring the organisation of $1/k$ of the blocks of the previous level, and this is a geometric series converging at $(k/(k-1))O(n)$. Given the fixed population size used in these experiments then the search performance is approximately linear in n.

6. CONCLUSIONS

In this paper we have introduced a new type of generative grammar and an offline inference method, and have shown that they are capable of accurately modelling the structure of shuffled modular and hierarchically modular test problems. We have additionally shown that these structures can be exploited using multi-scale hill climbing to find globally optimal solutions in approximately linear time, comparing favourably with other state-of-the-art approaches. We believe the key contribution of our work is that it demonstrates for the first time that generative grammar can be used to model combinatorial (as opposed to sequential) structure and solve challenging optimisation problems. This different approach affords new directions for future work.

We have produced some promising early results and we have a number of avenues of further investigation. Firstly we are keen to explore the application of schema grammar to problems with overlapping structure, as these are more difficult to model and are outside the capabilities of many model building search algorithms. Given the ability of the grammar to model complex overlap, this is a natural avenue for exploration. Secondly, we intend to study the application of schema grammar to different evolutionary problem solving frameworks. This includes EDA-style search in which the distribution of the compressed population could be probabilistically modelled and sampled to generate new offspring, and genetic algorithms, where the "language" of macro-mutation that the grammar provides could be used to facilitate variation in reproduction. Additionally, performance on larger and more realistic problems needs to be investigated to evaluate the suitability of schema grammar to more general problem solving.

7. REFERENCES

[1] M. Charikar, E. Lehman, and D. Liu. The smallest grammar problem. *IEEE Transactions on Information Theory*, 51(7):2554–2576, 2005.

[2] K. Deb and D. E. Goldberg. Analyzing deception in trap functions. In *Proceedings of the Second Workshop on Foundations of Genetic Algorithms*, pages 98–108, 1992.

[3] S. Forrest and M. Mitchell. Relative building-block fitness and the building-block hypothesis. *Ann Arbor*, 1001:48109, 1993.

[4] D. E. Goldberg. *Genetic Algorithms in Search, Optimization, and Machine Learning*. Addison-Wesley Professional, 1989.

[5] D. E. Goldberg, B. Korb, and K. Deb. Messy genetic algorithms: Motivation, analysis, and first results. *Complex Systems*, 3(5):493–530, 1989.

[6] G. R. Harik, F. G. Lobo, and K. Sastry. Linkage learning via probabilistic modeling in the extended compact genetic algorithm (ecga). *Scalable optimization via probabilistic modeling*, pages 39–61, 2006.

[7] M. Hauschild and M. Pelikan. An introduction and survey of estimation of distribution algorithms. *Swarm and Evolutionary Computation*, 1(3):111–128, 2011.

[8] J. H. Holland. *Adaptation in natural and artificial systems: An introductory analysis with applications to biology, control, and artificial intelligence*. U Michigan Press, 1975.

[9] D. Iclanzan and D. Dumitrescu. Overcoming hierarchical difficulty by hill-climbing the building block structure. *Proceedings of the 9th annual conference on Genetic and evolutionary computation*, pages 1256–1263, 2007.

[10] J. C. Kieffer and E. Yang. Grammar-based codes: a new class of universal lossless source codes. *IEEE Transactions on Information Theory*, 46(3):737 754, 2000.

[11] N. J. Larsson and A. Moffat. Off-line dictionary-based compression. *Proceedings of the IEEE*, 88(11):1722–1732, 2000.

[12] A. Lindenmayer. Mathematical models for cellular interactions in development I. Filaments with one-sided inputs. *Journal of Theoretical Biology*, 1968.

[13] R. Mills. *How micro-evolution can guide macro-evolution: Multi-scale search via evolved modular variation*. PhD thesis, University of Southampton, 2010.

[14] R. Mills, T. Jansen, and R. A. Watson. Transforming Evolutionary Search Into Higher-Level Evolutionary Search by Capturing Problem Structure. *IEEE Transactions on Evolutionary Computation*, To appear.

[15] H. Mühlenbein. *How genetic algorithms really work: I. mutation and hillclimbing*. PPSN, 1992.

[16] C. G. Nevill-Manning and I. H. Witten. Identifying hierarchical structure in sequences: A linear-time algorithm. *Journal of Artificial Intelligence Research*, 7:67–82, 1997.

[17] M. O'Neill and A. Brabazon. mGGA: The meta-grammar genetic algorithm. *Genetic Programming*, pages 311–320, 2005.

[18] M. Pelikan. *Bayesian optimization algorithm: From single level to hierarchy*. PhD thesis, University of Illinois at Urbana-Champaign, 2002.

[19] M. Pelikan and D. E. Goldberg. Escaping hierarchical traps with competent genetic algorithms. In *Proceedings of the Genetic and Evolutionary Computation Conference (GECCO-2001)*, pages 511 518, 2001.

[20] P. Prusinkiewicz, A. Lindenmayer, and J. Hanan. *The algorithmic beauty of plants*. Springer Verlag, 1990.

[21] K. J. Räihä and E. Ukkonen. The shortest common supersequence problem over binary alphabet is NP-complete. *Theoretical computer science*, 1981.

[22] C. Ryan, J. J. Collins, and M. O. Neill. Grammatical evolution: Evolving programs for an arbitrary language. *Genetic Programming*, pages 83–96, 1998.

[23] D. Thierens. The linkage tree genetic algorithm. *Parallel Problem Solving from Nature, PPSN XI*, pages 264–273, 2010.

[24] M. Toussaint. Compact representations as a search strategy: Compression EDAs. *Theoretical computer science*, 361(1):57–71, 2006.

[25] M. Toussaint and W. von Seelen. Complex adaptation and system structure. *Biosystems*, 90(3):769–782, 2007.

[26] R. A. Watson, G. S. Hornby, and J. B. Pollack. Modeling building-block interdependency. *Parallel Problem Solving from Nature—PPSN V*, pages 97–106, 1998.

Estimation of Distribution Algorithm using Factor Graph and Markov Blanket Canonical Factorization

B. Hoda Helmi
Iran University of Science and Technology
Tehran, Iran 13114-16846
helmi@iust.ac.ir

Adel T. Rahmani
Iran University of Science and Technology
Tehran, Iran 13114-16846
rahmani@iust.ac.ir

ABSTRACT

Finding a good model and efficiently estimating the distribution is still an open challenge in estimation of distribution algorithms (EDAs). Factorization encoded by models in most of the EDAs are constrained. However for optimization of many real-world problems, finding the model capable of representing complex interactions without much computational complexity overhead is the key challenge. On the other hand factor graph which is the most natural graphical model for representing additively decomposable functions is rarely employed in EDAs. In this paper we introduce Factor Graph based EDA (FGEDA) which learns factor graph as the model and estimate the probability distribution represented by the learned factor graph using Markov blanket canonical factorization. The class of factorization that is employed for approximation of distribution in FGEDA is expanded relative to famous EDAs. We have used matrix factorization for learning the factor graph of the problem based on the pairwise mutual information between pair of variables. Gibbs sampling and BB-wise crossover are used to generate new samples. Empirical evaluation as well as theoretical analysis of the approach show the efficiency and power of FGEDA in the optimization of functions with complex interactions. It is showed experimentally that FGEDA outperform other well-known EDAs.
GECCO track: Estimation of Distribution Algorithm.

Categories and Subject Descriptors

G.1.6 [**Numerical Analysis**]: Optimization

General Terms

Algorithm, Design, Experimentation, Performance

Keywords

Optimization problems, Estimation of distribution algorithms, Factor graph, Linkage learning, Mutual information, Matrix factorization

GECCO'14, July 12–16, 2014, Vancouver, BC, Canada.

http://dx.doi.org/10.1145/2576768.2598266 .

1. INTRODUCTION

Estimation of Distribution Algorithms (EDA) are algorithms that learn the variable's dependencies' structure and overcome the difficulty of optimization for problems with complex variable interactions. EDAs estimate the joint distribution of the multinomial data in order to generate new solutions. Encoding the joint distribution of the data is usually done using a graphical model. Bayesian networks [1] and Markov models [2] are widely used as the model in the model building process of EDAs, but factor graphs which are the ideal graphical model to encode the distribution of the data are rarely used possibly because there has been no efficient learning algorithm to learn this kind of graphical models.

In this paper, we introduce an efficient factor graph learning algorithm. To learn the factor graph we apply non-negative matrix factorization on mutual information matrix. After learning the factor graph, the joint probability distribution which is encoded by factor graph is approximated. New potential solutions are produced using Gibbs sampling based on the factor nodes and their Markov blankets. The process of model building and creating new samples are repeated until the optimum solution is found.

Utilizing the factor graph has some advantages over other models. First and most important of all, this graphical model explicitly shows the structure of the dependencies between variables of the problem. This human-readable information can easily be used by experts to analyze the problem and the results and the revealed structure of the problem can be used for analyzing similar problems. Second, knowing the linkage groups we can use this information to employ BB-wise genetic operators besides re-sampling the new potential solutions via Gibbs sampling which is a computationally expensive task.

The outline of this paper is as follows: In the next section, some related works are reviewed. In section 3 some related background information on factor graph and symmetric non-negative matrix factorization (SNMF) are reviewd. Section 4 introduces the proposed factor graph based estimation of distribution algorithm and explaines the model learning and sampling method used in the algorithm. In section 5, the behavior of the algorithm is analyzed. Section 6 presents the complexity of the algorithm. Section 8 presents the experimental results of the algorithm. To show the performance and efficiency of the proposed approach, it is tested on some benchmark problems and its effectiveness is discussed. Finally in section 9, some conclusion remarks, highlights of the algorithm and future directions are presented.

2. RELATED WORKS

Estimation of distribution algorithms (EDAs) [3] or Probabilistic Model Building Genetic Algorithms (PMBGAs) are algorithms that try to learn the structure of the problem in order to effectively explore the search space to find the optimum. Several EDAs are introduced [4], [1], [5], [6]. Most of these approaches are population based and generational search processes. Among all the methods used to learn and encode the distribution, graphical models like Bayesian networks and Markov networks are employed and investigated in many studies. There are pros and cons for using each of these graphical models in EDAs. On one hand learning Bayesian network from data is a computationally costly task, on the other hand sampling from undirected graphical models is difficult and requires Gibbs sampling which is computationally expensive.

Factor graphs are another type of undirected graphical models that subsume both Bayesian networks and Markov networks, in that every Bayesian network or Markov network can be converted to its corresponding factor graph of the same size [7]. These graphical models are the most natural graphical representations for the structure of Additively Decomposable Functions (ADF) [7]. Learning of factor graphs for ADF is more representative than learning of Bayesian networks because they match the ADF structure better [8]. Factor graph clearly shows the underlying structure of the problem and is readable for experts. This is an important property for the expert, when optimizing the problems with unknown dependency structure. But learning the structure of these kinds of graphical models and sampling using these distributions is difficult.

There are EDAs that utilize factor graphs to encode the distribution of the problem. Mühlenbein in [8] proposed using factor graphs as the model to represent the distribution of the problem in EDAs. In [9], an EDA approach is introduced in which the structure of the factor graph is learned using the Chi-square independence test. The Kikuchi approximation of the distribution is then used to approximate the distribution and finally Gibbs sampling is applied to sample new potential solutions. In [10], to search for the optimum, loopy belief propagation (LBF) is used to find the most probable configuration of the distribution. They first learn a Bayesian network from a population of potential solutions and then convert it to its corresponding factor graph to apply the LBF, and find the most probable configuration of the distribution.

Here, we introduce an EDA algorithm which directly learns factor graph from pair-wise statistics calculated from selected population and then samples new solutions based on the model learnt.

3. BACKGROUND

3.1 Factor Graph

A factor graph is a bipartite graph that describes the way a function of many variables factors into a product of several functions. For example, assume $g(x1, x2, x3, x4, x5)$ be a function with five variables. This function can be factored into a product of three functions as follows:

$$g(x_1, x_2, x_3, x_4, x_5) = f_1(x_1, x_2, x_4) f_2(x_2, x_3) f_3(x_4, x_5) \quad (1)$$

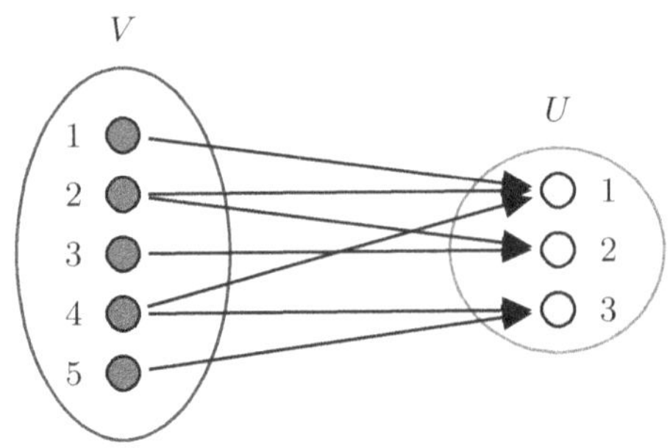

Figure 1: A factor graph that shows the factorization of equation (1)

The corresponding factor graph is illustrated in figure 1. The factor graph is consisted of variable nodes, factor nodes and the edges between these two kinds of nodes. For each variable of the function, there is a corresponding variable node in the factor graph. Each factor node corresponds to a factor. A variable node is connected to a factor node if and only if the variable is an argument of the corresponding function. In order to find the factor graph, we use a matrix factorization technique which has been mathematically proven to converge in polynomial time. To do so, we employ pair-wise variable dependencies to partition the variables probabilistically. Based on the concept of random walks on graphs, in our approach, the variable dependencies are modelled as empirical transitions generated by a mixture of latent factors.

3.2 Symmetric Non-Negative Matrix Factorization (SNMF)

Given a nonnegative matrix X, non-negative matrix factorization (NMF) is finding a lower-rank matrix approximation. Rank of a matrix is the number of linearly independent rows or columns of the matrix. So, NMF is formalized as:

$$X \approx CG^T \quad (2)$$

that can be achieved by calculating,

$$min||X - CG^T||, \quad (3)$$

where $||.||$ denotes a distance metric like divergence distance and $X \in \Re_+^{m*n}$, $C \in \Re_+^{m*k}$, $G \in \Re_+^{n*k}$.

The NMF can be applied to a similarity matrix. In this case the matrix factorization is a symmetric non-negative matrix factorization problem with the formulation:

$$\min_{H \geq 0} ||A - HH^T||_F^2 \quad (4)$$

where A is the similarity matrix of size $n \times n$ and H is a non-negative matrix of size $n \times m$ and the $||.||_F$ denotes the Forbenius norm. The largest entry in the ith row of H, indicates the factor/cluster of the ith item in A due to the non-negativity of H.

The symmetric non-negative matrix factorization is developed specially for soft clustering in data sets with non-linear clusters. There are algorithms for symmetric non-negative matrix factorization, which guarantee to produce stationary point solutions. The uniqueness of SNMF in terms of factorization quality, the independence on the eigenspace of A, and the sensitiveness to the fluctuation in the similarity matrix A, for soft clustering application is shown in [11].

4. FACTOR GRAPH BASED ESTIMATION OF DISTRIBUTION ALGORITHM

Variable dependencies can be encoded by an undirected graph, where vertices denote variables and edges' weights represent variable dependencies. In the proposed approach, this graph called mutual information matrix (MIM) is first constructed from a selected population of potential solutions using mutual information between every pair of variables. MIM is then factorized into a bipartite graph which represents the factor graph of the problem. So in the proposed approach, we are converting pair-wise dependencies to higher-order dependencies. After the factor graph is constructed new potential solutions are sampled using Gibbs sampling [12] and uniform BB-wise crossover [13].

The approach, as will be explained here, is capable of learning disjoint and overlapped linkage groups even for problems with linkage groups of varying size. The remainder of this section describes details of the proposed approach. First MIM is constructed by calculating MI between every pair of variables, then to accelerate the process of matrix factorization, some of the too small elements of MIM are pruned using a simple threshold. Based on our assumption of $k << n$, the threshold is set to μ, where μ is the mean of the elements in MIM. It should be noted that this pruning is by no means necessary for the algorithm.

Factorizing the MIM into a factor graph

Let $K(V, U, F)$ be the bipartite graph, where $V = \{v_i\}_{i=1}^{n}$ is a collection of variables and $U = \{u_p\}_{p=1}^{m}$ is a set of factor nodes (V and U are disjoint sets) and F contains all the edges connecting V and U. Let $B = \{b_{ip}\}$ denote the $n * m$ adjacency matrix with $b_{ip} \geq 0$ being the weight for edge $[v_i, u_p]$. To factorize the MIM and finding the corresponding bipartite graph, we use the similarity relation between v_i and v_j in the bipartite graph K presented in [14].

$$mim_{ij} = \sum_{p=1}^{m} \frac{b_{ip}b_{jp}}{\lambda_p} = (B\Lambda^{-1}B^T)_{ij}, \quad \Lambda = diag(\lambda_1, ..., \lambda_m) \tag{5}$$

Where $\lambda_p = \sum_{i=1}^{n} b_{ip}$ is the degree of vertex $u_p \in U$.

The above equation can be analyzed based on the random walks on graphs. e_{ij} is proportional to the stationary probability of transition between v_i and v_j, $p(v_i, v_j)$. All the paths between vertices in V, must go through vertices in U in the factor graph, therefore:

$$\begin{aligned} p(v_i, v_j) &= p(v_i)p(v_j|v_i) \\ &= d_i \sum_p p(u_p|v_i)p(v_j|u_p) \\ &= \sum_p \frac{p(v_i, u_p)p(u_p, v_j)}{\lambda_p}, \end{aligned} \tag{6}$$

where $d_i = p(v_i)$ is the degree of v_i. When $b_{ip} = p(v_i, u_p)$, equation (5) and equation (6) are the same. $p(u_p|v_i) = \frac{b_{ip}}{d_i}$ is the conditional probability of transitions from v_i to u_p and indicates how likely variable i belongs to factor nodes p.

Based on equation (5), the bipartite graph can be approximated by minimizing the $distance(MIM, B\Lambda^{-1}B^T)$. To make the problem easy we use $H = B\Lambda^{-1/2}$, then we have

$$\min_{H \in \Re_{+}^{n \times m}} distance(MIM, HH^T), \quad s.t. h_{ip} \geq 1, \tag{7}$$

This problem is a symmetric non-negative matrix factorization (SNMF) [15]. There are different numerical methods to find the local minima of this problem. Here we use the gradient descent method to minimize the divergence distance between the two adjacency matrices (equation (8)).

$$DD(X, Y) = \sum_{ij}(x_{ij}log\frac{x_{ij}}{y_{ij}} - x_{ij} + y_{ij}) \tag{8}$$

Theorem 4.1 *The distance is non-increasing under the following update rule*

$$\hat{h_{ip}} = \frac{h_{ip}}{\sum_j h_{jp}} \sum_j \frac{mim_{ij}}{(HH^T)_{ij}} h_{jp}. \tag{9}$$

The distance is invariant under the update rule if and only if H is at stationary point of the distance [16].

After H is calculated, B can be calculated using $B = H\Lambda^{1/2}$ and $\Lambda = diag(\lambda_1, ..., \lambda_m)$ where $\lambda_p = \sum_{i=1}^{n} h_{ip}$.

Proof of the convergence of the algorithm is available in [16]. We later use λ_p as the degree for factor node p. In order to provide an algorithmic scheme look at the following pseudo-code:

Algorithm 1 Learning the Factor Graph via SNMF

Input: A non-empty $|V| \times |V|$ matrix MIM. $maxFN = n$, $MN = k + \epsilon$

Output: factor graph

Initialize: Start with a $n \times m$ matrix H, where $m = maxFN$ and $H_{i \in V, j \in U} \in [0, 1]$ is randomly set.

repeat

Update H based on equation (9).

until H is invariant.

Construct $\Lambda = diag(\lambda_1, ..., \lambda_m)$ using $\lambda_p = \sum_{i=1}^{n} h_{ip}$.

Construct factor nodes. ($\forall i \in rows(H)$ create a factor node FN_i. Assign the MN largest rows of the $H[i]$ to the FN_i). Keep unique FNs as the set of factor nodes.

Parameter $maxFN$ is used to determine the dimensions of matrix H. For all the experiments this parameter is set to n which is number of variables in the problem. Parameter MN is the maximum allowed interactions between variables. This parameter is used to avoid an overly complex network. We do not set MN equal to the true value according to the problem structure. For each problem we add $\epsilon = 3$ to what is the true value of MN which is k. It should be noted that almost all the other methods also use such parameter to bound the size of the building blocks.

Generating new solutions

In this step, after learning the factor graphs and having the factors, the optimum value of the variables should be found. To do so, in order to be able to use Gibbs sampling we should approximate the distribution that is encoded in Factor Graph. We use the distribution approximation approach based on Markov blanket canonical factorization introduced in [17].

In [17] a new parameterization approach based on canonical parameterization and Markov blanket is presented in which every canonical factor can be calculated by local probabilities only. The Markov blanket canonical parameterization is defined relative to an arbitrary set of default assignments $\bar{\mathbf{x}} = (\bar{x}_1, ..., \bar{x}_n)$. Let $\mathbf{D} = \langle X_{i_1}, ..., X_{i_{|\mathbf{D}|}} \rangle$ be any subset of variables, and $\mathbf{d} = \langle x_{i_1}, ..., x_{i_{|\mathbf{D}|}} \rangle$ be any assignment to $\mathbf{D}$. For any $\mathbf{U} \subseteq \mathbf{D}$, ØŇ$\sigma_{\mathbf{U}:\mathbf{D}}[\mathbf{d}]$ is defined to be the restriction of the full instantiation $\sigma_{\mathbf{U}}[\mathbf{d}]$ of all variables in $\mathcal{X}$ to the corresponding instantiation of the subset $\mathbf{D}$. Let $\mathbf{D} \subseteq \mathcal{X}$ and $\mathbf{Y} \subseteq \mathcal{X} - \mathcal{D}$ then the Markov blanket canonical factor $f^*_{\mathbf{D}|\mathbf{Y}}$ is defined as equation (10).

$$f^*_{\mathbf{D}|\mathbf{Y}}(\mathbf{d}) = exp(\sum_{\mathbf{U} \subseteq \mathbf{D}} (-1)^{|\mathbf{D}-\mathbf{U}|} \log P(\sigma_{\mathbf{U}:\mathbf{D}}[\mathbf{d}] | \mathbf{Y} = \bar{\mathbf{y}})) \tag{10}$$

For positive Gibbs distribution and factor nodes with scopes $\{C_j\}_{j=1}^J$ (scopes of a factor node is the set of all the variables connected to it), and $\{C_j^*\}$ defined as $\{C_j^*\}_{j=1}^{J^*} = \cup_{j=1}^J 2^{C_j} - 0$, for any $\mathbf{D} \subseteq \mathcal{X}$

$$f^*_D = f^*_{\mathbf{D}|\mathcal{X}-\mathbf{D}} = f^*_{\mathbf{D}|MB(\mathbf{D})} \tag{11}$$

And

$$\begin{aligned} P(\mathbf{x}) &= P(\bar{\mathbf{x}}) \prod_{j=1}^{j^*} f^*_{C_j^*|(X)-C_j^*}(c_j^*) \\ &= P(\bar{\mathbf{x}}) \prod_{j=1}^{j^*} f^*_{C_j^*|MB(C_j^*)}(c_j^*), \end{aligned} \tag{12}$$

where c_j^* is the instantiation of C_j^* consistent with $\mathbf{x}$.

So according to equation (12), the joint probability distribution of a factor graph is approximated using probabilities over factor nodes and their Markov blankets only.

Now we can create new samples by performing Gibbs sampling. To create a new sample, we start with an initial state $x^0 = \{x_1^0, ..., x_n^0\}$. Based on the transition rule in (13), at each time t a variable i is to be updated. In one cycle of the Gibbs sampling all the n variables are updated.

$$\mathbf{X}^{t+1} = \begin{cases} x_j^{t+1} = x_j^t & \text{for } j \neq i \\ x_j^{t+1} \approx P(x_i^t | MB(x_i^t)) & \text{for } j = i \end{cases} \tag{13}$$

To generate L new solutions, Gibbs sampling should be applied L times. Instead of starting from random initial state, we select a high fitness solution from the population and repeat the Gibbs sampling C_n times.

Since we have learned the linkage groups in our model building phase, we can also perform BB-wise crossover and/or we can perform a search on each building block to find the optimum. In order to get advantage of both methods, we first generate $N/2$ samples by Gibbs sampling and then the other $N/2$ samples are generated by BB-wise crossover.

5. ALGORITHM ANALYSIS

In this section, we look closely at the SNMF approach by looking at the examples learned by this approach. In subsection 5.1, we see examples of SNMF performance for learning linkage groups in decomposable problems in the context of genetic algorithm and linkage learning. We analyze the matrix H with an example through different generations. In the second subsection, algorithm 1 is used to find the linkage groups in problems with overlapping building blocks to see if the approach is capable of finding the building blocks for additively decomposable problems with overlapping BBs or not. The next subsection is dedicated to the analysis of the effect of the $maxFN$ parameter used in algorithm 1 on the performance of the algorithm.

5.1 SNMF for learning the linkage groups in problems with non-overlapping BBs

In figure 2, the $MIM_{n \times n}$ ($n = 50$) matrix of mutual information, the matrix $H_{n \times maxFN}$ (SNMF resultant matrix, $maxFN = 50$) and linkage groups matrix for concatenated Trap-5 problem with 50 variables in different generations is depicted (concatenated trap function with tight linkage groups is used for the better visualization, algorithm is not sensitive to the place of variables in the string). The population size is set to 2600 and the $maxFN$ is set to n.

The rows show the information of the generations 1, 4 and 10 from top to bottom. The matrix H (second column in the figure), is an $n \times maxFN$ matrix that shows the value with which each variable (rows of the matrix) is related to each factor node (columns of the matrix). The intensity of each cell of the both matrices is relative to its value. Lighter cells have larger values and darker cells smaller values. The linkage groups matrix (third column in the figure), is an $n \times n$ matrix, which each of its entries correspond to memberships in the linkage groups. If the value of the ith row and j^{th} column is one(white), the ith and j^{th} variables are in a same linkage group and if zero (black), otherwise. Since we are solving a concatenated Trap-5 problem, we expect the error-free MIM to have ten 5×5 white squares along the main diagonal, while all other cells of the matrix are expected to be zero (black). For the matrix H, in the error-free case, for each of the linkage groups there should be at least one factor node (corresponding to the columns in the matrix H) with a light bar, without any other disconnected light cells in the same column.

As it is obvious in the figure, in the fourth generation (second row, third column) all the linkage groups are identified. But although the linkage groups are identified in the fourth generation, the optimum of the problem is not found up until the tenth generation (fourth row). That is due to the fact that some more generations are required after discovering the BBs, to search inside the BBs and mix the BBs in different individuals, in order to find the optimum solution. In this sample only BB-wise crossover is used to find the optimum configuration.

It is obvious from the figure that some of the columns (factor nodes) of the matrix H (second column of the figure 2) have very low degree (λ) (λ is used as the degree of the factor nodes and is defined in section 4), so that their corresponding cells are almost zero. Along with the generations, the amount of noise in the MIM and H are getting smaller. For the first generation, the number of the factor nodes is set to $maxFN = n = 50$. Along with the optimization algorithm, the number of unique and high-degree factor nodes approaches to its actual value which in this example is 10. The excess factor nodes (other 40 factor nodes) are either duplicates of the true factor nodes or have a very low degree. For example in the bottom row of the figure 2, 43 out of 50 columns have visually distinguishable degrees and these 43 columns are duplicate and there are no false factor nodes among them. Ten unique factor nodes out of these 43 factor

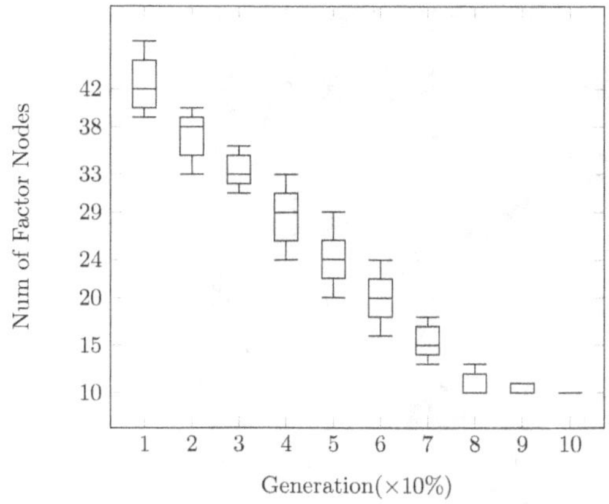

Figure 3: Number of factor nodes for the concatenated trap-5 problem with 50 variables over 100 runs.

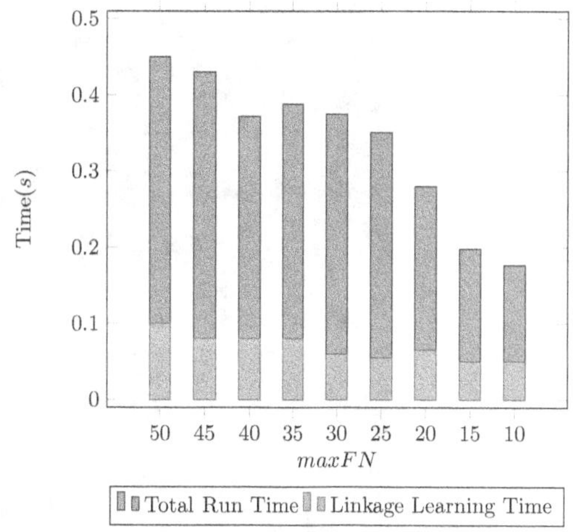

Figure 4: The effect of $maxFN$ on the total run time and linkage learning time for Trap5 problems with 50 variables.

nodes are the actual factor nodes which are utilized as the input to other steps of the algorithm.

Looking at the matrix H in the second row of the figure, it is obvious visually from the figure that there are almost no errors (disconnected light cells) at the columns with high degrees (columns with light bars). As it is shown in the figure, although we do not provide the algorithm with the actual number of factor nodes of the problem, our SNMF approach can find the necessary number of factor nodes and thus the linkage groups. Initially, the number of factor nodes is set equal to the number of variables of the problem. Again it is shown that the optimization search for the optimum value which is performed by BB-wise crossover takes some more generations after completely learning the linkage groups (in the example, from generation 4 to generation 10 that the optimum is found). We may be able to decrease the necessary generations by applying some other sampling method, instead of the simple BB-wise crossover. More research on this issue is left for the future work.

5.2 Parameter maxFN

In figure 3, the number of identified unique factor nodes during the algorithm for non-overlapping Trap-5 problem with 50 variables is averaged over 100 runs and depicted as box plots. During the algorithm, number of identified unique factor nodes converges to the actual number of BBs (figure 3). In figure 4, the total running time of the algorithm and the time spent on the factorization part of the algorithm for different initial value of $maxFN$ parameter is depicted. As it is expected, the running time gets lower when $maxFN$ is set closer to the real m.

5.3 SNMF for learning the linkage groups in overlapping problems

In this subsection, the learned factor graphs for problems with overlapping building blocks are presented. In figure 5, the MIM, H and linkage group matrices of a concatenated trap-5 problem with 32 variables and 10 building blocks is presented for the population size 20000. Each two neighbouring BBs have 2 variables in common. $maxFN$ is set to $n/2$ in this example. As it can be seen the SNMF approach have identified the linkage groups almost perfectly. As mentioned before because BB-wise genetic operators are unable to find optimum configuration for problems with overlapping BBs, we have applied the SNMF learning approach only for one generation for this problem.

6. COMPLEXITY ANALYSIS

In this section, the number of function evaluations and the time complexity of the proposed optimization algorithm are discussed. As explained above, the algorithm is comprised of three main steps of (1) constructing the MIM, (2) learning the factor graph (3) Generating new samples through Gibbs sampling and BB-wise crossover.

Number of evaluations: In the first step of the algorithm evaluations are done for constructing the MIM. Each individual in the population is evaluated exactly once in the first step. Therefore, if the population size is N, number of fitness evaluations in each iteration would be N and if number of generations is g, the overall number of evaluations of the algorithm would be $N \times g$.

Time: Pair-wise dependencies (mutual information) are computed by a pass through all the strings in the population. As MI values are calculated for each pair of variables therefore this computation is done in $O(n^2 \times N)$, where n is the problem size and N is the population size.

In the process of learning the factor graph, using the divergence distance for minimizing the distance between the two adjacency matrices (equation (8)), it is only needed to sum over all non-zero terms of matrix MIM for each update. So, If MIM is sparse, the time complexity of the equation (9) is $O(m^2 \times L)$, where L is the number of nonzero entries in MIM, m is the number of factor nodes. L is of order $O(n^2)$ in the worst case. The complexity of the sampling part of the algorithm is $N/2 \times C_n \times \sum_{i=1} n2^{MN} \approx N \times n \times 2^{MN}$. Therefore the overall time complexity of the algorithm is $O(n^2 \times N + m^2 \times n^2 + N \times n)$. Considering the worst case where $L = n^2$, time complexity of the FGEDA is $O(n^2 N + m^2 n^2)$.

7. REFERENCE ALGORITHMS

Two approaches are used as reference algorithms. Both are well studied optimization approaches in the category of

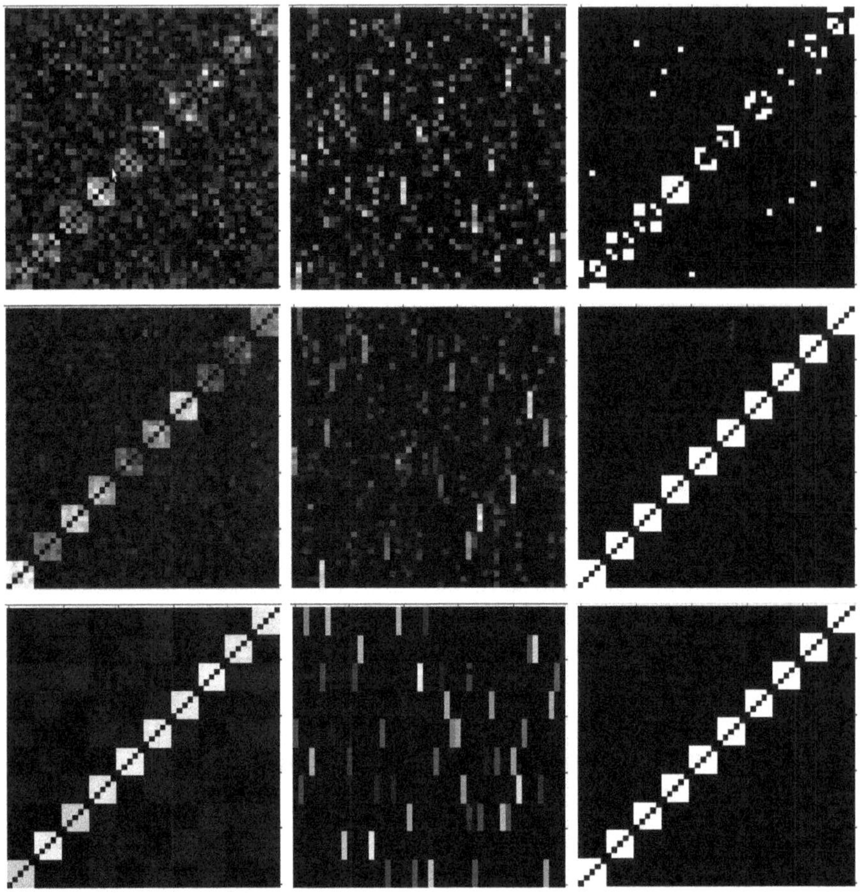

Figure 2: Matrix of MI, SNMF and linkage groups from left to right in generations 1, 4 and 10 from top to bottom for Trap-5 problem with 50 variables

estimation of distribution algorithms. Hierarchical Bayesian optimization algorithm (hBOA) [1] and dependency structure matrix genetic algorithm (DSMGA) [6] are used to compare the results. DSMGA uses mutual information to construct the dependency structure matrix and then cluster the DSM by an evolutionary strategy with a fit-to-data objective function. Here we have used DSMGA++ version [6] of the DSMGA which uses (s+w) algorithm for generating new solutions (for more information refer to [6]).

hBOA uses conditional probabilities of variables, a greedy algorithm and a scoring metric to learn a Bayesian network as the underlying probabilistic model of the problem. hBOA then uses the learned model and conditional probabilities to sample new potential solutions. For all the three algorithms, restricted tournament replacement is used to replace the population. For both DSMGA++ and hBOA parameters are set to their best configurations reported in [1, 6].

8. EXPERIMENTAL RESULTS

In this section, the experimental results are presented. First the experiments and test functions are explained and then the results are shown and analyzed.

Overlapping Trap

An additively decomposable Trap function (equation (14)) of order k is defined as the sum of single Trap functions of order k:

$$f(x) = \begin{cases} fHigh & \text{if } u(x) = k \\ fLow - u(x) * fLow/k & \text{else} \end{cases} \tag{14}$$

where $u(x)$ returns the number of 1s in string x. Usually $fHigh = 1$ and $fLow = 0.9$. Here we use overlap of order one between Trap sub-functions in which a variable in a block is common to the next block.

Neaest-neighbour NK landscape

An NK fitness landscape is defined by: (1) The number of bits, n. (2) The number of neighbours per bit, k. (3) A set of k neighbours $\Pi(X_i)$ for the i-th bit, X_i, for every $i \in \{0, ..., n-1\}$. (4) A sub-function g_i defining a real value for each combination of values of X_i and $\Pi(X_i)$ for every $i \in \{0, ..., n-1\}$. A look-up table with 2^{k+1} values defines each sub-function. Maximizing the objective function (15) is the goal.

$$f_{nk}(X_0, ..., X_{n-1}) = \sum_{i=0}^{n-1} g_i(X_i, \Pi(X_i)). \tag{15}$$

The four components of an NK problem instance affect the difficulty of optimizing NK landscapes. NK landscapes have attracted researchers in stochastic optimization because of their difficulties and properties.

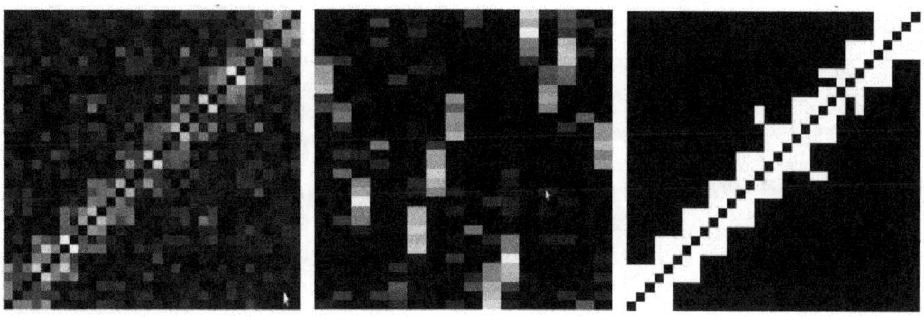

Figure 5: Left: 32×32 matrix of mutual information for trap5 problem of size 32 with overlapping building blocks (2 variables overlap). Middle: the matrix H. Right: the linkage groups constructed using SNMF

Algorithm 2 Algorithm of the proposed approach

Output: optimum solution

Create random population.
repeat
  Evaluate the population.
  Select population by tournament selection.
  {Computing the pairwise dependencies $e_{ij} \in E$ and constructing the MIM, $MIM(V, E)$}
  for all the individuals in the population **do**
    for each variable i and variable j, **do**
      Calculate $e_{ij} = MI(i, j)$
    end for
  end for
  Prune the MIM by threshold $= \mu_{MIM}$.
  Do the SNMF and find the factor nodes using the algorithm 1.
  Calculate the Markov blanket factors.
  Generate $N/2$ solutions by Gibbs sampling.
  Generate $N/2$ solutions by BB-wise crossover.
  Replace population.
until optimum found

Results

Each run is terminated either when the global optimum has been found or when the population has converged to a single solution or when the maximum number of iterations $g \approx n$ has been reached. The results are shown for the overlapping Trap functions with linkage groups of sizes 5 and 7. Population size is determined by bisection with 30 successful runs. The reported number of fitness evaluations are averaged over 30 independent runs. For the NK landscapes problem, we use $k = 5$. For each n, we use 1000 unique, independently generated instances.

To evaluate performance of the algorithm, the overall number of fitness evaluations is reported. The number of fitness evaluations for hBOA, DSMGA++ and FGEDA to solve overlapping Trap-5 and overlapping Trap-7 functions are depicted in figures 6 and 7. Results on NK-Landscape with $k = 5, 6$ are shown in figures 8 and 9. Comparing the results visually, the FGEDA needs smaller number of fitness evaluations and grows slower with regard to the problem size.

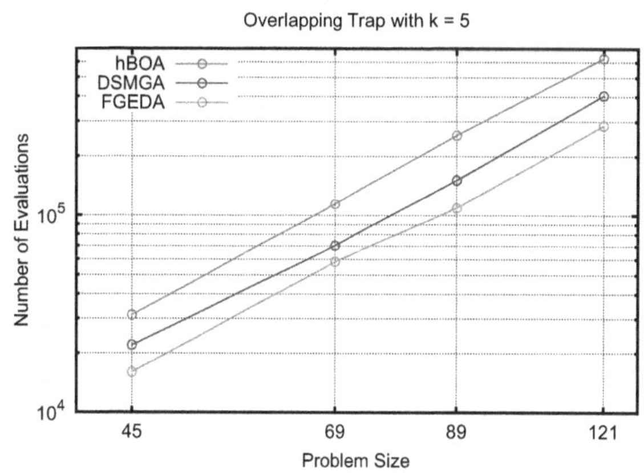

Figure 6: Number of fitness evaluations for hBOA, DSMGA++ and FGEDA to solve overlapping Trap-5.

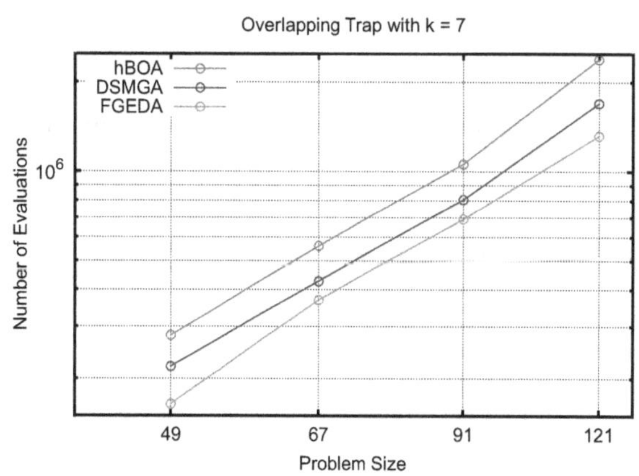

Figure 7: Number of fitness evaluations for hBOA, DSMGA++ and FGEDA to solve overlapping Trap-7.

9. SUMMARY AND CONCLUSION

This paper introduces a estimation distribution algorithm. We have used symmetric non-negative matrix factorization

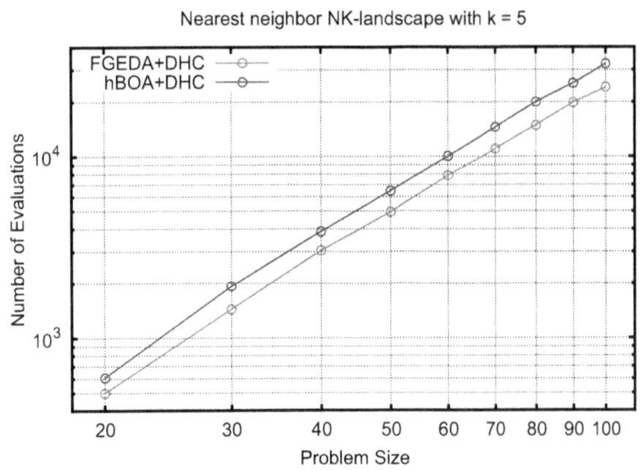

Figure 8: Number of fitness evaluations for nearest neighbor NK-Landscape with $k = 5$ for FGEDA and hBOA

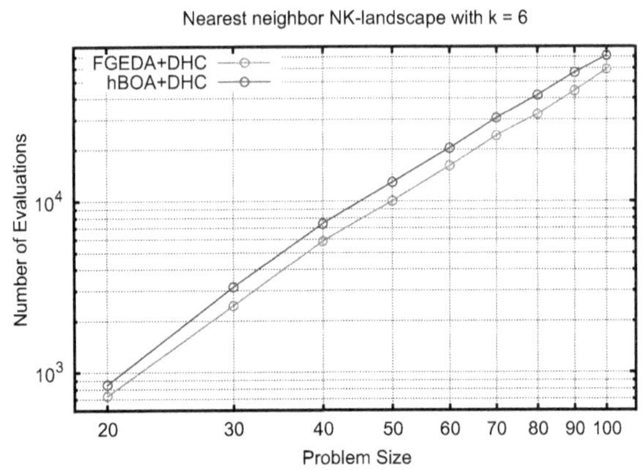

Figure 9: Number of fitness evaluations for nearest neighbor NK-Landscape with $k = 6$ for FGEDA and hBOA

for factorizing the matrix of mutual information and learning the factor graph of the problem. Markov blanket canonical parameterization is used to approximate the Gibbs distribution encoded by the factor graph. Having both the linkage groups and the joint distribution, new potential solutions are generated using Gibbs sampling and BB-wise crossover. To demonstrate the performance of the FGEDA, the results on overlapping Trap functions and NK-landscape problems are reported. It is shown that FGEDA can solve all the tested problems with polynomial number of fitness evaluations in polynomial time with respect to length of the problem. The results are compared to the results of two well-known reference approaches and it is shown that performance of the three methods is comparable in terms of the number of function evaluations. One of the advantages of FGEDA is that it learns the factor graph which is naturally the ideal model to encode the variable dependencies, in polynomial time. The algorithm description is easy and there is no black-box part in the algorithm. The learned model is simple to understand for humans. This can be a valuable property for the experts. The learning process has strong mathematical background and it is mathematically proved to converge. Having the factor graph we can also apply other methods like LBP to calculate the MAP for enhancing the sampling phase of the algorithm which is left for future works.

10. REFERENCES

[1] M. Pelikan. *Hierarchical Bayesian Optimization Algorithm*. Springer-Verlag Berlin Heidelberg, 2005.

[2] S. Shakya and A. Brownlee and J. McCall and F. Fournier and G. Owusu. A fully multivariate DEUM algorithm. *In (CEC-2009)*, pages 479-486. 2009.

[3] P. Larranaga and J. Lozano. *Estimation of Distribution Algorithms: A New Tool For Evolutionary Computation*. Kluwer Academic Pub, 2002.

[4] T. Mahnig and H. Muhlenbein. FDA - a scalable evolutionary algorithm for the optimization of additively decomposed functions. *Evol. Comput.*, 7(4):353–376, 1999.

[5] K. Sastry and D. E. Goldberg. *On Extended Compact Genetic Algorithm*. (IlliGAL Report No. 2000026), UIUC, Urbana, IL, 2000.

[6] T.-L. Yu. *A Matrix Approach for Finding Extrema: Problems With Modularity, Hierarchy, and Overlap*. PhD thesis, UIUC, Urbana, IL, 2006.

[7] F. R. Kschischang and B. J. Frey and H. A. Loeliger. Factor graphs and the sum-product algorithm. *IEEE Trans. Inf. Theory*, 47(2):498-519. 2001.

[8] H. Mühlenbein. *Convergence of Estimation of Distribution Algorithms for Finite Samples*. Technical Report. Germany: Fraunhofer Institute Autonomous intelligent Systems, 2008.

[9] R. Santana. Estimation of distribution algorithms with Kikuchi approximations. *Evol. Comput.*, 13(1):67-97. 2005.

[10] A. Mendiburu and R. Santana and Jose A. Lozano. *Introducing Belief Propagation in Estimation of Distribution Algorithms: A Parallel Approach*. Technical Report EHU-KAT-IK-11-07. Department of Computer Architecture and Technology, The University of the Basque Country, 2007.

[11] D. Kuang and H. Park and C. H. Q. Ding. Symmetric non-negative matrix factorization for graph clustering. *12th SIAM Int. Conf. on Data Mining*, pages 106-117. 2012.

[12] S. Geman and D. Geman. Stochastic relaxation, Gibbs distributions, and Bayesian rotation of images. *IEEE Trans. Pattern Anal. Mach. Intell.*, (6):721-741

[13] G. Harik. *Linkage Learning Via Probabilistic Modelling in the ECGA*. (IlliGAL Report No. 99010). UIUC, Urbana, IL, 1999.

[14] D. Zhou and B. SchÃűlkopf and T. Hofmann. Semi-supervised learning on directed graphs. In *(NIPS-2005)*, pages 1633-1640, 2005.

[15] D. D. Lee and H. S. Seung. Algorithms for Non-negative Matrix Factorization. In *(NIPS-2009)*, pages 556-562, 2009.

[16] K. Yu and S. Yu and V. Tresp. Soft clustering on graphs. In *(NIPS-2005)*, pages 0-5, 2005.

[17] P. Abbeel and D. Koller and A. Y. Ng. Learning factor graphs in polynomial time and sample complexity. *J. Mach. Learn. Res.*, 7:1743–1788. 2006.

Multi-objective Gene-pool Optimal Mixing Evolutionary Algorithms

Ngoc Hoang Luong
Centrum Wiskunde &
Informatica (CWI)
Amsterdam, The Netherlands
Hoang.Luong@cwi.nl

Han La Poutré
Centrum Wiskunde &
Informatica (CWI)
Amsterdam, The Netherlands
Han.La.Poutre@cwi.nl

Peter A.N. Bosman
Centrum Wiskunde &
Informatica (CWI)
Amsterdam, The Netherlands
Peter.Bosman@cwi.nl

ABSTRACT

The recently introduced Gene-pool Optimal Mixing Evolutionary Algorithm (GOMEA), with a lean, but sufficient, linkage model and an efficient variation operator, has been shown to be a robust and efficient methodology for solving single objective (SO) optimization problems with superior performance compared to classic genetic algorithms (GAs) and estimation-of-distribution algorithms (EDAs). In this paper, we bring the strengths of GOMEAs to the multi-objective (MO) optimization realm. To this end, we modify the linkage learning procedure and the variation operator of GOMEAs to better suit the need of finding the whole Pareto-optimal front rather than a single best solution. Based on state-of-the-art studies on MOEAs, we further pinpoint and incorporate two other essential components for a scalable MO optimizer. First, the use of an elitist archive is beneficial for keeping track of non-dominated solutions when the main population size is limited. Second, clustering can be crucial if different parts of the Pareto-optimal front need to be handled differently. By combining these elements, we construct a multi-objective GOMEA (MO-GOMEA). Experimental results on various MO optimization problems confirm the capability and scalability of our MO-GOMEA that compare favorably with those of the well-known GA NSGA-II and the more recently introduced EDA mohBOA.

Categories and Subject Descriptors

I.2.8 [**Artificial Intelligence**]: Problem Solving, Control Methods, and Search

General Terms

Algorithms, Performance, Experimentation

Keywords

Multi-objective optimization; Optimal Mixing; Linkage Tree Genetic Algorithm; Clustering

GECCO'14, July 12–16, Vancouver, BC, Canada.

http://dx.doi.org/10.1145/2576768.2598261.

1. INTRODUCTION

A multi-objective (MO) optimization problem of m objectives $f_i(\boldsymbol{x}), i \in \{0, 1, \dots, m-1\}$, is defined as, without loss of generality, to maximize all $f_i(\boldsymbol{x})$'s. The objective value vector of a solution $\boldsymbol{x}$ is $\boldsymbol{f}(\boldsymbol{x}) = (f_0(\boldsymbol{x}), f_1(\boldsymbol{x}), \dots, f_{m-1}(\boldsymbol{x}))$. A solution $\boldsymbol{x}^0$ *dominates* a solution $\boldsymbol{x}^1$ (denoted $\boldsymbol{x}^0 \succ \boldsymbol{x}^1$) if and only if $f_i(\boldsymbol{x}^0) \geq f_i(\boldsymbol{x}^1), \forall i \in \{0, 1, \dots, m-1\} \wedge \boldsymbol{f}(\boldsymbol{x}^0) \neq \boldsymbol{f}(\boldsymbol{x}^1)$. A solution $\boldsymbol{x}^0$ is Pareto optimal if and only if there does not exist a solution $\boldsymbol{x}^1$ such that $\boldsymbol{x}^1 \succ \boldsymbol{x}^0$. The Pareto-optimal set $\boldsymbol{\mathcal{P}_S}$ of the problem at hand is the set of all Pareto-optimal solutions. The Pareto-optimal front $\boldsymbol{\mathcal{P}_F}$ is the set of the objective value vectors of all Pareto-optimal solutions. The goal of MO optimization is to find a set of non-dominated solutions whose objective value vectors constitute a good approximation of the Pareto-optimal front [4].

It is known that MO evolutionary algorithms (MOEAs) are an effective methodology for solving MO optimization problems [4]. Most MOEAs studies focus on the capability to find a good approximation of the Pareto-optimal front. The quality of approximations is often assessed based on both proximity to the optimal front (i.e. as close as possible) and diversity along the front (i.e. as well-spread as possible) [4]. Commonly studied MOEAs, such as the Nondominated Sorting Genetic Algorithm II (NSGA-II) [5] and the improved Strength Pareto Evolutionary Algorithm (SPEA2) [13], have been demonstrated to be effective in achieving this two-fold goal for a wide range of problems. However, the important issue of scalability is often overlooked [10], which is typically highly dependent on the algorithms' capability for efficient and effective linkage learning. It has been shown that without detecting and exploiting the dependencies between problem variables (e.g. using classic crossover and mutation operators), MOEAs cannot solve some decomposable problems efficiently [7, 10]. Addressing scalability, there exist MO estimation-of-distribution algorithms (MOEDAs), such as the Multi-objective Adapted Maximum-Likelihood Model (MAMaLGaM) [1] for continuous variables and the Multi-objective Hierarchical Bayesian Optimization Algorithm (mohBOA) [10] for discrete variables. Similar to the advantages of EDAs in single objective (SO) optimization, MOEDAs attempt to bring these advantages to MO optimization by replacing classic variation operators with model-based variation operators [7, 9, 10].

Although EDAs (and MOEDAs) are robust optimizers, probabilistic model building procedure typically comes at the cost of larger population sizes and more CPU time as a result of large computational complexity for model building [9]. Furthermore, the estimation of complete probability distributions may be unnecessary if linkage information by itself suffices to perform variation effectively [12]. Such information is processed using an intensive, but effective, mixing procedure in the recently introduced class of Gene-pool Optimal Mixing Evolutionary Algorithms (GOMEAs) [12]. GOMEAs have been found to efficiently and reliably solve a variety of well-known SO benchmark problems, typically requiring far smaller population sizes and having better scalability in required function evaluations as compared to classic GAs and EDAs [12]. Moreover, certain classes of linkage models in GOMEA can be learned in $\mathcal{O}(nl^2)$ time [6] whereas learning comparable higher-order models in EDAs typically requires $\mathcal{O}(nl^3)$ time (where l is the problem size and n is the population size). It is these strengths of GOMEAs that we aim to transfer to MO optimization.

Studies on MOEAs have underlined important features for improving the capability of solving MO optimization problems. State-of-the-art MOEAs are characterized by implementations of the elitism concept in the context of MO optimization (i.e. when there exist multiple equally good trade-off solutions on the non-dominated Pareto front) [3]. A common elitism realization is the use of a secondary population, termed the elitist archive, for retaining non-dominated solutions found during the search. An archive can be beneficial because the sizes for the main population may be smaller than the number of solutions on the Pareto front and some non-dominated solutions can be lost due to selection [8].

The goal of MO optimization is two-fold: finding an approximation set of non-dominated solutions that is close to the Pareto-optimal front (i.e. proximity) and as diverse as possible (i.e. diversity, especially in the objective space) [4]. Standard MOEAs steer the population toward the optimal front while trying to preserve the diversity by different mechanisms, such as the selection based on crowding distance in NSGA-II [5] or the environmental selection in SPEA2 [13]. However, it has been showed that these mechanisms are insufficient for achieving a good scalability and that different parts of the optimal front should be processed separately [10]. State-of-the-art MOEDAs therefore often implement mixture probability distributions by clustering the selected solutions in the objective space and building a linkage model for each cluster separately (e.g. in mohBOA [10] and in MAMaLGaM [1]). Studies [10, 11] have noted the difficulty for finding the entire optimal front of some decomposable problems, especially the *extreme* regions of the optimal front, as for the studied problems the niches on the extremes become exponentially smaller than the niches in the *middle*. Furthermore, for MO optimization in general, selection tries to exploit all objectives simultaneously, thus reducing the pressure towards approaching the optimal front [1]. This problem was solved in MAMaLGaM-X$^+$ [1] by adding a separate SO optimizer for each objective and injecting the best solutions found by these SO optimizers into the elitist archive. In this paper, we adopt the idea of clustering from MAMaLGaM-X$^+$ but we adapt the process to fit well with the mechanism of GOMEA.

Having discussed the importance of elitist archiving, clustering, and linkage learning, in the remainder we will design and assemble these components into MO-GOMEA. Section 2 will describe these key components of MO-GOMEA. We presents benchmark problems and their characteristics in Section 3. Section 4 exhibits and discusses the experimental results. Finally, Section 5 concludes the paper.

```
MO-GOMEA  //population size n, k clusters
t ← 0; t^NIS ← 0
for i ∈ {0, 1, ..., n − 1} do
  P_i ← CreateRandomSolution()
  EvaluateFitness(P_i)
  A^t ← UpdateElitistArchive(P_i)
while ¬TerminationCriteriaSatisfied do
  t ← t + 1
  {C_0, C_1, ..., C_{k−1}} ← ClusterPopulation(P)
  for j ∈ {0, 1, ..., k − 1} do
    S_j ← TournamentSelection(C_j)
    F_j ← LearnLinkageModel(S_j)
  for i ∈ {0, 1, ..., n − 1} do
    C_j ← DetermineCluster(P_i, {C_0, C_1, ..., C_{k−1}})
    if ¬IsExtremeCluster(C_j) then
      O_i ← MO-OptimalMixing(P_i, C_j, F_j, A^t)
    else
      O_i ← SO-OptimalMixing(P_i, C_j, F_j, A^t)
  P ← O = {O_0, O_1, ..., O_{n−1}}
  if f(A^t) ≠ f(A^{t−1}) then
    t^NIS ← 0
  else
    t^NIS ← t^NIS + 1
```

Figure 1: Pseudo code for MO-GOMEA

2. MULTI-OBJECTIVE GOMEA

MO-GOMEA is started by randomly initializing a population $\mathcal{P}$ of n candidate solutions. All n solutions are evaluated to obtain their objective values. The population $\mathcal{P}$ is then clustered (in the objective space) into k clusters $\mathcal{C}_j$'s ($j \in \{0, 1, \ldots, k-1\}$) of equal sizes. For each cluster $\mathcal{C}_j$, selection is performed separately to obtain the corresponding selection set $\mathcal{S}_j$. From each $\mathcal{S}_j$, a separate linkage model $\mathcal{F}_j$ is learned. Finally, for each solution in the population $\mathcal{P}$, the cluster $\mathcal{C}_j$ that it belongs to is determined, and then variation is performed on the solution using the linkage relations captured by the corresponding linkage model $\mathcal{F}_j$ (see Section 2.4) where only the other solutions in the same cluster $\mathcal{C}_j$ are used as potential donors. This transforms each solution in the population into an offspring solution. These offspring complete replace the population. The pseudo-code for the outline of MO-GOMEA is given in Figure 1.

2.1 Elitist Archive

We use a basic, but effective, implementation of the elitist archive. We denote the elitist archive in generation t by $\mathcal{A}^t$ in decision-variable space and by $\boldsymbol{f}(\mathcal{A}^t)$ in objective space. Every newly generated solution is checked to see if it can be added into the archive. If the new solution is dominated by any archive member, it will be discarded. If it is a new non-dominated solution, it will be added into the archive, and archive members that are dominated by this new solution will be removed. In the case that there exists an archive member with the same objective values, the existing solution will be replaced by the new one if such replacement results in a diversity improvement for the archive in decision-variable space. We use a simple diversity metric for a solution: the Hamming distance to the nearest neighbor in the archive. Between the existing archive member and the new solution, the one having greater value for this metric will be chosen. How to ensure elitism for a bounded archive size is not our focus in this paper. Moreover, because of the nature of our benchmarks and experiment settings, we can assume that the elitist archive size is as large as the Pareto-optimal front.

2.2 Clustering

We use balanced k-leader-means clustering as previously used in MAMaLGaM [1] to cluster the population into k clusters of equal sizes. Note that clustering is performed in the objective space. First, a heuristic is used to select k leader solutions that are as well spread as possible. To do so, the first leader is the solution with maximum value in an arbitrary objective. The nearest-leader distances of all remaining solutions are computed as the distances to this first leader. The solution with the largest distance is chosen as the next leader. For every remaining solution, its nearest-leader distance is then updated if the distance to this new leader is smaller than the previous value. This process is repeated until k leaders are obtained. Second, k-means clustering is performed with the k leaders as the initial cluster means. Third, the distance from every solution to every final cluster mean is computed. Each cluster is then expanded to contain exactly c closest solutions, starting from each cluster mean. It was previously suggested to use $c = \frac{2}{k}|\boldsymbol{\mathcal{P}}|$, where $\boldsymbol{\mathcal{P}}$ are the solutions being clustered, resulting in overlap between neighboring clusters [1]. This reduces the probability that some solutions are not covered by any clusters. Moreover, it is beneficial to have equal-sized clusters so that a comparable amount of resources is used to handle each part of the Pareto-optimal front, to support obtaining an evenly-spread set of non-dominated solutions.

Instead of clustering the selection set as in mohBOA [10] and MAMaLGaM [1], in MO-GOMEA the whole population is clustered first, and selection is then performed for each cluster separately. This is done because MO-GOMEA does not generate offspring solutions by sampling new solutions from the learned models as is the case in MOEDAs. Instead, the variation operator in MO-GOMEA is used to improve each solution in the population in a more local-search like fashion (see Section 2.4). To do so, each solution in the population needs to be associated with a cluster.

Clustering helps to handle different parts of the Pareto-optimal front separately. This can be of major importance, especially for the extreme regions of the front where solutions maximize a single objective. This is because solutions from different extreme regions typically differ a lot. Moreover, in some problems the number of available solutions in the extreme regions can be much smaller than in the middle regions of the optimal front [11]. The additional use of separate SO optimizers to specifically obtain solutions in extreme regions of the front as used in MAMaLGaM-X$^+$ has been shown to be highly beneficial [1]. Although these separate optimizers can be tied in with the MOEA by running them generationally-synchronously parallel, putting the best solutions found by the separate optimizers into the elitist archive, and having the elitist archive participate in variation, such interaction between the populations of the SO and MO optimizers is still very limited. Therefore, instead of using external SO optimizers, in MO-GOMEA we use only a single population. In every generation, for each objective, in MO-GOMEA the cluster having the largest mean value in that objective is designated to perform only SO optimization in that objective during variation. If a single cluster happens to have the largest mean in more than one objective, we choose an objective arbitrarily. Moreover, while the selection procedure for learning linkage models in middle clusters is based on the Pareto-domination concept, the selection for extreme clusters is based on the single-objective only.

2.3 Linkage Learning

Linkage learning is performed for each cluster separately. Moreover, similar to the SO GOMEA, linkage learning is performed on a selection set that is obtained using tournament selection with tournament size 2 to have a beneficial bias in the model toward better fitness values.

Let $L = \{0, 1, \ldots, l-1\}$ be the set of indices of all l decision variables. To capture the interactions between these decision variables, GOMEAs use a general linkage model termed as the Family Of Subset (FOS). A FOS $\mathcal{F}$ consists of subsets of set L, i.e. $\mathcal{F} = \{\boldsymbol{F}^0, \boldsymbol{F}^1, \ldots, \boldsymbol{F}^{|\mathcal{F}|-1}\}$ where $\boldsymbol{F}^i \subseteq \{0, 1, \ldots, l-1\}$, $i \in \{0, 1, \ldots, |\mathcal{F}|-1\}$. A FOS $\mathcal{F}$ is thus a subset of the powerset of L, i.e. $\mathcal{F} \subseteq \mathcal{P}(L)$. Every subset $\boldsymbol{F}^i$ can be seen as a linkage group of problem variables that exhibit some degree of joint dependency and that should thus be copied jointly together when performing variation. Various GOMEA instances exist with different FOS structures [2, 12]. Here, we employ the Linkage Tree (LT) structure, which is the most commonly used in literature. In SO optimization, the GOMEA variant with LT is also known as the Linkage Tree Genetic Algorithm (LTGA) [12].

The LT contains all singleton subsets, i.e. $\boldsymbol{F}^i = \{i\}, i \in \{0, 1, \ldots, l-1\}$, capturing decision variables as being fully independent. The LT also contains combinations of variables, organized in a tree-like fashion. A branch node of the LT is a bivariate or multivariate subset $\boldsymbol{F}^i$, which is created by combining two subsets $\boldsymbol{F}^j$ and $\boldsymbol{F}^k$ such that $\boldsymbol{F}^j \cap \boldsymbol{F}^k = \emptyset, |\boldsymbol{F}^j| < |\boldsymbol{F}^i|, |\boldsymbol{F}^k| < |\boldsymbol{F}^i|$ and $\boldsymbol{F}^j \cup \boldsymbol{F}^k = \boldsymbol{F}^i$. The root node, which contains all the decision variable indices, is the set L itself and is discarded from the LT as it does not generate any new offspring solution when doing recombination. The LT has $2l-2$ linkage groups.

A full LT can be constructed by a procedure called Unweighted Pair Grouping Method with Arithmetic-mean (UPGMA [6]). Starting with all the singleton groups of univariate subsets (i.e. leaf nodes), multivariate groups (i.e. branch nodes) are created by consecutively combining two closest groups until the group containing all variable indices (i.e. root node) is created. Here, we use Mutual Information (MI) as the distance metric for UPGMA (i.e. a higher MI value indicates a closer distance). An optimal implementation of UPGMA exists that has $\mathcal{O}(nl^2)$ time complexity [6].

2.4 Optimal Mixing

Classic EAs use blind crossover and mutation to create offspring solutions. EDAs sample the learned probability distribution to generate new solutions. GOMEAs perform an intensive mixing procedure aimed at efficiently exploiting the FOS linkage model to improve all population members, one by one; the resulting solutions are offspring solutions.

Aimed at covering the whole Pareto-optimal front by discerning and exploiting different regions, the population is clustered in MO-GOMEA and for each cluster $\mathcal{C}_j$, a dedicated linkage model $\mathcal{F}_j$ is learned. Therefore, before improving a population member, we need to determine which cluster that solution belongs to. Although the clustering algorithm used here nicely constructs equally sized clusters, some solutions in $\mathcal{P}$ might actually not be covered by any cluster and some solutions may be covered by more than one cluster. Uncovered solutions are assigned to the cluster with the nearest mean. In case of multiple cluster assignments, ties are broken randomly. Every cluster thereby can be used to improve a more or less equal number of solutions.

Given cluster C_j that an existing solution $\boldsymbol{x}$ belongs to, and the corresponding FOS $\mathcal{F}_j$ of that cluster, MO-GOMEA changes $\boldsymbol{x}$, that we also refer to as the parent solution, incrementally by the Optimal Mixing (OM) procedure into an offspring solution as follows. First, the offspring solution $\boldsymbol{o}$ is created by cloning $\boldsymbol{x}$ and a backup $\boldsymbol{b}$ of $\boldsymbol{o}$ is created. We then traverse the linkage groups in FOS $\mathcal{F}_j$. For every $\boldsymbol{F}^i \in \mathcal{F}_j$, a donor solution $\boldsymbol{p}$ is randomly chosen from the same cluster C_j. The values of the problem variables whose indices are indicated by the linkage group $\mathcal{F}_i$ are copied from the donor $\boldsymbol{p}$ to the current solution $\boldsymbol{o}$. The objective values of this partially-altered solution $\boldsymbol{o}$ are evaluated and are compared with the backed-up state $\boldsymbol{b}$. If such mixing results in an improvement (i.e. the altered solution dominates the backed-up state $\boldsymbol{o} \succ \boldsymbol{b}$) or an equally good solution (i.e. the altered solution has the same objective values as the backed-up state $\boldsymbol{f}(\boldsymbol{o}) = \boldsymbol{f}(\boldsymbol{b})$) or a side step (i.e. the altered solution may not dominate the backed-up state but it is not dominated by any solutions in the elitist archive $\mathcal{A} \not\succ \boldsymbol{o}$), the changes are accepted and recorded as the new backup. Otherwise, the current solution is reverted to its backed-up state.

It can happen that all the mixing steps of OM do not improve nor at least change the parent solution or that there exist significant plateaus in the problem causing solutions to be changed back and forth. In SO GOMEA this problem was tackled by using a procedure termed Forced Improvement (FI) [2]. FI is essentially a second round of OM but the donor solution then is always the currently best found solution. In [2], FI is triggered when a parent solution is not changed after going through OM or when the number of subsequent generations that the best solution did not change, termed no-improvement stretch (NIS), exceeds the threshold $1 + \lfloor \log_{10}(n) \rfloor$. Here, we implement an MO version for FI through the following modifications. First, NIS is redefined as the number of consecutive generations that the Pareto front (in the objective space) formed by non-dominated solutions in the elitist archive stayed the same. Second, a new donor solution is now selected randomly from the elitist archive for each linkage group. Third, because FI aims to strictly improve the parent solution, a mixing step in the FI phase is only accepted if it results in a direct domination (i.e. $\boldsymbol{o} \succ \boldsymbol{b}$) or a Pareto-front improvement (i.e. a truly new non-dominated solution is found: $\mathcal{A}^t \not\succ \boldsymbol{o} \wedge \boldsymbol{f}(\boldsymbol{o}) \notin \boldsymbol{f}(\mathcal{A}^t)$). Similar to the SO version, rather than traversing the whole linkage tree, the FI procedure is stopped as soon as the first change is accepted. If the parent solution is still unchanged after FI, we simply replace it by a solution randomly chosen from the elitist archive. Pseudo-code is given in Figure 2.

OM in MO-GOMEA can be seen as a direct extension of OM in SO-GOMEA by replacing SO improvement checking with the Pareto-domination checking in every mixing step, and using multiple solutions from the elitist archive instead of a single best solution for the FI phase. MO-OM is employed for improving solutions that are determined as belonging to the middle region clusters. As discussed earlier however, having a mechanism that puts extra pressure on the individual objectives can be highly beneficial because the Pareto-domination improvement may not give enough pressure to find the extreme solutions (the solutions that maximize a single objective). Therefore, to improve solutions that belong to extreme region clusters, we employ SO-OM and SO-FI of the SO-GOMEA variant as reported in [2]. In other words, if a parent solution $\boldsymbol{x}$ belongs to the extreme cluster that is associated with optimizing single objective f_i, $\boldsymbol{x}$ will be improved by OM in the SO manner, and the solution $\boldsymbol{x}^{best}_{f_i}$ that stores the current maximum observed value for f_i will be considered as the single donor solution in FI. Note that, however, the NIS concept is still defined in the overall MO optimization context with regard to the Pareto front formed by the elitist archive members.

```
MO-OPTIMALMIXING(x, C, F, A^t)
b ← o ← x; f(b) ← f(o) ← f(x); changed ← false
for i ∈ {0, 1, ..., |F| − 1} do
  p ← RANDOM(C)
  o_{F^i} ← p_{F^i}
  if o_{F^i} ≠ b_{F^i} then
    f(o) ← EVALUATEFITNESS(o)
    A^t ← UPDATEELITISTARCHIVE(o)
    if (o ≻ b) or (f(o) = f(b)) or (A^t ⊁ o) then
      b_{F^i} ← o_{F^i}; f(b) ← f(o); changed ← true
    else
      o_{F^i} ← b_{F^i}; f(o) ← f(b)
if ¬changed or t^{NIS} > 1 + ⌊log_10(n)⌋ then
  changed ← false
  for i ∈ {0, 1, ..., |F| − 1} do
    p ← RANDOM(A^t)
    o_{F^i} ← p_{F^i}
    if o_{F^i} ≠ b_{F^i} then
      f(o) ← EVALUATEFITNESS(o)
      if (o ≻ b) or (A^t ⊁ o and f(o) ∉ f(A^t)) then
        b_{F^i} ← o_{F^i}; f(b) ← f(o); changed ← true
      else
        o_{F^i} ← b_{F^i}; f(o) ← f(b)
      A^t ← UPDATEELITISTARCHIVE(o)
    if changed then breakfor
if ¬changed then
  p ← RANDOM(A^t); o ← p; f(o) ← f(p)
```

Figure 2: Pseudo code for multi-objective Optimal Mixing

3. EXPERIMENTAL SETTINGS

3.1 Benchmark Problems

3.1.1 Zeromax - Onemax

Zeromax - Onemax [10] has two objectives that are defined over a binary string $\boldsymbol{x}$ of l bits as follows:

$$f_{\text{Onemax}}(\boldsymbol{x}) = \sum_{i=0}^{l-1} x_i; \quad f_{\text{Zeromax}}(\boldsymbol{x}) = l - f_{\text{Onemax}}(\boldsymbol{x}) \quad (1)$$

Objective f_{Onemax} counts the number of bits set to 1 while f_{Zeromax} counts the number of bits set to 0, making the objectives conflicting. Every candidate solution is a Pareto-optimal solution; any increase in the number of bits set to 1 will be a decrease in the number of bits set to 0, and vice versa. The Pareto-optimal front $\boldsymbol{\mathcal{P}_F}$ of Zeromax - Onemax consists of $l+1$ points $\boldsymbol{\mathcal{P}}_F = \{(i, l-i) \mid i \in \{0, 1, \dots l\}\}$, on a straight line. A point on $\boldsymbol{\mathcal{P}_F}$ can correspond to many different solutions, with the exception of the two extreme points that correspond to exactly a string of all 1s (maximizing Onemax) and a string of all 0s (maximizing Zeromax). It can be seen that the niches of the solutions having objective values in the middle regions of the front $\boldsymbol{\mathcal{P}_F}$ are exponentially larger than the niches in the extreme regions of $\boldsymbol{\mathcal{P}_F}$.

3.1.2 Trap-5 - Inverse Trap-5

Trap-5 - Inverse Trap-5 also has two objectives. Trap-5 is the well-known mutually exclusive, additively decomposable composition of the order-5 deceptive subfunctions:

$$f_{\text{Trap-5}}(\boldsymbol{x}) = \sum_{i=0}^{(l/5)-1} f^{\text{sub}}_{\text{Trap-5}}\left(\sum_{j=5i}^{5i+4} x_j\right) \quad (2)$$

where

$$f^{\text{sub}}_{\text{Trap-5}}(u) = \begin{cases} 5 & \text{if } u = 5 \\ 4 - u & \text{if } u < 5 \end{cases} \quad (3)$$

Inverse Trap-5 comprises the same partitions as Trap-5 but each partition is evaluated "inversely":

$$f^{\text{sub}}_{\text{Inverse-Trap-5}}(u) = \begin{cases} 5 & \text{if } u = 0 \\ u - 1 & \text{if } u > 0 \end{cases} \quad (4)$$

A candidate solution for which each partition has one objective subfunction that evaluates to 5 is Pareto-optimal. The Pareto-optimal front $\mathcal{P}_F$ consists of $l/5+1$ points $\mathcal{P}_F = \{(5i + 4(l/5 - i), 5(l/5 - i) + 4i) \mid i \in \{0, 1, \ldots l/5\}\}$, on a straight line. It is well-known known that in order to solve additively decomposable trap functions, it is crucial to preserve the linkage relations between problem variables during variation. Therefore, this benchmark is often used as a demonstration for the importance of linkage learning.

3.1.3 Leading Ones Trailing Zeros (LOTZ)

The Leading Ones Trailing Zeros (LOTZ) problem consists of two objectives: maximizing the number of consecutive bits set to 1 at the beginning and maximizing the number of consecutive bits set to zero at the end.

$$f_{\text{LO}}(\boldsymbol{x}) = \sum_{i=0}^{l-1}\prod_{j=0}^{i} x_j; \quad f_{\text{TZ}}(\boldsymbol{x}) = \sum_{i=0}^{l-1}\prod_{j=i}^{l-1}(1 - x_j) \quad (5)$$

A candidate solution that consists of a substring of all 1s followed by a substring of all 0s, i.e. having the form of $11\ldots100\ldots0$, is Pareto-optimal. The two extreme solutions are all 1s (maximizing Leading Ones) and all 0s (maximizing Trailing Zeros). The Pareto-optimal front $\mathcal{P}_F$ of LOTZ consists of $l+1$ points $\mathcal{P}_F^i = \{(i, l - i) \mid i \in \{0, 1, \ldots l\}\}$, on a straight line. However, different from the Zeromax - Onemax problem, any point on Pareto-optimal front $\mathcal{P}_F$ of LOTZ corresponds to exactly one Pareto-optimal solution.

3.1.4 Multi-objective MAXCUT

Weighted MAXCUT is defined over a weighted undirected graph $G = (V, E)$, where $V = (v_0, v_1, \ldots, v_{l-1})$ is the set of l vertices, and E is the set of edges (v_i, v_j) with corresponding weights w_{ij}'s. A maximum cut is a partition of l vertices into two disjoint subsets A and $B = V \backslash A$ such that the combined weight of all edges (v_i, v_j) having $v_i \in A$ and $v_j \in B$ is maximized. A cut can be encoded as a binary string $\boldsymbol{x}$ of l bits, in which each bit x_i corresponds to a vertex, and all 0-valued bits indicate vertices of set A while all 1-valued bits indicate vertices of set B. The objective function of the weighted MAXCUT problem is defined as follows

$$f_{\text{weighted MAXCUT}}(\boldsymbol{x}) = \sum_{(v_i, v_j) \in E} \begin{cases} w_{ij} & \text{if } x_i \neq x_j \\ 0 & \text{otherwise} \end{cases} \quad (6)$$

We construct an MO version of the weighted MAXCUT problem by optimizing a different MAXCUT instance in each objective. The instances have identical vertices but different edge weights. In our setup, each MAXCUT instance is a fully connected graph having $\frac{1}{2}l(l-1)$ edges.

3.2 Performance Indicator

To compare the performance of different MO optimizers, we employ the $\boldsymbol{D}_{\mathcal{P}_F \to \mathcal{S}}$ performance indicator, also known as inverse generational distance [1]:

$$\boldsymbol{D}_{\mathcal{P}_F \to \mathcal{S}}(\mathcal{S}) = \frac{1}{|\mathcal{P}_F|} \sum_{\boldsymbol{f}^0 \in \mathcal{P}_F} \min_{\boldsymbol{x} \in \mathcal{S}} \{d(\boldsymbol{f}(\boldsymbol{x}), \boldsymbol{f}^0)\} \quad (7)$$

where $\mathcal{P}_F$ is the Pareto-optimal front, $\mathcal{S}$ is the final approximation front (i.e. the outcome of that optimizer), and $d(\cdot,\cdot)$ computes the Euclidean distance. The $\boldsymbol{D}_{\mathcal{P}_F \to \mathcal{S}}$ performance indicator is the average distance from a point in $\mathcal{P}_F$ to its nearest point in $\mathcal{S}$. A smaller value of $\boldsymbol{D}_{\mathcal{P}_F \to \mathcal{S}}$ indicates a better performance result, and the value of 0 is achieved if and only if the approximation set equals the Pareto-optimal front. Note that calculating the average distance in "reversed order" yields a different indicator $\boldsymbol{D}_{\mathcal{S} \to \mathcal{P}_F}$, also known as generational distance. However, obtaining a low $\boldsymbol{D}_{\mathcal{S} \to \mathcal{P}_F}$ score does not mean that a good approximation front has been found since having a single Pareto-optimal point already gives a value of 0. The $\boldsymbol{D}_{\mathcal{P}_F \to \mathcal{S}}$ indicator is more useful because it balances both proximity (i.e. how close $\mathcal{S}$ is to the front $\mathcal{P}_F$) and diversity (i.e. how well-spread $\mathcal{S}$ is along the front $\mathcal{P}_F$) of the approximation set $\mathcal{S}$.

For the problems Zeromax - Onemax, Trap-5 - Inverse Trap-5, and LOTZ, $\mathcal{P}_F$ is known, as described in the previous section. For MO MAXCUT problem however, we can only construct $\mathcal{P}_F$ for small problem sizes $l \in \{6, 12, 25\}$ using enumerative methods. For $l \in \{50, 100\}$, we can only obtain reference fronts by consulting the results of [2] as follows. We use the maximum population sizes of LTGA, that reliably solve the single-objective MAXCUT, reported in [2] to set as the cluster size for MO-GOMEA. We then run 5 different instances of MO-GOMEA with different number of clusters $k \in \{1, 3, 5, 7, 10\}$. Each MO-GOMEA instance is run 100 times, each time with a budget of 20 million function evaluations. We take the Pareto front of all results in all these runs over all 5 instances of MO-GOMEA to be $\mathcal{P}_F$ in this case. A degree of reliability can be taken from the fact that the optimal extreme points were always found to be in the final reference fronts $\mathcal{P}_F$ so constructed by using a dedicated SO MAXCUT optimal solver from literature.

3.3 Experimental Setup

We compare the performance of MO-GOMEA with an commonly used instance of NSGA-II (2-point crossover with probability 0.9 and bit-flipping mutation with probability $1/l$). We also consider the best results obtained by the EDAs (MO-)UMDA and mohBOA as reported in [10]. We want to assess scalability, i.e. how the population size requirements and the required number of evaluations grow as the problem size increases. For the problems Zeromax - Onemax, Trap-5 - Inverse Trap-5, and LOTZ, the Pareto-optimal fronts are known, so to this end, we perform bisection. Bisection is a binary-search inspired procedure that aims to find the minimally required population size to solve a problem instance reliably. Here, we define reliable as achieving $\boldsymbol{D}_{\mathcal{P}_F \to \mathcal{S}} = 0$ (i.e. the entire Pareto-optimal front is found) in all 100 out of 100 independent runs. We perform 10 independent bisection searches for every problem size $l \in \{25, 50, 100, 200, 400\}$.

For MO-MAXCUT, because we do not know the Pareto-optimal front for certain, it is more difficult to perform bisection. Moreover, MO-MAXCUT is a (NP)-hard problem, for which polynomial scalability may not be expected, so

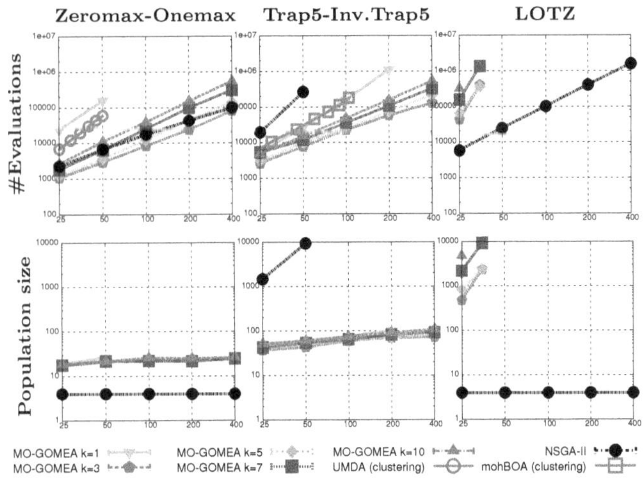

Figure 3: Scalability of MO-GOMEAs and competing optimizers. Horizontal axis: problem size.

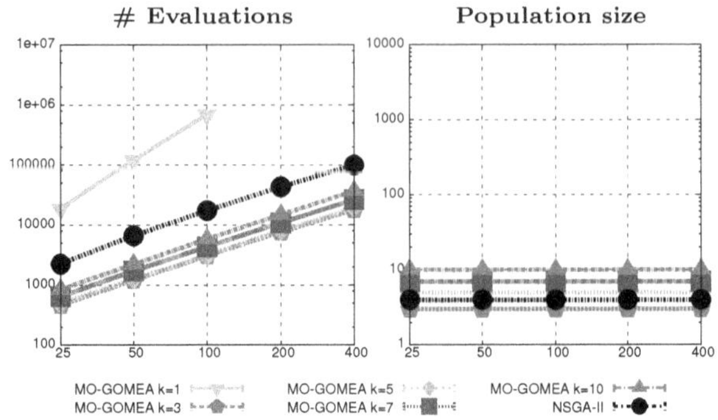

Figure 4: Scalability of MO-GOMEAs with mutation on Zeromax-Onemax. Horizontal axis: problem size.

we wish to observe how good of an approximation can be achieved. Therefore, we set the population sizes for MO-GOMEA and NSGA-II by consulting the results in [2], which solved SO-MAXCUT reliably. For each problem size, we use the average required population size of LTGA as the cluster size in MO-GOMEA and as the base population size in NSGA-II. We run MO-GOMEA with the number of clusters $k \in \{1, 3, 5, 7, 10\}$. Similarly, we run NSGA-II with the base population size scaled by 1, 2, 4, 8, and 16 times. For every MAXCUT problem instance $l \in \{6, 12, 25, 50, 100\}$, we perform 100 independent runs. We determine performance on the basis of the average convergence graph of the $\boldsymbol{D_{\mathcal{P}_F \to \mathcal{S}}}$ indicator. The budgets of function evaluations are also set by consulting [2]. For every problem size, we set the maximum number of evaluations to be 10 times the average number of evaluations that LTGA required to solve SO-MAXCUT (we multiply by 10 because we have a MO-GOMEA instance with at most $k = 10$ clusters). Note that we always consider 1 function evaluation to include evaluating both objectives.

4. RESULTS & DISCUSSIONS

4.1 Zeromax - Onemax

Figure 3 shows that MO-GOMEA with clustering (i.e. $k > 1$) outperforms UMDA with clustering in terms of number of evaluations as well as scalability. Note that, in [10], UMDA with clustering did not have an elitist archive and the required population size was not reported. It can be inferred however, that in order to cover all points of the Pareto-optimal front, the population size of UMDA without elitist archive must be at least as large as the Pareto-optimal front. Our MO-GOMEA instances require a smaller population size that grows quite slowly as the problem size increases. It can furthermore be observed that for solving this problem we do not really need many clusters in MO-GOMEA because all problem variables are independent from each other in all regions of the search space. That explains why MO-GOMEA with a number of clusters $k = 3$ has the best performance, and as we increase the number of clusters ($k = 5, 7, 10$), the number of evaluation also increases accordingly, but the scalability is relatively the same. However, MO-GOMEA without clustering ($k = 1$), and thus without internal SO optimizers, solves the problem much less efficiently. This is because the 2 extreme solutions (maximizing Zeromax vs. maximizing Onemax) are in very small niches that contain only 1 solution. Without clustering to distribute enough resources and without SO optimizers to approach these extreme regions efficiently, it is much harder to cover the entire Pareto-optimal front. In [10], an NSGA-II version without an elitist archive was found to hardly be able to solve the problem up to 50 problem variables. Here, being equipped with an elitist archive, NSGA-II can solve all Zeromax - Onemax instances with the smallest possible population size for NSGA-II of 4 individuals and with a performance much better than UMDA. This confirms the necessity of elitist archiving for scalable MO optimization.

NSGA-II does not have clustering nor SO optimizers. The fact that it can solve all Zeromax - Onemax of various problem sizes with such a small population size (and with slightly better scalability than MO-GOMEA) can be explained by its use of bit-wise mutation, which is not by default employed in MO-GOMEA. To validate this, we equip MO-GOMEA with a simple mutation operator: the mixing step at singleton linkage groups is replaced by randomly assigning a 0 or a 1 value (i.e. not genepool-based). The performance of MO-GOMEAs with this mutation operator is shown in Figure 4. With mutation, indeed the MO-GOMEAs now have a scalability relatively similar to NSGA-II. Moreover, the MO-GOMEAs need a fewer number of evaluations. The fact that MO-GOMEA with mutation but without clustering ($k = 1$, and thus without SO optimizers) still has worse performance indicates that clustering and internal SO optimizers are important features of MO-GOMEA. It is however also a result of the fact that mutation here is key to finding the extreme points. This however requires time in terms of generations and all higher-order mixing operations attempted by MO-GOMEA that follow from use of the full LT in the mean time are not useful. It would therefore be interesting in future work to look at techniques to filter out superfluous FOS sets as was recently done for the SO case [2].

4.2 Trap-5 - Inverse Trap-5

Figure 3 clearly demonstrates that MO-GOMEA outperforms both mohBOA and NSGA-II. Different from the Zeromax - Onemax benchmark of all-independent problem variables, Trap-5 - Inverse Trap-5 requires linkage learning to detect and preserve linkage relations between problem variables during recombination processes. Linkage learning is not employed in NSGA-II and even though it uses a recombination operator (two-point crossover) that is linkage friendly because we have encoded the trap functions tightly, it is still highly inefficient in finding the optimum. The strengths of the linkage model and optimal mixing procedure of GOMEA, which are known to contribute to its superior performance in solving the SO version of Trap-5 [12], is successfully extended to the MO realm. Given a properly learned linkage model, the OM procedure helps MO-GOMEA achieve successful mixing events which respect the dependencies between problem variables. The intensive local-search-inspired characteristic of the OM procedure moreover results in MO-GOMEA requiring only a small and slow-growth population size, similarly to the SO case [12].

The best results are again obtained with MO-GOMEA with 3 clusters. Using more clusters again leads to similar scalability but requires larger numbers of evaluations. This is again because the Pareto-optimal front of Trap-5 - Inverse Trap-5 has the same linkage structure (i.e. concatenated groups of 5 inter-dependent problem variables) in both objectives, resulting in redundant behavior when adding more clusters. However, MO-GOMEA with $k = 1$ clearly performs worse (but still better than NSGA-II) because the extreme regions of the front have again very small niches (similar to Zeromax - Onemax). Figure 3 also shows the performance of the MOEDA mohBOA with restricted tournament replacement and clustering, which had the best performance reported in [10]. Here, we obtain similar behavior for $k = 1$ but we obtain clearly better results for $k > 1$. Because in [10] mohBOA did not have an elitist archive, it is difficult to directly compare MO-GOMEA and mohBOA, which we did not re-implement. However, it has been reported in [12] that, in SO optimization for Trap-5, GOMEA had better performance than a typical EDA. Even if we assume that the probabilistic model building and sampling in mohBOA are as effective as the LT building and the OM procedure in MO-GOMEA, the elitist archive and internal SO optimizers cause MO-GOMEA to have better scalability.

4.3 LOTZ

Figure 3 shows that LOTZ is a challenge for MO-GOMEA. The reason is that we aim to cover the entire Pareto-optimal front reliably while LOTZ has a peculiar linkage structure. Only substrings of consecutive 1 bits at the beginning (Leading Ones) and the substring of consecutive 0 bits at the end (Trailing Zeros) contribute to the objective values. This means that all the mixing events of 0s and 1s in the middle are useless and can be considered as *noise*, affecting the effectiveness of linkage learning in MO-GOMEA. Moreover, the LT model fails to capture efficiently the type of operations needed to solve LOTZ. What further makes LOTZ a complicated problem is that selection pressure based on Pareto dominance makes it very difficult to obtain the extreme solutions of LOTZ (i.e. a string of all 1s and a string of all 0s). For example, a string $\boldsymbol{x}$ beginning with a 0 will be dominated by any strings beginning with a 1 and ending with a 0. This string $\boldsymbol{x}$ will therefore soon be deleted from of the population. The OM of GOMEA cannot improve $\boldsymbol{x}$ while still keeping the leading 0 bit because OM will prefer any dominating solutions $\boldsymbol{x}' \succ \boldsymbol{x}$ with a leading 1 bit. Even the SO version of OM in the extreme clusters cannot efficiently preserve this leading 0 bit because the leading 0 bit is only useful when it is combined with the substring of trailing 0s to create the extreme solution of all 0s. Figure 3 shows however that NSGA-II has little difficulty in solving LOTZ, requiring a population size of only 4. This is due to the

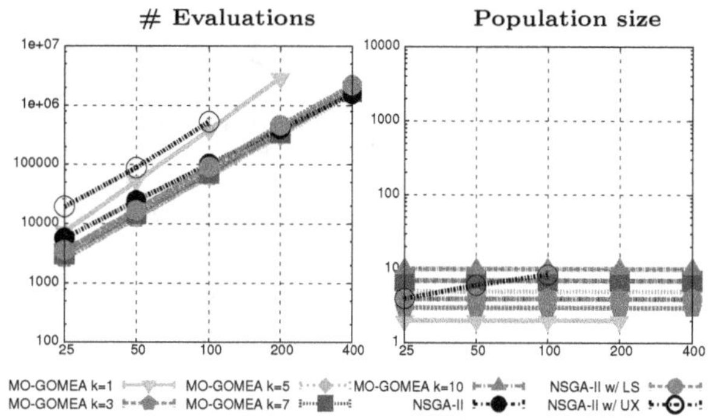

Figure 5: Scalability of MO-GOMEAs with local search and NSGA-IIs on LOTZ. Horizontal axis: problem size.

mutation operator of NSGA-II. It can be inferred from Figure 3 that, e.g. in order to solve LOTZ of 400 bits, NSGA-II needs to be run over than 300,000 generations, waiting for mutation to flip the right bit at the right time to obtain a Pareto-optimal solution. It should further be noted that the two-point crossover operator of NSGA-II has a favorable search bias here because it can preserve and recombine very large substrings of all 1s or all 0s at the beginning and end of a solution. Figure 5 validates this by showing that NSGA-II with uniform crossover performs worse.

LOTZ clearly poses additional challenges, which for MO-GOMEA include finding more appropriate linkage models and filtering useless subsets. However, LOTZ can still be solved fairly efficiently using a simple local search (LS) operator. Following the typical design of genetic local search, we apply LS at the end of every generation on each offspring solution by traversing the variables of a solution in a random order and flipping every variable, followed by a Pareto-improvement check. If a flip does not result in a solution dominated by the previous state nor dominated by the beginning state, it is accepted. Otherwise, it is reverted to the previous state. Figure 5 shows the performance of MO-GOMEA and NSGA-II with this LS. LS greatly improves the performance of MO-GOMEA, but not that of NSGA-II in terms of number of evaluations. These results underline just how beneficial it can be to use a proper LS operator to bring back diversity that might have gotten lost.

4.4 Multi-objective MAXCUT

Although Zeromax - Onemax, Trap-5 - Inverse Trap-5 and LOTZ are interesting benchmark problems with known Pareto-optimal fronts, they are fairly artificial in the sense that the Pareto-optimal fronts always have the shape of a straight line. We therefore also perform experiments the MO-MAXCUT problems where the Pareto-optimal front can be shaped very differently. The convergence graphs in Figure 6 show that for $l = 6$, NSGA-II performs slightly better than MO-GOMEA. For $l = 12$, only NSGA-II 16×, the one with the largest population size, outperforms MO-GOMEA. As the problem size increases however, the picture starts to change. For $l = 25$, only NSGA-II 16× has a convergence result as good as MO-GOMEA with $k = 5, 7$, but it is still outperformed by MO-GOMEA with $k = 10$. For larger problem sizes, $l = 50, 100$, MO-GOMEAs with clustering ($k > 1$) distinctly outperform all NSGA-II instances. The facts that MO-GOMEA with clustering exhibits better convergence for problem sizes $l > 25$ and that the bigger the problem, the wider the performance gap between the various

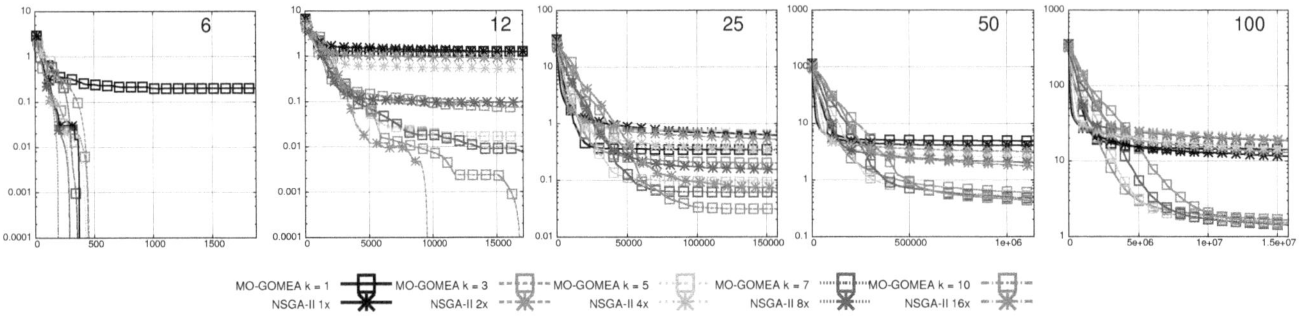

Figure 6: Average performance of instances of MO-GOMEA and instances of NSGA-II on multi-objective MAXCUT problems of different problem sizes. Horizontal axis: number of evaluations (both objectives per evaluation). Vertical axis: $D_{\mathcal{P}_F \to \mathcal{S}}$

MO-GOMEAs $k > 1$ and NSGA-IIs becomes, indicate the intrinsic superior scalability of MO-GOMEA over NSGA-II. MO-GOMEA without clustering ($k = 1$) has performance results relatively the same as those of NSGA-IIs, which do not have clustering either, on most problem sizes ($l > 6$). This emphasizes again the importance of clustering to handle different parts of the Pareto-optimal front separately. Also, although we did not perform bisection to find the minimally required population size for each instance (because the entire true Pareto-optimal front is unknown), it can be inferred, to a certain degree, from MAXCUT $l = 12, 25, 50$ that the more clusters MO-GOMEA have the better the convergence result is. This is because, different from the other benchmark problems, the structures of the objectives may now differ, causing different structures to require to be exploited along the front, which is supported by clustering.

5. CONCLUSIONS

In this paper, we have presented the MO-GOMEA framework. We have shown that for the combination with the LT FOS model, superior scalability for solving different classes of MO optimization problems can be achieved as compared to classic GAs (i.e. NSGA-II) and even state-of-the-art EDAs (i.e. mohBOA). Our experimental results further support that the key features of scalable MO optimizers that we identified and incorporated into MO-GOMEA are indeed responsible for the observed performance. These features are: an elitist archive to keep track of the Pareto front, clustering to process different regions of the Pareto front differently, linkage learning and an efficient mechanism for exploiting the learned linkage relations to generate offspring solutions. An elitist archive, even in a basic implementation, is beneficial for solving MO optimization problems. Clustering and the incorporation of an explicit, dedicated bias for SO optimization embedded in extreme clusters help MO-GOMEA to have better coverage of the Pareto-optimal front and to find extreme solutions more efficiently. Finally, the efficient and effective linkage learning and exploitation contribute to the scalability of MO-GOMEA in solving MO optimization problems. The experimental results have further indicated that diversity loss can easily play an important role in MO optimization and particularly for MO-GOMEA, for which reason diversity improving mechanisms such as mutation and local search should be studied in more detail in the future. Moreover, especially when multiple clusters are used, there is a clear need for filtering superfluous subsets in the FOS models and further improve scalability.

6. REFERENCES

[1] P. A. N. Bosman. The anticipated mean shift and cluster registration in mixture-based edas for multi-objective optimization. In *Proc. of the Genetic and Evolutionary Comp. Conf. - GECCO-2010*, pages 351–358. ACM, 2010.

[2] P. A. N. Bosman and D. Thierens. More concise and robust linkage learning by filtering and combining linkage hierarchies. In *Proc. of the Genetic and Evolutionary Comp. Conf. - GECCO-2013*, pages 359–366. ACM, 2013.

[3] C. Coello Coello, G. Pulido, and E. Montes. Current and future research trends in evolutionary multiobjective optimization. In *Information Processing with Evolutionary Algorithms*, Advanced Information and Knowledge Processing, pages 213–231. Springer London, 2005.

[4] K. Deb. *Multi-Objective Optimization Using Evolutionary Algorithms*. John Wiley & Sons, Inc., NY, USA, 2001.

[5] K. Deb, S. Agrawal, A. Pratap, and T. Meyarivan. A fast and elitist multiobjective genetic algorithm: NSGA-II. *IEEE Trans. on Evol. Computation*, 6(2):182–197, 2002.

[6] I. Gronau and S. Moran. Optimal implementations of UPGMA and other common clustering algorithms. *Information Processing Letters*, 104(6):205 – 210, 2007.

[7] N. Khan, D. E. Goldgerg, and M. Pelikan. Multi-objective bayesian optimization algorithm. IlliGAL Report No. 2002009. Technical report, University of Illinois at Urbana-Champaign, Illinois Genetic Algorithms Laboratory, Urbana, IL, 2002.

[8] J. D. Knowles and D. Corne. Properties of an adaptive archiving algorithm for storing nondominated vectors. *IEEE Trans. on Evol. Computation*, 7(2):100–116, 2003.

[9] M. Laumanns and J. Ocenasek. Bayesian optimization algorithms for multi-objective optimization. In *Parallel Problem Solving from Nature - PPSN VII*, pages 298–307. Springer, 2002.

[10] M. Pelikan, K. Sastry, and D. E. Goldberg. Multiobjective hboa, clustering, and scalability. In *Proc. of the Genetic and Evolutionary Comp. Conf. - GECCO-2005*, pages 663–670. ACM, 2005.

[11] K. Sastry, M. Pelikan, and D. E. Goldberg. Decomposable problems, niching, and scalability of multiobjective estimation of distribution algorithms. IlliGAL Report No. 2005004. Technical report, University of Illinois at Urbana-Champaign, Illinois Genetic Algorithms Laboratory, Urbana, IL, 2005.

[12] D. Thierens and P. A. N. Bosman. Optimal mixing evolutionary algorithms. In *Proceedings of the Genetic and Evolutionary Computation Conference - GECCO-2011*, pages 617–624. ACM, 2011.

[13] E. Zitzler, M. Laumanns, and L. Thiele. SPEA2: Improving the strength pareto evolutionary algorithm for multiobjective optimization. In *Evolutionary Methods for Design, Optimisation, and Control*, pages 95–100. CIMNE, Barcelona, Spain, 2002.

Multimodality and the Linkage-Learning Difficulty of Additively Separable Functions

Jean Martins
Institute of Mathematics and Computer Science
University of São Paulo, Brasil
jean@icmc.usp.br

Alexandre C. B. Delbem
Institute of Mathematics and Computer Science
University of São Paulo, Brasil
acbd@icmc.usp.br

ABSTRACT

Estimation of Distribution Algorithms (EDAs) have emerged from the synergy between machine-learning techniques and *Genetic Algorithms* (GAs). EDAs rely on probabilistic modeling for obtaining information about the underlying structure of optimization problems and implementing effective reproduction operators. The effectiveness of EDAs depends on the capacity of the model-building to extract reliable information about the problem. In this study we analyze additively separable functions and argue that the degree of multimodality of such functions defines their linkage-learning difficulty. Besides, by using entropy-based concepts and Jensen's inequality, we show how *allelic pairwise independence* may appear as a consequence of an increasing multimodality. The results characterize the linkage-learning difficulty of well-known functions, like the deceptive trap, bipolar and concatenated parity.

Categories and Subject Descriptors

G.1.6 [**Optimization**]: Global Optimization—*Estimation of Distribution Algorithms*

Keywords

Linkage-learning, Multimodality, Separable functions

1. INTRODUCTION

Nearly-decomposable systems and hierarchical structures were conceptually interpreted by Holland as an explanation for the performance of *Genetic Algorithms* (GAs) [15, 11]. From these ideas he developed the schema theorem and proposed the *Building-Block* (BB) hypothesis, which was further extended by Goldberg [6, 8]. Holland and Goldberg's theories led to the idea that as optimization problems are complex, their solutions may be composed of interacting substructures that should be considered by GAs in order to increase the efficiency of the search [15, 11].

GECCO'14, July 12–16, 2014, Vancouver, BC, Canada.

http://dx.doi.org/10.1145/2576768.2598281.

A large number of GAs have been developed so that such ideas can be effectively explored. Significant advances have been achieved under the umbrella of *Estimation of Distribution Algorithms* (EDAs) [12], which suggest that information can be extracted from the population of a GA (*Linkage Learning* (LL)) and used to guide the search. Such information is stored by linkage models and represents the statistical dependencies among decision variables. From such models, model-guided crossover or sampling can be performed for the generation of new solutions (see [16] and [14]).

Early studies on EDAs usually assumed the representativity of models as the key point for the effectiveness of EDAs. Therefore, univariate, bivariate and multivariate models were used to develop new EDAs. However, the model-complexity/effectiveness relation did not hold in all experimental results [1, 3]. On the contrary, studies have shown that useful information is hard to be extracted from population statistics and the use of a more complex model not necessarily leads to better results [5].

In recent years some studies have focused on characteristics of problems which impose such limitations on linkage-learning [4]. According to Coffin et al. [3], if separable *Concatenated Parity Functionss* (CPFs) are considered, the *Bayesian Optimization Algorithm* (BOA) [14], a state-of-the-art EDA, shows an exponential scaling. For the CPFs, LL procedures based on bivariate statistics (most of them) cannot find high-order linkages due to the intrinsic *allelic pairwise independence.* On the other hand, Chen et al. [1] showed that the *Compact Genetic Algorithm* (CGA) [9] and the *Extended Compact Genetic Algorithm* (ECGA) [10] can solve both, CPF and the *Concatenated Parity-Trap Functions* (CPTF) in polynomial time. It was argued that BOA's model-building is more susceptible to spurious linkages, which deteriorate its effectiveness as a whole. According to Echegoyen et al. [5], as the degree of interactions between decision variables increases, BOA's capacity to identify linkages deteriorates, proving that the complexity of the model is not sufficient to guarantee the effectiveness of an EDA. Martins and Delbem [13] also showed that, concerning *Multidimensional Knapsack Problems* (MKPs), useful linkages are hard to identify from bivariate statistics, implying low efficiency of the *Linkage Tree Genetic Algorithms* (LTGAs) used in the experiments.

Following this trend, we propose an information-theoretic framework for the analysis of the difficulties of linkage-learning in additively separable functions. We argue that multimodality may be decisive for making linkage-learning difficult. Furthermore, we show how multimodality affects the joint entropy between decision variables and how, in extreme cases, this fact makes linkage-learning mostly infeasible (implying *pairwise independence*). The analysis has shed some light on the importance of hybrid EDAs, i.e. there should be fall-back operators to support the limitations of model-building.

The paper is organized as follows: Section 2 reviews some concepts of information theory and interprets the multimodality from the perspective of linkage-learning; Section 3 describes some assumptions we made on multimodality linkage-learning difficulty and defines separability conditions according to entropy and mutual information; Section 4 describes the additive separable functions to be analyzed and verifies how the degree of multimodality is associated with the difficulty of learning; Section 5 summarizes the paper and draws some conclusions about the results.

2. BACKGROUND

2.1 Information Theory

This section reviews the basic information theory concepts used along the paper. Our aim is to clarify the connections between such theoretical concepts and the practical difficulties and limits faced by entropy-based linkage learning algorithms.

One of the most important concepts in information theory is *entropy*, which measures the uncertainty of a random variable X belonging to an alphabet $\xi = \{0, 1\}$. Denoting the probability of X to assume a value x as

$$p_X(x) = \Pr\{X = x\},\ x \in \xi,$$

the entropy is defined as follows:

DEFINITION 2.1 (ENTROPY). *Entropy $H(X)$ of a discrete random variable X is defined by*

$$H(X) = -\sum_{x \in \mathcal{S}_X} p_X(x) \log_2 p_X(x). \quad (1)$$

where $\mathcal{S}_X$ is the support of X, i.e. $\mathcal{S}_X = \{x \in \xi | p_X(x) > 0\}$.

As we are interested in pairwise measures of linkage, the previous definition must be extended for joint probability distributions and joint entropies:

DEFINITION 2.2 (JOINT ENTROPY). *The joint entropy of a pair of discrete random variables (X, Y) with a joint probability $p_{XY}(x, y)$ is defined by*

$$H(X, Y) = -\sum_{x \in \mathcal{S}_X} \sum_{y \in \mathcal{S}_Y} p_{XY}(x, y) \log_2 p_{XY}(x, y). \quad (2)$$

The joint and conditional entropies are of high importance for the analysis conducted in this paper. They enable the definition of a measure to quantify the amount of information a random variable contains about another, which is called the mutual information.

DEFINITION 2.3 (MUTUAL INFORMATION). *Considering X and Y discrete random variables, the mutual information is defined as*

$$I(X; Y) = H(X) + H(Y) - H(X, Y). \quad (3)$$

The mutual information $I(X; Y) \geq 0$, with equality occurring only if $p_{XY}(x, y) = p_X(x)p_Y(y)$, i.e. X and Y are independent. The mutual information can be used to measure dependence, however it is not strictly a metric and the variation of information is commonly used [16].

DEFINITION 2.4 (VARIATION OF INFORMATION). *The variation of information $VI(X; Y)$ is defined from the joint entropy $H(X, Y)$ and the mutual information $I(X; Y)$, as follows*

$$\begin{aligned} VI(X; Y) &= H(X, Y) - I(X; Y) \\ VI(X; Y) &= 2H(X, Y) - H(X) - H(Y). \quad (4) \end{aligned}$$

The variation of information, $VI(X; Y)$ decreases when $I(X; Y)$ grows, approaching zero for highly dependent variables. Therefore, $VI(X; Y)$ measures dissimilarities between X and Y – the minimum dissimilarity (maximum similarity) occurring when the random variables are identical. Although $VI(X; Y)$ is preferable to be used as a metric (as applied by the LTGA [16]), it can be inferred by $I(X; Y)$ and $H(X, Y)$ values. For simplicity, $I(X; Y)$ and $H(X, Y)$ will be used from now on.

In the next section we use the concepts defined above to describe how multimodality hampers the identification of statistical dependent variables. As statistical dependencies are the core for linkage-learning procedures, they are also useful for the understanding of the difficulties faced in building representative linkage-models.

3. METHODOLOGY

Most EDAs (except those with univariate models) rely on the measurement of statistical dependencies in their model-building step. Using the concepts defined in the previous section, here we describe how multimodality hampers the obtaining of accurate measurements of dependence. For the sake of simplicity, we have restricted the analysis to additive-separable pseudo-boolean functions.

3.1 Observable Separability Conditions

A function is said additively separable if its maximum (minimum) can be computed from the maximum (minimum) value from each m functions f_i, defined in disjoint subsets of $\{x_1, \ldots, x_\ell\}$.

$$f'(\mathbf{x}) = \sum_{i=0}^{m} f_i(x_{i*k}, \ldots, x_{i*k+k-1}),$$

Deceptive functions are well-known examples of separable functions commonly used to benchmark EDAs [8].

Assuming the context defined by separable functions of order k, we will show that as the number of local optima for each function f_i grows, it becomes harder to identify which variables are dependent or not. To illustrate our idea and define a basic separability condition, let us assume $k = 2$, where X and Y are variables from the same sub-function and Z is a variable from a different sub-function. From the mutual information, the correct identification of statistical dependence between X and Z will occur if the following general condition is observed:

$$I(X; Y) > I(X; Z)$$

From Equation (3), it follows that:

$$\begin{aligned} H(X) + H(Y) - H(X, Y) &> H(X) + H(Z) - H(X, Z) \\ H(Y) - H(X, Y) &> H(Z) - H(X, Z). \quad (5) \end{aligned}$$

In the simplest scenario, where all sub-functions f_i are equal, $H(Y) = H(Z)$, therefore:

$$H(X, Y) < H(X, Z). \quad (6)$$

In a linkage-learning procedure based on measures of bivariate statistics, it is clear that (5) and (6) are necessary conditions for a correct modeling, i.e. the pairwise joint entropy should reflect the separability of the fitness function. Besides it is worth noticing that, to a certain extent, they define valid necessary conditions for any linkage-learning algorithm.

3.2 Origins of Linkage-learning Difficulty in Separable Functions

In general, GAs start from a random population and in such a situation inequalities (5)-(6) do not hold. The probability of all possible pairs of values is the same, therefore the joint entropy is maximum and there is no mutual information (see Equation (2)). As selection and reproduction are performed, individuals in regions of better fitness survive, which changes the distribution of solutions in the search space. A decrease in the number of possible values assumed by decision variables is expected, which decreases the joint entropy among decision variables and makes statistical dependencies evident.

However, for some functions, even after selection and reproduction, the decrease in the pairwise joint entropy is too small. Therefore, linkage-learning cannot identify correct (useful) linkages and the search becomes less effective [1, 3].

Figure 1 shows two continuous fitness landscapes used to illustrate the effect of multimodality on linkage-learning. Figure 1(a) is a simple example in which the dependence between X and Y is easily observed. There are only four local attractors and after selection a large part of the search space becomes uninhabited. As a consequence, many pairs of values do not occur in the population, which decreases the joint entropy and increases the mutual information between X and Y. Figure 1(b) illustrates a more complex situation, with a larger number of local attractors. Even after selection, the pairs of values are very diversified, which implies a small decrease in the joint entropy and a more difficult verification of the statistical dependence between X and Y.

These small examples illustrate our basic hypothesis that multimodality imposes serious limitations on linkage-learning due to the difficulty in observing the correct linkages. The remainder of this paper deals with the analysis of different separable functions so as to verify the validity of our hypothesis and understand their consequences on the applicability of linkage-learning in a general black-box scenario.

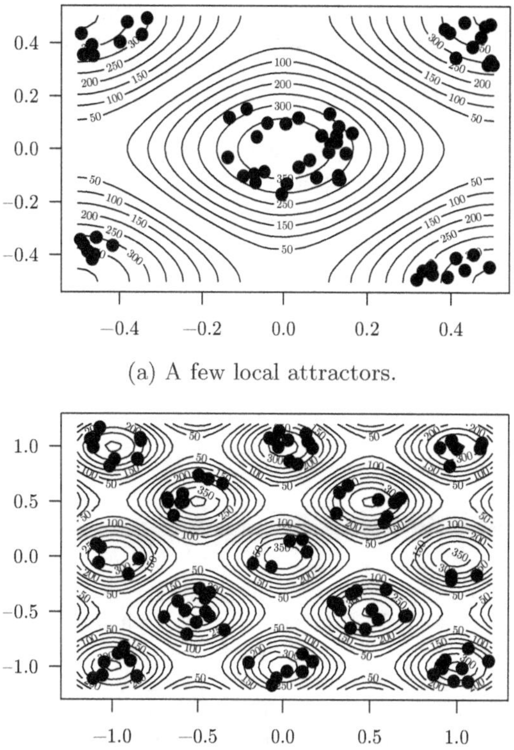

(a) A few local attractors.

(b) Many local attractors.

Figure 1: Population before and after selection. The crowding of solutions around local attractors induces statistical dependencies among decision variables.

4. ANALYSIS OF SEPARABLE FUNCTIONS

$H(X,Y)$ and $H(X,Z)$ were analyzed for different separable functions so as to verify the interpretation given in the previous section [1, 3]. Our validation is based on two criteria. For separable functions based on equal sub-functions we consider a problem easy for linkage-learning if δ_H is large:

$$\begin{aligned} H(X,Y) &< H(X,Z) \\ 0 &< H(X,Z) - H(X,Y) \\ \delta_H &= 1 - H(X,Y)/H(X,Z). \end{aligned} \tag{7}$$

For separable functions based on different sub-functions, like the mk-parity/trap, the same conclusion is based on δ_I:

$$\begin{aligned} I(X;Y) &> I(X;Z) \\ 0 &< I(X;Y) - I(X;Z) \\ \delta_I &= I(X;Y) - I(X;Z). \end{aligned} \tag{8}$$

However, in order to compute δ_H or δ_I, the distribution of pairs (X,Y) (intra-block variables) and (X,Z) (inter-block variables) must be known beforehand. Next sections discusses how to these probability distributions can be assessed.

4.1 Initial Population

The assessment of the probability distributions of decision variables in a population of candidate solutions is a complex task. A way to circumvent this difficulty is to consider a population generated by *deterministic Hill-Climbing* (dHC). From dHC we can simulate a situation in which a number of generations: crossover, mutation and selection steps has been performed. In this stage all disjoint subsets of variables would assume only optimal or local-optimal configurations and the model accuracy would highly influence the progress of the search.

The dHC decreases the intra-block entropy $H(X,Y)$, which improves the accuracy of linkage-models in separable functions in a simple and practical way [16]. Moreover, for being deterministic, we are able to know the real distributions of variables X, Y and Z in the population.

From now on we consider an initial population built as follows:

1. Generates n candidate solutions randomly,
2. Improves each solution by one-pass of dHC.

where dHC is performed from the leftmost variable, as follows: flip the current bit, if the fitness is not improved the bit is flipped back; proceeds until the rightmost variable is evaluated. The use of hill-climbing is known to improve model-building, as shown by Chen et al. [2], therefore we believe that a population built by dHC is realistic in a more general scenario.

4.2 Additive Separable Functions

Additive separable functions can be more easily solved by solving their components instead of attacking the problem as a whole. However, in a black-box context, GAs do not know the components of a separable function and linkage-learning must identify them. It is the role of GAs to mix such components appropriately in order to find better solutions [8]. The additive separable functions considered here are defined as follows:

$$\max f(\mathbf{x}, k),\ \mathbf{x} \in \{0,1\}^{\ell=m\times k}$$

$$f(\mathbf{x}, k) = \sum_{i=0}^{m-1} \texttt{subf}(x_{ki} + \cdots + x_{ki+k-1})$$

and they differ according to the definition of the functions `subf`. Next, we define the `subf` used in each case:

mk-**traps:** The *mk*-trap problem contains one global optimum and one local optimum solution (all-ones and all-zeros, respectively) and is defined as the maximization of a function composed of m components of size k. The fitness of a whole solution $\mathbf{x}$ is given by the summation of the results of each k-trap. Each k-trap takes the number of ones (unitation u) in its respective set of k variables as an argument and returns:

$$trap(u) = \begin{cases} k & \text{if } u = k, \\ k-1-u & \text{otherwise}. \end{cases}$$

Figure 2(a) illustrates the possible outcomes of $trap(u)$ for $k = 5$. There is a high probability that solutions randomly generated will be closer (in Hamming distance) to the suboptimal than the optimal configuration.

mk-**bipolar:** A different situation is observed for the *mk*-bipolar problem with blocks of size $2k$. For an $m = 5, k = 3$ problem, there are 32 global optimum solutions (combinations of all-ones and all-zeros components) and approximately three million local optimum solutions [7]. The k-bipolar function is defined as follows:

$$bipolar(u) = \begin{cases} 1 & \text{if } |u-k| = k, \\ 0.9 & \text{if } |u-k| = 0, \\ 0.8 & \text{if } |u-k| = 1. \end{cases}$$

Figure 2(b) shows the possible outcomes for a 6-bipolar function. Each component has two global optimum configurations and $\binom{6}{3}$ local optimum configurations. In the next sections we show how such difference impacts on linkage-learning and makes the *mk*-bipolar difficult for linkage-learning.

mk-**parity:** Like the *mk*-trap and the *mk*-bipolar, the CPF is also composed of the sum of m separable functions. However, it does not rely on deceptive functions; instead it uses m parity functions, defined as follows:

$$parity(u) = \begin{cases} C_{\text{even}}, & \text{if } u \text{ is even}, \\ C_{\text{odd}}, & \text{otherwise, with } C_{\text{even}} > C_{\text{odd}}. \end{cases}$$

For each parity function of size k, there are 2^{k-1} global optimum configurations, with ones and zeros showing the same probability distribution in a population. Since there are no observable pairwise dependencies, linkage-learning from bivariate statistics cannot identify the k-order dependencies in CPFs [3].

mk-**parity/trap:** This function is composed of concatenated k-parity and k-trap functions. It mixes two different difficulties, i.e. the high multimodality of parity functions with easier bimodal traps. Figure 2(d) illustrates two concatenated sub-functions (each of them contributes individually to the whole fitness).

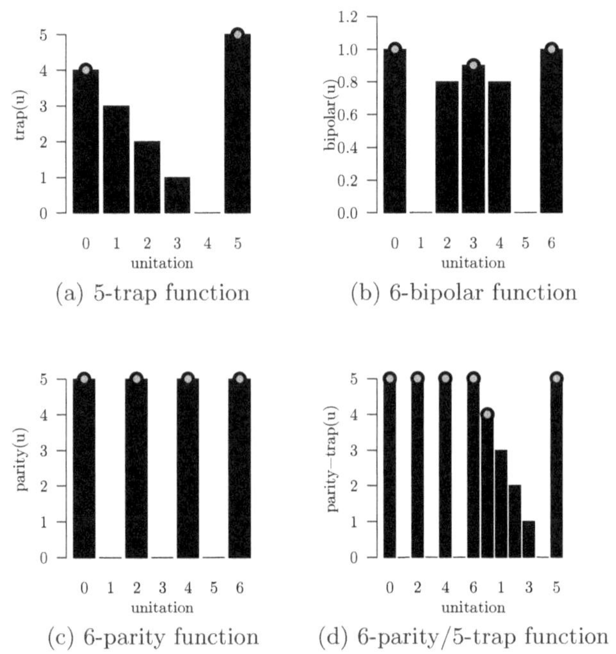

Figure 2: All possible outcomes of a trap function with $k = 5$ (a), a bipolar function with $k = 6$ (b), a parity function with $k = 6$ and a parity/trap function with $k = 6, 5$.

4.3 Probability Distributions after dHC

The dHC is performed on a 1-bit neighborhood. If each separable component is considered individually, their landscapes are similar to those illustrated in Figure 2(a)-2(d). As dHC is a greedy procedure, it will lead each component to different configurations, depending on the starting solution. However, the general result is predictable. The circles in Figures 2(a)-2(d) show the characteristic of all possible components after dHC.

To better understand the effects of dHC, let us describe in details the population used as base. Each component of k

binary variables can initially assume 2^k different configurations. In a random population, each of these configurations occurs with the same probability $1/2^k$. However, after dHC these probabilities change because the number of possible configurations for each pair of variables decreases according to the number of local-optimal.

The marginal and joint probabilities also depend on the number of global and local-optimum for each sub-function. In its general form the probability distribution of decision variables obeys the following equations:

$$\begin{aligned}
p_X(x) &= p_X(x|g) + p_X(x|q) \\
p_{XY}(y|x) &= p_{XY}(y|g \wedge x) + p_{XY}(y|q \wedge x) \\
p_{XY}(x,y) &= p_X(x)p_{XY}(y|x) \\
p_{XZ}(x,z) &= p_X(x)p_Z(z)
\end{aligned}$$

where g and q are, respectively, the probability of global and local optimal configurations. Next we describe the probability distributions after dHC for each of the functions previously defined:

k-trap: In a random population, the global optimal configuration for a k-trap function occurs with probability $1/2^k$. After dHC, configuration 01111 (for $k = 5$) will also become optimal, therefore, the global optimal configuration occurs with probability $g_t = 2/2^k$. Inversely, the probability of a local optimal configuration is $q_t = 1 - g_t$ and the probability distributions are defined by

$$\begin{aligned}
p_X(1) &= g_t \times 1 + q_t \times 0 = g_t \\
p_X(0) &= g_t \times 0 + q_t \times 1 = q_t \\
p_{XY}(1,1) &= g_t \times (1+0) = g_t \\
p_{XY}(1,0) &= g_t \times (0+0) = 0 \\
p_{XY}(0,1) &= q_t \times (0+0) = 0 \\
p_{XY}(0,0) &= q_t \times (0+1) = q_t
\end{aligned}$$

For k-trap, the multimodality does not depend on k, i.e. as k increases, the number of global and local-optimum is the same and equals 2.

k-bipolar: In this case, two global optimal configurations can be randomly generated, 000000 and 111111 (for $k = 3$) and two configurations which will become optimal after dHC, 100000 and 011111. Therefore, the global-optimum probability is $g_b = 4/2^{2k}$ and the local-optimum probability is $q_b = 1 - p_b$, from which the probability distributions are defined by

$$\begin{aligned}
p_X(1) &= g_b \times \frac{1}{2} + q_b \times \frac{k}{2k} = \frac{1}{2}(g_b + q_b) = \frac{1}{2} \\
p_X(0) &= p_X(1) \\
p_{XY}(1,1) &= \frac{1}{2} \times \left(g_b \frac{1}{2} \times 1 + q_b \times \frac{k-1}{2k-1}\right) \\
p_{XY}(1,0) &= \frac{1}{2} \times \left(g_b \frac{1}{2} \times 0 + q_b \times \frac{k}{2k-1}\right) \\
p_{XY}(0,1) &= p_{XY}(1,0) \\
p_{XY}(0,0) &= p_{XY}(1,1)
\end{aligned}$$

For k-bipolar, the multimodality depends on k and as k increases the number of global and local-optimum grows as $2 + \binom{2k}{k}$.

k-parity: For this function all configurations with even unitation are global optimal and there are no local optimal configurations, therefore, $g_p = 1$ and $q_p = 0$. In other words, for a block of size k, there are 2^{k-1} possible optimum configurations after dHC. Considering situations with even unitations, i.e. $u = 2i$, with $i = 0, 1, \ldots, \lfloor \frac{k}{2} \rfloor$, this condition provides:

$$\begin{aligned}
p_X(1) &= \frac{1}{2^{k-1}} \sum_{i=0}^{\lfloor \frac{k}{2} \rfloor} \binom{k}{2i} \frac{2i}{k} = \frac{1}{2} \\
p_X(0) &= \frac{1}{2^{k-1}} \sum_{i=0}^{\lfloor \frac{k}{2} \rfloor} \binom{k}{k-2i} \frac{k-2i}{k} = \frac{1}{2} \\
p_{XY}(1,1) &= \frac{1}{2} \times \sum_{i=1}^{\lfloor \frac{k}{2} \rfloor} \binom{k}{2i} \frac{2i}{k} = \frac{1}{4} \\
p_{XY}(1,0) &= \frac{1}{2} \times \sum_{i=1}^{\lfloor \frac{k}{2} \rfloor} \binom{k}{k-2i} \frac{k-2i}{k} = \frac{1}{4} \\
p_{XY}(0,1) &= p_{XY}(1,0) \\
p_{XY}(0,0) &= p_{XY}(1,1)
\end{aligned}$$

From the series defined for $p_X(1)$, all the other results can be derived by symmetry. For k-parity, the multimodality depends on k and as k increases, the number of global and local-optimum grows exponentially as 2^{k-1}.

k-parity/trap: The probability distribution for this concatenated function is defined from the distributions of its components, described above.

These functions constitute different levels of multimodality, therefore, by analyzing conditions (5)-(6) we can understand how multimodality affects δ_H, δ_I and the difficulty of linkage-learning.

4.4 Verifying the Separability Condition

From the probability distributions defined in the previous section, we can assess δ_H and δ_I in order to compare the difficulties from the perspective of linkage-learning. A large δ_H (δ_I) implies that the separable function in question is easy to be correctly modeled. This section shows the δ_I for all functions previously described, with a fixed k. After that, different values for k are considered and their influence on the learning difficulty of those functions is demonstrated.

To compute δ_I, values $H(X,Y)$ and $H(X,Z)$ are required for all functions. They can be obtained from the probability distributions, as follows:

δ_{I_t} (6-trap): Considering $k = 6$, $g_t = 2/2^6 = 0.03125$ and $q_t = 0.96875$, one has:

$$\begin{aligned}
H(X,Y) &= -g_t \log_2 g_t - q_t \log_2 q_t = 0.2006223 \\
I(X;Y) &= H(X) + H(Y) - H(X,Y) = 0.2006223 \\
H(X,Z) &= -g_t^2 \log_2 g_t^2 - g_t q_t \log_2 g_t q_t - q_t^2 \log_2 q_t^2 \\
&= 0.4012446 \\
I(X;Z) &= H(X) + H(Z) - H(X,Z) \\
&= 0.2006223 + 0.2006223 - 0.4012446 = 0 \\
\delta_{I_t} &= I(X;Y) - I(X;Z) = \mathbf{0.2006223}
\end{aligned}$$

δ_{I_b} **(3-bipolar):** Considering $k = 3$, $g_b = 4/2^6 = 0.0625$ and $q_b = 0.9375$, one has:

$$\begin{aligned}
H(X,Y) &= -2p_{XY}(1,1)\log_2 p_{XY}(1,1) \\
&\quad - 2p_{XY}(1,0)\log_2 p_{XY}(1,0) = 1.989727 \\
I(X;Y) &= H(X) + H(Y) - H(X,Y) \\
&= 1 + 1 - 1.989727 = 0.010273 \\
H(X,Z) &= -2p_X(1)^2 \log_2 p_X(1)^2 \\
&\quad - 2p_X(1)p_Z(0)\log_2 p_X(1)p_Z(0) = 2 \\
I(X;Z) &= H(X) + H(Z) - H(X,Z) \\
&= 1 + 1 - 2 = 0 \\
\delta_{I_b} &= I(X;Y) - I(X;Z) = \mathbf{0.010273}
\end{aligned}$$

δ_{I_p} **(6-parity):** Considering $k = 6$, $g_b = 1$ and $q_b = 0$, one has:

$$\begin{aligned}
H(X,Y) &= -2p_{XY}(1,1)\log_2 p_{XY}(1,1) \\
&\quad - 2p_{XY}(1,0)\log_2 p_{XY}(1,0) = 2 \\
I(X;Y) &= H(X) + H(Y) - H(X,Y) = 0 \\
H(X,Z) &= -2p_X(1)^2 \log_2 p_X(1)^2 \\
&\quad - 2p_X(1)p_Z(0)\log_2 p_X(1)p_Z(0) = 2 \\
I(X;Z) &= H(X) + H(Z) - H(X,Z) = 0 \\
\delta_{I_p} &= I(X;Y) - I(X;Z) = \mathbf{0}
\end{aligned}$$

$\delta_{I_{pt}}$ **(6-parity/trap):** Considering $k = 6$, X, Y variables from a trap function and Z a variable from a parity function. As two different functions are considered, we use δ_I

$$\begin{aligned}
I(X;Y) &= H(X) + H(Y) - H(X,Y) = 0.2006223 \\
H(X,Z) &= -p_X(0)p_Z(0)\log_2 p_X(0)p_Z(0) \\
&\quad - p_X(0)p_Z(1)\log_2 p_X(0)p_Z(1) \\
&\quad - p_X(1)p_Z(0)\log_2 p_X(1)p_Z(0) \\
&\quad - p_X(1)p_Z(1)\log_2 p_X(1)p_Z(1) = 1.200622 \\
I(X;Z) &= H(X) + H(Z) - H(X,Z) \\
&= 0.2006223 + 1 - 1.200622 = 0 \\
\delta_{I_{pt}} &= I(X;Y) - I(X;Z) = \mathbf{0.2006223}
\end{aligned}$$

Comparing the δ_H (δ_I) values, the difficulty in learning each of these functions is evident. The separability of the 6-trap is easy to learn from an appropriate population, i.e. variables X and Z will be wrongly considered as statistically dependent with a low probability. In fact, from the perspective of learning, k-trap is one of the easiest functions; after dHC each of the sub-functions assume only two different configurations, which implies a large decrease in the intra-block entropy.

For k-bipolar, on the other hand, such a decrease is very different. Since there are $\binom{2k}{k}$ possible configurations for the k decision variables, even after dHC, δ_{I_b} will be very small making difficult to identify the linkages with a certain confidence.

The situation is even worse for the k-parity function. Half of the 2^k configurations are possible after dHC and $\delta_{I_p} = 0$, which demonstrates the pairwise independence of intra-block variables, also shown by Coffin and Smith [3]. From the perspective of linkage-learning based on pairwise dependencies, learning the k-order dependencies of the parity function is infeasible.

The $\delta_{I_{pt}}$ for 6-parity/trap function confirms the results for the 6-parity and the 6-trap. In fact, it is easy to learn that variables from a trap function are dependent and variables from parity functions are pairwise-independent, which makes $\delta_{I_{pt}} = \delta_{I_t}$. Instead, if we had chosen X and Y from parity and Z from trap, then $\delta_{I_{pt}} = \delta_{I_p}$.

Figure 3 illustrates how δ_I values behave according to k. A large δ_I means that it is easy to identify linked variables. In summary, the difficulties in learning trap functions and parity/trap functions are the same, while the bipolar is harder to learn and the parity linkage-learning is infeasible ($\delta_I = 0$). For k-bipolar, as k grows, the number of configurations with fitness zero also grows, this fact decreases the accuracy of our model, as shown in Figure 3. However, as for $k = 3$ (the most common value used in literature) model and experiments agree, i.e. the discrepancy shown do not affect our conclusions.

As the search advances, some configurations might be lost, which decreases the intra-block entropy $H(X,Y)$ and increases the mutual information $I(X;Y)$. If all local optimal configurations have the same fitness contribution, this loss of diversity does not hampers the search, i.e. some configurations are lost but the global optimal can still be found by *mixing*. However, in more complex problems, pairwise independence can impose serious difficulties for EDAs.

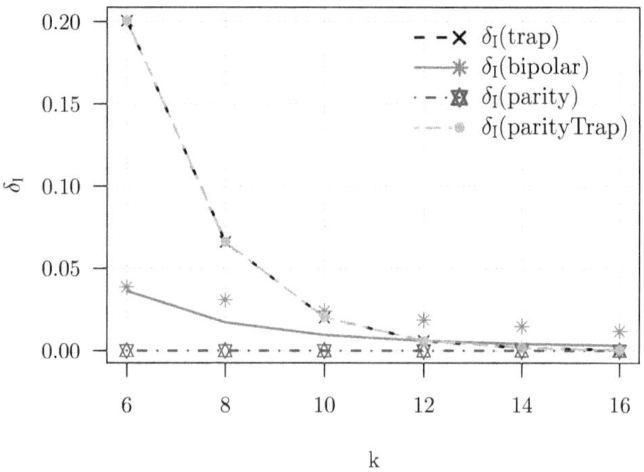

Figure 3: A correct linkage identification is harder for larger values of k, as shown by the decreasing δ_I. Additionally, k-bipolar is harder to learn than the k-trap and k-parity/trap, while the k-parity shows pairwise independence.

Figure 4 shows δ_H for all functions except parity/trap. Since δ_H is normalized we can see how k affects the difficulty of learning. As k-traps always have the same degree of multimodality, their difficulty does not increase with k. For k-bipolar and k-parity, on the other hand, the difficulty increases and very fast $\delta_H \approx 0$.

4.5 Using Jensen's Inequality Upper-bounds

Although the analysis above has correctly shown the differences in the difficulty in learning mk-traps and mk-bipolar functions, it is hard to extrapolate it for more general problems, because the real probability distributions are used in the calculation of the entropies.

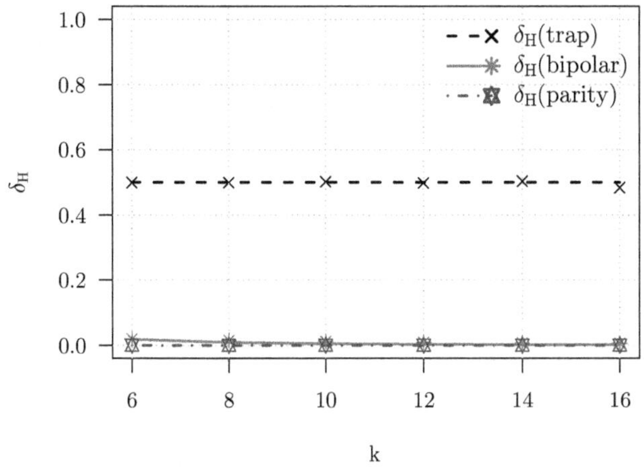

Figure 4: δ_H shows that the k-trap learning difficulty is stable as k grows. The same does not occurs for k-bipolar, whose degree of multimodality also depends on k.

In this section we show that, at the expense of some accuracy, entropy upper-bounds can also be used to infer δ_I, which facilitates the analysis of a larger class of separable functions. From Jensen's inequality, it follows that:

$$H(X) = \sum_{x \in \mathcal{S}_X} p_X(x) \log_2 \frac{1}{p_X(x)} \leq \log_2 \left(\sum_{x \in \mathcal{S}_X} p_X(x) \frac{1}{p_X(x)} \right)$$

where the right-hand side is the logarithm of a summation. This summation adds one for each value x with $p_X(x) > 0$, which results in an upper-bound in the entropy. Therefore, using the upper-bound given by the Jensen's inequality we need to know only the size of the support of (X, Y) and (X, Z), the conclusions become much easier. Let us repeat the analysis using this upper-bound. For simplicity, we use δ_I for the k-parity/trap and δ_H for all the other functions.

δ_{H_t} **(k-trap):** In mk-trap functions, after dHC has been performed, there are only two configurations in the population, i.e. blocks of $000000_{k=6}$, $111111_{k=6}$, therefore all the other $2^k - 2$ configurations have zero probability of occurrence. Using Jensen's inequality we can conclude:

$$H(X, Y) \leq \log_2(2) = 1.$$

Considering the inter-block entropy, all pair of values can occur, therefore the upper-bound is given by

$$H(X, Z) \leq \log_2(2^2) = 2,$$

from which we can conclude

$$\delta_H = 1 - H(X, Y)/H(X, Z) = 0.5,$$

which is the same normalized value previously obtained.

δ_{H_b} **(k-bipolar):** The conclusions are very similar if 6-bipolar functions are considered. In this case, there are 2 optimal, plus $\binom{6}{3} = 20$ local-optimum intra-block configurations, from which pair (X, Y) can assume any values. As the inter-block variables (X, Z) can also assume any pair of values:

$$(H(X, Y) = H(X, Z)) \leq \log_2(2^2) = 2,$$
$$\delta_H = 1 - H(X, Y)/H(X, Z) = \mathbf{0}.$$

In this case $\delta_H = 0$ and differently from the previous result only an approximation is obtained. However, we come to the same conclusion previously achieved, i.e. k-bipolar is harder than k-traps, considering linkage-learning of variables X, Y and Z.

δ_{H_p} **(k-parity):** The parity function is in the limit of separability, i.e. although there are well-defined blocks, they are not identifiable by low-order statistics. There are 2^{k-1} different possible configurations (all optimal, with even unitation) and no decreasing of intra-block entropy after dHC. Therefore, there is no mutual information and no way to discern dependent from independent variables. Using Jensen's inequality, the joint entropy between any pair of variables is limited above by:

$$(H(X, Y) = H(X, Z)) \leq \log_2(2^2) = 2,$$
$$\delta_H = 1 - H(X, Y)/H(X, Z) = \mathbf{0}.$$

However, it does not mean there are no higher-order linkages. For example, assume $k - 1$ dependencies are already known, composing a block called A. We need to decide which variable is dependent to this group. If we choose the correct variable Y, the number of possible configurations is 2^{k-1}, therefore:

$$H(AY) \leq \log_2(2^{k-1}) = k - 1$$

On the other hand, if we choose a wrong variable Z, the exact number of possible configurations is not known exactly, but it is surely $2^{k-1+\epsilon}$, with $\epsilon \in \mathbb{R}^+$, therefore:

$$H(AZ) \leq \log_2(2^{k-1+\epsilon}) = (k - 1 + \epsilon)$$

Since $H(AY) < H(AZ)$ in this case, δ_{H_p} would be greater than zero, which shows that, in fact, there are k-order linkages although there are no pairwise dependencies.

$\delta_{I_{pt}}$ **(k-parity/trap):** the concatenated parity/trap function is very similar to the trap. Assuming X, Y from a trap and Z from a parity function, there would be 2 possible configurations for (X, Y), therefore:

$$H(X, Y) \leq \log_2(2^1) = 1.$$

On the other hand, there would be $2 \times 2 = 2^2$ configurations for pair (X, Z), implying:

$$H(X, Z) \leq \log_2(2^2) = 2.$$

Consequently,

$$\delta_{I_{pt}} = H(Y) - H(X, Y) - H(Z) + H(X, Z)$$
$$= 1 - 1 - 1 + 2 = 1$$

and we conclude that it is easy to learn that variables from trap sub-functions are statistically dependent, while variables from parity function are not. It is also easy to see that if, instead, we had considered X and Y from a parity function and Z from a trap function, the situation would have been the opposite, with $\delta I_{pt} = 0$.

5. CONCLUSIONS

This paper addressed the use of concepts from information theory for the analysis of the limitations of linkage-learning. We argued that an increasing multimodality can lead to an observable allelic pairwise independence even in additively separable functions.

Using mutual information and joint entropy as references, we specified the necessary condition which makes the learning of bivariate dependencies feasible. This condition considers the degree of interactions among intra-block and inter-block variables, according to the probability distributions observed in the population. It was shown that additive separable functions composed of different sub-functions imply different degrees of observable separability, measured by δ_H and δ_I.

From these quantities, different benchmark functions, with different degrees of multimodality were compared according to their linkage-learning difficulty. The results clearly showed that the k-trap was the easiest functions for linkage-learning, followed by k-parity/trap and k-bipolar. We also confirmed that the learning of k-parity functions from bivariate statistics was infeasible due to its intrinsic allelic pairwise independence. Pairwise independence between decision variables may be very common in discrete optimization problems, where, besides multimodality, overlapping interactions strongly influence the variables' values in a population.

For a future analysis of more general problems, we also showed how entropy upper-bounds obtained by Jensen's inequality provide an easier way to approximate δ_H or δ_I. No true probability distributions are required in the analysis, but only the knowledge on the cardinality of the support of the random variables involved.

In a wide perspective, we have supported the idea that EDAs may have serious limitations on their capacity of learning in binary optimization problems. Fortunately, as in the case of parity functions, there must be ways to circumvent such difficulties. We believe, hybridization must be taken into account in order to guarantee that EDAs work when linkage-models are not reliable. EDAs like the LTGA, already exploits such an idea and even when only inaccurate linkage-models are available, the search can still progress. In future studies we aim at extending these ideas, analyzing how non-separable additive functions are related with multi-objective problems and how hybridization can contribute with model-based GAs.

Acknowledgments

The authors are indebted to *São Paulo Research Foundation* (FAPESP) for the financial support provided for this research (process number 2011/07792-4).

6. REFERENCES

[1] S.-C. Chen and T.-L. Yu. Difficulty of Linkage Learning in Estimation of Distribution Algorithms. In *Proceedings of the 11th Annual Conference on Genetic and Evolutionary Computation*, GECCO '09, pages 397–404, New York, NY, USA, 2009. ACM.

[2] W.-M. Chen, C.-Y. Hsu, T.-L. Yu, and W.-C. Chien. Effects of Discrete Hill Climbing on Model Building for Estimation of Distribution Algorithms. In *Proceeding of the Fifteenth Annual Conference on Genetic and Evolutionary Computation Conference*, GECCO '13, pages 367–374, New York, NY, USA, 2013. ACM.

[3] D. J. Coffin and R. E. Smith. The limitations of distribution sampling for linkage learning. In *Evolutionary Computation, 2007. CEC 2007. IEEE Congress on*, pages 364–369, 2007.

[4] C. Echegoyen, A. Mendiburu, R. Santana, and J. A. Lozano. On the Taxonomy of Optimization Problems Under Estimation of Distribution Algorithms. *Evol. Comput.*, 21(3):471–495, Sept. 2013.

[5] C. Echegoyen, Q. Zhang, A. Mendiburu, R. Santana, and J. Lozano. On the limits of effectiveness in estimation of distribution algorithms. In *Evolutionary Computation (CEC), 2011 IEEE Congress on*, pages 1573–1580, 2011.

[6] D. Goldberg. *Genetic algorithms in search, optimization, and machine learning.* Addison-wesley, 1989.

[7] D. Goldberg. Massive Multimodality, Deception, and Genetic Algorithms. *Parallel Problem Solving from Nature*, 2:37–46, 1992.

[8] D. Goldberg. *The design of innovation: Lessons from and for competent genetic algorithms.* Springer, 2002.

[9] G. Harik, F. Lobo, and D. Goldberg. The compact genetic algorithm. *Evolutionary Computation, IEEE Transactions on*, 3(4):287–297, nov 1999.

[10] G. Harik, F. Lobo, and K. Sastry. Linkage learning via probabilistic modeling in the extended compact genetic algorithm (ecga). *Scalable Optimization via Probabilistic Modeling*, pages 39–61, 2006.

[11] J. Holland. *Adaptation in natural and artificial systems.* MIT Press Cambridge, MA, USA, 1975.

[12] P. Larrañaga and J. Lozano. *Estimation of distribution algorithms: a new tool for evolutionary computation.* Springer Netherlands, 2002.

[13] J. P. Martins and A. C. B. Delbem. The Influence of Linkage-learning in the Linkage-tree GA when Solving Multidimensional Knapsack Problems. In *Proceeding of the Fifteenth Annual Conference on Genetic and Evolutionary Computation Conference*, GECCO '13, pages 821–828, New York, NY, USA, 2013. ACM.

[14] M. Pelikan. Bayesian Optimization Algorithm. In *Hierarchical Bayesian Optimization Algorithm*, volume 170 of *Studies in Fuzziness and Soft Computing*, pages 31–48. Springer Berlin / Heidelberg, 2005. 10.1007/978-3-540-32373-0_3.

[15] H. Simon. *The sciences of the artificial.* the MIT Press, 1996.

[16] D. Thierens and P. A. Bosman. Optimal Mixing Evolutionary Algorithms. In *Proceedings of the 13th Annual Conference on Genetic and Evolutionary Computation*, GECCO '11, pages 617–624, New York, NY, USA, 2011. ACM.

Comparison-Based Natural Gradient Optimization in High Dimension

Youhei Akimoto
Faculty of Engineering, Shinshu University
y_akimoto@shinshu-u.ac.jp

Anne Auger
INRIA, Research centre Saclay – Île-de-France
anne.auger@lri.fr

Nikolaus Hansen
INRIA, Research centre Saclay – Île-de-France
nikolaus.hansen@lri.fr

ABSTRACT

We propose a novel natural gradient based stochastic search algorithm, VD-CMA, for the optimization of high dimensional numerical functions. The algorithm is comparison-based and hence invariant to monotonic transformations of the objective function. It adapts a multivariate normal distribution with a restricted covariance matrix with twice the dimension as degrees of freedom, representing an arbitrarily oriented long axis and additional axis-parallel scaling. We derive the different components of the algorithm and show linear internal time and space complexity. We find empirically that the algorithm adapts its covariance matrix to the inverse Hessian on convex-quadratic functions with an Hessian with one short axis and different scaling on the diagonal. We then evaluate VD-CMA on test functions and compare it to different methods. On functions covered by the internal model of VD-CMA and on the Rosenbrock function, VD-CMA outperforms CMA-ES (having quadratic internal time and space complexity) not only in internal complexity but also in number of function calls with increasing dimension.

Categories and Subject Descriptors

G.1.6 [**Numerical Analysis**]: Optimization—*Global optimization, Gradient methods, Unconstrained optimization*; F.2.1 [**Analysis of Algorithms and Problem Complexity**]: Numerical Algorithms and Problems

Keywords

Covariance Matrix Adaptation, Natural Gradient, Hessian Matrix, Information Geometric Optimization, Theory

1. INTRODUCTION

Natural gradients, popularized in the context of machine learning by Amari [3], have been applied with success in various contexts like training of multilayer perceptron [4], variational inference [13], reinforcement learning [15, 16] or black-box optimization [14, 21]. In the setting of black-box optimization, given a family of probability distributions P_θ, a stochastic search algorithm is defined by an iterative update on P_θ. (This update should lead to convergence of P_θ towards a Dirac-delta distribution concentrated on optima of f.) The natural gradient can be elegantly used to define this update. Indeed, the original minimization problem of finding $\arg\min_{x\in\mathbb{R}^d} f(x)$ can be transformed into a joint optimization problem defined on Θ equipped with the Fisher metric. The joint problem can simply be minimization of the expectation of f over P_θ [7,21]. However this latter criterion is not invariant under monotonic transformations of f and can easily lead to unstable behavior. In order to achieve an invariant algorithm, a better choice for the joint problem is $\arg\max_{\theta\in\Theta} J(\theta)$ with $J(\theta) := \int_{x\in\mathbb{R}^d} W \circ f(x)\,\mathrm{d}P_\theta$, where $W \circ f$ is a θ-dependent rank-preserving transformation of f. The joint problem J is strictly comparison-based (or solely based on the f-ranks) and therefore invariant to monotonic transformations of f (see below for the precise definition) [5]. The natural gradient of $J(\theta)$, estimated by Monte Carlo samples from P_θ, governs the update of θ.

In contrast to some settings in machine learning where it is required to *estimate* the Fisher information matrix (FIM) and perform a numerical inversion in order to compute the natural gradient (e.g. for multi-layer perceptrons, see [4] for a discussion), in our context the inverse FIM can be explicitly derived provided a statistical model with known FIM is used. Consequently, efficient comparison-based optimization algorithms using natural gradients can be derived [1,5,7]. Interestingly, the covariance matrix adaptation evolution strategy (CMA-ES) [9, 10, 20]—a state-of-the-art evolutionary algorithm for continuous optimization—derives from the natural gradient framework sketched above when using the family of Gaussian distributions [1,5]. The CMA-ES algorithm was however introduced independently of the natural gradient approach.

The CMA-ES parametrizes a Gaussian model with full covariance matrix, i.e. θ encodes a mean vector and full covariance matrix. It achieves invariance to general linear transformation of the search space. However in consequence, its space complexity and its internal time complexity per f-call are quadratic (see details below). For optimizing functions in higher dimensions, quadratic scaling becomes quickly too time consuming and linear scaling is desirable. To achieve linear scaling, several "variants" of CMA-ES have been proposed compromising on the general invariance to linear transformation: sep-CMA [18] restricts C to a diagonal matrix, MVA [17] and R1-NES [19] parameterize C by

GECCO'14, July 12–16, 2014, Vancouver, BC, Canada.

ACM 978-1-4503-2662-9/14/07 ...$15.00.
http://dx.doi.org/10.1145/2576768.2598258.

$I + vv^{\mathrm{T}}$. We propose here a novel comparison-based algorithm with linear time and space complexity derived from the natural gradient. Instead of a full covariance matrix, we parametrize the covariance matrix as $D(I + vv^{\mathrm{T}})D$ where D is a diagonal matrix of size d and v a vector in $\mathbb{R}^d$. The parameter update follows the natural gradient and two further techniques from CMA-ES are borrowed: an evolution path that low pass filters the change of the distribution mean (additionally used for the natural gradient update) and cumulative step-size adaptation, based on a similar idea. Both mechanisms enhance the performance of CMA-ES considerably [8].

The reminder of the paper is organized as follows. Section 2 is devoted to the introduction to the IGO framework and the CMA-ES. In section 3, we derive the novel linear time and space algorithm from the IGO framework combined with the cumulation concept borrowed from the CMA-ES. The proposed method is called VD-CMA. In section 4, we compare VD-CMA with the CMA-ES on a standard benchmark testbed, both in terms of function evaluations and cpu time. It is also compared with other linear time variants of evolution strategies. We conclude this paper with summary and further discussion in Section 5.

2. INFORMATION GEOMETRIC OPTIMIZATION AND CMA-ES

Information Geometric Optimization (IGO) is a general framework for optimization in arbitrary search spaces. IGO is based on invariance and consequently leads to comparison and natural gradient based optimization algorithms [5]. We give now some background about IGO, explain how parts of the CMA-ES algorithm are instantiations of IGO on the family of Gaussian distributions and detail other important concepts of CMA-ES that we borrow to construct our novel algorithm. While the IGO framework applies to arbitrary search spaces, we describe it conveniently on $\mathbb{R}^d$.

2.1 Information Geometric Optimization

Given an objective function to be minimized, $f : \mathbb{R}^d \mapsto \mathbb{R}$, and a family of probability distributions, P_θ on $\mathbb{R}^d$ with $\theta \in \Theta$, equipped with the Fisher metric, a joint optimization problem is defined on Θ as the maximization of the expectation $J(\theta)$ of a nonlinear scaling W of the objective function f over P_θ. More specifically, we consider at a given iteration t the current parameter θ^t and define $W^f_{\theta^t}(x) := w\big(q^f_{\theta^t}(f(x))\big)$, where $w : [0, 1] \to \mathbb{R}$ is a non-increasing function and $q^f_{\theta^t}(\bar{f})$ is the probability of sampling a point from the current distribution given θ^t into the sub level set $\{x \in \mathbb{R}^d : f(x) \leq \bar{f}\}$, defined as $q^f_{\theta^t}(\bar{f}) := \int_{f(x)\leq\bar{f}} p_{\theta^t}(x)\,\mathrm{d}x$. Hence, the function J also depends on θ (denoted by J_{θ^t} in the sequel) and is defined as $J_{\theta^t}(\theta) := \int_{\mathbb{R}^d} W^f_{\theta^t}(x) p_\theta(x)\,\mathrm{d}x$. This q-quantile based transformation of f is invariant under monotonic transformations of f and leads to comparison-based algorithms that show the same performance on f as on any increasing transformation of f, e.g., $f(x) = a\|x\|^b + c$ is equivalent for all $a, b > 0$ and $c \in \mathbb{R}$. The IGO update consists in the gradient ascent step

$$\theta^{t+\delta t} = \theta^t + \delta t \tilde{\nabla} J_{\theta^t}(\theta)|_{\theta=\theta^t} \tag{1}$$

where $\tilde{\nabla} J_{\theta^t}(\theta)$ is the natural gradient of J_{θ^t} given by the product of the inverse of the FIM[1] $\mathcal{I}^{-1}(\theta)$ and the vanilla gradient $\nabla J_{\theta^t}(\theta)$. The gradient $\nabla J_{\theta^t}(\theta)$ is computed with the log-likelihood trick

$$\nabla J_{\theta^t}(\theta) = \int_{\mathbb{R}^d} W^f_{\theta^t}(x)\big(\nabla \ln p_\theta(x)\big) p_\theta(x)\,\mathrm{d}x \ . \tag{2}$$

The update (1) requires to evaluate the integral (2). This integral is naturally estimated by a Monte-Carlo method with λ samples drawn from the current distribution P_{θ^t}. Given a set of λ independent samples $x_i \sim P_{\theta^t}$, for $i = 1, \dots, \lambda$, the quantile function $q^f_{\theta^t}(f(x_i))$ is approximated by $(\mathrm{rk}(x_i) + 1/2)/\lambda$, with $\mathrm{rk}(x_i)$ the ranking of $f(x_i)$ among the λ samples, namely, $\mathrm{rk}(x_i) := |\{j : f(x_j) \leq f(x_i)\}|$. Hence $W^f_{\theta^t}(x_i)$ is approximated by $w_{\mathrm{rk}(x_i)} := w((\mathrm{rk}(x_i) + 1/2)/\lambda)$. With $w_i := w((i + 1/2)/\lambda)/\lambda$, the IGO algorithm update reads

$$\begin{aligned}\theta^{t+\delta t} - \theta^t &= \delta t \mathcal{I}^{-1}(\theta^t) \textstyle\sum_{i=1}^{\lambda} w_{\mathrm{rk}(x_i)} \nabla \ln p_{\theta^t}(x_i) \\ &= \delta t \mathcal{I}^{-1}(\theta^t) \textstyle\sum_{i=1}^{\lambda} w_i \nabla \ln p_{\theta^t}(x_{i:\lambda}) \ ,\end{aligned} \tag{3}$$

where $x_{i:\lambda}$ denotes the ith best point ranked according to f.

2.2 The CMA-ES Algorithm

The CMA-ES algorithm [9, 10, 20], considered as state-of-the-art method for stochastic numerical optimization, was recently found to derive from the natural gradient, and more precisely from the IGO framework described in the previous section [1, 5]. For CMA-ES, P_θ is the family of Gaussian distributions $\mathcal{N}(m, \sigma^2 C)$ parametrized with a mean vector $m \in \mathbb{R}^d$ and a covariance matrix $\sigma^2 C$, with $\sigma \in \mathbb{R}_>$ the so-called global step-size, and $C \in \mathbb{R}^{d\times d}$ a positive-definite symmetric matrix. Because Gaussian distributions are considered, the FIM and its inverse are well known and the IGO update (1) can be computed analytically [1]. The update of $\theta = (m, \sigma, C)$ in CMA-ES combines different ideas. The update of m and C uses the natural gradient as prescribed by the IGO algorithm (3), however also using the so-called cumulation concept that smoothens and accelerates this update without compromising its stability [8]. Then, different learning rates (corresponding to the step-size δt of the gradient ascent step) for the mean and the covariance matrix updates are used. Last, the global step-size σ is independently adapted in order to accelerate the search performance and prevent premature convergence.

We give in the sequel a compact but thorough definition of the CMA-ES algorithm. After the initialization of m, σ and $C = I$ and so-called evolution paths $p_\sigma = p_C = 0 \in \mathbb{R}^d$, the CMA-ES repeats the following steps until a termination criterion is satisfied.

Step 1. Matrix Decomposition. Compute the square root $\sqrt{C}$ of C, where $\sqrt{C}$ is symmetric and positive-definite, and satisfies $C = \sqrt{C}\sqrt{C}$.

Step 2. Sampling, Evaluation and Ranking. Sample λ candidate solutions $x_i \sim \mathcal{N}(m, \sigma^2 C)$, for $i \in [\![1, \lambda]\!]$, as follows. Generate d-variate standard normal random vectors $z_i \sim \mathcal{N}(0, I)$ and compute $x_i = m + \sigma\sqrt{C} z_i$. For the later use we keep $\{z_i\}$ as well as $\{x_i\}$. Then, evaluate their objective values $f(x_i)$ for all $i \in [\![1, \lambda]\!]$. Rank the solutions according to f. In the following steps the subscript $i : \lambda$ denotes the index of ith best solution among λ current samples.

[1]The Fisher information matrix, FIM, is defined as $\mathcal{I}(\theta) = \int_{\mathbb{R}^d} \nabla \ln p_\theta(x)(\nabla \ln p_\theta(x))^{\mathrm{T}} p_\theta(x)\,\mathrm{d}x$.

Step 3. Cumulation. Update the evolution paths p_σ and p_C as

$$p_\sigma \leftarrow (1 - c_\sigma)p_\sigma + \sqrt{c_\sigma(2 - c_\sigma)\mu_{\text{eff}}} \sum_{i=1}^{\mu} w_i z_{i:\lambda}$$
$$p_C \leftarrow (1 - c_c)p_C + \frac{h_\sigma\sqrt{c_c(2-c_c)\mu_{\text{eff}}}}{\sigma} \sum_{i=1}^{\mu} w_i(x_{i:\lambda} - m).$$

Here c_σ and c_c are the inverses of the backward time horizons for p_σ and p_C, respectively, and $\mu_{\text{eff}} = \left(\sum_{i=1}^{\mu} w_i^2\right)^{-1}$. We let $h_\sigma = 1$ if $\|p_\sigma\|^2/d < (2+4/(d+1))(1-(1-c_\sigma)^{2t})$, where t is the iteration number starting from one, and $h_\sigma = 0$ otherwise.

Step 4. Update Parameters. Compute the natural gradient and update the parameters as follows:

$$\begin{aligned} m &\leftarrow m + c_m \sum_{i=1}^{\mu} w_i \tilde{\nabla}_m \ln p_\theta(x_{i:\lambda}), \\ \sigma &\leftarrow \sigma \exp\left((c_\sigma/d_\sigma)\left(\|p_\sigma\|/\chi_d - 1\right)\right), \\ C &\leftarrow C + \underbrace{(1 - h_\sigma)c_1 c_c(2 - c_c)C}_{\text{make up for variance loss in case of } h_\sigma = 1} \\ &\quad + \underbrace{c_\mu \sum_{i=1}^{\mu} w_i \tilde{\nabla}_C \ln p_\theta(x_{i:\lambda})}_{\text{rank-}(\mu\wedge d)\text{ update}} + \underbrace{c_1 \tilde{\nabla}_C \ln p_\theta(m + \sigma p_C)}_{\text{rank-one update}} . \end{aligned}$$

Here c_m is the learning rate for the m update, c_μ and c_1 are the learning rates of the so-called rank-μ and rank-one updates for C. The damping parameter for the σ update is denoted by d_σ. The symbol χ_d denotes the expected value of $\|\mathcal{N}(0, I)\| = \sqrt{2}\Gamma((d+1)/2)/\Gamma(d/2) \approx \sqrt{d}(1 - 1/(4d) + 1/(21d^2))$. The approximated value is used in the algorithm. The natural gradient $\tilde{\nabla} = (\tilde{\nabla}_m, \tilde{\nabla}_C)$ of the log-likelihood of p_θ w.r.t. (m, C) is computed while σ is considered to be fixed.

When σ is fixed, the FIM $\mathcal{I}(\theta)$, where the parameter vector is $\theta = [m^{\mathrm{T}}, \operatorname{vec}(C)^{\mathrm{T}}]^{\mathrm{T}}$, becomes a block diagonal matrix $\operatorname{diag}(\mathcal{I}_m, \mathcal{I}_C)$ [2]. The diagonal blocks of $\mathcal{I}$ are given by $\mathcal{I}_m = \sigma^{-2}C^{-1}$ and $\mathcal{I}_C = 2^{-1}(C^{-1} \otimes C^{-1})$, where $\otimes$ denotes the Kronecker product. The vanilla gradients of the log-likelihood w.r.t. m and C are respectively $\nabla_m \ln p_\theta(x) = \sigma^{-2}C^{-1}(x - m)$ and $\nabla_C \ln p_\theta(x) = 2^{-1}C^{-1}(\sigma^{-2}(x - m)(x - m)^{\mathrm{T}} - C)C^{-1}$. Multiplying the inverse of $\mathcal{I}_m$ and $\mathcal{I}_C$ with the gradient $\nabla_m \ln p_\theta(x)$ and $\operatorname{vec}(\nabla_C \ln p_\theta(x))$, we have the natural gradient $\tilde{\nabla}_m \ln p_\theta(x) = (x - m)$ and $\tilde{\nabla}_C \ln p_\theta(x) = \sigma^{-2}(x - m)(x - m)^{\mathrm{T}} - C$. Therefore, the update equations for m and C read

$$\begin{aligned} C &\leftarrow C + c_\mu \sum_{i=1}^{\mu} w_i\left(\sigma^{-2}(x_{i:\lambda} - m)(x_{i:\lambda} - m)^{\mathrm{T}} - C\right) \\ &\quad + c_1\left(p_C p_C^{\mathrm{T}} - C\right), \\ m &\leftarrow m + c_m \sum_{i=1}^{\mu} w_i(x_{i:\lambda} - m) . \end{aligned}$$

The resulting m- and C-updates are similar to those used in the cross-entropy method (CEM) for continuous optimization [6] if $\sigma = 1$ and $c_1 = 0$, except that in CEM the m is updated first, which invariably leads to smaller variances in C and aggravates the problem of premature convergence.

The constants appearing in the algorithm are summarized in the following [8].

$$\begin{gathered} \lambda = 4 + \lfloor 3\ln(d) \rfloor, \quad \mu = \lfloor \lambda/2 \rfloor, \quad c_m = 1, \\ w_i = \frac{\ln((\lambda+1)/2) - \ln(i)}{\sum_{i=1}^{\mu}(\ln((\lambda+1)/2) - \ln(i))}, \quad c_\sigma = \frac{\mu_{\text{eff}}+2}{d+\mu_{\text{eff}}+5}, \\ d_\sigma = 1 + c_\sigma + 2\max(0, \sqrt{\tfrac{\mu_{\text{eff}}-1}{d+1}} - 1), \\ c_c = \frac{4+\mu_{\text{eff}}/d}{d+4+2\mu_{\text{eff}}/d}, \quad c_1 = \frac{2}{(d+1.3)^2+\mu_{\text{eff}}}, \\ c_\mu = \min\left(1 - c_1, \frac{2(\mu_{\text{eff}}-2+1/\mu_{\text{eff}})}{(d+2)^2+\mu_{\text{eff}}}\right) . \end{gathered} \tag{4}$$

The internal time complexity is $\mathcal{O}(d^3)$ for Step 1, $\mathcal{O}(\lambda d^2)$ for Step 2, $\mathcal{O}(\mu d)$ for Step 3 and $\mathcal{O}(\mu d^2)$ for Step 4. In practice, the matrix decomposition (Step 1) is done every $\lceil(10d(c_1+c_\mu))^{-1}\rceil$ iterations reducing the internal time complexity to $\mathcal{O}(d^2)$ per f-call. The space complexity is $\mathcal{O}(d^2 + \mu d)$.

3. VD-CMA: A LINEAR VARIANT OF CMA-ES FOR HIGH DIMENSION OPTIMIZATION

We derive in this section a novel comparison-based algorithm using the IGO framework and additional features of CMA-ES. The algorithm aims at optimizing functions in high dimensions and should thus scale linearly with dimension d for its internal time (per f-call) and memory requirements. For this purpose we restrict the covariance matrix of the Gaussian model $\{\mathcal{N}(m, \sigma^2 C)\}$ on $\mathbb{R}^d$ such that C has only $2d$ components to be adapted. More specifically, C is written in the form

$$C = D(I + vv^{\mathrm{T}})D \ , \tag{5}$$

where D is a diagonal matrix of dimension d and v is a vector in $\mathbb{R}^d$. This model is able to represent a scaling for each variable by D and a principle component, which is generally not parallel to an axis, by Dv. We parameterize the model by $\theta = (m \in \mathbb{R}^d, \sigma \in \mathbb{R}, \theta_C \in \mathbb{R}^{2d})$ where θ_C is composed of two parts: $\theta_D \in \mathbb{R}^d$ whose ith element is the ith diagonal element of D, and $v \in \mathbb{R}^d$.

3.1 Preliminaries

To derive the parameter update equation for the model based on the natural gradient, we first derive the gradient of the log-likelihood $\ln p_\theta(x)$ and the FIM of the model. When computing the gradient and the FIM, we suppose that σ is fixed and the parameter vector considered is $\theta = [m^{\mathrm{T}}, v^{\mathrm{T}}, \theta_D^{\mathrm{T}}]^{\mathrm{T}}$.

Notations. Let V be the diagonal matrix whose ith diagonal element is the $i$the component of v. The normalization of v by its Euclidean norm is denoted by $\bar{v} = v/\|v\|$. Analogously, $\bar{V} = V/\|v\|$. The determinant of $I + vv^{\mathrm{T}}$, namely $1+\|v\|^2$, is denoted γ_v. Let $\odot$ denote the element-wise product operator and $\bar{\bar{v}} = \bar{v} \odot \bar{v}$. The vector whose elements are all one is denoted by $\mathbf{1}$ for any dimension. The vector e_i is the unit vector whose ith component is one and the others are zero.

LEMMA 3.1. *Let $x \in \mathbb{R}^d$ and let $y = \sigma^{-1}D^{-1}(x - m)$. The gradients of the log-likelihood of our model w.r.t. m, v*

and θ_D are

$$\nabla_m \ln p_\theta(x) = \sigma^{-2}C^{-1}(x-m),$$
$$\nabla_{\theta_D} \ln p_\theta(x) = D^{-1}\left[y \odot y - \gamma_v^{-1}\langle y, v\rangle y \odot v - \mathbf{1}\right]$$
$$\nabla_v \ln p_\theta(x) = \gamma_v^{-1}\left[\langle y, v\rangle y - \gamma_v^{-1}(\langle y, v\rangle^2 + \gamma_v)v\right] .$$

PROOF IDEA. It is known from Eq. (20) in [2] that the partial derivative of the log-likelihood of the Gaussian model $\{\mathcal{N}(m,\Sigma)\}$ parameterized by θ given x w.r.t. θ_i is computed as

$$\frac{\partial \ln p_\theta(x)}{\partial\theta_i} = \frac{\partial m^{\mathrm{T}}}{\partial\theta_i}\Sigma^{-1}(x-m) + \frac{1}{2}\operatorname{Tr}\left(\Sigma^{-1}\frac{\partial\Sigma}{\partial\theta_i}\Sigma^{-1}\left[(x-m)(x-m)^{\mathrm{T}} - \Sigma\right]\right) ,$$

where Tr denotes the trace. Substituting the partial derivatives and simplifying the above equality, we have the gradients. The details are omitted due to the space limitation. □

LEMMA 3.2. *The Fisher information matrix of our model is a block diagonal matrix* $\operatorname{diag}(\mathcal{I}_m, \mathcal{I}_C)$, *where* $\mathcal{I}_m = \sigma^{-2}C^{-1}$ *and* $\mathcal{I}_C = \begin{bmatrix}\mathcal{I}_{v,v} & \mathcal{I}_{v,D}\\ \mathcal{I}_{D,v} & \mathcal{I}_{D,D}\end{bmatrix}$, *where* $\mathcal{I}_{v,D} = \mathcal{I}_{D,v}^{\mathrm{T}}$ *and*

$$\mathcal{I}_{v,v} = \gamma_v^{-1}\left[\|v\|^2 I + (1-\|v\|^2)\gamma_v^{-1}vv^{\mathrm{T}}\right],$$
$$\mathcal{I}_{D,v} = \gamma_v^{-1}D^{-1}V\left[(2+\|v\|^2)I - vv^{\mathrm{T}}\right],$$
$$\mathcal{I}_{D,D} = \gamma_v^{-1}D^{-1}\left[2\gamma_v I + \|v\|^2 V^2 - Vvv^{\mathrm{T}}V\right]D^{-1} .$$

PROOF IDEA. It is a well-know fact that the ijth element $[\mathcal{I}]_{i,j}$ of the FIM for the Gaussian distribution $\mathcal{N}(m,\Sigma)$ with parameter θ is $[\mathcal{I}]_{i,j} = \frac{\partial m}{\partial\theta_i}\Sigma^{-1}\frac{\partial m^{\mathrm{T}}}{\partial\theta_j} + \frac{1}{2}\operatorname{Tr}\left(\Sigma^{-1}\frac{\partial\Sigma}{\partial\theta_i}\Sigma^{-1}\frac{\partial\Sigma}{\partial\theta_j}\right)$. Remember $\theta = [m^{\mathrm{T}}, v^{\mathrm{T}}, \theta_D^{\mathrm{T}}]^{\mathrm{T}}$ and $\Sigma = \sigma^2 C = \sigma^2 D(I + vv^{\mathrm{T}})D$ in our case. The partial derivative $\partial m/\partial\theta_i = e_i$ if $\theta_i = m_i$ and $\partial m/\partial\theta_i = 0$ otherwise. On the other hand, $\partial\Sigma/\partial m_i = 0$. Therefore, the first term in the above equality appears only if both θ_i and θ_j are the elements of m, and the second term appears only if neither θ_i or θ_j is the element of m. This proves the block diagonal property of $\mathcal{I}$ and $\mathcal{I}_m = \Sigma^{-1} = \sigma^{-2}C^{-1}$ is an immediate consequence. The rests are derived from the second term by substituting the partial derivatives w.r.t. v and θ_D and simplifying it. □

To compute the natural gradient, the FIM must be invertible. Since $\mathcal{I}$ is block diagonal, the inverse is $\operatorname{diag}(\mathcal{I}_m^{-1}, \mathcal{I}_C^{-1})$ if both $\mathcal{I}_m$ and $\mathcal{I}_C$ are nonsingular. By Lemma 3.2 we know that $\mathcal{I}_m = (\sigma^2 C)^{-1}$ and it is nonsingular as long as C is nonsingular. The partitioned matrix inversion formula described in Theorem 8.5.11 in [12] shows that $\mathcal{I}_C$ is nonsingular if and only if the Schur complement $S_{v,v} = \mathcal{I}_{D,D} - \mathcal{I}_{D,v}\mathcal{I}_{v,v}^{-1}\mathcal{I}_{v,D}$ of $\mathcal{I}_{v,v}$ is nonsingular, where the invertibility of $\mathcal{I}_{v,v}$ is guaranteed by the Sherman-Morrison formula (e.g., Corollary 18.2.10 in [12]) as long as $v \neq 0$. The Schur complement $S_{v,v}$ is given in the following lemma, whose proof is straight forward from the partitioned matrix inversion formula, Sherman-Morrison formula and Lemma 3.2.

LEMMA 3.3. *The Schur complement of* $\mathcal{I}_{v,v}$ *in* $\mathcal{I}_C$ *appeared in Lemma 3.2 is* $S_{v,v} = 2D^{-1}[I - 2\overline{V}^2 + \overline{\overline{v}}\,\overline{\overline{v}}^{\mathrm{T}}]D^{-1}$.

Unfortunately, $S_{v,v}$ becomes singular for some $\overline{v}$. For example, $\overline{v} = e_i$ for any i is a typical case that causes the singularity of $S_{v,v}$. Moreover, $S_{v,v}$ becomes singular for any $\overline{v}$ (hence for any v) in the case of $d = 2$. Indeed, noting that $\|\overline{v}\|^2 = 1$, it is easy to see the determinant of $S_{v,v}$ is zero. Thus, the invertibility of $\mathcal{I}_C$ is not guaranteed. Theoretically one can use the pseudo inverse of the FIM to define the natural gradient everywhere. However, due to arbitrarily small eigenvalues of the FIM around singular points that lead to arbitrarily long natural gradients, the resulting parameter update becomes unstable when the parameter approaches a singular point. Therefore it does not essentially solve this difficulty.

3.2 Modified Fisher Information Matrix with Reduced Off-diagonal Blocks

A simple way to avoid singularity of the FIM is to restrict it to the principal diagonal blocks. Then, the natural gradient for each block of parameters is computed independently while the other parameters are fixed. In our case, the block diagonalized FIM is nonsingular since $\mathcal{I}_{v,v}$ and $\mathcal{I}_{D,D}$ are nonsingular according to the Scherman-Morrison formula, provided $v \neq 0$ and D is positive definite. However, this leads to poor behavior, for example, on the rotated Cigar function defined in Table 1, where the principle component of the covariance matrix should not be axis parallel and v has to be learned adequately. To get nonsingularity without significantly compromising the performance, we use $\operatorname{diag}(\mathcal{I}_m, \mathcal{I}_C^{(\alpha)})$ in place of $\operatorname{diag}(\mathcal{I}_m, \mathcal{I}_C)$, where

$$\mathcal{I}_C^{(\alpha)} = \begin{bmatrix}\mathcal{I}_{v,v} & \alpha\mathcal{I}_{v,D}\\ \alpha\mathcal{I}_{D,v} & \mathcal{I}_{D,D}\end{bmatrix}, \quad \alpha \in [0,1] . \tag{6}$$

If $\alpha = 1$, $\mathcal{I}_C^{(\alpha)}$ is the original FIM, if $\alpha = 0$, $\mathcal{I}_C^{(\alpha)}$ is block diagonal, and α must be tuned such that $\mathcal{I}_C^{(\alpha)}$ remains nonsingular for any v and D, with $\alpha = 1$ desired. Since $\mathcal{I}_{v,v}$ is nonsingular except for $v = 0$, according to the partitioned matrix inversion formula $\mathcal{I}_C^{(\alpha)}$ is invertible if and only if the Schur complement $S_{v,v} = \mathcal{I}_{D,D} - \alpha^2\mathcal{I}_{D,v}\mathcal{I}_{v,v}^{-1}\mathcal{I}_{v,D}$ of $\mathcal{I}_{v,v}$ is nonsingular.

LEMMA 3.4. *The Schur complement of* $\mathcal{I}_{v,v}$ *in (6) is* $S_{v,v} = D^{-1}(A + b\overline{\overline{v}}\,\overline{\overline{v}}^{\mathrm{T}})D^{-1}$, *where* $b = -(1-\alpha^2)\|v\|^4\gamma_v^{-1} + 2\alpha^2$ *and* $A = 2I - (b + 2\alpha)\overline{V}^2$.

The proof is straightforward from Lemma 3.2 and Scherman-Morrison formula. Although the necessary and sufficient condition for $S_{v,v}$ to be nonsingular is not provided, the next proposition shows a sufficient α which leads to numerically stable $S_{v,v}^{-1}$.

PROPOSITION 3.5. *Let* $\gamma = \gamma_v^{-1/2}$. *If we choose*

$$\alpha = \min\left(1, \frac{[\|v\|^4 + (2-\gamma)\gamma_v / \max_i(\overline{v}_i)]^{1/2}}{2 + \|v\|^2}\right) , \tag{7}$$

then $S_{v,v}$ *is nonsingular and its inverse is given by*

$$S_{v,v}^{-1} = D\left[A^{-1} - (1 + b\overline{\overline{v}}^{\mathrm{T}}A^{-1}\overline{\overline{v}})^{-1}bA^{-1}\overline{\overline{v}}\,\overline{\overline{v}}^{\mathrm{T}}A^{-1}\right]D .$$

PROOF IDEA. According to Lemma 3.4 and Scherman-Morrison formula, $S_{v,v}$ is invertible if A is nonsingular and $1 + b\overline{\overline{v}}^{\mathrm{T}}A^{-1}\overline{\overline{v}} \neq 0$. Then, Scherman-Morrison formula provides the above explicit form of $S_{v,v}^{-1}$. Thus, it suffices to show the nonsingularity of A and $1 + b\overline{\overline{v}}^{\mathrm{T}}A^{-1}\overline{\overline{v}} \neq 0$ under condition (7). Indeed, we prove $A_{i,i} \geq \gamma$ and $1 + b\overline{\overline{v}}^{\mathrm{T}}A^{-1}\overline{\overline{v}} \geq \gamma$. The necessary and sufficient condition for $A_{i,i} \geq \gamma$ is $\alpha^2 \leq [\|v\|^4 + (2-\gamma)(1+\|v\|^2)/\max(\overline{v}_j)]/(2+\|v\|^2)^2$. If this condition holds, we have $0 < \overline{\overline{v}}^{\mathrm{T}}A^{-1}\overline{\overline{v}} \leq \gamma^{-1}\sum_i \overline{\overline{v}}_i^2 \leq \gamma^{-1}\sum_i \overline{\overline{v}}_i = \gamma^{-1}$. Noting that $\gamma \leq 1$, we have that $1 + b\overline{\overline{v}}^{\mathrm{T}}A^{-1}\overline{\overline{v}} \geq \gamma$ holds if $b \geq \gamma(\gamma - 1)$. The necessary and sufficient condition for $b \geq$

$\gamma(\gamma-1)$ is $\alpha^2 \geq [\|v\|^4-(1-\gamma)\gamma(1+\|v\|^2)]/(\|v\|^4+2\|v\|^2+2)$. The α in (7) satisfies both inequalities. □

The following theorem provides $\mathcal{O}(d)$ computation of the modified natural gradient of the log-likelihood with α introduced in Proposition 3.5.

THEOREM 3.6. *The modified natural gradient is computed as follows. Let $y = D^{-1}(x-m)/\sigma$ as above. Let α, A and b be those which appear in Proposition 3.5 and Lemma 3.4. Compute s and t as follows.*

1. $s \leftarrow y \odot y - \|v\|^2 \langle y, \overline{v}\rangle \gamma_v^{-1} y \odot \overline{v} - \mathbf{1}$
2. $t \leftarrow \langle y, \overline{v}\rangle y - 2^{-1}(\langle y, \overline{v}\rangle^2 + \gamma_v)\overline{v}$
3. $s \leftarrow s - \alpha\gamma_v^{-1}\left((2+\|v\|^2)\overline{v}\odot t - \|v\|^2 \langle \overline{v}, t\rangle \overline{\overline{v}}\right)$
4. $s \leftarrow A^{-1}s - \left(1 + b\langle \overline{\overline{v}}, A^{-1}\overline{\overline{v}}\rangle\right)^{-1} b\langle s, A^{-1}\overline{\overline{v}}\rangle A^{-1}\overline{\overline{v}}$
5. $t \leftarrow t - \alpha\left[(2+\|v\|^2)\overline{v}\odot s - \langle s, \overline{\overline{v}}\rangle \overline{v}\right]$

Then, $\tilde{\nabla}_m \ln p_\theta(x) = x - m$, $\tilde{\nabla}_v \ln p_\theta(x) = \|v\|^{-1}t$ and $\tilde{\nabla}_{\theta_D} \ln p_\theta(x) = Ds$.

PROOF IDEA. The modified natural gradient is the product of the inverse of $\mathrm{diag}(\mathcal{I}_m, \mathcal{I}_C^{(\alpha)})$ and the vanilla gradient given in Lemma 3.1. The inverse of $\mathrm{diag}(\mathcal{I}_m, \mathcal{I}_C^{(\alpha)})$ is $\mathrm{diag}(\mathcal{I}_m^{-1}, (\mathcal{I}_C^{(\alpha)})^{-1})$. As is shown in Lemma 3.2, $\mathcal{I}_m = \sigma^{-2}C^{-1}$ and its inverse is $\mathcal{I}_m^{-1} = \sigma^2 C$. Premultiplying the vanilla gradient w.r.t. m by $\mathcal{I}_m^{-1}$, we have $\tilde{\nabla}_m \ln p_\theta(x) = x - m$. The inverse of $\mathcal{I}_C^{(\alpha)}$ with α in Proposition 3.5 can be computed by using the partitioned matrix inversion formula as

$$\begin{bmatrix} \mathcal{I}_{v,v} & \alpha\mathcal{I}_{v,D} \\ \alpha\mathcal{I}_{D,v} & \mathcal{I}_{D,D} \end{bmatrix}^{-1} = \begin{bmatrix} \mathcal{I}_{v,v}^{-1} & 0 \\ 0 & 0 \end{bmatrix} + \begin{bmatrix} -\alpha\mathcal{I}_{v,v}^{-1}\mathcal{I}_{v,D} \\ I \end{bmatrix} S_{v,v}^{-1}\begin{bmatrix} -\alpha\mathcal{I}_{D,v}\mathcal{I}_{v,v}^{-1} & I \end{bmatrix}$$

The inverse $\mathcal{I}_{v,v}^{-1}$ can be computed by the Scherman-Morrison formula and $S_{v,v}^{-1}$ is given in Proposition 3.5. Substituting them into the above equality and premultiplying the vanilla gradient given in Lemma 3.1 by the right hand side of the above equality, we obtain the natural gradient w.r.t. v and θ_D. The steps 2 to 7 are just a decomposition of the computation and can be computed in $\mathcal{O}(d)$. □

3.3 The VD-CMA Algorithm

The overall algorithm is as follows. Initialize m and σ depending on the problem search space. Initialize $D = I$ and $v \sim \mathcal{N}(0, I/d)$ and $p_C = p_\sigma = 0$.

Step 1. Sampling, Evaluation and Ranking. Sample λ candidate solutions x_i, for $i \in [\![1, \lambda]\!]$, as follows. Generate d-variate standard normal random vectors $z_i \sim \mathcal{N}(0, I)$, compute $y_i = z_i + (\sqrt{1+\|v\|^2} - 1)\langle z_i, \overline{v}\rangle \overline{v}$ and $x_i = m + \sigma D y_i$. Then, $y_i \sim \mathcal{N}(0, I + vv^\mathrm{T})$ and $x_i \sim \mathcal{N}(m, \sigma^2 D(I + vv^\mathrm{T})D)$. Evaluate their objective values $f(x_i)$ for all $i \in [\![1, \lambda]\!]$. Rank solutions according to f.

Step 2. Cumulation. The evolution paths p_σ and p_C are updated in the same way as the original CMA does (see Sec. 2.2). Note that $z_i = C^{-1/2}(x_i - m)/\sigma$ in the original CMA whereas $z_i = (I + vv^\mathrm{T})^{-1/2}D^{-1}(x_i - m)/\sigma \neq C^{-1/2}(x_i - m)/\sigma$ in our case. We use z_i rather than $C^{-1/2}(x_i - m)/\sigma$ in order to achieve linear time update. Then, compute h_σ in the same way as in the original CMA.

Step 3. Update Parameters. Update the parameters as follows:

$$\begin{aligned} m &\leftarrow m + c_m \textstyle\sum_{i=1}^{\mu} w_i \tilde{\nabla}_m \ln p_\theta(x_{i:\lambda}), \\ \sigma &\leftarrow \sigma \exp\left((c_\sigma/d_\sigma)\left(\|p_\sigma\|/\chi_d - 1\right)\right), \\ v &\leftarrow v + c_\mu \textstyle\sum_{i=1}^{\mu} w_i \tilde{\nabla}_v \ln p_\theta(x_{i:\lambda}) \\ &\quad + (1-h_\sigma)c_1 \tilde{\nabla}_v \ln p_\theta(m + \sigma p_C), \\ D &\leftarrow D + c_\mu \textstyle\sum_{i=1}^{\mu} w_i \tilde{\nabla}_D \ln p_\theta(x_{i:\lambda}) \\ &\quad + (1-h_\sigma)c_1 \tilde{\nabla}_D \ln p_\theta(m + \sigma p_C). \end{aligned}$$

Here the natural gradients are computed following Theorem 3.6. The (constant) parameters are taken from (4) except for c_σ, c_1 and c_μ. Since the degrees of freedom in the covariance matrix is $2d$ compared with $d(d+1)/2$ in the original CMA, we expect that the natural gradient estimate is more reliable and larger values for c_1 and c_μ can be taken. The learning rate c_σ for σ is modified as well to achieve better scale-up with d. Let c_1^{old} and c_μ^{old} be the settings given in (4). Then, we set

$$c_\sigma = \frac{\sqrt{\mu_{\mathrm{eff}}}}{2(\sqrt{d} + \sqrt{\mu_{\mathrm{eff}}})},\ c_1 = \frac{d-5}{6}c_1^{\mathrm{old}},\ c_\mu = \min\left(1 - c_1, \frac{d-5}{6}c_\mu^{\mathrm{old}}\right).$$

The internal space complexity decreases to $\mathcal{O}(\mu d)$, the internal time complexity for each objective function call to $\mathcal{O}(d)$ compared to $\mathcal{O}(\mu d + d^2)$ and $\mathcal{O}(d^2)$ in the standard CMA, respectively.

4. EXPERIMENTS

We evaluated the new VD-CMA on benchmark functions described in Table 1, where the number of variables varies from 10 to 10^4. The VD-CMA is comparison-based and has the same performance on any composition of the functions by a monotonic transformation. The initial mean vector obeys $\mathcal{N}(3 \cdot \mathbf{1}, 2^2 \cdot I)$, except for $f_{\mathrm{ros}}(x)$ and $f_{\mathrm{rosrot}}(x)$ where m obeys $\mathcal{N}(0, 2^2 \cdot I)$ to avoid the symmetry; the initial step-size is $\sigma = 2$. Runs are terminated as successful when a function value better than 10^{-10} is reached, otherwise when the number of function evaluations reached $10^5 \cdot d$. Only on the Rosenbrock functions about 15% of the runs were not successful due to the local minima and these are disregarded in the presentation. The code is implemented in Octave (single thread) and run on Debian 6.0 machine with Intel(R) Core(TM) i7-3770 3.4GHz CPU and 16 GB RAM.

Figure 1 shows a typical result on the 50 dimensional f_{ellcig} function, for which the inverse Hessian is proportional to $D_{\mathrm{ell}}^{-1}(I + (10^6 - 1)uu^\mathrm{T})D_{\mathrm{ell}}^{-1}$. First, D becomes proportional to D_{ell}^{-1}, then v starts to adapt, ending up with $v_i \approx \sqrt{(10^6-1)/d}$, such that $C = D(I + vv^\mathrm{T})D$ finally becomes closely proportional to the inverse Hessian. The reason of the later adaptation of v is that the function value is less sensitive to the direction of u than the coordinate-wise scaling by D_{ell} and the selection bias is only visible after $D \approx D_{\mathrm{ell}}^{-1}$. After learning the inverse Hessian, the speed of convergence is as fast as on f_{sph}. On the 50 dimensional f_{ellcig}, α is almost always one, whereas we observed a smaller α on lower dimensional functions (e.g., varying in $[0.75, 1]$ on the 10 dimensional f_{ellcig} and in $[0.65, 1]$ on the 10 dimensional f_{cig}).

Figure 2.(a) shows the number of function evaluations and CPU time in seconds, averaged over 10 independent runs on eight functions. The number of function evaluations scale up linearly on f_{sph}, f_{tab}, f_{cig}, f_{cigrot}, and slightly more than linear on f_{ell}, f_{ellcig}. On the Rosenbrock functions f_{ros} and

Table 1: **Test function definitions. R is an orthogonal matrix and u is a unit vector, both are randomly generated for each run; D_{ell} is a diagonal matrix whose ith diagonal element is $10^{3\frac{i-1}{d-1}}$. The global minimum point is located at $\mathbf{1}$, $R^{\mathrm{T}}\mathbf{1}$ and $\mathbf{0}$ for f_{ros}, f_{rosrot} and all other functions, respectively.**

Sphere	$f_{\text{sph}}(x) = \sum_{i=1}^{d} x_i^2$	Tablet	$f_{\text{tab}}(x) = 10^6 x_1^2 + \sum_{i=2}^{d} x_i^2$
Ellipsoid	$f_{\text{ell}}(x) = f_{\text{sph}}(D_{\text{ell}} x)$	Cigar	$f_{\text{cig}}(x) = x_1^2 + 10^6 \sum_{i=2}^{d} x_i^2$
Ellipsoid-Cigar	$f_{\text{ellcig}}(x) = f_{\text{cigrot}}(D_{\text{ell}} x)$	Rot-Tablet	$f_{\text{tabrot}}(x) = f_{\text{sph}}(x) + (10^6 - 1)\langle x, u\rangle^2$
Rot-Ellipsoid	$f_{\text{ellrot}}(x) = f_{\text{ell}}(Rx)$	Rot-Cigar	$f_{\text{cigrot}}(x) = 10^6 f_{\text{sph}}(x) + (1 - 10^6)\langle x, u\rangle^2$
Rot-Rosenbrock	$f_{\text{rosrot}}(x) = f_{\text{ros}}(Rx)$	Rosenbrock	$f_{\text{ros}}(x) = \sum_{i=1}^{d-1}\left[10^2(x_i^2 - x_{i+1})^2 + (x_i - 1)^2\right]$

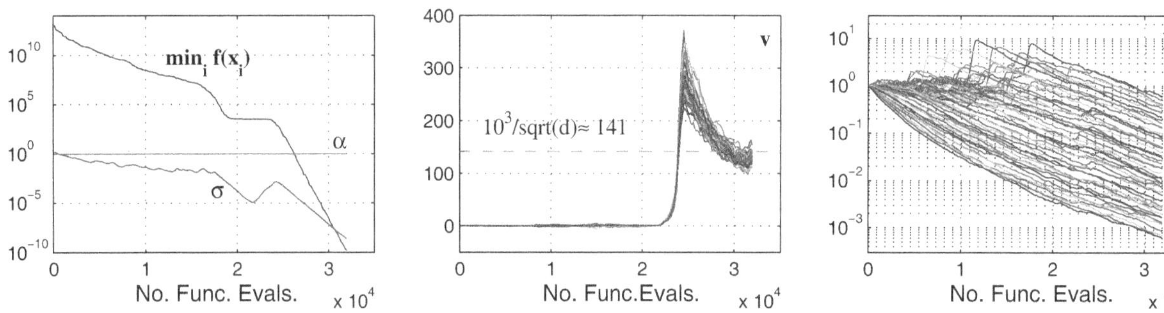

Figure 1: Single run on 50 dimensional f_{ellcig} with cigar axis $u = (1/\sqrt{d}, \ldots, 1/\sqrt{d})$. The minimum f-value at each iteration, α, σ (left), v values (center), and diagonal elements of D (right) are plotted.

f_{rosrot} the scale up is close to quadratic. On the other hand, it took 1.6e7, 1.0e7, 1.2e7 function evaluations on f_{tabrot} for $d = 10$, 20, 50, and 7.1e6, 1.3e7, 2.0e7 function evaluations on f_{ellrot} for $d = 10$, 20, 50, respectively, whereas the CMA requires 6.0e3, 1.6e4, 6.6e4 on f_{tabrot} and 6.2e3, 1.9e4, 1.0e5 function evaluations on f_{ellrot}. The inverse Hessian of these functions can not be well approximated by (5). Since the time complexity for each function evaluation is $\mathcal{O}(d)$, the total CPU time scales d times more than the number of function evaluations does.

Figure 2.(b) shows the speed up over the standard CMA. The reason of the speed up in terms of the number of function evaluations is the $(d-5)/6$ times larger learning rate for the C update. The effect is more pronounced on f_{ell}, f_{ellcig}, f_{tab} than on f_{cig} and f_{cigrot}, although they all have a Hessian matrix whose inverse can be represented by (5). This is because the standard CMA excels at learning single long components of C because of the cumulation in p_C. On f_{sph}, the performance does not differ much from standard CMA since C does not need to learn the shape and the σ update is dominative in determining the speed of convergence. When it comes to the total CPU time, our approach improves over the standard CMA for $d \geq 50$.

Figure 3 shows the scale up of VD-CMA, sep-CMA [18] and R1-NES [19], which are all linear time and space algorithms based on the same natural gradient principle.[2] Table 2 shows a comparison with the standard CMA, (1, 10)-AII [11] and (1, 10)-MVA [17]. The reason of better scale up of VD-CMA and sep-CMA than R1-NES even on f_{sph} is the cumulation employed to adapt σ. On f_{cig} and f_{cigrot} VD-CMA is more efficient than R1-NES, though both Gaussian models maintained by VD-CMA and R1-NES can adapt to the inverse Hessian. This is the effect of the cumulation for covariance adaptation. On f_{ell}, sep-CMA is faster than VD-CMA simply because the learning rate for the C update is higher. On the other hand, MVA and R1-NES, both of which restrict the covariance matrix to maintain only one long direction, do not solve f_{ell}, f_{ellcig} and f_{tab}. Since the model in our approach is richer than those maintained in sep-CMA and R1-NES, VD-CMA can solve more efficiently a larger class of functions including f_{ellcig}, f_{ros} and f_{rosrot} that are ill-conditioned and non-separable.

[2]The sep-CMA was introduced independently of the natural gradient, but later it was found in [2] to derive from the natural gradient framework.

Table 2: Average number of function evaluations to reach the target function value 10^{-9} on 20 dimensional functions among three runs except for MVA, where the average is computed over 70 runs. Data is taken from the references. Standard deviations are smaller than 3% of the average numbers except for MVA. On f_{ros}, no success was observed for MVA in 3.5×10^5 function evaluations.

	VD-CMA	CMA	(1, 10)-AII	(1, 10)-MVA
f_{ell}	9.4×10^3	2.0×10^4	1.2×10^4	no success
f_{ros}	2.0×10^4	2.1×10^4	2.1×10^4	5.7×10^4

5. DISCUSSION

Based on the IGO framework, we have derived a comparison-based stochastic search algorithm, VD-CMA, for continuous optimization in high dimension. To achieve internal computational time and space complexity linear in dimension, we have restricted the covariance matrix of the Gaussian distribution to $D(I + vv^{\mathrm{T}})D$. Since this model has singular

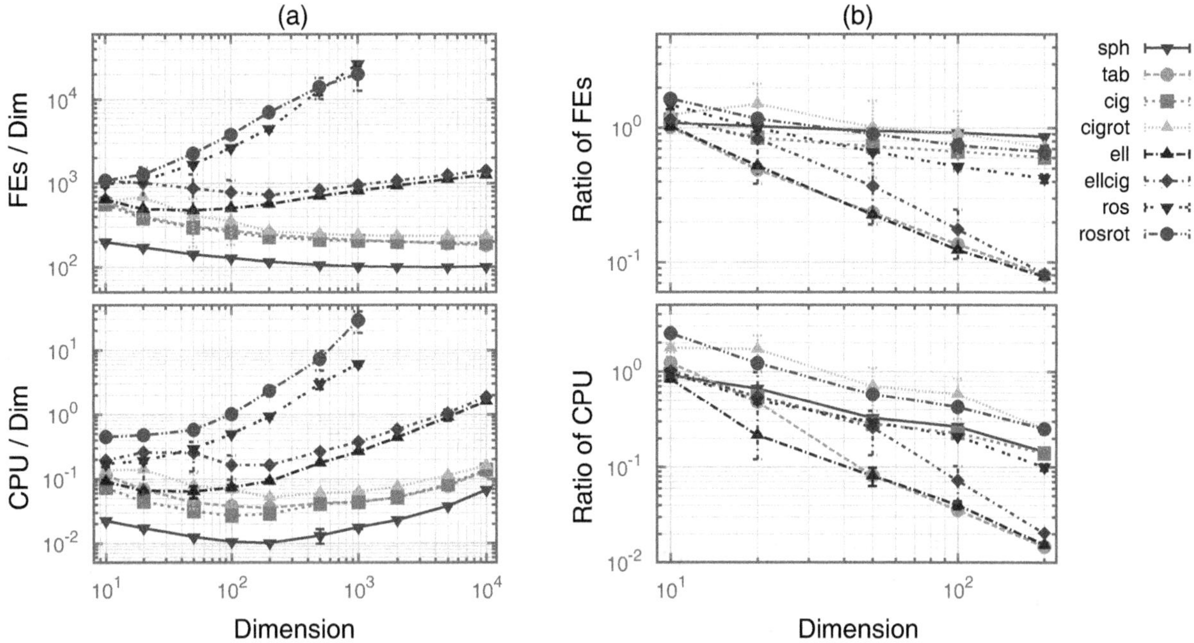

Figure 2: (a) Number of function evaluations (FEs) and CPU time [s] divided by d. (b) FEs and CPU time spent by VD-CMA divided by those spent by the CMA. Shown are average and standard deviation (error bar), from 10 independent runs.

points where the natural gradient is not defined and leads to unstable parameter update, we have defined a modified FIM to avoid the singularity and enable numerically stable computation of the natural gradient without significantly compromising the performance. Additionally to the natural gradient, we have incorporated the cumulation concept from the CMA-ES to make robust and accelerate the method.

We have shown the advantage of VD-CMA over the standard CMA in two aspects. One is the linear scaling of the internal time and memory usage w.r.t. the number of variables that is desired for optimizing functions in high dimension. The other is better scaling of the number of function evaluations thanks to the higher learning rates for the covariance update. The second aspect implies VD-CMA outperforms the standard CMA even on a low or moderate dimensional function where the inverse of the Hessian can be approximated by (5). On the other hand, if the model does not suit the inverse Hessian of a function, e.g., f_{ellrot} and f_{tabrot}, VD-CMA is inefficient compared to the standard-CMA. Compared to other linear time variants of the CMA-ES, it can solve a wider class of functions since we have a richer but linear number of elements of the covariance matrix.

We end with a remark on parallelization. As well as most evolutionary algorithms, one can benefit from parallelization. For the sake of simplicity we assume that λ processors are available. Then *sampling* and *evaluation* for each solution are performed in parallel. Moreover, step 2 and step 3 in Section 3.3 are parallelizable by computing $w_i z_{i:\lambda}$, $w_i(x_{i:\lambda} - m) = w_i \tilde{\nabla}_m \ln p_\theta(x_{i:\lambda})$, $w_i \tilde{\nabla}_v \ln p_\theta(x_{i:\lambda})$ and $w_i \tilde{\nabla}_D \ln p_\theta(x_{i:\lambda})$ for each $x_{i:\lambda}$ in parallel. Then, the number of floating point multiplications at each iteration on each processor reduces from $\mathcal{O}(\lambda d)$ to $\mathcal{O}(d)$. The other computation required is the sorting of $\mathcal{O}(\lambda)$ floating point numbers for ranking and the sum of $\mathcal{O}(\mu)$ floating point numbers for update, both of which are relatively cheap and can be also parallelized if needed. To further reduce the runtime, one can set the population size, λ, larger than the default value, which typically requires more function evaluations but smaller number of iterations. Large population also helps when the objective function is rugged.

Acknowledgements.

This work was supported by the ANR-2010-COSI-002 (SIMINOLE) and ANR-2012-MONU-0009 (NumBBO) grants of the French National Research Agency.

6. REFERENCES

[1] Y. Akimoto, Y. Nagata, I. Ono, and S. Kobayashi. Bidirectional Relation between CMA Evolution Strategies and Natural Evolution Strategies. In *Parallel Problem Solving from Nature – PPSN XI*, pages 154–163, 2010.

[2] Y. Akimoto, Y. Nagata, I. Ono, and S. Kobayashi. Theoretical Foundation for CMA-ES from Information Geometry Perspective. *Algorithmica*, 64:698–716, 2012.

[3] S. Amari. Natural Gradient Works Efficiently in Learning. *Neural Computation*, 10(2):251–276, 1998.

[4] S. Amari, H. Park, and K. Fukumizu. Adaptive method of realizing natural gradient learning for multilayer perceptrons. *Neural Computation*, 12:1399–1409, 2000.

[5] Y. Ollivier, L. Arnold, A. Auger, and N. Hansen. Information-Geometric Optimization Algorithms: A Unifying Picture via Invariance Principles. *arXiv:1106.3708*, 2011.

[6] P.-T. D. Boer, D. P. Kroese, S. Mannor, and R. Y. Rubinstein. A Tutorial on the Cross-Entropy Method. *Annals of Operations Research*, (134):19–67, 2005.

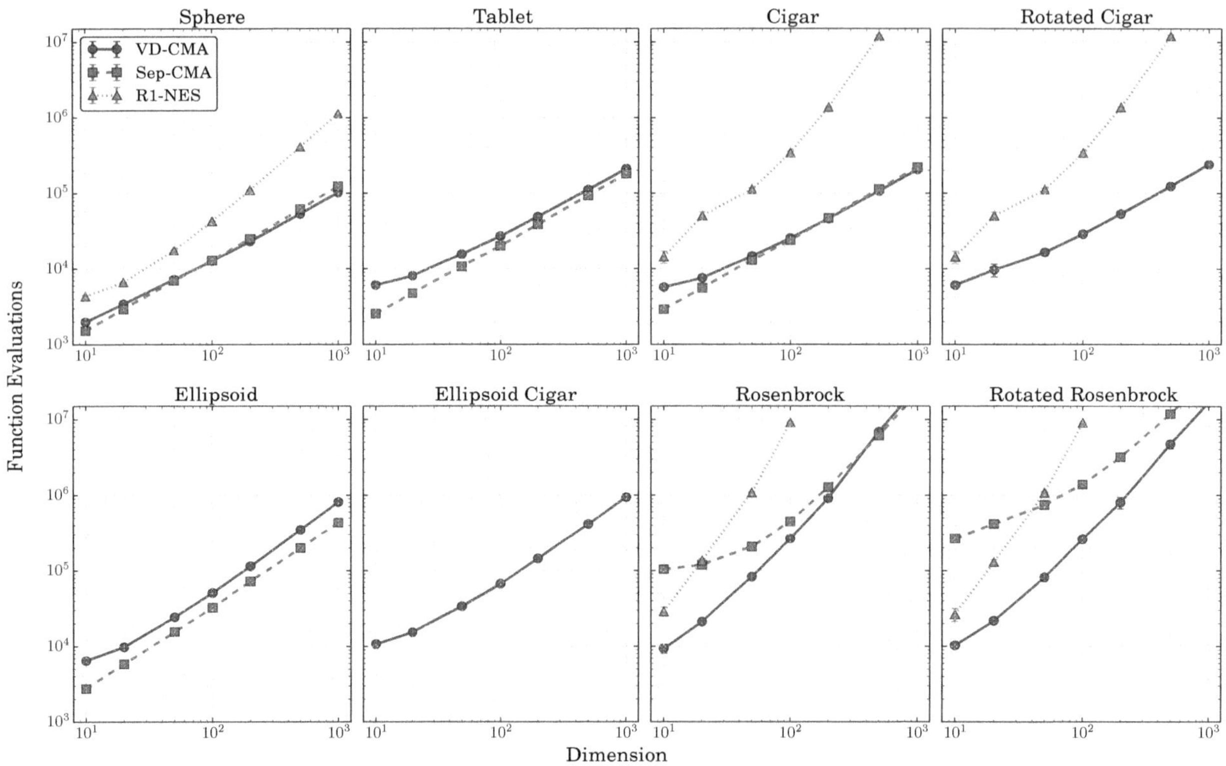

Figure 3: Number of function evaluations spent by VD-CMA, Sep-CMA and R1-NES. Shown are average and standard deviation (error bar), from 10 independe nt runs. Missing data implies it failed to reach the target within $2 \cdot 10^7$ function evaluations. Note that the error bars are hardly visible since the std. are small.

[7] T. Glasmachers, T. Schaul, Y. Sun, D. Wierstra, and J. Schmidhuber. Exponential Natural Evolution Strategies. In *Proceedings of Genetic and Evolutionary Computation Conference*, pages 393–400, 2010.

[8] N. Hansen and A. Auger. Principled Design of Continuous Stochastic Search: From Theory to Practice. In Y. Borenstein and A. Moraglio, editors, *Theory and Principled Methods for the Design of Metaheuristics*. Springer, 2013.

[9] N. Hansen, S. D. Muller, and P. Koumoutsakos. Reducing the time complexity of the derandomized evolution strategy with covariance matrix adaptation (CMA-ES). *Evolutionary Computation*, 11(1):1–18, 2003.

[10] N. Hansen and A. Ostermeier. Completely derandomized self-adaptation in evolution strategies. *Evolutionary Computation*, 9(2):159–195, 2001.

[11] N. Hansen, A. Ostermeier, and A. Gawelczyk. On the Adaptation of Arbitrary Normal Mutation Distributions in Evolution Strategies: The Generating set Adaptation. In *Proceedings of the Sixth International Conference on Genetic Algorithms*, pages 57–64, 1995.

[12] D. A. Harville. *Matrix Algebra from a Statistician's Perspective*. Springer-Verlag, 2008.

[13] A. Honkela, M. Tornio, T. Raiko, and J. Karhunen. Natural conjugate gradient in variational inference. In *Neural Information Processing, 14th International Conference, ICONIP 2007*, pages 305–314, 2008.

[14] L. Malagò, M. Matteucci, and G. Pistone. Towards the geometry of estimation of distribution algorithms based on the exponential family. In *Foundations of Genetic Algorithms*, pages 230–242. 2011.

[15] A. Miyamae, Y. Nagata, I. Ono, and S. Kobayashi. Natural Policy Gradient Methods with Parameter-based Exploration for Control Tasks. In *Advances in Neural Information Processing Systems 23*, pages 1660–1668, 2010.

[16] J. Peters and S. Schaal. Natural actor-critic. *Neurocomputing*, 71(7-9):1180–1190, 2008.

[17] J. Poland and A. Zell. Main vector adaptation: A CMA variant with linear time and space complexity. In *Proceedings of the Genetic and Evolutionary Computation Conference*, pages 1050–1055, 2001.

[18] R. Ros and N. Hansen. A simple modification in CMA-ES achieving linear time and space complexity. *Parallel Problem Solving from Nature–PPSN X*, pages 296–305, 2008.

[19] Y. Sun, F. Gomez, T. Schaul, and J. Schmidhuber. A Linear Time Natural Evolution Strategy for Non-Separable Functions. *GECCO'13 Companion*, pages 61–62, 2013.

[20] T. Suttorp, N. Hansen, and C. Igel. Efficient covariance matrix update for variable metric evolution strategies. *Machine Learning*, 75(2):167–197, 2009.

[21] D. Wierstra, T. Schaul, J. Peters, and J. Schmidhuber. Natural evolution strategies. In *IEEE Congress on Evolutionary Computation*, pages 3381–3387, 2008.

Halfspace Sampling in Evolution Strategies

Chun-Kit Au
Department of Computer Science & Eng.
The Chinese University of Hong Kong
Shatin, Hong Kong
auchunkit@cuhk.edu.hk

Ho-Fung Leung
Department of Computer Science & Eng.
The Chinese University of Hong Kong
Shatin, Hong Kong
lhf@cuhk.edu.hk

ABSTRACT

This paper presents a novel halfspace sampling method in single parent elitist evolution strategies (ESs) for unimodal functions. In halfspace sampling, the supporting hyperplane going through a parent separates the search space into a positive halfspace and a negative halfspace. If an offspring lies in the negative halfspace, it will be reflected with respect to the parent so that it lies in the positive halfspace. We derive the convergence rates of a scale-invariant step size (1+1)-ES with halfspace sampling on spherical functions in finite and infinite dimensions. We prove that the lower bounds of convergence rates are improved by a factor of 2 when strategies sample their offspring in the optimal positive halfspace. We also implement halfspace sampling into the (1+1) CMA-ES by introducing the concept of evolution halfspaces. Evolution halfspaces accumulate the significant information of the previous successful and unsuccessful steps in order to estimate the optimal positive halfspace. The (1+1)-CMA-ES with halfspace sampling is benchmarked on the BBOB noise-free testbed and experimentally compared with the standard (1+1)-CMA-ES.

Categories and Subject Descriptors

G.1.6 [**Numerical Analysis**]: Optimization—*global optimization, unconstrained optimization*; F.2.1 [**Analysis of Algorithms and Problem Complexity**]: Numerical Algorithms and Problems

General Terms

Algorithms, Theory

Keywords

Evolution Strategies, Halfspaces, Sampling, Plus Selection, Covariance Matrix Adaptation

GECCO'14, July 12–16, 2014, Vancouver, BC, Canada.

ACM 978-1-4503-2662-9/14/07 ...$15.00.
http://dx.doi.org/10.1145/2576768.2598335.

1. INTRODUCTION

Evolution Strategies (ESs) are robust random search algorithms. They are designed to minimise objective functions that map a continuous search space $\mathbb{R}^n$ into $\mathbb{R}$. In a $(1+1)$-ES, an offspring is created from a single parent $\mathbf{X}_k \in \mathbb{R}$ at iteration k. The offspring is generated by adding an *independent* random vector $\boldsymbol{\mathcal{N}}_k$ to $\mathbf{X}_k$. If the offspring is better than its parent, it is then selected to be the next parent $\mathbf{X}_{k+1}$. Otherwise, offspring are iteratively generated until a better solution is found.

The elitist $(1+1)$-ES is the most local and the fastest variant in the ES family, which has been studied in various literature [10, 3]. In the local search scenario, the $(1+1)$-ES outperforms its non-elitist counterparts. Conventionally, the $(1+1)$-ES implements a step size adaptation - the so-called one-fifth success rule. The basic idea is to increase a step size after a successful step and decrease it after a failure. A history of success probabilities is maintained as a threshold during the course of optimization so that the strategy increases its step size when the success probability is larger than 1/5, and decreases it otherwise. Intuitively, if "too many" steps are successful, this indicates that the search is too local. If "too few" steps are successful, this indicates that the step size used for sampling is too large. A recent development on $(1+1)$-ES is the implementation of the covariance matrix adaptation (CMA) with rank-one update [8]. In the (1+1)-CMA-ES, it adapts not only the step size σ_k but also the covariance matrix $\mathbf{C}_k \in \mathbb{R}^{n\times n}$ associated with the search distribution of mutation vectors based successful steps.

This paper introduces a novel sampling method that aims at improving the convergence rates of ES on *unimodal* functions. We propose to divide the search space into two halfspaces in $\mathbb{R}^n$ such that the hyperplane bounding the halfspaces passes through the parent $\mathbf{X}_k$. A proposed ES has a tendency to sample candidate solutions in the positive halfspace in which the previous successful steps are located. All the unsuccessful steps in the recent iterations are also used to estimate the positive halfspace. In order to estimate the optimal positive halfspace that contains as many better solutions as possible, we propose to maintain a new vector $\mathbf{n}_k \in \mathbb{R}^n$. This vector is a normal vector to the hyperplane bounding the halfspaces and is updated by exponential weighted sum of the previous successful and unsuccessful steps. The idea is similar to that of evolution paths in [7] but here it mainly focuses on the evolution of halfspaces by accumulating the significant information of steps in recent iterations.

We also investigate theoretically the gain we can expect from halfspace sampling on the spherical functions. Linear convergence of the scale-invariant step size $(1+1)$-ES with halfspace sampling is derived and its lower bounds are compared with those of the standard $(1+1)$-ES. We express the convergence rates in terms of expectations of random variables in finite dimensions of the search space. Lastly, we derive the expressions for the asymptotic normalised convergence rates when the dimension goes to infinity.

The objective of this paper is to present the concept of halfspace sampling in a $(1+1)$-ES. In details, the contributions of this paper are

- to introduce halfspace sampling in the elitist $(1+1)$-ES,
- to theoretically investigate algorithms' convergence rates on the spherical functions in finite and infinite dimensions,
- to experimentally compare convergence rates to evaluate the impact of halfspace sampling,
- to implement halfspace sampling in the $(1+1)$-CMA-ES and present the empirical performance results.

This paper is structured as follows. Section 2 explains in details how halfspace sampling works in a $(1+1)$-ES. Section 3 derives the linear convergence rates of a $(1+1)$-ES with halfspace sampling. Section 4 derives expressions for the asympotic normalized convergence rates. Numerical experiments are presented in Section 5 to evaluate the gain brought by halfspace sampling. In Section 6, we implement halfspace sampling in a $(1+1)$-CMA-ES and compare it with the standard $(1+1)$-CMA-ES. Lastly, we conclude this paper in Section 7.

2. HALFSPACE SAMPLING IN A (1+1)-ES

We start with formally defining halfspaces.

Definition 1. *Let* $\mathbf{n}$ *and* $\mathbf{x}_0$ *be two vectors in* $\mathbb{R}^n$. *The set* $H(\mathbf{n},\mathbf{x}_0) = \left\{\mathbf{x}\in\mathbb{R}^n : \mathbf{n}^T(\mathbf{x}-\mathbf{x}_0)=0\right\}$ *is a hyperplane in* $\mathbb{R}^n$ *passing through* $\mathbf{x}_0$ *and it has a normal vector* $\mathbf{n}$. *Corresponding to* H, *there is a pair of halfspaces: a positive closed halfsapce* $H_+(\mathbf{n},\mathbf{x}_0)$ *and a negative closed halfspace* $H_-(\mathbf{n},\mathbf{x}_0)$:

$$H_+(\mathbf{n},\mathbf{x}_0) = \left\{\mathbf{x}\in\mathbb{R}^n : \mathbf{n}^T(\mathbf{x}-\mathbf{x}_0)\geq 0\right\} \tag{1}$$

$$H_-(\mathbf{n},\mathbf{x}_0) = \left\{\mathbf{x}\in\mathbb{R}^n : \mathbf{n}^T(\mathbf{x}-\mathbf{x}_0)\leq 0\right\} \tag{2}$$

A halfspace is a convex set and its boundary is the hyperplane H that separates the space into two halfspaces. It defines a reflection that fixes the hyperplane and interchanges two halfspaces. By the definition, we can see that a hyperplane H is orthogonal to its normal vector $\mathbf{n}$. Any vector $\mathbf{x}$ with respect to the point $\mathbf{x}_0$ forms an acute angle with $\mathbf{n}$ when $\mathbf{x}$ lies in the positive closed halfspace, i.e. $\mathbf{x}\in H_+(\mathbf{n},\mathbf{x}_0)$. Similarly, it forms an obtuse angle if $\mathbf{x}$ lies in the negative closed halfspace, i.e. $\mathbf{x}\in H_-(\mathbf{n},\mathbf{x}_0)$. A positive closed halfspace can be derived from its respective negative closed halfspace by reversing the sign of the vector $\mathbf{n}$:

$$H_+(\mathbf{n},\mathbf{x}_0) = H_-(-\mathbf{n},\mathbf{x}_0) = -H_-(\mathbf{n},\mathbf{x}_0) \tag{3}$$

We can also derive similarly for a negative halfspace. Lastly, we define a lemma that is useful when we describe the optimal halfspaces in next section:

Lemma 1. *Let* $\mathbf{x},\mathbf{x}_0\in\mathbb{R}^n$ *be two vectors. Assume that* $\mathbf{x}_0+\mathbf{x}$ *lies in the positive closed halfspace* $H_+(\mathbf{n},\mathbf{x}_0)$ *with a normal vector* $\mathbf{n}\in\mathbb{R}^n$. *Then, the reflection* $\mathbf{x}_0-\mathbf{x}$ *with respect to* $\mathbf{x}_0$ *lies in the negative closed halfspace* $H_-(\mathbf{n},\mathbf{x}_0)$.

2.1 Halfspace Sampling

In halfspace sampling, the basic idea is to generate new candidate solutions in a halfspace where the previous successful samples are located. At iteration k, the positive halfspace $H_+(\mathbf{n},\mathbf{X}_k)$ with respect to the parent $\mathbf{X}_k$ is formed by accumulating the information of successful steps in recent iterations while the negative halfspace $H_-(\mathbf{n},\mathbf{X}_k)$ is formed from the information of unsuccessful steps. The two halfspaces have the same supporting hyperplanes that passes through the parent $\mathbf{X}_k$. Instead of sampling offspring that can lie in the whole search space $\mathbb{R}^n$, the $(1+1)$-ES with halfspace sampling generates offspring that lies in the positive halfspace $H_+(\mathbf{n},\mathbf{X}_k)$: If an offspring $\mathbf{X}_k+\boldsymbol{\mathcal{N}}$ lies in the positive halfspace, no action is required, where $\boldsymbol{\mathcal{N}}$ denotes a vector drawn from a standard multivariate normal distribution. Only if an offspring lies in the negative halfspace $\mathbf{X}_k+\boldsymbol{\mathcal{N}}\in H_-(\mathbf{n},\mathbf{X}_k)$, by Lemma 1, we reverse the direction of the random vector and the offspring will then lie in the positive halfspace i.e. $\mathbf{X}_k-\boldsymbol{\mathcal{N}}\in H_+(\mathbf{n},\mathbf{X}_k)$. Figure 1 illustrates the summary of the geometric interpretation for a parent, two halfspaces and the supporting hyperplane.

Algorithm 1 shows the pseudo code of the $(1+1)$-ES with halfspace sampling. We name the resulting strategy as $(1+1_{\rm hs})$-ES. Consider a scalar objective function $f:\mathbb{R}^n\mapsto\mathbb{R},\mathbf{x}\mapsto f(\mathbf{x})$ and $\mathbf{X}_k$ denotes the current parent at iteration k, and $\sigma_k\in\mathbb{R}_+$ is the step size. The vector $\mathbf{n}_k$ denotes the normal vector of the hyperplane H that passes through the parent $\mathbf{X}_k$. The algorithm starts by initialising $\mathbf{n}_k$ as a null vector $\mathbf{0}$. An instantiation of a multivariate normal distribution $\mathbf{Z}_k\sim\boldsymbol{\mathcal{N}}(\mathbf{0},\mathbf{I})$ with mean vector $\mathbf{0}$ and identity covariance matrix is generated. The vector $\mathbf{Z}_k$ is used if it lies in the positive halfspaces $H_+(\mathbf{n}_k,\mathbf{0})$, otherwise $-\mathbf{Z}_k$ is used.

2.2 Optimal Halfspaces in Convex Sublevel Sets

In a black box optimization scenario, the location of the optimum is unknown. It is necessary to understand the optimal halfspaces that contains as many better solutions as possible. Understanding the optimal halfspaces is also important for convergence analysis in next section as it affects the optimal bounds for convergence rates of the $(1+1_{\rm hs})$-ES. We now derive the optimal halfspaces at any point $\mathbf{x}\in\mathbb{R}^n$ when we optimise objective functions with convex sublevel sets. To achieve this, we first define the relationship between the supporting hyperplane and the tangent hyperplane at any point $\mathbf{x}$.

Definition 2. *Let* $f:\mathbb{R}^n\mapsto\mathbb{R},\mathbf{x}\mapsto f(\mathbf{x})$ *be an objective function with convex sublevel sets and* $\mathbf{x}_0\in\mathbb{R}^n$ *be a point in* n*-dimensional space. At the point* $\mathbf{x}_0$ *with an objective function value* $f(\mathbf{x}_0)$, *the supporting hyperplane contains all the points in the convex sublevel set* $C_-(\mathbf{x}_0) = \{\mathbf{x}\in\mathbb{R}^n : f(\mathbf{x})\leq f(\mathbf{x}_0)\}$ *with objective function values smaller than or equal to* $f(\mathbf{x}_0)$. *If* f *is differentiable at* $\mathbf{x}_0$, *then the tangent hyperplane* $T(\mathbf{x}_0)$ *at* $\mathbf{x}_0$ *is the supporting hyperplane.*

With this definition, we can derive the below lemma that the optimal halfspaces at a point $\mathbf{x}_0$ are delimited by the supporting hyperplane H at the point $\mathbf{x}_0$.

LEMMA 2. *Let f be an objective function with convex sublevel sets and assume f is differentiable. At the point $\mathbf{x}_0 \in \mathbb{R}^n$ with an objective function value $f(\mathbf{x}_0)$, the optimal halfspaces $H_+^*(\mathbf{n}^*, \mathbf{x}_0)$ and $H_-^*(\mathbf{n}^*, \mathbf{x}_0)$ with a normal vector $\mathbf{n}^*$ are delimited by the tangent hyperplane $T(\mathbf{x}_0)$. The optimal positive halfspace $H_+^*(\mathbf{n}^*, \mathbf{x}_0)$ contains all the points in $C_-(\mathbf{x}_0)$.*

By this lemma, the optimal positive halfspace delimited by the tangent hyperplane contains all the better solutions if we are optimising an objective function that has convex sublevel sets. We can additionally establish another lemma that the gradient descent direction at a point $\mathbf{x}_0$ is the normal of the supporting hyperplane for the optimal halfspaces at $\mathbf{x}_0$.

LEMMA 3. *Let $H_+^*(\mathbf{n}^*, \mathbf{x}_0)$ and $H_-^*(\mathbf{n}^*, \mathbf{x}_0)$ be the optimal halfspaces at the point $\mathbf{x}_0$ as in Lemma 2. If f is differentiable and has the convex sublevel sets, the normal vector $\mathbf{n}^*$ is in the form of $\left(-\frac{\partial f(\mathbf{x}_0)}{\partial x_1}, \ldots, -\frac{\partial f(\mathbf{x}_0)}{\partial x_n}\right)$ and it has the gradient descent direction at $\mathbf{x}_0$.*

Algorithm 1: Pseudo Code of a Simple (1+1)-ES with Halfspace Sampling

Initialise $\mathbf{X}_1$, σ_1, $\mathbf{n}_1 = \mathbf{0}, k = 1$
repeat
  $\mathbf{Z}_k \sim \mathcal{N}(\mathbf{0}, \mathbf{I})$
  if $\mathbf{Z}_k \notin H_+(\mathbf{n}_k, \mathbf{0})$ **then**
    $\mathbf{Z}_k = -\mathbf{Z}_k$
  $\mathbf{X}_k^{'} = \mathbf{X}_k + \sigma_k \mathbf{Z}_k$
  if $f(\mathbf{X}_k^{'}) \leq f(\mathbf{X}_k)$ **then**
    $\mathbf{X}_{k+1} \leftarrow \mathbf{X}_k^{'}$
  else
    $\mathbf{X}_{k+1} \leftarrow \mathbf{X}_k$
  $k = k + 1$
  `updateHalfSpaces`$(\mathbf{n}_k, \mathbf{Z}_k, f(\mathbf{X}_k^{'}), f(\mathbf{X}_k))$
until *termination condition is not met*;

3. LINEAR CONVERGENCE ON SPHERICAL FUNCTIONS

In this section, we theoretically investigate the gain brought by halfspace sampling. We are particularly interested in the linear convergence rates when the optimal halfspaces are used, i.e., $\mathbf{n}^*$ is known. In practice, the optimal halfspaces are not known and can be estimated only during the course of optimization. However, it is still of our interest as we can understand the maximum gain brought by halfspace sampling as well as the optimal bounds of convergence rates of the $(1 + 1_{\text{hs}})$-ES. We refer the resulting ES as the $(1 + 1_{\text{hs}})$-ES* where the optimal halfspaces are known.

Here we use the same definition of the linear convergence rate from [9, 2] and investigate convergence rates on spherical functions having the optimum in zero $g(||\mathbf{x}||), g \in \mathcal{M}$ where $\mathcal{M}$ denotes the set of functions $g : \mathbb{R} \mapsto \mathbb{R}$ that are strictly increasing. We study the case of the scale-invariant step size where $\sigma_k = \sigma||\mathbf{X}_k||$. We refer the resulting ES as scale-invariant step size ES. For different variants of algorithms with scale-invariant step size, the linear convergence is proved by the following reasons. First, there exists a CR $\in \mathbb{R}$ such that for all $k, k_0 \in \mathbb{R}$ with $k > k_0$

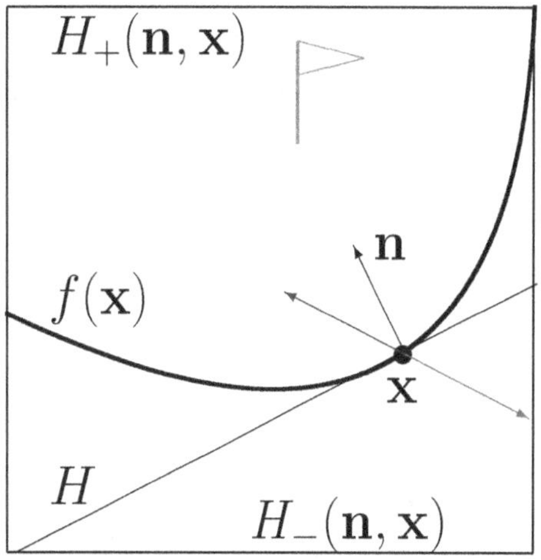

Figure 1: Halfspace sampling on an objective function f with convex sublevel sets. The flag in the diagram represents the optimum of the function. The curve represents the points having function value $f(\mathbf{x})$. The supporting hyperplane H (black solid line) with a normal vector n separates the space into the positive halfspace $H_+(\mathbf{n}, \mathbf{x})$ (the area above the line) and the negative halfspace $H_-(\mathbf{n}, \mathbf{x})$ (the area below the line). If a candidate solution (the red vector) lies in the negative halfspace, it will be discarded. Its reflection (the blue vector) with respect to x, which lies in the positive halfspace, will be used.

$$\frac{1}{\Lambda} \frac{1}{k - k_0} \mathrm{E}\left[-\ln \frac{||\mathbf{X}_k||}{||\mathbf{X}_{k_0}||}\right] = \mathrm{CR} \tag{4}$$

where Λ is the number of function evaluations in each iteration. This convergence rate CR of the algorithm is compatible with the almost sure convergence rate [2]. Therefore, we can prove that with scale-invariant step size, almost surely

$$-\frac{1}{\Lambda} \frac{1}{k - k_0} \ln \frac{||\mathbf{X}_k||}{||\mathbf{X}_{k_0}||} \xrightarrow[k \to \infty]{} \mathrm{CR}$$

For details of proof, please refer to [9, 2].

3.1 Preliminaries

Before establishing the main results, we derive some technical results and introduce some useful definitions. In a scale-invariant step size $(1 + 1)$-ES, in each iteration, a random independent vector following a standard multivariate normal distribution $\mathcal{N}$ is sampled to create an offspring $\mathbf{X}_k^{'} = \mathbf{X}_k + \sigma||\mathbf{X}_k||\mathcal{N}$. The distribution of $\sigma||\mathbf{X}_k||\mathcal{N}$ depends in prior on $\mathbf{X}_k$. However, since the distribution of $\mathcal{N}$ is spherical, the distribution of $\mathbf{X}_k + \sigma||\mathbf{X}_k||\mathcal{N}$ will be the same if we start from any vector with unit norm, so WLOG in the scale-invariant step size the distribution is independent of $\mathbf{X}_k$ and is determined by $||\mathbf{e}_1 + \sigma\mathcal{N}||$.

LEMMA 4. *Let $H_+^*(\mathbf{n}^*, \mathbf{e}_1)$ and $H_-^*(\mathbf{n}^*, \mathbf{e}_1)$ be the optimal halfspaces at the point $\mathbf{e}_1$. On spherical functions, the normalised normal vector $\mathbf{n}^*$ is $-\mathbf{e}_1$ and has the gradient descent direction to the optimum.*

The lemma establishes that the tangent hyperspace with a normal vector $-\mathbf{e}_1$ separates the space into two halfspaces and the convex sublevel sets $C_-(\mathbf{e}_1)$ lies in the positive halfspaces only. We now establish another lemma that simplifies the event of a candidate solution lying in the optimal halfspaces.

LEMMA 5. *Let $H_+^*(\mathbf{n}^*, \mathbf{e}_1)$ and $H_-^*(\mathbf{n}^*, \mathbf{e}_1)$ be the optimal halfspaces at the point $\mathbf{e}_1 = (1, 0, \ldots, 0)$ where $\mathbf{n}^*$ is the vector $-\mathbf{e}_1$. Let also $\mathbf{x}_{\mathbf{e}_1}^+$ be a candidate solution $\mathbf{x}_{\mathbf{e}_1}^+ = \mathbf{e}_1 + \sigma\boldsymbol{\mathcal{N}}$ sampled from the parent $\mathbf{e}_1$. On spherical functions, the two events $\{\mathbf{x}_{\mathbf{e}_1}^+ \in H_+^*(\mathbf{n}^*, \mathbf{e}_1)\}$ and $\{\mathbf{x}_{\mathbf{e}_1}^+ \in H_-^*(\mathbf{n}^*, \mathbf{e}_1)\}$ can be written as $\{\sigma[\boldsymbol{\mathcal{N}}]_1 \leq 0\}$ and $\{\sigma[\boldsymbol{\mathcal{N}}]_1 \geq 0\}$ respectively.*

We can establish a similar lemma for the candidate solution $\mathbf{x}_{\mathbf{e}_1}^- = \mathbf{e}_1 - \sigma\boldsymbol{\mathcal{N}}$.

LEMMA 6. *Let $\mathbf{x}_{\mathbf{e}_1}^-$ be a candidate solution $\mathbf{x}_{\mathbf{e}_1}^- = \mathbf{e}_1 - \sigma\boldsymbol{\mathcal{N}}$ sampled from the parent $\mathbf{e}_1$. On spherical functions, the two events $\{\mathbf{x}_{\mathbf{e}_1}^- \in H_+^*(\mathbf{n}^*, \mathbf{e}_1)\}$ and $\{\mathbf{x}_{\mathbf{e}_1}^- \in H_-^*(\mathbf{n}^*, \mathbf{e}_1)\}$ can be written as $\{\sigma[\boldsymbol{\mathcal{N}}]_1 \geq 0\}$ and $\{\sigma[\boldsymbol{\mathcal{N}}]_1 \leq 0\}$ respectively.*

With lemma 5 and 6, we can establish that on spherical functions, an offspring $\mathbf{x}_{\mathbf{e}_1}^+$ (or $\mathbf{x}_{\mathbf{e}_1}^-$) sampled from the parent $\mathbf{e}_1$ lies in the positive halfspace only if the scalar projection of $\sigma[\boldsymbol{\mathcal{N}}]_1$ onto the first coordinate $\mathbf{e}_1$ has a negative sign. That implies that a better solution is found only if $\sigma[\boldsymbol{\mathcal{N}}]_1$ is negative. Otherwise, a worse solution is sampled in the negative halfspace that does not contain the convex sublevel sets $C_-(\mathbf{e}_1)$.

We now need to use the indicator function for the event of an offspring lying in the optimal positive halfspace $H_+^*(\mathbf{n}^*, \mathbf{e}_1)$. We also need the indicator function for the event of an offspring being better than its parent $\mathbf{e}_1$. Therefore, we define the random variables U,V W^+ and W^-:

DEFINITION 3. *Let $U = \sigma[\boldsymbol{\mathcal{N}}]_1, V = -2|[\boldsymbol{\mathcal{N}}]_1| + \sigma||\boldsymbol{\mathcal{N}}||^2$, $W^+ = 2[\boldsymbol{\mathcal{N}}]_1 + \sigma||\boldsymbol{\mathcal{N}}||^2$ and $W^- = -2[\boldsymbol{\mathcal{N}}]_1 + \sigma||\boldsymbol{\mathcal{N}}||^2$*

We express the indicators for the events of $\mathbf{x}_{\mathbf{e}_1}^+$ or $\mathbf{x}_{\mathbf{e}_1}^-$ lying in the optimal positive halfspace with respect to $\mathbf{e}_1$ as

$$1_{\{\mathbf{x}_{\mathbf{e}_1}^+ \in H_+^*(\mathbf{n}^*, \mathbf{e}_1)\}} = 1_{\{U \leq 0\}} \tag{5}$$

$$1_{\{\mathbf{x}_{\mathbf{e}_1}^- \in H_+^*(\mathbf{n}^*, \mathbf{e}_1)\}} = 1_{\{U \geq 0\}} \tag{6}$$

and the indicator for the events of $\mathbf{x}_{\mathbf{e}_1}^+$ or $\mathbf{x}_{\mathbf{e}_1}^-$ being better than $\mathbf{e}_1$ as

$$1_{\{\mathbf{x}_{\mathbf{e}_1}^+ \text{ is better than } \mathbf{e}_1\}} = 1_{\{W^+ \leq 0\}} \tag{7}$$

$$1_{\{\mathbf{x}_{\mathbf{e}_1}^- \text{ is better than } \mathbf{e}_1\}} = 1_{\{W^- \leq 0\}} \tag{8}$$

We now establish one more technical lemma that is useful when we derive the linear convergence rate of $(1 + 1_{\text{hs}})$-ES*.

LEMMA 7. *The following two equations hold*

$$\begin{aligned} &\mathrm{E}\left[\ln(1 + \sigma W^+ 1_{\{U \leq 0, W^+ \leq 0\}} + \sigma W^- 1_{\{U > 0, W^- \leq 0\}})\right] \\ =&\mathrm{E}\left[\ln(1 + \sigma W^+ 1_{\{W^+ \leq 0\}} + \sigma W^- 1_{\{W^- \leq 0\}})\right] \end{aligned} \tag{9}$$

$$\begin{aligned} \mathrm{E}\left[\ln(1 + \sigma W^+ 1_{\{U \leq 0, W^+ \leq 0\}} + \sigma W^- 1_{\{U > 0, W^- \leq 0\}})\right] \\ = \mathrm{E}\left[\ln(1 + \sigma V 1_{\{V \leq 0\}})\right] \end{aligned} \tag{10}$$

where $U = \sigma[\boldsymbol{\mathcal{N}}]_1, V = -2|[\boldsymbol{\mathcal{N}}]_1| + \sigma||\boldsymbol{\mathcal{N}}||^2$, $W^+ = 2[\boldsymbol{\mathcal{N}}]_1 + \sigma||\boldsymbol{\mathcal{N}}||^2$ and $W^- = -2[\boldsymbol{\mathcal{N}}]_1 + \sigma||\boldsymbol{\mathcal{N}}||^2$ and $\boldsymbol{\mathcal{N}}$ is a random vector following a standard multivariate distribution.

3.2 The (1+1)-ES with Optimal Halfspaces

We now prove the linear convergence of the $(1 + 1_{\text{hs}})$-ES* with scale-invariant step size. We focus on investigation on the lower bounds of convergence rates for $(1 + 1_{\text{hs}})$-ES*. By comparing its lower bounds with those of a standard (1+1)-ES, we derive that the maximum gain brought by halfspace sampling is a factor of 2 in finite dimensions.

In a $(1 + 1_{\text{hs}})$-ES* with scale-invariant step size, a single offspring $\mathbf{X}_k^+ = \mathbf{X}_k + \sigma||\mathbf{X}_k||\boldsymbol{\mathcal{N}}$ is sampled from the parent $\mathbf{X}_k$, where $\boldsymbol{\mathcal{N}}$ is a standard multivariate normal distribution independent of $\mathbf{X}_k$. If the offspring $\mathbf{X}_k + \sigma||\mathbf{X}_k||\boldsymbol{\mathcal{N}}$ lies in the optimal negative halfspace $H_-^*(\mathbf{n}^*, \mathbf{X}_k)$, the direction of $\boldsymbol{\mathcal{N}}$ is reversed and the offspring becomes $\mathbf{X}_k^- = \mathbf{X}_k - \sigma||\mathbf{X}_k||\boldsymbol{\mathcal{N}}$. By Lemma 1, the new offspring lies in the optimal positive halfspace $H_+^*(\mathbf{n}^*, \mathbf{X}_k)$. Now, the update equation for $||\mathbf{X}_k||$ on spherical functions reads:

$$\begin{aligned} ||\mathbf{X}_{k+1}|| = &||\mathbf{X}_k^+|| \times 1_{\{\mathbf{X}_k^+ \in H_+^*(\mathbf{n}^*, \mathbf{X}_k), ||\mathbf{X}_k^+|| \leq ||\mathbf{X}_k||\}} \\ &+ ||\mathbf{X}_k^-|| \times 1_{\{\mathbf{X}_k^+ \notin H_+^*(\mathbf{n}^*, \mathbf{X}_k), ||\mathbf{X}_k^-|| \leq ||\mathbf{X}_k||\}} \\ &+ ||\mathbf{X}_k|| \times 1_{\{\mathbf{X}_k^+ \in H_+^*(\mathbf{n}^*, \mathbf{X}_k), ||\mathbf{X}_k^+|| > ||\mathbf{X}_k||\}} \\ &+ ||\mathbf{X}_k|| \times 1_{\{\mathbf{X}_k^+ \notin H_+^*(\mathbf{n}^*, \mathbf{X}_k), ||\mathbf{X}_k^-|| > ||\mathbf{X}_k||\}} \end{aligned} \tag{11}$$

where $\mathbf{X}_k^+ = \mathbf{X}_k + \sigma||\mathbf{X}_k||\boldsymbol{\mathcal{N}}$ and $\mathbf{X}_k^- = \mathbf{X}_k - \sigma||\mathbf{X}_k||\boldsymbol{\mathcal{N}}$. We now establish the following lemma before we prove the linear convergence of the $(1 + 1_{\text{hs}})$-ES* with scale-invariant step size:

LEMMA 8. *Let Z_k be the sequence of random variables*

$$\begin{aligned} Z_k = \frac{1}{2}\ln\Big[&||\mathbf{Y}_k^+||^2 \times 1_{\{\mathbf{Y}_k^+ \in H_+^*(\mathbf{n}^*, \mathbf{Y}_k), ||\mathbf{Y}_k^+|| \leq ||\mathbf{Y}_k||\}} \\ &+ ||\mathbf{Y}_k^-||^2 \times 1_{\{\mathbf{Y}_k^+ \notin H_+^*(\mathbf{n}^*, \mathbf{Y}_k), ||\mathbf{Y}_k^-|| \leq ||\mathbf{Y}_k||\}} \\ &+ ||\mathbf{Y}_k||^2 \times 1_{\{\mathbf{Y}_k^+ \in H_+^*(\mathbf{n}^*, \mathbf{Y}_k), ||\mathbf{Y}_k^+|| > ||\mathbf{Y}_k||\}} \\ &+ ||\mathbf{Y}_k||^2 \times 1_{\{\mathbf{Y}_k^+ \notin H_+^*(\mathbf{n}^*, \mathbf{Y}_k), ||\mathbf{Y}_k^-|| > ||\mathbf{Y}_k||\}}\Big] \end{aligned} \tag{12}$$

where $\mathbf{Y}_k = \mathbf{X}_k/||\mathbf{X}_k||$, $\mathbf{Y}_k^+ = \mathbf{X}_k/||\mathbf{X}_k|| + \sigma\boldsymbol{\mathcal{N}}$ and $\mathbf{Y}_k^- = \mathbf{X}_k/||\mathbf{X}_k|| - \sigma\boldsymbol{\mathcal{N}}$. Then Z_k are independent identically distributed as

$$Z^{(1+1_{\text{hs}})} = \frac{1}{2}\ln\left[1 + \sigma V 1_{\{V \leq 0\}}\right]$$

We are now ready to prove the linear convergence of the $(1 + 1_{\text{hs}})$-ES* and express its convergence rate in terms of $Z^{(1+1_{\text{hs}})}$.

THEOREM 1. *The $(1 + 1_{\text{hs}})$-ES* with scale-invariant step size ($\sigma_k = \sigma||\mathbf{X}_k||$) converge linearly on the class of spherical functions $g(||\mathbf{x}||), g \in \mathcal{M}$, and*

$$\lim_{k\to\infty}\frac{1}{k}\ln\frac{||\mathbf{X}_k||}{||\mathbf{X}_0||} = \mathrm{CR}_{(1+1_{\text{hs}})}(\sigma) = \frac{1}{2}\mathrm{E}\left[\ln(1 + \sigma V 1_{\{V \leq 0\}}\right] \tag{13}$$

where $V = -2|[\boldsymbol{\mathcal{N}}]_1| + \sigma||\boldsymbol{\mathcal{N}}||^2$ and $\boldsymbol{\mathcal{N}}$ follows a standard multivariate normal distribution.

PROOF. We start with the equation (11), square it and normalise the equation by $||\mathbf{X}_k||$ and take the logarithm. We get

$$\frac{1}{2}\ln\frac{||\mathbf{X}_{k+1}||^2}{||\mathbf{X}_k||^2} = \frac{1}{2}\ln\Big[||\mathbf{Y}_k^+||^2 \times 1_{\{\mathbf{Y}_k^+\in H_+^*(\mathbf{n}^*,\mathbf{Y}_k),||\mathbf{Y}_k^+||\le||\mathbf{Y}_k||\}} + ||\mathbf{Y}_k^-||^2 \times 1_{\{\mathbf{Y}_k^+\notin H_+^*(\mathbf{n}^*,\mathbf{Y}_k),||\mathbf{Y}_k^-||\le||\mathbf{Y}_k||\}} + ||\mathbf{Y}_k||^2 \times 1_{\{\mathbf{Y}_k^+\in H_+^*(\mathbf{n}^*,\mathbf{Y}_k),||\mathbf{Y}_k^+||>||\mathbf{Y}_k||\}} + ||\mathbf{Y}_k||^2 \times 1_{\{\mathbf{Y}_k^+\notin H_+^*(\mathbf{n}^*,\mathbf{Y}_k),||\mathbf{Y}_k^-||>||\mathbf{Y}_k||\}}\Big] \tag{14}$$

where $\mathbf{Y}_k = \mathbf{X}_k/||\mathbf{X}_k||$, $\mathbf{Y}_k^+ = \mathbf{X}_k/||\mathbf{X}_k|| + \sigma\mathcal{N}$ and $\mathbf{Y}_k^- = \mathbf{X}_k/||\mathbf{X}_k|| - \sigma\mathcal{N}$. According to Lemma 8, by isotropy of the standard multivariate normal distribution, the random variables in the RHS of equation (14) are independent and identically distributed as

$$Z^{(1+1_{\text{hs}})} = \frac{1}{2}\ln\left[1 + \sigma V 1_{\{V\le 0\}}\right].$$

By applying law of large number (LLN) for independent random variable,

$$\frac{1}{k}\ln\frac{||\mathbf{X}_k||}{||\mathbf{X}_0||} = \frac{1}{2k}\sum_{i=0}^{k-1}\ln\frac{||\mathbf{X}_{i+1}||^2}{||\mathbf{X}_i||^2}$$

and it converges to $\mathrm{E}\left[Z^{(1+1_{\text{hs}})}\right]$ and hence the result. □

We have derived the linear convergence rate of a $(1+1_{\text{hs}})$-ES*. We now derive the gain brought from halfspace sampling by considering the ratio of $\mathrm{CR}_{(1+1_{\text{hs}})}(\sigma)$ to $\mathrm{CR}_{(1+1)}(\sigma)$.

THEOREM 2. *The $(1+1_{\text{hs}})$-ES* with scale-invariant step size ($\sigma_k = \sigma||\mathbf{X}_k||$) converge linearly on the class of spherical functions $g(||\mathbf{x}||), g \in \mathcal{M}$, and the convergence rate is 2 times faster than that of the (1+1)-ES with scale-invariant step size, i.e.*

$$\frac{\mathrm{CR}_{(1+1_{\text{hs}})}(\sigma)}{\mathrm{CR}_{(1+1)}(\sigma)} = 2 \tag{15}$$

PROOF. First we refer the equation (7) in [1] for the definition of $\mathrm{CR}_{(1+1)}(\sigma)$. Consider the LHS of the equation (15) and by Lemma 7, we can substitute equations (9) into (15),

$$\begin{aligned}&\frac{\mathrm{CR}_{(1+1_{\text{hs}})}(\sigma)}{\mathrm{CR}_{(1+1)}(\sigma)}\\ =&\frac{\mathrm{E}\left[\ln(1+\sigma V 1_{\{V\le 0\}}\right]}{\mathrm{E}\left[\ln(1+\sigma W^+ 1_{\{W^+\le 0\}}\right]}\\ =&\frac{\mathrm{E}\left[\ln(1+\sigma W^+ 1_{\{W^+\le 0\}} + \sigma W^- 1_{\{W^-<0\}})\right]}{\mathrm{E}\left[\ln(1+\sigma W^+ 1_{\{W^+\le 0\}})\right]}\end{aligned} \tag{16}$$

By Lemma 8 in [1], we can further write the equation (16) as

$$\frac{\mathrm{E}\left[2\ln(1+\sigma W^+ 1_{\{W^+\le 0\}})\right]}{\mathrm{E}\left[\ln(1+\sigma W^+ 1_{\{W^+\le 0\}})\right]}$$

Hence the result holds. □

4. ASYMPTOTIC CONVERGENCE RATES

In this section, we study how the finite dimension convergence rates derived previously for $(1+1_{\text{hs}})$-ES* behave when the dimension goes infinity. We first derive the limit of the probability of success $p^s_{(1+1_{\text{hs}})}(\sigma/d)$ and a technical lemma.

LEMMA 9. *For all $\sigma > 0$,*

$$\lim_{n\to\infty} p^s_{(1+1_{\text{hs}})}\left(\frac{\sigma}{n}\right) = \Pr\left(|\,[\mathcal{N}]_1\,| \ge \sigma/2\right) = \bar{\Phi}_{\text{HN}}\left(\frac{\sigma}{2}\right) \tag{17}$$

where $\bar{\Phi}_{\text{HN}}$ is the complementary cumulative distribution of a standard half-normal distribution, $\bar{\Phi}_{\text{HN}}(x) = \sqrt{\frac{2}{\pi}}\int_x^\infty e^{-\frac{x^2}{2}}\,dx$ or, with the error function erf, $\bar{\Phi}_{\text{HN}}(x) = 1 - \mathrm{erf}\left(\frac{x}{\sqrt{2}}\right)$.

LEMMA 10. *The following equation holds for all $\sigma > 0$*

$$\mathrm{E}\left[|\,[\mathcal{N}]_1\,| 1_{\{|[\mathcal{N}]_1|\ge\sigma/2\}}\right] = \sqrt{\frac{2}{\pi}}\exp\left(-\frac{\sigma^2}{8}\right) \tag{18}$$

We now derive the asymptotic convergence rate of the $(1+1_{\text{hs}})$-ES* with scale-invariant step size.

THEOREM 3. *Assuming the uniform integrability, for $\sigma > 0$, the convergence rate of the $(1+1_{\text{hs}})$-ES* with scale-invariant step size on spherical functions satisfies at the limit*

$$\lim_{n\to\infty} n \times \mathrm{CR}_{(1+1_{\text{hs}})}\left(\frac{\sigma}{n}\right) = -\sqrt{\frac{2\sigma^2}{\pi}}\exp\left(-\frac{\sigma^2}{8}\right) + \frac{\sigma^2}{2}\bar{\Phi}_{\text{HN}}\left(\frac{\sigma}{2}\right) \tag{19}$$

PROOF. We start by investigating the limit of the random variable of

$$\mathrm{CR}_{(1+1_{\text{hs}})}\left(\frac{\sigma}{n}\right) = \frac{1}{2}\mathrm{E}\left[\ln\left(1 + \frac{\sigma}{n}\min\left(-2|\,[\mathcal{N}]_1\,| + \frac{\sigma}{n}||\mathcal{N}||^2, 0\right)\right)\right]$$

The following equation holds

$$\lim_{n\to\infty} n \times \frac{1}{2}\ln\left(1+\frac{\sigma}{n}\min\left(-2|\,[\mathcal{N}]_1\,| + \frac{\sigma}{n}||\mathcal{N}||^2, 0\right)\right) \xrightarrow[n\to\infty]{} \frac{1}{2}\sigma\min\left(-2|\,[\mathcal{N}]_1\,| + \sigma, 0\right) \tag{20}$$

We can further derive that

$$\begin{aligned}&\lim_{k\to\infty} n \times \mathrm{CR}_{(1+1_{\text{hs}})}\left(\frac{\sigma}{n}\right)\\ =&\frac{\sigma}{2}\mathrm{E}\left[\min\left(-2|\,[\mathcal{N}]_1\,| + \sigma, 0\right)\right]\\ =&\frac{\sigma}{2}\mathrm{E}\left[\left(-2|\,[\mathcal{N}]_1\,| + \sigma\right)1_{\{-2|[\mathcal{N}]_1|+\sigma\le 0\}}\right]\\ =&-\sigma\mathrm{E}\left[\left(|\,[\mathcal{N}]_1\,|\right)1_{\{-2|[\mathcal{N}]_1|+\sigma\le 0\}}\right] + \frac{\sigma^2}{2}\Pr\left(-2|\,[\mathcal{N}]_1\,| + \sigma \le 0\right)\\ =&-\sigma\mathrm{E}\left[\left(|\,[\mathcal{N}]_1\,|\right)1_{\{|[\mathcal{N}]_1|\ge\sigma/2\}}\right] + \frac{\sigma^2}{2}\Pr\left(|\,[\mathcal{N}]_1\,| \ge \sigma/2\right)\end{aligned} \tag{21}$$

By Lemma 9 and 10, we substitute equations (17) and (18) into (21), then the result follows. □

Putting together the expressions of asymptotic convergence rates and limits of probabilities of success, we can obtain the gain brought by halfspace sampling in the $(1+1_{\text{hs}})$-ES* when the dimension n goes to infinity. With Lemma 9, we first derive the limit of the probability of success in the $(1+1_{\text{hs}})$-ES* is 2 times that of the $(1+1)$-ES.

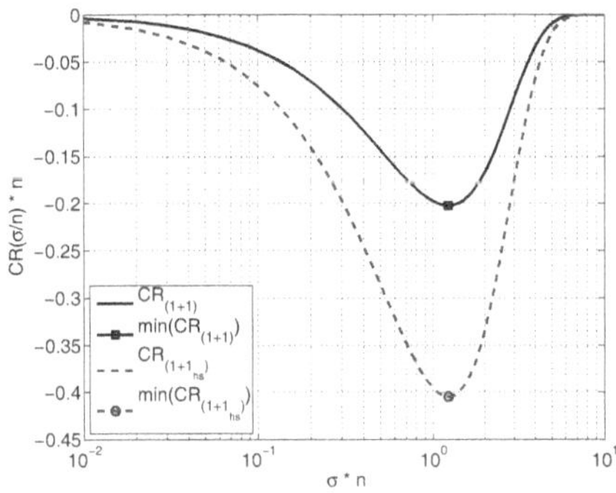

Figure 2: Theoretical limits results of the convergence rates for the $(1+1)$-ES in solid line (See Theorem 5 in [1]) and $(1+1_{\mathrm{hs}})$-ES* (Equation (19)) in dashed line if the dimension n goes to infinity.

THEOREM 4. *For all $\sigma > 0$,*

$$\lim_{n\to\infty} \frac{p^s_{(1+1_{\mathrm{hs}})}(\frac{\sigma}{n})}{p^s_{(1+1)}(\frac{\sigma}{n})} = 2 \tag{22}$$

where $p^s_{(1+1)}(\frac{\sigma}{n})$ is the limit of the probability of success of the $(1+1)$-ES.

PROOF. By Lemma 13 in [1], we can write the limit of the probability of success of the $(1+1)$-ES as

$$p^s_{(1+1)}(\frac{\sigma}{n}) = \Phi(-\frac{\sigma}{2}) = \frac{1}{2}\left(1+\mathrm{erf}(-\frac{\sigma}{2\sqrt{2}})\right) \tag{23}$$

Moreover, by Lemma 9, the LHS of equation (22) can be simplified into

$$\lim_{n\to\infty} \frac{p^s_{(1+1_{\mathrm{hs}})}(\frac{\sigma}{n})}{p^s_{(1+1)}(\frac{\sigma}{n})} = \frac{1-\mathrm{erf}(\frac{\sigma}{2\sqrt{2}})}{\frac{1}{2}\left(1+\mathrm{erf}(-\frac{\sigma}{2\sqrt{2}})\right)} \tag{24}$$

Since the error function has the property of

$$\mathrm{erf}(-\frac{\sigma}{2\sqrt{2}}) = -\mathrm{erf}(\frac{\sigma}{2\sqrt{2}}) \tag{25}$$

we substitute equation (25) into (24), we obtain the results. □

THEOREM 5. *Assuming the uniform integrability, for $\sigma > 0$, the convergence rate of the $(1+1_{\mathrm{hs}})$-ES* with scale-invariant step size on spherical functions converges at the rate that is twice faster than that of the $(1+1)$-ES with scale-invariant step size, i.e.*

$$\lim_{n\to\infty} \frac{\mathrm{CR}_{(1+1_{\mathrm{hs}})}\left(\frac{\sigma}{n}\right)}{\mathrm{CR}_{(1+1)}\left(\frac{\sigma}{n}\right)} = 2$$

PROOF. We start by substitute the CR into the expression into:

$$\begin{aligned}
&\lim_{n\to\infty} \frac{n \times \mathrm{CR}_{(1+1_{\mathrm{hs}})}\left(\frac{\sigma}{n}\right)}{n \times \mathrm{CR}_{(1+1)}\left(\frac{\sigma}{n}\right)} \\
&= \lim_{n\to\infty} \frac{n \ln(1+\frac{\sigma}{n}\min(-2|[\boldsymbol{\mathcal{N}}]_1| + \frac{\sigma}{n}||\boldsymbol{\mathcal{N}}||^2, 0))}{n \ln(1+\frac{\sigma}{n}\min(2[\boldsymbol{\mathcal{N}}]_1 + \frac{\sigma}{n}||\boldsymbol{\mathcal{N}}||^2, 0))} \\
&\xrightarrow[n\to\infty]{} \frac{\min(-2|[\boldsymbol{\mathcal{N}}]_1| + \sigma, 0)}{\min(2[\boldsymbol{\mathcal{N}}]_1 + \sigma, 0)}
\end{aligned} \tag{26}$$

Because of uniform integrability, we can write the equation into

$$\begin{aligned}
&\lim_{n\to\infty} \frac{\mathrm{CR}_{(1+1_{\mathrm{hs}})}\left(\frac{\sigma}{n}\right)}{\mathrm{CR}_{(1+1)}\left(\frac{\sigma}{n}\right)} = \frac{\mathrm{E}\left[\min\left(-2|[\boldsymbol{\mathcal{N}}]_1| + \sigma, 0\right)\right]}{\mathrm{E}\left[\min\left(2[\boldsymbol{\mathcal{N}}]_1 + \sigma, 0\right)\right]} \\
&= \frac{\mathrm{E}\left[\left(-2|[\boldsymbol{\mathcal{N}}]_1| + \sigma\right) 1_{\{-2|[\boldsymbol{\mathcal{N}}]_1|+\sigma \le 0\}}\right]}{\mathrm{E}\left[\left(2[\boldsymbol{\mathcal{N}}]_1 + \sigma\right) 1_{\{2[\boldsymbol{\mathcal{N}}]_1+\sigma \le 0\}}\right]} \\
&= \frac{\mathrm{E}\left[\left(-2|[\boldsymbol{\mathcal{N}}]_1| + \sigma\right) 1_{\{|[\boldsymbol{\mathcal{N}}]_1| \ge \sigma/2\}}\right]}{\mathrm{E}\left[\left(2[\boldsymbol{\mathcal{N}}]_1 + \sigma\right) 1_{\{[\boldsymbol{\mathcal{N}}]_1 \le -\sigma/2\}}\right]}
\end{aligned} \tag{27}$$

Since

$$\begin{aligned}
&\left(-2|[\boldsymbol{\mathcal{N}}]_1| + \sigma\right) 1_{\{|[\boldsymbol{\mathcal{N}}]_1| \ge \sigma/2\}} \\
&= \left(2[\boldsymbol{\mathcal{N}}]_1 + \sigma\right) 1_{\{[\boldsymbol{\mathcal{N}}]_1 \le -\sigma/2\}} + \left(-2[\boldsymbol{\mathcal{N}}]_1 + \sigma\right) 1_{\{[\boldsymbol{\mathcal{N}}]_1 \ge \sigma/2\}} \\
&= 2\left[\left(2[\boldsymbol{\mathcal{N}}]_1 + \sigma\right) 1_{\{[\boldsymbol{\mathcal{N}}]_1 \le -\sigma/2\}}\right]
\end{aligned} \tag{28}$$

Substitue equation (28) into (27), we obtain the result. □

Geometrically, we can interpret Theorems 2, 5 and 4 as follows: Consider a point $\mathbf{x} \in \mathbb{R}^n$ in the search space. A new sample is drawn from a standard multivariate normal distribution $\boldsymbol{\mathcal{N}}$ with its center located at $\mathbf{x}$. Since $\boldsymbol{\mathcal{N}}$ is isotropic, the probability of sampling a new point in any pairs of halfspaces with respect to $\mathbf{x}$ are the same. By Lemma 2, the optimal negative halfspace does not contain any points that are better than $\mathbf{x}$ if the underlying objective function has convex sublevel sets. With respect to the point $\mathbf{x}$, all the points in the negative halfspace are reflected into the positive halfspace. This is actually equivalent to *folding* over the probability mass in the negative halfspace and doubling the probability density in the positive halfspace.

We end this section by presenting a graph to compare the asymptotic convergence rate of a $(1+1)$-ES [1] and that of a $(1+1_{\mathrm{hs}})$-ES* (Equation (19)). Figure 2 shows the normal convergence rates of both algorithms. The minimal convergence rates of the $(1+1)$-ES and $(1+1_{\mathrm{hs}})$-ES* are approximately -0.202 and -0.404 respectively. By Theorem 5, halfspace sampling speeds up a single parent elitist evolution strategies by a factor of 2 regardless of step size σ chosen when the dimensions goes to infinity.

5. NUMERICAL SIMULATIONS ON CONVERGENCE RATES

We now compare the linear convergence rates of the $(1+1)$-ES with and without halfspace sampling. As the convergence rates are expressed in terms of the expectations of some random variables, we can simulate the convergence rates in finite dimensions by means of Monte-Carlo method. For every convergence rate expression, we simulate 10^6 times for each expectation of a random variable and averaged to obtain an estimate of the expectation and hence the convergence rates for different σ. The step size σ is chosen such that it is in the range of $0.01 \le \sigma \cdot n \le 10$ and with steps of 0.01 in $\sigma \cdot n$.

Figure 3 shows the resulting convergence rates in our simulations versus σ in the dimensions from 2 to 160. Overall in the simulations, the step sizes for the best measured convergence rates for $(1+1_{\mathrm{hs}})$-ES* are approximately the same as those in (1 + 1)-ES in the corresponding dimensions. Figure 3 also shows the best observed convergence rates for the $(1+1_{\text{hs}})$-ES* and the (1 + 1)-ES against the dimensions. By Theorem 2, $(1+1_{\text{hs}})$-ES* converges at a rate which is twice faster than that of a (1+)-ES. In all cases of our simulations in finite dimensions, the best observed convergence rates of the $(1+1_{\text{hs}})$-ES* approximately 2 times of those of the (1 + 1)-ES. The observed ratios of $\text{CR}_{(1+1_{\text{hs}})}\left(\frac{\sigma}{n}\right)/\text{CR}_{(1+1)}\left(\frac{\sigma}{n}\right)$ are constantly 2.

6. APPLICATIONS TO (1+1)-CMA-ES

In this section, we present the implementation of halfspace sampling in the (1+1)-CMA-ES [8]. The (1+1)-CMA-ES is basically an extension of the (1+1)-ES with one-fifth success rule where a covariance matrix of the search distribution is adapted during the course of optimization.

A (1 + 1)-CMA-ES consists of a parental candidate solution $\mathbf{X}_k \in \mathbb{R}$, the search path $\mathbf{p}_k \in \mathbb{R}^n$, a global step size $\sigma_k \in \mathbb{R}^+$, the success probability estimate $P^{\text{succ}} \in \mathbb{R}$ and the covariance matrix $\mathbf{C}_k \in \mathbb{R}^{n\times n}$. Consider an objective function $f: \mathbb{R}^n \mapsto \mathbb{R}, \mathbf{X} \mapsto f(\mathbf{X})$. At iteration k, the (1+1)-CMA-ES repeats the following steps until the termination condition is met:

1. Determine the Cholesky factor $\mathbf{A}_k \in \mathbb{R}^{n\times n}$ such that $\mathbf{C}_k = \mathbf{A}_k\mathbf{A}_k^{\text{T}}$.

2. Generate the offspring candidate solution $\mathbf{X}_k^{'} = \mathbf{X}_k + \sigma\mathbf{A}_k\mathbf{Z}_k$ where the vector $\mathbf{Z}_k$ is a n-dimensional random vector draw from a standard multivariate normal distribution.

3. If the offspring candidate solution is better than its parent $f(\mathbf{X}_k^{'}) \leq f(\mathbf{X}_k)$,

   (a) Assign $\mathbf{X}_k^{'}$ to $\mathbf{X}_k$.

   (b) Update the success probability estimate P_{k+1}^{succ} by $(1-c_p)P_k^{\text{succ}} + c_p$, where c_p is a learning rate $(0 < c_p \leq 1)$.

   (c) Update the search path $\mathbf{p}_{k+1}$ by $(1-c_c)\mathbf{p}_k + \mathbf{1}_{\{P_{k+1}^{\text{succ}} < P_{\text{thresh}}\}}\sqrt{c_c(2-c_c)}\mathbf{A}_k\mathbf{Z}_k$, where c_c is the learning rate for the search path and P_{thresh} is a threshold set to 0.44.

   (d) Update the covariance matrix $\mathbf{C}_{k+1}$ by

   $$(1 - c_{\text{cov}} + c_{\text{cov}}\mathbf{1}_{\{P_{k+1}^{\text{succ}} < P_{\text{thresh}}\}}c_c(2-c_c))\mathbf{C}_k + c_{\text{cov}}\mathbf{p}_k\mathbf{p}_k^{\text{T}}$$

   where c_{cov} is the learning rate for covariance matrix.

4. Otherwise,

   (a) Update the success probability estimate P_{k+1}^{succ} by $(1-c_p)P_k^{\text{succ}}$.

5. Update the global step size σ_{k+1} by $\sigma_k \exp\left(\frac{1}{d}\frac{P_{k+1}^{\text{succ}} - P_{\text{target}}}{1-P_{\text{target}}}\right)$, where $d > 0$ is damping constant and P_{target} is the target success probability.

Table 1: Parameter Settings

$d = 1 + \frac{n}{2}$	$c = \frac{2}{n+2}$	$P_{\text{target}} = \frac{2}{11}$	$c_{\text{p}} = \frac{1}{12}$
$c_{\text{cov}} = \frac{2}{n^2+6}$	$c_n^+ = \frac{4.06}{n^{1.85}+5.5}$	$c_n^- = \frac{0.87}{n^{1.47}-0.61}$	

6.1 Halfspace Sampling in (1+1)-CMA-ES

The basic assumption of theorems in previous sections is that the optimal halfspaces are known. In order to estimate the optimal halfspaces, we introduce the concept of evolution halfspaces. A new vector $\mathbf{n}_k \in \mathbb{R}^n$ is added to the (1 + 1)-CMA-ES with halfspace sampling . The update of the evolution halfspaces is done by updating $\mathbf{n}_k$ of the hyperplane $H_+(\mathbf{n}_k, \mathbf{X}_k)$. We do not keep track of the evolution of the negative halfspace since the positive and negative halfspaces are symmetric with respect to the parent $\mathbf{X}_k$. The positive halfspace $H_+(\mathbf{n}_k, \mathbf{X}_k)$ is updated whether a better solution is found or not. The constants c_n^+ and c_n^- are the learning rates for the evolution halfspaces when a successful step and a unsuccessful step is found respectively. Both the factors $\sqrt{c_n^+(2-c_n^+)}$ and $\sqrt{c_n^-(2+c_n^-)}$ normalise the variance of the $\mathbf{n}_k$. The new normal vector $\mathbf{n}_{k+1}$ is a weight mean of old normal vector $\mathbf{n}_k$ and either the successful step $\mathbf{A}_k\mathbf{Z}_k$ or the reverse of an unsuccessful step $-\mathbf{A}_k\mathbf{Z}_k$.

Altogether, the (1 + 1)-CMA-ES with halfspace sampling differs from the algorithm given in the previous subsection only in that the following steps are updated or added:

2) Generate the vector $\mathbf{Z}_k$ that is a n-dimensional random vector draw from a standard multivariate normal distribution. If $\mathbf{A}_k\mathbf{Z}_k \in H_+(\mathbf{n}_k, \mathbf{0})$, generate a candidate solution $\mathbf{X}_k^{'} = \mathbf{X}_k + \sigma_k\mathbf{A}_k\mathbf{Z}_k$. Otherwise $\mathbf{X}_k^{'} = \mathbf{X}_k - \sigma_k\mathbf{A}_k\mathbf{Z}_k$.

3e) Update the normal vector by $\mathbf{n}_{k+1} = (1-c_n^+)\mathbf{n}_k + \sqrt{c_n^+(2-c_n^+)}\mathbf{A}_k\mathbf{Z}_k$ where $c_n^+ \in \mathbb{R}^+$ $(0 < c_n^+ \leq 1)$ is the learning rate for the positive halfspace when a successful step is found.

4b) Update the normal vector by $\mathbf{n}_{k+1} = (1+c_n^-)\mathbf{n}_k - \sqrt{c_n^-(2+c_n^-)}\mathbf{A}_k\mathbf{Z}_k$, where $c_n^- \in \mathbb{R}^+$ $(0 < c_n^- \leq 1)$ is the learning rate for the positive halfspace when an unsuccessful step is found.

The values of the constants in the algorithms are summarised in the Table 1. All settings for the constants originally in the (1 + 1)-CMA-ES are the same as the default values in [8]. The two new learning rates c_n^+ and c_n^- are obtained by running experiments on sphere function of search space dimensionalities from $n = 2$ to $n = 40$, in each instance choosing the best median performance, and fitting the nonlinear regression curve through the resulting data points against the dimensions.

6.2 Results in Noiseless BBOB

In order to evaluate the benefit of halfspace sampling in (1 + 1)-CMA-ES, we compare it with the corresponding strategy that does not use halfspace sampling. The (1 + 1)-CMA-ES are tested on a set of noiseless black-box optimization problems from the BBOB-2013 framework [6]. Preliminary results from experiments follow those in [5] on

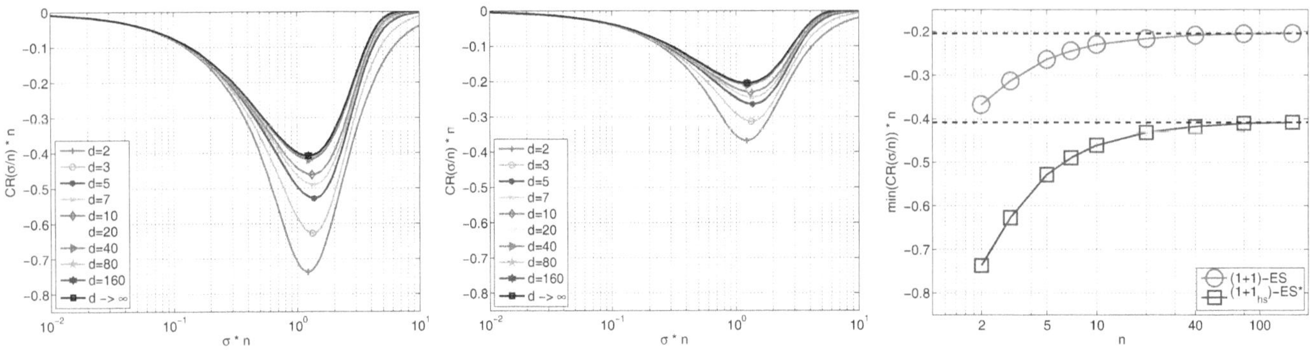

Figure 3: Convergence rates $\mathrm{CR}(\sigma)$ of the $(1+1_{\mathrm{hs}})$-ES* (left) and the $(1+1)$-ES (middle) for different dimensions n, all with scale-invariant step size. The right graph shows the best observed values of the convergence rates plotted against the dimensions and the dashed lines represent the theoretical limits when $n \to \infty$.

the benchmark functions given in [1, 6]. On unimodal functions, halfspace sampling shows a consistent improvement over the $(1+1)$-CMA-ES, except in the f_7 (Step-ellipsoid) and f_{12} (Bent Cigar). In 20D, we find statistically significant differences on f_2 (Ellipsoid Seperable), f_{10} (Ellipsoid) and f_{11} (Discus). In 5D, similar significant differences are found with an addition of f_{14} (Sum of Diff. Power). On multimodal function, halfspace sampling are neither harmful nor beneficial to $(1+1)$-CMA-ES, except in f_{21} (Gallagher 101 peaks) and f_{22} (Gallagher 21 peaks) where slight differences in success rate are observed in 20D. Generally, from these preliminary results, halfspace sampling is never observed to be significantly slower on any functions.

7. CONCLUSION

In this paper, we have analysed the $(1+1)$-ES with halfspace sampling. In halfspace sampling, the whole search space is divided into two halfspaces with respect to the parent. On the objective functions with convex sublevel sets, we prove that the positive halfspace contains the better candidate solutions while the negative halfspace contains worser candidate solutions. Therefore, in a $(1+1)$-ES with halfspace sampling, when an offspring lies in the negative halfspace, it will be discarded and its reflection with respect to the parent is used. We prove the linear convergence of a scale-invariant step size $(1+1)$-ES with optimal halfspaces and derive the convergence rates in finite and infinite dimensions. We prove that a $(1+1)$-ES with optimal halfspaces can converge twice faster than a $(1+1)$-ES. Lastly, we implement halfspace sampling in the $(1+1)$-CMA-ES. Our preliminary results in BBOB 2013 show that $(1+1)$-CMA-ES with halfspace sampling does not appear to be statistically slower than a standard $(1+1)$-CMA-ES.

There are a few aspects of future works for halfspace sampling. Firstly, we are interested in developing more robust methods of estimating the optimal halfspaces. Although the theorems have proven that a gain can be up to a factor 2, the basic assumption is on the use of optimal halfspaces at a given search point. It becomes a real challenge for ES to closely reach the theoretical gain when halfspace sampling is used. Secondly, we are particularly interested in developing strategies with the use of folded distributions. We have shown that given an objective function with convex sublevel sets, the positive halfspace with respect to a point $\mathbf{x} \in \mathbb{R}^n$ contains the better solution. With folded distributions, we can take advantages by sampling in the positive halfspace only. We also plan to incorporate halfspace sampling into population-based evolution strategies with the use of recombinations and to investigate the behavior of halfspace sampling in ES for noisy functions.

8. REFERENCES

[1] A. Auger, D. Brockhoff, and N. Hansen. Analyzing the impact of mirrored sampling and sequential selection in elitist evolution strategies. In *FOGA*, pages 127–138, 2011.

[2] A. Auger and N. Hansen. Reconsidering the progress rate theory for evolution strategies in finite dimensions. In *GECCO*, pages 445–452, 2006.

[3] H. Beyer. *The Theory of Evolution Strategies*. Natural Computing Series. Springer, 2001.

[4] S. Finck, N. Hansen, R. Ros, and A. Auger. Real-parameter black-box optimization benchmarking 2009: Presentation of the noiseless functions. Technical Report 2009/20, Research Center PPE, 2009. Updated February 2010.

[5] N. Hansen, A. Auger, S. Finck, and R. Ros. Real-parameter black-box optimization benchmarking 2012: Experimental setup. Technical report, INRIA, 2012.

[6] N. Hansen, S. Finck, R. Ros, and A. Auger. Real-parameter black-box optimization benchmarking 2009: Noiseless functions definitions. Technical Report RR-6829, INRIA, 2009. Updated February 2010.

[7] N. Hansen and A. Ostermeier. Completely derandomized self-adaptation in evolution strategies. *Evolutionary Computation*, 9(2):159–195, 2001.

[8] C. Igel, T. Suttorp, and N. Hansen. A computational efficient covariance matrix update and a (1+1)-cma for evolution strategies. In *GECCO*, pages 453–460, 2006.

[9] M. Jebalia, A. Auger, and P. Liardet. Log-linear convergence and optimal bounds for the (1+1)-es. In *Artificial Evolution*, pages 207–218, 2007.

[10] I. Rechenberg. *Evolutionsstrategie: Optimierung technischer Systeme nach Prinzipien der biologischen Evolution*. Problemata, 15. Frommann-Holzboog, 1973.

Handling Sharp Ridges with Local Supremum Transformations

Tobias Glasmachers
Institut für Neuroinformatik
Ruhr-Universität Bochum, Germany
tobias.glasmachers@ini.rub.de

ABSTRACT

A particular strength of many evolution strategies is their invariance against strictly monotonic and therefore rank-preserving transformations of the objective function. Their view onto a continuous fitness landscape is therefore completely determined by the shapes of the level sets. Most modern algorithms can cope well with diverse shapes as long as these are sufficiently smooth. In contrast, the sharp angles found in level sets of ridge functions can cause premature convergence to a non-optimal point. We propose a simple and generic family of transformation of the fitness function to avoid this effect. This allows general purpose evolution strategies to solve even extremely sharp ridge problems.

Categories and Subject Descriptors

[**Evolution Strategies and Evolutionary Programming**]

General Terms

Algorithms

Keywords

Evolution strategies, Robust Optimization, Ridge Functions

1. INTRODUCTION

In principle, evolution strategies (ES) are applicable to an extremely wide variety of optimization problems: with their direct search paradigm they interface the objective function as a black-box, and they do not presume any specific structure or even smoothness. Nowadays there is a rather modular repertoire of techniques available for handling different types of difficulties by means of online adaptation. The most prominent of these techniques is covariance matrix adaptation [8] which remedies otherwise slow convergence into ill-conditioned optima. Other challenges posed by multi-modality [2], fitness noise [7], and black-box constraints [1] have been approached with good success.

Here we focus on the challenge of non-smooth objectives. Although capable of handling non-smooth and even discontinuous objectives in principle it is well known that ES may fail on such problems. This was demonstrated recently for the extremely difficult "HappyCat" problem [4]. Since we are far from understanding the complete picture of which cases can and cannot be handled successfully by evolution strategies present analysis is limited to prototypical test cases such as ridge functions. We follow this approach in the present paper.

Our aim is to advance the optimization capabilities of evolution strategies (and possibly other optimizers) when facing difficult, non-smooth objectives. To this end we propose a rather generic technique that is based on performing a specific transformation to the objective function. This transformation alleviates the difficulty of sharp angles found in the shapes of non-smooth level sets. We make sure that the optimum of the untransformed objective can be located with arbitrarily good precision.

Ridges.

Ridge functions such as

$$f^{\text{ridge}}_{\alpha,d} : \mathbb{R}^N \to \mathbb{R}; \quad x = \begin{pmatrix} x_1 \\ \vdots \\ x_N \end{pmatrix} \mapsto x_1 + d \cdot \left(\sum_{i=2}^{N} x_i^2 \right)^{\alpha} \quad (1)$$

are a class or rather well investigated problems (see [9] for a systematic investigation for evolution strategies with isotropic search distributions, as well as [4] and references therein for an up-to-date discussion). They have been of some interest since they can be demonstrated to systematically misguide search strategy adaptation rules to the point where optimization breaks down completely. It should be noted that many gradient-based search schemes are facing similar problems, however, they are often considered inapplicable to non-smooth problems in the first place while ES remain a viable alternative.

In particular on sharp[1] ridges with $\alpha < 1/2$ the core mechanism of step size control is susceptible to cause premature convergence. This behavior can be understood qualitatively from the fact that rank-based algorithms "perceive"

[1]We refer to the cases $\alpha < 1/2$, $\alpha = 1/2$, and $\alpha > 1/2$ as sharp, linear, and smooth ridges, respectively. Note that in some previous work the case $\alpha = 1/2$ is already considered "sharp".

GECCO'14, July 12–16 2014, Vancouver, BC, Canada.

ACM 978-1-4503-2662-9/14/07 ...$15.00.
http://dx.doi.org/10.1145/2576768.2598215.

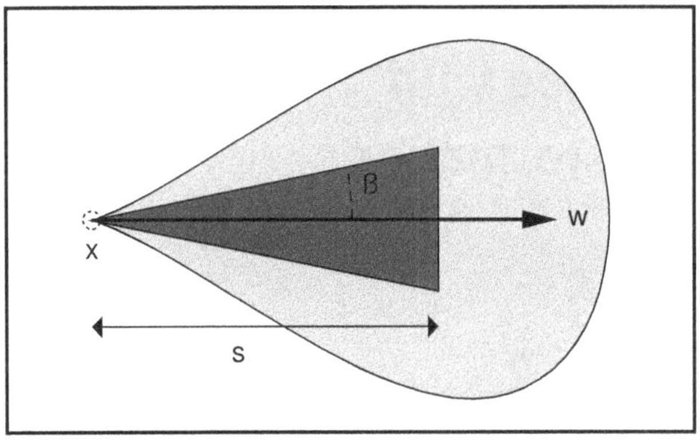

Figure 1: Illustration of the definition of the angle-based hardness measure for (sub-)level sets. The figure shows a non-smooth, connected level set with the corresponding sub-level set shaded in gray. The dark blue cone realizes the largest opening angle in the corner.

the objective landscape in terms of (sub-)level sets only, ignoring absolute function values.

Level sets and sub-level sets of ridge functions are connected but non-smooth. Their problem hardness or deceptiveness can be measured, e.g., by the inner angle of sub-level sets. We define the smallest inner angle of a sub-level set as the smallest opening angle of an infinitesimal cone that fits into the set. More precisely, let $w \in \mathbb{R}^N$ be a unit vector, $s > 0$, $\beta \in (0, \pi/2)$ and $x \in \mathbb{R}^N$ then we define the cone

$$C_{x,s,w,\beta} = \left\{ x + p \,\middle|\, p \in \mathbb{R}^N, \frac{\|p - (w^T p)w\|}{\tan(\beta)} \leq w^T p \leq s \right\}$$

at x with principal axis w, length s and opening angle β. We define the smallest opening angle of the set M as

$$\measuredangle(M) = \inf_{x \in M} \lim_{s \to 0} \sup_{w \in S^{N-1}} \left\{ \beta \in (0, \pi/2) \,\middle|\, C_{x,s,w,\beta} \subset M \right\}$$

where S^{N-1} denotes the unit sphere in $\mathbb{R}^N$, and for the positivity of β we define the infimum of an empty set as zero. Consequently we define the (maximal) hardness of an objective function $f : \mathbb{R}^N \to \mathbb{R}$ (to be minimized) as

$$\measuredangle(f) = \inf_{v \in \mathbb{R}} \measuredangle\big(\{x \in \mathbb{R}^N \mid f(x) < v\}\big) \ .$$

Figure 1 illustrates the concept.

For example, it holds $\measuredangle(f^{\text{ridge}}_{\alpha,d}) = \pi/2$ for smooth ridges with $\alpha > 1/2$, $0 < \measuredangle(f^{\text{ridge}}_{\alpha,d}) = \tan^{-1}(1/d) < \pi/2$ for linear ridges with $\alpha = 1/2$, and $\measuredangle(f^{\text{ridge}}_{\alpha,d}) = 0$ for sharp ridges with $\alpha < 1/2$.

Any positive angle can be opened up as widely as necessary by means of a linear transformation and therefore essentially by a CMA mechanism. Thus, an ES with CMA may handle ridges with $\alpha = 1/2$ for any value of d when given sufficient time to adapt the covariance matrix.

The same approach does not solve the problem for the arbitrarily sharp angles of level sets for $\alpha < 1/2$. The probability of sampling better offspring quickly decays to zero as the search distribution approaches the ridge. Consequently success-based step size adaptation (e.g., by means of the classic $1/5$ rule [10]) results in premature convergence. At the same time there is a trend for the most successful offspring to be sampled close to the ridge. This effect can result in convergence of estimation of distribution style approaches, including the cumulative step size control mechanisms used in many modern non-elitist ES (see e.g. [8]).

Furthermore, the problem can be made even harder by bending the ridge and by replacing the linear trend term x_1 along the ridge with a quadratic term (e.g., x_1^2). Then the relative impact of the trend along the ridge vanishes when approaching the optimum not only towards but also along the ridge. These two additional challenges have been combined in the so-called HappyCat benchmark problem [4] that turns out notoriously hard to solve for a number of well-established direct search algorithms.

Smoothing Difficult Level Sets.

In this paper we propose an approach to handling difficult shapes of level sets by optimizing a parameterized family of approximate objectives with more regularly shaped level sets. Since the question of what makes shapes of level sets difficult for optimization is hard to answer in general we focuses our analysis on the important aspect of ridges, which covers a large share of the difficulties arising in continuous, non-smooth objective functions.

Our approach does not tackle the problem by proposing novel search strategies tailored to the handling of ridges. In particular we do not touch existing step size and covariance matrix adaptation mechanisms. Instead our method can be understood as a family of transformations of the objective function, making the method generically applicable in principle to nearly every existing search algorithm. The only addition required to this search algorithm is a control mechanism for the parameter of the family of transformations, which can be set up as an additional outer loop.

In the following section we propose the aforementioned family of transformations and establish general properties that are of importance for optimization in general and for ES in particular. Then we investigate the impact of the transformations on different types of level sets, with a focus on ridge functions. We turn these insights into a meta optimization algorithm that can embrace many different types of optimizers as a module. Its performance is then evaluated on a number of standard benchmarks as well as on ridge functions of varying difficulty. We demonstrate how our approach enables an ES with CMA to successfully solve not only "standard" ridges of arbitrary difficulty but also more difficult variants. We close with our conclusions.

2. LOCAL SUPREMUM TRANSFORMS

In this section we introduce a number of non-linear transformations of objective (or fitness) functions. Let $f : \mathbb{R}^N \to \mathbb{R}$ be the objective function to be optimized. Without loss of generality we consider minimization in the following. For non-empty $\Delta \subset \mathbb{R}^N$ we define the new function

$$F_{f,\Delta}(x) = \sup \left\{ f(x + \delta) \,\middle|\, \delta \in \Delta \right\} \ .$$

We call $F_{f,\Delta}$ a *supremum transform* of the original fitness f. For maximization of f we replace the supremum with the infimum. Of course, in special cases such as for finite Δ or for continuous f and compact Δ the supremum is guaranteed to be attained and the supremum actually becomes a maximum.

The function $F_{f,\Delta}$ has a simple interpretation: it computes the worst case fitness over the set $x+\Delta = \{x+\delta \mid \delta \in \Delta\}$. For $\Delta = \{0\}$ it holds $F_{f,\Delta} = f$. If Δ is a small neighborhood of the origin then we can think of $F_{f,\Delta}$ as a "pessimistic" approximation to f, in the sense that minimizing $F_{f,\Delta}$ reveals the solution with best worst case behavior over its Δ-shaped neighborhood.

It is intuitive that for small enough Δ and under certain assumptions optimizing f and $F_{f,\Delta}$ will give similar results. The quality of the approximation will typically increase as Δ shrinks. We are interested in approximating an optimum of f, which can be achieved by optimizing $F_{f,\Delta}$ for a sequence of sets Δ with increasing concentration around the origin. For the time being we fix this approach and postpone the discussion why this may make sense to section 3. The simplest way to make the proceeding explicit is by means of an additional scaling parameter. For a fixed, bounded neighborhood Δ of the origin, all scaled versions $s \cdot \Delta$, $s > 0$, are also bounded neighborhoods of the origin. We define the family

$$F_{f,\Delta,s}(x) = \sup\left\{f(x + s \cdot \delta) \,\middle|\, \delta \in \Delta\right\} .$$

of *local supremum transforms (LSTs)* of f. We consider the set Δ fixed and vary only the scale parameter $s \geq 0$. Similar to filters in topology the emphasis in on the fact that for $s \to 0$ the sets $x + s \cdot \Delta$ over which the suprema are taken become arbitrarily concentrated around x.

Such families of LSTs have a number of properties with relevance in an optimization context. In the following we assume that the set Δ is bounded and contains the origin. Then it holds:

1. For a scale of $s = 0$ the transformation reduces to the original objective: $F_{f,\Delta,0} = f$.

2. For a continuous function f it holds
$$\lim_{s\to 0} F_{f,\Delta,s}(x) = f(x) \ ,$$
for all $x \in \mathbb{R}^N$, i.e., the family $F_{f,\Delta,s}$ of functions converges to the original objective in a point-wise manner. Furthermore, each $F_{f,\Delta,s}$ is a continuous function.

3. For a uniformly continuous function f it holds
$$\lim_{s\to 0} F_{f,\Delta,s} = f$$
with convergence in the maximum norm topology, i.e., the family $F_{f,\Delta,s}$ of functions converges uniformly to the original objective. Furthermore, each $F_{f,\Delta,s}$ is uniformly continuous. Note that this property holds automatically for continuous fitness f restricted to a compact subset of $\mathbb{R}^N$.

4. Assume that f is continuous and unimodal and that all of its level sets are bounded. Then the set X^* of optimizers of f as well as all sets $X^*_{f,\Delta,s}$ of optimizers of $F_{f,\Delta,s}$ are non-empty. Let $d(\cdot,\cdot)$ denote Euclidean distance between compact sets (with points as a special case). Then it holds
$$\lim_{s\to 0} \ \max\left\{d(x, X^*) \,\middle|\, x \in X^*_{f,\Delta,s}\right\} = 0 \ .$$

5. For a convex function f also all functions $F_{f,\Delta,s}$ are convex.

6. Let $\phi : \mathbb{R} \to \mathbb{R}$ be a strictly monotonically increasing function. Then it holds
$$F_{\phi\circ f,\Delta,s} = \phi \circ F_{f,\Delta,s} \ .$$

Proofs of these elementary properties are found in the supplementary material. The first property is of limited value when applying $F_{f,\Delta,s}$ for optimization. However, properties 2 and 3 indicate that shrinking s to zero over the course of the optimization turns the objective function gradually into the objective of original interest. This is useful when we are interested in solutions of approximately optimal quality. It is property 4 that ensures that minimization of LSTs of f results in convergence to a minimizer of f. Property 5 is a trivial consequence of convexity. Its importance lies in the fact that the LSTs do not destroy the polynomial time complexity of a convex optimization problem.

The last property is relevant in the context of rank-based algorithms, including most evolution strategies. It ensures that $F_{f,\Delta,s}$ is compatible with rank-based selection since it is invariant under rank-preserving transformations.

The supremum transformed fitness $F_{f,\Delta}$ is loosely connected to robust optimization [3] where the task is to find the solution with the best worst case behavior over a region of parameters that result, e.g., from parameter uncertainty. The uncertainty is often of a more complex nature than a Δ-shaped region, e.g., when parameters of constraints are uncertain. Our situation is quite different. We assume that values of f are reliable, thus we are not at all interested into optimizing worst case behavior. This allows us to drive s to zero, which does not make any sense in a robust optimization setting since uncertainty is not reduced during the optimization run.

3. ANALYSIS OF LEVEL SETS

The view of a direct search optimizer with invariance under rank-preserving transformations of objective values on the fitness landscape is completely determined by the shapes of the level sets. In this section we will investigate the effect of the (local) supremum transform on the shape of level sets. We will analyze three different models, namely the smooth, convex level sets of the ellipsoid function and the level sets of the ridge function (1) for $\alpha = 1/2$ and for $\alpha < 1/2$. For simplicity we assume that Δ is the closed unit ball $\Delta = \{\delta \in \mathbb{R}^N \mid \|\delta\| \leq 1\}$. Geometrically this means that the level sets of $F_{f,\Delta,s}$ originate from level sets of f but "inwards shifted" towards the optimum by a distance of s and possibly cut off appropriately. This will become more clear in the examples below.

Ellipsoid.

The standard ellipsoid function takes the form

$$f_\alpha^{\text{elli}}(x) = \sum_{i=1}^{N} \alpha^{\frac{i-1}{N-1}} x_i^2 \ .$$

For $\alpha = 1$ we obtain the sphere function $f^{\text{sphere}}(x) = \|x\|^2$. It is easy to see that it holds $F_{f,\Delta,s}(x) = (\|x\| + s)^2$ by means of which the level sets of $F_{f,\Delta,s}$ turn out to be also spheres around the origin. They originate from moving the level sets "inwards" by s. In other words even for fixed $s > 0$ optimization of f and $F_{f,\Delta,s}$ are equivalent.

The situation changes as we change the parameter α and with it the difficulty of the problem. A standard choice

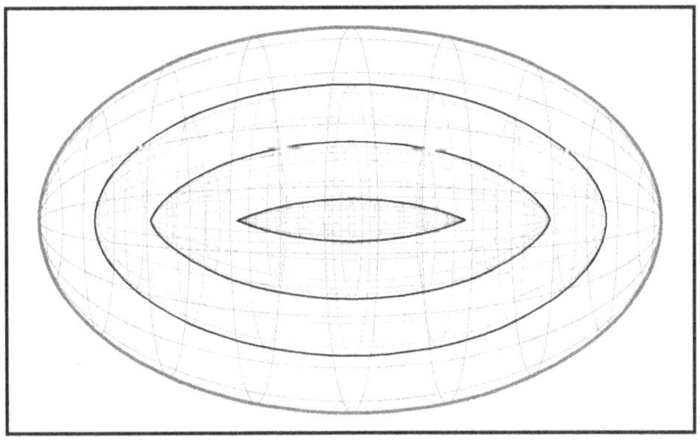

Figure 2: A prototypical level set of the ellipse function (outermost, red), with three inwards shifted level sets of LSTs. The angle $\measuredangle$ decreases from outer to inner (growing s), corresponding to increasing problem hardness.

for benchmarking is $\alpha = 10^{-6}$, resulting in ellipsoidal level sets with shortest principal axis 1000 times shorter than the longest principal axis. This is a linear transformation of the sphere that can be corrected for with a CMA mechanism. However, moving such a level sets inwards by a radius of s first results in ellipsoid-like shapes with even worse ratio of longest and shortest principal axis, and from some point on the outline becomes non-smooth. This effect is illustrated in figure 2. A level set of f with smallest principal axis length of $s + \epsilon$ shows up as a corresponding level set of $F_{f,\Delta,s}$ with shorted axis length of only ϵ. For $\epsilon \to 0$ the level set becomes arbitrarily eccentric, with increasing difficulty $\measuredangle \to 0$. Thus for a fixed value of s, when minimizing $F_{f,\Delta,s}$ we cannot expect to get systematically much closer to the optimum than reaching a level set with a smallest principal axis of about s. Of course, shrinking s to zero will allow a reasonable optimizer to make further progress and to locate the optimum with arbitrary precision.

Ridge.

For $\alpha > 1/2$ the level sets of the ridge function (1) are smooth. We do not consider this situation further since it is essentially covered by the ellipse case. For $\alpha = 1/2$ the level sets turn into cones with a singularity right on the ridge. The parameter d controls the opening angle $\measuredangle$ of these cones. For large d the angle decays towards zero which makes following the linear trend along the ridge increasingly hard. Since for fixed d the angle is always positive it can be opened up with a simple linear transformation which makes CMA mechanisms suitable for solving this type of problem.

Similar to the sphere, shifting the cone-shaped level sets towards the ridge does not change their shapes, see also figure 3. Therefore optimization of f and $F_{f,\Delta,s}$ are equivalent.

Sharp Ridge.

For $\alpha < 1/2$ the level sets of the ridge undergo a decisive change of shape: when approaching the ridge the opening angle quickly approaches zero. Figure 4 illustrates this property. In this situation CMA mechanisms can turn out to be insufficient if the search approaches the ridge faster

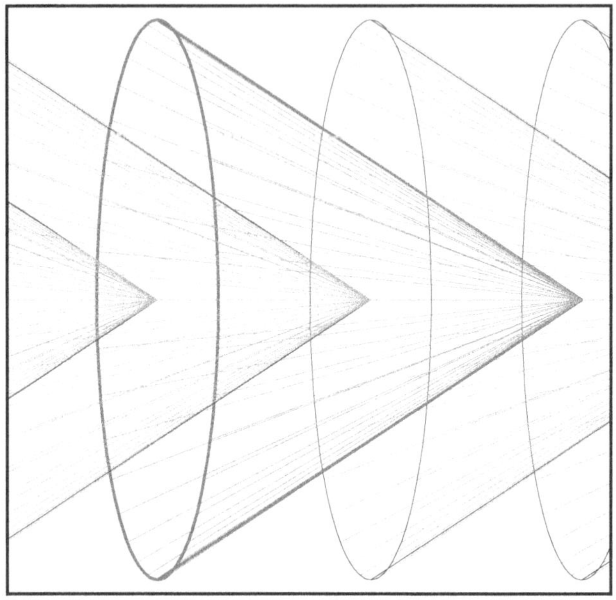

Figure 3: Level sets of the ridge function $f^{\text{ridge}}_{\alpha,d}$ for $\alpha = 1/2$ and $d = 1$. The level sets are cone shaped. The angle of the cone singularity becomes smaller for increasing values of the problem hardness parameter d. The level sets of all LSTs coincide with those of the ridge function.

than CMA can open up the angle, possibly resulting in premature convergence.

Interestingly, shifting the level sets of the sharp ridge inwards by any fixed distance $s > 0$ leaves us with a positive opening angle which can easily be opened up further with CMA, see figure 5. It is obvious that this property makes supremum transformations extremely valuable for the optimization of ridge functions.

On the sharp ridge the family of LSTs has a regularizing effect in a sense similar to, e.g., Tikhonov regularization: the problem of optimizing f is "ill-posed" (degenerate level sets), while for each fixed $s > 0$ optimizing $F_{f,\Delta,s}$ is "well-posed" (positive opening angle of the level set), and the solution of the ill-posed problem can be found by taking the limit $s \to 0$ of the solutions of the well-posed problems. Importantly, taking limits on the levels of problems and solutions commutes.

4. A META OPTIMIZATION STRATEGY

In this section we discuss a practical implementation of an optimization strategy based on LSTs. This is a rather conceptual algorithm, leaving many opportunities for improvement. At this point we are mostly interested in the difference between premature convergence and convergence to the optimum, which is a binary observable. The algorithm is by no means tuned for efficiency in terms of minimal number of queries to the black box fitness f.

The first question is for the shape of the set Δ. A ball shape is attractive for a number of reasons, including mathematical simplicity and invariance properties. However, this renders the practical evaluation of $F_{f,\Delta,s}$ intractable. Therefore we resort to a finite approximation. A reasonable set Δ should satisfy a few minimal requirements: its convex

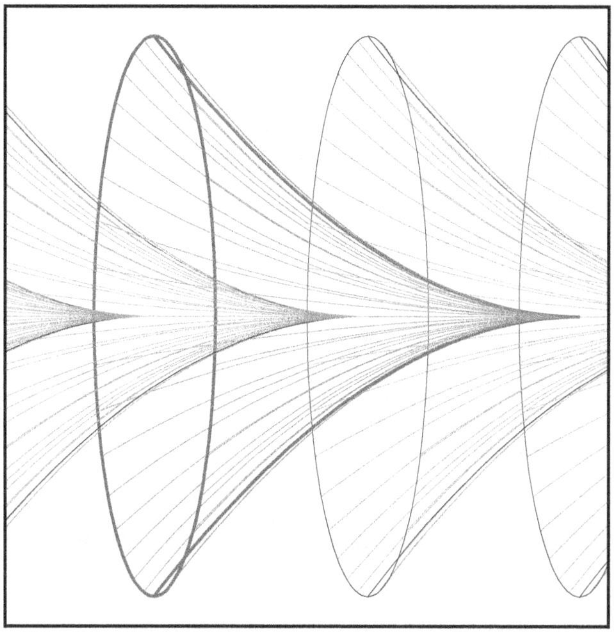

Figure 4: Level sets of the sharp ridge with parameter $\alpha = 1/4 < 1/2$. The sets originate (for $N = 3$) from rotating one branch of a parabula around the x_1 axis. Thus the opening angle of the sub-level set in the singularity becomes arbitrarily small when approaching the ridge. It is not possible to change this property by means of a linear transformation. Thus CMA techniques cannot fully resolve this issue.

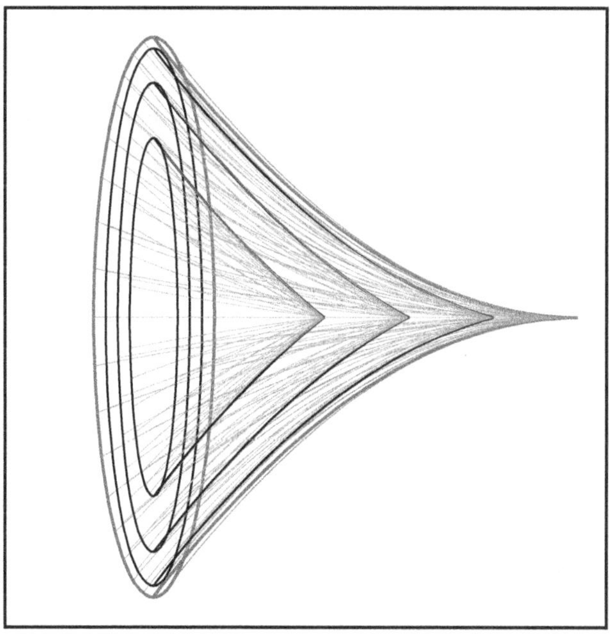

Figure 5: Level set of the sharp ridge with parameter $\alpha = 1/4$ (outermost, red), as well as three level sets of LSTs. Notice that the opening angle $\measuredangle$ of the singular point is positive for all $s > 0$. It increases (decreasing problem hardness) for growing s.

hull should be of full dimension, and it should contain the origin. Any such set is of size at least $N + 1$. One may further require symmetry of some sort as well as centering in some sense, e.g., with the origin forming the center of mass. Our intuition is that with these requirements fulfilled the exact choice of Δ should not play too much of a role. A simple choice fulfilling these requirements is

$$\Delta = \{0\} \cup \bigcup_{i=1}^{N} \{e_i, -e_i\}$$

where $e_i = (0, \dots, 1, \dots, 0) \in \mathbb{R}^N$ denotes the i-th unit vector. Due to $|\Delta| = 2N + 1$, the complexity of evaluating $F_{f,\Delta,s}$ is increased by a factor of $2N + 1 \in \mathcal{O}(N)$ as compared to the original fitness function f.

After fixing Δ it is straightforward to apply any black box optimizer A to the supremum transformed objective $F_{f,\Delta,s}$ for some fixed $s > 0$. Even if successful this will not result in the exact optimizer of f. Instead we need to drive s towards zero during the optimization run. This can be achieved trivially in an outer loop around the black box optimizer that shrinks s according to a predefined schedule. Starting with a rather large s and halving it in every iteration until some target accuracy is reached gives a straightforward implementation. Starting with large s is in accordance with a large initial variance of the search distribution so as to initially "cover" a large enough part of the search space.

It is worth noting that this proceeding requires the definition of a stopping criterion for the black box optimizer A after which the scale s can be reduced and the search can start over, typically starting from the position of the best-so-far solution. In many cases it is possible to leave some state variables of A in place when transitioning to a smaller value of s while other variables will need updating. This wrapper approach is formalized in algorithm 1.

Algorithm 1: Wrapper algorithm for LST optimization.

```
Input: s_0 > s_min > 0, search algorithm A
s = s_0
repeat
    update/reset state of A for fitness F_{f,Δ,s}
    repeat
        perform step of A with fitness F_{f,Δ,s}
    until stopping criterion of A is met
    s ← s/2
until s < s_min
```

At this point we specialize our considerations to an evolution strategy with adaptive step size parameter σ. This ES may additionally employ a CMA mechanism. We stop the inner loop as soon as the step size σ drops below then s-dependent threshold $c \cdot s$. Setting $c = 10^{-5}$ has proven sufficient in our experiments. Then the optimizer is re-initialized. Its position parameter (e.g., the parent in a (1+1)-ES) stays as is. Also the covariance matrix can be kept (or it may be regularized in order to undo adaptation for fine tuning). The step size σ is reset to the new value of s. Elitist strategies must reevaluate all parents since the fitness function has effectively changed. It is obvious that the concrete measures depend on the underlying algorithm and that many variations are possible.

N	2	4	8	16	32
xNES	339	1,064	3,985	16,374	70,084
LST wrapper	480	1,608	5,250	19,092	75,852

Table 1: Number of function evaluations for xNES with plain fitness and the xNES wrapper algorithm using local supremum transforms (LST) for the Ellipsoid function in different dimensions N. Note that supremum evaluations correspond to $2d+1$ black box fitness evaluations each. The optimum was successfully located within the target accuracy in all cases.

d	10^3	10^4	10^5	10^6	10^7	10^8	10^9
xNES	98	86	53	53	18	18	1
LST wrapper	100	100	100	100	100	100	100

Table 2: Number of successful runs out of 100 for both algorithms for the sharp ridge problem with $\alpha = 1/8$ in $N = 10$ dimensions for growing values of the parameter d, corresponding to increasing problem difficulty.

5. EXPERIMENTS

In this section we evaluate LST optimization empirically. We base our evaluation on the cases that have already been investigated in section 3. However, in this section we replace the ball-shaped set Δ with the finite version defined in the previous section. In addition we consider the extremely difficult ridge function known as HappyCat [4].

We implemented the wrapper algorithm described in the previous section with the xNES evolution strategy [6] as its inner loop optimization algorithm. We compare this approach to plain xNES without LST. xNES shares many properties with the well-known CMA-ES algorithm [8] with rank-μ update, but without evolution paths. In particular it adapts the covariance of its Gaussian search distribution to the problem at hand.

Our setup is as follows. Both optimizers are initialized with an isotropic search distribution with unit covariance matrix. The center of the distribution is randomly sampled in each run the from standard normal distribution.[2] For the wrapper algorithm the scale parameter is initialized to the same value as the global step size of xNES, in other words to $s_0 = 1$.

The algorithms are stopped as soon as a (problem dependent) target fitness value is reached. Premature convergence was detected by monitoring the smallest eigenvalue of the covariance matrix. If this value falls below the numerical accuracy of IEEE 64bit floating point ("double precition") numbers that were used for all experiments then the algorithm has converged prematurely.

All experiments were repeated 100 times. All numbers reported in this sections are medians over 100 independent runs.

5.1 Ellipsoid

It was shown in section 3 that for convex (sub-)level sets the supremum transform can increase problem difficulty. Here we investigate the severity of this effect. Therefore we have run the above algorithm on the ellipsoid problem with $\alpha = 10^{-6}$ in dimensions $N \in \{2, 4, 8, 16, 32\}$. The target fitness was set to 10^{-10}. The number of function evaluations is reported in table 1.

The difference between the two algorithms is surprisingly small. The LST wrapper requires between 10% to 75% more individuals to locate the optimum.[3] This is despite the fact that it can runs the inner optimizer several times for different scales s. We can conclude that the irregular level sets of the supremum transformed ellipsoid problem do not make the problem significantly more difficult.

5.2 Linear Ridge

For the ridge function (1) with $\alpha = 1/2$ both algorithms reliably manage to reach the target fitness value of -10^6 for virtually any value of the parameter $d > 0$. We have tested values up to one billion, where both algorithms are still capable of escaping the drag of the ridge in all 100 out of 100 runs.

5.3 Sharp Ridge

We perform a test similar to the previous one with the ridge function for $\alpha = 1/8$. The resulting ridge is sharp in the sense that the opening angles of the level sets become arbitrarily small when approaching the ridge. In successful runs the algorithms manages to quickly reach a target value of -10^6, while prematurely convergent runs usually get stuck far before reaching the target value. The number of successful runs out of 100 is reported in table 2.

The performance of default xNES slowly degrades with growing problem difficulty. Due to the analysis of section 3 and with the results on the linear ridge it is not surprising that the LST wrapper algorithm manages to solve the sharp ridge problem reliably even for extremely difficult instances with d as large as a billion. In other words, the theoretically predicted advantage is fully observable in practice.

5.4 Ridge with Corner

Until now both algorithms did profit from the symmetry of the test problems. For ellipse and ridge the optima of all supremum transforms for sufficiently symmetric Δ coincide with the optimum of the fitness, making it in principle unnecessary to shrink the scale parameter s (of course, the shape of the level sets of the ellipse function creates a necessity from a practical point of view). Now we consider less symmetric case for which the optima of $F_{d,\Delta,s}$ are indeed shifted away from the optimum of f

Further on, the above test problems do require an adaptation of the covariance matrix, but once the adaptation phase was successful no further adaptation is required. Next we test both algorithms on more difficult problems that require continuous adaptation of the covariance matrix.

We introduce a 90° corner into the ridge:

$$f_{\alpha,d}^{\text{corner}}(x) = x_1 + d \cdot \left((x_2 - |x_1|)^2 + \sum_{i=3}^{N} x_i^2 \right)^{\alpha}$$

Figure 6 illustrates this problem.

For this benchmark we sample the starting point with unit variance around $(10, 10, 0, \dots, 0) \in \mathbb{R}^N$ (i.e., close to

[2]For the HappyCat problem (see below) the distribution refers to the original problem formulation. In other words it is shifted by $(1, \dots, 1)^T$ in our experiments.

[3]The difference in number of black box queries grows linearly with problem dimension since the size of the set Δ does.

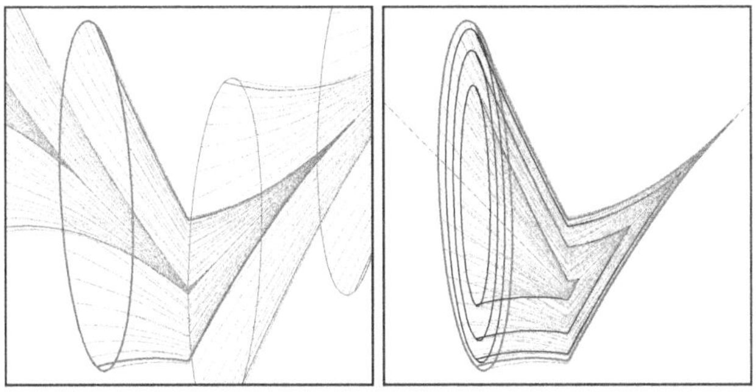

Figure 6: Left: level sets of the sharp ridge with corner with parameter $\alpha = 1/4$. Right: level sets of corresponding LSTs. The ridge is indicated by the dashed line.

d	10^1	10^2	10^3	10^4	10^5	10^6	10^7
xNES	100	1	0	0	0	0	0
LST wrapper	100	27	78	75	17	5	0

Table 3: Number of successful runs out of 100 for each of the algorithm for the sharp ridge with corner with $\alpha = 1/8$ in $N = 10$ dimensions for growing values of the parameter d, corresponding to increasing problem difficulty.

the ridge on the "worse" side of the corner). The additional difficulty of this problem is that a covariance matrix that is well adapted to the ridge hampers sampling a successful offspring around the corner. This effect becomes more pronounced with increasing eccentricity of the search distribution. Thus CMA algorithms may get stuck at the corner.

The results for both algorithms are found in table 3. The problem turns out to be much harder than without corner. Plain xNES breaks down already for rather low values of d. Compared to the sharp ridge without corner the performance of the LST wrapper algorithm is far less stable, but obviously the LST technique helps a lot also in this case. However, for extremely high values of d it fails completely.

5.5 HappyCat

The benchmark problem named HappyCat [4]

$$f_\alpha^{\text{hc}}(x) = \left[\left(\|x\|^2 - N\right)^2\right]^\alpha + \frac{1}{N}\left(\frac{1}{2}\|x\|^2 + \sum_{i=1}^{N} x_i\right) + \frac{1}{2}$$

is composed of a spherical ridge and a quadratic trend along this ridge. The naming of the function is due to its level lines for dimension $N = 2$, see figure 7. This is a unimodal function with unique optimum at $x^* = (-1, \dots, -1)$, with optimal value $f^* = f(x^*) = 0$. For $\alpha = 1$ the function is a fourth order polynomial, but for the default value of $\alpha = 1/8$ the ridge is rather sharp, while the quadratic trend within the ridge vanishes when approaching the optimum.

The visible trend towards the optimum decays while the impact of the ridge remains constant. Thus, this benchmark effectively tests the ability to solve the sharp ridge problem continuously for ever increasing values of d. At the same time the ridge is curved which requires a continuous adaptation of the covariance matrix. Both effects are active at the same time, making the problem extremely hard for most direct search algorithms.

Figure 7: Level lines of the HappyCat benchmark function for $\alpha = 1/8$ in the area $[-2, +2]^2 \subset \mathbb{R}^2$. The picture arising from the level lines explains the name. The lines for levels $f = 1$ and $f = 2$ exhibit sharp angles. They remain nearly parallel while the curvature of the ridge becomes already visible. This gives an idea of the hardness of the problem once the optimizer has arrived at the ridge.

In the original work [4] on the HappyCat function an ES-style algorithm based on line search (the so-called "Ray-ES") has been proposed as a possible conceptual solution. However, this algorithm is obviously tailored to the task of following a narrow valley or ridge while its performance on other objective was not evaluated. Here we test whether the supremum transform in conjunction with a general purpose ES can serve as an alternative algorithm for solving the HappyCat problem.

With the above formulation of the HappyCat function one quickly observes numerical problems. Assume some x close to x^* is represented with standard 64bit IEEE double precision floating point numbers (52 bits mantissa, 11 bits exponent, one sign bit). Then a distance of, say, $10^{-20} \approx 2^{-66}$ of x from the ridge is already far below the numerical resolution. Due to the small value of $\alpha = 1/8$ such a deviation results in a considerable cost of about $(10^{-20})^{2\alpha} = 10^{-5}$. For $N = 5$ the same penalty is received with the quadratic function in a distance of about $\sqrt{2N \cdot 10^{-5}} = 10^{-2}$ from the optimum. An ES with Gaussian sampling is essentially unable to avoid the minimal deviation of 10^{-20} while making steps in the order of 10^{-2} along the ridge, again because numerical accuracy limits the conditioning (multiplicative difference between eigen values) of the covariance matrix to about 10^{15}. Thus, with an ES with Gaussian sampling we cannot expect to obtain solutions systematically much closer than about 10^{-2} to the optimum, which is a poor resolution.

To alleviate the issue we shift the problem by $(1, \dots, 1)$, moving the optimum x^* into the origin. The shifted func-

N	2	3	5	10
(1+1)-xNES	$1.89 \cdot 10^{-1}$	$2.38 \cdot 10^{-1}$	$4.49 \cdot 10^{-1}$	$7.75 \cdot 10^{-1}$
LST wrapper	$2.11 \cdot 10^{-8}$	$1.52 \cdot 10^{-9}$	$1.21 \cdot 10^{-5}$	$2.14 \cdot 10^{-1}$

Table 4: Distance of the best search point from the optimum for the HappyCat problem with $\alpha = 1/8$.

tion can be expressed compactly as

$$f_\alpha^{\text{hc}}(x) = \left[Q^2 - 4QS + 4S^2\right]^\alpha + \frac{Q}{2N} \ .$$

with $Q = \|x\|^2$ and $S = \sum_{i=1}^N x_i$. This formulation can make good use of the increased precision of IEEE floating point numbers close to the origin. In theory this should enable solutions of extremely high precision. However, this arguments holds only for points very close to the origin, while in practice one has to follow the ridge already in some distance from the origin.

We have tested both algorithms on the HappyCat function for a number of different dimensions N. It turns out that the inner xNES instance of the LST wrapper regularly experiences numerical difficulties in its covariance update (due to its need for a matrix exponential, which turns out to be problematic in this case). Therefore we replace this algorithm with its (1+1)-ES counterpart (see [5]). The rank one updates of this variant can be computed in exponential form without the need for a matrix decomposition. For fairness of comparison we use this numerically stable algorithm also as a baseline method.

The algorithms were run until convergence and the distance of the best point to the optimum was recorded. The results are presented in table 4.

The results are clearly in favor of the LST wrapper approach. Plain (1+1)-xNES fails to locate the optimum to a satisfactory precision. Local supremum transforms do obviously help significantly. The algorithm manages to locate the optimum nearly exactly in low dimensions. However, for $N = 10$ performance degrades significantly. We conclude that the LST wrapper algorithm with (1+1)-xNES solves the HappyCat problem only in low dimensions.

6. CONCLUSION

We have introduced local supremum transforms, a family of parameterized transformations of the objective function. The transformations are compatible with the black box model since in practice they amount to simple maximization over a finite set of function evaluations. They interact nicely with rank-based algorithms since they are themselves invariant under rank-preserving transformations. The family of local supremum transforms has desirable properties that make it suitable as a replacement of the original optimization objective.

We have analyzed the impact of the supremum transformation on a class of objective functions that is notoriously difficult for black box direct search algorithms, namely sharp ridge functions. It was shown that the supremum transformed fitness is significantly easier to optimize than the ridge function itself. This enables an ES with covariance matrix adaptation to solve problems involving even extremely sharp ridges. In low search space dimensions the approach succeeds even on the HappyCat problem – a ridge-based benchmark problem that was designed to demonstrate the limitations of many direct search procedures.

We argue that the supremum transform is a principled approach to the otherwise problematic handling of sharp ridge functions with ES since it is completely agnostic to the underlying optimizer. Its disadvantages are a significant increase in the number of function evaluations and the need for an explicit mechanism controlling the scale parameter. Both shortcomings are worth addressing in future work, e.g., by means of online adaptation of the scale parameter and by adaptive switching between the optimization of plain fitness and its local supremum transformations.

7. REFERENCES

[1] D. V. Arnold and N. Hansen. A (1+1)-CMA-ES for constrained optimisation. In *Proceedings of the Genetic and Evolutionary Computation Conference (GECCO 2012)*, pages 297–304. ACM, 2012.

[2] A. Auger and N. Hansen. A restart CMA evolution strategy with increasing population size. In B. McKay et al., editors, *The 2005 IEEE International Congress on Evolutionary Computation (CEC'05)*, volume 2, pages 1769–1776, 2005.

[3] A. Ben-Tal, L. El Ghaoui, and A. Nemirovski. *Robust Optimization.* Princeton University Press, 2009.

[4] H.-G. Beyer and S. Finck. HappyCat – A Simple Function Class Where Well-Known Direct Search Algorithms Do Fail. In *Parallel Problem Solving from Nature (PPSN) XII*, pages 367–376. Springer, 2012.

[5] T. Glasmachers, T. Schaul, and J. Schmidhuber. A Natural Evolution Strategy for Multi-Objective Optimization. In *Parallel Problem Solving from Nature (PPSN) XI*, 2010.

[6] T. Glasmachers, T. Schaul, Y. Sun, D. Wierstra, and J. Schmidhuber. Exponential Natural Evolution Strategies. In *Genetic and Evolutionary Computation Conference (GECCO)*, Portland, OR, 2010.

[7] N. Hansen, S. P. N. Niederberger, L. Guzzella, and P. Koumoutsakos. A Method for Handling Uncertainty in Evolutionary Optimization with an Application to Feedback Control of Combustion. *IEEE Transactions on Evolutionary Computation*, 13(1):180–197, 2009.

[8] N. Hansen and A. Ostermeier. Completely derandomized self-adaptation in evolution strategies. *Evolutionary Computation*, 9(2):159–195, 2001.

[9] A. I. Oyman. *Convergence Behavior of Evolution Strategies on Ridge Functions.* PhD thesis, Universität Dortmund, 1999.

[10] I. Rechenberg. *Evolutionsstrategie: Optimierung technisher Systeme nach Prinzipien der biologischen Evolution.* Frommann-Holzboog, 1973.

A Computationally Efficient Limited Memory CMA-ES for Large Scale Optimization

Ilya Loshchilov
Laboratory of Intelligent Systems
École Polytechnique Fédérale de Lausanne, Switzerland
ilya.loshchilov@epfl.ch

ABSTRACT

We propose a computationally efficient limited memory Covariance Matrix Adaptation Evolution Strategy for large scale optimization, which we call the LM-CMA-ES. The LM-CMA-ES is a stochastic, derivative-free algorithm for numerical optimization of non-linear, non-convex optimization problems in continuous domain. Inspired by the limited memory BFGS method of Liu and Nocedal (1989), the LM-CMA-ES samples candidate solutions according to a covariance matrix reproduced from m direction vectors selected during the optimization process. The decomposition of the covariance matrix into Cholesky factors allows to reduce the time and memory complexity of the sampling to $O(mn)$, where n is the number of decision variables. When n is large (e.g., $n > 1000$), even relatively small values of m (e.g., $m = 20, 30$) are sufficient to efficiently solve fully non-separable problems and to reduce the overall run-time.

Categories and Subject Descriptors

I.2.8 [**Computing Methodologies**]: Artificial Intelligence Problem Solving, Control Methods, and Search

General Terms

Algorithms

Keywords

Evolution Strategies, CMA-ES, large scale optimization, Cholesky update

1. INTRODUCTION

The Covariance Matrix Adaptation Evolution Strategy (CMA-ES) is designed to learn dependencies between decision variables by adapting a covariance matrix which defines the sampling distribution of candidate solutions [6]. This algorithm constantly demonstrates good performance at various platforms for comparing continuous optimizers such as the Black-Box Optimization Benchmarking (BBOB) workshop [2, 18] and the Special Session at Congress on Evolutionary Computation [5, 16]. The CMA-ES was also extended to noisy [7], expensive [1, 17] and multi-objective optimization [12].

The principle advantage of the CMA-ES, the learning of dependencies between n decision variables, also forms its main practical limitations such as $O(n^2)$ memory storage and $O(n^2)$ computational complexity per function evaluation [21]. These limitations may preclude the use of the CMA-ES for computationally cheap but large scale optimization problems (e.g., with $n > 100$) if the internal computational cost of CMA-ES is greater than the cost of one function evaluation. On non-trivial large scale problems with $n > 10000$ not only the internal computational cost of the CMA-ES becomes significant but it is becoming simply impossible to efficiently store the covariance matrix in memory. One may argue that there are very few known continuous domain real-world problems of that huge dimensionality. This situation probably will not change much before practitioners have a set of tools that are able to efficiently search in such huge search spaces.

Several evolution strategies (ESs) have been proposed to deal with large scale optimization problems: $O(n)$ time and space complexity algorithms such as separable CMA-ES (sep-CMA-ES [21]) and linear time Natural Evolution Strategy (R1-NES [23]), L-CMA-ES [14] with $O(m^2n)$ time and $O(mn)$ space complexity, where only m dominant eigen-pairs of the covariance matrix are computed. The sep-CMA-ES learns only the scaling of variables. The R1-NES learns only the predominant eigen-direction. The L-CMA-ES learns m dominant eigen-pairs, but its $O(m^2n)$ sampling complexity practically ends up with $O(n^2)$ when $m = \sqrt{n}$ as studied in [14] for non-separable problems where multiple adaptation directions are required.

The problem of growing time and space complexity when optimizing large scale problems is not new. It was addressed in gradient-based optimization community when it became clear that for $n > 1000$ the storage of the approximate inverse Hessian matrix precludes the use of quasi-Newton methods such as Broyden–Fletcher-Goldfarb–Shanno (BFGS) method [22]. As a solution, it was proposed not to store the matrix but to reconstruct it using information from the last m iterations [19]. The final algorithm called the limited memory BFGS algorithm (L-BFGS or LM-BFGS) is still considered to be the state-of-the-art of large scale gradient-based optimization [15]. In this paper, we demonstrate that a very similar idea can be used to reconstruct the covari-

GECCO'14, July 12–16, 2014, Vancouver, BC, Canada.

http://dx.doi.org/10.1145/2576768.2598294 .

ance matrix in the CMA-ES to reduce the time and space complexity to $O(mn)$.

The paper is organized as follows. Section 2 reviews Evolution Strategies (ESs) proposed for large scale optimization. The LM-CMA-ES algorithm is described in section 3. The experimental validation of LM-CMA-ES is reported and discussed in section 4. Section 5 concludes the paper.

2. EVOLUTION STRATEGIES FOR LARGE SCALE OPTIMIZATION

Historically, first Evolution Strategies [20] were designed to perform the search without learning dependencies between variables which is a more recent development that gradually led to the CMA-ES algorithm [8, 6]. In this section, we discuss in detail the CMA-ES algorithm and its state-of-the-art derivatives for large scale optimization. For a recent comprehensive overview of Evolution Strategies, the interested reader is referred to [11].

2.1 The CMA-ES

The Covariance Matrix Adaptation Evolution Strategy [8, 9, 6] is probably the most popular and in overall the most efficient Evolution Strategy.

The $(\mu/\mu_w, \lambda)$-CMA-ES is outlined in **Algorithm** 1. At iteration t of CMA-ES, a mean $\boldsymbol{m}^t$ of the mutation distribution (can be interpreted as an estimation of the optimum) is used to generate its k-th out of λ candidate solution $\boldsymbol{x}_k \in \mathbb{R}^n$ (line 5) by adding a random Gaussian mutation defined by a (positive definite) covariance matrix $\mathbf{C}^t \in \mathbb{R}^{n\times n}$ as

$$\boldsymbol{x}_k^t = \mathcal{N}\left(\boldsymbol{m}^t, {\sigma^t}^2\mathbf{C}^t\right) = \boldsymbol{m}^t + \sigma^t\mathcal{N}(\mathbf{0}, \mathbf{C}^t), \qquad (1)$$

where σ^t is a mutation step-size. These λ solutions then should be evaluated on an objective function f (line 6). The old mean of the mutation distribution is stored in $\boldsymbol{m}^t$ and a new mean $\boldsymbol{m}^{t+1}$ is computed as a *weighted sum* of the best μ parent individuals selected among λ generated offspring individuals (line 7). The weights $\boldsymbol{w}$ are used to control the impact of selected individuals, weights are usually higher for better ranked individuals (line 1).

The procedure of the adaptation of the step-size σ^t in CMA-ES is inherited from the Cumulative Step-Size Adaptation Evolution Strategy (CSA-ES) [8] and is controlled by evolution path $\boldsymbol{p}_\sigma^{t+1}$. Successful mutation steps $\frac{\boldsymbol{m}^{t+1}-\boldsymbol{m}^t}{\sigma^t}$ (line 8) are tracked in the space of sampling, i.e., in the isotropic coordinate system defined by principal components of the covariance matrix $\mathbf{C}^t$. To update the evolution path $\boldsymbol{p}_\sigma^{t+1}$ a decay/relaxation factor c_σ is used to decrease the importance of previously performed steps with time. The step-size update rule increases the step-size if the length of the evolution path $\boldsymbol{p}_\sigma^{t+1}$ is longer than the expected length of the evolution path under random selection $\mathbb{E}\,\|\mathcal{N}(\mathbf{0},\mathbf{I})\|$, and decreases otherwise (line 13). Expectation of $\|\mathcal{N}(\mathbf{0},\mathbf{I})\|$ is approximated by $\sqrt{n}(1-\frac{1}{4n}+\frac{1}{21n^2})$. A damping parameter d_σ controls the change of the step-size.

The covariance matrix update consists of two parts (line 12): *rank-one update* [9] and *rank-μ update* [6]. The rank-one update computes evolution path $\boldsymbol{p}_c^{t+1}$ of successful moves of the mean $\frac{\boldsymbol{m}^{t+1}-\boldsymbol{m}^t}{\sigma^t}$ of the mutation distribution in the given coordinate system (line 10), in a similar way as the evolution path $\boldsymbol{p}_\sigma^{t+1}$ of the step-size. To stall the update of $\boldsymbol{p}_c^{t+1}$ when σ increases rapidly, a h_σ trigger is used (line 9).

Algorithm 1 The $(\mu/\mu_w, \lambda)$-CMA-ES

1: **given** $n \in \mathbb{N}_+$, $\lambda = 4 + \lfloor 3\ln n\rfloor$, $\mu = \lfloor\lambda/2\rfloor$, $\boldsymbol{w}_i = \frac{\ln(\mu+\frac{1}{2})-\ln i}{\sum_{j=1}^{\mu}(\ln(\mu+\frac{1}{2})-\ln j)}$ for $i = 1\ldots\mu$, $\mu_w = \frac{1}{\sum_{i=1}^{\mu} w_i^2}$, $c_\sigma = \frac{\mu_w+2}{n+\mu_w+3}$, $d_\sigma = 1 + c_\sigma + 2\max(0, \sqrt{\frac{\mu_w-1}{n+1}}-1)$, $c_c = \frac{4}{n+4}$, $c_1 = \frac{2\min(1,\lambda/6)}{(n+1.3)^2+\mu_w}$, $c_\mu = \frac{2\,(\mu_w-2+1/\mu_w)}{(n+2)^2+\mu_w}$

2: **initialize** $\boldsymbol{m}^{t=0} \in \mathbb{R}^n, \sigma^{t=0} > 0, \boldsymbol{p}_\sigma^{t=0} = \mathbf{0}, \boldsymbol{p}_c^{t=0} = \mathbf{0}, \mathbf{C}^{t=0} = \mathbf{I}, t \leftarrow 0$

3: **repeat**

4:   **for** $k = 1,\ldots,\lambda$ **do**

5:     $\boldsymbol{x}_k = \boldsymbol{m}^t + \sigma^t\mathcal{N}(\mathbf{0}, \mathbf{C}^t)$

6:     $\boldsymbol{f}_k = f(\boldsymbol{x}_k)$

7:   $\boldsymbol{m}^{t+1} \leftarrow \sum_{i=1}^{\mu}\boldsymbol{w}_i\boldsymbol{x}_{i:\lambda}$ // the symbol $i:\lambda$ denotes i-th best individual on f

8:   $\boldsymbol{p}_\sigma^{t+1} \leftarrow (1-c_\sigma)\boldsymbol{p}_\sigma^t + \sqrt{c_\sigma(2-c_\sigma)}\sqrt{\mu_w}\mathbf{C}^{t^{-\frac{1}{2}}}\frac{\boldsymbol{m}^{t+1}-\boldsymbol{m}^t}{\sigma^t}$

9:   $h_\sigma = \mathbb{1}_{\|p_\sigma^{t+1}\| < \sqrt{1-(1-c_\sigma)^{2(t+1)}}(1.4+\frac{2}{n+1})\,\mathbb{E}\|\mathcal{N}(\mathbf{0},\mathbf{I})\|}$

10:   $\boldsymbol{p}_c^{t+1} \leftarrow (1-c_c)\boldsymbol{p}_c^t + h_\sigma\sqrt{c_c(2-c_c)}\sqrt{\mu_w}\frac{\boldsymbol{m}^{t+1}-\boldsymbol{m}^t}{\sigma^t}$

11:   $\mathbf{C}_\mu = \sum_{i=1}^{\mu} w_i\frac{\boldsymbol{x}_{i:\lambda}-\boldsymbol{m}^t}{\sigma^t} \times \frac{(\boldsymbol{x}_{i:\lambda}-\boldsymbol{m}^t)^T}{\sigma^t}$

12:   $\mathbf{C}^{t+1} = (1-c_1-c_\mu)\mathbf{C}^t + c_1\underbrace{\boldsymbol{p}_c^{t+1}{\boldsymbol{p}_c^{t+1}}^T}_{\text{rank-one update}} + c_\mu\underbrace{\mathbf{C}_\mu^+}_{\text{rank-}\mu\text{ update}}$

13:   $\sigma^{t+1} \leftarrow \sigma^t\exp(\frac{c_\sigma}{d_\sigma}(\frac{\|p_\sigma^{t+1}\|}{\mathbb{E}\|\mathcal{N}(\mathbf{0},\mathbf{I})\|}-1))$

14:   $t \leftarrow t+1$

15: **until** *stopping criterion is met*

The rank-μ update computes a covariance matrix $\mathbf{C}_\mu$ as a weighted sum of covariances of successful steps of μ best individuals (line 11). The update of $\mathbf{C}$ itself is a replace of previously accumulated information by a new one with corresponding weights of importance (line 12): c_1 for covariance matrix $\boldsymbol{p}_c^{t+1}{\boldsymbol{p}_c^{t+1}}^T$ of rank-one update and c_μ for $\mathbf{C}_\mu$ of rank-μ update [6] such that $c_1 + c_\mu \leq 1$. Recently it was proposed to also take into account unsuccessful mutations in the *"active" rank-μ update* [10, 13].

In CMA-ES, the factorization of the covariance $\mathbf{C}$ into $\mathbf{A}\mathbf{A}^T = \mathbf{C}$ is needed to sample the multivariate normal distribution (line 5). The eigendecomposition with $O(n^3)$ complexity is used for the factorization. Already in the original CMA-ES it was proposed to perform the eigendecomposition every $n/10$ generations (not shown in **Algorithm** 1) to reduce the complexity per function evaluation to $O(n^2)$

2.2 Large Scale Variants

The original CMA-ES has $O(n^2)$ time and space complexity that precludes its applications for large scale optimization with $n \gg 100$. To enable the algorithm for large scale optimization, a linear time and space version called sep-CMA-ES was proposed in [21]. The algorithm does not learn dependencies but the scaling of variables by restraining the covariance matrix update to the diagonal elements:

$$c_{jj}^{t+1} = (1-c_{cov})c_{jj}^t + \frac{1}{\mu_{cov}}\left(\boldsymbol{p}_c^{t+1}\right)_j^2 + c_{ccov}\left(1-\frac{1}{\mu_{ccov}}\right)\sum_{i=1}^{\mu} w_i c_{jj}^t\left({z_{i:\lambda}}^{t+1}\right)_j^2, j = 1,\ldots,n \qquad (2)$$

where, for $j = 1,\ldots,n$ the c_{jj} are the diagonal elements of $\mathbf{C}^t$ and the $\left({z_{i:\lambda}}^{t+1}\right)_j = \left({x_{i:\lambda}}^{t+1}\right)_j/(\sigma^t\sqrt{(c_{jj})}$.

This update reduces the computational complexity to $O(n)$ and allows to exploit problem separability, thus the original property of being rotationally invariant is lost. The algorithm demonstrated good performance on separable problems and even outperformed CMA-ES on non-separable Rosenbrock function for $n > 100$.

A novel Natural Evolution Strategy (NES) variant, the Rank-One NES (R1-NES), which uses a low rank approximation of the search distribution covariance matrix was proposed recently by [23]. The algorithm adapts the search distribution according to the natural gradient with a particular parametrization of the covariance matrix,

$$\mathbf{C} = \sigma^2(\mathbf{I} + \boldsymbol{u}\boldsymbol{u}^T), \tag{3}$$

where u and σ are the parameters to be adjusted. The adaptation of the predominant eigen-direction $\boldsymbol{u}$ allows the algorithm to solve highly non-separable problems while maintaining only $O(n)$ time and space complexity.

A version of CMA-ES with a limited memory storage also called limited memory CMA-ES (L-CMA-ES) was proposed by [14]. The L-CMA-ES uses the m eigen-vectors and eigen-values spanning the m-dimensional dominant subspace of the n-dimensional covariance matrix $\mathbf{C}$. The authors adapted a singular value decomposition updating algorithm developed in [3] that allowed to avoid the explicit computation and storage of the covariance matrix. For $m < n$ the performance in terms of number of function evaluations gradually decreases while enabling the search in $\mathbb{R}^n$ for $n > 10000$. However, the computational complexity of $O(m^2 n)$ practically (for m in order of $\sqrt{n}$ [14]) leads to the same limitations as for the original CMA-ES.

The $(\mu/\mu_w, \lambda)$-Cholesky-CMA-ES proposed in [24] is of special interest in this paper because the LM-CMA-ES is based on this algorithm. The Cholesky-CMA represents a version of CMA-ES with rank-one update where instead of performing the factorization of the covariance matrix $\mathbf{C}^t$ into $\mathbf{A}^t{\mathbf{A}^t}^T = \mathbf{C}^t$, the Cholesky factor $\mathbf{A}^t$ and its inverse ${\mathbf{A}^t}^{-1}$ are iteratively updated. From **Theorem 1** [24] it follows that if $\mathbf{C}^t$ is updated as

$$\mathbf{C}^{t+1} = \alpha\mathbf{C}^t + \beta \boldsymbol{v}^t {\boldsymbol{v}^t}^T, \tag{4}$$

where $\boldsymbol{v} \in \mathbb{R}^n$ is given in the decomposition form $\boldsymbol{v}^t = \mathbf{A}^t\boldsymbol{z}^t$, and $\alpha, \beta \in \mathbb{R}^+$, then for $\boldsymbol{z} \neq \boldsymbol{0}$ a Cholesky factor of the matrix $\mathbf{C}^{t+1}$ can be computed by

$$\mathbf{A}^{t+1} = \sqrt{\alpha}\mathbf{A}^t + \frac{\sqrt{\alpha}}{\|\boldsymbol{z}^t\|^2}\left(\sqrt{1 + \frac{\beta}{\alpha}\|\boldsymbol{z}^t\|^2} - 1\right)[\mathbf{A}^t\boldsymbol{z}^t]{\boldsymbol{z}^t}^T, \tag{5}$$

for $\boldsymbol{z}_t = \boldsymbol{0}$ we have $\mathbf{A}^{t+1} = \sqrt{\alpha}\mathbf{A}^t$. From the **Theorem 2** [24] it follows that if ${\mathbf{A}^{-1}}^t$ is the inverse of $\mathbf{A}^t$, then the inverse of $\mathbf{A}^{t+1}$ can be computed by

$${\mathbf{A}^{-1}}^{t+1} = \frac{1}{\sqrt{\alpha}}{\mathbf{A}^{-1}}^t - \frac{1}{\sqrt{\alpha}\|\boldsymbol{z}^t\|^2}\left(1 - \frac{1}{\sqrt{1 + \frac{\beta}{\alpha}\|\boldsymbol{z}^t\|^2}}\right)\boldsymbol{z}^t[{\boldsymbol{z}^t}^T{\mathbf{A}^{-1}}^t] \tag{6}$$

for $\boldsymbol{z}^t \neq \boldsymbol{0}$ and by ${\mathbf{A}^{-1}}^{t+1} = \frac{1}{\sqrt{\alpha}}{\mathbf{A}^{-1}}^t$ for $\boldsymbol{z}^t = \boldsymbol{0}$.

The $(\mu/\mu_w, \lambda)$-Cholesky-CMA-ES is outlined in **Algorithm 2**. As well as in the original CMA-ES, Cholesky-CMA-ES

Algorithm 2 The $(\mu/\mu_w, \lambda)$-Cholesky-CMA-ES

1: **given** $n \in \mathbb{N}_+$, $\lambda = 4 + \lfloor 3\ln n \rfloor$, $\mu = \lfloor \lambda/2 \rfloor$, $w_i = \frac{\ln(\mu+1) - \ln(i)}{\mu\ln(\mu+1) - \sum_{j=1}^{\mu}\ln(j)}; i = 1 \ldots \mu$, $\mu_w = \frac{1}{\sum_{i=1}^{\mu} w_i^2}$, $c_\sigma = \frac{\sqrt{\mu_w}}{\sqrt{n} + \sqrt{\mu_w}}$, $d_\sigma = 1 + c_\sigma + 2\max(0, \sqrt{\frac{\mu_w - 1}{n+1}} - 1)$, $c_c = \frac{4}{n+4}$, $c_1 = \frac{2}{(n+\sqrt{2})^2}$
2: **initialize** $\boldsymbol{m}^{t=0} \in \mathbb{R}^n, \sigma^{t=0} > 0, \boldsymbol{p}_\sigma^{t=0} = \boldsymbol{0}, \boldsymbol{p}_c^{t=0} = \boldsymbol{0}, \mathbf{A}^{t=0} = \mathbf{I}, \mathbf{A}_{inv}^{t=0} = \mathbf{I}, t \leftarrow 0$
3: **repeat**
4:   **for** $k = 1, \ldots, \lambda$ **do**
5:     $\boldsymbol{z}_k = \mathcal{N}(\boldsymbol{0}, \mathbf{I})$
6:     $\boldsymbol{x}_k = \boldsymbol{m}^t + \sigma^t\mathbf{A}\boldsymbol{z}_k$
7:     $f_k = f(\boldsymbol{x}_k)$
8:   $\boldsymbol{m}^{t+1} \leftarrow \sum_{i=1}^{\mu} \boldsymbol{w}_i\boldsymbol{x}_{i:\lambda}$
9:   $\boldsymbol{z}_w \leftarrow \sum_{i=1}^{\mu} \boldsymbol{w}_i\boldsymbol{z}_{i:\lambda}$
10:   $\boldsymbol{p}_\sigma^{t+1} \leftarrow (1 - c_\sigma)\boldsymbol{p}_\sigma^t + \sqrt{c_\sigma(2 - c_\sigma)}\sqrt{\mu_w}\boldsymbol{z}_w$
11:   $\boldsymbol{p}_c^{t+1} \leftarrow (1 - c_c)\boldsymbol{p}_c^t + \sqrt{c_c(2 - c_c)}\sqrt{\mu_w}\mathbf{A}\boldsymbol{z}_w$
12:   $\boldsymbol{v} \leftarrow \mathbf{A}_{inv}^t\boldsymbol{p}_c$
13:   $\mathbf{A}^{t+1} = \sqrt{1 - c_1}\mathbf{A}^t + \frac{\sqrt{1-c_1}}{\|\boldsymbol{v}^t\|^2}\left(\sqrt{1 + \frac{c_1}{1-c_1}\|\boldsymbol{v}^t\|^2} - 1\right)\boldsymbol{p}_c{\boldsymbol{v}^t}^T$
14:   $\mathbf{A}_{inv}^{t+1} = \frac{1}{\sqrt{1-c_1}}\mathbf{A}_{inv}^t - \frac{1}{\sqrt{1-c_1}\|\boldsymbol{v}^t\|^2}\left(1 - \frac{1}{\sqrt{1 + \frac{c_1}{1-c_1}\|\boldsymbol{v}^t\|^2}}\right)\boldsymbol{v}^t[{\boldsymbol{v}^t}^T\mathbf{A}_{inv}^t]$,
15:   $\sigma^{t+1} \leftarrow \sigma^t\exp(\frac{c_\sigma}{d_\sigma}(\frac{\|\boldsymbol{p}_\sigma^{t+1}\|}{\mathbb{E}\|\mathcal{N}(\boldsymbol{0}, \mathbf{I})\|} - 1))$
16:   $t \leftarrow t + 1$
17: **until** *stopping criterion is met*

proceeds by sampling λ candidate solutions (lines 4 - 7) and taking into account the most successful μ out of λ solutions in the evolution paths adaptation (lines 10 and 11). However, the eigen-decomposition procedure is not required anymore because the Cholesky factor and its inverse are updated incrementally (line 13 and 14). This simplifies a lot the implementation of the algorithm and reduces its time complexity to $O(n^2)$. A postponed update of the Cholesky factors every $O(n)$ iterations would not reduce the asymptotic complexity further (as it does in the original CMA-ES) because the quadratic complexity will remain due to matrix-vector multiplications needed to sample new individuals.

The non-elitist Cholesky-CMA is a good alternative to the original CMA-ES and demonstrates a comparable performance [24]. While it has the same computational and memory complexity, the lack of rank-μ update may deteriorate its performance on problems where it is essential.

3. THE LM-CMA-ES

In this section, we first present main components of the computationally cheap limited memory CMA-ES and then introduce the algorithm itself. The components are: a procedure for reconstruction of Cholesky factors of a covariance matrix using stored direction vectors, a procedure to store these vectors and a new procedure for step-size adaptation.

3.1 Reconstruction of Cholesky factors

The idea to reconstruct the inverse Hessian matrix in the BFGS method [19] enabled its application for large scale gradient-based optimization. While the CMA-ES is a gradient-free algorithm, the two algorithms are indeed similar with a difference that the latter estimates the gradient in a stochas-

Algorithm 3 Az(): Cholesky factor - vector update

1: **given** $z \in \mathbb{R}^n, m \in \mathbb{Z}_+, \boldsymbol{j} \in \mathbb{Z}_+^m, \boldsymbol{P} \in \mathbb{R}^{m\times n}, \boldsymbol{V} \in \mathbb{R}^{m\times n}, \boldsymbol{b} \in \mathbb{R}^m, a \in [0,1]$
2: **initialize** $\boldsymbol{x} \leftarrow \boldsymbol{z}$
3: **for** $t = 1, \ldots, min(m, |\boldsymbol{j}|)$ **do**
4: $\quad k \leftarrow \boldsymbol{b}_{j_t} \boldsymbol{V}_{(j_t,:)} \cdot \boldsymbol{x}$
5: $\quad \boldsymbol{x} \leftarrow a\boldsymbol{x} + k\boldsymbol{P}_{(j_t,:)}$
6: **return** $\boldsymbol{x}$

Algorithm 4 Ainvz(): inverse Cholesky factor - vector update

1: **given** $z \in \mathbb{R}^n, m \in \mathbb{Z}_+, \boldsymbol{j} \in \mathbb{Z}^m, \boldsymbol{V} \in \mathbb{R}^{m\times n}, \boldsymbol{d} \in \mathbb{R}^m, c \in [0,1]$
2: **initialize** $\boldsymbol{x} \leftarrow \boldsymbol{z}$
3: **for** $t = 1, \ldots, min(m, |\boldsymbol{j}|)$ **do**
4: $\quad k \leftarrow \boldsymbol{d}_{j_t} \boldsymbol{V}_{(j_t,:)} \cdot \boldsymbol{x}$
5: $\quad \boldsymbol{x} \leftarrow c\boldsymbol{x} - k\boldsymbol{V}_{(j_t,:)}$
6: **return** $\boldsymbol{x}$

Algorithm 5 UpdateSet(): direction vectors selection

1: **given** $m \in \mathbb{R}^+, \boldsymbol{j} \in \mathbb{Z}_+^m, \boldsymbol{l} \in \mathbb{Z}_+^m, t \in \mathbb{Z}_+, N_{steps} \in \mathbb{Z}_+$
2: **if** $t < m$ **then**
3: $\quad \boldsymbol{j}_t \leftarrow t$
4: **else**
5: $\quad i_{min} \leftarrow 1 + argmin_i \left(\boldsymbol{l}_{\boldsymbol{j}_{i+1}} - \boldsymbol{l}_{\boldsymbol{j}_i}\right), |1 \le i \le (m-1)$
6: $\quad$ **if** $\boldsymbol{l}_{\boldsymbol{j}_{i_{min}}} - \boldsymbol{l}_{\boldsymbol{j}_{i_{min}-1}} \ge N_{steps}$ **then**
7: $\qquad i_{min}' \leftarrow 1$
8: $\quad$ **if** $i_{min} \ne m$ **then**
9: $\qquad \boldsymbol{j}_{tmp} \leftarrow \boldsymbol{j}_{i_{min}}$
10: $\qquad$ **for** $i = i_{min}, \ldots, m-1$ **do**
11: $\qquad\quad \boldsymbol{j}_i \leftarrow \boldsymbol{j}_{i+1}$
12: $\qquad \boldsymbol{j}_m \leftarrow \boldsymbol{j}_{tmp}$
13: $j_{cur} \leftarrow \boldsymbol{j}_{min(t+1,m)}$
14: $\boldsymbol{l}_{j_{cur}} \leftarrow t$
15: **return**: j_{cur}, $\boldsymbol{j}$, $\boldsymbol{l}$

tic way. This observation inspired us to investigate whether a similar matrix reconstruction procedure can be used in CMA-ES as well to reduce its time and space complexity.

As can be seen, the only use of Cholesky factor $\mathbf{A}^t$ in **Algorithm** 2 is for sampling of new solutions after $\mathbf{A}^t z_k$ or for its own update to $\mathbf{A}^{t+1}$. By setting $a = \sqrt{1-c_1}$ and $b^t = \frac{\sqrt{1-c_1}}{\|\boldsymbol{v}^t\|^2}\left(\sqrt{1 + \frac{c_1}{1-c_1}\|\boldsymbol{v}^t\|^2} - 1\right)$, one can rewrite the line (13) as

$$\mathbf{A}^{t+1} = a\mathbf{A}^t + b^t \boldsymbol{p}_c^t \boldsymbol{v}^{tT}, \tag{7}$$

In the following, we show how the vectors needed to sample new candidate solutions can be obtained without an explicit storage of Cholesky factors. At iteration $t = 0$, $\mathbf{A}^0 = \mathbf{I}$ and $\mathbf{A}^0 \boldsymbol{z} = \boldsymbol{z}$ in line (6) of **Algorithm** 2, the new updated Cholesky factor $\mathbf{A}^1 = a\mathbf{I} + b^0 \boldsymbol{p}_c^0 \boldsymbol{v}^{0T}$. At iteration $t = 1$, $\mathbf{A}^1 \boldsymbol{z} = (a\mathbf{I} + b^0 \boldsymbol{p}_c^0 \boldsymbol{v}^{0T})\boldsymbol{z} = a\boldsymbol{z} + b^0 \boldsymbol{p}_c^0 (\boldsymbol{v}^{0T}\boldsymbol{z})$ and $\mathbf{A}^2 = a(a\mathbf{I} + b^0 \boldsymbol{p}_c^0 \boldsymbol{v}^{0T}) + b^1 \boldsymbol{p}_c^1 \boldsymbol{v}^{1T}$. Thus, a very simple iterative procedure which scales as $O(mn)$ can be used to sample candidate solutions in $\mathbb{R}^n$ according to the Cholesky factor $\mathbf{A}^t$ reconstructed from m pairs of vectors $\boldsymbol{p}_c^t$ and $\boldsymbol{v}^t$.

The pseudo-code of the procedure to reconstruct $\boldsymbol{x} = \mathbf{A}^t \boldsymbol{z}$ from m direction vectors[1] is given in **Algorithm** 3. At each iteration of reconstruction of $\boldsymbol{x} = \mathbf{A}^t \boldsymbol{z}$ (lines 3 - 4), $\boldsymbol{x}$ is updated as a sum of a-weighted version of itself and b^t-weighted evolution path $\boldsymbol{p}_c^t$ scaled by the dot product of $\boldsymbol{v}^t$ and $\boldsymbol{x}$. As can be seen, the **Algorithm** uses $\boldsymbol{j}(t)$ indexation instead of t. This is simply a convenient way to have references to matrices $\boldsymbol{P}$ and $\boldsymbol{V}$ which store $\boldsymbol{p}_c^t$ and $\boldsymbol{v}^t$ vectors, respectively. In the next subsection, we will show how to efficiently manipulate these vectors.

A very similar approach can be used to reconstruct $\boldsymbol{x} = \mathbf{A}^{t-1}\boldsymbol{z}$, for the sake of reproducibility the pseudo-code is given in **Algorithm** 4 for $c = 1/\sqrt{1-c_1}$ and $d^t = \frac{1}{\sqrt{1-c_1}\|\boldsymbol{v}^t\|^2} \times \times \left(1 - \frac{1}{\sqrt{1 + \frac{c_1}{1-c_1}\|\boldsymbol{v}^t\|^2}}\right)$. The computational complexity of both procedures scales as $O(mn)$.

3.2 Direction Vectors Selection and Storage

It is an open question how to use only $m \ll n$ direction vectors to obtain a comparable amount of useful information as stored in the covariance matrix of the original CMA-ES. For large n and $\lambda \ll n$, evolution path vectors $\boldsymbol{p}_c^t$ from the last m iterations are likely to be quite similar and therefore to contain only some local information.

In this paper, we propose a simple approach which forces m selected vectors to be at approximately the same distance from each other in terms of number of iterations, but at most with the distance of N_{steps} from each other given that the m-th vector is the one from the last iteration. This selection procedure is outlined in **Algorithm** 5 which outputs an array of pointers $\boldsymbol{j}$ such that $\boldsymbol{j}_1$ points out to a row in matrices $\boldsymbol{P}$ and $\boldsymbol{V}$ with the oldest saved vectors $\boldsymbol{p}_c$ and $\boldsymbol{v}$ which will be taken into account during the reconstruction procedure. The higher the index i of $\boldsymbol{j}_i$ the more recent the corresponding direction vector is. The index j_{cur} points out to the oldest vector which will be replaced by the newest one in the same iteration when the procedure is called. The rule to choose a vector to be replaced is the following: find a pair of consecutively saved vectors with the closest distance (in terms of number of iterations, stored in $\boldsymbol{l}$) between each other (line 5), if this distance is smaller than N_{steps} then the most recent vector will be removed by assigning $j_{cur} \leftarrow i_{min}$, otherwise the oldest vector among m saved vectors should be removed. Thus, the procedure gradually replaces vectors in a way to keep them at approximately the same distance, but at most at distance of N_{steps} iterations.

3.3 Population Success Rule

An elegant success rule for step-size adaptation called the *median success rule* was recently proposed in [4]. It is applicable to non-elitist multi-recombinant evolution strategies. The median success rule compares the median fitness of the population to a fitness from the previous iteration. The comparison fitness is chosen to achieve a target success rate of 1/2. The empirical validation demonstrated that the median success rule is competitive to CSA [4].

In practice, one should count the number K_{succ} of individuals in the current population better than some j-th best individual of the previous population, where j depends on

[1] more precisely, we mean m evolution paths $\boldsymbol{p}_c$ and their inverses $\boldsymbol{v}$ but for brevity we say m direction vectors

n and λ but can be set to be 0.3λ [4]. Then, a normalized measurement

$$z \leftarrow \frac{2}{\lambda}\left(K_{succ} - \frac{\lambda+1}{2}\right) \quad (8)$$

can be computed such that $z \geq 0$ iff the median individual was successful.

The step-size is adapted as

$$\sigma \leftarrow \sigma \exp\left(\frac{s}{d_\sigma}\right), \quad (9)$$

where $s \leftarrow (1-c_\sigma)s + c_\sigma z$ and $d_s = 2(n-1)/n$.

We suppose that while being quite elegant the median success rule has a potential drawback that we will demonstrate on an example. Let us suppose that fitness values (to be minimized) of the previous population are say $\boldsymbol{f}_{t-1} = [2.1, 3.1, 4.1, 5.1, 6.1, 7.1, 8.1]$ while the fitness values of the current population are $\boldsymbol{f}_t = [1, 2, 3, 4, 5, 6, 7]$. According to the median success rule if j is chosen as, e.g., 3, the number of successful individual (with fitness values better than or equal to $\boldsymbol{f}_{t-1}(3) = 4.1$) is 4 (as $\boldsymbol{f}_t(1) = 1, \boldsymbol{f}_t(2) = 2, \boldsymbol{f}_t(3) = 3$ and $\boldsymbol{f}_t(4) = 4$). The computed value of K_{succ} is then will be used to adapt the step-size. However, its computation does not take into account the values of $\boldsymbol{f}_{t-1}(i)$ for $1 \leq i < j$ and even if all such $\boldsymbol{f}_{t-1}(i)$ are better than the best solution $\boldsymbol{f}_t(1)$, this information will not be taken into account.

This potential drawback is not the drawback in a sense that the *median* success rule was designed in this way. However, we suppose that the information omitted in the median success rule can be useful since it can provide a better estimate whether and by how much the new population is more successful than the previous one.

In this paper, we introduce *the population success rule* (PSR) for step-size adaptation for non-elitist multi-recombinant evolution strategies. To estimate the success of the current population we combine fitness function values from the previous and current population into a mixed set

$$\boldsymbol{f}_{mix} \leftarrow \boldsymbol{f}_{t-1} \cup \boldsymbol{f}_t \quad (10)$$

Then, we rank all individual in the mixed set to define two sets $\boldsymbol{r}_{t-1}$ and $\boldsymbol{r}_t$ containing ranks of individuals of the previous and current populations ranked in the mixed set.

We compute a normalized success measurement

$$z_{PSR} \leftarrow \frac{\sum_{i=1}^{\lambda} r_t(i) - r_{t-1}(i)}{\lambda^2} - z^*, \quad (11)$$

where z^* is a target success ratio. The step-size can be adapted as in (9).

The proposed *population success rule* takes into account all fitness function values from the previous and current generation. This success rule seems to represent a more general case of the 1/5th-rule which can be obtained when $\lambda = 1$.

3.4 The Algorithm

In the previous subsection we introduced all necessary components of the $(\mu/\mu_w, \lambda)$-LM-CMA-ES outlined in **Algorithm** 6. The algorithm represents a computationally efficient limited memory version of CMA-ES, where the Cholesky factor and its inverse are reconstructed from a set of stored direction vectors (lines 6 and 9). The mutation step-size is adapted using the population success rule (lines 15 - 13). The algorithm memory and time complexity scales as $O(mn)$.

Algorithm 6 The $(\mu/\mu_w, \lambda)$-LM-CMA-ES

1: **given** $n \in \mathbb{N}_+$, $\lambda = 4 + \lfloor 3 \ln n \rfloor$, $\mu = \lfloor \lambda/2 \rfloor$, $w_i = \frac{\ln(\mu+1) - \ln(i)}{\mu \ln(\mu+1) - \sum_{j=1}^{\mu} \ln(j)}; i = 1 \ldots \mu$, $\mu_w = \frac{1}{\sum_{i=1}^{\mu} w_i^2}$, $c_\sigma = 0.3$, $d_\sigma = 1$, $m = 4 + \lfloor 3 \ln n \rfloor$, $N_{steps} = m$, $c_c = \frac{1}{m}$, $c_1 = \frac{1}{10 ln(n+1)}$
2: **initialize** $\boldsymbol{m}^{t=0} \in \mathbb{R}^n, \sigma^{t=0} > 0, \boldsymbol{p}_c^{t=0} = \boldsymbol{0}, s \leftarrow 0, t \leftarrow 0$
3: **repeat**
4:     **for** $k = 1, \ldots, \lambda$ **do**
5:         $\boldsymbol{z}_k = \mathcal{N}(\boldsymbol{0}, \mathbf{I})$
6:         $\boldsymbol{x}_k = \boldsymbol{m}^t + \sigma^t Az(\boldsymbol{z}_k)$
7:         $\boldsymbol{f}_k^t = f(\boldsymbol{x}_k)$
8:     $\boldsymbol{m}^{t+1} \leftarrow \sum_{i=1}^{\mu} \boldsymbol{w}_i \boldsymbol{x}_{i:\lambda}$
9:     $\boldsymbol{p}_c^{t+1} \leftarrow (1-c_c)\boldsymbol{p}_c^t + \sqrt{c_c(2-c_c)}\sqrt{\mu_w}(\boldsymbol{m}^{t+1} - \boldsymbol{m}^t)/\sigma$
10:     $\boldsymbol{v} \leftarrow Ainvz(\boldsymbol{p}_c^{t+1})$
11:     $j_{cur} \leftarrow UpdateSet()$
12:     $\boldsymbol{V}_{(j_{cur},:)} \leftarrow \boldsymbol{v}; \boldsymbol{P}_{(j_{cur},:)} \leftarrow \boldsymbol{p}_c^{t+1}$
13:     $\boldsymbol{b}_{j_{cur}} \leftarrow \frac{\sqrt{1-c_1}}{\|\boldsymbol{v}^t\|^2}\left(\sqrt{1 + \frac{c_1}{1-c_1}\|\boldsymbol{v}^t\|^2} - 1\right)$
14:     $\boldsymbol{d}_{j_{cur}} = \frac{1}{\sqrt{1-c_1}\|\boldsymbol{v}^t\|^2}\left(1 - \frac{1}{\sqrt{1 + \frac{c_1}{1-c_1}\|\boldsymbol{v}^t\|^2}}\right)$,
15:     $\boldsymbol{r}^t, \boldsymbol{r}^{t-1} \leftarrow$ Ranks of $\boldsymbol{f}^t$ and $\boldsymbol{f}^{t-1}$ in $\boldsymbol{f}^t \cup \boldsymbol{f}^{t-1}$
16:     $z_{PSR} \leftarrow \frac{\sum_{i=1}^{\lambda} \boldsymbol{r}^t(i) - \boldsymbol{r}^{t-1}(i)}{\lambda^2} - z^*$
17:     $s \leftarrow (1-c_\sigma)s + c_\sigma z_{PSR}$
18:     $\sigma^{t+1} \leftarrow \sigma^t \exp(s/d_\sigma)$
19:     $t \leftarrow t+1$
20: **until** *stopping criterion is met*

4. SIMULATION RESULTS

In this section, we perform a set of numerical experiments to assess the performance of the proposed LM-CMA-ES on large scale optimization problem with $n = 128, 256, \ldots, 8096$. We investigate the performance on three basic problems: Sphere function $f_{Sphere}(\boldsymbol{x}) = \sum_{i=1}^{n} \boldsymbol{x}_i^2$, separable Ellipsoid function $f_{Elli}(\boldsymbol{x}) = \sum_{i=1}^{n} 10^{6\frac{i-1}{n-1}} \boldsymbol{x}_i^2$ and its rotated version $f_{ElliRot}(\boldsymbol{x}) = f_{Elli}(\boldsymbol{Qx})$, where $\boldsymbol{Q}$ is an orthogonal $n \times n$ matrix with each column vector $\boldsymbol{q}_i$ being a uniformly distributed unit vector implementing an angle-preserving transformation [21].

4.1 Experimental Setting

For the sake of reproducibility, the MATLAB/C++ source code of all tested algorithms is available at `https://sites.google.com/site/lmcmaeses/`.

In the order to estimate the performance of $(\mu/\mu_w, \lambda)$-LM-CMA-ES, we compare it with $(\mu/\mu_w, \lambda)$-Cholesky-CMA-ES and $(\mu/\mu_w, \lambda)$-Sep-CMA-ES. We use the default parameters for Cholesky-CMA-ES and Sep-CMA-ES as given in [24] and [21], respectively. The parameters of LM-CMA-ES are given in **Algorithm** 6. For all problems, the mean $\boldsymbol{m}^{t=0}$ is initialized in the range $[-5, 5]^n$, the population is sampled with initial step-size $\sigma^{t=0} = 5$ and using the same seed per run. Note that in all cases we use the default population size $\lambda = 4 + \lfloor 3 \ln n \rfloor$.

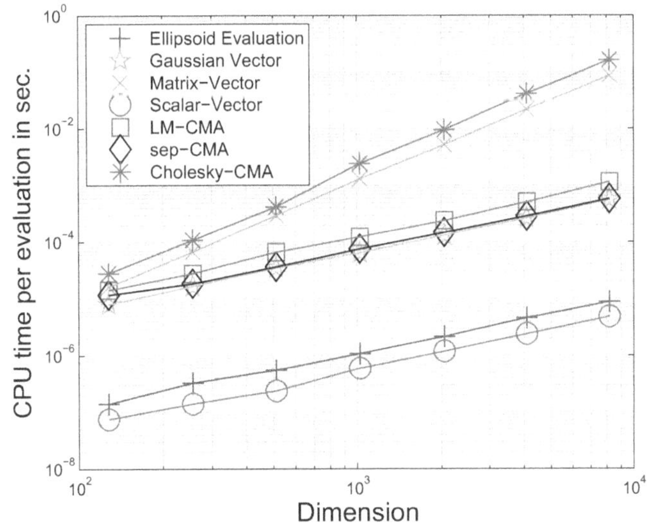

Figure 1: Timing results of LM-CMA-ES on the separable Ellipsoid compared to sep-CMA-ES and Cholesky-CMA-ES. The results were computed using at most 10^5 function evaluations for sep-CMA-ES and LM-CMA-ES and using at most 10^4 for Cholesky-CMA-ES.

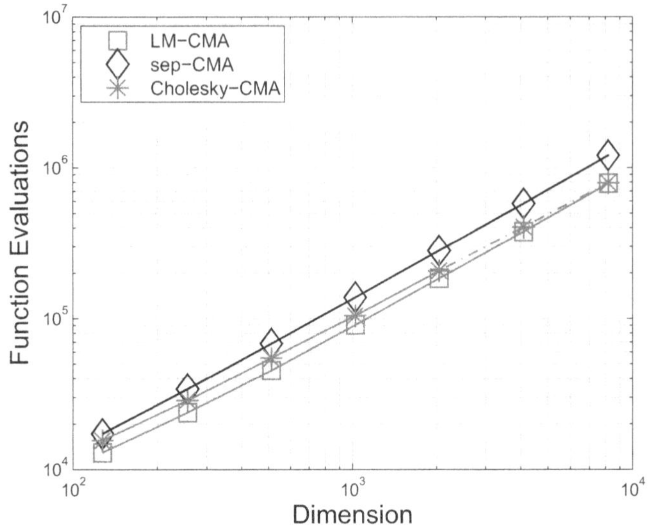

Figure 2: Results of LM-CMA-ES on the Sphere function compared to sep-CMA-ES and Cholesky-CMA-ES. Lines show the median of 11 runs for different problem dimensions to reach the target fitness value of 10^{-10}. The dotted line is an extrapolation.

4.2 Memory and Computational Complexity of LM-CMA-ES

The LM-CMA-ES has $O(mn)$ memory complexity and more specifically stores $\boldsymbol{Q} \in \mathbb{R}^{m \times n}$, $\boldsymbol{V} \in \mathbb{R}^{m \times n}$ and λ solution vectors $\boldsymbol{x}_i$. For large n and $m = \lambda_{default} = \lambda = 4 + \lfloor 3 \ln n \rfloor$ used in this paper, the algorithm stores approximately $3mn$ real-valued parameters. If a real-valued parameter requires 8 bytes of memory, then for $n = 8192$ the LM-CMA-ES will require 5.8 megabytes while the original CMA-ES would start to reach its limit by requiring 1 gigabyte of memory. Using the same amount of memory (more specifically, 1.03 gigabyte), the LM-CMA-ES will able to optimize a 1 million dimensional problem. Indeed, by taking $m = 1$ even less memory would be needed but the latter possibility makes sense only if the performance stays at a reasonable level.

Figure 1 shows how fast CPU time per evaluation scales for different operations (measured on a 2.0 GHz processor). Scalar-vector multiplication of a vector with n variables scales linearly with ca. $6 \cdot 10^{-10} n$ seconds, evaluation of the separable Ellipsoid is twice more expensive if a temporary data is used. Sampling of n normally distributed variables scales as ca. 100 vectors-scalar multiplications. As can be seen in Figure 1, sampling of $\boldsymbol{z}_k$ dominates the computational overhead of sep-CMA already after $n = 128$. The LM-CMA-ES scales almost linearly for $n \geq 1024$ as ca. $1.3 \cdot 10^{-7} n$ or ca. 200 scalar-vector multiplications. Matrix-vector multiplication scale quadratically with n and Cholesky-CMA-ES scales as ca. 1.5-2 matrix-vector multiplications.

Practically, the LM-CMA-ES is about 40 times faster (in terms of its internal computation cost per function evaluation) for $n = 2048$ and about 140 times faster for $n = 8192$ than Cholesky-CMA-ES. The LM-CMA-ES is only about 2 times slower than sep-CMA-ES, whose cost is dominated by sampling from normal distribution.

The computation cost of CMA-ES with full covariance matrix learning limits its applicability for $n \gg 100$ and makes it intractable because of memory for $n > 10000$.

4.3 Performance on Sphere and Ellipsoid

The Sphere function is often viewed in Evolutionary Computation to be the first function to look at when benchmarking evolutionary algorithms. Figure 2 demonstrates a comparable performance of LM-CMA-ES with population success rule, sep-CMA-ES with CSA and Cholesky-CMA-ES with CSA. It should be further studied what is the effect of the target population success rate (set to $z^* = 0.25$) whose value was chosen the same for all experiments in order to obtain a reasonable performance on Ellipsoid functions.

Figure 3-Left shows that both LM-CMA-ES and Cholesky-CMA-ES are rotationally invariant and therefore they optimization runs (one per function) are almost coincide (within the algorithm). The sep-CMA-ES is not rotationally invariant and therefore it performs better on the separable Ellipsoid than on its rotated version where the exploitation of the separability is not that useful. Importantly, the LM-CMA-ES often outperforms the Cholesky-CMA-ES in the beginning of optimization, while the adaptation of the full covariance matrix makes Cholesky-CMA-ES faster at later stages. Figure 3-Right shows that the loss of performance of LM-CMA-ES compared to Cholesky-CMA-ES is in order of a factor of 3-4 given that for $n = 2048$ the LM-CMA-ES uses only $m = 26$ direction vectors. It is important to keep in mind that for $n > 10000$ the Cholesky-CMA-ES becomes intractable both due to its memory and computational complexity. Then, the sep-CMA-ES becomes an alternative, however, it does not learn dependencies and might be therefore inefficient (see Figure 3-Left).

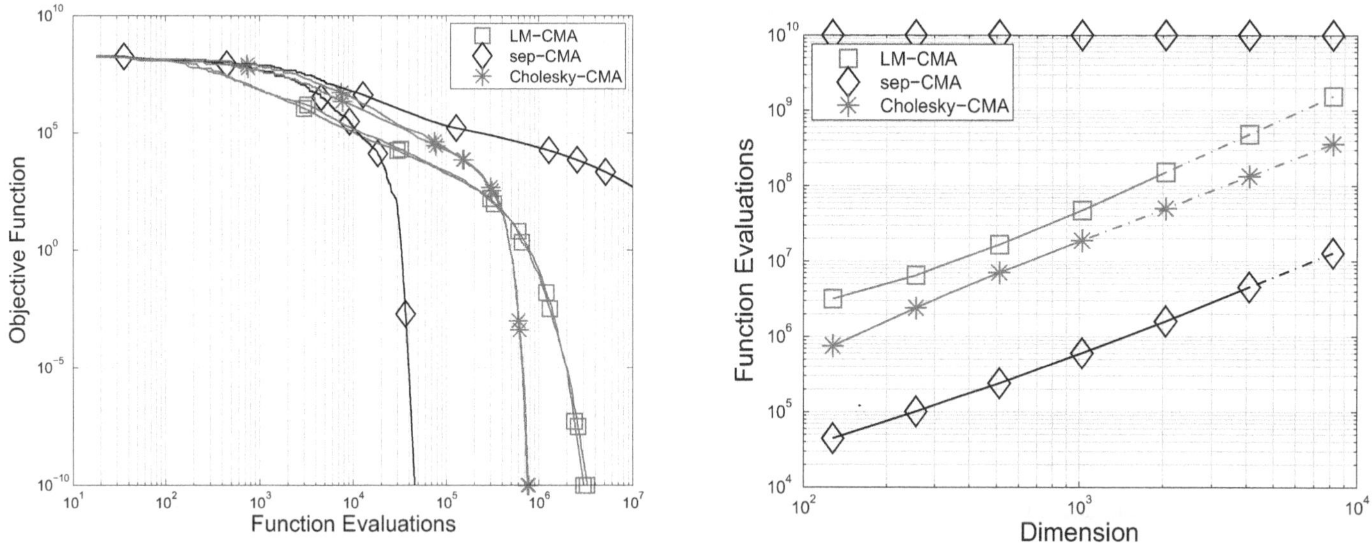

Figure 3: Left: Convergence plots of LM-CMA-ES, sep-CMA-ES and Cholesky-CMA-ES on 128-dimensional axis-parallel and rotated Ellipsoid functions. Right: The median of 11 runs on separable Ellipsoid function for different problem dimensions. The dotted lines correspond to extrapolated results by preserving the same scaling as between the last two actual estimations.

We discussed several large scale ESs in this paper: L-CMA-ES [14] and R1-NES [23]. We compared the LM-CMA-ES indirectly by analyzing the results from [14] and [23]. It takes about 6000 seconds for L-CMA-ES to solve 200-dimensional Ellipsoid after about $7e+6$ function evaluations with $m = \sqrt{n} = 14$ and 4000 seconds after $4e+6$ evaluations with $m = n/2 = 100$. The LM-CMA-ES solves the same problem after about 125 seconds and $5.3e+6$ function evaluations with $m = 19$. The performance is comparable while the LM-CMA-ES is about $32 - 48$ times faster that is unlikely to be only due to a different processor or implementation used. The L-CMA-ES has $O(m^2 n)$ computational complexity and therefore it is in order of m times computationally slower than LM-CMA-ES.

The R1-NES algorithm performs well on non-separable problems but tends to fail on problems where the learning of multiple principal components is essential, e.g., it fails on moderate dimensional rotated Ellipsoid function [23]. On Rosenbrock function the LM-CMA-ES is about 5 times faster (not shown) in terms of number of function evaluations for $n = 256, 512$. The R1-NES also samples from the normal distribution, and therefore the lower bound of its computational complexity is predefined (see Figure 1).

We performed an experiment on 100,000-dimensional separable Ellipsoid problems for 100,000 function evaluations (i.e., n evaluations). The original CMA-ES and Cholesky-CMA-ES cannot be applied due to memory requirements. The applicability of L-CMA-ES is also limited due to its $O(m^2 n)$ computational complexity. The results for sep-CMA-ES specifically designed for large scale optimization and the proposed LM-CMA-ES are shown in Figure 4. While the LM-CMA-ES gradually improves the fitness similarly as in Figure 3-Left, the sep-CMA-ES does not improve it because it diverges from the very first iterations. To investigate whether it is a mistake in our implementation, we launched the same experiment using the sep-CMA-ES author's MATLAB implementation where the divergence was also observed.

It should be noted that the separable Ellipsoid can be easily solved by various Evolutionary Algorithms which implicitly or explicitly exploit its separability, our purpose of its usage is to investigate how the LM-CMA-ES performs on problems with high dependencies between variables. Given that the LM-CMA-ES is rotationally invariant, its performance on both separable and non-separable problems is comparable, but the former is cheaper to compute.

5. DISCUSSION AND CONCLUSION

This paper presents a new approach to efficiently store and exploit the information about dependencies between decision variables of large scale optimization problems. It allows to reconstruct the Cholesky factor and its inverse using $m \ll n$ direction vectors that turns out to be sufficient to obtain good performance on large scale problems with highly-depended variables. The implementation of this approach in the LM-CMA-ES algorithm makes it possible to optimize a 1 million dimensional problem while learning dependencies between variables at a cost of about 0.1 second per function evaluation on an ordinary machine. Indeed, one should not plan to easily find a global optimum in such a huge search space, but some local optimization/tuning seems reasonable, e.g., in Machine Learning problems.

The proposed LM-CMA-ES algorithm is based on the *population success rule* which looks promising and requires further theoretical and empirical investigations. It should be studied as well whether it can be claimed to represent a general case of the 1/5th success rule. More experiments are required to investigate whether and when the lack of rank-μ update is a limitation.

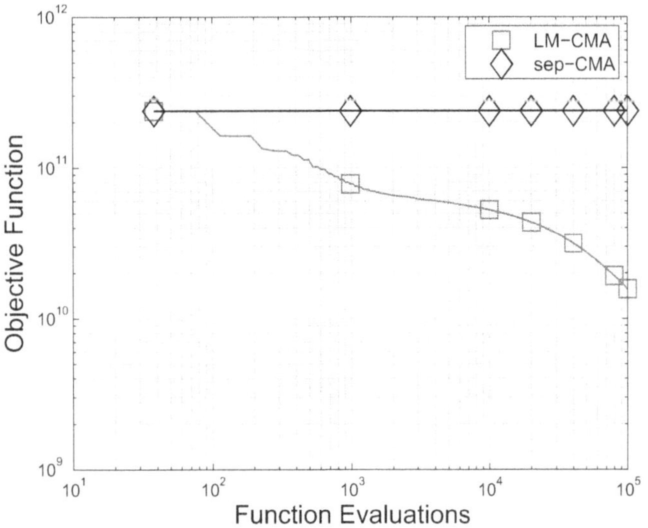

Figure 4: LM-CMA-ES and sep-CMA-ES on separable 100,000-dimensional Ellipsoid problem. The sep-CMA-ES divergences after the first generation (the best fitness is shown). Note that the LM-CMA-ES is rotationally invariant, therefore a similar performance is expected on 100,000-dimensional rotated Ellipsoid.

All parameters chosen for the algorithm were tuned only moderately and *specifically* for large n and might require a significant revision to address a wider set of optimization problems commonly used for EAs. However, we suppose that the performance on the Ellipsoid function is already worth a closer scientific investigation. We envision that several directions may further improve the algorithm: i) adaptation of m within a fixed range, the impact of m itself should be studied as well, ii) since the population success rule does not make any assumptions about the sampling distribution, the Gaussian sampling can be removed that would further speed-up the algorithm (e.g., to replace CSA by PSR in CMA-ES).

The speculations about a possibility of having CMA-ES like evolutionary processes going on in nature often end up around a hypothesis that there is no such a thing in natural evolution as a full covariance matrix and its update. One may suppose that only a limited number of direction vectors is stored to adjust the mutation in promising directions.

6. REFERENCES

[1] A. Auger, D. Brockhoff, N. Hansen, et al. Benchmarking the local metamodel CMA-ES on the noiseless BBOB'2013 test bed. In *GECCO (Companion), workshop on Black-Box Optimization Benchmarking (BBOB'2013)*, pages 1225–1232, 2013.

[2] A. Auger, S. Finck, N. Hansen, and R. Ros. BBOB 2010: Comparison Tables of All Algorithms on All Noiseless Functions. Technical Report RR-7215, INRIA, 2010.

[3] M. Brand. Fast low-rank modifications of the thin singular value decomposition. *Linear algebra and its applications*, 415(1):20–30, 2006.

[4] O. A. Elhara, A. Auger, and N. Hansen. A median success rule for non-elitist evolution strategies: Study of feasibility. In *Genetic and Evolutionary Computation Conference*, 2013.

[5] S. García, D. Molina, M. Lozano, and F. Herrera. A study on the use of non-parametric tests for analyzing the evolutionary algorithms' behaviour: a case study on the CEC'2005 Special Session on Real Parameter Optimization. *Journal of Heuristics*, 15:617–644, 2009.

[6] N. Hansen, S. Müller, and P. Koumoutsakos. Reducing the time complexity of the derandomized evolution strategy with covariance matrix adaptation (CMA-ES). *Evolutionary Computation*, 11(1):1–18, 2003.

[7] N. Hansen, A. S. Niederberger, L. Guzzella, and P. Koumoutsakos. A method for handling uncertainty in evolutionary optimization with an application to feedback control of combustion. *Evolutionary Computation, IEEE Transactions on*, 13(1):180–197, 2009.

[8] N. Hansen and A. Ostermeier. Adapting Arbitrary Normal Mutation Distributions in Evolution Strategies: The Covariance Matrix Adaptation. In *International Conference on Evolutionary Computation*, pages 312–317, 1996.

[9] N. Hansen and A. Ostermeier. Completely Derandomized Self-Adaptation in Evolution Strategies. *Evol. Comput.*, 9(2):159–195, June 2001.

[10] N. Hansen and R. Ros. Benchmarking a weighted negative covariance matrix update on the BBOB-2010 noiseless testbed. In *Genetic and Evolutionary Computation Conference*, pages 1673–1680. ACM, 2010.

[11] N. Hansen, D. V. Arnold, and A. Auger. Evolution Strategies. In J. Kacprzyk and W. Pedrycz, editors, *Handbook of Computational Intelligence*. Springer, 2013.

[12] C. Igel, N. Hansen, and S. Roth. Covariance matrix adaptation for multi-objective optimization. *Evolutionary computation*, 15(1):1–28, 2007.

[13] G. A. Jastrebski and D. V. Arnold. Improving Evolution Strategies through Active Covariance Matrix Adaptation. In *IEEE Congress on Evolutionary Computation*, pages 2814–2821, 2006.

[14] J. N. Knight and M. Lunacek. Reducing the space-time complexity of the CMA-ES. In *Genetic and Evolutionary Computation Conference*, pages 658–665. ACM, 2007.

[15] D. C. Liu and J. Nocedal. On the limited memory BFGS method for large scale optimization. *Mathematical programming*, 45(1-3):503–528, 1989.

[16] I. Loshchilov. CMA-ES with restarts for solving CEC 2013 benchmark problems. In *Evolutionary Computation (CEC), 2013 IEEE Congress on*, pages 369–376. IEEE, 2013.

[17] I. Loshchilov, M. Schoenauer, and M. Sebag. Self-adaptive surrogate-assisted covariance matrix adaptation evolution strategy. In *Genetic and Evolutionary Computation Conference*, pages 321–328. ACM, 2012.

[18] I. Loshchilov, M. Schoenauer, and M. Sebag. Bi-population CMA-ES agorithms with surrogate models and line searches. In *Genetic and Evolutionary Computation Conference*, pages 1177–1184. ACM, 2013.

[19] J. Nocedal. Updating quasi-newton matrices with limited storage. *Math. of computation*, 35(151):773–782, 1980.

[20] I. Rechenberg. *Evolutionsstrategie: optimierung technischer systeme nach prinzipien der biologischen evolution.* Frommann-Holzboog, 1973.

[21] R. Ros and N. Hansen. A simple modification in CMA-ES achieving and space complexity. In *Parallel Problem Solving from Nature–PPSN X*, pages 296–305. 2008.

[22] D. F. Shanno. Conditioning of Quasi-Newton Methods for Function Minimization. *Math. of Computation*, 24(111):647–656, 1970.

[23] Y. Sun, F. Gomez, T. Schaul, and J. Schmidhuber. A linear time natural evolution strategy for non-separable functions. *arXiv preprint arXiv:1106.1998*, 2011.

[24] T. Suttorp, N. Hansen, and C. Igel. Efficient covariance matrix update for variable metric evolution strategies. *Machine Learning*, 75(2):167–197, 2009.

Evolutionary Algorithms for Overlapping Correlation Clustering

Carlos E. Andrade
University of Campinas
Av. Albert Einstein, 1251
Campinas, SP, Brazil
andrade@ic.unicamp.br

Mauricio G. C. Resende
AT&T Labs Research
200 Laurel Avenue
Middletown, NJ 07748 USA
mgcr@research.att.com

Howard J. Karloff
Yahoo Labs
111 West 40th Street
New York, NY 10018 USA
karloff@yahoo-inc.com

Flávio K. Miyazawa
University of Campinas
Av. Albert Einstein, 1251
Campinas, SP, Brazil
fkm@ic.unicamp.br

ABSTRACT

In OVERLAPPING CORRELATION CLUSTERING (OCC), a number of objects are assigned to clusters. Two objects in the same cluster have correlated characteristics. As opposed to traditional clustering where objects are assigned to a single cluster, in OCC objects may be assigned to one or more clusters. In this paper, we present Biased Random-Key Genetic Algorithms for OCC. We present computational experiments such results outperformed the state of art methods for OCC.

Categories and Subject Descriptors

I.2.8 [Artificial Intelligence] [**Problem Solving, Control Methods, and Search**]: [Heuristic methods]

Keywords

Data mining; Correlation Clustering; Biased Random-Key Genetic Algorithm

1. INTRODUCTION

One of the most fundamental tasks in data analysis is to categorize objects in different sets such that two objects in the same set have certain characteristics that are correlated. This correlation is usually measured by a similarity value. The standard way of clustering is the creation of a partition of these objects. However, for some applications, it is natural that an object belong to two or more clusters since it can share characteristics with objects in more than one cluster. In this case, to partition the ground set does not make sense. Instead, it is more appropriate to assign the objects to clusters with possible overlapping. Several scenarios with these properties can be addressed: in social networks, a user belongs to several communities; in mobility analysis, persons share trajectories with respect to time and space; in biology, a protein belongs to several protein complexes having similar expressions.

We can model scenarios like these using OVERLAPPING CORRELATION CLUSTERING (OCC), introduced in [5]. This problem is closely related to Correlation Clustering (CC) [2] but allows overlapping of the clusters. Another major difference is in the relation among the objects. In OCC, this relation is expressed as a value in range $[0, 1]$ while in CC it takes on one of two discrete values in the set $\{0, 1\}$. This enables the utilization of different types of similarity functions leading to a more sophisticated analysis.

This paper presents Biased Random-Key Genetic Algorithms associated with local search procedures aiming to solve the overlapping correlation clustering problem under an optimization point of view. Section 2 formalizes the problem. Section 3 presents high level algorithms to deal with OCC. Section 4 depicts the experimental results and Section 5 presents the concluding remarks.

GECCO'14, July 12–16, 2014, Vancouver, BC, Canada.
Copyright 2014 ACM 978-1-4503-2662-9/14/07 ...$15.00.
http://dx.doi.org/10.1145/2576768.2598284.

2. DEFINITIONS

Let $V = \{v_1, \ldots, v_n\}$ be a set of n objects such that there exists a symmetric function $s : V \times V \to [0, 1]$ which gives the similarity $s(u, v)$ between two objects u and v in V. Let $L = \{1, \ldots, k\}$ be the set of k available labels (clusters). Since we allow an object to be in several clusters, we define $\ell : V \to 2^L \setminus \emptyset$ with $\ell(v)$ being the set of labels assigned to object v. Note that we require that each object have at least one label. If the set $\ell(v) = \{c_1, \ldots, c_s\}$ of labels is given to object v, then we assume that v is in clusters $c_1, \ldots, c_s$. Consider also $\mathcal{H} : 2^L \times 2^L \to [0, 1]$, a symmetric function which gives the similarity between two sets of labels. Higher "similarity" of E and F should correspond to higher $\mathcal{H}(E, F)$, and $\mathcal{H}(E, E)$ should be 1 for all E. In OVERLAPPING CORRELATION CLUSTERING (OCC), the task is to find a multi-labeling function ℓ that minimizes the cost function

$$\frac{1}{2} \sum_{(u,v) \in V \times V, u \neq v} |\mathcal{H}(\ell(u), \ell(v)) - s(u, v)|. \quad (1)$$

Note that Objective Function (1) represents the absolute error between the labeling and the similarity measure. In this sense, the objective is to find a labeling as close as possible to the given similarities.

This formulation enables the application in different contexts. However, we first need to measure the similarities that are context dependent. As the problem is general enough, we can use any type of comparison measure as long as it scales to the real interval $[0, 1]$. Another considerable task is to find the appropriate $\mathcal{H}$ function. As suggested in [5], we use two functions: The *Jaccard Similarity Coefficient* and the *Set-Intersection Indicator*. The Jaccard similarity coefficient, also known as the Jaccard index, is a well-known measure of similarity between two sample sets, widely used in biology and machine learning. Let E and F be two sets, not both empty. The Jaccard index of E and F is defined as $\mathcal{J}(E, F) = \frac{|E \cap F|}{|E \cup F|}$. The set-intersection indicator function is a simple function defined as $\mathcal{I}(E, F) = 1$ if $E \cap F \neq \emptyset$ or $\mathcal{I}(E, F) = 0$, otherwise.

Some scenarios require that objects be assigned a restricted number of labels among those available. A good example is in the analysis of mobility patterns, where in spite of the fact that trajectories can have a large number of characteristics, we restrict ourselves to only a few of the most meaningful ones. In these cases, we introduce a parameter p such that $|\ell(v)| \leq p$ for all $v \in V$.

It is easy to see that, if we consider $\mathcal{H} = \mathcal{I}$ and $p = 1$, each object will belong to a single cluster and the similarity between pairs of objects will be an indication as to whether they share the same cluster. In this case, if s follows the set-intersection function, we face the original correlation clustering problem, which is $\mathcal{NP}$-hard [2]. In [5], hardness proofs for the other cases are presented.

3. BIASED RANDOM KEY GENETIC ALGORITHM AND LOCAL SEARCH

To solve *Overlapping Correlation Clustering*, we opt to use a Biased Random-Key Genetic Algorithm (BRKGA) mainly because of its recent success in solving several problems, such as routing [1], packing [8], among others. The major features that distinguish BRKGAs from other genetic algorithms is the standard chromosome encoding and a well-defined and parameterized evolutionary process. The biased component of a BRKGA contributes to increasing the likelihood that high-quality solutions will pass down their genes to future generations. The decoding process links the genetic algorithm with the problem itself, indirectly mapping the chromosome space $[0, 1]^n$ onto the set of feasible solutions. See [8] for more details regarding BRKGAs.

3.1 Representation

In most BRKGA implementations, a chromosome is encoded as a real vector $\mathbf{x}' \in [0, 1]^n$, following the procedure given in [4]. However, other encodings are possible. In this paper, we use two forms of chromosomes to represent a labeling. Let n be the number of objects and k the number of available clusters. The first representation, called *compact*, is an integer vector $\mathbf{x^c} \in \mathbb{N}^n$, and the second, called *extended*, is a binary vector $\mathbf{x^e} \in \{0, 1\}^{nk}$.

For the compact chromosome $\mathbf{x^c}$, each $\mathbf{x}^\mathbf{c}_i$ is a positive integer that represents the clusters to which object v_i belongs. In this case, we consider each bit as a set indicator in which the least-significant bit corresponds to the first cluster, and so on. Although this representation limits the number of possible clusters ($k < 64$ on a 64-bit machine)[1], it enables very fast set operations since they are done bitwise, and for most applications, this limit is sufficient. In the extended chromosome $\mathbf{x^e}$, the subvector $\tilde{\mathbf{x}}^\mathbf{e} = \tilde{\mathbf{x}}^\mathbf{e}_{(i-1)k+1}, \ldots, \tilde{\mathbf{x}}^\mathbf{e}_{ik}$ is an indicator vector where, for each object v_i, $\tilde{\mathbf{x}}^\mathbf{e}_j$ is 1 if v_i is in cluster j, or 0 otherwise. This representation can be used with any $n > 1$ and $k > 1$.

Although both compact and extended representations are quite similar, they affect the evolutionary mechanism of BRKGA differently. In the compact representation, each allele is the full labeling of an object and therefore, in the mating process, the offspring inherits these full labelings. Learning occurs through the combination of entire sets of labels of each object. In the extended representation, each allele represents a specific label of an object. In the mating process, the offspring inherits each label individually, enabling learning to occur at the level of each label for each object.

3.2 Decoding a solution

To decode a solution from a chromosome using the representations of Section 3.1, we use a two-phase decoder in which the first phase extracts a solution and the second phase is committed to local search procedures. We assume that the input vector to the decoder is in compact representation. Note that in case of the extended representation, we need to "compactify" the vector obtaining from each subvector $\tilde{\mathbf{x}}^\mathbf{e} = \tilde{\mathbf{x}}^\mathbf{e}_{(i-1)k+1}, \ldots, \tilde{\mathbf{x}}^\mathbf{e}_{ik}$, for each object v_i, the integer that can be described by this sequence of bits. Algorithm 1 describes the first phase.

First of all, we must guarantee that the number of clusters of each object is limited to p. If the number $|\ell(v)|$ of clusters containing object v is greater than p, we repair the chromosome by removing $|\ell(v)| - p$ clusters from v uniformly at random. Lines 1–2 of Algorithm 1 summarize this procedure, in which by "$s \in \mathbf{x}$" we mean that "$s = x_h$ for some h," and by "$|s|$," the number of bits equal to one in the binary representation of s.

After the repair, we have a feasible solution whose value is computed in lines 4–11. We compare each pair of objects (u, v), calculating the Jaccard or set-intersection similarity and adding the error to the solution value, according to Equation (1). Note that in line 5 we abuse notation: $l(u) \leftarrow \mathbf{x}_u$ gets the labeling of object u. We also split the amount of error caused by u and v into two parts: the positive error e^+, indicating that labels assigned to u and v are too similar, and the negative error e^-, indicating otherwise. These errors are used in the local search phase to improve the solution. Note that vectors $e^+, e^- \in \mathbb{R}^+$. After local search, the solution may be improved and, in such case, we consolidate the change of the solution in the chromosome (line 13).

The running time complexity of the first phase is $O(kn^2)$ when k is unrestricted. Note that the repair phase runs in $O(kn)$ time. The solution value computation has a quadratic factor due to the comparison of each pair of objects. The time complexity of function $\mathcal{H}$ depends directly on k and the type of function. Assuming k is unrestricted, when $\mathcal{H} = \mathcal{J}$,

[1]If a specialized bitset structure like C++'s `bitset<>` template is used, this limitation can be overcome although at the expense of increased complexity.

Algorithm 1: Decoder – Phase 1

Input: a vector $\mathbf{x} \in \mathbb{N}^n$, integers $k, p \in \mathbb{N}$, and set V.
Output: modified $\mathbf{x}$ and the fitness $\mathcal{C}$ of $\mathbf{x}$.

foreach $s \in \mathbf{x}$ *such that* $|s| > p$ **do**
    Remove $|s| - p$ elements from s uniformly at random;
$\mathcal{C} \leftarrow 0$;
foreach *pair* $(u, v) \in V \times V$ **do**
    $l(u) \leftarrow \mathbf{x}_u$; $l(v) \leftarrow \mathbf{x}_v$;
    $error \leftarrow \mathcal{H}(\ell(u), \ell(v)) - s(u, v)$;
    $\mathcal{C} \leftarrow \mathcal{C} + \texttt{absval}(error)$;
    if $error > 0$ **then**
        $e_u^+ \leftarrow e_u^+ + error$; $e_v^+ \leftarrow e_v^+ + error$;
    else
        $e_u^- \leftarrow e_u^- - error$; $e_v^- \leftarrow e_v^- - error$;
`LocalSearch()`;
Rewrite the improved solution on the chromosome $\mathbf{x}$;
return *modified* $\mathbf{x}$ *and solution value* $\mathcal{C}$;

we need to compute the union and intersection of the two sets of labels, which takes O(k) time each. In the case of $\mathcal{H} = \mathcal{I}$, we only need to calculate the intersection, which takes O(k) time. However as observed in the previous section, for most practical applications, $k < 64$, which enables the representation using a 64-bit integer. The intersection can be implemented using a single machine `AND` operation, the union using a single machine `OR` operation, and the bit counting running in O(1) using a lookup table[2]. Using this implementation, the time complexity of phase 1 is O(n^2), if $k < 64$.

In the second phase, a local search procedure is applied to the solution found in phase 1. We developed a local search that explores neighborhood solutions based on error reduction. This procedure is detailed on Section 3.3. We also use the local search methods proposed in [5]. They developed two local searches, one for OCC using the Jaccard index as the $\mathcal{H}$ function and another using the set-intersection function. Section 3.4 details these algorithms.

3.3 Error Reduction Local Search

Algorithm 2 depicts the local search procedure based on error reduction, which we call `OLS`. In line 4, we sort the objects v in nonincreasing order of $e_v^+ + e_v^-$, such that we start with the object whose labeling leads to the most error in the entire clustering process. For the first given $\tau \leq n$ objects in this order, `OLS` attempts to reduce or augment the total similarity driven by the values of e^+ and e^-. This is done by removing or adding labels that impact total similarity. For a given object v, if $e_v^+ \geq e_v^-$, we try to find a most common label between v and all other objects, and remove it from v (line 16). Otherwise, if $e_v^+ < e_v^-$, we try to add to v a most common label that was not assigned to it (line 18). If none of these *add* or *remove* operations can be done, we remove a label from v uniformly at random and replace it with a label not assigned to v, also chosen uniformly at random (line 10–14). In this case, in each exchange we only select a new label not previously chosen in the previous iterations. In the worst case, we try all k labels. If an improvement is

[2]Another approach is to use the special hardware instruction `POPCNT` found in modern processors. For details, see [10].

Algorithm 2: Error Reduction Local Search – `OLS`

Input: labeling function ℓ; vectors $e^+, e^- \in \mathbb{R}^+$; integers $p, \tau \in \mathbb{N}$; set V.

1 Let $\mathcal{C}$ be the cost of ℓ computed with Obj. Func. (1);
2 $impr \leftarrow$ **True**;
3 **while** $impr =$ **True do**
4   Let V' be the set of objects $v \in V$, sorted in nonincreasing order of $e_v^+ + e_v^-$;
5     $impr \leftarrow$ **False**; $i \leftarrow 0$;
6   **while** $i \leq \tau$ **do**
7   Take the next $v \in V'$ in the given order;
8         $\hat{\ell}(v) \leftarrow \ell(v)$;
9         $local\_impr \leftarrow$ **True**;
10   **while** $local\_impr =$ **True do**
11             $\hat{\mathcal{C}} \leftarrow \mathcal{C}$;
12             $local\_impr \leftarrow$ **False**;
13   **if** $e_v^+ \geq e_v^-$ **and** $|\ell(v)| = 1$ **then**
14   Exchange the unique label $c \in \ell(v)$ for a $c' \notin \ell(v)$ chosen uniformly at random;
15   **if** $e_v^+ \geq e_v^-$ **and** $|\ell(v)| > 1$ **then**
16   Remove from $\ell(v)$ the $c \in \ell(v)$ which corresponds to the largest cluster containing v;
17   **if** $e_v^+ < e_v^-$ **and** $|\ell(v)| < p$ **then**
18   Add to $\ell(v)$ the c which corresponds to the largest cluster not containing v;
19   **foreach** $u \in V \setminus \{v\}$ **do**
20                 $\delta \leftarrow \mathcal{H}(\ell(u), \hat{\ell}(v)) - \mathcal{H}(\ell(u), \ell(v))$;
21   **if** $\delta > 0$ **then**
22                     $e^+(v) \leftarrow e^+(v) + \delta$; $e^+(u) \leftarrow e^+(u) + \delta$;
23   **else**
24                     $e^-(v) \leftarrow e^-(v) + \delta$; $e^-(u) \leftarrow e^-(u) + \delta$;
25                 $\mathcal{C} \leftarrow \mathcal{C} + \delta$;
26   **if** $\mathcal{C} \leq \hat{\mathcal{C}}$ **then**
27                 $impr \leftarrow$ **True**; $local\_impr \leftarrow$ **True**;
28   **else**
29                 $\mathcal{C} \leftarrow \hat{\mathcal{C}}$;
30   **if** $local\_impr =$ **True then** go to line 3; **else** $\ell(v) \leftarrow \hat{\ell}(v)$; i++;
31 **return** *labeling* ℓ *and solution value* $\mathcal{C}$;

reached, the solution value and the errors of each object are updated (lines 19–25) and a new iteration begins. After τ iterations without improvement, the local search stops.

The time complexity of `OLS` is tricky to compute since it depends on the starting solution. The innermost loop (starting in line 10) iterates at most k times since each label is added or removed only once. Note that adding (respectively, removing) a label that was removed (respectively, added) in earlier iterations (of the loop starting on line 10) does not lead to an improvement in solution quality. The exchange on line 14 can be done in O(1) time. The operations in lines 16 and 18 can be done in O($\log k$) time using a red-black tree [3] data structure for the histogram of labels that we use to keep track of the most used labels. However, note that for small values of k, it is worthwhile to use a naive linear approach running in time O(k). The update operations in lines 19–25 take O(n) time since we need to recalculate the function $\mathcal{H}$ for all pairs (v, w) with fixed v and $w \neq u \in V$. Therefore, the loop starting on line 6 has time complexity

$O(\tau(k \log k + kn))$. If $k < 64$ and $\tau \leq n$, then the time complexity is $O(n^2)$. As observed earlier, it is hard to estimate the complexity of the loop starting on line 3, but its main components are $O(n \log n)$ from line 4 and the complexity of the loop starting on line 6. Therefore, each iteration has time complexity $O(n^2)$.

3.4 Bonchi et al. Local Search

Bonchi et al. [5] propose two local search algorithms to deal with OCC using the Jaccard index and set-intersection functions. Their framework is based on the relabeling of objects, one at time, by solving a system of linear equations in the case of Jaccard, and by applying a simple greedy algorithm in the case of set intersection. The main idea is to find a good labeling of a single object given a fixed labeling of the other objects.

Let v be an object and ℓ be a labeling for all objects. The error incurred by v is defined as

$$C_v(\ell(v)|\ell) = \sum_{u \in V \setminus \{v\}} |\mathcal{H}(\ell(v), \ell(u)) - s(v,u)|, \quad (2)$$

and, consequently, the objective function (1) can be rewritten as

$$\frac{1}{2} \sum_{v \in V} C_v(\ell(v)|\ell). \quad (3)$$

Using these observations, Bonchi et al. proposed Algorithm 3, which is a simple local search algorithm.

In the case of the Jaccard index, the following approach is used. Let v be an object to be relabeled and ℓ be a fixed labeling for all $u \in V \setminus \{v\}$. Let x^v be an indicator vector such that $x^v_j = 1$ if label j is assigned to object v, and $x^v_j = 0$, otherwise. Assume that the number of labels assigned to v is t, that is,

$$\sum_{j \in L} x^v_j = t. \quad (4)$$

Ideally we would like to have $\mathcal{J}(\ell(v), \ell(u)) = s(v,u)$ for all $u \in V \setminus \{v\}$. This can be written as

$$\mathcal{J}(\ell(v), \ell(u)) = \frac{\sum_{j \in \ell(u)} x^v_j}{|\ell(u)| + t - \sum_{j \in \ell(u)} x^v_j} = s(v,u),$$

which is equivalent to

$$(1 + s(v,u)) \sum_{j \in \ell(u)} x^v_j - s(v,u)t = s(v,u)|\ell(u)| \quad (5)$$

for all $u \in V \setminus \{v\}$. Although Equations (4) and (5) are linear with respect to the unknowns x^v_j and t, these variables are integral and therefore the system seemingly cannot be solved in polynomial time. In [5], the authors applied a nonnegative least-squares optimization method which led to possibly fractional x^v and t values. They then sort x^v in nonincreasing order, breaking ties arbitrarily. Let π^v be the permutation of labels induced by this order and consider the p sets $\{\pi^v_1, \ldots, \pi^v_i\}$ for $i = 1, \ldots, p$. The new set of labels for v is the set $\{\pi^v_1, ..., \pi^v_i\}$ that minimizes Equation (2).

For the set-intersection indicator, Bonchi et al. present a greedy approach which starts from an empty labeling for a given object and fixes the labeling for the other objects as is done in the approach for the Jaccard index. In each iteration, the label that causes the least error while improving the solution value is chosen. If such a label cannot be found, the algorithm stops the search for this object and goes on to the next. In fact, this greedy search solves $C_v(\ell(v)|\ell)$ in line 6 of Algorithm 3.

Algorithm 3: Bonchi et al. Local Search – BSL

Input: labeling function ℓ; set V.

```
1  Let C be the cost of ℓ computed with Obj. Func. (1);
2  improvement ← True;
3  while improvement = True do
4      improvement ← False;
5      foreach v ∈ V do
6          Find the labeling L that minimizes C_v(L|ℓ);
7          Let Ĉ be the cost of (L|ℓ);
8          if Ĉ < C then
9              ℓ(v) ← L; Ĉ ← C;
10             improvement ← True;
11 return labeling ℓ and solution_value;
```

As in Algorithm 2, the time complexity of Algorithm 3 is tricky to determine because of its dependency on the starting solution. For the Jaccard function, the dominant factor is the nonnegative least squares that can be computed in $O(m^3)$ time, where m is the major dimension of the matrix [11]. Note that the matrix resulting from Equation (5) has dimension $n \times (k+1)$. As observed earlier, if $k < n$, then the complexity of an iteration of the main loop (starting on line 3) is $O(n^4)$. For the set-intersection function, each label search takes $O(k^2)$ time, which is done at most p times. As this operation is performed for each object, each iteration of the main loop takes $O(nk^3)$ time.

4. EXPERIMENTAL RESULTS

4.1 Instances

We used several datasets, grouped in two major categories, to evaluate our algorithms. The first category has instances with known multi-label assignments. For this case, we computed the similarities between the objects using the Jaccard index. These datasets were used to check the quality of the labelings produced by the algorithms when compared to the actual labelings. We used two datasets in this category. The first, named EMOTIONS, corresponds to psychological trials of people listening to music [17]. There are 593 objects (trials) and six available labels. The second dataset, named YEAST, is formed by micro-array expression data and phylogenetic profiles with 2417 genes in a learning set for which 14 functional classes (labels) are assigned [7].

The second category is instances with unknown multi-labelings. The first dataset in this category corresponds to animal trajectories from the Starkey Project [15][3]. We used an instance with 88 trajectories of elk, mule deer, and cattle, and classify them using five labels. To calculate the similarity between each trajectory, we used the approach presented in [6], which defines the *Edit Distance in Real Sequences* (EDR).[4] The similarity between two trajectories u and v is given by $s(u,v) = 1 - EDR(u,v)$.

The second group of instances in this category is from the field of biology. They consist of homologous groups of proteins from the SCOP taxonomy [13][5]. This taxonomy is a hand-made tree classification of functional proteins. We tested four databases with 669, 587, 567, and 654 proteins

[3]Available at http://www.fs.fed.us/pnw/starkey.

[4]Please, refer to the supplementary material for a comprehensive description.

[5]Available at http://scop.mrc-lmb.cam.ac.uk/scop.

(objects) for which we assigned at most with five labels. The similarities were calculated as follows: For a node u in the protein tree, let $d(u)$ be the depth of u in the tree. If u is the root, $d(u) = 0$. For any pair of nodes u and v, let $lca(u, v)$ denote the lowest common ancestor of u and v. Let V be the set of leaves of the classification tree. The similarity between different objects $u \in V$ and $v \in V$ is defined as

$$s(u, v) = \frac{d(lca(u, v))}{\max(d(u), d(v)) - 1}.$$

The third group in this category consists of 1,000 newsgroup messages spread over 20 newsgroups [14]. The similarities are calculated using a base dictionary of the 500 most common words excluding stop words and common names but keeping political and religious references. For each message, we construct a characteristic vector to reflect the *term frequency – inverse document frequency (TF-IDF)* of each word in the dictionary [12]. Using these vectors, we applied a radial basis function to obtain the similarities $s(u, v) = e^{||\mathbf{u}-\mathbf{v}||^2}$ where $\mathbf{u}$ and $\mathbf{v}$ are the characteristic vectors of messages u and v, respectively.

4.2 Evaluated algorithms

Using the two representations of Section 3.1 and decoders from Sections 3.3 and 3.4, we consider the following variations of BRKGAs:

- `OLS-Comp`: BRKGA using the compact representation and local search from Section 3.3;
- `OLS-Ext`: Same as above but using the extended representation;
- `BLS-Comp`: BRKGA using the compact representation and Bochi et al. local search from Section 3.4;
- `BLS-Ext`: Same as above but using the extended representation;

We also tested the algorithms from [5]. Originally, each run of those algorithms starts with a simple random vector and ends when Algorithm 3 cannot find improvements. To fortify these algorithms, we built multi-start approaches around them, allowing each run to take several iterations, each starting with a different random vector. We always keep the best solution and the algorithms stop when a stopping criterion is reached. These modifications have a great impact on the original algorithms in terms of solution quality. As expected, the multi-start approaches outperformed the original algorithms. Consequently, we use them in this paper but still refer to them as `Bonchi`.

4.3 Computational environment and parameters

The experiments were conducted on identical machines with two 6-core Intel Xeon 2.4 GHz CPUs (two threads per core) and 32 GBytes of RAM running GNU/Linux. Running times reported are UNIX real wall-clock times in seconds, excluding the effort to read the instance. The algorithms are implemented in C++ and we use the GNU `g++` compiler version 4.8. Random numbers were generated by an implementation of the Mersenne Twister.For the nonnegative least-squares method, we use the Householder rank-revealing QR decomposition [11] provided by the Eigen library [9].

For the BRKGAs, we set the parameters following the advise of [8]. The population size was set to $p = 500$, the elite size to $p_e = \lceil 0.30p \rceil$, and the number of mutants to $p_m = \lfloor 0.15p \rfloor$. The probability of inheriting each allele from the elite parent was $\rho_e = 0.70$. We used the island model [16] with three independent and concurrent populations where every 100 generations each population exports its two best solutions to the other populations. After 300 generations without improvement, all populations are reset to vectors of random keys. We set $\tau = 2\sqrt{n}$ after performing some short tuning trials and analyze the quality of solutions as a function of optimization time. We use 12 simultaneous cores for decoding.

Thirty independent runs were performed for all five algorithms. Each algorithm ran for a given maximum amount of time (instance dependent) or at for most 1,000 generations (or iterations) without improvement of the best solution.

4.4 Defining maximum running times for BRKGA

Since we have several types of problems, a significant variation in BRKGA running times is expected on each problem. We carried out some preliminary experiments and observed that the BRKGAs obtained a large number of small improvements in solution quality. In fact, in the first hour of optimization, the BRKGAs improved the solution about every two or three generations. In light of this, we performed one long run for an instance of each scenario. For these long runs we did not set a time limit but rather stopped after 1,000 generations without improvement of the best solution. As we only did one long run per scenario, we cannot draw any statistically significant conclusion about comparisons of the BRKGAs with the different $\mathcal{H}$ functions. We limit ourselves to observing the general behavior of these BRKGAs.

Figure 1 depicts the convergence of the cost value as a function of time and iterations for the EMOTIONS dataset. The Y-axis shows the cost value. The X-axis represents the time in seconds in Figure 1a and the number of iterations in Figure 1b. The solid red lines show the convergence for the BRKGA with the set-intersection function for values of p from one to six. The dashed blue line shows the same but for the Jaccard index function. We note that the BRKGA takes a long time with small improvements in the best solution and, after 30,000 seconds (about 8.3 hours), the improvements are even rarer. For the BRKGA with the Jaccard index function, values very close to zero, a lower bound on the optimum, are reached. Using the set-intersection indicator, the results are worse but the convergence behavior is similar. Looking at the number of iterations, one can note that the BRKGA with set-intersection function converges faster than it does with respect to time. We can conclude, therefore, that the local search spends more time using this function.

For other instances, the curves have the same behavior and they can be found in the supplementary material. For the YEAST dataset, running times are much larger than those on EMOTIONS. In this case, the BRKGA with the set-intersection function has slower convergence than it does with the Jaccard index but is able to obtain improvements even after running for 1,000,000 seconds (about 11 days). For the Starkey project dataset, the running times are very small for both $\mathcal{H}$ functions, mainly due to the size of the problem (88 objects). One notes that the BRKGA with set intersection is much worse than with the Jaccard index (except for the case of $p = 2$, in which they obtained similar

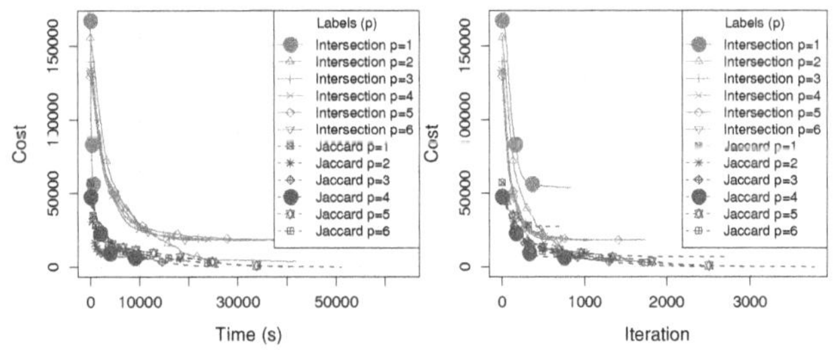

(a) (b)

Figure 1: Evolution of the cost for the EMOTIONS dataset.

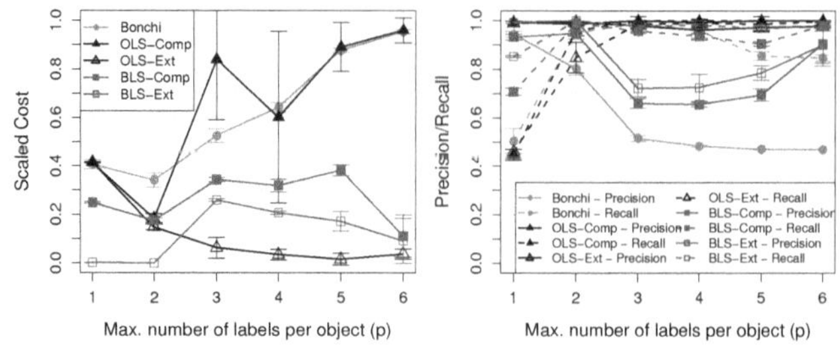

(a) Cost – Jaccard. (b) Prec./Rec. – Jaccard.

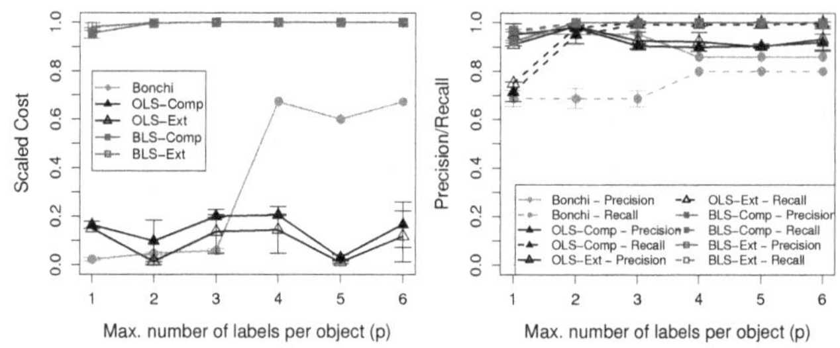

(c) Cost – Set-intersec. (d) Prec./Rec. – Set-intersec.

Figure 2: Comparison of costs, precision, and recall among the algorithms for the EMOTIONS dataset.

results). For the SCOP dataset 1, we observe different behavior: although the convergence is similar, running times are smaller than for the previous scenarios and, more importantly, the BRKGA with set intersection shows poor results when compared to EMOTIONS and YEAST. Later in this paper, we discuss these results in more detail. For newsgroup messages, we omitted the curves for the BRKGA with set intersection since it obtained results 20 times worse than with the Jaccard index but with convergence about 400 times faster. This may indicate that set intersection is not appropriate for clustering in this type of instance.

From these experiments, we can estimate the running times for each scenario and set time bounds for the experiments to follow. For EMOTIONS and YEAST, we limit the experiments to at most eight hours (28,800 seconds) trying to balance running time and solution quality. This limit is less favorable to the BRKGA with set intersection which still finds solution improvements after 15 days (1,250,000 seconds). For Starkey and SCOP, we set the maximum running time to one hour (3,600 seconds). For newsgroup messages, the maximum running time is set to seven days (604,800 seconds).

4.5 Evaluating the quality of the algorithms on ground-truth instances

To evaluate the quality of the algorithms, we first applied them on instances in which we know the actual labeling *a priori*. We compare the costs of the final solutions produced by the algorithms and also make use of two metrics, precision and recall. Define $P(x) = \{\{u,v\}, u \neq v : x(u) \cap x(v) \neq \emptyset\}$, the set of unordered pairs of objects with at least one common label in x. Let g be the labeling of the ground truth. The *precision* of a labeling ℓ is

$$Precision_g(\ell) = \frac{|P(\ell) \cap P(g)|}{|P(\ell)|}. \quad (6)$$

The *recall* of a labeling ℓ is

$$Recall_g(\ell) = \frac{|P(\ell) \cap P(g)|}{|P(g)|}. \quad (7)$$

Note that for $\ell = g$, $Precision_g(\ell) = Recall_g(\ell) = 1$.

Figure 2 shows the performance of the algorithms for the EMOTIONS dataset. The X-axis on all plots corresponds to the maximum number of allowed labels per object. For Figures 2a and 2c, the Y-axis corresponds to the scaled solution costs (wth lower being better). In the plots, the red line with circles shows results for `Bonchi`, the black lines with triangles for the BRKGAs with the `OLS` decoder, while the blue lines with squares show results for the BRKGAs with the `BLS` decoder. Solid symbols correspond to the compact chromosome representation and hollow symbols correspond to the extended representation. The description of Figures 2b and 2d is similar, but there, solid lines show precision and dashed lines, recall (with higher being better). Figures 2a and 2b correspond to the Jaccard index function and Figures 2c and 2d, to the set-intersection function.

The algorithms using the Jaccard index with $p = 1$ have similar performance. One notes that this case is very close to traditional clustering and results in a partition of the objects. But as more labels per object are allowed, the performance of `Bonchi` degrades while all but one of the BRKGAs perform well. The exception is `OLS-Comp`, which followed the performance of `Bonchi` and displayed a large variation in its results. The same decoder using the extended representation (`OLS-Ext`) obtained the best results on average. Analyzing Figure 2b, one can see that the precision and the recall of the BRKGAs are always above those of `Bonchi`. Even `OLS-Comp`, which obtained costs similar to those of `Bonchi`, showed better precision and recall. The algorithms that use the Bonchi et al. approach for set intersection showed worse performance than those using the `OLS` decoder. It is worthwhile to mention that the solutions obtained using the Jaccard index function have different cost values from those obtained using the set-intersection function, as the objective functions are different.

Figure 3 depicts results for the YEAST dataset. Its description is identical to that of Figure 2. Here, we observe a very different behavior for both the Jaccard index and set-intersection functions. For the Jaccard index, note that the algorithms using the `OLS` decoder perform poorly (Figure 3a) when the number of labels allowed for each object is small, while algorithms using `BLS` performed quite well. As p increases, `OLS` outperforms `BLS`. In particular, when p is between 8 and 11, the algorithms switch their behavior. However, it is interesting to notice that both precision and recall are relatively stable. For the set-intersection function,

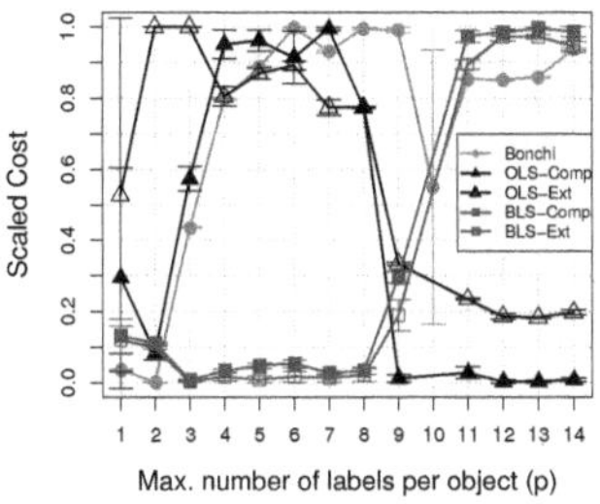

(a) Cost – Jaccard.

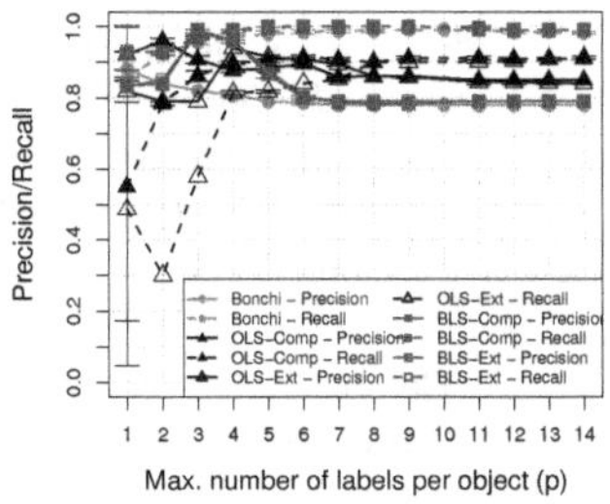

(b) Prec./Rec. – Jaccard.

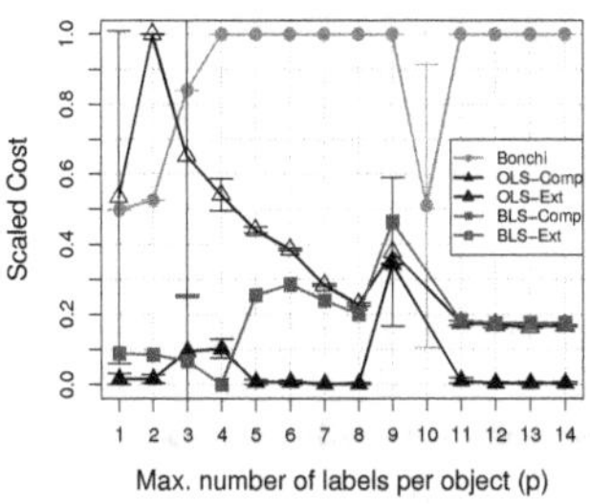

(c) Cost – Set-intersec.

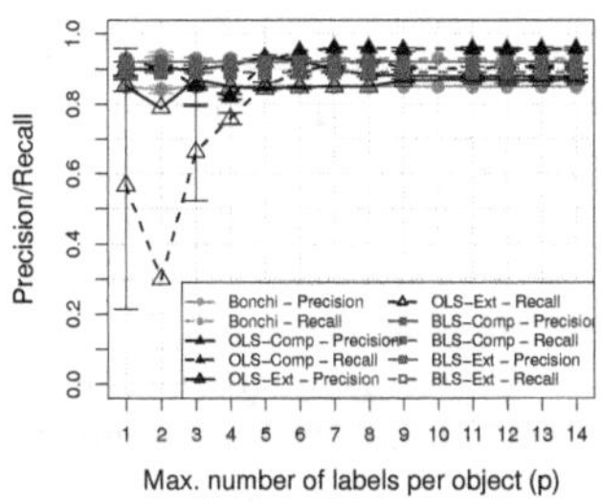

(d) Prec./Rec. – Set-intersec.

Figure 3: Comparison of costs, precision, and recall among the algorithms for the YEAST dataset.

the plots resemble the behavior of those for the Jaccard index function on the EMOTIONS dataset. Finally, note that the BRKGAs with BLS found better solutions on the YEAST dataset than they did on EMOTIONS. All BRKGAs obtained better precision on YEAST than they did on EMOTIONS.

4.6 Evaluating the algorithms for instances with unknown multi-labeling

To evaluate the algorithms on instances with no multi-labeling given *a priori*, we first consider the Starkey project dataset. The algorithms were run for labelings of size $p = 1, 2, 3$, from a total of $k = 5$ available labels. Figure 4 shows the costs of the labelings obtained by the algorithms. For each scenario (consisting of an $\mathcal{H}$ function and a value of p), we scaled the costs into the interval $[0, 1]$ using the minimum and maximum costs of all algorithms. The box plots show the smallest cost (lowest whiskers), the first quartile (bottom box), the median cost (filled circles), the third quartile (upper box), the largest cost (highest whiskers), and the outliers (gray hollow circles). We observe that the sizes of the boxes for all configurations are very small, indicating that similar costs were found for all runs on a given algorithm.

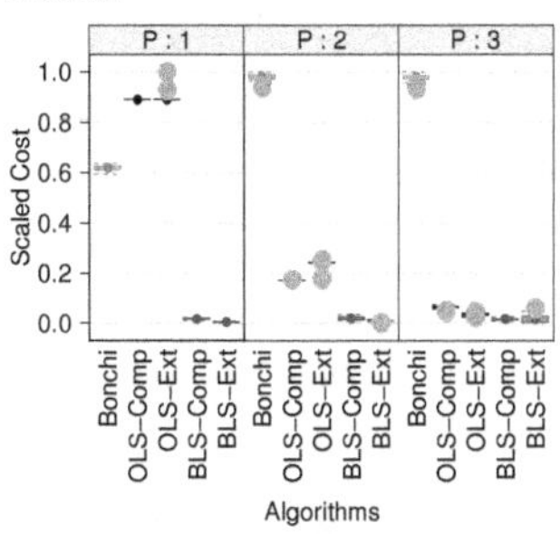

(a) Jaccard.

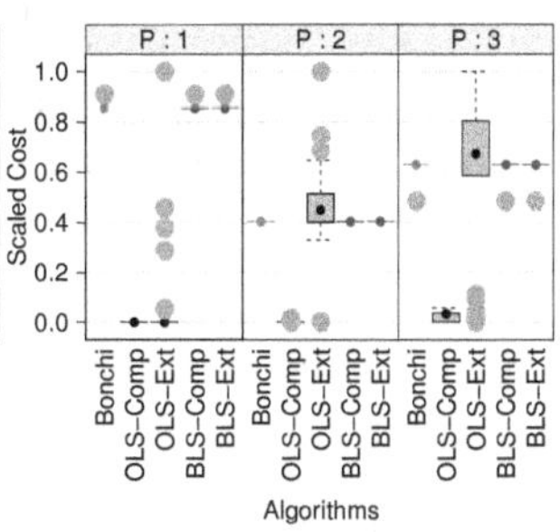

(b) Set-intersection.

Figure 4: Boxplot of median and quartiles for each algorithm in Starkey dataset.

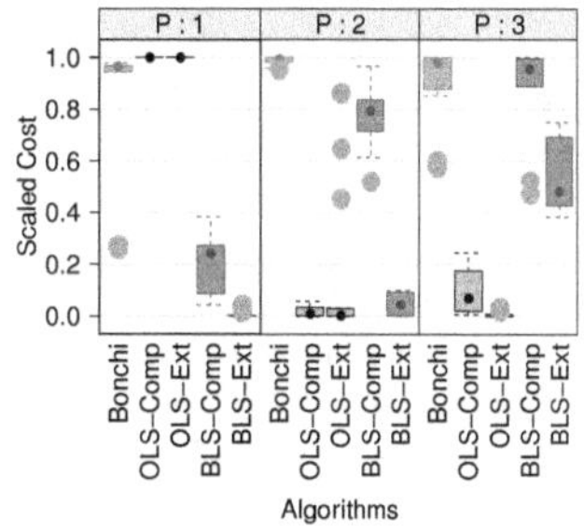

(a) Jaccard.

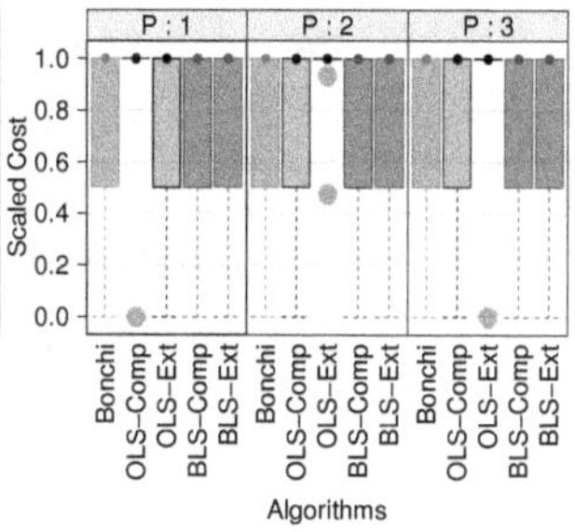

(b) Set-intersection.

Figure 5: Boxplot of median and quartiles for each algorithm in SCOP dataset.

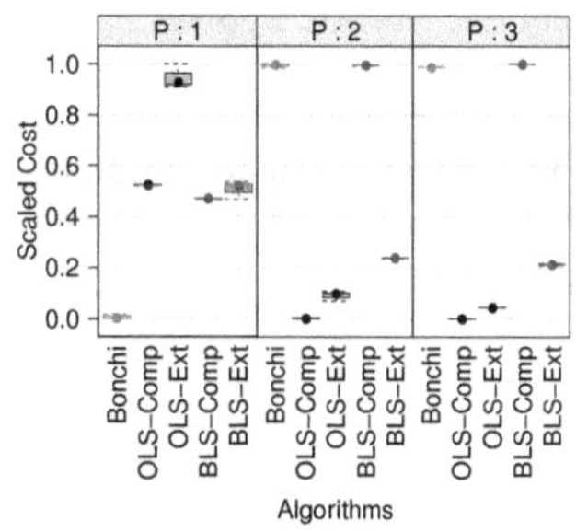

(a) Jaccard.

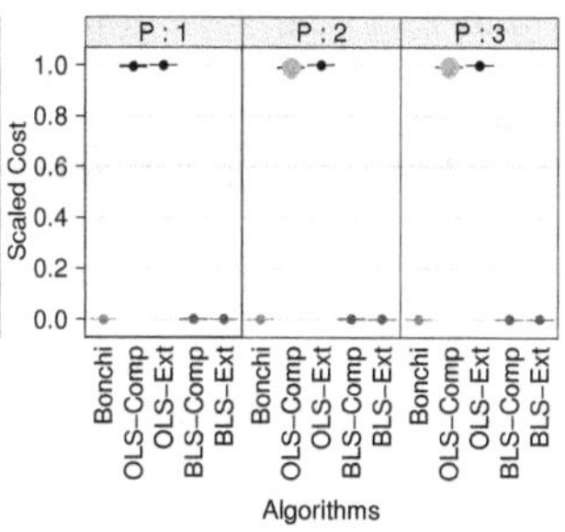

(b) Set-intersection.

Figure 6: Boxplot of median and quartiles for each algorithm in newsgroup messages.

For the Jaccard index, BLS-Comp and BLS-Ext were able to produce the best results, although slightly different. For set intersection, OLS-Comp found better solutions, although in some cases OLS-Ext also found good solutions as its outliers suggest. To confirm these results, we applied the Wilcoxon-Mann-Whitney U test.This test assumes as the null hypothesis that the location statistics are equal in both distributions. Assuming a confidence interval of 95%, almost all algorithms presented significant difference in their results when compared to each other for the Jaccard index. The exception is the pair BLS-Comp and BLS-Ext for $p = 3$, whose p-value is 0.67 and we cannot thus assure a significant difference. For the set-intersection function, OLS-Comp was significantly better than the other algorithms. Bonchi, BLS-Comp, and BLS-Ext found solutions having the same value on all runs. The complete results are presented in the supplementary material.

Figure 5 shows results on the four SCOP datasets. The structure is similar to that of Figure 4, except that the scaling was done for each dataset set separately and then combined in the plots for each configuration. For the Jaccard index, BLS-Comp and BLS-Ext found good solutions for $p = 1$, whereas OLS-Comp, OLS-Ext, and BLS-Ext had the best results for $p = 2$. In fact, the U test did not present significant difference among these three algorithms and value of p (for a confidence interval of 95%). For $p = 3$, OLS-Ext presented significantly better results than the other algorithms. For set intersection, the algorithms performed similarly and for most cases, no significant difference was found. Notice that the results are closer to 1.0 (worst solutions) which indicates that the algorithms converged to local minima frequently. But since the bottom whiskers are at 0.0, the algorithms did find a good solution. Again, refer to the supplementary material for the complete tests.

Figure 6 shows results for the instance from the newsgroup messages dataset. For the Jaccard index function, the behaviors of the algorithms are similar to those on the other instances. For $p = 1$, the algorithms using the Bonchi approach are able to find better results, but for $p \geq 2$, OLS-Comp found significantly better solutions. For set intersection, the algorithms using the Bonchi approach found the best results with no significant difference among them.

Table 1 lists the algorithms that obtained the best results for each dataset and configuration. For the Jaccard index, both OLS-Ext and BLS-Ext presented the best results for most cases, which indicates that algorithms using the extended representation are able to find better solutions than those using the compact representation. The OLS approach obtained more best solutions than did the BSL approach. For set intersection, the performances of the algorithms were similar, reaching the best solution at least once in most cases. In the Starkey dataset, the algorithms using OLS performed better than those which did not. For the newsgroup message dataset, Bonchi found the best solutions.

Table 1: Algorithms that computed the best results for each instance, $\mathcal{H}$ function, and p.

Inst.	p	Jaccard	Intersec	Inst.	p	Jaccard	Intersec
Starkey	1	BLS-Ext	OLS-Comp/ OLS-Ext	SCOP3	1	BLS-Ext	All
	2	BLS-Ext	OLS-Comp		2	OLS-Comp	Except OLS-Ext
	3	BLS-Ext	OLS-Comp/ OLS-Ext		3	OLS-Ext	All
SCOP1	1	BLS-Ext	All	SCOP4	1	BLS-Ext	All
	2	OLS-Ext	All		2	OLS-Ext	All
	3	OLS-Ext	All		3	OLS-Ext	All
SCOP2	1	BLS-Ext	All	News.	1	Bonchi	Bonchi
	2	OLS-Ext	All		2	OLS-Comp	Bonchi
	3	OLS-Ext	All		3	OLS-Comp	Bonchi

5. CONCLUDING REMARKS

In general, the BRKGAs are effective at finding good solutions and are able to beat the Bonchi et al. approach on most cases when using the Jaccard index in the objective function. For set intersection, the algorithms based on Bonchi et al. approach presented better results than other algorithms in most scenarios. Also, the extended representation allows the BRKGAs to obtain better results when compared to the compact representation on most cases. On the negative side, running times to convergence for the BRKGAs can be high. We believe that this is not a major issue, since most applications of OCC are prospective in nature and therefore do not require real-time response.

Acknowledgments

Carlos E. Andrade is supported by São Paulo Research Foundation (FAPESP) grants 2010/05233-5 and 2012/08222-0. Flávio K. Miyazawa is supported by National Council for Scientific and Technological Development (CNPq).

6. REFERENCES

[1] C. E. Andrade, F. K. Miyazawa, and M. G. C. Resende. Evolutionary algorithm for the k-Interconnected Multi-Depot Multi-Traveling Salesmen Problem. In *Proceeding of the Fifteenth Annual Conference on Genetic and Evolutionary Computation Conference*, GECCO '13, pages 463–470, New York, NY, USA, 2013. ACM.

[2] N. Bansal, A. Blum, and S. Chawla. Correlation clustering. *Machine Learning*, 56:89–113, 2004.

[3] R. Bayer. Symmetric binary B-Trees: Data structure and maintenance algorithms. *Acta Informatica*, 1:290–306, 1972.

[4] J. C. Bean. Genetic algorithms and random keys for sequencing and optimization. *ORSA Journal on Computing*, 2(6):154–160, 1994.

[5] F. Bonchi, A. Gionis, and A. Ukkonen. Overlapping correlation clustering. *Knowledge and Information Systems*, pages 1–32, 2012.

[6] L. Chen, M. T. Özsu, and V. Oria. Robust and fast similarity search for moving object trajectories. In *Proceedings of the 2005 ACM SIGMOD International Conference on Management of Data*, SIGMOD '05, pages 491–502, New York, NY, USA, 2005. ACM.

[7] A. Elisseeff and J. Weston. A kernel method for multi-labelled classification. In T. G. Dietterich, S. Becker, and Z. Ghahramani, editors, *Advances in Neural Information Processing Systems 14*, pages 681–687, 2001.

[8] J. F. Gonçalves and M. G. C. Resende. Biased random-key genetic algorithms for combinatorial optimization. *Journal of Heuristics*, 17:487–525, 2011.

[9] G. Guennebaud, B. Jacob, et al. Eigen v3. http://eigen.tuxfamily.org, 2010.

[10] I. S. Haque, V. S. Pande, and W. P. Walters. Anatomy of high-performance 2D similarity calculations. *Journal of Chemical Information and Modeling*, 51(9):2345–2351, 2011.

[11] A. S. Householder. Unitary triangularization of a nonsymmetric matrix. *Journal of the ACM*, 5(4):339–342, 1958.

[12] K. S. Jones. A statistical interpretation of term specificity and its application in retrieval. *Journal of Documentation*, 28(1):11–21, 1972.

[13] A. G. Murzin et al. SCOP: Structural classification of proteins, 2009. Accessed on Oct 16, 2013.

[14] J. Rennie et al. 20 newsgroups. http://qwone.com/~jason/20Newsgroups, 2008. Accessed on Oct 13, 2013.

[15] M. M. Rowland, P. K. Coe, R. J. Stussy, A. A. Ager, N. J. Cimon, B. K. Johnson, and M. J. Wisdom. The Starkey habitat database for ungulate research: Construction, documentation, and use. Technical report, U.S. Forest Service General Technical Report PNW-GTR-430, Portland, Oregon, USA, 1998.

[16] R. Tanese. Parallel genetic algorithms for a hypercube. In *Proceedings of the Second International Conference on Genetic Algorithms and their Application*, pages 177–183. L. Erlbaum Associates Inc., 1987.

[17] K. Trohidis, G. Tsoumakas, G. Kalliris, and I. Vlahavas. Multilabel classification of music into emotions. In *Proceedings of International Conference on Music Information Retrieval*, ISMIR 2008, pages 325–330, 2008.

On the Efficiency of Worst Improvement for Climbing NK-Landscapes

Matthieu Basseur
LERIA, Université d'Angers, France
matthieu.basseur@univ-angers.fr

Adrien Goëffon
LERIA, Université d'Angers, France
adrien.goeffon@univ-angers.fr

ABSTRACT

Climbers are often used in metaheuristics in order to intensify the search and identify local optima with respect to a neighborhood structure. Even if they constitute a central component of modern heuristics, their design principally consists in choosing the pivoting rule, which is often reduced to two alternative strategies: first improvement or best improvement. The conception effort of most metaheuristics belongs in proposing techniques to escape from local optima, and not necessarily on how to climb toward better local optima. In this paper, we are interested in attaining good local optima with basic hill-climbing techniques. The NK model will be used to evaluate a set of climbers proposed in this paper. By focusing on the pivoting rule definition, we show that choosing the worst improving neighbor often leads to attain better local optima. Moreover, by slightly modifying the worst improvement strategy, one can design efficient climbers which outperform first and best improvement in terms of tradeoff between quality and computational effort.

Categories and Subject Descriptors

I.2.8 [**Computing Methodologies**]: Artificial Intelligence—*Problem Solving, Control Methods, and Search*

Keywords

Local search, hill-climbing, fitness landscapes, NK-landscapes, first improvement, best improvement, worst improvement.

1. INTRODUCTION

Most metaheuristics are based on a neighborhood search technique, which consists in transforming an initial solution by application of local moves chosen from a neighborhood structure. During the last decades, a large panel of neighborhood searches have been designed, like hill-climbing, tabu search, simulated annealing, or iterated local search (see [3]). These metaheuristics mainly differ in the move selection heuristic employed. Hill-climbings are simple neighborhood search techniques and are widely used as basic elements of more sophisticated local search algorithms or advanced metaheuristics (including evolutionary and hybrid algorithms).

While designing a neighborhood search algorithm, three main conceptual issues have to be considered. First, the neighborhood structure design, which directly affects the fitness landscape to explore. This aspect is greatly problem-dependant and will not be discussed in this paper. Second, a method to choose the solution initiating or restarting the search has to be designed. This aspect is often debated, especially in iterated local search studies. Last, the *pivoting rule* defines the acceptance criterion of neighbors during the search. The paper focuses on this major aspect, which is rarely investigated, except for comparing first and best improvements on specific problems [2, 10].

In a previous study [1], we showed that first improvement tends to outperform best improvement on many landscapes derived from several combinatorial problems. An analysis of landscapes properties also indicated that first improvement is particularly efficient for climbing non-smooth landscapes. Intuitively, since best improvement systematically chooses the highest neighbor, it should conduce the search towards the nearest peak (local optima) of the landscape. On the contrary, first improvement often performs reduced improvements, which tends to drive progressively the search toward higher areas, where the potential local optima are also higher. To extrapolate, we believe that choosing the worst improving neighbor at each step of the search will allow to increase the number of steps and then the possibility to reach higher areas of landscapes by avoiding the climbing of small steepest peaks. In this paper, we aim at evaluating worst improvement as well as some other intermediate pivoting rules.

The paper is organized as follow. The next section focuses on fitness landscapes and NK model, and also recall hill-climbing principles. In section 3, we present alternative pivoting rules, including the underestimated worst improvement strategy. Results of empirical comparisons between 12 pivoting rules will be provided and analyzed in this section. In section 4, we propose refined pivoting rules, which allow to approximate the worst improvement strategy, with a reduced number of solution evaluations. Experiments and result analysis are also provided in order to evaluate the effectiveness of such approaches. In the last section we point out some conclusion and discuss on perspectives of this work.

GECCO'14, July 12–16, 2014, Vancouver, BC, Canada.

http://dx.doi.org/10.1145/2576768.2598268.

2. CLIMBING FITNESS LANDSCAPES

2.1 Combinatorial fitness landscapes

Fitness landscapes constitute a key concept in theoretical / evolutionary biology since the beginning of the 1930s. Originally, a fitness landscape is a genotype-phenotype mapping [11] which emphasizes the effect of mutations (genotype modifications) on fitness (lifetime reproductive success). Nowadays, this concept is frequently used to characterize combinatorial optimization problems within an evolutionary computation context [7, 6, 9].

Formally, a *combinatorial fitness landscape* is a triplet $(\mathcal{X},\mathcal{N},\mathfrak{f})$, where $\mathcal{X}$ is a set of *configurations* (or *candidate solutions*) called *search space*, $\mathcal{N} : \mathcal{X} \to 2^{\mathcal{X}}$ is a *neighborhood relation*, and $\mathfrak{f}$ is a *fitness function*. $\mathfrak{f}(x)$ is the *fitness* (or *height*) of a configuration $x \in \mathcal{X}$. $x' \in \mathcal{N}(x)$ is a *neighbor* of x. $\mathcal{N}(x)$ is called the *neighborhood* of x. In a maximization context, a *local optimum* is a configuration $x \in \mathcal{X}$ such that $\forall x' \in \mathcal{N}(x), \mathfrak{f}(x') \leqslant \mathfrak{f}(x)$, while a *global optimum* is a configuration $x^\star \in \operatorname{argmax}_{x\in\mathcal{X}} \mathfrak{f}(x)$.

A fitness landscape $(\mathcal{X},\mathcal{N},\mathfrak{f})$ is usually linked with a combinatorial optimization problem instance, where $\mathcal{X}$ represents a discrete set of feasible solutions, and $\mathfrak{f}$ corresponds to a scalar objective function or its estimation.

2.2 NK-landscapes

The NK family of landscapes has been proposed in [4] in order to generate artificial combinatorial landscapes with tunable shape properties: size and ruggedness. NK-landscapes use a basic search space, with binary strings as configurations and bit-flip (1-flip) as neighborhood. Characteristics of an NK-landscape are determined by means of two parameters N and K. N refers to the length of binary string configurations. $K \in \{0,\dots,N-1\}$ specifies the level of variables interdependency, which directly affects the ruggedness of the landscape. By increasing the value of K from 0 to $N-1$, NK-landscapes can be tuned from smooth to rugged. In particular, if $K=0$, the landscape contains only one local (global) optimum; on the contrary, setting K to $N-1$ leads to a random fitness assignment.

In NK-landscapes, the fitness function $F_{\rm NK} : \{0,1\}^N \to [0,1)$ to be maximized is defined as follows:

$$F_{\rm NK}(x) = \frac{1}{N}\sum_{i=1}^{N} C_i(x_i, \Pi_i(x)) \qquad (1)$$

x_i is the i-th bit of configuration x ($1 \leqslant i \leqslant N$). Subfunction Π_i defines the dependencies of bit i, with $\Pi_i(x) = \{x_{\pi_1(i)},\dots,x_{\pi_K(i)}\}$ such that $\pi_j(i) \in \{1,\dots,N\} \setminus \{i\}$ and $|\bigcup_{j=1}^{K} \pi_j(i)| = K$. Subfunction $C_i : \{0,1\}^{K+1} \to [0,1)$ defines the contribution value of x_i with respect to its set of dependencies $\Pi_i(x)$.

NK-landscape instances are both determined by the $(K+1)$-uples $(x_i, x_{\pi_1(i)}, \dots, x_{\pi_K(i)})$ and a fitness contribution matrix C describing the $2^N \times (K+1)$ possible contribution values. In standard NK-landscape instances considered here, dependencies between variables and contribution values are randomly generated from a uniform distribution.

2.3 Hill-climbing and Move Strategies

A *hill-climbing* algorithm (or *climber*) is a basic local search strategy which navigates through the search space thanks to non-deteriorating moves only. Given an initial configuration called *starting point*, a traditional climber iteratively moves to better neighbors, until a local optimum is reached. Such a search mechanism, also known as *iterative improvement*, allows to distinguish several variants which are discussed hereafter. To summarize, climbing a fitness landscape $(\mathcal{X},\mathcal{N},\mathfrak{f})$ consists actually in defining a move strategy which reaches a configuration as highest as possible.

Two commonly-used climbing move strategies, *first* and *best* improvement, constitute the widely used *pivoting rules*. These rules define how to select a better neighbor from a not locally optimal configuration [12]. More precisely, the *best improvement* strategy (or *greedy hill-climbing*) consists in selecting, at each iteration, a neighbor which achieves the best fitness. This implies to generate and evaluate the whole neighborhood at each step of the search. The *first improvement* strategy accepts the first evaluated neighbor which satisfies the moving condition and avoids the systematic generation of the entire neighborhood. *Worst improvement*, among other pivoting rules, can easily be considered but, to the best of our knowledge, is not really envisaged for the design of local search algorithms. This paper will focus on determining the actual efficiency of these underestimated move strategies, which are detailed in the next section.

A neutral move policy has to be established for climbing landscapes containing neutrality. We focus here on the evaluation of pivoting rules, then experimental comparisons will be realized on non-neutral NK-landscapes in order to prevent a possible impact of neutral move policies. Thus, climbers considered afterwards will respect the generic basic iterative improvement definition, allowing only stricly improving moves (see algorithm 1).

Algorithm 1 Generic basic iterative improvement algorithm

input: a starting point $x_s \in \mathcal{X}$
$x \leftarrow x_s$
while x is not a local optimum **do**
  $x \leftarrow x'$, x' choosen in $\{x^+ \in \mathcal{N}(x), \mathfrak{f}(x^+) > \mathfrak{f}(x)\}$ w.r.t. a pivoting rule
return x

3. FROM BEST TO WORST IMPROVEMENT

In a precedent study [1], we empirically show that first improvement allows to find better local optima than best improvement on most combinatorial landscapes, especially on difficult ones (fairly large and/or rugged landscapes). This result was observed on NK-landscapes and fitness landscapes derived from academic combinatorial problems: MAXSAT, QAP, and Flow-shop. In other words, this means that on difficult landscapes, selecting systematically the highest neighbor statistically leads to be trapped in local optimal of lower quality. It should be interesting to determine if strategies which favor the selection of improving neighbors of lower fitnesses conduct to higher local optima. In particular, it makes sense to consider the worst improvement pivoting rule, which selects the worst improving neighbor at each step of the search.

3.1 Considering Rank-based Pivoting Rules

Let $I_x = (x_1, x_2, \dots, x_w)$ a tuple constitued by all strictly (distincts) improving neighbors of $x \in \mathcal{X}$ sorted by decreasing fitnesses, ie. $\forall i \in \{1, \ldots, w\}, x_i \in \mathcal{N}(x)$, $\mathfrak{f}(x_i) > \mathfrak{f}(x)$ and $\mathfrak{f}(x_i) \geqslant \mathfrak{f}(x_{i+1})$ $(i < w)$.

Given a configuration x and an associated tuple $I_x = (x_1, x_2, \ldots, x_w)$, let us describe three generic ranking-based pivoting rules:

- $S_i^=$ selects at each step of the search the i-th best improving neighbor (x_i).
- $S_i^{\geqslant}$ selects randomly one of the i-th best improving neighbors (belonging to $\{x_1, x_2, \ldots, x_i\}$).
- $S_i^{\leqslant}$ selects randomly one of the $(w - i + 1)$-th worst improving neighbors (belonging to $\{x_i, x_{i+1}, \ldots, x_w\}$).

Let $q_1 = \lceil w/4 \rceil$, $m = \lceil w/2 \rceil$ and $q_3 = \lceil 3w/4 \rceil$ be respectively the indices of the first, second and third quartiles of I_x. $b = 1$ and w denote the indices corresponding to the best and the worst configurations of I_x. In the following, we will consider $S_i^=$, $S_i^{\geqslant}$ and $S_i^{\leqslant}$ combined with 5 ranking values: $i \in \{b, q_1, m, q_3, w\}$. Note that, as depicted in figure 1, some strategies are equivalent ($S_b^=$ and $S_b^{\geqslant}$, $S_b^{\leqslant}$ and $S_w^{\geqslant}$, $S_w^=$ and $S_w^{\leqslant}$). Obviously, $S_b^=$ corresponds to best improvement, $S_w^=$ to worst improvement, and $S_w^{\geqslant}$ to first improvement — despite the fact that the definition assumes that the whole neighborhood is systematically generated.

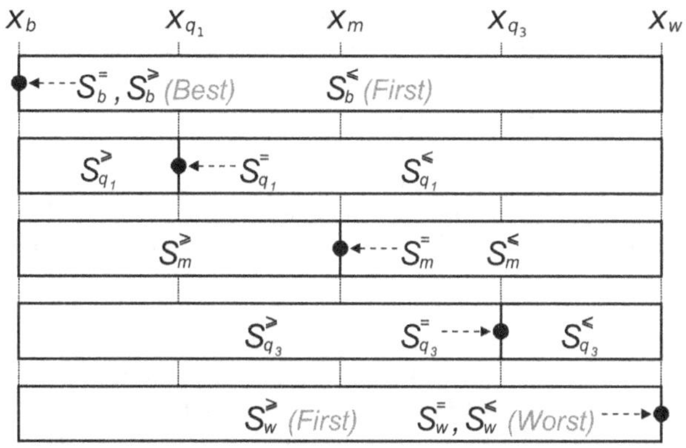

Figure 1: Illustration of different ranking-based pivoting rules. Improving neighbors are sorted from the best (x_b) to the worst (x_w). This ranking determines the candidate set of acceptable neighbors according to the pivoting rule. For instance, $S_{q3}^{\geqslant}$ consists in randomly selecting a configuration among the 75% most improving neighbors.

Consequently, we extracted 12 distinct ranking-based pivoting rules, which includes first, best and worst improvement move strategies. Their relative efficiency will be discussed below.

3.2 Experimentations

This section aims at competing climbers which use different ranking-based pivoting rules by measuring their respective ability to reach high local optima. Let us notice that this study mainly focus on the worst improvement performance. Other variants will help us to evaluate the impact of the move strategy in local searches.

Experimental process consists in the comparison of 12 hill-climbing versions, each one corresponding to a specific rank-based pivoting rule S (see section 3.1): $S_b^=$, $S_{q1}^=$, $S_m^=$, $S_{q3}^=$, $S_w^=$, $S_{q1}^{\geqslant}$, $S_m^{\geqslant}$, $S_{q3}^{\geqslant}$, $S_w^{\geqslant}$, $S_{q1}^{\leqslant}$, $S_m^{\leqslant}$, $S_{q3}^{\leqslant}$. All climbers are tested on various NK-landscapes. Recall that N and K parameters allow to build NK instances of different sizes and ruggednesses. In our experiments, we consider 28 (N, K) parametrizations, corresponding to all combinations of $N \in \{128, 256, 512, 1024\}$ and $K \in \{1, 2, 4, 6, 8, 10, 12\}$. For each couple (N, K), we generated 10 random landscapes. Consequently, 280 different NK-landscapes are considered here.

100 random configurations were generated for each NK-landscape, which will be used as starting points for hill-climbings. For each NK-landscape, 100 executions of the 12 hill-climbing versions were performed, using the same set of starting points in order to cancel the initialization bias. Searches are stopped when a local optimum is reached.

In this experiment analysis, we mainly focus on the quality of the local optima reached by all hill-climbings variants. For each triplet (N, K, S), we first compute the average fitness of the 1,000 local optima resulting from the corresponding searches. To increase readability, we only report on table 1 results for $S_i^=$ climbers as well as $S_w^{\geqslant}$ (first improvement) for comparison. Other intermediate variants are not outputted here, but will be discussed later. For each NK parametrization, we report the best average value in bold. The background is colored in grey if a method is not statistically outperformed by any other variant with respect to a binomial test (p-value 0.95) comparing, for a given pair of methods, both local optima obtained for each couple (instance,starting point). More precisely, if $\mathcal{S}$ denotes the number of successes of method A over method B, then A statistically outperforms B when $\frac{1}{2^{1000}} \sum_{i=0}^{\mathcal{S}} \binom{1000}{\mathcal{S}} \geqslant 0.95$, ie. $\mathcal{S} \geqslant 526$.

Numerical results given in table 1 allows to extract several clear conclusions. First, we observe that best improvement systematically achieves best average results on smooth instances ($K = \{1, 2\}$), while worst improvement outperforms other variants on all other landscapes. This observation is clearly confirmed by the statistical analysis. Previous work [1] already shown the superiority of best improvement against first improvement on smooth NK-landscapes, and the superiority of first improvement against best improvement on rugged ones. Here, experiments on rank-based pivoting rules show that worst improvement is clearly more efficient that first improvement each time first improvement outperforms best improvement. For reaching better local optima, it seems to be appropriate to choose only between best and worst improvement strategies, depending of the ruggedness of the landscape. This tendency is confirmed in figure 2, which shows the evolution of average fitness values according to the rank-based pivoting rule used. It indicates that the average quality of local optima is strongly correlated with the rank (quality) of selected neighbors, positively on smooth NK-landscapes and negatively on rugged ones.

Table 2 focus on the best local optima obtained by each strategy on each landscape. For each couple (strategy, instance), we first compute the best local optimum reached among the 100 executions. Given a (N,K) parametrization, values provided in the table corresponds to the average fitness of the best local optima obtained by each strategy on the 10 instances. Globally, observations reported for table 1 remain valid. We can then expect that the superiority of

N_K	$S_b^=$	$S_{q1}^=$	$S_m^=$	$S_{q3}^=$	$S_w^=$	$S_w^{\geqslant}$
128_1	**.6973**	.6916	.6877	.6845	.6809	.6896
256_1	**.7033**	.6986	.6966	.6944	.6918	.6980
512_1	**.6937**	.6886	.6856	.6828	.6803	.6872
1024_1	**.6997**	.6954	.6920	.6895	.6867	.6936
128_2	**.7169**	.7142	.7121	.7107	.7081	.7133
256_2	**.7130**	.7104	.7080	.7055	.7035	.7080
512_2	**.7120**	.7097	.7077	.7063	.7041	.7076
1024_2	**.7132**	.7109	.7092	.7073	.7052	.7088
128_4	.7216	.7214	.7231	.7230	**.7250**	.7207
256_4	.7211	.7224	.7237	.7247	**.7274**	.7218
512_4	.7228	.7238	.7255	.7268	**.7285**	.7232
1024_4	.7232	.7244	.7262	.7275	**.7298**	.7238
128_6	.7170	.7178	.7194	.7217	**.7251**	.7187
256_6	.7207	.7217	.7257	.7269	**.7313**	.7234
512_6	.7214	.7232	.7261	.7291	**.7338**	.7239
1024_6	.7223	.7243	.7276	.7302	**.7353**	.7250
128_8	.7124	.7135	.7150	.7166	**.7199**	.7136
256_8	.7147	.7163	.7201	.7214	**.7267**	.7179
512_8	.7163	.7190	.7220	.7256	**.7306**	.7200
1024_8	.7176	.7206	.7239	.7274	**.7330**	.7215
128_10	.7049	.7056	.7083	.7106	**.7115**	.7078
256_10	.7082	.7095	.7132	.7158	**.7197**	.7126
512_10	.7106	.7128	.7163	.7195	**.7244**	.7143
1024_10	.7121	.7150	.7185	.7223	**.7270**	.7165
128_12	.6970	.6980	.6996	.7022	**.7033**	.7009
256_12	.7015	.7026	.7062	.7087	**.7129**	.7053
512_12	.7045	.7066	.7104	.7133	**.7179**	.7082
1024_12	.7064	.7089	.7125	.7163	**.7209**	.7107

Table 1: Comparison of $S_i^=$ pivoting rules (average fitness of local optima reached from 1000 hill-climbings distributed on 10 instances). Recall that $S_b^=$ is best improvement, $S_w^=$ is worst improvement, and $S_w^{\geqslant}$, which is reported for comparison, is first improvement.

N_K	$S_b^=$	$S_{q1}^=$	$S_m^=$	$S_{q3}^=$	$S_w^=$	$S_w^{\geqslant}$
128_1	**.7103**	.7065	.7036	.7022	.6992	.7061
256_1	**.7127**	.7108	.7083	.7058	.7035	.7092
512_1	**.7011**	.6970	.6943	.6917	.6895	.6962
1024_1	**.7049**	.7013	.6981	.6954	.6930	.6998
128_2	**.7454**	.7419	.7418	.7382	.7386	.7397
256_2	**.7316**	.7288	.7273	.7257	.7233	.7279
512_2	**.7257**	.7240	.7219	.7196	.7182	.7220
1024_2	**.7233**	.7199	.7196	.7175	.7150	.7192
128_4	.7569	.7569	.7595	.7578	**.7604**	.7544
256_4	.7466	.7502	.7510	.7507	**.7544**	.7477
512_4	.7413	.7435	.7429	.7448	**.7470**	.7425
1024_4	.7363	.7366	.7389	.7410	**.7439**	.7372
128_6	.7569	.7575	.7579	.7589	**.7603**	.7554
256_6	.7449	.7512	.7524	.7536	**.7564**	.7507
512_6	.7425	.7420	.7443	.7476	**.7528**	.7435
1024_6	.7368	.7388	.7407	.7446	**.7478**	.7394
128_8	.7532	.7521	**.7562**	.7533	.7560	.7504
256_8	.7433	.7428	.7464	.7483	**.7524**	.7427
512_8	.7369	.7409	.7407	.7442	**.7486**	.7410
1024_8	.7308	.7343	.7371	.7395	**.7457**	.7365
128_10	.7432	.7447	**.7480**	.7436	.7471	.7448
256_10	.7356	.7344	.7380	.7420	**.7453**	.7373
512_10	.7317	.7315	.7348	.7377	**.7425**	.7337
1024_10	.7266	.7307	.7335	.7348	**.7401**	.7312
128_12	.7370	.7350	.7373	.7389	**.7400**	.7392
256_12	.7314	.7280	.7320	.7348	**.7375**	.7300
512_12	.7255	.7261	.7293	.7321	**.7360**	.7271
1024_12	.7228	.7222	.7264	.7307	**.7338**	.7238

Table 2: Average fitness of best local optima reached for each type of instance (10 instances per NK parametrization).

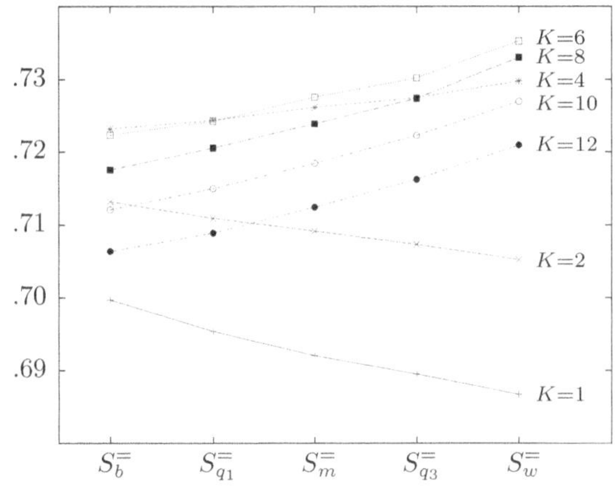

Figure 2: $S_i^=$ pivoting rules results with respect to landscape ruggedness, for a fixed size N=1024. Similar overall tendency is observed for other values of N (see table 1).

worst improvement should be observed also in an iterated local search context (considering a fixed number of local search realized).

In the graphic of figure 3, we report the average fitness values obtained by the 12 studied climbers versions (for $N = 1024$). Methods are ordered according to the average rank of solutions selected by the pivoting rule. For each ruggedness level (K), we observe a monotonic or nearly monotonic evolution of the average final fitnesses. This confirms that the local search efficiency is directly correlated (negatively or positively) with the fitness improvement realized at each step of the search. The table included in figure 3 reports numerical results for $K = 12$. This allows to visualize the monotonic evolution of results obtained by the generic ranking-based pivoting rules ($S^=$, $S^{\geqslant}$, and $S^{\leqslant}$).

The different results obtained and reported in tables 1 and 2, and in figure 3, show a clear interest in performing worst improvement hill-climbings while considering rugged landscapes. However, achieving a worst improvement search naturally requires most solution evaluations. When comparing worst improvement against best improvement, attaining a local optimum requires more moves: each best improvement step significantly increases the fitness value while worst improvement focus on minimizing the fitness benefit at each step of the search. First improvement naturally allows to avoid the systematic generation of the entire neighborhood, which drastically reduces the number of evaluations needed to reach the local optima. In the next section, we focus on the number of evaluations, and propose ways to keep advantages of worst improvement with a reduced number of solution evaluations.

4. APPROXIMATING WORST IMPROVEMENT

First results emphasizes that for climbing efficiently rugged landscapes, the search should focus on selecting the improving neighbors which achieve lower fitness values. However, such a strategy is time-consuming for two reasons. First, in

Strategy	b	q_1	m	q_3	w
$S^{=}$	.7064	.7089	.7125	.7163	**.7209**
$S^{\geqslant}$	.7064	.7072	.7083	.7094	.7107
$S^{\leqslant}$	.7107	.7133	.7158	.7185	.7209

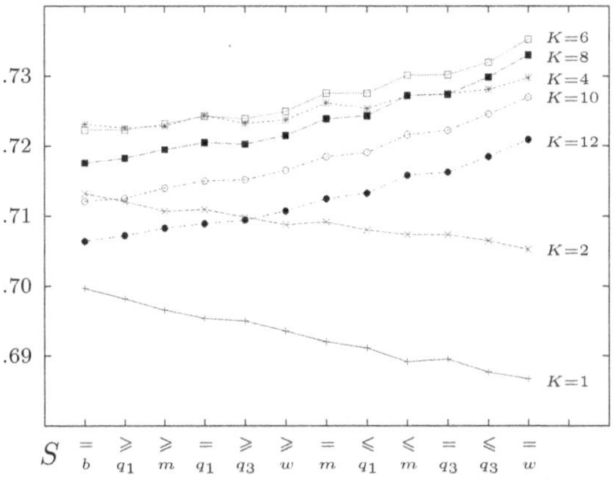

Figure 3: Performance of 12 ranking-based pivoting rules on 7 sets of NK-landscapes grouped by ruggedness (k=1 to 12, N=1024 only). Strategies are sorted according to the average ranking values $\frac{\text{avg\_rank\_of\_selected\_neighbor}-1}{\text{number\_of\_improving\_neighbors}-1}$ (from $S^{=}_{B}$ to $S^{=}_{W}$: 0, 1/8, 1/4, 1/4, 3/8, 1/2, 1/2, 5/8, 3/4, 3/4, 7/8, 1). Table (on top): numerical values for K=12.

minimizing the improvement realized at each step, we tend to greatly increase the number of steps needed to reach a local optimum. Second, as for best improvement, the whole neighborhood has to be generated for ensuring the selection of the worst neighbor — unless an incremental neighborhood evaluation is feasible.

Here, we propose to approximate the complete worst improvement strategy by generating the neighborhood partially. Such a mechanism is commonly used for approximating best improvement on large neighborhoods [8]. We propose here to select the worst improving neighbor of a solution within a subset of its neigborhood. More precisely, we introduce the *partial worst improvement* (denoted as $\mathcal{W}_\kappa$), which consists in stopping the neighborhood generation when κ improving neighbors are found (unless the whole neighborhood has been evaluated). At each step of the search, $\mathcal{W}_\kappa$ selects the configuration with the lowest fitness among the (at most) κ improving neighbors. As a consequence, the parameter κ directly affects the number of solution evaluations needed to perform a hill-climbing step. Note that $\mathcal{W}_1$ is first improvement, while $\mathcal{W}_N$ corresponds to the (complete) worst improvement.

In the experiments, several partial worst improvement versions have been tested: $\mathcal{W}_2$, $\mathcal{W}_4$, $\mathcal{W}_8$, $\mathcal{W}_{16}$, and also $\mathcal{W}_1$ and $\mathcal{W}_N$ for comparison. Experimental process consists then in the comparison of 6 hill-climbing versions which are competing on the set of 280 NK-landscapes used in the previous section. The experimental protocol remains also unchanged in terms of starting points, number of executions, and stopping criterion. Let us precise that neighbors are always generated in a random order. Table 3 reports results on rugged instances only ($K \geqslant 4$), where worst improvement dominates

N_K	Best	First	Partial Worst				Worst
	-	$\mathcal{W}_1$	$\mathcal{W}_2$	$\mathcal{W}_4$	$\mathcal{W}_8$	$\mathcal{W}_{16}$	$\mathcal{W}_N$
128_4	.7216 5k	.7207 1k	.7224 2k	.7237 4k	.7234 8k	.7243 16k	**.7250** 31k
256_4	.7211 19k	.7218 2k	.7233 5k	.7254 10k	.7257 21k	.7262 41k	**.7274** 136k
512_4	.7228 76k	.7232 5k	.7248 11k	.7262 23k	.7278 49k	.7281 97k	**.7285** 568k
1024_4	.7232 302k	.7238 12k	.7253 25k	.7270 54k	.7286 112k	.7291 223k	**.7298** 2336k
128_6	.7170 4k	.7187 1k	.7214 2k	.7228 5k	.7242 10k	.7240 21k	**.7251** 46k
256_6	.7207 15k	.7234 2k	.7264 5k	.7285 12k	.7301 26k	.7309 56k	**.7313** 221k
512_6	.7214 63k	.7239 5k	.7272 12k	.7298 28k	.7315 63k	.7328 135k	**.7338** 979k
1024_6	.7223 251k	.7250 13k	.7280 29k	.7310 65k	.7330 145k	.7343 311k	**.7353** 4151k
128_8	.7124 3k	.7136 1k	.7168 2k	.7194 5k	.7197 11k	.7192 24k	**.7199** 56k
256_8	.7147 13k	.7179 2k	.7218 5k	.7243 13k	.7259 30k	**.7267** 66k	**.7267** 284k
512_8	.7163 53k	.7200 5k	.7242 13k	.7266 31k	.7285 73k	.7297 163k	**.7306** 1324k
1024_8	.7176 214k	.7215 13k	.7251 31k	.7285 74k	.7306 172k	.7316 382k	**.7330** 5837k
128_10	.7049 3k	.7078 1k	.7103 2k	.7122 5k	.7116 11k	**.7127** 24k	.7115 59k
256_10	.7082 11k	.7126 2k	.7159 5k	.7176 13k	.7196 32k	**.7201** 71k	.7198 325k
512_10	.7106 46k	.7143 5k	.7190 13k	.7212 33k	.7232 81k	.7237 183k	**.7243** 1593k
1024_10	.7121 187k	.7165 14k	.7204 33k	.7235 80k	.7255 189k	.7265 439k	**.7270** 7325k
128_12	.6970 2k	.7009 1k	.7021 2k	.7035 5k	**.7037** 11k	.7028 24k	.7033 59k
256_12	.7015 10k	.7053 2k	.7089 5k	.7105 13k	.7124 33k	.7122 74k	**.7129** 346k
512_12	.7045 41k	.7082 5k	.7127 13k	.7151 34k	.7168 85k	**.7179** 199k	**.7179** 1816k
1024_12	.7064 166k	.7107 14k	.7150 34k	.7178 84k	.7197 206k	.7206 487k	**.7210** 8544k

Table 3: Comparison of first improvement, worst improvement, and partial worst improvement pivoting rules (average fitness of local optima reached from 1,000 hill-climbings distributed on 10 instances).

other strategies presented in the previous section. Average results and statistical significance are provided as described in section 3.2. We also report, for each instance, the average number of solution evaluations needed to reach a local optima (in thousands).

Let us recall that $\mathcal{W}_1$ and $\mathcal{W}_N$ were respectively denoted as $S^{=}_{w}$ and $S^{\geqslant}_{w}$ in table 1, then similar results can be retrieved for these methods in both tables, ie. worst improvement outperforms first improvement when $K \geqslant 4$. Globally, according to figure 4, which graphically summarizes results of table 3, $\mathcal{W}_N \succ \mathcal{W}_{16} \succ \mathcal{W}_8 \succ \mathcal{W}_4 \succ \mathcal{W}_2 \succ \mathcal{W}_1$, considering that $A \succ B$ denotes that hill-climbing algorithm A outperforms algorithm B in average on a particular set of instances. This confirms the overall tendency observed in the previous section, which states that when first improvement outperforms best improvement, the climbing efficiency is inversely proportional to the quality of the selected improving neighbors. Nevertheless, on most instances, a relatively low value of κ (regarding to N) is sufficient to obtain a partial worst improvement whose results are not statistically outperformed by the complete worst improvement.

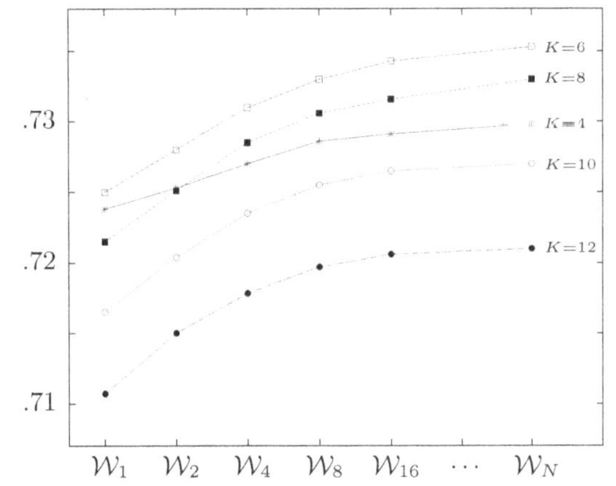

Figure 4: Average results of partial worst improvement strategies ($\mathcal{W}_\kappa$, with $\kappa \in \{1, 2, 4, 8, 16, 1024\}$) on rugged $N = 1024$ instances ($K \in \{4, 6, 8, 10, 12\}$).

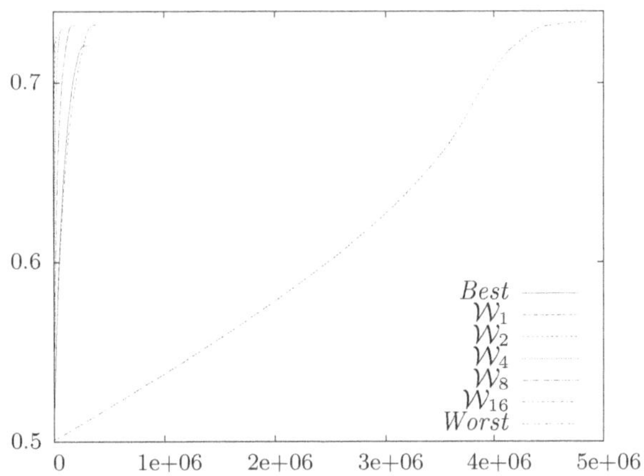

Figure 5: Average convergence of best, worst, and 4 partial worst improvements on a 1024_6 NK-landscape (number of evaluations in horizontal axis, average fitness in vertical axis).

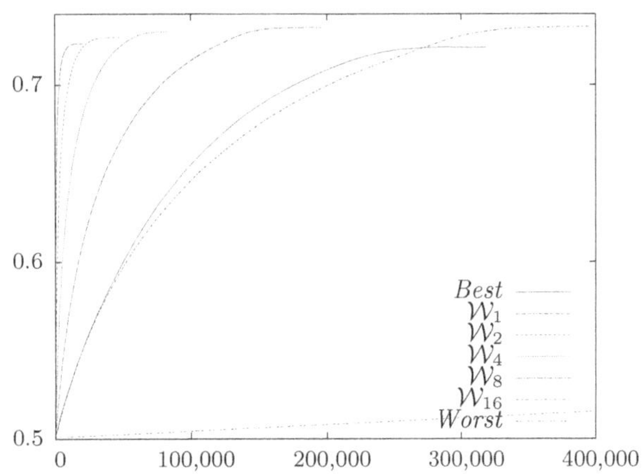

Figure 6: Average convergence of best, worst, and 4 partial worst improvements (focus on the first 400,000 evaluations).

The use of such technique is particularly interesting since it clearly requires less solution evaluations than worst improvement. In most cases, with an accurate κ value, a partial worst improvement can yield statistically comparable local optima while requiring significantly less solution evaluations than a complete worst improvement. Setting κ consists in determining the best compromise between hill-climbing efficiency and computational costs. Note that despite best and (complete) worst improvement both need to evaluate the whole neighborhood at each step of the search, the number of solution evaluations required by worst improvement is significantly greater than by best improvement since the number of (small) steps necessarily increases. The computational difference is especially observed during the first part of the search, when improving neighbors are numerous.

In figure 5, we report the average fitness evolution with respect to the number of solutions evaluated on a 1024_6 instance. This figure emphasizes that the computation cost of worst improvement is really high when compared to the other strategies. It is interesting to notice that although the convergence speed of worst improvement is low, it tends to increase during the search[1]. A similar evolution was observed for all instances.

Figure 6 reports the results outputted in figure 5 with a focus on the first 400,000 evaluations which suffice to terminate best and partial worst improvements. This figure allows us to visualize, on non-smooth NK-landscapes, the clear superiority of $\mathcal{W}_1$ (first improvement), $\mathcal{W}_2$, $\mathcal{W}_4$, $\mathcal{W}_8$, and $\mathcal{W}_{16}$ against best improvement. Moreover, the tradeoff between convergence speed and quality of obtained local optima is easy to observe. Increasing κ allows to reach better local optima but with higher computation costs. In particular, setting κ to 2 suffices to improve results obtained by first improvement ($\kappa = 1$) without increasing drastically the number of solution evaluations. When $\kappa = 16$, the observed convergence speed is similar to best improvement, but searches are trapped later in local optima.

5. CONCLUSION

Climbers are often considered as basic components of advanced search methods. However, influence of their conception choices are rarely discussed through advanced studies. In particular, most studies only focus on best and/or first improvement strategies. In this paper we focused on the design of hill-climbing pivoting rules, the aim being to reach high local optima in various landscapes. In particular, we first evaluate the ability of the worst improvement strategy to reach better configurations. Experiments show that worst improvement is more efficient than both first and best improvement strategies while exploring rugged NK-landscapes. Results also show that the average quality of the attained local optima is negatively correlated with the quality of selected neighbors: worst are the ranks of selected improving neighbors, better are the average local optima attained by the hill-climbing strategy. Results on smooth NK-landscapes lead to the opposite conclusion.

[1]For each worst improvement execution, note that the convergence speed increases during the whole search, and especially during the last steps. However, on figure 5, the worst improvement convergence seems slowing down after 4.10^6 average solution evaluations. It can be explained by the fact that the 100 executions reach a local optimum between 4.10^6 and 5.10^6 evaluations, but not simultaneously.

The second part of this study focused on reducing the computational cost induced by worst improvement. To this aim, we proposed intermediate pivoting rules between first and worst improvement. It mainly consists in combining the low computational cost of first improvement with the ability of worst improvement to reach good local optima. Experiments show that choosing the worst improving neighbor among a fixed number κ of potential improving moves leads to good tradeoffs between quickness (first improvement) and efficiency (worst improvement). In particular, choosing an adequate κ allows to define a partial worst improvement climber, whose results are statistically comparable to worst improvement ones while requiring a reduced computational effort.

Perspectives of this work include the application of worst-based improvement principle to classical combinatorial problems. In [1], we showed that first improvement outperforms best improvement in many cases when applied to flow-shop, QAP and MAXSAT problems. We can expect that worst improvement should outperforms both classical pivoting rules also on these problems. Naturally, some adaptation of this study have to be proposed in order to tackle combinatorial landscapes containing neutrality, which is a particularity of numerous landscapes derived from combinatorial problems.

Other perspective includes the extension of this analysis to Iterative Local Search methods [5]. Indeed, it should be interesting to determine if improving climbers can help to improve local search-based metaheuristics.

Acknowledgements

This work is partially supported by the Pays de la Loire Region (France) within the LigeRO project.

6. REFERENCES

[1] Matthieu Basseur and Adrien Goëffon. Hill-climbing strategies on various landscapes: an empirical comparison. In Christian Blum and Enrique Alba, editors, *GECCO*, pages 479–486. ACM, 2013.

[2] Pierre Hansen and Nenad Mladenović. First vs. best improvement: An empirical study. *Discrete Applied Mathematics*, 154(5):802–817, 2006.

[3] Holger Hoos and Thomas Stützle. *Stochastic Local Search: Foundations & Applications*. Morgan Kaufmann Publishers Inc., San Francisco, CA, USA, 2004.

[4] Stuart A. Kauffman. *The Origins of Order: Self-Organization and Selection in Evolution*. Oxford University Press, USA, 06 1993.

[5] Helena R. Lourenço, Olivier Martin, and Thomas Stützle. Iterated local search. In Fred Glover and Gary Kochenberger, editors, *Handbook of Metaheuristics*, volume 57 of *International Series in Operations Research & Management Science*, pages 321–353. Kluwer Academic Publishers, Norwell, Massachusetts, USA, 2002.

[6] Peter Merz and Bernd Freisleben. Fitness landscapes and memetic algorithm design. *New ideas in optimization*, pages 245–260, 1999.

[7] Melanie Mitchell, Stephanie Forrest, and John H Holland. The royal road for genetic algorithms: Fitness landscapes and GA performance. In *Proceedings of the first european conference on artificial life*, pages 245–254. Cambridge: The MIT Press, 1992.

[8] Nenad Mladenović and Pierre Hansen. Variable neighborhood search. *Computers & Operations Research*, 24(11):1097–1100, November 1997.

[9] Alain Ratle. Kriging as a surrogate fitness landscape in evolutionary optimization. *Artificial Intelligence for Engineering Design, Analysis and Manufacturing*, 15(01):37–49, 2001.

[10] Darrell Whitley, Adele E. Howe, and Doug Hains. Greedy or not? best improving versus first improving stochastic local search for MAXSAT. In *Proceedings of Twenty-Seventh Conference on Artificial Intelligence*. AAAI, 2013.

[11] S. Wright. The roles of mutation, inbreeding, crossbreeding and selection in evolution. *Proceedings of the VI International Congress of Genetics*, 1:356–366, 1932.

[12] Mihalis Yannakakis. The analysis of local search problems and their heuristics. In *Proceedings of the seventh annual symposium on Theoretical aspects of computer science*, STACS 90, pages 298–311, New York, NY, USA, 1990. Springer-Verlag New York, Inc.

Socially Inspired Algorithms for the Traveling Thief Problem

Mohammad Reza Bonyadi
School of Computer Science
The University of Adelaide
Adelaide, Australia
mrbonyadi@cs.adelaide.edu.au

Zbigniew Michalewicz
School of Computer Science
The University of Adelaide
Adelaide, Australia
zbyszek@cs.adelaide.edu.au

Michał Roman Przybyłek
Polish-Japanese Institute of Information Technology
Warsaw, Poland
mrp@pjwstk.edu.pl

Adam Wierzbicki
Polish-Japanese Institute of Information Technology
Warsaw, Poland
adamw@pjwstk.edu.pl

ABSTRACT

Many real-world problems are composed of two or more problems that are interdependent on each other. The interaction of such problems usually is quite complex and solving each problem separately cannot guarantee the optimal solution for the overall multi-component problem. In this paper we experiment with one particular 2-component problem, namely the Traveling Thief Problem (TTP). TTP is composed of the Traveling Salesman Problem (TSP) and the Knapsack Problem (KP). We investigate two heuristic methods to deal with TTP. In the first approach we decompose TTP into two sub-problems, solve them by separate modules/algorithms (that communicate with each other), and combine the solutions to obtain an overall approximated solution to TTP (this method is called CoSolver). The second approach is a simple heuristic (called density-based heuristic, DH) method that generates a solution for the TSP component first (a version of Lin-Kernighan algorithm is used) and then, based on the fixed solution for the TSP component found, it generates a solution for the KP component (associated with the given TTP). In fact, this heuristic ignores the interdependency between sub-problems and tries to solve the sub-problems sequentially. These two methods are applied to some generated TTP instances of different sizes. Our comparisons show that CoSolver outperforms DH specially in large instances.

GECCO'14, July 12–16, 2014, Vancouver, BC, Canada.

http://dx.doi.org/10.1145/2576768.2598367.

Categories and Subject Descriptors

G.1.6 [**Optimization**]: Constrained optimization
; I.2.8 [**Problem Solving, Control Methods, and Search**]: Scheduling

General Terms

Algorithms

Keywords

Traveling Thief Problem, Co-evolution, Heuristics, Metaheuristics, Multi-objective optimization, Non-separable problems, Real-world optimization problems

1. INTRODUCTION

In contemporary business enterprises the complexity of real-world problems has to be perceived as one of the greatest obstacles in achieving effectiveness. Even relatively small companies are frequently confronted — in their daily routines — with problems of very high complexity. There have been some studies to investigate sources of complexity (hardness) in real-world combinatorial optimization problems [9, 23, 15, 16]. For example, in [23] several reasons were identified that make optimization problems hard to solve. However, the reasons listed and discussed in that article (premature convergence, robustness, etc) were more related to the issues of the solvers rather than the hardness of the problems. Also, in [16], five main reasons behind the hardness of real-world problems were discussed: the size of the problem, modeling issues, noise, constraints, and some psychological pressures on the designer when problems are big. In [15], real-world problems were categorized into two groups: (1) design/static problems, and (2) operational/dynamic problems. The first category includes a variety of problems, such as traveling salesman problem (TSP), Vehicle Routing Problem (VRP), knapsack problem (KP), etc. The second category includes problems presented in the now-a-days industries (e.g. real-world supply chain). The author argued that, although some of the design/static problems (first category) are really hard and most of the current research has been concentrated on those problems, the problems from the second category (i.e. operational/dynamic problems) are much harder and represent a huge opportunity for Evolutionary Algorithms. It was also stated that the value of addressing the problems in the first category does not have significant influence on solving the problems in the second category [15].

The reason behind the aforementioned minimal influence was investigated in [9] where the authors claimed that the sources of complexity in real-world problems in the first group is somehow different from the ones in the second group. It was argued that most of real-world problems are multi-component problems (several potentially NP-Hard problems interact with each other) while most of the current researches have been concentrated on single component problems (traveling salesman problem, Knapsack problem, job shop scheduling, vehicle routing problem, etc). Also, it was stated that *interdependency* among components in operational/dynamic problems plays a key rule in the complexity of the problems. However, this interdependency is not found in design/static problems [9]. To illustrate the complexity that arises by interdependency in multi-component problems, a new test problem called Traveling Thief Problem (TTP) was introduced [9]. TTP was a composition of two well-known problems, TSP and KP (see section 2.3 for more details).

In this paper, a new algorithm (called CoSolver) for dealing with multi-component problems is proposed. CoSolver mimics the behavior of a corporation that has separate departments that specialize in solving some aspects of a multi-component problem. Each department is good in solving one component, like choosing a route or a schedule. On the other hand, departments need to work together to solve a real problem. They do so by communicating their partial solutions and negotiating with other departments. Also, we propose a simple heuristic (called Density-based Heuristic, DH) that first generates a solution for the TSP component of a given TTP and then it generates a solution for the found TSP so that the objective value is maximized. Note that DH ignores all interdependencies between the components. These two methods are compared through some generated benchmark TTPs. Results show that the performance of CoSolver is better than DH, which means that considering the interdependency between components in solving this multi-component problem (TTP) is beneficial.

The paper has been organized as follows. Section 2 gives some background information about combinatorial optimization problems, multi-component vs single component problems, and the description of the traveling thief problem. In section 3, we propose two methods to solve TTP. Section 4 gives some details for generating instances, and in section 5, the results of application of the proposed methods to the test problems are discussed. Section 6 concludes the paper.

2. BACKGROUND

In this section, some background information about Traveling Salesman Problem (TSP) and Knapsack Problem (KP) are given. Also, the Traveling Thief Problem (TTP) formulation is reviewed.

2.1 Traveling salesman and knapsack problems

Most of the real-world optimization problems are NP-complete[1], which means that they are *verifiable* in polynomial time, and every problem verifiable in polynomial time polynomially reduces to any of these problems. The question whether every polynomial-time-verifiable problem is polynomial-time-*solvable* is an old famous question in theoretical computer science [11, 3]. In particular, there are no known sub-exponential algorithms for any known NP-complete problem.

Two well-studied NP-complete problems in the literature are the Knapsack Problem (KP) and the Traveling Salesman Problem (TSP). In light of the above, there are no known polynomial algorithms to either of these problems.

State-of-the-art algorithm for TSP runs in $2^{n-\Omega(\sqrt{n/\log n})}$ time and exponential space [7], which is a huge improvement over classical algorithm described in [13] running in 2^n time[2]. Not only TSP is hard to solve, it is also hard to *approximate* — approximating TSP with a ratio bounded by a constant is polynomially equivalent to solving TSP. Moreover, almost every restriction of TSP that makes it non-trivial is also NP-complete. There are known, however, better algorithms and approximations in some special cases. For bounded-degree graphs with bounded weights there is an algorithm running in $(2-\epsilon)^n$ time and polynomial space [8]. For Euclidean TSP with bounded double dimension, there is a polynomial-time approximation scheme [6, 5]. The classical Christofides algorithm [10] computes a 1.5-approximation for metric TSP. Variety of heuristics were proposed to solve general TSP — this includes approaches based on genetic algorithms and ant colony optimization [12]. Two best available heuristics base on reformulation of TSP as Mixed Integer Linear Programming [1], and a generalization of k-opt heuristic [2].

Knapsack Problem can be solved in pseudo-polynomial time (i.e. polynomial in the unary coding of natural numbers) by using two obvious dynamic programming approaches: one with respect to weights of items, the other with respect to their profits. Also, the second approach gives rise to a fully-polynomial-time approximation scheme by simple truncation of profits. A survey on methods of solving Knapsack Problem found in Pisinger's PhD dissertation [17].

2.2 Multi vs single component problems

There have been many well-studied combinatorial optimization problems during the past years such as Vehicle Routing problem (VRP) and Capacitate VRP (CVRP) [22], TSP [14], and KP[18]. Most of these problems were inspired by some problems in industries such as transportation industry, mining industry, and supply chains. In fact, an efficient algorithm that is able to solve each of these problems were in a great value because it could be beneficial for some operations in an industry. However, during the past years, the need for problem solving in industries has been changed so that solving these problems have become in a less interest by industrial companies. In fact, none of these problems can be found as a single problem in an industry, so that solving each of these problems (even to optimality) is not that beneficial. This point was clarified in [15] and [9] where the main reason behind this lost of interest was introduced as new industries are after comprehensive solutions which covers the whole

[1]To be precise, the decision counterpart of these problems are NP-complete

[2]Up to a polynomial.

operation and not only a single part of the operation. As an example, international delivery companies are not only after finding the best routes for transportation (a VRP), but also they are after the best time-table for scheduling drivers for those vehicles, scheduling maintenance for the vehicles, and packing of items into vehicles at the same time. Note that all of these sub-problems (components) interdependent from each other, i.e. changing the transportation plan affects the best achievable solution for the scheduling drivers. Thus, it seems that the new industries are after optimization methods for multi-component problems and the methods that can only deal with single-component problems are not in interest.

This point was first investigated in [9] and a benchmark problem called Traveling Thief Problem (TTP) for multi-component optimization problems was introduced. TTP was a composition of two other well-studied problems (TSP and KP). It was shown [9] that, in TTP, solving each sub-problem to optimality does not guarantee locating the overall optimal solution.

2.3 Traveling thief problem

In the Traveling Thief Problem (TTP), there are n cities (i.e. nodes of a graph) together with a function d assigning to every pair i, j of cities a non-negative distance $d(i, j)$ from i to j ($d(i, j)$ plays the role of a weighted edge from a node i to a node j in the graph; $d(i, j) = +\infty$ means that there is no edge from i to j), and m items (each has a profit p_i and a weight w_i) distributed in the cities. The availability of items is given by a function $a_i = \{c_1, \dots, c_{k_i}\}$, which shows that item i is available at cities $c_1, c_2, \dots, c_{k_i}$, where c_i belongs to the set of cities $\{1, \dots, n\}$. It follows from our notation, that k_i copies of item i can be found over all cities. Additionally, we are given the following constants:

- a non-negative real number R — the rent ratio;
- a natural number W — the capacity of "the knapsack";
- two positive real numbers $v_{min} \leq v_{max}$ — the minimal and maximal speed of "the traveler".

The task is to find a complete tour Π visiting each city exactly once (i.e. a permutation Π of the initial segment of n positive natural numbers; abusing notation, we shall also write Π_{n+1} for Π_1; furthermore we assume that the permutation is stable on the first city — i.e. $\Pi_1 = 1$) and pick items from the cities x_i in a way that the total weight of the picked items does not exceed W, and the total profit (formulated in Eq. 1) is maximized.

$$P = \sum_{i=1}^{m} p_i \min(x_i, 1) - R \sum_{i=1}^{n} t_{i,i+1} \tag{1}$$

where P is the total profit, $x_i \in a_i \cup \{0\}$ represents the city that the item i should be picked from (0 refers to not picking the item at all), and $t_{i,j}$ is the time to travel from Π_i to Π_j assuming the weight of all picked items by city Π_i is W_{Π_i}, which is given by the formula:

$$t_{i,j} = \frac{d(\Pi_i, \Pi_j)}{v_{max} - W_{\Pi_i} \frac{v_{max} - v_{min}}{W}} \tag{2}$$

where W_{Π_i} is the total weight of the picked items from cities $\{\Pi_2, \Pi_3, \dots, \Pi_i\}$ (we assume that items from city $\Pi_1 = 1$ are picked at the end of the tour). Note that, if more items are picked while their total weight is smaller than W, the value of $t_{i,j}$ grows which causes reducing the value of P in Eq. 1. Also, by taking better tours in terms of total distance, some possibly high quality items (items which have a high profit) might only be available at the beginning of the tour and, hence, by picking those items, the travel time increases (items should be carried for a longer time), which causes reduction in the value of P. This shows that the interdependency between the two problems influences the optimum solutions for the whole problem. Also, solving each component in isolation does not necessarily lead to the optimum of the problem [9].

3. PROPOSED ALGORITHMS

In this section, we propose two algorithms to deal with TTP. The first algorithm (called Density-based Heuristic, DH) is a simple heuristic which ignores the interdependency between the components. The second algorithm is a socially inspired algorithm which mimics the behavior of groups of experts in solving multi-component problems in real-world.

3.1 Simple/DH heuristic

We propose a heuristic algorithm, called density-based heuristic, DH, for TTP. DH starts with generating a tour for the TSP (Asymmetric TSP, ATSP) that is as short as possible (according to the distances of the cities) and then, it tries to find the best picking plan for the found tour.

The Chained-Lin-Kernighan [4] method is used to generate TSP (ATSP)[3]. Once the tour Π is fixed, a $\overline{p}_i$ is calculated for each item i that estimates how good i is according to the tour. We propose the following function to calculate $\overline{p}_i$ for each item:

$$\overline{p}_i = p_i - Rt_i \tag{3}$$

where p_i is the value of item i, R is the rent rate, and t_i is given by:

$$t_i = \frac{L_i}{v_{max} - w_i \frac{v_{max} - v_{min}}{W}} \tag{4}$$

In Eq. 4, L_i is the total distance from the city where item i is picked from to the end of the tour, i.e.:

$$L_i = \begin{cases} 0 & \text{if } i = 1 \\ \sum_{k=i}^{n+1} d(\Pi_k, \Pi_{k+1}) & \text{if } i \neq 1 \end{cases} \tag{5}$$

In fact, the value of $\overline{p}_i$ is the total profit for the thief if only item i is picked during the whole tour [4]. Note that, to improve the time complexity of the algorithm, the L array is pre-calculated so that it is not recalculated for each item separately. After calculating $\overline{p}_i$ for all items, the items are sorted (descending according to their $\overline{p}_i$ for all i) and processed one by one in the sorted order. For each item i, if i fits into the knapsack and picking item i does not decrease the objective value then the item i is picked, otherwise, next item is processed. Algorithm 1 shows step by step process for DH.

[3] A C++ based implementation for this algorithm can be found in [2].

[4] Note that, in the case of repetitions of an item in different cities, the repetitive items can be assumed as another item and the $\overline{p}_i$ value is calculated for that as a new item

Algorithm 1: Simple Heuristic (SH)

```
1: Π ← solve TSP (ATSP) with given distances
2: Fill the array L
3: for i=1 to m do
4:     Calculate t_i by using Eq. 4
5:     p̄_i ← p_i − R t_i
6: sortedItems ← sort items according to p̄_i
7: W_c = 0, pickedItems = {}
8: P ← calcObj(pickedItems, Π)
9: for i=1 to m do
10:    if W_c + w_{sortedItems_i} < W then
11:        P' ← calcObj(pickedItems ∪ {sortedItems_i}, Π)
12:        if P' > P then
13:            W_c = W_c + w_{sortedItems_i}
14:            pickedItems = pickedItems ∪ {sortedItems_i}
15:            P ← P'
16:    if W_c ≥ W then
17:        break
18: return pickedItems, Π
```

Algorithm 2: CoSolver

```
d_k ← 0
W_k ← 0
P ← −∞
for r ← 1 to MaxIter do
    pickedItems' ← solve KRP with p_k, w_k, d_k and parameter W_k
    W_k ← Σ_{i∈pickedItems'} w_i[0 < x_i ≤ k]
    Π' ← solve TSKP with W_k, d
    P' ← calcObj(pickedItems', Π')
    if P' > P then
        P ← P'
        Π ← Π'
        pickedItems ← pickedItems'
        d_k ← d(Π_k, Π_{k+1})
    else
        break
return pickedItems, Π
```

In Algorithm 1, *calcObj* is a function that calculates the objective value according to a given set of items and tour. The time complexity for the algorithm for solving the knapsack part is in $O(nm^2)$. In fact, calculations for array L is in $O(n)$, calculations of $\overline{p}_i$ for all i is in $O(m)$, sorting the $\overline{p}_i$ for all i is in $O(m\log(m))$, and calculating objective value for each item is in $O(mn)$ in the worst case scenario (all items are picked).

A method similar to DH (called Simple Heuristic, SH) has been also proposed in [19]. In SH, it was proven that if picking a particular item i by itself results in worse objective value than picking no item, then picking item i is always disadvantageous if it is picked with any other combination of items. Thus, in SH, a measure u_i was calculated for each item that represented whether item i is disadvantageous. Then, rather than recalculating the objective value, the value of u_i was used in the condition for the *if* statement in line 11 of Algorithm 1. Note that calculating u_i is in $O(n)$, which can be done prior to the for loop in line 8. Thus, the time complexity of SH is in $O(mn)$, which is faster than DH. However, the solutions that SH was generating could still become even worse than the case that no item is picked. Also, the main aim of [19] was to propose a comprehensive benchmark set for TTP.

3.2 CoSolver: A Socially Inspired Algorithm

The main idea behind CoSolver is to decompose TTP into sub-problems, solve the sub-problems separately, with some communication between the sub-problems, and then compose the solutions back to obtain a solution to TTP. The general idea is shown on Fig 1.

We have identified the following sub-problems of TTP — one corresponding to a generalization of TSP, which we shall call Traveling Salesman with Knapsack Problem (TSKP), and another corresponding to a generalization of KP, which we shall call Knapsack on the Route Problem (KRP).

The Traveling Salesman with Knapsack Problem (TSKP) consists of n cities, a distance function d, a positive integer W (the capacity of the knapsack), a non-negative real number R (the rent rate) and a function w assigning to every node $i \in \{1, 2, \ldots, n\}$ the total weight w_i of items picked at i, and two positive real numbers $v_{min} \leq v_{max}$ corresponding to the minimal and the maximal speed of the traveler. The task is to find a complete tour Π visiting each city exactly once, such that the following is minimized:

$$T = -R\sum_{i=1}^{n} t_{i,i+1} \tag{6}$$

where $t_{i,i+1}$ is defined in the same way as in Eq. 2 from Section 2.

The Knapsack on the Route Problem (KRP) consists of n cities, a function d assigning to a city i the cost $d(i)$ of traveling from city i to city $i+1$ for $i < n$ and from city n to city 1 otherwise, and m items (each has a profit p_i and a weight w_i) distributed in the cities. The availability of items is given by a function $a_i = \{c_1, \ldots, c_{k_i}\}$. Additionally, we are given a natural number W (the capacity of the knapsack), a non-negative real number R (the rent ratio) and two positive real numbers $v_{min} \leq v_{max}$ corresponding to the minimal and the maximal speed of the traveler. The task is to find a function assigning to an item i a city $x_i \subseteq a_i \cup \{0\}$ where item i is picked (0 refers to not picking the item at all) such that the collective total weight of items does not exceed W, and the following is maximized:

$$P = \sum_{i=1}^{m} p_i \min(x_i, 1) - R\sum_{i=1}^{n} t_i \tag{7}$$

where:

$$t_i = \frac{d(i)}{v_{max} - W_i\frac{v_{max}-v_{min}}{W}} \tag{8}$$

and W_i is the total weight of the picked items from cities $\{2, \ldots, i\}$ (we assume that items from city 1 are picked at the end of the tour).

An iterative heuristic based on the above observation is presented as Algorithm 2.

Given an instance of TTP, CoSolver starts by creating an instance of KRP that consists of all items from all nodes and distances $d(k)$ equal zero. After finding a solution K' for this instance, it creates an instance of TSKP by assigning to each city a weight equal to the total weights of items picked at the city by KRP. A solution for TTP at the initial

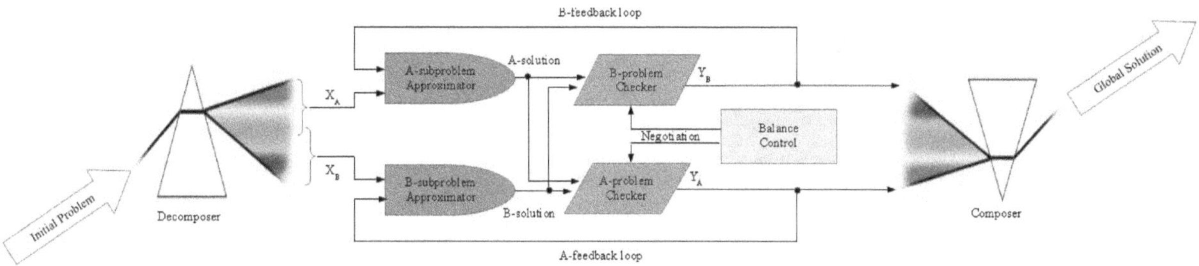

Figure 1: Decomposition of a problem on two sub-problems: A and B.

step consists of a pair K', Π', where Π' is the route found as a solution to the instance of TSKP. Then the profit P' of the solution is calculated. If profit P' is better than the best profit P that has been found so far, the process repeats with distances between nodes adjusted along tour Π'.

The current implementation of CoSolver uses an exact algorithm for TSKP, and the following heuristic for KRP. Let W_i denote the total weight of items picked at cities $\{2, \ldots, i\}$ according to some picking plan. We create an instance of KP with "relaxed profits" in the following way:

$$\overline{p}_i = p_i - R(t - t')$$

where t and t' are given by:

$$t_i = \frac{L_i}{v_{max} - (W_{i-1} + w_i)\frac{v_{max} - v_{min}}{W}} \quad (9)$$

$$t_i' = \frac{L_i}{v_{max} - W_{i-1}\frac{v_{max} - v_{min}}{W}} \quad (10)$$

and:

$$L_i = \begin{cases} 0 & \text{if } i = 1 \\ \sum_{k=i}^{n+1} d(k) & \text{if } i \neq 1 \end{cases} \quad (11)$$

Instances of KP are solved exactly by the usual dynamic programming method.

Note that the idea of decomposition and negotiation between modules was also mentioned [9]. In fact, the general idea of CoSolver is very similar to co-operational co-evolution proposed in [20] where a problem is divided to sub-problems and different parts of the problem are solved by different modules (potentially, each module is a population-based method). Then, the final solution is combined to create the solution for the original problem.

4. GENERATION OF INSTANCES

To compare performance of the proposed algorithms, we have prepared a generic framework for generating classes of TTP-instances. Each class is composed of three independent components: *meta*, *TSP* and *KP* that are explained in the rest of this section. Depending on parameters configuration of these components one is able to create separate classes of TTP-instances.

4.1 Meta-component

This subsection describes all parameters that are independent from the TSP graph and KP items — i.e. knapsack-capacity, rent rate, minimal-velocity and maximal-velocity. One can alter the importance of TSP or KP components in a TTP by tunning these parameters. As an example, a

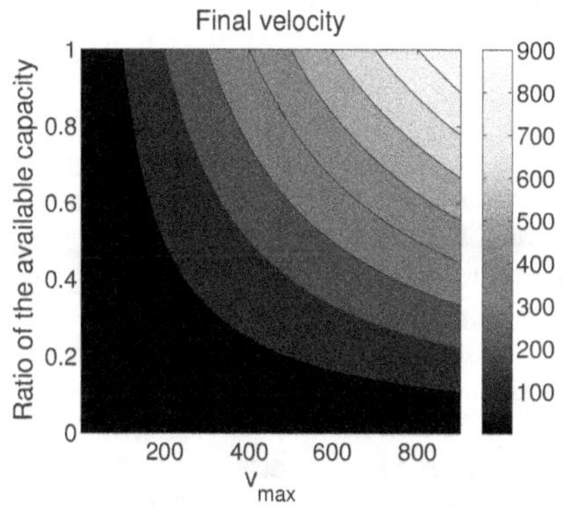

Figure 2: Impact of different values of the maximum velocity and ratio of the available capacity of the knapsack on the final velocity for a specific W.

reducing the value of the rent rate (w.r.t the profit of items) in fact reduces the contribution of the TSP component to the final objective value. In an extreme case, the TSP component is completely ignored if the rent rate is zero. Also, by increasing the value of the rent rate, total profit of items becomes less important in the final objective value and the speed of travel become more important (contribution of TSP in the final objective is increased). Consequently, the solution for the KP component have smaller impact on the total objective. This is also the same for the value of $v_{max} - v_{min}$. As an example, lets assume that v_{min} is a constant (0.1). If the value of $v_{max} - v_{min}$ becomes zero, the value of velocity, calculated by $v_{max} - (v_{max} - v_{min})\frac{W_c}{W}$ (W_c is the total weight of the picked items) becomes v_{max} for any $\frac{W_c}{W}$. Thus, picking any item has no impact on the speed of the travel, and hence, one can completely decompose TTP instance to two independent sub-problems (TSP component and KP-component) and solve them separately. Note that, with this setting, the optimal solution in isolation for each component in fact constructs the overall optimal solution for any given rent rate (see Fig 2). By making v_{max} larger (for a fixed v_{min}), the variability of the final velocity increases according to the ratio of the available capacity $(1 - \frac{W_c}{W})$. In fact, for a large v_{max}, the more items the thief pick, the faster the speed drops comparing to a smaller value for v_{max}. If the value of v_{max} is set to a very large value, the final velocity drops very fast and, for fixed values of other parameters (fixed profits and weights for items, rent rate, and distances), it would be better to have more available capacity in the knapsack to avoid significant drop of the travel speed. In fact, in this case, solving KP component to optimality is more harmful.

Algorithm 3: Generation of Instances

$V = \{0, 1, \ldots, n-1\}$
$E = \{\}$
for given number of iteration **do**
  perm ← random permutation of V
  add to E edges of the Hamiltonian cycle, that is defined by perm
return $G = (V, E)$

4.2 Methods of Generating *TSP-component*

By the *TSP-component* of a TTP-instance we define a weighted directed graph $G = (V, E, w)$, where V denotes the set of vertices, E denotes the set of edges and $w\colon E \to \mathbb{R}$ that assigns length (distance) to each of the edges.

Below we describe the classes of underlying graphs in greater depth. Both the class of *simple random graphs* and the class of *Euclidean random graphs* are based on the basic $G(n, p)$ model[5]; where $\boldsymbol{n}$ denotes the number of vertices in the graph G and $\boldsymbol{p}$ denotes probability that an edge e is — independently from other edges — included in $E(G)$.

Simple Random Graphs In this class we extend $G(n, p)$-model by an option of setting the length l of each edge $e \in E(G)$. Instances of this class are characterized by relatively high difficulty of the *TSP-component*. *Parameters:* $\boldsymbol{l_{min}}, \boldsymbol{l_{max}}$ — boundary values of an uniform distribution, from which lengths of edges are drawn.

Euclidean Random Graphs Vertices of the underlying graph G are embedded in some m-dimensional Euclidean space; i.e. there exists a function $\iota\colon V(G) \to \mathbb{R}^m$, such that for each $(n_1, n_2) \in E(G)$, the length of (n_1, n_2) is equal to Euclidean distance between $\iota(n_1)$ and $\iota(n_2)$. Although we allow m to be arbitrary large, up-to-now we have been concentrating mainly on cases for which $m = 2$, as graphs of this type resembles in highest degree most of the real-world problems and are the easiest to visualize. *Parameters:* m — number of dimensions of the Euclidean space; l_{max} — for each point from $\mathbb{R}^m$, that corresponds to some vertex from $V(G)$, values alongside each dimension are between 0 and l_{max} (in our case we draw them from a uniform distribution); $dist_{min}$ — minimal length of an edge (n_1, n_2).

Hamiltonian-Dense Graphs The main motivation behind this class of graphs is to make finding *Hamiltonian-cycles* relatively easy. Instances of this class are generated by Algorithm 3. *Parameters:* i — number of iterations; l_{min}, l_{max} — boundary values of the uniform distribution, from which lengths of edges are drawn.

4.3 Methods of Generating *KP-component*

KP-component of a TTP-instance is characterized by a set of all items I, each item being a pair $(weight, value)$ and a function $avail\colon I \times V(G) \to \{0, 1\}$ such that:

$$avail(i, v) = \begin{cases} 1 & \text{if item } i \text{ is available at vertex } v \\ 0 & \text{otherwise} \end{cases}$$

Uncorrelated Weights and Values Since *actual/global* valuableness of an item does strongly depend on the wider context in which the item is being considered[6] any sophisticated methods of generating the KP-component are rather hard to conceptualize. Therefore, we decided to generate *weight* and *value* of each item independently from one another, and control the hardness of the KP-component mainly by its size and the value of knapsack-capacity. *Parameters:* n is the number of items; $value_{min}, value_{max}$ are boundary values of the uniform distribution, from which *values* of items are drawn; $weight_{min}, weight_{max}$ are boundary values of an uniform distribution, from which *weights* of items are drawn; p is the probability with which each item is available at each vertex.

Greedy-proof Due to the fact that KP-instance in which values and weights of items are uncorrelated, are — in general — considered to be rather easy [18] and a greedy algorithm can solve them to high quality solutions, we propose a method of generating KP-component instances that are resistant against the greedy approach. As the first step of this *greedy-proof*-method we generate a number of items of relatively low weight and relatively high $\frac{value}{weight}$-ratio, whose total weight from all vertices constitutes some small fraction f of the knapsack-capacity W. As the second step we generate a relatively high amount of items, whose weights are drawn from the interval $[w - \frac{f}{2}, w]$. *Parameters: big* — number of heavy items; p — probability with which each heavy-item is available at each vertex; *small* — total number of small-items in all vertices; *fraction* — control parameter for bounds of total weight of small-items and weights of heavy-items.

4.4 Parameters of Benchmark Instances

The set of our benchmark instances counts 45 TTP-instances of different sizes[7] and levels of difficulty. The instances can be grouped into the following 6 classes according to the methods by which they were generated. Number in brackets indicates the actual number of instances of given type.

Euclidean (9) *meta-component*: $rent \in [1, 400]$, $capacity \in [200, 500]$, $velocity_{min} \in [25, 50]$, $velocity_{max} \in [60, 75]$; *TSP-component* — *Euclidean*: $n \in [15, 25]$, $p \in [0.1, 0.3]$, $l_{max} = 5000$, $dist_{min} = 10$; *KP-component* — *Uncorrelated*: $n \in [5, 10]$, $p \in [0.1, 0.3]$, $value \in [1, 10000]$, $weight \in [50, 100]$

Dense (3) *meta-component*: $rent \in [0.01, 100]$, $capacity \in [300, 600]$, $velocity_{min} \in [20, 40]$, $velocity_{max} \in [50, 90]$; *TSP-component* — *Hamiltonian-Dense*: $n \in [30, 35]$, $cycles = 3$; *KP-component* — *Uncorrelated*: $n \in [7, 10]$, $value \in [1, 10000]$, $weight \in [50, 100]$, $p = 0.47$

Random (8) *meta-component*: $rent \in [1, 1000]$, $capacity \in [200, 400]$, $velocity_{min} \in [25, 50]$, $velocity_{max} \in [60, 75]$; *TSP-component* — *Simple*: $n \in [15, 25]$, $p \in [0.1, 0.2]$, $length \in [1, 500]$; *KP-component* — *Uncorrelated*: $n \in [5, 10]$, $value \in [1, 500]$, $weight \in [30, 80]$, $p \in [0.1, 0.2]$

Small (5) *meta-component*: $rent \in [2, 5]$, $capacity \in [400, 800]$, $velocity_{min} \in [10, 100]$, $velocity_{max} \in [100, 200]$; *TSP-component* — *Simple*: $n \in [3, 6]$, $p = 1$, $length \in [1000, 5000]$; *KP-component* — *Uncorrelated*: $n \in [5, 10]$, $value \in [1, 1000]$, $weight \in [20, 80]$, $p \in [0.1, 0.3]$

Greedy-Proof (10) *meta-component*: $rent \in [0.05, 0.1]$, $capacity \in [10000, 20000]$, $velocity_{min} \in [25, 50]$, $velocity_{max} \in [60, 75]$; *TSP-component* — *Hamiltonian-Dense*: $n \in [4, 8]$,

[5]Introduced in [21], but named later after Erdős and Rényi.

[6]The main factors are: distance to last vertex on the tour, knapsack-rent, current load of knapsack, minimal and maximal velocity

[7]Because we were mainly interested in the question, how solutions obtained by our algorithms differ from the exact solutions, the sizes of instances are rather mediocre, as the latter need *exhaustive-search*.

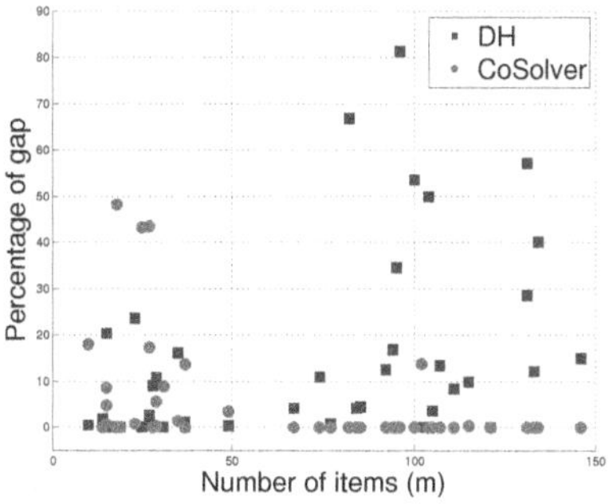

Figure 3: Performance of DH and CoSolver in solving the generated benchmark problems with regards to different number of items.

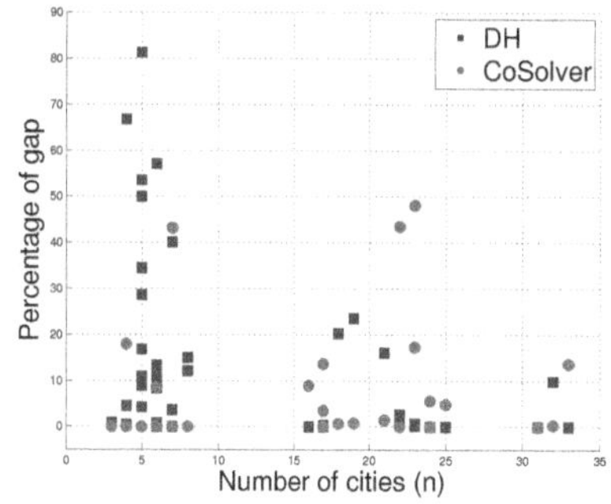

Figure 4: Performance of DH and CoSolver in solving the generated benchmark problems with regards to the different number of cities.

cycles = 3; *KP-component* — *Greedy-Proof*: $big \in [50, 70]$, $p \in [0.2, 0.25]$, $small \in [20, 25]$, $fraction \in [0.2, 0.25]$

KP-Centric (10) *meta-component*: $rent \in [1, 20]$, $capacity \in [5000, 10000]$, $velocity_{min} \in [25, 50]$, $velocity_{max} \in [60, 75]$; *TSP-component* — *Euclidean*: $n \in [4, 6]$, $p = 1$, $l_{max} = 100$, $dist_{min} = 10$; *KP-component* — *Uncorrelated*: $n \in [50, 100]$, $value \in [1, 10000]$, $weight \in [1, 10000]$, $p \in [0.2, 0.3]$

5. EXPERIMENTAL RESULTS

In order to compare DH and CoSolver, we generated 45 instances with different number of cities (from 3 to 33) and items (from 10 to 146) with the parameters mentioned in section 4.4. Both methods are applied to this set of benchmark problems and their results are compared. We also designed an exhaustive search that solves the generated benchmark set to optimality. In all comparisons, we use the percentage of the gap between the generated solution by each heuristic algorithm and the exact solution by $gap = 100\frac{z-z^*}{z^*}$, where z^* is the solution found by the exact solver and z is the solution found by a heuristic (DH or CoSolver). Note that the better the solution is, the lower the value of the gap will be.

The overall performance of the methods has been reported in Table 1. Clearly, CoSolver has a better performance than DH in average and also it has smaller standard deviation from the exact solution.

Table 1: Average and standard deviation of the gap for DH and CoSolver over all 45 instances.

	DH	CoSolver
Average	13.70	**5.16**
Std	20.03	**11.76**

Fig. 3 shows the scatter plot of the average value of the gap for CoSolver and DH from the exact solutions versus the number of items. It is clear in the figure that the CoSolver outperforms DH (smaller value for the gap is better) when the number of items is large. This was in fact expected as the strategy for picking items in DH for a given tour is very simple and intuitive. However, it seems that CoSolver has a good performance when the number of items is large (the value of gap is close to zero in most of the cases). This confirms that the negotiation between modules improves the ability of the method to make better decision to solve multi-component problems.

Fig. 4 shows scatter plot of the percentage of the gap versus the number of cities. It is clear from the figure that for a small number of cities, the performance of DH is much worse than CoSolver. The reason is that, when the number of cities is small, the contribution of the TSP part becomes minimal (the total distance for the whole tour is small). Thus, the picking plan for the items becomes very important. However, DH only uses a very simple rule to pick the items, which makes the algorithm ineffective. CoSolver however is equally effective when the number of cities is small or large.

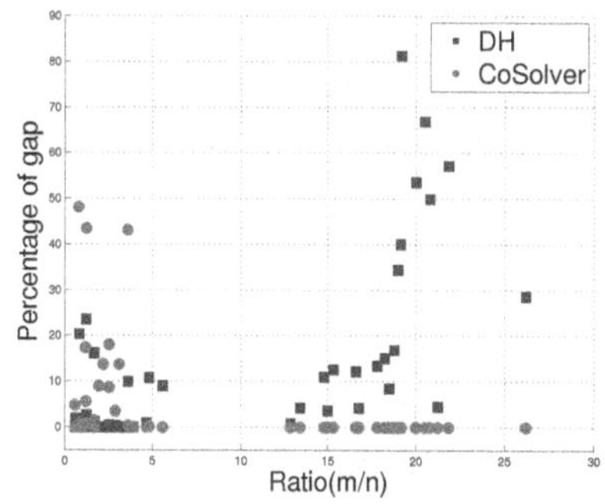

Figure 5: Performance of DH and CoSolver in solving the generated benchmark problems with regards to the number of items/number of cities.

Fig. 5 shows the gap vs ratio ($ratio = m/n$) for DH and CoSolver. Figure indicates that the higher this ratio is, the less effective DH is. In fact, when the number of cities is small and the number of items is large, DH is not that useful as the strategy for picking items in DH is not that effective in finding good solutions for the KP component to match with the found tour. However, CoSolver is way more effective especially for instances in which ration is high. This in fact confirms that the negotiation between modules can effectively address the multi-component problems. Note also that the algorithm for generating the tour in DH is one of the most effective known methods for solving TSP. However, CoSolver only utilizes problem knowledge to solve the given TTPs and no complex strategy in the algorithm were used.

Fig. 6 shows the gap vs rent rate for DH and CoSolver methods. Clearly, the performance of DH is lower than the performance of CoSolver when the rent rate is small. The reason is that (as discussed in section 4.1), for smaller values of the rent rate, the significance of the solution for the TSP component becomes smaller. As DH uses a simple heuristic to solve the KP component, it is actually expected that its performance is low when the rent rate is small. however,

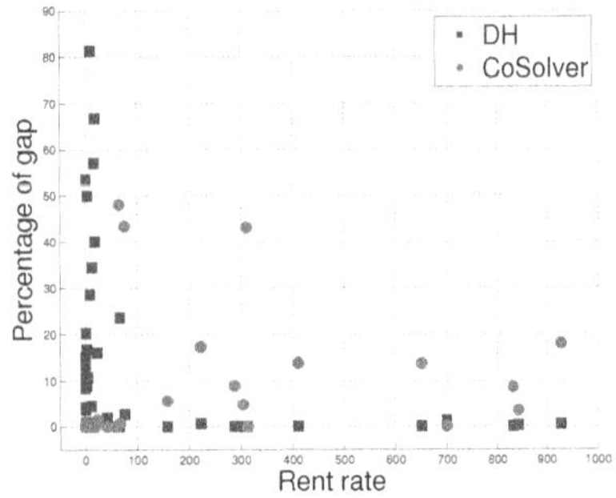

Figure 6: Performance of DH and CoSolver in solving the generated benchmark problems with regards to different rent rates.

when the rent rate is high, the contribution of TSP component becomes larger. As DH uses a good method to deal with the TSP component, its results become better when the rent rate increases.

6. CONCLUSIONS AND FUTURE WORK

In this paper, two methods for solving a multi-component problem (the Traveling Thief Problem, TTP) were proposed. The first method, called Density-based Heuristic (DH), bases on solving the components sequentially. The second method, called CoSolver, which was inspired by co-operational co-evolution, considers the interdependency among components. CoSolver mimics the behavior of group of experts who solve real-world problems in companies. In that method, the problem is decomposed and each component is solved by a module of CoSolver. The algorithm revises the solution through negotiation between its modules. This is done iteratively until no improvement is possible. We also generated some benchmark problems and applied the above two methods to the benchmarks. Results show that CoSolver outperforms DH in most of the cases, especially when the components are not decomposable (i.e. rent rate is larger than zero). This in fact confirms that considering interdependency is beneficial in solving multi-component problems. In future work, we will study other types of negotiation between modules of CoSolver, and develop algorithms based on other decompositions of TTP. Moreover, we will be interested in substituting exact algorithms for sub-problems of TTP with approximation algorithms.

7. REFERENCES

[1] A computer code for tsp. `http://www.math.uwaterloo.ca/tsp/concorde.html`.

[2] An effective implementation of the lk-heuristic. `http://www.akira.ruc.dk/~keld/research/LKH`.

[3] Millennium problems. `http://www.claymath.org/millenium-problems/p-vs-np-problem`.

[4] D. Applegate, W. Cook, and A. Rohe. Chained lin-kernighan for large traveling salesman problems. *INFORMS Journal on Computing*, 15(1):82–92, 2003.

[5] Y. Bartal and L.-A. Gottlieb. A linear time approximation scheme for euclidean tsp. *IEEE Annual Symp. on Found. of Comp. Sci.*, 0:698–706, 2013.

[6] Y. Bartal, L.-A. Gottlieb, and R. Krauthgamer. The traveling salesman problem: Low-dimensionality implies a polynomial time approximation scheme. In *Proc. of Symp. on Theory of Computing*, pages 663–672, New York, NY, USA, 2012. ACM.

[7] A. Björklund. Below all subsets for permutational counting problems. *CoRR*, abs/1211.0391, 2012.

[8] A. Björklund, T. Husfeldt, P. Kaski, and M. Koivisto. The traveling salesman problem in bounded degree graphs. *ACM Trans. on Algorithms*, 8(2):18, 2012.

[9] M. Bonyadi, Z. Michalewicz, and L. Barone. The travelling thief problem: The first step in the transition from theoretical problems to realistic problems. In *IEEE Congress on Evolutionary Computation (CEC)*, pages 1037–1044, 2013.

[10] N. Christofides. Worst-case analysis of a new heuristic for the travelling salesman problem. Technical Report 388, Graduate School of Industrial Administration, Carnegie Mellon University, 1976.

[11] S. A. Cook. The complexity of theorem-proving procedures. In *Proceedings of the Third Annual ACM Symposium on Theory of Computing*, STOC '71, pages 151–158, New York, NY, USA, 1971. ACM.

[12] M. Dorigo and L. M. Gambardella. Ant colony system: a cooperative learning approach to the traveling salesman problem. *IEEE Transactions on Evolutionary Computation*, 1(1):53–66, 1997.

[13] M. Held and R. M. Karp. A dynamic programming approach to sequencing problems. In *Proceedings of the 1961 16th ACM National Meeting*, ACM '61, pages 71.201–71.204, New York, NY, USA, 1961. ACM.

[14] E. L. Lawler, J. K. Lenstra, A. R. Kan, and D. B. Shmoys. *The traveling salesman problem: a guided tour of combinatorial optimization*, volume 3. Wiley Chichester, 1985.

[15] Z. Michalewicz. Quo vadis, evolutionary computation? In *Advances in Computational Intelligence*, pages 98–121. Springer, 2012.

[16] Z. Michalewicz and D. B. Fogel. *How to solve it: Modern Heuristics*. Springer New York, 2000.

[17] D. Pisinger. *Algorithms for Knapsack Problems*. PhD thesis, Dep. of Comp. Sci., Uni. of Copenhagen, 1995.

[18] D. Pisinger. Where are the hard knapsack problems? *Comp. & Op. Res.*, 32(9):2271–2284, 2005.

[19] S. Polyakovskiy, M. R. Bonyadi, M. Wagner, F. Neumann, and Z. Michalewicz. A comprehensive benchmark set and heuristics for the travelling thief problem. In *Genetic and Evolutionary Computation Conference (GECCO)*. ACM, 2014, To appear.

[20] M. A. Potter and K. A. De Jong. A cooperative coevolutionary approach to function optimization. In *Parallel Problem Solving from Nature—PPSN III*, pages 249–257. Springer, 1994.

[21] A. Rapoprt and R. Solomonof. Connectivity of random nets. *Bulletin of Mathematical Biology*, 13(2):107–117, 1951.

[22] P. Toth and D. Vigo. *The vehicle routing problem*, volume 9. Siam, 2002.

[23] T. Weise, M. Zapf, R. Chiong, and A. Nebro. Why is optimization difficult? In R. Chiong, editor, *Nature-Inspired Algorithms for Optimisation*, volume 193 of *Studies in Computational Intelligence*, pages 1–50. Springer Berlin Heidelberg, 2009.

NSGA-II with Iterated Greedy for a Bi-objective Three-stage Assembly Flowshop Scheduling Problem

Saulo Cunha Campos
Departamento de Informática
Universidade Federal de Viçosa (UFV)
Campus Universitário, Viçosa-MG
+55 (31) 3899-2394, Brazil, 36.570-000
saulo.campos@ufv.br

José Elias Claudio Arroyo
Departamento de Informática
Universidade Federal de Viçosa (UFV)
Campus Universitário, Viçosa-MG
+55 (31) 3899-2394, Brazil, 36.570-000
jarroyo@dpi.ufv.br

ABSTRACTT
In this paper we address a three-stage assembly flowshop scheduling problem where there are *m* machines at the first stage, a transportation machine at the second stage and an assembly machine at the third stage. At the first stage, different parts of a product are manufactured independently on parallel production lines. At the second stage, the manufactured parts are collected and transferred to the next stage. At the third stage, the parts are assembled into final products. The objective is to schedule *n* jobs on the machines so that total flowtime and the total tardiness of the jobs are minimized simultaneously. This problem has many applications in industry and belongs to the class of NP-Hard combinatorial optimization problems. In order to obtain near Pareto optimal solutions, we propose an Elitist Non-dominated Sorting Genetic Algorithm (NSGA-II) coupled with Iterated Greedy (IG) strategy. IG is a simple heuristic that has shown excellent results for different flowshop scheduling problems. A comparative study is presented between the results obtained using the standard NSGA-II, the enhanced NSGA-II with IG approach and a single-objective GRASP heuristic. Experimental results on both medium and large size of instances show the efficiency of the hybrid NSGA-II approach.

Keywords
Assembly Flowshop Scheduling, Multi-objective Optimization, Heuristics, Genetic Algorithms, Local Search.

1. INTRODUCTION
Jobs scheduling is a decision-making problem that occurs in manufacturing systems. This problem deals with the allocation of available resources to jobs over given time periods and the goal is to optimize one or more objectives (or criteria).

The scheduling problems have been thoroughly studied since the mid-50 [3]. Nowadays, scheduling problems are one of the most studied problems. It occurs mainly by two aspects: the first one concerns their practical importance, with various applications in several industries. The second aspect is about the difficulty for solving the majority problems of this class (these problems belong to the class NP-Hard).

The scheduling problem focused in this paper is the three-stage Assembly Flowshop Scheduling (3sAFS) problem. In this problem, *n* jobs (or products) are performed in three stages. At the first stage, the different parts of a job are manufactured independently on *m* parallel machines (each job has *m* parts), at the second stage the produced parts are collected and transferred from the production site to the assembly site, and at the last stage they are assembled into final products. At the second and third stages there is only a single machine. The production shop is composed of three stages that are disposed in series. Each job visits each stage in order, characterizing a permutation flowshop. This problem is NP-hard since its special case when $m = 1$ (which is a regular three-machine flowshop scheduling problem) is NP-hard [10].

In order to make the problem real, we consider sequence dependent setup times on machines of the first stage, transportation machine and assembly machine. Setup time is necessary to prepare the machine (for example, tooling, cleaning, positioning accessories, inspection of materials, among others) when a job *j* is processed immediately after another job *i*.

The 3sAFS problem addressed in this work is to find the processing sequence of jobs (schedule) in order to minimize simultaneously two objectives: the total flowtime and the total tardiness. The goal is to provide the decision maker with a set of efficient schedules (Pareto-optimal solutions) such that he may choose the most suitable schedule.

In the literature, other versions of the Assembly Flowshop Scheduling (AFS) problem have been studied by some authors. Some solution approaches have been proposed to solve the single objective two-stage AFS (2sAFS) problem. For the maximum job completion time (makespan) minimization some heuristics methods were developed by Potts et al. [23]. Al-Anzi and Allahverdi [1] consider the total completion time minimization and propose three metaheuristics, simulated annealing, tabu search, and a hybrid tabu search. Maximum lateness criterion is minimized by Allahverdi and Al-Anzi [2]. They consider sequence independent setup times and propose a self-adaptive differential evolution heuristic.

The single objective 3sAFS problem has been also addressed by some authors. For minimizing the makespan, Koulamas and Kyparisis [15] analyze the worst-case ratio bound for several constructive heuristics. Koulamas and Kyparisis [15] extended the 2sAFS problem to 3sAFS problem with the objective of minimizing the makespan. For the 3sAFS problem with sequence dependent setup times on first and third stages, a mathematical MIP model for minimizing the total completion time is proposed by Andrés and Hatami [4].

The 3sAFS problem with multi-objective optimization has been less studied. Some authors address bi-objectives problems but

GECCO'14, July 12–16, 2014, Vancouver, BC, Canada.

http://dx.doi.org/10.1145/2576768.2598324

they use weighted linear functions, that is, weights (preferences) are defined to each objective and them are combined in a linear function.

To minimize the weighted sum of the mean flowtime and maximum tardiness in a 3sAFS problem with sequence dependent set up times, a tabu search and a simulated annealing metaheuristic were developed by Hatami et al. [12]. For the same problem, a Greedy Randomized Adaptive Search Procedure (GRASP) was proposed by Campos et al. [7]. Maleki et al. [17] consider a 3sAFS problem with blocking and sequence dependent setup times with the objective to minimize the weighted mean completion time and makespan. These authors propose a metaheuristic based on simulated annealing.

Recently, Tajbakhsh et al. [26] apply multi-objective algorithms based on genetic algorithm and particle swarm optimization for a bi-objective 3sAFS problem with the objective to minimize the makespan and sum of the earliness and tardiness costs, simultaneously.

In this paper, multi-objective optimization is understood in its traditional form, which involves the generation of the Pareto-optimal or efficient solutions. To solve the bi-objective 3sAFS problem, we propose a hybrid algorithm based on NSGA-II (Elitist Non-dominated Sorting Genetic Algorithm) and Iterated Greedy (IG) algorithm.

NSGA-II proposed by [8] has been widely used for solving a variety of multi-objective optimization problems. IG algorithm, proposed by [25], is a powerful heuristic that has been applied to all sorts of scheduling problems obtaining high quality results. The main feature of the IG is its simplicity which is contrary to sophisticated algorithms that embed problem specific knowledge and that usually have many control parameters. Despite its simplicity, IG has shown state-of-the-art results under different flowshop variants and objectives [21].

In the literature, some authors show that the performance of the NSGA-II algorithm can be improved by using local search techniques [9] [11] [22]. To the best of our knowledge this is the first paper that combines NSGA-II with IG.

The rest of this paper is organized as follows. Section 2 presents the 3sAFS problem statement. In Section 3 we describe the proposed algorithm. The computational experiments and the statistical analyses of the obtained results are presented in Section 4. The last Section concludes the work.

2. PROBLEM STATEMENT

The 3sAFS problem investigated in this work consists in processing (or manufacturing) n jobs (products) on three stages production shop. Each job has m components (or parts) that are manufactured separately at the first stage (production line composed by m parallel machines). At the second stage, the produced parts of a job are collected and transported from production site to assembly machine. At the third stage, the parts are assembled into a final product. All jobs are available to be processed at time zero. All machines (including transportation and assembly machines) process only one job at a time without interruption or preemption. In addition, the sequence of jobs at all stages is the same (only permutation schedules are considered).

The processing time of a job j on machine k of the first stage is known and defined by $t_{[j,k]}$. This time corresponds to the manufacturing time of part k. The transportation time ($tt_{[j]}$), assembly time (at[j]) and the due date ($d_{[j]}$) of a job j also are known.

Between the processing of two consecutive jobs i and j, on a machine k of the first stage, a sequence dependent setup time $s1_{[k,i,j]}$ is considered. The setups times on the transportation and assembly machines are defined by $s2_{[i,j]}$ and $s3_{[i,j]}$, respectively, where i and j are two consecutive jobs.

The objective of the problem is to determine a permutation schedule s (sequence of the jobs) in order to minimize the total flowtime (F) and the total tardiness of the jobs (T).

The two objectives F and T are computed by the following equations:

$$f_1 = F = \sum_{j=1}^{n} C_{3[j]}$$

$$f_2 = T = \sum_{j=1}^{n} max\left\{0,\ C_{3[j]} - d_j\right\}$$

where, $C_{3[j]}$ is the completion time of job j at the third stage. $C_{3[j]}$ is calculated by the following equation:

$$C_{3[j]} = \max\left\{C_{2[j]},\ C_{3[j-1]}\right\} + s3_{[j-1,j]} + at_{[j]}\ ,$$

where, $C_{1[j]}$ and $C_{2[j]}$ are the completion times of job j at the first and second stage, respectively. j-1 is the immediately preceding job of job j in a sequence. $C_{1[j]}$ and $C_{2[j]}$ are calculated by the following equations:

$$C_{1[j]} = \max_{k=1,\dots,m}\left\{\sum_{i=1}^{j} s1_{[k,i-1,i]} + t_{[j,k]}\right\}$$

$$C_{2[j]} = max\left\{C_{1[j]},\ C_{2[j-1]}\right\} + s2_{[j-1,j]} + tt_{[j]}\ .$$

The optimized objectives are very important in manufacture systems. The first objective F is related to minimizing work-in-process inventories, while the second objective T is related to job due dates (customer service). These objectives are often of conflicting nature, usually there is not a single solution s optimizing F and T at once. Optimality in multi-objective optimization problems is therefore understood in the sense of Pareto-optimality, and the resolution of multi-objective optimization problems lies in the identification of all solutions belonging to the Pareto or efficient set, containing all alternatives s which are not dominated by any other alternative s'. To properly compare two solutions in a bi-objective minimization problem, the following definitions are used:

- A solution s dominates s' if the point $(f_1(s), f_2(s))$ dominates $(f_1(s'), f_2(s'))$, that is, $f_i(s) \le f_i(s')$ for i=1, 2, and $f_i(s) < f_i(s')$ for at least one i.
- A solution s is Pareto-optimal (or efficient) if there is no s' such that $(f_1(s'), f_2(s'))$ dominates $(f_1(s), f_2(s))$.

In Figure 1, we present two schedules (solutions) for an instance of the 3sAFS problem with n = 4 jobs. Dark blocks denote the required setup times. In this instance the first stage has m = 2 machines (M1 and M2). The transportation and assembly machines are Mt and Ma, respectively. The due date of jobs are d_1 = 20, d_2 = 15, d_3 = 43 and d_3 = 33. The processing times of jobs and the setups times are showed in the Figure 1. For this instance, the set of Pareto optimal solutions is formed by the following four job schedules: $s_1 = \{2, 1, 4, 3\}$, $s_2 = \{4, 2, 1, 3\}$, $s_3 = \{3, 4, 2, 1\}$ and $s_4 = \{4, 3, 2, 1\}$. The objective values of these schedules are $(F(s_1),T(s_1)) = (114, 6)$, $(F(s_2), T(s_2)) = (108, 16)$, $(F(s_3), T(s_3)) = (106, 28)$ and $(F(s_4), T(s_4)) = (104, 29)$, respectively. Note that the schedules s_1 and s_4 (showed in Figure 1) provide the minimum value of the total tardiness (T) and the total flowtime (F), respectively. Figure 2 shows the Pareto optimal front for the considered instance. Note that, the objectives F and T are conflicting, that is, there is not a single schedule that minimizes F and T at once.

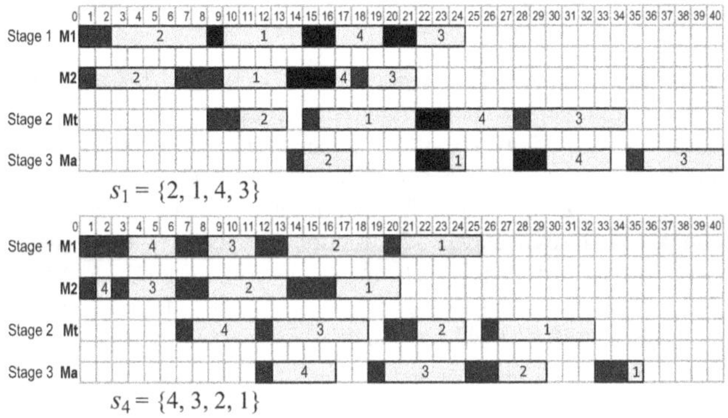

Figure 1: Two schedules for an instance of the 3sAFS problem.

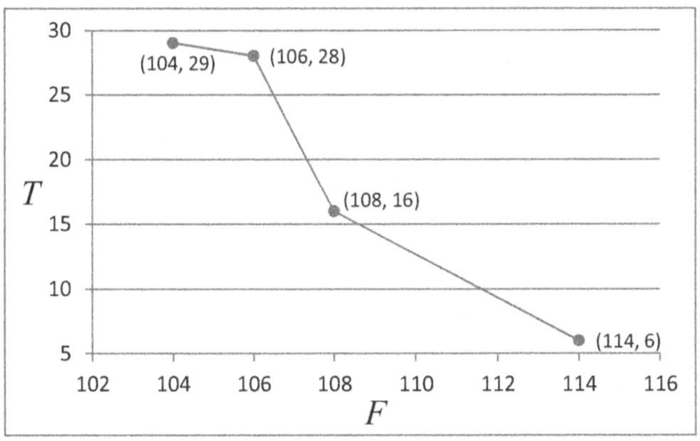

Figure 2: Pareto optimal front for an instance with n=4 jobs.

The goal of the bi-objective 3sAFS problem, addressed in this paper, is to determine the set of the Pareto-optimal permutation schedules in order to minimize F and T.

3. NSGA-II WITH ITERATED GREEDY

In this section we describe the proposed hybrid algorithm that combines the standard NSGA-II [8] with Iterated Greedy (IG) strategy. The proposed algorithm is named NSGA2-IG and is showed in Figure 3. The pseudocode description of NSGA2-IG is presented in Algorithm 1. The algorithm has three input parameters, N (size of a population), d (parameter used in the IG procedure) and *MaxCPUTime* (an amount of CPU time used as stopping criterion).

Initially (iteration $t = 0$), two solution populations P_t and Q_t, each of size N, are created. The solutions are generated randomly and by using a constructive heuristic.

The IG procedure begins with a non-dominated solution s selected randomly from P_t, executes a greedy local search and returns a population D' of non-dominated solutions. At the iteration $t = 0$, the IG procedure is not executed (D' = ∅).

The three populations P_t, Q_t and D' are combined to form a population R_t of size $2N + |D'|$, where $|P_t| = |Q_t| = N$. Next, a non-dominated sorting is used to classify the entire population $R_t = P_t \cup Q_t \cup D'$. Once, the non-dominated sorting is over, the population R_t becomes subdivided in k fronts ($F_1, F_2,\ldots, F_k$). All elements of the same front have the same non-domination rank. The best N solutions of the best non-dominated fronts are chosen to be the next generation parent solutions P_{t+1}. The N members of the parent population P_{t+1} are chosen from the first l non-dominated fronts $F_1, F_2,\ldots, F_{l-1}, F_l$ ($l \le k$), such that $|F_1 \cup F_2 \cup \ldots \cup F_{l-1}| < N$. If $|F_1 \cup F_2 \cup \ldots \cup F_l| = N$, the parent population is $P_{t+1} = F_1 \cup F_2 \cup \ldots \cup F_l$, and the solutions of $F_{l+1} \cup \ldots \cup F_k$ are rejected. If $|F_1 \cup F_2 \cup \ldots \cup F_l| > N$, the solutions of the last front F_l are sorted using the crowded distance comparison operator in descending order. The worst $|F_1 \cup F_2 \cup \ldots \cup F_l| - N$ solutions of front F_l are rejected. The solutions of $F_{l+1} \cup \ldots \cup F_k$ are also rejected. The new population P_{t+1} is now used for selection, crossover and mutation operators and to create a child population Q_{t+1} of size N. At next iteration (t=1), the IG procedure is executed. IG begins with a solution s selected randomly from F_1 ($F_1 \subset P_t$).

The above mentioned mechanism is continued until the stopping criterion is satisfied. The overall non-dominated solutions are kept as the final result.

```
Algorithm 1. NSGA2-IG(N, d, MaxCPUTime)
Inputs:
    N: Population size
    d: Parameter used in the IG strategy
    MaxCPUTime: Maximum CPU time that algorithm run
Output:
    D: Set of non-dominated solutions
Begin
   t ← 0; // iteration counter
   Pt ← ∅; //population of N solutions
   Qt ← ∅; //population of N child solutions
   D' ← ∅; //non-dominated solutions found by IG
   Rt ← ∅; //R=Pt∪Qt∪D', population to be classified
   CPUTime ← 0;
   Pt ← GenerateInitialPopulation(N);
   Qt ← GenerateInitialPopulation(N);
   while (CPUtime < MaxCPUTime) do
      if ( t ≥ 1) then
         s ← SolutionSelectedRandomly(F1);
         D' ← IG( s, d ); //IG method
      end-if
      Rt ← Pt ∪ Qt ∪ D';
      F1,F2...Fk ← Non_DominatedSorting( Rt );
      CrowdingDistanceSorting( Rt );
      Pt+1 ← Choose_The_Best_N_Solutions( Rt );
      Qt+1←SelectionCrossoverMutation(Pt+1, N);
      t ← t+1;
      updateCPUTime(CPUTime);
   end_while
   D ← F1;
   Return D;
End
```

In the next subsections, we describe in detail the population initialization phase, selection, crossover, mutation and the Iterated Greedy intensification.

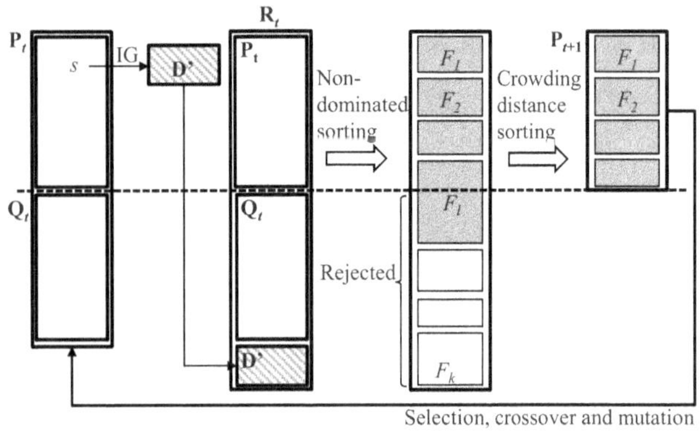

Figure 3. NSGA2-IG basic iteration.

3.1 Initialization

A solution (sequence of n jobs) is represented by an array with n elements. The NSGA2-IG algorithm begins with a population with $2N$ solutions. Part of this population is generated by the multi-objective partial enumeration heuristic (MOPE) proposed by Arroyo and Armentano [5]. The other part of the population was generated randomly.

MOPE heuristic is inspired on the NEH heuristics proposed by Nawaz [20]. MOPE uses the Pareto dominance concept to maintain not just one incomplete partial solution at each iteration (as in NEH), but a whole set of non-dominated partial solutions generated during the job insertion process. To minimize the combination of objectives total flowtime and total tardiness, the MOPE heuristic uses the following dispatching rules:

SPT (shortest processing time): the jobs are arranged in increasing order of the total processing time on the three stages.

TLB (tardiness lower bound): the jobs are arranged in decreasing order of a tardiness lower bound of job i [5].

The MOPE heuristic generates N_h ($<2N$) non-dominated solutions. Then, $2N$ - N_h solutions are generated randomly.

3.2 Selection, Crossover and Mutation

To create a child population Q_t, the following operators are executed: selection, recombination and mutation.

From two parent solutions, two child solutions are created. Each parent solution is selected from population P_t by using the binary tournament technique. This technique consists in choosing randomly two solutions of the population and the best one is selected. The solutions belonging to smaller fonts are always better. When comparing two solutions belonging to the same front, the one with the bigger crowding distance wins.

The crossover operator creates offspring solutions by coalescing two parents solutions. The aim is to generate better children, i.e. to generate better solutions after the crossover. Many different general and specific crossover operators have been proposed for the flowshop scheduling problems in the literature. In this paper, we use two effective operators: Two-Point Crossover (TPX) [13] and Similar Block 2-Point Order Crossover (SB2OX) [24].

The mutation operator used here is the interchange operator. This operator randomly choses two points along the child chromosome and swaps with each other and genes (jobs) in these two points are reversed. In each child solution, two swaps are performed with a mutation probability.

3.3 Iterated Greedy Intensification

To accelerate the convergence speed of the NSGA-II algorithm, we employ an intensification procedure based on the Iterated Greedy (IG) heuristic. IG is a simple method which has been applied to different sorts of single-objective scheduling problems. The first application of IG for flowshop scheduling problems was given by Ruiz and Stützle [25]. Minella, et al. [19] propose an adaptation of IG for multi-objective flowshop scheduling problems. Arroyo et al. [6] used the same intensification procedure in a multi-objective VNS heuristic to solve a single machine scheduling problem.

In this paper, the intensification procedure based on IG begins from a solution s selected randomly from the best set of non-dominated solutions (front F_1 obtained by the non-dominated sorting strategy). The pseudocode description of the used IG intensification is showed in Algorithm 2. The procedure is composed of two stages: destruction and construction. In the destruction stage, d jobs (selected randomly) are removed from s and a partial solution s_p (of size n-d) is obtained. The removed jobs are stored in J (where $J_{[i]}$, i=1,...,d, are the removed jobs). The construction stage has d steps. In step i=1, (n-d+1) partial solutions are constructed by inserting job $J_{[1]}$ in all possible positions of s_p. From the (n-d+1) partial solutions, the set D_i of non-dominated partial solutions are selected. In the next step, new solutions (of size n-d+2) are obtained by inserting job $J_{[2]}$ in each partial non-dominated solutions. From the solutions constructed in each step, the non-dominated solutions are always selected. In step d, a set D' of complete non-dominated solutions is determined. Figure 4 illustrates the idea of the greedy intensification procedure that starts from a solution s with n = 4 jobs and considering d =2.

```
Algorithm 2. IG (s, d)
Inputs:
   s: solution chosen randomly from F1
   d: number of jobs to be removed from s
Output:
   D': A set of non-dominated solutions obtained from s
begin
   J ← ∅
   //Destruction stage
   for (i ← 1 to d)
      J[i] ←remove a randomly selected job from s;
   sp ← s; //partial solution with n-d jobs
   //Construction stage:
   D' ← {sp}
   //Construction of non-dominated solution:
   for ( i ← 1 to d)
      Di ← ∅;
      for ( each partial solution s' of D')
          Ds' ← non-dominated solutions obtained
               after inserting job J[i] in all
               possible positions of s';
          Di ← non-dominated solution Di ∪ Ds';
      end-for
      D' ← Di;
   end-for
   Return D';
end
```

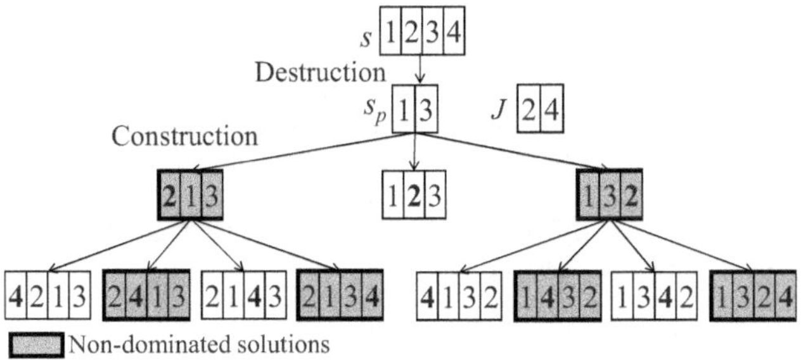

Figure 4. Iterated Greedy Intensification.

4. COMPUTATIONAL EXPERIMENTS

In this work, we analyze the efficiency of the IG intensification procedure used in the NSGA-II algorithm proposed by Deb et al. [8]. To solve the bi-objective three-stage assembly flowshop scheduling problem addressed in this work, we compare the hybrid NSGA2-IG algorithm with the standard NSGA-II and with a single-objective GRASP algorithm proposed by [7]. All algorithms were coded in C++ and executed on an Intel(R) Core Quad Q9400 2.67GHz and 8 GB of RAM.

The single-objective GRASP algorithm is based on the minimization of different weighted utility functions ($f_w = w_1 \times F + w_2 \times T$, where $w_1 + w_2 = 1$). To determinate a set of non-dominated solutions, the GRASP algorithm was executed with different weight vectors (w_1, w_2). We used the following eleven weights: (w_1, w_2) = (0, 1), (0.1, 0.9), (0.2, 0.8), (0.3, 0.7),…,(0.9, 0.1) and (1, 0). In each execution, a single solution was obtained. We selected the non-dominated solutions from the eleven obtained solutions.

In each execution of the algorithms NSGA2-IG, NSGA-II and GRASP, we use the same stopping criterion which is based on an amount of CPU time. This time was fixed in $110 \times n \times m$ milliseconds.

4.1 Benchmark Instances for the Problem

The instances of the problem were generated randomly according to Liefooghe et al. [16]. We considered test problems with number of jobs $n \in \{30, 50, 80, 100, 200\}$ and number of machines (at first stage) $m \in \{5, 10, 20\}$. The processing times are generated randomly, according to a uniform distribution: t_{ij}, tt_j, $ta_j \in U[0, 99]$. The setup times are uniformly distributed in the range [0–49]. The due dates for every jobs were generated randomly, with uniform distribution, over the interval $[3 \times p, (n+2) \times p]$, where p is the average value of previously generated processing times. We use the factor 3 because the 3sAFS problem can be considered as a flowshop with three machines. Thus, a due date d_i roughly lies between the average completion date of the first scheduled job and the average completion date of the last scheduled job [16]. For each configuration $n \times m$, 10 instances were generated. Therefore, a total of 150 instances were tested.

4.2 Performance Measures

In this work, to assess the quality of the non-dominated solutions attained by the three algorithms GRASP, NSGA-II and NSGA2-IG, two multi-objective performance measures are used: distance metric and hypervolume indicator.

We denoted by D_1, D_2 and D_3 the sets of non-dominated solutions (approximated Pareto fronts) obtained by the algorithms GRASP, NSGA-II and NSGA2-IG, respectively. We measure the quality of each set D_i (i =1,2,3) with relation to the reference set (*Ref*) constituted by gathering all non-dominated solutions obtained by the three algorithms, that is, *Ref* is the set of approximated non-dominated solutions obtained from ($D_1 \cup D_2 \cup D_3$). The *Ref* set is the best known Pareto-optimal front.

The used performance measures are defined as follow:

Average distance: measures the proximity between the solutions $s' \in D_i$ and the solutions $s \in Ref$. It also measures the solutions spreading on set D_i [14]. This metric is defined as follows:

$$d_{av}(D_i) = 100 \times \frac{1}{|Ref|} \sum_{s \in Ref} \min_{s' \in D_i} d(s, s')$$

where, $d(s,s') = \max\left\{\frac{f_1(s) - f_1(s')}{\Delta_1}, \frac{f_2(s) - f_2(s')}{\Delta_2}\right\}$,

and Δ_i is the difference between the biggest and smallest value of the objective f_i, considering the solutions of set *Ref*. Smaller values of $d_{av}(D_i)$ correspond to higher quality of the solutions in D_i.

Hypervolume indicator: measures the covered or dominated area by set D_i. In this paper, this metric is defined as follows:

$$H^*(D_i) = 100 \times \frac{H(Ref) - H(D_i)}{H(Ref)}$$

where, $H(X)$ is the hypervolume (area) of the solution space dominated by the solutions of the set X, i.e. the portion of the objective space that is dominated by X. Note that, we considered the relative percentage deviation of $H(D_i)$ with relation to $H(Ref)$. Smaller values of $H^*(D_i)$ correspond to higher quality of the solutions in D_i. The hypervolume indicator was introduced by Zitzler and Thiele [27].

4.3 Parameters of the Algorithms

The parameters of the algorithms NSGA-II and NGSA2-IG were experimentally fine-tuned. The algorithm GRASP was implemented following the original paper [7].

The best results of the standard NGSA-II were achieved using the following parameters: Population size N = 100. Crossover operator: TPX and SB2OX (to generate a child solution, a crossover operator is chosen randomly). Crossover probability: 100%. Mutation probability 30%.

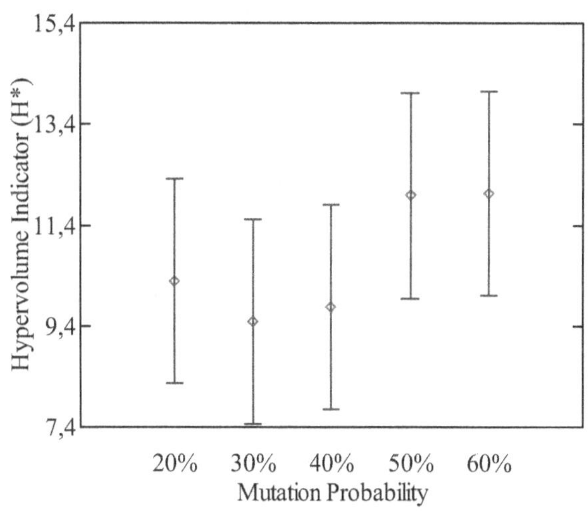

Figure 5. Means plot and Tukeys HSD intervals with 95% confidence level - Calibration of the mutation probability of the NSGA-II.

Figure 5 shows the performance of the NSGA-II algorithm (regarding the hypervolume indicator) for different mutation probabilities (20%, 30%, 40% and 50%). We performed the non-parametric Kruskal-Wallis Test [18] to validate the obtained results. The statistical analysis indicates that the obtained results are not significantly different for the five mutation probability values. However, we can see that the lowest average hypervolume was obtained for mutation probability 30%.

The NSGA2-IG uses the same parameters of NSGA-II. For the parameter d used the Iterated Greedy intensification, we tested different values. The best results were achieved using d =4 (for instances with $n \leq 100$) and $d = 2$ (for instances with $n = 200$).

4.4 Obtained Results

The non-dominated solutions obtained by the proposed hybrid algorithm NSGA2-IG are compared with the non-dominated solutions obtained by the other tested algorithms (GRASP and NSGA-II). To solve each test problem, the algorithms were run 10 times for all the 150 instances of the 3sAFS problem. The sets D_1, D_2 and D_3 contain the non-dominated solutions found among all the runs of the algorithms GRASP, NSGA-II and NSGA2-IG, respectively. For each instance, the reference set *Ref* is non-dominated solutions obtained from $(D_1 \cup D_2 \cup D_3)$.

We note that, for all the 150 instances tested, the algorithms NSGA2-IG and GRASP determine 94.66% and 5.49% of the reference solutions, respectively. The NSGA-II algorithm does not determine any reference solution.

The distance and hypervolume measures are calculated for each set D_i. In Table 1, results attained by the algorithms in relation to the average distance metric are presented. In this Table, the results (average values) are grouped according to the number of jobs and number of machines ($n \times m$) of the instances.

We can see that, for all groups of instances the NSGA2-IG algorithm is the one that produces lower average distances, that is, closer to zero. Then the proposed algorithm is notoriously better than the standard NSGA-II and GRASP. We can see also that the algorithm GRASP performs better than NSGA-II.

The distance metric measures the proximity between the solutions of a set D_i and the solutions of set *Ref*. Therefore, the higher the percentage of solutions of D_i in the *Ref* set, the lower tends to be the values of the distance metrics. The values of the distance metrics tend to be smaller, but those values also depend of the distance between D_i solutions and solutions belonging to *Ref* set obtained by other algorithms.

Table 2 presents the comparison of the algorithms regarding the hypervolume indicator. In this Table we can see again that NSGA2-IG algorithm presents lower average values of the relative percentage deviation of the hypervolume (H^*) for all group of instances.

4.5 Statistical Analysis

In order to validate the obtained results, we apply again a statistical analysis using the average distance (d_{av}) and hypervolume (H^*) measures as response variables.

First, to verify if the observed differences between the obtained results are statistically significant, we performed an analysis of variance (ANOVA) [18]. The three main assumptions of ANOVA were checked: normality, homoscedasticity and independence. Since the normality test was not satisfied, we performed the non-parametric Kruskal-Wallis Test. This test compares between the medians of the three algorithms to determine if there is a significant difference. The Kruskal-Wallis results (not shown in detail due to reasons of space) indicate that there is statistically significant difference between the obtained results at a 95% confidence level. It was observed that the computed P-value is less than 0.05 which shows that exist significant difference between the algorithms. The Kruskal Wallis Test does not specify which algorithms are different. So, we use a non-parametric Multiple Comparisons test to compare each pair of means with a 95% confidence level.

Table 1. Average distance (d_{av}) results.

n	m	GRASP	NSGA-II	NSGA2_IG
30	**5**	7.21	23.52	1.05
30	**10**	6.92	26.29	0,67
30	**20**	8.52	25.53	0.61
50	**5**	13.48	27.65	0.50
50	**10**	13.11	24.82	0.26
50	**20**	16.98	31.16	0.21
80	**5**	14.41	24.64	0.55
80	**10**	20.36	32.21	0.27
80	**20**	19.51	36.34	0.09
100	**5**	16.93	25.81	0.25
100	**10**	14.80	29.30	0.19
100	**20**	22.82	40.17	0.22
200	**5**	10.77	19.45	0.31
200	**10**	13.59	22.18	0.16
200	**20**	17.92	25.26	0.06
	Average	**14.49**	**27.62**	**0.36**

Table 2. Hypervolume indicator (H^*) results.

n	m	GRASP	NSGA-II	NSGA2_IG
30	**5**	13.75	37.68	3.66
30	**10**	15.92	36.15	3.74
30	**20**	16.63	34.48	3.81
50	**5**	23.25	43.07	3.82
50	**10**	18.28	39.27	3.25
50	**20**	22.46	36.88	3.28
80	**5**	19.34	39.68	2.89
80	**10**	28.00	43.45	2.70
80	**20**	23.12	40.88	2.59
100	**5**	22.90	41.37	2.77
100	**10**	19.71	40.10	2.06
100	**20**	23.55	41.34	2.03
200	**5**	15.29	38.62	2.03
200	**10**	19.60	34.96	2.17
200	**20**	23.24	29.03	2.18
	Average	**20.34**	**38.46**	**2.87**

The Tables 3 and 4 show the result of the Multiple Comparisons test regarding the average distance and hypervolume indicator metrics, respectively. The first column of these Tables shows the pairs of algorithms being compared. The "Difference" column displays the sample mean of the first algorithm minus that of the second. The "+/- Limits" column shows an uncertainty interval for the difference. Any pair of algorithms for which the absolute value of the difference exceeds the limit is statistically significant at the selected confidence level 95% and is indicated by an asterisk (*) in the "Significant" column. In Tables 3 and 4 we can see that there are significant differences between all the pairs of algorithms. The same statistical analysis can be displayed in Figures 6 and 7.

Table 3. Multiple Comparisons test - Average Distance.

Contrast	*Significant*	Difference	+/- Limits
GRASP ↔ NSGA-II	*	-13.1333	3.07722
GRASP ↔ NSGA2_IG	*	14.1287	3.07722
NSGA-II ↔ NSGA2_IG	*	27.262	3.07722

Table 4. Multiple Comparisons test - Hypervolume Indicator.

Contrast	*Significant*	Difference	+/- Limits
GRASP ↔ NSGA-II	*	-18.1287	1.46216
GRASP ↔ NSGA2_IG	*	18.6296	1.46216
NSGA-II ↔ NSGA2_IG	*	36.7583	1.46216

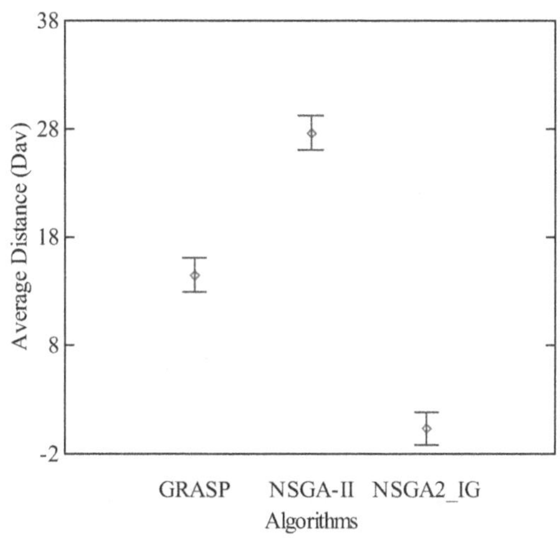

Figure 6. Means plot and Tukeys HSD intervals with 95% confidence level - Average Distance metric (d_{av}).

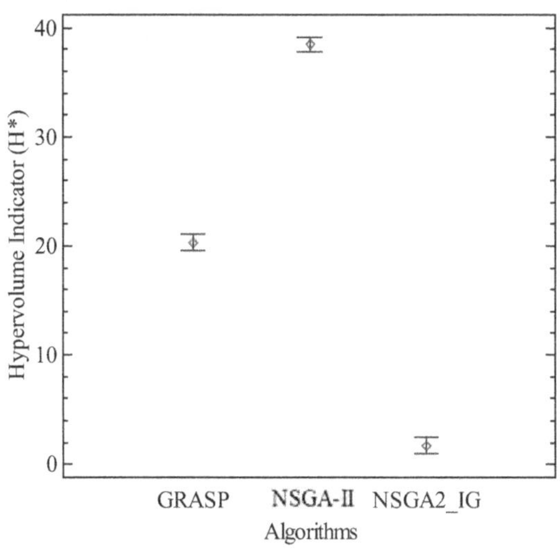

Figure 7. Means plot and Tukeys HSD intervals with 95% confidence level - Hypervolume Indicator (H^*).

Figures 6 and 7 show the means plot and Tukey's Honestly Signifiant Difference (HSD) intervals at 95% confidence level from the Multiple Comparisons test for two performance measures, respectively. Since the confidence interval of NSGA2-IG algorithm does not overlap any of the other intervals, the mean of NSGA2-IG is significantly different than that of the other two algorithms. So we can state that, on average, NSGA2-IG is better than NSGA-II and GRASP. We can see also that, on average, GRASP is better than NSGA-II.

The statistical analysis shows that the use of IG improves significantly the results of the basic NSGA-II algorithm.

5. CONCLUSIONS

This paper has proposed a hybrid algorithm for a bi-objective three-stage Assembly Flowshop Scheduling problem with sequence-dependent setup times. In order to find an approximation of the Pareto optimal set, the hybrid algorithm (NSGA2-IG) combines the basic NSGA-II [8] scheme with an intensification strategy based on Iterated Greedy.

We have performed a comparative study between the proposed algorithm and two other algorithms considering medium and large instances of the problem. According to the obtained results and the statistical analyses, the proposed NSGA2-IG algorithm performed better than the two algorithms, NSGA-II and GRASP. The results of NSGA-II were improved significantly by using IG intensification. After the computational experiments we can conclude that the proposed hybrid algorithm shows an excellent performance overcoming the original NSGA-II.

6. ACKNOWLEDGMENTS

This work was supported by Fundação de Amparo à Pesquisa do Estado de Minas Gerais (FAPEMIG), Conselho Nacional de Desenvolvimento Científico e Tecnológico (CNPq) and Coordenação de Aperfeiçoamento de Pessoal de Nível Superior (CAPES).

7. REFERENCES

[1] Al-Anzi, F. S., and Allahverdi, A. 2006. A hybrid tabu search heuristic for the two-stage assembly scheduling problem. *International Journal of Operations Research*, 3, 2 (2006), 109-119.

[2] Al-Anzi, F. S., and Allahverdi, A. 2007. A self-adaptive differential evolution heuristic for two-stage assembly scheduling problem to minimize maximum lateness with setup times. *European Journal of Operational Research*, 182, 1 (oct. 2007) 80-94.

[3] Allahverdi, A., Ng, C. T., Cheng, T. E., and Kovalyov, M. Y. 2008. A survey of scheduling problems with setup times or costs. *European Journal of Operational Research*, 187, 3 (2008), 985-1032.

[4] Andrés, C., and Hatami, S. 2011. The three stage assembly permutation flowshop scheduling problem. In *V international conference on industrial engineering and industrial management.* (Colombia, Cartagena, September 7-9, 2011). 867-875.

[5] Arroyo, J. E. C., and Armentano, V. A. 2004. A partial enumeration heuristic for multi-objective flowshop scheduling problems. *Journal of the Operational Research Society*, 55, 9 (sep. 2004), 1000-1007.

[6] Arroyo, J. E. C., Ottoni, R. S. and Oliveira, A. P. 2011. Multi-objective Variable Neighborhood Search Algorithms

for a Single Machine Scheduling Problem with Distinct due Windows. *Electronic Notes in Theoretical Computer Science*, 281 (Dec. 2011), 5-19.

[7] Campos, S. C., Arroyo, J. E. C., and Gonçalves, L. B. 2013. Uma heuristica grasp-vnd para o problema de sequenciamento de tarefas num ambiente assembly flowshop com três estágios e tempos de setup dependentes da sequência. In *Proceedings of the XLV Brazilian Symposium of Operational Research.* (Natal-RN, Brazil, Setember 16 - 19, 2013). 2147-2158.

[8] Deb, K., Pratap, A., Agarwal, S., and Meyarivan, T. A. M. T. 2002. A fast and elitist multiobjective genetic algorithm: NSGA-II. *Evolutionary Computation*, IEEE Transactions on, 6, 2 (Apr. 2002), 182-197.

[9] Deb, K., Steuer, R. E., Tewari, R., and Tewari, R. 2011. Bi-objective portfolio optimization using a customized hybrid NSGA-II procedure. In *Proceedings of the 6th international conference on Evolutionary Multi-criterion Optimization, EMO 2011.* (Ouro Preto-MG, Brazil, April 5-8, 2011). Springer Berlin Heidelberg, 358-373.

[10] Garey M.R., Johnson D.S., Sethi R. 1976. The complexity of flowshop and job shop scheduling. Mathematics and Operations Research, 1, 2 (May. 1976), 117–29.

[11] Guo, Y., Chen, Z. R., Ruan, Y. L., and Zhang, J. 2012. Application of NSGA-II with local search to multi-dock cross-docking sheduling problem. In *2012 IEEE International Conference on Systems, Man, and Cybernetics, SMC.* (Seoul, Korea, October 14-17, 2012). IEEE, 779-784.

[12] Hatami, S., Ebrahimnejad, S., Tavakkoli-Moghaddam, R., and Maboudian, Y. 2010. Two meta-heuristics for three-stage assembly flowshop scheduling with sequence-dependent setup times. *The International Journal of Advanced Manufacturing Technology*, 50, 9-12 (oct. 2010), 1153-1164.

[13] Ishibuchi, H., Yoshida, T., and Murata, T. 2003. Balance between genetic search and local search in memetic algorithms for multiobjective permutation flowshop scheduling. *IEEE Transactions on Evolutionary Computation*, 7, 2, (Apr. 2003), 204-223.

[14] Knowles, J., and Corne, D. 2002. On metrics for comparing nondominated sets. In *Proceedings of the 2002 Congress on Evolutionary Computation, CEC'02.* (Honolulu, HI, May 12-17, 2002). IEEE, 1, 711-716.

[15] Koulamas, C., and J Kyparisis, G. 2001. The three-stage assembly flowshop scheduling problem. *Computers & Operations Research*, 28, 7 (jun. 2001), 689-704.

[16] Liefooghe, A., Basseur, M., Humeau, J., Jourdan, L., and Talbi, E. G. 2012. On optimizing a bi-objective flowshop scheduling problem in an uncertain environment. *Computers & Mathematics with Applications*, 64, 12 (dec. 2012), 3747-3762.

[17] Maleki-Darounkolaei, A., Modiri, M., Tavakkoli-Moghaddam, R., and Seyyedi, I. 2012. A three-stage assembly flow shop scheduling problem with blocking and sequence-dependent set up times. *Journal of Industrial Engineering International*, 8, 8 (oct. 2012), 1-7.

[18] Montgomery, D. C., and Montgomery, D. C. 1997. *Design and analysis of experiments* (Vol. 7). New York: Wiley.

[19] Minella, G., Ruiz, R., and Ciavotta, M. 2011. Restarted Iterated Pareto Greedy algorithm for multi-objective flowshop scheduling problems. *Computers & Operations Research*, 38, 11 (Nov. 2011), 1521-1533.

[20] Nawaz, M., Enscore, E. E., and Ham, I. 1983. A heuristic algorithm for the m-machine, n-job flow-shop sequencing problem. *Omega*, 11, 1 (1983), 91-95.

[21] Pan, Q. K., and Ruiz, R. 2014. An effective iterated greedy algorithm for the mixed no-idle permutation flowshop scheduling problem. *Omega*, 44, (Apr. 2014), 41-50.

[22] Pires, D. F., Antunes, C. H., and Martins, A. G. 2012. NSGA-II with local search for a multi-objective reactive power compensation problem. *International Journal of Electrical Power & Energy Systems,* 43, 1 (dec. 2012), 313-324.

[23] Potts, C. N., Sevast'Janov, S. V., Strusevich, V. A., Van Wassenhove, L. N., and Zwaneveld, C. M. 1995. The two-stage assembly scheduling problem: complexity and approximation. *Operations Research*, 43, 2 (Apr. 1995), 346-355.

[24] Ruiz, R., Maroto, C., and Alcaraz, J. 2005. Solving the flowshop scheduling problem with sequence dependent setup times using advanced metaheuristics. *European Journal of Operational Research*, 165, 1 (Aug. 2005) 34-54.

[25] Ruiz, R., and Stützle, T. 2008. An iterated greedy heuristic for the sequence dependent setup times flowshop problem with makespan and weighted tardiness objectives. *European Journal of Operational Research*, 187, 3 (jun. 2008), 1143-1159.

[26] Tajbakhsh, Z., Fattahi, P., and Behnamian, J. 2013. Multi-objective assembly permutation flow shop scheduling problem: a mathematical model and a meta-heuristic algorithm. *Journal of the Operational Research Society*. (set. 2013).

[27] Zitzler, E., and Thiele, L. 1998. Multiobjective optimization using evolutionary algorithms – a comparative case study. In *Proceedings of the 5th International Conference Amsterdam on Parallel problem solving from nature (PPSN V).* (Amsterdam, The Netherlands, September 27–30, 1998). Springer Berlin Heidelberg, 1498, 292-301.

Efficient Identification of Improving Moves in a Ball for Pseudo-Boolean Problems

Francisco Chicano
Dept. de Lenguajes y Ciencias de la Computación
Universidad de Málaga, Andalucía Tech, Spain
chicano@lcc.uma.es

Darrell Whitley
Dept. of Computer Science
Colorado State University
Fort Collins CO, USA
whitley@cs.colostate.edu

Andrew M. Sutton
Fakultät für Mathematik und Informatik
Friedrich-Schiller-Universität Jena
07743 Jena, Germany
andrew.sutton@uni-jena.de

ABSTRACT

Hill climbing algorithms are at the core of many approaches to solve optimization problems. Such algorithms usually require the complete enumeration of a neighborhood of the current solution. In the case of problems defined over binary strings of length n, we define the r-ball neighborhood as the set of solutions at Hamming distance r or less from the current solution. For $r \ll n$ this neighborhood contains $\Theta(n^r)$ solutions. In this paper efficient methods are introduced to locate improving moves in the r-ball neighborhood for problems that can be written as a sum of a linear number of subfunctions depending on a bounded number of variables. NK-landscapes and MAX-kSAT are examples of these problems. If the number of subfunctions depending on any given variable is also bounded, then we prove that the method can explore the neighborhood in constant time, despite the fact that the number of solutions in the neighborhood is polynomial in n. We develop a hill climber based on our exploration method and we analyze its efficiency and efficacy using experiments with NKq-landscapes instances.

Categories and Subject Descriptors

I.2.8 [**Artificial Intelligence**]: Problem Solving, Control Methods, and Search

General Terms

Theory, Algorithms

Keywords

Hill Climbing, Local Search, NK-landscapes, Pseudo-Boolean Optimization

1. INTRODUCTION

Local search algorithms work by starting at an initial solution and then moving from one solution to a "neighboring" solution in the search space. The set of solutions that can be reached in one move from solution x is called the *neighborhood* of x, denoted with $N(x)$. Most modern forms of local search often use some form of Iterated Local Search [4]. Thus, any advance in local search algorithms can have an important impact in the solution of the problem.

A simple implementation of local search requires enumerating the entire neighborhood of the current solution. In *steepest ascent* local search, the algorithm moves to a solution providing the largest improvement of the objective function; in *next ascent* search moves to the first improving solution it finds in the neighborhood. For problems defined over a binary search space, the most common neighborhood is the "bit-flip" Hamming distance 1 neighborhood. Given inputs of binary strings of length n, the size of this neighborhood is n, and exactly n neighbors are examined to locate an improving move.

In the current paper, we introduce a next ascent local search algorithm that is capable of identifying improving moves within r steps for k-bounded Pseudo-Boolean optimization problems. In this case, the neighborhood is a radius r Hamming ball: the set of all solutions at most Hamming distance r from the current solution. The size of this neighborhood is $O(n^r)$. For specific distributions of variables, we prove that all new improving moves can be identified in $\Theta(1)$ time using $\Theta(n)$ space per move.

Whitley and Chen [8] proposed a steepest descent algorithm for NK-landscapes and MAX-kSAT with an average time complexity of $\Theta(1)$ per move for the Hamming distance 1 neighborhood. Their algorithm works n times faster than a naïve implementation of the neighborhood exploration. This result is expressed as average time complexity because the time required in one single move is not bounded by a constant but over m moves the time required for *next ascent* and for approximate *steepest ascent* is bounded by $O(m)$. Their algorithm is based on the Walsh decomposition of the objective function. The secret of the resulting speedup is based on the fact that on average a bit-flip affects only a constant number of terms in the Walsh decomposition of the objective function. For all k-bounded pseudo-Boolean functions, the time complexity of their steepest descent is $O(k^2 2^k)$. For MAX-kSAT the value of k is the number of literals per clause while for NK-landscapes $k = K + 1$.

In a later paper, Chen *et al.* [1] used the concept of second derivative of a pseudo-Boolean function to improve the computation time of the steepest descent for NK-landscapes for the Hamming distance 1 neighborhood. Using a second

GECCO'14, July 12–16, 2014, Vancouver, BC, Canada.

ACM 978-1-4503-2662-9/14/07 ...$15.00.
http://dx.doi.org/10.1145/2576768.2598304

derivative, they reduce the time needed to identify improving moves from $O(k^2 2^k)$ to $O(k^3)$. In addition, the new approach avoids the use of the Walsh transform, making the approach conceptually simpler.

In this paper, we generalize this result to present a local search algorithm that can look r moves ahead and identify all improving moves. This means that moves are being identified in a neighborhood containing all solutions that lie within a *Hamming ball* of radius r around the current solution. We assume that $r = O(1)$. If $r \ll n$, the number of solutions in such a neighborhood is $\Theta(n^r)$. New improving moves located up to r moves away can be identified in constant time. The memory required by our approach is $O(n)$. To achieve $O(1)$ time per move, the number of subfunctions in which any variable appears must be bounded by some constant c. We then prove that the resulting algorithm requires $O((3kc)^r n)$ space to track potential moves.

In order to evaluate our approach we perform an experimental study based on NKq-landscapes. The results reveal not only that the time required by the next ascent is independent of n, but also that increasing r we obtain a significant gain in the quality of the solutions found.

The rest of the paper is organized as follows. In the next section we introduce the pseudo-Boolean optimization problems. Section 3 defines the "Scores" of a solution and provide an algorithm to efficiently update them during a local search algorithm. We propose in Section 4 a next ascent hill climber with the ability to identify improving moves in a ball of radius r in constant time. Section 5 empirically analyzes this hill climber using NKq-landscapes instances and Section 6 outlines some conclusions and future work.

2. PSEUDO-BOOLEAN OPTIMIZATION

Our method for identifying improving moves in the radius r Hamming ball can be applied to all k-bounded pseudo-Boolean Optimization problems. This makes our method quite general: every compressible pseudo-Boolean Optimization problem can be transformed into a quadratic pseudo-Boolean Optimization problem with $k = 2$.

The family of k-bounded pseudo-Boolean Optimization problems have also been described as an *embedded landscape*. An *embedded landscape* [3] with *bounded epistasis* k is defined as a function $f(x)$ that can be written as the sum of m subfunctions, each one depending at most on k input variables. That is:

$$f(x) = \sum_{i=1}^{m} f^{(i)}(x), \tag{1}$$

where the subfunctions $f^{(i)}$ depend only on k components of x. Embedded Landscapes generalize NK-landscapes and the MAX-kSAT problem. We will consider in this paper that the number of subfunctions is linear in n, that is $m \in O(n)$. For NK-landscapes $m = n$ and is a common assumption in MAX-kSAT that $m \in O(n)$.

3. SCORES IN THE HAMMING BALL

For $v, x \in \mathbb{B}^n$, and a pseudo-Boolean function $f : \mathbb{B}^n \to \mathbb{R}$, we denote the *Score* of x with respect to *move* v as $S_v(x)$, defined as follows:[1]

$$S_v(x) = f(x \oplus v) - f(x), \tag{2}$$

[1]We omit the function f in $S_v(x)$ to simplify the notation.

where $\oplus$ denotes the exclusive OR bitwise operation. The Score $S_v(x)$ is the change in the objective function when we move from solution x to solution $x \oplus v$, that is obtained by flipping in x all the bits that are 1 in v.

All possible Scores for strings v with $|v| \leq r$ must be stored as a vector. The Score vector is updated as local search moves from one solution to another. This makes it possible to know where the improving moves are in a ball of radius r around the current solution. For next ascent, all of the improving moves can be buffered. An approximate form of steepest ascent local search can be implemented using multiple buffers [9].

If we naively use equation (2) to explicitly update this Score vector, we will have to evaluate all $\sum_{i=0}^{r} \binom{n}{i}$ neighbors in the Hamming ball. Instead, if the objective function satisfies some requirements described below, we can design an efficient next ascent hill climber for the radius r neighborhood that only stores a linear number of Score values and requires a constant time to update them. We next explain the theoretical foundations of this next ascent hill climber.

The first requirement for the objective function is that it must be written such that each subfunction depends only on k Boolean variables of x (k-bounded epistasis). In this case, we can write the scoring function $S_v(x)$ as an embedded landscape:

$$S_v(x) = \sum_{l=1}^{m} \left(f^{(l)}(x \oplus v) - f^{(l)}(x) \right) = \sum_{l=1}^{m} S_v^{(l)}(x), \tag{3}$$

where we use $S_v^{(l)}$ to represent the scoring functions of the subfunctions $f^{(l)}$. Let us define $w_l \in \mathbb{B}^n$ as the binary string such that the i-th element of w_l is 1 if and only if $f^{(l)}$ depends on variable x_i. The vector w_l can be considered as a mask that characterizes the variables that affect $f^{(l)}$. Since $f^{(l)}$ has bounded epistasis k, the number of ones in w_l, denoted with $|w_l|$, is at most k. By the definition of w_l, the next equalities immediately follow.

$$f^{(l)}(x \oplus v) = f^{(l)}(x) \quad \text{for all } v \in \mathbb{B}^n \text{ with } v \wedge w_l = 0, \tag{4}$$

$$S_v^{(l)}(x) = \begin{cases} 0 & \text{if } w_l \wedge v = 0, \\ S_{v \wedge w_l}^{(l)}(x) & \text{otherwise.} \end{cases} \tag{5}$$

Equation (5) claims that if none of the variables that change in the move characterized by v is an argument of $f^{(l)}$ the Score of this subfunction is zero, since the value of this subfunction will not change from $f^{(l)}(x)$ to $f^{(l)}(x \oplus v)$. On the other hand, if $f^{(l)}$ depends on variables that change, we only need to consider for the evaluation of $S_v^{(l)}(x)$ the changed variables that affect $f^{(l)}$. These variables are characterized by the mask vector $v \wedge w_l$. With the help of (5) we can write (3) as:

$$S_v(x) = \sum_{\substack{l=1 \\ w_l \wedge v \neq 0}}^{m} S_{v \wedge w_l}^{(l)}(x), \tag{6}$$

3.1 Scores Decomposition

The Score values in a ball of radius r give more information than just the change in the objective function for moves in that ball. Let us illustrate this idea with the moves in the balls of radius $r = 1$ and $r = 2$. Let us assume that x_i and x_j are two variables that do not appear together as arguments of any subfunction $f^{(l)}$. Then, the Score of the move

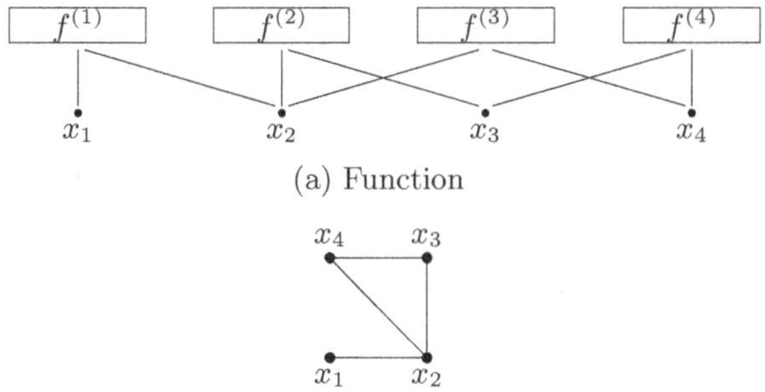

(b) Variable interaction graph

Figure 1: A function with $k = 2$ bounded epistasis, $n = 4$ variables and $m = 4$ subfunctions (top) and its corresponding variable interaction graph (bottom).

we obtain when we flip both variables is the sum of the Score values of the moves of each variable in isolation. To see this, let us denote with $\underline{i,j}$ the binary string with position i and j set to 1 and the rest set to 0. Similarly, we denote with $\underline{i}$ the binary string having 1 only in position i. According to (6) we can write:

$$S_{\underline{i,j}}(x) = \sum_{\substack{l=1 \\ w_l \wedge \underline{i,j} \neq 0}}^{m} S^{(l)}_{\underline{i,j} \wedge w_l}(x),$$

since x_i and x_j do not appear together in any subfunction, there is no w_l with 1s in both i and j positions, and we can write:

$$S_{\underline{i,j}}(x) = \sum_{\substack{l=1 \\ w_l \wedge \underline{i} \neq 0}}^{m} S^{(l)}_{\underline{i} \wedge w_l}(x) + \sum_{\substack{l=1 \\ w_l \wedge \underline{j} \neq 0}}^{m} S^{(l)}_{\underline{j} \wedge w_l}(x)$$
$$= S_{\underline{i}}(x) + S_{\underline{j}}(x),$$

which is the claimed result. This means that if $\underline{i}$ and $\underline{j}$ are not improving moves, then $\underline{i,j}$ cannot be an improving move. Thus, the Scores in the 1-ball are also implicitly providing information of higher order moves in which the involved variables do not interact. In our example, we only need to track and update all the 2-ball Scores $\underline{i,j}$ for which i and j appear together in at least one subfunction $f^{(l)}$.

This reasoning can be generalized to higher order moves. In order to do this let us introduce the *variable interaction graph* $G = (V, E)$, where V is the set of Boolean variables and E contains all the pairs of variables (x_i, x_j) that interact each other, that is, $(x_i, x_j) \in E$ if there exists a subfunction $f^{(l)}$ that depends on x_i and x_j. In Figure 1 we show a function with k-bounded epistasis and its corresponding variable interaction graph.

Let us consider the Score of the move with characteristic vector v. Abusing notation, we use v to represent also the set of variables that will be flipped in the move. Let us denote with $G[v]$ the subgraph of G induced by v, that is, the subgraph containing only the vertices in v and the edges of E between vertices in v. If $G[v]$ is connected then we cannot compute the Score of the move as the sum of Scores of lower order moves. If the graph is not connected, then we can decompose the Score as a sum of at least two Scores of lower order moves. These necessary lower order moves are determined by the connected components of $G[v]$. For example, in the function of Figure 1 the scoring function $S_{\underline{1,3,4}}$ can be written as the sum of the scoring functions $S_{\underline{1}}$ and $S_{\underline{3,4}}$. If we want to know if there is at least one improving move in a ball of radius r, we have to consider the Scores of all the moves v with $|v| \leq r$ for which $G[v]$ is a connected graph. We will denote this set of moves with M^r to simplify the notation in the following. In the next subsection we will address the question of how many of these Scores exist and what is the cost in time of updating them after a move.

3.2 Scores Update

Instead of computing the Scores from scratch using (6) after every move, it is more efficient in time to store the Scores $S_v(x)$ of the current solution x in memory and update only those that are affected by the move. We will consider in the next paragraphs the cost in time of this update and we will prove that it is independent of n if the number of subfunctions in which any variable appears is bounded by some constant c. Under the same assumptions, we will prove that the number of Scores we need to store in memory is linear in n.

When we flip a set of bits t, only the value of some subfunctions $f^{(l)}$ will be affected: exactly those subfunctions for which $w_l \wedge t \neq 0$. If subfunction $f^{(l)}$ is affected, all the $S^{(l)}_v(x)$ values with $v \wedge w_l \neq 0$ could also change and, as a consequence, we have to update the S_v stored Scores for $v \wedge w_l \neq 0$. For each of these Scores, the update related to subfunction $f^{(l)}$ can consist in computing the value $S^{(l)}_v(x \oplus t) = f^{(l)}(x \oplus t \oplus v) - f^{(l)}(x \oplus t)$, computing the value $S^{(l)}_v(x) = f^{(l)}(x \oplus v) - f^{(l)}(x)$ and updating the stored value of S_v by subtracting $S^{(l)}_v(x)$ and adding $S^{(l)}_v(x \oplus t)$. This procedure is shown in Algorithm 1, where the term S_v represents the Score of move v stored in memory.

Algorithm 1 Efficient algorithm for Scores update

Input: S, x, t
1: **for** $l = 1$ to m such that $w_l \wedge t \neq 0$ **do**
2:    **for** $v \in M^r$ such that $w_l \wedge v \neq 0$ **do**
3:       $S_v \leftarrow S_v + f^{(l)}(x \oplus t \oplus v) - f^{(l)}(x \oplus t)$ $- f^{(l)}(x \oplus v) + f^{(l)}(x)$
4:    **end for**
5: **end for**

Let us prove that Algorithm 1 is correct. First, we can observe that in the inner loop we can make variable v to take values for which $w_l \wedge v = 0$, since in this case $f^{(l)}(x \oplus t \oplus v) = f^{(l)}(x \oplus t)$ and $f^{(l)}(x \oplus v) = f^{(l)}(x)$, what means that the right hand side in line 3 is reduced to S_v (no update). For the same reason, we can make variable l in the first loop to take all values from 1 to m, even those for which $w_l \wedge t = 0$. The reason why we use the conditions $w_l \wedge t \neq 0$ and $w_l \wedge v \neq 0$ in Algorithm 1 is efficiency: each condition reduces the computational complexity of the algorithm by a factor of n (this will be clear later). But efficiency is irrelevant in the proof of correctness, so we will assume that the conditions are not there. Under this assumption lines 1 and 2 can be swapped in the algorithm. The result is shown in Algorithm 2.

The outer loop of Algorithm 2 is just iterating over all the possible moves $v \in M^r$ to update all the Scores. The inner

Algorithm 2 Simple algorithm for Scores update

```
Input: S, x, t
for v ∈ M^r do
    for l = 1 to m do
        S_v ← S_v + f^(l)(x ⊕ t ⊕ v) − f^(l)(x ⊕ t)
                  − f^(l)(x ⊕ v) + f^(l)(x)
    end for
end for
```

loop computes the new value for S_v using the expression:

$$\begin{aligned} S_v(x) &+ \sum_{l=1}^{m} \Big(f^{(l)}(x \oplus t \oplus v) - f^{(l)}(x \oplus t) \\ &- f^{(l)}(x \oplus v) + f^{(l)}(x) \Big) \\ &= S_v(x) + \sum_{l=1}^{m} \Big(S_v^{(l)}(x \oplus t) - S_v^{(l)}(x) \Big) \\ &= S_v(x) + \sum_{l=1}^{m} S_v^{(l)}(x \oplus t) - \sum_{l=1}^{m} S_v^{(l)}(x) \\ &= S_v(x \oplus t), \end{aligned}$$

where we used (3). This proves that Algorithm 1 (and Algorithm 2) are correct, since its goal is to compute $S_v(x \oplus t)$ starting from $S_v(x)$.

In the update of line 3 of Algorithm 1 only subfunction $f^{(l)}$ is involved. The time required to evaluate $f^{(l)}$ must be some function of k, since $f^{(l)}$ depends only on k bits of the input string. Let us call this function $b(k)$. In the case of NK-landscapes and MAX-kSAT, $b(k) \in O(k)$ (we should remember that in NK-landscapes $k = K + 1$).

Let us now count how many times the body of the outer loop in Algorithm 1 is executed. We do this by counting how many subfunctions $f^{(l)}$ have the property $w_l \wedge t \neq 0$.

We first introduce an additional assumption: *each Boolean variable x_i appears in at most c subfunctions.* Under this assumption, the number of subfunctions containing at least one of the bits in t (condition $w_l \wedge t \neq 0$) is at most $c|t|$. Since $|t|$ is bounded by the constant r, the inner loop is run at most cr times, which is a constant. It is common to have $m \in O(n)$, so the difference between including the condition $w_l \wedge t \neq 0$ or not in the first loop is a factor of n, as we mentioned earlier.

Once the outer loop has fixed a value for l, we need to compute how many moves $v \in M^r$ fulfill $w_l \wedge v \neq 0$ to end with a final expression for the time required by Algorithm 1. There is a way to enumerate all these moves v that also give us a bound for its cardinality. Since $G[v]$ must be a connected graph, we can always find a spanning tree of the graph. If we build all the possible trees of subgraphs of G having at most r variables and with root in each variable that appears in $f^{(l)}$, we are sure that we considered all the possible $v \in M^r$ such that $w_l \wedge v \neq 0$. In effect, let us suppose that there is a $v \in M^r$ such that $w_l \wedge v \neq 0$. Then, there is a variable x_i in w_l that is included in v and we can build a spanning tree of $G[v]$ with root x_i.

How many sets v we will find this way? We can easily give an upper bound. Given a variable x_i, the number of variables that interact with x_i (adjacent nodes in the variable interaction graph) is bounded by ck. Given a tree of r nodes with x_i in the root, we have to assign variables to the rest of the nodes in such a way that two connected nodes have interacting variables. The ways in which we can do this is bounded by $O((ck)^{r-1})$. We have to repeat the same operation for all the possible rooted trees and each of the k variables in subfunction $f^{(l)}$. Thus, a bound for the $v \in M^r$ such that $w_l \wedge v \neq 0$ is $O(k(ck)^{r-1}T_r)$, where T_r is the number of rooted trees with r vertices.

The number of rooted trees of r vertices can be computed using the following recurrence [2]:

$$T_{r+1} = \frac{1}{r} \sum_{l=1}^{r} \left(\sum_{d|l} d\, T_d \right) T_{r-l+1}, \tag{7}$$

$$T_1 = 1. \tag{8}$$

This series has the following asymptotic behaviour [5]:

$$\lim_{r \to \infty} \frac{T_r}{T_{r-1}} \approx 2.955765, \tag{9}$$

Using this property, a bound for the number of moves $v \in M^r$ such that $w_l \wedge v \neq 0$ is $O(c^{r-1}(3k)^r)$. This process must be repeated for all the subfunctions affected by t, which we proved to be bounded by $c|t|$. Taking into account that the time to evaluate each Score is $O(b(k))$ we finally have the total time $O(b(k)(3kc)^r|t|)$ to update all the Scores S_v for $v \in M^r$ when we flip $|t|$ bits. This time is independent of n, provided that neither k, r nor c depends on n. This result was already proved by Szeider for the MAX-kSAT and SAT problems [6]. We generalize Szeider's result and design an algorithm based on it. To the best of our knowledge there is no previous local search algorithm based on this result.

The number of Scores S_v we have to store is the cardinality of M^r. We can find a bound for this cardinality using the following argument. If we flip all the n variables in turn we will update all the Scores S_v with $v \in M^r$ at least once. According to the previous paragraph the time required to update all the affected Scores after 1 bit flip is $O(b(k)(3kc)^r)$. Dividing by the cost of evaluating a subfunction $b(k)$ and multiplying by the n bits that we flip, we have that the number of moves in M^r is $O((3kc)^r n)$. This means $O(n)$ space to store the Scores. This is the reason why in line 2 of Algorithm 1 removing the condition $w_l \wedge v \neq 0$ means executing line 3 around $O(n)$ more times.

Two other complexity issues should be noted. There is an up-front one-time initialization cost. The Score vector must be initialized and this also has cost $O((3kc)^r n)$. We also need to distinguish between "old" improving moves and "new" improving moves. After any set of bit flips unto radius r there are only a constant number of changes to the Score vector. Therefore there are at most a constant number of "new" improving moves that are created as a result of the most recent move. However, there can be a significant number of "old" improving moves that have already been identified. Just as there are at most a constant number of "new" improving moves after any update of the Score vector, there are also at most a constant number of "old" improving moves that are destroyed by any update of the Score vector.

We end this section providing a theorem with the main result of the paper. The proof of this theorem has been given in the previous paragraphs.

THEOREM 1. *Let f be a function defined over $\mathbb{B}^n$ that can be written in the form (1) where each subfunction $f^{(l)}$*

depends only on at most k Boolean variables and each variable appears in at most c subfunctions. Let the graph G be the variable interaction graph of f and M^r the set of moves $v \in \mathbb{B}^r$ up to order r such that $G[v]$ is a connected graph. Then:

- *The cardinality of M^r is $O((3kc)^r n)$.*
- *We only need to check the Scores $S_v(x)$ with $v \in M^r$ of the current solution x to determine the presence of an improving move in a ball of radius r around x. If the Scores are stored in memory this check requires constant time.*
- *The Scores $S_v(x)$ for $v \in M^r$ can be updated when we move from one solution x to $x \oplus t$ using Algorithm 1 in time $O(b(k)(3kc)^r|t|)$, where $b(k)$ is a bound of the time required to evaluate any subfunction $f^{(l)}$. This time is independent of n if k, r and c are independent of n.*

4. THE HAMMING-BALL HILL CLIMBER

The efficient Scores update of Algorithm 1 can be used in combination with any trajectory-based method like, Iterated Local Search or Tabu Search. In this section we describe a next ascent hill climber based on it. The proposed hill climber is shown in Algorithm 3. We assume maximization and for this reason we say that it is an "ascent" hill climber. However, the algorithm can consider minimization just changing the > operators in lines 5 and 10 by < operators. In the algorithm, variable *best* stores the best found solution at any given time. The algorithm starts by assigning the special value $\perp$, which means "no solution" to *best*. Next, it enters a loop that is repeated until the stopping condition is met. Each run of the loop body is an ascent starting from a random solution in the search space. In the loop, once a random solution has been selected and stored in x, the algorithm computes the Scores $S_v(x)$ for all $v \in M^r$ using the expression (6). The inner loop starting in line 5 implements the next ascent. While an improving move exists ($S_v > 0$ for some $v \in M^r$), the algorithm selects one of the improving moves t (line 6), updates the Scores using Algorithm 1 (line 7) and changes the current solution by the new one (line 8).

Algorithm 3 Hamming-ball next ascent.

```
1:  best ← ⊥
2:  while stop condition not met do
3:     x ← randomSolution();
4:     S ← computeScores(x);
5:     while S_v > 0 for some v ∈ M^r do
6:        t ← selectImprovingMove(S);
7:        updateScores(S,x,t);
8:        x ← x ⊕ t;
9:     end while
10:    if best = ⊥ or f(x) > f(best) then
11:       best ← x;
12:    end if
13: end while
```

Regarding the selection of the improving move, our approach in the experiments was to select always the one with the lowest Hamming distance to the current solution, that is, the lowest value of $|t|$. The main reason for selecting the nearest improving move is that, as stated by Theorem 1, the time required for updating the Scores is proportional to $|t|$. Thus, the nearest improving move is the fastest move in our algorithm. This selection can be done in constant time, since the classification of the moves as improving or non-improving can be done when the Scores are calculated and the Scores can be added to different lists depending on the distance to the current solution.

From the point of view of computation time, we expect the statements between lines 6 and 8 to run in a time that is independent of n. However, this time depends on k, c and r, where r is the only algorithm-dependent parameter (the others depend on the problem instance). According to Theorem 1, the time is exponential in r. Therefore, we have to be especially careful when we set the radius of the ball. Lines 3 and 4 are expected to run in linear time with respect to n, since the number of Scores (and variables) is linear.

Let us now consider the quality of the solutions obtained by the algorithm when we change r. Let us pick two radii for the ball: $r_1 < r_2$. Let us imagine that two ascents start from the same solution, one in each algorithm. Both instances of the algorithm will visit the same solutions until the algorithm with radius r_1 gets stuck in a local optimum or a plateau. In this case, however, the algorithm with r_2, which is considering a larger neighborhood, could find an improving move and could continue. Thus, we expect longer ascents and better quality solutions at the end of the ascents for larger values of r.

The fitness value of the best solution is a non-decreasing function of the time. As we increase r we expect better solutions at the end of the ascents, but the time spent in each ascent is also longer. It could happen that an instance of the algorithm with a lower value for r can reach better solutions earlier just because it is faster and finds an appropriate path joining lower distance moves. This fact makes impossible to set an *a priori* value for r that is valid for all the problems and instances. In the experimental section we will discuss this issue again on the results.

5. EXPERIMENTAL RESULTS

In this section we present experimental results obtained with the Hamming-ball next ascent. For the experiments we used NKq-landscapes. They are randomly generated functions that are specially interesting because it is possible to change their ruggedness and neutrality changing K and q, respectively. The objective function is:

$$f(x) = \sum_{l=1}^{n} f^{(l)}(x), \tag{10}$$

where each subfunction $f^{(l)}$ depends on variable x_l and other K variables and we have $k = K + 1$. These variables can be randomly selected from the remaining $n-1$, which yields the random-model NKq-landscapes. If the variables for subfunction $f^{(l)}$ are $\{x_l, x_{l+1}, \ldots, x_{l+K}\}$ with sum modulo n (and indices in the range 1 to n), then we have the adjacent-model NKq-landscapes. The latter has the advantage that a global optimum can be found in polynomial time using an algorithm proposed by Wright *et al.* [10], but also the number of subfunctions depending on a given variable is constant: $c = k = K + 1$. In the random-model there is no constant bound for the number of subfunctions in which the variables appear: a variable could appear in up to n subfunctions. The 2^{K+1} values that each subfunction $f^{(l)}$ can take in both, the adjacent and random models, are randomly generated from the set of integers $\{0, 1, \ldots, q-1\}$.

We proved in Section 3 that the Scores can be updated in a time that is independent of the size of the problem n. However, in a real implementation of Algorithm 3 there are two initialization procedures that require more than constant time. First, it is necessary to compute the set of moves M^r and allocate memory for the corresponding Scores. This is done only once for each problem instance and we call it *instance-dependent initialization*. Second, at the beginning of each ascent, a random solution has to be selected from the search space and the Scores for the solution have to be computed. We call this procedure *solution-dependent initialization*.

5.1 Illustrating Average Runtime

In a first experiment, we will estimate the average cost of each move empirically. We will do this by flipping *every variable the same number of times*; each individual flip results in a unique set of updates to the Score vector. This means we ignore improving moves and focus exclusively on the cost of updating the Score vector for every possible bit flip.

For a test problem we will use the adjacent-model NKq-landscape. We used instances of the problem with $n = 1,000$ to $n = 12,000$, $K = 1$ to $K = 4$ and $q = 2^{K+1}$. We generated 30 instances for each combination of values and averaged the results over the 30 instances. For r we used values $r = 1$ to 4. In each run we start from a random solution and flip each bit of the solution in turn until we reach $120,000$ flips. For instances with $n = 12,000$ this means flipping each bit exactly ten times. In order to have an unbiased distribution of bit flips only divisors of $12,000$ are allowed values for n. This way we ensure that each bit is flipped the same number of times in each instance.

In Figure 2 we can see the time required by the $120,000$ bit flips for $K = 3$ and all the values of r as a function of the size n. Except for some random fluctuations, the time is constant. Figure 3(a) shows the cardinality of M^r as a function of n. We can clearly see the predicted linear evolution. In Figures 3(b) and 3(c) we can observe the times required by the instance-dependent and solution-dependent initialization procedures. They increase more or less linearly with n. They can impose a time-limit to add to the memory-limit imposed by $|M^r|$ in the scalability of our proposal. The same behaviour can be observed for the other values of K (not shown). However, as we increase K, the times and $|M^r|$ also increase.

Since the time for performing the 120,000 moves is the same for all n, we have computed the mean time for all the values of n while K and r are fixed. Figure 4 shows how this time depends on K for different values of r. According to the results of Section 3 this time is exponential in r with K appearing in the base of the expression.

We repeated the previous experiment with the random-model NKq-landscape. In Figure 5(a) we can see the time required by the $120,000$ bit flips for $K = 3$, $q = 16$ and $r = 1$ to 3 as a function of the size n. Now we can observe a slight increase of the time with n. This is a consequence of the increasing number of subfunctions that depend on the same variable. Figure 5(c) shows the average (in the 30 instances) of the largest number of subfunctions a single

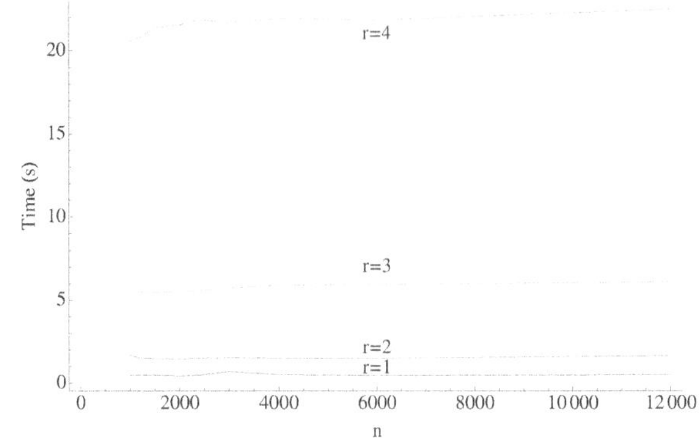

Figure 2: Time for Score updates in the adjacent-model NKq-landscapes.

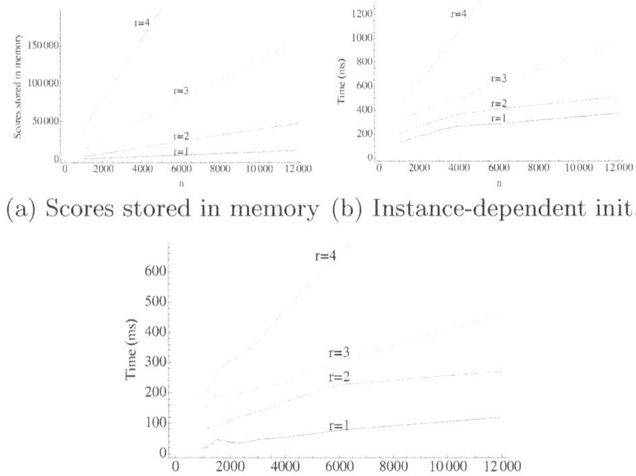

(a) Scores stored in memory (b) Instance-dependent init.

(c) Solution-dependent init.

Figure 3: Times and Scores for adjacent-model NKq-landscapes.

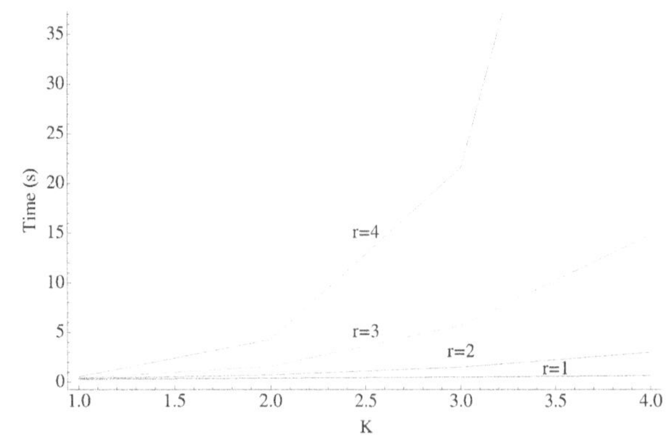

Figure 4: Time required for the 120,000 moves in the adjacent-model NKq-landscape as a function of K. Each curve corresponds to a different value of r.

variable affects. In the adjacent-model this number was constant, exactly $c = K + 1$. In the random-model this number is increasing with n and is not bounded by a constant. Regarding the cardinality of M^r, it still increases in a linear way with n as illustrated in Figure 5(b), although in theory the increase could be more than linear.

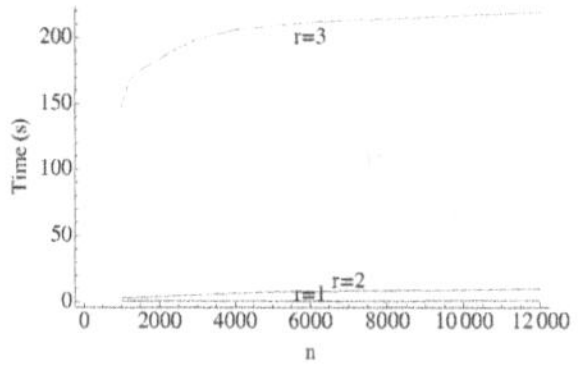

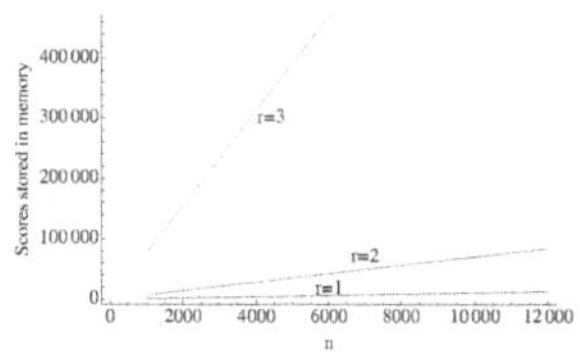

(a) Time for Score updates (b) Scores stored in memory

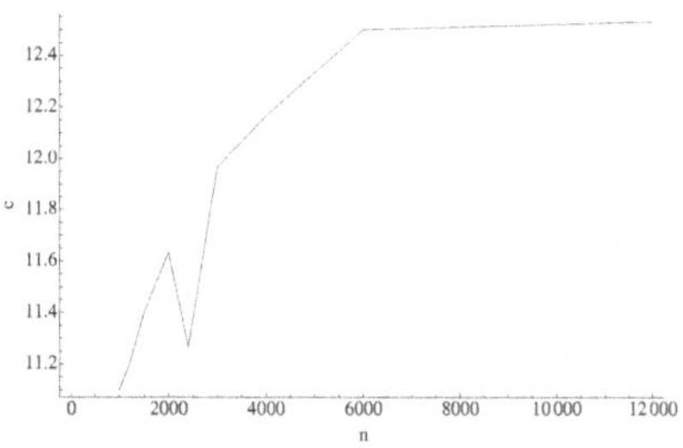

(c) Maximum subfunctions affected, c

Figure 5: Time, Scores and maximum number of subfunctions affected by a single variable for random-model NKq-landscapes.

5.2 On the Quality of the Solutions

In Section 4 we argued that an ascent of the Hamming-ball next ascent with radius $r_1 < r_2$ cannot obtain a better solution than an ascent starting from the same solution but using radius r_2. As a consequence, if the stopping condition of Algorithm 3 is to reach a fixed number of ascents, then we expect the quality of the solutions using r_2 to be no worse than the quality of the solutions when r_1 is the radius. However, larger radius also means longer execution time, not only for the Scores update but also for the different initialization procedures. If the stopping condition is to reach a fixed amount of time we cannot say which radius is the best option. The experiments in this section illustrate what happens in this case of NKq-landscapes.

Let us start analyzing the adjacent-model. We fix $n = 10,000$ and generated 30 instances for each combination of K used. We run the algorithm for 120 seconds in all the cases. Figure 6 shows the average fitness over the 30 instances of the best solution found by the algorithms against the elapsed time from the start of the search. The radius used are $r = 1$ to 6. In the figure $K = 2$ and $q = 8$. We can observe that using larger values for r the algorithm is able to find better solutions at any time. In the figure, it is clear that the algorithm with $r = 1$ cannot reach in 120 seconds the quality of the solutions found by the one with $r = 2$ at the beginning of its search. The same applies in the comparison with other radii. We can conclude that, in this example and for $r = 1$ to 6, increasing the value of r we obtain progressively better algorithms, even when the stopping condition is a time limit.

However, this improvement has also limitations. The gain in the quality of the solutions when we increase r from 1 to 2 is larger than the gain when we increase r from 2 to 3. Since the fitness value of the global optimum acts as a bound for the quality of the solutions, there must be an r value for which there is no gain. At this point, increasing r we can only penalize the efficacy of the algorithm because the run-

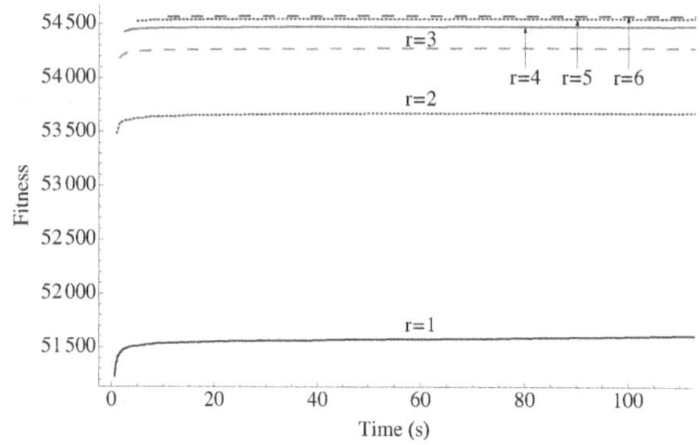

Figure 6: Best solution fitness over time for the Hamming-ball next ascent in adjacent-model NKq-landscapes.

time will still increase. To check this fact, we show in Figure 7 the normalized distance to the global optimum of the Hamming-ball next ascent for different radii (note that we are maximizing the objective function, but minimizing the distance to the global optimum). The points are averages over 30 random instances with $n = 10,000$, $K = 1$, $q = 4$ and $r = 1$ to 10. The algorithms were run for 120 seconds. The normalized distance to the optimum, n_d, is:

$$n_d(x) = \frac{f^* - f(x)}{f^*}, \qquad (11)$$

where f^* is the fitness value of the global optimum, computed using the algorithm by Wright *et al.* [10].

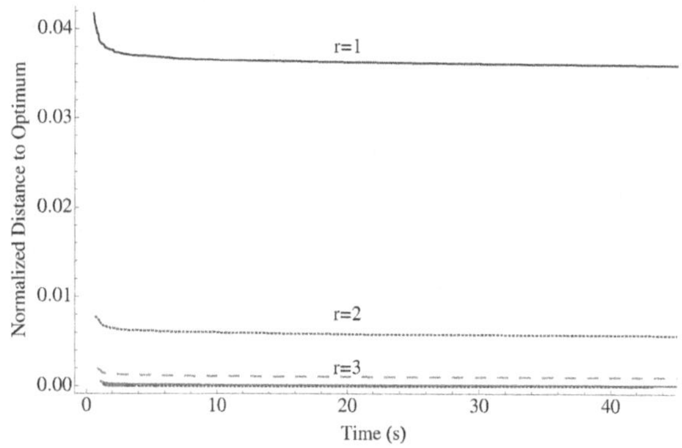

Figure 7: Normalized distance to the global optimum for the Hamming-ball next ascent.

With $r = 1$ the algorithm is approximately within 3.6% of the global optimum after 20 seconds. As we increase r, the algorithms get closer to the global optimum and the gains shrink. For $r = 3$ the results are withing 0.2% of the global optimum. For $r > 3$ the differences are so small that cannot be observed in the plot. For $r \geq 6$ an optimal solution is found in all the instances. For $r = 6$ the solution is found in 3.7 seconds. For $r = 7$ it is found in 2.1 seconds, and this is the fastest algorithm. For $r = 8, 9$ and 10 the algorithm requires 2.8 s, 3.4 s, and 5 s to find the optimal solution. For $r = 10$ the algorithm finds an optimal solution in the first ascent for all the instances.

Let us now consider a random NKq-Landscape, one that does not use adjacent interacting variables. In Figure 8 we plot the quality of the best solution as a function of time. The instance used has $n = 10,000$, $K = 2$ and $q = 8$. The plot shows the average over 30 randomly generated instances. We observe the same behaviour as in the adjacent-model. The only remarkable difference is that the instance dependent initialization is longer and this is why the curves are displaced in time as r increases.

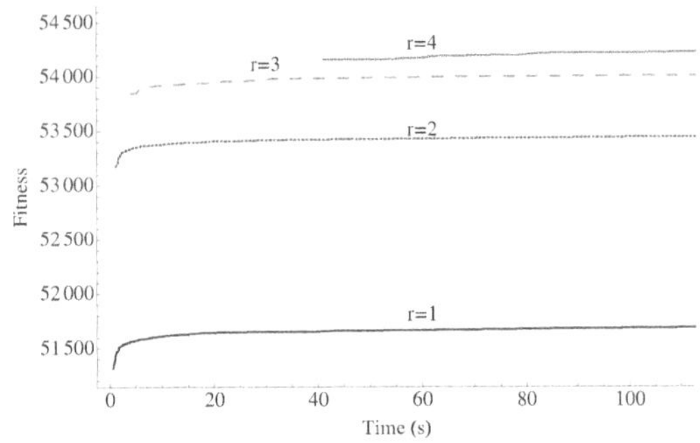

Figure 8: Best solution fitness over time for the Hamming-ball next ascent in random-model NKq-landscapes.

5.3 NKq-landscapes and MAX-kSAT

It has been empirically observed a common pattern in some industrial instances of MAX-3SAT. The number of clauses in which the same three variables appear is four with a high frequency. An hypothesis to explain this pattern is that these groups of clauses appear as a consequence of the Tseitin transformation [7], which is used to transform a general Boolean expression into CNF. The result is that these MAX-3SAT instances are similar in structure to NKq-landscapes instances with $K = 2$ and $q = 5$. Thus, we could expect the Hamming-ball next ascent to share the same behaviour in MAX-3SAT instances (and MAX-kSAT instances) as the NKq-landscape instances we have studied. In order to confirm this hypothesis we show in Figure 9 the fitness of the best solution against time for 30 randomly generated MAX-3SAT instances with groups of four clauses with the same variables. The number of variables is $n = 10,000$ and clauses are $m = 40,000$.

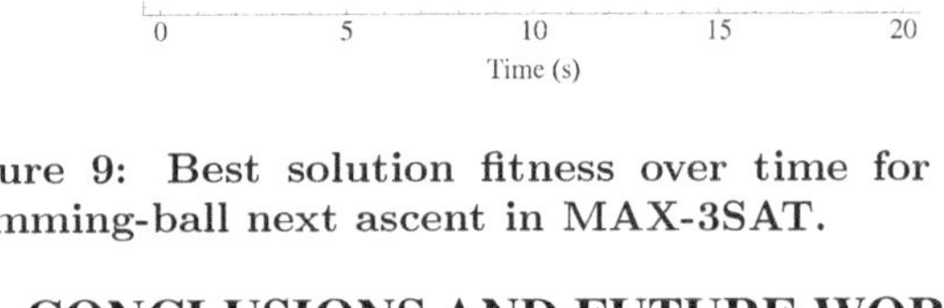

Figure 9: Best solution fitness over time for the Hamming-ball next ascent in MAX-3SAT.

6. CONCLUSIONS AND FUTURE WORK

In this paper we have provided an algorithm to efficiently identify improving moves in a Hamming ball of radius r around a solution of a k-bounded pseudo-Boolean optimization problem that can be written as a sum of subfunctions.

The empirical results on NKq-landscape instances show that increasing r improves the quality of the solutions found by next ascent local search. Further work is needed to study the benefits and limitations of using the Hamming Ball r-radius neighborhood for problems such as MAX-kSAT. The efficient algorithm for updating the Scores vector can also be combined with different strategies to escape from plateaus and local optima. In particular, a random walk flipping a small fraction of the decision variables could considerably reduce the computation time of the random restart.

7. ACKNOWLEDGMENTS

This research was sponsored by the Fulbright program, the Spanish Ministry of Education ("José Castillejo" mobility program), the Universidad de Málaga, Andalucía Tech, the Spanish Ministry of Science and Innovation and FEDER under contract TIN2011-28194, VSB-Technical University of Ostrava under contract OTRI 8.06/5.47.4142 and the Air Force Office of Scientific Research, Air Force Materiel Command, USAF, under grant number FA9550-11-1-0088. The U.S. Government is authorized to reproduce and distribute reprints for Governmental purposes notwithstanding any copyright notation thereon. The authors would also like to thank the organizers and participants of the seminar on Theory of Evolutionary Algorithms (13271) at Schloß Dagstuhl - Leibniz-Zentrum für Informatik.

8. REFERENCES

[1] W. Chen, D. Whitley, D. Hains, and A. Howe. Second order partial derivatives for NK-landscapes. In *Proceeding of GECCO*, pages 503–510. ACM, 2013.

[2] S. R. Finch. *Mathematical Constants*, chapter Otter's Tree Enumeration Constants, pages 295–316. Cambridge University Press, 2003.

[3] R. Heckendorn, S. Rana, and D. Whitley. Test function generators as embedded landscapes. In *FOGA*, pages 183–198. Morgan Kaufmann, 1999.

[4] H. H. Hoos and T. Stützle. *Stochastic Local Search: Foundations and Applications*. Morgan Kaufman, 2004.

[5] R. Otter. The number of trees. *Annals of Mathematics*, 49(3):583–599, 1948.

[6] S. Szeider. The parameterized complexity of k-flip local search for SAT and MAX SAT. *Discrete Optimization*, 8(1):139–145, 2011.

[7] G. S. Tseitin. On the complexity of derivations in the propositional calculus. *Studies in Mathematics and Mathematical Logic*, Part II:115–125, 1968.

[8] D. Whitley and W. Chen. Constant time steepest descent local search with lookahead for NK-landscapes and MAX-kSAT. In *Proceeding of GECCO*, pages 1357–1364. ACM, 2012.

[9] D. Whitley, A. Howe, and D. Hains. Greedy or not? best improving versus first improving stochastic local search for MAXSAT. In *Proc.of AAAI-2013*, 2013.

[10] A. Wright, R. Thompson, and J. Zhang. The computational complexity of NK fitness functions. *IEEE Trans. Evol. Comp.*, 4(4):373–379, 2000.

A Hybrid Incremental Genetic Algorithm for Subgraph Isomorphism Problem

HyukGeun Choi
School of Computer Science & Engineering
Seoul National University
1 Gwanak-ro, Gwanak-gu
Seoul, 151-744 Korea
hgchoi@soar.snu.ac.kr

Jinhyun Kim
School of Computer Science & Engineering
Seoul National University
1 Gwanak-ro, Gwanak-gu
Seoul, 151-744 Korea
jh@soar.snu.ac.kr

Byung-Ro Moon
School of Computer Science & Engineering
Seoul National University
1 Gwanak-ro, Gwanak-gu
Seoul, 151-744 Korea
moon@snu.ac.kr

ABSTRACT

Finding an isomorphic subgraph is a key problem in many real world applications modeled on graph. In this paper, we propose a new hybrid genetic algorithm(GA) for subgraph isomorphism problem which uses an incremental approach. We solve the problem with increasing the size of the subproblem step by step. The graph for which we search is gradually expanded from the empty structure to the entire one. We apply a hybrid GA to each subproblem, initialized with the evolved population of previous step. We present design issues for the incremental approach, and the effects of each design decision are analyzed by experiment. The proposed algorithm is tested on widely used dataset. With apposite vertex reordering along with moderate population diversity, incremental approach brought a significant performance improvement. Experimental results showed that our algorithm outperformed representative previous works.

Categories and Subject Descriptors

G.1.6 [**Numerical Analysis**]: Optimization—*Global optimization*; G.2.2 [**Discrete Mathematics**]: Graph Theory—*Graph algorithms*

General Terms

Algorithms

Keywords

Genetic algorithm, incremental genetic algorithm, subgraph isomorphism, vertex reordering

1. INTRODUCTION

Graphs are useful in universal and pervasive data representation models in various field. There are lots of interesting problems defined in terms of graphs including the subgraph isomorphism problem. Finding a common structure in two graphs is an important and general form of pattern matching, and common structures are often established by isomorphism or subgraph isomorphism. These problems arise in a number of real world applications such as pattern recognition [20], computer-aided design [18], image processing [14], bioinformatics [2], and cheminfomatics [12].

Given two graphs G_1 and G_2, the subgraph isomorphism problem is to determine whether G_2 contains a subgraph that is isomorphic to G_1. It is a generalization of the maximum clique problem, and is a well-known NP-hard problem [6]. The generalization of subgraph isomorphism problem is the maximum common subgraph isomorphism problem, which is to find the largest subgraph of two given graphs that are isomorphic to each other. This problem is also known to be NP-hard [10].

Many algorithms have been proposed for the subgraph isomorphism problem. But usually, these algorithms can solve the problem only for small-sized graphs or for those with notable restrictions [8, 15, 21, 23]. Some previous works used evolutionary approaches for the problem [3, 13, 25]. Among them, the one using a multi-objective approach showed notable performance [4].

In the subgraph isomorphism problem, the small subgraphs can be used to build solutions of the entire graph [17]. The optimal solutions on larger problem contain those of smaller problem as substructures. Previous works [1, 16, 24] proposed adaptive genetic algorithms dealing with dynamically changing problems by reusing the population, and Song and Victor [22] showed that the genetic algorithm starting with a high quality initial population and maintaining a moderate diversity led to good solutions. A better algorithm for the subgraph isomorphism problem could be derived by combining these ideas.

In this paper, we propose a new hybrid genetic algorithm for the subgraph isomorphism problem using an incremental approach. Starting from finding solutions of small subproblems, we gradually expand the problem size to the original problem. In each step of expansion, the results on a smaller problem in previous step are used as the initial population and a hybrid genetic algorithm evolves them over generations. Experimental results showed that the hybrid genetic algorithm with the incremental approach significantly improved the performance; we conclude that our new algorithm outperforms previous works.

GECCO'14, July 12–16, 2014, Vancouver, BC, Canada.
Copyright 2014 ACM 978-1-4503-2662-9/14/07 ...$15.00.
http://dx.doi.org/10.1145/2576768.2598382 .

The paper is organized as follows: Section 2 provides an overview of previous works. In Section 3, we describe an incremental approach and its related issues. Genetic framework and local heuristic are given in Section 4. Section 5 provides experimental results and discussions. Conclusions are in Section 6.

2. RELATED WORK

Given two graphs $G_1 = (V_1, E_1)$, $G_2 = (V_2, E_2)$, the subgraph isomorphism problem is to determine whether G_1 is isomorphic to a subgraph of G_2. Instead of tackling the problem directly, an optimization version of the problem is often solved. This problem asks to find a subgraph of G_2 which has the least number of different edges with G_1, or a subgraph which has the most number of common edges with G_1 [3, 13, 25]. If the graph found is the same as G_1, then it is a solution to the decision version of the problem. In this paper, we use the decision version and the optimization version of the problem interchangeably.

There are several algorithms dealing with the subgraph isomorphism problem. The recursive backtracking algorithm proposed by Ullmann [23] is one of the most commonly used for exact graph matching, which has exponential time complexity in general. Some approaches reduced the overall computational complexity by setting some limitations on the graphs [8, 15] or adopting domain specific knowledge [21]. Messmer and Bunke [17] studied a modified problem that detects subgraph isomorphisms from a number of a priori known graphs, so-called model graphs. They matched the decomposed model graphs onto the given input and the subgraph isomorphisms for the complete graphs are obtained by recombining this results.

For real-world applications, genetic algorithms also were used to solve the problem. Brown et al. [3] used GA in 2D chemical structure matching. Zhong et al. [25] applied GA for the subgraph isomorphism problem to compute resource assignment in real time digital simulators. Kim and Moon [13] proposed a malware detection system using a hybrid GA. They represented a malware as a directed dependency graph and transformed the malware detection problem into the subgraph isomorphism problem.

Choi et al. [4] suggested a multi-objective GA with a local search heuristic for this problem. Comparing the degrees of each vertex of two graphs that are mapped, they counted the number of mismatched vertices. Mapping a vertex v of G_1 to w of G_2 is mismatched, if either ingoing or outgoing degree of v is greater than that of w. They combined it with a commonly used fitness function counting the number of mismatched edges, which is the number of edges in G_1 but not in G_2 plus the number of edges in G_2 but not in G_1. The combined fitness function was $f = 0.1 \cdot f_1 + 0.9 \cdot f_2$ where f_1 denotes the number of mismatched edges and f_2 denotes the number of mismatched vertices. They showed that the new fitness function is more globally convex than that of previous studies and thereby improved the performance and efficiency.

3. THE PROPOSED ALGORITHM

3.1 Definition and Notation

Before proposing our new approach, the terms and notations are introduced for the subgraph isomorphism problem.

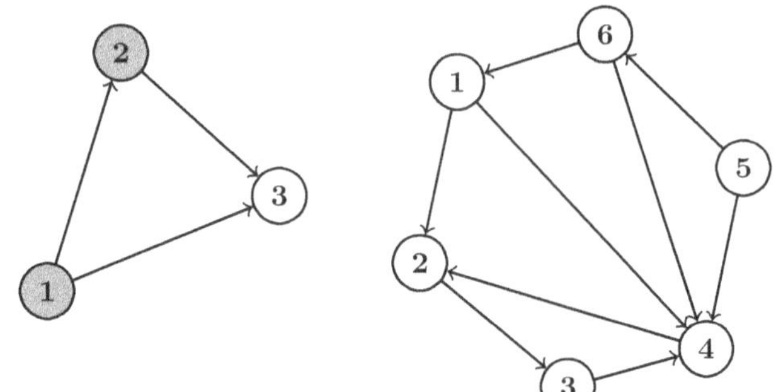

Figure 1: $G_1 = (V_1, E_1)$ and $G_2 = (V_2, E_2)$. Two vertices of G' is marked in gray.

First, we describe the formal definition of the following two terms.

DEFINITION 1. *An **isomorphism** from a graph $G_1 = (V_1, E_1)$ to a graph $G_2 = (V_2, E_2)$ is a bijection $g : V_1 \to V_2$ such that $(u, v) \in E_1$ if and only if $(g(u), g(v)) \in E_2$. We say that G_1 is **isomorphic** to G_2, if there is an isomorphism from G_1 to G_2.*

DEFINITION 2. *An injective function $g : V_1 \to V_2$ is a **subgraph isomorphism** from $G_1 = (V_1, E_1)$ to $G_2 = (V_2, E_2)$ if there exists a subgraph $G_s \subseteq G_2$ such that g is an isomorphism from G_1 to G_s.*

From this, we give the formal notation for the optimization problem for subgraph isomorphism.

DEFINITION 3. *Given two graphs $G_1 = (V_1, E_1)$ and $G_2 = (V_2, E_2)$ where $|V_1| \leq |V_2|$, the subgraph isomorphism problem, denoted by **SGIP**(G_1, G_2), is to find an injective function $g : V_1 \to V_2$ that minimizes the fitness function f. An optimal solution which has the fitness value of 0, is a subgraph isomorphism from G_1 to G_2.*

The function f introduced in section 2 is used as the fitness function of SGIP.

3.2 Main Idea

Suppose that g is a subgraph isomorphism from G_1 to G_2. If $G' = (V', E')$ is a subgraph of G_1, then $g|_{V'} : V' \to V_2$, a restriction of g on V', is a subgraph isomorphism from G' to G_2.

However, this does not mean that every subgraph isomorphism from G' to G_2 can be extended to a subgraph isomorphism from G_1 to G_2. Consider two graphs in Figure 1 and a subgraph G' of G_1 with two vertices 1 and 2. This subgraph consists of one directed edge from vertex 1 to 2. Two examples of subgraph isomorphism from V' to V_2 are illustrated in Figure 2. The isomorphism in Figure 2(a) cannot be extended, because there is no vertex in G_2 having edges both from vertex 2 and vertex 3. However, the isomorphism in Figure 2(b) could be extended by mapping vertex 3 in G_1 to vertex 4 in G_2.

To find a subgraph isomorphism for the problem SGIP(G_1, G_2), we first solve the subproblem SGIP(G', G_2). Solving the subproblem will be relatively easy if the size of the problem is smaller. We solve the subproblem by using a genetic algorithm, and produce various solutions of the problem. And these solutions are extended to initial solutions

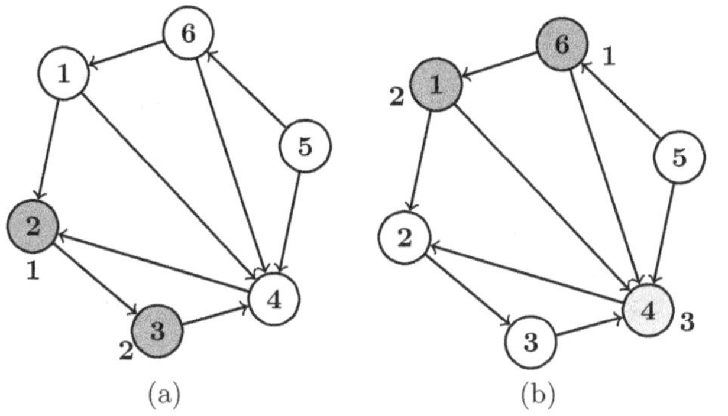

Figure 2: Two subgraph isomorphisms from V' to V_2. Mapping in (a) can not be extended to an isomorphism from V_1 to V_2, while mapping in (b) can.

for SGIP(G_1, G_2), which is also to be solved by a GA. If a genetic algorithm generates a solution of the subproblem which is extendable to an optimal solution of the original problem, then SGIP(G_1, G_2) could be solved rapidly by a GA.

3.3 The Structure of the Algorithm

We present a hybrid incremental genetic algorithm for the subgraph isomorphism problem in Algorithm 1.

Algorithm 1: Incremental Approach for subgraph isomorphism problem

---

Input: $G_1 = (V_1, E_1)$, $G_2 = (V_2, E_2)$
Output: A injective function $g : V_1 \rightarrow V_2$
$n \leftarrow$ the number of steps
for $i = 1$ **to** n **do**
  $m_i \leftarrow$ expansion size of i-th step
end for
$V' \leftarrow$ Reordering(V_1)
$G_{1,0} \leftarrow \varnothing$
$S_0 \leftarrow$ random initial solutions of SGIP($G_{1,0}, G_2$)
for $i = 1$ **to** n **do**
  $V_{curr} \leftarrow \{V'_1, \ldots, V'_{m_i}\}$
  $V' \leftarrow V' - V_{curr}$
  $G_{1,i} \leftarrow G_{1,i-1} \cup V_{curr}$ //adding m_i vertices
  $P_i \leftarrow$ initial solutions generated by S_{i-1}
  $S_i \leftarrow$ hybrid GA(P_i)
end for
return the best in S_n

First, we determine the number of steps n and the problem expansion size m_i, where $1 \leq i \leq n$ and $\sum_i m_i = |V_1|$. Next, the vertices in G_1 are rearranged to decide the order of problem expansion. Since this order is the most critical design issue in this incremental approach, we will discuss various reordering techniques and their performance in next subsection.

The incremental approach starts from the problem SGIP($G_{1,0}$, G_2) with an empty domain graph, $G_{1,0} = \varnothing$. For every i^{th} step, we expand the $G_{1,i-1}$ into $G_{1,i}$ by adding m_i vertices. And then, the hybrid genetic algorithm takes the results of the previous step to build an initial population of SGIP(G_1, G_2) and evolves it over generations. The solution of the original problem SGIP(G_1, G_2) is obtained from the results of the nth step.

The quality of an initial population is a prime determinant of the performance of genetic algorithm [22]. In the subgraph isomorphism problem, the optimal solution on a large problem contains those of smaller problems as substructures. Hence we expect that the initial population generated by this results may lead the algorithm to promising areas more efficiently than that of a randomly generated population. Hybridizing a good local search heuristic further helps concentrating on more promising areas.

3.4 Design Issues

We met three design issues in this algorithm: the order of vertices to be added at each step, the stopping criterion for each step, and the expansion size of each step. The details are explained below.

3.4.1 Vertex Reordering

The selection of vertices for the problem determines the search direction of the next step and affects the connection between solutions of each step. If vertices far away from the current subgraph is selected, the previous results is not very useful in the next step. Thus it makes sense to select vertices highly related to the current subgraph.

A graph search algorithm and vertex adjacency was used to measure the relation [11]. In addition, selecting an appropriate vertex in earlier steps may prune unnecessary search. The degree of vertex plays a key role in pruning the search space of the problem [7].

We applied three different schemes for reordering the vertices of G_1. The details of the reordering schemes are as follows:

- Max-degree reordering.

  We sort the vertices in non-increasing order of degree. The degree of a vertex is the sum of both ingoing and outgoing degrees.

- BFS reordering.

  We randomly select a starting vertex, and then run the breadth-first search on G_1. When the graph is disconnected and not all of the vertices are visited, we randomly choose another unvisited vertex and continue the procedure.

- Max-adjacency reordering.

  We randomly select a starting vertex, and repeatedly select one of the most attractive vertex in a greedy manner. The attractiveness of a vertex v is the number of adjacent vertices that are already ordered. Two vertices are adjacent to each other if there is an edge in any direction.

3.4.2 Stopping criterion

Basically, we used a fixed number of generations for all of the steps. But this may lead to excessive number of generations in earlier steps, because hybrid GA may converge very fast for relatively simple graphs. Moreover, keeping some solutions that are not converged in the population may preserve solution diversity. Both the quality and the diversity of solutions in the previous step have a decisive effect on the next step.

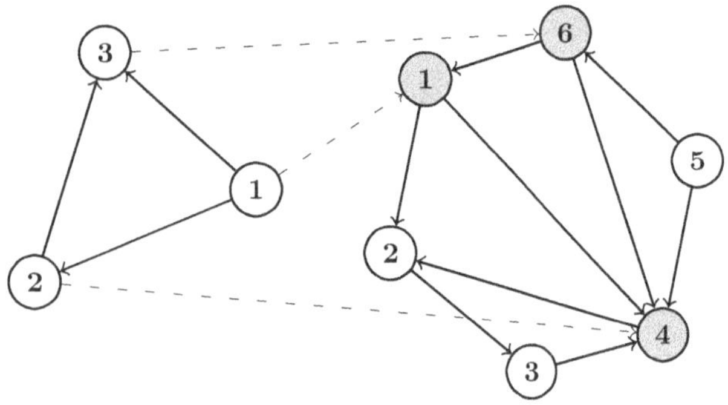

i	1	2	3	4	5	6
P[i]	1	4	6	3	5	2

Figure 3: Representation of a chromosome. Each vertex i in G_1 is mapped by a vertex $p[i]$ in G_2, drawn by dashed line.

We terminate each step if the population is sufficiently converged. We regard the number of the generations as the unit of time and distributed totally 100 generations equally to each step. Before starting each generation, we redistributed the remaining generations equally to next steps. By this procedure, more time is assigned to the later steps.

3.4.3 The expansion size

The number of vertices to be added at each step also determines the subproblem of each step. A naive way is to add a single vertex at each step. But it is a waste of time to run a GA when the expanded graph is too simple, for example, when an isolated vertex is added. Adding more vertices at that time enables efficient space search, but an immoderate expansion size may generate too much complicated graph. It is required to strike a balance between efficiency and difficulty by selecting a moderate expansion size.

4. GENETIC FRAMEWORK

The hybrid genetic algorithm we used in the incremental approach for the subgraph isomorphism problem is described below.

- Representation

  Given two graphs $G_1 = (V_1, E_1)$ and $G_2 = (V_2, E_2)$ where $|V_1| \leq |V_2|$, a chromosome represents a permutation of V_2 as an integer array. A subgraph isomorphism $g : V_1 \to V_2$, a solution of SGIP(V_1, V_2), is decoded by first $|V_1|$ genes in the chromosome. A vertex $v_{1,i} \in V_1$ is mapped to $v_{2,p[i]} \in V_2$ and an edge $(v_{1,i}, v_{1,j}) \in E_1$ is mapped to $(v_{2,p[i]}, v_{2,p[j]}) \in E_2$. Figure 3 shows an example. The main advantage of this representation is the flexibility toward the problem size expansion. Since a chromosome already has a full permutation of V_2, we can easily extend the mapping at each step without changing values of the genes.

- Fitness Function

  We use the function introduced in Section 2.

- Population

  The population size in each step of the incremental approach is 100. When GA starts, it takes the population evolved in the previous step as an initial population of the current step.

- Selection

  The tournament selection is used. We pick two chromosomes randomly and return better one with 80 percent of chance, otherwise return the worse one.

- Crossover

  We used cycle crossover [19].

- Mutation

  We select a number of genes to shuffle them in random order. Each of the gene independently has 40 percent of mutational chance.

- Local optimization algorithm

  We hybridize the local optimization algorithm with the incremental GA, by applying it to the initial population at the beginning, and to the offspring after crossover and mutation. We randomly swap two vertices when there is an improvement; this is repeated until there is no way to improve. The details are described in Algorithm 2.

Algorithm 2: Vertex swap local optimization algorithm

```
Input: A chromosome C of SGIP(G1, G2)
L ← {(i, j) | 1 ≤ i ≤ |V1|, i < j ≤ |V2|}
repeat
    flag ← false
    for all (i, j) ∈ L in random order do
        swap (C[i], C[j])
        calculate the difference
        if improved then
            flag ← true
        else
            swap(C[i], C[j]) // cancel
        end if
    end for
until flag
```

- Replacement

  We generate 50 offspring per generation and take 100 best solutions out of the existing solutions and the offspring.

- Stopping Criterion

  The hybrid GA stops when a certain ratio of population become the optimal solutions to the subproblem of ith step. We use the ratio values of 1%, 50% and 100%. In the last step, when the subproblem is same as the original one, the algorithm stops if an optimal solution is found. The fitness value of an optimal solution in the last step is always zero.

5. EXPERIMENTAL RESULTS

5.1 Dataset and Evaluation

We randomly generated 200 pairs of graphs by following a widely-used graph generation process [4, 5, 9]. We first generated the larger graph G_2. Exactly $\eta|V_2|^2$ directed edges are randomly generated without any other constraint, where η denotes the edge density. The graph may contain self-loops, and there may be two edges in both direction between two particular vertices. The smaller graph G_1 is generated from a subgraph of G_2. We randomly selected $|V_1|$ vertices from G_2, and the induced subgraph is taken as G_1. This means that there is always a subgraph isomorphism from G_1 to G_2 and the optimal fitness function value is always zero.

We used 4 different values for η and 5 different values for $|V_1|$ to generated 20 classes of graphs. For each of 20 classes, 10 pairs of graphs are independently generated. We used 0.01, 0.05, 0.1, 0.5 for η, and 10, 30, 50, 70, 90 for $|V_1|$. The number of vertices in the larger graph $|V_2|$ is fixed to 100.

We conducted 100 runs for each of 200 pairs of graphs to test an algorithm. This is 20000 runs in total. For each class, we averaged the results of 10 pairs of graphs. This is 1000 runs for each of the class. We measured the average fitness function value, the average running time, and the proportion of runs where an optimal solution was found. We wrote the program in C++ language and compiled it using g++ 4.6.3 with O3 option. We executed the program on servers with Intel Core i7 870 2.93GHz CPU and 4GB memory. We measured only the real running time of GA part of the program.

5.2 Baseline Results

Table 1: The result of traditional hybrid genetic algorithm.

$\|V_1\|$	η	f average	Ratio
10	0.01	0.0000	100.00%
	0.05	0.0000	100.00%
	0.1	**0.0005**	**99.50%**
	0.2	**0.0557**	**62.10%**
30	0.01	0.0000	100.00%
	0.05	**0.4813**	**51.00%**
	0.1	**0.7994**	**82.50%**
	0.2	**0.0718**	**99.40%**
50	0.01	**0.0094**	**91.30%**
	0.05	**0.0073**	**99.90%**
	0.1	0.0000	100.00%
	0.2	0.0000	100.00%
70	0.01	**0.0095**	**91.30%**
	0.05	0.0000	100.00%
	0.1	0.0000	100.00%
	0.2	0.0000	100.00%
90	0.01	0.0000	100.00%
	0.05	0.0000	100.00%
	0.1	0.0000	100.00%
	0.2	0.0000	100.00%

We tested a traditional hybrid genetic algorithm without using an incremental approach, to obtain a baseline results. Table 1 shows the average fitness value and the ratio of finding an optimal solution in percentage.

The baseline algorithm is an improved version of the multi-objective GA proposed by Choi et al. [4]. We modified some of the genetic operators and parameters in order to improve the performance. The ratio of finding an optimal solution slightly decreased for 2 out of twenty classes, and considerably increased for 8 classes.

For more than half of the classes, the GA found an optimal solution at every trial. Only 8 out of 20 classes were relatively difficult, and the result of these classes are marked in bold. Most of the difficult classes were when $|V_1|$ was not too small and not too big. For the later experiments, only these 8 classes will be used.

5.3 Effect of Vertex Reordering

Table 2 shows the average fitness function value of hybrid incremental genetic algorithms with four different reordering schemes mentioned. The expansion size of each step was 1, which means that a single vertex was added at each step. The schemes are no reordering(NO), Max-degree reordering(MD), BFS reordering(BFS), and Max-adjacency reordering(MA). The result of the traditional hybrid GA is also shown as the baseline(BASE). Adding an incremental approach to the hybrid GA without vertex reordering degraded the performance in all of the 8 classes. But this could be overcome by using vertex reordering schemes in most of the cases. The incremental approach using the most appropriate scheme, namely max-degree reordering(MD), even showed better performance than that of the baseline.

Table 2: The average fitness function value of hybrid incremental genetic algorithm with four different kinds of vertex reordering.

$\|V_1\|$	η	BASE	NO	MD	BFS	MA
10	0.1	0.0005	0.0015	**0.0002**	0.0010	**0.0002**
10	0.2	0.0557	0.0991	**0.0462**	0.0642	0.0573
30	0.05	0.4813	0.9318	**0.2431**	0.3969	0.3112
30	0.1	0.7994	1.1790	**0.3841**	0.8882	0.4475
30	0.2	0.0718	0.2802	**0.0364**	0.3812	0.1506
50	0.01	0.0094	0.1210	**0.0043**	0.0102	0.0098
50	0.05	0.0073	0.1973	**0.0000**	0.1440	0.0214
70	0.01	0.0095	0.1189	**0.0056**	0.0115	0.0106

5.4 Effect of Changing Stopping Criterion

Table 3 shows the average fitness function value of the hybrid incremental GAs with different stopping criteria. Each of the step is terminated when the count of optimal solutions in the population reaches a certain threshold. We used 100, 50, and 1 for the threshold value. The stopping criterion is applied to the algorithm with max-degree reordering and the algorithm without reordering. For each reordering scheme, we also showed the result of an algorithm without stopping criterion, which runs a fixed number of generations for each step, as the baseline. We marked the best result for each case with bold.

In general, reducing the threshold value gave better results for both schemes. In the case with max-degree reordering, using the lowest threshold value of one gave the best result in 5 out of 8 classes. And for the case without reordering, only one case was exceptional. Since reducing the threshold

Table 3: The average fitness function value of hybrid incremental genetic algorithm with stopping criteria for each step. The threshold values used are 100, 50, and 1. The two algorithms each with and without vertex reordering are tested.

$\lvert V_1 \rvert$	η	With max-degree reordering				Without reordering			
		Base	100	50	1	Base	100	50	1
10	0.1	0.0002	**0.0000**	0.0002	**0.0000**	0.0015	0.0006	**0.0001**	0.0003
10	0.2	0.0462	0.0374	**0.0315**	0.0365	0.0991	0.0823	0.0781	**0.0619**
30	0.05	0.2431	0.1719	0.1833	**0.1467**	0.9318	0.7545	0.7354	**0.6386**
30	0.1	0.3841	0.4699	0.3772	**0.3680**	1.1790	1.2363	1.1702	**1.0539**
30	0.2	0.0364	0.0335	0.0461	**0.0112**	**0.2802**	0.3493	0.5505	0.4196
50	0.01	0.0043	0.0046	**0.0040**	0.0058	0.1210	0.0719	0.0644	**0.0316**
50	0.05	**0.0000**	0.0210	0.0073	**0.0000**	0.1973	0.1538	0.1365	**0.1010**
70	0.01	0.0056	**0.0050**	0.0053	0.0060	0.1189	0.1123	0.1099	**0.0998**

value increases population diversity, focusing on exploration in intermediate steps seems to be more helpful than focusing on exploitation. Instead of evolving from a population full of local optima, it was better to evolve from a diverse population where only one of the solutions is locally optimal.

5.5 Effect of Changing Expansion Size

Table 4 shows the average fitness function value and the average running time of hybrid incremental GAs with different expansion size values. Since there are classes of graphs with $|V_1| = 10$, we used expansion sizes less than or equal to 5. We used max-degree reordering and stopping criterion with a threshold value of 1. Correlation coefficients between the averages and the expansion size are also calculated and presented. Among the five different cases, the best result for each classes is marked bold.

Generally, increasing the number of vertices to be added at each step was better in terms of fitness function value. However, the values does not have consistent and strong correlation with the expansion size. The expansion sizes of 4 and 5 each was the best choice for 3 classes. Large expansion size was also good in terms of average running time, and there was consistent and strong correlation. Changing the expansion size from 1 to 2 had the largest gap of running time, and the gap decreased afterwards. Therefore, it seems better to use a large expansion size since increasing the size reduces the running time without losing the solution quality.

5.6 Overall Result

We combined the best choices from the previous subsections in our hybrid incremental genetic algorithm. We used max-degree reordering, the stopping criterion with a threshold value of 1, and the expansion size value of 4. All of the 20 classes of graphs were tested by this algorithm and the result was compared to that of the traditional hybrid GA without incremental approach.

Table 5 shows the overall results. The average fitness function value, the standard deviation(SD) of the values, the average running time in seconds and the proportion of runs in which an optimal solution has found, are shown in the table, respectively

The table also contains p-values for each class computed by Welch's t-test. The alternative hypothesis is that the performance of the traditional algorithm is better than that of the incremental algorithm, where the performance is measured by the average fitness function value. Therefore, the p-value roughly denotes the probability that the incremental approach improves or retains the performance. Eleven out of twenty classes are marked as NA, which means that both algorithms always found an optimal solution and thus the p-value could not be defined. For the eight relatively difficult classes, the performance was significantly improved by the incremental approach. The minimum ratio of finding an optimal solution was dramatically increased from 51.00% to 70.10%. For the last class, when $|V_1| = 50$ and $\eta = 0.1$, the corresponding p-value was 0.0787. Since the average fitness of the incremental algorithm was greater than that of the other algorithm, the probability that two averages are the same is 0.8426. The result shows that using the incremental approach is significantly helpful to improve the performance of a hybrid genetic algorithm.

On the other hand, the average running time was not decreased by using the incremental approach. We observed the running time decrease in only seven classes. For relatively easy classes, the traditional GA found an optimal solution in earlier generation and terminates. However, the incremental GA runs at least one generation for each step. The increase in running time seemed to be caused by this basic cost.

6. CONCLUSIONS

In this paper, we proposed a new hybrid genetic algorithm with an incremental approach for the subgraph isomorphism problem. The incremental approach starts from finding a small-sized subgraph and it gradually expands the size of the problem. The prior results were used for an initial population of a hybrid genetic algorithm for the following step. We met several design issues for the new algorithms. First, we verified that the order of problem expansion dominates the direction of the overall search path and an elaborate vertex reordering scheme is essential for the incremental approach. Next, we observed that stopping criterion also have an influence on the performance. Focusing on exploration in intermediate step, it was better to evolve from a diverse population with few local optima. The size of problem expansion did not have an effect on the performance as much as a vertex reordering and stopping criterion did. However, increasing the expansion size of each step showed a tendency to improve the running time. By hybridizing a local optimization algorithm and maintaining moderate diversity, the hybrid incremental approach with appropriate schemes outperformed the previous works in the experimental results.

Although we traced the design issues for the incremental approach, there are still other issues that have to be figured

Table 4: The result of hybrid incremental genetic algorithm with five different expansion sizes ranging 1 through 5. The max-degree reordering and the stopping criterion with a threshold value of 1 are used.

$\|V_1\|$	η	Average fitness function value						Average running time in seconds					
		1	2	3	4	5	Corr.	1	2	3	4	5	Corr.
10	0.1	**0.0000**	0.0003	0.0003	0.0001	0.0004	0.5774	0.31	0.19	0.21	0.18	0.18	-0.8034
10	0.2	**0.0365**	0.0380	0.0386	0.0421	0.0506	0.9019	1.23	1.18	1.25	1.31	1.57	0.8377
30	0.05	0.1467	0.1467	0.1404	0.1395	**0.1389**	-0.9184	6.71	5.14	4.66	4.88	4.71	-0.7896
30	0.1	0.3680	0.2766	0.2936	**0.2731**	0.2755	-0.7393	6.28	3.97	3.27	3.10	2.69	-0.8910
30	0.2	0.0112	0.0221	0.0671	0.0223	**0.0111**	0.0000	6.08	3.94	3.18	2.93	2.33	-0.9247
50	0.01	0.0058	0.0054	0.0053	0.0065	**0.0050**	-0.1366	13.30	8.28	7.03	6.53	5.56	-0.8943
50	0.05	0.0000	0.0069	0.0000	**0.0000**	0.0074	0.3186	16.68	9.22	7.13	6.12	5.10	-0.8961
70	0.01	0.0060	0.0036	0.0035	**0.0029**	0.0035	-0.7472	33.38	19.52	16.20	14.03	12.36	-0.8926

Table 5: The overall result of hybrid genetic algorithm compared to traditional hybrid genetic algorithm.

$\|V_1\|$	η	Traditional hybrid GA				hybrid incremental GA				p-value
		f average	f SD	Time(s)	Ratio	f average	f SD	Time(s)	Ratio	
10	0.01	0.0000	0.0000	0.00	100.00%	0.0000	0.0000	0.09	100.00%	NA
	0.05	0.0000	0.0000	0.01	100.00%	0.0000	0.0000	0.12	100.00%	NA
	0.1	0.0005	0.0071	0.18	99.50%	0.0001	0.0032	0.18	99.90%	0.9489
	0.2	0.0557	0.0788	1.74	62.10%	0.0421	0.0712	1.31	70.10%	1.0000
30	0.01	0.0000	0.0000	0.14	100.00%	0.0000	0.0000	1.04	100.00%	NA
	0.05	0.4813	0.5788	12.30	51.00%	0.1395	0.3178	4.88	79.60%	1.0000
	0.1	0.7994	1.7404	9.98	82.50%	0.2731	1.1048	3.10	94.20%	1.0000
	0.2	0.0718	0.9258	3.26	99.40%	0.0223	0.4986	2.93	99.80%	0.9315
50	0.01	0.0094	0.0315	12.21	91.30%	0.0065	0.0247	6.53	93.50%	0.9890
	0.05	0.0073	0.2307	5.51	99.90%	0.0000	0.0000	6.12	100.00%	0.8412
	0.1	0.0000	0.0000	4.17	100.00%	0.0430	0.9610	7.43	99.80%	0.0787
	0.2	0.0000	0.0000	3.09	100.00%	0.0000	0.0000	10.34	100.00%	NA
70	0.01	0.0095	0.0319	26.58	91.30%	0.0029	0.0185	14.03	97.40%	1.0000
	0.05	0.0000	0.0000	0.12	100.00%	0.0000	0.0000	11.37	100.00%	NA
	0.1	0.0000	0.0000	0.25	100.00%	0.0000	0.0000	13.00	100.00%	NA
	0.2	0.0000	0.0000	1.17	100.00%	0.0000	0.0000	16.59	100.00%	NA
90	0.01	0.0000	0.0000	7.36	100.00%	0.0000	0.0000	18.89	100.00%	NA
	0.05	0.0000	0.0000	0.04	100.00%	0.0000	0.0000	21.40	100.00%	NA
	0.1	0.0000	0.0000	0.05	100.00%	0.0000	0.0000	24.91	100.00%	NA
	0.2	0.0000	0.0000	0.09	100.00%	0.0000	0.0000	29.67	100.00%	NA

out for a better performance. As shown in the experimental results, we only used manual tuning to set the parameter and settings of the incremental approach. In the future, we have in mind to incorporate adaptive features and use the dynamic configuration to select parameters and to apply different strategy. Also, we hope to try extensive experiments in the various size and types of the graphs and apply this approach to other combinatorial problems.

7. ACKNOWLEDGMENTS

This work was supported by the Engineering Research Center of Excellence Program of Korea Ministry of Science, ICT & Future Planning(MSIP) / National Research Foundation of Korea(NRF) (Grant NRF-2008-0062609). The ICT at Seoul National University provides research facilities for this study.

8. REFERENCES

[1] G. Bakirli, D. Birant, and A. Kut. An incremental genetic algorithm for classification and sensitivity analysis of its parameters. *Expert Systems with Applications*, 38(3):2609 – 2620, 2011.

[2] C. Borgelt and M. Berthold. Mining molecular fragments: finding relevant substructures of molecules. In *Data Mining, 2002. ICDM 2003. Proceedings. 2002 IEEE International Conference on*, pages 51–58, 2002.

[3] R. D. Brown, G. Jones, P. Willett, and R. C. Glen. Matching two-dimensional chemical graphs using genetic algorithms. *Journal of Chemical Information and Computer Sciences*, pages 63–70, 1994.

[4] J. Choi, Y. Yoon, and B.-R. Moon. An efficient genetic algorithm for subgraph isomorphism. In *Proceedings of the Fourteenth International Conference on Genetic and Evolutionary Computation Conference*, GECCO '12, pages 361–368, New York, NY, USA, 2012. ACM.

[5] D. Conte, P. Foggia, and M. Vento. Challenging complexity of maximum common subgraph detection algorithms: A performance analysis of three algorithms on a wide database of graphs. *Journal of Graph Algorithms and Applications*, 11(1):99–143, 2007.

[6] S. A. Cook. The complexity of theorem-proving procedures. In *Proceedings of the Third Annual ACM*

Symposium on Theory of Computing, STOC '71, pages 151–158, New York, NY, USA, 1971. ACM.

[7] D. G. Corneil and C. C. Gotlieb. An efficient algorithm for graph isomorphism. *J. ACM*, 17(1):51–64, Jan. 1970.

[8] D. Eppstein. Subgraph isomorphism in planar graphs and related problems. In *Proceedings of the Sixth Annual ACM-SIAM Symposium on Discrete Algorithms*, SODA '95, pages 632–640, Philadelphia, PA, USA, 1995. Society for Industrial and Applied Mathematics.

[9] P. Foggia, C. Sansone, and M. Vento. A Database of Graphs for Isomorphism and Sub-Graph isomorphism Benchmarking. *3rd IAPR-TC15 Workshop on Graph-based Representations in Pattern Recognition*, 2001.

[10] M. R. Garey and D. S. Johnson. *Computers and Intractability; A Guide to the Theory of NP-Completeness*. W. H. Freeman & Co., New York, NY, USA, 1990.

[11] I. Hwang, Y.-H. Kim, and B.-R. Moon. Multi-attractor gene reordering for graph bisection. In *Proceedings of the 8th Annual Conference on Genetic and Evolutionary Computation*, GECCO '06, pages 1209–1216, New York, NY, USA, 2006. ACM.

[12] A. Inokuchi, T. Washio, and H. Motoda. An apriori-based algorithm for mining frequent substructures from graph data. In D. Zighed, J. Komorowski, and J. Åżytkow, editors, *Principles of Data Mining and Knowledge Discovery*, volume 1910 of *Lecture Notes in Computer Science*, pages 13–23. Springer Berlin Heidelberg, 2000.

[13] K. Kim and B.-R. Moon. Malware detection based on dependency graph using hybrid genetic algorithm. In *Proceedings of the 12th Annual Conference on Genetic and Evolutionary Computation*, GECCO '10, pages 1211–1218, New York, NY, USA, 2010. ACM.

[14] J. Liu and Y. T. Lee. A graph-based method for face identification from a single 2d line drawing. *IEEE Trans. Pattern Anal. Mach. Intell.*, 23(10):1106–1119, Oct. 2001.

[15] E. M. Luks. Isomorphism of graphs of bounded valence can be tested in polynomial time. *Journal of Computer and System Sciences*, 25(1):42 – 65, 1982.

[16] N. Mansour, M. Awad, and K. El-fakih. Incremental genetic algorithm. *The International Arab Journal of Information Technology*, 3(1):42–47, 2006.

[17] B. Messmer and H. Bunke. Efficient subgraph isomorphism detection: a decomposition approach. *Knowledge and Data Engineering, IEEE Transactions on*, 12(2):307–323, 2000.

[18] M. Ohlrich, C. Ebeling, E. Ginting, and L. Sather. Subgemini: Identifying subcircuits using a fast subgraph isomorphism algorithm. In *Proceedings of the 30th International Design Automation Conference*, DAC '93, pages 31–37, New York, NY, USA, 1993. ACM.

[19] I. M. Oliver, D. J. Smith, and J. R. C. Holland. A study of permutation crossover operators on the traveling salesman problem. In *Proceedings of the Second International Conference on Genetic Algorithms on Genetic Algorithms and Their Application*, pages 224–230, Hillsdale, NJ, USA, 1987. L. Erlbaum Associates Inc.

[20] J. Rocha and T. Pavlidis. A shape analysis model with applications to a character recognition system. *IEEE Trans. Pattern Anal. Mach. Intell.*, 16(4):393–404, Apr. 1994.

[21] J. Rutgers, P. Wolkotte, P. HoÌĹlzenspies, J. Kuper, and G. J. M. Smit. An approximate maximum common subgraph algorithm for large digital circuits. In *Digital System Design: Architectures, Methods and Tools (DSD), 2010 13th Euromicro Conference on*, pages 699–705, 2010.

[22] B. Song and V. Li. A hybridization between memetic algorithm and semidefinite relaxation for the max-cut problem. In *Proceedings of the Fourteenth International Conference on Genetic and Evolutionary Computation Conference*, GECCO '12, pages 425–432, New York, NY, USA, 2012. ACM.

[23] J. R. Ullmann. An algorithm for subgraph isomorphism. *J. ACM*, 23(1):31–42, Jan. 1976.

[24] A. Wu, H. Yu, S. Jin, K.-C. Lin, and G. Schiavone. An incremental genetic algorithm approach to multiprocessor scheduling. *Parallel and Distributed Systems, IEEE Transactions on*, 15(9):824–834, 2004.

[25] Q. Zhong, Z. Wu, L. Lin, Y. Zhang, and Y. Zhang. Computing resources assignment in rtds simulators with subgraph isomorphism based on genetic algorithm. In *Electric Utility Deregulation and Restructuring and Power Technologies (DRPT), 2011 4th International Conference on*, pages 1144–1149, 2011.

Data-Driven Local Optima Network Characterization of QAPLIB Instances

David Iclănzan
david.iclanzan@gmail.com

Fabio Daolio
fabio.daolio@unil.ch

Marco Tomassini
marco.tomassini@unil.ch

Faculty of Business and Economics, University of Lausanne, Switzerland

ABSTRACT

Inherent networks of potential energy surfaces proposed in physical chemistry inspired a compact network characterization of combinatorial fitness landscapes. In these so-called Local Optima Networks (LON), the nodes correspond to the local optima and the edges quantify a measure of adjacency - transition probability between them.

Methods so far used an exhaustive search for extracting LON, limiting their applicability to small problem instances only. To increase scalability, in this paper a new data-driven methodology is proposed that approximates the LON from actual runs of search methods. The method enables the extraction and study of LON corresponding to the various types of instances from the Quadratic Assignment Problem Library (QAPLIB), whose search spaces are characterized in terms of local minima connectivity. Our analysis provides a novel view of the unified testbed of QAP combinatorial landscapes used in the literature, revealing qualitative inherent properties that can be used to classify instances and estimate search difficulty.

Categories and Subject Descriptors

F.2.m [**Analysis of Algorithms and Problem Complexity**]: Miscellaneous; G.2.2 [**Discrete Mathematics**]: Graph Theory—*Network problems*; I.2.8 [**Artificial Intelligence**]: Problem Solving, Control Methods, and Search—*Heuristic methods*

General Terms

Algorithms, Design, Theory

Keywords

Local Optima Networks, Quadratic Assignment Problem

1. INTRODUCTION

The performance of stochastic local search algorithms depends on structural aspects of the space being searched [12].

GECCO'14, July 12–16, 2014, Vancouver, BC, Canada.

ACM 978-1-4503-2662-9/14/07 ...$15.00.
http://dx.doi.org/10.1145/2576768.2598275 .

In particular, as the evaluation function guides the search towards better solutions, the number and distribution of local optima have an impact on problem difficulty. The search space analysis of a given problem instance routinely includes measures about the average distance between local minima, and the average distance of sampled solutions to the best-known minimum, together with correlation measures collected via random or adaptive walks. In this strand of research about fitness landscape analysis, the recently proposed Local Optima Networks (LON) model [26], aims to provide a compressed description of the search space at the level of local minima. This view has proved to be relevant for local search heuristics [8], the statistical features of the network being correlated with problem difficulty.

As originally envisioned, LON vertices are defined according to one-move deterministic hill-climbers and the connections are derived by exhaustively sampling all the solutions in the basins of attraction with regard to their one-mutant neighbors (*basin-transition* edges [26, 30]), or by performing a number of kick-moves from a local optimum and looking at the basin of the corresponding new solutions (*escape* edges [29]). The exhaustive sampling with one-move deterministic hill-climbers limits the applicability of LON to small problem instances.

Therefore, recently efforts have been made to overcome these limitations by replacing the costly exhaustive enumeration of the search space with more efficient and flexible sampling methods. These approaches rely on the critical assumption that approximated LON can still capture the essential features of the search space. Initial results are encouraging. In a first approach, by monitoring the search dynamics of a stochastic search method on a compressed view of NK landscapes facilitated by Self Organizing Maps, inherent networks retaining their descriptive power were successfully derived [13].

In this paper we investigate how a bounded sampling can alleviate the LON scalability issue, also addressing the trade-off between network size and the descriptive power of the resulting LON for Quadratic Assignment Problem (QAP) instances. The permutation-based search space of such a problem has been already the subject of many studies, especially when applied to the understanding and tuning of search performances, as for instance in [17, 23, 9, 2]. Models of problem hardness based on landscape characteristics have also been recently published [21]. The focus of this paper is to advance the LON model as a complementary and arguably richer characterization of these search space structures.

Local Optima Networks of QAP instances had been already extracted and analyzed, but for problem sizes of up to size 11 only [7, 6, 4] due to the super-exponential growth of the search space size. In order to be able to tackle larger problem instances, in this paper we propose a bounded sampling for LON modeling.

The paper is organized as follows: Section 2 gives the details of the proposed sampling method. Section 3 describes the experimental setup, while results are reported in Section 4. Section 5 concludes the paper, also outlining future lines of research.

2. DATA-DRIVEN LON EXTRACTION

2.1 Finding relevant vertices

The number of local optima in combinatorial optimization problems with regard to a simple move operator can grow exponentially with the size of the problem. The nodes of a reduced but still relevant LON should be solutions that are strong local optima, in the sense of a larger neighborhood structure, solutions that can not be improved very easily.

For the QAP problem, we accept as potential nodes of the LON solutions that are locally optima in the neighborhood of one and two swaps, random exchange moves. Therefore, the set of potential nodes corresponding to the instances studied in this paper were derived in the following way:

1. Starting from a random solution we perform an one-swap best-improvement hill-climbing to quickly locate a good solution.
2. If possible, this solution is further improved by a more costly best-improvement hill-climbing which explores the neighborhood of one and two swaps.
3. Steps 1 and 2 are repeated $2000n$ times, where n is the size of the problem.

The hill-climbers enumerate the neighborhood structure in a random order and accept solutions with better or equal cost. We accept changes at equal cost in order to increase the exploratory power of the sampling.

To assess the impact of vertex number on the properties of the resulting LON and its descriptive power, we used two network configurations. In the first one we included all potential nodes found by the above method, while in the second configuration, which we name "capped networks", the number of vertices was restricted to the fitness-wise top n^2 local optima, where n again denotes the problem size.

2.2 Approximating the reachability measures

As in a previous approach [13], we quantify the connectivity of the vertices empirically, running a local-search many times and counting the frequency with which it connects the nodes of the network.

For each vertex i the following procedure is applied:

1. Starting from the vertex, a random kick-move (consisting of k random swaps) is performed, which has the role of moving the solution out from the strong basin of attraction of that solution.
2. From the new state a hill-climbing is performed. If the result of the hill-climb is a node j of the network, we increment a reachability counter $C(i, j)$. When $i = j$ i.e the search returned to the starting vertex, the $C(i, j)$ counter accounts for the self-loop weight.
3. Steps 1 and 2 are repeated $20n^2$ times, where n is again the problem size.

The final adjacency matrix A of the LON is obtained by dividing the elements of C with the number of runs per node, therefore $A = C/(20n^2)$. As such, $A(i, j)$ quantifies the frequency with which node j was reached by the kick-move, hill-climb combination, when starting from node i.

As previous studies had shown [20] that search heuristics using the same move operator but slightly different exploitation strategies can induce different LON structures, in this paper we examined the outcome of using a first-improvement hill-climbing and a best-improvement hill-climbing strategy after the kick-move. As the nodes of the network are guaranteed local optima in the neighborhood of 2 swaps, we perform a random kick-move of 3 swaps.

3. EXPERIMENTS

3.1 QAP and QAPLIB

The QAP is a hard combinatorial problem that deals with the relative location of units interacting with one another. The objective is to minimize the total cost of interactions. In the problem statement, n units or facilities are to be assigned to n predefined locations, where each location can accommodate any one unit. Location i and location j are separated by a distance a_{ij}, generically representing the per-unit cost of interaction between the two locations. A flow of value b_{ij} has to go from unit i to unit j; the objective is to find an assignment, i.e. a bijection from the set of facilities onto the set of locations, which minimizes the sum of products flow $\times$ distance.

This bijection can naturally be encoded as a permutation π and the problem of cost assignment minimization can be formulated as: $\arg\min_{\pi \in P(n)} C(\pi)$, where $C(\pi) = \sum_{i=1}^{n} \sum_{j=1}^{n} b_{ij} a_{\pi_i \pi_j}$ is the cost function, $A = \{a_{ij}\}$ and $B = \{b_{ij}\}$ are the two $n \times n$ distance and flow matrixes, and π_i gives the location of facility i in permutation π. The structures of the distance and flow matrices characterize the class of instances of the QAP problem.

The most used, unified testbed for this problem is provided by the QAPLIB [3] collection. Since the computational effort of the proposed sampling method for the extraction of the LON edges is still proportional to the number of nodes, to effectively sample networks including all the potential nodes that were found in the first phase, we restrict this first analysis to all QAPLIB instances of size up to 32. This subset of 78 instances stemming from various sources and fields of application, covers already different classes of problems [25]: (i) the random, unstructured; (ii) the random, grid-based; (iii) examples from real life, and (iv) the real-life like, generated ones. For a detailed presentation, we refer the reader to the QAPLIB [3].

3.2 LON measures

Connectivity.

The order of the LON graph is given by the cardinality of its node set, the number of sampled strong local optima or points of interest $nPOIs$. The ratio of present to possible

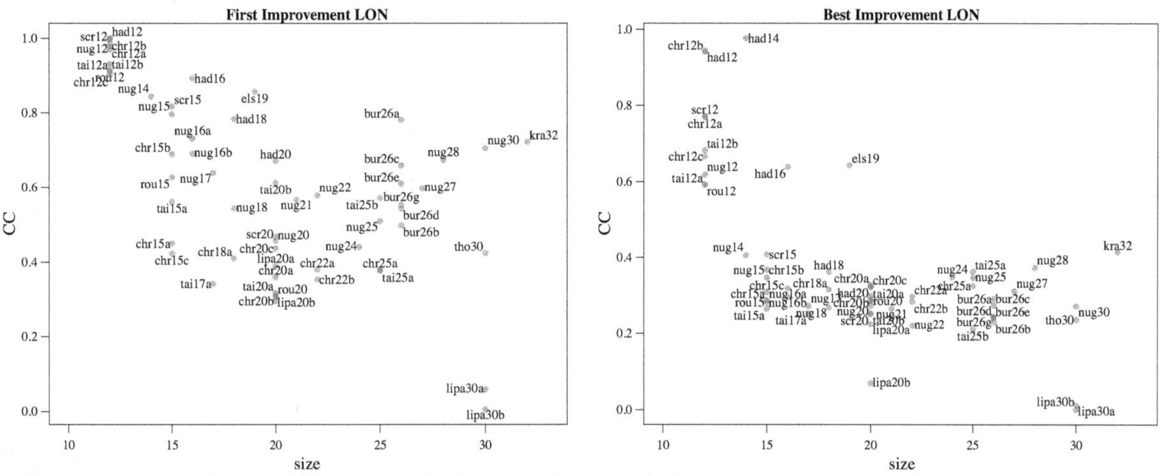

(a) clustering coefficient

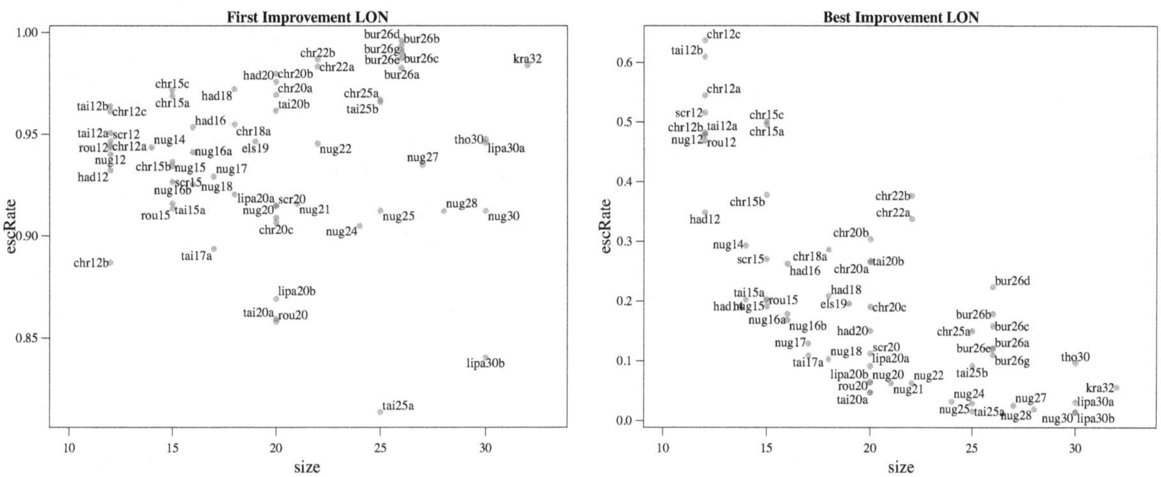

(b) escape rate

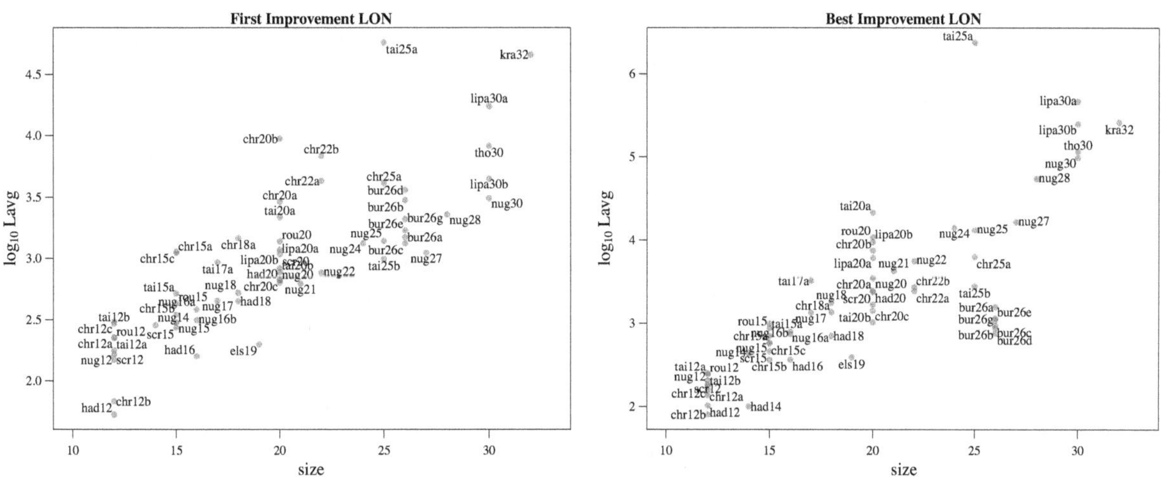

(c) average path length on a logarithmic scale

Figure 1: scatterplots of LON features with respect to problem size.

edges is the network *density*. In a random graph, all edges would be present with equal probability, but if there is a local structure to the connectivity, then the adjacent vertices of a vertex are connected with higher probability, which is measured by the clustering coefficient CC [18].

In a directed graph, though, connectivity is more subtle, as there can be a connection from node i to node j but not vice-versa; the measure of reciprocity, *recip*, defines the proportion of mutual connections. Then, there can be a path from i to j but not vice-versa; the $qLSCC$ variable gives the ratio of nodes in the largest strongly connected components, i.e. nodes that are connected through bidirectional paths.

Mixing patterns.

Transitions can bridge local optima that have similar or very diverse characteristics in terms of connectivity and fitness value, which in turns influences the dynamics of random and adaptive walks on the networks. We employ Newman's assortativity measure to gauge the correlation of degree, $degMix$, and fitness, $fitMix$, at each endpoint of LON edges [18].

Paths.

The escape rate, *escRate*, or more precisely its reciprocal, can be interpreted as the expected number of random kick-moves and hill-climb trials needed to escape the current local optimum [16]. By considering any two connected nodes i and j to be an expected number of moves apart that equals the reciprocal of their connection weight, we can calculate the LON average path length, *Lavg*, and the average length of paths leading to the best-known local optima, *Lopt*. Averages are computed as harmonic means because of possibly missing paths, disconnected components [18].

Communities.

Communities can be loosely defined as groups of nodes that are strongly connected between them and poorly connected with the rest of the graph. In order to find a suitable partitioning of nodes into community, we use a graph clustering algorithm that is based on the simulation of network flow [27], as in [6]. Then, to assess the level of community structure, we give Newman's modularity score, Q [19].

As we observed non-homogeneous partitioning, we also add the Gini coefficient, G, as a measure of inequality in the distribution of community sizes [10].

3.3 Hardness measure

To make a case for the LON characterization of the search space, the network features have to correlate with the performances of actual search heuristics. In the present work about QAP, Taillard's Robust Tabu Search (RoTS) [24] is a natural candidate, as its results are still state-of-the art on some problem instances. Moreover, even if Tabu Search appears to effectively restrict its search around local optima and close-by solutions [31], its search dynamics are not explicitly bounded to kick-moves and LON structure as in the Iterated Local Search case. For this reason also, the RoTS is a good choice to test the relevance of the LON study.

Thus, in order to assess the instance hardness, we use the expected number of Tabu iterations to find a solution with optimal cost (*Run-Length* [12]), in a scenario of independent restarts of the RoTS algorithm, so that both the success rate ($p_s \in (0, 1]$) and the convergence speed are taken into account [1]. In such setting, after $(N-1)$ unsuccessful runs stopped at T_{us}-steps and the final successful one running for T_s-steps, the total run-length would be $T = \sum_{k=1}^{N-1} (T_{us})_k + T_s$. Taking the expectation and considering that N follows a geometric distribution (Bernoulli trials) with parameter p_s, it gives: $\mathbb{E}(T) = \left(\frac{1-p_s}{p_s}\right)\mathbb{E}(T_{us}) + \mathbb{E}(T_s)$, where $\mathbb{E}(T_{us})$ equals the given maximum budget of RoTS iterations, the ratio of successful to total runs is an estimator for p_s, and $\mathbb{E}(T_s)$ can be estimated by the average running time of successful runs. We denote this estimated time to succeed *ets* in the following results presentation. As for the experimental setup, the RoTS is allowed a maximum of 10^5 unsuccessful iterations and is independently restarted 10^3 times on each problem instance.

4. RESULTS

We extracted the LON measures described in Section 3.2 for the networks containing all potential nodes and for the capped networks, with a maximum cardinality of n^2. When capped, networks lost on average approximately 85% of their nodes, resulting in a heavy shrinkage and much smaller network sizes. Therefore, we were surprised to find that network characteristics are very similar between full and capped networks. Indeed, by correlating element-wise all the observed measures and averaging the resulting coefficients, the correlation is 0.9838 for the first improvement LONs, and 0.9866 for the networks constructed with best improvement hill-climbing. In other words, the small networks accurately capture the same trends.

Due to space considerations we focus the analysis on the small, capped networks, which are also much more relevant from the scalability point of view. However the same trends are present in the bigger networks.

4.1 LON feature trends

Scatter plots of selected complex-network metrics with respect to problem size are presented in Figure 1 for the capped networks obtained through best-improvement, respectively first-improvement hill-climbing based sampling.

The clustering coefficient is inversely correlated with the problem size for both LON models, the networks becoming sparser as the size of the search space increases. However in the case of the networks obtained with first improvement hill-climbing we see a higher variance but also typically higher values, revealing an increased transitivity closure.

The trends for the escape rate are completely opposite in the case of the two models. The best improvement hill-climbing tends to return to the state prior to the kick-move much more often, an effect that increases with problem size - network sparseness. For this model the escape rate gradually decreases from around 0.65 to almost 0. In the case of first improvement hill-climbing, as the search space increases it is easier for the method to wander away from the basin of attraction of the original state, following a path of improving or neutral moves. This sampling results in networks with escape rate varying between 0.8 and almost 1.

The average path length correlates directly with the problem size for both models, meaning that distances between local optima increases. However, for the best-improvement based sampling it takes more trials to escape the basin of attraction of a local optima, therefore the path sizes increase

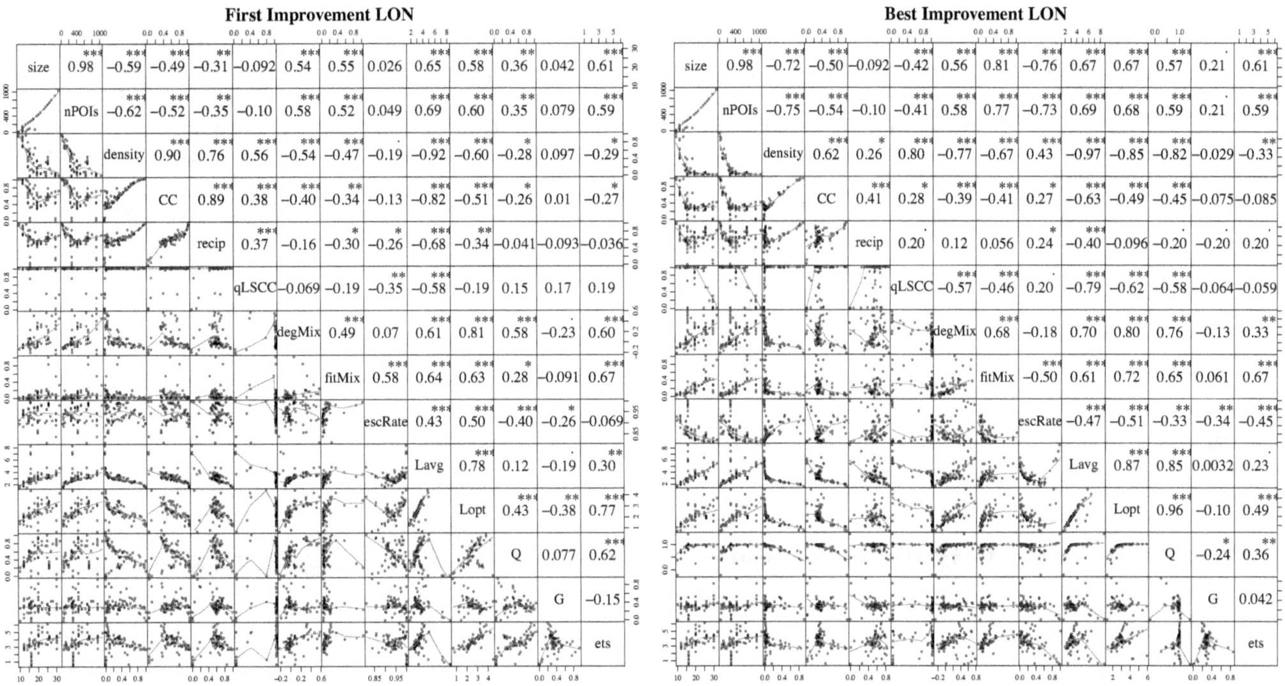

Figure 2: correlation diagrams for all pairs of observed variables, to be read from the diagonal. The lower panel displays scatter plots and smoothing splines for every possible pairing; the upper panel gives the corresponding Pearson correlation coefficient. In the lower panel, the smoothing is done through locally-weighted polynomial regressions [5]. In the upper panel, the correlation coefficient is tested against the null hypothesis and the resulting p-value is symbolically encoded at the levels of 0.1 (’), 0.05 (*), 0.01 (**), **and** 0.001 (***).

much faster, there being 2 order of magnitudes difference on the semi-logarithmic plots in Figure 1c.

The pairwise interplay and the correlation with estimated problem difficulty (last columns) between all studied metrics is presented in Figure 2 for both LON models. This reveals a complex picture, with many highly inter-correlated components, that might contribute in explaining and estimating problem hardness.

4.2 Regression model of the problem difficulty

In this section we take a closer at look what combinations of LON features are good candidates in predicting instance hardness for the RoTS [24], using both LON models. As depicted in Figure 3, problem difficulty naturally increases with the size of the instances. However, from the high variance exhibited from the scatter plot it is clear that problem size alone is far from enough to explain the inherent difficulty. For example, for problem size 20, the plot reveals that the expected running time is scattered along four orders of magnitude, ranging from very easy to very hard.

For the instances of size 20, Table 1 reports the determined LONs metrics and their possible role in explaining the variance exhibited by the performance measure. In the case of first-improvement LONs, the best individual predictors of search difficulty are the average length of paths leading to the global optimum, modularity, and cluster size inequality: these features are both significantly correlated with empirical difficulty and can also account for a high proportion of its variance. In the case of best-improvement LONs, the more relevant and more correlated metrics are degree assortativity, link reciprocity and clustering coefficient.

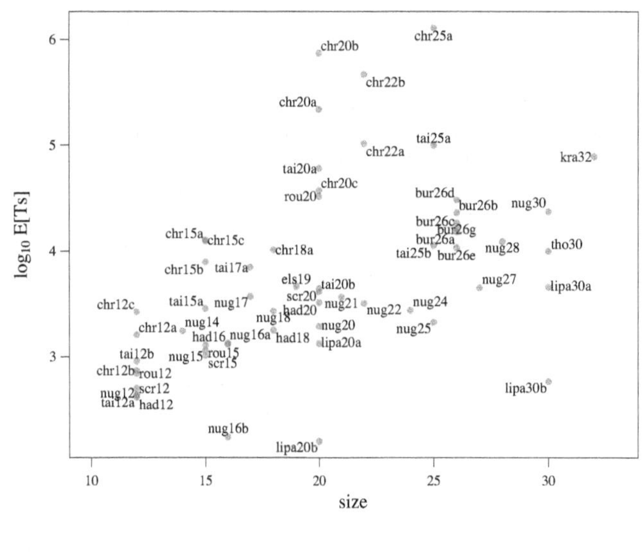

Figure 3: semi-logarithmic scatter plot of problem hardness versus instance size.

The rank correlations between instance hardness and each LON feature in turns for the whole data set, are given in

Table 1: subset of QAPLIB instances of size 20; rank correlation (ρ) of LON features and RoTS performance, and the proportion of performance variance ($\mathbf{R}^2$) that each feature could explain in a linear regression. Significant correlations are highlighted.

	First Impr.		Best Impr.	
	Spearman's ρ	R^2	Spearman's ρ	R^2
density	−0.54	0.16	−0.32	0.04
CC	−0.35	0.11	0.83**	0.62
recip	0.61*	0.45	0.89***	0.73
qLSCC	−0.67*	0.52	−0.11	0.00
degMix	0.65**	0.63	0.85***	0.75
fitMix	0.39	0.19	0.40	0.23
escRate	0.22	0.10	0.35·	0.30
Lavg	0.61*	0.54	0.05	0.01
Lopt	0.92***	0.84	0.64*	0.47
Q	0.79**	0.67	0.83*	0.36
G	−0.83**	0.65	−0.69*	0.52

$^{***}p < 0.001$, $^{**}p < 0.01$, $^{*}p < 0.05$

the last column of Fig. 2. In the LON sampled with first-improvement, the performance of RoTS seems to be associated the most with *Lopt*, modularity, and mixing patterns, confirming and extending the insights of Table 1. Correlation values are still significant albeit less high in the case of best-improvement sampling; mixing patterns with respect to local optima fitness values, length of paths to the best-known optimum, and escape rate, are the LON features mostly associated to RoTS search difficulty in this case.

In order to account for the high interplay between all these factors as revealed by Figure 2, we combine them into a multi-linear regression model. Admittedly, such data clearly suffer from multicollinearity, which inflates the variance of coefficient estimates making it harder to assess the individual contribution of each predictor. That does not invalidate the explanatory power of the whole group of predictors, though. Hence in the first columns of Table 2, we report regression models comprising all the LON metrics from both sampling methods. Indeed the amount of variance explained is high in both cases. Nonetheless we observe that best-improvement sampling of LON transitions produces networks that are less informative than those built by first-improvement sampling. This might be due to the fact that best-improvement hill-climbers tend to return to the starting point more often after the kick move.

Then we perform model selection by exhaustive search, retaining the model with the best explanatory power for any number of predictors; we choose the appropriate number of such variables by looking at the *Cp* statistic [15]. Next, from the selected models we drop each predictor in turns by performing a step-wise backward elimination until all the remaining predictors become statistically significant [28]. The last columns of Table 2 report the resulting regression models for both sampling methods. The relevant metrics are again different for the two models: it appears that connectivity metrics and mixing patterns are more critical to the best-improvement case, whereas in the first-improvement case there is a broader spectrum of significant features. With respect to the common ones, as for degree mixing easier instances notably present disassortative LONs, meaning that the problem is easier when there are frequent transitions between less connected optima and more connected ones. Escape rate is also positively associated with instance hardness in both cases. Finally, R^2 figures are particularly promising, especially for the LON constructed through first-improvement sampling: the multi-linear regression is able to explain almost 85% of the RoTS performance variance that we observe at the instance level.

Table 2: multiple linear regression models to explain the RoTS performance variance on all the considered QAPLIB instances, using LON metrics as predictors. Standard errors on the coefficients are in parenthesis. Significant coefficients are highlighted.

	All predictors		Selected predictors	
	First Impr.	Best Impr.	First Impr.	Best Impr.
density	0.95	−2.98	1.54*	
	(0.67)	(1.86)	(0.65)	
CC	−2.63**	1.27	−2.37**	
	(0.86)	(1.52)	(0.76)	
recip	0.31	1.14		
	(1.11)	(0.93)		
qLSCC	−0.63	0.81		1.83***
	(0.60)	(0.60)		(0.52)
degMix	2.12**	1.94*	2.23***	3.09***
	(0.72)	(0.74)	(0.54)	(0.53)
fitMix	0.07	0.45		1.14**
	(0.35)	(0.44)		(0.42)
escRate	7.02**	1.59*	7.49***	1.61*
	(2.12)	(0.63)	(1.71)	(0.61)
Lavg	−0.26	0.56		0.46*
	(0.42)	(0.33)		(0.20)
Lopt	0.42*	−0.40	0.45**	
	(0.19)	(0.32)	(0.14)	
Q	0.51	−0.04	0.92**	
	(0.38)	(1.13)	(0.33)	
G	−0.62	−2.02		
	(0.60)	(1.29)		
R^2	0.86	0.76	0.86	0.73
Adj. R^2	0.82	0.71	0.85	0.70

$^{***}p < 0.001$, $^{**}p < 0.01$, $^{*}p < 0.05$

4.3 Principal component and cluster analysis

Looking for further insight from the LON characterization, we start exploring the way in which QAP problem instances might be clustered according to their LON features. K. Smith-Miles and T. T. Tan already applied this idea of decomposing and clustering several problem features that correlate with problem hardness, in order to visualize instances and algorithm performance in a multidimensional feature space [22]. Equally, we employ principal component analysis (PCA) to derive a hopefully meaningful transformation of our observations [14].

The first column of table 3 contains the features that were used in the PCA analysis. All these properties are strictly derived network metrics: problem and network size are not encoded, neither is RoTS performance. The remaining columns report the feature scaling coefficients, which define the two principal components determined by the PCA for the two LON samplings. The principal components ac-

Table 3: variable loadings (coefficients) of the PCA.

	First Impr.		Best Impr.	
	Comp.1	Comp.2	Comp.1	Comp.2
density	−0.44	−0.07	0.37	−0.06
CC	−0.39	−0.23	0.32	−0.21
recip	−0.31	−0.36	0.13	−0.51
qLSCC	−0.20	−0.32	0.29	−0.16
degMix	0.33	−0.30	−0.34	−0.24
fitMix	0.15	−0.25	−0.27	−0.23
escRate	−0.06	−0.31	0.34	−0.10
Lavg	0.44	−0.02	−0.39	0.13
Lopt	0.30	−0.42	−0.38	−0.21
Q	0.31	−0.19	−0.24	−0.38
G	0.02	0.50	−0.05	0.58
Proportion of Variance	0.42	0.26	0.50	0.22
Cumulative Proportion	0.42	0.67	0.50	0.72

count for a combined 67% and 72% of all variance of the considered features from first-improvement and best-improvement LONs, respectively. This enable the transformation of the multidimensional LON feature space into a bivariate plane that should reveal the internal structure of the data.

On such a plane, Figure 4 depicts five clusters determined by a k-means algorithm [11]. From both first-improvement and best-improvement sampling a consistent picture emerges: the hardest problem instances, essentially those found in the upper half of Figure 3, are grouped together in the rightmost clusters. Further, "lipa*" instances, which are the easiest for their respective size, form a separate cluster in both cases, and "bur*" instances also tend to be grouped together. The leftmost cluster in both plots contains small and relatively easy problem instances, while the central cluster groups instances of moderate size and difficulty. Thus it seems that principal components from Table 3 mostly reconstruct problem size and instance hardness; indeed, some of the highest scaling coefficient are also significant predictors of search performance in Table 2.

As observed from the comparison of Figures 3 and 4, the k-means does a remarkable job in clustering the instances according to their size and *difficulty*, by using features expressing various aspects of network structure only. This provides further evidence that the LON characterization captures the relevant features of the problem search space.

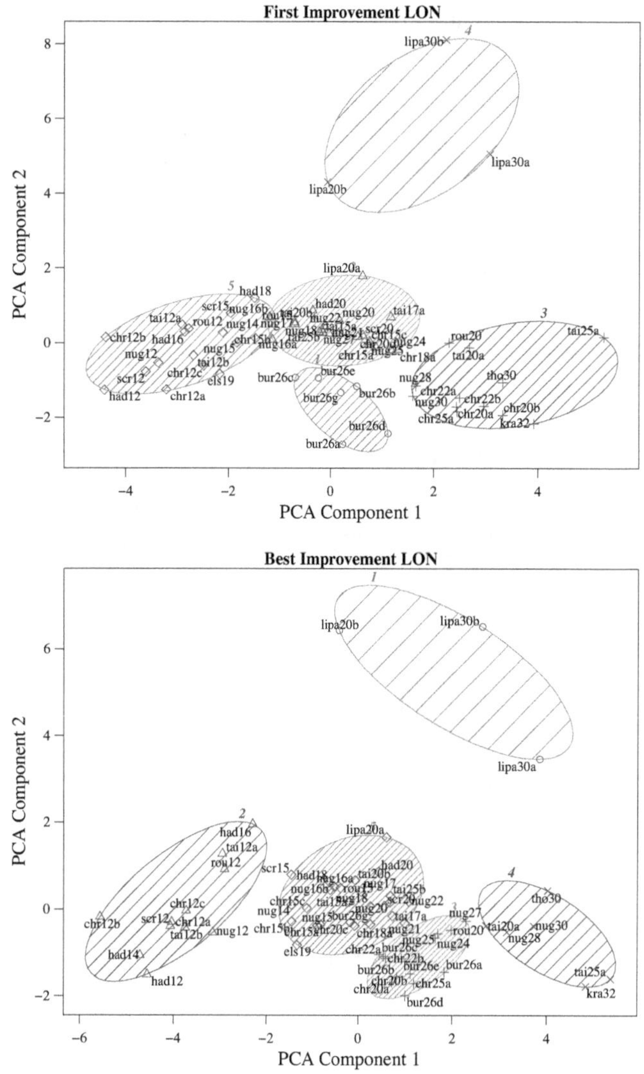

Figure 4: clustering plots. Points represent instances in the bivariate space that results from the scaling of principal component analysis [14] on the LON features only. Ellipses are drawn around the clusters obtained by the k-means algorithm [11].

5. CONCLUSIONS

Methods of fitness landscape analysis strive to characterize, understand and predict problem instance hardness. Classical definition and extraction methods for LON required the enumeration of the entire search space for exact identification of local optima, their basins of attraction, and the connecting structures that can be exploited by a search method. While providing the means for relevant fundamental analysis, the exhaustive nature of the sampling limited their applicability to problems of relatively small size. This paper proposes a two stage data-driven approximation for the LON extraction to alleviate this scalability issue. First, a search is performed to find strong local optima, solutions that are not trivial to improve. In a second stage, a vast sampling is conducted in order to empirically approximate the reachability relation between nodes of the LON.

The experimental and observational nature of this approach confers flexibility, as the move operator and sampling methods can be closely fitted to capture the effect of more complex search operators and their interplay or of different exploitation vs. exploration balances. While single fitness landscape measures are very unlikely to be able to explain problem hardness above a certain extent, the collection of network metrics derived from a LON have the potential to capture and express much more effectively the different facets of search difficulty, at least from the point of view of trajectory-based search metaheuristics.

Indeed, the analysis performed on QAPLIB problem instances confirms that the approximated LON provide an appropriate compressed description of their intrinsic properties related to their inherent hardness. The amount of instance hardness variability explained by these LON models is very high by static cost model standards [31], being up to 85%.

Also, the experiments revealed that landscape properties are accurately captured even in smaller networks, whose cardinality is capped to a low order polynomial of the problem size. The LON approximation in polynomial time (vs. exponential) opens up the possibility to apply this network characterization to other real-world problems.

Future work is still needed to analyze the presence of neutrality on these landscapes and its implications on network structure and on instance hardness.

Acknowledgments

This research is supported by the Sciex Fellowship nr. 12.061.

6. REFERENCES

[1] A. Auger and N. Hansen. Performance evaluation of an advanced local search evolutionary algorithm. In *CEC*, volume 2, pages 1777–1784. IEEE, 2005.

[2] U. Benlic and J.-K. Hao. Breakout local search for the quadratic assignment problem. *Applied Mathematics and Computation*, 2012.

[3] R. E. Burkard, S. E. Karisch, and F. Rendl. Qaplib–a quadratic assignment problem library. *Journal of Global Optimization*, 10(4):391–403, 1997.

[4] F. Chicano, F. Daolio, G. Ochoa, S. Vérel, M. Tomassini, and E. Alba. Local optima networks, landscape autocorrelation and heuristic search performance. In *Parallel Problem Solving from Nature-PPSN XII*, pages 337–347. Springer, 2012.

[5] W. Cleveland. Lowess: A program for smoothing scatterplots by robust locally weighted regression. *The American Statistician*, 35(1):54–54, 1981.

[6] F. Daolio, M. Tomassini, S. Vérel, and G. Ochoa. Communities of minima in local optima networks of combinatorial spaces. *Physica A Statistical Mechanics and its Applications*, 390:1684 1694, 2011.

[7] F. Daolio, S. Verel, G. Ochoa, and M. Tomassini. Local Optima Networks of the Quadratic Assignment Problem. In *CEC*, pages 1–8. IEEE, 2010.

[8] F. Daolio, S. Vérel, G. Ochoa, and M. Tomassini. Local optima networks and the performance of iterated local search. In T. Soule and J. H. Moore, editors, *GECCO*, pages 369–376. ACM, 2012.

[9] E. Gutiérrez and C. A. Brizuela. Ils-perturbation based on local optima structure for the qap problem. In *MICAI 2006: Advances in Artificial Intelligence*, pages 404–414. Springer, 2006.

[10] M. S. Handcock and M. Morris. Relative distribution methods in the social sciences (statistics for social science and behavorial sciences). 1999.

[11] J. A. Hartigan and M. A. Wong. Algorithm as 136: A k-means clustering algorithm. *Journal of the Royal Statistical Society. Series C (Applied Statistics)*, 28(1):100–108, 1979.

[12] H. H. Hoos and T. Stützle. *Stochastic Local Search: Foundations and Applications*. Morgan Kaufmann, San Francisco, CA, 2005.

[13] D. Iclănzan, F. Daolio, and M. Tomassini. Learning inherent networks from stochastic search methods. In *EvoStar 2014 (1)*, page (accepted), 2014.

[14] M. Maechler, P. Rousseeuw, A. Struyf, M. Hubert, and K. Hornik. *cluster: Cluster Analysis Basics and Extensions*, 2013. R package version 1.14.4.

[15] C. L. Mallows. Some comments on c p. *Technometrics*, 15(4):661–675, 1973.

[16] P. Merz. Advanced fitness landscape analysis and the performance of memetic algorithms. *Evolutionary Computation*, 12(3):303–325, 2004.

[17] P. Merz and B. Freisleben. Fitness landscape analysis and memetic algorithms for the quadratic assignment problem. *Evolutionary Computation, IEEE Transactions on*, 4(4):337–352, 2000.

[18] M. Newman. The structure and function of complex networks. *SIAM review*, pages 167–256, 2003.

[19] M. E. Newman and M. Girvan. Finding and evaluating community structure in networks. *Physical review E*, 69(2):026113, 2004.

[20] G. Ochoa, S. Verel, and M. Tomassini. First-improvement vs. best-improvement local optima networks of nk landscapes. In *Parallel Problem Solving from Nature, PPSN XI*, pages 104–113. Springer, 2010.

[21] E. Pitzer, A. Beham, and M. Affenzeller. Generic hardness estimation using fitness and parameter landscapes applied to robust taboo search and the quadratic assignment problem. In *GECCO conference companion*, pages 393–400. ACM, 2012.

[22] K. Smith-Miles and T. T. Tan. Measuring algorithm footprints in instance space. In *CEC*, pages 1–8. IEEE, 2012.

[23] T. Stützle. Iterated local search for the quadratic assignment problem. *European Journal of Operational Research*, 174(3):1519–1539, 2006.

[24] E. Taillard. Robust taboo search for the quadratic assignment problem. *Parallel computing*, 17(4):443–455, 1991.

[25] E. D. Taillard. Comparison of iterative searches for the quadratic assignment problem. *Location science*, 3(2):87–105, 1995.

[26] M. Tomassini, S. Verel, and G. Ochoa. Complex-network analysis of combinatorial spaces: The NK landscape case. *Physical Review E*, 78(6):066114, 2008.

[27] S. Van Dongen. Graph clustering via a discrete uncoupling process. *SIAM Journal on Matrix Analysis and Applications*, 30(1):121–141, 2008.

[28] W. N. Venables and B. D. Ripley. *Modern Applied Statistics with S*. Springer, New York, fourth edition, 2002. ISBN 0-387-95457-0.

[29] S. Vérel, F. Daolio, G. Ochoa, and M. Tomassini. Local optima networks with escape edges. In *Artificial Evolution. 10th International Conference, EA 2011. Revised Selected Papers*, number 7401 in LNCS, pages 49–60. Springer-Verlag, 2012.

[30] S. Verel, G. Ochoa, and M. Tomassini. Local optima networks of NK landscapes with neutrality. *IEEE Transactions on Evolutionary Computation*, 15(6):783–797, 2011.

[31] J.-P. Watson, L. D. Whitley, and A. E. Howe. Linking search space structure, run-time dynamics, and problem difficulty: A step toward demystifying tabu search. *J. Artif. Intell. Res.(JAIR)*, 24:221–261, 2005.

A Heuristic Approach to Schedule Reoptimization in the Context of Interactive Optimization

David Meignan
Institut für Informatik
Universität Osnabrück
Osnabrück, Deutschland
dmeignan@uni-osnabrueck.de

ABSTRACT

Optimization models used in planning and scheduling systems are not exempt from inaccuracies. These optimization systems often require an expert to assess solutions and to adjust them before taking decisions. However, adjusting a solution computed by an optimization procedure is difficult, especially because of the cascading effect. A small modification in a candidate solution may require to modify a large part of the solution. This obstacle to the adjustment of a solution can be overcome by interactive reoptimization. In this paper we analyze the impact of the cascading effect on a shift-scheduling problem and propose an efficient heuristic approach for reoptimizing solutions. The proposed approach is a local-search metaheuristic that has been adapted to the reoptimization. This approach is evaluated on a set of problem instances on which additional preferences are generated to simulate desired adjustments of a decision maker. Experimental results indicate that, even with a small perturbation, the cascading effect is manifest and cannot be efficiently tackled by applying recovery actions. Moreover, results show that the proposed reoptimization method provides significant cost gains within a short time while keeping a level of simplicity and modularity adequate for an implementation in a decision support system.

Categories and Subject Descriptors

I.2.8 [**Artificial Intelligence**]: Problem Solving, Control Methods, and Search—*Heuristic methods, Scheduling*

General Terms

Design, Algorithms, Human factors

Keywords

Reoptimization, interactive optimization, shift scheduling, heuristic

GECCO'14, July 12–16, 2014, Vancouver, BC, Canada.

ACM 978-1-4503-2662-9/14/07 ...$15.00.
http://dx.doi.org/10.1145/2576768.2598213.

1. INTRODUCTION

Optimization models used for decision support rarely consider all aspects of the real decision maker's problem [3, 20]. Several practical considerations explain this gap between an implemented optimization model and the real problem for which the decision maker has to take a decision. First, the optimization problem may be difficult to model, and tools and available resources to design complex models are often limited. For example in the domain of staff scheduling and rostering, optimization problems generally contain multiple objectives that are specific to the application area [9]. Some aspects such as stochastic demand or fairness between employees are difficult to model in a form appropriate for an optimization procedure. In addition to these difficulties inherent to the optimization problem, the knowledge required to model the problem may not be easily accessible. The transcription of expert knowledge into an optimization model may introduce some inaccuracies. Furthermore, it is common that secondary decision criteria are only identified when the real problem needs to be solved (i.e. at the time of the decision process and not during the initial design of the decision support tool). Consequently, in the context of decision aid, an optimization model is likely to present some simplifications and omissions. Interactive optimization may alleviate these inaccuracies and guarantee an efficient use of the optimization system.

In interactive optimization, the optimization system is adjusted through interactions with the decision maker in order to meet his preferences. The feedback of the decision maker on intermediate or previous optimization results can significantly modify the final solution or the performance of the optimization process. There are essentially two types of interactive optimization methods depending on the objective of the interaction. The first type of method uses interaction in order to improve the performance of the optimization process. This form of interaction appears, for instance, in human-guided search approaches [13], as well as interactive parameter tuning [12]. In the second type of interactive method, the objective is to "enrich" the optimization model. The decision maker interacts with the optimization system in order to obtain solutions that are more relevant to the real problem. This type of interaction is considered in interactive methods for multiobjective optimization [18] and interactive evolutionary algorithms [22]. In these two approaches, interactive enrichment concerns respectively the trade-offs between objectives and the fitness function. The interactive reoptimization approach investigated in this study is another form of interactive enrichment.

Reoptimization is the optimization of a problem instance that has been slightly perturbed and for which a solution has been previously found. The reoptimization problem is characterized, first, by the presence of an initial solution that has been obtained by solving the unperturbed problem instance. This initial solution can be used to improve the performance of the reoptimization procedure. Second, in addition to the initial objectives of the optimization problem, it is generally required to minimize the distance between the re-optimized solution and the initial solution. Finally, the requirements in terms of computation time for the reoptimization are usually stronger than for the initial optimization.

Reoptimization is of practical interest in various circumstances [1, 25, 21], and in particular, for tackling problems in dynamic environments. In the latter case, the problem instance changes over time and the current solution has to evolve with the updated problem instance. For example, on a staff scheduling problem, the absence of a staff member can be considered as a dynamic perturbation. In this case, a new schedule has to be found by reoptimizing the initial one. Reoptimization can also be useful in the context of optimization-based decision support systems for adjusting a solution interactively [19]. Unlike "dynamic optimization", a perturbation in interactive reoptimization is a modification made by the decision maker and not a real change in the environment. As explained previously, some inaccuracies in the problem model may necessitate an adjustment of the solution by the decision maker in order to reflect the real decision problem. Interactive re-optimization is a method that aims at solving several issues of a manual adjustment of a solution after the optimization process. Manually modifying a solution has major drawbacks if it is not assisted by an optimization procedure. First, it may be difficult for the user to apprehend all constraints and objectives of the optimization model when a solution is manually edited. In addition, due to the complexity of considered combinatorial optimization problems, it is generally difficult or impossible to reflect the modification to the whole solution. The fact that a local modification in a solution implies to adjust other parts of the solution is referred to as the cascading or propagation effect [19]. Interactive reoptimization aims at overcoming these obstacles. In this approach, solutions modified by the user are reoptimized. The reoptimization procedure globally optimizes a solution to take into account local modifications applied by the user.

Shift scheduling is an application for which reoptimization has a strong potential. The objective of a shift scheduling problem is to optimize the assignments of employees to shifts for a given planning period. A shift is a time interval in a day (e.g. early 7:00-15:00, late 15:00-22:00) over which employees have to be scheduled [5, 9]. A demand in terms of required employees is defined for each shift and day. A solution to the problem is a set of daily assignments of employees to shifts such as the required number of employees by shift and by day is satisfied. In addition, a solution must satisfy a set of legal constraints and meet as far as possible employees' preferences. In the literature, the reoptimization variant of the shift scheduling problem is mainly studied in the context of dynamic environments, i.e. for adjusting a schedule when an unexpected event has invalidated the initial planning. For example, an employee initially scheduled may be unavailable and a new planning has to be determined to satisfy the demand. A review of staff rerostering models and methods in the context of dynamic environments is presented in [17].

In contrast to existing studies, we present in this paper an approach for dealing with the reoptimization problem in the context of interactive optimization. The key aspects of the proposed method are the simplicity, modularity, and efficiency of the reoptimization method. Simplicity and modularity are essential for an integration in a decision support tool [5]. The method must be easy to implement, and the number of parameters has to be limited. In addition, modularity is essential to take into account the peculiarities of the application domain. Furthermore, the requirements in terms of computational time and solution's quality are critical in the context of interactive optimization. The reoptimization should take only few seconds to recover from a perturbation introduced by the decision maker. To achieve these objectives, we propose an Iterated Local-Search (ILS) [14] which is a conceptually simple metaheuristic with very few parameters. In addition, the proposed implementation makes use of high-level parallelism and delta-evaluation of the constraints to improve the performance of the metaheuristic. The reoptimization method is compared to recovery procedures in order to stress the importance of the cascading effect and to evaluate the proposed method.

The remainder of the paper is organized as follows. In Section 2, the shift scheduling problem and its reoptimization variant are presented. The proposed reoptimization method is detailed in Section 3. In Section 4, the method is evaluated. Conclusions are drawn in Section 5.

2. PROBLEM DEFINITION

2.1 Shift scheduling problem

The reoptimization problem considered in this paper is based on a shift scheduling problem that has been proposed for the International Nurse Rostering Competition held in 2010 (INRC2010) [11]. A formal definition of the INRC2010 problem model is given in [15]. The problem contains two types of constraints, namely hard and soft constraints. The hard constraints must be satisfied; otherwise, the solution is unfeasible and may lose its meaning. The soft constraints represent the objectives of the optimization problem, and the number of violations of these constraints has to be minimized.

Two hard constraints are defined:

H_1 *Shift demand coverage*: For each day, the number of employees assigned to a shift must be equal to the demand for the shift. Under-staffing and over-staffing is not allowed.

H_2 *Single shift assignment per day*: At most one shift can be assigned to an employee per day. A shift represents a complete working day.

We differentiate two types of soft constraints. The first set of constraints is related to work regulation and corresponds to the primary objectives, noted R. The second set, noted S, includes constraints that are more flexible and related to individual comfort. The problem model contains twelve soft constraints divided as follows:

R_1 *Maximum number of assignments*: The total number of assignments of an employee within the planning horizon should not exceed a given maximum value.

R_2 *Minimum number of assignments*: The total number of assignments of an employee within the planning horizon should not be less than a given minimum value.

R_3 *Maximum number of consecutive working days*: The number of consecutive working days of an employee should not exceed a given maximum value.

R_4 *Skill requirements*: The employee assigned to a shift should have the required skills for the shift (e.g. head or manager).

R_5 *Unwanted consecutive working shifts*: Some shifts should not be worked consecutively. Unwanted shift patterns consist of two or three shifts, e.g. *[Late; Early]*.

R_6 *Day-off and shift-off requests*: Assignments should satisfy day-off and shift-off requests of employees.

S_1 *Complete working weekends*: Weekends should be either entirely worked or completely free.

S_2 *Identical shifts during weekends*: During weekends completely worked, an employee should have the same shift assigned.

S_3 *Minimum number of consecutive working days*: The number of consecutive working days of an employee should not be less than a given minimum value.

S_4 *Maximum number of consecutive free days*: The number of consecutive day-offs of an employee should not exceed a given maximum value.

S_5 *Minimum number of consecutive free days*: The number of consecutive day-offs of an employee should not be less than a given minimum value.

S_6 *No free day before working weekends*: The day before a completely worked weekend should not be a day-off.

Except for R_4 and R_6, the parameters of these constraints are specified by type of contract and apply to a subset of the employees. For example, the maximum number of assignments may be set to 20 (on a four-weeks planning horizon) for full-time contracts, and limited to 10 for part-time contracts. For the constraint R_4 and R_6, skills, day-offs requests, and shift-offs requests are specified per employee.

2.2 Reoptimization problem

In the context of interactive optimization, the reoptimization problem appears when an initial solution is modified by the decision maker. These modifications aim at introducing aspects that are not modeled. For instance, the decision maker may want to reflect some parental constraints, or anticipate potential absences. The studied interactive scheduling process is summarized in Figure 1. First, an initial solution is obtained on the basis of the shift scheduling problem described in the previous section. Then, the decision maker specifies some preferences on assignments. Here, the schedule is not directly modified; instead, preferences on assignments are defined. An assignment preference is a shift that is preferred for a specific employee and day. Introducing these preferences result in a perturbed solution. A reoptimization procedure is applied on the perturbed solution to take into account the assignment preferences in addition to the initial constraints. The process of preference definition followed by the reoptimization can be iterated until a satisfactory schedule is obtained.

In comparison to the initial shift scheduling problem, the reoptimization problem contains two additional soft constraints. The first one corresponds to the modifications requested by the decision maker. The second additional soft constraint minimizes the distance between the reoptimized

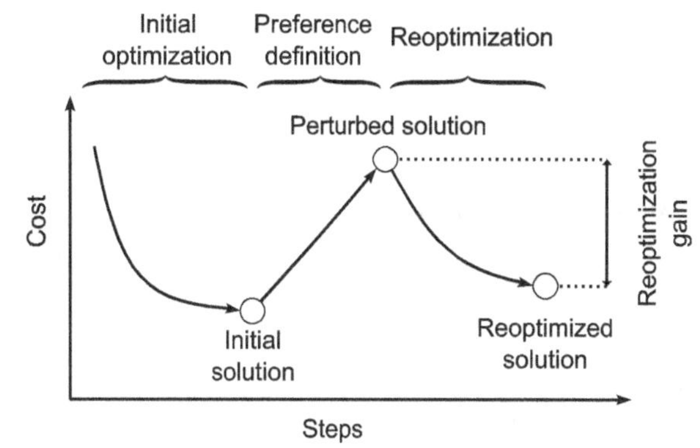

Figure 1: Principle of the interactive reoptimization process.

solution and the initial solution. For interactive reoptimization, these two constraints form the preferential model of the decision process, whereas the initial shift scheduling problem is the substantive model [24, 18]. In the following, the assignment preference constraint and the reoptimization distance constraint are described using the notation of [15]. In this notation, a candidate schedule is represented by the integer decision variables $x_{e,d} \in \mathcal{S}, \forall e \in \mathcal{E}, \forall d \in \mathcal{D}$, with $\mathcal{S}$ the set of shifts, $\mathcal{E}$ the set of employees, and $\mathcal{D}$ the set of day in the planning horizon.

2.2.1 Assignment preference constraint

An assignment preference is a tuple $\langle e, d, p\rangle \in \mathcal{P}$ indicating that, for the employee $e \in \mathcal{E}$ and day $d \in \mathcal{D}$, the shift $p \in \mathcal{S}$ is the preferred assignment. The assignment preference constraint, noted P, penalizes each assignment $x_{e,d}$ for which a preference is defined and not satisfied. The cost of the constraint is defined as follows:

$$f_P = \sum_{\langle e,d,p\rangle \in \mathcal{P}} \chi(x_{e,d} \neq p)$$

where χ is the function that maps a true proposition to the value 1 and a false one to 0.

2.2.2 Reoptimization distance constraint

In the proposed reoptimization model, a soft constraint has been introduced to minimize the distance between the initial solution and the reoptimized one. A similar constraint can be found in reoptimization models for dynamic environment, however the motivation of such a constraint for interactive reoptimization is different to that for dynamic optimization. The aim of the distance constraint in the case of dynamic optimization is to minimize the number of reassignments of employee according to the current planning [16]. In the context of interactive reoptimization, a schedule's modification is not a real reassignment of employees because the schedule has not yet been decided. However, a distance constraint is required to maintain coherence in the interactive process. If possible, the reoptimized solution should be similar to the initial solution because the preferences of the decision maker have been expressed on the basis of the initial solution. With a completely different reoptimized solution the preferences expressed on the initial solution may lose their meaning. This distance constraint favors the convergence toward a satisfactory solution for the decision maker.

Given an initial solution $x^0_{e,d}$, the cost of the distance constraint D is:

$$f_D = \sum_{e \in \mathcal{E}} \sum_{d \in \mathcal{D}} \chi(x_{e,d} \neq x^0_{e,d})$$

2.2.3 *Global objective*

Introducing two constraints in the initial problem raises the question of the relative importance of the soft constraints. In the INRC2010 problem model a weight is associated to each soft constraint and possibly varies according to the employee's contract. The objective is to minimize the weighted sum of the violation of constraints. For the proposed shift scheduling problem and reoptimization problem, a lexicographic ordering of the constraints is considered to introduce the two additional constraints. The resulting objective function combines weights and lexicographic order, i.e. some soft constraints have the same priority.

For the shift scheduling problem solved in the initial optimization step, work regulation constraints R_i have a higher priority than soft constraints S_i. The weights are maintained within these two set of constraints. The objective of the initial optimization step is:

$$minimize_{LEX}\left(\sum f_{R_i}, \sum f_{S_i}\right) \quad (1)$$

For the reoptimization step, the assignment preference constraint P has priority over soft constraints S_i but not over work regulation constraints R_i. The distance constraint has the lowest priority, as the role of the constraint is only related to the decision process. The objective of the reoptimization step is:

$$minimize_{LEX}\left(\sum f_{R_i}, f_P, \sum f_{S_i}, f_D\right) \quad (2)$$

In short, the work regulation constraints are the most important objectives, followed by the assignment preferences defined by the decision maker. The soft constraints related to individual "comfort" of employees come third. The distance constraint is the less important objective.

3. OPTIMIZATION PROCEDURES

3.1 Iterated local search

An Iterated Local Search (ILS) [14] is proposed for both optimization and reoptimization phases. This metaheuristic has the advantages of being simple and having few parameters. The ILS procedure used for the shift scheduling problem and the reoptimization of schedules is described in Algorithm 1.

ILS repeats two steps until a stopping criterion is met. Here, the stopping criterion is a time limit T (Algorithm 1, line 5). Starting from an initial solution that is provided or generated, the first step perturbs the solution to escape from local-optima (line 6). The second step improves the resulting solution by local search (line 7). An acceptance criterion is then applied to decide whether the newly improved solution is retained for the next iteration or not (lines 8-9). The implemented criterion only accepts better solutions. The next iteration thus always starts with the best solution found so far.

For the reoptimization, the procedure starts with the perturbed schedule. The perturbations come from the introduction of assignment preferences by the decision maker.

Algorithm 1: ILS procedure for shift scheduling and schedule reoptimization

```
Data: Time limit T, Initial solution s^0, Perturbation
      strength α
Result: Best found solution s*
// Generation/improvement of the initial solution
1  s ← s^0
2  if s = ∅ then s ← generateSolution()
3  s ← variableNeighborhoodDescent(s)
4  s* ← s
5  while time limit T not reached do
       // Perturbation
6      s ← randomPerturbation(s, α)
       // Local-search
7      s ← variableNeighborhoodDescent(s)
       // Acceptance criterion
8      if cost(s) < cost(s*) then s* ← s
9      s ← s*
10 end
```

This perturbed solution is an advantage for the search procedure if we assume that few assignment preferences have been added. For the initial optimization phase preceding the definition of assignment preferences, no solution is provided to the ILS procedure. In this case, an initial solution is generated using a greedy generation procedure.

The local-search step of the ILS procedure is a variable neighborhood descent [10] based on block-swap neighborhoods [7]. A block-swap is the exchange, between two employees, of blocks of consecutive shift-assignments on the same range of days. The variable neighborhood descent procedure uses block-swap neighborhoods with a block size varying between 1 and 7. The local-search procedure is described in Algorithm 2. The exploration starts with a block size of 1 for the neighborhood. If no solution in the neighborhood has a better cost than the current solution, then the block size is increased. When a better solution is found in the current neighborhood, the exploration continues from the neighborhood of this new solution, and the block size is reset to 1. The procedure ends when no improving solution is found in the 7-swap neighborhood. In this way, the solution is improved until a local-optimum (w.r.t. all 7 neighborhoods) is found.

The perturbation step of the ILS applies random block-rotations between three employees. The parameter α determines the strength of the perturbation. It corresponds to

Algorithm 2: Variable neighborhood descent procedure

```
Data: Solution to improve s
Result: Local minimum s
k ← 1
while k ≤ 7 do
    N ← SwapNeighborhood(k, s)
    while hasRemainingNeighbor(N) do
        if currentNeighborCost(N) < cost(s) then
            s ← currentNeighborSolution(N)
            k ← 1
            N ← SwapNeighborhood(k, s)
        else
            N ← nextNeighbor(N)
        end
    end
    k ← k + 1
end
```

the approximate ratio of assignments on which a rotation is applied.

3.2 Implementation details

The time restriction for reoptimizing a schedule is important for the interactive process. Reoptimization should last a few seconds. For computational experiments, the time limit is fixed to two seconds of computation on a standard computer. In order to meet this requirement and ensure good reoptimized solutions, two design features are considered for the implementation of the ILS procedure. First, high-level parallelism is used. Second, constraints are evaluated separately for computing the cost of solutions.

3.2.1 High-level parallelism

High-level parallelism is obtained from concurrent search processes [8]. The parallel version of ILS runs multiple concurrent ILS procedures that exchange asynchronously their best found solutions. This parallelism aims solely to speed up computation by using multi-thread strategy. Although the usage of multiple search-strategies or different parameter-settings could be beneficial, the choice of using the same ILS procedure has been motivated by the simplicity of the approach.

The procedure described in Algorithm 1 is the version of ILS when only one thread is used. The parallel version is obtained with very little modifications. After the application of the acceptance criterion, the ILS thread updates its best found solution with solutions possibly sent by other threads. If the best found solution has been obtained by the ILS thread during the last iteration, the thread sends its best found solution to other threads.

Using concurrent ILS threads may slightly favor diversification of the search in early iterations. However, no significant difference was found by varying the number of threads from 1 to 4 with the same cumulative computation time.

3.2.2 Constraints evaluation

To enhance further the performance of the ILS procedure, the method for evaluating the constraints has been tuned. In [11], the authors of the INRC2010 benchmark suggest an approach based on "numberings" [6] to evaluate the constraints. This evaluation method uses a set of counters to characterize a solution; then, the values of these counters are used to evaluate multiple constraints. By comparing different evaluation procedures, we came to the same conclusion as in [23], that the tested approach on "numberings" is less efficient than an evaluation method in which constraints are evaluated separately. Consequently, we opt for the latter.

Evaluating the constraints independently has two main advantages. First, it allows delta-evaluation of solutions for the exploration of neighborhoods. Delta-evaluation is a common method for evaluating the neighbors of a solution. During the local search, only the cost differences resulting from the moves are evaluated. Generally, the cost difference between two neighboring solutions is computed faster than a full evaluation of a solution. The second advantage concerns the modularity of the implementation. When constraints have independent evaluation (and delta-evaluation) procedures, it is easier to modify the problem model. The rank and weight of constraints can be easily modified. In addition, the introduction of a new constraint, such as the distance constraint and the preference constraint in the reoptimization model, does not necessitate any change in the initial evaluation procedures. Only a procedure for evaluating the new constraint is required.

4. COMPUTATIONAL EXPERIMENTS

The purpose of the experiments is twofold. The main point is to evaluate the proposed heuristic approach for solving the schedule reoptimization problem. In addition, the experiments aim at providing computational insights into the reoptimization problem and cascading effect.

Three aspects are examined in the computational experiments. In Section 4.1 the proposed heuristic approach is compared to existing results on the INRC2010 benchmark. In Section 4.2 the reoptimization procedure is compared to recovery procedures. The objective is to determine if the proposed global optimization approach is justified and efficient against local recovery procedures. Finally, in Section 4.3 the impact of the distance constraint introduced in the reoptimization problem is analysed.

The INRC2010 dataset[1] has been used for the experiments. This benchmark contains three classes of instances of increasing size called *Sprint*, *Medium* and *Long* instances. Only *Sprint* instances have been used as the number of assignments appears to be reasonable for the context of decision support. The benchmark contains 33 *Sprint* instances. For each instance, 10 employees have to be scheduled on a planning horizon of 28 days.

The problem instances in the INRC2010 benchmark are not reoptimization problems. The initial evaluation of the ILS procedure, in Section 4.1, is based on the original INRC2010 problem model; however, for the experiments presented in Sections 4.2 and 4.3, the benchmark has been adapted to the case of reoptimization.

All experiments were carried out on standard personal computer (Intel Core i5 2.5GHz, 8GB memory). The parameter α of the ILS procedure has been set to 5% for all tests.

4.1 Performance on INRC2010 benchmark

The ILS procedure has been evaluated first on the original INRC2010 problem model. The original INRC2010 problem model contains the constraints presented in Section 2.1, but does not use the reoptimization constraints and objectives introduced in Section 2.2.

In this section we present a comparison between the proposed heuristic and selected approaches from the literature. Three existing approaches have been selected based on the fact that, the average and standard deviation values are available, and the time limit for reported results has been adjusted with the INRC2010 time benchmark. The first method selected for the comparison is a hyper-heuristic presented in [4]. In the latter study, a set of 36 variants of a hyper-heuristic is evaluated. The best performing hyper-heuristic, namely *CF-GD-4* (Choice Function heuristic selection strategy, with a tournament size of 4, and Great Deluge acceptance criterion), has been retained for the comparison. The second method is a harmony search strategy proposed in [2]. The last method is an adaptive neighborhood search method presented in [15].

[1]The INRC2010 dataset is available at
`http://www.kuleuven-kulak.be/nrpcompetition`

The time limit obtained with the INRC2010 time benchmark for the ILS procedure is 9.5 seconds on *Sprint* instances. For the comparison of ILS with existing approaches, only one thread has been used, and 20 independent runs have been performed on each instance[2].

Figure 2 summarizes the results of pairwise comparisons by instance between ILS and the three selected methods. A t-test with a p-value of 5% has been used to determine if the results per instance are significantly different. A Welch correction is applied to the t-tests for taking into account the differences in sample sizes and variances. Note that the difference in the number of compared instances is due to the availability of the results. In [4], 23 out of 33 instances are considered for the evaluation of the hyper-heuristic, and 30 instances are considered for the adaptive neighborhood search approach in [15].

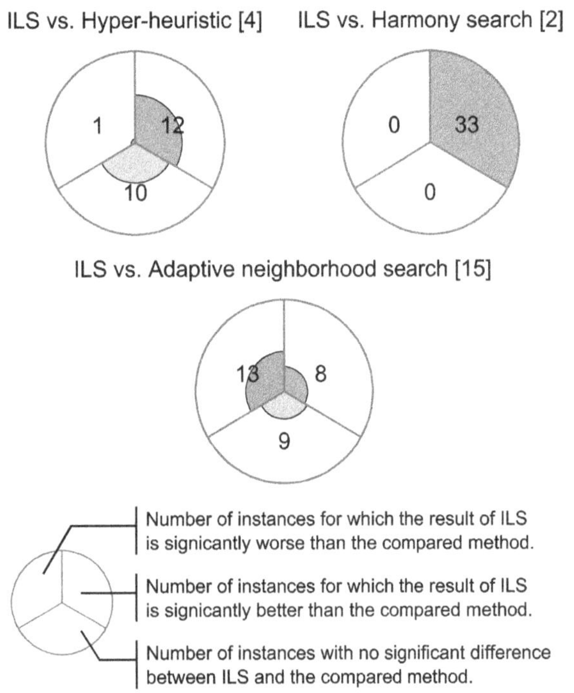

Figure 2: Comparative results of ILS on *Sprint* instances of the Inrc2010 benchmark.

The results reported in Figure 2 provide strong evidence that ILS outperforms the hyper-heuristic and the harmony search approach on *Sprint* instances of the INRC2010 benchmark. The ILS procedure obtains significantly better results than the hyper-heuristic on 12 instances, and for 1 instance ILS is worse than the hyper-heuristic. The t-tests between ILS and the harmony search indicates that ILS obtains significantly better results than the harmony search on all instances. The third circular chart in Figure 2 indicates that the results of ILS are globally worse than those of the adaptive neighborhood search procedure. However, the difference is less marked than for the two first charts.

This first experiment shows that the ILS procedure provides competitive results. Considering the simplicity of ILS and the modularity of the implementation, these results suggest that the proposed heuristic approach is a good basis for an interactive optimization approach.

4.2 Reoptimization versus recovery

4.2.1 Generation of reoptimization problems

As explained previously, instances of the INRC2010 benchmark have to be adapted to the reoptimization problem. The procedure for obtaining instances of reoptimization problem is the following. First, *Sprint* instances are solved with the ILS procedure. The objective considered for this optimization step is the lexicographic minimization of work regulation constraints and soft constraints as described in Equation 1 (Section 2.2). The obtained solutions are the initial (unperturbed) solutions. Then, random preferences are generated on these initial solutions in order to create the perturbed solutions. The perturbations correspond to 5 or 10 assignment preferences that are randomly generated. Note that the assignment preferences are generated so that they are not satisfied in the initial solutions. The resulting problems are the reoptimization of the perturbed solutions according to the objective presented in Equation 2 (Section 2.2). The latter objective contains, in addition to the work regulation constraints and soft constraints, an assignment preference constraint and a reoptimization distance constraint.

For each *Sprint* instance, 10 solutions to reoptimize are generated with 5 assignment preferences and 10 solutions with 10 assignment preferences. Initial solutions are obtained with 20 independent runs of the ILS procedure. To ensure good initial solutions, the parallel version of the ILS procedure is run on 4 threads with a time limit of 10 seconds.

4.2.2 Comparison between ILS and recovery

Considering the reoptimization problem, ILS is a "global" optimization approach in the sense that the search can potentially cover the whole search space thanks to the perturbation step. In concrete terms for the reoptimization, ILS is potentially able to optimize globally a perturbed solution instead of only applying local improvements to recover from the introduced perturbations. In this second experiment, ILS is compared to "pure" local-search procedures called recovery procedures. The objective is to determine if a global optimization approach is justified for the reoptimization when only small perturbations are introduced, and to evaluate the efficiency of ILS against recovery procedures.

For the reoptimization, the parallel version of the ILS procedure is run on 4 threads and the time limit is set to 2 seconds. The results are compared with those of two recovery procedures. The first recovery procedure is a 1-swap descent procedure. It is a local-descent procedure that improves the perturbed solution using the 1-swap neighborhood structure. Only improving moves within neighborhoods are accepted. The procedure stops when a local-optimum, w.r.t. the 1-swap neighborhood structure, is found. The second recovery procedure is a variable neighborhood descent procedure using block-swap neighborhood structures with block sizes of 1 to 7. This procedure corresponds to the local-search step of the ILS. These two recovery procedures only improve locally the perturbed solutions. In this way, the cost difference between ILS and recovery procedures would reflect the contribution of the global optimization.

[2]Detailed results of ILS for *Sprint* instances are provided as supplementary material.

Table 1 reports the average number of assignment preferences satisfied with the ILS reoptimization procedure, 1-swap recovery procedure, and 1-7-swap recovery procedure. In average, the reoptimization with ILS satisfied 2.81 and 5.49 preferences respectively for 5 and 10 introduced assignment preferences. The difference between 1-swap and ILS is substantial with an average gain of more than 2 preferences satisfied when 10 preferences are introduced. The difference between 1-7-swap and ILS is less important and necessitate a closer look at the cost of reoptimized solutions.

Table 1: Number of assignment preferences satisfied by recovery procedures and ILS

Introduced preferences	Average number of satisfied preferences		
	1-swap	1-7-swap	ILS
5	1.67	2.22	2.81
10	3.18	4.30	5.49

In Table 2 the cost of reoptimized solutions are compared between ILS and 1-swap, and between ILS and 1-7-swap. Note that it is not possible to report an average difference value due to the lexicographic objective function. (E.g. a solution with 3 unsatisfied preferences and 10 unsatisfied soft constraints, noted $\langle 3, 10\rangle$, is better than a solution with a cost $\langle 3, 12\rangle$, but worse than a solution $\langle 4, 8\rangle$. Here, it does not make sense to average the values of unsatisfied soft constraints.) In Table 2, the advantage of ILS against 1-7-swap is apparent. When 5 preferences are introduced, 63.94% of the solutions reoptimized with ILS are better than solutions obtained with 1-7-swap. Only 36.06% of resulting solutions have the same cost.

Table 2: Comparison of the cost of reoptimized solutions

Pref.	ILS vs. 1-swap		ILS vs. 1-7-swap	
	same cost	better cost	same cost	better cost
5	21.21%	78.79%	36.06%	63.94%
10	6.67%	93.33%	17.27%	82.73%

The reoptimization with ILS naturally outperformed the recovery procedures. However, the results reveal the difficulty of the reoptimization. The introduction of 5 assignment preferences is rather small considering the size of problem instances. In this context, the gain of ILS in Table 2 is substantial. These comparative results support the fact that a global optimization approach is justified to tackle the reoptimization problem, even though the perturbation is small.

4.3 Impact of the distance constraint

In this section we analyse the impact of the distance constraint on the results of ILS. The introduction of a distance constraint in the reoptimization problem raises two questions. First, considering that the constraint is ranked last in the objective function of the reoptimization problem, the distance between the initial solution and the reoptimized solution may not be significantly minimized. The second issue concerns the potential alteration of the local-search process. During the local-search step of the ILS procedure, the distance constraint guides the search towards the initial solution. This tendency may hinder the search to explore solutions that are far from the initial one. Consequently, the constraint may reduce the effectiveness of ILS.

These issues are investigated by comparing the result of ILS on reoptimization problems with and without the distance constraint. The set of reoptimization problems without distance constraint is obtained by removing the corresponding constraint from the problems considered in the previous section. The previous results of ILS are compared to the results obtained by the same procedure on problems without distance constraint.

Table 3 reports the average distance to initial solutions resulting from the reoptimization with and without distance constraint. When the distance constraint is taken into account, the distance to the initial solution is reduced by 43%. In addition, 86% of the solutions obtained with the distance constraint are closer or at equal distance to the initial solutions. These results confirm that the distance constraint significantly reduces the distance between the initial solution and the reoptimized solution, although the constraint is ranked last in the objective function.

Table 3: Average distances to initial solutions obtained with and without distance constraint

Introduced preferences	Average distance to initial solution	
	with constraint	without constraint
5	16.86	29.55
10	27.02	47.28

In order to examine the possible impact of the distance constraint on the cost of reoptimized solutions, a Wilcoxon signed-rank test has been performed. The test compares the costs with and without distance constraint (paired by problem instance). The results of the test, using a significance level of 5%, show no significant difference. This result supports the fact that the distance constraint has no significant impact on the effectiveness of ILS.

5. CONCLUSION

In this paper, we proposed a heuristic approach for the reoptimization of schedules in the context of interactive optimization. The objective was to design a method suitable for a decision support tool which implies to find a good balance between simplicity, modularity and efficiency of the reoptimization method.

The proposed problem model contains two constraints specific to the reoptimization that are added to an initial shift scheduling problem using a lexicographic ordering. This order between constraints is a convenient way to integrate the new constraints without introducing additional parameters such as weight values. The procedure for reoptimizing schedules is an ILS. This metaheuristic is conceptually simple, and the proposed implementation has only one parameter to be set. Two design features are considered to obtain appropriate performances for the interactive reoptimization process. First, high-level parallelism is used. Second, constraints are evaluated separately in order to allow a delta-evaluation of solutions and favor the modularity of the implementation.

A set of computational experiments has been performed to evaluate the effectiveness and adequacy of the proposed heuristic approach for reoptimizing schedules. The ILS procedure has been evaluated first on a shift scheduling problem and compared to three approaches from the literature. The results show that ILS provides competitive results in spite of the simplicity of the procedure. The second experiment compared ILS with two recovery procedures in order to determine if a global optimization approach is justified for the reoptimization of schedules. This comparison reveals that ILS provides significant cost gain, and support the fact that a global optimization approach is required to tackle the reoptimization problem, even though the perturbation is small. The last experiment analysed the impact of the distance constraint on the results of ILS. The results of the latter experiment show that the distance constraint allows to reduce significantly the distance between the initial solution and the reoptimized solution. In addition, the introduction of this constraint within the reoptimization problem model does not have significant impact on the effectiveness of ILS.

Future work will focus on the evaluation of the interactive reoptimization approach with real users and the analysis of usability aspects.

6. ACKNOWLEDGMENTS

This work was supported by the Deutsche Forschungsgemeinschaft (DFG), under grant ME 4045/2-1, for the project "Interactive metaheuristics for optimization-based decision support systems". The author wishes to thank Sigrid Knust for her suggestions on preparing the manuscript.

7. REFERENCES

[1] G. Ausiello, V. Bonifaci, and B. Escoffier. *Computability in Context: Computation and Logic in the Real World*, chapter Complexity and Approximation in Reoptimization, pages 101–129. Imperial College Press, 2007.

[2] M. A. Awadallah, A. T. Khader, M. A. Al-Betar, and A. L. Bolaji. Nurse rostering using modified harmony search algorithm. In *SEMCCO*. LNCS, 7077:27–37, Springer Berlin Heidelberg, 2011.

[3] J. P. Barthélemy, R. Bisdorff, and G. Coppin. Human centered processes and decision support systems. *European Journal of Operational Research*, 136(2):233–252, 2002.

[4] B. Bilgin, P. Demeester, M. Misir, W. Vancroonenburg, and G. V. Berghe. One hyper-heuristic approach to two timetabling problems in health care. *Journal of Heuristics*, 18:401–434, 2012.

[5] E. K. Burke, P. D. Causmaecker, G. V. Berghe, and H. V. Landeghem. The state of the art of nurse rostering. *Journal of Scheduling*, 7:441–499, 2004.

[6] E. K. Burke, P. D. Causmaecker, S. Petrovic, and G. V. Berghe. Fitness evaluation for nurse scheduling problems. In *CEC*. 2:1139–1146, 2001.

[7] E. K. Burke, T. Curtois, R. Qu, and G. V. Berghe. A time predefined variable depth search for nurse rostering. *INFORMS Journal on Computing*, 25(3):411–419, 2013.

[8] T. Crainic and M. Toulouse. *Handbook in Metaheuristics*, chapter Parallel Strategies for Meta-heuristics, pages 475–513. Springer, 2003.

[9] A. T. Ernst, H. Jiang, M. Krishnamoorthy, and D. Sier. Staff scheduling and rostering: A review of applications, methods and models. *European Journal of Operational Research*, 153(1):3–27, 2004.

[10] P. Hansen and N. Mladenović. *Handbook of Metaheuristics*, chapter Variable Neighborhood Search, pages 145–184. Kluwer Academic, 2003.

[11] S. Haspeslagh, P. D. Causmaecker, A. Schaerf, and M. Stølevik. The first international nurse rostering competition 2010. *Annals of Operations Research*, Online, DOI: 10.1007/s10479-012-1062-0, 2012.

[12] F. Hutter, T. Bartz-Beielstein, H. Hoos, K. Leyton-Brown, and K. Murphy. *Empirical Methods for the Analysis of Optimization Algorithms*, chapter Sequential Model-Based Parameter Optimisation: an Experimental Investigation of Automated and Interactive Approaches, pages 361–411. Springer, 2010.

[13] G. W. Klau, N. Lesh, J. Marks, and M. Mitzenmacher. Human-guided search. *Journal of Heuristics*, 16(3):289–310, 2010.

[14] H. R. Lourenço, O. C. Martin, and T. Stützle. *Handbook of Metaheuristics*, chapter Iterated Local Search, pages 321–353. Kluwer Academic, 2003.

[15] Z. Lü and J.-K. Hao. Adaptive neighborhood search for nurse rostering. *European Journal of Operational Research*, 218:865–876, 2012.

[16] B. Maenhout and M. Vanhoucke. An evolutionary approach for the nurse rerostering problem. *Computers & Operations Research*, 38(10):1400–1411, 2011.

[17] B. Maenhout and M. Vanhoucke. Reconstructing nurse schedules: Computational insights in the problem size parameters. *Omega*, 41(5):903–918, 2013.

[18] K. Miettinen, F. Ruiz, and A. P. Wierzbicki. *Multiobjective Optimization*, chapter Introduction to Multiobjective Optimization: Interactive Approaches, pages 27–58. Springer, 2008.

[19] M. L. Pinedo. *Scheduling Theory, Algorithms, and Systems*, chapter Design and Implementation of Scheduling Systems: Basic Concepts, pages 459–483. Springer, fourth edition, 2012.

[20] B. Roy. Main sources of inaccurate determination, uncertainty and imprecision in decision models. *Mathematical and Computer Modelling*, 12(10–11):1245–1254, 1989.

[21] H. Shachnai, G. Tamir, and T. Tamir. A theory and algorithms for combinatorial reoptimization. In *LATIN*. LNCS, 7256:618–630, Springer Berlin Heidelberg, 2012.

[22] H. Takagi. Interactive evolutionary computation: fusion of the capabilities of EC optimization and human evaluation. *Proceedings of the IEEE*, 89(9):1275–1296, 2001.

[23] C. Valouxis, C. Gogos, G. Goulas, P. Alefragis, and E. Housos. A systematic two phase approach for the nurse rostering problem. *European Journal of Operational Research*, 219(2):425–433, 2012.

[24] J. Wessels and A. P. Wierzbicki. *Model-Based Decision Support Methodology with Environmental Applications*, chapter Model-Based Decision Support, pages 9–28. Springer, 2000.

[25] A. Zych. *Reoptimization of NP-hard problems.* PhD thesis, ETH Zürich, 2012. Nr. 20257.

Static vs. Dynamic Populations in Genetic Algorithms for Coloring a Dynamic Graph

Cara Monical[1]
Centre College
600 W Walnut St
Danville, KY 40422
cmonica2@illinois.edu

Forrest Stonedahl[2]
Centre College
600 W Walnut St
Danville, KY 40422
forrest.stonedahl@centre.edu

ABSTRACT

We studied the performance of genetic algorithms for coloring dynamic graphs under a variety of experimental conditions, focusing on the relationship between the dynamics of the graph and that of the algorithm. Graph coloring is a well-studied NP-hard problem, while dynamic graphs are a natural way to model a diverse range of dynamic systems. Dynamic graph coloring can be applied to online scheduling in a changing environment, such as the online scheduling of conflicting tasks. As genetic algorithms (GAs) have been effective for graph coloring and are adaptable to dynamic environments, they are a promising choice for this problem. Thus, we compared the performance of three algorithms: a GA that maintained a single population adapting to the dynamic graph (DGA), a GA that restarted with a fresh population for the static graph of each time-step (SGA), and DSATUR, a well-known heuristic graph coloring algorithm re-applied at each time-step. We examined the relative performance of these algorithms for dynamic graphs of different sizes, edge densities, structures, and change rates, using different amounts of evolution between time-steps. Overall, the DGA consistently outperformed the SGA, being particularly dominant at low change rates, and under certain conditions was able to outperform DSATUR.

Categories and Subject Descriptors

I.28 [**Artificial Intelligence**]: Problem Solving, Control Methods, and Search; G.2.2 [**Discrete Mathematics**]: Graph Theory—*graph algorithms*

General Terms

Algorithms

Keywords

genetic algorithms, combinatorial optimization, dynamical optimization, dynamic graph, graph coloring

GECCO'14, July 12–16, 2014, Vancouver, BC, Canada.

ACM 978-1-4503-2662-9/14/07 ...$15.00.
http://dx.doi.org/10.1145/2576768.2598233.

1. INTRODUCTION AND RELATED WORK

The graph coloring problem is the well-known problem of assigning as few colors as possible to the vertices of a graph such that no two adjacent vertices are given the same color and is commonly used for scheduling applications [15, 13, 5]. Many real-world problems, however, are better modeled by a dynamic graph that can reflect a changing environment [8]. In the case of scheduling applications, this would allow for the online assignment of resources when only the current tasks are known, such as registers for the currently known values in program execution, frequencies for the currently connected devices in a mobile ad-hoc network, or batches for the currently tasked jobs in a job management system.

In the static model, a graph G has a set of vertices, V, and a set of edges, E. A dynamic graph adds the dimension of time, and so a dynamic graph varies either V (*vertex-dynamic or node-dynamic*) or E (*edge-dynamic*) or both [8]. We consider a discrete dynamic graph that is a succession of (related) static graphs; a *time step* is the time between the changes of the dynamic graph and G_k denotes the static graph at time k. The simplest extension of the static graph coloring problem to the dynamic graph coloring problem is to find a minimal coloring of the vertices of G at each time step. Because the static graph coloring decision problem is NP-complete [7] and the optimization problem is NP-hard, the dynamic graph coloring problem must be NP-hard also. In this work, we only consider vertex-dynamic graphs where edges are added and removed only when one of their endpoints is added or removed.

Two considerations for dynamic graph coloring problems are (1) whether the complete evolution (an offline problem) or only the current state (an online problem) of the dynamic graph is known during execution, and (2) whether vertices are allowed to change color as the graph changes. If a vertex color is fixed for the lifetime of the vertex, the offline dynamic graph coloring problem reduces to the static graph coloring problem on the graph constructed by taking the union of V and E over all time steps. Thus, this case is relatively uninteresting. While Lovász et al. [12] consider an online graph coloring problem where vertices' colors are fixed after assignment, we will consider a relaxed variant of the online dynamic graph coloring problem that allows color re-assignment at each time step.

The goal for our dynamic graph coloring problem is to minimize the cumulative (or equivalently, average) number

[1]Now at: University of Illinois Urbana-Champaign, Math Department, 1409 W. Green Street, Urbana, IL 61801
[2]Affiliated with Augustana College as of August 2014

of colors used to (properly) color the graph over time. Even if the color of a vertex can change between time steps, the coloring at time t is still a natural starting point for the coloring at time $t+1$. Therefore, we could also consider *color turnover*, or how many vertices change colors between time steps. Minimizing the number of colors and minimizing the amount of color turnover are potentially competing goals (as preventing the recoloring of a vertex could prevent finding an optimal coloring).

There may be practical situations where the cost of recoloring a vertex is greater than the cost of a slightly suboptimal coloring (such as in register allocation where values would need to be moved); however, in this work, we allow vertices to change colors freely and do not consider color turnover. In contrast, an ant-colony-inspired approach is given in [14], where vertices are only recolored when a conflict is created or when the degree saturation (the number of colors in the neighbors of a vertex) can be lowered. This approach will tend to have a lower rate of color turnover.

Genetic algorithms (GAs) [10] have frequently been used on the static graph coloring problem with reasonable success [3]. Additionally, in dealing with a dynamic environment, GAs are a natural choice because they mimic natural evolution, which occurs in a changing environment. However, one challenge with adapting GAs to dynamic problems is updating individuals in the population so they correspond to valid solutions of the changed problem [11]. While the most success in static graph coloring using genetic algorithms has occurred by hybridizing partition-based genetic algorithms with local search [6, 5], these algorithms present several challenges in adapting to dynamic graph coloring.

These algorithms commonly start by trying to find a k_0-coloring and when that is successful, search for a k_0-1 coloring and so on, until they find a suitable solution or reach the limits of available computational resources. This approach is not well-suited to a highly dynamic system where the goal is to find an optimal proper coloring at each time step and there may be a limited amount of evolution between changes in the graph. Furthermore, with edge-dynamic graphs, a change in the graph could break the independent sets of the individuals in the population, requiring costly rearrangement to restore individuals corresponding to a valid coloring. The genetic algorithm would need to actively detect changes in the graph (rather than just adapting to them) in order to update the population accordingly. Finally, even with just vertex-dynamic graphs, a small change in the graph could cause significant shifts in the vertices that should be colored the same color as new vertices will create new interactions between existing vertices.

The two other main classes of GAs for graph coloring are integer-based algorithms that encode and evolve colorings of the graphs directly and permutation-based algorithms that encode and evolve permutations of the graph's vertices (genotype), which are then decoded into colorings (phenotype) using the standard greedy coloring algorithm [9]. In integer-based algorithms the colorings are evolved directly and so a small change in the graph could require significant changes in the individuals to restore a proper coloring. However, with permutation-based algorithms, the changes to the graph are much more easily transferred to the individuals: vertices that have been removed from or added to the graph merely need to be removed from or added to the ordering encoded by each individual. Additionally, as the graph changes, it is likely that high fitness individuals will retain their high fitness—key vertices for early coloring in the graph at time t are likely still key in the changed graph at $t+1$, despite (possibly large) changes in the phenotypic coloring. Furthermore, permutation-based GAs do not require an active awareness of the algorithm to changes in the graph as the decoder will detect changes in the graph when using an individual to produce a coloring. Thus, we have focused exclusively on permutation-based GAs.

There are two genres of problems, traveling salesman-like problems and scheduling-like problems, that are typically tackled with permutation-based GAs, each with its own set of effective crossover and mutation operators [17]. In the former genre, preserving adjacency within an individual is important, while in the latter, preserving relative order of the vertices is key. Graph coloring clearly falls in the second class of problems, as it is frequently used for scheduling.

To our knowledge, we are the first to employ GAs for the dynamic graph coloring problem. As such, we focus on exploring the parameters of both the problem (Section 2.1) and the algorithm (Section 2.2) that affect the performance of a permutation-based GA. In Section 3, we discuss the effects on these parameters, including the edge density and graph structure of the graph (3.1), the rate at which the graph is changing (3.2), and the amount of evolution that can be done during each graph time step (3.3). While many variations to GAs, such as hybridizing with local search, seeding the initial population, or adapting the algorithm alongside the evolving solutions, have been shown to improve performance on graph coloring [2, 3], we seek to illuminate the relationship between the dynamic graph-coloring problem and GA performance, rather than determine the best possible algorithm. Consequently, we do not consider these improvements (or others), though we would recommend exploring these methods for real-world applications. Specifically, we focus on the relationship between the change rate of the graph, the amount of evolution done at each step, and the GAs' performance, as this relationship provides insight into the interaction between the two sources of dynamism: the dynamics of the problem and the dynamics of the algorithm.

2. METHODS

2.1 Graphs

We test our GAs on two different dynamic graph models. The first is a dynamic extension of $G(n,p)$ graphs developed by Erdős and Rényi [4]. In the static model, a $G(n,p)$ graph is a graph on n vertices where each edge appears with probability p. We define an extension of this model, $G(n,p,c_v)$ graphs, where c_v is the *vertex change rate.* To create a dynamic $G(n,p,c_v)$ graph, we start with a $G(n,p)$ graph for G_1, and at each successive time step, vertices in the graph G_t "die" (are removed in G_{t+1}) with probability c_v. To keep G at approximately n vertices, an expected nc_v vertices are added at each step. When a new vertex v is added, edges are added between v and each vertex already in the graph with probability p. Edges are only removed or added when their incident vertices are removed and added. Thus at any time t, G_t is a $G(n+\epsilon,p)$ graph, ϵ has high probability of being small, and an average of nc_v vertices change each step.

Our other dynamic graph model is a dynamic 2-D Euclidean graph. In a 2-D Euclidean graph, each vertex is assigned a random x and y coordinate in the unit square. Two vertices are adjacent if the Euclidean distance between them is less than some α threshold. For the dynamic Euclidean graph model, we mirrored the $G(n, p, c_v)$ model, where n and c_v act as above. The parameter p is used to calculate α such that two random points in the unit square have a probability p being a distance of α apart and thus will result in a graph with an edge density p. As we only examine vertex-dynamic graphs, vertices do not move between time steps (as this would change edges) but are deleted and added at new random (x, y) locations at a rate controlled by c_v. For both graph models, we varied n, p, and c_v in order to investigate how these parameters affected the GA performance.

2.2 Algorithms

Throughout our tests, we compared the performance of three algorithms:

- DSATUR [1], the standard graph coloring heuristic algorithm that colors vertices in order of degree saturation (used as a baseline for performance)
- DGA, a genetic algorithm with a dynamic population (single population evolves as the graph changes)
- SGA, a genetic algorithm with a static population (new random population is generated each time step).

The only difference between the DGA and SGA was how the population was handled as the graph changed. For both, we used an steady-state genetic algorithm [18] with elitism where the two children produced by crossover and mutation replace the two individuals with the worst fitness, regardless of the fitness of the new children.

Fitness was calculated by using the standard greedy coloring on the permutation specified by the individual. Using just the number of colors in the decoding offers little gradation in the fitness landscape as many individuals decode with the same number of colors. To break ties between these individuals, we examined the number of vertices assigned each of the three least used colors; an individual with only a few vertices of a color seemed closer to using fewer colors than one with a even distribution of vertices among the colors. Thus, we calculated fitness as $f = n^3c + n^2c_1 + nc_2 + c_3$, where c is the number of colors used, c_1 is the number of vertices colored the least used color, c_2 is the number colored the second least used color, and c_3 is the number colored the third least used color. As we wanted to minimize the number of colors used, our GAs sought to minimize fitness.

Six standard crossover operators for permutation-based GAs are described in [17]. These are edge, order 1 (OX1), order 2 (OX2), position, partially mapped (PMX), and cycle crossover. As edge crossover preserves adjacency, which is not important for graph coloring, we did not implement it. We did implement the other five and in preliminary experiments, saw no significant difference in the performance of the GAs with different crossover operators. As such, we used OX1 in our main experiments as it performed reasonably well and is a standard crossover operator.

Similarly we considered three mutation operators (RAR, SWAP, inversion) described in [9]. We found that RAR and SWAP performed noticeably better than inversion and having no mutation, but observed no significant difference between RAR and SWAP. We chose to use the SWAP operator. Our other constant parameters were chosen with reasonable default values based on the authors' previous experience; fine-tuning is unlikely to alter the main qualitative results:

- Population size: 100
- Tournament selection with tournament size: 3
- Crossover rate: 0.7
- Mutation chance per individual: 0.5.

For the initial dynamic population and the static population at each step, we simply generated 100 random permutations on the vertices in the current graph. To repair each individual in the dynamic population each time the graph changed, we removed all vertices that had been removed from the graph, and then independently added the new vertices at random positions in each individual.

The graph parameters (n, p, c_v) and number of individuals created (and fitness evaluations done) e, are all parameters determined by the nature of the problem being solved and computational resources available. Thus, in order to study the difference between the DGA and SGA for a wide variety of problems, we performed a univariate sensitivity analysis, in turn varying each of n, p, c_v, and e from the following default parameter values:

- Graph size, n: 100
- Edge density, p: 0.6
- Change rate, c_v: .01
- Individuals evolved per step, e: 1000.

2.3 Experiment

In our experiments, each run consisted of generating a random graph and a random initial dynamic population, and then letting the graph change 150 steps. For each step:

1. Add a vertex with probability c_v. Repeat n times.
2. Add new vertices to the DGA's population.
3. Run DSATUR on the current graph.
4. Evolve the DGA's population for e individuals.
5. Create the SGA's population and evolve e individuals.
6. Record the number of colors used by DSATUR and the best individual from the DGA and SGA.
7. Remove each vertex with probability c_v.
8. Remove "dead" vertices from the DGA's population.

Each test consisted of working with a single dynamic graph for 150 steps—running all three algorithms on the same graph so that we could compare their performance. For each set of parameters, we performed 200 replicate runs and took the mean of the cumulative number of colors used by each of the algorithms for the entire run of the graph.

3. RESULTS AND DISCUSSION

As the only difference between the DGA and the SGA is how the population is maintained, the two genetic algorithms do the same amount of work when the parameters are kept constant. DSATUR, relatively speaking, requires very little computational effort. However, our experiments show that the genetic algorithms can outperform DSATUR for certain values of n, p, c_v, and e. Furthermore, as seen in [16], there are 3-chromatic graphs on $O(n)$ vertices where DSATUR will use n colors, while GAs can theoretically find an optimal solution. Finally, the SGA does not outperform the DGA, though there are some parameter ranges where the two have indistinguishable performance.

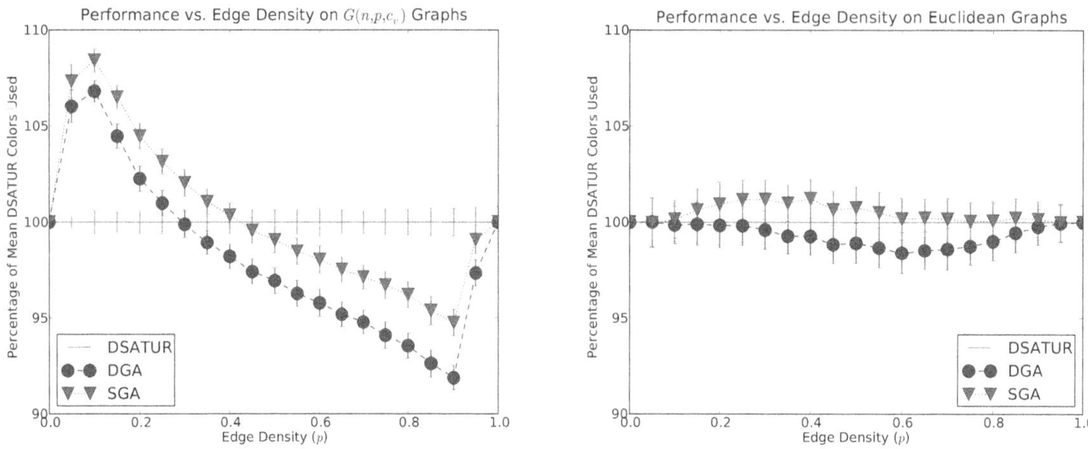

Figure 1: Performance of the genetic algorithms relative to DSATUR for varying edge densities, p, in $G(n, p, c_v)$ (left) and Euclidean (right) graphs. We can see that the DGA always outperformed SGA, and sometimes outperformed DSATUR, depending on edge density and graph structure.

In the figures that follow, we give performance values as a percentage of the mean number of colors DSATUR used so we can easily compare relative performance of the algorithms. Better performance occurs when the GAs use *fewer* colors relative to DSATUR. The error bars represent 95% confidence intervals estimated from the 200 replicate runs at each parameter setting and are scaled by the DSATUR mean. Despite the same number of replicate runs, the confidence intervals are much wider for the Euclidean graphs than for the $G(n, p, c_v)$ graphs, suggesting Euclidean graphs have a wider range of chromatic number than $G(n, p, c_v)$ graphs with the same parameters.

3.1 Edge Density (p)

As shown in Figure 1, the relative performance of the GAs to DSATUR depends strongly on p for $G(n, p, c_v)$ graphs. For $G(n, p, c_v)$ graphs with edge densities between .1 and .95, the relative genetic algorithm performance increases as edge density increases. Additionally, on $G(n, p, c_v)$ graphs, the DGA performance relative to SGA does not seem to depend on p, as there is a fairly consistent gap between their performance levels for almost all values of p.

For Euclidean graphs, the relative performance of the genetic algorithms to DSATUR is much less dependent on p. The DGA tends to slightly outperform DSATUR, while the SGA lags behind DSATUR. Higher edge densities in Euclidean graphs are likely to form cliques or near-cliques, which are colored effectively by prioritizing by degree saturation, and so DSATUR is able to do just as well as the GAs. However, in $G(n, p, c_v)$ graphs, the additional edges are more spread out through the entire graph, making graphs with higher edge densities harder to color. This provides the genetic algorithms more potential to improve on the DSATUR coloring, leading to a smaller percentage of colors used.

3.2 Change Rate (c_v) & Evolution Per Step (e)

The change rate of the graph, c_v, and the amount of evolution done per step, e, present an interesting relationship between the dynamic nature of the problem and the dynamic nature of the algorithm. As shown in Figure 2, more evolution leads to better performance of the GAs relative to DSATUR, especially on $G(n, p, c_v)$ graphs. This is not surprising since more evolution means more work is being done. However, on Euclidean graphs, more evolution (beyond $e \approx 1500$) does not substantially help the GAs improve its performance relative to DSATUR. Again, this suggests that DSATUR is able to get close to the optimal coloring on Euclidean graphs, whereas on the $G(n, p, c_v)$ DSATUR's coloring may be further from optimal, and more evolution allows the GAs to improve more compared against it.

In Figure 3, we observe that under constant evolution, the SGA and DSATUR performance differ by a constant percentage regardless of change rate. This is expected as the SGA does not interact with the changing graph and therefore its performance should not depend on the change rate. However, the DGA presents a very different picture. At low change rates, the DGA is able to noticeably outperform the SGA because small changes to the graph do not force substantial changes to the population and thus evolution can continue with minor disruption across graph changes. At higher change rates, there is much more upheaval in the dynamic population and so it offers less of an advantage over the SGA. Because new vertices are added to the individuals of the dynamic population randomly, the dynamic population is much closer to the fresh population of the SGA when there are lots of new vertices. Thus, the DGA starts to act more like the SGA as we have a more dynamic problem.

At very low levels of evolution, the DGA clearly offers better performance because the effects of evolution are allowed to accumulate. The SGA, on the other hand, starts with a new random population at every step, and thus does not have enough evolution to find a good solution. In contrast, at higher levels of evolution, the DGA performance only outperforms the SGA at very low change rates because with more evolution, the SGA has time to catch up with the evolution accumulated by the DGA.

While these trends are present in both $G(n, p, c_v)$ and Euclidean graphs, the gap between the DGA and SGA is much

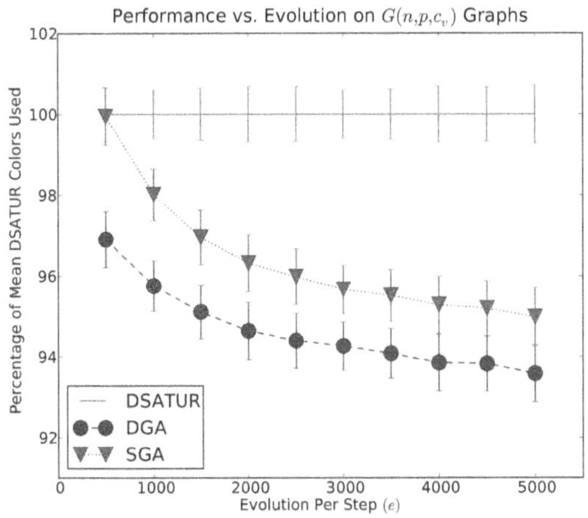

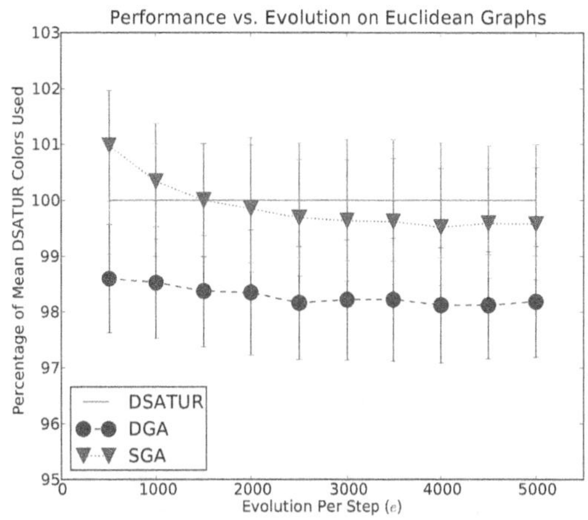

Figure 2: Performance of the GAs relative to DSATUR for varying evolution per step, e, in $G(n,p,c_v)$ (left) and Euclidean (right) graphs. As usual with GAs, there are diminishing returns on the GA performance as the amount of evolution done is increased. On $G(n,p,c_v)$ graphs, increasing evolution leads to better relative performance of the GAs. On Euclidean graphs, however, the benefit of more evolution levels off much faster.

wider for Euclidean graphs, and the DGA is better able to outperform the SGA. In a Euclidean graph, the edges are clustered locally and it is rare for a new vertex to connect two different sections of the graph. Thus changes in the graph are felt locally and we hypothesize that a good coloring is therefore more easily carried forward from the time step before. On $G(n,p,c_v)$ graphs, however, a new vertex can cause major disruptions in the coloring from the step before, and thus there is likely less benefit in keeping a dynamic population. This suggests that whenever changes are local rather than widespread, a dynamic population is better able to provide performance increases.

		e 500	1000	1500	2000
	100	5	10	15	20
	200	2.5	5	7.5	10
e_v	300	$\frac{5}{3}$	$\frac{10}{3}$	5	$\frac{20}{3}$
	400	1.25	2.5	3.75	5
	500	1	2	3	4

Table 1: nc_v values (the expected number of changed vertices each step) determined by e and e_v.

3.3 Individuals per Vertex

From our experiments with e and c_v, it is clear that problems the allow more evolution per graph time step and have low change rates are more solvable with dynamic GAs than problems with higher change rates or problems where the amount of evolution per graph time step is necessarily limited. For practical applications, however, it is likely that the amount of evolution is limited by the availability of computational resources and that the change rate is dictated by the how fast the situation being modeled is changing.

For example, we could imagine that we have 4 new tasks and the computational resources to evolve 1000 individuals per minute. We might ask: is it better to change 4 vertices every minute and evolve for 1000 fitness evaluations between changes, or is it better to change 1 vertex every 15 seconds and evolve for 250 fitness evaluations between each change? In the former case we have more evolution per step but a higher change rate, and in the latter case we have a lower change rate but less evolution between changes. Which will offer better performance?

To examine this question of trade-offs, we define a new parameter, $e_v = \frac{e}{nc_v}$, which represents the number of fitness evaluations *per changed vertex*. We then ran the same experiments as before on $G(n,p,c_v)$ graphs for various e_v values at different levels of evolution. The values for nc_v needed to achieve a given e_v with a given e value are given in Table 1. Instead of running for 150 time steps, we ran these graphs until 200 new vertices were added so all runs would process the same number of vertices. We examine the performance of the DGA at evolution rates of 500, 1000, 1500, and 2000 against DSATUR for varying e_v levels.

As seen in Figure 4, for this problem domain it is clearly better to choose longer time steps with more evolution and consequently higher change rates when possible, even though the DGA performance is generally better at lower change rates. This suggests that the effect of evolution is stronger than the effect of change rate in determining the performance of the GA. Frequent small changes are harder for the genetic algorithm to deal with than infrequent drastic ones, indicating that the time after a change that the genetic algorithm needs to adjust to the new problem is not linearly proportional to how much the graph has changed. It is better to change the problem as infrequently as possible so that you can maximize the amount of uninterrupted evolution.

3.4 Graph Size (n)

Finally, we experimented with the size of the graph n, while maintaining a constant amount of evolution ($e = 1000$). As seen in Figure 5, the GAs only outperform DSATUR for graphs with fewer than 200 vertices, and their performance

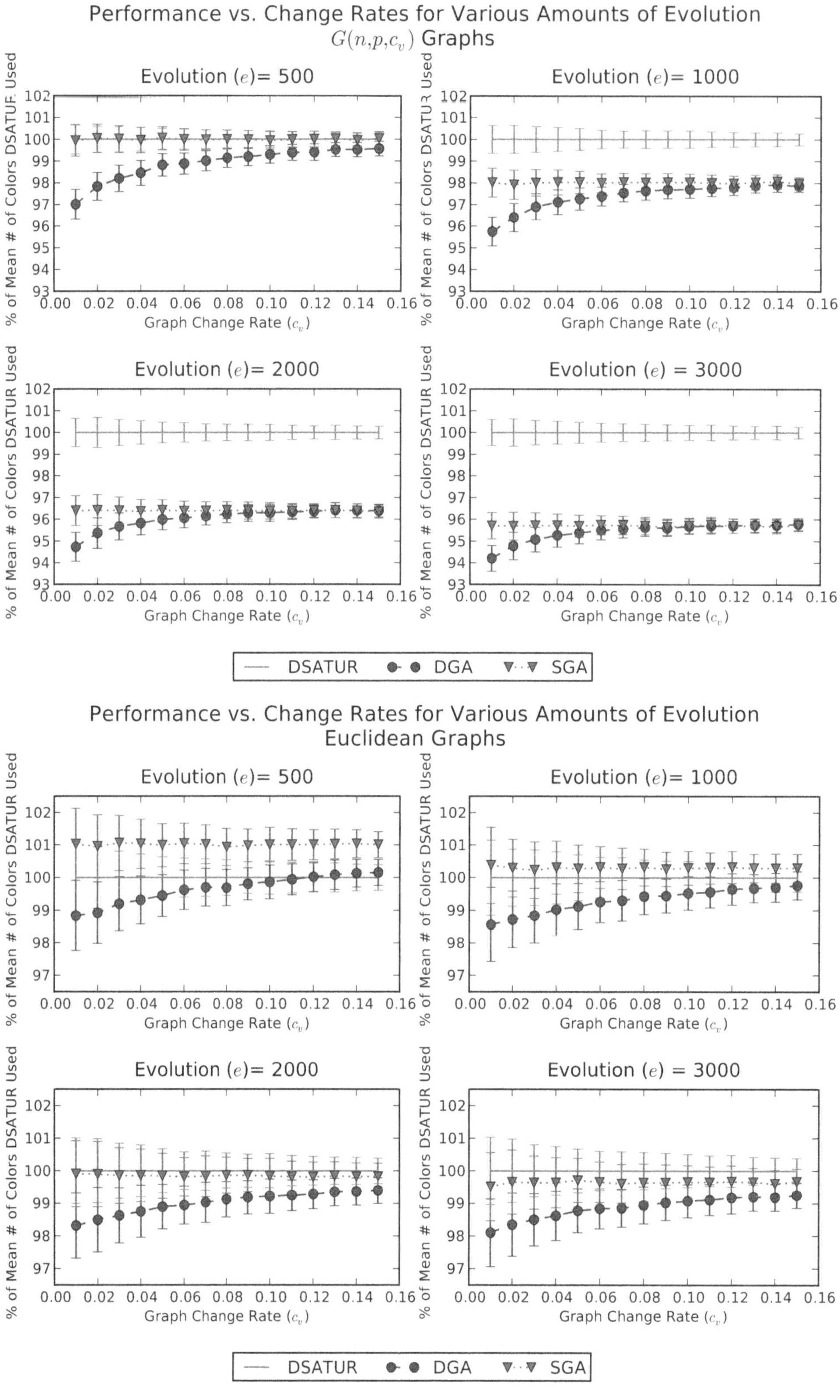

Figure 3: Performance of the genetic algorithms relative to DSATUR for varying change rates, c_v, and evolution, e, in $G(n, p, c_v)$ (top) and Euclidean (bottom) graphs. As change rates increase, DGA performance converges to SGA performance. This happens faster at higher rates of evolution. On Euclidean graphs, there is a much wider gap between DGA and SGA performance.

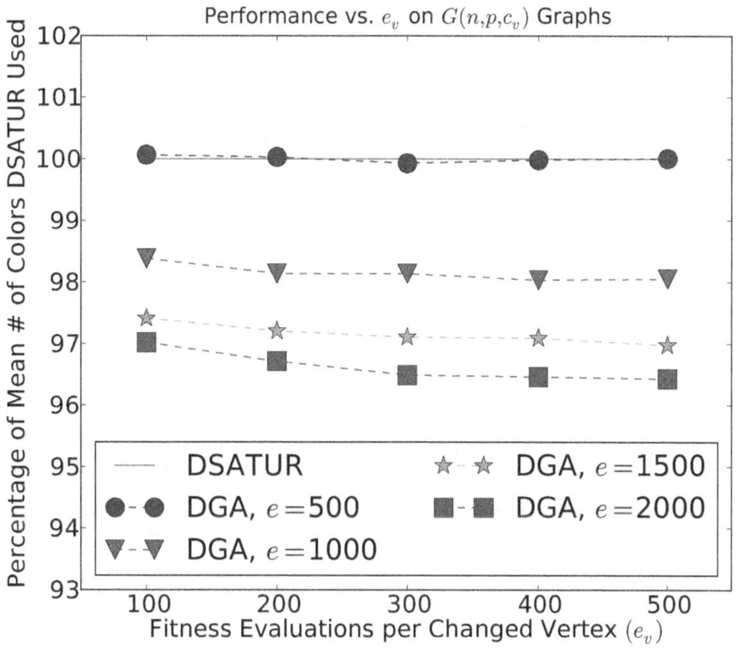

Figure 4: Performance of DGA relative to DSATUR at different amounts of evolution per step, e, for varying rates of individuals per changing vertex. Specific values for the expected number of changed vertices (nc_v) for a given e, e_v point are given in Table 1, but in general, higher levels of evolution at a fixed number of individuals per changed vertex require a higher number of changed vertices. Regardless of e_v, higher rates of evolution (and consequent higher change rates) have stronger relative performance to DSATUR.

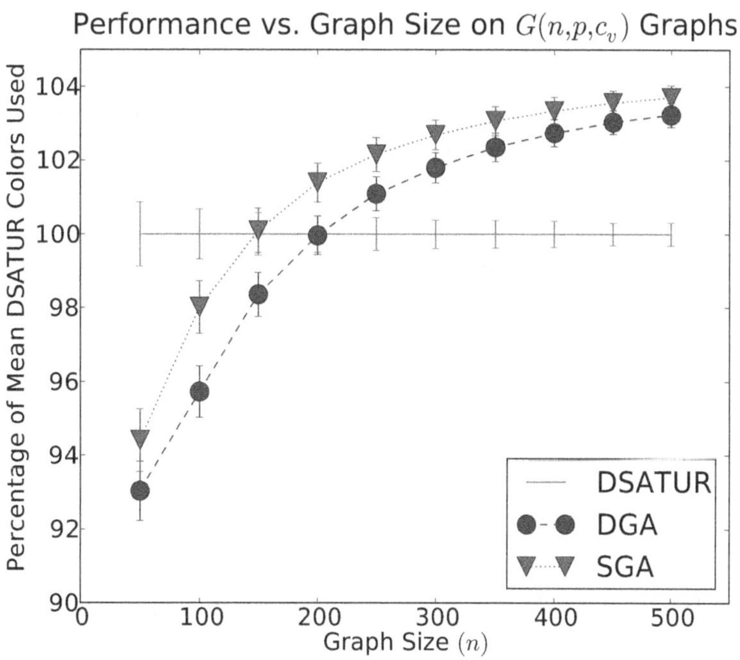

Figure 5: Performance of the genetic algorithms relative to DSATUR for varying sizes of $G(n, p, c_v)$ graphs. As graph sizes increase, the genetic algorithms' performance relative to DSATUR decreases. However, this trend levels off as graph sizes continue to increase.

relative to DSATUR decreases as the graph size increases. This suggests that a GA approach may not scale well to very large dynamic graphs. However, the worsening performance appears to be leveling off as graph sizes continue to increase, which is a good sign. It may also be possible to outperform DSATUR even at larger graph sizes if the GA is given sufficient computational resources. Furthermore, the dynamic graph coloring problem is still challenging for graphs with fewer than 200 vertices, so even if GA techniques do not scale well to large graphs, they could still serve many practical applications that fall into this size range.

4. CONCLUSIONS AND FUTURE WORK

With this work, we first described different variations of the dynamic graph coloring problem and defined two different dynamic graph models that extend classical random graph models. We then explored the effect of several different parameters on the performance of a genetic algorithm with a dynamic population and a genetic algorithm that starts with a new population at every step relative to DSATUR for the dynamic graph coloring problem. We are able to demonstrate conditions where a dynamic population is able to offer significant performance increases relative to both a genetic algorithm with a static population and to the standard graph coloring algorithm, DSATUR. Additionally, the added complexity/overhead of keeping a dynamic population while the graph changes is insignificant with a permutation based GA. In all circumstances, the dynamic population GA performed at least as well as the static population GA, and sometimes offered much better performance.

Broadly, this work supports the idea that the more dynamic a problem is, an algorithm is less able to utilize information from earlier time steps of the problem as these steps are less similar to the current problem. Then, highly dynamic problems reduce to a succession of static problems, while slightly dynamic problems are better tackled by a more dynamic algorithm. Future work is needed to explore graphs that are edge-dynamic, or both edge- and vertex-dynamic, as well as graphs with different structures from the two classes ($G(n, p, c_v)$ and Euclidean) examined here.

As mentioned early in the paper, some of the most successful static graph coloring algorithms use hybrid approaches, combining GAs with other heuristics or local search mechanisms, or use partition-based genetic algorithms. Since this paper presents the first application of genetic algorithms for the dynamic graph coloring problem, we chose to keep our genetic algorithms relatively pure and straightforward, but it would be interesting for follow-up papers to explore how much benefit could be gained through hybrid techniques. Further work also needs to be done in adapting more advanced static genetic algorithms to the problem of coloring a dynamic graph, There are also many variations of the graph coloring program that correspond to different practical applications, and future work could investigate if the techniques outlined here are applicable to dynamic versions of these problems.

5. REFERENCES

[1] BRÉLAZ, D. New methods to color the vertices of a graph. *Communications of the ACM 22*, 4 (Apr. 1979), 251–256.

[2] DAVIS, L. *Handbook of genetic algorithms*. VNR computer library. Van Nostrand Reinhold, 1991.

[3] EIBEN, A., VAN DER HAUW, J., AND VAN HEMERT, J. Graph coloring with adaptive evolutionary algorithms. *Journal of Heuristics 4* (1998), 25–46. 10.1023/A:1009638304510.

[4] ERDŐS, P., AND RÉNYI, A. On the evolution of random graphs. In *Publication of the Mathematical Institute of the Hungarian Academy of Sciences* (1960), pp. 17–61.

[5] GALINIER, P., HAMIEZ, J.-P., HAO, J.-K., AND PORUMBEL, D. Recent advances in graph vertex coloring. In *Handbook of Optimization*, I. Zelinka, V. Snášel, and A. Abraham, Eds., vol. 38 of *Intelligent Systems Reference Library*. Springer Berlin Heidelberg, 2013, pp. 505–528.

[6] GALINIER, P., AND HAO, J.-K. Hybrid evolutionary algorithms for graph coloring. *Journal of Combinatorial Optimization 3*, 4 (1999), 379–397.

[7] GAREY, M. R., AND JOHNSON, D. S. *Computers and Intractability: A Guide to the Theory of NP-Completeness*. W. H. Freeman & Co., New York, NY, USA, 1979.

[8] HARARY, F., AND GUPTA, G. Dynamic graph models. *Mathematical and Computer Modelling 25*, 7 (1997), 79–88.

[9] HAUW, K. V. D. Evaluating and Improving Steady State Evolutionary Algorithms on Constraint Satisfaction Problems. Master's thesis, Leiden University, 1996.

[10] HOLLAND, J. *Adaptation in natural and artificial systems: an introductory analysis with applications to biology, control, and artificial intelligence*. University of Michigan Press, 1975.

[11] JIN, Y., AND BRANKE, J. Evolutionary optimization in uncertain environments-a survey. *Trans. Evol. Comp 9*, 3 (June 2005), 303–317.

[12] LOVÁSZ, L., SAKS, M. E., AND TROTTER, W. T. An on-line graph coloring algorithm with sublinear performance ratio. *Discrete Mathematics 75*, 1-3 (1989), 319–325.

[13] MARX, D. Graph Coloring Problems and Their Applications in Scheduling. In *in Proc. John von Neumann PhD Students Conference* (2004), pp. 1–2.

[14] PREUVENEERS, D., AND BERBERS, Y. Acodygra: an agent algorithm for coloring dynamic graphs. In *Symbolic and Numeric Algorithms for Scientific Computing* (September 2004), vol. 6, pp. 381–390.

[15] SHIRINIVAS, S., VETRIVEL, S., AND ELANGO, N. Applications of Graph Theory in Computer Science An Overview. *International Journal of Engineering Science and Technology 2*, 9 (2010), 4610–4621.

[16] SPINRAD, J. P., AND VIJAYAN, G. Worst case analysis of a graph coloring algorithm. *Discrete Applied Mathematics 12*, 1 (1985), 89–92.

[17] STARKWEATHER, T., AND OF COMPUTER SCIENCE, C. S. U. D. *A Comparison of genetic sequencing operators*. No. 106 in Technical report (Colorado State University. Dept. of Computer Science). Colorado State University, Department of Computer Science, 1991.

[18] SYSWERDA, G. A study of reproduction in generational and steady-state genetic algorithms. *Foundation of Genetic Algorithms* (1991), 94–101.

A Comprehensive Benchmark Set and Heuristics for the Traveling Thief Problem

Sergey Polyakovskiy
School of Computer Science
The University of Adelaide

Mohammad Reza Bonyadi
School of Computer Science
The University of Adelaide

Markus Wagner
School of Computer Science
The University of Adelaide

Zbigniew Michalewicz
School of Computer Science
The University of Adelaide

Frank Neumann
School of Computer Science
The University of Adelaide

ABSTRACT

Real-world optimization problems often consist of several NP-hard optimization problems that interact with each other. The goal of this paper is to provide a benchmark suite that promotes a research of the interaction between problems and their mutual influence. We establish a comprehensive benchmark suite for the traveling thief problem (TTP) which combines the traveling salesman problem and the knapsack problem. Our benchmark suite builds on common benchmarks for the two sub-problems which grant a basis to examine the potential hardness imposed by combining the two classical problems. Furthermore, we present some simple heuristics for TTP and their results on our benchmark suite.

Categories and Subject Descriptors

G.1.6 [**Optimization**]: Miscellaneous; I.2.8 [**Problem Solving, Control Methods, and Search**]: Scheduling

General Terms

Experimentation, Algorithms

Keywords

Traveling thief problem, knapsack problem, interdependence, benchmarks

1. INTRODUCTION

Real-world optimization problems usually consist of several problems that interact with each other. In order to solve such problems it is important to understand and deal with these interactions. So far, the research literature is lacking systematic approaches for dealing with such interdependent problems.

In this paper, we consider the Traveling Thief Problem (TTP) [4] which is a combination of two of the most prominent combinatorial optimization problems, namely the traveling salesperson problem (TSP) and the knapsack problem (KP). Both problems have been considered in numerous theoretical and experimental studies, and very effective solvers are known that perform well on a variety of benchmarks.

We present a benchmark suite for TTP which is based on benchmark instances for the TSP and KP. The aim of this benchmark suite is to give researchers the opportunities

- to study TTP as a combination of TSP and KP,
- to compare the problem instances, and
- to provide algorithms that can effectively solve problems with interdependencies.

We systematically construct the benchmarks so that the resulting instances cover a wide range of features: from few cities with few items and small knapsacks to many cities with many items and large knapsacks. While we are confident that smaller instances can soon be solved to optimality, the larger ones most likely remain unsolved for the years to come.

It is important to note that the TTP is unlike many capacitated vehicle-routing problems in the area of Green Logistics (see, e.g., the survey article [8]). For example, the fuel consumption based on load or geographical features is considered in [6, 7] and the problem for several vehicles is solved using integer programming. In our case, we add to the routing problem not only a load-dependent feature, but also the NP-hard optimization problem of deciding which items are to be packed.

The remainder of this paper is organized as follows. First, we define the traveling thief problem in Section 2. In Section 3 we describe the systematic construction of the benchmark set. We present our heuristic algorithms in Section 4 and their results on the benchmarks in Section 5. We finish with some concluding remarks.

GECCO'14, July 12–16, 2014, Vancouver, BC, Canada.
Copyright 2014 ACM 978-1-4503-2662-9/14/07 ...$15.00.
http://dx.doi.org/10.1145/2576768.2598249.

2. TRAVELING THIEF PROBLEM

The Traveling Thief Problem is defined as follows. Given is a set of cities $N = \{1, \ldots, n\}$ for which a distance d_{ij}, $i, j \in N$ between any pair of cities is known. Every city i but the first contains a set of items $M_i = \{1, \ldots, m_i\}$. Each item k positioned in the city i is characterized by its value p_{ik} and weight w_{ik}, thus the item $I_{ik} \sim (p_{ik}, w_{ik})$. The thief must visit each of the cities exactly once starting from the first city and returning back to it in the end. Any item may be picked up into the knapsack in any city until the total weight of collected items does not exceed the maximum possible weight W. A renting rate R is to be paid per each time unit being on a way. υ_{max} and υ_{min} denote the maximal and minimum speeds that the thief can move, respectively. The goal is to find a tour of the maximal profit.

Let $y_{ik} \in \{0,1\}$ be a binary variable equal to one when the item k is picked up in the city i. In addition, let W_i denote the total weight of collected items when the thief leaves the city i. Therefore, the objective function for a tour $\Pi = (x_1, \ldots, x_n)$, $x_i \in N$ and a packing plan $P = (y_{21}, \ldots, y_{nm_i})$ takes the following form:

$$\begin{aligned} Z(\Pi, P) &= \sum_{i=1}^{n} \sum_{k=1}^{m_i} p_{ik} y_{ik} \\ &\quad - R \left(\frac{d_{x_n x_1}}{\upsilon_{max} - \nu W_{x_n}} + \sum_{i=1}^{n-1} \frac{d_{x_i x_{i+1}}}{\upsilon_{max} - \nu W_{x_i}} \right) \end{aligned}$$

where $\nu = \frac{\upsilon_{max} - \upsilon_{min}}{W}$ is a constant value. The minuend is the sum over all packed items' profits and the subtrahend is the amount that the thief pays for the knapsack's rent equal to the total traveling time along Π multiplied by R.

A numeric example of the TTP problem is provided via the graph given in Figure 1. Each node but the first has an assigned set of items, e.g. node 2 is associated with item I_{21} of profit $p_{21} = 20$ and weight $w_{21} = 2$, and with item I_{22} of profit $p_{22} = 30$ and weight $w_{22} = 3$. Let's assume that the maximum weight $W = 3$, the renting rate $R = 1$ and υ_{max} and υ_{min} are set as 1 and 0.1, respectively. Then the optimum objective value $Z(\Pi, P) = 50$ for $\Pi = (1, 2, 4, 3)$ and $P = (0, 0, 0, 1, 1, 0)$. Specifically, the thief collects no items traveling from city 1 to city 3 via cities 2 and 4. Therefore, this part of the tour costs 15. Only in the city 3 items I_{32} and I_{33} are picked up, that gives total profit of 80. However, on the way from city 3 back to city 1 the thief's knapsack has weight of 2. In fact, it reduces the speed and results in increased cost of 15. Consequently, the final objective value is $Z(\Pi, P) = 80 - 15 - 15 = 50$.

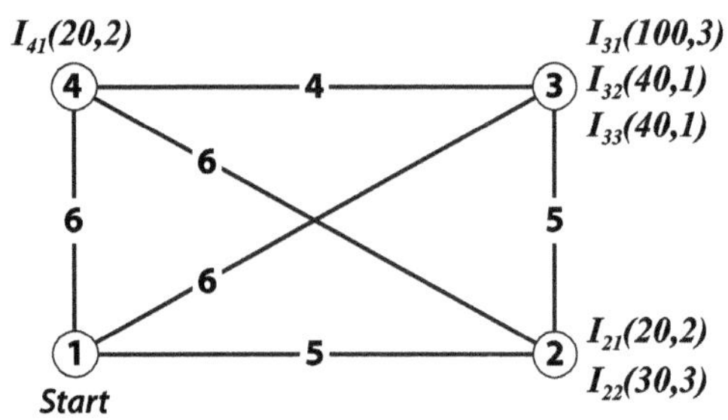

Figure 1: Illustrative Example

3. BENCHMARK SET

Herein we propose a new benchmark of instances in order to promote a correct comparison among different approaches to the TTP problem. It is mainly motivated by a desire to (1) have a combination of well-known test suites for each sub-problem, and (2) a correct adjustment of constant variables involved in the objective function. Specifically, from an experimental point of view, it is important to keep a balance between two components of the problem. It means that the near-optimal solution of one sub-problem must not dominate over the optimal solution of another sub-problem. Therefore, solving the shortest tour problem to optimality must not make the knapsack packing aspect negligible. Vice versa, the most profitable loading plan must not reduce the importance of a shorter tour.

To handle this task the most known set of test instances for each sub-problem was considered. The TSP library collected by Reinelt [2, 10] is to be the main departure point when one is going to evaluate his/her approach's performance on the TSP. It consists of over 100 instances with sizes ranging from 14 to 85,900 cities and is derived from industrial applications and geographic problems. Since its creation in 1990, an extensive investigation has been carried out and now all the symmetric TSP library instances are solved to optimality.

The knapsack problem was thoroughly studied by Martello, Pisinger and Toth [9]. Their work deals with the 0-1 knapsack and proposes the exact dynamic programming algorithm called `COMBO` to tackle it. Furthermore, they propose and investigate a test benchmark wealthy in ways to generate KP data. `COMBO` adopts a set of valid inequalities along with a new initial core problem that allows it to solve instances with up to 10,000 items in less than 0.2 seconds. The authors generated fifteen different types of KP varying weights and profits of items to investigate which aspects result in challenges for KP solvers in general and for their approach in particular. From their work, we pick several of the hardest cases and combine them with instances of the TSP library.

To generate our TTP instances we first consider the instances of the TSP library. First, we select the 81 instances that possess "EUC_2D" or "CEIL_2D" marks for their edge weight type tag. Despite the mark derived from the TSP library we assume that over the entire TTP benchmark suite all distances between the cities are integer values rounded up to the next integer. The resulting set has instances with the number of cities ranging from 51 and up to 85,900.

For each TSP instance, we generate a knapsack component using the code from [1]. Three ways to generate a KP data are selected respecting the evaluated hardness for solving and the recommendations reported in [9]. Each way results in a unique knapsack type. In the following, we distinguish between *uncorrelated*, *uncorrelated with similar weights* and *bounded strongly correlated* types.

For the uncorrelated type a weight w_{ik} and a profit p_{ik} of item k are uniformly distributed random integer values in $[1, 10^3]$. Loose correlation or no correlation among the profit and weight of each item makes an instance easy to solve to optimality even for large-sized problems [9]. However, this may be not straightforward for the TTP problem and a behavior of algorithms stays of a particular interest for research.

Addressing the uncorrelated type with similar weights we employ for w_{ik} and p_{ik} integer values uniformly distributed within $[10^3, 10^3 + 10]$ and $[1, 10^3]$ respectively. Producing items with similar weights complicates KP by increasing the core problem's size. It has already been shown that this type of 0-1 knapsack instances is more time consuming to be solved [9]. Consequently, having all items of almost equal weight but definitely different profit may require an additional effort to develop an algorithm which intelligently deal with this aspect in TTP, too.

Oppositely to the uncorrelated case, strongly correlated problems are typically very difficult. The bounded strongly correlated type adopts the bounded knapsack problem where multiple copies of an item are allowed to be selected complying with a maximum number restriction. As previously shown, its transformation to a 0-1 knapsack problem complicates the problem [9]. It significantly increases the computation time while it forces the cardinality constraints in COMBO to loose their effect. This indicates that specialized algorithms for the bounded version should be developed. To set up the initial bounded instance, we choose the interval $\left[1, 10^3\right]$ for an item's integer weight w_{ik} uniformly distributed generation and we set p_{ik} based on this as $w_{ik}+100$.

To diversify the size of the knapsack component, we distinguish between four values of an *item factor* $F \in \{1, 3, 5, 10\}$. In our benchmarks, F describes how many items per city are available. We use the same number of items for every city setting $F = m_i$ for any $i \in N$, $i \geq 2$. As assumed in the problem statement, the first city does not contain any item. Therefore, for a number of n cities we produce totally $F \times (n-1)$ items. Moreover, no correlation exists between the item's features and the features of the city it is assigned to, i.e. a simple many-to-one assignment between the set of cities and the set of items is performed, where each item $(i + f \times (n-1))$, $f \in \mathbb{N}^0$, $i \in \{1, \dots, n-1\}$, goes to the city $(i+1)$.

Next, for each TSP library instance, knapsack type and item factor we generate 10 instances. Each instance falls into its *capacity category* $C \in \{1, \dots, 10\}$ according to the instance number. The capacity category value C results in a unique maximum Knapsack weight value of $W = \left(\frac{C}{11}\right) \sum_{i=1}^{n} \sum_{k=1}^{F} w_{ik}$. Effectively, C is the factor by which the capacity of the smallest knapsack (in the set of 10) is multiplied.

As noted above, we try to manage the potential objective value by searching for a balance between TSP and KP components through the constant variables. Specifically, we set the same values for $v_{max} = 1$ and $v_{min} = 0.1$ over all instances. However, each instance gets its individual renting rate R defined as $R = \frac{Z\left(P^{OPT}\right)}{TIME\left(\Pi^{linkern}, P^{OPT}\right)}$, where $Z\left(P^{OPT}\right)$ corresponds to the optimal profit of the KP component and $TIME\left(\Pi^{linkern}, P^{OPT}\right)$ denotes the total traveling time along the near-optimal TSP tour $\Pi^{linkern}$ obtained via the Chained Lin-Kernighan heuristic [3][1] while picking the items according to the optimal KP component's solution P^{OPT}. Such selection of R guarantees the existence of at least one TTP solution with zero objective value.

Consequently, our final benchmark set based on 81 TSP instances, three KP types, four item factors and ten capacity categories contains $81 \times 3 \times 4 \times 10 = 9,720$ different TTP instances in total.[2]

4. HEURISTIC ALGORITHMS

Algorithm 1 Simple Heuristic (SH)

Fill the array D with values d_{x_i}, $x_i \in \{x_2, \dots, x_n\}$
Calculate the total traveling time t'.
for all items $I_{x_i k}$, $x_i \in \Pi$, $k \in M_{x_i}$ **do**
  Calculate $t_{x_i k}$ by using Equation 1
  Set $t'_{x_i k} := t' - d_{x_i} + t_{x_i k}$
  Set $score_{x_i k} := p_{x_i k} - R \times t_{x_i k}$
  Set $u_{x_i k} := R \times t' + (p_{x_i k} - R \times t'_{x_i k})$
Create the joint set of items I and sort them in descending order score values
Set the current used capacity variable $Wc := 0$
for all items $I_{x_i k} \in I$ **do**
  if $(Wc + w_{x_i k} < W)$ and $(u_{x_i k} > 0)$ **then**
    Add the item $I_{x_i k}$ to the packing plan P
    Increase the used capacity variable $Wc := Wc + w_{x_i k}$
  if $(Wc = W)$ **then**
    Exit the loop.
Set the resulting objective value $Z^* := max\,(Z(\Pi, P), -R \times t')$

We create solutions for TTP instances in two stages. First, we use the Chained Lin-Kernighan heuristic [3] to quickly construct a good TSP tour. We do this without considering the knapsack part of the TTP problem. Once we have this tour, it remains fixed for the duration of the subsequent optimization. Second, a heuristic creates a packing plan in order to achieve a good TTP objective value. The rest of the section presents our constructive and iterative heuristics.

4.1 Constructive Heuristic

This section describes a Simple Heuristic (SH) which constructs a solution by processing and picking the items that maximize the objective value according to a given tour. In SH, after generating a tour $\Pi = (x_1, \dots, x_n)$ for the TSP problem, a *score* value is calculated for each item to estimate how good it is according to Π. Let item $I_{x_i k}$ be positioned in city $x_i \in \Pi$. Subsequently, let d_{x_i} and $t_{x_i k}$ denote the total traveling distance and the total traveling time with $I_{x_i k}$ being collected from the city x_i to x_n and from x_n to the first city x_1, respectively. Then the function to calculate $score_{x_i k}$ is as follows:

$$score_{x_i k} = p_{x_i k} - R \times t_{x_i k}$$

where

$$t_{x_i k} = \frac{d_{x_i}}{v_{max} - \nu w_{x_i k}} \tag{1}$$

Specifically, $score_{x_i k}$ is the total profit that the thief gets if and only if item $I_{x_i k}$ is picked during the whole tour Π.

In SH we also use a strategy to eliminate so-called *disadvantageous* items which being taken cannot add any positive value to the resulting objective value. This strategy utilizes a fitness value $u_{x_i k}$ calculated for each item $I_{x_i k}$ as follows:

$$u_{x_i k} = R \times t' + (p_{x_i k} - R \times t'_{x_i k})$$

where $t'_{x_i k}$ and $t' = \sum_{i=1}^{n-1} d_{x_i x_{i+1}} + d_{x_n x_1}$ are the total traveling times over the tour Π when only item $I_{x_i k}$ is picked and when no items at all are picked (i.e. with maximal

[1]As available at http://www.tsp.gatech.edu/concorde/downloads/downloads.htm

[2]All instances and implementations of the objective function are available online: http://cs.adelaide.edu.au/~optlog/research/ttp.php

Algorithm 2 Random Local Search (RLS)

Initialize P^* such that no items are packed.
repeat until no improvement for X **iterations**
  Create P by inverting the packing status of a uniformly at random picked item of P^*.
  if $Z(\Pi, P) \geq Z(\Pi, P^*)$ and $w(P) \leq W$ **then**
    $P^* := P$

Algorithm 3 (1+1) Evolutionary Algorithm (EA)

Initialize P^* such that no items are packed.
repeat until no improvement for X **iterations**
  Create P by inverting the packing status of each item of P^* independently with probability $1/m$.
  if $Z(\Pi, P) \geq Z(\Pi, P^*)$ and $w(P) \leq W$ **then**
    $P^* := P$

possible speed v_{max}). Therefore, a negative value of $u_{x_i k}$ means that $I_{x_i k}$ must not be picked up despite any obtained score value. For a more detailed explanation, let us assume in the following that $u_{x_i k} \leq 0$ is the case. Let $\Delta\left(t'_{x_i k}, t'\right) = t'_{x_i k} - t'$ show the difference between the traveling times when $I_{x_i k}$ and no other item is selected. Then the inequality $p_{x_i k} \leq R \times \Delta\left(t'_{x_i k}, t'\right)$ holds. Subsequently, let I^* denote an arbitrary non-empty set of items that fit into the knapsack, while t'_{I^*} and $t'_{I^* \cup I_{x_i k}}$ be the total traveling times over the tour Π when only items of I^* are picked and when items of I^* along with item $I_{x_i k}$ are chosen, respectively. As the velocity depends linearly on the weight of the knapsack, the inequality $\Delta\left(t'_{x_i k}, t'\right) < \Delta\left(t'_{I^* \cup I_{x_i k}}, t'_{I^*}\right)$ is satisfied. Therefore, $p_{x_i k} < R \times \Delta\left(t'_{I^* \cup I_{x_i k}}, t'_{I^*}\right)$ proves that the preposition holds for any non-empty set I^* picked along with the disadvantageous item.

Once the computations of the $u_{x_i k}$ and $score_{x_i k}$ values for every item are finished, the joint set of all items I is sorted in descending order of the items' scores. Subsequently, each item of the joint set is considered one after another starting from the first element of I. If item $I_{x_i k}$ fits into the free capacity of the knapsack while its fitness value $u_{x_i k} > 0$ then it is taken to the packing plan P. Finally, SH obtains the resulting objective value as $Z^* = max\left(Z(\Pi, P), -R \times t'\right)$ that corresponds to the best choice between constructed solution and solution with no selected items (see Algorithm 1).

Let $m = |I|$ denote the total number of items of a TTP instance. Then the computational complexity of SH for constructing a packing plan P for a pre-set tour Π is in $O(n + m \log m)$. Specifically, it takes $O(n)$ to compute elements of array $D = \{d_{x_2}, \ldots, d_{x_n}\}$. Calculation of score and fitness values is in $O(m)$, while sorting of items and selecting items are in $O(m \log m)$ and $O(m)$, respectively.

4.2 Iterative Heuristics

Our iterative heuristics are a random local search (RLS) and a simple (1+1) evolutionary algorithm (EA). In stark contrast to the previously proposed constructive SH, the iterative heuristics do not use any domain knowledge whatsoever.

The heuristics work as follows. They record the best solution found so far, known as best-so-far. They then repeatedly create a single new solution. This solution is then compared against the current best-so-far and it replaces the previous best-so-far if the TTP objective value is not worse and if the knapsack capacity is not violated.

Formal descriptions are given in Algorithm 2 and 3, where P is a packing plan, m is the total number of items, $Z(\Pi, P)$ is the TTP objective value (assuming the given and fixed tour Π), and $w(P)$ is the total weight of all packed items.

5. EXPERIMENTS

The experimental setup is the follows. We run our heuristic algorithms from Section 4 on all 9,720 instances. The iterative heuristics are stopped when no improvement has been made for 10,000 iterations, or when a total runtime of 10 minutes for a run is reached. Due to their randomized nature, we perform 30 independent repetitions of the iterative heuristics on each instance.

First, to begin with our analyses, we show in Figure 2 a decision tree that is based on all gathered experimental data. It is generated with Matlab's Statistics Toolbox and we pruned the tree in order to get a compact tree that still contains valuable information to a practitioner. We observe the following:

- At first sight, it appears that the number of cities plays no role in this particular decision tree. However, this information is implicitly used via the number of items and the knapsack capacity category.
- In general, the evolutionary algorithm EA dominates small TTP instances with few cities and few items, as many of the leftmost leaves in the decision tree are labelled EA. It performs better than RLS since it can escape local optima.
- The random local search RLS performs well across mid-sized and several larger TTP instances. This is due to the fact that EA effectively wastes evaluations, as the packing status change of an item is not enforced. Consequently, RLS is more effective in reaching a local optima, as a change in the newly generated packing plan is enforced.
- The deterministic constructive heuristic SH can be found at the right-most leaf nodes of the decision tree. It is well suited for very large instances with many items. The reason is that SH quickly constructs a decent packing plan, whereas RLS and EA start from the empty packing plan and then cannot reach SH's performance within 10 minutes.

We show a representative excerpt of the results in Figure 3.[3] Note that we rescale the achieved objective values into the range $[0, 1]$: the objective value of packing no items at all is equivalent to 0, and the best to 1. We do this as the objective values are typically (but not always) negative. In addition, in some cases the worst value is negative and the best value positive, which makes the value ranges not suitable for a number of other visualisation techniques. The plots largely confirm our observations from the decision tree in Figure 2:

- RLS and EA perform best for a very wide range of TTP configurations.

[3] `http://cs.adelaide.edu.au/~optlog/research/ttp.php`

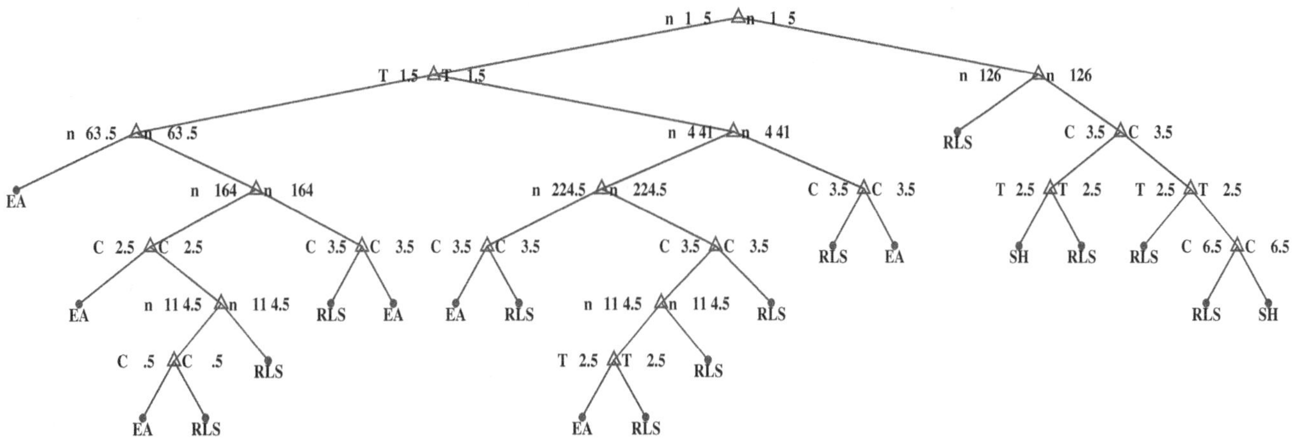

Figure 2: Decision tree based on all experimental results. n refers to the number of items, $C \in \{1, \ldots, 10\}$ to the capacity category, and T to the knapsack type. The values of $T \in \{1, 2, 3\}$ correspond to $\{bounded{-}strongly{-}corr, uncorr{-}similar{-}weights, uncorr\}$. Consequently, $T < 2.5$ is equivalent to $T \neq uncorr$.

- SH often is the best performing approach for very large TTP instances.

In addition, we notice the following interesting cases:

- For SH, the configuration of the TTP instance (what kind of items, how many, size of knapsack) seems to have a significant influence. In many cases, the achieved objective scores relative to RLS and EA are relatively stable. For example in the case of "uncorrelated item weight, $C = 10$, $F = 3$" (top right corner), all relative performances are at around 0.8. The reason for this behaviour that is relative to the starting point and relative to the performance of the iterative approaches is currently unclear.

- Compared to EA, RLS extends its good performance into larger TTP instances as it is more effective in reaching a local optimum. This can be seen in the plots as in most cases the EA marks decent before the RLS marks.

- The standard deviations for the iterative heuristics on instances with more than 5,000 cities are often quite significant. Consequently, we think that there is a lot of room left for smarter algorithms to explore the search space more efficiently.

As an example, let us have a closer look at the instances of the type "uncorrelated item weights, knapsack category 2, item factor 3" (top left plot in Figure 3). The underlying objective values are listed in Table 1 and the runtimes are shown in Figure 4. Note that we consider most of these to be "smaller" TTP instances.[4] PackNone refers to the solution where no item is packed along the tour from the Chained Lin-Kernighan algorithm; it serves as our first lower bound. SH is deterministic and we therefore do not report any standard deviations. Some observations are:

[4]Based on our observations and chosen ranges, we argue that for this F-value up to 3,000-5,000 cities result in small TTP instances.

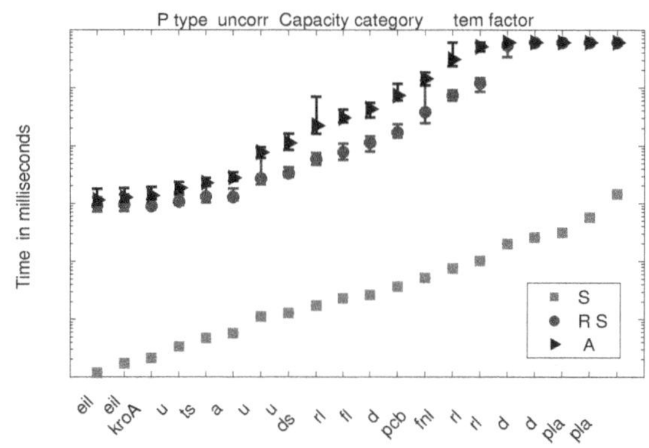

Figure 4: Subset of the results. Shown are the runtimes of the algorithms. The identifiers on the x-axis refer to the name of the underlying TSP instance.

- SH computes packing plans extremely quickly. It increases to just over 1s for the largest instance. On the other hand, the iterative RLS and EA hit the runtime limit of 10 minutes from about 6,000 cities onwards.

- It can be seen that EA's runtime is typically longer than that of RLS. The reasons are that, at times, either EA wastes time on re-evaluating solutions, or EA escapes local optima and subsequently climbs up to other optima again.

- On average, EA performs slightly better than RLS on small instances (up to 2,000-3,000 cities). RLS then clearly outperforms the other approaches on medium and larger instances. SH performs best in the case of the very largest city number.

- Iterative heuristics regularly pack items during an optimization run that are later unpacked again. The reason is that packing a heavy and invaluable item can increase the objective score temporarily during the optimization. However, as this slows down the thief, it can

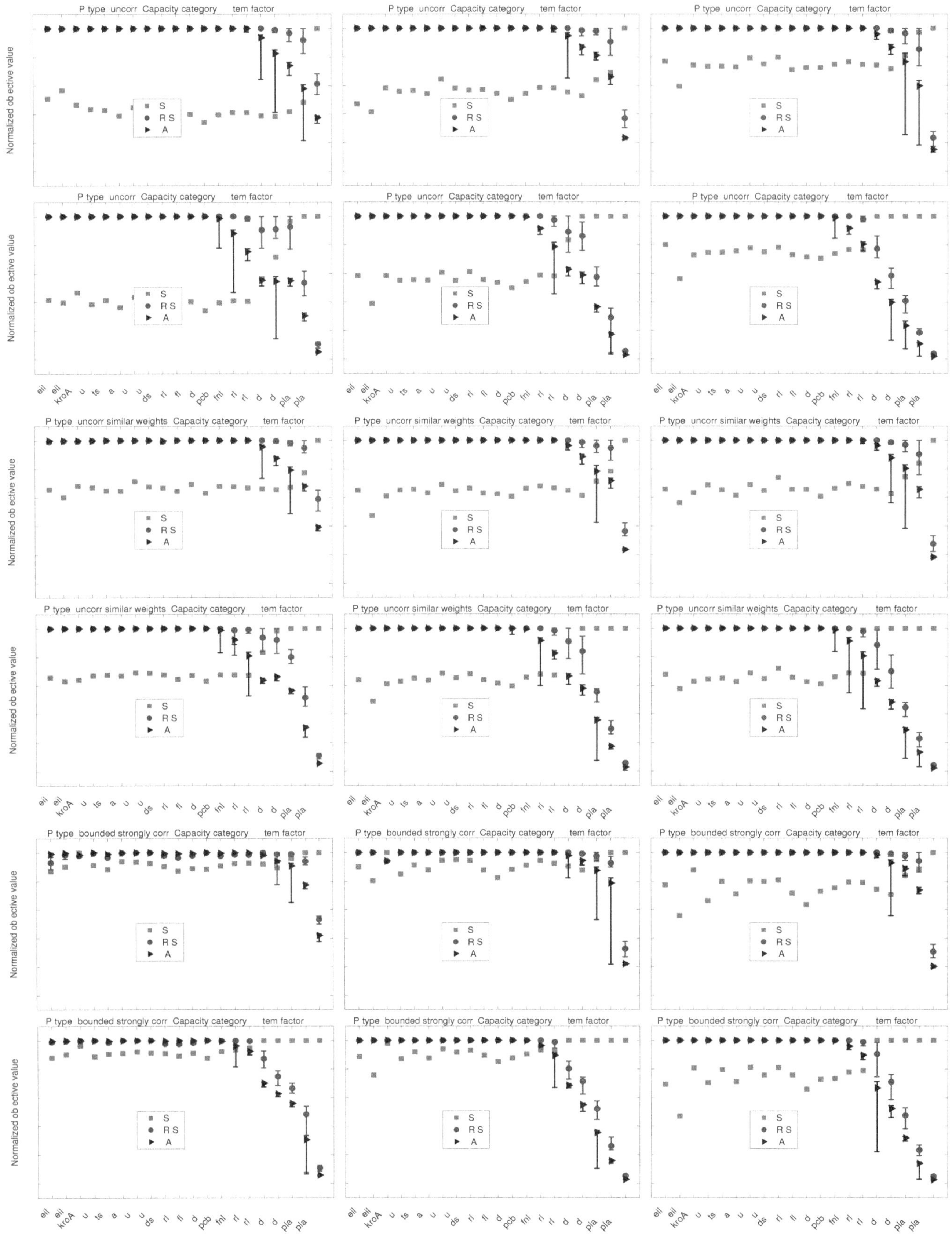

Figure 3: Subset of the results. Shown are the rescaled performances of our heuristics on a wide range of different instances. The identifiers on the x-axis refer to the name of the underlying TSP instance. Additional instance details are described in the plot titles. For example, the knapsack type is (f.t.t.b. in groups of six): uncorrelated, uncorrelated with similar weights, bounded strongly correlated.

Algorithm	eil51	eil76	kroA100	u159	ts225	a280	u574	u724	dsj1000	rl1304
RLS (mean)	8.21e3	1.16e4	1.93e4	4.03e4	5.70e4	6.32e4	1.36e5	1.67e5	1.11e5	3.12e5
RLS (std)	1.58e1	2.68e1	1.20e1	1.42e1	1.41e1	1.11e1	3.10	3.12	4.10e−1	6.23e1
EA (mean)	8.22e3	1.16e4	1.93e4	4.03e4	5.70e4	6.32e4	1.36e5	1.67e5	1.11e5	3.12e5
EA (std)	1.38e1	2.49e1	9.68	1.74e1	1.01e1	1.12e1	4.42	2.72	2.20e1	3.30e1
SH	−3.03e3	−3.65e3	−4.83e3	−5.37e3	−7.49e3	−2.05e4	−1.99e4	−5.16e4	−1.90e5	−9.69e4
PackNone	−1.46e4	−2.35e4	−2.58e4	−4.04e4	−5.57e4	−7.37e4	−1.46e5	−1.92e5	−3.75e5	−3.62e5

Algorithm	fl1577	d2103	pcb3038	fnl4461	rl5934	rl11849	d15112	d18512	pla33810	pla85900
RLS (mean)	3.57e5	4.80e5	6.50e5	9.08e5	1.44e6	2.69e6	3.44e6	3.53e6	2.02e6	−1.40e7
RLS (std)	1.66e2	1.55e2	2.21e2	1.99e2	5.11e2	1.51e3	4.96e4	1.82e5	4.61e5	6.18e5
EA (mean)	3.57e5	4.80e5	6.50e5	9.08e5	1.43e6	2.29e6	2.18e6	1.37e6	−2.16e6	−1.80e7
EA (std)	1.26e1	8.92e1	5.11e1	2.03e2	1.36e4	3.46e5	6.01e5	1.88e5	8.52e5	1.91e5
SH	−1.30e5	−2.17e5	−2.94e5	−4.23e5	−3.97e5	−1.07e6	−1.23e6	−1.74e6	−3.35e6	−7.49e6
PackNone	−4.53e5	−5.78e5	−9.09e5	−1.36e6	−1.67e6	−3.45e6	−4.17e6	−5.72e6	−9.28e6	−2.43e7

Table 1: Plot data for the instances "uncorrelated item weights, knapsack category 2, item factor 3" (see top left plot of Figure 3). Shown are the average objective values achieved and the corresponding standard deviations; the highest mean per instance is highlighted. The number of cities increases from left to right.

later become beneficial to deselect this item again due to the trade-off in knapsack renting cost vs. knapsack profit.

- The objective scores for the randomized algorithms vary hardly when the number of cities is less than 10,000. Even though different local optima are found, we conjecture that these local optima are all very close to the global optima for the chosen TSP tour.
- Interestingly, the objective values for one instance are (roughly) within one order of magnitude. This means that the packing plans have a significant influence on the TTP objective score, even though the TSP subproblem was solved almost to optimality by the used Chained Lin-Kernighan heuristic. It remains unknown by how much the achieved objective scores can be improved.

6. CONCLUSIONS

In this paper, we present a set of benchmarks for the travelling thief problem (TTP). The instances are systematically created to cover a wide range of features, and they are based on well-known instances for the travelling salesperson problem and for the knapsack problem. Our goal is to enable researches to investigate the hardness the two classical subproblems' combination. Even though we are confident that smaller instances can soon be optimally solved, we conjecture that the larger ones will remain unsolved for the years to come.

As a starting point, we provide a first set of structurally very different algorithms to effectively solve the problems. Our experiments show that a good and quick construction of a starting point is as important as an iterative search that can escape local optima.

In the future, we plan to intensively analyze the difficulty of the TTP through rigorous theoretical and experimental investigations. We plan to identify features that make instances easy or difficult to solve. The results can then be used to create problem-specific algorithms that are based on actual properties of the problem. Furthermore, we intend to discover inherent regularity in interaction between components and their mutual influence. The preliminary results have recently been obtained in [5], where the potential benefit of methods considering interdependency between components was studied.

Lastly, our instances can form the basis for many interpretations of the original TTP, such as, TTP with multiple thiefs, TTP without a restriction to visit every city, TTP with the option to sell items at specific locations, and so on.

Acknowledgements

This work was supported by ARC grants DP130104395 and DP140103400.

References

[1] Advanced generator for 0-1 Knapsack Problems. See `http://www.diku.dk/~pisinger/codes.html`.

[2] TSP Test Data. See `http://comopt.ifi.uni-heidelberg.de/software/TSPLIB95/index.html`.

[3] D. Applegate, W. J. Cook, and A. Rohe. Chained lin-kernighan for large traveling salesman problems. *INFORMS Journal on Computing*, 15:82–92, 2003.

[4] M. R. Bonyadi, Z. Michalewicz, and L. Barone. The travelling thief problem: The first step in the transition from theoretical problems to realistic problems. In *IEEE Congress on Evolutionary Computation*, pp. 1037–1044. IEEE, 2013.

[5] M. R. Bonyadi, Z. Michalewicz, M. R. Przybylek, and A. Wierzbicki. Socially inspired algorithms for the travelling thief problem. In *Genetic and Evolutionary Computation Conference, GECCO 2014*, 2014. to appear.

[6] I. Kara, B. Y. Kara, and M. K. Yetis. Energy minimizing vehicle routing problem. In A. Dress,

Y. Xu, and B. Zhu, editors, *Combinatorial Optimization and Applications*, Vol. 4616 of *Lecture Notes in Computer Science*, pp. 62–71. Springer Berlin Heidelberg, 2007.

[7] I. Kucukoglu, S. Ene, A. Aksoy, and N. Ozturk. Green capacitated vehicle routing problem fuel consumption optimization model. *Computational Engineering Research*, 3:16–23.

[8] C. Lin, K. Choy, G. Ho, S. Chung, and H. Lam. Survey of green vehicle routing problem: Past and future trends. *Expert Systems with Applications*, 41: 1118 – 1138, 2014.

[9] S. Martello, D. Pisinger, and P. Toth. Dynamic programming and strong bounds for the 0-1 knapsack problem. *Manage. Sci.*, 45:414–424, 1999.

[10] G. Reinelt. TSPLIB - A Traveling Salesman Problem Library. *ORSA Journal on Computing*, 3:376–384, 1991.

Performance of Metropolis Algorithm for the Minimum Weight Code Word Problem

Ajitha Shenoy K B
Department of Computer Science and Engineering
Indian Institute of Technology Kanpur, India.
ajith@cse.iitk.ac.in

Somenath Biswas
Department of Computer Science and Engineering
Indian Institute of Technology Kanpur, India.
sb@cse.iitk.ac.in

Piyush P Kurur
Department of Computer Science and Engineering
Indian Institute of Technology Kanpur, India.
ppk@cse.iitk.ac.in

ABSTRACT

We study the performance of the Metropolis algorithm for the problem of finding a code word of weight less than or equal to M, given a generator matrix of an $[n, k]$-binary linear code. The algorithm uses the set $\mathcal{S}_k$ of all $k \times k$ invertible matrices as its search space where two elements are considered adjacent if one can be obtained from the other via an elementary row operation (i.e by adding one row to another or by swapping two rows.) We prove that the Markov chains associated with the Metropolis algorithm mix rapidly for suitable choices of the temperature parameter T. We ran the Metropolis algorithm for a number of codes and found that the algorithm performed very well in comparison to previously known experimental results.

Categories and Subject Descriptors

G.1.6 [**Optimization**]: Simulated annealing; G.3 [**Probability and Statistics**]: Probabilistic algorithms (including Monte Carlo); H.1.1 [**Systems & Information Theory**]: Information Theory

General Terms

Theory, Algorithms

Keywords

Metropolis Algorithm; Minimum weight code word; search space; conductance; rapid mixing of Markov chain

1. INTRODUCTION

An $[n, k]$ binary linear code is a k-dimensional subspace of the vector space of n-dimensional binary vectors, its code words are the elements of the subspace, and a minimum weight code word of such a code is a non-zero code word with minimum number of 1's. (We provide the formal definitions in the next Section). Such a code can be succinctly presented by providing a basis of the k-dimensional subspace. The minimum weight code word problem requires one to find a minimum weight code word, given a basis of the code. This problem is important for several reasons: a minimum weight code word is a measure of the error correction capability of the code [9], also, codes with large minimum weight code words have applications in diverse areas such as cryptography [18, 17, 16], pseudorandom generators [1, 11].

The problem has been shown to be NP-hard [6], moreover, it remains hard even to obtain a constant factor approximation [10]. It is for this reason that researchers have proposed several probabilistic and heuristic algorithms to find low weight code words, given a basis of a binary linear code. Examples are: GA [4, 13, 5], hill climbing [4, 13, 5], tabu search [8], and ACO [7].

We study in this paper the efficacy of the Metropolis algorithm for solving the problem. Our Metropolis algorithm for an $[n, k]$ code uses the set of all $k \times k$ invertible binary matrices as its search space set. Two such elements are considered neighbours if one can be obtained from the other by an elementary row operation. We prove that the search space graph has large magnification and use this result to prove that the family of Markov chains, as defined by the Metropolis algorithm on an input instance, has a large conductance. It is known that [21] the Metropolis algorithm solves a combinatorial optimization problem like ours in polynomial time if and only if (1) the associated Markov chain family has high conductance (2) the probability of the favorable event in the stationary distribution is high. As our Metropolis algorithm tries to find a code word of weight less than or equal to M, where M is given as an input parameter, the algorithm will be efficient, in view of the conductance result, if the probability p_M of getting a code word of weight M is high in the stationary distribution. A good bound for p_M is difficult to estimate, this quantity closely related to the weight distribution of the binary linear codes. Therefore, to understand how well the Metropolis algorithm works for this problem, we experiment with a few codes. The codes that we use for our experiments are certain BCH codes and full dimensional codes of dimensions 50 and 100. We found that the Metropolis algorithm performed well for several BCH (Bose, Chaudhuri and Hocquenghem) codes [20], even obtaining the minimum in certain cases. For the full dimensional case, where the minimum weight is 1, the algorithm was able to converge quickly to a small weight code word. This compares favorably with previously known experimen-

GECCO'14, July 12–16, 2014, Vancouver, BC, Canada.
Copyright 2014 ACM 978-1-4503-2662-9/14/07 ...$15.00.
http://dx.doi.org/10.1145/2576768.2598274 .

tal results on BCH codes which used certain other search heuristics. Details are given in Section 5.

2. PRELIMINARIES

DEFINITION 2.1. ***(Binary Linear Codes)*** *An* $[n,k]$-binary linear code *is a* k*-dimensional vector subspace* C *of the* n*-dimensional vector space* $\mathbf{F}_2^n$ *over the finite field* $\mathbb{F}_2$*. The parameter* n *is called the* length *and* k *the* dimension *of the code* C*.*

A binary linear $[n,k]$-code C can be succinctly described by giving a basis for it. This is typically done by giving a *generator matrix* for the code C.

DEFINITION 2.2. ***(Generator Matrix)*** *A generator matrix for an* $[n,k]$ *linear code* C *is a* $k \times n$ *matrix* G *whose rows form a basis for* C*.*

This is called a generator matrix because a vector is a code word if and only if it is a linear combination of the rows of the generator matrix.

DEFINITION 2.3. ***(Elementary row operations)*** *For a* $k \times n$ *matrix* G *over the field* $\mathbb{F}_2$ *with rows* $\mathbf{g}_r$*,* $1 \leq r \leq k$*, the following are the elementary row operations for distinct* i *and* j*.*

1. $\mathbf{g}_i \leftarrow \mathbf{g}_i + \mathbf{g}_j$ *(the* j*-th row is added to the* i*-th row),*
2. $\mathbf{g}_i \leftrightarrow \mathbf{g}_j$ *(rows* i *and* j *are interchanged).*

DEFINITION 2.4. **(Minimum weight code word)** *For a code* C*, a non-zero vector* $\mathbf{v} \in C$ *of minimum Hamming weight is called a minimum weight code word. The* minimum weight code word *problem is to compute, given a generator matrix* G *of an* $[n,k]$*-code* C*, a minimum weight code word of* C*.*

The decision version of the minimum weight code word problem can be stated as follows.

DEFINITION 2.5. ***(Decision version)*** *Given* G*, a generator matrix for* C *and an integer* M*,* decide *whether there exists a non-zero vector in* C *of weight* M *or less.*

3. SEARCH SPACE

In this section, we define the search space which we use in our Metropolis algorithm. Our search space is similar to the search space defined for shortest lattice vector problem [2, 3]. The algorithm attempts to construct a generator matrix which has a minimum weight code word as one of its rows. It is easy to see that such a generator matrix always exists.

FACT 3.1. *[12] Let* G *be a generator matrix of the* $[n,k]$ *binary linear code* C*, then* G' *is a generator matrix for* C *if and only if there is a* $k \times k$ *invertible matrix* U *such that* $G' = UG$*.*

Consequently, for any input generator matrix G, the set of all matrices UG as U varies over $k \times k$ invertible matrices is precisely the set of all generator matrices of C. Therefore, the search space of our Metropolis algorithm will be the set $\mathcal{S}_k$ of all $k \times k$ invertible matrices and given a generator matrix G of C as input, our goal is to find a matrix U in $\mathcal{S}_k$ such that UG contains a minimum weight code word as one of its rows. A natural neighbourhood structure on the search spaces $\mathcal{S}_k$ can be defined in terms of elementary row operations on matrices in $\mathcal{S}_k$. We now formally define our search space.

DEFINITION 3.2. **(Search Space)** *Given an* $[n,k]$*-code* C *via a generator matrix* G *we define the search space as follows.*

Elements: *The elements of the search space* $\mathcal{S}_k$ *are the* $k \times k$ *invertible matrices* U *over* $GF(2)$*.*

Neighbourhood: *For a matrix* U *in* $\mathcal{S}_k$*, the set* $N(U)$ *of neighbours consists of matrices* V *that can be obtained from* U *by any of the following elementary operations:*

1. *add the* j*-th row to the* i*-th row,*
2. *swap the* i*-th and* j*-th rows,*

where i *and* j *are two distinct rows of* U*. This makes the underlying graph a* D*-regular graph where* D *is* $k(k-1)$*.*

Cost: *For an element* U *of the search space, the cost* $c(U)$ *is defined to be* w^α *where* w *is the minimum of the Hamming weights of rows of* UG *and* α *is a parameter which takes positive values.*

Convention: The elementary row operations that we defined above can be carried out on a matrix A by post multiplying by a suitable elementary matrix say E. We often identify a row operation with the corresponding elementary matrix. Note that $|\mathcal{S}_k|$ equal to number of binary $k \times k$ invertible matrices which is less than 2^{k^2}, the total number of $k \times k$ binary matrices.

We now show that the diameter of the search space graph is bounded by a polynomial in k.

PROPOSITION 3.3. *For any two matrices* U *and* V *in the search space* $\mathcal{S}_k$ *there is a path between them in the search space graph of length at most* k^2*.*

PROOF. The matrix $V^{-1}U$ is invertible as both U and V are. Therefore, $V^{-1}U$ can be transformed to the $k \times k$ identity matrix I_k by Gauss-Jordan elimination which uses a sequence of elementary row operations. This is done in k-stages one for each column. In the i-th stage, we transform the i-th column to the vector $\mathbf{e}_i$ which has a 1 at the i-th position and 0's elsewhere. Each of these stages can be carried out using at most k elementary row operations (more details in the proof of Lemma 3.4) and thus using $\ell \leq k^2$ elementary operations, $V^{-1}U$ gets transformed into I_k. Let $E_1, \ldots, E_\ell$ be the elementary matrices associated with the elementary row operations described above. Consequently, the product $V^{-1}UE_1 \cdots E_\ell$ is the identity matrix I_k. Therefore, V is the product $UE_1 \cdots E_\ell$. The sequence of matrices $U_i = U \cdot \prod_{j=1}^{i} E_i$ for $0 \leq i \leq \ell$ gives the path from matrix $U = U_0$ to $V = U_\ell$. $\square$

We prove next that our search space graph has large magnification. This will be used later to show that the family of Markov chains as defined by our Metropolis algorithm mixes rapidly. We now recall the definition of magnification [23]. Let $G = (V,E)$ be an undirected graph. Let S be a non-empty subset of V and let $\overline{S}$ denote its complement, i.e. $V \setminus S$. Let $E(S, \overline{S})$ denote the set of edges that go out of S. The magnification $\mu(S)$ is defined as

$$\mu(S) = \frac{|E(S, \overline{S})|}{|S|}.$$

The magnification for the graph G (also called as *edge expansion*), denoted by $\mu(G)$, is the minimum $\mu(S)$ where the minimization is done over all non-empty subsets S of V of cardinality at most $\frac{|V|}{2}$.

LEMMA 3.4. *A search space graph for minimum weight code word problem has magnification at least* $\frac{1}{2}$.

PROOF. We use the *canonical path method* [22] to lower-bound the magnification of the search graph. For this, we first canonize the Gauss-Jordan elimination procedure described in the proof of Proposition 3.3 that transforms an arbitrary $k \times k$ invertible matrix A to identity matrix. The procedure works in k-stages. The i-th stage starts with a matrix A_{i-1} whose r-th column, for any $r < i$ is the vector $\mathbf{e}_r$, the vector which has a 1 at r-th entry and 0 every where else. In the i-th stage, we convert the i-th column into $\mathbf{e}_i$ using elementary row operations. The stage begins with a swap of i-th row if and only if the (i, i)-th entry of A_{i-1} is a 0. In such a case, we choose to swap the i-th row and the j-th row, where j is the smallest integer greater than i such that the (j, i)-th entry is 1. There is always one such j because the matrix A_{i-1} is invertible. Having ensured that the (i, i)-th entry is 1, we convert each 1 in the i-th column, except the (i, i)-th entry to 0 by adding the i-th row. This gives us the matrix A_i. The elimination process ends when i is k and the resulting matrix A_k becomes identity. Let us call the sequence $E_1, \ldots, E_\ell$ of elementary operations used to reach the identity matrix from A in the above process as the *canonical Gauss-Jordan sequence* associated with the matrix A.

We show that canonical Gauss-Jordan sequences satisfy the following properties.

CLAIM 3.4.1. *1. There is a unique canonical Gauss-Jordan sequence associated with a given $k \times k$ invertible matrix-A. Moreover, two distinct matrices A and A' in $\mathcal{S}_k$ will have distinct canonical Gauss-Jordan sequences.*

2. The number of distinct canonical Gauss-Jordan sequences is equal to the cardinality of the search spaces $\mathcal{S}_k$.

3. If $E_1, \ldots, E_\ell$ is the canonical Gauss-Jordan sequence of some $k \times k$ matrix-A, then no two operators E_r and E_s in the sequence are the same.

PROOF. The way in which we have canonize the Gauss-Jordan elimination procedure above, it is clear that there is a unique canonical Gauss-Jordan sequence associated with a given $k \times k$ invertible matrix A. Now suppose that two distinct matrices A and A' in $\mathcal{S}_k$ have the same canonical Gauss-Jordan sequence, i.e $AE_1 \ldots E_\ell = I$ and $A'E_1 \ldots E_\ell = I$ which implies $A = A' = IE_\ell^{-1} \ldots E_1^{-1}$ which is a contradiction. Hence two distinct invertible matrices A and A' will have distinct canonical Gauss-Jordan sequences. This completes the proof of part 1 of our claim. To prove part 2 notice that the number of distinct canonical Gauss-Jordan sequences is equal to the number of invertible matrices in $\mathcal{S}_k$ which is equal to $|\mathcal{S}_k|$. Finally to prove part 3, consider any elementary row operation that occurs in the canonical Gauss-Jordan sequence. Either it is a row addition or a swap of two rows. It is clear that all the row additions are distinct as we add the row i only in the i-th stage of the procedure and that too to distinct rows in the i-th stage. A swap is used only to convert a 0-diagonal entry to 1. Consider such swap between rows i and j where $j > i$. This swap can happen only at the i-th stage and not at the j-th stage because to convert a 0 in the diagonal we use a row that is lower down in the matrix. This completes the proof of part 3. ☐

We now define the canonical path between two search graph elements U and V as follows: Let $E_1, \ldots, E_\ell$ be the canonical Gauss-Jordan sequence associated with the matrix $V^{-1}U$. Then the canonical path from U to V is the sequence $U = U_0, \ldots, U_\ell = V$ where $U_i = U \cdot \prod_{j=1}^{i} E_i$. Given U and V, by a slight abuse of notation, the canonical Gauss-Jordan sequence associated with $V^{-1}U$ is also called the *canonical Gauss-Jordan sequence associated with the canonical path*[1] from U to V.

Fix two neighbours C and D in the search space $\mathcal{S}_k$. We now estimate the number of canonical paths that go through the edge (C, D).

CLAIM 3.4.2. *For two neighbours C and D in $\mathcal{S}_k$ consider any canonical Gauss-Jordan sequence $E_1, \ldots, E_\ell$ containing the matrix $C^{-1}D$. There is a unique canonical path through the edge (C, D) that has $E_1, \ldots, E_\ell$ as its associated canonical Gauss-Jordan sequence.*

PROOF. Consider any canonical Gauss-Jordan sequence $E_1, \ldots, E_\ell$ such that $E_r = C^{-1}D$ for some $1 \le r \le \ell$. By Claim 3.4.1 all operators E_s, $s \ne r$, are different from $C^{-1}D$. Therefore, the only canonical path that passes through the edge (C, D) and has $E_1, \ldots, E_\ell$ as its associated canonical Gauss-Jordan sequence starts at $U = CE_{r-1}^{-1} \ldots E_1^{-1}$ and ends at $V = DE_{r+1} \ldots E_\ell$. ☐

We have the following consequence of the above claim.

CLAIM 3.4.3. *Let C and D be neighbours in the search space $\mathcal{S}_k$. Then the number of canonical paths passing through the edge (C, D) is bounded by the total number of points in the search space $\mathcal{S}_k$.*

This is because such a canonical path is uniquely determined by its canonical Gauss-Jordan sequence. The number of distinct Gauss-Jordan sequences is equal to the number of $k \times k$ invertible matrices which is the number of elements of the search space.

We now prove the bound on the magnification as given in the statement of the Lemma 3.4. Consider any non-empty subset S such that $|S| \le \frac{|\mathcal{S}_k|}{2}$. There are $|S| \times |\overline{S}|$ canonical paths that go from S to $\overline{S}$. Each of these paths passes through one of the edges in $E(S, \overline{S})$. As no edge can have more than $|\mathcal{S}_k|$ canonical paths passing through it by Claim 3.4.3, we have $|\mathcal{S}_k| \times |E(S, \overline{S})| \ge |S| \times |\overline{S}|$. As $|\overline{S}| \ge \frac{|\mathcal{S}_k|}{2}$ we have $|\mathcal{S}_k| \times |E(S, \overline{S})| \ge |S| \times \frac{|\mathcal{S}_k|}{2}$. Therefore, the magnification $\mu(S) = \frac{|E(S, \overline{S})|}{|S|}$ is greater than 1/2 for all

[1]We note that two different canonical paths may have the same associated Gauss-Jordan sequences: The canonical paths from U to V and from U' to V' will have the same associated canonical Gauss-Jordan sequence if and only if $U' = AU$ and $V' = AV$ for some invertible $k \times k$ matrix A

S of cardinality at most $|\mathcal{S}_k|/2$. Since magnification μ_k of the search space $\mathcal{S}_k$ is the minimum over all such $\mu(S)$'s, we have $\mu_k \geq \frac{1}{2}$. This completes the proof of Lemma 3.4.

4. MIXING TIME ANALYSIS

We use the Metropolis algorithm for the minimum weight code word problem. On a given input instance G, the Metropolis algorithm runs a Markov chain: the state space of the chain is the set $\mathcal{S}_k$ of $k \times k$ invertible matrices, which is the search space of our problem. Recall that the cost $c(U)$ associated with a search space element U, a matrix, is w^α where w is the minimum Hamming weight of the rows of UG. The Markov chain makes use of this cost function to define a random walk biased towards code words of lower weights. We now define the transition probabilities p_{UV}, the probability of making a transition to V given that the chain is at U.

$$p_{UV} = \begin{cases} 0 & \text{if } U \neq V, V \notin N(U) \\ \frac{1}{2D} \cdot \min\left(1, \exp\left(\frac{c(U)-c(V)}{T}\right)\right) & \text{if } V \in N(U) \\ 1 - \sum_{W \neq U} p_{UW} & \text{if } U = V. \end{cases}$$

In the above definition T stands for the temperature parameter, which remains fixed for the algorithm, and D is the degree of the underlying regular graph $\mathcal{S}_k$. Recall that D is $k(k-1)$. It is well known [19, Chapter: 10.4.1] that the above Markov chain has the stationary distribution given by

$$\pi_U = \frac{\exp\left(\frac{-c(U)}{T}\right)}{\sum_{V \in \mathcal{S}_k} \exp\left(\frac{-c(V)}{T}\right)}.$$

The complete algorithm (Algorithm 1) is given below:

Algorithm 1 Metropolis Algorithm

Input : The generator matrix G of linear code C and an integer M
Output : Matrix U such that UG contains a vector $\mathbf{v}$ with $w_H(\mathbf{v}) \leq M$.
Let U be the starting state in the search space as in Definition 3.2 and $c(U)$ denote its cost.
Set $BestWeight = c(U)$, steps=0
while $BestWeight > M$ and $steps < TSteps$ [$TSteps$ denotes Max. No. of steps specified by user] **do**
  Select any one of the neighbour U of V uniformly at random by performing one of the elementary operations as defined in Definition 3.2
  Set $U = V$ with probability

$$\alpha = \frac{1}{2}.\min\left(\frac{\exp\left(\frac{-c(V)}{T}\right)}{\exp\left(\frac{-c(U)}{T}\right)}, 1\right)$$

  if $BestWeight > c(U)$ **then**
    $BestWeight = c(U)$
  end if
  $steps = steps + 1$;
end while

We now show that the above Markov chain has large conductance for an appropriate choice of the temperature parameter T.

DEFINITION 4.1. **(Conductance)[23]** *For any non empty subset S of states in $\mathcal{S}_k$ with non empty complement $\overline{S}$, the* conductance *$\phi(S)$ of S is defined as*

$$\phi(S) = \frac{F_S}{C_S}$$

where

$$C_S = \sum_{U \in S} \pi_U$$

$$F_S = \sum_{U \in S, V \in \overline{S}} p_{UV}\pi_U$$

The conductance *ϕ_k of the Markov chain is defined to be*

$$\phi_k = \min_{S: C_S \leq \frac{1}{2}} \phi(S)$$

It is easy to see that $F_S = F_{\overline{S}}$ for all such sets S. This implies that $\phi(\overline{S}) = \phi(S)\frac{C_S}{1-C_S}$ (since $C_S + C_{\overline{S}} = \sum_{U \in \mathcal{S}_k} \pi_U = 1$ which implies $C_{\overline{S}} = 1 - C_S$), so we may equivalently write

$$\phi_k = \min_S\{\max(\phi(S), \phi(\overline{S}))\}$$

THEOREM 4.2. *The conductance ϕ_k of the Markov chain associated with our Metropolis algorithm for solving the minimum code word problem for an $[n,k]$-code satisfies*

$$\phi_k \geq \frac{1}{4D\exp\left(\frac{2(n^\alpha - 1)}{T}\right)},$$

where T is the temperature parameter and α is the exponent used in the cost function. In particular, when $T = \Omega(n^\alpha)$ the conductance is $\Omega\left(\frac{1}{D}\right)$, where D-denotes the number of neighbours for a node in the search graph.

PROOF. Consider any non-empty subset S of $\mathcal{S}_k$ such that $C_S \leq \frac{1}{2}$. There are two possibilities: either $|S| \leq \frac{|\mathcal{S}_k|}{2}$ or $|S| > \frac{|\mathcal{S}_k|}{2}$. We handle these cases separately.

First assume that $|S| \leq \frac{|\mathcal{S}_k|}{2}$. The flow out of S is bounded as follows.

$$F_S = \sum_{U \in S, V \in \overline{S}} p_{UV}\pi_U \geq \min(p_{UV})\min(\pi_U)|E(S, \overline{S})|$$

By Lemma 3.4, our search graph has magnification at least $1/2$ and hence $|E(S, \overline{S})| \geq \frac{1}{2}|S|$. As a result we have:

$$F_S \geq \min(p_{UV})\min(\pi_U)\frac{|S|}{2}. \quad (1)$$

We know that:

$$\pi_U = \frac{\exp\left(\frac{-c(U)}{T}\right)}{\sum_{V \in \mathcal{S}_k} \exp\left(\frac{-c(V)}{T}\right)} = \frac{\exp\left(\frac{-c(U)}{T}\right)}{Z}.$$

where Z is the partition function $\sum_{V \in \mathcal{S}_k} \exp\left(\frac{-c(V)}{T}\right)$. Let $c_{\max}$ and $c_{\min}$ denote the maxima and minima of the cost function $c(.)$ respectively. Notice that $c_{\max} \leq n^\alpha$ and $c_{\min} \geq 1$. Therefore, for any element U of the search space, its stationary probability π_U is bounded above and below as follows.

$$\frac{\exp\left(\frac{-n^\alpha}{T}\right)}{Z} \leq \pi_U \leq \frac{\exp\left(\frac{-1}{T}\right)}{Z} \quad (2)$$

Also, the transition probabilities p_{UV} satisfies

$$p_{UV} \geq \frac{1}{2D\exp\left(\frac{c_{\max}-c_{\min}}{T}\right)} \geq \frac{1}{2D\exp\left(\frac{n^\alpha-1}{T}\right)}. \quad (3)$$

From Equations (1),(2) and (3) we obtain

$$F_S \geq \frac{\exp\left(\frac{-n^\alpha}{T}\right)}{Z} \cdot \frac{1}{2D\exp\left(\frac{n^\alpha-1}{T}\right)} \cdot \frac{|S|}{2} \quad (4)$$

The capacity C_S is bounded as follows:

$$C_S = \sum_{U\in S} \pi_U \leq \max(\pi_U)\cdot|S| = \frac{\exp\left(\frac{-1}{T}\right)}{Z}\cdot|S| \quad (5)$$

Therefore from Equations (4) and (5), the conductance $\phi(S)$ of the subset S is lower bounded as:

$$\phi(S) = \frac{F_S}{C_S} \geq \frac{1}{4D\exp\left(\frac{2(n^\alpha-1)}{T}\right)} \quad (6)$$

Now consider the case when $|S| > \frac{|\mathcal{S}_k|}{2}$. Using Equation (6) for $\overline{S}$, we obtain:

$$\phi(\overline{S}) \geq \frac{1}{4D\exp\left(\frac{2(n^\alpha-1)}{T}\right)}.$$

Since $C_{\overline{S}} \geq \frac{1}{2}$ and $\frac{C_{\overline{S}}}{1-C_{\overline{S}}} \geq 1$, we have:

$$\phi(S) = \frac{C_{\overline{S}}}{1-C_{\overline{S}}}\phi(\overline{S}) \geq \frac{1}{4D\exp\left(\frac{2(n^\alpha-1)}{T}\right)}$$

Thus, we find that for both the cases, *viz.*, $|S| \leq \frac{|\mathcal{S}_k|}{2}$ and $|S| > \frac{|\mathcal{S}_k|}{2}$,

$$\phi(S) \geq \frac{1}{4D\exp\left(\frac{2(n^\alpha-1)}{T}\right)}.$$

As a result, the conductance ϕ_k of the Markov chain is bounded by

$$\phi_k \geq \frac{1}{4D\exp\left(\frac{2(n^\alpha-1)}{T}\right)}.$$

□

We use the above conductance result to show that the Markov chain for the Metropolis algorithm mixes rapidly, i.e., in time polynomial in n for an input $[n,k]$-code. Let $P^t(U_0,.)$ denote the probability distribution obtained by running the Markov chain for t steps starting the chain at U_0. As before π denotes the stationary probability distribution. To define mixing time we need the concept of total variation distance.

DEFINITION 4.3. **Total Variation Distance[15]** *Total variation distance between two probability distributions $P^t(U_0,.)$ and π is defined as:*

$$||P^t(U_0,.)-\pi||_{TV} = \frac{1}{2}\cdot\sum_{V\in\mathcal{S}_k}|P^t(U_0,V)-\pi(V)|$$

The mixing time $t_{\text{mix}}(\varepsilon)$ of the Markov chain is defined as

$$t_{\text{mix}}(\varepsilon) = \min\{t : \Delta(t) \leq \varepsilon\},$$

where $\Delta(t) = \max_{U_0\in\mathcal{S}_k}||P^t(U_0,.)-\pi||_{TV}$ denotes maximal variation distance between $P^t(U_0,.)$ and π as U_0 varies over the elements of the search space $\mathcal{S}_k$[15]. In other words, independent of the choice of the initial state U_0 to start the chain, if we run the Markov chain for $t \geq t_{\text{mix}}(\varepsilon)$ steps, we have the guarantee that in the resulting distribution, the probability $P^t(U_0,U)$ of obtaining the any state U is bounded above and below as follows.

$$\pi_U - \varepsilon \leq P^t(U_0,U) \leq \pi_U + \varepsilon.$$

A lower bound on the conductance ϕ_M of a Markov chain M translates to an upper bound on the mixing time as follows [23, Equation (2.13), page 58].

$$t^M_{\text{mix}}(\varepsilon) \leq \frac{2}{\phi_M^2}\left(\ln\varepsilon^{-1} + \ln\pi_{\min}^{-1}\right). \quad (7)$$

where $\pi_{\min}$ denotes the smallest of the stationary probabilities for the chain M and $t^M_{\text{mix}}(\varepsilon)$ denotes its mixing time. Using Theorem 4.2 we obtain the following bound on mixing time.

COROLLARY 4.4. *The mixing time $t_{\text{mix}}(\varepsilon)$, of the Markov chain associated with our Metropolis algorithm on an input $[n,k]$-code satisfies:*

$$t_{\text{mix}}(\varepsilon) \leq 32D^2\exp\left(\frac{4(n^\alpha-1)}{T}\right)\cdot(k^2\ln 2+\frac{n^\alpha-1}{T}+\ln\varepsilon^{-1}),$$

where D is the number of neighbours of any search point which we know to be $k(k-1)$.

In particular, when the temperature parameter T is $\Omega(n^\alpha)$, the mixing time $t_{\text{mix}}(\varepsilon)$ is $O(k^6 + k^4\ln\varepsilon^{-1})$.

PROOF. We first derive a bound on the probability $\pi_{\min}$ as follows. For any element U, we have

$$\pi_U = \frac{\exp\left(\frac{-c(U)}{T}\right)}{\sum_{V\in\mathcal{S}_k}\exp\left(\frac{-c(V)}{T}\right)}.$$

Using the bound $1 \leq c(U) \leq n^\alpha$ for the cost function $c(.)$, we obtain the following.

$$\pi_U \geq \frac{\exp\left(\frac{-n^\alpha}{T}\right)}{\sum_{V\in\mathcal{S}_k}\exp\left(\frac{-1}{T}\right)} = \frac{1}{\exp\left(\frac{n^\alpha-1}{T}\right)|\mathcal{S}_k|}.$$

The set $\mathcal{S}_k$ is the set of all $k\times k$ invertible matrices and hence $|\mathcal{S}_k| \leq 2^{k^2}$. Thus:

$$\pi_{\min} \geq \frac{1}{2^{k^2}\exp\left(\frac{n^\alpha-1}{T}\right)}. \quad (8)$$

Therefore, $\ln\pi_{\min}^{-1} \leq k^2\ln 2 + \frac{n^\alpha-1}{T}$.

The result follows from the above, Equation (7), and the bound on conductance given in Theorem 4.2. □

Given the generator matrix G of an $[n,k]$-code C and a bound M, our task is to find a code word of Hamming weight M or less if it exists. Every run of the Metropolis algorithm for $t_{\text{mix}}(\varepsilon)$ steps provides us with a sample U with probability at least $\pi_U - \varepsilon$. By taking the row of minimum weight in UG, we get a sample code word $\mathbf{x}$ of C. Let p_M be the probability that the sample code word $\mathbf{x}$ is of weight less than or equal to M. Then we have:

$$p_M \geq \sum_{U:\text{wt}(UG)\leq M}(\pi_U - \varepsilon),$$

where $\mathrm{wt}(UG)$ denotes the minimum of the Hamming weights of the rows of the matrix UG.

We take S samples $\mathbf{x}_1, \ldots, \mathbf{x}_S$ obtained through S runs of the Metropolis algorithm each for $t_{\mathrm{mix}}(\varepsilon)$ time and choose the one with the least Hamming weight. The probability that we fail to find a code word of weight M or less is upper bounded by $(1-p_M)^S$. Therefore, to obtain the such a code word with probability at least δ, we need $S \geq \frac{\log(1-\delta)}{\log(1-p_M)}$.

Let $N_M(G)$ denote the number of $k\times k$ invertible matrices U such that UG has a row of Hamming weight less than or equal to M. Choosing $\varepsilon = \frac{1}{2}\cdot\pi_{\min}$, we get p_M to be greater than $\frac{1}{2}\cdot N_M(G)\cdot\pi_{\min}$. Further, setting the temperature T to n^α we obtain, the mixing time $t_{\mathrm{mix}}(\varepsilon)$ to be $O(k^6)$ (Corollary 4.4) and $\pi_{\min}$ to be $\frac{1}{e2^{k^2}}$ (Equation (8)). Using these values, we have a bound on the total time $t_{\mathrm{total}}(\delta, M)$ as

$$t_{\mathrm{total}}(\delta, M) = S\cdot t_{\mathrm{mix}}(\varepsilon) = O\left(k^6\cdot\frac{\log(1-\delta)}{\log(1-p_M)}\right).$$

where p_M is $O\left(\frac{N_M(G)}{2^{k^2}}\right)$.

For a fixed code C if G and G' are two generator matrices of C we have $G' = UG$ for some U in $\mathcal{S}_k$. Therefore, $N_M(G) = N_M(G')$. As a result $N_M(G)$ is an invariant of the code C. We do not have an analytical expression for it. It is closely related to the well studied weight distribution function of the code.

The above discussions show that our algorithm will be able to find a code word of weight M or less in polynomial time if $N_M(G)$ is large at most a polynomial factor away from 2^{k^2}. Since we do not have a closed form expression for $N_M(G)$ for most codes, we run experiments to see how the algorithm performs on typical binary linear codes.

5. EXPERIMENTAL RESULTS

In the previous section, we proved that for the cost function $c(U) = \mathrm{w}^\alpha$, the family of Markov chains associated with the Metropolis algorithm is guaranteed to mix rapidly if we set the temperature T as n^α. To understand the performance as α varies, we performed experiments on two BCH codes BCH(511,58,183) and BCH(511,184,91) and the trivial $[50, 50, 1]$ and $[100, 100, 1]$ codes with α set as 1/2, 1, 2, 3, 5 and 7. We chose the trivial codes because their minimum weight code words are known: they are code words with a single 1. For $BCH(n, k, d)$ codes d stands for the *design distance* (see Section 7.3 in [14]) and it lower bounds the actual minimum weights. The performance is plotted in Figure 1 in which we observe that the performance is best for $\alpha = 1$. With α set to 1, we tested our algorithm on the set of 20 test cases given in six previous publications [4, 13, 8, 5, 7, 24]. The heuristic search algorithms used in these publications are Wallis's GA [4, 13], Askali's GA [4, 5], Tabu-search [4, 13, 8, 5], Hill Climbing [4, 13, 5], Ant colony optimization [7] and simulated annealing[7, 24]. Each of these heuristics use the same set, namely, the set of all length k binary words, as their search space.

We report the comparison of our algorithm against the algorithms cited above in Table 1, where the last two columns report the performance of our algorithm. The last but one column is for the case when our algorithm is run for k^2 steps and the best of 5000 samples is chosen. In the last column, we do the same with 500-steps, taking the best of 2000 samples. The other columns in the Table 1 give the performance of the previously studied algorithms. Based on the result, it can be seen that our Metropolis algorithm outperforms hill climbing, tabu search, Wallis's genetic algorithm and ant colony optimization [4, 13, 8, 5, 7] in all the twenty cases considered. When compared to the Askali's genetic algorithm [5, 4] on the twenty test cases, the performance was same in 9 cases, the genetic algorithm outperforms our algorithm in 4 test cases and our algorithm outperforms the genetic algorithm in 7 test cases.

We also compared the performance of our algorithm with that of the simulated annealing as reported in [7]. The paper [7] considered two BCH codes namely BCH(127, 64, 21) and BCH(255, 91, 51) and obtained code words of weight 27 and 75 respectively. In comparison, our algorithm was able to attain the minimum weight as 21 and 55 respectively.

6. CONCLUSION

In this paper, we studied the performance of the Metropolis algorithm for the minimum weight code word problem for binary linear codes. For an $[n, k]$-code, the algorithm uses a search space consisting of $k \times k$ invertible matrices and two such matrices are considered neighbours if one can be obtained from the other by an elementary row operation. We prove that the magnification of the search graph is large. Since this is the property of the search space, other random search heuristics can also possibly use the same search space profitably. Using the magnification result, we also prove that the Markov chain associated with a problem instance has large conductance, which is a necessary condition for the Metropolis algorithm to preform well on that instance. As simulated annealing (SA) has a close connection to the Metropolis algorithm, it would be instructive to try SA for this problem on our search space. We performed experiments to see how well does our algorithm perform on certain codes as against previously studied heuristics for the problem. The experimental results show that our algorithm performs quite well, it out-performs several previous heuristic algorithms used for this problem.

7. REFERENCES

[1] D. Ahmed and A. Asimi. A pseudo random generator efficient based on the decoding of the rational binary goppa code. *International Journal of Engineering Science and Technology (IJEST)*, 5(2):359–364, 2013.

[2] K. B. Ajitha Shenoy, S. Biswas, and P. P. Kurur. Metropolis algorithm for solving shortest lattice vector problem (svp). In *Hybrid Intelligent Systems (HIS), 2011 11th International Conference on*, pages 442–447, Dec 2011.

[3] K. B. Ajitha Shenoy, S. Biswas, and P. P. Kurur. Search graph formulation and hasting's generalization of metropolis algorithm for solving svp. *International Journal of Computer Information Systems and Industrial Management Applications*, 5:317–325, 2013.

[4] M. Askali, A. Azouaoui, S. Nouh, and M. Belkasmi. On the computing of the minimum distance of linear block codes by heuristic methods. *International Journal of Communications, Network and System Sciences*, 5(11):774–784, November 2012.

[5] M. Askali, S. Nouh, and M. Belkasmi. An efficient method to find the minimum distance of linear block

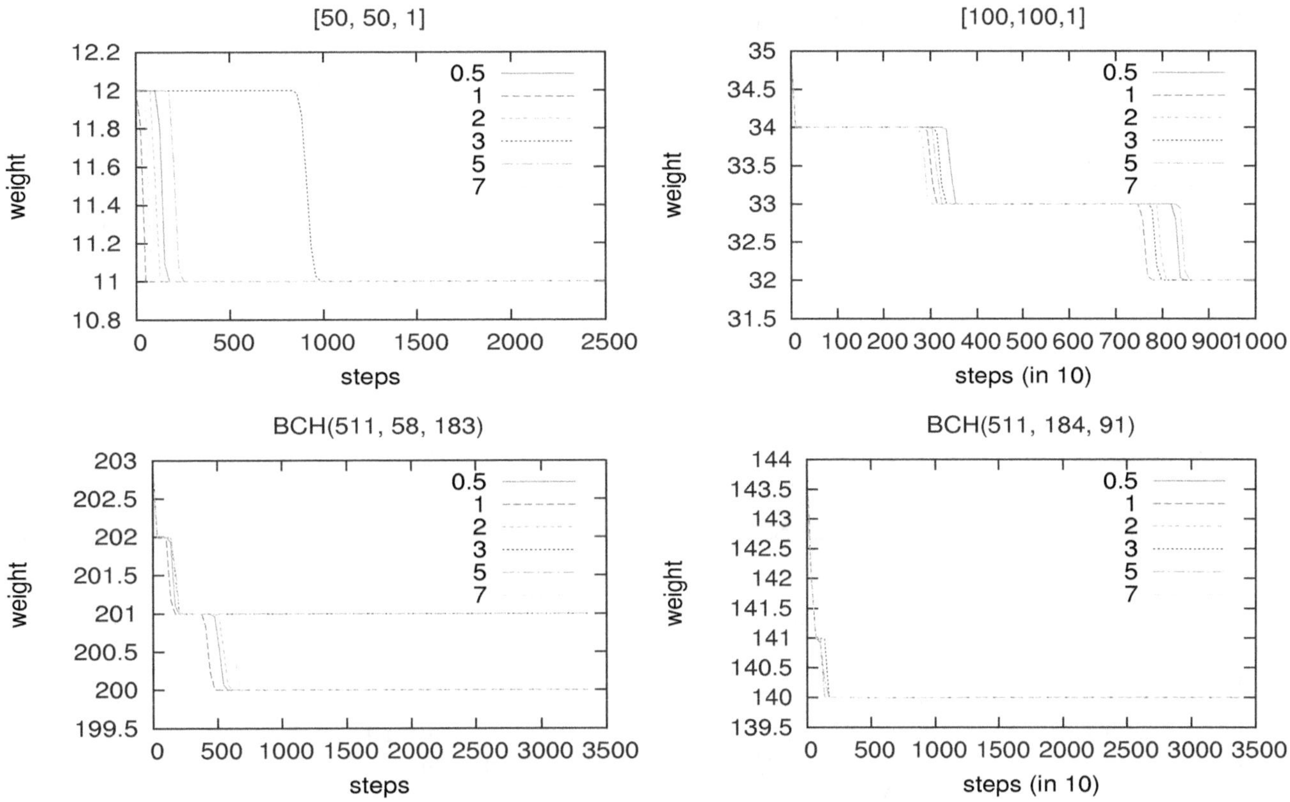

Figure 1: Varying α to choose best α: α set as 0.5, 1, 2, 3, 5 and 7 (k^2 steps, Average is taken over 1000 samples)

Table 1: Minimum Weight Code word found using Our Metropolis Algorithm Vs Different Methods given in papers [4, 13, 8, 5, 7]

Codes BCH ($n, k, d - design$)	Askali's GA [4, 5]	Wallis's GA [4, 13]	Hill Climbing [4, 5, 13]	Tabu Search [8, 4, 5, 13]	Ant Colony Optimization [7]	Metropolis Our Method k^2 steps 5000 Samples	Metropolis Our Method 500 steps 2000 samples
BCH (127, 64, 21)	**21**	**21**	28	24	24	**21**	**21**
BCH (127, 57, 23)	**23**	**23**	28	**23**	24	**23**	**23**
BCH (127, 50, 27)	**27**	**27**	32	31	**27**	**27**	**27**
BCH (255, 71, 59)	**63**	66	79	79	70	**63**	64
BCH (255, 79, 55)	**57**	60	74	64	69	**57**	**57**
BCH (255, 87, 53)	**57**	**57**	70	66	66	**57**	**57**
BCH (255, 91, 51)	**53**	59	72	69	68	54	54
BCH (255, 99, 47)	**51**	55	64	61	62	**51**	52
BCH (255, 107, 45)	**49**	51	64	62	60	50	50
BCH (255, 115, 43)	**45**	50	57	55	58	46	46
BCH (511, 304, 51)	74	79	90	85	–	**73**	74
BCH (511, 286, 55)	84	84	96	92	–	**78**	82
BCH (511, 238, 75)	103	105	118	112	–	102	**99**
BCH (511, 220, 79)	109	111	123	117	–	**108**	**108**
BCH (511, 184, 91)	**111**	128	135	140	–	120	127
BCH (511, 166, 95)	135	137	152	140	–	131	**128**
BCH (511, 121, 117)	155	152	163	163	–	151	**148**
BCH (511, 103, 123)	**160**	164	179	179	–	**160**	**160**
BCH (511, 76, 171)	176	176	195	184	–	**171**	175
BCH (511, 58, 183)	**183**	185	207	199	–	**183**	**183**

codes. In *IEEE International Conference on Multimedia Computing and Signal Processing*, pages 185 – 188. Tangles, May 2012.

[6] E. R. Berlekamp, R. J. McEliece, and H. C. A. van Tilborg. On the inherent intractability of certain coding problems. *IEEE Transactions on Information Theory*, 24(3):384–386, May 1978.

[7] J. A. Bland. Local search optimisation applied to the minimum distance problem. *Advanced Engineering Informatics*, 21(4):391–397, October 2007.

[8] J. A. Bland and A. T. Baylis. A tabu search approach to the minimum distance of error correcting codes. *International Journal of Electronics*, 79(6):829–837, 1995.

[9] R. Bose. *Information Theory Coding and Cryptography*. McGraw-Hill, New Delhi, India, 2008.

[10] I. Dumer, D. Micciancio, and M. Sudan. Hardness of approximating the minimum distance of a linear code. In *Foundations of Computer Science (FOCS), 40th Annual Symposium on*, pages 475–484, October 1999.

[11] J.-B. Fischer and J. Stern. An efficient pseudo-random generator provably as secure as syndrome decoding. In *Proceedings of the 15th Annual International Conference on Theory and Application of Cryptographic Techniques*, EUROCRYPT'96, pages 245–255, Berlin, Heidelberg, 1996.

[12] L. Hogben. *Handbook of Linear Algebra*. Champman and Hall/CRC, Taylor and Francis Group, USA, 2007.

[13] S. K. Houghten and J. L. Wallis. A comparative study of search techniques applied to the minimum distance problem of bch codes. In *In proceedings of sixth IASTED International Conference on Artificial Intelligence and Soft Computing*, pages 164–169. Brock University, May 2002.

[14] W. C. Huffman and V. Pless. *Fundamentals of Error Correcting Codes*. Cambridge University Press, Cambridge, United Kingdom, 2003.

[15] D. A. Levin, Y. Peres, and E. L. Wilmer. *Markov Chains and Mixing Times*. American Mathematical Society, Providence, RI, 2008.

[16] Z. H. Li, T. Xue, and H. Lai. Secret sharing schemes from binary linear codes. *Information Science*, 180(22):2265–2272, 1996.

[17] Z. Liu and X.-W. Wu. On a class of three-weight codes with cryptographic applications. In *Proceedings of 2012 IEEE International Symposium on Information Theory*, MIT, Cambridge, MA, USA, 2012.

[18] J. L. Massey. Some applications of coding theory in cryptography. In *Proceedings of the fourth IMA conference on Cryptography and Coding*, Cirencester, England, 1993.

[19] M. Mitzenmacher and E. Upfal. *Probability and Computing: Randomized Algorithms and Probabilistic Analysis*. Cambridge University Press, New York, USA, 2005.

[20] V. Pless. Bose Chaudhuri Hocquenghem (bch) codes. *Introduction to the Theory of Error-Correcting Codes, Third Edition*, pages 109–122, 1998.

[21] S. Sanyal, S. Raja, and S. Biswas. Necessary and sufficient conditions for success of the metropolis algorithm for optimization. In *Proceedings of the tenth ACM GECCO'10 Conference on Genetic and Evolutionary Computation*, pages 1417–1424. Portland, OR, USA, July 2010.

[22] A. Sinclair. Improved bounds for mixing rates of markov chains and multicommodity flow. *Combinatorics, Probability and Computing*, 1(4):351–370, 1992.

[23] A. Sinclair. *Algorithms for Ranodom Generation and Counting - A Markov Chain Approach*. Birkhauser Boston, Cambridge, MA 02139, U.S.A., 1993.

[24] M. Zhang and F. Ma. Simulated annealing approach to the minimum distance of error correcting codes. *Internation Journal of Electronics*, 76(3):377–384, 1994.

Asymmetric Quadratic Landscape Approximation Model

Alexandru-Adrian Tantar, Emilia Tantar
Interdisciplinary Centre for Security, Reliability and Trust
University of Luxembourg
6 Rue Richard Coudenhove-Kalergi
L-1359, Luxembourg, Luxembourg
{alexandru, emilia}.tantar@uni.lu

Oliver Schütze
Computer Science Department
CINVESTAV-IPN
Av. IPN 2508, Col. San Pedro Zacatenco
Mexico City, México
schuetze@cs.cinvestav.mx

ABSTRACT

This work presents an asymmetric quadratic approximation model and an ϵ-archiving algorithm. The model allows to construct, under local convexity assumptions, descriptors for local optima points in continuous functions. A descriptor can be used to extract confidence radius information. The ϵ-archiving algorithm is designed to maintain and update a set of such asymmetric descriptors, spaced at some given threshold distance. An in-depth analysis is conducted on the stability and performance of the asymmetric model, comparing the results with the ones obtained by a quadratic polynomial approximation. A series of different applications are possible in areas such as dynamic and robust optimization.

1. INTRODUCTION

Evolutionary algorithms and, more generally, heuristic methods, were and still are expected to offer solid results without relying on anything else besides direct sampling. Notable exceptions like, for example, quasi-Newton methods [8, 6] or the more recent CMA-ES [2], owe their success to the closer attention they paid to landscape. And while different other paradigms make use of derivatives, not all functions allow it. Also, most algorithms are by design not meant to exploit landscape information. A set of samples drawn from a local optimum's neighborhood, i.e. what an evolutionary algorithm is finally best at, is however sufficient to describe local landscape features. To this end, different studies looked at topology aspects, correlation or landscape approximation, among others [16, 12, 4, 11, 15, 17, 14, 9, 1, 7].

We propose in the following an asymmetric quadratic model and an ϵ-archiving algorithm that connect the optimization and landscape information ends. First, the model can be used to build a landscape descriptor based on a series of samples. The archiving algorithm, in turn, maintains and updates a list of such descriptors. If used from within a sampling algorithm, e.g. any standard evolutionary paradigm, the archiving techniques transparently builds a set of descriptors spaced at some specified distance.

GECCO'14, July 12–16, 2014, Vancouver, BC, Canada.

http://dx.doi.org/10.1145/2576768.2598381.

With respect to landscape alone, the studies of Wright [16], and later of Stadler [12], laid the foundation for a better understanding of a problem's difficulty. Others, like Kauffman [4], introduced the NK-landscape model. Theoretical biology also acknowledged advances in the area, e.g. [4], showing that high peaks are correlated in space and that peaks, in general, are not uniformly distributed. Furthermore, several fitness landscape classes were introduced, including fractal landscapes, see Sorkin *et al.* [11], nowadays covered by pedagogical materials and subject to detailed studies [15, 17]. Other works looked more at topology oriented information, discussing, for example, complex networks in combinatorial spaces [14]. A different class of approaches deals with modeling response as the realization of a stochastic process [9], also with studies that look into the multi-objective domain [1]. Last but not least, studies such as [7] focused on a more geometric type of descriptors where the global landscape is shaped by iterative quadratic approximations. For details on ϵ-archiving algorithms, using a multi-objective perspective, please refer to [10, 5].

For the remainder of this study, we assume a continuous function with convex (within a close neighborhood) local optima. With respect to this assumption, it should be straightforward to model the function's landscape in the neighborhood of an optimum by using a quadratic form. The resulting construct can serve (i) as an under- or over-approximation model, e.g. when dealing with complex or expensive to evaluate functions, (ii) as a simplified projection of the function's local geometry, or (iii) as a structural descriptor in dynamic problems. When used as a substitute model, landscape approximations act as predictors with new samples being evaluated via the approximation surface. In the second case, the model can be regarded as a descriptor that captures the function's (local) traits, e.g. including attributes related to covariance or principal components. Note that one is interested more in profiling the function's behavior near a local optimum, in this case, rather than in having a substitute model, i.e. not necessarily used for evaluating new samples. The last point assumes that local optima are roughly structure invariant over time, always with respect to a close neighborhood. Descriptors in this case can be used to map and track the optima at different time steps, based on their specific (geometric) attributes. A quadratic model is however likely to fail when the function is asymmetric. For a simple example of what asymmetry stands for within the limits of our study, please refer to Figure 1. It should be straightforward that any quadratic approximation would lead to either under or over approximation errors.

Algorithm 1: Asymmetric quadratic approximation.

Initialize the scaling vectors $\mathbf{\Lambda}^+ = \{\lambda_i^+ = 1\}^T_{1\leq i\leq n}$ and $\mathbf{\Lambda}^- = \{\lambda_i^- = 1\}^T_{1\leq i\leq n}$; draw a first sample x from the neighborhood of μ and initialize the covariance matrix estimation with $\mathbf{\Sigma} = [(x_i - \mu_i)(x_j - \mu_j)]_{1\leq i,j\leq n}$;

while *sampling not finished* **do**

  draw a new sample x and update the covariance matrix estimation, $\mathbf{\Lambda}^+$ and $\mathbf{\Lambda}^-$, knowing that $\mathbf{\Sigma} = [\mathbb{E}[(x_i - \mu_i)(x_j - \mu_j)]_{1\leq i,j\leq n}]$

  foreach $1 \leq i \leq n$ **do**

    $\lambda_i^+ = \big[(\mathrm{diag}(\mathrm{Z}_\alpha(\mathbf{v}_i + \mu))\mathbf{\Lambda}^+ + \mathrm{diag}(1 - \mathrm{Z}_\alpha(\mathbf{v}_i + \mu)\mathbf{\Lambda}^-)^T \mathrm{Z}_\beta^T(\mathbf{v}_i + \mu)/\Sigma\mathrm{Z}_\beta(\mathbf{v}_i + \mu)\big]$

    $\lambda_i^- = \big[(\mathrm{diag}(\mathrm{Z}_\alpha(\mu - \mathbf{v}_i))\mathbf{\Lambda}^+ + \mathrm{diag}(1 - \mathrm{Z}_\alpha(\mu - \mathbf{v}_i)\mathbf{\Lambda}^-)^T \mathrm{Z}_\beta^T(\mu - \mathbf{v}_i)/\Sigma\mathrm{Z}_\beta(\mu - \mathbf{v}_i)\big]$

  determine δ s.t. $\mathbf{\Lambda}\left[(x-\mu)^T\mathbf{\Sigma}^{-1}(x-\mu)\right] + \kappa = \epsilon + \kappa$

  $\delta = \left[y - \kappa - \Gamma(x)\right]\big\{[(\mathrm{diag}^2(\mathrm{Z}_\alpha)\mathrm{Z}_\beta^T/\Sigma\mathrm{Z}_\beta + \mathrm{diag}^2(1-\mathrm{Z}_\alpha)\mathrm{Z}_\beta^T/\Sigma\mathrm{Z}_\beta)^T\mathrm{Z}_\beta^T/\Sigma\mathrm{Z}_\beta][(x-\mu)^T\mathbf{\Sigma}^{-1}(x-\mu)]\big\}^{-1}$

  updated the scaling vectors w.r.t. the response err.:
  $\mathbf{\Lambda}^+ = 0.5(2.0\mathbf{\Lambda}^+ + \delta\mathrm{diag}(\mathrm{Z}_\alpha)\mathrm{Z}_\beta^T/\Sigma\mathrm{Z}_\beta)$
  $\mathbf{\Lambda}^- = 0.5(2.0\mathbf{\Lambda}^- + \delta\mathrm{diag}(1 - \mathrm{Z}_\alpha)\mathrm{Z}_\beta^T/\Sigma\mathrm{Z}_\beta)$

determine a confidence radius τ s.t. $\Gamma(\mu + \tau\bar{\mathrm{v}}) = \epsilon$:

$$\tau = \left\{\epsilon\left[\,[(\mathrm{diag}(\mathrm{Z}_\alpha(\bar{\mathrm{v}}))\mathbf{\Lambda}^+ + (1 - \mathrm{Z}_\alpha(\bar{\mathrm{v}}))\mathbf{\Lambda}^-)^T\mathrm{Z}_\beta^T(\bar{\mathrm{v}})/\Sigma\mathrm{Z}_\beta(\bar{\mathrm{v}})]\bar{\mathrm{v}}^T\bar{\mathrm{v}}\bar{v}\,\right]^{-1}\right\}^{0.5}$$

As a novel aspect, we thus consider landscape asymmetry which, to the best of our knowledge, was not previously addressed in an explicit manner in the literature.

The paper is organized as follows. The details of the proposed asymmetric model are presented in Section 2. The ϵ-archiving algorithm is outlined in Section 3, followed by a detailed discussion and comparison in Section 4. We end with conclusions and future directions.

2. ASYMMETRIC MODEL

The formalism presented in the following allows taking into account asymmetry along the main variance axes and can be generalized to outline secondary landscape features. As a side note, for the scope of our study, we limit ourselves only at describing local landscape characteristics. We consider in the following a quadratic form defined as:

$$\Gamma(x) = \mathbf{\Lambda}\left[(x-\mu)^T\mathbf{\Sigma}^{-1}(x-\mu)\right] + \kappa$$

where κ stands for a support constant; $\mathbf{\Lambda}$ is a matrix that maps a set of scalar values with respect to the eigenvectors $\mathbf{v}$ of $\mathbf{\Sigma}^{-1}$ at a local optimum μ. For the remainder of this section, we consider $\mathbf{\Lambda}$ to be defined as follows:

$$\mathbf{\Lambda} = \left[(\mathrm{diag}(\mathrm{Z}_\alpha(x))\mathbf{\Lambda}^+ + \mathrm{diag}(1-\mathrm{Z}_\alpha(x))\mathbf{\Lambda}^-)^T\mathrm{Z}_\beta^T(x)/\Sigma\mathrm{Z}_\beta(x)\right]$$

with $\mathbf{\Lambda}^+ = \{\lambda_i^+\}_{1\leq i\leq n}$, $\mathbf{\Lambda}^- = \{\lambda_i^-\}_{1\leq i\leq n}$ being scaling vectors associated with the eigenvectors $\mathbf{v}$, respectively with the reflected eigenvectors $-\mathbf{v}$; Z_α and Z_β are interpolation polynomials that allow defining a smooth transition among the scaling values specified by $\mathbf{\Lambda}^+$ and $\mathbf{\Lambda}^-$. As a notation convention, we will use Z_α and Z_β to refer to $\mathrm{Z}_\alpha(x)$, respectively to $\mathrm{Z}_\beta(x)$; $\Sigma\mathrm{Z}_\beta$ stands for the sum of all elements in Z_β. We assume in the following that both Z_α and Z_β are defined as normalized angle values:

$$\mathrm{Z}_\alpha(x) = 1 - \arccos\left[\frac{(x-\mu)^T\mathbf{v}}{((x-\mu)^T(x-\mu)\mathrm{diag}(\mathbf{v}^T\mathbf{v}))^{0.5}}\right]/\pi$$

$$\mathrm{Z}_\beta(x) = 1 - 2\arccos\left[\frac{|(x-\mu)^T\mathbf{v}|}{((x-\mu)^T(x-\mu)\mathrm{diag}(\mathbf{v}^T\mathbf{v}))^{0.5}}\right]/\pi$$

As a direct consequence of how Z_α and Z_β are defined, we obtain a linear scaling transition. Note that while this is sufficient w.r.t. the scope of our work, specific problems may nonetheless have different needs, namely in terms of more descriptive interpolation polynomials, e.g. including parameters that capture the traits that build into different landscape features. In order to obtain an accurate landscape approximation we thus need to have an estimate of the covariance matrix and of the scaling factors. As we will see later, most functions can be approximated to a reasonable extent by using a linear interpolation alone. If higher complexity polynomials should be specified, one may want to construct them by using any available insight about the function's (local) structure. Knowing that $\mathbf{\Sigma} = [\mathbb{E}[(x_i - \mu_i)(x_j - \mu_j)]_{1\leq i,j\leq n}]$, obtaining an estimate of the covariance matrix is only a matter of sampling and averaging over all points. Note that this estimation can be done online. After the covariance matrix is updated, we need to interpolate the scaling factors as to take into account the orientation of the updated eigenvectors:

$$\mathbf{\Lambda}^+ = \Big\{\lambda_i^+ = \big[(\mathrm{diag}(\mathrm{Z}_\alpha(\mathbf{v}_i + \mu))\mathbf{\Lambda}^+ + \mathrm{diag}(1 - \mathrm{Z}_\alpha(\mathbf{v}_i + \mu)\mathbf{\Lambda}^-)^T\mathrm{Z}_\beta^T(\mathbf{v}_i + \mu)/\Sigma\mathrm{Z}_\beta(\mathbf{v}_i + \mu)\big]\Big\}_{1\leq i\leq n}$$

$$\mathbf{\Lambda}^- = \Big\{\lambda_i^- = \big[(\mathrm{diag}(\mathrm{Z}_\alpha(\mu - \mathbf{v}_i))\mathbf{\Lambda}^+ + \mathrm{diag}(1 - \mathrm{Z}_\alpha(\mu - \mathbf{v}_i)\mathbf{\Lambda}^-)^T\mathrm{Z}_\beta^T(\mu - \mathbf{v}_i)/\Sigma\mathrm{Z}_\beta(\mu - \mathbf{v}_i)\big]\Big\}_{1\leq i\leq n}$$

A last step is to correct the error we observe between the approximation and the response (function) surface. If the scaling deviation is modeled with respect to a scalar δ, we can rewrite the initial quadratic equation as follows:

$$\Gamma^*(x) = \mathbf{\Lambda}^*\left[(x-\mu)^T\mathbf{\Sigma}^{-1}(x-\mu)\right] + \kappa$$

$$\mathbf{\Lambda}^* = \{[\mathrm{diag}(\mathrm{Z}_\alpha)(\mathbf{\Lambda}^+ + \delta\mathrm{diag}(\mathrm{Z}_\alpha)\mathrm{Z}_\beta^T/\Sigma\mathrm{Z}_\beta) + \mathrm{diag}(1 - \mathrm{Z}_\alpha)(\mathbf{\Lambda}^- + \delta\mathrm{diag}(1 - \mathrm{Z}_\alpha)\mathrm{Z}_\beta^T/\Sigma\mathrm{Z}_\beta)]^T\mathrm{Z}_\beta^T/\Sigma\mathrm{Z}_\beta\}$$

Assuming y to be the response value associated with the sample x, we can directly derive the value of the scalar δ:

$$\delta = \left[y - \kappa - \Gamma(x)\right]\big\{[(\mathrm{diag}^2(\mathrm{Z}_\alpha)\mathrm{Z}_\beta^T/\Sigma\mathrm{Z}_\beta + \mathrm{diag}^2(1 - \mathrm{Z}_\alpha)\mathrm{Z}_\beta^T/\Sigma\mathrm{Z}_\beta)^T\mathrm{Z}_\beta^T/\Sigma\mathrm{Z}_\beta][(x-\mu)^T\mathbf{\Sigma}^{-1}(x-\mu)]\big\}^{-1}$$

which allows us to obtain the updated scaling vectors:

$$\mathbf{\Lambda}^+ = 0.5(2.0\mathbf{\Lambda}^+ + \delta\mathrm{diag}(\mathrm{Z}_\alpha)\mathrm{Z}_\beta^T/\Sigma\mathrm{Z}_\beta)$$

$$\mathbf{\Lambda}^- = 0.5(2.0\mathbf{\Lambda}^- + \delta\mathrm{diag}(1 - \mathrm{Z}_\alpha)\mathrm{Z}_\beta^T/\Sigma\mathrm{Z}_\beta)$$

If considering aspects related to, for example, robustness or constraints imposed by a real-life problem as of interest, one may also want to compute a confidence radius, i.e. limit at which the function is expected to exceed a given (maximum accepted) threshold value ϵ. Or, in a more formal way, we would need to find a scalar τ for which $\Gamma(\mu + \tau\bar{\mathrm{v}}) = \epsilon$, where $\bar{\mathrm{v}}$ is the eigenvector that corresponds to the largest eigenvalue of the $\mathbf{\Sigma}^{-1}$ matrix, referred to hereafter as $\bar{\upsilon}$. We would thus have $\mathbf{\Lambda}\left[(\tau\bar{\mathrm{v}})^T\mathbf{\Sigma}^{-1}(\tau\bar{\mathrm{v}})\right] = \epsilon$, which leads to:

$$\tau = \left\{\epsilon\Big[\ [(\mathrm{diag}(\mathrm{Z}_\alpha(\bar{\mathrm{v}}))\mathbf{\Lambda}^+ + (1-\mathrm{Z}_\alpha(\bar{\mathrm{v}}))\mathbf{\Lambda}^-)^T\mathrm{Z}_\beta^T(\bar{\mathrm{v}})/\Sigma\mathrm{Z}_\beta(\bar{\mathrm{v}})]\bar{\mathrm{v}}^T\bar{\mathrm{v}}\bar{\upsilon}\ \Big]^{-1}\right\}^{0.5}$$

This last step only serves for obtaining a confidence radius and is therefore optional. A summary of all steps can be found in Algorithm 1; while we here use an internal sampling loop, the approximation model can be constructed based on samples provided by an external algorithm, e.g. any classical evolutionary technique. The first line corresponds to an *initialization* step while lines 3 to 10 form the actual *update* procedure. An offline model construction is also possible, starting from a collection of archived solutions.

A proof of convergence is outside the scope of this work. Note however that, if the function is locally quadratic, one can show that the model converges when the number of samples grows to infinity. Apart from asymptotic approximation errors, a misfit is obtained if either or both of the following are met: (i) the function is not convex within the area being sampled, or (ii) a non-linear scaling is needed in order to approximate the function's surface. Non-convexity may also be implied in this latter case. The first point can be addressed by sampling from a smaller region around the (local) optimum point, still under the assumption of local convexity; for the second point a different interpolation is however needed.

3. ARCHIVING ALGORITHM

Approximating the landscape of a local optimum has as main requirement having a set of samples from within a sufficient neighborhood of that optimum. We describe in the following an ϵ-archiving technique that, when used in conjunction with the asymmetric model, constructs an ϵ-set of solutions spaced at a given distance θ, corresponding (landscape) descriptors included. We would like to mention that both the ϵ and the θ parameters are problem dependent and supposed to reflect specific semantics like, for example, maximum allowed input error or, respectively, useful resolution of the parameters. For the remainder of this section, we denote by $\Delta_{\theta,\epsilon}$ an archive for which solutions are (i) spaced at a (minimum) distance θ, i.e. no two solutions can be closer than θ, and (ii) $\forall x \in \Delta_{\theta,\epsilon}$ we have that $f(x) \leq \Delta^*_{\theta,\epsilon} + \epsilon$, where $f(x)$ is the response value of x and $\Delta^*_{\theta,\epsilon} = f(x^*)$, $f(x^*) \leq f(\bar{x})$, $\forall \bar{x} \in \Delta_{\epsilon,\theta}$, is the best found (stored in the archive) value. For the remainder of this section, as a convention, we use $\{x\}$ to refer to a landscape descriptor centered in x. Removing a sample x from the archive is also regarded as being equivalent to removing the corresponding descriptor $\{x\}$.

The algorithm starts with an empty archive $\Delta_{\epsilon,\theta}$. All calls expect as input the archive and a sample point x. At output the algorithm provides an updated archive, i.e. that encloses the information carried by x, in the form of an additional landscape descriptor centered at x, or as an updated list of the existing descriptors. The algorithm starts by verifying if

Algorithm 2: ϵ-Archiving algorithm.

input : x, $\Delta_{\epsilon,\theta}$
output: $\Delta_{\epsilon,\theta}$

1 **if** $\neg\Delta^*_{\epsilon,\theta} \vee (\Delta^*_{\epsilon,\theta} \wedge y < \Delta^*_{\epsilon,\theta})$ **then**
2 $\quad \Delta^*_{\epsilon,\theta} \leftarrow y$, $\Delta_{\epsilon,\theta} = \{\bar{x} \in \Delta_{\epsilon,\theta} \mid f(\bar{x}) \leq \Delta^*_{\epsilon,\theta} + \epsilon\}$
3 **if** $|\Delta_{\epsilon,\theta}| = 0$ **then**
4 $\quad \Delta_{\epsilon,\theta} = \Delta_{\epsilon,\theta} \cup \{x\}$
5 **else if** $y < \Delta^*_{\epsilon,\theta} + \epsilon$ **then**
6 $\quad$ **foreach** $\bar{x} \in \Delta_{\epsilon,\theta} \mid f(\bar{x}) \leq y \wedge \|\hat{x} - x\| < \theta$ **do**
7 $\quad\quad \Delta_{\epsilon,\theta} \leftarrow \{\bar{x}, x\}$
8 $\quad$ **if** $|\{\bar{x} \in \Delta_{\epsilon,\theta} \mid f(\bar{x}) \leq y \wedge \|\hat{x} - x\| < \theta\}| = 0$ **then**
9 $\quad\quad \Delta_{\epsilon,\theta} = \Delta_{\epsilon,\theta} \cup \{x\}$
10 $\nabla = \{\varnothing\}$
11 **foreach** $\bar{x} \in \Delta_{\epsilon,\theta}$ **do**
12 $\quad \hat{\Delta}_{\epsilon,\theta} = \{\hat{x} \in \Delta_{\epsilon,\theta}/\nabla \mid f(\hat{x}) < f(\bar{x}) \wedge \|\hat{x} - \bar{x}\| < \theta\}$
13 $\quad$ **foreach** $\hat{x} \in \hat{\Delta}_{\epsilon,\theta}$ **do**
14 $\quad\quad \Delta_{\epsilon,\theta} \leftarrow \{\bar{x}, \hat{x}\}$, $\nabla = \nabla \cup \{\hat{x}\}$
15 $\Delta_{\epsilon,\theta} = \{\bar{x} \mid f(\bar{x}) \leq \Delta^*_{\epsilon,\theta} + \epsilon \wedge \bar{x} \notin \nabla\}$

$\Delta^*_{\epsilon,\theta}$ is defined (line 1). If not the case or if it is defined but $y = f(x)$ is below the best known support value $\Delta^*_{\epsilon,\theta}$ (the ϵ-region shifted down, also in line 1) then all non ϵ-solutions, if any, are removed. The following steps (lines 3-9) create a new descriptor if the archive does not contain any samples (lines 3-4) or if x is within the ϵ-region but (i) not within a θ distance from any other archived point, or (ii) within θ distance w.r.t. a subset of the archived points but strictly below the support of all points. If we have that x is within θ as compared to a given point $\bar{x}$ and, at the same time, above its support, the descriptor of $\bar{x}$ is updated to include the information carried by x. The $\Delta_{\epsilon,\theta} \leftarrow \{\bar{x}, x\}$ notation is used to indicate that the descriptor associated to a point $\bar{x}$ (from the archive) is updated by including the information enclosed by x. The last part of the algorithm (lines 10-15) updates the descriptors of any overlapping points, and removes all the descriptors that are no longer of interest, i.e. now falling outside the ϵ-region or that were used to update a different point in the archive (line 15).

A proof of convergence, as for the asymmetric approximation model, is outside the scope; it should be however straightforward that the algorithm constructs an (asymptotically) optimal ϵ-set of solutions if the probability of sampling from an arbitrarily small open ball at any given point is not null. Note that there may exist an infinite number of ϵ-optimal sets, e.g. see De Jong's function [13, 3].

4. ANALYSIS AND COMPARISON

A detailed analysis of the previously described asymmetric model was conducted on several classical benchmark functions [13, 3], presented in the following. A formal description of the benchmark functions can be found in Table 1; modified versions of the exponential and Mishra functions were used, with $f(x) = 1 - \exp(-x^T[0.55, 0.50; 0.50, 0.85]^{-1}x)$,

Table 1: An outline of the benchmark functions considered in this study; n stands for the number of variables.

Name		Function
De Jong	**f1**	$f(x) = \sum_{i=1}^{n} x_i^2$
Exponential†	**f2**	$f(x) = -\exp\left(-0.5 \sum_{i=1}^{n} x_i^2\right)$
Quadratic	**f3**	$f(x) = x^T [\mathbf{ABA}^T]^{-1} x$ $\mathbf{A} = \begin{bmatrix} \sin a & \cos a \\ \cos a & -\sin a \end{bmatrix}$ $\mathbf{B} = \begin{bmatrix} b & 0 \\ 0 & c \end{bmatrix}$ $a = 10.0,\ b = 2 \times 5^2,\ c = 2.0$
Hyper-Ellipsoid	**f4**	$f(x) = \sum_{i=1}^{n} i x_i$
Rastrigin	**f5**	$f(x) = 10n \sum_{i=1}^{n} (x_i^2 - 10\cos(2\pi x_i))$
Ackley	**f6**	$f(x) = -a \exp\left(-b\sqrt{1/n \sum_{i=1}^{n} x_i^2}\right)$ $- \exp\left(1/n \sum_{i=1}^{n} \cos(c x_i)\right) + a + \exp(1)$ $a = 20,\ b = 0.2,\ c = 2\pi$
Griewank	**f7**	$f(x) = \sum_{i=1}^{n} \frac{x_i^2}{4000} - \prod_{i=1}^{n} \cos\left(\frac{x_i}{\sqrt{i}}\right) + 1$
Alpine 1	**f8**	$f(x) = \sum_{i=1}^{n} \lvert x_i \sin(x_i) + 0.1 x_i \rvert$
Pinter	**f9**	$f(x) = \sum_{i=1}^{n} \{ i x_i^2 + 20 i \sin^2 a + i \log(1 + i b^2) \}$ $a = x_{i-1} \sin x_i + \sin x_{i+1}$ $b = x_{i-1}^2 - 2x_i + 3x_{i+1} - \cos x_i + 1$ $x_0 = x_n,\ x_{n+1} = x_1$
Bohachevsky	**f10**	$f(x) = \sum_{i=1}^{n-1} \{ x_i^2 + 2x_{i+1}^2 - 0.3\cos(3\pi x_i)$ $-0.4\cos(4\pi x_{i+1}) + 0.7 \}$
Mishra† 11	**f11**	$f(x) = \left\{ \frac{1}{n} \sum_{i=1}^{n} \lvert x_i \rvert - \left(\prod_{i=1}^{n} \lvert x_i \rvert\right)^{\frac{1}{n}} \right\}^2$
Price 04	**f12**	$f(x) = (2x_1^3 x_2 - x_2^3)^2 + (6x_1 - x_2^2 + x_2)^2$
Rosenbrock	**f13**	$f(x) = \sum_{i=1}^{n-1} \{ 100(x_i^2 - x_{i+1})^2 + (x_i - 1)^2 \}$
Wavy	**f14**	$f(x) = 1 - \frac{1}{n} \sum_{i}^{n} \cos(k x_i) e^{-\frac{x_i^2}{2}},\ k = 10$
Weierstrass	**f15**	$f(x) = \sum_{i}^{n} \left\{ \sum_{j=0}^{k} a^j \cos(2\pi b^j (x_i + 0.5)) \right.$ $\left. -n \sum_{j=0}^{k} a^j \cos(\pi b^j) \right\}$ $k = 20,\ a = 0.5,\ b = 3.0$

† a modified version of the function is used, details in text.

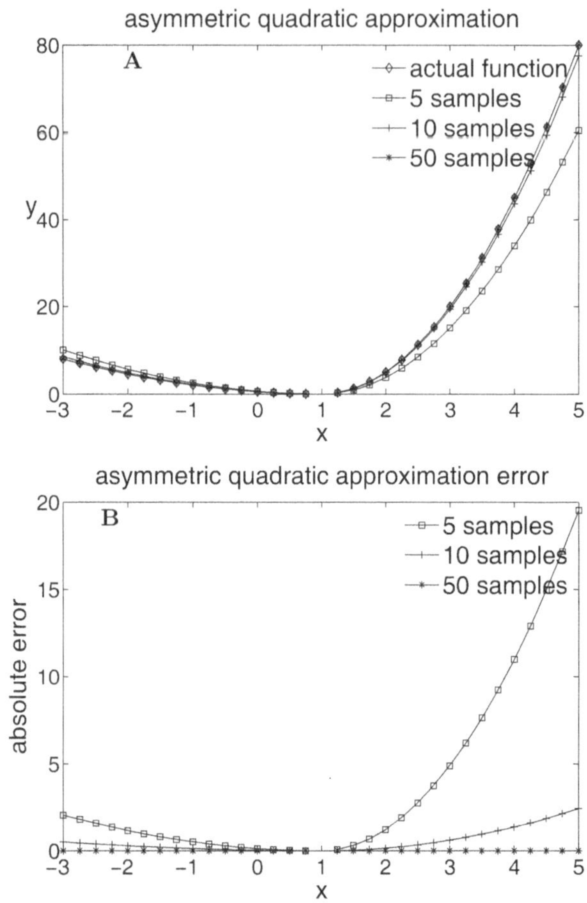

Figure 1: Approximation example (A) with 5, 10, respectively 50 samples, and the corresponding absolute error (B).

respectively $f(x) = \{\frac{1}{n}\sum_{i=1}^{n}|x_i| - (\prod_{i=1}^{n}|x_i|)^{0.05}\}^2$. Also, please mind that for the hereafter analysis and discussion, all functions, except the Rosenbrock, are shifted from the origin to $[\ 1\ 1\ ]$. All functions thus attain their (global) optimum value when $x = [\ 1\ 1\ ]$. The numerical results that follow are intended to describe the behaviour of the algorithm in terms of stability and approximation error, furthermore including a comparison with a quadratic polynomial model.

We start with a brief discussion of the ϵ-archiving technique followed by the approximation model results; a basic example can be found in Figure 1, with a close to perfect fit at less than 50 (uniform random) samples.

A series of complex archiving case studies can be found in Figure 2, for the Rosenbrock (f13, $\theta = 0.1$, $\epsilon = 10.0$) and Mishra (f11, $\theta = 0.1$, $\epsilon = 1.0e-3$) functions, running from an overall number of 100 to 10000 samples. While we here make use of random sampling exclusively, i.e. no selection or other similar mechanism, the chosen number of points can be regarded as being in direct relation with the main phases of, for example, an evolutionary algorithm. A random initialization step would, in a rather classical setup, result in 100 completely random samples. While it should be obvious that not much information can be gathered at this step, it may however be possible to construct an outline of how the ϵ-set is shaped. At 1000 samples, e.g. initial exploration phase, second row of Figure 2, a clear view of where the ϵ-optimal set lies is obtained. The following steps are expected to offer an asymptotic improvement with the archived points slowly stabilizing at a set of countable local optima points. We would like to recall that local landscape descriptors are constructed at each point and updated as new samples are drawn. Also, please mind that a completely random sampling is used; a different picture would result for an evolutionary algorithm as the search would be biased more towards the lower areas of the function's surface. The resulting ϵ-set is thus determined by the sampling process and the archiving parameters, i.e. the θ distance and the ϵ threshold. Depending on the nature of the sampling algorithm, asymptotic convergence to an optimal ϵ-set of solutions can be expected (the case for a completely random uniform sampling).

A summary of the results obtained for the approximation model can be found in Table 2; a number of 50 independent trials were run for each function. We are mainly interested in showing that the approximation algorithm is stable and that errors, with respect to the scale of each benchmark, are small. Also, in order to better assess the quality of the asymmetric approximation model, we compared the results to a quadratic polynomial approximation, defined by $Q(x) = xAx^T + Bx + c$, where A is a $(n+1) \times (n+1)$ matrix, B is a vector of $n+1$ elements and c is a scalar. We would

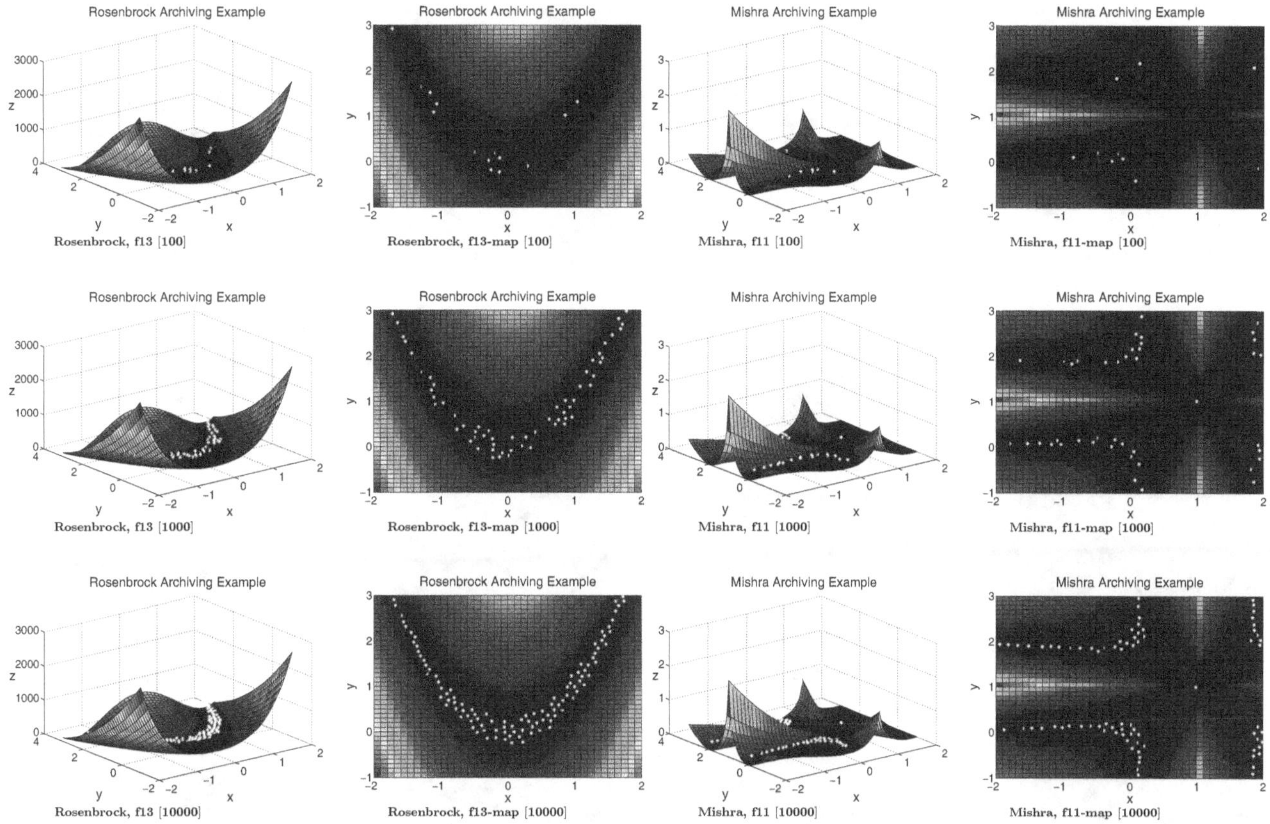

Figure 2: Archiving examples, given 100, 1000, respectively 10000 random samples, first, second and third row; Rosenbrock ($\theta = 0.1$, $\epsilon = 10.0$) and Mishra ($\theta = 0.1$, $\epsilon = 1.0e-3$) functions, surface and map representation.

Table 2: A summary of the results obtained for different benchmark functions, labels from f1 to f15, given 50 independent trial runs: r is the confidence radius at which y is expected to approach ϵ; $ierr$ and cnt stand for the absolute error, respectively number of points inside the confidence region with a value above ϵ. A root least squares error measure for the asymmetric and for the quadratic model are listed in the last four columns, err respectively $q.err$.

	ϵ	μ_r	σ_r	μ_y	σ_y	$\mu_{\lvert\epsilon-y\rvert}$	$\sigma_{\lvert\epsilon-y\rvert}$	μ_{ierr}	σ_{ierr}	μ_{cnt}	σ_{cnt}	μ_{err}	σ_{err}	W	$\mu_{q.err}$	$\sigma_{q.err}$
De Jong **f1**	0.1	0.314	0.001	0.099	0.001	0.001	0.001	0.000	0.000	0.000	0.000	2.039e-05	1.048e-05	-	2.530e-06	1.243e-08
Exponential **f2**	0.1	0.132	0.019	0.095	0.014	0.005	0.014	0.000	0.001	0.000	0.000	6.401e-05	2.288e-05	-	1.988e-05	2.898e-06
Quadratic **f3**	0.1	0.447	0.001	0.100	0.000	0.000	0.000	0.001	0.004	0.000	0.000	2.373e-05	9.273e-05	-	5.350e-07	1.777e-09
Hyper-Ellipsoid **f4**	0.1	0.223	0.001	0.100	0.001	0.001	0.001	0.001	0.001	0.000	0.000	3.946e-05	2.298e-05	-	7.357e-06	7.576e-08
Rastrigin **f5**	15.0	0.287	0.007	13.327	0.988	1.684	0.969	0.413	0.422	1.000	3.232	1.765e-02	2.165e-03	-	1.002e-02	6.303e-04
Ackley **f6**	1.5	0.171	0.015	1.115	0.129	0.385	0.129	0.124	0.158	4.820	10.548	7.477e-03	4.954e-03	-	3.210e-04	2.885e-05
Griewank **f7**	0.1	0.435	0.090	0.097	0.020	0.005	0.020	0.001	0.001	0.000	0.000	3.534e-05	1.305e-05	-	3.752e-06	7.900e-07
Alpine 1 **f8**	0.1	0.273	0.036	0.079	0.020	0.023	0.018	0.011	0.010	25.540	25.077	4.116e-04	1.597e-04	+	3.560e-03	1.348e-03
Pinter **f9**	15.0	0.483	0.137	10.154	3.486	4.883	3.433	1.885	1.952	21.040	40.159	5.380e-02	4.248e-02	+	5.357e-01	1.556e+00
Bohachevsky **f10**	0.5	0.366	0.103	0.771	0.198	0.294	0.163	0.370	0.249	21.040	59.416	8.187e-03	1.785e-03	+	2.659e-02	9.953e-02
Mishra 11 **f11**	0.01	0.290	0.031	0.008	0.003	0.003	0.002	0.002	0.002	7.960	24.758	8.327e-05	1.199e-05	+	1.369e-04	8.263e-06
Price 04 **f12**	1.5	0.193	0.040	1.412	0.312	0.153	0.285	0.073	0.081	0.000	0.000	6.418e-03	2.171e-03	+	6.715e-02	1.145e-01
Rosenbrock **f13**	15.0	0.159	0.041	15.155	3.972	2.026	3.408	0.654	0.686	0.000	0.000	7.559e-02	2.733e-02	-	5.737e-02	4.167e-02
Wavy **f14**	0.5	0.144	0.005	0.440	0.025	0.060	0.023	0.030	0.035	0.240	0.916	1.469e-03	9.148e-04	+	2.352e-02	6.471e-03
Weierstrass **f15**	5.0	0.382	0.127	4.096	0.860	1.003	0.740	1.774	1.764	93.860	140.130	4.605e-02	1.907e-02	+	6.636e-02	3.946e-02

like to mention that, as opposed to the asymmetric model, the quadratic polynomial approximation, while given with the (exact same) samples, is not constructed in an online mode, i.e. the algorithm works by considering the error of all samples in a single step (parameters obtained via singular value decomposition). In this listing, $\boldsymbol{r}$ is the confidence radius at which the response values, i.e. $y = f(x)$, are expected to approach $\boldsymbol{\epsilon}$; ***ierr*** and ***cnt*** stand for the absolute error, respectively number of points inside the confidence region with a value above $\boldsymbol{\epsilon}$. Root least squares error measures for the asymmetric and for the quadratic model are listed in the last five columns, ***err*** respectively ***q.err***. In addition, Figure 3 offers an equivalent graphical illustration of several asymmetric approximation models constructed at the global optimum of different benchmark functions, given 1000 samples. Note that the area depicted in the first column extends beyond the region we are concerned with; we nonetheless obtain an intuitive view of how the approxima-

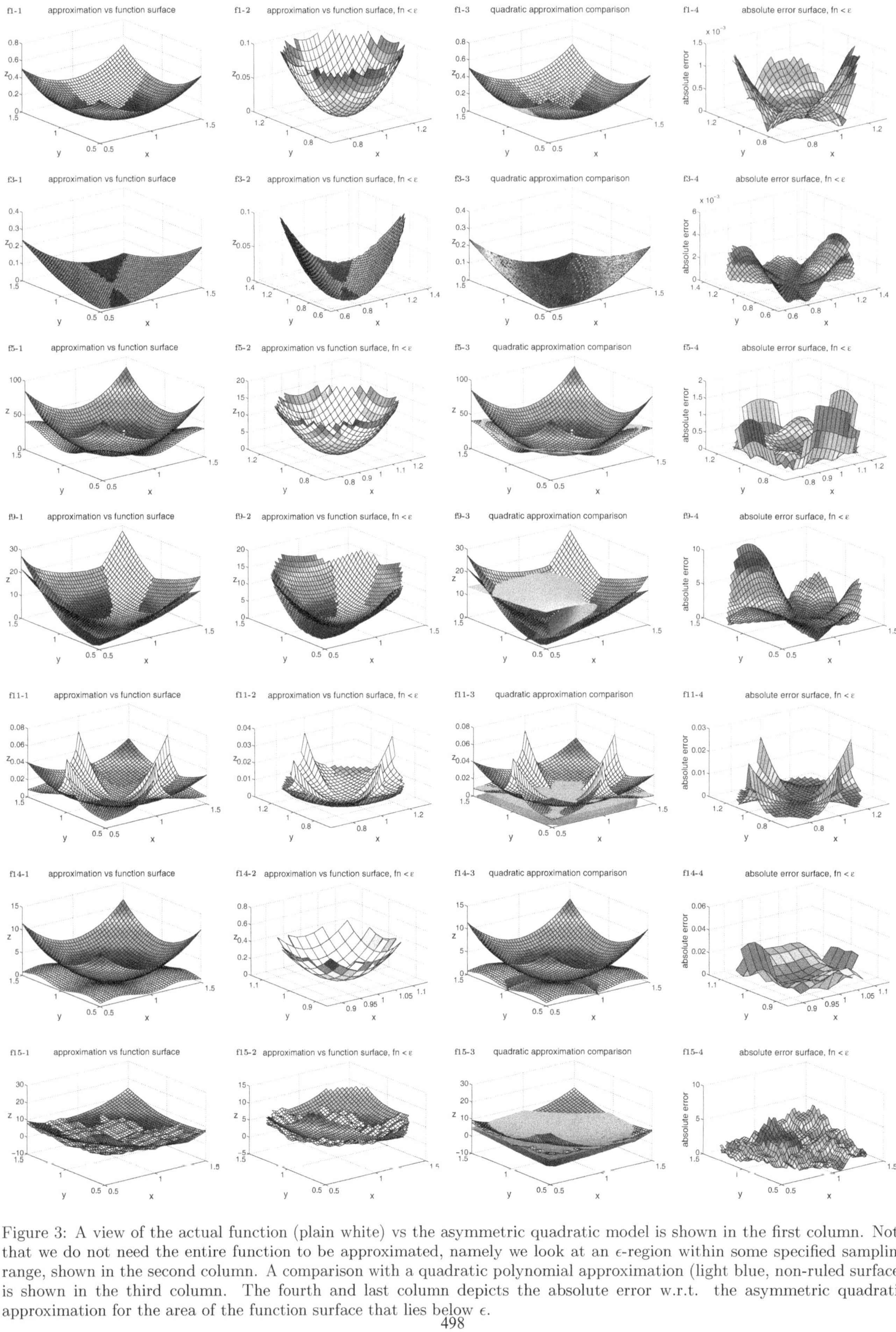

Figure 3: A view of the actual function (plain white) vs the asymmetric quadratic model is shown in the first column. Note that we do not need the entire function to be approximated, namely we look at an ϵ-region within some specified sampling range, shown in the second column. A comparison with a quadratic polynomial approximation (light blue, non-ruled surface) is shown in the third column. The fourth and last column depicts the absolute error w.r.t. the asymmetric quadratic approximation for the area of the function surface that lies below ϵ.

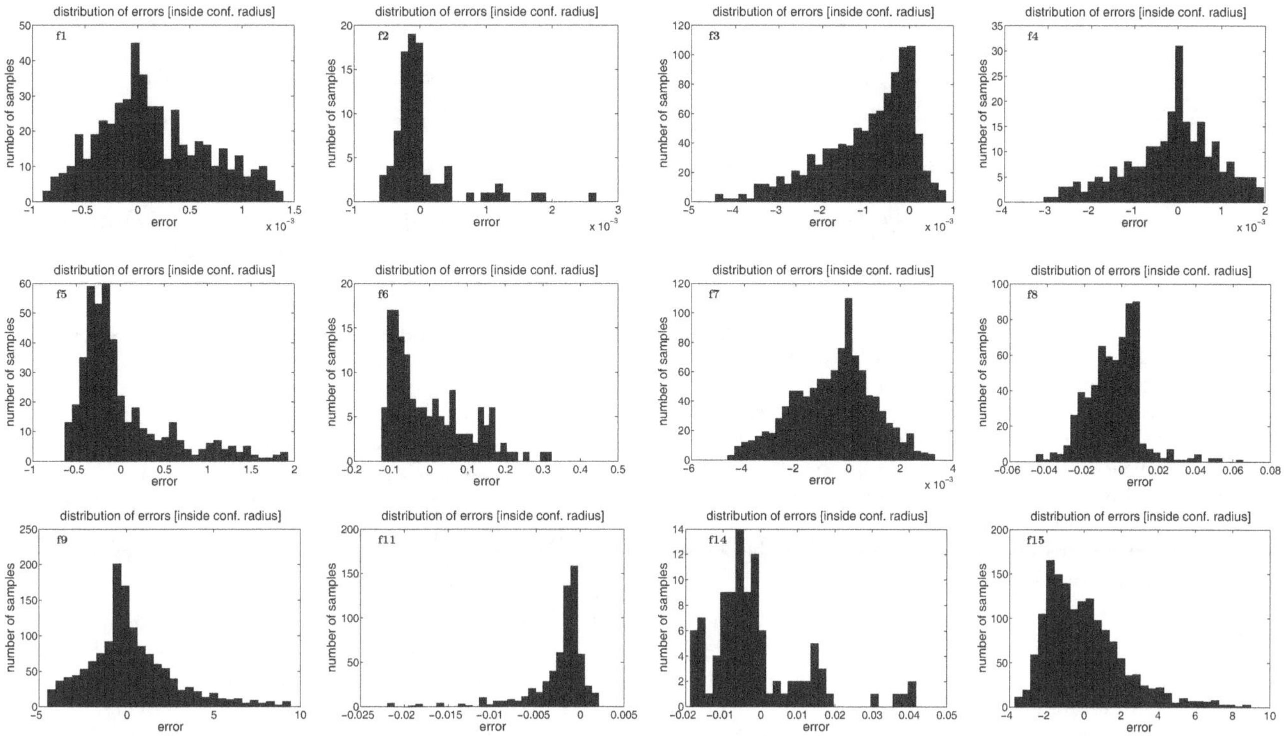

Figure 4: Approximation error histograms based on samples that are found inside the confidence radius.

tion model inserts into the convex local optimum region. Of more interest, the ϵ-region is shown in the second column. A comparative view of the function vs the asymmetric vs the polynomial model is offered in the third column (not always distinguishable given that results are, in some cases, extremely close; refer to Table 2 for a more meaningful comparison). The fourth and last column shows the absolute error surface of the asymmetric model when restricted to the ϵ-region alone. Error histograms based on samples from inside the confidence radius of each respective function are also available in Figure 4.

A particular attention should be paid to $\boldsymbol{\epsilon}$ and $\boldsymbol{\mu}_{\mathrm{y}}$ (average approximation surface value at $\boldsymbol{r}$); $\boldsymbol{\mu}_{\mathrm{y}}$ should yield values that are close to $\boldsymbol{\epsilon}$. Similarly, the value of $\boldsymbol{\mu}_{|\epsilon-y|}$ should be small when compared to the scale of the benchmark being used. A first, straightforward discussion can be made by looking at functions for which the confidence radius can be obtained analytically. De Jong's function is such an example. Knowing that we used an ϵ equal to 0.1, we have that the confidence radius is, in this case, $\boldsymbol{\epsilon}^{0.5} \approx 0.316$. For comparison, the result provided by the algorithm (average value) is of $\boldsymbol{\mu}_{\mathrm{r}} = 0.314$, with a variance $\boldsymbol{\sigma}_{\mathrm{r}} = 0.001$. For a real life scenario however, one is likely not to be able to calculate the confidence radius directly. A similar problem would appear if the function in itself is too complex or difficult to handle. Second, from a numerical point of view, the results in Table 2 indicate that the approximation errors are comparable for most of the benchmarks considered, with a bias for the quadratic polynomial model. As a specific remark, please mind that no meaningful normalization of the benchmarks can be made and, as such, it is not possible to directly compare the results obtained for one function as opposed to another. A Mann-Whitney U test (w column) w.r.t. the average least squares error of the models has been used to assess the extent at which the results of the asymmetric and polynomial models differ, using a significance α level of 0.01. A + sign is used to indicate that the asymmetric model ranked better when compared to the polynomial one; a - sign indicates that the model was outranked.

As an overall conclusion, the asymmetric model outperforms the polynomial one and best fits when irregularities or non-convex features need to be dealt with. Examples are the modified Mishra (**f11**), Wavy (**f14**) or Weierstrass (**f15**) function. Also, it compares well against benchmarks such as De Jong's (**f1**), the Hyper-Ellipsoid (**f4**), or the Rosenbrock (**f13**) function. The histograms in Figure 4 also show that large deviations, i.e. in terms of scale as opposed to a specific benchmark, are less likely to be seen. Furthermore, some remarks have to be made. First, as the asymmetric model is not given with all samples at once, errors are introduced due to having only partial information. Second, and most important, the quadratic polynomial model fails when the local landscape of the optimum does not shape into a convex form. A clear example can be found in Figure 3 for **f11** and **f15** (double surface approximation). From a numerical point of view, the error of the quadratic polynomial model is reasonably low in these cases though the parameters lead to a hyperboloid approximation. Furthermore, the low radius and confidence radius response value variance ($\boldsymbol{\sigma}_r$, respectively $\boldsymbol{\sigma}_y$, w.r.t. the scale of each respective function) show that the algorithm is stable.

5. CONCLUSIONS

The results obtained for the different benchmarks used in this paper show that the asymmetric quadratic approximation model, with respect to confidence radius and response surface approximation, is stable. Furthermore, when used in conjunction with the ϵ-archiving technique presented in Section 3, one is provided with a powerful tool that can be transparently used from within any sampling algorithm.

Future directions include a study where functions are categorized in order to understand better the strength of the asymmetric model. With respect to the scope of this study we preferred to look at some of the benchmark functions most used in the literature. Also, while not explored in this article, the eigenvectors and corresponding scaling information deserve a more attentive look. Another interesting aspect concerns the additional error control (or descriptive strength) that can be obtained by using different interpolation polynomials. While the linear interpolation sufficed with respect to this proof of concept, one can still notice non-smooth transitions along the main axes of the approximation surface. A further possible improvement may thus come from investigating how interpolation polynomials can be used (i) in order to reduce errors, (ii) construct a smoother transition, or (iii) address specific cases where the landscape is known to fall within a given class.

Remarks

A full listing of the code and an additional document detailing the results obtained for each function can be found online at http://www.exscientia.org.

Acknowledgements

This study is supported by the National Research Fund (Fonds National de la Recherche, FNR), Luxembourg, and the Centre National de la Recherche Scientifique (CNRS), France, in the framework of the Multi-Objective Metaheuristics for Energy-Aware Scheduling in Cloud Computing Systems INTER/CNRS/11/03 Green@Cloud project. The main expected outcome of this project is to construct an energy-aware scheduling framework, able to reduce the energy needed for high-performance computing and networking operations, namely for large-scale distributed systems.

Fonds National de la Recherche Luxembourg

National Research Fund, Luxembourg, http://www.fnr.lu.

6. REFERENCES

[1] D. Biermann, K. Weinert, and T. Wagner. Model-based optimization revisited: Towards real-world processes. In *Evolutionary Computation, 2008. CEC 2008. (IEEE World Congress on Computational Intelligence). IEEE Congress on*, pages 2975–2982, June 2008.

[2] N. Hansen and S. Kern. Evaluating the CMA evolution strategy on multimodal test functions. In *Proceedings of Parallel Problem Solving From Nature (PPSN VIII)*, pages 282–291, 2004.

[3] M. Jamil and X.-S. Yang. A literature survey of benchmark functions for global optimization problems. *CoRR*, abs/1308.4008, 2013.

[4] S. A. Kauffman. *The Origins of Order: Self-Organization and Selection in Evolution.* Oxford University Press, USA, 1 edition, June 1993.

[5] J. D. Knowles and D. Corne. Approximating the nondominated front using the pareto archived evolution strategy. *Evolutionary Computation*, 8(2):149–172, 2000.

[6] D. C. Liu and J. Nocedal. On the limited memory bfgs method for large scale optimization. *Math. Program.*, 45(3):503–528, Dec. 1989.

[7] R. Marcia, J. Mitchell, and J. Rosen. Iterative convex quadratic approximation for global optimization in protein docking. *Computational Optimization and Applications*, 32(3):285–297, 2005.

[8] J. Nocedal. Updating quasi-newton matrices with limited storage. *Mathematics of Computation*, 35(151):773–782, 1980.

[9] J. Sacks, W. J. Welch, T. J. Mitchell, and H. P. Wynn. Design and analysis of computer experiments. *Statistical Science*, 4(4):409–423, 11 1989.

[10] O. Schütze, C. A. C. Coello, E. Tantar, and E.-G. Talbi. Computing a finite size representation of the set of approximate solutions of an MOP. *CoRR*, abs/0804.0581, 2008.

[11] G. B. Sorkin. Efficient simulated annealing on fractal energy landscapes. *Algorithmica*, 6(3):367–418, 1991.

[12] P. F. Stadler. Towards a theory of landscapes. In R. López-Peña, H. Waelbroeck, R. Capovilla, R. García-Pelayo, and F. Zertuche, editors, *Complex Systems and Binary Networks*, volume 461-461 of *Lecture Notes in Physics*, pages 78–163. Springer Berlin Heidelberg, 1995.

[13] K. Táng, X. Lǐ, P. N. Suganthan, Z. Yáng, and T. Weise. Benchmark functions for the CEC'2010 special session and competition on large-scale global optimization. Technical report, University of Science and Technology of China (USTC), School of Computer Science and Technology, Nature Inspired Computation and Applications Laboratory (NICAL): Héféi, Ānhuī, China, Jan. 8, 2010.

[14] M. Tomassini and F. Daolio. A complex-networks view of hard combinatorial search spaces. In E. Tantar, A.-A. Tantar, P. Bouvry, P. Del Moral, P. Legrand, C. A. Coello Coello, and O. Schütze, editors, *EVOLVE – A Bridge between Probability, Set Oriented Numerics and Evolutionary Computation*, volume 447 of *Studies in Computational Intelligence*, pages 223–245. Springer Berlin Heidelberg, 2013.

[15] E. D. Weinberger and P. F. Stadler. Why some fitness landscapes are fractal. *Journal of Theoretical Biology*, 163(2):255–275, July 1993.

[16] S. Wright. The roles of mutation, inbreeding, crossbreeding and selection in evolution. *Proc.Int.Cong.Gen.*, 1:356–366, 1932.

[17] I. Zelinka, O. Zmeskal, and P. Saloun. Fractal analysis of fitness landscapes. In H. Richter and A. Engelbrecht, editors, *Recent Advances in the Theory and Application of Fitness Landscapes*, volume 6 of *Emergence, Complexity and Computation*, pages 427–456. Springer Berlin Heidelberg, 2014.

Generalized Asymmetric Partition Crossover (GAPX) for the Asymmetric TSP

Renato Tinós
Department of Computing and Mathematics
University of São Paulo
Ribeirão Preto, SP, Brazil
rtinos@ffclrp.usp.br

Darrell Whitley
Department of Computer Science
Colorado State University
Fort Collins, CO, USA
whitley@cs.colostate.edu

Gabriela Ochoa
Department of Computing Science and Mathematics
University of Stirling
Stirling, FK9 4LA, Scotland
gabriela.ochoa@cs.stir.ac.uk

ABSTRACT

The Generalized Partition Crossover (GPX) constructs new solutions for the Traveling Salesman Problem (TSP) by finding recombining partitions with one entry and one exit in the graph composed by the union of two parent solutions. If there are k recombining partitions in the union graph, $2^k - 2$ solutions are simultaneously exploited by GPX. Generalized Asymmetric Partition Crossover (GAPX) is introduced; it finds more recombining partitions and can also find partitions for the asymmetric TSP. GAPX does this by locating partitions that cut vertices of degree 4 in the union graph and by finding partitions with multiple entry and exit points, both in $O(n)$ time. GAPX can improve the quality of solutions generated by the Lin-Kernighan-Helsgaun heuristic and improve the state of the art for the asymmetric TSP.

Categories and Subject Descriptors

I.2.8 [**Artificial Intelligence**]: [Problem Solving, Control Methods, and Search]

Keywords

Asymmetric Traveling Salesman Problem, Recombination Operator, Evolutionary Combinatorial Optimization

1. INTRODUCTION

An instance of the Traveling Salesman Problem (TSP) can be defined by a complete weighted graph $G(V, E)$, where $V = \{v_1, v_2, \dots, v_n\}$ is a set of n vertices (or cities) and E contains edges between every pair of vertices in V. Each edge $e_{i,j} \in E$ between vertices $v_i, v_j \in V$ is associated with a weight $w_{i,j} \in \mathbb{R}^+$, generally indicating the distance or travel cost between the two cities. All candidate solutions for a TSP are Hamiltonian circuits in G, and thus each solution $x \in X$ is typically represented as permutations over the set of vertices in graph G. Considering the vertex v_{x_1} as the fixed start and end point, then the evaluation of a particular solution $\mathbf{x} = [x_1, x_2, \dots, x_n]^{\mathrm{T}} \in X$, specifying a permutation on $n - 1$ vertices, is given by:

$$f(\mathbf{x}) = w_{x_n,x_1} + \sum_{i=1}^{n-1} w_{x_i,x_{i+1}} \qquad (1)$$

The objective of the optimization process is to find $\mathbf{x} \in X$ with the minimum evaluation $f(\mathbf{x})$. The TSP can be symmetric or asymmetric. For example, the *distance* between two cities is typically a symmetric cost; however, the travel time from city A to city B might be different from the travel time from city B to city A depending on traffic patterns or time of day.

An amazing number of optimization algorithms have been proposed for the TSP. One of the best heuristics is the Lin-Kernighan-Helsgaun (LKH) algorithm [5]. The core of LKH is a variable depth local search (LK heuristic). In LKH, a number of improvements have been added to the original LK heuristic, like the use of sensitive analysis to estimate the probability of an edge appearing in an optimal solution. LKH is also a form of iterated local search which uses soft restarts. In addition, LKH includes a recombination operator, called Iterative Partial Transcription (IPT) [7], which is similar in effect to the Generalized Partition Crossover (GPX) operator independently developed by Whitley et al. [13] [12]. Both GPX and IPT are 1) respectful and 2) transmits genes. Respectful operators transfer all common features (edges) found in both parents to the offspring. Operators that "transmit genes" generate offspring that are composed only of features (edges) contained in the parent solutions. GPX has $O(n)$ complexity while IPT as described has $O(n^2)$ complexity.

Hains et al. [4] improved multi-trail LKH by using GPX. However, due to the similarity of Helsgaun's IPT recombination operator and GPX, the improvement was not a result of using GPX, rather the improvement was a result of using respectful recombination more frequently. Hains et al. recombined each new locally optimal solution with *all* of the previously discovered local optima. LKH with IPT only recombined each new locally optimal solution with the current best so far solution. By accumulating *all* of the local optima encountered, Hains et al. incrementally constructed a population on the fly which could be exploited by recombination.

In this paper, we add three enhancements to GPX. First, GPX is adapted for use with the asymmetric TSP (ATSP). The new operator is called *GAPX: Generalized Asymmetric Partition Crossover*. This means that GAPX considers the direction in which the tour (solution) is moving along each

GECCO'14, July 12–16, 2014, Vancouver, BC, Canada.
Copyright 2014 ACM 978-1-4503-2662-9/14/07 ...$15.00.
http://dx.doi.org/10.1145/2576768.2598245.

edge during recombination. GAPX can still be applied to the symmetric TSP. Second, GAPX exploits cuts that break nodes of degree 4 of the union graph between two parent solutions as a site for crossover. IPT also exploits "cuts" at vertices of degree 4 during recombination. While IPT appears to have $O(n^2)$ complexity in the worst case, Helsgaun's implementation of IPT is often efficient because recombination can only occur at common edges, or at vertices of degree four. The third enhancement allows GAPX to identify partitions with multiple entries and exits, i.e., subgraphs with more that two points connecting the partition to the rest of the union graph. Both the original GPX operator and the IPT operator exploit only subgraphs with 1 entry and 1 exit. These three enhancements do not change the complexity of the original GPX; the cost of recombination is $O(n)$, where n is the number of cities in the TSP. GAPX can find more feasible recombinations than GPX or IPT, and thus, it can exploit a larger number of possible offspring.

In Section 3, GAPX is evaluated in two ways: first, as a recombination operator inside a Genetic Algorithm (GA) using local search based on 3-opt moves; second, as a recombination operator used to improve solutions generated by multi-trial LKH. The experimental results indicate that the GAPX can be employed to produce very competitive algorithms for the ATSP. This paper is concluded in Section 4 with a discussion of future work.

2. GAPX

Whitley et al. [13] presented the GPX operator for the symmetric TSP. Both GPX and GAPX recombine solutions by exchanging subpaths that contain edges not shared by the parents. The subpaths are identified by removing the common edges of the union graph $G_u = G_1 \cup G_2$, where $G_1 = (V, E_1)$ and $G_2 = (V, E_2)$ are the parent solutions, and connected components are found using Breadth First Search in the remaining graph. The solutions generated by partition crossover (PX, GPX or GAPX) are always Hamiltonian circuits [12]. If there are k connected components representing feasible partitions, then $2^k - 2$ offspring different from the parents can be generated by crossover [13]. As the evaluation of a Hamiltonian cycle length is the sum of the subpaths inside and outside the recombining partitions in the TSP, the best of the $2^k - 2$ offspring solutions is found by selecting the best partial solution for each subgraph partition. In practice, the GPX operator has been observed to exploit as much as 27 partitions, and the set of reachable offspring contained more than $2^{26} = 64$ million local optima. GPX, IPT, and GAPX all return the best of the 2^k offspring; GAPX is guaranteed to yield a larger value of k than GPX or IPT.

Previous work has also shown that if the parent solutions are local optima, the majority of the offspring are also local optima [12]. This is due to the fact that no feasible partition can be further improved by local search; if this is true for the parents, it must also be true for the offspring. The only local search move than can improve a solution after GAPX (or GPX) is one that moves multiple cities distributed across multiple partitions, and this type of improving move is rare.

Figure 1 illustrates two ideas: it illustrates how recombination exploits partitions of the graph G_u and it also illustrates how a graph can be divided at a vertex of degree 4. Let the red (dashed) lines represent parent one and blue (solid) lines represent parent two. First consider the middle graph. A partition exists which cuts only 2 common edges. This creates a single entry and exit from each subgraph. Given one entry and exit, a tour can be broken at these "cuts" and recombination will always yield new distinct and feasible offspring [12]. If there are multiple partitions that cut 2 common edges, this process can be repeated (i.e., iterated). The leftmost graph illustrates another idea: nodes of degree 4 can be "split". If vertex 6 in Figure 1 is broken into vertices 6 and 6', with a zero cost on the new edge, the graph can again be partitioned by cutting common edges. We will denote 6' as a *ghost* vertex. Ghost vertices are removed after recombination.

One possible challenge with creating *ghost* vertices is that every vertex of degree 4 can be split in two ways, because the ghost vertex might be inserted before or after the original vertex. Thus, if there are $O(n)$ vertices of degree 4, there are potentially $O(2^n)$ different graphs that might be generated by splitting vertices of degree 4. In practice, this problem is resolved by recognizing that the desired graph is obtained by doing the insertion consistently. All vertices of degree 4 are split by consistently inserting the ghost vertex immediately after the original vertex. In the ATSP this is sufficient to correctly split all of the vertices of degree 4 because all solutions are directional. In the symmetric TSP, each solution can be thought of as being bi-directional since the tour can be navigated in a clockwise or counter-clockwise fashion. Luckily, it does not matter which direction is chosen as long as the insertion of ghost vertices is done consistently after (or before) the original vertex.

We will refer to the direction of movement from one vertex to the next as the "flow" of the Hamiltonian circuit. The direction of "flow" is particularly important for the ATSP. This process is captured in the following procedure.

Procedure 1: *Create a ghost vertex in G_1 and G_2 for each vertex with degree 4 in G_u. Determine the direction of flow. Insert the ghost vertex immediately after the original vertex of degree 4 in both G_1 and G_2. The common edge between the original vertex and the ghost vertex is assigned weight 0.*

After *ghost* vertices are inserted, we ask which common edges partition the graph. If a partition yields a single entry and exit point, then recombination can occur and will yield a new Hamiltonian circuit. The properties of GPX are explained in more detail by Whitley et al. [12, 13]. Using GAPX to split vertices of degree 4 is illustrated in the following example (see Figure 1). The * symbol illustrates the (only) location where respectful recombination is feasible.

```
  Parent 1:   11 * 1 2 3 4 5 6 * 6' 7 8 9 10
  Parent 2:   11 * 1 3 2 5 4 6 * 6' 8 7 10 9
Offspring 1:  11 * 1 2 3 4 5 6 * 6' 8 7 10 9
Offspring 2:  11 * 1 3 2 5 4 6 * 6' 7 8 9 10
```

GAPX is illustrated on a more complex example in Figure 2. In this case, there are 3 partitions and thus there are $2^k - 2 = 8 - 2 = 6$ possible offspring. It is not necessary to generate all offspring; the best possible offspring is obtained by selecting the best subpaths inside each subgraph [12].

Splitting a vertex of degree 4 does not necessarily divide the graph into connected subgraphs. This can be seen by considering the vertices 10, 10', 13, 13', 15 and 15' in Figure 2. These nodes are also split but do not yield common edges that can be used to divide graph G_u.

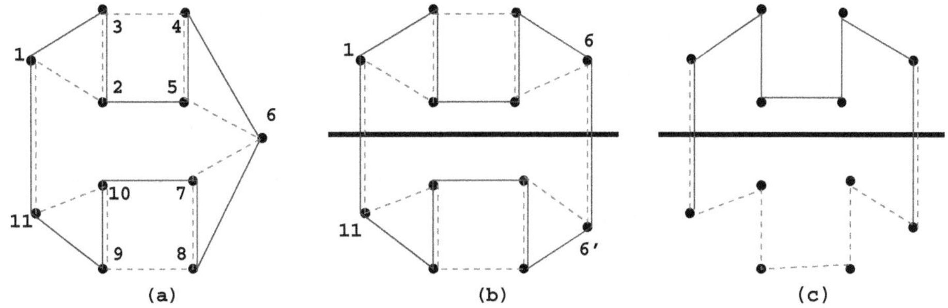

Figure 1: Recombination by breaking vertices of degree 4. a) The blue (solid) and red (dashed) solutions can be recombined by breaking the graph into two subgraphs, where each subgraph has only one entry and exit for both tours. b) Vertices of degree 4 (vertex 6 in this case) are split into two vertices (6 and 6'), with a dummy (zero cost) edge between them. The graph is then cut or "partitioned" using common edges. c) One of the offspring generated by recombination.

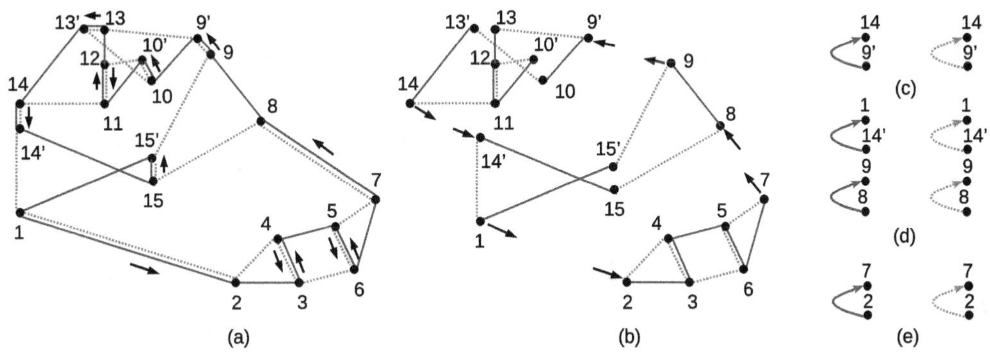

Figure 2: GAPX applied to an example with 15 vertices. a) Insertion of the ghost nodes after vertices with degree 4 with nodes 9', 10', 13', 14' and 15' being ghost nodes; b) After removing the common edges three connected components are identified; c), d), e) Because the simplified graphs are equal for both solutions, the three candidate partitions are feasible partitions for recombination.

2.1 GAPX for the ATSP

For the ATSP, GAPX considers an edge as a common edge only if the respective edges in both parents have the same flow direction, e.g., the union of edge (1,2) and (1,2) is a common edge, while the union of edge (1,2) and (2,1) is not a common edge. GAPX also recognizes more complex partitions that can have multiple entries and exits.

GAPX generates offspring in the following way. 1) Generate graph G_u by merging the parents, G_1 and G_2. 2) Split vertices of degree 4 by inserting ghost vertices after the original vertex; denote the new graph as G'_u. 3) Delete the common edges from G'_u and identify the connected subgraphs; copy the common edges to the offspring. 4) Determine if the connected subgraphs are *feasible partitions*. 5) Copy the edges from the shortest subpath for each *feasible partition*.

A *feasible partition* is one where both tours enter at the same entry points, both tours visit all of the vertices of the partition, and both tours exit at the same exit points. Both IPT and the original GPX use only partitions with a single entry and exit, with one exception: the "residual graph" can have multiple entry and exit points. For example, in Figure 2 there are two partitions with a single entry and exit. After the feasible partitions are processed, the *remainder* of the graph has multiple entries and exits. After feasible partitions are identified, the remainder of the graph is also considered a feasible partition for recombination.

GAPX can be applied to the symmetric TSP by arbitrarily selecting the direction of flow. Thus, the label of entry or exit is arbitrary (i.e. exchangable) but fixed.

2.2 Multiple Entries and Exits Partitions

The second major contribution of this paper is a procedure to identify feasible partitions with multiple entries and exists. After identifying the connected components in the graph obtained from removing the common edges of G'_u, the obtained partitions must be tested. Denote these as *candidate partitions.* The candidate partitions are connected components of G'_u after all of the common edges are deleted. All of the vertices in a candidate partition must be reachable by traversing single edges (not common edges). If a vertex has only one edge that connects to another vertex in the connected components, then it is a potential entry or exit.

If a partition subgraph is not a feasible partition for recombination, it cannot be used to generate a Hamiltonian cycle. To test if a candidate partition is a feasible partition, the following test is applied.

Procedure 2:

i) *For each candidate partition, create a simplified directed graph G_{in} for each Hamiltonian cycle (parent)* *containing only the entry and exit vertices found in each candidate partition. Replace the path inside the candidate partition between each entry and respective exit vertices by only one edge;*

ii *Verify if the simplified graphs inside the candidate partition are equal for both parents. If the simplified graphs are equal, the candidate partition is a feasible partition under recombination.*

The identification of the entry and exit vertices, as well the edges connecting them, can be done by visiting each vertex of G'_u following the paths given by G_1 and G_2. Therefore, all simplified graphs G_{in} can be constructed in $O(n)$ time.

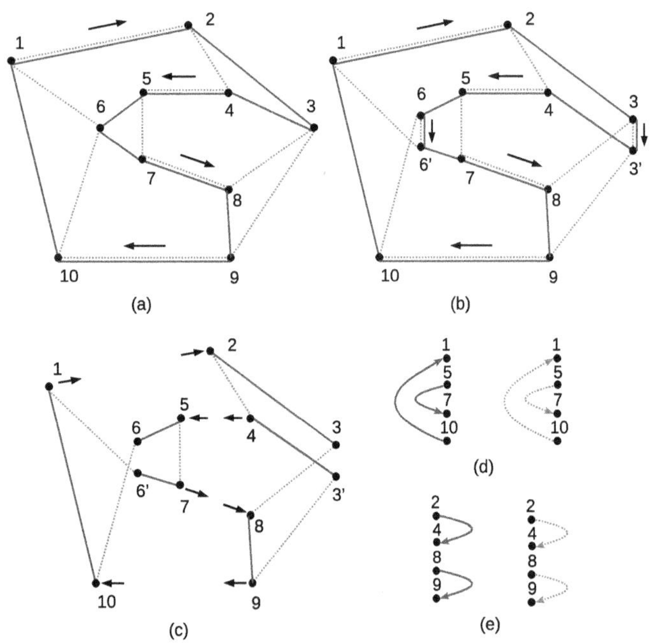

Figure 3: GAPX applied to an example with partitions with multiple entries and exits. a) Assume we know the direction of "flow"; b) Ghost vertices are inserted after vertices with degree 4 (Procedure 1); c) After removing the common edges, the two connected components are identified; d), e) Each candidate partition generates two simplified graphs, one for each solution. Because the simplified graphs are equal, the two candidate partitions are feasible partitions for recombination (Procedure 2). If the paths inside one partition are exchanged, the offspring must be Hamiltonian cycles.

Examples of the application of procedures 1 and 2 are given in figures 2 and 3. In Figure 2 GAPX identifies the 2 feasible cuts yielding 3 feasible partitions. In Figure 3, there are two entry points and two exit points and two feasible partitions. Note that vertices 1, 5, 7 and 10 are all connected vertices reachable by single edges; similarly, 2, 4, 8 and 9 are all connected vertices. Thus GAPX identifies a feasible cut that cross 4 instead of 2 common edges. The implementation of GAPX is described in Algorithm 1.

When compared to the original GPX, the following differences can be observed: i) Step 1 is not present; ii) The common edges are independent of the flow direction (Step 3); iii) The identification of recombining partitions (Step 5) is made by testing if the candidate partition has one entry and one exit.

Algorithm 1 GAPX

Step 1. Insert a ghost vertex immediately after each vertex with degree 4 in both Hamiltonian cycles. The common edge between the original vertex and the ghost vertex has weight 0 (Procedure 1). The graphs G_1 and G_2 (parents) with the added ghost vertices are respectively denoted G'_1 and G'_2.
Step 2. Create a union graph $G'_u = G'_1 \cup G'_2$.
Step 3. Remove all common edges (with same flow direction) of $G'_u = G'_1 \cup G'_2$.
Step 4. Use Breadth First Search to find the connected components of G_u to identify the candidate partitions for recombination.
Step 5. Determine if the candidate recombining partitions are feasible partitions for recombination. To test each candidate partition, create 2 simplified graphs, one for each parent. The simplified graphs should contain as vertices only the entry and exit vertices of the candidate partition. Inside the partition, replace the path between each entry and respective exit vertex by a single edge. Verify if the two simplified graphs are equal (Procedure 2). If the graphs are equal, the candidate partition is a feasible partition for recombination.
Step 6. Apply crossover by finding the shortest path inside each feasible partition.

2.3 Analysis

In this section, we present a theorem stating that recombination using GAPX results in offspring that are Hamiltonian circuits. Recall that GAPX cuts only common edges with same flow direction for both parents. For the symmetric TSP, the flow directions can be the same, or exactly the opposite. The following lemmas are about the identification of the cutting points for the candidate partitions.

LEMMA 2.1. *The direction of flow across a common (cut) edge separating feasible partitions is the same for both Hamiltonian cycles (parents) for the ATSP. In the case of the symmetric TSP, the direction of flow must be* consistent *across cuts.*

PROOF. Edges must be copied to the offspring in the same order that they appear in the parents. A cutting point that is an entry for the path given by one parent and an exit for the path given by the other parent would cause the inversion of the paths in the offspring for an ATSP. For the symmetric TSP, if all of the "cut" common edges consistently have reversed flow, the flow direction of one of the parents (which parent is arbitrary) can be reversed. □

LEMMA 2.2. *A entry or exit of a recombining partition in $G'_u = G'_1 \cup G'_2$, where G'_1 and G'_2 are created from graphs G_1 and G_2 using Procedure 1, can only be a common edge of G'_1 and G'_2.*

PROOF. Entry and exit points must connect all of the feasible partitions. The procedure that creates ghost vertices removed all vertices with degree 4 in the union graph. Thus, all cut points in the graph must cut both Hamiltonian cycles in the same place, and this only happens when common edges are cut. □

THEOREM 2.3. *The candidate partitions identified using Procedure 2 are feasible partitions for recombination. The result of recombination using these feasible partitions yield Hamiltonian circuits.*

PROOF. For the previous lemmas, one can observe that the entry and exit vertices of a candidate partition are entries or exits for both Hamiltonian cycles (parents). However, the order in which the entry/exit pairs are visited can be different for the paths given by each parent.

Let $G_{in}^{p1} = (V_s, E_{in}^{p1})$ and $G_{in}^{p2} = (V_s, E_{in}^{p2})$ denote the simplified graphs for the parents with edges representing the paths **inside** the partition, where V_s contains the entry/exit vertices of the partition and $E_{in}^{p_i}$ are edges representing the paths inside the partition for parent p_i. Let $G_{out}^{p1} = (V_s, E_{out}^{p1})$ and $G_{out}^{p2} = (V_s, E_{out}^{p2})$ denote the simplified graphs for the parents with the edges representing paths **outside** the partition, where $E_{out}^{p_i}$ are edges representing the paths outside the partition for parent p_i. Then the combined simplified graphs in the two offspring o_i are $G_s^{o1} = (V_s, E_{in}^{p1} \cup E_{out}^{p2})$ and $G_s^{o2} = (V_s, E_{in}^{p2} \cup E_{out}^{p1})$.

If $E_{in}^{p1} = E_{in}^{p2}$, then the combined graphs of the offspring are equal to the simplified combined graphs for the parents, i.e., $G_s^{p1} = G_{in}^{p1} \cup G_{out}^{p1}$ and $G_s^{p2} = G_{in}^{p2} \cup G_{out}^{p2}$. Since the simplified combined graphs for both parents are Hamiltonian cycles, the offspring generated in this way are also Hamiltonian cycles. One can observe that the same procedure cannot be adopted for testing if G_{out}^{p1} is equal to G_{out}^{p2} because these simplified graphs can be changed by other recombining partitions. □

THEOREM 2.4. *The time complexity of the GAPX operator is $O(n)$.*

PROOF. Procedure 1 generates vectors with size equal to the number of vertices of degree 4 (n_{v4}) plus the number of cities (n). As $n_{v4} < n$, the procedure is $O(n)$. The same complexity $O(n)$ is observed in steps 2, 3, 4, and in the procedure used to identify the entries and exits in the partitions. When Procedure 2 is applied to test the i-th candidate partition, two simplified graphs with size $n_{io}(i)$ are built, where $n_{io}(i)$ is the number of entries and exits in the i-th candidate partition. As the sum of $n_{io}(i)$ for all candidate partitions is equal or less than the number of nodes in the union graph, then the procedure is $O(n)$. □

2.3.1 Observations and Opportunities

Using GAPX, all feasible partitions for recombination in graph G_u must cut an even number of common edges. However, one can prove that not all partitions that cut an even number of common edges yields a feasible partition for recombination. In some cases there are connected subgraphs that do not yield feasible partitions and cannot be combined to yield feasible partitions. In other cases, two non-feasible partitions can be unioned to create a feasible partition; we ignore this in the current implementation because in the worse case these unions appears to require $O(n^2)$ time. This points to two lines of future research: 1) we have still not exploited all of the ways in which respectful and transmitting recombination can be used to find improved solutions and 2) we continue to explore how to identify more of these partitions in $O(n)$ time.

3. EXPERIMENTS

The GAPX can be applied as a recombination operator in different algorithms employed to generate improved solutions for the ATSP. This section demonstrates the ability of the GAPX to find superior solutions in two different approaches.

3.1 Genetic Algorithm with GAPX

We apply the GAPX as a recombining operator inside a Genetic Algorithm (GA) that uses local search based on the 3-opt moves (ls3opt).

In Algorithm 2, ls3opt is applied to random solutions in order to generate the initial population. Elitism is used to preserve the current best solution, while tournament selection (where two individuals are randomly chosen and the best is selected with probability 0.8) is used to select parents for crossover. If crossover did not improve the best solution, mutation is applied. In the mutation operator, the solution is transformed, with same probability, by: a 2-opt move, a double bridge move and ls3opt. While 3-opt and double bridge moves keep the order between cities, 2-opt moves allow the inversion of subpaths between two cities in the solution. In order to reduce the computational time of the local search procedure, the ls3opt employed here uses a limited number of neighbor vertices in the 3-opt moves, and "don't look bits" and "first found solution" strategies (we use the same procedure employed in [8]). In the GA, if the best solution is not improved in the last 20 generations, the neighborhood size employed by ls3opt is increased (starting with 10 cities until a limit of 150 cities or n if it is smaller than 150). Then, all solutions, with exception of the best solution, are replaced by random solutions optimized by ls3opt (immigration). The parameters employed here are: population size equal to 300 individuals, number of runs equal to 25, and execution until the optimal solution is found or until a maximum number of 1500 generations.

The GA with GAPX is here compared to 2 other approaches. All algorithms are exactly the same, except that they use different crossover operators. This means that differences in the results are due to the effectiveness of recombination. The only difference between GPX and GAPX is that GAPX finds more feasible partitions for recombination. The three crossover operators were the following:

i) Same-site-copy-first crossover (SSCFX) [11]. SSCFX was used in the evolutionary algorithm applied to the ATSP by [14]. This operator has similarities to several operators from the 1990s that emphasized the inheritance of location and relative position.

ii) GPX adapted to the ATSP. Only partitions with 2 cutting points are used, and vertices with degree 4 are not considered as possible cutting points. To be applied to the ATSP, the direction of flow of the common edges is considered when determining if a connected subgraph is a feasible partition for recombination.

iii) GAPX. The operator splits nodes of degree 4 and finds partitions with multiple entries and exits.

Table 1 presents the obtained results for the asymmetric instances of the TSPLIB [9] (the instances generated from ftv170 were not employed here). Note that all instances of the ATSP in the TSPLIB contain less than 500 cities. In order to allow the comparison to the results obtained by other algorithms (e.g., the results compiled in [8]), Table 1 presents the follow measures: *success*, that indicates the percentage of runs where the global optimum was found; *a-err*, that is the average percentage excess with respect to the global optimum evaluation; *a-T*, that is the average computation time for each run in seconds. The experiments were performed on a Core 2 Quad 2.83 GHz processor.

Algorithm 2 GA with GAPX

```
P=popInit();
while termination condition is not satisfied do
  Q(1)=bestSolution(P);
  for i=2 to maxpop do
    (p1,p2)=selection(P);
    Q(i)=crossover(p1,p2);
    if crossover did not improve the solutions then
      Q(i)=mutation(Q(i));
    end if
  end for
  if best solution did not improve in last 20 gen. then
    increase the neighborhood size used in ls3opt;
    Q=immigration();
  end if
  P=Q;
end while
```

Of the three operators, the GA with GAPX shows the best performance; it is the only operator that resulted in an optimal solution in every case. SSCFX is a disruptive operator that will often introduce new edges during recombination and there is little to ensure these edges are likely to be found in competitive solutions. While it was the poorest of the 3 operators, it did surprisingly well, solving 10 of the 24 test problems with 100 percent success. When we analyze the final evaluation produced by the GA using SSCFX, we found that the GA with SSCFX was sometimes trapped in local optima from which it was not able to escape.

Table 1 shows that GAPX produced better results than GPX adapted to the ATSP. We know the operators are doing basically the same thing; the only difference is that the new operator is able to find more feasible partitions for recombination. This means that GAPX is breaking the parent solutions into more and smaller subgraphs; both operators make greedy choices when selecting the best solutions from each subgraph. In the worst case, i.e., when GAPX cannot find any additional feasible partition for crossover, both operators generate the same offspring. In the best case, the new operator finds additional offspring that are *guaranteed* to be as good or better than the offspring produced by GPX; GAPX can generate all of the offspring found by GPX, plus more offspring not found by GPX.

When compared to the results of state-of-art evolutionary computation approaches compiled in [8], the GA with GAPX presents better performance for *a-err* (and *success*) than the GA in [2], the Memetic Algorithm (MA) in [1], and the MA in [14]. The GA with GAPX displays similar performance to the GA using the edge assembly crossover (EAX) of Nagata [8]. The GA with EAX had 100 percent success on 23 of 24 instances, while the GA with GAPX displayed 100 percent success on all instances. However, the runtime costs (labeled *a-T* in our Table 1) reported by Nagata et al. [8] were significantly lower.

The GA with EAX uses the concept of AB-cycles to copy the edges of the parents to the offspring and, in order to produce Hamiltonian cycles, introduces new edges not present in the parents. The results presented in [8] are generated by the consecutive application of the EAX crossover operator from a initial population of 300 individuals generated by ls3opt. It would appear that the lower runtime cost is due to the fact that ls3opt (which is costly) is not used by the GA with EAX after the population is initialized.

EAX and GAPX should be viewed as being complementary rather than competitive. EAX is more explorative, and generally exploration is costly. An application of the EAX operator is more expensive that applying GAPX. However EAX is less expensive that the ls3opt local search operations; the results of Nagata suggest that EAX could be used instead of ls3opt to provide the exploration that is needed. GAPX is more exploitative than EAX, because GAPX aggressively finds the best local optima reachable from the available set of solutions that are undergoing recombination. But GAPX can only utilize the edges that are available in the set of solutions that are undergoing recombination, it does not create or destroy new edges.

In the next section, we illustrate other ways in which GAPX can be used as a low cost exploitive operator.

3.2 Lin-Kernighan-Helsgaun (LKH) and LKH using GAPX

While not initially developed for the ATSP, the LKH algorithm is capable of yielding very impressive results for the ATSP. This is accomplished by transforming the ATSP into a symmetric TSP by doubling the size of the original problem. Both LKH and the *Concorde* Branch and Bound use this transformation. If city A appears in the symmetric TSP, then two cities A_1 and A_2 created from A will appear in the ATSP. A_1 can only be a destination and A_2 can only be a point of origination, and the cost of going from A_1 to A_2 is zero, while the cost of going from A_2 to A_1 is infinite (or prohibitively large).

LHK [5] is able to find the optimal solution for all asymmetric instances of the TSPLIB. As with the GA with EAX, LHK results in an optimal solution with lower frequency than the GA with GAPX (i.e., *a-err* and *success* are better for GAPX compared to LKH), but LKH displays lower runtime costs (as measured by *a-T*). The LKH results also appear to be superior to EAX: EAX solved 121 out of the 126 instances [8] presented in [10] in at least one of 100 runs, while LKH solved all 126 instances [6].

This section uses GAPX to improve solutions generated by the multi-trial LKH using the default parameters [6]. Hains et al. [4] describe two ways to do this for the symmetric TSP: i) generate solutions from LKH across runs representing multiple runs of LKH, or ii) generating solutions from LKH across restarts of the same run.

Applying GAPX "across runs" means that multiple runs of LKH are being used, and as local optima are found by the different runs, GAPX recombines the solutions to look for better solutions. When using GAPX across runs, the new solutions found by GAPX are not re-inserted into the search process. This means that GAPX runs as an isolated side process recombining the solutions found by LKH, but it does not influence LKH in any way.

LKH is a form of iterated local search that uses a "kick" operator to escape local optima. LKH already uses IPT before applying the kick operator. In the version of LKH we have investigated, IPT recombines the current local optimum with the previous best local optimum. Applying GAPX "across restarts" means that when LKH would normally apply IPT, we apply GAPX instead; also, instead of just recombining the current local optimum with the previous best local optimum, we save all of the previously discovered local optima and recombine the best solution so far with *all* of the other local optima.

Table 1: Results for the GA with: same-site-copy-first crossover (SSCFX) [11]; adapted GPX; GAPX.

Problem	SSCFX [11]			adapted GPX			GAPX		
	success	*a-err*	*a-T*	*success*	*a-err*	*a-T*	*success*	*a-err*	*a-T*
br17	100	0.000	0.02	100	0.000	0.03	100	0.000	0.03
ftv33	100	0.000	0.36	100	0.000	0.34	100	0.000	0.21
ftv35	88	0.016	24.55	92	0.011	23.00	100	0.000	0.75
ftv38	52	0.063	57.87	92	0.010	45.05	100	0.000	1.83
p43	100	0.000	16.31	100	0.000	16.05	100	0.000	7.02
ftv44	100	0.000	4.34	100	0.000	1.42	100	0.000	1.08
ftv47	76	0.081	76.32	100	0.000	28.67	100	0.000	2.45
ry48p	52	0.265	114.08	100	0.000	29.79	100	0.000	2.82
ft53	100	0.000	33.15	100	0.000	27.83	100	0.000	3.57
ftv55	100	0.000	21.06	100	0.000	11.70	100	0.000	1.10
ftv64	92	0.065	70.72	100	0.000	57.66	100	0.000	3.19
ft70	64	0.032	242.90	92	0.004	169.61	100	0.000	16.26
ftv70	72	0.068	249.84	64	0.074	313.30	100	0.000	10.98
kro124p	56	0.124	954.02	92	0.002	606.14	100	0.000	34.84
ftv170	44	0.501	4600.13	40	0.672	5270.10	100	0.000	1243.55
rbg323	100	0.000	32.05	100	0.000	39.13	100	0.000	31.68
rbg358	100	0.000	390.60	100	0.000	432.25	100	0.000	301.12
rbg403	100	0.000	74.23	100	0.000	80.05	100	0.000	78.85
rbg443	100	0.000	31.83	100	0.000	26.97	100	0.000	29.97

success: % of successful runs; *a-err*: average % excess; *a-T*: average computation time (in sec.).

In the experiments presented here, we used LKH applying GAPX "across runs." In this case, GAPX does not interfere in the LKH heuristic. Also, GAPX can be applied to the original ATSP without needing to transform it into the (twice as large) symmetric TSP.

We again use the controlled experiments similar to those used by Hains et al. [4]. The experiments were executed 25 times, each time with a different random seed for LKH. For each execution, LKH was run with 10 hard restarts, and each run was allowed 50 soft restarts; thus a total of 500 locally optimal solutions are generated for each execution. Assume the 10 hard restarts are being executed as 10 parallel runs. After the ith soft restart, we obtain 10 solutions from each parallel run. After the first restart, we add the best solution found so far by GAPX to this set. In this way, we do not lose the best solution found by GAPX until the last soft restart. This means there are 11 solutions at each soft restart. The best of the 11 solutions is selected, and it is recombined with the other 10 solutions. For each execution of LKH, this process is repeated 50 times, once for each soft restart. This means that the GAPX operator is applied 500 times for each execution of LKH. Thus, LKH will sample 500 locally optimal solutions, and GAPX will generate an additional 500 locally optimal solutions. By adding GAPX in this way, we can never do worse than multi-trial LKH, but GAPX can potentially find better solutions.

Table 2 shows results over 25 executions for the best solutions in 4 real ATSP instances with more than 800 cities [3] and for instances generated by inserting random Gaussian deviations (with standard deviation equal to $0.2w_{ij}$) to each weight w_{ji} in the symmetric TSPs generated from cities randomly distributed according to uniform distribution (E1k and E3k) or clusters of cities (C1k and C3k) [3]. Also, the statistical comparison using the non-parametric Wilcoxon signed-rank test with significance level 0.02 is presented.

GAPX presented better average results for 15 out of 16 instances, and improved the best solution found by LKH 12 times. In the multi-trial LKH, IPT is employed to recombine the solution found in the current trial to the best solution found in the run and to recombine the final best solutions between runs. Thus even after the application of IPT, GAPX was still able to recombine the solutions and generate improved solutions. It is important to observe that GAPX is dependent on the quality and diversity of the solutions produced in the different runs of LKH. When the diversity of the solutions produced in different runs of LKH is low, there is less diversity to exploit and GAPX generally produces fewer improvement. In the experiments shown in Table 2, the lowest diversity between the evaluations across the runs (in each execution) was produced for the instance td1000. For problems were LKH finds good solutions very fast, GAPX is not capable to improve the results because the diversity across the runs is low after a few trials of LKH.

4. CONCLUSIONS

In this paper, a new version of partition crossover is presented. The major contributions are mechanisms that allow GAPX to: i) consider vertices of degree 4 as potential cutting points for the feasible partitions for recombination; ii) exploiting feasible partitions with any even number of cutting points; iii) performing these operators in $O(n)$ time. The original GPX operator only recombined partitions with one entry and exit point, and only cut common edges. The IPT operator does recombination by exploiting vertices of degree 4, but the description of the operator results in $O(n^2)$ complexity. These properties result in a high probability of generating locally optimal solutions if the parents are local optima, which is very helpful in escaping from local optima. Also, our search strategies apply recombination much more frequently than does the LKH algorithm.

GAPX exploits and explores more solutions than GPX or IPT. Given k feasible partitions, $2^k - 2$ solutions different from the parent solutions are generated by any partition crossover operator. This is true for GPX, IPT and GAPX. Because GAPX finds more partitions, the number of solutions explored by GAPX increases exponentially.

Very competitive results were generated using the GAPX in the experiments performed here. The GAPX can be used in combination with other search methods. This was demonstrated by applying it in two different approaches: i) as a

Table 2: Results for LKH and LKH+GAPX. The last column shows the results of the statistical comparison (+ indicates better performance for LKH+GAPX and = indicates similar performance).

Problem	n	LKH		LKH+GAPX		Statistical Test
		mean+std	best	mean+std	best	
dc849	849	37570.8 ±10.5	37556	37569.7 ±10.7	37552	+
dc895	895	108247.0 ±53.2	108130	108217.2 ±59.1	108050	+
dc932	932	481413.6 ±115.7	481178	481340.9 ±119.0	481123	+
td1000	1001	1242210.6 ±108.2	1242183	1242210.6 ±108.2	1242183	=
C1k0a	1000	10114604.9 ±20532.7	10082973	10113136.2 ±20950.2	10080354	+
C1k1a	1000	10032272.4 ±12865.5	10018188	10031731.7 ±12922.4	10018188	+
C1k2a	1000	9475235.9 ±40639.6	9432171	9472372.2 ±41076.8	9427838	+
C3k0a	3162	17387429.6 ±27973.5	17337642	17386118.9 ±28121.6	17335639	+
C3k1a	3162	16977847.2 ±51494.6	16900660	16976991.4 ±51012.3	16900660	+
C3k2a	3162	17584664.4 ±60515.7	17459990	17584018.6 ±60703.9	17459508	+
E1k0a	1000	22107830.2 ±35056.4	22041858	22102500.2 ±34363.0	22041858	+
E1k1a	1000	21807800.6 ±34677.8	21760078	21803461.9 ±30111.9	21754715	+
E1k2a	1000	22002493.0 ±38596.9	21932612	21990489.1 ±40564.8	21924819	+
E3k0a	3162	39062713.8 ±66376.4	38945473	39030295.6 ±68831.6	38916452	+
E3k1a	3162	38859134.2 ±97705.1	38659539	38832147.1 ±98882.3	38647128	+
E3k2a	3162	38841077.8 ±65879.6	38705784	38803683.3 ±68168.7	38660737	+

recombination operator in a GA, it was able to find the global optimum in all runs for instances in TSPLIB; ii) as an external-improvement operator used to improve locally optimal solutions produced by multi-trial LKH, GAPX was able to improve solutions in 12 out of 16 instances with more than 800 cities.

GAPX can be used to improve the results of any iterative method that generates multiple local optima; it collects these local optima into a population and then recombines the best solution with the other solutions in the population. This can also be done online or offline.

We know that GAPX still does not exploit all possible partitions. We can prove that there exits non-feasible partitions that can be merged or "fused" into a feasible partition for recombination. In this worse case, this "fusion" could have $O(n^2)$ cost, but it is possible this complexity can be reduced by developing more efficient methods to recognize which non-feasible partitions should be fused and which non-feasible partition should not be fused. Finally, GAPX can be used for other types of TSPs, including dynamic TSPs and symmetric TSPs. Applying GAPX to the symmetric TSP is a natural future step of this work.

5. ACKNOWLEDGMENTS

Renato Tinós was a visiting researcher in the Department of Computer Science at CSU. The visit of the researcher was made possible by the support provided by FAPESP (under grant 2012/22200-9), USP, and CSU. This research was sponsored by the Air Force Office of Scientific Research, Air Force Materiel Command, USAF (under grant FA9550-11-1-0088). The U.S. Government is authorized to reproduce and distribute reprints for Governmental purposes notwithstanding any copyright notation thereon.

6. REFERENCES

[1] L. Buriol, P. M. França, and P. Moscato. A new memetic algorithm for the asymmetric TSP. *Journal of Heuristics*, 10(5):483–506, 2004.

[2] I.-C. Choi, S.-I. Kim, and H.-S. Kim. A genetic algorithm with a mixed region search for the asymmetric TSP. *Comp. & Op. Res.*, 30(5):773–786, 2003.

[3] J. Cirasella, D. S. Johnson, L. A. McGeoch, and W. Zhang. The asymmetric TSP: algorithms, instance generators, and tests. In *Alg. Eng. and Experimentation*, pages 32–59. Springer, 2001.

[4] D. Hains, D. Whitley, and A. Howe. Improving Lin-Kernighan-Helsgaun with crossover on clustered instances of the TSP. In *Proc. of PPSN XII*, pages 388–397. Springer, 2012.

[5] K. Helsgaun. An effective implementation of the Lin-Kernighan traveling salesman heuristic. *European Journal of Oper. Res.*, 126(1):106–130, 2000.

[6] K. Helsgaun. LKH results for Soler's ATSP instances. http://www.akira.ruc.dk/ keld/research/LKH/, April 2012.

[7] A. Möbius, B. Freisleben, P. Merz, and M. Schreiber. Combinatorial optimization by iterative partial transcription. *Phys. Rev. E*, 59(4):4667, 1999.

[8] Y. Nagata and D. Soler. A new genetic algorithm for the asymmetric TSP. *Expert Syst. with Applications*, 39(10):8947–8953, 2012.

[9] G. Reinelt. TSPLIB 95. http://www.iwr.uni-heidelberg.de/groups/comopt/software/TSPLIB95/, 1995.

[10] D. Soler, E. Martínez, and J. Micó. A transformation for the mixed general routing problem with turn penalties. *Journal of the Oper. Res. Soc.*, 59(4):540–547, 2007.

[11] H.-F. Wang and K.-Y. Wu. Hybrid genetic algorithm for optimization problems with permutation property. *Comp. & Op. Res.*, 31(14):2453–2471, 2004.

[12] D. Whitley, D. Hains, and A. Howe. Tunneling between optima: partition crossover for the TSP. In *Proc. of GECCO'09*, pages 915–922, 2009.

[13] D. Whitley, D. Hains, and A. Howe. A hybrid genetic algorithm for the TSP using generalized partition crossover. In *Proc. of PPSN XI*. Springer, 2010.

[14] L.-N. Xing, Y.-W. Chen, K.-W. Yang, F. Hou, X.-S. Shen, and H.-P. Cai. A hybrid approach combining an improved genetic algorithm and optimization strategies for the asymmetric TSP. *Eng. Applications of Art. Int.*, 21(8):1370–1380, 2008.

Revised Analysis of the (1+1) EA for the Minimum Spanning Tree Problem

Carsten Witt
DTU Compute
Technical University of Denmark
2800 Kgs. Lyngby
Denmark

ABSTRACT

We revisit the classical analysis of the (1+1) EA for the minimum spanning tree problem in the case that nothing is known about the weights of the underlying graph. Here the original upper bound on the expected running time by Neumann and Wegener [Theor. Comput. Sci. 378(1), 32–40, 2007], which depends on the largest weight of the graph, is of no use. The best upper bound available before in this case is due to Reichel and Skutella [FOGA 2009, 21–28] and is of order $O(m^3 \log n)$, where m is the number of edges and n the number of vertices. Using an adaptive drift analysis, we show the improved bound $O(m^2(\sqrt{c(G)} + \log n))$, where $c(G)$ is the circumference (length of the longest cycle) of the graph. This is only by an asymptotic factor of at most $\sqrt{n}/\log n$ away from the classical lower bound. Furthermore, an alternative fitness function leading to the bound $O(m^2 \log n)$ is proposed, and limitations of the adaptive drift analysis are pointed out.

Categories and Subject Descriptors

F.2 [**Theory of Computation**]: Analysis of Algorithms and Problem Complexity

General Terms

Theory, Algorithms

Keywords

Evolutionary Algorithms, Minimum Spanning Tree Problem, Runtime Analysis

1. INTRODUCTION

The running time analysis of randomized search heuristics, in particular evolutionary algorithms (EAs), on problems on combinatorial optimization has advanced considerably in the last decade [11]. This line of research gives theoretically founded insight into what choice of algorithms and parameters allows for efficient solution of a problem and what choice is inefficient. One conclusion is that even very simple EAs and local search algorithms find optimal or approximate solutions to several combinatorial optimization in expected polynomial time. This applies to both "easy" problems from the class P of polynomial-time solvable problems as well as (in terms of approximate solutions) to several NP-hard problems.

Recently developed analytical tools such as multiplicative and adaptive drift analysis [4] enable us to prove very exact running time statements for EAs on pseudo-boolean example functions such as OneMax and LeadingOnes [3] and even the whole class of linear functions [15]. Here even the exact constant in the leading term of the polynomial describing the running time is known. In contrast, results in combinatorial optimization are often of asymptotic nature, i. e., use O-notation, and are not necessarily tight, i. e., only upper and lower bounds on the running time are known, which may differ by large factors. In particular, there is a collection of analyses (e. g., [2, 10, 13]) leading to polynomial lower bounds, whereas the upper bounds are pseudo-polynomial in that they depend on a certain problem parameter such as the largest weight of a graph. While it is believed that the dependence on the largest weight is only an artefact of the analyses and there has been some progress on selected problems (outlined below), it is an outstanding problem to prove tight bounds. With the recently developed analytical toolbox, it is worth revisiting the combinatorial problems and studying whether we can obtain improved bounds.

In this paper, we focus on how a simple (1+1) EA and randomized local search (RLS) solve the well-known minimum spanning tree (MST) problem. This is one of the earliest (originally published at GECCO 2004) and very influential running time results of EAs in combinatorial optimization. Given an undirected, weighted and connected graph $G = (V, E, w)$, Neumann and Wegener [10] study a canonical fitness function returning the total edge weight of a search point, provided it encodes a tree. Otherwise the fitness functions contains penalty terms leading to trees. With respect to the (1+1) EA, they obtain an upper bound on the expected running time of $O(m^2(\log n + \log w_{\max}))$, where $n := |V|$, $m = |E|$, and $w_{\max}$ is the largest edge weight of the graph, and a lower bound of $\Omega(m^2 \log n)$. Hence, if nothing is known about the weights, upper and lower bounds can be arbitrarily far apart. This is in sharp contrast to the analysis of RLS, where Reichel and Skutella [13] could show the tight result $\Theta(m^2 \log n)$. Briefly speaking, a major diffi-

GECCO'14, July 12–16, Vancouver, BC, Canada.

ACM 978-1-4503-2662-9/14/07... $15.00.
http://dx.doi.org/10.1145/2576768.2598237.

culty is introduced to the analysis due to the ability of the (1+1) EA to exchange many edges in a step.

There is a single prior work by Reichel and Skutella [12] which aims at removing the dependence on $w_{\max}$ from the running time bound for the (1+1) EA on the MST problem. The idea is to replace the fitness function by another one having smaller weights but leading to the same acceptance behavior of the (1+1) EA. In this way, it is seen that $w_{\max}$ need not exceed $m^{m/2}$, hence $\log(w_{\max}) \le m \ln m$, which implies the general upper bound $O(m^3 \log n)$ on the expected running time. Note that there still is a gap of order m between upper and lower bound.

Our contribution narrows this gap to at most $\sqrt{n}/\log n$. More precisely, we show the upper bound $O(m^2(\log n + \sqrt{c(G)}))$, where $c(G)$ is the circumference (length of the longest cycle) of the underlying graph. Hence, if the graph has circumference up to $O(\log^2 n)$, the bound is asymptotically tight. The result is obtained by adaptive drift analysis along with a carefully chosen potential function. Moreover, the analysis reveals structural insights into the behavior of (1+1) EA on the problem, which allow us to define an alternative fitness function whose set of global optima still coincides with the MSTs of the graph. Somewhat surprisingly, the expected running time can be bounded by $O(m^2 \log n)$ in this case, which corresponds to the bound for RLS and the lower bound w. r. t. the classical fitness function.

This paper is structured as follows. In Section 2, we give formal definitions of the algorithms and problems studied. In Section 3, we describe the structural insights that lead to the alternative fitness function and that are fundamental for the forthcoming drift analysis. This analysis implies the new result w. r. t. the original fitness function and is presented in Section 4. Limitations of the technique, in particular why the factor $\sqrt{c(G)}$ could not be avoided, are discussed in Section 5. We finish with some conclusions.

2. PRELIMINARIES

We consider two classical randomized search heuristics called RLS and (1+1) EA, see Algorithms 1 and 2, which are intensively studied in the theory of randomized search heuristics [1,8]. The search space is $\{0,1\}^m$ since subsets of edges will be encoded by their characteristic vector. The (1+1) EA is a globally searching hillclimber, whereas RLS samples from a neighborhood of size 2. Steps changing two bits are crucial for the MST problem since all MSTs have the same number of edges. The running time (synonymously, optimization time) of the algorithms is defined as the random number of iterations until an optimal search point has been sampled.

Algorithm 1 (1+1) EA

```
t := 0.
Choose uniformly at random x_0 ∈ {0,1}^m.
repeat
   Create x' by flipping each bit in x_t independently with
   probability 1/m.
   x_{t+1} := x' if f(x') ≤ f(x_t), and x_{t+1} := x_t otherwise.
   t := t + 1.
until some stopping criterion is fulfilled.
```

Recall that we, throughout the paper, assume an arbitrary but fixed connected, undirected and weighted graph $G = (V, E, w)$, where $w\colon E \to \mathbb{N}$, for which an MST has to be found. We denote the edges by $e_1, \dots, e_m$ and their associated weights by $w_1, \dots, w_m$. Neumann and Wegener [10] propose the following fitness function. Let $x \in \{0,1\}^m$ be a search point describing a selection of edges, i. e., a subgraph of G, by identifying one-bits with selected edges. We define $c(x)$ to be the number of connected components (CCs) in this subgraph. If the current search point does not encode a spanning tree, the first aim of the function is to reduce the number of CCs to 1 and the second one is to arrive at a spanning subtree, i. e., a subgraph choosing exactly $n-1$ edges. These two aims are encoded in the fitness function by appropriate penalty terms. Afterwards, the most difficult phase of optimization begins. From the set of trees, one of smallest total weight has to be found by mutations swapping edges.

Algorithm 2 Randomized local search (RLS)

```
t := 0.
Choose uniformly at random x_0 ∈ {0,1}^m.
repeat
   Choose b ∈ {1,2} uniformly. Flip b bits in x_t chosen
   uniformly at random.
   x_{t+1} := x' if f(x') ≤ f(x_t), and x_{t+1} := x_t otherwise..
   t := t + 1.
until some stopping criterion is fulfilled.
```

Let $M \ge m w_{\max}$, where $w_{\max} := \max\{w_1, \dots, w_m\}$, be a number that is chosen so large that unconnected graphs always have worse fitness than connected ones and cyclic subgraphs worse fitness than trees. The fitness function is defined by

$$f(x) = M^2(c(x)-1) + M\left(\sum_{i=1}^{m} x_i - (n-1)\right) + \left(\sum_{i=1}^{m} w_i x_i\right).$$

Hence, if x encodes a tree, its weight is returned. Once a search point of the (1+1) EA or RLS describes a tree, the algorithm will never accept non-trees. It is not too difficult to show (similar to the OneMax problem) that the algorithms quickly arrive at trees.

Theorem 1 ([10]). *The expected time until RLS or (1+1) EA working on the fitness function f have constructed a (not necessarily minimal) spanning tree is $O(m \log n)$.*

Hence, in light of the overall bound $O(m^2(\log n + \sqrt{c(G)}))$ we want to prove, the time until a tree has been found is asymptotically negligible. In the remainder of the paper, we assume that (1+1) EA/RLS has already constructed a tree and analyze the progress towards MSTs. Assuming x to encode a tree, we denote by $w(x) := \sum_{i=1}^{m} w_i x_i$ its weight and define w_{opt} as the weight of an MST.

Finally, we list one important drift theorem used to capture this progress. It is taken from [4] except for the trivial adaptation to arbitrary positive $s_{\min}$-values, which can be found in [5].

Theorem 2 (Multiplicative Drift). *Let $S \subseteq \mathbb{R}$ be a finite set of positive numbers with minimum $s_{\min} > 0$. Let $\{X^{(t)}\}_{t \ge 0}$ be a sequence of random variables over $S \cup \{0\}$. Let T be the random first point in time $t \ge 0$ for which $X^{(t)} = 0$.*

Suppose that there exists a $\delta > 0$ *such that*

$$E(X^{(t)} - X^{(t+1)} \mid X^{(t)} = s) \geq \delta s$$

for all $s \in S$ *with* $\Pr(X^{(t)} = s) > 0$. *Then for all* $s_0 \in S$ *with* $\Pr(X^{(0)} = s_0) > 0$,

$$E(T \mid X^{(0)} = s_0) \leq \frac{\ln(s_0/s_{\min}) + 1}{\delta}.$$

Moreover, it holds that $\Pr(T > (\ln(s_0/s_{\min}) + r)/\delta)) \leq e^{-r}$ *for any* $r > 0$.

3. LOCAL SEARCH, STRUCTURAL PROPERTIES OF SPANNING TREES, AND ALTERNATIVE FITNESS FUNCTIONS

Once the (1+1) EA has created a search point describing a spanning tree, it is necessary for an improvement to flip some one-bits, corresponding to the removal of edges, and the same number of zero-bits, corresponding to the inclusion of edges; otherwise the resulting graph would not contain $n-1$ edges. RLS is dependent on steps flipping exactly two bits, and these yield a relative progress towards the optimum, as the following lemma describes.

LEMMA 3 ([10]). *Let* x *be a search point describing a non-minimum spanning tree. Then there exist some* $k \in \{1, \dots, n-1\}$ *and* k *accepted 2-bit flips such that the average weight decrease of these flips is at least* $(w(x) - w_{\text{opt}})/k$.

The multiplicative drift theorem (Theorem 2) can now be used to prove that the final phase of optimization, i. e., until RLS and (1+1) EA have converted an arbitrary tree to an MST, takes time $O(m^2(\log n + \log w_{\max}))$. The key arguments are that a two-bit flip has probability $\Omega(1/m^2)$, which accounts for the factor $O(m^2)$, and that $w(x) - w_{\text{opt}} \leq m w_{\max}$. Taking the logarithm, the last bound accounts for the factor $\log n + \log w_{\max}$. (Note that $\log m = O(\log n)$ since $m \leq n^2$.)

The proof of Lemma 3 goes back to the following structural result.

LEMMA 4 ([9]). *Let* T *be a minimum spanning tree and* S *be an arbitrary (possibly also minimal) spanning tree. Then there exists a bijection* $\Phi\colon T \setminus S \to S \setminus T$ *such that for every edge* $e \in T \setminus S$, $\Phi(e)$ *closes a cycle in* S *and* $w(e) \leq w(\Phi(e))$.

The previous two lemmas were also used in the prior work by Reichel and Skutella [12] that aims at removing the dependence on $w_{\max}$ from the running time bound for the (1+1) EA. As already mentioned, they replace the objective function by another one with bounded weights but leading to the same acceptance behavior of the algorithm. Since the acceptance behavior of RLS and (1+1) EA only depends on the ordering of fitness values of the search points considered for selection (they are so-called ranking-based algorithms), the following definition, inspired by [12], comes in handy. It also takes into account the maximum Hamming distance $H(x, x')$ of two search points compared in a selection step.

DEFINITION 5. *Let* $d \in \{1, \dots, n\}$. *Two pseudo-boolean functions* $f, g \in \{0,1\}^n \to \mathbb{R}$ *are called* neighborhood-d rank-equivalent, *for short* neighborhood-d equivalent, *if for all* x, x' *such that* $H(x, x') \leq d$, *it holds* $\operatorname{sgn}(f(x) - f(x')) = \operatorname{sgn}(g(x) - g(x'))$.

The formulation that for all x, x' we have $\operatorname{sgn}(f(x) - f(x')) = \operatorname{sgn}(g(x) - g(x'))$ is equivalent to that for all x, x' we have $f(x) \leq f(x')$ if and only if $g(x) \leq g(x')$. We prefer the first formulation since it immediately points out that equal function values are also preserved.

The observation made in the following lemma implies for RLS that $w_{\max}$ may be replaced by m on any MST problem. This result is proved in [13]. Roughly speaking, it is sufficient to replace every weight w_i of the linear weight function $w(x)$ by the rank of the i-th weight in the increasing sequence (with equals weights getting equal ranks). For the sake of completeness, we supply the simple arguments here.

LEMMA 6. *Let* $f(x) = f_m x_m + \dots + f_1 x_1$ *be a linear function and assume w. l. o. g. that* $f_m \geq \dots \geq f_1 > 0$. *Then* f *and the function* $r(x) = r_m x_m + \dots + r_1 x_1$, *where* $r_i := |\{f_1, \dots, f_i\}|$, *are neighborhood-2 equivalent.*

PROOF. Let $x \in \{0,1\}^n$ be arbitrary but fixed. Let x' be another search point satisfying $H(x, x') \leq 1$. Consider the function r from this lemma. If $H(x, x') = 1$, then $f(x') > f(x)$ if and only if $r(x') > r(x)$ since all weights are positive in both functions. Analogously the case $f(x') < f(x)$ and $r(x') < r(x)$ is treated. The case $f(x') = f(x)$ is not possible.

Suppose now $H(x, x') = 2$ and let $i > j$ be the two indices where the search points differ. If i and j are both 0-bits or 1-bits in x, we argue as before. Otherwise, $f(x') > f(x)$ if i is a 0-bit, j a 1-bit in x and $f_i > f_j$. By construction of the r_i, $r(x') > r(x)$ follows. Analogously, $f(x') < f(x)$ implies $r(x') < r(x)$. Finally, the case $f(x') = f(x)$ is equivalent to $f_i = f_j$. Then also $r_i = r_j$ and $r(x') = r(x)$ follows. □

The linear function $r(x)$ from Lemma 6 can be understood as a "surrogate function" on which RLS can be run instead of $w(x)$ when searching for MSTs, without changing its stochastic behavior. As a result, the $O(\log w_{\max} + \log n)$ factor from the running time bound is replaced by the logarithm of the largest r-value, i. e., $\log(r_1 + \dots + r_m) \leq \log((m^2 + m)/2)$, which is $O(\log m) = O(\log n)$. This completes the argument from [13] and proves that the running time of RLS, which only considers neighborhoods of size at most 2, is $O(m^2 \log n)$. Note that this matches the lower bound from [10].

The structure of the function $r(x)$ from Lemma 6 allows us further insights on the optimization process during the search for MSTs, which in the end will lead to the alternative fitness function for the (1+1) EA. We start with another definition.

DEFINITION 7. *Two linear functions* $f(x) = f_m x_m + \dots + f_1 x_1$ *and* $g(x) = g_m x_m + \dots + g_1 x_1$ *are called* weight-rank equivalent *if for all* $i, j \in \{1, \dots, n\}$ *it holds* $\operatorname{sgn}(f_i - f_j) = \operatorname{sgn}(g_i - g_j)$.

The function $r(x)$ from Lemma 6 is the unique weight-rank equivalent function to $w(x)$ which minimizes the maximal weight in natural numbers. Interestingly, the function $r(x)$ makes sense as a "surrogate" function also for the (1+1) EA on the MST problem even though it is not necessarily neighborhood-d equivalent to the actual fitness function for $d > 2$. In fact, every function that is weight-rank equivalent to the classical fitness function for the MST (assuming trees as search points) preserves the location of global optima, as the following lemma shows.

LEMMA 8. *Suppose $g(x) = g_m x_m + \cdots + g_1 x_1$ is weight-rank equivalent to the function $w(x) = w_m x_m + \cdots + w_1 x_1$ obtained from an MST instance. Let x_{opt} describe a minimum spanning tree with respect to the weight function w. Then for every $x \in \{0,1\}^m$ describing a spanning tree it holds $g(x) \geq g(x_{\mathrm{opt}}) =: g_{\mathrm{opt}}$. Moreover, $g(x) = g_{\mathrm{opt}}$ if and only if x describes an MST w. r. t. w.*

If x does not describe an MST, there exists some $k \in \{1, \ldots, n-1\}$ and k accepted 2-bit flips such that the average weight decrease of these flips is at least $(g(x) - g_{\mathrm{opt}})/k$.

PROOF. The analysis from Lemma 6 shows that two functions being weight rank-equivalent are also neighborhood-2 rank-equivalent. Hence, improving 2-bit flips with respect to w are improving 2-bit flips with respect to g and vice versa. Lemma 4 is in force with respect to the g-weights and thereby also Lemma 3. In particular, non-optimal trees (w. r. t. w) must have a larger g-value than minimum spanning trees (w. r. t. w).

All minimum spanning trees w. r. t. w have the same w-value and can be converted into each other by two-bit flips due to Lemma 4. Hence, they must all have the same g-value, too. □

Hence, if the search for minimum spanning trees takes place on the graph with weight function g instead of f, and additionally $g(x) \geq g(x_{\mathrm{opt}}) + 1$ is guaranteed for non-MSTs x (to maintain $s_{\min} = 1$ in Theorem 2), we can redo the analysis by Neumann and Wegener [10] to obtain the following result.

THEOREM 9. *Given an undirected weighted connected graph $G = (V, E, w)$, let the fitness function $g\colon \{0,1\}^m \to \mathbb{R}$ be defined by*

$$g(x) = M^2(c(x) - 1) + M\left(\sum_{i=1}^{m} x_i - (n-1)\right) + \sum_{i=1}^{m} x_i \cdot \mathit{rank}(w_i),$$

where $M := m^2$ and $\mathit{rank}(w_i)$ denotes the rank of weight w_i in the increasingly sorted sequence. The expected time until the (1+1) EA finds an optimum for $g(x)$ is bounded by $O(m^2 \log n)$, and every such optimum describes an MST in G.

The "surrogate" function g from the preceding theorem can be used instead of the classical function f and guarantees polynomial running time. However, it is based on non-trivial problem knowledge about the MST problem. In fact, the required structural results from Lemma 4 are shown using the ideas underlying the correctness proof of Kruskal's algorithm, which also considers the ranks of the edge weights only. See also the characterization of the set of MSTs by weight ranks in Section 6 of [14]. So with this level of problem knowledge, no evolutionary algorithm would have to be applied.

Otherwise, without knowing Kruskal's algorithm or related structural insights, one would probably have come up with the original fitness function f as defined in [10]. Therefore, it is still interesting to analyze whether the time to find an optimum for f (in case of large weights) is less than the $O(m^3 \log n)$ bound that was obtained by Reichel and Skutella [12]. This is dealt with in the next section.

4. IMPROVED UPPER BOUND FOR THE (1+1) EA

In this section, we show our improved upper bound on the running time of the (1+1) EA for the MST problem, using the classical fitness function f. In the following theorem, the circumference (length of the longest cycle) of an undirected graph is denoted by $c(G)$. If G is acyclic (in which case the MST problem is trivial anyway), we define $c(G) := 0$.

THEOREM 10. *Given an arbitrary MST instance, the running time of the (1+1) EA on the corresponding fitness function f is upper bounded by $O(m^2(\log n + \sqrt{c(G)}))$ both in expectation and with probability $1 - O(n^{-c})$ for any constant $c > 0$.*

To prove the theorem, we conduct an adaptive drift analysis, where the underlying potential function $h(x)$, to be minimized, depends on both the weight function w and the circumference $c(G)$. The exact definition of the potential function is inspired by the techniques developed in [15] and further applied in [6] and [7]. More precisely, we apply drift analysis using a potential function that will be defined below in accordance with the definition of weight-rank equivalence. However, this is not a straightforward application of the above-mentioned literature but includes non-trivial modifications in the potential function and the drift analysis due to the characteristics of the underlying MST problem.

Once having defined the potential function, the idea is to analyze the potential $X^{(t)} := h(x^{(t)})$ of the random search point $x^{(t)}$ maintained by the (1+1) EA on f at time t. We first bound its expected one-step change $E(X^{(t)} - X^{(t+1)} \mid X^{(t)})$, i. e., the expected decrease of distance from time t to time $t+1$. The following lemma states this bound as well as a bound on the maximum value of the potential function, which is required in the multiplicative drift theorem (Theorem 2).

LEMMA 11.

1. $E(X^{(t)} - X^{(t+1)} \mid X^{(t)}) \geq \frac{X^{(t)}}{2e^2 m^2}$.
2. $\ln(X^{(t)}/s_{\min}) \leq O(\log n) + \sqrt{2ec(G)}$.

Deferring the definition of h and the proof of the previous lemma, we obtain our theorem.

PROOF OF THEOREM 10. We will argue later that $h(x) = 0$ if x encodes an MST and $h(x) \geq s_{\min}$ for some $s_{\min} > 0$ otherwise. The expected running time now follows immediately by plugging the two statements of Lemma 11 into Theorem 2. The tail bound is obtained by setting $r = c \ln n$. □

In the following, we unroll the proofs of the drift statements. The proof of Lemma 11 relies on the analysis of the one-step drift of the potential function $h\colon \{0,1\}^m \to \mathbb{R}$. We now introduce the setup required to define $h(x)$. Without loss of generality, we assume $w_m \geq \cdots \geq w_1 > 0$ and write search points as $x_m \ldots x_1$, calling x_m the leftmost and x_1 the rightmost bit. To reduce the number of cases needed in the forthcoming drift analysis, we assume that for all $i, j \in [m] := \{1, \ldots, m\}$

$$i > j \quad \Rightarrow \quad w_i = w_j \vee w_i - w_j \geq W^*$$

for some W^* defined below. This holds without loss of generality since we can simply multiply all (integral) weights by W^* without changing the acceptance behavior of the (1+1) EA.

DEFINITION 12. *Let an undirected weighted graph G be given and let x^* denote an arbitrary but fixed MST. For $i \in [m]$, let*

$$\gamma_i := (1+\Phi)^{i-1},$$

where

$$\Phi := \frac{\sqrt{2ec(G)}}{m}$$

Based on this, let

$$g_i := \min\{\gamma_i, g_{i-1} + w_i - w_{i-1}\}$$

for all $1 < i \le m$, $g_1 := \gamma_1 := 1$ and $g(x) := \sum_{i=1}^m g_i x_i$. Finally, let the potential function $h\colon \{0,1\}^m \to \mathbb{R}$ be defined by

$$h(x) := g(x) - g(x^*).$$

For any $i \in [m]$, we also define:

- $\kappa(i) := \max\{j \le i \mid g_j = \gamma_j\}$, *the most significant index right of i (possibly i itself) capping according to the sequence γ_i,*
- $\eta(i) := \min\{j \ge i \mid g_j = \gamma_j\}$, *the least significant index left of i (possibly i itself) capping according to the sequence γ_i,*
- $L(i) := \{m, \dots, \kappa(i)\}$, *the indices left of $\kappa(i)$,*
- $R(i) := \{\kappa(i)-1, \dots, 1\}$, *the indices right of $\kappa(i)$.*

The idea of the potential function, reflected by the minimum operator in the definition of g_i, is to cap the original weights at γ_i in case they are "too steeply increasing" and to rebuild the slope of original weights otherwise by letting $g_i - g_{i-1} = w_i - w_{i-1}$. The variable $\kappa(i)$ is intuitively a "breaking point" and denotes the most significant index right of i where g_j equals γ_j. The intuition is that the potential function will underestimate the progress made at indices being at least as significant as i. In all less significant indices (those in $R(i)$), we will pessimistically assume that they contribute a loss, and the choice of $\kappa(i)$ guarantees that this loss is overestimated.

Clearly, $w(x)$ and $g(x)$ are weight-rank equivalent. Hence, by Lemma 8, the set of search points x where $h(x) = 0$ equals the set of MSTs with respect to w. We now list another useful property related to the $\kappa(i)$, which means that the g_i-weights are constant between two different κ-indices if W^* is chosen large enough (more details below). This will simplify the case analysis in the main proof.

LEMMA 13. *If $W^* \ge \gamma_m$ then for any $i \in [m]$: $g_i = \gamma_{\kappa(i)}$*

PROOF. Recall that for any $i \ge 2$ there only are the two cases $w_i - w_{i-1} = 0$ and $w_i - w_{i-1} \ge W^* \ge \gamma_m$. If $w_i - w_{i-1} \ge \gamma_m$ then $g_{i-1} + w_i - w_{i-1} \ge 1 + \gamma_m$, hence the minimum in the definition of g_i is obtained at γ_i, implying $i = \kappa(i)$. In the other case, since $\gamma_i > \gamma_{i-1} \ge g_{i-1}$, the minimum is taken at g_{i-1} and the claim follows (inductively decreasing i until it equals $\kappa(i)$). □

From now on, assume W^* to be sufficiently large for the previous lemma to hold. We obtain the following observation.

OBSERVATION 14. *Sort the set of all different κ-values decreasingly as $\kappa_\ell > \cdots > \kappa_1$. Then for $j \in \{2, \dots, \ell\}$ we have $g_{\kappa_j} > g_{\kappa_j - 1} = g_{\kappa_j - 2} = \cdots = g_{\kappa_{j-1}}$, i. e., there is a plateau of constant g-weights between two subsequent κ-indices and an increase in g-weight at the next κ-index.*

The following lemma allows us to set $s_{\min} = \Phi$ in the multiplicative drift theorem.

LEMMA 15. *For any $x \in \{0,1\}^m$, $h(x) = 0$ or $h(x) \ge \Phi$.*

PROOF. Since $g(x)$ and $w(x)$ are weight-rank equivalent, Lemma 8 is in force. The non-negativity now follows from the lemmma since $h(x) = g(x) - g(x^*)$ for an arbitrary MST x^* w.r.t. w. Moreover, if x is not optimal, $g(x)$ and thus $h(x)$ can be written as the sum of k positive differences of edges weights (resulting from the edge swaps). Each such difference is at least $\gamma_2 - \gamma_1 = \Phi$. □

As mentioned above, we will analyze the stochastic process $X_{t\ge0}^{(t)}$ where $X^{(t)} = h(x^{(t)})$ for all t, and define $\Delta_t := X^{(t)} - X^{(t+1)}$. Recall that we are interested in the first point in time t where $X^{(t)} = 0$ holds. The one-step drift $E(\Delta_t \mid X^{(t)})$ of the potential function will be worked out conditioned on certain events depending on two flipping bits. The following notions prepare the definition of these events.

DEFINITION 16. *Given $x^{(t)} \in \{0,1\}^n$, denote by x' the random search point created by mutation of $x^{(t)}$ (before selection). We define*

- $I := \{i \in [m] \mid x_i^{(t)} = 1\}$ *the one-bits in $x^{(t)}$,*
- $I^* := \{i \in I \mid x_i' = 0\}$ *the one-bits flipping to 0,*
- $Z := \{i \in [m] \mid x_i^{(t)} = 0\}$ *the zero-bits in $x^{(t)}$,*
- $Z^* := \{i \in Z \mid x_i' = 1\}$ *the zero-bits flipping to 1.*

Note that the random sets I^* and Z^* are disjoint and that the remaining bits in $[m]$ contribute nothing to the Δ_t-value.

Obviously, for $\Delta_t \ne 0$ it is necessary that $x^{(t+1)} \ne x^{(t)}$. We fix an arbitrary search point $x^{(t)}$ and let A be the event that $x^{(t+1)} \ne x^{(t)}$. The event A requires that

$$I^* \ne \emptyset \text{ and } \sum_{j\in I^*} w_j - \sum_{j \in Z^*} w_j \ge 0.$$

Hence, for A to occur it is necessary that for at least one $i \in I^*$

$$\sum_{j\in I^*} w_j - \sum_{j \in Z^* \cap L(i)} w_j \ge 0,$$

since we only ignore the loss due to the bits in $R(i)$. We decompose the event A according to two indices i and j, where i denotes the leftmost flipping one-bit and and j the leftmost flipping zero-bit right of $\eta(i)$.

DEFINITION 17. *The event $A_{i,j}$, where $i, j \in [m]$, occurs iff the following five conditions hold simultaneously.*

1. $I^* \ne \emptyset$ *and* $Z^* \ne \emptyset$.
2. $i = \max I^*$.
3. $j = \max(Z^* \cap \{1, \dots, \eta(i) - 1\})$.
4. $\sum_{k \in I^*} w_k - \sum_{k \in Z^* \cap L(i)} w_k \ge 0$.
5. *A spanning tree is obtained by flipping the bits from $I^* \cup Z^*$ in $x^{(t)}$.*

Obviously, all events $A_{i,j}$ are disjoint. Note that each accepted mutation must flip as many zero-bits as one-bits to maintain spanning trees. In particular, each accepted mutation flips at least one pair of bits (i, j), where i is a one-bit, j a zero-bit and j weighs at most as much as i. If bit j weights strictly less, then j is right of i. Otherwise, j must be of same weight of i and hence in $\eta(i) - 1, \ldots, \kappa(i)$. Hence, the disjoint union of the events $A_{i,j}$ is a superset of A (in other words, is necessary for A). The key inequality used to bound the one-step drift is stated in the following lemma.

LEMMA 18. *$E(\Delta_t \mid A_{i,j}) \geq \frac{g_i - g_j}{2e}$ for all $i, j \in [m]$ such that $\Pr(A_{i,j}) > 0$ and all $t \geq 0$.*

Before we prove Lemma 18, let us show how it can be used to prove Lemma 11.

PROOF OF LEMMA 11. We still fix an arbitrary search point $x^{(t)}$, denote by $X^{(t)} = h(x^{(t)})$ its potential and investigate the following step. As observed above, in the step the potential remains either unchanged or a certain event $A_{i,j}$ occurs. The total drift can then be expressed as

$$E(X^{(t)} - X^{(t+1)} \mid X^{(t)}) = \sum_{i \in I, j \in Z \cap \{1, \ldots, \eta(i)-1\}, \Pr(A_{i,j}>0)} E(\Delta_t \mid A_{i,j}) \cdot \Pr(A_{i,j}).$$

Using Lemma 18, the last expression is at least

$$\sum_{i \in I, j \in Z \cap \{1, \ldots, \eta(i)-1\}, \Pr(A_{i,j})>0} \frac{g_i - g_j}{2e} \Pr(A_{i,j}).$$

Note that $\Pr(A_{i,j}) \geq (1/m^2)(1 - 1/m)^{m-2} \geq 1/(em^2)$ if $A_{i,j}$ is possible since it is sufficient to flip bits i and j and not to flip the rest to accept the mutation. Note also that $g_i - g_j \geq 0$ since $j \leq \eta(i) - 1$, so that we may omit terms from the sum to obtain a lower bound.

For every accepted two-bit flip there is an event $A_{i,j}$ corresponding to the two flipping bits. By Lemma 8, there are k accepted two-bit flips $(i_1, j_1), \ldots, (i_k, j_k)$, where $j_r \leq \eta(i_r) - 1$ for $r \in [k]$. Consequently,

$$\begin{aligned} E(X^{(t)} - X^{(t+1)} \mid X^{(t)}) &\geq \sum_{r=1}^{k} (g_{i_r} - g_{j_r}) \Pr(A_{i_r, j_r}) \\ &\geq \sum_{r=1}^{k} \frac{(g_{i_r} - g_{j_r})}{2e} \frac{1}{em^2} \\ &= \frac{g(X^{(t)}) - g(x^*)}{2e^2 m^2}, \end{aligned}$$

where the equality holds since the i_r denote the one-bits in $X^{(t)} \setminus x^*$ and the j_r the one-bits in $x^* \setminus X^{(t)}$. Hence, we get

$$E(X^{(t)} - X^{(t+1)} \mid X^{(t)}) \geq \frac{h(X^{(t)})}{2e^2 m^2},$$

which proves the first statement of Lemma 11.

For the second statement of Lemma 11, we use that for every t it holds $X^{(t)} \leq \sum_{i=1}^{m} \gamma_i$. Using the geometric series and the inequality $1 + x \leq e^x$, the latter is at most

$$\frac{\left(1 + \frac{\sqrt{2ec(G)}}{m}\right)^m}{\frac{\sqrt{2ec(G)}}{m}} \leq \frac{m e^{m\sqrt{2ec(G)}/m}}{\sqrt{2ec(G)}} \leq m e^{\sqrt{2ec(G)}}.$$

From this we obtain

$$\ln(X^{(0)}) \leq \sqrt{2ec(G)} + \ln m.$$

Finally, $\ln(s_{\min}) = \ln(\Phi) \geq \ln(1/m)$, which altogether proves $\ln(X^{(0)}/\ln(s_{\min})) \leq \sqrt{2ec(G)} + O(\log n)$. □

The still outstanding proof of Lemma 18 requires a careful analysis of the one-step drift, taking into account the specific structure of the drift function.

PROOF OF LEMMA 18. Recall that we want to condition on the event $A_{i,j}$ (Definition 17), where i is the leftmost flipping one-bit and j a flipping zero-bit right of $\eta(i)$. Moreover, recall the notions introduced in Definitions 12 and 16. Let

$$\Delta_L(i) := \left(\sum_{k \in I^*} g_k - \sum_{\ell \in Z^* \cap L(i)} g_\ell\right) \cdot \mathbb{1}_A,$$

$$\Delta_R(i) := \left(\sum_{k \in Z^* \cap R(i)} g_k\right) \cdot \mathbb{1}_A,$$

where $\mathbb{1}_A$ denotes the indicator random variable of event A. Recall that $\Delta_t = 0$ if A does not occur. Otherwise, $\Delta_t = \sum_{k \in I^*} g_k - \sum_{\ell \in Z^*} g_\ell$. Hence, we have $\Delta_t = (\Delta_L(i) - \Delta_R(i))$ regardless of i. By linearity of expectation, we obtain

$$E(\Delta_t \mid A_{i,j}) = E(\Delta_L(i) \mid A_{i,j}) - E(\Delta_R(i) \mid A_{i,j}). \quad (1)$$

We first show that $(\Delta_L(i) \mid A_{i,j})$ is a nonnegative random variable, i. e., the probability of any negative outcome is 0. To prove this, assume that $A_{i,j}$ holds, which implies that no bit left of i flips to 0. We inspect the two sums from the definition of $\Delta_L(i)$. Since only spanning trees are accepted, any accepted mutation changes as many zero- as one-bits. Hence, it must hold that $|I^*| \geq |Z^* \cap L(i)|$. Pessimistically (with the aim of proving a lower bound on $\Delta_L(i)$), we assume that equality holds for the size of the two sets. Then there are r pairs $(k_1, \ell_1), \ldots, (k_r, \ell_r)$, where $k_s \in I^*$ and $\ell_s \in Z^* \cap L(i)$, such that

$$(\Delta_L(i) \mid A_{i,j}) = \left(\sum_{s=1}^{r} g_{k_s} - g_{\ell_s}\right) \cdot \mathbb{1}_A.$$

Note that for any s we have $\ell_s \geq \kappa(i)$ and $k_s \leq i$ since i is the leftmost flipping one-bit. By definition,

$$g_k - g_\ell \geq w_k - w_\ell \text{ for } k < \ell, \quad (2)$$

$$g_k - g_\ell = w_k - w_\ell = 0 \text{ for } i \geq k > \ell \geq \kappa(i). \quad (3)$$

Hence,

$$\begin{aligned} (\Delta_L(i) \mid A_{i,j}) &= \left(\sum_{s=1}^{r} g_{k_s} - g_{\ell_s}\right) \cdot \mathbb{1}_A \\ &\geq \left(\sum_{s=1}^{r} w_{k_s} - w_{\ell_s}\right) \cdot \mathbb{1}_A \\ &= \left(\sum_{k \in I^*} w_k - \sum_{\ell \in Z^* \cap L(i)} w_\ell\right) \cdot \mathbb{1}_A \geq 0 \end{aligned}$$

where the first inequality uses (2) and (3) and the last inequality holds by definition of $A_{i,j}$.

Now let $S_{i,j}$ be the event that $|Z^* \cap L(i) \setminus \{j\}| = 0$, that is, that no bit in $L(i)$ (possibly except j) flips to 1. We have

$$E(\Delta_L(i) \mid A_{i,j}) = E(\Delta_L(i) \mid A_{i,j} \cap S_{i,j}) \cdot \Pr(S_{i,j} \mid A_{i,j}) + E(\Delta_L(i) \mid A_{i,j} \cap \bar{S}_i) \cdot \Pr(\bar{S}_i \mid A_{i,j})$$

by the law of total probability. Since the random variable $(\Delta_L(i) \mid A_{i,j})$ cannot have any negative outcomes, all these conditional expectations are non-negative as well. From (1) we thus derive

$$E(\Delta_t \mid A_{i,j}) \geq E(\Delta_L(i) \mid A_{i,j} \cap S_{i,j}) \cdot \Pr(S_{i,j} \mid A_{i,j}) - E(\Delta_R(i) \mid A_{i,j}). \quad (4)$$

We will now bound the terms from (4) from below to obtain our result. For $(S_{i,j} \mid A_{i,j})$ to occur, it is sufficient that all bits in $L(i)$ except i and j do not flip (note that bits i and j flip by assumption). Consequently, $\Pr(S_{i,j} \mid A_{i,j}) \geq (1 - 1/m)^{m-2} \geq e^{-1}$. According to the definition of $A_{i,j}$, the mutation flipping only i and j is accepted. Hence, we estimate $E(\Delta_L(i) \mid A_{i,j} \cap S_{i,j}) \geq g_i - g_j$. Altogether,

$$E(\Delta_L(i) \mid A_{i,j} \cap S_{i,j}) \cdot \Pr(S_{i,j} \mid A_{i,j}) \geq \frac{g_i - g_j}{e}. \quad (5)$$

Finally, we need a bound on $E(\Delta_R(i))$, which is determined by the bits in $R(i)$ that flip to 1. Here we distinguish two cases with respect to j.

Case 1: $j < \kappa(i)$. By definition of $A_{i,j}$, not all bits in $Z \cap R(i)$ but only those of index at most at j can flip to 1, and bit j is forced to flip. Since only spanning trees are accepted, each flipping zero-bit requires another one-bit to flip to 0. If only bit $k \in Z$ was flipped to 1, the resulting search point would contain a cycle, say edges $e_1, \ldots, e_\ell$, one of which is denoted by bit k. For a spanning tree to be obtained, it is necessary that one of the bits associated with edges $e_1, \ldots, e_\ell$ flips to 0 simultaneously with k flipping to 1.

Clearly, $\ell \leq c(G)$. Event $A_{i,j}$ already occurs if only bits i and j flip. Moreover, bits are flipped independently. Hence, on $A_{i,j}$, the probability that $k \in Z \cap R(i) \cap \{1, \ldots, j-1\}$ flips is bounded from above by $\frac{1}{m} \cdot \frac{c(G)}{m} = \frac{c(G)}{m^2}$. Pessimistically, we assume that A occurs in such a mutation. By linearity of expectation, it follows that

$$E(\Delta_R(i) \mid A_{i,j}) \leq \sum_{k=1}^{j-1} \frac{c(G)}{m^2} g_k.$$

Along with (4) and (5), we get

$$E(\Delta_t \mid A_{i,j}) \geq \frac{g_i - g_j}{e} - \frac{c(G)}{m^2} \sum_{k=1}^{j-1} g_k \geq \frac{g_i - g_j}{e} - \frac{c(G)}{m^2} \left(\sum_{k=1}^{\kappa(j)-1} \gamma_k + (j - \kappa(j))\gamma_{\kappa(j)} \right), \quad (6)$$

where we used Lemma 13 to bound $g_k \leq \gamma_k$ for $k \leq \kappa(j) - 1$. Since $j < \kappa(i)$, Observation 14 yields that

$$g_i - g_j = \gamma_{\kappa(i)} - \gamma_{\kappa(j)} > 0,$$

hence

$$g_i - g_j = (1 + \Phi)^{\kappa(i)} - (1 + \Phi)^{\kappa(j)} \geq (1 + \Phi)^{\kappa(j)}((1 + \Phi)^{\kappa(i) - \kappa(j)} - 1) \geq \gamma_{\kappa(j)}(\kappa(i) - \kappa(j))\Phi, \quad (7)$$

where we used Bernoulli's inequality.

We are left with the sum over k. Plugging in the definition of γ_k in the geometric series, this is estimated by

$$\sum_{k=1}^{\kappa(j)-1} \gamma_k = \sum_{k=1}^{\kappa(j)-1} (1 + \Phi)^{k-1} = \frac{(1 + \Phi)^{\kappa(j)-1} - 1}{\Phi} \leq \frac{\gamma_{\kappa(j)}}{\Phi},$$

so that the term in parentheses from (6) is bounded according to

$$\sum_{k=1}^{\kappa(j)-1} \gamma_k + (j - \kappa(j))\gamma_{\kappa(j)} \leq \frac{j + 1 - \kappa(j)}{\Phi} \gamma_{\kappa(j)} \leq \frac{\kappa(i) - \kappa(j)}{\Phi} \gamma_{\kappa(j)},$$

where we used $\Phi < 1$ and $j < \kappa(i)$. Since by definition $c(G)/m^2 = \Phi^2/(2e)$, we bound the whole negative term in (6) as

$$\frac{c(G)}{m^2} \frac{\kappa(i) - \kappa(j)}{\Phi} \gamma_{\kappa(j)} \leq \frac{\Phi \gamma_{\kappa(j)}(\kappa(i) - \kappa(j))}{2e} \leq \frac{g_i - g_j}{2e},$$

using (7).

Hence, finally,

$$E(\Delta_t \mid A_{i,j}) \geq \frac{g_i - g_j}{e} - \frac{g_i - g_j}{2e} = \frac{g_i - g_j}{2e}.$$

Case 2: $j \geq \kappa(i)$. Then by definition of $A_{i,j}$, we get $g_i - g_j = 0$, so we only need to prove $E(\Delta_t \mid A_{i,j}) \geq 0$. If i and j are the only flipping bits, nothing is to show. Otherwise, we remove i and j from I^* and Z^*, respectively, and recompute i and j according to event $A_{i,j}$. Possibly repeating this process, we either arrive at a pair (i, j) satisfying Case 1, which proves a positive drift, or run out of flipping bits, which means that the drift is 0. □

5. LIMITATIONS OF THE TECHNIQUE

The drift analysis done in the proof of Theorem 10 requires that a result in the style of Lemma 18 can be obtained. Roughly speaking, the lemma says that the multiplicative drift w. r. t. the g-function is in the same order as if only two-bit flips were allowed (more precisely, order $\Omega(1/m^2)$). This leads to a factor $O(\sqrt{c(G)})$ in the running time bound for the following reason. Each flipping zero-bit, say bit k, must be compensated by a flipping one-bit for the spanning tree property to be maintained. Now, if the flipping zero-bit closes a cycle of length ℓ, there are $\ell - 1$ ways of flipping a one-bit, all of which are accepted. Pessimistically, the proof assumes $\ell = \Omega(n)$. In addition, it pessimistically assumes $\Omega(m)$ different choices for the flipping zero-bit k. The math in the analysis of Case 1 in the proof of Lemma 18 only works under these pessimistic assumptions if subsequent g_i-values are by a factor of at least $1 + \Omega(\sqrt{c(G)}/m)$ apart.

The situation pessimistically assumed in the drift analysis cannot be excluded during the optimization. Consider a subgraph on $n' + 1$ vertices, where $n' = \Omega(n)$, and assume that a path of length n' through the vertices $v_1, \ldots, v_{n'}$, forms a spanning tree for the subgraph. Let $V_L := \{v_1, \ldots, v_{n'/4}\}$ and $V_R := \{v_{3n'/4}, \ldots, v_{n'}\}$ be the first resp. last $n'/4$ vertices on the path. Each of the $(n')^2/4 = \Omega(m)$ edges between V_L and V_R closes a cycle of length at least $n'/4 = \Omega(n)$, which is in accordance with the pessimistic assumptions. Hence, the analysis of the one-step drift does not yield immediate room for improvement here.

Of course, looking at the scenario just described, a uniform flipping zero-bit would probably lead to shorter cycles in the next steps. So a drift analysis over several steps, keeping track of the stochastic change of the longest path in the current spanning tree, might help further improve the upper bound on the expected running time.

Finally, it seems not too difficult to obtain from the drift analysis the bound $O(m^2c(G)\log(n))$ if the mutation probability of the (1+1) EA is reduced from $1/m$ to $1/(m\sqrt{c(G)})$. The lower bound by Neumann and Wegener [10] could also be adapted to this case, altogether resulting in a tight bound $\Theta(m^2c(G)\log n)$. We consider this not to be particularly interesting since the decreased mutation probability simply would result in many steps not flipping bits at all.

Conclusions

We have revisited the classical analysis of the (1+1) EA for the minimum spanning tree problem and the case of unbounded edge weights. By an adaptive drift analysis, we have obtained the bound $O(m^2(\log n + \sqrt{c(G)}))$, which improves the previous result from [12] by an asymptotic factor of $m/\sqrt{c(G)}$. Furthermore, we have gained structural insights into the problem. These allowed us to define an alternative fitness function on which the running time for the (1+1) EA matches the one of RLS and asymptotically does not depend on the weights of the graph.

We have also pointed out reasons why the gap between upper and lower running time bound could not be closed. Future research on this problem seems necessary. Furthermore, there are other results in combinatorial optimization such as the single-source shortest path problem [2], where the best upper bound on the running time of the (1+1) EA depends on the largest weight in the underlying problem and the analysis from [12] does not apply. Additional insight into the problem structure seems required to come up with any improved bound here.

6. REFERENCES

[1] Anne Auger and Benjamin Doerr. *Theory of Randomized Search Heuristics – Foundations and Recent Developments*. World Scientific Publishing, 2011.

[2] Surender Baswana, Somenath Biswas, Benjamin Doerr, Tobias Friedrich, Piyush P. Kurur, and Frank Neumann. Computing single source shortest paths using single-objective fitness functions. In *Proc. of FOGA '09*, pages 59–66. ACM Press, 2009.

[3] Süntje Böttcher, Benjamin Doerr, and Frank Neumann. Optimal fixed and adaptive mutation rates for the LeadingOnes problem. In *Proc. of PPSN 2010*, volume 6238 of *Lecture Notes in Computer Science*, pages 1–10. Springer, 2010.

[4] Benjamin Doerr and Leslie Ann Goldberg. Adaptive drift analysis. *Algorithmica*, 65(1):224–250, 2013.

[5] Benjamin Doerr, Daniel Johannsen, and Carola Winzen. Multiplicative drift analysis. *Algorithmica*, 64(4):673–697, 2012.

[6] Benjamin Doerr and Sebastian Pohl. Run-time analysis of the (1+1) evolutionary algorithm optimizing linear functions over a finite alphabet. In *Proc. of GECCO '12*, pages 1317–1324. ACM Press, 2012.

[7] Benjamin Doerr, Dirk Sudholt, and Carsten Witt. When do evolutionary algorithms optimize separable functions in parallel? In *Proc. of FOGA '13*, pages 51–64. ACM Press, 2013.

[8] Thomas Jansen. *Analyzing Evolutionary Algorithms - The Computer Science Perspective*. Natural Computing Series. Springer, 2013.

[9] Ernst W. Mayr and C. Greg Plaxton. On the spanning trees of weighted graphs. *Combinatorica*, 12(4):433–447, 1992.

[10] Frank Neumann and Ingo Wegener. Randomized local search, evolutionary algorithms, and the minimum spanning tree problem. *Theoretical Computer Science*, 378(1):32–40, 2007.

[11] Frank Neumann and Carsten Witt. *Bioinspired Computation in Combinatorial Optimization – Algorithms and Their Computational Complexity*. Natural Computing Series. Springer, 2010.

[12] Joachim Reichel and Martin Skutella. On the size of weights in randomized search heuristics. In *Proc. of FOGA '09*, pages 21–28. ACM Press, 2009.

[13] Joachim Reichel and Martin Skutella. Evolutionary algorithms and matroid optimization problems. *Algorithmica*, 57(1):187–206, 2010.

[14] Ingo Wegener. Simulated annealing beats metropolis in combinatorial optimization. In *Proc. of ICALP '05*, volume 3580 of *Lecture Notes in Computer Science*, pages 589–601. Springer, 2005.

[15] Carsten Witt. Tight bounds on the optimization time of a randomized search heuristic on linear functions. *Combinatorics, Probability and Computing*, 22(2):294–318, 2013.

Simultaneous Generation of Prototypes and Features Through Genetic Programming

Mauricio García-Limón, Hugo Jair Escalante, Eduardo Morales, Alicia Morales-Reyes
Instituto Nacional de Astrofísica, Óptica y Electrónica
Computer Science Department
Luis Enrique Erro No. 1, Tonantzintla,
Puebla, 72840, Mexico
{mauricio.garcia,hugojair,emorales,a.morales}@inaoep.mx

ABSTRACT

Nearest-neighbor (NN) methods are highly effective and widely used pattern classification techniques. There are, however, some issues that hinder their application for large scale and noisy data sets; including, its high storage requirements, its sensitivity to noisy instances, and the fact that test cases must be compared to all of the training instances. Prototype (PG) and feature generation (FG) techniques aim at alleviating these issues to some extent; where, traditionally, both techniques have been implemented separately. This paper introduces a genetic programming approach to tackle the simultaneous generation of prototypes and features to be used for classification with a NN classifier. The proposed method learns to combine instances and attributes to produce a set of prototypes and a new feature space for each class of the classification problem via genetic programming. An heterogeneous representation is proposed together with ad-hoc genetic operators. The proposed approach overcomes some limitations of NN without degradation in its classification performance. Experimental results are reported and compared with several other techniques. The empirical assessment provides evidence of the effectiveness of the proposed approach in terms of classification accuracy and instance/feature reduction.

Categories and Subject Descriptors

I.5.2 [**Pattern recognition**]: Design Methodology—*Classifier design and evaluation, Feature evaluation and selection*

Keywords

Prototype Generation, Feature Extraction, NN Classifier, Genetic Programming, Pattern Recognition.

1. INTRODUCTION

Pattern classification is concerned with the construction of predictive models that can map instances to a predefined set of classes or labels. This is one of the main problems in machine learning and pattern recognition and it has been a widely studied field [9]. Among the variety of classification models proposed so far, nearest-neighbors (NN) methods are among the most popular ones [23]. This type of classifiers store all training instances and when classifying a new object, they compare it to all cases in the training set. The label for the test object is obtained by processing the labels associated to its nearest training instances.

Although NN methods are highly effective, and easy to implement/understand, they present some issues that hinder their application to certain types of problems. First, NN methods have interesting convergence properties as the size of the training set increases, however, storing large training sets consumes significantly more resources. Second, when classifying a new test object it has to be compared to every instance in the training set, which becomes computationally expensive for large data sets. Third, similar to other classification models, NN techniques are susceptible to the curse of dimensionality. Finally, another important issue of NN methods is that they are sensitive to noisy instances (e.g., misclassified instances and outliers).

These weaknesses of NN methods have been tackled with different approaches, mainly with two variants of instance reduction, namely, instance selection [7] and prototype generation [21]. Instance reduction techniques select a subset of instances to substitute the original training set. Prototype generation (PG) methods produce artificial instances and can represent better the input space, therefore are more general. Both methods diminish the storage requirements for NN classifiers and make more efficient the labeling process. However, instance reduction techniques do not deal with high-dimensionality and noisy data issues in NN methods. For dealing with these shortcomings, feature selection and construction can be applied; these methodologies aim at reducing the dimensionality of data and extracting informative data representations [8]. Although, instance and feature reduction approaches are beneficial for NN classifiers, both methodologies are commonly applied separately. Hence, not all NN's concerns are addressed by existing methods.

This paper introduces SGPFGP: *Simultaneous Generation of Prototypes and Features through Genetic Programming*, a novel approach to simultaneous feature and prototype generation for NN-based classification. SGPFGP learns how to combine instances and attributes to generate a set of prototypes and a new feature space for classification tasks via genetic programming. An heterogeneous repre-

GECCO'14, July 12–16, 2014, Vancouver, BC, Canada.
Copyright 2014 ACM 978-1-4503-2662-9/14/07 ...$15.00.
http://dx.doi.org/10.1145/2576768.2598356.

sentation is proposed and appropriate genetic operators are introduced. To the best of our knowledge, this is the first approach that aims at learning simultaneously class-specific prototypes and features to be used for NN-based classification. The effectiveness of the proposed method is evaluated and its performance is compared to alternative techniques. Experimental results show that SGPFGP compares favorably to state-of-the-art PG methods in terms of accuracy and reduction, with the additional benefit of dimensionality reduction.

The rest of this paper is organized as follows. Next section reviews related work on instance and feature reduction. Section 3 describes in detail the proposed SGPFGP approach. Section 4 presents the experimental framework to assess SGPFGP. Section 5 reports experimental results obtained by the proposed method. Finally, Section 6 outlines conclusions and discusses future work directions.

2. RELATED WORK

The PG problem has been approached in several ways, for a comprehensive study we refer the reader to [21], where Triguero et al. review and classify most of the existing PG methods up to 2012, additionally, a taxonomy and experimental comparison of these methods is also reported.

Most PG methods are iterative, they start with a set of prototypes (either randomly selected from the data set or artificially generated) and these are refined trying to maximize the classification performance. A classical representative of iterative PG methods is learning vector quantization (LVQ) [9], although many alternative methods have been proposed. For instance, in [21] the best method for PG in terms of classification performance was GENN (Generalized Editing using NN) [11]. GENN is a detrimental method that iteratively removes and re-labels instances. GENN achieves substantially better results than any other PG method compared in [21], although it was among the worse in terms of reduction of instances. On the other hand, PSCSA (Prototype Selection Clonal Selection Algorithm) obtained the best performance in terms of reduction [6]. PSCSA models the PG problem as an optimization one and uses an artificial immune system, the clonal selection algorithm, to solve it. This method is able to exactly select a single example per class, achieving the best reduction performance among the other 24 methods considered in [21]. However, its performance in terms of accuracy was worse than many other strategies. Other effective methods are based on bio-inspired optimization as well, see e.g., [5, 15, 2, 4, 19]. All of these methods evolve a population of individuals (codifying prototypes) trying to maximize the classification performance.

Although very effective PG methods have been proposed so far, it is somewhat disappointing that these methods have been developed independently of feature reduction techniques. Nevertheless, a few efforts in this direction have been proposed. Cagné et al. propose co-evolutionary approaches to simultaneously learn prototypes and neighborhood distance measure [1]. Both, competitive and cooperative schemes, are evaluated. Hussein et al. propose a genetic algorithm for instance selection, and feature weighting [10]. The main conclusion from [10] is that NN performance increases when one combines both types of methods. Paredes et al. used gradient descend to tackle the same problem, resulting in a very effective model [16]. More recently, Triguero et al. proposed a differential evolution technique that combines PG with feature weighting [22]. The above methods perform instance selection and feature weighting, allowing a reduction in the number of instances of the training set; however, they do not reduce data dimensionality.

Kuncheva and Jain propose a genetic algorithm for instance and feature selection [14]. Pedrajas et al. propose a similar evolutionary algorithm but put more emphasis on efficiency [17]. More recently, Chen et al. propose a multi-objective evolutionary algorithm for instance and feature selection [3]. Although being effective, these methods are still limited in terms of not being able to learn or to generate new features. Besides, as stated above, instance selection methods are a special case of PG, and therefore, generating prototypes is advantageous over selection (see partial/early evidence in [13]). Finally, it should be noted that the simultaneous methods from [14, 3] have only been evaluated on very small data sets.

This paper proposes SGPFGP, a method for simultaneous prototype and feature generation based on genetic programming. Contrary to previous hybrid approaches (instance + feature reduction) for selection, the proposed approach is completely based on the generation paradigm. That is, the aim is to build artificial instances and new features to improve NN classification performance. Escalante et al. have recently proposed a PG method based on genetic programming that combines instances to produce prototypes [4]. The proposed method extends that work by also allowing features generation, and by proposing a modeling framework that selects class-specific prototypes and features.

3. SIMULTANEOUS GENERATION OF PROTOTYPES AND FEATURES

Genetic programming is one of the youngest evolutionary algorithms [12], it has the distinctive feature that programs, codified in elaborated data structures, are evolved to solve complex modeling problems. Herein, a method for Simultaneous Generation of Prototypes and Features through Genetic Programming (SGPFGP) is introduced. The goal is to learn class-specific prototypes and features for pattern classification by NN.

The underlying hypotheses of SGPFGP are that prototypes for a class are formed by combining training instances that belong to that class; likewise, the generated features for a particular class are formed by combining features of instances that belong to that class. By considering a tree-structure for codifying prototypes and features, and letting leaf nodes to denote instances (resp. features) while non-terminal nodes to denote operators between leaf nodes, it is quite natural to use genetic programming to evolve a population of tree-prototypes and tree-features trying to maximize the classification performance of an NN classifier. The rest of this section provides a detailed description of the proposed method.

3.1 Considered scenario

Let $\mathcal{T} = \{(\mathbf{x}_1, y_1) \ldots, (\mathbf{x}_N, y_N)\}$ be a training set of labeled instances, with $\mathbf{x}_i \in \mathbb{R}^d$ and $y_i \in \mathcal{C} = \{1, \ldots, K\}$, where d is the problem dimensionality and K is the number of classes in the considered problem. The goal is to generate a set of sets of prototypes $\mathcal{P}^* = \{\mathcal{P}_1, \ldots, \mathcal{P}_K\}$ (one set of prototypes per class) where each set of prototypes is defined as follows: $\mathcal{P}_k = \{(\mathbf{w}_1^k, y_1^k), \ldots, (\mathbf{w}_{L_k}^k, y_{L_k}^k)\}$, for $k = 1, \ldots, K$

such that $L_k << N$, where L_k is the number of prototypes for class k, $\mathbf{w}_i^k \in \mathbb{R}^{d_k}$, and d_k is dimensionality of the feature space for prototypes in set $\mathcal{P}_k$. This means that each set of prototypes $\mathcal{P}_k$ is associated to a single class k and the prototypes of this class have the same dimensionality d_k, which is not necessarily the same for different classes.

3.2 Representation

For learning $\mathcal{P}^*$ a genetic program is proposed where each individual codifies a possible solution to this problem, see Figure 1. Specifically, individuals are represented by a set of trees pairs: $\{(\mathcal{S}_p^1, \mathcal{S}_f^1), \ldots, (\mathcal{S}_p^K, \mathcal{S}_f^K)\}$, where $\mathcal{S}_p^k = \{s_{p,1}^k, \ldots, s_{p,L_k}^k\}$ is a set of trees for generating class k prototypes and $\mathcal{S}_f^k = \{s_{f,1}^k, \ldots, s_{f,d_k}^k\}$ is a set of trees for generating class k features. Each tree is associated to a single prototype $(s_{p,i}^k)$ or feature $(s_{f,j}^k)$, and both sets of trees are dependent to each other: prototypes generated via $\mathcal{S}_p^k$ use features generated with $\mathcal{S}_f^k$. In this way, pairs $(\mathcal{S}_p^k, \mathcal{S}_f^k)$ are associated to a set of prototypes: $\mathcal{P}_k = \{(\mathbf{w}_1^k, y_1^k), \ldots, (\mathbf{w}_{L_k}^k, y_{L_k}^k)\}$.

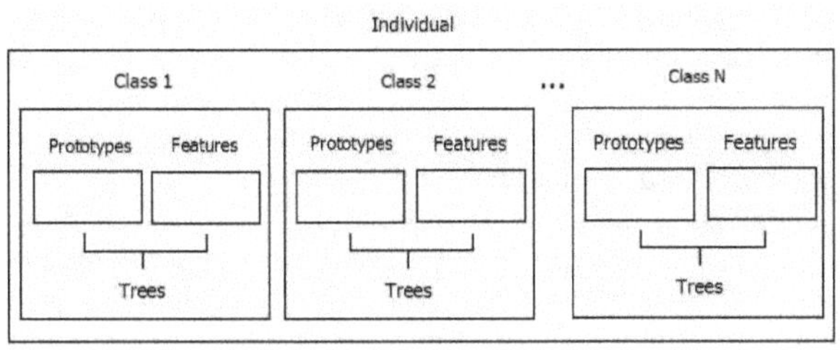

Figure 1: Representation of an individual: class-specific prototype-feature trees.

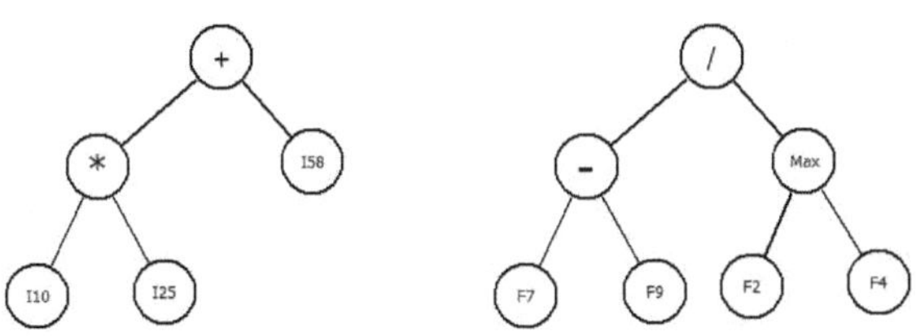

Figure 2: Prototype representation ($s_{p,i}^k$, left): instances are combined; and feature representation ($s_{p,i}^k$, right): features are combined.

Hence, in SGPFGP individuals are encoded as trees $s_{p,i}^k$ and $s_{f,j}^k$ in the genetic program (see Figure 2). Each tree $s_{p,i}^k$ (resp. $s_{f,j}^k$) can generate a prototype (resp. feature) by combining instances (resp. features) taken from the training set $\mathcal{T}$. That is, the terminal set for prototype-trees $s_{p,i}^k$ is the subset of instances from the training set $\mathcal{T}$ that are labeled with class k. Likewise, the terminal set for feature-trees $s_{f,j}^k$ is the set of $d-$dimensional feature vectors of instances in $\mathcal{T}$ that belong to class k.

The function set for combining instances and features is the following set of operators: $\{+, -, *, /, Min, Max\}$, all of them with arity two. In a preliminary study, other operators were evaluated (including operators of arity 1); however, better results were observed with the above mentioned function set.

3.3 Fitness function

The proposed representation is implemented into a standard genetic program [18], with the aim of maximizing the classification performance of a 1NN[1] classifier when using prototypes and features induced by different individuals. Accordingly, the fitness function for the genetic program is simply the classification performance obtained by a 1NN when classifying all instances in a validation set. Instances in the validation set are not considered in the terminal set of prototype trees (i.e., the validation set and $\mathcal{T}$ are disjoint). The motivation behind this hold-out split is to avoid, to some extent, generating overfitted prototypes/features.

More specifically, to assess the quality of every individual, the next procedure is followed: the prototypes induced by prototype-trees are obtained using the input space of feature-trees for each class. Next, every instance to be classified with the prototypes is first projected into the features learned by the genetic program for each class, and then it is compared to the prototypes of different classes (each comparison in the corresponding input space). The test instance is assigned to the class of the nearest prototype. One should note that by proceeding in this way, the 1NN classifier is allowed to learn specific features and prototypes for each of the considered classes.

3.4 Genetic program and considered operators

Algorithm 1 presents the details of the proposed SGPFGP method. The population was initialized with ramped-half-and-half considering a maximum tree deep of *D_max*. For initializing prototype-trees per class half of the trees are initialized with the full method, and the other half with the grow technique, with the restriction of using instances of the same class. Feature-trees were initialized similarly, but without the class-restriction, because features are initially common to all instances. For initialization, the proposed method takes as input PP and PF parameters, which specify the number of initial prototype-trees and feature-trees, respectively. One should notice that, although the user has to specify PP and PG, after initialization, the genetic program automatically determines/adjust the final number of prototypes and features.

Generic genetic operators and ad-hoc ones are considered for the SGPFGP method. An extensive preliminary experimentation was conducted to determine the best operators combination, here the ones that provided the best results are described (individuals are selected via tournament):

- **Crossover**: given two individuals, a prototype (resp. feature) tree from each parent is randomly selected, then a subtree of each selected tree is chosen and ex-

[1]One should note that the selection of 1NN (instead of any other KNN classifier) is not arbitrary. Most previous studies on PG for NN classification have used 1NN as well, see [21]. This is, in part, motivated by the fact that using 1NN allows PG methods to be able (at least theoretically) to reach the optimal number of prototypes (1 per class). Nevertheless, the proposed method can also work with other KNN classifiers.

Algorithm 1 Simultaneous Generation of Prototypes and Features through Genetic Programming.

Require: :
  $\mathcal{T}$: Training Set;
  $\mathcal{V}$: Validation Set;
  Generations : Number of Generations
  Population : Number of Individuals
  PP : Proportion of initial prototypes
  PF : Proportion of initial features
Ensure: $Best_x$: The best individual, the solution that obtains the highest accuracy in $\mathcal{V}$.
  $P \Leftarrow$ *Ramped-half-and-half*$(PP, PF, \mathcal{T})$
  $Best_x \Leftarrow \emptyset$
  $FBest \Leftarrow -Inf$
  $i = 0$
  while $i <= Generations$ **do**
    for $j = 1 \rightarrow Population$ **do**
      $f(j) \leftarrow fitness(P_j, \mathcal{V})$
      if $f(j) > FBest$ **then**
        $FBest \leftarrow f(j)$
        $Best_x \Leftarrow P_j$
      end if
    end for
    $Pool \Leftarrow Sampling(P)$
    $Offspring \Leftarrow MultiCrossover(Pool)$
    $Offspring \Leftarrow Crossover(Offspring)$
    $Offspring \Leftarrow Mutation(Offspring)$
    $P \Leftarrow Selection(P, Offspring)$
    $i \leftarrow i + 1$
  end while
  return X_p

changed. The outputs of this operator are two offspring. This process is repeated for each class associated to the classification problem. The operator is applied to all classes because the representation is complex and affecting a class at a time would not have a significant effect in the overall population.

- **Mutation**: given an individual, for each class, a randomly selected tree is eliminated and a new one is generated (using the same process as in the initialization). This procedure is similar for both prototype and feature trees.
- **Multi-Crossover**: a new crossover operator is introduced due to the representation complexity. Given two individuals, a new offspring is generated by combining trees from the parents. The offspring tree, for each class, is selected from the corresponding trees of the parents with uniform probability. This procedure is similar for both prototype and feature trees.

Genetic operators are applied with certain probabilities and in a predefined order (see Algorithm 1). A population of trees is evolved and the best individual found during the search process is returned. In the rest of the paper the performance of the proposed method is evaluated for simultaneous prototype and feature generation.

4. EXPERIMENTAL FRAMEWORK

For the experimental evaluation of the proposed method, the suite of data sets introduced by Triguero et al. [21] is considered. This benchmark consists of 59 data sets associated to different classification problems. Table 1 describes the considered data sets.

This suite comprises classification problems with varied characteristics in terms of number of classes, number/type of attributes (nominal and numeric), and number of instances. Table 2 summarizes the main features of the benchmark. This suite has been widely used for benchmarking GP methods [21, 4]. Commonly, results of PG methods are reported separately for **small** (data sets with less than 2,000 instances) and **large** (data sets with at least 2,000 instances) data sets. Accordingly, results for both types of data sets are reported. Different aspects of the proposed method are assessed through this benchmark and a performance comparison to other approaches using the same suite is carried out.

The evaluation methodology adopted in [21] consists of applying PG methods to each data set in a 10-fold cross validation scheme. That is, each data set is split into 10 subsets, and 10 rounds of training and testing are performed; in each round 9 subsets are used as training set and 1 subset is used for testing, the process is repeated 10 times using a different subset for testing each time. This means that for each data set the proposed PG method is applied 10 times, every time the method learns prototypes and features using the training subsets and the generated prototypes/features are evaluated in the test set.

For the evaluation process, a 1NN rule is used by the generated prototypes[2]. One should note that a single run of the proposed method over the whole benchmark represents 590 executions (10 times per data set). It is important to emphasize this because the same evaluation methodology as in [21] has been adopted (using exactly the same data partitions for training and testing in each of the 10-folds per data set), thus results are directly comparable to those reported by Triguero et al. and other authors that have used the same collection.

The following experimental settings are defined to assess the proposed approach: the number of generations is set to 50, the population size is set to 100, and the maximum tree depth is fixed to 3. The values of these parameters were determined after a brief preliminary study on parameter selection. Finally, to compare results obtained from different methods, a Wilcoxon signed-rank test is used to determine if the difference in performance is statistically significant, with a confidence level of 95%.

5. EXPERIMENTAL RESULTS

This section reports experimental results to show the effectiveness of the proposed method. The performance of SGPFGP is compared against 24 other PG techniques that have been evaluated with the same benchmark. The analysis starts by visually analyzing the positioning of the learned prototypes for a 2D data set. Next, the SGPFGP performance is evaluated in terms of classification accuracy, and instance/feature reduction rates.

[2]One should note that since there is a subset of prototypes and features per class. Every test-instance has to be represented and compared using the set of prototypes and features learned for each class. The test-instance is labeled with the class of the nearest prototype.

Table 1: **Description of the data sets used for the experimental study [21]. The number of samples, the number of attributes and the number of classes are shown per data set.**

Data set	Samples	Attributes	Classes
Abalone	4174	8	28
Appendicitis	106	7	2
Australian	690	14	2
Autos	205	25	6
Balance	624	4	3
Banana	5300	2	2
Bands	539	19	2
Breast-Cancer	286	9	2
Bupa	345	6	2
Car	1728	6	4
Chess	3196	36	2
Cleveland	297	13	5
Coil2000	9822	85	2
Contraceptive	1473	9	3
Crx	125	15	2
Dermatology	366	33	6
Ecoli	336	7	8
Flare-Solar	1066	9	2
German	1000	20	2
Glass	214	9	7
Haberman	306	3	2
Hayes-Roth	133	4	3
Heart	270	13	2
Hepatitis	155	19	2
Housevotes	435	16	2
Iris	150	4	3
Led7digit	500	7	10
Lymphography	148	18	2
Magic	19020	10	2
Mammographic	961	5	2
Marketing	8993	13	9
Monks	432	6	2
Movements-libras	360	90	15
Newthyroid	215	5	3
Nursey	12960	8	5
Pageblocks	5472	10	5
Penbased	10992	16	10
Phoneme	5404	5	2
Pima	768	8	2
Ring	7400	20	2
Saheart	462	9	2
Satimage	6435	36	7
Segment	2310	19	7
Sonar	208	60	2
Spambase	4597	57	2
Spectheart	267	44	2
Splice	3190	60	3
Tae	151	5	3
Texture	5500	40	11
Thyroid	7200	21	3
Tic-tac-toe	958	9	2
Titanic	2201	3	2
Twonorm	7400	20	2
Vehicle	846	18	4
Vowel	990	13	11
Wine	178	13	3
Wisconsin	683	9	2
Yeast	1484	8	10
Zoo	101	16	7

Table 2: Summary of features for the 59 data sets of the considered benchmark [21].

	Small	Large
# data sets	40	19
# Classes	[2, 15]	[2, 28]
# Instances	[101, 1,728]	[2,201, 19,020]
# Attributes	[3, 90]	[2, 85]
# BDs w. Nominal atts.	7	3
# BDs w. Numerical atts.	22	14
# BDs w. Mixed atts.	11	2

5.1 Visualization learned prototypes

In this section, the prototypes generated with SGPFGP using a 2D-data set are presented. The goal of this experiment is to analyze how the prototypes learned by SGPFGP are distributed in the input space for a complex classification problem. The banana data set is associated to a binary classification task (2-classes) that contains 5300 instances described by 2 attributes. Figure 3 shows a subsampling of the original data set; it can be seen that the decision surface for this problem is non linear and very complex to capture.

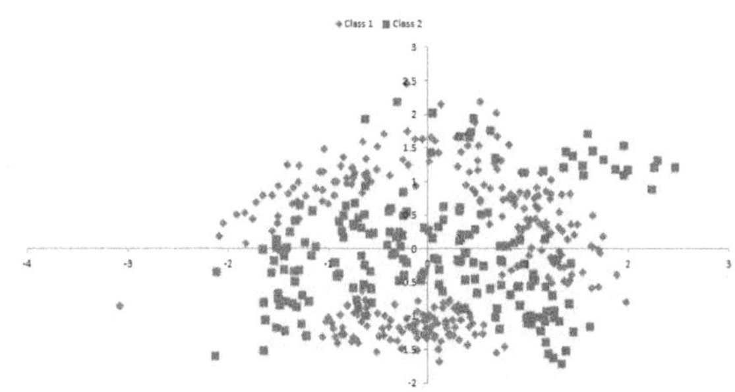

Figure 3: Banana data set.

Recall that the proposed method generates specific features for each class, hence, for this data set the SGPFGP output is two sets of prototypes/features. Figures 4 and 5 show a subsampling of the banana data set projected into the feature spaces of each of the classes. In each figure the corresponding prototypes are also plotted. From these figures, it can be seen that features for different classes result in very different projections of the training data. The projection induced by features from class 2 (Figure 5) somewhat preserves the structure of the original problem, while the projection for features from class 1 (Figure 4) is totally different. In both projections, one can see that the generated prototypes effectively capture the distribution of training examples of the respective class, i.e., prototypes of a class are closer to instances of its own class than to those of different classes.

For this particular example, the SGPFGP method selects 7 and 6 prototypes for classes 1 and 2, respectively; which represents a reduction performance of 0.9975. SGPFGP achieves an average classification performance of 0.8628 for this data set, which is very close to the performance of the best method for this data set in the comparative study of [21] (the DEPUR method obtained 0.896 [20]).

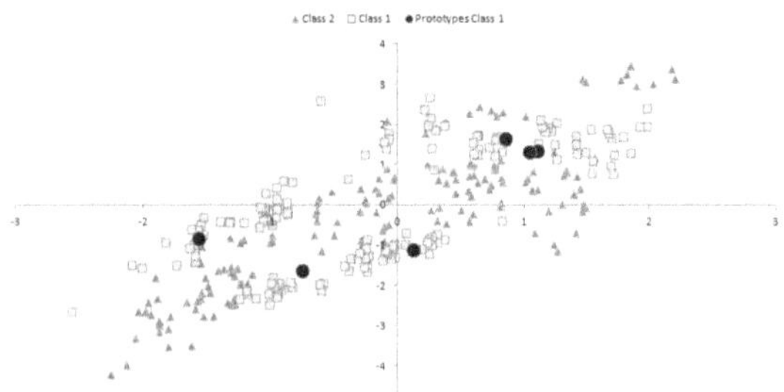

Figure 4: Feature space and prototypes of class 1 for the Banana data set.

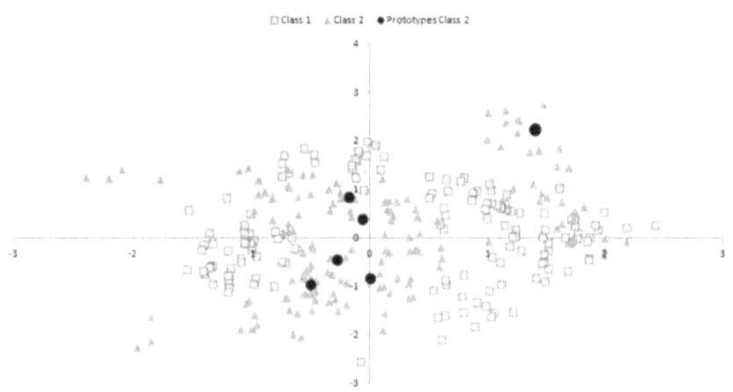

Figure 5: Feature space and prototypes of class 2 for the Banana data set.

5.2 Classification performance of prototypes

Table 3 shows the average classification performance obtained by the SGPFGP approach for small and large data sets, for comparison the corresponding results for 1NN using the whole training set are included as well as the performances (from [21]) obtained by the best methods in terms of accuracy (GENN [11]) and reduction (PSCSA [6]).

Table 3: Average classification accuracy for SGPFGP and reference methods.

	SGPFGP	GENN [11]	PSCSA [6]	1NN
Small	0.719 ± 0.06	***0.756*** ± 0.05	$0.668 \pm 0.07\star$	0.734 ± 0.05
Large	0.802 ± 0.01	***0.813*** ± 0.01	$0.670 \pm 0.02\star$	0.80 ± 0.01

$\star$ statistically significant difference.

From Table 3, it is observed that prototypes and features generated by SGPFGP do not degrade significantly the classification performance obtained with 1NN when using the whole data set. Therefore, data dimensionality and number of training instances are reduced without compromising the classification performance.

The proposed method outperforms PSCSA by a large margin over both small and large data sets, the differences are statistically significant. On the other hand, GENN outperforms SGPFGP by about 4% and 1% for small and large data sets, however these differences are not statistically significant. These results confirm that SGPFGP is a very competitive method in terms of accuracy, achieving similar performance as the best PG methods that were evaluated in [21]. Interestingly, better results were obtained by SGPFGP for large data sets; this is a very positive result because PG methods are precisely designed to deal with large data sets.

It is important to mention that SGPFGP classification performance is similar to that obtained by another PG method based on genetic programming [4]. However, SGPFGP obtains substantially better instance-reduction performance and is able to reduce data dimensionality.

Table 4 shows the average execution time (in seconds) for the classification phase of SGPFGP, compared against the execution time of 1NN over the large data sets. We can appreciate that the proposal is far more efficient, it reduces a 98.45% of the time in the classification. One should note that the execution time in SGPFGP includes the processes of projecting data into different feature spaces and estimating distances.

Table 4: Average execution time (seconds) in the classification step.

Dataset	SGPFGP	1NN
Large	0.0067	0.1695

5.3 Reduction performance of prototypes

Table 5 shows the average instance-reduction rates for SGPFGP, GENN, PSCSA and 1NN. From this table, it is observed that SGPFGP performance is very competitive as well. SGPFGP significantly outperforms GENN (improvements higher than 80%) and achieves virtually the same reduction performance as PSCSA, which is the best method in terms of reduction evaluated in [21]. In fact, SGPFGP offers a better tradeoff between accuracy (Table 3) and reduction (Table 5) than the referenced methods. These results can be better appreciated in Figures 6 and 7, where accuracy vs. reduction are plotted for the 24 methods considered in [21] for small and large data sets, respectively.

Table 5: Average reduction rates obtained by the considered methods.

	SGPFGP	GENN	PSCSA	1NN
Small	0.983 ± 0.0007	$0.186 \pm 0.0205\star$	***0.985*** ± 0.0001	0 ± 0
Large	0.994 ± 0.0005	$0.157 \pm 0.0049\star$	***0.998*** ± 0.0001	0 ± 0

$\star$ statistically significant difference

5.4 Accuracy vs. reduction tradeoff

It can be seen from Figure 6 that for small data sets, the performance in reduction of SGPFGP is among the best ones; although its accuracy is lower than several other techniques (e.g., PSO [15]). However, as depicted in Figure 7, for large data sets the proposed approach offers the best tradeoff between accuracy and reduction. Achieving similar accuracy as ENPC [5] and DEPUR [20] (two highly effective PG techniques), but with much better reduction performance. Also the fact that GENN obtains highly accurate prototypes at the expense of poor reduction performance is confirmed.

If the Pareto front is constructed using the reduction and accuracy performances for all of the considered PG methods, SGPFGP would be part of it (i.e., it *dominates* many other PG methods in both figures). SGPFGP would be located in the upper right corner of the Pareto front, making it an ideal solution that fulfills the accuracy vs. reduction tradeoff.

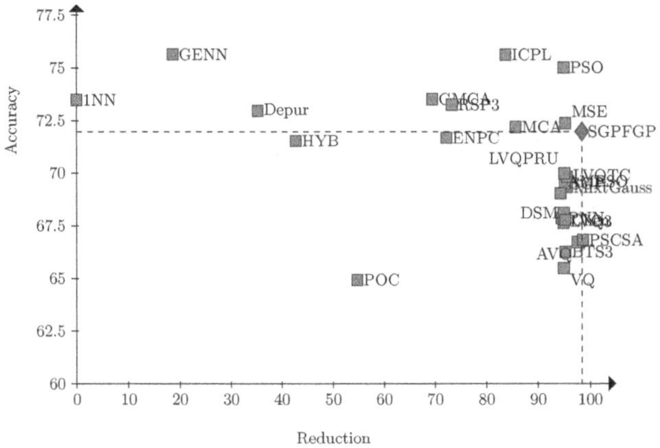

Figure 6: Average reduction ($x-$axis) vs. accuracy ($y-$axis) for small data sets.

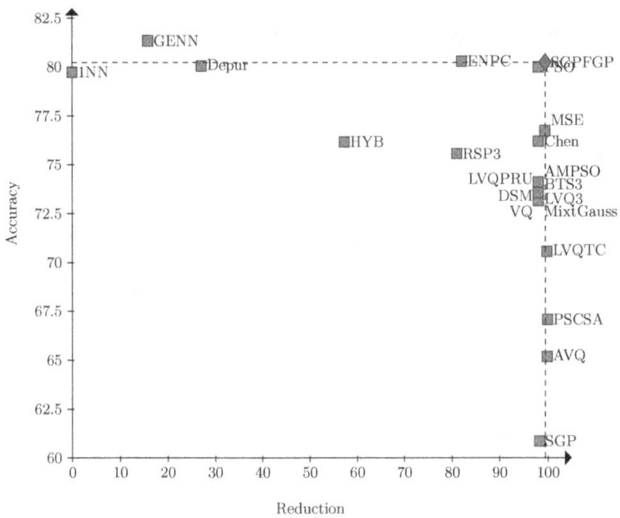

Figure 7: Average reduction ($x-$axis) vs. accuracy ($y-$axis) for large data sets.

Therefore, it is possible to conclude that SGPFGP is a very competitive method in terms of the accuracy and instance reduction tradeoff, mainly for large data sets.

5.5 Feature generation

The proposed PG method has demonstrated to be a competitive approach. Moreover, experimental results have shown the additional benefit of dimensionality reduction. In this regard, the average feature reduction rates were of 0.418 and 0.41 for small and large data sets, respectively. Thus, SGPFGP generates representations that account for only 60% of the original dimensionality and yet it is able to obtain state-of-the-art performance. The combined reduction of instances and features results in speeding up 1NN when classifying test instances. As future work we will compare the performance of SGPFGP with that of alternative feature selection/extraction techniques.

5.6 Performance over different attribute types

Because the considered data sets can have nominal, numeric or mixed attributes, it is worth analyzing SGPFGP performance for these different types of attributes. Table 6 shows the average accuracy obtained by the proposed method for different attribute types using small and large data sets. Nominal attributes are better exploited by the proposed approach for both small and large data sets (please note that there are only 10 data sets with only-nominal attributes, 7 small and 3 large ones). Although for large data sets the performance is virtually the same when using nominal or numeric attributes.

It is interesting that better performance is obtained by the proposed method when a single attribute type was considered (either nominal or numeric) and that SGPFGP has problems for data sets with mixed attributes. This result could be due to the nature of the proposed approach which combines attributes to generate new features: combining attributes of different nature does not necessarily result in a better feature.

Table 6: Average accuracy for different data types.

	Nominal	Numerical	Mixed
Small	***0.768*** ± 0.04	0.724 ± 0.07	0.671 ± 0.06
Large	***0.828*** ± 0.02	0.823 ± 0.01	0.613 ± 0.01

6. CONCLUSIONS AND FUTURE WORK

This paper introduced SGPFGP a novel approach to simultaneous feature and prototype generation for NN-based classification. SGPFGP learns to combine instances and attributes to generate class-specific prototypes and features via genetic programming. A heterogeneous representation is proposed and appropriate genetic operators are applied. To the best of our knowledge, this is the first approach that aims at learning simultaneously prototypes and features for every class used in NN-based classification. The performance of the proposed method is evaluated and compared with a wide variety of other PG methods. Experimental results show that SGPFGP compares favorably to state-of-the-art PG methods in terms of accuracy and reduction, with the additional benefit of reducing data sets dimensionality.

Conclusions of this work can be summarized as follows:

- SGPFGP is able to reduce data dimensionality and the number of training instances without compromising the classification performance. In fact, SGPFGP obtains similar performance as the most effective PG methods proposed so far.
- Better results are obtained by SGPFGP for large data sets, making it suitable for large scale classification problems.
- Instance-reduction performance of SGPFGP is very close to the optimal reduction rates (i.e., one instance per class). SGPFGP outperforms most of the reference methods considered in the study in terms of instance reduction.
- SGPFGP reduces about 40% data sets dimensionality. Building new features that are more informative for designing NN classifiers.
- SGPFGP obtains better results when data sets attributes are of the same type (either nominal or nu-

meric). This is possibly due to the fact that the current representation and operators are not designed to combine heterogeneous attributes.

- During the search SGPFGP tries to balance the number of instances per class. This is good for database problems with unbalanced data.

Current and future work include approaching the problem of simultaneous feature-prototype generation with a multi-objective genetic program that can result in solutions with better tradeoffs among the objectives involved in the problem (e.g., accuracy + instance-reduction + dimensionality-reduction). We would also like to compare the proposed approach with feature extraction/construction methods in the state-of-art. Finally, the proposed approach is currently being assessed on real and large scale data sets, including object recognition and image annotation data.

Acknowledgements. This work was partially supported by the LACCIR programm under project ID R1212LAC006. Mauricio García-Limón was supported by CONACyT with scholarship No. 345683.

7. REFERENCES

[1] C. Carné and M. Parizeau. Coevolution of nearest neighbot classifiers. *International Journal of Pattern Recognition and Artificial Intelligence*, 21(5):921–946, 2007.

[2] A. Cervantes, I. M. Galvan, and P. Isasi. AMPSO: a new particle swarm method for nearest neighborhood classification. *IEEE Transactions on Systems Man and Cybernetics part B*, 39(5):1082–1091, 2009.

[3] J. H. Chen, H. M. Chen, and S. Y. Ho. Design of nearest neighbor classifiers: multi-objective approach. *International Journal of Approximate Reasoning*, 40:3–22, 2005.

[4] H. J. Escalante, K. M. Mendoza, M. Graff, and A. Morales-Reyes. Genetic programming of prototypes for pattern classification. In *Proceedings of IbPRIA 2013*, volume 7887 of *LNCS*, pages 100–107. Springer, 2013.

[5] F. Fernandez and P. Isasi. Evolutionary design of nearest prototype classifiers. *Journal fo Heuristics*, 10:431–454, 2004.

[6] U. Garain. Prototype reduction using an artificial immune system. *Pattern Analysis and Applications*, 11(3–4):353–363, 2008.

[7] S. García, J. Derrac, J. R. Cano, and F. Herrera. Prototype selection for nearest neighbor classification: Taxonomy and empirical study. *IEEE Transactions on Pattern Analysis and Machine Intelligence*, 34(3):417–435, 2012.

[8] I. Guyon, S. Gunn, M. Nikravesh, and L. Zadeh, editors. *Feature extraction, foundations and applications*, volume 207 of *Studies in fuzzines and soft computing*. Springer, 2006.

[9] T. Hastie, R. Tibshirani, and J. Friedman. *The Elements of Statistical Learning*. Springer New York Inc., New York, NY, USA, 2001.

[10] F. Hussein, N. Kharma, and R. Ward. Genetic algorithms for feature selection and weighting a review and study. *Document Analysis and Recognition*, pages 1240–1244, 2001.

[11] J. Koplowitz and T. Brown. On the relation of performance to editing in nearest neighbor rules. *Pattern Recognition*, 13(3):251–255, 1981.

[12] J. R. Koza. *Genetic Programming: On the Programming of Computers by Means of Natural Selection*. The MIT Press, 1992.

[13] L. Kuncheva and J. Bezdek. Nearest prototype classification: Clustering, genetic algorithms or random search. *IEEE Transations on Systems Man and Cybernetics part C*, 28(1):160–164, 1998.

[14] L. Kuncheva and L. C. Jain. Nearest neighbor classifier: Simultaneous editing and feature selection. *Pattern recognition letters*, 20:1149–1156, 1999.

[15] L. Nanni and A. Lumini. Particle swarm optimization for prototype reduction. *Neurocomputing*, 72(4–6):1092–1097, 2008.

[16] R. Paredes and E. Vidal. Learning prototypes and distances: A prototype reduction technique based on nearest neighbor error minimization. *Pattern Recognition*, 39:180–188, 2006.

[17] N. G. Pedrajas, A.H. García, and J. P. Rodríguez. A scalable approach to simultaneous evolutionary instance and feature selection. *Information Sciences*, 228:150–174, 2012.

[18] R. Poli, W. B. Langdon, and N. Freitag McPhee. *A field guide to genetic programming*. Published via `http://lulu.com` and freely available at `http://www.gp-field-guide.org.uk`, 2008.

[19] A. Rosales-Perez H. J. Escalante, C. A. Coello, J. A. Gonzalez and C. A. Reyes-Garcia. An Evolutionary Multi-Objective Approach for Prototype Generation. Proccedigns of the World Congress on Computational Intelligence, to appear, 2014.

[20] J. S. Sanchez, R. Barandela, A. I. Marques, R. Alejo, and J. Badenas. Analysis of new techniques to obtain quality training sets. *Pattern Recognition Letters*, 24(7):1015–1022, 2003.

[21] I. Triguero, J. Derrac, S. García, and F.Herrera. A taxonomy and experimental study on prototype generation for nearest neighbor classification. *IEEE Transations on Systems Man and Cybernetics part C*, 42(1):86–100, 2012.

[22] I. Triguero, J. Derrac, S. García, and F. Herrera. Integrating a differential evolution feature weighting scheme into prototype generation. *Neurocomputing*, 37:332–343, 2012.

[23] X. Wu, V. Kumar, R. Quinlan, J. Ghosh, Q. Yang, H. Motoda, G. J. McLachlan, A. Ng, B. Liu, P. S. Yu, Z.-H. Zhou, M. Steinbach, D. J. Hand, and D. Steinberg. Top 10 algorithms in data mining. *Knowledge Information Systems*, 14(1):1–37, 2007.

Salient Object Detection Using Learning Classifier Systems that Compute Action Mappings

Muhammad Iqbal, Syed Saud Naqvi, Will N. Browne,
Christopher Hollitt and Mengjie Zhang
Victoria University of Wellington, NZ @ecs.vuw.ac.nz
muhammad.iqbal@,syed.saud.naqvi@,will.browne@,christopher.hollitt@,mengjie.zhang@

ABSTRACT

Learning classifier systems (LCSs) are rule-based online evolutionary machine learning techniques that solve a problem by interacting with an environment. LCSs have been successfully used in various applications such as data mining, robot control and computer vision systems. Salient object detection is the task of automatically localizing the objects of interests in a scene by suppressing the background information, which facilitates various machine learning applications such as object segmentation, recognition and tracking. It is a difficult problem as natural scenes can often have objects with cluttered backgrounds (making it difficult to distinguish the object from background based on its features) or other complicating factors such as multiple objects. Existing saliency learning methods learn a single weight vector emphasizing the importance of each feature/attribute for the whole image dataset, hence losing generalization in the test phase when considering unseen images. LCS technique has the ability to learn weight sets for different types of images automatically. Hence, this paper investigates the application of LCS for learning image dependent feature fusion strategies for the task of salient object detection. Our LCS approach evolves generalized rules for a well known benchmark dataset consisting of 1000 images, of various types and difficulty levels, and outperforms a genetic algorithm based system that was previously state-of-the-art.

Categories and Subject Descriptors

F.1.1 [**Models of Computation**]: Genetics-Based Machine Learning, Learning Classifier Systems

General Terms

Algorithms, Performance

Keywords

Learning Classifier Systems, XCS, Genetic Algorithms, Saliency, Object Detection, Pattern Recognition

GECCO'14, July 12–16, 2014, Vancouver, BC, Canada.

http://dx.doi.org/10.1145/2576768.2598371.

1. INTRODUCTION

Visual attention is a fundamental research problem in psychology, neuroscience and computer vision literature. Salient object detection designated a sub-problem of visual attention, is the task of marking regions of interest in a scene, which facilitates various computer vision applications, e.g. object recognition [39] and image compression [25]. Typical methods used to detect salient objects in an image concentrate on constructing deterministic tailor-made features [16, 27]. Recently, Naqvi et al. [34] used a genetic algorithm (GA) based system to find optimal parameters to build a bottom-up saliency map[1] for eye-fixation prediction. The obtained results by GA were promising, but it evolved a single weight vector for the whole image dataset, hence losing generalization in the test phase when considering unseen images.

A learning classifier system (LCS) is a rule-based learning system [8, 18] that adaptively learns a task by interacting with an unknown environment and uses evolutionary computing to evolve the rules, which collectively solve the problem. Due to cooperative nature of the evolved rules, an LCS has an inherent capability to learn weight sets for different types of images automatically, which could result in improved performance of the system. GAs are purely competitive with the whole population aiming to converge to the optimal solution, whereas LCSs are competitive only in niches, i.e. separable subsolutions of the problem domain that when combined cover the complete space of the problem. The LCS technique has been successfully applied to a wide range of problems including data mining, control, modeling, image processing and optimization problems [4, 7, 28, 37].

In the work presented here, an accuracy-based LCS model will be adopted to compute saliency maps in order to detect salient objects in an image. The proposed LCS-based systems are to be tested on the MSRA salient object database [31] using the labeled ground truth[2] from [1] (see Section 5). The results are to be compared with the GA-based system [34].

2. BACKGROUND

2.1 Salient Object Detection

Researchers have built computational models of visual attention to predict where humans are likely to fixate [6,26,34]. Recently, it has been expanded to identify regions of interest

[1] A saliency map is a computed image designed to emphasize the object to be detected, over its background.

[2] A ground truth is a manually segmented binary image that emphasizes the object to be detected.

for object detection and localization. Salient object detection is the task of marking regions of interest in a scene. It is a difficult problem in computer vision as natural scenes can have objects with cluttered backgrounds (making it difficult to distinguish the object from background based on its features) and can contain multiple objects. Deterministic methods include humanly constructed features and are usually combined in a linear manner, neglecting the relative importance of individual features. Machine learning approaches have the ability to learn feature importance during combination, which enhances their performance in challenging cases such as scenes with cluttered backgrounds and multiple objects. 1) Salient object detection finds applications in object recognition [39], salient object segmentation [12] and image compression [25].

Judd et al. [26] learned a model of saliency from 33 features (including low, mid and high level features) to predict human eye fixations. They used Support Vector Machines (SVMs) with linear kernels to learn feature weightings. Zhao et al. [44] used least square regression to learn eye fixation prediction using basic saliency features (i.e., color, intensity and orientation). Borji et al. [6] in a later work also tested linear regression to learn a model of saliency from eye tracking data. All the above mentioned approaches achieve reasonably good results, however lose generalization as they only a learn a single set of weights for all image types.

AdaBoost [6, 45] learns the task of salient object detection using an assembly of weak learners (hence increasing generalization). However the quality of final solution depends upon the performance of individual learners and can be affected drastically by one of the learners in the decision tree, which badly affects the generalization of the overall system. Once again, AdaBoost does not divide the image set into domains depending upon image type, which degrades generalization on unseen images.

2.2 Learning Classifier Systems

Traditionally, an LCS represents a rule-based agent that incorporates evolutionary computing and machine learning to solve a given task by interacting with a previously unknown environment. After observing the current state of the environment, the agent performs an action and the environment provides a reward. The generalization property in LCS allows a single rule to cover more than one state provided that the action-reward mapping is similar.

XCS [40] is a formulation of LCS that uses accuracy-based fitness to learn the problem by forming a complete mapping of states and actions to rewards. In XCS, the learning agent evolves a population $[P]$ of classifiers, where each classifier consists of a rule and a set of associated parameters estimating the quality of the rule. Each rule is of the form 'if *condition* then *action*'. Commonly, the condition is represented by a fixed length bitstring defined over the ternary alphabet $\{0, 1, \#\}$ where '#' is the 'don't care' symbol which can be either 0 or 1; and the action is represented by a numeric constant.

Various richer encoding schemes have been investigated to represent high level knowledge in LCS in an attempt to obtain compact classifier rules [14, 21, 22], to solve overlapping problems [19, 23], to approximate functions [9, 42], to develop useful feature extractors [2], to tackle problems involving large number of discrete actions [29,32], to compute continuous actions [20, 38, 43], and to identify and process building blocks of knowledge [10, 24].

The following two XCS-based classifier systems, i.e. XCSCA (XCS with Computed Action) [29] and XCSRCFA (XCSR with Code-Fragment Actions) [20] are directly related to the work to be presented here.

2.2.1 XCS with Computed Action

XCSCA [29] is a supervised learning system, which computes action mappings using the input message x and a weight vector w. XCSCA borrows the idea of supervised learning from UCS [5], and the idea of action mappings from XCSF [42]. In XCSCA, classifiers have no prediction since, as in UCS, there is no incoming reward. Consequently, XCSCA does not produce a complete action map, rather it only evolves the correct output function.

The reported experimental results show that XCSCA can evolve accurate and compact representations of various binary functions, which would be difficult to be solve using the base XCS technique [29].

2.2.2 XCSR with Code-Fragment Actions

XCSRCFA extends the typical XCSR system [41] to tackle problems involving continuous actions [20]. In XCSRCFA, the typically used numeric action is replaced by a code fragment, which is a binary tree. The function set for the tree is problem dependent such as $\{+,-,*,/...\}$ for symbolic regression problems, and {AND,OR,NOT...} for Boolean problems. The terminal set is {D0,D1,D2,...,Dn-1} where n is the length of the environmental input message.

The action value of a classifier is determined by loading the terminal symbols in the action tree with the corresponding environmental instance's values. Thus the action is continuous with respect to the input state in XCSRCFA. XCSRCFA has been successfully applied to solve various continuous action problems as well as function approximation problems [20].

3. SALIENT OBJECT DETECTION USING LEARNING CLASSIFIER SYSTEMS

Commonly, salient objects in an image are detected by determining a saliency map for the input image, which is a computed image that attempts to emphasize the object to be detected. We have adopted a supervised approach, similar to XCSCA, where the target saliency map (i.e. the ground truth) is also provided along with the input image during training. The goal of LCS is to evolve saliency maps for each input image such that the error between the computed saliency map and the target saliency map is minimum. The learnt rules can then be applied to select appropriate learned maps for previously unseen test images. The error function used in this work is given in Equation 1:

$$\epsilon = 1 - \frac{\mathcal{TP} + \mathcal{TN}}{\mathcal{TP} + \mathcal{FP} + \mathcal{TN} + \mathcal{FN}}, \quad (1)$$

where $\mathcal{TP}$ and $\mathcal{TN}$ are the number of correctly classified positive and negative pixel values, in a single image, between the computed saliency map (after segmentation as described in Section 5.2) and the ground truth, respectively. $\mathcal{FP}$ and $\mathcal{FN}$ represents the falsely classified pixel values.

Instead of matching the input image at pixel-level against conditions of classifier rules, we will compute the following nine saliency-based features, which are two-dimensional real-valued matrices, for each input image (see Figure 2). We carefully select potential features from previous work [3, 12, 15, 31, 33] that are suited for the task of salient object detection and have been previously shown to correlate with visual attention in different experimental settings. To thoroughly evaluate the learning performance of models, we have chosen features that complement each other well, with each one performing better than others for a particular image type.

- $f0$: A feature that computes the spatial variance of colors to highlight the salient object based on the work of Liu et al. [31].
- $f1$: A feature capturing the feature contrast based on distance between cluster centers, inspired by the work of Fu et al. [15]. The initial clusters are obtained from k-means segmentation.
- $f2$: A feature computing the spatial distribution of pixels in a cluster with respect to image center again inspired by the work of Fu et al. [15].
- $f3$: A region based feature that takes into account the global contrast of a region to all other spatial neighboring regions [12].
- $f4$: A global region-based color feature based on the work of Naqvi et al. [33], where it computes the object based global contrast taking into account only the neighboring super-pixels. The distance between regions is computed using the earth movers distance (EMD) [36].
- $f5$: A global region-based color feature which is similar to $f4$ but the distance between regions is the L2 distance, based on the work of Naqvi et al. [33].
- $f6$: A feature that captures the objectness measure of image windows, based on the work of Alexe et al. [3].
- $f7$: A feature that clusters information based on objectness of image regions [3].
- $f8$: A feature capturing local pattern distinctness, based on the work of Naqvi et al. [33].

If classifiers' conditions in an LCS are matched directly to the computed image features, then it will be hard to evolve any generalized classifier rules due to the large-sized two-dimensional image features [28]. Therefore, in order to enable generalization, we introduce a novel encoding scheme to match an input image against classifier conditions. In this encoding scheme, each computed image feature f_i will be encoded as a real-valued constant d_i to be matched against classifiers' conditions. The real-valued constant for a feature is computed using earth mover's distance (EMD) [36] from a two-dimensional artificial feature consisting of all 1s. EMD is a way of converting an image into a number, which is defined as the minimum cost for transforming one histogram into the other such that there exists a ground distance between the features.[3] Consequently, conditions in classifier rules will be encoded as concatenation of real-valued intervals so that the system can evolve generalized classifiers, see Figure 1.

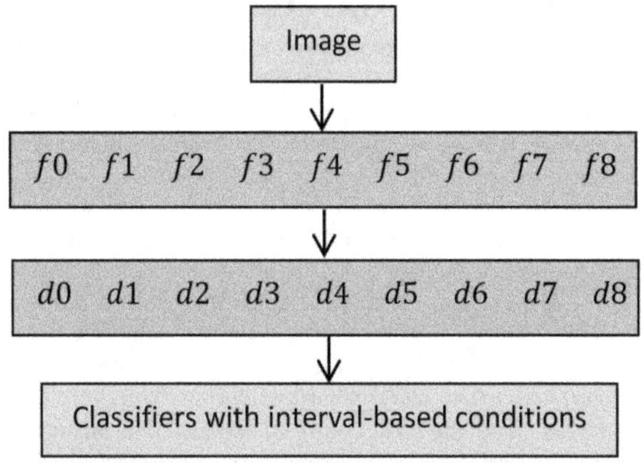

Figure 1: The novel encoding scheme to match an input image against the classifier population in order to enable generalization in classifier rules.

Usually an LCS evolves rules having fixed scalar actions. However, in the problem domains having large number of discrete actions and/or continuous actions, it is beneficial to *compute* actions instead of *mapping* actions [20, 29]. In this work, we have used the following two approaches to compute the action, i.e. the saliency map, in a classifier rule: (1) using a linear combination function, similar to XCSCA [29], and (2) using a code-fragment action, similar to XCSRCFA [20]. It is to be noted that the XCSCA-based system seeks feature selection, where as the XCSRCFA-based system seeks feature construction.

3.1 Computing Saliency using Linear Combination Functions (XCSCA)

In this approach, a saliency map is computed as a linear function of the input image and a weight vector w. In this function, the computed two-dimensional features are linearly combined with the evolved weights to produce the required saliency map for the matched input image, as given in Equation 2. Here x_0 denotes a constant input parameter. The weights are evolved using recursive least squares, as described by Lanzi et al. [30].

$$SaliencyMap = w_0x_0 + \sum w_{i+1}f_i; \qquad i = 0, 1, 2...8. \quad (2)$$

3.2 Computing Saliency using Code-Fragment Actions (XCSRCFA)

Each code-fragment action is a binary tree of maximum depth two, which is set to limit the tree size. Code-fragment actions are evolved using the GP-based crossover and mutation operations, as described in [20, 23]. To evaluate a code-fragment action, a terminal in the action tree will be loaded with the corresponding two-dimensional feature matrix computed for the input image. The evaluation of a code-fragment action will result in a two-dimensional matrix, which will be used as the computed saliency map by the system for the matched input image.

It is to be noted in both methods that to form a match set, we use the real-valued distance (denoted by d) for each

[3]We used the fast implementation of EMD with thresholded ground distances based on the work of Pele and Werman [35].

of the two-dimensional features, but to compute the saliency map the corresponding feature (denoted by f) itself is used.

4. SALIENT OBJECT DETECTION USING GENETIC ALGORITHMS

In order to utilize an equivalent benchmark (i.e., GA), which has shown state-of-the-art performance (at saliency prediction) compared with several other specialized visual attention models [34], we implement a novel GA based technique, similar to [34], to learn optimal feature weights in comparison to our LCS techniques. To this end we learn the feature weightings for combining various features from different modalities using GA. We use a real-coded representation of the GA as all of the decision variables are real. The initial population is randomly chosen within the specified bounds, i.e. [-1, 1], for all variables. We empirically determined the most appropriate selection function to be roulette wheel and the elite count to be six. The number of generations of the GA is the sole stopping criteria.

The problem of saliency learning can be effectively modeled as a binary classification problem, by comparing the thresholded saliency map with the binary ground truth (see Section 5.2). The objective of the GA is to maximize the number of truly labeled examples out of the total number of examples. Hence the fitness function used for the GA is the same as the error function of the LCS as given by Equation 1. By doing this, we also remove any biases and make the comparison fairer.

The crossover function used in the GA is the standard uniform crossover operation [17]. Mutation generates random search directions and steps which have the ability to adapt according to the result of the last generation. The steps and search directions are forced to remain in the feasible region by imposing bounds on variables. A combination of step size s, scale sc and direction vector $\mathbf{d}$ are added to the selected parent $\mathcal{P}$ to compute the offspring $\mathcal{O}$, as shown in Equation 3.

$$\mathcal{O} = \mathcal{P}_i^{(1)} + s \times sc \times \mathbf{d} \tag{3}$$

5. EXPERIMENTAL DESIGN

5.1 Data Set

This work employs the MSRA salient object database [31] using the labeled ground truth from [1]. The MSRA data set is comprised of 25,000 images in total, a common benchmark dataset in the field and represents many types of dataset as it contains many classes of image. The MSRA data set includes ground truth annotations in form of labeled rectangles from multiple users. These ground-truth annotations classify multiple objects as one by putting them in a single rectangle and also do not cater for pixel-wise accuracy. To remedy these effects, a set of 1000 images are manually segmented by a single user to obtain binary masks [1]. These ground truth masks consider the effect of pixel-wise accuracy and multiple objects (the details about the ground truth database can be found in [1]), and is widely accepted in the field of computer vision as a standard benchmark for saliency evaluation. The data set includes examples having the following classes of images increasing its diversity and making it difficult for techniques that use a single set of learned parameters: (1) images with cluttered background, (2) images with multiple objects, (3) images with large salient objects, (4) images with small salient objects, and (5) images with faces, persons, objects and text.

Figure 2 shows some example images with their ground truth and respective features from the data set employed [31]. It is to be noted that all images and respective ground truth are resized to 200×200 pixels to leverage computational efficiency. Consequently the computed feature maps are of the same size.

5.2 Performance Measure

As the performance of saliency models depends upon the number of truly classified pixels compared with the total number of pixel seen by the system for a particular image, we use the classification accuracy of the predicted saliency maps as the performance measure. The classification accuracy of a particular saliency map is computed by comparing it with the ground truth data for a particular image. In order to compare a real valued saliency map with corresponding binary ground truth, it must be first segmented. In order to segment the saliency map, we use the standard benchmark method reported in [1]. According to this method, the saliency map is first over-segmented using some segmentation algorithm, i.e. mean-shift segmentation [13] in our implementation. Afterward, average saliency is computed for each segment. The saliency map is finally thresholded by comparing the average saliency per segment with a threshold set to be two times the mean saliency value of the saliency map. The segments having average saliency greater than the threshold are assigned 1 in the resulting segmented saliency map, while zeros are assigned to the rest of the map. The binary saliency map obtained after the above-mentioned process is then compared pixel by pixel with the binary ground truth to acquire the number of truly classified pixels ($\mathcal{TP}$ and $\mathcal{TN}$) out of the total number of pixels ($\mathcal{TP}, \mathcal{FP}, \mathcal{TN}, \mathcal{FN}$) and finally the classification accuracy.

5.3 Experimental Setup

The XCS-based systems use the following parameter values, commonly used in the literature, as suggested by Butz and Wilson in [11]: learning rate $\beta = 0.2$; fitness fall-off rate $\alpha = 0.1$; error threshold $\epsilon_0 = 10$; fitness exponent $\nu = 5$; threshold for GA application in the action set $\theta_{GA} = 25$; two-point crossover with probability $\chi = 0.8$; mutation probability $\mu = 0.01$; experience threshold for classifier deletion $\theta_{del} = 20$; fraction of mean fitness for deletion $\delta = 0.1$; classifier experience threshold for subsumption $\theta_{sub} = 20$; reduction of the fitness $fitnessReduction = 0.1$; $r_0 = 0.7$; $m_0 = 0.5$; and the selection method is tournament selection with tournament size ratio 0.4. GA subsumption is activated whereas action set subsumption is deactivated. The number of classifiers used is 2000 and the number of training instances is $20,000$, in all the experiments conducted here. Explore and exploit problem instances are alternated.

For the code-fragment action based approach, the used function set is $\{+, -, *, /\}$. For the linear combination function based approach, the constant input parameter $x_0 = 0.5$; and $\delta_{rls} = 100$.

The population size of the GA is 570 and the number of generations used is 100 so that the number of evaluations in the GA and the XCS-based systems are approximately equal. The crossover fraction is set to 0.8.

All the experiments have been repeated 30 times with a

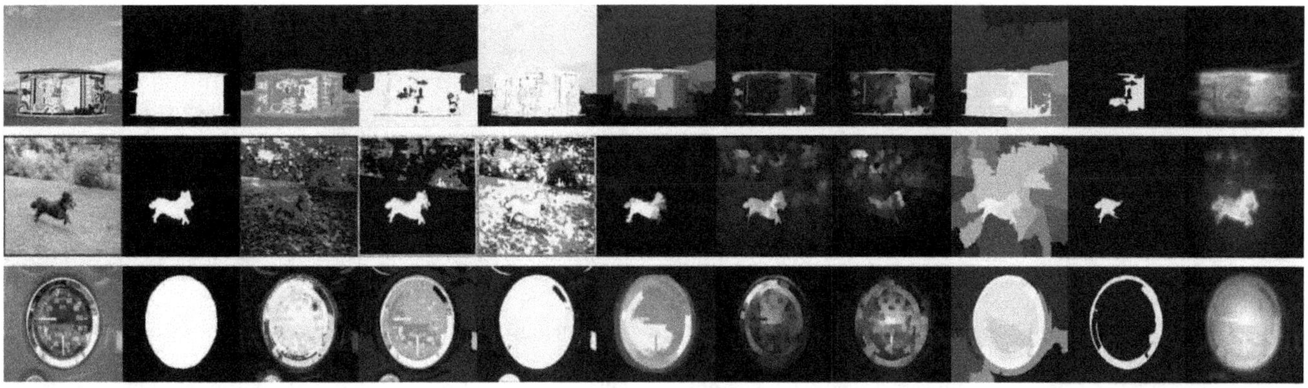

Figure 2: From left to right: image, ground truth, features $f0 - f8$ in the same order as listed in Section 3.

different seed in each run, where the image data set has been randomly divided into a training set of 700 and a testing set of 300 images in each experiment. Each result reported in this work is the average of the 30 runs.

6. RESULTS

The performance of two XCS-based classifier systems and a GA-based system for detecting salient objects in the training process is shown in Figure 3. In Figure 3(a), the X-axis is the number of problem instances used as training examples, the Y-axis is the performance measured as the percentage of correct classification during the last 50 exploit problem instances. In Figure 3(b), the X-axis is the number of generations of the GA, whereas Y-axis is the measured performance in terms of classification accuracy. The error bars show standard deviation in the 30 runs.

The GA-based system learned the weights and increased the performance gradually (effectively in a staircase fashion). The maximum increase in training performance is observed between the generations 20 to 30 with increase in small steps for the remaining of the training phase.

The code-fragment based XCS system struggles during the first 3000 problem instances, then it gradually improves to reach approximately 93% performance. The linear combination based XCS system outperformed the code-fragment based approach by quickly learning in the early stages and reached approximately 96% performance. The error bars confirmed that the linear combination based XCS system is more consistent than the code-fragment based system.

The performance of two XCS-based classifier systems and a GA-based system for detecting salient objects in the testing process is shown in Table 1. The linear combination based XCS system outperformed the code-fragment based XCS approach as well as the GA-based approach in the testing by reaching approximately 94.33% performance. Smaller standard deviation value in the linear combination based XCS system indicates that this approach is more consistent than the other two systems. To test the statistical significance of our methods, we performed an unpaired two-tailed t-test. The linear combination based XCS system was found to be statistically significant over the others with two-tailed p-values equal to 0.0001 and 0.0002 respectively. The code-fragment action based XCS system and the GA based system were found to be statistically similar in performance with a two-tailed p-value equal to 0.3773.

It is worth noting that the performance of the GA-based

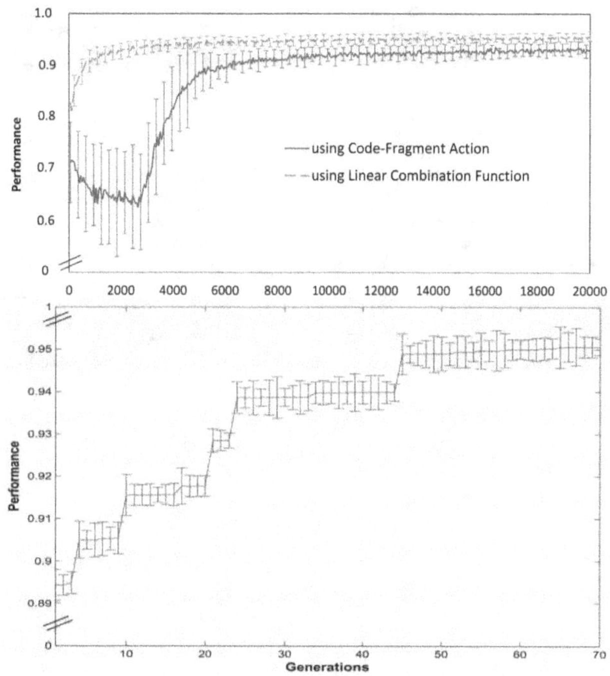

Figure 3: Comparison of two XCS-based classifier systems and a GA-based system during training process for detecting salient objects. The GA-based system performs batch learning with 700 instances per generation.

Table 1: Comparison of two XCS-based classifier systems and a GA-based system during testing process for detecting salient objects.

Method	Performance
LCS with Code-Fragment Actions	89.11 ± 3.34
LCS with Linear Combination Functions	94.33 ± 0.51
Genetic Algorithm	87.51 ± 9.26

system in the testing phase is noticeably worse than its performance in the training phase, i.e. GA suffered from overfitting. This may be due to the reason that the GA-based system produced a single individual, that is a set of feature weights, as the final solution. This single set of weights may not be good enough for all types of images in the test set due to the expected difference between training images and testing images from a real-world domain. The XCS-based systems did not suffer from over-fitting in this way because they divided the search space into different niches and evolved appropriate classifier rules for each niche.

Figure 4 presents the visual comparison of saliency maps generated by the GA and XCS based systems. Higher intensity values mean higher saliency and vice versa. It is noted that the saliency output of the GA based system highlights the salient objects appropriately but is affected by background clutter. Although, the code-fragment based XCS system does not uniformly highlight the salient objects but effectively suppresses the background information to the minimal. The linear combination based XCS system generates balanced saliency maps by uniformly highlighting salient objects and ensuring the inclusion of background to the minimum.

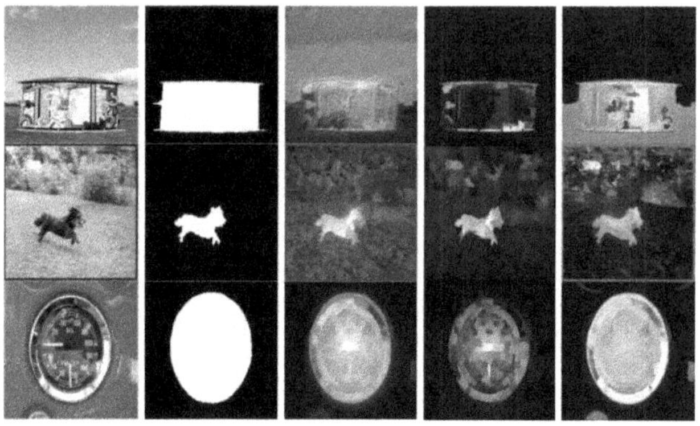

Figure 4: Visual comparison of saliency techniques. From left to right: input image, ground truth, GA, XCSRCFA, XCSCA

7. ANALYSIS OF EVOLVED SOLUTIONS

Table 2 shows the weighting parameters learned by the GA during four different selected runs on different training image sets. Weight vector number 1 and 2 are the ones having high accuracies above 94% (highest accuracies), whereas vector number 3 and 4 shown here have less than 75% accuracy (lowest accuracies). It is anticipated that having too many negatively weighted features (as in the case of weight vectors 3 and 4) generally degrades performance as the features having negative values can suppress important features (having salient peaks), when combined linearly through addition. Feature $f4$ is generally weighted heavily (with positive values), supporting our findings in the XCS-based system that computes saliency maps using code-fragmented actions, shown in Table 4. Features $f3$ and $f5$ are also heavily weighted in comparison to other features and always have positive values.

Table 2: The weight vectors learned by the GA. The results for the four indicative runs are shown here.

No.	Weight Vector								
	$w0$	$w1$	$w2$	$w3$	$w4$	$w5$	$w6$	$w7$	$w8$
1	0.61	0.08	0.79	0.50	0.70	0.57	0.77	0.54	0.70
2	0.72	0.15	0.03	0.51	0.77	0.41	0.16	0.20	0.51
3	-0.04	0.23	-0.15	0.83	1.00	0.63	-0.70	-0.81	0.37
4	-0.34	-0.16	-0.88	0.65	0.67	0.61	0.06	-0.06	0.67

A sample of the experienced (i.e. $exp \geq 1/\beta$) and accurate (i.e. $\epsilon \leq \epsilon_0$) classifier rules evolved in a typical run of code-fragment based system are shown in Table 3. The evolved rules in code-fragment based classifier system indicate that the computed saliency map in this approach mostly consists of a single feature. This approach could not find a relation between different features possibly due to the empirically chosen good features, the lack of any weighting of the features, and/or the less descriptive function set used to generate a code-fragment action. All of these points will be further investigated in future work.

In order to get an insight of the importance of different features in the code-fragment action based classifier system, we calculated the number of occurrences of each feature in the code-fragment actions of experienced and accurate classifier rules obtained in the final solutions. The calculated frequency of each features' occurrences is shown in Table 4. It is observed that the features $f7$ and $f8$ are the least common ones as they occurred, only six and three times in the code-fragment actions, respectively. It is worth noting that the feature $f8$ only occurred in combination with the features $f2$ and $f4$ and not as an individual. Feature $f4$ is the most important feature in this approach as it occurred 413 times, which is twice the total occurrences of all other features, i.e. 208, the next most occurring features are $f2$, $f5$, and $f6$.

Table 4: Frequency of features' occurrences in the experienced and accurate classifiers evolved in the XCS-based system that computes saliency maps using code-fragment actions.

Feature	Description	Frequency
$f0$	spatial variance of colors	31
$f1$	feature contrast	14
$f2$	spatial distribution of pixels	44
$f3$	the global contrast of a region	30
$f4$	object based global contrast using EMD	413
$f5$	object based global contrast using L2	36
$f6$	objectness measure of image windows	44
$f7$	clusters information	6
$f8$	local pattern distinctness	3

A sample of the experienced and accurate classifier rules evolved in a typical run of linear combination based system are shown in Table 5. The linear combination based system evolved weights for each feature in each classifier, see Table 5. It is to be noted that there are 10 weights in each classifier, the first on the left side corresponding to the constant input x_0 and the remaining nine corresponding to the nine computed saliency features. This approach is more efficient and robust than the code-fragment based approach because in this method, different features can be combined in different classifiers according to the evolved weights. For example, in classifier number two shown in Table 5, the features $f3$, $f5$, and $f8$ have larger weights than the other features. Therefore, the classifier number two is giving more importance to the features $f3$, $f5$, and $f8$ while combining all the features using a linear combination. Similarly, in classifier number eight, the features $f4$, $f5$, $f6$, and $f8$ are more important than the other features. This was not common in the code-fragment based approach, which mostly computed saliency maps using just one feature at a time.

8. CONCLUSIONS

The designed XCS-based systems outperformed the GA-based system in computing saliency maps in order to de-

Table 3: **A sample of the experienced (i.e. $exp \geq 1/\beta$) and accurate (i.e. $\epsilon \leq \epsilon_0$) classifier rules, obtained in a typical run, using code-fragment action based XCS system.**

No.	Condition									Action
1	[0.48,0.63]	[0.49,0.62]	[0.39,0.81]	[0.17,0.94]	[0.31,0.75]	[0.22,0.51]	[0.64,1.00]	[0.25,0.86]	[0.00,0.00]	D3
2	[0.07,0.84]	[0.79,1.00]	[0.00,0.98]	[0.71,0.83]	[0.50,1.00]	[0.00,0.46]	[0.06,1.00]	[0.00,0.64]	[0.23,1.00]	D4
3	[0.48,0.63]	[0.49,0.62]	[0.39,0.81]	[0.17,0.94]	[0.31,0.75]	[0.22,0.51]	[0.15,1.00]	[0.25,0.86]	[0.00,0.00]	D3
4	[0.00,1.00]	[0.00,0.24]	[0.00,1.00]	[0.02,0.07]	[0.00,1.00]	[0.00,0.43]	[0.76,1.00]	[0.00,0.64]	[0.03,0.31]	D4
5	[0.00,0.51]	[0.00,0.24]	[0.00,0.25]	[0.00,0.07]	[0.00,0.23]	[0.00,0.06]	[0.93,1.00]	[0.05,0.30]	[0.03,0.51]	D4
6	[0.00,0.23]	[0.00,0.24]	[0.00,0.25]	[0.02,0.07]	[0.00,0.66]	[0.00,0.43]	[0.00,1.00]	[0.05,0.64]	[0.03,0.31]	D4
7	[0.00,1.00]	[0.05,0.91]	[0.00,0.75]	[0.00,0.77]	[0.00,0.42]	[0.13,0.43]	[0.93,1.00]	[0.00,0.34]	[0.03,0.31]	D5
8	[0.00,0.51]	[0.00,0.57]	[0.00,0.25]	[0.00,0.77]	[0.00,0.23]	[0.00,0.06]	[0.83,1.00]	[0.05,0.30]	[0.03,0.73]	D4
9	[0.78,1.00]	[0.12,0.32]	[0.00,0.84]	[0.00,0.41]	[0.00,0.37]	[0.00,0.33]	[0.00,0.65]	[0.00,0.24]	[0.00,0.60]	D4D2D8/+
10	[0.00,0.23]	[0.00,1.00]	[0.00,0.25]	[0.00,0.07]	[0.00,0.66]	[0.00,0.43]	[0.00,1.00]	[0.05,0.30]	[0.03,0.73]	D4

Table 5: **A sample of the experienced (i.e. $exp \geq 1/\beta$) and accurate (i.e. $\epsilon \leq \epsilon_0$) classifier rules, obtained in a typical run, using linear combination based XCS system.**

No.	Condition									Weight Vector
1	[0.74,1.00]	[0.14,0.25]	[0.09,0.72]	[0.00,0.82]	[0.00,0.56]	[0.00,0.49]	[0.00,1.00]	[0.00,0.68]	[0.00,0.98]	35.2,46.3,25.6,-5.5,29.8,26.9,5.7,96.4,1.7,3.3
2	[0.00,0.74]	[0.12,0.64]	[0.14,0.59]	[0.00,0.70]	[0.19,0.36]	[0.00,0.56]	[0.59,1.00]	[0.00,0.02]	[0.00,1.00]	-335.6,192.0,181.7,-3.3,369.8,-329.2,691.8,343.7,38.5,733.5
3	[0.19,1.00]	[0.08,1.00]	[0.08,1.00]	[0.61,0.82]	[0.19,1.00]	[0.50,1.00]	[0.83,1.00]	[0.00,0.50]	[0.20,1.00]	-799.9,606.6,-138.0,117.5,2.9,441.2,-243.8,200.4,540.2,491.1
4	[0.19,1.00]	[0.74,1.00]	[0.62,1.00]	[0.50,0.68]	[0.35,0.80]	[0.00,0.36]	[0.41,1.00]	[0.00,0.47]	[0.54,1.00]	-674.4,594.2,-155.8,150.3,-116.7,560.0,-225.9,124.4,475.7,583.8
5	[0.18,1.00]	[0.12,1.00]	[0.00,0.59]	[0.42,0.70]	[0.00,0.53]	[0.00,0.46]	[0.59,1.00]	[0.18,0.47]	[0.25,1.00]	-145.1,-28.5,-1.9,914.7,994.3,-509.5,488.0,-39.4,349.3,-499.8
6	[0.00,0.74]	[0.12,0.51]	[0.00,0.59]	[0.00,0.68]	[0.00,0.60]	[0.14,0.46]	[0.59,1.00]	[0.00,0.02]	[0.28,0.34]	40.8,-243.6,-83.5,606.9,532.6,611.4,672.0,69.7,-142.0,174.7
7	[0.00,1.00]	[1.00,1.00]	[0.08,1.00]	[0.00,1.00]	[0.00,1.00]	[0.00,0.38]	[0.41,0.66]	[0.00,0.52]	[0.53,1.00]	-629.4,774.4,-697.0,177.8,-8.2,1081.5,660.1,1532.2,101.5,647.9
8	[0.43,0.83]	[0.87,1.00]	[0.46,0.97]	[0.05,1.00]	[0.47,1.00]	[0.00,0.02]	[0.23,1.00]	[0.38,0.90]	[0.00,0.31]	-635.9,390.7,-542.2,216.3,-2.9,1077.3,699.7,1604.1,300.7,654.2
9	[0.43,0.83]	[0.87,1.00]	[0.00,0.97]	[0.05,1.00]	[0.47,1.00]	[0.00,0.02]	[0.23,1.00]	[0.00,0.73]	[0.00,1.00]	-631.1,391.6,-542.4,214.5,-2.7,1081.2,694.4,1601.3,301.1,656.2
10	[0.37,0.87]	[0.50,0.74]	[0.56,1.00]	[0.61,1.00]	[0.00,1.00]	[0.00,1.00]	[0.23,1.00]	[0.00,0.50]	[0.44,1.00]	-931.3,260.1,-342.5,457.2,-3.9,931.7,403.5,1284.7,381.8,730.4

tect salient objects in an image. It is found that the GA-based system suffered from over-fitting in the real-world domain experimented in this work where as the XCS-based systems avoid this over-fitting by dividing the search space into niches and evolving appropriate classifier rules for each niche. Further, the linear combination based XCS system is found to be superior, due to its feature selection property, to the code-fragment based system in computing saliency maps.

The code-fragment based system could not find a relation between the empirically chosen good image features, so it often produced a single feature as the computed saliency map. The feature $f4$, which computes the object based global contrast using the earth movers distance and taking into account only the neighboring super-pixels, is found to be most important in this approach. Even with each map consisting of a single feature, this approach outperformed the GA-based system in the testing phase due to the cooperative nature of the evolved classifier rules.

Future work includes the introduction of a mechanism to generate feature weights and using more expressive functions for the code-fragment based classifier system.

9. REFERENCES

[1] R. Achanta, S. Hemami, F. Estrada, and S. Süsstrunk. Frequency-tuned Salient Region Detection. In *Proc of IEEE Conference on Computer Vision and Pattern Recognition*, pages 1597–1604, 2009.

[2] M. Ahluwalia and L. Bull. A Genetic Programming Based Classifier System. In *Proc of the Genetic and Evolutionary Computation Conference*, pages 11–18, 1999.

[3] B. Alexe, T. Deselaers, and V. Ferrari. What is an Object? In *Proc of IEEE Conference on Computer Vision and Pattern Recognition*, pages 73–80, 2010.

[4] M. Behdad, L. Barone, T. French, and M. Bennamoun. On XCSR for Electronic Fraud Detection. *Evolutionary Intelligence*, 5(2):139–150, 2012.

[5] E. Bernadó-Mansilla and J. M. Garrell-Guiu. Accuracy-Based Learning Classifier Systems: Models, Analysis and Applications to Classification Tasks. *Evolutionary Computation*, 11(3):209–238, 2003.

[6] A. Borji. Boosting Bottom-Up and Top-Down Visual Features for Saliency Estimation. In *Proc of IEEE Conference on Computer Vision and Pattern Recognition*, pages 438–445, 2012.

[7] L. Bull. *Applications of Learning Classifier Systems.* Springer, 2004.

[8] L. Bull and T. Kovacs. *Foundations of Learning Classifier Systems: An Introduction.* Springer, 2005.

[9] M. V. Butz, P. L. Lanzi, and S. W. Wilson. Function Approximation With XCS: Hyperellipsoidal Conditions, Recursive Least Squares, and Compaction. *IEEE Transactions on Evolutionary Computation*, 12(3):355–376, 2008.

[10] M. V. Butz, M. Pelikan, X. Llorà, and D. E. Goldberg. Automated Global Structure Extraction for Effective Local Building Block Processing in XCS. *Evolutionary Computation*, 14(3):345–380, 2006.

[11] M. V. Butz and S. W. Wilson. An Algorithmic Description of XCS. *Soft Computing*, 6(3-4):144–153, 2002.

[12] M.-M. Cheng, G.-X. Zhang, N. J. Mitra, X. Huang, and S.-M. Hu. Global Contrast based Salient Region Detection. In *Proc of IEEE Conference on Computer Vision and Pattern Recognition*, pages 409–416, 2011.

[13] D. Comaniciu and P. Meer. Mean shift: A robust approach toward feature space analysis. *IEEE Transactions on Pattern Analysis and Machine Intelligence*, 24(5):603–619, 2002.

[14] H. H. Dam, H. A. Abbass, C. Lokan, and X. Yao. Neural-Based Learning Classifier Systems. *IEEE Transactions on Knowledge and Data Engineering*, 20(1):26–39, 2008.

[15] H. Fu, X. Cao, and Z. Tu. Cluster-Based Co-Saliency

Detection. *IEEE Transactions on Image Processing*, 22(10):3766–3778, 2013.

[16] S. Goferman, L. Zelnik-Manor, and A. Tal. Context-Aware Saliency Detection. *IEEE Transactions on Pattern Analysis and Machine Intelligence*, 34(10):1915–1926, 2012.

[17] D. E. Goldberg. *Genetic Algorithms in Search, Optimization and Machine Learning*. Addison Wesley, 1989.

[18] J. H. Holland, L. B. Booker, M. Colombetti, M. Dorigo, D. E. Goldberg, S. Forrest, R. L. Riolo, R. E. Smith, P. L. Lanzi, W. Stolzmann, and S. W. Wilson. What Is a Learning Classifier System? In *Learning Classifier Systems, From Foundations to Applications*, pages 3–32. Springer, 2000.

[19] C. Ioannides, G. Barrett, and K. Eder. Improving XCS Performance on Overlapping Binary Problems. In *Proc of the IEEE Congress on Evolutionary Computation*, pages 1420–1427, 2011.

[20] M. Iqbal, W. N. Browne, and M. Zhang. XCSR with Computed Continuous Action. In *Proc of the Australasian Joint Conference on Artificial Intelligence*, pages 350–361, 2012.

[21] M. Iqbal, W. N. Browne, and M. Zhang. Evolving Optimum Populations with XCS Classifier Systems. *Soft Computing*, 17(3):503–518, 2013.

[22] M. Iqbal, W. N. Browne, and M. Zhang. Extending Learning Classifier System with Cyclic Graphs for Scalability on Complex, Large-Scale Boolean Problems. In *Proc of the Genetic and Evolutionary Computation Conference*, pages 1045–1052, 2013.

[23] M. Iqbal, W. N. Browne, and M. Zhang. Learning Complex, Overlapping and Niche Imbalance Boolean Problems Using XCS-Based Classifier Systems. *Evolutionary Intelligence*, 6(2):73–91, 2013.

[24] M. Iqbal, W. N. Browne, and M. Zhang. Reusing Building Blocks of Extracted Knowledge to Solve Complex, Large-Scale Boolean Problems. *IEEE Transactions on Evolutionary Computation*, 2013. `http://dx.doi.org/10.1109/TEVC.2013.2281537`.

[25] L. Itti. Automatic Foveation for Video Compression Using a Neurobiological Model of Visual Attention. *IEEE Transactions on Image Processing*, 13(10):1304–1318, 2004.

[26] T. Judd, K. Ehinger, F. Durand, and A. Torralba. Learning to Predict Where Humans Look. In *Proc of International Conference on Computer Vision*, pages 2106–2113, 2009.

[27] D. A. Klein and S. Frintrop. Center-surround Divergence of Feature Statistics for Salient Object Detection. In *Proc of International Conference on Computer Vision*, pages 2214–2219, 2011.

[28] I. Kukenys, W. N. Browne, and M. Zhang. Transparent, Online Image Pattern Classification Using a Learning Classifier System. In *Applications of Evolutionary Computation*, volume 6624 of *Lecture Notes in Computer Science*, pages 183–193. Springer Berlin Heidelberg, 2011.

[29] P. L. Lanzi and D. Loiacono. Classifier Systems That Compute Action Mappings. In *Proc of the Genetic and Evolutionary Computation Conference*, pages 1822–1829, 2007.

[30] P. L. Lanzi, D. Loiacono, S. W. Wilson, and D. E. Goldberg. Generalization in the XCSF Classifier System: Analysis, Improvement, and Extension. *Evolutionary Computation*, 15(2):133–168, 2007.

[31] T. Liu, Z. Yuan, J. Sun, J. Wang, N. Zheng, X. Tang, and H.-Y. Shum. Learning to Detect a Salient Object. *IEEE Transactions on Pattern Analysis and Machine Intelligence*, 33(2):353–367, 2011.

[32] D. Loiacono, A. Marelli, and P. L. Lanzi. Support Vector Machines for Computing Action Mappings in Learning Classifier Systems. In *Proc of the IEEE Congress on Evolutionary Computation*, pages 2141–2148, 2007.

[33] S. S. Naqvi, W. N. Browne, and C. Hollitt. Combining Object-Based Local and Global Feature Statistics for Salient Object Search. In *Proc of International Conference on Image and Vision Computing New Zealand*, page 6, 2013.

[34] S. S. Naqvi, W. N. Browne, and C. Hollitt. Optimizing Visual Attention Models for Predicting Human Fixations Using Genetic Algorithms. In *Proc of IEEE Congress on Evolutionary Computation*, pages 1302–1309, 2013.

[35] O. Pele and M. Werman. Fast and Robust Earth Mover's Distances. In *Proc of International Conference on Computer Vision*, pages 460–467, 2009.

[36] Y. Rubner, C. Tomasi, and L. J. Guibas. The Earth Mover's Distance as a Metric for Image Retrieval. *International Journal of Computer Vision*, 40(2):99–121, 2000.

[37] K. Shafi, T. Kovacs, H. A. Abbass, and W. Zhu. Intrusion Detection with Evolutionary Learning Classifier Systems. *Natural Computing*, 8(1):3–27, 2009.

[38] T. H. Tran, C. Sanza, Y. Duthen, and D. T. Nguyen. XCSF with Computed Continuous Action. In *Proc of the Genetic and Evolutionary Computation Conference*, pages 1861–1869, 2007.

[39] D. Walther and C. Koch. Modeling Attention to Salient Proto-Objects. *Neural Networks*, 19(9):1395–1407, 2006.

[40] S. W. Wilson. Classifier Fitness Based on Accuracy. *Evolutionary Computation*, 3(2):149–175, 1995.

[41] S. W. Wilson. Get Real! XCS with Continuous-Valued Inputs. In *Learning Classifier Systems*, pages 209–219. Springer, 2000.

[42] S. W. Wilson. Classifiers that Approximate Functions. *Natural Computing*, 1:211–233, 2002.

[43] S. W. Wilson. Three Architectures for Continuous Action. In *Learning Classifier Systems*, pages 239–257. Springer, 2007.

[44] Q. Zhao and C. Koch. Learning a Saliency Map Using Fixated Locations in Natural Scenes. *Journal of Vision*, 11(3):1–15, 2011.

[45] Q. Zhao and C. Koch. Learning Visual Saliency by Combining Feature Maps in a Nonlinear Manner Using AdaBoost. *Journal of Vision*, 12(6):1–15, 2012.

SAX-EFG: An Evolutionary Feature Generation Framework for Time Series Classification

Uday Kamath
George Mason University
Fairfax, Virginia USA
ukamath@gmu.edu

Jessica Lin
George Mason University
Fairfax, Virginia USA
jessica@gmu.edu

Kenneth De Jong
George Mason University
Fairfax, Virgina USA
kdejong@gmu.edu

ABSTRACT

A variety of real world applications fit into the broad definition of time series classification. Using traditional machine learning approaches such as treating the time series sequences as high dimensional vectors have faced the well known "curse of dimensionality" problem. Recently, the field of time series classification has seen success by using preprocessing steps that discretize the time series using a Symbolic Aggregate ApproXimation technique (SAX) and using recurring subsequences ("motifs") as features.

In this paper we explore a feature construction algorithm based on genetic programming that uses SAX-generated motifs as the building blocks for the construction of more complex features. The research shows that the constructed complex features improve the classification accuracy in a statistically significant manner for many applications.

Track: Evolutionary Machine Learning

Categories and Subject Descriptors

I.2.6 [**Computing Methodologies**]: Artificial Intelligence—*Learning*[Knowledge acquisition]

General Terms

Algorithms

Keywords

machine learning; time-series classification; genetic programming; evolutionary computation

1. INTRODUCTION

Many real-world applications such as motion detection in robotics, climate change detection based on anthropogenic measurements, and financial market predictions based on stock price variations fit into a broad definition of time series classification. In time series classification, individual instances are sequences of numeric values associated with labels. Using traditional machine learning approaches such as treating the time series sequences as high-dimensional vectors have faced with the well known "curse of dimensionality" problem [25]. Most data mining techniques typically involve some form of transformation on the existing real-valued time-ordered data. The complex structural characteristics of real-world time series data such as high-dimensionality, feature correlation, and measurement-induced noise render classic data mining algorithms ineffective and inefficient for these representations. In contrast, symbolic transformations such as Symbolic Aggregate approXimation (SAX) have been shown to be very effective for a large number of time series applications [31]. SAX, in addition to performing mapping from time series to discrete symbols, also performs dimensionality reduction.

Unlike other data types, there are no "explicit" features or signals in discretized sequence data that can help traditional machine learning algorithms learn and predict from the data. In sequence-based classification, the immediate goal becomes the discovery of signals or features in the sequence data that correlate with the desired property, as well as discrimination between sequences that contain such property and those that do not. Sequence data exhibit interrelationships in the elements that are important in understanding and predicting future sequences. However, finding these relationships is proven to be an NP-hard problem [34]. When we use naïve enumerations for defining these features they often result in poor predictions. Some algorithms that perform well in prediction lack transparency, i.e., the discriminating features generated by these methods are not easily identifiable. Recently, an evolutionary algorithm based feature generation (EFG) technique was introduced to generate discriminating features for DNA sequence classification [16, 17]. It was shown that the EFG-based approach was able to generate features in human-readable manner that biologists are interested in, while achieving good predictive performance [16, 17].

In this paper, the SAX and EFG algorithms are combined to produce an effective time series classification methodology. SAX performs the high level transformation of converting real-valued time series to discretized alphabet-based sequences. EFG uses these transformed sequences to find complex patterns as discriminating features that can be used with any generic classifiers. We first provide a brief introduction to time series representations, SAX, and EFG in section 2. We then describe how EFG and SAX can be combined to-

GECCO'14, July 12–16, 2014, Vancouver, BC, Canada.

ACM 978-1-4503-2662-9/14/07 ...$15.00.
http://dx.doi.org/10.1145/2576768.2598321.

gether in sections 3 and 4. In section 5 we describe the evaluation experiments that were performed on publicly available real-world datasets. Finally, we conclude with some overall observations and directions for future work.

2. BACKGROUND

Time series data have been analyzed in various data mining tasks such as classification, clustering, indexing, and summarization. In this paper we focus only on the classification task; however, the proposed approach is general and can be applied to other tasks as well.

For the purposes of this research a time series is assumed to be an ordered set of real-valued variables, and a time series classification problem is a set of labeled time series instances to be used as training data to construct a predictive model for classifying unseen time series instances.

Most time series classification approaches first perform some transformation that converts the real-valued ordered data to an approximate representation of the data. Many transformations like Discrete Fourier Transform (DFT) [12], Discrete Wavelet Transform (DWT) [5], Piecewise Linear, and Piecewise Constant models (PAA) [20], (APCA) [14, 19], Singular Value Decomposition (SVD), and symbolic representations [25] have been proposed. Each of these techniques can be considered to be approximating the signal using linear combinations of some basis functions. In similarity-based classification of time series, a distance function or a similarity function is defined to measure the distance or similarity between a pair of sequences. Given such a distance function, one can use existing classification methods such as k-nearest neighbor classifiers (KNNs) or support vector machines (SVMs) with local alignment kernels [42, 7]. Time series shapelets using subsequence patterns and logical combinations of these patterns have recently been proposed and are gaining popularity for classification [29, 45]. Many statistical representation based techniques such as position-specific scoring matrix (PSSM)—also known as the position-weight matrix (PWM)—method, which assumes symbols at all positions are drawn independently [39, 13], the weight array model (WAM) which relaxes assumptions of independence by additionally modeling dependencies on a previous position [40], higher-order Markov models, which model more dependencies and outperform PSSMs [43, 18], and even more complex models like Bayesian networks [4, 1] and Markov Random Fields (MRFs) [44, 2] have been successfully employed in sequence classification. String based kernels in SVM, the weighted position kernel (similar to positional features), and the spectrum kernel (similar to the spectrum features) [36, 37] have been widely used in bioinformatics sequence classification applications.

3. METHODOLOGY

3.1 Symbolic Aggregate approXimation

SAX is a transformation technique that allows a time series of arbitrary length n to be reduced to a string of user-defined length w, ($w \ll n$). The alphabet size is also a user-defined integer α, where $\alpha \geq 2$. SAX performs the discretization using two distinct steps: 1) transform the data into the Piecewise Aggregate Approximation (PAA) representation, and 2) map the PAA representation into a discrete string representation. SAX can be performed repeatedly via

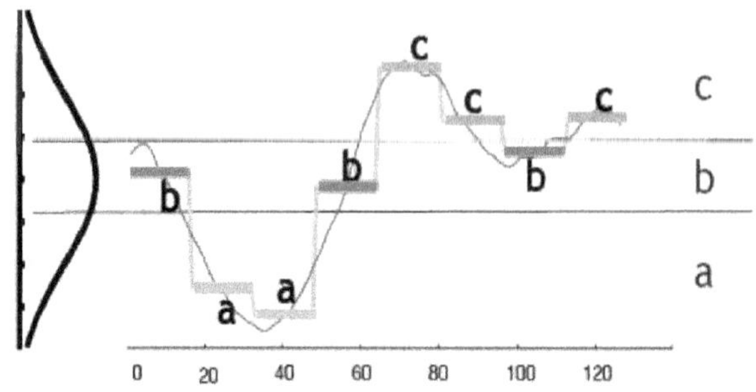

Figure 1: PAA approximations with predetermined breakpoints mapped to symbols. In the example above, with n = 128, w = 8 and a = 3, the time series is mapped to the word baabccbc [26]

a sliding window on subsequences from a longer time series, in which case a third, optional step may be employed: numerosity reduction of the data.

3.1.1 Piecewise Aggregate Approximation (PAA)

A time series T of length n can be represented in a w-dimensional space by a vector C. The ith element of C is calculated by the following equation:

$$\bar{c_i} = \frac{w}{n} \sum_{j=\frac{n}{w}(i-1)+1}^{\frac{n}{w}i} c_j \tag{1}$$

First, each time series is normalized to have a mean zero and standard deviation of one. The normalized time series data T is then divided into w equal sized "frames". The mean value of the data falling within a frame is calculated and a vector of these values becomes the reduced representation. The representation can be visualized as an approximation of the original time series with a linear combination of box basis functions. PAA has been considered to be a simple yet effective technique compared to more sophisticated ones like DWT and DFT [21, 20].

3.1.2 Discrete Symbolization

In the symbolization step, each PAA coefficient is mapped to a symbol based on a set of breakpoints. Ideally, we want the distribution of symbols to be equiprobable. Since normalized short time series tend to have a Gaussian distribution, we can define the breakpoints as the boundaries that will produce equal-sized areas under the Gaussian curve [28, 26]. A symbolic transformation table could thus be created by defining breakpoints that would result in regions of equal-probability on the Gaussian distribution. These breakpoints (or the z-values) may be determined by looking them up in statistical tables. Once the breakpoints are obtained, the mapping of a PAA coefficient to symbol is straight-forward. Figure 1 summarizes the process.

3.1.3 Numerosity Reduction

Most time series data have a large number of values, and one common technique is to consider a sliding window of length n (user defined parameter) subjected to SAX. Each subsequence of length n is normalized with mean zero and unit standard deviation and converted to a SAX string.

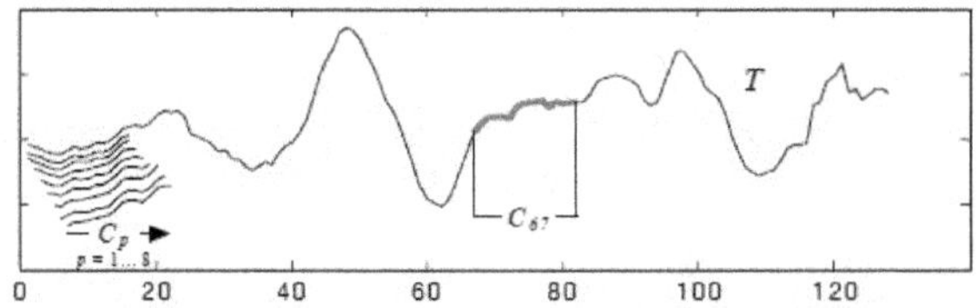

Figure 2: Timeseries of length 128, showing overlapping signals starting at different positions from p 1 to 8 [26].

Thus a set of SAX strings are obtained which correspond to the original time series. It was found that a SAX subsequence S_i is likely to be very similar to its neighboring subsequences S_{i+1} and S_{i-1}, especially when the sequence is in a smooth region, as depicted in Figure 2. Typically only the first of the repeating sequence of identical strings is recorded to avoid artificial over-representation of patterns. Such technique is called numerosity reduction.

As an example, suppose we have the following sequence of SAX strings with the sliding window technique:

$S = aac\ \ aac\ \ abc\ \ abb\ \ abb\ \ abb\ \ abb\ \ bac\ \ baa$

With the numerosity reduction option, we would get the following sequence instead:

$S_{nr} = aac_1\ \ abc_3\ \ abb_4\ \ bac_8\ \ baa_9$

The subscripts denote the offsets of the strings in the original sequence. In some datasets and applications, including these omitted subsequences may be useful, as they might carry important signals. But in most datasets, it was found that excluding these repeating subsequences resulted in a more accurate representation and classification accuracy [26].

3.2 Evolutionary Feature Generation (EFG)

EFG uses a Genetic Programming (GP) algorithm to explore a large, complex space of potentially useful features from the given training dataset [23]. Features are represented as standard GP trees, and a population of features is evolved over time using standard GP mechanisms of mutation and crossover. EFG uses a surrogate filter-based fitness function to estimate the usefulness of the GP-generated features, since the wrapper methodology to find effectiveness of the features is costly. A *hall of fame* mechanism incrementally collects the best estimated features for subsequent use with a classifier. Next, we present details of all the evolutionary elements and constructs that are used in the EFG algorithm.

3.2.1 Feature Representation

Various researchers, as highlighted in the related work section, have individually discovered many building blocks that can be very effective in finding the patterns in sequence classification. The novelty of the EFG algorithm is that it not only defines many new building blocks, but it also gives a structure through strongly-typed GP evolution, combining various building blocks in an effective and human-understandable manner. This structured way of searching a vast feature space involves building a complex structure given the constraints defined from simpler ones. Strongly-typed GP plays the role of giving structure and guidance to the vast search space of features. Next, we highlight the building blocks from the simplest short subsequence known as a motif, which becomes the common building block to the complex higher-order signals that can be constructed through the algorithm. We have arranged the explanation at various levels of complexity starting from Level 1 (the simplest) to Level 3 (the most complex).

Name	Args	Return Type
`and`	2 non-terminal boolean	boolean
`or`	2 non-terminal boolean	boolean
`not`	2 non-terminal boolean	boolean
`matches`	motif	boolean
`matchesAtPosition`	motif, position	boolean
`positionalShift`	motif, position,Shift	boolean
`correlational`	motif, motif, position, close	boolean
`motif-*`	ERC-chars	motif
`position`	ERC-int	Integer
`shift`	ERC-int	Integer
`close`	ERC-int	Integer
`region`	ERC-int,ERC-int	Integer
ERC-char	{Symbols}	Character
ERC-int	$\{1, \ldots, length\}$	Integer

Table 1: A table of the non-terminals and terminal nodes employed by EFG.

Level 1: Motif.

The most common building block is the presence of a short subsequence of strings of a given length, which are constructed as parse trees from the given alphabets. These motifs are used as a building block in all the second level constructs.

Level 2: Pattern Matching Functions.

Using the motifs as basic building blocks, EFG constructs features corresponding to patterns to be matched using a set of predefined functions, `matches`, `matchesAtPosition`, `positionalShift` and `correlational` as indicated in Table 1. The `matches` captures the simple compositional pattern. The `matchesAtPosition` allows constructing simple positional features from the motifs at a given position.The `positionalShift` allows constructing positional features that may be displaced in either direction by a small shift given as a parameter. The `correlational` operator captures the presence of positional features adjacent to each other, within a distance.

Level 3: Complex Higher Order Signals.

Many statistical learning approaches, such as Bayesian networks and Markov-chain models, rely on higher order elements formed from lower order signals as the discriminative features [24]. The approach of having logical combinatorial operators like `and`, `or`, and `not` acts in a similar way to construct more complex features combining the simple Level 1 motifs, Level 2 elements, or even the Level 3 features to form any level of complex patterns from simpler conjuncts or disjuncts.

3.2.2 *Genetic Operators*

As in most evolutionary algorithms, individuals have to undergo some modifications through genetic breeding operators to generate a new representation from the existing population individual(s). Studies have shown robust evolutionary algorithms incorporate both mutation and crossover as the breeding operators [38]. In this research, we explored forming problem-specific mutations as small, incremental operators. These mutation operators are motif mutation, positional mutation, shift mutation and adjacency mutation. In this work, the standard subtree crossover, one of the most common genetic recombination operators used in GP [23] is employed.

3.2.3 *Bloat Control*

One common problem with evolving variable-length or tree-structured individuals in EAs is that as the generation progresses, the individuals become complex in structure or length without any changes to fitness, commonly referred to as "bloat". One of the ways to control bloat is to have structural elements that reduce the chance of forming larger trees without much improvement to the fitness. By making specific building blocks, such as the `correlational` feature, rather than leaving it for evolution to form complex trees with two positional features capturing adjacent positional information is one such example. Another method that is used in EFG to combat increase in length and complexity is to employ a lexicographic tournament selection: if multiple individuals have the same fitness, the selection chooses the individual with the smaller tree depth [23].

3.2.4 *Population and Generation Mechanism*

The EFG algorithm creates individuals in generation 0 consisting of N randomly generated features using the well-known *ramped half-and-half* generative method [23]. The population size for GP is generally large, and we have employed a size of 10000. Instead of keeping the population size fixed for every generation, we employed the well known strategy of population implosion to reduce the size of population by 10% in every generation [27].

3.2.5 *Fitness Function*

A surrogate fitness function, or a "filter" approach, which is considered to be fast and effective way for feature evaluation [22] is employed in EFG. Since most sequence classification data are imbalanced and have very few positives and a large number of negatives, the goal is to improve precision while managing the discriminating power of features. We formulate the fitness function: $\text{Fitness}(f) = \frac{C_{+,f}}{C_+} * |\hat{C_{+,f}} - \hat{C_{-,f}}|$. In this equation, f refers to a feature, $C_{+,f}$ and $C_{-,f}$ are the number of positive and negative training sequences that contain the feature f, respectively. C_+ and C_- are the total number of positive training sequences. $\hat{C_{+,f}}$ and $\hat{C_{-,f}}$ are the normalized count of positive and negative sequences. This fitness function tracks the occurrence of a feature in positive sequences, as negative sequences may not have any common features or signals. The fitness function additionally penalizes non-discriminating features; that is, features that are equally found in positive and negative training sequences.

The goal is to maximize the fitness function, but the standard fitness formulated for GP aims for minimization [23]. So, the standard fitness of a feature is defined by f as $\text{Standard}(f) = 1/(\text{Fitness}(f))$. EFG then converts the standard fitness back into the GP-adjusted fitness $1/(1 + \text{Koza}(f))$ to select fit individuals. Note that the GP-adjusted fitness takes values in $[0, 1]$.

3.2.6 *Hall of Fame*

Since GP is a generational EA, i.e., the parents die after producing the offspring, there can be a "genetic drift" and convergence to a local optimum [8]. This can result in the loss of some of the best individuals, which can be useful discriminating features for classification. Introducing elitism, i.e., the ability to keep some of the best individuals in the population helps to overcome this at the expense of introducing strong selection pressure. To maintain this balance of not losing the best individuals in every generation and not introducing elitism for strong selection pressure, external storage has been found to be the ideal design decision [8]. The EFG algorithm will use this external storage of features known as *hall of fame*, and at the end of the EA run, these highly fit feature sets chosen from each generation become the feature set that constitutes the solution.

4. SAX-EFG FRAMEWORK

The overall framework for employing EFG along with SAX for time series is shown in Figure 4. SAX performs the preprocessing to convert the time series data to a sequence of SAX strings, and EFG does the feature generation task while any discriminating classifier like Naïve Bayes can be used to learn models from these features.

The mapping of time series to SAX strings requires various user-defined parameters like the sliding-window length n, PAA frame reduction size w, and alphabet size α for discretizing. In the experiments in this paper an alphabet of size 4 was used for all the experiments. The sliding window size and PAA size were used from standard SAX based runs from previous research and is mentioned along with results in the table.

The EFG algorithm used a default motif length range of 1 to 8 characters. Ideally, a motif should be restricted to contain only whole SAX strings. That is, in theory a motif should not be allowed to break up a string (pattern). In our experiments, however, we find that enforcing such restriction via the use of N (don't care or gap symbol) between SAX strings results in very little difference in accuracy. This may be due to the sparsity of the patterns, as well as the fact that a pattern needs to be both overrepresented *and* discriminative in order to be included in the feature set. The shift parameter for positional matching with error is set to 3 and closeness for capturing correlation between motifs is set to 4. The mutation and crossover parameters are also set to default of 0.1 each and 0.7 respectively. The hall of fame capture of features per generation is set to 250. The EFG algorithm is run for 30 generations.

4.1 Datasets

The datasets chosen for this task are some standard time series datasets with binary class labels from the real-world time series data. GunPoint dataset comes from the video surveillance domain and has two classes, containing 50 training and 150 testing examples with time series length of 150 [33]. The electrocardiogram (ECG) dataset contains measurements of cardiac electrical activity as recorded from electrodes at various locations on the body; each instance in

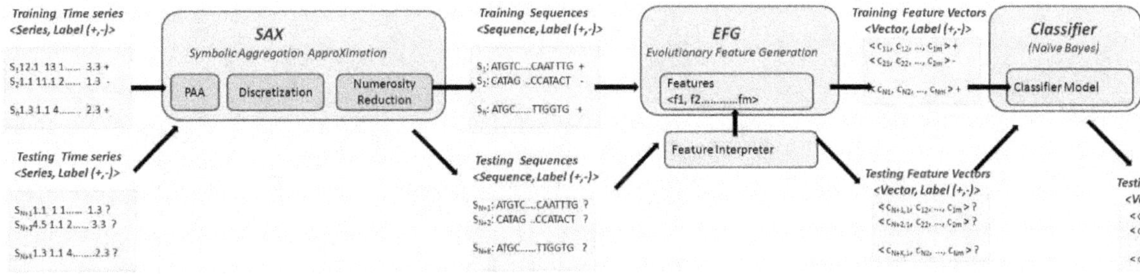

Figure 3: The EFG algorithm with the SAX algorithm

Dataset	Time Series Length	Train Size	Test Size
GunPoint	150	50	150
ECG200	96	100	100
Coffee	286	28	28
Lightning2	637	60	61
SonyAIBOSurface	70	20	601

Table 2: Dataset characteristics giving time series length, training and test size.

the ECG database contains the measurements recorded by one electrode during one heartbeat [30]. The Coffee dataset comes from food spectrograms domain [32]. The Lightning2 dataset comes from the geographic and satellite-based monitoring domain [11]. The SonyAIBOSurface dataset comes from the robotics and surface detection domain [41]. Table 2 gives the details of each dataset in terms of the time series length, training data size and the testing data size.

5. EXPERIMENTS

5.1 Comparing Time Series Algorithms

For our method, the SAX parameters like the sliding window length n and the PAA reduction length w are set based on previous studies done on SAX and outlined in Table 3. The choice of an alphabet of size 4 was a self-imposed restriction to allow some additional comparisons with our DNA sequence research. In future work, this can be changed and explored with higher numbers.

It has been shown that for time series classification, 1NN on the raw time series using standard distance measures like Euclidean Distance (L_2) or Dynamic Time Warping (DTW) [3] outperforms many more sophisticated classifiers [10]. Therefore, to follow literature standard, we compare our approach to 1NN as the classifier, with the following variations: (1) Euclidean Distance as the distance measure on the raw data, (2) DTW as the distance measure on the raw data, (3) SAX as the representation using the same parameters as EFG-SAX (the column labeled SAX), and (4) trained SAX as the representation where the best parameters are learned from the training set for each dataset (the column labeled SAX-BEST). In addition to the 1NN methods, we also compare with the shapelet and the logical shapelet algorithms.

During the testing phase, the same parameters of SAX are applied to the time series for SAX conversion and the trained model is used for predicting. The error rate measured as $(1 - accuracy)$, the standard metric used in all time series studies, is used as the comparison metric. Accuracy is defined as the percentage of correct predictions.

The implementations using Euclidean Distance (L_2), DTW, and SAX were obtained from the authors [26, 3]. The shapelet and logical shapelet were obtained from the work [29, 45]. EFG implementation was also obtained from the authors [16]. The SAX-BEST, SAX and EFG have parameters of sliding window size, segment size and the alphabet size for each experiment in the Table 3 and both the shapelet methods used the best parameters as noted in [29, 45]. All the experiments are run 30 times, comparisons made using paired-t tests and the statistically significant results with 95% confidence are reported in bold-faced and underlined in Table 3.

It can be observed that EFG-SAX gives performance comparable to many time series based algorithms for most datasets. For the Coffee and the GunPoint datasets EFG-SAX gives the statistically significantly better results. More importantly, it can be seen that in 4 out of 5 datasets SAX with EFG performs better than plain SAX. We could not run the Lightning2 dataset with either shapelet or logical shapelet implementations due to memory related issues.

5.2 Comparing Sequence Classification Algorithms

If SAX is used for discretizing the time series classification datasets, can EFG be comparable to other techniques known for handling discrete sequence-based data? A comparison of EFG with feature-based, statistical and kernel methods on some subset of datasets with the same preprocessing from time series to symbolic discrete set using SAX will be the next research goal. Two datasets, GunPoint and SonyAiBoSurface from above, which were statistically best and sightly worse respectively were considered for this comparison. We used an SVM with WeightedDegreePosition Kernel as the string kernel implementation, K-mer for feature based, and Homogeneous HMM and MSP as statistical discriminative and generative techniques.

The kernel parameters such as motif length or order were kept same as that of EFG at 8, while other parameters for the SVM and the HMM were chosen using cross-validation using a default ranges in the grid search. The implementation of the statistical methods employed for comparison is in Java, based on the publicly-available Jstacs package [15]. The kernel-based methods are implemented using the publicly-available Shogun toolkit [35] with the standard SVM implementation provided in the publicly-available LibSVM package [6]. The feature-based methods employed for a baseline validation are implemented in Java. The methods

Dataset	Euclidean	DTW	Shapelet	Logical	SAX-BEST	SAX	EFG-SAX	Rank
GunPoint	0.09	0.08	0.11	0.14	0.18 (32,4,10)	0.20 (32,4,4)	**0.032** (32,4,4)	1
ECG200	0.15	0.22	0.15	0.14	0.12(32,8,4)	0.12 (32,8,4)	0.13(32,8,4)	2
Coffee	0.16	0.12	0.04	0.04	0.46(48,4,3)	0.18(48,4,4)	**0.01**(48,4,4)	1
Lightning2	0.29	**0.17**	-	-	0.313 (128,8,4)	0.313 (128,8,4)	0.22(128,8,4)	2
SonyAIBOSurface	0.30	0.30	0.15	**0.14**	0.38 (10,8,5)	0.38 (10,8,4)	0.32 (10,8,4)	3

Table 3: Error Rate comparing EFG-SAX with the state-of-the-art algorithms and the last column giving an overall rank in the comparison.

Methodology	Feature		Kernel	Statistical	
Datasets	K-Mer	EFG-SAX	WD-S	HMM	MSP
Gun	0.07	**0.032**	0.05	0.12	0.04
Sony	0.52	**0.32**	0.52	0.47	0.39

Table 4: Error Rate comparing EFG-SAX with feature, statistical, and kernel methods

that have randomness are run 30 times, and the mean error is noted and the significance is calculated using paired-t tests with 95% confidence intervals and shown in bold-faced and underlined in Table 4.

Interestingly, it can be seen that SAX based discretized symbolic representation works well with EFG as compared to other techniques. The dataset SonyAIBOSurface, for which SAX-EFG achieved a bit worse performance as compared to using other state-of-the-art, shows even worse performance using all other techniques like WD-S kernel, K-mer, HMM and MSP.

5.3 Multi-class Time Series Classification

Finally, some of the time series applications are multi-class in nature. EFG in general is a binary-classification-based framework as it tries to find features which are discriminating to one class as compared to the other, evident from the fitness function. There are two broadly different ways to address the multi-class datasets: 1) change the EFG algorithm or the fitness function to accommodate the multi-class discrimination using something like entropy, 2) without changing the EFG algorithm, use machine learning strategies to adapt the binary-class problems to multi-class problems. There have been many machine learning strategies to adapt the binary-class problems to multi-class problems as one-vs.-one or one-vs.-rest problems, creating many binary classification problems.

In this work, we use the second approach and adapt the one-vs.-one strategy in the methodology to create many binary classification problems. We create binary classification models using EFG features for these and combine the models using simple vote mechanism in an ensemble.

The dataset adopted for experimentation is the cylinder-bell-funnel (CBF) time series data [9]. The time series for CBF is defined from the following equations, where $c(t)$, $b(t)$ and $f(t)$ define cylinder, bell, and funnel respectively.

$$c(t) = (6+\eta) * \chi[a,b](t) + \varepsilon(t) \quad (2)$$

$$b(t) = (6+\eta) * \chi[a,b](t) * (t-a)/(b-a) + \varepsilon(t) \quad (3)$$

$$f(t) = (6+\eta) * \chi[a,b](t) * (b-t)/(b-a) + \varepsilon(t) \quad (4)$$

$$\chi[a,b](t) = \left\{ \begin{array}{l} 0, t < a \\ 1, a < t < b \\ 0, t > b \end{array} \right\} \quad (5)$$

Figure 4 illustrates instances of CBF, showing the cylinder class having a plateau from a to b, the bell class having a gradual increase from a to b and the funnel class having sudden increase at a and gradual decrease to b. The time series is of length 128 and is considered a model characterizing the properties of temporal domains. Various characteristics of CBF such as random amplitude variation as a result of η, random noise as a result of ε and large variations at start and end make it really suitable as a model complex classification problem [9].

The implementation of EFG-SAX was trained on three models for cylinder-bell, cylinder-funnel, and bell-funnel using EFG-SAX as before with a Naïve Bayes classifier. The voting ensemble using average function for the probability estimate was chosen to combine the outputs for each models and give classification and confidence to the unseen test data.

We compare EFG-SAX with the following methods: 1NN with Euclidean Distance on the raw data, 1NN with DTW on the raw data, 1NN with SAX using the same parameters as EFG-SAX, 1NN with SAX using trained alphabet size, and two shapelet methods. The results are shown in Table 5. The methods that have randomness are run 30 times, and the mean error is noted and the significance is calculated using paired-t tests with 95% confidence intervals and shown in bold-faced underlined. EFG-SAX outperforms all the traditional time series classification algorithms in a significant way, recording the lowest error rate.

6. CONCLUSION

In this paper, the SAX-EFG framework for time series classification was implemented and studied. It is clear that for binary classification applications, the EFG-SAX framework performs better or close to the best algorithms for time series classification.

It was also interesting to note that EFG-SAX outperforms the traditional feature, kernel, and statistical methods with

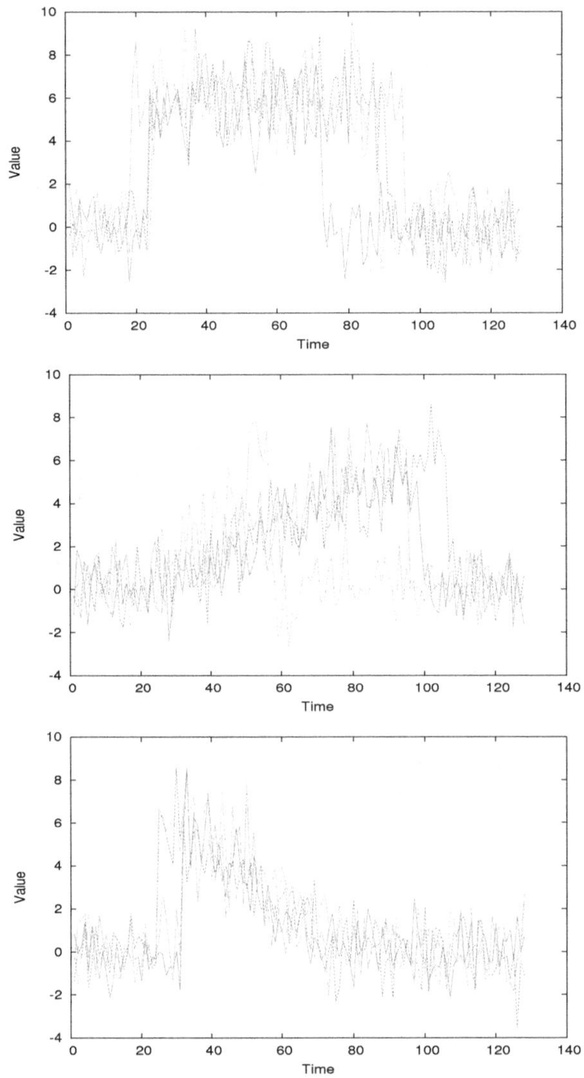

Figure 4: Showing Cylinder, Bell and Funnel as three classes from top to bottom as time series.

same SAX based discretization confirming the generic nature of EFG to find more complex patterns in sequences. Finally, applying EFG for multi-class algorithms using ensemble methodology with one-vs.-one shows relative strength of EFG in finding discriminative features and enhancing the ensemble classification accuracy. In future, we also want to study in-depth the correlation between the discriminative features found in the discretized sequences to the real-valued patterns in the time series.

7. REFERENCES

[1] I. Ben-Gal, A. Shani, A. Gohr, J. Grau, S. Arviv, A. Shmilovici, S. Posch, and I. Grosse. Identification of transcription factor binding sites with variable-order bayesian networks. *Bioinformatics*, 21(11):2657–2666, 2005.

[2] A. Bernal, K. Crammer, A. Hatzigeorgiou, and F. Pereira. Global discriminative learning for higher-accuracy computational gene prediction. *PLoS Comp Biol*, 3(3):e54, 2003.

Algorithm	Error
Euclidean	0.14
DTW	0.05
SAX-BEST (32,4,10)	0.10
SAX (32,4,4)	0.11
EFG-SAX (32,4,4)	**0.02**
Shapelet	0.10
Logical	0.33

Table 5: Comparison of EFG-SAX with different algorithms on the CBF dataset

[3] D. J. Berndt and J. Clifford. Using Dynamic Time Warping to Find Patterns in Time Series. In *KDD Workshop*, pages 359–370, 1994.

[4] D. Cai, A. Delcher, B. Kao, and S. Kasif. Modeling splice sites with bayes networks. *Bioinformatics*, 16(2):152–158, 2000.

[5] K.-P. Chan and A. W.-C. Fu. Efficient time series matching by wavelets. In *Data Engineering, 1999. Proceedings., 15th International Conference on*, pages 126–133. IEEE, 1999.

[6] C. C. Chang and C. J. Lin. *LIBSVM: a library for support vector machines*. Online, 2001.

[7] T. Cover and P. Hart. Nearest neighbor pattern classification. *Information Theory, IEEE Transactions on*, 13(1):21 -27, january 1967.

[8] K. A. De Jong. *Evolutionary computation: a unified approach*. MIT Press, Cambridge, MA, 2001.

[9] J. J. R. Diez, C. A. GonzÃąlez, and H. BostrÃűm. Learning first order logic time series classifiers: Rules and boosting. In *PKDD*, page 299, 2000.

[10] H. Ding, G. Trajcevski, P. Scheuermann, X. Wang, and E. Keogh. Querying and mining of time series data: Experimental comparison of representations and distance measures. *Proc. VLDB Endow.*, 1(2):1542–1552, Aug. 2008.

[11] D. Eads, D. Hillb, S. Davisa, S. Perkinsa, J. Maa, R. Portera, and J. Theilera. Genetic algorithms and support vector machines for time series classification. In *Proc. of SPIE Vol*, volume 4787, page 75, 2002.

[12] C. Faloutsos, M. Ranganathan, and Y. Manolopoulos. *Fast subsequence matching in time-series databases*, volume 23. ACM, 1994.

[13] N. I. Gershenzon, G. D. Stormo, and I. P. Ioshikhes. Computational technique for improvement of the position-weight matrices for the DNA/protein binding sites. *Nucl. Acids Res.*, 33(7):2290–2301, 2005.

[14] P. Geurts. Pattern extraction for time series classification. In *Principles of Data Mining and Knowledge Discovery*, pages 115–127. Springer, 2001.

[15] J. Grau, J. Keilwagen, A. Gohr, B. Haldemann, S. Posch, and I. Grosse. A java framework for statistical analysis and classification of biological sequences. *J. Mach. Learn. Res.*, 13:1967–1971, 2012.

[16] U. Kamath, J. Compton, R. Islamaj Dogan, K. De Jong, and A. Shehu. An evolutionary algorithm approach for feature generation from sequence data and its application to dna splice site prediction. *IEEE/ACM Transactions on Computational Biology and Bioinformatics (TCBB)*, 9(5):1387–1398, 2012.

[17] U. Kamath, K. A. De Jong, and A. Shehu. An evolutionary-based approach for feature generation: Eukaryotic promoter recognition. In *Evolutionary Computation (CEC), 2011 IEEE Congress on*, pages 277–284. IEEE, 2011.

[18] J. Keilwagen, J. Grau, I. A. Paponov, S. Posch, M. Strickert, and I. Grosse. De-novo discovery of differentially abundant transcription factor binding sites including their positional preference. *PLoS Comp Biol*, 7(2):e1001070, 2011.

[19] E. Keogh, K. Chakrabarti, M. Pazzani, and S. Mehrotra. Dimensionality reduction for fast similarity search in large time series databases. *Knowledge and information Systems*, 3(3):263–286, 2001.

[20] E. Keogh, K. Chakrabarti, M. Pazzani, and S. Mehrotra. Locally adaptive dimensionality reduction for indexing large time series databases. In *ACM SIGMOD Record*, volume 30, pages 151–162. ACM, 2001.

[21] E. Keogh and S. Kasetty. On the need for time series data mining benchmarks: a survey and empirical demonstration. *Data Mining and Knowledge Discovery*, 7(4):349–371, 2003.

[22] R. Kohavi and G. H. John. Wrappers for feature subset selection. *Artificial Intelligence*, 97(1-2):273–324, 1997.

[23] J. Koza. *On the Programming of Computers by Means of Natural Selection.* MIT Press, Boston, MA, 1992.

[24] J. Lasserre and C. M. Bishop. Generative or Discriminative? Getting the Best of Both Worlds. *BAYESIAN STATISTICS*, 8:3–24, 2007.

[25] J. Lin, E. Keogh, S. Lonardi, and B. Chiu. A symbolic representation of time series, with implications for streaming algorithms. In *Proceedings of the 8th ACM SIGMOD workshop on Research issues in data mining and knowledge discovery*, DMKD '03, pages 2–11, New York, NY, USA, 2003. ACM.

[26] J. Lin, E. Keogh, L. Wei, and S. Lonardi. Experiencing sax: A novel symbolic representation of time series. *Data Min. Knowl. Discov.*, 15(2):107–144, Oct. 2007.

[27] S. Luke, G. C. Balan, and L. Panait. Population implosion in genetic programming. in genetic and evolutionary computation. In *Genetic and Evolutionary Computation Conference*, 2003.

[28] M. L. Marx and R. J. Larsen. *Introduction to mathematical statistics and its applications.* Pearson/Prentice Hall, 2006.

[29] A. Mueen, E. Keogh, and N. Young. Logical-shapelets: An expressive primitive for time series classification. In *Proceedings of the 17th ACM SIGKDD International Conference on Knowledge Discovery and Data Mining*, KDD '11, pages 1154–1162, 2011.

[30] R. T. Olszewski. Generalized feature extraction for structural pattern recognition in time-series data. Technical report, DTIC Document, 2001.

[31] P. Patel, E. Keogh, J. Lin, and S. Lonardi. Mining motifs in massive time series databases. In *In Proceedings of IEEE International Conference on Data Mining (ICDM)*, pages 370–377, 2002.

[32] C. Ratanamahatana, E. Keogh, A. J. Bagnall, and S. Lonardi. A novel bit level time series representation with implication of similarity search and clustering. In *Advances in Knowledge Discovery and Data Mining*, pages 771–777. Springer, 2005.

[33] C. A. Ratanamahatana and E. Keogh. Making time-series classification more accurate using learned constraints. In *Proceedings of SIAM international conference on data mining*, pages 11–22. Lake Buena Vista, Florida, 2004.

[34] R. Riviere, D. Barth, C. J., and A. Denise. Shuffling biological sequences with motif constraints. *J. Discrete Algo.*, 6(2):192–204, 2007.

[35] S. Sonnenburg, G. Rätsch, S. Henschel, C. Widmer, J. Behr, A. Zien, and F. de Bona. The SHOGUN machine learning toolbox. *J. Mach. Learn. Res.*, 11:1799–1802, 2010.

[36] S. Sonnenburg, G. Schweikert, P. Philips, J. Behr, and G. Rätsch. Accurate splice site prediction using support vector machines. *BMC Bioinformatics*, 8(10):S7, 2007.

[37] S. Sonnenburg, A. Zien, P. Philips, and G. Rätsch. Poims: positional oligomer importance matrices - understanding support vector machine-based signal detectors. In *ISMB*, pages 6–14, 2008.

[38] W. M. Spears. Crossover or mutation. In *FOGA*, pages 221–237, 1992.

[39] R. Staden. Methods to locate signals in nucleic acid sequences. *Nucl. Acids Res.*, 12(1):505–519, 1984.

[40] L. Taher, P. Meinicke, and B. Morgensten. On splice site prediction using weight array models: a comparison of smoothing techniques. *J. of Physics: Conference Series*, 90(1):012004, 2007.

[41] D. L. Vail, M. M. Veloso, and J. D. Lafferty. Conditional random fields for activity recognition. In *Proceedings of the 6th international joint conference on Autonomous agents and multiagent systems*, page 235. ACM, 2007.

[42] V. N. Vapnik. *The Nature of Statistical Learning Theory.* Springer, 1995.

[43] E. P. Xing, M. I. Jordan, R. M. Karp, and S. Russell. A hierarchical Bayesian Markovian model for motifs in biopolymer sequences. In S. Becker, S. Thrun, and O. K., editors, *Advances in Neural Information Processing Systems*, pages 200–207, 2002.

[44] O. Yakhnenko, A. Silvescu, and V. Honavar. Discriminatively trained Markov model for sequence classification. In *IEEE Intl Conf on Data Mining (ICDM)*, pages 1–8, November 2005.

[45] L. Ye and E. Keogh. Time series shapelets: A new primitive for data mining. In *Proceedings of the 15th ACM SIGKDD International Conference on Knowledge Discovery and Data Mining*, KDD '09, pages 947–956, 2009.

Evolving Deep Unsupervised Convolutional Networks for Vision-Based Reinforcement Learning

Jan Koutník Jürgen Schmidhuber Faustino Gomez
IDSIA, USI-SUPSI
Galleria 2
Manno-Lugano, CH 6928
{hkou, juergen, tino}@idsia.ch

ABSTRACT

Dealing with high-dimensional input spaces, like visual input, is a challenging task for reinforcement learning (RL). Neuroevolution (NE), used for continuous RL problems, has to either reduce the problem dimensionality by (1) compressing the representation of the neural network controllers or (2) employing a pre-processor (*compressor*) that transforms the high-dimensional raw inputs into low-dimensional features. In this paper, we are able to evolve extremely small *recurrent neural network* (RNN) controllers for a task that previously required networks with over a million weights. The high-dimensional visual input, which the controller would normally receive, is first transformed into a compact feature vector through a deep, max-pooling convolutional neural network (MPCNN). Both the MPCNN preprocessor and the RNN controller are evolved successfully to control a car in the TORCS racing simulator using only visual input. This is the first use of deep learning in the context evolutionary RL.

Categories and Subject Descriptors

I.2.6 [**Artificial Intelligence**]: Learning—*Connectionism and neural nets*

Keywords

deep learning; neuroevolution; vision-based TORCS; reinforcement learning; games

1. INTRODUCTION

Most approaches to scaling neuroevolution to tasks that require large networks, such as those processing video input, have focused on indirect encodings where relatively small neural network descriptions are transformed via a complex mapping into networks of arbitrary size [4, 7, 10, 12, 14, 21].

A different approach to dealing with high-dimensional input which has been studied in the context of single-agent RL (i.e. TD [23], policy gradients [22], etc.), is to combine action learning with an unsupervised learning (UL) preprocessor or "compressor" which provides a lower-dimensional feature vector that the agent receives as input instead of the raw observation [5, 8, 11, 15, 17, 18, 19]. The UL compressor is trained on the high-dimensional observations generated by the learning agent's actions, that the agent then uses as a state representation to learn a value function.

In [3], the first combination of UL and evolutionary reinforcement learning was introduced where a single UL module is trained on data generated by entire population as it interacts with environment (which would normally be discarded) to build a representation that allows evolution to search in a relatively low-dimensional feature space. This approach attacks the problem of high-dimensionality from the opposite direction compared to indirect encoding: instead of compressing large networks into short genomes, the inputs are compressed so that smaller networks can be used.

In this paper, this Unsupervised Learning – Evolutionary Reinforcement Learning (UL-ERL) approach is scaled up to the much more challenging reinforcement learning problem of driving a car in the TORCS simulator using vision from the driver's perspective as input. The only work to successfully solve this task to date [13] did so using an indirect encoding that searches for networks in a low-dimensional frequency domain representation that effectively compresses over 1 million weights down to just a few hundred Fourier coefficients.

Here, a Max-Pooling Convolutional Neural Network (MPCNN; [2, 20]) is used as an unsupervised sensory preprocessor that reduces the input dimensionality of images to the point where an extremely small (only 33 weights) recurrent neural network controller can be evolved to drive the car successfully. MPCNNs are normally trained using a classifier output layer and backpropagation, meaning that a training set of class-labeled examples is required. Here, instead, the MPCNN without the classifier layer is evolved to maximize variance in the output representations of a small set of images collected at random from the environment. This quickly provides a small number of useful features, without the need for supervision (constructing a training set), that are used as inputs to the evolving recurrent neural network controllers. To our knowledge, this is the first use of a deep learning feedforward architecture for evolutionary reinforcement learning.

The next section describes the MPCNN architecture that is used to compress the high-dimensional vision inputs. Sec-

GECCO'14, July 12–16, 2014, Vancouver, BC, Canada.

http://dx.doi.org/10.1145/2576768.2598358.

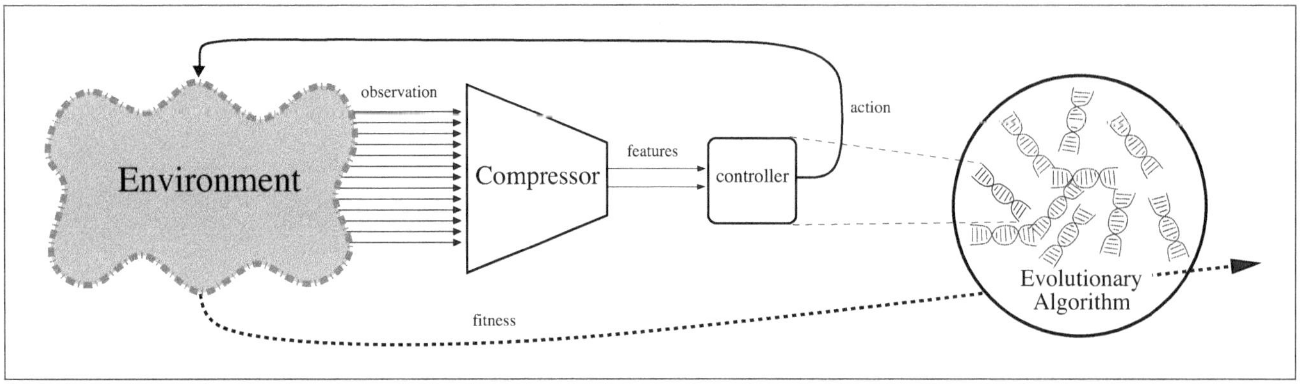

Figure 1: The Unsupervised Learning – Evolutionary Reinforcement Learning (UL-ERL) framework. Controllers (e.g. neural networks) are evolved as in conventional ERL except that the controller receives input from an unsupervised "compressor" that reduces the dimensionality of the raw observations into a compact feature vector. The compressor is trained using images generated by the interactions of candidate controllers with the environment.

tion 3 covers the overall UL-ERL framework. Section 4 presents the experiments in the TORCS race car driving domain, which are discussed in section 5.

2. MAX-POOLING CONVOLUTIONAL NEURAL NETWORKS

Convolution Neural Networks [6, 16] are deep hierarchical networks that have recently become the state of the art in pattern recognition and image processing due to the advent of fast implementations on graphics card multiprocessors (GPU) [1]. CNNs have two parts: (1) a deep feature detector consisting of alternating *convolutional* and *downsampling* layers, and (2) a classifier that receives the output of the final layer of the feature detector.

Each convolutional layer ℓ, has a bank of $m^\ell \times n^\ell$ filters, F^ℓ, where m^ℓ is the number input maps (images), I^ℓ, to the layer, and n^ℓ is the number of output maps (inputs to the next layer). Each output map is computed by:

$$I^{\ell+1} = \sigma\left(\sum_{j=1}^{m^\ell} I_j^\ell * F_{ij}^\ell\right), \quad i = 1..n^\ell, \ell = 1, 3, 5...,$$

where $*$ is the convolution operator, F_{ij}^ℓ is the i-th filter for the j-th map and σ is a non-linear squashing function (e.g. sigmoid). Note that ℓ is always odd because of the subsampling layers between each of the convolutional layers.

The downsampling layers reduce resolution of each map. Each map is partitioned into non-overlapping blocks and a value of each block is used in the output map. The max-pooling operation used here subsamples the map by simply taking the maximum value in the block as the output, making these networks Max-Pooling CNNs [2, 20].

The stacked alternating layers transform the input into progressively lower dimensional abstract representations that are then classified typically using a standard feed-forward neural network that has an output neuron for each class. The entire network is usually trained using a large training set of class-labeled images via backpropagation [16]. Figure 6 illustrates the particular MPCNN architecture used in this paper. It should be clear from the figure that each convolution layer is just a matrix product where the matrix entries are filters and the convolution is used instead of multiplication.

3. METHOD: MPC-RNN

Figure 1 shows the general framework used in this paper to evolve small neural network controllers for tasks with high-dimensional inputs such as vision. The controller itself is evolved in the usual way (i.e. neuroevolution; [24]) except that during evaluation the candidate networks do not receive observations directly from the environment. Instead they receive a feature vector of much lower dimensionality provided by the unsupervised compressor. The compressor is trained on observations (images) generated by the actions taken by candidate controllers as they interact with the environment. Training can either by conducted on-line using images generated from the evolving controllers, or off-line, collected by some other means and trained in batch mode.

Deep neural processors such as MPCNNs are normally trained to perform image classification through supervised learning using enormous training sets. Of course, this requires *a priori* knowledge of what constitutes a class. In a general RL setting, we may not know how the space of images should be partitioned. For example, how many classes should there be for images perceived from the first-person perspective while driving the TORCS car? We could study the domain in detail to construct a training set that could then be used to train the MPCNN with backpropagation. However, we do not want the learning system to rely on task-specific domain knowledge, so, instead, the MPCNN is *evolved* without using a labeled training set. A set of k images is collected from the environment, and then MPCNNs are evolved to maximize the fitness:

$$f_{\text{kernels}} = \min(D) + \text{mean}(D), \quad (1)$$

where D is a list of all Euclidean distances,

$$d_{i,j} = \|\mathbf{f}_i - \mathbf{f}_j\|, \forall i > j,$$

between k normalized feature vectors $\{\mathbf{f}_1 \ldots \mathbf{f}_k\}$ generated

(a) (b) (c)

Figure 2: Visual TORCS environment. (a) The 1st-person perspective used as input to the RNN controllers (figure 3) to drive the car around the track. (b), a 3rd-person perspective of car. The controllers were evolved using a track (c) of length of 714.16 m and road width of 10 m, that consists of straight segments of length 50 and 100 m and curves with radius of 25 m. The car starts at the bottom (start line) and has to drive counter-clockwise. The track boundary has a width of 14 m.

from k images in the training set by the MPCNN encoded in the genome.

This fitness function forces the evolving MPCNNs to output feature vectors that are spread out in feature space, so that when the final, evolved MPCNN processes images for the evolving controllers, it will provide enough discriminative power to allow them to take correct actions.

4. VISUAL TORCS EXPERIMENTS

The goal of the task is to evolve a recurrent neural network controller that can drive the car around a race track using the compressed representation provided by the MPCNN which is evolved separately.

The visual TORCS environment is based on TORCS version 1.3.1. The simulator had to be modified to provide images as input to the controllers. At each time-step during a network evaluation, an image rendered in OpenGL is captured in the car code (C++), and passed via UDP to the client (Java), that contains the RNN controller. The client is wrapped into a Java class that provides methods for setting up the RNN weights, executing the evaluation, and returning the fitness score. These methods are called from Mathematica which is used to implement the evolutionary search.

The Java wrapper allows multiple controllers to be evaluated in parallel in different instances of the simulator via different UDP ports. This feature is critical for the experiments presented below since, unlike the non-vision-based TORCS, the costly image rendering, required for vision, cannot be disabled. The main drawback of the current implementation is that the images are captured from the screen buffer and, therefore, have to actually be rendered to the screen.

Other tweaks to the original TORCS include changing the control frequency from 50 Hz to 5 Hz, and removing the "*3-2-1-GO*" waiting sequence from the beginning of each race. The image passed in the UDP is encoded as a message chunk with *image* prefix, followed by *unsigned byte* values of the image pixels.

4.1 Setup

In each fitness evaluation, the candidate controller is tested in two trials, one on the track shown in figure 2(c), and one on its mirror image. A trial consists of placing the car at the starting line and driving it for 25 s of simulated time, resulting in a maximum of 125 time-steps at the 5 Hz control frequency. At each control step (see figure 3), a raw 64×64 pixel image, taken from the driver's perspective is split into three color planes (hue, saturation and brightness). The saturation plane is passed through the MPCNN compressor which generates a 3-dimensional feature vector that is fed into a simple recurrent neural network (SRN) with 3 hidden neurons, and 3 output neurons. The first two outputs, o_1, o_2, are averaged, $(o_1+o_2)/2$, to provide the steering signal (-1 =full left lock, 1 =full right lock), and the third neuron, o_3, controls the brake and throttle (-1 = full brake, 1 = full throttle). All neurons use sigmoidal activation functions.

The 33 network weights were directly encoded in real-valued genomes and evolved using CoSyNE [9] with population size of 100, a mutation rate of 0.8, and each of the two trials is scored using the following function:

$$f = d - \frac{3m}{1000} + \frac{v_{max}}{5} - 100c\ , \qquad (2)$$

where d is the distance along the track axis measured from the starting line, v_{max} is maximum speed, m is the cumulative damage, and c is the sum of squares of the control signal differences, divided by the number of control variables, 3, and the number simulation control steps, T:

$$c = \frac{1}{3T}\sum_{i}^{3}\sum_{t}^{T}[o_i(t) - o_i(t-1)]^2. \qquad (3)$$

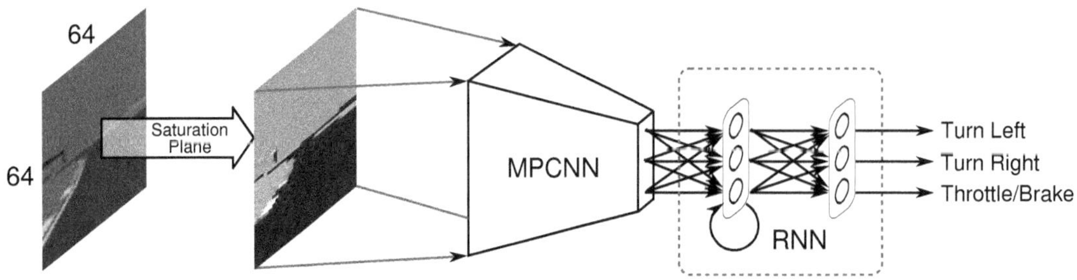

Figure 3: Visual TORCS network controller pipeline. At each time-step a raw 64×64 pixel image, taken from the driver's perspective, is split into three planes (hue, saturation and brightness). The saturation plane is fed into the max-pooling convolutional network (MPCNN), that generates features for the recurrent neural network (RNN) controller, that drives the car by controlling the steering, brakes, and accelerator. See Figure 6 for the details of the MPCNN network.

Layer	Type	m	n	#maps	map size
1	C	1	10	10	63×63
2	MP	-	-	10	21×21
3	C	10	10	10	20×20
4	MP	-	-	10	10×10
5	C	10	10	10	9×9
6	MP	-	-	10	3×3
7	C	10	10	3	2×2
8	MP	-	-	3	1×1

Table 1: MPCNN topology. The table summarizes the MPCNN architecture used; type of a layer, where C is for convolutional, MP for max-pooling, dimensions of the filter bank m and n, number of output maps and their resolution.

The maximum speed component in equation (2) forces the controllers to accelerate and brake efficiently, while the damage component favors controllers that drive safely, and c encourages smoother driving. Fitness scores roughly correspond to the distance traveled along the race track axis.

Each individual is evaluated both on the track and its mirror image to prevent the RNN from blindly memorizing the track without using the visual input. The original track starts with a left turn, while the mirrored track starts with a right turn, forcing the network to use the visual input to distinguish between tracks. The final fitness score is the minimum of the two track scores (equation 2).

Before the RNN controllers can be evolved, the MPCNN that will provide them with inputs while driving, is first itself evolved off-line at the beginning of each run. A set of 20 images was collected by taking snapshots from the driver's perspective (i.e. figure 2a) at regular intervals while manually driving the car once around the track. These images were then mirrored horizontally to form a training set of 40 images that were used to evolve MPCNNs that maximized the fitness function in equation (1).

The MPCNNs had 8 layers alternating between convolution and max-pooling operations, as shown in figure 6 and Table 1. The first step in processing a 64×64 pixel image from TORCS is to convolve it with each of the 10 filters in layer 1, to produce 10 63×63 feature maps, each of which is reduced down to 21×21 by the first max-pooling layer (2). These 10 features are convolved again by layer 3, max-pooled in layer 4, and so on, until the image is reduced down to just 3 1-dimensional features which are fed to the controller. This architecture has a total of 993 weights that were directly encoded in a real-valued genome, and also evolved using CoSyNE [9] with, a population size of 100, and mutation rate of 0.8.

4.2 Results

The average fitness of 3 runs after 300 CoSyNE generations reached 531. Evolving one controller for 300 generations (which involves 45,000 fitness evaluations) takes almost 40 hours on an 8-core machine[1] (running 8 evaluations in parallel).

Table 2 compares the distance travelled and maximum speed of the best MPC-RNN controller with the published results in [13] (a large RNN controller evolved in frequency domain and hand-coded controllers that come with the TORCS package).

The performance of MPC-RNN is not as good as the other controllers, but the car can complete a lap and continue driving without crashing. The hand-coded controllers drive better since they have access to the car state variables such as velocities, accelerations along axes, and some high-level features such as the distance from the car to the edge of the track. The Visual RNN also drives better but requires networks with over 1 million weights and image preprocessing—edge detection, dilation. The Robert's edge detector it uses convolves the input image with two 2×2 kernels ($\left[\begin{smallmatrix} 1 & 0 \\ 0 & -1 \end{smallmatrix}\right]$ and $\left[\begin{smallmatrix} 0 & 1 \\ -1 & 0 \end{smallmatrix}\right]$), whereas MPCNN is capable of performing edge detection as well, using the evolved convolutional layers.

In a typical run, 20 generations is required for evolution to overcome a local optima (fitness around 150) where controllers just drive straight and crash to the barrier at maximum speed. Later, the controllers start to distinguish between the left and right turns and the fitness quickly jumps above 300. After reaching fitness of 500, the controllers start to drive more smoothly, accelerate on straight sections and optimize the driving path to complete a lap and keep from crashing.

Figure 4 shows the evolution of the MPCNN feature vectors for each of the 40 images in the training set, in one of the three runs. As the features evolve they very quickly move

[1]AMD FX 8120 8-core, 16 GB RAM, nVidia GTX-570

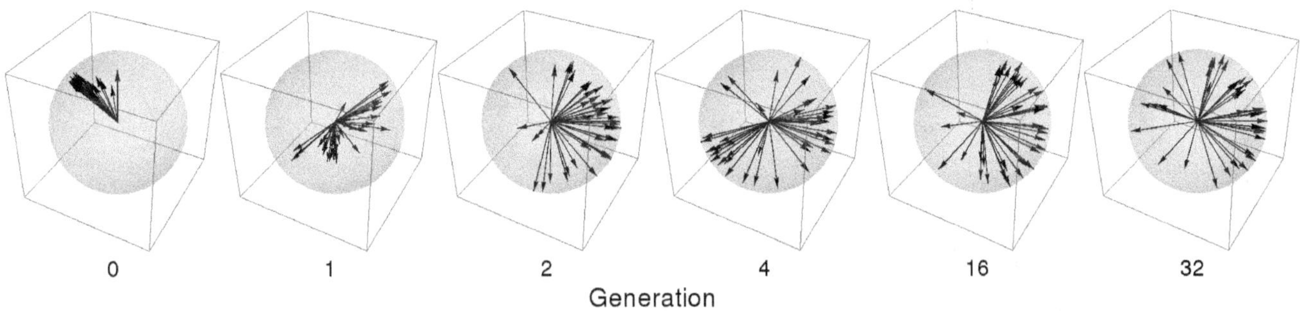

Figure 4: Evolving MPCNN features. Each plot shows the feature vectors for each of the 40 training images on the unit sphere. Initially (generation 0), the features are clustered together. After just a few generations spread out so that the MPCNN discriminates more clearly between the images.

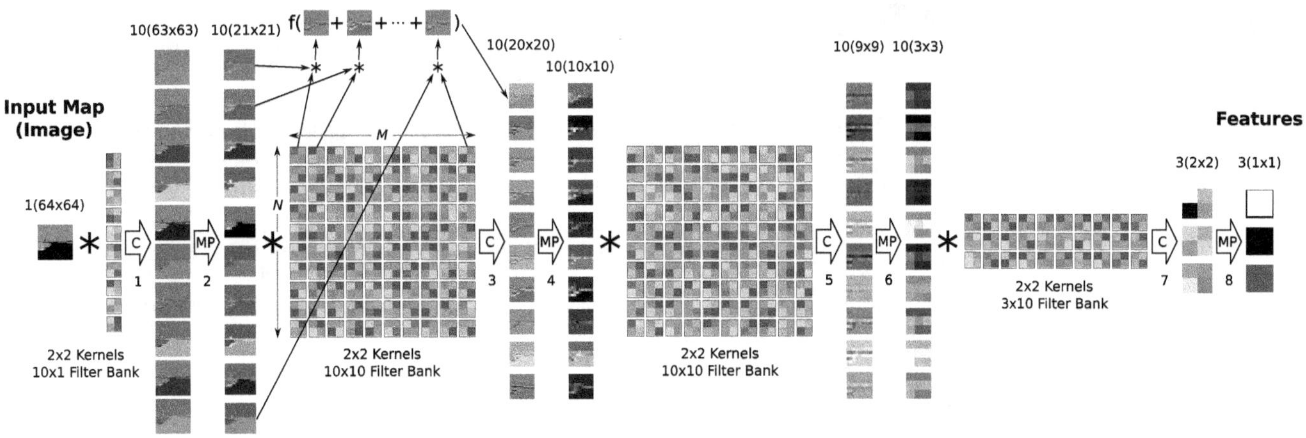

Figure 6: Max-Pooling Convolutional Neural Network (MPCNN) with 8 layers alternating between convolution (C) and downsampling (MP; using max-pooling). The first layer convolves the input 64×64 pixel image with a bank of 10×10 filters producing 10 maps of size 63×63, that are down-sampled to 21×21 by MP layer 2. Layer 3 convolves each of these 10 maps with a filter, sums the results and passes them through the nonlinear function f, producing 10 maps of 20×20 pixels each, and so on until the input image is transformed to just 3 features that are passed to the RNN controller, see Figure 3.

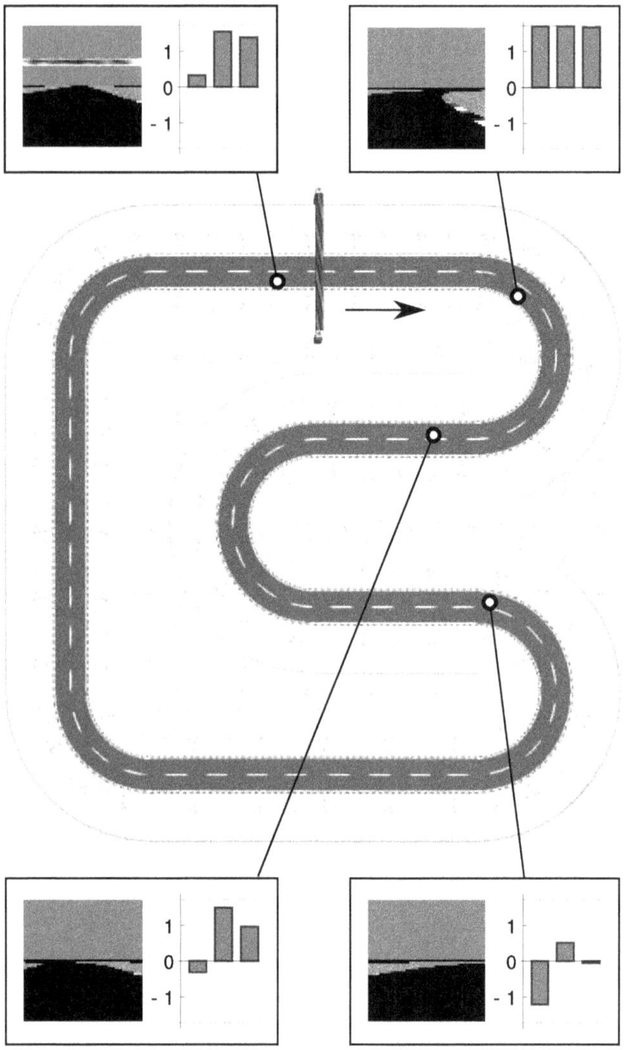

Figure 5: Evolved visual features. Each inset shows the image at a particular point on the track and the 3-dimensional feature vector produced by the evolved MPCNN.

controller	d [m]	v_{max} [km/h]
olethros	570	147
bt	613	141
berniw	624	149
tita	657	150
inferno	682	150
visual RNN[13]	625	144
MPC-RNN	547	97

Table 2: Maximum distance, d, in meters and maximum speed, v_{max}, in kilometers per hour achieved by hand-coded controllers that come with TORCS which enjoy access to the state variables (the five upper table entries), a million-weight RNN controller that drives using pre-processed 64×64 pixel images as input, evolved indirectly in the Fourier domain, and the MPC-RNN agent with just 33 weights in its RNN controller.

away from each other in feature space. While simply pushing the feature vectors apart is no guarantee of achieving maximally informative compressed representations, this simple, unsupervised training procedure provides enough discriminative power in practice to get the car safely across the finish line.

4.3 Generalization

The generalization ability of the controllers was tested on three different tracks constructed from components (e.g. curve with the same radius) from the track used to evolve them, see table 3. Track 1 is a very long oval that tests whether the network is able to accelerate beyond the maximum speed observed during evolution. The two other tracks are shorter and test whether the controllers can cope with different combinations of corners.

The maximum and average distance, and top speed (over 20 tests) achieved by the controllers in 500 seconds of driving is shown in table 3. For track 1, the best controller achieved a maximum speed above 150 km/h and was able to brake soon enough to slow down in front of the hairpin, in order to complete a lap within the allotted time. For tracks 2 and 3, the best controller was only able to complete about half a lap on average.

5. DISCUSSION

The results show that it is possible to circumvent the indirect encoding approach by shifting the computational burden to a deep image processor that removes the redundancy in the environment so that almost trivially small networks can be evolved efficiently to solve a complex control task. The driving performance is not yet as good as the only other method to tackle this problem [13], and the generalization ability of the driver networks needs to be more thoroughly tested (e.g. using more realistic, irregular tracks).

So far the feature generating MPCNN has been evolved off-line. A better approach might be to interleave the compressor evolution with controller evolution so that the compressor is trained continually using images generated by the controller as they become more and more proficient in the task as in [3].

As general approach MPC-RNN harnesses the power of deep learning for RL without having to train a deep network in a supervised manner. Future work will extend the approach to higher-dimensional action spaces like the 41-DOF iCub humanoid, to perform manipulation tasks using vision.

Acknowledgments

This research was supported by Swiss National Science Foundation grant #138219: "Theory and Practice of Reinforcement Learning 2", and EU FP7 project: "NAnoSCale Engineering for Novel Computation using Evolution" (NASCENCE), grant agreement #317662.

References

[1] D. C. Ciresan, U. Meier, L. M. Gambardella, and J. Schmidhuber. Deep big simple neural nets for handwritten digit recognition. *Neural Computation*, 22(12):3207–3220, 2010.

				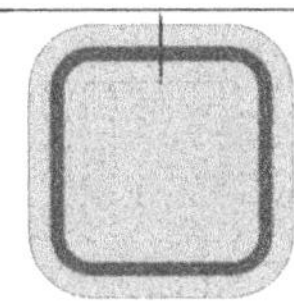			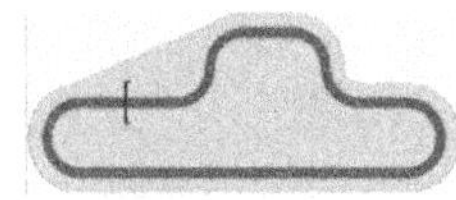		
	Track 1 (4514 m)			**Track 2** (557 m)			**Track 3** (980 m)		
	d [m]	**laps**	v_{max} [km/h]	d [m]	**laps**	v_{max} [km/h]	d [m]	**laps**	v_{max} [km/h]
Maximum	5214.2	1.16	154.2	391.2	0.70	106.0	906.0	0.92	122.0
Average	2711.4	0.60	150.7	274.4	0.49	98.0	547.7	0.56	102.2
Std. dev.	1831.5	0.41	2.13	112.6	0.20	9.5	320.8	0.33	16.1

Table 3: Generalization results. The best overall driver from the three runs was tested on three other tracks, different from the one used during evolution.

[2] D. C. Ciresan, U. Meier, J. Masci, L. M. Gambardella, and J. Schmidhuber. Flexible, high performance convolutional neural networks for image classification. In *Proceedings of the International Joint Conference on Artificial Intelligence (IJCAI)*, pages 1237–1242, 2011.

[3] G. Cuccu, M. Luciw, J. Schmidhuber, and F. Gomez. Intrinsically motivated evolutionary search for vision-based reinforcement learning. In *Proceedings of the IEEE Conference on Development and Learning, and Epigenetic Robotics*, 2011.

[4] D. B. D'Ambrosio and K. O. Stanley. A novel generative encoding for exploiting neural network sensor and output geometry. In *Proceedings of the 9th Conference on Genetic and Evolutionary Computation*, (GECCO), pages 974–981, New York, NY, USA, 2007. ACM.

[5] F. Fernández and D. Borrajo. Two steps reinforcement learning. *International Journal of Intelligent Systems*, 23(2):213–245, 2008.

[6] K. Fukushima. Neocognitron: A self-organizing neural network for a mechanism of pattern recognition unaffected by shift in position. *Biological Cybernetics*, 36(4):193–202, 1980.

[7] J. Gauci and K. Stanley. Generating large-scale neural networks through discovering geometric regularities. In *Proceedings of the Conference on Genetic and Evolutionary Computation*, (GECCO), pages 997–1004, New York, NY, USA, 2007. ACM.

[8] L. Gisslén, M. Luciw, V. Graziano, and J. Schmidhuber. Sequential Constant Size Compressors and Reinforcement Learning. In *Proceedings of the Fourth Conference on Artificial General Intelligence*, 2011.

[9] F. Gomez, J. Schmidhuber, and R. Miikkulainen. Accelerated neural evolution through cooperatively coevolved synapses. *Journal of Machine Learning Research*, 9(May):937–965, 2008.

[10] F. Gruau. Cellular encoding of genetic neural networks. Technical Report RR-92-21, Ecole Normale Superieure de Lyon, Institut IMAG, Lyon, France, 1992.

[11] S. R. Jodogne and J. H. Piater. Closed-loop learning of visual control policies. *Journal of Artificial Intelligence Research*, 28:349–391, 2007.

[12] H. Kitano. Designing neural networks using genetic algorithms with graph generation system. *Complex Systems*, 4:461–476, 1990.

[13] J. Koutník, G. Cuccu, J. Schmidhuber, and F. Gomez. Evolving large-scale neural networks for vision-based reinforcement learning. In *Proceedings of the Genetic and Evolutionary Computation Conference (GECCO)*, Amsterdam, 2013.

[14] J. Koutník, F. Gomez, and J. Schmidhuber. Evolving neural networks in compressed weight space. In *Proceedings of the Conference on Genetic and Evolutionary Computation (GECCO-10)*, 2010.

[15] S. Lange and M. Riedmiller. Deep auto-encoder neural networks in reinforcement learning. In *International Joint Conference on Neural Networks (IJCNN 2010), Barcelona, Spain*, 2010.

[16] Y. LeCun, L. Bottou, Y. Bengio, and P. Haffner. Gradient-based learning applied to document recognition. *Proceedings of the IEEE*, 86(11):2278–2324, November 1998.

[17] R. Legenstein, N. Wilbert, and L. Wiskott. Reinforcement Learning on Slow Features of High-Dimensional Input Streams. *PLoS Computational Biology*, 6(8), 2010.

[18] D. Pierce and B. Kuipers. Map learning with uninterpreted sensors and effectors. *Artificial Intelligence*, 92:169–229, 1997.

[19] M. Riedmiller, S. Lange, and A. Voigtlaender. Autonomous reinforcement learning on raw visual input data in a real world application. In *Proceedings of the International Joint Conference on Neural Networks (IJCNN)*, pages 1–8, Brisbane, Australia, 2012.

[20] D. Scherer, A. Müller, and S. Behnke. Evaluation of pooling operations in convolutional architectures for object recognition. In *Proceedings of the International Conference on Artificial Neural Networks*, ICANN, 2010.

[21] J. Schmidhuber. Discovering neural nets with low Kolmogorov complexity and high generalization capability. *Neural Networks*, 10(5):857–873, 1997.

[22] R. S. Sutton, D. A. McAllester, S. P. Singh, and Y. Mansour. Policy gradient methods for reinforcement learning with function approximation. In *Advances in Neural Information Processing Systems 12 (NIPS)*, pages 1057–1063, 1999.

[23] G. Tesauro. Practical issues in temporal difference learning. In D. S. Lippman, J. E. Moody, and D. S. Touretzky, editors, *Advances in Neural Information Processing Systems 4 (NIPS)*, pages 259–266. Morgan Kaufmann, 1992.

[24] X. Yao. Evolving artificial neural networks. *Proceedings of the IEEE*, 87(9):1423–1447, 1999.

Three-Cornered Coevolution Learning Classifier Systems for Classification Tasks

Syahaneim Marzukhi
Faculty of Science and Defence Technology
National Defence University Malaysia (NDUM), KL, Malaysia
syahaneim@upnm.edu.my

Will N. Browne
Faculty of Engineering
Victoria University of Wellington (VUW), Wellington, New Zealand
will.browne@vuw.ac.nz

Mengjie Zhang
Faculty of Engineering
Victoria University of Wellington (VUW), Wellington, New Zealand
mengjie.zhang@ecs.vuw.ac.nz

ABSTRACT

The Three-Cornered Coevolution concept describes a framework where artificial problems may be generated in concert with classification agents in order to provide insight into their relationships. This is unlike standard studies where humans set a problem's difficulty, which may have bias or lack understanding of the multiple interactions of a problem's characteristics, such as noise in conjunction with class imbalance. Previous studies have shown that it is feasible to generate problems with one agent in relation to a single classification agent's performance, but when to adjust the problem difficulty was manually set.

This paper introduces a second classification agent to trigger the coevolutionary process within the system, where its functionality and effect on the system requires investigation. The classification agents, in this case Learning Classifier Systems, use different styles of learning techniques (e.g. supervised or reinforcement learning techniques) to learn the problems. Experiments show that the realised system is capable of autonomously generating various problems, triggering learning and providing insight into each learning system's ability by determining the problem domains where they perform relatively well - this is in contrast to humans having to determine the problem domains.

Categories and Subject Descriptors

I.2.6 [**Computing Methodologies**]: ARTIFICIAL INTELLIGENCE, Learning, Concept learning

General Terms

Algorithm, Performance

Keywords

Classification, Learning Classifier Systems

GECCO'14, July 12–16, 2014, Vancouver, BC, Canada.
Copyright 2014 ACM 978-1-4503-2662-9/14/07 ...$15.00.
http://dx.doi.org/10.1145/2576768.2598371 .

1. INTRODUCTION

Recently the theoretical framework of *Three-Cornered Coevolution* was proposed by Wilson [25]. Wilson suggested an automatic system for image transformation with a pattern generator and pattern recognizers. This is to be a human-independent system that may provide a new insight into the pattern recognition problem.

The name 'three-cornered' derives from having one problem generation agent, one favoured classification agent, where the system seeks to maximize its performance and one classification agent to monitor (i.e. intercept) the learning between the first two agents in case it becomes stagnated. However, this theoretical framework has not yet been implemented and tested. It is therefore unclear how well the framework will work to drive the coevolution within the system.

Three-Cornered Coevolution is an important concept in evolutionary computation (EC) as it addresses both how computers can solve interesting problems and how to find interesting problems to solve, which was previously the human investigators' task. This shifts the onus from defining the problem data and associated parameters set-up, to defining the characteristics of the problem that are likely to affect its difficulty, e.g. noise, dimensionality and so forth. The goal is to automatically discover the connection between problem characteristics and the ability of methods within an EC technique, which affect performance (e.g. classification accuracy). This reduces human effort, the need for human knowledge of the problem/technique and hence any associated biases. Ultimately, the Three-Cornered Coevolution could determine the maximum difficulty in an identified type of problem domain that can be solved by an algorithm together with automatically tuned methods and parameters, but for this work, the aim is to simply determine if the framework is practical.

This paper presents a realised implementation of the *Three-Cornered Coevolution Framework* [25] for addressing the classification problems, albeit practical design decisions were made that have resulted in differences from the originally envisioned system. The work focuses on addressing the artificial data for classification (rather than image patterns) in a *coadaptive manner* (e.g. each agent adapts and learns the problems while evolving the individual's rules).

Previously, Marzukhi et al., introduced the *Two-Cornered Coevolution System* [12] where a generation agent and a classification agent autonomously evolved problems of interest.

This work showed the ability of the generation agent to create classification problems based on the classification agent's ability, but learning was triggered through human set limits and not as Wilson's *Three-Cornered Coevolution Framework* envisaged.

One reason why the Three-Cornered Coevolution System is preferred over the Two-Cornered Coevolution System is that both the rate of convergence to a classification performance level and the maximum achievable performance level itself are not known *a priori*, so it is difficult to determine when the generation agent should adjust the problem. The rate is complex as EC techniques may have an exponential, non-monotonic or punctuated equilibrium rise to maximum performance, so setting a predefined level for a single classification agent to reach is difficult. By introducing a similar third agent (i.e. the Interceptor), the classification performance difference can be used to trigger the change in problem complexity when necessary, i.e. one agent's performance has stagnated and then the other agent's follows a similar pattern. This does not overcome all problems, but does avoid the necessity of setting an absolute level that must be reached. The third agent can also assist in determining whether the problem should be made 'harder' or 'easier' when the agents' performance have stagnated. This is because it helps separate whether a current non-optimal performance level is likely due to the problem or to the techniques' abilities, i.e. the former when the agents' performances are similar and the latter when there is a difference. Problems with low performing, stagnated agents could be made easier (and vice versa), whilst a difference in performance encourages exploration of problem difficulty.

There are three main objectives in designing the system.

1. Develop a *Three-Cornered Coevolution LCSs* for classification which consists of three main agents: the generation agent (i.e. the Sender) and the classification agents (i.e. the Receiver and the Interceptor).

2. Investigate the effect of triggering change in the learning of agents.

3. Investigate whether there is any insight into the learning capabilities of the agents.

2. BACKGROUND

2.1 Classification

The field of *pattern recognition* is concerned with an automatic discovery of regularities in data through the use of computer algorithms for further actions such as classifying the data into different categories [3]. An example of pattern recognition is *classification*, which is a task of assigning one of several predefined categories to each object in previously unseen data [5].

Classification is a data mining task which resolves the class of an object by assigning a collection of objects (data) to the target classes (categories). The goal of classification is to accurately predict the target class for each case in the collection of objects (data). The simplest type of classification problem is binary classification, where the target class has only two possible labels.

2.2 Types of Learning

Machine learning (ML) is generally categorized according to the type of learning procedure used to generate the output value. Learning methods in machine learning can be distinguished into: supervised, unsupervised and reinforcement learning [14]. In this work we are dealing with the supervised learning and reinforcement learning techniques for addressing the non-sequential task (i.e. classification).

2.3 Learning Classifier Systems (LCSs)

Learning Classifier Systems (LCSs) [7] are a subset of Evolutionary Machine Learning systems, which are machine learning techniques that incorporate reinforcement learning (RL) and evolutionary computation (e.g. genetic algorithm (GA)) in its main component. The RL component is applied to the classifier's predictions to evaluate the classifiers [8] for the identification of the best rules, while the EC component is responsible for discovering potentially better rules [4].

In LCSs, knowledge is commonly represented as a set of condition-action rules called classifiers, where the rules are usually in the form of 'IF <condition> THEN <action>'. The *condition* specifies the state which the rule matches, and the *action* specifies the selected action to be sent to the environment when the condition is satisfied. Typical LCSs learn by interacting with an environment.

Accuracy-based LCSs, e.g. XCS, have been recognized as one of the main representatives of LCSs 'to date' [2], the most universal being 'Michigan-style' LCSs [23, 22]. The success of XCS is due to two main aspects of its architecture: the classifier's fitness is based on the accuracy of the prediction and 'niche-based' GA. XCS uses a form of restricted mating called 'niche-based' GA which focuses genetic search and provides a strong generalisation to the system [10]. Other interesting features in XCS include [10]: 1) *subsumption* that provides another bias towards generalisated rules, 2) *deletion and GA invocation* to balance rule allocation between niches, and 3) *macroclassifiers* which are classifiers with a numerosity parameter (parameter is used to indicate the number of identical virtual classifiers), which decreases the run-time and provides an important statistic on the worth of each unique rule.

UCS [2] is a learning classifier system derived from XCS that works under a supervised learning scheme [18]. As UCS is specifically designed for *supervised learning*, it benefits directly from known labels during training [21]. The main difference between UCS and XCS is as follows [18]. First, the Performance Component is adjusted based on a supervised learning scheme. Thus, UCS only evolves high-rewarded classifiers (i.e. the best action map). Secondly, UCS calculates accuracy as the percentage of correct classification. The Reinforcement Component and the Discovery Component of the system work similar to XCS.

UCS uses the same classifiers' representation as in XCS, and 'niche-based' GA is implemented as the main search mechanism. However, niches in UCS are defined by the correct rule-set [C], and it is expected that UCS will generalize over the search space of correct rule-sets [2]. During learning, UCS perceives a set of labeled examples which consists of a set of instances $x = (x_1, ..., x_n)$ and its corresponding class c. Therefore, UCS is being presented with an input example together with the associated class, $x : c$. UCS works as in Algorithm 1.

Algorithm 1: Algorithmic description of UCS during *learning* (adapted from [18]).

```
begin
    Perceive an input example x with the associated class c.
    Scan the population [P].
    Create a match set [M] consisting of those classifiers whose
    conditions match the input x.
    Form a correct set [C] consisting of those classifiers in the
    match set [M] which predict the class c.
    if [C] is empty then
        Activate the covering operator, creating a new classifier
        with a generalized condition matching x and class c.
    end
end
```

At each time the classifier participates in the match set [M] in the learning mode, the classifier parameters are updated as follows [17, 18]. The accuracy *acc* is computed as the percentage of correct classification:

$$acc = \frac{NumberOfCorrectClassification}{experience} \tag{1}$$

Note, since the classifiers' parameters are updated in the match set [M], the classifiers' experience *exp* is increased by one every time the classifier participates in the match set [M]. The niche size *cs* store the average number of classifiers that participates in the correct set [C]. The niche size *cs* is updated whenever the classifier belongs to the correct set [C]. The rest of the parameters in UCS (i.e. the accuracy κ, the relative accuracy κ' and the fitness F) are updated in the same way as in XCS.

2.4 Coevolution

According to the Darwinian theory [1], an individual evolves through interaction with the environment. Coevolution is the complementary evolution between closely associated species (individuals) [6], in a situation where two different species interact with each other. In *evolutionary algorithms* (EAs), evolution is viewed as the process that enables the population to adapt in a fixed simulated environment [6]. Further, in *Coevolutionary Algorithms* (CEAs), evolution is influenced by other independently acting populations in the simulated environment [6]. Often in natural evolution, the evolution is not just locally within each population, but also in response to environmental changes as caused by each population. As a consequence, natural evolution actually implies coevolution, which is reflected in the Three-Cornered Coevolution framework as the environment of the learning agents changes as the problem domain changes based on the agents' performance.

2.5 Two-Cornered Coevolution System

The *Two-Cornered Coevolution Learning Classifier System* for pattern classification is a new human independent adjustable system capable of producing various classification problems and testing the learning algorithm [12]. The Two-Cornered Coevolution System has shown that LCSs are able to generate interesting problems for classification. The system was able to automatically create image-based data [12] and artificial data [13] to test the learning techniques for solving classification tasks.

The system consisted of two main agents, a generation agent (i.e. the Sender (`S`)) and a classification agent (i.e. the Receiver (`R`)), which form the basis of the current work. `S`'s rules consist of a condition with a starting state ($state_1$) and the subsequent state ($state_2$), see table 1, where each state is encoded in a real value range to enable generalisation if possible. The action encodes whether the problem is made harder or easier by transitioning from $state_1$ to $state_2$ for the classification algorithm, based on whether `R`'s performance decreases or increases, respectively. The search space from $state_1$ could have been transversed randomly, but this would be inefficient due to revisiting solutions. Considering that the direction of search is known (e.g. attempting to discover harder problems until the performance is minimized) as it is set *a priori*, Tabu search is utilised considering the performance of the classification agent.

The system was able to generate different types of problems for classification, where the problem's difficulty could be tuned and adjusted automatically based on the classification agent's ability to learn (i.e. either increasing or decreasing the problem's difficulty depending on the classification performance). The results suggested that the Two-Cornered Coevolution System had modified the traditional process for classification, as now both the problem and the solution adapt in parallel rather than independently. Further, the detailed analysis showed that the evolved problems can easily be interpreted in order to understand the effect of features in the problem that altered the classification agent's performance.

3. METHODS

The focus of this study is to develop a *Three-Cornered Coevolution System* where `S` creates various evolved problems for classification, whilst the classification agents `R` and the Interceptor (`I`) learn the problems and adapt to different feedback returns from the generation agent. Here, the classification agents use different techniques of learning (e.g. either supervised learning or reinforcement learning technique) to learn the problems.

Setting the task of `S` *a priori* has the problem that `R` may become stagnated. The new classification agent `I` is introduced to automatically activate the coevolutionary process within the system. This new agent is termed the 'Interceptor' as analogy to a spy intercepting a message, which forces the communicating agents to change patterns. When the difference in performance between `R` and `I` is below a certain threshold value, `S` changes the problem's difficulty (e.g. increases the difficulty levels) based on `R's` and `I's` learning ability (e.g. both high).

3.1 Framework Design

Figure 1 illustrates the overall design of the system. In this setup, the Three-Cornered Coevolution System is implemented as a *coadaptive coevolution* where each agent learns to adapt to the changes of the problem (two-way learning) as the parameters setting for each agent are fixed, while the individuals in each agent (i.e. `S's` rule-set, `R's` rules and `I's` rules) evolve. `S` generates various evolved problems for classification (i.e. a set of artificial data based on the evolved problem) that will need to be solved by `R` and `I`. Therefore, `S` activates a program for problem generation, while `R` and `I` activate a program for classification.

The action of `I` may or may not always be competitive with `R`, as `R` and `I` use different techniques of learning. When the difference in performance between `R` and `I` is small (see Figure 2) the coevolutionary process is activated so that

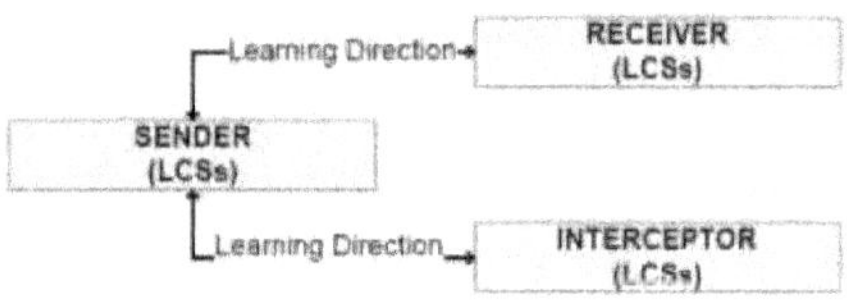

Figure 1: Three-Cornered Coevolution System.

S can change the problem's difficulty (e.g. to make the problem 'harder') based on the classification agents' learning ability.

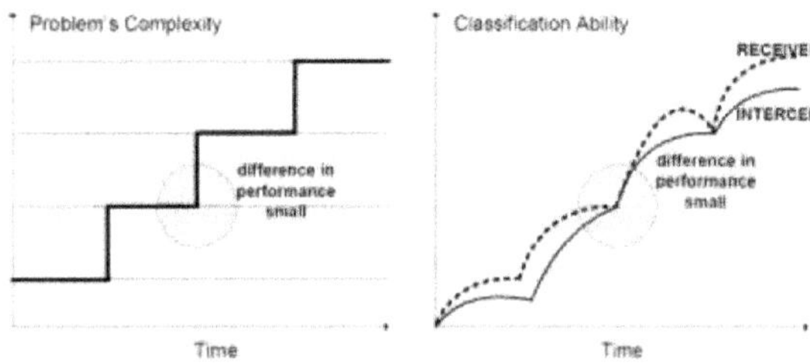

Figure 2: The difference in performance between R and I will trigger the learning process.

3.2 Knowledge Representation

S needs to generate various evolved problems for classification (i.e. where the *problem* is a list of of features F such as [Fn Fc Fd Fi Fr Fan Fcn Fcbl Fcbd]) (see [13] for details), while R and I learn the artificial data that is generated based on the evolved problem. Table 1 illustrates S's *condition-action* rule format. The *condition* specifies the problem containing $state_1$ and $state_2$. Each $state_n$ contains a list of features F for the problem. Each feature F in $state_n$ is encoded to be real valued at $real_n = (l_n, u_n)$, with a lower bound and an upper bound within a specified interval.

Feature F is defined and can take a certain value within the specified interval as follows. Fn is number of data features in each instance (i.e. if Fn=2, then the instance contains of two data features f1 and f2), where Fn from 2 to 5. Fc is number of data features that apply conjunction (Fc at least 1/2 of Fn). Fd is number of data features that apply disjunction (Fn $\geq$ Fd $\geq$ 0). Fi is number of irrelevant data features in each instance (Fn $\geq$ Fi $\geq$ 0 and Fi $\neq$ Fc $\neq$ Fd). Fr is number of redundant data features in each instance (Fn $\geq$ Fr $\geq$ 0). Fan is percentage of noise that apply to class (Fan from 0% to 50%). Fcn is percentage of noise that apply to data features (Fcn from 0% to 50%). Fcbl is percentage of class balance that apply to dataset (i.e. 50% Class 1,50% Class 0), where Fcbl from 0% to 100%. Fcbd is percentage of decision boundary (i.e. wide or small decision boundary), where Fcbd from 0% to 50%.

S's *action* (i.e *ProblemDifficulty*) can be either '1' for a 'harder' problem, or '0' for an 'easier' problem. If the classification performance for the problem defined by $state_2$ is greater than the classification performance for the problem defined by $state_1$, then the problem's difficulty is considered 'easier', otherwise 'harder'.

Table 1: S's condition-action rule format.

IF<*condition*>THEN<*action*>
IF<*condition* : $state_1, state_2$>THEN<*ProblemDifficulty*> $state_n$ is a list of features F containing: [Fc Fd Fi Fr Fan Fcn Fcbl Fcbd]
$state_1, state_2$: *ProblemDifficulty* $state_1$: $[l_1, u_1], [l_2, u_2], ..., [l_8, u_8]$
given a problem: [1, 0, 0, 0, 20, 20, 80, 20] $state_1$:[0,1], [0,1], [0,1], [0,1], [0,5], [45,50], [70,100], [0,25] *ProblemDifficulty* is predicted to be: **0** (easier)

Table 2 illustrates R's and I's *condition-action* rule format. The *condition* specifies each data feature for the instance in the dataset, while the *action* is the class. The *condition* is encoded to be real-value of $real_n = (l_n, u_n)$, where l_n is the lower bound and u_n is the upper bound within the interval $[0, 1]$. The last row illustrates R's and I's rules to specify one instance that contains of two data features $f1$ and $f2$ where the value of each data feature is within the interval of lower bound l_n and upper bound u_n (i.e. [0,1]). The action can be either '1' for 'Class 1', otherwise '0' for 'Class 0'. R and I will receive a reward of '1000' for correct classification or '0' for incorrect classification.

Table 2: R's and I's condition-action rule format.

IF<*condition*>THEN<*action*>
IF<*instance*>THEN<*class*> *instance* is a list of data feature f containing: *instance*:$[f1, f2, ..., fn]$, where $f1 : [l_1, u_1]$
given an instance with two data features: [0.5, 0.6] *instance*: [0.3,0.6], [0.5,0.8] *class* is predicted to be: **0** ('Class 0')

3.3 Data Generation and Classification

The process of *artificial data generation* and *classification* between S, R and I are provided as follows. First, S generates variants of problems for classification (i.e. how to generate a population of problems can be thought of as *meta-problem*). In order to create a set of artificial data for an individual problem, S is initialized with a problem state containing a list of features (i.e [Fn Fc Fd Fi Fr Fan Fcn Fcbl Fcbd]. Next, S creates a set of artificial data for an individual problem and sends each instance in the dataset to R and I.

Secondly, R and I need to classify each instance in the dataset as either belonging to 'Class 1' or 'Class 0' and send either '1' for 'Class 1' or '0' for 'Class 0'. However, R will use a different technique (or methods) for learning compared to I, for classifying the instances. In response, S sends a numerical reward to R and I of '1000' for correct classification else '0' independently.

Thirdly, S evolves the problems to generate a new problem at appropriate levels of difficulty (i.e. increasing the problem's difficulty). The first problem in a sequence could be set randomly, but to facilitate comparison between R and I it is manually set, see row 0, table 1. Next, tabu search, set for 100 steps, is used to maximize the performance of R (irrespective of I's performance). S's rule-set is then updated based on its ability to predict the effect of the state transition (from initial state to final state discovered by the tabu search) on R's performance.

In subsequent problems it is the difference between R's and I's performance that triggers how tabu search functions in S. If the difference is positive and greater than a set threshold, e.g. 10 percentage points, then the search will maximize R's performance (as before). Alternatively, if the problem becomes 'too easy' such that both R and I can solve it to within the threshold difference the tabu search is used to minimize the performance of I (irrespective of R's performance), effectively making the problem harder. Note: for true coevolution to occur there would need to be a population of each classification agent type so that parameters as well as rules could evolve.

4. EXPERIMENTAL DESIGN

Two sets of experiments have been performed in order to verify the Three-Cornered Coevolution System for addressing classification tasks. In *Experiment 1*, the effect of triggering change in the learning of agents (i.e. R and I use different types of learning systems) was investigated when S consistently increased the problem's difficulty. In *Experiment 2*, the learning capabilities of the agents (i.e. any improvement in the learning of agents when R and I used different methods of selection) was further investigated.

S generates various problems containing a list of parameters F (features of the problem) and hence creates a sequence of n instances (i.e. n is set to 2,000) for each problem in turn. Each value (i.e. associated class) of an instance is created 'on-the-fly' within the interval $[0, 1]$ and labeled accordingly (i.e. either 'Class 0' or 'Class 1', as set as a binary problem).

Both R and I are executed following *Wilson's explore/exploit scheme* [24], which has become the standard approach in accuracy-based LCSs. If the classification agent uses the reinforcement learning technique (i.e. XCS system), the parameters are set according to [9]. However, if the classification agent is a supervised learner (i.e. UCS system), the parameters are set according to [21, 15, 16] and is implemented as suggested in [11].

The population size N was limited to 500 classifiers for R and I to learn each problem, where R and I learn 2,000 instances (i.e. R and I run for the 2,000 iterations of each problem). Both values are low for the standard LCSs in order to reduce training times as the overall *meta-problem* task is time consuming. There will be many iterations of R and I for each iteration of S. After 2,000 instances (a single instance of a generating problem in S), R's and I's classification performances are recorded to measure R's and I's performance on the specified problem. The threshold for considering the performances as different was empirically set as 10 percentage points (values up to 20% worked well). S's success (i.e. S's performance) is to correctly predict the effect of a change in problem characteristic on R and I's classification performance.

It is a standard practice to take the average of 30 independent runs in assessing the results of EC experiments in order to avoid outliers and assist in statistical analysis. However, this makes the assumption that each problem remains the same for 30 independent runs, which is not the case here, as S varies the problem to R and I stochastically. Although the patterns of performance may be similar between all the runs, the phase between performance improvements or decreases may (often) differ, which render taking the average at any given instance meaningless. Therefore, the results only illustrate R's and I's classification performance from a single run out of 30 runs conducted to verify consistency in performance for learning a number of problems. The classification performance is recorded from the average of every 100 exploit trials.

5. RESULTS

R and I were applied to the four problem domains (i.e. Fn=2 to Fn=5), where the results of R and I (i.e. the classification performance), and S (i.e. changes of features F in the problem) are presented. In the original *Two-Cornered Coevolution System*, S could tune the problem either to be 'harder' or 'easier'. Here, we are interested in identifying which problems are 'hard' for a learning system (e.g. XCS) compared with an alternative system (e.g. UCS) and importantly, vice versa.

5.1 Experiment 1 Results

In this experiment, the capability of XCS system (i.e. the reinforcement learning system) and UCS system (i.e. the supervised learning system) which use the same selection method (i.e. tournament selection) to learn the problems is investigated. First, S is tasked to *maximize XCS's performance* (i.e. R-XCS) if the performance is different or *minimize UCS's performance* (i.e. I-UCS) if performance is similar. Second, the roles are swapped with S tasked to *minimize XCS's performance*, while *maximizing UCS's performance*. Figure 3 and Figure 4 depict the classification performance between XCS system and UCS system for Fn=2.

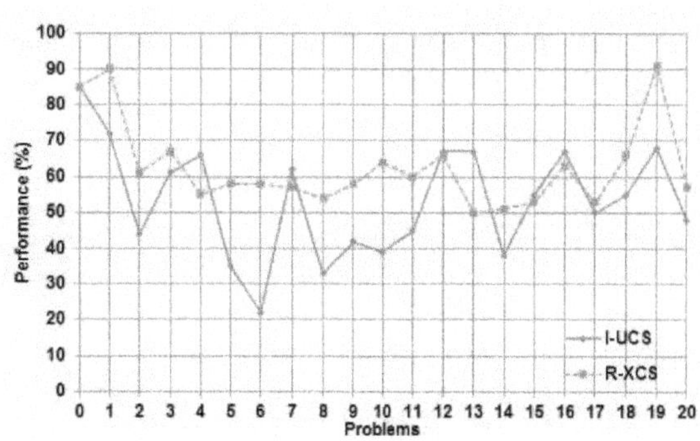

Figure 3: R-XCS's versus I-UCS's performance when S tunes the problems' difficulty to favour R-XCS, Fn=2.

The plots show that the difference in performance between R and I is able to trigger the coevolutionary process within the system. S successfully adjusts the problem's difficulty and creates various difficult problems while maximizing/minimizing either XCS/UCS's or UCS/XCS's performance. The results indicate that in certain problems UCS outperforms XCS or XCS outperforms UCS, where these results are discussed in more detail in Table 3 and Table 4. The final column shows the relative classification performance of R and I, which can be greater than the threshold ('+'), positive but less than the threshold difference ('=') or inverted when I outperforms R ('-'). S starts with the initial problem (the first row), where R-XCS's and I-UCS's classification performances are shown in the last two columns. The initial

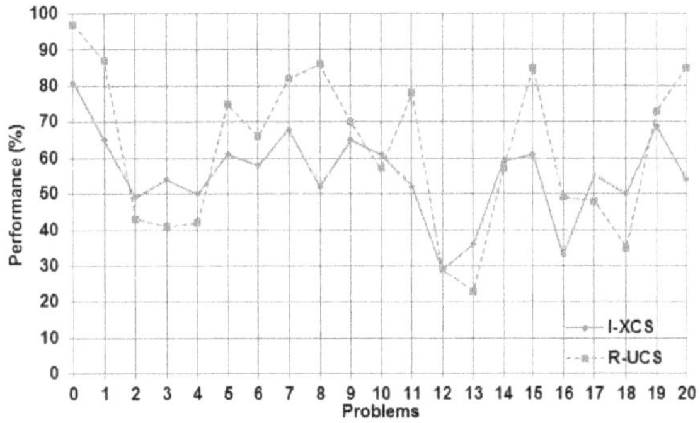

Figure 4: R-UCS's versus I-XCS's performance when S tunes the problems' difficulty to favour R-UCS.

Table 4: Changes of features F when S tunes the problems' difficulty to favour R-UCS for 11 problems.

	Fi	Fr	Fan	Fcn	Fcbl	Fcbd	R-I
0	0	1	5	5	50	5	+
1	**0**	**0**	**15**	**3**	**3**	**1**	**+**
2	1	1	45	46	72	36	-
3	1	1	4	0	75	4	-
4	0	1	1	0	79	1	-
5	1	1	2	1	60	3	+
6	1	0	1	1	67	2	=
7	**1**	**0**	**4**	**2**	**15**	**32**	**+**
8	1	1	1	2	58	3	+
9	**1**	**1**	**35**	**1**	**3**	**0**	**=**
10	1	1	2	0	53	28	=

problem is then adjusted to the next problem (the second row) by S to be 'harder' as the difference in performance was below the threshold, which decreases I-UCS's performance (the last column), and so on. It is noted that when Fn=2 and S is tasked to make the problem 'harder', S sets Fc to be 0 (i.e. from Fc=1 to Fc=0) which is not shown in the tables. Here, Fc=1 means a single conjunction resulting in both data features f1 and f2 being tied together, which simplifies the problem.

In general R-XCS achieves better results compared to I-UCS as the favoured agent as S uses tabu search to maximize its performance or to minimize I-UCS's performance. However, I-UCS outperforms R-XCS specifically for problems with class imbalance and action noise (e.g. *problem 7*. The results from the other problem domains (i.e. Fn=3, Fn=4 and Fn=5) show the same pattern so are not shown here for the sake of brevity.

Table 3: Changes of features F when S tunes the problems' difficulty to favour R-XCS for 11 problems.

	Fi	Fr	Fan	Fcn	Fcbl	Fcbd	R-I
0	0	1	5	5	50	5	=
1	1	1	9	12	44	12	+
2	1	1	12	2	54	29	+
3	1	1	0	4	65	4	=
4	0	1	0	2	58	26	-
5	1	1	3	2	82	4	+
6	0	1	0	0	86	4	+
7	**0**	**0**	**25**	**0**	**25**	**31**	**-**
8	1	0	3	1	69	33	+
9	1	0	3	1	73	1	+
10	0	0	2	1	63	41	+

Table 4 describes the changes of features F in the problem for the initial problem up to 10 problems, when favouring R-UCS's classification performance for Fn=2. R-UCS outperforms I-XCS for addressing class imbalance (i.e. *problem 1, 7* and *9*), including condition noise and a small decision boundary (i.e. *problem 1* and *9*). The results from the other problem domains (i.e. Fn=3, Fn=4 and Fn=5) again show the same pattern.

The findings showed that XCS performed better than UCS when the class balance (Fcbl) was tuned to be greater than 50%, while the noise that applied to the action (Fan) and condition (Fcn) was low. However, when the values of the class balance (Fcbl) was decreased and the noise that applied to the action (Fan) and condition (Fcn) were increased, UCS achieved better performance than XCS.

5.2 Experiment 2 Results

In this experiment, the capability of roulette-wheel selection (RW) or tournament selection (T) to learn different types of problems is investigated. First, S is tasked to favour R-XCS-RW (i.e. XCS system that uses roulette-wheel selection) again by maximizing R's performance while the difference is above the threshold (i.e. 10%) and minimizing I's (I-XCS-T) when similar. Second, tournament selection is used by R and roulette-wheel selection by I.

Figure 5 depicts the classification performance between R-XCS-RW and I-XCS-T for Fn=2 when S increases the problem's difficulty while *minimizing I-XCS-T's performance.* The plots illustrate that I-XCS-T often achieves better performance compared to R-XCS-RW even though S is tasked to minimize I-XCS-T's performance.

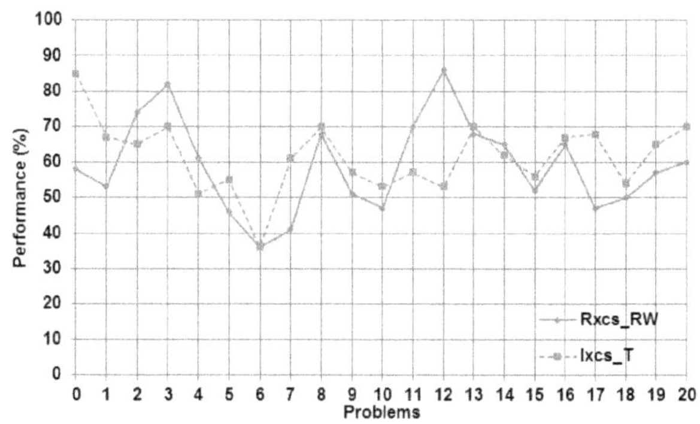

Figure 5: R-XCS-RW's versus I-XCS-T's performance. Note: RW does not often outperform T even though favoured.

Figure 6 depicts R-XCS-T's and I-XCS-RW's performance for Fn=2 when S increases the problem's difficulty while *minimizing I-XCS-RW's performance.* The plots illustrate that for almost all of the problems R-XCS-T outperforms I-XCS-RW. S successfully adjusts the problem's difficulty and creates various difficult problems while minimizing I-XCS-RW's performance.

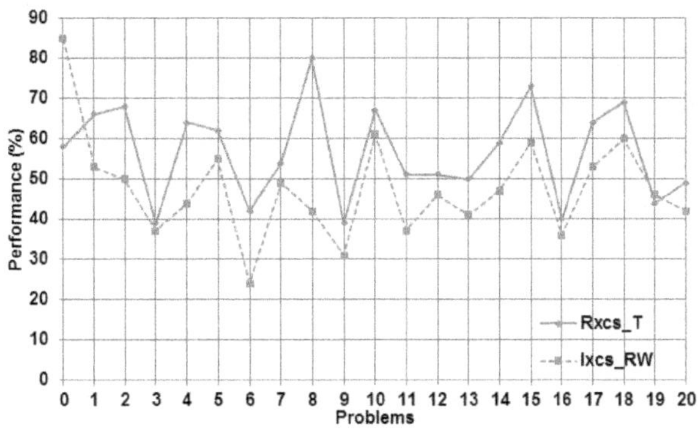

Figure 6: R-XCS-T's versus I-XCS-RW's performance. Note: T often outperforms RW when favoured.

To further illustrate the difference between T and RW methods three problem dimensions (Fan, Fcn, Fcbl) were selected to plot, with two views shown in figure 7. Note the 5, 5, 50 starting position for both experiments. S could have explored any part of the search space to separate XCS-RW from XCS-T (shown as red star if no positive difference or red plus if difference is above the threshold) or vice versa. XCS-RW's performs relatively well when the levels of noise is low (i.e. Fan and Fcn are low), regardless of class imbalance. This is likely due to the explorative nature of the method. XCS-T has been determined to perform better compared with XCS-RW for addressing noisy problems.

6. DISCUSSIONS

The overall aim of this work was to develop the *Three-Cornered Coevolution System*, where three different agents evolve to adapt to the changes of the problem. The goal has been advanced as the coevolutionary process was triggered autonomously between the participating agents in the system. S coevolves to tune and adjust the problem's difficulty autonomously based on the difference in performance between R and I, while R and I also learn each new problem. However, the realised system is *coadaptive evolution* rather than pure coevolution as the classification agents do not evolve themselves, e.g. parameters such as mutation rate do not change in an experiment.

The capability of the classification agents (i.e. R and I) that used different types of learning systems (i.e. either UCS or XCS) on 'hard' problems was investigated. The results indicated that UCS was more robust than XCS for addressing the class imbalance problems and less sensitive to noise, most likely due its supervised nature. In addition, the results also confirmed that the capability of the classification agents (i.e. R and I) can be adjusted when different techniques of selection within the same agent type were applied. The results showed that the classification agent that used tournament selection was more robust to noisy environment compared to roulette-wheel selection, which is not surprising due to its rank-based nature [9]. Conversely, in low noise problem domains with class imbalance, roulette-wheel selection is preferable due to its exploration capabilities.

It was found that both systems (i.e. UCS and XCS) did not achieve 100% performance for solving certain 'hard' problems created by S due to the *non-tuned parameter* settings being used for XCS and UCS for all of the experiments. In [15, 16], the papers provide a few resampling techniques that allow UCS to deal with the class imbalance problems more effectively. However, these techniques were not applied for this work. In [19, 20], the authors report that there are two critical parameters in XCS for optimal performance (i.e. the learning rate and the GA triggering threshold θ_{GA}). Here, the same learning rate and the GA triggering threshold θ_{GA} were used in XCS. In future, if XCS is configured appropriately (e.g. adaptive tuning on the two critical parameters), it is hypothesized that a significant improvement of XCS's performance can be achieved, but again the parameter tuning was not the main objective of this paper, so this is left to future work.

7. CONCLUSIONS

The *Three-Cornered Coevolution System* was executed in a coadaptive manner. In the Three-Cornered Coevolution System S using tabu search consecutively adjusted the problem's difficulty and generated a wide range of problems for classification. R and I attempted to solve the classification tasks where the classification performance were varied. Findings showed that the classification performance was related to the type and degree of the noise, the class imbalance ratio and the characteristics of the artificial data. Furthermore, this new approach identified both strengths and weaknesses of the learning capabilities of different agents autonomously. This includes determining where XCS can outperform UCS (high class imbalance with low noise) and when roulette wheel can outperform tournament selection (class imbalance with low noise), which has not been widely reported in the literature.

Future work should consider *true coevolution* such that multiple agents could be evolved (i.e. adaptive tuning to set parameters), albeit the stepped coadaptive evolution adopted here is worthwhile model.

8. REFERENCES

[1] T. Bäck, D. B. Fogel, and Z. Michalewicz. *Evolutionary Computation 1: Basic Algorithms and Operators.* Institute of Physics Publishing, 2000.

[2] E. Bernadó-Mansilla and J. M. Garrell-Guiu. Accuracy-Based Learning Classifier Systems: Models, Analysis and Applications to Classification Tasks. *Evolutionary Computation*, 11(3):209–238, 2003.

[3] C. Bishop. *Pattern Recognition and Machine Learning.* Springer, Natural Computing Series, 2006.

[4] M. V. Butz. *Rule-Based Evolutionary Online Learning Systems: A Principal Approach to LCS Analysis and Design.* Springer, Berlin Heidelberg, 2006.

[5] R. O. Duda, P. Hart, and D. Stork. *Pattern Classification 2nd Edition.* John Wiley, 2001.

[6] A. Engelbrecht. *Computational Intelligence, An Introduction, 2nd Edition.* John Wiley, 2005.

[7] J. H. Holland and J. Reitman. Cognitive Systems based on Adaptive Algorithms. *Pattern-directed inference systems*, page 313Ű329, 1978.

[8] P. J. Jiadong Yang, Hua Xu. Effective Search for Pittsburgh Learning Classifier Systems via Estimation

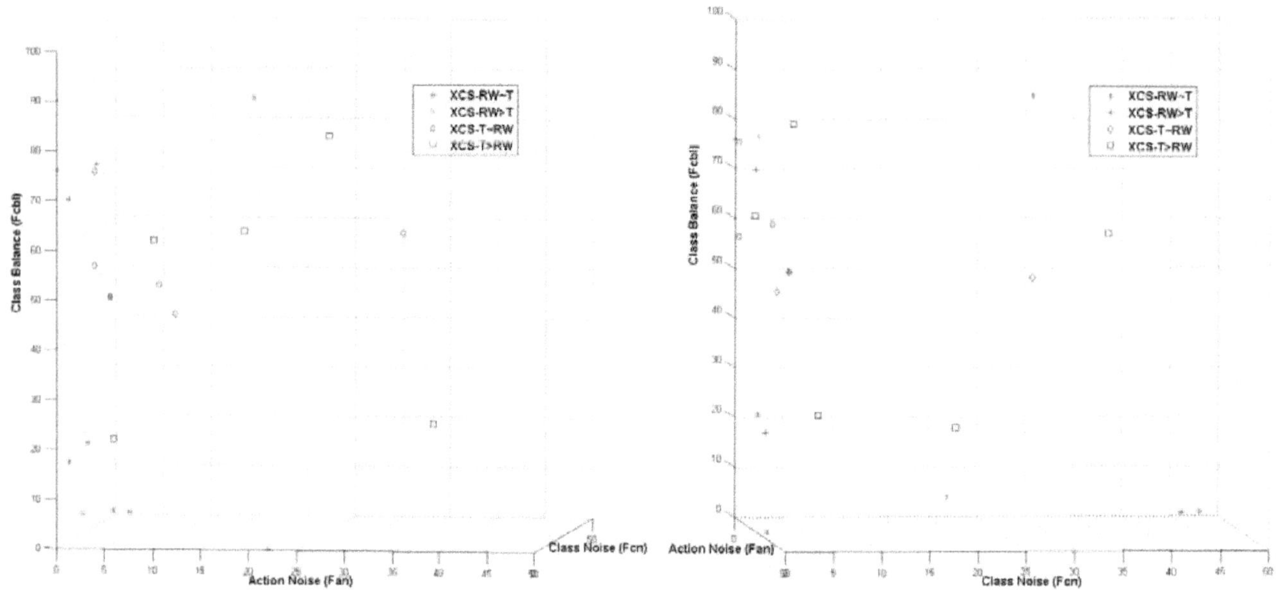

Figure 7: XCS-T's versus XCS-RW's performance when S consistently tunes the problem's difficulty by adjusting features F. XCS-RW∼T means the RW was the favoured method (i.e. R), but did not reach the threshold, whereas XCS-RW>T did obtain the threshold. This is two views of the same plot.

of Distribution Algorithms. *Information Sciences*, 2012(198):100–117, 2012.

[9] F. Kharbat, L. Bull, and M. Odeh. Revisiting Genetic Selection in the XCS Learning Classifier System. In *The 2005 IEEE Congress on Evolutionary Computation, 2005*, volume 3, pages 2061–2068, Sept 2005.

[10] T. Kovacs. Strength or Accuracy : Credit Assignment in Learning Classifier System. *Evolutionary Computation*, 12:99–135, 2004. Massachusetts Institute of Technology.

[11] I. Kukenys, W. N. Browne, and M. Zhang. Transparent, Online Image Pattern Classification using a Learning Classier System. In *The 13th European Event on Evolutionary Computation in Image Analysis and Signal Processing (EvoApplications 2011)*. Springer-Verlag, 2011.

[12] S. Marzukhi, W. N. Browne, and M. Zhang. Two-Cornered Learning Classifier Systems for Pattern Generation and Classification. In *The 12th Genetic and Evolutionary Computation Conference (GECCO 2012)*, pages 895–902. ACM, 2012.

[13] S. Marzukhi, W. N. Browne, and M. Zhang. Adaptive artificial datasets through learning classifier systems for classification tasks. In *International Workshop in Learning Classifier Systems 2013 (IWLCS 2013)*, pages 1243–1250. ACM, 2013.

[14] A. R. Mehryar Mohri and A. Talwalkar. *Foundations of Machine Learning*. MIT Press, 2012.

[15] A. Orriols-Puig and E. Bernadó-Mansilla. The Class Imbalance Problem in UCS Classifier System: A Preliminary Study. In *IWLCS*, pages 161–180, 2005.

[16] A. Orriols-Puig and E. Bernadó-Mansilla. Class Imbalance Problem in UCS Classifier System: Fitness Adaptation. In *Congress on Evolutionary Computation*, pages 604–611, 2005.

[17] A. Orriols-Puig and E. Bernadó-Mansilla. A Further Look at UCS Classifier System. *The 6th Genetic and Evolutionary Computation Conference (GECCO 2006)*, 2006.

[18] A. Orriols-Puig and E. Bernadó-Mansilla. Revisiting UCS: Description, Fitness Sharing, and Comparison with XCS. In *IWLCS*, pages 96–116, 2007.

[19] A. Orriols-Puig and E. Bernadó-Mansilla. Evolutionary Rule-based Systems for Imbalanced Data Sets. *Soft Computing*, 13(3):213–225, 2009.

[20] A. Orriols-Puig, E. Bernadó-Mansilla, D. E. Goldberg, K. Sastry, and P. L. Lanzi. Facetwise Analysis of XCS for Problems with Class Imbalances. *IEEE Trans. Evolutionary Computation*, 13(5):1093–1119, 2009.

[21] K. Shafi. *An Online and Adaptive Signature-based Approach for Intrusion Detection Using Learning Classifier Systems*. PhD thesis, School of Information Technology and Electrical Engineering, University of New South Wales, Australian Defence Force Academy, Australia, 2008.

[22] M. Troc and O. Unold. Self-Adaptation of Parameters in A Learning Classifier System Ensemble Machine. *Application in Mathematics Computer Science*, 20(1):157–174, 2010.

[23] O. Unold. Self-Adaptive Learning Classifier System. *Journal of Circuits, Systems, and Computers*, 19(1):275–296, 2010.

[24] S. W. Wilson. Classifier Fitness Based on Accuracy. *Evolutionary Computation*, 3(2):149–175, 1995. Massachusetts Institute of Technology.

[25] S. W. Wilson. Coevolution of Pattern Generators and Recognizers. In *GECCO '09*. ACM, New York, 2009.

Complete Action Map or Best Action Map in Accuracy -based Reinforcement Learning Classifier Systems

Masaya Nakata
The University of Electro-Communications
Tokyo, Japan
m.nakata@cas.hc.uec.ac.jp

Pier Luca Lanzi
Politecnico di Milano
Milano, Italy
pierluca.lanzi@polimi.it

Tim Kovacs
University of Bristol
Bristol, UK
kovacs@cs.bris.ac.uk

Keiki Takadama
The University of Electro-Communications
Tokyo, Japan
keiki@inf.uec.ac.jp

ABSTRACT

We study two existing Learning Classifier Systems (LCSs): XCS, which has a *complete map* (which covers all actions in each state), and XCSAM, which has a *best action map* (which covers only the highest-return action in each state). This allows XCSAM to learn with a smaller population size limit (but larger population size) and to learn faster than XCS on well-behaved tasks. However, many tasks have difficulties like noise and class imbalances. XCS and XCSAM have not been compared on such problems before. This paper aims to discover which kind of map is more robust to these difficulties. We apply them to a classification problem (the multiplexer problem) with class imbalance, Gaussian noise or alternating noise (where we return the reward for a different action). We also compare them on real-world data from the UCI repository without adding noise. We analyze how XCSAM focuses on the best action map and introduce a novel deletion mechanism that helps to evolve classifiers towards a best action map. Results show the best action map is more robust (has higher accuracy and sometimes learns faster) in all cases except small amounts of alternating noise.

Categories and Subject Descriptors

I.2.6 [**Artificial Intelligence**]: Learning—*knowledge acquisition, concept learning*

General Terms

Algorithms, Experimentation, Performance

Keywords

Learning Classifier System, XCS, XCSAM, complete action map, best action map, classification

GECCO'14, July 12–16, 2014, Vancouver, BC, Canada.
Copyright 2014 ACM 978-1-4503-2662-9/14/07 ...$15.00.
http://dx.doi.org/10.1145/2576768.2598351.

1. INTRODUCTION

Learning Classifier Systems (LCSs) [7] are rule-based learning systems that evolve general rules (called classifiers) using Genetic Algorithms [6] to represent human-readable solutions. The accuracy-based LCSs [21] [1] are the most popular classifier system model so far and have been successfully applied to a wide range of problem domains [2] such as classification [8], regression [5], and sequential decision making problems [4]. Accuracy-based LCSs can be classified to two types according to a difference of learning mechanisms that they employ: Accuracy-based Reinforcement Learning Classifier Systems (ARLCS) which employ reinforcement learning (RL) [18], i.e., the XCS classifier system [21], and Accuracy-based Supervised Learning Classifier Systems (ASLCS) which employ supervised learning instead of RL, i.e., the UCS classifier system [1]. While ASLCS is a useful and robust model in supervised learning tasks [14], it is not designed to be suitable for RL tasks.

When we design ARLCS for given problems, we have to choose either one of two learning strategies: a *complete action map* which predicts the rewards of all actions in each state and a *best action map* which in contrast covers only the highest-return action in each state. Most real world applications have difficulties like noise and class imbalances in their state-space and reward functions. Accordingly, a key which can help to design LCS is to understand which strategy (complete or best-action map) is more robust to which kind of difficulties.

Orriols-Puig shows that UCS (with a best action map) can derive better performance than XCS (with a complete map) on a class-imbalanced classification problem [14]. Stone and Bull show the ZCS classifier system [20] (which is a strength-based LCS and employs a best action map) exceeds performance of XCS on noisy problems [17]. Also, Fani shows a revised ZCS for data mining can derive higher classification accuracy than XCS in a classification problem with real world data [19]. These results may suggest the best action map is a more robust strategy than the complete action map. However, ZCS and UCS are not ARLCS. Specifically, as noted previously, UCS can successfully identify a highest-return action (i.e., a correct class) using supervised data. ZCS, like ARLCS, employs reinforcement learning, but it may not correctly generalize classifiers because of its strength-based fitness. Strength-based fitness directly estimates reward (i.e., high fitness means high estimated reward). This is useful to identify the best action map but is less useful to find accurate classifiers. In contrast, the accuracy-based fitness of ARLCS is calculated from an error in estimated prediction; it is useful to accurately generalize classifiers but is very sensitive to noise (especially noise which is added to a reward). This means accuracy-based fitness mistakenly leads to incorrect generalization in noisy problems. Accordingly, best action maps may not be robust in class-imbalanced, noisy and real-world classification.

In summary, previous studies have found ZCS and UCS were more robust than XCS on class-imbalanced and noisy tasks, but it is not clear if this is due to their best-action maps, or due to their definition of fitness. This paper compares complete and best maps in systems with the same definition of fitness; specifically, we compare two ARLCSs; XCS and XCSAM [12] [11]. XCS evolves a complete action map while XCSAM is a variation of XCS which evolves best action maps. We apply them to versions of a classification problem (the multiplexer) with class imbalance, Gaussian noise or alternating noise. We also compare them on real world data from the UCI repository [16]. From experimental results we analyze how XCSAM focuses on the best action map. We also introduce a novel deletion mechanism [9] that helps to evolve classifiers towards the best action map.

The remainder of this paper is organized as follows: In sections 2 and 3 we describe mechanisms of XCS and XCSAM. In section 4 we show experimental results of XCS and XCSAM on problems with noise and class-imbalance, and real wold data. In section 5 we analyze the results of the XCSAM and introduce the deletion mechanism for XCSAM. In section 6 we show experimental results for XCSAM with the deletion mechanism. Finally, in section 7, we conclude this paper by summarizing the contributions.

2. XCS CLASSIFIER SYSTEM

The XCS classifier system maintains a population of rules ("classifiers") which represent the solution to a reinforcement learning problem [10]. The following sub-sections explain the classifiers and mechanisms of XCS.

2.1 Classifier

A classifier is a *condition-action* rule; a condition C is coded by $C \in \{0, 1, \#\}^L$, where L is the length of condition, and the symbol '#' is the *don't care symbol* which matches all input values (*i.e.*, 0 or 1). Classifiers consist of a condition, an action, and four main parameters [21, 3]: (i) the prediction p, which estimates the relative payoff that the system expects when the classifier is used; (ii) the prediction error ε, which estimates the error of the prediction p; (iii) the fitness F, which estimates the accuracy of the payoff prediction given by p; and (iv) the numerosity *num*, which indicates how many copies of classifiers with the same condition and the same action are present in the population.

2.2 Mechanism

At time t, XCS builds a *match set* [M] containing the classifiers in the population [P] whose condition matches the current sensory input s_t; if [M] does not contain all the feasible actions *covering* takes place and creates a set of classifiers that matches s_t and cover all the missing actions. This process ensures that XCS can evolve a complete mapping so that in any state it can predict the effect of every possible action in terms of expected returns.[1]

For each possible action a in [M], XCS computes the *system prediction* $P(s_t, a)$ which estimates the payoff that XCS expects if action a is performed in s_t. The system prediction $P(s_t, a)$ is computed as the fitness weighted average of the predictions of classifiers in [M] which advocate action a:

$$P(s_t, a) = \sum_{cl_k \in [M](a)} p_k \times \frac{F_k}{\sum_{cl_i \in [M](a)} F_i} \tag{1}$$

where, [M](a) represents the subset of classifiers of [M] with action a, p_k identifies the prediction of classifier cl_k, and F_k identifies the fitness of classifier cl_k. Then XCS selects an action to perform; the classifiers in [M] which advocate the selected action form the current *action set* [A].

The selected action a_t is performed, and a scalar reward r_{t+1} is returned to XCS together with a new input s_{t+1}. When the reward r_{t+1} is received, the estimated payoff $P(t)$ is computed as follows:

$$P(t) = r_{t+1} + \gamma \max_{a \in [M]} P(s_{t+1}, a) \tag{2}$$

where γ is the discount factor [18], which is 0 for single-step tasks such as those in this work. Next, the parameters of the classifiers in [A] are updated in the following order [3]: prediction, prediction error, and finally fitness. Prediction p is updated with learning rate β ($0 \leq \beta \leq 1$):

$$p_k \leftarrow p_k + \beta(P(t) - p_k) \tag{3}$$

Then, the prediction error ϵ and classifier fitness are updated with the absolute accuracy κ:

$$\epsilon_k \leftarrow \epsilon_k + \beta(|P(t) - p_k| - \epsilon_k) \tag{4}$$

$$\kappa_k = \begin{cases} 1 & \text{if } \epsilon_k \leq \epsilon_0, \\ \alpha(\epsilon_k/\epsilon_0)^{-\nu} & \text{otherwise.} \end{cases} \tag{5}$$

$$F_k \leftarrow F_k + \beta\left(\frac{\kappa_k \times num_k}{\sum_{cl_j \in [A]} \kappa_j \times num_j} - F_k\right) \tag{6}$$

The GA is applied to classifiers in [A] [21]. It selects two classifiers, copies them, and with probability χ performs crossover on the copies; then it mutates each element in its condition with probability μ.

3. XCSAM CLASSIFIER SYSTEM

XCS [21] evolves classifiers that represent complete action maps which are composed of all available actions in every possible situation, but the complete action map increases the population size required to evolve an optimal solution. UCS [1] deals with the best action map and is trained using supervised learning, unlike XCS which uses reinforcement learning. Therefore, UCS is limited in that it cannot be applied to reinforcement learning applications. XCS with Adaptive Action Mapping (or XCSAM), provides a trade-off between XCS and UCS. Like XCS, it can solve both reinforcement learning (multi-step) and supervised classification (one-step) problems; like UCS, XCSAM does not evolve a

[1] In the algorithmic description [3], covering is activated when the match set contains less than θ_{mna} actions; however, θ_{mna} is always set to the number of available actions so that the match covers all the actions.

complete action map but tries to focus on the best actions only while learning proceeds. XCSAM extends the original XCS by (i) including a mechanism to adaptively identify the redundant actions from those that should be included in a best action map and by (ii) getting rid of redundant actions while still exploring the space of viable optimal solutions.

3.1 Identification of the Best Action Map

Firstly, XCSAM identifies the best action when the selected action is performed. In a typical reinforcement learning problem involving delayed rewards, the expected future reward at the current state $maxP(s_t, a)$ (Equation 2), tends to be higher than the expected future reward at the previous state $maxP(s_{t-1}, a)$ (because of the discount factor γ). Accordingly, since the action corresponding to a higher reward also tends to correspond to a shorter state sequence, the best actions will tend to have a value of $maxP(s_t, a)$ larger than $maxP(s_{t-1}, a)$. More precisely, $maxP(s_{t-1}, a)$ converges to $\gamma maxP(s_t, a)$ at the next state, while $maxP(s_t, a)$ converges to the $maxP(s_{t-1}, a)/\gamma$. Thus, when an executed action is a best action, in XCS the predictions of the accurate classifiers in [A] tend to converge to $maxP(s_{t-1}, a)/\gamma$. For this reason, XCSAM can identify the actions that are likely to be part of the best action map by comparing $maxP(s_t, a)$ against $\zeta \times maxP(s_{t-1}, a)/\gamma$ (where ζ is a learning rate added to guarantee convergence). If $maxP(s_t, a)$ is greater than the threshold $\zeta \times maxP(s_{t-1}, a)/\gamma$, then a is a good candidate for the best action map and should be maintained.

After having identified good action candidates for the best action map, XCSAM needs to adaptively identify classifiers that may be good candidate for the final best action map. Accordingly, XCSAM adds a parameter *eam* to classifiers, or *effect of adaptive mapping*, that for classifier cl_i is updated according to Equation 7, where *nma* represents the number of available actions. The value of *eam* of classifiers advocating the selected action converges to 1 if the classifier is a good candidate for the final best action map; otherwise, *eam* converges to *nma*. Therefore, classifiers with an *eam* close to one are good candidates to represent the final best action map while classifiers with an *eam* close to *nma* are less likely to be maintained as they are probably advocating actions with lower expected return.

$$eam_i \leftarrow \begin{cases} eam_i + \beta(1 - eam_i) \\ \qquad \text{if} \quad maxP(s_t, a) \geq \zeta \times maxP(s_{t-1}, a)/\gamma \\ eam_i + \beta(nma - eam_i) \qquad \text{otherwise.} \end{cases} \tag{7}$$

3.2 Evolution on the Best Actions

To focus evolution on the best actions, XCSAM acts on the covering operator to prevent the generation of classifiers that are not likely to be included in the final solution. In particular, XCSAM tunes the covering threshold θ_{mna} based on the actions' predicted reward and the *eam* parameters. Initially, θ_{mna} is set to the number of feasible actions (the same value as in XCS). When $[M]$ is generated, XCSAM computes the prediction array before covering is applied (whereas XCS computes it only after covering). Then, XCSAM computes the current θ_{mna} as the average *eam* of the classifiers in [M] weighted for the expected future return $maxP(s_t, a)$. If the number of different actions in $[M]$ is smaller than the computed θ_{mna}, covering is called and the prediction array is computed again to update the prediction array.

If solving a single-step problem, as in the current work, XCSAM computes a *selection array* $S(a)$ that associates a selection probability to each action as follows:

$$S(a_j) = \frac{\sum_{cl_k \in [M]|a_j} p_k \times F_k}{\sum_{cl_k \in [M]} F_k} \tag{8}$$

After action selection is performed, XCSAM generates both the action set [A] (as XCS) and also the *not action set* $[\bar{A}]$ consisting of the classifiers in $[M]$ not advocating the selected action. The selection probability is calculated from the fitness F and parameter *eam* [13] When the executed action is considered a candidate best action, the parents in the GA are selected from $[A]$ to promote the evolution of classifiers that are likely to be in the final best action map while the deleted classifiers are selected from $[\bar{A}]$ to get rid of classifiers that are not likely to be part of the final solution. Otherwise, if there is not enough information about the executed action, or $[\bar{A}]$ is empty, XCSAM applies deletion in $[P]$ as in XCS. When the executed action is not identified as a candidate best action, the parents are selected from $[\bar{A}]$ to explore the solution space even further and deletion is applied to the population as in XCS.

4. EXPERIMENT: XCS VS XCSAM

We apply XCS and XCSAM to the multiplexer and a classification problem with real world data. We add three kinds of problem difficulty to the multiplexer: class-imbalance, Gaussian noise or alternating noise. Class-imbalance can be observed in many real world data such as oil spills in satellite images, failures in manufacturing process, and rare medical diagnosis [15]. Gaussian noise simulates real-world-like reward functions which sometimes return a different reward value when the same action is executed in the same state. Alternating noise simulates the dataset having several aliasing states which have the same input but different class. All three conditions can occur in real world problems.

4.1 Experiments on Multiplexer Problems

4.1.1 Multiplexer problem and Experimental design

Multiplexer problem. The multiplexer (MP) [21] is defined over a binary string of $k + 2^k$ bits; the first k bits represent an address pointing to the remaining 2^k bits. For instance, the 6-multiplexer function ($k = 2$) applied to the input string 110001 will return 1 as an *answer* (i.e., class), while when applied to 110110 it will return 0. We compare XCS and XCSAM using the 11MP ($k = 3$). Following XCS tradition [21] we generate inputs randomly, so the train and test sets are the same.

Experimental design. During *learning* problems, the system selects actions randomly from those represented in the match set. During *evaluation* problems, the system selects the action with highest expected return. When the system performs the correct action, it receives a 1000 reward, otherwise it receives 0. The genetic algorithm is enabled only during *learning* problems, and it is turned off during *evaluation* problems. The covering operator is always enabled, but operates only if needed. Learning problems and test problems alternate. The performance is reported as the moving average over the last 50000 (the class imbalance) or 5000 (Gaussian noise and alternating noise) evaluation problems. All the plots are averages over 20 experiments.

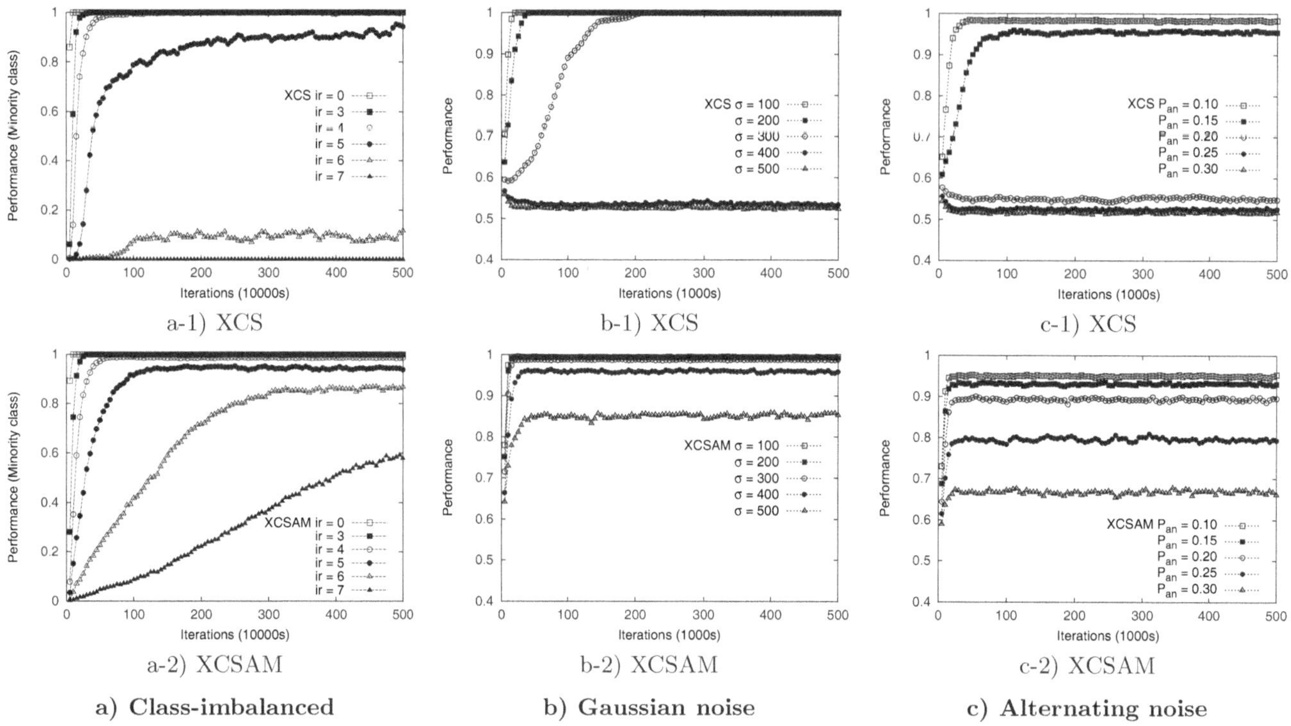

Figure 1: Performances of XCS and XCSAM on the multiplexer problem.

4.1.2 Class-imbalance

In our first set of experiments we use the class-imbalanced multiplexer problem (IMP) [15], which generates a binary string of $k + 2^k$ bits as an instance. If the answer of its instance, which is computed as in the normal MP, belongs to the *minority class*, then this instance is accepted as an input with probability $1/2^{ir}$, where ir denotes the imbalance level of the dataset. If the answer belongs to the *majority class*, this instance is accepted as the input at all times. Accepted inputs are sent to the LCS. Note $ir = 0$ represents the usual balanced multiplexer. We set the minority class to 0 and the majority class to 1. We use the following parameter settings [15]:[2] $N = 800$, $\epsilon_0 = 1$, $\mu = 0.04$, $P_{\#} = 0.6$, $\chi = 0.8$, $\beta = 0.2$, $\alpha = 0.1$, $\delta = 0.1$, $\nu = 5$, $\theta_{GA} = 25$, $\theta_{del} = 20$, $\theta_{sub} = 200$, GA subsumption is turned on while AS subsumption is turned off; in XCSAM, we set $\zeta = 0.99$. We set different imbalance levels ir to $= 0$, 3, 4, 5, 6, and 7. The maximum iteration is set to 5,000,000 as in [15].

Figure 1-a) shows the performances of XCS and XCSAM on the class-imbalanced 11-bit multiplexer problem. Each performance curve shows the rate of correct answers for the minority class only (the performance for the majority class reaches optimally with all ir in both systems). XCS reaches optimality with $ir = 0$, 3 and 4; it reaches near-optimal performance (0.94) with $ir = 5$, but it fails to reach near-optimal performance with $ir = 6$ and 7 because in XCS overgeneralized classifiers remain in the population. Specifically, in the class-imbalanced multiplexer problem, both systems have a tendency to overgeneralize classifiers for the majority class. Overgeneralized classifiers have relatively high fitness because inputs where they are wrong (minority-class inputs) happen with very low frequency. Since XCS deletes classifiers based on their fitness, XCS mistakenly keeps the overgeneralized classifiers as good classifiers. XCSAM also reaches optimality with $ir = 0$, 3 and 4. XCSAM with $ir = 5$ reaches 0.94 faster than XCS. With $ir = 6$ and 7 XCSAM clearly has better performances than XCS. While in XCSAM overgeneralized classifiers are also generated, it can detect and delete them in contrast with XCS. This is because XCSAM deletes classifiers which are not candidates for the best action map when it identifies overgeneralized classifiers (which have incorrect best actions) using the reward signal. These results suggest that the best action map can enhance the performance of ARLCS in class-imbalanced problems, because the evolution of the best action map works to detect and quickly delete overgeneralized classifiers.

4.1.3 Gaussian noise

In our second set of experiments we add Gaussian noise to the reward on the (normal) multiplexer [21]. Gaussian noise is added with mean zero and standard deviation σ to the environment reward. The parameter settings are the same as the previous experiment. We set σ to different values: 100, 200, 300, 400 and 500. The maximum iteration is 500,000.

Figure 1-b) shows the performances of XCS and XCSAM on the 11-bit multiplexer problem with Gaussian noise. XCS reaches optimality with $\sigma = 100$, 200 and 300. However, it suddenly fails to reach optimal performance with higher σ. In contrast, XCSAM reaches optimality faster than XCS with $\sigma = 200$ and 300. Even with a large noise ($\sigma = 400$ and 500), XCSAM reaches about 0.96 and 0.85 respectively.

[2][15] also adapts XCS parameter settings to optimize it for class-imbalanced problems but we use the unadapted settings from [15] because we want to compare best-action and complete maps without optimisations, and over all three problem conditions (not just class imbalance). Future work could consider parameter optimization for all cases.

With Gaussian noise, the fitness of a classifier is much lower because the prediction error ϵ which is used to calculate the fitness becomes large. This means most classifiers are inaccurate, hence XCS cannot select a correct action using the inaccurate system predictions (which are calculated from the fitness). In XCSAM most classifiers are also inaccurate but XCSAM can identify classifiers which are candidates for the best action map. This is because the reward signal, even with added noise, is still useful to identify best action rules; a *positive* reward, which is returned when a best action is executed, is usually larger than a *negative* reward, which is returned when a *not*-best action is executed. That is, the reward signal still indicates the best action even with Gaussian noise. Hence, XCSAM can select the best action classifiers, which remain in the population, by deleting redundant classifiers which are not candidate for the best action map. These results suggest that the best action map contributes to stably derive high performance by deleting redundant classifiers in Gaussian noise where the positive reward is larger than the negative reward. In the next experiments we test the case of noise where the positive reward is sometimes equal to the negative reward.

4.1.4 Alternating noise

In our third set of experiments we add *alternating noise* to the reward on the (normal) multiplexer problem. With alternating noise, the reward is swapped with a certain probability P_{an}. Specifically, the positive reward (1000) is replaced by the negative reward, which means this noise simulates a state space which includes aliasing states. For instance, an instance of 6MP "00100" has a best action "1"; however, when a learner executes an action "1", 1-P_{an} % of all instances "00100" returns the positive reward 1000 but P_{an} % instance return the negative reward 0 even. The parameter settings are the same as the previous experiment. We use different P_{an} to 0.10, 0.15, 0.20, 0.25 and 0.30. The maximum iteration is set to 500,000.

Figure 1-c) shows the performance of XCS and XCSAM on the 11-bit multiplexer problem with alternating noise. With P_{an} = 0.10 and 0.15, XCS reaches 0.98 and 0.95 respectively; it fails to reach optimal performance with P_{an} = 0.20, 0.25 and 0.30. The performance of XCSAM with P_{an} = 0.10 and 0.15 are worse than XCS, in fact they converge to 0.95 and 0.93 respectively. However, with P_{an} = 0.20, 0.25 and 0.30, XCSAM clearly improves on the performances of XCS. With alternating noise, XCSAM has a tendency to delete classifiers which are candidates for the best action map, because XCSAM mistakenly identifies them as redundant classifiers when the returned reward is 0 (i.e., reward 0 represents that executed action is not the best action). In contrast, XCS keeps them even with the added noise (XCS deletes classifiers based on their fitness), because they have relatively high fitness in the case of small noise. Hence, with small noise P_{an} = 0.10 and 0.15, the performance of XCSAM is lower than that of XCS. However, with large noises P_{an} = 0.20, 0.25 and 0.30, the fitness of classifiers is much low, hence, XCS cannot select actions using the incorrect system prediction (which is the same reason of Gaussian noise).

4.2 Experiment on Real World Data

To evaluate performance of XCS and XCSAM on a real world application, we apply both systems to classification tasks with real world data from the UCI repository [16]. As shown in Table 1 we use 20 datasets. In the Table, #len denotes the length of input in each dataset and #cls denotes the number of classes in each dataset. As in previous work [1], if the attributes are binary, the data is codified in the ternary alphabet. If the attributes are real, the data is codified as an interval range. For simplicity, all real attributes are normalized to the range [0,1). Nominal attributes are translated into numeric values, and so considered as real attributes. The datasets are run on a stratified ten-fold cross-validation test. To test the differences between the both systems, we use a paired t-test from the ten-fold cross-validation results. The parameter settings are the same as previously except the population size limit N = 6400. The maximum iteration is 100,000.

Table 1: Datasets and Results of XCS and XCSAM (Bold text indicates p<0.05). •/° indicates a positive significant difference of XCS/XCSAM respectively.

DataName	#len	#cls	XCS	XCSAM	p value
Audiology	69	24	0.46	0.59	**0.002**°
A.C.card	14	2	0.84	0.84	0.531
Balance S.	4	3	0.83	0.80	**0.026•**
Bupa	6	2	0.69	0.67	0.530
Breast_w	9	2	0.91	0.89	0.152
Breast_wd	32	2	0.96	0.97	0.088
Cmc	9	3	0.53	0.51	**0.010•**
Glass	9	6	0.74	0.70	0.207
Heart-c	13	5	0.48	0.51	0.091
Heart-h	13	5	0.64	0.68	0.154
Hepatitis	19	2	0.88	0.83	**0.035•**
Iris	4	3	0.96	0.94	0.081
Libras	91	15	0.15	0.17	0.253
Segment	19	7	0.94	0.95	0.293
Soybean	35	19	0.21	0.45	**6.6E-08**°
Vehicle	18	4	0.72	0.71	0.407
Vowel	13	19	0.62	0.63	0.854
Vote	16	2	0.96	0.96	0.988
Wine	13	3	0.96	0.96	0.985
Zoo	17	7	0.95	0.92	0.081
			XCS•-XCSAM°:		3 - 2

The classification accuracies of XCS and XCSAM are shown in Table 1. We note XCS is significantly better (p<0.05) than XCSAM on *Balance S.*, *Cmc* and *Hepatitis* while XCSAM is significantly better *Audiology* and *Soybean* which have longer inputs and more classes than other datasets. Overall, we cannot find a clear advantage for either system.

5. ANALYSIS

To understand why XCSAM does not derive higher classification accuracies than XCS, we analyze how XCSAM focuses on the best action map. From the analysis, we introduce a deletion strategy for XCSAM which can help to evolve the best action map.

5.1 Analysis

Specifically, we analyze the parameters *eam* (effectiveness of adaptive action mapping) and ϵ (prediction error) of classifiers in the population when XCSAM is applied to the real dataset *Vowel*. The reason for focusing on *Vowel* is that XCSAM did not derive a better performance than XCS although *Vowel* has many classes like *Audiology* and *Soybean*

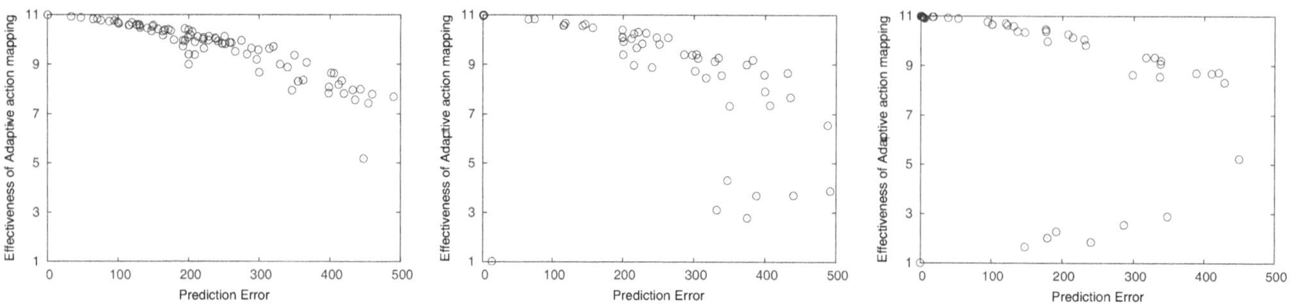

a) 10,000th iteration b) 50,000th iteration c) 100,000th iteration

Figure 2: Classifies in the population when XCSAM is applied to *Vowel*

where XCSAM clearly derived higher classification accuracy than XCS. In *Vowel*, the number of available actions nma is 11, which is the same as the number of classes of *Vowel*.

Figure 2 shows the classifiers in the population when XCSAM is applied to *Vowel*. The vertical and horizontal axes indicate the classifiers' eam and ϵ parameters. A classifier has the best action if its eam is close to 1, while a not-best action if its eam is close to 11 (nma). Similarly, a classifier is accurate if its ϵ is close to 0, while inaccurate if its ϵ is close to 500. For instance, classifiers which are placed at the left-top corner are accurate but not candidates for the best action map; classifiers which are placed at the left-bottom corner are accurate and candidates for the best action map. From figure a), at the 10,000th iteration, XCSAM generates redundant classifiers which are inaccurate (large ϵ) or not candidates for the best action map (large eam). At the 50,000th iteration, XCSAM gradually generates classifiers which have large ϵ but small eam; on the other hand many redundant classifiers remain. At the 100,000th as the final iteration, XCSAM successfully learns several accurate classifiers (left-bottom corner) which have a best action ($eam = 1$); however many inaccurate classifiers and redundant classifiers (left-bottom corner) still remain. This analysis suggests XCSAM can partially learn the best action map, but it has many redundant classifiers which are inaccurate or are not best action map candidates. Hence, XCSAM sometimes fails to efficiently evolve the best action map.

5.2 Deletion mechanism

From the analysis, to efficiently focus on the best action map, XCSAM needs to delete many redundant classifiers. However, using a steady-state GA, XCSAM deletes only two classifiers in each generation, hence many redundant classifiers remain in the population. Here, we introduce a new deletion mechanism that deletes more than two classifiers as necessary. Specifically, in XCSAM, θ_{mna}, which is calculated from the parameter eam, is the number of actions which should be in the matchset [M]. When $\theta_{mna} = nma$ (number of action types), classifiers in [M] should not be removed because XCSAM does not detect the best action in its state. In contrast, when $\theta_{mna} = 1$ (which means XCSAM correctly identified the best action), classifiers will be redundant if [M] has more than one type of action. More generally, if the number of action types in [M] ($nma_{[M]}$) is larger than θ_{mna}, we can suspect there are some redundant classifiers in [M]. For this reason, the new deletion mechanism deletes classifiers if $nma_{[M]} > \theta_{mna}$. The new deletion mechanism is called when the executed action is identified as the best action. First, the average eam $EAM(a)$ is computed from classifiers with action a. Then XCSAM builds a *maximum eam set* [E] composed of classifiers in [M] which advocate the $maxEAM(a)$ (i.e., they are not even close to the best action map); and deletes all classifiers in [E] if $nma_{[M]} > \theta_{mna}$. XCSAM repeats this process while $nma_{[M]} > \theta_{mna}$.

6. EXPERIMENT: REVISED XCSAM

We apply the revised XCSAM with the new deletion mechanism to the multiplexer and real world data.

6.1 Experiments on Multiplexer Problems

The experimental settings are the same as the previous experiments (Section 4.1). Figure 3 shows the performance of the revised XCSAM on the 11-bit multiplexer with class-imbalance, Gaussian noise or alternating noise. With class-imbalance (Figure 3 a)), the revised XCSAM reaches optimality with $ir = 0$, 3 and 4; with $ir = 5$ and 6 it reaches 0.99 and 0.96 respectively, which is higher accuracy than the standard XCSAM which reaches to 0.94 and 0.87 respectively (see Figure 1-a)). With Gaussian noise (Figure 3 b)), with $\sigma = 100$, 200, 300 and 400, the performance is as good as that of the standard XCSAM. With $\sigma = 500$, the revised XCSAM reaches 0.90 while standard XCSAM reaches 0.85 (see Figure 1-b)). In contrast, with alternating noise (Figure 3 b)), the performance of revised XCSAM is lower than the standard XCSAM. For instance, with $P_{an} = 0.10$ and 0.15, the revised XCSAM reaches 0.89 and 0.84 respectively, while the standard XCSAM reaches 0.95 and 0.93. As noted in Section 4.1, with class-imbalance and Gaussian noise, since XCSAM can identify the best action map, the new deletion mechanism correctly deletes redundant classifiers. Hence, the revised XCSAM can successfully focus on the best action map and evolve them toward accurate classifiers. However, with alternating noise, XCSAM sometimes mistakenly identifies redundant classifier as the best action map due to noise. This causes the new deletion mechanism to mistakenly delete even classifiers which are candidates for the best action map. Hence, the revised XCSAM does not perform better than the standard XCSAM. This suggests that, if ARLCS can evolve only best action maps and have no redundant classifiers in their population, the best action map is more robust than the complete action map for class-imbalance and Gaussian noise; in contrast, robustness with alternating noise is worse than the complete action map.

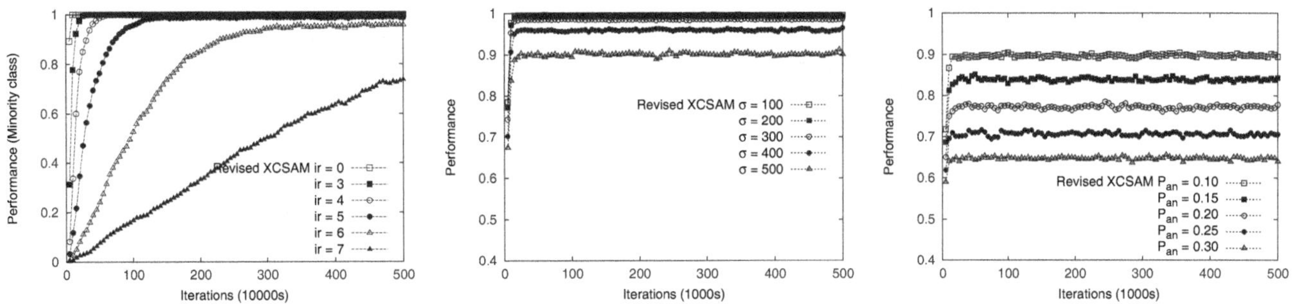

a) Class-imbalance   b) Gaussian noise   c) Alternating noise

Figure 3: Performance of revised XCSAM on the multiplexer problem

Table 2: Results of Revised XCSAM (Bold text indicates p<0.05). p_1 value indicates the difference between XCS and revised XCSAM. •/° indicates a positive significant difference of XCS/Revised XCSAM respectively. p_2 value indicates it between XCSAM and revised XCSAM. ♦/◇ indicates a positive significant difference of XCSAM/ RevisedXCSAM respectively.

DataName	Revised XCSAM	p_1 value	p_2 value
Audiology	0.57	**0.031**°	0.554
A.C.card	0.84	0.755	0.726
Balance S.	0.85	**0.003**°	**0.001**◇
Bupa	0.67	0.260	0.812
Breast_w	0.89	0.258	0.891
Breast_wd	0.97	0.152	0.811
Cmc	0.52	0.375	0.423
Glass	0.69	0.228	0.879
Heart-c	0.49	0.678	0.304
Heart-h	0.61	0.377	0.055
Hepatitis	0.83	**0.020**°	0.838
Iris	0.95	0.343	0.168
Libras	0.22	**0.002**°	**0.005**◇
Segment	0.95	**0.040**°	0.231
Soybean	0.40	**1.1E-04**°	0.065
Vehicle	0.70	0.179	0.657
Vowel	0.85	**2.6E-0.5**°	**5.3E-0.7**◇
Vote	0.95	**0.044**•	0.227
Wine	0.96	0.999	0.988
Zoo	0.95	0.972	0.343
	XCS•-Revised XCSAM°:		1 - 7
	XCSAM♦-Revised XCSAM◇:		0 - 3

6.2 Experiment on Real World Data

We test the revised XCSAM on classifying the real world datasets from Section 4.2, using the same parameter settings. Table 2 shows the classification accuracy of XCS and p values between XCS and the revised XCSAM and between the standard XCSAM and revised XCSAM. The revised XCSAM clearly improves on the classification accuracy of XCSAM (see Table 1). We also found seven positive significant differences of revised XCSAM from XCS. In particular, the revised XCSAM derives high classification accuracy on the datasets *Audiology*, *Libras*, *Soybean* and *Vowel*, where their input-lengths are relatively long and there are many possible classes. Additionally, since three positive significant differences of revised XCSAM from the standard XCSAM are noted, the revised XCSAM successfully improves on the performance of XCSAM on the real world data. From these results, the best action map is more effective on the classification of data where an input has many elements (i.e., it is high-dimensional) and many classes.

Finally, to understand how the revised XCSAM focuses on the best action map, we analyze the classifiers of revised XCSAM when it is applied to dataset *Vowel*; see figure 4. At the 10,000th iteration, like the standard XCSAM, revised XCSAM generates redundant classifiers which are inaccurate (large ϵ) or not candidates for the best action map (large eam). At the 50,000th iteration, the revised XCSAM gradually learns only the classifiers which have small eam parameters. Note in the standard XCSAM, many classifiers which have large eam remain, but the revised XCSAM successfully deletes them. At the 100,000th iteration, many accurate classifiers (which have $\epsilon = 0$ and $eam = 1$) are generated and the classifiers which have large eam do not remain. From these results, the revised XCSAM successfully deletes classifies which are not best action map candidates, hence, the revised XCSAM can derive high performance.

7. SUMMARY AND CONCLUSION

This paper compares XCS [20] with XCSAM [11, 12] on multiplexer problems and classification of real world data. Specifically, firstly, we test both system on the multiplexer problem with the three problem difficulties: class-imbalance, Gaussian noise and alternating noise. Experimental results show that XCSAM can derive better performance (higher accuracy and sometimes faster learning) than XCS with class-imbalance and Gaussian noise, where XCSAM can identify classifiers which are best action map candidates. Hence, XCSAM can efficiently evolve classifiers toward a best action map. In contrast, XCSAM sometimes derives lower accuracy than XCS when the alternating noise is small. From analysing this we introduce a new deletion mechanism. While original XCSAM sometimes fails to focus on the best action map in real world data, we show our new deletion mechanism can focus on it with real world data. The revised XCSAM which employs the new deletion mechanism can derive higher accuracy than XCSAM on the class-imbalanced and Gaussian noise problems; however with alternating noise, its accuracy degrades more than XCSAM. On classification with real world data, the revised XCSAM can derive higher classification accuracy on data which have a high-dimensional input and many possible classes. These

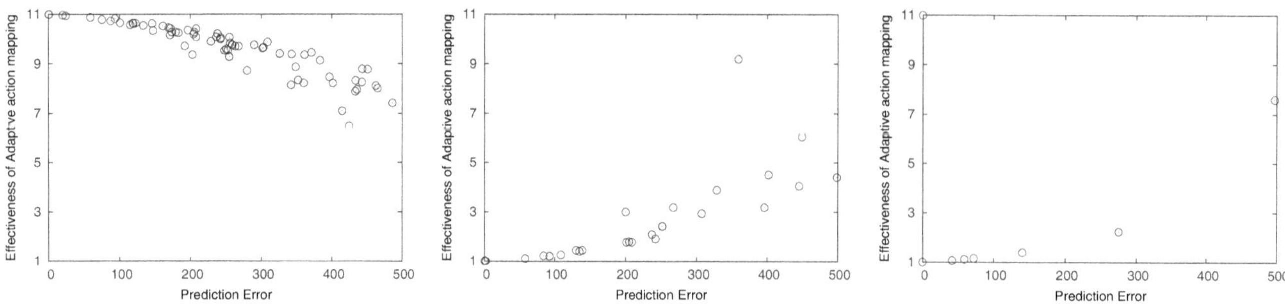

a) 10,000th iteration b) 50,000th iteration c) 100,000th iteration

Figure 4: Classifies in the population when revised XCSAM is applied to *Vowel*

result suggest that the best action map is more robust to the class-imbalance and Gaussian noise, since the evolution of best action maps works to detect and quickly delete over-generalized classifiers and classifiers which do not have a best action map. Note, despite these problem difficulties, the reward signal is still useful to guide the LCS to the best action. The alternating noise causes XCSAM to mistakenly identify a not-best action as best action. Accordingly, XCSAM deletes accurate classifiers which have a best action by wrongly identifying them as not-best actions. Hence, the best action map is less robust than the complete action map in noise where the best action is mistakenly evaluated as the not-best action, i.e., in aliased states.

Our conclusion is that the best action map is a powerful strategy in problems which distinctively return a positive reward for the best action with a negative reward for the not-best action (i.e., the positive reward is always larger than the negative reward). Additionally, if ARLCS can successfully focus on only the best action map, the best action map contributes to high performance on a complex problem which has a high-dimensional input and many possible classes. The complete action map is a better strategy than the best action map when given problems include the aliasing states. Results with RL problems could be different from classification problems but we leave this for future work.

8. REFERENCES

[1] E. Bernadó-mansilla and J. M.Garrell-Guiu. Accuracy-based Learning Classifier Systems: Models, Analysis and Applications to Classification Tasks. *Evolutionary Computation*, 11:209–238, 2003.

[2] Larry Bull, Ester Bernadó-Mansilla, and John H. Holmes, editors. *Learning Classifier Systems in Data Mining*, volume 125 of *Studies in Computational Intelligence*. Springer, 2008.

[3] M. V. Butz and S. W. Wilson. An algorithmic description of XCS. *Journal of Soft Computing*, 6(3–4):144–153, 2002.

[4] M. V. Butz, D. E. Goldberg, and P. L. Lanzi. Gradient descent methods in learning classifier systems: Improving XCS performance in multistep problems. *IEEE Trans. on Evol. Comp.*, 9(5):452–473, October 2005.

[5] M. V. Butz, P. L. Lanzi, and S. W. Wilson. Function approximation with XCS: Hyperellipsoidal conditions, recursive least squares, and compaction. *IEEE Trans. on Evol. Comp.*, 12(3):355–376, 2008.

[6] D. E. Goldberg. Genetic Algorithms in Search, Optimization, and Machine Learning. *Addison Wesley*, 1989.

[7] J. H. Holland. Escaping Brittleness: The Possibilities of General Purpose Learning Algorithms Applied to Parallel Rule-based system. *Machine Learning*, 2:593–623, 1986.

[8] F. Kharbat, L. Bull, and M. Odeh. Mining breast cancer data with XCS. GECCO2007, pages 2066–2073, 2007.

[9] T. Kovacs. Deletion schemes for classifier systems. GECCO1999, pages 329–336, 1999.

[10] Pier Luca Lanzi. Learning classifier systems from a reinforcement learning perspective. *Soft Computing - A Fusion of Foundations, Methodologies and Applications*, 6(3):162–170, 2002.

[11] M. Nakata, P. L. Lanzi, and K. Takadama. Enhancing Learning Capabilities by XCS with Best Action Mapping. In *PPSN XII*, volume 7491 of *LNCS*, pages 256–265. Springer, 2012.

[12] M. Nakata, P. L. Lanzi, and K. Takadama. XCS with Adaptive Action Mapping. In *SEAL2012*, volume 7673 of *LNCS*, pages 138–147. Springer, 2012.

[13] Masaya Nakata, Pier Luca Lanzi, and Keiki Takada ma. Selection strategy for XCS with adaptive action mapping. In *GECCO2013*, p. 1085–1092. ACM, 2013.

[14] A. Orriols and E. Bernadó-Mansilla. Class imbalance problem in UCS classifier system: fitness adaptation. In *CEC2005*, vol. 1, p. 604–611. IEEE, 2005.

[15] A. Orriols-Puig and E. Bernadó-Mansilla. Bounding XCS's parameters for unbalanced datasets. In *GECCO2006*, pages 1561–1568. ACM, 2006.

[16] UCIrvine Machine Learning Repository. http://archive.ics.uci.edu/ml/.

[17] C. Stone and L. Bull. Comparing XCS and ZCS on noisy continuous valued environments. In *ETechnical Report. UWE*, 2005.

[18] R. S. Sutton and A. G. Barto. *Reinforcement Learning – An Introduction*. MIT Press, 1998.

[19] Fani A. Tzima and Pericles A. Mitkas. ZCS Revisited: Zeroth-level Classifier Systems for Data Mining. *ICDM Workshops*, pages 700–709, 2008.

[20] S. W. Wilson. ZCS: A Zeroth Level Classifier System. *Evolutionary Computation*, 2(1):1–18, 1994.

[21] S. W. Wilson. Classifier fitness based on accuracy. *Evolutionary Computation*, 3(2):149–175, June 1995.

A Modified XCS Classifier System for Sequence Labeling

Masaya Nakata
The University of
Electro-Communications
Tokyo, Japan
m.nakata@cas.hc.uec.ac.jp

Tim Kovacs
University of Bristol
Bristol, UK
kovacs@cs.bris.ac.uk

Keiki Takadama
The University of
Electro-Communications
Tokyo, Japan
keiki@inf.uec.ac.jp

ABSTRACT

This paper introduces XCS-SL, an extension of XCS for sequence labeling, a form of time-series classification where every input has a class label. In sequence labeling the correct class of an input may depend on data received on previous time stamps, so a learner may need to refer to data at previous time stamps. That is, some classification rules (called "classifiers" here) must include conditions on previous inputs (a kind of memory). We assume the agent does not know how many conditions on previous inputs are needed to classify the current input, and the number of conditions/memories needed may be different for each input. Hence, using a fixed number of conditions is not a good solution. A novel idea we introduce is classifiers that have a variable-length condition to refer back to data at previous times. The condition can grow and shrink to find a suitable memory size. On a benchmark problem XCS-SL can learn optimal classifiers, and on a real-world sequence labeling task, it derived high classification accuracy and discovered interesting knowledge that shows dependencies between inputs at different times.

Categories and Subject Descriptors

I.2.6 [**Artificial Intelligence**]: Learning—*knowledge acquisition, concept learning*

General Terms

Algorithms, Experimentation, Performance

Keywords

Learning Classifier System, XCS, generalization, time series data, sequence labeling, classification

GECCO'14, July 12–16, 2014, Vancouver, BC, Canada.
Copyright 2014 ACM 978-1-4503-2662-9/14/07 ...$15.00.
http://dx.doi.org/10.1145/2576768.2598352.

1. INTRODUCTION

Many real world applications, such as stock exchange, inventory control, and the observation of natural phenomena, generate time-series data, in which data points have a natural sequence [6]. Classification of time-series data has attracted great interest in the machine learning field. The goals of classification are to find a model or a function that classifies data to predefined classes [6] and to discover important patterns as knowledge that help to understand why data is classified to the class. For the latter case, while the model or function can be variously represented by *IF-THEN rules*, *decision trees*, *mathematical formulae* and *neural networks* [6], to be human-readable the representation should generate simple, compact, and understandable patterns. IF-THEN rules are a human-readable representation and they can be extracted directly from data using, for example, a Learning Classifier System (LCS) [7]. An LCS is an IF-THEN rule-based learning system based on a Genetic Algorithm [5], which has been successful as a classification tool [17] [18]. LCS can discover human-readable patterns by the generalization of rules (called "classifiers") using a simple symbol (i.e., don't care symbol #) to represent features which are not relevant to the classifiers. We study LCS for learning human-readable rules from time-series data.

In normal (i.e., not time-series) classification, each data point in a given dataset is an independent observation for an object, hence the dataset has no sequential or time-oriented relationships between data. Even if these are the relationships, i.e., the order of data in dataset is sequential or time-series, the conventional classification tools do not consider them to find patterns. Typical time-series data is a sequence of values or observed events [6] such as EEG (electroencephalography) data and spoken sound data as in [4] [9]. In typical time-series classification a whole sequence of data is given one class label, e.g., a whole series of EEG readings is given one label "normal" or "abnormal". Preen has proposed an extension of XCS for financial time-series data [13]. In contrast, this paper considers a kind of time-series classification called *sequence labeling* [10], in which every input in the sequence is given a class, e.g., in part of speech tagging each word in a sentence is classified as a noun, verb etc. As the field of time-series data mining matures, a wider range of real world sequence labeling applications has been studied, such as the observation of natural phenomena [22], part of speech tagging [15] and care support for human daily activity [8]. To classify the input to the correct class, a learner may need to refer back to inputs at previous time stamps to disambiguate the current input. However, in most real world applications, the learner does not know where and how many previous inputs are needed to classify the current input. In addition, each input may need a different number of previous inputs.

This paper introduces an extension of the XCS classifier system [20] for sequence labeling called XCS-SL. A novel idea is a classifier that has a *variable-length* condition which is composed of sub-conditions as a kind of memory to refer back to previous inputs. The classifier condition can *grow* and *shrink* by evolution of classifiers to explore the suitable memory size for classifying the current input to the correct class. Accordingly, we also address the questions of how XCS-SL should evolve classifiers to efficiently find out the suitable memory size for each input and what are the advantages of variable-length conditions over fixed-length conditions, in which the memory size is a fixed value.

The remainder of this paper is organized as follows: In section 2 we explain the sequence labeling task in detail. In section 3 we present the related works of LCSs that use memory in brief and introduce the mechanism of XCS-SL. In section 4 we test XCS-SL on a novel benchmark problem (the Layered Multiplexer problem) and compare two evolutionary algorithms in XCS-SL. In section 5 we apply XCS-SL to Activity of Daily Living (ADL) recognition [12] as a real world application. Finally, in section 6, we conclude this paper by summarizing the contributions and discussing the possible future directions.

2. SEQUENCE LABELING

In normal (non-time-series) classification, the data consists of *input/class* pairs: $\langle \boldsymbol{x} : y \rangle$, where $\boldsymbol{x}$ is an input vector and y is a class of the data. For example, if we are predicting hobbies, the data could be in this format: ⟨*male*, *twenties* : *likes-football*⟩. Alternatively, if we are predicting engine failure from diagnostic tests the data could be in this format: ⟨0.6, 0.5, 0.3 : *defect*⟩. Typically, each element $x_i \in \boldsymbol{x}$ of the input is a different observed event from other elements such as x_1 = *male* and x_2 = *twenties*. The class of an input is not dependent on any other input since they are independently observed events. Hence the dataset has no sequential or time-oriented relationships between data.

In contrast, while data for time-series classification has input/class pairs, the input is a *sequence* of values from one event: $\langle (t_0, \boldsymbol{x}_0), (t_1, \boldsymbol{x}_1), \cdots, (t_n, \boldsymbol{x}_n){:}y \rangle$ where t denotes a time stamp. Since the time-series data is the sequence of one event, all elements of the input are values of the same observed event at different time stamps e.g., ⟨(t_0,*breakfast*), (t_1, *exercise*), (t_2, *shower*):*good-sleep*⟩ or e.g. ⟨(t_0, 0.3), (t_1, 0.5), (t_2, 0.2):*defect*⟩. Note that there is only one class label y which classifies the whole sequence.

Sequence labeling is a kind of time-series classification in which there is a class for *every* time stamp: $\langle (t_0, \boldsymbol{x}_0){:}y_0 \rangle$, $\langle (t_1, \boldsymbol{x}_1){:}y_1 \rangle$, $\cdots$, $\langle (t_n, \boldsymbol{x}_n){:}y_n \rangle$. In sequence labeling, the data is similar to both normal classification, since every input has a class, and to time-series classification, since the inputs represent a sequence. For example, the data can be: ⟨(t_0, *bathroom*):*shower*⟩, ⟨(t_1, *kitchen*):*breakfast*⟩, or e.g. ⟨(t_1, 0.4, 0.2):*buy*⟩, ⟨(t_2, 0.6, 0.2):*sell*⟩.

In predicting the class of an input, it may in general be useful to consider data from past or future events. For example, in part of speech tagging, to classify a word it may be useful to know the class of words that come both before and after the current word. We are interested in a specific

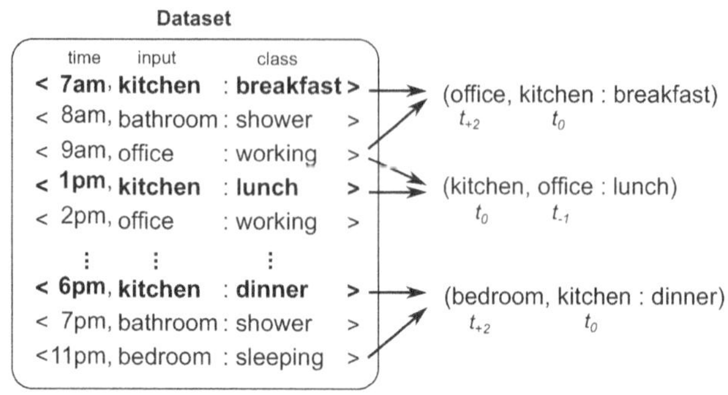

Figure 1: Example of data for sequence labeling.

sequence labeling application called Activity of Daily Living (see section 5). In this problem, like many problems, we have a training set of labeled data, but we also want to be able to classify new unlabeled data. For this reason we will learn patterns in the inputs but not in the actions of the learner, because on unlabeled data we do not know if the actions were correct. (In future work we will evaluate action patterns too.) In this work we do not use the time stamps except to order the inputs. We do not pass the time stamp as a feature to XCS-SL, so it cannot learn patterns such as "If time is between 2 and 4pm THEN...".

Figure 1 gives an example of how sequence information can help classify inputs. The left half of the figure shows part of an activity recognition dataset which records where a person was at a certain time and what activity they were doing. In this data the input "*kitchen*" is placed at different time stamps "*7am*", "*1pm*" and "*6pm*" but it has the different classes "*breakfast*", "*lunch*", or "*dinner*" respectively. Hence, the input "*kitchen*" does not unambiguously identify the current class. To borrow a term from reinforcement learning, we could say there are a set of activity classes ("*breakfast*", "*lunch*", and "*dinner*") which are *perceptually aliased* and which appear the same (as "*kitchen*") to the learner. In non-time-series classification, a learner considers only the current input, hence he probably fails to classify "*kitchen*" to the correct class. However, the learner can successfully classify it when considers current, previous and future inputs. That is, he can disambiguate the aliased input by considering inputs at other times. The right half of figure 1 and the arrows in the middle of the figure show combination of inputs which can identify the current activity (class) correctly. For example, if the person is in the kitchen at the current timet_0 and they are in the office at time t_{+1} then we predict they are having breakfast at t_0. While many patterns can be accurate, optimal patterns should be composed of minimum elements. For instance, the pattern for the class "*lunch*" may be {(t_{+1}, *office*), (t_0, *kitchen*), (t_{-1}, *office*), (t_{-2}, *bathroom*)} but this is not the minimal representations. A minimal one is {(t_0, *kitchen*), (t_{-1}, *office*)}.

A difficulty of sequence labeling is that the leaner does not know where and how many previous and future inputs are needed to classify the current input. The learner explores many possible patterns to find optimal patterns, hence it may need many memories to refer back or forward to data at different time stamps. In many tasks, such as online learning, we want to predict the current or future class strictly from the past, and so we consider only past data.

3. XCS FOR SEQUENCE LABELING

Classifiers require memory to refer back to the previous data to find patterns in sequence labeling tasks. Specifically, the additional memories can be added to the "IF" part (i.e., condition C). Some LCS papers e.g. [11] [19] have added memory to classifiers, but to our knowledge they were all used to solve POMDP (Partially Observable Markov Decision Process) or Semi-MDP problems, which are sequential decision making tasks, unlike the classification task in this paper. These works used small numbers of memories, or short memory lengths (a few time steps), but we are interested in more difficult problems which need a lot of memories, some of which must be quite old. Also, most previous methods used fixed-length memories, which, as we will see, as not as suitable as variable-length.

One possible way to represent the condition structure is, like the previous works [11] [19], with a *fixed-length condition* where the memory size has a fixed value. In our system each memory is sub-condition C_n for the corresponding previous time t_{-n} from the current time t_0. Accordingly, classifiers can be represented as $\{C_0, C_{-1}, \cdots, C_{-M}$:A$\}$, where A is a class ("THEN" part) and M is the maximum memory size. For example, some classifiers cl with M=2:

$$cl_{11} = \{kitchen,\ office,\ bathroom{:}lunch\}$$
$$cl_{12} = \{kitchen,\ office,\ \ \#\ \ {:}lunch\}$$

While the classifier cl_{11} is not the minimum representation for the class "*lunch*" (see Figure 1), by employing the *don't care symbol* # which matches any input, we can represent the more general and optimal classifier cl_{12}. The limitation of a fixed-length condition is that it is requires to set a fixed value although the LCS does not know how many memories are needed to find disambiguating patterns. If we underestimate the memory required then classification accuracy will suffer. If we overestimate it then the LCS needs a huge population size to explore many possible patterns, which needs a long run-time and a lot of training.

The novel idea introduced here is a *variable-length* condition so the memory size can be changed adaptively to fit the memories that are needed for each input. As a similar idea, a *chain* of classifiers which is a kind of variable length-condition is introduced by DACS [3] and CCS [16]. Classifiers can be connected with other classifiers as a chain. Our idea also requires the maximum memory size as a fixed value, but the memory size of classifier can reduce in during learning. For example new classifiers can be:

$$cl_{31} = \{kitchen,\ office,\ bathroom{:}lunch\}$$
$$cl_{32} = \{kitchen,\ office{:}lunch\}$$

Variable-length conditions can be not only the same the fixed-length conditions (classifier cl_{31}) but also more compact than fixed-length conditions (classifier cl_{32}). Accordingly, the classifier is required to explore the suitable memory size for each input. Classifiers with fewer conditions are more general and we want to find compact conditions that have as few memories as possible.

This paper proposes an extension of the XCS classifier system [20] for sequence labeling (XCS-SL), which employs classifiers that have variable-length conditions. In XCS-SL, classifiers can *grow* and *shrink* by evolution to explore a suitable memory size for data that are matched to its classifier condition. Hence, the evolution mechanism of XCS-SL is important in learning optimal memory patterns. XCS-SL

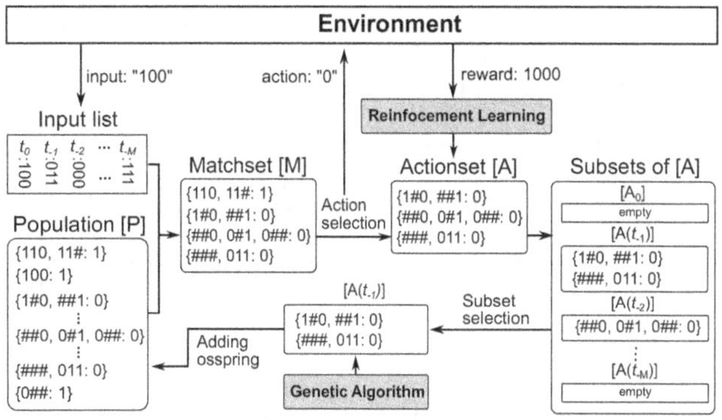

Figure 2: Overview of XCS-SL

almost works the same as standard XCS [2] but some mechanisms in the performance and the discovery components [2] are modified. In the remainder of this section we describe classifiers and the extended components. We also explain *subsumption* [21] and the *shrinker* mechanism we introduce, which can help to find compact conditions.

3.1 XCS-SL Classifiers

Like standard XCS classifiers [2], classifiers in XCS-SL consist of a condition C, an action A, and four main parameters [2]. Additionally, in XCS-SL, classifiers have a new parameter which is the memory size m to determine the condition length; the condition is composed of sub-conditions $C_0, C_{-1}, \cdots, C_{-m}$. Each sub-condition C_{-n} corresponds to the input at the time stamp t_{-n}. The memory size is determined and fixed when the classifier is generated but the maximum memory size for all classifiers M is set to a fixed value.

3.2 XCS-SL Mechanisms

This section details how the mechanisms of XCS-SL are different from those of XCS.

3.2.1 *Performance component*

As shown in Figure 2, at the current time t_0, XCS-SL stacks the input to the *input list*. When the number of inputs in the list is larger than the maximum memory size M, XCS-SL deletes the input at the oldest time stamp t_{-M}. Next, XCS-SL builds a *match set* [M] containing the classifiers in the population [P] whose sub-conditions each match C_{-n} the stacked input at the corresponding time t_{-n}. If [M] does not contain all the possible actions *covering* [2] takes place and generates classifiers; their memory size m is set uniform randomly but the maximum value is the number of inputs in the input list. Each sub-condition C_{-n} is copied from the corresponding input at the time stamp t_{-n} but each element of the sub-condition is replaced by the don't care symbol # with a probability $P_{\#}$. From here, XCS-SL works the same as XCS in the performance component. Specifically, for each possible action in [M], XCS-SL computes the *system prediction*, which estimates the payoff that XCS-SL expects if action a is performed on the current input (see [2] for more detail). Then, XCS-SL selects an action to perform; the classifiers in [M] which advocate the selected action form the current *action set* [A]. Finally, the selected action is performed, and a scalar reward is returned to XCS-SL together with an input at a next time stamp at t_{+1}. After the performance component, the reinforcement component [2] using Reinforcement Learning is performed the same way as in XCS to update the classifier parameters.

3.2.2 *Discovery component*

After the reinforcement component is performed, XCS-SL evolves classifiers using a Genetic Algorithm (GA) [5]. In the sequence labeling, each input can have its own suitable memory size (i.e., each input may need a different number of previous inputs). Hence, XCS-SL is required to evolve classifiers which have suitable memory size. Accordingly, XCS-SL builds *subsets* $[A(t_{-n})]$ of the action set which each consist of classifiers in [A] whose memory size m is equal to n. Then XCS-SL selects one subset from among the subsets $[A(t_0)] \cdots [A(t_{-M})]$ to perform the GA on. After selection, the GA is applied to classifiers in the selected subset. Two offspring are generated as copies of two selected parents and the crossover and mutation operators are applied to the offspring with probability χ and μ respectively. In crossover, each sub-condition is recombined with the corresponding sub-condition of the other offspring. Mutation changes elements in each sub-condition. After that, it also changes the memory size m of a classifier to a random value with probability μ. If the memory size is reduced, the extra sub-conditions C_{-n} $(n > m)$ are removed. If the memory size grows, new sub-conditions C_{-n} $(n > m)$ are added which are copies of the corresponding input at the time stamp t_{-n} in the input list.

The subset-selection method is important in finding suitable memory sizes. We have compared two selection methods: random selection and fitness-based selection. In fitness-based selection, the selection probability of subset $[A(t_{-n})]$ is the average of the fitness of the classifiers in it. We hypothesise that subsets with necessary memory will have higher average fitness than subsets with more memory than they need, which should make fitness-based selection successful. We hypothesise this because if a subset has a classifier that is accurate but has more memory than it needs, this classifier should be subsumed by an accurate classifier with less memory (see Section 3.2.3). Hence, the only classifiers with more memory than they need will tend to be inaccurate and have low fitness. We compare fitness-based selection and random selection in section 4. If fitness-based selection is superior that suggests our hypothesis is correct.

3.2.3 *Subsumption*

Subsumption is an generalization operator that helps to decrease the population size by subsuming a classifier to a more general classifier. Subsumption comes in two forms: *Action set subsumption* and *GA subsumption* [21] [2]. In XCS-SL, subsumption applies to classifiers which have different condition lengths from each other. To compare the generality of these classifiers, we assume the shorter classifier has extra virtual maximally general sub-conditions (that have only #) to fit the condition length of the longer classifier. For instance, as shown in Figure 3, to compare the generalities of the classifiers cl_a and cl_b, we consider that cl_a has one maximally general sub-condition "####" added. Accordingly, the sub-conditions C_0 and C_{-1} of cl_a are more general than the corresponding sub-condition of cl_b, hence, cl_a is more general than cl_b. In the other case, cl_c is not more general than cl_d because the sub-condition C_0 of cl_c is not more general than the C_0 of cl_d.

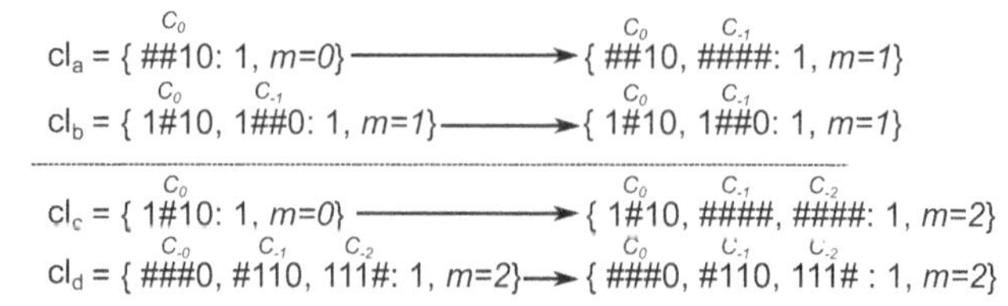

Figure 3: Example of subsumption

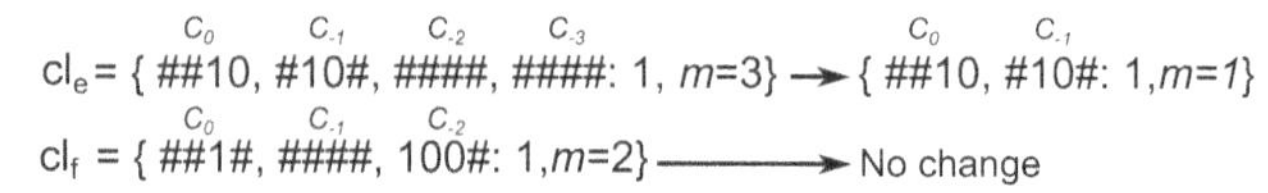

Figure 4: Example of shrinker

3.2.4 *Shrinker*

The shrinker is a compaction operator that helps to find compact conditions; it decreases the memory size of classifiers whose sub-conditions are maximally general. Specifically, if the sub-condition C_{-m} for the oldest time stamp is coded by only #, then its sub-condition is removed and the memory size m is decreased by 1. This process is repeated recursively. Note that the shrinker is not applied to classifiers whose memory size is 0 (i.e., the condition is composed only one sub-condition C_0). For instance, as shown in Figure 4, the sub-condition C_{-3} of classifier cl_e is removed, since C_{-3} is the maximally general condition "####", and the memory size of cl_e is reduced to 2. Iterating, the sub-condition C_{-2} is then removed. In the other case, the sub-condition C_{-2} of classifier cl_f is not the maximally general condition, hence C_{-2} is not removed. The shrinker is applied to classifiers generating by covering and the Genetic Algorithm.

4. TEST ON BENCHMARK PROBLEM

We test XCS-SL on the layered multiplexer problem as a benchmark sequence labeling task. From the test, we derive answers for two key questions on XCS-SL; (i) how XCS-SL should evolve classifiers to efficiently find a suitable memory size for each input? That is, which is the better evolutional algorithm: random selection or fitness-based selection? (ii) what are the advantages of the variable-length condition over the fixed-length condition?

4.1 Layered Multiplexer Problem

4.1.1 *Problem Definition*

This paper introduces a new kind of multiplexer problem [20], which we call n-Layered l-bit Multiplexer Problem (n-l LMP). The length l of input is determined from the length of the *address bits* k as $l = k + 2^k$. In the LMP, the class of an input at time t may depend on inputs at previous time stamps. The LMP defines a Boolean function on a sequence of l-bit strings. We make a dataset of D random binary strings. We send them as inputs to the LCS in sequence from t_0 to t_D and then repeat. The class of the current input is decided by referring to a previous input at a *reference time rt*; the reference time is calculated from the current input. XCS-SL stores M inputs to the input list before the start of the experiment, so there is a history for the first classifiers if they need it. Also, we consider the dataset to wrap

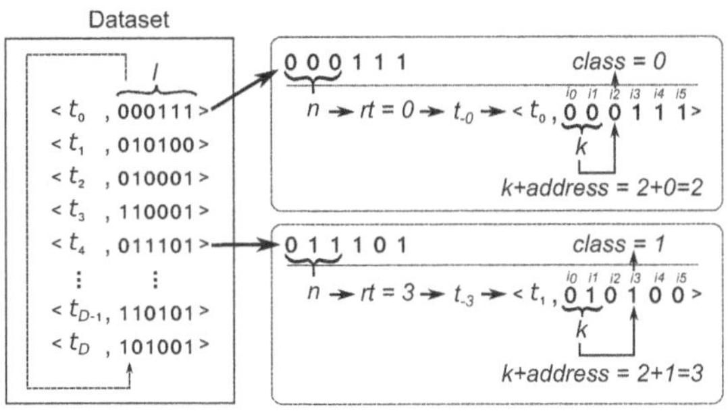

Figure 5: Example of 3-Layered 6-Multiplexer problem (3-6 LMP)

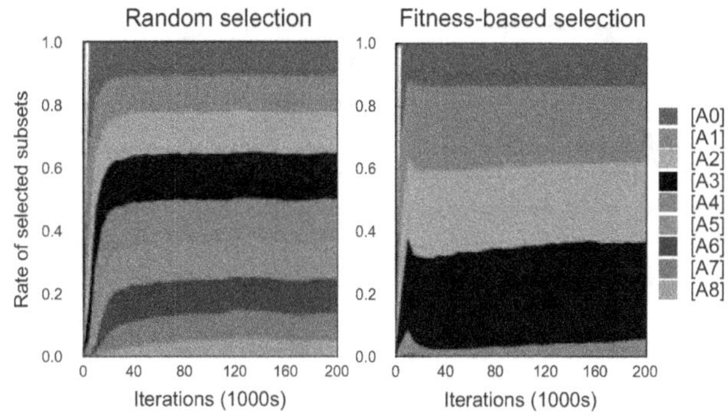

Figure 8: Rates of selected subsets for GA

around, so if the reference time would be negative then we start counting backwards from the end of the dataset to find the reference input i.e., if $t_{-rt} < t_0$ then we wrap around to the end of the dataset and use t_{D-rt} as the reference input. Specifically, the first n bits of the current input is converted to a decimal number as the reference time. Next, the class of the current input is set to an *answer* bit of the previous input at t_{-rt} which is computed as in the normal l-bit multiplexer problem [20]. In detail, the first k bits of input t_{-rt} represent an address bit pointing to the remaining 2^k bits. The answer is the bit at $k + address$ where $address$ is a decimal number which is converted from the address bits. Figure 5 shows an example of the 3-Layered 6-bit ($k = 2$) Multiplexer Problem (which we denote 3-6LMP). In the input at time t_0, the reference time rt is equal to 0 (which is computed from the first n=3 bits "000"). The class of the current input is determined by the previous input at t_{-0} i.e., in this case the current input determines its own class. The class of the current input is found by applying the normal multiplexer function to the input at the reference time: since k=2 we compute the $address$ 0 from the first two bits ("00"). The data bits are 0111, of which the 0th bit has value 0. Hence the class of the current input is 0. As another example, the class of input at time t_4 is 1, because the rt is 3 (which is computed from "011") and the answer of the previous input at t_{-3}=t_1 is the bit at 3 (=2+1). The LMP sends a reward of 1000 when the LCS performs a correct action, otherwise 0. We use $D = 50000$ in this paper, and employ the set of {0, 1, 2, 3}-Layered 3-bit ($k = 1$) Multiplexer Problems ({0, 1, 2, 3}-3 LMP). Note 0-3 LMP is the normal 3-bit multiplexer.

4.2 Random vs. Fitness-based Set Selection

We test XCS-SL and XCS on the LMP from section 4.1, and compare the two strategies for subset selection in XCS-SL: random selection and average fitness-based selection. Each experiment consists of a number of problems that the system must solve. In each problem as one iteration, the LCS alternatively solves a *learning* problem and an *evaluation* problem (see [20]). During *learning* problems, the system selects an action randomly from those represented in the match set. During *evaluation* problems, to evaluate the system performance, the system selects the action with highest expected return but does not apply the reinforcement and discovery components. We use the standard parameter settings [2]: $N = 3000$, $\epsilon_0 = 1$, $\mu = 0.04$, $P_\# = 0.33$, $\chi = 0.8$, $\beta = 0.2$, $\alpha = 0.1$, $\delta = 0.1$, $\nu = 5$, $\theta_{GA} = 25$, $\theta_{del} = 20$, $\theta_{sub} = 20$ and Action set subsumption and GA subsumption are turned on. For XCS-SL, we set the maximum memory size $M = 8$. The maximum iteration is 200,000. The *performance*, which is the rate of correct actions the system executed, and the *population size*, which is the number of (macro) classifiers [20] in the population, are reported as the moving average over the last 5000 evaluation problems. All the plots are averages over 20 experiments.

Figures 6 and 7 compare the performance and population size of XCS and XCS-SL with random and fitness-based selection on {0, 1, 2, 3}-3 LMP. Note the scale of the vertical axis for XCS is different from that of XCS-SL. XCS reaches optimal performance on 0-3 LMP and successfully decreases the population size to about 15 classifiers. As can be expected, XCS fails to reach optimal performance on other LMP problems, since it has no memory. XCS-SL with random selection reaches optimal performance on all LMP problems except for the 3-3 LMP. However, the population size is larger than with fitness-based selection (and XCS's population), even on 0-3 LMP where it is about 1160 classifiers. In contrast, XCS-SL with average-fitness selection reaches optimal performance on all LMP problems successfully decreases the population size. In particular, the population size 0-3 LMP is about 98 classifiers, although that is larger than XCS's. From these results, by employing fitness selection in XCS-SL, it can derive the better performance than the random selection. Also, XCS-SL successfully learns classifiers for inputs that are depend on the previous inputs.

We now analyze why fitness-based selection works to reduce the population size compared to random selection. Figure 8 shows the rates of selected subsets by random selection and fitness-based selection on 2-3 LMP. Note the maximum memory size M in XCS-SL is 8 while in 2-3 LMP the maximum necessary memory size is 3 (since maximum reference time is $3 = 2^2 - 1$). Hence, classifiers in $[A(t_{-4})] \cdots [A(t_{-8})]$ are redundant and the rates of selected subsets $[A(t_{-4})] \cdots [A(t_{-8})]$ should preferably converge to 0. From Figure 8, the random selection evenly selects all subsets. In contrast, the fitness-based selection intensively selects the subsets of $[A(t_0)] \cdots [A(t_{-3})]$, while the rates of $[A(t_{-4})] \cdots [A(t_{-8})]$ are clearly reduced. From these results, random selection generates many redundant classifiers whose memory size is larger than the necessary memory size. Fitness-based selection successfully focuses on the classifiers which have a suitable memory size. In the remainder of this paper we employ fitness-based selection on XCS-SL.

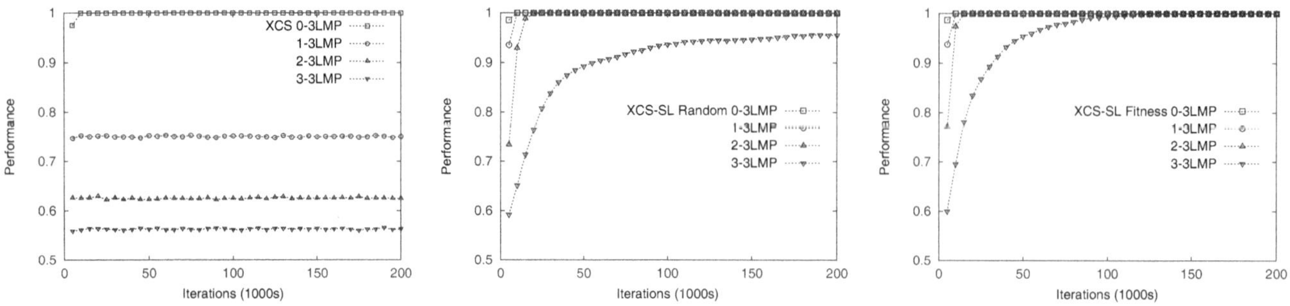

a) XCS　　b) XCS-SL Random selection　　c) XCS-SL Fitness-based selection

Figure 6: Performance of XCS and XCS-SL with the random selection and the fitness-based selection

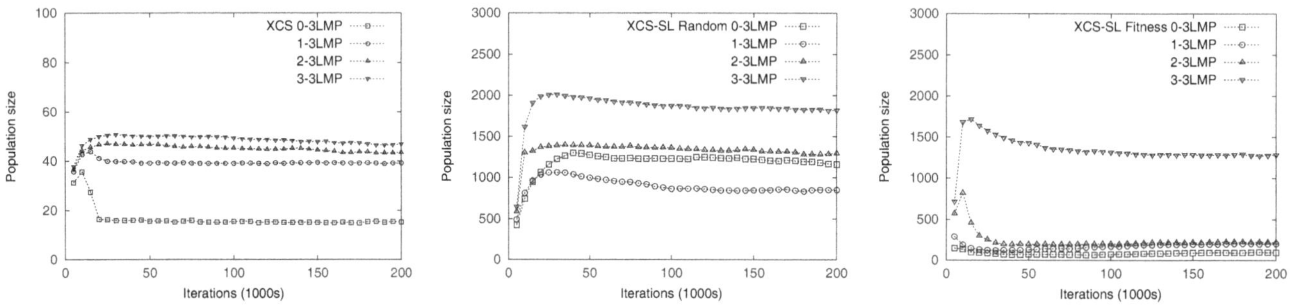

a) XCS　　b) XCS-SL Random selection　　c) XCS-SL Fitness-based selection

Figure 7: Population size of XCS and XCS-SL with the random selection and the fitness-based selection

4.3 Fixed length vs. Variable length

Here we test the standard XCS-SL (using the variable-length condition) and Fix-XCS-SL (using a fixed-length condition). Specifically, we modify XCS-SL to Fix-XCS-SL where the memory size m of all classifiers is set to the maximum memory size M, i.e., the condition length is fixed. The experimental settings are the same as the previous test. We apply both systems to 3-3 LMP, and we set M = 8, 9, 10, 11, 20, 30. Both systems store M inputs in the input list before the start of experiment.

As shown in Figure 9, XCS-SL stably reaches optimal performance with different maximum memory size M. This suggests that, even with a much larger maximum memory than necessary, XCS-SL can successfully find out the suitable memory size, and it can adaptively tune condition length to fit the memory size the problem requires. Fix-XCS-SL reaches optimal performance faster than XCS-SL on M=8, 9. This is because Fix-XCS-SL starts with the right amount of memory but XCS-SL has to find the right amount. However, Fix-XCS-SL fails to reach optimality on M=10, 11, and it does not show any sign of adapting on M=20, 30. With the larger memory sizes, the search space is too large for Fix-XCS-SL to explore effectively. These results suggest that the fixed-length condition is useful in problems where we can estimate how many and where previous inputs are needed to classify data to a class. However, in most real applications we do not know how many and where, hence the maximum memory size must be set to a "large enough" value. Accordingly, the variable-length condition is more useful in most problems since it works well even when the maximum memory length is much bigger than is needed. In other words, the overhead for overestimating the maximum memory size is small when we use variable-length conditions.

5. APPLICATION TO ADL RECOGNITION

Activity of Daily Living (ADL) recognition [12] is a classification task to recognize the human activity from binary sensors. ADL data is available in UCI repository [14] as a classification problem. We modify the data (OrdonezA) to be a sequence labeling task. As shown in Figure 10, the format of each data point is a timestamp/input/class; an input in the form of binary sensor data consists of 3 elements (*sensor*, *sensor type* and *room*); a class indicates a human activity. Specifically, the *sensor* input can be one of 12 sensors: *Shower*, *Basin*, *Cooktop*, *Maindoor*, *Fridge*, *Cabinet*, *Cupboard*, *Toilet*, *Seat*, *Bed*, *Microwave* and *Toaster*; the sensor type can be one of 5 types: *PIR*, *Magnetic*, *Flush*, *Pressure* and *Electric*; the room can be one of 5 rooms: *Bedroom*, *Bathroom*, *Living*, *Entrance* and *Kitchen*; the class can be one of 10 human activities: *Sleeping*, *Showering*, *Breakfast*, *Lunch*, *Dinner*, *Snack*, *Grooming*, *Leaving*, *Toileting* and *Spare_Time/TV*. The dataset has 397 data points and contains some aliasing data that has the same input but a different class. For example, some aliasing data is:

⟨ t_a, *Toaster*, *Electronic*, *Kitchen*:*Breakfast* ⟩
⟨ t_b, *Toaster*, *Electronic*, *Kitchen*:*Lunch* ⟩
⟨ t_c, *Basin*, *PIR*, *Bathroom*:*Toileting* ⟩
⟨ t_d, *Basin*, *PIR*, *Bathroom*:*Grooming* ⟩

We set the first 70% of the data to training data and the last 30% of the data to test data. Each experiment consists of a *training* phase and *test* phase. The *training* phase is composed of *learning* problems and *evaluation* problems the same as previous tests in Section 4, and the system uses

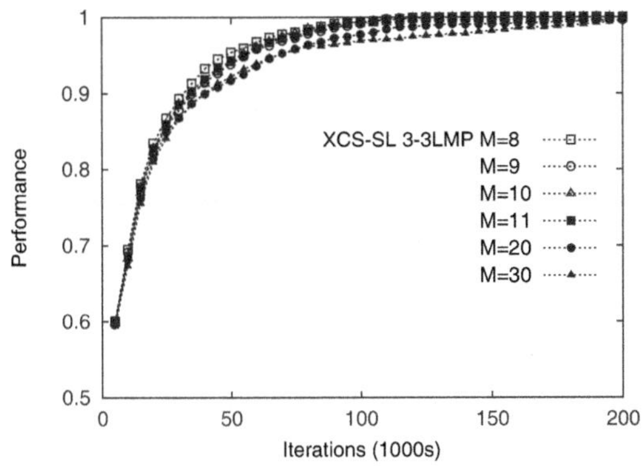

a) XCS-SL

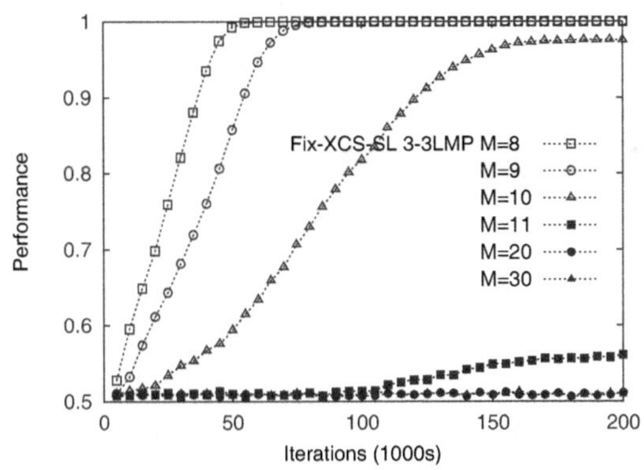

b) Fix-XCS-SL

Figure 9: Results of XCS-SL and Fix-XCS-SL on 3-3 LMP

	input			class
timestamp	, sensor	, sensor type	, room	: activity
< 2011-11-28 02:27:59 - 10:18:11	, Bed	, Pressure	, Bedroom	: Sleeping >
< 2011-11-28 10:21:24 - 10:21:31	, Cabinet	, Magnetic	, Bathroom	: Toileting >
< 2011-11-28 10:21:44 - 10:23:31	, Basin	, PIR	, Bathroom	: Toileting >
< 2011-11-28 10:23:02 - 10:23:36	, Toilet	, Flush	, Bathroom	: Toileting >
< 2011-11-28 10:25:44 - 10:32:06	, Shower	, PIR	, Bathroom	: Showering>
< 2011-11-28 10:34:23 - 10:34:41	, Fridge	, Magnetic	, Kitchen	: Breakfast >
⋮	⋮	⋮	⋮	⋮
< 2011-12-11 15:29:03 - 15:30:14	, Toilet	, Flush	, Bathroom	, Toileting >
< 2011-12-11 15:41:34 - 15:43:30	, Basin,	, PIR	, Bathroom	, Grooming >

Figure 10: Dataset of ADL

the training data. The test phase happens after the training phase. During the *test* phase, the system must solve the test data and, as in the evaluation phase, does not apply the reinforcement and discovery components. We compare XCS, XCS-SL and Fix-XCS-SL on the ADL recognition task, and we employ the same parameter settings of the previous tests except for $N = 5000$ and Action Set subsumption was turned off to avoid overly strong generalization pressure which has been noted in other papers e.g., [1]. Also we use a different maximum memory size M=8 and 12. The maximum iteration is 200,000. The *performance on training data* which is the classification accuracy during the training phase is reported as the moving average over the last 5000 evaluation problems. We also calculate the *classification accuracy* during the test phase. All the plots are averages over 20

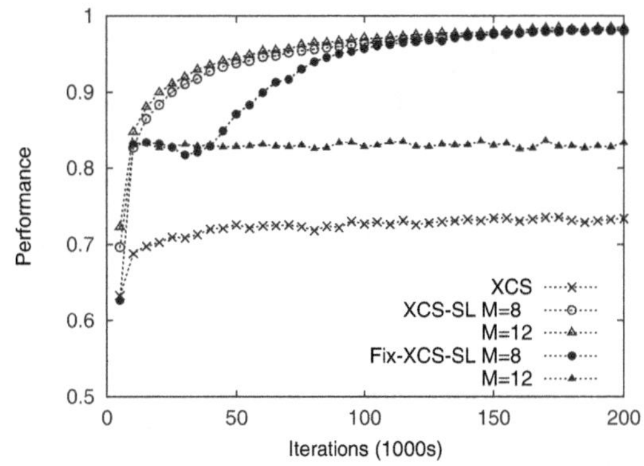

Figure 11: Performance on training data in ADL recognition

experiments. XCS-SL and Fix-XCS-SL store M inputs to the input list before the start of experiment.

Figure 11 shows the performance on training data of XCS, XCS-SL, and Fix-XCS-SL. As can be expected, XCS cannot reach the optimal performance because of the aliasing data. XCS-SL reaches about 97% performance faster than Fix-XCS-SL, and with different memory sizes M. While Fix-XCS-SL slowly reaches to 97% with M=8, it cannot reach close to optimal performance and converges to 83% with M=12. Tables 1 and 2 shows the classification accuracies on test data and p values of XCS, XCS-SL and Fix-XCS-SL. The classification accuracies of XCS-SL (M=8, 12) are better than XCS, the positive significant differences ($p < 0.001$) between XCS and XCS-SL (M=8, 12) are noted, and no significant difference between M=8 and 12 on XCS-SL was found. This result shows that XCS-SL stably derives high classification accuracy even with large memory size. Similarly, the classification accuracy of Fix-XCS-SL (M=8) is also better than XCS, the positive significant difference ($p < 0.001$) between XCS and Fix-XCS-SL (M=8) is noted. However, the classification accuracy of Fix-XCS-SL (M=12) is much lower than XCS and XCS-SL. This is because Fix-XCS-SL fails to learn correct classifiers due to the large memory size.

Figure 12 shows examples of interesting classifiers that XCS-SL (M=8) learned on the ADL task. The classifier cl_a represents "the subject cooks breakfast after the shower". Notice that the condition for the current time is fully general: no matter what the current input is, the classifier predicts breakfast. The current condition effectively aliases many possible states (sensor inputs), but the memory of the shower disambiguates the current state and predicts the subject is having breakfast. This is an example of the kind of human-readable pattern mentioned in the introduction.

Classifier cl_b, "subject cooks lunch after Spare_time/TV" also uses memory to disambiguate the current state. The current condition matches when the cooktop is used, but breakfast, lunch and dinner all use the cooktop, so they are aliased. This classifier uses memory of the *seat* sensor, which indicates a unique human activity *Spare_time/TV*, to disambiguate the current state.

Classifiers cl_c and cl_d use the *Entrance* room category, which represents the human activity *Leaving* (the house). There is no sensor to represent returning to the house, but any sensor after *Leaving* indicates the subject has returned.

Table 1: **Classification accuracies of XCS, XCS-SL and Fix-XCS-SL**

XCS		0.750
XCS-SL	M=8	0.853
	M=12	0.853
Fix-XCS-SL	M=8	0.850
	M=12	0.187

Table 2: p values of XCS, XCS-SL and Fix-XCS-SL (Bold text indicates p<0.001)

		XCS-SL		Fix-XCS-SL	
		M=8	M=12	M=8	M=12
XCS		**8.05E-05**	**8.93E-05**	**4.14E-04**	**2.33E-16**
XCS-SL	M=8	-	9.50E-01	7.53E-01	**1.87E-26**
	M=12	-	-	7.87E-01	**4.13E-24**
Fix-XCS-SL	M=8	-	-	-	**6.61E-22**

cl_a = { (#, #, #), (#, #, #), (Shower, #, #): Breakfast}
cl_b = { (Cooktop, #, #), (#, #, #), (Seat, #, #):Lunch}
cl_c = { (Fridge, #, #), (#, #, Living), (#, #, Entrance):Snack}
cl_d = { (Basin, PIR, Bathroom), (Maindoor, #, Entrance):Grooming}

Figure 12: Examples classifiers on ADL recognition

Classifiers cl_c represents "the subject eats a snack after he/she came back home". Classifier cl_d represents "the subject grooms after he/she came back home".

6. CONCLUSION

This paper introduced XCS for sequence labeling (XCS-SL). We introduced the Layered Multiplexer problem as a benchmark for sequence labeling. From the test on the LMP we showed XCS-SL successfully learns correct classifiers which have suitable memory size for given problems. Specifically, we showed that the fitness-based selection as an evolutionary algorithm can enhance XCS-SL to efficiently find out the suitable memory size. We also showed that the fixed-length condition is useful for problems where we know the suitable memory size; the variable-length condition, in contrast, is useful in most problems since it can handle a larger memory size than the fixed-length condition. In future work we will consider messy-coding, learning patterns on both actions and inputs, comparisons with other memory-using LCS.

7. REFERENCES

[1] E. Bernadó-Mansilla & J. M. Garrell-Guiu. Accuracy-based Learning Classifier Systems: Models, Analysis and Applications to Classification Tasks. *Evolutionary Computation*, 11:209–238, 2003.

[2] M. V. Butz & S. W. Wilson. An algorithmic description of XCS. *Journal of Soft Computing*, 6(3–4):144–153, 2002.

[3] B. Carse & T.C. Fogarty. A Delayed-Action Classifier System for Learning in Temporal Environments. In *Evolutionary Computation, 1994. IEEE World Congress on Comp. Int.*, p. 670–673, 1994.

[4] W. A. Chaovalitwongse, O. A. Prokopyev, & P. M. Pardalos. Electroencephalogram (EEG) time series classification: Applications in epilepsy. *Annals of Operations Research*, 148(1):227–250, 2006.

[5] D. E. Goldberg. Genetic Algorithms in Search, Optimization, and Machine Learning. *Addison Wesley*, 1989.

[6] J. Han. *Data Mining:Concepts and Techniques.* Morgan Kaufmann, 2005.

[7] J. H. Holland. Escaping Brittleness: The Possibilities of General Purpose Learning Algorithms Applied to Parallel Rule-based system. *Machine Learning*, 2:593–623, 1986.

[8] B. Kaluža, V. Mirchevska, E. Dovgan, M. Luštrek, & M. Gams. An agent-based approach to care in independent living. In *Ambient Intelligence, LNCS* 6439, p. 177–186. Springer, 2010.

[9] M. Kudo, J. Toyama, & M. Shimbo. Multidimensional curve classification using passing-through regions. *Pattern Recogn. Lett.*, 20(11-13):1103–1111, 1999.

[10] J. D. Lafferty, A. McCallum, & F. C. N. Pereira. Conditional random fields: Probabilistic models for segmenting and labeling sequence data. In *ICML2001*, pages 282–289, 2001.

[11] P. L. Lanzi & S. W. Wilson. Toward Optimal Classifier System Performance in Non-Markov Environments. *Evolutionary Computation*, 8(4):393–418, 2000.

[12] F. J. Ordóñez, P. de Toledo, & A. Sanchis. Activity Recognition Using Hybrid Generative/Discriminative Models on Home Environments Using Binary Sensors. *Sensors*, 13(5):5460–5477, 2013.

[13] R. Preen. An XCS Approach to Forecasting Financial Time Series. In *GECCO2009*, p. 2625–2632. ACM, 2009.

[14] UCIrvine Machine Learning Repository. http://archive.ics.uci.edu/ml/.

[15] H. Schmid. Probabilistic Part-of-Speech Tagging Using Decision Trees. In *Inter. Conference on New Methods in Language Processing*, pages 44–49, 1994.

[16] Andy Tomlinson & Larry Bull. An accuracy based corporate classifier system. *Soft Computing*, 6(3-4):200–215, 2002.

[17] Fani A. Tzima & Pericles A. Mitkas. ZCS Revisited: Zeroth-level Classifier Systems for Data Mining. *ICDM Workshops*, pages 700–709, 2008.

[18] Fani A. Tzima & Pericles A. Mitkas. Strength-based learning classifier systems revisited: Effective rule evolution in supervised classification tasks. *Eng. Appl. Artif. Intell.*, 26(2):818–832, February 2013.

[19] A. Webb, E. Hart, P. Ross, & A. Lawson. Controlling a Simulated Khepera with an XCS Classifier System with Memory. In *ECAL2003*, pages 885–892, 2003.

[20] S. W. Wilson. Classifier fitness based on accuracy. *Evolutionary Computation*, 3(2):149–175, June 1995.

[21] S. W. Wilson. Generalization in the XCS classifier system. In *In Proceedings of 3rd the Third Annual Genetic Programming Conf.*, pages 665–674, 1998.

[22] K. Zhang & W. Fan. Forecasting skewed biased stochastic ozone days: Analyses, solutions and beyond. *Knowl. Inf. Syst.*, 14(3):299–326, 2008.

A Memetic Algorithm to Select Training Data for Support Vector Machines

Jakub Nalepa
Institute of Informatics
Silesian University of Technology
Akademicka 16
44-100 Gliwice, Poland
jakub.nalepa@polsl.pl

Michal Kawulok
Institute of Informatics
Silesian University of Technology
Akademicka 16
44-100 Gliwice, Poland
michal.kawulok@polsl.pl

ABSTRACT

In this paper we propose a new memetic algorithm (MASVM) for fast and efficient selection of a valuable training set for support vector machines (SVMs). This is a crucial step especially in case of large and noisy data sets, since the SVM training has high time and memory complexity. The majority of state-of-the-art methods exploit the data geometry analysis, both in the input and kernel space. Although evolutionary algorithms have been proven to be very efficient for this purpose, they have not been extensively studied so far. Here, we propose a new method employing an adaptive genetic algorithm enhanced by some refinement techniques. The refinements are based on utilizing a pool of the support vectors identified so far at various steps of the algorithm. Extensive experimental study performed on the well-known benchmark, real-world and artificial data sets clearly confirms the efficacy, robustness and convergence capabilities of the proposed approach, and shows that it is competitive compared with other state-of-the-art techniques.

Categories and Subject Descriptors

I.2.8 [**Artificial Intelligence**]: Problem Solving, Control Methods, and Search—*Heuristic methods*; I.2.0 [**Artificial Intelligence**]: General

General Terms

Algorithms

Keywords

Memetic algorithm; self-adaptation; support vector machines; training data selection

1. INTRODUCTION

Support vector machines (SVMs) [5] is a supervised classifier which has been successfully applied to a variety of pattern recognition problems. However, its main limitation lies in high training complexity, which makes it virtually inapplicable in case of huge training sets. SVM training is a constrained quadratic programming (QP) problem of $O(n^3)$ time and $O(n^2)$ memory complexity, where n is the cardinality of the training set. During training, SVMs determine a hyperplane that linearly separates two classes in higher-dimensional kernel spaces, and it is later used to classify the data. The hyperplane is defined by the *support vectors* (SVs), which are selected from the entire training set.

The number of SVs is usually small compared with the number of vectors in the training set. Taking that into account, some attempts have been made to reduce the training sets and use only those samples, from which the SVs are predicted to be selected. State-of-the-art techniques are focused either on random selection or analysis of the data geometry in the input or kernel spaces. An alternative approach is to use a genetic algorithm (GA) for selecting the training data [11]. It is an effective method, but requires that the size of the refined set is given prior to the GA optimization. In practice, it is difficult to determine the optimal size, and the GA should be run for various sizes of the reduced set.

Our contribution lies in introducing a new memetic algorithm (MASVM) to select a good training set. We introduce a concept of the support vectors pool, in which valuable samples identified so far are stored. They are used to enhance other individuals for guiding the search. We propose to generate *super individuals* representing training sets composed of SVs only. A new selection scheme is incorporated to balance the exploitation and exploration of the solution space. Since MASVM adapts its parameters, including the training set size, it is not necessary to determine it *a priori*. The experiments show that MASVM is very robust and competitive compared with other state-of-the-art techniques.

The paper is organized as follows. State of the art regarding training set reduction techniques is outlined in Section 2. The details of the proposed memetic algorithm are detailed in Section 3, and the results obtained in our experimental study are presented and discussed in Section 4. Conclusions and directions for our future work are given in Section 5.

2. RELATED LITERATURE

There were numerous approaches proposed over the years towards dealing with large data sets in SVM training. Their purpose was to decrease the training time or to make it feasible in some cases, but also to select valuable data from noisy or poorly labeled data sets. The initial efforts were aimed at reducing the time complexity of the QP optimization by

GECCO'14, July 12–16, 2014, Vancouver, BC, Canada.

http://dx.doi.org/10.1145/2576768.2598370.

splitting it into a number of sub-problems [10]. Although this substantially reduces the training time, the size of many real-world data sets is too large to make this method applicable. It concerns various domains, including bioinformatics, genomics, document categorization, and more [25]. In such cases, the solution is to select a subset of training samples from the entire set, and train SVM using the reduced set.

There exist approaches for dealing with large sets based on approximating the answer of a non-linear kernel machine [23, 24]. Here, the input data are mapped into a low-dimensional randomized feature space, and fast linear learning methods are applied to estimate the answer of the corresponding non-linear kernel machine. The approximation of the decision function by means of multiplying the input with a Gaussian random matrix and applying a non-linearity was the basis of the recently proposed *Fastfood* algorithm [13].

A simple, yet effective, approach to reduce a training set size is to sample a subset of a large set randomly [2]. This method was the basis for other sampling algorithms, including reduced support vector machines (RSVMs) [14], later applied and enhanced in many works [3,7]. RSVMs select a small subset randomly to build a thin rectangular kernel matrix instead of the full kernel matrix, which significantly reduces the training computational complexity. It means that the SVs are chosen from a small random subset, but the optimization is performed using the entire training set.

Randomized methods proved to be quite effective, however they ignore the relations between the training set vectors. Active sampling procedures emerged to take advantage of the data geometry. Crisp clusters were applied to reject samples, which are positioned inside the clusters formed by the vectors with the same class label. The vectors inside the uniformly-labeled clusters are seldom determined as SVs [12]. The k-means clustering and an iterative process were used to reduce the number of misclassified samples [4]. Hierarchical clustering is applied as the initial step of sample reduction by data structure analysis (SR-DSA) [30], which was used for comparisons in the research reported here. It is executed for each class separately, and the interior samples from each cluster are removed based on the Mahalanobis distance in the kernel space. The exterior samples that are far from the opposite class clusters are discarded, since they should not influence the decision boundary [26].

Some methods use alternative clustering techniques to analyze the data geometry. In [31], convex hulls embedding the training data are determined, and the samples are selected using Hausdorff distance between the convex hulls of opposite classes. A method based on the convex-concave hull analysis was recently discussed [16]. In [33], the points from the training set are interpreted as a graph and subject to β-skeleton algorithm. It enables to reduce both training and testing time while being almost as effective as utilizing the entire set. The minimum enclosing and the smallest enclosing ball with a ring region analyses were applied in [29,32].

There are methods which predict the location of the separating hyperplane and select those vectors for RSVM training that are positioned close to it. This hyperplane may be estimated based on the samples heterogeneity measured by entropy [28] or using preliminary classification based on Mahalanobis distances [1]. Training sets can also be selected using active learning, which operates on a large unlabeled set, and dynamically determines labels for the samples [19]. It was shown that these approaches select the labels near the hyperplane [27]. Overall, the mentioned geometry-based methods are dependent on the training set size, which is a significant drawback in case of very large data sets.

Evolutionary algorithms (EAs) have not been extensively explored for selecting SVM training sets. In our earlier work we proposed a genetic algorithm (GA) [11], which consists in evolving a population of N solutions that define small training sets. Each solution, i.e., a *chromosome*, represents a subset of $2K$ samples from the entire training set. The population is successively improved in the biologically-inspired algorithm, in which chromosomes are selected, crossed-over and mutated. The *fitness* of each individual corresponds to the classification accuracy. The most important shortcoming of the GA is an unclear selection of the chromosome size ($2K$) to ensure the proper convergence speed, exploration and exploitation capabilities. We addressed this problem recently [21] using an adaptive approach. Here, the GA process is initiated with a set of individuals of a small chromosome size, which is subsequently increased.

Memetic algorithms (MAs), also referred to as hybrid genetic algorithms, are built upon the population-based approach. They combine EAs to explore the solution space with local refinement procedures applied for expoiting the solutions already found [18]. Due to their high convergence capabilities and wide practical applicability, a number of MAs have been proposed for solving various pattern recognition and optimization problems [8,9,15,17,20].

3. MEMETIC ALGORITHM

In this section we elaborate on the proposed MA to select training set for SVM (MASVM). We discuss the concept of the support vectors pool $\boldsymbol{P}$, containing valuable samples used in refining solutions and creating *super individuals* (SIs) that are composed of SVs only, and are likely to be well-fitted. A new adaptive selection scheme balancing the exploration and exploitation of the solution space is presented.

3.1 Algorithm outline

Let $\boldsymbol{T}$ denote the entire training set containing $t = t_A + t_B$ samples ($t_A \neq t_B$ e.g., for imbalanced sets), each belonging to one out of two classes, C_A and C_B, respectively. We aim at reducing the entire set $\boldsymbol{T}$ and finding a refined set $\boldsymbol{T}'$ with $t' = t'_A + t'_B$ valuable samples, where $t' \ll t$. Clearly, t' is not known *a priori* and should be determined carefully.

3.1.1 Chromosomes

In MASVM (Alg. 1), each individual (*chromosome*) p_i, $i \in \{1, 2, \ldots, N\}$, represents a refined training set $\boldsymbol{T}'$. The initial population of N individuals is drawn using random sampling (line 1). A new individual p_i contains $t^{(i)}$ (which is independent from t, and $t^{(i)} \ll t$) distinct samples taken from the entire training set $\boldsymbol{T}$ (see Fig. 1). Initially, the same number of samples from both classes are selected ($t_A^{(i)} = t_B^{(i)} = K$ thus $t^{(i)} = 2K$, where K is small at the beginning and increases during the MA execution) to avoid biasing $\boldsymbol{T}'$ with vectors from the more numerous class. Importantly, the MA is not dependent on the training set size t, which may be enormously large for real-life data, and making SVMs inapplicable for such sets in practice. Finding a fitness η of an individual p_i consists in training the SVM using the refined set $\boldsymbol{T}'$, and determining the area under receiver operating characteristic curve (AUC) for the entire set $\boldsymbol{T}$.

Algorithm 1 A memetic algorithm to select refined SVM training set (MASVM).

```
1: Initialize population of size $N$;                    ▷ Random sampling
2: $c_s \leftarrow 0$; $p_B \leftarrow$ null; $\boldsymbol{P} \leftarrow \emptyset$;
3: $\eta_I \leftarrow 0$; $\eta_P \leftarrow 0$; $\eta_B \leftarrow 0$;
4: regenerate ← false;                                   ▷ Re-generation condition
5: repeat
6:     Determine $N$ pairs $(p_a, p_b)$;                  ▷ Pre-selection
7:     for all $(p_a, p_b)$ do
8:         $p_c' \leftarrow$ Crossover$(p_a, p_b, K)$;
9:         $p_c'' \leftarrow$ Compensate$(p_c', \boldsymbol{T}, K)$;
10:        $p_c''' \leftarrow$ Educate$(p_c'', \boldsymbol{P})$;   ▷ With probability $\mathcal{P}_e$
11:        $p_c \leftarrow$ Mutate$(p_c''')$;             ▷ With probability $\mathcal{P}_m$
12:        $\eta(p_c) \leftarrow$ FindFitness$(p_c, \boldsymbol{T})$;
13:        if $(\eta(p_c) > \eta_B)$ then
14:            $\eta_B \leftarrow \eta(p_c)$; $p_B \leftarrow p_c$;   ▷ Update best fitness
15:        end if
16:    end for
17:    Update support vectors pool $\boldsymbol{P}$;
18:    Generate and assess $\alpha \cdot N$ super individuals;
19:    Form the next generation $G$;                      ▷ Post-selection
20:    $\Delta_T \leftarrow \eta_B - \eta_I$;             ▷ Improvement after increase
21:    $\Delta_R \leftarrow \eta_B - \eta_P$;             ▷ Recent improvement
22:    if $(c_s < \mathcal{T}_s)$ or $(\Delta_R \geq 0.5 \cdot \Delta_T)$
23:        or $(\varrho_{SV}(p_B) < \mathcal{T}_{SV})$ or $(\Delta_T = 0)$ then
24:        $c_s \leftarrow c_s + 1$;                      ▷ $K$ is not increased
25:    else if (LGA mode is local) then
26:        Set LGA mode to global;
27:    else
28:        $\delta_K \leftarrow 1 + |\varrho_{SV}(p_B) - \mathcal{T}_{SV}| \,/\, (1 - \mathcal{T}_{SV})$;
29:        $K \leftarrow \delta_K \cdot K$; $\eta_I \leftarrow \eta_B$; $c_s \leftarrow 0$;
30:        Set LGA mode to local;
31:    end if
32:    $\eta_P \leftarrow \eta_B$;
33:    regenerate ← CheckRegenerationCondition();
34:    if (regenerate) then
35:        Re-generate population;
36:    end if
37: until StopCondition();
38: return $p_B$ with the highest $\eta_B$;               ▷ $t' = t^{(B)}$
```

3.1.2 Selection

The population of solutions evolves in time. First, N pairs of individuals from the *i-th* generation G_i are selected (Alg. 1, line 6) to create the $(i+1)$-*th* generation G_{i+1} using a new *local-global adaptation* (LGA) scheme. In this scheme, the individuals are sorted according to their η values. Afterwards, the population is divided into two parts: one containing $\epsilon \cdot N$ well-fitted individuals, and the other $(N - \epsilon \cdot N)$ less-fitted ones. Finally, $\epsilon \cdot N$ pairs (p_a, p_b) are selected from the fittest individuals along with the $(N - \epsilon \cdot N)$ pairs drawn from the less-fitted part of the population (the local mode). Thus, both parts of the population are exploited independently. Finally, if the MA reaches the steady state (e.g., the improvement of the best individual is neglectable), the parent p_a is selected from the fittest part, whereas p_b from the other one to increase the exploration capabilities (the global mode). The mode can be changed back to exploit a promising part of the solution space. Here, we incorporated the LGA into the proposed MA and compared its performance with our multi-parent selection (AMPC) [21], which outperformed well-known high-low fit (HLF) pre-selection scheme [6]. The latter was proved to be asymptotically best for optimizing SVM training sets [11].

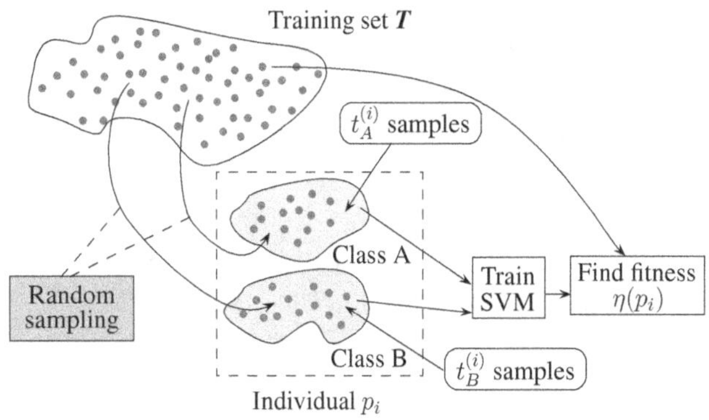

Figure 1: Creation and evaluation of an individual p_i in MASVM.

3.1.3 Crossover

For each pair (p_a, p_b), a new individual p_c is generated using crossover (line 8) with compensation (line 9) if necessary (see Fig. 2). The individuals p_a and p_b create an intermediate child p_c' with $(t^{(a)} + t^{(b)})$ inherited vectors. The size of p_c is determined randomly ($\max(t^{(a)}, t^{(b)}) \leq t^{(c)} \leq 2K$), and the number of samples is equal for both classes. It is easy to see that the sum of distinct parent samples may be less than $t^{(c)}$. In this case, the compensation (Alg. 1, line 9) is performed to select remaining samples from $\boldsymbol{T}$ randomly.

3.1.4 Education and mutation

In the education procedure (line 10), each p_c'' sample which was not selected as a SV during the last SVM training is treated as a "weak sample". Each weak sample is substituted by a SV drawn from the support vectors pool $\boldsymbol{P}$ with the probability $\mathcal{P}_e$. Clearly, only those vectors from $\boldsymbol{P}$ that are not included into p_c'' already are considered. p_c''' is mutated with the probability $\mathcal{P}_m$. It consists in random selection of the p_c''' vectors from both classes and substituting them with new samples drawn from the entire set $\boldsymbol{T}$. The fitness of the final p_c is found as discussed earlier (line 12), and the best fitness in the population η_B is updated if necessary (line 14).

3.1.5 Super individuals

Once the children are generated, the newly determined SVs are added to the support vectors pool $\boldsymbol{P}$ (line 17). Then, we generate and assess $\alpha \cdot N$, $\alpha < 1$, SIs (line 18). They contain at most K samples from each class that were selected as SVs and reside in $\boldsymbol{P}$. The number of samples from each class is not necessarily the same in case of the SIs, since the number of class A and B vectors kept in $\boldsymbol{P}$ may be different (and less than K). The individuals from the set $\boldsymbol{P}$, those from the current generation G_i, and the children are used to form the next generation G_{i+1} (line 19). The best N solutions out of $(2N + \alpha \cdot N)$ ones are chosen.

3.1.6 Self-adaptation

After the post-selection, it is verified whether the number of samples K is to be increased (line 23). In order to bal-

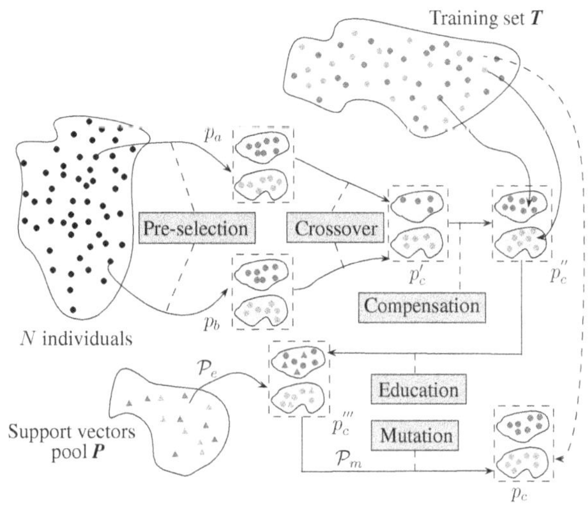

Figure 2: Creation of a child p_c in MASVM.

ance the exploitation and exploration of the solution space, we assume that it can be increased once in $\mathcal{T}_s$ consecutive generations. Also, K is not changed, if the fitness did not grow since the last increase ($\Delta_T = 0$), or the fitness improvement Δ_R was significant (i.e., greater than $0.5 \cdot \Delta_T$). If the LGA mode is local, then it is swapped to global (line 26) before K is updated to further explore the solution space.

The increase factor δ_K is determined based on the ratio $\varrho_{SV} = s/t'$, where s is the number of SVs in the best individual p_B, and $t' = t^{(B)}$ (line 28). Clearly, if this ratio is relatively small (below a threshold $\mathcal{T}_{SV}$), then the current refined set size has not been exploited. Once the value of K is updated (line 29), the LGA mode is set back to local for intensive exploitation of the population (line 30).

3.1.7 *Re-generation*

To diversify the search, we re-generate the population if necessary (line 35), based on analyzing the change of the best individual's fitness η_B and the population diversity ϕ [21]. Here, $r \cdot N$ best individuals are copied, and $(N - r \cdot N)$ ones are drawn randomly from $\boldsymbol{T}$ to keep N constant. The MA may be stopped when the fitness does not grow in a given number of consecutive generations, K is not further increased or the desired fitness is reached.

4. EXPERIMENTAL VALIDATION

Extensive experiments were conducted to compare the performance of the proposed MA with the following state-of-the-art techniques: 1) random sampling [2], 2) data structure analysis method (SR-DSA) [30], 3) genetic algorithm (GASVM) [11], and 4) adaptive genetic algorithm (AGA) [21]. The considered data sets include: 1) *Adult* benchmark set from the UCI repository[1], 2) *Skin* – real-world set derived from the ECU skin image database [22], and 3) *2D* – an artificially generated set of 6371 points positioned on a 500×500 surface. This set of points was used for both training and validation. *Skin* set consists of the training set $\boldsymbol{T}$ with $4 \cdot 10^6$ pixels in the RGB color space and the validation set $\boldsymbol{V}$ with 97560 pixels. For *Adult*, we omitted the samples with missing data, and the set was split into training $\boldsymbol{T}$ (15082 vectors) and validation $\boldsymbol{V}$ (15080 vectors) sets. The presented scores were obtained for $\boldsymbol{V}$. The validation sets were not used during the MASVM set selection for *Adult* and *Skin*.

[1] `http://archive.ics.uci.edu/ml/datasets.html`

Table 1: Settings used for different data sets.

Data set ↓	γ	C	τ (seconds)
2D	100	10	30
Skin	1	10	300
Adult	0.1	0.1	300

4.1 Experimental settings

In this study, we used the LIBSVM for SVM implementation, while the remaining methods were implemented in C++. The experiments were run on an Intel Xeon 3.2 GHz computer with 16 GB RAM. We used SVMs with the RBF kernel: $K(\boldsymbol{u}, \boldsymbol{v}) = \exp\left(-\gamma \|\boldsymbol{u} - \boldsymbol{v}\|^2\right)$. The SVM parameters (i.e., C and γ) were set relying on a grid search with an exponential step [21]. They are summarized in Tab. 1, along with the maximum MASVM execution time τ. Its parameters were set as follows: $N = 10$ (population size), $K = 10$ (initial number of samples per class), $\mathcal{P}_m = 0.3$ (mutation probability), $\mathcal{P}_e = 0.3$ (education probability), $\epsilon = 0.5$ (LGA selection coefficient), $\mathcal{T}_s = 3$ (minimal number of generations without the K increase), $r = 0.1$ (re-generation coefficient), S–10 re-generation (see Section 4.3), $\alpha = 0.2$ (SIs generation coefficient). N and K are relatively small to decrease the MA execution time. We used $\mathcal{T}_{SV} = 0.25$ (SVs ratio) to balance the exploitation and exploration of the solution space (increasing $\mathcal{T}_{SV}$ causes converging to local minima).

In the hierarchical clustering (the first step in the SR-DSA), the distance between clusters to merge increases with the decrease of the number of clusters [30]. It is worth to note that the selection of the SR-DSA parameters is not trivial and strongly influences its performance, especially in case of imbalanced data sets. The following numbers of clusters were used: $c = 255$ for *2D*, $c = 505$ for *Adult*, and $c = 4048$ for *Skin*. Once the clusters are found, $\lambda|M_i|$ samples are removed from each cluster M_i (along with the samples that are distant from the other class vectors), where $|M_i|$ is the number of its samples. In this study, we used $\lambda = 0.8$ for *2D* set, $\lambda = 0.92$ for *Adult* set, and $\lambda = 0.9995$ for *Skin* set.

4.2 Analysis and discussion

In this section we present the results obtained using the proposed MASVM along with the state-of-the-art techniques. All tests for GASVM [11], AGA [21] and MASVM were run 30 times and terminated after τ seconds (see Tab. 1). Their execution time includes the SVM training time for each individual to find its fitness. Contrary to that, in case of the random sampling and SR-DSA, this training is omitted.

In Figs. 3–5, we compare AUC obtained for *Adult*, *Skin* and *2D* data sets for g_M generations ($g_M = 100$, $g_M = 40$ and $g_M = 60$, respectively). The plots present the AUC value of the best individual (averaged over 30 runs) along with its standard deviation. We investigated the performance of two variants of GASVM for each data set, termed GASVM-K, where K is the number of samples per class in the refined set $\boldsymbol{T}'$. Since this value is not modified during the GASVM execution, it should be carefully selected beforehand [21]. We compare the efficacy of the approach for two values of K: 1) $K = 10$ (which is the initial K value in MASVM), and 2) $K = \bar{t}'/2$ ($\bar{t}'$ is the average size of the refined set of the best individual obtained using MASVM).

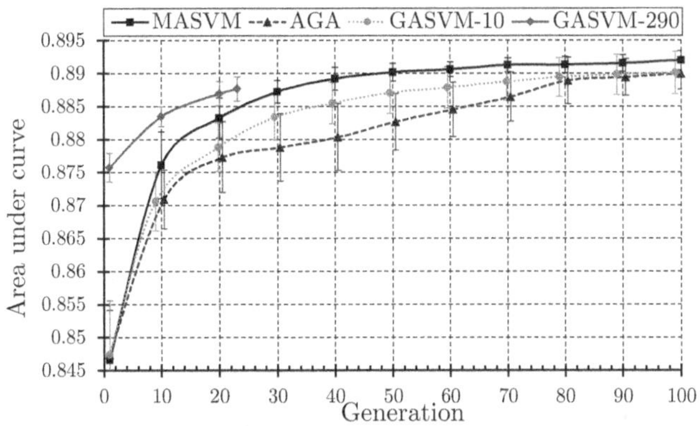

Figure 3: AUC obtained using different methods for *Adult* data set.

It is clear that the best initial AUC is strongly dependent on the training set size (see GASVM–290, GASVM–24 and GASVM–253 in Figs. 3–5). However, it can be noted that GASVM has been terminated after a relatively small number of generations, which indicates a high computational cost in case of large K's (the execution time exceeded τ). Although MASVM, which utilizes the adaptive approach for K tuning, starts from a relatively poor AUC, it is much faster and converges to the initial GASVM (with large K) results rapidly. The desired K is unknown *a priori*, and selecting an improper, i.e., too large, K will drastically increase the execution time of GASVM. Thus, it would have to be run multiple times to determine a reasonable size of $\boldsymbol{T}'$ [11]. This issue is resolved in the AGA and MASVM by the adaptive setting of K according to the current search state. It is easy to see that GASVM with small K has large exploitation capabilities, but lacks the exploration abilities (it converges fast to the steady state). Since MASVM balances the exploitation and exploration, it delivers the best asymptotic results among all investigated techniques.

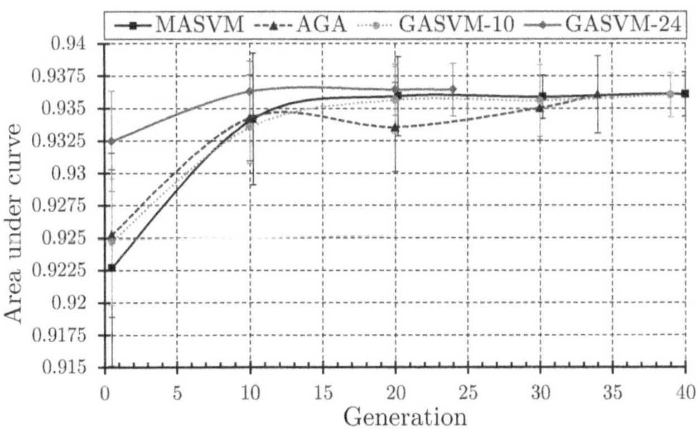

Figure 4: AUC obtained using different methods for *Skin* data set.

Selecting valuable training vectors is crucial for noisy data sets. The results obtained for *Skin* set using the AGA

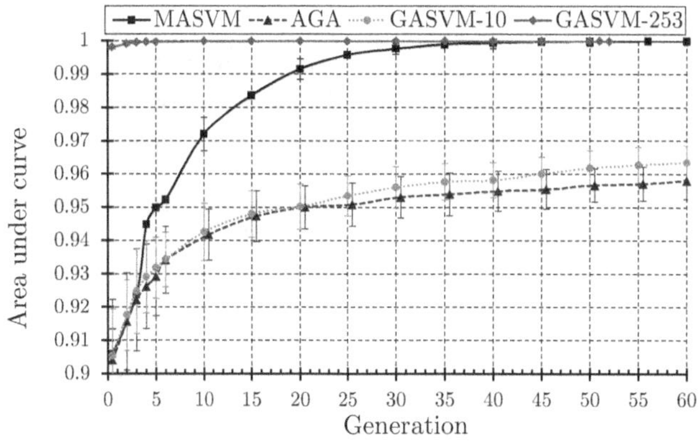

Figure 5: AUC obtained using different methods for *2D* data set.

(Fig. 4) show that the performance may be affected by misleading vectors (see generations 10–30), but the adaptive approach copes well with this problem and converges to the high-quality results. K is increased by a larger factor in AGA than in MASVM, and getting rid of "bad" samples takes more time. The same issue is illustrated in Fig. 6, showing the AUC obtained by random sampling. The bars indicate the minimal and maximal AUC values for various sizes of $\boldsymbol{T}'$. Its performance substantially drops for *Skin* set when t' is large. It confirms the noisiness of the data.

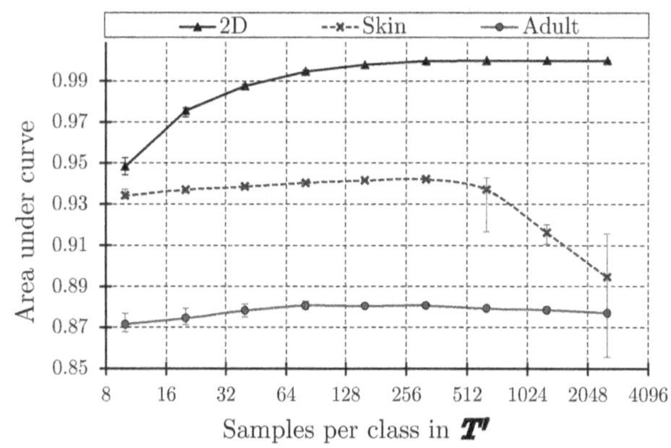

Figure 6: AUC obtained using random sampling for various numbers of samples per class in T'.

In Fig. 7, we visualized the exemplary refined training sets obtained by SR-DSA, GASVM, AGA and MASVM. Black and white points indicate the $\boldsymbol{T}$ vectors, and those marked with white and black crosses show the data selected to the set $\boldsymbol{T}'$ (the colors are swapped for clarity). MASVM gives the best AUC and maximizes the ratio ϱ_{SV} in $\boldsymbol{T}'$.

In Tab. 2, we compare the detailed results obtained using the evaluated algorithms. Also, we trained the SVM using $\boldsymbol{T}$. It was not possible in the case of *Skin* set because of its size. MASVM outperformed other state-of-the-art algorithms and delivered the largest AUC scores. It is easy to see that the number of support vectors s is kept small without lowering the score. Thus, it allows for faster SVM classification. The ϱ_{SV} values are slightly smaller in case of MASVM compared with the AGA. The higher AUC for

Table 2: Comparison of AUC (in %) obtained using various methods.

Set		SVM	SR-DSA [30]	GASVM (t_1/t_2) [11]	AGA [21]	MASVM
Adult	AUC	88.7607	82.7171	$88.7532 \pm 57.24 \cdot 10^{-4}$/ $88.7508 \pm 18.25 \cdot 10^{-4}$	$88.7580 \pm 56.05 \cdot 10^{-4}$	**89.0854** $\pm 19.63 \cdot 10^{-4}$
	t'	15082	751	20/290	36	290 ± 101
	s	7536	369	20/290	36	281 ± 95
	ϱ_{SV}(%)	49.97	49.13	100/100	100	96.90
	g	–	–	195/22	94	50
	τ (s)	71	16.2	300/300	300	300
Skin	AUC	–	92.4454	$93.5859 \pm 22.14 \cdot 10^{-4}$/ $93.6365 \pm 16.91 \cdot 10^{-4}$	$93.6285 \pm 33.11 \cdot 10^{-4}$	**93.6471** $\pm 23.47 \cdot 10^{-4}$
	t'	$4 \cdot 10^6$	58	20/48	20	47 ± 14
	s	–	4	$17 \pm 2/38 \pm 5$	17 ± 3	37 ± 12
	ϱ_{SV}(%)	–	6.70	85/79.17	85	78.72
	g	–	–	38/23	34	25
	τ (s)	–	162.99	300/300	300	300
2D	AUC	99.9980	99.5733	$96.8038 \pm 46.04 \cdot 10^{-4}$/ $99.9906 \pm 26.18 \cdot 10^{-6}$	$97.8285 \pm 51.71 \cdot 10^{-4}$	**99.9999** $\pm 24.22 \cdot 10^{-7}$
	t'	6371	573	20/506	38 ± 6	506 ± 72
	s	279	142	$20/184 \pm 6$	36 ± 6	239 ± 11
	ϱ_{SV}(%)	46.50	24.78	100/36.36	94.74	47.23
	g	–	–	302/26	50	59
	τ (s)	0.6	1.07	30/30	30	30

MASVM shows that the training set is increased too slowly in case of the AGA. It is confirmed by the average number of generations g, which indicates that the small sized individuals were exploited too long by the AGA. It should be noted that SR-DSA executes quite fast and delivers reasonable scores for each considered data set. However, if its parameters are not selected very carefully (in a time-consuming process) then the performance drastically decays.

4.3 Sensitivity analysis on method components

Here, we analyze the role of several MASVM components and assess their impact on the average AUC and number of SVs found in the refined training sets obtained using the proposed MA. The investigated MASVM variants are summarized in Tab. 3. The population diversity ϕ is measured by the metric proposed in [21]. The s_ϕ value indicates the number of consecutive generations with the same ϕ.

Table 3: Abbreviations of the MASVM variants.

No–R	MASVM without the re-generation
CCR	Re-generation applied after each increase of K
DR–0.03	Re-generation applied if $\phi < 0.03$
DR–0.05	Re-generation applied if $\phi < 0.05$
S–5	Re-generation applied if $s_\phi = 5$
S–10	Re-generation applied if $s_\phi = 10$
AMPC	MASVM with the AMPC selection
No–SI	MASVM without the super individuals
No–E	MASVM without the education procedure
E–30%	MASVM with $\mathcal{P}_e = 0.3$
E–50%	MASVM with $\mathcal{P}_e = 0.5$

In Tab. 4, we present the results obtained for *Adult* data set sampled in various time moments τ. As the baseline for this investigation we assume $\mathcal{P}_e = 0.8$, DR–0.05 re-generation and the LGA selection scheme (the other settings as described in Section 4.1). The results confirm that too frequent re-generation of the population affects the MASVM exploitation capabilities (see CCR, DR–0.03 and DR–0.05). Also, in case of the AMPC variant the solutions are not intensively optimized. On the other hand, too intensive exploitation of a small subset of training samples may cause getting stuck in the local minima (see E–50% compared with No–E). Clearly, balancing both the exploitation and exploration of the solution space, and utilizing the available knowledge determined so far, result in the best AUC scores (E–30%). Fig. 8 shows the average number of support vectors visualized in various time intervals. It is easy to note that the number of training samples increased very fast in case of the AMPC variant. This highlights its exploration tendency, since the small sets were not analyzed properly and were quickly increased. It is also worth to mention that tuning the MASVM parameters may slightly change its efficacy, and setting them incorrectly will not degrade its performance significantly. Thus, MASVM is robust for various (not necessarily optimal) values of its parameters.

5. CONCLUSIONS AND FUTURE WORK

In this paper we proposed a new memetic algorithm for SVM training set selection (MASVM), which adapts itself according to the current search state, and exploits the available knowledge. It is capable of determining the size of a valuable training set in short time, and balances the exploitation and exploration of the solution space. We introduced a concept of the *super individuals* composed of the SVs only, and the support vectors pool, in which the valuable training samples are stored. They are used for enhancing other individuals to guide the search. Also, MASVM copes well with various (not necessarily optimal) parameters settings. An extensive experimental study clearly confirms the competitiveness of the proposed approach.

Our ongoing works are focused on combining MASVM with the data structure analysis for local search and the

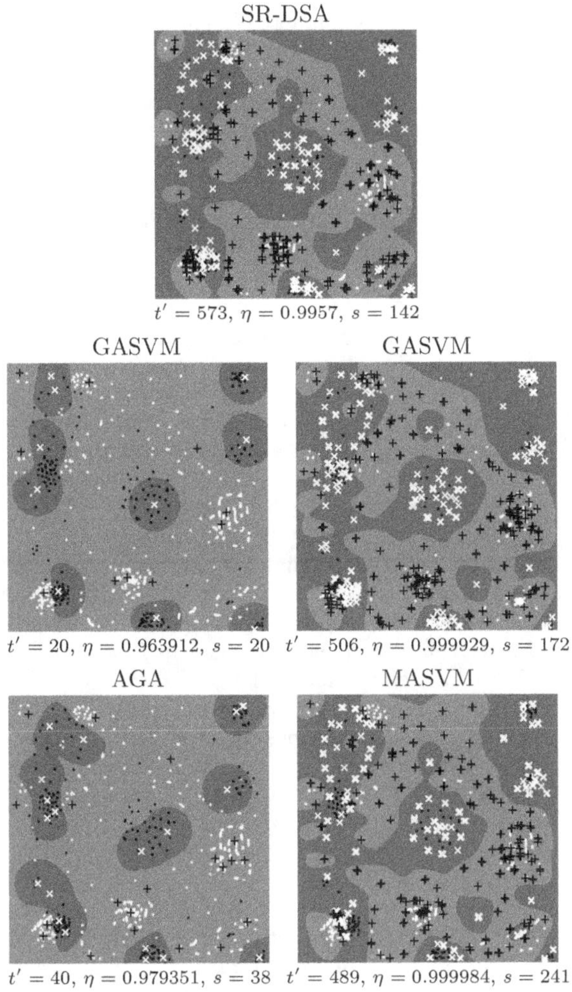

Figure 7: Training set selected using SR-DSA [30], GASVM [11], AGA [21] and MASVM.

initial assessment of training samples. Also, we aim at implementing the parallel MASVM for further decreasing the execution time, and evaluating MASVM on more data sets.

6. ACKNOWLEDGMENTS

This work has been supported by the Polish Ministry of Science and Higher Education under research grant no. IP2012 026372 from the Science Budget 2013–2015. The work was performed using the infrastructure supported by POIG.02.03.01-24-099/13 grant: "GeCONiI–Upper Silesian Center for Computational Science and Engineering".

7. REFERENCES

[1] S. Abe and T. Inoue. Fast training of support vector machines by extracting boundary data. In *Proc. Int. Conf. on ANNs*, pages 308–313. Springer, 2001.

[2] J. L. Balcázar, Y. Dai, and O. Watanabe. A random sampling technique for training support vector machines. In *Proc. ALT*, pages 119–134. Springer, 2001.

[3] C.-C. Chang, H.-K. Pao, and Y.-J. Lee. An RSVM based two-teachers-one-student semi-supervised learning algorithm. *Neural Networks*, 25:57–69, 2012.

Table 4: AUC (in %) and s in time points τ (in seconds) for *Adult* data set.

	τ	AUC	s
No–R	0	$84.9053 \pm 76.52 \cdot 10^{-4}$	20
	120	$88.7224 \pm 27.16 \cdot 10^{-4}$	122 ± 37
	240	$88.8838 \pm 22.43 \cdot 10^{-4}$	192 ± 73
	360	$88.9680 \pm 19.90 \cdot 10^{-4}$	248 ± 90
	600	$89.0527 \pm 19.06 \cdot 10^{-4}$	362 ± 126
CCR	0	$84.8515 \pm 88.16 \cdot 10^{-4}$	20
	120	$88.3508 \pm 20.43 \cdot 10^{-4}$	98 ± 24
	240	$88.5961 \pm 18.21 \cdot 10^{-4}$	171 ± 42
	360	$88.6822 \pm 19.96 \cdot 10^{-4}$	248 ± 66
	600	$88.8230 \pm 14.45 \cdot 10^{-4}$	367 ± 78
DR–0.03	0	$84.6004 \pm 81.18 \cdot 10^{-4}$	20
	120	$88.6934 \pm 25.21 \cdot 10^{-4}$	107 ± 38
	240	$88.8770 \pm 22.08 \cdot 10^{-4}$	181 ± 79
	360	$88.9368 \pm 25.00 \cdot 10^{-4}$	225 ± 109
	600	$88.9914 \pm 25.48 \cdot 10^{-4}$	305 ± 146
DR–0.05	0	$85.0717 \pm 10.10 \cdot 10^{-3}$	20
	120	$88.5571 \pm 25.06 \cdot 10^{-4}$	111 ± 36
	240	$88.7672 \pm 19.96 \cdot 10^{-4}$	192 ± 78
	360	$88.8533 \pm 18.62 \cdot 10^{-4}$	270 ± 99
	600	$88.9116 \pm 17.35 \cdot 10^{-4}$	381 ± 139
S–5	0	$84.4017 \pm 10.87 \cdot 10^{-3}$	20
	120	$88.6967 \pm 24.14 \cdot 10^{-4}$	119 ± 37
	240	$88.8635 \pm 19.55 \cdot 10^{-4}$	200 ± 74
	360	$88.9419 \pm 19.39 \cdot 10^{-4}$	270 ± 106
	600	$89.0218 \pm 18.33 \cdot 10^{-4}$	393 ± 144
S–10	0	$84.8044 \pm 80.72 \cdot 10^{-4}$	20
	120	$88.6699 \pm 33.03 \cdot 10^{-4}$	129 ± 42
	240	$88.8490 \pm 28.43 \cdot 10^{-4}$	213 ± 86
	360	$88.9642 \pm 26.61 \cdot 10^{-4}$	286 ± 122
	600	$89.0450 \pm 22.75 \cdot 10^{-4}$	352 ± 156
AMPC	0	$84.7725 \pm 91.62 \cdot 10^{-4}$	20
	120	$88.5639 \pm 22.07 \cdot 10^{-4}$	162 ± 55
	240	$88.7418 \pm 19.96 \cdot 10^{-4}$	277 ± 95
	360	$88.8085 \pm 20.53 \cdot 10^{-4}$	361 ± 124
	600	$88.8793 \pm 18.62 \cdot 10^{-4}$	452 ± 147
No–SI	0	$84.8012 \pm 99.60 \cdot 10^{-4}$	20
	120	$\mathbf{88.7303} \pm 25.94 \cdot 10^{-4}$	154 ± 39
	240	$88.8755 \pm 19.77 \cdot 10^{-4}$	228 ± 60
	360	$88.9460 \pm 19.20 \cdot 10^{-4}$	297 ± 98
	600	$89.0499 \pm 22.73 \cdot 10^{-4}$	420 ± 147
No–E	0	$84.8580 \pm 95.82 \cdot 10^{-4}$	20
	120	$88.7162 \pm 24.33 \cdot 10^{-4}$	134 ± 27
	240	$\mathbf{88.9087} \pm 20.98 \cdot 10^{-4}$	234 ± 59
	360	$88.9739 \pm 20.71 \cdot 10^{-4}$	305 ± 93
	600	$89.0561 \pm 18.25 \cdot 10^{-4}$	394 ± 123
E–30%	0	$84.6679 \pm 97.00 \cdot 10^{-4}$	20
	120	$88.6598 \pm 26.44 \cdot 10^{-4}$	120 ± 35
	240	$88.8911 \pm 20.71 \cdot 10^{-4}$	231 ± 75
	360	$\mathbf{89.0041} \pm 18.53 \cdot 10^{-4}$	284 ± 84
	600	$\mathbf{89.0789} \pm 19.95 \cdot 10^{-4}$	362 ± 124
E–50%	0	$84.8592 \pm 11.17 \cdot 10^{-3}$	20
	120	$88.6674 \pm 22.35 \cdot 10^{-4}$	140 ± 34
	240	$88.8710 \pm 22.34 \cdot 10^{-4}$	245 ± 76
	360	$88.9452 \pm 20.40 \cdot 10^{-4}$	321 ± 124
	600	$89.0575 \pm 20.85 \cdot 10^{-4}$	410 ± 170

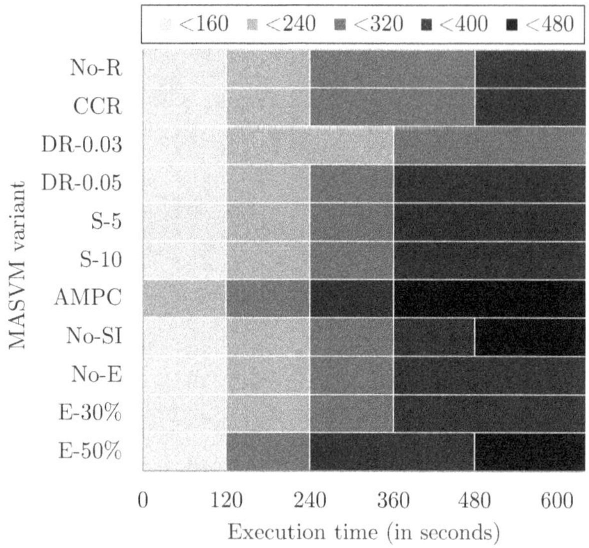

Figure 8: Average number of SVs obtained by various MASVM variants for *Adult* data set.

[4] L.-J. Chien, C.-C. Chang, and Y.-J. Lee. Variant methods of reduced set selection for reduced support vector machines. *JISE*, 26(1):183–196, 2010.

[5] C. Cortes and V. Vapnik. Support-Vector Networks. *Mach. Learn.*, 20(3):273–297, 1995.

[6] E. E. A. Elamin. A proposed genetic algorithm selection method. In *Proc. 1st NITS*, pages 1–8, 2006.

[7] E. Ferragut and J. Laska. Randomized sampling for large data applications of SVM. In *Proc. IEEE ICMLA*, volume 1, pages 350–355, 2012.

[8] X. Guan, X. Zhang, D. Han, Y. Zhu, J. Lv, and J. Su. A strategic flight conflict avoidance approach based on a memetic algorithm. *Chinese J. of Aeronautics*, 27(1):93 – 101, 2014.

[9] Y. Jin, J.-K. Hao, and J.-P. Hamiez. A memetic algorithm for the minimum sum coloring problem. *Comput. Oper. Res.*, 43:318 – 327, 2014.

[10] T. Joachims. Making large-scale SVM learning practical. In B. Schölkopf, C. J. C. Burges, and A. J. Smola, editors, *Adv. in kernel methods*, pages 169–184. MIT Press, 1999.

[11] M. Kawulok and J. Nalepa. Support vector machines training data selection using a genetic algorithm. In *Proc. S+SSPR 2012*, volume 7626 of *LNCS*, pages 557–565. Springer, 2012.

[12] R. Koggalage and S. Halgamuge. Reducing the number of training samples for fast support vector machine classification. *Neural Information Process. – Lett. and Reviews*, 2(3):57–65, 2004.

[13] Q. Le, T. Sarlos, and A. Smola. Fastfood – approximating kernel expansions in loglinear time. In *Proc. ICML*, 2013.

[14] Y.-J. Lee and S.-Y. Huang. Reduced support vector machines: A statistical theory. *IEEE T. Neural Networ.*, 18(1):1–13, 2007.

[15] Y. Li, P. Li, B. Wu, L. Jiao, and R. Shang. Kernel clustering using a hybrid memetic algorithm. *Natural Comput.*, 12(4):605–615, 2013.

[16] A. Lopez-Chau, X. Li, and W. Yu. Convex-concave hull for classification with SVM. In *Proc. IEEE ICDMW*, pages 431–438, 2012.

[17] M. Marinaki and Y. Marinakis. An island memetic differential evolution algorithm for the feature selection problem. In *Proc. NICSO*, volume 512 of *SCI*, pages 29–42. Springer, 2014.

[18] P. Moscato. On Evolution, Search, Optimization, Genetic Algorithms and Martial Arts – Towards Memetic Algorithms. Technical Report 158-79, California Institute of Technology, 1989.

[19] D. R. Musicant and A. Feinberg. Active set support vector regression. *IEEE T. on Neural Networ.*, 15(2):268–275, 2004.

[20] J. Nalepa and Z. J. Czech. New selection schemes in a memetic algorithm for the vehicle routing problem with time windows. In *Proc. ICANNGA*, volume 7824 of *LNCS*, pages 396–405. Springer, 2013.

[21] J. Nalepa and M. Kawulok. Adaptive genetic algorithm to select training data for support vector machines. In *EvoApp.*, LNCS. Springer, 2014. in press.

[22] S. L. Phung, D. Chai, and A. Bouzerdoum. Adaptive skin segmentation in color images. In *Proc. IEEE ICASSP*, pages 353–356, 2003.

[23] A. Rahimi and B. Recht. Random features for large-scale kernel machines. In *Proc. NIPS*, pages 1177–1184. 2008.

[24] A. Rahimi and B. Recht. Weighted sums of random kitchen sinks: Replacing minimization with randomization in learning. In *Proc. NIPS*, pages 1313–1320. 2009.

[25] I. Rodriguez-Lujan, C. S. Cruz, and R. Huerta. Hierarchical linear support vector machine. *Patt. Recogn.*, 45(12):4414 – 4427, 2012.

[26] S. Salvador and P. Chan. Determining the number of clusters / segments in hierarchical clustering / segmentation algorithms. In *Proc. IEEE ICTAI*, pages 576–584, 2004.

[27] G. Schohn and D. Cohn. Less is more: Active learning with support vector machines. In *Proc. ICML*, pages 839–846, 2000.

[28] H. Shin and S. Cho. Neighborhood property–based pattern selection for SVMs. *Neural Comput.*, 19(3):816–855, 2007.

[29] I. W. Tsang, J. T. Kwok, and P.-M. Cheung. Core vector machines: Fast SVM training on very large data sets. *J. of Mach. Learn. Res.*, 6:363–392, 2005.

[30] D. Wang and L. Shi. Selecting valuable training samples for SVMs via data structure analysis. *Neurocomputing*, 71:2772–2781, 2008.

[31] J. Wang, P. Neskovic, and L. N. Cooper. Training data selection for SVMs. In *Adv. in Natural Comp.*, pages 554–564. Springer, 2005.

[32] Z.-Q. Zeng, H.-R. Xu, Y.-Q. Xie, and J. Gao. A geometric approach to train SVM on very large data sets. In *Proc. ISKE*, volume 1, pages 991–996, 2008.

[33] W. Zhang and I. King. Locating support vectors via β-skeleton technique. In *Proc. ICONIP*, pages 1423–1427, 2002.

Steady State IBEA Assisted by MLP Neural Networks for Expensive Multi-Objective Optimization Problems

Nessrine Azzouz
SOIE lab, University of Tunis, Tunisia
azouznessrine@gmail.com

Slim Bechikh
SOIE lab, University of Tunis, Tunisia
slim.bechikh@gmail.com

Lamjed Ben Said
SOIE lab, University of Tunis, Tunisia
lamjed.bensaid@isg.rnu.tn

ABSTRACT

Several engineering problems involve simultaneously several objective functions where at least one of them is expensive to evaluate. This fact has yielded to a new class of Multi-Objective Problems (MOPs) called expensive MOPs. Several attempts have been conducted in the literature with the goal to minimize the number of expensive evaluations by using surrogate models stemming from the machine learning field. Usually, researchers substitute the expensive objective function evaluation by an estimation drawn from the used surrogate. In this paper, we propose a new way to tackle expensive MOPs. The main idea is to use Neural Networks (NNs) within the Indicator-Based Evolutionary Algorithm (IBEA) in order to estimate the contribution of each generated offspring in terms of hypervolume. After that, only fit individuals with respect to the estimations are exactly evaluated. Our proposed algorithm called NN-SS-IBEA (Neural Networks assisted Steady State IBEA) have been demonstrated to provide good performance with a low number of function evaluations when compared against the original IBEA and MOEA/D-RBF on a set of benchmark problems in addition to the airfoil design problem.

Categories and Subject Descriptors

I.2.8 [**Computing Methodologies**]: Articial Intelligence—*Problem Solving, Control Method, and Search.*

General Terms

Algorithms

Keywords

Multi-objective optimization, Surrogate model, fitness approximation, Neural networks.

GECCO'14, July 12–16, Vancouver, BC, Canada.
Copyright 2014 ACM 978-1-4503-2662-9/14/07 ...$15.00.
http://dx.doi.org/10.1145/2576768.2598271.

1. INTRODUCTION

Several engineering problems (such as aeronautical and aerodynamic design, etc.) involve multiple and often conflicting objective functions to be optimized simultaneously. These problems are known as Multi-objective Optimization Problems (MOPs), and their solution gives rise to a set of trade-off solutions, called the Pareto optimal set. In the last decade, Evolutionary Algorithms (EA) have been proved efficient and well suitable for dealing with MOPs, mainly because of their ability to provide multiple Pareto-optimal solutions on a single run and they are insensitive to the shape and continuity of the Pareto front. One of the major difficulties in applying EAs to real problems is the large number of fitness evaluations necessary to obtain a good approximation of the Pareto front. In some real world situations, it is often the case that fitness evaluation of the solution is not always readily available, too costly or hazardous to be constructed or the evaluation is extremely computationally intensive which pose a particular challenge to EA and make them an unaffordable choice (computationally speaking) in some cases. We label such category of problems as "Expensive Problems". The time required to solve these problems is still a challenge for the methods and algorithms. The evaluation of a single design can take a long time, from several hours up to days or week's of computational time. Thus, there is an evident need to find a reliable and efficient method, which is able to produce reasonably good solutions within a given budget on computational cost/time by reducing the number of computational evaluations.

To alleviate the problem of converging time of computationally expensive optimization problems, several attempts have been conducted in the literature [14]. Recently, researchers have developed techniques to achieve an effective reduction of fitness function evaluations by exploiting knowledge acquired during the solution process. This knowledge can, for instance, be used to adapt the recombination and mutation operators in order to sample offspring in promising areas of the search space (as done through the use of cultural algorithms). Knowledge of past evaluations can also be used to predict promising new solutions at a smaller evaluation cost than that of the original problem and thus by using surrogate models, also known as metamodels, stemming from the machine learning field. Usually, researchers substitute the expensive objective function evaluation by an estimation drawn from the used surrogate [4], [7], [9], [12], [17], [19]. Despite the significant progress made in the last decades, the study on existing surrogate-assisted evolutionary frameworks remains open for further improvements.

Particularly, present surrogate-assisted evolutionary frameworks proposed are typically flawed by the introduction of false optima, since it is difficult to model the expensive problem accurately.
A promising approach to the search for non-dominated solutions over the entire Pareto front of the expensive MOP is a class of Indicator-Based Evolutionary Algorithms (IBEAs) where selection is based on solution contribution to a certain quality indicator. The main critical point in this type of algorithms is the required computational effort for: (1) computing the quality indicator values for a certain non-dominated solution set and (2) updating the solution set. To tackle these difficulties of IBEAs in order to improve their applicability to expensive MOPs, we propose a new idea called NN-SS-IBEA (Neural Networks assisted Steady State IBEA). The key ingredient of our work lies in the use of Neural Networks (NNs) within IBEA in order to estimate the contribution of each generated offspring in terms of hypervolume. After that, only fit individuals with respect to the estimations are exactly evaluated. In this study, we use a steady-state approach that employs a simple replacement strategy, which avoids most of the computational overload caused by operations other than fitness evaluations. This method has been shown to be beneficial for EAs [11]. We believe that the steady-state approach should also be effective in the context of expensive MOPs. Our proposed approach is assessed through experimental studies including comparative experiments against the most prominent recent works (MOEA/D-RBF) and the original IBEA by utilizing academic benchmark problems commonly used by the community in addition to the airfoil design problem. The remainder of this paper is structured as follows. Section 2 deals with the basic concepts. Section 3 is dedicated to present our proposed approach NN-SS-IBEA and details its components. Section 4 deals with the detailed experimental study. Finally, section 5 concludes the paper and gives some avenues for future research.

2. BASIC CONCEPTS

2.1 Multi-Objective Optimization

The MOP (also called Multi-criteria optimization or vector optimization problem) that can be defined as the problem of finding [13] a vector of decision variables which satisfies constraints and optimizes a vector function whose elements represent the objective functions. A MOP can be formally defined as [2]:

$$\begin{cases} Minimizing \quad F(s) = [f_1(s), f_2(s), \ldots, f_M(s)]^T \\ g_j(s) \leq 0 \quad j \in 1, \ldots, J \\ h_k(s) \leq 0 \quad k \in 1, \ldots, K \\ s_i^L \leq s_i \leq s_i^U, \quad i \in \{1, ..., n\} \end{cases} \tag{1}$$

Where M is the number of objective functions; J is the number of inequality constraints, K is the number of equality constraints and s_i^L and s_i^U correspond respectively to the lower and upper bounds of the variable s_i. $S = (s_1, s_2, ..., s_n)$ is a vector of decision variables, where n is the number of independent variables s_i. The evaluation function F is a mapping from the vector of decision variables $S = (s_1, s_2, ..., s_n)$ to a set of objective values $y = (a_1, a_2, ..., a_n)$.

In the following, we give some background definitions related to MOP:
Definition 1: We say that a solution $s^* \in S$ (S is the feasible region) is Pareto optimal if there does not exist another $s \in S$ such that:

$$\begin{cases} f_i(s) \leq f_i(s^*) & for\ all \quad i = 1, ...k \\ f_j(s) < f_j(s^*) & for\ at\ least\ one\ j \end{cases} \tag{2}$$

Definition 2: Given two solutions $s = (s_1, s_2, ..., s_n)$ and $t = (t_1, t_2, ..., t_n)$, we say that s dominate t (denoted by $f(s) \leq f(t)$) if and only if:

$$\begin{cases} \forall m \in \{1, ..., M\} & f_m(s) < f_m(t) \\ \exists m \in \{1, ..., M\} & where \quad f_m(s) < f_m(t) \end{cases} \tag{3}$$

Definition 3: The pareto optimal set P^* is defined by:

$$P^* = \left\{ s \in S | \neg \exists s' \in S\,,\ f(s') \leq f(s) \right\} \tag{4}$$

Definition 4: The pareto front PF^* is defined by:

$$PF^* = \{f(s)\,,\ s \in P^*\} \tag{5}$$

2.2 Multi-Layer Perceptron Neural Network (MLP-NN)

The MLP-NN is a multilayer feed forward network that has been widely used in several meta-modeling applications [5], [8]. An MLP is composed of neurons and the output (y) of each neuron is thus:

$$y = \phi(\sum_{i=1}^{n} w_i\, a_i + b) \tag{6}$$

Where, w denotes the vector of weights, a is the vector of inputs, b is the bias and ϕ is the activation function.
The activation function is chosen to be the logistic sigmoid function $1/(1+e^{-\alpha})$, where α is a slope parameter, although other activation functions are also possible. This function is used because it is mathematically convenient. It is well-known that MLPs are universal approximators, which makes them attractive for modeling black box functions for which little information about their form is known. The development of the back-propagation learning algorithm for determining weights in a MLP has made these networks the most popular among researchers and users of neural networks.

2.3 Latin Hypercube Sampling Method (LHS)

LHS is a statistical method, providing an efficient way of sampling variables from multidimensional distribution [6]. Let N be the number of variables $(x_1, ..., x_N)$. The range of each variable is divided into k equiprobable intervals $\{(x_{11}, ..., x_{1K}), ..., (x_{N1}, ..., x_{NK})\}$. A value is selected randomly from each interval. The N values obtained for each variable are paired randomly with the other variables. The LHS can be summarized as:

- Divide the range of each variable into K equiprobable invervals;
- From each interval select a value randomly, for the ith interval, the sampled cumulative probability can be written as [18]:

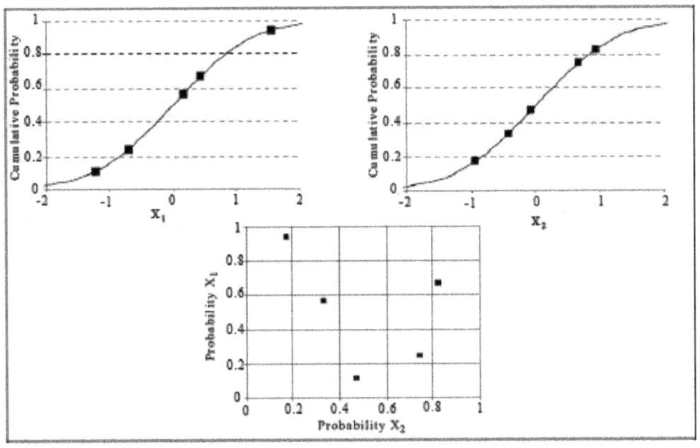

Figure 1: Example of LHS: Random stratified sampling of variables x_1 and x_2 at 5 intervals (Top) and random pairing of sampled x_1 and x_2 forming a Latin hypercube (Down).

$Prob_i = (1/K)r_u + (i-1)/K$

Where $r_u \in [0, 1]$;

- Transform the probability values sampled into the value x :

  $x = F^{-1}(Prob)$;

- The K values obtained for each variable x are paired randomly with the n values of the other variables.

Figure 1 illustrates an example of LHS for the case of $N = 2$ and $k = 5$.
The main advantage of this sampling scheme is that coverage more efficiently the shape of the entire distribution sample than the random samples.

3. OUR PROPOSED APPROACH

3.1 Overview

The well known IBEA algorithm is employed here and is modified to satisfy the role of the main optimizer. The approximation of the objective functions is implemented via a global MLP model, chosen because of its reported simplicity and efficiency to solve complex engineering problems. Initially, a population of individual is initialized using a Design of Experiment (DoE) method . The fitness of each individual in the population is then evaluated using the original objective function. NN-SS-IBEA uses an external archive to store the best solutions found so far in the evolutionary process. This archive is initialized with the non-dominated solutions found in P. For each IBEA search generation, the best solutions with the highest fitness value are archived in the database. After some evaluations' E of performing the classical IBEA search, specifically when ample data points for surrogate building have been collected in the database, the MLP will be constructed. The key ingredient of our work is the construction of surrogates (MLP) that directly predict the contribution in term of hypervolume indicator value of the offspring instead of calculating the fitness values using the original objective function. The predictions produced by the surrogate model thus serves to pre-screen the offspring

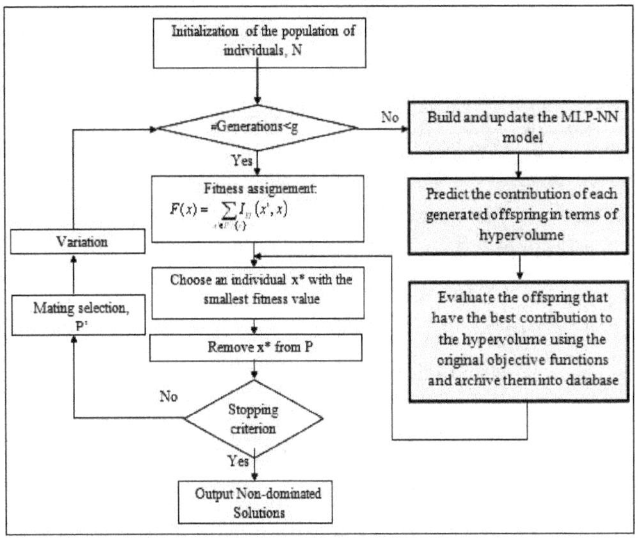

Figure 2: The basic workflow of NN-SS-IBEA.

such that only the elite solution individuals, i.e., those offspring that have the best contribution to the hypervolume indicator are more worthy to undergo exact assessments or evaluations based on the original "expensive" objectives f and will be added to the database. This reduces the unnecessary "expensive" evaluations of inferior offspring whose contribution to the hypervolume are anticipated to be poor, thus arriving at near the true Pareto front more efficiently. Using the archived solutions in the database, the MLP surrogate model M is subsequently trained. We propose to define a maximum allowable number of training points to hold in the database . Once this upper limit is reached, we still allow the insertion of new points, but the database is pruned until reaching again the maximum allowable number of solutions. The motivation for defining a maximum number of points to be kept in the database is to reduce the computational cost associated to the training process, and to adapt the model in the neighborhood of the Pareto front approximation, as the evolution progresses. This process then continues until the computational budget set is exhausted or some other user specified termination criteria are met. When the algorithm ends, the nondominated solutions are attained.
For a better understanding of the proposed approach, Algorithm 1 and Figure 2 show the basic workflow of the proposed NN-SS-IBEA.

3.2 Details

3.2.1 Initialization

Initially, a training set $T_{set} = s_i, \ldots, s_N$ of N well-spread solutions is generated using the LHS method. The set of solutions T_{set} is evaluated by using the real fitness function. The number of current fitness function evaluations n_{eval} is initially set as $n_{eval} = N$. NN-SS-IBEA uses an external archive A to store the nondominated solutions found so far in the evolutionary process. This archive is initialized with the nondominated solutions found in T_{set} . At the beginning, a new offspring is generated from the population P by performing crossover and mutation operator. The stopping criterion considered in NN-SS-IBEA is the number of fitness

Algorithm 1 Pseudo code of the NN-SS-IBEA

INPUT:
N (population size);
N_{max} (maximum number of evaluations);
n (number of evaluations);
K (fitness scaling factor);
OUTPUT:
A (Archive population):
BEGIN
Initialization:
Set $n = 0$; /* the evaluation counter */
An initial population P is generated and then
evaluated using $f()$;
Set $A = P$; /*An archive to store the best
solutions*/
While $(n \leq N_{max})$ **do**
Perform crossover and mutation to generate new
solution z from P;
$Q = P \cup \{z\}$;
If $(n \geq E)$ **Then**
Build and **update** the MLP surrogate model
M based on training points;
$\forall x \in Q$ Calculate the approximated
hypervolume contributions $F^{'}(x)$
of individuals in Q;
Else
$\forall x \in Q : F(x^1) = \sum_{x^2 \in P \setminus \{x^1\}} e^{-I(\{x^2\},\{x^1\})/k}$
/*Calculate the true fitness values of individuals
in Q*/
End if
Choose the S individuals $S = x_1, \ldots, x_s \in Q$
with the highest fitness value,
i.e.$\forall x \in Q\, F(x_1, ..., x_n) \geq F(x)$;
Evaluate S using $f()$; /*Calculate the true fitness
values of the best individuals*/
$n = n + size(S)$;
$A = A \cup S$;
While (size$(A) > N$) **do**
Choose an individual $x^{'} \in A$ with the smallest
fitness value, i.e. $\forall x \in A\, F(x^{'}) \leq F(x)$;
$A = A \setminus \{x^{'}\}$;
End
End
Return A;
END

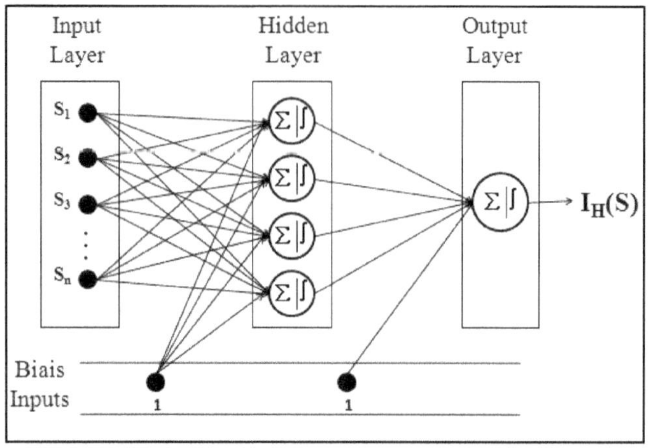

Figure 3: A typical three-layer feed forward Multi-layer Perceptron Neural Network.

function evaluations and, therefore, the stopping criterion is initially set as false, i.e. stopping criterion $= FALSE$.

3.2.2 *Building The Model*

As previously indicated, we use an MLP surrogate model to assess and categorize individuals of the offspring. In general, an MLP with one sufficient large hidden layer is capable of approximating any continuous function to any given accuracy. Here, the activation function is often chosen to be the logistic sigmoid $1/(1 + e^{-x})$ (Note however that other types of activation function can also be adopted).
Using the archived solutions N, an MLP surrogate model M is subsequently built. The backbone of our scheme includes the back-propagation algorithm to build and learn the surrogate M from N that models the contribution to the hypervolume indicator value of the offspring for the current IBEA search generation. Let $\{(s^1, I_H(s^1)), (s^2, I_H(s^2)), ..., (s^n, I_H(s^n))\}$ be a set of n training patterns (input-output pairs), where $s^i \in S$ is the input vector in the n-dimensional pattern space, and $I_H(s^i)$ is the desired output vector (see Figure3). Before training, all network weights must be initialized to small random numbers. This ensures that the network is not saturated by large values of the weights. An MLP network may be described by the following steps:

1. Apply the current training pair (i.e input vector and desired output vector) from the training set.
2. Calculate the actual network output.
3. Calculate the error between the actual output and the desired output.
4. Adjust the network weights to minimize the error.
5. Repeat steps 1 to 4 for each vector pair in the training set until the error E for the entire set is acceptably low.

Using the MLP surrogate model, the hypervolume indicator predicted value of a given offspring s is predicted as: $I^{'}_H(s) = \sum w_j h_j(s)$ where h is the activation function.

3.2.3 Selecting Points To Evaluate

A set $S = \{s_1, ..., s_N\}$ of N solutions taken from P chosen to be evaluated using the real fitness function. Each solution in S is selected such that it has the best contribution to the hypervolume indicator. No solution in S should be duplicated. If this is the case, the repeated solution should be removed from S.

3.2.4 Termination Criterion

For each new evaluated solution, we set $n_{eval} = n_{eval}+1$, if $n_{eval} \geq E_{max}$ then we set stopping criterion $= TRUE$, where n_{eval} and E_{max} are the current and the maximum number of fitness function evaluations, respectively.

4. EXPERIMENTAL STUDY

4.1 Research Questions

The main objective of this paper is to design a MLP Neural Networks assisted Steady State IBEA for dealing with expensive MOP, in order to reduce the number of fitness function evaluations that are required to produce reasonably good approximations of MOPs of different complexity. Compared to many other EA's, the steady state approach has the advantage of being computationally less expensive. We attempt to answer following research questions:

- **RQ1.** Is the proposed NN-SS-IBEA algorithm able to conduct an effective and computationally efficient search?
- **RQ2.** Can our approach yield useful insights into the trade-offs between objectives for real world problems?

4.2 Used Benchmark Problems

In order to assess the performance of our proposed approach NN-SS-IBEA, we compare its results with respect to those obtained by the original IBEA and by MOEA/D-RBF, which uses the well-known MOEA/D assisted by RBF neural networks. We adopted the ZDT test problems except for ZDT5 (which is a discrete problem) and DTLZ1 to DTLZ7. In order to evaluate the capabilities of NN-SS-IBEA when dealing with computationally expensive problems, we also tested its performance using a real-world problem, as a case study.
Next, we describe the ZDT, DTLZ and airfoil problem, which was adopted to validate our proposed approach.

4.2.1 Standard Test Problems

4.2.1.1 Two-objective Test Problems: (ZDT) Benchmark.

The ZDT test functions are introduced by [20] and are widely employed as a benchmark test problems in the EA literature. The set of ZDT problems consists of six test functions, each of these test functions contains a particular feature that is representative of a real world optimization problem such as a convex/non-convex, discontinuous or a non-uniform distributed Pareto-optimal front, that could cause difficulty in converging to the pareto front.

4.2.1.2 Three-objective Test Problems: (DTLZ) Benchmark.

The DTLZ test functions are introduced by [3]. This set includes seven different test functions; each of these test functions contains particular features that are representative of a real world optimization problem such as linear, spherical or disconnected.
Note that the set of DTLZ test problems are actually a collection of scalable test functions, that is, all DTLZ test functions are scalable to have any number of decision-variables and any number of objectives. We focus only on three-objective test problems because they are easier to visualize. Next, we describe the airfoil problem, which was adopted to validate our proposed approach.

4.2.2 Airfoil Shape Optimization: A Case Study

Our case study consists of the multi-objective optimization of an airfoil shape problem adapted from [16] (called here MOPRW). This problem corresponds to the airfoil shape optimization of a standard-class glider, aiming to obtain an optimum performance for a sailplane.

4.2.2.1 Problem Statement.

Two conflicting objective functions are defined in terms of a sailplane average weight and operating conditions. They are defined as:

- Minimize C_D/C_L

  s.t. $C_L = 0.63, \quad Re = 2.04\ 10^6, \quad M = 0.12$

- Minimize $C_D/C_L^{3/2}$

  s.t. $C_L = 1.05, \quad Re = 1.29\ 10^6, \quad M = 0.08$

Where $C_D/C_L$is the inverse of the glider's gliding ratio, $C_D/C_L^{3/2}$correspond to the sink rate. Both are important performance measures for this aerodynamic optimization problem. C_D and C_L are the drag and lift coefficients, respectively. Re and M are the Reynolds, and Mach numbers, respectively.
Each of these objectives is evaluated at different prescribed flight conditions, given in terms of Mach and Reynolds numbers. The aim of solving this MOP is to find a better airfoil shape, which improves a reference design. Constraints:

- Maximal $C_L \geq 1.05 \quad for \quad Re = 106, \quad M = 0.06$;
- Maximum airfoil thickness 13.0;
- Trailing edge thickness 0.25%.

4.2.2.2 Geometry Parametrization.

In the present case study, a modified variant of PARSEC-functions (gPARSEC functions) [15] representation was adopted. The function is governed by eleven parameters (Their allowable range are defined in Table 1); r_{le} leading edge radius, X_{up}/X_{lo} location of maximum thickness for upper/lower surfaces, Z_{up}/Z_{lo} maximum thickness for upper/lower surfaces, Z_{xxup}/Z_{xxlo} curvature for upper/lower surfaces, at maximum thickness locations, Z_{te} trailing edge coordinate, ΔZ_{te} trailing edge thickness, α_{te} trailing edge direction, and β_{te} trailing edge wedge angle, to generate different classes of airfoils and is mathematically represented as follows:

Table 1: Parameter ranges for our modified Parsec airfoil representation.

Design Variable	Lower Bound	Upper Bound
r_{leup}	0.0085	0.0126
r_{lelo}	0.0020	0.0040
α_{te}	7.0000	10.0000
β_{te}	10.0000	14.0000
Z_{te}	-0.0060	-0.0030
$\triangle Z_{te}$	0.0025	0.0050
X_{up}	0.4100	0.4600
Z_{up}	0.1100	0.1300
Z_{xxup}	-0.9000	-0.7000
X_{lo}	0.2000	0.2600
Z_{lo}	-0.0230	-0.0150
Z_{xxlo}	0.0500	0.2000

$$Z_{upper} = \sum_{n=1}^{6} a_n x^{\frac{n-1}{2}}, \qquad Z_{lower} = \sum_{n=1}^{6} b_n x^{\frac{n-1}{2}},$$

where a_n , and b_n are the real coefficients which are determined as functions of the 12 described geometric parameters.

A system of equations are used to equate the coefficients as a function of variables and solved simultaneously. The coefficients a_n , and b_n serve as intermediate variables for interpolating the airfoil's coordinates, which are used by the CFD solver (we used the Xfoil CFD code) for its discretization process. The optimizer perturbs the geometrical variables to generate different classes of airfoils, until a convergence criterion is satisfied.

4.3 Used Metrics

Evaluating the performance of optimization algorithms is a crucial task, particularly for MOEAs that attempt to converge to the true Pareto-optimal front while maintaining a good distribution of the solutions found. Several performance measures are proposed in the EMO literature to evaluate one or both of these goals [21]. In order to evaluate the performance of our proposed approach NN-SS-IBEA, we compared its results with respect to those obtained by the original IBEA and by MOEA/D-RBF. For comparing these algorithms, we adopted, in our experimental study, the I_H^- performance measure.

Let P^* be a set of uniformly distributed points in the objective space along the PF. Let P be an approximation to the PF, the I_H^- performance measure is defined as:

$$I_H^-(P^*, P) = I_H(P^*) - I_H(P) \qquad (7)$$

Where $I_H(P^*)$ is the hypervolume between the Pareto optimal front P^* and a reference point r.

The idea of the I_H^- performance measure is that the lower I_H^- value, the better the found solution set is. The advantage of this measure is that the diversity and the convergence of found solutions can be expressed by just one numerical value.

In our experiments, as in [10] we select 500 evenly distributed points in PF and let these points be P^* for each test instance with 2 objectives, and 990 points for each test instance with 3 objectives.

Table 2: Parameters of the multiobjective algorithms.

Parameter	MOEA value
Stopping criterion	200 fitness function evaluations (ZDT problem using 8 decision variables) 1000 fitness function evaluations (ZDT problem using 10 and 30 decision variables)
Crossover probability	0.9
Crossover operator	SBX
Mutation probability	1/n (where n denotes the number of decision variables)
Mutation operator	Polynomial
Mutation index	20
Population size	100
Archive size	100

Table 3: Parameters of the surrogate model.

Parameter	MLP-NN
Activation function	Sigmoid
Architecture	3-5-1
Learning rate	0.00006
Number of training cycle	50000

4.4 Adopted Statistical Methodology

For the validation of significance of results and comparison between the classical IBEA, NN-SS-IBEA and MOEA/D-RBF, we carried out the parametric student t-test using the statistical toolbox provided in Matlab. The test was performed using the results of 50 runs.

It is important to note that we have verified the normality of data using the Kolmogorov-Smirnov test and we obtained that all data sets are normally distributed. This fact allowed us using the t-test.

Tables 4-6 show results of a Student's t-test study, when comparing our proposed approach againts the classical IBEA. [*] means a significant difference between results, with at least a 95% confidence level.

4.5 Parameter Tuning And Settings

In this subsection, we present the parameter settings used for all subsequent tests. See Table 2 for the parameters of the algorithms used and Table 3 for the parameters of the metamodel used. For each MOP, 50 independent runs were performed with each algorithm. The termination criterion of an algorithm is a predefined number of evaluations. As previously indicated, the algorithms were evaluated using the I_H^- metrics. The results obtained are summarized in Tables 4-7. These tables display the average and the standard deviation (in the parentheses) of the I_H^- indicators for each MOP. The reference vector r used for computing the performance measures, for each MOP, is shown in each table of results. For an easier interpretation, the best results are presented in boldface for each test problem adopted.

4.6 Result Analysis And Discussion

This section presents the results obtained from our experiments for RQs 1 and 2 set out in Sub Section 4.1.

Table 4: Results of the I_H^- performance measure for NN-SS-IBEA, IBEA and MOEA/D-RBF, using eight decision variables on ZDT problems.

	NN-SS-IBEA	IBEA	MOEA/D-RBF	Reference point (r)
ZDT1	**0.9E-03*** (0.9E-04)	10.209 (3.310)	9.1E-03 (0.8E-03)	$(10, 10)^T$
ZDT2	**0.8E-03*** (0.1E-03)	13.223 (3.945)	9.7E-03 (1.5E-03)	$(10, 10)^T$
ZDT3	**0.9E-01*** (6.7E-01)	21.218 (7.307)	0.115 (0.898)	$(20, 20)^T$
ZDT4	**1.5E+03** (0.3E+03)	1.7E+03 (0.4E+03)	1.6E+03 (0.4E+03)	$(50, 50)^T$
ZDT6	**0.958*** (1.873)	32.134 (2.672)	1.690 (2.006)	$(10, 10)^T$

Table 5: Results of the I_H^- performance measure for NN-SS-IBEA, IBEA and MOEA/D-RBF, using 30 and 10 decision variables, respectively on ZDT problems.

	NN-SS-IBEA	IBEA	MOEA/D-RBF	Reference point (r)
ZDT1	**0.8E-03*** (0.9E-04)	9.758 (1.235)	0.4E-02 (0.3E-03)	$(5, 5)^T$
ZDT2	**0.5E-03*** (0.1E-03)	0.1E+02 (0.1E+01)	0.6E-02 (0.7E-03)	$(5, 5)^T$
ZDT3	**1.928*** (0.795)	0.1E+02 (0.1E+01)	2.298 (0.952)	$(5, 5)^T$
ZDT4	1.2E+03 (0.2E+03)	**0.5E+03** (0.1E+03)	1.8E+03 (0.3E+03)	$(50, 50)^T$
ZDT6	**0.985*** (0.754)	22.057 (2.385)	1.244 (0.996)	$(5, 5)^T$

Table 6: Results of the I_H^- performance measure for NN-SS-IBEA and the classical IBEA on DTLZ problems.

	NN-SS-IBEA	IBEA
DTLZ1	**0.2E-05*** (0.8E-06)	0.1E-07(0.7E-08)
DTLZ2	**0.192***(0.005)	0.340(0.024)
DTLZ3	0.1E-09 (0.9E-10)	**0.3E-08**(0.1E-08)
DTLZ4	**0.138***(0.085)	0.964(0.658)
DTLZ5	**0.192***(0.005)	0.352(0.030)
DTLZ6	0.9E-14(0.4E-14)	**0.6E-10**(0.1E-09)
DTLZ7	**0.053***(0.023)	0.087(0.053)

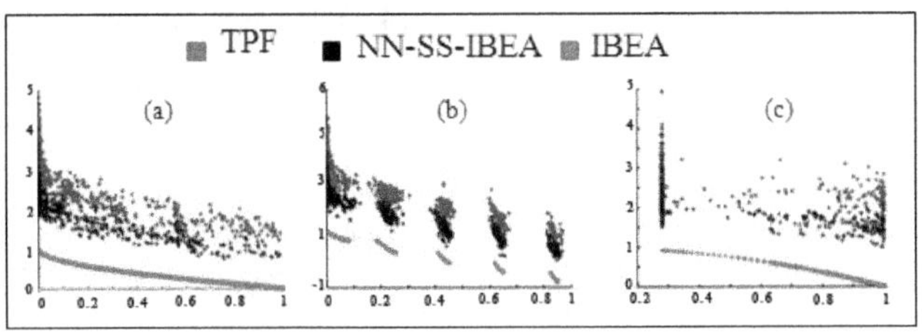

Figure 4: The non-dominated solutions of IBEA and NN-SS-IBEA for all 50 runs on the various problems; ZDT1, ZDT3 et ZDT6 respectively, after 1000 evaluations.

Results of RQ1 (Effectiveness and Computationally Efficient Search): To answer RQ1, we compared our approach against the original IBEA and MOEA/D-RBF on a set of benchmark problems.

- **Standard test problems**

Table 4 shows the results obtained for the I_H^- performance measure when the algorithms are tested on the ZDT test problems using eight decision variables. From this table, it can be clearly seen that the best results were obtained by NN-SS-IBEA. With respect to our proposed approach and MOEA/D-RBF, it is possible to see that NN-SS-IBEA obtained better results than those obtained by MOEA/D-RBF in all of the adopted MOPs.

In Table 5, we show the results obtained by NN-SS-IBEA, the classical IBEA and MOEA/D-RBF in the ZDT test problems using 30 and 10 decision variables, respectively. From this table it is possible to see that NN-SS-IBEA obtained a better approximation to PF than the one achieved by MOEA/D-RBF in most of the test problems adopted. This comparison was performed in order to show the effectiveness of our proposed NN-SS-IBEA in terms of the quality of the solutions that it reached with respect to the solutions obtained by the classical IBEA and MOEA/D-RBF. As we can see, NN-SS-IBEA significantly outperformed the classical IBEA and MOEA/D-RBF in most of the ZDT test problems.

From the results in table 6, it can be observed that the classical IBEA, fared significantly poorer than the NN-SS-IBEA on at least 4 out of the 7 problems considered.

In the Figure 4, we present the converged non-dominated solutions obtained by the classical IBEA and our proposed approach NN-SS-IBEA at 1000 evaluations for some problems that are considered in the study, with Subfigures 5(a), 5(b) and 5(c) depicting the representative convex, concave and discontinuous test problems. TPF denotes the true Pareto front. From the figure, it can be observed that overall the non-dominated solutions attained by NN-SS-IBEA are closer to the true Pareto front than those of the classical IBEA.

Results of RQ2 (Real World Problems): To answer RQ2, we compared our approach against the original IBEA and MOEA/D-RBF using an airfoil design problem.

- **Airfoil design problem**

According to Table 7, we can see that NN-SS-IBEA obtained better hypervolume values than the classical IBEA and MOEA/D-RBF. The classical IBEA and MOEA/D-RBF employed, repectively, on average, 4,550 and 2,000 seconds to achieve the value reported in Table 7 in the I_H performance measure, while our NN-SS-IBEA required 1,250 seconds to achieve a similar value. Thus, we argue that our proposed NN-SS-IBEA is a good choice for dealing with computationally expensive MOPs.

5. CONCLUSIONS AND FUTURE WORKS

This paper aims at developing a method called NN-SS-IBEA, for approximating the Pareto front of an expensive MOP. The core novelty of our work lies in the construction of surrogates MLP-NN that directly predict the hypervolume indicator value of the offspring instead of calculate the fitness values using the original objective function. Experimental results on a set of standard test problems have shown

Table 7: Results of the I_H performance measure for NN-SS-IBEA, IBEA and MOEA/D-RBF on the airfoil design problem.

MOP	NN-SS-IBEA	IBEA	MOEA/D-RBF	Reference point (r)
MOPR	**2.9E-07***(8.1E-09)	2.3E-07 (1.9E-08)	2.4E-07 (6.4E-09)	$(0.007610, 0.005236)^T$

that NN-SS-IBEA is able to outperform both to the classical IBEA and to MOEA/D-RBF when performing only 200 and 1,000 fitness function evaluations. We also validated our proposed approach with a real-world computationally expensive MOP: airfoil design. This illustrates the potential of our proposed approach for solving computationally expensive MOPs.
As part of our future work, we plan to use our approach in problems having three or more objectives. Also, we pretend to couple to our approach a local search mechanism, so that, while NN-SS-IBEA obtains candidate solutions to be evaluated with the real fitness function, the local search refines these solutions, thus accelerating the convergence towards the true Pareto front. In addition, we plan to incorporate decision's maker preference information in expensive MOPs[1]. Finally, we are also interested in testing our approach with more real-world problems having more decision variables, and that is indeed part of our ongoing research.

6. REFERENCES

[1] S. Bechikh. *Incorporating Decision Maker's Preference Information in Evolutionary Multi-objective Optimization.* PhD thesis, High Institute of Management of Tunis, University of Tunis, Tunisia, 2013.

[2] K. Deb. *Multi-Objective Optimization using Evolutionary Algorithms.* Wiley-Interscience Series in Systems and Optimization. John Wiley and Sons, Chichester, 2001.

[3] K. Deb, L. Thiele, M. Laumanns, and E. Zitzler. Scalable multi-objective optimization test problems. volume 1, pages 825–830, 2002.

[4] M.T. Emmerich, K. Giannakoglou, and B. Naujoks. Single- and multiobjective evolutionary optimization assisted by gaussian random field metamodels. *IEEE Trans. Evolutionary Computation*, 10(4):421–439, 2006.

[5] A. Gaspar-Cunhaa and A. Vieira. A multi-objective evolutionary algorithm using neural networks to approximate fitness evaluations. *International Journal of Computers, Systems, and Signals*, 6(1):18–36, 2005.

[6] R. L. Iman and W. J. Conover. A distribution-free approach to inducing rank correlation among input variables. *Communication in Statistics*, B11(3):311–334, 1982.

[7] Y. Jin. A comprehensive survey of fitness approximation in evolutionary computation. *Soft Computing*, 9(1):3–12, 2005.

[8] Y. Jin, M. Olhofer, and B. Sendhoff. Managing approximate models in evolutionary aerodynamic design optimization. In *In Proceedings of IEEE Congress on Evolutionary Computation*, pages 592–599. IEEE Press, 2001.

[9] Y. Jin, M. Olhofer, and B. Sendhoff. A framework for evolutionary optimization with approximate fitness functions. *IEEE Transactions on Evolutionary Computation*, 6(5):481–494, 2002.

[10] S. Z. Martinez and C. A. Coello Coello. Moea/d assisted by rbf networks for expensive multi-objective optimization problems. In Christian Blum and Enrique Alba, editors, *GECCO*, pages 1405–1412. ACM, 2013.

[11] C. L. Mumford. Simple population replacement strategies for a steady-state multi-objective evolutionary algorithm. In *Genetic and Evolutionary Computation Conference*, pages 1389–1400. Springer, juin 2004.

[12] Y. S. Ong, A. J. Keane, and P. B. Nair. Evolutionary optimization of computationally expensive problems via surrogate modeling. *American Institute of Aeronautics and Astronautics Journal*, 41(4):687–696, 2003.

[13] A. OSYCZKA. Multicriteria optimization for engineering design. *In Design Optimization, J. S. Gero, Ed. Academic Press, Inc., New York, NY,*, pages 193–227, 1985.

[14] L. V. Santana-Quintero, A. A. Montano, and C. A. Coello Coello. *A review of techniques for handling expensive functions in evolutionary multi-objective optimization*, chapter 1, pages 29–59. Berlin: Springer-Verlag, 2010.

[15] H. Sobieczky. Parametric airfoils and wings. In Kozo Fujii and GeorgeS Dulikravich, editors, *Recent Development of Aerodynamic Design Methodologies*, volume 65 of *Notes on Numerical Fluid Mechanics (NNFM)*, pages 71–87. Vieweg+Teubner Verlag, 1999.

[16] A. Szollos, M. Smid, and J. Hajek. Aerodynamic optimization via multi-objective micro-genetic algorithm with range adaptation, knowledge-based reinitialization, crowding and epsilon-dominance. *Advances in Engineering Software*, 40:419–430, 2009.

[17] D. Verbeeck, F. Maes, K. D. Grave, and H. Blockeel. Multi-objective optimization with surrogate trees. In *GECCO*, pages 679–686. ACM, 2013.

[18] G. D. Wyss and K. H. Jorgensen. A user's guide to lhs: Sandia's latin hypercube sampling software. Technical report, SAND98-0210. Sandia National Laboratories, Albuquerque, NM., 1998.

[19] Q. Zhang, W. Liu, E. Tsang, and B. Virginas. Expensive multiobjective optimization by moea/d with gaussian process model. *IEEE Trans. Evolutionary Computation*, 14(3):456–474, 2010.

[20] E. Zitzler, K. Deb, and L. Thiele. Comparison of multiobjective evolutionary algorithms: Empirical results. *Evolutionary Computation*, 8:173–195, 2000.

[21] E. Zitzler, L. Thiele, M. Laumanns, C. M. Fonseca, and V. G. da Fonseca. Performance assessment of multiobjective optimizers: An analysis and review. *IEEE Transactions on Evolutionary Computation*, 7(2):117–132, 2003.

Two-dimensional Subset Selection for Hypervolume and Epsilon-Indicator

Karl Bringmann
Max Planck Institute for Informatics
Saarbrücken, Germany

Tobias Friedrich
Friedrich-Schiller-Universität Jena
Jena, Germany

Patrick Klitzke
Universität des Saarlandes
Saarbrücken, Germany

ABSTRACT

The goal of bi-objective optimization is to find a small set of good compromise solutions. A common problem for bi-objective evolutionary algorithms is the following subset selection problem (SSP): Given n solutions $P \subset \mathbb{R}^2$ in the objective space, select k solutions P^* from P that optimize an indicator function. In the hypervolume SSP we want to select k points P^* that maximize the hypervolume indicator $\mathcal{I}_{\text{hyp}}(P^*, r)$ for some reference point $r \in \mathbb{R}^2$. Similarly, the ε-indicator SSP aims at selecting k points P^* that minimize the ε-indicator $\mathcal{I}_{\text{eps}}(P^*, R)$ for some reference set $R \subset \mathbb{R}^2$ of size m (which can be $R = P$).

We first present a new algorithm for the hypervolume SSP with runtime $\mathcal{O}(n\,(k + \log n))$. Our second main result is a new algorithm for the ε-indicator SSP with runtime $\mathcal{O}(n \log n + m \log m)$. Both results improve the current state of the art runtimes by a factor of (nearly) n and make the problems tractable for new applications. Preliminary experiments confirm that the theoretical results translate into substantial empirical runtime improvements.

Categories and Subject Descriptors

F.2 [**Theory of Computation**]:
Analysis of Algorithms and Problem Complexity

General Terms

Measurement, Archiving Algorithms, Performance, Hypervolume-Indicator, Epsilon-Indicator

1. INTRODUCTION

In the general Subset Selection Problem (SSP) we are given a set $P \subset \mathbb{R}^d$ of size n and a positive integer k. The task is to select a subset $P^* \subseteq P$ of size k that maximizes (or minimizes) $\mathcal{I}(P^*)$ for some indicator function $\mathcal{I}$. We study the two-dimensional case $d = 2$ and present new results for two common indicator functions.

The hypervolume indicator $\mathcal{I}_{\text{hyp}}(P^*, r)$ of a set P^* measures the volume of the space dominated by P^* up to some fixed reference point r (for formal definitions see Section 2). The aim of the *Hypervolume Subset Selection Problem* (HYPSSP) is to maximize $\mathcal{I}_{\text{hyp}}(P^*, r)$. The second indicator we consider is the ε-indicator $\mathcal{I}_{\text{eps}}(P^*, R)$, which is defined relative to a reference set $R \subset \mathbb{R}^d$ of size m (one may choose $P = R$) and measures how well P^* approximates R. The aim of the *ε-Indicator Subset Selection Problem* (EPSSSP) is to minimize $\mathcal{I}_{\text{eps}}(P^*, R)$.

Motivation. Subset selection problems occur frequently in all population-based search heuristics. We describe two specific applications. First, consider a hypervolume-based $(\mu + \lambda)$-evolutionary multiobjective algorithm (EMOA) such as SIBEA [20], SMS-EMOA [5], or the generational MO-CMA-ES [13, 14]. In every generation we have μ parents and generate λ offspring. From these $\mu + \lambda$ solutions we want to select the next population of size μ. Since our overall goal is to maximize the hypervolume indicator, we want to choose these μ points such that they maximize the hypervolume among all size-μ sets, which is an instance of HYPSSP by choosing $k = \mu$ and $n = \mu + \lambda$. Typically, $\lambda \approx \mu$ so that $k \approx n/2$. For a discussion why in general a greedy approach with $\lambda = 1$ cannot find a set with maximal hypervolume, see [7, 8].

Similarly, there are ε-indicator-based algorithms such as AGE [9], where we have a reference set R (that changes over time) and want to select the next generation such that we minimize the ε-indicator with respect to R.

A second motivation lies in the evaluation of indicator-based EMOAs by running them on test problems. When running many different EMOAs on a test problem, it would be nice to be able to compare them with the optimal set of μ points. Now, test problems are often designed in such a way that we know the Pareto front explicitly, but this does not directly yield the optimal hypervolume achievable with μ points. To compute this number, we may discretize the Pareto front, to get a good finite approximation P of the Pareto front. Solving HYPSSP on the point set P with $k = \mu$ now yields (an approximation of) the desired value, the optimal hypervolume achievable with μ points on this test problem. Note that in this situation we want to choose $n = |P|$ as large as possible to get a good approximation, while $k = \mu \ll n$.

Results on Hypervolume Subset Selection. For 2 dimensions there are algorithms which solve HYPSSP in time $\mathcal{O}(n^3)$ [4], $\mathcal{O}(kn^2)$ [3] and $\mathcal{O}(n^2)$ [16]. The only known lower bound is the trivial $\Omega(n)$. Note that the lower bounds of $\Omega(n \log n)$ for computing the hypervolume [6] and computing all contributions [12] in two dimensions do not imply a lower bound for HYPSSP as we are computing a set of points and not volumes. In higher dimensions, no algorithm is known that is faster than enumerating all $\binom{n}{k}$ subsets of P of size k (see, e.g., [8]). In Section 3 we present a novel algorithm that shows the following.

Theorem 1. *Two-dimensional* HYPSSP *can be solved in time*

$$\mathcal{O}(n\,(k + \log n)).$$

GECCO'14, July 12–16, 2014, Vancouver, BC, Canada.

ACM 978-1-4503-2662-9/14/07 ...$15.00.
http://dx.doi.org/10.1145/2576768.2598276.

This improves all previous algorithms by roughly a factor n. Our preliminary experiments practically confirm this theoretical improvement (cf. [1]). Our algorithmic improvement is based on a rarely cited, but very useful idea of Brucker [10]. In programming contests this approach is known as the *convex hull trick* [2].

Results on ε-Indicator Subset Selection. EPSSSP was first studied by Ponte, Paquete, and Figueira [18], who gave an $\mathcal{O}(nm\log(nm))$ time algorithm for dimension $d = 2$. Recently, Vaz, Paquete, and Ponte [19] slightly improved this algorithm by lowering the log-factor, however, the runtime remains $\Omega(nm)$. Again, in higher dimensions, no algorithm is known that is faster than enumerating all subsets of P of size k.

In a different community, Koltun and Papadimitriou [15] studied a variant of EPSSSP (under the name of "approximately dominating representatives" of "skylines"). In their variant they do not fix a bound k on the size of the selected set $|P^*|$, but they fix a bound ε on the quality $\mathcal{I}_{\text{eps}}(P^*, R)$ and minimize $|P^*|$ with respect to this bound. Moreover, they only consider the case $P = R$. They showed that in 2 dimensions their variant can be solved in $\mathcal{O}(n)$ time (after sorting). Intuitively, their problem variant is simpler than ours, since any algorithm for our variant yields an algorithm for their variant (with roughly the same runtime) by using a binary search over $k \in \{1, \ldots, n\}$. In the opposite direction, such a reduction does not work, since the quantity $\varepsilon^* := \mathcal{I}_{\text{eps}}(P^*, R)$ is a real number. Hence binary search for ε^* may go on forever, computing better and better approximations of ε^*, but never the correct value. In this sense, we are tackling a harder problem in this paper.

We present in Section 4 a novel algorithm for EPSSSP in 2 dimensions. It is randomized in that its runtime is a random variable that is small in expectation and with high probability (i.e., with probability $1 - n^{-c}$ for any fixed $c > 0$). The result of our randomized algorithm is guaranteed to be correct. We use an extension of the result of Koltun and Papadimitriou [15] as a subroutine.

Theorem 2. *Two-dimensional* EPSSSP *can be solved with a randomized algorithm in time (in expectation and with high probability)*

$$\mathcal{O}(n\log n + m\log m).$$

This answers an open problem of Vaz et al. [19], of whether there is a subquadratic time algorithm for EPSSSP (although they might have intended a deterministic algorithm, while we present a randomized one). Again, this improves the state of the art by roughly a factor of n (at least if $n = m$), which is confirmed by preliminary experiments (cf. [1]).

2. PRELIMINARIES

We consider maximization problems with vector-valued objective functions $f\colon \mathcal{X} \to \mathbb{R}^d$, where $\mathcal{X}$ denotes an arbitrary search space. The feasible points $\mathcal{Y} := f(\mathcal{X})$ are called the objective space. In this paper we *only work in the objective space*, i.e., we always consider points in $\mathbb{R}^d$ and may ignore that these points stem from a search space $\mathcal{X}$.

We say that a point $p = (p_1, \ldots, p_d) \in \mathbb{R}^d$ *(weakly) dominates* a point $q = (q_1, \ldots, q_d) \in \mathbb{R}^d$ ($q \preceq p$) iff $p_i \geqslant q_i$ for all $1 \leqslant i \leqslant d$.

In the definitions in this Section 2 we consider the general case of $d \in \mathbb{N}, d \geqslant 2$. We note, however, that in all subsequent sections we will work in dimension $d = 2$.

2.1 Hypervolume indicator

For a set $P \subset \mathbb{R}^d$ the *hypervolume indicator* (with respect to the reference point $r \in \mathbb{R}^d$) is defined defined as

$$\mathcal{I}_{\text{hyp}}(P, r) := \int_{\mathbb{R}^d} A(z)\, dz,$$

where $A\colon \mathbb{R}^d \to \{0, 1\}$ is the *attainment function* and $A(z) = 1$ if and only if $r \preceq z$ and there is a point $p \in P$ with $z \preceq p$. Thus, $\mathcal{I}_{\text{hyp}}(P, r)$ measures the volume of the space "between" r and P.

We study the following problem:

> **Problem HYPSSP:** Given $k \in \mathbb{N}$, $r \in \mathbb{R}^d$, and a set $P \subset \mathbb{R}^d$ of size n, compute a subset $P^* \subseteq P$ of size at most k that maximizes $\mathcal{I}_{\text{hyp}}(P^*, r)$.

We note three *standard simplifications*. First, we can without loss of generality assume that $r = (0, \ldots, 0)$, since translation of P by $-r$ reduces to this situation. We write

$$\mathcal{I}_{\text{hyp}}(P) := \mathcal{I}_{\text{hyp}}(P, (0, \ldots, 0))$$

for short. Then we can assume that $P \subset \mathbb{R}^d_{>0}$, since points with non-positive coordinates do not contribute to the hypervolume.

Second, we can assume that there are no two points $p, q \in P$ with $p \preceq q$ (in which case we say that P is *non-dominating*), since there is an optimal solution containing no dominated point: In any solution $P' \subseteq P$ that contains p we can replace p by q (or simply delete p, if P' already contains q) without increasing the size of P' or decreasing $\mathcal{I}_{\text{hyp}}(P')$. Thus, we may simply delete any dominated point in P. We note that in 2 dimensions we can delete all dominated points from P in $\mathcal{O}(n\log n)$ time [17], so this assumption can be ensured in our alloted runtime.

Finally, in 2 dimensions we can assume that the points $P = \{p_1, \ldots, p_n\}$ are *sorted* by increasing x-coordinate. It is not hard to see that, since P is non-dominating, in this case the points are also sorted by decreasing y-coordinate. Again this can be ensured in time $\mathcal{O}(n\log n)$.

In 2 dimensions, we denote the x- and y-coordinates of a point $p \in \mathbb{R}^2$ by p_x and p_y. Then for reference point $(0, 0)$ and for a sorted non-dominating set $P = \{p^1, \ldots, p^n\} \subset \mathbb{R}^d_{>0}$ we have $0 < p^1_x < \ldots < p^n_x$ and $p^1_y > \ldots > p^n_y > 0$.

2.2 ε-Indicator

In this paper we consider additive approximation. By taking the logarithm, our algorithm also works in the multiplicative setting. For points $p = (p_1, \ldots, p_d)$, $r = (r_1, \ldots, r_d) \in \mathbb{R}^d$, we set

$$\mathcal{I}_{\text{eps}}(p, r) := \max_{1 \leqslant i \leqslant d} r_i - p_i.$$

This denotes the minimal number ε by which we have to increase p in all coordinates so that it dominates q. This number measures how well p approximates q. For finite sets of points $P, R \subset \mathbb{R}^d$ the ε-indicator is defined as

$$\mathcal{I}_{\text{eps}}(P, R) := \max_{r \in R} \min_{p \in P} \mathcal{I}_{\text{eps}}(p, r).$$

This denotes the minimal number ε by which we have to increase all points in P in all coordinates so that every point in R is dominated by some point in P. It measures how well P approximates R. We say that P ε-approximates R if $\mathcal{I}_{\text{eps}}(P, R) \leqslant \varepsilon$.

In the following, we consider R as a fixed reference set and want to select a subset P^* of P that best approximates R subject to a size constraint. Note that it is allowed to set $P = R$.

> **Problem EPSSSP:** Given $k \in \mathbb{N}$, $R \subset \mathbb{R}^d$ of size m, and a set $P \subset \mathbb{R}^d$ of size n, compute a subset $P^* \subseteq P$ of size at most k that minimizes $\mathcal{I}_{\text{eps}}(P^*, R)$.

Similar to the simplifications for HYPSSP, we may delete all dominated points in P (since there is an optimal solution containing no dominated point) and in R (since if we approximate the dominating point then we also approximate the dominated one). Additionally, we can assume that P and R are sorted. In 2 dimensions, this can again be ensured in the alloted runtime $\mathcal{O}(n \log n + m \log m)$. In the remainder of the paper we always work in $d = 2$ dimensions.

3. ALGORITHM FOR HYPSSP

After the standard simplifications described above in Section 2, we are given a set $P = \{p^1, \dots, p^n\}$ with $0 < p_x^1 < \dots < p_x^n$ and $p_y^1 > \dots > p_y^n > 0$, and an integer k. Recall that our goal is to compute a set $P^* \subseteq P$ of size at most k that maximizes $\mathcal{I}_{\text{hyp}}(P^*) = \mathcal{I}_{\text{hyp}}(P^*, (0,0))$. We first present an algorithm that computes $\mathcal{I}_{\text{hyp}}(P^*)$, i.e., the maximal hypervolume instead of a set of points achieving the maximal hypervolume. In Section 3.3 we then explain how we can reconstruct P^* from our computation of $\mathcal{I}_{\text{hyp}}(P^*)$.

3.1 The Algorithm

Note that our reference point for $\mathcal{I}_{\text{hyp}}$ is $(0,0)$ (which we can assume by transforming the problem instance accordingly). During our computation we will, however, consider hypervolumes with respect to other reference points, as follows.

We define H_i^ℓ as the maximum hypervolume achievable with at most ℓ points and reference point $(p_x^i, 0)$, for any $0 \leqslant \ell \leqslant k$ and $1 \leqslant i \leqslant n$. Since the points $p^1, \dots, p^i$ do not contribute anything when the reference point is $(p_x^i, 0)$, we have

$$H_i^\ell = \max_{Q \subseteq_\ell \{p^{i+1}, \dots, p^n\}} \mathcal{I}_{\text{hyp}}(Q, (p_x^i, 0)),$$

where we use $A \subseteq_\ell B$ as a shorthand for $A \subseteq B$, $|A| \leqslant \ell$. We extend the definition of H_i^ℓ to $i = 0$ by setting $p_x^0 := 0$. Note that H_0^k is the maximal hypervolume of any k points in P with reference point $(0,0)$. In other words, $H_0^k = \mathcal{I}_{\text{hyp}}(P^*)$ is what we want to compute.

Moreover, we define $F_i^\ell(x)$ as the maximum hypervolume achievable with at most ℓ points, with p^i being the first of these points, and reference point $(x, 0)$, for any $1 \leqslant \ell \leqslant k$, $1 \leqslant i \leqslant n$, and $x \leqslant p_x^i$. Formally, we have

$$F_i^\ell(x) = \max_{\substack{Q \subseteq_\ell \{p^i, \dots, p^n\} \\ p^i \in Q}} \mathcal{I}_{\text{hyp}}(Q, (x, 0))$$

We will use the functions $F_i^\ell(x)$ in order to compute the values $H_{i'}^{\ell'}$, and vice versa, on our way of computing H_0^k. The next lemma shows how to compute $H_0^\ell, \dots, H_{n-1}^\ell$ from $F_1^\ell(x), \dots, F_n^\ell(x)$.

Lemma 3. *For any* $0 \leqslant i < n$ *and* $1 \leqslant \ell \leqslant k$ *we have*

$$H_i^\ell = \max_{i < j \leqslant n} F_j^\ell(p_x^i).$$

Proof. If the selected set Q is empty then the hypervolume is $\mathcal{I}_{\text{hyp}}(Q, r) = 0$ (for any reference point r). Otherwise Q contains at least one point; let p^j be the leftmost of these points. We obtain

$$\begin{aligned} H_i^\ell &= \max_{Q \subseteq_\ell \{p^{i+1}, \dots, p^n\}} \mathcal{I}_{\text{hyp}}(Q, (p_x^i, 0)) \\ &= \max\Big\{0, \max_{i < j \leqslant n} \max_{\substack{Q \subseteq_\ell \{p^j, \dots, p^n\} \\ p^j \in Q}} \mathcal{I}_{\text{hyp}}(Q, (p_x^i, 0))\Big\} \\ &= \max\{0, \max_{i < j \leqslant n} F_j^\ell(p_x^i)\}. \end{aligned}$$

We finish the proof by noting that $F_j^\ell(p_x^i) \geqslant 0$. □

The second relation shows how to compute $F_i^\ell(x)$ from $H_i^{\ell-1}$.

Lemma 4. *For any* $1 \leqslant i \leqslant n$, $1 \leqslant \ell \leqslant k$, *and* $x \leqslant p_x^i$ *we have*

$$F_i^\ell(x) = -p_y^i \cdot x + \left(p_y^i p_x^i + H_i^{\ell-1}\right).$$

In particular, the above lemma shows that $F_i^\ell(x)$ is a linear function $a \cdot x + b$ in variable x. Its coefficients a and b can be read of Lemma 4 once we have computed $H_i^{\ell-1}$. Note that the slope of $F_i^\ell(x)$ is $\text{slope}(F_i^\ell(x)) = -p_y^i$ so that the functions $F_1^\ell, \dots, F_n^\ell$ are sorted by increasing slope. Moreover, we can store the function $F_i^\ell(x)$ succinctly by only storing its coefficients a, b. This allows to evaluate F_i^ℓ at any given point x in constant time.

Proof of Lemma 4. Recall that in the definition of $F_i^\ell(x)$ the point p^i is required to be in the chosen set Q. We can split the hypervolume $F_i^\ell(x)$ into a part to the left of p_x^i (which is simply $\mathcal{I}_{\text{hyp}}(\{p^i\}, (x, 0))$) and a part to the right of p_x^i (which can be expressed as a hypervolume of at most $\ell - 1$ points with reference point $(p_x^i, 0)$, since we cut off at p_x^i). Formally, we have

$$\begin{aligned} F_i^\ell(x) &= \max_{\substack{Q \subseteq_\ell \{p^i, \dots, p^n\} \\ p^i \in Q}} \mathcal{I}_{\text{hyp}}(Q, (x, 0)) \\ &= \mathcal{I}_{\text{hyp}}(\{p^i\}, (x, 0)) + \max_{Q \subseteq_{\ell-1} \{p^{i+1}, \dots, p^n\}} \mathcal{I}_{\text{hyp}}(Q, (p_x^i, 0)). \end{aligned}$$

We finish the proof by noting that the first summand on the right hand side equals $p_y^i(p_x^i - x)$ and the second summand is $H_i^{\ell-1}$. □

Plugging these two lemmas together yields an algorithm for computing the desired maximal hypervolume $\mathcal{I}_{\text{hyp}}(P^*) = H_0^k$, see Algorithm 1. Observe that for initialization we can use $H_i^0 = H_n^\ell = 0$ for all $0 \leqslant i \leqslant n$ and $1 \leqslant \ell \leqslant k$.

Concerning runtime, note that the trivial evaluation of Lemma 3 (line 6 of Algorithm 1) takes $\Theta(n^2)$ time (as we have to iterate over $1 \leqslant i < j \leqslant n$). In the next section we present a faster evaluation method, Algorithm 2, that runs in time $\mathcal{O}(n)$. This speedup is the core trick of our new algorithm. It is easy to see that then Algorithm 1 runs in time $\mathcal{O}(nk)$. Since we have to ensure that the input P is non-dominating and sorted, which takes time $\mathcal{O}(n \log n)$, we obtain a total runtime of $\mathcal{O}(n(k + \log n))$ to solve HYPSSP. The space requirement is $\mathcal{O}(n)$, since we can forget $H_0^{\ell-1}, \dots, H_n^{\ell-1}$ and $F_1^{\ell-1}, \dots, F_n^{\ell-1}$ once we have computed $H_0^\ell, \dots, H_n^\ell$ and $F_1^\ell, \dots, F_n^\ell$.

3.2 Upper Envelope

We want to find a linear time algorithm for the following problem: Given a sequence of linear functions with increasing slopes and a set of x-coordinates given in increasing order, compute the maximal value of all those functions for each coordinate. More formally we are given $F_1^\ell(x), \dots, F_n^\ell(x)$ with $\text{slope}(F_1^\ell) < \dots < \text{slope}(F_n^\ell)$ and coordinates $p_x^0 < \dots < p_x^{n-1}$ and want to compute the values

$$H_i^\ell = \max_{i < j \leqslant n} F_j^\ell(p_x^i) \quad \text{for all } 0 \leqslant i < n.$$

Algorithm 1: HYPSSP in 2 dimensions

Input: set $P = \{p^1, .., p^n\}$ with $0 < p_x^1 < ... < p_x^n$ and $p_y^1 > ... > p_y^n > 0$

$p_x^0 := 0$

for $i = 0$ **to** n **do** $H_i^0 := 0$

for $\ell = 1$ **to** k **do**

  for $i = 1$ **to** n **do** compute (the coefficients of) the linear function $F_i^\ell(x) := -p_y^i \cdot x + \left(p_y^i p_x^i + H_i^{\ell-1}\right)$

  $H_n^\ell := 0$

  $H_i^\ell := \max_{i<j\leqslant n} F_j^\ell(p_x^i)$ for $0 \leqslant i < n$ (using Algorithm 2)

return H_0^k

Algorithm 2: Upper Envelope

Input: coordinates $x_1 < .. < x_n$, linear functions $f_1, ..., f_n$ with slope$(f_1) < ... <$ slope(f_n)

1 Dequeue $S := \emptyset$

2 **for** $i = 1$ **to** n **do**

3   **while** $|S| > 1$ **and** $\otimes(f_i, S_{|S|-1}) \leqslant \otimes(S_{|S|}, S_{|S|-1})$ **do**

4   S.popBack() *// delete $S_{|S|}$*

5   S.append(f_i)

6   **while** $|S| > 1$ **and** $\otimes(S_1, S_2) \leqslant x_i$ **do**

7   S.popFront() *// delete S_1*

8   $h_i := S_1(x_i)$ *// evaluate function S_1 at position x_i*

9 return $h_1, \ldots, h_n$

Note that the function $\max_{i<j\leqslant n} F_j^\ell(x)$ is an *upper envelope* of linear functions. Since the space above such an upper envelope is convex, the technique of reducing a problem to evaluations of upper envelopes is known as the *convex hull trick* [2].

For the sake of readability, we mirror x and all indices so that from now on we consider $f_1, \ldots, f_n$ and $x_1, \ldots, x_n$ with $f_i(x) := F_{n+1-i}(-x)$ and $x_i := -p_x^{n-i}$. Then we have $x_1 < \ldots < x_n$ and slope$(f_1) < \ldots <$ slope(f_n), and the goal is to compute $h_i = \max_{1\leqslant j\leqslant i} f_j(x_i)$, which equals the desired value H_i^ℓ. Since each function f_j describes a line, the function

$$U_i(x) := \max_{1\leqslant j\leqslant i} f_j(x)$$

describes the *upper envelope* of those lines. Hence, our goal is to evaluate (incremental) upper envelopes of lines at given positions. Since U_i is an upper envelope, it describes an x-monotone polygonal chain (since the part of U_i, where a particular f_j is maximal, is a line segment). By following the upper envelope from left to right, we first follow $f_{j(1)}$, then $f_{j(2)}$, and so on, until we finally follow $f_{j(h)}$. We represent this upper envelope by the sequence $(f_{j(1)}, \ldots, f_{j(h)})$. With slight abuse of notation we write $U_i = (f_{j(1)}, \ldots, f_{j(h)})$.

Computing the upper envelope of lines is a standard task in computational geometry and can be done in linear time (since our functions f_j are already sorted by slope) [11]. You can find the standard algorithm for this task by considering lines 1–5 of Algorithm 2. Here, we use a standard dequeue S containing linear functions, and we denote the elements of S by $S_1, \ldots, S_{|S|}$. Moreover, we denote the x-coordinate of the intersection of two linear functions f and g by $\otimes(f, g)$; this can be computed in constant time. If we deleted lines 6–8 from Algorithm 2, then after the i-th iteration the dequeue S would contain exactly the upper envelope U_i, in our representation as a sequence $(f_{j(1)}, \ldots, f_{j(h)})$.

Through lines 6–8 of Algorithm 2 we have adapted the standard upper envelope algorithm as follows. In every iteration, we search for the element of the upper envelope $U_i = (f_{j(1)}, \ldots, f_{j(h)})$ that is maximal at position x_i. Say, $f_{j(v)}(x_i)$ is maximal among all $f_j(x_i)$, $1 \leqslant j \leqslant i$. Since $x_1, \ldots, x_n$ are sorted ascendingly, any function $f_{j(v')}$, $v' < v$, can be deleted, since it will not be of importance to any x_j, $j > i$. Finally, we evaluate $f_{j(v)}$ at x_i, which yields h_i. This explains lines 6–8 of Algorithm 2.

Runtime. The runtime of Algorithm 2 is linear, since we can amortize the append() operations and deletions. There are exactly n append() operations, since in each iteration of the loop we add one element to S. Thus, we can perform at most n deletions in total, and the overall runtime is $\mathcal{O}(n)$.

Correctness. Intuitively, we prove that in the i-th iteration the dequeue S contains all functions (in sorted order) that appear in the upper envelope of $f_1, \ldots, f_i$ restricted to the halfplane $\{(x, y) \in \mathbb{R}^2 \mid x \geqslant x_i\}$. Thus, indeed the first entry S_1 corresponds to the segment of the upper envelope of $f_1, \ldots, f_i$ that contains x_i, so we correctly compute h_i.

In the previous section we defined $U_i = (f_{j(1)}, \ldots, f_{j(h)})$ as the upper envelope of $f_1, \ldots, f_i$. Note that the function $f_{j(v)}$ is maximal among all f_j for any x between the intersections of $f_{j(v-1)}$ and $f_{j(v)}$ and the intersection of $f_{j(v)}$ and $f_{j(v+1)}$. More formally, for all $1 < v < h$ the value $f_{j(v)}(x)$ is maximal among all $f_j(x)$ for any $x \in [\otimes(f_{j(v-1)}, f_{j(v)}), \otimes(f_{j(v)}, f_{j(v+1)})] =: I_v(U_i)$, and $f_{j(1)}(x)$ is maximal for any $x \in (-\infty, \otimes(f_{j(1)}, f_{j(2)})] =: I_1(U_i)$, and $f_{j(h)}(x)$ is maximal for any $x \in [\otimes(f_{j(h-1)}, f_{j(h)}), \infty) =: I_h(U_i)$. This way, the real line is partitioned into $I_1(U_i) \cup \ldots \cup I_h(U_i)$, such that function $f_{j(v)}$ is maximal among all f_j, $1 \leqslant j \leqslant i$, in interval $I_v(U_i)$.

For proving correctness we show that at the end of the i-th iteration the following invariant holds.

Lemma 5. *Let $U_i = (f_{j(1)}, f_{j(2)}, \ldots, f_{j(h)})$ be the upper envelope of $f_1, \ldots, f_i$ and let a be such that $x_i \in I_a(U_i)$. Then after the end of the i-th iteration the dequeue S is*

$$S = (f_{j(a)}, f_{j(a+1)}, \ldots, f_{j(h)}).$$

Note that this invariant implies correctness of the computed value h_i: Since $x_i \in I_a(U_i)$, function $f_{j(a)}$ is maximal among $f_1, \ldots, f_i$ at position x_i. Hence, we have

$$h_i = \max_{1\leqslant j\leqslant i} f_j(x_i) = f_{j(a)}(x_i) = S_1(x_i).$$

Proof. We argue that the invariant holds true. By induction, we can assume that it is true at the end of iteration $i - 1$, so that $S = (f_{j(a)}, f_{j(a+1)}, \ldots, f_{j(h)})$, where $U_{i-1} = (f_{j(1)}, f_{j(2)}, \ldots, f_{j(h)})$ is the upper envelope of $f_1, \ldots, f_{i-1}$, and $x_{i-1} \in I_a(U_{i-1})$. We show that it also holds after iteration i.

Observe that $S = (f_{j(a)}, \ldots, f_{j(h)})$, being a subsequence of an upper envelope, is itself the upper envelope of $\{f_{j(a)}, f_{j(a)+1} \ldots, f_{i-2}, f_{i-1}\}$. Hence, lines 3–5 of Algorithm 2 correctly compute the upper envelope $U' = (f_{j'(1)}, f_{j'(2)}, \ldots, f_{j'(g)})$ of $\{f_{j(a)}, f_{j(a)+1} \ldots, f_{i-1}, f_i\}$, since this is the well-known algorithm for computing upper envelopes (for a proof of correctness of this algorithm we essentially show that we can delete $S_{|S|}$ if and only if it lies underneath f_i in the interval $(\otimes(S_{|S|}, S_{|S|-1}), \infty)$, and this happens if and only if $\otimes(f_i, S_{|S|-1}) \leqslant \otimes(S_{|S|}, S_{|S|-1})$).

Since we know that $f_1, \ldots, f_{j(a)-1}$ are less than $f_{j(a)}$ at position $x_{i-1} \leqslant x_i$, they are also less than $f_{j(a)}$ at position x_i, since the slopes are increasing. Hence, the maximum of $f_1, \ldots, f_i$ at x_i is attained by $U' = (f_{j'(1)}, f_{j'(2)}, \ldots, f_{j'(g)})$. It remains to find the interval of U' containing x_i, which can be done by throwing away all $f_{j'(v)}$ with $\otimes(f_{j'(v)}, f_{j'(v+1)}) \leqslant x_i$, since $f_{j'(v+1)}$ is bigger than $f_{j'(v)}$ to the right of $\otimes(f_{j'(v)}, f_{j'(v+1)})$, so that it is also bigger at x_i. This is done by lines 6–7 of Algorithm 2. More formally, let b such that $x_i \in I_b(U')$. Then in lines 6–7 we delete the functions $f_{j'(1)}, \ldots, f_{j'(b-1)}$ from $S = U' = (f_{j'(1)}, f_{j'(2)}, \ldots, f_{j'(g)})$, thereby restoring the invariant. □

3.3 Reconstruction of P^*

As is the case for many dynamic-programming-like algorithms, from the computation of the optimal value $\mathcal{I}_{\text{hyp}}(P^*)$ we can efficiently reconstruct an optimal solution P^* achieving the optimal value $\mathcal{I}_{\text{hyp}}(P^*)$.

To this end, we augment our dequeue S to not only store linear functions f_j, but tuples (f_j, j), so that we know the index j of every linear function in S. With this, in the computation of H_i^ℓ we not only compute its value, but also find some $j > i$ such that $H_i^\ell = F_j^\ell(p_x^i)$. This tells us that when we selected point p^i and want to select ℓ more points, then the next point should be j. Let us store

$$\text{Next}_i^\ell := j.$$

Then an optimal solution P^* can be reconstructed as

$$\{p^{i_1}, \ldots, p^{i_k}\}$$

by setting $i_0 := 0$ and $i_{\ell+1} := \text{Next}_{i_\ell}^{k-\ell}$.

We remark that this increases the space requirement from $\mathcal{O}(n)$ to $\mathcal{O}(k\,n)$, as we now have to store the full table Next.

4. ALGORITHM FOR EPSSSP

We start with an outline of the algorithm. Let (k, P, R) be a EPSSSP instance with (unknown) optimal value ε^*. We assume that P and R are non-dominating and sorted. We first design a test to check for any given $\varepsilon \in \mathbb{R}$ whether $\varepsilon \geqslant \varepsilon^*$. In other words, we want to check whether there exists a subset $P' \subseteq P$ of size k with $\mathcal{I}_{\text{eps}}(P', R) \leqslant \varepsilon$. We call this an *$\varepsilon$-test*. Extending an algorithm by Koltun and Papadimitriou [15] (who consider the case $P = R$) we show the following lemma.

Lemma 6. *An ε-test can be performed in time $\mathcal{O}(n + m)$.*

We could try to use ε-tests directly for a binary search for the optimal approximation ratio $\varepsilon^* \in \mathbb{R}$. This could yield arbitrarily good approximations to ε^*, but would not allow to compute ε^* exactly, as it can be any real number. However, ε^* is by definition among the $n \cdot m$ values $S = \{\mathcal{I}_{\text{eps}}(p, r) \mid p \in P, r \in R\}$. We obtain a simple $\mathcal{O}(nm\log(nm))$ time algorithm by sorting S and then doing a binary search for ε^* in S, incurring $\log(nm)$ ε-tests, see Algorithm 3.

Algorithm 3: EPSSSP in 2 dimensions, $\mathcal{O}(nm\log(nm))$ time

Input: integer k, non-dominating and sorted sets P, R

sort $S = \{\mathcal{I}_{\text{eps}}(p, r) \mid p \in P, r \in R\}$
binary search for $\varepsilon^* \in S$ using ε-tests (see Algorithm 4)

To get quasi-linear runtime, we observe that one can partition the possible values for ε^* into $2n$ sorted sequences $S_1, \ldots, S_{2n}$ of length at most m each. Note that running a binary search on each sorted sequence using ε-tests still yields a runtime of $\Omega(nm)$, which is not quasilinear. Instead, we search over the sorted sequences S_i with a more intelligent randomized algorithm as follows. In each iteration we take a random pivot element ε_p from $S = \bigcup_i S_i$. We do an ε-test with ε_p. Say, we get the answer $\varepsilon_p \geqslant \varepsilon^*$. This allows to delete all values in the sequences S_i that are at least ε_p. Deleting these values takes time $\mathcal{O}(n\log m)$: in every sequence S_i we do a binary search for ε_p to determine the cut-off point. Similarly, if the answer of the ε-test was $\varepsilon_p < \varepsilon^*$ then we can delete all values in the sequences S_i that are at most ε_p in time $\mathcal{O}(n\log m)$. The crucial observation now is that the expected size of $\bigcup_i S_i$ drops by a constant factor in each iteration. Since in the beginning we have $|\bigcup_i S_i| = \mathcal{O}(nm)$, after $\mathcal{O}(\log(nm))$ iterations (in expectation and with high probability[1]) we have deleted all elements of the sequences S_i and found ε^* on the way. This yields a total runtime of $\mathcal{O}((n\log m + m)\log(nm))$.

We present an improvement to runtime $\mathcal{O}((n+m)\log(nm)) = \mathcal{O}(n\log n + m\log m)$ in Section 4.3, which is more of theoretical interest, as indicated by our preliminary experiments.

In the remainder of this section, we work out these ideas in detail.

4.1 ε-Test

In this section we prove Lemma 6. Recall that, given an EPSSSP instance (k, P, R) with (unknown) optimal value ε^* and given $\varepsilon \in \mathbb{R}$, an ε-test determines whether $\varepsilon \geqslant \varepsilon^*$. We present a greedy algorithm with runtime $\mathcal{O}(n + m)$ (cf. Algorithm 4).

Recall that $P = \{p^1, \ldots, p^n\}$ and $R = \{r^1, \ldots, r^m\}$ are already sorted and non-dominating, so that they are sorted by increasing x-coordinates as well as decreasing y-coordinates.

The rightmost point r^m of R (i.e., the one with largest x-coordinate) has to be approximated by some point in the chosen subset $P' \subseteq P$. Consider the leftmost point p^i in P with $p_x^i + \varepsilon \geqslant r_x^m$. The point p^i approximates r^m in x-direction. If it does not approximate r^m in y-direction, then *no* point in P ε-approximates r^m, since, among all points $p \in P$ with sufficiently large x-coordinate to approximate r^m, p^i is the point with largest y-coordinate (because it is leftmost). Thus, in this case we can safely answer $\varepsilon < \varepsilon^*$.

If, on the other hand, p^i ε-approximates r^m then we may greedily pick p^i into our selected set $P' \subseteq P$. To argue this, we show that p^i ε-approximates a superset of any other point p^h that ε-approximates r^m. Formally, for any h with $\mathcal{I}_{\text{eps}}(p^h, r^m) \leqslant \varepsilon$ we have $\{r \in R \mid \mathcal{I}_{\text{eps}}(p^h, r) \leqslant \varepsilon\} \subseteq \{r \in R \mid \mathcal{I}_{\text{eps}}(p^i, r) \leqslant \varepsilon\}$. Note that $h \geqslant i$, since p^i is the leftmost point ε-approximating r^m. Now, if $r \in R$ is ε-approximated by p^h then $p_y^i + \varepsilon \geqslant p_y^h + \varepsilon \geqslant r_y$ (since $h \geqslant i$ and p^h ε-approximates r) and $p_x^i + \varepsilon \geqslant r_x^m \geqslant r_x$ (since p^i ε-approximates r^m and r^m is rightmost in R). Thus, p^i also ε-approximates r. Hence, if there is at all a set $P' \subseteq P$ of size k that ε-approximates R, then there is such a set containing p^i, and we may greedily pick p^i to be included in P' without violating optimality.

Now consider the leftmost point r^j with $r_y^j \leqslant p_y^i + \varepsilon$. Since we also have $p_x^i + \varepsilon \geqslant r_x^m \geqslant r_x^j$, the points $r^j, r^{j+1}, \ldots, r^m$ are ε-approximated by p^i, and these are all points that are ε-approximated by p^i. Since these points are already covered by picking p^i, we may delete them from R, i.e., set $m := j - 1$. Moreover, since p^i approximates a superset of all points to its right, we may delete $p^i, p^{i+1}, \ldots, p^n$ from P, i.e., set $n := i - 1$; these points no longer approximate any points in R. We are left with a new instance of EPSSSP on new sets P, R with k reduced by one, so we may repeat this procedure.

[1] I.e., with probability $\geqslant 1 - n^{-c}$ for any $c > 0$, where the constant hidden in the $\mathcal{O}$-notation of the number of iterations depends on c.

For termination, we know that $\varepsilon \geqslant \varepsilon^*$ if after choosing any $\ell \leqslant k$ points we have $m = 0$, meaning that the points picked so far ε-approximate all points in R already. Moreover, if after choosing k points we do not yet approximate all of R (i.e., $m > 0$), then we have $\varepsilon < \varepsilon^*$.

Algorithm 4: ε-Test

```
Input: real ε, integer k, non-dominating and sorted sets
       P = {p^1, ..., p^n}, R = {r^1, ..., r^m}
1  P' := ∅
2  for ℓ ← 1 to k do
3      let i be the minimal i ∈ {1, ..., n} with p^i_x + ε ≥ r^m_x
4      if I_eps(p^i, r^m) > ε then return "ε < ε*"
5      P' := P' ∪ {p^i}
6      let j be the minimal j ∈ {1, ..., m} with r^j_y ≤ p^i_y + ε
7      m := j − 1    // delete r^j, ..., r^m from R
8      n := i − 1    // delete p^i, ..., p^n from P
9      if m = 0 then return "ε ≥ ε*"
10 return "ε < ε*"
```

We now argue that Algorithm 4 can be implemented in time $\mathcal{O}(n+m)$. To this end, we implement the search for i in line 3 by a linear scan over $n, n-1, \ldots, i+1, i$. Observe that every element that is touched by this linear scan is deleted later in the same iteration. Thus, in total we touch every point in P at most once. Similarly, we search for j by considering $m, m-1, \ldots, j+1, j$, so that we touch every point in R at most once. This yields a runtime bound of $\mathcal{O}(n+m)$.

4.2 Subset Selection

In this section, we show how to use the ε-test from the last section to solve EPSSSP in time $\mathcal{O}((n \log m + m)\log(nm))$, proving a weaker version of Theorem 2.

Sorted Sequences. As has been observed in [18, 19], ε^* is among the values $\mathcal{I}_{\text{eps}}(p, r)$ with $p \in P$, $r \in R$, since at least one pair (p, r) prevents us from further decreasing ε^*. We can split these values into sorted sequences as follows. Write $R = \{r^1, \ldots, r^m\}$ and recall that this sequence of points is sorted by increasing x-coordinate and decreasing y-coordinate. Observe that this implies that R is also sorted according to increasing $r_x - r_y$ values. Now fix a point $p \in P$. Determine the largest index $1 \leqslant i_p \leqslant m$ such that $r_x^{i_p} - r_y^{i_p} \leqslant p_x - p_y$. Since R is sorted by $r_x - r_y$, a binary search does this in time $\mathcal{O}(\log m)$. Then the following sequences are sorted (this is essentially the same property as [19, Proposition 3.2]).

Lemma 7. *For any $p \in P$, the following sequences are sorted:*

$$S_p^y := \left(\mathcal{I}_{\text{eps}}(p, r^1), \ldots, \mathcal{I}_{\text{eps}}(p, r^{i_p})\right),$$
$$S_p^x := \left(\mathcal{I}_{\text{eps}}(p, r^{i_p+1}), \ldots, \mathcal{I}_{\text{eps}}(p, r^m)\right).$$

Proof. Since R is sorted by increasing values of $r_x - r_y$ and i_p is the largest index with $r_x^{i_p} - r_y^{i_p} \leqslant p_x - p_y$, we have $r_x^i - r_y^i \leqslant p_x - p_y$ for all $1 \leqslant i \leqslant i_p$ and $r_x^i - r_y^i > p_x - p_y$ for all $i_p + 1 \leqslant i \leqslant m$. Let us focus on $1 \leqslant i \leqslant i_p$, or equivalently the sequence S_p^y. Note that $r_x^i - r_y^i \leqslant p_x - p_y$ is equivalent to $r_x^i - p_x \leqslant r_y^i - p_y$. Hence, we have $\mathcal{I}_{\text{eps}}(p, r^i) = \max\{r_x^i - p_x, r_y^i - p_y\} = r_y^i - p_y$. Since p is fixed and $\{r^1, \ldots, r^{i_p}\}$ is sorted by y-coordinates, also the values $r_y^i - p_y$ are sorted, proving that the sequence S_p^y is sorted. An analogous argument shows the claim for S_p^x. □

Note that the sequences S_p^x, S_p^y, $p \in P$, form $2n$ sequences with at most m elements each. We will denote these sequences by $S_1, \ldots, S_{2n}$ from now on. These sequences are all of the form $\{\mathcal{I}_{\text{eps}}(p, r^s), \mathcal{I}_{\text{eps}}(p, r^{s+1}), \ldots, \mathcal{I}_{\text{eps}}(p, r^t)\}$ for some $p \in P$ and $1 \leqslant s, t \leqslant m$. Note that we can store such a sequence implicitly by only storing p, s, t, and do not have to explicitly store all its elements. This implicit representation allows us to efficiently support the following operations on $S_i = (p_i, s_i, t_i)$:

(1) Compute the j-th element: This is $\mathcal{I}_{\text{eps}}(p_i, r^{s_i+j-1})$.
(2) Compute the size $|S_i|$: This is $t_i - s_i + 1$.
(3) Delete the first j elements: Change S_i to $(p_i, s_i + j, t_i)$.
(4) Delete the last j elements: Change S_i to $(p_i, s_i, t_i - j)$.

As a final remark, note that some of the sequences $S_1, \ldots, S_{2n}$ are ordered ascendingly and some descendingly. For the sake of readability, we want to assume from now on that *all sequences $S_1, \ldots, S_{2n}$ are sorted in increasing order*. To achieve this, we may augment the implicit representation of a sequence by a bit specifying whether it is sorted ascendingly or descendingly. In case it is sorted descendingly, we then mirror indices appropriately, e.g., when accessing the j-th element of $S_i = (p_i, s_i, t_i)$ that is sorted descendingly we return $\mathcal{I}_{\text{eps}}(p_i, r^{t_i-j+1})$.

In summary, we obtain $2n$ sequences $S_1, \ldots, S_{2n}$ sorted ascendingly and of size at most m each, such that ε^* is among these sequences. Computing (an implicit representation of) these sequences takes time $\mathcal{O}(n \log m)$, see also Algorithm 5.

Algorithm 5: Computing sorted sequences

```
Input: non-dominating, sorted sets P and R = {r^1, ..., r^m}
foreach p ∈ P do
    binary search for the largest 1 ≤ i_p ≤ m with
        r^{i_p}_x − r^{i_p}_y ≤ p_x − p_y
the sorted sequences are {I_eps(p, r^1), ..., I_eps(p, r^{i_p})}
(represented as (p, 1, i_p)) and
{I_eps(p, r^{i_p+1}), ..., I_eps(p, r^m)} (represented as
(p, i_p + 1, m)) for each p ∈ P.
```

Binary Search over Many Sequences. We are left with the following abstract problem. Given sorted sequences $S_1, \ldots, S_{2n}$ of length at most m containing an unknown target value ε^*, and access to an ε-test that computes for a given ε whether $\varepsilon \geqslant \varepsilon^*$ and runs in time $\mathcal{O}(n+m)$, compute ε^*.

Denote by $S := \bigcup_i S_i$ the concatenation of the sequences S_i. In every iteration we pick a uniformly random pivot element ε_p in S (which can be done in $\mathcal{O}(n)$ time) and do an ε-test with ε_p. If $\varepsilon_p \geqslant \varepsilon^*$ we memorize ε_p as a candidate for ε^*; we only have to store the smallest among all candidates. Then we delete all values $\varepsilon \geqslant \varepsilon_p$ in all the sequences S_i (as we already found a better candidate for ε^* than all these values). Note that these deletions can be done in $\mathcal{O}(\log m)$ time per sequence S_i by running a binary search for ε_p in S_i and then deleting all greater elements – all necessary operations are supported by our implicit representation of the sequences S_i. Otherwise, if $\varepsilon_p < \varepsilon^*$ then we instead delete all values $\varepsilon \leqslant \varepsilon_p$ (as all these values are smaller than ε^*). The crucial property now is the following:

> In each iteration, with constant probability we reduce the size of S by a constant factor. (*)

Since $|S| = \mathcal{O}(nm)$ in the beginning, this property implies that after $\mathcal{O}(\log(nm))$ iterations (in expectation and with high probability) the set S is empty. Since we must have deleted ε^* at some point, our current candidate is equal to ε^*, and the algorithm has a correct output, see Algorithm 6.

Since in each iteration we do one ε-test and $\mathcal{O}(n)$ binary searches in the S_i's, we obtain a total runtime of $\mathcal{O}((n \log m + m)\log(nm))$ (in expectation and with high probability).

Algorithm 6: EPSSSP in 2 dimensions, slower version

```
Input: integer k, non-dominating and sorted sets P, R
1  compute sorted sequences S_1, ..., S_2n containing ε* using
   Algorithm 5
2  ε_cand := ∞
3  while not all sets S_i empty do
4      choose ε_p uniformly at random over all sequences S_i
5      ε-test with ε_p using Algorithm 4
6      if ε_p ⩾ ε* then
7          ε_cand := min{ε_cand, ε_p}
8          for 1 ⩽ i ⩽ n do
9              delete all ε ⩾ ε_p from S_i using a binary search
10     else
11         for 1 ⩽ i ⩽ n do
12             delete all ε ⩽ ε_p from S_i using a binary search
13 return ε_cand
14 the corresponding set of points P* is the set computed by an
   ε-test with ε = ε_cand
```

Proof of Property (*) for Algorithm 6. Denote by U_i the number of elements of S_i that are at least ε_p, and by L_i the number of elements of S_i that are smaller than ε_p. Let

$$U := \sum_i U_i \quad \text{and} \quad L := \sum_i L_i.$$

Observe that, independent of the value of ε^*, we delete at least $\min\{U, L+1\}$ elements from $S = \bigcup_i S_i$: If $\varepsilon_p \geqslant \varepsilon^*$ we delete the U elements that are at least ε_p, and if $\varepsilon_p < \varepsilon^*$ we delete the L smaller elements and ε_p itself.

Since we pick ε_p uniformly at random in S, we pick ε_p in the middle third of S with probability 1/3. More precisely, we have $\lceil \frac{1}{3}|S| \rceil \leqslant U \leqslant \lceil \frac{2}{3}|S| \rceil$ with probability $\frac{1}{|S|}(\lceil \frac{2}{3}|S| \rceil - \lceil \frac{1}{3}|S| \rceil + 1) \geqslant \frac{1}{3}$. If this event occurs, then $\min\{U, L+1\} \geqslant \frac{1}{3}|S|$. Thus, with constant probability we delete at least a constant fraction of S. □

4.3 Theoretical Improvement

In this section, we reduce the runtime to $\mathcal{O}(n \log n + m \log m)$. To this end, we show that for having Property (*) it is not necessary to do a full binary search for the pivot ε_p in each sequence S_i.

Again, in each iteration of the algorithm we choose a uniformly random pivot ε_p in $S = \bigcup_i S_i$ and do an ε-test with ε_p. Assume first that $\varepsilon_p \geqslant \varepsilon^*$. Again we store ε_p as a candidate in this case. Now we consider the $\lceil \frac{2}{3}|S_i| \rceil$-th element ε_i of S_i; as S_i is sorted we can access this element in constant time. If $\varepsilon_i \geqslant \varepsilon_p$ then we delete all elements in S_i to the right of ε_i (including ε_i, these values are at least as large as our current candidate). Otherwise S_i stays as is. If, on the other hand, $\varepsilon_p < \varepsilon^*$ then we consider the $\lceil \frac{1}{3}|S_i| \rceil$-th element ε_i of S_i. If $\varepsilon_i \leqslant \varepsilon_p$ then we delete all elements to the left of ε_i (including ε_i). Otherwise S_i stays as is. Note that now an iteration only takes time $\mathcal{O}(n+m)$. Again, we repeat these iterations until all sequences are empty, in this case the candidate we stored for ε^* is finally correct. These changes result in Algorithm 7.

Algorithm 7: EPSSSP in 2 dimensions, faster version

```
Input: integer k, non-dominating and sorted sets P, R
The algorithm is the same as Algorithm 6, except that we
replace line 9 by:
9a         let ε_i be the ⌈(2/3)|S_i|⌉-th element of S_i
9b         if ε_i ⩾ ε_p then
9c             delete ε_i and all elements to its right from S_i
replace line 12 by:
12a        let ε_i be the ⌈(1/3)|S_i|⌉-th element of S_i
12b        if ε_i ⩽ ε_p then
12c            delete ε_i and all elements to its left from S_i
```

To bound the runtime of Algorithm 7, it remains to show that Property (*) is still satisfied. If this is the case, then we again need $\mathcal{O}(\log(nm))$ iterations and obtain a total runtime of $\mathcal{O}((n + m)\log(nm)) = \mathcal{O}(n \log n + m \log m)$ (in expectation and with high probability).

Proof of Property (*) for Algorithm 7. Again, let $U_i := \{s \in S_i \mid s \geqslant \varepsilon_p\}$, $L_i := \{s \in S_i \mid s < \varepsilon_p\}$ and $U := \sum_i U_i$, $L := \sum_i L_i$.

Claim 8. *In the current iteration, Algorithm 7 deletes at least* $\min\{\frac{1}{3}U - \frac{1}{6}L, \frac{1}{3}(L+1) - \frac{1}{6}(U-1)\}$ *elements.*

Proof. First assume that $\varepsilon_p \geqslant \varepsilon^*$. We prove that in any set S_i we delete at least $\frac{1}{3}U_i - \frac{1}{6}L_i$ elements. Summing over all $1 \leqslant i \leqslant 2n$ then yields the result. Consider Algorithm 7 and note that if $\varepsilon_i \geqslant \varepsilon_p$ then we delete all elements to the right of ε_i (including ε_i). Thus, we delete at least $\frac{1}{3}|S_i|$ elements. As $U_i \leqslant |S_i|$ and $L_i \geqslant 0$, we delete at least

$$\tfrac{1}{3}|S_i| \geqslant \tfrac{1}{3}U_i - \tfrac{1}{6}L_i$$

elements. If, on the other hand, $\varepsilon_i < \varepsilon_p$, then we do not delete any elements from S_i. In this case we have $L_i \geqslant \frac{2}{3}|S_i|$ and $U_i \leqslant \frac{1}{3}|S_i|$, so that

$$0 \geqslant \tfrac{1}{3}U_i - \tfrac{1}{6}L_i.$$

Hence, also in this case we delete at least $\frac{1}{3}U_i - \frac{1}{6}L_i$ elements, because this number is non-positive.

In summary, we obtain that if $\varepsilon_p \geqslant \varepsilon^*$ we delete at least $\frac{1}{3}U - \frac{1}{6}L$ elements. In the case $\varepsilon_p < \varepsilon^*$, a symmetric argument using $L' := \{s \in S \mid s \leqslant \varepsilon_p\}$ and $U' := \{s \in S \mid s > \varepsilon_p\}$ shows that we delete at least $\frac{1}{3}L' - \frac{1}{6}U'$ elements of S. Recalling the definition of $L = \{s \in S \mid s < \varepsilon_p\}$ and $U = \{s \in S \mid s \geqslant \varepsilon_p\}$, we see that $L' \geqslant L + 1$ and $U' \leqslant U - 1$. Hence, in this case we delete at least $\frac{1}{3}(L+1) - \frac{1}{6}(U-1)$ elements of S. □

To finish the proof of Property (*), note that since ε_p is uniformly random in S we have $\lceil \frac{2}{5}|S| \rceil \leqslant U \leqslant \lceil \frac{3}{5}|S| \rceil$ with probability at least $\frac{1}{5}$. If this event occurs, then $\min\{\frac{1}{3}U - \frac{1}{6}L, \frac{1}{3}(L+1) - \frac{1}{6}(U-1)\} \geqslant \frac{1}{3} \cdot \frac{2}{5}|S| - \frac{1}{6} \cdot \frac{3}{5}|S| = \frac{1}{30}|S|$. Thus, with constant probability we delete at least a constant fraction of S. □

5. EXPERIMENTS

All the presented algorithms for the hypervolume indicator as well as the epsilon indicator have been implemented and are available at the homepage of the second author [1].

We experimentally compared our algorithm for HYPSSP with runtime $\mathcal{O}(n \cdot k)$ (Algorithm 1) with the dynamic programming approach of Auger et al. [3] with runtime $\mathcal{O}(n^2 k)$. For the ε-indicator we set $P = R$ so that $n = m$. We implemented the $\mathcal{O}(n^2 \log n)$ algorithm (Algorithm 3), which has the same asymptotic runtime as [18, 19], and compared it with both algorithms we described (Algorithm 6 and Algorithm 7).

We tested instances for increasing $10^2 \leqslant n \leqslant 10^7$ and $k \in \{10, 20, 50, n/2\}$. These values for k have been chosen with the motivations in mind that we sketched in the introduction. The algorithm runtimes was averaged over 30 runs for n randomly sampled points or points with equal distance taken from the fronts $f_1(x) = 1 - x$, $f_2(x) = \sqrt{1 - x^2}$, and $f_3(x) = \frac{1}{x}$.

All experiments showed a similar behavior. We observed no differences in the algorithms' runtime behavior for the three fronts and the two ways of sampling. The measured runtimes fit very well to the asymptotic guarantees, meaning that all hidden constants are reasonably small. However, Algorithm 6 was as fast as Algorithm 7 in our experiments, i.e., this minor runtime improvement is only of theoretical nature. The experiments showed that our new algorithms are empirically faster by several orders of magnitude than the previous state of the art. Details will be provided in an extended version of this paper.

Acknowledgments

The research leading to these results has received funding from the Australian Research Council (ARC) under grant agreement DP140103400 and from the European Union Seventh Framework Programme (FP7/2007-2013) under grant agreement no 618091 (SAGE). Karl Bringmann is a recipient of the *Google Europe Fellowship in Randomized Algorithms*, and this research is supported in part by this Google Fellowship.

References

[1] `http://docs.theinf.uni-jena.de/code/ssp.zip`.

[2] `http://wcipeg.com/wiki/Convex_hull_trick`.

[3] A. Auger, J. Bader, D. Brockhoff, and E. Zitzler. Investigating and exploiting the bias of the weighted hypervolume to articulate user preferences. In *11th Annual Conference on Genetic and Evolutionary Computation (GECCO '09)*, pp. 563–570. ACM Press, 2009.

[4] J. M. Bader. *Hypervolume-Based Search for Multiobjective Optimization: Theory and Methods*. PhD thesis, Eidgen?ssische Technische Hochschule ETH Z?rich, 2009.

[5] N. Beume, B. Naujoks, and M. T. M. Emmerich. SMS-EMOA: Multiobjective selection based on dominated hypervolume. *European Journal of Operational Research*, 181:1653–1669, 2007.

[6] N. Beume, C. M. Fonseca, M. López-Ibáñez, L. Paquete, and J. Vahrenhold. On the complexity of computing the hypervolume indicator. *IEEE Trans. Evolutionary Computation*, 13:1075–1082, 2009.

[7] N. Beume, B. Naujoks, M. Preuss, G. Rudolph, and T. Wagner. Effects of 1-greedy $\mathcal{S}$-metric-selection on innumerably large Pareto fronts. In *5th International Conference on Evolutionary Multi-Criterion Optimization (EMO '09)*, Vol. 5467 of *LNCS*, pp. 21–35, 2009.

[8] K. Bringmann and T. Friedrich. An efficient algorithm for computing hypervolume contributions. *Evolutionary Computation*, 18:383–402, 2010.

[9] K. Bringmann, T. Friedrich, F. Neumann, and M. Wagner. Approximation-guided evolutionary multi-objective optimization. In *22nd International Joint Conference on Artificial Intelligence (IJCAI '11)*, pp. 1198–1203. IJCAI/AAAI, 2011.

[10] P. Brucker. Efficient algorithms for some path partitioning problems. *Discrete Applied Mathematics*, 62:77–85, 1995.

[11] M. de Berg, O. Cheong, M. van Kreveld, and M. Overmars. *Computational Geometry*. Springer, 2008.

[12] M. T. M. Emmerich and C. M. Fonseca. Computing hypervolume contributions in low dimensions: Asymptotically optimal algorithm and complexity results. In *6th International Conference on Evolutionary Multi-Criterion Optimization (EMO '11)*, Vol. 6576 of *LNCS*, pp. 121–135. Springer, 2011.

[13] C. Igel, N. Hansen, and S. Roth. Covariance matrix adaptation for multi-objective optimization. *Evolutionary Computation*, 15:1–28, 2007.

[14] C. Igel, T. Suttorp, and N. Hansen. Steady-state selection and efficient covariance matrix update in the multi-objective CMA-ES. In *4th International Conference on Evolutionary Multi-Criterion Optimization (EMO '07)*, Vol. 4403 of *LNCS*, pp. 171–185. Springer, 2007.

[15] V. Koltun and C. H. Papadimitriou. Approximately dominating representatives. *Theoretical Computer Science*, 371:148–154, 2007.

[16] T. Kuhn, C. M. Fonseca, L. Paquete, S. Ruzika, and J. R. Figueira. Hypervolume subset selection in two dimensions: Formulations and algorithms. Technical report, Fachbereich Mathematik, TU Kaiserslautern, 2014.

[17] H. T. Kung, F. Luccio, and F. P. Preparata. On finding the maxima of a set of vectors. *Journal of the ACM*, 22: 469–476, 1975.

[18] A. Ponte, L. Paquete, and J. R. Figueira. On beam search for multicriteria combinatorial optimization problems. In *9th International Conference in Integration of AI and OR Techniques in Contraint Programming for Combinatorial Optimzation Problems (CPAIOR '12)*, Vol. 7298 of *LNCS*, pp. 307–321. Springer, 2012.

[19] D. Vaz, L. Paquete, and A. Ponte. A note on the ε-indicator subset selection. *Theoretical Computer Science*, 499: 113–116, 2013.

[20] E. Zitzler, D. Brockhoff, and L. Thiele. The hypervolume indicator revisited: On the design of Pareto-compliant indicators via weighted integration. In *4th International Conference on Evolutionary Multi-Criterion Optimization (EMO '07)*, Vol. 4403 of *LNCS*, pp. 862–876. Springer, 2007.

Improving Many-Objective Optimization Performance by Sequencing Evolutionary Algorithms

Martin Dohr
Institute of Electronics
Graz University of Technology
Austria
martin.dohr@tugraz.at

Bernd Eichberger
Institute of Electronics
Graz University of Technology
Austria
bernd.eichberger@tugraz.at

ABSTRACT

Evolutionary multiobjective optimization (EMO) has been successfully applied to various real-world scenarios with usually two or three contradicting optimization goals. However, several studies have pointed out a great deterioration of computational performance when handling more than three objectives. In order to improve the scalability of multiobjective evolutionary algorithms (MOEAs) onto higher-dimensional objective spaces, techniques using e.g. scalarizing functions and preference- or indicator-based guidance have been proposed. Most of those proposals require a-priori information or a decision maker during optimization, which increases the complexity of the algorithms.

In this paper, we propose a divide and conquer method for many-objective optimization. First, we partition a problem into lower-dimensional subproblems for which standard algorithms are known to perform very well. Our key improvement is the sequential usage of MOEAs, utilizing the results of one suboptimization as initial population for another MOEA. This technique allows modular optimization phases and can be applied to common evolutionary algorithms. We test our enhanced method on the hard to solve multiobjective Quadratic Assignment Problem (mQAP), using a variety of established MOEAs.

Categories and Subject Descriptors

I.2.8 [**ARTIFICIAL INTELLIGENCE**]: Problem Solving, Control Methods, and Search—*Heuristic methods*

General Terms

Algorithms, Performance, Experimentation

Keywords

Multiobjective Evolutionary Algorithms, many-objective optimization, multiobjective quadratic assignment problem

GECCO'14, July 12–16, 2014, Vancouver, BC, Canada.

ACM 978-1-4503-2662-9/14/07 ...$15.00.
http://dx.doi.org/10.1145/2576768.2598326.

1. INTRODUCTION

Multiobjective Optimization has been a very popular research topic in the field of evolutionary computation over the last decades. This is due to the fact, that most real-world optimization problems are defined by multiple contradicting objective functions. Solutions can be seen as good tradeoffs between those optimization goals. A vast amount of Multiobjective Evolutionary Algorithms (MOEAs) has therefore been proposed and successfully applied to various applications. However, most of those algorithms have been designed for problems consisting of two or three objective functions. For more complex problems, modeled by four or more objective functions, the search performance of standard MOEAs is greatly reduced [9, 6]. The well-known 'curse of dimensionality' leads to huge objective spaces accompanied by the following problems:

- The principle of Pareto-dominance becomes ineffective as the amount of non-dominated solutions in random samples increases with the number of dimensions in objective space [8].
- In order to maintain a selection pressure towards the Pareto front, the sizes for current populations and archives in MOEAs have to be increased drastically.
- Consequently, as the amount of function evaluations required to step ahead one generation in the evolutionary algorithm rises, the algorithm becomes more computationally intensive.
- One further issue is that the visualization of optimization results can be very challenging for more than 3-dimensional problems.

According to [7], approaches to improve the scalability of algorithms can be categorized into several techniques:

1. Attempts to reduce the objective dimensionality and therefore simplifying the problem, e.g. [2]
2. Focusing the search on a smaller region of the Pareto front defined by preference information from a decision maker, e.g. [15]
3. Improving ranking mechanisms or definitions of dominance to increase selection pressure, e.g. [3]
4. Using multiobjective quality indicators for fitness evaluation instead of Pareto dominance, e.g. [1, 17]

The drawback of those techniques is that they induce additional complexity or custom parameters to the optimization process.

In this paper, we propose a divide and conquer approach for many-objective optimization. First, the objective space is explored by solving lower-dimensional subproblems. This can be done very fast using known evolutionary algorithms. The results of those explorations are then used as input for the main optimization phase. Our technique allows modular optimization phases and can be applied to common evolutionary algorithms. In comparison to previous techniques, our method does not require a-priori knowledge of the problem, the shape of the pareto front or regions of interest for the decision maker.

The rest of this paper is organized as follows: in Section 2, we will give a detailed explanation of our method and different ways of implementation. We will test our approach on the 4-, 6-and 12-dimensional multiobjective quadratic assignment problem using four well-established MOEAs in Section 3. The results of those experiments are then discussed in the concluding Section 4.

2. SEQUENCING MOEAS

Nearly every evolutionary algorithm in literature initializes the first population using random values. Those values are usually picked without any information of the problem or shape of the Pareto front. The only information available are upper and lower bounds for each decision variable and possible optimization constraints. While this can be handled very well for 2- and 3-objective problems, it represents a serious performance issue for higher-dimensional problems.

We propose to break up many-objective optimization tasks into low-dimensional subproblems. Usually, optimization problems with k objectives are given in the form:

$$\begin{aligned} &\min_{\vec{x}} \vec{f}(\vec{x}) = \{f_1(\vec{x}), f_2(\vec{x}), \ldots, f_k(\vec{x})\} \\ &\text{subject to: } \vec{x} \in \mathbf{X} \end{aligned} \tag{1}$$

where the decision vector $\vec{x}$ is chosen out of the feasible region $\mathbf{X}$. We can now define subproblems $\vec{f}_{s1}(\vec{x}), \ldots, \vec{f}_{sn}(\vec{x})$ consisting of two or three objective functions from the main problem as for example:

$$\begin{aligned} \vec{f}_{s1}(\vec{x}) &= \{f_1(\vec{x}), f_2(\vec{x}), f_3(\vec{x})\} \\ \vec{f}_{s2}(\vec{x}) &= \{f_4(\vec{x}), f_5(\vec{x}), f_6(\vec{x})\} \\ &\ldots \\ \vec{f}_{sn}(\vec{x}) &= \{f_{k-2}(\vec{x}), f_{k-1}(\vec{x}), f_k(\vec{x})\} \end{aligned} \tag{2}$$

Partitioning can be done arbitrarily or by including available information on correlation of objective functions or regions of special interest. In any case, we suggest not to exceed three objectives per partition in order to maintain the performance advantage. The subproblems can be handled very efficiently by standard algorithms and are solved in modular (exploring) optimization phases. The resulting solutions represent the initial population for the many-objective (master) optimization algorithm. We expect the run time of the exploring algorithms to be negligible compared to the master. Also, population sizes can be much smaller while still achieving a high coverage of the selected objective subspace. On the other hand, we assume the initial population of the master algorithm to be very close to some regions of the Pareto front. Therefore, we expect a significantly better search performance of the master algorithm.

2.1 Methods

We distinguish between two methods for our approach. The *sequential* method initializes one random population for the first subproblem. The results of the first exploration phase are then used to initialize the second algorithm, which optimizes the next subproblem and so forth. The resulting populations of all exploration phases are accumulated and represent the initial population for the master algorithm.

In the second approach, called *parallel* method, all exploring algorithms initialize with a random population. The results are merged into a starting population for the master algorithm. We indicate those two methods by adding 'S' or 'P' prefixes respectively to the MOEA under test. Principal flow diagrams of both methods are depicted in Figures 1 and 2 for a 4-objective problem.

The exploring phases handle only low-dimensional problems. Therefore, the population sizes for those algorithms can be quite small compared to the master algorithm. In order to achieve good performance, the population size of the master algorithm should be at least large enough to accommodate the Pareto front of each exploration algorithm. It is even advisable for the master algorithm to incorporate all exploring populations as each individual reflects some knowledge of the selected subproblem. If the capacity of the master population exceeds the amount of incoming solutions, the rest of the population is initialized using random values.

To provide an example, we have taken 'snapshots' of the fitness values for all objectives during one optimization run of the sequential and parallel adaptions of NSGSAII. The visualization was done using hierarchical box plots [1]. To improve the readability, we normalized the fitness values for each objective individually and indicated exploring and master phases. It can be seen that the master phase, starting at 5400 evaluations, contains some very good fitness values while the exploring phases show a fast convergence toward their respective optimization goals within 2500 evaluations each. The significantly lower values of objective 4 are due to the characteristics of the generated benchmark problem.

3. EXPERIMENT SETUP

3.1 Benchmark Problems

In order to test our method and provide statistical analysis, we have chosen the multiobjective Quadratic Assignment Problem (mQAP) [11] as benchmark. The single objective QAP [12] variant is known to be NP-hard [14] and also considered to be one of the hardest combinatorial problems in this class. It is defined by two $n \times n$ matrices $\mathbf{A}$ and $\mathbf{B}$, representing the distance between locations and flow between facilities. The goal is to find a permutation π that maps facilities onto locations such that the corresponding product of flow and distance is minimized:

$$\min_{\pi} f(\pi) = \sum_{i=1}^{n} (\sum_{j=1}^{n} a_{ij} \times b_{\pi(i)\pi(j)}) \tag{3}$$

[1]http://www.mathworks.com/matlabcentral/fileexchange/40878-hierarchically-grouped-boxplot

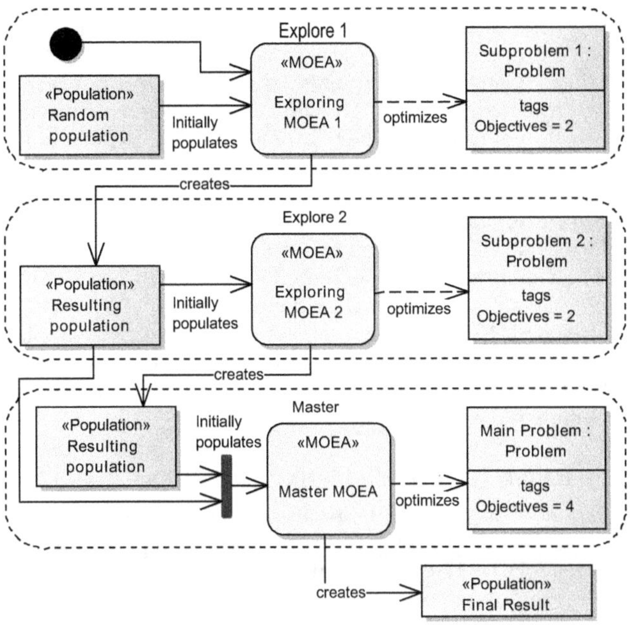

Figure 1: Flowchart for sequential approach

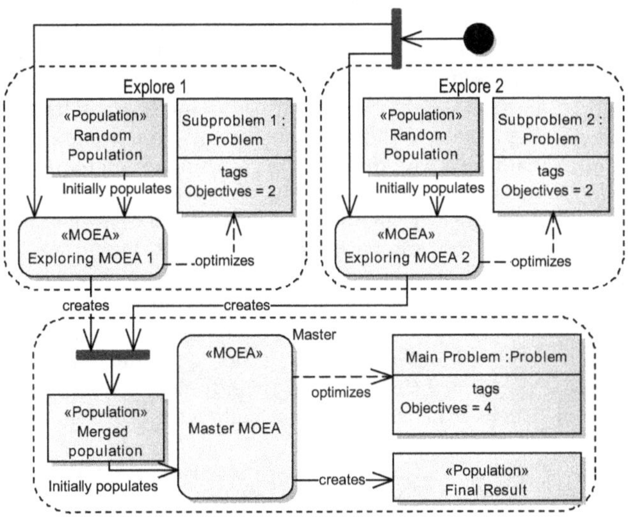

Figure 2: Flowchart for parallel approach

The multiobjective variant considers k flow matrices $\mathbf{B}^1 \dots \mathbf{B}^k$ and leads to k objective functions:

$$
\begin{aligned}
&\min_{\pi} \vec{f}(\pi) = \{f_1(\pi), \dots, f_k(\pi)\} \\
&\text{with } f_m(\pi) = \sum_{i=1}^{n} (\sum_{j=1}^{n} a_{ij} \times b^m_{\pi(i)\pi(j)}) \qquad (4) \\
&\text{and } 1 \leq m \leq k
\end{aligned}
$$

While most publications study this problem with two or three objectives, we created 4- and 6- and 12- dimensional test instances using the generator from [10]. The parameters used are summarized in Table 1.

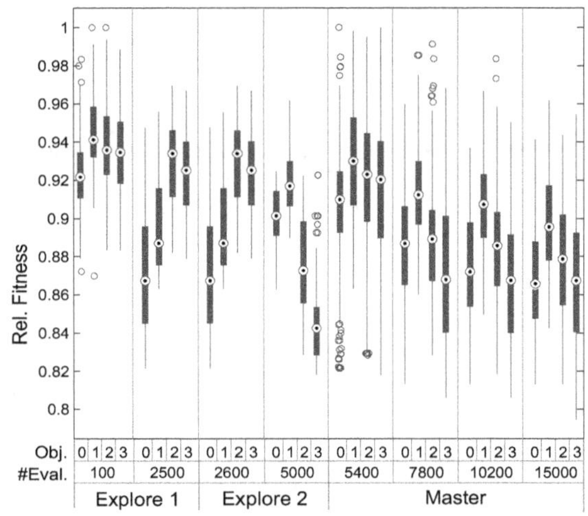

Figure 3: Relative Fitness Values of Population during SNSGAII Execution

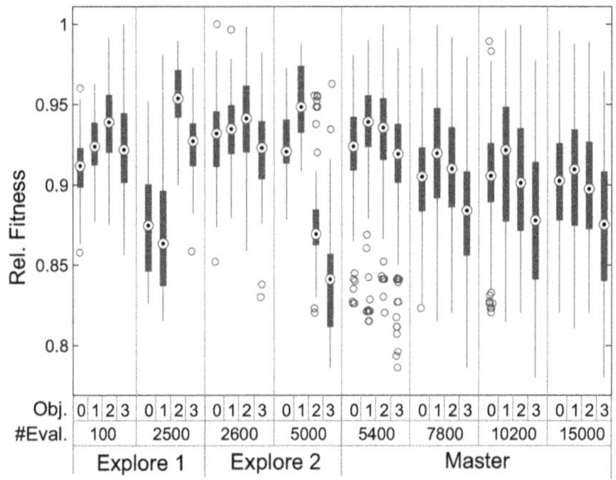

Figure 4: Relative Fitness Values of Population during PNSGAII Execution

3.2 MOEAs and parameters

We want to test our technique using four established evolutionary algorithms with different fitness assignment and selection strategies. For each algorithm, we implemented parallel and sequential methods and compare their performance to the unaltered reference algorithm using the same number of total function evaluations. Further, we evaluate each problem with small and large evaluation budgets.

NSGAII [4] ranks solutions by the number of dominated individuals in the current population and SPEA2 [18] also uses Pareto dominance to fill an external archive. With increased objective dimensionality, we expect both algorithms to degrade in performance as current populations will consist solely of non dominated individuals and selection pressure will therefore decrease.

We compare their performance to a hypervolume-based IBEA [17], which we expect to perform better on many-objective problems. However, calculating the hypervolume for high dimensions could have a serious impact on compu-

Table 1: Parameters for benchmark problems

Name	20-4fl-uni	10-6fl-uni	15-12fl-uni
Facilities	20	10	15
Objectives	4	6	12
Subproblems	2 × 2 Obj.	2 × 3 Obj.	4 × 3 Obj.
maxFlow	100		
Correlation	0		
Seed	23453464		

Table 2: Parameters for algorithms

			SMOEA/PMOEA		Ref.
20-4fl-uni	Population Size		Explorer:	100	400
			Master:	400	
	Evaluation Budget	Small	Explorer:	2500	15000
			Master:	10000	
		Large	Explorer:	3000	30000
			Master:	24000	
10-6fl-uni	Population Size		Explorer:	120	500
			Master:	500	
	Evaluation Budget	Small	Explorer:	2500	15000
			Master:	10000	
		Large	Explorer:	10000	75000
			Master:	55000	
15-12fl-uni	Population Size		Explorer:	120	1200
			Master:	1200	
	Evaluation Budget	Small	Explorer:	5000	120000
			Master:	100000	
		Large	Explorer:	15000	300000
			Master:	240000	

tational performance. For reasons of simplicity, we assume the archive size in IBEA and SPEA2 to be identical with the respective population size.

Finally, all algorithms have to compete with MOEA/D [16], which decomposes the problem into a large number of single objective subproblems and optimizes them in parallel. We use Tchebycheff aggregation functions and uniformly distributed weight vectors for all experiments. Note the population size in MOEA/D equals the number of weight vectors as explained in [16]. In our experiments, we chose the granularity of weight distributions in order to obtain population sizes as similar to the other algorithms as possible.

For all algorithms, we use PMX crossover ($p_{crossover} = 1$) and swap mutation ($p_{mutation} = 0.3$) operators. All relevant parameters are listed in Table 2.

3.3 Quality Indicators

To measure the performance of our method, we compare different quality indicators for each problem. Hypervolume (HV) [19] is used to evaluate the general performance while the additive ϵ-indicator [20] focuses on the convergence behavior towards the Pareto front. These indicators are used for the 4- and 6-objective problem instances. When evaluating the 12-objective problem, we experienced serious performance issues using SPEA2 and IBEA. This was expected due to the heavy computational load of high dimensional hypervolumes and SPEA2 fitness assignments for large populations. Therefore, the 12-objective problem was only evaluated using NSGAII and MOEA/D algorithms with Inverse Generational Distance (IGD)[13] replacing the hypervolume performance indicator.

Since the true Pareto front for our benchmark problem instances is not known, we assume the overall dominating solutions of all experimental runs as surrogates.

The experiments were executed on an Intel Core i5-3320 at 2.6 GHz and 4 GB RAM running Microsoft Windows 7 and Java SE Runtime Environment 1.7. The software implementations of all used algorithms and indicators are based on jMetal, the 'Metaheuristic Algorithms in Java' framework, version 4.4 [5].

4. RESULTS AND CONCLUSION

Figures 5 to 10 show the resulting quality indicators after 100 independent runs for 4- and 6-dimensional problems and 30 runs for the 12-dimensional problem respectively.

For the 4-objective problem, we can see a significant improvement of the hypervolume and ϵ-indicator for the NSGAII and SPEA2 algorithms as well as for the sequential method of IBEA when using a small evaluation budget. Increasing the number of total evaluations shows the same improvements for SPEA2 and NSGAII while no significant change can be seen for the IBEA. However, MOEA/D does not significantly benefit from our method with either evaluation budget and the ϵ-indicator reveals some inferior results for the parallel adaption and large number of evaluations.

For the 6-objective problem, the performance increases of SPEA2 and NSGAII are less distinct but still noticeable. As before, the sequential method outperforms the parallel implementation. However, the results of MOEA/D and IBEA reveal a slight deterioration due to our methods. Considering the performance gain in terms of execution time, this drawback might be negligible when comparing constant run time instead of total number of evaluations. Interestingly, NSGAII performed the worst for this problem instance and did not benefit from the considerably larger evaluation budget.

As stated before, the 12-objective problem was only evaluated using the MOEA/D and NSGAII implementations due to performance issues. The results show a very slight improvement for the IGD indicator, especially for the parallel method. Also, all MOEA/D runs clearly outperform NSGAII on such a high-dimensional problem instance.

4.1 Execution Time

Tables 3 and 4 summarize the average execution times of all experimental runs. As expected, the efficient usage of exploring MOEAs improves the overall execution time of all our algorithms. This speed improvement lies between 15% and 20% for most algorithms.

4.2 Conclusion

We have shown that our proposed method can clearly improve the convergence behavior and execution time of common MOEAs for many-objective optimization. The biggest improvement has been achieved for dominance-based SPEA2 and NSGAII algorithms, optimizing four and six objectives. Extending the objective space even showed minor improvements for MOEA/D while decreasing the execution time by

Table 3: Average Execution times of all algorithms for the 20-4fl-uni and 10-6fl-uni problems

Algorithm	Execution Time [ms]			
	20-4fl-uni		10-6fl-uni	
	Small	Large	Small	Large
MOEA/D	365	679	347	1606
SMOEA/D	293	613	268	1354
PMOEA/D	291	617	277	1319
SPEA2	7523	15684	32262	183520
SSPEA2	5563	14468	25040	149691
PSPEA2	6315	13524	23791	140072
NSGAII	1292	2575	1507	7848
SNSGAII	919	2117	1097	6127
PNSGAII	931	2087	1096	6158
IBEA	13534	27494	25648	139279
SIBEA	9209	22530	17149	104388
PIBEA	9364	22617	17306	103805

Table 4: Average Execution times of NSGAII and MOEA/D for the 15-12fl-uni problem

Algorithm	Exec. Time [ms]		Improvement [%]	
	Small	Large	Small	Large
MOEA/D	26627	105893		
SMOEA/D	23114	79105	13.2	25.3
PMOEA/D	23034	77300	13.5	27.0
NSGAII	69475	187793		
SNSGAII	58082	155548	16.4	17.2
PNSGAII	56872	156898	18.1	16.5

25%. Given constant run time, we can expect the performance gains to be even better.

For lower objective spaces, our experiment showed that the proposed sequential method outperforms it's parallel counterpart. However, this can not be said with certainty for the 12-objective problem instance where the parallel implementation of MOEA/D performed best. We suggest that the optimal strategy strongly depends on internal mechanics of the corresponding algorithm.

Summarizing, our method can clearly improve SPEA2 and NSGAII optimization performance on many-objective problems. For MOEA/D, we have achieved reduced execution time as the low-dimensional subproblems are faster to evaluate. We could even show minor performance improvements for the 12-objective problem instance.

Further research will focus on problems with higher objective space dimensions and according decomposition strategies. We also want to optimize the ratio between exploring and master phases and respective population sizes to improve the overall performance of our method. Additional performance gains are expected by implementing an adaptive heuristic for mutation and crossover probabilities.

5. REFERENCES

[1] N. Beume, B. Naujoks, and M. Emmerich. SMS-EMOA: Multiobjective selection based on dominated hypervolume. *European Journal of Operational Research*, 181(3):1653 – 1669, 2007.

[2] D. Brockhoff and E. Zitzler. Are all objectives necessary? on dimensionality reduction in evolutionary multiobjective optimization. In *Proceedings of the 9th International Conference on Parallel Problem Solving from Nature*, PPSN'06, pages 533–542, Berlin, Heidelberg, 2006. Springer-Verlag.

[3] D. W. Corne and J. D. Knowles. Techniques for highly multiobjective optimisation: Some nondominated points are better than others. In *Proceedings of the 9th Annual Conference on Genetic and Evolutionary Computation*, GECCO '07, pages 773–780, New York, NY, USA, 2007. ACM.

[4] K. Deb, A. Pratap, S. Agarwal, and T. Meyarivan. A fast and elitist multiobjective genetic algorithm: NSGA-II. *Evolutionary Computation, IEEE Transactions on*, 6(2):182–197, 2002.

[5] J. J. Durillo and A. J. Nebro. jMetal: A java framework for multi-objective optimization. *Advances in Engineering Software*, 42:760–771, 2011.

[6] E. Hughes. Evolutionary many-objective optimisation: many once or one many? In *Evolutionary Computation, 2005. The 2005 IEEE Congress on*, volume 1, pages 222–227 Vol.1, 2005.

[7] H. Ishibuchi, N. Akedo, H. Ohyanagi, and Y. Nojima. Behavior of EMO algorithms on many-objective optimization problems with correlated objectives. In *Evolutionary Computation (CEC), 2011 IEEE Congress on*, pages 1465–1472, 2011.

[8] H. Ishibuchi, N. Tsukamoto, and Y. Nojima. Evolutionary many-objective optimization: A short review. In *IEEE Congress on Evolutionary Computation*, pages 2419–2426, 2008.

[9] V. Khare, X. Yao, and K. Deb. Performance scaling of multi-objective evolutionary algorithms. In C. Fonseca, P. Fleming, E. Zitzler, L. Thiele, and K. Deb, editors, *Evolutionary Multi-Criterion Optimization*, volume 2632 of *Lecture Notes in Computer Science*, pages 376–390. Springer Berlin Heidelberg, 2003.

[10] J. Knowles and D. Corne. Instance generators and test suites for the multiobjective quadratic assignment problem. In C. Fonseca, P. Fleming, E. Zitzler, L. Thiele, and K. Deb, editors, *Evolutionary Multi-Criterion Optimization*, volume 2632 of *Lecture Notes in Computer Science*, pages 295–310. Springer Berlin Heidelberg, 2003.

[11] J. D. Knowles and D. Corne. Towards landscape analyses to inform the design of hybrid local search for the multiobjective quadratic assignment problem. In A. Abraham, J. R. del Solar, and M. Köppen, editors, *HIS*, volume 87 of *Frontiers in Artificial Intelligence and Applications*, pages 271–279. IOS Press, 2002.

[12] T. C. Koopmans and M. Beckmann. Assignment problems and the location of economic activities. *Econometrica: journal of the Econometric Society*, pages 53–76, 1957.

[13] M. N. Le, Y.-S. Ong, S. Menzel, C.-W. Seah, and B. Sendhoff. Multi co-objective evolutionary optimization: Cross surrogate augmentation for computationally expensive problems. In *Evolutionary Computation (CEC), 2012 IEEE Congress on*, pages 1–8, June 2012.

[14] S. Sahni and T. Gonzalez. P-complete approximation problems. *J. ACM*, 23(3):555–565, July 1976.

[15] L. Thiele, K. Miettinen, P. J. Korhonen, and J. Molina. A preference-based evolutionary algorithm for multi-objective optimization. *Evol. Comput.*, 17(3):411–436, Sept. 2009.

[16] Q. Zhang and H. Li. MOEA/D: A multiobjective evolutionary algorithm based on decomposition. *Evolutionary Computation, IEEE Transactions on*, 11(6):712–731, 2007.

[17] E. Zitzler and S. Künzli. Indicator-based selection in multiobjective search. In *in Proc. 8th International Conference on Parallel Problem Solving from Nature (PPSN VIII*, pages 832–842. Springer, 2004.

[18] E. Zitzler, M. Laumanns, and L. Thiele. SPEA2: Improving the strength pareto evolutionary algorithm for multiobjective optimization. In *Evolutionary Methods for Design, Optimisation, and Control*, pages 95–100. CIMNE, Barcelona, Spain, 2002.

[19] E. Zitzler and L. Thiele. Multiobjective evolutionary algorithms: a comparative case study and the strength pareto approach. *Evolutionary Computation, IEEE Transactions on*, 3(4):257–271, 1999.

[20] E. Zitzler, L. Thiele, M. Laumanns, C. M. Fonseca, and V. G. da Fonseca. Performance assessment of multiobjective optimizers: An analysis and review. *IEEE Transactions on Evolutionary Computation*, 7:117–132, 2002.

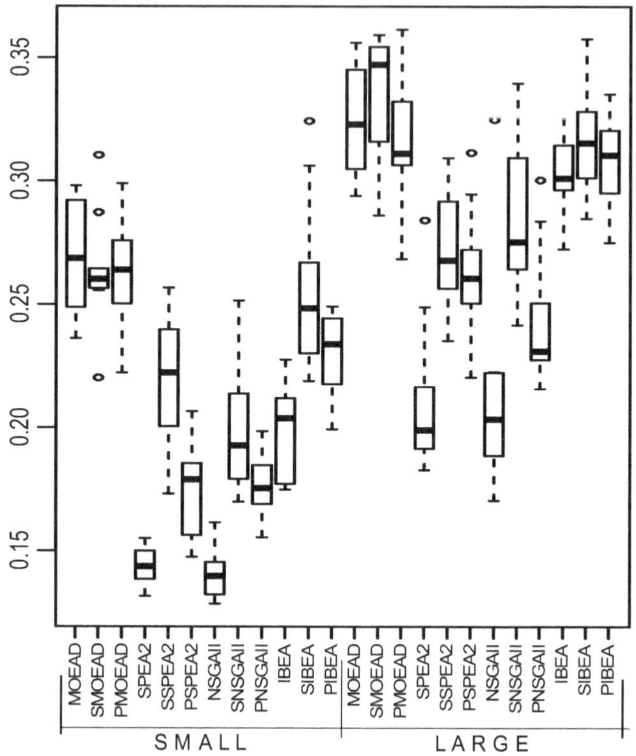

Figure 5: Boxplot of hypervolume for the 20-4fl-uni problem

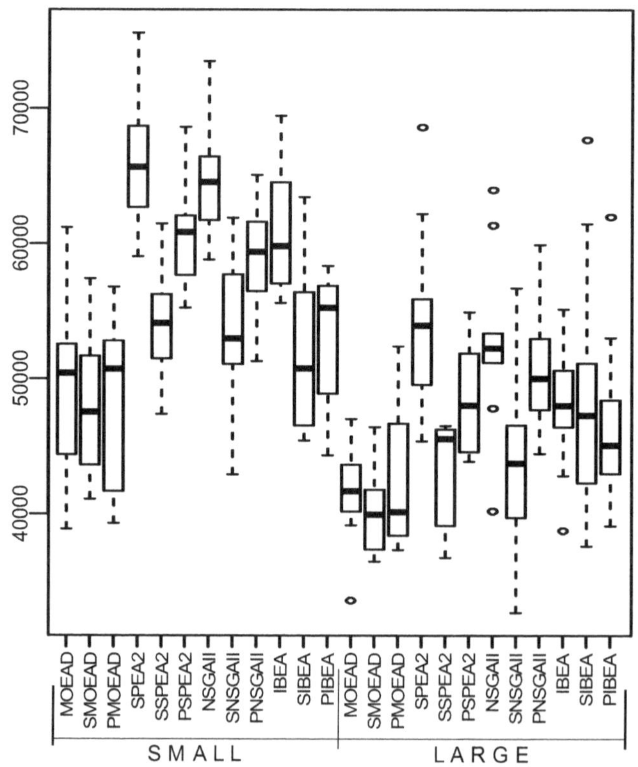

Figure 6: Boxplot of ϵ-indicators for the 20-4fl-uni problem

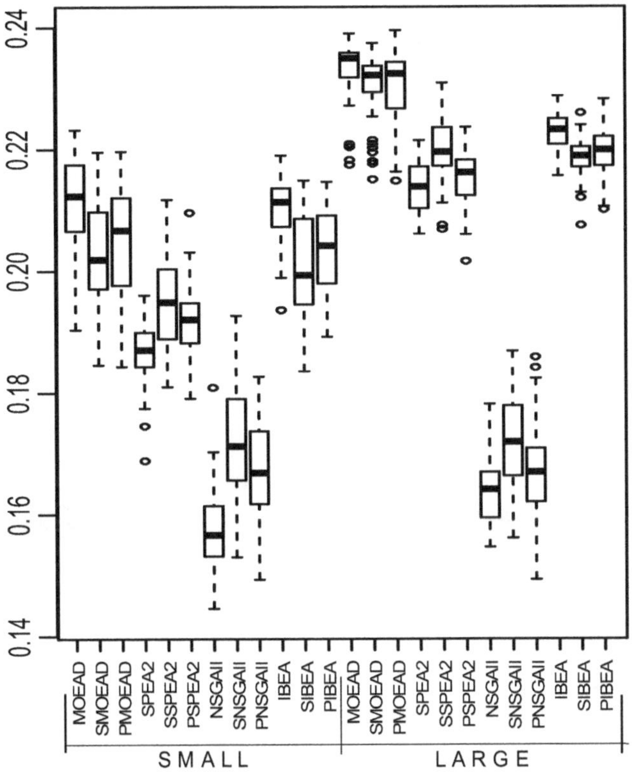

Figure 7: Boxplot of hypervolume for the 10-6fl-uni problem

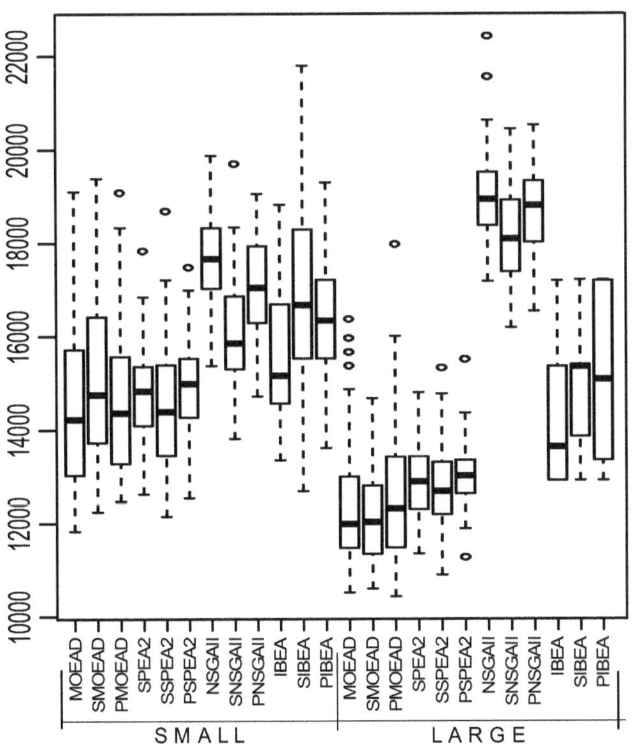

Figure 8: Boxplot of ϵ-indicators for the 10-6fl-uni problem

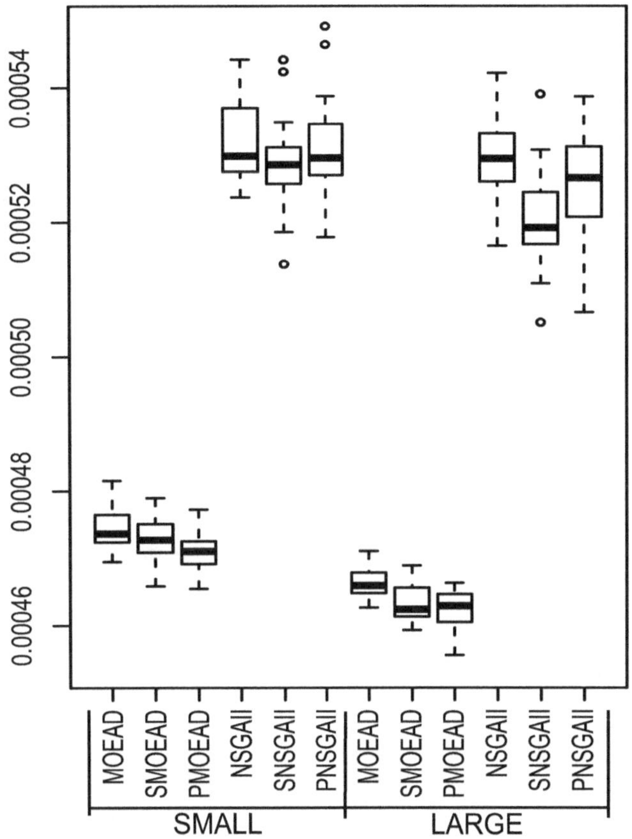

Figure 9: Boxplot of IGD for the 15-12fl-uni problem

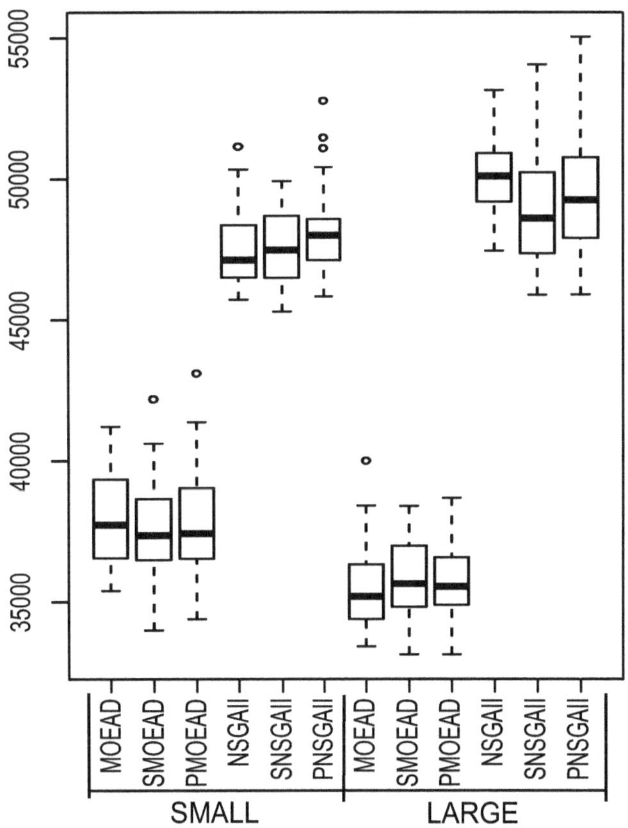

Figure 10: Boxplot of ϵ-indicators for the 15-12fl-uni problem

Efficiently Identifying Pareto Solutions when Objective Values Change

Jonathan E. Fieldsend*
Computer Science
University of Exeter, UK
J.E.Fieldsend@exeter.ac.uk

Richard M. Everson
Computer Science
University of Exeter, UK
R.M.Everson@exeter.ac.uk

ABSTRACT

In many multi-objective problems the objective values assigned to a particular design can change during the course of an optimisation. This may be due to dynamic changes in the problem itself, or updates to estimated objectives in noisy problems. In these situations, designs which are non-dominated at one time step may become dominated later not just because a new and better solution has been found, but because the existing solution's performance has degraded. Likewise, a dominated solution may later be identified as non-dominated because its objectives have comparatively improved. We propose management algorithms based on recording single "guardian dominators" for each solution which allow rapid discovery and updating of the non-dominated subset of solutions evaluated by an optimiser. We examine the computational complexity of our proposed approach, and compare the performance of different ways of selecting the guardian dominators.

Categories and Subject Descriptors

E.1 [**Data**]: Data Structures—*Graphs and networks*; G.1.6 [**Mathematics of Computing**]: Numerical Analysis—*Optimization, Global optimization*

General Terms

Algorithms, Experimentation, Performance, Theory

Keywords

Multi-objective optimisation, dynamic problems, uncertainty

1. INTRODUCTION

A typical assumption when performing an optimisation is that the evaluation of a solution does not vary unless the solution itself is modified. A number of data structures exist for efficiently maintaining and querying sets of multi-objective solutions in this situation (see [1] for a recent review). In the worst case, the number of domination comparisons required before a solution can be classified as non-dominated is equal to the size of the current non-dominated set. However, this assumes that a domination relationship between two solutions at time t will persist at all future time steps. If this does not hold it becomes necessary to track dominated as well as non-dominated solutions as the search progresses if we want to guarantee access at a particular time step to the best estimate of the non-dominated subset of solutions visited by an optimiser. How to efficiently maintain an elite archive when the assigned objectives are susceptible to change has not been widely addressed in the literature. We present here data structures and algorithms to facilitate the efficient identification of the non-dominated subset of solutions, when the *assigned* objectives to previously evaluated solutions may vary over time. This work is based on our recent technical report [5].

Assigned objectives may vary in a number of circumstances. In dynamic optimisation problems the problem itself changes over time, meaning that the objective vectors of all solutions evaluated at any time may vary if reassessed at a later time [10]. In noisy problems repeated evaluation of the same solution leads to different values for the objectives [8, 7]. Finally, an objective evaluation may be updated or refined at some later point due to the receipt of new information [4]. In all these cases, the objective vector $\mathbf{y}$ associated with the design vector $\mathbf{x}$ at some time t, may not be the same as the objective vector associated with $\mathbf{x}$ at $t+1$.

We now briefly review the ideas of dominance and Pareto optimality in Section 2 before discussing in Section 3 the computational complexity of managing a set where at each time step a previously evaluated solution may have its objectives changed, or a brand new solution may be evaluated. We introduce a data structure and algorithms to efficiently maintain the set of evaluated solutions and identify the non-dominated subset in Section 4. In Section 5 we provide empirical assessments of different algorithms. The paper concludes with a discussion in Section 6.

2. MULTI-OBJECTIVE OPTIMISATION

In multi-objective optimisation problems the optimiser seeks to simultaneously extremise D objectives, $f_d(\mathbf{x}), d = 1, \ldots, D$, where each objective depends upon an L-dimensional solution vector $\mathbf{x}$ of parameters or design variables. The parameters may also be subject to equality and inequality constraints which, for simplicity, we assume can be evalu-

*Corresponding author.

GECCO'14, July 12–16, 2014, Vancouver, BC, Canada.
Copyright 2014 ACM 978-1-4503-2662-9/14/07 ...$15.00.
http://dx.doi.org/10.1145/2576768.2598279.

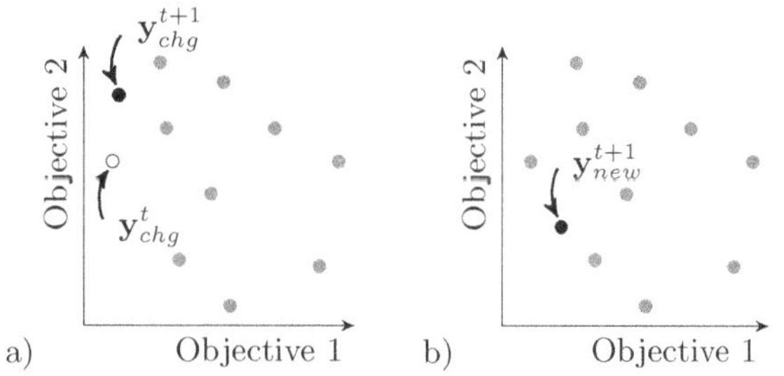

Figure 1: Two possible transitions from Y^t to Y^{t+1}. *a:* a single member of Y^t has had its value shifted from $\mathbf{y}^t_{chg}$ to $\mathbf{y}^{t+1}_{chg}$. *b:* a new solution has been evaluated with objective vector $\mathbf{y}^{t+1}_{new}$.

ated precisely. When the objectives are to be minimised the multi-objective optimisation problem may be expressed as: minimse $\mathbf{y} = \mathbf{f}(\mathbf{x}) = (f_1(\mathbf{x}), \ldots, f_D(\mathbf{x}))$ with $\mathbf{x} \in \mathcal{X} \subseteq \mathbb{R}^L$. The feasible domain $\mathcal{X}$ is defined by any design constraints. When there is more than one objective to be minimised, solutions may exist for which performance on one objective cannot be improved without reducing performance on at least one other. Such solutions are *Pareto optimal*.

The notion of *dominance* may be used to make Pareto optimality clearer. Assuming, without loss of generality, that the goal is to minimise the objectives, and given two *objective vectors*, $\mathbf{v}$ and $\mathbf{u}$, then $\mathbf{u}$ is said to *dominate* $\mathbf{v}$ iff $\mathbf{u}_d \le \mathbf{v}_d, \forall d = 1, \ldots, D$ and $\mathbf{u} \neq \mathbf{v}$. This is denoted as $\mathbf{u} \prec \mathbf{v}$.[1] Furthermore, we denote by $U \prec \mathbf{v}$ the situation where at least one member of the set U dominates $\mathbf{v}$. A set of objective vectors is said to be a *mutually non-dominating set* if no member of the set is dominated by any other member. A solution to a multi-objective optimisation problem is thus *Pareto optimal* if it is not dominated by any other feasible solution. The set of all Pareto optimal solutions is the Pareto set, and its image in objective space is the Pareto front. We denote the estimated Pareto front (the non-dominated subset of objective vectors associated with the solutions evaluated by an optimiser) by E.

Here we address problems in which the objectives associated with a solution may *vary* from one time step to the next. As such we effectively have a solution whose associated objective vector $\mathbf{y}$ is dependent on the time t at which it is evaluated; we indicate this with $\mathbf{y}^t$. We denote by Y^t the set of all objective vectors that have been evaluated at time t. An illustration is provided in Figure 1. In the left panel a single member $\mathbf{y}^t_{chg}$ of Y^t has a new objective value at time $t+1$, namely $\mathbf{y}^{t+1}_{chg}$. This new objective value is associated with the same solution as $\mathbf{y}^t_{chg}$. Also in this illustration all other $\mathbf{y}_i \in Y^t$, $i \neq chg$ are unaltered so that $\mathbf{y}^t_i = \mathbf{y}^{t+1}_i$, and $|Y^t| = |Y^{t+1}|$. In the right panel a new solution has been evaluated, resulting in $\mathbf{y}^{t+1}_{new}$, meaning that $|Y^{t+1}| = |Y^t| + 1$.

3. UPDATING ON A SINGLE TIME STEP

Consider a general set Y^t. At time $t+1$ either a single solution has had its associated objective vector in Y^t *changed* or a new solution has been evaluated for the first time, which is added to Y^t to form Y^{t+1}. In a situation where more than one member of Y^t has its value changed or there is more than a single new solution added to Y^t, each individual modification to the set may be viewed as a distinct time step and the order these are processed is immaterial to the final states of the solutions and the elite set.

The non dominated members E^t of Y^t may be selected via the `nondom` function defined below:

$$A = \texttt{nondom}(Z) = \{\mathbf{z} \in Z \,|\, \nexists \mathbf{v} \in Z, \mathbf{v} \prec \mathbf{z}\}. \tag{1}$$

The estimated Pareto front at time t may therefore be identified as $E^t = \texttt{nondom}(Y^t)$. E^t is also known as the elite set or archive. It is also useful to define a function which returns the subset of a population whose members dominate an objective vector $\mathbf{u}$:

$$B = \texttt{dom\_members}(\mathbf{u}, Z) = \{\mathbf{z} \in Z \,|\, \mathbf{z} \prec \mathbf{u}\}. \tag{2}$$

If $\mathbf{v}^t \in Y^t$ and $\texttt{dom\_members}(\mathbf{v}^t, Y^t) = \emptyset$, then $\mathbf{v}^t \in E^t$. Conversely if $\texttt{dom\_members}(\mathbf{v}^t, Y^t) \neq \emptyset$, then $\mathbf{v}^t \notin E^t$. E^t may thus be alternatively defined as:

$$E^t = \{\mathbf{y}^t \in Y^t \,|\, \texttt{dom\_members}(\mathbf{y}^t, Y^t) = \emptyset\}. \tag{3}$$

This may seem a slightly convoluted route to defining the non-dominated set, however it is a useful formulation for determining which solutions need to be compared to E^t for possible entry into E^{t+1}

3.1 Changing a dominated member of Y^t

Consider the effect of changing the objective vector of a dominated member of Y^t, $\mathbf{y}^t_{chg}$. If $\mathbf{y}^t_{chg} \notin E^t$, then the change to $\mathbf{y}^{t+1}_{chg}$ (from $\mathbf{y}^t_{chg}$) means that it should now enter E^{t+1} if $\texttt{dom\_members}(\mathbf{y}^{t+1}, E^t) = \emptyset$. However, there are no other members of Y^{t+1} that can enter E^{t+1} as a result of the movement of $\mathbf{y}^t_{chg}$ to $\mathbf{y}^{t+1}_{chg}$, because if they were dominated by members of E^t, they will still be dominated by the same members at $t+1$. That is, because $\mathbf{y}^t_{chg} \notin E^t$, then there is at least one $\mathbf{e}^t \in E^t$ which dominates $\mathbf{y}^t_{chg}$. At time $t+1$ this $\mathbf{e}^t$ therefore also dominates *all* solutions that $\mathbf{y}^t_{chg}$ dominated at time t.

Existing members of E^t will require removal from E^{t+1} if they are dominated by $\mathbf{y}^{t+1}_{chg}$, so if $\mathbf{y}^{t+1}_{chg}$ enters E^{t+1}, then each $\mathbf{e}^t_i \in E^t$ should be compared to $\mathbf{y}^{t+1}_{chg}$, and if $\mathbf{y}^{t+1}_{chg} \prec \mathbf{e}^t_i$ then $\mathbf{e}^t_i$ cannot be a member of E^{t+1}. As long as the domination comparison results are stored when $\mathbf{y}^{t+1}_{chg}$ is compared to E^t for entry into E^{t+1}, this stage will not require any additional domination calculations. Consequently a maximum of $|E^t|$ domination comparisons are required when the objective vector of a dominated member of Y^t is changed.

3.2 Changing a non-dominated member of Y^t

If prior to varying its objective values $\mathbf{y}^t_{chg} \in E^t$, then its change in location may mean it should not be in E^{t+1}. However, *even* if it does enter E^{t+1}, as illustrated in Figure 1a, solutions in Y^t that it dominated may enter E^{t+1} because the change in location to $\mathbf{y}^{t+1}_{chg}$ from $\mathbf{y}^t_{chg}$ may mean solutions in Y^t that were previously dominated by $\mathbf{y}^t_{chg}$ are no longer dominated in Y^{t+1}.

If $\texttt{dom\_members}(\mathbf{y}^{t+1}_{chg}, E^t) = \emptyset$, then $\mathbf{y}^{t+1}_{chg}$ will enter E^{t+1}; otherwise it will be excluded and E^{t+1} is initially set as

[1]As we are only concerned with the objective space representation of solutions here, we restrict our dominance notation to this space.

$E^t \setminus \{\mathbf{y}^t_{chg}\}$. If $\mathbf{y}^{t+1}_{chg}$ does enter E^{t+1}, then all other $\mathbf{e}^t_i \in E^t$ must be assessed to discover whether they are dominated by $\mathbf{y}^{t+1}_{chg}$. If $\mathbf{y}^{t+1}_{chg} \prec \mathbf{e}^t_i$, then $\mathbf{e}^t_i$ will not be a member of E^{t+1}. The members $\mathbf{y}^t_i$ of Y^t which are dominated by $\mathbf{y}^t_{chg}$ need to be compared to $\mathbf{y}^{t+1}_{chg}$ only if they are dominated exclusively by $\mathbf{y}^t_{chg}$ at time t; that is $\texttt{dom\_members}(\mathbf{y}^t_i, Y^t) = \{\mathbf{y}^t_{chg}\}$. This is because if a $\mathbf{y}^t_i$ is dominated by members of Y^t other than $\mathbf{y}^t_{chg}$, then it will still be dominated by them at $t+1$ since these members are unchanged.

We denote by K the number of solutions in Y^t which are dominated *exclusively* by $\mathbf{y}^t_{chg}$. In practise K is typically small (often zero); in order to be exclusively dominated by a single member of Y^t it is necessary (but not sufficient) for a solution to lie in the level 2 Pareto shell, namely those solutions that are non-dominated in the set $Y^t \setminus E^t$ (see [2]).

In the worst case $|E^t| + K - 1$ domination comparisons are required before the membership of E^{t+1} is determined. That is, $\mathbf{y}^{t+1}_{chg}$ will, at worst, need to be compared with all members of E^t bar itself ($|E^t| - 1$ comparisons) and the K solutions dominated only by $\mathbf{y}^t_{chg}$ must be compared to $\mathbf{y}^{t+1}_{chg}$, requiring K domination comparisons. If a solution is not dominated by $\mathbf{y}^{t+1}_{chg}$ it may enter $E^t + 1$ directly without any other domination comparisons required because if $\mathbf{y}^t_{chg}$ was the *only* dominating member in Y^t, then by definition no other members of E^t can dominate it. This comparison may also result in $\mathbf{y}^{t+1}_{chg}$ being removed from E^{t+1}.

3.3 Evaluating a new location

Finally, a completely new location, $\mathbf{y}^{t+1}_{new}$, may be suggested due to evaluation of a new solution. In this case determination of membership of E^{t+1} is made by domination comparison of this proposal with the members of E^t. From this we can see the computational complexity of determining the elite set of solutions when adding a new location into Y^{t+1} is in the worst case $|E^t|$ domination comparisons.

3.4 Multiple sequential updates

The cost of determining the elite set E^{t+1} of Y^{t+1} from a single changed member of Y^t, when all domination relations between members of Y^t have been recorded, is the sum of two components: $|E^t|$ domination comparisons plus an additional $K - 1$ domination comparisons when Y^t_{chg} is non-dominated. This complexity depends on the dominance relations between elements of Y^t being stored, which in itself is computationally expensive.

However, even if all the domination relations between members of Y^t are stored and the $|E^t|$ or $|E^t|+K-1$ domination comparisons necessary to determine the elite set E^{t+1} when a member of Y^t is changed are computed, this fails to update all the domination relations between elements of Y^{t+1}. In particular, the domination relations between elements of Y^t which are dominated by more than one element of Y^t are not updated. For instance, the updating scheme described in Section 3.3 relies on knowing *which* members of Y^t a solution is dominated by. We also need to compare a new solution $\mathbf{y}^{t+1}_{new}$ against $Y^t \setminus E^t$ to keep track of this information. Specifically, if $\mathbf{y}^{t+1}_{new}$ enters E^{t+1}, then the members of Y^t that it dominates will need to be identified (requiring at worst $|Y^{t+1} \setminus E^{t+1}|$ domination comparisons). If $\mathbf{y}^{t+1}_{new}$ is dominated by E_t, then we can utilise the observation that $\mathbf{y}^{t+1}_{new}$ can at most dominate the subset of Y^{t+1} which is dominated by *every* member of $\texttt{dom\_members}$ $(\mathbf{y}^{t+1}_{new}, E^{t+1})$, but in the worst case this too is also $Y^{t+1} \setminus E^{t+1}$.

We think of two solutions being *linked* if one dominates the other. Maintaining all domination links between members of Y^t as new solutions enter and existing solutions change is exorbitant for any $|Y^t|$ larger than a modest size. As such, it is impractical to use the approach outlined in Section 3 directly. However, efficient updates are possible by recording the information for just a *single* solution that dominates each member of $Y^t \setminus E^t$. The storage requirement of $\mathcal{O}(|Y^t|)$ is vastly reduced in comparison with the $\mathcal{O}(|Y^t|^2)$ needed to store all links, and the computational cost of maintaining these single links is also far superior to maintaining all domination links. We will now outline this proposed approach.

4. GUARDIAN DOMINATORS

Instead of keeping track of *all* domination relations between members of Y^t, here we suggest that for each member $\mathbf{y}^t_i$ of $Y^t \setminus E^t$ a *single* other solution in Y^t is recorded which dominates it: its *guardian dominator*. As we show below, tracking these links as search progresses is computationally inexpensive, and permits Y^t and E^t to be cheaply updated.

The guardian dominator of the ith member of Y^t is labelled $\mathbf{y}^{t,\star}_i$ for convenience (therefore $\mathbf{y}^{t,\star}_i \prec \mathbf{y}^t_i$). By definition there is no solution in Y^t which dominates any members of E^t, and as such the elements of E^t are not assigned guardian dominators. Figure 2 illustrates the ways in which these single relationships are maintained for $D = 2$ objectives. Figure 2b shows the 43 domination relationships between the 14 solutions plotted in Figure 2a; domination links are shown as edges between each dominating and dominated solution. Figure 2c shows the same set, but with only domination links between members of $Y^t \setminus E^t$ and their guardian dominators, which are selected from E^t, making 10 edges in total as $|Y^t \setminus E^t| = 10$. Figure 2d again shows Y^t, but this time with the $\mathbf{y}^{t,\star}_i$ selected arbitrarily from the set of all potential candidates, not just those in E^t, which again results in 10 edges. Finally, Figure 2e shows the links between each element of $Y^t \setminus E^t$ and their guardian dominator, with the $\mathbf{y}^{t,\star}_i$ assigned as the *closest* dominating member of Y^t. Here we have used the Euclidean distance to determine the proximity of solutions, but other distance measures might be more useful in other situations.

As can be seen in Figure 2, a substantial number of domination relations can exist between the elements of a general set of data. The minimum number is $|Y^t \setminus E^t|$, which corresponds to each element of $Y^t \setminus E^t$ being dominated by a single element of E^t; that is, there are two Pareto shells, with each element of E^t dominating non-intersecting subsets of the second shell. The maximum is $\binom{|Y^t|}{2}$, which corresponds to the situation where the number of Pareto shells equals the number of elements in Y^t so that the element forming the first shell dominates $|Y^t|-1$ solutions, the next shell element dominates $|Y^t| - 2$ solutions, and so on.

The minimum number of guardian dominators and corresponding domination links needed for a set Y^t is $|Y^t \setminus E^t|$, because each member of $Y^t \setminus E^t$ must be assigned a guardian.

On inspection of Figures 2d-e, it can be seen that if the guardian dominator $\mathbf{y}^{t,\star}_i$ of an element $\mathbf{y}^t_i$ is itself dominated, then there is a chain of domination links which eventually reaches a member of E^t. This is inevitable, because all el-

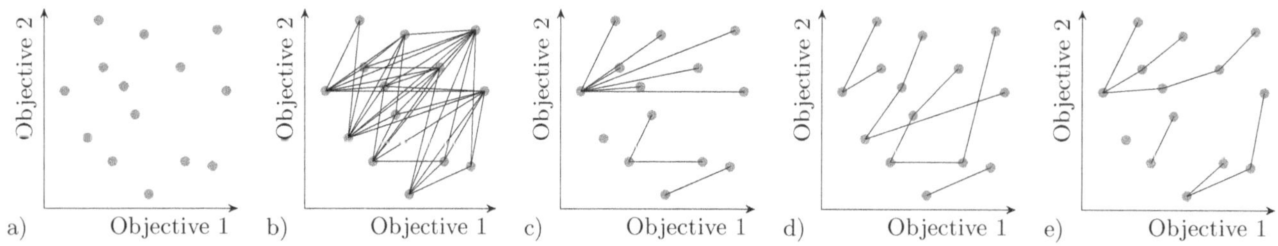

Figure 2: *a:* Graph representations of a general set of 14 solutions, plotted via their objective values in Y^t. *b:* All domination relations between solutions shown via edges. *c:* Single domination relation edge plotted per solution, only members of E^t selected as guardian dominators. *d:* Single domination relation edge shown per solution, guardian dominator selected arbitrarily from valid candidates in Y^t. *e:* Single domination relation edge shown per solution, closest dominating member selected as guardian dominator.

Algorithm 1 Methods for determining E^{t+1} and for assigning guardian dominator when a new solution is generated. Best case and worst case domination comparisons required are indicated at the right using $\mathcal{B}$ and $\mathcal{W}$ respectively. Best case varies for options 2.1-2.4 depending on whether option 1.1 is selected or options 1.2-1.3 to obtain $\mathbf{e}^t_{dom}$. It is possible to combine this approach with data structures suggested in [1] to reduce the number of domination comparisons required for line 2.

1: **if** $E^t \not\prec \mathbf{y}^{t+1}_{new}$ **then** — *New solution $\mathbf{y}^{t+1}_{new}$ is not dominated by any element of E^t*
2: $\quad E^{t+1} := E^t \cup \{\mathbf{y}^{t+1}_{new}\}$; $E^{t+1} := E^{t+1} \setminus \{\mathbf{e}^t \in E^t \,|\, \mathbf{y}^{t+1}_{new} \prec \mathbf{e}^t\}$ — *Ensure E^{t+1} is a non-dominated set*
3: $\quad$ Assign $\mathbf{y}^{t+1}_{new}$ as guardian dominator for $\{\mathbf{e}^t \in E^t \,|\, \mathbf{y}^{t+1}_{new} \prec \mathbf{e}^t\}$ — $\mathcal{B} = \mathcal{W} = |E^t|$
4: **else** — *New solution $\mathbf{y}^{t+1}_{new}$ is dominated by an element of E^t*
5: $\quad E^{t+1} := E^t$
6: $\quad$ **option 1.1:** $\mathbf{e}^{t+1}_{dom}$:= the first element in E^{t+1} which dominates $\mathbf{y}^{t+1}_{new}$
7: $\quad$ **option 1.2:** $\mathbf{e}^{t+1}_{dom}$:= the closest element in E^{t+1} which dominates $\mathbf{y}^{t+1}_{new}$
8: $\quad$ **option 1.3:** $\mathbf{e}^{t+1}_{dom}$:= as the element in E^{t+1} which dominates $\mathbf{y}^{t+1}_{new}$ and which guards the fewest others
9: $\quad$ **option 2.1:** $\mathbf{y}^{t+1,\star}_{new} := \mathbf{e}^{t+1}_{dom}$ — $\mathcal{B} = 1$ *or* $|E^t|$, $\mathcal{W} = |E^t|$
10: $\quad$ **option 2.2:** $\mathbf{y}^{t+1,\star}_{new}$:= the first dominating element of $Y^t_{dom} \cup \{\mathbf{e}^{t+1}_{dom}\}$ — $\mathcal{B} = 1$ *or* $|E^t| + 1$, $\mathcal{W} = |E^t \cup Y^t_{dom}|$
11: $\quad$ **option 2.3:** $\mathbf{y}^{t+1,\star}_{new}$:= the closest dominating element of $Y^t_{dom} \cup \{\mathbf{e}^{t+1}_{dom}\}$ — $\mathcal{B} = |Y^t_{dom}| + 1$ *or* $\mathcal{B} = \mathcal{W} = |E^t \cup Y^t_{dom}|$
12: $\quad$ **option 2.4:** $\mathbf{y}^{t+1,\star}_{new}$:= the dominating element of $Y^t_{dom} \cup \{\mathbf{e}^{t+1}_{dom}\}$ which guards the fewest — $\mathcal{B}$ *&* $\mathcal{W}$ *as option 2.3*
13: **end if**

ements of Y^t have a dominating member associated with them except the members of E^t themselves. As such all chains *must* end with an E^t solution. Chains may join together as they approach E^t, but it is impossible for a dominated solution not to have a direct sequence to one of the elements of E^t via the guardian dominator links. This property is extremely useful, and we exploit it in our proposed approach for maintaining Y^t and identifying E^t. We denote the subset of Y^t for which $\mathbf{y}^t_i$ acts as the guardian dominator by Y^t_i. Note that $\mathbf{y}^t_i$ may not be the only element in Y^t which dominates members of Y^t_i, it is merely the dominator that is *recorded*.

4.1 Selecting and updating guardians

At first sight it appears desirable to minimise the number of solutions for which any solution is the guardian dominator; that is to prefer arrangements like Figure 2d and 2e to Figure 2c. This sort of configuration minimises the number of domination comparisons that must be made if a guardian itself is changed. However, to achieve this more domination comparisons are required than, for example, assigning the first solution dominating $\mathbf{y}^{t+1}$ to be $\mathbf{y}^{t+1,\star}$ the guardian dominator of $\mathbf{y}^{t+1}$. We suggest a number of different methods for selecting and updating guardian dominators in Algorithms 1 and 2 which span the range of low domination cost for assigning guardians, but potentially high domination cost when elements of Y^t are changed, through to higher domination cost for guardian assignment, but fewer domination comparisons when a solution is changed. It should be noted that it is generally impossible to ensure $|Y^t_i| \leq 1$ for all members of Y^t, because if there are more solutions in Pareto shell 2 than shell 1, then some members of E^t will inevitably be the guardian dominator for more than one element of Y^t.

Algorithm 1 presents the options we consider when a new solution $\mathbf{y}^{t+1}_{new}$ is evaluated at time $t+1$. If it is not dominated by the non-dominated subset of Y^t (line 1) then it is added to E^{t+1}, and any members of E^t which $\mathbf{y}^{t+1}_{new}$ dominates are assigned $\mathbf{y}^{t+1}_{new}$ as their guardian dominator. On the other hand, if $\mathbf{y}^{t+1}_{new}$ is dominated, we consider a number of options to assign its guardian. First, one of the members of E^t which dominates $\mathbf{y}^{t+1}_{new}$ must be selected (options 1.1-1.3), and labelled as $\mathbf{e}^{t+1}_{dom}$. Computationally the quickest option is to assign $\mathbf{y}^{t+1,\star}_{new}$ as the first element found in E^t which dominates $\mathbf{y}^{t+1}_{new}$ (lines 6 & 9). At worst this requires E^t domination comparisons, but in the best case just a single domination comparison is required. However, this approach may result in non-dominated members of Y^t being the guardian dominators for many solutions (c.f. Figure 2c), so that many comparisons are required should the value of one of these guardians change later.

The idea underlying option 2.2 is to promote longer chains of domination links by assigning a guardian dominator from solutions that are not in the elite archive. Rather than searching through all Y^{t+1}, a greedy assignment is made.

Algorithm 2 Methods for determining E^{t+1} when objective values of a member of Y^t change, and for assigning/updating guardian dominators. Best and worst case domination comparisons required are indicated using $\mathcal{B}$ and $\mathcal{W}$.

if $\mathbf{y}^t_{chg} \in E^t$ **then** — *Non-dominated solution being changed*
  if $\{E^t \cup Y^t_{chg} \setminus \{\mathbf{y}^t_{chg}\}\} \nprec \mathbf{y}^{t+1}_{chg}$ **then** — *Changed solution is still non-dominated*
    $U = \{\mathbf{e}^t \in E^t | \mathbf{y}^{t+1}_{chg} \prec \mathbf{e}^t\}$ — *Identify dominated members of previous elite set*
    $E^{t+1} = \{\mathbf{y}^{t+1}_{chg}\} \cup E^t \setminus U$
    Set $\mathbf{y}^{t+1}_{chg}$ as guardian dominator for all elements in U — $\mathcal{B} = \mathcal{W} = |E^t \cup Y^t_{chg}| - 1$
  else — *changed solution is now dominated*
    $E^{t+1} = E^t \setminus \{\mathbf{y}^t_{chg}\}$
    option 3.1: $\mathbf{y}^{t+1,\star}_{chg} :=$ first dominating element of $E^t \cup Y^t_{chg}$ — $\mathcal{B} = 1, \mathcal{W} = |E^t \cup Y^t_{chg}|$
    option 3.2: $\mathbf{y}^{t+1,\star}_{chg} :=$ closest dominating element of $E^t \cup Y^t_{chg}$ — $\mathcal{B} = \mathcal{W} = |E^t \cup Y^t_{chg}|$
    option 3.3: $\mathbf{y}^{t+1,\star}_{chg} :=$ dominating element of $E^t \cup Y^t_{chg}$ which guards the fewest — $\mathcal{B} = \mathcal{W} = |E^t \cup Y^t_{chg}|$
  end if
  for each $\mathbf{y}^t_i \in Y^t_{chg}$ **do** — *Check all solutions that $\mathbf{y}^t_{chg}$ was a guardian dominator for*
    if $\{E^{t+1} \cup Y^t_{chg}\} \nprec \mathbf{y}^t_i$ **then** — *Previously dominated solution is now non-dominated*
      $E^{t+1} := E^{t+1} \cup \{\mathbf{y}^t_i\}$ — $\mathcal{W} = |E^{t+1} \cup Y^t_{chg}|$
    else
      option 4.1: if $\mathbf{y}^{t+1}_{chg} \prec \mathbf{y}^t_i$ then $\mathbf{y}^{t+1,\star}_i := \mathbf{y}^{t+1}_{chg}$, else assign first dominating element of E^{t+1} — $\mathcal{B} = 1, \mathcal{W} = |E^{t+1}|$
      option 4.2: $\mathbf{y}^{t+1,\star}_i :=$ first dominating element of $S = Y^t_{chg} \cup \{\mathbf{y}^{t+1}_{chg}\} \cup E^{t+1}$ — $\mathcal{B} = 1, \mathcal{W} = |S|$
      option 4.3: $\mathbf{y}^{t+1,\star}_i :=$ closest dominating element of $S = Y^t_{chg} \cup \{\mathbf{y}^{t+1}_{chg}\} \cup E^{t+1}$ — $\mathcal{B} = \mathcal{W} = |S|$
      option 4.4: $\mathbf{y}^{t+1,\star}_i :=$ dominating element of $S = Y^t_{chg} \cup \{\mathbf{y}^{t+1}_{chg}\} \cup E^{t+1}$ which guards the fewest — $\mathcal{B} = \mathcal{W} = |S|$
    end if
  end for
else — *Dominated solution being changed*
  if $E^t \nprec \mathbf{y}^{t+1}_{chg}$ **then** — *Changed solution is now non-dominated*
    $U = \{\mathbf{e}^t \in E^t | \mathbf{y}^{t+1}_{chg} \prec \mathbf{e}^t\}$ — *Identify dominated members of previous elite set*
    Set $\mathbf{y}^{t+1}_{chg}$ as the guardian dominator for all elements in U
    $E^{t+1} = \{\mathbf{y}^{t+1}_{chg}\} \cup E^t \setminus U$ — $\mathcal{W} = |E^t|$
  else — *Changed solution is still dominated*
    $E^{t+1} := E^t$ — $\mathcal{B} = 1, \mathcal{W} = |E^t|$
    option 5.1: $\mathbf{y}^{t+1,\star}_{chg} :=$ first dominating element of $\mathbf{y}^{t,\star}_{chg} \cup E^{t+1}$ — $\mathcal{B} = 1, \mathcal{W} = |E^{t+1}| + 1$
    option 5.2: $\mathbf{y}^{t+1,\star}_{chg} :=$ first dominating element of $S = Y^t_{chg} \cup \mathbf{y}^{t,\star}_{chg} \cup E^{t+1}$ — $\mathcal{B} = 1, \mathcal{W} = |S|$
    option 5.3: $\mathbf{y}^{t+1,\star}_{chg} :=$ closest dominating element of $S = Y^t_{chg} \cup \mathbf{y}^{t,\star}_{chg} \cup E^{t+1}$ — $\mathcal{B} = \mathcal{W} = |S|$
    option 5.4: $\mathbf{y}^{t+1,\star}_{chg} :=$ dominating element of $S = Y^t_{chg} \cup \mathbf{y}^{t,\star}_{chg} \cup E^{t+1}$ which guards the fewest — $\mathcal{B} = \mathcal{W} = |S|$
  end if
  for each $\mathbf{y}^t_i \in Y^t_{chg}$ **do** — *Check all solutions that $\mathbf{y}^t_{chg}$ was a guardian dominator for*
    option 6.1: if $\mathbf{y}^{t+1}_{chg} \prec \mathbf{y}^t_i$ then $\mathbf{y}^{t+1,\star}_i := \mathbf{y}^{t+1}_{chg}$, else $\mathbf{y}^{t+1,\star}_i := \mathbf{y}^{t,\star}_{chg}$ — $\mathcal{B} = \mathcal{W} = 1$
    option 6.2: $\mathbf{y}^{t+1,\star}_i :=$ first dominating element of $S = Y^t_{chg} \cup \{\mathbf{y}^{t+1}_{chg}\} \cup \{\mathbf{y}^{t,\star}_{chg}\}$ — $\mathcal{B} = 1, \mathcal{W} = |S|$
    option 6.3: $\mathbf{y}^{t+1,\star}_i :=$ closest dominating element of $S = Y^t_{chg} \cup \{\mathbf{y}^{t+1}_{chg}\} \cup \{\mathbf{y}^{t,\star}_{chg}\} \cup E^{t+1}$ — $\mathcal{B} = \mathcal{W} = |S|$
    option 6.4: $\mathbf{y}^{t+1,\star}_i :=$ dom'ing element of $S = Y^t_{chg} \cup \{\mathbf{y}^{t+1}_{chg}\} \cup \{\mathbf{y}^{t,\star}_{chg}\} \cup E^{t+1}$ which guards the fewest — $\mathcal{B} = \mathcal{W} = |S|$
  end for
end if

$\mathbf{y}^{t+1,\star}_{new}$ is taken as the first element of Y^t which has as a guardian the selected member of the elite archive which dominates $\mathbf{y}^{t+1}_{new}$. Specifically $\mathbf{y}^{t+1,\star}_{new}$ is assigned to be the first element in $Y^t_{dom} \cup \{\mathbf{e}^{t+1}_{dom}\}$ which dominates $\mathbf{y}^{t+1}_{new}$.

Extending the idea of promoting long chains of domination links, in option 2.3 we seek to attach a changed element to an existing chain at a location distant from E^t. The new guardian is then chosen to be the closest (using the Euclidean metric) dominating member of the subset of Y^t for which $\mathbf{e}^{t+1}_{dom}$ was the guardian, namely Y^t_{dom}. Choosing the closest ensures that the guardian cannot dominate any of the valid alternatives in $Y^t_{dom} \cup \{\mathbf{e}^{t+1}_{dom}\}$.

Finally, in option 2.4, the dominating member of $Y^t_{dom} \cup \{\mathbf{e}^{t+1}_{dom}\}$ which is the currently guardian dominator for the fewest elements of Y^t is selected as $\mathbf{y}^{t+1,\star}_{new}$. This attempts to reduce the total number of domination links from a solution, but does not ensure that the selected guardian is at the end of a chain in $Y^t_{dom} \cup \{\mathbf{e}^{t+1}_{dom}\}$. Option combination 1.1 and 2.1 has the lowest best case cost, but is less effective at generating long chains. Options 2.2-2.4 require the same number of domination comparisons.

Algorithm 2 presents the options we consider when an existing solution $\mathbf{y}^t_{chg}$ is changed at time $t+1$. If $\mathbf{y}^t_{chg} \in E^t$ then the fact that $\mathbf{y}^{t+1}_{chg}$ is not dominated by any element of E^t is insufficient to determine whether $\mathbf{y}^{t+1}_{chg}$ should enter E^{t+1} because it may have moved to a position where it is dominated by a solution that it dominated at time t. Therefore it must also be compared to the elements of Y^t_{chg} to determine whether it belongs to E^{t+1}. If it is not dominated by any elements of Y^t_{chg}, it joins E^{t+1}, and any elements of E^t which it now dominates do not enter E^{t+1} and are assigned $\mathbf{y}^{t+1}_{chg}$ as their guardian dominator. If it does not enter E^{t+1} then we consider three options for assigning its guardian $\mathbf{y}^{t+1,\star}_{chg}$. The first (line 8) assigns the first element of $E^t \cup Y^t_{chg}$ found which dominates it, the second selects the Euclidean closest from the same set, and the third selects the dominating member from the set which currently guards the fewest members of Y^t.

Irrespective of the assignment of $\mathbf{y}^{t+1}_{chg}$, the solutions for which it was guardian dominator must now be checked to discover whether they are in E^{t+1}. If they are not elite, then we examine four options for assigning their guardian dominator. In the first option (line 16) $\mathbf{y}^{t+1}_{chg}$ remains the guardian if its changed position still dominates the solution, otherwise the first dominating member of E^{t+1} is selected. The other options use $Y^t_{chg} \cup \{\mathbf{y}^{t+1}_{chg}\} \cup E^{t+1}$, selecting either the first dominating member identified, the closest dominating member, or the dominating member guarding the fewest.

In the situation where $\mathbf{y}^t_{chg} \notin E^t$, $\mathbf{y}^{t+1}_{chg}$ only needs to be compared to E^t to determine if it is non-dominated or not. The options we consider for guardian dominator assignment to $\mathbf{y}^{t+1}_{chg}$ if it is dominated are: $\mathbf{y}^{t,\star}_{chg}$ if it still dominates, otherwise the first dominating from E^t; the first dominating element of $Y^t_{chg} \cup \{\mathbf{y}^{t,\star}_{chg}\} \cup E^{t+1}$; the closest dominating member of this set; or the dominating member guarding the fewest. As in the earlier case, the guardian dominators for the elements of Y^t_{chg} may also need to be reassigned. In the first option $\mathbf{y}^{t+1}_{chg}$ is kept as guardian dominator if its changed position still dominates the solution, if not the previous guardian dominator of $\mathbf{y}^{t+1}_{chg}$ itself is selected, as this *must* dominate all members of Y^t_{chg}. The next three options use $Y^t_{chg} \cup \{\mathbf{y}^{t+1}_{chg}\} \cup \{\mathbf{y}^{t,\star}_{chg}\} \cup E^{t+1}$, the first selecting the first dominating member identified, the second selecting the closest dominating member, and the last selecting the dominating member which guards the fewest in Y^t.

5. EMPIRICAL ANALYSIS

Although we give the worst case numbers of domination comparisons needed for the different updating options, many of them are determined by the size of Y^t_{chg}, which is determined by the particular problem being optimised and how guardians were chosen earlier. We therefore illustrate how these various methods perform on synthetic data which is generated to mimic the behaviour of different convergence/search types, and on a running optimiser. We follow a general procedure in which, at alternate time steps, either the objective vector for an existing member of Y^t is changed or a new location $\mathbf{y}^{t+1}_{new}$ is added.

In the simulation, for each member of Y^t we store an underlying 'true' objective location, which is never observed directly. Instead, an evaluation of a solution results in a noisy version of the true objective vector obtained by adding Gaussian noise. The $\mathbf{y}$ of a solution is the mean of the noisy objective vector samples taken thus far. This mimics the refinement of objectives in noisy optimisation (see e.g. [9, 6]). We model the iterative generating process of Y^t in four distinct ways, based on two solution generation models, and two selection models. These mimic both how an optimiser may progress over time, and how there may be bias in the solution selected for changing.

For solution generation the two regimes are:

1. The underlying 'true' objective locations of new solutions are drawn at random from a unit variance Gaussian. This emulates a search problem where the objective vector of a new solution bears little relation to fitness of the best members evaluated thus far (the likely parents), or one that is already well-converged and therefore rarely finds a better solution.

2. The underlying 'true' objective locations of new solutions are set as a perturbed value close to the 'true' objective vector of a randomly selected member of E^t (perturbed by additive multivariate isotropic Gaussian noise with $\sigma_{mut} = 0.25$). This simulates a search where the evolved solutions are in the general region of objective space as previously discovered good solutions.

For selecting which $\mathbf{y}^t$ to vary at a time step:

1. $\mathbf{y}^t_{chg}$ is selected at random from Y^t. Any solution may have its objective vector changed.

2. $\mathbf{y}^t_{chg}$ is selected at random from E^t. Only estimated Pareto solutions have their objective vector changed.

Combining a solution generation procedure with a selection procedure creates four distinct simulations. $\mathcal{S}_1$: random new solutions, random changed solutions; $\mathcal{S}_2$: random new solutions, random elite changed solutions; $\mathcal{S}_3$: new solutions in vicinity of E^t, random changed solutions; $\mathcal{S}_4$: new solutions in vicinity of E^t, random elite changed solutions.

We initialised Y^1 with a single location in objective space, whose true objective vector is $\mathbf{0}$, which is perturbed by additive multivariate isotropic Gaussian noise with $\sigma_{noise} = 0.1$. The simulations reported here used two objectives and were run for 100,000 time steps. We use the option configurations detailed in Table 1, which cover a wide range of the methods described in Algorithms 1 and 2.

Figure 3 shows how key measures of complexity develop using the different methods of guardian selection on the simulations as $|Y^t|$ increases. The top row shows the cumulative moving average size of selected Y^t_{chg}, averaged over 50 runs. This is recorded every time step where a member of Y^t is changed (and therefore a Y^t_{chg} was used). The middle row shows the (cumulative) mean number of domination comparisons required at each time step to identify E^t. Finally, the bottom row shows the ratio between the number of domination comparisons required, and the size of E^t, thus allowing us to discount the effect of different elite population sizes in the different simulations. A few key points may be observed. Although the methods which compare fewer solutions when assigning a guardian dominator to new locations ($\mathcal{C}_{1-3}$) tend to require fewer domination comparisons on some simulations (notably $\mathcal{S}_1$ and $\mathcal{S}_3$), these methods require orders of magnitude more domination comparisons on $\mathcal{S}_2$ (randomly chosen new solutions and randomly chosen elite changed solutions). This is because the elite members tend to act as the guardian dominators for many members of Y^t, compared with the other methods, and these heavily-loaded elements are also changed relatively frequently. Therefore, this combination of methods appears to be a poor choice when an algorithm is only advancing its Pareto front estimate slowly,

Label	Option combinations	Description of guardian assignment
$\mathcal{C}_1$	1.1, 2.1, 3.1, 4.1, 5.1, 6.1	Assigns first dominating to $\mathbf{y}_{new}^{t+1}$, and first dominating to $\mathbf{y}_{chg}^{t+1}$
$\mathcal{C}_2$	1.2, 2.1, 3.1, 4.1, 5.1, 6.1	Assigns closest elite to $\mathbf{y}_{new}^{t+1}$, and first dominating to $\mathbf{y}_{chg}^{t+1}$
$\mathcal{C}_3$	1.3, 2.1, 3.1, 4.1, 5.1, 6.1	Assigns dominating elite which guards fewest to $\mathbf{y}_{new}^{t+1}$, and first dominating to $\mathbf{y}_{chg}^{t+1}$
$\mathcal{C}_4$	1.1, 2.2, 3.1, 4.2, 5.2, 6.2	Assigns first dominating found – always searching through Y_{chg}^t first for $\mathbf{y}_{chg}^{t+1}$
$\mathcal{C}_5$	1.2, 2.3, 3.2, 4.3, 5.3, 6.3	Assigns closest dominating solution from comparison sets
$\mathcal{C}_6$	1.3, 2.4, 3.3, 4.4, 5.4, 6.4	Assigns dominating solution with fewest guarded solutions from comparison sets

Table 1: Methods combinations tested empirically. Options refer to Algorithms 1 and 2.

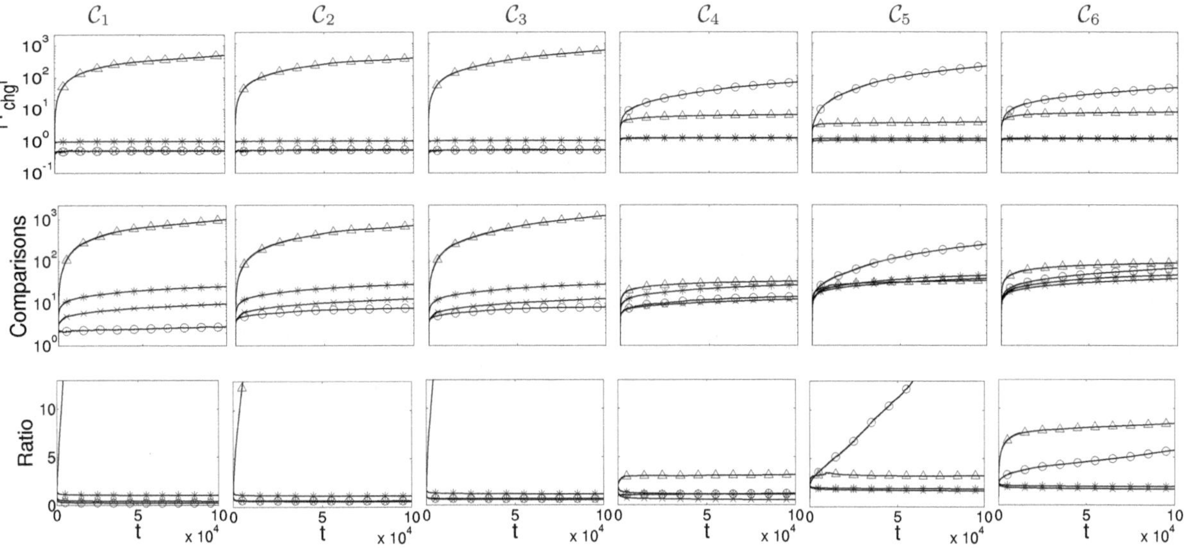

Figure 3: Growth of $|Y_{chg}^t|$ and number of domination comparisons using different guardian selection methods. Top row (log scale): $|Y_{chg}^t|$. Middle row (log scale) number of domination comparisons. Bottom row: ratio of number of dominations to elite archive size. Each panel shows the cumulative moving average over 100,000 time steps, averaged over 50 runs. Circles denote simulation $\mathcal{S}_1$, triangles: $\mathcal{S}_2$, crosses: $\mathcal{S}_3$ and stars: $\mathcal{S}_4$.

and where there is a bias towards changing elite solutions. Across the simulation types, the combination $\mathcal{C}_4$ appears to give the best overall performance, having a slightly worse ratio on simulation $\mathcal{S}_1$, than $\mathcal{C}_{1-3}$, but a vastly better ratio on $\mathcal{S}_2$, and on all simulations the average number of comparisons per time step required is 0.5-3 times $|E^t|$.

In detail, $\mathcal{C}_4$ behaves as follows. If a new proposal is dominated it selects the guardian from the set of solutions guarded by the first member in E^t which dominates $\mathbf{y}_{new}^{t+1}$. If an existing elite member is changed and moved to a dominated location, its guardian is selected as the first dominating member of $E^t \cup Y_{chg}^t$. The new guardian of each Y_{chg}^t element in this case is selected as the first dominating member of $Y_{chg}^t \cup \{\mathbf{y}_{chg}^{t+1}\} \cup E^{t+1}$ (otherwise, the element enters E^{t+1}). If a *dominated* member of Y^t is moved to a non-dominated location, it is set as the guardian for any newly dominated elements E^t. If instead it moves to another still dominated location, its guardian dominator is kept the same (if it still dominates) or replaced with the first dominating member of E^{t+1} identified. All elements of Y^{t+1} for which $\mathbf{y}_{chg}^t$ was guardian are compared to each other, the new location of the changed solution, $\mathbf{y}_{chg}^{t+1}$, and the location of the guardian dominator of $\mathbf{y}_{chg}^t$ ($\mathbf{y}_{chg}^{t,\star}$). The first dominating element of this set is assigned as the guardian dominator for each previously guarded solution.

We also examined the effect of the methods in a simple multi-objective optimiser, applied to two of the DTLZ test problems [3], where objective values are subject to change. We use two and three objective versions of DTLZ1, which has multiple deceptive fronts, the majority of which are distant from the Pareto front, and DTLZ2, where random solutions are in the general vicinity of the Pareto front. We chose these two as they nicely span a range of expected population behaviours. We modified the DTLZ problems so that isotropic Gaussian noise with $\sigma = 0.1$ contaminated the objectives. The problems were optimised with a $(|E^t|+1)$-Evolution Strategy (ES), in which at each iteration (time step) a member of E^t was selected at random. This member was either mutated on a single design parameter (using Gaussian mutation with $\sigma = 0.1$), creating $\mathbf{y}_{new}^{t+1}$, or reevaluated to update its mean objective vector estimate, resulting in $\mathbf{y}_{chg}^{t+1}$, using an accumulative resampling approach to improve the objective estimate [9, 6].

Figure 4 shows the empirical results of using the different methods to identify E^t for this optimiser. Note that the elite archives E^t identified by each method are identical, as is the ES's behaviour (when started with the same random number generator seed). We are concerned solely with the cost of finding E^t at each time step. As with the synthetic data, we average results over 50 different runs for each method combination. Again, combination $\mathcal{C}_4$ is the best choice, having

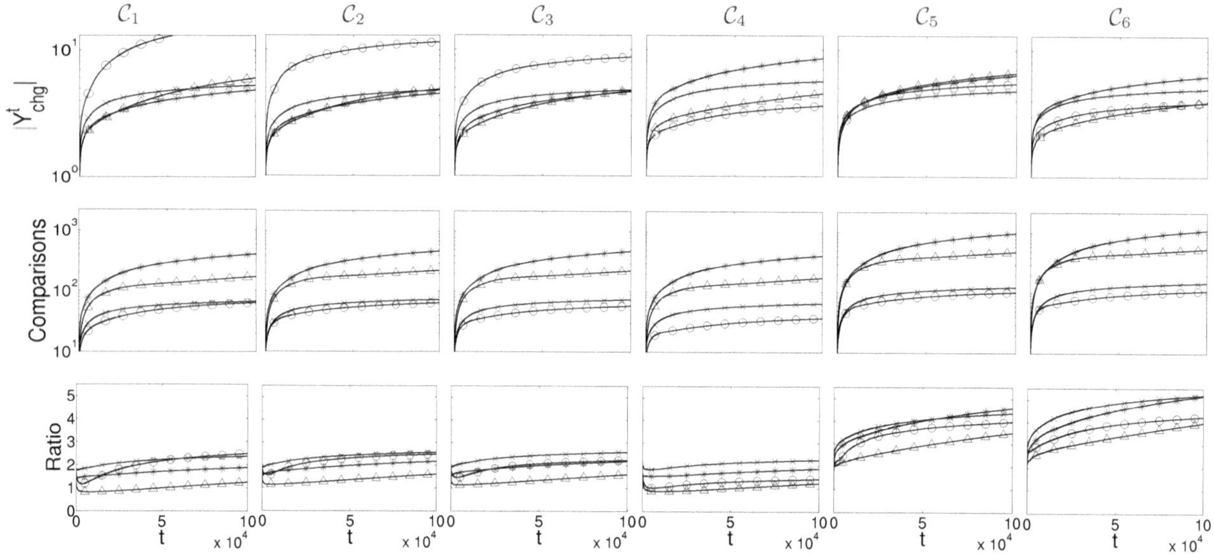

Figure 4: Growth of $|Y^t_{chg}|$ and number of domination comparisons using different guardian selection methods for noisy DTLZ problems. Top row (log scale): $|Y^t_{chg}|$. Middle row (log scale) number of domination comparisons. Bottom row: ratio of number of dominations to elite archive size. Each panel shows the cumulative moving average over 100,000 time steps, averaged over 50 runs. Circles: DTLZ1, $D = 2$. Triangles: DTLZ1, $D = 3$. Crosses: DTLZ2, $D = 2$. Stars: DTLZ2, $D = 3$.

better or equivalent comparison costs across problems, with the average number of comparison requires ranging from 1 to 2.2 times $|E^t|$.

6. DISCUSSION

This paper has presented a new method for rapidly discovering the non-dominated elite sets in evolving populations, considering both when new solutions are added to the population and when the objective values of solutions change during the optimisation. This latter case is particularly important for dynamic and noisy optimisation. The method relies on the assignment of a *guardian dominator* to every non-elite solution. Although a full average case complexity analysis is not available because it depends on the nature of the set being tracked, we show that guardian dominators can allow rapid location of the elite set in a changing population. Performance of the scheme depends on the way in which the population of solutions evolves and empirically we have found the different guardian assignment method perform differently in different situations. This opens up a future avenue of work on dynamically adapting the assignment method as a population evolves. Nonetheless, even a fixed assignment method vastly reduces the number of domination comparisons need to maintain the elite set and will allow noisy and dynamic problems to be efficiently handled.

We have exploited the time-cost improvements it provides in a state-of-the-art noisy optimiser [6], and example MATLAB code is available from `https://github.com/fieldsend`.

7. REFERENCES

[1] N. Altwaijry and M. Menai. Data structures in multi-objective evolutionary algorithms. *J. Computer Science and Technology*, 27(6):1197–1210, 2012.

[2] K. Deb, S. Agrawal, A. Pratap, and T. Meyarivan. A Fast Elitist Non-Dominated Sorting Genetic Algorithm for Multi-Objective Optimization: NSGA-II. In *Parallel Problem Solving from Nature*, pages 849–858. Springer, 2000.

[3] K. Deb, L. Thiele, M. Laumanns, and E. Zitzler. Scalable Multi–Objective Optimization Test Problems. In *IEEE Congress on Evolutionary Computation*, volume 1, pages 825–830, 2002.

[4] J. Fieldsend and R. Everson. On the efficient use of uncertainty when performing expensive ROC optimisation. In *IEEE Congress on Evolutionary Computation*, pages 3984–3991, 2008.

[5] J. Fieldsend and R. Everson. On the efficient maintenance and updating of Pareto solutions when assigned objectives values may change. Technical report, University of Exeter, UK, December 2013.

[6] J. Fieldsend and R. Everson. The Rolling Tide Evolutionary Algorithm: A Multi-Objective Optimiser for Noisy Optimisation Problems. *IEEE Transactions on Evolutionary Computation*, in press.

[7] C.-K. Goh and K. Tan. *Evolutionary Multi-objective Optimization in Uncertain Environments*. Springer, 2009.

[8] J. Horn and N. Nafpliotis. Multiobjective Optimization Using the Niched Pareto Genetic Algorithm. Technical Report 93005, Illinois Genetic Algorithms Laboratory, University of Illinois at Urbana-Champaign, 1993.

[9] T. Park and K. Ryu. Accumulative Sampling for Noisy Evolutionary Multi-Objective Optimization. In *Proceeding of the Genetic and Evolutionary Computation Conference*, pages 793–800, 2011.

[10] S. Yang, Y. Ong, and Y. Jin. *Evolutionary computation in dynamic and uncertain environments.* Springer, 2007.

The Parameter Optimization of Kalman Filter Based on Multi-Objective Memetic Algorithm

Yu-Dan Huo
Department of Computer Science
China University of Geosciences
Wuhan, China
yudanhuo@163.com

Zhi-Hua Cai
Department of Computer Science
China University of Geosciences
Wuhan, China
zhcai@cug.edu.cn

Wen-Yin Gong
Department of Computer Science
China University of Geosciences
Wuhan, China
wygong@cug.edu.cn

Qin Liu
Department of Computer Science
China University of Geosciences
Wuhan, China
lq8738@126.com

ABSTRACT

Generally, there are two objectives in the optimization of the measurement noise covariance matrix R of Kalman filter. However, most of the traditional optimization methods of Kalman filter only focus on one objective. In this paper, we proposed a new method to optimize the parameter R based on Multi-Objective Memetic Algorithm (MOMA). Compared with traditional methods, it can optimize multiple objectives simultaneously. In this method, the decision vector is the diagonal elements of matrix R, the first objective function f_1 is the mean of the residual vectors, and the second objective function f_2 is the degree of mismatching between the actual value of the residual covariance with its theoretical value. In the MOMA, the global search based on NSGA-II is utilized to minimize the two objective functions, and the local search based on Simulated Annealing (SA) is just used to minimize the f_1. The experimental results demonstrate that the Kalman filter optimized by MOMA, namely MOMA-Kalman, can get much smaller filtering error than regular Kalman filter and other adaptive filter algorithms, such as SageHusa-Kalman and Fuzzy-Kalman.

Categories and Subject Descriptors

G.1.6 [**Numerical Analysis**]: Optimization—*global optimization*; I.2.8 [**Artificial Intelligence**]: Problem Solving, Control Methods, and Search—*control theory*

GECCO'14, July 12–16, 2014, Vancouver, BC, Canada.

http://dx.doi.org/10.1145/2576768.2598242.

Keywords

Kalman filter; parameter optimization; multi-objective optimization; memetic algorithm

1. INTRODUCTION

Kalman Filter (KF) [1] is one of the well-known and efficient methods for estimating the state of dynamic system from an incomplete and noisy measurement. Since it was proposed in 1960s, Kalman filter has been widely applied in many fields, such as navigation, signal processing, control system and information fusion. It also has many improved variants like Extended Kalman Filter (EKF) [2] and Unscented Kalman Filter (UKF) [3] which are utilized in nonlinear system. The Kalman filter works well in the condition that the *a priori* statistics of the stochastic errors in both dynamic process and measurement models are assumed to be available, which is very difficult in practical applications, especially the measurement noise covariance matrix R. To solve this problem, many adaptive mechanisms are used into Kalman filter, which is called Adaptive Kalman Filter (AKF). According to the filtering performance, adaptive Kalman filter can optimize or estimate its noise statistics parameters adaptively to adjust to the change of process or measurement noise. Mehra [4] classified the different methods of adaptive filter into four categories: Bayesian, maximum likelihood, correlation and covariance matching.

The traditional adaptive Kalman filter algorithms include Sage-Husa Kalman [5] based on maximum *a posteriori* probability estimation, Fuzzy Kalman [6] based on fuzzy logic and covariance matching, Bayes adaptive filter [7] based on Bayesian estimation, Robust Kalman [8] and so on. In recent years, more and more people start to use Evolutionary Algorithms (EA) into adaptive Kalman filter. In literature, Szabat [9], Salvatore [10], Jatoth [11], and Mosavi [12] published some of the earlier work on using evolutionary algorithms to optimize the initial parameter value of Kalman filter. Generally, there are two objectives in the parameter optimization of Kalman filter. One is to reduce the filtering error ,and the other one is to estimate the actual value of the parameters. However, all the adaptive Kalman filter methods mentioned above only focus on one objective. For example, Sage-Husa Kalman focuses on the error reduction and Fuzzy Kalman focuses on the actual parameter estimation. Even the adaptive Kalman filter based on single-objective evolutionary algorithm, just can optimize one objective each time.

In this paper, we proposed to utilize multi-objective memetic algorithm (MOMA) to optimize the parameter R of Kalman filter, which can optimize the two objectives mentioned above simultaneously. MOMA [13, 14] is the multi-objective optimization version of memetic algorithm (MA) [15]. It has been successfully applied to many fields, such as knapsack problems [16], dynamic location problems [17], art classifiers [18], transmission network expansion planning [19] and environmental power unit commitment [20]. The MOMA used in this paper is a combination of NSGA-II [21] and Simulated Annealing (SA) [22]. In the optimization, The first objective function f_1 is the mean value of the residual vectors of Kalman filter. In certain extend it symbolizes the filtering error. The second objective function f_2 is the degree of mismatching between the actual value of the residual covariance with its theoretical value. It can be used to find the actual value of R. For the purpose of getting smaller error under the premise that the optimized value of R is close to its actual value, the local search based on SA just minimizes the first objective function.

The rest of this paper is organized as follows: Section II introduces the Kalman filter and its parameter optimization problem. Section III introduces the new method of optimizing the parameter R of Kalman filter based on multi-objective memetic algorithm. Some simulation results are presented in Section IV to show its performance. Finally, Section V concludes the paper.

2. PARAMETER OPTIMIZATION OF KALMAN FILTER

2.1 Kalman Filter

Kalman filter is one of the most popular algorithms in the control area. It is always used to estimate the state of a dynamic system. The system model and measurement model for a simple linear discrete-time Kalman filter are represented as:

$$x_k = \Phi x_{k-1} + \omega_k \tag{1}$$

$$z_k = H x_k + \nu_k \tag{2}$$

where $x_k \in R^n$ is the system state vector, $\omega_k \in R^n$ is the system noise vector, $z_k \in R^m$ is the measurement vector to system state, and $\nu_k \in R^m$ is the measurement noise vector. Φ is the state transition matrix, which reflects the mathematical or physical relationship between system state x_k and x_{k-1}. H is the measurement matrix, which represents the relationship between the measurement z_k and system state x_k. The vector ω_k and ν_k are both white noise sequences with zero means and mutually independent

$$E[\omega_k \omega_i^T] = \begin{cases} Q, & i = k \\ 0, & i \neq k \end{cases}; \tag{3}$$

$$E[\nu_k \nu_i^T] = \begin{cases} R, & i = k \\ 0, & i \neq k \end{cases}; \tag{4}$$

$$E[\omega_k \nu_i^T] = 0, \text{for all } i \text{ and } k. \tag{5}$$

where non-negative definite matrix Q is the system noise covariance matrix, positive definite matrix R is the measurement noise covariance matrix, $E[\bullet]$ represents expectation, and superscript "T" denotes matrix transpose.

The purpose of Kalman filter is to estimate the actual value of x_k in equation (1). Based on the model equations (1)-(5), the key five equations of discrete-time Kalman filter is summarized as follows:

$$\hat{x}_k^- = \Phi \hat{x}_{k-1}; \tag{6}$$

$$P_k^- = \Phi P_{k-1} \Phi^T + Q; \tag{7}$$

$$K_k = P_k^- H^T (H P_k^- H^T + R)^{-1}; \tag{8}$$

$$\hat{x}_k = \hat{x}_k^- + K_k (z_k - H \hat{x}_k^-); \tag{9}$$

$$P_k = (I - K_k H) P_k^-. \tag{10}$$

Equations (6)-(7) are the time update equations of Kalman filter from step $k-1$ to k. These equations generate *a priori* estimation of system state at step k. Equations (8)-(10) are the measurement update equations of the algorithm. They incorporate the measurement value z_k into *a priori* estimation to obtain an improved *a posteriori* estimation, which is the output of Kalman filter at step k. In the above equations, $\hat{x}_k$ is the estimation value of the system state x_k, P_k is the error covariance matrix defined by $E[(x_k - \hat{x}_k)(x_k - \hat{x}_k)^T]$, and weighting matrix K_k is the Kalman gain matrix. The Kalman filter algorithm starts with an initial condition value $\hat{x}_0$ and P_0.

The procedure of Kalman filter algorithm is showed by Algorithm 1.

Algorithm 1 Kalman Filter

```
Set the parameters Φ, H, Q and R;
Initialize the x̂_0, P_0, k = 1;
while (need to estimate the system state) do
    Time Update:
        x̂_k^- = Φ x̂_{k-1};
        P_k^- = Φ P_{k-1} Φ^T + Q;
    Get the measurement z_k;
    Measurement Update:
        K_k = P_k^- H^T (H P_k^- H^T + R)^{-1};
        x̂_k = x̂_k^- + K_k (z_k - H x̂_k^-);
        P_k = (I - K_k H) P_k^-;
    k = k + 1;
end while
```

2.2 Parameter Optimization of Kalman Filter

Kalman filter is a very powerful method to estimate the system state. But it only works well in the condition that the parameters Φ, H, Q and R in the equations (6)-(10) are precisely known. Inaccurate values of these parameters will reduce the filtering accuracy, increase the filtering error, and even cause filter divergence. There have been many works on optimizing these parameters.

We can get the Φ and H by building accurate system and measurement models. The value of Q is generally stable in a system, although there is no direct method to get it. The most difficult, and also important is to estimate the value of R, because of its variability. For example in the navigation system, one very important application of Kalman filter, once the external environment of the target which is being navigated has changed, the value of R will change immediately. So a multi-objective memetic algorithm (MOMA) is used in this paper to optimize the parameter R of Kalman filter. It can minimize two objective functions simultaneously, compared to the other methods which can just minimize only one objective function each time.

2.3 Selection of Objective Functions

In the optimization of parameter R, generally there are two objectives. The first one is to decrease the root mean square error (RMSE) of filtering. We use the mean of residual vectors as the first objective function [23]. For Kalman filter, at filter step k, the residual ε_k is defined as follows:

$$\varepsilon_k = \tilde{z}_k = z_k - \hat{z}_k^- = z_k - H\hat{x}_k^- \tag{11}$$

where z_k is the measurement at step k, H is the measurement matrix, $\hat{x}_k^-$ is the predictive value of state vector x_k, and $\hat{z}_k^-$ defined by $H\hat{x}_k^-$ is the estimation of measurement z_k. From the definition we can see that the ε_k includes the new information from measurement z_k. From equation (9), if $\varepsilon_k = 0$, then the predictive value of state vector x_k is the estimation value. That means the estimation at step $k-1$ is very accurate. So the residual ε_k symbolizes the filter error in certain extend. Then we can define the first objective function as follows:

$$f_1(x) = \frac{1}{S}\sum_{k=1}^{S} \varepsilon_k^T \varepsilon_k \tag{12}$$

where S is the total step number of filtering.

The second objective is to estimate the actual value of R. Based on covariance-matching techniques [24], we designed the second objective function. The basic idea behind the covariance-matching techniques is to make the actual value of the covariance of the residual ε_k consistent with its theoretical value. From Kalman filter equations, the theoretical covariance of residual ε_k is

$$C_t = HP_k^- H^T + R. \tag{13}$$

The actual covariance of residual ε_k is approximated by its sample covariance

$$C_a = \frac{1}{M}\sum_{i=1}^{M} \varepsilon_i \varepsilon_i^T \tag{14}$$

where M is the window size which is chosen empirically to give some statistical smoothing. When filtering, if the value of R is accurate, C_t and C_a are basically the same. So we can define the second objective function based on the degree of mismatching between C_t and C_a:

$$f_2(x) = \left| \frac{trace(C_a)}{trace(C_t)} - 1 \right| \tag{15}$$

where $trace(\bullet)$ represents calculating the trace of the matrix in the bracket. The closer the estimation of parameter R to its actual value, the closer the value of $f_2(x)$ to zero.

The function $f_1(x)$ defined in equation (12) and the function $f_2(x)$ defined in equation (15) are the objective functions we used in the multi-objective memetic algorithm to optimize the parameter R of Kalman filter.

3. OPTIMIZATION OF R BASED ON MULTI-OBJECTIVE MEMETIC ALGORITHM

3.1 Multi-Objective Optimization Model

Without loss of the generality, a multi-objective optimization problem with a set of m decision variables, a set of n constrains and a set of k objective functions can be described as follow:

$$\begin{aligned} &minimize: y = f(x) = (f_1(x), ..., f_k(x)) \\ &subject\ to: e(x) = (e_1(x), ..., e_n(x)) \leq 0 \end{aligned}$$

where $x = (x_1, x_2, ..., x_m) \in D$ is the decision vector, $y = (y_1, y_2, ..., y_k) \in Y$ is the objective vector, D denotes as the decision space, and Y means the objective space. Generally, for each decision vector, it satisfies the constrain functions. In most instances, there are contradictions between objective functions. The reduction of one objective function may cause a increase of another objective function. And generally, it's impossible to make all the objective functions to reach the optimal value.

In a certain sense, the problem of optimizing parameter R is a kind of multi-objective optimization problem. R is a positive definite matrix, so only the diagonal elements need to be optimized. Assume R is a m-dimensional square matrix, so the decision vector can be assumed as $\mathbf{x} = (r_{11}, r_{22}, ..., r_{mm})$, where $r_{ii}(i = 1, \ldots, m)$ is the i-th diagonal element of matrix R. Then this optimization problem can be abstracted to a multi-objective optimization problem:

$$\begin{aligned} &minimize: y = f(x) = (f_1(x), f_2(x)) \\ &subject\ to: minR \leq r_{ii} \leq maxR, i = 1, 2, \ldots, m \\ &where: x = (r_{11}, r_{22}, ..., r_{mm}) \end{aligned}$$

where $minR$ and $maxR$ are the lower limit and upper limit to the elements of R, objective functions $f_1(x)$ and $f_2(x)$ are defined in equation (12) and (15). In general, one possible value of R can't make both the $f_1(x)$ and $f_2(x)$ to reach the minimum.

3.2 Memetic Algorithm

Memetic algorithm (MA), inspired by both Darwinian principle of natural evolution and Dawkins' notion of cultural evolution, is a metaheuristic search method [25]. In general, MA can be viewed as a combination of a population-based global optimization technique and a individual-based local heuristic search method, which improves the capability of global optimization algorithms like GA for finding optimal solutions in the optimization problems with higher convergence speed. Like GA, memetic algorithm is also a population-based algorithm. Its unique aspect is that the individuals are promoted to get some experiences from the others in the population by a local search process between traditional evolutionary process [25]. In some problem domains, MA has been shown to be both more efficient and more effective than traditional evolutionary algorithm [26]. In a MA, the initial population is generated randomly, and then the fitness of every individual is improved by local search. In each generation, original genetic operators, such as selection, crossover and mutation, are applied like in the GA, and then, local search is executed again to improve the population quality. Algorithm 2 explains the procedure of a simple single-objective memetic algorithm:

Algorithm 2 Simple Memetic Algorithm

t:=0;
$P(t)$:=initPop();
$P(t)$:=localSearch($P(t)$);
evaluateFitness($P(t)$);
while (stoping criteria not met) **do**
    $P^{'}(t)$:=selectForVariation($P(t)$);
    $P^{'}(t)$:=recombine($P^{'}(t)$);
    $P^{'}(t)$:=mutate($P^{'}(t)$);
    $P^{'}(t)$:=localSearch($P^{'}(t)$);
    evaluateFitness($P^{'}(t)$);
    $P(t+1)$:=selectNewPop($P(t)$,$P^{'}(t)$);
    t:=t+1;
end while

3.3 Multi-Objective Memetic Algorithm (M-OMA)

In the optimization of parameter R, when the two objective functions are minimized simultaneously, we hope to reduce the filtering error as much as we can. So the objective function $f_1(x)$ should get more attention in the optimization process. Multi-objective memetic algorithm (MOMA) is a perfect choice for this purpose. Using MOMA, we can minimize the function $f_1(x)$ and $f_2(x)$ simultaneously at the global search, and then only minimize $f_1(x)$ at the local search. The MOMA we used in this paper is a combination of NSGA-II and Simulated Annealing (SA). NSGA-II is used for global search and SA is used for local search.

Proposed by Prof. Kalyanmoy Deb [21], NSGA-II is a very famous algorithm for solving multi-objective optimization problems. In the fast non-dominated sort of NSGA-II, the individuals are sorted into each front. The individuals in the first front are completely non-dominant and the ones in the second front are dominated by the individuals in the first front only and the front goes so on. Each individual are assigned rank values as the fitness. The rank value of the individuals in first front is 1 and the rank value of the individuals in second front is 2 and so on. Besides of the rank value, crowding distance is calculated for each individual to measure how close it is to its neighbors. The mechanism of crowding distance is utilized to improve the diversity of the solutions. In each generation, tournament selection is used to select parents based on the rank value and crowding distance. And then, crossover and mutation operators are utilized on parents to generate offsprings. At last, merger the parents and offsprings, and select the best N individuals based on rank value and crowding distance to generate the population for the next generation, where N is the size of population. The pseudo-code of MOMA based on NSGA-II is showed by Algorithm 3.

Simulated Annealing (SA) [22] is utilized in the MOMA proposed for local search. SA is a generic probabilistic metaheuristic for the global optimization problem. It comes from annealing in metallurgy, a approach to heat and control cooling of a material to increase the size of its crystals and reduce

Algorithm 3 Multi-Objective Memetic Algorithm

Initialize the population Pop randomly;
Local search by Simulated Annealing on Pop;
Sort Pop by non-domination sort and crowding distance;
while (stopping criteria not met) **do**
    Generate parents $P \leftarrow$ tournament selection on Pop;
    Generate offspring $O \leftarrow$ genetic operator on P;
    Local search by Simulated Annealing on O every five generations;
    Generate intermediate population $I \leftarrow P \cup O$;
    Sort I by non-domination sort and crowding distance;
    $Pop \leftarrow$ select previous $sizePop$ individuals of I;
end while

their defects. It has been proven that, for any given finite problem, the probability that the SA get the global optimal solution approaches 1 if there is enough annealing time. The SA used in MOMA is showed by Algorithm 4.

Algorithm 4 Simulated Annealing on Pop

Initialize $T_0 = 10, kmax = 8, ratio = 0.9$;
for $i = 1$ to $sizePop \times 0.1$ **do**
    $x \leftarrow Pop(i), T \leftarrow 10^6, k \leftarrow 0$;
    while $k < kmax$ and $T > T_0$ **do**
        $x^{'} \leftarrow neighbour(x)$;
        $\Delta f_1 \leftarrow f_1(x^{'}) - f_1(x), \Delta f_2 \leftarrow f_2(x^{'}) - f_2(x)$;
        if $\Delta f_1 < 0$ and $\Delta f_2 < 0$ **then**
            $x \leftarrow x$';
        end if
        if $\Delta f_1 < 0$ and $\Delta f_2 \geq 0$ **then**
            if $e^{-\frac{\Delta f_2}{T}} \geq rand(1)$ **then**
                $x \leftarrow x$';
            end if
        end if
        $k \leftarrow k + 1, T \leftarrow T * ratio$;
    end while
end for

In MOMA, the balance of global search and local search is a very important issue [27]. Considering both the simplicity and the balance of global search and local search, the SA is applied to only the 10 percent best individuals of each generation after every 5 generations of global search.

3.4 Optimization of R based on MOMA

The MOMA is an iterative algorithm and it spends a lot of time for running. However, Kalman filter is a real-time approach, and it has high demands on the running time. So the optimization of parameter R using MOMA must be in offline mode. That means the parameter R is optimized by MOMA at first, and then the optimal value is used in a regular Kalman filter.

The schematics of optimizing R in one generation is described by Figure. 1. In Figure. 1, there are N Kalman filters, representing the N individuals in a population with different values of parameter R. Using their own parameter R, the filters run on the historical data, and evaluate the objective functions f_1 and f_2 based on the filter results. Then the generation begins, including non-dominated sort, calculating crowding distance, selection, crossover, mutation and local search. After the generation, the old values of R are updated by new values. Repeat this process until the stopping criteria is reached. At last, N optimal values of R are obtained.

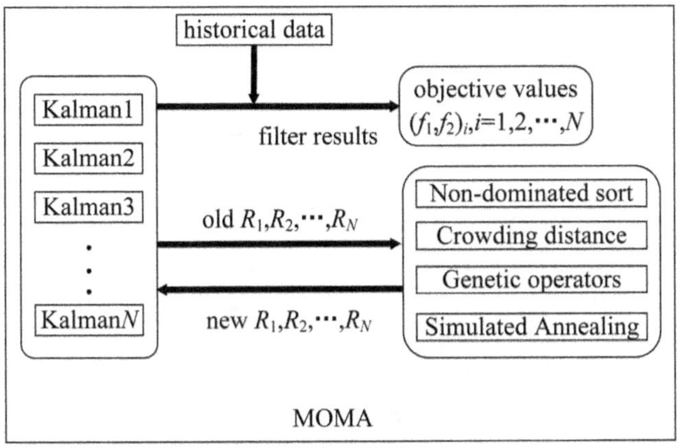

Figure 1: The process of optimizing parameter R in one generation.

4. SIMULATION EXPERIMENTS

In this section, simulation experiments have been carried out to compare the performance of MOMA-Kalman, whose parameter R is optimized by multi-objective memetic algorithm, with the other variants of Kalman filter.

4.1 Simulation Model Based on Target Tracking

The experiments are based on a simulation of rocket target tracking. Assume a rocket is doing uniformly accelerated motion escaping from the Earth. Its acceleration is $20m/s^2$. The fluctuations of engine thrust always cause some fluctuations of the acceleration. A radar on the ground is tracking the rocket and it gives the observation of the distance of the rocket from the ground every second. The observations are noisy. Now we need to estimate the displacement, velocity and acceleration of the rocket every second using Kalman filter.

So the system state at k-th second is $x_k = [d_k, v_k, a_k]^T$, where d_k indicates the displacement of the rocket at k-th second, v_k indicates the velocity and a_k indicates the acceleration. According to the physical model of uniformly accelerated motion, the system model is

$$x_k = \begin{bmatrix} 1 & 1 & 0.5 \\ 0 & 1 & 1 \\ 0 & 0 & 1 \end{bmatrix} \times x_{k-1} + \omega_{k-1} \quad (16)$$

where ω_{k-1} is zero-mean Gaussian white noise with covariance matrix $Q = diag([0, 0, 0.1])$ caused by engine thrust fluctuations. The measurement model is

$$z_k = [1 \ \ 0 \ \ 0] \times x_k + \nu_k \quad (17)$$

where z_k is the observation of the rocket displacement at k-th second and ν_k is the measurement noise with covariance matrix R. The initial conditions in the simulation are assumed to be $x_0 = [1000, 50, 20]^T$, $\hat{x}_0 = [990, 0, 0]^T$ and the initial error covariance matrix is given by $P_0 = diag([30, 20, 10])$. The rocket state is estimated by Kalman filter from 0 to 200s.

4.2 Experiment Results and Analysis

In practice, the value of R is unknown. Based on the measurement information, MOMA-Kalman uses the multi-objective memetic algorithm we proposed in this paper to optimize the R at first, and then uses the optimal value into regular Kalman filter to estimate the state of the rocket. Set the population size of MOMA is 20, and the pareto front of optimizing the parameter R we get is showed in Figure. 2. From Figure. 2 we can see that, the MOMA well minimized the objective function $f_1(x)$ and $f_2(x)$ simultaneously.

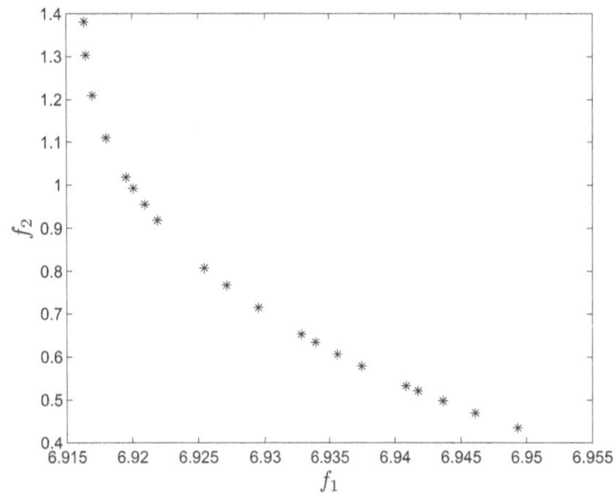

Figure 2: The pareto front of R obtained by MOMA.

The comparison results of the MOMA-Kalman with other Kalman filter algorithms on root mean square error(RMSE) of filtering are listed in Table 1, where Regular-Kalman represents the regular Kalman filter algorithm, SageHusa-Kalman [5] is an adaptive Kalman filter based on maximum *a posteriori* probability estimation, and Fuzzy-Kalman [6] is an adaptive Kalman filter based on fuzzy logic. In MOMA-Kalman, the initial value of R is optimized by MOMA, and in NSGA-Kalman, the initial value of R is optimized by NSGA-II. Each Kalman filter algorithm run 30 times, and each time Regular-Kalman, SageHusa-Kalman and Fuzzy-Kalman share a same initial value of R which is selected randomly, each time MOMA-Kalman and NSGA-Kalman stop the optimization until 500 times of evaluation. In the experiment, MOMA-Kalman and NSGA-Kalman chose the first individual of the pareto set as the optimal value of parameter R. However, in practical applications, the optimal value can be chosen by actual demand. If the first objective function is paid more attention on than the second one, then the individual which has the smallest value of $f_1(x)$ can be chosen as the final optimal value of R. Conversely, if the second objective function is paid more attention on, then the individual which has the smallest value of $f_2(x)$ is chosen.

In Table 1, the smallest error of each time is marked in bold. It is clear that, MOMA-Kalman got the smallest error 25 times in comparison. It has been proven that the method of optimizing the parameter R of Kalman filter by MOMA is very effective.

Table 1: The comparison results on root mean square error.

Run time	Regular-Kalman	SageHusa-Kalman	Fuzzy-Kalman	NSGA-Kalman	MOMA-Kalman
1	6.1378	6.3661	6.1053	5.2829	**5.2384**
2	5.8159	6.4088	5.7881	5.4019	**5.2855**
3	5.8083	6.4101	5.7809	5.2729	**5.2384**
4	7.0481	6.3114	7.0048	**5.2854**	**5.2854**
5	5.9855	6.3841	5.9533	**5.2384**	**5.2384**
6	5.9878	6.3838	5.9555	5.6242	**5.2384**
7	6.6822	6.3250	6.6350	5.2851	**5.2384**
8	6.4088	6.3418	6.3734	**5.2854**	5.2855
9	5.7981	6.4117	5.7711	5.2895	**5.2384**
10	7.1010	6.3101	7.0559	**5.2854**	**5.2854**
11	7.4249	6.3052	7.3691	**5.2384**	**5.2384**
12	6.8134	6.3191	6.7778	**5.2854**	**5.2854**
13	5.3235	6.5312	5.2737	**5.2853**	5.2854
14	6.0743	6.3732	6.0437	5.3629	**5.2863**
15	6.2531	6.3547	6.2176	5.3003	**5.2851**
16	6.9887	6.3130	6.9473	5.2855	**5.2854**
17	6.4267	6.3405	6.3906	5.3888	**5.2384**
18	5.2686	6.6102	**5.1176**	5.2855	5.2854
19	7.2080	6.3079	7.1595	5.3271	**5.2384**
20	6.8654	6.3171	6.8281	**5.2384**	**5.2384**
21	5.4331	6.6228	**5.2015**	5.2384	5.2384
22	7.4014	6.3054	7.3463	**5.2384**	**5.2384**
23	6.3580	6.3458	6.3185	5.3163	**5.2384**
24	5.3481	6.5214	5.3046	5.2869	**5.2384**
25	6.0218	6.3795	5.9930	**5.2853**	5.2854
26	7.1491	6.3090	7.1025	**5.2384**	**5.2384**
27	5.6307	6.4432	5.5969	5.2839	**5.2384**
28	7.0224	6.3121	6.9799	**5.2384**	**5.2384**
29	7.0324	6.3118	6.9896	**5.2384**	**5.2384**
30	7.5263	6.3046	7.4673	5.2602	**5.2383**
mean	6.4114	6.3760	6.3616	5.2958	**5.2556**
variance	4.777×10^{-1}	7.8×10^{-3}	4.940×10^{-1}	5.6×10^{-3}	$\mathbf{5.3250\times10^{-4}}$

The comparison results of MOMA-Kalman and Regular-Kalman at 22-th run are visualized in Figure. 3, with the x-coordinate being the filter time from 0 to 200s and y-coordinate being filter error. At k-th second, the filter error is defined by

$$Filter\ error = \sqrt{(\hat{d}_k - d_k)^2 + (\hat{v}_k - v_k)^2 + (\hat{a}_k - a_k)^2}$$

where d_k, v_k and a_k are the real value of the rocket displacement, velocity and acceleration at k-th second, $\hat{d}_k$, $\hat{v}_k$ and $\hat{a}_k$ are the estimated value obtained by Kalman filter. From Figure. 3, it is obvious that the MOMA-Kalman has a much greater convergence speed than Regular-Kalman.

The comparison results on estimating the real value of rocket displacement, velocity and acceleration are also shown in Figure. 4, Figure. 5 and Figure. 6. From these figures we can see, the estimates of MOMA-Kalman converge to the real value much faster than the estimates of Regular-Kalman.

5. CONCLUSIONS

A new method to optimize the measurement noise covariance matrix R of Kalman filter based on multi-objective memetic algorithm (MOMA) is developed in this paper. Compared with traditional optimization methods of Kalman filter, which only focus on one objective function in the process of optimization, this new method can optimize multiple objective functions simultaneously. The experimental results based on a simulation of target tracking demonstrated its effectiveness. The Kalman filter optimized by MOMA, namely MOMA-Kalman, can get much smaller filtering error than regular Kalman filter, SageHusa-Kalman, Fuzzy-Kalman and NSGA-Kalman.

6. ACKNOWLEDGMENTS

This work is supported in part by the National Natural Science Foundation of China under Grant No.61203307, and

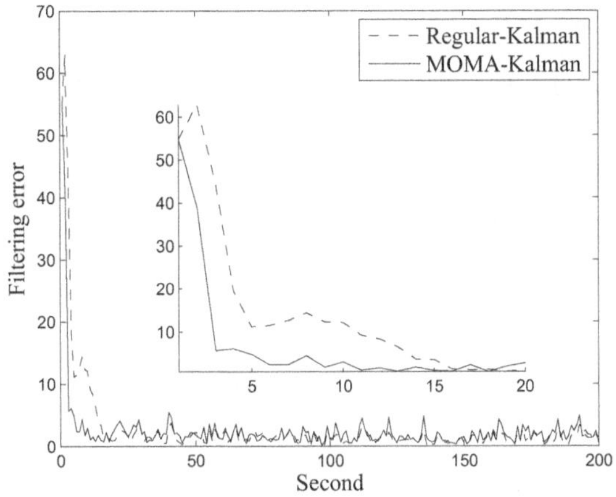

Figure 3: Comparison of MOMA-Kalman and Regular-Kalman on the filtering error at k-th second.

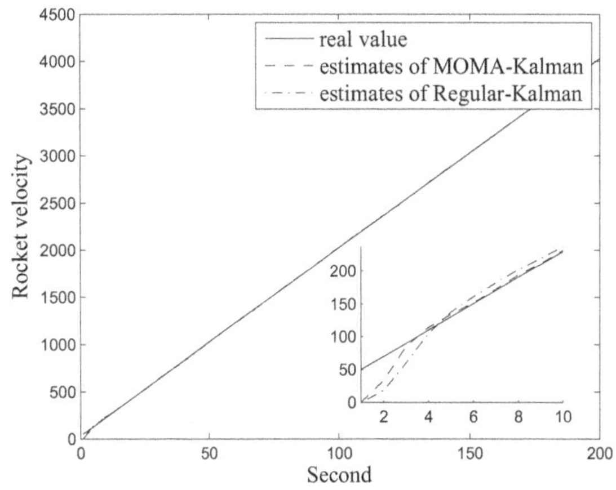

Figure 5: Comparison on estimating the rocket velocity.

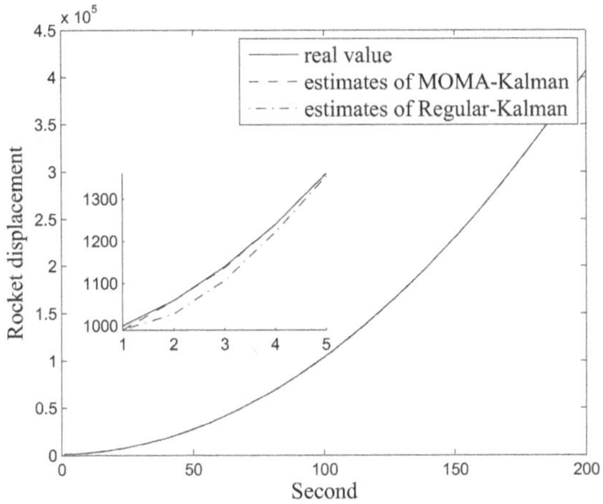

Figure 4: Comparison on estimating the rocket displacement.

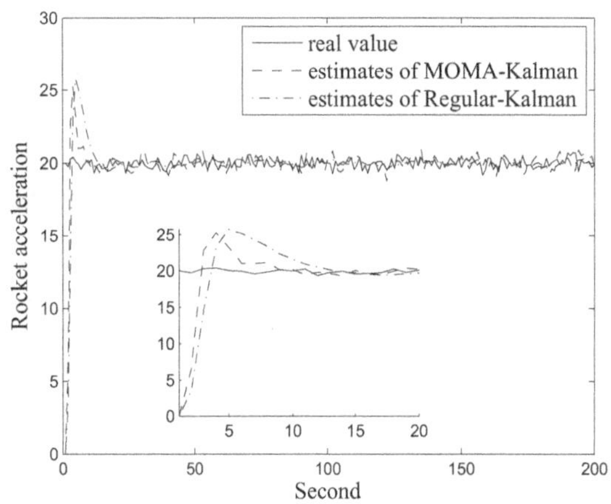

Figure 6: Comparison on estimating the rocket acceleration.

the Natural Science Foundation of Hubei Province under Grant No. 2013CFA004.

7. REFERENCES

[1] R. E. Kalman et al. A new approach to linear filtering and prediction problems. *Journal of Basic Engineering*, 82(1):35–45, 1960.

[2] R. Dhaouadi, N. Mohan, and L. Norum. Design and implementation of an extended kalman filter for the state estimation of a permanent magnet synchronous motor. *IEEE Transactions on Power Electronics*, 6(3):491–497, 1991.

[3] S. Julier, J. Uhlmann, and H. F. Durrant-Whyte. A new method for the nonlinear transformation of means and covariances in filters and estimators. *IEEE Transactions on Automatic Control*, 45(3):477–482, 2000.

[4] R. Mehra. Approaches to adaptive filtering. *IEEE Transactions on Automatic Control*, 17(5):693–698, 1972.

[5] M. Narasimhappa, P. Rangababu, S. L. Sabat, and J. Nayak. A modified sage-husa adaptive kalman filter for denoising fiber optic gyroscope signal. In *2012 Annual IEEE India Conference*, pages 1266–1271. IEEE, 2012.

[6] B. Talel and B. H. Faycal. Fuzzy kalman filter for non linear stochastic systems. In *10th International Multi-Conference on Systems, Signals & Devices*, pages 1–7. IEEE, 2013.

[7] S. Sarkka and J. Hartikainen. Non-linear noise adaptive kalman filtering via variational bayes. In *IEEE International Workshop on Machine Learning for Signal Processing*, pages 1–6. IEEE, 2013.

[8] X. M. Qu. Robust kalman track fusion in target tracking with uncertainties. In *International Conference on Computational Problem-Solving*, pages 1–4. IEEE, 2011.

[9] K. Szabat and T. Orlowska-Kowalska. Performance improvement of industrial drives with mechanical elasticity using nonlinear adaptive kalman filter. *IEEE*

Transactions on Industrial Electronics, 55(3):1075–1084, 2008.

[10] N. Salvatore, A. Caponio, F. Neri, S. Stasi, and G. L. Cascella. Optimization of delayed-state kalman-filter-based algorithm via differential evolution for sensorless control of induction motors. *IEEE Transactions on Industrial Electronics*, 57(1):385–394, 2010.

[11] R. K. Jatoth, D. N. Rao, and K. S. Kumar. Particle swarm optimization aided unscented kalman filter for ballistic target tracking. In *IEEE International Conference on Communication Control and Computing Technologies*, pages 455–460. IEEE, 2010.

[12] M. Mosavi, M. Sadeghian, and S. Saeidi. Increasing dgps navigation accuracy using kalman filter tuned by genetic algorithm. *International Journal of Computer Science Issues*, 8(6), 2011.

[13] J. D. Knowles and D. W. Corne. M-paes: A memetic algorithm for multiobjective optimization. In *2000 Congress on Evolutionary Computation*, volume 1, pages 325–332. IEEE, 2000.

[14] D. Liu, K. C. Tan, C. K. Goh, and W. K. Ho. A multiobjective memetic algorithm based on particle swarm optimization. *IEEE Transactions on Systems, Man, and Cybernetics, Part B: Cybernetics*, 37(1):42–50, 2007.

[15] X. S. Chen, Y. S. Ong, M. H. Lim, and K. C. Tan. A multi-facet survey on memetic computation. *IEEE Transactions on Evolutionary Computation*, 15(5):591–607, 2011.

[16] H. Ishibuchi and S. Kaige. Implementation of simple multiobjective memetic algorithms and its application to knapsack problems. *International Journal of Hybrid Intelligent Systems*, 1(1):22–35, 2004.

[17] J. Dias, M. E. Captivo, and J. Clímaco. A memetic algorithm for multi-objective dynamic location problems. *Journal of Global Optimization*, 42(2):221–253, 2008.

[18] R. Li, T. R. Mersch, O. X. Wen, A. Kaylani, and G. C. Anagnostopoulos. Multi-objective memetic evolution of art-based classifiers. In *IEEE Congress on Evolutionary Computation*, pages 1–8. IEEE, 2010.

[19] H. Kakuta and H. Mori. A multi-objective memetic algorithm for probabilistic transmission network expansion planning. In *IEEE International Conference on Systems Man and Cybernetics*, pages 1414–1419. IEEE, 2010.

[20] Y. F. Li, N. Pedroni, and E. Zio. A memetic evolutionary multi-objective optimization method for environmental power unit commitment. *IEEE Transactions on Power Systems*, 28(3):2660–2669, 2013.

[21] K. Deb, A. Pratap, S. Agarwal, and T. Meyarivan. A fast and elitist multiobjective genetic algorithm: Nsga-ii. *IEEE Transactions on Evolutionary Computation*, 6(2):182–197, 2002.

[22] F. J. Rodriguez, C. Garcia-Martinez, and M. Lozano. Hybrid metaheuristics based on evolutionary algorithms and simulated annealing: Taxonomy, comparison, and synergy test. *IEEE Transactions on Evolutionary Computation*, 16(6):787–800, 2012.

[23] L. Han, Z. R. Jing, M. M. Wei, and L. X. Zhang. Adaptive extended kalman filter based on genetic algorithm for tightly-coupled integrated inertial and gps navigation. In *Second International Conference on Intelligent Computation Technology and Automation*, volume 1, pages 520–524. IEEE, 2009.

[24] D. J. Jwo and F. C. Chung. Fuzzy adaptive unscented kalman filter for ultra-tight gps/ins integration. In *International Symposium on Computational Intelligence and Design*, volume 2, pages 229–235. IEEE, 2010.

[25] Q. H. Nguyen, Y. S. Ong, and N. Krasnogor. A study on the design issues of memetic algorithm. In *IEEE Congress on Evolutionary Computation*, pages 2390–2397. IEEE, 2007.

[26] N. Krasnogor and J. Smith. A tutorial for competent memetic algorithms: model, taxonomy, and design issues. *IEEE Transactions on Evolutionary Computation*, 9(5):474–488, 2005.

[27] H. Ishibuchi, T. Yoshida, and T. Murata. Balance between genetic search and local search in memetic algorithms for multiobjective permutation flowshop scheduling. *IEEE Transactions on Evolutionary Computation*, 7(2):204–223, 2003.

A Framework for the Study of Preference Incorporation in Multiobjective Evolutionary Algorithms

Raluca Iordache
Dept. of Computer Science
University POLITEHNICA
Bucharest, Romania
riordache@outlook.com

Serban Iordache
SCOOP Software GmbH
Cologne, Germany
siordache@acm.org

Florica Moldoveanu
Dept. of Computer Science
University POLITEHNICA
Bucharest, Romania
florica.moldoveanu@cs.pub.ro

ABSTRACT

We present a formal framework for the study of user preference incorporation into multiobjective evolutionary algorithms. This framework can accommodate virtually any preference model, including those that violate the independence of irrelevant alternatives. We also introduce the Preferanto notation, which permits the specification of a large variety of preference models. A number of properties and indicators are proposed for characterizing preference models. We report the results of a case study experiment assessing the impact of incorporating different preference models into an NSGA-II algorithm.

Categories and Subject Descriptors

Computing methodologies [**Artificial intelligence**]: Search methodologies—*Heuristic function construction*

General Terms

Algorithms

Keywords

preference incorporation, many objective optimization

1. INTRODUCTION

A multiobjective optimization problem (MOP) involves several objectives to be achieved. In most cases, these objectives are conflicting and there is no solution that simultaneously optimizes all of them. Instead, there exists a set of so-called *Pareto-optimal* solutions, which are not dominated by any other feasible solution. Therefore, multiobjective optimizers produce approximation sets consisting of solutions close to the Pareto optimal front. Choosing the best solution from a set of feasible alternatives is not possible without additional preference information, which has to be provided by a decision maker. Depending on the moment when these preferences are articulated, multiobjective optimization methods are based on *a priori*, *a posteriori* or *interactive* approaches [10].

A priori methods involve expressing user preferences before performing the search. Most of these methods are based on aggregating the multiple objectives into a single objective. Typical examples include the *weighted sum* or the *lexicographic* approach. A priori approaches are very appealing, because they transform the multiple optimization problem into a single objective one. However, for real-world complex problems it is in general very difficult or even impossible to aggregate the multiple objectives in a way that accurately reflects the user's preferences.

Interactive methods involve the progressive articulation of preferences. At each generation, the decision makers are asked to provide preference information that will be used to guide the subsequent search. These methods take into account that usually, the decision makers are initially not fully aware of their preferences. However, they gain insight gradually during the solution process, by being exposed to different sets of candidate solutions.

A posteriori methods are concerned with constructing a set of alternative solutions from which the decision makers will choose the one they prefer. The goal of these methods is to provide a set of alternatives that is relatively small, but nonetheless contains all solutions that are most likely of interest to the decision maker. In most cases, this means offering a set of solutions that are well distributed on the Pareto front.

Multiobjective evolutionary algorithms (MOEA) are currently the preferred way to tackle multioptimization problems that are too complex to be solved with traditional operations research techniques. Most research on MOEA focuses on a posteriori methods, and, in particular, on efficient ways of constructing a good set of alternative solutions from which the decision maker will choose the preferred one. In many approaches, the selection pressure is provided only by the Pareto dominance. Such approaches are usually not suitable for many-objective problems, that is, problems involving four or more objectives [11]. When the number of objectives increases, the selection pressure becomes too weak, because the number of non-dominated solutions grows exponentially. The number of solutions needed to approximate the Pareto front also grows exponentially, which makes it very difficult for the decision maker to choose the best alternative.[1]

[1]There are, however, a few approaches able to deal with many-objective problems. See, for example, [2].

GECCO'14, July 12–16, 2014, Vancouver, BC, Canada.
Copyright 2014 ACM 978-1-4503-2662-9/14/07 ...$15.00.
http://dx.doi.org/10.1145/2576768.2598380.

In the recent years, a number of approaches for incorporating user preference information in MOEA have been proposed in order to overcome the above mentioned problems [6, 4, 13]. User preferences refine the partial order induced by the Pareto dominance, focusing the search on the region of interest to the decision maker. Comparing different preference incorporation approaches and deciding which one is the most suitable for a particular problem is a very difficult task. In this paper, we introduce a framework for the study of preference incorporation in MOEA. Our framework can accommodate virtually any preference scheme, including those that violate the independence of irrelevant alternatives. In order to be able to analyze a large variety of preference models, we also introduce the *Preferanto* notation, which is a simple and intuitive language for specifying complex user preferences. A number of properties and indicators are proposed for characterizing preference models. As a proof of concept, we conduct a case study experiment using our framework, in order to assess the impact of incorporating different preference models into an NSGA-II algorithm.

The remaining of this paper is organized as follows. In Section 2 we introduce our preference incorporation framework by formalizing concepts such as *preference model* and *multiobjective problem with preferences*, we describe several properties that may characterize a preference model and we propose a number of preference indicators. In Section 3 we present the Preferanto notation and the methodology of transforming a Preferanto specification into a preference model. In Section 4 we describe the approach used to incorporate preference information into an NSGA-II algorithm, the design of our experiments and their outcome. The last section concludes the paper and outlines future research directions.

2. THE PREFERENCE INCORPORATION FRAMEWORK

In this section, we introduce a formal framework for incorporating preferences into MOEA. Before describing the proposed framework, we briefly review some of the basic concepts and terminology related to multiobjective problems and MOEA.

2.1 Basic concepts

Definition 1. Given a decision space $X \subseteq \mathbb{R}^n$, an objective space $Z \subseteq \mathbb{R}^k$ and a vector of k objective functions $f = (f_1, ..., f_k) : X \to Z$, the *general multiobjective problem* (general MOP) [7] is defined as minimizing $\mathrm{f(x)} = (f_1(\mathrm{x}), ..., f_k(\mathrm{x}))$ subject to:
$g_i(\mathrm{x}) \leq 0,\ i = 1, ..., m$
$h_j(\mathrm{x}) = 0,\ j = 1, ..., p$
where $g_i, h_j : X \to \mathbb{R}$ are the constraint functions of the problem.

Usually, there is no decision vector x that minimizes all the objective functions. Therefore, the solution of a MOP is given by a set of non-dominated decision vectors. A solution $\mathrm{x} \in X$ is said to be *Pareto optimal* with respect to X if $f(\mathrm{x})$ is not dominated by any objective vector $\mathrm{z} \in Z$. The set of all Pareto optimal solutions constitutes the *Pareto optimal set*, while its image in the objective space constitutes the *Pareto optimal front*. These notions can be formalized as follows:

- An objective vector $\mathrm{z} \in Z$ *dominates* an objective vector $\mathrm{z}' \in Z$ (denoted $\mathrm{z} \prec \mathrm{z}'$) iff:
  $z_i \leq z'_i, \forall i \in \{1, ..., k\} \wedge \exists i \in \{1, ..., k\}$ such that $z_i < z'_i$.
- An objective vector $\mathrm{z} \in Z$ *weakly dominates* an objective vector $\mathrm{z}' \in Z$ (denoted $\mathrm{z} \preceq \mathrm{z}'$) iff:
  $z_i \leq z'_i, \forall i \in \{1, ..., k\}$.
- The *Pareto optimal set* $\mathcal{P}^*$ is defined as:
  $\mathcal{P}^* = \{\mathrm{x} \in X \mid \nexists \mathrm{x}' \in X, \text{ such that } f(\mathrm{x}') \prec f(\mathrm{x})\}$
- The *Pareto optimal front* $\mathcal{PF}^*$ is defined as:
  $\mathcal{PF}^* = \{\mathrm{f(x)} \mid \mathrm{x} \in \mathcal{P}^*\}$

2.2 Preference incorporation

In order to give multiobjective evolutionary algorithms (MOEA) the possibility to focus the search on the region of interest, we need to incorporate user preferences in the definition of the MOP. Throughout this paper, we use the term *multiobjective problem with preferences* (MOPP) to denote a MOP enhanced with preference information. Each preference incorporation scheme involves a preference model, for which we propose the following definition:

Definition 2. A function $\mathscr{P} : 2^Z \to 2^{Z \times Z}$ is called a *preference model* over the objective space Z, iff $\forall A \subseteq Z$, $\mathscr{P}(A)$ is a strict partial order on A.

Given a set $A \subseteq Z$ and two objective vectors $\mathrm{u}, \mathrm{v} \in A$, we say that the vector u *preferentially dominates* the vector v with respect to A (denoted $\mathrm{u} \underset{A}{\prec\!\cdot} \mathrm{v}$), if $(\mathrm{u}, \mathrm{v}) \in \mathscr{P}(A)$.

Definition 3. Given a preference model $\mathscr{P}$ over an objective space Z and a set $A \subseteq Z$, the *preferential front* of A (denoted $\mathcal{F}^*_A$) is defined as the set of preferentially non-dominated vectors with respect to A:
$$\mathcal{F}^*_A = \{\mathrm{u} \in A \mid \nexists \mathrm{v} \in A, \text{ such that } \mathrm{v} \underset{A}{\prec\!\cdot} \mathrm{u}\}$$

A preference model can be attached to a MOP only if it does not violate the Pareto dominance relation imposed by its objective functions.

Definition 4. A preference model $\mathscr{P}$ is *Pareto compliant* with a given MOP iff
$\forall A \subseteq Z, \forall \mathrm{u}, \mathrm{v} \in A, \mathrm{u} \underset{A}{\prec\!\cdot} \mathrm{v} \Rightarrow \mathrm{v} \nprec \mathrm{u}$.

We propose the following definition, which describes a multiobjective problem with preferences (MOPP) as a MOP together with a Pareto compliant preference model.

Definition 5. Given a decision space $X \subseteq \mathbb{R}^n$, an objective space $Z \subseteq \mathbb{R}^k$, a vector of k objective functions $f = (f_1, ..., f_k) : X \to Z$ and a Pareto compliant preference model $\mathscr{P}$ over the objective space Z, the *general multiobjective problem with preferences* (general MOPP) is defined as minimizing $\mathrm{f(x)} = (f_1(\mathrm{x}), ..., f_k(\mathrm{x}))$, with $f(x) \in \mathcal{F}^*_Z$, subject to:
$g_i(\mathrm{x}) \leq 0,\ i = 1, ..., m$
$h_j(\mathrm{x}) = 0,\ j = 1, ..., p$
where $\mathcal{F}^*_Z$ is the preferential front of the objective space Z and $g_i, h_j : X \to \mathbb{R}$ are the constraint functions of the problem.

It can be noticed that the above definition could be rewritten without referring to a preferential model, because $\mathcal{F}_Z^*$ only involves the preferential dominance relation with respect to Z. This means that a partial order on Z would be sufficient to define the MOPP. The reason for formulating the definition in terms of a preferential model is our interest in evolutionary algorithms for the MOPP. Such algorithms deal with populations of candidate solutions at each generation step. A preference model is useful in evaluating the fitness of the individuals in a population. It also helps assessing the performance of different evolutionary algorithms for the MOPP.

- A preference model $\mathscr{P}$ is *Pareto complete* with respect to a given MOP iff:
  $\forall A \subseteq Z, \forall \mathrm{u}, \mathrm{v} \in A, \mathrm{u} \prec \mathrm{v} \Rightarrow \mathrm{u} \underset{A}{\prec\!\cdot} \mathrm{v}$.
- A preference model $\mathscr{P}$ is called *total* with respect to a given MOP iff:
  $\forall A \subseteq Z, \mathscr{P}(A)$ is a strict total order on A.
- A preference model $\mathscr{P}$ is *weakly consistent* with respect to a given MOP iff:
  $\forall A, B \subseteq Z, \forall \mathrm{u}, \mathrm{v} \in A \cap B, \mathrm{u} \underset{A}{\prec\!\cdot} \mathrm{v} \Rightarrow \mathrm{v} \underset{B}{\not\prec\!\cdot} \mathrm{u}$.
- A preference model $\mathscr{P}$ is *strongly consistent* with respect to a given MOP iff:
  $\forall A, B \subseteq Z, \forall \mathrm{u}, \mathrm{v} \in A \cap B, \mathrm{u} \underset{A}{\prec\!\cdot} \mathrm{v} \Rightarrow \mathrm{u} \underset{B}{\prec\!\cdot} \mathrm{v}$.

Non-consistent preferences violate the *independence of irrelevant alternatives* (IIA). The concept of IIA has been introduced by Arrow [1], and is one of the criteria considered in his *Impossibility theorem.* The violation of the IIA is also known as the *rank reversal* phenomenon. We can illustrate the problem addressed by the IIA considering the following scenario:

Faced with two alternatives A and B, a person prefers A to B. After introducing a third alternative C, the person prefers B to A.

The person in the above scenario expresses preferences that do not satisfy the IIA criterion.

To our best knowledge, non-consistent preferences have not been studied in the context of MOEA, although there are several multicriteria decision making (MCDM) approaches affected by rank reversal (see [18] for an illustration of the rank reversal phenomenon in 5 popular MCDM approaches). The legitimacy of rank reversal in MCDM is a controversial issue [14] and, obviously, having to deal with rank reversal is not desirable. However, in many real world situations, it may be impossible to avoid this phenomenon. Experimental evidence indicates that the IIA is often violated by decision makers [16]. Therefore, it is important that our framework also accommodates non-consistent preferences.

2.3 Preference indicators

In the previous subsection we have defined a number of possible traits of a preference model (Pareto completeness, totalness, consistency). A more accurate characterization can be obtained by defining scalar measures associated with a preference model.

Definition 6. A *preference indicator* is a function
$I_{\text{pref}} : \mathscr{P} \to \mathbb{R}$
that associates numerical values to preference models.

The preference indicators we propose in this subsection are based on the properties of the partially ordered sets (posets) obtained by applying a preference model to a given set. Therefore, it is helpful to have corresponding scalar measures associated with posets.

Definition 7. A *poset indicator* is a function
$I_{poset} : 2^{Z \times Z} \to \mathbb{R}$
that associates numerical values to strict partial orders:
$\forall R \subseteq Z \times Z$, such that R is a strict partial order,
$I_{\text{poset}}(R) \in \mathbb{R}$ is the *poset indicator* of R.

In the context of our preference incorporation framework, the strict partial orders R referred in the above definition are obtained by applying a preference model to an approximation set A. Therefore, if $u, v \in A$ and uRv, we can say that solution u preferentially dominates solution v.

2.3.1 Selectivity indicators

We are interested in assessing the degree of refinement introduced by a preference model, by analyzing the strict posets which it produces. We will refer this property of a preference model as its *selectivity* and we introduce the following 3 *poset selectivity indicators*:

1. **The dominance poset indicator**
   Defined as the number of solutions that are preferentially dominated by at least one other element, divided by the number of solutions.
   $\forall A \subseteq Z, \forall R \subseteq A \times A,$
   $I_{\text{poset}}^{\text{dominance}}(R) = |\{u \in A \mid \exists v \in A, vRu\}| \;/\; |A|$
2. **The relation poset indicator**
   Defined as the number of preferentially domination relations divided by the maximum number of possible preferentially domination relations.
   $\forall A \subseteq Z, \forall R \subseteq A \times A,$
   $I_{\text{poset}}^{\text{relation}}(R) = |\{(u, v) \in A \times A \mid uRv\}| \;/\; M,$
   where $M = \frac{|A| * (|A|-1)}{2}$.
3. **The front poset indicator**
   Defined as the number of fronts generated by the non-dominating sorting procedure used by the NSGA algorithms [15] minus 1, divided by the number of solutions.
   $\forall A \subseteq Z, \forall R \subseteq A \times A,$
   $I_{\text{poset}}^{\text{front}}(R) = (\text{number-of-fronts} - 1) \;/\; |A|.$

Intuitively, we can define the *selectivity* I_{pref}^{sel} of a preference model $\mathscr{P}$ with respect to a poset selectivity indicator I_{poset}^{sel} as the average poset selectivity value over the set of all non-dominated subsets of Z. However, such a definition is not mathematically rigorous and, in the general case, it is also not a reliable measure. We define instead a procedure for estimating the selectivity of a preference model, which is appropriate for our preference incorporation framework.

The selectivity of a preference model is considered a reliable indicator only if the poset selectivity values considered for computing its value have low variance. For the three poset selectivity indicators introduced above, our experiments show that their values are affected by the size of the approximation sets considered. However, these values have low variance for approximation sets of the same size. Therefore, the estimation procedure presented in Algorithm 1 provides a reliable measure for the selectivity of a preference model, for a given approximation set size. Choosing the size to be used in estimating the selectivity of a preference model is usually straightforward, because most MOEA use a fixed population size during their evolution. If this is not the case, a value close to the maximum population size should be chosen.

Algorithm 1 Estimate the selectivity of a preference model

```
procedure COMPUTESELECTIVITY(𝒫, I^sel_poset, N, S)
    generate N approximations of the Pareto front,
                        each set having the cardinality S
    sum ← 0
    for each approximation set A do
        sum ← sum + I^sel_poset(𝒫(A))
    end for
    selectivity ← sum/N
end procedure
```

2.3.2 *Inconsistency indicators*

In many cases, non-consistent preferences are unavoidable, although they lead to the undesirable rank reversal phenomenon. This means that the preference for a solution over another is context dependent, that is, it is affected by the other solutions present in the candidate set. We consider that a few occurrences of this phenomenon are acceptable, but we discourage the incorporation of preference models with a high rate of rank reversals, because they have a rather chaotic character.

In order to measure the degree of inconsistency exhibited by a preference model, we introduce a class of preference indicators called *inconsistency indicators*. As in the case of selectivity indicators, we offer a procedure for estimating the value of an inconsistency indicator for a given approximation set size. This procedure makes use of a *discrepancy operator* $\delta : 2^{Z\times Z} \times 2^{Z\times Z} \rightarrow [0,1]$. For two strict posets R and Q on a set A, $\delta(R,Q)$ gives the discrepancy between these posets.

Various discrepancy operators can be defined. A simple one, based on the number of differences between the compared posets is presented below:

$\delta_{\text{diff}}(R,Q) = |\{(u,v) \in A \times A \mid uRv \neq uQv\}| \;/\; (|A| * (|A|-1))$

Given an approximation set A and a discrepancy operator δ, the poset inconsistency indicator is defined as:

$I^{\text{inconsist}}_{\text{poset}}(A,\delta) = (\sum_{z\in A} \delta(\mathscr{P}(A) \restriction_{(A\setminus\{z\})}, \mathscr{P}(A\setminus\{z\}))) \;/\; |A|$

The symbol $\restriction$ in the above equation denotes the restriction of a binary relation: given a poset R on a set A and a subset $B \subset A$, $R\restriction_B$ is the restriction of R to the subset B.

The Algorithm 1 can be reused to estimate the inconsistency indicator of a preference model, by replacing the $I^{\text{sel}}_{\text{poset}}$ with the $I^{\text{inconsist}}_{\text{poset}}$.

3. THE PREFERANTO NOTATION

Current approaches of incorporating decision maker preferences into MOEA are constrained to a particular formulation of preferences [12]. The method of dealing with the particular preference scheme is perceived as part of the search methodology, although, in many cases, the search algorithm is independent of the preference scheme used and could be adapted straightforwardly to work with any preference model.

The theoretical framework introduced in the previous section treats the preference model as a parameter of the optimization problem. This view fosters an approach that clearly separates the search-related aspects from those concerning the handling of some particular preference scheme, thus allowing algorithm designers to concentrate on the core of their work. This is in line with recent efforts to separate the algorithm-specific part of an optimizer from the application-specific part (see, for example, the PISA framework [3]).

Since the preference model is treated as a parameter of the optimization problem, it would be useful to have a standard way to specify it. The benefit of a unified way of expressing preferences has been recognized by Purshouse et al. [12] and a first step in this direction has been made by Wang et al. [17]. In this section, we propose a specification language called *Preferanto*, which allows describing a large variety of preference models using a simple but powerful notation. Preferanto can be easily integrated into existing multiobjective test problem toolkits in order to provide multiobjective problems with preferences. Therefore, Preferanto is a useful companion tool to our theoretical framework, which allows experimenting with various preference models and incorporation schemes.

3.1 Notation

We introduce the Preferanto notation gradually, starting with a preference model using the lexicographic approach. In this approach, the objectives are ranked by their importance. When comparing two solutions sol_1 and sol_2, their objectives are compared in the order of their ranks. If, for the first objective at which their values differ, sol_1 is better than sol_2, then sol_1 preferentially dominates sol_2 ($sol_1 \prec\!\cdot\; sol_2$).

Let us consider a MOP with the objectives z_1, z_2 and z_3, which are ranked in the order: z_3, z_1, z_2. Preferanto is a rule based specification language, which requires each rule to be written on a separate line, in the order of their priorities. Our simple preference model will therefore consist of 3 rules, expressed in the Preferanto notation as follows:

```
preferences {
  z3;
  z1;
  z2;
}
```

A Preferanto rule may involve several objectives, combined in a mathematical expression. This way, a weighted sum preference model can be expressed using a single rule, containing the aggregation formula. A weighted sum preferential model with the weights 0.1, 0.2 and 0.3 can be represented as:

```
preferences {
  0.1 · z1 + 0.2 · z2 + 0.3 · z3;
}
```

Moreover, a Preferanto rule is not restricted to a single mathematical expression. Instead, it can contain a tuple of such expressions, as in the following specification:

```
preferences {
  < z1 + 0.5 · z2, z3 >;
  < z2, z3 + 0.7 · z1, z1 · z2 >;
}
```

In the above example, the comparison of two solutions sol_1 and sol_2 starts with the first rule, which implies computing the values of $z_1+0.5\cdot z_2$ and z_3 for both solutions. If, for both expressions the values of sol_1 are better than the ones of sol_2, then sol_1 preferentially dominates sol_2. Conversely, if for both expressions the values of sol_2 are better than the ones of sol_1, then sol_2 preferentially dominates sol_1. Otherwise, the second rule is considered in an analogous way.

User preferences such as those considered in the Guided Multi-Objective Evolutionary Algorithm (G-MOEA) [5] can be easily expressed in Preferanto by using a single rule specification with a tuple with two elements:

```
preferences {
  < z1 + a12 · z2, a21 · z1 + z2 >;
}
```

A Preferanto rule having a single mathematical expression can be seen as a rule with a tuple that contains only one element. Therefore, all Preferanto rules involve tuples. The angle brackets are optional for tuples with only one element.

A Preferanto rule can also have attached a condition. The effect of the condition is that the rule is taken into consideration only if the condition evaluates to *true*. This allows expressing the fact that some rules become important only in a given context. Let us consider a hypothetical e-commerce company confronted with a multiobjective problem involving shipping goods to its customers. Two objectives are relevant for the company in choosing the best shipping alternative for a product: the shipping cost and the delivery time. The company sees the shipping cost as the most important objective. However, the company has to pay a substantial penalty if the good is not delivered within 7 days. Therefore, the delivery time becomes the most important objective, if one of the solutions compared has a delivery time greater than 7 days.

In order to express conditions as the one needed in the above scenario, Preferanto makes use of three *preferential operators*, as seen in Table 1. The preferential operators

Table 1: Preference operators

Preference operator	Meaning
AT_LEAST_ONE(cond)	cond(sol_1) OR cond(sol_2)
EXACTLY_ONE(cond)	cond(sol_1) XOR cond(sol_2)
ALL(cond)	cond(sol_1) AND cond(sol_2)

take as argument a boolean formula, which usually involves one or many objectives. The formula is evaluated twice, once for each of the solutions to be compared. The two resulting boolean values are passed as arguments to the boolean operator (OR, XOR, or AND) associated with the given preference operator, in order to decide whether the corresponding rule should be taken into consideration or skipped.

In the e-commerce company scenario discussed above, the delivery time becomes the most important objective only if exactly one of the two solutions compared has a delivery time greater than 7 days. If both solutions have lower delivery times, there is no penalty. If both have greater delivery times, the penalty must be paid no matter which solution is chosen. Therefore, the preferences for this scenario can be expressed using the EXACTLY_ONE operator as shown below:

```
preferences {
  [EXACTLY_ONE(deliveryTime > 7)] deliveryTime;
  cost;
  deliveryTime;
}
```

As seen above, the condition attached to a rule is written in brackets. It is allowed to construct conditions that combine several preferential operators, as in the following example involving the quality of service of a network:

```
preferences {
  [AT_LEAST_ONE(availability < 0.98) &
          ALL(cost < 5)] availability:high;
  <cost, responseTime>;
}
```

For convenience, Preferanto also defines two *direction operators*: *low* and *high*. In the example above, the *high* operator is used to indicate that *availability* is a maximization objective. The *low* operator is default and can be omitted, but using it to specify preferences that combine minimization and maximization objectives improves readability.

3.2 Transforming a Preferanto specification into a preference model

Our goal in this subsection is to devise a general procedure for converting a Preferanto specification into a preference model. Taking into account the definition of a preference model, this goal can be reformulated as devising a general procedure such that: for any Preferanto specification and any population A, the procedure constructs a strict partial order on A, which is in accordance with the Preferanto specification.

We start by describing an algorithm for pairwise comparisons based on a Preferanto specification (Algorithm 2).

Algorithm 2 Pairwise comparison of two solutions

function PAIRWISECOMPARE($sol_1, sol_2, preferences$)
  for each rule $r \in preferences$ **do**
    if $cond_r$ is null OR $cond_r(sol_1, sol_2) = true$ **then**
      $result \leftarrow compare(tuple_r(sol_1), tuple_r(sol_2))$
      if $result \neq 0$ **then return** $result$
      end if
    end if
  end for
  return 0
end function

The pairwise comparison is implemented as a function returning -1 if sol_1 is preferred to sol_2, 1 if sol_2 is preferred to sol_1 and 0 if there is no preference relation between the two solutions. The `pairwiseCompare` function processes the rules in the order of their priorities. If the current rule has no condition or its condition evaluates to true, the tuples corresponding to sol_1 and sol_2 for this rule are compared using the function `compare`. This function returns -1 if all elements in the tuple of sol_1 have better values than the elements in the tuple of sol_2, 1 if all elements in the tuple of sol_2 have better values than the elements in the tuple of sol_1, and 0 otherwise. If `compare` returns a non-zero value, this value is used as the return value of `pairwiseCompare`. If the tuple comparisons performed by `compare` return 0 for all rules, `pairwiseCompare` returns 0.

The pairwise comparisons performed by Algorithm 2 impose a binary relation on the set of individuals in a population A. In what follows, such a relation will be referred as the *pairwise comparison relation on* A, denoted PCR_A. It can be easily proved that in the case of a Preferanto specification having only unconditional rules, PCR_A is a strict partial order, $\forall A$. Therefore, a Preferanto specification having only unconditional rules can be transformed into a preference model by using its pairwise comparison relations as follows: $\forall A, \mathscr{P}(A) = PCR_A$.

For a Preferanto specification having at least one conditional rule, PCR_A is in general not transitive and therefore it is not a strict partial order. We exemplify this by considering the following Preferanto specification:

```
preferences {
  [ALL(z1 < 0.5)] z1;
  z2;
}
```

We consider a set A containing three solutions (sol_1, sol_2, sol_3), with the objective values given in Table 2.

Table 2: Objective values for a set of solutions A leading to an intransitive PCR_A

Objective	sol_1	sol_2	sol_3
z_1	0.2	0.4	0.6
z_2	0.7	0.3	0.5

The PCR for these values and the above Preferanto specification includes the following intransitive preferences: $sol_1 \prec\cdot\, sol_2$, $sol_2 \prec\cdot\, sol_3$, $sol_3 \prec\cdot\, sol_1$.

Since PCR is not transitive in general, another approach has to be taken in order to transform a Preferanto specification having conditional rules into a preference model. This approach will be discussed in the remaining of this subsection.

For any Preferanto specification having conditional rules and any approximation set A, we need to construct a strict partial order on A. If A has n solutions, any relation on A can be represented by a matrix R with $n \times n$ elements. Therefore, our goal is to devise a function `getPoset`, which takes as arguments an approximation set A and a preference specification, and returns a matrix R representing the strict partial order induced on A. The matrix R used in our approach stores not only information about the preference relation between solutions, but also about the preference rule that has been decisive in establishing this relationship:

$R_{ij} = r$, iff $sol_i \prec\cdot\, sol_j$ due to the rule r.
$R_{ij} = -r$, iff $sol_j \prec\cdot\, sol_i$ due to the rule r.

In order to ensure that at each step the matrix R corresponds to a strict partial order, all changes to R will be made through the function `setTrans` presented in Algorithm 3.

The function `setTrans` returns $false$ if by adding the preference relation given as argument and taking the transitive closure, R is no longer a partial order (for example, because the newly added preference relation has produced a cycle).

The basic idea for implementing the `getPoset` function is to iterate through the preference rules and at each step to create a list with the candidate preference relations induced by the current rule. Then, the preference relations from this list will be added sequentially to R using the `setTrans` function, until all preference relations have been added or a preference relation that would break the strict partial order has been found. After founding a preference rule that breaks the partial order, this preference relation and all the remaining ones in the list will be skipped and the next preference rule will be considered.

If used in the above form, the outcome of `getPoset` would depend on the order in which the preference relations have

Algorithm 3 Adding a preference relation to R and ensuring that R remains a strict partial order

```
function SETTRANS(R, i, j, r)
    if R_ij ≠ 0 then
        if R_ij = r then
            return true
        else
            return false
        end if
    end if
    R_ij ← r
    R_ji ← −r
    R ← transitive closure of R
    if R is not a strict partial order then
        return false
    else
        return true
    end if
end function
```

been added to the current list, that is, on the order in which the pairwise comparisons have been performed. Since this is not admissible, we need a method of sorting the list of candidate preference relations. To this end, we store additional information in the list of candidate preference relations, in the form of an array of differences between the expressions defining each element in the tuple of the current rule. Specifically, let us consider that the current rule has a tuple $< expr_1, expr_2, ..., expr_m >$. During the pair comparison of two solutions sol_i and sol_j, we create an m-dimensional array `diffs`, such that:

$\texttt{diffs}[k] = expr_k(sol_i) - expr_k(sol_j), \forall k = 1..m$ The elements of the list of candidate preference relations will be data structures of the type `PrefRel`, which contains the following fields: (`from`, `to`, `diffs`). The field `from` gives the index of the dominating solution, the field `to` gives the index of the dominated solution and the field `diffs` is the array mentioned before. The list of candidate preference relations can now be sorted lexicographically based on the values in the `diffs` arrays.

The pseudocode of the `getPoset` function is presented in Algorithm 4 and the pseudocode of the `getCandidatePreferenceRelations` function is presented in Algorithm 5.

In general, the preference models constructed using the function `getPoset` are not consistent, that is, they are affected by the rank reversal phenomenon. Preferanto is thus a powerful notation, capable to express both consistent preference models (by using only unconditional rules) and preference models that violate the independence of irrelevant alternatives (by including at least one conditional rule).

4. CASE STUDY

In order to illustrate the usefulness of our framework, we devise an experiment for assessing the impact of incorporating different preference models into an NSGA-II algorithm [8]. NSGA-II uses a nondominated sorting algorithm in order to construct a series of fronts. Each individual in the front i is dominated by all individuals in any front $p < i$ and dominates all individuals in any front $q > i$. No domination relation exists between individuals in the same front. The fitness of an individual is given by the front on which it re-

Algorithm 4 Obtaining a strict poset for A in accordance with the Preferanto *preferences*

```
function GETPOSET(A, preferences)
    initialize R
    for each rule r ∈ preferences do
        list ← getCandidatePreferenceRelations(R, r)
        sort list lexicographically based on the diffs field
        Q ← R
        lastDiffs ← null
        for each prefRel ∈ list do
            if lastDiffs ≠ null AND lastDiffs ≠ diffs then
                R ← Q
            end if
            ok ← setTrans(Q, prefRel_from, prefRel_to, r)
            if ok = false then
                Skip the remaining elements in list
                Continue with the next rule
            end if
        end for
    end for
    return R
end function
```

Algorithm 5 Creating the list of candidate preference relations

```
function GETCANDIDATEPREFERENCERELATIONS(R, r)
    initialize list
    for i ← 1, n − 1 do
        for j ← i + 1, n do
            diffs ← null
            if cond_r is null OR cond_r(sol_i, sol_j)=true then
                diffs ← tuple_r(sol_i) − tuple_r(sol_j)
                if all elements of diffs are negative then
                    list ← list + PrefRel(i, j, -diffs))
                end if
                if all elements of diffs are positive then
                    list ← list + PrefRel(j, i, diffs))
                end if
            end if
        end for
    end for
    return R
end function
```

sides. The NSGA-II algorithm uses the Pareto dominance in order to construct the fitness fronts. In order to incorporate user preferences, we replace the Pareto dominance with a dominance relation that chains Pareto dominance and preferential dominance:
$\forall A, \forall u, v \in A, u$ dominates v iff $u \prec v$ or ($v \nprec u$ and $u \underset{A}{\prec\!\cdot} v$).

In what follows, we will use the acronym NSGAP (NSGA with preferences) to refer to our NSGA-II algorithm enhanced with preference information. In order to implement the NSGAP algorithm, we have used the MOEA Framework (`http://www.moeaframework.org/`). The source code of our implementation is freely available at `https://github.com/preferanto/preferanto`.

Our goal is to study how preference models with different selectivities affect the performance of the NSGAP relative to the NSGA-II. In all experiments we use the *dominance selectivity indicator* and a population size of 100. The problem considered is DTLZ2 [9], which is scalable to any number of decision variables and to any number of objectives. For both algorithms we have considered all DTLZ2 problems with the number of objectives between 2 and 10 and we have used as termination condition a number of 5000 function evaluations. The number of decision variables has been set as 9 + the number of objectives.

Our first step is to produce for each number of objectives sets of preference models with the following selectivities: 0.1, 0.2, ..., 0.9. By using a simple genetic algorithm that generates preference models and evaluates their selectivity, we have produced for each selectivity in the considered range a set of 10 different preferential models. The preference models used as individuals by the genetic algorithm have been obtained by generating Preferanto notations with only unconditional rules. Each rule is a tuple with a variable number of elements. Each element in a tuple is a weighted sum of a variable number of objectives. The genetic algorithm has therefore to solve a single objective optimization problem, where the objective is given by the desired selectivity and the decision variables are the parameters of the Preferanto notations: the number of rules, the number of elements in a tuple, the number and weights of the terms in an element of a tuple.

In a second step, we have generated and stored reference sets for both NSGA-II and NSGAP. For each number of objectives we have produced 10 approximation sets using the NSGA-II algorithm. For each number of objectives, for each selectivity and for each of their 10 associated preference models, we have generated a reference set using the NSGAP algorithm.

In the final step we have computed for each objective count and each selectivity a *nondominance ratio indicator*, using the following procedure: For a given preference model and a given reference set produced by the NSGA-II algorithm, we preferentially compare each solution in the NSGA-II approximation set with each solution in the NSGAP approximation set and we count how many of the solutions in the NSGA-II front are not dominated by any solution in the NSGAP approximation front. This value is then divided by the number of solutions in the NSGA-II front in order to obtain the *nondominance ratio indicator*. Finally, for each number of objectives and each selectivity we average the nondominance ratio indicators computed for their corresponding 10 different preference models.

In the absence of preference information, which corresponds to a selectivity with value 0, all solutions are preferentially nondominated, and the nondominance ratio indicator has the value 1.

Figure 1 shows how the nondominance ratio indicator is affected by the selectivity for 2, 3 and 10 objectives. It can be observed that the impact of incorporating user preferences becomes more significant when the number of objectives increases. For 10 objectives, even a small value of selectivity such as 0.1 leads to an abrupt fall of the nondominance ratio. This means that even when preference information is scarce, the incorporation of this information in MOEA may lead to a dramatic performance boost.

5. CONCLUSIONS

We have introduced a framework for the study of user preference incorporation in MOEA and a preference speci-

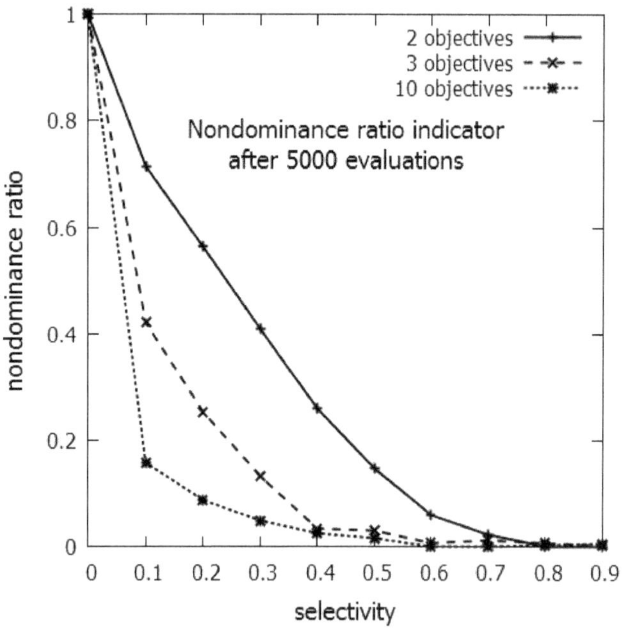

Figure 1: Nondominance ratio indicator after 5000 function evaluations.

fication notation that allows expressing complex preference models. The case study shows that the selectivity indicators defined by our framework are reliable and useful measures for characterizing preference models.

We have devised a method of transforming a Preferanto specification into a preference model. For specifications containing only unconditional rules, the method produces a consistent preference model, while for specifications that contain at least one conditional rule, the resulting preference model may be affected by the rank reversal phenomenon.

Incorporating non-consistent preferences and assessing the performance of the algorithms using such preferences are tasks that pose a series of challenges, due to the rank reversal problem. Further research has to be done in order to analyze different characteristics of non-consistent preference models, such as the impact of set size and selectivity on the rate of rank reversals and how these rank reversals are distributed among the most preferred and least preferred solutions.

Future research directions also include: devising more sophisticated preference indicators; developing faster methods of estimating the value of a preference indicator (for example, based on the Preferanto specification of a preference model); finding methods to determine whether a Preferanto specification with conditional rules is affected by the rank reversal phenomenon.

6. REFERENCES

[1] K. J. Arrow. *Social Choice and Individual Values.* John Wiley and Sons, New York, NY, 1951.

[2] J. Bader and E. Zitzler. HypE: An Algorithm for Fast Hypervolume-Based Many-Objective Optimization. *Evolutionary Computation*, 19(1):45–76, Spring, 2011.

[3] S. Bleuler, M. Laumanns, L. Thiele, and E. Zitzler. PISA—A Platform and Programming Language Independent Interface for Search Algorithms. In *EMO 2003*, pages 494–508, Faro, Portugal, 2003. Springer. LNCS. Volume 2632.

[4] J. Branke and K. Deb. Integrating user preferences into evolutionary multi-objective optimization. In Y. Jin, editor, *Knowledge Incorporation in Evolutionary Computation*, pages 461–478. Springer, October 2004.

[5] J. Branke, T. Kaußler, and H. Schmeck. Guidance in evolutionary multi-objective optimization. *Advances in Engineering Software*, 32:499–507, 2001.

[6] C. A. C. Coello. Handling preferences in evolutionary multiobjective optimization: a survey. In *Evolutionary Computation, 2000. Proceedings of the 2000 Congress on*, volume 1, 2000.

[7] C. A. C. Coello, G. B. Lamont, and D. A. V. Veldhuizen. *Evolutionary Algorithms for Solving Multi-Objective Problems (Genetic and Evolutionary Computation).* Springer-Verlag New York, Inc., Secaucus, NJ, USA, 2006.

[8] K. Deb, A. Pratap, S. Agarwal, and T. Meyarivan. A fast and elitist multiobjective genetic algorithm: NSGA-II. *IEEE Transactions on Evolutionary Computation*, 6:182–197, 2002.

[9] K. Deb, L. Thiele, M. Laumanns, and E. Zitzler. Scalable Test Problems for Evolutionary Multi-Objective Optimization. Technical report, Computer Engineering and Networks Laboratory (TIK), Swiss Federal Institute of Technology (ETH Zurich), 2001.

[10] J. Horn. *Handbook of Evolutionary Computation*, chapter Multicriterion decision making. IOP Press, Oxford, 1997.

[11] R. Purshouse and P. Fleming. Evolutionary many-objective optimisation: An exploratory analysis. In *IEEE Congress on Evolutionary Computation, CEC'03*, volume 3, pages 2066–2073, 2003.

[12] R. C. Purshouse, K. Deb, M. M. Mansor, S. Mostaghim, and R. Wang. A review of hybrid evolutionary multiple criteria decision making methods. *COIN Report*, (2014005), January 2014.

[13] L. Rachmawati and D. Srinivasan. Preference incorporation in multi-objective evolutionary algorithms: A survey. In *IEEE Congress on Evolutionary Computation (CEC 2006)*, pages 962–968, Vancouver, BC, 2006.

[14] T. L. Saaty and L. G. Vargas. The legitimacy of rank reversal. *Omega*, 12(5):513–516, 1984.

[15] N. Srinivas and K. Deb. Multiobjective optimization using nondominated sorting in genetic algorithms. *Evolutionary Computation*, 2(3):221–248, 1994.

[16] A. Tversky and I. Simonson. Context-Dependent preferences. *Manage Sci Manage Sci*, 39(10):1179–1189, 1993.

[17] R. Wang, R. C. Purshouse, and P. J. Fleming. "Whatever Works Best for You"- A New Method for a Priori and Progressive Multi-objective Optimisation. In *EMO 2013*, pages 337–351. Springer. LNCS Vol. 7811, Sheffield, UK, 2013.

[18] Y.-M. Wang and Y. Luo. On rank reversal in decision analysis. *Mathematical and Computer Modelling*, 49(5-6):1221–1229, 2009.

Controlling Selection Area of Useful Infeasible Solutions and Their Archive for Directed Mating in Evolutionary Constrained Multiobjective Optimization

Minami Miyakawa
The University of Electro-Communications
1-5-1 Chofugaoka, Chofu,Tokyo, Japan
miyakawa@hs.hc.uec.ac.jp

Keiki Takadama
The University of Electro-Communications
1-5-1 Chofugaoka, Chofu,Tokyo, Japan
keiki@inf.uec.ac.jp

Hiroyuki Sato
The University of Electro-Communications
1-5-1 Chofugaoka, Chofu,Tokyo, Japan
sato@hc.uec.ac.jp

ABSTRACT

As an evolutionary approach to solve constrained multi-objective optimization problems (CMOPs), recently a MOEA using the two-stage non-dominated sorting and the directed mating (TNSDM) has been proposed. In TNSDM, the directed mating utilizes infeasible solutions dominating feasible solutions to generate offspring. Although the directed mating contributes to improve the search performance of TNSDM in CMOPs, there are two problems. First, since the number of infeasible solutions dominating feasible solutions in the population depends on each CMOP, the effectiveness of the directed mating also depends on each CMOP. Second, infeasible solutions utilized in the directed mating are discarded in the selection process of parents (elites) population and cannot be utilized in the next generation. To overcome these problems and further improve the effectiveness of the directed mating in TNSDM, in this work we propose an improved TNSDM introducing a method to control selection area of infeasible solutions and an archiving strategy of useful infeasible solutions for the directed mating. The experimental results on m objectives k knapsacks problems shows that the improved TNSDM improves the search performance by controlling the directionality of the directed mating and increasing the number of directed mating executions in the solution search.

Categories and Subject Descriptors

I.2.8 [**Artificial Intelligence**]: Problem Solving, Control Methods, and Search—*Heuristic methods*; G.1.6 [**Numerical Analysis**]: Optimization

General Terms

Algorithms, Design, Performance

Keywords

multi-objective optimization, constraint-handling, directed mating

1. INTRODUCTION

Multi-objective evolutionary algorithms (MOEAs) try to find Pareto optimal solutions (POS) showing the trade-off among objective functions in multi-objective optimization problems (MOPs) [1]. MOEAs are particularly suited to solve MOPs since they can obtain a set of Pareto optimal solutions (POS) from the population in a single run of the algorithm. When we address constrained MOPs (CMOPs) involving several constraints, we need to consider how to handle infeasible solutions in MOEAs.

GECCO'14, July 12–16, 2014, Vancouver, BC, Canada.

ACM 978-1-4503-2662-9/14/07 ...$15.00.
http://dx.doi.org/10.1145/2576768.2598313 .

So far, several constraint-handling methods studied for single-objective optimization have been extended for solving CMOPs [2]. As an approach to avoid special handling of infeasible solutions in the process of evolution, death penalty methods [3, 4] eliminating infeasible solutions from the population have been introduced in MOEAs [5]. Repairing methods modifying infeasible solutions to satisfy all constraints by using problem specific procedures have also been investigated for multi-objective problems [6, 7]. On the other hand, there is another approach to evolve infeasible solutions into feasible ones. The representative penalty methods [8, 9, 10] have been extended for MOEAs [11, 12, 13]. In these methods, a penalty value (e.g., constraint violation values multiplied by a penalty parameter) is added to each objective function value, and the combined values are used for a parent selection. However, generally, an appropriate penalty parameter depends on each CMOP [14]. Other methods evolving infeasible solutions into feasible ones by independently treating objective and constraint violation values have been studied, and the constrained NSGA-II (CNSGA-II) [15] has been known as a representative MOEA employing this approach. Recently, as the same approach, a MOEA using the two-stage non-dominated sorting and the directed mating (TNSDM) [16] has been proposed.

TNSDM introduces a parents selection based on the two-stage non-dominated sorting of solutions and the directed mating to improve the convergence of solutions toward the Pareto front. In the parents selection, first, we classify the entire population into several fronts by the non-dominated sorting based on constraint violation values. Then, we re-classify each obtained front by the non-dominated sorting based on objective function values, and select the parents population from upper fronts. In this way, the superiority of solutions on the same non-dominance level of constraint violation values is determined by the non-dominance level of objective function values. It leads to find feasible solutions having better objective function values in the evolutionary process of infeasible solutions. Also, to generate one offspring, after we select a primary parent, we pick solutions $\mathcal{M}$ dominating the primary parent from the entire population including infeasible solutions. Then we select a secondary parent from the picked solutions $\mathcal{M}$ and apply genetic operators. In this way, the directed mating utilizes valuable genetic information of infeasible solutions to enhance the con-

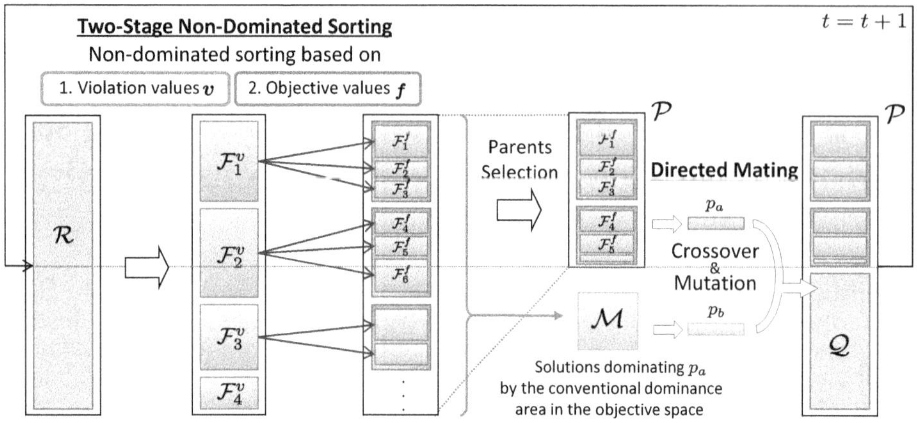

Figure 1: The block diagram of the conventional TNSDM [16]

vergence of each primary parent toward its search direction in the objective space.

The search performance of TNSDM has been verified on several benchmark CMOPs [16]. The results showed that the directed mating significantly contributed to improve the search performance of TNSDM in CMOPs. However, the conventional directed mating has two problems. First, since the number of infeasible solutions dominating feasible solutions in the population depends on the feasibility of solutions in each CMOP, the effectiveness of the directed mating also depends on each CMOP. Second, infeasible solutions utilized in the directed mating are discarded in the selection process of parents (elites) population and cannot be utilized in the next generation.

To overcome the two problems in the conventional directed mating and further improve the effectiveness of the directed mating in TNSDM, in this work we propose an improved TNSDM introducing a method to control selection area of solutions $\mathcal{M}$ and an archiving strategy of useful infeasible solutions for the directed mating. These methods introduced in the improved TNSDM encourage further utilization of infeasible solutions in evolutionary constrained multi-objective optimization. In this work, we focus on combinatorial constrained multi-objective optimization problems, and we verify the search performance of the improved TNSDM and compare its search performance with the conventional constrained CNSGA-II [15] on m objectives k knapsack problems [17] with $m = \{2, 4, 6\}$ objectives and feasibility ratio of solutions $\phi = \{0.1, 0.3, 0.5\}$ in the solution space.

2. EVOLUTIONARY CONSTRAINED MULTI-OBJECTIVE OPTIMIZATION

2.1 Constrained MOPs

Constrained MOPs (CMOPs) are concerned with finding solution(s) $\boldsymbol{x}$ maximizing (or minimizing) m kinds of objective functions f_i $(i = 1, 2, \ldots, m)$ subject to satisfy k kinds of constraints g_j $(j = 1, 2, \ldots, k)$. CMOP is defined as

$$\begin{cases} \text{Maximize/Minimize} & f_i(\boldsymbol{x}) \quad (i = 1, 2, \ldots, m) \\ \text{subject to} & g_j(\boldsymbol{x}) \geq 0 \quad (j = 1, 2, \ldots, k). \end{cases} \tag{1}$$

Solutions satisfying all k constraints are said to be *feasible*, and solutions satisfying not all k constraints are said to be *infeasible*. The constraint violation vector $\boldsymbol{v}(\boldsymbol{x})$ is defined as

$$v_j(\boldsymbol{x}) = \begin{cases} |g_j(\boldsymbol{x})|, & \text{if } g_j(\boldsymbol{x}) < 0 \\ 0, & \text{otherwise} \end{cases} \quad (j = 1, 2, \ldots, k). \tag{2}$$

Also, the sum of constraint violation values is $\Omega(\boldsymbol{x}) = \sum_{j=1}^{k} v_j(\boldsymbol{x})$. Next, *Pareto dominance* between $\boldsymbol{x}$ and $\boldsymbol{y}$ in maximization problems is defined as follows: If

$$\forall i : f_i(\boldsymbol{x}) \geq f_i(\boldsymbol{y}) \ \wedge \ \exists i : f_i(\boldsymbol{x}) > f_i(\boldsymbol{y}) \ (i = 1, 2, \ldots, m) \tag{3}$$

is satisfied, $\boldsymbol{x}$ dominates $\boldsymbol{y}$ on objective function values, which is denoted by $\boldsymbol{x} \succ_f \boldsymbol{y}$ in the following. In the case of minimization problems, the inequalities of **Eq. (3)** are reversed. Also, a feasible solution $\boldsymbol{x}$ not dominated by any other feasible solutions is said to be a non-dominated solution. A set of non-dominated solutions is called Pareto optimal solutions (POS), and the trade-off among objective functions represented by POS in the objective space is called the Pareto front.

2.2 MOEAs for Solving CMOPs

To solve CMOPs by using MOEAs, we need to introduce a mechanism to obtain feasible solutions from infeasible ones in the evolutionary process. In this work, we focus on an approach to evolve infeasible solutions into feasible ones, and we pick the constrained NSGA-II (CNSGA-II) [15] as a representative constrained MOEA employing this approach. CNSGA-II is an extended NSGA-II for solving CMOPs. CNSGA-II uses *constraint-dominance* [15] instead of *Pareto dominance* using only objective function values defined in **Eq. (3)**. Since CNSGA-II uses *constraint-dominance*, only the sum of constraint violation values is considered in the evolutionary process of infeasible solutions. Consequently, objective function values of obtained feasible solutions would be worse. Also, since infeasible solutions have less chance to generate offspring than feasible ones, valuable genetic information of infeasible solutions would not be utilized in the solution search.

To overcome the problems in the conventional CNSGA-II, a MOEA using the two-stage non-dominated sorting and the directed mating (TNSDM) has been proposed [16].

3. TNSDM

The block diagram of the conventional TNSDM [16] is shown in **Fig. 1**. TNSDM is designed based on the framework of NSGA-II [15] where the parents (elites) population $\mathcal{P}$ and the offspring population $\mathcal{Q}$ construct the entire population $\mathcal{R}$ $(= \mathcal{P} \cup \mathcal{Q})$.

3.1 Two-Stage Non-Dominated Sorting

To select the parents population $\mathcal{P}$ from the entire population $\mathcal{R}$, TNSDM classifies $\mathcal{R}$ into several fronts by using the two-stage non-dominated sorting based on constraint violation values and objective function values. TNSDM employs dominance based on

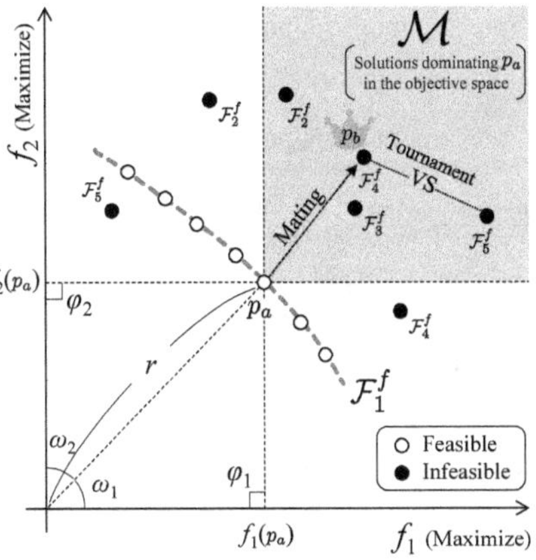

Figure 2: The directed mating (the conventional selection area with $S = 0.5$) [16]

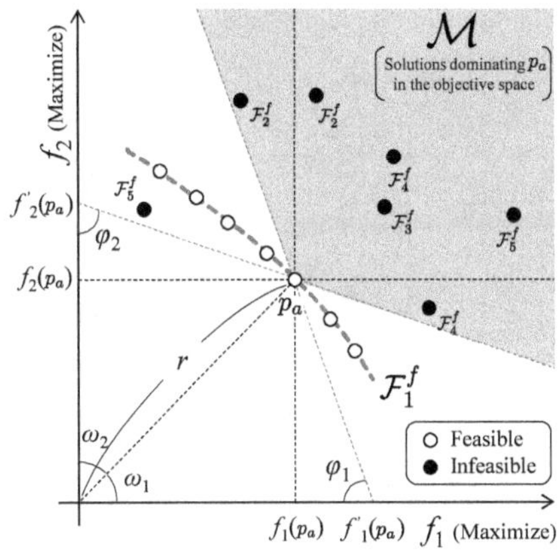

Figure 3: Expanded selection area with $S < 0.5$

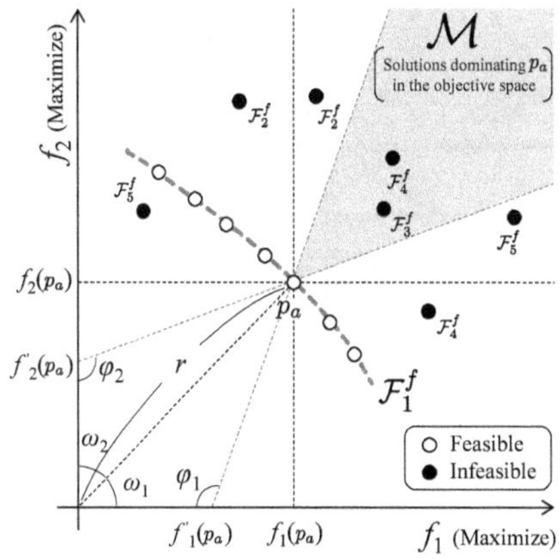

Figure 4: Contracted selection area with $S > 0.5$

constraint violation values [18, 19]. If the following equation is satisfied, $\boldsymbol{x}$ dominates $\boldsymbol{y}$ on constraint violation values ($\boldsymbol{x} \succ_v \boldsymbol{y}$).

$$\forall j : v_j(\boldsymbol{x}) \leq v_j(\boldsymbol{y}) \ \wedge \ \exists j : v_j(\boldsymbol{x}) < v_j(\boldsymbol{y}) \ (j = 1, 2, \dots, k) \quad (4)$$

First the entire population $\mathcal{R}$ is classified into several fronts ($\mathcal{F}_1^v$, $\mathcal{F}_2^v, \dots$) based on the non-dominance level of constraint violation values by using **Eq. (4)**. Since all constraint violation values of feasible solutions are zero ($\boldsymbol{v}(\boldsymbol{x}) = \{0, 0, \dots, 0\}$), feasible solutions are always classified into the uppermost front $\mathcal{F}_1^v$. Then, each front $\mathcal{F}_i^v$ $(i = 1, 2, \dots)$ is re-classified into sub-fronts ($\mathcal{F}_1^f, \mathcal{F}_2^f, \dots$) based on the non-dominance level of objective function values by using **Eq. (3)**. **Fig. 1** shows an example of that $\mathcal{F}_1^v$ is re-classified into $\mathcal{F}_1^f, \mathcal{F}_2^f$ and $\mathcal{F}_3^f$, and $\mathcal{F}_2^v$ is re-classified into $\mathcal{F}_4^f, \mathcal{F}_5^f$ and $\mathcal{F}_6^f$. Thus, the superiority of solutions decided by the non-dominance level of constraint violation values is maintained even after the re-classification of solutions by the non-dominance level of objective function values. Next, similar to the conventional NSGA-II, TNSDM selects the half of solutions in the entire population $\mathcal{R}$ as the parents population $\mathcal{P}$ from upper fronts whilst considering the crowding distance (CD) [15].

In this way, the superiority of solutions on the same non-dominance level of constraint violation values is determined by the non-dominance level of objective function values. It leads to find feasible solutions having better objective function values from infeasible ones.

3.2 Directed Mating

TNSDM introduces the directed mating to improve the convergence of each solution toward its search direction in the objective space. **Fig. 2** shows a conceptual figure of the directed mating. In this figure, all solutions in the entire population $\mathcal{R}$ are distributed in the objective space, and feasible solutions belonging to $\mathcal{F}_1^f$ are the parents population $\mathcal{P}$.

First, we select a primary parent p_a from the parents population $\mathcal{P}$ by using the crowded tournament selection used in [15]. In the tournament, two solutions are randomly chosen from $\mathcal{P}$, and the solution belonging to an upper front becomes parent p_a. If both of them belong to the same front, the solution having a larger CD becomes parent p_a. Next, we pick a set of solutions $\mathcal{M}$ $(= \{\boldsymbol{x} \in \mathcal{R} \mid \boldsymbol{x} \succ_f p_a\})$ dominating p_a in the objective space from the entire population $\mathcal{R}$ including infeasible solutions. If p_a is infeasible or the size of $\mathcal{M}$ is less than two ($|\mathcal{M}| < 2$), we cannot perform the directed mating, and a secondary parent p_b is selected from $\mathcal{P}$ by using the crowded tournament in the same way of NSGA-II. Otherwise, we perform the directed mating. In this case, a secondary parent p_b is selected from $\mathcal{M}$ dominating the primary parent p_a. To select p_b from $\mathcal{M}$, the crowded tournament selection [15] is also applied in this work. In the example of **Fig. 2**, two solutions belonging to $\mathcal{F}_4^f$ and $\mathcal{F}_5^f$ are randomly chosen from $\mathcal{M}$, and the solution belonging to $\mathcal{F}_4^f$ becomes p_b to mate with p_a.

In the case of the conventional CNSGA-II, all mating are performed in the parents population $\mathcal{P}$, and all parents are feasible after the total number of feasible solutions exceeds the half size of the entire population $\mathcal{R}$. On the other hand, in the directed mating, all primary parents are selected from $\mathcal{P}$ but secondary parents are selected even from infeasible solutions discarded in the selection of $\mathcal{P}$ if they dominate their primary parents in the objective space. As example in **Fig. 2**, although secondary p_b is infeasible, there is a possibility that p_b has valuable genetic information to enhance the convergence of primary p_a toward the true Pareto front since p_b dominates p_a in the objective space.

3.3 Two Problems in Directed Mating

The search performance of the conventional TNSDM has been verified on several benchmark CMOPs [16]. The results showed that the directed mating significantly contributed to improve the search performance of TNSDM in CMOPs. However, the conventional directed mating has two problems.

First, since the number of solutions $\mathcal{M}$ dominating each primary parent depends on the feasibility of solutions in each CMOP, the effectiveness of the directed mating also depends on each CMOP. In CMOPs with high feasibility, the number of infeasible solutions in the population is low. In this case, the most of primary parents cannot perform the directed mating. Consequently, the effectiveness of the directed mating cannot be obtained. Therefore, for CMOPs with high feasibility, it is desirable to expand the selection area of $\mathcal{M}$ in order to perform the directed mating. Contrary, in CMOPs with low feasibility, the number of infeasible solutions in the population is high. In this case, since the number of solutions $\mathcal{M}$ dominating each primary parent become large, the selection pressure to select its secondly parent by the crowded tournament selection in the directed mating will become low. Therefore, for CMOPs with low feasibility, it is desirable to contract the selection area of $\mathcal{M}$ in order to restrict the size of $\mathcal{M}$ by selecting only solutions having similar search direction.

Second, when the number of feasible solutions exceeds the half size of the entire population, since most of solutions in $\mathcal{M}$ are infeasible solutions, they are discarded in the selection process of parents (elites) population $\mathcal{P}$ and cannot be utilized in the next gen-

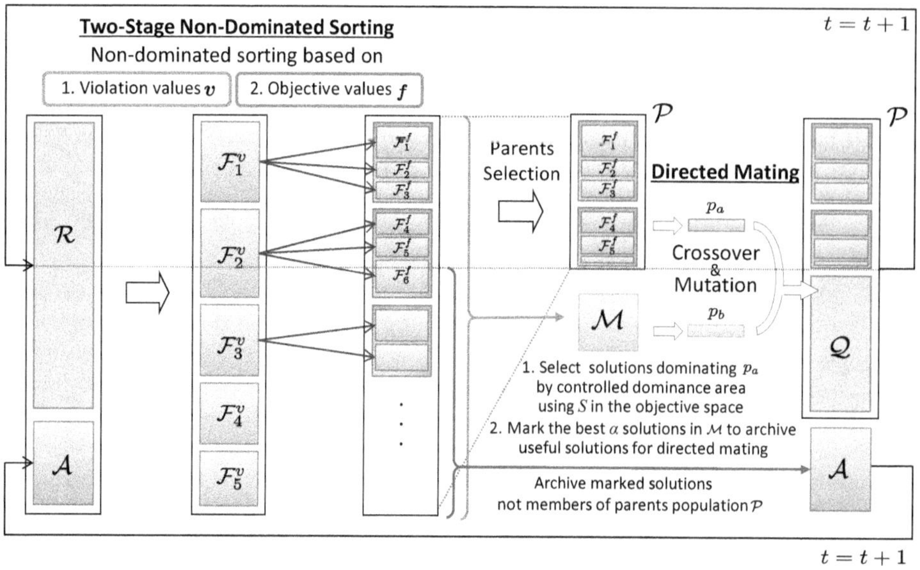

Figure 5: The block diagram of the improved TNSDM using the archive population $\mathcal{A}$

eration. Therefore, the framework of TNSDM has a potential to further improve the search performance by archiving useful solutions selected in $\mathcal{M}$ to the next generation and repeatedly utilizing them in the directed mating.

4. PROPOSAL: IMPROVED TNSDM

To overcome the two problems described in Section 3.3 and further improve the effectiveness of the directed mating in TNSDM, in this work we propose an improved TNSDM introducing a method to control selection area of solutions $\mathcal{M}$ and an archiving strategy of useful solutions for the directed mating. These methods introduced in the improved TNSDM encourage further utilization of infeasible solutions in evolutionary constrained multi-objective optimization.

4.1 Controlling Selection Area of Solutions $\mathcal{M}$

To overcome the first problem described in Section 3.3, the improved TNSDM introduces a method to control selection area of $\mathcal{M}$ by controlling dominance area of solutions (CDAS) [20].

In the improved TNSDM, we pick solutions $\mathcal{M}$ based on the dominance area controlled by CDAS. In CDAS, we modify each objective function value by using the user defined parameter S in the following equation.

$$f_i^{'}(\boldsymbol{x}) = \frac{r \cdot \sin(\omega_i + S \cdot \pi)}{\sin(S \cdot \pi)} \quad (i = 1, 2, \cdots, m), \tag{5}$$

where, $S = \varphi_i/\pi$. **Figs. 2-4** show examples of the modification of the objective function values of $\boldsymbol{x}$ $(= p_a)$ with different S, where r is the norm of $\boldsymbol{f}(\boldsymbol{x})$, $f_i(\boldsymbol{x})$ is the i-th objective function value, ω_i is the declination angle between $\boldsymbol{f}(\boldsymbol{x})$ and $f_i(\boldsymbol{x})$, and φ_i is the controlled angle by S. In the following, $\boldsymbol{x}$ dominates $\boldsymbol{y}$ based on the controlled dominance area is denoted by $\boldsymbol{x} \succ_{f'} \boldsymbol{y}$.

Fig. 2 shows a case of $S = 0.5$. In this case, the dominance area is equivalent to the conventional dominance area, and the selection area of solutions $\mathcal{M}$ is equivalent to the conventional directed mating [16]. In the example of **Fig. 2**, four solutions are picked as $\mathcal{M}$. **Fig. 3** shows a case of $S < 0.5$. In this case, the selection area of solutions $\mathcal{M}$ is expanded. Although the directionality of the directed mating is deteriorated, more solutions can be picked as $\mathcal{M}$. In the example of **Fig. 3**, six solutions are picked as $\mathcal{M}$. In this case, we can expect to increase the number of the directed mating exe-

Algorithm 1 The improved TNSDM

Randomly generate initial solutions ($\mathcal{R}$)
$\mathcal{A} = \emptyset$
for $t = 1$ to T **do**
  $\boldsymbol{\mathcal{F}^v} = \boldsymbol{\mathcal{F}^f} = \emptyset$
  $\boldsymbol{\mathcal{F}^v}$ $(= \{\mathcal{F}_1^v, \mathcal{F}_2^v, ...\})$ =Non-dominated sort ($\mathcal{R} \cup \mathcal{A}$, $\succ_v$)
  for $i = 1$ to $|\boldsymbol{\mathcal{F}^v}|$ **do**
    $j = 1 + |\boldsymbol{\mathcal{F}^f}|$
    $\boldsymbol{\mathcal{F}^f} = \boldsymbol{\mathcal{F}^f} \cup \{\mathcal{F}_j^f, \mathcal{F}_{j+1}^f, \ldots\}$ =Non-dominated sort ($\mathcal{F}_i^v$, $\succ_f$)
  end for
  Crowding distance ($\boldsymbol{\mathcal{F}^f}$)
  $\mathcal{P}$ = Truncation ($\mathcal{R} \cup \mathcal{A}$, $|\mathcal{R}|/2$)
  for $j = 1$ to $|\mathcal{Q}|$ **do**
    p_a = Tournament selection ($\mathcal{P}$)
    $\mathcal{M} = \{\boldsymbol{x} \in \mathcal{R} \cup \mathcal{A} \mid \boldsymbol{x} \succ_{f'} p_a\}$
    Mark best α solutions selected in $\mathcal{M}$ $(\{\boldsymbol{x} \in \mathcal{R} \cup \mathcal{A} \mid \boldsymbol{x} \succ_{f'} p_a\})$
    if p_a is infeasible or $|\mathcal{M}| < 2$ **then**
      p_b = Tournament selection ($\mathcal{P}$)
    else
      p_b = Tournament selection ($\mathcal{M}$)
    end if
    Q_j = Crossover and Mutation (p_a, p_b)
  end for
  $\mathcal{A} = \{\boldsymbol{x} \in \mathcal{R} \cup \mathcal{A} \mid \boldsymbol{x}$ is a marked solution $\wedge\ \boldsymbol{x} \notin \mathcal{P}\}$
  $\mathcal{R} = \mathcal{P} \cup \mathcal{Q}$
end for
$\mathcal{POS} = \{\boldsymbol{x} \in \mathcal{R}^{feasible} \mid \neg\exists \boldsymbol{y} \in \mathcal{R}^{feasible} : \boldsymbol{y} \succ_f \boldsymbol{x}\}$

cutions especially in problems with high feasibility. **Fig. 4** shows a case of $S > 0.5$. in this case, the selection area of solutions $\mathcal{M}$ is contracted. Since only solutions having similar search direction to the primary parent p_a are selected as $\mathcal{M}$, we can expect to emphasize the directionality of the solution search in the directed mating. However, in this case, since the number of solutions in $\mathcal{M}$ is decreased, some primary parents cannot perform the directed mating, then the effectiveness of the directed mating cannot be obtained.

4.2 Archive of Useful Infeasible Solutions

To overcome the second problem described in Section 3.3, the improved TNSDM introduces an archiving strategy of useful solutions for the directed mating. **Algorithm 1** and **Fig. 5** show the

Table 1: Symbols used in the pseudo code

$\mathcal{P}$	The parents population. The size is $\lvert\mathcal{P}\rvert$ (=$\lvert\mathcal{R}\rvert/2$).
$\mathcal{Q}$	The offspring population. The size is $\lvert\mathcal{Q}\rvert$ (=$\lvert\mathcal{R}\rvert/2$). Offspring are $\{Q_1, Q_2, \ldots, Q_{\lvert\mathcal{Q}\rvert}\}$ $(=\mathcal{Q})$.
$\mathcal{R}$	The entire population, $\mathcal{P} \cup \mathcal{Q}$.
$\mathcal{A}$	The proposed archive population for directed mating.
$\mathcal{F}^v$	A set of fronts classified by violation values $\boldsymbol{v}$. $\mathcal{F}^v = \{\mathcal{F}_1^v, \mathcal{F}_2^v, \ldots, \mathcal{F}^v_{\lvert\mathcal{F}^v\rvert}\}$.
$\mathcal{F}^f$	A set of fronts classified by objective values $\boldsymbol{f}$. $\mathcal{F}^f = \{\mathcal{F}_1^f, \mathcal{F}_2^f, \ldots, \mathcal{F}^f_{\lvert\mathcal{F}^f\rvert}\}$.
p_a, p_b	A pair of parents to generate one offspring.
$\mathcal{M}$	Solutions dominating p_a in the objective space.
T	The total number of generation.
$\mathcal{R}^{feasible}$	Feasible solutions in $\mathcal{R}$. $\mathcal{R}^{feasible} \subseteq \mathcal{R}$.
$\mathcal{POS}$	Pareto optimal solutions (POS), the output of MOEA.

pseudo-code and the block diagram of the improved TNSDM including the archiving strategy, respectively. Also, **Table 1** shows symbols used in **Algorithm 1** and **Fig. 5**. The improved TNSDM introduces the archive population $\mathcal{A}$ to maintain useful solutions for the directed mating. In **Algorithm 1**, codes of the conventional TNSDM are written in black, and additional codes for the improved TNSDM are written in red.

First, the improved TNSDM classifies the combined solutions $\mathcal{R} \cup \mathcal{A}$ into several fronts by the two-stage non-dominated sorting, and selects the parents population $\mathcal{P}$. In the directed mating, a primary parent p_a is selected by the crowded tournament selection in the same manner of the conventional TNSDM. Then, in the improved TNSDM, solutions $\mathcal{M}$ dominating p_a based on the controlled dominance area are selected from the combined solutions $\mathcal{R} \cup \mathcal{A}$ ($\mathcal{M} = \{\boldsymbol{x} \in \mathcal{R} \cup \mathcal{A} \mid \boldsymbol{x} \succ_{f'} p_a\}$). Also, in the improved TNSDM, to archive useful solutions for the directed mating, we mark the best α solutions in $\mathcal{M}$ in order of solution belonging to upper front. The superiority of solutions belonging to the same front are decided by CD. This mark on solutions in $\mathcal{R} \cup \mathcal{A}$ is used to select the archive population $\mathcal{A}$. Next, we select a secondly parents p_b from $\mathcal{M}$, and generate an offspring by applying crossover and mutation. This process is repeated until filling up the offspring population $\mathcal{Q}$.

Next, we select the archive population $\mathcal{A}$. In the combined solutions $\mathcal{R}\cup\mathcal{A}$, we select marked solutions not members of the parents population $\mathcal{P}$ as the archive population $\mathcal{A}$ (the 23th line of **Algorithm 1**). In other words, $\mathcal{A}$ is all marked solutions in the discarded solutions by the selection process of the parents population $\mathcal{P}$.

In the improved TNSDM, we can control the size of archive by varying the parameter α. The size of archive is increased by increasing α.

5. EXPERIMENTAL SETUP

5.1 Benchmark Problem

In this work, we use m objectives k knapsacks problems (mk-KP) [17]. mk-KP is different from multi-objective 0/1 knapsack problems [6] often used as a benchmark problem of MOEAs in that mk-KP can independently vary the number of objectives m and knapsacks (constraints) k. mk-KP is defined as

$$\begin{cases} \text{Maximize} & f_i(\boldsymbol{x}) = \sum_{l=1}^{n} p_{li} \cdot x_l \quad (i = 1, 2, \ldots, m) \\ \text{subject to} & \sum_{l=1}^{n} w_{lj} \cdot x_l \leq c_j \quad (j = 1, 2, \ldots, k). \end{cases} \tag{6}$$

In this problem, there are n items and k knapsacks (constraints). Each item l has m kinds of profits p_{li} ($i = 1, 2, \ldots, m$) and k kinds of weights w_{lj} ($j = 1, 2, \ldots, k$). The task is to find combinations of items $\boldsymbol{x} = \{x_1, x_2, \ldots, x_n\} \in \{0, 1\}^n$ which maximizes the total of profits on m kinds of objectives subject to the total of weights does not exceed k kinds of knapsack capacities c_j. The capacities of knapsacks c_j are defined as

$$c_j = \phi_j \cdot \sum_{l=1}^{n} w_{lj} \quad (j = 1, 2, \ldots, k), \tag{7}$$

where, ϕ_j is the feasibility ratio for each knapsack (constraint), we can control the difficulty of each constraint by varying ϕ_j. In this work, we use a constant ϕ for all knapsacks (i.e., $\phi = \phi_1 = \phi_2 = \ldots = \phi_k$).

5.2 Parameters and Metrics

We use mk-KP with n = 500 items (bits), $m = \{2, 4, 6\}$ objectives, k = 6 knapsacks (constraints) and feasibility $\phi = \{0.1, 0.3, 0.5\}$. We set profits and weights of each item to random integers in the interval [10,100]. As genetic parameters, we use uniform crossover with crossover ratio $P_c = 1.0$, bit-flip mutation with mutation ratio $P_m = 1/n$, and the population size is set to $\lvert\mathcal{R}\rvert = 200$ ($\lvert\mathcal{P}\rvert = \lvert\mathcal{Q}\rvert = 100$). As the termination criterion of optimization, the total number of generations is set to $T = 10^4$ for each run. Although the computational cost of the improved TNSDM using the archive is increased by increasing its parameter α, to clarify the effects of the proposed archive, we compare the search performance of each algorithm under the condition of the same total number of generations T (the same total number of evaluations of solutions) in this work. In the following experiments, we show average (mean) results of 50 runs.

To evaluate the obtained POS, we use Hypervolume (HV) [21] as a comprehensive metric evaluating both the convergence and the diversity of the obtained POS. HV measures m-dimensional volume covered by obtained POS and a reference point $\boldsymbol{r}$ in the objective space. Obtained POS showing a higher value of HV can be considered as a better set of solutions in term of both the convergence and the diversity toward the true Pareto front. In this work, $\boldsymbol{r}$ is set to the origin point in the objective space ($\boldsymbol{r} = \{0, 0, \ldots, 0\}$).

6. RESULTS AND DISCUSSION

6.1 The Increase of Directed Mating Executions

Before we verify the search performance of the improved TNSDM, here we observe the number of directed mating executions in the improved TNSDM. **Figs. 6-8** show the percentage of directed mating executions in all matings during the solution search in mk-KPs with $m = \{2, 4, 6\}$ objectives and feasibilities $\phi = \{0.1, 0.3, 0.5\}$. In each figure, we plot results of the improved TNSDMs when the parameters S and α are varied. The selection area of $\mathcal{M}$ is expanded by decreasing S from 0.5. Contrary, the selection area of $\mathcal{M}$ is contracted by increasing S from 0.5. In addition, the archive size of the improved TNSDM is increased by increasing α. In each figure, the case using $S = 0.5$ and $\alpha = 0$ is equivalent to the conventional TNSDM [16] using the conventional selection area of $\mathcal{M}$ and no archive.

6.1.1 *Effects of Controlling Selection Area of $\mathcal{M}$*

First, we focus on the effects of the controlling selection area of $\mathcal{M}$ in the improved TNSDM. As general tendency in **Figs. 6-8**, we can see that the number of directed mating executions is decreased by increasing S. This is because the number of primary parents being able to perform the directed mating is decreased by contracting the selection area of $\mathcal{M}$. Contrary, the number of primary parents being able to perform the directed mating is increased by increasing S and expanding the selection area of $\mathcal{M}$. Also, we can see the tendency that the number of directed mating executions is decreased by increasing feasibility ϕ. This is because the number of infeasible

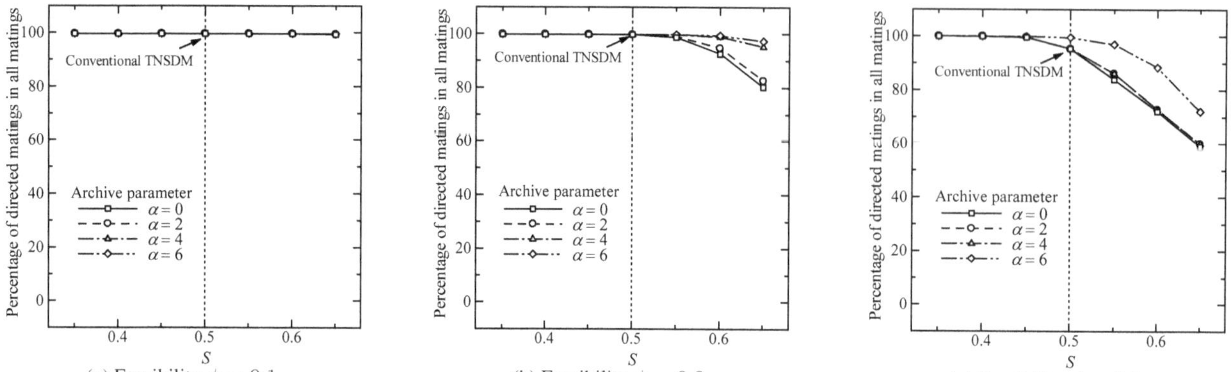

(a) Feasibility $\phi = 0.1$ (b) Feasibility $\phi = 0.3$ (c) Feasibility $\phi = 0.5$

Figure 6: Percentage of directed mating executions in all matings in $m = 2$ objective problems

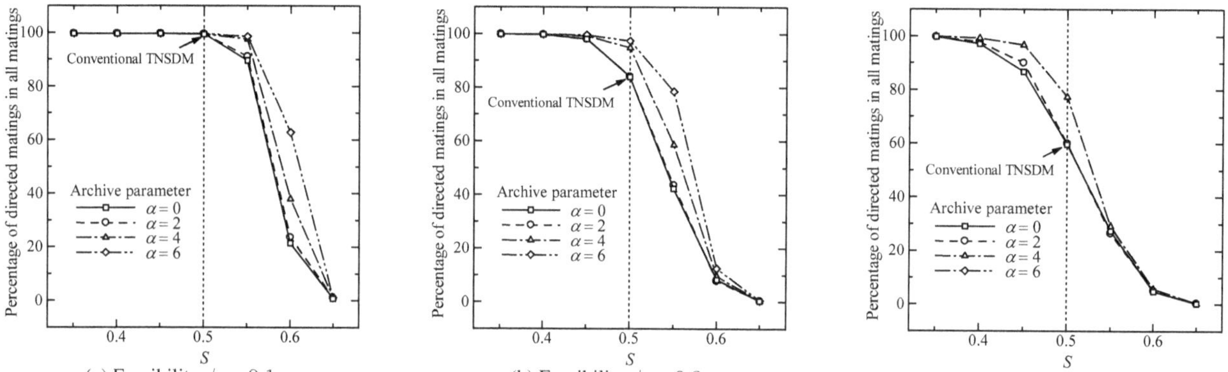

(a) Feasibility $\phi = 0.1$ (b) Feasibility $\phi = 0.3$ (c) Feasibility $\phi = 0.5$

Figure 7: Percentage of directed mating executions in all matings in $m = 4$ objective problems

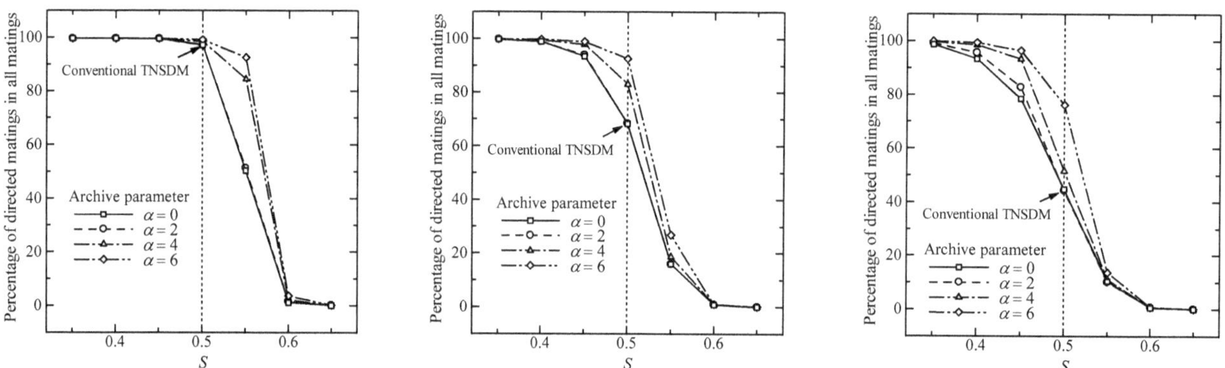

(a) Feasibility $\phi = 0.1$ (b) Feasibility $\phi = 0.3$ (c) Feasibility $\phi = 0.5$

Figure 8: Percentage of directed mating executions in all matings in $m = 6$ objective problems

solutions in the population is decreased by increasing ϕ. However, even in problems with high feasibility, we can see that the number of directed mating executions can be improved by expanding the selection area of $\mathcal{M}$ with $S < 0.5$.

6.1.2 *Effects of Archiving Useful Infeasible Solutions*

Next, we focus on the effects of the archive in the improved TNSDM. As we can see in **Figs. 6-8**, the number of directed mating executions is increased by increasing the size of archive α. These results reveal that the archive strategy in the improved TNSDM contributes to increase the number of directed matings by maintaining more candidates of secondary parents in the archive $\mathcal{A}$.

6.2 The Search Performance Verification

To verify the search performance of the improved TNSDM, **Figs. 9-11** show the results of HV achieved by the improved TNSDM at the final generation in mk-KPs with $m = \{2, 4, 6\}$ objectives and feasibilities $\phi = \{0.1, 0.3, 0.5\}$. In each figure, we plot the results of the improved TNSDMs when the parameters S and α are varied. Similar to **Figs. 6-8**, the improved TNSDM using $S = 0.5$ and $\alpha = 0$ is equivalent to the conventional TNSDM [16], and its HV is shown as horizontal red line in each figure. All the results are normalized by the results obtained by the conventional CNSGA-II [15].

6.2.1 *Effects of Controlling Selection Area of $\mathcal{M}$*

First, we focus on the effects of the controlling selection area of $\mathcal{M}$ in the improved TNSDM. To discuss the effects of only the controlling selection area of $\mathcal{M}$, here we will focus on the results achieved by the improved TNSDMs without the archive $\alpha = 0$ (the solid line and the rectangle marker) in **Figs. 9-11**.

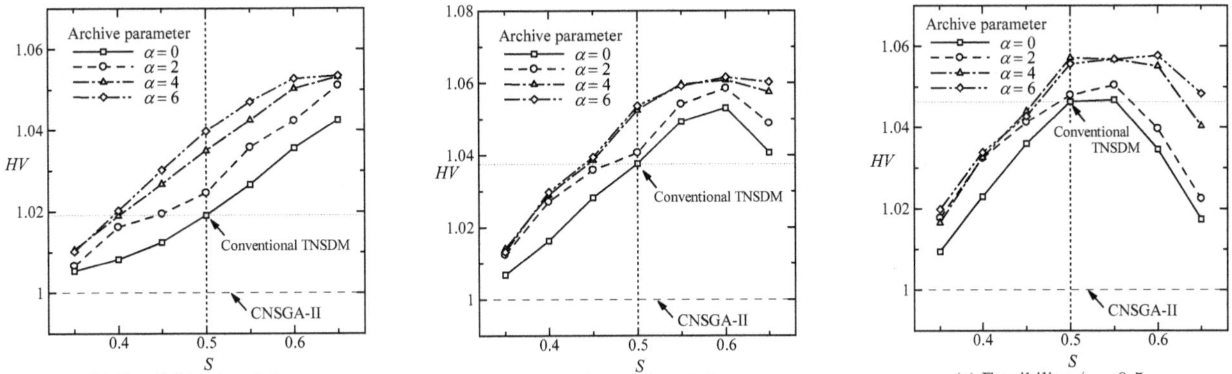

(a) Feasibility $\phi = 0.1$ (b) Feasibility $\phi = 0.3$ (c) Feasibility $\phi = 0.5$

Figure 9: Results of HV in $m = 2$ objective problems

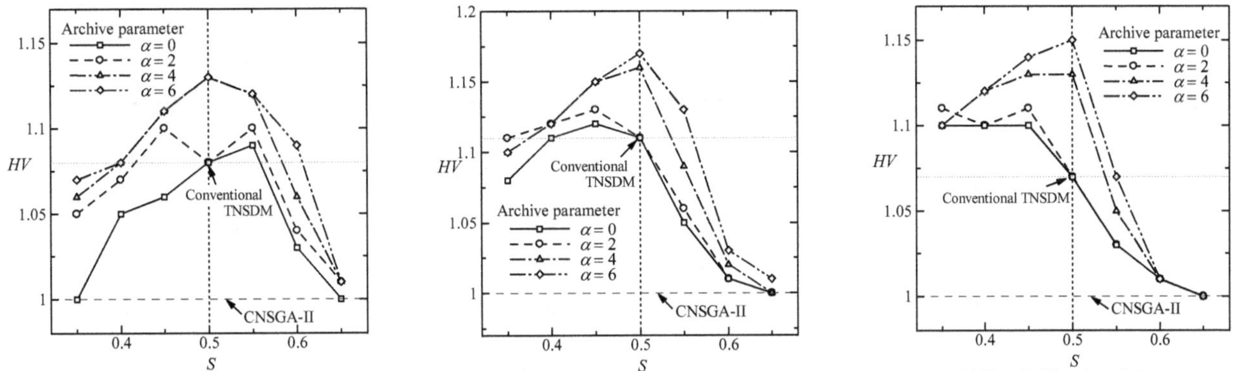

(a) Feasibility $\phi = 0.1$ (b) Feasibility $\phi = 0.3$ (c) Feasibility $\phi = 0.5$

Figure 10: Results of HV in $m = 4$ objective problems

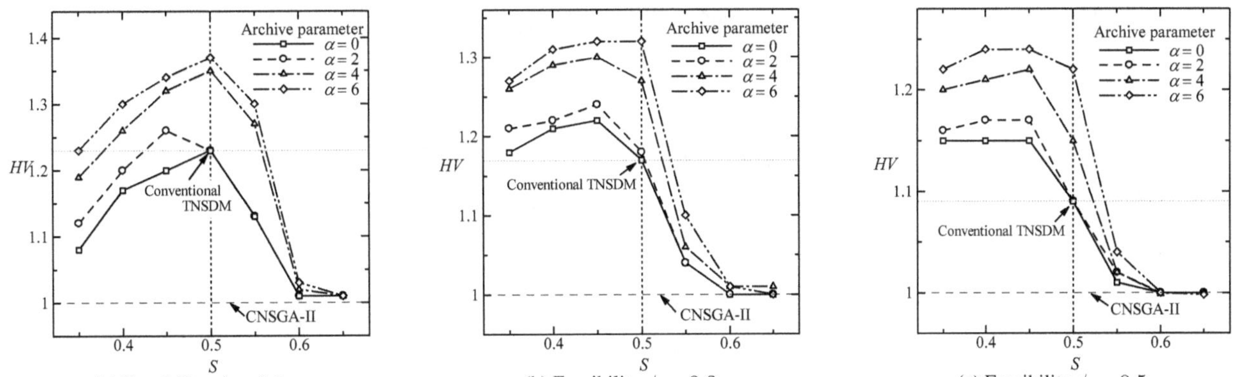

(a) Feasibility $\phi = 0.1$ (b) Feasibility $\phi = 0.3$ (c) Feasibility $\phi = 0.5$

Figure 11: Results of HV in $m = 6$ objective problems

First, we discuss the results of **Fig. 9** in $m = 2$ objective problems. From the results of **Fig. 9 (a)** in the problem with feasibility ratio $\phi = 0.1$, we can see that values of HV are monotonically increased by increasing S. In this case, as shown in **Fig. 6 (a)**, almost 100% of offspring are generated by the directed mating. Thus, in case of the number of infeasible solutions in the population is large in problems with low feasibility ϕ, we can see that the directed mating emphasizing the directionality of the solution search by contracting the selection area of solutions $\mathcal{M}$ achieves high HV. Next, from the results of **Fig. 9 (c)** in the problem with feasibility $\phi = 0.5$, we can see that there is the optimal parameter $S^* = 0.55$ to maximize HV. Since HV is decreased by setting $S > 0.55$, we can see that too large S deteriorates the search performance. In this case, as shown in **Fig. 6 (c)**, the number of directed mating executions is decreased by increasing S since the selection area of solutions $\mathcal{M}$ is contracted. These results suggest that the deterioration of HV in $S > 0.55$ is caused by the decrease of the number of directed mating executions. These results reveal that a large S has a positive effect to emphasize the directionality of the solution search in the directed mating and a negative effect to reduce the number of directed mating executions in the solution search. Also, although methods with $S < 0.5$ maintain almost 100% of directed mating executions, values of HV are deteriorated. This is caused by deterioration of the directionality of the directed mating using too large selection area of $\mathcal{M}$ with too small S. Therefore, there is an appropriate S^* maximizing HV depending on the feasibility of each problems.

Next, we discuss the results of **Figs. 10** and **11** in $m = \{4, 6\}$ objectives problems. From the results in the problems with high feasibility ratio $\phi = \{0.3, 0.5\}$, we can see that the optimal parameters to maximize HV become $S^* < 0.5$. That is, in these problems, values of HV are improved when the selection area of solutions $\mathcal{M}$ is expanded. As shown in **Figs. 7** and **8**, the number of directed mating executions is decreased by increasing the number of objectives m and feasibility ratio ϕ. Therefore, the expanded selection area of solutions $\mathcal{M}$ contributes to increase the number of directed mating executions, and it leads to improve the search perfromance.

6.2.2 *Effects of Archiving Useful Infeasible Solutions*

To verify the effects of the archive of useful solutions in the improved TNSDM, we focus on the parameter of archive size α. From all results in **Figs. 9-11**, the improved TNSDMs with $\alpha > 0$ achieves higher HV than the one without the archive ($\alpha = 0$), and values of HV are improved by increasing the archive size α. Also, in some problems, when the archive size α is increased, the optimal parameter of the controlling selection area S^* is moved to a larger value, and it allows to further emphasize the directionality of the solution search in the directed mating. These results reveal that the archive of useful solutions for the directed mating contributes to improve the search performance of the improved TNSDM.

Thus, we can see that both the controlling selection area of $\mathcal{M}$ and the archive improve the search performance of TNSDM, and the highest search performance is achieved when we combined them in the improved TNSDM. Also, the search performance improvement from CNSGA-II becomes more significant by increasing the number of objectives. This may be caused by the performance deterioration of the conventional dominance-based MOEAs such as CNSGA-II in many-objective optimization.

7. CONCLUSIONS

To further improve the effectiveness of the directed mating in TNSDM for solving CMOPs, in this work we proposed the improved TNSDM introducing the controlling selection area of solutions $\mathcal{M}$ and the archive of useful solutions for the directed mating. The experimental results showed that HV is improved by controlling selection area of solutions $\mathcal{M}$ and archiving useful solutions for the directed mating. Although each of them contribute to improve the search performance of TNSDM, the highest search performance is achieved when we combine them in the improved TNSDM.

As future works, we will verify the search performance of the improved TNSDM on continuous CMOPs. Also, we will study an adaptive control of S in the controlling selection area of $\mathcal{M}$ by detecting a characteristic of CMOP during the solutions search.

8. REFERENCES

[1] K. Deb, *Multi-Objective Optimization using Evolutionary Algorithms*, John Wiley & Sons, 2001.

[2] E. Mezura-Montes, *Constraint-Handling in Evolutionary Optimization*, Springer, 2009.

[3] F. Hoffmeister and J. Sprave, "Problem-independent handling of constraints by use of metric penalty functions," *Proc. of the 5th Annual Conference on Evolutionary Programming (EP 1996)*, pp. 289–294, 1996.

[4] T. Bäck, F. Hoffmeister and H. Schwefel, "A Survey of Evolution Strategies," *Proc. of the 4th International Conference on Genetic Algorithms*, pp. 2–9, 1991.

[5] C. A. C. Coello and A. D. Christiansen, "MOSES: A Multiobjective Optimization Tool for Engineering Design," *Engineering Optimization*, 31 (3), pp.337–368, 1999.

[6] E. Zitzler and L. Thiele, "Multiobjective Evolutionary Algorithms: A Comparative Case Study and the Strength Pareto Approach," *IEEE Trans. on Evolutionary Computation*, Vol.3 (4), pp.257–271, 1999.

[7] H. Ishibuchi and S. Kaige, "Effects of Repair Procedures on the Performance of EMO Algorithms for Multiobjective 0/1 Knapsack Problems," *Proc. of the 2003 Congress on Evolutionary Computation (CEC'2003)*, Vol. 4, pp.2254–2261, 2003.

[8] A. Homaifar, S. H. Y. Lai and X. Qi, "Constrained Optimization via Genetic Algorithms," *Trans. of The Society for Modeling and Simulation International - SIMULATION*, 62 (4), pp.242–254, 1994.

[9] J. Joines and C. Houck, "On the Use of Non-Stationary Penalty Functions to Solve Nonlinear Constrained Optimization Problems with Gas," *Proc. of the First IEEE Conference on Evolutionary Computation*, pp.579–584, 1994.

[10] R. Farmani and J.A. Wright, "Self-Adaptive Fitness Formulation for Constrained Optimization," *IEEE Trans. on Evolutionary Computation*, 7 (5), pp.445–455, 2003.

[11] K. Deb. "Evolutionary Algorithms for Multi-Criterion Optimization in Engineering Design," *Evolutionary Algorithms in Engineering and Computer Science*, chapter 8, pp.135–161, John Wiley & Sons, 1999.

[12] J. Hazra and A. K. Sinha, "A multi-objective optimal power flow using particle swarm optimization," *European Trans. on Electrical Power*, Vol. 21, Issue 1, pp. 1028–1045, 2011.

[13] Y. G. Woldesenbet, G. G. Yen and B. G. Tessema, "Constraint Handling in Multiobjective Evolutionary Optimization," *IEEE Trans. on Evolutionary Computation*, Vol. 13, Issue 3, pp. 514–525, 2009.

[14] E. Mezura-Montes and C. A. C. Coello, "Constrained Optimization via Multiobjective Evolutionary Algorithms," *Multiobjective Problem Solving from Nature*, Part I, Springer, pp. 53–75, 2008.

[15] K. Deb, A. Pratap, S. Agarwal and T. Meyarivan, "A Fast and Elitist Multi-Objective Genetic Algorithm: NSGA-II," *IEEE Trans. on Evolutionary Computation*, Vol. 6, pp.182–197, 2002.

[16] M. Miyakawa, K. Takadama, and H. Sato, "Two-Stage Non-Dominated Sorting and Directed Mating for Solving Problems with Multi-Objectives and Constraints," *Proc. of 2013 Genetic and Evolutionary Computation Conference (GECCO 2013)*, pp. 647-654, 2013.

[17] H. Kellerer, U. Pferschy and D. Pisinger, *Knapsack Problems*, Springer, 2004.

[18] T. Ray, K. Tai and C. Seow, "An evolutionary algorithm for multiobjective optimization," *Eng. Optim.*, Vol. 33, no. 3, pp. 399–424, 2001.

[19] S. Kukkonen, J. Lampinen, "Constrained Real-Parameter Optimization with Generalized Differential Evolution," *Proc. of 2006 IEEE Congress on Evolutionary Computation (CEC2006)*, pp. 911–918, 2006.

[20] H. Sato, H. Aguirre and K. Tanaka, "Controlling Dominance Area of Solutions and Its Impact on the Performance of MOEAs," *Proc. of the 4th Int'l Conf. on Evolutionary Multi-Criterion Optimization (EMO2007)*, LNCS, Springer, Vol. 4403, pp.5–20, 2007.

[21] E. Zitzler, *Evolutionary Algorithms for Multiobjective Optimization: Methods and Applications*, PhD thesis, Swiss Federal Institute of Technology, Zurich, 1999.

Hypervolume-Based Local Search in Multi-Objective Evolutionary Optimization

Martin Pilát
Charles University in Prague
Faculty of Mathematics and Physics
Malostranské náměstí 25
118 01 Prague, Czech Republic
Martin.Pilat@mff.cuni.cz

Roman Neruda
Institute of Computer Science
Academy of Sciences of the Czech Republic
Pod Vodárenskou věží 271/2
182 07 Prague, Czech Republic
roman@cs.cas.cz

ABSTRACT

This paper describes a surrogate based multi-objective evolutionary algorithm with hyper-volume contribution-based local search. The algorithm switches between an NSGA-II phase and a local search phase. In the local search phase, a model for each of the objectives is trained and CMA-ES is used to optimize the hyper-volume contribution of each individual with respect to its two neighbors on the non-dominated front. The performance of the algorithm is evaluated using the well known ZDT and WFG benchmark suites.

Categories and Subject Descriptors

I.2.8 [**Artificial Intelligence**]: Problem Solving, Control Methods, and Search—*heuristic methods*; I.6.3 [**Simulation and Modeling**]: Applications

Keywords

Multi-objective optimization, surrogate modeling, NSGA-II, hyper-volume

General Terms

Algorithms

1. INTRODUCTION

Multi-objective evolutionary algorithms have been widely accepted as one of the best multi-objective optimizers. However, their usefulness for solving real-life tasks is rather limited by the huge number of objective function evaluations they require to find a good approximation of the Pareto front – and these evaluations may be expensive both in terms of computational complexity and money. This problem have been intensively solved in the last decade and two approaches have been commonly employed: one of them is based on parallelization, the other is based on surrogate modeling.

The parallelization-based approach relies on large number of processing units (either CPUs or, more recently, even GPUs) to spread the computational load, and thus reduce the wall-clock time needed to find a good approximation of the Pareto front. Although this approach can be used for some of the optimization tasks, there are also problems with financially expensive functions. Parallelization also usually does not lower the number of function evaluations. In such cases, the parallelization approach can lower the wall-clock time of the optimization, but the financial costs remain the same.

The other approach – the surrogate-modeling based one – aims at lowering the number of objective function evaluations directly. It builds a surrogate model (a cheap approximation of the real expensive objective) whose goal is to learn the structure of the problem and to assist the evolutionary algorithm during the optimization. The algorithm then exploits the information obtained from the surrogate model to find new solutions during a local search, or to filter the not-promising solutions, so they are never evaluated with the real objective. The surrogate model is usually based on a machine-learning or statistical regression technique and it is trained using some previously evaluated individuals.

In this work, we present a novel surrogate-based multi-objective algorithm that uses the surrogate models during a local search phase. It tries to maximize the hyper-volume contribution of individuals in the population with respect to their neighbors on the non-dominated front.

In the rest of the paper, we first provide overview of related work in the field of evolutionary multi-objective optimization. Then, we describe the new algorithm. Further, the algorithm is compared to NSGA-II and ASM-MOMA on two sets of benchmark functions and the results are presented and discussed. Finally, we provide ideas for possible further improvements of the algorithm.

GECCO'14, July 12–16, 2014, Vancouver, BC, Canada.

http://dx.doi.org/10.1145/2576768.2598332.

2. RELATED WORK

Surrogate-based evolutionary multi-objective optimization has gained a lot of attention in the last decade. Among the first multi-objective evolutionary algorithms which used surrogate models were two versions of NSGA-II [4]. The version by Voutchkov and Keane [17] creates surrogate model for each of the objectives. This model is optimized for several generations, and in the end, some evenly spaced points are selected and added to an archive of individuals. Eventually, this archive is truncated, if a pre-defined size is exceeded. On the other hand, the surrogate-based NSGA-II by Nain and Deb [13] switches between two phases, in one of them the surrogate models are employed, while in the other the real objectives are optimized directly.

Loshchilov et al. [12] present a surrogate-based multi-objective algorithm with aggregated surrogate model. It uses only a single surrogate model which predicts the quality of each individual as a whole instead of using all the objectives. In this case, an approach based on the combination of OneClass SVM and support vector regression [5] is used to identify parts of the search space which may contain new non-dominated individuals. In each generation a large number of individuals is generated and only some of them, based on the surrogate model, are selected for evaluation with the real objective function. An improved version of the algorithm [11] is based on ranking SVM [8].

Lim et al. [10] use a single-objective surrogate assisted evolutionary algorithm in the local search phase together with two different surrogate models. One of the models is a low order polynomial, while the other is a more complicated ensemble model. Each of these models is optimized using the single-objective evolution, the resulting solutions are evaluated with the real objective, and then a selection procedure is executed which decides which of the newly found individuals are added back to the population.

Ponweiser et al. [16] used a hyper-volume based local search inspired by the efficient global optimization approach [9]. Their approach, SMS-EGO, uses the hyper-volume contribution of each individual and the expected improvement is optimized.

Pilát and Neruda also presented an evolutionary algorithm with aggregated surrogate model – ASM-MOMA [14]. The surrogate model used in this algorithm is based on the distance from the set of current non-dominated points (the distance is computed in the objective space) and a (evolutionary algorithm based) local search is executed to optimize some of the individuals in the population. The local search starts with an initial population generated close to the optimized individual in order to encourage a more local search in the area around the initial point. The best solution found during the local search replaces the original individual in the population.

Algorithm 1 HO-MOMA

require $[R_x, R_y]$ – hyper-volume reference point
require *popSize* – the population size
require p_{loc} – probability of local search

1: $P_0 :=$ random initial population
2: $A_0 := \emptyset$ {the archive}
3: $t := 0$
4: **while** termination condition not met **do**
5: $\quad P^*_{t+1} := \emptyset$
6: $\quad$ **if** $t \bmod 2 = 0$ **then** {perform the NSGA-II phase}
7: $\quad\quad$ **for** $i := 1$ to *popSize*/2 **do**
8: $\quad\quad\quad p_1 :=$TournamentSelection(P_t);
9: $\quad\quad\quad p_2 :=$TournamentSelection(P_t);
10: $\quad\quad\quad [o_1, o_2] :=$Crossover$(p_1,p_2)$;
11: $\quad\quad\quad o_1 :=$Mutation(o_1);
12: $\quad\quad\quad o_2 :=$Mutation(o_2);
13: $\quad\quad\quad$ Evaluate(o_1);
14: $\quad\quad\quad$ Evaluate(o_2);
15: $\quad\quad\quad P^*_{t+1} = P^*_{t+1} \cup \{o_1, o_2\}$
16: $\quad\quad$ **end for**
17: $\quad$ **else** {perform the local search phase}
18: $\quad\quad m_1 :=$TrainModel$(A_t, 1)$ {model for f_1}
19: $\quad\quad m_2 :=$TrainModel$(A_t, 2)$ {model for f_2}
20: $\quad\quad$ **for** each non-dominated front N **do**
21: $\quad\quad\quad$ sort(N) {according to f_1, ascending}
22: $\quad\quad\quad$ **for** $i := 1$ to size(N) **do**
23: $\quad\quad\quad\quad$ **if** rand(0,1) $< p_{loc}$ **then**
24: $\quad\quad\quad\quad\quad o :=$Optimize$(N, i, R_x, R_y, m_1, m_2)$
25: $\quad\quad\quad\quad\quad$ Evaluate(o)
26: $\quad\quad\quad\quad\quad P^*_{t+1} := P^*_{t+1} \cup \{o\}$
27: $\quad\quad\quad\quad$ **end if**
28: $\quad\quad\quad$ **end for**
29: $\quad\quad$ **end for**
30: $\quad$ **end if** {phases}
31: $\quad P_{t+1} :=$NSGA2Selection$(P_t \cup P^*_{t+1})$
32: $\quad A_{t+1} :=$Truncate$(A_t \cup P^*_{t+1})$
33: $\quad t := t + 1$
34: **end while**

3. ALGORITHM DESCRIPTION

In this section, we describe HO-MOMA – a new multi-objective surrogate-based memetic algorithm based on the optimization of hyper-volume contribution. It can be currently used only for bi-objective problems, the generalization of the algorithm to problems with more objectives is left as a future work. The limitation is given mainly by the way the reference point for the scalarization in the local search phase is selected.

During the development of the algorithm, a preliminary version was used for comparison of different local search techniques in multi-objective optimization and the results were presented in [15]. The version presented here contains a different fitness function in the local search phase, and also the individuals which are optimized are selected in a different way.

HO-MOMA (cf. Algorithm 1) periodically switches between two phases. In one of the phases (lines 7–16), an iteration of NSGA-II [4] is executed. In the other phase (lines 18–29), a local search algorithm, based only on surrogate model evaluations, is run. After each of the phases (lines 31-33), the NSGA-II selection is executed, and also an archive of evaluated individuals is updated and truncated, if necessary.

The NSGA-II phase is rather simple, only a single iteration of NSGA-II main loop (the crossover and mutation) is executed. The only addition is the keeping of the archive of evaluated individuals – newly created individuals are added to the archive and, if necessary, the archive is truncated to a pre-defined size.

The described (and tested) version of HO-MOMA uses NSGA-II in some of the iterations. The algorithm was chosen rather arbitrarily as it is a well known and well tested algorithm with known characteristics. However, any other multi-objective algorithm with similar structure can also be used instead of NSGA-II.

3.1 Local search

The local search phase is much more interesting. First (lines 18 and 19), surrogate model for each of the objectives is trained based on the previously evaluated objective val-

Algorithm 2 TrainModel(A, i)

```
1: T := ∅
2: for j := 1 to size(A) do
3:     T := T ∪ ⟨A[j].vars, A[j].value(j)⟩
4: end for
5: m := SVR-Train(T)
6: return m
```

Algorithm 3 Optimize(N, i, R_x, R_y,m_1,m_2)

```
[r_x, r_y] := DetermineRef(N, i, R_x, R_y, m_1, m_2)
fit(x) := fitness(x, r_x, r_y, m_1, m_2)
initalPoint := I
CMAES-Initialize(I, popSize_L, σ, fit);
for i :=1 to iter_L do
    CMAES-Iteration()
end for
return CMAES-BestIndividual()
```

ues of the individuals in the archive (cf. Algorithm 2). To this end, a training set is created from the archive (lines 1–4 of TrainModel). The training set assigns the value of the given objective to the values of the variables of the individuals. Then, the surrogate model, support vector regression, is trained to predict the values from the training set. The model basically learns the objective function of the given problem.

After the model training, the population is divided into non-dominated fronts, and the local search is executed for each individual in each front with a given probability (lines 22–24). First, each of the fronts is sorted according to the values of the first objective in ascending order (this means it is also sorted by the second objective in the descending order). Then, the local search procedure is executed.

The local search procedure (cf. Algorithm 3) first determines the correct reference point for the hyper-volume contribution computation. The values of the reference point are based on the second objective of the individual preceding the optimized one on the non-dominated front, and on the value of the first objective of the individual right after the optimized one. If the optimized individual is the first or the last individual in a given non-dominated front, the values of the reference point used for the algorithm evaluation is used (see also Algorithm 4 for details of the reference determination).

Finally, a fitness function, based on the coordinates of the reference point $[r_x, r_y]$ and the models of the two objectives m_1 and m_2 is constructed in the following way:

$$\text{fitness}(x, r_x, r_y, m_1, m_2) =$$
$$\begin{cases} (r_x - m_1(x))(r_y - m_2(x)) & m_1(x) < r_x \wedge m_2(x) < r_y \\ r_x - m_1(x) & m_1(x) > r_x \wedge m_2(x) < r_y \\ r_y - m_2(x) & m_1(x) < r_x \wedge m_2(x) > r_y \\ -\text{dist}([r_x, r_y], [m_1(x), m_2(x)]) & \text{otherwise,} \end{cases}$$

where $\text{dist}(a, b)$ is the Euclidean distance of the two points a and b in the objective space. The definition of the fitness function may seem complicated, but it is in fact a simple, continuous, uni-modal function, see Figure 1 for a plot of

Algorithm 4 DetermineRef(N, i, R_x,R_y,m_1,m_2)

```
if i = 1 then {leftmost point}
    r_y := R_y
else
    r_y := m_1(N[i − 1])
end if
if i = size(N) then {rightmost point}
    r_x := R_x
else
    r_x := m_2(N[i + 1])
end if
return [r_x, r_y]
```

Figure 1: Plot of the local search fitness function with reference $[r_x, r_y] = [1, 1]$ and models m_1 and m_2.

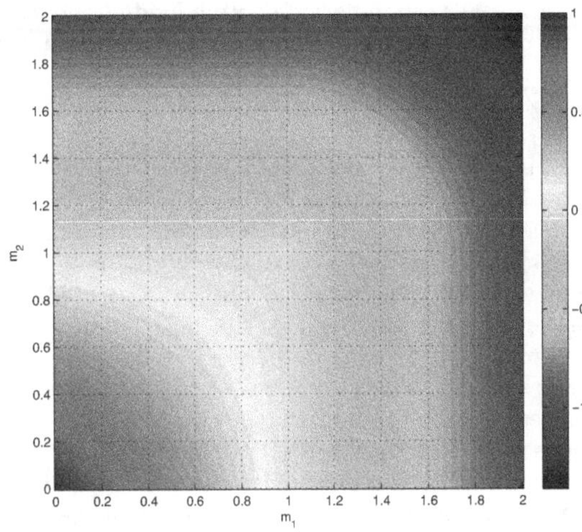

this function with the reference point $[r_x, r_y] = [1.0, 1.0]$ as the function of the value of models m_1 and m_2.

The fitness function is negative in cases where the point x is dominated by the reference $[r_x, r_y]$ and also if x and the reference are mutually non-dominated. The only situation, in which it is positive, is if x dominates the reference. In this case, the value is equal to the hyper-volume dominated only by the point x (in the current non-dominated front). This fitness function is then optimized (cf. Algorithm 3) with the CMA evolution strategy [6]. Starting with a relatively low step size, and with the initial population generated in the neighborhood of the optimized individual ensures the search is rather local.

After the CMA-ES finishes, the best individual found (the one which maximizes the fitness defined above) is added to the population of the multi-objective algorithm. This, as with the NSGA-II phase, the population is then merged with the previous population and the NSGA-II selection is executed. The newly created individuals are also added to the archive, and the archive is truncated.

For the archive truncation we use a random approach – random individuals are removed from the archive as long as the size of the archive is larger than a pre-defined value. In our earlier work, we also experimented with different truncation strategies, but this one works the best.

We have also experimented with different types of local search algorithms, like gradient search, random search, and an evolutionary algorithm with the same operators ad those used in the NSGA-II phase, however, CMA-ES provides the most robust results among these algorithms.

4. RESULTS

We compared HO-MOMA to NSGA-II [4], and ASM-MOMA [14]. All the algorithms use the SBX crossover [2] with probability 0.9 and polynomial mutation [3] with probability $1.0/N$, where N is the number of variables of the given problem. The population size is set to 100. The surrogate-based algorithms use an archive of at most 800 individuals and the models are build using support vector regression [5] with RBF kernel with bandwidth parameter 0.01. The algorithms were stopped after 30,000 evaluations.

In the local search phase, ASM-MOMA uses an evolutionary algorithm with SBX crossover and polynomial mutation. The algorithm has a population of 50 individuals generated from the optimized one by performing the polynomial mutation 100 times on each of them, and it runs for 30 generations. 25% of the individuals are optimized with the local search operator.

In HO-MOMA, the local search phase uses the CMA evolution strategy [6]. It has a population of 10 individuals and is run for at most 200 iterations. The initial step size σ is different for each variable set to 0.01 times the range of the particular variable. This rather small σ was selected to encourage the local search around the optimized individual. In some preliminary tests, we used larger σ but we found out that the lower values work better. The individuals undergo the local search with probability 0.5.

Previous experiments indicate that in the case of ASM-MOMA, there is no significant difference among different local search optimizers (EA, CMA-ES, random search and gradient search), whereas in the case of HO-MOMA, CMA-ES provides the most robust results, and the other optimizers do not work that well. This is the reason, why different local search optimizers were used in ASM-MOMA and HO-MOMA in the comparison (together with the fact, that EA is the optimizer originally used in ASM-MOMA).

The algorithms were tested on the ZDT [18] and WFG [7] benchmarks. We used 30 variables for ZDT1-3, 10 variables for ZDT4, and ZDT6, and 24 variables for the WFG problems (4 of the variables are position based and 20 are distance based). The reference point $[R_x, R_y]$ was set to [11,11] for the ZDT problems, and to [3,5] for the WFG problems. We compare the difference between the hyper-volume of μ-optimal distribution [1] for $\mu = 100$ for the given problem and the hyper-volume of the non-dominated set found by the algorithm. We denote this metric as ΔH. The results are presented in the form of graphs which represent the median ΔH obtained after a number of objective function evaluations. The median was obtained from 15 independent runs. We also added error bars to the graphs which represent the first and third quartile of the ΔH reached by the algorithm.

The sources of ASM-MOMA and HO-MOMA are included as a supplementary material, together with the $\mu-$optimal fronts used during the testing.

The results (graphically represented in Figures 2-4) indicate that HO-MOMA is able to outperform both NSGA-II and ASM-MOMA on most of the benchmark functions. This is true especially in the first 5,000 function evaluations. This means, HO-MOMA is suitable particularly for problems limited to rather low numbers of function evaluations.

For the ZDT problems, HO-MOMA is able to reduce the number of function evaluations needed to reach a given ΔH significantly, usually around 20 times compared to NSGA-II. In fact, it can reach $\Delta\text{H} = 0.001$ in around 2,000 evaluations for all problems except ZDT4. Such low value of ΔH signifies almost perfect solution, and there are probably no practical differences between the values of $\Delta\text{H} = 0.001$ and $\Delta\text{H} = 0.0001$, which is the best value the algorithm is able to obtain. For ZDT6 we can observe a largely improved performance, as HO-MOMA is able to reach the value of $\Delta\text{H} = 0.0001$, while NSGA-II (and in most cases even ASM-MOMA) only reach $\Delta\text{H} = 0.01$. The combination of NSGA-II operators with CMA-ES works well in this case, which leads to the improved performance. On the other hand, the surrogate modeling itself (as used in ASM-MOMA) does not improve the results to such a large extent. The ZDT4 problem contains a lot of local Pareto optimal fronts which makes it hard for surrogate-based algorithms. This translates to worse results of both ASM-MOMA and HO-MOMA.

The WFG problems are more complicated than the ZDT ones. Also, the ΔH values are not directly comparable between these two benchmark sets as the Pareto fronts of the WFG problems are around 10 times longer than those of the ZDT problems, this also translates to one order of magnitude larger ΔH values.

Nevertheless, HO-MOMA still compares well with both ASM-MOMA and NSGA-II on the WFG benchmark. For WFG1 and WFG2, HO-MOMA gives the best results of the three algorithms for the whole run. On WFG1, the convergence of HO-MOMA is much faster especially in the first generations, where the ΔH quickly drops. Values around $\Delta\text{H} = 7$ are reached after only 1,000 evaluations, whereas both ASM-MOMA and NSGA-II need more than 10,000 evaluations to obtain similar quality of solutions. After this initial quick improvement, the convergence rate of all the algorithms is similar.

For WFG2, the difference between HO-MOMA and the other two algorithms is even larger. HO-MOMA is able to attain $\Delta\text{H} = 0.1$, while the other algorithms reach only $\Delta\text{H} = 0.9$ and converge very slowly afterward. In WFG2 the objectives are non-separable functions, so the CMA-ES is more suitable for their optimization than NSGA-II, which leads to this significantly improved performance.

The differences among the algorithms are much lower for the rest of the WFG benchmark. For WFG5 and WFG6, HO-MOMA converges much faster in the beginning (first 5,000 evaluations), however, the other algorithms are similarly good after approx. 7,000 evaluations. For WFG6, NSGA-II and ASM-MOMA even outperform HO-MOMA after more than 10,000 evaluations, as HO-MOMA converges to a local optima. For WFG3 and WFG4, there is almost no difference among the three algorithms. For WFG7 and WFG8, ASM-MOMA and HO-MOMA perform similarly, however, they are both slightly worse than NSGA-II. Finally, for WFG9, both HO-MOMA and ASM-MOMA are slower than NSGA-II in the beginning (first 5,000 evaluations), however they are able to find better solutions later (only in less than half of the runs, as the median is the same as for NSGA-II).

Figure 2: Comparison of NSGA-II, ASM-MOMA, and HO-MOMA on ZDT1-5, ZDT6, and WFG1. The results are aggregated over 15 runs. The error bars indicate the line indicates the median, the error bars are the first and third quartile.

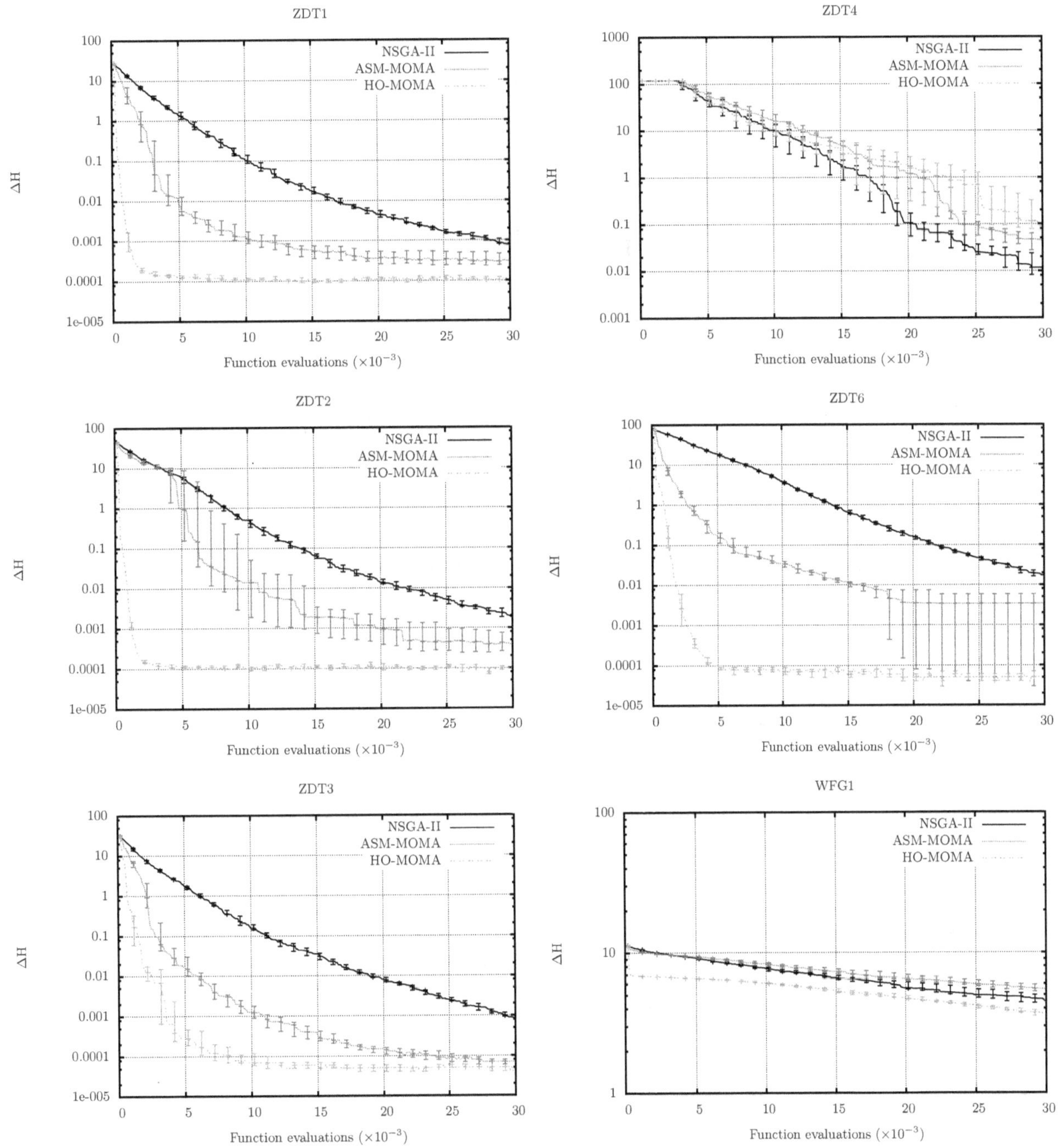

Figure 3: Comparison of NSGA-II, ASM-MOMA, and HO-MOMA on WFG2-7. The results are aggregated over 15 runs. The error bars indicate the line indicates the median, the error bars are the first and third quartile.

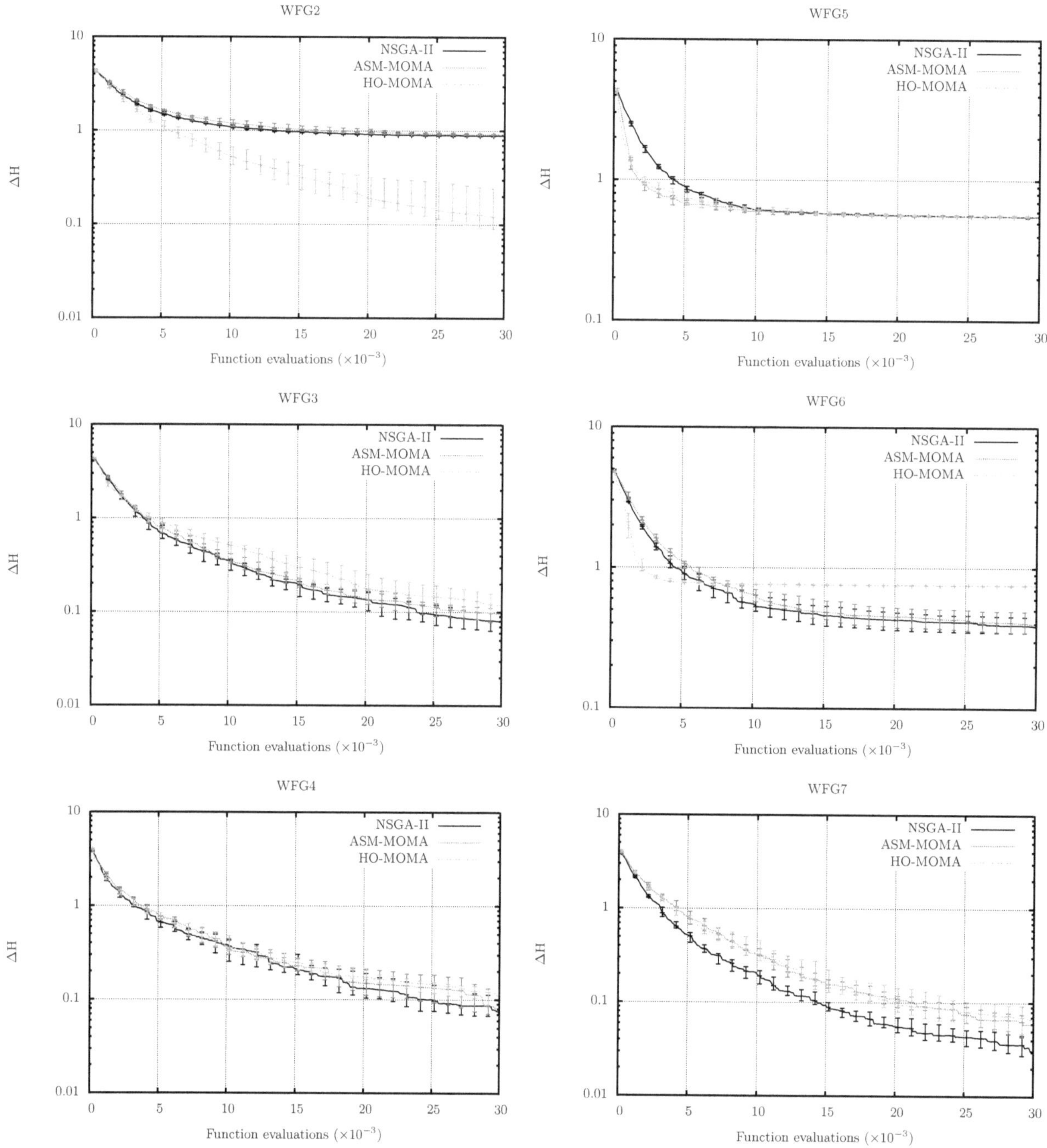

Figure 4: Comparison of NSGA-II, ASM-MOMA, and HO-MOMA on WFG8 and WFG9. The results are aggregated over 15 runs. The error bars indicate the line indicates the median, the error bars are the first and third quartile.

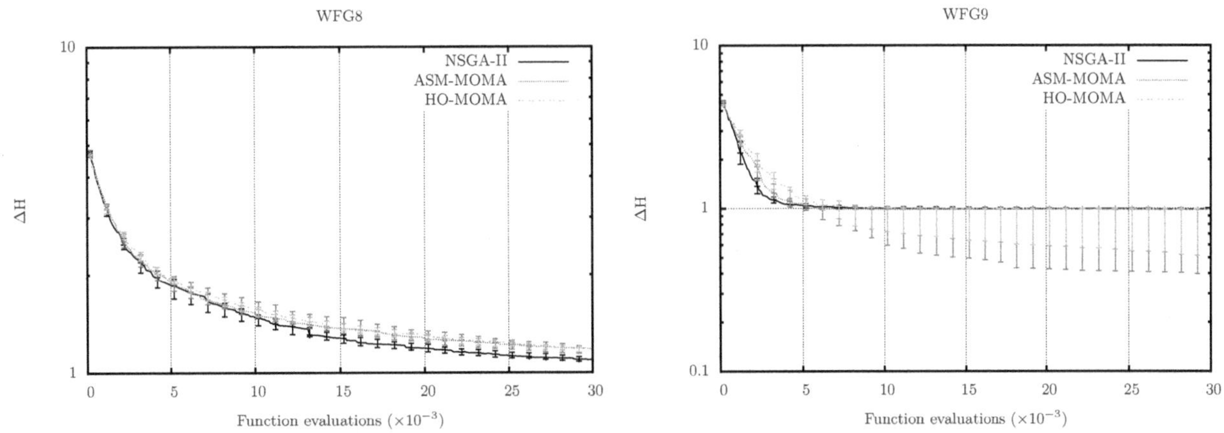

5. CONCLUSIONS AND FUTURE WORK

We have presented a novel surrogate-based multi-objective evolutionary algorithm. The most important contribution is the local search phase of the algorithm, which is based on the maximization of the hyper-volume contribution of some individuals in the population with respect to their neighbors on their non-dominated front.

The algorithm performs better than both NSGA-II and ASM-MOMA on most of the tested functions, especially during the first 5,000 function evaluations. This makes the algorithm suitable for solving tasks, where only thousands of objective function evaluations are available. HO-MOMA also shows that the combination of NSGA-II with evolution strategies, like CMA-ES, may be a prospective way to improve the performance of multi-objective optimizers further.

In some cases, we have observed a pre-mature convergence, or a slow down when compared to NSGA-II. Making the number of individuals optimized by the local search adaptive – increasing it when the local search improves the convergence, and decreasing it when it degrades the performance may help to obtain better results in the future. Also, the use of support vector regression should be re-evaluated – although it was among the best methods for ASM-MOMA, the models may be too simple to grasp the more difficult functions which HO-MOMA models.

In the future, the algorithm should be evaluated on some real-life problems and compared to different multi-objective optimizers. The generalization to problems with more than two objectives is another challenging task left for a future work.

6. ACKNOWLEDGMENTS

Roman Neruda has been partially supported by The Ministry of Education of the Czech Republic project COST LD 13002.

7. REFERENCES

[1] A. Auger, J. Bader, D. Brockhoff, and E. Zitzler. Theory of the hypervolume indicator: optimal μ-distributions and the choice of the reference point. In *Proceedings of the tenth ACM SIGEVO workshop on Foundations of genetic algorithms*, FOGA '09, pages 87–102, New York, NY, USA, 2009. ACM.

[2] K. Deb and R. B. Agrawal. Simulated binary crossover for continuous search space. *Complex Systems*, 9:1–34, 1994.

[3] K. Deb and M. Goyal. A combined genetic adaptive search (geneas) for engineering design. *Computer Science and Informatics*, 26(4):30–45, 1996.

[4] K. Deb, A. Pratap, S. Agarwal, and T. Meyarivan. A fast and elitist multiobjective genetic algorithm: Nsga-ii. *Evolutionary Computation, IEEE Transactions on*, 6(2):182–197, 2002.

[5] H. Drucker, C. J. C. Burges, L. Kaufman, A. J. Smola, and V. Vapnik. Support vector regression machines. In M. Mozer, M. I. Jordan, and T. Petsche, editors, *NIPS*, pages 155–161. MIT Press, 1996.

[6] N. Hansen and A. Ostermeier. Completely derandomized self-adaptation in evolution strategies. *Evol. Comput.*, 9(2):159–195, June 2001.

[7] S. Huband, P. Hingston, L. Barone, and L. While. A review of multiobjective test problems and a scalable test problem toolkit. *Evolutionary Computation, IEEE Transactions on*, 10(5):477–506, 2006.

[8] T. Joachims. A support vector method for multivariate performance measures. In *Proceedings of the 22nd international conference on Machine learning*, ICML '05, pages 377–384, New York, NY, USA, 2005. ACM.

[9] D. R. Jones, M. Schonlau, and W. J. Welch. Efficient global optimization of expensive black-box functions. *J. of Global Optimization*, 13(4):455–492, Dec. 1998.

[10] D. Lim, Y. Jin, Y.-S. Ong, and B. Sendhoff. Generalizing surrogate-assisted evolutionary computation. *Trans. Evol. Comp*, 14(3):329–355, June 2010.

[11] I. Loshchilov, M. Schoenauer, and M. Sebag. Dominance-based pareto-surrogate for multi-objective optimization. In K. Deb, A. Bhattacharya, N. Chakraborti, P. Chakroborty, S. Das, J. Dutta, S. K. Gupta, A. Jain, V. Aggarwal, J. Branke, S. J. Louis, and K. C. Tan, editors, *SEAL*, volume 6457 of

Lecture Notes in Computer Science, pages 230–239. Springer, 2010.

[12] I. Loshchilov, M. Schoenauer, and M. Sebag. A mono surrogate for multiobjective optimization. In M. Pelikan and J. Branke, editors, *GECCO*, pages 471–478. ACM, 2010.

[13] P. K. Nain and K. Deb. A multi-objective optimization procedure with successive approximate models. *KanGAL report*, (2005002), 2005.

[14] M. Pilát and R. Neruda. Aggregate meta-models for evolutionary multiobjective and many-objective optimization. *Neurocomputing*, 116:392–402, 2013.

[15] M. Pilát and R. Neruda. The effect of different local search algorithms on the performance of multi-objective optimizers. In *IEEE Congress on Evolutionary Computation 2014*, 2014. accepted.

[16] W. Ponweiser, T. Wagner, D. Biermann, and M. Vincze. Multiobjective optimization on a limited budget of evaluations using model-assisted $\mathcal{S}$-metric selection. In *Proceedings of the 10th International Conference on Parallel Problem Solving from Nature. PPSN X*, pages 784–794, Berlin, Heidelberg, 2008. Springer-Verlag.

[17] I. Voutchkov and A. Keane. Multiobjective optimization using surrogates. In *Proceedings of the 7th International Conference on Adaptive Computing in Design and Manufacture*, pages 167–175. The M.C.Escher Company, April 2006.

[18] E. Zitzler, K. Deb, and L. Thiele. Comparison of multiobjective evolutionary algorithms: Empirical results. *Evol. Comput.*, 8(2):173–195, June 2000.

Inverted PBI in MOEA/D and its Impact on the Search Performance on Multi and Many-Objective Optimization

Hiroyuki Sato
The University of Electro-Communications
1-5-1 Chofugaoka, Chofu,Tokyo, 182-8585 Japan
sato@hc.uec.ac.jp

ABSTRACT

MOEA/D decomposes a multi-objective optimization problem into a number of single objective optimization problems. Each single objective optimization problem is defined by a scalarizing function using a weight vector. In MOEA/D, there are several scalarizing approaches such as the weighted Tchebycheff, the weighted sum, and the PBI (penalty-based boundary intersection). However, these conventional scalarizing approaches face a difficulty to approximate a widely spread Pareto front in some problems. To enhance the spread of Pareto optimal solutions in the objective space and improve the search performance of MOEA/D especially in many-objective optimization problems, in this work we propose the inverted PBI scalarizing approach which is an extension of the conventional PBI. We use many-objective knapsack problems and WFG4 problems with 2∼8 objectives, and compare the search performance of NSGA-III and four MOEA/Ds using the weighted Tchebycheff, the weighted sum, the PBI and the inverted PBI. As results, we show that MOEA/D using the inverted PBI achieves higher search performance than other algorithms in problems with many-objectives and the difficulty to obtain a widely spread Pareto front in the objective space.

Categories and Subject Descriptors

I.2.8 [**Artificial Intelligence**]: Problem Solving, Control Methods, and Search—*Heuristic methods*; G.1.6 [**Numerical Analysis**]: Optimization

General Terms

Algorithms, Design, Performance

Keywords

multi-objective optimization, MOEA/D, scalarizing functions

1. INTRODUCTION

MOEA/D (MOEA based on decomposition), one of the representative evolutionary algorithms for multi-objective optimization, decomposes a multi-objective optimization problem (MOP) into a number of single-objective optimization problems [1]. Each single-objective optimization problem is defined by a scalarizing function using a weight vector. Recently, the framework of MOEA/D has been increasingly investigated, and a number of its variants have been proposed so far [2, 3, 4, 5]. Also, the decomposition of the objective space in MOEA/D is an effective approach especially for many-objective optimization problems (MaOPs) which optimizes four or more objective functions simultaneously. In MaOPs, Pareto dominance-based MOEAs such as NSGA-II [6] and SPEA2 [7] have a problem to rank solutions in the population, i.e., most of the solutions become non-dominated and the same rank is assigned to them, which seriously spoils proper selection pressure required in the evolution process [8]. On the other hand, MOEA/D uses a scalar value aggregated from multiple objective function values instead of Pareto dominance when solutions are compared. Therefore, MOEA/D can easily determine the superiority of solutions even in MaOPs. NSGA-III, an improved NSGA-II, has also introduced the concept of decomposition of the objective space [9].

In MOEA/D, there are several scalarizing approaches such as the weighted Tchebycheff, the weighted sum and the PBI (penalty-based boundary intersection). However, the conventional scalarizing approaches face a difficulty to approximate a widely spread Pareto front in some MOPs. The weighted Tchebycheff and the PBI evolve solutions toward the obtained ideal point $\boldsymbol{z}$ in the objective space. Generally, each element of $\boldsymbol{z}$ is the best objective function value for each objective function found during the solution search. If the obtained ideal point $\boldsymbol{z}$ is close to the true ideal point $\boldsymbol{z}^*$ of Pareto front, a wide range of Pareto front can be approximated. However, the distance between the obtained $\boldsymbol{z}$ and the true $\boldsymbol{z}^*$ becomes large in some MOPs with a characteristic that solutions in the population tend to be distributed in a specific region of Pareto front. In this case, if solutions are evolved toward the obtained ideal point $\boldsymbol{z}$, the entire Pareto front cannot be approximated. To overcome this problem, the first aim of this work is to design a scalarizing function which can approximate a widely spread Pareto front in the objective space. Also, the second aim is to design a scalarizing function effective for many-objective optimization. A recent study [10] showed that the weighted sum approach achieved higher search performance than other scalarizing approaches in many-objective knapsack problems [11]. Therefore, in this work we design a scalarizing function by considering a characteristic of the weighted sum.

Thus, to enhance the spread of Pareto optimal solutions (POS) in the objective space and improve the search performance of MOEA/D in MaOPs, in this work we propose the inverted PBI function which is an extension of the conventional PBI function. The conventional PBI evolves solutions toward the obtained ideal point $\boldsymbol{z}$ by minimizing scalarizing function value. On the other hand, the inverted PBI evolves solutions from the current nadir point $\boldsymbol{n}$ by maximizing scalarizing function value. Each element of $\boldsymbol{n}$ is set to the worst

GECCO'14, July 12–16, 2014, Vancouver, BC, Canada.

ACM 978-1-4503-2662-9/14/07 ...$15.00.
http://dx.doi.org/10.1145/2576768.2598297 .

(a) PBI [1] (b) Inverted PBI

Figure 1: Difference between the conventional PBI and the proposed inverted PBI

objective function value for each objective function in the population. The inverted PBI uses the parameter θ similar to the conventional PBI. The inverted PBI using $\theta = 0$ has the similar effect to the conventional weighted sum. That is, the inverted PBI involves the weighted sum achieving high search performance in MaOPs [10] as the case of $\theta = 0$. Also, the inverted PBI can emphasize the directivity for the search direction determined by weight vector by increasing θ. We use discrete many-objective knapsack problems [11] and WFG4 problems [12] with m =2∼8 objectives, and compare the search performance of NSGA-III [9] and four MOEA/Ds using the weighted Tchebycheff, the weighted sum, the PBI and the inverted PBI.

2. MOEA/D

2.1 Algorithm

MOEA/D decomposes a multi-objective optimization problem into a number of single-objective optimization problems. The single-objective optimization problems are defined by scalarizing functions g using uniformly distributed weight vectors $\boldsymbol{\lambda}^i$ $(i = 1, 2, \ldots, N)$. Each weight vector $\boldsymbol{\lambda}^i$ determines a search direction in the m-dimensional objective space. Each element λ^i_j $(j = 1, 2, \ldots, m)$ is one of $\{0/H, 1/H, \ldots, H/H\}$ based on the decomposition parameter H, and $N = C^{m-1}_{H+m-1}$ kinds of weight vectors satisfying $\sum_{j=1}^{m} \lambda^i_j = 1.0$ are used for solution search. In the following, the algorithm of MOEA/D [1] is briefly described.

Step 1) Initialization:

Step 1-1) Compute the Euclidean distances between any two weight vectors and find the T nearest weight vectors to each weight vector. For each $i = 1, 2, \ldots, N$, set $B(i) = \{i_1, \ldots, i_T\}$, where $\boldsymbol{\lambda}^{i_1}, \ldots, \boldsymbol{\lambda}^{i_T}$ are the T nearest weight vectors to $\boldsymbol{\lambda}^i$.

Step 1-2) Randomly generate the population $(\boldsymbol{x}^1, \boldsymbol{x}^2, \ldots, \boldsymbol{x}^N)$.

Step 2) Solution Search:

For $i = 1, 2, \ldots, N$, perform the following procedure.

Step 2-1) Randomly choose two indexes k and l from $B(i)$, and then generate a new offspring $\boldsymbol{y}$ from parents $\boldsymbol{x}^k$ and $\boldsymbol{x}^l$ by applying genetic operators.

Step 2-2) For each index $j \in B(i)$, if $g(\boldsymbol{y}|\boldsymbol{\lambda}^j)$ is better than $g(\boldsymbol{x}^j|\boldsymbol{\lambda}^j)$, then the current solution $\boldsymbol{x}^j$ is replaced by the generated offspring $\boldsymbol{y}$ $(\boldsymbol{x}^j = \boldsymbol{y})$.

Step 3) Stopping Criteria:

If the termination criteria is satisfied, then stop and pick POS from the population $(\boldsymbol{x}^1, \boldsymbol{x}^2, \ldots, \boldsymbol{x}^N)$ as the output of the optimization. Otherwise, go to **Step 2**.

2.2 Scalarizing Functions

In MOEA/D, there are several scalarizing approaches to aggregate m kinds of objective function values [1]. In the following, we introduce the weighted Tchebycheff, the weighted sum and the PBI approaches.

Tchebycheff

The scalar optimization problem of the weighted Tchebycheff function g^{tch} [13] is defined by

$$\text{Minimize } g^{tch}(\boldsymbol{x}|\boldsymbol{\lambda}) = \max_{1 \le j \le m} \{\lambda_j \cdot |f_j(\boldsymbol{x}) - z_j|\}, \tag{1}$$

where, $\boldsymbol{z}$ is the obtained ideal point. In this work, each element z_j $(j = 1, 2, \ldots, m)$ is set to the minimum (best) objective function value f_j in the population. The weighted Tchebycheff approach searches a solution minimizing g^{tch} toward $\boldsymbol{z}$. The weighted Tchebycheff has an advantage that both convex and concave Pareto front can be approximated.

Weighted Sum

The scalar optimization problem of the weighted sum function g^{ws} is defined by

$$\text{Maximize } g^{ws}(\boldsymbol{x}|\boldsymbol{\lambda}) = \sum_{j=1}^{m} \lambda_j \cdot (n_j - f_j(\boldsymbol{x})), \tag{2}$$

where, $\boldsymbol{n}$ is the current nadir point. In this work, each element n_j $(j = 1, 2, \ldots, m)$ is set to the maximum (worst) objective function value f_j in the population. The weighted sum approach searches a solution maximizing g^{ws} from $\boldsymbol{n}$. A recent study [10] reported that the weighted sum approach achieves higher search performance than the weighted Tchebycheff approach in MaOPs. However, the weighted sum approach has a problem that the entire concave Pareto front cannot be approximated [1].

PBI

The scalar optimization problem of the PBI (penalty-based boundary intersection) function g^{pbi} [1] is defined by

$$\text{Minimize } g^{pbi}(\boldsymbol{x}|\boldsymbol{\lambda}) = d_1 + \theta d_2, \tag{3}$$

where,

$$d_1 = \frac{||(\boldsymbol{f}(\boldsymbol{x}) - \boldsymbol{z})^T \boldsymbol{\lambda}||}{||\boldsymbol{\lambda}||}, \tag{4}$$

$$d_2 = ||\boldsymbol{f}(\boldsymbol{x}) - (\boldsymbol{z} - d_1 \boldsymbol{\lambda})||. \tag{5}$$

θ is the parameter of the PBI, and its range is $\theta \ge 0$. **Fig. 1 (a)** shows d_1 and d_2 of a solution $\boldsymbol{x}$ for a weight vector $\boldsymbol{\lambda} = \{0.5, 0.5\}$

PBI:

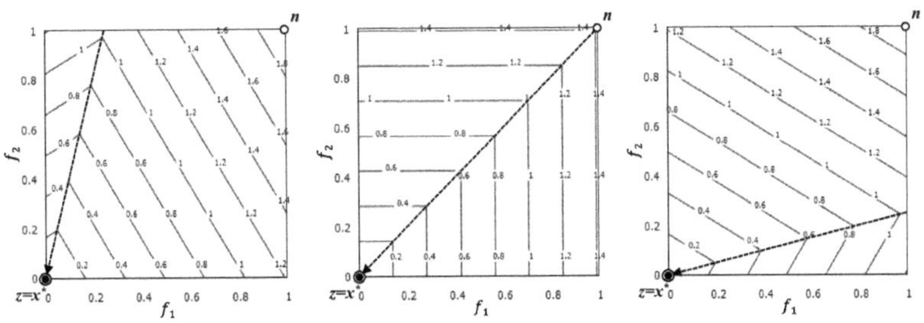

(a) $\boldsymbol{\lambda} = \{0.2, 0.8\}$ (b) $\boldsymbol{\lambda} = \{0.5, 0.5\}$ (c) $\boldsymbol{\lambda} = \{0.8, 0.2\}$

Figure 2: Contour lines of the conventional PBI using $\theta = 1.0$

Inverted PBI:

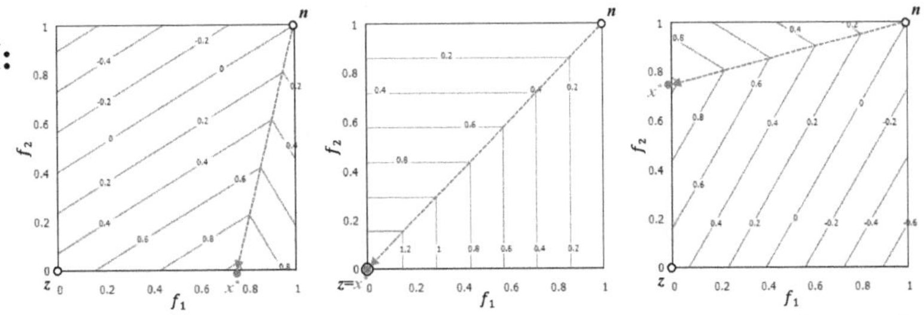

(a) $\boldsymbol{\lambda} = \{0.2, 0.8\}$ (b) $\boldsymbol{\lambda} = \{0.5, 0.5\}$ (c) $\boldsymbol{\lambda} = \{0.8, 0.2\}$

Figure 3: Contour lines of the proposed inverted PBI using $\theta = 1.0$

in $m = 2$ dimensional objective space of a minimization problem. In the PBI approach, a solution having a small d_1 is considered as a better solution close to Pareto front. Also, distance d_2 from weight vector $\boldsymbol{\lambda}$ is considered. Finally, g^{pbi} is calculated by adding the value of d_2 multiplied by θ to d_1. That is, a solution having a small d_1 and d_2 is considered as a better solution. The balance between d_1 and d_2 in g^{pbi} is controlled by the parameter θ. Thus, the PBI approach searches a solution toward the obtained ideal point $\boldsymbol{z}$ by minimizing g^{pbi}.

2.3 Problem and Design Principle

Each scalarizing approach has its own characteristics, it makes an impact on the search performance of MOEA/D.

In some MOPs, the conventional scalarizing approaches face a difficulty to approximate a widely spread Pareto front in the objective space. In the case of the weighted Tchebycheff and the PBI approaches, solutions are evolved toward $\boldsymbol{z}$ in the objective space. Generally, $\boldsymbol{z}$ is the obtained ideal point found during the solution search. When the obtained $\boldsymbol{z}$ is close to the true ideal point $\boldsymbol{z}^*$ of Pareto front, a wide range of Pareto front can be approximated. However, the distance between the obtained $\boldsymbol{z}$ and the true $\boldsymbol{z}^*$ becomes large in some MOPs with a characteristic that solutions in the population tend to be distributed in a specific area of Pareto front. In this case, if solutions are evolved toward the obtained $\boldsymbol{z}$ which is far from the true $\boldsymbol{z}^*$, a wide range of Pareto front cannot be approximated. This tendency can be observed especially in multi and many-objective knapsack problems [11]. The knapsack problems have the difficulty to approximate the entire Pareto front widely spread in the objective space. To overcome this problem, the first aim of this work is to design a scalarizing function to approximate a widely spread Pareto front.

Additionally, the second aim of this work is to design an effective scalarizing function for many-objective optimization. Recent study [10] reported that the weighted sum approach achieves higher search performance than other scalarizing approaches in many-objective knapsack problems [11]. Therefore, in this work we design a novel scalarizing function by considering a characteristic of the weighted sum function. Also, we consider to approximate the entire concave Pareto front since the conventional weighted sum cannot approximate the entire concave Pareto front [1].

3. PROPOSED METHOD

3.1 Concept

To enhance the spread of POS in the objective space and improve the search performance of MOEA/D in MaOPs, in this work we propose the inverted PBI function which is an extension of the conventional PBI function. The conventional PBI evolves solutions toward the obtained ideal point $\boldsymbol{z}$ by minimizing scalarizing function value. Contrary, the inverted PBI evolves solutions from the current nadir point $\boldsymbol{n}$ by maximizing scalarizing function value. Similar to the conventional PBI, the inverted PBI also uses the parameter θ. The inverted PBI using $\theta = 0$ has the similar effect to the weighted sum. Also, the directivity for the search direction determined by weight vector is emphasized by increasing θ.

3.2 Inverted PBI Function

The scalar optimization problem of the inverted PBI function g^{ipbi} is defined by

$$\text{Maximize } g^{ipbi}(\boldsymbol{x}|\boldsymbol{\lambda}) = d_1 - \theta d_2, \tag{6}$$

where,

$$d_1 = \frac{||(\boldsymbol{n} - \boldsymbol{f}(\boldsymbol{x}))^T \boldsymbol{\lambda}||}{||\boldsymbol{\lambda}||}, \tag{7}$$

$$d_2 = ||(\boldsymbol{n} - \boldsymbol{f}(\boldsymbol{x})) - d_1 \boldsymbol{\lambda}||. \tag{8}$$

θ is the parameter of the inverted PBI, and its range is $\theta \geq 0$. Although the conventional PBI searches a solution toward the obtained ideal point $\boldsymbol{z}$ by minimizing g^{pbi}, the inverted PBI searches a solution from the current nadir point $\boldsymbol{n}$ by maximizing g^{ipbi}. Similar to the example of the PBI shown in **Fig. 1 (a)**, **Fig. 1 (b)** shows d_1 and d_2 of a solution $\boldsymbol{x}$ for a weight vector $\boldsymbol{\lambda} = \{0.5, 0.5\}$ in the case of the inverted PBI. In the inverted PBI approach, a solution

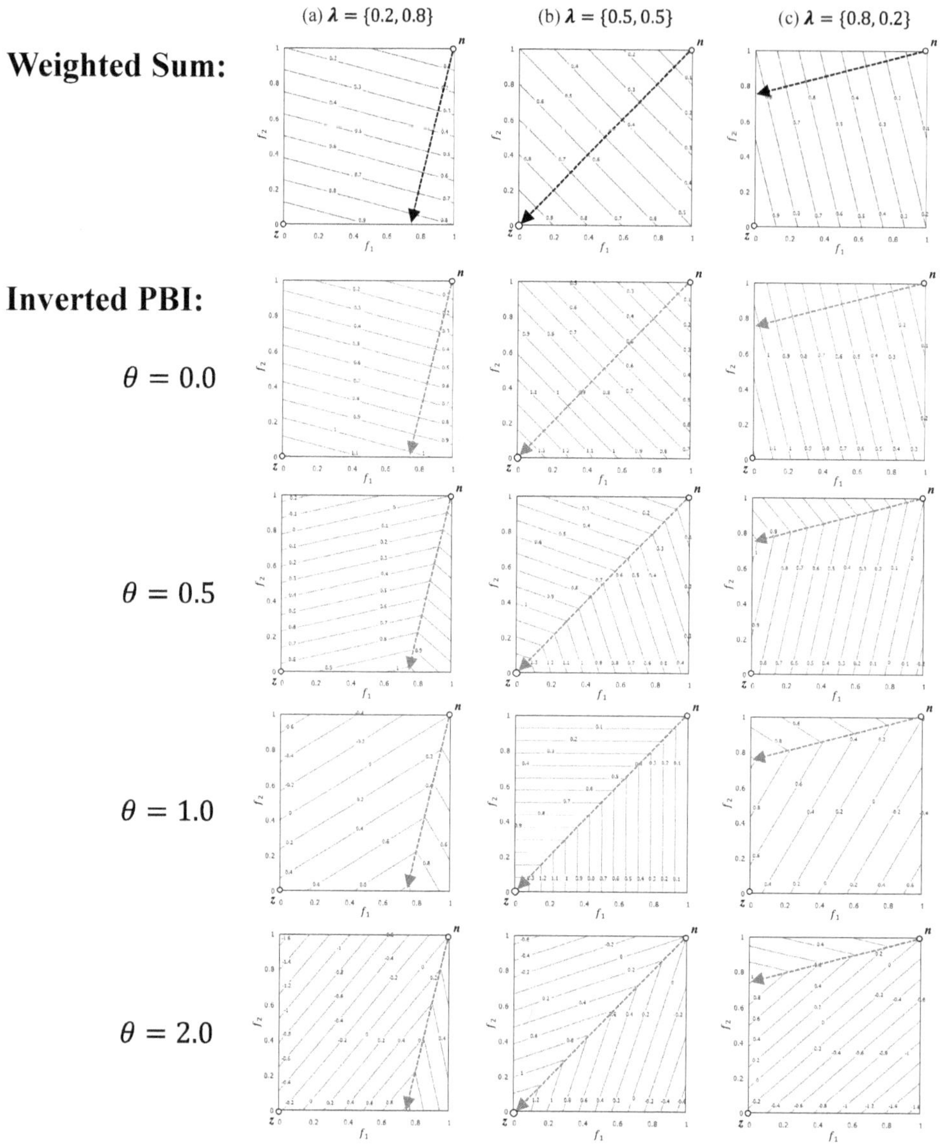

Figure 4: Contour lines of the conventional weighted sum and the proposed inverted PBI

having a large d_1 is considered as a better solution close to Pareto front. Also, distance d_2 from weight vector $\boldsymbol{\lambda}$ is considered. Finally, g^{ipbi} is calculated by subtracting the value of d_2 multiplied by θ from d_1. That is, a solution having a large d_1 and a small d_2 is considered as a better solution. Similar to the conventional PBI, the balance between d_1 and d_2 in g^{ipbi} is controlled by θ.

3.3 Difference from PBI

First, we explain the difference between the PBI and the inverted PBI. **Fig. 2** shows contour lines of the PBI function g^{pbi} in $m = 2$ dimensional minimization problem. Similarly, **Fig. 3** shows contour lines of the inverted PBI function g^{ipbi}. For both functions, three patterns of contour lines with different $\boldsymbol{\lambda}$ are shown. In these figure, the ideal point is set to $\boldsymbol{z} = \{0, 0\}$, and the nadir point is set to $\boldsymbol{n} = \{1, 1\}$. Also, the best point $\boldsymbol{x}^*$ achieving the best value of g^{pbi} or g^{ipbi} is plotted in each figure.

The conventional PBI approach tries to minimize g^{pbi}. As shown in **Fig. 2**, the shape of contour lines of g^{pbi} is changed by varying $\boldsymbol{\lambda}$. However, $\boldsymbol{x}^*$ achieving the best (minimum) g^{pbi} is not changed by varying $\boldsymbol{\lambda}$, and $\boldsymbol{x}^* = \boldsymbol{z}$ for any $\boldsymbol{\lambda}$. That is, the goal points $\boldsymbol{x}^*$ of g^{pbi} with any $\boldsymbol{\lambda}$ are the same point $\boldsymbol{z}$. Generally, $\boldsymbol{z}$ is the obtained ideal point found during the solution search. If the obtained $\boldsymbol{z}$ is close to the true $\boldsymbol{z}^*$ of Pareto front, the conventional PBI can approximate a wide range of Pareto front. Otherwise, the conventional PBI face the difficulty to approximate a wide range of Pareto front because all solutions are evolved toward the single point $\boldsymbol{z}$ in the objective space even if the obtained $\boldsymbol{z}$ is far from the true $\boldsymbol{z}^*$

The inverted PBI approach tries to maximize g^{ipbi}. As shown in **Fig. 3**, the shape of contour lines of g^{ipbi} is changed by varying $\boldsymbol{\lambda}$. In the inverted PBI approach, $\boldsymbol{x}^*$ achieving the best (maximum) g^{ipbi} is also changed by varying $\boldsymbol{\lambda}$. That is, the goal points $\boldsymbol{x}^*$ of g^{ipbi} with different $\boldsymbol{\lambda}$ are not the same point and widely distributed in the objective space. Since the goal points $\boldsymbol{x}^*$ are different depending on $\boldsymbol{\lambda}$, we can expect that the inverted PBI search a wide range of the objective space.

3.4 Difference from Weighted Sum

Next, we explain the difference between the weighted sum and the inverted PBI. **Fig. 4** shows contour lines of the weighted sum function g^{ws} and the inverted PBI functions g^{ipbi} with $\theta = \{0.0, 0.5,$

$1.0, 2.0\}$ in $m = 2$ dimensional minimization problem. For all functions, three patterns of contour lines with different $\boldsymbol{\lambda}$ are shown.

Both the weighted sum and the inverted PBI are functions which are maximized from the nadir point $\boldsymbol{n}$. First, we compare the contour lines of the weighted sum and the inverted PBI using $\theta = 0.0$. Although their degrees of slope are different, their directions and shapes of slope are the same. Since the inverted PBI using $\theta = 0.0$ does not consider the distance d_2, its effect becomes similar to the weighted sum. Next, we can see that the contour lines of the inverted PBI functions are changed by varying θ. The directivity for the search direction determined by weight vector is emphasized by increasing θ.

Thus, the inverted PBI using $\theta = 0$ has the similar effect to the weighted sum. That is, the inverted PBI involves the weighted sum achieving high search performance in MaOPs [10] as the case of $\theta = 0$. Furthermore, the inverted PBI extends the effect of the weighted sum to emphasize the directivity for the search direction by increasing θ.

4. EXPERIMENTAL SETUP

4.1 Five Algorithms

In this work, we compare five algorithms. Four algorithms are MOEA/Ds using the weighted Tchebycheff, the weighted sum, the PBI and the inverted PBI, respectively. The last one is NSGA-III [9] proposed by Prof. Deb. NSGA-III is an improved version of NSGA-II and tries to approximate Pareto front by decomposing the objective space similar to MOEA/D. To maintain the distribution of solutions in the objective space, NSGA-III uses distance between solutions and weight vectors instead of the crowding distance used in NSGA-II.

4.2 Test Problems and Parameters

As test problems, we use discrete many-objective knapsack problem (MOKP) [11] and continuous WFG4 [12]. MOKP is a maximization problem and WFG4 is a minimization problem.

MOKP is formulated by

$$\begin{cases} \text{Maximize } f_j(\boldsymbol{x}) = \sum_{i=1}^{n} x_i \cdot p_{i,j} \\ \text{subject to } g_j(\boldsymbol{x}) = \sum_{i=1}^{n} x_i \cdot w_{i,j} \le c_j \end{cases} (j = 1, \dots, m), \quad (9)$$

where, $p_{i,j}$ and $w_{i,j} (j = 1, 2, \cdots, m)$ denote profit and weight of item i according to knapsack (objective) j. c_j is the capacity of knapsack j. The capacity of knapsack is given by $c_j = \phi \cdot \sum_{i=1}^{n} w_{i,j}$ based on the feasibility ratio ϕ. To use the same implementation of algorithms for both MOKP and WFG4, we solve MOKP as a minimization problem formulated by

$$\begin{cases} \text{Minimize } f_j'(\boldsymbol{x}) = \sum_{i=1}^{n} p_{i,j} - f_j(\boldsymbol{x}) \\ \text{subject to } g_j(\boldsymbol{x}) = \sum_{i=1}^{n} x_i \cdot w_{i,j} \le W_j \end{cases} (j = 1, \cdots, m). \quad (10)$$

We use MOKPs with $m = \{2, 3, 4, 5, 6, 7, 8\}$ objectives, $n = 500$ items (bits), and feasibility ratio $\phi = 0.5$. To deal with infeasible solutions we use the greedy repair mechanism [11]. Similar to [11], $p_{i,j}$ and $w_{i,j}$ are generated as random integers in the interval $[10, 100]$. To generate offspring, we adopt uniform crossover with a crossover rate 1.0, and apply bit-flipping mutation with a mutation rate $4/n$. The termination criterion is set to 10^4 generations.

WFG4 [12] has concave Pareto front. In WFG4, two kinds of difficulties can be controlled by the distance-related parameter L and the position-related parameter K. The difficulty of the convergence toward Pareto front is increased by increasing L. In this work, a fixed $L = 10$ is used. Also, the difficulty to cover the entire Pareto front is increased by increasing K. In this work, we verify the search performance in WFG4 problems with different K. Since assignable values of K in WFG4 is restricted, we set $K = k + (m - 1) - k \mod (m-1)$ by varying $k = \{10, 50, 100, 200, 400\}$. Therefore, the number of variables is $n = L + K$. Also, the number of objectives is set to $m = \{2, 4, 6, 8\}$. To generate offspring, we adopt SBX with a crossover rate 0.8 and $\eta_c = 15$, and apply polynomial mutation with a mutation rate $4/n$ and $\eta_m = 20$. The termination criterion is set to $3,000$ generations.

The decomposition parameters to generate weight vectors in MOEA/D are set to $H = \{200, 19, 9, 6, 5, 4, 4\}$ for $m = \{2, 3, 4, 5, 6, 7, 8\}$ objectives, respectively. Therefore, the population sizes are $N = \{201, 210, 220, 210, 252, 210, 330\}$ for $m = \{2, 3, 4, 5, 6, 7, 8\}$, respectively. MOEA/Ds and NSGA-III use the same weight vectors and the population size. In MOEA/Ds, the neighborhood size is set to $T = 20$. In the following experiments, we show the average performance with 30 runs.

4.3 Performance Metrics

To evaluate the search performance, we use Hypervolume (HV) [14], which measures the m-dimensional volume of the region enclosed by the obtained POS and a dominated reference point $\boldsymbol{r}$ in the objective space. Higher HV indicates better POS in terms of both convergence and diversity. In MOKPs, we use $\boldsymbol{r} = \{0, 0, \dots, 0\}$. In WFG4 problems, after we normalize the objective function values of POS by $f_j'(\boldsymbol{x}) = f_j(\boldsymbol{x})/2j$ $(j = 1, 2, \dots, m)$, we calculate HV with $\boldsymbol{r} = \{1.1, 1.1, \dots, 1.1\}$.

To provide additional information separately on convergence and diversity of the obtained POS, we also use $Norm$ [15] and Maximum Spread (MS) [14], respectively. Higher value of $Norm$ generally means higher convergence to the true POS. Although $Norm$ cannot precisely reflect local features of the distribution of the obtained POS, we can observe the general tendency of convergence for POS from their values. On the other hand, higher MS indicates better diversity in POS, i.e. a widely spread Pareto front.

5. RESULTS AND DISCUSSION

5.1 HV by Varying θ in MOKPs

Fig. 5 shows HV of MOEA/Ds using the PBI and the inverted PBI at the final generation when we vary the parameter θ. In these figures, we also plot the values of HV achieved by MOEA/D using the weighted sum as horizontal lines.

First, we can see that the values of HV achieved by the PBI using $\theta = 0.0$ and the inverted PBI using $\theta = 0.0$ are similar to the HV achieved by the weighted sum. This result reveals that the search performance of the inverted PBI using $\theta = 0.0$ is similar to the one of the weighted sum. For the PBI, the optimal parameter maximizing HV is $\theta^* = 0.0$ for all objectives m. For the inverted PBI, the optimal parameters are $\theta^* = \{0.6, 0.2, 0.2, 0.1\}$ for $m = \{2, 4, 6, 8\}$ objectives, respectively. Also, we can see that the values of HV achieved by the inverted PBI using θ^* are higher than the conventional weighted sum and PBI using θ^* for all objectives m.

5.2 The Search Performance in MOKPs

Fig. 6 shows the search performance of five algorithms at the final generation in MOKPs when we vary the number of objectives m. For the PBI and inverted PBI, we plot the results using the optimal θ^* maximizing HV. For the PBI, the optimal parameter is $\theta^* = 0$ for all objectives m. For the inverted PBI, the optimal parameters are $\theta^* = \{0.6, 0.3, 0.2, 0.2, 0.2, 0.1, 0.1\}$ for $m = \{2, 3, 4, 5, 6, 7, 8\}$ objectives, respectively. All the results are normalized by the result achieved by the weighted Tchebycheff.

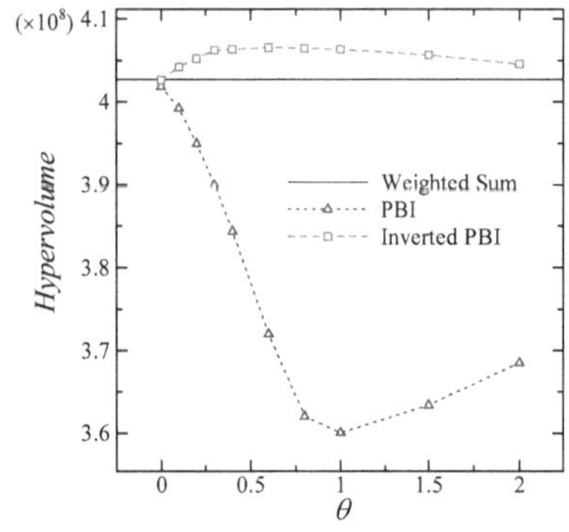

(a) $m = 2$ objectives

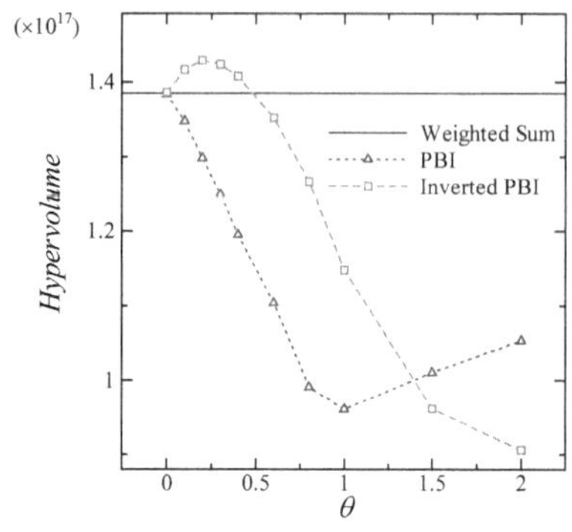

(b) $m = 4$ objectives

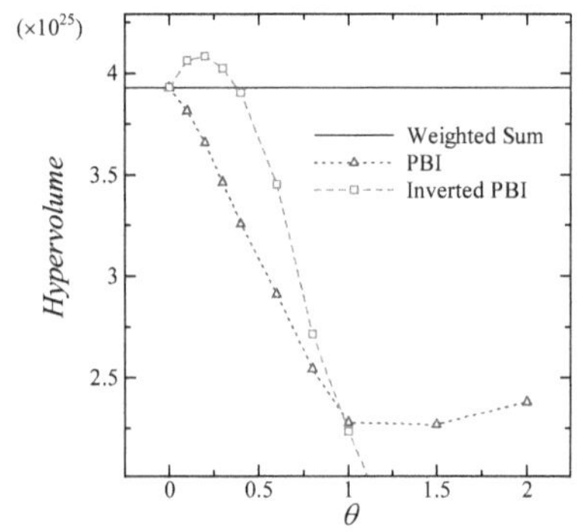

(c) $m = 6$ objectives

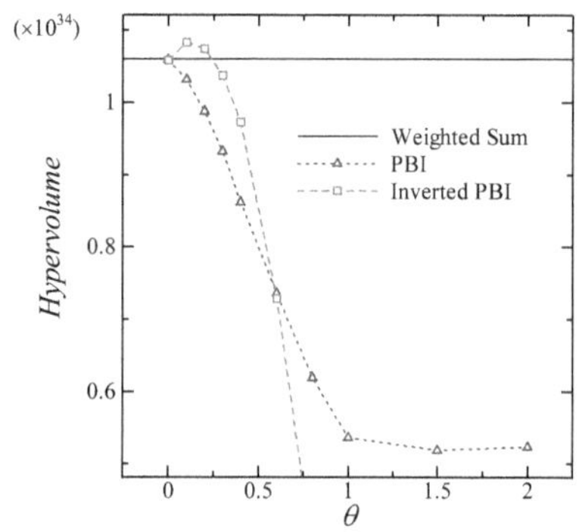

(d) $m = 8$ objectives

Figure 5: Results of HV in MOKPs when the parameter θ is varied

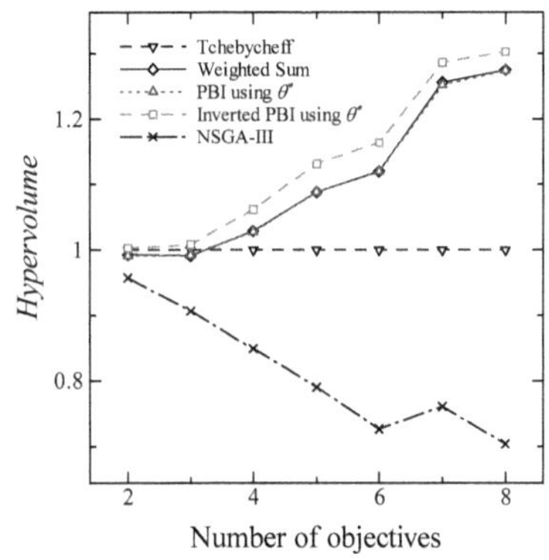

(a) $Hypervolume$ (Comprehensive metric)

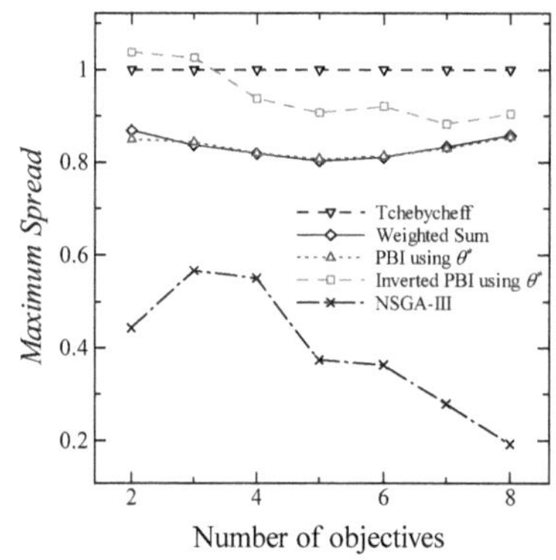

(b) $MaximumSpread$ (Diversity metric)

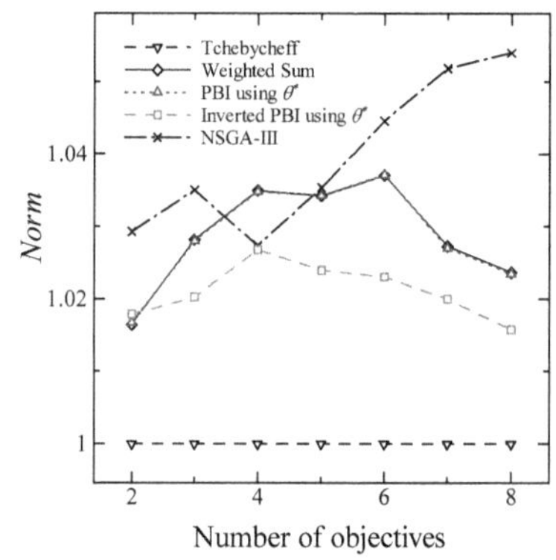

(c) $Norm$ (Convergence metric)

Figure 6: The search performance in MOKPs when the number of objectives is varied

Fig. 6 (a) shows results of HV. In the problems with $m = \{2, 3\}$ objectives, we can see that the weighted Tchebycheff achieves higher HV than the weighted sum and the PBI. However, in the problems with $m \geq 4$ objectives, the weighted sum and the PBI achieve higher HV than the weighted Tchebycheff. This result reveals that the weighed sum and the PBI show higher search performance than the weighted Tchebycheff in MaOPs. On the other hand, we can see that the inverted PBI improves HV from the weighted sum and the PBI, and achieves the highest HV among five algorithms for all objectives m.

Next, to clarify the gain of the improvement of HV by the inverted PBI, **Fig. 6 (b)** shows the results of MS to evaluate the spread of the obtained POS in the objective space, and **Fig. 6 (c)** shows the results of $Norm$ to evaluate the convergence of the obtained POS toward Pareto front. Here, we compare the weighted sum, the PBI and the inverted PBI. From the results in **Fig. 6 (b)**, for all objectives m, we can see that the inverted PBI achieves higher MS than the weighted sum and the PBI. On the other hand, from the results in **Fig. 6 (c)**, for the problems with $m \geq 3$ objectives, the values of $Norm$ achieved by the inverted PBI are lower than the weighted sum and the PBI. These results clarify that the gain of the improvement of HV by the inverted PBI is brought by the improvement of the spread of the obtained POS in the objective space.

5.3 Distribution of the Population in MOKP

Here, we observe the distribution of the obtained population at the final generation in MOKP with $m = 2$ objectives. **Fig. 7** shows the true POS [16] and four populations obtained by the weighted

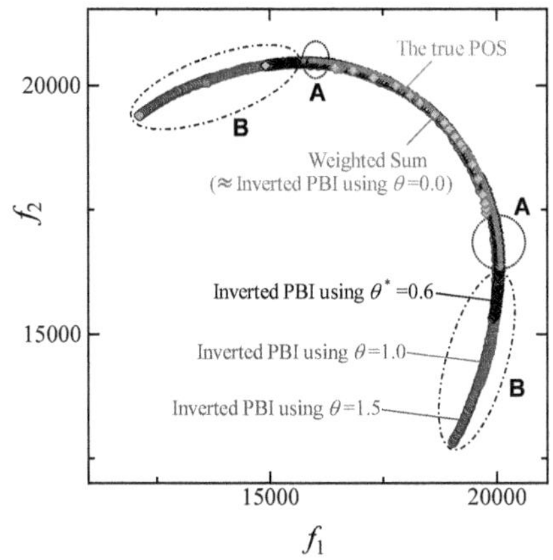

Figure 7: The obtained populations in MOKP with $m = 2$ objectives

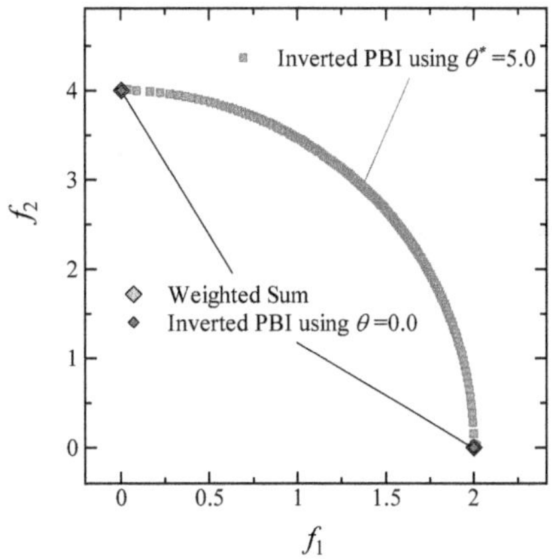

Figure 8: The obtained POS in WFG4 with $m = 2$ objectives and $k = 10$

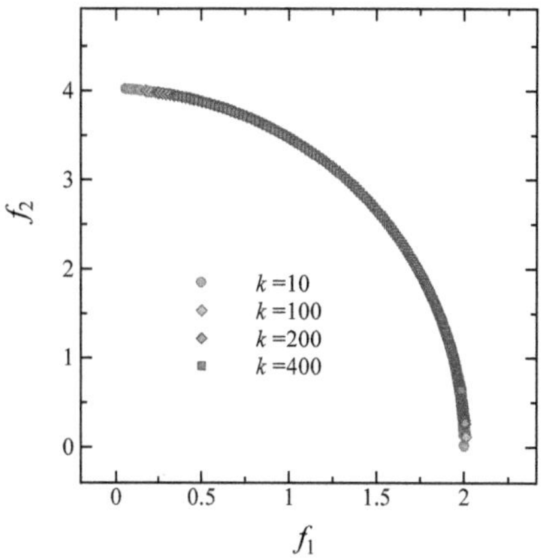

Figure 9: The obtained POS in four WFG4 problems with different k

sum and the inverted PBIs with $\theta = \{0.6, 1.0, 1.5\}$. Note that the distribution of the population obtained by the weighted sum is similar to the one obtained by the inverted PBI using $\theta = 0.0$.

First, we can see that the population evolved by the conventional weighted sum cannot cover the entire Pareto front. To approximate the entire Pareto front, the regions A in **Fig. 7** must be searched. In the case of the inverted PBI, we can see that the spread of the population in the objective space is significantly improved by increasing θ. Actually, there is no true POS in the regions B. However, the inverted PBI can obtain POS in the regions A by searching the regions B. In this work, the highest HV is achieved by the inverted PBI using $\theta^* = 0.6$. The inverted PBIs using $\theta > 0.6$ search a wider range of the objective space even if the range is dominated region by other solutions in the population. Therefore, the number of POS in the population is decreased by increasing θ, and HV is deteriorated.

This result reveals that the inverted PBI can obtain a widely spread POS by searching a wide range of objective space which cannot be searched by the weighted sum.

5.4 Approximation of Concave Pareto Front

Here, we observe the obtained POS in WFG4 problem having concave Pareto front. **Fig. 8** shows three sets of POS obtained by the weighted sum, the inverted PBI using $\theta = 0$ and the inverted PBI using $\theta^* = 5$ at the final generation in WFG4 with $m = 2$ objectives. The optimal $\theta^* = 5$ in the inverted PBI is experimentally obtained by the parameter tuning in the range $\theta = [0, 10]$.

It has been known that the weighted sum cannot approximate the entire concave Pareto front [1]. As shown in **Fig. 8**, the POS obtained by the weighted sum are distributed in both extreme regions of the Pareto front. Since the inverted PBI using $\theta = 0$ has the similar effect to the weighted sum, its POS are also distributed in both extreme regions. On the other hand, we can see that the inverted PBI using $\theta^* = 5$ can approximate the entire concave Pareto front by emphasizing the directivity for each search direction.

5.5 The Search Performance in WFG4s

Finally, we compare the search performance of five algorithms in WFG4 problems by varying the problem parameter k. In order to briefly know the impact of the parameter k in WFG4 problems, **Fig. 9** shows four sets of POS obtained by the weighted Tchebycheff approach in $m = 2$ dimensional WFG4 problems with $k = \{10, 100, 200, 400\}$. From the results, we can see that the difficulty to obtain a widely spread POS is increased by increasing the parameter k in WFG4 problems.

Fig. 10 shows the results of HV at the final generation when the problem parameter k is varied. From the results, we can see that the weighted sum shows the lowest HV in almost all WFG4 problems. This is because, the weighted sum cannot approximate the entire concave Pareto front. In the problems with $m = 2$ objectives, the weighed Tchebycheff achieves the highest HV for all k. In the problems with $m = 4$ objectives, the inverted PBI using θ^* achieves the highest HV for all k. In problems with $m = \{6, 8\}$ and a small k, we can see that NSGA-III and PBI using θ^* achieve higher HV than inverted PBI using θ^*. Since NSGA-III is designed especially for solving MaOPs, its search performance becomes high in $m = \{6, 8\}$ objective problems. However, we can see the tendency that the values of HV achieved by NSGA-III and PBI using θ^* are gradually deteriorated by increasing k and the difficulty to obtain a widely spread POS in WFG4 problems. On the other hand, we can see that the inverted PBI using θ^* achieves the highest HV among five algorithms in problems with $m = \{6, 8\}$ objectives and $k \geq 100$.

These results reveal that the inverted PBI using θ^* shows high search performance especially in problems with many-objectives and the difficulty to obtain a widely spread POS in the objective space.

6. CONCLUSIONS

To enhance the spread of POS in the objective space and improve the search performance of MOEA/D in MaOPs, in this work we have proposed the inverted PBI function which is an extension of the PBI function. We compared the search performance of five algorithms in discrete MOKPs and continuous WFG4 problems with 2∼8 objectives. Four algorithms were MOEA/Ds using the weighted Tchebycheff, the weighted sum, the PBI and the inverted PBI, respectively. The last one was NSGA-III employing the decomposition approach of the objective space similar to MOEA/D. The experimental results showed that the inverted PBI approach using an appropriate θ^* achieved the highest HV among five algorithms for all MOKPs used in this work. Also, in WFG4 problems, we showed that the inverted PBI using θ^* achieved the highest search performance in problems with many-objectives and the difficulty to obtain a widely spread POS in the objective space.

As future works, we will study an automatic control of the parameter θ in the inverted PBI. Also, we will study a method to independently control θ for each weight vector $\boldsymbol{\lambda}$.

7. REFERENCES

[1] Q. Zhang and H. Li, "MOEA/D: A Multi-objective Evolutionary Algorithm Based on Decomposition," *IEEE*

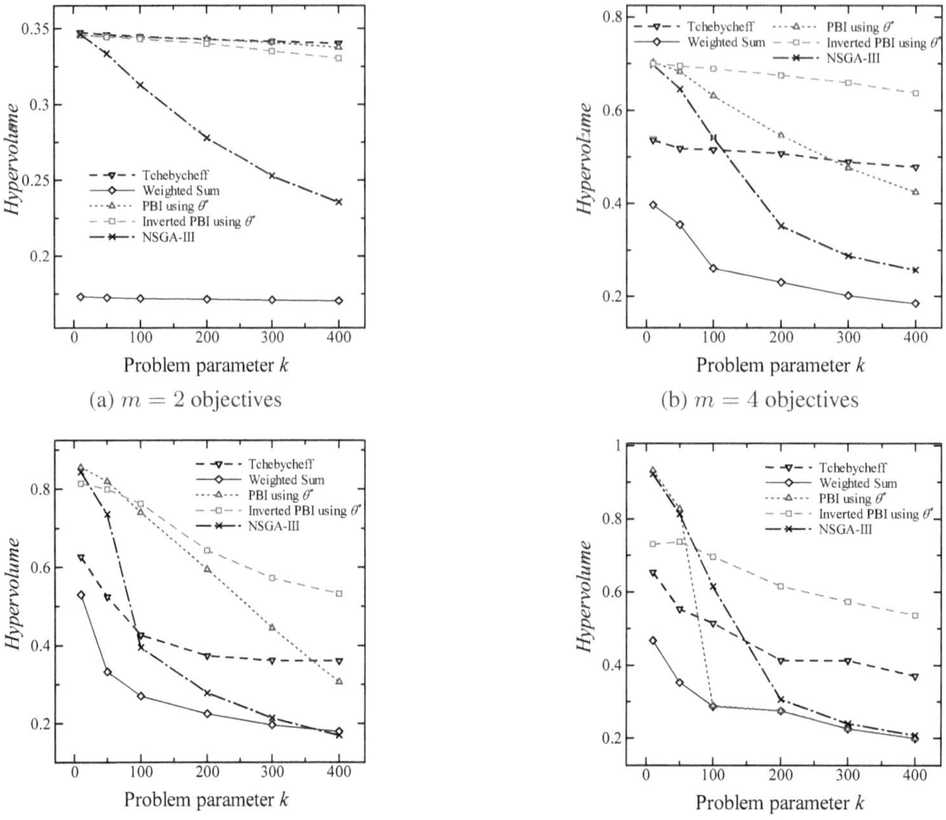

(a) $m = 2$ objectives (b) $m = 4$ objectives (c) $m = 6$ objectives (d) $m = 8$ objectives

Figure 10: Results of HV on WFG4 problems

Trans. on Evolutionary Computation, Vol.11, No. 6, pp.712–731, 2007.

[2] Q. Zhang, W. Liu and Hui Li, "The Performance of a New Version of MOEA/D on CEC09 Unconstrained MOP Test Instances," *Proc. of 2009 IEEE Congress on Evolutionary Computation (CEC'2009)*, pp. 203–208, 2009.

[3] Q. Zhang, W. Liu, E. Tsang and B. Virginas, "Expensive Multiobjective Optimization by MOEA/D with Gaussian Process Model," *IEEE Transactions on Evolutionary Computation*, Vol. 14, No. 3, pp. 456–474, 2010.

[4] H. Ishibuchi, Y. Sakane, N. Tsukamoto and Y. Nojima, "Simultaneous Use of Different Scalarizing Functions in MOEA/D," *Proc. of the 12th annual conference on Genetic and Evolutionary Computation (GECCO'2010)*, pp. 519–526, ACM Press, 2010.

[5] S. Z. Martinez and C. A. C. Coello, "A Hybridization of MOEA/D with the Nonlinear Simplex Search Algorithm," *Proc. of the 2013 IEEE Symposium on Computational Intelligence in Multicriteria Decision Making (MCDM'2013)*, pp. 48–55, IEEE Press, 2013.

[6] K. Deb, A. Pratap, S. Agarwal, T. Meyarivan, "A Fast Elitist Multi-Objective Genetic Algorithm: NSGA-II," *IEEE Trans. on Evolutionary Computation*, Vol.6, pp.182–197, 2002.

[7] E. Zitzler, M. Laumanns and L. Thiele, "SPEA2: Improving the Strength Pareto Evolutionary Algorithm," *TIK-Report*, No.103, 2001.

[8] H. Ishibuchi, N. Tsukamoto, and Y. Nojima, "Evolutionary many-objective optimization: A short review," *Proc. of 2008 IEEE Congress on Evolutionary Computation (CEC2008)*, pp. 2424-2431, 2008.

[9] K. Deb and H. Jain, "An Evolutionary Many-Objective Optimization Algorithm Using Reference-point Based Non-dominated Sorting Approach, Part I: Solving Problems with Box Constraints," *IEEE Transactions on Evolutionary Computation*, Volume:PP, Issue:99, pp.1-23, 2013.

[10] H. Ishibuchi, N. Akedo, and Y. Nojima, "A Study on the Specification of a Scalarizing Function in MOEA/D for Many-Objective Knapsack Problems," *Proc. of Learning and Intelligent Optimization 7 (LION 7)*, LNCS 7997, pp. 231–246, 2013.

[11] E. Zitzler and L. Thiele, "Multiobjective Evolutionary Algorithms: A Comparative Case Study and the Strength Pareto Approach," *IEEE Trans. on Evolutionary Computation*, Vol.3 (4), pp. 257–271, 1999.

[12] S. Huband, P. Hingston, L. Barone, and L. While, "A Review of Multi-objective Test Problems and a Scalable Test Problem Toolkit," *IEEE Transactions on Evolutionary Computation*, Vol. 10, No 5, pp. 477–506, 2006.

[13] K. Miettinen, *Nonlinear Multiobjective Optimization*, Norwell, MA:Kluwer, 1999.

[14] E.Zitzler, *Evolutionary Algorithms for Multiobjective Optimization: Methods and Applications*, PhD thesis, Swiss Federal Institute of Technology, Zurich, 1999.

[15] M. Sato, H. Aguirre and K. Tanaka, "Effects of δ-Similar Elimination and Controlled Elitism in the NSGA-II Multiobjective Evolutionary Algorithm," *Proc. of 2006 IEEE Congress on Evolutionary Computation (CEC2006)*, pp. 1164–1171, 2006.

[16] http://www.tik.ee.ethz.ch/sop/download/supplementary/testProblemSuite/

Hybridization of Electromagnetism with Multi-objective Evolutionary Algorithms for RCPSP

Jing Xiao
School of Computer Science
South China Normal University
Guangzhou 510631, China
xiaojing@scnu.edu.cn

Zhou Wu
School of Computer Science
South China Normal University
Guangzhou 510631, China
wz30230@163.com

Jian-Chao Tang
School of Computer Science
South China Normal University
Guangzhou 510631, China
michealtang@163.com

ABSTRACT

As one of the most challenging combinatorial optimization problems in scheduling, the resource-constrained project scheduling problem (RCPSP) has attracted numerous scholars' interest resulting in considerable research in the past few decades. However, most of these papers focused on the single objective RCPSP; only a few papers concentrated on the multi-objective resource-constrained project scheduling problem (MORCPSP). Inspired by a procedure called electromagnetism (EM), which can help a generic population-based evolutionary search algorithm to obtain good results for single objective RCPSP, in this paper we attempt to extend EM and hybridize it with three reputable state-of-the-art multi-objective evolutionary algorithms (MOEAs) i.e. NSGA-II, SPEA2 and MOEA/D, for MORCPSP. Our two objectives are minimizing makespan and total tardiness. We perform computational experiments on standard benchmark datasets. Empirical comparison and analysis of the results obtained by the hybridization versions of EM with NSGA-II, SPEA2 and MOEA/D are conducted. The results demonstrate that EM can improve the performance of NSGA-II and SPEA2.

Categories and Subject Descriptors

I.2.8 [**Problem Solving, Control Methods, and Search**]: Scheduling; G.1.6 [**ptimization**]: Constrained optimization

Keywords

Resource-constrained project scheduling; Multi-objective optimization; Electromagnetism; Evolutionary algorithms

1. INTRODUCTION

The research on the classical resource-constrained project scheduling problem (RCPSP) has been widely expanded over the past several decades. An overview of RCPSP can be stated as follows. A set of activities N numbered from 0 to n is to be scheduled without preemption. Activity i has a duration d_i and needs some resources which are limited during every moment to be completed. We assume that the renewable resources set is R and the availability of each resource type k, $k \in R$, which is a constant a_k throughout the project horizon. Each activity i needs r_{ik} units of resource k during each period of its duration, $i \in N, k \in R$. The dummy start and end activities 0 and n have zero duration and do not require any resources. The precedence relation between the activities is that one activity can not start until all its predecessors have been finished, so a solution for RCPSP is feasible if and only if the precedence and resource constraints are satisfied. In general, a solution of RCPSP is represented as a schedule or a list of start times $s = (s_0, \cdots, s_n)$ that implies a list of corresponding finishing times $f = (f_0, \cdots, f_n)$. Obviously, as every manager usually wants to finish projects as quickly as possible with minimum cost and high quality, RCPSP is a multi-objective optimization problem. According to [19] and [4], the primary objectives of a multi-objective resource-constrained project scheduling problem (MORCPSP) include makespan, activity tardiness, net present value (NPV), resource investment (RI) and robustness.

MORCPSP is strongly NP-hard due to the difficulty of its solution method; there has been a growing interest in this field in the recent years. Słowiński presented the first multi-objective RCPSP framework that applied multi-objective linear programming to a MORCPSP with splittable activities, multiple modes, renewable, non-renewable and doubly constrained resources [19]. Furthermore, Słowiński proposed a decision support system to optimize several objectives by using parallel priority rules, simulated annealing, branch and bound [20]. The multi-mode project scheduling problem under multi-category resource constraints with fuzzy time parameters of activities was considered in [10, 12, 18]. These three papers were partial to the fuzzy version of MORCPSP and Pareto simulated annealing (PSA) was frequently used. Hapke proposed a two-stage interactive search over a non-dominated solution space to handle a multiple-criteria PSP with multiple modes, renewable, non-renewable and doubly constrained resources [11]. Nabrzyski described a decision support system that could generate a set of feasible schedules using tabu search (TS) for individual criteria [15]. In [16], the authors presented a knowledge-based multi-objective project scheduling system that handled a class of non-preemptive scheduling problems. The makespan, resource utilization smoothness, maximum lateness, NPV and project cost were considered in [11, 15, 16]. In order to min-

GECCO'14, July 12–16, 2014, Vancouver, BC, Canada.

http://dx.doi.org/10.1145/2576768.2598228

imize makespan, "weighted" lateness of activities and violation of resource constraints, multi-objective versions of simulated annealing (MOPSA) and tabu search (MOTS) were applied for RCPSP [21]. A MOTS, which consisted of running a single objective TS with a different linear aggregated function, was implemented to minimize makespan and maximize robustness in [3]. Abbasi did similar research which aggregated the two objectives of minimizing makespan and maximizing robustness into a linear objective and applied SA to solve it [1].

Most of the aforementioned papers applied SA and TS to solve MORCPSP, but failed to obtain enough Pareto solutions. As we know, many state-of-the-art multi-objective evolutionary algorithms (MOEAs) such as NSGA-II [7], SPEA2 [23], MOEA/D [22], have been developed rapidly and widely applied to multi-objective problems in the past two decades. Certainly some MOEAs have been applied to MORCPSP. NSGA-II and a mathematical model proposed by Kazemi were applied to MORCPSP with discounted cash flows that aimed at minimizing makespan and maximizing net present value [13]. Aboutalebi compared the performance of NSGA-II with Multi-objective Particle Swarm Optimization (MOPSO) for the bi-objective RCPSP in terms of makespan and NPV [2]. Ballest́n focused on theoretical study and gave some proofs for MOPSP with regular objective functions(ROFs) [4]. Comparisons among NSGA-II, SPEA2 and PSA in several performance measures were presented. Five multi-objective metaheuristic algorithms were implemented to optimize makespan and total weighted start time of the activities in [9], in which four performance measures were used for comparisons and a detailed experimental analysis was given.

From the aforementioned papers, we can see that the research on MORCPSP is still limited; only a few papers applied MOEAs to MORCPSP. Meanwhile, many excellent hybrid algorithms have been presented and successfully applied to single objective RCPSP. For example, since electromagnetism (EM) heuristics has been applied to many unconstrained global optimization problems, Debels et al. extended the EM heuristics and integrated it into scatter search (SS) frame for a single objective RCPSP [8]. By utilizing the principle that the EM force generated by two solutions would guide the search direction, scatter search integrated with EM outperformed other state-of-the art heuristics for single objective RCPSP. However, to the best of our knowledge, no paper was found in literature integrating EM heuristics into MOEAs to solve MORCPSP. Inspired by the method presented by Debels, we have modified EM heuristics to make it suitable for MORCPSP and combined it with NSGA-II, SPEA2 and MOEA/D.

The remainder of the paper is organized as follows: in Section 1, some basic concepts concerning multi-objective problems are introduced and the representation and evaluation of MORCPSP are defined. In Section 3, we show how the EM methodology can be modified for MORCPSP and then hybridized with MOEAs. Section 4 shows experiment results and comparison analysis. Concluding remarks are given in Section 5.

2. PROBLEM STATEMENT

A multi-objective optimization problem (MOP) can be stated as following:

$$minimize\ F(x) = (f_1(x), \cdots, f_m(x))\ subject\ to\ x \in \Omega \quad (1)$$

where Ω is the decision (variable) space; R^m is the objective space, and $F : \Omega \to R^m$ consists of m objective functions. Very often, no solution in Ω can minimize all the objectives simultaneously since the objectives in (1) contradict with each other. The tradeoffs among the objectives have usually been taken into consideration by the decision maker. The best tradeoffs among the objectives can be defined in terms of Pareto optimality.

Let $x_a, x_b \in R^m$, x_a dominates x_b ($x_a \prec x_b$) if and only if

$$\begin{aligned} &\forall i = 1, 2, \cdots, m,\ f_i(x_a) \le f_i(x_b) \wedge \\ &\exists j = 1, 2, \cdots, m,\ f_i(x_a) < f_i(x_b) \end{aligned} \quad (2)$$

A solution $x^* \in \Omega$ is Pareto optimal (non-dominated) if and only if

$$\neg \exists x \in \Omega\, x \prec x^* \quad (3)$$

$F(x^*)$ is then called a Pareto optimal (objective) vector. The set of all the Pareto optimal solutions (non-dominated solutions) is called the Pareto set (PS) and the set of all the Pareto optimal objective vectors is the Pareto front (PF).

In MORCPSP, the precedence relationship between activities is illustrated by a directed acyclic graph; every node in the graph has a series of attributes associated with time and resource constraints. There are many objective functions of interest for managers. In this paper, using x as a feasible solution, we focus on two objectives of minimizing the makespan $f_1(x)$ (f_n is the finishing time of end activity)and minimizing the total tardiness $f_2(x)$ which can be defined as follows:

$$f_1(x) = f_n \quad (4)$$

$$f_2(x) = \sum_{i=0}^{n} max\{0,\ f_i - dd_i\} \quad (5)$$

where f_i is the finishing time of activity i, and dd_i represents the due date of activity i.

Once the fundamental definitions of MORCPSP have been established, we discuss the representation scheme and evaluation procedure of solutions for RCPSP. Random-key (RK) and activity-list (AL) are the most important representations for schedules of heuristics for the RCPSP. In order to avoid that a single schedule can be represented by different activity lists or random keys, Debels [8] studied scaling in Euclidean space, precedence constraints, timing anomalies and activities with the same starting times. They proposed a unique standardised random key (SRK) representation to guarantee that each solution in SRK form is uniquely associated with a schedule. Taking the project depicted in Figure 1, for example, we illustrate the SRK scheme that we will adopt in this paper. Assuming that activity i needs only one kind of renewable resource r_i. The duration and due date of activity i is d_i and dd_i respectively; a feasible schedule could be depicted as in Figure 2 if each type of resource availability is 2 (we omit the dummy start and end activity; the horizontal axis represents time, the vertical axis resources). The activity with the earliest start time receives the highest priority denoted by 1, so a unique SRK vector $x = [1; 4; 3; 1; 4; 6; 7; 8; 9]$ for schedule in Figure 2 can be gained when we attribute the lowest priority to all activities starting at the same time such as 1 for activity 1 and activity 4, 4 for activity 2 and activity 5. Each SRK vector can be transformed into a schedule by a serial scheduled

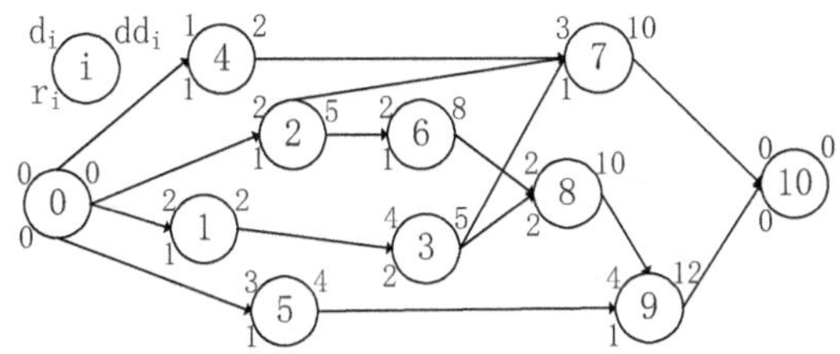

Figure 1: Project example

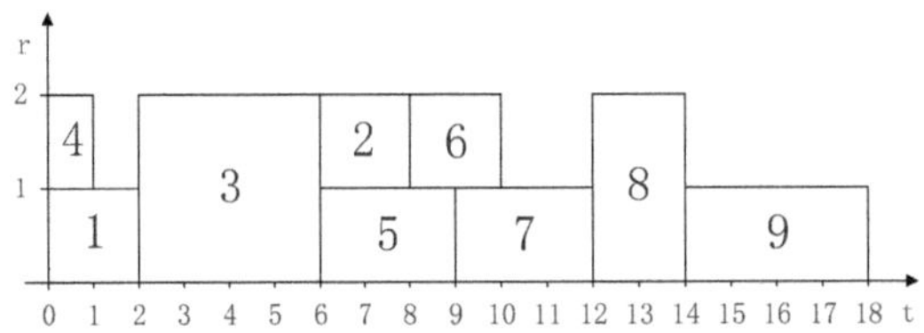

Figure 2: A schedule for the example project

generation scheme (SGS), and vice versa. Based on [17], it is proved that the schedule makespan obtained by backward and forward shifts is never higher than the makespan of the schedule without shifting. In this paper, we iteratively perform backward and forward shifts until no further improvement can be found.

3. MOEAS HYBRIDIZED WITH EM HEURISTICS FOR MORCPSP

Electromagnetism (EM) optimization heuristics for unconstrained global optimization problems is proposed by Birril [6]. Each point representing a solution has a charge related to an objective function value in a multi-objective solution space by analogy with electromagnetism. Two arbitrary points in a population of solutions generate a force with each other. In an evolutionary search algorithm, each point (solution) in the population attracts or repels on other points with a force that is proportional to the product of the charges and inversely proportional to the distance between the points. The principle of the algorithm guiding the search is that a point with a relatively good objective function value attracts others and the points with inferior objective values repel the other population members. Based on the research of [6] and [8], we extend EM heuristics for MORCPSP.

Let x_i and x_j be two feasible solutions of MORCPSP, which are represented by SRK. The charge between x_i and x_j can be defined as:

$$q_{ij} = \sum_{k=1}^{m} \varphi_k \frac{f_k(x_i) - f_k(x_j)}{f_k^{worst} - f_k^{best}} \tag{6}$$

where m is the number of objectives, $f_k(x_i)$ is the k-th objective value of x_i, f_k^{worst} and f_k^{best} are the worst and best values of k-th objective, and φ_k is a constant factor. q_{ij} is positive, and x_j attracts x_i in its direction if x_i is dominated by x_j. On the contrary, x_j repels x_i when x_i dominates x_j. The force exerted on solution x_i by solution x_j can be defined as:

$$F_{ij} = (x_j - x_i) \cdot q_{ij} \tag{7}$$

Finally, the search can move from solution x_i to $x_i + F_{ij}$ in the direction of x_j. For example, x_j will guide the move direction of x_i with the attractive force F_{ij} when x_j dominates x_i as shown in Figure 3.

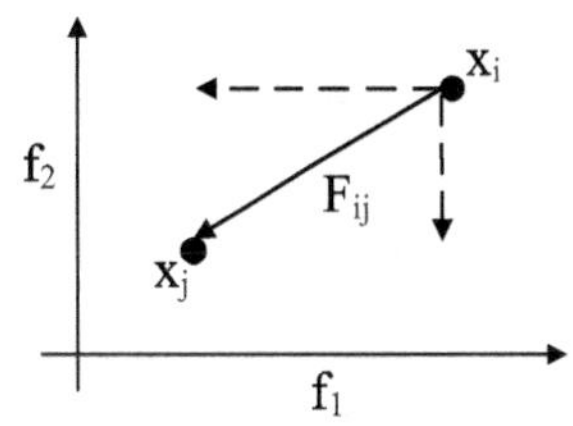

Figure 3: x_j attracts x_i

For the MORCPSP, forces are exerted in changing in the priority of each activity. Two boundaries $p_{min} \in [1; n-1]$ and $p_{max} \in [2; n]$ (n denotes the total number of activities) are selected randomly and the SRK values between p_{min} and p_{max} are updated according to the force exerted in these dimensions. We preserve the priority structures of the activities with SRK values between p_{min} and p_{max} by subtracting a large constant from all SRK values that are lower than p_{min} and adding a large constant to those larger than p_{max}. The last step transforms the resulting RK vector into the SRK format. A hybrid two-point/EM crossover operator can be described briefly as follows:

1. $SRK < p_{min}$: a large constant value is subtracted from the priority.
2. $p_{min} \leq SRK \leq p_{max}$: a force calculated by EM is added to the priority value.
3. $SRK > p_{max}$: a large constant value is added to the priority value.

Using the project example depicted in Figure 1, we demonstrate how to implement the hybrid two-point/EM crossover operation. Let $x_1 = [1;3;6;1;5;4;7;8;9]$ and $x_2 = [1;1;3;6;4;4;8;7;8]$; tehy are two feasible SRK vectors associated with the two schedules depicted in Figure 4 and Figure 5. With the due data set $dd = [2;5;5;2;4;8;10;10;12]$, two bi-objective solutions $f(x_1) = (19,22)$ and $f(x_2) = (15,21)$ can be computed with the objective functions. The first objective is makespan; total tardiness value is the second objective. We assume that 22 and 15 are the worst and best values of makespan, and the worst and best values of total tardiness are 25 and 18, so that the charge of $q_{12} = 5/7 \approx 0.71$. According to $F_{12} = q_{12}(x_2 - x_1)$, force F_{12} on x_1 can be calculated. In Table 1 (an adaptation of [8]), the components of x_1 between $[p_{min}; p_{max}]$ are italic and we can obtain a new schedule x_1' with $x_1' = x_1 + F_{12}'$ where the force F_{12}' added to x_1 is represented as a vector. Finally, x_1' can be converted to its SRK form x_1'' by using SGS. The schedule corresponding to x_1'' is depicted in Figure 6, with $f(x_1'') = (18,21)$. This hybrid two-point/EM crossover operator on x_1 not only preserves the part of SRK vector larger than p_{max} and lower than p_{min}, but also results in the middle part between p_{min} and p_{max} being attracted by x_2. Meanwhile, we can reproduce another offspring that copies the lowest and highest priorities from x_2, with a middle part repelled by x_1.

The hybrid EM/two point crossover operator illustrated above is used for generating offspring instead of the traditional two-point crossover in the recombination steps when we integrate EM heuristics into MOEAs. NSGA-II, SPEA2 and MOEA/D integrated with EM heuristics are abbrevi-

Table 1: Illustration of the execution of hybrid two-point/EM crossover operator

Activities	1	2	3	4	5	6	7	8	9
x_1	1	*3*	*6*	1	*5*	*4*	*7*	8	9
x_2	1	1	3	6	4	4	8	7	8
F_{12}	0	-1.42	-2.13	3.55	-0.71	0	0.71	-0.71	-0.71
F'_{12}	-10	-1.42	-2.13	-10	-0.71	0	0.71	+10	+10
x'_1	-9	1.58	3.87	-9	4.29	4	7.71	18	19
x''_1	1	3	4	1	5	5	7	8	9

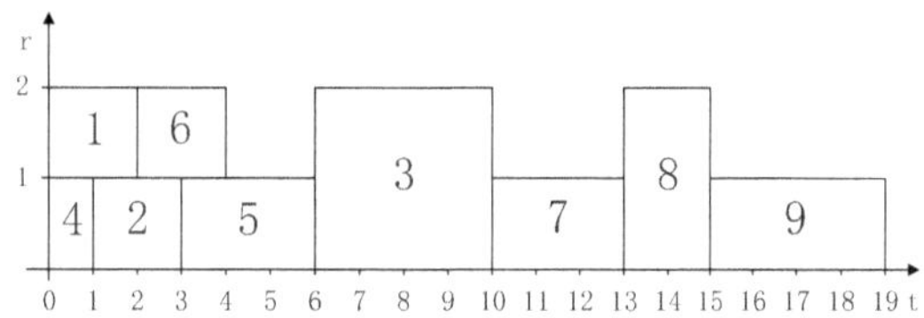

Figure 4: A schedule for the example project (associated with vector x_1)

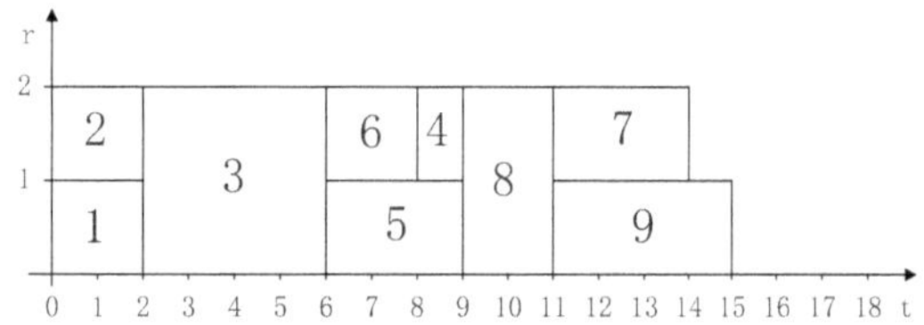

Figure 5: A schedule for the example project (associated with vector x_2)

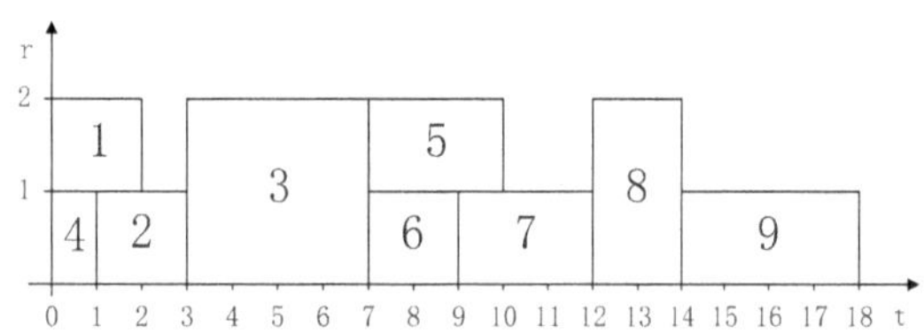

Figure 6: The resulting schedule after two-point/EM crossover operator(x'')

ated as NSGA-II_EM, SPEA2_EM and MOEA/D_EM respectively.

4. COMPUTATIONAL EXPERIMENTS

We implement NSGA-II, SPEA2, MOEA/D and the EM integration versions of these three algorithms in C for Windows. The performances of these algorithms are compared and analyzed. For test instances, we have chosen 20 instances from the standard j120 set introduced in [14] for the RCPSP and borrow the due date data generated by [5], where the procedure to generate the due date data in j120 datasets was presented.

4.1 Performance measures

In our experiments, C-Metric and D-Metric are two performance measures that have been adopted to evaluate the solution sets produced by different evolutionary algorithms. Set Coverage (C-Metric) computes the percentage of solutions of one set dominated by solutions of another set. Let A and B be two sets of solutions. The set coverage is defined as:

$$C(A, B) = \frac{|\{u \in B \mid \exists v \in A : v \prec u\}|}{|B|} \times 100\% \quad (8)$$

The value $C(A, B) = 100\%$ means that all solutions of B are dominated by solutions of A, and $C(A, B) = 0$ implies no solution of B is dominated by solution of A. It is notable that $C(A, B)$ is not necessarily equal to $100\% - C(B, A)$.

Distance from the PF (D-Metirc) is a value representing how "far" an approximation set is from the pareto front. We assume that P^* is a set of uniformly distributed points along the PF. Let A be a set of solutions, the average distance from A to P^* is defined as:

$$D(A, p^*) = \frac{\forall_{v \in A} d(v, p^*)}{|A|} \quad (9)$$

where $d(v, p^*)$ is the minimum Euclidean distance between v and the points in P^*. If P^* is large enough to represent the PF very well, set A must be very close to the PF when $D(A, p^*)$ is low enough. In our experiments, we do not know the actual PF. The non-dominated solutions obtained from all algorithms are used as the reference set P^* for each instance. On the other hand, we incorporate a simple objective normalization technique into D-metric measure since the difference between two objectives is large in the MOR-CPSP. A simple normalization method is to replace objective $f_i (i = 1, \cdots, m)$ by

$$\overline{f_i} = \frac{f_i - z_i^{min}}{z_i^{max} - z_i^{min}} \quad (10)$$

where z_i^{max} and z_i^{min} are the maximum and minimum values of i-th objective in reference set P^*.

4.2 Results and discussion

In our experiments, the population size for NSGA-II, SPEA2 and MOEA/D is 400. The value of φ_k for every objective in formula (6) is equal to 1.0. We use the Tchebycheff approach and set neighborhood size T to 10 for MOEA/D. The mutation rate of 0.06 is considered for all algorithms. 10 runs are performed for each algorithm on each instance. All algorithms stop after 50000 schedules (the limit of the generated solutions) for each run.

Table 2 presents the mean and standard deviation (in parentheses) of D-Metric values of the final solutions obtained by each algorithm for each test instance. The lowest D-Metric value for each instance is highlighted in bold. This table reveals that both NSGA-II_EM and SPEA2_EM always obtain lower D-Metric values than the original NSGA-II and SPEA2 for every test instance. MOEA/D_EM outperforms MOEA/D only in some cases. For most of the test

Table 2: **D-Metric values of the solutions found by all algorithms**

Instance	NGSA-II_EM	NSGA-II	SPEA2_EM	SPEA2	MOEA/D_EM	MOEA/D
j1201_1	0.163200 (0.110843)	0.268415 (0.042091)	**0.162228 (0.043900)**	0.246307 (0.081313)	0.288599 (0.100944)	0.328420 (0.159503)
j1203_1	**0.100523 (0.020825)**	0.246516 (0.103831)	0.157168 (0.035272)	0.185046 (0.031415)	0.403337 (0.041520)	0.419340 (0.042296)
j1207_1	**0.223809 (0.030841)**	0.409326 (0.043008)	0.267419 (0.035742)	0.407949 (0.028567)	0.408074 (0.078571)	0.439741 (0.046970)
j1207_2	**0.172999 (0.042994)**	0.311869 (0.032037)	0.218184 (0.033647)	0.315638 (0.036806)	0.305533 (0.087398)	0.274949 (0.082346)
j1207_3	**0.121832 (0.025514)**	0.183532 (0.022284)	0.144873 (0.017190)	0.194366 (0.017873)	0.159975 (0.024960)	0.149186 (0.050367)
j1208_2	**0.212596 (0.028920)**	0.320349 (0.013728)	0.270112 (0.037019)	0.345120 (0.025097)	0.432038 (0.060652)	0.366119 (0.065073)
j1209_1	**1.686167 (0.355045)**	1.951842 (0.312715)	2.342359 (0.378472)	2.512612 (0.309398)	8.040846 (0.527713)	7.849065 (0.346391)
j12013_1	**0.293799 (0.037316)**	0.302950 (0.052840)	0.311022 (0.040043)	0.339106 (0.018104)	0.345289 (0.068257)	0.332394 (0.035339)
j12013_3	**0.340263 (0.051045)**	0.483405 (0.045561)	0.472029 (0.056875)	0.558730 (0.060322)	0.565930 (0.143919)	0.635762 (0.145453)
j12014_1	**0.455602 (0.091126)**	0.580738 (0.037406)	0.638889 (0.094932)	0.651105 (0.041320)	1.092641 (0.106771)	1.074799 (0.116551)
j12014_4	**0.246730 (0.028484)**	0.307940 (0.006683)	0.261719 (0.025531)	0.318058 (0.027928)	0.302034 (0.054704)	0.334357 (0.035912)
j12017_1	0.308155 (0.051928)	0.424944 (0.037152)	0.376482 (0.042306)	0.488073 (0.023985)	**0.306448 (0.050745)**	0.327213 (0.050698)
j12018_1	0.910386 (0.17314)	1.083189 (0.100957)	**0.856226 (0.081337)**	0.956120 (0.072537)	1.034924 (0.157626)	1.073031 (0.163138)
j12018_2	**0.703001 (0.128390)**	1.092111 (0.067413)	0.858761 (0.091567)	1.043556 (0.065132)	1.143381 (0.115887)	1.154931 (0.071703)
j12020_1	**0.338100 (0.042221)**	0.417025 (0.027627)	0.401242 (0.045097)	0.462683 (0.027333)	0.505591 (0.057957)	0.501293 (0.046469)
j12033_1	**0.224643 (0.028424)**	0.249478 (0.029008)	0.257060 (0.058417)	0.291789 (0.021613)	0.271421 (0.039278)	0.306213 (0.065989)
j12038_1	**0.334125 (0.035588)**	0.416374 (0.037037)	0.363426 (0.033379)	0.442106 (0.028688)	0.469018 (0.067336)	0.491434 (0.065547)
j12039_1	**0.180294 (0.02602)**	0.224459 (0.009225)	0.193497 (0.018230)	0.232667 (0.014423)	0.268164 (0.035207)	0.263108 (0.035121)
j12040_1	**0.480312 (0.057485)**	0.552961 (0.023166)	0.680385 (0.195961)	0.617951 (0.045947)	1.526790 (0.120499)	1.494150 (0.113586)
j12040_2	**0.278632 (0.031901)**	0.327046 (0.016825)	0.417558 (0.092951)	0.349108 (0.045680)	0.572834 (0.053188)	0.568823 (0.068758)

instances, NSGA-II_EM achieves the lowest D-Metric values among all algorithms.

Figure 7 shows the potential non-dominated solutions obtained by 10 runs of each algorithm on 5 instances. Clearly almost all solutions obtained by NSGA-II are dominated by solutions obtained by NSGA-II_EM. SPEA2_EM works out a majority of the solutions that dominate the solutions obtained by SPEA2, but most of the solutions obtained by MOEA/D and MOEA/D_EM are dominated by each other. It means that the EM heuristics can not help to improve the performance of MOEA/D. The potential non-dominated solutions plotted by NSGA-II_EM are probably the closest to the reference Pareto front.

In order to evaluate the convergence of all algorithms, Figure 8 presents the average D-Metric values of the current population to p^* with the number of schedules on 5 test instances. These results indicate that MOEAs integrated with EM heuristics converge faster than their original versions in most cases. NSGA-II_EM is the most effective one among all algorithms.

Figure 9 shows that in terms of the C-Metric, the final solutions obtained by NSGA-II_EM are better than those achieved by NSGA-II in most cases. SPEA2_EM gets similar results but MOEA/D_EM cannot achieve better performance than MOEA/D.

From the experimental results shown above, combing EM heuristics with NSGA-II and SPEA2 improves performances, especially for NSGA-II. NSGA-II_EM outperforms NSGA-II in terms of solution quality and convergence; as does SPEA2_EM. Compared with MOEA/D, MOEA/D_EM is not effective. The reason that EM plays different roles in these three algorithms is explained by the different individual selection for crossover operator. In NSGA-II, the whole population is used for selection and crossover. For SPEA2, the mating pool used for recombination and mutation is constructed with the individuals selected from the archive population. According to the principle of EM, the larger the difference between two individuals used for crossover, the more obvious the effect. Because EM will guide the search direction in terms of the objective values, EM can hardly work when the two individuals used for crossover have similar objective values. In NSGA-II, all individuals in population take part in crossover operator, so the diversity and differences in individuals can be guaranteed for EM. SPEA2 selects only individuals from the archive population for crossover, so EM heuristics integrated into SPEA2 can

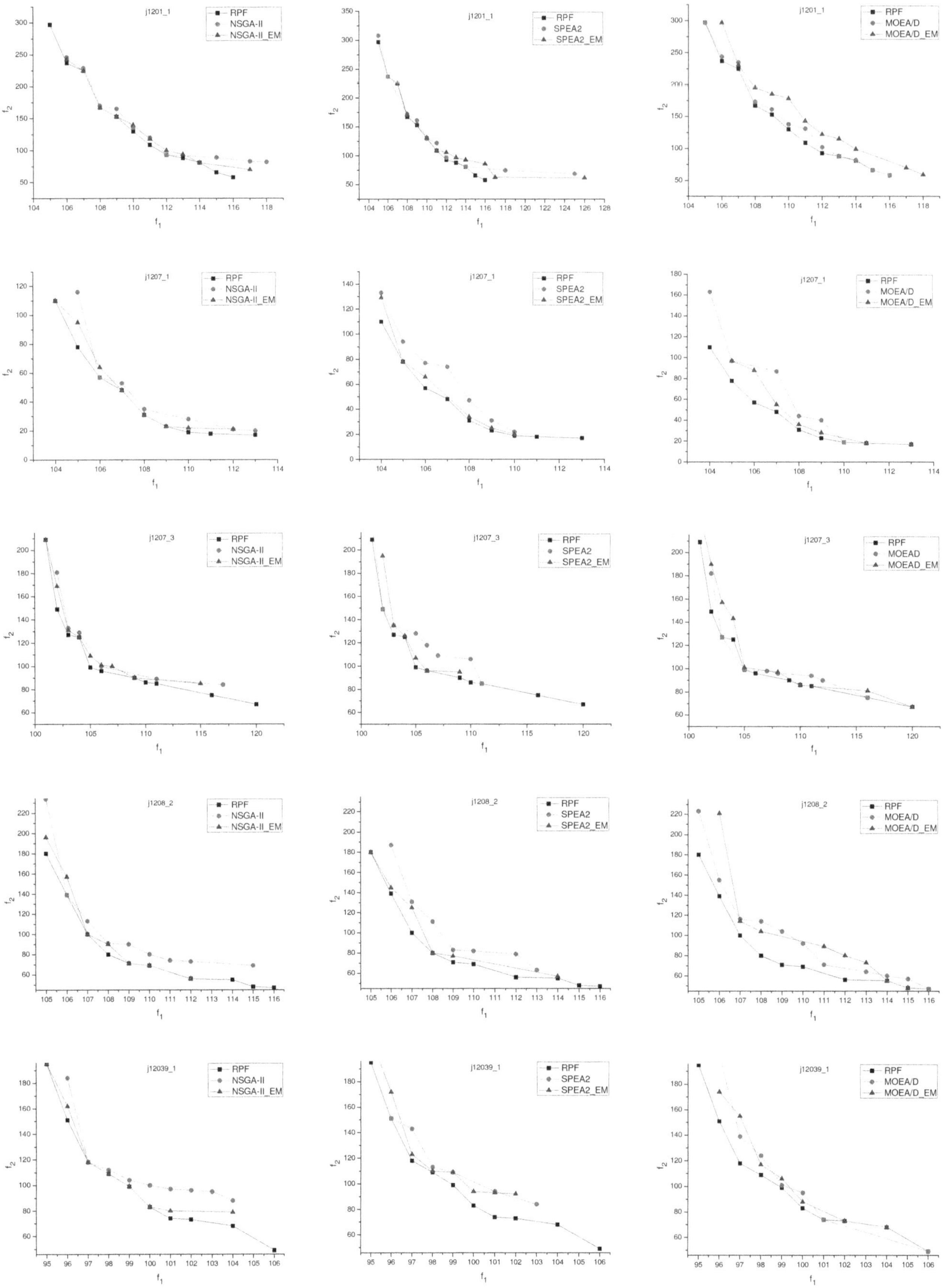

Figure 7: Non-dominated solutions obtained by 10 runs of each algorithm on some test instances

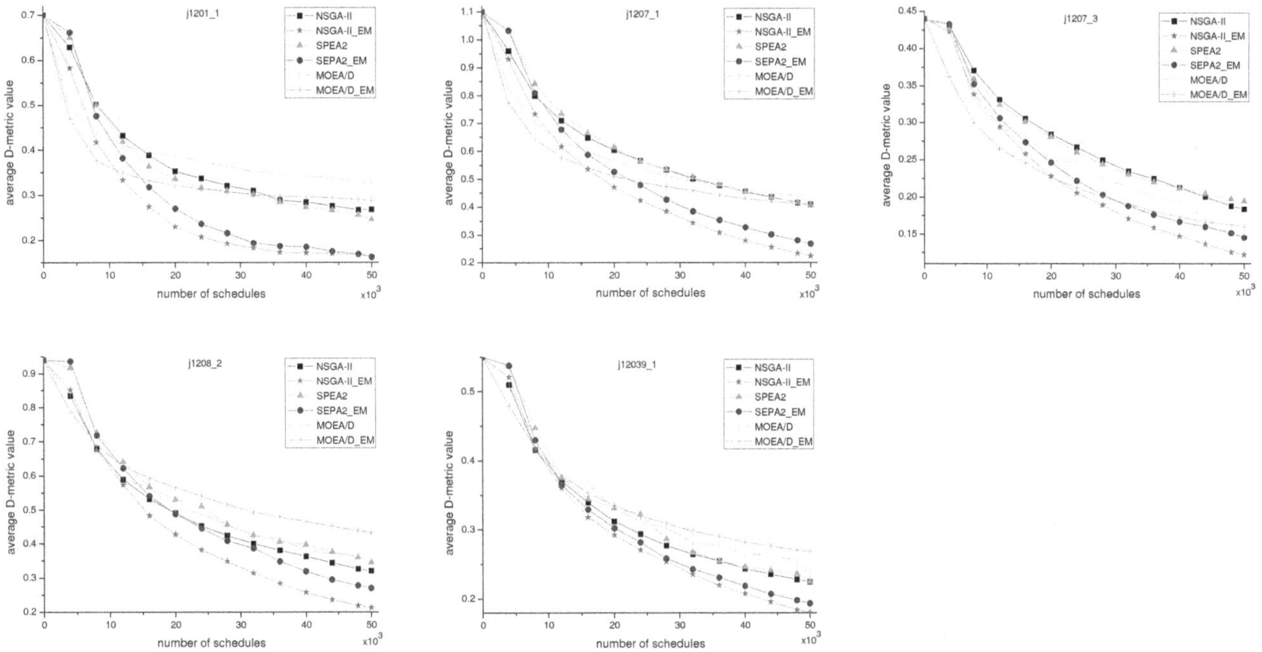

Figure 8: The average D-Metric values of all algorithms for some test instances

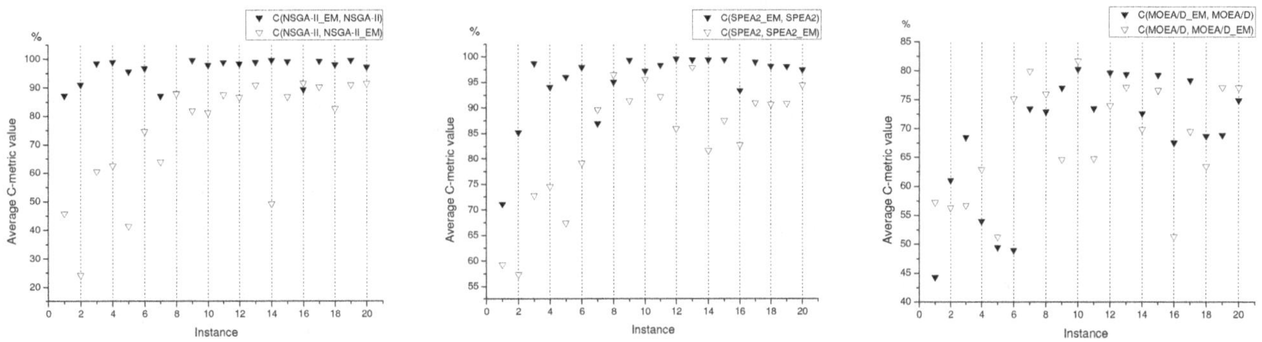

Figure 9: Average set coverage between algorithms hybridized with EM and their original versions for all test instances

not work as well as in NSGA-II because individuals in the archive are elitist, and the similarities among them reduce the effectiveness of the EM heuristics. Nevertheless, the approach to generate new solutions in MOEA/D is quite different from NSGA-II and SPEA2. In the recombination step of MOEA/D, a new solution is generated from two neighborhoods which are similar by using crossover and mutation operators. Furthermore, updating the neighboring solutions with this new solution will make the neighboring individuals more similar in MOEA/D. This may explain why EM could not improve performance of MOEA/D. To sum up, NSGA-II_EM is the most effective algorithm for the MORCPSP among the algorithms we have studied.

5. CONCLUSIONS

In this paper, we have studied if the electromagnetism (EM) heuristic procedure could be effectively hybridized with multi-objective evolutionary algorithms (MOEAs) for the multi-objective resource-constrained project scheduling problem (MORCPSP), one of the most challenging combinatorial optimization problems in scheduling. Not only the approach of extending EM heuristics to apply to MORCPSP, but also how to combine EM with MOEAs framework have been introduced. We have hybridized EM heuristics with three state-of-the-art MOEAs, including NSGA-II, SPEA2 and MOEA/D, and compared them with their corresponding original versions on some test instances. The experimental results show that hybridizing EM heuristics with NSGA-II and SPEA2, especially for NSGA-II, can improve various aspects of performances; it is not effective to combine EM with MOEA/D. Finally, we also give a brief explanation why EM plays different roles in these three algorithms and the conclude that NSGA-II integrated with EM heuristics is the most effective algorithm for the MORCPSP. Further research will focus on doing research on the other objectives mentioned in this paper and developing appropriate algorithms capable of calculating the real Pareto front for MORCPSP.

6. ACKNOWLEDGMENTS

This work was partially supported by the National Natural Science Foundation of China (NSFC) projects No. 6120 2296 and 71102146, the National High-Technology Research and Development Program ("863"Program) of China under Grant No.2013$AA01A$212, the Natural Science Foundation of Guangdong Province project No.S2012030006242, the State Key Laboratory of Software Engineering project No. SKLSE2012-09-08, the Research Fund for Young Teachers of South China Normal University No.2012KJ009 and the Scientific Research Foundation of the Graduate School of South China Normal University No. 2012kyjj229.

7. REFERENCES

[1] B. Abbasi, S. Shadrokh, and J. Arkat. Bi-objective resource-constrained project scheduling with robustness and makespan criteria. *Applied Mathematics and Computation*, 180(1):146–152, 2006.

[2] R. Aboutalebi, A. Najafi, and B. Ghorashi. Solving multi-mode resource-constrained project scheduling problem using two multi-objective evolutionary algorithms. *Afr J Bus Manage*, 6(11):4057–65, 2012.

[3] M. A. Al-Fawzan and M. Haouari. A bi-objective model for robust resource-constrained project scheduling. *International Journal of Production Economics*, 96(2):175–187, 2005.

[4] F. Ballest´n and R. Blanco. Theoretical and practical fundamentals for multi-objective optimisation in resource-constrained project scheduling problems. *Computers & Operations Research*, 38(1):51–62, 2011.

[5] F. Ballest´n, V. Valls, and S. Quintanilla. Due dates and rcpsp. In J. Józefowska and J. Węglarz, editors, *Perspectives in Modern Project Scheduling*, volume 92 of *International Series in Operations Research & Management Science*, chapter 4, pages 79–104. Springer US, 2006.

[6] Ş. İ. Birbil and S.-C. Fang. An electromagnetism-like mechanism for global optimization. *Journal of global optimization*, 25(3):263–282, 2003.

[7] K. Deb, A. Pratap, S. Agarwal, and T. Meyarivan. A fast and elitist multiobjective genetic algorithm: Nsga-ii. *Evolutionary Computation, IEEE Transactions on*, 6(2):182–197, 2002.

[8] D. Debels, B. De Reyck, R. Leus, and M. Vanhoucke. A hybrid scatter search/electromagnetism meta-heuristic for project scheduling. *European Journal of Operational Research*, 169(2):638–653, 2006.

[9] H. C. Gomes, F. de Assis das Neves, and M. J. F. Souza. Multi-objective metaheuristic algorithms for the resource-constrained project scheduling problem with precedence relations. *Computers & Operations Research*, 44(0):92 – 104, 2014.

[10] M. Hapke, A. Jaszkiewicz, and R. Slowinski. Fuzzy project scheduling with multiple criteria. In *Fuzzy Systems, 1997., Proceedings of the Sixth IEEE International Conference on*, volume 3, pages 1277–1282. IEEE, 1997.

[11] M. Hapke, A. Jaszkiewicz, and R. Słowiński. Interactive analysis of multiple-criteria project scheduling problems. *European Journal of Operational Research*, 107(2):315–324, 1998.

[12] M. Hapke, A. Jaszkiewicz, and R. Słowiński. Fuzzy multi-mode resource-constrained project scheduling with multiple objectives. In J. Węglarz, editor, *Project Scheduling*, volume 14 of *International Series in Operations Research & Management Science*, chapter 16, pages 353–380. Springer US, 1999.

[13] F. Kazemi and R. Tavakkoli-Moghaddan. Solving a multi-objective multi-mode resource-constrained project scheduling with discounted cash flows. In *Proceedings of the 6th international management conference*, 2008.

[14] R. Kolisch, A. Sprecher, and A. Drexl. Characterization and generation of a general class of resource-constrained project scheduling problems. *Management science*, 41(10):1693–1703, 1995.

[15] J. Nabrzyski and J. Węglarz. On an expert system with tabu search for multiobjective project scheduling. In *Emerging Technologies and Factory Automation, 1995. ETFA '95, Proceedings., 1995 INRIA/IEEE Symposium on*, volume 3, pages 87–94. IEEE, 1995.

[16] J. Nabrzyski and J. Węglarz. Knowledge-based multiobjective project scheduling problems. In J. Węglarz, editor, *Project Scheduling*, volume 14 of *International Series in Operations Research & Management Science*, chapter 17, pages 383–411. Springer US, 1999.

[17] L. Özdamar and G. Ulusoy. A note on an iterative forward/backward scheduling technique with reference to a procedure by li and willis. *European Journal of Operational Research*, 89(2):400–407, 1996.

[18] H. Pan and C.-H. Yeh. A metaheuristic approach to fuzzy project scheduling. In V. Palade, R. Howlett, and L. Jain, editors, *Knowledge-Based Intelligent Information and Engineering Systems*, volume 2773 of *Lecture Notes in Computer Science*, chapter 145, pages 1081–1087. Springer Berlin Heidelberg, 2003.

[19] R. Słowiński. Multiobjective network scheduling with efficient use of renewable and nonrenewable resources. *European Journal of Operational Research*, 7(3):265–273, 1981.

[20] R. Słowiński, B. Soniewicki, and J. Węglarz. Dss for multiobjective project scheduling. *European Journal of Operational Research*, 79(2):220–229, 1994.

[21] A. Viana and J. Pinho de Sousa. Using metaheuristics in multiobjective resource constrained project scheduling. *European Journal of Operational Research*, 120(2):359–374, 2000.

[22] Q. Zhang and H. Li. Moea/d: A multiobjective evolutionary algorithm based on decomposition. *Evolutionary Computation, IEEE Transactions on*, 11(6):712–731, 2007.

[23] E. Zitzler, M. Laumanns, and L. Thiele. Spea2: Improving the strength pareto evolutionary algorithm. Technical Report 103, Computer Engineering and Networks Laboratory (TIK), (ETH) Zurich, Switzerland, 2001.

An Improved NSGA-III Procedure for Evolutionary Many-Objective Optimization

Yuan Yuan, Hua Xu, Bo Wang
State Key Laboratory of Intelligent Technology and Systems
Tsinghua National Laboratory for Information Science and Technology
Department of Computer Science and Technology, Tsinghua University, Beijing 100084, P.R.China
yyxhdy@gmail.com, xuhua@tsinghua.edu.cn, wbthu@outlook.com

ABSTRACT

Many-objective (four or more objectives) optimization problems pose a great challenge to the classical Pareto-dominance based multi-objective evolutionary algorithms (MOEAs), such as NSGA-II and SPEA2. This is mainly due to the fact that the selection pressure based on Pareto-dominance degrades severely with the number of objectives increasing. Very recently, a reference-point based NSGA-II, referred as NSGA-III, is suggested to deal with many-objective problems, where the maintenance of diversity among population members is aided by supplying and adaptively updating a number of well-spread reference points. However, NSGA-III still relies on Pareto-dominance to push the population towards Pareto front (PF), leaving room for the improvement of its convergence ability. In this paper, an improved NSGA-III procedure, called θ-NSGA-III, is proposed, aiming to better tradeoff the convergence and diversity in many-objective optimization. In θ-NSGA-III, the non-dominated sorting scheme based on the proposed θ-dominance is employed to rank solutions in the environmental selection phase, which ensures both convergence and diversity. Computational experiments have shown that θ-NSGA-III is significantly better than the original NSGA-III and MOEA/D on most instances no matter in convergence and overall performance.

Categories and Subject Descriptors

I.2.8 [**Artificial Intelligence**]: Problem Solving, Control Methods, and Search—*Heuristic methods*; G.1.6 [**Numerical Analysis**]: Optimization

General Terms

Algorithms, Performance

Keywords

Many-objective optimization, NSGA-III, θ-NSGA-III, θ-dominance, non-dominated sorting

GECCO'14, July 12–16, 2014, Vancouver, BC, Canada.
Copyright 2014 ACM 978-1-4503-2662-9/14/07 ...$15.00.
http://dx.doi.org/10.1145/2576768.2598342 .

1. INTRODUCTION

Recently, many-objective optimization, typically referring to the optimization of problems having four or more objectives, has attracted increasing attention in evolutionary multi-objective optimization (EMO) community. The boom of the research on evolutionary many-objective optimization is mainly inspired from two aspects. On the one hand, the optimization problems involving a high number of objectives indeed appear widely in many real-world applications, e.g., control system design [17], industrial scheduling [27], software engineering [26]. Hence, the practitioners are in need of effective optimizer to solve these problems at hand. On the other hand, the popular Pareto-dominance based multi-objective evolutionary algorithms (MOEAs), such as NSGA-II [9] and SPEA2 [31], have encountered great difficulties in many-objective optimization, although they have shown excellent performance on problems with two or three objectives. The primary reason is that almost all the solutions in each population become non-dominated with the number of objectives increasing, which would lead to the severe loss of Pareto-based selection pressure towards the Pareto front (PF).

To overcome the drawback of Pareto-dominance based MOEAs, some efforts have been made in the literature. In summary, the developing techniques can be roughly classified into the following two types:

1) Adoption of new preference relations: Since the Pareto-dominance relation scales poorly in many-objective optimization, it is natural to use other preference relations, including modified Pareto-dominance and different ranking schemes, so as to produce fine selection pressure towards PF. Up to now, many alternative preference relations have been proposed, such as favour relation [13], ϵ-dominance [22], fuzzy Pareto-dominance [15] and so on [21, 12, 25].

2) Adoption of new diversity promotion mechanisms: In many-objective optimization, Pareto-dominance could not provide sufficient selection pressure to make progress in a given population, so the diversity criterion begins to play a key role in such cases. However, the existing diversity-preservation criteria, such as crowding distance [9], are not suitable for many-objective problems [19, 20]. Thus, a new mechanism promoting the diversity is needed. In the work [1], two mechanisms for managing diversity were proposed to investigate their impact on overall convergence in many-objective optimization. The recently proposed NSGA-III [8] replaced the crowding distance operator in NSGA-II with a clustering operator which is aided by a set of well-distributed reference points.

It is worthy noting that, unlike Pareto-dominance based MOEAs, another two class of approaches, decomposition-based and indicator-based approaches, have been found very promising in many-objective optimization. The former decomposes a problem with multiple objectives into a set of single-objective subproblems through scalarizing functions, and then solves these subproblems simultaneously by evolving a population of solutions. MOEA/D [29, 23] is the most typical implementation of this class. The indicator-based approach employs a single performance indicator, such as hypervolume [30, 3], to optimize a desired property of evolutionary population. Regarding the exact calculation of hypervolume is especially computational expensive in high-dimensional objective space, the fast algorithm [2] that uses Monte Carlo simulation to approximate the exact hypervolume values has been developed.

This paper proposes an improved NSGA-III procedure, called θ-NSGA-III, for evolutionary many-objective optimization. θ-NSGA-III inherits the characteristic ideas in the original NSGA-III, including the adaptive normalization and diversity-preservation aided by well-spread reference points. However, quite different from NSGA-III, a new preference relation, referred as θ-dominance, is used instead of Pareto-dominance in the proposed θ-NSGA-III. Our motivation is based on the following consideration. NSGA-III emphasizes population members which are Pareto non-dominated yet close to the reference line of each reference point. Nevertheless, when the number of objectives is high, Pareto-dominance lacks enough selection pressure to pull the population towards PF, so NSGA-III indeed emphasizes diversity more than convergence in such cases. We want to improve the convergence of NSGA-III for many-objective problems but without much deterioration of its good diversity maintenance ability. The proposed θ-dominance could well serve this goal. In the θ-dominance, the solutions are allocated into different clusters represented by well-distributed reference points. Only the solutions within the same cluster have the competitive relationship, where a fitness function similar to penalty-based boundary intersection (PBI) function [29] is defined. When conducting the environmental selection, the non-dominated sorting scheme [16] based on θ-dominance not only prefers solutions with better fitness values in each cluster, but also ensures that the solutions distribute as evenly as possible between these clusters. In the experimental studies, the impact of the parameter θ on the performance of θ-NSGA-III is first investigated. Further, θ-NSGA-III is compared with NSGA-III and MOEA/D on well-known test problems, the results indicate that θ-NSGA-III significantly outperforms the other two algorithms in most cases.

The remainder of this paper is organized as follows. Section 2 presents the background knowledge of this paper. The proposed θ-NSGA-III is described in detail in Section 3. Experimental studies on well known test problems are carried out in Section 4. Finally, our conclusions are drawn in Section 5.

2. BACKGROUND

In this section, some basic definitions in multi-objective optimization are first given. Then, we will briefly introduce the original NSGA-III.

2.1 Basic Definitions

The multi-objective optimization problem (MOP) can be mathematically defined as follows:

$$\begin{aligned} \min \mathbf{f}(\mathbf{x}) &= (f_1(\mathbf{x}), f_2(\mathbf{x}), \ldots, f_m(\mathbf{x}))^{\mathrm{T}} \\ &\text{subject to } \mathbf{x} \in \Omega \subseteq \mathbb{R}^n \end{aligned} \tag{1}$$

where $\mathbf{x} = (x_1, x_2, ..., x_n)^{\mathrm{T}}$ is a n-dimensional decision variable vector from the decision space Ω; $\mathbf{f} : \Omega \rightarrow \Theta \subseteq \mathbb{R}^m$ consists a set of m objective functions, and is a mapping from n-dimensional decision space Ω to m-dimensional objective space Θ.

DEFINITION 1. *Given two decision vectors $\mathbf{x}, \mathbf{y} \in \Omega$, $\mathbf{x}$ is said to Pareto dominate $\mathbf{y}$, denoted by $\mathbf{x} \prec \mathbf{y}$, if $f_i(\mathbf{x}) \leq f_i(\mathbf{y})$, for every $i \in \{1, 2, \ldots, m\}$, and $f_j(\mathbf{x}) < f_j(\mathbf{y})$, for at least one index $j \in \{1, 2, \ldots, m\}$.*

DEFINITION 2. *A decision vector $\mathbf{x}^* \in \Omega$ is Pareto optimal if there is no $\mathbf{x} \in \Omega$ such that $\mathbf{x} \prec \mathbf{x}^*$.*

DEFINITION 3. *The Pareto set, PS, is defined as:*

$$PS = \{\mathbf{x} \in \Omega | \mathbf{x} \text{ is Pareto optimal}\} \tag{2}$$

DEFINITION 4. *The Pareto front, PF, is defined as:*

$$PF = \{\mathbf{f}(\mathbf{x}) \in \mathbb{R}^m | \mathbf{x} \in PS\} \tag{3}$$

DEFINITION 5. *The ideal point $\mathbf{z}^*$ is a vector $\mathbf{z}^* = (z_1^*, z_2^*, \ldots, z_m^*)^{\mathrm{T}}$, where z_i^* is the infimum of f_i for every $i \in \{1, 2, \ldots, m\}$.*

The goal of MOEAs is to move the non-dominated objective vectors towards PF (convergence), and also generate a good distribution of these vectors over the PF (diversity).

2.2 Original NSGA-III

The basic framework of NSGA-III remains similar to the established NSGA-II [9] with significant changes in its selection mechanism. The main procedure of NSGA-III can be briefly described below.

NSGA-III starts with the definition of a set of reference points. Then an initial population with N members is randomly generated, where N is the population size. The next steps are iterated until the termination criterion is satisfied. At the t-th generation, the current parent population P_t is used to produce an offspring population Q_t by using randomly selection, simulated binary crossover (SBX) operator and polynomial mutation [7]. The size of P_t and Q_t are both N. Thereafter, the two populations P_t and Q_t are merged together to form a new population $R_t = P_t \cup Q_t$ (of size $2N$). To choose the best N members from R_t for the next generation, the non-dominated sorting based on usual domination principle [4] is first used, which classifies R_t into different non-domination levels (F_1, F_2, and so on). Then, a new population S_t is constructed by filling members of different non-domination levels one at a time, starting from F_1, until the size of S_t equals to N or for the first time becomes greater than N. Let us suppose that the last level included is the l-th level. Hence, the solutions from the level $l+1$ onwards are simply rejected. Members in $S_t \setminus F_l$ are already chosen for P_{t+1}, and the remaining population slots are chosen from F_l such that a desired diversity is maintained in the population. In the original NSGA-II, the solutions in

F_l with the largest crowding distance values are selected. However, the crowding distance measure does not perform well for many-objective problems [20]. Thus, the selection mechanism in NSGA-III is modified by conducting a more systematic analysis of members in S_t with respect to the supplied reference points.

To achieve this, objective values and supplied reference points are first normalized so that they have an identical range. After normalization, the ideal point of the set S_t is the zero vector. Thereafter, the perpendicular distance between a member in S_t and each of the reference lines (joining the ideal point with a reference point) is calculated. Each member in S_t is then associated with a reference point having the minimum perpendicular distance. Next, the niche count ρ_j for the j-th reference point, defined as the number of members in $S_t \setminus F_l$ that are associated with the j-th reference point, can be obtained based on the above process. Further, a niche-preservation operation is executed to select members from F_l, and it works as follows. First, the reference point set $J_{\min} = \{j : \text{argmin}_j \rho_j\}$ having the minimum ρ_j value is identified. In case of $|J_{\min}| > 1$, one $\bar{j} \in J_{\min}$ is randomly chosen. If $\rho_{\bar{j}} = 0$, we choose the one having the shortest perpendicular distance to the j-th reference line among members associated with the j-th reference point in F_l, and add it to P_{t+1}. The count of $\rho_{\bar{j}}$ is then increased by one. In the event $\rho_j \geq 1$, a randomly chosen member from front F_l that is associated with the j-th reference point is added to P_{t+1}, and the count of $\rho_{\bar{j}}$ also needs increasing by one. In both of the two cases, once there exists no such member to be selected, the j-th reference point is excluded from further consideration for the current generation. After niche counts are updated, the above niche operation is repeated for a total of $K = N - |S_t \setminus F_l|$ times to fill the remaining population slots of P_{t+1}. For more details of NSGA-III, please refer to [8].

3. PROPOSED ALGORITHM

3.1 Overview

The framework of the proposed θ-NSGA-III can be described in Algorithm 1. First, a set of K reference points is generated, which is denoted as $\boldsymbol{\Lambda} = \{\boldsymbol{\lambda}_1, \boldsymbol{\lambda}_2, \ldots, \boldsymbol{\lambda}_K\}$. For an m-objective problem, $\boldsymbol{\lambda}_j$ ($j \in \{1, 2, \ldots, K\}$) is an m-dimensional vector represented by $\boldsymbol{\lambda}_j = (\lambda_{j,1}, \lambda_{j,2}, \ldots, \lambda_{j,m})^{\mathrm{T}}$, where $\lambda_{j,k} \geq 0, k = 1, 2, \ldots, m$ and $\sum_{k=1}^{m} \lambda_{j,k} = 1$. Next, the initial population with N members is randomly produced. For the ideal point $\mathbf{z}^*$, it is often very time-consuming to compute exact z_i^*, so it is indeed estimated by the minimum value found so far for objective f_i, and is updated during the search. Steps 5-21 are iterated until the termination criterion is satisfied. In Step 6, the offspring population Q_t is produced by using the same genetic operators with those in NSGA-III. And like wise, Q_t is combined with the current population P_t, and form a new population R_t. Thereafter, R_t is normalized using the ideal point $\mathbf{z}^*$. After normalization, the clustering operator is used to split the members in R_t into a set of K clusters $\mathcal{C} = \{C_1, C_2, \ldots, C_K\}$, where the cluster C_j is represented by the reference point $\boldsymbol{\lambda}_j$. Then, the non-dominated sorting based on θ-dominance (not Pareto-dominance) is employed to classify R_t into different θ-non-domination levels (F_1, F_2, and so on). θ-dominance, which is the key concept in θ-NSGA-III, would be introduced later. Once θ-non-dominated-sorting has been finished, the remaining steps fill the population slots in P_{t+1} using one level at a time, starting from F_1. Unlike both NSGA-II and NSGA-III, we just randomly select solutions in the last accepted level F_l in θ-NSGA-III, because θ-dominance has stressed both convergence and diversity. Surely, some strategies to enhance the diversity could also be used as well in Step 18.

Algorithm 1 Framework of the proposed θ-NSGA-III

```
1: Λ ← GenerateReferencePoints()
2: P_0 ← InitializePopulation()
3: z* ← InitializeIdealPoint()
4: t ← 0
5: while the termination criterion is not met do
6:    Q_t ← MakeOffspringPopulation(P_t)
7:    UpdateIdealPoint(Q_t)
8:    R_t ← P_t ∪ Q_t
9:    Normalize(R_t, z*)
10:   C ← Clustering(R_t, Λ)
11:   {F_1, F_2, ...} ← θ-Non-dominated-sort(R_t, C)
12:   P_{t+1} ← ∅
13:   i ← 1
14:   while |P_{t+1}| + |F_i| ≤ N do
15:      P_{t+1} ← P_{t+1} ∪ F_i
16:      i ← i + 1
17:   end while
18:   RandomSort(F_i)
19:   P_{t+1} ← P_{t+1} ∪ F_i[1 : (N − |P_{t+1}|)]
20:   t ← t + 1
21: end while
```

Although θ-NSGA-III borrows several ideas of NSGA-III such as adaptive normalization and association operation, they differ a lot in some aspects. First, we adopt a simpler method that could generate any number of reference points, further resulting in an arbitrary population size. Second, the normalization and association (clustering) procedures occur in different occasions that can be seen in Algorithm 1, and the implementation details are also a little modified. Above all, we replace the original Pareto dominance used in NSGA-III with the proposed θ-dominance, which could well balance the convergence and diversity in many-objective optimization. In the following subsections, the important procedures of θ-NSGA-III are to be described in detail, and the motivation behind them will also be mentioned.

3.2 Reference Points Generation

In the original NSGA-III, the Das and Dennis's systematic approach [6] is adopted to generate structured reference points. However, in this approach, the number of reference points K would be controlled by a parameter H, where $K = C_{H+m-1}^{m-1}$. NSGA-III uses a population size N that is set as the smallest even number greater than or equal to K, so N indirectly depends on H. When the number of objectives m is high, N would become very large even if there exist only one intermediate reference point [8].

In the proposed θ-NSGA-III, we adopt a simpler approach [18] but with more flexibility to produce K uniformly distributed points, which can be depicted in Algorithm 2, where $rand(0, 1)$ is a random function returning a real number between 0 and 1 with uniform distribution.

3.3 Adaptive Normalization

In the original NSGA-III, the authors presented a normalization procedure, which is claimed to lead to more appropriate normalization values. However, the procedure is

Algorithm 2 GenerateReferencePoints()

for $j \leftarrow 1$ to K **do**
  $s \leftarrow 0$
  for $k \leftarrow 1$ to m **do**
    if $k < m$ **then**
      $r \leftarrow rand(0, 1)$
      $\lambda_{j,k} \leftarrow (1 - s)(1 - r^{\frac{1}{m-k}})$
      $s \leftarrow s + \lambda_{j,k}$
    else
      $\lambda_{j,k} \leftarrow 1 - s$
    end if
  end for
end for

a little computational expensive since it would involve the solving of linear system of equations. Moreover, although the procedure could work well on problems with not too many objectives, we find that it sometimes results in abnormal normalization results on problems having a high number of objectives.

In θ-NSGA-III, we just use an usual way to normalize the population. Suppose $\mathbf{z}^{\max} = (z_1^{\max}, z_2^{\max}, \ldots, z_m^{\max})^{\mathrm{T}}$, where $z_i^{\max}$ is the maximum value for objective f_i in the population to be normalized. Then, for a solution $\mathbf{x}$, the normalized objective value $\tilde{f}_i(\mathbf{x})$ can be computed as $\tilde{f}_i(\mathbf{x}) = (f_i(\mathbf{x}) - z_i^*)/(z_i^{\max} - z_i^*)$. The overall procedure is summarized in Algorithm 3.

Algorithm 3 Normalize(R_t, $\mathbf{z}^*$)

$(z_1^{\max}, z_2^{\max}, \ldots, z_m^{\max})^{\mathrm{T}} \leftarrow (-\infty, -\infty, \ldots, -\infty)^{\mathrm{T}}$
for each solution $\mathbf{x}$ in R_t **do**
  for $i \leftarrow 1$ to m **do**
    if $f_i(\mathbf{x}) > z_i^{\max}$ **then**
      $z_i^{\max} \leftarrow f_i(\mathbf{x})$
    end if
  end for
end for
for each solution $\mathbf{x}$ in R_t **do**
  for $i \leftarrow 1$ to m **do**
    $\tilde{f}_i(\mathbf{x}) \leftarrow (f_i(\mathbf{x}) - z_i^*)/(z_i^{\max} - z_i^*)$
  end for
end for

3.4 Clustering Operator

In the proposed θ-NSGA-III, the clustering operator is similar to that in NSGA-III, but it is run on different populations. In the original NSGA-III, the operator is done to S_t, while in θ-NSGA-III, is to R_t. The clustering works in the normalized objective space, where the ideal point is the origin. In Figure 1, $\tilde{\mathbf{f}}(\mathbf{x}) = (\tilde{f}_1(\mathbf{x}), \tilde{f}_2(\mathbf{x}), \ldots, \tilde{f}_m(\mathbf{x}))^{\mathrm{T}}$ is the normalized objective vector for the solution $\mathbf{x}$, L is a line passing through the origin with direction $\boldsymbol{\lambda}_j$, and $\mathbf{u}$ is the projection of $\tilde{\mathbf{f}}(\mathbf{x})$ on L. Let $d_{j,1}(\mathbf{x})$ be the distance between the origin and $\mathbf{u}$, and $d_{j,2}(\mathbf{x})$ be the perpendicular distance between $\tilde{\mathbf{f}}(\mathbf{x})$ and L. They can be computed respectively as follows

$$d_{j,1}(\mathbf{x}) = \|\tilde{\mathbf{f}}(\mathbf{x})^{\mathrm{T}}\boldsymbol{\lambda}_j\|/\|\boldsymbol{\lambda}_j\| \quad (4)$$

$$d_{j,2}(\mathbf{x}) = \left\|\tilde{\mathbf{f}}(\mathbf{x}) - d_{j,1}(\mathbf{x})(\boldsymbol{\lambda}_j/\|\boldsymbol{\lambda}_j\|)\right\| \quad (5)$$

For the clustering operator, only $d_{j,2}$ will be concerned, $d_{j,1}$ will be involved later in the definition of θ-dominance.

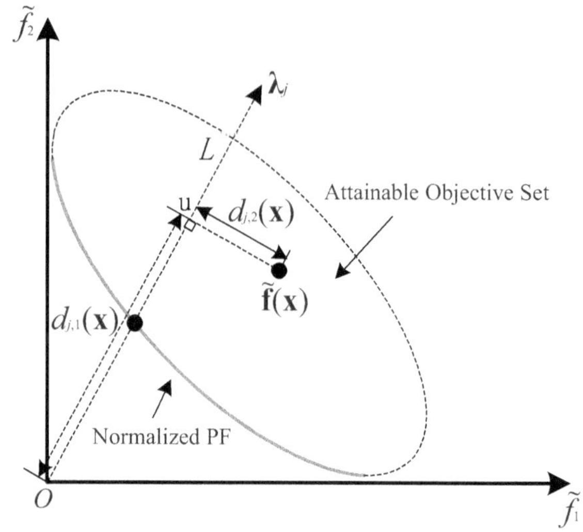

Figure 1: Illustration of distances $d_{j,1}$ and $d_{j,2}$.

We assign a solution $\mathbf{x}$ to the cluster C_j with the minimum $d_{j,2}(\mathbf{x})$ value. The detail process of clustering is shown in Algorithm 4.

Algorithm 4 Clustering(R_t, $\boldsymbol{\Lambda}$)

$\{C_1, C_2, \ldots, C_K\} \leftarrow \{\emptyset, \emptyset, \ldots, \emptyset\}$
for each solution $\mathbf{x}$ in R_t **do**
  $k \leftarrow 1$
  $\min \leftarrow d_{1,2}(\mathbf{x})$
  for $j \leftarrow 2$ to K **do**
    if $d_{j,2}(\mathbf{x}) < \min$ **then**
      $\min \leftarrow d_{j,2}(\mathbf{x})$
      $k \leftarrow j$
    end if
  end for
  $C_k \leftarrow C_k \cup \{\mathbf{x}\}$
end for

3.5 θ-dominance

Let $\mathcal{F}_j(\mathbf{x}) = d_{j,1}(\mathbf{x}) + \theta d_{j,2}(\mathbf{x})$, $j \in \{1, 2, \ldots, K\}$, where θ is a predefined penalty parameter. The form of $\mathcal{F}_j(x)$ is the same with that of PBI function [29]. But here, the distances $d_{j,1}$ and $d_{j,2}$ are both computed in the normalized objective space. It is clear that $d_{j,2}(\mathbf{x}) = 0$ ensures that $\tilde{\mathbf{f}}(\mathbf{x})$ is always in L resulting in perfect diversity, while smaller $d_{j,1}$ value means better convergence. With the definition of $\mathcal{F}_j$, several concepts related with θ-dominance can be defined as follows

DEFINITION 6. *Given two solutions $\mathbf{x}, \mathbf{y} \in \Omega$, $\mathbf{x}$ is said to θ-dominate $\mathbf{y}$, denoted by $\mathbf{x} \prec_\theta \mathbf{y}$, if $\mathbf{x} \in C_j$, $\mathbf{y} \in C_j$, and $\mathcal{F}_j(\mathbf{x}) < \mathcal{F}_j(\mathbf{y})$, where $j \in \{1, 2, \ldots, K\}$.*

DEFINITION 7. *A solution $\mathbf{x}^* \in \Omega$ is θ-optimal if there is no other solution $\mathbf{x} \in \Omega$ such that $\mathbf{x} \prec_\theta \mathbf{x}^*$*

DEFINITION 8. *All feasible solutions that are θ-optimal form the θ-optimal set (θ-OS), and the corresponding mappings of θ-OS in the objective space Θ is called θ-optimal front (θ-OF).*

Based on the definition of θ-dominance, we have the following two properties, which respectively illustrate that the relation $\prec_\theta$ is asymmetric and transitive.

PROPERTY 1. *If two solutions* $\mathbf{x}, \mathbf{y} \in \Omega$ *satisfy* $\mathbf{x} \prec_\theta \mathbf{y}$, *then* $\mathbf{y} \not\prec_\theta \mathbf{x}$

PROOF. Suppose $\mathbf{y} \prec_\theta \mathbf{x}$, then $\exists j \in \{1, 2, \ldots, K\}$, $\mathbf{y} \in C_j$, $\mathbf{x} \in C_j$, and $\mathcal{F}_j(\mathbf{y}) < \mathcal{F}_j(\mathbf{x})$. However, according to $\mathbf{x} \prec_\theta \mathbf{y}$, $\mathcal{F}_j(\mathbf{x}) < F_j(\mathbf{y})$. So, the supposition is invalid, and the proposition is true. □

PROPERTY 2. *If three solutions* $\mathbf{x}, \mathbf{y}, \mathbf{z} \in \Omega$ *satisfy* $\mathbf{x} \prec_\theta \mathbf{y}$ *and* $\mathbf{y} \prec_\theta \mathbf{z}$, *then* $\mathbf{x} \prec_\theta \mathbf{z}$

PROOF. By $\mathbf{x} \prec_\theta \mathbf{y}$, we have that $\exists j \in \{1, 2, \ldots, K\}$, $\mathbf{x} \in C_j$, $\mathbf{y} \in C_j$, and $\mathcal{F}_j(\mathbf{x}) < \mathcal{F}_j(\mathbf{y})$. And according to $\mathbf{y} \prec_\theta \mathbf{z}$, then $\mathbf{z} \in C_j$, $\mathcal{F}_j(\mathbf{y}) < \mathcal{F}_j(\mathbf{z})$. Overall, $\mathbf{x} \in C_j$, $\mathbf{z} \in C_j$ and $\mathcal{F}_j(\mathbf{x}) < \mathcal{F}_j(\mathbf{z})$. Thus, $\mathbf{x} \prec_\theta \mathbf{z}$ □

Due to Property 1 and 2, the fast non-dominated sorting approach [9] can be directly used in θ-dominance sense, and the population R_t would be partitioned into different θ-non-domination levels.

4. EXPERIMENTAL STUDIES

4.1 Experimental Setup

The proposed θ-NSGA-III is implemented in the jMetal framework [14]. The well-known DTLZ1-4 problems [10] are used as test functions, where the number of objectives is varied by us between 4 to 20. In Figure 2, the PFs of DTLZ1 and DTLZ2 for three objectives are shown. The PFs of DTLZ3 and DTLZ4 are the same with DTLZ2, which only differ in the mapping from the decision space to the objective space. In order to evaluate the performance of the concerned algorithms, the generational distance (GD)[28] and inverted generational distance (IGD) [5] would be involved as performance metrics in our experiments, which can be explained as the following. Let P^* be a set of uniformly distributed points along the PF. Let A be an approximation to the PF. The metrics GD and IGD of the set A are respectively defined as:

$$\mathrm{GD}(A, P^*) = \frac{1}{|A|}\sqrt{\sum_{i=1}^{|A|} d_i^2} \tag{6}$$

$$\mathrm{IGD}(A, P^*) = \frac{1}{|P^*|}\sqrt{\sum_{i=1}^{|P^*|} \tilde{d}_i^2} \tag{7}$$

where d_i ($\tilde{d}_i$) is the Euclidean distance between the i-th member in the set A (P^*) and its nearest member in the set P^* (A). GD can only reflect the convergence of an algorithm, while IGD could measure both convergence and diversity in a sense. For both of two metrics, smaller value means better quality.

To verify the effectiveness of proposed θ-NSGA-III, we compare its performance to the original NSGA-III [8] and MOEA/D [23]. In both NSGA-III and MOEA/D, the population size N is controlled by a parameter H ($N = C_{H+m-1}^{m-1}$), while in θ-NSGA-III, the population size can be arbitrary. But for ensuring a fair comparison, we adopt the uniform population size and the maximum number of fitness evaluations in all the three considered algorithms, which are listed in Table 1.

The other parameters of θ-NSGA-III are shown in Table 2. Here, we haven't decided the parameter θ, which would be further investigated in Section 4.2. As for NSGA-III and MOEA/D, their other parameters are just set according to the original papers. Each algorithm is run 30 times independently for each case, and average results are recoded.

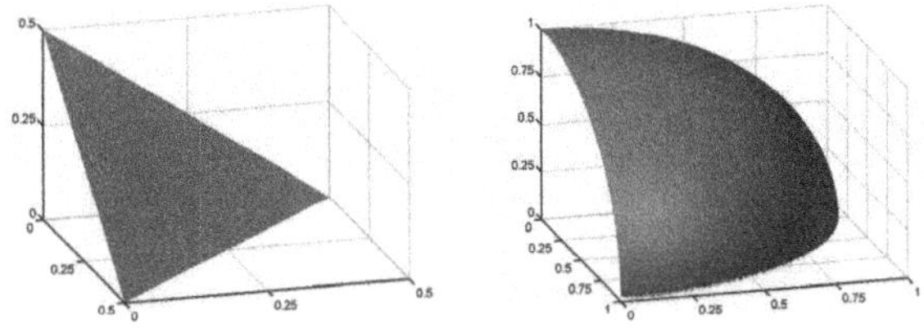

(a) DTLZ1. (b) DTLZ2.

Figure 2: Visualization of PFs of DTLZ1 and DTLZ2 for three objectives.

Table 1: The population size and the maximum number of fitness evaluations.

m	H	N	Fitness Evaluations
4	9	220	100,100
5	6	210	99,960
6	5	252	100,044
8	4	330	99,990
10	3	220	100,100
12	3	364	100,100
14	3	560	100,240
16	3	816	100,368
18	3	1140	100,320
20	2	210	99,960

Table 2: The other parameters of θ-NSGA-III

Parameter	Value
Number of reference points (K)	N
Crossover probability (p_c)	0.9
Mutation probability (p_m)	$1/n$
Distribution index for crossover (η_c)	30
Distribution index for mutation (η_m)	20

4.2 Influence of Parameter θ

Compared to the original NSGA-III, θ-NSGA-III has an additional parameter θ. In this subsection, we will examine the influence of θ on the performance of θ-NSGA-III. IGD metric is used here, since it can reflect overall performance including both convergence and diversity. We consider the situation $m \in \{4, 8, 12, 16\}$ and $0 \leq \theta \leq 20$. Figure 3 shows that how the performance of θ-NSGA-III varies over the change of θ.

From Figure 3, it can be seen that, for DTLZ1, the IGD value presents slight fluctuations except for the 12-objective instance, where the IGD change seems more instable roughly between $\theta = 2$ and $\theta = 7$. For both DTLZ2 and DTLZ4, the variation trend of IGD is similar. That is, $\theta = 0$ would result in a relative poor performance, and when $\theta > 0$, IGD value is maintained nearly at the same level all through. As for DTLZ3, the IGD for 12-objective and 16-objective instances decreases smoothly at the beginning (approximately from $\theta = 0$ to $\theta = 5$), then the value become stable; the IGD for 4-objective instance has almost no variation all the while; the IGD for 8-objective instance is the worst when $\theta = 0$,

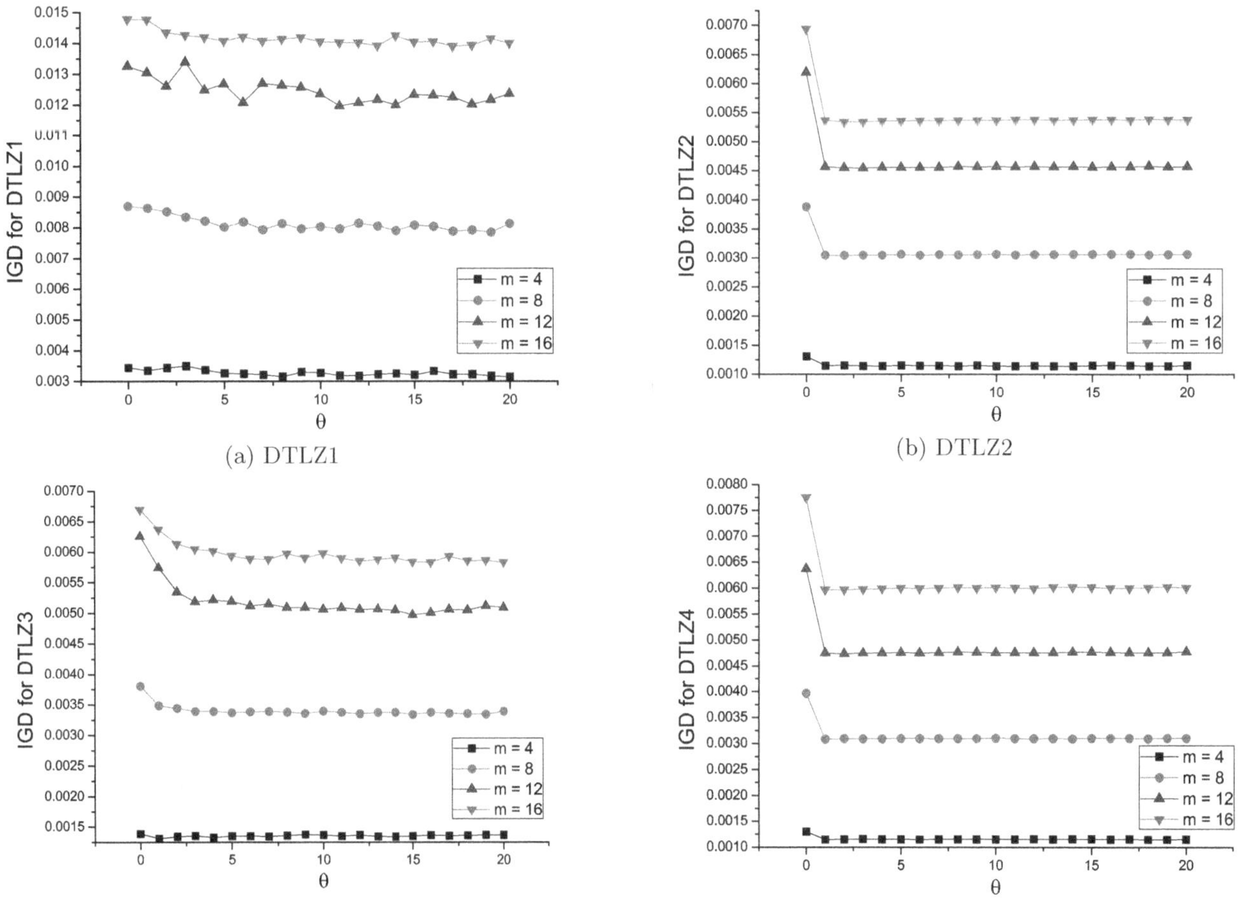

(a) DTLZ1 (b) DTLZ2 (c) DTLZ3 (d) DTLZ4

Figure 3: Investigation of the influence of θ on the performance of θ-NSGA-III for DTLZ 1-4 problems with varying number of objectives m. The figures show the average of 30 independent runs each.

and stays almost unchanged at the remaining θ values. To sum up, $\theta = 0$ is not recommended in our θ-NSGA-III since it nearly always leads to the worst IGD result, and the performance of θ-NSGA-III is robust over a wide range of θ values which is beneficial to the practical use of θ-NSGA-III. In the following experiments, θ is just set to be 5.

4.3 Comparison Results

In this subsection, we will present the comparison results between the proposed θ-NSGA-III, the original NSGA-III and MOEA/D. Table 3 provides the average GD and IGD of each compared algorithm for DTLZ1-4 problems having 4 to 20 objectives. In order to draw statistically sound conclusions, the Wilcoxon signed-rank test [11] at a 5% significance level is further carried out on the three average GD or IGD results obtained by three algorithms respectively for each instance, and the one that is significantly better than the other two is marked in bold face.

From Table 3, regarding GD metric, θ-NSGA-III performs significant better than NSGA-III and MOEA/D on 9 out of 10 DTLZ1 instances except for the 4-objective instance, where NSGA-III has the smallest GD value but there exists no statistical significance. For DTLZ2 and DTLZ4 problems, θ-NSGA-III exhibits obvious superiority since it is always significant better than NSGA-III and MOEA/D on all the concerned instances. As for DTLZ3, θ-NSGA-III significantly outperforms NSGA-III and MOEA/D on 6 out of 10 instances; NSGA-III performs best significantly only on 4-objective and 5-objective instances; on the remaining two instances, θ-NSGA-III still obtains the best GD values although the results are without significance. Since GD metric purely measures the convergence of an algorithm, it can be safely concluded that θ-NSGA-III generally shows the best convergence ability for many-objective problems among all the three algorithms. Specially, the fact θ-NSGA-III outperforms NSGA-III on GD metric illustrates that the proposed θ-dominance indeed improves the convergence of original NSGA-III in replace of the Pareto-dominance, which partly confirms the motivation for this study.

When it comes to IGD metric, θ-NSGA-III is significant better than NSGA-III and MOEA/D in most instances, including 7 DTLZ1 instances, 9 DTLZ2 instances, 8 DTLZ3 instances, and 9 DTLZ4 instances. θ-NSGA-III is significantly outperformed by NSGA-III on all 4-objective instances and the 5-objective DTLZ1 instance, but the gap between them seems not so clear, and θ-NSGA-III still performs better than MOEA/D on these instances. Because IGD metric combines the information of convergence and diversity into a whole, the results indicate that θ-NSGA-III has the best overall performance and is very promising in

Table 3: Comparison between θ-NSGA-III, NSGA-III, and MOEA/D

Problem	m	GD			IGD		
		θ-NSGA-III	NSGA-III	MOEA/D	θ-NSGA-III	NSGA-III	MOEA/D
DTLZ1	4	7.147367E-02	1.194571E-02	3.030940E-01	3.233821E-03	**2.622568E-03**	6.569777E-03
	5	**7.953799E-03**	8.694054E-03	1.421262E+00	4.897804E-03	**4.326618E-03**	1.731600E-02
	6	**9.282109E-03**	1.175294E-02	1.331502E+00	5.795215E-03	6.000549E-03	2.018833E-02
	8	**1.530516E-02**	3.414592E-02	5.305738E-01	**8.056204E-03**	1.260810E-02	2.805876E-02
	10	**5.432319E-02**	9.316793E-02	4.252602E-01	**1.170874E-02**	1.841571E-02	3.272573E-02
	12	**1.819230E-02**	1.195657E-01	4.218465E-01	**1.199624E-02**	2.745254E-02	2.854125E-02
	14	**1.721140E-02**	1.834626E-01	6.101847E-01	**1.307193E-02**	4.125902E-02	6.028564E-02
	16	**1.757701E-02**	1.215636E+00	1.194802E+00	**1.415559E-02**	7.177616E-02	1.097786E-01
	18	**2.242161E-02**	2.744731E+00	2.045014E+00	**1.542844E-02**	1.039266E-01	1.159088E-01
	20	**4.587515E-02**	8.450395E-01	1.285424E-01	**2.396450E-02**	6.738313E-02	3.351446E-02
DTLZ2	4	**2.046303E-03**	2.538939E-03	3.967537E-03	1.149039E-03	**1.100917E-03**	1.742903E-03
	5	**4.396954E-03**	6.125664E-03	7.795486E-03	**1.780862E-03**	2.012950E-03	3.415192E-03
	6	**6.410115E-03**	9.267768E-03	1.033922E-02	**2.256722E-03**	2.806871E-03	3.747893E-03
	8	**9.823255E-03**	1.478273E-02	1.363422E-02	**3.060328E-03**	4.321556E-03	4.677150E-03
	10	**1.693581E-02**	2.632225E-02	2.101903E-02	**4.075165E-03**	6.385276E-03	5.588852E-03
	12	**1.686319E-02**	2.612782E-02	2.019314E-02	**4.564802E-03**	7.338915E-03	6.308985E-03
	14	**1.598765E-02**	2.466134E-02	1.895783E-02	**4.929844E-03**	8.454116E-03	6.580670E-03
	16	**1.536926E-02**	2.353691E-02	1.818666E-02	**5.356541E-03**	9.205518E-03	6.930945E-03
	18	**1.451685E-02**	2.206333E-02	1.773535E-02	**5.704462E-03**	9.864807E-03	7.981181E-03
	20	**3.816497E-02**	5.874783E-02	4.465366E-02	**7.239501E-03**	1.277330E-02	1.010432E-02
DTLZ3	4	6.660327E-03	**3.028080E-03**	8.312969E-03	1.343317E-03	**1.145557E-03**	1.751199E-03
	5	9.058163E-03	**6.806226E-03**	1.063779E+00	2.042259E-03	2.096937E-03	6.577953E-03
	6	**9.159316E-03**	9.180469E-03	9.678572E-01	**2.533024E-03**	2.804483E-03	7.353213E-03
	8	**1.331580E-02**	1.707303E-02	3.425063E-01	**3.424340E-03**	5.141099E-03	8.537354E-03
	10	3.429092E-02	6.045586E-02	1.783019E-01	**4.742726E-03**	7.866186E-03	8.268878E-03
	12	**2.711708E-02**	1.241488E-01	5.711991E-02	**5.219557E-03**	1.000520E-02	9.794224E-03
	14	**2.158932E-02**	3.559196E-01	1.556527E-01	**5.538358E-03**	1.336140E-02	1.270166E-02
	16	**2.040819E-02**	1.209573E+00	5.214353E-01	**5.954946E-03**	2.165244E-02	2.516194E-02
	18	**3.284361E-02**	1.958558E+00	1.287473E+00	**6.616016E-03**	3.365187E-02	3.213193E-02
	20	7.879964E-02	2.509615E-01	1.026432E-01	**1.109914E-02**	1.566994E-02	1.168683E-02
DTLZ4	4	**2.037898E-03**	2.542045E-03	4.283030E-03	1.147480E-03	**1.100780E-03**	2.527278E-03
	5	**4.415283E-03**	6.123178E-03	7.945216E-03	**1.789928E-03**	2.014448E-03	4.075787E-03
	6	**6.433575E-03**	9.272363E-03	1.086709E-02	**2.270834E-03**	2.809236E-03	4.605452E-03
	8	**1.008925E-02**	1.475719E-02	1.450697E-02	**3.096551E-03**	4.316074E-03	5.951227E-03
	10	**1.740289E-02**	2.641742E-02	2.395872E-02	**4.139658E-03**	6.162423E-03	7.316202E-03
	12	**1.795626E-02**	2.614657E-02	2.346515E-02	**4.752917E-03**	7.073280E-03	8.515172E-03
	14	**1.782045E-02**	2.504145E-02	2.249369E-02	**5.313945E-03**	7.828505E-03	9.323785E-03
	16	**1.785509E-02**	2.457113E-02	2.277746E-02	**5.990658E-03**	8.725350E-03	1.029241E-02
	18	**1.756051E-02**	2.358901E-02	2.209823E-02	**6.667148E-03**	9.509864E-03	1.090675E-02
	20	**4.253799E-02**	6.011912E-02	5.007374E-02	**7.821877E-03**	1.133464E-02	1.152812E-02

many-objective optimization compared with state-of-the-art algorithms.

5. CONCLUSION

In this paper, we have presented a new many-objective evolutionary algorithm, referred as θ-NSGA-III, whose selection mechanism is based on θ-dominance. θ-NSGA-III aims to improve the convergence ability of the original NSGA-III, so as to better balance the convergence and diversity in many-objective optimization. To achieve this goal, a new preference relation, θ-dominance, is introduced into the proposed algorithm, which emphasizes both convergence and diversity. Through the experiments, the performance of θ-NSGA-III is found to be insensitive to the parameter θ, which could perform well over a wide range of θ values. We validate the effectiveness of θ-NSGA-III using well-known test problems having 4 to 20 objectives. The comparison results with two established algorithms (NSGA-III and MOEA/D) shows that θ-NSGA-III significantly outperforms NSGA-III and MOEA/D on most instances no matter in convergence and overall performance. In the future, we will incorporate the diversity enhancement strategy into θ-NSGA-III. And also, we would like to apply θ-NSGA-III to more benchmark problems and real-world problems.

Acknowledgment

This work is supported by National Natural Science Foundation of China (Grant No. 61175110), National Basic Research Program of China (973 Program) (Grant No. 2012CB 316305), National S&T Major Projects of China (Grant No. 2011ZX02101-004) and National Banking Information Technology Risk Management Projects of China.

6. REFERENCES

[1] S. F. Adra and P. J. Fleming. Diversity management in evolutionary many-objective optimization. *IEEE Transactions on Evolutionary Computation*, 15(2):183–195, 2011.

[2] J. Bader and E. Zitzler. Hype: An algorithm for fast hypervolume-based many-objective optimization. *Evolutionary Computation*, 19(1):45–76, 2011.

[3] N. Beume, B. Naujoks, and M. Emmerich. SMS-EMOA: Multiobjective selection based on dominated hypervolume. *European Journal of Operational Research*, 181(3):1653–1669, 2007.

[4] V. Chankong and Y. Y. Haimes. *Multiobjective Decision Making Theory and Methodology*. New York: North-Holland, 1983.

[5] C. A. C. Coello and N. C. Cortés. Solving multiobjective optimization problems using an artificial immune system. *Genetic Programming and Evolvable Machines*, 6(2):163–190, 2005.

[6] I. Das and J. E. Dennis. Normal-boundary intersection: A new method for generating the pareto surface in nonlinear multicriteria optimization problems. *SIAM Journal on Optimization*, 8(3):631–657, 1998.

[7] K. Deb and R. B. Agrawal. Simulated binary crossover for continuous search space. *Complex Systems*, 9:1–34, 1994.

[8] K. Deb and J. Himanshu. An evolutionary many-objective optimization algorithm using reference-point based non-dominated sorting approach, part I: Solving problems with box constraints. *IEEE Transactions on Evolutionary Computation*, in press.

[9] K. Deb, A. Pratap, S. Agarwal, and T. Meyarivan. A fast and elitist multiobjective genetic algorithm: NSGA-II. *IEEE Transactions on Evolutionary Computation*, 6(2):182–197, 2002.

[10] K. Deb, L. Thiele, M. Laumanns, and E. Zitzler. *Scalable test problems for evolutionary multiobjective optimization*. TIK-Technical Report No. 112, 2001.

[11] J. Demšar. Statistical comparisons of classifiers over multiple data sets. *The Journal of Machine Learning Research*, 7:1–30, 2006.

[12] F. di Pierro, S.-T. Khu, and D. A. Savic. An investigation on preference order ranking scheme for multiobjective evolutionary optimization. *IEEE Transactions on Evolutionary Computation*, 11(1):17–45, 2007.

[13] N. Drechsler, R. Drechsler, and B. Becker. Multi-objective optimisation based on relation favour. In *Evolutionary multi-criterion optimization*, pages 154–166. Springer, 2001.

[14] J. J. Durillo and A. J. Nebro. jmetal: A java framework for multi-objective optimization. *Advances in Engineering Software*, 42(10):760–771, 2011.

[15] M. Farina and P. Amato. A fuzzy definition of "optimality" for many-criteria optimization problems. *IEEE Transactions on Systems, Man and Cybernetics, Part A: Systems and Humans*, 34(3):315–326, 2004.

[16] D. E. Goldberg. *Genetic algorithms in search, optimization, and machine learning*. Addison-wesley Reading Menlo Park, 1989.

[17] J. G. Herrero, A. Berlanga, and J. M. M. Lopez. Effective evolutionary algorithms for many-specifications attainment: application to air traffic control tracking filters. *IEEE Transactions on Evolutionary Computation*, 13(1):151–168, 2009.

[18] A. Jaszkiewicz. Momh multiple-objective metaheuristics. Apr. 2013. [Online]. Available: http://home.gna.org/momh/index.html.

[19] M. Köppen and K. Yoshida. Substitute distance assignments in nsga-ii for handling many-objective optimization problems. In *Evolutionary Multi-Criterion Optimization*, pages 727–741. Springer, 2007.

[20] S. Kukkonen and K. Deb. Improved pruning of non-dominated solutions based on crowding distance for bi-objective optimization problems. In *IEEE Congress on Evolutionary Computation (CEC) 2006*, pages 1179–1186. IEEE, 2006.

[21] S. Kukkonen and J. Lampinen. Ranking-dominance and many-objective optimization. In *IEEE Congress on Evolutionary Computation (CEC) 2007*, pages 3983–3990. IEEE, 2007.

[22] M. Laumanns, L. Thiele, K. Deb, and E. Zitzler. Combining convergence and diversity in evolutionary multiobjective optimization. *Evolutionary computation*, 10(3):263–282, 2002.

[23] H. Li and Q. Zhang. Multiobjective optimization problems with complicated pareto sets, MOEA/D and NSGA-II. *IEEE Transactions on Evolutionary Computation*, 13(2):284–302, 2009.

[24] M. Li, J. Zheng, K. Li, Q. Yuan, and R. Shen. Enhancing diversity for average ranking method in evolutionary many-objective optimization. In *Parallel Problem Solving from Nature, PPSN XI*, pages 647–656. Springer, 2010.

[25] A. López, C. A. C. Coello, A. Oyama, and K. Fujii. An alternative preference relation to deal with many-objective optimization problems. In *Evolutionary Multi-Criterion Optimization*, pages 291–306. Springer, 2013.

[26] W. Mkaouer, M. Kessentini, S. Bechikh, K. Deb, and M. Ó. Cinnéide. High dimensional search-based software engineering: Finding tradeoffs among 15 objectives for automating software refactoring using NSGA-III. COIN Report No. 2013002, 2013.

[27] A. Sülflow, N. Drechsler, and R. Drechsler. Robust multi-objective optimization in high dimensional spaces. In *Evolutionary multi-criterion optimization*, pages 715–726. Springer, 2007.

[28] D. A. Van Veldhuizen. Multiobjective evolutionary algorithms: classifications, analyses, and new innovations. Technical report, DTIC Document, 1999.

[29] Q. Zhang and H. Li. MOEA/D: A multiobjective evolutionary algorithm based on decomposition. *IEEE Transactions on Evolutionary Computation*, 11(6):712–731, 2007.

[30] E. Zitzler and S. Künzli. Indicator-based selection in multiobjective search. In *Parallel Problem Solving from Nature-PPSN VIII*, pages 832–842. Springer, 2004.

[31] E. Zitzler, M. Laumanns, and L. Thiele. SPEA2: Improving the strength pareto evolutionary algorithm. In *Proceedings of Evolutionary Methods for Design, Optimisation and Control with Application to Industrial Problems*, pages 95–100, 2001.

Evolutionary Many-Objective Optimization Using Ensemble Fitness Ranking

Yuan Yuan, Hua Xu, Bo Wang
State Key Laboratory of Intelligent Technology and Systems
Tsinghua National Laboratory for Information Science and Technology
Department of Computer Science and Technology, Tsinghua University, Beijing 100084, P.R.China
yyxhdy@gmail.com, xuhua@tsinghua.edu.cn, wbthu@outlook.com

ABSTRACT

In this paper, a new framework, called ensemble fitness ranking (EFR), is proposed for evolutionary many-objective optimization that allows to work with different types of fitness functions and ensemble ranking schemes. The framework aims to rank the solutions in the population more appropriately by combing the ranking results from many simple individual rankers. As to the form of EFR, it can be regarded as an extension of average and maximum ranking methods which have been shown promising for many-objective problems. The significant change is that EFR adopts more general fitness functions instead of objective functions, which would make it easier for EFR to balance the convergence and diversity in many-objective optimization. In the experimental studies, the influence of several fitness functions and ensemble ranking schemes on the performance of EFR is fist investigated. Afterwards, EFR is compared with two state-of-the-art methods (MOEA/D and NSGA-III) on well-known test problems. The computational results show that EFR significantly outperforms MOEA/D and NSGA-III on most instances, especially for those having a high number of objectives.

Categories and Subject Descriptors

I.2.8 [**Artificial Intelligence**]: Problem Solving, Control Methods, and Search—*Heuristic methods*; G.1.6 [**Numerical Analysis**]: Optimization

General Terms

Algorithms, Performance

Keywords

Many-objective optimization, ensemble fitness ranking, average ranking, maximum ranking, fitness function, NSGA-III, MOEA/D

GECCO'14, July 12–16, 2014, Vancouver, BC, Canada.

http://dx.doi.org/10.1145/2576768.2598345 .

1. INTRODUCTION

During the past several decades, multi-objective optimization problems (MOPs) have stirred much interest in the evolutionary computation community. In a MOP, there exist several objectives that should be optimized simultaneously. Generally, these objectives are in conflict to each other to some extent, and no single solution can be found to best satisfy all of them. When solving MOPs, we aim to seek for a set of solutions in the decision space achieving the best trade-offs between each objective, known as *Pareto Set* (PS). The mapping of PS in the objective space is referred as *Pareto Front* (PF). Evolutionary algorithms (EAs) have been recognized as especially desirable for handing MOPs, mainly because they can obtain an approximation of PF in a single simulation run. Up to present, various of multi-objective evolutionary algorithms (MOEAs) have been proposed to effectively solve MOPs. However, most of these algorithms have been evaluated and applied to MOPs with only two or three objectives, despite the fact that optimization problems involving a large number of objectives indeed appear widely in real-world applications [13]. In the literature, such MOPs having more than three objectives are often termed as *many-objective* optimization problems.

Unfortunately, experimental and analytical results [15, 24] have indicated that many-objective optimization problems would pose serious difficulties to the existing MOEAs, particulary for the popular Pareto-based MOEAs, such as NSGA-II [8] and SPEA2 [28]. The primary reason for this is that the proportion of non-dominated solutions in a population increases rapidly with the number of objectives, and it would lead to the severe loss of Pareto dominance-based selection pressure toward the PF. To overcome this shortage, it is key to devising alternative approaches to rank individuals in the population instead of using the original Pareto dominance. In the light of this direction, some efforts have been made and the proposed approaches can be roughly classified into three types. The first class of approaches focuses on adopting new preference relations that could induce finer grain order in the objective space than that induced by Pareto dominance relation, for example, weighted sum, average and maximum ranking [3], flavour relation [11] and ϵ-dominance [20]. The second class of methods decomposes a MOP into a set of single-objective subproblems through scalarizing functions, and then solves these subproblems simultaneously by evolving a population of solutions. MOEA/D [26, 21] is probably the most representative implementation of this class. The last class is based on the use of performance indicators. It is intended to perform solution selection by directly optimizing a single indicator such as hypervolume [27, 4]. Besides the above mentioned three classes, it is necessary to note that there is another different type of research, aiming to promote the diversity in many-objective optimization, including the work in [1] and recently proposed NSGA-III [7], although there has not been much study in this respect yet.

The average ranking (AR) and maximum ranking (MR) preference relations are both originally proposed by Bentley and Wakefield [3]. In spite of the simplicity, they have been found to perform well in converging to the PF in many-objective optimization. Corne and Knowles [6] reported that AR is highly effective in comparison with other more complicated ranking schemes, covering problems with 5 to 20 objectives and differing amounts of inter-objective correlation. Kukkonen and Lampinen [19] specially examined AR and MR, and implemented them in an MOEA called GDE3 [18]. They concluded that AR and MR appear to be a promising alternative to Pareto dominance relation for many-objective problems. In several similar researches [23, 16, 14], the comparative studies of different preference relations or ranking methods,including AR and MR, are carried out to deal with problems with a high number of objectives. It is worth noting that although AR and MR have shown their potential, both of them often converge into a subset of PF due to the lack of diversity maintenance mechanism [19, 16]. As for MR, there also exists the particular downside that it tends to favor extreme solutions, i.e., it prefers solutions with high performance in some objectives, but without taking into account the especially poor performance in the rest of the objectives. To our knowledge, the efforts to improve AR or MR are rather limited. Recently, Li et al. [22] proposed a diversity enhancement strategy for AR to balance convergence and diversity during evolution process. But overall, the potential of AR and MR in many-objective optimization is still far from being fully explored.

This paper proposes a new framework, called *ensemble fitness ranking* (EFR), for evolutionary many-objective optimization. EFR assigns the global rank to each solution by combining a set of ranking lists, each of which is collected according to a unique fitness function. Our motivation is to improve ranking reliability and rationality by integrating multiple ranking results produced by different simple individual rankers (fitness functions). With regard to the form, EFR can be viewed as the extension of AR and MR. The significant difference lies in that EFR employs more general fitness functions instead of objective functions. Unlike the single objective function, a suitable fitness function can indicate the "closeness" of the solution to the PF in a sense. A number of different fitness functions may have an active effect on the diversity maintenance. So, compared with AR and MR, it is easier for the proposed EFR to balance the convergence and diversity in many-objective optimization. To instantiate the proposed framework, we provide three kinds of alternative fitness functions and three kinds of ensemble ranking schemes, and several EFR variants are involved to investigate their influence to the convergence ability and overall performance. Further, we compare one EFR variant with MOEA/D and NSGA-III on many-objective problems, the computational results indicate that EFR performs significantly better than the other two in most cases.

In the remainder of this paper, some background knowledge is first provided in Section 2. Thereafter, in Section 3, the proposed EFR methods are described in detail. The experimental studies are conducted in Section 4. Finally, Section 5 concludes this study.

2. BACKGROUND

In this section, some necessary definitions in multi-objective optimization are first given. Then, we will briefly introduce the average ranking (AR) and maximum ranking (MR) which are the important basis of our work.

2.1 Basic Definitions

A MOP can be mathematically defined as follows:

$$\begin{aligned} \min \mathbf{f}(\mathbf{x}) = (f_1(\mathbf{x}), f_2(\mathbf{x}), \dots, f_m(\mathbf{x}))^{\mathrm{T}} \\ \text{subject to } \mathbf{x} \in \Omega \subseteq \mathbb{R}^n \end{aligned} \quad (1)$$

where $\mathbf{x} = (x_1, x_2, ..., x_n)^{\mathrm{T}}$ is a n-dimensional decision variable vector from the decision space Ω; $\mathbf{f} : \Omega \to \Lambda \subseteq \mathbb{R}^m$ consists a set of m objective functions, and is a mapping from n-dimensional decision space Ω to m-dimensional objective space Λ.

Definition 1. *Given $\mathbf{x}, \mathbf{y} \in \Omega$, $\mathbf{x}$ is said to Pareto dominate $\mathbf{y}$, denoted by $\mathbf{x} \prec \mathbf{y}$, if $f_i(\mathbf{x}) \le f_i(\mathbf{y})$, for every $i \in \{1, 2, \dots, m\}$, and $f_j(\mathbf{x}) < f_j(\mathbf{y})$, for at least one index $j \in \{1, 2, \dots, m\}$.*

Definition 2. *A decision vector $\mathbf{x}^* \in \Omega$ is Pareto optimal if there is no $\mathbf{x} \in \Omega$ such that $\mathbf{x} \prec \mathbf{x}^*$.*

Definition 3. *The Pareto set, PS, is defined as:*

$$PS = \{\mathbf{x} \in \Omega | \mathbf{x} \text{ is Pareto optimal}\} \quad (2)$$

Definition 4. *The Pareto front, PF, is defined as:*

$$PF = \{\mathbf{f}(\mathbf{x}) \in \mathbb{R}^m | \mathbf{x} \in PS\} \quad (3)$$

Definition 5. *The ideal vector $\mathbf{z}^*$ is a vector $\mathbf{z}^* = (z_1^*, z_2^*, \dots, z_m^*)^{\mathrm{T}}$, where z_i^* is the infimum of f_i for every $i \in \{1, 2, \dots, m\}$.*

The goal of MOEAs is to move the non-dominated objective vectors towards PF (convergence), and also generate a good distribution of these vectors over the PF (diversity).

2.2 Average and Maximum Ranking

The AR and MR methods consider each objective independently. For an objective $f_j, j \in \{1, 2, \dots, m\}$, the solutions in the population are sorted in the non-decreasing order in accordance with values of such objective, and a ranking list is built where each solution has its own ranking position. When all the objectives are concerned, we totaly have m ranking lists corresponding to m objectives. For each solution $\mathbf{x}$, it has m ranking positions, and can be represented by the vector $\mathbf{R}(\mathbf{x}) = (r_1(\mathbf{x}), r_2(\mathbf{x}), \dots, r_m(\mathbf{x}))^{\mathrm{T}}$, where $r_j(\mathbf{x})$ is the rank of $\mathbf{x}$ for the objective f_j. Once $\mathbf{R}(\mathbf{x})$ is calculated, a single rank is obtained for each solution by combing the m ranking positions, which is used to reflect the overall quality of solutions. To be specific, AR gives the global rank to a solution $\mathbf{x}$ in this way:

$$R_{avg}(\mathbf{x}) = \sum_{j=1}^{m} r_j(\mathbf{x}) \quad (4)$$

while MR computes the global rank as the following:

$$R_{max}(\mathbf{x}) = \min_{j=1}^{m} r_j(\mathbf{x}) \tag{5}$$

In Table 1, AR and MR are demonstrated with a small example of six 3-objective solutions.

Table 1: An example of average ranking and maximum ranking.

Solution	(f_1, f_2, f_3)	r_1	r_2	r_3	AR	MR
A	$(5, 2, 4)$	3	3	4	10	3
B	$(2, 3, 6)$	1	4	6	11	1
C	$(7, 1, 1)$	4	2	1	7	1
D	$(8, 6, 5)$	5	5	5	15	5
E	$(9, 0, 2)$	6	1	2	9	1
F	$(4, 7, 3)$	2	6	3	11	2

Based on R_{avg} or R_{max}, we can further define preference relations. A solution $\mathbf{x}$ dominates solution $\mathbf{y}$ with respect to AR relation, denoted by $\mathbf{x} \prec_{avg} \mathbf{y}$, if and only if $R_{avg}(\mathbf{x}) < R_{avg}(\mathbf{y})$. Similarly, a solution $\mathbf{x}$ dominates solution $\mathbf{y}$ with respect to MR relation, denoted by $\mathbf{x} \prec_{max} \mathbf{y}$, if and only if $R_{max}(\mathbf{x}) < R_{max}(\mathbf{y})$. It is apparent that both $\prec_{avg}$ and $\prec_{max}$ are transitive relations, so both of them can be easily used to discriminate solutions within the same population unambiguously.

3. PROPOSED METHODS

3.1 Overview

Instead of considering each objective f_j, we introduce the fitness functions in our proposed ensemble fitness ranking (EFR) methods. For a fitness function $\mathcal{F}_j$, it assigns the value $\mathcal{F}_j(\mathbf{x})$ to each solution $\mathbf{x}$, which can reflect how well the solution is in a certain aspect. Without loss of generality, the smaller $\mathcal{F}_j(x)$ value means better quality of $\mathbf{x}$ according to $\mathcal{F}_j$. Suppose we have K different fitness functions $\mathcal{F}_1, \mathcal{F}_2, \ldots, \mathcal{F}_K$. Then similar to average and maximum ranking, for each solution $\mathbf{x}$, it has K ranking positions, denoted by the vector $\mathbf{R}(\mathbf{x}) = (r_1(\mathbf{x}), r_2(\mathbf{x}), \ldots, r_K(\mathbf{x}))^{\mathrm{T}}$, here $r_j(\mathbf{x})$ is the rank of $\mathbf{x}$ for the fitness function $\mathcal{F}_j$. After obtaining $\mathbf{R}(\mathbf{x})$ for all solutions, the ensemble ranking is used to give the global rank $R_g(\mathbf{x})$ to each solution $\mathbf{x}$ based on $\mathbf{R}(\mathbf{x})$. Obviously, we can compute $R_g(\mathbf{x})$ in the same way with respect to AR or MR scheme as follows:

$$R_g(\mathbf{x}) = \sum_{j=1}^{K} r_j(\mathbf{x}) \tag{6}$$

$$R_g(\mathbf{x}) = \min_{j=1}^{K} r_j(\mathbf{x}) \tag{7}$$

It should be noted that some solutions may be assigned the same global rank. So, according to R_g, the considered population can be partitioned into a number of solution sets $\{F_1, F_2, \ldots\}$, where the solutions in F_i have the i-th minimum R_g value.

The basic framework of our proposed EFR methods is similar to NSGA-II [8], which is described in Algorithm 1. First, an initial population with N solutions is randomly produced, where N is the population size. Second, K different fitness functions are generated. Finally, Steps 4-21 are iterated until the termination criterion is satisfied. In each generation t, the binary tournament selection based on R_g, the simulated binary crossover (SBX) operator and polynomial mutation [2] are first performed to produce the offspring population Q_t. In Step 6, the populations P_t, Q_t are merged as the population R_t. In Steps 7-10, $\mathbf{R}(\mathbf{x})$ is calculated for each solution $\mathbf{x}$. In Step 11, the global ranks are assigned and R_t is further classified into some solution sets (analogous to "fronts" in NSGA-II), just as stated in the previous paragraph. In the remaining steps, exactly N solutions are selected from F_i in order. When reaching the last considered F_i, another selection criterion is used to sort it (see Step 18), and the best solutions needed are chosen to fill all population slots. In this paper, we mainly emphasize the ensemble ranking, so the random sort is indeed used in Step 18 for simplicity.

Algorithm 1 Framework of the proposed EFR methods

1: $P_0 \leftarrow$ InitializePopulation()
2: $\{\mathcal{F}_1, \mathcal{F}_2, \ldots, \mathcal{F}_K\} \leftarrow$ GenerateFitnessFunctions()
3: $t \leftarrow 0$
4: **while** the termination criterion is not met **do**
5: $\quad Q_t \leftarrow$ MakeOffspringPopulation(P_t)
6: $\quad R_t \leftarrow P_t \cup Q_t$
7: $\quad$**for** $i \leftarrow 1$ to K **do**
8: $\quad\quad$sort R_t according to $\mathcal{F}_i$ in non-decreasing order
9: $\quad\quad$set r_i for each individual in R_t
10: $\quad$**end for**
11: $\quad \{F_1, F_2, \ldots\} \leftarrow$ EnsembleRanking(R_t, $\mathbf{R}$)
12: $\quad P_{t+1} \leftarrow \emptyset$
13: $\quad i \leftarrow 1$
14: $\quad$**while** $|P_{t+1}| + |F_i| \leq N$ **do**
15: $\quad\quad P_{t+1} \leftarrow P_{t+1} \cup F_i$
16: $\quad\quad i \leftarrow i + 1$
17: $\quad$**end while**
18: $\quad$Sort(F_i)
19: $\quad P_{t+1} \leftarrow P_{t+1} \cup F_i[1 : (N - |P_{t+1}|)]$
20: $\quad t \leftarrow t + 1$
21: **end while**

From Algorithm 1, it can be seen that there exist two critical issues to implement the framework. One is how to choose suitable fitness functions, and the other is how to perform the ensemble ranking. In Section 3.2, several possible fitness functions that can be used in our framework are introduced. In Section 3.3, we will also present another available ensemble ranking scheme in addition to AR and MR to assign global ranks, referred to as *layering ranking* (LR) in this paper.

3.2 Alternative Fitness Functions

The fitness function $\mathcal{F}_j$ used in our framework would better meet the condition that the calculation of $\mathcal{F}_j(\mathbf{x})$ for solution $\mathbf{x}$ should not depend on the other solutions in R_t. Otherwise, F_j values will make no sense in the selected next population P_{t+1} from R_t. Hence, the assignment of $\mathcal{F}_j$ values would be aided by some external means. In this paper, three kinds of alternative fitness functions are to be investigated: L^p norm, Tchebycheff function, and penalty-based boundary intersection (PBI) function [26]. Let $\boldsymbol{\lambda}_j = (\lambda_{j,1}, \lambda_{j,2}, \ldots, \lambda_{j,m})^{\mathrm{T}}$, where $\lambda_{j,k} \geq 0, k = 1, 2, \ldots, m$ and $\sum_{k=1}^{m} \lambda_{j,k} = 1$, then they can be respectively described as follows

1) L^p *Norm*:

$$\mathcal{F}_j(\mathbf{x}) = \{\sum_{k=1}^{m}(\lambda_{j,k}|f_k(\mathbf{x}) - z_k^*|^p)\}^{\frac{1}{p}} \quad (8)$$

where $p \geq 1$. When $p = 1$, it degenerates to weighted sum, which has difficulty in capturing non-convex PFs. However, large p value would greatly increase the computation load, although it may work well on more complex PFs.

2) *Tchebycheff Function*:

$$\mathcal{F}_j(\mathbf{x}) = \max_{k=1}^{m}\{\frac{1}{\lambda_{j,k}}|f_k(\mathbf{x}) - z_k^*|\} \quad (9)$$

It is worth noting that the adopted form is a little different from that in [26, 21], where $\mathcal{F}_j$ is defined as $\mathcal{F}_j(\mathbf{x}) = \max_{k=1}^{m}\{\lambda_{j,k}|f_k(\mathbf{x}) - z_k^*|\}$. The modification is based on the following theorem:

THEOREM 1. *If the line going through* $\mathbf{z}^*$ *with direction* $\boldsymbol{\lambda}_j$ *has an intersection with the PF, then the intersection point is the optimal solution to* $\mathcal{F}_j$ *defined in Equation (9).*

PROOF. Let $\mathbf{f}(\mathbf{x})$ be the intersection point with the PF, then we have the following equality

$$\frac{f_1(\mathbf{x}) - z_1^*}{\lambda_{j,1}} = \frac{f_2(\mathbf{x}) - z_2^*}{\lambda_{j,2}} = \ldots = \frac{f_m(\mathbf{x}) - z_m^*}{\lambda_{j,m}} = C \quad (10)$$

where C is a constant. Suppose $\mathbf{f}(\mathbf{x})$ is not the optimal solution to $\mathcal{F}_j$, then $\exists\mathbf{f}(\mathbf{y})$ satisfies $\mathcal{F}_j(\mathbf{y}) < \mathcal{F}_j(\mathbf{x})$. According to Equation (10), $\mathcal{F}_j(\mathbf{x}) = C$. Then $\forall k \in \{1, 2, \ldots, m\}$, we have

$$\frac{f_k(\mathbf{y}) - z_k^*}{\lambda_{j,k}} \leq \mathcal{F}_j(\mathbf{y}) < C = \frac{f_k(\mathbf{x}) - z_k^*}{\lambda_{j,k}} \quad (11)$$

Hence, $f_k(\mathbf{y}) < f_k(\mathbf{x})$. This is is contradicted with the condition that $\mathbf{f}(\mathbf{x})$ is located on the PF and the supposition is invalid. □

According to Theorem 1, the form used in this paper can produce more uniformly distributed solutions in the objective space if uniformly distributed $\boldsymbol{\lambda}_j$, $j = 1, 2, \ldots$, are generated.

3) *PBI Function*:

$$\mathcal{F}_j(\mathbf{x}) = d_{j,1} + \theta d_{j,2}; \quad (12)$$

where $\theta > 0$ is a user-defined penalty parameter, $d_{j,1} = \|(\mathbf{f}(\mathbf{x})-\mathbf{z}^*)^{\mathrm{T}}\boldsymbol{\lambda}_j\|/\|\boldsymbol{\lambda}_j\|$ and $d_{j,2} = \|\mathbf{f}(\mathbf{x})-\mathbf{z}^*-d_{j,1}(\boldsymbol{\lambda}_j/\|\boldsymbol{\lambda}_j\|)\|$. As shown in Figure 1, L is a line passing through $\mathbf{z}^*$ with direction $\boldsymbol{\lambda}_j$, and $\mathbf{u}$ is the projection of $\mathbf{f}(\mathbf{x})$ on L. $d_{j,1}$ is the distance between $\mathbf{z}^*$ and $\mathbf{u}$, and $d_{j,2}$ is the perpendicular distance between $\mathbf{f}(\mathbf{x})$ and L. The decreasing of $\mathcal{F}_j$ would push $\mathbf{f}(\mathbf{x})$ as low as possible so that it reaches the the boundary of attainable objective set.

Certainly, K fitness functions can be comprised of all three kinds mentioned above. However, in this paper, we only investigate the situation that K fitness functions belong to the same type. To ensure the diversity, K uniformly distributed vectors $\boldsymbol{\lambda}_1, \boldsymbol{\lambda}_2, \ldots, \boldsymbol{\lambda}_K$ are generated [17] so as to obtain K fitness functions $\mathcal{F}_1, \mathcal{F}_2, \ldots, \mathcal{F}_K$, whose procedure is described Algorithm 2, where $rand(0, 1)$ is a random function returning a real number between 0 and 1 with uniform distribution. Moreover, it should be mentioned that it is often very time-consuming to compute exact z_k^*, so it is indeed approximated by the minimum value found so far for objective f_k in our methods.

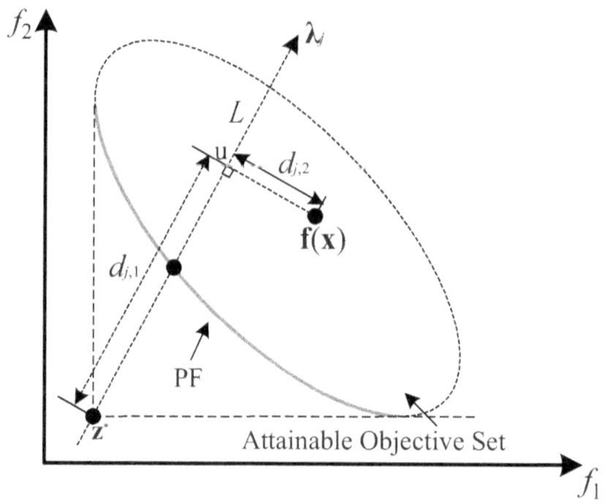

Figure 1: Illustration of PBI function.

Algorithm 2 Generate K uniformly distributed vectors

```
for j ← 1 to K do
   s ← 0
   for k ← 1 to m do
      if k < m then
         r ← rand(0, 1)
         λ_{j,k} ← (1 − s)(1 − r^{1/(m−k)})
         s ← s + λ_{j,k}
      else
         λ_{j,k} ← 1 − s
      end if
   end for
end for
```

3.3 Ensemble Ranking

In this subsection, we will provide another ensemble ranking scheme, called layering ranking (LR), to assign global ranks. The procedure of LR can be depicted in Algorithm 3, where the population P is to be given global ranks. Take the solutions shown in Table 1 for instance, LR assigns the global ranks as follows: $A(2)$, $B(1)$, $C(1)$, $D(3)$, $E(1)$, $F(2)$. It can be seen that, different from AR and MR, LR gives the consecutive ranks to solutions.

Algorithm 3 LayeringRanking(P, $\mathbf{R}$)

```
rank ← 1
while P ≠ ∅ do
   Q ← ∅
   for j ← 1 to K do
      choose solution x in P with minimum r_j value
      R_g(x) ← rank
      Q ← Q ∪ {x}
   end for
   remove all solutions in Q from P
   rank ← rank + 1
end while
```

4. EXPERIMENTAL STUDIES

The proposed methods are all implemented in the jMetal framework [12]. The well-known DTLZ1, DTLZ2, DTLZ3, and DTLZ4 problems [9] are considered. We vary the number of objectives between 2 to 20. In order to assess the performance of the proposed algorithms, the generational distance (GD) [25] and inverted generational distance (IGD)

[5] are involved as metrics in our experiments. They can be expressed as follows: Let P^* be a set of uniformly distributed points along the PF. Let A be an approximation to the PF. The metrics GD and IGD of the set A are respectively defined as:

$$\mathrm{GD}(A, P^*) = \frac{1}{|A|}\sqrt{\sum_{i=1}^{|A|} d_i^2} \tag{13}$$

$$\mathrm{IGD}(A, P^*) = \frac{1}{|P^*|}\sqrt{\sum_{i=1}^{|P^*|} \tilde{d}_i^2} \tag{14}$$

where d_i ($\tilde{d}_i$) is the Euclidean distance between the i-th member in the set A (P^*) and its nearest member in the set P^* (A). GD can only reflect the convergence of an algorithm, while IGD combines the information of convergence and diversity into a whole. For both of two metrics, smaller values means better quality.

Because there are different fitness functions and ensemble ranking schemes that could be used, several variants of the implemented methods will be concerned in the experiments, which are listed in Table 2. All the algorithms are run 30 times independently for each problem, and average results are recoded.

Table 2: Variants of the implemented methods.

Variant	Fitness Function	Ensemble Ranking
EFR-1	L^p Norm	LR
EFR-2	Tchebycheff	LR
EFR-3	PBI	LR
EFR-4	PBI	MR
EFR-5	PBI	AR

4.1 Comparison between EFR methods

In this subsection, we will make the comparison between EFR variants to examine the influence of alternative fitness functions and ensemble ranking schemes. The shared parameters of EFR methods are shown in Table 3. Specially, for L^p norm, p is set to be 3, and for PBI function, θ is set to be 5. To ensure a fair comparison, for each problem, we limit the number of objective function evaluations to a maximum of 100,000 for all algorithms.

Table 3: Parameter settings of EFR variants

Parameter	Value
Population size (N)	200
Number of fitness functions (K)	200
Crossover probability (p_c)	0.9
Mutation probability (p_m)	$1/n$
Distribution index for crossover (η_c)	20
Distribution index for mutation (η_m)	20

Figures 2 and 3 present the average GD and IGD results for DTLZ 1-4 problems respectively. First, it is interesting to note that EFR-3 and EFR-4 nearly always have the same performance on all the considered cases. It may be because the preference of MR and LR is roughly consistent in the situation selecting half of the solutions from a population, although they lead to different subtle rankings.

From Figure 2, for DTLZ1 and DTLZ2, EFR-5 performs the best while EFR-2 seems to be the worst; EFR-3 is merely better than EFR-2 and they differs only a bit for DTLZ2. For DTLZ3, EFR-5 still exhibits the advantage for the instances that the number of objective is not very high; but for instances more than 8 objectives, EFR-1 and EFR-3 are the winners while EFR-5 becomes the worst except for the 14-objective instance, where EFR-5 outperforms EFR-1 and EFR-2; the results of EFR-1 and EFR-2 are distinguishable only for instances having more than 14 objectives, where EFR-2 is outperformed by EFR-1 very weakly. For DTLZ4, the situation is similar to that for DTLZ3; but EFR-5 performs worst for instances with more than 6 objectives all the while; for instances with more than 14 objectives, EFR-2 appears sightly better than EFR-1 on the contrary to that in DTLZ3.

From Figure 3, for DTLZ1, there is no obvious difference between EFR-1, EFR-3 and EFR-4 and they perform better overall than the other two; EFR-2 is better than EFR-5 for instances with less than 16 objectives, but is outperformed by EFR-5 when the number of objectives further increases. For DTLZ2, the performance of EFR-5 is almost the worst when the number of objectives is no more than 14, but when the objective gets larger, EFR-2 outperforms both EFR-1 and EFR-2; EFR-1 seems better than EFR-2 for instances with high number of objectives; EFR-3 and EFR-4 still show the superiority over the others. For both DTLZ3 and DTLZ4, the performance of EFR variants can be roughly ranked. Specially, for DTLZ3, EFR-3 and EFR-4 perform best, following by EFR-1 and EFR-2, while EFR-5 is the worst. For DTLZ4, the variants can be separated into three groups, EFR-3 and EFR-4 form the first group which are ranked first; EFR-1 and EFR-2 have the similar performance and are ranked second; EFR-5 still ranks last.

Because GD is a convergence metric and IGD is the metric considering both convergence and diversity, we can make the following summary based on the above results. For fitness functions, PBI seems to be the best choice, L^p norm and Tchebycheff function have no distinct difference on DTLZ 2-4, but for DTLZ1, L^p norm leads to better convergence. As for ensemble ranking schemes, MR and LR nearly show the equivalent overall performance and are better than AR, but AR achieves the best convergence in DTLZ1. It can be safely inferred that the diversity of AR in our framework still needs to be further enhanced.

4.2 Comparison with other methods

In this subsection, we will compare the variant EFR-3 (in the following, call it EFR for short), with two established MOEAs, named as MOEA/D [21] and NSGA-III [7]. MOEA/D is the MOEA based on decomposing a MOP into a number of scalar optimization problems that are simultaneously optimized, which could be easily scaled up for many-objective problems. NSGA-III is a very recent MOEA particulary for many-objective optimization, whose framework is similar to NSGA-II with significant changes in its selection mechanism. The population size N of MOEA/D and NSGA-III are both controlled by an integer H, where $N = C_{H+m-1}^{m-1}$. The chosen value of H for problems with different number of objectives, the resulting population size, and the maximum objective function evaluations are given in Table 4. The settings of the other parameters of MOEA/D and NSGA-III are just according to the original papers. For

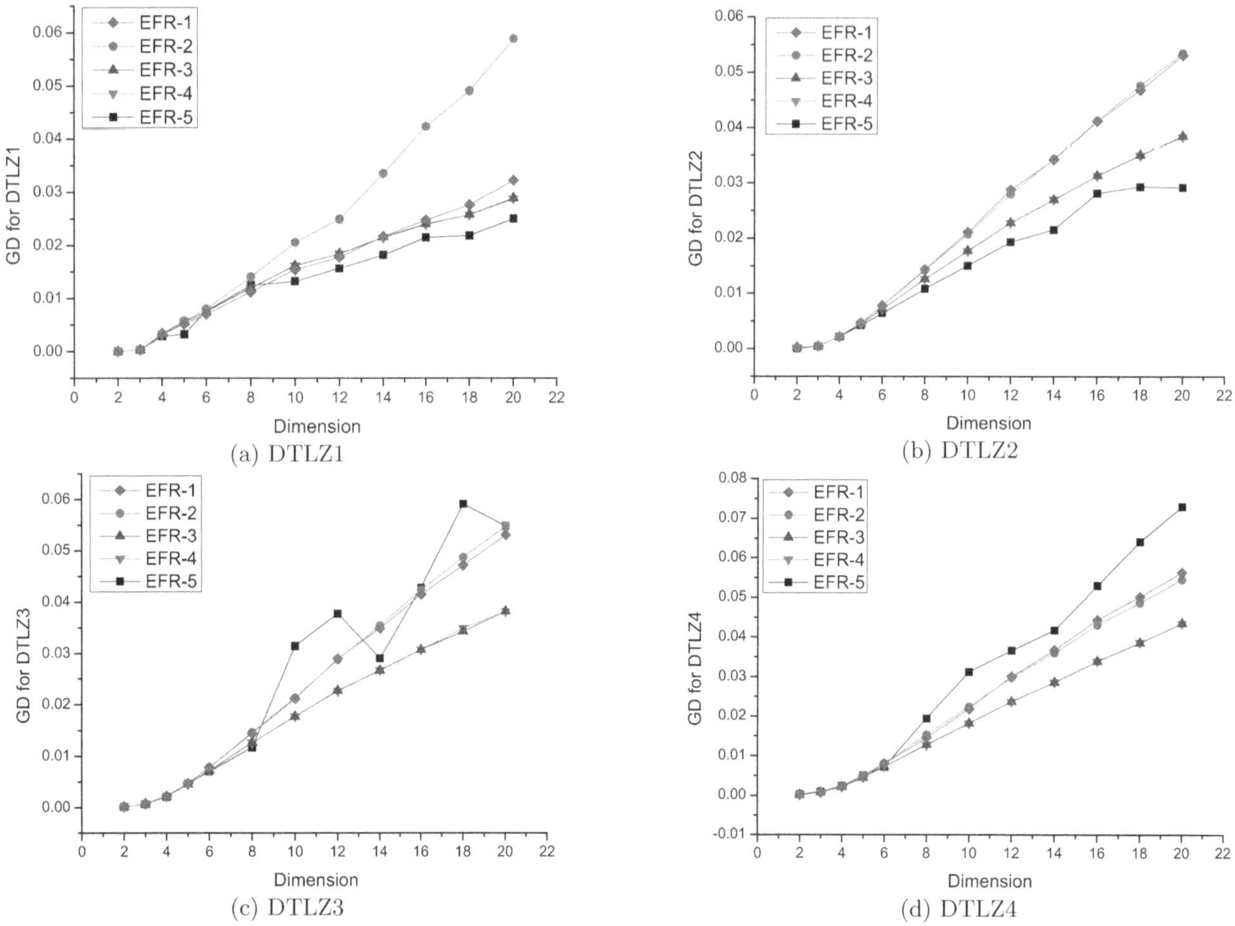

Figure 2: Comparison of the performance of EFR variants on GD metric for DTLZ 1-4 problems with varying number of objectives (dimension). The figures show the average of 30 independent runs each.

the EFR, the population size and maximum objective function evaluations are reset to the same with those in the compared algorithms, the number of fitness functions is set equal to the population size, and the other parameters remain the same with those shown in Table 3. Since IGD could measure both the diversity and convergence in a sense, it is adopted as comparison metric here.

Table 4: Parameters of MOEA/D and NSGA-III.

m	H	N	Function Evaluations
3	19	210	99,960
4	9	220	100,100
5	6	210	99,960
6	5	252	100,044
8	4	330	99,990
10	3	220	100,100
12	3	364	100,100
14	3	560	100,240

Table 5 provides the average IGD of each compared algorithm for DTLZ 1-4 having 3 to 14 objectives. In order to find significant differences, the Wilcoxon signed-rank test [10] is further carried out on the three average results respectively obtained by three algorithms for each instance, and the one that is significantly better than the other two (with the significance level of 0.05) is marked in bold. From Table 5, it can be seen that the proposed EFR significantly outperforms MOEA/D and NSGA-III on all the considered problems with more than four objectives. NSGA-III shows superiority in problems with three and four objectives. To be specific, NSGA-III is significantly better than EFR and MOEA/D on all 3-objective problems, and it is still the winner on all 4-objective problems except for DTLZ3, where EFR is a little better than NSGA-III but there exists no significance. For 3-objective problems, although EFR is worse than NSGA-III, it achieves the competitive performance with respect to MOEA/D. EFR is significantly outperformed by NSGA-III for 4-objective DTLZ1, DTLZ2 and DTLZ4, but the gap between them is not so obvious. In summary, EFR is a very promising alternative for many-objective problems compared with existing state-of-the-art methods.

5. CONCLUSION AND FUTURE WORK

In this paper, we have presented an ensemble fitness ranking (EFR) framework for solving many-objective optimization problems. This framework allows to work with different kinds alternative fitness functions and ensemble ranking schemes. Through the experiments, PBI is found to be the most ideal fitness function, while MR and LR are ranking

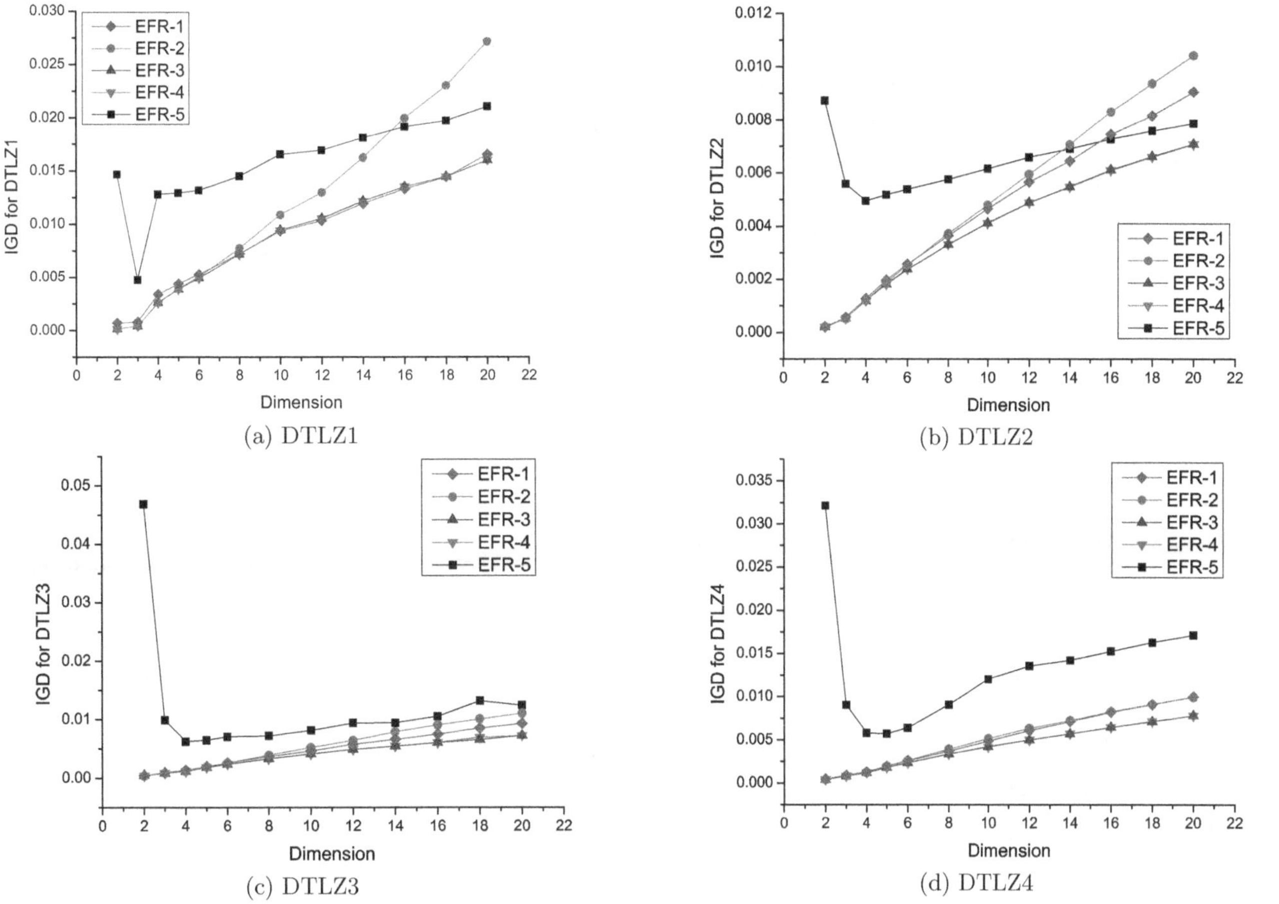

(a) DTLZ1 (b) DTLZ2 (c) DTLZ3 (d) DTLZ4

Figure 3: Comparison of the performance of EFR variants on IGD metric for DTLZ 1-4 problems with varying number of objectives (dimension). The figures show the average of 30 independent runs each.

schemes resulting in similar performance. AR shows good convergence ability as a whole, but its maintenance of diversity needs to be further improved. To verify the effectiveness of our framework, the proposed EFR is compared with MOEA/D and NSGA-III on problems having varying number of objectives. The results show that EFR significantly outperforms MOEA/D and NSGA-III on most instances, e-specially for those with high number of objectives. In the future, we will continue this study in the following aspects. First, we would develop strategies to enhance the diversity of AR in our framework, where the work in [22] may be a useful reference. Second, we want to incorporate the preference into our framework by weighting raking results from different rankers. Lastly, EFR would be tested on broader range of problems to further demonstrate its effectiveness.

Acknowledgment

This work is supported by National Natural Science Foundation of China (Grant No. 61175110), National Basic Research Program of China (973 Program) (Grant No. 2012CB 316305), National S&T Major Projects of China (Grant No. 2011ZX02101-004) and National Banking Information Technology Risk Management Projects of China.

6. REFERENCES

[1] S. F. Adra and P. J. Fleming. Diversity management in evolutionary many-objective optimization. *IEEE Transactions on Evolutionary Computation*, 15(2):183–195, 2011.

[2] R. B. Agrawal, K. Deb, and R. B. Agrawal. Simulated binary crossover for continuous search space. *Complex Systems*, 9(2): 115-148, 1995

[3] P. J. Bentley and J. P. Wakefield. Finding acceptable solutions in the pareto-optimal range using multiobjective genetic algorithms. In *Soft Computing in Engineering Design and Manufacturing*, pages 231–240. Springer, 1998.

[4] N. Beume, B. Naujoks, and M. Emmerich. Sms-emoa: Multiobjective selection based on dominated hypervolume. *European Journal of Operational Research*, 181(3):1653–1669, 2007.

[5] C. A. C. Coello and N. C. Cortés. Solving multiobjective optimization problems using an artificial immune system. *Genetic Programming and Evolvable Machines*, 6(2):163–190, 2005.

[6] D. W. Corne and J. D. Knowles. Techniques for highly multiobjective optimisation: some nondominated points are better than others. In *Proceedings of the 9th annual conference on Genetic and evolutionary computation (GECCO)*, 2007.

Table 5: Comparison of EFR, MOEA/D and NSGA-III on IGD metric.

Problem	m	EFR	MOEA/D	NSGA-III
DTLZ1	3	4.136483E-04	4.633166E-04	**2.938980E-04**
	4	2.522413E-03	5.807972E-03	**2.419834E-03**
	5	**3.795216E-03**	1.678922E-02	4.304645E-03
	6	**4.673733E-03**	2.593178E-02	5.930539E-03
	8	**6.549155E-03**	2.712590E-02	1.384594E-02
	10	**9.327998E-03**	2.383760E-02	2.599091E-02
	12	**9.740158E-03**	3.214111E-02	3.320180E-02
	14	**1.091462E-02**	6.116184E-02	5.230736E-02
DTLZ2	3	5.036636E-04	5.009822E-04	**3.775795E-04**
	4	1.152701E-03	1.739747E-03	**1.100574E-03**
	5	**1.797095E-03**	3.423462E-03	2.013230E-03
	6	**2.256326E-03**	3.751035E-03	2.806929E-03
	8	**3.061871E-03**	4.696051E-03	4.321507E-03
	10	**4.065464E-03**	5.611757E-03	6.315871E-03
	12	**4.552580E-03**	6.117158E-03	7.338335E-03
	14	**4.908524E-03**	6.358814E-03	8.367192E-03
DTLZ3	3	8.184213E-04	8.055299E-04	**6.094970E-04**
	4	1.160800E-03	1.753353E-03	1.170746E-03
	5	**1.793648E-03**	6.031817E-03	2.036958E-03
	6	**2.274413E-03**	6.667546E-03	2.886499E-03
	8	**3.074188E-03**	8.369069E-03	4.811574E-03
	10	**4.086756E-03**	7.918472E-03	9.017786E-03
	12	**4.530450E-03**	9.876872E-03	1.145193E-02
	14	**4.875834E-03**	1.293029E-02	1.817348E-02
DTLZ4	3	8.228233E-04	1.005974E-03	**6.085986E-04**
	4	1.147441E-03	2.509969E-03	**1.100826E-03**
	5	**1.780017E-03**	4.127854E-03	2.014415E-03
	6	**2.266260E-03**	4.587130E-03	2.808462E-03
	8	**3.091705E-03**	5.988025E-03	4.317174E-03
	10	**4.128603E-03**	7.270253E-03	6.161857E-03
	12	**4.734533E-03**	8.459775E-03	7.074542E-03
	14	**5.267423E-03**	9.364443E-03	7.829817E-03

[7] K. Deb and J. Himanshu. An evolutionary many-objective optimization algorithm using reference-point based non-dominated sorting approach, part I: Solving problems with box constraints. *IEEE Transactions on Evolutionary Computation*, in press.

[8] K. Deb, A. Pratap, S. Agarwal, and T. Meyarivan. A fast and elitist multiobjective genetic algorithm: NSGA-II. *IEEE Transactions on Evolutionary Computation*, 6(2):182–197, 2002.

[9] K. Deb, L. Thiele, M. Laumanns, and E. Zitzler. *Scalable test problems for evolutionary multiobjective optimization.* In Evolutionary multi-objective optimization, pages 105–145 Springer, 2005.

[10] J. Demšar. Statistical comparisons of classifiers over multiple data sets. *The Journal of Machine Learning Research*, 7:1–30, 2006.

[11] N. Drechsler, R. Drechsler, and B. Becker. Multi-objective optimisation based on relation favour. In *Evolutionary multi-criterion optimization*, pages 154–166. Springer, 2001.

[12] J. J. Durillo and A. J. Nebro. jmetal: A java framework for multi-objective optimization. *Advances in Engineering Software*, 42(10):760–771, 2011.

[13] P. J. Fleming, R. C. Purshouse, and R. J. Lygoe. Many-objective optimization: An engineering design perspective. In *Evolutionary multi-criterion optimization*, pages 14–32. Springer, 2005.

[14] M. Garza-Fabre, G. T. Pulido, and C. A. C. Coello. Ranking methods for many-objective optimization. In *MICAI 2009: Advances in Artificial Intelligence*, pages 633–645. Springer, 2009.

[15] K. Ikeda, H. Kita, and S. Kobayashi. Failure of pareto-based MOEAs: Does non-dominated really mean near to optimal? In *Proceedings of the IEEE Congress on Evolutionary Computation (CEC)*, 2001.

[16] A. L. Jaimes, L. V. S. Quintero, and C. A. C. Coello. Ranking methods in many-objective evolutionary algorithms. In *Nature-inspired algorithms for optimisation*, pages 413–434. Springer, 2009.

[17] A. Jaszkiewicz. MOMH multiple-objective metaheuristics. Apr. 2013. [Online]. Available: http://home.gna.org/momh/index.html.

[18] S. Kukkonen and J. Lampinen. GDE3: The third evolution step of generalized differential evolution. In *IEEE Congress on Evolutionary Computation (CEC)*, 2005.

[19] S. Kukkonen and J. Lampinen. Ranking-dominance and many-objective optimization. In *IEEE Congress on Evolutionary Computation (CEC)*, 2007.

[20] M. Laumanns, L. Thiele, K. Deb, and E. Zitzler. Combining convergence and diversity in evolutionary multiobjective optimization. *Evolutionary computation*, 10(3):263–282, 2002.

[21] H. Li and Q. Zhang. Multiobjective optimization problems with complicated pareto sets, MOEA/D and NSGA-II. *IEEE Transactions on Evolutionary Computation*, 13(2):284–302, 2009.

[22] M. Li, J. Zheng, K. Li, Q. Yuan, and R. Shen. Enhancing diversity for average ranking method in evolutionary many-objective optimization. In *Parallel Problem Solving from Nature, PPSN XI*, pages 647–656. Springer, 2010.

[23] A. López Jaimes and C. A. Coello Coello. Study of preference relations in many-objective optimization. In *Proceedings of the 11th Annual conference on Genetic and evolutionary computation (GECCO)*, 2009.

[24] R. C. Purshouse and P. J. Fleming. On the evolutionary optimization of many conflicting objectives. *IEEE Transactions on Evolutionary Computation*, 11(6):770–784, 2007.

[25] D. A. Van Veldhuizen. Multiobjective evolutionary algorithms: classifications, analyses, and new innovations. Technical report, DTIC Document, 1999.

[26] Q. Zhang and H. Li. MOEA/D: A multiobjective evolutionary algorithm based on decomposition. *IEEE Transactions on Evolutionary Computation*, 11(6):712–731, 2007.

[27] E. Zitzler and S. Künzli. Indicator-based selection in multiobjective search. In *Parallel Problem Solving from Nature-PPSN VIII*, pages 832–842. Springer, 2004.

[28] E. Zitzler, M. Laumanns, and L. Thiele. SPEA2: Improving the strength pareto evolutionary algorithm. In *Proceedings of Evolutionary Methods for Design, Optimisation and Control with Application to Industrial Problems*, pages 95–100, 2001.

There and Back Again: Gene-Processing Hardware for the Evolution and Robotic Deployment of Robust Navigation Strategies

David M. Bryson*
BEACON Center
Michigan State University
East Lansing, Michigan, USA
+1 (517) 884-2555
brysonda@egr.msu.edu

Aaron P. Wagner*
BEACON Center
Michigan State University
East Lansing, Michigan, USA
+1 (517) 884-2555
wagner@metsci.com

Charles Ofria
Computer Science and Engineering
Michigan State University
East Lansing, Michigan, USA
+1 (517) 884-2562
ofria@egr.msu.edu

ABSTRACT

Navigation strategies represent some of the most intriguing examples of complex and intelligent behaviors in nature. Accordingly, they have been the focus of extensive research in animal behavior and in evolutionary robotics. However, engineering successes in harnessing the evolutionary dynamics that shape sophisticated navigation strategies remain limited. Here we describe a novel gene-processing architecture for digital organisms that enables the evolution of central-place-foraging strategies, such as those seen in honeybees and striped hyena. While previous studies have evolved navigation de novo, the resulting algorithms have been relatively fragile and difficult to translate into physical systems. In contrast, the strategies evolved in this study are highly congruous with those seen in nature: a single evolved foraging strategy incorporates periods of directed travel, fixed pattern search, cue response, and reorientation when outcomes do not match expected results. Additionally, the genetic architecture enabled rapid extraction of the underlying behavioral algorithm and transference to a robotic system, proving to be robust to issues of noise and scale that commonly plague such attempts. Accordingly, we demonstrate that the flexibility and interpretability of the new gene-processing hardware readily facilitate the creation, study, and utilization of naturalistic and deployable algorithms for functionally complex behaviors.

Categories and Subject Descriptors

D.2.2 [**Software Engineering**]: Design Tools and Techniques – *Evolutionary prototyping.* I.2.9 [**Computing Methodologies**]: Robotics – *Autonomous vehicles.*

General Terms

Algorithms, Design, Reliability.

*These authors contributed equally to this work.

GECCO'14, July 12–16, 2014, Vancouver, BC, Canada.
ACM 978-1-4503-2662-9/14/07.
http://dx.doi.org/10.1145/2576768.2598363

Keywords

Genetic architecture. Robustness. Navigation. Avida. Robotics. Autonomy. Behavior.

1. INTRODUCTION

Engineering has a long tradition of attempting to emulate the behaviors and intellectual capacities of biological organisms in robotic and autonomous systems [1]. Evolutionary computation takes the next step: instead of mimicking the specific behaviors, it replicates the process that produced those behaviors, with a goal of finding solutions that work more effectively with their hardware. However, it remains challenging to evolve engineered systems with the complexity and flexibility of the biological systems that originally inspired them. For example, if one attempts to evolve navigation strategies to a fixed target, fixed travel paths tend to emerge, instead of something more flexible and responsive [2,3]. Even when there is variability in the requirements, static strategies still often dominate, even if they produce only limited success [4]. While such results do offer insights into potential approaches for addressing highly specified engineering tasks, they do little in the way of contributing broadly applicable algorithms or toward furthering our understanding of intelligent behaviors. Consequently, such results fail to fully capture the potential of evolution for furthering engineering, and determining a method to consistently produce flexible and intelligent responses has become an important goal.

Similarly, a major goal of biological research is to understand the processes that favor the evolutionary emergence of adaptive complexity and modulate the functional expression of responsive behaviors. Thus, studies that contribute to the aims of both biology and engineering are those focused on the patterns and processes involved in the evolutionary emergence of responsive traits (e.g., navigation), not purely functional ones (e.g., locomotion or motility). For example, what are the most effective architectures that permit or promote the evolution of truly intelligent systems, such as systems that can predict and respond to conditions beyond those they are explicitly engineered to deal with? Can we evolve these systems in an open-ended manner, avoiding the assumptions and inherent restraints of engineering them? If so, what environments favor their evolution?

As a flexible platform for investigating the evolutionary patterns and processes involved in producing complex traits, the digital evolution software platform Avida [5] remains the most widely used. One advantage of Avida is that the von Neumann style genetic architectures of the agents in the evolving populations provide easier algorithmic transparency, enabling a deep understanding of the evolved solutions. Accordingly, Avida has been used to study the evolution of, and algorithms supporting, simple forms of memory [3], gradient and path following [4,6], cooperation [7,8], division of labor [9], and other complex behaviors [10-13].

The genetic hardware of an evolving system is critical in determining the evolutionary potential of populations [14]. Digital evolution in Avida has been shown to be incredibly robust to minor changes in genetic architecture [15], allowing for fruitful exploration of new design approaches. Accordingly, prior work has shown that some architectural modifications can allow populations to better adapt to their environment, both more quickly and with greater long-term success. For example, hardware traits such as enhanced evolvable control of regulatory interactions between genetic instructions and portions of genomes, can allow populations to better adapt to their environment, both more quickly and with greater long-term success [16].

Here we describe a new genetic architecture for Avida incorporating design elements for the evolutionary creation of more flexible and modular genomes. In particular, the design includes enhanced capacities for genetic execution flow control, parallel operations, and coordination. This design philosophy was predicated on the idea that, just as regulatory mechanisms support complex behaviors in nature, incorporating these elements into Avida would better enable the selective execution of genomic code based on environmental stimuli. Thus these architectural features were expected to advance the evolution of intelligent stimulus-response behavioral algorithms and facilitate high levels of cognitive decision-making. We show that these expanded regulation capabilities do support the rapid evolution of more sophisticated, intelligent, naturalistic, and responsive behaviors in a dynamic and challenging foraging and navigation environment. Moreover, the algorithms underlying these behaviors were readily transferred to a simple real-world robot, seemingly unaffected by the typical 'reality-gap' issues of over-fit strategies.

2. DESIGN

In order to describe and measure the performance of the gene-based 'GP8' hardware, we compare it to three other Avida architectures, described here.

2.1 Heads Architecture

The Heads instruction set architecture is the default virtual CPU design in Avida. It consists of a von Neumann style design, featuring a single memory space containing the instructions of the genomic program. The 26 standard instructions operate on three 32-bit registers, four memory space pointers (called heads), two stacks, and input/output buffers. Accordingly, a typical organism consists of a virtual CPU executing a genomic program that interacts with the environment to collect resources and produces an instruction-by-instruction copy of itself, after which the copy is split to create an offspring organism. The virtual CPU in the Heads architecture executes a single instruction per cycle. Each organism is granted 30 CPU cycles per update.

2.2 Threaded Heads-EX Hardware

The Heads-EX hardware [16] extends Heads architecture, adding additional registers, enhanced instruction argument semantics, and multiple new conditional and flow control instructions. The instruction set options include additional instructions such as those enabling thread creation and coordination, environment sensing, and movement [e.g., as in 17-19]. The threading instructions allow genomic programs to activate multiple threads of execution in the virtual CPU by executing the 'fork' instruction. Each thread maintains its own set of registers and a local stack. During each cycle, the CPU executes a single instruction for each thread, in the order that the threads are created. The thread coordination instructions allow threads to pause their own execution until certain values appeared in the registers of other threads.

2.3 BCR (Behavioral Co-Routine) Hardware

The BCR hardware extends the Heads-EX hardware, adding co-routine pre-processing, instruction functional classes, and CPU cycle micro-operations. The BCR virtual CPU pre-processes the genomic program into discrete co-routines in independent memory spaces. Each co-routine is executed in its own thread. We modified the existing genomic execution hardware to allow for separate regulatory control mechanisms for distinct functional classes. Specifically, instructions governing reproduction, sensory input, and behavioral actions were grouped into the three functional classes, respectively. Behaviorally distinct co-routines, for example a routine dedicated exclusively to reproduction, can run completely in parallel with other operations. Execution of functionally classed instructions is limited such that only one co-routine can execute an instruction from each class per cycle. Subsequent attempts to execute a functionally classed instruction during a given CPU cycle cause the thread to block until the next cycle. We altered CPU cycle processing to execute up to 20 non-classed instructions (micro-operations) per cycle, permitting data processing and decision-making to be more environmentally responsive.

2.4 GP8 (Gene-Processing) Hardware

The GP8 gene-processing hardware relaxes many execution restrictions from the BCR hardware, resulting in the pre-processed genome segments performing as multiple independent subprograms (genes) that are concurrently executed on independent threads. Each thread executes up to 20 micro-operations that may perform any combination of computation, decision-making, sensing, action queuing, and regulation instructions. Three actions, heading rotation, forward movement, and resource intake (eating), may be queued during micro-operation execution. These actions, which interact with and can alter the environment, remain limited to once per CPU cycle. The queued actions are performed at the end of a given cycle, so that any number of genes may manipulate organism behavior without stalling, and as such preventing the starvation of certain threads that could occur with functionally classed instructions in the BCR hardware.

3. APPLICATION

Our explicit goal in this work was to test the potential of gene-based genetic architectures for facilitating the evolution of cognitive decision makers. Specifically, we targeted the evolutionary development of behaviorally plastic organisms that could navigate using strategies that include modifying activities in response to changing conditions. To that end, we evolved BCR and GP8 digital populations challenged with a central-place foraging problem, in which foragers must travel to find food and return to a central place for reproduction (Fig. 1A) [20]. We then developed and used new tools to dissect the evolved behavioral algorithms. Finally, we demonstrated the effectiveness of those algorithms via deployment in a real-world robot.

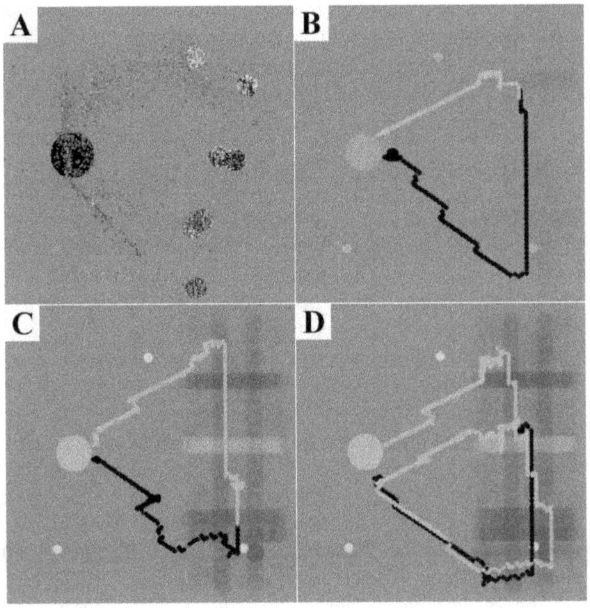

Fig. 1. Modular genetic architectures facilitate the evolution of naturalistic foraging and navigation strategies. (**A**) the full BCR population from Box 1, showing agents traveling from the central birth den (large black circle) out to distant food resources (mid-sized grey and white circles), returning home to reproduce (see also Supplementary Movie 1). Organisms (small points) are colored to reflect their current food preferences. Shading of the food resources reflects the current balance between consumption by the foraging organisms and regrowth. While the organism can evolve to look for and process information about the food resource it targets, the central den is not detectable from afar. **B-D** show foraging paths for single organisms pulled from the population. Outbound paths are shown in black (traces began shortly after the organisms left the den), while the inbound path after feeding is white. Each of the seven available food resources move along semi-random paths within the rightmost third of the environment. Cumulative travel paths are shown as colored bands. The darker resource bands apparent in C and D reflect the longer time the agents spent foraging. Note that the organism in D discovered the den only after returning to the resource field a second time to reorient and recalibrate its approach.

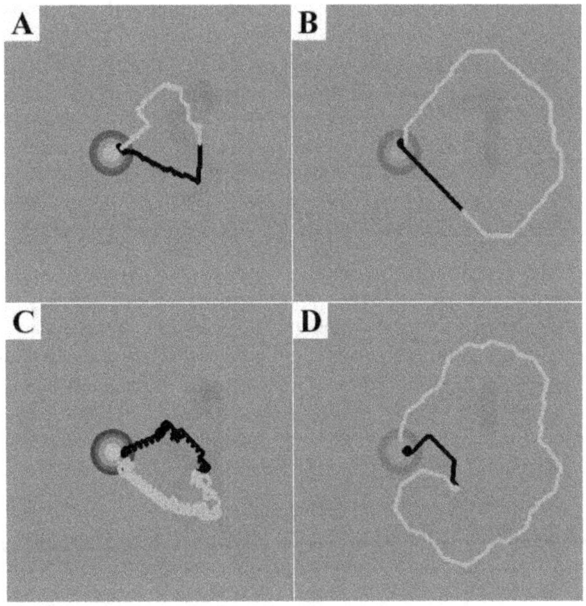

Fig. 2. Greater independence of gene execution flows improved the evolvability and robustness of behavioral algorithms. Shown are example foraging route traces for four organisms from different GP8 populations that evolved to look for, process, and respond to information about distant food resources (colored points and bands), and then reliably return to a den site (multi-ringed target) where they can reproduce. The den was not detectable from afar, requiring organisms to navigate back to it without direct sensory input. A and B correspond with the dissected organisms in Box 2 (A = from population 117, B = from population 178). The lighter shading of the food resources reflects the shorter foraging times for these organisms relative to the BCR populations. Overall, navigation strategies incorporated an exceptionally naturalistic and robust mix of fixed pattern search, response to cues, and context-dependent behaviors.

3.1 Evolutionary Environment

Each of the 90 evolutionary trials of each genetic architecture was conducted for 200,000 updates in a simulated environment containing spatio-temporally dynamic food resources ($\approx$ 2,200 generations for BCR populations and 2,000 for GP8 populations). Mutation rates were set to 0.0015 per site per divide with 0.00075 insertion and deletion probabilities. Populations were limited to 2000 organisms. When a birth would have caused the population to exceed that limit, another member of the population was removed. Maximum age limits were set to 30,000 classed operations (defined in the hardware descriptions, above) before organisms were removed. New organisms were born into the cell faced by their parent, with a random orientation. An unlimited number of organisms could occupy any cell.

World sizes in BCR trials were set to 251 X 251 cells. In the GP8 populations, the world was extended to 501 X 501 cells to repress any evolved behaviors dependent on using the walls around the world boundary edges as navigational cues (though this behavior was never detected). Similarly, in BCR, there were an additional three 'landmark' resources included in the environment (visible in Fig. 1). As with the boundary walls, we detected no evolved strategies that relied on these landmarks. Each evolutionary world contained seven discrete food resources and one 'den' resource. Each food resource had a diameter of 19 cells, while the den resource had a diameter of 39 cells. Each cell of a food resource could contain up to one full unit of food. When an organism fed from a full cell, the resource was fully consumed (depleted to a value of zero), regrowing at a rate of 0.05 units per update. Food values were independent across cells. Den and landmark resources were not consumable.

In addition to the effects of depletion, food resource conditions were kept dynamic by placing them in motion within a set boundary area. Initially, in order to allow the naïve ancestor to survive, each food resource was centered over the den. Over evolutionary time, however, the boundary area was periodically moved to the east of the den. Simultaneously, the width and height of the boundary area was slowly expanded. The final boundary area, reached after 52,500 updates of progressive change, was the area between 65 and 170 cells west of the den, extending 125 cells above and below the world vertical centerline.

Movement of each resource was semi-random and independent. At the start of each update, a resource was moved 10 cells along its current direction of travel. If movement would push the outer edge of a resource beyond the boundary area, that resource would 'bounce' by reversing travel direction. Additionally, every 100 updates, the direction of movement would be randomly reassigned, including from options for no change and for no movement. Full descriptions of these relatively new resource options in Avida are available in the code documentation.

In order to feed from a resource, organisms had to set an internal 'forage-target' state to the value that matched the targeted food resource (0 thru 6). By default, all organisms are born into a neutral 'juvenile' state with a forage-target not matching any resource. Execution of a 'set-forage-target' instruction changed the organism's forage-target to that specified by the value in the instruction's modifying register. Organisms' could reset this forage preference state at any time during their lifetime.

To permit the evolution of behavioral algorithms for finding food, each hardware included a visual sensor instruction. Dependent on the instruction mutating into the genome and supporting mutations for controlling sensing behavior, via these sensors, organisms could collect data about their surrounding environment, including characteristics of visible resources, objects (walls, landmarks), and other organisms within a 45-degree cone in the faced direction. However, the den site was never visible to these sensors (GP8 organisms did have a simple instruction for returning true/false for whether they were currently standing on a den cell). Sensor distances were limited to a maximum of 100 cells.

Box 1. BCR & Robot Evolved Algorithm

```
while (true) {
  if not resource in front:
    rotate counter-clockwise 45 degrees
  if not resource in front:
    rotate counter-clockwise 45 degrees
  if not resource in front:
    move
    rotate counter-clockwise 45 degrees
  else:
    move
  switch (current heading):
    north:      keep current heading
    northeast:  rotate to face east
    east:       rotate to face south
    southeast:  rotate to face southwest
    south:      rotate to face north
    southwest:  rotate to face east
    west:       rotate to face south
    northwest:  rotate to face west
  if not resource in front:
    rotate counter-clockwise 45 degrees
  else:
    switch (current heading):
      north:      keep current heading
      northeast:  rotate to face east
      east:       rotate to face south
      southeast:  rotate to face southwest
      south:      rotate to face north
      southwest:  rotate to face east
      west:       rotate to face south
      northwest:  rotate to face west
  move
  move
  move
}
```

The full behavior of the visual sensor is described in the Avida documentation. In brief, the sensor mechanism was explicitly designed to allow high levels of flexibility in terms of evolved visual strategies and expressed visual behaviors. Thus, evolution could produce capacities for selectively collecting data on different resource types (including food and other organisms) and at different distances, while also choosing between counts of visible objects (of the specified type), or simply gathering data on the closest visible object or a specific instance of the object type (e.g., food resource #1). As outputs, among other data, the sensor returned integers representing counts of objects, values of objects (e.g., level of food resource), and distance to the nearest of the objects. In effect, the sensors were designed to allow evolution to produce organisms that could selectively process a perfect representation of the visual field. In practice, however, these sensory capacities are extremely complex. Thus, most initial evolutionary attempts to collect sensory data are certain to involve collection of irrelevant data, not to mention the challenge of appropriately processing data once gathered.

We initialized each evolutionary trial with two simple, identical organisms that randomly moved about the environment, blindly attempting to collect resources, copy their genomes, and reproduce. In BCR, movement was limited to one step per update. Organisms were required to have consumed one unit of any food resource before reproducing. Additionally, they were required to be in one of the communal den cells. Thus, all organisms were faced with the challenges of being born at the den, needing to find and move to food resources, successfully consuming resources from a 'full' cell, and returning back to a den they could not see.

We used Avida version 2.13 for all experiments. Data were post-processed using Python 2.7.1. Plots were generated using R version 2.15.2 using the ggplot2 and boot libraries.

3.2 Robot Description

Our test robot was an Arduino UNO controlled DFRobot two-wheel drive 'turtle' platform driven with a Seeedstudio Motor Shield V2.0, using a Freescale Semiconductor MAG3110 triple axis magnetometer (SparkFun SEN-10619 breakout board) for cardinal direction mapping. The 'visual' sensor was emulated with a MaxBotix LV-MaxSonar-EZ0 ultrasonic range finder.

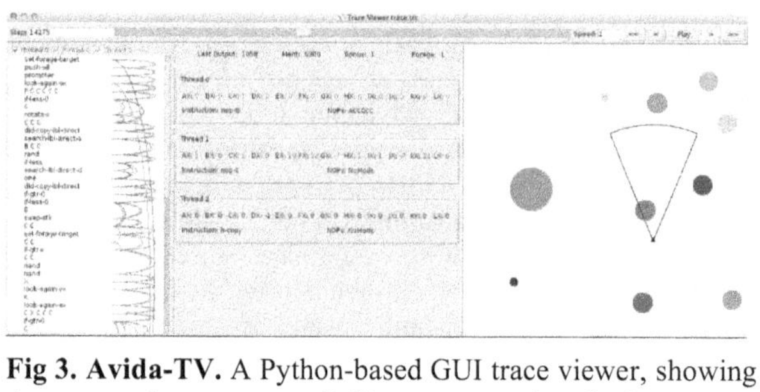

Fig 3. Avida-TV. A Python-based GUI trace viewer, showing the genomic program (left), current virtual CPU state (middle), and current environment state (right). The environment view shows the organism (black arrow) and its visual field (black outline), the resources (medium colored circles), the nest (large gray circle), and stationary landmarks (small colored circles).

3.3 Algorithm Extraction

Avida contains flexible recording methods that enable experimenters to collect detailed information about instruction execution, organism location, and resource availability. We used these recording tools to gather full lifetime traces of organisms from successful populations. We stepped through these instruction traces using Avida-TV (a GUI trace viewer, see Fig. 3), analyzing information intake, decision making, and actions. The resulting distilled behavioral algorithms from a BCR organism and two GP8 organisms are shown in Boxes 1 and 2, respectively.

3.4 Results with New Architectures

The central-place foraging task presented by the environment posed formidable challenges, from evolving vision for finding food to evolving navigation skills to get back to the den. When utilizing the Heads-EX architecture, all 90 trial populations invariably failed to survive the initial boundary area expansions. The BCR architecture demonstrated the first surviving populations, with 10 out of the 90 trials. Of those ten surviving populations, eight utilized fixed-pattern, non-responsive strategies that remain constant regardless of resource conditions. Two of the populations exhibited truly responsive strategies, with organisms actively altering navigational trajectories based on the environment. The GP8 architecture dramatically increased the frequency survival (73 out of 90), as well as the frequency of the evolution of responsive strategies (42 out of 73).

Analysis of the algorithms underlying these evolved foraging behaviors quickly revealed that they are remarkably lightweight, both behaviorally and computationally. For example, the navigation strategy from the BCR organism shown in Figure 1 can be broken into four spatial-context-dependent stages: (1) traveling southeast while resources are visible ahead and to the upper left. (2) Heading due north, feeding along the way, while resources are consistently visible ahead. (3) Alternating between stepping north, west, and south while resources are visible to the south. (4) Heading southwest toward the den provided that resources remain visible to the east. If the den isn't reached by the time all food resources are completely out of sight, the organism recalibrates and reorients itself by returning to the resource field. While this behavior is functionally complex, all actions are governed by reactions to only two values: the current heading and the visibility of resources.

Box 2. GP8 Evolved Behavioral Algorithms

Pop 117:

```
while (true) {
  if resource in front: rotate counter-clockwise 45 degrees
  move
  if resource in front: rotate counter-clockwise 45 degrees
  move
  if resource in front: rotate counter-clockwise 45 degrees
  else:
    switch (current heading):
      north:      keep current heading
      northeast:  rotate to face east
      east:       rotate to face south
      southeast:  rotate to face southwest
      south:      rotate to face north
      southwest:  rotate to face east
      west:       rotate to face south
      northwest:  rotate to face west
  move
}
```

Pop 178:

```
loop_count = 0
while (true) {
  loop_count += 1
  rotate clockwise 45 degrees
  move
  if have eaten: rotate clockwise 45 degrees
  move
  if resource in front: rotate counter-clockwise 45 degrees
  else: rotate counter-clockwise 90 degrees
  move
  if loop_count == 15:
    loop_count = 0
    if resource in front: rotate counter-clockwise 45 degrees
    else: rotate counter-clockwise 90 degrees
    move
  if have eaten: rotate clockwise 45 degrees
  move
}
```

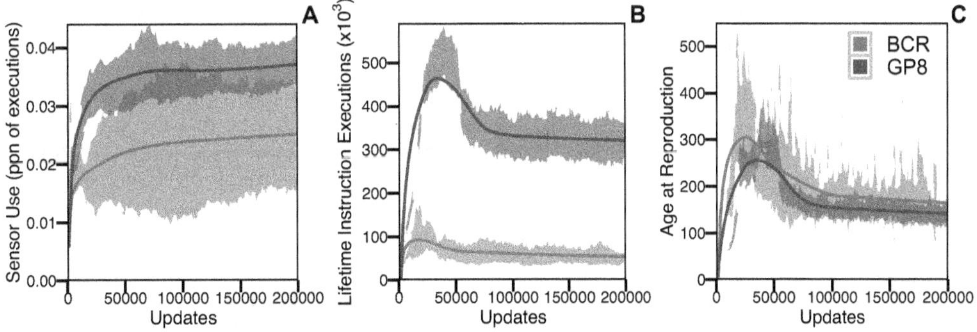

Fig. 4. Flexibility in genetic architectures permits rapid evolution of informed strategies. While sensory intake increased steadily over evolutionary time (A) for both hardwares, evolved strategies were progressively more effective at reducing the duration of foraging trips, as measured by age at reproduction (C; in updates) or number of instructions executed (B). Note that the design of the GP8 architectures enables more instruction executions per update because of instruction queuing vs gene stalling in BCR. Lines are LOESS fits. Shaded regions indicate bootstrapped 95% confidence intervals. The resource field boundary area, which was moved progressively farther from the den, reached its furthest and final point at 52,500 updates.

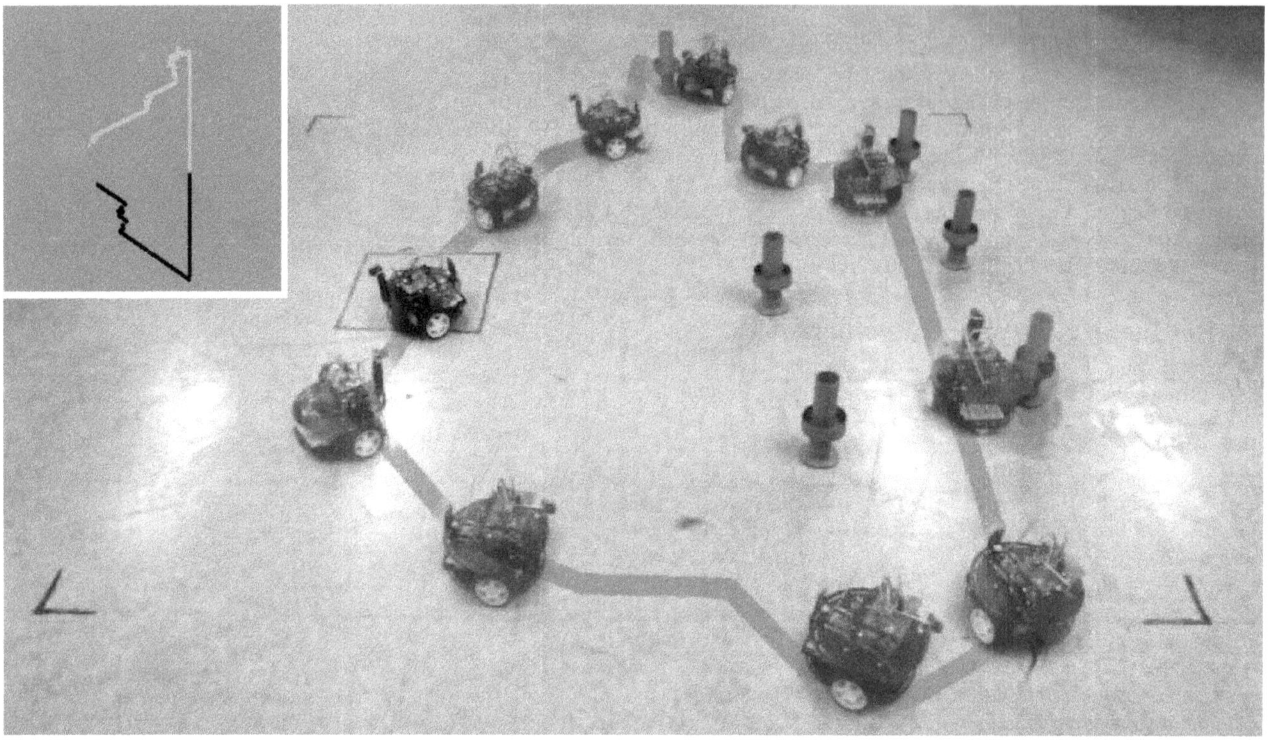

Fig. 5. Composite depiction of the test robot's navigation path. The robot starts off in the nest (outlined square), navigating toward and through the resource field (green towers), following the blue highlighted path. The corner symbols demarcate the ultrasonic sensor interference buffer zone. The inset depicts a path followed by the source organism within the Avida environment.

The GP8 hardware exhibited populations with similarly lightweight, yet robust navigational strategies. Additionally, two general strategies appeared. The first was similar to the BCR algorithm (Figure 2a and 2c, see also the algorithm for Pop 117 in Box 2 and supplemental Movie 2). The second general approach was state-full, navigating into the resource field prior to successful resource collection, and keeping the resource field at the edge of sight after consumption (Figure 2b and 2d, the algorithm for Pop 178 in Box 2, and supplemental Movie 3).

In general, organisms evolved with the GP8 hardware exhibited substantially increased usage of lifetime CPU cycles compared to the BCR hardware due to the reduction in thread starvation potential (Figure 4b). The increased computation of GP8 organisms allowed for notably increased intake of environment information through the sensor instruction (Figure 4a). This likely contributed substantially to the increased success of GP8 populations. Additionally, GP8 organisms had a somewhat reduced gestation time (Figure 4c), likely conferring a competitive advantage to such organisms.

3.5 Robot Deployment

We directly implemented the algorithm displayed in Box 1 within our test robot using Arduino C++. The robot was then tested in a 6-foot square area (see Figure 5), using lightweight circular towers to emulate resources. The towers obstructed the ultrasonic distance, thus were 'visible' to the robot when the measured distance was less than a set threshold (30 inches north/south or east/west, 42 inches diagonally). Bumping into one of the resource towers was counted as a successful collection. The robot was started in the nest, marked as the black outlined square. Because the robot could not reproduce, as an organism would in Avida, crossing over the nest outline was treated as a successful return to the nest.

A depiction of a successful run is shown in Figure 5 (see supplemental Video 4). The evolved algorithm enabled the robot to successfully navigate southeast from the nest until it was position below the field of resources. At that point, the robot travels north, 'consuming' a resource along the way, until it has left the resource field. The robot reorients and travels southwest until it returns to the nest. The high-level navigation behavior was based completely on the current surroundings, demonstrating robustness to disturbance and noise. For example, when we picked up the robot and moved it into the center of the resources, it reoriented and proceeded back to the nest (see supplemental Video 5). Similarly, the robot was still able to navigate back to the nest when the resource towers were moved during a run (supplemental Video 5). The relative scale of the physical robot to the test environment is vastly different from the evolutionary environment, indicating that the algorithm exhibits a surprising robustness to changes in scale. We confirmed this by testing the robot in a larger, 15-foot square environment, increasing only the ultrasonic detection distance threshold and the length of unit movement (see supplemental Video 6).

4. CONCLUSION

We have shown that flexible hardware architectures, combined with dynamic environments can create pathways for the evolution of intelligent, responsive, and robust navigation strategies. Overall, the new Avida features provided a valuable and viable platform for (1) creating robust and intelligent behavioral rules for robots, (2) testing the efficacy of genetic architectures for favoring behavioral flexibility, and (3) evaluating the effectiveness of environmental designs in evolving functionally and adaptively complex behaviors. Most importantly, in addition to resolving the posed navigation challenge, the strategies evolved here were highly congruous with their natural analogs: in multiple populations, dominant foraging strategies incorporated periods of directed travel, fixed pattern search, cue response, and recalibration and reorientation when outcomes did not match expected results (Fig. 1 & Fig. 2). Many readers who have ever lost a car in a parking lot may appreciate the value of this strategic combination.

Additionally, while many previous studies have also attempted to evolve navigation strategies *de novo*, the resulting algorithms have proved difficult to translate into physical robotic systems. This difficulty is often attributed to the so-called 'reality gap', wherein physical systems diverge from their approximations in simulation. In contrast, using the new Avida architectures developed here, because the evolved navigation behaviors were responsive to general rules about the environment and not fixed to the details of the environment, they were readily transferred to a simple robotic system, proving to be robust to reality gap issues of noise and scale commonly plaguing such attempts.

In natural systems, the most successful solutions are those that ensure survival, regardless of situational noise and variation in the environment. Indeed, evolution is a rich source of robust behaviors in natural systems. Developing reliable methods for such discovery of effective, deployable, and lightweight algorithms in robotics could revolutionize the field. Importantly, the approach demonstrated here reveals that open-ended evolution has the potential to achieve that goal when left unburdened by the biases of human perspective. In particular, considering the simplicity of the deployed hardware and evolved algorithms, our approach highlights the potential of evolving gene-based architectures to generate practical solutions, while also greatly simplifying software and hardware requirements, and associated costs.

5. ACKNOWLEDGMENTS

We thank Matt Allen for developing Avida-TV used in the extraction of the algorithm. We also thank Cliff Bohm for providing the facility used in testing and filming the robot in the large-scale environment. Finally, we would like to thank members of the Michigan State University Digital Evolution Laboratory for fruitful discussions and funding from the BEACON Center for the Study of Evolution in Action.

This material is based in part upon work supported by the National Science Foundation under Cooperative Agreement No. DBI-0939454. Any opinions, findings, and conclusions or recommendations expressed in this material are those of the author(s) and do not necessarily reflect the views of the National Science Foundation.

6. REFERENCES

[1] Nelson AL, Barlow GJ, and Doitsidis L. 2009. Fitness functions in evolutionary robotics: A survey and analysis. *Robotics and Autonomous Systems* 57:345-370.

[2] Elsberry WR, Grabowski LM, Ofria C & Pennock RT. 2009. Cockroaches, drunkards, and climbers: Modeling the evolution of simple movement strategies using digital organisms. *Proceedings of the IEEE Symposium on Artificial Life*, pp. 92-99.

[3] Grabowski LM, Bryson DM, Dyer F, Pennock RT, Ofria C. 2010. Early evolution of memory usage in digital organisms. *Proceedings of the 12th International Conference on Artificial Life*. Odense, Denmark.

[4] Clune J, Ofria C, and Pennock RT. 2007. Investigating the Emergence of Phenotypic Plasticity in Evolving Digital Organisms, *Proceedings of the 2007 European Conference on Artificial Life*, 4648:74-83.

[5] Ofria C, Bryson DM, Wilke CO. 2009. Avida: A software platform for research in computational evolutionary biology. In: Adamatzky A, Komosinski M, editors. *Artificial Life Models in Software*. London, UK: Springer Verlag, London, UK. Second edition.

[6] Grabowski LM, Bryson DM, Dyer FC, Pennock RT, and Ofria C. 2011. Clever creatures: Case studies of evolved digital organisms. *Proceedings of the Proceedings of the 2011 European Conference on Artificial Life*.

[7] Beckmann BE, McKinley PK, Knoester DB, and Ofria C. 2007. Evolution of cooperative information gathering in self-replicating digital organisms. *Proceedings of the First IEEE International Conference on Self-Adaptive and Self-Organizing Systems (SASO)*. Boston, Massachusetts, pp. 65-76.

[8] Knoester DB, McKinley PK, Beckmann B, and Ofria C. 2007. Directed evolution of communication and cooperation in digital organisms, Lecture Notes in Computer Science (*Proceedings of the 2007 European Conference on Artificial Life*) 4648:384-394.

[9] Goldsby HJ, Dornhaus A, Kerr B, and Ofria C. 2013. Task-switching costs promote the evolution of division of labor and shifts in individuality. *Proceedings of the National Academy of Science*.

[10] Beckmann B, Grabowski L, McKinley PK, and Ofria C. 2008. Autonomic software development methodology based on Darwinian evolution (Abstract), *Proceedings of the 5th IEEE International Conference on Autonomic Computing*. Chicago IL, June 2008, pp. 203-204.

[11] Grabowski LM, Elsberry WR, Pennock RT, and Ofria C. 2008. On the evolution of motility and intelligent tactic response. *Proceedings of the ACM Genetic and Evolutionary Computation Conference (GECCO-2008)*. Atlanta GA, pp. 209-216.

[12] Knoester DB, McKinley PK, and Ofria C. 2008. Cooperative network construction using digital germlines, *Proceedings of the ACM Genetic and Evolutionary Computation Conference (GECCO-2008)*. Atlanta GA, July 2008, pp. 217-224.

[13] Beckmann BE & McKinley PK. 2008. Evolution of adaptive population control in multi-agent systems. *Proceedings of the Second IEEE International Conference on Self-Adaptive and Self- Organizing Systems (SASO)*. Venice, Italy, pp. 181–190.

[14] Bryson DM. 2012. The evolutionary potential of populations on complex fitness landscapes. Michigan State University. Ph.D Thesis.

[15] Bryson DM and Ofria C. 2012. Digital evolution exhibits surprising robustness to poor design decisions. *Artificial Life 13: Proceedings of the 13th International Conference on the Simulation and Synthesis of Living Systems*. July 2012, East

Lansing, MI, USA, pages 19-26. MIT Press, Cambridge, MA.

[16] Bryson DM, Ofria C. 2013. Understanding evolution potential in virtual CPU architectures. *PLoS ONE* 8: e83242.

[17] Fortuna MA, Zaman L, Wagner AP, Ofria C. 2013. Evolving Digital Ecological Networks. PLoS Comput Biol 9: e1002928.

[18] Wagner AP, Zaman L, Dworkin I, Ofria C. 2013. Behavioral strategy chases promote the evolution of prey intelligence. *arXiv:1310.1369*.

[19] Lehmann K, Goldman BW, Dworkin I, Bryson DM, Wagner AP. 2013. From cues to signals: evolution of interspecific communication via aposematism and mimicry in a predator-prey system. *arXiv:1309.2852*.

[20] Orians, G. H , and N. E. Pearson. 1979. On the theory of central place foraging. Pages 155-177 in D. J. Horn, R. D. Mitchell, and G. R. Stairs, eds. Analysis of ecological systems. Ohio State University Press, Columbus.

Evolving Neural Networks That Are Both Modular and Regular: HyperNeat Plus the Connection Cost Technique

Joost Huizinga
Evolving AI Lab
Department of Computer Science
University of Wyoming
jhuizing@uwyo.edu

Jean-Baptiste Mouret
ISIR, Université Pierre et Marie Curie-Paris 6
CNRS UMR 7222
Paris, France
mouret@isir.upmc.fr

Jeff Clune
Evolving AI Lab
Department of Computer Science
University of Wyoming
jeffclune@uwyo.edu

ABSTRACT

One of humanity's grand scientific challenges is to create artificially intelligent robots that rival natural animals in intelligence and agility. A key enabler of such animal complexity is the fact that animal brains are *structurally organized* in that they exhibit *modularity* and *regularity*, amongst other attributes. Modularity is the localization of function within an encapsulated unit. Regularity refers to the compressibility of the information describing a structure, and typically involves symmetries and repetition. These properties improve evolvability, but they rarely emerge in evolutionary algorithms without specific techniques to encourage them. It has been shown that (1) modularity can be evolved in neural networks by adding a cost for neural connections and, separately, (2) that the HyperNEAT algorithm produces neural networks with complex, functional regularities. In this paper we show that adding the connection cost technique to HyperNEAT produces neural networks that are significantly more modular, regular, and higher performing than HyperNEAT without a connection cost, even when compared to a variant of HyperNEAT that was specifically designed to encourage modularity. Our results represent a stepping stone towards the goal of producing artificial neural networks that share key organizational properties with the brains of natural animals.

Categories and Subject Descriptors

I.2.6 [**Artificial Intelligence**]: Learning—*Connectionism and neural nets*

Keywords

Artificial Neural Networks; Modularity; Regularity; HyperNEAT; NSGA-II

GECCO'14, July 12–16, 2014, Vancouver, BC, Canada.

ACM 978-1-4503-2662-9/14/07 ...$15.00.
http://dx.doi.org/10.1145/2576768.2598232.

1. INTRODUCTION

An open and ambitious question in the field of evolutionary robotics is how to produce robots that possess the intelligence, versatility, and agility of natural animals. A major enabler of such complexity in animals lies in the fact that their bodies and brains are *structurally organized* in that they exhibit *modularity* and *regularity*, amongst other attributes [22,30].

A network is considered modular if it contains groups of highly interconnected nodes, called modules, which are only sparsely connected to nodes outside the module [8,17,22]. In addition to such topological modularity, an even stronger case for modularity can be made if such topological modules correspond to the performance of sub-functions, a property called *functional modularity* [22].

Theoretical and empirical evidence suggests that modularity speeds up *evolvability*, which is the rate of evolutionary adaptation [1,8,17–19]. Modularity improves evolvability by allowing building blocks (modules) to be rewired for new functions and—because the effects of mutations tend to be confined within a module—by allowing evolution to tinker with one module without global effects [17].

Regularity can be defined as: "the compressibility of the description of the structure" [22]; as a structure becomes more regular, less information is required to describe it. Common forms of regularity include repetition, symmetry and self-similarity. It has been shown that regularity improves both performance and evolvability [5,7,14,15], and increasingly does so on more regular problems [10]. Legged locomotion, for example, can greatly benefit from the reuse of information [5,10,14–16].

Despite the advantages of modularity and regularity, these properties do not naturally emerge in evolutionary algorithms without special techniques to encourage them [8–10, 17]. While these properties enhance evolvability and ultimately performance, such long-term advantages do not typically grant an immediate fitness boost to individuals that exhibit them. Evolution has been shown to forgo long-term benefits in performance and evolvability if there is no short-term benefit [7,37,38].

Encouraging the evolution of modularity has been a longstanding interest in the field, yielding a variety of strategies to promote it [8,12,14,15,17,31,32,35,36]. One general strategy is to design developmental systems featuring encodings biased towards modular structures [14,15,31,32,35]. While effective, these heavily biased encodings often produce networks that adhere very closely to a specific structure, leaving little room to adapt when circumstances require a different topology. Another method was demonstrated by Kashtan and Alon [17], who showed that alternating environments with modularly varying goals can give rise to modular networks. Unfortunately, it can be difficult to define modularly varying goals for many tasks. Moreover, the frequency of alternating between these environments must be finely tuned for the effect to emerge [8, 12]. Espinosa-Soto and Wagner [12] found that modularity can be evolved by selecting for a new task while retaining selection for previously acquired functionalities. However, it is non-trivial to decide on a sequence of sub-tasks that will eventually provide a complex, functionally modular solution to a specific task.

In this paper we will build upon a different, recently published method that yields the evolution of modular networks. In 2013, Clune, Mouret and Lipson showed that applying a cost for network connections leads to modular networks [8], and does so in a wider range of environments than a previous leading method [17]. This *connection-cost technique* (CCT) is biologically plausible, as many connection costs exist in natural networks, such as the cost to build and maintain connections, slower propagation through long connections, and the physical space occupied by long connections [30]. Connection costs may thus help explain the ubiquitous modularity found in natural networks [8, 30]. Furthermore, the CCT is computationally inexpensive and can be easily incorporated into the fitness of any evolutionary algorithm, especially multi-objective algorithms [11].

The most common method for producing regular networks is to use a generative encoding (also called an indirect or developmental encoding) [10, 14–16, 27, 29, 31]. The encoding of an individual defines how its genotype is mapped to its phenotype, and a generative encoding implies an indirect mapping such that elements in the genotype might describe more than just a single element in the phenotype. Generative encodings are often based on natural developmental systems, such as gene regulatory networks, cell division, or chemical gradients, making them more biologically plausible than direct encodings [29]. In generative encodings, compact genomes describe a much larger phenotype via the reuse of genomic information, giving rise to regular structures. In fact, if we consider the genotype as a compression of the phenotype, large phenotypes encoded by small genotypes are regular by definition [22].

To generate regularity we employ the HyperNEAT [27] algorithm, which encodes neural networks with a generative encoding called Compositional Pattern Producing Networks (CPPNs) [26]. CPPNs produce spatial patterns that exhibit regularity with variation (Fig. 1a). These spatial patterns define the connectivity across the geometric layout of nodes, enabling HyperNEAT to produce networks that exhibit structural regularity [9]. This paper demonstrates that the combination of HyperNEAT with the Connection Cost Technique –HyperNEAT-CCT– produces networks that are both modular and regular.

2. METHODS

2.1 HyperNEAT

To generate a network, HyperNEAT requires a geometric layout of nodes (see Fig. 1b-d for the layouts for problems in this paper). Given one of these layouts and a CPPN, the

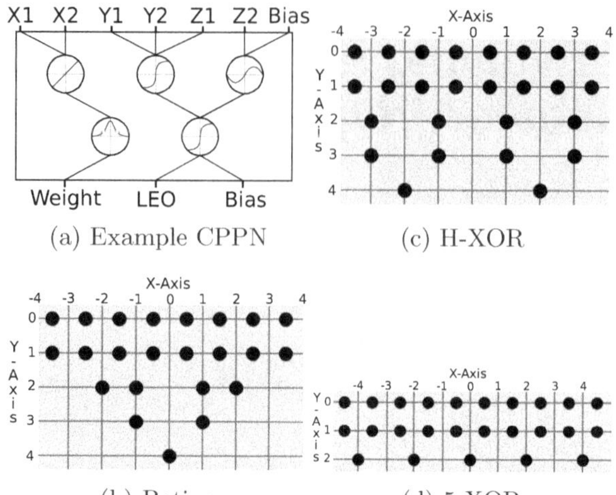

(a) Example CPPN (b) Retina (c) H-XOR (d) 5-XOR

Figure 1: Example CPPN and geometric layouts. *(a)* A CPPN example (see section 2.1). *(b)* Geometric layout for the Retina Problem. *(c)* Geometric layout for the **H-XOR** problem. *(d)* Geometric layout for the **5-XOR** problem. Note that, the z coordinates of all nodes are 0.

connectivity of a network is determined by supplying the x, y, and, z coordinates of two neurons as inputs to the CPPN, after which the weight of the connection between those neurons is set to the *weight* output of the CPPN (Fig. 1a). To set the biases of neurons, the x, y and z coordinates of a single node are supplied to the CPPN together with a null position for the other inputs, and the bias is read from a separate *bias* output node (Fig. 1a).

Because it has been demonstrated that the original HyperNEAT has trouble creating modular networks [4], we have implemented HyperNEAT with the Link-Expression Output (LEO) [36], an additional output neuron determining whether connections are expressed (Fig. 1a). This extension allows HyperNEAT to separate network connectivity from weight patterns, enhancing its ability to evolve sparsely connected, yet functional, sub-units. Connecting a *Gaussian seed* to LEO further increases HyperNEAT's ability to produce modular networks [36].

The Gaussian seed consists of an additional hidden node with a Gaussian activation function, added to the network upon initialization. This node is connected to two inputs by one inhibitory and one excitatory connection, such that their sum represents the difference along one axis. Because the Gaussian activation function produces strong activations only for values close to 0, it will 'fire' only when distances between nodes are short, thus encouraging shorter connections, which may help in discovering modular solutions [36].

However, by planting the Gaussian seed inside the CPPN, there is no guarantee that the seed will be preserved throughout evolution. Whenever there is no immediate benefit for shorter connections, which may occur at any point in a run, the Gaussian seed might disappear completely from the population. We believe that, due to its persistence as a selection pressure, the CCT will generally outperform the locality seed. That is because there exist many situations in which the advantages of short connections are not immediate while solving problems in challenging or changing environments. To test that hypothesis we include a treatment featuring HyperNEAT, LEO, and the Gaussian seed.

In our implementation the seed is exclusively employed for the x inputs, which was reported to be the most successful variant [36]. The weights from the input to the Gaussian seed are -0.6 and 0.6, respectively. The LEO node starts with a sigmoid activation function (a hyperbolic tangent) and a negative bias (-1). A link is expressed when the LEO node returns a value ≥ 0, which provides a behavior similar to the step function used in [36].

HyperNEAT evolves CPPNs genomes via the NeuroEvolution of Augmenting Topologies (NEAT) algorithm [28]. The three important parts of the NEAT algorithm are (1) an intelligent method for crossover between networks, (2) protecting diversity through speciation and (3) complexification, which means starting with networks that have few nodes and connections, and adding them across evolutionary time. In this paper we have implemented HyperNEAT within the PNSGA algorithm from [8], which is programmed within the Sferes2[1] platform [23]. The resulting algorithm differs from NEAT in two ways. First, speciation, which encourages genomic diversity in NEAT, is replaced by a behavioral diversity objective, an adaptation employed in several other publications [20,33]. Second, crossover has been removed for simplicity. We follow previous publications by the authors of HyperNEAT in maintaining the name HyperNEAT to algorithmic variants that have its key components (e.g. CPPNs, complexification, and diversity) [20,33].

2.2 Experiments

There are four different treatments: (1) HyperNEAT, (2) HyperNEAT with the Gaussian Seed (HyperNEAT-GS) [36], (3) HyperNEAT with the Connection Cost Technique (HyperNEAT-CCT), and (4) a direct encoding with the Connection Cost Technique (DirectEncoding-CCT), which is the main algorithm from [8]. Each HyperNEAT treatment features LEO (explained above). All treatments are evolved according to the same evolutionary algorithm described in section 2.3, and every treatment optimizes at least two objectives: performance on the test problem and behavioral diversity. Treatments employing CCT add minimizing connection costs as a third objective.

Behavioral diversity of an individual is calculated by storing the output for every possible input in a binary vector (< 0 is false, ≥ 0 is true) and then taking the average Hamming distance to the binary vector of all other individuals in the population. The connection-cost is calculated as the sum of squared lengths of all connections in the phenotype [8].

2.3 Evolutionary Algorithm

We incorporate the CCT into the multi-objective PNSGA algorithm [8], an extended version of NSGA-II [11]. These algorithms optimize individuals on several tasks at once, and try to preserve and select for all individuals that have some unique trade-off between between objectives, such as being very good at one task but terrible at the others, or being average at all tasks. PNSGA extends NSGA-II by assigning a probability to an objective, which determines the frequency that this objective will factor into selection. By assigning a lower probability to the connection cost objective, we can implement the intuition that performance on the task is more important than a low connection cost. For these experiments, following [8], the probability of the connection cost factoring into a fitness comparison is 25%.

The population is initialized with randomly generated, fully connected networks without hidden nodes, as is prescribed for NEAT [28]. Parents are chosen via tournament selection (tournament size of 2), where the winner is the one that dominates the other, with ties broken randomly.

Parents are copied and the copies are mutated following [8]. The mutation operators: add connection (9%), remove connection (8%), add node (5%), and remove node (4%), are executed at most once. Change weight (10%) and, for CPPNs, change activation function (10%) mutations are performed on a per connection and per node basis. Mutation rates were chosen as the result of a preliminary parameter sweep for high performance. For CPPN-based treatments the activation functions are randomly selected from the following set: Gaussian, linear, sigmoid and sine. Biases are handled by an additional input that always has an activation of 1, meaning the connection between a node and this input determines the bias for that node.

Survivors were selected from the mixed population of offspring and parents. For all experiments the population size was 1000 and the only stopping condition was the maximum number of generations, which was either 25000 or 50000, depending on the problem.

2.4 Test problems

We have tested all treatments on three modular and regular problems from [8]: the **Retina Problem** (originally introduced in [17]), the **5-XOR problem**, and the **Hierarchical XOR problem**.

The **Retina Problem** simulates a simple retina that receives visual input from 8 pixels (Fig. 2a). The left and right halves of the retina may each contain a pattern of interest known as an "object". The patterns, shown in figure 2b, are flattened versions of those from [8] and are defined such that each pattern has a mirror image on the other side of the retina, providing at least one symmetry that can be discovered. The network is tested on all 256 possible patterns and the task for the network is to indicate whether there is (> 0) or is not (< 0) an object present at both the left and the right side of the retina. Note that, while the problem is modularly decomposable, there also exist perfect-performing, nonmodular solutions [8,17].

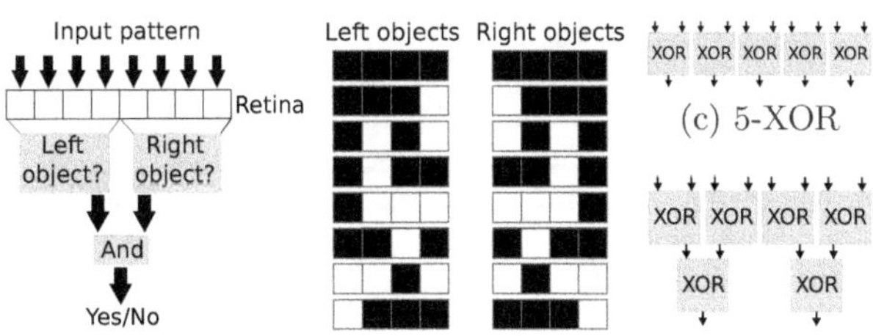

(a) Retina (b) Retina objects (c) 5-XOR (d) H-XOR

Figure 2: Experimental Problems. *(a)* The general structure of the Retina Problem, where the network has to answer whether there is both a left and a right object present. *(b)* The patterns that count as objects for the Retina Problem. *(c)* The **H-XOR** problem, consisting of 2 identical, hierarchically nested XOR problems. *(d)* The **5-XOR** problem, which contains 5 separate XOR problems.

[1]All of the source code used to perform these experiments is available on EvolvingAI.com.

The **5-XOR problem** (Fig. 2c) includes five independent XOR problems that a network must solve in parallel. Performance on this task is the average performance over all five XOR tasks. The problem has regularity because of the repeated XORs and it is modularly decomposable because each XOR can be solved separately.

The **Hierarchical XOR problem** (**H-XOR**) (Fig. 2d) consist of two separable, hierarchically nested XOR problems (the XOR of two XORs). As with the **5-XOR** problem, separability and repetition make that both modularity and regularity are expected to be beneficial in this problem.

2.5 Metrics and Visualizations

When reporting the performance across runs we always consider the 'best' individual of the population, where 'best' means the first individual when sorting on performance first and modularity second. Ties are broken arbitrarily.

The structural modularity of our networks is measured by the widely-used modularity Q-score [24]. For functional modularity we use two measures from [8]: *modular decomposition* and *sub-problems solved*. To calculate modular decomposition we split the network to maximize modularity, as described in [24], with the maximum number of allowed splits equal to the number of sub-problems, and test whether inputs corresponding to different sub-problems end up in different modules. To calculate the number of sub-problems solved we check, for every sub-problem, whether there exists a node in the network that linearly separates the positive and negative classes of that sub-problem. If such a node exists the sub-problem is considered solved.

Following [8], we visualize modularity by moving nodes to the location that minimizes the summed length of their connections, while holding inputs and outputs fixed (Fig. 3c). This optimal neural placement (ONP) visualization is inspired by the fact that neurons in some natural organisms are located optimally to minimize the summed length of the connections between them [2,3]. Nodes in the ONP visualizations are colored according to the best modular split. The maximum number of splits performed depends on the problem: the Retina Problem and **H-XOR** problems are split in two parts, while the **5-XOR** problem is split in 5 parts. Nodes that solve one of the sub-problems are depicted with a large colored border surrounding them. Because modularity differences are not visually apparent at the lower and higher levels (all treatments produce some modular and some non-modular networks) the networks within each treatment are sorted according to their modularity and those around the middle of this list are depicted in this paper.

As mentioned in section 1, regularity can be defined as the compressibility of the data describing a structure. However, since this minimum description length is impossible to calculate exactly [21], we approximate the regularity by compressing the network using the Lempel-Ziv-Welch compression algorithm. To approximate regularity, we write the network weights and biases to an ASCII string, compress it, and test by which fraction the string size was reduced. Because order matters, we repeat this process for 500 different permutations of the weights and biases and take the average as the regularity value.

When visualizing regularity we leave nodes in their actual geometric locations so as not to distort regularities (e.g. Fig. 4). In this visualization we color excitatory connections green and inhibitory connections red. The width of the connection indicates the strength of that connection. Similarly, we depict the bias of each node as a circle inside each node, where green circles indicate a positive bias, red circles indicate a negative bias, and the size of the circle indicates the strength of the bias.

Statistical tests are performed with the Mann-Withney-U rank sum test, unless otherwise specified. Shaded areas in graphs represent 95% bootstrapped confidence intervals of the median, generated by sampling the data 5000 times. Triangles below graphs indicate when values for HyperNEAT-CCT are significantly higher than for the treatment with the corresponding symbol and treatment color ($p < 0.05$).

3. RESULTS

3.1 The Retina Problem

In the retina experiment, the performance of HyperNEAT-CCT is significantly higher at nearly every generation than both HyperNEAT and HyperNEAT-GS (Fig. 3a); even after the medians of all treatments have reached perfect performance, lower-performing runs in the HyperNEAT and HyperNEAT-GS treatments make those treatments perform significantly worse than HyperNEAT-CCT. In terms of modularity, the level for HyperNEAT hardly changes over time, while the modularity of HyperNEAT-CCT progressively increases; the difference becomes significant after 12000 generations (Fig. 3b). The modularity of HyperNEAT-GS, on the other hand, spikes during the first few generations, but then it decreases over time to a significantly lower level than HyperNEAT-CCT (Fig. 3b). This behavior is evidence for our hypothesis that the Gaussian seed may not be an effective way to promote modularity in cases where there is no immediate fitness benefit.

To examine functional modularity we look at the best networks produced after 50000 generations. Our test for problem decomposition, which in this case is having the inputs for the left and right sub-problems in different modules (section 2.5), shows that 75% of the HyperNEAT-CCT runs are left-right modular, which is higher than HyperNEAT, for which 64% of the networks are left-right modular, but the difference is not significant ($p = 0.124$ Fisher's exact test). In addition, when considering the number of sub-problems solved (section 2.5), HyperNEAT-CCT networks solve an average of 0.67 (out of 2) sub-problems, which is significantly ($p = 0.024$) higher than HyperNEAT networks, which solve an average of 0.41 sub-problems.

The differences in modularity are also visually apparent (Fig. 3c). The networks of HyperNEAT-CCT look more modular, demonstrate left-right modularity more often, and have more nodes that solve sub-problems than the HyperNEAT and HyperNEAT-GS networks.

The reason HyperNEAT-CCT performs better is probably because the problem is modular. Additionally, by guiding evolution towards the space of networks with fewer connections, fewer weights need to be optimized. As analyses in [8] revealed, the reason treatments that select for performance alone do not produce modularity despite its benefits is because the benefits of modularity come in the long term, whereas selection acts on immediate fitness benefits. Interestingly, most of the modularity increases occur after the majority of HyperNEAT-CCT runs have achieved near-perfect performance. That is likely because once performance is perfect, or nearly so, the only way a network

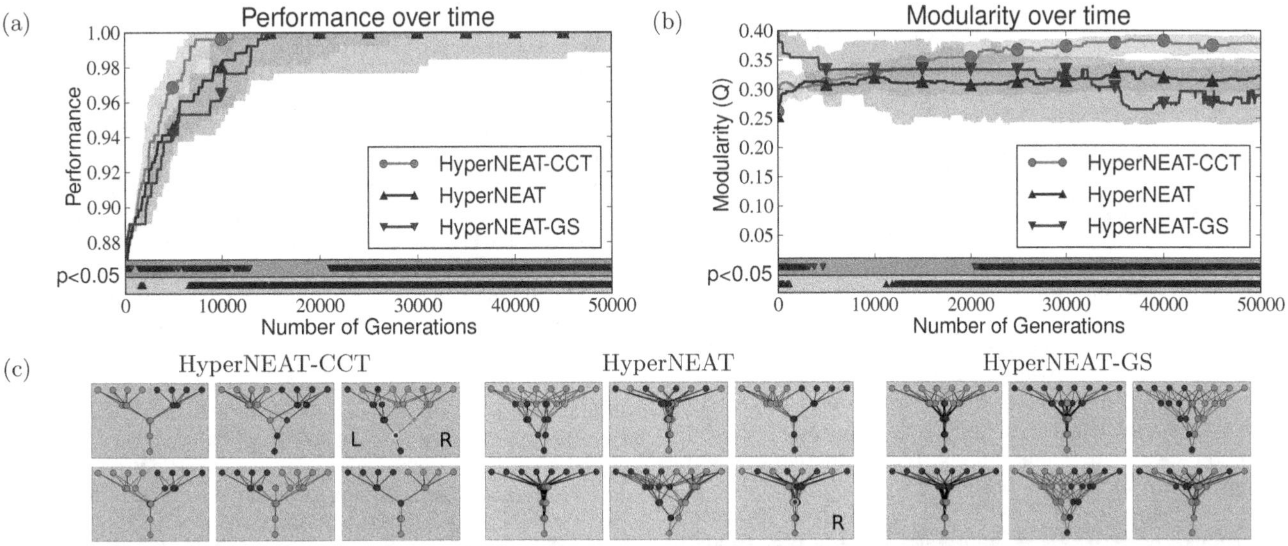

Figure 3: Results for the Retina Problem. HyperNEAT-CCT significantly *(a)* outperforms and *(b)* has higher modularity than both HyperNEAT and HyperNEAT-GS. *(c)* ONP visualizations (see section 2.5) for networks 54 to 60 (out of 100) for HyperNEAT and HyperNEAT-CCT and networks 27 to 33 (out of 50) for HyperNEAT-GS (sorted on modularity). Colored rings indicate neurons that solve the right (orange) and left (blue) sub-problems. HyperNEAT-CCT networks are visually more modular, exhibit left-right modularity more often, and solve significantly more sub-problems than HyperNEAT or HyperNEAT-GS networks.

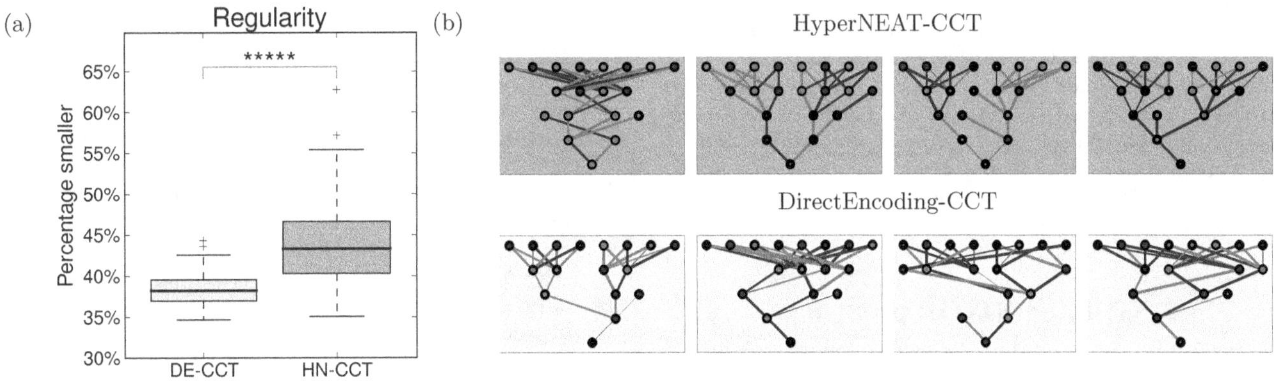

Figure 4: HyperNEAT-CCT networks are more regular than DirectEncoding-CCT networks. *(a)* HyperNEAT-CCT networks compress significantly more ($p < 0.00001$). *(b)* Four perfectly-performing networks with the highest modularity scores from HyperNEAT-CCT and DirectEncoding-CCT. All four networks of HyperNEAT-CCT show some form of symmetry with variation, including switching excitatory and inhibitory connections. The DirectEncoding-CCT networks are irregular.

can be selected over others is by reducing connection costs, which tends to increase modularity [8].

While the results of HyperNEAT-GS are lower than expected, the figures shown are for the highest-performing version of it that we found after experimenting with its key parameters (Fig 4a, b and c). Initially we ran HyperNEAT-GS with the default settings for the Gaussian seed [36] and a negative bias on the LEO output of -2, which resulted in fewer connections by enforcing stronger spatial constraints. After analyzing our results, we hypothesized that the poor performance of HyperNEAT-GS might have been because the distances between our nodes are greater than in [36], so we switched to settings (described in section 2.2) that compensate for the increased distances. These settings significantly improved performance ($p < 0.05$ for most generations), but did not improve modularity. We subsequently changed the bias from -2 to -1, which is more suitable when applying locality to only a single axis, and while this change improved modularity to the level reported in Fig. 3b, the overall results are still worse than those reported in [36]. This difference in performance is likely due to differences in the evolutionary algorithm (section 2.1) and in the problem definition (in [36] the sub-problems did not have to be combined into a single answer).

Since changing its seed improved the performance obtained by HyperNEAT-GS, it is possible that it can be improved to a level where it outperforms HyperNEAT-CCT. However, the weights of the Gaussian seed were free to evolve, yet evolution was unable to adapt the seed to improve either performance or modularity, which shows that HyperNEAT-GS can fail to produce modularity in absence of direct rewards.

The differences between the treatments with and without a connection-cost are not as pronounced as those demonstrated by Clune, Mouret and Lipson [8], indicating that the beneficial effects of CCT on HyperNEAT are not as great as was the case for the direct encoding. The reason for this is probably that HyperNEAT, even with the Link-Expression Output, has trouble pruning individual connections.

Comparing HyperNEAT-CCT with DirectEncoding-CCT (the main algorithm from [8]), the direct encoding is significantly higher performing in early generations and significantly more modular throughout evolution. The indirect encoding of HyperNEAT seems to struggle more with the irregularities of this problem and is not as good at pruning connections. That is expected, since removing connections in the direct encoding is easy compared to doing so in HyperNEAT, which has to adapt the patterns produced by the LEO node such that it cuts off the redundant parts while keeping the rest of the network intact.

A main advantage of HyperNEAT is its ability to produce regular patterns [9, 10, 27]. Compression tests (see methods, section 2.5) reveal that HyperNEAT-CCT networks are significantly more regular than the DirectEncoding-CCT (Figure 4): the direct encoding with CCT becomes 38% smaller upon compression, but HyperNEAT-CCT compresses further down by 43%, making it significantly more compressible ($p < 0.00001$). Thus, HyperNEAT-CCT networks are regular in addition to being modular.

The regularity of HyperNEAT-CCT is also visually apparent (Fig. 4b). In many of its networks, the left side is mirrored on the right side, even though the signs of the connections are sometimes switched. Other networks feature alternating or mirrored patterns in the biases or connections. While HyperNEAT-CCT networks also exhibit some clear variations in each of its patterns, on balance they are much more regular than the DirectEncoding-CCT networks (Fig. 4b), which do not show any discernible patterns.

3.2 The 5-XOR and H-XOR problems

On the **5-XOR** problem the treatments differ only slightly until after 25000 generations, where the performance and modularity of HyperNEAT-CCT becomes significantly better than HyperNEAT (Fig. 5a,b). The visual difference in modularity is also clear for networks of intermediate modularity (Fig. 5c); HyperNEAT-CCT networks perfectly divide the problem into five individual networks while the networks produced by HyperNEAT are entangled.

On the **H-XOR** problem, HyperNEAT-CCT significantly outperforms HyperNEAT in both performance and modularity for most of the first 15000 generations (Fig. 5d,e). HyperNEAT eventually catches up, erasing the significant differences. Network visualizations reveal clear examples where HyperNEAT-CCT networks modularly decompose the problem, whereas HyperNEAT networks have not managed to disentangle the left and right problems (Figure 5f).

Due to computational and time constraints, we did not test HyperNEAT-GS on the **5-XOR** and **H-XOR** problem. Given the results presented in section 3.1, it is likely that HyperNEAT-GS would underperform HyperNEAT and HyperNEAT-CCT. Also, because splitting the sub-problems is necessary to obtain perfect performance on these problems, there is no need to test for sub-problems solved as this will be directly reflected in performance.

4. FUTURE WORK

While we have shown the advantages of HyperNEAT-CCT on simple diagnostic problems, the real power of this method lies in its ability to create large-scale, modular networks. HyperNEAT can create functional neural networks with millions of connections, but the networks and tasks performed were simple [13, 27]. In future research we will increase the scale of networks that have both regularity and modularity and test whether these properties improve the ability to perform more complex tasks.

An other area to explore is to allow HyperNEAT to evolve the number and geometric location of its hidden neurons [25]. Because the patterns of neural connectivity HyperNEAT produces depend on the geometric location of nodes [9], adding the CCT to Evolvable-Substrate HyperNEAT [25] may further increase HyperNEAT's ability to create functional neural modularity and could reduce the need for users to create geometric node layouts that encourage the appropriate modular decomposition of problems.

Lastly, a recent technique showed that the regular patterns produced by a generative encoding, such as HyperNEAT, aids the learning capabilities of networks [34]. We will combine our method with intra-life learning algorithms to investigate whether learning is improved when it occurs in structurally organized neural networks. Such learning may also ameliorate HyperNEAT's inability to cope with irregularity [6, 10].

5. CONCLUSION

One strategy to make robots more intelligent and agile is to evolve neural network controllers that emulate the structural organization of animal brains, including their modularity and regularity. Because these properties do not naturally emerge in evolutionary algorithms, some techniques have to be employed to encourage them to evolve. We have demonstrated how HyperNEAT with the connection-cost technique (HyperNEAT-CCT) can evolve networks that are both modular and regular, which increases performance on modular, regular problems compared to both the default HyperNEAT algorithm and a variant of HyperNEAT specifically designed to encourage modularity. We have also shown that networks produced by HyperNEAT-CCT are more regular than networks produced by adding the CCT to a direct encoding.

While other methods that lead to modular and regular networks exist, this work demonstrates a powerful, general way to promote modularity in the HyperNEAT algorithm, which has recently become one of the leading generative encodings due to its ability to produce complex regularities, evolve extremely large-scale neural networks, and exploit the geometry of problems. Our work thus merges separate lines of research into evolving regularity and modularity, allowing them to be combined into a potentially powerful algorithm that can produce large-scale neural networks that exhibit key properties of structural organization in animal brains. Our work thus represents a step towards the day in which we can evolve computational brains that rival natural brains in complexity and intelligence.

6. ACKNOWLEDGMENTS

We thank Kai Olav Ellefsen and the members of the Evolving AI Lab. JBM is supported by an ANR young researchers grant (Creadapt, ANR-12-JS03-0009).

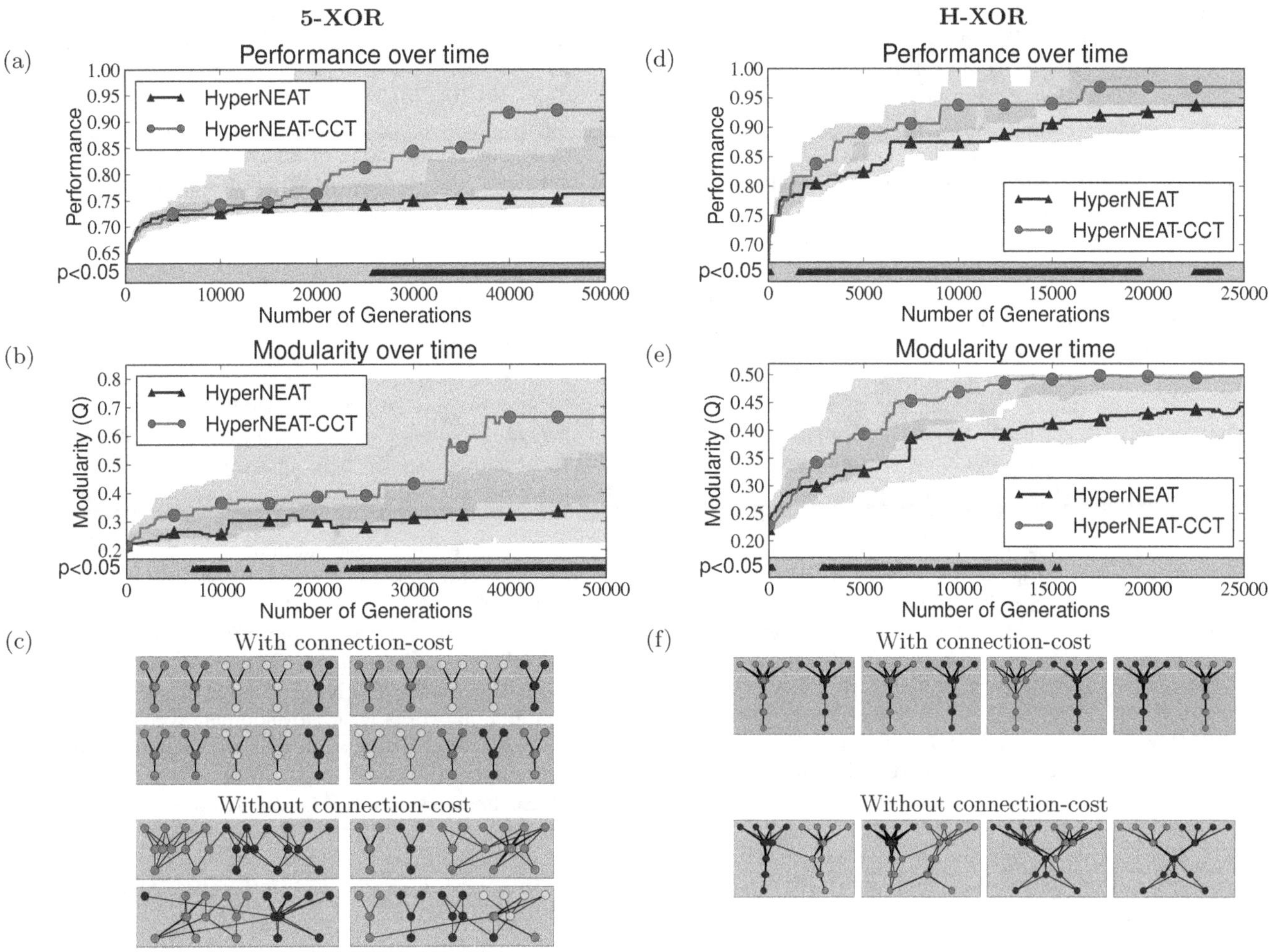

Figure 5: A Connection Cost Also Increases Modularity and Regularity on the 5-XOR and H-XOR Problems. *(a)* Median performance over time for the **5-XOR** experiment. HyperNEAT-CCT performs significantly better than HyperNEAT after 25000 generations. *(b)* Median modularity over time for the **5-XOR** problem. HyperNEAT-CCT is significantly more modular than HyperNEAT after around 22000 generations (and for periods prior). *(c)* A comparison of **5-XOR** networks 18-22 (sorted on modularity) showing ONP visualizations (see methods). HyperNEAT-CCT networks decompose the problem into the appropriate five modules while HyperNEAT without a connection cost makes unnecessary connections between the separate XOR problems. *(d)* On the **H-XOR** problem, HyperNEAT-CCT performs significantly better than HyperNEAT for most of the run. *(e)* HyperNEAT-CCT is significantly more modular for most early generations before HyperNEAT catches up. *(f)* A visual comparison of **H-XOR** networks 24-28 (sorted on modularity) showing ONP visualizations (see methods). HyperNEAT-CCT splits the problem perfectly while HyperNEAT makes unnecessary connections between the left and the right problems.

7. REFERENCES

[1] S.B. Carroll. Chance and necessity: the evolution of morphological complexity and diversity. *Nature*, 409(6823):1102–1109, 2001.

[2] C. Cherniak, Z. Mokhtarzada, R. Rodriguez-Esteban, and K. Changizi. Global optimization of cerebral cortex layout. *Proceedings of the National Academy of Sciences*, 101(4):1081–6, January 2004.

[3] D.B. Chklovskii, T. Schikorski, and C.F. Stevens. Wiring optimization in cortical circuits. *Neuron*, 34(3):341–347, 2002.

[4] J. Clune, B.E. Beckmann, P.K. McKinley, and C. Ofria. Investigating whether HyperNEAT produces modular neural networks. In *Proceedings of the Genetic and Evolutionary Computation Conference*, pages 635–642. ACM, 2010.

[5] J. Clune, B.E. Beckmann, C. Ofria, and R.T. Pennock. Evolving coordinated quadruped gaits with the HyperNEAT generative encoding. In *Proceedings of the IEEE Congress on Evolutionary Computation*, pages 2764–2771, 2009.

[6] J. Clune, B.E. Beckmann, R.T. Pennock, and C. Ofria. HybrID: A Hybridization of Indirect and Direct Encodings for Evolutionary Computation. In *Proceedings of the European Conference on Artificial Life*, 2009.

[7] J. Clune, D. Misevic, C. Ofria, R.E. Lenski, S.F. Elena, and R. Sanjuán. Natural selection fails to

optimize mutation rates for long-term adaptation on rugged fitness landscapes. *PLoS Computational Biology*, 4(9):e1000187, 2008.

[8] J. Clune, J-B. Mouret, and H. Lipson. The evolutionary origins of modularity. *Proceedings of the Royal Society B*, 280(20122863), 2013.

[9] J. Clune, C. Ofria, and R.T. Pennock. The sensitivity of HyperNEAT to different geometric representations of a problem. In *Proceedings of the Genetic and Evolutionary Computation Conference*, pages 675–682, 2009.

[10] J. Clune, K.O. Stanley, R.T. Pennock, and C. Ofria. On the performance of indirect encoding across the continuum of regularity. *IEEE Transactions on Evolutionary Computation*, 15(4):346–367, 2011.

[11] K. Deb, A. Pratap, S. Agarwal, and T.A.M.T. Meyarivan. A fast and elitist multiobjective genetic algorithm: Nsga-ii. *Evolutionary Computation, IEEE Transactions on*, 6(2):182–197, 2002.

[12] C. Espinosa-Soto and A. Wagner. Specialization can drive the evolution of modularity. *PLoS Computational Biology*, 6(3):e1000719, 2010.

[13] J. Gauci and K.O. Stanley. Generating large-scale neural networks through discovering geometric regularities. In *Proceedings of the Genetic and Evolutionary Computation Conference*, pages 997–1004. ACM, 2007.

[14] G.S. Hornby, H. Lipson, and J.B. Pollack. Generative representations for the automated design of modular physical robots. *IEEE Transactions on Robotics and Automation*, 19(4):703–719, 2003.

[15] G.S. Hornby and J. B. Pollack. Evolving L-systems to generate virtual creatures. *Computers & Graphics*, 25(6):1041–1048, December 2001.

[16] B. Inden, Y. Jin, R. Haschke, and H. Ritter. Exploiting inherent regularity in control of multilegged robot locomotion by evolving neural fields. *2011 Third World Congress on Nature and Biologically Inspired Computing*, pages 401–408, October 2011.

[17] N. Kashtan and U. Alon. Spontaneous evolution of modularity and network motifs. *Proceedings of the National Academy of Sciences*, 102(39):13773–13778, September 2005.

[18] N. Kashtan, E. Noor, and U. Alon. Varying environments can speed up evolution. *Proceedings of the National Academy of Sciences*, 104(34):13711–13716, August 2007.

[19] C.P. Klingenberg. Developmental constraints, modules and evolvability. *Variation: A central concept in biology*, pages 1–30, 2005.

[20] J. Lehman, S. Risi, D.B. D'Ambrosio, and K.O. Stanley. Encouraging reactivity to create robust machines. *Adaptive Behavior*, 21(6):484–500, August 2013.

[21] M. Li. *An introduction to Kolmogorov complexity and its applications*. Springer, 1997.

[22] H. Lipson. Principles of modularity, regularity, and hierarchy for scalable systems. *Journal of Biological Physics and Chemistry*, 7(December):125–128, 2007.

[23] J-B. Mouret and S. Doncieux. Sferes v2: Evolvin' in the multi-core world. *IEEE Congress on Evolutionary Computation*, (2):1–8, July 2010.

[24] M.E.J. Newman. Modularity and community structure in networks. *Proceedings of the National Academy of Sciences*, 103(23):8577–8582, 2006.

[25] S. Risi, J. Lehman, and K.O. Stanley. Evolving the placement and density of neurons in the hyperneat substrate. *Proceedings of the 12th annual conference on Genetic and evolutionary computation - GECCO '10*, (Gecco):563, 2010.

[26] K.O. Stanley. Compositional pattern producing networks: A novel abstraction of development. *Genetic Programming and Evolvable Machines*, 8(2):131–162, 2007.

[27] K.O. Stanley, D.B. D'Ambrosio, and J. Gauci. A hypercube-based encoding for evolving large-scale neural networks. *Artificial Life*, 15(2):185–212, 2009.

[28] K.O. Stanley and R. Miikkulainen. Evolving neural networks through augmenting topologies. *Evolutionary Computation*, 10(2):99–127, 2002.

[29] K.O. Stanley and R. Miikkulainen. A taxonomy for artificial embryogeny. *Artificial Life*, 9(2):93–130, 2003.

[30] G.F. Striedter. *Principles of brain evolution*. Sinauer Associates Sunderland, MA, 2005.

[31] M. Suchorzewski. Evolving scalable and modular adaptive networks with Developmental Symbolic Encoding. *Evolutionary intelligence*, 4(3):145–163, September 2011.

[32] M. Suchorzewski and J. Clune. A novel generative encoding for evolving modular, regular and scalable networks. In *Proceedings of the Genetic and Evolutionary Computation Conference*, pages 1523–1530, 2011.

[33] P. Szerlip and K.O. Stanley. Indirectly Encoded Sodarace for Artificial Life. *Advances in Artificial Life, ECAL 2013*, pages 218–225, September 2013.

[34] P. Tonelli and J-B. Mouret. On the relationships between generative encodings, regularity, and learning abilities when evolving plastic, artificial neural networks. *PLoS One*, page To appear, 2013.

[35] V.K. Valsalam and R. Miikkulainen. Evolving symmetric and modular neural networks for distributed control. *Proceedings of the 11th Annual conference on Genetic and evolutionary computation - GECCO '09*, page 731, 2009.

[36] P. Verbancsics and K.O. Stanley. Constraining connectivity to encourage modularity in hyperneat. In *Proceedings of the 13th annual conference on Genetic and evolutionary computation*, pages 1483–1490. ACM, 2011.

[37] G.P. Wagner, J. Mezey, and R. Calabretta. *Modularity. Understanding the development and evolution of complex natural systems*, chapter Natural selection and the origin of modules. MIT Press, 2001.

[38] G.P. Wagner, M. Pavlicev, and J.M. Cheverud. The road to modularity. *Nature Reviews Genetics*, 8(12):921–31, December 2007.

Trading Control Intelligence for Physical Intelligence: Muscle Drives in Evolved Virtual Creatures

Dan Lessin
Dept. of Computer Science
The Univ. of Texas at Austin
Austin, Texas, USA
dlessin@cs.utexas.edu

Don Fussell
Dept. of Computer Science
The Univ. of Texas at Austin
Austin, Texas, USA
fussell@cs.utexas.edu

Risto Miikkulainen
Dept. of Computer Science
The Univ. of Texas at Austin
Austin, Texas, USA
risto@cs.utexas.edu

ABSTRACT

Traditional evolved virtual creatures [12] are actuated using unevolved, uniform, invisible drives at joints between rigid segments. In contrast, this paper shows how such conventional actuators can be replaced by evolvable muscle drives that are a part of the creature's physical structure. Such a muscle-drive system replaces control intelligence with meaningful morphological complexity. For instance, the experiments in this paper show that control intelligence sufficient for locomotion or jumping can be moved almost entirely from the brain into the musculature of evolved virtual creatures.

This design is important for two reasons: First, the control intelligence is made visible in the purposeful development of muscle density, orientation, attachment points, and size. Second, the complexity that needs to be evolved for the brain to control the actuators is reduced, and in some cases can be essentially eliminated, thus freeing brain power for higher-level functions. Such designs may thus make it possible to create more complex behavior than would otherwise be achievable.

Categories and Subject Descriptors

I.2.6 [**Artificial Intelligence**]: Learning—*connectionism and neural nets*; I.6.8 [**Simulation and Modeling**]: Types of Simulation—*animation*; I.2.1 [**Artificial Intelligence**]: Applications and Expert Systems—*games*; I.3.7 [**Computer Graphics**]: Three-Dimensional Graphics and Realism—*animation*

Keywords

evolved virtual creatures; artificial life; muscle drives; physics-based character animation; physical intelligence; morphological complexity

GECCO'14, July 12–16, Vancouver, BC, Canada.

http://dx.doi.org/10.1145/2576768.2598290.

Figure 1: A creature evolved for jumping (Section 4.2.5) using the method described in this paper, demonstrating the morphological complexity that results from replacing implicit joint-motor drives with an evolvable musculature. As with all other examples in this work, the physical intelligence embodied by these muscle drives enables this creature to perform a useful task essentially without control intelligence (Section 3.2). Video of this and all other results can be viewed at http://youtu.be/csZ9JZcuBfE.

1. INTRODUCTION

Morphological complexity is an important goal for evolved virtual creatures (or *EVCs*; Figure 1) [2]. How can it be increased to approach the morphological complexity of creatures evolved in the real world? Traditional segmented EVCs [12, 3, 10, 8] achieve some measure of complexity through the placement, dimensions, and types of their rigid segments and joints. More recently, creatures with morphology based on implicit definitions such as CPPNs and gene regulatory networks [2, 6, 4] have demonstrated a different–and arguably greater morphological complexity, albeit based on indirect developmental mechanisms. In contrast, this paper demonstrates that it is possible to increase the complexity of the rigid-bodied model directly by employing a more advanced approach to actuation.

In a conventional EVC, actuation is provided by implicit joint motors. Such motors are completely uniform, i.e., present at every free axis of every joint, and fixed over time.

They are also typically unseen, perhaps because their uniformity would provide little reward for making them visible.

However, our recent work [9] has demonstrated that EVCs can also be successfully actuated by a simple form of simulated muscle–a variable-strength linear spring attached to two segments across a joint. Although, in that implementation, the muscles were controlled by a complex brain, one particularly interesting property of such drives is that they do not actually require this control complexity. As will be shown in this paper, these muscles are able to embody and replace a significant portion of the control intelligence that would normally be provided by the creature's brain. In fact, creatures that are almost entirely without control intelligence can still develop sufficient *physical* intelligence (in the form of their evolved musculature) to perform rudimentary, yet useful tasks, such as jumping and simple locomotion.

One particularly beneficial result of this shifting of intelligence from brain to body is the fact that, where the control intelligence was externally invisible, the physical intelligence that replaces it is visible in the morphological complexity of the muscles. And although the muscle-drive model described in this work is in some ways simple, it nevertheless communicates meaningful complexity through its evolved characteristics: the density or lack of muscles at a joint, their size (with rendered thickness indicating strength), orientation (indicating direction of force application), and their attachment points.

In addition, this effective obviation of control logic could ultimately prove useful as an evolutionary robotics application if mechanisms similar to the simple simulated muscles used here can be implemented in the real world, especially where control intelligence is at a premium. Robots that need to be particularly small, for example, might benefit from replacing a relatively complex controller with a properly evolved actuator musculature.

Even traditional EVC applications could benefit from this easing of the demands on brainpower. By removing the cognitive load that can now be borne by the muscle drives, this implementation frees the brain to devote equivalent computational power to achieving more complex behavioral goals.

In the balance of this paper, this new step on the biologically inspired path to meaningful morphological complexity and reduced control loads is described, and successful results are presented and evaluated.

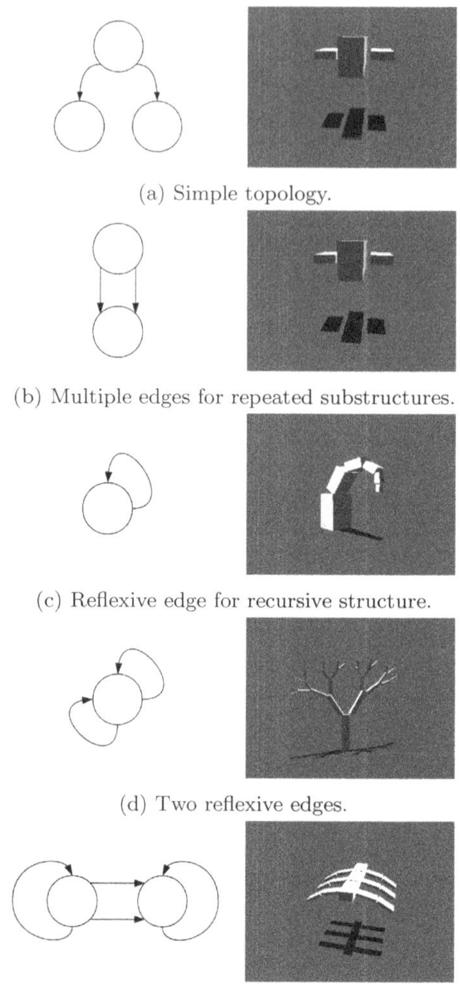

(a) Simple topology.

(b) Multiple edges for repeated substructures.

(c) Reflexive edge for recursive structure.

(d) Two reflexive edges.

(e) Multiple and reflexive edges together.

Figure 2: Hand-designed genotype/phenotype pairs (after those of Sims [12]) demonstrate the encoding power of EVC systems.

2. BASIC EVC SYSTEM

The basic EVC system described in this paper is in large part built on a traditional EVC framework [12, 3, 7, 10]. This section briefly sets out the components of this system, which—while not the primary focus of this paper—are nevertheless fundamental.

2.1 Evolutionary Algorithm

The specifics of the evolutionary algorithm are largely conventional, making use of elitism, fitness-proportionate selection, and rank selection [11]. In addition, some degree of shaping [13] is employed, as described in Sections 4.2 and 4.3. Fitness is evaluated in a physically simulated virtual environment implemented with NVIDIA PhysX.

New individuals are created through crossover followed by mutation. The directed graph genotypes used (see Section 2.2) are sufficiently tree-like that crossover can be implemented by choosing a random point in each of the parent graphs and swapping sub-trees at those points. This produces two child graphs, one of which is randomly discarded. Mutation mechanisms and probabilities vary by attribute type.

2.2 Morphology

As with most EVCs, creature morphology is described by a graph-based genotype, with graph nodes representing body segments, and graph edges representing joints between segments. By starting at the root and traversing the graph's edges, the phenotype is expressed. Reflexive edges as well as multiple edges between the same node pair are allowed, making it possible to define recursive and repeated body substructures easily, as illustrated in Figure 2. In addition, reflection of body parts as well as body symmetry are made readily available to evolution.

In the implementation of EVCs in this paper, all PhysX primitives are made available for use as body segments: boxes, spheres, and capsules. Joints between segments may be of most of the types offered by PhysX, specifically: fixed, revolute, spherical, prismatic, and cylindrical. (Note that, consistent with this paper's focus on muscle drives, the joints themselves are omitted from all renderings.) In contrast to the typical technique of separately evolving explicit joint limits, most limitations on joint movement are provided implicitly by creature structure through natural collisions between adjacent segments.

3. EVOLVABLE MUSCULATURE

The evolvable musculature described in this section makes it possible to transfer control intelligence to physical intelligence, which is the focus of this paper. First, the implementation of the muscle drives themselves is described, then the extremely minimal control that it enables is specified.

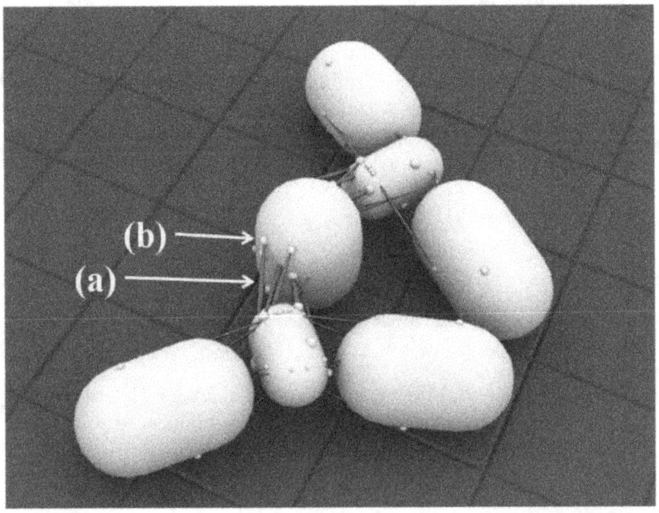

Figure 3: Evolvable musculature, with example muscle body (a) and attachment point (b) indicated. The density of muscles at a joint, their thickness (indicating strength and activation), orientation, and attachment points all contribute meaningfully to the creature's morphological complexity.

3.1 Muscle Drives

The muscle drives are implemented as simple linear springs. Each muscle (Figure 3(a)) is completely described by its attachment points and maximum strength. An attachment point (Figure 3(b)) may be placed anywhere on a rigid body segment, and each pair of attachment points must exist across a joint connecting two such segments. Muscles may be added and removed by evolution, and their attachment points and maximum strength are evolvable. During simulation, a muscle's activation (in [0,1]) determines what portion of its maximum strength that muscle will apply.

The muscle is implemented using a standard PhysX joint called a *distance joint*, modifying its attributes so that it acts as a simple linear spring. A PhysX distance joint allows the specification of a maximum distance between two attachment points, and this maximum is enforced by spring-like behavior when exceeded. By setting the distance joint's maximum distance to zero, only the spring-like enforcements are applied. The spring constant is adjusted during simulation to reflect the tension that results from combining the muscle's activation with its maximum force value. Note that this implementation–with numerous joints of varying types between a single pair of rigid body segments–is probably not typical for PhysX, and initial results with normal settings resulted in simulations that were not sufficiently stable. All experiments presented in this paper rely on a much smaller simulation step–1/240th of a second–as well as other configuration settings, all of which can significantly affect simulation efficiency.

From the three evolvable properties of each muscle (two attachment points and the maximum strength), as well as the fact that muscles may be added or removed at any joint, a great degree of visually obvious meaningful morphological complexity emerges. This design also has the potential to embody sufficient physical intelligence to perform basic behaviors with only a trivial degree of control intelligence required, as will be described next.

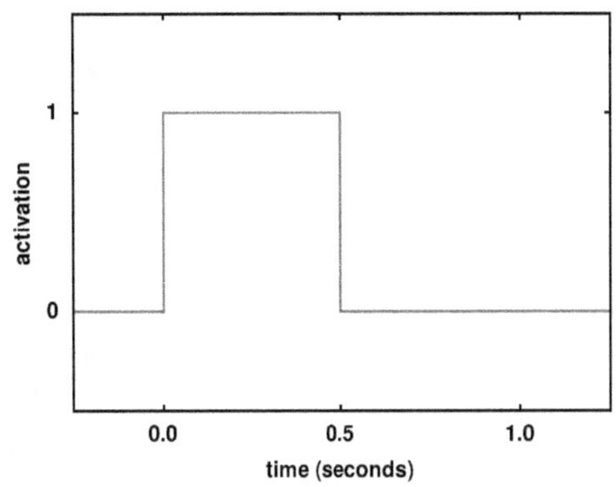

(a) Jump activation (single square pulse).

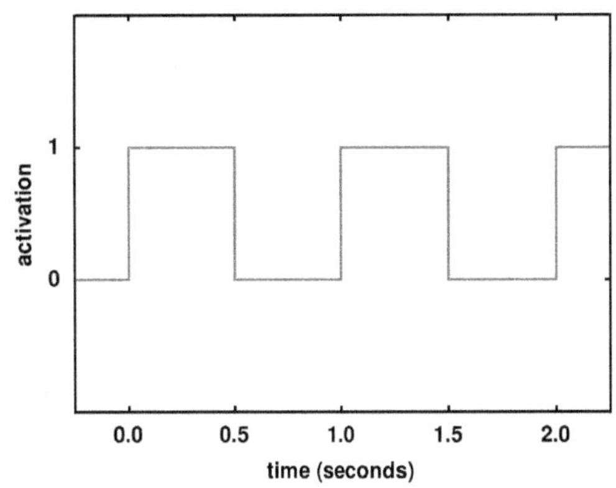

(b) Locomotion activation (repeating square wave).

Figure 4: With the muscle drives' capacity for physical intelligence, simple but useful behaviors can be performed effectively without control intelligence. Here, the fixed global muscle activations that replace the typical EVC's relatively complex brain for all experiments in this work are illustrated.

3.2 Minimal Control

As a demonstration of approximately how much physical intelligence the evolvable musculature can embody, the examples in this paper all function almost entirely without control intelligence (Figure 4).

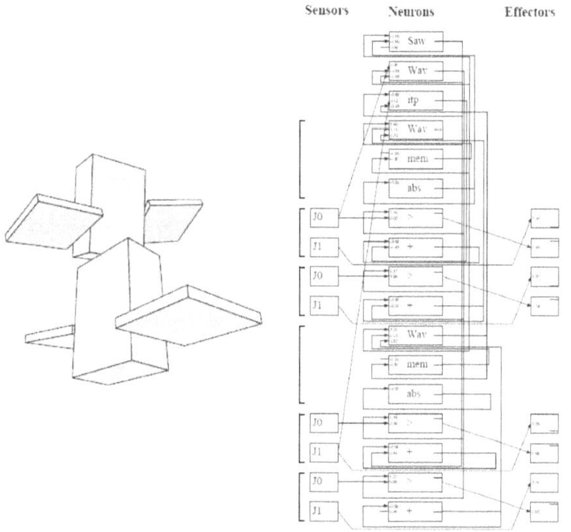

Figure 5: For comparison, this figure illustrates a body and brain from one of Sims' conventional EVCs–this one evolved for locomotion [12]. Note the different balance of control and physical intelligence, with greater complexity hidden in the brain, while the morphology is less elaborate.

In a conventional evolved virtual creature, control intelligence is implemented as a neural network [10] or a directed graph of simple computing nodes [12], as shown in Figure 5. In the creatures in this paper, far less is required. For these new creatures, the typical brain is replaced by a single activation function, which is applied to all muscles simultaneously. This activation function was arbitrarily chosen and fixed before each experiment began, being neither evolved nor hand-tuned for suitability. These functions (a half-second unit-amplitude square pulse for jumping, and a 1-Hz unit-amplitude square wave for locomotion) are illustrated in Figure 4.

4. EXPERIMENTS

In this section, the results of two experiments are presented, in which creatures evolve body and musculature for the tasks of jumping and locomotion. In each case, the potential for physical intelligence in the muscle drives effectively obviates control intelligence and also demonstrates the muscle drives' potential to exhibit meaningful morphological complexity. All of the results described here can be seen in motion in the accompanying video[1].

4.1 Experimental Setup

For all of the results in this paper (Sections 4.2 and 4.3), a typical population size was on the order of 100. Between 221 and 500 generations were used to obtain all of the jump results shown, and between 1000 and 2000 generations were used for the locomotion results. In both the locomotion and jumping tasks, 10 copies of the experiment would be executed in parallel, each with its own random seed. The champions of these 10 runs typically form a diverse collection of successful results, although certain variations of morphological themes tend to recur. Illustrative examples are presented in the subsections below.

The variety demonstrated in these results suggests fertile ground for the future development of new, more challenging tasks, as discussed in Section 5.

4.2 Jump Results

The following five subsections illustrate the various solutions found for a simple jumping task. For this skill, fitness is defined using a number of intermediate shaping steps, resulting in a sequence of fitness goals like the one below. Each stage is complete when a sufficient fraction of the population–on the order of 5%–has achieved full fitness. At that point, that percentage having full fitness is replicated to fill a new population, and evolution continues in the next stage.

A useful concept in defining these goals is the axis-aligned bounding box (AABB)–particularly its top and bottom, which describe the creature's highest and lowest extents. Both static (i.e., at rest) and highest (as measured throughout a single fitness evaluation) AABB measures are employed.

1. **static AABB top**
   (to encourage a static size requiring multiple segments)
2. **static AABB top + highest AABB top**
   (to encourage muscles and upward action, while maintaining static size)
3. **highest AABB top + highest AABB bottom**
   (to encourage ground clearance, while maintaining upward action)

For all jump evolution experiments, control consists solely of the single fixed global activation signal depicted in Figure 4(a), with all other required intelligence residing entirely within the body, including the evolvable musculature.

In each result illustration (Figures 6-10), the left and right sides show the creature before and during its jump, respectively.

4.2.1 Jump Result 1

Figure 6: Two-armed swing (repeatable).

The creature in Figure 6 adapts its morphology to the given minimal control signal by developing heavy arms that are swung up by appropriately placed muscles. The upward momentum of these limbs is then sufficient to make the creature airborne.

Foreshadowing a common technique observed in the locomotion results, this creature happens to end its jump in the same configuration from which it began, demonstrating a potential for repeated action.

[1] http://youtu.be/csZ9JZcuBfE

4.2.2 Jump Result 2

Figure 7: Two-armed swing (non-repeatable).

The creature in Figure 7 applies the same basic limb-swinging strategy to a different morphology, resulting in a strong jump that does not happen to end in the same pose from which it began.

4.2.3 Jump Result 3

Figure 8: One-armed swing.

The strategy in Figure 8 is similar to that of the previous two, but it works here with a single limb instead of a symmetrical pair of limbs. As with Jump Result 1, this creature's consistent begin and end poses foreshadow the successful technique seen in the locomotion results–in this case matching almost exactly the morphology and behavior of Locomotion Result 2.

4.2.4 Jump Result 4

Figure 9: Four-legged push.

The creature in Figure 9 employs the far less common (for this experiment) technique of pushing off the ground rather than swinging limbs up. This bias may result from the particular method of fitness shaping used for this skill, in which an initial upward extension of the creature's axis-aligned bounding box is rewarded as an intermediate goal on the way to a true jumping behavior.

4.2.5 Jump Result 5

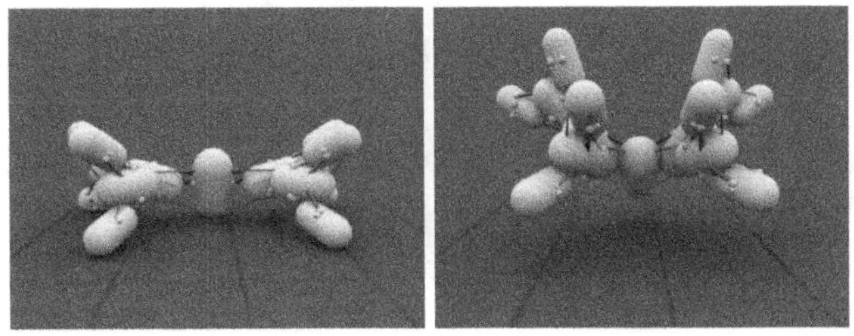

Figure 10: Complex-arm swing.

In Figure 10–the most morphologically elaborate of the jump results–a particularly complex collection of segments, joints, and muscles is applied to the work of swinging heavy arms up to induce a successful leap. (See Figure 1 for a more detailed illustration.)

4.3 Locomotion Results

In this section, results from a locomotion experiment are presented, in which the single fixed square-pulse control signal of Figure 4(a) was replaced with the repeating fixed square-wave signal of Figure 4(b), and the ultimate fitness function was changed from jump height to distance traveled in a given amount of time. A sequence of fitness goals like the one below–with the first three the same as in the jump results–is used for shaping. Note that in the fourth step, only a modest amount of horizontal travel is required for success. Once that initial degree of locomotion has been established, and the final stage begins, the previous requirement for jumping fitness is removed, and evolution is allowed to focus solely on optimizing horizontal travel towards an effectively unlimited distance goal.

1. **static AABB top**
2. **static AABB top + highest AABB top**
3. **highest AABB top + highest AABB bottom**
4. **highest AABB bottom + (modest) horizontal distance traveled**
   (to encourage locomotion while ground clearance (jumping) is maintained)
5. **horizontal distance traveled (unlimited)**
   (to optimize locomotion alone once it has begun to develop.)

In each of the following eight examples, the left image is a closeup of the creature with muscles relaxed (as during the trough of the activation square wave), and the right image depicts the creature with muscles activated, during locomotion, with approximate direction of movement indicated by the arrow.

4.3.1 Locomotion Result 1

Figure 11: Double front-armed swing hop.

In Figure 11, the square-wave activation of muscles is used to swing the front limbs up, accumulating momentum which produces forward translation during repeated jumps.

4.3.2 Locomotion Result 2

Figure 12: Single front-armed swing hop.

With morphology and action very similar to that of Jump Result 3, the creature in Figure 12 also employs a repeating forward-translating jump for simple but highly effective locomotion.

4.3.3 Locomotion Result 3

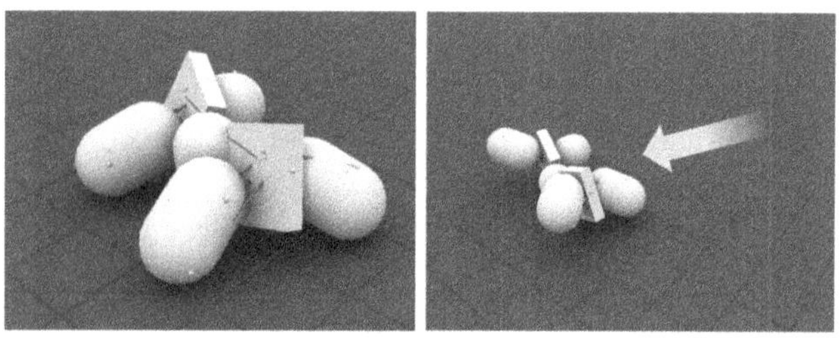

Figure 13: Front-armed swing step.

The mode of locomotion of the creature in Figure 13 is surprisingly complex and subtle, given the abrupt simplicity of the global activation signal. In a two-stage sequence of actions, this creature swings front legs up, which causes the middle box segments first to tip forward, then step ahead, pulling the back limbs along with them.

4.3.4 Locomotion Result 4

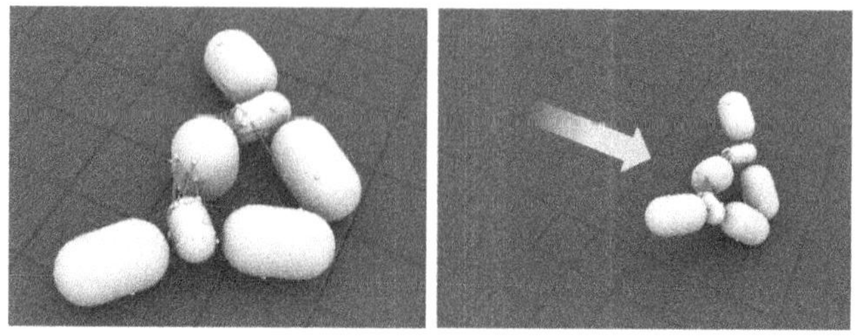

Figure 14: Delta wheelbarrow.

The creature in Figure 14 employs a dense concentration of muscles at its central joints to produce upward and forward momentum, which results in a wheelbarrowing forward slide.

4.3.5 Locomotion Result 5

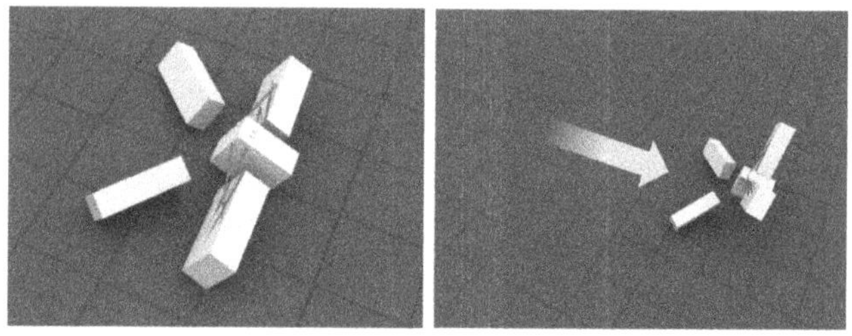

Figure 15: Front-hinged swing drag.

In Figure 15, muscles sharply raise forward segments that are hinged so as to provide a lifting and forward-moving impulse, which drags the stabilizing rear legs along the ground.

4.3.6 Locomotion Result 6

Figure 16: Square wheelbarrow.

In Figure 16, a different morphology employs the same basic technique as Locomotion Result 4 to again produce a sliding wheelbarrow-like forward movement.

4.3.7 *Locomotion Result 7*

Figure 17: Complex swing step.

In Figure 17, the most morphologically complex of the locomotion results, one cluster of segments forms a stable base, while another such cluster is swung up to produce an elegant raise-tip-and-step sequence of actions, resulting in forward motion.

4.3.8 *Locomotion Result 8*

Figure 18: High hop.

In one of the simplest yet most effective locomotion results (Figure 18), the creature uses clusters of strong muscles to swing up heavy limbs, lifting its comparatively small root segment in a high-jumping locomotive technique.

5. DISCUSSION AND FUTURE WORK

It is important to note that the claimed benefits of the evolved muscle drives–removing a measure of the burden from control intelligence and embodying that intelligence as functional morphological complexity–are not expected to be limited to this particular form of adaptable drive. Any sufficiently inhomogeneous evolvable drive system should be able to accomplish the same goal. For example, if traditional EVC joint-motor drives had evolvable strengths, a similar transfer of intelligence from brain to body should be possible. The increase in morphological complexity in that case might be smaller (perhaps variable motor sizes displayed at a joint, rather than the varied number, orientation and attachment points exhibited by muscle drives), but still useful.

Another important point is that the work presented here is intended to establish that this evolvable musculature can embody *some* useful degree of control complexity, but does not yet include a quantification of that amount. This topic is worthy of a more systematic examination in the future.

Although the main goal of this work is to trade control intelligence for physical intelligence, the evolved muscle drives also make it possible to meaningfully increase morphological complexity. This goal can be advanced in several ways in the future.

One obvious next step would be to replace the current system's simulated linear springs with a more complex model employing simulated soft bodies or pressurized cloth for the bulk of the muscles. Previous work with simulated muscles [5] already demonstrated that such an approach is feasible, and has done so specifically within PhysX. Allowing muscles to help define the distribution of the body's mass, as they do in real creatures, would significantly advance the process of biologically inspired purposeful complexification of morphology. Also, the meaningful change of such muscles' shape during simulation–indicating the degree of their extension and activation–would add an additional layer of realistic detail.

Another biologically inspired refinement of the rigid-segment EVC model would be to simulate skin, as anticipated by Sims 20 years ago [12]. With powerful cloth simulation widely available (including in PhysX), this extension has become a conceivable next step on the path of life-like morphological complexification. In particular, combining simulated-cloth skin with massed muscles (as described above) might produce a particularly rich simulation, with a skin stretching and sliding over muscles as they extend and contract.

Looking even further into the future, if evolved creatures can embody the right kinds of morphological complexity, perhaps externally imposed joint mechanisms could be replaced by more realistic and more expressive joints whose properties arise directly from their morphology. By allowing the shape of the rigid-body segments to evolve [1], and permitting the inclusion of other necessary anatomical elements such as tendons and ligaments, it may be possible for rich and useful joint properties to emerge naturally, adding yet another layer of purpose-driven morphological complexity to evolved virtual creatures.

Similarly, although on a somewhat different path, the ability to evolve sufficiently detailed exoskeleton segments, along with the necessary muscles and connecting elements, could permit the development of exoskeleton-based virtual creatures. In this style of morphology–where again, body function follows from its form–meaningful complexity should emerge.

Moving forward into more demanding tasks in the future, the diversity of results displayed in Sections 4.2 and 4.3 is encouraging. The variety of available solutions for these simple behaviors promises greater opportunity for continued success as new constraints are applied.

6. CONCLUSION

This paper has described a version of evolved virtual creatures in which traditional joint-motor drives are replaced by a simple yet powerful evolvable musculature. The results presented here have demonstrated that this new substrate can support a significant degree of physical intelligence, sufficient to almost entirely replace the control intelligence that would normally be used for basic but useful tasks such as jumping and locomotion. The process of shifting this intelligence into a new complexity in the body makes it visible, enabling progress toward the goal of meaningful morphological complexity. And the fact that this can make (for these basic tasks) the typical EVC brain essentially superfluous, gives some indication of how much of a control burden these muscle drives can embody, and the degree to which they can liberate the brain's computational resources for other, more complex work. In addition, it demonstrates that, in some real-world applications, where these simple tasks are useful, but brains are difficult to support, a sufficiently evolvable drive system like this one may enable an entirely new class of solutions to emerge.

7. ACKNOWLEDGEMENTS

This research was supported by NSF grants DBI-0939454 and IIS-0915038, by NIH grant R01-GM105042, and by equipment donations from Intel's Visual Computing Program.

8. REFERENCES

[1] J. E. Auerbach and J. C. Bongard. Evolving CPPNs to grow three-dimensional physical structures. In *Proceedings of the 12th Annual Conference on Genetic and Evolutionary Computation*, GECCO '10, pages 627–634, New York, NY, USA, 2010. ACM.

[2] J. E. Auerbach and J. C. Bongard. On the relationship between environmental and morphological complexity in evolved robots. In *Proceedings of the Fourteenth International Conference on Genetic and Evolutionary Computation Conference*, GECCO '12, pages 521–528, New York, NY, USA, 2012. ACM.

[3] N. Chaumont, R. Egli, and C. Adami. Evolving virtual creatures and catapults. *Artificial Life*, 13(2):139–157, 2007.

[4] N. Cheney, R. MacCurdy, J. Clune, and H. Lipson. Unshackling evolution: Evolving soft robots with multiple materials and a powerful generative encoding. In *Proceeding of the Fifteenth Annual Conference on Genetic and Evolutionary Computation Conference*, GECCO '13, pages 167–174, New York, NY, USA, 2013. ACM.

[5] K. Glette and M. Hovin. Evolution of artificial muscle-based robotic locomotion in PhysX. In *Intelligent Robots and Systems (IROS), 2010 IEEE/RSJ International Conference on*, pages 1114–1119. IEEE, 2010.

[6] M. Joachimczak and B. Wróbel. Co-evolution of morphology and control of soft-bodied multicellular animats. In *Proceedings of the Fourteenth International Conference on Genetic and Evolutionary Computation Conference*, GECCO '12, pages 561–568, New York, NY, USA, 2012. ACM.

[7] N. Lassabe, H. Luga, and Y. Duthen. A new step for artificial creatures. In *Artificial Life, 2007. ALIFE'07. IEEE Symposium on*, pages 243–250. IEEE, 2007.

[8] J. Lehman and K. Stanley. Evolving a diversity of virtual creatures through novelty search and local competition. In *Proceedings of the 13th annual conference on Genetic and evolutionary computation*, pages 211–218. ACM, 2011.

[9] D. Lessin, D. Fussell, and R. Miikkulainen. Open-ended behavioral complexity for evolved virtual creatures. In *Proceeding of the Fifteenth Annual Conference on Genetic and Evolutionary Computation Conference*, GECCO '13, pages 335–342, New York, NY, USA, 2013. ACM.

[10] T. Miconi. In silicon no one can hear you scream: Evolving fighting creatures. *Genetic Programming*, pages 25–36, 2008.

[11] M. Mitchell. *An Introduction to Genetic Algorithms*. MIT Press, Cambridge, MA, USA, 1998.

[12] K. Sims. Evolving virtual creatures. In *Proceedings of the 21st annual conference on Computer graphics and interactive techniques*, SIGGRAPH '94, pages 15–22, New York, NY, USA, 1994. ACM.

[13] B. Skinner. The behavior of organisms: An experimental analysis. *The Century psychology series*, 1938.

Guided Self-Organization in Indirectly Encoded and Evolving Topographic Maps

Sebastian Risi
Center for Computer Games Research
IT University of Copenhagen
Copenhagen, Denmark
sebr@itu.dk

Kenneth O. Stanley
Department of EECS
University of Central Florida
Orlando, FL 32816, USA
kstanley@eecs.ucf.edu

ABSTRACT

An important phenomenon seen in many areas of biological brains and recently in deep learning architectures is a process known as self-organization. For example, in the primary visual cortex, color and orientation maps develop based on lateral inhibitory connectivity patterns and Hebbian learning dynamics. These *topographic maps*, which are found in all sensory systems, are thought to be a key factor in enabling abstract cognitive representations. This paper shows for the first time that the Hypercube-based NeuroEvolution of Augmenting Topologies (HyperNEAT) method can be seeded to begin evolution with such lateral connectivity, enabling genuine self-organizing dynamics. The proposed approach draws on HyperNEAT's ability to generate a pattern of weights across the connectivity of an artificial neural network (ANN) based on a function of its geometry. Validating this approach, the afferent weights of an ANN self-organize in this paper to form a genuine topographic map of the input space for a simple line orientation task. Most interestingly, this seed can then be evolved further, providing a method to guide the self-organization of weights in a specific way, much as evolution likely guided the self-organizing trajectories of biological brains.

Categories and Subject Descriptors

I.2.6 [**Artificial Intelligence**]: Learning – connectionism and neural nets

General Terms

Algorithms

Keywords

Self-Organization; Topographic Maps; Plastic Neural Networks; Adaptation; Learning; Neuroevolution; CPPNs; HyperNEAT

GECCO'14, July 12–16, 2014, Vancouver, BC, Canada.
Copyright 2014 ACM 978-1-4503-2662-9/14/07 ...$15.00.
http://dx.doi.org/10.1145/2576768.2598369.

1. INTRODUCTION

While *neuroevolution* (NE), i.e. evolving artificial neural networks (ANNs) through evolutionary algorithms, has produced significant results in a variety of different domains [7, 28, 33], the ANNs evolved through NE still often do not include some of the important features seen in natural brains. One example of such a feature is neural plasticity, which allows a plastic ANN to change its internal connection weights during its lifetime based on Hebbian learning. This synaptic plasticity underlies the ability of real brains to learn and to adapt to sudden environmental changes. While there has been progress in incorporating plasticity into NE algorithms [6, 14, 16, 19, 23], so far these approaches are only applied to simple toy problems and do not exhibit many of the important plasticity-enabled features seen in natural brains.

One such "hallmark feature of vertebrate brains" [31] is topographic maps, which are areas of the brain that are spatially organized based on some feature of sensory input from the environment. In topographic maps neurons that respond to related sensory input are located near each other. For example the primary visual cortex (like many other areas in the neocortex) includes a topographic map [30], which means that it is organized such that adjacent neurons respond to adjacent regions of the visual field. Thivierge and Marcus [31] suggest that a key function of topographic maps is to enable abstract cognitive representations.

The topographic maps in the brain are themselves the result of a self-organizing process of synaptic connection weights, in which lateral inhibitory synapses and competitive learning play an important role [13]. As Miikkulainen [13] showed, a biologically realistic *hand-designed* ANN with short range excitatory and long range inhibitory connectivity allows the synaptic weights to self-organize to form a topographic map of the sensory stimuli. The lateral connections between neurons help to focus the initial activation pattern into a localized (winner-take-all) response on the map after which the connection weight are modified based on Hebbian learning.

Because evolving such plastic ANNs from scratch is likely a highly deceptive task [19], the new idea introduced in this paper is that the Hypercube-based NeuroEvolution of Augmenting Topologies (HyperNEAT) method [5, 8, 29] can be seeded to directly begin with the necessary lateral connectivity. This advance is enabled by HyperNEAT's ability to generate a pattern of weights across the connectivity of an evolving neural network based on a function of its geometry.

HyperNEAT employs an indirect encoding called compositional pattern producing networks (CPPNs) [25], which can compactly encode connectivity patterns with regularities such as symmetry, repetition, and repetition with variation. It also showed that giving neurons actual *locations* within the coordinate space of the evolving neural network allows evolution to exploit *topography* (i.e. not just topology), thereby allowing the geometry of sensors to align sensibly with the geometry of neurons in the brain. This type of geometric placement of neurons is missing from many ANN models, yet it is known to be essential to the organization and function of biological brains [24]. Because of this insight, HyperNEAT is able to evolve high-dimensional ANNs with regularities appropriate to the problem domain [4, 8, 9, 29], which is in the case of this paper a self-organizing topographic map.

More importantly, a seeded such structure can than be evolved further, allowing HyperNEAT (1) to guide the self-organization of weights towards a particular target configuration and (2) to accelerate the self-organizing process compared to a uniform weight baseline approach. To demonstrate the potential of this method, experiments in a simple line orientation task are performed, revealing that the seeded HyperNEAT approach is able to form a genuine topographic map of the input space. The main results is that seeding HyperNEAT with a connectivity pattern that encourages the emergence of topographic maps could allow NE approaches to expand the scope of neural structures that evolution can discover to dynamic structures heretofore only seen in neuroscience.

2. BACKGROUND AND RELATED WORK

This section reviews the Neuroevolution of Augmenting Topologies (NEAT) and HyperNEAT methods behind the new approach presented in this paper.

2.1 Neuroevolution of Augmenting Topologies (NEAT)

The HyperNEAT method is itself an extension of the original NEAT algorithm for evolving ANNs. NEAT starts with a population of simple neural networks and then *adds complexity* over generations by adding new nodes and connections through mutations. By evolving networks in this way, the topology of the network does not need to be known a priori; NEAT searches through increasingly complex networks to find a suitable level of complexity. Because it starts simply and gradually adds complexity, it tends to find a solution network close to the minimal necessary size. However, as explained next, it turns out that directly representing connections and nodes as explicit genes in the genome cannot scale up to very large networks. For a complete overview of NEAT see Stanley and Miikkulainen [26].

2.2 HyperNEAT

NEAT is called a *direct encoding* because each part of the solution's representation (i.e. each connection weight in the genome) maps to a single piece of structure in the final solution network [7]. The significant disadvantage of this approach is that even when different parts of the solution are similar, they must be encoded and therefore discovered separately. Thus HyperNEAT introduces an *indirect* encoding instead, which means that the description of the solution is compressed such that information can be reused, allowing the final solution to contain more components than the description itself. Indirect encodings allow solutions to be represented as a *pattern* of parameters, rather than requiring each parameter to be represented individually [1, 9, 25, 27]. HyperNEAT, reviewed in this section, is an indirect encoding extension of NEAT that is proven in a number of challenging domains that require discovering regularities [3, 8, 9, 29]. For a full description see Stanley et al. [29] and Gauci and Stanley [9].

In HyperNEAT, NEAT is altered to evolve an indirect encoding called *compositional pattern producing networks* (CPPNs; [25]) *instead* of ANNs. The CPPN in HyperNEAT plays the role of DNA in nature, but at a much higher level of abstraction; in effect it encodes a pattern of weights that is painted across the geometry of a network. Yet the convenient trick in HyperNEAT is that this encoding is *itself* a network, which means that CPPNs can be evolved by NEAT. A CPPN is a *compositions of functions*, wherein each function loosely corresponds to a useful regularity. For example, a Gaussian function induces symmetry and a periodic function such as sine creates segmentation through repetition. In effect, the indirect CPPN encoding can compactly encode patterns with regularities such as symmetry, repetition, and repetition with variation [20, 25]. Thus as the CPPN increases in complexity, it encodes increasingly complex amalgamations of regularities and symmetries that are projected across the connectivity of a network [8, 9].

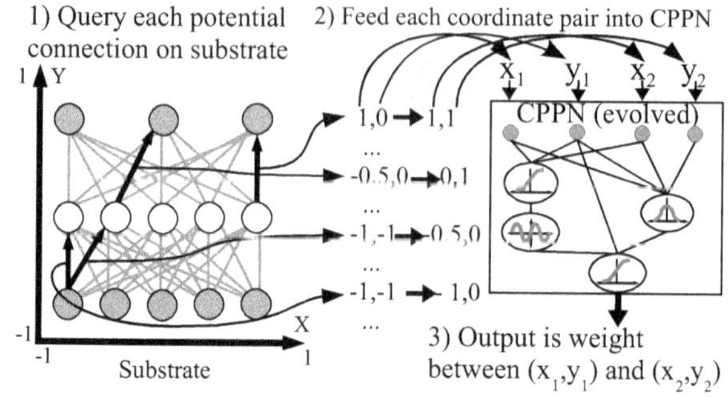

Figure 1: HyperNEAT Geometric Connectivity Pattern Interpretation. A collection of nodes, called the *substrate*, is assigned coordinates that range from -1 to 1 in all dimensions. (1) Every potential connection in the substrate is queried to determine its presence and weight; the dark directed lines in the substrate depicted in the figure represent a sample of connections that are queried. (2) Internally, the CPPN (which is evolved) is a graph that determines which activation functions are connected. As in an ANN, the connections are weighted such that the output of a function is multiplied by the weight of its outgoing connection. For each query, the CPPN takes as input the positions of the two endpoints and (3) outputs the weight of the connection between them. Thus, CPPNs can produce regular patterns of connections in space.

Unlike in many common neural network formalisms, in HyperNEAT neurons exist at *locations* in space. That way, connectivity is expressed across a geometry, like in a natural brain. Formally, CPPNs are *functions* that input the locations of nodes (i.e. the *geometry* of a network) and output weights between those locations. That way, when queried for many pairs of nodes situated in n dimensions, the result is a topographic connectivity pattern in that space. Consider a CPPN that takes four inputs labeled x_1, y_1, x_2, and y_2; this point in four-dimensional space *also* denotes the connection between the two-dimensional points (x_1, y_1) and (x_2, y_2), and the output of the CPPN for that input thereby represents the weight of that connection (figure 1). Because the connections are produced by a function of their endpoints, the final structure is produced with *knowledge* of its geometry. In effect, the CPPN is painting a pattern on the inside of a four-dimensional hypercube that is interpreted as the isomorphic connectivity pattern, which explains the origin of the name *hypercube-based NEAT* (HyperNEAT). Connectivity patterns produced by a CPPN in this way are called *substrates* so that they can be verbally distinguished from the CPPN itself, which is also a network.

Each queried point in the substrate is a node in an ANN. The experimenter defines both the location and role (i.e. hidden, input, or output) of each such node. As a rule of thumb, nodes are placed on the substrate to reflect the geometry of the task [3, 29]. That way, the connectivity of the substrate is a function of the task structure. For example, the sensors of a robot can be placed from left to right on the substrate in the same order that they exist on the robot. Outputs for moving left or right can also be placed in the same order, allowing HyperNEAT to understand from the outset the correlation of sensors to effectors. In this way, knowledge about the problem geometry can be injected into the search and HyperNEAT can exploit the regularities of a problem that are invisible to traditional neural network encodings.

In summary, the HyperNEAT method evolves the internal topology and weights of the CPPN that compactly *encodes* ANN weight patterns. The capabilities of HyperNEAT are important for the approach presented in this paper because the lateral connectivity patterns necessary for the self-organization of connection weights can also be expressed as a function of geometry. As explained next, an extension to HyperNEAT called adaptive HyperNEAT [16], allows not only patterns of weights across the connectivity of an ANN to be generated by a function of its geometry, but also patterns of local learning rules.

2.3 Adaptive HyperNEAT

Unlike traditional static ANNs in neuroevolution whose weights do not change during their lifetime, plastic ANNs [6, 14, 23] that play an important role in the formation of topographic maps [13, 22] can *adapt* by changing their internal connection strengths according to a Hebbian learning rule that modifies synaptic weights based on pre- and postsynaptic neuron activity.

The main idea in adaptive HyperNEAT [16] is that CPPNs can not only encode connectivity patterns but also *patterns of plasticity rules*. As in the brain, different *regions* of the ANN should be more or less plastic and employ different learning rules, which HyperNEAT can facilitate because it sees the ANN geometry. This idea is based on the insight that if a CPPN can paint a pattern of connection weights across network geometry, then it should also be able to paint a pattern of varying *plasticity rules* across the same geometry. That way, it does not need to encode each rule separately (i.e. because the CPPN is an indirect encoding). To facilitate this capability, instead of outputting only a *weight*, the Adaptive HyperNEAT variant in paper has one additional output that encodes the learning rate η of the Hebbian Rule:

$$\Delta w_{ij} = \eta \cdot o_i o_j \, . \qquad (1)$$

In this way, the CPPN computes an entire pattern of Hebbian rules with different learning rates as a function of the neural geometry in a regular pattern across the network. In this paper, adaptive HyperNEAT will be compared to a HyperNEAT variant that assigns learning rate η for every afferent connection uniformly. This comparison is designed to investigate the minimal sufficient adaptive dynamics that allow the automatic self-organization of a topographic map.

3. APPROACH: SEEDING HYPERNEAT WITH LATERAL INHIBITORY CONNECTIVITY PATTERNS

The new idea in this paper is that because the lateral connectivity patterns in topographic maps are related to their geometry, evolution in HyperNEAT can be seeded with geometric principles that bias the pattern of connectivity in a similar way. The hope is that the weights of the resulting ANNs should also self-organize, forming a genuine topographic map of the input stimuli. Additionally, this seed can then be evolved further, providing a method to guide the self-organization of weights in a specific way, much as evolution likely guided the self-organizing trajectories of biological brains (i.e. part of the specific mechanisms for structure formation in biological brains is genetically determined and shaped by evolution [10]).

For example, Miikkulainen [13] modeled the lateral connectivity patterns of a self-organizing ANN, also called self-organizing map (SOM), in form of a "Mexican hat", in which the connections to the closest neurons are excitatory and inhibitory to neurons farther away. Such a connectivity pattern can easily also be expressed by a CPPN, by also including a Mexican hat function to the set of activation functions for HyperNEAT. Because the Mexican hat function peaks when its input is 0.0, inputting a difference between coordinates, e.g. Δx, achieves the highest value when the coordinates are the same and negative values for coordinates further apart than some threshold. The Mexican hat function employed in this paper is described as follows:

$$\gamma(x) = \begin{cases} 0.1, & |x| < 0.6 \\ -0.0125, & |x| > 0.6 \text{ and } |x| < 1.8 \\ 0.0, & \text{otherwise.} \end{cases} \qquad (2)$$

Figure 2 shows an example of such a *SOM-generating CPPN seed* together with the HyperNEAT substrate employed in this paper. The substrate contains a two-dimensional input layer (A) and an output layer (B). The two CPPNs are depictions of the same CPPN being queried to determine the weights and learning rates of two different substrate connections. The CPPN at the bottom receives as input the x and y coordinates of a node in A and a node in B and returns the weight of that connection from its AB output node and the corresponding Hebbian learning rate η of that connection. Note that only the afferent connection weights are adapted during the training of the network. The CPPN on top is the *SOM seed* (i.e. the lateral weights within the SOM in the first generation of evolution), which describes the lateral connectivity pattern of the hidden layer with short range excitatory and long range inhibitory connections. This setup in effect means that the CPPN encodes both the initial starting weights and the temporal dynamics of the plastic component of the network (i.e. the AB connections in Figure 2, yielding the ability to evolve the entire temporal dynamics and starting point for a self-organizing system.

3.1 ANN Activation and Weight Adaptation

The plastic ANN encoded by HyperNEAT is activated for each training input and, following Miikkulainen [13], allowed to settle until it reaches a stable state. The number of activations for the experiments in this paper is set to 15. After the initial network activation the afferent weights are updated based on the Hebbian learning rule (Equation 1) and then normalized to keep the sum of weights constant [2].

The next section introduces the experiments in this paper designed to test HyperNEAT's ability to produce topographic map-like structures that develop through a process of self-organization of connection weights. Additionally, a property common to most abstract implementations of SOMs [12] and more biologically plausible computational models [13, 22] is that the afferent connection weights are normally initialized to small random numbers (such an example is shown in Figure 3a). Therefore, an interesting unexplored question is whether this self-organization could be guided and potentially accelerated by indirectly encoding the initial afferent neural weight patterns. This intriguing possibility is now enabled by HyperNEAT's ability to describe large-scale ANN connectivity patterns as a function of neural geometry.

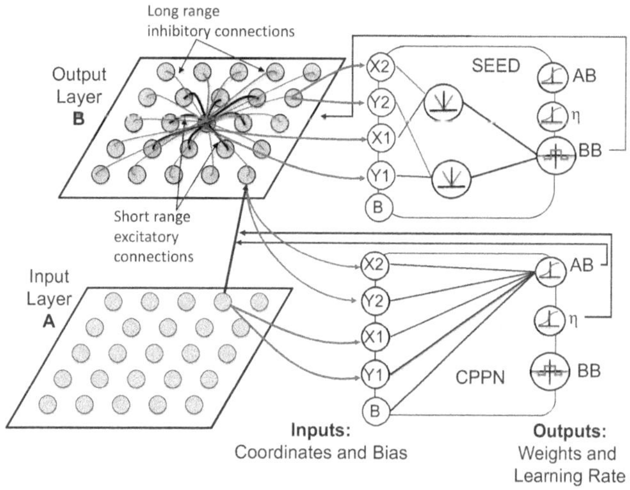

Figure 2: HyperNEAT Substrate and Lateral Connectivity CPPN Seed. The substrate contains a two-dimensional input layer (A) and an output layer (B). The two CPPNs are depictions of the same CPPN being queried to determine the weights and learning rates of two different substrate connections. The CPPN at the bottom receives as input the x and y coordinates of a node in A and a node in B and returns the weight of that connection from its AB output node, as well as the corresponding Hebbian learning rate η of that connection from its η output. The CPPN at the top is being queried simply for the static weight of a connection entirely within the B layer, i.e. a BB connection.

4. EXPERIMENTS

The experiment in this paper tests the ability of the HyperNEAT approach to guide self-organization of connection weights in a line orientation task. In this task, differently-oriented lines are projected onto the ANN retina of 7×7 input neurons. The ANN output layer has the same number and layout of neurons. The substrate structure corresponds to the setup shown in Figure 2 (though the resolution shown in the figure is lower for clarity). At each learning step, one out of eight differently-orientated lines are selected in a *random order* and projected on the retina. This process is repeated for a total of 250 input presentations (following the network activation described in Section 3.1). Topographic maps of visual features such as line orientation are well studied in computational models of self-organization [21] and therefore provide a good first proof of concept for the ability of HyperNEAT to evolve a guided self-organizing process.

To asses the potential advantage of further evolving the initial SOM-generating CPPN seed shown in Figure 2, it is important first to test the self-organization capabilities of the initial seed itself. Figure 3 shows an example of randomly initialized weight patterns from the input neurons to the computational layer (before self-organization) and the weight pattern after training (i.e. 250 input presentations) for the seed-CPPN. The afferent connection weights self-organized such that neurons near each other respond to similar features of the sensory input (i.e. some neurons respond more strongly to particular line orientations than other neurons). The line orientation to which each neuron maximally responds is also shown before and after training with varying orientation increments (Figure 4). This figure shows how the self-organizing process responds to different orientation increments and consequently different number of training samples (eight compared to 30). The weight vectors

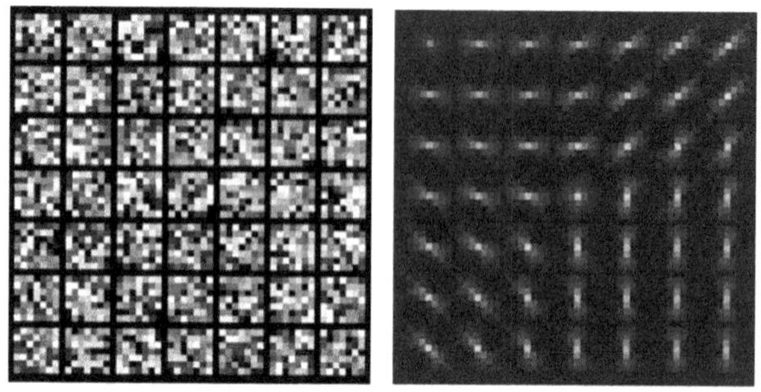

(a) Before Training (b) After Training

Figure 3: Weight Pattern Before and After Self-organization. This figure shows the weight patterns from each input node to all the 7×7 nodes in the output layer before (a) and (b) after self-organization . For example, the square to the top left depicts the connection weights from all 49 (7×7) input nodes to this particular output node.

form a topographic map that correctly reflects the distribution of input stimuli.

Now that the viability of the CPPN seed is established the question in this paper is whether evolution can provide a boost beyond the self-organizing functionality that the seed already provides. To test the hypothesis that HyperNEAT can guide the self-organizing process through indirectly encoded afferent connection weights, the evolved CPPNs are tested on their ability to create ANNs that can self-organize into a *particular* weight configuration *independently of the order of presented input samples*. It is important to note that the aim of this study is not to suggest that the particular final configuration is inherently important in its own right, but rather to make the point that evolution can shape the self-organizing process to push it in a particular direction. In effect, choosing an explicit final target configuration in this experiment makes it easier to show definitively and explicitly that such shaping is possible. In the future this principle can then be applied to more subtle and less explicit endpoints for self-organizing processes. The fitness of a network for this purpose is determined based on:

$$\Phi = 1.0 - \frac{1}{N}\sum_{i=0}^{N} |w_i - c(t)_i|, \qquad (3)$$

where **w** is the weight vector produced by the CPPN seed (as seen in Figure 3b), **c** is the current weight vector at time t and N are the total number of connections in the ANN. This function is evaluated every ten training steps and the resulting values are summed to determine the fitness for one trial. To encourage solutions that match as closely as possible to the final target pattern, a value of 5.0 is added to the fitness each time step that the pattern is within a margin of 0.1% to the target pattern. This fitness function encourages self-organization of connectivity weights into the final configuration as fast as possible. To encourage robust solutions that do not depend on a particular order of input samples, each network is evaluated on five independent trials and the final fitness is the average performance across these trials.

Five different approaches are compared to determine the role of different initial afferent weight patterns and indirectly encoded learning rates on the self-organizing progress:

- In the **Seeded HyperNEAT** approach the initial weights from the input to the output layer of the ANN are determined by the HyperNEAT approach described in Section 2.3 in which

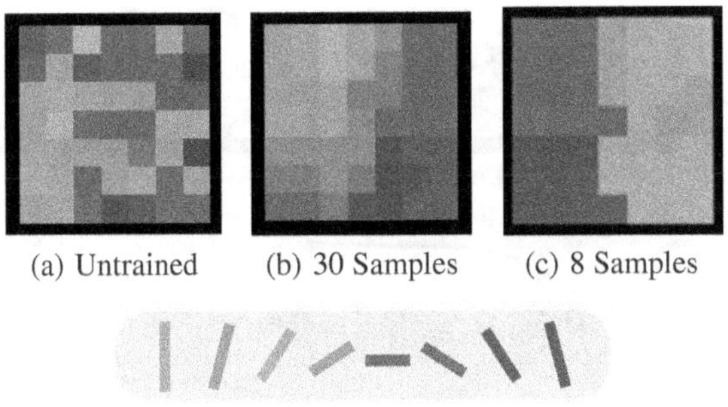

(a) Untrained (b) 30 Samples (c) 8 Samples

(d) Line Orientations

Figure 4: Neuron Orientation Sensitivity. Line orientations (d) are shown to which the neurons in the output layer maximally respond before the self-organization of afferent connection (a), and after the training with different orientation increments and therefore different-sized training samples (30 compared to eight) in (b) and (c). The corresponding self-organized afferent weight patterns for (c) are shown in Figure 3b. The main results is that the weight vectors form a topographic map that correctly reflects the distribution of input stimuli.

evolution is seeded with a lateral connectivity pattern (Figure 2). The Hebbian learning rate for the weights from the input to the outputs nodes are uniformly set to 1.0.

- The **Seeded Uniform** approach follows the Seeeded HyperNEAT approach but the weights from the input to the output layer are all set to an intermediate inform value of 0.5 instead of being determined by HyperNEAT.
- **Seeded Random** tests the influence of starting with random weights in the range [0, 1] from the inputs to the output nodes. This approach reflects the conventional approach initializing the afferent weights in SOMs [12, 13].
- The **Seeded Adaptive HyperNEAT** approach follows the Seeded HyperNEAT approach but in addition to the weights the learning rates are also generated by HyperNEAT (Section 2.3). This approach tests the hypothesis that distributing the learning rules in a pattern could provide an additional advantage.
- In the **Unseeded HyperNEAT** approach in this paper evolution is not seeded (i.e. the initial CPPNs do not contain any hidden nodes). This variant is designed to test the influence of seeding HyperNEAT with a SOM-like connectivity pattern. It is important to note that HyperNEAT can theoretically discover a CPPN similar to the seed CPPN by itself (e.g. a Mexican Hat function can be added during node addition) that would encode a lateral connectivity pattern necessary for self-organization.

4.1 Experimental Parameters

The size of each HyperNEAT population was 50 with 10% elitism and a termination criterion of 50 generations. Sexual offspring (75%) did not undergo mutation. Asexual offspring (25%) had 0.6 probability of weight mutation, 0.06 chance of link addition, and 0.005 chance of node addition. The available CPPN activation functions were sigmoid, Gaussian, absolute value, cosine, Mexican hat, and sine, all with equal probability of being added.

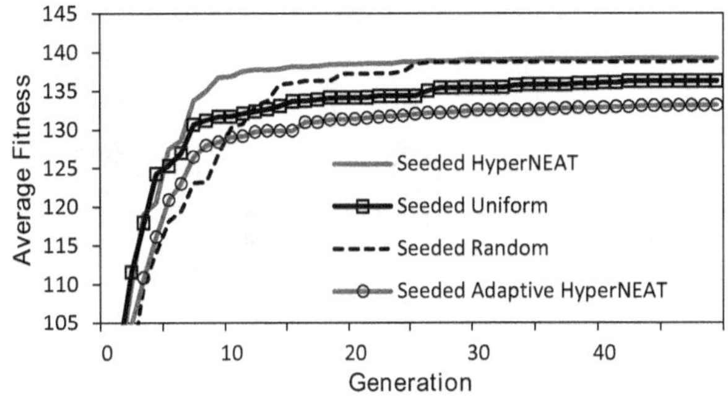

Figure 5: Training Performance. The average best fitness over generations is shown for the different HyperNEAT variants, which are averaged over 30 runs. The main result is that Seeded HyperNEAT and Seeded Random reach a significantly higher average fitness than all other approaches.

5. RESULTS

Each of the HyperNEAT approaches is evaluated over 30 independent runs consisting of 50 generations of evolution. Figure 5 shows the training performance over generations for the different HyperNEAT variants. While the seeded HyperNEAT and Seeded Random approaches reach a similar average maximum fitness of 139.24 ($\sigma = 0.49$) and 138.82 ($\sigma = 0.77$), respectively, the Uniform setup and seeded Adaptive HyperNEAT reach significantly lower average maximum fitness values ($p < 0.05$ according to the Student's t-test). The Unseeded HyperNEAT fails to achieve high average performance and only reaches a fitness of 24.16 ($\sigma = 0.01$) (data not shown).

It is important to note that while the differences in average fitness between the investigated HyperNEAT methods appear relatively small, the number of generations it took them on average to find a solution paints a clearer picture (Figure 6). A network counts as a solution if the error between its final weight pattern (after self-organization) and the training weight pattern is less than 0.01%. Seeded HyperNEAT finds a solution in 7.5 generations on average ($\sigma = 3.01$), which is significantly faster ($p < 0.05$) than any of the other approaches (Figure 6). In fact, the unseeded version fails to find a solution in all 30 runs, confirming the necessity of the initial CPPN seed and the deceptiveness of rediscovering the necessary lateral connectivity pattern through evolution alone. It is interesting to note that Seeded Adaptive HyperNEAT performs significantly worse than Seeded HyperNEAT alone ($p < 0.001$), suggesting that a uniform learning rate is already optimal for this particular task.

Because one motivation for this paper is to investigate the robustness of evolved networks in self-organizing into a particular target configuration, a generalization test was devised to measure how well an evolved solution would perform under different random orders of training samples. The generalization test consists of 30 trials and measures whether solutions get within a margin of 1% and 0.1% to the final weight target configuration shown in Figure 3b. The score on the generalization test reflects the probability that a solution evolved by a particular HyperNEAT variant self-organizes correctly (Figure 7). Seeded HyperNEAT, Seeded Adaptive HyperNEAT and the Uniform approach do not perform significantly different and are able to get within a margin of 1% to the target pattern in 50%, 46% and 56% of the time, respectively. However, all three methods perform significantly better than the Random approach ($p < 0.05$), which only solves the task 35% of the time. The

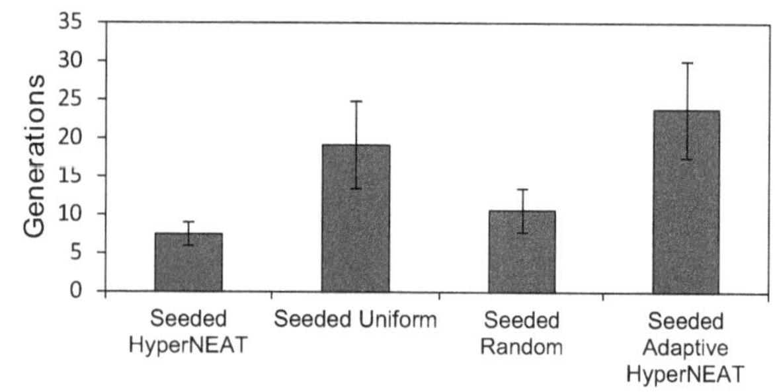

Figure 6: Average Generations to Solution (lower is better). The average number of generations over 30 runs that it took the different HyperNEAT variants to reach the final target configuration (Figure 3b) is shown. The unseeded version fails to find a solution in all 30 runs (data not shown). The main result is that Seeded HyperNEAT finds a solution significantly faster than all the other approaches.

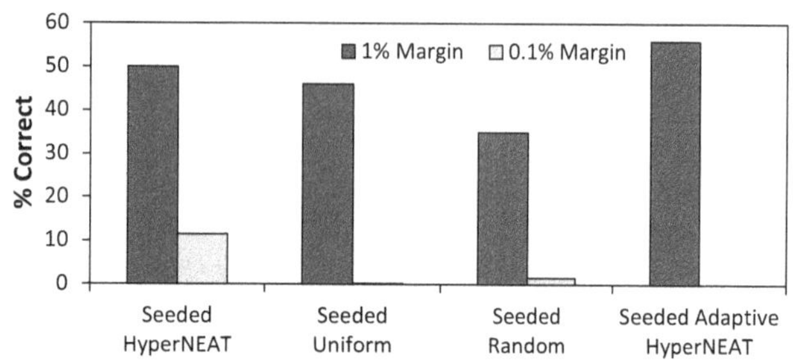

Figure 7: Generalization Test Results. This chart depicts how often the final champions from each of the 30 runs are able to reach the target configuration averaged over 30 independent trials (with different orders of training examples). Higher values are better.

final performance decreases significantly for all approaches if solutions are required get within a margin of 0.1% to the target pattern ($p < 0.001$). Seeded HyperNEAT only passes this stricter generalization test 15% of the times, which is however significantly higher than for the Uniform and Random approach ($p < 0.001$). Interestingly, these results indicate that the Random approach is less reliable in producing the final target configuration and that determining the initial afferent weights through HyperNEAT allows it to self-organize into the target configuration with a greater accuracy.

5.1 Self-Organization Analysis

Because both the Seeded HyperNEAT and the Seeded Uniform approach are able to reach the correct target pattern – within a margin of 1% error – about the same number of times how can their significant difference in final average performance (Figure 5) be explained? A closer look at typical learning curves for both approaches during self-organization of the map (Figure 8) suggest that while the seeded HyperNEAT and Uniform approach ultimately reach a similar accuracy, HyperNEAT reaches it more quickly (and therefore reaches a higher fitness). One way to analyze the reason behind these different progressions is to observe the development of the orientation sensitivity of the output neurons. From Figure 8 it becomes clear that the Seeded HyperNEAT approach is able to establish the correct orientation pattern more quickly than the Uniform approach. Initial uniform weights seem to hinder the self-organizing progress, which could potentially be explained by the increased local competition between neurons (i.e. by starting

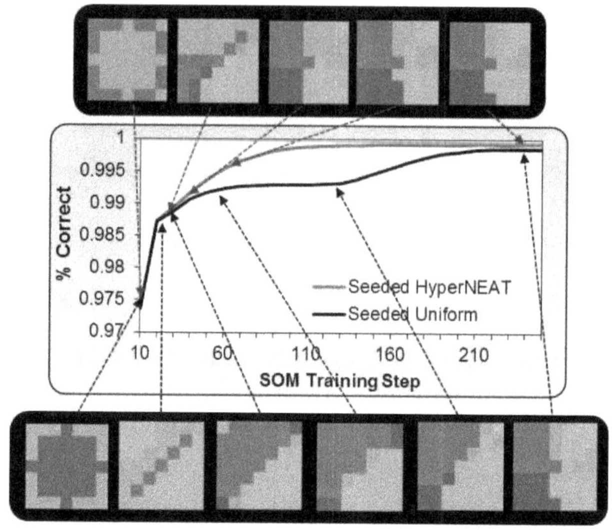

Figure 8: Development of Orientation Preferences. The development of the orientation preferences of the output neurons over time is shown for the Seeded HyperNEAT approach (top) and the Uniform approach (bottom). The initial non-uniform weights (Figure 9) allow the Seeded HyperNEAT approach to self-organize into the target configuration in fewer training steps.

Table 1: Training and Generalization Results. The Seeded HyperNEAT approach often performs significantly better than the other HyperNEAT variants and never significantly worse.

Method	Fitness	Generations	1% Margin
HyperNEAT	**139.2** ($\sigma = 0.49$)	**7.5** ($\sigma = 3.01$)	50%
Random	138.8 ($\sigma = 0.77$)	10.6 ($\sigma = 5.9$)	34%
Uniform	136.2 ($\sigma = 1.70$)	19.1 ($\sigma = 11.4$)	46%
Adaptive	133.1 ($\sigma = 1.82$)	23.8 ($\sigma = 12.5$)	**56%**
Unseeded	24.1 ($\sigma = 0.03$)	-	-

with uniform weights each neuron will initially respond similarly to the same input stimuli). The Seeded HyperNEAT approach on the other hand creates a smooth initial weight pattern (Figure 9) that likely reduces the initial competition among neurons (similarly to a random initialization).

The main result is that while HyperNEAT and the Random setup reach a similar final performance, HyperNEAT is able to reproduce the final target weight pattern significantly more often. Additionally, the Uniform setup reaches an average lower maximum fitness because the self-organization process is delayed when all the weights are initially the same. Overall then the Seeded HyperNEAT approach combines the speed of the Random setup with the reproducibility of the Uniform setup. The results are summarized in Table 1.

6. DISCUSSION AND FUTURE WORK

While the domain presented in this paper is simple, it helps to demonstrate that it is indeed possible to seed HyperNEAT with lateral connectivity that allows the network to self-organize into a genuine topographic map of the input space. Also importantly, self-organization can be guided and accelerated by indirectly encoding the initial afferent neural weight patterns with the HyperNEAT method. While this study does not suggest that a particular final configuration of weights is inherently important in its own

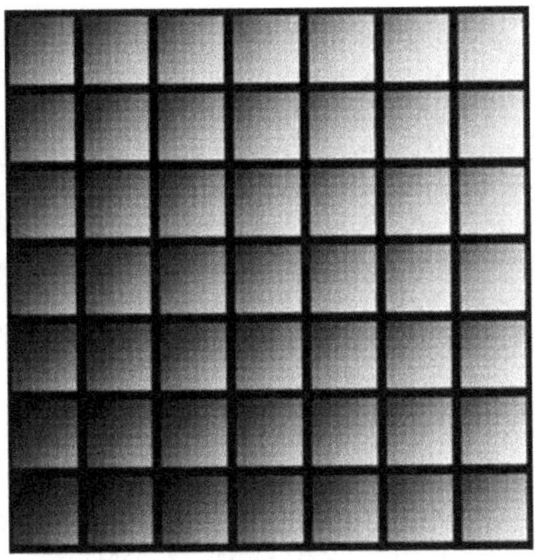

Figure 9: Evolved Initial Weight Pattern for Seeded HyperNEAT. The initial weight pattern from the input nodes to the output nodes is shown that was determined by the Seeded HyperNEAT approach. This pattern provides the self-organizing process with a bias towards a particular target configuration and accelerates the self-organizing process compared to a uniform initialization of connection weights.

right, it nevertheless establishes that such guided self-organization is possible. In effect evolving towards a final target facilitated the analysis of the role of different initial afferent weight patterns and indirectly encoded learning rates on the self-organizing progress.

Interestingly, the poor performance of the unseeded version (Figure 6) suggests that the path through the search space to encoding such lateral connectivity patterns necessary for self-organizing dynamics to emerge is inherently deceptive. Similar results indicating that discovering particular kinds of structures is deceptive were also observed by Verbancsics and Stanley [32] and Risi and Stanley [17] on seeding HyperNEAT with the concept of locality. This growing body of evidence suggests that such deception might be common when geometric principles such as lateral connectivity or locality are essential to achieving the desired behavior but fitness does not reward the intermediate stepping stones that lead to that final objective. Thus manually constructing an appropriate starting seed may prove an important tool to avert deception in many domains. In the future it might also be possible to automatically *compile* a seed that directly satisfies some user-imposed properties [15].

Furthermore, while prior results in a T-Maze learning task suggest the benefit of indirectly encoded learning rules [16], Seeded Adaptive HyperNEAT's performance in this domain is less consistent. It reaches a significantly lower maximum fitness than Seeded HyperNEAT (Figure 5), which could suggest that a uniform learning rate is already optimal for this particular task. However, it performs better on the generalization test (1% margin) than Seeded HyperNEAT (though not significantly), and interestingly, the three most general solutions that solve the task in 80% of the time are all evolved by the Seeded Adaptive HyperNEAT approach. Figure 10 shows the initial weight and learning rate pattern from the most general evolved Adaptive HyperNEAT solution. Although a more detailed analysis is warranted in the future, this result indicates that (1) both learning rate *and* weight pattern can work together to robustly guide the self-organizational process and (2) finding such a solution is harder because the right learning rate pattern also has to be discovered.

In the future it might be possible to combine a SOM-generating seed with a recent HyperNEAT extension called adaptive evolvable-substrate HyperNEAT [17, 18]. Adaptive ES-HyperNEAT can automatically determine the placement, density and plasticity of neurons in the HyperNEAT substrate. Thus seeding the adaptive ES-HyperNEAT approach with the right lateral connectivity could in principle allow structures reminiscent of deep learning architectures [11] to evolve, in which the internal layers self-organize into topographic maps that in each successive layer form higher and higher abstract representations of the input space.

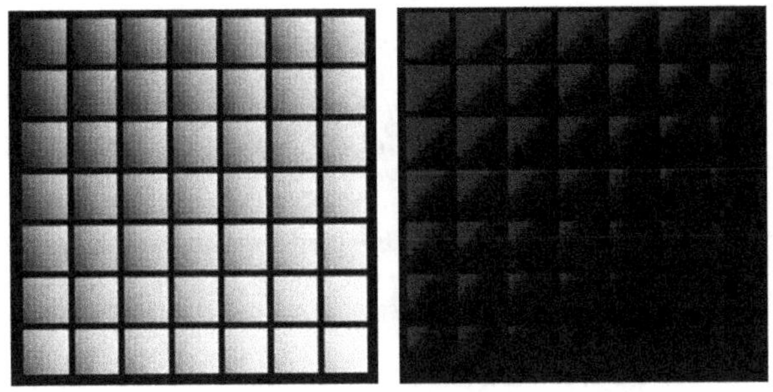

(a) Weight Pattern (b) Learning Rate Pattern

Figure 10: Evolved Initial Weight and Learning Rate Pattern for Seeded Adaptive HyperNEAT. The initial weight and learning rate pattern for the afferent connections are shown that were determined by the Seeded Adaptive HyperNEAT approach. The very robust performance of this evolved solution on the generalization test suggests that both weights *and* learning rate patterns can work together to bias the self-organizing process.

7. CONCLUSION

This paper introduced the idea that the indirect HyperNEAT encoding can be seeded with a lateral inhibitory connectivity pattern, which then allows the weights from the inputs to the hidden layer to self-organize to form a genuine topographic map of the input space. The benefit of this new approach is that the initial seed can be evolved further to accelerate the self-organizing process and to bias it towards a specific target configuration. An interesting implication is that enabling HyperNEAT to capture this key feature of natural systems might now allow us to evolve architectures resembling deep learning networks that also rely on unsupervised learning processes.

References

[1] J. C. Bongard. Evolving modular genetic regulatory networks. In *Proc. of the 2002 Congress on Evolutionary Computation*, 2002.

[2] Y. Choe, J. Sirosh, and R. Miikkulainen. Laterally interconnected self-organizing maps in hand-written digit recognition. *Advances in neural information processing systems*, pages 736–742, 1996.

[3] J. Clune, B. E. Beckmann, C. Ofria, and R. T. Pennock. Evolving coordinated quadruped gaits with the HyperNEAT generative encoding. In *Proceedings of the IEEE Congress on Evolutionary Computation (CEC-2009) Special Session on Evolutionary Robotics*, Piscataway, NJ, USA, 2009. IEEE Press.

[4] J. Clune, K. O. Stanley, R. T. Pennock, and C. Ofria. On the performance of indirect encoding across the continuum of regularity. *Evolutionary Computation, IEEE Transactions on*, 15(3):346–367, 2011.

[5] D. D'Ambrosio and K. O. Stanley. A novel generative encoding for exploiting neural network sensor and output geometry. In *Proceedings of the Genetic and Evolutionary Computation Conference (GECCO 2007)*, New York, NY, 2007. ACM Press.

[6] D. Floreano and J. Urzelai. Evolutionary robots with online self-organization and behavioral fitness. *Neural Networks*, 13:431–443, 2000.

[7] D. Floreano, P. Dürr, and C. Mattiussi. Neuroevolution: from architectures to learning. *Evolutionary Intelligence*, 1(1): 47–62, 2008.

[8] J. Gauci and K. O. Stanley. A case study on the critical role of geometric regularity in machine learning. In *Proceedings of the Twenty-Third AAAI Conference on Artificial Intelligence (AAAI-2008)*, Menlo Park, CA, 2008. AAAI Press.

[9] J. Gauci and K. O. Stanley. Autonomous evolution of topographic regularities in artificial neural networks. *Neural Computation*, 22:1860–1898, 2010.

[10] C. S. Goodman and C. J. Shatz. Developmental mechanisms that generate precise patterns of neuronal connectivity. *Cell*, 72:77–98, 1993.

[11] G. E. Hinton, S. Osindero, and Y.-W. Teh. A fast learning algorithm for deep belief nets. *Neural computation*, 18(7): 1527–1554, 2006.

[12] T. Kohonen. *Self-organizing maps*, volume 30. Springer, 2001.

[13] R. Miikkulainen. Self-organizing process based on lateral inhibition and synaptic resource redistribution. In *Proceedings of the International Conference on Artificial Neural Networks*, pages 415–420, 1991.

[14] Y. Niv, D. Joel, I. Meilijson, and E. Ruppin. Evolution of reinforcement learning in uncertain environments: A simple explanation for complex foraging behaviors. *Adaptive Behavior*, 10(1):5–24, 2002. ISSN 1059-7123.

[15] S. Risi. A Compiler for CPPNs: Transforming Phenotypic Descriptions Into Genotypic Representations. In *Proceedings of the 2013 AAAI Fall Symposium on How Should Intelligence be Abstracted in AI Research*, 2013.

[16] S. Risi and K. O. Stanley. Indirectly encoding neural plasticity as a pattern of local rules. In S. Doncieux, B. Girard, A. Guillot, J. Hallam, J.-A. Meyer, and J.-B. Mouret, editors, *From Animals to Animats 11*, volume 6226 of *Lecture Notes in Computer Science*, pages 533–543. Springer Berlin / Heidelberg, 2010.

[17] S. Risi and K. O. Stanley. An enhanced hypercube-based encoding for evolving the placement, density, and connectivity of neurons. *Artificial Life*, 18(4):331–363, 2012.

[18] S. Risi and K. O. Stanley. A unified approach to evolving plasticity and neural geometry. In *Neural Networks (IJCNN), The 2012 International Joint Conference on*. IEEE, 2012.

[19] S. Risi, C. E. Hughes, and K. O. Stanley. Evolving plastic neural networks with novelty search. *Adaptive Behavior - Animals, Animats, Software Agents, Robots, Adaptive Systems*, 18:470–491, December 2010. ISSN 1059-7123.

[20] J. Secretan, N. Beato, D. B. D'Ambrosio, A. Rodriguez, A. Campbell, and K. O. Stanley. Picbreeder: Evolving pictures collaboratively online. In *CHI '08: Proceedings of the twenty-sixth annual SIGCHI conference on Human factors in computing systems*, pages 1759–1768, New York, NY, USA, 2008. ACM.

[21] J. Sirosh and R. Miikkulainen. Cooperative self-organization of afferent and lateral connections in cortical maps. *Biological Cybernetics*, 71(1):65–78, 1994.

[22] J. Sirosh and R. Miikkulainen. Topographic receptive fields and patterned lateral interaction in a self-organizing model of the primary visual cortex. *Neural Computation*, 9(3): 577–594, 1997.

[23] A. Soltoggio, J. A. Bullinaria, C. Mattiussi, P. Dürr, and D. Floreano. Evolutionary advantages of neuromodulated plasticity in dynamic, reward-based scenarios. In *Artificial Life XI*, pages 569–576, Cambridge, MA, 2008. MIT Press.

[24] O. Sporns. Network analysis, complexity, and brain function. *Complexity*, 8(1):56–60, 2002.

[25] K. O. Stanley. Compositional pattern producing networks: A novel abstraction of development. *Genetic Programming and Evolvable Machines Special Issue on Developmental Systems*, 8(2):131–162, 2007.

[26] K. O. Stanley and R. Miikkulainen. Evolving neural networks through augmenting topologies. *Evolutionary Computation*, 10:99–127, 2002.

[27] K. O. Stanley and R. Miikkulainen. A taxonomy for artificial embryogeny. *Artificial Life*, 9(2):93–130, 2003.

[28] K. O. Stanley and R. Miikkulainen. Competitive coevolution through evolutionary complexification. *Journal of Artificial Intelligence Research*, 21:63–100, 2004.

[29] K. O. Stanley, D. B. D'Ambrosio, and J. Gauci. A hypercube-based indirect encoding for evolving large-scale neural networks. *Artificial Life*, 15(2):185–212, 2009.

[30] N. Swindale. The development of topography in the visual cortex: A review of models. *Network: Computation in neural systems*, 7(2):161–247, 1996.

[31] J.-P. Thivierge and G. F. Marcus. The topographic brain: from neural connectivity to cognition. *Trends in neurosciences*, 30(6):251–259, 2007.

[32] P. Verbancsics and K. O. Stanley. Constraining Connectivity to Encourage Modularity in HyperNEAT. In *Proceedings of the Genetic and Evolutionary Computation Conference (GECCO 2011)*, New York, NY, 2011. ACM.

[33] X. Yao. Evolving artificial neural networks. *Proceedings of the IEEE*, 87(9), September 1999.

Some Distance Measures for Morphological Diversification in Generative Evolutionary Robotics

Eivind Samuelsen
Institute of Informatics, University of Oslo
Postboks 1080 Blindern
0316 Oslo, Norway
eivinsam@ifi.uio.no

Kyrre Glette
Institute of Informatics, University of Oslo
Postboks 1080 Blindern
0316 Oslo, Norway
kyrrehg@ifi.uio.no

ABSTRACT

Evolutionary robotics often involves optimization in large, complex search spaces, requiring good population diversity. Recently, measures to actively increase diversity or novelty have been employed in order to get sufficient exploration of the search space either as the sole optimization objective or in combination with some performance measurement.

When evolving morphology in addition to the control system, it can be difficult to construct a measure that sufficiently captures the qualitative differences between individuals. In this paper we investigate four diversity measures, applied in a set of evolutionary robotics experiments using an indirect encoding for evolving robot morphology. In the experiments we optimize forward locomotion capabilities of symmetrical legged robots in a physics simulation.

Two distance measures in Cartesian phenotype feature spaces are compared with two methods operating in the space of possible morphology graphs. These measures are used for computing a diversity objective in a multi-objective evolutionary algorithm, and compared to a control case with no diversity objective.

For the given task one of the distance measures shows a clear improvement over the control case in improving the main objectives, while others display better ability to diversify, underlining the difficulty of designing good, general measures of morphological diversity.

Categories and Subject Descriptors

I.2.9 [**Computing Methodologies**]: Artificial Intelligence—*Robotics*

General Terms

Design, experimentation

Keywords

Evolutionary robotics, indirect encoding, multiple solutions / niching

GECCO'14, July 12–16, 2014, Vancouver, BC, Canada.

ACM 978-1-4503-2662-9/14/07 ...$15.00.
http://dx.doi.org/10.1145/2576768.2598325.

1. INTRODUCTION

In situations where human intervention is difficult or impossible, automatic robot adaptation or repair would be desirable. With the recent and frequent advances in 3D printing technology, such as an increasing number of materials, higher speeds, and portability, new possibilities open up for the design or repair of robotic systems. For example, one could imagine a team of robots including a mobile 3D printer, capable of repairing or producing new robot morphologies in situ [21].

Evolutionary robotics (ER) approaches the challenge of automatic design and adaptation of robotic systems through the use of evolutionary algorithms (EAs) - population-based search algorithms inspired by evolution in nature [20]. While ER research has mainly been concentrated on the optimization of robotic control systems, e.g. for legged robots [9], using software simulations it is also possible to address the challenge of simultaneously optimizing robot morphology and control [16].

Automated robot design without a fixed topology introduces an encoding challenge, as more complex data structures are needed to describe the space of possible solutions. Thus, ER research has produced a wide variety of coding schemes for describing morphology. In [13] a tree-based structure is used, where each node represents one of several possible standard modules like joints or variable sized rigid elements. A wide variety of relatively realistic robotic tasks are optimized for, starting from initial populations of hand-made designs.

In [16], simulated locomoting robots with co-evolved morphology and control were reproduced and tested in real life. The reproduction was done using 3D-printing and standard actuator components. The encoding used is direct, and very low-level: The control system is a fully connected, variable size artificial neural network, and the morphology is represented as a number of rigid bars or linear actuators connecting points in space. While this approach succeeded in creating real-life robots capable of forward locomotion, the encoding lacked support for the kind of modularity and structural regularity seen in nature.

In generative and developmental systems, complex phenotypes are generated from simpler genotypes through some sort of indirect encoding. This encoding is used as a developmental program, or set of instructions that can be evaluated to produce the phenotype. These encodings are highly productive - they can produce highly complex and structured results from very terse information [10] and are known to outperform direct encoding in simple morphology optimization tasks [11].

In the perhaps most well-known example of generative co-evolution of morphology and control [24], animal-like creatures are evolved in a virtual environment using a graph-based representation. Morphology is described by means of a directed graph, which may also contain cycles, and advanced morphologies with repeating or fractal structures are achieved. The control system is a network with nodes representing mathematical functions. A variety of behaviors like walking, swimming and following are evolved.

Other generative approaches to evolution of robot morphology and control in virtual environments include gene regulatory network encodings [3], producing robot morphologies consisting of smaller building blocks, and compositional pattern producing network methods [1, 2], resulting in morphologies with complex surfaces.

A generative co-evolutionary approach which also takes the step of producing the evolved results in the real world is presented in [10]. Here, robots are encoded with initial values and production rules for an L-system, which are then interpreted into morphology and control components. The resulting robots display aspects of symmetry and modularity, and have a higher complexity and fitness than directly encoded robots.

While EAs are effective on large and complex search spaces, they may still suffer from premature convergence and thus it is of interest to encourage an exploratory search based on a diverse population of solutions. Several approaches exist to encourage population diversity, such as niching or fitness sharing [23]. Another efficient approach is to include a diversity measure as a separate objective in a multi-objective setting [4]. This approach has also shown to be efficient in ER, where an added diversity objective can help overcome the so-called bootstrap problem [18]. Another recent approach to evolutionary search is the novelty search, which abandons fitness objectives altogether and explores purely based on new behavior [14], e.g. solutions which are different than those already explored. This approach can also be combined with performance objectives in hybrid approaches [17, 15].

Common for all of the methods is the need for a distance measure which defines the distance between two solutions. While such a distance can easily be defined as e.g. the Euclidean distance between two constant-sized real-value genomes, it is less straightforward to define in genotype space where the solutions have developed to various sizes and structures, like a neural network graph. Further, for the evolution of robot control systems, the links between the genotypic description, the phenotypic controller structure, and the final behavior may be complex, and thus approaches based on comparing the differences in the resulting behavior may be preferred. In [19], a behavior-based distance outperformed a neural network structure distance in the phenotype space.

While there are some approaches to general distance measures based on behavior [8, 6], these methods assume a fixed robot morphology and operate on clearly defined behavior vectors such as sensory-motor values or leg-ground contact. It is less obvious how such measures would be defined in a context where the morphology changes, e.g. when new limbs with new motors are generated and radically different locomotion strategies appear.

On the other hand, with generative mappings specifying morphology there is an interest for differentiating the solutions on a phenotypic level, as the mapping from genotype to phenotype may be highly nonlinear. One approach to this would be to quantify some properties of the morphologies, such as width, height, and number of joints. These properties were applied in the evolution of virtual creatures in [15], using a novelty search approach.

However, such a list of properties does not necessarily distinguish well between different structural differences. One approach may be to implement more specific morphology descriptors, such as e.g. the number of legs, if this kind of information is available. As several morphology constructions can be seen as graphs, a general graph distance metric could be applied, such as graph probing [19] or the graph edit distance (GED) [7]. However, finding the general GED is an NP-hard problem, and may thus easily become a computational challenge.

In this paper we investigate some distance measures for generative robot morphologies. The distance measures are evaluated in an evolutionary robotics setting, where we evolve simulated robot morphologies for a relatively simple locomotion task, using two different control strategies. We compare a diversity-neutral search with the different distance measures, employed in the diversity objective of a multi-objective evolutionary algorithm (MOEA).

The first measure is similar to the one proposed in [15], which operates in a three-dimensional Cartesian morphology space. We then define a second measure which also operates in a three-dimensional Cartesian space, but gives a more detailed description of the topology of the body. The next two distances are graph-based measures, one morphology-specific and one which builds on a restricted case of the graph edit distance.

The remainder of this paper is organized as follows: In Section 2 an overview of the generative coding is given, followed by a definition of the distance measures, and then the experimental setup. The results of the experiments are shown in Section 3. Section 4 contains discussion of the results, before a conclusion and pointers for future work are given in Section 5.

2. METHODS

To examine the performance of the four diversity measures, a set of experiments were performed in which an MOEA was to maximize forward movement, while minimizing mass and maximizing one of the diversity measures. The four measures were also compared to the base case of optimizing forward movement and mass alone, with no diversity objective. All five cases were run with two different control system encodings to reduce any bias introduced by the control system.

The EA used is NSGA-II [5], and the evaluations were done using the PhysX physics simulation engine. The encoding that is used will be described in Subsection 2.1, followed by a description of the physical parameters and control system parameters that are evolved, in Subsection 2.2. Then the evaluation and objective functions are described in Subsection 2.3, before the diversity measures are detailed in Subsection 2.4. Finally, the general setup of the experiments is explained in Subsection 2.5.

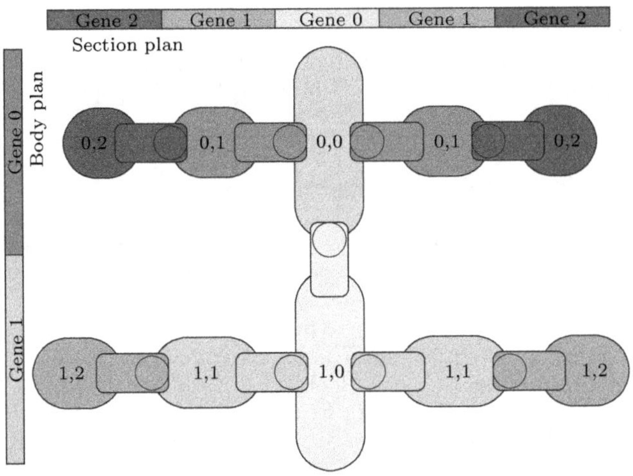

Figure 1: Morphological encoding. The two sets of genes are expressed in different combinations in different parts of the phenotype.

2.1 Encoding

The encoding used in the experiments is based on the Hox-gene inspired encoding used in [22]. Inspired by how morphology is encoded in animals, the encoding is restricted to creating symmetric bodies with a spine-limb structure by describing a single limb-generating program and a set of parameters specific to each spinal section. To generate the complete morphology, the limb-generating program, or section plan, is instanced once for each spinal section, generating a unique limb consisting of a spinal segment and one or more limb segments by using that sections parameters, as illustrated in Figure 1.

As in [22], the limb-generating program is simply a variable-length list of genes, where each gene encodes the parameters used to describe the morphology of one segment. However, here a more generalized method is used to apply the section parameters during phenotype development. The body plan genes for each section k contain a fixed number of values $h_1^{(k)}, h_2^{(k)}, \ldots, h_N^{(k)}$. These genes encode the values that differentiate between sections; each value $H_i^{(k)}$ of section k is calculated as

$$H_i^{(k)} = \begin{cases} h_i^{(k)} + H_i^{(k-1)} & \text{if } k > 0 \\ h_i^{(k)} & \text{else} \end{cases}$$

The parameters in the section plan genes are encoded as $N + 1$-dimensional vectors $[p_0, p_1, p_2, \ldots, p_N]$ in the genotype. Each expressed value $p^{(j,k)}$ of segment j in section k is then calculated as

$$p^{(j,k)} = p_0^{(j)} + \sum_{i=1}^{N} H_i^{(k)} p_i^{(j)}$$

Crossover is done by cloning each parent and matching up genes in each clone by their historical markers. Each gene contains one such marker; they are always inherited unchanged, and new marker values only appear when a mutation causes new genes to appear. Unmatched genes are left untouched by the crossover operator. Crossover of the parameters in a gene is done by whole arithmetic recombination.

Table 1: Evolution parameters

Parameter function	Symbol	Value
Population size	μ	200
Body plan parameter mutation size	σ_H	0.2
Control system parameter mutation size	σ_C	0.1
Morphology parameter mutation size	σ_M	0.05
Gene insertion probability	p_I	0.0025
Gene deletion probability	p_D	0.005

Mutation is done by by applying a normal-distributed random variable with a zero mean to each parameter. The various parameters were mutated using three different standard deviation values, as summarized in Table 1.

During mutation, each gene also has a probability of having a new gene inserted behind it or having its next gene deleted. In these experiments the maximum number of genes in the body plan and section plan is set to 3. This limits the outcomes to a maximum of 3 pairs of limbs and 2 joints in each limb. Which limits the size of the morphology search space, and stops the diversity measures from promoting individuals with an increasingly large number of joints.

This was done partly because we wanted to focus the search on robots that were easy, and not too costly, to construct in real life; partly because initial experiments indicated that removing these limits would require an increase in population size beyond what could be afforded for the experiments presented here.[1] The limits are implemented by setting the insert probability to 0 when the number of genes has reached its maximum. Otherwise the insertion and deletion probabilities are as shown in Table 1.

2.2 Parameters and Control Systems

The section plan genes encode a small number of physical parameters. The spine segment, of which there is always exactly one in the section plan, has two parameters: the segment length l and the side offset o that decides how far along the side of the spine segment the first limb segment will appear, if present. The limb segments, which constitute the rest of the section plan, has three parameters: the segment length l, the axis-of-rotation angle A_ϕ that controls the twist of the limb joint compared to the previous joint, and the rest angle A_ψ that adds an offset to the angle which the joint will start the simulation in, which is considered the zero point in the control systems.

As all parameters were coded as real numbers with no limits, the segment length and the side offset were translated using the formulas

$$\begin{aligned} L &= L' \cdot \exp(l) \\ O &= 1/(1 + \exp(-o)) \end{aligned}$$

This was done in order to map them onto more suitable ranges ($(0, \infty)$ and $(0, 1)$ respectively). Here, L' is the length

[1]The two graph-based measures, at least, will intuitively strive to spread the population evenly out across all $\sum_{n=1}^{N} M^n$ possible topologies. Here, N is the maximum number of sections and M is the maximum number of segments in each section, including the spine. $N = 3$, $M = 3$ gives 39 possibilities. Increasing both by only 1 would result in 340 possibilities, so the population would have to be increased dramatically to ensure that candidates from the 39 topologies in the smaller search space are properly represented.

of the previous limb or spine segment. In the case of the first spine segment L' was set to 0.1 m. If the segment length is less than what is required to contain the necessary servo motor, the segment, and any following segments in the section plan, would not be expressed. This mechanism enables different sections to have different number of limb segments. Subsequently, if the infeasibly short segment is a spine segment, the following sections in the body plan would not be expressed either.

One of two control systems was used in the experiments. Both are simple open-loop systems, and produce periodical signals with a frequency of 1 Hz. The first control system is a simple amplitude-phase system, as used in [12], which can be expressed as

$$C_{\alpha\phi}(t) = \alpha \tanh\left(4 \sin\left(2\pi\left(t + \phi\right)\right)\right)$$

In principle, this control system has two parameters per joint, but in this case the amplitude is coded symmetrically along with the morphology, and the phases are coded differentially, reducing it to three parameters per joint pair: amplitude, phase, and phase offset for the second joint in the pair.

The second control system is a cyclic cubic B-spline with four knots, located at $t_0 = 0$, $t_1 = 0.25$, $t_2 = 0.5$ and $t_3 = 0.75$, with a period of one. Strictly speaking the B-spline then only needs four control values to be fully defined, but here two differentially coded phase parameters are added to be able to ensure that smooth phase changes are likely to occur during mutation. The encoding is symmetrical like the amplitude-offset system, resulting in six parameters per joint pair.

2.3 Evaluation

Each individual in the population is evaluated by simulating its behavior for 8 simulated seconds. After 1 s of settling time has passed, the position of the robot is reset to a fixed starting point in the environment. After the remaining 7 s have passed, the distance traveled by the robot is measured as the displacement of the tip of the front spine segment along the axis that segment was pointing at the beginning of the simulation. The mass objective value uses the mass calculated by the simulator.[2]

In order to make the task more challenging, low, wide obstacles were placed in the simulated environment at regular intervals. The obstacles were 2 cm tall and 2 cm deep, and extended 10 m in each direction. The first obstacle was put 0.5 m in front of the robot, with a new obstacle appearing every half meter after that. The thickness of the robot limbs were set to 4 cm, so the obstacles only add a degree of unevenness to the ground, forcing the robots to lift themselves up slightly to move forward past the first half meter.

The morphology of the robots was variable to a very large degree, making infeasible constructions probable. To minimize this problem robots that had no joints, or that clearly did not simulate properly (e.g. robots that resulted in movement scores $\geq$ 1 km) were removed before the survival selection.

[2]The simulations was done using PhysX version 3.3 beta-2, with a fixed timestep of 1/128 s. The robot models and obstacles were constructed with capsule and box primitives and the joints were free 1D revolute joints with additional custom constraints to simulate internal friction and torque exerted by a basic DC motor model.

2.4 Diversity

The diversity of an individual x in the population P_n is the average distance to all other individuals in the population, which can be written as:

$$D_d(x) = \frac{1}{|P_n| - 1} \sum_{y \in P_n} d(x, y)$$

Here, d is the distance measure used. This paper compares four different distance measures, operating in different phenotype spaces. Two of these are Cartesian spaces, both mapping the robot morphology to points in $\mathbb{R}^3$, with each of the three axes corresponding to a scalar feature of the morphology. In the first measure, the three features are the height, mass and number of joints (HMJ), as seen in [15], except the Euclidean distance is used as the distance value instead of its square:

$$d_{HMJ}(x, y) = \|HMJ(x) - HMJ(y)\|$$

The three features in the second measure, length-branches-depth (LBD), is the sum of segment lengths, the number of branches in the robot topology (i.e. the number of sections with at least one limb segment), and the depth of the longest branch (i.e., the maximum number of joints in any limb). As with the first measure, the Euclidean distance is used:

$$d_{LBD}(x, y) = \|LBD(x) - LBD(y)\|$$

The phenotype space of the other two is a graph space, so other distance metrics have to be used. The first measure is the degree-2 graph edit distance (GED), as explained in [25], which limits the graph edit distance search to only inserting and removing nodes with no more than two neighbors. The insert and remove costs are $\gamma(\Lambda \to v) = 1$ and $\gamma(u \to \Lambda) = 1$, and the relabel cost is

$$\gamma(u \to v) = 1 - \exp\left(-|L_u - L_v|\right)$$

where l_x is the length of segment x. This way the differences between two matched segments can never be greater than the difference from removing or inserting a segment. The time complexity of this algorithm is bounded by $O\left(NME^2\right)$, where N and M are the number of nodes in the two graphs and E is the maximum number of outgoing nodes in any node in the two graphs. Here, E is guaranteed to be less or equal to 3, resulting in a time complexity of $O(NM)$, but with a large constant factor, because each of the NM operations are quite expensive.

The second graph measure exploits the fact that all evolvable morphologies are symmetric and can be laid out in two dimensions with coordinates as shown in Figure 1. By doing a topology sweep (TS), an approximation of the graph edit distance can be found as the best correlation between two-dimensional images of the topologies. Each segment is given a coordinate (i, j), where i is the index of the body section the link belongs to (e.g. all segments in the head section have $i = 0$), and $|j|$ is the number of segments to the spine. The sign of j is positive on the right side and negative on the right. This finds the difference of the best match between the two morphologies by summing up the cost of replacing the segments in the first morphology with the segments of the second, displaced by some k along the i axis:

$$d_{TS}(x, y) = \min_k \sum_i \sum_j \gamma\left(s^x_{i,j} \to s^y_{i+k,j}\right)$$

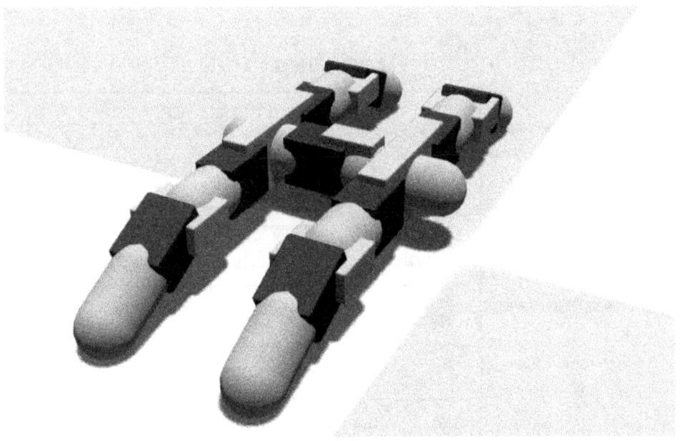

Figure 2: The initial prototype robot.

if body x has no segment at position i, j then $s^x_{i,j} = \Lambda$, and $\gamma(\Lambda \rightarrow \Lambda)$ is naturally zero. The implementation used is not very efficient, using $O(NMS)$ time, where S is the number of sections in the longest robot. Since S here is less or equal to 3, this reduces to the same complexity as the GED, however, the operations are much cheaper in this case, resulting in run times comparable to that of the Cartesian measures.

2.5 Experimental Setup

Each diversity measure, along with the control case without any diversity measure, was tested with both control systems in order to reduce any bias introduced by the specific control system used. To simplify implementation, the runs with no diversity measure were run with a third dummy objective, which would always evaluate to zero, that in effect reduce the algorithm to two-objective optimization. In total, there is 10 different combinations of diversity measures and control systems. In these experiments, each combination was run 21 times. At the end of each generation, the objective values of each surviving individual were recorded. The number of branches and the depth features of each individual, as used in d_{LBD}, was also recorded for later analysis. Each run was terminated after the 600th generation. At the end of each run, the average diversity of the final population is recorded, as measured by all four diversity measures.

The population was initialized with genotypes based on a prototype with two body plan genes and three section plan genes. The segment length parameters were $l_0 = 1$, $l_1 = 0.9$ and $l_1 = 1.1$, resulting in segment lengths of 10 cm, 9 cm and 9.9 cm respectively. The other parameters of the first two segments were zero, while the parameters were $A_\phi = \pi/2$ and $A_\psi = -\pi/6$ for the outer limb segment. The robot generated by these parameters is shown in Figure 2. All control system parameters are initialized to zero. To generate the initial population, this prototype was then cloned μ times, and then each of the clones were mutated 10 times.

To measure how the diversity measures affects the main objective of forward locomotion, a linear regression model is estimated that predicts the 90th percentile forward moving individual[3] of the population at a given generation. Even though considerable effort has been spent to implement con-

[3]Since the population size was 200 in all the experiments, this corresponds to the 20th best individual ranked by that objective.

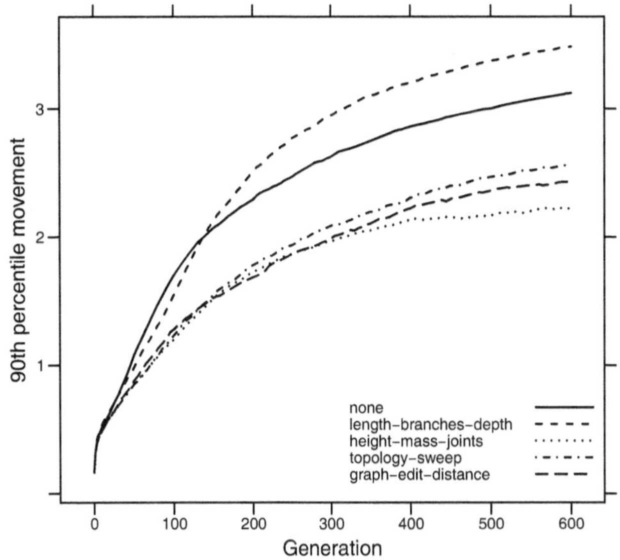

Figure 3: (Expected) average performance of the algorithm as measured by the 90th percentile forward moving individual for the different diversity measures after different generations.

straints so that impractical or faulty solutions are not scored well, some will always slip through[4] and appear as outliers on the fringes of the population. The 90th percentile is more robust against outliers than the single best individual, while still being a good indication of the performance achieved by the best individuals . The model is on the form

$$\hat{s}_U(C, V) = \alpha_0 + \alpha_C C + \alpha_V$$

Here, U is the diversity case (i.e. one of the diversity measures or no diversity measure) used as the basis for the model and V is the diversity case we want to model the performance of. α_0 is the expected score of diversity case U with the amplitude-phase control system, and α_V is the expected difference between cases U and V. This model is robust in the sense that when applied the predicted score will be the same regardless of the choice of U.

When fitting the model, C is set to one for all runs with the cubic spline control system, and zero otherwise. The $\alpha_C C$ term of the model accounts for systematic differences in score between the two control systems. Setting $C = 0.5$ gives a model for the average expected score for the two control systems.

3. RESULTS

The expected forward locomotion performance of the different diversity measures over generations are shown in Figure 3. Table 2 shows the p-values of the T-test on the pairwise differences in performance, as found by calculating $\hat{s}_U$ for all cases. The matrix is symmetric, so only the lower triangular part is supplied.

[4]For example, the runs using the HMJ measure were vulnerable to extremely tall robots that just tilted very slowly forward, since the height component of the diversity measure encouraged very tall designs.

Table 2: P-values of pairwise T-tests on diversity measure forward movement performance differences after generation 600

	None	LBD	HMJ	TS	GED
LBD	0.0001				
HMJ	<0.0001	<0.0001			
TS	<0.0001	<0.0001	0.0002		
GED	<0.0001	<0.0001	0.0221	0.1553	

Table 3: Mean cross-measure diversity of the final populations

		Measured by			
		LBD	HMJ	TS	GED
Evolved with	None	1.69	3.14	1.22	1.54
	LBD	3.66	9.00	3.05	3.17
	HMJ	8.18	8.94	5.90	6.28
	TS	5.62	6.76	5.74	5.80
	GED	5.54	5.99	5.23	5.71

The control case performs better ($p < 0.01$) than the cases with a diversity measure approximately from generation 50 to generation 100, where the LBD measure catches up. This measure then outperforms the control case approximately from generation 200 until termination, and has been measurably better than the other measures since generation 10. The other measures remain inseparable until generation 450, when the HMJ measure becomes measurably worse than TS. HMJ becomes different only by a weak significance to GED, with p-values in the range of 0.02 to 0.05, after generation 480. TS and GED distance remain inseparable, statistically speaking, until the end.

Figure 4 shows the distribution of number of branches and depth of the different diversity cases. The values are found using regression models similar to the one used for the forward movement score for each branch or depth value, but with a quasibinomial model instead of a linear one because the numbers are proportions. It can be seen that while HMJ, TS and GED all have a large proportion of 1 and 3-branched robots (i.e. bipeds and hexapods) and a smaller proportion of 2-branched robots, the diversity-less case and LBD produce dominantly 2-branched robots. Similarly, when looking at the depth distribution the control case and LBD mostly produce robots with two-jointed limbs, while for the other three cases the distribution between one and two-jointed limbs is much more even.

The final population diversity in the different cases as measured by all four diversity measures is shown in Table 3. In all measures the diversity of the control case is much lower than in the other cases. The diversity measured by TS and GED are similar in all cases, and the runs with these two measures also result in similar values in all measurements. The two Cartesian distance measures show a different behavior. Both measures rate runs with HMJ diversity highly, and conversely runs with both HMJ and LBD are rated highly by HMJ, but runs with LBD rate much lower with itself.

Figure 5 shows three examples of robots produced by the algorithm. The robot in Figure 5a has 1 branch and a depth of 2, and locomotes using a rolling motion. Since the obstacles are wide and relatively low, the robot is able to roll over it and stay on course. Figure 5b shows a tripod morphology

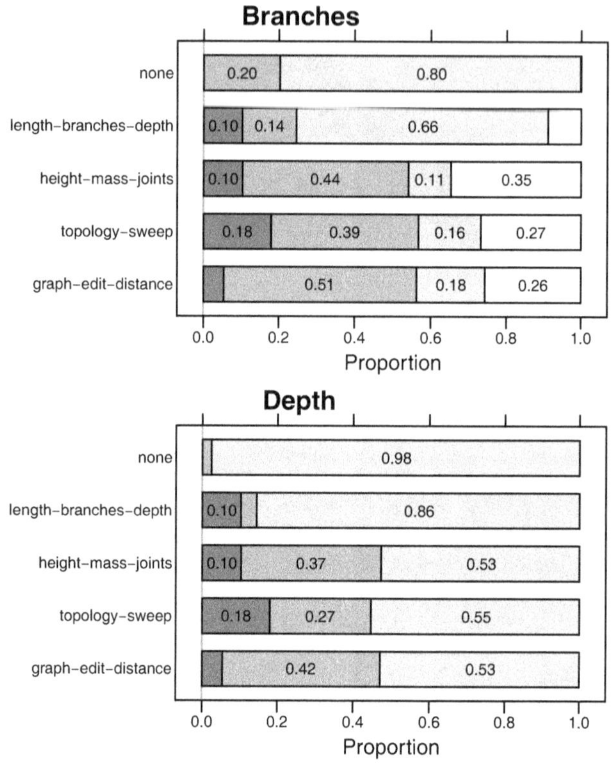

Figure 4: Limb length and branch count distribution - dark gray is 0, middle gray is 1, light gray is 2 and white is 3. The number inside the boxes is the corresponding proportion, no number means less than 0.10.

(1 branch, depth 1) were the limbless rear spine segments are used as a third leg that helps push the robot forward. In Figure 5c one can see a much larger morphology with 2 branches and a limb depth of 2. This robot uses a gait where all four limbs move synchronously to lift the body up and forward. When the robot reaches the obstacles it gains extra traction from pushing against them with the rear limbs. Some variants of this morphology is able to propel itself far enough forward to grab on to a new obstacle each period, thus reaching a speed of 0.5 m/s.

4. DISCUSSION

From the experimental results, we can make the following observations:

- Measuring diversity with the LBD distance gives the best-performing forward movement results, as seen in Figure 3, and thus LBD-based diversity search seems to explore most efficiently the set of useful morphologies for the given task. We hypothesize the following: In the given scenario, the most efficient solutions tend to be quadruped configurations, as seen in Figure 4. Optimization of the LBD diversity may lead to a larger variation in the total length of the robot limbs, as there is a limited number of topologies available for

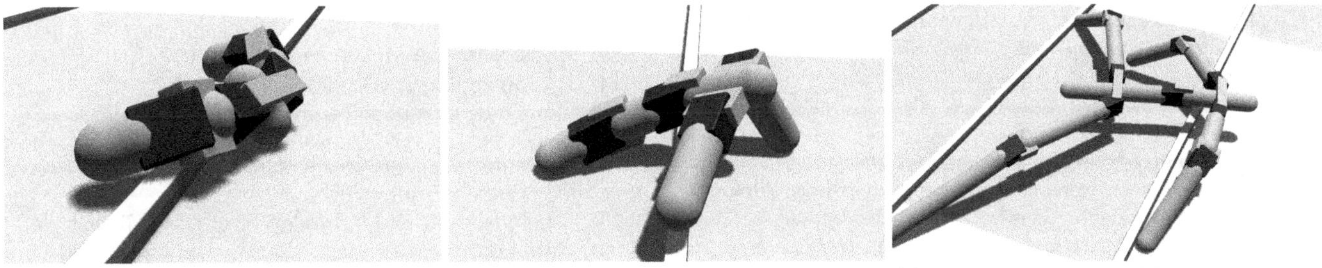

(a) Rolling robot climbing the low obstacles (b) Robot with successful tripod gait (c) Robot pushing itself from the obstacle behind it

Figure 5: Some example results

the branches and depth combinations. The LBD measure may thus tend to explore different lengths within a quadruped configuration, leading to efficient solutions for the task, as opposed to the other measures which may emphasize less significant components.

- For the given task, it is clear from Figure 3 that even though LBD diversity gives the best forward movement performance, the control case still gives significantly better performance than diversity using any of the other measures. One reason for this may be that the more complex distances lead to a wider exploration of the search space, and thus limit exploitation, while in the current task such a wide exploration is not necessary in order to achieve good results. It is however possible that more complex and deceptive tasks may require a wider search and thus favor search based on diversity with the more complex, topology-based distances.

- While the GED distance gives a theoretically better measure of difference between topology graphs than the TS distance, we can see from Table 3 that the two distances produce relatively similar values, with TS being slightly higher on all measures. The slight favor of TS is also indicated by the even distributions in Figure 4. The preferable graph-based distance metric would therefore be TS, also taking into consideration that GED is computationally much more complex. As an example, the evolutionary experiments using GED diversity required about three times longer runtime than the other diversity experiments.

- From Table 3 one can observe that there are complex interactions between the distance metrics. For instance, evolving with the HMJ diversity will lead to high diversity scores over all measures, even outperforming the results of evolving directly with other measures. At the same time, evolving with LBD gives a very high HMJ score, but poor scores in the other measures. The mechanisms behind this seem complex; however we relate it to different morphology components getting different emphasis depending on the distance measure, directing the search in different directions.

5. CONCLUSION AND FUTURE WORK

In this paper, we have presented some distance measures for a generative robot morphology encoding, and analyzed their performance across two control systems in a simulated environment. For the given locomotion task with small obstacles, one of the distance measures shows a clear improvement over the plain evolutionary approach. Since the performances of the different methods vary considerably, an evaluation of the distance measure to employ according to the task at hand seems appropriate.

Most of the measures are morphology-specific, in principle requiring a rigid, acyclic graph-like morphology, limiting the scope of these results somewhat. However, the restrictions may not be as strict as they appear; many rigid generative morphologies should be translatable into acyclic structures on a functional level (e.g. by collapsing rigid structures and then collapsing duplicate edges (joints) between nodes), with differences in rigid structures handled by relabeling costs, and techniques may possibly be found to do the same for non-rigid morphologies as well (some Voronoi diagram-inspired approach, perhaps).

While the proposed diversity measures indeed show promising results, the search was limited to a relatively small set of possible topologies. It would be perhaps be prudent to verify the results with looser restrictions on the number of limbs and joints per limb. There are also other aspects about the morphological phenotype spaces that could be explored. For instance, the current distance measures do not take into account the joint angles, which may for otherwise similar topologies have a great impact on the resulting behavior. Similarly, the control systems are co-evolved with the morphology and should thus be taken into consideration. While there is no obvious approach to measuring behavior together with generative morphologies, as mentioned in Section 1, it would be highly interesting to explore measures which would give more information of the combined morphology and control.

In order to fully explore the possibilities and limitations of the diversity methods, and the capabilities of the generative system, it would be necessary to experiment with even more complex tasks, such as environments with more difficult obstacles. This could again lead to more complex morphologies, as indicated in [2]. Furthermore, the generality of the results should be verified for a range of different encodings, environments and tasks, and also over a wider range of control systems.

6. REFERENCES

[1] J. E. Auerbach and J. C. Bongard. Evolving cppns to grow three-dimensional physical structures. In *Proceedings of the 12th annual conference on Genetic and evolutionary computation*, pages 627–634. ACM, 2010.

[2] J. E. Auerbach and J. C. Bongard. On the relationship between environmental and morphological complexity in evolved robots. In *Proceedings of the fourteenth international conference on Genetic and evolutionary computation conference*, GECCO '12, pages 521–528, New York, NY, USA, 2012. ACM.

[3] J. Bongard. Evolving modular genetic regulatory networks. In *Evolutionary Computation, 2002. CEC'02. Proceedings of the 2002 Congress on*, volume 2, pages 1872–1877. IEEE, 2002.

[4] E. D. de Jong, R. A. Watson, and J. B. Pollack. Reducing bloat and promoting diversity using multi-objective methods. In *Proceedings of the Genetic and Evolutionary Computation Conference (GECCO-2001)*, pages 11–18. Morgan Kaufmann, 2001.

[5] K. Deb, A. Pratap, S. Agarwal, and T. Meyarivan. A fast and elitist multiobjective genetic algorithm: Nsga-ii. *Evolutionary Computation, IEEE Transactions on*, 6(2):182 –197, apr 2002.

[6] S. Doncieux and J.-B. Mouret. Behavioral diversity measures for evolutionary robotics. In *Evolutionary Computation (CEC), 2010 IEEE Congress on*, pages 1–8. IEEE, 2010.

[7] X. Gao, B. Xiao, D. Tao, and X. Li. A survey of graph edit distance. *Pattern Analysis and applications*, 13(1):113–129, 2010.

[8] J. C. Gomes and A. L. Christensen. Generic behaviour similarity measures for evolutionary swarm robotics. In *Proceedings of the Genetic and Evolutionary Computation Conference (GECCO) 2013*, pages 199–206. ACM, 2013.

[9] G. Hornby, S. Takamura, J. Yokono, O. Hanagata, T. Yamamoto, and M. Fujita. Evolving robust gaits with aibo. In *Robotics and Automation, 2000. Proceedings. ICRA '00. IEEE International Conference on*, volume 3, pages 3040 –3045 vol.3, 2000.

[10] G. S. Hornby, H. Lipson, and J. B. Pollack. Generative representations for the automated design of modular physical robots. *Robotics and Automation, IEEE Transactions on*, 19(4):703–719, 2003.

[11] M. Komosinski and A. Rotaru-Varga. Comparison of different genotype encodings for simulated three-dimensional agents. *Artificial Life*, 7(4):395–418, 2001.

[12] S. Koos, A. Cully, and J.-B. Mouret. Fast damage recovery in robotics with the t-resilience algorithm. *International Journal of Robotics Research*, 32(14):1700–1723, 2013.

[13] C. Leger. *Automated synthesis and optimization of robot configurations: an evolutionary approach*. PhD thesis, Carnegie Mellon University, 1999.

[14] J. Lehman and K. O. Stanley. Exploiting open-endedness to solve problems through the search for novelty. In *Proceedings of the Eleventh International Conference on Artificial Life (ALIFE XI)*, pages 329–336, 2008.

[15] J. Lehman and K. O. Stanley. Evolving a diversity of virtual creatures through novelty search and local competition. In *Proceedings of the 13th annual conference on Genetic and evolutionary computation*, pages 211–218. ACM, 2011.

[16] H. Lipson and J. Pollack. Automatic design and manufacture of robotic lifeforms. *Nature*, 406:974–978, 2000.

[17] J.-B. Mouret. Novelty-based multiobjectivization. In *New Horizons in Evolutionary Robotics*, pages 139–154. Springer, 2011.

[18] J.-B. Mouret and S. Doncieux. Overcoming the bootstrap problem in evolutionary robotics using behavioral diversity. In *Evolutionary Computation, 2009. CEC'09. IEEE Congress on*, pages 1161–1168. IEEE, 2009.

[19] J.-B. Mouret and S. Doncieux. Using behavioral exploration objectives to solve deceptive problems in neuro-evolution. In *Proceedings of the 11th Annual conference on Genetic and evolutionary computation*, pages 627–634. ACM, 2009.

[20] S. Nolfi, D. Floreano, and D. Floreano. *Evolutionary robotics: The biology, intelligence, and technology of self-organizing machines*, volume 26. MIT press Cambridge, 2000.

[21] S. Revzen, M. Bhoite, A. Macasieb, and M. Yim. Structure synthesis on-the-fly in a modular robot. In *Intelligent Robots and Systems (IROS), 2011 IEEE/RSJ International Conference on*, pages 4797–4802. IEEE, 2011.

[22] E. Samuelsen, K. Glette, and J. Torresen. A hox gene inspired generative approach to evolving robot morphology. In *Proceedings of the 15th annual conference on Genetic and evolutionary computation*, pages 751–758. ACM, 2013.

[23] B. Sareni and L. Krahenbuhl. Fitness sharing and niching methods revisited. *Evolutionary Computation, IEEE Transactions on*, 2(3):97–106, 1998.

[24] K. Sims. Evolving virtual creatures. In *Proceedings of the 21st annual conference on Computer graphics and interactive techniques*, SIGGRAPH '94, pages 15–22, New York, NY, USA, 1994. ACM.

[25] K. Zhang, J. T.-L. Wang, D. Shasha, et al. On the editing distance between undirected acyclic graphs. *International Journal of Foundations of Computer Science*, 7(1):43–58, 1996.

www.ingramcontent.com/pod-product-compliance
Lightning Source LLC
LaVergne TN
LVHW080108011026
849160LV00013B/1056

* 9 7 8 1 4 5 0 3 3 2 6 6 8 *